The Holy Bible

REVISED STANDARD VERSION

SECOND CATHOLIC EDITION

THE HOLY BIBLE

Revised Standard Version | *Second Catholic Edition*

TRANSLATED FROM THE ORIGINAL TONGUES
BEING THE VERSION SET FORTH A.D. 1611

OLD AND NEW TESTAMENTS REVISED A.D. 1881–1885 AND A.D. 1901
(APOCRYPHA REVISED A.D. 1894)

COMPARED WITH THE MOST ANCIENT AUTHORITIES
AND REVISED A.D. 1946, 1952, AND 1965
(APOCRYPHA REVISED A.D. 1957 AND 1966)

THE ORIGINAL CATHOLIC EDITION OF THE RSV TRANSLATION
WAS PREPARED BY THE
CATHOLIC BIBLICAL ASSOCIATION OF GREAT BRITAIN

THIS EDITION WAS REVISED ACCORDING TO
LITURGIAM AUTHENTICAM, 2001

IGNATIUS PRESS
San Francisco

With ecclesiastical approval
Nihil Obstat: Thomas Hanlon, S.T.L., L.S.S., Ph.L.
Imprimatur: +Peter W. Bartholome, D.D.
Bishop of Saint Cloud, Minnesota, May 11, 1966

Cover art: *The Four Evangelists*, by Christopher J. Pelicano
Cover design by Roxanne Mei Lum

Maps by David Notley
Camway Creative Limited, Somerset, England

Printed in India ∞

INTRODUCTION

(TO THE 1966 EDITION)

THIS EDITION of the Revised Standard Version of the Bible has been prepared for the use of Catholics by a committee of the Catholic Biblical Association of Great Britain. It is published with ecclesiastical approval and by agreement with the Standard Bible Committee and the Division of Christian Education of the National Council of the Churches of Christ in the United States of America.

The Revised Standard Version itself needs no lengthy introduction, being already well known and widely read. It is, as its Preface states, "an authorized revision of the American Standard Version, published in 1901, which was a revision of the King James Version, published in 1611." In Britain, the King James Version is more commonly called the Authorized Version. It occupies a unique place in English Biblical and indeed literary tradition. The Standard Bible of 1901 was the work of an American committee revising it in the light of modern textual criticism. In 1937 it was decided to make a revision of the Standard Version which should "embody the best results of modern scholarship as to the meaning of the Scriptures, and express this meaning in English diction which is designed for use in public and private worship and preserves those qualities which have given to the King James Version a supreme place in English literature." The New Testament in this new version was published in 1946 and the whole Bible in 1952.

The remarkable success which attended the new revision on its appearance seems to be ample justification of the revisers' aims and it has been acclaimed on all sides as a translation which combines accuracy and clarity of meaning with beauty of language and traditional diction.

For four hundred years, following upon the great upheaval of the Reformation, Catholics and Protestants have gone their separate ways and suspected each other's translations of the Bible of having been in some way manipulated in the interests of doctrinal presuppositions. It must be admitted that these suspicions were not always without foundation. At the present time, however, the sciences of textual criticism and philology, not to mention others, have made such great advances that the Bible text used by translators is substantially the same for all—Protestants and Catholics alike.

Today, and indeed since the appearance in 1943 of the Encyclical Letter *Divino Afflante Spiritu,* encouraging Biblical studies, Catholics like every one else go back to the original languages and base their translations on the same critical principles.

With the improvement in interdenominational relations and the advance of Biblical knowledge, the possibility of producing a Bible common to all Christians was mooted as far back as 1953. It was felt that, if such a thing could be achieved, it would be of incalculable benefit in wiping away remaining misconceptions and prejudices and in fostering still further good relations between the Churches. The Word of God would then not only be our common heritage and unifying link but be recognized as such, and those engaged in theological discussion could appeal to the same authoritative text. A decisive step toward this objective could be made by editing the Revised Standard Version for Catholic use.

A small committee of members of the Catholic Biblical Association was formed and permission obtained to examine this translation and suggest any changes that might be required to make it acceptable to Catholics. The Standard Bible Committee of the U.S.A. was then approached and they gave warm welcome to the proposal. Here was a wonderful opportunity to make a real step forward in the field of ecumenical relations. However, ideas of this kind take time to penetrate all levels and many difficulties and delays ensued. But a change of mind has taken place and what seemed to many in 1953 to be a novel idea of doubtful value or even of no value at all is now generally recognized to be a legitimate and desirable goal.

In the present edition the aim has not been to improve the translation as such. No doubt there are many places where a different rendering might have been chosen on critical grounds. This has been avoided. But there are other places where, the critical evidence being evenly balanced, considerations of Catholic tradition have favored a particular rendering or the inclusion of a passage omitted by the RSV translators.

In the Old Testament it has not been thought necessary to make any changes in the text. There is, however, the very important difference in the number of books. Catholic Bibles include seven extra books and parts of two others. These are known to Catholics as "deuterocanonical" and are regarded as an integral part of the Canon of the Old Testament. They are here printed in the order in which they appear in the Latin Vulgate, with the exception of the extra parts of the Book of Esther. As these parts do not occur in the Hebrew text of Esther, St. Jerome extracted them from their place in the Greek in deference to the view favoring their canonicity and included them in his translation of Esther. But not regarding them as canonical he put them together at the end of the Hebrew text regardless of their historical or logical sequence. In this edition of the RSV they have been restored to their proper place in the narrative. These books and parts of books are regarded by Protestants as apocryphal.

This question of the "Apocrypha" is the one big problem left and needs to be carefully considered when discussing the possibility of a common Bible. The books known as the Apocrypha are: 1 and 2 Esdras (3 and 4 Esdras), Tobit, Judith, Wisdom, Sirach (Ecclesiasticus), Baruch with the Letter of Jeremiah, 1 and 2 Maccabees, Additions to Daniel and to Esther, and the Prayer of Manasseh. Since the time of the Reformation these books have been regarded as noncanonical by Protestants and either grouped at the end of the Old Testament or left out altogether. Roman Catholics, on the other hand, have continued to regard them as inspired and canonical, with the following exceptions. There are three items in the Apocrypha which are not included in the deuterocanonical books, namely, 1 and 2 Esdras (3 and 4 Esdras) and the Prayer of Manasseh, and which in consequence are not printed in this Bible. The other books are given in the translation of the Revised Standard Version, which was published in 1957. A word must be said here about the origin of these books. In the days of Jesus Christ, the Jews had no precisely defined (in the sense of officially closed) Canon of the Scriptures. Besides the books of the Hebrew Canon as we now know it, there were others of more recent origin (mostly of the first and second centuries b.c.) which were held in great esteem but whose exact status had not been finally determined. Though many of them had been written in Hebrew and Aramaic they seem to have circulated mainly outside Palestine, in a Greek translation or text, among the Greek-speaking Jews of the Dispersion, especially in Egypt. The books were less acceptable to the Jews of the Pharisaic tradition in Jerusalem, but many fragments of them in Hebrew and Aramaic have been found at Qumran where there was a religious community distinct from the Pharisees.

The first Christians were Aramaic-speaking Jews of Palestine and they used the Hebrew Scriptures. Very soon the Greek-speaking Jewish and Gentile converts outnumbered those of Aramaic speech; and consequently the Bible they used, namely, the Greek Septuagint translation which included the books referred to above, came into general use. The books thus came to be implicitly accepted by the Christians of the first centuries, though no attempt was made to issue an official decree defining the limits of the Old Testament Canon.

With the virtual disappearance of the priestly class as a force in Judaism after the destruction of the Temple in A.D. 70, and the rise of the Pharisees to a position of dominance as champions of the national heritage, the Jews set about the task of consolidating their tradition and defining the limits of their sacred writings. Toward the end of the first century A.D. at Jamnia, they decided that their Bible consisted only of books written up to the time of Ezra, when prophecy was deemed to have ceased; and this criterion, though not applied uniformly, excluded the books of more recent origin which were on the whole less in accord with the Pharisaic outlook. The need for a decision was forced upon the Jews because of the growing controversies with Christians; and besides delimiting the Canon of Scripture they also not long afterward condemned the Greek Septuagint translation as inaccurate. Though the decision about the Canon was not of course binding upon the Christians, it did have some influence on them in the course of centuries and various writers expressed doubts about the extra books of the Greek Bible which had come into general use. This was especially so in the fourth century A.D. when, for example, St. Jerome regarded them as noncanonical. Eventually official decrees confirming the longer Canon were issued toward the end of the fourth and beginning of the fifth centuries in the West at Hippo and Carthage and in the East during the eighth and ninth centuries at Nicaea and Constantinople. But doubts and adverse opinions continued to be expressed in various quarters and by prominent writers.

In the sixteenth century the Reformers rejected the extra books, partly, perhaps, because some of the teaching contained in them seemed to favor Roman doctrine, but chiefly because they were not in the Hebrew Canon. Finally, the Council of Trent Issued its decree on the Canon of Scripture in 1546 declaring that all the books which it had been the custom to read in the Catholic Church and which were contained in the ancient Latin Vulgate Bible must be accepted as sacred and canonical. The decree gave the list of the books in question which in fact coincided with the lists issued by earlier Councils in the West. It is interesting to note that though 3 and 4 Esdras and the Prayer of Manasseh were excluded from the list they were printed at the end of many subsequent Latin Bibles *"ne prorsus interirent"*—"lest they altogether perish."

The positions taken up in the sixteenth century with regard to the Old Testament Canon are substantially the same as those held today. The aim of this edition is to show that there is more common ground for the practical purpose of Bible reading than perhaps may appear at first sight. Thus, there is an increasing tendency on the part of Protestants to include the "Apocrypha" in their Bibles without necessarily admitting their inspired and canonical character. On the other hand, Roman Catholics do not today attach the same significance to the traditional order of books in the Old Testament as they once did. There seems room for some accommodation here. This is an important development and it must be taken in conjunction with another equally important, namely, the steadily diminishing number of textual differences, as may be seen in the present edition.

To turn now to the text of the "Apocrypha." There is in the first place a striking contrast between the uniformity imposed on the Hebrew text by the rabbis and the lack of it in the Greek text of the Christian Bible. The other ancient versions add to the variety. The consequence of this is that there are often substantial differences between the English translations of these books according to which Greek recension or version has been used. Thus, for example, in the case of the Book of Sirach (Ecclesiasticus), the Latin, on which the Douay Version is based, is notably longer than the Revised Standard Version which is based on the Greek. It is generally agreed that the Greek underlying the RSV is better than the recension underlying the Latin. On critical principles therefore we should accept the RSV text as preferable to the Douay. It is admitted today that the decree of Trent declaring that Catholics must accept the books contained in the Latin Vulgate with all their parts does not oblige us to accept passages which have been judged, according to the best critical principles, not to be part of the original text. Thus the passage known as the "Three Heavenly Witnesses" or the "Comma Johanneum" (1 John 5:7–8), which is in the Latin Vulgate and in versions based on it, does not appear in recent Catholic editions of the New Testament. This procedure is in accordance with the directives given in *Divino Afflante Spiritu.*

The aim of the translator must be to render into intelligible language, as faithfully as possible, what he regards on solid critical grounds as the original text or the closest possible approximation to it. In some cases the original has not come down to us, but it is still incumbent on the translator to try to get as near as possible to it by a study of the most ancient versions.

In conclusion, a tribute of thanks must be paid to the Catholic bishops who have approved this edition and to the American Standard Bible Committee who have throughout given their unfailing and generous support in spite of difficulties and delays. Thanks are due also to all those who throughout the years of waiting have been inspired by the ideal of Christian unity to persevere in the work of producing this Bible. Its appearance coincides in time with a development in relations between Christian bodies which no one could have foreseen ten years ago, a development which offers great promise of the fulfilment of our Savior's words, "that they may all be one" (John 17:21).

Abbreviations for the Books of the Bible

OLD TESTAMENT

Gen	Genesis
Ex	Exodus
Lev	Leviticus
Num	Numbers
Deut	Deuteronomy
Josh	Joshua
Judg	Judges
Ruth	Ruth
1 Sam	1 Samuel
2 Sam	2 Samuel
1 Kings	1 Kings
2 Kings	2 Kings
1 Chron	1 Chronicles
2 Chron	2 Chronicles
Ezra	Ezra
Neh	Nehemiah
Tob	Tobit
Jud	Judith
Esther	Esther
Job	Job
Ps	Psalms
Prov	Proverbs
Eccles	Ecclesiastes
Song	Song of Solomon
Wis	Wisdom
Sir	Sirach (Ecclesiasticus)
Is	Isaiah
Jer	Jeremiah
Lam	Lamentations
Bar	Baruch
Ezek	Ezekiel
Dan	Daniel
Hos	Hosea
Joel	Joel
Amos	Amos
Obad	Obadiah
Jon	Jonah
Mic	Micah
Nahum	Nahum
Hab	Habakkuk
Zeph	Zephaniah
Hag	Haggai
Zech	Zechariah
Mal	Malachi
1 Mac	1 Maccabees
2 Mac	2 Maccabees

NEW TESTAMENT

Mt	Matthew
Mk	Mark
Lk	Luke
Jn	John
Acts	Acts of the Apostles
Rom	Romans
1 Cor	1 Corinthians
2 Cor	2 Corinthians
Gal	Galatians
Eph	Ephesians
Phil	Philippians
Col	Colossians
1 Thess	1 Thessalonians
2 Thess	2 Thessalonians
1 Tim	1 Timothy
2 Tim	2 Timothy
Tit	Titus
Philem	Philemon
Heb	Hebrews
Jas	James
1 Pet	1 Peter
2 Pet	2 Peter
1 Jn	1 John
2 Jn	2 John
3 Jn	3 John
Jude	Jude
Rev	Revelation (Apocalypse)

The
OLD TESTAMENT

Revised Standard Version | *Second Catholic Edition*

TRANSLATED FROM THE ORIGINAL TONGUES
BEING THE VERSION SET FORTH A.D. 1611
REVISED A.D. 1881 AND A.D. 1901

COMPARED WITH THE MOST ANCIENT AUTHORITIES
AND REVISED A.D. 1946, 1952, AND 1965
(APOCRYPHA REVISED A.D. 1957 AND 1966)

THE ORIGINAL CATHOLIC EDITION OF THE RSV TRANSLATION
WAS PREPARED BY THE
CATHOLIC BIBLICAL ASSOCIATION OF GREAT BRITAIN

THIS EDITION WAS REVISED ACCORDING TO
LITURGIAM AUTHENTICAM, 2001

The Names and Order of the Books of
THE OLD TESTAMENT

	Page		Page
Genesis	1	Song of Solomon (Canticle of Canticles)	517
Exodus	40	The Wisdom of Solomon (Wisdom)	522
Leviticus	73	Sirach (Ecclesiasticus)	538
Numbers	96	Isaiah (Isaias)	581
Deuteronomy	129	Jeremiah (Jeremias)	633
Joshua (Josue)	159	Lamentations	683
Judges	178	Baruch	689
Ruth	198	Ezekiel (Ezechiel)	695
1 Samuel (1 Kings)	201	Daniel	736
2 Samuel (2 Kings)	226	Hosea (Osee)	754
1 Kings (3 Kings)	248	Joel	763
2 Kings (4 Kings)	273	Amos	767
1 Chronicles (1 Paralipomenon)	297	Obadiah (Abdias)	774
2 Chronicles (2 Paralipomenon)	319	Jonah (Jonas)	776
Ezra (1 Esdras)	346	Micah (Michaeas)	778
Nehemiah (2 Esdras)	354	Nahum	783
Tobit (Tobias)	365	Habakkuk (Habacuc)	786
Judith	374	Zephaniah (Sophonias)	789
Esther	386	Haggai (Aggeus)	792
Job	395	Zechariah (Zacharias)	794
Psalms	421	Malachi (Malachias)	801
Proverbs	489	1 Maccabees (1 Machabees)	803
Ecclesiastes	511	2 Maccabees (2 Machabees)	828

The books of the Apocrypha and the Deuterocanonical Books of the Catholic Old Testament
are related as follows:

APOCRYPHA	DEUTEROCANONICAL BOOKS
1 (3) Esdras	Not included
2 (4) Esdras	Not included
Tobit	Tobit
Judith	Judith
Additions to Esther	Esther (part of)
The Wisdom of Solomon	The Wisdom of Solomon
Sirach	Sirach
Baruch	Baruch 1–5
The Letter of Jeremiah	Baruch 6
The Prayer of Azariah and the Song of the Three Young Men	Daniel 3 (part of)
Susanna	Daniel 13
Bel and the Dragon	Daniel 14
The Prayer of Manasseh	Not included
1 Maccabees	1 Maccabees
2 Maccabees	2 Maccabees

Abbreviations in the Notes

In the notes to the books of the Old Testament, the following abbreviations are used: Ms for manuscript; Mss for manuscripts. Heb denotes the Hebrew of the consonantal Masoretic Text of the Old Testament; and MT denotes the Hebrew of the pointed Masoretic Text of the Old Testament. The ancient versions of the Old Testament are indicated by:

Gk	Septuagint Greek Version of Old Testament
Lat	Latin Version of Tobit, Judith, and 2 Maccabees
Sam	Samaritan Hebrew text of Old Testament
Syr	Syriac Version of Old Testament
Tg	Targum
Vg	Vulgate, Latin Version of Old Testament

Cn indicates a correction made where the text has suffered in transmission and the versions provide no satisfactory restoration but the Committee agrees with the judgment of competent scholars as to the most probable reconstruction of the original text.

References to quoted and parallel passages are given following the textual notes on pages where these are relevant.

THE OLD TESTAMENT

THE FIRST BOOK OF MOSES COMMONLY CALLED

GENESIS

Six Days of Creation and the Sabbath

1 * In the beginning God created [a] the heavens and the earth. [2]The earth was without form and void, and darkness was upon the face of the deep; and the Spirit [b] of God was moving over the face of the waters.

3 And God said, "Let there be light"; and there was light. [4]And God saw that the light was good; and God separated the light from the darkness. [5]God called the light Day, and the darkness he called Night. And there was evening and there was morning, one day.

6 And God said, "Let there be a firmament in the midst of the waters, and let it separate the waters from the waters." [7]And God made the firmament and separated the waters which were under the firmament from the waters which were above the firmament. And it was so. [8]And God called the firmament Heaven. And there was evening and there was morning, a second day.

9 And God said, "Let the waters under the heavens be gathered together into one place, and let the dry land appear." And it was so. [10]God called the dry land Earth, and the waters that were gathered together he called Seas. And God saw that it was good. [11]And God said, "Let the earth put forth vegetation, plants yielding seed, and fruit trees bearing fruit in which is their seed, each according to its kind, upon the earth." And it was so. [12]The earth brought forth vegetation, plants yielding seed according to their own kinds, and trees bearing fruit in which is their seed, each according to its kind. And God saw that it was good. [13]And there was evening and there was morning, a third day.

14 And God said, "Let there be lights in the firmament of the heavens to separate the day from the night; and let them be for signs and for seasons and for days and years, [15]and let them be lights in the firmament of the heavens to give light upon the earth." And it was so. [16]And God made the two great lights, the greater light to rule the day, and the lesser light to rule the night; he made the stars also. [17]And God set them in the firmament of the heavens to give light upon the earth, [18]to rule over the day and over the night, and to separate the light from the darkness. And God saw that it was good. [19]And there was evening and there was morning, a fourth day.

20 And God said, "Let the waters bring forth swarms of living creatures, and let birds fly above the earth across the firmament of the heavens." [21]So God created the great sea monsters and every living creature that moves, with which the waters swarm, according to their kinds, and every winged bird according to its kind. And God saw that it was good. [22]And God blessed them, saying, "Be fruitful and multiply and fill the waters in the seas, and let birds multiply on the earth." [23]And there was evening and there was morning, a fifth day.

24 And God said, "Let the earth bring forth living creatures according to their kinds: cattle and creeping things and beasts of the earth according to their kinds." And it was so. [25]And God made the beasts of the earth according to their kinds and the cattle according to their kinds, and everything that creeps upon the ground according to its kind. And God saw that it was good.

26 Then God said, "Let us make man in our image, after our likeness; and let them have dominion over the fish of the sea, and over the birds of the air, and over the cattle, and over all the earth, and over every creeping thing that creeps upon the earth." [27]So God created man in his own image, in the image of God he created him; male and female he created them. [28]And God blessed them, and God said to them, "Be fruitful and multiply, and fill the earth and subdue it; and have dominion over the fish of the sea and over the birds of the air and over every living thing that moves upon the earth." [29]And God said, "Behold, I have given you every plant yielding seed which is upon the face of all the earth, and every tree with seed in its fruit; you shall have them for food. [30]And to every beast of the earth, and to every bird of the air, and to everything that creeps on the earth, everything that has the breath of life, I have given every green plant for food." And it was so. [31]And God saw everything

---

[a] Or *When God began to create.*
[b] Or *wind.*
1:1: Jn 1:1.
1:26, 27: Gen 5:1; Mt 19:4; Mk 10:6; Col 3:10; Jas 3:9.
* 1:1—2:4a: The aim of this narrative is not to present a scientific picture but to teach religious truth, especially the dependence of all creation on God and its consecration to him through the homage rendered by man, who is the climax of creation. Hence its strong liturgical character and the concluding emphasis on the sabbath. It serves as a prologue to the whole of the Old Testament.

that he had made, and behold, it was very good. And there was evening and there was morning, a sixth day.

2 Thus the heavens and the earth were finished, and all the host of them. [2]And on the seventh day God finished his work which he had done, and he rested on the seventh day from all his work which he had done. [3]So God blessed the seventh day and hallowed it, because on it God rested from all his work which he had done in creation.

Another Account of Creation

4 These are the generations of the heavens and the earth when they were created.

[*] In the day that the LORD God made the earth and the heavens, [5]when no plant of the field was yet in the earth and no herb of the field had yet sprung up—for the LORD God had not caused it to rain upon the earth, and there was no man to till the ground; [6]but a mist [c] went up from the earth and watered the whole face of the ground—[7]then the LORD God formed man of dust from the ground, and breathed into his nostrils the breath of life; and man became a living soul. [8]And the LORD God planted a garden in Eden, in the east; and there he put the man whom he had formed. [9]And out of the ground the LORD God made to grow every tree that is pleasant to the sight and good for food, the tree of life also in the midst of the garden, and the tree of the knowledge of good and evil.

10 A river flowed out of Eden to water the garden, and there it divided and became four rivers. [11]The name of the first is Pi'shon; it is the one which flows around the whole land of Hav'ilah, where there is gold; [12]and the gold of that land is good; bdellium and onyx stone are there. [13]The name of the second river is Gi'hon; it is the one which flows around the whole land of Cush. [14]And the name of the third river is Tigris, which flows east of Assyria. And the fourth river is the Euphra'tes.

15 The LORD God took the man and put him in the garden of Eden to till it and keep it. [16]And the LORD God commanded the man, saying, "You may freely eat of every tree of the garden; [17]but of the tree of the knowledge of good and evil you shall not eat, for in the day that you eat of it you shall die."

18 Then the LORD God said, "It is not good that the man should be alone; I will make him a helper fit for him." [19]So out of the ground the LORD God formed every beast of the field and every bird of the air, and brought them to the man to see what he would call them; and whatever the man called every living creature, that was its name. [20]The man gave names to all cattle, and to the birds of the air, and to every beast of the field; but for the man there was not found a helper fit for him. [21]So the LORD God caused a deep sleep to fall upon the man, and while he slept took one of his ribs and closed up its place with flesh; [22]and the rib which the LORD God had taken from the man he made into a woman and brought her to the man. [23]Then the man said,

"This at last is bone of my bones
 and flesh of my flesh;
she shall be called Woman,[d]
 because she was taken out of Man." [e]

[24]Therefore a man leaves his father and his mother and clings to his wife, and they become one flesh. [25]And the man and his wife were both naked, and were not ashamed.

The Fall of Man

3 Now the serpent was more subtle than any other wild creature that the LORD God had made. He said to the woman, "Did God say, 'You shall not eat of any tree of the garden'?" [2]And the woman said to the serpent, "We may eat of the fruit of the trees of the garden; [3]but God said, 'You shall not eat of the fruit of the tree which is in the midst of the garden, neither shall you touch it, lest you die.'" [4]But the serpent said to the woman, "You will not die. [5]For God knows that when you eat of it your eyes will be opened, and you will be like God, knowing good and evil." [6]So when the woman saw that the tree was good for food, and that it was a delight to the eyes, and that the tree was to be desired to make one wise, she took of its fruit and ate; and she also gave some to her husband, and he ate. [7]Then the eyes of both were opened, and they knew that they were naked; and they sewed fig leaves together and made themselves aprons.

8 And they heard the sound of the LORD God walking in the garden in the cool of the day, and the man and his wife hid themselves from the presence of the LORD God among the trees of the garden. [9]But the LORD God called to the man, and said to him, "Where are you?" [10]And he said, "I heard the sound of you in the garden, and I was afraid, because I was naked; and I hid myself." [11]He said, "Who told you that you were naked? Have you eaten of the tree of which I commanded you not to eat?" [12]The man said, "The woman whom you gave to be with me, she gave me fruit

---

[c] Or *flood*.
[d] Heb *ishshah*.
[e] Heb *ish*.
2:1-3: Ex 20:11.
2:2: Heb 4:4, 10.
2:7: 1 Cor 15:45, 47.
2:9: Rev 2:7; 22:2, 14, 19.
2:24: Mt 19:5; Mk 10:7; 1 Cor 6:16; Eph 5:31.
3:1: Rev 12:9; 20:2.
3:4: 2 Cor 11:3.
[*] 2:4b ff: This account of the state of the world at the beginning, which introduces the story of the first sin, comes from a different and earlier source and is composed in a very different style. There is nothing in these early chapters that commits us to any particular scientific view of the origins of the world or man, or that would exclude the evolution hypothesis.

of the tree, and I ate." [13]Then the LORD God said to the woman, "What is this that you have done?" The woman said, "The serpent beguiled me, and I ate." [14]The LORD God said to the serpent,

"Because you have done this,
    cursed are you above all cattle,
    and above all wild animals;
upon your belly you shall go,
    and dust you shall eat
    all the days of your life.
[15]I will put enmity between you and the woman,
    and between your seed and her seed;
he shall bruise your head, *
    and you shall bruise his heel."

[16]To the woman he said,

"I will greatly multiply your pain in
    childbearing;
    in pain you shall bring forth children,
yet your desire shall be for your husband,
    and he shall rule over you."

[17]And to Adam he said,

"Because you have listened to the voice of your
    wife,
    and have eaten of the tree
of which I commanded you,
    'You shall not eat of it,'
cursed is the ground because of you;
    in toil you shall eat of it all the days of your
    life;
[18]thorns and thistles it shall bring forth to you;
    and you shall eat the plants of the field.
[19]In the sweat of your face
    you shall eat bread
till you return to the ground,
    for out of it you were taken;
you are dust,
    and to dust you shall return."

20 The man called his wife's name Eve, [f] because she was the mother of all living. [21]And the LORD God made for Adam and for his wife garments of skins, and clothed them.

22 Then the LORD God said, "Behold, the man has become like one of us, knowing good and evil; and now, lest he put forth his hand and take also of the tree of life, and eat, and live for ever"— [23]therefore the LORD God sent him forth from the garden of Eden, to till the ground from which he was taken. [24]He drove out the man; and at the east of the garden of Eden he placed the cherubim, and a flaming sword which turned every way, to guard the way to the tree of life.

Cain and Abel

4 [†] Now Adam knew Eve his wife, and she conceived and bore Cain, saying, "I have gotten [g] a man with the help of the LORD." [2]And again, she bore his brother Abel. Now Abel was a keeper of sheep, and Cain a tiller of the ground. [3]In the course of time Cain brought to the LORD an offering of the fruit of the ground, [4]and Abel brought

some of the firstlings of his flock and of their fat portions. And the LORD had regard for Abel and his offering, [5]but for Cain and his offering he had no regard. So Cain was very angry, and his countenance fell. [6]The LORD said to Cain, "Why are you angry, and why has your countenance fallen? [7]If you do well, will you not be accepted? And if you do not do well, sin is lurking at the door; its desire is for you, but you must master it."

8 Cain said to Abel his brother, "Let us go out to the field." [h] And when they were in the field, Cain rose up against his brother Abel, and killed him. [9]Then the LORD said to Cain, "Where is Abel your brother?" He said, "I do not know; am I my brother's keeper?" [10]And the LORD said, "What have you done? The voice of your brother's blood is crying to me from the ground. [11]And now you are cursed from the ground, which has opened its mouth to receive your brother's blood from your hand. [12]When you till the ground, it shall no longer yield to you its strength; you shall be a fugitive and a wanderer on the earth." [13]Cain said to the LORD, "My punishment is greater than I can bear. [14]Behold, you have driven me this day away from the ground; and from your face I shall be hidden; and I shall be a fugitive and a wanderer on the earth, and whoever finds me will slay me." [15]Then the LORD said to him, "Not so! [i] If any one slays Cain, vengeance shall be taken on him sevenfold." And the LORD put a mark on Cain, lest any who came upon him should kill him. [16]Then Cain went away from the presence of the LORD, and dwelt in the land of Nod, [j] east of Eden.

Beginnings of Civilization

17 Cain knew his wife, and she conceived and bore E'noch; and he built a city, and called the name of the city after the name of his son, Enoch. [18]To E'noch was born I'rad; and Irad was the father of Mehu'ja-el, and Mehuja-el the father of Methu'sha-el, and Methusha-el the father of

---

[f] The name in Hebrew resembles the word for *living*.
[g] Heb *qanah*, get.
[h] Sam Gk Syr Compare Vg: Heb lacks *Let us go out to the field*.
[i] Gk Syr Vg: Heb *Therefore*.
[j] That is *Wandering*.
3:13: 2 Cor 11:3.
3:14, 15: Rev 12:9; 20:2.
3:17, 18: Heb 6:8.
3:22, 24: Rev 2:7; 22:2, 14, 19.
4:4: Heb 11:4.
4:8: 1 Jn 3:12.
* 3:15, *he shall bruise your head:* i.e., the seed of the woman, that is, mankind descended from Eve, will eventually gain the victory over the powers of evil. This victory will, of course, be gained through the work of the Messiah who is *par excellence* the seed of the woman.
The Latin Vulgate has the reading *ipsa conteret,* "she shall bruise." Some Old Latin manuscripts have this reading, and it occurs also in St. Augustine, *De Genesi contra Manichaeos,* II, which is earlier than St. Jerome's translation. It could be due originally to a copyist's mistake, which was then seen to contain a genuine meaning—namely, that Mary, too, would have her share in the victory, inasmuch as she was mother of the Savior.
† 4:1: The story of Cain and Abel has the purpose of showing the effects of sin within society, the fratricide of Cain leading to the vengeance of Lamech and so to the Flood. We are, however, no longer in the first age of humanity, as can be seen from verses 14, 17, etc.

La'mech. [19]And La'mech took two wives; the name of the one was A'dah, and the name of the other Zillah. [20]A'dah bore Ja'bal; he was the father of those who dwell in tents and have cattle. [21]His brother's name was Ju'bal; he was the father of all those who play the lyre and pipe. [22]Zillah bore Tu'bal-cain; he was the forger of all instruments of bronze and iron. The sister of Tubal-cain was Na'amah.

23 La'mech said to his wives:
"A'dah and Zillah, hear my voice;
you wives of Lamech, hearken to what I say:
I have slain a man for wounding me,
a young man for striking me.
[24]If Cain is avenged sevenfold,
truly La'mech seventy-sevenfold."

25 And Adam knew his wife again, and she bore a son and called his name Seth, for she said, "God has appointed for me another child instead of Abel, for Cain slew him." [26]To Seth * also a son was born, and he called his name E'nosh. At that time men began to call upon the name of the LORD.

Adam's Descendants to Noah

5 This is the book of the generations † of Adam. When God created man, he made him in the likeness of God. [2]Male and female he created them, and he blessed them and named them Man when they were created. [3]When Adam had lived a hundred and thirty years, he became the father of a son in his own likeness, after his image, and named him Seth. [4]The days of Adam after he became the father of Seth were eight hundred years; and he had other sons and daughters. [5]Thus all the days that Adam lived were nine hundred and thirty years; and he died.

6 When Seth had lived a hundred and five years, he became the father of E'nosh. [7]Seth lived after the birth of E'nosh eight hundred and seven years, and had other sons and daughters. [8]Thus all the days of Seth were nine hundred and twelve years; and he died.

9 When E'nosh had lived ninety years, he became the father of Ke'nan. [10]E'nosh lived after the birth of Ke'nan eight hundred and fifteen years, and had other sons and daughters. [11]Thus all the days of E'nosh were nine hundred and five years; and he died.

12 When Ke'nan had lived seventy years, he became the father of Ma-hal'alel. [13]Ke'nan lived after the birth of Ma-hal'alel eight hundred and forty years, and had other sons and daughters. [14]Thus all the days of Ke'nan were nine hundred and ten years; and he died.

15 When Ma-hal'alel had lived sixty-five years, he became the father of Jar'ed. [16]Ma-hal'alel lived after the birth of Jar'ed eight hundred and thirty years, and had other sons and daughters. [17]Thus all the days of Ma-hal'alel were eight hundred and ninety-five years; and he died.

18 When Jar'ed had lived a hundred and sixty-two years he became the father of E'noch. [19]Jared lived after the birth of E'noch eight hundred years, and had other sons and daughters. [20]Thus all the days of Jar'ed were nine hundred and sixty-two years; and he died.

21 When E'noch had lived sixty-five years, he became the father of Methu'selah. [22]E'noch walked with God after the birth of Methu'selah three hundred years, and had other sons and daughters. [23]Thus all the days of E'noch were three hundred and sixty-five years. [24]E'noch walked with God; and he was not, for God took him.

25 When Methu'selah had lived a hundred and eighty-seven years, he became the father of La'mech. [26]Methu'selah lived after the birth of La'mech seven hundred and eighty-two years, and had other sons and daughters. [27]Thus all the days of Methu'selah were nine hundred and sixty-nine years; and he died.

28 When La'mech had lived a hundred and eighty-two years, he became the father of a son, [29]and called his name Noah, saying, "Out of the ground which the LORD has cursed this one shall bring us relief from our work and from the toil of our hands." [30]La'mech lived after the birth of Noah five hundred and ninety-five years, and had other sons and daughters. [31]Thus all the days of La'mech were seven hundred and seventy-seven years; and he died.

32 After Noah was five hundred years old, Noah became the father of Shem, Ham, and Ja'pheth.

The Wickedness of Mankind

6 When men began to multiply on the face of the ground, and daughters were born to them, [2]the sons of God ‡ saw that the daughters of men were fair; and they took to wife such of them as they chose. [3]Then the LORD said, "My spirit shall not abide in man for ever, for he is flesh, but his days shall be a hundred and twenty years." [4]The Neph'ilim were on the earth in those days, and also afterward, when the sons of God came in to the daughters of men, and they bore children to them. These were the mighty men that were of old, the men of renown.

5 The LORD saw that the wickedness of man

5:1: Gen 1:27.
5:24: Heb 11:5.
6:4: Num 13:33.
* 4:26: *Seth* takes the place of the murdered Abel and is the ancestor of Noah. In Ex 3:14 and 6:2–3 we find another account of the origins of Yahwism.
† 5:1, *generations:* It should be noted that these genealogies are selective and schematic, and the numbers, as often in the Old Testament, are symbolic.
‡ 6:2, *sons of God* could mean simply "divine beings," as elsewhere in the Old Testament. The writer, however, may be using an old story or myth to point out the progressive degradation of mankind before the Flood and to warn against the evil effects of intermarriage either of the descendants of Seth with the Kenites or, more probably, of the Israelites with the native populations of Canaan.

was great in the earth, and that every imagination of the thoughts of his heart was only evil continually. [6]And the LORD was sorry that he had made man on the earth, and it grieved him to his heart. [7]So the LORD said, "I will blot out man whom I have created from the face of the ground, man and beast and creeping things and birds of the air, for I am sorry that I have made them." [8]But Noah found favor in the eyes of the LORD.

9 These are the generations of Noah. Noah was a righteous man, blameless in his generation; Noah walked with God. [10]And Noah had three sons, Shem, Ham, and Ja'pheth.

Noah Makes the Ark as God Commands

11 * Now the earth was corrupt in God's sight, and the earth was filled with violence. [12]And God saw the earth, and behold, it was corrupt; for all flesh had corrupted their way upon the earth. [13]And God said to Noah, "I have determined to make an end of all flesh; for the earth is filled with violence through them; behold, I will destroy them with the earth. [14]Make yourself an ark of gopher wood; make rooms in the ark, and cover it inside and out with pitch. [15]This is how you are to make it: the length of the ark three hundred cubits, its breadth fifty cubits, and its height thirty cubits. [16]Make a roof [k] for the ark, and finish it to a cubit above; and set the door of the ark in its side; make it with lower, second, and third decks. [17]For behold, I will bring a flood of waters upon the earth, to destroy all flesh in which is the breath of life from under heaven; everything that is on the earth shall die. [18]But I will establish my covenant with you; and you shall come into the ark, you, your sons, your wife, and your sons' wives with you. [19]And of every living thing of all flesh, you shall bring two of every sort into the ark, to keep them alive with you; they shall be male and female. [20]Of the birds according to their kinds, and of the animals according to their kinds, of every creeping thing of the ground according to its kind, two of every sort shall come in to you, to keep them alive. [21]Also take with you every sort of food that is eaten, and store it up; and it shall serve as food for you and for them." [22]Noah did this; he did all that God commanded him.

The Great Flood

7 Then the LORD said to Noah, "Go into the ark, you and all your household, for I have seen that you are righteous before me in this generation. [2]Take with you seven pairs of all clean animals, the male and his mate; and a pair of the animals that are not clean, the male and his mate; [3]and seven pairs of the birds of the air also, male and female, to keep their kind alive upon the face of all the earth. [4]For in seven days I will send rain upon the earth forty days and forty nights; and every living thing that I have made I will blot out

from the face of the ground." [5]And Noah did all that the LORD had commanded him.

6 Noah was six hundred years old when the flood of waters came upon the earth. [7]And Noah and his sons and his wife and his sons' wives with him went into the ark, to escape the waters of the flood. [8]Of clean animals, and of animals that are not clean, and of birds, and of everything that creeps on the ground, [9]two and two, male and female, went into the ark with Noah, as God had commanded Noah. [10]And after seven days the waters of the flood came upon the earth.

11 In the six hundredth year of Noah's life, in the second month, on the seventeenth day of the month, on that day all the fountains of the great deep burst forth, and the windows of the heavens were opened. [12]And rain fell upon the earth forty days and forty nights. [13]On the very same day Noah and his sons, Shem and Ham and Ja'pheth, and Noah's wife and the three wives of his sons with them entered the ark, [14]they and every beast according to its kind, and all the cattle according to their kinds, and every creeping thing that creeps on the earth according to its kind, and every bird according to its kind, every bird of every sort. [15]They went into the ark with Noah, two and two of all flesh in which there was the breath of life. [16]And they that entered, male and female of all flesh, went in as God had commanded him; and the LORD shut him in.

17 The flood continued forty days upon the earth; and the waters increased, and bore up the ark, and it rose high above the earth. [18]The waters prevailed and increased greatly upon the earth; and the ark floated on the face of the waters. [19]And the waters prevailed so mightily upon the earth that all the high mountains under the whole heaven were covered; [20]the waters prevailed above the mountains, covering them fifteen cubits deep. [21]And all flesh died that moved upon the earth, birds, cattle, beasts, all swarming creatures that swarm upon the earth, and every man; [22]everything on the dry land in whose nostrils was the breath of life died. [23]He blotted out every living thing that was upon the face of the ground, man and animals and creeping things and birds of the air; they were blotted out from the earth. Only Noah was left, and those that were with him in the ark. [24]And the waters prevailed upon the earth a hundred and fifty days.

The Flood Subsides

8 But God remembered Noah and all the beasts and all the cattle that were with him in the ark. And God made a wind blow over the earth,

---

k Or *window*.
7:7: Mt 24:38; Lk 17:27.
* 6:11: Here begins the Flood narrative formed of two almost parallel accounts. This fact explains the existence of repetitions and discrepancies. It is, in places, remarkably similar to other Flood stories from the ancient Near East.

and the waters subsided; ²the fountains of the deep and the windows of the heavens were closed, the rain from the heavens was restrained, ³and the waters receded from the earth continually. At the end of a hundred and fifty days the waters had abated; ⁴and in the seventh month, on the seventeenth day of the month, the ark came to rest upon the mountains of Ar'arat. ⁵And the waters continued to abate until the tenth month; in the tenth month, on the first day of the month, the tops of the mountains were seen.

6 At the end of forty days Noah opened the window of the ark which he had made, ⁷and sent forth a raven; and it went to and fro until the waters were dried up from the earth. ⁸Then he sent forth a dove from him, to see if the waters had subsided from the face of the ground; ⁹but the dove found no place to set her foot, and she returned to him to the ark, for the waters were still on the face of the whole earth. So he put forth his hand and took her and brought her into the ark with him. ¹⁰He waited another seven days, and again he sent forth the dove out of the ark; ¹¹and the dove came back to him in the evening, and behold, in her mouth a freshly plucked olive leaf; so Noah knew that the waters had subsided from the earth. ¹²Then he waited another seven days, and sent forth the dove; and she did not return to him any more.

13 In the six hundred and first year, in the first month, the first day of the month, the waters were dried from off the earth; and Noah removed the covering of the ark, and looked, and behold, the face of the ground was dry. ¹⁴In the second month, on the twenty-seventh day of the month, the earth was dry. ¹⁵Then God said to Noah, ¹⁶"Go forth from the ark, you and your wife, and your sons and your sons' wives with you. ¹⁷Bring forth with you every living thing that is with you of all flesh—birds and animals and every creeping thing that creeps on the earth—that they may breed abundantly upon the earth, and be fruitful and multiply upon the earth." ¹⁸So Noah went forth, and his sons and his wife and his sons' wives with him. ¹⁹And every beast, every creeping thing, and every bird, everything that moves upon the earth, went forth by families out of the ark.

God's Promise to Noah

20 Then Noah built an altar to the LORD, and took of every clean animal and of every clean bird, and offered burnt offerings on the altar. ²¹And when the LORD smelled the pleasing odor, the LORD said in his heart, "I will never again curse the ground because of man, for the imagination of man's heart is evil from his youth; neither will I ever again destroy every living creature as I have done. ²²While the earth remains, seedtime and harvest, cold and heat, summer and winter, day and night, shall not cease."

The Covenant with Noah

9 And God blessed Noah and his sons, and said to them, "Be fruitful and multiply, and fill the earth. ²The fear of you and the dread of you shall be upon every beast of the earth, and upon every bird of the air, upon everything that creeps on the ground and all the fish of the sea; into your hand they are delivered. ³Every moving thing that lives shall be food for you; and as I gave you the green plants, I give you everything. ⁴Only you shall not eat flesh with its life, that is, its blood. ⁵For your lifeblood I will surely require a reckoning; of every beast I will require it and of man; of every man's brother I will require the life of man. ⁶Whoever sheds the blood of man, by man shall his blood be shed; for God made man in his own image. ⁷And you, be fruitful and multiply, bring forth abundantly on the earth and multiply in it."

8 Then God said to Noah and to his sons with him, ⁹ "Behold, I establish my covenant with you and your descendants after you, ¹⁰and with every living creature that is with you, the birds, the cattle, and every beast of the earth with you, as many as came out of the ark.¹ ¹¹I establish my covenant with you, that never again shall all flesh be cut off by the waters of a flood, and never again shall there be a flood to destroy the earth." ¹²And God said, "This is the sign of the covenant which I make between me and you and every living creature that is with you, for all future generations: ¹³I set my bow in the cloud, and it shall be a sign of the covenant between me and the earth. ¹⁴When I bring clouds over the earth and the bow is seen in the clouds, ¹⁵I will remember my covenant which is between me and you and every living creature of all flesh; and the waters shall never again become a flood to destroy all flesh. ¹⁶When the bow is in the clouds, I will look upon it and remember the everlasting covenant between God and every living creature of all flesh that is upon the earth." ¹⁷God said to Noah, "This is the sign of the covenant which I have established between me and all flesh that is upon the earth."

Noah and His Sons

18 The sons of Noah who went forth from the ark were Shem, Ham, and Ja'pheth. Ham was the father of Canaan. ¹⁹These three were the sons of Noah; and from these the whole earth was peopled.

20 Noah was the first tiller of the soil. He planted a vineyard; ²¹and he drank of the wine, and became drunk, and lay uncovered in his tent. ²²And Ham, the father of Canaan, saw the nakedness of his father, and told his two brothers outside. ²³Then Shem and Ja'pheth took a garment,

---

¹ Gk: Heb repeats *every beast of the earth.*
9:4: Lev 7:26, 27; 17:10–14; Deut 12:16, 23.

6

laid it upon both their shoulders, and walked backward and covered the nakedness of their father; their faces were turned away, and they did not see their father's nakedness. [24]When Noah awoke from his wine and knew what his youngest son had done to him, [25]he said,

"Cursed be Canaan;
   a slave of slaves shall he be to his brothers."
[26]He also said,

"Blessed by the Lord my God be Shem;[m]
   and let Canaan be his slave.
[27]God enlarge Ja'pheth,
   and let him dwell in the tents of Shem;
   and let Canaan be his slave."

28 After the flood Noah lived three hundred and fifty years. [29]All the days of Noah were nine hundred and fifty years; and he died.

Nations Descended from Noah

10 These are the generations[*] of the sons of Noah, Shem, Ham, and Ja'pheth; sons were born to them after the flood.

2 The sons of Ja'pheth: Gomer, Ma'gog, Ma'dai, Ja'van, Tu'bal, Me'shech, and Ti'ras. [3]The sons of Gomer: Ash'kenaz, Ri'phath, and Togar'mah. [4]The sons of Ja'van: Eli'shah, Tar'shish, Kittim, and Do'danim. [5]From these the coastland peoples spread. These are the sons of Ja'pheth[n] in their lands, each with his own language, by their families, in their nations.

6 The sons of Ham: Cush, Egypt, Put, and Canaan. [7]The sons of Cush: Seba, Hav'ilah, Sabtah, Ra'amah, and Sab'teca. The sons of Raamah: Sheba and De'dan. [8]Cush became the father of Nimrod; he was the first on earth to be a mighty man. [9]He was a mighty hunter before the Lord; therefore it is said, "Like Nimrod a mighty hunter before the Lord." [10]The beginning of his kingdom was Ba'bel, E'rech, and Accad, all of them in the land of Shi'nar. [11]From that land he went into Assyria, and built Nin'eveh, Reho'both-Ir, Ca'lah, and [12]Re'sen between Nin'eveh and Ca'lah; that is the great city. [13]Egypt became the father of Lu'dim, An'amim, Leha'bim, Naph'tuhim, [14]Pathru'sim, Caslu'him (whence came the Philis'tines), and Caph'torim.

15 Canaan became the father of Si'don his firstborn, and Heth, [16]and the Jeb'usites, the Am'orites, the Gir'gashites, [17]the Hi'vites, the Arkites, the Si'nites, [18]the Ar'vadites, the Zem'arites, and the Ha'mathites. Afterward the families of the Canaanites spread abroad. [19]And the territory of the Canaanites extended from Si'don, in the direction of Ge'rar, as far as Gaza, and in the direction of Sodom, Gomor'rah, Admah, and Zeboi'im, as far as La'sha. [20]These are the sons of Ham, by their families, their languages, their lands, and their nations.

21 To Shem also, the father of all the children of E'ber, the elder brother of Ja'pheth, children were born. [22]The sons of Shem: E'lam, Asshur, Arpach'shad, Lud, and Ar'am. [23]The sons of Ar'am: Uz, Hul, Ge'ther, and Mash. [24]Arpach'shad became the father of She'lah; and Shelah became the father of E'ber. [25]To E'ber were born two sons: the name of the one was Pe'leg,[o] for in his days the earth was divided, and his brother's name was Joktan. [26]Joktan became the father of Almo'dad, She'leph, Haz"arma'veth, Je'rah, [27]Hador'am, U'zal, Diklah, [28]O'bal, Abim'a-el, Sheba, [29]O'phir, Hav'ilah, and Jo'bab; all these were the sons of Joktan. [30]The territory in which they lived extended from Me'sha in the direction of Se'phar to the hill country of the east. [31]These are the sons of Shem, by their families, their languages, their lands, and their nations.

32 These are the families of the sons of Noah, according to their genealogies, in their nations; and from these the nations spread abroad on the earth after the flood.

The Tower of Babel

11 [†]Now the whole earth had one language and few words. [2]And as men migrated from the east, they found a plain in the land of Shinar and settled there. [3]And they said to one another, "Come, let us make bricks, and burn them thoroughly." And they had brick for stone, and bitumen for mortar. [4]Then they said, "Come, let us build ourselves a city, and a tower with its top in the heavens, and let us make a name for ourselves, lest we be scattered abroad upon the face of the whole earth." [5]And the Lord came down to see the city and the tower, which the sons of men had built. [6]And the Lord said, "Behold, they are one people, and they have all one language; and this is only the beginning of what they will do; and nothing that they propose to do will now be impossible for them. [7]Come, let us go down, and there confuse their language, that they may not understand one another's speech." [8]So the Lord scattered them abroad from there over the face of all the earth, and they left off building the city. [9]Therefore its name was called Ba'bel, because there the Lord confused[p] the language of all the earth; and from there the Lord scattered them abroad over the face of all the earth.

Descendants of Shem

10 These are the descendants of Shem. When Shem was a hundred years old, he became the

---

[m] Or *Blessed be the Lord, the God of Shem.*
[n] Compare verses 20, 31. Heb lacks *These are the sons of Japheth.*
[o] That is *Division.*
[p] Compare Heb *balal*, confuse.
[*] 10:1, *generations:* This "table of the nations" makes use of old material to show how all the nations of the world as then known have descended from the generation that survived the Flood. It was from this world that Abraham was called to be the father of the chosen people.
[†] 11:1–9: The tower of Babel (= Babylon) is taken as a symbol of political power, empire-building, and the civilization that opposes God's plan. The tower was probably a ziggurat, i.e., Babylonian temple.

7

father of Arpach'shad two years after the flood; [11]and Shem lived after the birth of Arpach'shad five hundred years, and had other sons and daughters.

12 When Arpach'shad had lived thirty-five years, he became the father of She'lah; [13]and Arpach'shad lived after the birth of She'lah four hundred and three years, and had other sons and daughters.

14 When She'lah had lived thirty years, he became the father of E'ber; [15]and She'lah lived after the birth of E'ber four hundred and three years, and had other sons and daughters.

16 When E'ber had lived thirty-four years, he became the father of Pe'leg; [17]and E'ber lived after the birth of Pe'leg four hundred and thirty years, and had other sons and daughters.

18 When Pe'leg had lived thirty years, he became the father of Re'u; [19]and Pe'leg lived after the birth of Re'u two hundred and nine years, and had other sons and daughters.

20 When Re'u had lived thirty-two years, he became the father of Se'rug; [21]and Re'u lived after the birth of Se'rug two hundred and seven years, and had other sons and daughters.

22 When Se'rug had lived thirty years, he became the father of Na'hor; [23]and Se'rug lived after the birth of Na'hor two hundred years, and had other sons and daughters.

24 When Na'hor had lived twenty-nine years, he became the father of Te'rah; [25]and Na'hor lived after the birth of Te'rah a hundred and nineteen years, and had other sons and daughters.

26 When Te'rah had lived seventy years, he became the father of Abram, Na'hor, and Haran.

Descendants of Terah

27 Now these are the descendants of Te'rah. Terah was the father of Abram, Na'hor, and Haran; and Haran was the father of Lot. [28]Haran died before his father Te'rah in the land of his birth, in Ur of the Chalde'ans. [29]And Abram and Na'hor took wives; the name of Abram's wife was Sar'ai, and the name of Nahor's wife, Milcah, the daughter of Haran the father of Milcah and Is'cah; [30]Now Sar'ai was barren; she had no child.

31 Te'rah took Abram his son and Lot the son of Haran, his grandson, and Sar'ai his daughter-in-law, his son Abram's wife, and they went forth together from Ur of the Chalde'ans to go into the land of Canaan; but when they came to Haran, they settled there. [32]The days of Te'rah were two hundred and five years; and Terah died in Haran.

The Call of Abram

12 * Now the Lord said to Abram, "Go from your country and your kindred and your father's house to the land that I will show you. [2]And I will make of you a great nation, and I will bless you, and make your name great, so that you will be a blessing. [3]I will bless those who bless

you, and him who curses you I will curse; and by you all the families of the earth shall bless themselves." [q]

4 So Abram went, as the Lord had told him; and Lot went with him. Abram was seventy-five years old when he departed from Haran. [5]And Abram took Sar'ai his wife, and Lot his brother's son, and all their possessions which they had gathered, and the persons that they had gotten in Haran; and they set forth to go to the land of Canaan. When they had come to the land of Canaan, [6]Abram passed through the land to the place at She'chem, to the Oak [r] of Mo'reh. At that time the Canaanites were in the land. [7]Then the Lord appeared to Abram, and said, "To your descendants I will give this land." So he built there an altar to the Lord, who had appeared to him. [8]Thence he removed to the mountain on the east of Bethel, and pitched his tent, with Bethel on the west and Ai on the east; and there he built an altar to the Lord and called on the name of the Lord. [9]And Abram journeyed on, still going toward the Neg'eb.

Abram and Sarai in Egypt

10 Now there was a famine in the land. So Abram went down to Egypt to sojourn there, for the famine was severe in the land. [11]When he was about to enter Egypt, he said to Sar'ai his wife, "I know that you are a woman beautiful to behold; [12]and when the Egyptians see you, they will say, 'This is his wife'; then they will kill me, but they will let you live. [13]Say you are my sister, that it may go well with me because of you, and that my life may be spared on your account." [14]When Abram entered Egypt the Egyptians saw that the woman was very beautiful. [15]And when the princes of Pharaoh saw her, they praised her to Pharaoh. And the woman was taken into Pharaoh's house. [16]And for her sake he dealt well with Abram; and he had sheep, oxen, he-donkeys, menservants, maidservants, she-donkeys, and camels.

17 But the Lord afflicted Pharaoh and his house with great plagues because of Sar'ai, Abram's wife. [18]So Pharaoh called Abram, and said, "What is this you have done to me? Why did you not tell me that she was your wife? [19]Why did you say, 'She is my sister,' so that I took her for my wife? Now then, here is your wife, take her,

---

[q] Or in you all the families of the earth shall be blessed.
[r] Or Terebinth.
12:1: Acts 7:3; Heb 11:8.
12:2: Gen 15:5; 17:4, 5; 18:18; 22:17; 28:14; 32:12; 35:11; 46:3.
12:3: Gen 18:18; 22:17, 18; 26:4; 28:14; Gal 3:8.
12:7: Gen 13:15; 15:18; 17:8; 24:7; 26:3; 28:4, 13; 35:12; 48:4; Acts 7:5; Gal 3:16.
12:10–20: Gen 20:1–18; 26:7–11.
13:15: Acts 7:5; Gal 3:16.
* 12:1–3: With Abraham's call, sacred history in the strict sense begins. The promise theme runs through the whole patriarchal history, e.g., 18:18; 28:14.

and be gone." [20]And Pharaoh gave men orders concerning him; and they set him on the way, with his wife and all that he had.

Abram and Lot Separate

13 So Abram went up from Egypt, he and his wife, and all that he had, and Lot with him, into the Neg'eb.

2 Now Abram was very rich in cattle, in silver, and in gold. [3]And he journeyed on from the Neg'eb as far as Bethel, to the place where his tent had been at the beginning, between Bethel and Ai, [4]to the place where he had made an altar at the first; and there Abram called on the name of the LORD. [5]And Lot, who went with Abram, also had flocks and herds and tents, [6]so that the land could not support both of them dwelling together; for their possessions were so great that they could not dwell together, [7]and there was strife between the herdsmen of Abram's cattle and the herdsmen of Lot's cattle. At that time the Canaanites and the Per'izzites dwelt in the land.

8 Then Abram said to Lot, "Let there be no strife between you and me, and between your herdsmen and my herdsmen; for we are kinsmen. [9]Is not the whole land before you? Separate yourself from me. If you take the left hand, then I will go to the right; or if you take the right hand, then I will go to the left." [10]And Lot lifted up his eyes, and saw that the Jordan valley was well watered everywhere like the garden of the LORD, like the land of Egypt, in the direction of Zoar; this was before the LORD destroyed Sodom and Gomor'rah. [11]So Lot chose for himself all the Jordan valley, and Lot journeyed east; thus they separated from each other. [12]Abram dwelt in the land of Canaan, while Lot dwelt among the cities of the valley and moved his tent as far as Sodom. [13]Now the men of Sodom were wicked, great sinners against the LORD.

14 The LORD said to Abram, after Lot had separated from him, "Lift up your eyes, and look from the place where you are, northward and southward and eastward and westward; [15]for all the land which you see I will give to you and to your descendants for ever. [16]I will make your descendants as the dust of the earth; so that if one can count the dust of the earth, your descendants also can be counted. [17]Arise, walk through the length and the breadth of the land, for I will give it to you." [18]So Abram moved his tent, and came and dwelt by the Oaks s of Mamre, which are at He'bron; and there he built an altar to the LORD.

Lot's Captivity and Rescue

14 In the days of Am'raphel king of Shi'nar, Ar'ioch king of Ella'sar, Ched"-or-lao'mer king of E'lam, and Ti'dal king of Goi'im, [2]these kings made war with Be'ra king of Sodom, Birsha king of Gomor'rah, Shi'nab king of Admah, She-me'ber king of Zeboi'im, and the king of Be'la

(that is, Zoar). [3]And all these joined forces in the Valley of Siddim (that is, the Salt Sea). [4]Twelve years they had served Ched"-or-lao'mer, but in the thirteenth year they rebelled. [5]In the fourteenth year Ched"-or-lao'mer and the kings who were with him came and subdued the Reph'aim in Ash'teroth-karna'im, the Zu'zim in Ham, the E'mim in Sha'veh-kir"iatha'im, [6]and the Horites in their Mount Se'ir as far as El-par'an on the border of the wilderness; [7]then they turned back and came to Enmish'pat (that is, Ka'desh), and subdued all the country of the Amal'ekites, and also the Am'orites who dwelt in Haz'azon-ta'mar. [8]Then the king of Sodom, the king of Gomor'rah, the king of Admah, the king of Zeboi'im, and the king of Be'la (that is, Zoar) went out, and they joined battle in the Valley of Siddim [9]with Ched"-or-lao'mer king of E'lam, Ti'dal king of Goi'im, Am'raphel king of Shi'nar, and Ar'ioch king of Ella'sar, four kings against five. [10]Now the Valley of Siddim was full of bitumen pits; and as the kings of Sodom and Gomor'rah fled, some fell into them, and the rest fled to the mountain. [11]So the enemy took all the goods of Sodom and Gomor'rah, and all their provisions, and went their way; [12]they also took Lot, the son of Abram's brother, who dwelt in Sodom, and his goods, and departed.

13 Then one who had escaped came, and told Abram the Hebrew, who was living by the Oaks s of Mamre the Am'orite, brother of Eshcol and of A'ner; these were allies of Abram. [14]When Abram heard that his kinsman had been taken captive, he led forth his trained men, born in his house, three hundred and eighteen of them, and went in pursuit as far as Dan. [15]And he divided his forces against them by night, he and his servants, and routed them and pursued them to Ho'bah, north of Damascus. [16]Then he brought back all the goods, and also brought back his kinsman Lot with his goods, and the women and the people.

Melchizedek Blesses Abram

17 After his return from the defeat of Ched"-or-lao'mer and the kings who were with him, the king of Sodom went out to meet him at the Valley of Sha'veh (that is, the King's Valley). [18]And Melchiz'edek * king of Salem brought out bread and wine; he was priest of God Most High. [19]And he blessed him and said,

"Blessed be Abram by God Most High,
      maker of heaven and earth;
[20]and blessed be God Most High,
      who has delivered your enemies into your
            hand!"

---

s Or *Terebinths.*
14:17-20: Heb 7:1-10.
* 14:18, *Melchizedek* was later taken as a Messianic figure (Ps 110:4) and interpreted in the New Testament as foreshadowing Christ, whose priesthood (including the offering of bread and wine) exceeds that of the Old Testament; cf. Heb 7:1-7.

And Abram gave him a tenth of everything. [21]And the king of Sodom said to Abram, "Give me the persons, but take the goods for yourself." [22]But Abram said to the king of Sodom, "I have sworn to the LORD God Most High, maker of heaven and earth, [23]that I would not take a thread or a sandal-thong or anything that is yours, lest you should say, 'I have made Abram rich.' [24]I will take nothing but what the young men have eaten, and the share of the men who went with me; let A'ner, Eshcol, and Mamre take their share."

God's Covenant with Abram

15 After these things the word of the LORD came to Abram in a vision, "Fear not, Abram, I am your shield; your reward shall be very great." * [2]But Abram said, "O Lord GOD, what will you give me, for I continue childless, and the heir of my house is Elie'zer of Damascus?" [3]And Abram said, "Behold, you have given me no offspring; and a slave born in my house will be my heir." [4]And behold, the word of the LORD came to him, "This man shall not be your heir; your own son shall be your heir." [5]And he brought him outside and said, "Look toward heaven, and number the stars, if you are able to number them." Then he said to him, "So shall your descendants be." [6]And he believed the LORD; and he reckoned it to him as righteousness.

7 And he said to him, "I am the LORD who brought you from Ur of the Chalde'ans, to give you this land to possess." [8]But he said, "O Lord GOD, how am I to know that I shall possess it?" [9]He said to him, "Bring me a heifer three years old, a she-goat three years old, a ram three years old, a turtledove, and a young pigeon." [10]And he brought him all these, cut them in two, and laid each half over against the other; but he did not cut the birds in two. [11]And when birds of prey came down upon the carcasses, Abram drove them away.

12 As the sun was going down, a deep sleep fell on Abram; and behold, a dread and great darkness fell upon him. [13]Then the LORD said to Abram, "Know of a surety that your descendants will be sojourners in a land that is not theirs, and will be slaves there, and they will be oppressed for four hundred years; [14]but I will bring judgment on the nation which they serve, and afterward they shall come out with great possessions. [15]As for yourself, you shall go to your fathers in peace; you shall be buried in a good old age. [16]And they shall come back here in the fourth generation; for the iniquity of the Am'orites is not yet complete."

17 When the sun had gone down and it was dark, behold, a smoking fire pot and a flaming torch passed between these pieces. [18]On that day the LORD made a covenant with Abram, saying, "To your descendants I give this land, from the river of Egypt to the great river, the river Euphra'-tes, [19]the land of the Kenites, the Ken'izzites, the Kad'monites, [20]the Hittites, the Per'izzites, the Reph'aim, [21]the Am'orites, the Canaanites, the Gir'gashites and the Jeb'usites."

The Birth of Ishmael

16 Now Sar'ai, Abram's wife, bore him no children. She had an Egyptian maid whose name was Hagar; [2]and Sar'ai said to Abram, "Behold now, the LORD has prevented me from bearing children; go in to my maid; it may be that I shall obtain children by her." And Abram listened to the voice of Sar'ai. [3]So, after Abram had dwelt ten years in the land of Canaan, Sar'ai, Abram's wife, took Hagar the Egyptian, her maid, and gave her to Abram her husband as a wife. [4]And he went in to Hagar, and she conceived; † and when she saw that she had conceived, she looked with contempt on her mistress. [5]And Sar'ai said to Abram, "May the wrong done to me be on you! I gave my maid to your embrace, and when she saw that she had conceived, she looked on me with contempt. May the LORD judge between you and me!" [6]But Abram said to Sar'ai, "Behold, your maid is in your power; do to her as you please." Then Sarai dealt harshly with her, and she fled from her.

7 The angel of the LORD found her by a spring of water in the wilderness, the spring on the way to Shur. [8]And he said, "Hagar, maid of Sar'ai, where have you come from and where are you going?" She said, "I am fleeing from my mistress Sarai." [9]The angel of the LORD said to her, "Return to your mistress, and submit to her." [10]The angel of the LORD also said to her, "I will so greatly multiply your descendants that they cannot be numbered for multitude." [11]And the angel of the LORD said to her, "Behold, you are with child, and shall bear a son; you shall call his name Ish'mael; [t] because the LORD has given heed to your affliction. [12]He shall be a wild donkey of a man, his hand against every man and every man's hand against him; and he shall dwell over against all his kinsmen." [13]So she called the name of the LORD who spoke to her, "You are a God of seeing"; for she said, "Have I really seen God and remained alive after seeing him?" [u] [14]Therefore the well was called Be'er-la'hai-roi; [v] it lies between Ka'desh and Be'red.

---

[t] That is *God hears*.
[u] Cn: Heb *have I even here seen after him who sees me?*
[v] That is *the well of one who sees and lives*.
15:4: Gen 17:16, 21; 18:10; 21:2.
15:5: Rom 4:18; Heb 11:12.
15:6: Rom 4:3, 9, 22, 23; Gal 3:6.
15:13, 14: Acts 7:6, 7.
15:18: Gen 17:2, 7, 9–14, 21.
* 15:1: The Vulgate has "I am thy protector, and thy reward exceeding great." There was, however, at this stage, no idea of a reward in a future life.
† 16:1–4: The practice suggested by Sarai, involving as it did polygamy, was in accord with moral standards at that time and is referred to in legal codes of the period.

15 And Hagar bore Abram a son; and Abram called the name of his son, whom Hagar bore, Ish'mael. [16]Abram was eighty-six years old when Hagar bore Ish'mael to Abram.

The Sign of the Covenant

17 When Abram was ninety-nine years old the LORD appeared to Abram, and said to him, "I am God Almighty;[w] walk before me, and be blameless. [2]And I will make my covenant between me and you, and will multiply you exceedingly." [3]Then Abram fell on his face; and God said to him, [4]"Behold, my covenant is with you, and you shall be the father of a multitude of nations. [5]No longer shall your name be Abram,[x] but your name shall be Abraham;[y] for I have made you the father of a multitude of nations. [6]I will make you exceedingly fruitful; and I will make nations of you, and kings shall come forth from you. [7]And I will establish my covenant between me and you and your descendants after you throughout their generations for an everlasting covenant, to be God to you and to your descendants after you. [8]And I will give to you, and to your descendants after you, the land of your sojournings, all the land of Canaan, for an everlasting possession; and I will be their God."

9 And God said to Abraham, "As for you, you shall keep my covenant, you and your descendants after you throughout their generations. [10]This is my covenant, which you shall keep, between me and you and your descendants after you: Every male among you shall be circumcised. [11]You shall be circumcised in the flesh of your foreskins, and it shall be a sign of the covenant between me and you. [12]He that is eight days old among you shall be circumcised; every male throughout your generations, whether born in your house, or bought with your money from any foreigner who is not of your offspring, [13]both he that is born in your house and he that is bought with your money, shall be circumcised. So shall my covenant be in your flesh an everlasting covenant. [14]Any uncircumcised male who is not circumcised in the flesh of his foreskin shall be cut off from his people; he has broken my covenant."

15 And God said to Abraham, "As for Sar'ai your wife, you shall not call her name Sarai, but Sarah shall be her name. [16]I will bless her, and moreover I will give you a son by her; I will bless her, and she shall be a mother of nations; kings of peoples shall come from her." [17]Then Abraham fell on his face and laughed, and said to himself, "Shall a child be born to a man who is a hundred years old? Shall Sarah, who is ninety years old, bear a child?" [18]And Abraham said to God, "O that Ish'mael might live in your sight!" [19]God said, "No, but Sarah your wife shall bear you a son, and you shall call his name Isaac.[z] I will establish my covenant with him as an everlasting covenant for his descendants after him. [20]As for Ish'mael, I have heard you; behold, I will bless him and make him fruitful and multiply him exceedingly; he shall be the father of twelve princes, and I will make him a great nation. [21]But I will establish my covenant with Isaac, whom Sarah shall bear to you at this season next year."

22 When he had finished talking with him, God went up from Abraham. [23]Then Abraham took Ish'mael his son and all the slaves born in his house or bought with his money, every male among the men of Abraham's house, and he circumcised the flesh of their foreskins that very day, as God had said to him. [24]Abraham was ninety-nine years old when he was circumcised in the flesh of his foreskin. [25]And Ish'mael his son was thirteen years old when he was circumcised in the flesh of his foreskin. [26]That very day Abraham and his son Ish'mael were circumcised; [27]and all the men of his house, those born in the house and those bought with money from a foreigner, were circumcised with him.

A Son Promised to Abraham and Sarah

18 And the LORD appeared to him by the Oaks [a] of Mamre, as he sat at the door of his tent in the heat of the day. [2]He lifted up his eyes and looked, and behold, three men stood in front of him. When he saw them, he ran from the tent door to meet them, and bowed himself to the earth, [3]and said, "My lord, if I have found favor in your sight, do not pass by your servant. [4]Let a little water be brought, and wash your feet, and rest yourselves under the tree, [5]while I fetch a morsel of bread, that you may refresh yourselves, and after that you may pass on—since you have come to your servant." So they said, "Do as you have said." [6]And Abraham hastened into the tent to Sarah, and said, "Make ready quickly three measures [b] of fine meal, knead it, and make cakes." [7]And Abraham ran to the herd, and took a calf, tender and good, and gave it to the servant, who hastened to prepare it. [8]Then he took curds, and milk, and the calf which he had prepared, and set it before them; and he stood by them under the tree while they ate.

9 They said to him, "Where is Sarah your wife?" And he said, "She is in the tent." [10]The LORD said, "I will surely return to you in the spring, and Sarah your wife shall have a son." And Sarah was

---

[w] Heb *El Shaddai*.
[x] That is *exalted father*.
[y] Here taken to mean *father of a multitude*.
[z] That is *he laughs*.
[a] Or *Terebinths*.
[b] Heb *seahs*.
17:5: Rom 4:17.
17:7: Lk 1:55; Gal 3:16.
17:8: Acts 7:5.
17:10: Acts 7:8.
17:11–14: Gen 17:24; 21:4.
18:10: Rom 9:9.

listening at the tent door behind him. [11]Now Abraham and Sarah were old, advanced in age; it had ceased to be with Sarah after the manner of women. [12]So Sarah laughed to herself, saying, "After I have grown old, and my husband is old, shall I have pleasure?" [13]The LORD said to Abraham, "Why did Sarah laugh, and say, 'Shall I indeed bear a child, now that I am old?' [14]Is anything too hard [c] for the LORD? At the appointed time I will return to you, in the spring, and Sarah shall have a son." [15]But Sarah denied, saying, "I did not laugh"; for she was afraid. He said, "No, but you did laugh."

Abraham Intercedes for Sodom

16 Then the men set out from there, and they looked toward Sodom; and Abraham went with them to set them on their way. [17]The LORD said, "Shall I hide from Abraham what I am about to do, [18]seeing that Abraham shall become a great and mighty nation, and all the nations of the earth shall bless themselves by him? [d] [19]No, for I have chosen [e] him, that he may charge his children and his household after him to keep the way of the LORD by doing righteousness and justice; so that the LORD may bring to Abraham what he has promised him." [20]Then the LORD said, "Because the outcry against Sodom and Gomor'rah is great and their sin is very grave, [21]I will go down to see whether they have done altogether according to the outcry which has come to me; and if not, I will know."

22 So the men turned from there, and went toward Sodom; but Abraham still stood before the LORD. [23]Then Abraham drew near, and said, "Will you indeed destroy the righteous with the wicked? [24]Suppose there are fifty righteous within the city; will you then destroy the place and not spare it for the fifty righteous who are in it? [25]Far be it from you to do such a thing, to slay the righteous with the wicked, so that the righteous fare as the wicked! Far be that from you! Shall not the Judge of all the earth do right?" [26]And the LORD said, "If I find at Sodom fifty righteous in the city, I will spare the whole place for their sake." [27]Abraham answered, "Behold, I have taken upon myself to speak to the Lord, I who am but dust and ashes. [28]Suppose five of the fifty righteous are lacking? Will you destroy the whole city for lack of five?" And he said, "I will not destroy it if I find forty-five there." [29]Again he spoke to him, and said, "Suppose forty are found there." He answered, "For the sake of forty I will not do it." [30]Then he said, "Oh let not the Lord be angry, and I will speak. Suppose thirty are found there." He answered, "I will not do it, if I find thirty there." [31]He said, "Behold, I have taken upon myself to speak to the Lord. Suppose twenty are found there." He answered, "For the sake of twenty I will not destroy it." [32]Then he said, "Oh let not the Lord be angry, and I will speak again but this

once. Suppose ten are found there." He answered, "For the sake of ten I will not destroy it." [33]And the LORD went his way, when he had finished speaking to Abraham; and Abraham returned to his place.

The Immorality of Sodom

19 [*] The two angels came to Sodom in the evening; and Lot was sitting in the gate of Sodom. When Lot saw them, he rose to meet them, and bowed himself with his face to the earth, [2]and said, "My lords, turn aside, I pray you, to your servant's house and spend the night, and wash your feet; then you may rise up early and go on your way." They said, "No; we will spend the night in the street." [3]But he urged them strongly; so they turned aside to him and entered his house; and he made them a feast, and baked unleavened bread, and they ate. [4]But before they lay down, the men of the city, the men of Sodom, both young and old, all the people to the last man, surrounded the house; [5]and they called to Lot, "Where are the men who came to you tonight? Bring them out to us, that we may know them." [6]Lot went out of the door to the men, shut the door after him, [7]and said, "I beg you, my brothers, do not act so wickedly. [8]Behold, I have two daughters who have not known man; let me bring them out to you, and do to them as you please; only do nothing to these men, for they have come under the shelter of my roof." [9]But they said, "Stand back!" And they said, "This fellow came to sojourn, and he would play the judge! Now we will deal worse with you than with them." Then they pressed hard against the man Lot, and drew near to break the door. [10]But the men put forth their hands and brought Lot into the house to them, and shut the door. [11]And they struck with blindness the men who were at the door of the house, both small and great, so that they wearied themselves groping for the door.

Sodom and Gomorrah Destroyed

12 Then the men said to Lot, "Have you any one else here? Sons-in-law, sons, daughters, or any one you have in the city, bring them out of the place; [13]for we are about to destroy this place, because the outcry against its people has become great before the LORD, and the LORD has sent us to destroy it." [14]So Lot went out and said to his sons-in-law, who were to marry his daughters, "Up, get out of this place; for the LORD is about to destroy the city." But he seemed to his sons-in-law to be jesting.

---

[c] Or *wonderful.*
[d] Or *in him all the nations of the earth shall be blessed.*
[e] Heb *known.*
18:12: 1 Pet 3:6.
18:14: Mt 19:26; Mk 10:27; Lk 1:37; Rom 9:9.
18:18: Gen 12:3; Acts 3:25; Gal 3:8.
[*] 19:1: The Sodom episode, so often referred to in the Old and New Testaments, expresses the abhorrence of the true Israelite for unnatural sin and the violation of the sacred duty of hospitality, cf. Judg 19:11-30.

15 When morning dawned, the angels urged Lot, saying, "Arise, take your wife and your two daughters who are here, lest you be consumed in the punishment of the city." ¹⁶But he lingered; so the men seized him and his wife and his two daughters by the hand, the LORD being merciful to him, and they brought him forth and set him outside the city. ¹⁷And when they had brought them forth, they ᶠ said, "Flee for your life; do not look back or stop anywhere in the valley; flee to the hills, lest you be consumed." ¹⁸And Lot said to them, "Oh, no, my lords; ¹⁹behold, your servant has found favor in your sight, and you have shown me great kindness in saving my life; but I cannot flee to the hills, lest the disaster overtake me, and I die. ²⁰Behold, yonder city is near enough to flee to, and it is a little one. Let me escape there—is it not a little one? —and my life will be saved!" ²¹He said to him, "Behold, I grant you this favor also, that I will not overthrow the city of which you have spoken. ²²Make haste, escape there; for I can do nothing till you arrive there." Therefore the name of the city was called Zoar. ᵍ ²³The sun had risen on the earth when Lot came to Zoar.

24 Then the LORD rained on Sodom and Gomor'rah brimstone and fire from the LORD out of heaven; ²⁵and he overthrew those cities, and all the valley, and all the inhabitants of the cities, and what grew on the ground. ²⁶But Lot's wife behind him looked back, and she became a pillar of salt. ²⁷And Abraham went early in the morning to the place where he had stood before the LORD; ²⁸and he looked down toward Sodom and Gomor'rah and toward all the land of the valley, and beheld, and behold, the smoke of the land went up like the smoke of a furnace.

29 So it was that, when God destroyed the cities of the valley, God remembered Abraham, and sent Lot out of the midst of the overthrow, when he overthrew the cities in which Lot dwelt.

The Shameful Origin of the Moabites and Ammonites

30 Now Lot went up out of Zoar, and dwelt in the hills with his two daughters, for he was afraid to dwell in Zoar; so he dwelt in a cave with his two daughters. ³¹And the first-born said to the younger, "Our father is old, and there is not a man on earth to come in to us after the manner of all the earth. ³²Come, let us make our father drink wine, and we will lie with him, that we may preserve offspring through our father." ³³So they made their father drink wine that night; and the first-born went in, and lay with her father; he did not know when she lay down or when she arose. ³⁴And on the next day, the first-born said to the younger, "Behold, I lay last night with my father; let us make him drink wine tonight also; then you go in and lie with him, that we may preserve offspring through our father." ³⁵So they made their

father drink wine that night also; and the younger arose, and lay with him; and he did not know when she lay down or when she arose. ³⁶Thus both the daughters of Lot were with child by their father. ³⁷The first-born bore a son, and called his name Moab; he is the father of the Moabites to this day. ³⁸The younger also bore a son, and called his name Ben-am'mi; he is the father of the Am'monites to this day.

Abraham and Sarah at Gerar

20 From there Abraham journeyed toward the territory of the Neg'eb, and dwelt between Ka'desh and Shur; and he sojourned in Ge'rar. ²And Abraham said of Sarah his wife, "She is my sister." And Abim'elech king of Ge'rar sent and took Sarah. ³But God came to Abim'elech in a dream by night, and said to him, "Behold, you are a dead man, because of the woman whom you have taken; for she is a man's wife." ⁴Now Abim'elech had not approached her; so he said, "Lord, will you slay an innocent people? ⁵Did he not himself say to me, 'She is my sister'? And she herself said, 'He is my brother.' In the integrity of my heart and the innocence of my hands I have done this." ⁶Then God said to him in the dream, "Yes, I know that you have done this in the integrity of your heart, and it was I who kept you from sinning against me; therefore I did not let you touch her. ⁷Now then restore the man's wife; for he is a prophet, and he will pray for you, and you shall live. But if you do not restore her, know that you shall surely die, you, and all that are yours."

8 So Abim'elech rose early in the morning, and called all his servants, and told them all these things; and the men were very much afraid. ⁹Then Abim'elech called Abraham, and said to him, "What have you done to us? And how have I sinned against you, that you have brought on me and my kingdom a great sin? You have done to me things that ought not to be done." ¹⁰And Abim'elech said to Abraham, "What were you thinking of, that you did this thing?" ¹¹Abraham said, "I did it because I thought, There is no fear of God at all in this place, and they will kill me because of my wife. ¹²Besides she is indeed my sister, the daughter of my father but not the daughter of my mother; and she became my wife. ¹³And when God caused me to wander from my father's house, I said to her, 'This is the kindness you must do me: at every place to which we come, say of me, He is my brother.'" ¹⁴Then Abim'elech took sheep and oxen, and male and female slaves, and gave them to Abraham, and restored Sarah his wife to him. ¹⁵And Abim'elech said, "Behold, my land is before you; dwell

---

ᶠ Gk Syr Vg: Heb *he*.
ᵍ That is *Little*.
19:24, 25: Lk 17:29.
19:26: Lk 17:32.
19:28: Rev 9:2.

where it pleases you." [16]To Sarah he said, "Behold, I have given your brother a thousand pieces of silver; it is your vindication in the eyes of all who are with you; and before every one you are righted." [17]Then Abraham prayed to God; and God healed Abim'elech, and also healed his wife and female slaves so that they bore children. [18]For the LORD had closed all the wombs of the house of Abim'elech because of Sarah, Abraham's wife.

The Birth of Isaac

21 The LORD visited Sarah as he had said, and the LORD did to Sarah as he had promised. [2]And Sarah conceived, and bore Abraham a son in his old age at the time of which God had spoken to him. [3]Abraham called the name of his son who was born to him, whom Sarah bore him, Isaac. [4]And Abraham circumcised his son Isaac when he was eight days old, as God had commanded him. [5]Abraham was a hundred years old when his son Isaac was born to him. [6]And Sarah said, "God has made laughter for me; every one who hears will laugh over me." [7]And she said, "Who would have said to Abraham that Sarah would suckle children? Yet I have borne him a son in his old age."

Hagar and Ishmael Sent Away

8 And the child grew, and was weaned; and Abraham made a great feast on the day that Isaac was weaned. [9]But Sarah saw the son of Hagar the Egyptian, whom she had borne to Abraham, playing with her son Isaac.[h] [10]So she said to Abraham, "Cast out this slave woman with her son; for the son of this slave woman shall not be heir with my son Isaac." [11]And the thing was very displeasing to Abraham on account of his son. [12]But God said to Abraham, "Be not displeased because of the lad and because of your slave woman; whatever Sarah says to you, do as she tells you, for through Isaac shall your descendants be named. [13]And I will make a nation of the son of the slave woman also, because he is your offspring." [14]So Abraham rose early in the morning, and took bread and a skin of water, and gave it to Hagar, putting it on her shoulder, along with the child, and sent her away. And she departed, and wandered in the wilderness of Be'er-she'ba.

15 When the water in the skin was gone, she cast the child under one of the bushes. [16]Then she went, and sat down over against him a good way off, about the distance of a bowshot; for she said, "Let me not look upon the death of the child." And as she sat over against him, the child lifted up his voice[i] and wept. [17]And God heard the voice of the lad; and the angel of God called to Hagar from heaven, and said to her, "What troubles you, Hagar? Fear not; for God has heard the voice of the lad where he is. [18]Arise, lift up the lad, and hold him fast with your hand; for I will make him a great nation." [19]Then God opened her eyes, and

she saw a well of water; and she went, and filled the skin with water, and gave the lad a drink. [20]And God was with the lad, and he grew up; he lived in the wilderness, and became an expert with the bow. [21]He lived in the wilderness of Par'an; and his mother took a wife for him from the land of Egypt.

Abraham and Abimelech Make a Covenant

22 At that time Abim'elech and Phi'col the commander of his army said to Abraham, "God is with you in all that you do; [23]now therefore swear to me here by God that you will not deal falsely with me or with my offspring or with my posterity, but as I have dealt loyally with you, you will deal with me and with the land where you have sojourned." [24]And Abraham said, "I will swear."

25 When Abraham complained to Abim'elech about a well of water which Abimelech's servants had seized, [26]Abim'elech said, "I do not know who has done this thing; you did not tell me, and I have not heard of it until today." [27]So Abraham took sheep and oxen and gave them to Abim'elech, and the two men made a covenant. [28]Abraham set seven ewe lambs of the flock apart. [29]And Abim'elech said to Abraham, "What is the meaning of these seven ewe lambs which you have set apart?" [30]He said, "These seven ewe lambs you will take from my hand, that you may be a witness for me that I dug this well." [31]Therefore that place was called Be'er-she'ba;[j] because there both of them swore an oath. [32]So they made a covenant at Be'er-she'ba. Then Abim'elech and Phi'col the commander of his army rose up and returned to the land of the Philis'tines. [33]Abraham planted a tamarisk tree in Be'er-she'ba, and called there on the name of the LORD, the Everlasting God. [34]And Abraham sojourned many days in the land of the Philis'tines.

God Tests Abraham

22 * After these things God tested Abraham, and said to him, "Abraham!" And he said, "Here am I." [2]He said, "Take your son, your only-begotten son Isaac, whom you love, and go to the land of Mori'ah, and offer him there as a burnt offering upon one of the mountains of which I shall tell you." [3]So Abraham rose early in the morning, saddled his donkey, and took two of his young men with him, and his son Isaac; and he cut the wood for the burnt offering, and arose and went to the place of which God had told him. [4]On the third day Abraham lifted up his eyes and saw

---

h Gk Vg: Heb lacks *with her son Isaac.*
i Gk: Heb *she lifted up her voice.*
j That is *Well of seven* or *Well of the oath.*
21:4: Acts 7:8.
21:10: Gal 4:30.
21:12: Rom 9:7; Heb 11:18.
21:31: Gen 26:33.
22:1–18: Heb 11:17–19.
* 22:1–19: The sacrifice of Isaac, while reprobating the practice of human sacrifice then in use among the Canaanites, gives a magnificent example of Abraham's faith and obedience, as also does 18:1–15; cf. Rom 4 and Heb 11:8–12.

the place afar off. [5]Then Abraham said to his young men, "Stay here with the donkey; I and the lad will go yonder and worship, and come again to you." [6]And Abraham took the wood of the burnt offering, and laid it on Isaac his son; * and he took in his hand the fire and the knife. So they went both of them together. [7]And Isaac said to his father Abraham, "My father!" And he said, "Here am I, my son." He said, "Behold, the fire and the wood; but where is the lamb for a burnt offering?" [8]Abraham said, "God will provide himself the lamb for a burnt offering, my son." So they went both of them together.

9 When they came to the place of which God had told him, Abraham built an altar there, and laid the wood in order, and bound Isaac his son, and laid him on the altar, upon the wood. [10]Then Abraham put forth his hand, and took the knife to slay his son. [11]But the angel of the LORD called to him from heaven, and said, "Abraham, Abraham!" And he said, "Here am I." [12]He said, "Do not lay your hand on the lad or do anything to him; for now I know that you fear God, seeing you have not withheld your son, your only-begotten son, from me." [13]And Abraham lifted up his eyes and looked, and behold, behind him was a ram, caught in a thicket by his horns; and Abraham went and took the ram, and offered it up as a burnt offering instead of his son. [14]So Abraham called the name of that place The LORD will provide; [k] as it is said to this day, "On the mount of the LORD it shall be provided." [1]

15 And the angel of the LORD called to Abraham a second time from heaven, [16]and said, "By myself I have sworn, says the LORD, because you have done this, and have not withheld your son, your only-begotten son, [17]I will indeed bless you, and I will multiply your descendants as the stars of heaven and as the sand which is on the seashore. And your descendants shall possess the gate of their enemies, [18]and by your descendants shall all the nations of the earth bless themselves, because you have obeyed my voice." [19]So Abraham returned to his young men, and they arose and went together to Be'er-she'ba; and Abraham dwelt at Beer-sheba.

The Children of Nahor

20 Now after these things it was told Abraham, "Behold, Milcah also has borne children to your brother Na'hor: [21]Uz the first-born, Buz his brother, Ke'muel the father of Ar'am, [22]Che'sed, Ha'zo, Pildash, Jidlaph, and Bethu'el." [23]Bethu'el became the father of Rebekah. These eight Milcah bore to Na'hor, Abraham's brother. [24]Moreover, his concubine, whose name was Reu'mah, bore Te'bah, Ga'ham, Ta'hash, and Ma'acah.

Sarah's Death and Burial

23 Sarah lived a hundred and twenty-seven years; these were the years of the life of Sarah. [2]And Sarah died at Kir'iath-ar'ba (that is, He'bron) in the land of Canaan; and Abraham went in to mourn for Sarah and to weep for her. [3]And Abraham rose up from before his dead, and said to the Hittites, [4]"I am a stranger and a sojourner among you; give me property among you for a burying place, that I may bury my dead out of my sight." [5]The Hittites answered Abraham, [6]"Hear us, my lord; you are a mighty prince among us. Bury your dead in the choicest of our sepulchres; none of us will withhold from you his sepulchre, or hinder you from burying your dead." [7]Abraham rose and bowed to the Hittites, the people of the land. [8]And he said to them, "If you are willing that I should bury my dead out of my sight, hear me, and entreat for me E'phron the son of Zo'har, [9]that he may give me the cave of Mach-pe'lah, which he owns; it is at the end of his field. For the full price let him give it to me in your presence as a possession for a burying place." [10]Now E'phron was sitting among the Hittites; and Ephron the Hittite answered Abraham in the hearing of the Hittites, of all who went in at the gate of his city, [11]"No, my lord, hear me; I give you the field, and I give you the cave that is in it; in the presence of the sons of my people I give it to you; bury your dead." [12]Then Abraham bowed down before the people of the land. [13]And he said to E'phron in the hearing of the people of the land, "But if you will, hear me; I will give the price of the field; accept it from me, that I may bury my dead there." [14]E'phron answered Abraham, [15]"My lord, listen to me; a piece of land worth four hundred shekels of silver, what is that between you and me? Bury your dead." [16]Abraham agreed with E'phron; and Abraham weighed out for Ephron the silver which he had named in the hearing of the Hittites, four hundred shekels of silver, according to the weights current among the merchants.

17 So the field of E'phron in Mach-pe'lah, which was to the east of Mamre, the field with the cave which was in it and all the trees that were in the field, throughout its whole area, was made over [18]to Abraham as a possession in the presence of the Hittites, before all who went in at the gate of his city. [19]After this, Abraham buried Sarah his wife in the cave of the field of Mach-pe'lah east of Mamre (that is, He'bron) in the land of Canaan. [20]The field and the cave that is in it were made over to Abraham as a possession for a burying place by the Hittites.

[k] Or see.
[1] Or he will be seen.
22:9, 10, 12: Jas 2:21.
22:16, 17: Lk 1:73; Heb 6:13, 14; 11:11, 12.
22:18: Acts 3:25; Gal 3:16.
23:4: Heb 11:9, 13.
23:16, 17: Acts 7:16.
* 22:6: Isaac, carrying the wood up the mountain for the sacrifice, has often been seen as a figure of Christ carrying his cross to die on Golgotha.

The Marriage of Isaac and Rebekah

24 Now Abraham was old, well advanced in years; and the LORD had blessed Abraham in all things. ²And Abraham said to his servant, the oldest of his house, who had charge of all that he had, "Put your hand under my thigh, ³and I will make you swear by the LORD, the God of heaven and of the earth, that you will not take a wife for my son from the daughters of the Canaanites, among whom I dwell, ⁴but will go to my country and to my kindred, and take a wife for my son Isaac." ⁵The servant said to him, "Perhaps the woman may not be willing to follow me to this land; must I then take your son back to the land from which you came?" ⁶Abraham said to him, "See to it that you do not take my son back there. ⁷The LORD, the God of heaven, who took me from my father's house and from the land of my birth, and who spoke to me and swore to me, 'To your descendants I will give this land,' he will send his angel before you, and you shall take a wife for my son from there. ⁸But if the woman is not willing to follow you, then you will be free from this oath of mine; only you must not take my son back there." ⁹So the servant put his hand under the thigh of Abraham his master, and swore to him concerning this matter.

10 Then the servant took ten of his master's camels and departed, taking all sorts of choice gifts from his master; and he arose, and went to Mesopota′mia, to the city of Na′hor. ¹¹And he made the camels kneel down outside the city by the well of water at the time of evening, the time when women go out to draw water. ¹²And he said, "O LORD, God of my master Abraham, grant me success today, I beg you, and show mercy to my master Abraham. ¹³Behold, I am standing by the spring of water, and the daughters of the men of the city are coming out to draw water. ¹⁴Let the maiden to whom I shall say, 'Please let down your jar that I may drink,' and who shall say, 'Drink, and I will water your camels'—let her be the one whom you have appointed for your servant Isaac. By this I shall know that you have shown mercy to my master."

15 Before he had done speaking, behold, Rebekah, who was born to Bethu′el the son of Milcah, the wife of Na′hor, Abraham's brother, came out with her water jar upon her shoulder. ¹⁶The maiden was very fair to look upon, a virgin, whom no man had known. She went down to the spring, and filled her jar, and came up. ¹⁷Then the servant ran to meet her, and said, "Please give me a little water to drink from your jar." ¹⁸She said, "Drink, my lord"; and she quickly let down her jar upon her hand, and gave him a drink. ¹⁹When she had finished giving him a drink, she said, "I will draw for your camels also, until they have done drinking." ²⁰So she quickly emptied her jar into the trough and ran again to the well to draw, and she drew for all his camels. ²¹The man gazed at her in silence to learn whether the LORD had prospered his journey or not.

22 When the camels had done drinking, the man took a gold ring weighing a half shekel, and two bracelets for her arms weighing ten gold shekels, ²³and said, "Tell me whose daughter you are. Is there room in your father's house for us to lodge in?" ²⁴She said to him, "I am the daughter of Bethu′el the son of Milcah, whom she bore to Na′hor." ²⁵She added, "We have both straw and food enough, and room to lodge in." ²⁶The man bowed his head and worshiped the LORD, ²⁷and said, "Blessed be the LORD, the God of my master Abraham, who has not forsaken his mercy and his faithfulness toward my master. As for me, the LORD has led me in the way to the house of my master's kinsmen."

28 Then the maiden ran and told her mother's household about these things. ²⁹Rebekah had a brother whose name was La′ban; and Laban ran out to the man, to the spring. ³⁰When he saw the ring, and the bracelets on his sister's arms, and when he heard the words of Rebekah his sister, "Thus the man spoke to me," he went to the man; and behold, he was standing by the camels at the spring. ³¹He said, "Come in, O blessed of the LORD; why do you stand outside? For I have prepared the house and a place for the camels." ³²So the man came into the house; and La′ban ungirded the camels, and gave him straw and food for the camels, and water to wash his feet and the feet of the men who were with him. ³³Then food was set before him to eat; but he said, "I will not eat until I have told my errand." He said, "Speak on."

34 So he said, "I am Abraham's servant. ³⁵The LORD has greatly blessed my master, and he has become great; he has given him flocks and herds, silver and gold, menservants and maidservants, camels and donkeys. ³⁶And Sarah my master's wife bore a son to my master when she was old; and to him he has given all that he has. ³⁷My master made me swear, saying, 'You shall not take a wife for my son from the daughters of the Canaanites, in whose land I dwell, ³⁸but you shall go to my father's house and to my kindred, and take a wife for my son.' ³⁹I said to my master, 'Perhaps the woman will not follow me.' ⁴⁰But he said to me, 'The LORD, before whom I walk, will send his angel with you and prosper your way; and you shall take a wife for my son from my kindred and from my father's house; ⁴¹then you will be free from my oath, when you come to my kindred; and if they will not give her to you, you will be free from my oath.'

42 "I came today to the spring, and said, 'O LORD, the God of my master Abraham, if now you

will prosper the way which I go, [43]behold, I am standing by the spring of water; let the young woman who comes out to draw, to whom I shall say, "Please give me a little water from your jar to drink," [44]and who will say to me, "Drink, and I will draw for your camels also," let her be the woman whom the LORD has appointed for my master's son.'

45 "Before I had done speaking in my heart, behold, Rebekah came out with her water jar on her shoulder; and she went down to the spring, and drew. I said to her, 'Please let me drink.' [46]She quickly let down her jar from her shoulder, and said, 'Drink, and I will give your camels drink also.' So I drank, and she gave the camels drink also. [47]Then I asked her, 'Whose daughter are you?' She said, 'The daughter of Bethu'el, Na'hor's son, whom Milcah bore to him.' So I put the ring on her nose, and the bracelets on her arms. [48]Then I bowed my head and worshiped the LORD, and blessed the LORD, the God of my master Abraham, who had led me by the right way to take the daughter of my master's kinsman for his son. [49]Now then, if you will deal loyally and truly with my master, tell me; and if not, tell me; that I may turn to the right hand or to the left."

50 Then La'ban and Bethu'el answered, "The thing comes from the LORD; we cannot speak to you bad or good. [51]Behold, Rebekah is before you, take her and go, and let her be the wife of your master's son, as the LORD has spoken." 52 When Abraham's servant heard their words, he bowed himself to the earth before the LORD. [53]And the servant brought forth jewelry of silver and of gold, and raiment, and gave them to Rebekah; he also gave to her brother and to her mother costly ornaments. [54]And he and the men who were with him ate and drank, and they spent the night there. When they arose in the morning, he said, "Send me back to my master." [55]Her brother and her mother said, "Let the maiden remain with us a while, at least ten days; after that she may go." [56]But he said to them, "Do not delay me, since the LORD has prospered my way; let me go that I may go to my master." [57]They said, "We will call the maiden, and ask her." [58]And they called Rebekah, and said to her, "Will you go with this man?" She said, "I will go." [59]So they sent away Rebekah their sister and her nurse, and Abraham's servant and his men. [60]And they blessed Rebekah, and said to her, "Our sister, be the mother of thousands of ten thousands; and may your descendants possess the gate of those who hate them!" [61]Then Rebekah and her maids arose, and rode upon the camels and followed the man; thus the servant took Rebekah, and went his way.

62 Now Isaac had come from [n] Be'er-la'hai-roi, and was dwelling in the Neg'eb. [63]And Isaac went out to meditate in the field in the evening; and he lifted up his eyes and looked, and behold, there were camels coming. [64]And Rebekah lifted up her eyes, and when she saw Isaac, she alighted from the camel, [65]and said to the servant, "Who is the man yonder, walking in the field to meet us?" The servant said, "It is my master." So she took her veil and covered herself. [66]And the servant told Isaac all the things that he had done. [67]Then Isaac brought her into the tent,[o] and took Rebekah, and she became his wife; and he loved her. So Isaac was comforted after his mother's death.

Abraham Marries Keturah

25 Abraham took another wife, whose name was Ketu'rah. [2]She bore him Zimran, Jokshan, Me'dan, Mid'ian, Ishbak, and Shuah. [3]Jokshan was the father of Sheba and De'dan. The sons of Dedan were Asshu'rim, Letu'shim, and Le-um'mim. [4]The sons of Mid'ian were E'phah, E'pher, Ha'noch, Abi'da, and Elda'ah. All these were the children of Ketu'rah. [5]Abraham gave all he had to Isaac. [6]But to the sons of his concubines Abraham gave gifts, and while he was still living he sent them away from his son Isaac, eastward to the east country.

The Death of Abraham

7 These are the days of the years of Abraham's life, a hundred and seventy-five years. [8]Abraham breathed his last and died in a good old age, an old man and full of years, and was gathered to his people. [9]Isaac and Ish'mael his sons buried him in the cave of Mach-pe'lah, in the field of E'phron the son of Zo'har the Hittite, east of Mamre, [10]the field which Abraham purchased from the Hittites. There Abraham was buried, with Sarah his wife. [11]After the death of Abraham God blessed Isaac his son. And Isaac dwelt at Be'er-la'hai-roi.

The Descendants of Ishmael

12 These are the descendants of Ish'mael, Abraham's son, whom Hagar the Egyptian, Sarah's maid, bore to Abraham. [13]These are the names of the sons of Ish'mael, named in the order of their birth: Neba'ioth, the first-born of Ishmael; and Ke'dar, Ad'beel, Mibsam, [14]Mishma, Du'mah, Massa, [15]Ha'dad, Te'ma, Je'tur, Na'phish, and Ked'emah. [16]These are the sons of Ish'mael and these are their names, by their villages and by their encampments, twelve princes according to their tribes. [17](These are the years of the life of Ish'mael, a hundred and thirty-seven years; he breathed his last and died, and was gathered to his kindred.) [18]They dwelt from Hav'ilah to Shur, which is opposite Egypt in the direction of Assyria; he settled [p] over against all his people.

---

[n] Syr Tg: Heb *from coming to.*
[o] Heb adds *of Sarah his mother.*
[p] Heb *fell.*
25:13-16: 1 Chron 1:29–31.

17

The Birth of Esau and Jacob

19 * These are the descendants of Isaac, Abraham's son: Abraham was the father of Isaac, [20]and Isaac was forty years old when he took to wife Rebekah, the daughter of Bethu'el the Arame'an of Pad'dan-ar'am, the sister of La'ban the Aramean. [21]And Isaac prayed to the Lord for his wife, because she was barren; and the Lord granted his prayer, and Rebekah his wife conceived. [22]The children struggled together within her; and she said, "If it is thus, why do I live?" ^q So she went to inquire of the Lord. [23]And the Lord said to her,

"Two nations are in your womb,
and two peoples, born of you, shall be
divided;
the one shall be stronger than the other,
the elder shall serve the younger."

[24]When her days to be delivered were fulfilled, behold, there were twins in her womb. [25]The first came forth red, all his body like a hairy mantle; so they called his name Esau. [26]Afterward his brother came forth, and his hand had taken hold of Esau's heel; so his name was called Jacob.^r Isaac was sixty years old when she bore them.

Esau Sells His Birthright

27 When the boys grew up, Esau was a skilful hunter, a man of the field, while Jacob was a quiet man, dwelling in tents. [28]Isaac loved Esau, because he ate of his game; but Rebekah loved Jacob.

29 Once when Jacob was boiling pottage, Esau came in from the field, and he was famished. [30]And Esau said to Jacob, "Let me eat some of that red pottage, for I am famished!" (Therefore his name was called E'dom.) ^s [31]Jacob said, "First sell me your birthright." [32]Esau said, "I am about to die; of what use is a birthright to me?" [33]Jacob said, "Swear to me first." ^t So he swore to him, and sold his birthright to Jacob. [34]Then Jacob gave Esau bread and pottage of lentils, and he ate and drank, and rose and went his way. Thus Esau despised his birthright.

Isaac and Abimelech

26 Now there was a famine in the land, besides the former famine that was in the days of Abraham. And Isaac went to Ge'rar, to Abim'elech king of the Philis'tines. [2]And the Lord appeared to him, and said, "Do not go down to Egypt; dwell in the land of which I shall tell you. [3]Sojourn in this land, and I will be with you, and will bless you; for to you and to your descendants I will give all these lands, and I will fulfil the oath which I swore to Abraham your father. [4]I will multiply your descendants as the stars of heaven, and will give to your descendants all these lands; and by your descendants all the nations of the earth shall bless themselves: [5]because Abraham obeyed my voice and kept my charge, my commandments, my statutes, and my laws."

6 So Isaac dwelt in Ge'rar. [7]When the men of the place asked him about his wife, he said, "She is my sister"; for he feared to say, "My wife," thinking, "lest the men of the place should kill me for the sake of Rebekah"; because she was fair to look upon. [8]When he had been there a long time, Abim'elech king of the Philis'tines looked out of a window and saw Isaac fondling Rebekah his wife. [9]So Abim'elech called Isaac, and said, "Behold, she is your wife; how then could you say, 'She is my sister'?" Isaac said to him, "Because I thought, 'Lest I die because of her.'" [10]Abim'elech said, "What is this you have done to us? One of the people might easily have lain with your wife, and you would have brought guilt upon us." [11]So Abim'elech warned all the people, saying, "Whoever touches this man or his wife shall be put to death."

12 And Isaac sowed in that land, and reaped in the same year a hundredfold. The Lord blessed him, [13]and the man became rich, and gained more and more until he became very wealthy. [14]He had possessions of flocks and herds, and a great household, so that the Philis'tines envied him. [15](Now the Philis'tines had stopped and filled with earth all the wells which his father's servants had dug in the days of Abraham his father.) [16]And Abim'elech said to Isaac, "Go away from us; for you are much mightier than we."

17 So Isaac departed from there, and encamped in the valley of Ge'rar and dwelt there. [18]And Isaac dug again the wells of water which had been dug in the days of Abraham his father; for the Philis'tines had stopped them after the death of Abraham; and he gave them the names which his father had given them. [19]But when Isaac's servants dug in the valley and found there a well of springing water, [20]the herdsmen of Ge'rar quarreled with Isaac's herdsmen, saying, "The water is ours." So he called the name of the well E'sek,^u because they contended with him. [21]Then they dug another well, and they quarreled over that also; so he called its name Sitnah.^v [22]And he moved from there and dug another well, and over that they did not quarrel; so he called its name Reho'both,^w saying, "For now the Lord has made room for us, and we shall be fruitful in the land."

23 From there he went up to Be'er-she'ba. [24]And the Lord appeared to him the same night and said, "I am the God of Abraham your father; fear not, for I am with you and will bless you and

---

^q Syr: Heb obscure.
^r That is *He takes by the heel* or *He supplants.*
^s That is *Red.*
^t Heb *today.*
^u That is *Contention.*
^v That is *Enmity.*
^w That is *Broad places* or *Room.*
* 25:19: With the birth of Esau and Jacob we enter a new narrative cycle. Jacob, renamed Israel, is represented as the ancestor of the twelve tribes and, therefore, of the whole people; cf. Deut 26:5.

multiply your descendants for my servant Abraham's sake." ²⁵So he built an altar there and called upon the name of the LORD, and pitched his tent there. And there Isaac's servants dug a well.

26 Then Abim'elech went to him from Ge'rar with Ahuz'zath his adviser and Phi'col the commander of his army. ²⁷Isaac said to them, "Why have you come to me, seeing that you hate me and have sent me away from you?" ²⁸They said, "We see plainly that the LORD is with you; so we say, let there be an oath between you and us, and let us make a covenant with you, ²⁹that you will do us no harm, just as we have not touched you and have done to you nothing but good and have sent you away in peace. You are now the blessed of the LORD." ³⁰So he made them a feast, and they ate and drank. ³¹In the morning they rose early and took oath with one another; and Isaac set them on their way, and they departed from him in peace. ³²That same day Isaac's servants came and told him about the well which they had dug, and said to him, "We have found water." ³³He called it Shi'bah; therefore the name of the city is Be'er-she'ba to this day.

Esau's Hittite Wives

34 When Esau was forty years old, he took to wife Judith the daughter of Bee'ri the Hittite, and Bas'emath the daughter of E'lon the Hittite; ³⁵and they made life bitter for Isaac and Rebekah.

Isaac Blesses Jacob

27 When Isaac was old and his eyes were dim so that he could not see, he called Esau his older son, and said to him, "My son"; and he answered, "Here I am." ²He said, "Behold, I am old; I do not know the day of my death. ³Now then, take your weapons, your quiver and your bow, and go out to the field, and hunt game for me, ⁴and prepare for me savory food, such as I love, and bring it to me that I may eat; that I may bless you before I die."

5 Now Rebekah was listening when Isaac spoke to his son Esau. So when Esau went to the field to hunt for game and bring it, ⁶Rebekah said to her son Jacob, "I heard your father speak to your brother Esau, ⁷'Bring me game, and prepare for me savory food, that I may eat it, and bless you before the LORD before I die.' ⁸Now therefore, my son, obey my word as I command you. ⁹Go to the flock, and fetch me two good kids, that I may prepare from them savory food for your father, such as he loves; ¹⁰and you shall bring it to your father to eat, so that he may bless you before he dies." ¹¹But Jacob said to Rebekah his mother, "Behold, my brother Esau is a hairy man, and I am a smooth man. ¹²Perhaps my father will feel me, and I shall seem to be mocking him, and bring a curse upon myself and not a blessing." ¹³His mother said to him, "Upon me be your curse, my son; only obey my word, and go, fetch them to

me." ¹⁴So he went and took them and brought them to his mother; and his mother prepared savory food, such as his father loved. ¹⁵Then Rebekah took the best garments of Esau her older son, which were with her in the house, and put them on Jacob her younger son; ¹⁶and the skins of the kids she put upon his hands and upon the smooth part of his neck; ¹⁷and she gave the savory food and the bread, which she had prepared, into the hand of her son Jacob.

18 So he went in to his father, and said, "My father"; and he said, "Here I am; who are you, my son?" ¹⁹Jacob said to his father, "I am Esau your first-born. I have done as you told me; now sit up and eat of my game, that you may bless me." ²⁰But Isaac said to his son, "How is it that you have found it so quickly, my son?" He answered, "Because the LORD your God granted me success." ²¹Then Isaac said to Jacob, "Come near, that I may feel you, my son, to know whether you are really my son Esau or not." ²²So Jacob went near to Isaac his father, who felt him and said, "The voice is Jacob's voice, but the hands are the hands of Esau." ²³And he did not recognize him, because his hands were hairy like his brother Esau's hands; so he blessed him. ²⁴He said, "Are you really my son Esau?" He answered, "I am." ²⁵Then he said, "Bring it to me, that I may eat of my son's game and bless you." So he brought it to him, and he ate; and he brought him wine, and he drank. ²⁶Then his father Isaac said to him, "Come near and kiss me, my son." ²⁷So he came near and kissed him; and he smelled the smell of his garments, and blessed him, and said,

"See, the smell of my son
　is as the smell of a field which the LORD has
　　blessed!
²⁸May God give you of the dew of heaven,
　and of the fatness of the earth,
　　and plenty of grain and wine.
²⁹Let peoples serve you,
　and nations bow down to you.
Be lord over your brothers,
　and may your mother's sons bow down to
　　you.
Cursed be every one who curses you,
　and blessed be every one who blesses you!"

Esau's Lost Blessing

30 As soon as Isaac had finished blessing Jacob, when Jacob had scarcely gone out from the presence of Isaac his father, Esau his brother came in from his hunting. ³¹He also prepared savory food, and brought it to his father. And he said to his father, "Let my father arise, and eat of his son's game, that you may bless me." ³²His father Isaac said to him, "Who are you?" He

26:33: Gen 21:31.
27:5: Gen 12:3; Num 24:9.

answered, "I am your son, your first-born, Esau." [33]Then Isaac trembled violently, and said, "Who was it then that hunted game and brought it to me, and I ate it all* before you came, and I have blessed him?—yes, and he shall be blessed." [34]When Esau heard the words of his father, he cried out with an exceedingly great and bitter cry, and said to his father, "Bless me, even me also, O my father!" [35]But he said, "Your brother came with guile, and he has taken away your blessing." [36]Esau said, "Is he not rightly named Jacob? For he has supplanted me these two times. He took away my birthright; and behold, now he has taken away my blessing." Then he said, "Have you not reserved a blessing for me?" [37]Isaac answered Esau, "Behold, I have made him your lord, and all his brothers I have given to him for servants, and with grain and wine I have sustained him. What then can I do for you, my son?" [38]Esau said to his father, "Have you but one blessing, my father? Bless me, even me also, O my father." And Esau lifted up his voice and wept.

39 Then Isaac his father answered him:

"Behold, away from ʸ the fatness of the earth
   shall your dwelling be,
and away from ʸ the dew of heaven on high.
[40]By your sword you shall live,
   and you shall serve your brother;
but when you break loose
   you shall break his yoke from your neck."

Jacob Escapes Esau's Fury

41 Now Esau hated Jacob because of the blessing with which his father had blessed him, and Esau said to himself, "The days of mourning for my father are approaching; then I will kill my brother Jacob." [42]But the words of Esau her older son were told to Rebekah; so she sent and called Jacob her younger son, and said to him, "Behold, your brother Esau comforts himself by planning to kill you. [43]Now therefore, my son, obey my voice; arise, flee to La'ban my brother in Haran, [44]and stay with him a while, until your brother's fury turns away; [45]until your brother's anger turns away, and he forgets what you have done to him; then I will send, and fetch you from there. Why should I be bereft of you both in one day?"

46 Then Rebekah said to Isaac, "I am weary of my life because of the Hittite women. If Jacob marries one of the Hittite women such as these, one of the women of the land, what good will my life be to me?"

28 Then Isaac called Jacob and blessed him, and charged him, "You shall not marry one of the Canaanite women. [2]Arise, go to Pad'dan-ar'am to the house of Bethu'el your mother's father; and take as wife from there one of the daughters of La'ban your mother's brother. [3]God Almighty ᶻ bless you and make you fruitful and multiply you, that you may become a company of peoples. [4]May he give the blessing of Abraham to you and to your descendants with you, that you may take possession of the land of your sojournings which God gave to Abraham!" [5]Thus Isaac sent Jacob away; and he went to Pad'dan-ar'am to La'ban, the son of Bethu'el the Arame'an, the brother of Rebekah, Jacob's and Esau's mother.

Esau Marries Ishmael's Daughter

6 Now Esau saw that Isaac had blessed Jacob and sent him away to Pad'dan-ar'am to take a wife from there, and that as he blessed him he charged him, "You shall not marry one of the Canaanite women," [7]and that Jacob had obeyed his father and his mother and gone to Pad'dan-ar'am. [8]So when Esau saw that the Canaanite women did not please Isaac his father, [9]Esau went to Ish'mael and took to wife, besides the wives he had, Maha'lath the daughter of Ishmael Abraham's son, the sister of Neba'ioth.

Jacob's Dream at Bethel

10 * Jacob left Be'er-she'ba, and went toward Haran. [11]And he came to a certain place, and stayed there that night, because the sun had set. Taking one of the stones of the place, he put it under his head and lay down in that place to sleep. [12]And he dreamed that there was a ladder set up on the earth, and the top of it reached to heaven; and behold, the angels of God were ascending and descending on it! [13]And behold, the LORD stood above it ᵃ and said, "I am the LORD, the God of Abraham your father and the God of Isaac; the land on which you lie I will give to you and to your descendants; [14]and your descendants shall be like the dust of the earth, and you shall spread abroad to the west and to the east and to the north and to the south; and by you and your descendants shall all the families of the earth bless themselves. ᵇ [15]Behold, I am with you and will keep you wherever you go, and will bring you back to this land; for I will not leave you until I have done that of which I have spoken to you." [16]Then Jacob awoke from his sleep and said, "Surely the LORD is in this place; and I did not know it." [17]And he was afraid, and said, "How awesome is this place! This is none other than the house of God, and this is the gate of heaven."

18 So Jacob rose early in the morning, and he took the stone which he had put under his head and set it up for a pillar and poured oil on the top

---

* Cn: Heb *of all.*
ʸ Or *of.*
ᶻ Heb *El Shaddai.*
ᵃ Or *beside him.*
ᵇ Or *be blessed.*
* 28:10–22: This narrative explains and justifies the use of what had formerly been a Canaanite sanctuary, Bethel. The ladder seems to represent the ziggurat, which was a temple with steps leading to a platform at the top.

of it. [19]He called the name of that place Bethel;[c] but the name of the city was Luz at the first. [20]Then Jacob made a vow, saying, "If God will be with me, and will keep me in this way that I go, and will give me bread to eat and clothing to wear, [21]so that I come again to my father's house in peace, then the Lord shall be my God, [22]and this stone, which I have set up for a pillar, shall be God's house; and of all that you give me I will give the tenth to you."

Jacob Meets Rachel

29 Then Jacob went on his journey, and came to the land of the people of the east. [2]As he looked, he saw a well in the field, and behold, three flocks of sheep lying beside it; for out of that well the flocks were watered. The stone on the well's mouth was large, [3]and when all the flocks were gathered there, the shepherds would roll the stone from the mouth of the well, and water the sheep, and put the stone back in its place upon the mouth of the well.

4 Jacob said to them, "My brothers, where do you come from?" They said, "We are from Haran." [5]He said to them, "Do you know La'ban the son of Na'hor?" They said, "We know him." [6]He said to them, "Is it well with him?" They said, "It is well; and see, Rachel his daughter is coming with the sheep!" [7]He said, "Behold, it is still high day, it is not time for the animals to be gathered together; water the sheep, and go, pasture them." [8]But they said, "We cannot until all the flocks are gathered together, and the stone is rolled from the mouth of the well; then we water the sheep."

9 While he was still speaking with them, Rachel came with her father's sheep; for she kept them. [10]Now when Jacob saw Rachel the daughter of La'ban his mother's brother, and the sheep of Laban his mother's brother, Jacob went up and rolled the stone from the well's mouth, and watered the flock of Laban his mother's brother. [11]Then Jacob kissed Rachel, and wept aloud. [12]And Jacob told Rachel that he was her father's kinsman, and that he was Rebekah's son; and she ran and told her father.

13 When La'ban heard the tidings of Jacob his sister's son, he ran to meet him, and embraced him and kissed him, and brought him to his house. Jacob told Laban all these things, [14]and La'ban said to him, "Surely you are my bone and my flesh!" And he stayed with him a month.

Jacob Marries Laban's Daughters

15 Then La'ban said to Jacob, "Because you are my kinsman, should you therefore serve me for nothing? Tell me, what shall your wages be?" [16]Now La'ban had two daughters; the name of the older was Leah, and the name of the younger was Rachel. [17]Leah's eyes were weak, but Rachel was beautiful and lovely. [18]Jacob loved Rachel; and he said, "I will serve you seven years for your younger daughter Rachel." [19]La'ban said, "It is better that I give her to you than that I should give her to any other man; stay with me." [20]So Jacob served seven years for Rachel, and they seemed to him but a few days because of the love he had for her.

21 Then Jacob said to La'ban, "Give me my wife that I may go in to her, for my time is completed." [22]So La'ban gathered together all the men of the place, and made a feast. [23]But in the evening he took his daughter Leah and brought her to Jacob; and he went in to her. [24](La'ban gave his maid Zilpah to his daughter Leah to be her maid.) [25]And in the morning, behold, it was Leah; and Jacob said to La'ban, "What is this you have done to me? Did I not serve with you for Rachel? Why then have you deceived me?" [26]La'ban said, "It is not so done in our country, to give the younger before the first-born. [27]Complete the week of this one, and we will give you the other also in return for serving me another seven years." [28]Jacob did so, and completed her week; then La'ban gave him his daughter Rachel to wife. [29](La'ban gave his maid Bilhah to his daughter Rachel to be her maid.) [30]So Jacob went in to Rachel also, and he loved Rachel more than Leah, and served La'ban for another seven years.

31 When the Lord saw that Leah was hated, he opened her womb; but Rachel was barren. [32]And Leah conceived and bore a son, and she called his name Reuben;[d] for she said, "Because the Lord has looked upon my affliction; surely now my husband will love me." [33]She conceived again and bore a son, and said, "Because the Lord has heard [e] that I am hated, he has given me this son also"; and she called his name Simeon. [34]Again she conceived and bore a son, and said, "Now this time my husband will be joined [f] to me, because I have borne him three sons"; therefore his name was called Levi. [35]And she conceived again and bore a son, and said, "This time I will praise [g] the Lord"; therefore she called his name Judah; then she ceased bearing.

30 When Rachel saw that she bore Jacob no children, she envied her sister; and she said to Jacob, "Give me children, or I shall die!" [2]Jacob's anger was kindled against Rachel, and he said, "Am I in the place of God, who has withheld from you the fruit of the womb?" [3]Then she said, "Here is my maid Bilhah; go in to her, that she may bear upon my knees, and even I may have children through her." [4]So she gave him her maid Bilhah as a wife; and Jacob went in to her. [5]And Bilhah conceived and bore Jacob a son.

---

[c] That is *The house of God*.
[d] That is *See, a son*.
[e] Heb *shama*.
[f] Heb *lawah*.
[g] Heb *hodah*.

[6]Then Rachel said, "God has judged me, and has also heard my voice and given me a son"; therefore she called his name Dan.[h] [7]Rachel's maid Bilhah conceived again and bore Jacob a second son. [8]Then Rachel said, "With mighty wrestlings I have wrestled[i] with my sister, and have prevailed"; so she called his name Naph'tali.

9 When Leah saw that she had ceased bearing children, she took her maid Zilpah and gave her to Jacob as a wife. [10]Then Leah's maid Zilpah bore Jacob a son. [11]And Leah said, "Good fortune!" so she called his name Gad.[j] [12]Leah's maid Zilpah bore Jacob a second son. [13]And Leah said, "Blessed am I! For the women will call me blessed"; so she called his name Asher.[k]

14 In the days of wheat harvest Reuben went and found mandrakes in the field, and brought them to his mother Leah. Then Rachel said to Leah, "Give me, I pray, some of your son's mandrakes." [15]But she said to her, "Is it a small matter that you have taken away my husband? Would you take away my son's mandrakes also?" Rachel said, "Then he may lie with you tonight for your son's mandrakes." [16]When Jacob came from the field in the evening, Leah went out to meet him, and said, "You must come in to me; for I have hired you with my son's mandrakes." So he lay with her that night. [17]And God hearkened to Leah, and she conceived and bore Jacob a fifth son. [18]Leah said, "God has given me my hire[l] because I gave my maid to my husband"; so she called his name Is'sachar. [19]And Leah conceived again, and she bore Jacob a sixth son. [20]Then Leah said, "God has endowed me with a good dowry; now my husband will honor[m] me, because I have borne him six sons"; so she called his name Zeb'ulun. [21]Afterwards she bore a daughter, and called her name Dinah. [22]Then God remembered Rachel, and God hearkened to her and opened her womb. [23]She conceived and bore a son, and said, "God has taken away my reproach"; [24]and she called his name Joseph,[n] saying, "May the LORD add to me another son!"

Jacob Prospers

25 When Rachel had borne Joseph, Jacob said to La'ban, "Send me away, that I may go to my own home and country. [26]Give me my wives and my children for whom I have served you, and let me go; for you know the service which I have given you." [27]But La'ban said to him, "If you will allow me to say so, I have learned by divination that the LORD has blessed me because of you; [28]name your wages, and I will give it." [29]Jacob said to him, "You yourself know how I have served you, and how your cattle have fared with me. [30]For you had little before I came, and it has increased abundantly; and the LORD has blessed you wherever I turned. But now when shall I provide for my own household also?" [31]He said,

"What shall I give you?" Jacob said, "You shall not give me anything; if you will do this for me, I will again feed your flock and keep it: [32]let me pass through all your flock today, removing from it every speckled and spotted sheep and every black lamb, and the spotted and speckled among the goats; and such shall be my wages. [33]So my honesty will answer for me later, when you come to look into my wages with you. Every one that is not speckled and spotted among the goats and black among the lambs, if found with me, shall be counted stolen." [34]La'ban said, "Good! Let it be as you have said." [35]But that day La'ban removed the he-goats that were striped and spotted, and all the she-goats that were speckled and spotted, every one that had white on it, and every lamb that was black, and put them in charge of his sons; [36]and he set a distance of three days' journey between himself and Jacob; and Jacob fed the rest of La'ban's flock.

37 Then Jacob took fresh rods of poplar and almond and plane, and peeled white streaks in them, exposing the white of the rods. [38]He set the rods which he had peeled in front of the flocks in the runnels, that is, the watering troughs, where the flocks came to drink. And since they bred when they came to drink, [39]the flocks bred in front of the rods and so the flocks brought forth striped, speckled, and spotted. [40]And Jacob separated the lambs, and set the faces of the flocks toward the striped and all the black in the flock of La'ban; and he put his own droves apart, and did not put them with Laban's flock. [41]Whenever the stronger of the flock were breeding Jacob laid the rods in the runnels before the eyes of the flock, that they might breed among the rods, [42]but for the feebler of the flock he did not lay them there; so the feebler were La'ban's, and the stronger Jacob's. [43]Thus the man grew exceedingly rich, and had large flocks, maidservants and menservants, and camels and donkeys.

Jacob Flees with His Family and Flocks

31 Now Jacob heard that the sons of La'ban were saying, "Jacob has taken all that was our father's; and from what was our father's he has gained all this wealth." [2]And Jacob saw that La'ban did not regard him with favor as before. [3]Then the LORD said to Jacob, "Return to the land of your fathers and to your kindred, and I will be with you." [4]So Jacob sent and called Rachel and Leah into the field where his flock was, [5]and said to them, "I see that your father does not regard me with favor as he did before. But the God of

---

[h] That is *He judged.*
[i] Heb *niphtal.*
[j] That is *Fortune.*
[k] That is *Blessed.*
[l] Heb *sakar.*
[m] Heb *zabal.*
[n] That is *He adds.*

my father has been with me. ⁶You know that I have served your father with all my strength; ⁷yet your father has cheated me and changed my wages ten times, but God did not permit him to harm me. ⁸If he said, 'The spotted shall be your wages,' then all the flock bore spotted; and if he said, 'The striped shall be your wages,' then all the flock bore striped. ⁹Thus God has taken away the cattle of your father, and given them to me. ¹⁰In the mating season of the flock I lifted up my eyes, and saw in a dream that the he-goats which leaped upon the flock were striped, spotted, and mottled. ¹¹Then the angel of God said to me in the dream, 'Jacob,' and I said, 'Here I am!' ¹²And he said, 'Lift up your eyes and see, all the goats that leap upon the flock are striped, spotted, and mottled; for I have seen all that La'ban is doing to you. ¹³I am the God of Bethel, where you anointed a pillar and made a vow to me. Now arise, go forth from this land, and return to the land of your birth.'" ¹⁴Then Rachel and Leah answered him, "Is there any portion or inheritance left to us in our father's house? ¹⁵Are we not regarded by him as foreigners? For he has sold us, and he has been using up the money given for us. ¹⁶All the property which God has taken away from our father belongs to us and to our children; now then, whatever God has said to you, do."

17 So Jacob arose, and set his sons and his wives on camels; ¹⁸and he drove away all his cattle, all his livestock which he had gained, the cattle in his possession which he had acquired in Pad'dan-ar'am, to go to the land of Canaan to his father Isaac. ¹⁹La'ban had gone to shear his sheep, and Rachel stole her father's household gods. ²⁰And Jacob outwitted La'ban the Arame'an, in that he did not tell him that he intended to flee. ²¹He fled with all that he had, and arose and crossed the Euphra'tes, and set his face toward the hill country of Gilead.

Laban Overtakes Jacob

22 When it was told La'ban on the third day that Jacob had fled, ²³he took his kinsmen with him and pursued him for seven days and followed close after him into the hill country of Gilead. ²⁴But God came to La'ban the Arame'an in a dream by night, and said to him, "Take heed that you say not a word to Jacob, either good or bad."

25 And La'ban overtook Jacob. Now Jacob had pitched his tent in the hill country, and Laban with his kinsmen encamped in the hill country of Gilead. ²⁶And La'ban said to Jacob, "What have you done, that you have cheated me, and carried away my daughters like captives of the sword? ²⁷Why did you flee secretly, and cheat me, and did not tell me, so that I might have sent you away with mirth and songs, with tambourine and lyre? ²⁸And why did you not permit me to kiss my sons and my daughters farewell? Now you have done

foolishly. ²⁹It is in my power to do you harm; but the God of your father spoke to me last night, saying, 'Take heed that you speak to Jacob neither good nor bad.' ³⁰And now you have gone away because you longed greatly for your father's house, but why did you steal my gods?" ³¹Jacob answered La'ban, "Because I was afraid, for I thought that you would take your daughters from me by force. ³²Any one with whom you find your gods shall not live. In the presence of our kinsmen point out what I have that is yours, and take it." Now Jacob did not know that Rachel had stolen them.

33 So La'ban went into Jacob's tent, and into Leah's tent, and into the tent of the two maidservants, but he did not find them. And he went out of Leah's tent, and entered Rachel's. ³⁴Now Rachel had taken the household gods and put them in the camel's saddle, and sat upon them. La'ban felt all about the tent, but did not find them. ³⁵And she said to her father, "Let not my lord be angry that I cannot rise before you, for the way of women is upon me." So he searched, but did not find the household gods.

36 Then Jacob became angry, and upbraided La'ban; Jacob said to Laban, "What is my offense? What is my sin, that you have hotly pursued me? ³⁷Although you have felt through all my goods, what have you found of all your household goods? Set it here before my kinsmen and your kinsmen, that they may decide between us two. ³⁸These twenty years I have been with you; your ewes and your she-goats have not miscarried, and I have not eaten the rams of your flocks. ³⁹That which was torn by wild beasts I did not bring to you; I bore the loss of it myself; of my hand you required it, whether stolen by day or stolen by night. ⁴⁰Thus I was; by day the heat consumed me, and the cold by night, and my sleep fled from my eyes. ⁴¹These twenty years I have been in your house; I served you fourteen years for your two daughters, and six years for your flock, and you have changed my wages ten times. ⁴²If the God of my father, the God of Abraham and the Fear of Isaac, had not been on my side, surely now you would have sent me away empty-handed. God saw my affliction and the labor of my hands, and rebuked you last night."

Laban and Jacob Make a Covenant

43 Then La'ban answered and said to Jacob, "The daughters are my daughters, the children are my children, the flocks are my flocks, and all that you see is mine. But what can I do this day to these my daughters, or to their children whom they have borne? ⁴⁴Come now, let us make a covenant, you and I; and let it be a witness between you and me." ⁴⁵So Jacob took a stone, and set it up as a pillar. ⁴⁶And Jacob said to his kinsmen, "Gather stones," and they took stones, and made a

heap; and they ate there by the heap. ⁴⁷La'ban called it Je'gar-sahadu'tha:° but Jacob called it Gale'ed.ᴾ ⁴⁸La'ban said, "This heap is a witness between you and me today." Therefore he named it Gale'ed, ⁴⁹and the pillar ᑫ Mizpah, ᴿ for he said, "The Lᴏʀᴅ watch between you and me, when we are absent one from the other. ⁵⁰If you ill-treat my daughters, or if you take wives besides my daughters, although no man is with us, remember, God is witness between you and me."

51 Then La'ban said to Jacob, "See this heap and the pillar, which I have set between you and me. ⁵²This heap is a witness, and the pillar is a witness, that I will not pass over this heap to you, and you will not pass over this heap and this pillar to me, for harm. ⁵³The God of Abraham and the God of Na'hor, the God of their father, judge between us." So Jacob swore by the Fear of his father Isaac, ⁵⁴and Jacob offered a sacrifice on the mountain and called his kinsmen to eat bread; and they ate bread and tarried all night on the mountain.

55 ˢEarly in the morning La'ban arose, and kissed his grandchildren and his daughters and blessed them; then he departed and returned home.

32 Jacob went on his way and the angels of God met him; ²and when Jacob saw them he said, "This is God's army!" So he called the name of that place Ma"hana'im. ᵗ

Jacob Sends Gifts to Appease Esau

3 And Jacob sent messengers before him to Esau his brother in the land of Se'ir, the country of Edom, ⁴instructing them, "Thus you shall say to my lord Esau: Thus says your servant Jacob, 'I have sojourned with La'ban, and stayed until now; ⁵and I have oxen, donkeys, flocks, menservants, and maidservants; and I have sent to tell my lord, in order that I may find favor in your sight.'"

6 And the messengers returned to Jacob, saying, "We came to your brother Esau, and he is coming to meet you, and four hundred men with him." ⁷Then Jacob was greatly afraid and distressed; and he divided the people that were with him, and the flocks and herds and camels, into two companies, ⁸thinking, "If Esau comes to the one company and destroys it, then the company which is left will escape."

9 And Jacob said, "O God of my father Abraham and God of my father Isaac, O Lᴏʀᴅ who said to me, 'Return to your country and to your kindred, and I will do you good,' ¹⁰I am not worthy of the least of all the mercy and all the faithfulness which you have shown to your servant, for with only my staff I crossed this Jordan; and now I have become two companies. ¹¹Deliver me, I beg you, from the hand of my brother, from the hand of Esau, for I fear him, lest he come and slay us all, the mothers with the children. ¹²But you said,

'I will do you good, and make your descendants as the sand of the sea, which cannot be numbered for multitude.'"

13 So he lodged there that night, and took from what he had with him a present for his brother Esau, ¹⁴two hundred she-goats and twenty he-goats, two hundred ewes and twenty rams, ¹⁵thirty milch camels and their colts, forty cows and ten bulls, twenty she-donkeys and ten he-donkeys. ¹⁶These he delivered into the hand of his servants, every drove by itself, and said to his servants, "Pass on before me, and put a space between drove and drove." ¹⁷He instructed the foremost, "When Esau my brother meets you, and asks you, 'To whom do you belong? Where are you going? And whose are these before you?' ¹⁸then you shall say, 'They belong to your servant Jacob; they are a present sent to my lord Esau; and moreover he is behind us.'" ¹⁹He likewise instructed the second and the third and all who followed the droves, "You shall say the same thing to Esau when you meet him, ²⁰and you shall say, 'Moreover your servant Jacob is behind us.'" For he thought, "I may appease him with the present that goes before me, and afterwards I shall see his face; perhaps he will accept me." ²¹So the present passed on before him; and he himself lodged that night in the camp.

Jacob Wrestles at Peniel

22 The same night he arose and took his two wives, his two maids, and his eleven children, and crossed the ford of the Jabbok. ²³He took them and sent them across the stream, and likewise everything that he had. ²⁴And Jacob was left alone; and a man wrestled with him until the breaking of the day. ²⁵When the man saw that he did not prevail against Jacob, he touched the hollow of his thigh; and Jacob's thigh was put out of joint as he wrestled with him. ²⁶Then he said, "Let me go, for the day is breaking." But Jacob said, "I will not let you go, unless you bless me." ²⁷And he said to him, "What is your name?" And he said, "Jacob." ²⁸Then he said, "Your name shall no more be called Jacob, but Israel, ᵁ for you have striven with God and with men, and have prevailed." ²⁹Then Jacob asked him, "Tell me, I pray, your name." But he said, "Why is it that you ask my name?" And there he blessed him. ³⁰So Jacob called the name of the place Peni'el, ⱽ saying, "For I have seen God face to face, and yet my life is preserved." ³¹The sun rose upon him as he passed Penu'el, limping because of his thigh. ³²Therefore to this day the

---

° In Aramaic *The heap of witness.*
ᴾ In Hebrew *The heap of witness.*
ᑫ Compare Sam: Heb lacks *the pillar.*
ᴿ That is *Watchpost.*
ˢ Ch 32:1 in Heb.
ᵗ Here taken to mean *Two armies.*
ᵁ That is *He who strives with God* or *God strives.*
ⱽ That is *The face of God.*

Israelites do not eat the sinew of the hip which is upon the hollow of the thigh, because he touched the hollow of Jacob's thigh on the sinew of the hip.*

Jacob and Esau Meet

33 And Jacob lifted up his eyes and looked, and behold, Esau was coming, and four hundred men with him. So he divided the children among Leah and Rachel and the two maids. ²And he put the maids with their children in front, then Leah with her children, and Rachel and Joseph last of all. ³He himself went on before them, bowing himself to the ground seven times, until he came near to his brother.

4 But Esau ran to meet him, and embraced him, and fell on his neck and kissed him, and they wept. ⁵And when Esau raised his eyes and saw the women and children, he said, "Who are these with you?" Jacob said, "The children whom God has graciously given your servant." ⁶Then the maids drew near, they and their children, and bowed down; ⁷Leah likewise and her children drew near and bowed down; and last Joseph and Rachel drew near, and they bowed down. ⁸Esau said, "What do you mean by all this company which I met?" Jacob answered, "To find favor in the sight of my lord." ⁹But Esau said, "I have enough, my brother; keep what you have for yourself." ¹⁰Jacob said, "No, I beg you, if I have found favor in your sight, then accept my present from my hand; for truly to see your face is like seeing the face of God, with such favor have you received me. ¹¹Accept, I beg you, my gift that is brought to you, because God has dealt graciously with me, and because I have enough." Thus he urged him, and he took it.

12 Then Esau said, "Let us journey on our way, and I will go before you." ¹³But Jacob said to him, "My lord knows that the children are frail, and that the flocks and herds giving suck are a care to me; and if they are overdriven for one day, all the flocks will die. ¹⁴Let my lord pass on before his servant, and I will lead on slowly, according to the pace of the cattle which are before me and according to the pace of the children, until I come to my lord in Se'ir."

15 So Esau said, "Let me leave with you some of the men who are with me." But he said, "What need is there? Let me find favor in the sight of my lord." ¹⁶So Esau returned that day on his way to Se'ir. ¹⁷But Jacob journeyed to Succoth,ʷ and built himself a house, and made booths for his cattle; therefore the name of the place is called Succoth.

Jacob Comes to Shechem

18 And Jacob came safely to the city of She'chem, which is in the land of Canaan, on his way from Pad'dan-ar'am; and he camped before the city. ¹⁹And from the sons of Ha'mor, She'chem's father, he bought for a hundred pieces of money* the piece of land on which he had pitched his tent. ²⁰There he erected an altar and called it El-El'ohe-Israel. ʸ

Shechem Defiles Dinah

34 Now Dinah the daughter of Leah, whom she had borne to Jacob, went out to visit the women of the land; ²and when She'chem the son of Ha'mor the Hi'vite, the prince of the land, saw her, he seized her and lay with her and humbled her. ³And his soul was drawn to Dinah the daughter of Jacob; he loved the maiden and spoke tenderly to her. ⁴So She'chem spoke to his father Ha'mor, saying, "Get me this maiden for my wife." ⁵Now Jacob heard that he had defiled his daughter Dinah; but his sons were with his cattle in the field, so Jacob held his peace until they came. ⁶And Ha'mor the father of She'chem went out to Jacob to speak with him. ⁷The sons of Jacob came in from the field when they heard of it; and the men were indignant and very angry, because he had wrought folly in Israel by lying with Jacob's daughter, for such a thing ought not to be done.

8 But Ha'mor spoke with them, saying, "The soul of my son She'chem longs for your daughter; I beg you, give her to him in marriage. ⁹Make marriages with us; give your daughters to us, and take our daughters for yourselves. ¹⁰You shall dwell with us; and the land shall be open to you; dwell and trade in it, and get property in it." ¹¹She'chem also said to her father and to her brothers, "Let me find favor in your eyes, and whatever you say to me I will give. ¹²Ask of me ever so much as marriage present and gift, and I will give according as you say to me; only give me the maiden to be my wife."

13 The sons of Jacob answered She'chem and his father Ha'mor deceitfully, because he had defiled their sister Dinah. ¹⁴They said to them, "We cannot do this thing, to give our sister to one who is uncircumcised, for that would be a disgrace to us. ¹⁵Only on this condition will we consent to you: that you will become as we are and every male of you be circumcised. ¹⁶Then we will give our daughters to you, and we will take your daughters to ourselves, and we will dwell with you and become one people. ¹⁷But if you will not listen to us and be circumcised, then we will take our daughter, and we will be gone."

18 Their words pleased Ha'mor and Hamor's son She'chem. ¹⁹And the young man did not delay to do the thing, because he had delight in Jacob's daughter. Now he was the most honored of all his family. ²⁰So Ha'mor and his son She'chem came

---

ʷ That is *Booths.*
ˣ Heb *a hundred qesitah.*
ʸ That is *God, the God of Israel.*
* 32:24–32: The meaning of this, one of the oldest and most mysterious narratives in Genesis, remains obscure. It is intended to explain the place name Penuel, which means "face of God."

to the gate of their city and spoke to the men of their city, saying, [21]"These men are friendly with us; let them dwell in the land and trade in it, for behold, the land is large enough for them; let us take their daughters in marriage, and let us give them our daughters. [22]Only on this condition will the men agree to dwell with us, to become one people: that every male among us be circumcised as they are circumcised. [23]Will not their cattle, their property and all their beasts be ours? Only let us agree with them, and they will dwell with us." [24]And all who went out of the gate of his city hearkened to Ha'mor and his son She'chem; and every male was circumcised, all who went out of the gate of his city.

Dinah Is Avenged by Her Brothers

25 On the third day, when they were sore, two of the sons of Jacob, Simeon and Levi, Dinah's brothers, took their swords and came upon the city unawares, and killed all the males. [26]They slew Ha'mor and his son She'chem with the sword, and took Dinah out of Shechem's house, and went away. [27]And the sons of Jacob came upon the slain, and plundered the city, because their sister had been defiled; [28]they took their flocks and their herds, their donkeys, and whatever was in the city and in the field; [29]all their wealth, all their little ones and their wives, all that was in the houses, they captured and made their prey. [30]Then Jacob said to Simeon and Levi, "You have brought trouble on me by making me odious to the inhabitants of the land, the Canaanites and the Per'izzites; my numbers are few, and if they gather themselves against me and attack me, I shall be destroyed, both I and my household." [31]But they said, "Should he treat our sister as a harlot?"

Jacob Returns to Bethel

35 God said to Jacob, "Arise, go up to Bethel, and dwell there; and make there an altar to the God who appeared to you when you fled from your brother Esau." [2]So Jacob said to his household and to all who were with him, "Put away the foreign gods that are among you, and purify yourselves, and change your garments; [3]then let us arise and go up to Bethel, that I may make there an altar to the God who answered me in the day of my distress and has been with me wherever I have gone." [4]So they gave to Jacob all the foreign gods that they had, and the rings that were in their ears; and Jacob hid them under the oak which was near She'chem.

5 And as they journeyed, a terror from God fell upon the cities that were round about them, so that they did not pursue the sons of Jacob. [6]And Jacob came to Luz (that is, Bethel), which is in the land of Canaan, he and all the people who were with him, [7]and there he built an altar, and called the place El-beth'el,[z] because there God had re- vealed himself to him when he fled from his

brother. [8]And Deborah, Rebekah's nurse, died, and she was buried under an oak below Bethel; so the name of it was called Al'lon-bac'uth. [a]

9 God appeared to Jacob again, when he came from Pad'dan-ar'am, and blessed him. [10]And God said to him, "Your name is Jacob; no longer shall your name be called Jacob, but Israel shall be your name." So his name was called Israel. [11]And God said to him, "I am God Almighty:[b] be fruitful and multiply; a nation and a company of nations shall come from you, and kings shall spring from you. [12]The land which I gave to Abraham and Isaac I will give to you, and I will give the land to your descendants after you." [13]Then God went up from him in the place where he had spoken with him. [14]And Jacob set up a pillar in the place where he had spoken with him, a pillar of stone; and he poured out a drink offering on it, and poured oil on it. [15]So Jacob called the name of the place where God had spoken with him, Bethel.

The Birth of Benjamin and the Death of Rachel

16 Then they journeyed from Bethel; and when they were still some distance from Eph'rath, Rachel went into labor, and she had hard labor. [17]And when she was in her hard labor, the mid- wife said to her, "Fear not; for now you will have another son." [18]And as her soul was departing (for she died), she called his name Ben-o'ni;[c] but his father called his name Benjamin.[d] [19]So Rachel died, and she was buried on the way to Eph'rath (that is, Bethlehem), [20]and Jacob set up a pillar upon her grave; it is the pillar of Rachel's tomb, which is there to this day. [21]Israel journeyed on, and pitched his tent beyond the tower of E'der.

22 While Israel dwelt in that land Reuben went and lay with Bilhah his father's concubine; and Israel heard of it.

Now the sons of Jacob were twelve. [23]The sons of Leah: Reuben (Jacob's first-born), Simeon, Levi, Judah, Is'sachar, and Zeb'ulun. [24]The sons of Rachel: Joseph and Benjamin. [25]The sons of Bilhah, Rachel's maid: Dan and Naph'tali. [26]The sons of Zilpah, Leah's maid: Gad and Asher. These were the sons of Jacob who were born to him in Pad'dan-ar'am.

The Death of Isaac

27 And Jacob came to his father Isaac at Mamre, or Kir'iath-ar'ba (that is, He'bron), where Abraham and Isaac had sojourned. [28]Now the days of Isaac were a hundred and eighty years. [29]And Isaac breathed his last; and he died and was gathered to his people, old and full of days; and his sons Esau and Jacob buried him.

---

[z] That is God of Bethel.
[a] That is Oak of weeping.
[b] Heb El Shaddai.
[c] That is Son of my sorrow.
[d] That is Son of the right hand or Son of the South.

Esau's Descendants

36 These are the descendants of Esau (that is, E'dom). [2]Esau took his wives from the Canaanites: A'dah the daughter of E'lon the Hittite, Oholiba'mah the daughter of An'ah the son * of Zib'eon the Hi'vite, [3]and Bas'emath, Ish'mael's daughter, the sister of Neba'ioth. [4]And A'dah bore to Esau, Eli'phaz; Bas'emath bore Reu'el; [5]and Oholiba'mah bore Je'ush, Ja'lam, and Ko'rah. These are the sons of Esau who were born to him in the land of Canaan.

6 Then Esau took his wives, his sons, his daughters, and all the members of his household, his cattle, all his beasts, and all his property which he had acquired in the land of Canaan; and he went into a land away from his brother Jacob. [7]For their possessions were too great for them to dwell together; the land of their sojournings could not support them because of their cattle. [8]So Esau dwelt in the hill country of Se'ir; Esau is E'dom.

9 These are the descendants of Esau the father of the E'domites in the hill country of Se'ir. [10]These are the names of Esau's sons: Eli'phaz the son of A'dah the wife of Esau, Reu'el the son of Bas'emath the wife of Esau. [11]The sons of Eli'phaz were Te'man, Omar, Ze'pho, Ga'tam, and Ke'naz. [12](Timna was a concubine of Eli'phaz, Esau's son; she bore Am'alek to Eliphaz.) These are the sons of A'dah, Esau's wife. [13]These are the sons of Reu'el: Na'hath, Ze'rah, Shammah, and Mizzah. These are the sons of Bas'emath, Esau's wife. [14]These are the sons of Oholiba'mah the daughter of An'ah the son f of Zib'eon, Esau's wife: she bore to Esau Je'ush, Ja'lam, and Ko'rah.

Chiefs and Kings of Edom

15 These are the chiefs of the sons of Esau. The sons of Eli'phaz the first-born of Esau: the chiefs Te'man, Omar, Ze'pho, Ke'naz, [16]Ko'rah, Ga'tam, and Am'alek; these are the chiefs of Eli'phaz in the land of E'dom; they are the sons of A'dah. [17]These are the sons of Reu'el, Esau's son: the chiefs Na'hath, Ze'rah, Shammah, and Mizzah; these are the chiefs of Reu'el in the land of E'dom; they are the sons of Bas'emath, Esau's wife. [18]These are the sons of Oholiba'mah, Esau's wife: the chiefs Je'ush, Ja'lam, and Ko'rah; these are the chiefs born of Oholiba'mah the daughter of An'ah, Esau's wife. [19]These are the sons of Esau (that is, E'dom), and these are their chiefs.

20 These are the sons of Se'ir the Horite, the inhabitants of the land: Lo'tan, Sho'bal, Zib'eon, An'ah, [21]Di'shon, E'zer, and Di'shan; these are the chiefs of the Horites, the sons of Se'ir in the land of E'dom. [22]The sons of Lo'tan were Ho'ri and He'man; and Lo'tan's sister was Timna. [23]These are the sons of Sho'bal: Alvan, Man'ahath, E'bal, She'pho, and Onam. [24]These are the sons of Zib'eon: A'iah and An'ah; he is the Anah who found the hot springs in the wilderness, as he pastured the donkeys of Zibeon his father. [25]These are the children of An'ah: Di'shon and Oholiba'mah the daughter of Anah. [26]These are the sons of Di'shon: Hemdan, Eshban, Ithran, and Che'ran. [27]These are the sons of E'zer: Bilhan, Za'avan, and A'kan. [28]These are the sons of Di'shan: Uz and Ar'an. [29]These are the chiefs of the Horites: the chiefs Lo'tan, Sho'bal, Zib'eon, An'ah, [30]Di'shon, E'zer, and Di'shan; these are the chiefs of the Horites, according to their clans in the land of Se'ir.

31 These are the kings who reigned in the land of E'dom, before any king reigned over the Israelites. [32]Be'la the son of Beor reigned in E'dom, the name of his city being Din'habah. [33]Be'la died, and Jo'bab the son of Ze'rah of Bozrah reigned in his stead. [34]Jo'bab died, and Hu'sham of the land of the Te'manites reigned in his stead. [35]Hu'sham died, and Ha'dad the son of Be'dad, who defeated Mid'ian in the country of Moab, reigned in his stead, the name of his city being A'vith. [36]Ha'dad died, and Samlah of Masre'kah reigned in his stead. [37]Samlah died, and Sha'ul of Reho'both on the Euphra'tes reigned in his stead. [38]Sha'ul died, and Ba'al-ha'nan the son of Achbor reigned in his stead. [39]Ba'al-ha'nan the son of Achbor died, and Hadar reigned in his stead, the name of his city being Pa'u; his wife's name was Mehet'abel, the daughter of Ma'tred, daughter of Me'zahab.

40 These are the names of the chiefs of Esau, according to their families and their dwelling places, by their names: the chiefs Timna, Alvah, Je'theth, [41]Oholiba'mah, E'lah, Pi'non, [42]Ke'naz, Te'man, Mibzar, [43]Mag'diel, and I'ram; these are the chiefs of E'dom (that is, Esau, the father of Edom), according to their dwelling places in the land of their possession.

Joseph Dreams of Greatness

37 Jacob dwelt in the land of his father's sojournings, in the land of Canaan. [2]This is the history of the family of Jacob.

* Joseph, being seventeen years old, was shepherding the flock with his brothers; he was a lad with the sons of Bilhah and Zilpah, his father's wives; and Joseph brought an ill report of them to their father. [3]Now Israel loved Joseph more than any other of his children, because he was the son of his old age; and he made him a long robe with sleeves. [4]But when his brothers saw that their father loved him more than all his brothers, they hated him, and could not speak peaceably to him.

---

* Sam Gk Syr: Heb *daughter*.
f Gk Syr: Heb *daughter*.
36:2: Gen 26:34; 28:9.
36:20–28: 1 Chron 1:38–42.
36:31–43: 1 Chron 1:43–53.
* 37:2: From this point the book of Genesis is chiefly concerned with the Joseph story, which is full of the sense of divine providence. It has, as might be expected, a markedly Egyptian character.

5 Now Joseph had a dream, and when he told it to his brothers they only hated him the more. [6]He said to them, "Hear this dream which I have dreamed: [7]behold, we were binding sheaves in the field, and behold, my sheaf arose and stood upright; and behold, your sheaves gathered round it, and bowed down to my sheaf." [8]His brothers said to him, "Are you indeed to reign over us? Or are you indeed to have dominion over us?" So they hated him yet more for his dreams and for his words. [9]Then he dreamed another dream, and told it to his brothers, and said, "Behold, I have dreamed another dream; and behold, the sun, the moon, and eleven stars were bowing down to me." [10]But when he told it to his father and to his brothers, his father rebuked him, and said to him, "What is this dream that you have dreamed? Shall I and your mother and your brothers indeed come to bow ourselves to the ground before you?" [11]And his brothers were jealous of him, but his father kept the saying in mind.

Joseph Is Sold by His Brothers

12 Now his brothers went to pasture their father's flock near She'chem. [13]And Israel said to Joseph, "Are not your brothers pasturing the flock at She'chem? Come, I will send you to them." And he said to him, "Here I am." [14]So he said to him, "Go now, see if it is well with your brothers, and with the flock; and bring me word again." So he sent him from the valley of He'bron, and he came to She'chem. [15]And a man found him wandering in the fields; and the man asked him, "What are you seeking?" [16]"I am seeking my brothers," he said, "tell me, I beg you, where they are pasturing the flock." [17]And the man said, "They have gone away, for I heard them say, 'Let us go to Do'than.'" So Joseph went after his brothers, and found them at Dothan. [18]They saw him afar off, and before he came near to them they conspired against him to kill him. [19]They said to one another, "Here comes this dreamer. [20]Come now, let us kill him and throw him into one of the pits; then we shall say that a wild beast has devoured him, and we shall see what will become of his dreams." [21]But when Reuben heard it, he delivered him out of their hands, saying, "Let us not take his life." [22]And Reuben said to them, "Shed no blood; cast him into this pit here in the wilderness, but lay no hand upon him"—that he might rescue him out of their hand, to restore him to his father. [23]So when Joseph came to his brothers, they stripped him of his robe, the long robe with sleeves that he wore; [24]and they took him and cast him into a pit. The pit was empty, there was no water in it.

25 Then they sat down to eat; and looking up they saw a caravan of Ish'maelites coming from Gilead, with their camels bearing gum, balm, and myrrh, on their way to carry it down to Egypt. [26]Then Judah said to his brothers, "What profit is it if we slay our brother and conceal his blood? [27]Come, let us sell him to the Ish'maelites, and let not our hand be upon him, for he is our brother, our own flesh." And his brothers heeded him. [28]Then Mid'ianite traders passed by; and they drew Joseph up and lifted him out of the pit, and sold him to the Ish'maelites for twenty shekels of silver; and they took Joseph to Egypt.

29 When Reuben returned to the pit and saw that Joseph was not in the pit, he tore his clothes [30]and returned to his brothers, and said, "The lad is gone; and I, where shall I go?" [31]Then they took Joseph's robe, and killed a goat, and dipped the robe in the blood; [32]and they sent the long robe with sleeves and brought it to their father, and said, "This we have found; see now whether it is your son's robe or not." [33]And he recognized it, and said, "It is my son's robe; a wild beast has devoured him; Joseph is without doubt torn to pieces." [34]Then Jacob tore his garments, and put sackcloth upon his loins, and mourned for his son many days. [35]All his sons and all his daughters rose up to comfort him; but he refused to be comforted, and said, "No, I shall go down to Sheol to my son, mourning." Thus his father wept for him. [36]Meanwhile the Mid'ianites had sold him in Egypt to Pot'iphar, an officer of Pharaoh, the captain of the guard.

Judah and Tamar

38 It happened at that time that Judah went down from his brothers, and turned in to a certain Adul'lamite, whose name was Hi'rah. [2]There Judah saw the daughter of a certain Canaanite whose name was Shua; he married her and went in to her, [3]and she conceived and bore a son, and he called his name Er. [4]Again she conceived and bore a son, and she called his name O'nan. [5]Yet again she bore a son, and she called his name She'lah. She [g] was in Che'zib when she bore him. [6]And Judah took a wife for Er his first-born, and her name was Ta'mar. [7]But Er, Judah's first-born, was wicked in the sight of the Lord; and the Lord slew him. [8]Then Judah said to O'nan, "Go in to your brother's wife, and perform the duty of a brother-in-law to her, and raise up offspring for your brother." [9]But O'nan knew that the offspring would not be his; so when he went in to his brother's wife he spilled the semen on the ground, lest he should give offspring to his brother. [10]And what he did was displeasing in the sight of the Lord, and he slew him also. [11]Then Judah said to Ta'mar his daughter-in-law, "Remain a widow in your father's house, till She'lah my son grows up"—for he feared that he would die, like his brothers. So Ta'mar went and dwelt in her father's house.

---

g Gk: Heb He.
37:11, 28: Acts 7:9.

12 In course of time the wife of Judah, Shua's daughter, died; and when Judah was comforted, he went up to Timnah to his sheepshearers, he and his friend Hi′rah the Adul′lamite. [13]And when Tamar was told, "Your father-in-law is going up to Timnah to shear his sheep," [14]she put off her widow's garments, and put on a veil, wrapping herself up, and sat at the entrance to Enaim, which is on the road to Timnah; for she saw that She′lah was grown up, and she had not been given to him in marriage. [15]When Judah saw her, he thought her to be a harlot, for she had covered her face. [16]He went over to her at the road side, and said, "Come, let me come in to you," for he did not know that she was his daughter-in-law. She said, "What will you give me, that you may come in to me?" [17]He answered, "I will send you a kid from the flock." And she said, "Will you give me a pledge, till you send it?" [18]He said, "What pledge shall I give you?" She replied, "Your signet and your cord, and your staff that is in your hand." So he gave them to her, and went in to her, and she conceived by him. [19]Then she arose and went away, and taking off her veil she put on the garments of her widowhood.

20 When Judah sent the kid by his friend the Adul′lamite, to receive the pledge from the woman's hand, he could not find her. [21]And he asked the men of the place, "Where is the harlot [h] who was at Ena′im by the wayside?" And they said, "No harlot [h] has been here." [22]So he returned to Judah, and said, "I have not found her; and also the men of the place said, 'No harlot [h] has been here.' " [23]And Judah replied, "Let her keep the things as her own, lest we be laughed at; you see, I sent this kid, and you could not find her."

24 About three months later Judah was told, "Ta′mar your daughter-in-law has played the harlot; and moreover she is with child by harlotry." And Judah said, "Bring her out, and let her be burned." [25]As she was being brought out, she sent word to her father-in-law, "By the man to whom these belong, I am with child." And she said, "Mark, I beg you, whose these are, the signet and the cord and the staff." [26]Then Judah acknowledged them and said, "She is more righteous than I, inasmuch as I did not give her to my son She′lah." And he did not lie with her again.

27 When the time of her delivery came, there were twins in her womb. [28]And when she was in labor, one put out a hand; and the midwife took and bound on his hand a scarlet thread, saying, "This came out first." [29]But as he drew back his hand, behold, his brother came out; and she said, "What a breach you have made for yourself!" Therefore his name was called Per′ez.[i] [30]Afterward his brother came out with the scarlet thread upon his hand; and his name was called Ze′rah.

Joseph and Potiphar's Wife

39 Now Joseph was taken down to Egypt, and Pot′iphar, an officer of Pharaoh, the captain of the guard, an Egyptian, bought him from the Ish′maelites who had brought him down there. [2]The LORD was with Joseph, and he became a successful man; and he was in the house of his master the Egyptian, [3]and his master saw that the LORD was with him, and that the LORD caused all that he did to prosper in his hands. [4]So Joseph found favor in his sight and attended him, and he made him overseer of his house and put him in charge of all that he had. [5]From the time that he made him overseer in his house and over all that he had the LORD blessed the Egyptian's house for Joseph's sake; the blessing of the LORD was upon all that he had, in house and field. [6]So he left all that he had in Joseph's charge; and having him he had no concern for anything but the food which he ate.

Now Joseph was handsome and good-looking. [7]And after a time his master's wife cast her eyes upon Joseph, and said, "Lie with me." [8]But he refused and said to his master's wife, "Behold, having me my master has no concern about anything in the house, and he has put everything that he has in my hand; [9]he is not greater in this house than I am; nor has he kept back anything from me except yourself, because you are his wife; how then can I do this great wickedness, and sin against God?" [10]And although she spoke to Joseph day after day, he would not listen to her, to lie with her or to be with her. [11]But one day, when he went into the house to do his work and none of the men of the house was there in the house, [12]she caught him by his garment, saying, "Lie with me." But he left his garment in her hand, and fled and got out of the house. [13]And when she saw that he had left his garment in her hand, and had fled out of the house, [14]she called to the men of her household and said to them, "See, he has brought among us a Hebrew to insult us; he came in to me to lie with me, and I cried out with a loud voice; [15]and when he heard that I lifted up my voice and cried, he left his garment with me, and fled and got out of the house." [16]Then she laid up his garment by her until his master came home, [17]and she told him the same story, saying, "The Hebrew servant, whom you have brought among us, came in to me to insult me; [18]but as soon as I lifted up my voice and cried, he left his garment with me, and fled out of the house."

19 When his master heard the words which his wife spoke to him, "This is the way your servant treated me," his anger was kindled. [20]And Joseph's master took him and put him into the

---

[h] Or *cult prostitute.*
[i] That is *A breach.*
39:1, 2, 21: Acts 7:9.

prison, the place where the king's prisoners were confined, and he was there in prison. [21]But the LORD was with Joseph and showed him mercy, and gave him favor in the sight of the keeper of the prison. [22]And the keeper of the prison committed to Joseph's care all the prisoners who were in the prison; and whatever was done there, he was the doer of it; [23]the keeper of the prison paid no heed to anything that was in Joseph's care, because the LORD was with him; and whatever he did, the LORD made it prosper.

The Dreams of Two Prisoners

40 Some time after this, the butler of the king of Egypt and his baker offended their lord the king of Egypt. [2]And Pharaoh was angry with his two officers, the chief butler and the chief baker, [3]and he put them in custody in the house of the captain of the guard, in the prison where Joseph was confined. [4]The captain of the guard charged Joseph with them, and he waited on them; and they continued for some time in custody. [5]And one night they both dreamed—the butler and the baker of the king of Egypt, who were confined in the prison—each his own dream, and each dream with its own meaning. [6]When Joseph came to them in the morning and saw them, they were troubled. [7]So he asked Pharaoh's officers who were with him in custody in his master's house, "Why are your faces downcast today?" [8]They said to him, "We have had dreams, and there is no one to interpret them." And Joseph said to them, "Do not interpretations belong to God? Tell them to me, I beg you."

9 So the chief butler told his dream to Joseph, and said to him, "In my dream there was a vine before me, [10]and on the vine there were three branches; as soon as it budded, its blossoms shot forth, and the clusters ripened into grapes. [11]Pharaoh's cup was in my hand; and I took the grapes and pressed them into Pharaoh's cup, and placed the cup in Pharaoh's hand." [12]Then Joseph said to him, "This is its interpretation: the three branches are three days; [13]within three days Pharaoh will lift up your head and restore you to your office; and you shall place Pharaoh's cup in his hand as formerly, when you were his butler. [14]But remember me, when it is well with you, and do me the kindness, I beg you, to make mention of me to Pharaoh, and so get me out of this house. [15]For I was indeed stolen out of the land of the Hebrews; and here also I have done nothing that they should put me into the dungeon."

16 When the chief baker saw that the interpretation was favorable, he said to Joseph, "I also had a dream: there were three cake baskets on my head, [17]and in the uppermost basket there were all sorts of baked food for Pharaoh, but the birds were eating it out of the basket on my head." [18]And Joseph answered, "This is its interpreta-

tion: the three baskets are three days; [19]within three days Pharaoh will lift up your head—from you!—and hang you on a tree; and the birds will eat the flesh from you."

20 On the third day, which was Pharaoh's birthday, he made a feast for all his servants, and lifted up the head of the chief butler and the head of the chief baker among his servants. [21]He restored the chief butler to his butlership, and he placed the cup in Pharaoh's hand; [22]but he hanged the chief baker, as Joseph had interpreted to them. [23]Yet the chief butler did not remember Joseph, but forgot him.

Joseph Interprets Pharaoh's Dream

41 After two whole years, Pharaoh dreamed that he was standing by the Nile, [2]and behold, there came up out of the Nile seven cows sleek and fat, and they fed in the reed grass. [3]And behold, seven other cows, gaunt and thin, came up out of the Nile after them, and stood by the other cows on the bank of the Nile. [4]And the gaunt and thin cows ate up the seven sleek and fat cows. And Pharaoh awoke. [5]And he fell asleep and dreamed a second time; and behold, seven ears of grain, plump and good, were growing on one stalk. [6]And behold, after them sprouted seven ears, thin and blighted by the east wind. [7]And the thin ears swallowed up the seven plump and full ears. And Pharaoh awoke, and behold, it was a dream. [8]So in the morning his spirit was troubled; and he sent and called for all the magicians of Egypt and all its wise men; and Pharaoh told them his dream, but there was none who could interpret it [j] to Pharaoh.

9 Then the chief butler said to Pharaoh, "I remember my faults today. [10]When Pharaoh was angry with his servants, and put me and the chief baker in custody in the house of the captain of the guard, [11]we dreamed on the same night, he and I, each having a dream with its own meaning. [12]A young Hebrew was there with us, a servant of the captain of the guard; and when we told him, he interpreted our dreams to us, giving an interpretation to each man according to his dream. [13]And as he interpreted to us, so it came to pass; I was restored to my office, and the baker was hanged."

14 Then Pharaoh sent and called Joseph, and they brought him hastily out of the dungeon; and when he had shaved himself and changed his clothes, he came in before Pharaoh. [15]And Pharaoh said to Joseph, "I have had a dream, and there is no one who can interpret it; and I have heard it said of you that when you hear a dream you can interpret it." [16]Joseph answered Pharaoh, "It is not in me; God will give Pharaoh a favorable answer." [17]Then Pharaoh said to Joseph, "Behold,

---

[j] Gk: Heb *them.*

in my dream I was standing on the banks of the Nile; [18]and seven cows, fat and sleek, came up out of the Nile and fed in the reed grass; [19]and seven other cows came up after them, poor and very gaunt and thin, such as I had never seen in all the land of Egypt. [20]And the thin and gaunt cows ate up the first seven fat cows, [21]but when they had eaten them no one would have known that they had eaten them, for they were still as gaunt as at the beginning. Then I awoke. [22]I also saw in my dream seven ears growing on one stalk, full and good; [23]and seven ears, withered, thin, and blighted by the east wind, sprouted after them, [24]and the thin ears swallowed up the seven good ears. And I told it to the magicians, but there was no one who could explain it to me."

25 Then Joseph said to Pharaoh, "The dream of Pharaoh is one; God has revealed to Pharaoh what he is about to do. [26]The seven good cows are seven years, and the seven good ears are seven years; the dream is one. [27]The seven lean and gaunt cows that came up after them are seven years, and the seven empty ears blighted by the east wind are also seven years of famine. [28]It is as I told Pharaoh, God has shown to Pharaoh what he is about to do. [29]There will come seven years of great plenty throughout all the land of Egypt, [30]but after them there will arise seven years of famine, and all the plenty will be forgotten in the land of Egypt; the famine will consume the land, [31]and the plenty will be unknown in the land by reason of that famine which will follow, for it will be very grievous. [32]And the doubling of Pharaoh's dream means that the thing is fixed by God, and God will shortly bring it to pass. [33]Now therefore let Pharaoh select a man discreet and wise, and set him over the land of Egypt. [34]Let Pharaoh proceed to appoint overseers over the land, and take the fifth part of the produce of the land of Egypt during the seven plenteous years. [35]And let them gather all the food of these good years that are coming, and lay up grain under the authority of Pharaoh for food in the cities, and let them keep it. [36]That food shall be a reserve for the land against the seven years of famine which are to befall the land of Egypt, so that the land may not perish through the famine."

Joseph's Rise to Power in Egypt

37 This proposal seemed good to Pharaoh and to all his servants. [38]And Pharaoh said to his servants, "Can we find such a man as this, in whom is the Spirit of God?" [39]So Pharaoh said to Joseph, "Since God has shown you all this, there is none so discreet and wise as you are; [40]you shall be over my house, and all my people shall order themselves as you command; only as regards the throne will I be greater than you." [41]And Pharaoh said to Joseph, "Behold, I have set you over all the land of Egypt." [42]Then Pharaoh took his signet ring from his hand and put it on Joseph's hand, and arrayed him in garments of fine linen, and put a gold chain about his neck; [43]and he made him to ride in his second chariot; and they cried before him, "Bow the knee!" [k] Thus he set him over all the land of Egypt. [44]Moreover Pharaoh said to Joseph, "I am Pharaoh, and without your consent no man shall lift up hand or foot in all the land of Egypt." [45]And Pharaoh called Joseph's name Zaph'enath-pane'ah; and he gave him in marriage As'enath, the daughter of Poti'phera priest of On. So Joseph went out over the land of Egypt.

46 Joseph was thirty years old when he entered the service of Pharaoh king of Egypt. And Joseph went out from the presence of Pharaoh, and went through all the land of Egypt. [47]During the seven plenteous years the earth brought forth abundantly, [48]and he gathered up all the food of the seven years when there was plenty [l] in the land of Egypt, and stored up food in the cities; he stored up in every city the food from the fields around it. [49]And Joseph stored up grain in great abundance, like the sand of the sea, until he ceased to measure it, for it could not be measured.

50 Before the year of famine came, Joseph had two sons, whom As'enath, the daughter of Poti'-phera priest of On, bore to him. [51]Joseph called the name of the first-born Manas'seh, [m] "For," he said, "God has made me forget all my hardship and all my father's house." [52]The name of the second he called E'phraim, [n] "For God has made me fruitful in the land of my affliction."

53 The seven years of plenty that prevailed in the land of Egypt came to an end; [54]and the seven years of famine began to come, as Joseph had said. There was famine in all lands; but in all the land of Egypt there was bread. [55]When all the land of Egypt was famished, the people cried to Pharaoh for bread; and Pharaoh said to all the Egyptians, "Go to Joseph; what he says to you, do." [56]So when the famine had spread over all the land, Joseph opened all the storehouses, [o] and sold to the Egyptians, for the famine was severe in the land of Egypt. [57]Moreover, all the earth came to Egypt to Joseph to buy grain, because the famine was severe over all the earth.

Joseph's Brothers Go to Egypt

42 When Jacob learned that there was grain in Egypt, he said to his sons, "Why do you look at one another?" [2]And he said, "Behold, I

---

[k] *Abrek*, probably an Egyptian word similar in sound to the Hebrew word meaning *to kneel*.
[l] Sam Gk: Heb *which were*.
[m] That is *Making to forget*.
[n] From a Hebrew word meaning *to be fruitful*.
[o] Gk Vg Compare Syr: Heb *all that was in them*.

41:38–45: Acts 7:10.
41:54: Acts 7:11.
42:2: Acts 7:12.

have heard that there is grain in Egypt; go down and buy grain for us there, that we may live, and not die." [3]So ten of Joseph's brothers went down to buy grain in Egypt. [4]But Jacob did not send Benjamin, Joseph's brother, with his brothers, for he feared that harm might befall him. [5]Thus the sons of Israel came to buy among the others who came, for the famine was in the land of Canaan.

6 Now Joseph was governor over the land; he it was who sold to all the people of the land. And Joseph's brothers came, and bowed themselves before him with their faces to the ground. [7]Joseph saw his brothers, and knew them, but he treated them like strangers and spoke roughly to them. "Where do you come from?" he said. They said, "From the land of Canaan, to buy food." [8]Thus Joseph knew his brothers, but they did not know him. [9]And Joseph remembered the dreams which he had dreamed of them; and he said to them, "You are spies, you have come to see the weakness of the land." [10]They said to him, "No, my lord, but to buy food have your servants come. [11]We are all sons of one man, we are honest men, your servants are not spies." [12]He said to them, "No, it is the weakness of the land that you have come to see." [13]And they said, "We, your servants, are twelve brothers, the sons of one man in the land of Canaan; and behold, the youngest is this day with our father, and one is no more." [14]But Joseph said to them, "It is as I said to you, you are spies. [15]By this you shall be tested: by the life of Pharaoh, you shall not go from this place unless your youngest brother comes here. [16]Send one of you, and let him bring your brother, while you remain in prison, that your words may be tested, whether there is truth in you; or else, by the life of Pharaoh, surely you are spies." [17]And he put them all together in prison for three days.

18 On the third day Joseph said to them, "Do this and you will live, for I fear God: [19]if you are honest men, let one of your brothers remain confined in your prison, and let the rest go and carry grain for the famine of your households, [20]and bring your youngest brother to me; so your words will be verified, and you shall not die." And they did so. [21]Then they said to one another, "In truth we are guilty concerning our brother, in that we saw the distress of his soul, when he begged us and we would not listen; therefore is this distress come upon us." [22]And Reuben answered them, "Did I not tell you not to sin against the lad? But you would not listen. So now there comes a reckoning for his blood." [23]They did not know that Joseph understood them, for there was an interpreter between them. [24]Then he turned away from them and wept; and he returned to them and spoke to them. And he took Simeon from them and bound him before their eyes. [25]And Joseph gave orders to fill their bags with grain, and to replace every man's money in his sack, and to give them provisions for the journey. This was done for them.

Joseph's Brothers Return to Canaan

26 Then they loaded their donkeys with their grain, and departed. [27]And as one of them opened his sack to give his donkey food at the lodging place, he saw his money in the mouth of his sack; [28]and he said to his brothers, "My money has been put back; here it is in the mouth of my sack!" At this their hearts failed them, and they turned trembling to one another, saying, "What is this that God has done to us?"

29 When they came to Jacob their father in the land of Canaan, they told him all that had befallen them, saying, [30]"The man, the lord of the land, spoke roughly to us, and took us to be spies of the land. [31]But we said to him, 'We are honest men, we are not spies; [32]we are twelve brothers, sons of our father; one is no more, and the youngest is this day with our father in the land of Canaan.' [33]Then the man, the lord of the land, said to us, 'By this I shall know that you are honest men: leave one of your brothers with me, and take grain for the famine of your households, and go your way. [34]Bring your youngest brother to me; then I shall know that you are not spies but honest men, and I will deliver to you your brother, and you shall trade in the land.' "

35 As they emptied their sacks, behold, every man's bundle of money was in his sack; and when they and their father saw their bundles of money, they were dismayed. [36]And Jacob their father said to them, "You have bereaved me of my children: Joseph is no more, and Simeon is no more, and now you would take Benjamin; all this has come upon me." [37]Then Reuben said to his father, "Slay my two sons if I do not bring him back to you; put him in my hands, and I will bring him back to you." [38]But he said, "My son shall not go down with you, for his brother is dead, and he only is left. If harm should befall him on the journey that you are to make, you would bring down my gray hairs with sorrow to Sheol."

Joseph's Brothers Bring Benjamin to Egypt

43 Now the famine was severe in the land. [2]And when they had eaten the grain which they had brought from Egypt, their father said to them, "Go again, buy us a little food." [3]But Judah said to him, "The man solemnly warned us, saying, 'You shall not see my face, unless your brother is with you.' [4]If you will send our brother with us, we will go down and buy you food; [5]but if you will not send him, we will not go down, for the man said to us, 'You shall not see my face, unless your brother is with you.' " [6]Israel said, "Why did you treat me so ill

42:5: Acts 7:11.

as to tell the man that you had another brother?" [7]They replied, "The man questioned us carefully about ourselves and our kindred, saying, 'Is your father still alive? Have you another brother?' What we told him was in answer to these questions; could we in any way know that he would say, 'Bring your brother down'?" [8]And Judah said to Israel his father, "Send the lad with me, and we will arise and go, that we may live and not die, both we and you and also our little ones. [9]I will be surety for him; of my hand you shall require him. If I do not bring him back to you and set him before you, then let me bear the blame for ever; [10]for if we had not delayed, we would now have returned twice."

11 Then their father Israel said to them, "If it must be so, then do this: take some of the choice fruits of the land in your bags, and carry down to the man a present, a little balm and a little honey, gum, myrrh, pistachio nuts, and almonds. [12]Take double the money with you; carry back with you the money that was returned in the mouth of your sacks; perhaps it was an oversight. [13]Take also your brother, and arise, go again to the man; [14]may God Almighty [p] grant you mercy before the man, that he may send back your other brother and Benjamin. If I am bereaved of my children, I am bereaved." [15]So the men took the present, and they took double the money with them, and Benjamin; and they arose and went down to Egypt, and stood before Joseph.

16 When Joseph saw Benjamin with them, he said to the steward of his house, "Bring the men into the house, and slaughter an animal and make ready, for the men are to dine with me at noon." [17]The man did as Joseph bade him, and brought the men to Joseph's house. [18]And the men were afraid because they were brought to Joseph's house, and they said, "It is because of the money, which was replaced in our sacks the first time, that we are brought in, so that he may seek occasion against us and fall upon us, to make slaves of us and seize our donkeys." [19]So they went up to the steward of Joseph's house, and spoke with him at the door of the house, [20]and said, "Oh, my lord, we came down the first time to buy food; [21]and when we came to the lodging place we opened our sacks, and there was every man's money in the mouth of his sack, our money in full weight; so we have brought it again with us, [22]and we have brought other money down in our hand to buy food. We do not know who put our money in our sacks." [23]He replied, "Rest assured, do not be afraid; your God and the God of your father must have put treasure in your sacks for you; I received your money." Then he brought Simeon out to them. [24]And when the man had brought the men into Joseph's house, and given them water, and they had washed their feet, and when he had

given their donkeys food, [25]they made ready the present for Joseph's coming at noon, for they heard that they should eat bread there.

26 When Joseph came home, they brought into the house to him the present which they had with them, and bowed down to him to the ground. [27]And he inquired about their welfare, and said, "Is your father well, the old man of whom you spoke? Is he still alive?" [28]They said, "Your servant our father is well, he is still alive." And they bowed their heads and made obeisance. [29]And he lifted up his eyes, and saw his brother Benjamin, his mother's son, and said, "Is this your youngest brother, of whom you spoke to me? God be gracious to you, my son!" [30]Then Joseph made haste, for his heart yearned for his brother, and he sought a place to weep. And he entered his chamber and wept there. [31]Then he washed his face and came out; and controlling himself he said, "Let food be served." [32]They served him by himself, and them by themselves, and the Egyptians who ate with him by themselves, because the Egyptians might not eat bread with the Hebrews, for that is an abomination to the Egyptians. [33]And they sat before him, the first-born according to his birthright and the youngest according to his youth; and the men looked at one another in amazement. [34]Portions were taken to them from Joseph's table, but Benjamin's portion was five times as much as any of theirs. So they drank and were merry with him.

Joseph Detains Benjamin

44 Then he commanded the steward of his house, "Fill the men's sacks with food, as much as they can carry, and put each man's money in the mouth of his sack, [2]and put my cup, the silver cup, in the mouth of the sack of the youngest, with his money for the grain." And he did as Joseph told him. [3]As soon as the morning was light, the men were sent away with their donkeys. [4]When they had gone but a short distance from the city, Joseph said to his steward, "Up, follow after the men; and when you overtake them, say to them, 'Why have you returned evil for good? Why have you stolen my silver cup? [q] [5]Is it not from this that my lord drinks, and by this that he divines? You have done wrong in so doing.'"

6 When he overtook them, he spoke to them these words. [7]They said to him, "Why does my lord speak such words as these? Far be it from your servants that they should do such a thing! [8]Behold, the money which we found in the mouth of our sacks, we brought back to you from the land of Canaan; how then should we steal silver or gold from your lord's house? [9]With whomever

[p] Heb El Shaddai.
[q] Gk Compare Vg: Heb lacks Why have you stolen my silver cup?

of your servants it be found, let him die, and we also will be my lord's slaves." [10]He said, "Let it be as you say: he with whom it is found shall be my slave, and the rest of you shall be blameless." [11]Then every man quickly lowered his sack to the ground, and every man opened his sack. [12]And he searched, beginning with the eldest and ending with the youngest; and the cup was found in Benjamin's sack. [13]Then they tore their clothes, and every man loaded his donkey, and they returned to the city.

14 When Judah and his brothers came to Joseph's house, he was still there; and they fell before him to the ground. [15]Joseph said to them, "What deed is this that you have done? Do you not know that such a man as I can indeed divine?" [16]And Judah said, "What shall we say to my lord? What shall we speak? Or how can we clear ourselves? God has found out the guilt of your servants; behold, we are my lord's slaves, both we and he also in whose hand the cup has been found." [17]But he said, "Far be it from me that I should do so! Only the man in whose hand the cup was found shall be my slave; but as for you, go up in peace to your father."

Judah Pleads for Benjamin's Release

18 Then Judah went up to him and said, "O my lord, let your servant, I beg you, speak a word in my lord's ears, and let not your anger burn against your servant; for you are like Pharaoh himself. [19]My lord asked his servants, saying, 'Have you a father, or a brother?' [20]And we said to my lord, 'We have a father, an old man, and a young brother, the child of his old age; and his brother is dead, and he alone is left of his mother's children; and his father loves him.' [21]Then you said to your servants, 'Bring him down to me, that I may set my eyes upon him.' [22]We said to my lord, 'The lad cannot leave his father, for if he should leave his father, his father would die.' [23]Then you said to your servants, 'Unless your youngest brother comes down with you, you shall see my face no more.' [24]When we went back to your servant my father we told him the words of my lord. [25]And when our father said, 'Go again, buy us a little food,' [26]we said, 'We cannot go down. If our youngest brother goes with us, then we will go down; for we cannot see the man's face unless our youngest brother is with us.' [27]Then your servant my father said to us, 'You know that my wife bore me two sons; [28]one left me, and I said, Surely he has been torn to pieces; and I have never seen him since. [29]If you take this one also from me, and harm befalls him, you will bring down my gray hairs in sorrow to Sheol.' [30]Now therefore, when I come to your servant my father, and the lad is not with us, then, as his life is bound up in the lad's life, [31]when he sees that the lad is not with us, he will die; and your servants will bring down the gray hairs of

your servant our father with sorrow to Sheol. [32]For your servant became surety for the lad to my father, saying, 'If I do not bring him back to you, then I shall bear the blame in the sight of my father all my life.' [33]Now therefore, let your servant, I beg you, remain instead of the lad as a slave to my lord; and let the lad go back with his brothers. [34]For how can I go back to my father if the lad is not with me? I fear to see the evil that would come upon my father."

Joseph Makes Himself Known to His Brothers

45 Then Joseph could not control himself before all those who stood by him; and he cried, "Make every one go out from me." So no one stayed with him when Joseph made himself known to his brothers. [2]And he wept aloud, so that the Egyptians heard it, and the household of Pharaoh heard it. [3]And Joseph said to his brothers, "I am Joseph; is my father still alive?" But his brothers could not answer him, for they were dismayed at his presence.

4 So Joseph said to his brothers, "Come near to me, I beg you." And they came near. And he said, "I am your brother, Joseph, whom you sold into Egypt. [5]And now do not be distressed, or angry with yourselves, because you sold me here; for God sent me before you to preserve life. [6]For the famine has been in the land these two years; and there are yet five years in which there will be neither plowing nor harvest. [7]And God sent me before you to preserve for you a remnant on earth, and to keep alive for you many survivors. [8]So it was not you who sent me here, but God; and he has made me a father to Pharaoh, and lord of all his house and ruler over all the land of Egypt. [9]Make haste and go up to my father and say to him, 'Thus says your son Joseph, God has made me lord of all Egypt; come down to me, do not tarry; [10]you shall dwell in the land of Go'shen, and you shall be near me, you and your children and your children's children, and your flocks, your herds, and all that you have; [11]and there I will provide for you, for there are yet five years of famine to come; lest you and your household, and all that you have, come to poverty.' [12]And now your eyes see, and the eyes of my brother Benjamin see, that it is my mouth that speaks to you. [13]You must tell my father of all my splendor in Egypt, and of all that you have seen. Make haste and bring my father down here." [14]Then he fell upon his brother Benjamin's neck and wept; and Benjamin wept upon his neck. [15]And he kissed all his brothers and wept upon them; and after that his brothers talked with him.

16 When the report was heard in Pharaoh's house, "Joseph's brothers have come," it pleased

---

45:1: Acts 7:13.

Pharaoh and his servants well. [17]And Pharaoh said to Joseph, "Say to your brothers, 'Do this: load your beasts and go back to the land of Canaan; [18]and take your father and your households, and come to me, and I will give you the best of the land of Egypt, and you shall eat the fat of the land.' [19]Command them ˣ also, 'Do this: take wagons from the land of Egypt for your little ones and for your wives, and bring your father, and come. [20]Give no thought to your goods, for the best of all the land of Egypt is yours.'"

21 The sons of Israel did so; and Joseph gave them wagons, according to the command of Pharaoh, and gave them provisions for the journey. [22]To each and all of them he gave festal garments; but to Benjamin he gave three hundred shekels of silver and five festal garments. [23]To his father he sent as follows: ten donkeys loaded with the good things of Egypt, and ten she-donkeys loaded with grain, bread, and provision for his father on the journey. [24]Then he sent his brothers away, and as they departed, he said to them, "Do not quarrel on the way." [25]So they went up out of Egypt, and came to the land of Canaan to their father Jacob. [26]And they told him, "Joseph is still alive, and he is ruler over all the land of Egypt." And his heart fainted, for he did not believe them. [27]But when they told him all the words of Joseph, which he had said to them, and when he saw the wagons which Joseph had sent to carry him, the spirit of their father Jacob revived; [28]and Israel said, "It is enough; Joseph my son is still alive; I will go and see him before I die."

Jacob Brings His Whole Family to Egypt

46 So Israel took his journey with all that he had, and came to Be'er-she'ba, and offered sacrifices to the God of his father Isaac. [2]And God spoke to Israel in visions of the night, and said, "Jacob, Jacob." And he said, "Here am I." [3]Then he said, "I am God, the God of your father; do not be afraid to go down to Egypt; for I will there make of you a great nation. [4]I will go down with you to Egypt, and I will also bring you up again; and Joseph's hand shall close your eyes." [5]Then Jacob set out from Be'er-she'ba; and the sons of Israel carried Jacob their father, their little ones, and their wives, in the wagons which Pharaoh had sent to carry him. [6]They also took their cattle and their goods, which they had gained in the land of Canaan, and came into Egypt, Jacob and all his offspring with him, [7]his sons, and his sons' sons with him, his daughters, and his sons' daughters; all his offspring he brought with him into Egypt.

8 Now these are the names of the descendants of Israel, who came into Egypt, Jacob and his sons. Reuben, Jacob's first-born, [9]and the sons of Reuben: Ha'noch, Pallu, Hezron, and Carmi. [10]The sons of Simeon: Jemu'el, Ja'min, O'had, Ja'chin, Zo'har, and Sha'ul, the son of a Canaanitish woman. [11]The sons of Levi: Gershon, Ko'hath, and Merar'i. [12]The sons of Judah: Er, O'nan, She'lah, Per'ez, and Ze'rah (but Er and Onan died in the land of Canaan); and the sons of Perez were Hezron and Ha'mul. [13]The sons of Is'sachar: To'la, Pu'vah, I'ob, and Shimron. [14]The sons of Zeb'ulun: Se'red, E'lon, and Jah'leel [15](these are the sons of Leah, whom she bore to Jacob in Pad'dan-ar'am, together with his daughter Dinah; altogether his sons and his daughters numbered thirty-three). [16]The sons of Gad: Ziph'ion, Haggi, Shu'ni, Ezbon, E'ri, Aro'di, and Are'li. [17]The sons of Asher: Imnah, Ishvah, Ishvi, Beri'ah, with Se'rah their sister. And the sons of Beriah: He'ber and Mal'chi-el [18](these are the sons of Zilpah, whom La'ban gave to Leah his daughter; and these she bore to Jacob—sixteen persons). [19]The sons of Rachel, Jacob's wife: Joseph and Benjamin. [20]And to Joseph in the land of Egypt were born Manas'seh and E'phraim, whom As'enath, the daughter of Poti'phera the priest of On, bore to him. [21]And the sons of Benjamin: Be'la, Be'cher, Ashbel, Ge'ra, Na'aman, E'hi, Rosh, Muppim, Huppim, and Ard [22](these are the sons of Rachel, who were born to Jacob—fourteen persons in all). [23]The sons of Dan: Hu'shim. [24]The sons of Naph'tali: Jah'zeel, Gu'ni, Je'zer, and Shillem [25](these are the sons of Bilhah, whom La'ban gave to Rachel his daughter, and these she bore to Jacob—seven persons in all). [26]All the persons belonging to Jacob who came into Egypt, who were his own offspring, not including Jacob's sons' wives, were sixty-six persons in all; [27]and the sons of Joseph, who were born to him in Egypt, were two; all the persons of the house of Jacob, that came into Egypt, were seventy.

Jacob Dwells in the Land of Goshen

28 He sent Judah before him to Joseph, to appear ˢ before him in Go'shen; and they came into the land of Goshen. [29]Then Joseph made ready his chariot and went up to meet Israel his father in Go'shen; and he presented himself to him, and fell on his neck, and wept on his neck a good while. [30]Israel said to Joseph, "Now let me die, since I have seen your face and know that you are still alive." [31]Joseph said to his brothers and to his father's household, "I will go up and tell Pharaoh, and will say to him, 'My brothers and my father's household, who were in the land of Canaan, have come to me; [32]and the men are shepherds, for they have been keepers of cattle; and they have brought their flocks, and their herds, and all that they have.' [33]When Pharaoh calls you,

---

ˣ Compare Gk Vg: Heb *you are commanded.*
ˢ Sam Syr Compare Gk Vg: Heb *to show the way.*
46:6: Acts 7:14, 15.
46.8–27: Ex 1:1–4; Num 26:4–50.
46:27: Acts 7:14.

and says, 'What is your occupation?' [34]you shall say, 'Your servants have been keepers of cattle from our youth even until now, both we and our fathers,' in order that you may dwell in the land of Go′shen; for every shepherd is an abomination to the Egyptians."

47 So Joseph went in and told Pharaoh, "My father and my brothers, with their flocks and herds and all that they possess, have come from the land of Canaan; they are now in the land of Go′shen." [2]And from among his brothers he took five men and presented them to Pharaoh. [3]Pharaoh said to his brothers, "What is your occupation?" And they said to Pharaoh, "Your servants are shepherds, as our fathers were." [4]They said to Pharaoh, "We have come to sojourn in the land; for there is no pasture for your servants' flocks, for the famine is severe in the land of Canaan; and now, we pray you, let your servants dwell in the land of Go′shen." [5]Then Pharaoh said to Joseph, "Your father and your brothers have come to you. [6]The land of Egypt is before you; settle your father and your brothers in the best of the land; let them dwell in the land of Go′shen; and if you know any able men among them, put them in charge of my cattle."

7 Then Joseph brought in Jacob his father, and set him before Pharaoh, and Jacob blessed Pharaoh. [8]And Pharaoh said to Jacob, "How many are the days of the years of your life?" [9]And Jacob said to Pharaoh, "The days of the years of my sojourning are a hundred and thirty years; few and evil have been the days of the years of my life, and they have not attained to the days of the years of the life of my fathers in the days of their sojourning." [10]And Jacob blessed Pharaoh, and went out from the presence of Pharaoh. [11]Then Joseph settled his father and his brothers, and gave them a possession in the land of Egypt, in the best of the land, in the land of Ram′eses, as Pharaoh had commanded. [12]And Joseph provided his father, his brothers, and all his father's household with food, according to the number of their dependents.

The Famine in Egypt and Canaan

13 Now there was no food in all the land; for the famine was very severe, so that the land of Egypt and the land of Canaan languished by reason of the famine. [14]And Joseph gathered up all the money that was found in the land of Egypt and in the land of Canaan, for the grain which they bought; and Joseph brought the money into Pharaoh's house. [15]And when the money was all spent in the land of Egypt and in the land of Canaan, all the Egyptians came to Joseph, and said, "Give us food; why should we die before your eyes? For our money is gone." [16]And Joseph answered, "Give your cattle, and I will give you food in exchange for your cattle, if your money is

gone." [17]So they brought their cattle to Joseph; and Joseph gave them food in exchange for the horses, the flocks, the herds, and the donkeys: and he supplied them with food in exchange for all their cattle that year. [18]And when that year was ended, they came to him the following year, and said to him, "We will not hide from my lord that our money is all spent; and the herds of cattle are my lord's; there is nothing left in the sight of my lord but our bodies and our lands. [19]Why should we die before your eyes, both we and our land? Buy us and our land for food, and we with our land will be slaves to Pharaoh; and give us seed, that we may live, and not die, and that the land may not be desolate."

20 So Joseph bought all the land of Egypt for Pharaoh; for all the Egyptians sold their fields, because the famine was severe upon them. The land became Pharaoh's; [21]and as for the people, he made slaves of them [t] from one end of Egypt to the other. [22]Only the land of the priests he did not buy; for the priests had a fixed allowance from Pharaoh, and lived on the allowance which Pharaoh gave them; therefore they did not sell their land. [23]Then Joseph said to the people, "Behold, I have this day bought you and your land for Pharaoh. Now here is seed for you, and you shall sow the land. [24]And at the harvests you shall give a fifth to Pharaoh, and four fifths shall be your own, as seed for the field and as food for yourselves and your households, and as food for your little ones." [25]And they said, "You have saved our lives; may it please my lord, we will be slaves to Pharaoh." [26]So Joseph made it a statute concerning the land of Egypt, and it stands to this day, that Pharaoh should have the fifth; the land of the priests alone did not become Pharaoh's.

The Last Days of Jacob

27 Thus Israel dwelt in the land of Egypt, in the land of Go′shen; and they gained possessions in it, and were fruitful and multiplied exceedingly. [28]And Jacob lived in the land of Egypt seventeen years; so the days of Jacob, the years of his life, were a hundred and forty-seven years.

29 And when the time drew near that Israel must die, he called his son Joseph and said to him, "If now I have found favor in your sight, put your hand under my thigh, and promise to deal loyally and truly with me. Do not bury me in Egypt, [30]but let me lie with my fathers; carry me out of Egypt and bury me in their burying place." He answered, "I will do as you have said." [31]And he said, "Swear to me"; and he swore to him. Then Israel bowed himself upon the head of his bed.

Jacob Blesses Joseph and His Sons

48 After this Joseph was told, "Behold, your father is ill"; so he took with him his two

---

[t] Sam Gk Compare Vg: Heb *he removed them to the cities.*

sons, Manas'seh and E'phraim. [2]And it was told to Jacob, "Your son Joseph has come to you"; then Israel summoned his strength, and sat up in bed. [3]And Jacob said to Joseph, "God Almighty [u] appeared to me at Luz in the land of Canaan and blessed me, [4]and said to me, 'Behold, I will make you fruitful, and multiply you, and I will make of you a company of peoples, and will give this land to your descendants after you for an everlasting possession.' [5]And now your two sons, who were born to you in the land of Egypt before I came to you in Egypt, are mine; E'phraim and Manas'seh shall be mine, as Reuben and Simeon are. [6]And the offspring born to you after them shall be yours; they shall be called by the name of their brothers in their inheritance. [7]For when I came from Paddan, Rachel to my sorrow died in the land of Canaan on the way, when there was still some distance to go to Eph'rath; and I buried her there on the way to Ephrath (that is, Bethlehem)."

8 When Israel saw Joseph's sons, he said, "Who are these?" [9]Joseph said to his father, "They are my sons, whom God has given me here." And he said, "Bring them to me, I pray you, that I may bless them." [10]Now the eyes of Israel were dim with age, so that he could not see. So Joseph brought them near him; and he kissed them and embraced them. [11]And Israel said to Joseph, "I had not thought to see your face; and behold, God has let me see your children also." [12]Then Joseph removed them from his knees, and he bowed himself with his face to the earth. [13]And Joseph took them both, E'phraim in his right hand toward Israel's left hand, and Manas'seh in his left hand toward Israel's right hand, and brought them near him. [14]And Israel stretched out his right hand and laid it upon the head of E'phraim, who was the younger, and his left hand upon the head of Manas'seh, crossing his hands, for Manasseh was the first-born. [15]And he blessed Joseph, and said,

"The God before whom my fathers Abraham
  and Isaac walked,
the God who has led me all my life long to this
    day,
[16]the angel who has redeemed me from all evil,
    bless the lads;
and in them let my name be perpetuated, and
    the name of my fathers Abraham and
    Isaac;
and let them grow into a multitude in the midst
    of the earth."

17 When Joseph saw that his father laid his right hand upon the head of E'phraim, it displeased him; and he took his father's hand, to remove it from Ephraim's head to Manas'seh's head. [18]And Joseph said to his father, "Not so, my father; for this one is the first-born; put your right hand upon his head." [19]But his father refused, and said, "I know, my son, I know; he also shall be-

come a people, and he also shall be great; nevertheless his younger brother shall be greater than he, and his descendants shall become a multitude of nations." [20]So he blessed them that day, saying,
  "By you Israel will pronounce blessings, saying,
    'God make you as E'phraim and as
      Manas'seh'";
and thus he put Ephraim before Manasseh. [21]Then Israel said to Joseph, "Behold, I am about to die, but God will be with you, and will bring you again to the land of your fathers. [22]Moreover I have given to you rather than to your brothers one mountain slope [v] which I took from the hand of the Am'orites with my sword and with my bow."

Jacob's Last Words to His Sons

49 [*] Then Jacob called his sons, and said, "Gather yourselves together, that I may tell you what shall befall you in days to come. [2]Assemble and hear, O sons of Jacob,
    and hearken to Israel your father.

[3]Reuben, you are my first-born,
    my might, and the first fruits of my
      strength,
    pre-eminent in pride and pre-eminent in
      power.
[4]Unstable as water, you shall not have pre-
    eminence
    because you went up to your father's bed;
    then you defiled it—you [w] went up to my
      couch!

[5]Simeon and Levi are brothers;
    weapons of violence are their swords.
[6]O my soul, come not into their council;
    O my spirit, [x] be not joined to their
      company;
for in their anger they slay men,
    and in their wantonness they hamstring
      oxen.
[7]Cursed be their anger, for it is fierce;
    and their wrath, for it is cruel!
I will divide them in Jacob
    and scatter them in Israel.

[8]Judah, your brothers shall praise you;
    your hand shall be on the neck of your
      enemies;
    your father's sons shall bow down before
      you.
[9]Judah is a lion's whelp;
    from the prey, my son, you have gone up.

---

[u] Heb *El Shaddai*.
[v] Heb *shekem*, shoulder.
[w] Gk Syr Tg: Heb *he*.
[x] Or *glory*.
49:9, 10: Num 24:9; Rev 5:5.
[*] 49:1–27; In their present form these "Oracles of Jacob," blessings pronounced upon his sons as epitomizing the twelve tribes, date from the period of the early monarchy.

He stooped down, he lurked as a lion,
and as a lioness; who dares rouse him up?
[10]The scepter shall not depart from Judah,
nor the ruler's staff from between his feet,
until he comes to whom it belongs;[y]
and to him shall be the obedience of the
peoples.
[11]Binding his foal to the vine
and his donkey's colt to the choice vine,
he washes his garments in wine
and his vesture in the blood of grapes;
[12]his eyes shall be red with wine,
and his teeth white with milk.

[13]Zeb'ulun shall dwell at the shore of the sea;
he shall become a haven for ships,
and his border shall be at Si'don.

[14]Is'sachar is a strong donkey,
crouching between the sheepfolds;
[15]he saw that a resting place was good,
and that the land was pleasant;
so he bowed his shoulder to bear,
and became a slave at forced labor.

[16]Dan shall judge his people
as one of the tribes of Israel.
[17]Dan shall be a serpent in the way,
a viper by the path,
that bites the horse's heels
so that his rider falls backward.
[18]I wait for your salvation, O LORD.

[19]Raiders[z] shall raid Gad,
but he shall raid at their heels.

[20]Asher's food shall be rich,
and he shall yield royal dainties.

[21]Naph'tali is a deer let loose,
that bears comely fawns.[a]

[22]Joseph is a fruitful bough,
a fruitful bough by a spring;
his branches run over the wall.
[23]The archers fiercely attacked him,
shot at him, and harassed him sorely;
[24]yet his bow remained unmoved,
his arms[b] were made agile
by the hands of the Mighty One of Jacob
(by the name of the Shepherd, the Rock of
Israel),
[25]by the God of your father who will help you,
by God Almighty[u] who will bless you
with blessings of heaven above,
blessings of the deep that lies beneath,
blessings of the breasts and of the womb.
[26]The blessings of your father
are mighty beyond the blessings of the
eternal mountains,[c]

the bounties of the everlasting hills;
may they be on the head of Joseph,
and on the brow of him who was separate
from his brothers.

[27]Benjamin is a ravenous wolf,
in the morning devouring the prey,
and at evening dividing the spoil."

Jacob's Death and Burial

28 All these are the twelve tribes of Israel; and
this is what their father said to them as he
blessed them, blessing each with the blessing
suitable to him. [29]Then he charged them, and said
to them, "I am to be gathered to my people; bury
me with my fathers in the cave that is in the field
of E'phron the Hittite, [30]in the cave that is in the
field at Mach-pe'lah, to the east of Mamre, in
the land of Canaan, which Abraham bought with
the field from E'phron the Hittite to possess as a
burying place. [31]There they buried Abraham and
Sarah his wife; there they buried Isaac and
Rebekah his wife; and there I buried Leah—[32]the
field and the cave that is in it were purchased
from the Hittites." [33]When Jacob finished charging his sons, he drew up his feet into the bed, and
breathed his last, and was gathered to his people.

50 Then Joseph fell on his father's face, and
wept over him, and kissed him. [2]And Joseph commanded his servants the physicians to
embalm his father. So the physicians embalmed
Israel; [3]forty days were required for it, for so
many are required for embalming. And the Egyptians wept for him seventy days.

4 And when the days of weeping for him were
past, Joseph spoke to the household of Pharaoh,
saying, "If now I have found favor in your eyes,
speak, I beg you, in the ears of Pharaoh, saying,
[5]My father made me swear, saying, 'I am about to
die: in my tomb which I hewed out for myself in
the land of Canaan, there shall you bury me.'
Now therefore let me go up, I beg you, and bury
my father; then I will return." [6]And Pharaoh answered, "Go up, and bury your father, as he made
you swear." [7]So Joseph went up to bury his father; and with him went up all the servants of
Pharaoh, the elders of his household, and all
the elders of the land of Egypt, [8]as well as all
the household of Joseph, his brothers, and his
father's household; only their children, their
flocks, and their herds were left in the land of
Go'shen. [9]And there went up with him both chariots and horsemen; it was a very great company.

---

[y] Syr Compare Tg: Heb *until Shiloh comes* or *until he comes to Shiloh.*
[z] Heb *gedud,* a raiding troop.
[a] Or *who gives beautiful words.*
[b] Heb *the arms of his hands.*
[u] Heb *El Shaddai.*
[c] Compare Gk: Heb *of my progenitors to.*

[10]When they came to the threshing floor of Atad, which is beyond the Jordan, they lamented there with a very great and sorrowful lamentation; and he made a mourning for his father seven days. [11]When the inhabitants of the land, the Canaanites, saw the mourning on the threshing floor of Atad, they said, "This is a grievous mourning to the Egyptians." Therefore the place was named A'bel-miz'raim;[d] it is beyond the Jordan. [12]Thus his sons did for him as he had commanded them; [13]for his sons carried him to the land of Canaan, and buried him in the cave of the field at Machpe'lah, to the east of Mamre, which Abraham bought with the field from E'phron the Hittite, to possess as a burying place. [14]After he had buried his father, Joseph returned to Egypt with his brothers and all who had gone up with him to bury his father.

Joseph Forgives His Brothers

15 When Joseph's brothers saw that their father was dead, they said, "It may be that Joseph will hate us and pay us back for all the evil which we did to him." [16]So they sent a message to Joseph, saying, "Your father gave this command before he died, [17]'Say to Joseph, Forgive, I beg you, the transgression of your brothers and their sin, because they did evil to you.' And now, we pray you, forgive the transgression of the servants of the God of your father." Joseph wept when they spoke to him. [18]His brothers also came and fell down before him, and said, "Behold, we are your servants." [19]But Joseph said to them, "Fear not, for am I in the place of God? [20]As for you, you meant evil against me; but God meant it for good, to bring it about that many people should be kept alive, as they are today. [21]So do not fear; I will provide for you and your little ones." Thus he reassured them and comforted them.

Joseph's Last Days and Death

22 So Joseph dwelt in Egypt, he and his father's house; and Joseph lived a hundred and ten years. [23]And Joseph saw E'phraim's children of the third generation; the children also of Ma'chir the son of Manas'seh were born upon Joseph's knees. [24]And Joseph said to his brothers, "I am about to die; but God will visit you, and bring you up out of this land to the land which he swore to Abraham, to Isaac, and to Jacob." [25]Then Joseph took an oath of the sons of Israel, saying, "God will visit you, and you shall carry up my bones from here." [26]So Joseph died, being a hundred and ten years old; and they embalmed him, and he was put in a coffin in Egypt.

---

[d] That is *meadow* (or *mourning*) of Egypt.
50:13: Acts 7:16.

EXODUS

The Sons of Israel

1 These are the names of the sons of Israel who came to Egypt with Jacob, each with his household: [2]Reuben, Simeon, Levi, and Judah, [3]Is'sachar, Zeb'ulun, and Benjamin, [4]Dan and Naph'tali, Gad and Asher. [5]All the offspring of Jacob were seventy persons; Joseph was already in Egypt. [6]Then Joseph died, and all his brothers, and all that generation. [7]But the descendants of Israel were fruitful and increased greatly; they multiplied and grew exceedingly strong; so that the land was filled with them.

The Israelites Are Oppressed by the Egyptians

8 Now there arose a new king over Egypt, who did not know Joseph. [9]And he said to his people, "Behold, the sons of Israel are too many and too mighty for us. [10]Come, let us deal shrewdly with them, lest they multiply, and, if war befall us, they join our enemies and fight against us and escape from the land." [11]Therefore they set taskmasters over them to afflict them with heavy burdens; and they built for Pharaoh store-cities, Pithom and Ra-am'ses. [12]But the more they were oppressed, the more they multiplied and the more they spread abroad. And the Egyptians were in dread of the sons of Israel. [13]So they made the sons of Israel serve with rigor, [14]and made their lives bitter with hard service, in mortar and brick, and in all kinds of work in the field; in all their work they made them serve with rigor.

15 Then the king of Egypt said to the Hebrew midwives, one of whom was named Shiphrah and the other Puah, [16]"When you serve as midwife to the Hebrew women, and see them upon the birthstool, if it is a son, you shall kill him; but if it is a daughter, she shall live." [17]But the midwives feared God, and did not do as the king of Egypt commanded them, but let the male children live. [18]So the king of Egypt called the midwives, and said to them, "Why have you done this, and let the male children live?" [19]The midwives said to Pharaoh, "Because the Hebrew women are not like the Egyptian women; for they are vigorous and are delivered before the midwife comes to them." [20]So God dealt well with the midwives; and the people multiplied and grew very strong. [21]And because the midwives feared God he gave them families. [22]Then Pharaoh commanded all his people, "Every son that is born to the Hebrews [a]

you shall cast into the Nile, but you shall let every daughter live."

Birth and Youth of Moses

2 Now a man from the house of Levi went and took to wife a daughter of Levi. [2]The woman conceived and bore a son; and when she saw that he was a goodly child, she hid him three months. [3]And when she could hide him no longer she took for him a basket made of bulrushes, and daubed it with bitumen and pitch; and she put the child in it and placed it among the reeds at the river's brink. [4]And his sister stood at a distance, to know what would be done to him. [5]Now the daughter of Pharaoh came down to bathe at the river, and her maidens walked beside the river; she saw the basket among the reeds and sent her maid to fetch it. [6]When she opened it she saw the child; and behold, the baby was crying. She took pity on him and said, "This is one of the Hebrews' children." [7]Then his sister said to Pharaoh's daughter, "Shall I go and call you a nurse from the Hebrew women to nurse the child for you?" [8]And Pharaoh's daughter said to her, "Go." So the girl went and called the child's mother. [9]And Pharaoh's daughter said to her, "Take this child away, and nurse him for me, and I will give you your wages." So the woman took the child and nursed him. [10]And the child grew, and she brought him to Pharaoh's daughter, and he became her son; and she named him Moses, [b] for she said, "Because I drew him out [c] of the water."

Moses Flees to Midian

11 One day, when Moses had grown up, he went out to his people and looked on their burdens; and he saw an Egyptian beating a Hebrew, one of his people. [12]He looked this way and that, and seeing no one he killed the Egyptian and hid him in the sand. [13]When he went out the next day, behold, two Hebrews were struggling together; and he said to the man that did the wrong, "Why do you strike your fellow?" [14]He answered, "Who made you a prince and a judge over us? Do you mean to kill me

---

This book, made up of various traditions of different dates, deals with two events, the deliverance from Egypt and the Sinai covenant, which, closely linked together, form the basis of Old Testament faith. It is dominated by the personality of Moses.

[a] Sam Gk Tg: Heb lacks *to the Hebrews.*
[b] Heb *Mosheh.* [c] Heb *mashah.*

1:1-4: Gen 46:8–27; Num 26:4–50. **1:5-8:** Acts 7:14–18.
1:10, 11, 22: Acts 7:19. **2:2:** Acts 7:20; Heb 11:23.
2:5, 10: Acts 7:21. **2:11:** Acts 7:23; Heb 11:24.
2:12: Acts 7:24. **2:14:** Acts 7:27, 28.

as you killed the Egyptian?" Then Moses was afraid, and thought, "Surely the thing is known." [15]When Pharaoh heard of it, he sought to kill Moses.

But Moses fled from Pharaoh, and stayed in the land of Mid′ian; and he sat down by a well. [16]Now the priest of Mid′ian had seven daughters; and they came and drew water, and filled the troughs to water their father's flock. [17]The shepherds came and drove them away; but Moses stood up and helped them, and watered their flock. [18]When they came to their father Reu′el, he said, "How is it that you have come so soon today?" [19]They said, "An Egyptian delivered us out of the hand of the shepherds, and even drew water for us and watered the flock." [20]He said to his daughters, "And where is he? Why have you left the man? Call him, that he may eat bread." [21]And Moses was content to dwell with the man, and he gave Moses his daughter Zippo′rah. [22]She bore a son, and he called his name Gershom; for he said, "I have been a sojourner [d] in a foreign land."

23 In the course of those many days the king of Egypt died. And the sons of Israel groaned under their bondage, and cried out for help, and their cry under bondage came up to God. [24]And God heard their groaning, and God remembered his covenant with Abraham, with Isaac, and with Jacob. [25]And God saw the sons of Israel, and God knew their condition.

Moses and the Burning Bush

3 Now Moses was keeping the flock of his father-in-law, Jethro, the priest of Mid′ian; and he led his flock to the west side of the wilderness, and came to Horeb, the mountain of God. [2]And the angel of the LORD appeared to him in a flame of fire out of the midst of a bush; and he looked, and behold, the bush was burning, yet it was not consumed. [3]And Moses said, "I will turn aside and see this great sight, why the bush is not burnt." [4]When the LORD saw that he turned aside to see, God called to him out of the bush, "Moses, Moses!" And he said, "Here am I." [5]Then he said, "Do not come near; put off your shoes from your feet, for the place on which you are standing is holy ground." [6]And he said, "I am the God of your father, the God of Abraham, the God of Isaac, and the God of Jacob." And Moses hid his face, for he was afraid to look at God.

7 Then the LORD said, "I have seen the affliction of my people who are in Egypt, and have heard their cry because of their taskmasters; I know their sufferings, [8]and I have come down to deliver them out of the hand of the Egyptians, and to bring them up out of that land to a good and broad land, a land flowing with milk and honey, to the place of the Canaanites, the Hittites, the Am′orites, the Per′izzites, the Hi′vites, and the Jeb′usites. [9]And now, behold, the cry of the sons of Israel has come to me, and I have seen the oppression with which the Egyptians oppress them. [10]Come, I will send you to Pharaoh that you may bring forth my people, the sons of Israel, out of Egypt." [11]But Moses said to God, "Who am I that I should go to Pharaoh, and bring the sons of Israel out of Egypt?" [12]He said, "But I will be with you; and this shall be the sign for you, that I have sent you: when you have brought forth the people out of Egypt, you shall serve God upon this mountain."

God Reveals His Name

13 Then Moses said to God, "If I come to the sons of Israel and say to them, 'The God of your fathers has sent me to you,' and they ask me, 'What is his name?' what shall I say to them?" [14]God said to Moses, "I AM WHO I AM." [e] * And he said, "Say this to the sons of Israel, 'I AM has sent me to you.'" [15]God also said to Moses, "Say this to the sons of Israel, 'The LORD, [f] the God of your fathers, the God of Abraham, the God of Isaac, and the God of Jacob, has sent me to you': this is my name for ever, and thus I am to be remembered throughout all generations. [16]Go and gather the elders of Israel together, and say to them, 'The LORD, the God of your fathers, the God of Abraham, of Isaac, and of Jacob, has appeared to me, saying, "I have observed you and what has been done to you in Egypt; [17]and I promise that I will bring you up out of the affliction of Egypt, to the land of the Canaanites, the Hittites, the Am′orites, the Per′izzites, the Hi′vites, and the Jeb′usites, a land flowing with milk and honey."' [18]And they will listen to your voice; and you and the elders of Israel shall go to the king of Egypt and say to him, 'The LORD, the God of the Hebrews, has met with us; and now, we beg you, let us go a three days' journey into the wilderness, that we may sacrifice to the LORD our God.' [19]I know that the king of Egypt will not let you go unless compelled by a mighty hand. [g] [20]So I will stretch out my hand and strike Egypt with all the wonders which I will do in it; after that he will let you go. [21]And I will give this people favor in the sight of the Egyptians; and when you go, you shall not go empty, [22]but each woman shall ask of her neighbor, and of her who sojourns in her house, jewelry of silver and of gold, and clothing, and you shall put them on your sons and on your daughters; thus you shall despoil the Egyptians."

[d] Heb ger.

[e] Or I AM WHAT I AM or I WILL BE WHAT I WILL BE.

[f] The word LORD when spelled with capital letters, stands for the divine name, YHWH, which is here connected with the verb hayah, to be.

[g] Gk Vg: Heb no, not by a mighty hand.

2:15, 22: Acts 7:29.   2:24: Acts 7:34.
3:1–4:17: Ex 6:2–13.   3:2: Acts 7:30.   3:5: Acts 7:33.
3:6: Mt 22:32; Mk 12:26; Lk 20:37; Acts 3–13; 7:32.
* 3:14: The translation is uncertain; it is, therefore, difficult to decide whether this is a refusal to disclose the name or an explanation of the divine title Yahweh revealed immediately afterward.

God Gives Moses Help for His Mission

4 Then Moses answered, "But behold, they will not believe me or listen to my voice, for they will say, 'The Lord did not appear to you.'" ²The Lord said to him, "What is that in your hand?" He said, "A rod." ³And he said, "Cast it on the ground." So he cast it on the ground, and it became a serpent; and Moses fled from it. ⁴But the Lord said to Moses, "Put out your hand, and take it by the tail"—so he put out his hand and caught it, and it became a rod in his hand—⁵"that they may believe that the Lord, the God of their fathers, the God of Abraham, the God of Isaac, and the God of Jacob, has appeared to you." ⁶Again, the Lord said to him, "Put your hand into your bosom." And he put his hand into his bosom; and when he took it out, behold, his hand was leprous, as white as snow. ⁷Then God said, "Put your hand back into your bosom." So he put his hand back into his bosom; and when he took it out, behold, it was restored like the rest of his flesh. ⁸"If they will not believe you," God said, "or heed the first sign, they may believe the latter sign. ⁹If they will not believe even these two signs or heed your voice, you shall take some water from the Nile and pour it upon the dry ground; and the water which you shall take from the Nile will become blood upon the dry ground."

10 But Moses said to the Lord, "Oh, my Lord, I am not eloquent, either heretofore or since you have spoken to your servant; but I am slow of speech and of tongue." ¹¹Then the Lord said to him, "Who has made man's mouth? Who makes him mute, or deaf, or seeing, or blind? Is it not I, the Lord? ¹²Now therefore go, and I will be with your mouth and teach you what you shall speak." ¹³But he said, "Oh, my Lord, send, I pray, some other person." ¹⁴Then the anger of the Lord was kindled against Moses and he said, "Is there not Aaron, your brother, the Levite? I know that he can speak well; and behold, he is coming out to meet you, and when he sees you he will be glad in his heart. ¹⁵And you shall speak to him and put the words in his mouth; and I will be with your mouth and with his mouth, and will teach you what you shall do. ¹⁶He shall speak for you to the people; and he shall be a mouth for you, and you shall be to him as God. ¹⁷And you shall take in your hand this rod, with which you shall do the signs."

Moses Returns to Egypt

18 Moses went back to Jethro his father-in-law and said to him, "Let me go back, I beg, to my kinsmen in Egypt and see whether they are still alive." And Jethro said to Moses, "Go in peace." ¹⁹And the Lord said to Moses in Mid'ian, "Go back to Egypt; for all the men who were seeking your life are dead." ²⁰So Moses took his wife and his sons and set them on a donkey, and went back to the land of Egypt; and in his hand Moses took the rod of God.

21 And the Lord said to Moses, "When you go back to Egypt, see that you do before Pharaoh all the miracles which I have put in your power; but I will harden his heart, so that he will not let the people go. ²²And you shall say to Pharaoh, 'Thus says the Lord, Israel is my first-born son, ²³and I say to you, "Let my son go that he may serve me"; if you refuse to let him go, behold, I will slay your first-born son.'"

24 At a lodging place on the way the Lord met him and sought to kill him. ²⁵Then Zippo'rah took a flint and cut off her son's foreskin, and touched Moses' feet with it, and said, "Surely you are a bridegroom of blood to me!" ²⁶So he let him alone. Then it was that she said, "You are a bridegroom of blood," because of the circumcision.

27 The Lord said to Aaron, "Go into the wilderness to meet Moses." So he went, and met him at the mountain of God and kissed him. ²⁸And Moses told Aaron all the words of the Lord with which he had sent him, and all the signs which he had charged him to do. ²⁹Then Moses and Aaron went and gathered together all the elders of the sons of Israel. ³⁰And Aaron spoke all the words which the Lord had spoken to Moses, and did the signs in the sight of the people. ³¹And the people believed; and when they heard that the Lord had visited the sons of Israel and that he had seen their affliction, they bowed their heads and worshiped.

Bricks without Straw

5 Afterward Moses and Aaron went to Pharaoh and said, "Thus says the Lord, the God of Israel, 'Let my people go, that they may hold a feast to me in the wilderness.'" ²But Pharaoh said, "Who is the Lord, that I should heed his voice and let Israel go? I do not know the Lord, and moreover I will not let Israel go." ³Then they said, "The God of the Hebrews has met with us; let us go, we beg, a three days' journey into the wilderness, and sacrifice to the Lord our God, lest he fall upon us with pestilence or with the sword." ⁴But the king of Egypt said to them, "Moses and Aaron, why do you take the people away from their work? Get to your burdens." ⁵And Pharaoh said, "Behold, the people of the land are now many and you make them rest from their burdens!" ⁶The same day Pharaoh commanded the taskmasters of the people and their foremen, ⁷"You shall no longer give the people straw to make bricks, as heretofore; let them go and gather straw for themselves. ⁸But the number of bricks which they made heretofore you shall lay upon them, you shall by no means lessen it; for they are idle; therefore they cry, 'Let us go and offer

4:19: Acts 7:34.

sacrifice to our God.' ⁹Let heavier work be laid upon the men that they may labor at it and pay no regard to lying words."

10 So the taskmasters and the foremen of the people went out and said to the people, "Thus says Pharaoh, 'I will not give you straw. ¹¹Go yourselves, get your straw wherever you can find it; but your work will not be lessened in the least.' " ¹²So the people were scattered abroad throughout all the land of Egypt, to gather stubble for straw. ¹³The taskmasters were urgent, saying, "Complete your work, your daily task, as when there was straw." ¹⁴And the foremen of the sons of Israel, whom Pharaoh's taskmasters had set over them, were beaten, and were asked, "Why have you not done all your task of making bricks today, as before?"

15 Then the foremen of the sons of Israel came and cried to Pharaoh, "Why do you deal thus with your servants? ¹⁶No straw is given to your servants, yet they say to us, 'Make bricks!' And behold, your servants are beaten; but the fault is in your own people." ¹⁷But he said, "You are idle, you are idle; therefore you say, 'Let us go and sacrifice to the LORD.' ¹⁸Go now, and work; for no straw shall be given you, yet you shall deliver the same number of bricks." ¹⁹The foremen of the sons of Israel saw that they were in evil plight, when they said, "You shall by no means lessen your daily number of bricks." ²⁰They met Moses and Aaron, who were waiting for them, as they came forth from Pharaoh; ²¹and they said to them, "The LORD look upon you and judge, because you have made us offensive in the sight of Pharaoh and his servants, and have put a sword in their hand to kill us."

22 Then Moses turned again to the LORD and said, "O LORD, why have you done evil to this people? Why did you ever send me? ²³For since I came to Pharaoh to speak in your name, he has done evil to this people, and you have not delivered your people at all." ¹But the Lord said to Moses, "Now you shall see what I will do to Pharaoh; for with a strong hand he will send them out, yes, with a strong hand he will drive them out of his land."

God Promises Deliverance

2 And God said to Moses, "I am the LORD. ³I appeared to Abraham, to Isaac, and to Jacob, as God Almighty,ʰ but by my name the LORD I did not make myself known to them. ⁴I also established my covenant with them, to give them the land of Canaan, the land in which they dwelt as sojourners. ⁵Moreover I have heard the groaning of the sons of Israel whom the Egyptians hold in bondage and I have remembered my covenant. ⁶Say therefore to the sons of Israel, 'I am the LORD, and I will bring you out from under the burdens of the Egyptians, and I will deliver you

from their bondage, and I will redeem you with an outstretched arm and with great acts of judgment, ⁷and I will take you for my people, and I will be your God; and you shall know that I am the LORD your God, who has brought you out from under the burdens of the Egyptians. ⁸And I will bring you into the land which I swore to give to Abraham, to Isaac, and to Jacob; I will give it to you for a possession. I am the LORD.' " ⁹Moses spoke thus to the sons of Israel; but they did not listen to Moses, because of their broken spirit and their cruel bondage.

10 And the LORD said to Moses, ¹¹"Go in, tell Pharaoh king of Egypt to let the sons of Israel go out of his land." ¹²But Moses said to the LORD, "Behold, the sons of Israel have not listened to me; how then shall Pharaoh listen to me, who am a man of uncircumcised lips?" ¹³But the LORD spoke to Moses and Aaron, and gave them a charge to the sons of Israel and to Pharaoh king of Egypt to bring the sons of Israel out of the land of Egypt.

The Genealogy of Moses and Aaron

14 These are the heads of their fathers' houses: the sons of Reuben, the first-born of Israel: Ha'noch, Pallu, Hezron, and Carmi; these are the families of Reuben. ¹⁵The sons of Simeon: Jemu'el, Ja'min, O'had, Ja'chin, Zo'har, and Sha'ul, the son of a Canaanite woman; these are the families of Simeon. ¹⁶These are the names of the sons of Levi according to their generations: Gershon, Ko'hath, and Merar'i, the years of the life of Levi being a hundred and thirty-seven years. ¹⁷The sons of Gershon: Libni and Shim'e-i, by their families. ¹⁸The sons of Ko'hath: Amram, Izhar, He'bron, and Uz'ziel, the years of the life of Kohath being a hundred and thirty-three years. ¹⁹The sons of Merar'i: Mah'li and Mu'shi. These are the families of the Levites according to their generations. ²⁰Amram took to wife Joch'ebed his father's sister and she bore him Aaron and Moses, the years of the life of Amram being one hundred and thirty-seven years. ²¹The sons of Izhar: Ko'rah, Ne'pheg, and Zich'ri. ²²And the sons of Uz'ziel: Mish'a-el, El'zaphan, and Sithri. ²³Aaron took to wife Eli'sheba, the daughter of Ammin'adab and the sister of Nahshon; and she bore him Na'dab, Abi'hu, Elea'zar, and Ith'amar. ²⁴The sons of Ko'rah: Assir, Elka'nah, and Abi'a-saph; these are the families of the Ko'rahites. ²⁵Elea'zar, Aaron's son, took to wife one of the daughters of Pu'ti-el; and she bore him Phin'e-has. These are the heads of the fathers' houses of the Levites by their families.

ʰ Heb El Shaddai.
6:1, 6: Acts 13:17.
6:14–16: Gen 46:8–11; Num 26:5–14.
6:16–19: Num 3:15–20; 26:57–58; 1 Chron 6:1, 16–19.
6:20–23: Num 26:58–60.

26 These are the Aaron and Moses to whom the LORD said: "Bring out the sons of Israel from the land of Egypt by their hosts." [27]It was they who spoke to Pharaoh king of Egypt about bringing out the sons of Israel from Egypt, this Moses and this Aaron.

Moses and Aaron Obey God's Commands

28 On the day when the LORD spoke to Moses in the land of Egypt, [29]the LORD said to Moses, "I am the LORD; tell Pharaoh king of Egypt all that I say to you." [30]But Moses said to the LORD, "Behold, I am of uncircumcised lips; how then shall Pharaoh listen to me?" [1]And the LORD said to Moses, "See, I make you as God to Pharaoh; and Aaron your brother shall be your prophet. [2]You shall speak all that I command you; and Aaron your brother shall tell Pharaoh to let the sons of Israel go out of his land. [3]But I will harden Pharaoh's heart, and though I multiply my signs and wonders in the land of Egypt, [4]Pharaoh will not listen to you; then I will lay my hand upon Egypt and bring forth my hosts, my people the sons of Israel, out of the land of Egypt by great acts of judgment. [5]And the Egyptians shall know that I am the LORD, when I stretch forth my hand upon Egypt and bring out the sons of Israel from among them." [6]And Moses and Aaron did so; they did as the LORD commanded them. [7]Now Moses was eighty years old, and Aaron eighty-three years old, when they spoke to Pharaoh.

Aaron's Miraculous Rod

8 And the LORD said to Moses and Aaron, [9]"When Pharaoh says to you, 'Prove yourselves by working a miracle,' then you shall say to Aaron, 'Take your rod and cast it down before Pharaoh, that it may become a serpent.'" [10]So Moses and Aaron went to Pharaoh and did as the LORD commanded; Aaron cast down his rod before Pharaoh and his servants, and it became a serpent. [11]Then Pharaoh summoned the wise men and the sorcerers; and they also, the magicians of Egypt, did the same by their secret arts. [12]For every man cast down his rod, and they became serpents. But Aaron's rod swallowed up their rods. [13]Still Pharaoh's heart was hardened, and he would not listen to them; as the LORD had said.

The First Plague: Water of the Nile
Turned to Blood

14 * Then the LORD said to Moses, "Pharaoh's heart is hardened, he refuses to let the people go. [15]Go to Pharaoh in the morning, as he is going out to the water; wait for him by the river's brink, and take in your hand the rod which was turned into a serpent. [16]And you shall say to him, 'The LORD, the God of the Hebrews, sent me to you, saying, "Let my people go, that they may serve me in the wilderness; and behold, you have not yet obeyed." [17]Thus says the LORD, "By this you shall know that I am the LORD: behold, I will strike the water

that is in the Nile with the rod that is in my hand, and it shall be turned to blood, [18]and the fish in the Nile shall die, and the Nile shall become foul, and the Egyptians will loathe to drink water from the Nile."'" [19]And the LORD said to Moses, "Say to Aaron, 'Take your rod and stretch out your hand over the waters of Egypt, over their rivers, their canals, and their ponds, and all their pools of water, that they may become blood; and there shall be blood throughout all the land of Egypt, both in vessels of wood and in vessels of stone.'"

20 Moses and Aaron did as the LORD commanded; in the sight of Pharaoh and in the sight of his servants, he lifted up the rod and struck the water that was in the Nile, and all the water that was in the Nile turned to blood. [21]And the fish in the Nile died; and the Nile became foul, so that the Egyptians could not drink water from the Nile; and there was blood throughout all the land of Egypt. [22]But the magicians of Egypt did the same by their secret arts; so Pharaoh's heart remained hardened, and he would not listen to them; as the LORD had said. [23]Pharaoh turned and went into his house, and he did not lay even this to heart. [24]And all the Egyptians dug round about the Nile for water to drink, for they could not drink the water of the Nile.

The Second Plague: Frogs

25 Seven days passed after the LORD had [i]struck the Nile. [1]Then the LORD said to Moses, "Go in to Pharaoh and say to him, 'Thus says the LORD, "Let my people go, that they may serve me. [2]But if you refuse to let them go, behold, I will plague all your country with frogs; [3]the Nile shall swarm with frogs which shall come up into your house, and into your bedchamber and on your bed, and into the houses of your servants and of your people, [j] and into your ovens and your kneading bowls; [4]the frogs shall come up on you and on your people and on all your servants."'" [5][k] And the LORD said to Moses, "Say to Aaron, 'Stretch out your hand with your rod over the rivers, over the canals, and over the pools, and cause frogs to come upon the land of Egypt!'" [6]So Aaron stretched out his hand over the waters of Egypt; and the frogs came up and covered the land of Egypt. [7]But the magicians did the same by their secret arts, and brought frogs upon the land of Egypt.

8 Then Pharaoh called Moses and Aaron, and said, "Entreat the LORD to take away the frogs

---

[i] Ch 7:26 in Heb.
[j] Gk: Heb *upon your people*.
[k] Ch 8:1 in Heb.
7:3: Acts 7:36.
* 7:14: Here begins the story of the ten plagues. Again, the narrative is composite, and originally different traditions knew of different numbers of plagues. All, however, lead up to the climax of the death of the first-born. Some of the plagues correspond to natural phenomena that are known to occur, or to have occurred in the past, in Egypt.

from me and from my people; and I will let the people go to sacrifice to the Lord." [9]Moses said to Pharaoh, "Be pleased to command me when I am to entreat, for you and for your servants and for your people, that the frogs be destroyed from you and your houses and be left only in the Nile." [10]And he said, "Tomorrow." Moses said, "Be it as you say, that you may know that there is no one like the Lord our God. [11]The frogs shall depart from you and your houses and your servants and your people; they shall be left only in the Nile." [12]So Moses and Aaron went out from Pharaoh; and Moses cried to the Lord concerning the frogs, as he had agreed with Pharaoh.[1] [13]And the Lord did according to the word of Moses; the frogs died out of the houses and courtyards and out of the fields. [14]And they gathered them together in heaps, and the land stank. [15]But when Pharaoh saw that there was a respite, he hardened his heart, and would not listen to them; as the Lord had said.

The Third Plague: Gnats

[16] Then the Lord said to Moses, "Say to Aaron, 'Stretch out your rod and strike the dust of the earth, that it may become gnats throughout all the land of Egypt.'" [17]And they did so; Aaron stretched out his hand with his rod, and struck the dust of the earth, and there came gnats on man and beast; all the dust of the earth became gnats throughout all the land of Egypt. [18]The magicians tried by their secret arts to bring forth gnats, but they could not. So there were gnats on man and beast. [19]And the magicians said to Pharaoh, "This is the finger of God." But Pharaoh's heart was hardened, and he would not listen to them; as the Lord had said.

The Fourth Plague: Swarms of Flies

[20] Then the Lord said to Moses, "Rise up early in the morning and wait for Pharaoh, as he goes out to the water, and say to him, 'Thus says the Lord, "Let my people go, that they may serve me. [21]Else, if you will not let my people go, behold, I will send swarms of flies on you and your servants and your people, and into your houses; and the houses of the Egyptians shall be filled with swarms of flies, and also the ground on which they stand. [22]But on that day I will set apart the land of Goshen, where my people dwell, so that no swarms of flies shall be there; that you may know that I am the Lord in the midst of the earth. [23]Thus I will put a division[m] between my people and your people. By tomorrow shall this sign be."'" [24]And the Lord did so; there came great swarms of flies into the house of Pharaoh and into his servants' houses, and in all the land of Egypt the land was ruined by reason of the flies.

[25] Then Pharaoh called Moses and Aaron, and said, "Go, sacrifice to your God within the land."

[26]But Moses said, "It would not be right to do so; for we shall sacrifice to the Lord our God offerings abominable to the Egyptians. If we sacrifice offerings abominable to the Egyptians before their eyes, will they not stone us? [27]We must go three days' journey into the wilderness and sacrifice to the Lord our God as he will command us." [28]So Pharaoh said, "I will let you go, to sacrifice to the Lord your God in the wilderness; only you shall not go very far away. Make entreaty for me." [29]Then Moses said, "Behold, I am going out from you and I will pray to the Lord that the swarms of flies may depart from Pharaoh, from his servants, and from his people, tomorrow; only let not Pharaoh deal falsely again by not letting the people go to sacrifice to the Lord." [30]So Moses went out from Pharaoh and prayed to the Lord. [31]And the Lord did as Moses asked, and removed the swarms of flies from Pharaoh, from his servants, and from his people; not one remained. [32]But Pharaoh hardened his heart this time also, and did not let the people go.

The Fifth Plague: Death of the Egyptians' Livestock

9 Then the Lord said to Moses, "Go in to Pharaoh, and say to him, 'Thus says the Lord, the God of the Hebrews, "Let my people go, that they may serve me. [2]For if you refuse to let them go and still hold them, [3]behold, the hand of the Lord will fall with a very severe plague upon your cattle which are in the field, the horses, the donkeys, the camels, the herds, and the flocks. [4]But the Lord will make a distinction between the cattle of Israel and the cattle of Egypt, so that nothing shall die of all that belongs to the sons of Israel."'" [5]And the Lord set a time, saying, "Tomorrow the Lord will do this thing in the land." [6]And the next day the Lord did this thing; all the cattle of the Egyptians died, but of the cattle of the sons of Israel not one died. [7]And Pharaoh sent, and behold, not one of the cattle of the Israelites was dead. But the heart of Pharaoh was hardened, and he did not let the people go.

The Sixth Plague: Boils

[8] And the Lord said to Moses and Aaron, "Take handfuls of ashes from the kiln, and let Moses throw them toward heaven in the sight of Pharaoh. [9]And it shall become fine dust over all the land of Egypt, and become boils breaking out in sores on man and beast throughout all the land of Egypt." [10]So they took ashes from the kiln, and stood before Pharaoh, and Moses threw them toward heaven, and it became boils breaking out in sores on man and beast. [11]And the magicians could not stand before Moses because of the boils, for the boils were upon the magicians and upon all the Egyptians. [12]But the Lord hardened the

---

[1] Or which he had brought upon Pharaoh.
[m] Gk Vg: Heb set redemption.

heart of Pharaoh, and he did not listen to them; as the LORD had spoken to Moses.

The Seventh Plague: Thunder and Hail

13 Then the LORD said to Moses, "Rise up early in the morning and stand before Pharaoh, and say to him, 'Thus says the LORD, the God of the Hebrews, "Let my people go, that they may serve me. [14]For this time I will send all my plagues upon your heart, and upon your servants and your people, that you may know that there is none like me in all the earth. [15]For by now I could have put forth my hand and struck you and your people with pestilence, and you would have been cut off from the earth; [16]but for this purpose have I let you live, to show you my power, so that my name may be declared throughout all the earth. [17]You are still exalting yourself against my people, and will not let them go. [18]Behold, tomorrow about this time I will cause very heavy hail to fall, such as never has been in Egypt from the day it was founded until now. [19]Now therefore send, get your cattle and all that you have in the field into safe shelter; for the hail shall come down upon every man and beast that is in the field and is not brought home, and they shall die." '" [20]Then he who feared the word of the LORD among the servants of Pharaoh made his slaves and his cattle flee into the houses; [21]but he who did not regard the word of the LORD left his slaves and his cattle in the field.

22 And the LORD said to Moses, "Stretch forth your hand toward heaven, that there may be hail in all the land of Egypt, upon man and beast and every plant of the field, throughout the land of Egypt." [23]Then Moses stretched forth his rod toward heaven; and the LORD sent thunder and hail, and fire ran down to the earth. And the LORD rained hail upon the land of Egypt; [24]there was hail, and fire flashing continually in the midst of the hail, very heavy hail, such as had never been in all the land of Egypt since it became a nation. [25]The hail struck down everything that was in the field throughout all the land of Egypt, both man and beast; and the hail struck down every plant of the field, and shattered every tree of the field. [26]Only in the land of Goshen, where the sons of Israel were, there was no hail.

27 Then Pharaoh sent, and called Moses and Aaron, and said to them, "I have sinned this time; the LORD is in the right, and I and my people are in the wrong. [28]Entreat the LORD; for there has been enough of this thunder and hail; I will let you go, and you shall stay no longer." [29]Moses said to him, "As soon as I have gone out of the city, I will stretch out my hands to the LORD; the thunder will cease, and there will be no more hail, that you may know that the earth is the LORD's. [30]But as for you and your servants, I know that you do not yet fear the LORD God." [31](The flax and the barley were ruined, for the barley was in the ear and the flax was in bud. [32]But the wheat and the spelt were not ruined, for they are late in coming up.) [33]So Moses went out of the city from Pharaoh, and stretched out his hands to the LORD; and the thunder and the hail ceased, and the rain no longer poured upon the earth. [34]But when Pharaoh saw that the rain and the hail and the thunder had ceased, he sinned yet again, and hardened his heart, he and his servants. [35]So the heart of Pharaoh was hardened, and he did not let the sons of Israel go; as the LORD had spoken through Moses.

The Eighth Plague: Locusts

10 Then the LORD said to Moses, "Go in to Pharaoh; for I have hardened his heart and the heart of his servants, that I may show these signs of mine among them, [2]and that you may tell in the hearing of your son and of your son's son how I have made sport of the Egyptians and what signs I have done among them; that you may know that I am the LORD."

3 So Moses and Aaron went in to Pharaoh, and said to him, "Thus says the LORD, the God of the Hebrews, 'How long will you refuse to humble yourself before me? Let my people go, that they may serve me. [4]For if you refuse to let my people go, behold, tomorrow I will bring locusts into your country, [5]and they shall cover the face of the land, so that no one can see the land; and they shall eat what is left to you after the hail, and they shall eat every tree of yours which grows in the field, [6]and they shall fill your houses, and the houses of all your servants and of all the Egyptians; as neither your fathers nor your grandfathers have seen, from the day they came on earth to this day.' " Then he turned and went out from Pharaoh.

7 And Pharaoh's servants said to him, "How long shall this man be a snare to us? Let the men go, that they may serve the LORD their God; do you not yet understand that Egypt is ruined?" [8]So Moses and Aaron were brought back to Pharaoh; and he said to them, "Go, serve the LORD your God; but who are to go?" [9]And Moses said, "We will go with our young and our old; we will go with our sons and daughters and with our flocks and herds, for we must hold a feast to the LORD." [10]And he said to them, "The LORD be with you, if ever I let you and your little ones go! Look, you have some evil purpose in mind. [n] [11]No! Go, the men among you, and serve the LORD, for that is what you desire." And they were driven out from Pharaoh's presence.

12 Then the LORD said to Moses, "Stretch out your hand over the land of Egypt for the locusts, that they may come upon the land of Egypt, and

---

[n] Heb *before your face*.
9:16: Rom 9:17.

eat every plant in the land, all that the hail has left." ¹³So Moses stretched forth his rod over the land of Egypt, and the LORD brought an east wind upon the land all that day and all that night; and when it was morning the east wind had brought the locusts. ¹⁴And the locusts came up over all the land of Egypt, and settled on the whole country of Egypt, such a dense swarm of locusts as had never been before, nor ever shall be again. ¹⁵For they covered the face of the whole land, so that the land was darkened, and they ate all the plants in the land and all the fruit of the trees which the hail had left; not a green thing remained, neither tree nor plant of the field, through all the land of Egypt. ¹⁶Then Pharaoh called Moses and Aaron in haste, and said, "I have sinned against the LORD your God, and against you. ¹⁷Now therefore, forgive my sin, I beg you, only this once, and entreat the LORD your God only to remove this death from me." ¹⁸So he went out from Pharaoh, and entreated the LORD. ¹⁹And the LORD turned a very strong west wind, which lifted the locusts and drove them into the Red Sea; not a single locust was left in all the country of Egypt. ²⁰But the LORD hardened Pharaoh's heart, and he did not let the children of Israel go.

The Ninth Plague: Darkness

21 Then the LORD said to Moses, "Stretch out your hand toward heaven that there may be darkness over the land of Egypt, a darkness to be felt." ²²So Moses stretched out his hand toward heaven, and there was thick darkness in all the land of Egypt three days; ²³they did not see one another, nor did any rise from his place for three days; but all the sons of Israel had light where they dwelt. ²⁴Then Pharaoh called Moses, and said, "Go, serve the LORD; your children also may go with you; only let your flocks and your herds remain behind." ²⁵But Moses said, "You must also let us have sacrifices and burnt offerings, that we may sacrifice to the LORD our God. ²⁶Our cattle also must go with us; not a hoof shall be left behind, for we must take of them to serve the LORD our God, and we do not know with what we must serve the LORD until we arrive there." ²⁷But the LORD hardened Pharaoh's heart, and he would not let them go. ²⁸Then Pharaoh said to him, "Get away from me; take heed to yourself; never see my face again; for in the day you see my face you shall die." ²⁹Moses said, "As you say! I will not see your face again."

Warning of the Final Plague

11 The LORD said to Moses, "Yet one plague more I will bring upon Pharaoh and upon Egypt; afterwards he will let you go from here; when he lets you go, he will drive you away completely. ²Speak now in the hearing of the people, that they ask, every man of his neighbor and every woman of her neighbor, jewelry of silver

and of gold." ³And the LORD gave the people favor in the sight of the Egyptians. Moreover, the man Moses was very great in the land of Egypt, in the sight of Pharaoh's servants and in the sight of the people.

4 And Moses said, "Thus says the LORD: About midnight I will go forth in the midst of Egypt; ⁵and all the first-born in the land of Egypt shall die, from the first-born of Pharaoh who sits upon his throne, even to the first-born of the maidservant who is behind the mill; and all the first-born of the cattle. ⁶And there shall be a great cry throughout all the land of Egypt, such as there has never been, nor ever shall be again. ⁷But against any of the sons of Israel, either man or beast, not a dog shall growl; that you may know that the LORD makes a distinction between the Egyptians and Israel. ⁸And all these your servants shall come down to me, and bow down to me, saying, 'Get you out, and all the people who follow you.' And after that I will go out." And he went out from Pharaoh in hot anger. ⁹Then the LORD said to Moses, "Pharaoh will not listen to you; that my wonders may be multiplied in the land of Egypt."

10 Moses and Aaron did all these wonders before Pharaoh; and the LORD hardened Pharaoh's heart, and he did not let the sons of Israel go out of his land.

The Passover Instituted

12 * The LORD said to Moses and Aaron in the land of Egypt, ²"This month shall be for you the beginning of months; it shall be the first month of the year for you. ³Tell all the congregation of Israel that on the tenth day of this month they shall take every man a lamb according to their fathers' houses, a lamb for a household; ⁴and if the household is too small for a lamb, then a man and his neighbor next to his house shall take according to the number of persons; according to what each can eat you shall make your count for the lamb. ⁵Your lamb shall be without blemish, a male a year old; you shall take it from the sheep or from the goats; ⁶and you shall keep it until the fourteenth day of this month, when the whole assembly of the congregation of Israel shall kill their lambs in the evening.° ⁷Then they shall take some of the blood, and put it on the two doorposts and the lintel of the houses in which they eat them. ⁸They shall eat the flesh that night, roasted; with unleavened bread and bitter herbs they shall eat it. ⁹Do not eat any of it raw or boiled with water, but roasted, its head with its legs and its inner parts. ¹⁰And you shall let none of it remain until the

---

° Heb *between the two evenings.*
* 12:1: The feast of the Passover, the regulations for which are given here, commemorates the deliverance from Egypt. The feast of unleavened bread would probably have been added only after the entry into Canaan. The Passover foreshadows the sacrifice of Jesus (1 Cor 5:7).

morning, anything that remains until the morning you shall burn. [11]In this manner you shall eat it: your loins girded, your sandals on your feet, and your staff in your hand; and you shall eat it in haste. It is the LORD's Passover. [12]For I will pass through the land of Egypt that night, and I will strike all the first-born in the land of Egypt, both man and beast; and on all the gods of Egypt I will execute judgments: I am the LORD. [13]The blood shall be a sign for you, upon the houses where you are; and when I see the blood, I will pass over you, and no plague shall fall upon you to destroy you, when I strike the land of Egypt.

14 "This day shall be for you a memorial day, and you shall keep it as a feast to the LORD; throughout your generations you shall observe it as an ordinance for ever. [15]Seven days you shall eat unleavened bread; on the first day you shall put away leaven out of your houses, for if any one eats what is leavened, from the first day until the seventh day, that person shall be cut off from Israel. [16]On the first day you shall hold a holy assembly, and on the seventh day a holy assembly; no work shall be done on those days; but what every one must eat, that only may be prepared by you. [17]And you shall observe the feast of unleavened bread, for on this very day I brought your hosts out of the land of Egypt: therefore you shall observe this day, throughout your generations, as an ordinance for ever. [18]In the first month, on the fourteenth day of the month at evening, you shall eat unleavened bread, and so until the twenty-first day of the month at evening. [19]For seven days no leaven shall be found in your houses; for if any one eats what is leavened, that person shall be cut off from the congregation of Israel, whether he is a sojourner or a native of the land. [20]You shall eat nothing leavened; in all your dwellings you shall eat unleavened bread."

21 Then Moses called all the elders of Israel, and said to them, "Select lambs for yourselves according to your families, and kill the Passover lamb. [22]Take a bunch of hyssop and dip it in the blood which is in the basin, and touch the lintel and the two doorposts with the blood which is in the basin; and none of you shall go out of the door of his house until the morning. [23]For the LORD will pass through to slay the Egyptians; and when he sees the blood on the lintel and on the two doorposts, the LORD will pass over the door, and will not allow the destroyer to enter your houses to slay you. [24]You shall observe this rite as an ordinance for you and for your sons for ever. [25]And when you come to the land which the LORD will give you, as he has promised, you shall keep this service. [26]And when your children say to you, 'What do you mean by this service?' [27]you shall say, 'It is the sacrifice of the LORD's Passover, for he passed over the houses of the sons of Israel in Egypt, when he slew the Egyptians but spared our houses.'" And the people bowed their heads and worshiped.

28 Then the sons of Israel went and did so; as the LORD had commanded Moses and Aaron, so they did.

The Tenth Plague: The Death of Egypt's First-born

29 At midnight the LORD struck all the first-born in the land of Egypt, from the first-born of Pharaoh who sat on his throne to the first-born of the captive who was in the dungeon, and all the first-born of the cattle. [30]And Pharaoh rose up in the night, he, and all his servants, and all the Egyptians; and there was a great cry in Egypt, for there was not a house where one was not dead. [31]And he summoned Moses and Aaron by night, and said, "Rise up, go forth from among my people, both you and the sons of Israel; and go, serve the LORD, as you have said. [32]Take your flocks and your herds, as you have said, and be gone; and bless me also!"

The Exodus: From Rameses to Succoth

33 And the Egyptians were urgent with the people, to send them out of the land in haste; for they said, "We are all dead men." [34]So the people took their dough before it was leavened, their kneading bowls being bound up in their mantles on their shoulders. [35]The sons of Israel had also done as Moses told them, for they had asked of the Egyptians jewelry of silver and of gold, and clothing; [36]and the LORD had given the people favor in the sight of the Egyptians, so that they let them have what they asked. Thus they despoiled the Egyptians.

37 And the sons of Israel journeyed from Ram'eses to Succoth, about six hundred thousand men on foot, besides women and children. [38]A mixed multitude also went up with them, and very many cattle, both flocks and herds. [39]And they baked unleavened cakes of the dough which they had brought out of Egypt, for it was not leavened, because they were thrust out of Egypt and could not tarry, neither had they prepared for themselves any provisions.

40 The time that the sons of Israel dwelt in Egypt was four hundred and thirty years. [41]And at the end of four hundred and thirty years, on that very day, all the hosts of the LORD went out from the land of Egypt. [42]It was a night of watching by the LORD, to bring them out of the land of Egypt; so this same night is a night of watching kept to the LORD by all the sons of Israel throughout their generations.

The Ordinance of the Passover

43 And the LORD said to Moses and Aaron, "This is the ordinance of the Passover: no for-

12:13: Heb 11:28.   12:40: Acts 7:6.

eigner shall eat of it; [44]but every slave that is bought for money may eat of it after you have circumcised him. [45]No sojourner or hired servant may eat of it. [46]In one house shall it be eaten; you shall not carry forth any of the flesh outside the house; and you shall not break a bone of it. [47]All the congregation of Israel shall keep it. [48]And when a stranger shall sojourn with you and would keep the Passover to the LORD, let all his males be circumcised, then he may come near and keep it; he shall be as a native of the land. But no uncircumcised person shall eat of it. [49]There shall be one law for the native and for the stranger who sojourns among you."

50 Thus did all the sons of Israel; as the LORD commanded Moses and Aaron, so they did. [51]And on that very day the LORD brought the sons of Israel out of the land of Egypt by their hosts.

13 The LORD said to Moses, [2] "Consecrate to me all the first-born; whatever is the first to open the womb among the sons of Israel, both of man and of beast, is mine."

The Feast of Unleavened Bread

3 And Moses said to the people, "Remember this day, in which you came out from Egypt, out of the house of bondage, for by strength of hand the LORD brought you out from this place; no leavened bread shall be eaten. [4]This day you are to go forth, in the month of Abib. [5]And when the LORD brings you into the land of the Canaanites, the Hittites, the Am'orites, the Hi'vites, and the Jeb'usites, which he swore to your fathers to give you, a land flowing with milk and honey, you shall keep this service in this month. [6]Seven days you shall eat unleavened bread, and on the seventh day there shall be a feast to the LORD. [7]Unleavened bread shall be eaten for seven days; no leavened bread shall be seen with you, and no leaven shall be seen with you in all your territory. [8]And you shall tell your son on that day, 'It is because of what the LORD did for me when I came out of Egypt.' [9]And it shall be to you as a sign on your hand and as a memorial between your eyes, that the law of the LORD may be in your mouth; for with a strong hand the LORD has brought you out of Egypt. [10]You shall therefore keep this ordinance at its appointed time from year to year.

The Consecration of First-born Males

11 "And when the LORD brings you into the land of the Canaanites, as he swore to you and your fathers, and shall give it to you, [12]you shall set apart to the LORD all that first opens the womb. All the firstlings of your cattle that are males shall be the LORD's. [13]Every firstling of a donkey you shall redeem with a lamb, or if you will not redeem it you shall break its neck. Every first-born of man among your sons you shall redeem. [14]And when in time to come your son asks you, 'What does this mean?' you shall say to him, 'By

strength of hand the LORD brought us out of Egypt, from the house of bondage. [15]For when Pharaoh stubbornly refused to let us go, the LORD slew all the first-born in the land of Egypt, both the first-born of man and the first-born of cattle. Therefore I sacrifice to the LORD all the males that first open the womb; but all the first-born of my sons I redeem.' [16]It shall be as a mark on your hand or frontlets between your eyes; for by a strong hand the LORD brought us out of Egypt."

The Pillar of Cloud and the Pillar of Fire

17 When Pharaoh let the people go, God did not lead them by way of the land of the Philis'tines, although that was near; for God said, "Lest the people repent when they see war, and return to Egypt." [18]But God led the people round by the way of the wilderness toward the Red Sea. And the sons of Israel went up out of the land of Egypt equipped for battle. [19]And Moses took the bones of Joseph with him; for Joseph had solemnly sworn the sons of Israel, saying, "God will visit you; then you must carry my bones with you from here." [20]And they moved on from Succoth, and encamped at Etham, on the edge of the wilderness. [21]And the LORD went before them by day in a pillar of cloud to lead them along the way, and by night in a pillar of fire to give them light, that they might travel by day and by night; [22]the pillar of cloud by day and the pillar of fire by night did not depart from before the people.

Crossing the Red Sea

14 Then the LORD said to Moses, [2] "Tell the sons of Israel to turn back and encamp in front of Piha-hi'roth, between Migdol and the sea, in front of Ba'al-ze'phon; you shall encamp over against it, by the sea. [3]For Pharaoh will say of the sons of Israel, 'They are entangled in the land; the wilderness has shut them in.' [4]And I will harden Pharaoh's heart, and he will pursue them and I will get glory over Pharaoh and all his host; and the Egyptians shall know that I am the LORD." And they did so.

5 When the king of Egypt was told that the people had fled, the mind of Pharaoh and his servants was changed toward the people, and they said, "What is this we have done, that we have let Israel go from serving us?" [6]So he made ready his chariot and took his army with him, [7]and took six hundred picked chariots and all the other chariots of Egypt with officers over all of them. [8]And the LORD hardened the heart of Pharaoh king of Egypt and he pursued the sons of Israel as they went forth defiantly. [9]The Egyptians pursued them, all Pharaoh's horses and

12:46: Num 9:12; Jn 19:36.
12:49: Lev 24:22; Num 9:14; 15:15, 16, 29.
13:2, 12, 15: Lk 2:23.
13:19: Gen 50:25.
14:8: Acts 13:17.

49

chariots and his horsemen and his army, and overtook them encamped at the sea, by Piha-hi'roth, in front of Ba'al-ze'phon.

10 When Pharaoh drew near, the sons of Israel lifted up their eyes, and behold, the Egyptians were marching after them; and they were in great fear. And the sons of Israel cried out to the Lord; [11]and they said to Moses, "Is it because there are no graves in Egypt that you have taken us away to die in the wilderness? What have you done to us, in bringing us out of Egypt? [12]Is not this what we said to you in Egypt, 'Let us alone and let us serve the Egyptians'? For it would have been better for us to serve the Egyptians than to die in the wilderness." [13]And Moses said to the people, "Fear not, stand firm, and see the salvation of the Lord, which he will work for you today; for the Egyptians whom you see today, you shall never see again. [14]The Lord will fight for you, and you have only to be still." [15]The Lord said to Moses, "Why do you cry to me? Tell the sons of Israel to go forward. [16]Lift up your rod, and stretch out your hand over the sea and divide it, that the sons of Israel may go on dry ground through the sea. [17]And I will harden the hearts of the Egyptians so that they shall go in after them, and I will get glory over Pharaoh and all his host, his chariots, and his horsemen. [18]And the Egyptians shall know that I am the Lord, when I have gotten glory over Pharaoh, his chariots, and his horsemen."

19 Then the angel of God who went before the host of Israel moved and went behind them; and the pillar of cloud moved from before them and stood behind them, [20]coming between the host of Egypt and the host of Israel. And there was the cloud and the darkness; and the night passed[p] without one coming near the other all night.

21 Then Moses stretched out his hand over the sea; and the Lord drove the sea back by a strong east wind all night, and made the sea dry land, and the waters were divided. [22]And the sons of Israel went into the midst of the sea on dry ground, the waters being a wall to them on their right hand and on their left. [23]The Egyptians pursued, and went in after them into the midst of the sea, all Pharaoh's horses, his chariots, and his horsemen. [24]And in the morning watch the Lord in the pillar of fire and of cloud looked down upon the host of the Egyptians, and discomfited the host of the Egyptians, [25]clogging[q] their chariot wheels so that they drove heavily; and the Egyptians said, "Let us flee from before Israel; for the Lord fights for them against the Egyptians."

The Egyptians Drown in the Sea

26 Then the Lord said to Moses, "Stretch out your hand over the sea, that the water may come back upon the Egyptians, upon their chariots, and upon their horsemen." [27]So Moses stretched forth his hand over the sea, and the sea returned to its usual flow when the morning appeared; and the Egyptians fled into it, and the Lord routed[r] the Egyptians in the midst of the sea. [28]The waters returned and covered the chariots and the horsemen and all the host[s] of Pharaoh that had followed them into the sea; not so much as one of them remained. [29]But the sons of Israel walked on dry ground through the sea, the waters being a wall to them on their right hand and on their left.

30 Thus the Lord saved Israel that day from the hand of the Egyptians; and Israel saw the Egyptians dead upon the seashore. [31]And Israel saw the great work which the Lord did against the Egyptians, and the people feared the Lord; and they believed in the Lord and in his servant Moses.

The Songs of Moses and Miriam

15 Then Moses and the sons of Israel sang this song to the Lord, saying,
"I will sing to the Lord, for he has triumphed
    gloriously;
    the horse and his rider[t] he has thrown into
      the sea.
[2]The Lord is my strength and my song,
    and he has become my salvation;
this is my God, and I will praise him,
    my father's God, and I will exalt him.
[3]The Lord is a man of war;
    the Lord is his name.

[4]"Pharaoh's chariots and his host he cast into
    the sea;
    and his picked officers are sunk in the Red
    Sea.
[5]The floods cover them;
    they went down into the depths like a stone.
[6]Your right hand, O Lord, glorious in power,
    your right hand, O Lord, shatters the
    enemy.
[7]In the greatness of your majesty you
    overthrow your adversaries;
    you send forth your fury, it consumes them
    like stubble.
[8]At the blast of your nostrils the waters piled
    up,
    the floods stood up in a heap;
    the deeps congealed in the heart of the sea.
[9]The enemy said, 'I will pursue, I will overtake,
    I will divide the spoil, my desire shall have
    its fill of them.
    I will draw my sword, my hand shall
    destroy them.'

---

[p] Gk: Heb *and it lit up the night.*
[q] Or *binding.* Sam Gk Syr: Heb *removing.*
[r] Heb *shook off.*
[s] Gk Syr: Heb *to all the host.*
[t] Or *its chariot.*
14:12: Ex 16:3; 17:3.

¹⁰You blew with your wind, the sea covered them;
  they sank as lead in the mighty waters.

¹¹"Who is like you, O Lᴏʀᴅ, among the gods?
  Who is like you, majestic in holiness,
  terrible in glorious deeds, doing wonders?
¹²You stretched out your right hand,
  the earth swallowed them.

¹³"You have led in your merciful love the people
    whom you have redeemed,
  you have guided them by your strength to
    your holy abode.
¹⁴The peoples have heard, they tremble;
  pangs have seized on the inhabitants of
    Philistia.
¹⁵Now are the chiefs of Edom dismayed;
  the leaders of Moab, trembling seizes them;
  all the inhabitants of Canaan have melted
    away.
¹⁶Terror and dread fall upon them;
  because of the greatness of your arm, they
    are as still as a stone,
  till your people, O Lᴏʀᴅ, pass by,
  till the people pass by whom you have
    purchased.
¹⁷You will bring them in, and plant them on your
    own mountain,
  the place, O Lᴏʀᴅ, which you have made for
    your abode,
  the sanctuary, O Lᴏʀᴅ, which your hands
    have established.
¹⁸The Lᴏʀᴅ will reign for ever and ever."

19 For when the horses of Pharaoh with his chariots and his horsemen went into the sea, the Lᴏʀᴅ brought back the waters of the sea upon them; but the sons of Israel walked on dry ground in the midst of the sea. ²⁰Then Miriam, the prophetess, the sister of Aaron, took a timbrel in her hand; and all the women went out after her with timbrels and dancing. ²¹And Miriam sang to them:

"Sing to the Lord, for he has triumphed
    gloriously;
  the horse and his rider he has thrown into the
    sea."

Bitter Water Is Made Sweet

22 Then Moses led Israel onward from the Red Sea, and they went into the wilderness of Shur; they went three days in the wilderness and found no water. ²³When they came to Marah, they could not drink the water of Marah because it was bitter; therefore it was named Marah.ᵘ ²⁴And the people murmured against Moses, saying, "What shall we drink?" ²⁵And he cried to the Lᴏʀᴅ; and the Lᴏʀᴅ showed him a tree, and he threw it into the water, and the water became sweet.

There the Lᴏʀᴅ ᵛ made for them a statute and an ordinance and there he tested them, ²⁶saying, "If you will diligently listen to the voice of the

Lᴏʀᴅ your God, and do that which is right in his eyes, and give heed to his commandments and keep all his statutes, I will put none of the diseases upon you which I put upon the Egyptians; for I am the Lᴏʀᴅ, your healer."

27 Then they came to E'lim, where there were twelve springs of water and seventy palm trees; and they encamped there by the water.

Manna from Heaven

16 They set out from E'lim, and all the congregation of the sons of Israel came to the wilderness of Sin, which is between Elim and Sinai, on the fifteenth day of the second month after they had departed from the land of Egypt. ²And the whole congregation of the sons of Israel murmured against Moses and Aaron in the wilderness, ³and said to them, "Would that we had died by the hand of the Lᴏʀᴅ in the land of Egypt, when we sat by the fleshpots and ate bread to the full; for you have brought us out into this wilderness to kill this whole assembly with hunger."

4 Then the Lᴏʀᴅ said to Moses, "Behold, I will rain bread from heaven for you; and the people shall go out and gather a day's portion every day, that I may test them, whether they will walk in my law or not. ⁵On the sixth day, when they prepare what they bring in, it will be twice as much as they gather daily." ⁶So Moses and Aaron said to all the sons of Israel, "At evening you shall know that it was the Lᴏʀᴅ who brought you out of the land of Egypt, ⁷and in the morning you shall see the glory of the Lᴏʀᴅ, because he has heard your murmurings against the Lᴏʀᴅ. For what are we, that you murmur against us?" ⁸And Moses said, "When the Lᴏʀᴅ gives you in the evening flesh to eat and in the morning bread to the full, because the Lᴏʀᴅ has heard your murmurings which you murmur against him—what are we? Your murmurings are not against us but against the Lᴏʀᴅ."

9 And Moses said to Aaron, "Say to the whole congregation of the sons of Israel, 'Come near before the Lᴏʀᴅ, for he has heard your murmurings.'" ¹⁰And as Aaron spoke to the whole congregation of the sons of Israel, they looked toward the wilderness, and behold, the glory of the Lᴏʀᴅ appeared in the cloud. ¹¹And the Lᴏʀᴅ said to Moses, ¹²"I have heard the murmurings of the sons of Israel; say to them, 'At twilight you shall eat flesh, and in the morning you shall be filled with bread; then you shall know that I am the Lᴏʀᴅ your God.'"

13 In the evening quails came up and covered the camp; and in the morning dew lay round about

ᵘ That is *Bitterness*.
ᵛ Heb *he*.
16:3: Ex 14:12; 17:3.
16:4, 13: Jn 6:31.

the camp. [14]And when the dew had gone up, there was on the face of the wilderness a fine, flake-like thing, fine as hoarfrost on the ground.* [15]When the sons of Israel saw it, they said to one another, "What is it?" [w] For they did not know what it was. And Moses said to them, "It is the bread which the LORD has given you to eat. [16]This is what the LORD has commanded: 'Gather of it, every man of you, as much as he can eat; you shall take an omer apiece, according to the number of the persons whom each of you has in his tent.' " [17]And the sons of Israel did so; they gathered, some more, some less. [18]But when they measured it with an omer, he that gathered much had nothing over, and he that gathered little had no lack; each gathered according to what he could eat. [19]And Moses said to them, "Let no man leave any of it till the morning." [20]But they did not listen to Moses; some left part of it till the morning, and it bred worms and became foul; and Moses was angry with them. [21]Morning by morning they gathered it, each as much as he could eat; but when the sun grew hot, it melted.

22 On the sixth day they gathered twice as much bread, two omers apiece; and when all the leaders of the congregation came and told Moses, [23]he said to them, "This is what the LORD has commanded: 'Tomorrow is a day of solemn rest, a holy sabbath to the LORD; bake what you will bake and boil what you will boil, and all that is left over lay by to be kept till the morning.' " [24]So they laid it by till the morning, as Moses bade them; and it did not become foul, and there were no worms in it. [25]Moses said, "Eat it today, for today is a sabbath to the LORD; today you will not find it in the field. [26]Six days you shall gather it; but on the seventh day, which is a sabbath, there will be none." [27]On the seventh day some of the people went out to gather, and they found none. [28]And the LORD said to Moses, "How long do you refuse to keep my commandments and my laws? [29]See! The LORD has given you the sabbath, therefore on the sixth day he gives you bread for two days; remain every man of you in his place, let no man go out of his place on the seventh day." [30]So the people rested on the seventh day.

31 Now the house of Israel called its name manna; it was like coriander seed, white, and the taste of it was like wafers made with honey. [32]And Moses said, "This is what the LORD has commanded: 'Let an omer of it be kept throughout your generations, that they may see the bread with which I fed you in the wilderness, when I brought you out of the land of Egypt.' " [33]And Moses said to Aaron, "Take a jar, and put an omer of manna in it, and place it before the LORD, to be kept throughout your generations." [34]As the LORD commanded Moses, so Aaron placed it before the covenant, to be kept. [35]And the sons of Israel ate the manna forty years, till they came to a habitable land; they ate the manna, till they came to the border of the land of Canaan. [36](An omer is the tenth part of an ephah.)

Water from the Rock

17 All the congregation of the sons of Israel moved on from the wilderness of Sin by stages, according to the commandment of the LORD, and camped at Reph'idim; but there was no water for the people to drink. [2]Therefore the people found fault with Moses, and said, "Give us water to drink." And Moses said to them, "Why do you find fault with me? Why do you put the LORD to the test?" [3]But the people thirsted there for water, and the people murmured against Moses, and said, "Why did you bring us up out of Egypt, to kill us and our children and our cattle with thirst?" [4]So Moses cried to the LORD, "What shall I do with this people? They are almost ready to stone me." [5]And the LORD said to Moses, "Pass on before the people, taking with you some of the elders of Israel; and take in your hand the rod with which you struck the Nile, and go. [6]Behold, I will stand before you there on the rock at Horeb; and you shall strike the rock, and water shall come out of it, that the people may drink." And Moses did so, in the sight of the elders of Israel. [7]And he called the name of the place Massah [x] and Mer'ibah, [y] because of the fault-finding of the sons of Israel, and because they put the LORD to the test by saying, "Is the LORD among us or not?"

Amalek Attacks Israel and Is Defeated

8 Then came Am'alek and fought with Israel at Reph'idim. [9]And Moses said to Joshua, "Choose for us men, and go out, fight with Am'alek; tomorrow I will stand on the top of the hill with the rod of God in my hand." [10]So Joshua did as Moses told him, and fought with Am'alek; and Moses, Aaron, and Hur went up to the top of the hill. [11]Whenever Moses held up his hand, Israel prevailed; and whenever he lowered his hand, Am'alek prevailed. [12]But Moses' hands grew weary; so they took a stone and put it under him, and he sat upon it, and Aaron and Hur held up his hands, one on one side, and the other on the other side; so his hands were steady until the going down of the sun. [13]And Joshua mowed down Am'alek and his people with the edge of the sword.

14 And the LORD said to Moses, "Write this as a memorial in a book and recite it in the ears of

---

[w] Or "It is manna." Heb man hu.
[x] That is Proof.
[y] That is Contention.
16:18: 2 Cor 8:15.
17:3: 14:12; 16:3.
17:14: Deut 25:17–19; 1 Sam 15:2–9.
* 16:14: The mysterious manna may have been a substance secreted by the tamarisk or perhaps by an insect that feeds on its leaves and is edible. In the New Testament it is a type of the Eucharist; cf. Jn 6:31–35, 48–51.

Joshua, that I will utterly blot out the remembrance of Am'alek from under heaven." [15]And Moses built an altar and called the name of it, The LORD is my banner, [16]saying, "A hand upon the banner of the LORD! [z] The LORD will have war with Am'alek from generation to generation."

Jethro's Counsel to Moses

18 Jethro, the priest of Mid'ian, Moses' father-in-law, heard of all that God had done for Moses and for Israel his people, how the LORD had brought Israel out of Egypt. [2]Now Jethro, Moses' father-in-law, had taken Zippo'rah, Moses' wife, after he had sent her away, [3]and her two sons, of whom the name of the one was Gershom (for he said, "I have been a sojourner [a] in a foreign land"), [4]and the name of the other, Elie'zer [b] (for he said, "The God of my father was my help, and delivered me from the sword of Pharaoh"). [5]And Jethro, Moses' father-in-law, came with his sons and his wife to Moses in the wilderness where he was encamped at the mountain of God. [6]And when one told Moses, "Behold, [c] your father-in-law Jethro is coming to you with your wife and her two sons with her," [7]Moses went out to meet his father-in-law, and did obeisance and kissed him; and they asked each other of their welfare, and went into the tent. [8]Then Moses told his father-in-law all that the LORD had done to Pharaoh and to the Egyptians for Israel's sake, all the hardship that had come upon them in the way, and how the LORD had delivered them. [9]And Jethro rejoiced for all the good which the LORD had done to Israel, in that he had delivered them out of the hand of the Egyptians.

10 And Jethro said, "Blessed be the LORD, who has delivered you out of the hand of the Egyptians and out of the hand of Pharaoh. [11]Now I know that the LORD is greater than all gods, because he delivered the people from under the hand of the Egyptians, [d] when they dealt arrogantly with them." [12]And Jethro, Moses' father-in-law, offered [e] a burnt offering and sacrifices to God; and Aaron came with all the elders of Israel to eat bread with Moses' father-in-law before God.

13 The next day Moses sat to judge the people, and the people stood about Moses from morning till evening. [14]When Moses' father-in-law saw all that he was doing for the people, he said, "What is this that you are doing for the people? Why do you sit alone, and all the people stand about you from morning till evening?" [15]And Moses said to his father-in-law, "Because the people come to me to inquire of God; [16]when they have a dispute, they come to me and I decide between a man and his neighbor, and I make them know the statutes of God and his decisions." [17]Moses' father-in-law said to him, "What you are doing is not good. [18]You and the people with you will wear yourselves out, for the thing is too heavy for you; you

are not able to perform it alone. [19]Listen now to my voice; I will give you counsel, and God be with you! You shall represent the people before God, and bring their cases to God; [20]and you shall teach them the statutes and the decisions, and make them know the way in which they must walk and what they must do. [21]Moreover choose able men from all the people, such as fear God, men who are trustworthy and who hate a bribe; and place such men over the people as rulers of thousands, of hundreds, of fifties, and of tens. [22]And let them judge the people at all times; every great matter they shall bring to you, but any small matter they shall decide themselves; so it will be easier for you, and they will bear the burden with you. [23]If you do this, and God so commands you, then you will be able to endure, and all this people also will go to their place in peace."

24 So Moses gave heed to the voice of his father-in-law and did all that he had said. [25]Moses chose able men out of all Israel, and made them heads over the people, rulers of thousands, of hundreds, of fifties, and of tens. [26]And they judged the people at all times; hard cases they brought to Moses, but any small matter they decided themselves. [27]Then Moses let his father-in-law depart, and he went his way to his own country.

The Israelites Reach Mount Sinai

19 On the third new moon after the sons of Israel had gone forth out of the land of Egypt, on that day they came into the wilderness of Sinai. [2]And when they set out from Reph'idim and came into the wilderness of Sinai, they encamped in the wilderness; and there Israel encamped before the mountain. [3]And Moses went up to God, and the LORD called to him out of the mountain, saying, "Thus you shall say to the house of Jacob, and tell the sons of Israel: [*] [4]You have seen what I did to the Egyptians, and how I bore you on eagles' wings and brought you to myself. [5]Now therefore, if you will obey my voice and keep my covenant, you shall be my own possession among all peoples; for all the earth is mine, [6]and you shall be to me a kingdom of priests and a holy nation. These are the words which you shall speak to the children of Israel."

7 So Moses came and called the elders of the people, and set before them all these words which the LORD had commanded him. [8]And all the people answered together and said, "All that the LORD

---

[z] Cn: Heb obscure.
[a] Heb *ger*.
[b] Heb *Eli*, my God, *ezer*, help.
[c] Sam Gk Syr: Heb *I*.
[d] Transposing the last clause of v. 10 to v. 11.
[e] Syr Tg Vg: Heb *took*.
18:3, 4: Acts 7.29.
19:5, 6: Deut 7.6; 14.2, 21; 26.19; Tit 2.14; 1 Pet 2.9; Rev 1.6; 5.10.
[*] 19:3: The covenant makes Israel the people of God and binds them to the fulfilment of the commandments; it is concluded in chapter 24.

has spoken we will do." And Moses reported the words of the people to the LORD. ⁹And the LORD said to Moses, "Behold, I am coming to you in a thick cloud, that the people may hear when I speak with you, and may also believe you for ever."

Then Moses told the words of the people to the LORD. ¹⁰And the LORD said to Moses, "Go to the people and consecrate them today and tomorrow, and let them wash their garments, ¹¹and be ready by the third day; for on the third day the LORD will come down upon Mount Sinai in the sight of all the people. ¹²And you shall set bounds for the people round about, saying, 'Take heed that you do not go up into the mountain or touch the border of it; whoever touches the mountain shall be put to death; ¹³no hand shall touch him, but he shall be stoned or shot; whether beast or man, he shall not live.' When the trumpet sounds a long blast, they shall come up to the mountain." ¹⁴So Moses went down from the mountain to the people, and consecrated the people; and they washed their garments. ¹⁵And he said to the people, "Be ready by the third day; do not go near a woman."

God Speaks to Moses on the Mountain

16 On the morning of the third day there was thunder and lightning, and a thick cloud upon the mountain, and a very loud trumpet blast, so that all the people who were in the camp trembled. ¹⁷Then Moses brought the people out of the camp to meet God; and they took their stand at the foot of the mountain. ¹⁸And Mount Sinai was wrapped in smoke, because the LORD descended upon it in fire; and the smoke of it went up like the smoke of a kiln, and the whole mountain quaked greatly. ¹⁹And as the sound of the trumpet grew louder and louder, Moses spoke, and God answered him in thunder. ²⁰And the LORD came down upon Mount Sinai, to the top of the mountain; and the LORD called Moses to the top of the mountain, and Moses went up. ²¹And the LORD said to Moses, "Go down and warn the people, lest they break through to the LORD to gaze and many of them perish. ²²And also let the priests who come near to the LORD consecrate themselves, lest the LORD break out upon them." ²³And Moses said to the LORD, "The people cannot come up to Mount Sinai; for you yourself charged us, saying, 'Set bounds about the mountain, and consecrate it.'" ²⁴And the LORD said to him, "Go down, and come up bringing Aaron with you; but do not let the priests and the people break through to come up to the LORD, lest he break out against them." ²⁵So Moses went down to the people and told them.

The Ten Commandments

20 And God spoke all these words, saying,*
2 "I am the LORD your God, who brought you out of the land of Egypt, out of the house of bondage.

3 "You shall have no other gods before ᶠ me.

4 You shall not make for yourself a graven image, or any likeness of anything that is in heaven above, or that is in the earth beneath, or that is in the water under the earth; ⁵you shall not bow down to them or serve them; for I the LORD your God am a jealous God, visiting the iniquity of the fathers upon the children to the third and the fourth generation of those who hate me, ⁶but showing mercy to thousands of those who love me and keep my commandments.

7 "You shall not take the name of the LORD your God in vain; for the LORD will not hold him guiltless who takes his name in vain.

8 "Remember the sabbath day, to keep it holy. ⁹Six days you shall labor, and do all your work; ¹⁰but the seventh day is a sabbath to the LORD your God; in it you shall not do any work, you, or your son, or your daughter, your manservant, or your maidservant, or your cattle, or the sojourner who is within your gates; ¹¹for in six days the LORD made heaven and earth, the sea, and all that is in them, and rested the seventh day; therefore the LORD blessed the sabbath day and hallowed it.

12 "Honor your father and your mother, that your days may be long in the land which the LORD your God gives you.

13 "You shall not kill.

14 "You shall not commit adultery.

15 "You shall not steal.

16 "You shall not bear false witness against your neighbor.

17 "You shall not covet your neighbor's house; you shall not covet your neighbor's wife, or his manservant, or his maidservant, or his ox, or his donkey, or anything that is your neighbor's."

18 Now when all the people perceived the thunder and the lightning and the sound of the trumpet and the mountain smoking, the people were afraid and trembled; and they stood afar off, ¹⁹and said to Moses, "You speak to us, and we will hear; but let not God speak to us, lest we die." ²⁰And

---

ᶠ Or *besides*.
19:12-19: Heb 12:18–20.
20:2-17: Deut 5:6–21.
20:3: Ex 20:23; Deut 5:7.
20:4: Ex 20:23; 34:17; Lev 19:4; 26:1; Deut 4:15–19; 5:8; 27:15.
20:5, 6: Ex 23:24; 34:6, 7, 14; Deut 4:24; 5:9, 10; 7:9.
20:7: Lev 19:12; Deut 5:11.
20:8: Ex 23:12; 31:12–17; 34:21; 35:2, 3; Lev 19:3; Deut 5:12–15.
20:12-16: Mt 19:18, 19; Mk 10:19; Lk 18:20.
20:12: Lev 19:3; Deut 5:16; Mt 15:4; Mk 7:10; Eph 6:2.
20:13: Gen 9:6; Ex 21:12; Lev 24:17; Deut 5:17; Mt 5:21; Jas 2:11.
20:13-17: Rom 13:9.
20:14: Lev 20:10; Deut 5:18; Mt 5:27; Rom 7:7.
20:15: Lev 19:11; Deut 5:19.
20:16: Ex 23:1; Deut 5:20.
20:17: Deut 5:21; Rom 7:7.
* 20:1–17: The Ten Commandments, in their original form even briefer than here, are found in a different version in Deut 5:6–21.

Moses said to the people, "Do not fear; for God has come to test you, and that the fear of him may be before your eyes, that you may not sin."

God Gives Moses Laws about Sacrifice

21 And the people stood afar off, while Moses drew near to the thick darkness where God was. ²²And the LORD said to Moses, "Thus you shall say to the people of Israel: 'You have seen for yourselves that I have talked with you from heaven. ²³You shall not make gods of silver to be with me, nor shall you make for yourselves gods of gold. ²⁴An altar of earth you shall make for me and sacrifice on it your burnt offerings and your peace offerings, your sheep and your oxen; in every place where I cause my name to be remembered I will come to you and bless you. ²⁵And if you make me an altar of stone, you shall not build it of hewn stones; for if you wield your tool upon it you profane it. ²⁶And you shall not go up by steps to my altar, that your nakedness be not exposed on it.'

Laws concerning Slaves

21 "Now these are the ordinances which you shall set before them. ²When you buy a Hebrew slave, he shall serve six years, and in the seventh he shall go out free, for nothing. ³If he comes in single, he shall go out single; if he comes in married, then his wife shall go out with him. ⁴If his master gives him a wife and she bears him sons or daughters, the wife and her children shall be her master's and he shall go out alone. ⁵But if the slave plainly says, 'I love my master, my wife, and my children; I will not go out free,' ⁶then his master shall bring him to God, and he shall bring him to the door or the doorpost; and his master shall bore his ear through with an awl; and he shall serve him for life.

7 "When a man sells his daughter as a slave, she shall not go out as the male slaves do. ⁸If she does not please her master, who has designated her ^g for himself, then he shall let her be redeemed; he shall have no right to sell her to a foreign people, since he has dealt faithlessly with her. ⁹If he designates her for his son, he shall deal with her as with a daughter. ¹⁰If he takes another wife to himself, he shall not diminish her food, her clothing, or her marital rights. ¹¹And if he does not do these three things for her, she shall go out for nothing, without payment of money.

Laws concerning Violence and Harm

12 "Whoever strikes a man so that he dies shall be put to death. ¹³But if he did not lie in wait for him, but God let him fall into his hand, then I will appoint for you a place to which he may flee. ¹⁴But if a man willfully attacks another to kill him treacherously, you shall take him from my altar, that he may die.

15 "Whoever strikes his father or his mother shall be put to death.

16 "Whoever steals a man, whether he sells him or is found in possession of him, shall be put to death.

17 "Whoever curses his father or his mother shall be put to death.

18 "When men quarrel and one strikes the other with a stone or with his fist and the man does not die but keeps his bed, ¹⁹then if the man rises again and walks abroad with his staff, he that struck him shall be clear; only he shall pay for the loss of his time, and shall have him thoroughly healed.

20 "When a man strikes his slave, male or female, with a rod and the slave dies under his hand, he shall be punished. ²¹But if the slave survives a day or two, he is not to be punished; for the slave is his money.

22 "When men strive together, and hurt a woman with child, so that there is a miscarriage, and yet no harm follows, the one who hurt her shall ^h be fined, according as the woman's husband shall lay upon him; and he shall pay as the judges determine. ²³If any harm follows, then you shall give life for life, ²⁴eye for eye, tooth for tooth, hand for hand, foot for foot, ²⁵burn for burn, wound for wound, stripe for stripe.

26 "When a man strikes the eye of his slave, male or female, and destroys it, he shall let the slave go free for the eye's sake. ²⁷If he knocks out the tooth of his slave, male or female, he shall let the slave go free for the tooth's sake.

28 "When an ox gores a man or a woman to death, the ox shall be stoned, and its flesh shall not be eaten; but the owner of the ox shall be clear. ²⁹But if the ox has been accustomed to gore in the past, and its owner has been warned but has not kept it in, and it kills a man or a woman, the ox shall be stoned, and its owner also shall be put to death. ³⁰If a ransom is laid on him, then he shall give for the redemption of his life whatever is laid upon him. ³¹If it gores a man's son or daughter, he shall be dealt with according to this same rule. ³²If the ox gores a slave, male or female, the owner shall give to their master thirty shekels of silver, and the ox shall be stoned.

33 "When a man leaves a pit open, or when a man digs a pit and does not cover it, and an ox or a donkey falls into it, ³⁴the owner of the pit shall make it good; he shall give money to its owner, and the dead beast shall be his.

---

^g Another reading is *so that he has not designated her.*
^h Heb *he shall.*
20:23: Ex 20:3, 4; 34:17; Deut 27:15.
20:24: Ex 27:1–8; Deut 12:5; 26:2.
20:25: Deut 27:5, 6.
21:2–11: Lev 25:39–46; Deut 15:12–18.
21:12: Ex 20:13; Lev 24:17; Deut 5:17; Mt 5:21.
21:13: Num 35:10–34; Deut 19:1–13; Josh 20:1–9.
21:16: Deut 24:7.
21:17: Lev 20:9; Mt 15:4; Mk 7:10.
21:23–25: Lev 24:19–20; Deut 19:21; Mt 5:38.

35 "When one man's ox hurts another's, so that it dies, then they shall sell the live ox and divide the price of it; and the dead beast also they shall divide. ³⁶Or if it is known that the ox has been accustomed to gore in the past, and its owner has not kept it in, he shall pay ox for ox, and the dead beast shall be his.

Laws of Restitution

22 ¹ "If a man steals an ox or a sheep, and kills it or sells it, he shall pay five oxen for an ox, and four sheep for a sheep. ʲ He shall make restitution; if he has nothing, then he shall be sold for his theft. ⁴If the stolen beast is found alive in his possession, whether it is an ox or a donkey or a sheep, he shall pay double.

2 ᵏ "If a thief is found breaking in, and is struck so that he dies, there shall be no bloodguilt for him; ³but if the sun has risen upon him, there shall be bloodguilt for him.

5 "When a man causes a field or vineyard to be grazed over, or lets his beast loose and it feeds in another man's field, he shall make restitution from the best in his own field and in his own vineyard.

6 "When fire breaks out and catches in thorns so that the stacked grain or the standing grain or the field is consumed, he that kindled the fire shall make full restitution.

7 "If a man delivers to his neighbor money or goods to keep, and it is stolen out of the man's house, then, if the thief is found, he shall pay double. ⁸If the thief is not found, the owner of the house shall come near to God, to show whether or not he has put his hand to his neighbor's goods.

9 "For every breach of trust, whether it is for ox, for donkey, for sheep, for clothing, or for any kind of lost thing, of which one says, 'This is it,' the case of both parties shall come before God; he whom God shall condemn shall pay double to his neighbor.

10 "If a man delivers to his neighbor a donkey or an ox or a sheep or any beast to keep, and it dies or is hurt or is driven away, without any one seeing it, ¹¹an oath by the LORD shall be between them both to see whether he has not put his hand to his neighbor's property; and the owner shall accept the oath, and he shall not make restitution. ¹²But if it is stolen from him, he shall make restitution to its owner. ¹³If it is torn by beasts, let him bring it as evidence; he shall not make restitution for what has been torn.

14 "If a man borrows anything of his neighbor, and it is hurt or dies, the owner not being with it, he shall make full restitution. ¹⁵If the owner was with it, he shall not make restitution; if it was hired, it came for its hire. ˡ

Social and Religious Laws

16 "If a man seduces a virgin who is not betrothed, and lies with her, he shall give the marriage present for her, and make her his wife. ¹⁷If her father utterly refuses to give her to him, he shall pay money equivalent to the marriage present for virgins.

18 "You shall not permit a sorceress to live.

19 "Whoever lies with a beast shall be put to death.

20 "Whoever sacrifices to any god, save to the LORD only, shall be utterly destroyed.

21 "You shall not wrong a stranger or oppress him, for you were strangers in the land of Egypt. ²²You shall not afflict any widow or orphan. ²³If you do afflict them, and they cry out to me, I will surely hear their cry; ²⁴and my wrath will burn, and I will kill you with the sword, and your wives shall become widows and your children fatherless.

25 "If you lend money to any of my people with you who is poor, you shall not be to him as a creditor, and you shall not exact interest from him. ²⁶If ever you take your neighbor's garment in pledge, you shall restore it to him before the sun goes down; ²⁷for that is his only covering, it is his mantle for his body; in what else shall he sleep? And if he cries to me, I will hear, for I am compassionate.

28 "You shall not revile God, nor curse a ruler of your people.

29 "You shall not delay to offer from the fulness of your harvest and from the outflow of your presses.

"The first-born of your sons you shall give to me. ³⁰You shall do likewise with your oxen and with your sheep: seven days it shall be with its dam; on the eighth day you shall give it to me.

31 "You shall be men consecrated to me; therefore you shall not eat any flesh that is torn by beasts in the field; you shall cast it to the dogs.

Laws concerning Justice

23 "You shall not utter a false report. You shall not join hands with a wicked man, to be a malicious witness. ²You shall not follow a multitude to do evil; nor shall you bear witness in a suit, turning aside after a multitude, so as to

---

ⁱ Ch 21:37 in Heb.
ʲ Restoring the second half of verse 3 and the whole of verse 4 to their place immediately following verse 1.
ᵏ Ch 22:1 in Heb.
ˡ Or *it is reckoned in* (Heb *comes into*) *its hire.*
22:7–15: Lev 5:14—6:7; Num 5:5–8.
22:16–17: Deut 22:28, 29.
22:18: Lev 20:27; Deut 18:10.
22:19: Lev 18:23; 20:15, 16; Deut 27:21.
22:21: Ex 23:9; Lev 19:33, 34; Deut 27:19.
22:22: Deut 24:17.
22:25–27: Lev 25:36, 37; Deut 23:19, 20.
22:28: Acts 23:5.
22:29: Ex 23:16, 19; Deut 26:2–11; Ex 13:2, 11–16.
22:31: Ex 19:6; Lev 11:44; 19:1; 7:24; 17:15.
23:1: Ex 20:16; 23:7; Deut 5:20; 19:15–21.

pervert justice; [3]nor shall you be partial to a poor man in his suit.

4 "If you meet your enemy's ox or his donkey going astray, you shall bring it back to him. [5]If you see the donkey of one who hates you lying under its burden, you shall refrain from leaving him with it, you shall help him to lift it up. [m]

6 "You shall not pervert the justice due to your poor in his suit. [7]Keep far from a false charge, and do not slay the innocent and righteous, for I will not acquit the wicked. [8]And you shall take no bribe, for a bribe blinds the officials, and subverts the cause of those who are in the right.

9 "You shall not oppress a stranger; you know the heart of a stranger, for you were strangers in the land of Egypt.

The Sabbatical Year and the Sabbath

10 "For six years you shall sow your land and gather in its yield; [11]but the seventh year you shall let it rest and lie fallow, that the poor of your people may eat; and what they leave the wild beasts may eat. You shall do likewise with your vineyard, and with your olive orchard.

12 "Six days you shall do your work, but on the seventh day you shall rest; that your ox and your donkey may have rest, and the son of your maidservant, and the alien, may be refreshed. [13]Take heed to all that I have said to you; and make no mention of the names of other gods, nor let such be heard out of your mouth.

Annual Feasts

14 "Three times in the year you shall keep a feast to me. [15]You shall keep the feast of unleavened bread; as I commanded you, you shall eat unleavened bread for seven days at the appointed time in the month of Abib, for in it you came out of Egypt. None shall appear before me empty-handed. [16]You shall keep the feast of harvest, of the first fruits of your labor, of what you sow in the field. You shall keep the feast of ingathering at the end of the year, when you gather in from the field the fruit of your labor. [17]Three times in the year shall all your males appear before the Lord God.

18 "You shall not offer the blood of my sacrifice with leavened bread, or let the fat of my feast remain until the morning.

19 "The first of the first fruits of your ground you shall bring into the house of the LORD your God.

"You shall not boil a kid in its mother's milk.

The Conquest of Canaan Promised

20 "Behold, I send an angel before you, to guard you on the way and to bring you to the place which I have prepared. [21]Give heed to him and listen to his voice, do not rebel against him, for he will not pardon your transgression; for my name is in him.

22 "But if you listen attentively to his voice

and do all that I say, then I will be an enemy to your enemies and an adversary to your adversaries.

23 "When my angel goes before you, and brings you in to the Am′orites, and the Hittites, and the Per′izzites, and the Canaanites, the Hi′vites, and the Jeb′usites, and I blot them out, [24]you shall not bow down to their gods, nor serve them, nor do according to their works, but you shall utterly overthrow them and break their pillars in pieces. [25]You shall serve the LORD your God, and I [n] will bless your bread and your water; and I will take sickness away from the midst of you. [26]None shall cast her young or be barren in your land; I will fulfil the number of your days. [27]I will send my terror before you, and will throw into confusion all the people against whom you shall come, and I will make all your enemies turn their backs to you. [28]And I will send hornets before you, which shall drive out Hi′vite, Canaanite, and Hittite from before you. [29]I will not drive them out from before you in one year, lest the land become desolate and the wild beasts multiply against you. [30]Little by little I will drive them out from before you, until you are increased and possess the land. [31]And I will set your bounds from the Red Sea to the sea of the Philis′tines, and from the wilderness to the Euphra′tes; for I will deliver the inhabitants of the land into your hand, and you shall drive them out before you. [32]You shall make no covenant with them or with their gods. [33]They shall not dwell in your land, lest they make you sin against me; for if you serve their gods, it will surely be a snare to you."

The Blood of the Covenant

24 And he said to Moses, "Come up to the LORD, you and Aaron, Na′dab, and Abi′hu, and seventy of the elders of Israel, and worship afar off. [2]Moses alone shall come near to the LORD; but the others shall not come near, and the people shall not come up with him."

3 Moses came and told the people all the words of the LORD and all the ordinances; and all the people answered with one voice, and said, "All the words which the LORD has spoken we will do." [4]And Moses wrote all the words of the LORD. And he rose early in the morning, and built an altar at the foot of the mountain, and twelve pillars, according to the twelve tribes of Israel. [5]And he sent young men of the sons of Israel,

---

[m] Gk: Heb obscure.
[n] Gk Vg: Heb *he.*
23:3, 6: Lev 19:15.
23:7: Ex 20:16; 23:1.
23:8: Deut 16:19.
23:9: Ex 22:21; Lev 19:33, 34; Deut 27:19.
23:10, 11: Lev 25:1–7.
23:12: Ex 20:8–11; 31:15–17; 34:21; 35:2; Deut 5:12–15.
23:14–17: Ex 34:22–24; Lev 23:1–44; Deut 16:1–17.
23:18: Ex 12:10; 34:25; Lev 2:11; 7:15.
23:19: Ex 22:29; 34:26; Deut 26:2–11; 14:21.

who offered burnt offerings and sacrificed peace offerings of oxen to the Lord. [6]And Moses took half of the blood and put it in basins, and half of the blood he threw against the altar. [7]Then he took the book of the covenant, and read it in the hearing of the people; and they said, "All that the Lord has spoken we will do, and we will be obedient." [8]And Moses took the blood and threw it upon the people, and said, "Behold the blood of the covenant which the Lord has made with you in accordance with all these words."

On the Mountain of God

9 Then Moses and Aaron, Na'dab, and Abi'hu, and seventy of the elders of Israel went up, [10]and they saw the God of Israel; and there was under his feet as it were a pavement of sapphire stone, like the very heaven for clearness. [11]And he did not lay his hand on the chief men of the people of Israel; they beheld God, and ate and drank.

12 The Lord said to Moses, "Come up to me on the mountain, and wait there; and I will give you the tables of stone, with the law and the commandment, which I have written for their instruction." [13]So Moses rose with his servant Joshua, and Moses went up into the mountain of God. [14]And he said to the elders, "Wait here for us, until we come to you again; and, behold, Aaron and Hur are with you; whoever has a cause, let him go to them."

15 Then Moses went up on the mountain, and the cloud covered the mountain. [16]The glory of the Lord settled on Mount Sinai, and the cloud covered it six days; and on the seventh day he called to Moses out of the midst of the cloud. [17]Now the appearance of the glory of the Lord was like a devouring fire on the top of the mountain in the sight of the sons of Israel. [18]And Moses entered the cloud, and went up on the mountain. And Moses was on the mountain forty days and forty nights.

Offerings for the Tabernacle

25 The Lord said to Moses, [2] "Speak to the sons of Israel, that they take for me an offering; from every man whose heart makes him willing you shall receive the offering for me. [3]And this is the offering which you shall receive from them: gold, silver, and bronze, [4]blue and purple and scarlet stuff and fine twined linen, goats' hair, [5]tanned rams' skins, goatskins, acacia wood, [6]oil for the lamps, spices for the anointing oil and for the fragrant incense, [7]onyx stones, and stones for setting, for the ephod and for the breastpiece. [8]And let them make me a sanctuary, that I may dwell in their midst. [9]According to all that I show you concerning the pattern of the tabernacle, and of all its furniture, so you shall make it.

The Ark of the Covenant

10 "They shall make an ark of acacia wood; two cubits and a half shall be its length, a cubit and a half its breadth, and a cubit and a half its height. [11]And you shall overlay it with pure gold, within and without shall you overlay it, and you shall make upon it a molding of gold round about. [12]And you shall cast four rings of gold for it and put them on its four feet, two rings on the one side of it, and two rings on the other side of it. [13]You shall make poles of acacia wood, and overlay them with gold. [14]And you shall put the poles into the rings on the sides of the ark, to carry the ark by them. [15]The poles shall remain in the rings of the ark; they shall not be taken from it. [16]And you shall put into the ark the covenant which I shall give you. [17]Then you shall make a mercy seat° of pure gold; two cubits and a half shall be its length, and a cubit and a half its breadth. [18]And you shall make two cherubim of gold; of hammered work shall you make them, on the two ends of the mercy seat. [19]Make one cherub on the one end, and one cherub on the other end; of one piece with the mercy seat shall you make the cherubim on its two ends. [20]The cherubim shall spread out their wings above, overshadowing the mercy seat with their wings, their faces one to another; toward the mercy seat shall the faces of the cherubim be. [21]And you shall put the mercy seat on the top of the ark; and in the ark you shall put the covenant that I shall give you. [22]There I will meet with you, and from above the mercy seat, from between the two cherubim that are upon the ark of the covenant, I will speak with you of all that I will give you in commandment for the sons of Israel.

The Table for the Bread of the Presence

23 "And you shall make a table of acacia wood; two cubits shall be its length, a cubit its breadth, and a cubit and a half its height. [24]You shall overlay it with pure gold, and make a molding of gold around it. [25]And you shall make around it a frame a handbreadth wide, and a molding of gold around the frame. [26]And you shall make for it four rings of gold, and fasten the rings to the four corners at its four legs. [27]Close to the frame the rings shall lie, as holders for the poles to carry the table. [28]You shall make the poles of acacia wood, and overlay them with gold, and the table shall be carried with these. [29]And you shall make its plates and dishes for incense, and its flagons and bowls with which to pour libations; of pure gold you shall make them. [30]And you shall set the bread of the Presence on the table before me always.

° Or cover.

24:8: Mt 26:28; Mk 14:24; Lk 22:20; 1 Cor 11:25; Heb 9:20; 10:29.
24:12: 2 Cor 3:3.
25-31: Ex 35–40.
25:2-8: Ex 35:4–9.
25:10-22: Ex 37:1–9.
25:23-30: Ex 37:10–15.
25:30: Ex 39:36; 40:23; Lev 24:5–9.

The Lampstand

31 "And you shall make a lampstand of pure gold. The base and the shaft of the lampstand shall be made of hammered work; its cups, its capitals, and its flowers shall be of one piece with it; ³²and there shall be six branches going out of its sides, three branches of the lampstand out of one side of it and three branches of the lampstand out of the other side of it; ³³three cups made like almonds, each with capital and flower, on one branch, and three cups made like almonds, each with capital and flower, on the other branch—so for the six branches going out of the lampstand; ³⁴and on the lampstand itself four cups made like almonds, with their capitals and flowers, ³⁵and a capital of one piece with it under each pair of the six branches going out from the lampstand. ³⁶Their capitals and their branches shall be of one piece with it, the whole of it one piece of hammered work of pure gold. ³⁷And you shall make the seven lamps for it; and the lamps shall be set up so as to give light upon the space in front of it. ³⁸Its snuffers and their trays shall be of pure gold. ³⁹Of a talent of pure gold shall it be made, with all these utensils. ⁴⁰And see that you make them after the pattern for them, which is being shown you on the mountain.

The Tabernacle

26 "Moreover you shall make the tabernacle with ten curtains of fine twined linen and blue and purple and scarlet stuff; with cherubim skilfully worked shall you make them. ²The length of each curtain shall be twenty-eight cubits, and the breadth of each curtain four cubits; all the curtains shall have one measure. ³Five curtains shall be coupled to one another; and the other five curtains shall be coupled to one another. ⁴And you shall make loops of blue on the edge of the outmost curtain in the first set; and likewise you shall make loops on the edge of the outmost curtain in the second set. ⁵Fifty loops you shall make on the one curtain, and fifty loops you shall make on the edge of the curtain that is in the second set; the loops shall be opposite one another. ⁶And you shall make fifty clasps of gold, and couple the curtains one to the other with the clasps, that the tabernacle may be one whole.

7 "You shall also make curtains of goats' hair for a tent over the tabernacle; eleven curtains shall you make. ⁸The length of each curtain shall be thirty cubits, and the breadth of each curtain four cubits; the eleven curtains shall have the same measure. ⁹And you shall couple five curtains by themselves, and six curtains by themselves, and the sixth curtain you shall double over at the front of the tent. ¹⁰And you shall make fifty loops on the edge of the curtain that is outmost in one set, and fifty loops on the edge of the curtain which is outmost in the second set.

11 "And you shall make fifty clasps of bronze, and put the clasps into the loops, and couple the tent together that it may be one whole. ¹²And the part that remains of the curtains of the tent, the half curtain that remains, shall hang over the back of the tabernacle. ¹³And the cubit on the one side, and the cubit on the other side, of what remains in the length of the curtains of the tent shall hang over the sides of the tabernacle, on this side and that side, to cover it. ¹⁴And you shall make for the tent a covering of tanned rams' skins and goatskins.

The Framework

15 "And you shall make upright frames for the tabernacle of acacia wood. ¹⁶Ten cubits shall be the length of a frame, and a cubit and a half the breadth of each frame. ¹⁷There shall be two tenons in each frame, for fitting together; so shall you do for all the frames of the tabernacle. ¹⁸You shall make the frames for the tabernacle: twenty frames for the south side; ¹⁹and forty bases of silver you shall make under the twenty frames, two bases under one frame for its two tenons, and two bases under another frame for its two tenons; ²⁰and for the second side of the tabernacle, on the north side twenty frames, ²¹and their forty bases of silver, two bases under one frame, and two bases under another frame; ²²and for the rear of the tabernacle westward you shall make six frames. ²³And you shall make two frames for corners of the tabernacle in the rear; ²⁴they shall be separate beneath, but joined at the top, at the first ring; thus shall it be with both of them; they shall form the two corners. ²⁵And there shall be eight frames, with their bases of silver, sixteen bases; two bases under one frame, and two bases under another frame.

26 "And you shall make bars of acacia wood, five for the frames of the one side of the tabernacle, ²⁷and five bars for the frames of the other side of the tabernacle, and five bars for the frames of the side of the tabernacle at the rear westward. ²⁸The middle bar, halfway up the frames, shall pass through from end to end. ²⁹You shall overlay the frames with gold, and shall make their rings of gold for holders for the bars; and you shall overlay the bars with gold. ³⁰And you shall erect the tabernacle according to the plan for it which has been shown you on the mountain.

The Veil and the Screen

31 "And you shall make a veil of blue and purple and scarlet stuff and fine twined linen; in skilled work shall it be made, with cherubim; ³²and you shall hang it upon four pillars of acacia

25:31-40: Ex 37:17-24.
25:40: Acts 7:44; Heb 8:5.
26:1-14: Ex 36:8-19.
26:15-29: Ex 36:20-34.
26:31-37: Ex 36:35-38.

overlaid with gold, with hooks of gold, upon four bases of silver. [33]And you shall hang the veil from the clasps, and bring the ark of the covenant in there within the veil; and the veil shall separate for you the holy place from the most holy. [34]You shall put the mercy seat upon the ark of the covenant in the most holy place. [35]And you shall set the table outside the veil, and the lampstand on the south side of the tabernacle opposite the table; and you shall put the table on the north side.

36 "And you shall make a screen for the door of the tent, of blue and purple and scarlet stuff and fine twined linen, embroidered with needlework. [37]And you shall make for the screen five pillars of acacia, and overlay them with gold; their hooks shall be of gold, and you shall cast five bases of bronze for them.

The Altar of Burnt Offering

27 "You shall make the altar of acacia wood, five cubits long and five cubits broad; the altar shall be square, and its height shall be three cubits. [2]And you shall make horns for it on its four corners; its horns shall be of one piece with it, and you shall overlay it with bronze. [3]You shall make pots for it to receive its ashes, and shovels and basins and forks and firepans; all its utensils you shall make of bronze. [4]You shall also make for it a grating, a network of bronze; and upon the net you shall make four bronze rings at its four corners. [5]And you shall set it under the ledge of the altar so that the net shall extend half way down the altar. [6]And you shall make poles for the altar, poles of acacia wood, and overlay them with bronze; [7]and the poles shall be put through the rings, so that the poles shall be upon the two sides of the altar, when it is carried. [8]You shall make it hollow, with boards; as it has been shown you on the mountain, so shall it be made.

The Court and Its Hangings

9 "You shall make the court of the tabernacle. On the south side the court shall have hangings of fine twined linen a hundred cubits long for one side; [10]their pillars shall be twenty and their bases twenty, of bronze, but the hooks of the pillars and their fillets shall be of silver. [11]And likewise for its length on the north side there shall be hangings a hundred cubits long, their pillars twenty and their bases twenty, of bronze, but the hooks of the pillars and their fillets shall be of silver. [12]And for the breadth of the court on the west side there shall be hangings for fifty cubits, with ten pillars and ten bases. [13]The breadth of the court on the front to the east shall be fifty cubits. [14]The hangings for the one side of the gate shall be fifteen cubits, with three pillars and three bases. [15]On the other side the hangings shall be fifteen cubits, with three pillars and three bases. [16]For the gate of the court there shall be a screen twenty cubits long, of blue and purple and scarlet

stuff and fine twined linen, embroidered with needlework; it shall have four pillars and with them four bases. [17]All the pillars around the court shall be filleted with silver; their hooks shall be of silver, and their bases of bronze. [18]The length of the court shall be a hundred cubits, the breadth fifty, and the height five cubits, with hangings of fine twined linen and bases of bronze. [19]All the utensils of the tabernacle for every use, and all its pegs and all the pegs of the court, shall be of bronze.

The Oil for the Lamp

20 "And you shall command the sons of Israel that they bring to you pure beaten olive oil for the light, that a lamp may be set up to burn continually. [21]In the tent of meeting, outside the veil which is before the covenant, Aaron and his sons shall tend it from evening to morning before the LORD. It shall be a statute for ever to be observed throughout their generations by the sons of Israel.

Holy Garments for the Priests

28 "Then bring near to you Aaron your brother, and his sons with him, from among the sons of Israel, to serve me as priests— Aaron and Aaron's sons, Na'dab and Abi'hu, Elea'zar and Ith'amar. [2]And you shall make holy garments for Aaron your brother, for glory and for beauty. [3]And you shall speak to all who have ability, whom I have endowed with an able mind, that they make Aaron's garments to consecrate him for my priesthood. [4]These are the garments which they shall make: a breastpiece, an ephod, a robe, a coat of checker work, a turban, and a sash; they shall make holy garments for Aaron your brother and his sons to serve me as priests.

The Ephod

5 "They shall receive gold, blue and purple and scarlet stuff, and fine twined linen. [6]And they shall make the ephod of gold, of blue and purple and scarlet stuff, and of fine twined linen, skilfully worked. [7]It shall have two shoulder-pieces attached to its two edges, that it may be joined together. [8]And the skilfully woven band upon it, to belt it on, shall be of the same workmanship and materials, of gold, blue and purple and scarlet stuff, and fine twined linen. [9]And you shall take two onyx stones, and engrave on them the names of the sons of Israel, [10]six of their names on the one stone, and the names of the remaining six on the other stone, in the order of their birth. [11]As a jeweler engraves signets, so shall you engrave the two stones with the names of the sons of Israel; you shall enclose them in settings of gold filigree. [12]And you shall set the two stones upon

27:1–8: Ex 38:1–7.
27:9–19: Ex 38:9–20.
27:20–21: Lev 24:1–4.
28:6–12: Ex 39:2–7.

60

the shoulder-pieces of the ephod, as stones of remembrance for the sons of Israel; and Aaron shall bear their names before the Lord upon his two shoulders for remembrance. [13]And you shall make settings of gold filigree, [14]and two chains of pure gold, twisted like cords; and you shall attach the corded chains to the settings.

The Breastpiece of Judgment

15 "And you shall make a breastpiece of judgment, in skilled work; like the work of the ephod you shall make it; of gold, blue and purple and scarlet stuff, and fine twined linen shall you make it. [16]It shall be square and double, a span its length and a span its breadth. [17]And you shall set in it four rows of stones. A row of sardius, topaz, and carbuncle shall be the first row; [18]and the second row an emerald, a sapphire, and a diamond; [19]and the third row a jacinth, an agate, and an amethyst; [20]and the fourth row a beryl, an onyx, and a jasper; they shall be set in gold filigree. [21]There shall be twelve stones with their names according to the names of the sons of Israel; they shall be like signets, each engraved with its name, for the twelve tribes. [22]And you shall make for the breastpiece twisted chains like cords, of pure gold; [23]and you shall make for the breastpiece two rings of gold, and put the two rings on the two edges of the breastpiece. [24]And you shall put the two cords of gold in the two rings at the edges of the breastpiece; [25]the two ends of the two cords you shall attach to the two settings of filigree, and so attach it in front to the shoulder-pieces of the ephod. [26]And you shall make two rings of gold, and put them at the two ends of the breastpiece, on its inside edge next to the ephod. [27]And you shall make two rings of gold, and attach them in front to the lower part of the two shoulder-pieces of the ephod, at its joining above the skilfully woven band of the ephod. [28]And they shall bind the breastpiece by its rings to the rings of the ephod with a lace of blue, that it may lie upon the skilfully woven band of the ephod, and that the breastpiece shall not come loose from the ephod. [29]So Aaron shall bear the names of the sons of Israel in the breastpiece of judgment upon his heart, when he goes into the holy place, to bring them to continual remembrance before the Lord. [30]And in the breastpiece of judgment you shall put the U'rim and the Thummim, and they shall be upon Aaron's heart, when he goes in before the Lord; thus Aaron shall bear the judgment of the sons of Israel upon his heart before the Lord continually.

The Robe of the Ephod

31 "And you shall make the robe of the ephod all of blue. [32]It shall have in it an opening for the head, with a woven binding around the opening, like the opening in a garment, [p] that it may not be torn. [33]On its skirts you shall make pomegranates of blue and purple and scarlet stuff, around its skirts, with bells of gold between them, [34]a golden bell and a pomegranate, a golden bell and a pomegranate, round about on the skirts of the robe. [35]And it shall be upon Aaron when he ministers, and its sound shall be heard when he goes into the holy place before the Lord, and when he comes out, lest he die.

Other Priestly Garments

36 "And you shall make a plate of pure gold, and engrave on it, like the engraving of a signet, 'Holy to the Lord.' [37]And you shall fasten it on the turban by a lace of blue; it shall be on the front of the turban. [38]It shall be upon Aaron's forehead, and Aaron shall take upon himself any guilt incurred in the holy offering which the sons of Israel hallow as their holy gifts; it shall always be upon his forehead, that they may be accepted before the Lord.

39 "And you shall weave the coat in checker work of fine linen, and you shall make a turban of fine linen, and you shall make a sash embroidered with needlework.

40 "And for Aaron's sons you shall make coats and sashes and caps; you shall make them for glory and beauty. [41]And you shall put them upon Aaron your brother, and upon his sons with him, and shall anoint them and ordain them and consecrate them, that they may serve me as priests. [42]And you shall make for them linen breeches to cover their naked flesh; from the loins to the thighs they shall reach; [43]and they shall be upon Aaron, and upon his sons, when they go into the tent of meeting, or when they come near the altar to minister in the holy place; lest they bring guilt upon themselves and die. This shall be a perpetual statute for him and for his descendants after him.

The Ordination of Priests

29 "Now this is what you shall do to them to consecrate them, that they may serve me as priests. Take one young bull and two rams without blemish, [2]and unleavened bread, unleavened cakes mixed with oil, and unleavened wafers spread with oil. You shall make them of fine wheat flour. [3]And you shall put them in one basket and bring them in the basket, and bring the bull and the two rams. [4]You shall bring Aaron and his sons to the door of the tent of meeting, and wash them with water. [5]And you shall take the garments, and put on Aaron the coat and the robe of the ephod, and the ephod, and the breastpiece, and belt him with the skilfully woven band of the ephod; [6]and you shall set the turban on his head, and put the holy crown upon the turban. [7]And you shall take the anointing oil, and

---

[p] The Hebrew word is of uncertain meaning.
28:15–28: Ex 39:8–21.
28:31–34: Ex 39:22–26.
28:36, 37: Ex 39:30, 31.
28:39, 40, 42: Ex 39:27–29.
29:1–37: Lev 8:1–34.

pour it on his head and anoint him. [8]Then you shall bring his sons, and put coats on them, [9]and you shall belt them with sashes [q] and bind caps on them; and the priesthood shall be theirs by a perpetual statute. Thus you shall ordain Aaron and his sons.

10 "Then you shall bring the bull before the tent of meeting. Aaron and his sons shall lay their hands upon the head of the bull, [11]and you shall kill the bull before the Lord, at the door of the tent of meeting, [12]and shall take part of the blood of the bull and put it upon the horns of the altar with your finger, and the rest of [r] the blood you shall pour out at the base of the altar. [13]And you shall take all the fat that covers the entrails, and the appendage of the liver, and the two kidneys with the fat that is on them, and burn them upon the altar. [14]But the flesh of the bull, and its skin, and its dung, you shall burn with fire outside the camp; it is a sin offering.

15 "Then you shall take one of the rams, and Aaron and his sons shall lay their hands upon the head of the ram, [16]and you shall slaughter the ram, and shall take its blood and throw it against the altar round about. [17]Then you shall cut the ram into pieces, and wash its entrails and its legs, and put them with its pieces and its head, [18]and burn the whole ram upon the altar; it is a burnt offering to the Lord; it is a pleasing odor, an offering by fire to the Lord.

19 "You shall take the other ram; and Aaron and his sons shall lay their hands upon the head of the ram, [20]and you shall kill the ram, and take part of its blood and put it upon the tip of the right ear of Aaron and upon the tips of the right ears of his sons, and upon the thumbs of their right hands, and upon the great toes of their right feet, and throw the rest of the blood against the altar round about. [21]Then you shall take part of the blood that is on the altar, and of the anointing oil, and sprinkle it upon Aaron and his garments, and upon his sons and his sons' garments with him; and he and his garments shall be holy, and his sons and his sons' garments with him.

22 "You shall also take the fat of the ram, and the fat tail, and the fat that covers the entrails, and the appendage of the liver, and the two kidneys with the fat that is on them, and the right thigh (for it is a ram of ordination), [23]and one loaf of bread, and one cake of bread with oil, and one wafer, out of the basket of unleavened bread that is before the Lord; [24]and you shall put all these in the hands of Aaron and in the hands of his sons, and wave them for a wave offering before the Lord. [25]Then you shall take them from their hands, and burn them on the altar in addition to the burnt offering, as a pleasing odor before the Lord; it is an offering by fire to the Lord.

26 "And you shall take the breast of the ram of Aaron's ordination and wave it for a wave offering before the Lord; and it shall be your portion. [27]And you shall consecrate the breast of the wave offering, and the thigh of the priests' portion, which is waved, and which is offered from the ram of ordination, since it is for Aaron and for his sons. [28]It shall be for Aaron and his sons as a perpetual debt from the sons of Israel, for it is the priests' portion to be offered by the sons of Israel from their peace offerings; it is their offering to the Lord.

29 "The holy garments of Aaron shall be for his sons after him, to be anointed in them and ordained in them. [30]The son who is priest in his place shall wear them seven days, when he comes into the tent of meeting to minister in the holy place.

31 "You shall take the ram of ordination, and boil its flesh in a holy place; [32]and Aaron and his sons shall eat the flesh of the ram and the bread that is in the basket, at the door of the tent of meeting. [33]They shall eat those things with which atonement was made, to ordain and consecrate them, but an outsider shall not eat of them, because they are holy. [34]And if any of the flesh for the ordination, or of the bread, remain until the morning, then you shall burn the remainder with fire; it shall not be eaten, because it is holy.

35 "Thus you shall do to Aaron and to his sons, according to all that I have commanded you; through seven days shall you ordain them, [36]and every day you shall offer a bull as a sin offering for atonement. Also you shall offer a sin offering for the altar, when you make atonement for it, and shall anoint it, to consecrate it. [37]Seven days you shall make atonement for the altar, and consecrate it, and the altar shall be most holy; whatever touches the altar shall become holy.

The Daily Offerings

38 "Now this is what you shall offer upon the altar: two lambs a year old day by day continually. [39]One lamb you shall offer in the morning, and the other lamb you shall offer in the evening; [40]and with the first lamb a tenth measure of fine flour mingled with a fourth of a hin of beaten oil, and a fourth of a hin of wine for a libation. [41]And the other lamb you shall offer in the evening, and shall offer with it a cereal offering and its libation, as in the morning, for a pleasing odor, an offering by fire to the Lord. [42]It shall be a continual burnt offering throughout your generations at the door of the tent of meeting before the Lord, where I will meet with you, to speak there to you. [43]There I will meet with the sons of Israel, and it shall be sanctified by my glory; [44]I will consecrate the tent

---

[q] Gk: Heb *girdles, Aaron and his sons.*
[r] Heb *all.*
29:18: Eph 5:2; Phil 4:18.
29:38–42: Num 28:3–10.

of meeting and the altar; Aaron also and his sons I will consecrate, to serve me as priests. [45]And I will dwell among the sons of Israel, and will be their God. [46]And they shall know that I am the LORD their God, who brought them forth out of the land of Egypt that I might dwell among them; I am the LORD their God.

The Altar of Incense

30 "You shall make an altar to burn incense upon; of acacia wood shall you make it. [2]A cubit shall be its length, and a cubit its breadth; it shall be square, and two cubits shall be its height; its horns shall be of one piece with it. [3]And you shall overlay it with pure gold, its top and its sides round about and its horns; and you shall make for it a molding of gold round about. [4]And two golden rings shall you make for it; under its molding on two opposite sides of it shall you make them, and they shall be holders for poles with which to carry it. [5]You shall make the poles of acacia wood, and overlay them with gold. [6]And you shall put it before the veil that is by the ark of the covenant, before the mercy seat that is over the covenant, where I will meet with you. [7]And Aaron shall burn fragrant incense on it; every morning when he dresses the lamps he shall burn it, [8]and when Aaron sets up the lamps in the evening, he shall burn it, a perpetual incense before the LORD throughout your generations. [9]You shall offer no unholy incense thereon, nor burnt offering, nor cereal offering; and you shall pour no libation thereon. [10]Aaron shall make atonement upon its horns once a year; with the blood of the sin offering of atonement he shall make atonement for it once in the year throughout your generations; it is most holy to the LORD."

The Half Shekel for the Sanctuary

11 The LORD said to Moses, [12]"When you take the census of the sons of Israel, then each shall give a ransom for himself to the LORD when you number them, that there be no plague among them when you number them. [13]Each who is numbered in the census shall give this: half a shekel according to the shekel of the sanctuary (the shekel is twenty gerahs), half a shekel as an offering to the LORD. [14]Every one who is numbered in the census, from twenty years old and upward, shall give the LORD's offering. [15]The rich shall not give more, and the poor shall not give less, than the half shekel, when you give the LORD's offering to make atonement for yourselves. [16]And you shall take the atonement money from the sons of Israel, and shall appoint it for the service of the tent of meeting; that it may bring the sons of Israel to remembrance before the LORD, so as to make atonement for yourselves."

The Bronze Laver

17 The LORD said to Moses, [18]"You shall also make a laver of bronze, with its base of bronze, for washing. And you shall put it between the tent of meeting and the altar, and you shall put water in it, [19]with which Aaron and his sons shall wash their hands and their feet. [20]When they go into the tent of meeting, or when they come near the altar to minister, to burn an offering by fire to the LORD, they shall wash with water, lest they die. [21]They shall wash their hands and their feet, lest they die: it shall be a statute for ever to them, even to him and to his descendants throughout their generations."

The Anointing Oil and Incense

22 Moreover, the LORD said to Moses, [23]"Take the finest spices: of liquid myrrh five hundred shekels, and of sweet-smelling cinnamon half as much, that is, two hundred and fifty, and of aromatic cane two hundred and fifty, [24]and of cassia five hundred, according to the shekel of the sanctuary, and of olive oil a hin; [25]and you shall make of these a sacred anointing oil blended as by the perfumer; a holy anointing oil it shall be. [26]And you shall anoint with it the tent of meeting and the ark of the covenant, [27]and the table and all its utensils, and the lampstand and its utensils, and the altar of incense, [28]and the altar of burnt offering with all its utensils and the laver and its base; [29]you shall consecrate them, that they may be most holy; whatever touches them will become holy. [30]And you shall anoint Aaron and his sons, and consecrate them, that they may serve me as priests. [31]And you shall say to the sons of Israel, 'This shall be my holy anointing oil throughout your generations. [32]It shall not be poured upon the bodies of ordinary men, and you shall make no other like it in composition; it is holy, and it shall be holy to you. [33]Whoever compounds any like it or whoever puts any of it on an outsider shall be cut off from his people.'"

34 And the LORD said to Moses, "Take sweet spices, stacte, and onycha, and galbanum, sweet spices with pure frankincense (of each shall there be an equal part), [35]and make an incense blended as by the perfumer, seasoned with salt, pure and holy; [36]and you shall beat some of it very small, and put part of it before the covenant in the tent of meeting where I shall meet with you; it shall be for you most holy. [37]And the incense which you shall make according to its composition, you shall not make for yourselves; it shall be for you holy to the LORD. [38]Whoever makes any like it to use as perfume shall be cut off from his people."

Bezalel and Oholiab

31 The LORD said to Moses, [2]"See, I have called by name Bez'alel the son of Uri, son

---

30:1-5: Ex 37:25-29.
30:11-16: Ex 38:25, 26.
30:18: Ex 38:8.
30:22-33: Ex 37:29.
31:1-6: Ex 35:30—36:1.

of Hur, of the tribe of Judah: [3]and I have filled him with the Spirit of God, with ability and intelligence, with knowledge and all craftsmanship, [4]to devise artistic designs, to work in gold, silver, and bronze, [5]in cutting stones for setting, and in carving wood, for work in every craft. [6]And behold, I have appointed with him Oho'liab, the son of Ahis'amach, of the tribe of Dan; and I have given to all able men ability, that they may make all that I have commanded you: [7]the tent of meeting, and the ark of the covenant, and the mercy seat that is thereon, and all the furnishings of the tent, [8]the table and its utensils, and the pure lampstand with all its utensils, and the altar of incense, [9]and the altar of burnt offering with all its utensils, and the laver and its base, [10]and the finely worked garments, the holy garments for Aaron the priest and the garments of his sons, for their service as priests, [11]and the anointing oil and the fragrant incense for the holy place. According to all that I have commanded you they shall do."

The Sabbath Law

12 And the LORD said to Moses, [13] "Say to the sons of Israel, 'You shall keep my sabbaths, for this is a sign between me and you throughout your generations, that you may know that I, the LORD, sanctify you. [14]You shall keep the sabbath, because it is holy for you; every one who profanes it shall be put to death; whoever does any work on it, that soul shall be cut off from among his people. [15]Six days shall work be done, but the seventh day is a sabbath of solemn rest, holy to the LORD; whoever does any work on the sabbath day shall be put to death. [16]Therefore the sons of Israel shall keep the sabbath, observing the sabbath throughout their generations, as a perpetual covenant. [17]It is a sign for ever between me and the sons of Israel that in six days the LORD made heaven and earth, and on the seventh day he rested, and was refreshed.'"

The Tables of the Covenant

18 And he gave to Moses, when he had made an end of speaking with him upon Mount Sinai, the two tables of the covenant, tables of stone, written with the finger of God.

The Golden Calf

32 When the people saw that Moses delayed to come down from the mountain, the people gathered themselves together to Aaron, and said to him, "Up, make us gods, who shall go before us; as for this Moses, the man who brought us up out of the land of Egypt, we do not know what has become of him." [2]And Aaron said to them, "Take off the rings of gold which are in the ears of your wives, your sons, and your daughters, and bring them to me." [3]So all the people took off the rings of gold which were in their ears, and brought them to Aaron. [4]And he received the gold at their hand, and fashioned it with a graving tool, and made a molten calf; and they said, "These are your gods, O Israel, who brought you up out of the land of Egypt!" [5]When Aaron saw this, he built an altar before it; and Aaron made proclamation and said, "Tomorrow shall be a feast to the LORD." [6]And they rose up early the next day, and offered burnt offerings and brought peace offerings; and the people sat down to eat and drink, and rose up to play.

7 And the LORD said to Moses, "Go down; for your people, whom you brought up out of the land of Egypt, have corrupted themselves; [8]they have turned aside quickly out of the way which I commanded them; they have made for themselves a molten calf, and have worshiped it and sacrificed to it, and said, 'These are your gods, O Israel, who brought you up out of the land of Egypt!' " [9]And the LORD said to Moses, "I have seen this people, and behold, it is a stiff-necked people; [10]now therefore let me alone, that my wrath may burn hot against them and I may consume them; but of you I will make a great nation."

11 But Moses begged the LORD his God, and said, "O LORD, why does your wrath burn hot against your people, whom you have brought forth out of the land of Egypt with great power and with a mighty hand? [12]Why should the Egyptians say, 'With evil intent he brought them forth, to slay them in the mountains, and to consume them from the face of the earth'? Turn from your fierce wrath, and repent of this evil against your people. [13]Remember Abraham, Isaac, and Israel, your servants, to whom you swore by your own self, and said to them, 'I will multiply your descendants as the stars of heaven, and all this land that I have promised I will give to your descendants, and they shall inherit it for ever.' " [14]And the LORD repented of the evil which he thought to do to his people.

15 And Moses turned, and went down from the mountain with the two tables of the covenant in his hands, tables that were written on both sides; on the one side and on the other were they written. [16]And the tables were the work of God, and the writing was the writing of God, graven upon the tables. [17]When Joshua heard the noise of the people as they shouted, he said to Moses, "There is a noise of war in the camp." [18]But he said, "It is not the sound of shouting for victory, or the sound of the cry of defeat, but the sound of singing that I hear." [19]And as soon as he came near the camp and saw the calf and the dancing, Moses' anger burned hot, and he threw the tables out of his hands and broke them at the foot of the

31:12-17: Ex 20:8; 23:12; 35:2; Deut 5:12-15.
32:1-6: Acts 7:40, 41.
32:6: 1 Cor 10:7.
32:9-14: Ex 32:31-35; Num 14:11-25.

mountain. [20]And he took the calf which they had made, and burnt it with fire, and ground it to powder, and scattered it upon the water, and made the sons of Israel drink it.

21 And Moses said to Aaron, "What did this people do to you that you have brought a great sin upon them?" [22]And Aaron said, "Let not the anger of my lord burn hot; you know the people, that they are set on evil. [23]For they said to me, 'Make us gods, who shall go before us; as for this Moses, the man who brought us up out of the land of Egypt, we do not know what has become of him.' [24]And I said to them, 'Let any who have gold take it off'; so they gave it to me, and I threw it into the fire, and there came out this calf."

25 And when Moses saw that the people had broken loose (for Aaron had let them break loose, to their shame among their enemies), [26]then Moses stood in the gate of the camp, and said, "Who is on the Lord's side? Come to me." And all the sons of Levi gathered themselves together to him. [27]And he said to them, "Thus says the Lord God of Israel, 'Put every man his sword on his side, and go back and forth from gate to gate throughout the camp, and slay every man his brother, and every man his companion, and every man his neighbor.' " [28]And the sons of Levi did according to the word of Moses; and there fell of the people that day about three thousand men. [29]And Moses said, "Today you have ordained yourselves **s** for the service of the Lord, each one at the cost of his son and of his brother, that he may bestow a blessing upon you this day."

30 The next day Moses said to the people, "You have sinned a great sin. And now I will go up to the Lord; perhaps I can make atonement for your sin." [31]So Moses returned to the Lord and said, "Alas, this people has sinned a great sin; they have made for themselves gods of gold. [32]But now, if you will forgive their sin—and if not, blot me, I beg you, out of your book which you have written." [33]But the Lord said to Moses, "Whoever has sinned against me, him will I blot out of my book. [34]But now go, lead the people to the place of which I have spoken to you; behold, my angel shall go before you. Nevertheless, in the day when I visit, I will visit their sin upon them."

35 And the Lord sent a plague upon the people, because they made the calf which Aaron made.

The Command to Leave Sinai

33 The Lord said to Moses, "Depart, go up from here, you and the people whom you have brought up out of the land of Egypt, to the land of which I swore to Abraham, Isaac, and Jacob, saying, 'To your descendants I will give it.' [2]And I will send an angel before you, and I will drive out the Canaanites, the Am'orites, the Hittites, the Per'izzites, the Hi'vites, and the Jeb'usites. [3]Go up to a land flowing with milk and honey; but I will not go up among you, lest I consume you in the way, for you are a stiff-necked people."

4 When the people heard these evil tidings, they mourned; and no man put on his ornaments. [5]For the Lord had said to Moses, "Say to the sons of Israel, 'You are a stiff-necked people; if for a single moment I should go up among you, I would consume you. So now put off your ornaments from you, that I may know what to do with you.' " [6]Therefore the sons of Israel stripped themselves of their ornaments, from Mount Horeb onward.

The Tent of Meeting

7 Now Moses used to take the tent and pitch it outside the camp, far off from the camp; and he called it the tent of meeting. And every one who sought the Lord would go out to the tent of meeting, which was outside the camp. [8]Whenever Moses went out to the tent, all the people rose up, and every man stood at his tent door, and looked after Moses, until he had gone into the tent. [9]When Moses entered the tent, the pillar of cloud would descend and stand at the door of the tent, and the Lord would speak with Moses. [10]And when all the people saw the pillar of cloud standing at the door of the tent, all the people would rise up and worship, every man at his tent door. [11]Thus the Lord used to speak to Moses face to face, as a man speaks to his friend. When Moses turned again into the camp, his servant Joshua the son of Nun, a young man, did not depart from the tent.

Moses' Intercession

12 Moses said to the Lord, "See, you say to me, 'Bring up this people'; but you have not let me know whom you will send with me. Yet you have said, 'I know you by name, and you have also found favor in my sight.' [13]Now therefore, I beg you, if I have found favor in your sight, show me now your ways, that I may know you and find favor in your sight. Consider too that this nation is your people." [14]And he said, "My presence will go with you, and I will give you rest." [15]And he said to him, "If your presence will not go with me, do not carry us up from here. [16]For how shall it be known that I have found favor in your sight, I and your people? Is it not in your going with us, so that we are distinct, I and your people, from all other people that are upon the face of the earth?"

17 And the Lord said to Moses, "This very thing that you have spoken I will do; for you have found favor in my sight, and I know you by name." [18]Moses said, "I beg you, show me your glory." [19]And he said, "I will make all my goodness pass before you, and will proclaim before you my name

---

s Gk Vg See Tg: Heb *ordain yourselves*.
32:23: Acts 7:40.
32:32, 33: Rev 3:5.
33:3: Acts 7:51.
33:11: Num 12:8; Deut 34:10.
33:19: Rom 9:15.

'The LORD'; and I will be gracious to whom I will be gracious, and will show mercy on whom I will show mercy. [20]But," he said, "you cannot see my face; for man shall not see me and live." [21]And the LORD said, "Behold, there is a place by me where you shall stand upon the rock; [22]and while my glory passes by I will put you in a cleft of the rock, and I will cover you with my hand until I have passed by; [23]then I will take away my hand, and you shall see my back; but my face shall not be seen."

New Tables of Stone

34 The LORD said to Moses, "Cut two tables of stone like the first; and I will write upon the tables the words that were on the first tables, which you broke. [2]Be ready in the morning, and come up in the morning to Mount Sinai, and present yourself there to me on the top of the mountain. [3]No man shall come up with you, and let no man be seen throughout all the mountain; let no flocks or herds feed before that mountain." [4]So Moses cut two tables of stone like the first; and he rose early in the morning and went up on Mount Sinai, as the LORD had commanded him, and took in his hand two tables of stone. [5]And the LORD descended in the cloud and stood with him there, and proclaimed the name of the LORD. [6]The LORD passed before him, and proclaimed, "The LORD, the LORD, a God merciful and gracious, slow to anger, and abounding in mercy and faithfulness, [7]keeping merciful love for thousands, forgiving iniquity and transgression and sin, but who will by no means clear the guilty, visiting the iniquity of the fathers upon the children and the children's children, to the third and the fourth generation." [8]And Moses made haste to bow his head toward the earth, and worshiped. [9]And he said, "If now I have found favor in your sight, O Lord, let the Lord, I beg you, go in the midst of us, although it is a stiff-necked people; and pardon our iniquity and our sin, and take us for your inheritance."

The Covenant Renewed

10 And he said, "Behold, I make a covenant. Before all your people I will do marvels, such as have not been wrought in all the earth or in any nation; and all the people among whom you are shall see the work of the LORD; for it is a terrible thing that I will do with you. [11]"Observe what I command you this day. Behold, I will drive out before you the Am'orites, the Canaanites, the Hittites, the Per'izzites, the Hi'vites, and the Jeb'usites. [12]Take heed to yourself, lest you make a covenant with the inhabitants of the land where you go, lest it become a snare in your midst. [13]You shall tear down their altars, and break their pillars, and cut down their Ashe'rim [14](for you shall worship no other god, for the LORD, whose name is Jealous, is a jealous God), [15]lest you make a covenant with the inhabitants of the land, and when they play the harlot after their gods and sacrifice to their gods and one invites you, you eat of his sacrifice, [16]and you take of their daughters for your sons, and their daughters play the harlot after their gods and make your sons play the harlot after their gods.

17 "You shall make for yourself no molten gods.

18 "The feast of unleavened bread you shall keep. Seven days you shall eat unleavened bread, as I commanded you, at the time appointed in the month Abib; for in the month of Abib you came out from Egypt. [19]All that opens the womb is mine, all your male[x] cattle, the firstlings of cow and sheep. [20]The firstling of a donkey you shall redeem with a lamb, or if you will not redeem it you shall break its neck. All the first-born of your sons you shall redeem. And none shall appear before me empty.

21 "Six days you shall work, but on the seventh day you shall rest; in plowing time and in harvest you shall rest. [22]And you shall observe the feast of weeks, the first fruits of wheat harvest, and the feast of ingathering at the year's end. [23]Three times in the year shall all your males appear before the LORD God, the God of Israel. [24]For I will cast out nations before you, and enlarge your borders; neither shall any man desire your land, when you go up to appear before the LORD your God three times in the year.

25 "You shall not offer the blood of my sacrifice with leaven; neither shall the sacrifice of the feast of the Passover be left until the morning. [26]The first of the first fruits of your ground you shall bring to the house of the LORD your God. You shall not boil a kid in its mother's milk."

27 And the LORD said to Moses, "Write these words; in accordance with these words I have made a covenant with you and with Israel." [28]And he was there with the LORD forty days and forty nights; he neither ate bread nor drank water. And he wrote upon the tables the words of the covenant, the ten commandments.[t]

The Shining Face of Moses

29 When Moses came down from Mount Sinai, with the two tables of the covenant in his hand as he came down from the mountain, Moses did not know that the skin of his face shone because he had been talking with God. [30]And when Aaron

---

[x] Gk Theodotion Vg Tg: Heb uncertain.
[t] Heb *words*.
34:6: Num 14:18; Neh 9:17; Ps 86:15; 103:8; 145:8; Jon 4:2.
34:14: Ex 20:5; 34:7; Deut 4:24; 5:9.
34:17: Ex 20:4.
34:18: Ex 12:15–20.
34:19–20: Ex 13:2, 11–16.
34:21: Ex 20:8–10; 23:12; 31:12–17; 35:2; Deut 5:12–15.
34:22–24: Ex 23:14–17; Lev 23:1–44; Deut 16:1–17.
34:25: Ex 23:18; Lev 2:11; Ex 12:10.
34:26: Ex 23:19; Deut 14:21; 26:2–11.
34:29–35: 2 Cor 3:7–16.

and all the sons of Israel saw Moses, behold, the skin of his face shone, and they were afraid to come near him. ³¹But Moses called to them; and Aaron and all the leaders of the congregation returned to him, and Moses talked with them. ³²And afterward all the sons of Israel came near, and he gave them in commandment all that the Lord had spoken with him in Mount Sinai. ³³And when Moses had finished speaking with them, he put a veil on his face; ³⁴but whenever Moses went in before the Lord to speak with him, he took the veil off, until he came out; and when he came out, and told the sons of Israel what he was commanded, ³⁵the sons of Israel saw the face of Moses, that the skin of Moses' face shone; and Moses would put the veil upon his face again, until he went in to speak with him.

Sabbath Regulations

35 Moses assembled all the congregation of the sons of Israel, and said to them, "These are the things which the Lord has commanded you to do. ²Six days shall work be done, but on the seventh day you shall have a holy sabbath of solemn rest to the Lord; whoever does any work on it shall be put to death; ³you shall kindle no fire in all your habitations on the sabbath day."

Preparations for Making the Tabernacle

4 Moses said to all the congregation of the sons of Israel, "This is the thing which the Lord has commanded. ⁵Take from among you an offering to the Lord; whoever is of a generous heart, let him bring the Lord's offering: gold, silver, and bronze; ⁶blue and purple and scarlet stuff and fine twined linen; goats' hair, ⁷tanned rams' skins, and goatskins; acacia wood, ⁸oil for the light, spices for the anointing oil and for the fragrant incense, ⁹and onyx stones and stones for setting, for the ephod and for the breastpiece.

10 "And let every able man among you come and make all that the Lord has commanded: the tabernacle, ¹¹its tent and its covering, its hooks and its frames, its bars, its pillars, and its bases; ¹²the ark with its poles, the mercy seat, and the veil of the screen; ¹³the table with its poles and all its utensils, and the bread of the Presence; ¹⁴the lampstand also for the light, with its utensils and its lamps, and the oil for the light; ¹⁵and the altar of incense, with its poles, and the anointing oil and the fragrant incense, and the screen for the door, at the door of the tabernacle; ¹⁶the altar of burnt offering, with its grating of bronze, its poles, and all its utensils, the laver and its base; ¹⁷the hangings of the court, its pillars and its bases, and the screen for the gate of the court; ¹⁸the pegs of the tabernacle and the pegs of the court, and their cords; ¹⁹the finely wrought garments for ministering in the holy place, the holy garments for Aaron the priest, and the garments of his sons, for their service as priests."

Offerings Brought for the Tabernacle

20 Then all the congregation of the sons of Israel departed from the presence of Moses. ²¹And they came, every one whose heart stirred him, and every one whose spirit moved him, and brought the Lord's offering to be used for the tent of meeting, and for all its service, and for the holy garments. ²²So they came, both men and women; all who were of a willing heart brought brooches and earrings and signet rings and armlets, all sorts of gold objects, every man dedicating an offering of gold to the Lord. ²³And every man with whom was found blue or purple or scarlet stuff or fine linen or goats' hair or rams' skins or goatskins, brought them. ²⁴Every one who could make an offering of silver or bronze brought it as the Lord's offering; and every man with whom was found acacia wood of any use in the work, brought it. ²⁵And all women who had ability spun with their hands, and brought what they had spun in blue and purple and scarlet stuff and fine twined linen; ²⁶all the women whose hearts were moved with ability spun the goats' hair. ²⁷And the leaders brought onyx stones and stones to be set, for the ephod and for the breastpiece, ²⁸and spices and oil for the light, and for the anointing oil, and for the fragrant incense. ²⁹All the men and women, the sons of Israel, whose heart moved them to bring anything for the work which the Lord had commanded by Moses to be done, brought it as their freewill offering to the Lord.

Bezalel and Oholiab Receive the Offerings

30 And Moses said to the sons of Israel, "See, the Lord has called by name Bez′alel the son of Uri, son of Hur, of the tribe of Judah; ³¹and he has filled him with the Spirit of God, with ability, with intelligence, with knowledge, and with all craftsmanship, ³²to devise artistic designs, to work in gold and silver and bronze, ³³in cutting stones for setting, and in carving wood, for work in every skilled craft. ³⁴And he has inspired him to teach, both him and Oho′liab the son of Ahis′amach of the tribe of Dan. ³⁵He has filled them with ability to do every sort of work done by a craftsman or by a designer or by an embroiderer in blue and purple and scarlet stuff and fine twined linen, or by a weaver—by any sort of workman or skilled **36** designer. ¹Bez′alel and Oho′liab and every able man in whom the Lord has put ability and intelligence to know how to do any work in the construction of the sanctuary shall work in accordance with all that the Lord has commanded."

2 And Moses called Bez′alel and Oho′liab and every able man in whose mind the Lord had put

35:2, 3: Ex 23:12; 31:12–17; 34:21; Deut 5:12–15.
35:4–9: Ex 25:1–9.
35:30–36:1: Ex 31:1–6.

ability, every one whose heart stirred him up to come to do the work; [3]and they received from Moses all the freewill offering which the sons of Israel had brought for doing the work on the sanctuary. They still kept bringing him freewill offerings every morning, [4]so that all the able men who were doing every sort of task on the sanctuary came, each from the task that he was doing, [5]and said to Moses, "The people bring much more than enough for doing the work which the LORD has commanded us to do." [6]So Moses gave command, and word was proclaimed throughout the camp, "Let neither man nor woman do anything more for the offering for the sanctuary." So the people were restrained from bringing; [7]for the stuff they had was sufficient to do all the work, and more.

Construction of the Tabernacle

8 And all the able men among the workmen made the tabernacle with ten curtains; they were made of fine twined linen and blue and purple and scarlet stuff, with cherubim skilfully worked. [9]The length of each curtain was twenty-eight cubits, and the breadth of each curtain four cubits; all the curtains had the same measure.

10 And he coupled five curtains to one another, and the other five curtains he coupled to one another. [11]And he made loops of blue on the edge of the outmost curtain of the first set; likewise he made them on the edge of the outmost curtain of the second set; [12]he made fifty loops on the one curtain, and he made fifty loops on the edge of the curtain that was in the second set; the loops were opposite one another. [13]And he made fifty clasps of gold, and coupled the curtains one to the other with clasps; so the tabernacle was one whole.

14 He also made curtains of goats' hair for a tent over the tabernacle; he made eleven curtains. [15]The length of each curtain was thirty cubits, and the breadth of each curtain four cubits; the eleven curtains had the same measure. [16]He coupled five curtains by themselves, and six curtains by themselves. [17]And he made fifty loops on the edge of the outmost curtain of the one set, and fifty loops on the edge of the other connecting curtain. [18]And he made fifty clasps of bronze to couple the tent together that it might be one whole. [19]And he made for the tent a covering of tanned rams' skins and goatskins.

20 Then he made the upright frames for the tabernacle of acacia wood. [21]Ten cubits was the length of a frame, and a cubit and a half the breadth of each frame. [22]Each frame had two tenons, for fitting together; he did this for all the frames of the tabernacle. [23]The frames for the tabernacle he made thus: twenty frames for the south side; [24]and he made forty bases of silver under the twenty frames, two bases under one frame for its two tenons, and two bases under another frame for its two tenons. [25]And for the second side of the tabernacle, on the north side, he made twenty frames [26]and their forty bases of silver, two bases under one frame and two bases under another frame. [27]And for the rear of the tabernacle westward he made six frames. [28]And he made two frames for corners of the tabernacle in the rear. [29]And they were separate beneath, but joined at the top, at the first ring; he made two of them thus, for the two corners. [30]There were eight frames with their bases of silver: sixteen bases, under every frame two bases.

31 And he made bars of acacia wood, five for the frames of the one side of the tabernacle, [32]and five bars for the frames of the other side of the tabernacle, and five bars for the frames of the tabernacle at the rear westward. [33]And he made the middle bar to pass through from end to end halfway up the frames. [34]And he overlaid the frames with gold, and made their rings of gold for holders for the bars, and overlaid the bars with gold.

35 And he made the veil of blue and purple and scarlet stuff and fine twined linen; with cherubim skilfully worked he made it. [36]And for it he made four pillars of acacia, and overlaid them with gold; their hooks were of gold, and he cast for them four bases of silver. [37]He also made a screen for the door of the tent, of blue and purple and scarlet stuff and fine twined linen, embroidered with needlework; [38]and its five pillars with their hooks. He overlaid their capitals, and their fillets were of gold, but their five bases were of bronze.

Making the Ark of the Covenant

37 Bez'alel made the ark of acacia wood; two cubits and a half was its length, a cubit and a half its breadth, and a cubit and a half its height. [2]And he overlaid it with pure gold within and without, and made a molding of gold around it. [3]And he cast for it four rings of gold for its four corners, two rings on its one side and two rings on its other side. [4]And he made poles of acacia wood, and overlaid them with gold, [5]and put the poles into the rings on the sides of the ark, to carry the ark. [6]And he made a mercy seat of pure gold; two cubits and a half was its length, and a cubit and a half its breadth. [7]And he made two cherubim of hammered gold; on the two ends of the mercy seat he made them, [8]one cherub on the one end, and one cherub on the other end; of one piece with the mercy seat he made the cherubim on its two ends. [9]The cherubim spread out their wings above, overshadow-

---

36:8-19: Ex 26:1-14.
36:20-34: Ex 26:15-29.
36:35-38: Ex 26:31-37.
37:1-9: Ex 25:10-22.

ing the mercy seat with their wings, with their faces one to another; toward the mercy seat were the faces of the cherubim.

Making the Table

10 He also made the table of acacia wood; two cubits was its length, a cubit its breadth, and a cubit and a half its height; ¹¹and he overlaid it with pure gold, and made a molding of gold around it. ¹²And he made around it a frame a handbreadth wide, and made a molding of gold around the frame. ¹³He cast for it four rings of gold, and fastened the rings to the four corners at its four legs. ¹⁴Close to the frame were the rings, as holders for the poles to carry the table. ¹⁵He made the poles of acacia wood to carry the table, and overlaid them with gold. ¹⁶And he made the vessels of pure gold which were to be upon the table, its plates and dishes for incense, and its bowls and flagons with which to pour libations.

Making the Lampstand

17 He also made the lampstand of pure gold. The base and the shaft of the lampstand were made of hammered work; its cups, its capitals, and its flowers were of one piece with it. ¹⁸And there were six branches going out of its sides, three branches of the lampstand out of one side of it and three branches of the lampstand out of the other side of it; ¹⁹three cups made like almonds, each with capital and flower, on one branch, and three cups made like almonds, each with capital and flower, on the other branch—so for the six branches going out of the lampstand. ²⁰And on the lampstand itself were four cups made like almonds, with their capitals and flowers, ²¹and a capital of one piece with it under each pair of the six branches going out of it. ²²Their capitals and their branches were of one piece with it; the whole of it was one piece of hammered work of pure gold. ²³And he made its seven lamps and its snuffers and its trays of pure gold. ²⁴He made it and all its utensils of a talent of pure gold.

Making the Altar of Incense

25 He made the altar of incense of acacia wood; its length was a cubit, and its breadth was a cubit; it was square, and two cubits was its height; its horns were of one piece with it. ²⁶He overlaid it with pure gold, its top, and its sides round about, and its horns; and he made a molding of gold round about it, ²⁷and made two rings of gold on it under its molding, on two opposite sides of it, as holders for the poles with which to carry it. ²⁸And he made the poles of acacia wood, and overlaid them with gold.

Making the Anointing Oil and Incense

29 He made the holy anointing oil also, and the pure fragrant incense, blended as by the perfumer.

Making the Altar of Burnt Offering

38 He made the altar of burnt offering also of acacia wood; five cubits was its length, and five cubits its breadth; it was square, and three cubits was its height. ²He made horns for it on its four corners; its horns were of one piece with it, and he overlaid it with bronze. ³And he made all the utensils of the altar, the pots, the shovels, the basins, the forks, and the firepans: all its utensils he made of bronze. ⁴And he made for the altar a grating, a network of bronze, under its ledge, extending halfway down. ⁵He cast four rings on the four corners of the bronze grating as holders for the poles; ⁶he made the poles of acacia wood, and overlaid them with bronze. ⁷And he put the poles through the rings on the sides of the altar, to carry it with them; he made it hollow, with boards.

Making the Laver and the Court

8 And he made the laver of bronze and its base of bronze, from the mirrors of the ministering women who ministered at the door of the tent of meeting.

9 And he made the court; for the south side the hangings of the court were of fine twined linen, a hundred cubits; ¹⁰their pillars were twenty and their bases twenty, of bronze, but the hooks of the pillars and their fillets were of silver. ¹¹And for the north side a hundred cubits, their pillars twenty, their bases twenty, of bronze, but the hooks of the pillars and their fillets were of silver. ¹²And for the west side were hangings of fifty cubits, their pillars ten, and their sockets ten; the hooks of the pillars and their fillets were of silver. ¹³And for the front to the east, fifty cubits. ¹⁴The hangings for one side of the gate were fifteen cubits, with three pillars and three bases. ¹⁵And so for the other side; on this hand and that hand by the gate of the court were hangings of fifteen cubits, with three pillars and three bases. ¹⁶All the hangings round about the court were of fine twined linen. ¹⁷And the bases for the pillars were of bronze, but the hooks of the pillars and their fillets were of silver; the overlaying of their capitals was also of silver, and all the pillars of the court were filleted with silver. ¹⁸And the screen for the gate of the court was embroidered with needlework in blue and purple and scarlet stuff and fine twined linen; it was twenty cubits long and five cubits high in its breadth, corresponding to the hangings of the court. ¹⁹And their pillars were four; their four bases were of bronze, their hooks of silver, and the overlaying of their capitals and their fillets of silver. ²⁰And all the pegs

---

37:10–16: Ex 25:23–29.
37:17–24: Ex 25:31–39.
37:25–29: Ex 30:1–5.
38:1–7: Ex 27:1–8.
38:8: Ex 30:18.
38:9–20: Ex 27:9–19.

for the tabernacle and for the court round about were of bronze.

Materials of the Tabernacle

21 This is the sum of the things for the tabernacle, the tabernacle of the covenant, as they were counted at the commandment of Moses, for the work of the Levites under the direction of Ith'amar the son of Aaron the priest. ²²Bez'alel the son of Uri, son of Hur, of the tribe of Judah, made all that the LORD commanded Moses; ²³and with him was Oho'liab the son of Ahis'amach, of the tribe of Dan, a craftsman and designer and embroiderer in blue and purple and scarlet stuff and fine twined linen.

24 All the gold that was used for the work, in all the construction of the sanctuary, the gold from the offering, was twenty-nine talents and seven hundred and thirty shekels, by the shekel of the sanctuary. ²⁵And the silver from those of the congregation who were numbered was a hundred talents and a thousand seven hundred and seventy-five shekels, by the shekel of the sanctuary: ²⁶a beka a head (that is, half a shekel, by the shekel of the sanctuary), for every one who was numbered in the census, from twenty years old and upward, for six hundred and three thousand, five hundred and fifty men. ²⁷The hundred talents of silver were for casting the bases of the sanctuary, and the bases of the veil; a hundred bases for the hundred talents, a talent for a base. ²⁸And of the thousand seven hundred and seventy-five shekels he made hooks for the pillars, and overlaid their capitals and made fillets for them. ²⁹And the bronze that was contributed was seventy talents, and two thousand and four hundred shekels; ³⁰with it he made the bases for the door of the tent of meeting, the bronze altar and the bronze grating for it and all the utensils of the altar, ³¹the bases round about the court, and the bases of the gate of the court, all the pegs of the tabernacle, and all the pegs round about the court.

Making the Priests' Garments

39 And of the blue and purple and scarlet stuff they made finely wrought garments, for ministering in the holy place; they made the holy garments for Aaron; as the LORD had commanded Moses.

2 And he made the ephod of gold, blue and purple and scarlet stuff, and fine twined linen. ³And gold leaf was hammered out and cut into threads to work into the blue and purple and the scarlet stuff, and into the fine twined linen, in skilled design. ⁴They made for the ephod shoulder-pieces, joined to it at its two edges. ⁵And the skilfully woven band upon it, to belt it on, was of the same materials and workmanship, of gold, blue and purple and scarlet stuff, and fine twined linen; as the LORD had commanded Moses.

6 The onyx stones were prepared, enclosed in settings of gold filigree and engraved like the engravings of a signet, according to the names of the sons of Israel. ⁷And he set them on the shoulder-pieces of the ephod, to be stones of remembrance for the sons of Israel; as the LORD had commanded Moses.

8 He made the breastpiece, in skilled work, like the work of the ephod, of gold, blue and purple and scarlet stuff, and fine twined linen. ⁹It was square; the breastpiece was made double, a span its length and a span its breadth when doubled. ¹⁰And they set in it four rows of stones. A row of sardius, topaz, and carbuncle was the first row; ¹¹and the second row, an emerald, a sapphire, and a diamond; ¹²and the third row, a jacinth, an agate, and an amethyst; ¹³and the fourth row, a beryl, an onyx, and a jasper; they were enclosed in settings of gold filigree. ¹⁴There were twelve stones with their names according to the names of the sons of Israel; they were like signets, each engraved with its name, for the twelve tribes. ¹⁵And they made on the breastpiece twisted chains like cords, of pure gold; ¹⁶and they made two settings of gold filigree and two gold rings, and put the two rings on the two edges of the breastpiece; ¹⁷and they put the two cords of gold in the two rings at the edges of the breastpiece. ¹⁸Two ends of the two cords they had attached to the two settings of filigree; thus they attached it in front to the shoulder-pieces of the ephod. ¹⁹Then they made two rings of gold, and put them at the two ends of the breastpiece, on its inside edge next to the ephod. ²⁰And they made two rings of gold, and attached them in front to the lower part of the two shoulder-pieces of the ephod, at its joining above the skilfully woven band of the ephod. ²¹And they bound the breastpiece by its rings to the rings of the ephod with a lace of blue, so that it should lie upon the skilfully woven band of the ephod, and that the breastpiece should not come loose from the ephod; as the LORD had commanded Moses.

22 He also made the robe of the ephod woven all of blue; ²³and the opening of the robe in it was like the opening in a garment, with a binding around the opening, that it might not be torn. ²⁴On the skirts of the robe they made pomegranates of blue and purple and scarlet stuff and fine twined linen. ²⁵They also made bells of pure gold, and put the bells between the pomegranates upon the skirts of the robe round about, between the pomegranates; ²⁶a bell and a pomegranate, a bell and a pomegranate round about upon the skirts of the robe for ministering; as the LORD had commanded Moses.

38:25, 26: Ex 30:11–16.
39:2–7: Ex 28:6–12.
39:8–21: Ex 28:15–28.
39:22–26: Ex 28:31–34.

27 They also made the coats, woven of fine linen, for Aaron and his sons, ²⁸and the turban of fine linen, and the caps of fine linen, and the linen breeches of fine twined linen, ²⁹and the sash of fine twined linen and of blue and purple and scarlet stuff, embroidered with needlework; as the LORD had commanded Moses.

30 And they made the plate of the holy crown of pure gold, and wrote upon it an inscription, like the engraving of a signet, "Holy to the LORD." ³¹And they tied to it a lace of blue, to fasten it on the turban above; as the LORD had commanded Moses.

The Work Finished

32 Thus all the work of the tabernacle of the tent of meeting was finished; and the sons of Israel had done according to all that the LORD had commanded Moses; so had they done. ³³And they brought the tabernacle to Moses, the tent and all its utensils, its hooks, its frames, its bars, its pillars, and its bases; ³⁴the covering of tanned rams' skins and goatskins, and the veil of the screen; ³⁵the ark of the covenant with its poles and the mercy seat; ³⁶the table with all its utensils, and the bread of the Presence; ³⁷the lampstand of pure gold and its lamps with the lamps set and all its utensils, and the oil for the light; ³⁸the golden altar, the anointing oil and the fragrant incense, and the screen for the door of the tent; ³⁹the bronze altar, and its grating of bronze, its poles, and all its utensils; the laver and its base; ⁴⁰the hangings of the court, its pillars, and its bases, and the screen for the gate of the court, its cords, and its pegs; and all the utensils for the service of the tabernacle, for the tent of meeting; ⁴¹the finely worked garments for ministering in the holy place, the holy garments for Aaron the priest, and the garments of his sons to serve as priests. ⁴²According to all that the LORD had commanded Moses, so the sons of Israel had done all the work. ⁴³And Moses saw all the work, and behold, they had done it; as the LORD had commanded, so had they done it. And Moses blessed them.

Erection of the Tabernacle

40 The LORD said to Moses, ² "On the first day of the first month you shall erect the tabernacle of the tent of meeting. ³And you shall put in it the ark of the covenant, and you shall screen the ark with the veil. ⁴And you shall bring in the table, and set its arrangements in order; and you shall bring in the lampstand, and set up its lamps. ⁵And you shall put the golden altar for incense before the ark of the covenant, and set up the screen for the door of the tabernacle. ⁶You shall set the altar of burnt offering before the door of the tabernacle of the tent of meeting, ⁷and place the laver between the tent of meeting and the altar, and put water in it. ⁸And you shall set up the court round about, and hang up the screen for the gate of the court. ⁹Then you shall take the anointing oil, and anoint the tabernacle and all that is in it, and consecrate it and all its furniture; and it shall become holy. ¹⁰You shall also anoint the altar of burnt offering and all its utensils, and consecrate the altar; and the altar shall be most holy. ¹¹You shall also anoint the laver and its base, and consecrate it. ¹²Then you shall bring Aaron and his sons to the door of the tent of meeting, and shall wash them with water, ¹³and put upon Aaron the holy garments, and you shall anoint him and consecrate him, that he may serve me as priest. ¹⁴You shall bring his sons also and put coats on them, ¹⁵and anoint them, as you anointed their father, that they may serve me as priests: and their anointing shall admit them to a perpetual priesthood throughout their generations."

16 Thus did Moses; according to all that the LORD commanded him, so he did. ¹⁷And in the first month in the second year, on the first day of the month, the tabernacle was erected. ¹⁸Moses erected the tabernacle; he laid its bases, and set up its frames, and put in its poles, and raised up its pillars; ¹⁹and he spread the tent over the tabernacle, and put the covering of the tent over it, as the LORD had commanded Moses. ²⁰And he took the covenant and put it into the ark, and put the poles on the ark, and set the mercy seat above on the ark; ²¹and he brought the ark into the tabernacle, and set up the veil of the screen, and screened the ark of the covenant; as the LORD had commanded Moses. ²²And he put the table in the tent of meeting, on the north side of the tabernacle, outside the veil, ²³and set the bread in order on it before the LORD; as the LORD had commanded Moses. ²⁴And he put the lampstand in the tent of meeting, opposite the table on the south side of the tabernacle, ²⁵and set up the lamps before the LORD; as the LORD had commanded Moses. ²⁶And he put the golden altar in the tent of meeting before the veil, ²⁷and burnt fragrant incense upon it; as the LORD had commanded Moses. ²⁸And he put in place the screen for the door of the tabernacle. ²⁹And he set the altar of burnt offering at the door of the tabernacle of the tent of meeting, and offered upon it the burnt offering and the cereal offering; as the LORD had commanded Moses. ³⁰And he set the laver between the tent of meeting and the altar, and put water in it for washing, ³¹with which Moses and Aaron and his sons washed their hands and their feet; ³²when they went into the tent of meeting, and when they approached the altar, they washed; as the LORD commanded Moses. ³³And he

39:27-29: Ex 28:39, 40, 42.
39:30-31: Ex 28:36, 37.
39:36: Ex 25:30; 40:23; Lev 24:5–9.
40:23: Ex 25:30; 39:36; Lev 24:5–9.
40:30-32: Ex 30:18–21.

erected the court round the tabernacle and the altar, and set up the screen of the gate of the court. So Moses finished the work.

The Cloud and the Glory of the Lord

34 Then the cloud* covered the tent of meeting, and the glory of the Lord filled the tabernacle. [35]And Moses was not able to enter the tent of meeting, because the cloud abode upon it, and the glory of the Lord filled the tabernacle. [36]Throughout all their journeys, whenever the cloud was taken up from over the tabernacle, the sons of Israel would go onward; [37]but if the cloud was not taken up, then they did not go onward till the day that it was taken up. [38]For throughout all their journeys the cloud of the Lord was upon the tabernacle by day, and fire was in it by night, in the sight of all the house of Israel.

40:34: Rev 15:8.
* 40:34: *the cloud* and the fire, that is, the *glory,* are ways of representing at the same time the presence and the transcendence of God.

LEVITICUS

Burnt Offerings

1 The Lord called Moses, and spoke to him from the tent of meeting, saying, [2] "Speak to the sons of Israel, and say to them, When any man of you brings an offering to the Lord, you shall bring your offering of cattle from the herd or from the flock.

3 "If his offering is a burnt offering from the herd, he shall offer a male without blemish; he shall offer it at the door of the tent of meeting, that he may be accepted before the Lord; [4]he shall lay his hand upon the head of the burnt offering, and it shall be accepted for him to make atonement for him. [5]Then he shall kill the bull before the Lord; and Aaron's sons the priests shall present the blood, and throw the blood round about against the altar that is at the door of the tent of meeting. [6]And he shall flay the burnt offering and cut it into pieces; [7]and the sons of Aaron the priest shall put fire on the altar, and lay wood in order upon the fire; [8]and Aaron's sons the priests shall lay the pieces, the head, and the fat, in order upon the wood that is on the fire upon the altar; [9]but its entrails and its legs he shall wash with water. And the priest shall burn the whole on the altar, as a burnt offering, an offering by fire, a pleasing odor to the Lord.

10 "If his gift for a burnt offering is from the flock, from the sheep or goats, he shall offer a male without blemish; [11]and he shall kill it on the north side of the altar before the Lord, and Aaron's sons the priests shall throw its blood against the altar round about. [12]And he shall cut it into pieces, with its head and its fat, and the priest shall lay them in order upon the wood that is on the fire upon the altar; [13]but the entrails and the legs he shall wash with water. And the priest shall offer the whole, and burn it on the altar; it is a burnt offering, an offering by fire, a pleasing odor to the Lord.

14 "If his offering to the Lord is a burnt offering of birds, then he shall bring his offering of turtledoves or of young pigeons. [15]And the priest shall bring it to the altar and wring off its head, and burn it on the altar; and its blood shall be drained out on the side of the altar; [16]and he shall take away its crop with the feathers, and cast it beside the altar on the east side, in the place for ashes; [17]he shall tear it by its wings, but shall not divide it asunder. And the priest shall burn it on

the altar, upon the wood that is on the fire; it is a burnt offering, an offering by fire, a pleasing odor to the Lord.

Cereal Offerings

2 "When any one brings a cereal offering as an offering to the Lord, his offering shall be of fine flour; he shall pour oil upon it, and put frankincense on it, [2]and bring it to Aaron's sons the priests. And he shall take from it a handful of the fine flour and oil, with all of its frankincense; and the priest shall burn this as its memorial portion upon the altar, an offering by fire, a pleasing odor to the Lord. [3]And what is left of the cereal offering shall be for Aaron and his sons; it is a most holy part of the offerings by fire to the Lord.

4 "When you bring a cereal offering baked in the oven as an offering, it shall be unleavened cakes of fine flour mixed with oil, or unleavened wafers spread with oil. [5]And if your offering is a cereal offering baked on a griddle, it shall be of fine flour unleavened, mixed with oil; [6]you shall break it in pieces, and pour oil on it; it is a cereal offering. [7]And if your offering is a cereal offering cooked in a pan, it shall be made of fine flour with oil. [8]And you shall bring the cereal offering that is made of these things to the Lord; and when it is presented to the priest, he shall bring it to the altar. [9]And the priest shall take from the cereal offering its memorial portion and burn this on the altar, an offering by fire, a pleasing odor to the Lord. [10]And what is left of the cereal offering shall be for Aaron and his sons; it is a most holy part of the offerings by fire to the Lord.

11 "No cereal offering which you bring to the Lord shall be made with leaven; for you shall burn no leaven nor any honey as an offering by fire to the Lord. [12]As an offering of first fruits you may bring them to the Lord, but they shall not be offered on the altar for a pleasing odor. [13]You shall season all your cereal offerings with salt; you shall not let the salt of the covenant with your God be lacking from your cereal offering; with all your offerings you shall offer salt.

14 "If you offer a cereal offering of first fruits to the Lord, you shall offer for the cereal offering

---

As the name suggests, this book is almost exclusively concerned with the regulation of the religious life of Israel by the Levitical priesthood. Although its underlying concept of Israel as a holy people contains an element of permanent importance, the law as such, except for those parts that Christ expressly sanctioned, is not binding on Christians.

of your first fruits crushed new grain from fresh ears, parched with fire. [15]And you shall put oil upon it, and lay frankincense on it; it is a cereal offering. [16]And the priest shall burn as its memorial portion part of the crushed grain and of the oil with all of its frankincense; it is an offering by fire to the LORD.

Peace Offerings

3 "If a man's offering is a sacrifice of peace offering, if he offers an animal from the herd, male or female, he shall offer it without blemish before the LORD. [2]And he shall lay his hand upon the head of his offering and kill it at the door of the tent of meeting; and Aaron's sons the priests shall throw the blood against the altar round about. [3]And from the sacrifice of the peace offering, as an offering by fire to the LORD, he shall offer the fat covering the entrails and all the fat that is on the entrails, [4]and the two kidneys with the fat that is on them at the loins, and the appendage of the liver which he shall take away with the kidneys. [5]Then Aaron's sons shall burn it on the altar upon the burnt offering, which is upon the wood on the fire; it is an offering by fire, a pleasing odor to the LORD.

6 "If his offering for a sacrifice of peace offering to the LORD is an animal from the flock, male or female, he shall offer it without blemish. [7]If he offers a lamb for his offering, then he shall offer it before the LORD, [8]laying his hand upon the head of his offering and killing it before the tent of meeting; and Aaron's sons shall throw its blood against the altar round about. [9]Then from the sacrifice of the peace offering as an offering by fire to the LORD he shall offer its fat, the fat tail entire, taking it away close by the backbone, and the fat that covers the entrails, and all the fat that is on the entrails, [10]and the two kidneys with the fat that is on them at the loins, and the appendage of the liver which he shall take away with the kidneys. [11]And the priest shall burn it on the altar as food offered by fire to the LORD.

12 "If his offering is a goat, then he shall offer it before the LORD, [13]and lay his hand upon its head, and kill it before the tent of meeting; and the sons of Aaron shall throw its blood against the altar round about. [14]Then he shall offer from it, as his offering for an offering by fire to the LORD, the fat covering the entrails, and all the fat that is on the entrails, [15]and the two kidneys with the fat that is on them at the loins, and the appendage of the liver which he shall take away with the kidneys. [16]And the priest shall burn them on the altar as food offered by fire for a pleasing odor. All fat is the LORD's. [17]It shall be a perpetual statute throughout your generations, in all your dwelling places, that you eat neither fat nor blood."

Sin Offerings

4 And the LORD said to Moses, [2]"Say to the sons of Israel, If any one sins unwittingly in any of the things which the LORD has commanded not to be done, and does any one of them, [3]if it is the anointed priest who sins, thus bringing guilt on the people, then let him offer for the sin which he has committed a young bull without blemish to the LORD for a sin offering. [4]He shall bring the bull to the door of the tent of meeting before the LORD, and lay his hand on the head of the bull, and kill the bull before the LORD. [5]And the anointed priest shall take some of the blood of the bull and bring it to the tent of meeting; [6]and the priest shall dip his finger in the blood and sprinkle part of the blood seven times before the LORD in front of the veil of the sanctuary. [7]And the priest shall put some of the blood on the horns of the altar of fragrant incense before the LORD which is in the tent of meeting, and the rest of the blood of the bull he shall pour out at the base of the altar of burnt offering which is at the door of the tent of meeting. [8]And all the fat of the bull of the sin offering he shall take from it, the fat that covers the entrails and all the fat that is on the entrails, [9]and the two kidneys with the fat that is on them at the loins, and the appendage of the liver which he shall take away with the kidneys [10](just as these are taken from the ox of the sacrifice of the peace offerings), and the priest shall burn them upon the altar of burnt offering. [11]But the skin of the bull and all its flesh, with its head, its legs, its entrails, and its dung, [12]the whole bull he shall carry forth outside the camp to a clean place, where the ashes are poured out, and shall burn it on a fire of wood; where the ashes are poured out it shall be burned.

13 "If the whole congregation of Israel commits a sin unwittingly and the thing is hidden from the eyes of the assembly, and they do any one of the things which the LORD has commanded not to be done and are guilty; [14]when the sin which they have committed becomes known, the assembly shall offer a young bull for a sin offering and bring it before the tent of meeting; [15]and the elders of the congregation shall lay their hands upon the head of the bull before the LORD, and the bull shall be killed before the LORD. [16]Then the anointed priest shall bring some of the blood of the bull to the tent of meeting, [17]and the priest shall dip his finger in the blood and sprinkle it seven times before the LORD in front of the veil. [18]And he shall put some of the blood on the horns of the altar which is in the tent of meeting before the LORD; and the rest of the blood he shall pour

3:1-17: Lev 7:11-18.
4:2-12: Num 15:27-29.
4:13-21: Num 15:22-26.

out at the base of the altar of burnt offering which is at the door of the tent of meeting. ¹⁹And all its fat he shall take from it and burn upon the altar. ²⁰Thus shall he do with the bull; as he did with the bull of the sin offering, so shall he do with this; and the priest shall make atonement for them, and they shall be forgiven. ²¹And he shall carry forth the bull outside the camp, and burn it as he burned the first bull; it is the sin offering for the assembly.

22 "When a ruler sins, doing unwittingly any one of all the things which the LORD his God has commanded not to be done, and is guilty, ²³if the sin which he has committed is made known to him, he shall bring as his offering a goat, a male without blemish, ²⁴and shall lay his hand upon the head of the goat, and kill it in the place where they kill the burnt offering before the LORD; it is a sin offering. ²⁵Then the priest shall take some of the blood of the sin offering with his finger and put it on the horns of the altar of burnt offering, and pour out the rest of its blood at the base of the altar of burnt offering. ²⁶And all its fat he shall burn on the altar, like the fat of the sacrifice of peace offerings; so the priest shall make atonement for him for his sin, and he shall be forgiven.

27 "If any one of the common people sins unwittingly in doing any one of the things which the LORD has commanded not to be done, and is guilty, ²⁸when the sin which he has committed is made known to him he shall bring for his offering a goat, a female without blemish, for his sin which he has committed. ²⁹And he shall lay his hand on the head of the sin offering, and kill the sin offering in the place of burnt offering. ³⁰And the priest shall take some of its blood with his finger and put it on the horns of the altar of burnt offering, and pour out the rest of its blood at the base of the altar. ³¹And all its fat he shall remove, as the fat is removed from the peace offerings, and the priest shall burn it upon the altar for a pleasing odor to the LORD; and the priest shall make atonement for him, and he shall be forgiven.

32 "If he brings a lamb as his offering for a sin offering, he shall bring a female without blemish, ³³and lay his hand upon the head of the sin offering, and kill it for a sin offering in the place where they kill the burnt offering. ³⁴Then the priest shall take some of the blood of the sin offering with his finger and put it on the horns of the altar of burnt offering, and pour out the rest of its blood at the base of the altar. ³⁵And all its fat he shall remove as the fat of the lamb is removed from the sacrifice of peace offerings, and the priest shall burn it on the altar, upon the offerings by fire to the LORD; and the priest shall make atonement for him for the sin which he has committed, and he shall be forgiven.

5 "If any one sins in that he hears a public adjuration to testify and though he is a witness, whether he has seen or come to know the matter, yet does not speak, he shall bear his iniquity. ²Or if any one touches an unclean thing, whether the carcass of an unclean beast or a carcass of unclean cattle or a carcass of unclean swarming things, and it is hidden from him, and he has become unclean, he shall be guilty. ³Or if he touches human uncleanness, of whatever sort the uncleanness may be with which one becomes unclean, and it is hidden from him, when he comes to know it he shall be guilty. ⁴Or if any one utters with his lips a rash oath to do evil or to do good, any sort of rash oath that men swear, and it is hidden from him, when he comes to know it he shall in any of these be guilty. ⁵When a man is guilty in any of these, he shall confess the sin he has committed, ⁶and he shall bring his guilt offering to the LORD for the sin which he has committed, a female from the flock, a lamb or a goat, for a sin offering; and the priest shall make atonement for him for his sin.

7 "But if he cannot afford a lamb, then he shall bring, as his guilt offering to the LORD for the sin which he has committed, two turtledoves or two young pigeons, one for a sin offering and the other for a burnt offering. ⁸He shall bring them to the priest, who shall offer first the one for the sin offering; he shall wring its head from its neck, but shall not sever it, ⁹and he shall sprinkle some of the blood of the sin offering on the side of the altar, while the rest of the blood shall be drained out at the base of the altar; it is a sin offering. ¹⁰Then he shall offer the second for a burnt offering according to the ordinance; and the priest shall make atonement for him for the sin which he has committed, and he shall be forgiven.

11 "But if he cannot afford two turtledoves or two young pigeons, then he shall bring, as his offering for the sin which he has committed, a tenth of an ephah of fine flour for a sin offering; he shall put no oil upon it, and shall put no frankincense on it, for it is a sin offering. ¹²And he shall bring it to the priest, and the priest shall take a handful of it as its memorial portion and burn this on the altar, upon the offerings by fire to the LORD; it is a sin offering. ¹³Thus the priest shall make atonement for him for the sin which he has committed in any one of these things, and he shall be forgiven. And the remainder shall be for the priest, as in the cereal offering."

Guilt Offerings

14 The LORD said to Moses, ¹⁵ "If any one commits a breach of faith and sins unwittingly in any of the holy things of the LORD, he shall bring, as his guilt offering to the LORD, a ram without blemish out of the flock, valued by you in shekels of silver, according to the shekel of the sanctuary; it

is a guilt offering. [16]He shall also make restitution for what he has done amiss in the holy thing, and shall add a fifth to it and give it to the priest; and the priest shall make atonement for him with the ram of the guilt offering, and he shall be forgiven.

[17] "If any one sins, doing any of the things which the LORD has commanded not to be done, though he does not know it, yet he is guilty and shall bear his iniquity. [18]He shall bring to the priest a ram without blemish out of the flock, valued by you at the price for a guilt offering, and the priest shall make atonement for him for the error which he committed unwittingly, and he shall be forgiven. [19]It is a guilt offering; he is guilty before the LORD."

6 [a] The LORD said to Moses, [2] "If any one sins and commits a breach of faith against the LORD by deceiving his neighbor in a matter of deposit or security, or through robbery, or if he has oppressed his neighbor [3]or has found what was lost and lied about it, swearing falsely—in any of all the things which men do and sin therein, [4]when one has sinned and become guilty, he shall restore what he took by robbery, or what he got by oppression, or the deposit which was committed to him, or the lost thing which he found, [5]or anything about which he has sworn falsely; he shall restore it in full, and shall add a fifth to it, and give it to him to whom it belongs, on the day of his guilt offering. [6]And he shall bring to the priest his guilt offering to the LORD, a ram without blemish out of the flock, valued by you at the price for a guilt offering; [7]and the priest shall make atonement for him before the LORD, and he shall be forgiven for any of the things which one may do and thereby become guilty."

The Law of Offerings

[8] [b] The LORD said to Moses, [9] "Command Aaron and his sons, saying, This is the law of the burnt offering. The burnt offering shall be on the hearth upon the altar all night until the morning, and the fire of the altar shall be kept burning on it. [10]And the priest shall put on his linen garment, and put his linen breeches upon his body, and he shall take up the ashes to which the fire has consumed the burnt offering on the altar, and put them beside the altar. [11]Then he shall put off his garments, and put on other garments, and carry forth the ashes outside the camp to a clean place. [12]The fire on the altar shall be kept burning on it, it shall not go out; the priest shall burn wood on it every morning, and he shall lay the burnt offering in order upon it, and shall burn on it the fat of the peace offerings. [13]Fire shall be kept burning upon the altar continually; it shall not go out.

[14] "And this is the law of the cereal offering. The sons of Aaron shall offer it before the LORD, in front of the altar. [15]And one shall take from it a handful of the fine flour of the cereal offering with its oil and all the frankincense which is on the cereal offering, and burn this as its memorial portion on the altar, a pleasing odor to the LORD. [16]And the rest of it Aaron and his sons shall eat; it shall be eaten unleavened in a holy place; in the court of the tent of meeting they shall eat it. [17]It shall not be baked with leaven. I have given it as their portion of my offerings by fire; it is a thing most holy, like the sin offering and the guilt offering. [18]Every male among the children of Aaron may eat of it, as decreed for ever throughout your generations, from the LORD's offerings by fire; whoever touches them shall become holy."

[19] The LORD said to Moses, [20] "This is the offering which Aaron and his sons shall offer to the LORD on the day when he is anointed: a tenth of an ephah of fine flour as a regular cereal offering, half of it in the morning and half in the evening. [21]It shall be made with oil on a griddle; you shall bring it well mixed, in baked [c] pieces like a cereal offering, and offer it for a pleasing odor to the LORD. [22]The priest from among Aaron's sons, who is anointed to succeed him, shall offer it to the LORD as decreed for ever; the whole of it shall be burned. [23]Every cereal offering of a priest shall be wholly burned; it shall not be eaten."

[24] The LORD said to Moses, [25] "Say to Aaron and his sons, This is the law of the sin offering. In the place where the burnt offering is killed shall the sin offering be killed before the LORD; it is most holy. [26]The priest who offers it for sin shall eat it; in a holy place it shall be eaten, in the court of the tent of meeting. [27]Whatever [d] touches its flesh shall be holy; and when any of its blood is sprinkled on a garment, you shall wash that on which it was sprinkled in a holy place. [28]And the earthen vessel in which it is boiled shall be broken; but if it is boiled in a bronze vessel, that shall be scoured, and rinsed in water. [29]Every male among the priests may eat of it; it is most holy. [30]But no sin offering shall be eaten from which any blood is brought into the tent of meeting to make atonement in the holy place; it shall be burned with fire.

7 "This is the law of the guilt offering. It is most holy; [2]in the place where they kill the burnt offering they shall kill the guilt offering, and its blood shall be thrown on the altar round about. [3]And all its fat shall be offered, the fat tail, the fat that covers the entrails, [4]the two kidneys with the fat that is on them at the loins, and the appendage of the liver which he shall take away with the kidneys; [5]the priest shall burn them on the altar as an offering by fire to the LORD; it is a

---

[a] Ch 5:20 in Heb.
[b] Ch 6:1 in Heb.
[c] Meaning of Heb is uncertain.
[d] Or Whoever.
6:1–7: Ex 22:7–15; Num 5:5–8.

guilt offering. [6]Every male among the priests may eat of it; it shall be eaten in a holy place; it is most holy. [7]The guilt offering is like the sin offering, there is one law for them; the priest who makes atonement with it shall have it. [8]And the priest who offers any man's burnt offering shall have for himself the skin of the burnt offering which he has offered. [9]And every cereal offering baked in the oven and all that is prepared on a pan or a griddle shall belong to the priest who offers it. [10]And every cereal offering, mixed with oil or dry, shall be for all the sons of Aaron, one as well as another.

Further Instructions

[11] "And this is the law of the sacrifice of peace offerings which one may offer to the LORD. [12]If he offers it for a thanksgiving, then he shall offer with the thank offering unleavened cakes mixed with oil, unleavened wafers spread with oil, and cakes of fine flour well mixed with oil. [13]With the sacrifice of his peace offerings for thanksgiving he shall bring his offering with cakes of leavened bread. [14]And of such he shall offer one cake from each offering, as an offering to the LORD; it shall belong to the priest who throws the blood of the peace offerings. [15]And the flesh of the sacrifice of his peace offerings for thanksgiving shall be eaten on the day of his offering; he shall not leave any of it until the morning. [16]But if the sacrifice of his offering is a votive offering or a freewill offering, it shall be eaten on the day that he offers his sacrifice, and the next day what remains of it shall be eaten, [17]but what remains of the flesh of the sacrifice on the third day shall be burned with fire. [18]If any of the flesh of the sacrifice of his peace offering is eaten on the third day, he who offers it shall not be accepted, neither shall it be credited to him; it shall be an abomination, and he who eats of it shall bear his iniquity.

[19] "Flesh that touches any unclean thing shall not be eaten; it shall be burned with fire. All who are clean may eat flesh, [20]but the person who eats of the flesh of the sacrifice of the LORD's peace offerings while an uncleanness is on him, that person shall be cut off from his people. [21]And if any one touches an unclean thing, whether the uncleanness of man or an unclean beast or any unclean abomination, and then eats of the flesh of the sacrifice of the LORD's peace offerings, that person shall be cut off from his people."

[22] The LORD said to Moses, [23] "Say to the people of Israel, You shall eat no fat, of ox, or sheep, or goat. [24]The fat of an animal that dies of itself, and the fat of one that is torn by beasts, may be put to any other use, but on no account shall you eat it. [25]For every person who eats of the fat of an animal of which an offering by fire is made to the LORD shall be cut off from his people. [26]Moreover you shall eat no blood whatever, whether of fowl or of animal, in any of your dwellings. [27]Whoever eats any blood, that person shall be cut off from his people."

[28] The LORD said to Moses, [29] "Say to the sons of Israel, He that offers the sacrifice of his peace offerings to the LORD shall bring his offering to the LORD; from the sacrifice of his peace offerings [30]he shall bring with his own hands the offerings by fire to the LORD; he shall bring the fat with the breast, that the breast may be waved as a wave offering before the LORD. [31]The priest shall burn the fat on the altar, but the breast shall be for Aaron and his sons. [32]And the right thigh you shall give to the priest as an offering from the sacrifice of your peace offerings; [33]he among the sons of Aaron who offers the blood of the peace offerings and the fat shall have the right thigh for a portion. [34]For the breast that is waved and the thigh that is offered I have taken from the sons of Israel, out of the sacrifices of their peace offerings, and have given them to Aaron the priest and to his sons, as a perpetual debt from the sons of Israel. [35]This is the portion of Aaron and of his sons from the offerings made by fire to the LORD, consecrated to them on the day they were presented to serve as priests of the LORD; [36]the LORD commanded this to be given them by the sons of Israel, on the day that they were anointed; it is a perpetual debt throughout their generations."

[37] This is the law of the burnt offering, of the cereal offering, of the sin offering, of the guilt offering, of the consecration, and of the peace offerings, [38]which the LORD commanded Moses on Mount Sinai, on the day that he commanded the sons of Israel to bring their offerings to the LORD, in the wilderness of Sinai.

The Rites of Ordination

8 The LORD said to Moses, [2] "Take Aaron and his sons with him, and the garments, and the anointing oil, and the bull of the sin offering, and the two rams, and the basket of unleavened bread; [3]and assemble all the congregation at the door of the tent of meeting." [4]And Moses did as the LORD commanded him; and the congregation was assembled at the door of the tent of meeting.

[5] And Moses said to the congregation, "This is the thing which the LORD has commanded to be done." [6]And Moses brought Aaron and his sons, and washed them with water. [7]And he put on him the coat, and girded him with the sash, and clothed him with the robe, and put the ephod upon him, and girded him with the skilfully woven band of the ephod, binding it to him therewith. [8]And he placed the breastpiece on him, and in the breastpiece he put the U'rim and the Thummim. [9]And he set the turban upon his head, and on the turban, in front, he set the

8:1–36: Ex 29:1–37.

golden plate, the holy crown, as the LORD commanded Moses.

10 Then Moses took the anointing oil, and anointed the tabernacle and all that was in it, and consecrated them. [11]And he sprinkled some of it on the altar seven times, and anointed the altar and all its utensils, and the laver and its base, to consecrate them. [12]And he poured some of the anointing oil on Aaron's head, and anointed him, to consecrate him. [13]And Moses brought Aaron's sons, and clothed them with coats, and girded them with sashes, and bound caps on them, as the LORD commanded Moses.

14 Then he brought the bull of the sin offering; and Aaron and his sons laid their hands upon the head of the bull of the sin offering. [15]And Moses killed it, and took the blood, and with his finger put it on the horns of the altar round about, and purified the altar, and poured out the blood at the base of the altar, and consecrated it, to make atonement for it. [16]And he took all the fat that was on the entrails, and the appendage of the liver, and the two kidneys with their fat, and Moses burned them on the altar. [17]But the bull, and its skin, and its flesh, and its dung, he burned with fire outside the camp, as the LORD commanded Moses.

18 Then he presented the ram of the burnt offering; and Aaron and his sons laid their hands on the head of the ram. [19]And Moses killed it, and threw the blood upon the altar round about. [20]And when the ram was cut into pieces, Moses burned the head and the pieces and the fat. [21]And when the entrails and the legs were washed with water, Moses burned the whole ram on the altar, as a burnt offering, a pleasing odor, an offering by fire to the LORD, as the LORD commanded Moses.

22 Then he presented the other ram, the ram of ordination; and Aaron and his sons laid their hands on the head of the ram. [23]And Moses killed it, and took some of its blood and put it on the tip of Aaron's right ear and on the thumb of his right hand and on the great toe of his right foot. [24]And Aaron's sons were brought, and Moses put some of the blood on the tips of their right ears and on the thumbs of their right hands and on the great toes of their right feet; and Moses threw the blood upon the altar round about. [25]Then he took the fat, and the fat tail, and all the fat that was on the entrails, and the appendage of the liver, and the two kidneys with their fat, and the right thigh; [26]and out of the basket of unleavened bread which was before the LORD he took one unleavened cake, and one cake of bread with oil, and one wafer, and placed them on the fat and on the right thigh; [27]and he put all these in the hands of Aaron and in the hands of his sons, and waved them as a wave offering before the LORD. [28]Then Moses took them from their hands, and burned them on the altar with the burnt offering, as an ordination offering, a pleasing odor, an offering by fire to the LORD. [29]And Moses took the breast, and waved it for a wave offering before the LORD; it was Moses' portion of the ram of ordination, as the LORD commanded Moses.

30 Then Moses took some of the anointing oil and of the blood which was on the altar, and sprinkled it upon Aaron and his garments, and also upon his sons and his sons' garments; so he consecrated Aaron and his garments, and his sons and his sons' garments with him.

31 And Moses said to Aaron and his sons, "Boil the flesh at the door of the tent of meeting, and there eat it and the bread that is in the basket of ordination offerings, as I commanded, saying, 'Aaron and his sons shall eat it'; [32]and what remains of the flesh and the bread you shall burn with fire. [33]And you shall not go out from the door of the tent of meeting for seven days, until the days of your ordination are completed, for it will take seven days to ordain you. [34]As has been done today, the LORD has commanded to be done to make atonement for you. [35]At the door of the tent of meeting you shall remain day and night for seven days, performing what the LORD has charged, lest you die; for so I am commanded." [36]And Aaron and his sons did all the things which the LORD commanded by Moses.

Aaron's Priesthood Inaugurated

9 On the eighth day Moses called Aaron and his sons and the elders of Israel; [2]and he said to Aaron, "Take a bull calf for a sin offering, and a ram for a burnt offering, both without blemish, and offer them before the LORD. [3]And say to the sons of Israel, 'Take a male goat for a sin offering, and a calf and a lamb, both a year old without blemish, for a burnt offering, [4]and an ox and a ram for peace offerings, to sacrifice before the LORD, and a cereal offering mixed with oil; for today the LORD will appear to you.'" [5]And they brought what Moses commanded before the tent of meeting; and all the congregation drew near and stood before the LORD. [6]And Moses said, "This is the thing which the LORD commanded you to do; and the glory of the LORD will appear to you." [7]Then Moses said to Aaron, "Draw near to the altar, and offer your sin offering and your burnt offering, and make atonement for yourself and for the people; and bring the offering of the people, and make atonement for them; as the LORD has commanded."

8 So Aaron drew near to the altar, and killed the calf of the sin offering, which was for himself. [9]And the sons of Aaron presented the blood to him, and he dipped his finger in the blood and put it on the horns of the altar, and poured out the blood at the base of the altar; [10]but the fat and the kidneys and the appendage of the liver from

the sin offering he burned upon the altar, as the LORD commanded Moses. [11]The flesh and the skin he burned with fire outside the camp.

12 And he killed the burnt offering; and Aaron's sons delivered to him the blood, and he threw it on the altar round about. [13]And they delivered the burnt offering to him, piece by piece, and the head; and he burned them upon the altar. [14]And he washed the entrails and the legs, and burned them with the burnt offering on the altar.

15 Then he presented the people's offering, and took the goat of the sin offering which was for the people, and killed it, and offered it for sin, like the first sin offering. [16]And he presented the burnt offering, and offered it according to the ordinance. [17]And he presented the cereal offering, and filled his hand from it, and burned it upon the altar, besides the burnt offering of the morning.

18 He killed the ox also and the ram, the sacrifice of peace offerings for the people; and Aaron's sons delivered to him the blood, which he threw upon the altar round about, [19]and the fat of the ox and of the ram, the fat tail, and that which covers the entrails, and the kidneys, and the appendage of the liver; [20]and they put the fat upon the breasts, and he burned the fat upon the altar, [21]but the breasts and the right thigh Aaron waved for a wave offering before the LORD; as Moses commanded.

22 Then Aaron lifted up his hands toward the people and blessed them; and he came down from offering the sin offering and the burnt offering and the peace offerings. [23]And Moses and Aaron went into the tent of meeting; and when they came out they blessed the people, and the glory of the LORD appeared to all the people. [24]And fire came forth from before the LORD and consumed the burnt offering and the fat upon the altar; and when all the people saw it, they shouted, and fell on their faces.

Nadab and Abihu

10 Now Na'dab and Abi'hu, the sons of Aaron, each took his censer, and put fire in it, and laid incense on it, and offered unholy fire before the LORD, such as he had not commanded them. [2]And fire came forth from the presence of the LORD and devoured them, and they died before the LORD. [3]Then Moses said to Aaron, "This is what the LORD has said, 'I will show myself holy among those who are near me, and before all the people I will be glorified.'" And Aaron held his peace.

4 And Moses called Mish'a-el and El'zaphan, the sons of Uz'ziel the uncle of Aaron, and said to them, "Draw near, carry your brethren from before the sanctuary out of the camp." [5]So they drew near, and carried them in their coats out of the camp, as Moses had said. [6]And Moses said to

Aaron and to Elea'zar and Ith'amar, his sons, "Do not let the hair of your heads hang loose, and do not rend your clothes, lest you die, and lest wrath come upon all the congregation; but your brethren, the whole house of Israel, may bewail the burning which the LORD has kindled. [7]And do not go out from the door of the tent of meeting, lest you die; for the anointing oil of the LORD is upon you." And they did according to the word of Moses.

8 And the LORD spoke to Aaron, saying, [9]"Drink no wine nor strong drink, you nor your sons with you, when you go into the tent of meeting, lest you die; it shall be a statute for ever throughout your generations. [10]You are to distinguish between the holy and the common, and between the unclean and the clean; [11]and you are to teach the sons of Israel all the statutes which the LORD has spoken to them by Moses."

12 And Moses said to Aaron and to Elea'zar and Ith'amar, his sons who were left, "Take the cereal offering that remains of the offerings by fire to the LORD, and eat it unleavened beside the altar, for it is most holy; [13]you shall eat it in a holy place, because it is your due and your sons' due, from the offerings by fire to the LORD; for so I am commanded. [14]But the breast that is waved and the thigh that is offered you shall eat in any clean place, you and your sons and your daughters with you; for they are given as your due and your sons' due, from the sacrifices of the peace offerings of the sons of Israel. [15]The thigh that is offered and the breast that is waved they shall bring with the offerings by fire of the fat, to wave for a wave offering before the LORD, and it shall be yours, and your sons' with you, as a debt for ever; as the LORD has commanded."

16 Now Moses diligently inquired about the goat of the sin offering, and behold, it was burned! And he was angry with Elea'zar and Ith'amar, the sons of Aaron who were left, saying, [17]"Why have you not eaten the sin offering in the place of the sanctuary, since it is a thing most holy and has been given to you that you may bear the iniquity of the congregation, to make atonement for them before the LORD? [18]Behold, its blood was not brought into the inner part of the sanctuary. You certainly ought to have eaten it in the sanctuary, as I commanded." [19]And Aaron said to Moses, "Behold, today they have offered their sin offering and their burnt offering before the LORD; and yet such things as these have befallen me! If I had eaten the sin offering today, would it have been acceptable in the sight of the LORD?" [20]And when Moses heard that, he was content.

9:18–21: Lev 3:1–11.
10:8: Ezek 44:21.
10:12, 13: Lev 6:14–18.
10:14, 15: Lev 7:30–34.

Clean and Unclean Foods

11 * And the LORD said to Moses and Aaron, 2 "Say to the sons of Israel, These are the living things which you may eat among all the beasts that are on the earth. 3Whatever parts the hoof and is cloven-footed and chews the cud, among the animals, you may eat. 4Nevertheless among those that chew the cud or part the hoof, you shall not eat these: The camel, because it chews the cud but does not part the hoof, is unclean to you. 5And the rock badger, because it chews the cud but does not part the hoof, is unclean to you. 6And the hare, because it chews the cud but does not part the hoof, is unclean to you. 7And the swine, because it parts the hoof and is cloven-footed but does not chew the cud, is unclean to you. 8Of their flesh you shall not eat, and their carcasses you shall not touch; they are unclean to you.

9 "These you may eat, of all that are in the waters. Everything in the waters that has fins and scales, whether in the seas or in the rivers, you may eat. 10But anything in the seas or the rivers that has not fins and scales, of the swarming creatures in the waters and of the living creatures that are in the waters, is an abomination to you. 11They shall remain an abomination to you; of their flesh you shall not eat, and their carcasses you shall have in abomination. 12Everything in the waters that has not fins and scales is an abomination to you.

Unclean Creatures

13 "And these you shall have in abomination among the birds, they shall not be eaten, they are an abomination: the eagle, the vulture, the osprey, 14the kite, the falcon according to its kind, 15every raven according to its kind, 16the ostrich, the nighthawk, the sea gull, the hawk according to its kind, 17the owl, the cormorant, the ibis, 18the water hen, the pelican, the carrion vulture, 19the stork, the heron according to its kind, the hoopoe, and the bat.

20 "All winged insects that go upon all fours are an abomination to you. 21Yet among the winged insects that go on all fours you may eat those which have legs above their feet, with which to leap on the earth. 22Of them you may eat: the locust according to its kind, the bald locust according to its kind, the cricket according to its kind, and the grasshopper according to its kind. 23But all other winged insects which have four feet are an abomination to you.

24 "And by these you shall become unclean; whoever touches their carcass shall be unclean until the evening, 25and whoever carries any part of their carcass shall wash his clothes and be unclean until the evening. 26Every animal which parts the hoof but is not cloven-footed or does not chew the cud is unclean to you; every one who touches them shall be unclean. 27And all that go on their paws, among the animals that go on all fours, are unclean to you; whoever touches their carcass shall be unclean until the evening, 28and he who carries their carcass shall wash his clothes and be unclean until the evening; they are unclean to you.

29 "And these are unclean to you among the swarming things that swarm upon the earth: the weasel, the mouse, the great lizard according to its kind, 30the gecko, the land crocodile, the lizard, the sand lizard, and the chameleon. 31These are unclean to you among all that swarm; whoever touches them when they are dead shall be unclean until the evening. 32And anything upon which any of them falls when they are dead shall be unclean, whether it is an article of wood or a garment or a skin or a sack, any vessel that is used for any purpose; it must be put into water, and it shall be unclean until the evening; then it shall be clean. 33And if any of them falls into any earthen vessel, all that is in it shall be unclean, and you shall break it. 34Any food in it which may be eaten, upon which water may come, shall be unclean; and all drink which may be drunk from every such vessel shall be unclean. 35And everything upon which any part of their carcass falls shall be unclean; whether oven or stove, it shall be broken in pieces; they are unclean, and shall be unclean to you. 36Nevertheless a spring or a cistern holding water shall be clean; but whatever touches their carcass shall be unclean. 37And if any part of their carcass falls upon any seed for sowing that is to be sown, it is clean; 38but if water is put on the seed and any part of their carcass falls on it, it is unclean to you.

39 "And if any animal of which you may eat dies, he who touches its carcass shall be unclean until the evening, 40and he who eats of its carcass shall wash his clothes and be unclean until the evening; he also who carries the carcass shall wash his clothes and be unclean until the evening.

41 "Every swarming thing that swarms upon the earth is an abomination; it shall not be eaten. 42Whatever goes on its belly, and whatever goes on all fours, or whatever has many feet, all the swarming things that swarm upon the earth, you shall not eat; for they are an abomination. 43You shall not make yourselves abominable with any swarming thing that swarms; and you shall not defile yourselves with them, lest you become unclean. 44For I am the LORD your God; consecrate yourselves therefore, and be holy, for I am holy.

11:2-47: Deut 14:3–21.
11:44-45: Lev 19:2; 20:7, 26; 1 Pet 1:16.
* 11:1: These regulations concerning what is ritually pure or impure depend, for the most part, on circumstances peculiar to that time; e.g., animals, such as the pig, used in pagan sacrifices. Some correspond to ancient taboos.

You shall not defile yourselves with any swarming thing that crawls upon the earth. [45]For I am the Lord who brought you up out of the land of Egypt, to be your God; you shall therefore be holy, for I am holy."

46 This is the law pertaining to beast and bird and every living creature that moves through the waters and every creature that swarms upon the earth, [47]to make a distinction between the unclean and the clean and between the living creature that may be eaten and the living creature that may not be eaten.

Purification of Women

12 The Lord said to Moses, [2]"Say to the sons of Israel, If a woman conceives, and bears a male child, then she shall be unclean seven days; as at the time of her menstruation, she shall be unclean. [3]And on the eighth day the flesh of his foreskin shall be circumcised. [4]Then she shall continue for thirty-three days in the blood of her purifying; she shall not touch any hallowed thing, nor come into the sanctuary, until the days of her purifying are completed. [5]But if she bears a female child, then she shall be unclean two weeks, as in her menstruation; and she shall continue in the blood of her purifying for sixty-six days.

6 "And when the days of her purifying are completed, whether for a son or for a daughter, she shall bring to the priest at the door of the tent of meeting a lamb a year old for a burnt offering, and a young pigeon or a turtledove for a sin offering, [7]and he shall offer it before the Lord, and make atonement for her; then she shall be clean from the flow of her blood. This is the law for her who bears a child, either male or female. [8]And if she cannot afford a lamb, then she shall take two turtledoves or two young pigeons, one for a burnt offering and the other for a sin offering; and the priest shall make atonement for her, and she shall be clean."

Skin Diseases

13 The Lord said to Moses and Aaron, [2]"When a man has on the skin of his body a swelling or an eruption or a spot, and it turns into a leprous disease on the skin of his body, then he shall be brought to Aaron the priest or to one of his sons the priests, [3]and the priest shall examine the diseased spot on the skin of his body; and if the hair in the diseased spot has turned white and the disease appears to be deeper than the skin of his body, it is a leprous disease; when the priest has examined him he shall pronounce him unclean. [4]But if the spot is white in the skin of his body, and appears no deeper than the skin, and the hair in it has not turned white, the priest shall shut up the diseased person for seven days; [5]and the priest shall examine him on the seventh day, and if in his eyes the disease is checked and the disease has not spread in the

skin, then the priest shall shut him up seven days more; [6]and the priest shall examine him again on the seventh day, and if the diseased spot is dim and the disease has not spread in the skin, then the priest shall pronounce him clean; it is only an eruption; and he shall wash his clothes, and be clean. [7]But if the eruption spreads in the skin, after he has shown himself to the priest for his cleansing, he shall appear again before the priest; [8]and the priest shall make an examination, and if the eruption has spread in the skin, then the priest shall pronounce him unclean; it is leprosy.

9 "When a man is afflicted with leprosy, he shall be brought to the priest; [10]and the priest shall make an examination, and if there is a white swelling in the skin, which has turned the hair white, and there is quick raw flesh in the swelling, [11]it is a chronic leprosy in the skin of his body, and the priest shall pronounce him unclean; he shall not shut him up, for he is unclean. [12]And if the leprosy breaks out in the skin, so that the leprosy covers all the skin of the diseased person from head to foot, so far as the priest can see, [13]then the priest shall make an examination, and if the leprosy has covered all his body, he shall pronounce him clean of the disease; it has all turned white, and he is clean. [14]But when raw flesh appears on him, he shall be unclean. [15]And the priest shall examine the raw flesh, and pronounce him unclean; raw flesh is unclean, for it is leprosy. [16]But if the raw flesh turns again and is changed to white, then he shall come to the priest, [17]and the priest shall examine him, and if the disease has turned white, then the priest shall pronounce the diseased person clean; he is clean.

18 "And when there is in the skin of one's body a boil that has healed, [19]and in the place of the boil there comes a white swelling or a reddish-white spot, then it shall be shown to the priest; [20]and the priest shall make an examination, and if it appears deeper than the skin and its hair has turned white, then the priest shall pronounce him unclean; it is the disease of leprosy, it has broken out in the boil. [21]But if the priest examines it, and the hair on it is not white and it is not deeper than the skin, but is dim, then the priest shall shut him up seven days; [22]and if it spreads in the skin, then the priest shall pronounce him unclean; it is diseased. [23]But if the spot remains in one place and does not spread, it is the scar of the boil; and the priest shall pronounce him clean.

24 "Or, when the body has a burn on its skin and the raw flesh of the burn becomes a spot, reddish-white or white, [25]the priest shall examine it, and if the hair in the spot has turned white and it appears deeper than the skin, then it is leprosy;

11:46: Num 5:2, 3.
12:1–8: Lk 2:22–24.

it has broken out in the burn, and the priest shall pronounce him unclean; it is a leprous disease. [26]But if the priest examines it, and the hair in the spot is not white and it is no deeper than the skin, but is dim, the priest shall shut him up seven days, [27]and the priest shall examine him the seventh day; if it is spreading in the skin, then the priest shall pronounce him unclean; it is a leprous disease. [28]But if the spot remains in one place and does not spread in the skin, but is dim, it is a swelling from the burn, and the priest shall pronounce him clean; for it is the scar of the burn.

29 "When a man or woman has a disease on the head or the beard, [30]the priest shall examine the disease; and if it appears deeper than the skin, and the hair in it is yellow and thin, then the priest shall pronounce him unclean; it is an itch, a leprosy of the head or the beard. [31]And if the priest examines the itching disease, and it appears no deeper than the skin and there is no black hair in it, then the priest shall shut up the person with the itching disease for seven days, [32]and on the seventh day the priest shall examine the disease; and if the itch has not spread, and there is in it no yellow hair, and the itch appears to be no deeper than the skin, [33]then he shall shave himself, but the itch he shall not shave; and the priest shall shut up the person with the itching disease for seven days more; [34]and on the seventh day the priest shall examine the itch, and if the itch has not spread in the skin and it appears to be no deeper than the skin, then the priest shall pronounce him clean; and he shall wash his clothes, and be clean. [35]But if the itch spreads in the skin after his cleansing, [36]then the priest shall examine him, and if the itch has spread in the skin, the priest need not seek for the yellow hair; he is unclean. [37]But if in his eyes the itch is checked, and black hair has grown in it, the itch is healed, he is clean; and the priest shall pronounce him clean.

38 "When a man or a woman has spots on the skin of the body, white spots, [39]the priest shall make an examination, and if the spots on the skin of the body are of a dull white, it is tetter that has broken out in the skin; he is clean.

40 "If a man's hair has fallen from his head, he is bald but he is clean. [41]And if a man's hair has fallen from his forehead and temples, he has baldness of the forehead but he is clean. [42]But if there is on the bald head or the bald forehead a reddish-white diseased spot, it is leprosy breaking out on his bald head or his bald forehead. [43]Then the priest shall examine him, and if the diseased swelling is reddish-white on his bald head or on his bald forehead, like the appearance of leprosy in the skin of the body, [44]he is a leprous man, he is unclean; the priest must pronounce him unclean; his disease is on his head.

45 "The leper who has the disease shall wear torn clothes and let the hair of his head hang loose, and he shall cover his upper lip and cry, 'Unclean, unclean.' [46]He shall remain unclean as long as he has the disease; he is unclean; he shall dwell alone in a habitation outside the camp.

47 "When there is a leprous disease in a garment, whether a woolen or a linen garment, [48]in warp or woof of linen or wool, or in a skin or in anything made of skin, [49]if the disease shows greenish or reddish in the garment, whether in warp or woof or in skin or in anything made of skin, it is a leprous disease and shall be shown to the priest. [50]And the priest shall examine the disease, and shut up that which has the disease for seven days; [51]then he shall examine the disease on the seventh day. If the disease has spread in the garment, in warp or woof, or in the skin, whatever be the use of the skin, the disease is a malignant leprosy; it is unclean. [52]And he shall burn the garment, whether diseased in warp or woof, woolen or linen, or anything of skin, for it is a malignant leprosy; it shall be burned in the fire.

53 "And if the priest examines, and the disease has not spread in the garment in warp or woof or in anything of skin, [54]then the priest shall command that they wash the thing in which is the disease, and he shall shut it up seven days more; [55]and the priest shall examine the diseased thing after it has been washed. And if the diseased spot has not changed color, though the disease has not spread, it is unclean; you shall burn it in the fire, whether the leprous spot is on the back or on the front.

56 "But if the priest examines, and the disease is dim after it is washed, he shall tear the spot out of the garment or the skin or the warp or woof; [57]then if it appears again in the garment, in warp or woof, or in anything of skin, it is spreading; you shall burn with fire that in which is the disease. [58]But the garment, warp or woof, or anything of skin from which the disease departs when you have washed it, shall then be washed a second time, and be clean."

59 This is the law for a leprous disease in a garment of wool or linen, either in warp or woof, or in anything of skin, to decide whether it is clean or unclean.

The Cleansing of Lepers

14 The LORD said to Moses, [2]"This shall be the law of the leper for the day of his cleansing. He shall be brought to the priest; [3]and the priest shall go out of the camp, and the priest shall make an examination. Then, if the leprous disease is healed in the leper, [4]the priest shall command them to take for him who is to be cleansed two living clean birds and cedarwood

14:2-32: Mt 8:4; Mk 1:44; Lk 5:14; 17:14.

and scarlet stuff and hyssop; [5]and the priest shall command them to kill one of the birds in an earthen vessel over running water. [6]He shall take the living bird with the cedarwood and the scarlet stuff and the hyssop, and dip them and the living bird in the blood of the bird that was killed over the running water; [7]and he shall sprinkle it seven times upon him who is to be cleansed of leprosy; then he shall pronounce him clean, and shall let the living bird go into the open field. [8]And he who is to be cleansed shall wash his clothes, and shave off all his hair, and bathe himself in water, and he shall be clean; and after that he shall come into the camp, but shall dwell outside his tent seven days. [9]And on the seventh day he shall shave all his hair off his head; he shall shave off his beard and his eyebrows, all his hair. Then he shall wash his clothes, and bathe his body in water, and he shall be clean.

10 "And on the eighth day he shall take two male lambs without blemish, and one ewe lamb a year old without blemish, and a cereal offering of three tenths of an ephah of fine flour mixed with oil, and one log of oil. [11]And the priest who cleanses him shall set the man who is to be cleansed and these things before the Lord, at the door of the tent of meeting. [12]And the priest shall take one of the male lambs, and offer it for a guilt offering, along with the log of oil, and wave them for a wave offering before the Lord; [13]and he shall kill the lamb in the place where they kill the sin offering and the burnt offering, in the holy place; for the guilt offering, like the sin offering, belongs to the priest; it is most holy. [14]The priest shall take some of the blood of the guilt offering, and the priest shall put it on the tip of the right ear of him who is to be cleansed, and on the thumb of his right hand, and on the great toe of his right foot. [15]Then the priest shall take some of the log of oil, and pour it into the palm of his own left hand, [16]and dip his right finger in the oil that is in his left hand, and sprinkle some oil with his finger seven times before the Lord. [17]And some of the oil that remains in his hand the priest shall put on the tip of the right ear of him who is to be cleansed, and on the thumb of his right hand, and on the great toe of his right foot, upon the blood of the guilt offering; [18]and the rest of the oil that is in the priest's hand he shall put on the head of him who is to be cleansed. Then the priest shall make atonement for him before the Lord. [19]The priest shall offer the sin offering, to make atonement for him who is to be cleansed from his uncleanness. And afterward he shall kill the burnt offering; [20]and the priest shall offer the burnt offering and the cereal offering on the altar. Thus the priest shall make atonement for him, and he shall be clean.

21 "But if he is poor and cannot afford so much, then he shall take one male lamb for a guilt offering to be waved, to make atonement for him, and a tenth of an ephah of fine flour mixed with oil for a cereal offering, and a log of oil; [22]also two turtledoves or two young pigeons, such as he can afford; the one shall be a sin offering and the other a burnt offering. [23]And on the eighth day he shall bring them for his cleansing to the priest, to the door of the tent of meeting, before the Lord; [24]and the priest shall take the lamb of the guilt offering, and the log of oil, and the priest shall wave them for a wave offering before the Lord. [25]And he shall kill the lamb of the guilt offering; and the priest shall take some of the blood of the guilt offering, and put it on the tip of the right ear of him who is to be cleansed, and on the thumb of his right hand, and on the great toe of his right foot. [26]And the priest shall pour some of the oil into the palm of his own left hand; [27]and shall sprinkle with his right finger some of the oil that is in his left hand seven times before the Lord; [28]and the priest shall put some of the oil that is in his hand on the tip of the right ear of him who is to be cleansed, and on the thumb of his right hand, and the great toe of his right foot, in the place where the blood of the guilt offering was put; [29]and the rest of the oil that is in the priest's hand he shall put on the head of him who is to be cleansed, to make atonement for him before the Lord. [30]And he shall offer, of the turtledoves or young pigeons such as he can afford, [31]one * for a sin offering and the other for a burnt offering, along with a cereal offering; and the priest shall make atonement before the Lord for him who is being cleansed. [32]This is the law for him in whom is a leprous disease, who cannot afford the offerings for his cleansing."

Cleansing of Leprous Houses

33 The Lord said to Moses and Aaron, [34]"When you come into the land of Canaan, which I give you for a possession, and I put a leprous disease in a house in the land of your possession, [35]then he who owns the house shall come and tell the priest, 'There seems to me to be some sort of disease in my house.' [36]Then the priest shall command that they empty the house before the priest goes to examine the disease, lest all that is in the house be declared unclean; and afterward the priest shall go in to see the house. [37]And he shall examine the disease; and if the disease is in the walls of the house with greenish or reddish spots, and if it appears to be deeper than the surface, [38]then the priest shall go out of the house to the door of the house, and shut up the house seven days. [39]And the priest shall come again on the seventh day, and look; and if the disease has spread in the walls of the house, [40]then the priest shall command that they take out the stones in

---

* Gk Syr: Heb *afford,* [31]*such as he can afford, one.*

which is the disease and throw them into an unclean place outside the city; [41]and he shall cause the inside of the house to be scraped round about, and the plaster that they scrape off they shall pour into an unclean place outside the city; [42]then they shall take other stones and put them in the place of those stones, and he shall take other plaster and plaster the house.

43 "If the disease breaks out again in the house, after he has taken out the stones and scraped the house and plastered it, [44]then the priest shall go and look; and if the disease has spread in the house, it is a malignant leprosy in the house; it is unclean. [45]And he shall break down the house, its stones and timber and all the plaster of the house; and he shall carry them forth out of the city to an unclean place. [46]Moreover he who enters the house while it is shut up shall be unclean until the evening; [47]and he who lies down in the house shall wash his clothes; and he who eats in the house shall wash his clothes.

48 "But if the priest comes and makes an examination, and the disease has not spread in the house after the house was plastered, then the priest shall pronounce the house clean, for the disease is healed. [49]And for the cleansing of the house he shall take two small birds, with cedarwood and scarlet stuff and hyssop, [50]and shall kill one of the birds in an earthen vessel over running water, [51]and shall take the cedarwood and the hyssop and the scarlet stuff, along with the living bird, and dip them in the blood of the bird that was killed and in the running water, and sprinkle the house seven times. [52]Thus he shall cleanse the house with the blood of the bird, and with the running water, and with the living bird, and with the cedarwood and hyssop and scarlet stuff; [53]and he shall let the living bird go out of the city into the open field; so he shall make atonement for the house, and it shall be clean."

54 This is the law for any leprous disease: for an itch, [55]for leprosy in a garment or in a house, [56]and for a swelling or an eruption or a spot, [57]to show when it is unclean and when it is clean. This is the law for leprosy.

Concerning Men's Bodily Discharges

15 The LORD said to Moses and Aaron, [2] "Say to the sons of Israel, When any man has a discharge from his body, his discharge is unclean. [3]And this is the law of his uncleanness for a discharge: whether his body runs with his discharge, or his body is stopped from discharge, it is uncleanness in him. [4]Every bed on which he who has the discharge lies shall be unclean; and everything on which he sits shall be unclean. [5]And any one who touches his bed shall wash his clothes, and bathe himself in water, and be unclean until the evening. [6]And whoever sits on anything on which he who has the discharge has sat

shall wash his clothes, and bathe himself in water, and be unclean until the evening. [7]And whoever touches the body of him who has the discharge shall wash his clothes, and bathe himself in water, and be unclean until the evening. [8]And if he who has the discharge spits on one who is clean, then he shall wash his clothes, and bathe himself in water, and be unclean until the evening. [9]And any saddle on which he who has the discharge rides shall be unclean. [10]And whoever touches anything that was under him shall be unclean until the evening; and he who carries such a thing shall wash his clothes, and bathe himself in water, and be unclean until the evening. [11]Any one whom he that has the discharge touches without having rinsed his hands in water shall wash his clothes, and bathe himself in water, and be unclean until the evening. [12]And the earthen vessel which he who has the discharge touches shall be broken; and every vessel of wood shall be rinsed in water.

13 "And when he who has a discharge is cleansed of his discharge, then he shall count for himself seven days for his cleansing, and wash his clothes; and he shall bathe his body in running water, and shall be clean. [14]And on the eighth day he shall take two turtledoves or two young pigeons, and come before the LORD to the door of the tent of meeting, and give them to the priest; [15]and the priest shall offer them, one for a sin offering and the other for a burnt offering; and the priest shall make atonement for him before the LORD for his discharge.

16 "And if a man has an emission of semen, he shall bathe his whole body in water, and be unclean until the evening. [17]And every garment and every skin on which the semen comes shall be washed with water, and be unclean until the evening. [18]If a man lies with a woman and has an emission of semen, both of them shall bathe themselves in water, and be unclean until the evening.

Concerning Women's Bodily Discharges

19 "When a woman has a discharge of blood which is her regular discharge from her body, she shall be in her impurity for seven days, and whoever touches her shall be unclean until the evening. [20]And everything upon which she lies during her impurity shall be unclean; everything also upon which she sits shall be unclean. [21]And whoever touches her bed shall wash his clothes, and bathe himself in water, and be unclean until the evening. [22]And whoever touches anything upon which she sits shall wash his clothes, and bathe himself in water, and be unclean until the evening; [23]whether it is the bed or anything upon which she sits, when he touches it he shall be unclean until the evening. [24]And if any man lies

15:24: Lev 18:19; 20:18.

84

with her, and her impurity is on him, he shall be unclean seven days; and every bed on which he lies shall be unclean.

25 "If a woman has a discharge of blood for many days, not at the time of her impurity, or if she has a discharge beyond the time of her impurity, all the days of the discharge she shall continue in uncleanness; as in the days of her impurity, she shall be unclean. [26]Every bed on which she lies, all the days of her discharge, shall be to her as the bed of her impurity; and everything on which she sits shall be unclean, as in the uncleanness of her impurity. [27]And whoever touches these things shall be unclean, and shall wash his clothes, and bathe himself in water, and be unclean until the evening. [28]But if she is cleansed of her discharge, she shall count for herself seven days, and after that she shall be clean. [29]And on the eighth day she shall take two turtledoves or two young pigeons, and bring them to the priest, to the door of the tent of meeting. [30]And the priest shall offer one for a sin offering and the other for a burnt offering; and the priest shall make atonement for her before the LORD for her unclean discharge.

The Law concerning Discharges

31 "Thus you shall keep the sons of Israel separate from their uncleanness, lest they die in their uncleanness by defiling my tabernacle that is in their midst."

32 This is the law for him who has a discharge and for him who has an emission of semen, becoming unclean thereby; [33]also for her who is sick with her impurity; that is, for any one, male or female, who has a discharge, and for the man who lies with a woman who is unclean.

The Day of Atonement

16 The LORD spoke to Moses, after the death of the two sons of Aaron, when they drew near before the LORD and died; [2]and the LORD said to Moses, "Tell Aaron your brother not to come at all times into the holy place within the veil, before the mercy seat which is upon the ark, lest he die; for I will appear in the cloud upon the mercy seat. [3]But thus shall Aaron come into the holy place: with a young bull for a sin offering and a ram for a burnt offering. [4]He shall put on the holy linen coat, and shall have the linen breeches on his body, be girded with the linen sash, and wear the linen turban; these are the holy garments. He shall bathe his body in water, and then put them on. [5]And he shall take from the congregation of the sons of Israel two male goats for a sin offering, and one ram for a burnt offering.

6 "And Aaron shall offer the bull as a sin offering for himself, and shall make atonement for himself and for his house. [7]Then he shall take the two goats, and set them before the LORD at the door of the tent of meeting; [8]and Aaron shall cast

lots upon the two goats, one lot for the LORD and the other lot for Aza'zel. [9]And Aaron shall present the goat on which the lot fell for the LORD, and offer it as a sin offering; [10]but the goat on which the lot fell for Aza'zel shall be presented alive before the LORD to make atonement over it, that it may be sent away into the wilderness to Azazel.

11 "Aaron shall present the bull as a sin offering for himself, and shall make atonement for himself and for his house; he shall kill the bull as a sin offering for himself. [12]And he shall take a censer full of coals of fire from the altar before the LORD, and two handfuls of sweet incense beaten small; and he shall bring it within the veil [13]and put the incense on the fire before the LORD, that the cloud of the incense may cover the mercy seat which is upon the covenant, lest he die; [14]and he shall take some of the blood of the bull, and sprinkle it with his finger on the front of the mercy seat, and before the mercy seat he shall sprinkle the blood with his finger seven times.

15 "Then he shall kill the goat of the sin offering which is for the people, and bring its blood within the veil, and do with its blood as he did with the blood of the bull, sprinkling it upon the mercy seat and before the mercy seat; [16]thus shall make atonement for the holy place, because of the uncleannesses of the sons of Israel, and because of their transgressions, all their sins; and so he shall do for the tent of meeting, which abides with them in the midst of their uncleannesses. [17]There shall be no man in the tent of meeting when he enters to make atonement in the holy place until he comes out and has made atonement for himself and for his house and for all the assembly of Israel. [18]Then he shall go out to the altar which is before the LORD and make atonement for it, and shall take some of the blood of the bull and of the blood of the goat, and put it on the horns of the altar round about. [19]And he shall sprinkle some of the blood upon it with his finger seven times, and cleanse it and hallow it from the uncleannesses of the sons of Israel.

20 "And when he has made an end of atoning for the holy place and the tent of meeting and the altar, he shall present the live goat; [21]and Aaron shall lay both his hands upon the head of the live goat, and confess over him all the iniquities of the sons of Israel, and all their transgressions, all their sins; and he shall put them upon the head of the goat, and send him away into the wilderness by the hand of a man who is in readiness. [22]The goat shall bear all their iniquities upon him to a solitary land; and he shall let the goat go in the wilderness.

23 "Then Aaron shall come into the tent of meeting, and shall put off the linen garments

---

16:2, 12: Heb 6:19; 9:7, 25.

which he put on when he went into the holy place, and shall leave them there; [24]and he shall bathe his body in water in a holy place, and put on his garments, and come forth, and offer his burnt offering and the burnt offering of the people, and make atonement for himself and for the people. [25]And the fat of the sin offering he shall burn upon the altar. [26]And he who lets the goat go to Aza′zel shall wash his clothes and bathe his body in water, and afterward he may come into the camp. [27]And the bull for the sin offering and the goat for the sin offering, whose blood was brought in to make atonement in the holy place, shall be carried forth outside the camp; their skin and their flesh and their dung shall be burned with fire. [28]And he who burns them shall wash his clothes and bathe his body in water, and afterward he may come into the camp.

[29] "And it shall be a statute to you for ever that in the seventh month, on the tenth day of the month, you shall afflict yourselves, and shall do no work, either the native or the stranger who sojourns among you; [30]for on this day shall atonement be made for you, to cleanse you; from all your sins you shall be clean before the Lord. [31]It is a sabbath of solemn rest to you, and you shall afflict yourselves; it is a statute for ever. [32]And the priest who is anointed and consecrated as priest in his father's place shall make atonement, wearing the holy linen garments; [33]he shall make atonement for the sanctuary, and he shall make atonement for the tent of meeting and for the altar, and he shall make atonement for the priests and for all the people of the assembly. [34]And this shall be an everlasting statute for you, that atonement may be made for the sons of Israel once in the year because of all their sins." And Moses did as the Lord commanded him.

The Slaughter of Animals

17 * And the Lord said to Moses, [2]"Say to Aaron and his sons, and to all the sons of Israel, This is the thing which the Lord has commanded. [3]If any man of the house of Israel kills an ox or a lamb or a goat in the camp, or kills it outside the camp, [4]and does not bring it to the door of the tent of meeting, to offer it as a gift to the Lord before the tabernacle of the Lord, bloodguilt shall be imputed to that man; he has shed blood; and that man shall be cut off from among his people. [5]This is to the end that the sons of Israel may bring their sacrifices which they slay in the open field, that they may bring them to the Lord, to the priest at the door of the tent of meeting, and slay them as sacrifices of peace offerings to the Lord; [6]and the priest shall sprinkle the blood on the altar of the Lord at the door of the tent of meeting, and burn the fat for a pleasing odor to the Lord. [7]So they shall no more slay their sacrifices for satyrs, after whom they play the harlot. This shall be a statute for ever to them throughout their generations.

[8] "And you shall say to them, Any man of the house of Israel, or of the strangers that sojourn among them, who offers a burnt offering or sacrifice, [9]and does not bring it to the door of the tent of meeting, to sacrifice it to the Lord; that man shall be cut off from his people.

Eating of Blood Forbidden

[10] "If any man of the house of Israel or of the strangers that sojourn among them eats any blood, I will set my face against that person who eats blood, and will cut him off from among his people. [11]For the life of the flesh is in the blood; and I have given it for you upon the altar to make atonement for your souls; for it is the blood that makes atonement, by reason of the life. [12]Therefore I have said to the sons of Israel, No person among you shall eat blood, neither shall any stranger who sojourns among you eat blood. [13]Any man also of the sons of Israel, or of the strangers that sojourn among them, who takes in hunting any beast or bird that may be eaten shall pour out its blood and cover it with dust.

[14] "For the life of every creature is the blood of it; • therefore I have said to the sons of Israel, You shall not eat the blood of any creature, for the life of every creature is its blood; whoever eats it shall be cut off. [15]And every person that eats what dies of itself or what is torn by beasts, whether he is a native or a sojourner, shall wash his clothes, and bathe himself in water, and be unclean until the evening; then he shall be clean. [16]But if he does not wash them or bathe his flesh, he shall bear his iniquity."

18 And the Lord said to Moses, [2]"Say to the sons of Israel, I am the Lord your God. [3]You shall not do as they do in the land of Egypt, where you dwelt, and you shall not do as they do in the land of Canaan, to which I am bringing you. You shall not walk in their statutes. [4]You shall do my ordinances and keep my statutes and walk in them. I am the Lord your God. [5]You shall therefore keep my statutes and my ordinances, by doing which a man shall live: I am the Lord.

Laws concerning Sexual Relations

[6] "None of you shall approach any one near of kin to him to uncover nakedness. I am the Lord. [7]You shall not uncover the nakedness of your father, which is the nakedness of your mother; she is your mother, you shall not uncover her nakedness. [8]You shall not uncover the nakedness

---

• Gk Syr Compare Vg: Heb *for the life of all flesh, its blood is in its life.*
16:27: Heb 13:11.
17:10–16: Lev 3:17; 7:26, 27; 19:26; Deut 12:16, 23–25.
18:5: Lk 10:28; Rom 10:5; Gal 3:12.
18:7: Lev 20:11.
* 17:1: The so-called "Code of Holiness" (chapters 17–26) implies an exalted idea of the holiness and otherness of the God of Israel.

of your father's wife; it is your father's nakedness. [9]You shall not uncover the nakedness of your sister, the daughter of your father or the daughter of your mother, whether born at home or born abroad. [10]You shall not uncover the nakedness of your son's daughter or of your daughter's daughter, for their nakedness is your own nakedness. [11]You shall not uncover the nakedness of your father's wife's daughter, begotten by your father, since she is your sister. [12]You shall not uncover the nakedness of your father's sister; she is your father's near kinswoman. [13]You shall not uncover the nakedness of your mother's sister, for she is your mother's near kinswoman. [14]You shall not uncover the nakedness of your father's brother, that is, you shall not approach his wife; she is your aunt. [15]You shall not uncover the nakedness of your daughter-in-law; she is your son's wife, you shall not uncover her nakedness. [16]You shall not uncover the nakedness of your brother's wife; she is your brother's nakedness. [17]You shall not uncover the nakedness of a woman and of her daughter, and you shall not take her son's daughter or her daughter's daughter to uncover her nakedness; they are your [f] near kinswomen; it is wickedness. [18]And you shall not take a woman as a rival wife to her sister, uncovering her nakedness while her sister is yet alive.

19 "You shall not approach a woman to uncover her nakedness while she is in her menstrual uncleanness. [20]And you shall not lie carnally with your neighbor's wife, and defile yourself with her. [21]You shall not give any of your children to devote them by fire to Mo'lech, and so profane the name of your God: I am the LORD. [22]You shall not lie with a male as with a woman; it is an abomination. [23]And you shall not lie with any beast and defile yourself with it, neither shall any woman give herself to a beast to lie with it: it is perversion.

24 "Do not defile yourselves by any of these things, for by all these the nations I am casting out before you defiled themselves; [25]and the land became defiled, so that I punished its iniquity, and the land vomited out its inhabitants. [26]But you shall keep my statutes and my ordinances and do none of these abominations, either the native or the stranger who sojourns among you [27](for all of these abominations the men of the land did, who were before you, so that the land became defiled); [28]lest the land vomit you out, when you defile it, as it vomited out the nation that was before you. [29]For whoever shall do any of these abominations, the persons that do them shall be cut off from among their people. [30]So keep my charge never to practice any of these abominable customs which were practiced before you, and never to defile yourselves by them: I am the LORD your God."

Ritual and Moral Holiness

19 And the LORD said to Moses, [2]"Say to all the congregation of the sons of Israel, You shall be holy; for I the LORD your God am holy. [3]Every one of you shall revere his mother and his father, and you shall keep my sabbaths: I am the LORD your God. [4]Do not turn to idols or make for yourselves molten gods: I am the LORD your God.

5 "When you offer a sacrifice of peace offerings to the LORD, you shall offer it so that you may be accepted. [6]It shall be eaten the same day you offer it, or on the next day; and anything left over until the third day shall be burned with fire. [7]If it is eaten at all on the third day, it is an abomination; it will not be accepted, [8]and every one who eats it shall bear his iniquity, because he has profaned a holy thing of the LORD; and that person shall be cut off from his people.

9 "When you reap the harvest of your land, you shall not reap your field to its very border, neither shall you gather the gleanings after your harvest. [10]And you shall not strip your vineyard bare, neither shall you gather the fallen grapes of your vineyard; you shall leave them for the poor and for the sojourner: I am the LORD your God.

11 "You shall not steal, nor deal falsely, nor lie to one another. [12]And you shall not swear by my name falsely, and so profane the name of your God: I am the LORD.

13 "You shall not oppress your neighbor or rob him. The wages of a hired servant shall not remain with you all night until the morning. [14]You shall not curse the deaf or put a stumbling block before the blind, but you shall fear your God: I am the LORD.

15 "You shall do no injustice in judgment; you shall not be partial to the poor or defer to the great, but in righteousness shall you judge your neighbor. [16]You shall not go up and down as a slanderer among your people, and you shall not stand forth against the life [g] of your neighbor: I am the LORD.

---

[f] Gk: Heb lacks *your*.
[g] Heb *blood*.
18:9, 11: Lev 20:17; Deut 27:22.
18:12: Lev 20:19.
18:14: Lev 20:20.
18:15: Lev 20:12.
18:16: Lev 20:21.
18:17: Lev 20:14.
18:19: Lev 15:24; 20:18.
18:21: Lev 20:2–5.
18:22: Lev 20:13; Deut 23:18.
18:23: Ex 22:19; Lev 20:15, 16; Deut 27:21.
19:2: Lev 11:44, 45; 20:7, 26; 1 Pet 1:16.
19:3, 30: Ex 20:12; Deut 5:16; Ex 20:8; 23:12; 34:21; 35:23; Deut 5:12–15.
19:4: Ex 20:4; Lev 26:1; Deut 4:15–19; 27:15.
19:9, 10: Lev 23:22; Deut 24:20, 21.
19:11: Ex 20:15, 16; Deut 5:19.
19:12: Ex 20:7; Deut 5:11; Mt 5:33.
19:13: Deut 24:15; Jas 5:4.
19:14: Deut 27:18.
19:15: Ex 23:6; Deut 1:17.

17 "You shall not hate your brother in your heart, but you shall reason with your neighbor, lest you bear sin because of him. [18]You shall not take vengeance or bear any grudge against the sons of your own people, but you shall love your neighbor as yourself: I am the LORD.

19 "You shall keep my statutes. You shall not let your cattle breed with a different kind; you shall not sow your field with two kinds of seed; nor shall there come upon you a garment of cloth made of two kinds of stuff.

20 "If a man lies carnally with a woman who is a slave, betrothed to another man and not yet ransomed or given her freedom, an inquiry shall be held. They shall not be put to death, because she was not free; [21]but he shall bring a guilt offering for himself to the LORD, to the door of the tent of meeting, a ram for a guilt offering. [22]And the priest shall make atonement for him with the ram of the guilt offering before the LORD for his sin which he has committed; and the sin which he has committed shall be forgiven him.

23 "When you come into the land and plant all kinds of trees for food, then you shall count their fruit as forbidden; [h] three years it shall be forbidden to you, it must not be eaten. [24]And in the fourth year all their fruit shall be holy, an offering of praise to the LORD. [25]But in the fifth year you may eat of their fruit, that they may yield more richly for you: I am the LORD your God.

26 "You shall not eat any flesh with the blood in it. You shall not practice augury or witchcraft. [27]You shall not round off the hair on your temples or mar the edges of your beard. [28]You shall not make any cuttings in your flesh on account of the dead or tattoo any marks upon you: I am the LORD.

29 "Do not profane your daughter by making her a harlot, lest the land fall into harlotry and the land become full of wickedness. [30]You shall keep my sabbaths and reverence my sanctuary: I am the LORD.

31 "Do not turn to mediums or wizards; do not seek them out, to be defiled by them: I am the LORD your God.

32 "You shall rise up before the hoary head, and honor the face of an old man, and you shall fear your God: I am the LORD.

33 "When a stranger sojourns with you in your land, you shall not do him wrong. [34]The stranger who sojourns with you shall be to you as the native among you, and you shall love him as yourself; for you were strangers in the land of Egypt: I am the LORD your God.

35 "You shall do no wrong in judgment, in measures of length or weight or quantity. [36]You shall have just balances, just weights, a just ephah, and a just hin: I am the LORD your God, who brought you out of the land of Egypt. [37]And you shall observe all my statutes and all my ordinances, and do them: I am the LORD."

Penalties for Violations

20 The LORD said to Moses, [2] "Say to the sons of Israel, Any man of the sons of Israel, or of the strangers that sojourn in Israel, who gives any of his children to Mo'lech shall be put to death; the people of the land shall stone him with stones. [3]I myself will set my face against that man, and will cut him off from among his people, because he has given one of his children to Mo'lech, defiling my sanctuary and profaning my holy name. [4]And if the people of the land do at all hide their eyes from that man, when he gives one of his children to Mo'lech, and do not put him to death, [5]then I will set my face against that man and against his family, and will cut them off from among their people, him and all who follow him in playing the harlot after Mo'lech.

6 "If a person turns to mediums and wizards, playing the harlot after them, I will set my face against that person, and will cut him off from among his people. [7]Consecrate yourselves therefore, and be holy; for I am the LORD your God. [8]Keep my statutes, and do them; I am the LORD who sanctify you. [9]For every one who curses his father or his mother shall be put to death; he has cursed his father or his mother, his blood is upon him.

10 "If a man commits adultery with the wife of [i] his neighbor, both the adulterer and the adulteress shall be put to death. [11]The man who lies with his father's wife has uncovered his father's nakedness; both of them shall be put to death, their blood is upon them. [12]If a man lies with his daughter-in-law, both of them shall be put to death; they have committed incest, their blood is upon them. [13]If a man lies with a male as with a woman, both of them have committed an abomination; they shall be put to death, their blood is upon them. [14]If a man takes a wife and her mother also, it is wickedness; they shall be burned with fire, both he and they, that there may be no wickedness among you. [15]If a man lies with a beast, he

---

[h] Heb their uncircumcision.
[i] Heb repeats if a man commits adultery with the wife of.
19:18: Mt 5:43; 19:19; 22:39; Mk 12:31; Lk 10:27; Rom 13:9; Gal 5:14; Jas 2:8.
19:19: Deut 22:9, 11.
19:26: Lev 3:17; 7:26, 27; 17:10–16; Deut 12:16, 23–25; 18:10.
19:27: Lev 21:5; Deut 14:1.
19:29: Deut 23:17, 18.
19:30: Ex 20:8–11; 23:12; 34:21; 35:2, 3; Lev 19:3; 26:2; Deut 5:12–15.
19:31: Lev 20:6, 27.
19:33: Ex 22:21.
20:2–5: Lev 18:21.
20:6: Lev 19:31.
20:7: Lev 11:44, 45; 19:2; 20:26; 1 Pet 1:16.
20:9: Ex 21:17; Deut 27:16.
20:10: Ex 20:14; Lev 18:20; Deut 5:18.
20:11: Lev 18:7, 8.
20:12: Lev 18:15.
20:13: Lev 18:22.
20:14: Lev 18:17; Deut 27:23.
20:15, 16: Lev 18:23.

shall be put to death; and you shall kill the beast. [16]If a woman approaches any beast and lies with it, you shall kill the woman and the beast; they shall be put to death, their blood is upon them.

17 "If a man takes his sister, a daughter of his father or a daughter of his mother, and sees her nakedness, and she sees his nakedness, it is a shameful thing, and they shall be cut off in the sight of the children of their people; he has uncovered his sister's nakedness, he shall bear his iniquity. [18]If a man lies with a woman having her sickness, and uncovers her nakedness, he has made naked her fountain, and she has uncovered the fountain of her blood; both of them shall be cut off from among their people. [19]You shall not uncover the nakedness of your mother's sister or of your father's sister, for that is to make naked one's near kin; they shall bear their iniquity. [20]If a man lies with his uncle's wife, he has uncovered his uncle's nakedness; they shall bear their sin, they shall die childless. [21]If a man takes his brother's wife, it is impurity; he has uncovered his brother's nakedness, they shall be childless.

22 "You shall therefore keep all my statutes and all my ordinances, and do them; that the land where I am bringing you to dwell may not vomit you out. [23]And you shall not walk in the customs of the nation which I am casting out before you; for they did all these things, and therefore I abhorred them. [24]But I have said to you, 'You shall inherit their land, and I will give it to you to possess, a land flowing with milk and honey.' I am the Lord your God, who have separated you from the peoples. [25]You shall therefore make a distinction between the clean beast and the unclean, and between the unclean bird and the clean; you shall not make yourselves abominable by beast or by bird or by anything with which the ground teems, which I have set apart for you to hold unclean. [26]You shall be holy to me; for I the Lord am holy, and have separated you from the peoples, that you should be mine.

27 "A man or a woman who is a medium or a wizard shall be put to death; they shall be stoned with stones, their blood shall be upon them."

The Holiness of Priests

21 And the Lord said to Moses, "Speak to the priests, the sons of Aaron, and say to them that none of them shall defile himself for the dead among his people, [2]except for his nearest of kin, his mother, his father, his son, his daughter, his brother, [3]or his virgin sister (who is near to him because she has had no husband; for her he may defile himself). [4]He shall not defile himself as a husband among his people and so profane himself. [5]They shall not make tonsures upon their heads, nor shave off the edges of their beards, nor make any cuttings in their flesh. [6]They shall be holy to their God, and not profane the name of their God; for they offer the offerings by fire to the Lord, the bread of their God; therefore they shall be holy. [7]They shall not marry a harlot or a woman who has been defiled; neither shall they marry a woman divorced from her husband; for the priest is holy to his God. [8]You shall consecrate him, for he offers the bread of your God; he shall be holy to you; for I the Lord, who sanctify you, am holy. [9]And the daughter of any priest, if she profanes herself by playing the harlot, profanes her father; she shall be burned with fire.

10 "The priest who is chief among his brethren, upon whose head the anointing oil is poured, and who has been consecrated to wear the garments, shall not let the hair of his head hang loose, nor tear his clothes; [11]he shall not go in to any dead body, nor defile himself, even for his father or for his mother; [12]neither shall he go out of the sanctuary, nor profane the sanctuary of his God; for the consecration of the anointing oil of his God is upon him: I am the Lord. [13]And he shall take a wife in her virginity. [14]A widow, or one divorced, or a woman who has been defiled, or a harlot, these he shall not marry; but he shall take to wife a virgin of his own people, [15]that he may not profane his children among his people; for I am the Lord who sanctify him."

16 And the Lord said to Moses, [17]"Say to Aaron, None of your descendants throughout their generations who has a blemish may approach to offer the bread of his God. [18]For no one who has a blemish shall draw near, a man blind or lame, or one who has a mutilated face or a limb too long, [19]or a man who has an injured foot or an injured hand, [20]or a hunchback, or a dwarf, or a man with a defect in his sight or an itching disease or scabs or crushed testicles; [21]no man of the descendants of Aaron the priest who has a blemish shall come near to offer the Lord's offerings by fire; since he has a blemish, he shall not come near to offer the bread of his God. [22]He may eat the bread of his God, both of the most holy and of the holy things, [23]but he shall not come near the veil or approach the altar, because he has a blemish, that he may not profane my sanctuaries; for I am the Lord who sanctify them." [24]So Moses spoke to Aaron and to his sons and to all the sons of Israel.

The Use of Holy Things

22 And the Lord said to Moses, [2]"Tell Aaron and his sons to keep away from the holy things of the sons of Israel, which they dedicate

20:17: Lev 18:9.
20:18: Lev 15:24; 18:19.
20:19: Lev 18:12, 13.
20:20: Lev 18:14.
20:21: Lev 18:16.
20:26: Lev 20:7.
20:27: Lev 19:31; 20:6.
21:1–3: Ezek 44:25.
21:5: Lev 19:27; Deut 14:1.

to me, so that they may not profane my holy name: I am the LORD. ³Say to them, 'If any one of all your descendants throughout your generations approaches the holy things, which the sons of Israel dedicate to the LORD, while he has an uncleanness, that person shall be cut off from my presence: I am the LORD. ⁴None of the line of Aaron who is a leper or suffers a discharge may eat of the holy things until he is clean. Whoever touches anything that is unclean through contact with the dead or a man who has had an emission of semen, ⁵and whoever touches a creeping thing by which he may be made unclean or a man from whom he may take uncleanness, whatever his uncleanness may be—⁶the person who touches any such shall be unclean until the evening and shall not eat of the holy things unless he has bathed his body in water. ⁷When the sun is down he shall be clean; and afterward he may eat of the holy things, because such are his food. ⁸That which dies of itself or is torn by beasts he shall not eat, defiling himself by it: I am the LORD.' ⁹They shall therefore keep my charge, lest they bear sin for it and die thereby when they profane it: I am the LORD who sanctify them.

10 "An outsider shall not eat of a holy thing. A sojourner of the priest's or a hired servant shall not eat of a holy thing; ¹¹but if a priest buys a slave as his property for money, the slave may eat of it; and those that are born in his house may eat of his food. ¹²If a priest's daughter is married to an outsider she shall not eat of the offering of the holy things. ¹³But if a priest's daughter is a widow or divorced, and has no child, and returns to her father's house, as in her youth, she may eat of her father's food; yet no outsider shall eat of it. ¹⁴And if a man eats of a holy thing unwittingly, he shall add the fifth of its value to it, and give the holy thing to the priest. ¹⁵The priests shall not profane the holy things of the sons of Israel, which they offer to the LORD, ¹⁶and so cause them to bear iniquity and guilt, by eating their holy things: for I am the LORD who sanctify them."

Acceptable Offerings

17 And the LORD said to Moses, ¹⁸"Say to Aaron and his sons and all the people of Israel, When any one of the house of Israel or of the sojourners in Israel presents his offering, whether in payment of a vow or as a freewill offering which is offered to the LORD as a burnt offering, ¹⁹to be accepted you shall offer a male without blemish, of the bulls or the sheep or the goats. ²⁰You shall not offer anything that has a blemish, for it will not be acceptable for you. ²¹And when any one offers a sacrifice of peace offerings to the LORD, to fulfil a vow or as a freewill offering, from the herd or from the flock, to be accepted it must be perfect; there shall be no blemish in it. ²²Animals blind or disabled or mutilated or having a discharge or an

itch or scabs, you shall not offer to the LORD or make of them an offering by fire upon the altar to the LORD. ²³A bull or a lamb which has a part too long or too short you may present for a freewill offering; but for a votive offering it cannot be accepted. ²⁴Any animal which has its testicles bruised or crushed or torn or cut, you shall not offer to the LORD or sacrifice within your land; ²⁵neither shall you offer as the bread of your God any such animals gotten from a foreigner. Since there is a blemish in them, because of their mutilation, they will not be accepted for you."

26 And the LORD said to Moses, ²⁷"When a bull or sheep or goat is born, it shall remain seven days with its mother; and from the eighth day on it shall be acceptable as an offering by fire to the LORD. ²⁸And whether the mother is a cow or a ewe, you shall not kill both her and her young in one day. ²⁹And when you sacrifice a sacrifice of thanksgiving to the LORD, you shall sacrifice it so that you may be accepted. ³⁰It shall be eaten on the same day, you shall leave none of it until morning: I am the LORD.

31 "So you shall keep my commandments and do them: I am the LORD. ³²And you shall not profane my holy name, but I will be hallowed among the sons of Israel; I am the LORD who sanctify you, ³³who brought you out of the land of Egypt to be your God: I am the LORD."

The Sabbath

23 The LORD said to Moses, ²"Say to the sons of Israel, The appointed feasts of the LORD which you shall proclaim as holy convocations, my appointed feasts, are these. ³Six days shall work be done; but on the seventh day is a sabbath of solemn rest, a holy convocation; you shall do no work; it is a sabbath to the LORD in all your dwellings.

The Passover

4 "These are the appointed feasts of the LORD, the holy convocations, which you shall proclaim at the time appointed for them. ⁵In the first month, on the fourteenth day of the month in the evening,ʲ is the LORD's Passover. ⁶And on the fifteenth day of the same month is the feast of unleavened bread to the LORD; seven days you shall eat unleavened bread. ⁷On the first day you shall have a holy convocation; you shall do no laborious work. ⁸But you shall present an offering by fire to the LORD seven days; on the seventh day is a holy convocation; you shall do no laborious work."

The Offering of First Fruits

9 And the LORD said to Moses, ¹⁰"Say to the sons of Israel, When you come into the land which I give you and reap its harvest, you shall bring the sheaf of the first fruits of your harvest

---

ʲ Heb *between the two evenings.*
22:12: Lev 7:31–36.
23:1–44: Ex 23:14–17; 34:22–24; Deut 16:1–17.

to the priest; [11]and he shall wave the sheaf before the Lord, that you may find acceptance; on the day after the sabbath the priest shall wave it. [12]And on the day when you wave the sheaf, you shall offer a male lamb a year old without blemish as a burnt offering to the Lord. [13]And the cereal offering with it shall be two tenths of an ephah of fine flour mixed with oil, to be offered by fire to the Lord, a pleasing odor; and the drink offering with it shall be of wine, a fourth of a hin. [14]And you shall eat neither bread nor grain parched or fresh until this same day, until you have brought the offering of your God: it is a statute for ever throughout your generations in all your dwellings.

The Feast of Weeks

15 "And you shall count from the day after the sabbath, from the day that you brought the sheaf of the wave offering; seven full weeks shall they be, [16]counting fifty days to the day after the seventh sabbath; then you shall present a cereal offering of new grain to the Lord. [17]You shall bring from your dwellings two loaves of bread to be waved, made of two tenths of an ephah; they shall be of fine flour, they shall be baked with leaven, as first fruits to the Lord. [18]And you shall present with the bread seven lambs a year old without blemish, and one young bull, and two rams; they shall be a burnt offering to the Lord, with their cereal offering and their drink offerings, an offering by fire, a pleasing odor to the Lord. [19]And you shall offer one male goat for a sin offering, and two male lambs a year old as a sacrifice of peace offerings. [20]And the priest shall wave them with the bread of the first fruits as a wave offering before the Lord, with the two lambs; they shall be holy to the Lord for the priest. [21]And you shall make proclamation on the same day; you shall hold a holy convocation; you shall do no laborious work: it is a statute for ever in all your dwellings throughout your generations.

22 "And when you reap the harvest of your land, you shall not reap your field to its very border, nor shall you gather the gleanings after your harvest; you shall leave them for the poor and for the stranger: I am the Lord your God."

The Feast of Trumpets

23 And the Lord said to Moses, [24] "Say to the sons of Israel, In the seventh month, on the first day of the month, you shall observe a day of solemn rest, a memorial proclaimed with blast of trumpets, a holy convocation. [25]You shall do no laborious work; and you shall present an offering by fire to the Lord."

The Day of Atonement

26 And the Lord said to Moses, [27] "On the tenth day of this seventh month is the day of atonement; it shall be for you a time of holy convocation, and you shall afflict yourselves and present

an offering by fire to the Lord. [28]And you shall do no work on this same day; for it is a day of atonement, to make atonement for you before the Lord your God. [29]For whoever is not afflicted on this same day shall be cut off from his people. [30]And whoever does any work on this same day, that person I will destroy from among his people. [31]You shall do no work: it is a statute for ever throughout your generations in all your dwellings. [32]It shall be to you a sabbath of solemn rest, and you shall afflict yourselves; on the ninth day of the month beginning at evening, from evening to evening shall you keep your sabbath."

The Feast of Booths

33 And the Lord said to Moses, [34] "Say to the sons of Israel, On the fifteenth day of this seventh month and for seven days is the feast of booths [k] to the Lord. [35]On the first day shall be a holy convocation; you shall do no laborious work. [36]Seven days you shall present offerings by fire to the Lord; on the eighth day you shall hold a holy convocation and present an offering by fire to the Lord; it is a solemn assembly; you shall do no laborious work.

37 "These are the appointed feasts of the Lord, which you shall proclaim as times of holy convocation, for presenting to the Lord offerings by fire, burnt offerings and cereal offerings, sacrifices and drink offerings, each on its proper day; [38]besides the sabbaths of the Lord, and besides your gifts, and besides all your votive offerings, and besides all your freewill offerings, which you give to the Lord.

39 "On the fifteenth day of the seventh month, when you have gathered in the produce of the land, you shall keep the feast of the Lord seven days; on the first day shall be a solemn rest, and on the eighth day shall be a solemn rest. [40]And you shall take on the first day the fruit of goodly trees, branches of palm trees, and boughs of leafy trees, and willows of the brook; and you shall rejoice before the Lord your God seven days. [41]You shall keep it as a feast to the Lord seven days in the year; it is a statute for ever throughout your generations; you shall keep it in the seventh month. [42]You shall dwell in booths for seven days; all that are native in Israel shall dwell in booths, [43]that your generations may know that I made the sons of Israel dwell in booths when I brought them out of the land of Egypt: I am the Lord your God."

44 Thus Moses declared to the sons of Israel the appointed feasts of the Lord.

The Lamp

24 The Lord said to Moses, [2] "Command the sons of Israel to bring you pure oil from beaten olives for the lamp, that a light may be

---

[k] Or *tabernacles*.
23:22: Lev 19:9, 10; Deut 24:20, 21.
24:1-4: Ex 27:20, 21.

kept burning continually. [3]Outside the veil of the covenant, in the tent of meeting, Aaron shall keep it in order from evening to morning before the LORD continually; it shall be a statute for ever throughout your generations. [4]He shall keep the lamps in order upon the lampstand of pure gold before the LORD continually.

Bread for the Tabernacle

5 "And you shall take fine flour, and bake twelve cakes of it; two tenths of an ephah shall be in each cake. [6]And you shall set them in two rows, six in a row, upon the table of pure gold. [7]And you shall put pure frankincense with each row, that it may go with the bread as a memorial portion to be offered by fire to the LORD. [8]Every sabbath day Aaron shall set it in order before the LORD continually on behalf of the sons of Israel as a covenant for ever. [9]And it shall be for Aaron and his sons, and they shall eat it in a holy place, since it is for him a most holy portion out of the offerings by fire to the LORD, a perpetual debt."

Blasphemy and Its Punishment

10 Now an Israelite woman's son, whose father was an Egyptian, went out among the sons of Israel; and the Israelite woman's son and a man of Israel quarreled in the camp, [11]and the Israelite woman's son blasphemed the Name, and cursed. And they brought him to Moses. His mother's name was Shelo'mith, the daughter of Dibri, of the tribe of Dan. [12]And they put him in custody, till the will of the LORD should be declared to them.

13 And the LORD said to Moses, [14]"Bring out of the camp him who cursed; and let all who heard him lay their hands upon his head, and let all the congregation stone him. [15]And say to the sons of Israel, Whoever curses his God shall bear his sin. [16]He who blasphemes the name of the LORD shall be put to death; all the congregation shall stone him; the sojourner as well as the native, when he blasphemes the Name, shall be put to death. [17]He who kills a man shall be put to death. [18]He who kills a beast shall make it good, life for life. [19]When a man causes a disfigurement in his neighbor, as he has done it shall be done to him, [20]fracture for fracture, eye for eye, tooth for tooth; as he has disfigured a man, he shall be disfigured. [21]He who kills a beast shall make it good; and he who kills a man shall be put to death. [22]You shall have one law for the sojourner and for the native; for I am the LORD your God." [23]So Moses spoke to the sons of Israel; and they brought him who had cursed out of the camp, and stoned him with stones. Thus the sons of Israel did as the LORD commanded Moses.

The Sabbatical Year

25 The LORD said to Moses on Mount Sinai, [2]"Say to the sons of Israel, When you come into the land which I give you, the land shall keep a sabbath to the LORD. [3]Six years you shall sow your field, and six years you shall prune your vineyard, and gather in its fruits; [4]but in the seventh year there shall be a sabbath of solemn rest for the land, a sabbath to the LORD; you shall not sow your field or prune your vineyard. [5]What grows of itself in your harvest you shall not reap, and the grapes of your undressed vine you shall not gather; it shall be a year of solemn rest for the land. [6]The sabbath of the land shall provide food for you, for yourself and for your male and female slaves and for your hired servant and the sojourner who lives with you; [7]for your cattle also and for the beasts that are in your land all its yield shall be for food.

The Year of Jubilee

8 "And you shall count seven weeks [1] of years, seven times seven years, so that the time of the seven weeks of years shall be to you forty-nine years. [9]Then you shall send abroad the loud trumpet on the tenth day of the seventh month; on the day of atonement you shall send abroad the trumpet throughout all your land. [10]And you shall hallow the fiftieth year, and proclaim liberty throughout the land to all its inhabitants; it shall be a jubilee for you, when each of you shall return to his property and each of you shall return to his family. [11]A jubilee shall that fiftieth year be to you; in it you shall neither sow, nor reap what grows of itself, nor gather the grapes from the undressed vines. [12]For it is a jubilee; it shall be holy to you; you shall eat what it yields out of the field.

13 "In this year of jubilee each of you shall return to his property. [14]And if you sell to your neighbor or buy from your neighbor, you shall not wrong one another. [15]According to the number of years after the jubilee, you shall buy from your neighbor, and according to the number of years for crops he shall sell to you. [16]If the years are many you shall increase the price, and if the years are few you shall diminish the price, for it is the number of the crops that he is selling to you. [17]You shall not wrong one another, but you shall fear your God; for I am the LORD your God.

18 "Therefore you shall do my statutes, and keep my ordinances and perform them; so you will dwell in the land securely. [19]The land will yield its fruit, and you will eat your fill, and dwell in it securely. [20]And if you say, 'What shall we eat in the seventh year, if we may not sow or gather in our crop?' [21]I will command my blessing upon you in the sixth year, so that it will bring forth fruit for three years. [22]When you sow in the eighth

---

[1] Or *sabbaths.*

24:5–9: Ex 25:30; 39:36; 40:23; Mt 12:4; Mk 2:26; Lk 6:4.
24:19, 20: Ex 21:23–25; Deut 19:21; Mt 5:38.
24:22: Ex 12:49; Num 9:14; 15:15, 16, 29.
25:2–7: Ex 23:10, 11.

year, you will be eating old produce; until the ninth year, when its produce comes in, you shall eat the old. [23]The land shall not be sold in perpetuity, for the land is mine; for you are strangers and sojourners with me. [24]And in all the country you possess, you shall grant a redemption of the land.

25 "If your brother becomes poor, and sells part of his property, then his next of kin shall come and redeem what his brother has sold. [26]If a man has no one to redeem it, and then himself becomes prosperous and finds sufficient means to redeem it, [27]let him reckon the years since he sold it and pay back the overpayment to the man to whom he sold it; and he shall return to his property. [28]But if he has not sufficient means to get it back for himself, then what he sold shall remain in the hand of him who bought it until the year of jubilee; in the jubilee it shall be released, and he shall return to his property.

29 "If a man sells a dwelling house in a walled city, he may redeem it within a whole year after its sale; for a full year he shall have the right of redemption. [30]If it is not redeemed within a full year, then the house that is in the walled city shall be made sure in perpetuity to him who bought it, throughout his generations; it shall not be released in the jubilee. [31]But the houses of the villages which have no wall around them shall be reckoned with the fields of the country; they may be redeemed, and they shall be released in the jubilee. [32]Nevertheless the cities of the Levites, the houses in the cities of their possession, the Levites may redeem at any time. [33]And if one of the Levites does not exercise[m] his right of redemption, then the house that was sold in a city of their possession shall be released in the jubilee; for the houses in the cities of the Levites are their possession among the sons of Israel. [34]But the fields of common land belonging to their cities may not be sold; for that is their perpetual possession.

35 "And if your brother becomes poor, and cannot maintain himself with you, you shall maintain him; as a stranger and a sojourner he shall live with you. [36]Take no interest from him or increase, but fear your God; that your brother may live beside you. [37]You shall not lend him your money at interest, nor give him your food for profit. [38]I am the LORD your God, who brought you forth out of the land of Egypt to give you the land of Canaan, and to be your God.

39 "And if your brother becomes poor beside you, and sells himself to you, you shall not make him serve as a slave: [40]he shall be with you as a hired servant and as a sojourner. He shall serve with you until the year of the jubilee; [41]then he shall go out from you, he and his children with him, and go back to his own family, and return to the possession of his fathers. [42]For they are my

servants, whom I brought forth out of the land of Egypt; they shall not be sold as slaves. [43]You shall not rule over him with harshness, but shall fear your God. [44]As for your male and female slaves whom you may have: you may buy male and female slaves from among the nations that are round about you. [45]You may also buy from among the strangers who sojourn with you and their families that are with you, who have been born in your land; and they may be your property. [46]You may bequeath them to your sons after you, to inherit as a possession for ever; you may make slaves of them, but over your brethren the sons of Israel you shall not rule, one over another, with harshness.

47 "If a stranger or sojourner with you becomes rich, and your brother beside him becomes poor and sells himself to the stranger or sojourner with you, or to a member of the stranger's family, [48]then after he is sold he may be redeemed; one of his brothers may redeem him, [49]or his uncle, or his cousin may redeem him, or a near kinsman belonging to his family may redeem him; or if he grows rich he may redeem himself. [50]He shall reckon with him who bought him from the year when he sold himself to him until the year of jubilee, and the price of his release shall be according to the number of years; the time he was with his owner shall be rated as the time of a hired servant. [51]If there are still many years, according to them he shall refund out of the price paid for him the price for his redemption. [52]If there remain but a few years until the year of jubilee, he shall make a reckoning with him; according to the years of service due from him he shall refund the money for his redemption. [53]As a servant hired year by year shall he be with him; he shall not rule with harshness over him in your sight. [54]And if he is not redeemed by these means, then he shall be released in the year of jubilee, he and his children with him. [55]For to me the sons of Israel are servants, they are my servants whom I brought forth out of the land of Egypt: I am the LORD your God.

Rewards for Obedience

26 "You shall make for yourselves no idols and erect no graven image or pillar, and you shall not set up a figured stone in your land, to bow down to them; for I am the LORD your God. [2]You shall keep my sabbaths and reverence my sanctuary: I am the LORD.

3 "If you walk in my statutes and observe my commandments and do them, [4]then I will give

---

[m] Compare Vg: Heb *exercises*.
25:35: Deut 15:7–11.
25:36: Ex 22:25; Deut 23:19, 20.
25:39–43: Ex 21:2–6; Deut 15:12–18.
26:1: Lev 19:4; Ex 20:4, 23; Deut 4:15–18; 27:15.
26:2: Ex 20:8; 23:12; 34:21; 35:2, 3; Lev 19:3, 30; Deut 5:12–15.
26:3–13: Deut 7:12–26; 28:1–14.

you your rains in their season, and the land shall yield its increase, and the trees of the field shall yield their fruit. [5]And your threshing shall last to the time of vintage, and the vintage shall last to the time for sowing; and you shall eat your bread to the full, and dwell in your land securely. [6]And I will give peace in the land, and you shall lie down, and none shall make you afraid; and I will remove evil beasts from the land, and the sword shall not go through your land. [7]And you shall chase your enemies, and they shall fall before you by the sword. [8]Five of you shall chase a hundred, and a hundred of you shall chase ten thousand; and your enemies shall fall before you by the sword. [9]And I will have regard for you and make you fruitful and multiply you, and will confirm my covenant with you. [10]And you shall eat old store long kept, and you shall clear out the old to make way for the new. [11]And I will make my abode among you, and my soul shall not abhor you. [12]And I will walk among you, and will be your God, and you shall be my people. [13]I am the LORD your God, who brought you forth out of the land of Egypt, that you should not be their slaves; and I have broken the bars of your yoke and made you walk erect.

Punishment for Disobedience

[14] "But if you will not listen to me, and will not do all these commandments, [15]if you spurn my statutes, and if your soul abhors my ordinances, so that you will not do all my commandments, but break my covenant, [16]I will do this to you: I will appoint over you sudden terror, consumption and fever that waste the eyes and cause life to pine away. And you shall sow your seed in vain, for your enemies shall eat it; [17]I will set my face against you, and you shall be struck down before your enemies; those who hate you shall rule over you, and you shall flee when none pursues you. [18]And if in spite of this you will not listen to me, then I will chastise you again sevenfold for your sins, [19]and I will break the pride of your power, and I will make your heavens like iron and your earth like brass; [20]and your strength shall be spent in vain, for your land shall not yield its increase, and the trees of the land shall not yield their fruit.

[21] "Then if you walk contrary to me, and will not listen to me, I will bring more plagues upon you, sevenfold as many as your sins. [22]And I will let loose the wild beasts among you, which shall rob you of your children, and destroy your cattle, and make you few in number, so that your ways shall become desolate.

[23] "And if by this discipline you are not turned to me, but walk contrary to me, [24]then I also will walk contrary to you, and I myself will strike you sevenfold for your sins. [25]And I will bring a sword upon you, that shall execute vengeance for the

covenant; and if you gather within your cities I will send pestilence among you, and you shall be delivered into the hand of the enemy. [26]When I break your staff of bread, ten women shall bake your bread in one oven, and shall deliver your bread again by weight; and you shall eat, and not be satisfied.

[27] "And if in spite of this you will not listen to me, but walk contrary to me, [28]then I will walk contrary to you in fury, and chastise you myself sevenfold for your sins. [29]You shall eat the flesh of your sons, and you shall eat the flesh of your daughters. [30]And I will destroy your high places, and cut down your incense altars, and cast your dead bodies upon the dead bodies of your idols; and my soul will abhor you. [31]And I will lay your cities waste, and will make your sanctuaries desolate, and I will not smell your pleasing odors. [32]And I will devastate the land, so that your enemies who settle in it shall be astonished at it. [33]And I will scatter you among the nations, and I will unsheathe the sword after you; and your land shall be a desolation, and your cities shall be a waste.

[34] "Then the land shall enjoy [n] its sabbaths as long as it lies desolate, while you are in your enemies' land; then the land shall rest, and enjoy [n] its sabbaths. [35]As long as it lies desolate it shall have rest, the rest which it had not in your sabbaths when you dwelt upon it. [36]And as for those of you that are left, I will send faintness into their hearts in the lands of their enemies; the sound of a driven leaf shall put them to flight, and they shall flee as one flees from the sword, and they shall fall when none pursues. [37]They shall stumble over one another, as if to escape a sword, though none pursues; and you shall have no power to stand before your enemies. [38]And you shall perish among the nations, and the land of your enemies shall eat you up. [39]And those of you that are left shall pine away in your enemies' lands because of their iniquity; and also because of the iniquities of their fathers they shall pine away like them.

[40] "But if they confess their iniquity and the iniquity of their fathers in their treachery which they committed against me, and also in walking contrary to me, [41]so that I walked contrary to them and brought them into the land of their enemies; if then their uncircumcised heart is humbled and they make amends for their iniquity; [42]then I will remember my covenant with Jacob, and I will remember my covenant with Isaac and my covenant with Abraham, and I will remember the land. [43]But the land shall be left by them, and enjoy [n] its

---

[n] Or *pay for.*
26:11, 12: 2 Cor 6:16.
26:14–45: Deut 28:16–68.
26:40, 41: Acts 7:51.

sabbaths while it lies desolate without them; and they shall make amends for their iniquity, because they spurned my ordinances, and their soul abhorred my statutes. [44]Yet for all that, when they are in the land of their enemies, I will not spurn them, neither will I abhor them so as to destroy them utterly and break my covenant with them; for I am the LORD their God; [45]but I will for their sake remember the covenant with their forefathers, whom I brought forth out of the land of Egypt in the sight of the nations, that I might be their God: I am the LORD."

46 These are the statutes and ordinances and laws which the LORD made between him and the sons of Israel on Mount Sinai by Moses.

Votive Offerings

27 The LORD said to Moses, [2] "Say to the sons of Israel, When a man makes a special vow of persons to the LORD at your valuation, [3]then your valuation of a male from twenty years old up to sixty years old shall be fifty shekels of silver, according to the shekel of the sanctuary. [4]If the person is a female, your valuation shall be thirty shekels. [5]If the person is from five years old up to twenty years old, your valuation shall be for a male twenty shekels, and for a female ten shekels. [6]If the person is from a month old up to five years old, your valuation shall be for a male five shekels of silver, and for a female your valuation shall be three shekels of silver. [7]And if the person is sixty years old and upward, then your valuation for a male shall be fifteen shekels, and for a female ten shekels. [8]And if a man is too poor to pay your valuation, then he shall bring the person before the priest, and the priest shall value him; according to the ability of him who vowed the priest shall value him.

9 "If it is an animal such as men offer as an offering to the LORD, all of such that any man gives to the LORD is holy. [10]He shall not substitute anything for it or exchange it, a good for a bad, or a bad for a good; and if he makes any exchange of beast for beast, then both it and that for which it is exchanged shall be holy. [11]And if it is an unclean animal such as is not offered as an offering to the LORD, then the man shall bring the animal before the priest, [12]and the priest shall value it as either good or bad; as you, the priest, value it, so it shall be. [13]But if he wishes to redeem it, he shall add a fifth to the valuation.

14 "When a man dedicates his house to be holy to the LORD, the priest shall value it as either good or bad; as the priest values it, so it shall stand. [15]And if he who dedicates it wishes to redeem his house, he shall add a fifth of the valuation in money to it, and it shall be his.

16 "If a man dedicates to the LORD part of the land which is his by inheritance, then your valuation shall be according to the seed for it; a sow-

ing of a homer of barley shall be valued at fifty shekels of silver. [17]If he dedicates his field from the year of jubilee, it shall stand at your full valuation; [18]but if he dedicates his field after the jubilee, then the priest shall compute the money-value for it according to the years that remain until the year of jubilee, and a deduction shall be made from your valuation. [19]And if he who dedicates the field wishes to redeem it, then he shall add a fifth of the valuation in money to it, and it shall remain his. [20]But if he does not wish to redeem the field, or if he has sold the field to another man, it shall not be redeemed any more; [21]but the field, when it is released in the jubilee, shall be holy to the LORD, as a field that has been devoted; the priest shall be in possession of it. [22]If he dedicates to the LORD a field which he has bought, which is not a part of his possession by inheritance, [23]then the priest shall compute the valuation for it up to the year of jubilee, and the man shall give the amount of the valuation on that day as a holy thing to the LORD. [24]In the year of jubilee the field shall return to him from whom it was bought, to whom the land belongs as a possession by inheritance. [25]Every valuation shall be according to the shekel of the sanctuary: twenty gerahs shall make a shekel.

26 "But a firstling of animals, which as a firstling belongs to the LORD, no man may dedicate; whether ox or sheep, it is the LORD's. [27]And if it is an unclean animal, then he shall buy it back at your valuation, and add a fifth to it; or, if it is not redeemed, it shall be sold at your valuation.

28 "But no devoted thing that a man devotes to the LORD, of anything that he has, whether of man or beast, or of his inherited field, shall be sold or redeemed; every devoted thing is most holy to the LORD. [29]No one devoted, who is to be utterly destroyed from among men, shall be ransomed; he shall be put to death.

30 "All the tithe of the land, whether of the seed of the land or of the fruit of the trees, is the LORD's; it is holy to the LORD. [31]If a man wishes to redeem any of his tithe, he shall add a fifth to it. [32]And all the tithe of herds and flocks, every tenth animal of all that pass under the herdsman's staff, shall be holy to the LORD. [33]A man shall not inquire whether it is good or bad, neither shall he exchange it; and if he exchanges it, then both it and that for which it is exchanged shall be holy; it shall not be redeemed."

34 These are the commandments which the LORD commanded Moses for the sons of Israel on Mount Sinai.

27:28: Num 18:14.

95

THE FOURTH BOOK OF MOSES COMMONLY CALLED

NUMBERS

The First Census of Israel

1 The LORD spoke to Moses in the wilderness of Sinai, in the tent of meeting, on the first day of the second month, in the second year after they had come out of the land of Egypt, saying, ²"Take a census of all the congregation of the sons of Israel, by families, by fathers' houses, according to the number of names, every male, head by head; ³from twenty years old and upward, all in Israel who are able to go forth to war, you and Aaron shall number them, company by company. ⁴And there shall be with you a man from each tribe, each man being the head of the house of his fathers. ⁵And these are the names of the men who shall attend you. From Reuben, Eli'zur the son of Shed'eur; ⁶from Simeon, Shelu'mi-el the son of Zurishad'dai; ⁷from Judah, Nahshon the son of Ammin'adab; ⁸from Is'sachar, Nethan'el the son of Zu'ar; ⁹from Zeb'ulun, Eli'ab the son of He'lon; ¹⁰from the sons of Joseph, from E'phraim, Elish'ama the son of Ammi'hud, and from Manas'seh, Gama'li-el the son of Pedah'zur; ¹¹from Benjamin, Abi'dan the son of Gideo'ni; ¹²from Dan, Ahie'zer the son of Ammishad'dai; ¹³from Asher, Pa'giel the son of Ochran; ¹⁴from Gad, Eli'asaph the son of Deu'el; ¹⁵from Naph'tali, Ahi'ra the son of E'nan." ¹⁶These were the ones chosen from the congregation, the leaders of their ancestral tribes, the heads of the clans of Israel.

17 Moses and Aaron took these men who have been named, ¹⁸and on the first day of the second month, they assembled the whole congregation together, who registered themselves by families, by fathers' houses, according to the number of names from twenty years old and upward, head by head, ¹⁹as the LORD commanded Moses. So he numbered them in the wilderness of Sinai.

20 The people of Reuben, Israel's first-born, their generations, by their families, by their fathers' houses, according to the number of names, head by head, every male from twenty years old and upward, all who were able to go forth to war: ²¹the number of the tribe of Reuben was forty-six thousand five hundred.

22 Of the people of Simeon, their generations, by their families, by their fathers' houses, those of them that were numbered, according to the number of names, head by head, every male from twenty years old and upward, all who were able to go forth to war: ²³the number of the

tribe of Simeon was fifty-nine thousand three hundred.

24 Of the people of Gad, their generations, by their families, by their fathers' houses, according to the number of the names, from twenty years old and upward, all who were able to go forth to war: ²⁵the number of the tribe of Gad was forty-five thousand six hundred and fifty.

26 Of the people of Judah, their generations, by their families, by their fathers' houses, according to the number of names, from twenty years old and upward, every man able to go forth to war: ²⁷the number of the tribe of Judah was seventy-four thousand six hundred.

28 Of the people of Is'sachar, their generations, by their families, by their fathers' houses, according to the number of names, from twenty years old and upward, every man able to go forth to war: ²⁹the number of the tribe of Is'sachar was fifty-four thousand four hundred.

30 Of the people of Zeb'ulun, their generations, by their families, by their fathers' houses, according to the number of names, from twenty years old and upward, every man able to go forth to war: ³¹the number of the tribe of Zeb'ulun was fifty-seven thousand four hundred.

32 Of the people of Joseph, namely, of the people of E'phraim, their generations, by their families, by their fathers' houses, according to the number of names, from twenty years old and upward, every man able to go forth to war: ³³the number of the tribe of E'phraim was forty thousand five hundred.

34 Of the people of Manas'seh, their generations, by their families, by their fathers' houses, according to the number of names, from twenty years old and upward, every man able to go forth to war: ³⁵the number of the tribe of Manas'seh was thirty-two thousand two hundred.

36 Of the people of Benjamin, their generations, by their families, by their fathers' houses, according to the number of names, from twenty years old and upward, every man able to go forth to war: ³⁷the number of the tribe of Benjamin was thirty-five thousand four hundred.

38 Of the people of Dan, their generations, by

The title of this book is explained by the census with which it opens. It is composed of both history and legislation, and, though edited finally by the priests after the Exile, it contains much ancient material.
1:1–46: Num 26:1–51.

their families, by their fathers' houses, according to the number of names, from twenty years old and upward, every man able to go forth to war: [39]the number of the tribe of Dan was sixty-two thousand seven hundred.

40 Of the people of Asher, their generations, by their families, by their fathers' houses, according to the number of names, from twenty years old and upward, every man able to go forth to war: [41]the number of the tribe of Asher was forty-one thousand five hundred.

42 Of the people of Naph'tali, their generations, by their families, by their fathers' houses, according to the number of names, from twenty years old and upward, every man able to go forth to war: [43]the number of the tribe of Naph'tali was fifty-three thousand four hundred.

44 These are those who were numbered, whom Moses and Aaron numbered with the help of the leaders of Israel, twelve men, each representing his fathers' house. [45]So the whole number of the sons of Israel, by their fathers' houses, from twenty years old and upward, every man able to go forth to war in Israel—[46]their whole number was six hundred and three thousand five hundred and fifty.

47 But the Levites were not numbered by their ancestral tribe along with them. [48]For the LORD said to Moses, [49]"Only the tribe of Levi you shall not number, and you shall not take a census of them among the sons of Israel; [50]but appoint the Levites over the tabernacle of the covenant, and over all its furnishings, and over all that belongs to it; they are to carry the tabernacle and all its furnishings, and they shall tend it, and shall encamp around the tabernacle. [51]When the tabernacle is to be set out, the Levites shall take it down; and when the tabernacle is to be pitched, the Levites shall set it up. And if any one else comes near, he shall be put to death. [52]The sons of Israel shall pitch their tents by their companies, every man by his own camp and every man by his own standard; [53]but the Levites shall encamp around the tabernacle of the covenant, that there may be no wrath upon the congregation of the sons of Israel; and the Levites shall keep charge of the tabernacle of the covenant." [54]Thus did the sons of Israel; they did according to all that the LORD commanded Moses.

Order of Encampment and Marching

2 The LORD said to Moses and Aaron, [2]"The sons of Israel shall encamp each by his own standard, with the ensigns of their fathers' houses; they shall encamp facing the tent of meeting on every side. [3]Those to encamp on the east side toward the sunrise shall be of the standard of the camp of Judah by their companies, the leader of the people of Judah being Nahshon the son of Ammin'adab, [4]his host as numbered being seventy-four thousand six hundred. [5]Those to en-

camp next to him shall be the tribe of Is'sachar, the leader of the people of Issachar being Nethan'el the son of Zu'ar, [6]his host as numbered being fifty-four thousand four hundred. [7]Then the tribe of Zeb'ulun, the leader of the people of Zebulun being Eli'ab the son of He'lon, [8]his host as numbered being fifty-seven thousand four hundred. [9]The whole number of the camp of Judah, by their companies, is a hundred and eighty-six thousand four hundred. They shall set out first on the march.

10 "On the south side shall be the standard of the camp of Reuben by their companies, the leader of the people of Reuben being Eli'zur the son of Shed'eur, [11]his host as numbered being forty-six thousand five hundred. [12]And those to encamp next to him shall be the tribe of Simeon, the leader of the people of Simeon being Shelu'-mi-el the son of Zurishad'dai, [13]his host as numbered being fifty-nine thousand three hundred. [14]Then the tribe of Gad, the leader of the people of Gad being Eli'asaph the son of Reu'el, [15]his host as numbered being forty-five thousand six hundred and fifty. [16]The whole number of the camp of Reuben, by their companies, is a hundred and fifty-one thousand four hundred and fifty. They shall set out second.

17 "Then the tent of meeting shall set out, with the camp of the Levites in the midst of the camps; as they encamp, so shall they set out, each in position, standard by standard.

18 "On the west side shall be the standard of the camp of E'phraim by their companies, the leader of the people of Ephraim being Elish'ama the son of Ammi'hud, [19]his host as numbered being forty thousand five hundred. [20]And next to him shall be the tribe of Manas'seh, the leader of the people of Manasseh being Gama'liel the son of Pedah'zur, [21]his host as numbered being thirty-two thousand two hundred. [22]Then the tribe of Benjamin, the leader of the people of Benjamin being Abi'dan the son of Gideo'ni, [23]his host as numbered being thirty-five thousand four hundred. [24]The whole number of the camp of E'phraim, by their companies, is a hundred and eight thousand one hundred. They shall set out third on the march.

25 "On the north side shall be the standard of the camp of Dan by their companies, the leader of the people of Dan being Ahie'zer the son of Ammishad'dai, [26]his host as numbered being sixty-two thousand seven hundred. [27]And those to encamp next to him shall be the tribe of Asher, the leader of the people of Asher being Pa'giel the son of Ochran, [28]his host as numbered being forty-one thousand five hundred. [29]Then the tribe

---

1:47: Num 2:33.
1:50–53: Num 3:5–8, 21–37; 4:1–33; 8:19; 18:3, 4, 23.

of Naph'tali, the leader of the people of Naphtali being Ahi'ra the son of E'nan, [30]his host as numbered being fifty-three thousand four hundred. [31]The whole number of the camp of Dan is a hundred and fifty-seven thousand six hundred. They shall set out last, standard by standard."

[32] These are the sons of Israel as numbered by their fathers' houses; all in the camps who were numbered by their companies were six hundred and three thousand five hundred and fifty. [33]But the Levites were not numbered among the sons of Israel, as the LORD commanded Moses. [34] Thus did the sons of Israel. According to all that the LORD commanded Moses, so they encamped by their standards, and so they set out, every one in his family, according to his fathers' house.

Sons of Aaron

3 These are the generations of Aaron and Moses at the time when the LORD spoke with Moses on Mount Sinai. [2]These are the names of the sons of Aaron: Na'dab the first-born, and Abi'hu, Elea'zar, and Ith'amar; [3]these are the names of the sons of Aaron, the anointed priests, whom he ordained to minister in the priest's office. [4]But Na'dab and Abi'hu died before the LORD when they offered unholy fire before the LORD in the wilderness of Sinai; and they had no children. So Elea'zar and Ith'amar served as priests in the lifetime of Aaron their father.

Duties of the Levites

[5] And the LORD said to Moses, [6] "Bring the tribe of Levi near, and set them before Aaron the priest, that they may minister to him. [7]They shall perform duties for him and for the whole congregation before the tent of meeting, as they minister at the tabernacle; [8]they shall have charge of all the furnishings of the tent of meeting, and attend to the duties for the sons of Israel as they minister at the tabernacle. [9]And you shall give the Levites to Aaron and his sons; they are wholly given to him from among the sons of Israel. [10]And you shall appoint Aaron and his sons, and they shall attend to their priesthood; but if any one else comes near, he shall be put to death."

[11] And the LORD said to Moses, [12] "Behold, I have taken the Levites from among the sons of Israel instead of every first-born that opens the womb among the sons of Israel. The Levites shall be mine, [13]for all the first-born are mine; on the day that I slew all the first-born in the land of Egypt, I consecrated for my own all the first-born in Israel, both of man and of beast; they shall be mine: I am the LORD."

Census of the Levites

[14] And the LORD said to Moses in the wilderness of Sinai, [15] "Number the sons of Levi, by fathers' houses and by families; every male from a month old and upward you shall number." [16]So Moses numbered them according to the word of the LORD, as he was commanded. [17]And these were the sons of Levi by their names: Gershon and Ko'hath and Merar'i. [18]And these are the names of the sons of Gershon by their families: Libni and Shim'e-i. [19]And the sons of Ko'hath by their families: Amram, Izhar, He'bron, and Uz'ziel. [20]And the sons of Merar'i by their families: Mah'li and Mu'shi. These are the families of the Levites, by their fathers' houses.

[21] Of Gershon were the family of the Libnites and the family of the Shim'eites; these were the families of the Ger'shonites. [22]Their number according to the number of all the males from a month old and upward was [a] seven thousand five hundred. [23]The families of the Ger'shonites were to encamp behind the tabernacle on the west, [24]with Eli'asaph, the son of La'el as head of the fathers' house of the Ger'shonites. [25]And the charge of the sons of Gershon in the tent of meeting was to be the tabernacle, the tent with its covering, the screen for the door of the tent of meeting, [26]the hangings of the court, the screen for the door of the court which is around the tabernacle and the altar, and its cords; all the service pertaining to these.

[27] Of Ko'hath were the family of the Am'ramites, and the family of the Iz'harites, and the family of the He'bronites, and the family of the Uz'zielites; these are the families of the Ko'hathites. [28]According to the number of all the males, from a month old and upward, there were eight thousand six hundred, attending to the duties of the sanctuary. [29]The families of the sons of Ko'-hath were to encamp on the south side of the tabernacle, [30]with Eliza'phan the son of Uz'ziel as head of the fathers' house of the families of the Ko'hathites. [31]And their charge was to be the ark, the table, the lampstand, the altars, the vessels of the sanctuary with which the priests minister, and the screen; all the service pertaining to these. [32]And Elea'zar the son of Aaron the priest was to be chief over the leaders of the Levites, and to have oversight of those who had charge of the sanctuary.

[33] Of Merar'i were the family of the Mah'lites and the family of the Mu'shites: these are the families of Merari. [34]Their number according to the number of all the males from a month old and upward was six thousand two hundred. [35]And the head of the fathers' house of the families of Merar'i was Zu'riel the son of Abiha'il; they were to encamp on the north side of the tabernacle.

---

[a] Heb *their number was.*
3:2: Num 26:60.
3:5–13: Num 8:6–26.
3:5–8: Num 1:50–53; 3:21–37; 4:1–33; 8:19.
3:11–13: Num 3:45; 8:18.
3:15–34: Num 4:34–49.
3:17–20: Ex 6:16, 22.

³⁶And the appointed charge of the sons of Merar′i was to be the frames of the tabernacle, the bars, the pillars, the bases, and all their accessories; all the service pertaining to these; ³⁷also the pillars of the court round about, with their bases and pegs and cords.

38 And those to encamp before the tabernacle on the east, before the tent of meeting toward the sunrise, were Moses and Aaron and his sons, having charge of the rites within the sanctuary, whatever had to be done for the sons of Israel; and any one else who came near was to be put to death. ³⁹All who were numbered of the Levites, whom Moses and Aaron numbered at the commandment of the LORD, by families, all the males from a month old and upward, were twenty-two thousand.

Redemption of the First-born

40 And the LORD said to Moses, "Number all the first-born males of the sons of Israel, from a month old and upward, taking their number by names. ⁴¹And you shall take the Levites for me—I am the LORD—instead of all the first-born among the sons of Israel, and the cattle of the Levites instead of all the firstlings among the cattle of the sons of Israel." ⁴²So Moses numbered all the first-born among the sons of Israel, as the LORD commanded him. ⁴³And all the first-born males, according to the number of names, from a month old and upward as numbered were twenty-two thousand two hundred and seventy-three.

44 And the LORD said to Moses, ⁴⁵"Take the Levites instead of all the first-born among the sons of Israel, and the cattle of the Levites instead of their cattle; and the Levites shall be mine: I am the LORD. ⁴⁶And for the redemption of the two hundred and seventy-three of the first-born of the sons of Israel, over and above the number of the male Levites, ⁴⁷you shall take five shekels apiece; reckoning by the shekel of the sanctuary, the shekel of twenty gerahs, you shall take them, ⁴⁸and give the money by which the excess number of them is redeemed to Aaron and his sons." ⁴⁹So Moses took the redemption money from those who were over and above those redeemed by the Levites; ⁵⁰from the first-born of the sons of Israel he took the money, one thousand three hundred and sixty-five shekels, reckoned by the shekel of the sanctuary; ⁵¹and Moses gave the redemption money to Aaron and his sons, according to the word of the LORD, as the LORD commanded Moses.

The Kohathites

4 The LORD said to Moses and Aaron, ² "Take a census of the sons of Ko′hath from among the sons of Levi, by their families and their fathers' houses, ³from thirty years old up to fifty years old, all who can enter the service, to do the work in the tent of meeting. ⁴This is the service of the sons of Ko′hath in the tent of meeting: the most holy things. ⁵When the camp is to set out,

Aaron and his sons shall go in and take down the veil of the screen, and cover the ark of the covenant with it; ⁶then they shall put on it a covering of goatskin, and spread over that a cloth all of blue, and shall put in its poles. ⁷And over the table of the bread of the Presence they shall spread a cloth of blue, and put upon it the plates, the dishes for incense, the bowls, and the flagons for the drink offering; the continual bread also shall be on it; ⁸then they shall spread over them a cloth of scarlet, and cover the same with a covering of goatskin, and shall put in its poles. ⁹And they shall take a cloth of blue, and cover the lampstand for the light, with its lamps, its snuffers, its trays, and all the vessels for oil with which it is supplied: ¹⁰and they shall put it with all its utensils in a covering of goatskin and put it upon the carrying frame. ¹¹And over the golden altar they shall spread a cloth of blue, and cover it with a covering of goatskin, and shall put in its poles; ¹²and they shall take all the vessels of the service which are used in the sanctuary, and put them in a cloth of blue, and cover them with a covering of goatskin, and put them on the carrying frame. ¹³And they shall take away the ashes from the altar, and spread a purple cloth over it; ¹⁴and they shall put on it all the utensils of the altar, which are used for the service there, the firepans, the forks, the shovels, and the basins, all the utensils of the altar; and they shall spread upon it a covering of goatskin, and shall put in its poles. ¹⁵And when Aaron and his sons have finished covering the sanctuary and all the furnishings of the sanctuary, as the camp sets out, after that the sons of Ko′hath shall come to carry these, but they must not touch the holy things, lest they die. These are the things of the tent of meeting which the sons of Kohath are to carry.

16 "And Elea′zar the son of Aaron the priest shall have charge of the oil for the light, the fragrant incense, the continual cereal offering, and the anointing oil, with the oversight of all the tabernacle and all that is in it, of the sanctuary and its vessels."

17 The LORD said to Moses and Aaron, ¹⁸"Let not the tribe of the families of the Ko′hathites be destroyed from among the Levites; ¹⁹but deal thus with them, that they may live and not die when they come near to the most holy things: Aaron and his sons shall go in and appoint them each to his task and to his burden, ²⁰but they shall not go in to look upon the holy things even for a moment, lest they die."

The Gershonites and Merarites

21 The LORD said to Moses, ²²"Take a census of the sons of Gershon also, by their families and

---

3:45: Num 3:11–13; 8:18.
4:1–33: Num 1:50–53; 3:5–8, 21–37; 8:19; 18:3, 4, 23.

their fathers' houses; [23]from thirty years old up to fifty years old, you shall number them, all who can enter for service, to do the work in the tent of meeting. [24]This is the service of the families of the Ger'shonites, in serving and bearing burdens: [25]they shall carry the curtains of the tabernacle, and the tent of meeting with its covering, and the covering of goatskin that is on top of it, and the screen for the door of the tent of meeting, [26]and the hangings of the court, and the screen for the entrance of the gate of the court which is around the tabernacle and the altar, and their cords, and all the equipment for their service; and they shall do all that needs to be done with regard to them. [27]All the service of the sons of the Ger'shonites shall be at the command of Aaron and his sons, in all that they are to carry, and in all that they have to do; and you shall assign to their charge all that they are to carry. [28]This is the service of the families of the sons of the Ger'shonites in the tent of meeting, and their work is to be under the oversight of Ith'amar the son of Aaron the priest.

29 "As for the sons of Merar'i, you shall number them by their families and their fathers' houses; [30]from thirty years old up to fifty years old, you shall number them, every one that can enter the service, to do the work of the tent of meeting. [31]And this is what they are charged to carry, as the whole of their service in the tent of meeting: the frames of the tabernacle, with its bars, pillars, and bases, [32]and the pillars of the court round about with their bases, pegs, and cords, with all their equipment and all their accessories; and you shall assign by name the objects which they are required to carry. [33]This is the service of the families of the sons of Merar'i, the whole of their service in the tent of meeting, under the hand of Ith'amar the son of Aaron the priest."

Census of the Levites

34 And Moses and Aaron and the leaders of the congregation numbered the sons of the Ko'hathites, by their families and their fathers' houses, [35]from thirty years old up to fifty years old, every one that could enter the service, for work in the tent of meeting; [36]and their number by families was two thousand seven hundred and fifty. [37]This was the number of the families of the Ko'hathites, all who served in the tent of meeting, whom Moses and Aaron numbered according to the commandment of the LORD by Moses.

38 The number of the sons of Gershon, by their families and their fathers' houses, [39]from thirty years old up to fifty years old, every one that could enter the service for work in the tent of meeting—[40]their number by their families and their fathers' houses was two thousand six hundred and thirty. [41]This was the number of the families of the sons of Gershon, all who served in the tent of meeting, whom Moses and Aaron

numbered according to the commandment of the LORD.

42 The number of the families of the sons of Merar'i, by their families and their fathers' houses, [43]from thirty years old up to fifty years old, every one that could enter the service, for work in the tent of meeting—[44]their number by families was three thousand two hundred. [45]These are those who were numbered of the families of the sons of Merar'i, whom Moses and Aaron numbered according to the commandment of the LORD by Moses.

46 All those who were numbered of the Levites, whom Moses and Aaron and the leaders of Israel numbered, by their families and their fathers' houses, [47]from thirty years old up to fifty years old, every one that could enter to do the work of service and the work of bearing burdens in the tent of meeting, [48]those who were numbered of them were eight thousand five hundred and eighty. [49]According to the commandment of the LORD through Moses they were appointed, each to his task of serving or carrying; thus they were numbered by him, as the LORD commanded Moses.

Unclean Persons

5 The LORD said to Moses, [2]"Command the sons of Israel that they put out of the camp every leper, and every one having a discharge, and every one that is unclean through contact with the dead; [3]you shall put out both male and female, putting them outside the camp, that they may not defile their camp, in the midst of which I dwell." [4]And the sons of Israel did so, and drove them outside the camp; as the LORD said to Moses, so the sons of Israel did.

Confession and Restitution

5 And the LORD said to Moses, [6]"Say to the sons of Israel, When a man or woman commits any of the sins that men commit by breaking faith with the LORD, and that person is guilty, [7]he shall confess his sin which he has committed; and he shall make full restitution for his wrong, adding a fifth to it, and giving it to him to whom he did the wrong. [8]But if the man has no kinsman to whom restitution may be made for the wrong, the restitution for wrong shall go to the LORD for the priest, in addition to the ram of atonement with which atonement is made for him. [9]And every offering, all the holy things of the sons of Israel, which they bring to the priest, shall be his; [10]and every man's holy things shall be his; whatever any man gives to the priest shall be his."

An Unfaithful Wife or Jealous Husband

11 And the LORD said to Moses, [12]"Say to the sons of Israel, If any man's wife goes astray and

---

4:34–49: Num 3:15–34.
5:2, 3: Num 12:14, 15.
5:5–8: Ex 22:7–15; Lev 6:1–7.

acts unfaithfully against him, [13]if a man lies with her carnally, and it is hidden from the eyes of her husband, and she is undetected though she has defiled herself, and there is no witness against her, since she was not taken in the act; [14]and if the spirit of jealousy comes upon him, and he is jealous of his wife who has defiled herself; or if the spirit of jealousy comes upon him, and he is jealous of his wife, though she has not defiled herself; [15]then the man shall bring his wife to the priest, and bring the offering required of her, a tenth of an ephah of barley meal; he shall pour no oil upon it and put no frankincense on it, for it is a cereal offering of jealousy, a cereal offering of remembrance, bringing iniquity to remembrance.

16 "And the priest shall bring her near, and set her before the LORD; [17]and the priest shall take holy water in an earthen vessel, and take some of the dust that is on the floor of the tabernacle and put it into the water. [18]And the priest shall set the woman before the LORD, and unbind the hair of the woman's head, and place in her hands the cereal offering of remembrance, which is the cereal offering of jealousy. And in his hand the priest shall have the water of bitterness that brings the curse. [19]Then the priest shall make her take an oath, saying, 'If no man has lain with you, and if you have not turned aside to uncleanness, while you were under your husband's authority, be free from this water of bitterness that brings the curse. [20]But if you have gone astray, though you are under your husband's authority, and if you have defiled yourself, and some man other than your husband has lain with you, [21]then' (let the priest make the woman take the oath of the curse, and say to the woman) 'the LORD make you an execration and an oath among your people, when the LORD makes your thigh fall away and your body swell; [22]may this water that brings the curse pass into your bowels and make your body swell and your thigh fall away.' And the woman shall say, 'Amen, Amen.'

23 "Then the priest shall write these curses in a book, and wash them off into the water of bitterness; [24]and he shall make the woman drink the water of bitterness that brings the curse, and the water that brings the curse shall enter into her and cause bitter pain. [25]And the priest shall take the cereal offering of jealousy out of the woman's hand, and shall wave the cereal offering before the LORD and bring it to the altar; [26]and the priest shall take a handful of the cereal offering, as its memorial portion, and burn it upon the altar, and afterward shall make the woman drink the water. [27]And when he has made her drink the water, then, if she has defiled herself and has acted unfaithfully against her husband, the water that brings the curse shall enter into her and cause bitter pain, and her body shall swell, and her thigh

shall fall away, and the woman shall become an execration among her people. [28]But if the woman has not defiled herself and is clean, then she shall be free and shall conceive children.

29 "This is the law in cases of jealousy, when a wife, though under her husband's authority, goes astray and defiles herself, [30]or when the spirit of jealousy comes upon a man and he is jealous of his wife; then he shall set the woman before the LORD, and the priest shall execute upon her all this law. [31]The man shall be free from iniquity, but the woman shall bear her iniquity."

The Nazirites

6 And the LORD said to Moses, [2]"Say to the sons of Israel, When either a man or a woman makes a special vow, the vow of a Naz'i-rite,[b] to separate himself to the LORD, [3]he shall separate himself from wine and strong drink; he shall drink no vinegar made from wine or strong drink, and shall not drink any juice of grapes or eat grapes, fresh or dried. [4]All the days of his separation[c] he shall eat nothing that is produced by the grapevine, not even the seeds or the skins.

5 "All the days of his vow of separation no razor shall come upon his head; until the time is completed for which he separates himse i to the LORD, he shall be holy; he shall let the locks of hair of his head grow long.

6 "All the days that he separates himself to the LORD he shall not go near a dead body. [7]Neither for his father nor for his mother, nor for brother or sister, if they die, shall he make himself unclean; because his separation to God is upon his head. [8]All the days of his separation he is holy to the LORD.

9 "And if any man dies very suddenly beside him, and he defiles his consecrated head, then he shall shave his head on the day of his cleansing; on the seventh day he shall shave it. [10]On the eighth day he shall bring two turtledoves or two young pigeons to the priest to the door of the tent of meeting, [11]and the priest shall offer one for a sin offering and the other for a burnt offering, and make atonement for him, because he sinned by reason of the dead body. And he shall consecrate his head that same day, [12]and separate himself to the LORD for the days of his separation, and bring a male lamb a year old for a guilt offering; but the former time shall be void, because his separation was defiled.

13 "And this is the law for the Naz'irite, when the time of his separation has been completed: he shall be brought to the door of the tent of meeting, [14]and he shall offer his gift to the LORD, one male

---

[b] That is *one separated* or *one consecrated.*
[c] Or *Naziriteship.*
6:3: Lk 1:15.
6:13–21: Acts 21:24, 26.

lamb a year old without blemish for a burnt offering, and one ewe lamb a year old without blemish as a sin offering, and one ram without blemish as a peace offering, [15]and a basket of unleavened bread, cakes of fine flour mixed with oil, and unleavened wafers spread with oil, and their cereal offering and their drink offerings. [16]And the priest shall present them before the LORD and offer his sin offering and his burnt offering, [17]and he shall offer the ram as a sacrifice of peace offering to the LORD, with the basket of unleavened bread; the priest shall offer also its cereal offering and its drink offering. [18]And the Naz'irite shall shave his consecrated head at the door of the tent of meeting, and shall take the hair from his consecrated head and put it on the fire which is under the sacrifice of the peace offering. [19]And the priest shall take the shoulder of the ram, when it is boiled, and one unleavened cake out of the basket, and one unleavened wafer, and shall put them upon the hands of the Naz'irite, after he has shaven the hair of his consecration, [20]and the priest shall wave them for a wave offering before the LORD; they are a holy portion for the priest, together with the breast that is waved and the thigh that is offered; and after that the Naz'irite may drink wine.

21 "This is the law for the Naz'irite who takes a vow. His offering to the LORD shall be according to his vow as a Nazirite, apart from what else he can afford; in accordance with the vow which he takes, so shall he do according to the law for his separation as a Nazirite."

The Priestly Benediction

22 The LORD said to Moses, [23]"Say to Aaron and his sons, Thus you shall bless the sons of Israel: you shall say to them,

[24]The LORD bless you and keep you:

[25]The LORD make his face to shine upon you, and be gracious to you:

[26]The LORD lift up his countenance upon you, and give you peace.

27 "So shall they put my name upon the sons of Israel, and I will bless them."

Offerings of the Leaders

7 On the day when Moses had finished setting up the tabernacle, and had anointed and consecrated it with all its furnishings, and had anointed and consecrated the altar with all its utensils, [2]the leaders of Israel, heads of their fathers' houses, the leaders of the tribes, who were over those who were numbered, [3]offered and brought their offerings before the LORD, six covered wagons and twelve oxen, a wagon for every two of the leaders, and for each one an ox; they offered them before the tabernacle. [4]Then the LORD said to Moses, [5]"Accept these from them, that they may be used in doing the service of the tent of meeting, and give them to the Levites, to each man according to his service." [6]So Moses

took the wagons and the oxen, and gave them to the Levites. [7]Two wagons and four oxen he gave to the sons of Gershon, according to their service; [8]and four wagons and eight oxen he gave to the sons of Merar'i, according to their service, under the direction of Ith'amar the son of Aaron the priest. [9]But to the sons of Ko'hath he gave none, because they were charged with the care of the holy things which had to be carried on the shoulder. [10]And the leaders offered offerings for the dedication of the altar on the day it was anointed; and the leaders offered their offering before the altar. [11]And the LORD said to Moses, "They shall offer their offerings, one leader each day, for the dedication of the altar."

12 He who offered his offering the first day was Nahshon the son of Ammin'adab, of the tribe of Judah; [13]and his offering was one silver plate whose weight was a hundred and thirty shekels, one silver basin of seventy shekels, according to the shekel of the sanctuary, both of them full of fine flour mixed with oil for a cereal offering; [14]one golden dish of ten shekels, full of incense; [15]one young bull, one ram, one male lamb a year old, for a burnt offering; [16]one male goat for a sin offering; [17]and for the sacrifice of peace offerings, two oxen, five rams, five male goats, and five male lambs a year old. This was the offering of Nahshon the son of Ammin'adab.

18 On the second day Nethan'el the son of Zu'ar, the leader of Is'sachar, made an offering; [19]he offered for his offering one silver plate, whose weight was a hundred and thirty shekels, one silver basin of seventy shekels, according to the shekel of the sanctuary, both of them full of fine flour mixed with oil for a cereal offering; [20]one golden dish of ten shekels, full of incense; [21]one young bull, one ram, one male lamb a year old, for a burnt offering; [22]one male goat for a sin offering; [23]and for the sacrifice of peace offerings, two oxen, five rams, five male goats, and five male lambs a year old. This was the offering of Nethan'el the son of Zu'ar.

24 On the third day Eli'ab the son of He'lon, the leader of the men of Zeb'ulun: [25]his offering was one silver plate, whose weight was a hundred and thirty shekels, one silver basin of seventy shekels, according to the shekel of the sanctuary, both of them full of fine flour mixed with oil for a cereal offering; [26]one golden dish of ten shekels, full of incense; [27]one young bull, one ram, one male lamb a year old, for a burnt offering; [28]one male goat for a sin offering; [29]and for the sacrifice of peace offerings, two oxen, five rams, five male goats, and five male lambs a year old. This was the offering of Eli'ab the son of He'lon.

30 On the fourth day Eli'zur the son of Shed'eur, the leader of the men of Reuben: [31]his offering was one silver plate whose weight was a

hundred and thirty shekels, one silver basin of seventy shekels, according to the shekel of the sanctuary, both of them full of ine flour mixed with oil for a cereal offering; ³²one golden dish of ten shekels, full of incense; ³³one young bull, one ram, one male lamb a year old, for a burnt offering; ³⁴one male goat for a sin offering; ³⁵and for the sacrifice of peace offerings, two oxen, five rams, five male goats, and five male lambs a year old. This was the offering of Eli′zur the son of Shed′eur.

36 On the fifth day Shelu′mi-el the son of Zurishad′dai, the leader of the men of Simeon: ³⁷his offering was one silver plate, whose weight was a hundred and thirty shekels, one silver basin of seventy shekels, according to the shekel of the sanctuary, both of them full of fine flour mixed with oil for a cereal offering; ³⁸one golden dish of ten shekels, full of incense; ³⁹one young bull, one ram, one male lamb a year old, for a burnt offering; ⁴⁰one male goat for a sin offering; ⁴¹and for the sacrifice of peace offerings, two oxen, five rams, five male goats, and five male lambs a year old. This was the offering of Shelu′mi-el the son of Zurishad′dai.

42 On the sixth day Eli′asaph the son of Deu′el, the leader of the men of Gad: ⁴³his offering was one silver plate, whose weight was a hundred and thirty shekels, one silver basin of seventy shekels, according to the shekel of the sanctuary, both of them full of fine flour mixed with oil for a cereal offering; ⁴⁴one golden dish of ten shekels, full of incense; ⁴⁵one young bull, one ram, one male lamb a year old, for a burnt offering; ⁴⁶one male goat for a sin offering; ⁴⁷and for the sacrifice of peace offerings, two oxen, five rams, five male goats, and five male lambs a year old. This was the offering of Eli′asaph the son of Deu′el.

48 On the seventh day Elish′ama the son of Ammi′hud, the leader of the men of E′phraim: ⁴⁹his offering was one silver plate, whose weight was a hundred and thirty shekels, one silver basin of seventy shekels, according to the shekel of the sanctuary, both of them full of fine flour mixed with oil for a cereal offering; ⁵⁰one golden dish of ten shekels, full of incense; ⁵¹one young bull, one ram, one male lamb a year old, for a burnt offering; ⁵²one male goat for a sin offering; ⁵³and for the sacrifice of peace offerings, two oxen, five rams, five male goats, and five male lambs a year old. This was the offering of Elish′ama the son of Ammi′hud.

54 On the eighth day Gama′liel the son of Pedah′zur, the leader of the men of Manas′seh: ⁵⁵his offering was one silver plate, whose weight was a hundred and thirty shekels, one silver basin of seventy shekels, according to the shekel of the sanctuary, both of them full of fine flour mixed

with oil for a cereal offering; ⁵⁶one golden dish of ten shekels, full of incense; ⁵⁷one young bull, one ram, one male lamb a year old, for a burnt offering; ⁵⁸one male goat for a sin offering; ⁵⁹and for the sacrifice of peace offerings, two oxen, five rams, five male goats, and five male lambs a year old. This was the offering of Gama′liel the son of Pedah′zur.

60 On the ninth day Abi′dan the son of Gideo′ni, the leader of the men of Benjamin: ⁶¹his offering was one silver plate, whose weight was a hundred and thirty shekels, one silver basin of seventy shekels, according to the shekel of the sanctuary, both of them full of fine flour mixed with oil for a cereal offering; ⁶²one golden dish of ten shekels, full of incense; ⁶³one young bull, one ram, one male lamb a year old, for a burnt offering; ⁶⁴one male goat for a sin offering; ⁶⁵and for the sacrifice of peace offerings, two oxen, five rams, five male goats, and five male lambs a year old. This was the offering of Abi′dan the son of Gideo′ni.

66 On the tenth day Ahie′zer the son of Ammishad′dai, the leader of the men of Dan: ⁶⁷his offering was one silver plate, whose weight was a hundred and thirty shekels, one silver basin of seventy shekels, according to the shekel of the sanctuary, both of them full of fine flour mixed with oil for a cereal offering; ⁶⁸one golden dish of ten shekels, full of incense; ⁶⁹one young bull, one ram, one male lamb a year old, for a burnt offering; ⁷⁰one male goat for a sin offering; ⁷¹and for the sacrifice of peace offerings, two oxen, five rams, five male goats, and five male lambs a year old. This was the offering of Ahie′zer the son of Ammishad′dai.

72 On the eleventh day Pa′giel the son of Ochran, the leader of the men of Asher: ⁷³his offering was one silver plate, whose weight was a hundred and thirty shekels, one silver basin of seventy shekels, according to the shekel of the sanctuary, both of them full of fine flour mixed with oil for a cereal offering; ⁷⁴one golden dish of ten shekels, full of incense; ⁷⁵one young bull, one ram, one male lamb a year old, for a burnt offering; ⁷⁶one male goat for a sin offering; ⁷⁷and for the sacrifice of peace offerings, two oxen, five rams, five male goats, and five male lambs a year old. This was the offering of Pa′giel the son of Ochran.

78 On the twelfth day Ahi′ra the son of E′nan, the leader of the men of Naph′tali: ⁷⁹his offering was one silver plate, whose weight was a hundred and thirty shekels, one silver basin of seventy shekels, according to the shekel of the sanctuary, both of them full of fine flour mixed with oil for a cereal offering; ⁸⁰one golden dish of ten shekels, full of incense; ⁸¹one young bull, one ram, one male lamb a year old, for a burnt offering; ⁸²one

male goat for a sin offering; [83]and for the sacrifice of peace offerings, two oxen, five rams, five male goats, and five male lambs a year old. This was the offering of Ahi'ra the son of E'nan.

84 This was the dedication offering for the altar, on the day when it was anointed, from the leaders of Israel: twelve silver plates, twelve silver basins, twelve golden dishes, [85]each silver plate weighing a hundred and thirty shekels and each basin seventy, all the silver of the vessels two thousand four hundred shekels according to the shekel of the sanctuary, [86]the twelve golden dishes, full of incense, weighing ten shekels apiece according to the shekel of the sanctuary, all the gold of the dishes being a hundred and twenty shekels; [87]all the cattle for the burnt offering twelve bulls, twelve rams, twelve male lambs a year old, with their cereal offering; and twelve male goats for a sin offering; [88]and all the cattle for the sacrifice of peace offerings twenty-four bulls, the rams sixty, the male goats sixty, the male lambs a year old sixty. This was the dedication offering for the altar, after it was anointed.

89 And when Moses went into the tent of meeting to speak with the LORD, he heard the voice speaking to him from above the mercy seat that was upon the ark of the covenant, from between the two cherubim; and it spoke to him.

The Seven Lamps

8 Now the LORD said to Moses, [2]"Say to Aaron, When you set up the lamps, the seven lamps shall give light in front of the lampstand." [3]And Aaron did so; he set up its lamps to give light in front of the lampstand, as the LORD commanded Moses. [4]And this was the workmanship of the lampstand, hammered work of gold; from its base to its flowers, it was hammered work; according to the pattern which the LORD had shown Moses, so he made the lampstand.

The Levites' Consecration and Service

5 And the LORD said to Moses, [6]"Take the Levites from among the sons of Israel, and cleanse them. [7]And thus you shall do to them, to cleanse them: sprinkle the water of expiation upon them, and let them go with a razor over all their body, and wash their clothes and cleanse themselves. [8]Then let them take a young bull and its cereal offering of fine flour mixed with oil, and you shall take another young bull for a sin offering. [9]And you shall present the Levites before the tent of meeting, and assemble the whole congregation of the sons of Israel. [10]When you present the Levites before the LORD, the sons of Israel shall lay their hands upon the Levites, [11]and Aaron shall offer the Levites before the LORD as a wave offering from the sons of Israel, that it may be theirs to do the service of the LORD. [12]Then the Levites shall lay their hands upon the heads of the bulls; and you shall offer the one for a sin

offering and the other for a burnt offering to the LORD, to make atonement for the Levites. [13]And you shall cause the Levites to attend Aaron and his sons, and shall offer them as a wave offering to the LORD.

14 "Thus you shall separate the Levites from among the sons of Israel, and the Levites shall be mine. [15]And after that the Levites shall go in to do service at the tent of meeting, when you have cleansed them and offered them as a wave offering. [16]For they are wholly given to me from among the sons of Israel; instead of all that open the womb, the first-born of all the sons of Israel, I have taken them for myself. [17]For all the first-born among the sons of Israel are mine, both of man and of beast; on the day that I slew all the first-born in the land of Egypt I consecrated them for myself, [18]and I have taken the Levites instead of all the first-born among the sons of Israel. [19]And I have given the Levites as a gift to Aaron and his sons from among the sons of Israel, to do the service for the sons of Israel at the tent of meeting, and to make atonement for the sons of Israel, that there may be no plague among the sons of Israel in case the sons of Israel should come near the sanctuary."

20 Thus did Moses and Aaron and all the congregation of the sons of Israel to the Levites; according to all that the LORD commanded Moses concerning the Levites, the sons of Israel did to them. [21]And the Levites purified themselves from sin, and washed their clothes; and Aaron offered them as a wave offering before the LORD, and Aaron made atonement for them to cleanse them. [22]And after that the Levites went in to do their service in the tent of meeting in attendance upon Aaron and his sons; as the LORD had commanded Moses concerning the Levites, so they did to them.

23 And the LORD said to Moses, [24]"This is what pertains to the Levites: from twenty-five years old and upward they shall go in to perform the work in the service of the tent of meeting; [25]and from the age of fifty years they shall withdraw from the work of the service and serve no more, [26]but minister to their brethren in the tent of meeting, to keep the charge, and they shall do no service. Thus shall you do to the Levites in assigning their duties."

The Passover Kept at Sinai

9 And the LORD spoke to Moses in the wilderness of Sinai, in the first month of the second year after they had come out of the land of Egypt, saying, [2]"Let the sons of Israel keep the Passover at its appointed time. [3]On the fourteenth day of this month, in the evening, you shall keep it at its appointed time; according to all its statutes and

8:6–26: Num 3:5–13.
8:18: Num 3:11–13, 45.
9:1–5: Ex 12:1–14, 21–28.

all its ordinances you shall keep it." ⁴So Moses told the sons of Israel that they should keep the Passover. ⁵And they kept the Passover in the first month, on the fourteenth day of the month, in the evening, in the wilderness of Sinai; according to all that the LORD commanded Moses, so the sons of Israel did. ⁶And there were certain men who were unclean through touching the dead body of a man, so that they could not keep the Passover on that day; and they came before Moses and Aaron on that day; ⁷and those men said to him, "We are unclean through touching the dead body of a man; why are we kept from offering the LORD's offering at its appointed time among the sons of Israel?" ⁸And Moses said to them, "Wait, that I may hear what the LORD will command concerning you."

9 The LORD said to Moses, ¹⁰ "Say to the sons of Israel, If any man of you or of your descendants is unclean through touching a dead body, or is afar off on a journey, he shall still keep the Passover to the LORD. ¹¹In the second month on the fourteenth day in the evening they shall keep it; they shall eat it with unleavened bread and bitter herbs. ¹²They shall leave none of it until the morning, nor break a bone of it; according to all the statute for the Passover they shall keep it. ¹³But the man who is clean and is not on a journey, yet refrains from keeping the Passover, that person shall be cut off from his people, because he did not offer the LORD's offering at its appointed time; that man shall bear his sin. ¹⁴And if a stranger sojourns among you, and will keep the Passover to the LORD, according to the statute of the Passover and according to its ordinance, so shall he do; you shall have one statute, both for the sojourner and for the native."

The Cloud and the Fire

15 On the day that the tabernacle was set up, the cloud covered the tabernacle, the tent of the covenant; and at evening it was over the tabernacle like the appearance of fire until morning. ¹⁶So it was continually; the cloud covered it by day, ᵈ and the appearance of fire by night. ¹⁷And whenever the cloud was taken up from over the tent, after that the sons of Israel set out; and in the place where the cloud settled down, there the sons of Israel encamped. ¹⁸At the command of the LORD the sons of Israel set out, and at the command of the LORD they encamped; as long as the cloud rested over the tabernacle, they remained in camp. ¹⁹Even when the cloud continued over the tabernacle many days, the sons of Israel kept the charge of the LORD, and did not set out. ²⁰Sometimes the cloud was a few days over the tabernacle, and according to the command of the LORD they remained in camp; then according to the command of the LORD they set out. ²¹And sometimes the cloud remained from evening until morning; and when the cloud was taken up in the morning, they set out, or if it continued for a day and a night, when the cloud was taken up they set out. ²²Whether it was two days, or a month, or a longer time, that the cloud continued over the tabernacle, abiding there, the sons of Israel remained in camp and did not set out; but when it was taken up they set out. ²³At the command of the LORD they encamped, and at the command of the LORD they set out; they kept the charge of the LORD, at the command of the LORD by Moses.

The Silver Trumpets

10 The LORD said to Moses, ² "Make two silver trumpets; of hammered work you shall make them; and you shall use them for summoning the congregation, and for breaking camp. ³And when both are blown, all the congregation shall gather themselves to you at the entrance of the tent of meeting. ⁴But if they blow only one, then the leaders, the heads of the tribes of Israel, shall gather themselves to you. ⁵When you blow an alarm, the camps that are on the east side shall set out. ⁶And when you blow an alarm the second time, the camps that are on the south side shall set out. An alarm is to be blown whenever they are to set out. ⁷But when the assembly is to be gathered together, you shall blow, but you shall not sound an alarm. ⁸And the sons of Aaron, the priests, shall blow the trumpets. The trumpets shall be to you for a perpetual statute throughout your generations. ⁹And when you go to war in your land against the adversary who oppresses you, then you shall sound an alarm with the trumpets, that you may be remembered before the LORD your God, and you shall be saved from your enemies. ¹⁰On the day of your gladness also, and at your appointed feasts, and at the beginnings of your months, you shall blow the trumpets over your burnt offerings and over the sacrifices of your peace offerings; they shall serve you for remembrance before your God; I am the LORD your God."

Departure from Sinai

11 In the second year, in the second month, on the twentieth day of the month, the cloud was taken up from over the tabernacle of the covenant, ¹²and the sons of Israel set out by stages from the wilderness of Sinai; and the cloud settled down in the wilderness of Par'an. ¹³They set out for the first time at the command of the LORD by Moses. ¹⁴The standard of the camp of the men of Judah set out first by their companies; and over their host was Nahshon the son of Ammin'adab. ¹⁵And over the host of the tribe of the men of Is'sachar was Nethan'el the son of Zu'ar. ¹⁶And

ᵈ Gk Syr Vg: Heb lacks *by day*.
9:12: Ex 12:46; Jn 19:36.
9:15–23: Ex 40:36–38.

105

over the host of the tribe of the men of Zeb'ulun was Eli'ab the son of He'lon.

17 And when the tabernacle was taken down, the sons of Gershon and the sons of Merar'i, who carried the tabernacle, set out. [18]And the standard of the camp of Reuben set out by their companies; and over their host was Eli'zur the son of Shed'eur. [19]And over the host of the tribe of the men of Simeon was Shelu'mi-el the son of Zurishad'dai. [20]And over the host of the tribe of the men of Gad was Eli'asaph the son of Deu'el.

21 Then the Ko'hathites set out, carrying the holy things, and the tabernacle was set up before their arrival. [22]And the standard of the camp of the men of E'phraim set out by their companies; and over their host was Elish'ama the son of Ammi'hud. [23]And over the host of the tribe of the men of Manas'seh was Gama'liel the son of Pedah'zur. [24]And over the host of the tribe of the men of Benjamin was Abi'dan the son of Gideo'ni.

25 Then the standard of the camp of the men of Dan, acting as the rear guard of all the camps, set out by their companies; and over their host was Ahie'zer the son of Ammishad'dai. [26]And over the host of the tribe of the men of Asher was Pa'giel the son of Ochran. [27]And over the tribe of the men of Naph'tali was Ahi'ra the son of E'nan. [28]This was the order of march of the sons of Israel according to their hosts, when they set out.

29 And Moses said to Ho'bab the son of Reu'el the Mid'ianite, Moses' father-in-law, "We are setting out for the place of which the Lord said, 'I will give it to you'; come with us, and we will do you good; for the Lord has promised good to Israel." [30]But he said to him, "I will not go; I will depart to my own land and to my kindred." [31]And he said, "Do not leave us, I beg you, for you know how we are to encamp in the wilderness, and you will serve as eyes for us. [32]And if you go with us, whatever good the Lord will do to us, the same will we do to you."

33 So they set out from the mount of the Lord three days' journey; and the ark of the covenant of the Lord went before them three days' journey, to seek out a resting place for them. [34]And the cloud of the Lord was over them by day, whenever they set out from the camp.

35 And whenever the ark set out, Moses said, "Arise, O Lord, and let your enemies be scattered; and let them who hate you flee before you." [36]And when it rested, he said, "Return, O Lord, to the ten thousand thousands of Israel."

Complaining in the Desert

11 And the people complained in the hearing of the Lord about their misfortunes; and when the Lord heard it, his anger was kindled, and the fire of the Lord burned among them, and consumed some outlying parts of the camp. [2]Then the people cried to Moses; and Moses prayed to the Lord, and the fire abated. [3]So the name of that place was called Tab'erah,* because the fire of the Lord burned among them.

4 Now the rabble that was among them had a strong craving; and the people of Israel also wept again, and said, "O that we had meat to eat! [5]We remember the fish we ate in Egypt for nothing, the cucumbers, the melons, the leeks, the onions, and the garlic; [6]but now our strength is dried up, and there is nothing at all but this manna to look at."

7 Now the manna was like coriander seed, and its appearance like that of gum resin. [8]The people went about and gathered it, and ground it in mills or beat it in mortars, and boiled it in pots, and made cakes of it; and the taste of it was like the taste of cakes baked with oil. [9]When the dew fell upon the camp in the night, the manna fell with it.

10 Moses heard the people weeping throughout their families, every man at the door of his tent; and the anger of the Lord blazed hotly, and Moses was displeased. [11]Moses said to the Lord, "Why have you dealt ill with your servant? And why have I not found favor in your sight, that you lay the burden of all this people upon me? [12]Did I conceive all this people? Did I bring them forth, that you should say to me, 'Carry them in your bosom, as a nurse carries the sucking child,' to the land which you swore to give their fathers? [13]Where am I to get meat to give to all this people? For they weep before me and say, 'Give us meat, that we may eat.' [14]I am not able to carry all this people alone, the burden is too heavy for me. [15]If you will deal thus with me, kill me at once, if I find favor in your sight, that I may not see my wretchedness."

The Seventy Elders

16 And the Lord said to Moses, "Gather for me seventy men of the elders of Israel, whom you know to be the elders of the people and officers over them; and bring them to the tent of meeting, and let them take their stand there with you. [17]And I will come down and talk with you there; and I will take some of the spirit which is upon you and put it upon them; and they shall bear the burden of the people with you, that you may not bear it yourself alone. [18]And say to the people, 'Consecrate yourselves for tomorrow, and you shall eat meat; for you have wept in the hearing of the Lord, saying, "Who will give us meat to eat? For it was well with us in Egypt." Therefore the Lord will give you meat, and you shall eat. [19]You shall not eat one day, or two days, or five days, or ten days, or twenty days, [20]but a whole month, until it

---

* That is *Burning*.
10:35: Ps 68:1, 2.
11:4: 1 Cor 10:6.

comes out at your nostrils and becomes loath-some to you, because you have rejected the Lᴏʀᴅ who is among you, and have wept before him, saying, "Why did we come forth out of Egypt?" ' " ²¹But Moses said, "The people among whom I am number six hundred thousand on foot; and you have said, 'I will give them meat, that they may eat a whole month!' ²²Shall flocks and herds be slaughtered for them, to satisfy them? Or shall all the fish of the sea be gathered together for them, to satisfy them?" ²³And the Lᴏʀᴅ said to Moses, "Is the Lᴏʀᴅ's hand shortened? Now you shall see whether my word will come true for you or not."

24 So Moses went out and told the people the words of the Lᴏʀᴅ; and he gathered seventy men of the elders of the people, and placed them round about the tent. ²⁵Then the Lᴏʀᴅ came down in the cloud and spoke to him, and took some of the spirit that was upon him and put it upon the seventy elders; and when the spirit rested upon them, they prophesied. But they did so no more.

26 Now two men remained in the camp, one named Eldad, and the other named Medad, and the spirit rested upon them; they were among those registered, but they had not gone out to the tent, and so they prophesied in the camp. ²⁷And a young man ran and told Moses, "Eldad and Medad are prophesying in the camp." ²⁸And Joshua the son of Nun, the minister of Moses, one of his chosen men, said, "My lord Moses, forbid them." ²⁹But Moses said to him, "Are you jealous for my sake? Would that all the Lᴏʀᴅ's people were prophets, that the Lᴏʀᴅ would put his spirit upon them!" ³⁰And Moses and the elders of Israel returned to the camp.*

The Quails

31 And there went forth a wind from the Lᴏʀᴅ, and it brought quails from the sea, and let them fall beside the camp, about a day's journey on this side and a day's journey on the other side, round about the camp, and about two cubits above the face of the earth. ³²And the people rose all that day, and all night, and all the next day, and gath-ered the quails; he who gathered least gathered ten homers; and they spread them out for them-selves all around the camp. ³³While the meat was yet between their teeth, before it was consumed, the anger of the Lᴏʀᴅ was kindled against the people, and the Lᴏʀᴅ struck the people with a very great plague. ³⁴Therefore the name of that place was called Kib′roth-hatta′avah, ᶠ because there they buried the people who had the craving. ³⁵From Kib′roth-hatta′avah the people journeyed to Haze′roth; and they remained at Hazeroth.

Aaron and Miriam Speak against Moses

12 Miriam and Aaron spoke against Moses because of the Cushite woman whom he had married, for he had married a Cushite woman; ²and they said, "Has the Lᴏʀᴅ indeed spoken only

through Moses? Has he not spoken through us also?" And the Lᴏʀᴅ heard it. ³Now the man Moses was very meek, more than all men that were on the face of the earth. ⁴And suddenly the Lᴏʀᴅ said to Moses and to Aaron and Miriam, "Come out, you three, to the tent of meeting." And the three of them came out. ⁵And the Lᴏʀᴅ came down in a pillar of cloud, and stood at the door of the tent, and called Aaron and Miriam; and they both came forward. ⁶And he said, "Hear my words: If there is a prophet among you, I the Lᴏʀᴅ make myself known to him in a vision, I speak with him in a dream. ⁷Not so with my servant Moses; he is en-trusted with all my house. ⁸With him I speak mouth to mouth, clearly, and not in dark speech; and he beholds the form of the Lᴏʀᴅ. Why then were you not afraid to speak against my servant Moses?"

9 And the anger of the Lᴏʀᴅ was kindled against them, and he departed; ¹⁰and when the cloud removed from over the tent, behold, Miriam was leprous, as white as snow. And Aaron turned towards Miriam, and behold, she was leprous. ¹¹And Aaron said to Moses, "Oh, my lord, do not ᵍ punish us because we have done foolishly and have sinned. ¹²Let her not be as one dead, of whom the flesh is half consumed when he comes out of his mother's womb." ¹³And Moses cried to the Lᴏʀᴅ, "Heal her, O God, I beg you." ¹⁴But the Lᴏʀᴅ said to Moses, "If her father had but spit in her face, should she not be shamed seven days? Let her be shut up outside the camp seven days, and after that she may be brought in again." ¹⁵So Miriam was shut up outside the camp seven days; and the people did not set out on the march till Miriam was brought in again. ¹⁶After that the people set out from Haze′roth, and encamped in the wilderness of Par′an.

Spies Sent into Canaan

13 The Lᴏʀᴅ said to Moses, ² "Send men to spy out the land of Canaan, which I give to the sons of Israel; from each tribe of their fathers shall you send a man, every one a leader among them." ³So Moses sent them from the wil-derness of Par′an, according to the command of the Lᴏʀᴅ, all of them men who were heads of the sons of Israel. ⁴And these were their names: From the tribe of Reuben, Sham′mu-a the son of Zaccur; ⁵from the tribe of Simeon, Sha′phat the son of Ho′ri; ⁶from the tribe of Judah, Caleb the son of Jephun′neh; ⁷from the tribe of Is′sachar, I′gal the son of Joseph; ⁸from the tribe of E′phraim, Hoshe′a the son of Nun; ⁹from the tribe

---

ᶠ That is *Graves of craving.*
ᵍ Heb *lay not sin upon us.*
* 11:16–30: The account of the election of the seventy elders emphasizes the charismatic or prophetic basis of authority in the community.
11:34: 1 Cor 10:6.
12:7: Heb 3:2, 5, 6.
12:8: Ex 33:11; Deut 34:10.

of Benjamin, Palti the son of Ra'phu; [10]from the tribe of Zeb'ulun, Gad'diel the son of Sodi; [11]from the tribe of Joseph (that is from the tribe of Manas'seh), Gaddi the son of Susi; [12]from the tribe of Dan, Am'miel the son of Gemal'li; [13]from the tribe of Asher, Seth'ur the son of Michael; [14]from the tribe of Naph'tali, Nahbi the son of Voph'si; [15]from the tribe of Gad, Geu'el the son of Machi. [16]These were the names of the men whom Moses sent to spy out the land. And Moses called Hoshe'a the son of Nun Joshua.

[17] Moses sent them to spy out the land of Canaan, and said to them, "Go up into the Neg'eb yonder, and go up into the hill country, [18]and see what the land is, and whether the people who dwell in it are strong or weak, whether they are few or many, [19]and whether the land that they dwell in is good or bad, and whether the cities that they dwell in are camps or strongholds, [20]and whether the land is rich or poor, and whether there is wood in it or not. Be of good courage, and bring some of the fruit of the land." Now the time was the season of the first ripe grapes.

[21] So they went up and spied out the land from the wilderness of Zin to Re'hob, near the entrance of Ha'math. [22]They went up into the Neg'eb, and came to He'bron; and Ahi'man, Sheshai, and Talmai, the descendants of A'nak, were there. (Hebron was built seven years before Zoan in Egypt.) [23]And they came to the Valley of Eshcol, and cut down from there a branch with a single cluster of grapes, and they carried it on a pole between two of them; they brought also some pomegranates and figs. [24]That place was called the Valley of Eshcol,[h] because of the cluster which the men of Israel cut down from there.

[25] At the end of forty days they returned from spying out the land. [26]And they came to Moses and Aaron and to all the congregation of the sons of Israel in the wilderness of Par'an, at Ka'desh; they brought back word to them and to all the congregation, and showed them the fruit of the land. [27]And they told him, "We came to the land to which you sent us; it flows with milk and honey, and this is its fruit. [28]Yet the people who dwell in the land are strong, and the cities are fortified and very large; and besides, we saw the descendants of A'nak there. [29]The Amal'ekites dwell in the land of the Neg'eb; the Hittites, the Jeb'usites, and the Am'orites dwell in the hill country; and the Canaanites dwell by the sea, and along the Jordan."

[30] But Caleb quieted the people before Moses, and said, "Let us go up at once, and occupy it; for we are well able to overcome it." [31]Then the men who had gone up with him said, "We are not able to go up against the people; for they are stronger than we." [32]So they brought to the sons of Israel an evil report of the land which they had spied

out, saying, "The land, through which we have gone to spy it out, is a land that devours its inhabitants; and all the people that we saw in it are men of great stature. [33]And there we saw the Neph'ilim (the sons of A'nak, who come from the Nephilim); and we seemed to ourselves like grasshoppers, and so we seemed to them."

The People Rebel

14 Then all the congregation raised a loud cry; and the people wept that night. [2]And all the sons of Israel murmured against Moses and Aaron; the whole congregation said to them, "Would that we had died in the land of Egypt! Or would that we had died in this wilderness! [3]Why does the LORD bring us into this land, to fall by the sword? Our wives and our little ones will become a prey; would it not be better for us to go back to Egypt?"

[4] And they said to one another, "Let us choose a captain, and go back to Egypt." [5]Then Moses and Aaron fell on their faces before all the assembly of the congregation of the sons of Israel. [6]And Joshua the son of Nun and Caleb the son of Jephun'neh, who were among those who had spied out the land, tore their clothes, [7]and said to all the congregation of the sons of Israel, "The land, which we passed through to spy it out, is an exceedingly good land. [8]If the LORD delights in us, he will bring us into this land and give it to us, a land which flows with milk and honey. [9]Only, do not rebel against the LORD; and do not fear the people of the land, for they are bread for us; their protection is removed from them, and the LORD is with us; do not fear them." [10]But all the congregation said to stone them with stones.

Then the glory of the LORD appeared at the tent of meeting to all the sons of Israel. [11]And the LORD said to Moses, "How long will this people despise me? And how long will they not believe in me, in spite of all the signs which I have wrought among them? [12]I will strike them with the pestilence and disinherit them, and I will make of you a nation greater and mightier than they."

Moses Intercedes for the People

[13] But Moses said to the LORD, "Then the Egyptians will hear of it, for you brought up this people in your might from among them, [14]and they will tell the inhabitants of this land. They have heard that you, O LORD, are in the midst of this people; for you, O LORD, are seen face to face, and your cloud stands over them and you go before them, in a pillar of cloud by day and in a pillar of fire by night. [15]Now if you kill this people as one man, then the nations who have heard your fame will say, [16]'Because the LORD was not able to

---

h That is *Cluster*.
13:33: Gen 6:4.
14:3: Acts 7:39.
14:11–25: Ex 32:9–14, 31–35.

bring this people into the land which he swore to give to them, therefore he has slain them in the wilderness.' [17]And now, I beg you, let the power of the LORD be great as you have promised, saying, [18] 'The LORD is slow to anger, and abounding in mercy, forgiving iniquity and transgression, but he will by no means clear the guilty, visiting the iniquity of fathers upon children, upon the third and upon the fourth generation.' [19]Pardon the iniquity of this people, I beg you, according to the greatness of your mercy, and according as you have forgiven this people, from Egypt even until now."

20 Then the LORD said, "I have pardoned, according to your word; [21]but truly, as I live, and as all the earth shall be filled with the glory of the LORD, [22]none of the men who have seen my glory and my signs which I wrought in Egypt and in the wilderness, and yet have put me to the proof these ten times and have not hearkened to my voice, [23]shall see the land which I swore to give to their fathers; and none of those who despised me shall see it. [24]But my servant Caleb, because he has a different spirit and has followed me fully, I will bring into the land into which he went, and his descendants shall possess it. [25]Now, since the Amal'ekites and the Canaanites dwell in the valleys, turn tomorrow and set out for the wilderness by the way to the Red Sea."

God's Punishment of the Disobedient

26 And the LORD said to Moses and to Aaron, [27] "How long shall this wicked congregation murmur against me? I have heard the murmurings of the sons of Israel, which they murmur against me. [28]Say to them, 'As I live,' says the LORD, 'what you have said in my hearing I will do to you: [29]your dead bodies shall fall in this wilderness; and of all your number, numbered from twenty years old and upward, who have murmured against me, [30]not one shall come into the land where I swore that I would make you dwell, except Caleb the son of Jephun'neh and Joshua the son of Nun. [31]But your little ones, who you said would become a prey, I will bring in, and they shall know the land which you have despised. [32]But as for you, your dead bodies shall fall in this wilderness. [33]And your children shall be shepherds in the wilderness forty years, and shall suffer for your faithlessness, until the last of your dead bodies lies in the wilderness. [34]According to the number of the days in which you spied out the land, forty days, for every day a year, you shall bear your iniquity, forty years, and you shall know my displeasure.' [35]I, the LORD, have spoken; surely this will I do to all this wicked congregation that are gathered together against me: in this wilderness they shall come to a full end, and there they shall die."

36 And the men whom Moses sent to spy out the land, and who returned and made all the congregation to murmur against him by bringing up an evil report against the land, [37]the men who brought up an evil report of the land, died by plague before the LORD. [38]But Joshua the son of Nun and Caleb the son of Jephun'neh remained alive, of those men who went to spy out the land.

39 And Moses told these words to all the sons of Israel, and the people mourned greatly. [40]And they rose early in the morning, and went up to the heights of the hill country, saying, "See, we are here, we will go up to the place which the LORD has promised; for we have sinned." [41]But Moses said, "Why now are you transgressing the command of the LORD, for that will not succeed? [42]Do not go up lest you be struck down before your enemies, for the LORD is not among you. [43]For there the Amal'ekites and the Canaanites are before you, and you shall fall by the sword; because you have turned back from following the LORD, the LORD will not be with you." [44]But they presumed to go up to the heights of the hill country, although neither the ark of the covenant of the LORD, nor Moses, departed out of the camp. [45]Then the Amal'ekites and the Canaanites who dwelt in that hill country came down, and defeated them and pursued them, even to Hormah.

Various Offerings

15 The LORD said to Moses, [2] "Say to the sons of Israel, When you come into the land you are to inhabit, which I give you, [3]and you offer to the LORD from the herd or from the flock an offering by fire or a burnt offering or a sacrifice, to fulfil a vow or as a freewill offering or at your appointed feasts, to make a pleasing odor to the LORD, [4]then he who brings his offering shall offer to the LORD a cereal offering of a tenth of an ephah of fine flour, mixed with a fourth of a hin of oil; [5]and wine for the drink offering, a fourth of a hin, you shall prepare with the burnt offering, or for the sacrifice, for each lamb. [6]Or for a ram, you shall prepare for a cereal offering two tenths of an ephah of fine flour mixed with a third of a hin of oil; [7]and for the drink offering you shall offer a third of a hin of wine, a pleasing odor to the LORD. [8]And when you prepare a bull for a burnt offering, or for a sacrifice, to fulfil a vow, or for peace offerings to the LORD, [9]then you shall offer with the bull a cereal offering of three tenths of an ephah of fine flour, mixed with half a hin of oil, [10]and you shall offer for the drink offering half a hin of wine, as an offering by fire, a pleasing odor to the LORD.

11 "Thus it shall be done for each bull or ram, or for each of the male lambs or the kids. [12]According to the number that you prepare, so shall

---

14:22, 23: Heb 3:18.
14:29: Heb 3:17.
14:33: Acts 7:36.

you do with every one according to their number. [13]All who are native shall do these things in this way, in offering an offering by fire, a pleasing odor to the LORD. [14]And if a stranger is sojourning with you, or any one is among you throughout your generations, and he wishes to offer an offering by fire, a pleasing odor to the LORD, he shall do as you do. [15]For the assembly, there shall be one statute for you and for the stranger who sojourns with you, a perpetual statute throughout your generations; as you are, so shall the sojourner be before the LORD. [16]One law and one ordinance shall be for you and for the stranger who sojourns with you."

17 The LORD said to Moses, [18]"Say to the sons of Israel, When you come into the land to which I bring you [19]and when you eat of the food of the land, you shall present an offering to the LORD. [20]Of the first of your coarse meal you shall present a cake as an offering; as an offering from the threshing floor, so shall you present it. [21]Of the first of your coarse meal you shall give to the LORD an offering throughout your generations.

22 "But if you err, and do not observe all these commandments which the LORD has spoken to Moses, [23]all that the LORD has commanded you by Moses, from the day that the LORD gave commandment, and onward throughout your generations, [24]then if it was done unwittingly without the knowledge of the congregation, all the congregation shall offer one young bull for a burnt offering, a pleasing odor to the LORD, with its cereal offering and its drink offering, according to the ordinance, and one male goat for a sin offering. [25]And the priest shall make atonement for all the congregation of the sons of Israel, and they shall be forgiven; because it was an error, and they have brought their offering, an offering by fire to the LORD, and their sin offering before the LORD, for their error. [26]And all the congregation of the sons of Israel shall be forgiven, and the stranger who sojourns among them, because the whole population was involved in the error.

27 "If one person sins unwittingly, he shall offer a female goat a year old for a sin offering. [28]And the priest shall make atonement before the LORD for the person who commits an error, when he sins unwittingly, to make atonement for him; and he shall be forgiven. [29]You shall have one law for him who does anything unwittingly, for him who is native among the sons of Israel, and for the stranger who sojourns among them. [30]But the person who does anything with a high hand, whether he is native or a sojourner, reviles the LORD, and that person shall be cut off from among his people. [31]Because he has despised the word of the LORD, and has broken his commandment, that person shall be utterly cut off; his iniquity shall be upon him."

Punishment for Violating the Sabbath

32 While the sons of Israel were in the wilderness, they found a man gathering sticks on the sabbath day. [33]And those who found him gathering sticks brought him to Moses and Aaron, and to all the congregation. [34]They put him in custody, because it had not been made plain what should be done to him. [35]And the LORD said to Moses, "The man shall be put to death; all the congregation shall stone him with stones outside the camp." [36]And all the congregation brought him outside the camp, and stoned him to death with stones, as the LORD commanded Moses.

Tassels on Garments

37 The LORD said to Moses, [38]"Speak to the sons of Israel, and bid them to make tassels on the corners of their garments throughout their generations, and to put upon the tassel of each corner a cord of blue; [39]and it shall be to you a tassel to look upon and remember all the commandments of the LORD, to do them, not to follow after your own heart and your own eyes, which you are inclined to go after wantonly. [40]So you shall remember and do all my commandments, and be holy to your God. [41]I am the LORD your God, who brought you out of the land of Egypt, to be your God: I am the LORD your God."

Revolt of Korah, Dathan, and Abiram

16 Now Ko'rah the son of Iz'har, son of Ko'hath, son of Levi, and Da'than and Abi'ram the sons of Eli'ab, and On the son of Pe'leth, sons of Reuben, [2]took men; and they rose up before Moses, with a number of the sons of Israel, two hundred and fifty leaders of the congregation, chosen from the assembly, well-known men; [3]and they assembled themselves together against Moses and against Aaron, and said to them, "You have gone too far! For all the congregation are holy, every one of them, and the LORD is among them; why then do you exalt yourselves above the assembly of the LORD?" [4]When Moses heard it, he fell on his face; [5]and he said to Ko'rah and all his company, "In the morning the LORD will show who is his, and who is holy, and will cause him to come near to him; him whom he will choose he will cause to come near to him. [6]Do this: take censers, Ko'rah and all his company; [7]put fire in them and put incense upon them before the LORD tomorrow, and the man whom the LORD chooses shall be the holy one. You have gone too far, sons of Levi!" [8]And Moses said to Ko'rah, "Hear now, you sons of Levi: [9]is it too small a thing for you that the God of Israel has separated you from the congregation of Israel, to

15:14: Ex 12:49; Lev 24:22; Num 15:15, 16, 29.
15:17-21: Ex 34:26; Lev 23:14.
15:22-26: Lev 4:13–21.
15:27-29: Lev 4:2–12.
15:38-40: Deut 22:12.
16:5: 2 Tim 2:19.

bring you near to himself, to do service in the tabernacle of the Lord, and to stand before the congregation to minister to them; ¹⁰and that he has brought you near him, and all your brethren the sons of Levi with you? And would you seek the priesthood also? ¹¹Therefore it is against the Lord that you and all your company have gathered together; what is Aaron that you murmur against him?"

12 And Moses sent to call Da'than and Abi'ram the sons of Eli'ab; and they said, "We will not come up. ¹³Is it a small thing that you have brought us up out of a land flowing with milk and honey, to kill us in the wilderness, that you must also make yourself a prince over us? ¹⁴Moreover you have not brought us into a land flowing with milk and honey, nor given us inheritance of fields and vineyards. Will you put out the eyes of these men? We will not come up."

15 And Moses was very angry, and said to the Lord, "Do not respect their offering. I have not taken one donkey from them, and I have not harmed one of them." ¹⁶And Moses said to Ko'rah, "Be present, you and all your company, before the Lord, you and they, and Aaron, tomorrow; ¹⁷and let every one of you take his censer, and put incense upon it, and every one of you bring before the Lord his censer, two hundred and fifty censers; you also, and Aaron, each his censer." ¹⁸So every man took his censer, and they put fire in them and laid incense upon them, and they stood at the entrance of the tent of meeting with Moses and Aaron. ¹⁹Then Ko'rah assembled all the congregation against them at the entrance of the tent of meeting. And the glory of the Lord appeared to all the congregation.

Korah, Dathan, and Abiram Are Punished

20 And the Lord said to Moses and to Aaron, ²¹"Separate yourselves from among this congregation, that I may consume them in a moment." ²²And they fell on their faces, and said, "O God, the God of the spirits of all flesh, shall one man sin, and will you be angry with all the congregation?" ²³And the Lord said to Moses, ²⁴"Say to the congregation, Get away from about the dwelling of Ko'rah, Da'than, and Abi'ram."

25 Then Moses rose and went to Da'than and Abi'ram; and the elders of Israel followed him. ²⁶And he said to the congregation, "Depart, I beg you, from the tents of these wicked men, and touch nothing of theirs, lest you be swept away with all their sins." ²⁷So they got away from about the dwelling of Ko'rah, Da'than, and Abi'ram; and Dathan and Abiram came out and stood at the door of their tents, together with their wives, their sons, and their little ones. ²⁸And Moses said, "Hereby you shall know that the Lord has sent me to do all these works, and that it has not been of my own accord. ²⁹If these men die the common

death of all men, or if they are visited by the fate of all men, then the Lord has not sent me. ³⁰But if the Lord creates something new, and the ground opens its mouth, and swallows them up, with all that belongs to them, and they go down alive into Sheol, then you shall know that these men have despised the Lord."

31 And as he finished speaking all these words, the ground under them split asunder; ³²and the earth opened its mouth and swallowed them up, with their households and all the men that belonged to Ko'rah and all their goods. ³³So they and all that belonged to them went down alive into Sheol; and the earth closed over them, and they perished from the midst of the assembly. ³⁴And all Israel that were round about them fled at their cry; for they said, "Lest the earth swallow us up!" ³⁵And fire came forth from the Lord, and consumed the two hundred and fifty men offering the incense.

36¹ Then the Lord said to Moses, ³⁷"Tell Elea'zar the son of Aaron the priest to take up the censers out of the blaze; then scatter the fire far and wide. For they are holy, ³⁸the censers of these men who have sinned at the cost of their lives; so let them be made into hammered plates as a covering for the altar, for they offered them before the Lord; therefore they are holy. Thus they shall be a sign to the sons of Israel." ³⁹So Elea'zar the priest took the bronze censers, which those who were burned had offered; and they were hammered out as a covering for the altar, ⁴⁰to be a reminder to the sons of Israel, so that no one who is not a priest, who is not of the descendants of Aaron, should draw near to burn incense before the Lord, lest he become as Ko'rah and as his company—as the Lord said to Elea'zar through Moses.

A Plague Strikes the Rebels

41 But the next day all the congregation of the sons of Israel murmured against Moses and against Aaron, saying, "You have killed the people of the Lord." ⁴²And when the congregation had assembled against Moses and against Aaron, they turned toward the tent of meeting; and behold, the cloud covered it, and the glory of the Lord appeared. ⁴³And Moses and Aaron came to the front of the tent of meeting, ⁴⁴and the Lord said to Moses, ⁴⁵"Get away from the midst of this congregation, that I may consume them in a moment." And they fell on their faces. ⁴⁶And Moses said to Aaron, "Take your censer, and put fire therein from off the altar, and lay incense on it, and carry it quickly to the congregation, and make atonement for them; for wrath has gone forth from the Lord, the plague has begun." ⁴⁷So Aaron took it as Moses said, and ran into the midst of the assembly; and behold, the plague had already

---

¹ Ch 17:1 in Heb.

begun among the people; and he put on the incense, and made atonement for the people. [48]And he stood between the dead and the living; and the plague was stopped. [49]Now those who died by the plague were fourteen thousand seven hundred, besides those who died in the affair of Ko′rah. [50]And Aaron returned to Moses at the entrance of the tent of meeting, when the plague was stopped.

The Blossoming of Aaron's Rod

17 [j] The Lord said to Moses, [2] "Speak to the sons of Israel, and get from them rods, one for each fathers' house, from all their leaders according to their fathers' houses, twelve rods. Write each man's name upon his rod, [3]and write Aaron's name upon the rod of Levi. For there shall be one rod for the head of each fathers' house. [4]Then you shall deposit them in the tent of meeting before the covenant, where I meet with you. [5]And the rod of the man whom I choose shall sprout; thus I will make to cease from me the murmurings of the sons of Israel, which they murmur against you." [6]Moses spoke to the sons of Israel; and all their leaders gave him rods, one for each leader, according to their fathers' houses, twelve rods; and the rod of Aaron was among their rods. [7]And Moses deposited the rods before the Lord in the tent of the covenant.

8 And the next day Moses went into the tent of the covenant; and behold, the rod of Aaron for the house of Levi had sprouted and put forth buds, and produced blossoms, and it bore ripe almonds. [9]Then Moses brought out all the rods from before the Lord to all the sons of Israel; and they looked, and each man took his rod. [10]And the Lord said to Moses, "Put back the rod of Aaron before the covenant, to be kept as a sign for the rebels, that you may make an end of their murmurings against me, lest they die." [11]Thus did Moses; as the Lord commanded him, so he did.

12 And the sons of Israel said to Moses, "Behold, we perish, we are undone, we are all undone. [13]Every one who comes near, who comes near to the tabernacle of the Lord, shall die. Are we all to perish?"

Duties of Priests and Levites

18 So the Lord said to Aaron, "You and your sons and your fathers' house with you shall bear iniquity in connection with the sanctuary; and you and your sons with you shall bear iniquity in connection with your priesthood. [2]And with you bring your brethren also, the tribe of Levi, the tribe of your father, that they may join you, and minister to you while you and your sons with you are before the tent of the covenant. [3]They shall attend you and attend to all duties of the tent; but shall not come near to the vessels of the sanctuary or to the altar, lest they, and you, die. [4]They shall join you, and attend to the tent of meeting, for all the service of the tent; and no one

else shall come near you. [5]And you shall attend to the duties of the sanctuary and the duties of the altar, that there be wrath no more upon the sons of Israel. [6]And behold, I have taken your brethren the Levites from among the sons of Israel; they are a gift to you, given to the Lord, to do the service of the tent of meeting. [7]And you and your sons with you shall attend to your priesthood for all that concerns the altar and that is within the veil; and you shall serve. I give your priesthood as a gift, [k] and any one else who comes near shall be put to death."

The Priest's Portion

8 Then the Lord said to Aaron, "And behold, I have given you whatever is kept of the offerings made to me, all the consecrated things of the sons of Israel; I have given them to you as a portion, and to your sons as a perpetual debt. [9]This shall be yours of the most holy things, reserved from the fire; every offering of theirs, every cereal offering of theirs and every sin offering of theirs and every guilt offering of theirs, which they render to me, shall be most holy to you and to your sons. [10]In a most holy place shall you eat of it; every male may eat of it; it is holy to you. [11]This also is yours, the offering of their gift, all the wave offerings of the sons of Israel; I have given them to you, and to your sons and daughters with you, as a perpetual debt; every one who is clean in your house may eat of it. [12]All the best of the oil, and all the best of the wine and of the grain, the first fruits of what they give to the Lord, I give to you. [13]The first ripe fruits of all that is in their land, which they bring to the Lord, shall be yours; every one who is clean in your house may eat of it. [14]Every devoted thing in Israel shall be yours. [15]Everything that opens the womb of all flesh, whether man or beast, which they offer to the Lord, shall be yours; nevertheless the firstborn of man you shall redeem, and the firstling of unclean beasts you shall redeem. [16]And their redemption price (at a month old you shall redeem them) you shall fix at five shekels in silver, according to the shekel of the sanctuary, which is twenty gerahs. [17]But the firstling of a cow, or the firstling of a sheep, or the firstling of a goat, you shall not redeem; they are holy. You shall sprinkle their blood upon the altar, and shall burn their fat as an offering by fire, a pleasing odor to the Lord; [18]but their flesh shall be yours, as the breast that is waved and as the right thigh are yours. [19]All the holy offerings which the sons of Israel present to the Lord I give to you, and to your sons and daughters with you, as a perpetual debt; it is a

[j] Ch 17:16 in Heb.
[k] Heb *service of gift.*
18:3, 4, 23: Num 1:50–53; 3:5–8, 21–37; 4:1–33; 8:19.
18:14: Lev 27:28.
18:19: 2 Chron 13:5.

covenant of salt for ever before the LORD for you and for your offspring with you." 20And the LORD said to Aaron, "You shall have no inheritance in their land, neither shall you have any portion among them; I am your portion and your inheritance among the sons of Israel.

21 "To the Levites I have given every tithe in Israel for an inheritance, in return for their service which they serve, their service in the tent of meeting. 22And henceforth the sons of Israel shall not come near the tent of meeting, lest they bear sin and die. 23But the Levites shall do the service of the tent of meeting, and they shall bear their iniquity; it shall be a perpetual statute throughout your generations; and among the sons of Israel they shall have no inheritance. 24For the tithe of the sons of Israel, which they present as an offering to the LORD, I have given to the Levites for an inheritance; therefore I have said of them that they shall have no inheritance among the sons of Israel."

25 And the LORD said to Moses, 26"Moreover you shall say to the Levites, 'When you take from the sons of Israel the tithe which I have given you from them for your inheritance, then you shall present an offering from it to the LORD, a tithe of the tithe. 27And your offering shall be reckoned to you as though it were the grain of the threshing floor, and as the fulness of the wine press. 28So shall you also present an offering to the LORD from all your tithes, which you receive from the sons of Israel; and from it you shall give the LORD's offering to Aaron the priest. 29Out of all the gifts to you, you shall present every offering due to the LORD, from all the best of them, giving the hallowed part from them.' 30Therefore you shall say to them, 'When you have offered from it the best of it, then the rest shall be reckoned to the Levites as produce of the threshing floor, and as produce of the wine press; 31and you may eat it in any place, you and your households; for it is your reward in return for your service in the tent of meeting. 32And you shall bear no sin by reason of it, when you have offered the best of it. And you shall not profane the holy things of the sons of Israel, lest you die.'"

Ceremony of the Red Heifer

19 Now the LORD said to Moses and to Aaron, 2"This is the statute of the law which the LORD has commanded: Tell the sons of Israel to bring you a red heifer without defect, in which there is no blemish, and upon which a yoke has never come. 3And you shall give her to Elea'zar the priest, and she shall be taken outside the camp and slaughtered before him; 4and Elea'zar the priest shall take some of her blood with his finger, and sprinkle some of her blood toward the front of the tent of meeting seven times. 5And the heifer shall be burned in his sight; her skin, her flesh,

and her blood, with all her dung, shall be burned; 6and the priest shall take cedarwood and hyssop and scarlet stuff, and cast them into the midst of the burning of the heifer. 7Then the priest shall wash his clothes and bathe his body in water, and afterwards he shall come into the camp; and the priest shall be unclean until evening. 8He who burns the heifer shall wash his clothes in water and bathe his body in water, and shall be unclean until evening. 9And a man who is clean shall gather up the ashes of the heifer, and deposit them outside the camp in a clean place; and they shall be kept for the congregation of the sons of Israel for the water for impurity, for the removal of sin. 10And he who gathers the ashes of the heifer shall wash his clothes, and be unclean until evening. And this shall be to the sons of Israel, and to the stranger who sojourns among them, a perpetual statute.

Laws concerning the Dead

11 "He who touches the dead body of any person shall be unclean seven days; 12he shall cleanse himself with the water on the third day and on the seventh day, and so be clean; but if he does not cleanse himself on the third day and on the seventh day, he will not become clean. 13Whoever touches a dead person, the body of any man who has died, and does not cleanse himself, defiles the tabernacle of the LORD, and that person shall be cut off from Israel; because the water for impurity was not thrown upon him, he shall be unclean; his uncleanness is still on him.

14 "This is the law when a man dies in a tent: every one who comes into the tent, and every one who is in the tent, shall be unclean seven days. 15And every open vessel, which has no cover fastened upon it, is unclean. 16Whoever in the open field touches one who is slain with a sword, or a dead body, or a bone of a man, or a grave, shall be unclean seven days. 17For the unclean they shall take some ashes of the burnt sin offering, and running water shall be added in a vessel; 18then a clean person shall take hyssop, and dip it in the water, and sprinkle it upon the tent, and upon all the furnishings, and upon the persons who were there, and upon him who touched the bone, or the slain, or the dead, or the grave; 19and the clean person shall sprinkle upon the unclean on the third day and on the seventh day; thus on the seventh day he shall cleanse him, and he shall wash his clothes and bathe himself in water, and at evening he shall be clean.

20 "But the man who is unclean and does not cleanse himself, that person shall be cut off from the midst of the assembly, since he has defiled the sanctuary of the LORD; because the water for impurity has not been thrown upon him, he is unclean. 21And it shall be a perpetual statute for them. He who sprinkles the water for impurity

shall wash his clothes; and he who touches the water for impurity shall be unclean until evening. ²²And whatever the unclean person touches shall be unclean; and any one who touches it shall be unclean until evening."

The Waters of Meribah

20 And the sons of Israel, the whole congregation, came into the wilderness of Zin in the first month, and the people stayed in Ka'desh; and Miriam died there, and was buried there.

2 Now there was no water for the congregation; and they assembled themselves together against Moses and against Aaron. ³And the people contended with Moses, and said, "Would that we had died when our brethren died before the LORD! ⁴Why have you brought the assembly of the LORD into this wilderness, that we should die here, both we and our cattle? ⁵And why have you made us come up out of Egypt, to bring us to this evil place? It is no place for grain, or figs, or vines, or pomegranates; and there is no water to drink." ⁶Then Moses and Aaron went from the presence of the assembly to the door of the tent of meeting, and fell on their faces. And the glory of the LORD appeared to them, ⁷and the LORD said to Moses, ⁸ "Take the rod, and assemble the congregation, you and Aaron your brother, and tell the rock before their eyes to yield its water; so you shall bring water out of the rock for them; so you shall give drink to the congregation and their cattle." ⁹And Moses took the rod from before the LORD, as he commanded him.

10 And Moses and Aaron gathered the assembly together before the rock, and he said to them, "Hear now, you rebels; shall we bring forth water for you out of this rock?" ¹¹And Moses lifted up his hand and struck the rock with his rod twice; and water came forth abundantly, and the congregation drank, and their cattle. ¹²And the LORD said to Moses and Aaron, "Because you did not believe in me, to sanctify me in the eyes of the sons of Israel, therefore you shall not bring this assembly into the land which I have given them." ¹³These are the waters of Mer'ibah, ¹ where the sons of Israel contended with the LORD, and he showed himself holy among them.

Passage through Edom Refused

14 Moses sent messengers from Ka'desh to the king of E'dom, "Thus says your brother Israel: You know all the adversity that has befallen us: ¹⁵how our fathers went down to Egypt, and we dwelt in Egypt a long time; and the Egyptians dealt harshly with us and our fathers; ¹⁶and when we cried to the LORD, he heard our voice, and sent an angel and brought us forth out of Egypt; and here we are in Ka'desh, a city on the edge of your territory. ¹⁷Now let us pass through your land. We will not pass through field or vineyard, neither will we drink water from a well; we will go along

the King's Highway, we will not turn aside to the right hand or to the left, until we have passed through your territory." ¹⁸But E'dom said to him, "You shall not pass through, lest I come out with the sword against you." ¹⁹And the sons of Israel said to him, "We will go up by the highway; and if we drink of your water, I and my cattle, then I will pay for it; let me only pass through on foot, nothing more." ²⁰But he said, "You shall not pass through." And E'dom came out against them with many men, and with a strong force. ²¹Thus E'dom refused to give Israel passage through his territory; so Israel turned away from him.

The Death of Aaron

22 And they journeyed from Ka'desh, and the sons of Israel, the whole congregation, came to Mount Hor. ²³And the LORD said to Moses and Aaron at Mount Hor, on the border of the land of E'dom, ²⁴ "Aaron shall be gathered to his people; for he shall not enter the land which I have given to the sons of Israel, because you rebelled against my command at the waters of Mer'ibah. ²⁵Take Aaron and Elea'zar his son, and bring them up to Mount Hor; ²⁶and strip Aaron of his garments, and put them upon Elea'zar his son; and Aaron shall be gathered to his people, and shall die there." ²⁷Moses did as the LORD commanded; and they went up Mount Hor in the sight of the congregation. ²⁸And Moses stripped Aaron of his garments, and put them upon Elea'zar his son; and Aaron died there on the top of the mountain. Then Moses and Eleazar came down from the mountain. ²⁹And when all the congregation saw that Aaron was dead, all the house of Israel wept for Aaron thirty days.

The Bronze Serpent

21 When the Canaanite, the king of Ar'ad, who dwelt in the Neg'eb, heard that Israel was coming by the way of Ath'arim, he fought against Israel, and took some of them captive. ²And Israel vowed a vow to the LORD, and said, "If you will indeed give this people into my hand, then I will utterly destroy their cities." ³And the LORD listened to the voice of Israel, and gave over the Canaanites; and they utterly destroyed them and their cities; so the name of the place was called Hormah. ^m

4 From Mount Hor they set out by the way to the Red Sea, to go around the land of E'dom; and the people became impatient on the way. ⁵And the people spoke against God and against Moses, "Why have you brought us up out of Egypt to die in the wilderness? For there is no food and no water, and we loathe this worthless food." ⁶Then

---

¹ That is *Contention*.
^m Heb *Destruction*.
20:2–13: Ex 17:2–7.
20:25–29: Num 33:38, 39.
21:1: Num 33:40.

the LORD sent fiery serpents among the people, and they bit the people, so that many sons of Israel died. [7]And the people came to Moses, and said, "We have sinned, for we have spoken against the LORD and against you; pray to the LORD, that he take away the serpents from us." So Moses prayed for the people. [8]And the LORD said to Moses, "Make a fiery serpent, and set it up as a sign; and every one who is bitten, when he sees it, shall live." [9]So Moses made a bronze serpent, and set it up as a sign; and if a serpent bit any man, he would look at the bronze serpent and live.*

The Journey to Moab

10 And the sons of Israel set out, and encamped in O'both. [11]And they set out from O'both, and encamped at I'ye-ab'arim, in the wilderness which is opposite Moab, toward the sunrise. [12]From there they set out, and encamped in the Valley of Ze'red. [13]From there they set out, and encamped on the other side of the Arnon, which is in the wilderness that extends from the boundary of the Am'orites; for the Arnon is the boundary of Moab, between Moab and the Amorites. [14]Wherefore it is said in the Book of the Wars of the LORD,

"Wa'heb in Su'phah,
  and the valleys of the Arnon,
[15]and the slope of the valleys
  that extends to the seat of Ar,
  and leans to the border of Moab."

16 And from there they continued to Be'er;[n] that is the well of which the LORD said to Moses, "Gather the people together, and I will give them water." [17]Then Israel sang this song:

"Spring up, O well!—Sing to it!—
[18]the well which the princes dug,
  which the nobles of the people delved,
  with the scepter and with their staves."

And from the wilderness they went on to Mat'tanah, [19]and from Mat'tanah to Nahal'iel, and from Nahaliel to Ba'moth, [20]and from Ba'moth to the valley lying in the region of Moab by the top of Pisgah which looks down upon the desert.[o]

Sihon the King of the Amorites Defeated

21 Then Israel sent messengers to Si'hon king of the Am'orites, saying, [22]"Let me pass through your land; we will not turn aside into field or vineyard; we will not drink the water of a well; we will go by the King's Highway, until we have passed through your territory." [23]But Si'hon would not allow Israel to pass through his territory. He gathered all his men together, and went out against Israel to the wilderness, and came to Ja'haz, and fought against Israel. [24]And Israel slew him with the edge of the sword, and took possession of his land from the Arnon to the Jabbok, as far as to the Am'monites; for Ja'zer was the boundary of the Ammonites.[p] [25]And Israel took all these cities, and Israel settled in all

the cities of the Am'orites, in Heshbon, and in all its villages. [26]For Heshbon was the city of Si'hon the king of the Am'orites, who had fought against the former king of Moab and taken all his land out of his hand, as far as the Arnon. [27]Therefore the ballad singers say,

"Come to Heshbon, let it be built,
  let the city of Si'hon be established.
[28]For fire went forth from Heshbon,
  flame from the city of Si'hon.
It devoured Ar of Moab,
  the lords of the heights of the Arnon.
[29]Woe to you, O Moab!
  You are undone, O people of Che'mosh!
He has made his sons fugitives, and his
    daughters captives, to an Am'orite king,
    Si'hon.
[30]So their posterity perished from Heshbon,[q] as
    far as Di'bon,
  and we laid waste until fire spread to
    Med'eba."[r]

Og the King of Bashan Defeated

31 Thus Israel dwelt in the land of the Am'orites. [32]And Moses sent to spy out Ja'zer; and they took its villages, and dispossessed the Am'orites that were there. [33]Then they turned and went up by the way to Bashan; and Og the king of Bashan came out against them, he and all his people, to battle at Ed're-i. [34]But the LORD said to Moses, "Do not fear him; for I have given him into your hand, and all his people, and his land; and you shall do to him as you did to Si'hon king of the Am'orites, who dwelt at Heshbon." [35]So they slew him, and his sons, and all his people, until there was not one survivor left to him; and they possessed his land.

Balak Summons Balaam

22 Then the sons of Israel set out, and encamped in the plains of Moab beyond the Jordan at Jericho. [2]And Balak the son of Zippor saw all that Israel had done to the Am'orites. [3]And Moab was in great dread of the people, because they were many; Moab was overcome with fear of the sons of Israel. [4]And Moab said to the elders of Mid'ian, "This horde will now lick up all that is round about us, as the ox licks up the grass of the field." So Balak the son of Zippor, who was king of Moab at that time, [5]sent messengers to Balaam the son of Beor at

---

[n] That is Well.
[o] Or Jeshimon.
[p] Gk: Heb the boundary of the Ammonites was strong.
[q] Gk: Heb we have shot at them. Heshbon has perished.
[r] Compare Sam and Gk: Heb we have laid waste to Nophah which to Medeba.
21:21–30: Deut 2:26–37.
21:33–35: Deut 3:1–7.
22:1: Num 33:48.
* 21:4–9: The bronze serpent may have been the standard or symbol of the tribe of Levi, to which Moses and Aaron belonged. In Jn 3:14 it becomes a type of the saving cross of Christ.

Pe'thor, which is near the River, in the land of Am'aw to call him, saying, "Behold, a people has come out of Egypt; they cover the face of the earth, and they are dwelling opposite me. ⁶Come now, curse this people for me, since they are too mighty for me; perhaps I shall be able to defeat them and drive them from the land; for I know that he whom you bless is blessed, and he whom you curse is cursed."

7 So the elders of Moab and the elders of Mid'ian departed with the fees for divination in their hand; and they came to Balaam, and gave him Balak's message. ⁸And he said to them, "Lodge here this night, and I will bring back word to you, as the Lord speaks to me"; so the princes of Moab stayed with Balaam. ⁹And God came to Balaam and said, "Who are these men with you?" ¹⁰And Balaam said to God, "Balak the son of Zippor, king of Moab, has sent to me, saying, ¹¹'Behold, a people has come out of Egypt, and it covers the face of the earth; now come, curse them for me; perhaps I shall be able to fight against them and drive them out.'" ¹²God said to Balaam, "You shall not go with them; you shall not curse the people, for they are blessed." ¹³So Balaam rose in the morning, and said to the princes of Balak, "Go to your own land; for the Lord has refused to let me go with you." ¹⁴So the princes of Moab rose and went to Balak, and said, "Balaam refuses to come with us."

15 Once again Balak sent princes, more in number and more honorable than they. ¹⁶And they came to Balaam and said to him, "Thus says Balak the son of Zippor: 'Let nothing hinder you from coming to me; ¹⁷for I will surely do you great honor, and whatever you say to me I will do; come, curse this people for me.'" ¹⁸But Balaam answered and said to the servants of Balak, "Though Balak were to give me his house full of silver and gold, I could not go beyond the command of the Lord my God, to do less or more. ¹⁹Please, now, tarry here this night also, that I may know what more the Lord will say to me." ²⁰And God came to Balaam at night and said to him, "If the men have come to call you, rise, go with them; but only what I bid you, that shall you do."

Balaam, His Donkey, and the Angel

21 * So Balaam rose in the morning, and saddled his donkey, and went with the princes of Moab. ²²But God's anger was kindled because he went; and the angel of the Lord took his stand in the way as his adversary. Now he was riding on the donkey, and his two servants were with him. ²³And the donkey saw the angel of the Lord standing in the road, with a drawn sword in his hand; and the donkey turned aside out of the road, and went into the field; and Balaam struck the donkey, to turn her into the road. ²⁴Then the

angel of the Lord stood in a narrow path between the vineyards, with a wall on either side. ²⁵And when the donkey saw the angel of the Lord, she pushed against the wall, and pressed Balaam's foot against the wall; so he struck her again. ²⁶Then the angel of the Lord went ahead, and stood in a narrow place, where there was no way to turn either to the right or to the left. ²⁷When the donkey saw the angel of the Lord, she lay down under Balaam; and Balaam's anger was kindled, and he struck the donkey with his staff. ²⁸Then the Lord opened the mouth of the donkey, and she said to Balaam, "What have I done to you, that you have struck me these three times?" ²⁹And Balaam said to the donkey, "Because you have made sport of me. I wish I had a sword in my hand, for then I would kill you." ³⁰And the donkey said to Balaam, "Am I not your donkey, upon which you have ridden all your life long to this day? Was I ever accustomed to do so to you?" And he said, "No."

31 Then the Lord opened the eyes of Balaam, and he saw the angel of the Lord standing in the way, with his drawn sword in his hand; and he bowed his head, and fell on his face. ³²And the angel of the Lord said to him, "Why have you struck your donkey these three times? Behold, I have come forth to withstand you, because your way is perverse before me; ³³and the donkey saw me, and turned aside before me these three times. If she had not turned aside from me, surely just now I would have slain you and let her live." ³⁴Then Balaam said to the angel of the Lord, "I have sinned, for I did not know that you stood in the road against me. Now therefore, if it is evil in your sight, I will go back again." ³⁵And the angel of the Lord said to Balaam, "Go with the men; but only the word which I bid you, that shall you speak." So Balaam went on with the princes of Balak.

36 When Balak heard that Balaam had come, he went out to meet him at the city of Moab, on the boundary formed by the Arnon, at the extremity of the boundary. ³⁷And Balak said to Balaam, "Did I not send to you to call you? Why did you not come to me? Am I not able to honor you?" ³⁸Balaam said to Balak, "Behold, I have come to you! Have I now any power at all to speak anything? The word that God puts in my mouth, that must I speak." ³⁹Then Balaam went with Balak, and they came to Kir'iath-hu'zoth. ⁴⁰And Balak sacrificed oxen and sheep, and sent to Balaam and to the princes who were with him.

Balaam's First Oracle

41 And the next day Balak took Balaam and brought him up to Ba'moth-ba'al; and from there

---

* 22:21–35: The story of Balaam and his donkey is of popular origin. The oracles of this foreign seer, especially the fourth (24:15–19), refer to the Messianic king of the future, of whom David is the type.

23

he saw the nearest of the people. ¹And Balaam said to Balak, "Build for me here seven altars, and provide for me here seven bulls and seven rams." ²Balak did as Balaam had said; and Balak and Balaam offered on each altar a bull and a ram. ³And Balaam said to Balak, "Stand beside your burnt offering, and I will go; perhaps the LORD will come to meet me; and whatever he shows me I will tell you." And he went to a bare height. ⁴And God met Balaam; and Balaam said to him, "I have prepared the seven altars, and I have offered upon each altar a bull and a ram." ⁵And the LORD put a word in Balaam's mouth, and said, "Return to Balak, and thus you shall speak." ⁶And he returned to him, and behold, he and all the princes of Moab were standing beside his burnt offering. ⁷And Balaam took up his discourse, and said,

"From Ar'am Balak has brought me,
    the king of Moab from the eastern
        mountains:
'Come, curse Jacob for me,
    and come, denounce Israel!'
⁸How can I curse whom God has not cursed?
    How can I denounce whom the LORD has not
        denounced?
⁹For from the top of the mountains I see him,
    from the hills I behold him;
behold, a people dwelling alone,
    and not reckoning itself among the nations!
¹⁰Who can count the dust of Jacob,
    or number the fourth part ᵃ of Israel?
Let me die the death of the righteous,
    and let my end be like his!"

11 And Balak said to Balaam, "What have you done to me? I took you to curse my enemies, and behold, you have done nothing but bless them." ¹²And he answered, "Must I not take heed to speak what the LORD puts in my mouth?"

Balaam's Second Oracle

13 And Balak said to him, "Come with me to another place, from which you may see them; you shall see only the nearest of them, and shall not see them all; then curse them for me from there." ¹⁴And he took him to the field of Zophim, to the top of Pisgah, and built seven altars, and offered a bull and a ram on each altar. ¹⁵Balaam said to Balak, "Stand here beside your burnt offering, while I meet the LORD yonder." ¹⁶And the LORD met Balaam, and put a word in his mouth, and said, "Return to Balak, and thus shall you speak." ¹⁷And he came to him, and, behold, he was standing beside his burnt offering, and the princes of Moab with him. And Balak said to him, "What has the LORD spoken?" ¹⁸And Balaam took up his discourse, and said,

"Rise, Balak, and hear;
    hearken to me, O son of Zippor:
¹⁹God is not man, that he should lie,
    or a son of man, that he should repent.
Has he said, and will he not do it?
    Or has he spoken, and will he not fulfil it?
²⁰Behold, I received a command to bless:
    he has blessed, and I cannot revoke it.
²¹He has not beheld misfortune in Jacob;
    nor has he seen trouble in Israel.
The LORD their God is with them,
    and the shout of a king is among them.
²²God brings them out of Egypt;
    they have as it were the horns of the
        wild ox.
²³For there is no enchantment against Jacob,
    no divination against Israel;
now it shall be said of Jacob and Israel,
    'What has God wrought!'
²⁴Behold, a people! As a lioness it rises up
    and as a lion it lifts itself;
it does not lie down till it devours the prey,
    and drinks the blood of the slain."

25 And Balak said to Balaam, "Neither curse them at all, nor bless them at all." ²⁶But Balaam answered Balak, "Did I not tell you, 'All that the LORD says, that I must do'?" ²⁷And Balak said to Balaam, "Come now, I will take you to another place; perhaps it will please God that you may curse them for me from there." ²⁸So Balak took Balaam to the top of Peor, that overlooks the desert. ᵗ ²⁹And Balaam said to Balak, "Build for me here seven altars, and provide for me here seven bulls and seven rams." ³⁰And Balak did as Balaam had said, and offered a bull and a ram on each altar.

Balaam's Third Oracle

24

When Balaam saw that it pleased the LORD to bless Israel, he did not go, as at other times, to look for omens, but set his face toward the wilderness. ²And Balaam lifted up his eyes, and saw Israel encamping tribe by tribe. And the Spirit of God came upon him, ³and he took up his discourse, and said,

"The oracle of Balaam the son of Beor,
    the oracle of the man whose eye is opened, ᵘ
⁴the oracle of him who hears the words of God,
    who sees the vision of the Almighty,
        falling down, but having his eyes
            uncovered:
⁵How fair are your tents, O Jacob,
    your encampments, O Israel!
⁶Like valleys that stretch afar,
    like gardens beside a river,
like aloes that the LORD has planted,
    like cedar trees beside the waters.
⁷Water shall flow from his buckets,
    and his seed shall be in many waters,
his king shall be higher than Agag,
    and his kingdom shall be exalted.

ᵃ Or *dust clouds.*
ᵗ Or *Jeshimon.*
ᵘ Or *closed* or *perfect.*

8God brings him out of Egypt;
  he has as it were the horns of the wild ox,
 he shall eat up the nations his adversaries,
    and shall break their bones in pieces,
    and pierce them through with his arrows.
9He lurked, he lay down like a lion,
    and like a lioness; who will rouse him up?
Blessed be every one who blesses you,
    and cursed be every one who curses you."

Balaam's Fourth Oracle

10 And Balak's anger was kindled against Balaam, and he struck his hands together; and Balak said to Balaam, "I called you to curse my enemies, and behold, you have blessed them these three times. 11Therefore now flee to your place; I said, 'I will certainly honor you,' but the LORD has held you back from honor." 12And Balaam said to Balak, "Did I not tell your messengers whom you sent to me, 13'If Balak should give me his house full of silver and gold, I would not be able to go beyond the word of the LORD, to do either good or bad of my own will; what the LORD speaks, that will I speak'? 14And now, behold, I am going to my people; come, I will let you know what this people will do to your people in the latter days." 15And he took up his discourse, and said,

"The oracle of Balaam the son of Beor,
    the oracle of the man whose eye is
    opened, ᵛ
16the oracle of him who hears the words of
    God,
    and knows the knowledge of the Most
    High,
who sees the vision of the Almighty,
    falling down, but having his eyes
    uncovered:
17I see him, but not now;
    I behold him, but not near:
a star shall come forth out of Jacob,
    and a scepter shall rise out of Israel;
it shall crush the forehead ʷ of Moab,
    and break down all the sons of Sheth.
18E'dom shall be dispossessed,
    Se'ir also, his enemies, shall be
    dispossessed,
    while Israel does valiantly.
19By Jacob shall dominion be exercised,
    and the survivors of cities be destroyed!"

20 Then he looked on Am'alek, and took up his discourse, and said,

"Amalek was the first of the nations,
    but in the end he shall come to destruction."

21 And he looked on the Kenite, and took up his discourse, and said,

"Enduring is your dwelling place,
    and your nest is set in the rock;
22nevertheless Kain shall be wasted.
    How long shall Asshur take you away
    captive?"

23 And he took up his discourse, and said,
"Alas, who shall live when God does this?
24   But ships shall come from Kittim
and shall afflict Asshur and E'ber;
    and he also shall come to destruction."

25 Then Balaam rose, and went back to his place; and Balak also went his way.

Worship of Baal of Peor

25 While Israel dwelt in Shittim the people began to play the harlot with the daughters of Moab. 2These invited the people to the sacrifices of their gods, and the people ate, and bowed down to their gods. 3So Israel yoked himself to Ba'al of Peor. And the anger of the LORD was kindled against Israel; 4and the LORD said to Moses, "Take all the chiefs of the people, and hang them in the sun before the LORD, that the fierce anger of the LORD may turn away from Israel." 5And Moses said to the judges of Israel, "Every one of you slay his men who have yoked themselves to Ba'al of Peor."

6 And behold, one of the sons of Israel came and brought a Mid'ianite woman to his family, in the sight of Moses and in the sight of the whole congregation of the sons of Israel, while they were weeping at the door of the tent of meeting. 7When Phin'ehas the son of Elea'zar, son of Aaron the priest, saw it, he rose and left the congregation, and took a spear in his hand 8and went after the man of Israel into the inner room, and pierced both of them, the man of Israel and the woman, through her body. Thus the plague was stayed from the sons of Israel. 9Nevertheless those that died by the plague were twenty-four thousand.

10 And the LORD said to Moses, 11"Phin'ehas the son of Elea'zar, son of Aaron the priest, has turned back my wrath from the sons of Israel, in that he was jealous with my jealousy among them, so that I did not consume the sons of Israel in my jealousy. 12Therefore say, 'Behold, I give to him my covenant of peace; 13and it shall be to him, and to his descendants after him, the covenant of a perpetual priesthood, because he was jealous for his God, and made atonement for the sons of Israel.'"

14 The name of the slain man of Israel, who was slain with the Mid'ianite woman, was Zimri the son of Sa'lu, head of a fathers' house belonging to the Simeonites. 15And the name of the Mid'ianite woman who was slain was Cozbi the daughter of Zur, who was the head of the people of a fathers' house in Mid'ian.

16 And the LORD said to Moses, 17"Harass the Mid'ianites, and strike them; 18for they have harassed you with their wiles, with which they

ᵛ Or closed or perfect.
ʷ Heb corners (of the head).
24:9: Gen 49:9.

beguiled you in the matter of Peor, and in the matter of Cozbi, the daughter of the prince of Mid'ian, their sister, who was slain on the day of the plague on account of Peor."

Another Census of Israel

26 After the plague the Lord said to Moses and to Elea'zar the son of Aaron, the priest, ² "Take a census of all the congregation of the sons of Israel, from twenty years old and upward, by their fathers' houses, all in Israel who are able to go forth to war." ³And Moses and Elea'zar the priest spoke with them in the plains of Moab by the Jordan at Jericho, saying, ⁴"Take a census of the people,* from twenty years old and upward," as the Lord commanded Moses. The sons of Israel, who came forth out of the land of Egypt, were:

5 Reuben, the first-born of Israel; the sons of Reuben: of Ha'noch, the family of the Ha'nochites; of Pallu, the family of the Pal'luites; ⁶of Hezron, the family of the Hez'ronites; of Carmi, the family of the Carmites. ⁷These are the families of the Reubenites; and their number was forty-three thousand seven hundred and thirty. ⁸And the sons of Pallu: Eli'ab. ⁹The sons of Eli'ab: Nem'u-el, Da'than, and Abi'ram. These are the Dathan and Abiram, chosen from the congregation, who contended against Moses and Aaron in the company of Ko'rah, when they contended against the Lord, ¹⁰and the earth opened its mouth and swallowed them up together with Ko'rah, when that company died, when the fire devoured two hundred and fifty men; and they became a warning. ¹¹Notwithstanding, the sons of Ko'rah did not die.

12 The sons of Simeon according to their families: of Nem'u-el, the family of the Nem'u-elites; of Ja'min, the family of the Ja'minites; of Ja'chin, the family of the Ja'chinites; ¹³of Ze'rah, the family of the Ze'rahites; of Sha'ul, the family of the Sha'ulites. ¹⁴These are the families of the Simeonites, twenty-two thousand two hundred.

15 The sons of Gad according to their families: of Ze'phon, the family of the Ze'phonites; of Hag'gi, the family of the Haggites; of Shu'ni, the family of the Shu'nites; ¹⁶of Ozni, the family of the Oznites; of E'ri, the family of the E'rites; ¹⁷of Ar'od, the family of the Ar'odites; of Are'li, family of the Are'lites. ¹⁸These are the families of the sons of Gad according to their number, forty thousand five hundred.

19 The sons of Judah were Er and O'nan; and Er and Onan died in the land of Canaan. ²⁰And the sons of Judah according to their families were: of She'lah, the family of the She'lanites; of Per'ez, the family of the Per'ezites; of Ze'rah, the family of the Ze'rahites. ²¹And the sons of Per'ez were: of Hezron, the family of the Hez'ronites; of Ha'mul, the family of the Ha'mulites. ²²These are

the families of Judah according to their number, seventy-six thousand five hundred.

23 The sons of Is'sachar according to their families: of To'la, the family of the To'laites; of Pu'vah, the family of the Pu'nites; ²⁴of Jash'ub, the family of the Jash'ubites; of Shimron, the family of the Shim'ronites. ²⁵These are the families of Is'sachar according to their number, sixty-four thousand three hundred.

26 The sons of Zeb'ulun, according to their families: of Se'red, the family of the Se'redites; of E'lon, the family of the E'lonites; of Jah'leel, the family of the Jah'leelites. ²⁷These are the families of the Zeb'ulunites according to their number, sixty thousand five hundred.

28 The sons of Joseph according to their families: Manas'seh and E'phraim. ²⁹The sons of Manas'seh: of Ma'chir, the family of the Ma'-chirites; and Machir was the father of Gilead; of Gilead, the family of the Gileadites. ³⁰These are the sons of Gilead: of Iez'er, the family of the Iez'erites; of He'lek, the family of the He'lekites; ³¹and of As'riel, the family of the As'rielites; and of She'chem, the family of the She'chemites; ³²and of Shemi'da, the family of the Shemi'daites; and of He'pher, the family of the He'pherites. ³³Now Zeloph'ehad the son of He'pher had no sons, but daughters: and the names of the daughters of Zelophehad were Mahlah, Noah, Hoglah, Milcah, and Tirzah. ³⁴These are the families of Manas'seh; and their number was fifty-two thousand seven hundred.

35 These are the sons of E'phraim according to their families: of Shu'thelah, the family of the Shu''thela'hites; of Be'cher, the family of the Be'-cherites; of Ta'han, the family of the Ta'hanites. ³⁶And these are the sons of Shu'thelah: of E'ran, the family of the E'ranites. ³⁷These are the families of the sons of E'phraim according to their number, thirty-two thousand five hundred. These are the sons of Joseph according to their families.

38 The sons of Benjamin according to their families: of Be'la, the family of the Be'laites; of Ash'bel, the family of the Ash'belites; of Ahi'-ram, the family of the Ahi'ramites; ³⁹of Shephu'pham, the family of the Shephu'phamites; of Hu'pham, the family of the Hu'phamites. ⁴⁰And the sons of Be'la were Ard and Na'aman: of Ard, the family of the Ardites; of Naaman, the family of the Na'amites. ⁴¹These are the sons of Benjamin according to their families; and their number was forty-five thousand six hundred.

42 These are the sons of Dan according to their families: of Shu'ham, the family of the Shu'hamites. These are the families of Dan according to their families. ⁴³All the families of the

---

* Supplying *take a census of the people.* Compare verse 2.
26:5–51: Num 1:22–46.

Shu'hamites, according to their number, were sixty-four thousand four hundred.

44 The sons of Asher according to their families: of Imnah, the family of the Imnites; of Ishvi, the family of the Ishvites; of Beri'ah, the family of the Beri'ites. ⁴⁵Of the sons of Beri'ah: of He'ber, the family of the He'berites; of Mal'chi-el, the family of the Mal'chi-elites. ⁴⁶And the name of the daughter of Asher was Se'rah. ⁴⁷These are the families of the sons of Asher according to their number, fifty-three thousand four hundred.

48 The sons of Naph'tali according to their families: of Jah'zeel, the family of the Jah'zeelites; of Gu'ni, the family of the Gu'nites; ⁴⁹of Je'zer, the family of the Je'zerites; of Shillem, the family of the Shil'lemites. ⁵⁰These are the families of Naph'tali according to their families; and their number was forty-five thousand four hundred.

51 This was the number of the sons of Israel, six hundred and one thousand seven hundred and thirty.

52 The LORD said to Moses: ⁵³"To these the land shall be divided for inheritance according to the number of names. ⁵⁴To a large tribe you shall give a large inheritance, and to a small tribe you shall give a small inheritance; every tribe shall be given its inheritance according to its numbers. ⁵⁵But the land shall be divided by lot; according to the names of the tribes of their fathers they shall inherit. ⁵⁶Their inheritance shall be divided according to lot between the larger and the smaller."

57 These are the Levites as numbered according to their families: of Gershon, the family of the Ger'shonites; of Ko'hath, the family of the Ko'hathites; of Merar'i, the family of the Merar'ites. ⁵⁸These are the families of Levi: the family of the Libnites, the family of the He'bronites, the family of the Mahlites, the family of the Mu'shites, the family of the Ko'rahites. And Ko'hath was the father of Amram. ⁵⁹The name of Amram's wife was Joch'ebed the daughter of Levi, who was born to Levi in Egypt; and she bore to Amram Aaron and Moses and Miriam their sister. ⁶⁰And to Aaron were born Na'dab, Abi'hu, Elea'zar and Ith'amar. ⁶¹But Na'dab and Abi'hu died when they offered unholy fire before the LORD. ⁶²And those numbered of them were twenty-three thousand, every male from a month old and upward; for they were not numbered among the sons of Israel, because there was no inheritance given to them among the sons of Israel.

63 These were those numbered by Moses and Elea'zar the priest, who numbered the sons of Israel in the plains of Moab by the Jordan at Jericho. ⁶⁴But among these there was not a man of those numbered by Moses and Aaron the priest, who had numbered the sons of Israel in the wilderness of Sinai. ⁶⁵For the LORD had said of them, "They shall die in the wilderness." There was not left a man of them, except Caleb the son of Jephun'neh and Joshua the son of Nun.

The Daughters of Zelophehad

27 Then drew near the daughters of Zeloph'ehad the son of He'pher, son of Gilead, son of Ma'chir, son of Manas'seh, from the families of Manasseh the son of Joseph. The names of his daughters were: Mahlah, Noah, Hoglah, Milcah, and Tirzah. ²And they stood before Moses, and before Elea'zar the priest, and before the leaders and all the congregation, at the door of the tent of meeting, saying, ³"Our father died in the wilderness; he was not among the company of those who gathered themselves together against the LORD in the company of Ko'rah, but died for his own sin; and he had no sons. ⁴Why should the name of our father be taken away from his family, because he had no son? Give to us a possession among our father's brethren."

5 Moses brought their case before the LORD. ⁶And the LORD said to Moses, ⁷"The daughters of Zeloph'ehad are right; you shall give them possession of an inheritance among their father's brethren and cause the inheritance of their father to pass to them. ⁸And you shall say to the sons of Israel, 'If a man dies, and has no son, then you shall cause his inheritance to pass to his daughter. ⁹And if he has no daughter, then you shall give his inheritance to his brothers. ¹⁰And if he has no brothers, then you shall give his inheritance to his father's brothers. ¹¹And if his father has no brothers, then you shall give his inheritance to his kinsman that is next to him of his family, and he shall possess it. And it shall be to the sons of Israel a statute and ordinance, as the LORD commanded Moses.'"

Joshua Appointed Moses' Successor

12 The LORD said to Moses, "Go up into this mountain of Ab'arim, and see the land which I have given to the sons of Israel. ¹³And when you have seen it, you also shall be gathered to your people, as your brother Aaron was gathered, ¹⁴because you rebelled against my word in the wilderness of Zin during the strife of the congregation, to sanctify me at the waters before their eyes." (These are the waters of Mer'ibah of Ka'desh in the wilderness of Zin.) ¹⁵Moses said to the LORD, ¹⁶"Let the LORD, the God of the spirits of all flesh, appoint a man over the congregation, ¹⁷who shall go out before them and come in before them, who shall lead them out and bring them in; that the congregation of the LORD may not be as sheep which have no shepherd." ¹⁸And the LORD said to Moses, "Take Joshua the son of Nun, a

26:57-62: Num 1:47–49.
26:64, 65: Num 14:26–35.
27:1-11: Num 36:1–12.
27:12-14: Deut 3:23–27; 32:48–52.
27:18-23: Deut 3:28.

man in whom is the spirit, and lay your hand upon him; [19]cause him to stand before Elea′zar the priest and all the congregation, and you shall commission him in their sight. [20]You shall invest him with some of your authority, that all the congregation of the sons of Israel may obey. [21]And he shall stand before Elea′zar the priest, who shall inquire for him by the judgment of the U′rim before the Lord; at his word they shall go out, and at his word they shall come in, both he and all the sons of Israel with him, the whole congregation." [22]And Moses did as the Lord commanded him; he took Joshua and caused him to stand before Elea′zar the priest and the whole congregation, [23]and he laid his hands upon him, and commissioned him as the Lord directed through Moses.

Daily Offerings

28 The Lord said to Moses, [2]"Command the sons of Israel, and say to them, 'My offering, my food for my offerings by fire, my pleasing odor, you shall take heed to offer to me in its due season.' [3]And you shall say to them, This is the offering by fire which you shall offer to the Lord: two male lambs a year old without blemish, day by day, as a continual offering. [4]The one lamb you shall offer in the morning, and the other lamb you shall offer in the evening; [5]also a tenth of an ephah of fine flour for a cereal offering, mixed with a fourth of a hin of beaten oil. [6]It is a continual burnt offering, which was ordained at Mount Sinai for a pleasing odor, an offering by fire to the Lord. [7]Its drink offering shall be a fourth of a hin for each lamb; in the holy place you shall pour out a drink offering of strong drink to the Lord. [8]The other lamb you shall offer in the evening; like the cereal offering of the morning, and like its drink offering, you shall offer it as an offering by fire, a pleasing odor to the Lord.

Sabbath Offerings

9 "On the sabbath day two male lambs a year old without blemish, and two tenths of an ephah of fine flour for a cereal offering, mixed with oil, and its drink offering: [10]this is the burnt offering of every sabbath, besides the continual burnt offering and its drink offering.

Monthly Offerings

11 "At the beginnings of your months you shall offer a burnt offering to the Lord: two young bulls, one ram, seven male lambs a year old without blemish; [12]also three tenths of an ephah of fine flour for a cereal offering, mixed with oil, for each bull; and two tenths of fine flour for a cereal offering, mixed with oil, for the one ram; [13]and a tenth of fine flour mixed with oil as a cereal offering for every lamb; for a burnt offering of pleasing odor, an offering by fire to the Lord. [14]Their drink offerings shall be half a hin of wine for a bull, a third of a hin for a ram, and a fourth of a hin for a lamb; this is the burnt offering of each

month throughout the months of the year. [15]Also one male goat for a sin offering to the Lord; it shall be offered besides the continual burnt offering and its drink offering.

Offerings at Passover

16 "On the fourteenth day of the first month is the Lord's Passover. [17]And on the fifteenth day of this month is a feast; seven days shall unleavened bread be eaten. [18]On the first day there shall be a holy convocation: you shall do no laborious work, [19]but offer an offering by fire, a burnt offering to the Lord: two young bulls, one ram, and seven male lambs a year old; see that they are without blemish; [20]also their cereal offering of fine flour mixed with oil; three tenths of an ephah shall you offer for a bull, and two tenths for a ram; [21]a tenth shall you offer for each of the seven lambs; [22]also one male goat for a sin offering, to make atonement for you. [23]You shall offer these besides the burnt offering of the morning, which is for a continual burnt offering. [24]In the same way you shall offer daily, for seven days, the food of an offering by fire, a pleasing odor to the Lord; it shall be offered besides the continual burnt offering and its drink offering. [25]And on the seventh day you shall have a holy convocation; you shall do no laborious work.

Offerings at the Feast of Weeks

26 "On the day of the first fruits, when you offer a cereal offering of new grain to the Lord at your feast of weeks, you shall have a holy convocation; you shall do no laborious work, [27]but offer a burnt offering, a pleasing odor to the Lord: two young bulls, one ram, seven male lambs a year old; [28]also their cereal offering of fine flour mixed with oil, three tenths of an ephah for each bull, two tenths for one ram, [29]a tenth for each of the seven lambs; [30]with one male goat, to make atonement for you. [31]Besides the continual burnt offering and its cereal offering, you shall offer them and their drink offering. See that they are without blemish.

Offerings at the Feast of Trumpets

29 "On the first day of the seventh month you shall have a holy convocation; you shall do no laborious work. It is a day for you to blow the trumpets, [2]and you shall offer a burnt offering, a pleasing odor to the Lord: one young bull, one ram, seven male lambs a year old without blemish; [3]also their cereal offering of fine flour mixed with oil, three tenths of an ephah for the bull, two tenths for the ram, [4]and one tenth for each of the seven lambs; [5]with one male goat for a sin offering, to make atonement for you; [6]besides the burnt offering of the new moon, and its

28:3–8: Ex 29:38–42.
28:16: Ex 12:1–14, 21–27; Lev 23:5; Deut 16:1, 2, 5–7.
28:17–25: Ex 12:15–20; Lev 23:6–8; Deut 16:3, 4, 8.
28:26–31: Ex 23:16; 34:22; Lev 23:15–21; Deut 16:9–12.
29:1–6: Ex 23:16; 34:22; Lev 23:23–25.

cereal offering, and the continual burnt offering and its cereal offering, and their drink offering, according to the ordinance for them, a pleasing odor, an offering by fire to the LORD.

Offerings on the Day of Atonement

7 "On the tenth day of this seventh month you shall have a holy convocation, and afflict yourselves; you shall do no work, [8]but you shall offer a burnt offering to the LORD, a pleasing odor: one young bull, one ram, seven male lambs a year old; they shall be to you without blemish; [9]and their cereal offering of fine flour mixed with oil, three tenths of an ephah for the bull, two tenths for the one ram, [10]a tenth for each of the seven lambs: [11]also one male goat for a sin offering, besides the sin offering of atonement, and the continual burnt offering and its cereal offering, and their drink offerings.

Offerings at the Feast of Booths

12 "On the fifteenth day of the seventh month you shall have a holy convocation; you shall do no laborious work, and you shall keep a feast to the LORD seven days; [13]and you shall offer a burnt offering, an offering by fire, a pleasing odor to the LORD, thirteen young bulls, two rams, fourteen male lambs a year old; they shall be without blemish; [14]and their cereal offering of fine flour mixed with oil, three tenths of an ephah for each of the thirteen bulls, two tenths for each of the two rams, [15]and a tenth for each of the fourteen lambs; [16]also one male goat for a sin offering, besides the continual burnt offering, its cereal offering and its drink offering.

17 "On the second day twelve young bulls, two rams, fourteen male lambs a year old without blemish, [18]with the cereal offering and the drink offerings for the bulls, for the rams, and for the lambs, by number, according to the ordinance; [19]also one male goat for a sin offering, besides the continual burnt offering and its cereal offering, and their drink offerings.

20 "On the third day eleven bulls, two rams, fourteen male lambs a year old without blemish, [21]with the cereal offering and the drink offerings for the bulls, for the rams, and for the lambs, by number, according to the ordinance; [22]also one male goat for a sin offering, besides the continual burnt offering and its cereal offering and its drink offering.

23 "On the fourth day ten bulls, two rams, fourteen male lambs a year old without blemish, [24]with the cereal offering and the drink offerings for the bulls, for the rams, and for the lambs, by number, according to the ordinance; [25]also one male goat for a sin offering, besides the continual burnt offering, its cereal offering and its drink offering.

26 "On the fifth day nine bulls, two rams, fourteen male lambs a year old without blemish, [27]with the cereal offering and the drink offerings for the bulls, for the rams, and for the lambs, by number, according to the ordinance; [28]also one male goat for a sin offering; besides the continual burnt offering and its cereal offering and its drink offering.

29 "On the sixth day eight bulls, two rams, fourteen male lambs a year old without blemish, [30]with the cereal offering and the drink offerings for the bulls, for the rams, and for the lambs, by number, according to the ordinance; [31]also one male goat for a sin offering; besides the continual burnt offering, its cereal offering, and its drink offerings.

32 "On the seventh day seven bulls, two rams, fourteen male lambs a year old without blemish, [33]with the cereal offering and the drink offerings for the bulls, for the rams, and for the lambs, by number, according to the ordinance; [34]also one male goat for a sin offering; besides the continual burnt offering, its cereal offering, and its drink offering.

35 "On the eighth day you shall have a solemn assembly: you shall do no laborious work, [36]but you shall offer a burnt offering, an offering by fire, a pleasing odor to the LORD: one bull, one ram, seven male lambs a year old without blemish, [37]and the cereal offering and the drink offerings for the bull, for the ram, and for the lambs, by number, according to the ordinance; [38]also one male goat for a sin offering; besides the continual burnt offering and its cereal offering and its drink offering.

39 "These you shall offer to the LORD at your appointed feasts, in addition to your votive offerings and your freewill offerings, for your burnt offerings, and for your cereal offerings, and for your drink offerings, and for your peace offerings."

40 [y] And Moses told the sons of Israel everything just as the LORD had commanded Moses.

The Keeping of Vows

30 Moses said to the heads of the tribes of the sons of Israel, "This is what the LORD has commanded. [2]When a man vows a vow to the LORD, or swears an oath to bind himself by a pledge, he shall not break his word; he shall do according to all that proceeds out of his mouth. [3]Or when a woman vows a vow to the LORD, and binds herself by a pledge, while within her father's house, in her youth, [4]and her father hears of her vow and of her pledge by which she has bound herself, and says nothing to her; then all her vows shall stand, and her every pledge by which she has bound herself shall stand. [5]But if her father expresses disapproval to her on the day

---

y Ch 30:1 in Heb.
29:7-11: Lev 16:29–34; 23:26–32.
29:12-34: Lev 23:33–35.
29:35-38: Lev 23:36.
30:2-16: Deut 23:21–23.
30:2: Mt 5:33.

that he hears of it, no vow of hers, no pledge by which she has bound herself, shall stand; and the Lord will forgive her, because her father opposed her. [6]And if she is married to a husband, while under her vows or any thoughtless utterance of her lips by which she has bound herself, [7]and her husband hears of it, and says nothing to her on the day that he hears; then her vows shall stand, and her pledges by which she has bound herself shall stand. [8]But if, on the day that her husband comes to hear of it, he expresses disapproval, then he shall make void her vow which was on her, and the thoughtless utterance of her lips, by which she bound herself; and the Lord will forgive her. [9]But any vow of a widow or of a divorced woman, anything by which she has bound herself, shall stand against her. [10]And if she vowed in her husband's house, or bound herself by a pledge with an oath, [11]and her husband heard of it, and said nothing to her, and did not oppose her; then all her vows shall stand, and every pledge by which she bound herself shall stand. [12]But if her husband makes them null and void on the day that he hears them, then whatever proceeds out of her lips concerning her vows, or concerning her pledge of herself, shall not stand: her husband has made them void, and the Lord will forgive her. [13]Any vow and any binding oath to afflict herself, her husband may establish, or her husband may make void. [14]But if her husband says nothing to her from day to day, then he establishes all her vows, or all her pledges, that are upon her; he has established them, because he said nothing to her on the day that he heard of them. [15]But if he makes them null and void after he has heard of them, then he shall bear her iniquity."

16 These are the statutes which the Lord commanded Moses, as between a man and his wife, and between a father and his daughter, while in her youth, within her father's house.

War against Midian

31 The Lord said to Moses, [2]"Avenge the sons of Israel on the Mid'ianites; afterward you shall be gathered to your people." [3]And Moses said to the people, "Arm men from among you for the war, that they may go against Mid'ian, to execute the Lord's vengeance on Midian. [4]You shall send a thousand from each of the tribes of Israel to the war." [5]So there were provided, out of the thousands of Israel, a thousand from each tribe, twelve thousand armed for war. [6]And Moses sent them to the war, a thousand from each tribe, together with Phin'ehas the son of Elea'zar the priest, with the vessels of the sanctuary and the trumpets for the alarm in his hand. [7]They warred against Mid'ian, as the Lord commanded Moses, and slew every male. [8]They slew the kings of Mid'ian with the rest of their

slain, E'vi, Re'kem, Zur, Hur, and Reba, the five kings of Midian; and they also slew Balaam the son of Beor with the sword. [9]And the sons of Israel took captive the women of Mid'ian and their little ones; and they took as booty all their cattle, their flocks, and all their goods. [10]All their cities in the places where they dwelt, and all their encampments, they burned with fire, [11]and took all the spoil and all the booty, both of man and of beast. [12]Then they brought the captives and the booty and the spoil to Moses, and to Elea'zar the priest, and to the congregation of the sons of Israel, at the camp on the plains of Moab by the Jordan at Jericho.

Return from the War

13 Moses, and Elea'zar the priest, and all the leaders of the congregation, went forth to meet them outside the camp. [14]And Moses was angry with the officers of the army, the commanders of thousands and the commanders of hundreds, who had come from service in the war. [15]Moses said to them, "Have you let all the women live? [16]Behold, these caused the sons of Israel, by the counsel of Balaam, to act treacherously against the Lord in the matter of Peor, and so the plague came among the congregation of the Lord. [17]Now therefore, kill every male among the little ones, and kill every woman who has known man by lying with him. [18]But all the young girls who have not known man by lying with him, keep alive for yourselves. [19]Encamp outside the camp seven days; whoever of you has killed any person, and whoever has touched any slain, purify yourselves and your captives on the third day and on the seventh day. [20]You shall purify every garment, every article of skin, all work of goats' hair, and every article of wood."

21 And Elea'zar the priest said to the men of war who had gone to battle: "This is the statute of the law which the Lord has commanded Moses: [22]only the gold, the silver, the bronze, the iron, the tin, and the lead, [23]everything that can stand the fire, you shall pass through the fire, and it shall be clean. Nevertheless it shall also be purified with the water of impurity; and whatever cannot stand the fire, you shall pass through the water. [24]You must wash your clothes on the seventh day, and you shall be clean; and afterward you shall come into the camp."

Division of the Booty

25 The Lord said to Moses, [26]"Take the count of the booty that was taken, both of man and of beast, you and Elea'zar the priest and the heads of the fathers' houses of the congregation; [27]and divide the booty into two parts, between the warriors who went out to battle and all the congregation. [28]And levy for the Lord a tribute from the

31:16: Rev 2:14.

men of war who went out to battle, one out of five hundred, of the persons and of the oxen and of the donkeys and of the flocks; [29]take it from their half, and give it to Elea′zar the priest as an offering to the LORD. [30]And from the sons of Israel's half you shall take one drawn out of every fifty, of the persons, of the oxen, of the donkeys, and of the flocks, of all the cattle, and give them to the Levites who have charge of the tabernacle of the LORD." [31]And Moses and Elea′zar the priest did as the LORD commanded Moses.

[32] Now the booty remaining of the spoil that the men of war took was: six hundred and seventy-five thousand sheep, [33]seventy-two thousand cattle, [34]sixty-one thousand donkeys, [35]and thirty-two thousand persons in all, women who had not known man by lying with him. [36]And the half, the portion of those who had gone out to war, was in number three hundred and thirty-seven thousand five hundred sheep, [37]and the LORD's tribute of sheep was six hundred and seventy-five. [38]The cattle were thirty-six thousand, of which the LORD's tribute was seventy-two. [39]The donkeys were thirty thousand five hundred, of which the LORD's tribute was sixty-one. [40]The persons were sixteen thousand, of which the LORD's tribute was thirty-two persons. [41]And Moses gave the tribute, which was the offering for the LORD, to Elea′zar the priest, as the LORD commanded Moses.

[42] From the sons of Israel's half, which Moses separated from that of the men who had gone to war—[43]now the congregation's half was three hundred and thirty-seven thousand five hundred sheep, [44]thirty-six thousand cattle, [45]and thirty thousand five hundred donkeys, [46]and sixteen thousand persons—[47]from the sons of Israel's half Moses took one of every fifty, both of persons and of beasts, and gave them to the Levites who had charge of the tabernacle of the LORD; as the LORD commanded Moses.

[48] Then the officers who were over the thousands of the army, the captains of thousands and the captains of hundreds, came near to Moses, [49]and said to Moses, "Your servants have counted the men of war who are under our command, and there is not a man missing from us. [50]And we have brought the LORD's offering, what each man found, articles of gold, armlets and bracelets, signet rings, earrings, and beads, to make atonement for ourselves before the LORD." [51]And Moses and Elea′zar the priest received from them the gold, all wrought articles. [52]And all the gold of the offering that they offered to the LORD, from the commanders of thousands and the commanders of hundreds, was sixteen thousand seven hundred and fifty shekels. [53](The men of war had taken booty, every man for himself.) [54]And Moses and Elea′zar the priest received the gold from the commanders of thousands and of hundreds, and

brought it into the tent of meeting, as a memorial for the sons of Israel before the LORD.

Conquest and Division of the Trans-Jordan Lands

[32] Now the sons of Reuben and the sons of Gad had a very great multitude of cattle; and they saw the land of Ja′zer and the land of Gilead, and behold, the place was a place for cattle. [2]So the sons of Gad and the sons of Reuben came and said to Moses and to Elea′zar the priest and to the leaders of the congregation, [3]"At′aroth, Di′bon, Ja′zer, Nimrah, Heshbon, E″lea′leh, Sebam, Nebo, and Beon, [4]the land which the LORD struck before the congregation of Israel, is a land for cattle; and your servants have cattle." [5]And they said, "If we have found favor in your sight, let this land be given to your servants for a possession; do not take us across the Jordan."

[6] But Moses said to the sons of Gad and to the sons of Reuben, "Shall your brethren go to the war while you sit here? [7]Why will you discourage the heart of the sons of Israel from going over into the land which the LORD has given them? [8]Thus did your fathers, when I sent them from Ka′desh-bar′nea to see the land. [9]For when they went up to the Valley of Eshcol, and saw the land, they discouraged the heart of the sons of Israel from going into the land which the LORD had given them. [10]And the LORD's anger was kindled on that day, and he swore, saying, [11]'Surely none of the men who came up out of Egypt, from twenty years old and upward, shall see the land which I swore to give to Abraham, to Isaac, and to Jacob, because they have not wholly followed me; [12]none except Caleb the son of Jephun′neh the Ken′izzite and Joshua the son of Nun, for they have wholly followed the LORD.' [13]And the LORD's anger was kindled against Israel, and he made them wander in the wilderness forty years, until all the generation that had done evil in the sight of the LORD was consumed. [14]And behold, you have risen in your fathers' stead, a brood of sinful men, to increase still more the fierce anger of the LORD against Israel! [15]For if you turn away from following him, he will again abandon them in the wilderness; and you will destroy all this people."

[16] Then they came near to him, and said, "We will build sheepfolds here for our flocks, and cities for our little ones, [17]but we will take up arms, ready to go before the sons of Israel, until we have brought them to their place; and our little ones shall live in the fortified cities because of the inhabitants of the land. [18]We will not return to our homes until the sons of Israel have inherited each his inheritance. [19]For we will not inherit with them on the other side of the Jordan and beyond; because our inheritance has come to us on this side of the Jordan to the east." [20]So Moses

said to them, "If you will do this, if you will take up arms to go before the LORD for the war, ²¹and every armed man of you will pass over the Jordan before the LORD, until he has driven out his enemies from before him ²²and the land is subdued before the LORD; then after that you shall return and be free of obligation to the LORD and to Israel; and this land shall be your possession before the LORD. ²³But if you will not do so, behold, you have sinned against the LORD; and be sure your sin will find you out. ²⁴Build cities for your little ones, and folds for your sheep; and do what you have promised." ²⁵And the sons of Gad and the sons of Reuben said to Moses, "Your servants will do as my lord commands. ²⁶Our little ones, our wives, our flocks, and all our cattle, shall remain there in the cities of Gilead; ²⁷but your servants will pass over, every man who is armed for war, before the LORD to battle, as my lord orders."

28 So Moses gave command concerning them to Elea′zar the priest, and to Joshua the son of Nun, and to the heads of the fathers' houses of the tribes of the sons of Israel. ²⁹And Moses said to them, "If the sons of Gad and the sons of Reuben, every man who is armed to battle before the LORD, will pass with you over the Jordan and the land shall be subdued before you, then you shall give them the land of Gilead for a possession; ³⁰but if they will not pass over with you armed, they shall have possessions among you in the land of Canaan." ³¹And the sons of Gad and the sons of Reuben answered, "As the LORD has said to your servants, so we will do. ³²We will pass over armed before the LORD into the land of Canaan, and the possession of our inheritance shall remain with us beyond the Jordan."

33 And Moses gave to them, to the sons of Gad and to the sons of Reuben and to the half-tribe of Manas′seh the son of Joseph, the kingdom of Si′hon king of the Am′orites and the kingdom of Og king of Bashan, the land and its cities with their territories, the cities of the land throughout the country. ³⁴And the sons of Gad built Di′bon, At′aroth, Aro′er, ³⁵At′roth-sho′phan, Ja′zer, Jog′behah, ³⁶Beth-nim′rah and Beth-har′an, fortified cities, and folds for sheep. ³⁷And the sons of Reuben built Heshbon, E″lea′leh, Kir″iatha′im, ³⁸Nebo, and Ba′al-me′on (their names to be changed), and Sibmah; and they gave other names to the cities which they built. ³⁹And the sons of Ma′chir the son of Manas′seh went to Gilead and took it, and dispossessed the Am′orites who were in it. ⁴⁰And Moses gave Gilead to Ma′chir the son of Manas′-seh, and he settled in it. ⁴¹And Ja′ir the son of Manas′seh went and took their villages, and called them Hav′voth-ja′ir.ᶻ ⁴²And No′bah went and took Ke′nath and its villages, and called it Nobah, after his own name.

The Stages of Israel's Journey from Egypt

33 These are the stages of the sons of Israel, when they went forth out of the land of Egypt by their hosts under the leadership of Moses and Aaron. ²Moses wrote down their starting places, stage by stage, by command of the LORD; and these are their stages according to their starting places. ³They set out from Ram′eses in the first month, on the fifteenth day of the first month; on the day after the Passover the sons of Israel went out triumphantly in the sight of all the Egyptians, ⁴while the Egyptians were burying all their first-born, whom the LORD had struck down among them; upon their gods also the LORD executed judgments.

5 So the sons of Israel set out from Ram′eses, and encamped at Succoth. ⁶And they set out from Succoth, and encamped at E′tham, which is on the edge of the wilderness. ⁷And they set out from E′tham, and turned back to Pi-hahi′roth, which is east of Ba′al-ze′phon; and they encamped before Migdol. ⁸And they set out from before Hahi′roth, and passed through the midst of the sea into the wilderness, and they went a three days' journey in the wilderness of E′tham, and encamped at Marah. ⁹And they set out from Marah, and came to E′lim; at Elim there were twelve springs of water and seventy palm trees, and they encamped there. ¹⁰And they set out from E′lim, and encamped by the Red Sea. ¹¹And they set out from the Red Sea, and encamped in the wilderness of Sin. ¹²And they set out from the wilderness of Sin, and encamped at Dophkah. ¹³And they set out from Dophkah, and encamped at A′lush. ¹⁴And they set out from A′lush, and encamped at Reph′idim, where there was no water for the people to drink. ¹⁵And they set out from Reph′idim, and encamped in the wilderness of Sinai. ¹⁶And they set out from the wilderness of Sinai, and encamped at Kib′roth-hatta′avah. ¹⁷And they set out from Kib′roth-hatta′avah, and encamped at Haze′roth. ¹⁸And they set out from Haze′roth, and encamped at Rithmah. ¹⁹And they set out from Rithmah, and encamped at Rim′mon-per′ez. ²⁰And they set out from Rim′mon-per′ez, and encamped at Libnah. ²¹And they set out from Libnah, and encamped at Rissah. ²²And they set out from Rissah, and encamped at Kehela′thah. ²³And they set out from Kehela′thah, and encamped at Mount She′pher. ²⁴And they set out from Mount She′pher, and encamped at Hara′dah. ²⁵And they set out from Hara′dah, and encamped at Makhe′loth. ²⁶And they set out from Makhe′loth, and encamped at Ta′hath. ²⁷And they set out from Ta′hath, and encamped at Te′rah. ²⁸And they set out from Te′rah, and encamped at Mithkah. ²⁹And they set

---

ᶻ That is the *villages of Jair.*

out from Mithkah, and encamped at Hashmo′nah. [30]And they set out from Hashmo′nah, and encamped at Mose′roth. [31]And they set out from Mose′roth, and encamped at Be′ne-ja′akan. [32]And they set out from Be′ne-ja′akan, and encamped at Hor-haggid′gad. [33]And they set out from Hor-haggid′gad, and encamped at Jot′bathah. [34]And they set out from Jot′bathah, and encamped at Abro′nah. [35]And they set out from Abro′nah, and encamped at E′zion-ge′ber. [36]And they set out from E′zion-ge′ber, and encamped in the wilderness of Zin (that is, Ka′desh). [37]And they set out from Ka′desh, and encamped at Mount Hor, on the edge of the land of E′dom.

38 And Aaron the priest went up Mount Hor at the command of the Lord, and died there, in the fortieth year after the sons of Israel had come out of the land of Egypt, on the first day of the fifth month. [39]And Aaron was a hundred and twenty-three years old when he died on Mount Hor.

40 And the Canaanite, the king of Ar′ad, who dwelt in the Neg′eb in the land of Canaan, heard of the coming of the sons of Israel.

41 And they set out from Mount Hor, and encamped at Zalmo′nah. [42]And they set out from Zalmo′nah, and encamped at Pu′non. [43]And they set out from Pu′non, and encamped at O′both. [44]And they set out from O′both, and encamped at I′ye-ab′arim, in the territory of Moab. [45]And they set out from I′yim, and encamped at Di′bon-gad. [46]And they set out from Di′bon-gad, and encamped at Al′mon-diblatha′im. [47]And they set out from Al′mon-diblatha′im, and encamped in the mountains of Ab′arim, before Nebo. [48]And they set out from the mountains of Ab′arim, and encamped in the plains of Moab by the Jordan at Jericho; [49]they encamped by the Jordan from Beth-jesh′imoth as far as A′bel-shit′tim in the plains of Moab.

Instructions for the Conquest of Canaan

50 And the Lord said to Moses in the plains of Moab by the Jordan at Jericho, [51]"Say to the sons of Israel, When you pass over the Jordan into the land of Canaan, [52]then you shall drive out all the inhabitants of the land from before you, and destroy all their figured stones, and destroy all their molten images, and demolish all their high places; [53]and you shall take possession of the land and settle in it, for I have given the land to you to possess it. [54]You shall inherit the land by lot according to your families; to a large tribe you shall give a large inheritance, and to a small tribe you shall give a small inheritance; wherever the lot falls to any man, that shall be his; according to the tribes of your fathers you shall inherit. [55]But if you do not drive out the inhabitants of the land from before you, then those of them whom you let remain shall be as pricks in your eyes and thorns in your sides, and they shall trouble you in the land where you dwell. [56]And I will do to you as I thought to do to them."

Boundaries of the Land of Canaan

34 The Lord said to Moses, [2]"Command the sons of Israel, and say to them, When you enter the land of Canaan (this is the land that shall fall to you for an inheritance, the land of Canaan in its full extent), [3]your south side shall be from the wilderness of Zin along the side of E′dom, and your southern boundary shall be from the end of the Salt Sea on the east; [4]and your boundary shall turn south of the ascent of Akrab′bim, and cross to Zin, and its end shall be south of Ka′desh-bar′nea; then it shall go on to Ha′zar-ad′dar, and pass along to Azmon; [5]and the boundary shall turn from Azmon to the Brook of Egypt, and its termination shall be at the sea.

6 "For the western boundary, you shall have the Great Sea and its [a] coast; this shall be your western boundary.

7 "This shall be your northern boundary: from the Great Sea you shall mark out your line to Mount Hor; [8]from Mount Hor you shall mark it out to the entrance of Ha′math, and the end of the boundary shall be at Ze′dad; [9]then the boundary shall extend to Ziphron, and its end shall be at Ha′zar-e′nan; this shall be your northern boundary.

10 "You shall mark out your eastern boundary from Ha′zar-e′nan to She′pham; [11]and the boundary shall go down from She′pham to Rib′lah on the east side of A′in; and the boundary shall go down, and reach to the shoulder of the sea of Chin′nereth on the east; [12]and the boundary shall go down to the Jordan, and its end shall be at the Salt Sea. This shall be your land with its boundaries all round."

13 Moses commanded the sons of Israel, saying, "This is the land which you shall inherit by lot, which the Lord has commanded to give to the nine tribes and to the half-tribe; [14]for the tribe of the sons of Reuben by fathers' houses and the tribe of the sons of Gad by their fathers' houses have received their inheritance, and also the half-tribe of Manas′seh; [15]the two tribes and the half-tribe have received their inheritance beyond the Jordan at Jericho eastward, toward the sunrise."

Tribal Leaders

16 The Lord said to Moses, [17]"These are the names of the men who shall divide the land to you for inheritance: Elea′zar the priest and Joshua the son of Nun. [18]You shall take one leader of every tribe, to divide the land for inheritance.

---

[a] Syr: Heb lacks *its.*
33:38, 39: Num 20:23–29; Deut 10:6.
33:52: Ex 23:24; Deut 7:5; 12:3.
34:3–5: Josh 15:1–4.
34:13–15: Josh 14:1–5.

¹⁹These are the names of the men: Of the tribe of Judah, Caleb the son of Jephun'neh. ²⁰Of the tribe of the sons of Simeon, Shemu'el the son of Ammi'hud. ²¹Of the tribe of Benjamin, Eli'dad the son of Chis'lon. ²²Of the tribe of the sons of Dan a leader, Bukki the son of Jogli. ²³Of the sons of Joseph: of the tribe of the sons of Manas'seh a leader, Han'niel the son of E'phod. ²⁴And of the tribe of the sons of E'phraim a leader, Ke'muel the son of Shiph'tan. ²⁵Of the tribe of the sons of Zeb'ulun a leader, Eliza'phan the son of Parnach. ²⁶Of the tribe of the sons of Is'sachar a leader, Pal'ti-el the son of Azzan. ²⁷And of the tribe of the sons of Asher a leader, Ahi'hud the son of Shelo'mi. ²⁸Of the tribe of the sons of Naph'tali a leader, Pedah'el the son of Ammi'hud. ²⁹These are the men whom the Lord commanded to divide the inheritance for the sons of Israel in the land of Canaan."

Cities for the Levites

35 The Lord said to Moses in the plains of Moab by the Jordan at Jericho, ²"Command the sons of Israel, that they give to the Levites, from the inheritance of their possession, cities to dwell in; and you shall give to the Levites pasture lands round about the cities. ³The cities shall be theirs to dwell in, and their pasture lands shall be for their cattle and for their livestock and for all their beasts. ⁴The pasture lands of the cities, which you shall give to the Levites, shall reach from the wall of the city outward a thousand cubits all round. ⁵And you shall measure, outside the city, for the east side two thousand cubits, and for the south side two thousand cubits, and for the west side two thousand cubits, and for the north side two thousand cubits, the city being in the middle; this shall belong to them as pasture land for their cities. ⁶The cities which you give to the Levites shall be the six cities of refuge, where you shall permit the manslayer to flee, and in addition to them you shall give forty-two cities. ⁷All the cities which you give to the Levites shall be forty-eight, with their pasture lands. ⁸And as for the cities which you shall give from the possession of the sons of Israel, from the larger tribes you shall take many, and from the smaller tribes you shall take few; each, in proportion to the inheritance which it inherits, shall give of its cities to the Levites."

Cities of Refuge

9 And the Lord said to Moses, ¹⁰"Say to the sons of Israel, When you cross the Jordan into the land of Canaan, ¹¹then you shall select cities to be cities of refuge for you, that the manslayer who kills any person without intent may flee there. ¹²The cities shall be for you a refuge from the avenger, that the manslayer may not die until he stands before the congregation for judgment. ¹³And the cities which you give shall be your six cities of refuge. ¹⁴You shall give three cities beyond the Jordan, and three cities in the land of Canaan, to be cities of refuge. ¹⁵These six cities shall be for refuge for the sons of Israel, and for the stranger and for the sojourner among them, that any one who kills any person without intent may flee there.

Concerning Murder and Revenge

16 "But if he struck him down with an instrument of iron, so that he died, he is a murderer; the murderer shall be put to death. ¹⁷And if he struck him down with a stone in the hand, by which a man may die, and he died, he is a murderer; the murderer shall be put to death. ¹⁸Or if he struck him down with a weapon of wood in the hand, by which a man may die, and he died, he is a murderer; the murderer shall be put to death. ¹⁹The avenger of blood shall himself put the murderer to death; when he meets him, he shall put him to death. ²⁰And if he stabbed him from hatred, or hurled at him, lying in wait, so that he died, ²¹or in enmity struck him down with his hand, so that he died, then he who struck the blow shall be put to death; he is a murderer; the avenger of blood shall put the murderer to death, when he meets him.

22 "But if he stabbed him suddenly without enmity, or hurled anything on him without lying in wait, ²³or used a stone, by which a man may die, and without seeing him cast it upon him, so that he died, though he was not his enemy, and did not seek his harm; ²⁴then the congregation shall judge between the manslayer and the avenger of blood, in accordance with these ordinances; ²⁵and the congregation shall rescue the manslayer from the hand of the avenger of blood, and the congregation shall restore him to his city of refuge, to which he had fled, and he shall live in it until the death of the high priest who was anointed with the holy oil. ²⁶But if the manslayer shall at any time go beyond the bounds of his city of refuge to which he fled, ²⁷and the avenger of blood finds him outside the bounds of his city of refuge, and the avenger of blood slays the manslayer, he shall not be guilty of blood. ²⁸For the man must remain in his city of refuge until the death of the high priest; but after the death of the high priest the manslayer may return to the land of his possession.

29 "And these things shall be for a statute and ordinance to you throughout your generations in all your dwellings. ³⁰If any one kills a person, the murderer shall be put to death on the evidence of witnesses; but no person shall be put to death on the testimony of one witness. ³¹Moreover you shall accept no ransom for the life of a murderer,

35:1-8: Lev 25:32–34; Josh 21:1–42.
35:6, 9-34: Deut 19:1–13.

who is guilty of death; but he shall be put to death. [32]And you shall accept no ransom for him who has fled to his city of refuge, that he may return to dwell in the land before the death of the high priest. [33]You shall not thus pollute the land in which you live; for blood pollutes the land, and no expiation can be made for the land, for the blood that is shed in it, except by the blood of him who shed it. [34]You shall not defile the land in which you live, in the midst of which I dwell; for I the LORD dwell in the midst of the sons of Israel."

Concerning Married Women's Inheritance

36 The heads of the fathers' houses of the families of the sons of Gilead the son of Ma'chir, son of Manas'seh, of the fathers' houses of the sons of Joseph, came near and spoke before Moses and before the leaders, the heads of the fathers' houses of the sons of Israel; [2]they said, "The LORD commanded my lord to give the land for inheritance by lot to the sons of Israel; and my lord was commanded by the LORD to give the inheritance of Zeloph'ehad our brother to his daughters. [3]But if they are married to any of the sons of the other tribes of the sons of Israel then their inheritance will be taken from the inheritance of our fathers, and added to the inheritance of the tribe to which they belong; so it will be taken away from the lot of our inheritance. [4]And when the jubilee of the sons of Israel comes, then their inheritance will be added to the inheritance of the tribe to which they belong; and their inher-

itance will be taken from the inheritance of the tribe of our fathers."

[5] And Moses commanded the sons of Israel according to the word of the LORD, saying, "The tribe of the sons of Joseph is right. [6]This is what the LORD commands concerning the daughters of Zeloph'ehad, 'Let them marry whom they think best; only, they shall marry within the family of the tribe of their father. [7]The inheritance of the sons of Israel shall not be transferred from one tribe to another; for every one of the sons of Israel shall cling to the inheritance of the tribe of his fathers. [8]And every daughter who possesses an inheritance in any tribe of the sons of Israel shall be wife to one of the family of the tribe of her father, so that every one of the sons of Israel may possess the inheritance of his fathers. [9]So no inheritance shall be transferred from one tribe to another; for each of the tribes of the sons of Israel shall cling to its own inheritance.'"

[10] The daughters of Zeloph'ehad did as the LORD commanded Moses; [11]for Mahlah, Tirzah, Hoglah, Milcah, and Noah, the daughters of Zeloph'ehad, were married to sons of their father's brothers. [12]They were married into the families of the sons of Manas'seh the son of Joseph, and their inheritance remained in the tribe of the family of their father.

[13] These are the commandments and the ordinances which the LORD commanded by Moses to the sons of Israel in the plains of Moab by the Jordan at Jericho.

THE FIFTH BOOK OF MOSES COMMONLY CALLED
DEUTERONOMY

Events at Horeb Recalled

1 These are the words that Moses spoke to all Israel beyond the Jordan in the wilderness, in the Ar′abah over against Suph, between Par′an and To′phel, La′ban, Haze′roth, and Di′zahab. ²It is eleven days' journey from Horeb by the way of Mount Se′ir to Ka′desh-bar′nea. ³And in the fortieth year, on the first day of the eleventh month, Moses spoke to the sons of Israel according to all that the LORD had given him in commandment to them, ⁴after he had defeated Si′hon the king of the Am′orites, who lived in Heshbon, and Og the king of Bashan, who lived in Ash′taroth and in Ed′re-i. ⁵Beyond the Jordan, in the land of Moab, Moses undertook to explain this law, saying, ⁶"The LORD our God said to us in Horeb, 'You have stayed long enough at this mountain; ⁷turn and take your journey, and go to the hill country of the Am′orites, and to all their neighbors in the Ar′abah, in the hill country and in the lowland, and in the Neg′eb, and by the seacoast, the land of the Canaanites, and Lebanon, as far as the great river, the river Euphrates. ⁸Behold, I have set the land before you; go in and take possession of the land which the LORD swore to your fathers, to Abraham, to Isaac, and to Jacob, to give to them and to their descendants after them.'

Appointment of Heads of the Tribes

9 "At that time I said to you, 'I am not able alone to bear you; ¹⁰the LORD your God has multiplied you, and behold, you are this day as the stars of heaven for multitude. ¹¹May the LORD, the God of your fathers, make you a thousand times as many as you are, and bless you, as he has promised you! ¹²How can I bear alone the weight and burden of you and your strife? ¹³Choose wise, understanding, and experienced men, according to your tribes, and I will appoint them as your heads.' ¹⁴And you answered me, 'The thing that you have spoken is good for us to do.' ¹⁵So I took the heads of your tribes, wise and experienced men, and set them as heads over you, commanders of thousands, commanders of hundreds, commanders of fifties, commanders of tens, and officers, throughout your tribes. ¹⁶And I charged your judges at that time, 'Hear the cases between your brethren, and judge righteously between a man and his brother or the alien that is with him. ¹⁷You shall not be partial in judgment; you shall hear the small and the great alike; you shall not be

afraid of the face of man, for the judgment is God's; and the case that is too hard for you, you shall bring to me, and I will hear it.' ¹⁸And I commanded you at that time all the things that you should do.

Israel's Refusal to Enter the Land

19 "And we set out from Horeb, and went through all that great and terrible wilderness which you saw, on the way to the hill country of the Am′orites, as the LORD our God commanded us; and we came to Ka′desh-bar′nea. ²⁰And I said to you, 'You have come to the hill country of the Am′orites, which the LORD our God gives us. ²¹Behold, the LORD your God has set the land before you; go up, take possession, as the LORD, the God of your fathers, has told you; do not fear or be dismayed.' ²²Then all of you came near me, and said, 'Let us send men before us, that they may explore the land for us, and bring us word again of the way by which we must go up and the cities into which we shall come.' ²³The thing seemed good to me, and I took twelve men of you, one man for each tribe; ²⁴and they turned and went up into the hill country, and came to the Valley of Eshcol and spied it out. ²⁵And they took in their hands some of the fruit of the land and brought it down to us, and brought us word again, and said, 'It is a good land which the LORD our God gives us.'

26 "Yet you would not go up, but rebelled against the command of the LORD your God; ²⁷and you murmured in your tents, and said, 'Because the LORD hated us he has brought us forth out of the land of Egypt, to give us into the hand of the Am′orites, to destroy us. ²⁸Where are we going up? Our brethren have made our hearts melt, saying, "The people are greater and taller than we; the cities are great and fortified up to heaven; and moreover we have seen the sons of the An′akim there."' ²⁹Then I said to you, 'Do not be in dread or afraid of them. ³⁰The LORD your God who goes before you will himself fight for you, just as he

---

The title comes from the mistranslation of 17:18 in the Greek version (the Septuagint) and really means "a second copy of the law." The book comprises the so-called "Deuteronomic Code of Law" (chapters 12–26), edited within the framework of two discourses attributed to Moses represented as prophet and lawgiver. The whole is rounded off with a third discourse, a psalm, and an account of Moses' death and burial. The central theme of Deuteronomy is the election of Israel as the people of God by means of the covenant.
1:9-15: Num 11:10–25.
1:16-18: Ex 18:25, 26.
1:22-46: Num 13:1—14:45; 32:8–13.

did for you in Egypt before your eyes, [31]and in the wilderness, where you have seen how the LORD your God bore you, as a man bears his son, in all the way that you went until you came to this place.' [32]Yet in spite of this word you did not believe the LORD your God, [33]who went before you in the way to seek you out a place to pitch your tents, in fire by night, to show you by what way you should go, and in the cloud by day.

Punishment for Israel's Rebellion

34 "And the LORD heard your words, and was angered, and he swore, [35]'Not one of these men of this evil generation shall see the good land which I swore to give to your fathers, [36]except Caleb the son of Jephun'neh; he shall see it, and to him and to his children I will give the land upon which he has trodden, because he has wholly followed the LORD!' [37]The LORD was angry with me also on your account, and said, 'You also shall not go in there; [38]Joshua the son of Nun, who stands before you, he shall enter; encourage him, for he shall cause Israel to inherit it. [39]Moreover your little ones, who you said would become a prey, and your children, who this day have no knowledge of good or evil, shall go in there, and to them I will give it, and they shall possess it. [40]But as for you, turn, and journey into the wilderness in the direction of the Red Sea.'

41 "Then you answered me, 'We have sinned against the LORD; we will go up and fight, just as the LORD our God commanded us.' And every man of you belted on his weapons of war, and thought it easy to go up into the hill country. [42]And the LORD said to me, 'Say to them, Do not go up or fight, for I am not in the midst of you; lest you be defeated before your enemies.' [43]So I spoke to you, and you would not listen; but you rebelled against the command of the LORD, and were presumptuous and went up into the hill country. [44]Then the Am'orites who lived in that hill country came out against you and chased you as bees do and beat you down in Se'ir as far as Hormah. [45]And you returned and wept before the LORD; but the LORD did not listen to your voice or give ear to you. [46]So you remained at Ka'desh many days, the days that you remained there.

The Years in the Wilderness

2 "Then we turned, and journeyed into the wilderness in the direction of the Red Sea, as the LORD told me; and for many days we went about Mount Se'ir. [2]Then the LORD said to me, [3]'You have been going about this mountain country long enough; turn northward. [4]And command the people, You are about to pass through the territory of your brethren the sons of Esau, who live in Se'ir; and they will be afraid of you. So take good heed; [5]do not contend with them; for I will not give you any of their land, no, not so much as for the sole of the foot to tread on, because I have given Mount

Se'ir to Esau as a possession. [6]You shall purchase food from them for money, that you may eat; and you shall also buy water of them for money, that you may drink. [7]For the LORD your God has blessed you in all the work of your hands; he knows your going through this great wilderness; these forty years the LORD your God has been with you; you have lacked nothing.' [8]So we went on, away from our brethren the sons of Esau who live in Se'ir, away from the Ar'abah road from E'lath and E'zion-ge'ber.

"And we turned and went in the direction of the wilderness of Moab. [9]And the LORD said to me, 'Do not harass Moab or contend with them in battle, for I will not give you any of their land for a possession, because I have given Ar to the sons of Lot for a possession.' [10](The E'mim formerly lived there, a people great and many, and tall as the An'akim; [11]like the An'akim they are also known as Reph'aim, but the Moabites call them E'mim. [12]The Horites also lived in Se'ir formerly, but the sons of Esau dispossessed them, and destroyed them from before them, and settled in their stead; as Israel did to the land of their possession, which the LORD gave to them.) [13]'Now rise up, and go over the brook Ze'red.' So we went over the brook Zered. [14]And the time from our leaving Ka'desh-bar'nea until we crossed the brook Ze'red was thirty-eight years, until the entire generation, that is, the men of war, had perished from the camp, as the LORD had sworn to them. [15]For indeed the hand of the LORD was against them, to destroy them from the camp, until they had perished.

16 "So when all the men of war had perished and were dead from among the people, [17]the LORD said to me, [18]'This day you are to pass over the boundary of Moab at Ar; [19]and when you approach the frontier of the sons of Ammon, do not harass them or contend with them, for I will not give you any of the land of the sons of Ammon as a possession, because I have given it to the sons of Lot for a possession.' [20](That also is known as a land of Reph'aim; Rephaim formerly lived there, but the Am'monites call them Zamzum'mim, [21]a people great and many, and tall as the An'akim; but the LORD destroyed them before them; and they dispossessed them, and settled in their stead; [22]as he did for the sons of Esau, who live in Se'ir, when he destroyed the Horites before them, and they dispossessed them, and settled in their stead even to this day. [23]As for the Avvim, who lived in villages as far as Gaza, the Caphtorim, who came from Caphtor, destroyed them and settled in their stead.) [24]'Rise up, take your journey, and go over the valley of

---

1:31: Acts 13:18.
2:1-8: Num 21:4-20.

the Arnon; behold, I have given into your hand Si'hon the Am'orite, king of Heshbon, and his land; begin to take possession, and contend with him in battle. [25]This day I will begin to put the dread and fear of you upon the peoples that are under the whole heaven, who shall hear the report of you and shall tremble and be in anguish because of you.'

The Defeat of Sihon the King of Heshbon

26 "So I sent messengers from the wilderness of Ked'emoth to Si'hon the king of Heshbon, with words of peace, saying, [27]'Let me pass through your land; I will go only by the road, I will turn aside neither to the right nor to the left. [28]You shall sell me food for money, that I may eat, and give me water for money, that I may drink; only let me pass through on foot, [29]as the sons of Esau who live in Se'ir and the Moabites who live in Ar did for me, until I go over the Jordan into the land which the Lord our God gives to us.' [30]But Si'hon the king of Heshbon would not let us pass by him; for the Lord your God hardened his spirit and made his heart obstinate, that he might give him into your hand, as at this day. [31]And the Lord said to me, 'Behold, I have begun to give Si'hon and his land over to you; begin to take possession, that you may occupy his land.' [32]Then Si'hon came out against us, he and all his people, to battle at Ja'haz. [33]And the Lord our God gave him over to us; and we defeated him and his sons and all his people. [34]And we captured all his cities at that time and utterly destroyed every city, men, women, and children; we left none remaining; [35]only the cattle we took as spoil for ourselves, with the booty of the cities which we captured. [36]From Aro'er, which is on the edge of the valley of the Arnon, and from the city that is in the valley, as far as Gilead, there was not a city too high for us; the Lord our God gave all into our hands. [37]Only to the land of the sons of Ammon you did not draw near, that is, to all the banks of the river Jabbok and the cities of the hill country, and wherever the Lord our God forbade us.

The Defeat of Og the King of Bashan

3 "Then we turned and went up the way to Bashan; and Og the king of Bashan came out against us, he and all his people, to battle at Ed're-i. [2]But the Lord said to me, 'Do not fear him; for I have given him and all his people and his land into your hand; and you shall do to him as you did to Si'hon the king of the Am'orites, who dwelt at Heshbon.' [3]So the Lord our God gave into our hand Og also, the king of Bashan, and all his people; and we struck him until no survivor was left to him. [4]And we took all his cities at that time—there was not a city which we did not take from them—sixty cities, the whole region of Argob, the kingdom of Og in Bashan.

[5]All these were cities fortified with high walls, gates, and bars, besides very many unwalled villages. [6]And we utterly destroyed them, as we did to Si'hon the king of Heshbon, destroying every city, men, women, and children. [7]But all the cattle and the spoil of the cities we took as our booty. [8]So we took the land at that time out of the hand of the two kings of the Am'orites who were beyond the Jordan, from the valley of the Arnon to Mount Hermon [9](the Sido'nians call Hermon Sir'ion, while the Am'orites call it Se'nir), [10]all the cities of the tableland and all Gilead and all Bashan, as far as Sal'ecah and Ed're-i, cities of the kingdom of Og in Bashan. [11](For only Og the king of Bashan was left of the remnant of the Reph'aim; behold, his bedstead was a bedstead of iron; is it not in Rabbah of the Am'monites? Nine cubits was its length, and four cubits its breadth, according to the common cubit. [a])

12 "When we took possession of this land at that time, I gave to the Reubenites and the Gadites the territory beginning at Aro'er, which is on the edge of the valley of the Arnon, and half the hill country of Gilead with its cities; [13]the rest of Gilead, and all Bashan, the kingdom of Og, that is, all the region of Argob, I gave to the half-tribe of Manas'seh. (The whole of that Bashan is called the land of Reph'aim. [14]Ja'ir the Manas'site took all the region of Argob, that is, Bashan, as far as the border of the Gesh'urites and the Ma-ac'athites, and called the villages after his own name, Hav'voth-ja'ir, as it is to this day.) [15]To Ma'chir I gave Gilead, [16]and to the Reubenites and the Gadites I gave the territory from Gilead as far as the valley of the Arnon, with the middle of the valley as a boundary, as far over as the river Jabbok, the boundary of the Am'monites; [17]the Ar'abah also, with the Jordan as the boundary, from Chin'nereth as far as the sea of the Arabah, the Salt Sea, under the slopes of Pisgah on the east.

18 "And I commanded you at that time, saying, 'The Lord your God has given you this land to possess; all your men of valor shall pass over armed before your brethren the sons of Israel. [19]But your wives, your little ones, and your cattle (I know that you have many cattle) shall remain in the cities which I have given you, [20]until the Lord gives rest to your brethren, as to you, and they also occupy the land which the Lord your God gives them beyond the Jordan; then you shall return every man to his possession which I have given you.' [21]And I commanded Joshua at that time, 'Your eyes have seen all that the Lord your God has done to these two kings; so will the Lord

---

a Heb cubit of a man.
2:26–37: Num 21:21–32.
3:1–11: Num 21:33–35.
3:12–20: Num 32.

do to all the kingdoms into which you are going over. [22]You shall not fear them; for it is the LORD your God who fights for you.'

Moses Views Canaan from Pisgah

23 "And I begged the LORD at that time, saying, [24] 'O Lord GOD, you have only begun to show your servant your greatness and your mighty hand; for what god is there in heaven or on earth who can do such works and mighty acts as yours? [25]Let me go over, I pray, and see the good land beyond the Jordan, that excellent hill country, and Lebanon.' [26]But the LORD was angry with me on your account, and would not listen to me; and the LORD said to me, 'Let it satisfy you; speak no more to me of this matter. [27]Go up to the top of Pisgah, and lift up your eyes westward and northward and southward and eastward, and behold it with your eyes; for you shall not go over this Jordan. [28]But charge Joshua, and encourage and strengthen him; for he shall go over at the head of this people, and he shall put them in possession of the land which you shall see.' [29]So we remained in the valley opposite Beth-pe'or.

Moses Commands Obedience to God

4 "And now, O Israel, give heed to the statutes and the ordinances which I teach you, and do them; that you may live, and go in and take possession of the land which the LORD, the God of your fathers, gives you. [2]You shall not add to the word which I command you, nor take from it; that you may keep the commandments of the LORD your God which I command you. [3]Your eyes have seen what the LORD did at Ba'al-pe'or; for the LORD your God destroyed from among you all the men who followed the Ba'al of Peor; [4]but you who held fast to the LORD your God are all alive this day. [5]Behold, I have taught you statutes and ordinances, as the LORD my God commanded me, that you should do them in the land which you are entering to take possession of it. [6]Keep them and do them; for that will be your wisdom and your understanding in the sight of the peoples, who, when they hear all these statutes, will say, 'Surely this great nation is a wise and understanding people.' [7]For what great nation is there that has a god so near to it as the LORD our God is to us, whenever we call upon him? [8]And what great nation is there, that has statutes and ordinances so righteous as all this law which I set before you this day?

9 "Only take heed, and keep your soul diligently, lest you forget the things which your eyes have seen, and lest they depart from your heart all the days of your life; make them known to your children and your children's children—[10]how on the day that you stood before the LORD your God at Horeb, the LORD said to me, 'Gather the people to me, that I may let them hear my words, so that they may learn to fear me all the days that they

live upon the earth, and that they may teach their children so.' [11]And you came near and stood at the foot of the mountain, while the mountain burned with fire to the heart of heaven, wrapped in darkness, cloud, and gloom. [12]Then the LORD spoke to you out of the midst of the fire; you heard the sound of words, but saw no form; there was only a voice. [13]And he declared to you his covenant, which he commanded you to perform, that is, the ten commandments; [b] and he wrote them upon two tables of stone. [14]And the LORD commanded me at that time to teach you statutes and ordinances, that you might do them in the land which you are going over to possess.

15 "Therefore take good heed to yourselves. Since you saw no form on the day that the LORD spoke to you at Horeb out of the midst of the fire, [16]beware lest you act corruptly by making a graven image for yourselves, in the form of any figure, the likeness of male or female, [17]the likeness of any beast that is on the earth, the likeness of any winged bird that flies in the air, [18]the likeness of anything that creeps on the ground, the likeness of any fish that is in the water under the earth. [19]And beware lest you lift up your eyes to heaven, and when you see the sun and the moon and the stars, all the host of heaven, you be drawn away and worship them and serve them, things which the LORD your God has allotted to all the peoples under the whole heaven. [20]But the LORD has taken you, and brought you forth out of the iron furnace, out of Egypt, to be a people of his own possession, as at this day. [21]Furthermore the LORD was angry with me on your account, and he swore that I should not cross the Jordan, and that I should not enter the good land which the LORD your God gives you for an inheritance. [22]For I must die in this land, I must not go over the Jordan; but you shall go over and take possession of that good land. [23]Take heed to yourselves, lest you forget the covenant of the LORD your God, which he made with you, and make a graven image in the form of anything which the LORD your God has forbidden you. [24]For the LORD your God is a devouring fire, a jealous God.

25 "When you beget children and children's children, and have grown old in the land, if you act corruptly by making a graven image in the form of anything, and by doing what is evil in the sight of the LORD your God, so as to provoke him to anger, [26]I call heaven and earth to witness against you this day, that you will soon utterly perish from the land which you are going over the Jordan to possess; you will not live long upon it,

---

[b] Heb *words*.

3:23–27: Num 27:12–14; Deut 32:48–52.
4:2: Rev 22:18, 19.
4:9–14: Ex 19:1–20, 21.
4:24: Heb 12:29.

but will be utterly destroyed. [27]And the LORD will scatter you among the peoples, and you will be left few in number among the nations where the LORD will drive you. [28]And there you will serve gods of wood and stone, the work of men's hands, that neither see, nor hear, nor eat, nor smell. [29]But from there you will seek the LORD your God, and you will find him, if you search after him with all your heart and with all your soul. [30]When you are in tribulation, and all these things come upon you in the latter days, you will return to the LORD your God and obey his voice, [31]for the LORD your God is a merciful God; he will not fail you or destroy you or forget the covenant with your fathers which he swore to them.

[32] "For ask now of the days that are past, which were before you, since the day that God created man upon the earth, and ask from one end of heaven to the other, whether such a great thing as this has ever happened or was ever heard of. [33]Did any people ever hear the voice of God speaking out of the midst of the fire, as you have heard, and still live? [34]Or has God ever attempted to go and take a nation for himself from the midst of another nation, by trials, by signs, by wonders, and by war, by a mighty hand and an outstretched arm, and by great terrors, according to all that the LORD your God did for you in Egypt before your eyes? [35]To you it was shown, that you might know that the LORD is God; there is no other besides him. [36]Out of heaven he let you hear his voice, that he might discipline you; and on earth he let you see his great fire, and you heard his words out of the midst of the fire. [37]And because he loved your fathers and chose their descendants after them, and brought you out of Egypt with his own presence, by his great power, [38]driving out before you nations greater and mightier than yourselves, to bring you in, to give you their land for an inheritance, as at this day; [39]know therefore this day, and lay it to your heart, that the LORD is God in heaven above and on the earth beneath; there is no other. [40]Therefore you shall keep his statutes and his commandments, which I command you this day, that it may go well with you, and with your children after you, and that you may prolong your days in the land which the LORD your God gives you for ever." *

Cities of Refuge East of the Jordan

[41] † Then Moses set apart three cities in the east beyond the Jordan, [42]that the manslayer might flee there, who kills his neighbor unintentionally, without being at enmity with him in time past, and that by fleeing to one of these cities he might save his life: [43]Bezer in the wilderness on the tableland for the Reubenites, and Ramoth in Gilead for the Gadites, and Golan in Bashan for the Manas'sites.

Moses Sets Forth the Law

[44] This is the law which Moses set before the children of Israel; [45]these are the decrees, the statutes, and the ordinances, which Moses spoke to the children of Israel when they came out of Egypt, [46]beyond the Jordan in the valley opposite Beth-pe'or, in the land of Si'hon the king of the Am'orites, who lived at Heshbon, whom Moses and the children of Israel defeated when they came out of Egypt. [47]And they took possession of his land and the land of Og the king of Bashan, the two kings of the Am'orites, who lived to the east beyond the Jordan; [48]from Aro'er, which is on the edge of the valley of the Arnon, as far as Mount Sir'ion [c] (that is, Hermon), [49]together with all the Ar'abah on the east side of the Jordan as far as the Sea of the Arabah, under the slopes of Pisgah.

The Ten Commandments

5 And Moses summoned all Israel, and said to them, "Hear, O Israel, the statutes and the ordinances which I speak in your hearing this day, and you shall learn them and be careful to do them. [2]The LORD our God made a covenant with us in Horeb. [3]Not with our fathers did the LORD make this covenant, but with us, who are all of us here alive this day. [4]The LORD spoke with you face to face at the mountain, out of the midst of the fire, [5]while I stood between the LORD and you at that time, to declare to you the word of the LORD; for you were afraid because of the fire, and you did not go up into the mountain. He said:

[6] "'I am the LORD your God, who brought you out of the land of Egypt, out of the house of bondage.

[7] "'You shall have no other gods before [d] me.

[8] You shall not make for yourself a graven image, or any likeness of anything that is in heaven above, or that is on the earth beneath, or that is in the water under the earth; [9]you shall not bow down to them or serve them; for I the LORD your God am a jealous God, visiting the iniquity of the fathers upon the children to the third and fourth generation of those who hate me, [10]but showing merciful love to thousands of those who love me and keep my commandments.

[11] "'You shall not take the name of the LORD your God in vain: for the LORD will not hold him guiltless who takes his name in vain.

[12] "'Observe the sabbath day, to keep it holy, as the LORD your God commanded you. [13]Six days

---

[c] Syr: Heb *Sion*.
[d] Or *besides*.
4:41–43: Num 35:6, 9–34; Deut 19:2–13; Josh 20:7–9.
4:35: Mk 12:32.
5:6–21: Ex 20:2–17.
* 4:32–40: This passage gives the clearest and most eloquent expression of Israel's consciousness of its election as the people of God.
† 4:41: The beginning of the second discourse of Moses containing the Deuteronomic version of the Ten Commandments; cf. Ex 20:1–17.

you shall labor, and do all your work; ¹⁴but the seventh day is a sabbath to the LORD your God; in it you shall not do any work, you, or your son, or your daughter, or your manservant, or your maidservant, or your ox, or your donkey, or any of your cattle, or the sojourner who is within your gates, that your manservant and your maidservant may rest as well as you. ¹⁵You shall remember that you were a servant in the land of Egypt, and the LORD your God brought you out from there with a mighty hand and an outstretched arm; therefore the LORD your God commanded you to keep the sabbath day.

16 "'Honor your father and your mother, as the LORD your God commanded you; that your days may be prolonged, and that it may go well with you, in the land which the LORD your God gives you.

17 "'You shall not kill.

18 "'Neither shall you commit adultery.

19 "'Neither shall you steal.

20 "'Neither shall you bear false witness against your neighbor.

21 "'Neither shall you covet your neighbor's wife; and you shall not desire your neighbor's house, his field, or his manservant, or his maidservant, his ox, or his donkey, or anything that is your neighbor's.'

Moses the Mediator of God's Will

22 "These words the LORD spoke to all your assembly at the mountain out of the midst of the fire, the cloud, and the thick darkness, with a loud voice; and he added no more. And he wrote them upon two tables of stone, and gave them to me. ²³And when you heard the voice out of the midst of the darkness, while the mountain was burning with fire, you came near to me, all the heads of your tribes, and your elders; ²⁴and you said, 'Behold, the LORD our God has shown us his glory and greatness, and we have heard his voice out of the midst of the fire; we have this day seen God speak with man and man still live. ²⁵Now therefore why should we die? For this great fire will consume us; if we hear the voice of the LORD our God any more, we shall die. ²⁶For who is there of all flesh, that has heard the voice of the living God speaking out of the midst of fire, as we have, and has still lived? ²⁷Go near, and hear all that the LORD our God will say; and speak to us all that the LORD our God will speak to you; and we will hear and do it.'

28 "And the LORD heard your words, when you spoke to me; and the LORD said to me, 'I have heard the words of this people, which they have spoken to you; they have rightly said all that they have spoken. ²⁹Oh that they had such a mind as this always, to fear me and to keep all my commandments, that it might go well with them and with their children for ever! ³⁰Go and say to them,

"Return to your tents." ³¹But you, stand here by me, and I will tell you all the commandment and the statutes and the ordinances which you shall teach them, that they may do them in the land which I give them to possess.' ³²You shall be careful to do therefore as the LORD your God has commanded you; you shall not turn aside to the right hand or to the left. ³³You shall walk in all the way which the LORD your God has commanded you, that you may live, and that it may go well with you, and that you may live long in the land which you shall possess.

The Great Commandment

6 "Now this is the commandment, the statutes and the ordinances which the LORD your God commanded me to teach you, that you may do them in the land to which you are going over, to possess it; ²that you may fear the LORD your God, you and your son and your son's son, by keeping all his statutes and his commandments, which I command you, all the days of your life; and that your days may be prolonged. ³Hear therefore, O Israel, and be careful to do them; that it may go well with you, and that you may multiply greatly, as the LORD, the God of your fathers, has promised you, in a land flowing with milk and honey.

4 * "Hear, O Israel: The LORD our God is one LORD; ● ⁵and you shall love the LORD your God with all your heart, and with all your soul, and with all your might. ⁶And these words which I command you this day shall be upon your heart; ⁷and you shall teach them diligently to your children, and shall talk of them when you sit in your house, and when you walk by the way, and when you lie down, and when you rise. ⁸And you shall bind them as a sign upon your hand, and they shall be as frontlets between your eyes. ⁹And you shall write them on the doorposts of your house and on your gates.

Caution against Disobedience

10 "And when the LORD your God brings you into the land which he swore to your fathers, to Abraham, to Isaac, and to Jacob, to give you, with great and excellent cities, which you did not build, ¹¹and houses full of all good things, which you did

---

● Or the LORD our God, the LORD is one.
Or the LORD is our God, the LORD is one.
Or the LORD is our God, the LORD alone.
5:14: Ex 20:8–11; 23:12.
5:16–20: Mt 19:18, 19; Mk 10:19; Lk 18:20.
5:16: Mt 15:4; Mk 7:10; Eph 6:3.
5:17, 18: Jas 2:11.
5:17–21: Rom 13:9.
5:18: Mt 5:27; Rom 7:7.
5:21: Rom 7:7.
5:22–27: Ex 20:18–21.
6:4, 5: Mt 22:37; Mk 12:29, 30; Lk 10:27.
6:6–9: Deut 6:20–25; 11:18–20.
6:8: Ex 13:9, 16; Deut 11:18.
* 6:4–9: The recital thrice daily of this text, plus two others, is the principal practice of piety of the religious Jew; it is called the Shema ("Hear"). It contains the greatest commandment of the Law, that is, the love of the covenant-God (cf. Mt 22:37), and a clear statement of monotheism.

not fill, and cisterns hewn out, which you did not hew, and vineyards and olive trees, which you did not plant, and when you eat and are full, [12]then take heed lest you forget the LORD, who brought you out of the land of Egypt, out of the house of bondage. [13]You shall fear the LORD your God; you shall serve him, and swear by his name. [14]You shall not go after other gods, of the gods of the peoples who are round about you; [15]for the LORD your God in the midst of you is a jealous God; lest the anger of the LORD your God be kindled against you, and he destroy you from off the face of the earth.

16 "You shall not put the LORD your God to the test, as you tested him at Massah. [17]You shall diligently keep the commandments of the LORD your God, and his decrees, and his statutes, which he has commanded you. [18]And you shall do what is right and good in the sight of the LORD, that it may go well with you, and that you may go in and take possession of the good land which the LORD swore to give to your fathers [19]by thrusting out all your enemies from before you, as the LORD has promised.

20 "When your son asks you in time to come, 'What is the meaning of the decrees and the statutes and the ordinances which the LORD our God has commanded you?' [21]then you shall say to your son, 'We were Pharaoh's slaves in Egypt; and the LORD brought us out of Egypt with a mighty hand; [22]and the LORD showed signs and wonders, great and grievous, against Egypt and against Pharaoh and all his household, before our eyes; [23]and he brought us out from there, that he might bring us in and give us the land which he swore to give to our fathers. [24]And the LORD commanded us to do all these statutes, to fear the LORD our God, for our good always, that he might preserve us alive, as at this day. [25]And it will be righteousness for us, if we are careful to do all this commandment before the LORD our God, as he has commanded us.'

A Chosen People

7 "When the LORD your God brings you into the land which you are entering to take possession of it, and clears away many nations before you, the Hittites, the Gir'gashites, the Am'orites, the Canaanites, the Per'izzites, the Hi'vites, and the Jeb'usites, seven nations greater and mightier than yourselves, [2]and when the LORD your God gives them over to you, and you defeat them; then you must utterly destroy them; you shall make no covenant with them, and show no mercy to them. [3]You shall not make marriages with them, giving your daughters to their sons or taking their daughters for your sons. [4]For they would turn away your sons from following me, to serve other gods; then the anger of the LORD would be kindled against you, and he would destroy you quickly.

[5]But thus shall you deal with them: you shall break down their altars, and dash in pieces their pillars, and hew down their Ashe'rim, and burn their graven images with fire.

6 "For you are a people holy to the LORD your God; the LORD your God has chosen you to be a people for his own possession, out of all the peoples that are on the face of the earth. [7]It was not because you were more in number than any other people that the LORD set his love upon you and chose you, for you were the fewest of all peoples; [8]but it is because the LORD loves you, and is keeping the oath which he swore to your fathers, that the LORD has brought you out with a mighty hand, and redeemed you from the house of bondage, from the hand of Pharaoh king of Egypt. [9]Know therefore that the LORD your God is God, the faithful God who keeps covenant and merciful love with those who love him and keep his commandments, to a thousand generations, [10]and repays to their face those who hate him, by destroying them; he will not be slack with him who hates him, he will repay him to his face. [11]You shall therefore be careful to do the commandment, and the statutes, and the ordinances, which I command you this day.

Blessing for Obedience

12 "And because you listen to these ordinances, and keep and do them, the LORD your God will keep with you the covenant and the merciful love which he swore to your fathers to keep; [13]he will love you, bless you, and multiply you; he will also bless the fruit of your body and the fruit of your ground, your grain and your wine and your oil, the increase of your cattle and the young of your flock, in the land which he swore to your fathers to give you. [14]You shall be blessed above all peoples; there shall not be male or female barren among you, or among your cattle. [15]And the LORD will take away from you all sickness; and none of the evil diseases of Egypt, which you knew, will he inflict upon you, but he will lay them upon all who hate you. [16]And you shall destroy all the peoples that the LORD your God will give over to you, your eye shall not pity them; neither shall you serve their gods, for that would be a snare to you.

17 "If you say in your heart, 'These nations are greater than I; how can I dispossess them?' [18]you shall not be afraid of them, but you shall remember what the LORD your God did to Pharaoh and to all Egypt, [19]the great trials which your eyes saw, the signs, the wonders, the mighty hand,

---

6:13: Mt 4:10; Lk 4:8.
6:16: Mt 4:7; Lk 4:12.
7:1: Acts 13:19.
7:2-4: Ex 23:32, 33; 34:12, 15, 16.
7:3: Ex 34:15, 16.
7:5: Ex 23:24; 34:13; Num 33:52; Deut 12:3.
7:6: Ex 19:5; 22:31; Lev 11:44, 45; 19:2; 20:7, 26; Num 15:40; Deut 14:2, 21; 26:19; 28:9.

and the outstretched arm, by which the Lord your God brought you out; so will the Lord your God do to all the peoples of whom you are afraid. ²⁰Moreover the Lord your God will send hornets among them, until those who are left and hide themselves from you are destroyed. ²¹You shall not be in dread of them; for the Lord your God is in the midst of you, a great and terrible God. ²²The Lord your God will clear away these nations before you little by little; you may not make an end of them at once, ᶠ lest the wild beasts grow too numerous for you. ²³But the Lord your God will give them over to you, and throw them into great confusion, until they are destroyed. ²⁴And he will give their kings into your hand, and you shall make their name perish from under heaven; not a man shall be able to stand against you, until you have destroyed them. ²⁵The graven images of their gods you shall burn with fire; you shall not covet the silver or the gold that is on them, or take it for yourselves, lest you be ensnared by it; for it is an abomination to the Lord your God. ²⁶And you shall not bring an abominable thing into your house, and become accursed like it; you shall utterly detest and abhor it; for it is an accursed thing.

A Warning Not to Forget God

8 "All the commandment which I command you this day you shall be careful to do, that you may live and multiply, and go in and possess the land which the Lord swore to give to your fathers. ²And you shall remember all the way which the Lord your God has led you these forty years in the wilderness, that he might humble you, testing you to know what was in your heart, whether you would keep his commandments, or not. ³And he humbled you and let you hunger and fed you with manna, which you did not know, nor did your fathers know; that he might make you know that man does not live by bread alone, but that man lives by everything that proceeds out of the mouth of the Lord. ⁴Your clothing did not wear out upon you, and your foot did not swell, these forty years. ⁵Know then in your heart that, as a man disciplines his son, the Lord your God disciplines you. ⁶So you shall keep the commandments of the Lord your God, by walking in his ways and by fearing him. ⁷For the Lord your God is bringing you into a good land, a land of brooks of water, of fountains and springs, flowing forth in valleys and hills, ⁸a land of wheat and barley, of vines and fig trees and pomegranates, a land of olive trees and honey, ⁹a land in which you will eat bread without scarcity, in which you will lack nothing, a land whose stones are iron, and out of whose hills you can dig copper. ¹⁰And you shall eat and be full, and you shall bless the Lord your God for the good land he has given you.

¹¹ "Take heed lest you forget the Lord your God, by not keeping his commandments and his ordinances and his statutes, which I command you this day: ¹²lest, when you have eaten and are full, and have built excellent houses and live in them, ¹³and when your herds and flocks multiply, and your silver and gold is multiplied, and all that you have is multiplied, ¹⁴then your heart be lifted up, and you forget the Lord your God, who brought you out of the land of Egypt, out of the house of bondage, ¹⁵who led you through the great and terrible wilderness, with its fiery serpents and scorpions and thirsty ground where there was no water, who brought you water out of the flinty rock, ¹⁶who fed you in the wilderness with manna which your fathers did not know, that he might humble you and test you, to do you good in the end. ¹⁷Beware lest you say in your heart, 'My power and the might of my hand have gotten me this wealth.' ¹⁸You shall remember the Lord your God, for it is he who gives you power to get wealth; that he may confirm his covenant which he swore to your fathers, as at this day. ¹⁹And if you forget the Lord your God and go after other gods and serve them and worship them, I solemnly warn you this day that you shall surely perish. ²⁰Like the nations that the Lord makes to perish before you, so shall you perish, because you would not obey the voice of the Lord your God.

Consequences of Rebelling against God

9 "Hear, O Israel; you are to pass over the Jordan this day, to go in to dispossess nations greater and mightier than yourselves, cities great and fortified up to heaven, ²a people great and tall, the sons of the An'akim, whom you know, and of whom you have heard it said, 'Who can stand before the sons of A'nak?' ³Know therefore this day that he who goes over before you as a devouring fire is the Lord your God; he will destroy them and subdue them before you; so you shall drive them out, and make them perish quickly, as the Lord has promised you.

4 "Do not say in your heart, after the Lord your God has thrust them out before you, 'It is because of my righteousness that the Lord has brought me in to possess this land'; whereas it is because of the wickedness of these nations that the Lord is driving them out before you. ⁵Not because of your righteousness or the uprightness of your heart are you going in to possess their land; but because of the wickedness of these nations the Lord your God is driving them out from before you, and that he may confirm the word which the Lord swore to your fathers, to Abraham, to Isaac, and to Jacob.

6 "Know therefore, that the Lord your God is not giving you this good land to possess because

---

ᶠ Or *quickly.*
8:3: Mt 4:4; Lk 4:4.
9:3: Heb 12:29.

of your righteousness; for you are a stubborn people. [7]Remember and do not forget how you provoked the Lord your God to wrath in the wilderness; from the day you came out of the land of Egypt, until you came to this place, you have been rebellious against the Lord. [8]Even at Horeb you provoked the Lord to wrath, and the Lord was so angry with you that he was ready to destroy you. [9]When I went up the mountain to receive the tables of stone, the tables of the covenant which the Lord made with you, I remained on the mountain forty days and forty nights; I neither ate bread nor drank water. [10]And the Lord gave me the two tables of stone written with the finger of God; and on them were all the words which the Lord had spoken with you on the mountain out of the midst of the fire on the day of the assembly. [11]And at the end of forty days and forty nights the Lord gave me the two tables of stone, the tables of the covenant. [12]Then the Lord said to me, 'Arise, go down quickly from here; for your people whom you have brought from Egypt have acted corruptly; they have turned aside quickly out of the way which I commanded them; they have made themselves a molten image.'

13 "Furthermore the Lord said to me, 'I have seen this people, and behold, it is a stubborn people; [14]let me alone, that I may destroy them and blot out their name from under heaven; and I will make of you a nation mightier and greater than they.' [15]So I turned and came down from the mountain, and the mountain was burning with fire; and the two tables of the covenant were in my two hands. [16]And I looked, and behold, you had sinned against the Lord your God; you had made yourselves a molten calf; you had turned aside quickly from the way which the Lord had commanded you. [17]So I took hold of the two tables, and cast them out of my two hands, and broke them before your eyes. [18]Then I lay prostrate before the Lord as before, forty days and forty nights; I neither ate bread nor drank water, because of all the sin which you had committed, in doing what was evil in the sight of the Lord, to provoke him to anger. [19]For I was afraid of the anger and hot displeasure which the Lord bore against you, so that he was ready to destroy you. But the Lord listened to me that time also. [20]And the Lord was so angry with Aaron that he was ready to destroy him; and I prayed for Aaron also at the same time. [21]Then I took the sinful thing, the calf which you had made, and burned it with fire and crushed it, grinding it very small, until it was as fine as dust; and I threw the dust of it into the brook that descended out of the mountain.

22 "At Tab'erah also, and at Massah, and at Kib'roth-hatta'avah, you provoked the Lord to wrath. [23]And when the Lord sent you from Ka'desh-bar'nea, saying, 'Go up and take posses-sion of the land which I have given you,' then you rebelled against the commandment of the Lord your God, and did not believe him or obey his voice. [24]You have been rebellious against the Lord from the day that I knew you.

25 "So I lay prostrate before the Lord for these forty days and forty nights, because the Lord had said he would destroy you. [26]And I prayed to the Lord, 'O Lord God, do not destroy your people and your heritage, whom you have redeemed through your greatness, whom you have brought out of Egypt with a mighty hand. [27]Remember your servants, Abraham, Isaac, and Jacob; do not regard the stubbornness of this people, or their wickedness, or their sin, [28]lest the land from which you brought us say, "Because the Lord was not able to bring them into the land which he promised them, and because he hated them, he has brought them out to slay them in the wilderness." [29]For they are your people and your heritage, whom you brought out by your great power and by your outstretched arm.'

The Second Pair of Stone Tables

10 "At that time the Lord said to me, 'Hew two tables of stone like the first, and come up to me on the mountain, and make an ark of wood. [2]And I will write on the tables the words that were on the first tables which you broke, and you shall put them in the ark.' [3]So I made an ark of acacia wood, and hewed two tables of stone like the first, and went up the mountain with the two tables in my hand. [4]And he wrote on the tables, as at the first writing, the ten commandments [g] which the Lord had spoken to you on the mountain out of the midst of the fire on the day of the assembly; and the Lord gave them to me. [5]Then I turned and came down from the mountain, and put the tables in the ark which I had made; and there they are, as the Lord commanded me.

6 "(The sons of Israel journeyed from Be-er'oth Be'ne-ja'akan [h] to Mose'rah. There Aaron died, and there he was buried; and his son Elea'zar ministered as priest in his stead. [7]From there they journeyed to Gud'godah, and from Gudgodah to Jot'bathah, a land with brooks of water. [8]At that time the Lord set apart the tribe of Levi to carry the ark of the covenant of the Lord, to stand before the Lord to minister to him and to bless in his name, to this day. [9]Therefore Levi has no portion or inheritance with his brothers; the Lord is his inheritance, as the Lord your God said to him.)

10 "I stayed on the mountain, as at the first time, forty days and forty nights, and the Lord listened to me that time also; the Lord was

---

[g] Heb words.
[h] Or the wells of the Bene-jaakan.
9:8-21: Ex 32:7-20.
9:25-29: Ex 32:11-14.

unwilling to destroy you. [11]And the LORD said to me, 'Arise, go on your journey at the head of the people, that they may go in and possess the land, which I swore to their fathers to give them.'

The Essence of the Law

12 "And now, Israel, what does the LORD your God require of you, but to fear the LORD your God, to walk in all his ways, to love him, to serve the LORD your God with all your heart and with all your soul, [13]and to keep the commandments and statutes of the LORD, which I command you this day for your good? [14]Behold, to the LORD your God belong heaven and the heaven of heavens, the earth with all that is in it; [15]yet the LORD set his heart in love upon your fathers and chose their descendants after them, you above all peoples, as at this day. [16]Circumcise therefore the foreskin of your heart, and be no longer stubborn. [17]For the LORD your God is God of gods and Lord of lords, the great, the mighty, and the terrible God, who is not partial and takes no bribe. [18]He executes justice for the fatherless and the widow, and loves the sojourner, giving him food and clothing. [19]Love the sojourner therefore; for you were sojourners in the land of Egypt. [20]You shall fear the LORD your God; you shall serve him and cling to him, and by his name you shall swear. [21]He is your praise; he is your God, who has done for you these great and terrible things which your eyes have seen. [22]Your fathers went down to Egypt seventy persons; and now the LORD your God has made you as the stars of heaven for multitude.

Rewards for Obedience

11 "You shall therefore love the LORD your God, and keep his charge, his statutes, his ordinances, and his commandments always. [2]And consider this day (since I am not speaking to your children who have not known or seen it), consider the discipline [1] of the LORD your God, his greatness, his mighty hand and his outstretched arm, [3]his signs and his deeds which he did in Egypt to Pharaoh the king of Egypt and to all his land; [4]and what he did to the army of Egypt, to their horses and to their chariots; how he made the water of the Red Sea overflow them as they pursued after you, and how the LORD has destroyed them to this day; [5]and what he did to you in the wilderness, until you came to this place; [6]and what he did to Da'than and Abi'ram the sons of Eli'ab, son of Reuben; how the earth opened its mouth and swallowed them up, with their households, their tents, and every living thing that followed them, in the midst of all Israel; [7]for your eyes have seen all the great work of the LORD which he did.

8 "You shall therefore keep all the commandment which I command you this day, that you may be strong, and go in and take possession of the land which you are going over to possess,

[9]and that you may live long in the land which the LORD swore to your fathers to give to them and to their descendants, a land flowing with milk and honey. [10]For the land which you are entering to take possession of it is not like the land of Egypt, from which you have come, where you sowed your seed and watered it with your feet, like a garden of vegetables; [11]but the land which you are going over to possess is a land of hills and valleys, which drinks water by the rain from heaven, [12]a land which the LORD your God cares for; the eyes of the LORD your God are always upon it, from the beginning of the year to the end of the year.

13 "And if you will obey my commandments which I command you this day, to love the LORD your God, and to serve him with all your heart and with all your soul, [14]he [j] will give the rain for your land in its season, the early rain and the later rain, that you may gather in your grain and your wine and your oil. [15]And he [j] will give grass in your fields for your cattle, and you shall eat and be full. [16]Take heed lest your heart be deceived, and you turn aside and serve other gods and worship them, [17]and the anger of the LORD be kindled against you, and he shut up the heavens, so that there be no rain, and the land yield no fruit, and you perish quickly off the good land which the LORD gives you.

18 "You shall therefore lay up these words of mine in your heart and in your soul; and you shall bind them as a sign upon your hand, and they shall be as frontlets between your eyes. [19]And you shall teach them to your children, talking of them when you are sitting in your house, and when you are walking by the way, and when you lie down, and when you rise. [20]And you shall write them upon the doorposts of your house and upon your gates, [21]that your days and the days of your children may be multiplied in the land which the LORD swore to your fathers to give them, as long as the heavens are above the earth. [22]For if you will be careful to do all this commandment which I command you to do, loving the LORD your God, walking in all his ways, and clinging to him, [23]then the LORD will drive out all these nations before you, and you will dispossess nations greater and mightier than yourselves. [24]Every place on which the sole of your foot treads shall be yours; your territory shall be from the wilderness and Lebanon and from the River, the river Euphrates, to the western sea. [25]No man shall be able to stand against you; the LORD your God will lay the fear of you and the dread of you upon all the land that you shall tread, as he promised you.

---

[1] Or *instruction*.
[j] Sam Gk Vg: Heb *I*.
10:17: Acts 10:34; Gal 2:6; Rev 17:14; 19:16.
10:19: Ex 22:21; 23:9; Lev 19:34.
10:22: Acts 7:14.

26 "Behold, I set before you this day a blessing and a curse: [27]the blessing, if you obey the commandments of the LORD your God, which I command you this day, [28]and the curse, if you do not obey the commandments of the LORD your God, but turn aside from the way which I command you this day, to go after other gods which you have not known. [29]And when the LORD your God brings you into the land which you are entering to take possession of it, you shall set the blessing on Mount Ger'izim and the curse on Mount E'bal. [30]Are they not beyond the Jordan, west of the road, toward the going down of the sun, in the land of the Canaanites who live in the Ar'abah, over against Gilgal, beside the Oak [k] of Mo'reh? [31]For you are to pass over the Jordan to go in to take possession of the land which the LORD your God gives you; and when you possess it and live in it, [32]you shall be careful to do all the statutes and the ordinances which I set before you this day.

Pagan Shrines to Be Destroyed

12 "These are the statutes and ordinances which you shall be careful to do in the land which the LORD, the God of your fathers, has given you to possess, all the days that you live upon the earth. [2]*You shall surely destroy all the places where the nations whom you shall dispossess served their gods, upon the high mountains and upon the hills and under every green tree; [3]you shall tear down their altars, and dash in pieces their pillars, and burn their Ashe'rim with fire; you shall hew down the graven images of their gods, and destroy their name out of that place. [4]You shall not do so to the LORD your God. [5]But you shall seek the place which the LORD your God will choose out of all your tribes to put his name and make his habitation there; there you shall go, [6]and there you shall bring your burnt offerings and your sacrifices, your tithes and the offering that you present, your votive offerings, your freewill offerings, and the firstlings of your herd and of your flock; [7]and there you shall eat before the LORD your God, and you shall rejoice, you and your households, in all that you undertake, in which the LORD your God has blessed you. [8]You shall not do according to all that we are doing here this day, every man doing whatever is right in his own eyes; [9]for you have not as yet come to the rest and to the inheritance which the LORD your God gives you. [10]But when you go over the Jordan, and live in the land which the LORD your God gives you to inherit, and when he gives you rest from all your enemies round about, so that you live in safety, [11]then to the place which the LORD your God will choose, to make his name dwell there, there you shall bring all that I command you: your burnt offerings and your sacrifices, your tithes and the offering that you present, and all your votive offerings which you vow to

the LORD. [12]And you shall rejoice before the LORD your God, you and your sons and your daughters, your menservants and your maidservants, and the Levite that is within your towns, since he has no portion or inheritance with you. [13]Take heed that you do not offer your burnt offerings at every place that you see; [14]but at the place which the LORD will choose in one of your tribes, there you shall offer your burnt offerings, and there you shall do all that I am commanding you.

Concerning Eating

15 "However, you may slaughter and eat flesh within any of your towns, as much as you desire, according to the blessing of the LORD your God which he has given you; the unclean and the clean may eat of it, as of the gazelle and as of the deer. [16]Only you shall not eat the blood; you shall pour it out upon the earth like water. [17]You may not eat within your towns the tithe of your grain or of your wine or of your oil, or the firstlings of your herd or of your flock, or any of your votive offerings which you vow, or your freewill offerings, or the offering that you present; [18]but you shall eat them before the LORD your God in the place which the LORD your God will choose, you and your son and your daughter, your manservant and your maidservant, and the Levite who is within your towns; and you shall rejoice before the LORD your God in all that you undertake. [19]Take heed that you do not forsake the Levite as long as you live in your land.

20 "When the LORD your God enlarges your territory, as he has promised you, and you say, 'I will eat flesh,' because you crave flesh, you may eat as much flesh as you desire. [21]If the place which the LORD your God will choose to put his name there is too far from you, then you may kill any of your herd or your flock, which the LORD has given you, as I have commanded you; and you may eat within your towns as much as you desire. [22]Just as the gazelle or the deer is eaten, so you may eat of it; the unclean and the clean alike may eat of it. [23]Only be sure that you do not eat the blood; for the blood is the life, and you shall not eat the life with the flesh. [24]You shall not eat it; you shall pour it out upon the earth like water. [25]You shall not eat it; that all may go well with you and with your children after you, when you do what is right in the sight of the LORD. [26]But the holy things which are due from you, and your votive offerings, you shall take, and you shall go to the place which the LORD will choose, [27]and offer your burnt offerings, the flesh and the blood,

---

[k] Gk Syr: See Gen 12:6. Heb *Oaks* or *Terebinths*.
12:1–28: Ex 20:24.
12:16, 23: Lev 17:10–14; 19:26.
* 12:2: This law, enforcing one single place of worship, connects historically with the religious reform of Josiah just before the Exile in the opinion of many scholars; cf. 2 Kings 22–23.

on the altar of the LORD your God; the blood of your sacrifices shall be poured out on the altar of the LORD your God, but the flesh you may eat. [28]Be careful to heed all these words which I command you, that it may go well with you and with your children after you for ever, when you do what is good and right in the sight of the LORD your God.

Warning against Idolatry

29 "When the LORD your God cuts off before you the nations whom you go in to dispossess, and you dispossess them and dwell in their land, [30]take heed that you be not ensnared to follow them, after they have been destroyed before you, and that you do not inquire about their gods, saying, 'How did these nations serve their gods?—that I also may do likewise.' [31]You shall not do so to the LORD your God; for every abominable thing which the LORD hates they have done for their gods; for they even burn their sons and their daughters in the fire to their gods.

[32] [1] "Everything that I command you you shall be careful to do; you shall not add to it or take from it.

13 "If a prophet arises among you, or a dreamer of dreams, and gives you a sign or a wonder, [2]and the sign or wonder which he tells you comes to pass, and if he says, 'Let us go after other gods,' which you have not known, 'and let us serve them,' [3]you shall not listen to the words of that prophet or to that dreamer of dreams; for the LORD your God is testing you, to know whether you love the LORD your God with all your heart and with all your soul. [4]You shall walk after the LORD your God and fear him, and keep his commandments and obey his voice, and you shall serve him and cling to him. [5]But that prophet or that dreamer of dreams shall be put to death, because he has taught rebellion against the LORD your God, who brought you out of the land of Egypt and redeemed you out of the house of bondage, to make you leave the way in which the LORD your God commanded you to walk. So you shall purge the evil from the midst of you.

6 "If your brother, the son of your mother, or your son, or your daughter, or the wife of your bosom, or your friend who is as your own soul, entices you secretly, saying, 'Let us go and serve other gods,' which neither you nor your fathers have known, [7]some of the gods of the peoples that are round about you, whether near you or far off from you, from the one end of the earth to the other, [8]you shall not yield to him or listen to him, nor shall your eye pity him, [1.]or shall you spare him, nor shall you conceal him; [9]but you shall kill him; your hand shall be first against him to put him to death, and afterwards the hand of all the people. [10]You shall stone him to death with stones, because he sought to draw you away from the LORD your God, who brought you out of the

land of Egypt, out of the house of bondage. [11]And all Israel shall hear, and fear, and never again do any such wickedness as this among you.

12 "If you hear in one of your cities, which the LORD your God gives you to dwell there, [13]that certain base fellows have gone out among you and have drawn away the inhabitants of the city, saying, 'Let us go and serve other gods,' which you have not known, [14]then you shall inquire and make search and ask diligently; and behold, if it be true and certain that such an abominable thing has been done among you, [15]you shall surely put the inhabitants of that city to the sword, destroying it utterly, all who are in it and its cattle, with the edge of the sword. [16]You shall gather all its spoil into the midst of its open square, and burn the city and all its spoil with fire, as a whole burnt offering to the LORD your God; it shall be a heap for ever, it shall not be built again. [17]None of the devoted things shall cling to your hand; that the LORD may turn from the fierceness of his anger, and show you mercy, and have compassion on you, and multiply you, as he swore to your fathers, [18]if you obey the voice of the LORD your God, keeping all his commandments which I command you this day, and doing what is right in the sight of the LORD your God.

Pagan Practices Forbidden

14 "You are the sons of the LORD your God; you shall not cut yourselves or make any baldness on your foreheads for the dead. [2]For you are a people holy to the LORD your God, and the LORD has chosen you to be a people for his own possession, out of all the peoples that are on the face of the earth.

3 "You shall not eat any abominable thing. [4]These are the animals you may eat: the ox, the sheep, the goat, [5]the deer, the gazelle, the roebuck, the wild goat, the ibex, the antelope, and the mountain-sheep. [6]Every animal that parts the hoof and has the hoof cloven in two, and chews the cud, among the animals, you may eat. [7]Yet of those that chew the cud or have the hoof cloven you shall not eat these: The camel, the hare, and the rock badger, because they chew the cud but do not part the hoof, are unclean for you. [8]And the swine, because it parts the hoof but does not chew the cud, is unclean for you. Their flesh you shall not eat, and their carcasses you shall not touch.

9 "Of all that are in the waters you may eat these: Whatever has fins and scales you may eat. [10]And whatever does not have fins and scales you shall not eat; it is unclean for you.

---

[1] Ch 13:1 in Heb.
12:29–32: Ex 23:24; 34:12–14; Num 33:52.
14:1: Lev 19:28.
14:2: Ex 19:5, 6; Deut 26:19; Tit 2:14; 1 Pet 2:9; Rev 1:6; 5:10.
14:3–20: Lev 11:2–23.

11 "You may eat all clean birds. ¹²But these are the ones which you shall not eat: the eagle, the vulture, the osprey, ¹³the buzzard, the kite, after their kinds; ¹⁴every raven after its kind; ¹⁵the ostrich, the nighthawk, the sea gull, the hawk, after their kinds; ¹⁶the little owl and the great owl, the water hen ¹⁷and the pelican, the carrion vulture and the cormorant, ¹⁸the stork, the heron, after their kinds; the hoopoe and the bat. ¹⁹And all winged insects are unclean for you; they shall not be eaten. ²⁰All clean winged things you may eat.

21 "You shall not eat anything that dies of itself; you may give it to the alien who is within your towns, that he may eat it, or you may sell it to a foreigner; for you are a people holy to the Lord your God.

"You shall not boil a kid in its mother's milk.

Regulations concerning Tithes

22 "You shall tithe all the yield of your seed, which comes forth from the field year by year. ²³And before the Lord your God, in the place which he will choose, to make his name dwell there, you shall eat the tithe of your grain, of your wine, and of your oil, and the firstlings of your herd and flock; that you may learn to fear the Lord your God always. ²⁴And if the way is too long for you, so that you are not able to bring the tithe, when the Lord your God blesses you, because the place is too far from you, which the Lord your God chooses, to set his name there, ²⁵then you shall turn it into money, and bind up the money in your hand, and go to the place which the Lord your God chooses, ²⁶and spend the money for whatever you desire, oxen, or sheep, or wine or strong drink, whatever your appetite craves; and you shall eat there before the Lord your God and rejoice, you and your household. ²⁷And you shall not forsake the Levite who is within your towns, for he has no portion or inheritance with you.

28 "At the end of every three years you shall bring forth all the tithe of your produce in the same year, and lay it up within your towns; ²⁹and the Levite, because he has no portion or inheritance with you, and the sojourner, the fatherless, and the widow, who are within your towns, shall come and eat and be filled; that the Lord your God may bless you in all the work of your hands that you do.

Concerning the Sabbatical Year

15 "At the end of every seven years you shall grant a release. ²And this is the manner of the release: every creditor shall release what he has lent to his neighbor; he shall not exact it of his neighbor, his brother, because the Lord's release has been proclaimed. ³Of a foreigner you may exact it; but whatever of yours is with your brother your hand shall release. ⁴But there will be no poor among you (for the Lord will bless you in

the land which the Lord your God gives you for an inheritance to possess), ⁵if only you will obey the voice of the Lord your God, being careful to do all this commandment which I command you this day. ⁶For the Lord your God will bless you, as he promised you, and you shall lend to many nations, but you shall not borrow; and you shall rule over many nations, but they shall not rule over you.

7 "If there is among you a poor man, one of your brethren, in any of your towns within your land which the Lord your God gives you, you shall not harden your heart or shut your hand against your poor brother, ⁸but you shall open your hand to him, and lend him sufficient for his need, whatever it may be. ⁹Take heed lest there be a base thought in your heart, and you say, 'The seventh year, the year of release is near,' and your eye be hostile to your poor brother, and you give him nothing, and he cry to the Lord against you, and it be sin in you. ¹⁰You shall give to him freely, and your heart shall not be grudging when you give to him; because for this the Lord your God will bless you in all your work and in all that you undertake. ¹¹For the poor will never cease out of the land; therefore I command you, You shall open wide your hand to your brother, to the needy and to the poor, in the land.

12 "If your brother, a Hebrew man, or a Hebrew woman, is sold to you, he shall serve you six years, and in the seventh year you shall let him go free from you. ¹³And when you let him go free from you, you shall not let him go empty-handed; ¹⁴you shall furnish him liberally out of your flock, out of your threshing floor, and out of your wine press; as the Lord your God has blessed you, you shall give to him. ¹⁵You shall remember that you were a slave in the land of Egypt, and the Lord your God redeemed you; therefore I command you this today. ¹⁶But if he says to you, 'I will not go out from you,' because he loves you and your household, since he fares well with you, ¹⁷then you shall take an awl, and thrust it through his ear into the door, and he shall be your bondman for ever. And to your bondwoman you shall do likewise. ¹⁸It shall not seem hard to you, when you let him go free from you; for at half the cost of a hired servant he has served you six years. So the Lord your God will bless you in all that you do.

Regulations concerning Livestock

19 "All the firstling males that are born of your herd and flock you shall consecrate to the Lord your God; you shall do no work with the firstling of your herd, nor shear the firstling of your flock.

14:21: Lev 11:39, 40; 17:15; Ex 23:19; 34:26.
14:22-29: Lev 27:30-33; Num 18:21-32.
15:12-18: Ex 21:2-11; Lev 25:39-46.
15:19-23: Ex 13:11, 12; 22:30; 34:19; Num 18:17, 18.

²⁰You shall eat it, you and your household, before the Lord your God year by year at the place which the Lord will choose. ²¹But if it has any blemish, if it is lame or blind, or has any serious blemish whatever, you shall not sacrifice it to the Lord your God. ²²You shall eat it within your towns; the unclean and the clean alike may eat it, as though it were a gazelle or a deer. ²³Only you shall not eat its blood; you shall pour it out on the ground like water.

Keeping the Passover

16 "Observe the month of A'bib, and keep the Passover to the Lord your God; for in the month of Abib the Lord your God brought you out of Egypt by night. ²And you shall offer the Passover sacrifice to the Lord your God, from the flock or the herd, at the place which the Lord will choose, to make his name dwell there. ³You shall eat no leavened bread with it; seven days you shall eat it with unleavened bread, the bread of affliction—for you came out of the land of Egypt in hurried flight—that all the days of your life you may remember the day when you came out of the land of Egypt. ⁴No leaven shall be seen with you in all your territory for seven days; nor shall any of the flesh which you sacrifice on the evening of the first day remain all night until morning. ⁵You may not offer the Passover sacrifice within any of your towns which the Lord your God gives you; ⁶but at the place which the Lord your God will choose, to make his name dwell in it, there you shall offer the Passover sacrifice, in the evening at the going down of the sun, at the time you came out of Egypt. ⁷And you shall boil it and eat it at the place which the Lord your God will choose; and in the morning you shall turn and go to your tents. ⁸For six days you shall eat unleavened bread; and on the seventh day there shall be a solemn assembly to the Lord your God; you shall do no work on it.

Keeping the Feast of Weeks

9 "You shall count seven weeks; begin to count the seven weeks from the time you first put the sickle to the standing grain. ¹⁰Then you shall keep the feast of weeks to the Lord your God with the tribute of a freewill offering from your hand, which you shall give as the Lord your God blesses you; ¹¹and you shall rejoice before the Lord your God, you and your son and your daughter, your manservant and your maidservant, the Levite who is within your towns, the sojourner, the fatherless, and the widow who are among you, at the place which the Lord your God will choose, to make his name dwell there. ¹²You shall remember that you were a slave in Egypt; and you shall be careful to observe these statutes.

Keeping the Feast of Booths

13 "You shall keep the feast of booths seven days, when you make your ingathering from your threshing floor and your wine press; ¹⁴you shall rejoice in your feast, you and your son and your daughter, your manservant and your maidservant, the Levite, the sojourner, the fatherless, and the widow who are within your towns. ¹⁵For seven days you shall keep the feast to the Lord your God at the place which the Lord will choose; because the Lord your God will bless you in all your produce and in all the work of your hands, so that you will be altogether joyful.

16 "Three times a year all your males shall appear before the Lord your God at the place which he will choose: at the feast of unleavened bread, at the feast of weeks, and at the feast of booths. They shall not appear before the Lord empty-handed; ¹⁷every man shall give as he is able, according to the blessing of the Lord your God which he has given you.

Appointing Judges and Officers

18 "You shall appoint judges and officers in all your towns which the Lord your God gives you, according to your tribes; and they shall judge the people with righteous judgment. ¹⁹You shall not pervert justice; you shall not show partiality; and you shall not take a bribe, for a bribe blinds the eyes of the wise and subverts the cause of the righteous. ²⁰Justice, and only justice, you shall follow, that you may live and inherit the land which the Lord your God gives you.

Forbidden Forms of Worship

21 "You shall not plant any tree as an Ashe'rah beside the altar of the Lord your God which you shall make. ²²And you shall not set up a pillar, which the Lord your God hates.

17 "You shall not sacrifice to the Lord your God an ox or a sheep in which is a blemish, any defect whatever; for that is an abomination to the Lord your God.

2 "If there is found among you, within any of your towns which the Lord your God gives you, a man or woman who does what is evil in the sight of the Lord your God, in transgressing his covenant, ³and has gone and served other gods and worshiped them, or the sun or the moon or any of the host of heaven, which I have forbidden, ⁴and it is told you and you hear of it; then you shall inquire diligently, and if it is true and certain that such an abominable thing has been done in Israel, ⁵then you shall bring forth to your gates that man or woman who has done this evil thing, and you shall stone that man or woman to death with stones. ⁶On the evidence of two witnesses or of three witnesses he that is to die shall

16:1–17: Ex 23:14–17; Lev 23; Num 28–29.
16:19: Ex 23:6–9; Lev 19:15.
16:21, 22: Lev 26:1.
17:1: Lev 22:17–24.
17:2–7: Ex 22:20.
17:6: Num 35:30; Deut 19:15; Mt 18:16; 2 Cor 13:1; 1 Tim 5:19; Heb 10:28.

be put to death; a person shall not be put to death on the evidence of one witness. [7]The hand of the witnesses shall be first against him to put him to death, and afterward the hand of all the people. So you shall purge the evil from the midst of you.

Legal Decisions by Priests and Judges

8 "If any case arises requiring decision between one kind of homicide and another, one kind of legal right and another, or one kind of assault and another, any case within your towns which is too difficult for you, then you shall arise and go up to the place which the LORD your God will choose, [9]and coming to the Levitical priests, and to the judge who is in office in those days, you shall consult them, and they shall declare to you the decision. [10]Then you shall do according to what they declare to you from that place which the LORD will choose; and you shall be careful to do according to all that they direct you; [11]according to the instructions which they give you, and according to the decision which they pronounce to you, you shall do; you shall not turn aside from the verdict which they declare to you, either to the right hand or to the left. [12]The man who acts presumptuously, by not obeying the priest who stands to minister there before the LORD your God, or the judge, that man shall die; so you shall purge the evil from Israel. [13]And all the people shall hear, and fear, and not act presumptuously again.

Limitations of Royal Authority

14 "When you come to the land which the LORD your God gives you, and you possess it and dwell in it, and then say, 'I will set a king over me, like all the nations that are round about me'; [15]you may indeed set as king over you him whom the LORD your God will choose. One from among your brethren you shall set as king over you; you may not put a foreigner over you, who is not your brother. [16]Only he must not multiply horses for himself, or cause the people to return to Egypt in order to multiply horses, since the LORD has said to you, 'You shall never return that way again.' [17]And he shall not multiply wives for himself, lest his heart turn away; nor shall he greatly multiply for himself silver and gold.

18 "And when he sits on the throne of his kingdom, he shall write for himself in a book a copy of this law, from that which is in the charge of the Levitical priests; [19]and it shall be with him, and he shall read in it all the days of his life, that he may learn to fear the LORD his God, by keeping all the words of this law and these statutes, and doing them; [20]that his heart may not be lifted up above his brethren, and that he may not turn aside from the commandment, either to the right hand or to the left; so that he may continue long in his kingdom, he and his children, in Israel.

Privileges of Priests and Levites

18 "The Levitical priests, that is, all the tribe of Levi, shall have no portion or inheritance with Israel; they shall eat the offerings by fire to the LORD, and his rightful dues. [2]They shall have no inheritance among their brethren; the LORD is their inheritance, as he promised them. [3]And this shall be the priests' due from the people, from those offering a sacrifice, whether it be ox or sheep: they shall give to the priest the shoulder and the two cheeks and the stomach. [4]The first fruits of your grain, of your wine and of your oil, and the first of the fleece of your sheep, you shall give him. [5]For the LORD your God has chosen him out of all your tribes, to stand and minister in the name of the LORD, him and his sons for ever.

6 "And if a Levite comes from any of your towns out of all Israel, where he lives—and he may come when he desires—to the place which the LORD will choose, [7]then he may minister in the name of the LORD his God, like all his fellow Levites who stand to minister there before the LORD. [8]They shall have equal portions to eat, besides what he receives from the sale of his patrimony.[m]

Abominable Practices Prohibited

9 "When you come into the land which the LORD your God gives you, you shall not learn to follow the abominable practices of those nations. [10]There shall not be found among you any one who burns his son or his daughter as an offering,[n] any one who practices divination, a soothsayer, or an augur, or a sorcerer, [11]or a charmer, or a medium, or a wizard, or a necromancer. [12]For whoever does these things is an abomination to the LORD; and because of these abominable practices the LORD your God is driving them out before you. [13]You shall be blameless before the LORD your God. [14]For these nations, which you are about to dispossess, give heed to soothsayers and to diviners; but as for you, the LORD your God has not allowed you so to do.

15 "The LORD your God will raise up for you a prophet like me from among you, from your brethren—him you shall heed—[16]just as you desired of the LORD your God at Horeb on the day of the assembly, when you said, 'Let me not hear again the voice of the LORD my God, or see this great fire any more, lest I die.' [17]And the LORD said to me, 'They have rightly said all that they have spoken. [18]I will raise up for them a prophet *

[m] Heb obscure.
[n] Heb makes his son or his daughter pass through the fire.
17:7: Deut 19:19; 1 Cor 5:13.
18:1-8: Num 18:20-24.
18:10, 11: Ex 22:18; Lev 19:26, 31; 20:6, 27.
18:13: Mt 5:48.
18:15-19: Acts 3:22, 23; 7:37.
* 18:18: The prophet like Moses mentioned here refers either to the prophetic movement as a whole or to an individual, either Joshua (successor of Moses) or Samuel. The New Testament sees here a reference to the Messiah; cf. Jn 1:21; Acts 3:22; 7:37.

like you from among their brethren; and I will put my words in his mouth, and he shall speak to them all that I command him. [19]And whoever will not give heed to my words which he shall speak in my name, I myself will require it of him. [20]But the prophet who presumes to speak a word in my name which I have not commanded him to speak, or who speaks in the name of other gods, that same prophet shall die.' [21]And if you say in your heart, 'How may we know the word which the LORD has not spoken?'—[22]when a prophet speaks in the name of the LORD, if the word does not come to pass or come true, that is a word which the LORD has not spoken; the prophet has spoken it presumptuously, you need not be afraid of him.

Cities of Refuge

19 "When the LORD your God cuts off the nations whose land the LORD your God gives you, and you dispossess them and dwell in their cities and in their houses, [2]you shall set apart three cities for you in the land which the LORD your God gives you to possess. [3]You shall prepare the roads, and divide into three parts the area of the land which the LORD your God gives you as a possession, so that any manslayer can flee to them.

4 "This is the provision for the manslayer, who by fleeing there may save his life. If any one kills his neighbor unintentionally without having been at enmity with him in time past—[5]as when a man goes into the forest with his neighbor to cut wood, and his hand swings the axe to cut down a tree, and the head slips from the handle and strikes his neighbor so that he dies—he may flee to one of these cities and save his life; [6]lest the avenger of blood in hot anger pursue the manslayer and overtake him, because the way is long, and wound him mortally, though the man did not deserve to die, since he was not at enmity with his neighbor in time past. [7]Therefore I command you, You shall set apart three cities. [8]And if the LORD your God enlarges your border, as he has sworn to your fathers, and gives you all the land which he promised to give to your fathers—[9]provided you are careful to keep all this commandment, which I command you this day, by loving the LORD your God and by walking ever in his ways—then you shall add three other cities to these three, [10]lest innocent blood be shed in your land which the LORD your God gives you for an inheritance, and so the guilt of bloodshed be upon you.

11 "But if any man hates his neighbor, and lies in wait for him, and attacks him, and wounds him mortally so that he dies, and the man flees into one of these cities, [12]then the elders of his city shall send and fetch him from there, and hand him over to the avenger of blood, so that he may die. [13]Your eye shall not pity him, but you shall purge the guilt of innocent blood° from Israel, so that it may be well with you.

Concerning Landmarks

14 "In the inheritance which you will hold in the land that the LORD your God gives you to possess, you shall not remove your neighbor's landmark, which the men of old have set.

Concerning Witnesses

15 "A single witness shall not prevail against a man for any crime or for any wrong in connection with any offense that he has committed; only on the evidence of two witnesses, or of three witnesses, shall a charge be sustained. [16]If a malicious witness rises against any man to accuse him of wrongdoing, [17]then both parties to the dispute shall appear before the LORD, before the priests and the judges who are in office in those days; [18]the judges shall inquire diligently, and if the witness is a false witness and has accused his brother falsely, [19]then you shall do to him as he had meant to do to his brother; so you shall purge the evil from the midst of you. [20]And the rest shall hear, and fear, and shall never again commit any such evil among you. [21]Your eye shall not pity; it shall be life for life, eye for eye, tooth for tooth, hand for hand, foot for foot.

Concerning Warfare

20 "When you go forth to war against your enemies, and see horses and chariots and an army larger than your own, you shall not be afraid of them; for the LORD your God is with you, who brought you up out of the land of Egypt. [2]And when you draw near to the battle, the priest shall come forward and speak to the people, [3]and shall say to them, 'Hear, O Israel, you draw near this day to battle against your enemies: let not your heart faint; do not fear, or tremble, or be in dread of them; [4]for the LORD your God is he that goes with you, to fight for you against your enemies, to give you the victory.' [5]Then the officers shall speak to the people, saying, 'What man is there that has built a new house and has not dedicated it? Let him go back to his house, lest he die in the battle and another man dedicate it. [6]And what man is there that has planted a vineyard and has not enjoyed its fruit? Let him go back to his house, lest he die in the battle and another man enjoy its fruit. [7]And what man is there that has betrothed a wife and has not taken her? Let him go back to his house, lest he die in the battle and another man take her.' [8]And the officers shall speak further to the people, and say, 'What man is there that is fearful and fainthearted? Let him

---

° Or *the blood of the innocent.*
19:1-13: Ex 21:12–14; Num 35.
19:15: Num 35:30; Deut 17:6; Mt 18:16; 2 Cor 13:1; 1 Tim 5:19; Heb 10:28.
19:16-20: Ex 20:16; 23:1; Lev 19:16; Deut 5:20.
19:19: 1 Cor 5:13.
19:21: Ex 21:23–26; Lev 24:20; Mt 5:38.

go back to his house, lest the heart of his fellows melt as his heart.' ⁹And when the officers have made an end of speaking to the people, then commanders shall be appointed at the head of the people.

10 "When you draw near to a city to fight against it, offer terms of peace to it. ¹¹And if its answer to you is peace and it opens to you, then all the people who are found in it shall do forced labor for you and shall serve you. ¹²But if it makes no peace with you, but makes war against you, then you shall besiege it; ¹³and when the LORD your God gives it into your hand you shall put all its males to the sword, ¹⁴but the women and the little ones, the cattle, and everything else in the city, all its spoil, you shall take as booty for yourselves; and you shall enjoy the spoil of your enemies, which the LORD your God has given you. ¹⁵Thus you shall do to all the cities which are very far from you, which are not cities of the nations here. ¹⁶But in the cities of these peoples that the LORD your God gives you for an inheritance, you shall save alive nothing that breathes, ¹⁷but you shall utterly destroy them, the Hittites and the Am'orites, the Canaanites and the Per'izzites, the Hi'vites and the Jeb'usites, as the LORD your God has commanded; ¹⁸that they may not teach you to do according to all their abominable practices which they have done in the service of their gods, and so to sin against the LORD your God.

19 "When you besiege a city for a long time, making war against it in order to take it, you shall not destroy its trees by wielding an axe against them; for you may eat of them, but you shall not cut them down. Are the trees in the field men that they should be besieged by you? ²⁰Only the trees which you know are not trees for food you may destroy and cut down that you may build siegeworks against the city that makes war with you, until it falls.

Concerning the Slain

21 "If in the land which the LORD your God gives you to possess, any one is found slain, lying in the open country, and it is not known who killed him, ²then your elders and your judges shall come forth, and they shall measure the distance to the cities which are around him that is slain; ³and the elders of the city which is nearest to the slain man shall take a heifer which has never been worked and which has not pulled in the yoke. ⁴And the elders of that city shall bring the heifer down to a valley with running water, which is neither plowed nor sown, and shall break the heifer's neck there in the valley. ⁵And the priests the sons of Levi shall come forward, for the LORD your God has chosen them to minister to him and to bless in the name of the LORD, and by their word every dispute and every assault shall be settled. ⁶And all the elders of that

city nearest to the slain man shall wash their hands over the heifer whose neck was broken in the valley; ⁷and they shall testify, 'Our hands did not shed this blood, neither did our eyes see it shed. ⁸Forgive, O LORD, your people Israel, whom you have redeemed, and set not the guilt of innocent blood in the midst of your people Israel; but let the guilt of blood be forgiven them.' ⁹So you shall purge the guilt of innocent blood from your midst, when you do what is right in the sight of the LORD.

Women Taken Captive

10 "When you go forth to war against your enemies, and the LORD your God gives them into your hands, and you take them captive, ¹¹and see among the captives a beautiful woman, and you have desire for her and would take her for yourself as wife, ¹²then you shall bring her home to your house, and she shall shave her head and pare her nails. ¹³And she shall put off her captive's garb, and shall remain in your house and bewail her father and her mother a full month; after that you may go in to her, and be her husband, and she shall be your wife. ¹⁴Then, if you have no delight in her, you shall let her go where she will; but you shall not sell her for money, you shall not treat her as a slave, since you have humiliated her.

Right of the First-born Son

15 "If a man has two wives, the one loved and the other disliked, and they have borne him children, both the loved and the disliked, and if the first-born son is hers that is disliked, ¹⁶then on the day when he assigns his possessions as an inheritance to his sons, he may not treat the son of the loved as the first-born in preference to the son of the disliked, who is the first-born, ¹⁷but he shall acknowledge the first-born, the son of the disliked, by giving him a double portion of all that he has, for he is the first issue of his strength; the right of the first-born is his.

Rebellious Sons

18 "If a man has a stubborn and rebellious son, who will not obey the voice of his father or the voice of his mother, and, though they chastise him, will not give heed to them, ¹⁹then his father and his mother shall take hold of him and bring him out to the elders of his city at the gate of the place where he lives, ²⁰and they shall say to the elders of his city, 'This our son is stubborn and rebellious, he will not obey our voice; he is a glutton and a drunkard.' ²¹Then all the men of the city shall stone him to death with stones; so you shall purge the evil from your midst; and all Israel shall hear, and fear.

Miscellaneous Laws

22 "And if a man has committed a crime punishable by death and he is put to death, and you

21:18–21: Ex 20:12; 21:15, 17; Lev 20:9; Deut 5:16; 27:16.
21:22: Acts 5:30; 10:39.

hang him on a tree, [23]his body shall not remain all night upon the tree, but you shall bury him the same day, for a hanged man is accursed by God; you shall not defile your land which the LORD your God gives you for an inheritance.

22 "You shall not see your brother's ox or his sheep go astray, and withhold your help[p] from them; you shall take them back to your brother. [2]And if he is not near you, or if you do not know him, you shall bring it home to your house, and it shall be with you until your brother seeks it; then you shall restore it to him. [3]And so you shall do with his donkey; so you shall do with his garment; so you shall do with any lost thing of your brother's, which he loses and you find; you may not withhold your help. [4]You shall not see your brother's donkey or his ox fallen down by the way, and withhold your help[p] from them; you shall help him to lift them up again.

5 "A woman shall not wear anything that pertains to a man, nor shall a man put on a woman's garment; for whoever does these things is an abomination to the LORD your God.

6 "If you chance to come upon a bird's nest, in any tree or on the ground, with young ones or eggs and the mother sitting upon the young or upon the eggs, you shall not take the mother with the young; [7]you shall let the mother go, but the young you may take to yourself; that it may go well with you, and that you may live long.

8 "When you build a new house, you shall make a parapet for your roof, that you may not bring the guilt of blood upon your house, if any one fall from it.

9 "You shall not sow your vineyard with two kinds of seed, lest the whole yield be forfeited to the sanctuary,[q] the crop which you have sown and the yield of the vineyard. [10]You shall not plow with an ox and a donkey together. [11]You shall not wear a mingled stuff, wool and linen together.

12 "You shall make yourself tassels on the four corners of your cloak with which you cover yourself.

Concerning Sexual Relations

13 "If any man takes a wife, and goes in to her, and then spurns her, [14]and charges her with shameful conduct, and brings an evil name upon her, saying, 'I took this woman, and when I came near her, I did not find in her the tokens of virginity,' [15]then the father of the young woman and her mother shall take and bring out the tokens of her virginity to the elders of the city in the gate; [16]and the father of the young woman shall say to the elders, 'I gave my daughter to this man to wife, and he spurns her; [17]and behold, he has made shameful charges against her, saying, "I did not find in your daughter the tokens of virginity."

And yet these are the tokens of my daughter's virginity.' And they shall spread the garment before the elders of the city. [18]Then the elders of that city shall take the man and whip him; [19]and they shall fine him a hundred shekels of silver, and give them to the father of the young woman, because he has brought an evil name upon a virgin of Israel; and she shall be his wife; he may not put her away all his days. [20]But if the thing is true, that the tokens of virginity were not found in the young woman, [21]then they shall bring out the young woman to the door of her father's house, and the men of her city shall stone her to death with stones, because she has wrought folly in Israel by playing the harlot in her father's house; so you shall purge the evil from the midst of you.

22 "If a man is found lying with the wife of another man, both of them shall die, the man who lay with the woman, and the woman; so you shall purge the evil from Israel.

23 "If there is a betrothed virgin, and a man meets her in the city and lies with her, [24]then you shall bring them both out to the gate of that city, and you shall stone them to death with stones, the young woman because she did not cry for help though she was in the city, and the man because he violated his neighbor's wife; so you shall purge the evil from the midst of you.

25 "But if in the open country a man meets a young woman who is betrothed, and the man seizes her and lies with her, then only the man who lay with her shall die. [26]But to the young woman you shall do nothing; in the young woman there is no offense punishable by death, for this case is like that of a man attacking and murdering his neighbor; [27]because he came upon her in the open country, and though the betrothed young woman cried for help there was no one to rescue her.

28 "If a man meets a virgin who is not betrothed, and seizes her and lies with her, and they are found, [29]then the man who lay with her shall give to the father of the young woman fifty shekels of silver, and she shall be his wife, because he has violated her; he may not put her away all his days.

[30][r] "A man shall not take his father's wife, nor shall he uncover her who is his father's. [s]

---

[p] Heb *hide yourself.*
[q] Heb *become holy.*
[r] Ch 23:1 in Heb.
[s] Heb *uncover his father's skirt.*
21:23: Gal 3:13.
22:1-4: Ex 23:4, 5.
22:9-11: Lev 19:19.
22:12: Num 15:37–41.
22:21: 1 Cor 5:13.
22:22-27: Ex 20:14; Lev 18:20; 20:10; Deut 5:18.
22:24: 1 Cor 5:13.
22:28, 29: Ex 22:16, 17.

Exclusion from the Assembly

23 "He whose testicles are crushed or whose male member is cut off shall not enter the assembly of the LORD.

2 "No bastard shall enter the assembly of the LORD; even to the tenth generation none of his descendants shall enter the assembly of the LORD.

3 "No Am'monite or Moabite shall enter the assembly of the LORD; even to the tenth generation none belonging to them shall enter the assembly of the LORD for ever; ⁴because they did not meet you with bread and with water on the way, when you came forth out of Egypt, and because they hired against you Balaam the son of Beor from Pe'thor of Mesopota'mia, to curse you. ⁵Nevertheless the LORD your God would not listen to Balaam; but the LORD your God turned the curse into a blessing for you, because the LORD your God loved you. ⁶You shall not seek their peace or their prosperity all your days for ever.

7 "You shall not abhor an E'domite, for he is your brother; you shall not abhor an Egyptian, because you were a sojourner in his land. ⁸The children of the third generation that are born to them may enter the assembly of the LORD.

Sanitary, Ritual, and Humanitarian Precepts

9 "When you go forth against your enemies and are in camp, then you shall keep yourself from every evil thing.

10 "If there is among you any man who is not clean by reason of a nocturnal emission, then he shall go outside the camp, he shall not come within the camp; ¹¹but when evening comes on, he shall bathe himself in water, and when the sun is down, he may come within the camp.

12 "You shall have a place outside the camp and you shall go out to it; ¹³and you shall have a stick with your weapons; and when you relieve yourself outside, you shall dig a hole with it, and turn back and cover up your excrement. ¹⁴Because the LORD your God walks in the midst of your camp, to save you and to give up your enemies before you, therefore your camp must be holy, that he may not see anything indecent among you, and turn away from you.

15 "You shall not give up to his master a slave who has escaped from his master to you; ¹⁶he shall dwell with you, in your midst, in the place which he shall choose within one of your towns, where it pleases him best; you shall not oppress him.

17 "There shall be no cult prostitute of the daughters of Israel, neither shall there be a cult prostitute of the sons of Israel. ¹⁸You shall not bring the hire of a harlot, or the wages of a dog, ᵗ into the house of the LORD your God in payment for any vow; for both of these are an abomination to the LORD your God.

19 "You shall not lend upon interest to your brother, interest on money, interest on victuals, interest on anything that is lent for interest. ²⁰To a foreigner you may lend upon interest, but to your brother you shall not lend upon interest; that the LORD your God may bless you in all that you undertake in the land which you are entering to take possession of it.

21 "When you make a vow to the LORD your God, you shall not be slack to pay it; for the LORD your God will surely require it of you, and it would be sin in you. ²²But if you refrain from vowing, it shall be no sin in you. ²³You shall be careful to perform what has passed your lips, for you have voluntarily vowed to the LORD your God what you have promised with your mouth.

24 "When you go into your neighbor's vineyard, you may eat your fill of grapes, as many as you wish, but you shall not put any in your vessel. ²⁵When you go into your neighbor's standing grain, you may pluck the ears with your hand, but you shall not put a sickle to your neighbor's standing grain.

Laws concerning Marriage and Divorce

24 * "When a man takes a wife and marries her, if then she finds no favor in his eyes because he has found some indecency in her, and he writes her a bill of divorce and puts it in her hand and sends her out of his house, and she departs out of his house, ²and if she goes and becomes another man's wife, ³and the latter husband dislikes her and writes her a bill of divorce and puts it in her hand and sends her out of his house, or if the latter husband dies, who took her to be his wife, ⁴then her former husband, who sent her away, may not take her again to be his wife, after she has been defiled; for that is an abomination before the LORD, and you shall not bring guilt upon the land which the LORD your God gives you for an inheritance.

Various Laws

5 "When a man is newly married, he shall not go out with the army or be charged with any business; he shall be free at home one year, to be happy with his wife whom he has taken.

6 "No man shall take a mill or an upper millstone in pledge; for he would be taking a life in pledge.

7 "If a man is found stealing one of his brethren, the sons of Israel, and if he treats him as a slave or sells him, then that thief shall die; so you shall purge the evil from the midst of you.

ᵗ Or *male prostitute.*
23:19: Ex 22:26; Lev 25:35–37.
23:21-23: Num 30:2–16.
24:1: Mt 5:31; 19:7; Mk 10:4.
24:6, 10-13: Ex 22:26, 27.
24:7: Ex 21:16; 1 Cor 5:13.
24:1: Divorce was permitted in Old Testament times on account of "hardness of heart"; Jesus, however, insists that it was not in the original plan of God (Mt 19:7–9).

8 "Take heed, in an attack of leprosy, to be very careful to do according to all that the Levitical priests shall direct you; as I commanded them, so you shall be careful to do. [9]Remember what the LORD your God did to Miriam on the way as you came forth out of Egypt.

10 "When you make your neighbor a loan of any sort, you shall not go into his house to fetch his pledge. [11]You shall stand outside, and the man to whom you make the loan shall bring the pledge out to you. [12]And if he is a poor man, you shall not sleep in his pledge; [13]when the sun goes down, you shall restore to him the pledge that he may sleep in his cloak and bless you; and it shall be righteousness to you before the LORD your God.

14 "You shall not oppress a hired servant who is poor and needy, whether he is one of your brethren or one of the sojourners who are in your land within your towns; [15]you shall give him his hire on the day he earns it, before the sun goes down (for he is poor, and sets his heart upon it); lest he cry against you to the LORD, and it be sin in you.

16 "The fathers shall not be put to death for the children, nor shall the children be put to death for the fathers; every man shall be put to death for his own sin.

17 "You shall not pervert the justice due to the sojourner or to the fatherless, or take a widow's garment in pledge; [18]but you shall remember that you were a slave in Egypt and the LORD your God redeemed you from there; therefore I command you to do this.

19 "When you reap your harvest in your field, and have forgotten a sheaf in the field, you shall not go back to get it; it shall be for the sojourner, the fatherless, and the widow; that the LORD your God may bless you in all the work of your hands. [20]When you beat your olive trees, you shall not go over the boughs again; it shall be for the sojourner, the fatherless, and the widow. [21]When you gather the grapes of your vineyard, you shall not glean it afterward; it shall be for the sojourner, the fatherless, and the widow. [22]You shall remember that you were a slave in the land of Egypt; therefore I command you to do this.

25 "If there is a dispute between men, and they come into court, and the judges decide between them, acquitting the innocent and condemning the guilty, [2]then if the guilty man deserves to be beaten, the judge shall cause him to lie down and be beaten in his presence with a number of stripes in proportion to his offense. [3]Forty stripes may be given him, but not more; lest, if one should go on to beat him with more stripes than these, your brother be degraded in your sight.

4 "You shall not muzzle an ox when it treads out the grain.

Duty to a Brother's Widow

5 "If brothers dwell together, and one of them dies and has no son, the wife of the dead shall not be married outside the family to a stranger; her husband's brother shall go in to her, and take her as his wife, and perform the duty of a husband's brother to her. [6]And the first son whom she bears shall succeed to the name of his brother who is dead, that his name may not be blotted out of Israel. [7]And if the man does not wish to take his brother's wife, then his brother's wife shall go up to the gate to the elders, and say, 'My husband's brother refuses to perpetuate his brother's name in Israel; he will not perform the duty of a husband's brother to me.' [8]Then the elders of his city shall call him, and speak to him: and if he persists, saying, 'I do not wish to take her,' [9]then his brother's wife shall go up to him in the presence of the elders, and pull his sandal off his foot, and spit in his face; and she shall answer and say, 'So shall it be done to the man who does not build up his brother's house.' [10]And the name of his house [u] shall be called in Israel, The house of him that had his sandal pulled off.

Various Commands

11 "When men fight with one another, and the wife of the one draws near to rescue her husband from the hand of him who is beating him, and puts out her hand and seizes him by the private parts, [12]then you shall cut off her hand; your eye shall have no pity.

13 "You shall not have in your bag two kinds of weights, a large and a small. [14]You shall not have in your house two kinds of measures, a large and a small. [15]A full and just weight you shall have, a full and just measure you shall have; that your days may be prolonged in the land which the LORD your God gives you. [16]For all who do such things, all who act dishonestly, are an abomination to the LORD your God.

17 "Remember what Am'alek did to you on the way as you came out of Egypt, [18]how he attacked you on the way, when you were faint and weary, and cut off at your rear all who lagged behind you; and he did not fear God. [19]Therefore when the LORD your God has given you rest from all your enemies round about, in the land which the LORD your God gives you for an inheritance to possess, you shall blot out the remembrance of Am'alek from under heaven; you shall not forget.

---

u Heb *its name*.
24:8, 9: Lev 13–14.
24:14, 15: Lev 19:13; Jas 5:4.
24:17, 18: Ex 22:21–24; 23:9; Lev 19:33, 34.
24:19–22: Lev 19:9, 10; 23:22.
25:4: 1 Cor 9:9; 1 Tim 5:18.
25:5, 6: Mt 22:24; Mk 12:19; Lk 20:28.
25:13–16: Lev 19:35, 36.
25:17–19: Ex 17:14; 1 Sam 15.

First Fruits and Tithes

26 "When you come into the land which the LORD your God gives you for an inheritance, and have taken possession of it, and live in it, [2]you shall take some of the first of all the fruit of the ground, which you harvest from your land that the LORD your God gives you, and you shall put it in a basket, and you shall go to the place which the LORD your God will choose, to make his name to dwell there. [3]And you shall go to the priest who is in office at that time, and say to him, 'I declare this day to the LORD your God that I have come into the land which the LORD swore to our fathers to give us.' [4]Then the priest shall take the basket from your hand, and set it down before the altar of the LORD your God.

5 "And you shall make response before the LORD your God, 'A wandering Arame'an was my father; and he went down into Egypt and sojourned there, few in number; and there he became a nation, great, mighty, and populous. [6]And the Egyptians treated us harshly, and afflicted us, and laid upon us hard bondage. [7]Then we cried to the LORD the God of our fathers, and the LORD heard our voice, and saw our affliction, our toil, and our oppression; [8]and the LORD brought us out of Egypt with a mighty hand and an outstretched arm, with great terror, with signs and wonders; [9]and he brought us into this place and gave us this land, a land flowing with milk and honey. [10]And behold, now I bring the first of the fruit of the ground, which you, O LORD, have given me.' And you shall set it down before the LORD your God, and worship before the LORD your God; [11]and you shall rejoice in all the good which the LORD your God has given to you and to your house, you, and the Levite, and the sojourner who is among you.

12 "When you have finished paying all the tithe of your produce in the third year, which is the year of tithing, giving it to the Levite, the sojourner, the fatherless, and the widow, that they may eat within your towns and be filled, [13]then you shall say before the LORD your God, 'I have removed the sacred portion out of my house, and moreover I have given it to the Levite, the sojourner, the fatherless, and the widow, according to all your commandment which you have commanded me; I have not transgressed any of your commandments, neither have I forgotten them; [14]I have not eaten of the tithe while I was mourning, or removed any of it while I was unclean, or offered any of it to the dead; I have obeyed the voice of the LORD my God, I have done according to all that you have commanded me. [15]Look down from your holy habitation, from heaven, and bless your people Israel and the ground which you have given us, as you swore to our fathers, a land flowing with milk and honey.'

Concluding Exhortation

16 "This day the LORD your God commands you to do these statutes and ordinances; you shall therefore be careful to do them with all your heart and with all your soul. [17]You have declared this day concerning the LORD that he is your God, and that you will walk in his ways, and keep his statutes and his commandments and his ordinances, and will obey his voice; [18]and the LORD has declared this day concerning you that you are a people for his own possession, as he has promised you, and that you are to keep all his commandments, [19]that he will set you high above all nations that he has made, in praise and in fame and in honor, and that you shall be a people holy to the LORD your God, as he has spoken."

The Inscribed Stones and Altar on Mount Ebal

27 Now Moses and the elders of Israel commanded the people, saying, "Keep all the commandment which I command you this day. [2]And on the day you pass over the Jordan to the land which the LORD your God gives you, you shall set up large stones, and plaster them with plaster; [3]and you shall write upon them all the words of this law, when you pass over to enter the land which the LORD your God gives you, a land flowing with milk and honey, as the LORD, the God of your fathers, has promised you. [4]And when you have passed over the Jordan, you shall set up these stones, concerning which I command you this day, on Mount E'bal, and you shall plaster them with plaster. [5]And there you shall build an altar to the LORD your God, an altar of stones; you shall lift up no iron tool upon them. [6]You shall build an altar to the LORD your God of unhewn [v] stones; and you shall offer burnt offerings on it to the LORD your God; [7]and you shall sacrifice peace offerings, and shall eat there; and you shall rejoice before the LORD your God. [8]And you shall write upon the stones all the words of this law very plainly."

9 And Moses and the Levitical priests said to all Israel, "Keep silence and hear, O Israel: this day you have become the people of the LORD your God. [10]You shall therefore obey the voice of the LORD your God, keeping his commandments and his statutes, which I command you this day."

Twelve Curses at Mount Ebal

11 And Moses charged the people the same day, saying, [12]"When you have passed over the Jordan, these shall stand upon Mount Ger'izim to bless the people: Simeon, Levi, Judah, Is'sachar, Joseph, and Benjamin. [13]And these shall stand upon Mount E'bal for the curse: Reuben, Gad, Asher, Zeb'ulun, Dan, and Naph'tali. [14]And the

---

[v] Heb whole.
26:1–11: Ex 22:29; 23:19; 34:26; Num 18:12, 13.

Levites shall declare to all the men of Israel with a loud voice:

15 " 'Cursed be the man who makes a graven or molten image, an abomination to the Lord, a thing made by the hands of a craftsman, and sets it up in secret.' And all the people shall answer and say, 'Amen.'

16 " 'Cursed be he who dishonors his father or his mother.' And all the people shall say, 'Amen.'

17 " 'Cursed be he who removes his neighbor's landmark.' And all the people shall say, 'Amen.'

18 " 'Cursed be he who misleads a blind man on the road.' And all the people shall say, 'Amen.'

19 " 'Cursed be he who perverts the justice due to the sojourner, the fatherless, and the widow.' And all the people shall say, 'Amen.'

20 " 'Cursed be he who lies with his father's wife, because he has uncovered her who is his father's.' ʷ And all the people shall say, 'Amen.'

21 " 'Cursed be he who lies with any kind of beast.' And all the people shall say, 'Amen.'

22 " 'Cursed be he who lies with his sister, whether the daughter of his father or the daughter of his mother.' And all the people shall say, 'Amen.'

23 " 'Cursed be he who lies with his mother-in-law.' And all the people shall say, 'Amen.'

24 " 'Cursed be he who slays his neighbor in secret.' And all the people shall say, 'Amen.'

25 " 'Cursed be he who takes a bribe to slay an innocent person.' And all the people shall say, 'Amen.'

26 " 'Cursed be he who does not confirm the words of this law by doing them.' And all the people shall say, 'Amen.'

Blessing for Obedience

28 "And if you obey the voice of the Lord your God, being careful to do all his commandments which I command you this day, the Lord your God will set you high above all the nations of the earth. ²And all these blessings shall come upon you and overtake you, if you obey the voice of the Lord your God. ³Blessed shall you be in the city, and blessed shall you be in the field. ⁴Blessed shall be the fruit of your body, and the fruit of your ground, and the fruit of your beasts, the increase of your cattle, and the young of your flock. ⁵Blessed shall be your basket and your kneading-trough. ⁶Blessed shall you be when you come in, and blessed shall you be when you go out.

7 "The Lord will cause your enemies who rise against you to be defeated before you; they shall come out against you one way, and flee before you seven ways. ⁸The Lord will command the blessing upon you in your barns, and in all that you undertake; and he will bless you in the land which the Lord your God gives you. ⁹The Lord will establish you as a people holy to himself, as he has sworn to you, if you keep the commandments

of the Lord your God, and walk in his ways. ¹⁰And all the peoples of the earth shall see that you are called by the name of the Lord; and they shall be afraid of you. ¹¹And the Lord will make you abound in prosperity, in the fruit of your body, and in the fruit of your cattle, and in the fruit of your ground, within the land which the Lord swore to your fathers to give you. ¹²The Lord will open to you his good treasury the heavens, to give the rain of your land in its season and to bless all the work of your hands; and you shall lend to many nations, but you shall not borrow. ¹³And the Lord will make you the head, and not the tail; and you shall tend upward only, and not downward; if you obey the commandments of the Lord your God, which I command you this day, being careful to do them, ¹⁴and if you do not turn aside from any of the words which I command you this day, to the right hand or to the left, to go after other gods to serve them.

Warnings against Disobedience

15 "But if you will not obey the voice of the Lord your God or be careful to do all his commandments and his statutes which I command you this day, then all these curses shall come upon you and overtake you. ¹⁶Cursed shall you be in the city, and cursed shall you be in the field. ¹⁷Cursed shall be your basket and your kneading-trough. ¹⁸Cursed shall be the fruit of your body, and the fruit of your ground, the increase of your cattle, and the young of your flock. ¹⁹Cursed shall you be when you come in, and cursed shall you be when you go out.

20 "The Lord will send upon you curses, confusion, and frustration, in all that you undertake to do, until you are destroyed and perish quickly, on account of the evil of your doings, because you have forsaken me. ²¹The Lord will make the pestilence cling to you until he has consumed you off the land which you are entering to take possession of it. ²²The Lord will strike you with consumption, and with fever, inflammation, and fiery heat, and with drought, ˣ and with blasting, and with mildew; they shall pursue you until you perish. ²³And the heavens over your head shall be brass, and the earth under you shall be iron. ²⁴The Lord will make the rain of your land powder and dust; from heaven it shall come down upon you until you are destroyed.

ʷ Heb *uncovered his father's skirt*.
ˣ Another reading is *sword*.
27:15: Ex 20:4, 23; 34:17; Lev 19:4; 26:1; Deut 4:16, 23, 25; 5:8; 7:25.
27:16: Ex 20:12; 21:15, 17; Lev 20:9; Deut 5:16; 21:18–21.
27:18: Lev 19:14.
27:19: Ex 22:21–24; 23:9; Lev 19:33, 34; Deut 24:17, 18.
27:20: Lev 18:8; 20:11; Deut 22:30.
27:21: Ex 22:19; Lev 18:23; 20:15.
27:22: Lev 18:9; 20:17.
27:23: Lev 18:17; 20:14.
27:26: Gal 3:10.
28: Lev 26:3–45.

25 "The LORD will cause you to be defeated before your enemies; you shall go out one way against them, and flee seven ways before them; and you shall be a horror to all the kingdoms of the earth. ²⁶And your dead body shall be food for all birds of the air, and for the beasts of the earth; and there shall be no one to frighten them away. ²⁷The LORD will strike you with the boils of Egypt, and with the ulcers and the scurvy and the itch, of which you cannot be healed. ²⁸The LORD will strike you with madness and blindness and confusion of mind; ²⁹and you shall grope at noonday, as the blind grope in darkness, and you shall not prosper in your ways; and you shall be only oppressed and robbed continually, and there shall be no one to help you. ³⁰You shall betroth a wife, and another man shall lie with her; you shall build a house, and you shall not dwell in it; you shall plant a vineyard, and you shall not use the fruit of it. ³¹Your ox shall be slain before your eyes, and you shall not eat of it; your donkey shall be violently taken away before your face, and shall not be restored to you; your sheep shall be given to your enemies, and there shall be no one to help you. ³²Your sons and your daughters shall be given to another people, while your eyes look on and fail with longing for them all the day; and it shall not be in the power of your hand to prevent it. ³³A nation which you have not known shall eat up the fruit of your ground and of all your labors; and you shall be only oppressed and crushed continually; ³⁴so that you shall be driven mad by the sight which your eyes shall see. ³⁵The LORD will strike you on the knees and on the legs with grievous boils of which you cannot be healed, from the sole of your foot to the crown of your head.

36 "The LORD will bring you, and your king whom you set over you, to a nation that neither you nor your fathers have known; and there you shall serve other gods, of wood and stone. ³⁷And you shall become a horror, a proverb, and a byword, among all the peoples where the LORD will lead you away. ³⁸You shall carry much seed into the field, and shall gather little in; for the locust shall consume it. ³⁹You shall plant vineyards and dress them, but you shall neither drink of the wine nor gather the grapes; for the worm shall eat them. ⁴⁰You shall have olive trees throughout all your territory, but you shall not anoint yourself with the oil; for your olives shall drop off. ⁴¹You shall beget sons and daughters, but they shall not be yours; for they shall go into captivity. ⁴²All your trees and the fruit of your ground the locust shall possess. ⁴³The sojourner who is among you shall mount above you higher and higher; and you shall come down lower and lower. ⁴⁴He shall lend to you, and you shall not lend to him; he shall be the head, and you shall be the tail.

⁴⁵All these curses shall come upon you and pursue you and overtake you, till you are destroyed, because you did not obey the voice of the LORD your God, to keep his commandments and his statutes which he commanded you. ⁴⁶They shall be upon you as a sign and a wonder, and upon your descendants for ever.

47 "Because you did not serve the LORD your God with joyfulness and gladness of heart, by reason of the abundance of all things, ⁴⁸therefore you shall serve your enemies whom the LORD will send against you, in hunger and thirst, in nakedness, and in want of all things; and he will put a yoke of iron upon your neck, until he has destroyed you. ⁴⁹The LORD will bring a nation against you from afar, from the end of the earth, as swift as the eagle flies, a nation whose language you do not understand, ⁵⁰a nation of stern countenance, who shall not regard the person of the old or show favor to the young, ⁵¹and shall eat the offspring of your cattle and the fruit of your ground, until you are destroyed; who also shall not leave you grain, wine, or oil, the increase of your cattle or the young of your flock, until they have caused you to perish. ⁵²They shall besiege you in all your towns, until your high and fortified walls, in which you trusted, come down throughout all your land; and they shall besiege you in all your towns throughout all your land, which the LORD your God has given you. ⁵³And you shall eat the offspring of your own body, the flesh of your sons and daughters, whom the LORD your God has given you, in the siege and in the distress with which your enemies shall distress you. ⁵⁴The man who is the most tender and delicately bred among you will grudge food to his brother, to the wife of his bosom, and to the last of the children who remain to him; ⁵⁵so that he will not give to any of them any of the flesh of his children whom he is eating, because he has nothing left him, in the siege and in the distress with which your enemy shall distress you in all your towns. ⁵⁶The most tender and delicately bred woman among you, who would not venture to set the sole of her foot upon the ground because she is so delicate and tender, will grudge to the husband of her bosom, to her son and to her daughter, ⁵⁷her afterbirth that comes out from between her feet and her children whom she bears, because she will eat them secretly, for want of all things, in the siege and in the distress with which your enemy shall distress you in your towns.

58 "If you are not careful to do all the words of this law which are written in this book, that you may fear this glorious and awesome name, the LORD your God, ⁵⁹then the LORD will bring on

28:49: 1 Cor 14:21.

you and your offspring extraordinary afflictions, afflictions severe and lasting, and sicknesses grievous and lasting. [60]And he will bring upon you again all the diseases of Egypt, which you were afraid of; and they shall cling to you. [61]Every sickness also, and every affliction which is not recorded in the book of this law, the LORD will bring upon you, until you are destroyed. [62]Whereas you were as the stars of heaven for multitude, you shall be left few in number; because you did not obey the voice of the LORD your God. [63]And as the LORD took delight in doing you good and multiplying you, so the LORD will take delight in bringing ruin upon you and destroying you; and you shall be plucked off the land which you are entering to take possession of it. [64]And the LORD will scatter you among all peoples, from one end of the earth to the other; and there you shall serve other gods, of wood and stone, which neither you nor your fathers have known. [65]And among these nations you shall find no ease, and there shall be no rest for the sole of your foot; but the LORD will give you there a trembling heart, and failing eyes, and a languishing soul; [66]your life shall hang in doubt before you; night and day you shall be in dread, and have no assurance of your life. [67]In the morning you shall say, 'Would it were evening!' and at evening you shall say, 'Would it were morning!' because of the dread which your heart shall fear, and the sights which your eyes shall see. [68]And the LORD will bring you back in ships to Egypt, a journey which I promised that you should never make again; and there you shall offer yourselves for sale to your enemies as male and female slaves, but no man will buy you."

The Covenant Renewed in Moab

29 [y] These are the words of the covenant which the LORD commanded Moses to make with the sons of Israel in the land of Moab, besides the covenant which he had made with them at Horeb.

[2][z] And Moses summoned all Israel and said to them: "You have seen all that the LORD did before your eyes in the land of Egypt, to Pharaoh and to all his servants and to all his land, [3]the great trials which your eyes saw, the signs, and those great wonders; [4]but to this day the LORD has not given you a mind to understand, or eyes to see, or ears to hear. [5]I have led you forty years in the wilderness; your clothes have not worn out upon you, and your sandals have not worn off your feet; [6]you have not eaten bread, and you have not drunk wine or strong drink; that you may know that I am the LORD your God. [7]And when you came to this place, Si'hon the king of Heshbon and Og the king of Bashan came out against us to battle, but we defeated them; [8]we took their land, and gave it for an inheritance to the Reu-

benites, the Gadites, and the half-tribe of the Manas'sites. [9]Therefore be careful to do the words of this covenant, that you may prosper [a] in all that you do.

10 "You stand this day all of you before the LORD your God; the heads of your tribes, [b] your elders, and your officers, all the men of Israel, [11]your little ones, your wives, and the sojourner who is in your camp, both he who hews your wood and he who draws your water, [12]that you may enter into the sworn covenant of the LORD your God, which the LORD your God makes with you this day; [13]that he may establish you this day as his people, and that he may be your God, as he promised you, and as he swore to your fathers, to Abraham, to Isaac, and to Jacob. [14]Nor is it with you only that I make this sworn covenant, [15]but with him who is not here with us this day as well as with him who stands here with us this day before the LORD our God.

16 "You know how we dwelt in the land of Egypt, and how we came through the midst of the nations through which you passed; [17]and you have seen their detestable things, their idols of wood and stone, of silver and gold, which were among them. [18]Beware lest there be among you a man or woman or family or tribe, whose heart turns away this day from the LORD our God to go and serve the gods of those nations; lest there be among you a root bearing poisonous and bitter fruit, [19]one who, when he hears the words of this sworn covenant, blesses himself in his heart, saying, 'I shall be safe, though I walk in the stubbornness of my heart.' This would lead to the sweeping away of moist and dry alike. [20]The LORD would not pardon him, but rather the anger of the LORD and his jealousy would smoke against that man, and the curses written in this book would settle upon him, and the LORD would blot out his name from under heaven. [21]And the LORD would single him out from all the tribes of Israel for calamity, in accordance with all the curses of the covenant written in this book of the law. [22]And the generation to come, your children who rise up after you, and the foreigner who comes from a far land, would say, when they see the afflictions of that land and the sicknesses with which the LORD has made it sick—[23]the whole land brimstone and salt, and a burnt-out waste, unsown, and growing nothing, where no grass can sprout, an overthrow like that of Sodom and Gomor'rah, Admah and Zeboi'im, which the LORD overthrew in his anger and wrath—[24]yes, all the nations would say, 'Why

---

[y] Ch 28:69 in Heb.
[z] Ch 29:1 in Heb.
[a] Or *deal wisely.*
[b] Gk Syr: Heb *your heads, your tribes.*
29:4: Rom 11:8.
29:18: Acts 8:23; Heb 12:15.

has the LORD done thus to this land? What means the heat of this great anger?' [25]Then men would say, 'It is because they forsook the covenant of the LORD, the God of their fathers, which he made with them when he brought them out of the land of Egypt, [26]and went and served other gods and worshiped them, gods whom they had not known and whom he had not allotted to them; [27]therefore the anger of the LORD was kindled against this land, bringing upon it all the curses written in this book; [28]and the LORD uprooted them from their land in anger and fury and great wrath, and cast them into another land, as at this day.'

29 "The secret things belong to the LORD our God; but the things that are revealed belong to us and to our children for ever, that we may do all the words of this law.

God's Fidelity Assured

30 "And when all these things come upon you, the blessing and the curse, which I have set before you, and you call them to mind among all the nations where the LORD your God has driven you, [2]and return to the LORD your God, you and your children, and obey his voice in all that I command you this day, with all your heart and with all your soul; [3]then the LORD your God will restore your fortunes, and have compassion upon you, and he will gather you again from all the peoples where the LORD your God has scattered you. [4]If your outcasts are in the uttermost parts of heaven, from there the LORD your God will gather you, and from there he will fetch you; [5]and the LORD your God will bring you into the land which your fathers possessed, that you may possess it; and he will make you more prosperous and numerous than your fathers. [6]And the LORD your God will circumcise your heart and the heart of your offspring, so that you will love the LORD your God with all your heart and with all your soul, that you may live. [7]And the LORD your God will put all these curses upon your foes and enemies who persecuted you. [8]And you shall again obey the voice of the LORD, and keep all his commandments which I command you this day. [9]The LORD your God will make you abundantly prosperous in all the work of your hand, in the fruit of your body, and in the fruit of your cattle, and in the fruit of your ground; for the LORD will again take delight in prospering you, as he took delight in your fathers, [10]if you obey the voice of the LORD your God, to keep his commandments and his statutes which are written in this book of the law, if you turn to the LORD your God with all your heart and with all your soul.

Exhortation to Choose Life

11 "For this commandment which I command you this day is not too hard for you, neither is it far off. [12]It is not in heaven, that you should say,

'Who will go up for us to heaven, and bring it to us, that we may hear it and do it?' [13]Neither is it beyond the sea, that you should say, 'Who will go over the sea for us, and bring it to us, that we may hear it and do it?' [14]But the word is very near you; it is in your mouth and in your heart, so that you can do it.

15 "See, I have set before you this day life and good, death and evil. [16]If you obey the commandments of the LORD your God [c] which I command you this day, by loving the LORD your God, by walking in his ways, and by keeping his commandments and his statutes and his ordinances, then you shall live and multiply, and the LORD your God will bless you in the land which you are entering to take possession of it. [17]But if your heart turns away, and you will not hear, but are drawn away to worship other gods and serve them, [18]I declare to you this day, that you shall perish; you shall not live long in the land which you are going over the Jordan to enter and possess. [19]I call heaven and earth to witness against you this day, that I have set before you life and death, blessing and curse; therefore choose life, that you and your descendants may live, [20]loving the LORD your God, obeying his voice, and clinging to him; for that means life to you and length of days, that you may dwell in the land which the LORD swore to your fathers, to Abraham, to Isaac, and to Jacob, to give them."

Joshua Becomes Moses' Successor

31 So Moses continued to speak these words to all Israel. [2]And he said to them, "I am a hundred and twenty years old this day; I am no longer able to go out and come in. The LORD has said to me, 'You shall not go over this Jordan.' [3]The LORD your God himself will go over before you; he will destroy these nations before you, so that you shall dispossess them; and Joshua will go over at your head, as the LORD has spoken. [4]And the LORD will do to them as he did to Si'hon and Og, the kings of the Am'orites, and to their land, when he destroyed them. [5]And the LORD will give them over to you, and you shall do to them according to all the commandment which I have commanded you. [6]Be strong and of good courage, do not fear or be in dread of them: for it is the LORD your God who goes with you; he will not fail you or forsake you."

7 Then Moses summoned Joshua, and said to him in the sight of all Israel, "Be strong and of good courage; for you shall go with this people into the land which the LORD has sworn to their fathers to give them; and you shall put them in

---

[c] Gk: Heb lacks *If you obey the commandments of the* LORD *your God.*
30:4: Mt 24:31; Mk 13:27.
30:12, 13: Rom 10:6, 7.
30:14: Rom 10:8.
31:6, 8: Heb 13:5.

possession of it. [8]It is the LORD who goes before you; he will be with you, he will not fail you or forsake you; do not fear or be dismayed."

Rereading of the Law Commanded

9 And Moses wrote this law, and gave it to the priests the sons of Levi, who carried the ark of the covenant of the LORD, and to all the elders of Israel. [10]And Moses commanded them, "At the end of every seven years, at the set time of the year of release, at the feast of booths, [11]when all Israel comes to appear before the LORD your God at the place which he will choose, you shall read this law before all Israel in their hearing. [12]Assemble the people, men, women, and little ones, and the sojourner within your towns, that they may hear and learn to fear the LORD your God, and be careful to do all the words of this law, [13]and that their children, who have not known it, may hear and learn to fear the LORD your God, as long as you live in the land which you are going over the Jordan to possess."

Moses and Joshua Receive God's Charge

14 And the LORD said to Moses, "Behold, the days approach when you must die; call Joshua, and present yourselves in the tent of meeting, that I may commission him." And Moses and Joshua went and presented themselves in the tent of meeting. [15]And the LORD appeared in the tent in a pillar of cloud; and the pillar of cloud stood by the door of the tent.

16 And the LORD said to Moses, "Behold, you are about to sleep with your fathers; then this people will rise and play the harlot after the strange gods of the land, where they go to be among them, and they will forsake me and break my covenant which I have made with them. [17]Then my anger will be kindled against them in that day, and I will forsake them and hide my face from them, and they will be devoured; and many evils and troubles will come upon them, so that they will say in that day, 'Have not these evils come upon us because our God is not among us?' [18]And I will surely hide my face in that day on account of all the evil which they have done, because they have turned to other gods. [19]Now therefore write this song, and teach it to the sons of Israel; put it in their mouths, that this song may be a witness for me against the sons of Israel. [20]For when I have brought them into the land flowing with milk and honey, which I swore to give to their fathers, and they have eaten and are full and grown fat, they will turn to other gods and serve them, and despise me and break my covenant. [21]And when many evils and troubles have come upon them, this song shall confront them as a witness (for it will live unforgotten in the mouths of their descendants); for I know the purposes which they are already forming, before I have brought them into the land that I swore to give." [22]So Moses wrote this song the same day, and taught it to the sons of Israel.

23 And the LORD commissioned Joshua the son of Nun and said, "Be strong and of good courage; for you shall bring the children of Israel into the land which I swore to give them: I will be with you."

24 When Moses had finished writing the words of this law in a book, to the very end, [25]Moses commanded the Levites who carried the ark of the covenant of the LORD, [26]"Take this book of the law, and put it by the side of the ark of the covenant of the LORD your God, that it may be there for a witness against you. [27]For I know how rebellious and stubborn you are; behold, while I am yet alive with you, today you have been rebellious against the LORD; how much more after my death! [28]Assemble to me all the elders of your tribes, and your officers, that I may speak these words in their ears and call heaven and earth to witness against them. [29]For I know that after my death you will surely act corruptly, and turn aside from the way which I have commanded you; and in the days to come evil will befall you, because you will do what is evil in the sight of the LORD, provoking him to anger through the work of your hands."

The Song of Moses

30 Then Moses spoke the words of this song until they were finished, in the ears of all the assembly of Israel:

32 "Give ear, O heavens, and I will speak;
and let the earth hear the words of my
mouth.
[2]May my teaching drop as the rain,
my speech distil as the dew,
as the gentle rain upon the tender grass,
and as the showers upon the herb.
[3]For I will proclaim the name of the LORD.
Ascribe greatness to our God!

[4]"The Rock, his work is perfect;
for all his ways are justice.
A God of faithfulness and without iniquity,
just and right is he.
[5]They have dealt corruptly with him,
they are no longer his children because of
their blemish;
they are a perverse and crooked generation.
[6]Do you thus repay the LORD,
you foolish and senseless people?
Is not he your father, who created you,
who made you and established you?
[7]Remember the days of old,
consider the years of many generations;
ask your father, and he will show you;
your elders, and they will tell you.

32:5: Phil 2:15.

⁸When the Most High gave to the nations their
    inheritance,
    when he separated the sons of men,
he fixed the bounds of the peoples
    according to the number of the sons of
        Israel. ᵈ
⁹For the LORD's portion is his people,
    Jacob his allotted heritage.

¹⁰"He found him in a desert land,
    and in the howling waste of the
        wilderness;
he encircled him, he cared for him,
    he kept him as the apple of his eye.
¹¹Like an eagle that stirs up its nest,
    that flutters over its young,
spreading out its wings, catching them,
    bearing them on its pinions,
¹²the LORD alone did lead him,
    and there was no foreign god with him.
¹³He made him ride on the high places of the
        earth,
    and he ate the produce of the field;
and he made him suck honey out of the rock,
    and oil out of the flinty rock.
¹⁴Curds from the herd, and milk from the flock,
    with fat of lambs and rams,
    herds of Bashan and goats,
with the finest of the wheat—
    and of the blood of the grape you drank
        wine.

¹⁵"But Jesh'urun waxed fat, and kicked;
    you waxed fat, you grew thick, you became
        sleek;
then he forsook God who made him,
    and scoffed at the Rock of his salvation.
¹⁶They stirred him to jealousy with strange
        gods;
    with abominable practices they provoked
        him to anger.
¹⁷They sacrificed to demons which were no
        gods,
    to gods they had never known,
to new gods that had come in of late,
    whom your fathers had never dreaded.
¹⁸You were unmindful of the Rock that begot ᵉ
    you,
    and you forgot the God who gave you birth.

¹⁹"The LORD saw it, and spurned them,
    because of the provocation of his sons and
        his daughters.
²⁰And he said, 'I will hide my face from them,
    I will see what their end will be,
for they are a perverse generation,
    children in whom is no faithfulness.
²¹They have stirred me to jealousy with what is
    no god;

they have provoked me with their idols.
So I will stir them to jealousy with those who
    are no people;
    I will provoke them with a foolish nation.
²²For a fire is kindled by my anger,
    and it burns to the depths of Sheol,
devours the earth and its increase,
    and sets on fire the foundations of the
        mountains.

²³" 'And I will heap evils upon them;
    I will spend my arrows upon them;
²⁴they shall be wasted with hunger,
    and devoured with burning heat
    and poisonous pestilence;
and I will send the teeth of beasts against
    them,
    with venom of crawling things of the dust.
²⁵In the open the sword shall bereave,
    and in the chambers shall be terror,
destroying both young man and virgin,
    the sucking child with the man of gray
        hairs.
²⁶I would have said, "I will scatter them afar,
    I will make the remembrance of them cease
        from among men,"
²⁷had I not feared provocation by the enemy,
    lest their adversaries should judge amiss,
lest they should say, "Our hand is triumphant,
    the LORD has not wrought all this." '

²⁸"For they are a nation void of counsel,
    and there is no understanding in them.
²⁹If they were wise, they would understand this,
    they would discern their latter end!
³⁰How should one chase a thousand,
    and two put ten thousand to flight,
unless their Rock had sold them,
    and the LORD had given them up?
³¹For their rock is not as our Rock,
    even our enemies themselves being judges.
³²For their vine comes from the vine of Sodom,
    and from the fields of Gomor'rah;
their grapes are grapes of poison,
    their clusters are bitter;
³³their wine is the poison of serpents,
    and the cruel venom of asps.

³⁴"Is not this laid up in store with me,
    sealed up in my treasuries?
³⁵Vengeance is mine, and recompense,
    for the time when their foot shall slip;
for the day of their calamity is at hand,
    and their doom comes swiftly.

ᵈ Or *God.*
ᵉ Or *bore.*
32:17: 1 Cor 10:20.
32:21: Rom 10:19; 11:11; 1 Cor 10:22.
32:35: Rom 12:19; Heb 10:30.

[36] For the LORD will vindicate his people
 and have compassion on his servants,
when he sees that their power is gone,
 and there is none remaining, bond or free.
[37] Then he will say, 'Where are their gods,
 the rock in which they took refuge,
[38] who ate the fat of their sacrifices,
 and drank the wine of their drink
 offering?
Let them rise up and help you,
 let them be your protection!

[39] " 'See now that I, even I, am he,
 and there is no god beside me;
I kill and I make alive;
 I wound and I heal;
 and there is none that can deliver out of my
 hand.
[40] For I lift up my hand to heaven,
 and swear, As I live for ever,
[41] if I sharpen my glittering sword, [f]
 and my hand takes hold on judgment,
I will take vengeance on my adversaries,
 and will repay those who hate me.
[42] I will make my arrows drunk with blood,
 and my sword shall devour flesh—
with the blood of the slain and the captives,
 from the long-haired heads of the enemy.'

[43] "Praise his people, O you nations;
 for he avenges the blood of his servants,
and takes vengeance on his adversaries,
 and makes expiation for the land of his
 people." [g]

44 Moses came and recited all the words of this
song in the hearing of the people, he and Joshua [h]
the son of Nun. [45] And when Moses had finished
speaking all these words to all Israel, [46] he said to
them, "Lay to heart all the words which I enjoin
upon you this day, that you may command them
to your children, that they may be careful to do all
the words of this law. [47] For it is no trifle for you,
but it is your life, and thereby you shall live long
in the land which you are going over the Jordan to
possess."

Moses' Death Foretold

48 And the LORD said to Moses that very day,
[49] "Ascend this mountain of the Ab'arim, Mount
Nebo, which is in the land of Moab, opposite Jericho; and view the land of Canaan, which I give to
the sons of Israel for a possession; [50] and die on
the mountain which you ascend, and be gathered
to your people, as Aaron your brother died in
Mount Hor and was gathered to his people; [51] because you broke faith with me in the midst of the
sons of Israel at the waters of Mer'ibath-ka'desh,
in the wilderness of Zin; because you did not
revere me as holy in the midst of the sons of
Israel. [52] For you shall see the land before you; but

you shall not go there, into the land which I give
to the sons of Israel."

Moses' Final Blessing

33 This is the blessing with which Moses the
 man of God blessed the children of Israel
before his death. [2] He said,
"The LORD came from Sinai,
 and dawned from Se'ir upon us; [i]
 he shone forth from Mount Par'an,
he came from the ten thousands of holy ones,
 with flaming fire [j] at his right hand.
[3] Yes, he loved his people; [k]
 all those consecrated to him were in his [x]
 hand;
so they followed [j] in your steps,
 receiving direction from you,
[4] when Moses commanded us a law,
 as a possession for the assembly of Jacob.
[5] Thus the LORD became king in Jesh'urun,
 when the heads of the people were
 gathered,
 all the tribes of Israel together.

[6] "Let Reuben live, and not die,
 nor let his men be few."

[7] And this he said of Judah:
"Hear, O LORD, the voice of Judah,
 and bring him in to his people.
With your hands contend [l] for him,
 and be a help against his adversaries."

[8] And of Levi he said,
"Give to Levi [m] your Thummim,
 and your U'rim to your godly one,
 whom you tested at Massah,
 with whom you strove at the waters of
 Mer'ibah;
[9] who said of his father and mother,
 'I regard them not';
he disowned his brothers,
 and ignored his children.
For they observed your word,
 and kept your covenant.
[10] They shall teach Jacob your ordinances,
 and Israel your law;
they shall put incense before you,
 and whole burnt offering upon your altar.
[11] Bless, O LORD, his substance,
 and accept the work of his hands;

---

[f] Heb *the lightning of my sword.*
[g] Gk Vg: Heb *his land his people.*
[h] Gk Syr Vg: Heb *Hoshea.*
[i] Gk Syr Vg: Heb *them.*
[j] The meaning of the Hebrew word is uncertain.
[k] Gk: Heb *peoples.*
[x] Heb *your.*
[l] Cn: Heb *with his hands he contended.*
[m] Gk: Heb lacks *Give to Levi.*
32:43: Rom 15:10; Heb 1:6 (Septuagint); Rev 6:10; 19:2.

crush the loins of his adversaries,
of those that hate him, that they rise not
again."

¹²Of Benjamin he said,
"The beloved of the Lord,
he dwells in safety by him;
he encompasses him all the day long,
and makes his dwelling between his
shoulders."

¹³And of Joseph he said,
"Blessed by the Lord be his land,
with the choicest gifts of heaven above,ⁿ
and of the deep that lies beneath,
¹⁴with the choicest fruits of the sun,
and the rich yield of the months,
¹⁵with the finest produce of the ancient
mountains,
and the abundance of the everlasting
hills,
¹⁶with the best gifts of the earth and its fulness,
and the favor of him that dwelt in the
bush.
Let these come upon the head of Joseph,
and upon the crown of the head of him that
is prince among his brothers.
¹⁷His firstling bull has majesty,
and his horns are the horns of a wild ox;
with them he shall push the peoples,
all of them, to the ends of the earth;
such are the ten thousands of E'phraim,
and such are the thousands of Manas'seh."

¹⁸And of Zeb'ulun he said,
"Rejoice, Zebulun, in your going out;
and Is'sachar, in your tents.
¹⁹They shall call peoples to their mountain;
there they offer right sacrifices;
for they suck the affluence of the seas
and the hidden treasures of the sand."

²⁰And of Gad he said,
"Blessed be he who enlarges Gad!
Gad lurks like a lion,
he tears the arm, and the crown of the
head.
²¹He chose the best of the land for himself,
for there a commander's portion was
reserved;
and he came to the heads of the people,
with Israel he executed the commands
and just decrees of the Lord."

²²And of Dan he said,
"Dan is a lion's whelp,
that leaps forth from Bashan."

²³And of Naph'tali he said,

"O Naphtali, satisfied with favor,
and full of the blessing of the Lord,
possess the lake and the south."

²⁴And of Asher he said,
"Blessed above sons be Asher;
let him be the favorite of his brothers,
and let him dip his foot in oil.
²⁵Your bars shall be iron and bronze;
and as your days, so shall your strength be.

²⁶"There is none like God, O Jesh'urun,
who rides through the heavens to your help,
and in his majesty through the skies.
²⁷The eternal God is your dwelling place,
and underneath are the everlasting arms.
And he thrust out the enemy before you,
and said, Destroy.
²⁸So Israel dwelt in safety,
the fountain of Jacob alone,
in a land of grain and wine;
yes, his heavens drop down dew.
²⁹Happy are you, O Israel! Who is like you,
a people saved by the Lord,
the shield of your help,
and the sword of your triumph!
Your enemies shall come fawning to you;
and you shall tread upon their high places."

The Death of Moses

34 And Moses went up from the plains of
Moab to Mount Nebo, to the top of Pisgah, which is opposite Jericho. And the Lord
showed him all the land, Gilead as far as Dan,
²all Naph'tali, the land of E'phraim and Manas'-
seh, all the land of Judah as far as the western
sea, ³the Neg'eb, and the Plain, that is, the valley
of Jericho the city of palm trees, as far as Zoar.
⁴And the Lord said to him, "This is the land of
which I swore to Abraham, to Isaac, and to
Jacob, 'I will give it to your descendants.' I have
let you see it with your eyes, but you shall not go
over there." ⁵So Moses the servant of the Lord
died there in the land of Moab, according to the
word of the Lord, ⁶and he buried him in the valley in the land of Moab opposite Beth-pe'or; but
no man knows the place of his burial to this day.
⁷Moses was a hundred and twenty years old
when he died; his eye was not dim, nor his natural force abated. ⁸And the sons of Israel wept for
Moses in the plains of Moab thirty days; then
the days of weeping and mourning for Moses
were ended.

9 And Joshua the son of Nun was full of the
spirit of wisdom, for Moses had laid his hands
upon him; so the sons of Israel obeyed him, and
did as the Lord had commanded Moses. ¹⁰And

ⁿ Two Heb Mss and Tg: Heb *with the dew.*
34:10: Num 12:6–8.

there has not arisen a prophet since in Israel like Moses, whom the LORD knew face to face, [11]none like him for all the signs and the wonders which the LORD sent him to do in the land of Egypt, to Pharaoh and to all his servants and to all his land, [12]and for all the mighty power and all the great and terrible deeds which Moses wrought in the sight of all Israel.

THE BOOK OF

JOSHUA

God Commissions Joshua

1 After the death of Moses the servant of the LORD, the LORD said to Joshua the son of Nun, Moses' minister, [2] "Moses my servant is dead; now therefore arise, go over this Jordan, you and all this people, into the land which I am giving to them, to the sons of Israel. [3] Every place that the sole of your foot will tread upon I have given to you, as I promised to Moses. [4] From the wilderness and this Lebanon as far as the great river, the river Euphrates, all the land of the Hittites to the Great Sea toward the going down of the sun shall be your territory. [5] No man shall be able to stand before you all the days of your life; as I was with Moses, so I will be with you; I will not fail you or forsake you. [6] Be strong and of good courage; for you shall cause this people to inherit the land which I swore to their fathers to give them. [7] Only be strong and very courageous, being careful to do according to all the law which Moses my servant commanded you; turn not from it to the right hand or to the left, that you may have good success wherever you go. [8] This book of the law shall not depart out of your mouth, but you shall meditate on it day and night, that you may be careful to do according to all that is written in it; for then you shall make your way prosperous, and then you shall have good success. [9] Have I not commanded you? Be strong and of good courage; be not frightened, neither be dismayed; for the LORD your God is with you wherever you go."

Preparations for Taking Over the Land

10 Then Joshua commanded the officers of the people, [11] "Pass through the camp, and command the people, 'Prepare your provisions; for within three days you are to pass over this Jordan, to go in to take possession of the land which the LORD your God gives you to possess.'"

12 And to the Reubenites, the Gadites, and the half-tribe of Manas'seh Joshua said, [13] "Remember the word which Moses the servant of the LORD commanded you, saying, 'The LORD your God is providing you a place of rest, and will give you this land.' [14] Your wives, your little ones, and your cattle shall remain in the land which Moses gave you beyond the Jordan; but all the men of valor among you shall pass over armed before your brethren and shall help them, [15] until the LORD gives rest to your brethren as well as to you, and

they also take possession of the land which the LORD your God is giving them; then you shall return to the land of your possession, and shall possess it, the land which Moses the servant of the LORD gave you beyond the Jordan toward the sunrise." [16] And they answered Joshua, "All that you have commanded us we will do, and wherever you send us we will go. [17] Just as we obeyed Moses in all things, so we will obey you; only may the LORD your God be with you, as he was with Moses! [18] Whoever rebels against your commandment and disobeys your words, whatever you command him, shall be put to death. Only be strong and of good courage."

Spies Sent to Jericho

2 And Joshua the son of Nun sent two men secretly from Shittim as spies, saying, "Go, view the land, especially Jericho." And they went, and came into the house of a harlot whose name was Ra'hab, and lodged there. [2] And it was told the king of Jericho, "Behold, certain men of Israel have come here tonight to search out the land." [3] Then the king of Jericho sent to Ra'hab, saying, "Bring forth the men that have come to you, who entered your house; for they have come to search out all the land." [4] But the woman had taken the two men and hidden them; and she said, "True, men came to me, but I did not know where they came from; [5] and when the gate was to be closed, at dark, the men went out; where the men went I do not know; pursue them quickly, for you will overtake them." [6] But she had brought them up to the roof, and hid them with the stalks of flax which she had laid in order on the roof. [7] So the men pursued after them on the way to the Jordan as far as the fords; and as soon as the pursuers had gone out, the gate was shut.

8 Before they lay down, she came up to them on the roof, [9] and said to the men, "I know that the LORD has given you the land, and that the fear of you has fallen upon us, and that all the inhabitants of the land melt away before you. [10] For we

---

This book continues the narrative from the death of Moses (Deut 34), through the conquest of Canaan, down to the great covenant-renewal at Shechem. The account of the conquest is stylized and summarized: thus, not all the tribes entered the land together as here described, the operation was not so free of difficulties and even failures as we might assume after a reading of this book, and the occupation of the whole country could not have been carried out by Joshua in person. Judges 1 gives a somewhat different and complementary version.
1:5: Heb 13:5.
1:12-18: Josh 22:1-34; Num 32:20-22.

159

have heard how the LORD dried up the water of the Red Sea before you when you came out of Egypt, and what you did to the two kings of the Am′orites that were beyond the Jordan, to Si′hon and Og, whom you utterly destroyed. [11]And as soon as we heard it, our hearts melted, and there was no courage left in any man, because of you; for the LORD your God is he who is God in heaven above and on earth beneath. [12]Now then, swear to me by the LORD that as I have dealt kindly with you, you also will deal kindly with my father's house, and give me a sure sign, [13]and save alive my father and mother, my brothers and sisters, and all who belong to them, and deliver our lives from death." [14]And the men said to her, "Our life for yours! If you do not tell this business of ours, then we will deal kindly and faithfully with you when the LORD gives us the land."

15 Then she let them down by a rope through the window, for her house was built into the city wall, so that she dwelt in the wall. [16]And she said to them, "Go into the hills, lest the pursuers meet you; and hide yourselves there three days, until the pursuers have returned; then afterward you may go your way." [17]The men said to her, "We will be guiltless with respect to this oath of yours which you have made us swear. [18]Behold, when we come into the land, you shall bind this scarlet cord in the window through which you let us down; and you shall gather into your house your father and mother, your brothers, and all your father's household. [19]If any one goes out of the doors of your house into the street, his blood shall be upon his head, and we shall be guiltless; but if a hand is laid upon any one who is with you in the house, his blood shall be on our head. [20]But if you tell this business of ours, then we shall be guiltless with respect to your oath which you have made us swear." [21]And she said, "According to your words, so be it." Then she sent them away, and they departed; and she bound the scarlet cord in the window.

22 They departed, and went into the hills, and remained there three days, until the pursuers returned; for the pursuers had made search all along the way and found nothing. [23]Then the two men came down again from the hills, and passed over and came to Joshua the son of Nun; and they told him all that had befallen them. [24]And they said to Joshua, "Truly the LORD has given all the land into our hands; and moreover all the inhabitants of the land are fainthearted because of us."

Israel Passes over the Jordan

3 Early in the morning Joshua rose and set out from Shittim, with all the sons of Israel; and they came to the Jordan, and lodged there before they passed over. [2]At the end of three days the officers went through the camp [3]and commanded the people, "When you see the ark of the cov-

enant of the LORD your God being carried by the Levitical priests, then you shall set out from your place and follow it, [4]that you may know the way you shall go, for you have not passed this way before. Yet there shall be a space between you and it, a distance of about two thousand cubits; do not come near it." [5]And Joshua said to the people, "Sanctify yourselves; for tomorrow the LORD will do wonders among you." [6]And Joshua said to the priests, "Take up the ark of the covenant, and pass on before the people." And they took up the ark of the covenant, and went before the people.

7 And the LORD said to Joshua, "This day I will begin to exalt you in the sight of all Israel, that they may know that, as I was with Moses, so I will be with you. [8]And you shall command the priests who bear the ark of the covenant, 'When you come to the brink of the waters of the Jordan, you shall stand still in the Jordan.'" [9]And Joshua said to the sons of Israel, "Come here, and hear the words of the LORD your God." [10]And Joshua said, "Hereby you shall know that the living God is among you, and that he will without fail drive out from before you the Canaanites, the Hittites, the Hi′vites, the Per′izzites, the Gir′gashites, the Am′orites, and the Jeb′usites. [11]Behold, the ark of the covenant of the Lord of all the earth is to pass over before you into the Jordan. [12]Now therefore take twelve men from the tribes of Israel, from each tribe a man. [13]And when the soles of the feet of the priests who bear the ark of the LORD, the Lord of all the earth, shall rest in the waters of the Jordan, the waters of the Jordan shall be stopped from flowing, and the waters coming down from above shall stand in one heap."

14 So, when the people set out from their tents, to pass over the Jordan with the priests bearing the ark of the covenant before the people, [15]and when those who bore the ark had come to the Jordan, and the feet of the priests bearing the ark were dipped in the brink of the water (the Jordan overflows all its banks throughout the time of harvest), [16]the waters coming down from above stood and rose up in a heap far off, at Adam, the city that is beside Zar′ethan, and those flowing down toward the sea of the Ar′abah, the Salt Sea, were wholly cut off; and the people passed over opposite Jericho. [17]And while all Israel were passing over on dry ground, the priests who bore the ark of the covenant of the LORD stood on dry ground in the midst of the Jordan, until all the nation finished passing over the Jordan. *

Twelve Stones Set Up at Gilgal

4 When all the nation had finished passing over the Jordan, the LORD said to Joshua, [2] "Take twelve men from the people, from each tribe a

* 3:7-17: The crossing of the Jordan is described in such a way as to bring out the theological parallelism with the crossing of the Red Sea (or, Sea of Reeds); both are seen as due to the direct intervention of God.

man, [3]and command them, 'Take twelve stones from here out of the midst of the Jordan, from the very place where the priests' feet stood, and carry them over with you, and lay them down in the place where you lodge tonight.'" [4]Then Joshua called the twelve men from the sons of Israel, whom he had appointed, a man from each tribe; [5]and Joshua said to them, "Pass on before the ark of the LORD your God into the midst of the Jordan, and take up each of you a stone upon his shoulder, according to the number of the tribes of the sons of Israel, [6]that this may be a sign among you, when your children ask in time to come, 'What do those stones mean to you?' [7]Then you shall tell them that the waters of the Jordan were cut off before the ark of the covenant of the LORD; when it passed over the Jordan, the waters of the Jordan were cut off. So these stones shall be to the sons of Israel a memorial for ever."

8 And the men of Israel did as Joshua commanded, and took up twelve stones out of the midst of the Jordan, according to the number of the tribes of the sons of Israel, as the LORD told Joshua; and they carried them over with them to the place where they lodged, and laid them down there. [9]And Joshua set up twelve stones in the midst of the Jordan, in the place where the feet of the priests bearing the ark of the covenant had stood; and they are there to this day. [10]For the priests who bore the ark stood in the midst of the Jordan, until everything was finished that the LORD commanded Joshua to tell the people, according to all that Moses had commanded Joshua.

The people passed over in haste; [11]and when all the people had finished passing over, the ark of the LORD and the priests passed over before the people. [12]The sons of Reuben and the sons of Gad and the half-tribe of Manas'seh passed over armed before the sons of Israel, as Moses had bidden them; [13]about forty thousand ready armed for war passed over before the LORD for battle, to the plains of Jericho. [14]On that day the LORD exalted Joshua in the sight of all Israel; and they stood in awe of him, as they had stood in awe of Moses, all the days of his life.

15 And the LORD said to Joshua, [16]"Command the priests who bear the ark of the covenant to come up out of the Jordan." [17]Joshua therefore commanded the priests, "Come up out of the Jordan." [18]And when the priests bearing the ark of the covenant of the LORD came up from the midst of the Jordan, and the soles of the priests' feet were lifted up on dry ground, the waters of the Jordan returned to their place and overflowed all its banks, as before.

19 The people came up out of the Jordan on the tenth day of the first month, and they encamped in Gilgal on the east border of Jericho. [20]And those twelve stones, which they took out of the Jordan, Joshua set up in Gilgal. [21]And he said to the sons of Israel, "When your children ask their fathers in time to come, 'What do these stones mean?' [22]then you shall let your children know, 'Israel passed over this Jordan on dry ground.' [23]For the LORD your God dried up the waters of the Jordan for you until you passed over, as the LORD your God did to the Red Sea, which he dried up for us until we passed over, [24]so that all the peoples of the earth may know that the hand of the LORD is mighty; that you may fear the LORD your God for ever."

The Sons of Israel Are Circumcised

5 When all the kings of the Am'orites that were beyond the Jordan to the west, and all the kings of the Canaanites that were by the sea, heard that the LORD had dried up the waters of the Jordan for the sons of Israel until they had crossed over, their heart melted, and there was no longer any spirit in them, because of the sons of Israel.

2 At that time the LORD said to Joshua, "Make flint knives and circumcise the sons of Israel again the second time." [3]So Joshua made flint knives, and circumcised the sons of Israel at Gib'eath-haar'aloth. [a] [4]And this is the reason why Joshua circumcised them: all the males of the people who came out of Egypt, all the men of war, had died on the way in the wilderness after they had come out of Egypt. [5]Though all the people who came out had been circumcised, yet all the people that were born on the way in the wilderness after they had come out of Egypt had not been circumcised. [6]For the sons of Israel walked forty years in the wilderness, till all the nation, the men of war that came forth out of Egypt, perished, because they did not listen to the voice of the LORD; to them the LORD swore that he would not let them see the land which the LORD had sworn to their fathers to give us, a land flowing with milk and honey. [7]So it was their children, whom he raised up in their stead, that Joshua circumcised; for they were uncircumcised, because they had not been circumcised on the way.

8 When the circumcising of all the nation was done, they remained in their places in the camp till they were healed. [9]And the LORD said to Joshua, "This day I have rolled away the reproach of Egypt from you." And so the name of that place is called Gilgal [b] to this day.

The Passover at Gilgal

10 While the sons of Israel were encamped in Gilgal they kept the Passover on the fourteenth day of the month at evening in the plains of Jericho. [11]And on the next day after the Passover,

---

[a] That is the hill of the foreskins.
[b] From Heb galal to roll.

on that very day, they ate of the produce of the land, unleavened cakes and parched grain. [12]And the manna ceased on the next day, when they ate of the produce of the land; and the sons of Israel had manna no more, but ate of the fruit of the land of Canaan that year.

Joshua's Vision

13 When Joshua was by Jericho, he lifted up his eyes and looked, and behold, a man stood before him with his drawn sword in his hand; and Joshua went to him and said to him, "Are you for us, or for our adversaries?" [14]And he said, "No; but as commander of the army of the LORD I have now come." And Joshua fell on his face to the earth, and worshiped, and said to him, "What does my lord bid his servant?" [15]And the commander of the LORD's army said to Joshua, "Put off your shoes from your feet; for the place where you stand is holy." And Joshua did so.

Jericho Taken and Destroyed

6 * Now Jericho was shut up from within and from without because of the sons of Israel; none went out, and none came in. [2]And the LORD said to Joshua, "See, I have given into your hand Jericho, with its king and mighty men of valor. [3]You shall march around the city, all the men of war going around the city once. Thus shall you do for six days. [4]And seven priests shall bear seven trumpets of rams' horns before the ark; and on the seventh day you shall march around the city seven times, the priests blowing the trumpets. [5]And when they make a long blast with the ram's horn, as soon as you hear the sound of the trumpet, then all the people shall shout with a great shout; and the wall of the city will fall down flat, and the people shall go up every man straight before him." [6]So Joshua the son of Nun called the priests and said to them, "Take up the ark of the covenant, and let seven priests bear seven trumpets of rams' horns before the ark of the LORD." [7]And he said to the people, "Go forward; march around the city, and let the armed men pass on before the ark of the LORD."

8 And as Joshua had commanded the people, the seven priests bearing the seven trumpets of rams' horns before the LORD went forward, blowing the trumpets, with the ark of the covenant of the LORD following them. [9]And the armed men went before the priests who blew the trumpets, and the rear guard came after the ark, while the trumpets blew continually. [10]But Joshua commanded the people, "You shall not shout or let your voice be heard, neither shall any word go out of your mouth, until the day I bid you shout; then you shall shout." [11]So he caused the ark of the LORD to compass the city, going about it once; and they came into the camp, and spent the night in the camp.

12 Then Joshua rose early in the morning, and the priests took up the ark of the LORD. [13]And the seven priests bearing the seven trumpets of rams' horns before the ark of the LORD passed on, blowing the trumpets continually; and the armed men went before them, and the rear guard came after the ark of the LORD, while the trumpets blew continually. [14]And the second day they marched around the city once, and returned into the camp. So they did for six days.

15 On the seventh day they rose early at the dawn of day, and marched around the city in the same manner seven times: it was only on that day that they marched around the city seven times. [16]And at the seventh time, when the priests had blown the trumpets, Joshua said to the people, "Shout; for the LORD has given you the city. [17]And the city and all that is within it shall be devoted to the LORD for destruction; † only Ra′hab the harlot and all who are with her in her house shall live, because she hid the messengers that we sent. [18]But you, keep yourselves from the things devoted to destruction, lest when you have devoted them you take any of the devoted things and make the camp of Israel a thing for destruction, and bring trouble upon it. [19]But all silver and gold, and vessels of bronze and iron, are sacred to the LORD; they shall go into the treasury of the LORD." [20]So the people shouted, and the trumpets were blown. As soon as the people heard the sound of the trumpet, the people raised a great shout, and the wall fell down flat, so that the people went up into the city, every man straight before him, and they took the city. [21]Then they utterly destroyed all in the city, both men and women, young and old, oxen, sheep, and donkeys, with the edge of the sword.

22 And Joshua said to the two men who had spied out the land, "Go into the harlot's house, and bring out from it the woman, and all who belong to her, as you swore to her." [23]So the young men who had been spies went in, and brought out Ra′hab, and her father and mother and brothers and all who belonged to her; and they brought all her kindred, and set them outside the camp of Israel. [24]And they burned the city with fire, and all within it; only the silver and gold, and the vessels of bronze and of iron, they put into the treasury of the house of the LORD. [25]But Ra′hab the harlot, and her father's household, and all who belonged to her, Joshua saved alive; and she dwelt in Israel to this day, because she hid the messengers whom Joshua sent to spy out Jericho.

---

* 6:1: Here, as elsewhere, the history has been worked over in accordance with certain theological ideas.

† 6:17: Following the indications elsewhere in the Old Testament, it would appear that the ban, that is, the physical destruction of the enemy in obedience to the Deity, was practiced much less than a reading of Joshua might suggest. Despite the high religious principles that motivated it, it must be seen in the light of the imperfect stage of moral development reached at that time.

26 Joshua laid an oath upon them at that time, saying, "Cursed before the Lord be the man that rises up and rebuilds this city, Jericho.

At the cost of his first-born shall he lay its foundation,

and at the cost of his youngest son shall he set up its gates."

27 So the Lord was with Joshua; and his fame was in all the land.

The Sin of Achan and Its Punishment

7 But the sons of Israel broke faith in regard to the devoted things; for A'chan the son of Carmi, son of Zabdi, son of Ze'rah, of the tribe of Judah, took some of the devoted things; and the anger of the Lord burned against the sons of Israel.

2 Joshua sent men from Jericho to Ai, which is near Beth-a'ven, east of Bethel, and said to them, "Go up and spy out the land." And the men went up and spied out Ai. ³And they returned to Joshua, and said to him, "Let not all the people go up, but let about two or three thousand men go up and attack Ai; do not make the whole people toil up there, for they are but few." ⁴So about three thousand went up there from the people; and they fled before the men of Ai, ⁵and the men of Ai killed about thirty-six men of them, and chased them before the gate as far as Sheb'arim, and slew them at the descent. And the hearts of the people melted, and became as water.

6 Then Joshua tore his clothes, and fell to the earth upon his face before the ark of the Lord until the evening, he and the elders of Israel; and they put dust upon their heads. ⁷And Joshua said, "Alas, O Lord God, why have you brought this people over the Jordan at all, to give us into the hands of the Am'orites, to destroy us? Would that we had been content to dwell beyond the Jordan! ⁸O Lord, what can I say, when Israel has turned their backs before their enemies! ⁹For the Canaanites and all the inhabitants of the land will hear of it, and will surround us, and cut off our name from the earth; and what will you do for your great name?"

10 The Lord said to Joshua, "Arise, why have you thus fallen upon your face? ¹¹Israel has sinned; they have transgressed my covenant which I commanded them; they have taken some of the devoted things; they have stolen, and lied, and put them among their own stuff. ¹²Therefore the sons of Israel cannot stand before their enemies; they turn their backs before their enemies, because they have become a thing for destruction. I will be with you no more, unless you destroy the devoted things from among you. ¹³Up, sanctify the people, and say, 'Sanctify yourselves for tomorrow; for thus says the Lord, God of Israel, "There are devoted things in the midst of you, O Israel; you cannot stand before your

enemies, until you take away the devoted things from among you." ¹⁴In the morning therefore you shall be brought near by your tribes; and the tribe which the Lord takes shall come near by families; and the family which the Lord takes shall come near by households; and the household which the Lord takes shall come near man by man. ¹⁵And he who is taken with the devoted things shall be burned with fire, he and all that he has, because he has transgressed the covenant of the Lord, and because he has done a shameful thing in Israel.' "

16 So Joshua rose early in the morning, and brought Israel near tribe by tribe, and the tribe of Judah was taken; ¹⁷and he brought near the families of Judah, and the family of the Ze'rahites was taken; and he brought near the family of the Zerahites man by man, and Zabdi was taken; ¹⁸and he brought near his household man by man, and A'chan the son of Carmi, son of Zabdi, son of Ze'rah of the tribe of Judah, was taken. ¹⁹Then Joshua said to A'chan, "My son, give glory to the Lord God of Israel, and render praise to him; and tell me now what you have done; do not hide it from me." ²⁰And A'chan answered Joshua, "Of a truth I have sinned against the Lord God of Israel, and this is what I did: ²¹when I saw among the spoil a beautiful mantle from Shi'nar, and two hundred shekels of silver, and a bar of gold weighing fifty shekels, then I coveted them, and took them; and behold, they are hidden in the earth inside my tent, with the silver underneath."

22 So Joshua sent messengers, and they ran to the tent; and behold, it was hidden in his tent with the silver underneath. ²³And they took them out of the tent and brought them to Joshua and all the sons of Israel; and they laid them down before the Lord. ²⁴And Joshua and all Israel with him took A'chan the son of Ze'rah, and the silver and the mantle and the bar of gold, and his sons and daughters, and his oxen and donkeys and sheep, and his tent, and all that he had; and they brought them up to the Valley of A'chor. ²⁵And Joshua said, "Why did you bring trouble on us? The Lord brings trouble on you today." And all Israel stoned him with stones; they burned them with fire, and stoned them with stones. ²⁶And they raised over him a great heap of stones that remains to this day; then the Lord turned from his burning anger. Therefore to this day the name of that place is called the Valley of A'chor. ᶜ

Capture and Destruction of Ai

8 And the Lord said to Joshua, "Do not fear or be dismayed; take all the fighting men with you, and arise, go up to Ai; see, I have given into your hand the king of Ai, and his people, his city,

ᶜ That is *Trouble*.
6:26: 1 Kings 16:34.

and his land; [2]and you shall do to Ai and its king as you did to Jericho and its king; only its spoil and its cattle you shall take as booty for yourselves; lay an ambush against the city, behind it."

3 So Joshua arose, and all the fighting men, to go up to Ai; and Joshua chose thirty thousand mighty men of valor, and sent them forth by night. [4]And he commanded them, "Behold, you shall lie in ambush against the city, behind it; do not go very far from the city, but hold yourselves all in readiness; [5]and I, and all the people who are with me, will approach the city. And when they come out against us, as before, we shall flee before them; [6]and they will come out after us, till we have drawn them away from the city; for they will say, 'They are fleeing from us, as before.' So we will flee from them; [7]then you shall rise up from the ambush, and seize the city; for the LORD your God will give it into your hand. [8]And when you have taken the city, you shall set the city on fire, doing as the LORD has bidden; see, I have commanded you." [9]So Joshua sent them forth; and they went to the place of ambush, and lay between Bethel and Ai, to the west of Ai; but Joshua spent that night among the people.

10 And Joshua arose early in the morning and mustered the people, and went up, with the elders of Israel, before the people to Ai. [11]And all the fighting men who were with him went up, and drew near before the city, and encamped on the north side of Ai, with a ravine between them and Ai. [12]And he took about five thousand men, and set them in ambush between Bethel and Ai, to the west of the city. [13]So they stationed the forces, the main encampment which was north of the city and its rear guard west of the city. But Joshua spent that night in the valley. [14]And when the king of Ai saw this he and all his people, the men of the city, made haste and went out early to the descent [d] toward the Arabah to meet Israel in battle; but he did not know that there was an ambush against him behind the city. [15]And Joshua and all Israel made a pretense of being beaten before them, and fled in the direction of the wilderness. [16]So all the people who were in the city were called together to pursue them, and as they pursued Joshua they were drawn away from the city. [17]There was not a man left in Ai or Bethel, who did not go out after Israel; they left the city open, and pursued Israel.

18 Then the LORD said to Joshua, "Stretch out the javelin that is in your hand toward Ai; for I will give it into your hand." And Joshua stretched out the javelin that was in his hand toward the city. [19]And the ambush rose quickly out of their place, and as soon as he had stretched out his hand, they ran and entered the city and took it; and they made haste to set the city on fire. [20]So when the men of Ai looked back, behold, the smoke of the city went up to heaven; and they had no power to flee this way or that, for the people that fled to the wilderness turned back upon the pursuers. [21]And when Joshua and all Israel saw that the ambush had taken the city, and that the smoke of the city went up, then they turned back and struck the men of Ai. [22]And the others came forth from the city against them; so they were in the midst of Israel, some on this side, and some on that side; and Israel struck them, until there was left none that survived or escaped. [23]But the king of Ai they took alive, and brought him to Joshua.

24 When Israel had finished slaughtering all the inhabitants of Ai in the open wilderness where they pursued them, and all of them to the very last had fallen by the edge of the sword, all Israel returned to Ai, and struck it with the edge of the sword. [25]And all who fell that day, both men and women, were twelve thousand, all the people of Ai. [26]For Joshua did not draw back his hand, with which he stretched out the javelin, until he had utterly destroyed all the inhabitants of Ai. [27]Only the cattle and the spoil of that city Israel took as their booty, according to the word of the LORD which he commanded Joshua. [28]So Joshua burned Ai, and made it for ever a heap of ruins, as it is to this day. [29]And he hanged the king of Ai on a tree until evening; and at the going down of the sun Joshua commanded, and they took his body down from the tree, and cast it at the entrance of the gate of the city, and raised over it a great heap of stones, which stands there to this day.

Joshua Sacrifices and Reads the Law at Mount Ebal

30 Then Joshua built an altar on Mount E′bal to the LORD, the God of Israel, [31]as Moses the servant of the LORD had commanded the sons of Israel, as it is written in the book of the law of Moses, "an altar of unhewn stones, upon which no man has lifted an iron tool"; and they offered on it burnt offerings to the LORD, and sacrificed peace offerings. [32]And there, in the presence of the sons of Israel, he wrote upon the stones a copy of the law of Moses, which he had written. [33]And all Israel, sojourner as well as homeborn, with their elders and officers and their judges, stood on opposite sides of the ark before the Levitical priests who carried the ark of the covenant of the LORD, half of them in front of Mount Ger′izim and half of them in front of Mount E′bal, as Moses the servant of the LORD had commanded at the first, that they should bless the sons of Israel. [34]And afterward he read all the words of the law, the blessing and the curse, according to

---

[d] Cn: Heb appointed time.
8:30-35: Deut 27:2-8.

all that is written in the book of the law. ³⁵There was not a word of all that Moses commanded which Joshua did not read before all the assembly of Israel, and the women, and the little ones, and the sojourners who lived among them.

The Gibeonites' Stratagem

9 When all the kings who were beyond the Jordan in the hill country and in the lowland all along the coast of the Great Sea toward Lebanon, the Hittites, the Am'orites, the Canaanites, the Per'izzites, the Hi'vites, and the Jeb'usites, heard of this, ²they gathered together with one accord to fight Joshua and Israel.

3 But when the inhabitants of Gib'eon heard what Joshua had done to Jericho and to Ai, ⁴they on their part acted with cunning, and went and made ready provisions, and took worn-out sacks upon their donkeys, and wineskins, worn-out and torn and mended, ⁵with worn-out, patched sandals on their feet, and worn-out clothes; and all their provisions were dry and moldy. ⁶And they went to Joshua in the camp at Gilgal, and said to him and to the men of Israel, "We have come from a far country; so now make a covenant with us." ⁷But the men of Israel said to the Hi'vites, "Perhaps you live among us; then how can we make a covenant with you?" ⁸They said to Joshua, "We are your servants." And Joshua said to them, "Who are you? And where do you come from?" ⁹They said to him, "From a very far country your servants have come, because of the name of the Lord your God; for we have heard a report of him, and all that he did in Egypt, ¹⁰and all that he did to the two kings of the Am'orites who were beyond the Jordan, Si'hon the king of Heshbon, and Og king of Bashan, who dwelt in Ash'taroth. ¹¹And our elders and all the inhabitants of our country said to us, 'Take provisions in your hand for the journey, and go to meet them, and say to them, "We are your servants; come now, make a covenant with us." ' ¹²Here is our bread; it was still warm when we took it from our houses as our food for the journey, on the day we set forth to come to you, but now, behold, it is dry and moldy; ¹³these wineskins were new when we filled them, and behold, they are burst; and these garments and shoes of ours are worn out from the very long journey." ¹⁴So the men partook of their provisions, and did not ask direction from the Lord. ¹⁵And Joshua made peace with them, and made a covenant with them, to let them live; and the leaders of the congregation swore to them.

16 At the end of three days after they had made a covenant with them, they heard that they were their neighbors, and that they dwelt among them. ¹⁷And the sons of Israel set out and reached their cities on the third day. Now their cities were Gib'eon, Chephi'rah, Be-er'oth, and Kir'iath-je'arim. ¹⁸But the sons of Israel did not kill them, because the leaders of the congregation had sworn to them by the Lord, the God of Israel. Then all the congregation murmured against the leaders. ¹⁹But all the leaders said to all the congregation, "We have sworn to them by the Lord, the God of Israel, and now we may not touch them. ²⁰This we will do to them, and let them live, lest wrath be upon us, because of the oath which we swore to them." ²¹And the leaders said to them, "Let them live." So they became hewers of wood and drawers of water for all the congregation, as the leaders had said of them.

22 Joshua summoned them, and he said to them, "Why did you deceive us, saying, 'We are very far from you,' when you dwell among us? ²³Now therefore you are cursed, and some of you shall always be slaves, hewers of wood and drawers of water for the house of my God." ²⁴They answered Joshua, "Because it was told to your servants for a certainty that the Lord your God had commanded his servant Moses to give you all the land, and to destroy all the inhabitants of the land from before you; so we feared greatly for our lives because of you, and did this thing. ²⁵And now, behold, we are in your hand: do as it seems good and right in your sight to do to us." ²⁶So he did to them, and delivered them out of the hand of the sons of Israel; and they did not kill them. ²⁷But Joshua made them that day hewers of wood and drawers of water for the congregation and for the altar of the Lord, to continue to this day, in the place which he should choose.

The Sun Stands Still

10 When Ado'ni-ze'dek king of Jerusalem heard how Joshua had taken Ai, and had utterly destroyed it, doing to Ai and its king as he had done to Jericho and its king, and how the inhabitants of Gib'eon had made peace with Israel and were among them, ²he * feared greatly, because Gib'eon was a great city, like one of the royal cities, and because it was greater than Ai, and all its men were mighty. ³So Ado'ni-ze'dek king of Jerusalem sent to Hoham king of He'bron, to Piram king of Jarmuth, to Japhi'a king of La'chish, and to De'bir king of Eg'lon, saying, ⁴"Come up to me, and help me, and let us strike Gib'eon; for it has made peace with Joshua and with the sons of Israel." ⁵Then the five kings of the Am'orites, the king of Jerusalem, the king of He'bron, the king of Jarmuth, the king of La'chish, and the king of Eg'lon, gathered their forces, and went up with all their armies and encamped against Gib'eon, and made war against it.

6 And the men of Gib'eon sent to Joshua at the camp in Gilgal, saying, "Do not relax your hand

---

* Heb *they.*

from your servants; come up to us quickly, and save us, and help us; for all the kings of the Am'orites that dwell in the hill country are gathered against us." [7]So Joshua went up from Gilgal, he and all the people of war with him, and all the mighty men of valor. [8]And the LORD said to Joshua, "Do not fear them, for I have given them into your hands; there shall not a man of them stand before you." [9]So Joshua came upon them suddenly, having marched up all night from Gilgal. [10]And the LORD threw them into a panic before Israel, who slew them with a great slaughter at Gib'eon, and chased them by the way of the ascent of Beth-ho'ron, and struck them as far as Aze'kah and Makke'dah. [11]And as they fled before Israel, while they were going down the ascent of Beth-ho'ron, the LORD threw down great stones from heaven upon them as far as Aze'kah, and they died; there were more who died because of the hailstones than the men of Israel killed with the sword.

[12] Then spoke Joshua to the LORD in the day when the LORD gave the Am'orites over to the men of Israel; and he said in the sight of Israel,

"Sun, stand still at Gib'eon,

and you Moon in the valley of Ai'jalon."

[13]And the sun stood still, and the moon stayed,

until the nation took vengeance on their

enemies.

Is this not written in the Book of Jash'ar? The sun stayed in the midst of heaven, and did not hasten to go down for about a whole day. [14]There has been no day like it before or since, when the LORD listened to the voice of a man; for the LORD fought for Israel. *

[15] Then Joshua returned, and all Israel with him, to the camp at Gilgal.

Five Kings Defeated

[16] These five kings fled, and hid themselves in the cave at Makke'dah. [17]And it was told Joshua, "The five kings have been found, hidden in the cave at Makke'dah." [18]And Joshua said, "Roll great stones against the mouth of the cave, and set men by it to guard them; [19]but do not stay there yourselves, pursue your enemies, fall upon their rear, do not let them enter their cities; for the LORD your God has given them into your hand." [20]When Joshua and the men of Israel had finished slaying them with a very great slaughter, until they were wiped out, and when the remnant which remained of them had entered into the fortified cities, [21]all the people returned safe to Joshua in the camp at Makke'dah; not a man moved his tongue against any of the sons of Israel.

[22] Then Joshua said, "Open the mouth of the cave, and bring those five kings out to me from the cave." [23]And they did so, and brought those five kings out to him from the cave, the king of Jerusalem, the king of He'bron, the king of Jarmuth, the king of La'chish, and the king of Eg'lon. [24]And when they brought those kings out to Joshua, Joshua summoned all the men of Israel, and said to the chiefs of the men of war who had gone with him, "Come near, put your feet upon the necks of these kings." Then they came near, and put their feet on their necks. [25]And Joshua said to them, "Do not be afraid or dismayed; be strong and of good courage; for thus the LORD will do to all your enemies against whom you fight." [26]And afterward Joshua struck them and put them to death, and he hung them on five trees. And they hung upon the trees until evening; [27]but at the time of the going down of the sun, Joshua commanded, and they took them down from the trees, and threw them into the cave where they had hidden themselves, and they set great stones against the mouth of the cave, which remain to this very day.

[28] And Joshua took Makke'dah on that day, and struck it and its king with the edge of the sword; he utterly destroyed every person in it, he left none remaining; and he did to the king of Makkedah as he had done to the king of Jericho.

[29] Then Joshua passed on from Makke'dah, and all Israel with him, to Libnah, and fought against Libnah; [30]and the LORD gave it also and its king into the hand of Israel; and he struck it with the edge of the sword, and every person in it; he left none remaining in it; and he did to its king as he had done to the king of Jericho.

[31] And Joshua passed on from Libnah, and all Israel with him, to La'chish, and laid siege to it, and assaulted it: [32]and the LORD gave La'chish into the hand of Israel, and he took it on the second day, and struck it with the edge of the sword, and every person in it, as he had done to Libnah.

[33] Then Horam king of Gezer came up to help La'chish; and Joshua struck him and his people, until he left none remaining.

[34] And Joshua passed on with all Israel from La'chish to Eg'lon; and they laid siege to it, and assaulted it; [35]and they took it on that day, and struck it with the edge of the sword; and every person in it he utterly destroyed that day, as he had done to La'chish.

[36] Then Joshua went up with all Israel from Eg'lon to He'bron; and they assaulted it, [37]and took it, and struck it with the edge of the sword, and its king and its towns, and every person in it; he left none remaining, as he had done to Eg'lon, and utterly destroyed it with every person in it.

[38] Then Joshua, with all Israel, turned back to

---

* 10:12–14: Joshua's apostrophe to the sun occurs in a fragment quoted from an old collection of epic material, and the quotation goes on beyond verse 12. This would make a literal interpretation of this event undesirable. It appears from the narrative that a great storm occurred at the same time as the attack and powerfully helped toward the Israelite victory (verse 11). It is this sign of divine aid that is so graphically apostrophized in the following poetic fragment (verses 12–13).

De'bir and assaulted it, ³⁹and he took it with its king and all its towns; and they struck them with the edge of the sword, and utterly destroyed every person in it; he left none remaining; as he had done to Heb'ron and to Libnah and its king, so he did to De'bir and to its king.

40 So Joshua defeated the whole land, the hill country and the Neg'eb and the lowland and the slopes, and all their kings; he left none remaining, but utterly destroyed all that breathed, as the LORD God of Israel commanded. ⁴¹And Joshua defeated them from Ka'desh-bar'nea to Gaza, and all the country of Go'shen, as far as Gib'eon. ⁴²And Joshua took all these kings and their land at one time, because the LORD God of Israel fought for Israel. ⁴³Then Joshua returned, and all Israel with him, to the camp at Gilgal.

The United Kings of Northern Canaan Defeated

11 When Jabin king of Ha'zor heard of this, he sent to Jo'bab king of Madon, and to the king of Shimron, and to the king of Ach'shaph, ²and to the kings who were in the northern hill country, and in the Ar'abah south of Chin'neroth, and in the lowland, and in Na'photh-dor on the west, ³to the Canaanites in the east and the west, the Am'orites, the Hittites, the Per'izzites, and the Jeb'usites in the hill country, and the Hi'vites under Hermon in the land of Mizpah. ⁴And they came out, with all their troops, a great host, in number like the sand that is upon the seashore, with very many horses and chariots. ⁵And all these kings joined their forces, and came and encamped together at the waters of Me'rom, to fight with Israel.

6 And the LORD said to Joshua, "Do not be afraid of them, for tomorrow at this time I will give over all of them, slain, to Israel; you shall hamstring their horses, and burn their chariots with fire." ⁷So Joshua came suddenly upon them with all his people of war, by the waters of Me'rom, and fell upon them. ⁸And the LORD gave them into the hand of Israel, who struck them and chased them as far as Great Sidon and Mis'rephoth-ma'im, and eastward as far as the valley of Mizpeh; and they struck them, until they left none remaining. ⁹And Joshua did to them as the LORD bade him; he hamstrung their horses, and burned their chariots with fire.

10 And Joshua turned back at that time, and took Ha'zor, and struck its king with the sword; for Hazor formerly was the head of all those kingdoms. ¹¹And they put to the sword all who were in it, utterly destroying them; there was none left that breathed, and he burned Ha'zor with fire. ¹²And all the cities of those kings, and all their kings, Joshua took, and struck them with the edge of the sword, utterly destroying them, as Moses the servant of the LORD had commanded. ¹³But none of the cities that stood on mounds did Israel burn, except Ha'zor only; that Joshua burned. ¹⁴And all the spoil of these cities and the cattle, the sons of Israel took for their booty; but every man they struck with the edge of the sword, until they had destroyed them, and they did not leave any that breathed. ¹⁵As the LORD had commanded Moses his servant, so Moses commanded Joshua, and so Joshua did; he left nothing undone of all that the LORD had commanded Moses.

Summary of Joshua's Conquests

16 So Joshua took all that land, the hill country and all the Neg'eb and all the land of Go'shen and the lowland and the Ar'abah and the hill country of Israel and its lowland ¹⁷from Mount Ha'lak, that rises toward Se'ir, as far as Ba'al-gad in the valley of Lebanon below Mount Hermon. And he took all their kings, and struck them, and put them to death. ¹⁸Joshua made war a long time with all those kings. ¹⁹There was not a city that made peace with the sons of Israel, except the Hi'vites, the inhabitants of Gib'eon; they took all in battle. ²⁰For it was the LORD's doing to harden their hearts that they should come against Israel in battle, in order that they should be utterly destroyed, and should receive no mercy but be exterminated, as the LORD commanded Moses.

21 And Joshua came at that time, and wiped out the An'akim from the hill country, from Heb'ron, from De'bir, from A'nab, and from all the hill country of Judah, and from all the hill country of Israel; Joshua utterly destroyed them with their cities. ²²There was none of the An'akim left in the land of the sons of Israel; only in Gaza, in Gath, and in Ashdod, did some remain. ²³So Joshua took the whole land, according to all that the LORD had spoken to Moses; and Joshua gave it for an inheritance to Israel according to their tribal allotments. And the land had rest from war.

The Kings Conquered by Moses

12 Now these are the kings of the land, whom the sons of Israel defeated, and took possession of their land beyond the Jordan toward the sunrising, from the valley of the Arnon to Mount Hermon, with all the Ar'abah eastward: ²Si'hon king of the Am'orites who dwelt at Heshbon, and ruled from Aro'er, which is on the edge of the valley of the Arnon, and from the middle of the valley as far as the river Jabbok, the boundary of the Am'monites, that is, half of Gilead, ³and the Ar'abah to the Sea of Chin'neroth eastward, and in the direction of Bethjesh'imoth, to the sea of the Arabah, the Salt Sea, southward to the foot of the slopes of Pisgah; ⁴and Og [•] king of Bashan, one of the remnant of the Reph'aim, who dwelt at Ash'taroth and at Ed're-i ⁵and ruled over Mount Hermon and

[•] Gk: Heb the boundary of Og.

Sal'ecah and all Bashan to the boundary of the Gesh'urites and the Ma-ac'athites, and over half of Gilead to the boundary of Si'hon king of Heshbon. [6]Moses, the servant of the LORD, and the sons of Israel defeated them; and Moses the servant of the LORD gave their land for a possession to the Reubenites and the Gadites and the half-tribe of Manas'seh.

The Kings Conquered by Joshua

7 And these are the kings of the land whom Joshua and the sons of Israel defeated on the west side of the Jordan, from Ba'al-gad in the valley of Lebanon to Mount Ha'lak, that rises toward Se'ir (and Joshua gave their land to the tribes of Israel as a possession according to their allotments, [8]in the hill country, in the lowland, in the Ar'abah, in the slopes, in the wilderness, and in the Neg'eb, the land of the Hittites, the Am'orites, the Canaanites, the Per'izzites, the Hi'vites, and the Jeb'usites): [9]the king of Jericho, one; the king of Ai, which is beside Bethel, one; [10]the king of Jerusalem, one; the king of He'bron, one; [11]the king of Jarmuth, one; the king of La'chish, one; [12]the king of Eg'lon, one; the king of Gezer, one; [13]the king of De'bir, one; the king of Geder, one; [14]the king of Hormah, one; the king of Ar'ad, one; [15]the king of Libnah, one; the king of Adul'lam, one; [16]the king of Makke'dah, one; the king of Bethel, one; [17]the king of Tap'pu-ah, one; the king of He'pher, one; [18]the king of A'phek, one; the king of Lashar'on, one; [19]the king of Madon, one; the king of Ha'zor, one; [20]the king of Shim'ronme'ron, one; the king of Ach'shaph, one; [21]the king of Ta'anach, one; the king of Megid'do, one; [22]the king of Ke'desh, one; the king of Jok'ne-am in Carmel, one; [23]the king of Dor in Na'phath-dor, one; the king of Goi'im in Galilee, [f] one; [24]the king of Tirzah, one: in all, thirty-one kings.

Still Unconquered Parts of Canaan

13 * Now Joshua was old and advanced in years; and the LORD said to him, "You are old and advanced in years, and there remains yet very much land to be possessed. [2]This is the land that yet remains: all the regions of the Philis'tines, and all those of the Gesh'urites [3](from the Shi'hor, which is east of Egypt, northward to the boundary of Ek'ron, it is reckoned as Canaanite; there are five rulers of the Philis'tines, those of Gaza, Ash'dod, Ash'kelon, Gath, and Ek'ron), and those of the Avvim, [4]in the south, all the land of the Canaanites, and Me-ar'ah which belongs to the Sido'nians, to A'phek, to the boundary of the Am'orites, [5]and the land of the Geb'alites, and all Lebanon, toward the sunrising, from Ba'al-gad below Mount Hermon to the entrance of Ha'math, [6]all the inhabitants of the hill country from Lebanon to Mis'rephoth-ma'im, even all the Sido'nians. I will myself drive them out from before the sons of

Israel; only allot the land to Israel for an inheritance, as I have commanded you. [7]Now therefore divide this land for an inheritance to the nine tribes and half the tribe of Manas'seh."

8 With the other half of the tribe of Manas'seh [g] the Reubenites and the Gadites received their inheritance, which Moses gave them, beyond the Jordan eastward, as Moses the servant of the LORD gave them: [9]from Aro'er, which is on the edge of the valley of the Arnon, and the city that is in the middle of the valley, and all the tableland of Med'eba as far as Di'bon; [10]and all the cities of Si'hon king of the Am'orites, who reigned in Heshbon, as far as the boundary of the Am'monites; [11]and Gilead, and the region of the Gesh'urites and Ma-ac'athites, and all Mount Hermon, and all Bashan to Sal'ecah; [12]all the kingdom of Og in Bashan, who reigned in Ash'taroth and in Ed're-i (he alone was left of the remnant of the Reph'aim); these Moses had defeated and driven out. [13]Yet the sons of Israel did not drive out the Gesh'urites or the Ma-ac'athites; but Ge'shur and Ma'acath dwell in the midst of Israel to this day.

14 To the tribe of Levi alone Moses gave no inheritance; the offerings by fire to the LORD God of Israel are their inheritance, as he said to him.

The Territory of Reuben

15 And Moses gave an inheritance to the tribe of the Reubenites according to their families. [16]So their territory was from Aro'er, which is on the edge of the valley of the Arnon, and the city that is in the middle of the valley, and all the tableland by Med'eba; [17]with Heshbon, and all its cities that are in the tableland; Di'bon, and Ba'moth-ba'al, and Beth-ba'al-me'on, [18]and Ja'haz, and Ked'emoth, and Meph'a-ath, [19]and Kir"iatha'im, and Sibmah, and Ze'reth-sha'har on the hill of the valley, [20]and Beth-pe'or, and the slopes of Pisgah, and Beth-jesh'imoth, [21]that is, all the cities of the tableland, and all the kingdom of Si'hon king of the Am'orites, who reigned in Heshbon, whom Moses defeated with the leaders of Mid'ian, E'vi and Re'kem and Zur and Hur and Reba, the princes of Si'hon, who dwelt in the land. [22]Balaam also, the son of Beor, the soothsayer, the sons of Israel killed with the sword among the rest of their slain. [23]And the border of the people of Reuben was the Jordan as a boundary. This was the inheritance of the Reubenites, according to their families with their cities and villages.

The Territory of Gad

24 And Moses gave an inheritance also to the tribe of the Gadites, according to their families.

---

[f] Gk: Heb Gilgal.
[g] Cn: Heb With it.
* 13-21: This section consists of topographical indications: the possessions and boundaries of the tribes and other ethnic groups, and a list of the cities of refuge.

25Their territory was Ja'zer, and all the cities of Gilead, and half the land of the Am'monites, to Aro'er, which is east of Rabbah, 26and from Heshbon to Ra'math-miz'peh and Bet'onim, and from Ma"hana'im to the territory of De'bir, h 27and in the valley Beth-ha'ram, Beth-nim'rah, Succoth, and Za'phon, the rest of the kingdom of Si'hon king of Heshbon, having the Jordan as a boundary, to the lower end of the Sea of Chin'nereth, eastward beyond the Jordan. 28This is the inheritance of the Gadites according to their families, with their cities and villages.

The Territory of the Half-tribe
of Manasseh (East)

29 And Moses gave an inheritance to the half-tribe of Manas'seh; it was allotted to the half-tribe of the Manas'sites according to their families. 30Their region extended from Ma"hana'im, through all Bashan, the whole kingdom of Og king of Bashan, and all the towns of Ja'ir, which are in Bashan, sixty cities, 31and half Gilead, and Ash'taroth, and Ed're-i, the cities of the kingdom of Og in Bashan; these were allotted to the people of Ma'chir the son of Manas'seh for the half of the Ma'chirites according to their families.

32 These are the inheritances which Moses distributed in the plains of Moab, beyond the Jordan east of Jericho. 33But to the tribe of Levi Moses gave no inheritance; the LORD God of Israel is their inheritance, as he said to them.

The Distribution of Territory
West of the Jordan

14 And these are the inheritances which the sons of Israel received in the land of Canaan, which Elea'zar the priest, and Joshua the son of Nun, and the heads of the fathers' houses of the tribes of the sons of Israel distributed to them. 2Their inheritance was by lot, as the LORD had commanded Moses for the nine and one-half tribes. 3For Moses had given an inheritance to the two and one-half tribes beyond the Jordan; but to the Levites he gave no inheritance among them. 4For the people of Joseph were two tribes, Manas'seh and E'phraim; and no portion was given to the Levites in the land, but only cities to dwell in, with their pasture lands for their cattle and their substance. 5The sons of Israel did as the LORD commanded Moses; they allotted the land.

Hebron Allotted to Caleb

6 Then the people of Judah came to Joshua at Gilgal; and Caleb the son of Jephun'neh the Ken'izzite said to him, "You know what the LORD said to Moses the man of God in Ka'desh-bar'nea concerning you and me. 7I was forty years old when Moses the servant of the LORD sent me from Ka'desh-bar'nea to spy out the land; and I brought him word again as it was in my heart. 8But my brethren who went up with me made the heart of the people melt; yet I wholly followed the LORD my God. 9And Moses swore on that day, saying, 'Surely the land on which your foot has trodden shall be an inheritance for you and your children for ever, because you have wholly followed the LORD my God.' 10And now, behold, the LORD has kept me alive, as he said, these forty-five years since the time that the LORD spoke this word to Moses, while Israel walked in the wilderness; and now, behold, I am this day eighty-five years old. 11I am still as strong to this day as I was in the day that Moses sent me; my strength now is as my strength was then, for war, and for going and coming. 12So now give me this hill country of which the LORD spoke on that day; for you heard on that day how the An'akim were there, with great fortified cities: it may be that the LORD will be with me, and I shall drive them out as the LORD said."

13 Then Joshua blessed him; and he gave He'bron to Caleb the son of Jephun'neh for an inheritance. 14So He'bron became the inheritance of Caleb the son of Jephun'neh the Ken'izzite to this day, because he wholly followed the LORD, the God of Israel. 15Now the name of He'bron formerly was Kir'iath-ar'ba; i this Arba was the greatest man among the An'akim. And the land had rest from war.

The Territory of Judah

15 The lot for the tribe of the people of Judah according to their families reached southward to the boundary of E'dom, to the wilderness of Zin at the farthest south. 2And their south boundary ran from the end of the Salt Sea, from the bay that faces southward; 3it goes out southward of the ascent of Akrab'bim, passes along to Zin, and goes up south of Ka'desh-bar'nea, along by Hezron, up to Addar, turns about to Karka, 4passes along to Azmon, goes out by the Brook of Egypt, and comes to its end at the sea. This shall be your south boundary. 5And the east boundary is the Salt Sea, to the mouth of the Jordan. And the boundary on the north side runs from the bay of the sea at the mouth of the Jordan; 6and the boundary goes up to Beth-hog'lah, and passes along north of Beth-ar'abah; and the boundary goes up to the stone of Bohan the son of Reuben; 7and the boundary goes up to De'bir from the Valley of A'chor, and so northward, turning toward Gilgal, which is opposite the ascent of Adum'mim, which is on the south side of the valley; and the boundary passes along to the waters of En-she'mesh, and ends at En-ro'gel; 8then the boundary goes up by the valley of the son of Hinnom at the southern shoulder of the Jeb'usite (that is, Jerusalem); and the

---

h Gk Syr Vg: Heb Lidebir.
i That is The city of Arba.
14:6–15: Num 13:6, 30; 14:6, 24, 30.

boundary goes up to the top of the mountain that lies over against the valley of Hinnom, on the west, at the northern end of the valley of Reph'aim; ⁹then the boundary extends from the top of the mountain to the spring of the Waters of Nephto'ah, and from there to the cities of Mount E'phron; then the boundary bends round to Ba'alah (that is, Kir'iath-je'arim); ¹⁰and the boundary circles west of Ba'alah to Mount Se'ir, passes along to the northern shoulder of Mount Je'arim (that is, Ches'alon), and goes down to Beth-she'mesh, and passes along by Timnah; ¹¹the boundary goes out to the shoulder of the hill north of Ek'ron, then the boundary bends round to Shik'keron, and passes along to Mount Ba'alah, and goes out to Jab'neel; then the boundary comes to an end at the sea. ¹²And the west boundary was the Great Sea with its coast-line. This is the boundary round about the people of Judah according to their families.

Caleb Occupies His Portion

13 According to the commandment of the Lord to Joshua, he gave to Caleb the son of Jephun'neh a portion among the people of Judah, Kir'iath-ar'ba, that is, He'bron (Arba was the father of A'nak). ¹⁴And Caleb drove out from there the three sons of A'nak, She'shai and Ahi'man and Talmai, the descendants of Anak. ¹⁵And he went up from there against the inhabitants of De'bir; now the name of Debir formerly was Kir'iath-se'pher. ¹⁶And Caleb said, "Whoever strikes Kir'iath-se'pher, and takes it, to him will I give Ach'sah my daughter as wife." ¹⁷And Oth'ni-el the son of Ke'naz, the brother of Caleb, took it; and he gave him Ach'sah his daughter as wife. ¹⁸When she came to him, she urged him to ask her father for a field; and she alighted from her donkey, and Caleb said to her, "What do you wish?" ¹⁹She said to him, "Give me a present; since you have set me in the land of the Neg'eb, give me also springs of water." And Caleb gave her the upper springs and the lower springs.

The Towns of Judah

20 This is the inheritance of the tribe of the people of Judah according to their families. ²¹The cities belonging to the tribe of the people of Judah in the extreme South, toward the boundary of E'dom, were Kab'zeel, E'der, Jagur, ²²Kinah, Dimo'nah, Ada'dah, ²³Ke'desh, Ha'zor, Ithnan, ²⁴Ziph, Telem, Be-a'loth, ²⁵Ha'zor-hadat'tah, Ker'i-oth-hez'ron (that is, Ha'zor), ²⁶A'mam, Shema, Mo'ladah, ²⁷Ha'zar-gad'dah, Heshmon, Beth-pel'et, ²⁸Ha'zar-shu'al, Be'er-she'ba, Biziothi'ah, ²⁹Ba'alah, I'im, E'zem, ³⁰Elto'lad, Che'sil, Hormah, ³¹Zik'lag, Madman'nah, Sansan'nah, ³²Leba'oth, Shilhim, A'in, and Rimmon: in all, twenty-nine cities, with their villages.

33 And in the lowland, Esh'ta-ol, Zorah, Ash'nah, ³⁴Zano'ah, En-gan'nim, Tap'pu-ah, E'nam,

³⁵Jarmuth, Adul'lam, Socoh, Aze'kah, ³⁶Sha"a-ra'im, Aditha'im, Gede'rah, Gede'rotha"im: fourteen cities with their villages.

37 Ze'nan, Hadash'ah, Mig'dal-gad, ³⁸Di'lean, Mizpeh, Jok'the-el, ³⁹La'chish, Bozkath, Eg'lon, ⁴⁰Cabbon, Lahmam, Chitlish, ⁴¹Gede'roth, Beth-da'gon, Na'amah, and Makke'dah: sixteen cities with their villages.

42 Libnah, E'ther, A'shan, ⁴³Iphtah, Ash'nah, Nezib, ⁴⁴Kei'lah, Ach'zib, and Mare'shah: nine cities with their villages.

45 Ek'ron, with its towns and its villages; ⁴⁶from Ek'ron to the sea, all that were by the side of Ash'dod, with their villages.

47 Ash'dod, its towns and its villages; Gaza, its towns and its villages; to the Brook of Egypt, and the Great Sea with its coast-line.

48 And in the hill country, Sha'mir, Jat'tir, Socoh, ⁴⁹Dannah, Kir'iath-san'nah (that is, De'bir), ⁵⁰A'nab, Esh'temoh, A'nim, ⁵¹Goshen, Holon, and Giloh: eleven cities with their villages.

52 A'rab, Du'mah, E'shan, ⁵³Ja'nim, Beth-tap'pu-ah, Aphe'kah, ⁵⁴Humtah, Kir'iath-ar'ba (that is, He'bron), and Zior: nine cities with their villages.

55 Maon, Carmel, Ziph, Juttah, ⁵⁶Jezre'el, Jok'de-am, Zano'ah, ⁵⁷Kain, Gib'e-ah, and Timnah: ten cities with their villages.

58 Halhul, Beth-zur, Gedor, ⁵⁹Ma'arath, Beth-a'noth, and El'tekon: six cities with their villages.

60 Kir'iath-ba'al (that is, Kir'iath-je'arim), and Rabbah: two cities with their villages.

61 In the wilderness, Beth-ar'abah, Middin, Seca'cah, ⁶²Nibshan, the City of Salt, and En-ge'di: six cities with their villages.

63 But the Jeb'usites, the inhabitants of Jerusalem, the people of Judah could not drive out; so the Jebusites dwell with the people of Judah at Jerusalem to this day.

The Territory of Ephraim

16 The allotment of the descendants of Joseph went from the Jordan by Jericho, east of the waters of Jericho, into the wilderness, going up from Jericho into the hill country to Bethel; ²then going from Bethel to Luz, it passes along to At'aroth, the territory of the Ar'chites; ³then it goes down westward to the territory of the Japh'letites, as far as the territory of Lower Beth-ho'ron, then to Gezer, and it ends at the sea.

4 The people of Joseph, Manas'seh and E'phraim, received their inheritance.

5 The territory of the E'phraimites by their families was as follows: the boundary of their inheritance on the east was At'aroth-ad'dar as far as Upper Beth-ho'ron, ⁶and the boundary goes

15:14–19: Judg 1:10–15, 20.
15:63: Judg 1:21; 2 Sam 5:6.

thence to the sea; on the north is Michme'thath; then on the east the boundary turns round toward Ta'anath-shi'loh, and passes along beyond it on the east to Jano'ah, [7]then it goes down from Jano'ah to At'aroth and to Na'arah, and touches Jericho, ending at the Jordan. [8]From Tap'pu-ah the boundary goes westward to the brook Kanah, and ends at the sea. Such is the inheritance of the tribe of the E'phraimites by their families, [9]together with the towns which were set apart for the E'phraimites within the inheritance of the Manas'sites, all those towns with their villages. [10]However they did not drive out the Canaanites that dwelt in Gezer: so the Canaanites have dwelt in the midst of E'phraim to this day but have become slaves to do forced labor.

The Territory of the Half-tribe of Manasseh (West)

17 Then allotment was made to the tribe of Manas'seh, for he was the first-born of Joseph. To Ma'chir the first-born of Manasseh, the father of Gilead, were allotted Gilead and Bashan, because he was a man of war. [2]And allotments were made to the rest of the tribe of Manas'seh, by their families, Abi-e'zer, He'lek, As'ri-el, She'chem, He'pher, and Shemi'da; these were the male descendants of Manasseh the son of Joseph, by their families.

3 Now Zeloph'ehad the son of He'pher, son of Gilead, son of Ma'chir, son of Manas'seh, had no sons, but only daughters; and these are the names of his daughters: Mahlah, Noah, Hoglah, Milcah, and Tirzah. [4]They came before Elea'zar the priest and Joshua the son of Nun and the leaders, and said, "The LORD commanded Moses to give us an inheritance along with our brethren." So according to the commandment of the LORD he gave them an inheritance among the brethren of their father. [5]Thus there fell to Manas'seh ten portions, besides the land of Gilead and Bashan, which is on the other side of the Jordan; [6]because the daughters of Manas'seh received an inheritance along with his sons. The land of Gilead was allotted to the rest of the Manas'sites.

7 The territory of Manas'seh reached from Asher to Michme'thath, which is east of She'chem; then the boundary goes along southward to the inhabitants of En-tap'pu-ah. [8]The land of Tap'pu-ah belonged to Manas'seh, but the town of Tappu-ah on the boundary of Manasseh belonged to the sons of E'phraim. [9]Then the boundary went down to the brook Kanah. The cities here, to the south of the brook, among the cities of Manas'seh, belong to E'phraim. Then the boundary of Manasseh goes on the north side of the brook and ends at the sea; [10]the land to the south being E'phraim's and that to the north being Manas'seh's, with the sea forming its boundary; on the north Asher is reached,

and on the east Is'sachar. [11]Also in Is'sachar and in Asher Manas'seh had Beth-she'an and its villages, and Ib'leam and its villages, and the inhabitants of Dor and its villages, and the inhabitants of En-dor and its villages, and the inhabitants of Ta'anach and its villages, and the inhabitants of Megid'do and its villages; the third is Na'phath. [j] [12]Yet the sons of Manas'seh could not take possession of those cities; but the Canaanites persisted in dwelling in that land. [13]But when the sons of Israel grew strong, they put the Canaanites to forced labor, and did not utterly drive them out.

The Tribe of Joseph Protests

14 And the tribe of Joseph spoke to Joshua, saying, "Why have you given me but one lot and one portion as an inheritance, although I am a numerous people, since hitherto the LORD has blessed me?" [15]And Joshua said to them, "If you are a numerous people, go up to the forest, and there clear ground for yourselves in the land of the Per'izzites and the Reph'aim, since the hill country of E'phraim is too narrow for you." [16]The tribe of Joseph said, "The hill country is not enough for us; yet all the Canaanites who dwell in the plain have chariots of iron, both those in Beth-she'an and its villages and those in the Valley of Jezre'el." [17]Then Joshua said to the house of Joseph, to E'phraim and Manas'seh, "You are a numerous people, and have great power; you shall not have one lot only, [18]but the hill country shall be yours, for though it is a forest, you shall clear it and possess it to its farthest borders; for you shall drive out the Canaanites, though they have chariots of iron, and though they are strong."

The Territories of the Remaining Tribes

18 Then the whole congregation of the sons of Israel assembled at Shiloh, and set up the tent of meeting there; the land lay subdued before them.

2 There remained among the sons of Israel seven tribes whose inheritance had not yet been apportioned. [3]So Joshua said to the sons of Israel, "How long will you be slack to go in and take possession of the land, which the LORD, the God of your fathers, has given you? [4]Provide three men from each tribe, and I will send them out that they may set out and go up and down the land, writing a description of it with a view to their inheritances, and then come to me. [5]They shall divide it into seven portions, Judah continuing in his territory on the south, and the house of Joseph in their territory on the north. [6]And you shall describe the land in seven divisions and

---

[j] Heb obscure.
16:10: Judg 1:29.
17:3, 4: Num 26:33; 27:1–7.
17:11–13: Judg 1:27–28.

bring the description here to me; and I will cast lots for you here before the LORD our God. [7]The Levites have no portion among you, for the priesthood of the LORD is their heritage; and Gad and Reuben and half the tribe of Manas'seh have received their inheritance beyond the Jordan eastward, which Moses the servant of the LORD gave them."

8 So the men started on their way; and Joshua charged those who went to write the description of the land, saying, "Go up and down and write a description of the land, and come again to me; and I will cast lots for you here before the LORD in Shiloh." [9]So the men went and passed up and down in the land and set down in a book a description of it by towns in seven divisions; then they came to Joshua in the camp at Shiloh, [10]and Joshua cast lots for them in Shiloh before the LORD; and there Joshua apportioned the land to the sons of Israel, to each his portion.

The Territory of Benjamin

11 The lot of the tribe of Benjamin according to its families came up, and the territory allotted to it fell between the tribe of Judah and the tribe of Joseph. [12]On the north side their boundary began at the Jordan; then the boundary goes up to the shoulder north of Jericho, then up through the hill country westward; and it ends at the wilderness of Beth-a'ven. [13]From there the boundary passes along southward in the direction of Luz, to the shoulder of Luz (the same is Bethel), then the boundary goes down to At'aroth-ad'dar, upon the mountain that lies south of Lower Beth-ho'ron. [14]Then the boundary goes in another direction, turning on the western side southward from the mountain that lies to the south, opposite Beth-ho'ron, and it ends at Kir'iath-ba'al (that is, Kir'iath-je'arim), a city belonging to the tribe of Judah. This forms the western side. [15]And the southern side begins at the outskirts of Kir'iath-je'arim; and the boundary goes from there to E'phron,[k] to the spring of the Waters of Nephto'ah; [16]then the boundary goes down to the border of the mountain that overlooks the valley of the son of Hinnom, which is at the north end of the valley of Reph'aim; and it then goes down the valley of Hinnom, south of the shoulder of the Jeb'usites, and downward to En-ro'gel; [17]then it bends in a northerly direction going on to En-she'mesh, and thence goes to Geli'loth, which is opposite the ascent of Adum'mim; then it goes down to the stone of Bohan the son of Reuben; [18]and passing on to the north of the shoulder of Beth-ar'abah [l] it goes down to the Ar'abah; [19]then the boundary passes on to the north of the shoulder of Beth-hog'lah; and the boundary ends at the northern bay of the Salt Sea, at the south end of the Jordan: this is the southern border. [20]The Jordan forms its boundary on the eastern

side. This is the inheritance of the tribe of Benjamin, according to its families, boundary by boundary round about.

21 Now the cities of the tribe of Benjamin according to their families were Jericho, Beth-hog'lah, E'mek-ke'ziz, [22]Beth-ar'abah, Zemara'im, Bethel, [23]Avvim, Par'ah, Oph'rah, [24]Che'pharam'moni, Ophni, Ge'ba—twelve cities with their villages: [25]Gib'eon, Ra'mah, Be-er'oth, [26]Mizpeh, Chephi'rah, Mozah, [27]Re'kem, Ir'peel, Tar'alah, [28]Ze'la, Ha-e'leph, Je'bus[m] (that is, Jerusalem), Gib'e-ah [n] and Kir'iath-je'arim [o]—fourteen cities with their villages. This is the inheritance of the tribe of Benjamin according to its families.

The Territory of Simeon

19 The second lot came out for Simeon, for the tribe of Simeon, according to its families; and its inheritance was in the midst of the inheritance of the tribe of Judah. [2]And it had for its inheritance Be'er-she'ba, Sheba, Mo'ladah, [3]Ha'zar-shu'al, Balah, E'zem, [4]Elto'lad, Be'thul, Hormah, [5]Zik'lag, Beth-mar'caboth, Ha'zar-su'sah, [6]Beth-leba'oth, and Sharu'hen—thirteen cities with their villages; [7]En-rim'mon, E'ther, and A'shan—four cities with their villages; [8]together with all the villages round about these cities as far as Ba'alath-be'er, Ra'mah of the Neg'eb. This was the inheritance of the tribe of Simeon according to its families. [9]The inheritance of the tribe of Simeon formed part of the territory of Judah; because the portion of the tribe of Judah was too large for them, the tribe of Simeon obtained an inheritance in the midst of their inheritance.

The Territory of Zebulun

10 The third lot came up for the tribe of Zeb'ulun, according to its families. And the territory of its inheritance reached as far as Sa'rid; [11]then its boundary goes up westward, and on to Mar'eal, and touches Dab'besheth, then the brook which is east of Jok'ne-am; [12]from Sa'rid it goes in the other direction eastward toward the sunrise to the boundary of Chis'loth-ta'bor; thence it goes to Dab'erath, then up to Japhi'a; [13]from there it passes along on the east toward the sunrise to Gath-he'pher, to Eth-ka'zin, and going on to Rimmon it bends toward Ne'ah; [14]then on the north the boundary turns about to Hanna'thon, and it ends at the valley of Iph'tahel; [15]and Kattath, Nahal'al, Shimron, I'dalah, and Bethlehem—twelve cities with their villages. [16]This is the inheritance of the tribe of Zeb'ulun, according to its families—these cities with their villages.

---

[k] Cn See 15:9. Heb *westward.*
[l] Gk: Heb *to the shoulder over against the Arabah.*
[m] Gk Syr Vg: Heb *the Jebusite.*
[n] Heb *Gibeath.*
[o] Gk: Heb *Kiriath.*

The Territory of Issachar

17 The fourth lot came out for Is'sachar, for the tribe of Issachar, according to its families. [18]Its territory included Jezre'el, Chesul'loth, Shunem, [19]Haph'ara-im, Shi'on, Ana'harath, [20]Rabbith, Kish'ion, E'bez, [21]Re'meth, En-gan'nim, En-had'-dah, Beth-paz'zez; [22]the boundary also touches Tabor, Shahazu'mah, and Beth-she'mesh, and its boundary ends at the Jordan—sixteen cities with their villages. [23]This is the inheritance of the tribe of Is'sachar, according to its families—the cities with their villages.

The Territory of Asher

24 The fifth lot came out for the tribe of Asher according to its families. [25]Its territory included Helkath, Ha'li, Be'ten, Ach'shaph, [26]Allam'melech, A'mad, and Mi'shal; on the west it touches Carmel and Shihorlib'nath, [27]then it turns eastward, it goes to Beth-da'gon, and touches Zeb'ulun and the valley of Iph'tahel northward to Beth-e'mek and Nei'el; then it continues in the north to Ca'bul, [28]E'bron, Re'hob, Hammon, Kanah, as far as Sidon the Great; [29]then the boundary turns to Ra'mah, reaching to the fortified city of Tyre; then the boundary turns to Ho'sah, and it ends at the sea; Maha'lab, [P] Ach'-zib, [30]Ummah, A'phek and Re'hob—twenty-two cities with their villages. [31]This is the inheritance of the tribe of Asher according to its families—these cities with their villages.

The Territory of Naphtali

32 The sixth lot came out for the tribe of Naph'tali, for the tribe of Naphtali, according to its families. [33]And its boundary ran from He'leph, from the oak in Za-anan'nim, and Ad'ami-nek'eb, and Jab'neel, as far as Lakkum; and it ended at the Jordan; [34]then the boundary turns westward to Az'noth-ta'bor, and goes from there to Hukkok, touching Zeb'ulun at the south, and Asher on the west, and Judah on the east at the Jordan. [35]The fortified cities are Ziddim, Zer, Hammath, Rakkath, Chin'nereth, [36]Ad'amah, Ra'mah, Ha'zor, [37]Ke'desh, Ed're-i, En-ha'zor, [38]Yi'ron, Mig'dal-el, Horem, Beth-a'nath, and Beth-she'mesh—nineteen cities with their villages. [39]This is the inheritance of the tribe of Naph'tali according to its families—the cities with their villages.

The Territory of Dan

40 The seventh lot came out for the tribe of Dan, according to its families. [41]And the territory of its inheritance included Zorah, Esh'ta-ol, Irshe'mesh, [42]Sha-alab'bin, Ai'jalon, Ithlah, [43]E'lon, Timnah, Ek'ron, [44]El'tekeh, Gib'bethon, Ba'alath, [45]Je'hud, Ben'e-be'rak, Gath-rim'mon, [46]and Me-jar'kon and Rakkon with the territory over against Joppa. [47]When the territory of the Da'nites was lost to them, the Danites went up and fought against Le'shem, and after capturing it and putting it to the sword they took possession of it and settled in it, calling Leshem, Dan,

after the name of Dan their ancestor. [48]This is the inheritance of the tribe of Dan, according to their families—these cities with their villages.

The Inheritance of Joshua

49 When they had finished distributing the several territories of the land as inheritances, the sons of Israel gave an inheritance among them to Joshua the son of Nun. [50]By command of the LORD they gave him the city which he asked, Tim'nath-se'rah in the hill country of E'phraim; and he rebuilt the city, and settled in it.

51 These are the inheritances which Elea'zar the priest and Joshua the son of Nun and the heads of the fathers' houses of the tribes of the sons of Israel distributed by lot at Shiloh before the LORD, at the door of the tent of meeting. So they finished dividing the land.

The City of Refuge

20 Then the LORD said to Joshua, [2]"Say to the sons of Israel, 'Appoint the cities of refuge, of which I spoke to you through Moses, [3]that the manslayer who kills any person without intent or unwittingly may flee there; they shall be for you a refuge from the avenger of blood. [4]He shall flee to one of these cities and shall stand at the entrance of the gate of the city, and explain his case to the elders of that city; then they shall take him into the city, and give him a place, and he shall remain with them. [5]And if the avenger of blood pursues him, they shall not give up the slayer into his hand; because he killed his neighbor unwittingly, having had no enmity against him in times past. [6]And he shall remain in that city until he has stood before the congregation for judgment, until the death of him who is high priest at the time: then the slayer may go again to his own town and his own home, to the town from which he fled.'"

7 So they set apart Ke'desh in Galilee in the hill country of Naph'tali, and She'chem in the hill country of E'phraim, and Kir'iath-ar'ba (that is, He'bron) in the hill country of Judah. [8]And beyond the Jordan east of Jericho, they appointed Be'zer in the wilderness on the tableland, from the tribe of Reuben, and Ra'moth in Gilead, from the tribe of Gad, and Golan in Bashan, from the tribe of Manas'seh. [9]These were the cities designated for all the sons of Israel, and for the stranger sojourning among them, that any one who killed a person without intent could flee there, so that he might not die by the hand of the avenger of blood, till he stood before the congregation.

Cities of the Levites

21 Then the heads of the fathers' houses of the Levites came to Elea'zar the priest and

---

P Cn Compare Gk: Heb *Mehebel*.
19:47: Judg 18:27–31.
20:2–9: Num 35:6–34; Deut 4:41–43; 19:1–13.
21:1–42: Num 35:1–8; 1 Chron 6:54–81.

to Joshua the son of Nun and to the heads of the fathers' houses of the tribes of the sons of Israel; ²and they said to them at Shiloh in the land of Canaan, "The LORD commanded through Moses that we be given cities to dwell in, along with their pasture lands for our cattle." ³So by command of the LORD the sons of Israel gave to the Levites the following cities and pasture lands out of their inheritance.

4 The lot came out for the families of the Ko'hathites. So those Levites who were descendants of Aaron the priest received by lot from the tribes of Judah, Simeon, and Benjamin, thirteen cities.

5 And the rest of the Ko'hathites received by lot from the families of the tribe of E'phraim, from the tribe of Dan and the half-tribe of Manas'seh, ten cities.

6 The Ger'shonites received by lot from the families of the tribe of Is'sachar, from the tribe of Asher, from the tribe of Naph'tali, and from the half-tribe of Manas'seh in Bashan, thirteen cities.

7 The Merar'ites according to their families received from the tribe of Reuben, the tribe of Gad, and the tribe of Zeb'ulun, twelve cities.

8 These cities and their pasture lands the sons of Israel gave by lot to the Levites, as the LORD had commanded through Moses.

9 Out of the tribe of Judah and the tribe of Simeon they gave the following cities mentioned by name, ¹⁰which went to the descendants of Aaron, one of the families of the Ko'hathites who belonged to the Levites; since the lot fell to them first. ¹¹They gave them Kir'iath-ar'ba (Arba being the father of A'nak), that is He'bron, in the hill country of Judah, along with the pasture lands round about it. ¹²But the fields of the city and its villages had been given to Caleb the son of Jephun'neh as his possession.

13 And to the descendants of Aaron the priest they gave He'bron, the city of refuge for the slayer, with its pasture lands, Libnah with its pasture lands, ¹⁴Jat'tir with its pasture lands, Eshtemo'a with its pasture lands, ¹⁵Ho'lon with its pasture lands, De'bir with its pasture lands, ¹⁶A'in with its pasture lands, Juttah with its pasture lands, Beth-she'mesh with its pasture lands—nine cities out of these two tribes; ¹⁷then out of the tribe of Benjamin, Gib'eon with its pasture lands, Ge'ba with its pasture lands, ¹⁸An'athoth with its pasture lands, and Al'mon with its pasture lands—four cities. ¹⁹The cities of the descendants of Aaron, the priests, were in all thirteen cities with their pasture lands.

20 As to the rest of the Ko'hathites belonging to the Kohathite families of the Levites, the cities allotted to them were out of the tribe of E'phraim. ²¹To them were given She'chem, the city of refuge for the slayer, with its pasture lands in the hill country of E'phraim, Gezer with its pasture lands, ²²Kib'za-im with its pasture lands, Beth-ho'ron with its pasture lands—four cities; ²³and out of the tribe of Dan, El'teke with its pasture lands, Gib'bethon with its pasture lands, ²⁴Ai'jalon with its pasture lands, Gath-rim'mon with its pasture lands—four cities; ²⁵and out of the half-tribe of Manas'seh, Ta'anach with its pasture lands, and Gath-rim'mon with its pasture lands—two cities. ²⁶The cities of the families of the rest of the Ko'hathites were ten in all with their pasture lands.

27 And to the Ger'shonites, one of the families of the Levites, were given out of the half-tribe of Manas'seh, Golan in Bashan with its pasture lands, the city of refuge for the slayer, and Be-eshte'rah with its pasture lands—two cities; ²⁸and out of the tribe of Is'sachar, Kish'ion with its pasture lands, Dab'erath with its pasture lands, ²⁹Jarmuth with its pasture lands, En-gan'nim with its pasture lands—four cities; ³⁰and out of the tribe of Asher, Mishal with its pasture lands, Abdon with its pasture lands, ³¹Helkath with its pasture lands, and Re'hob with its pasture lands—four cities; ³²and out of the tribe of Naph'tali, Ke'desh in Galilee with its pasture lands, the city of refuge for the slayer, Ham'moth-dor with its pasture lands, and Kartan with its pasture lands—three cities. ³³The cities of the several families of the Ger'shonites were in all thirteen cities with their pasture lands.

34 And to the rest of the Levites, the Merar'ite families, were given out of the tribe of Zeb'ulun, Jok'ne-am with its pasture lands, Kartah with its pasture lands, ³⁵Dimnah with its pasture lands, Nahal'al with its pasture lands—four cities; ³⁶and out of the tribe of Reuben, Be'zer with its pasture lands, Ja'haz with its pasture lands, ³⁷Ked'emoth with its pasture lands, and Meph'a-ath with its pasture lands—four cities; ³⁸and out of the tribe of Gad, Ra'moth in Gilead with its pasture lands, the city of refuge for the slayer, Ma"hana'im with its pasture lands, ³⁹Heshbon with its pasture lands, Ja'zer with its pasture lands—four cities in all. ⁴⁰As for the cities of the several Merar'ite families, that is, the remainder of the families of the Levites, those allotted to them were in all twelve cities.

41 The cities of the Levites in the midst of the possession of the sons of Israel were in all forty-eight cities with their pasture lands. ⁴²These cities had each its pasture lands round about it; so it was with all these cities.

43 Thus the LORD gave to Israel all the land which he swore to give to their fathers; and having taken possession of it, they settled there. ⁴⁴And the LORD gave them rest on every side just as he had sworn to their fathers; not one of all

their enemies had withstood them, for the Lord had given all their enemies into their hands. [45]Not one of all the good promises which the Lord had made to the house of Israel had failed; all came to pass.

The Eastern Tribes Return

22 Then Joshua summoned the Reubenites, and the Gadites, and the half-tribe of Manas′seh, [2]and said to them, "You have kept all that Moses the servant of the Lord commanded you, and have obeyed my voice in all that I have commanded you; [3]you have not forsaken your brethren these many days, down to this day, but have been careful to keep the charge of the Lord your God. [4]And now the Lord your God has given rest to your brethren, as he promised them; therefore turn and go to your home in the land where your possession lies, which Moses the servant of the Lord gave you on the other side of the Jordan. [5]Take good care to observe the commandment and the law which Moses the servant of the Lord commanded you, to love the Lord your God, and to walk in all his ways, and to keep his commandments, and to cling to him, and to serve him with all your heart and with all your soul." [6]So Joshua blessed them, and sent them away; and they went to their homes.

7 Now to the one half of the tribe of Manas′seh Moses had given a possession in Bashan; but to the other half Joshua had given a possession beside their brethren in the land west of the Jordan. And when Joshua sent them away to their homes and blessed them, [8]he said to them, "Go back to your homes with much wealth, and with very many cattle, with silver, gold, bronze, and iron, and with much clothing; divide the spoil of your enemies with your brethren." [9]So the Reubenites and the Gadites and the half-tribe of Manas′seh returned home, parting from the sons of Israel at Shiloh, which is in the land of Canaan, to go to the land of Gilead, their own land of which they had possessed themselves by command of the Lord through Moses.

An Altar of Witness by the Jordan

10 And when they came to the region about the Jordan, that lies in the land of Canaan, the Reubenites and the Gadites and the half-tribe of Manas′seh built there an altar by the Jordan, an altar of great size. [11]And the sons of Israel heard say, "Behold, the Reubenites and the Gadites and the half-tribe of Manas′seh have built an altar at the frontier of the land of Canaan, in the region about the Jordan, on the side that belongs to the sons of Israel." [12]And when the sons of Israel heard of it, the whole assembly of the sons of Israel gathered at Shiloh, to make war against them.

13 Then the sons of Israel sent to the Reubenites and the Gadites and the half-tribe of Manas′-

seh, in the land of Gilead, Phin′ehas the son of Elea′zar the priest, [14]and with him ten chiefs, one from each of the tribal families of Israel, every one of them the head of a family among the clans of Israel. [15]And they came to the Reubenites, the Gadites, and the half-tribe of Manas′seh, in the land of Gilead, and they said to them, [16]"Thus says the whole congregation of the Lord, 'What is this treachery which you have committed against the God of Israel in turning away this day from following the Lord, by building yourselves an altar this day in rebellion against the Lord? [17]Have we not had enough of the sin at Peor from which even yet we have not cleansed ourselves, and for which there came a plague upon the congregation of the Lord, [18]that you must turn away this day from following the Lord? And if you rebel against the Lord today he will be angry with the whole congregation of Israel tomorrow. [19]But now, if your land is unclean, pass over into the Lord's land where the Lord's tabernacle stands, and take for yourselves a possession among us; only do not rebel against the Lord, or make us as rebels by building yourselves an altar other than the altar of the Lord our God. [20]Did not A′chan the son of Ze′rah break faith in the matter of the devoted things, and wrath fell upon all the congregation of Israel? And he did not perish alone for his iniquity.'"

21 Then the Reubenites, the Gadites, and the half-tribe of Manas′seh said in answer to the heads of the families of Israel, [22]"The Mighty One, God, the Lord! The Mighty One, God, the Lord! He knows; and let Israel itself know! If it was in rebellion or in breach of faith toward the Lord, spare us not today [23]for building an altar to turn away from following the Lord; or if we did so to offer burnt offerings or cereal offerings or peace offerings on it, may the Lord himself take vengeance. [24]No, but we did it from fear that in time to come your children might say to our children, 'What have you to do with the Lord, the God of Israel? [25]For the Lord has made the Jordan a boundary between us and you, you Reubenites and Gadites; you have no portion in the Lord.' So your children might make our children cease to worship the Lord. [26]Therefore we said, 'Let us now build an altar, not for burnt offering, nor for sacrifice, [27]but to be a witness between us and you, and between the generations after us, that we do perform the service of the Lord in his presence with our burnt offerings and sacrifices and peace offerings; lest your children say to our children in time to come, "You have no portion in the Lord."' [28]And we thought, If this should be said to us or to our descendants in time to come, we should say, 'Behold the copy of the altar of the Lord,

22:1–34: 1:12–18; Num 32:20–22.

175

which our fathers made, not for burnt offerings, nor for sacrifice, but to be a witness between us and you.' [29]Far be it from us that we should rebel against the LORD, and turn away this day from following the LORD by building an altar for burnt offering, cereal offering, or sacrifice, other than the altar of the LORD our God that stands before his tabernacle!"

30 When Phin'ehas the priest and the chiefs of the congregation, the heads of the families of Israel who were with him, heard the words that the Reubenites and the Gadites and the Manas'sites spoke, it pleased them well. [31]And Phin'ehas the son of Elea'zar the priest said to the Reubenites and the Gadites and the Manas'sites, "Today we know that the LORD is in the midst of us, because you have not committed this treachery against the LORD; now you have saved the sons of Israel from the hand of the LORD."

32 Then Phin'ehas the son of Elea'zar the priest, and the chiefs, returned from the Reubenites and the Gadites in the land of Gilead to the land of Canaan, to the sons of Israel, and brought back word to them. [33]And the report pleased the sons of Israel; and the sons of Israel blessed God and spoke no more of making war against them, to destroy the land where the Reubenites and the Gadites were settled. [34]The Reubenites and the Gadites called the altar Witness; "For," said they, "it is a witness between us that the LORD is God."

Joshua Exhorts the People

23 A long time afterward, when the LORD had given rest to Israel from all their enemies round about, and Joshua was old and well advanced in years, [2]Joshua summoned all Israel, their elders and heads, their judges and officers, and said to them, "I am now old and well advanced in years; [3]and you have seen all that the LORD your God has done to all these nations for your sake, for it is the LORD your God who has fought for you. [4]Behold, I have allotted to you as an inheritance for your tribes those nations that remain, along with all the nations that I have already cut off, from the Jordan to the Great Sea in the west. [5]The LORD your God will push them back before you, and drive them out of your sight; and you shall possess their land, as the LORD your God promised you. [6]Therefore be very steadfast to keep and do all that is written in the book of the law of Moses, turning aside from it neither to the right hand nor to the left, [7]that you may not be mixed with these nations left here among you, or make mention of the names of their gods, or swear by them, or serve them, or bow down yourselves to them, [8]but cling to the LORD your God as you have done to this day. [9]For the LORD has driven out before you great and strong nations; and as for you, no man has been

able to withstand you to this day. [10]One man of you puts to flight a thousand, since it is the LORD your God who fights for you, as he promised you. [11]Take good heed to yourselves, therefore, to love the LORD your God. [12]For if you turn back, and join the remnant of these nations left here among you, and make marriages with them, so that you marry their women and they yours, [13]know assuredly that the LORD your God will not continue to drive out these nations before you; but they shall be a snare and a trap for you, a scourge on your sides, and thorns in your eyes, till you perish from off this good land which the LORD your God has given you.

14 "And now I am about to go the way of all the earth, and you know in your hearts and souls, all of you, that not one thing has failed of all the good things which the LORD your God promised concerning you; all have come to pass for you, not one of them has failed. [15]But just as all the good things which the LORD your God promised concerning you have been fulfilled for you, so the LORD will bring upon you all the evil things, until he has destroyed you from off this good land which the LORD your God has given you, [16]if you transgress the covenant of the LORD your God, which he commanded you, and go and serve other gods and bow down to them. Then the anger of the LORD will be kindled against you, and you shall perish quickly from off the good land which he has given to you."

The Tribes Renew the Covenant

24 * Then Joshua gathered all the tribes of Israel to She'chem, and summoned the elders, the heads, the judges, and the officers of Israel; and they presented themselves before God. [2]And Joshua said to all the people, "Thus says the LORD, the God of Israel, 'Your fathers lived of old beyond the Euphrates, Te'rah, the father of Abraham and of Na'hor; and they served other gods. [3]Then I took your father Abraham from beyond the River and led him through all the land of Canaan, and made his offspring many. I gave him Isaac; [4]and to Isaac I gave Jacob and Esau. And I gave Esau the hill country of Se'ir to possess, but Jacob and his children went down to Egypt. [5]And I sent Moses and Aaron, and I plagued Egypt with what I did in the midst of it; and afterwards I brought you out. [6]Then I brought your fathers out of Egypt, and you came to the sea; and the Egyptians pursued your fathers with chariots and horsemen to the Red Sea. [7]And when they cried to the LORD, he put darkness between you and the Egyptians, and made the sea come upon them and cover them; and your eyes saw what I did to

---

* 24:1: The full gathering of the tribes at Shechem for a renewal of the covenant sealed the conquest and the final apportioning of the land. It seems to indicate the conversion to the worship of Yahweh of those Hebrews who did not go down to Egypt.

Egypt; and you lived in the wilderness a long time. [8]Then I brought you to the land of the Am'orites, who lived on the other side of the Jordan; they fought with you, and I gave them into your hand, and you took possession of their land, and I destroyed them before you. [9]Then Balak the son of Zippor, king of Moab, arose and fought against Israel; and he sent and invited Balaam the son of Beor to curse you, [10]but I would not listen to Balaam; therefore he blessed you; so I delivered you out of his hand. [11]And you went over the Jordan and came to Jericho, and the men of Jericho fought against you, and also the Am'orites, the Per'izzites, the Canaanites, the Hittites, the Gir'gashites, the Hi'vites, and the Jeb'usites; and I gave them into your hand. [12]And I sent the hornet before you, which drove them out before you, the two kings of the Am'orites; it was not by your sword or by your bow. [13]I gave you a land on which you had not labored, and cities which you had not built, and you dwell therein; you eat the fruit of vineyards and oliveyards which you did not plant.'

14 "Now therefore fear the LORD, and serve him in sincerity and in faithfulness; put away the gods which your fathers served beyond the River, and in Egypt, and serve the LORD. [15]And if you be unwilling to serve the LORD, choose this day whom you will serve, whether the gods your fathers served in the region beyond the River, or the gods of the Am'orites in whose land you dwell; but as for me and my house, we will serve the LORD."

16 Then the people answered, "Far be it from us that we should forsake the LORD, to serve other gods; [17]for it is the LORD our God who brought us and our fathers up from the land of Egypt, out of the house of bondage, and who did those great signs in our sight, and preserved us in all the way that we went, and among all the peoples through whom we passed; [18]and the LORD drove out before us all the peoples, the Am'orites who lived in the land; therefore we also will serve the LORD, for he is our God."

19 But Joshua said to the people, "You cannot serve the LORD; for he is a holy God; he is a jealous God; he will not forgive your transgressions or your sins. [20]If you forsake the LORD and serve foreign gods, then he will turn and do you harm,

and consume you, after having done you good." [21]And the people said to Joshua, "No; but we will serve the LORD." [22]Then Joshua said to the people, "You are witnesses against yourselves that you have chosen the LORD, to serve him." And they said, "We are witnesses." [23]He said, "Then put away the foreign gods which are among you, and incline your heart to the LORD, the God of Israel." [24]And the people said to Joshua, "The LORD our God we will serve, and his voice we will obey." [25]So Joshua made a covenant with the people that day, and made statutes and ordinances for them at She'chem. [26]And Joshua wrote these words in the book of the law of God; and he took a great stone, and set it up there under the oak in the sanctuary of the LORD. [27]And Joshua said to all the people, "Behold, this stone shall be a witness against us; for it has heard all the words of the LORD which he spoke to us; therefore it shall be a witness against you, lest you deal falsely with your God." [28]So Joshua sent the people away, every man to his inheritance.

The Death of Joshua and Eleazar

29 After these things Joshua the son of Nun, the servant of the LORD, died, being a hundred and ten years old. [30]And they buried him in his own inheritance at Tim'nath-se'rah, which is in the hill country of E'phraim, north of the mountain of Ga'ash.

31 And Israel served the LORD all the days of Joshua, and all the days of the elders who outlived Joshua and had known all the work which the LORD did for Israel.

32 The bones of Joseph which the sons of Israel brought up from Egypt were buried at She'chem, in the portion of ground which Jacob bought from the sons of Ha'mor the father of She'chem for a hundred pieces of money; q it became an inheritance of the descendants of Joseph.

33 And Elea'zar the son of Aaron died; and they buried him at Gib'e-ah, the town of Phin'ehas his son, which had been given him in the hill country of E'phraim.

---

q Heb qesitah.
24:32: Gen 50:24, 25; Ex 13:19; Acts 7:16.

THE BOOK OF

JUDGES

Israel's Failure to Complete the Conquest

1 * After the death of Joshua the sons of Israel inquired of the LORD, "Who shall go up first for us against the Canaanites, to fight against them?" [2]The LORD said, "Judah shall go up; behold, I have given the land into his hand." [3]And Judah said to Simeon his brother, "Come up with me into the territory allotted to me, that we may fight against the Canaanites; and I likewise will go with you into the territory allotted to you." So Simeon went with him. [4]Then Judah went up and the LORD gave the Canaanites and the Per'izzites into their hand; and they defeated ten thousand of them at Be'zek. [5]They came upon Ado'ni-be'zek at Be'zek, and fought against him, and defeated the Canaanites and the Per'izzites. [6]Ado'ni-be'zek fled; but they pursued him, and caught him, and cut off his thumbs and his great toes. [7]And Ado'ni-be'zek said, "Seventy kings with their thumbs and their great toes cut off used to pick up scraps under my table; as I have done, so God has repaid me." And they brought him to Jerusalem, and he died there.

8 And the men of Judah fought against Jerusalem, and took it, and struck it with the edge of the sword, and set the city on fire. [9]And afterward the men of Judah went down to fight against the Canaanites who dwelt in the hill country, in the Neg'eb, and in the lowland. [10]And Judah went against the Canaanites who dwelt in He'bron (now the name of Hebron was formerly Kir'iath-ar'ba); and they defeated Sheshai and Ahi'man and Talmai.

11 From there they went against the inhabitants of De'bir. The name of Debir was formerly Kir'iath-se'pher. [12]And Caleb said, "He who attacks Kir'iath-se'pher and takes it, I will give him Ach'sah my daughter as wife." [13]And Oth'niel the son of Ke'naz, Caleb's younger brother, took it; and he gave him Ach'sah his daughter as wife. [14]When she came to him, she urged him to ask her father for a field; and she alighted from her donkey, and Caleb said to her, "What do you wish?" [15]She said to him, "Give me a present; since you have set me in the land of the Neg'eb, give me also springs of water." And Caleb gave her the upper springs and the lower springs.

16 And the descendants of the Ken'ite, Moses' father-in-law, went up with the people of Judah from the city of palms into the wilderness of Judah, which lies in the Negeb near Ar'ad; and they went and settled with the people. [17]And Judah went with Simeon his brother, and they defeated the Canaanites who inhabited Ze'phath, and utterly destroyed it. So the name of the city was called Hormah. [18]Judah also took Gaza with its territory, and Ash'kelon with its territory, and Ek'ron with its territory. [19]And the LORD was with Judah, and he took possession of the hill country, but he could not drive out the inhabitants of the plain, because they had chariots of iron. [20]And He'bron was given to Caleb, as Moses had said; and he drove out from it the three sons of A'nak. [21]But the people of Benjamin did not drive out the Jeb'usites who dwelt in Jerusalem; so the Jebusites have dwelt with the people of Benjamin in Jerusalem to this day.

22 The house of Joseph also went up against Bethel; and the LORD was with them. [23]And the house of Joseph sent to spy out Bethel. (Now the name of the city was formerly Luz.) [24]And the spies saw a man coming out of the city, and they said to him, "Please, show us the way into the city, and we will deal kindly with you." [25]And he showed them the way into the city; and they struck the city with the edge of the sword, but they let the man and all his family go. [26]And the man went to the land of the Hittites and built a city, and called its name Luz; that is its name to this day.

27 Manas'seh did not drive out the inhabitants of Beth-she'an and its villages, or Ta'anach and its villages, or the inhabitants of Dor and its villages, or the inhabitants of Ib'leam and its villages, or the inhabitants of Megid'do and its villages, but the Canaanites persisted in dwelling in that land. [28]When Israel grew strong, they put the Canaanites to forced labor, but did not utterly drive them out.

This book, which has been edited at least twice, fills in the period from the settlement to the monarchy. This was a period of crisis that gave rise to "saviors" raised up by God to meet these critical situations. The deeds of six of these are recounted at some length: Othniel, Ehud, Deborah (and Barak), Gideon, Jephthah, Samson; there are also six "minor" judges who are given only a short notice: Shamgar, Tola, Jair, Ibzan, Elon, Abdon. The book ends with two appendixes (chapters 17–21).

1:10: Josh 15:13–19.
1:10-15: Josh 15:14–19.
1:20: Josh 15:14.
1:21: Josh 15:63.
1:27, 28: Josh 17:11–13.
* 1:1: This first chapter describes the difficulties and defeats of the conquest.

29 And E'phraim did not drive out the Canaanites who dwelt in Gezer; but the Canaanites dwelt in Gezer among them.

30 Zeb'ulun did not drive out the inhabitants of Kitron, or the inhabitants of Nahal'ol; but the Canaanites dwelt among them, and became subject to forced labor.

31 Asher did not drive out the inhabitants of Ac'co, or the inhabitants of Si'don, or of Ahlab, or of Ach'zib, or of Helbah, or of A'phik, or of Re'hob; [32]but the Ash'erites dwelt among the Canaanites, the inhabitants of the land; for they did not drive them out.

33 Naph'tali did not drive out the inhabitants of Beth-she'mesh, or the inhabitants of Beth-a'nath, but dwelt among the Canaanites, the inhabitants of the land; nevertheless the inhabitants of Beth-shemesh and of Beth-anath became subject to forced labor for them.

34 The Am'orites pressed the Da'nites back into the hill country, for they did not allow them to come down to the plain; [35]the Am'orites persisted in dwelling in Har-he'res, in Ai'jalon, and in Sha-al'bim, but the hand of the house of Joseph rested heavily upon them, and they became subject to forced labor. [36]And the border of the Am'orites ran from the ascent of Akrab'bim, from Se'la and upward.

Israel's Disobedience

2 Now the angel of the LORD went up from Gilgal to Bochim. And he said, "I brought you up from Egypt, and brought you into the land which I swore to give to your fathers. I said, 'I will never break my covenant with you, [2]and you shall make no covenant with the inhabitants of this land; you shall break down their altars.' But you have not obeyed my command. What is this you have done? [3]So now I say, I will not drive them out before you; but they shall become adversaries [a] to you, and their gods shall be a snare to you." [4]When the angel of the LORD spoke these words to all the sons of Israel, the people lifted up their voices and wept. [5]And they called the name of that place Bochim; [b] and they sacrificed there to the LORD.

Death of Joshua

6 When Joshua dismissed the people, the sons of Israel went each to his inheritance to take possession of the land. [7]And the people served the LORD all the days of Joshua, and all the days of the elders who outlived Joshua, who had seen all the great work which the LORD had done for Israel. [8]And Joshua the son of Nun, the servant of the LORD, died at the age of one hundred and ten years. [9]And they buried him within the bounds of his inheritance in Tim'nath-he'res, in the hill country of E'phraim, north of the mountain of Ga'ash. [10]And all that generation also were gathered to their fathers; and there arose another generation

after them, who did not know the LORD or the work which he had done for Israel.

Israel's Unfaithfulness

11 And the sons of Israel did what was evil in the sight of the LORD and served the Ba'als; [12]and they forsook the LORD, the God of their fathers, who had brought them out of the land of Egypt; they went after other gods, from among the gods of the peoples who were round about them, and bowed down to them; and they provoked the LORD to anger. [13]They forsook the LORD, and served the Ba'als and the Ash'taroth. [14]So the anger of the LORD was kindled against Israel, and he gave them over to plunderers, who plundered them; and he sold them into the power of their enemies round about, so that they could no longer withstand their enemies. [15]Whenever they marched out, the hand of the LORD was against them for evil, as the LORD had warned, and as the LORD had sworn to them; and they were in great distress.

16 Then the LORD raised up judges, who saved them out of the power of those who plundered them. [17]And yet they did not listen to their judges; for they played the harlot after other gods and bowed down to them; they soon turned aside from the way in which their fathers had walked, who had obeyed the commandments of the LORD, and they did not do so. [18]Whenever the LORD raised up judges for them, the LORD was with the judge, and he saved them from the hand of their enemies all the days of the judge; for the LORD was moved to pity by their groaning because of those who afflicted and oppressed them. [19]But whenever the judge died, they turned back and behaved worse than their fathers, going after other gods, serving them and bowing down to them; they did not drop any of their practices or their stubborn ways. * [20]So the anger of the LORD was kindled against Israel; and he said, "Because this people have transgressed my covenant which I commanded their fathers, and have not obeyed my voice, [21]from now on I will not drive out before them any of the nations that Joshua left when he died, [22]that by them I may test Israel, whether they will take care to walk in the way of the LORD as their fathers did, or not." [23]So the LORD left those nations, not driving them out at once, and he did not give them into the power of Joshua.

Nations Remaining in the Land

3 Now these are the nations which the LORD left, to test Israel by them, that is, all in Israel who had no experience of any war in Canaan; [2]it

---

[a] Vg Old Latin Compare Gk: Heb *sides*.
[b] That is *Weepers*.
1:29: Josh 16:10.
2:6–9: Josh 24:28–31.
* 2:11–19: This passage gives the theological scheme of the book according to which the episodic history is presented. It comes from an editor inspired by the ideas of Deuteronomy and resembles closely the scheme according to which the kings, beginning with Solomon, are assessed and judged.

was only that the generations of the sons of Israel might know war, that he might teach war to such at least as had not known it before. ³These are the nations: the five lords of the Philis'tines, and all the Canaanites, and the Sido'nians, and the Hi'vites who dwelt on Mount Lebanon, from Mount Ba'al-her'mon as far as the entrance of Ha'math. ⁴They were for the testing of Israel, to know whether Israel would obey the commandments of the LORD, which he commanded their fathers by Moses. ⁵So the sons of Israel dwelt among the Canaanites, the Hittites, the Am'orites, the Per'izzites, the Hi'vites, and the Jeb'usites; ⁶and they took their daughters to themselves for wives, and their own daughters they gave to their sons; and they served their gods.

Othni-el

7 And the sons of Israel did what was evil in the sight of the LORD, forgetting the LORD their God, and serving the Ba'als and the Ashe'roth. ⁸Therefore the anger of the LORD was kindled against Israel, and he sold them into the hand of Cu'shan-rishatha'im king of Mesopota'mia; and the sons of Israel served Cushan-rishathaim eight years. ⁹But when the sons of Israel cried to the LORD, the LORD raised up a deliverer for the sons of Israel, who delivered them, Oth'ni-el the son of Ke'naz, Caleb's younger brother. ¹⁰The Spirit of the LORD came upon him, and he judged Israel; he went out to war, and the LORD gave Cu'shan-rishatha'im king of Mesopota'mia into his hand; and his hand prevailed over Cushan-rishathaim. ¹¹So the land had rest forty years. Then Oth'ni-el the son of Ke'naz died.

Ehud

12 And the sons of Israel again did what was evil in the sight of the LORD; and the LORD strengthened Eg'lon the king of Moab against Israel, because they had done what was evil in the sight of the LORD. ¹³He gathered to himself the Am'monites and the Amal'ekites, and went and defeated Israel; and they took possession of the city of palms. ¹⁴And the sons of Israel served Eg'lon the king of Moab eighteen years.

15 But when the sons of Israel cried to the LORD, the LORD raised up for them a deliverer, E'hud, the son of Gera, the Benjaminite, a left-handed man. The sons of Israel sent tribute by him to Eg'lon the king of Moab. ¹⁶And E'hud made for himself a sword with two edges, a cubit in length; and he girded it on his right thigh under his clothes. ¹⁷And he presented the tribute to Eg'lon king of Moab. Now Eglon was a very fat man. ¹⁸And when E'hud had finished presenting the tribute, he sent away the people that carried the tribute. ¹⁹But he himself turned back at the sculptured stones near Gilgal, and said, "I have a secret message for you, O king." And he commanded, "Silence." And all his attendants went out from his presence. ²⁰And E'hud came to him, as he was sitting alone in his cool roof chamber. And Ehud said, "I have a message from God for you." And he arose from his seat. ²¹And E'hud reached with his left hand, took the sword from his right thigh, and thrust it into his belly; ²²and the hilt also went in after the blade, and the fat closed over the blade, for he did not draw the sword out of his belly; and the dirt came out. ²³Then E'hud went out into the vestibule, ᶜ and closed the doors of the roof chamber upon him, and locked them.

24 When he had gone, the servants came; and when they saw that the doors of the roof chamber were locked, they thought, "He is only relieving himself in the closet of the cool chamber." ²⁵And they waited till they were utterly at a loss; but when he still did not open the doors of the roof chamber, they took the key and opened them; and there lay their lord dead on the floor.

26 E'hud escaped while they delayed, and passed beyond the sculptured stones, and escaped to Se-i'rah. ²⁷When he arrived, he sounded the trumpet in the hill country of E'phraim; and the sons of Israel went down with him from the hill country, having him at their head. ²⁸And he said to them, "Follow after me; for the LORD has given your enemies the Moabites into your hand." So they went down after him, and seized the fords of the Jordan against the Moabites, and allowed no man to pass over. ²⁹And they killed at that time about ten thousand of the Moabites, all strong, able-bodied men; not a man escaped. ³⁰So Moab was subdued that day under the hand of Israel. And the land had rest for eighty years.

Shamgar

31 After him was Shamgar the son of A'nath, who killed six hundred of the Philis'tines with an oxgoad; and he too delivered Israel.

Deborah and Barak

4 And the sons of Israel again did what was evil in the sight of the LORD, after E'hud died. ²And the LORD sold them into the hand of Ja'bin king of Canaan, who reigned in Ha'zor; the commander of his army was Sis'era, who dwelt in Haro'sheth-ha-goi'im. ³Then the sons of Israel cried to the LORD for help; for he had nine hundred chariots of iron, and oppressed the sons of Israel cruelly for twenty years.

4 Now Deborah, a prophetess, the wife of Lap'pidoth, was judging Israel at that time. ⁵She used to sit under the palm of Deborah between Ra'mah and Bethel in the hill country of E'phraim; and the sons of Israel came up to her for judgment. ⁶She sent and summoned Barak the son of Abin'o-am from Ke'desh in Naph'tali, and said to him, "The LORD, the God of Israel,

---

ᶜ The meaning of the Hebrew word is unknown.

commands you, 'Go, gather your men at Mount Ta'bor, taking ten thousand from the tribe of Naphtali and the tribe of Zeb'ulun. ⁷And I will draw out Sis'era, the general of Ja'bin's army, to meet you by the river Ki'shon with his chariots and his troops; and I will give him into your hand.'" ⁸Barak said to her, "If you will go with me, I will go; but if you will not go with me, I will not go." ⁹And she said, "I will surely go with you; nevertheless, the road on which you are going will not lead to your glory, for the LORD will sell Sis'era into the hand of a woman." Then Deborah arose, and went with Barak to Ke'desh. ¹⁰And Barak summoned Zeb'ulun and Naph'tali to Ke'desh; and ten thousand men went up at his heels; and Deborah went up with him.

11 Now He'ber the Kenite had separated from the Kenites, the descendants of Ho'bab the father-in-law of Moses, and had pitched his tent as far away as the oak in Za-anan'nim, which is near Ke'desh.

12 When Sis'era was told that Barak the son of Abin'o-am had gone up to Mount Ta'bor, ¹³Sis'era called out all his chariots, nine hundred chariots of iron, and all the men who were with him, from Haro'sheth-ha-goi'im to the river Ki'shon. ¹⁴And Deborah said to Barak, "Up! For this is the day in which the LORD has given Sis'era into your hand. Does not the LORD go out before you?" So Barak went down from Mount Ta'bor with ten thousand men following him. ¹⁵And the LORD routed Sis'era and all his chariots and all his army before Barak at the edge of the sword; and Sisera alighted from his chariot and fled away on foot. ¹⁶And Barak pursued the chariots and the army to Haro'sheth-ha-goi'im, and all the army of Sis'era fell by the edge of the sword; not a man was left.

Jael Kills Sisera

17 But Sis'era fled away on foot to the tent of Ja'el, the wife of He'ber the Kenite; for there was peace between Ja'bin the king of Ha'zor and the house of Heber the Kenite. ¹⁸And Ja'el came out to meet Sis'era, and said to him, "Turn aside, my lord, turn aside to me; have no fear." So he turned aside to her into the tent, and she covered him with a rug. ¹⁹And he said to her, "Please, give me a little water to drink; for I am thirsty." So she opened a skin of milk and gave him a drink and covered him. ²⁰And he said to her, "Stand at the door of the tent, and if any man comes and asks you, 'Is any one here?' say, No." ²¹But Ja'el the wife of He'ber took a tent peg, and took a hammer in her hand, and went softly to him and drove the peg into his temple, till it went down into the ground, as he was lying fast asleep from weariness. So she died. ²²And behold, as Barak pursued Sis'era, Ja'el went out to meet him, and said to him, "Come, and I will show you the man whom you are seeking." So he

went in to her tent; and there lay Sisera dead, with the tent peg in his temple.

23 So on that day God subdued Ja'bin the king of Canaan before the sons of Israel. ²⁴And the hand of the sons of Israel bore harder and harder on Ja'bin the king of Canaan, until they destroyed Jabin king of Canaan.

The Song of Deborah

5 Then sang Deborah and Barak the son of Abin'o-am on that day: *

²"That the leaders took the lead in Israel,
    that the people offered themselves willingly,
    bless ᵈ the LORD!

³"Hear, O kings; give ear, O princes;
    to the LORD I will sing,
    I will make melody to the LORD, the God of Israel.

⁴"LORD, when you went forth from Se'ir,
    when you marched from the region of E'dom,
the earth trembled,
    and the heavens dropped,
    yes, the clouds dropped water.
⁵The mountains quaked before the LORD,
    the One of Sinai, before the LORD, the God of Israel.

⁶"In the days of Shamgar, son of A'nath,
    in the days of Ja'el, caravans ceased
    and travelers kept to the byways.
⁷The peasantry ceased in Israel, they ceased
    until you arose, Deborah,
    arose as a mother in Israel.
⁸When new gods were chosen,
    then war was in the gates.
Was shield or spear to be seen
    among forty thousand in Israel?
⁹My heart goes out to the commanders of Israel
    who offered themselves willingly among the people.
    Bless the LORD.

¹⁰"Tell of it, you who ride on tawny donkeys,
    you who sit on rich carpets ᵉ
    and you who walk by the way.
¹¹To the sound of musicians ᵉ at the watering places,
    there they repeat the triumphs of the LORD,
    the triumphs of his peasantry in Israel.

"Then down to the gates marched
    the people of the LORD.

ᵈ Or *You who offered yourselves willingly among the people, bless.*
ᵉ The meaning of the Hebrew word is uncertain.
* 5:1: The song of Deborah gives an alternative to the prose account of the previous chapter. Though touched up by later editors, it is very ancient and gives a valuable picture of the state of Israel in the thirteenth century B.C.

12"Awake, awake, Deborah!
  Awake, awake, utter a song!
Arise, Barak, lead away your captives,
  O son of Abin'o-am.
13Then down marched the remnant of the
    noble;
  the people of the LORD marched down for
    him f against the mighty.
14From E'phraim they set out there ˣ into the
    valley, ᵍ
  following you, Benjamin, with your
    kinsmen;
from Ma'chir marched down the commanders,
  and from Zeb'ulun those who bear the
    marshal's staff;
15the princes of Is'sachar came with Deborah,
  and Issachar faithful to Barak;
  into the valley they rushed forth at his
    heels.
Among the clans of Reuben
  there were great searchings of heart.
16Why did you tarry among the sheepfolds,
  to hear the piping for the flocks?
Among the clans of Reuben
  there were great searchings of heart.
17Gilead stayed beyond the Jordan;
  and Dan, why did he abide with the ships?
Asher sat still at the coast of the sea,
  settling down by his landings.
18Zeb'ulun is a people that jeoparded their lives
    to the death;
  Naph'tali too, on the heights of the field.

19"The kings came, they fought;
  then fought the kings of Canaan,
at Ta'anach, by the waters of Megid'do;
  they got no spoils of silver.
20From heaven fought the stars,
  from their courses they fought against
    Sis'era.
21The torrent Ki'shon swept them away,
  the onrushing torrent, the torrent Kishon.
March on, my soul, with might!

22"Then loud beat the horses' hoofs
  with the galloping, galloping of his steeds.

23"Curse Me'roz, says the angel of the LORD,
  curse bitterly its inhabitants,
because they came not to the help of the LORD,
  to the help of the LORD against the mighty.

24"Most blessed of women be Ja'el,
  the wife of He'ber the Kenite,
  of tent-dwelling women most blessed.
25He asked for water and she gave him milk,
  she brought him curds in a lordly bowl.
26She put her hand to the tent peg
  and her right hand to the workmen's mallet;

she struck Sis'era a blow,
  she crushed his head,
  she shattered and pierced his temple.
27He sank, he fell,
  he lay still at her feet;
at her feet he sank, he fell;
  where he sank, there he fell dead.

28"Out of the window she peered,
  the mother of Sis'era gazed ʰ through the
    lattice:
'Why is his chariot so long in coming?
  Why do the hoofbeats of his chariots
    tarry?'
29Her wisest ladies make answer,
  no, she gives answer to herself,
30'Are they not finding and dividing the spoil?—
  A maiden or two for every man;
spoil of dyed stuffs for Sis'era,
  spoil of dyed stuffs embroidered,
  two pieces of dyed work embroidered for
    my neck as spoil?'

31"So perish all your enemies, O LORD!
  But your friends be like the sun as he rises
    in his might."

And the land had rest for forty years.

The Midianite Oppression

6 The sons of Israel did what was evil in the
sight of the LORD; and the LORD gave them
into the hand of Mid'ian seven years. 2And the
hand of Mid'ian prevailed over Israel; and because of Midian the sons of Israel made for themselves the dens which are in the mountains, and
the caves and the strongholds. 3For whenever the
Israelites put in seed the Mid'ianites and the
Amal'ekites and the people of the East would
come up and attack them; 4they would encamp
against them and destroy the produce of the land,
as far as the neighborhood of Gaza, and leave no
sustenance in Israel, and no sheep or ox or donkey. 5For they would come up with their cattle
and their tents, coming like locusts for number;
both they and their camels could not be counted;
so that they wasted the land as they came in.
6And Israel was brought very low because of
Mid'ian; and the sons of Israel cried for help to
the LORD.

7 When the sons of Israel cried to the LORD on
account of the Mid'ianites, 8the LORD sent a
prophet to the sons of Israel; and he said to them,
"Thus says the LORD, the God of Israel: I led you
up from Egypt, and brought you out of the house

---

f Gk: Heb *me*.
ˣ Cn: Heb *From Ephraim their root*.
ᵍ Gk: Heb *in Amalek*.
ʰ Gk Compare Tg: Heb *exclaimed*.
5:31: Rev 1:16.

of bondage; [9]and I delivered you from the hand of the Egyptians, and from the hand of all who oppressed you, and drove them out before you, and gave you their land; [10]and I said to you, 'I am the LORD your God; you shall not pay reverence to the gods of the Am'orites, in whose land you dwell.' But you have not given heed to my voice."

The Call of Gideon

11 Now the angel of the LORD came and sat under the oak at Oph'rah, which belonged to Jo'ash the Abiez'rite, as his son Gideon was beating out wheat in the wine press, to hide it from the Mid'ianites. [12]And the angel of the LORD appeared to him and said to him, "The LORD is with you, you mighty man of valor." [13]And Gideon said to him, "Please, sir, if the LORD is with us, why then has all this befallen us? And where are all his wonderful deeds which our fathers recounted to us, saying, 'Did not the LORD bring us up from Egypt?' But now the LORD has cast us off, and given us into the hand of Mid'ian." [14]And the LORD turned to him and said, "Go in this might of yours and deliver Israel from the hand of Mid'ian; do not I send you?" [15]And he said to him, "Please, Lord, how can I deliver Israel? Behold, my clan is the weakest in Manas'seh, and I am the least in my family." [16]And the LORD said to him, "But I will be with you, and you shall strike the Mid'ianites as one man." [17]And he said to him, "If now I have found favor with you, then show me a sign that it is you who speak with me. [18]Do not depart from here, I beg you, until I come to you, and bring out my present, and set it before you." And he said, "I will stay till you return."

19 So Gideon went into his house and prepared a kid, and unleavened cakes from an ephah of flour; the meat he put in a basket, and the broth he put in a pot, and brought them to him under the oak and presented them. [20]And the angel of God said to him, "Take the meat and the unleavened cakes, and put them on this rock, and pour the broth over them." And he did so. [21]Then the angel of the LORD reached out the tip of the staff that was in his hand, and touched the meat and the unleavened cakes; and there sprang up fire from the rock and consumed the flesh and the unleavened cakes; and the angel of the LORD vanished from his sight. [22]Then Gideon perceived that he was the angel of the LORD; and Gideon said, "Alas, O Lord GOD! For now I have seen the angel of the LORD face to face." [23]But the LORD said to him, "Peace be to you; do not fear, you shall not die." [24]Then Gideon built an altar there to the LORD, and called it, The LORD is peace. To this day it still stands at Oph'rah, which belongs to Abiez'rites.

25 That night the LORD said to him, "Take your father's bull, the second bull seven years old, and pull down the altar of Ba'al which your father has, and cut down the Ashe'rah that is beside it; [26]and build an altar to the LORD your God on the top of the stronghold here, with stones laid in due order; then take the second bull, and offer it as a burnt offering with the wood of the Ashe'rah which you shall cut down." [27]So Gideon took ten men of his servants, and did as the LORD had told him; but because he was too afraid of his family and the men of the town to do it by day, he did it by night.

Gideon Destroys the Altar of Baal

28 When the men of the town rose early in the morning, behold, the altar of Ba'al was broken down, and the Ashe'rah beside it was cut down, and the second bull was offered upon the altar which had been built. [29]And they said to one another, "Who has done this thing?" And after they had made search and inquired, they said, "Gideon the son of Jo'ash has done this thing." [30]Then the men of the town said to Jo'ash, "Bring out your son, that he may die, for he has pulled down the altar of Ba'al and cut down the Ashe'rah beside it." [31]But Jo'ash said to all who were arrayed against him, "Will you contend for Ba'al? Or will you defend his cause? Whoever contends for him shall be put to death by morning. If he is a god, let him contend for himself, because his altar has been pulled down." [32]Therefore on that day he was called Jerubba'al, that is to say, "Let Ba'al contend against him," because he pulled down his altar.

33 Then all the Mid'ianites and the Amal'ekites and the people of the East came together, and crossing the Jordan they encamped in the Valley of Jezre'el. [34]But the Spirit of the LORD took possession of Gideon; and he sounded the trumpet, and the Abiez'rites were called out to follow him. [35]And he sent messengers throughout all Manas'seh; and they too were called out to follow him. And he sent messengers to Asher, Zeb'ulun, and Naph'tali; and they went up to meet them.

The Sign of the Fleece

36 Then Gideon said to God, "If you will deliver Israel by my hand, as you have said, [37]behold, I am laying a fleece of wool on the threshing floor; if there is dew on the fleece alone, and it is dry on all the ground, then I shall know that you will deliver Israel by my hand, as you have said." [38]And it was so. When he rose early next morning and squeezed the fleece, he wrung enough dew from the fleece to fill a bowl with water. [39]Then Gideon said to God, "Let not your anger burn against me, let me speak but this once; please, let me make trial only this once with the fleece; please, let it be dry only on the fleece, and on all the ground let there be dew." [40]And God did so that night; for it was dry on the fleece only, and on all the ground there was dew.

Gideon's Army Selected

7 Then Jerubba'al (that is, Gideon) and all the people who were with him rose early and encamped beside the spring of Harod; and the camp of Mid'ian was north of them, by the hill of Mo'reh, in the valley.

2 The Lord said to Gideon, "The people with you are too many for me to give the Mid'ianites into their hand, lest Israel vaunt themselves against me, saying, 'My own hand has delivered me.' ³Now therefore proclaim in the ears of the people, saying, 'Whoever is fearful and trembling, let him return home.'" And Gideon tested them; [i] twenty-two thousand returned, and ten thousand remained.

4 And the Lord said to Gideon, "The people are still too many; take them down to the water and I will test them for you there; and he of whom I say to you, 'This man shall go with you,' shall go with you; and any of whom I say to you, 'This man shall not go with you,' shall not go." ⁵So he brought the people down to the water; and the Lord said to Gideon, "Every one that laps the water with his tongue, as a dog laps, you shall set by himself; likewise every one that kneels down to drink." ⁶And the number of those that lapped, putting their hands to their mouths, was three hundred men; but all the rest of the people knelt down to drink water. ⁷And the Lord said to Gideon, "With the three hundred men that lapped I will deliver you and give the Mid'ianites into your hand; and let all the others go every man to his home." ⁸So he took the jars of the people from their hands, [j] and their trumpets; and he sent all the rest of Israel every man to his tent, but retained the three hundred men; and the camp of Mid'ian was below him in the valley.

Gideon Routs the Midianites

9 That same night the Lord said to him, "Arise, go down against the camp; for I have given it into your hand. ¹⁰But if you fear to go down, go down to the camp with Pu'rah your servant; ¹¹and you shall hear what they say, and afterward your hands shall be strengthened to go down against the camp." Then he went down with Pu'rah his servant to the outposts of the armed men that were in the camp. ¹²And the Mid'ianites and the Amal'ekites and all the people of the East lay along the valley like locusts for multitude; and their camels were without number, as the sand which is upon the seashore for multitude. ¹³When Gideon came, behold, a man was telling a dream to his comrade; and he said, "Behold, I dreamed a dream; and a cake of barley bread tumbled into the camp of Mid'ian, and came to the tent, and struck it so that it fell, and turned it upside down, so that the tent lay flat." ¹⁴And his comrade answered, "This is no other than the sword of Gideon the son of Jo'ash, a man of Israel; into his hand God has given Mid'ian and all the host."

15 When Gideon heard the telling of the dream and its interpretation, he worshiped; and he returned to the camp of Israel, and said, "Arise; for the Lord has given the host of Mid'ian into your hand." ¹⁶And he divided the three hundred men into three companies, and put trumpets into the hands of all of them and empty jars, with torches inside the jars. ¹⁷And he said to them, "Look at me, and do likewise; when I come to the outskirts of the camp, do as I do. ¹⁸When I blow the trumpet, I and all who are with me, then blow the trumpets also on every side of all the camp, and shout, 'For the Lord and for Gideon.'"

19 So Gideon and the hundred men who were with him came to the outskirts of the camp at the beginning of the middle watch, when they had just set the watch; and they blew the trumpets and smashed the jars that were in their hands. ²⁰And the three companies blew the trumpets and broke the jars, holding in their left hands the torches, and in their right hands the trumpets to blow; and they cried, "A sword for the Lord and for Gideon!" ²¹They stood every man in his place round about the camp, and all the army ran; they cried out and fled. ²²When they blew the three hundred trumpets, the Lord set every man's sword against his fellow and against all the army; and the army fled as far as Beth-shit'tah toward Zer'erah, [k] as far as the border of Abel-meho'lah, by Tabbath. ²³And the men of Israel were called out from Naph'tali and from Asher and from all Manas'seh, and they pursued after Mid'ian.

24 And Gideon sent messengers throughout all the hill country of E'phraim, saying, "Come down against the Mid'ianites and seize the waters against them, as far as Beth-bar'ah, and also the Jordan." So all the men of Ephraim were called out, and they seized the waters as far as Beth-barah, and also the Jordan. ²⁵And they took the two princes of Mid'ian, Or'eb and Ze'eb; they killed Oreb at the rock of Oreb, and Zeeb they killed at the wine press of Zeeb, as they pursued Midian; and they brought the heads of Oreb and Zeeb to Gideon beyond the Jordan.

Gideon's Triumph

8 And the men of E'phraim said to him, "What is this that you have done to us, not to call us when you went to fight with Mid'ian?" And they upbraided him violently. ²And he said to them, "What have I done now in comparison with you? Is not the gleaning of the grapes of E'phraim better than the vintage of Abie'zer? ³God has

---

[i] Cn: Heb *and depart from Mount Gilead.*
[j] Cn: Heb *the people took provisions in their hands.*
[k] Another reading is *Zeredah.*

given into your hands the princes of Mid'ian, Or'eb and Ze'eb; what have I been able to do in comparison with you?" Then their anger against him was abated, when he had said this.

4 And Gideon came to the Jordan and passed over, he and the three hundred men who were with him, faint yet pursuing. ⁵So he said to the men of Succoth, "Please, give loaves of bread to the people who follow me; for they are faint, and I am pursuing after Zebah and Zalmun'na, the kings of Mid'ian." ⁶And the officials of Succoth said, "Are Zebah and Zalmun'na already in your hand, that we should give bread to your army?" ⁷And Gideon said, "Well then, when the Lord has given Zebah and Zalmun'na into my hand, I will flail your flesh with the thorns of the wilderness and with briers." ⁸And from there he went up to Penu'el, and spoke to them in the same way; and the men of Penuel answered him as the men of Succoth had answered. ⁹And he said to the men of Penu'el, "When I come again in peace, I will break down this tower."

10 Now Zebah and Zalmun'na were in Karkor with their army, about fifteen thousand men, all who were left of all the army of the people of the East; for there had fallen a hundred and twenty thousand men who drew the sword. ¹¹And Gideon went up by the caravan route east of No'bah and Jog'behah, and attacked the army; for the army was off its guard. ¹²And Zebah and Zalmun'na fled; and he pursued them and took the two kings of Mid'ian, Zebah and Zalmunna, and he threw all the army into a panic.

13 Then Gideon the son of Jo'ash returned from the battle by the ascent of He'res. ¹⁴And he caught a young man of Succoth, and questioned him; and he wrote down for him the officials and elders of Succoth, seventy-seven men. ¹⁵And he came to the men of Succoth, and said, "Behold Zebah and Zalmun'na, about whom you taunted me, saying, 'Are Zebah and Zalmunna already in your hand, that we should give bread to your men who are faint?'" ¹⁶And he took the elders of the city and he took thorns of the wilderness and briers and with them taught the men of Succoth. ¹⁷And he broke down the tower of Penu'el, and slew the men of the city.

18 Then he said to Zebah and Zalmun'na, "Where are the men whom you slew at Ta'bor?" They answered, "As you are, so were they, every one of them; they resembled the sons of a king." ¹⁹And he said, "They were my brothers, the sons of my mother; as the Lord lives, if you had saved them alive, I would not slay you." ²⁰And he said to Je'ther his first-born, "Rise, and slay them." But the youth did not draw his sword; for he was afraid, because he was still a youth. ²¹Then Zebah and Zalmun'na said, "Rise yourself, and fall upon us; for as the man is, so is his strength." And

Gideon arose and slew Zebah and Zalmunna; and he took the crescents that were on the necks of their camels.

Gideon's Ephod Becomes a Snare

22 Then the men of Israel said to Gideon, "Rule over us, you and your son and your grandson also; for you have delivered us out of the hand of Mid'ian." ²³Gideon said to them, "I will not rule over you, and my son will not rule over you; the Lord will rule over you." * ²⁴And Gideon said to them, "Let me make a request of you; give me every man of you the earrings of his spoil." (For they had golden earrings, because they were Ish'maelites.) ²⁵And they answered, "We will willingly give them." And they spread a garment, and every man cast in it the earrings of his spoil. ²⁶And the weight of the golden earrings that he requested was one thousand seven hundred shekels of gold; besides the crescents and the pendants and the purple garments worn by the kings of Mid'ian, and besides the collars that were about the necks of their camels. ²⁷And Gideon made an ephod of it and put it in his city, in Oph'rah; and all Israel played the harlot after it there, and it became a snare to Gideon and to his family. ²⁸So Mid'ian was subdued before the sons of Israel, and they lifted up their heads no more. And the land had rest forty years in the days of Gideon.

The Death of Gideon

29 Jerubba'al the son of Jo'ash went and dwelt in his own house. ³⁰Now Gideon had seventy sons, his own offspring, for he had many wives. ³¹And his concubine who was in She'chem also bore him a son, and he called his name Abim'elech. ³²And Gideon the son of Jo'ash died in a good old age, and was buried in the tomb of Jo'ash his father, at Oph'rah of the Abiez'rites.

33 As soon as Gideon died, the sons of Israel turned again and played the harlot after the Ba'als, and made Ba'al-be'rith their god. ³⁴And the sons of Israel did not remember the Lord their God, who had rescued them from the hand of all their enemies on every side; ³⁵and they did not show kindness to the family of Jerubba'al (that is, Gideon) in return for all the good that he had done to Israel.

Abimelech Tries to Establish a Monarchy

9 Now Abim'elech the son of Jerubba'al went to She'chem to his mother's kinsmen and said to them and to the whole clan of his mother's family, ²"Say in the ears of all the citizens of She'chem, 'Which is better for you, that all seventy of the sons of Jerubba'al rule over you, or that one rule over you?' Remember also that I am your bone and your flesh." ³And his mother's

---

* 8:23: It appears from the sequel that Gideon did in fact become a king even if he refused the title; but the idea of an hereditary monarchy was still unacceptable, as the following history of Abimelech shows.

kinsmen spoke all these words on his behalf in the ears of all the men of She'chem; and their hearts inclined to follow Abim'elech, for they said, "He is our brother." [4]And they gave him seventy pieces of silver out of the house of Ba'al-be'rith with which Abim'elech hired worthless and reckless fellows, who followed him. [5]And he went to his father's house at Oph'rah, and slew his brothers the sons of Jerubba'al, seventy men, upon one stone; but Jo'tham the youngest son of Jerubbaal was left, for he hid himself. [6]And all the citizens of She'chem came together, and all Beth-mil'lo, and they went and made Abim'elech king, by the oak of the pillar at Shechem.

Jotham's Parable
of the Trees, Vine, and Bramble

[7] When it was told to Jo'tham, he went and stood on the top of Mount Ger'izim, and cried aloud and said to them, "Listen to me, you men of She'chem, that God may listen to you. [8]The trees once went forth to anoint a king over them; and they said to the olive tree, 'Reign over us.' [9]But the olive tree said to them, 'Shall I leave my fatness, by which gods and men are honored, and go to sway over the trees?' [10]And the trees said to the fig tree, 'Come you, and reign over us.' [11]But the fig tree said to them, 'Shall I leave my sweetness and my good fruit, and go to sway over the trees?' [12]And the trees said to the vine, 'Come you, and reign over us.' [13]But the vine said to them, 'Shall I leave my wine which cheers gods and men, and go to sway over the trees?' [14]Then all the trees said to the bramble, 'Come you, and reign over us.' [15]And the bramble said to the trees, 'If in good faith you are anointing me king over you, then come and take refuge in my shade; but if not, let fire come out of the bramble and devour the cedars of Lebanon.'

[16] "Now therefore, if you acted in good faith and honor when you made Abim'elech king, and if you have dealt well with Jerubba'al and his house, and have done to him as his deeds deserved—[17]for my father fought for you, and risked his life, and rescued you from the hand of Mid'ian; [18]and you have risen up against my father's house this day, and have slain his sons, seventy men on one stone, and have made Abim'elech, the son of his maidservant, king over the citizens of She'chem, because he is your kinsman—[19]if you then have acted in good faith and honor with Jerubba'al and with his house this day, then rejoice in Abim'elech, and let him also rejoice in you; [20]but if not, let fire come out from Abim'elech, and devour the citizens of She'chem, and Beth-mil'lo; and let fire come out from the citizens of Shechem, and from Beth-millo, and devour Abimelech." [21]And Jo'tham ran away and fled, and went to Be'er and dwelt there, for fear of Abim'elech his brother.

The Downfall of Abimelech

[22] Abim'elech ruled over Israel three years. [23]And God sent an evil spirit between Abim'elech and the men of She'chem; and the men of Shechem dealt treacherously with Abimelech; [24]that the violence done to the seventy sons of Jerubba'al might come and their blood be laid upon Abim'elech their brother, who slew them, and upon the men of She'chem, who strengthened his hands to slay his brothers. [25]And the men of She'chem put men in ambush against him on the mountain tops, and they robbed all who passed by them along that way; and it was told Abim'elech.

[26] And Ga'al the son of E'bed moved into She'-chem with his kinsmen; and the men of Shechem put confidence in him. [27]And they went out into the field, and gathered the grapes from their vineyards and trod them, and held festival, and went into the house of their god, and ate and drank and reviled Abim'elech. [28]And Ga'al the son of E'bed said, "Who is Abim'elech, and who are we of She'chem, that we should serve him? Did not the son of Jerubba'al and Ze'bul his officer serve the men of Ha'mor the father of Shechem? Why then should we serve him? [29]Would that this people were under my hand! then I would remove Abim'e-lech. I would say [1] to Abimelech, 'Increase your army, and come out.'"

[30] When Ze'bul the ruler of the city heard the words of Ga'al the son of E'bed, his anger was kindled. [31]And he sent messengers to Abim'elech at Aru'mah,[m] saying, "Behold, Ga'al the son of E'bed and his kinsmen have come to She'chem, and they are stirring up [n] the city against you. [32]Now therefore, go by night, you and the men that are with you, and lie in wait in the fields. [33]Then in the morning, as soon as the sun is up, rise early and rush upon the city; and when he and the men that are with him come out against you, you may do to them as occasion offers."

[34] And Abim'elech and all the men that were with him rose up by night, and laid wait against She'chem in four companies. [35]And Ga'al the son of E'bed went out and stood in the entrance of the gate of the city; and Abim'elech and the men that were with him rose from the ambush. [36]And when Ga'al saw the men, he said to Ze'bul, "Look, men are coming down from the mountain tops!" And Zebul said to him, "You see the shadow of the mountains as if they were men." [37]Ga'al spoke again and said, "Look, men are coming down from the center of the land, and one company is coming from the direction of the Diviners' Oak." [38]Then Ze'bul said to him, "Where is your mouth now, you who said, 'Who is Abim'elech, that we should serve him?' Are not

[1] Gk: Heb and he said.
[m] Cn See 9:41. Heb Tormah.
[n] Cn: Heb besieging.

these the men whom you despised? Go out now and fight with them." [39]And Ga′al went out at the head of the men of She′chem, and fought with Abim′elech. [40]And Abim′elech chased him, and he fled before him; and many fell wounded, up to the entrance of the gate. [41]And Abim′elech dwelt at Aru′mah; and Ze′bul drove out Ga′al and his kinsmen, so that they could not live on at She′chem.

42 On the following day the men went out into the fields. And Abim′elech was told. [43]He took his men and divided them into three companies, and laid wait in the fields; and he looked and saw the men coming out of the city, and he rose against them and slew them. [44]Abim′elech and the company° that was with him rushed forward and stood at the entrance of the gate of the city, while the two companies rushed upon all who were in the fields and slew them. [45]And Abim′elech fought against the city all that day; he took the city, and killed the people that were in it; and he razed the city and sowed it with salt.

46 When all the people of the Tower of She′-chem heard of it, they entered the stronghold of the house of El-be′rith. [47]Abim′elech was told that all the people of the Tower of She′chem were gathered together. [48]And Abim′elech went up to Mount Zalmon, he and all the men that were with him; and Abimelech took an axe in his hand, and cut down a bundle of brushwood, and took it up and laid it on his shoulder. And he said to the men that were with him, "What you have seen me do, make haste to do, as I have done." [49]So every one of the people cut down his bundle and following Abim′-elech put it against the stronghold, and they set the stronghold on fire over them, so that all the people of the Tower of She′chem also died, about a thousand men and women.

50 Then Abim′elech went to The′bez, and encamped against Thebez, and took it. [51]But there was a strong tower within the city, and all the people of the city fled to it, all the men and women, and shut themselves in; and they went to the roof of the tower. [52]And Abim′elech came to the tower, and fought against it, and drew near to the door of the tower to burn it with fire. [53]And a certain woman threw an upper millstone upon Abim′elech's head, and crushed his skull. [54]Then he called hastily to the young man his armor-bearer, and said to him, "Draw your sword and kill me, lest men say of me, 'A woman killed him.'" And his young man thrust him through, and he died. [55]And when the men of Israel saw that Abim′elech was dead, they departed every man to his home. [56]Thus God repaid the crime of Abim′elech, which he committed against his father in killing his seventy brothers; [57]and God also made all the wickedness of the men of She′chem fall back upon their heads, and upon

them came the curse of Jo′tham the son of Jerubba′al.

Tola and Jair

10 After Abim′elech there arose to deliver Israel Tola the son of Puah, son of Dodo, a man of Is′sachar; and he lived at Sha′mir in the hill country of E′phraim. [2]And he judged Israel twenty-three years. Then he died, and was buried at Sha′mir.

3 After him arose Ja′ir the Gileadite, who judged Israel twenty-two years. [4]And he had thirty sons who rode on thirty donkeys; and they had thirty cities, called Hav′voth-ja′ir to this day, which are in the land of Gilead. [5]And Ja′ir died, and was buried in Kamon.

Oppression by the Philistines and Ammonites

6 And the sons of Israel again did what was evil in the sight of the Lord, and served the Ba′als and the Ash′taroth, the gods of Syria, the gods of Sidon, the gods of Moab, the gods of the Am′monites, and the gods of the Philis′tines; and they forsook the Lord, and did not serve him. [7]And the anger of the Lord was kindled against Israel, and he sold them into the hand of the Philis′tines and into the hand of the Am′monites, [8]and they crushed and oppressed the children of Israel that year. For eighteen years they oppressed all the sons of Israel that were beyond the Jordan in the land of the Am′orites, which is in Gilead. [9]And the Am′monites crossed the Jordan to fight also against Judah and against Benjamin and against the house of E′phraim; so that Israel was sorely distressed.

10 And the sons of Israel cried to the Lord, saying, "We have sinned against you, because we have forsaken our God and have served the Ba′als." [11]And the Lord said to the sons of Israel, "Did I not deliver you from the Egyptians and from the Am′orites, from the Am′monites and from the Philis′tines? [12]The Sido′nians also, and the Amal′ekites, and the Ma′onites, oppressed you; and you cried to me, and I delivered you out of their hand. [13]Yet you have forsaken me and served other gods; therefore I will deliver you no more. [14]Go and cry to the gods whom you have chosen; let them deliver you in the time of your distress." [15]And the sons of Israel said to the Lord, "We have sinned; do to us whatever seems good to you; only deliver us, we beg you, this day." [16]So they put away the foreign gods from among them and served the Lord; and he became indignant over the misery of Israel.

17 Then the Am′monites were called to arms, and they encamped in Gilead; and the sons of Israel came together, and they encamped at Mizpah. [18]And the people, the leaders of Gilead, said one to another, "Who is the man that will

° Vg and some Mss of Gk: Heb *companies*.

begin to fight against the Am'monites? He shall be head over all the inhabitants of Gilead."

Jephthah

11 Now Jephthah the Gileadite was a mighty warrior, but he was the son of a harlot. Gilead was the father of Jephthah. ²And Gilead's wife also bore him sons; and when his wife's sons grew up, they thrust Jephthah out, and said to him, "You shall not inherit in our father's house; for you are the son of another woman." ³Then Jephthah fled from his brothers, and dwelt in the land of Tob; and worthless fellows collected round Jephthah, and went raiding with him.

4 After a time the Am'monites made war against Israel. ⁵And when the Am'monites made war against Israel, the elders of Gilead went to bring Jephthah from the land of Tob; ⁶and they said to Jephthah, "Come and be our leader, that we may fight with the Am'monites." ⁷But Jephthah said to the elders of Gilead, "Did you not hate me, and drive me out of my father's house? Why have you come to me now when you are in trouble?" ⁸And the elders of Gilead said to Jephthah, "That is why we have turned to you now, that you may go with us and fight with the Am'monites, and be our head over all the inhabitants of Gilead." ⁹Jephthah said to the elders of Gilead, "If you bring me home again to fight with the Am'monites, and the LORD gives them over to me, I will be your head." ¹⁰And the elders of Gilead said to Jephthah, "The LORD will be witness between us; we will surely do as you say." ¹¹So Jephthah went with the elders of Gilead, and the people made him head and leader over them; and Jephthah spoke all his words before the LORD at Mizpah.

12 Then Jephthah sent messengers to the king of the Am'monites and said, "What have you against me, that you have come to me to fight against my land?" ¹³And the king of the Am'monites answered the messengers of Jephthah, "Because Israel on coming from Egypt took away my land, from the Arnon to the Jabbok and to the Jordan; now therefore restore it peaceably." ¹⁴And Jephthah sent messengers again to the king of the Am'monites ¹⁵and said to him, "Thus says Jephthah: Israel did not take away the land of Moab or the land of the Am'monites, ¹⁶but when they came up from Egypt, Israel went through the wilderness to the Red Sea and came to Ka'desh. ¹⁷Israel then sent messengers to the king of E'dom, saying, 'Let us pass, we beg, through your land'; but the king of Edom would not listen. And they sent also to the king of Moab, but he would not consent. So Israel remained at Ka'desh. ¹⁸Then they journeyed through the wilderness, and went around the land of E'dom and the land of Moab, and arrived on the east side of the land of Moab, and camped on the other

side of the Arnon; but they did not enter the territory of Moab, for the Arnon was the boundary of Moab. ¹⁹Israel then sent messengers to Si'hon king of the Am'orites, king of Heshbon; and Israel said to him, 'Let us pass, we beg, through your land to our country.' ²⁰But Si'hon did not trust Israel to pass through his territory; so Sihon gathered all his people together, and encamped at Ja'haz, and fought with Israel. ²¹And the LORD, the God of Israel, gave Si'hon and all his people into the hand of Israel, and they defeated them; so Israel took possession of all the land of the Am'orites, who inhabited that country. ²²And they took possession of all the territory of the Am'orites from the Arnon to the Jabbok and from the wilderness to the Jordan. ²³So then the LORD, the God of Israel, dispossessed the Am'orites from before his people Israel; and are you to take possession of them? ²⁴Will you not possess what Che'mosh your god gives you to possess? And all that the LORD our God has dispossessed before us, we will possess. ²⁵Now are you any better than Balak the son of Zippor, king of Moab? Did he ever strive against Israel, or did he ever go to war with them? ²⁶While Israel dwelt in Heshbon and its villages, and in Aro'er and its villages, and in all the cities that are on the banks of the Arnon, three hundred years, why did you not recover them within that time? ²⁷I therefore have not sinned against you, and you do me wrong by making war on me; the LORD, the Judge, decide this day between the sons of Israel and the people of Ammon." ²⁸But the king of the Am'monites did not heed the message of Jephthah which he sent to him.

Jephthah's Vow

29 Then the Spirit of the LORD came upon Jephthah, and he passed through Gilead and Manas'seh, and passed on to Mizpah of Gilead, and from Mizpah of Gilead he passed on to the Am'monites. ³⁰And Jephthah made a vow to the LORD, and said, "If you will give the Am'monites into my hand, ³¹then whoever comes forth from the doors of my house to meet me, when I return victorious from the Am'monites, shall be the LORD's, and I will offer him up for a burnt offering." ³²So Jephthah crossed over to the Am'monites to fight against them; and the LORD gave them into his hand. ³³And he struck them from Aro'er to the neighborhood of Minnith, twenty cities, and as far as A'bel-ker'amim, with a very great slaughter. So the Am'monites were subdued before the sons of Israel.

Jephthah's Daughter

34 Then Jephthah came to his home at Mizpah; and behold, his daughter came out to meet him with timbrels and with dances; she was his only child; beside her he had neither son nor daughter. ³⁵And when he saw her, he tore his clothes, and

said, "Alas, my daughter! you have brought me very low, and you have become the cause of great trouble to me; for I have opened my mouth to the LORD, and I cannot take back my vow." [36]And she said to him, "My father, if you have opened your mouth to the LORD, do to me according to what has gone forth from your mouth, now that the LORD has avenged you on your enemies, on the Am'monites." [37]And she said to her father, "Let this thing be done for me; let me alone two months, that I may go and wander [p] on the mountains, and bewail my virginity, I and my companions." [38]And he said, "Go." And he sent her away for two months; and she departed, she and her companions, and bewailed her virginity upon the mountains. [39]And at the end of two months, she returned to her father, who did with her according to his vow which he had made. * She had never known a man. And it became a custom in Israel [40]that the daughters of Israel went year by year to lament the daughter of Jephthah the Gileadite four days in the year.

Intertribal Fighting

12 The men of E'phraim were called to arms, and they crossed to Za'phon and said to Jephthah, "Why did you cross over to fight against the Am'monites, and did not call us to go with you? We will burn your house over you with fire." [2]And Jephthah said to them, "I and my people had a great feud with the Am'monites; and when I called you, you did not deliver me from their hand. [3]And when I saw that you would not deliver me, I took my life in my hand, and crossed over against the Am'monites, and the LORD gave them into my hand; why then have you come up to me this day, to fight against me?" [4]Then Jephthah gathered all the men of Gilead and fought with E'phraim; and the men of Gilead struck Ephraim, because they said, "You are fugitives of Ephraim, you Gileadites, in the midst of Ephraim and Manas'seh." [5]And the Gileadites took the fords of the Jordan against the E'phraimites. And when any of the fugitives of E'phraim said, "Let me go over," the men of Gilead said to him, "Are you an Ephraimite?" When he said, "No," [6]they said to him, "Then say Shib'boleth," and he said, "Sib'boleth," for he could not pronounce it right; then they seized him and slew him at the fords of the Jordan. And there fell at that time forty-two thousand of the E'phraimites.

[7]Jephthah judged Israel six years. Then Jephthah the Gileadite died, and was buried in his city in Gilead. [q]

Ibzan, Elon, and Abdon

[8]After him Ibzan of Bethlehem judged Israel. [9]He had thirty sons; and thirty daughters he gave in marriage outside his clan, and thirty daughters he brought in from outside for his sons. And he judged Israel seven years. [10]Then Ibzan died, and was buried at Bethlehem.

11 After him E'lon the Zeb'ulunite judged Israel; and he judged Israel ten years. [12]Then E'lon the Zeb'ulunite died, and was buried at Ai'jalon in the land of Zeb'ulun.

13 After him Abdon the son of Hillel the Pir'athonite judged Israel. [14]He had forty sons and thirty grandsons, who rode on seventy donkeys; and he judged Israel eight years. [15]Then Abdon the son of Hillel the Pir'athonite died, and was buried at Pir'athon in the land of E'phraim, in the hill country of the Amal'ekites.

The Birth of Samson

13 [†] And the sons of Israel again did what was evil in the sight of the LORD; and the LORD gave them into the hand of the Philis'tines for forty years.

2 And there was a certain man of Zorah, of the tribe of the Da'nites, whose name was Mano'ah; and his wife was barren and had no children. [3]And the angel of the LORD appeared to the woman and said to her, "Behold, you are barren and have no children; but you shall conceive and bear a son. [4]Therefore beware, and drink no wine or strong drink, and eat nothing unclean, [5]for behold, you shall conceive and bear a son. No razor shall come upon his head, for the boy shall be a Naz'irite to God from birth; and he shall begin to deliver Israel from the hand of the Philis'tines." [6]Then the woman came and told her husband, "A man of God came to me, and his countenance was like the countenance of the angel of God, very terrible; I did not ask him where he was from, and he did not tell me his name; [7]but he said to me, 'Behold, you shall conceive and bear a son; so then drink no wine or strong drink, and eat nothing unclean, for the boy shall be a Naz'irite to God from birth to the day of his death.'"

8 Then Mano'ah entreated the LORD, and said, "O, LORD, I beg you, let the man of God whom you sent come again to us, and teach us what we are to do with the boy that will be born." [9]And God listened to the voice of Mano'ah, and the angel of God came again to the woman as she sat in the field; but Manoah her husband was not with her. [10]And the woman ran in haste and told her husband, "Behold, the man who came to me the other day has appeared to me." [11]And Mano'ah arose and went after his wife and came to the man and said to him, "Are you the man

---

[p] Cn: Heb *go down.*
[q] Gk: Heb *in the cities of Gilead.*
13:4, 5: Lk 1:15.
* 11:39: Human sacrifice, common in Canaan and surrounding lands, was never permitted in Israel; cf. Lev 18:21. The few cases we find were due to foreign influence or to an erroneous conscience; cf. 2 Sam 21:4–6; 2 Kings 23:10.
† 13:1: The "Samson cycle" (chapters 13–16) is built on the theme of the broken vow; cf. 13:4–5. This gives a religious character to what otherwise has the appearance of profane literature.

who spoke to this woman?" And he said, "I am." [12]And Mano'ah said, "Now when your words come true, what is to be the boy's manner of life, and what is he to do?" [13]And the angel of the Lord said to Mano'ah, "Of all that I said to the woman let her beware. [14]She may not eat of anything that comes from the vine, neither let her drink wine or strong drink, or eat any unclean thing; all that I commanded her let her observe."

15 Mano'ah said to the angel of the Lord, "Please, let us detain you, and prepare a kid for you." [16]And the angel of the Lord said to Mano'ah, "If you detain me, I will not eat of your food; but if you make ready a burnt offering, then offer it to the Lord." (For Manoah did not know that he was the angel of the Lord.) [17]And Mano'ah said to the angel of the Lord, "What is your name, so that, when your words come true, we may honor you?" [18]And the angel of the Lord said to him, "Why do you ask my name, seeing it is wonderful?" [19]So Mano'ah took the kid with the cereal offering, and offered it upon the rock to the Lord, to him who works ˣ wonders.ˢ [20]And when the flame went up toward heaven from the altar, the angel of the Lord ascended in the flame of the altar while Mano'ah and his wife looked on; and they fell on their faces to the ground.

21 The angel of the Lord appeared no more to Mano'ah and to his wife. Then Manoah knew that he was the angel of the Lord. [22]And Mano'ah said to his wife, "We shall surely die, for we have seen God." [23]But his wife said to him, "If the Lord had meant to kill us, he would not have accepted a burnt offering and a cereal offering at our hands, or shown us all these things, or now announced to us such things as these." [24]And the woman bore a son, and called his name Samson; and the boy grew, and the Lord blessed him. [25]And the Spirit of the Lord began to stir him in Ma'haneh-dan, between Zorah and Esh'ta-ol.

Samson's Marriage at Timnah

14 Samson went down to Timnah, and at Timnah he saw one of the daughters of the Philis'tines. [2]Then he came up, and told his father and mother, "I saw one of the daughters of the Philis'tines at Timnah; now get her for me as my wife." [3]But his father and mother said to him, "Is there not a woman among the daughters of your kinsmen, or among all our people, that you must go to take a wife from the uncircumcised Philis'tines?" But Samson said to his father, "Get her for me; for she pleases me well."

4 His father and mother did not know that it was from the Lord; for he was seeking an occasion against the Philis'tines. At that time the Philistines had dominion over Israel.

5 Then Samson went down with his father and mother to Timnah, and he came to the vineyards of Timnah. And behold, a young lion roared against him; [6]and the Spirit of the Lord came mightily upon him, and he tore the lion asunder as one tears a kid; and he had nothing in his hand. But he did not tell his father or his mother what he had done. [7]Then he went down and talked with the woman; and she pleased Samson well. [8]And after a while he returned to take her; and he turned aside to see the carcass of the lion, and behold, there was a swarm of bees in the body of the lion, and honey. [9]He scraped it out into his hands, and went on, eating as he went; and he came to his father and mother, and gave some to them, and they ate. But he did not tell them that he had taken the honey from the carcass of the lion.

10 And his father went down to the woman, and Samson made a feast there; for so the young men used to do. [11]And when the people saw him, they brought thirty companions to be with him. [12]And Samson said to them, "Let me now put a riddle to you; if you can tell me what it is, within the seven days of the feast, and find it out, then I will give you thirty linen garments and thirty festal garments; [13]but if you cannot tell me what it is, then you shall give me thirty linen garments and thirty festal garments." And they said to him, "Put your riddle, that we may hear it." [14]And he said to them,

"Out of the eater came something to eat.

Out of the strong came something sweet."
And they could not in three days tell what the riddle was.

15 On the fourth ᵗ day they said to Samson's wife, "Entice your husband to tell us what the riddle is, lest we burn you and your father's house with fire. Have you invited us here to impoverish us?" [16]And Samson's wife wept before him, and said, "You only hate me, you do not love me; you have put a riddle to my countrymen, and you have not told me what it is." And he said to her, "Behold, I have not told my father nor my mother, and shall I tell you?" [17]She wept before him the seven days that their feast lasted; and on the seventh day he told her, because she pressed him hard. Then she told the riddle to her countrymen. [18]And the men of the city said to him on the seventh day before the sun went down,

"What is sweeter than honey?

What is stronger than a lion?"
And he said to them,

"If you had not plowed with my heifer,

you would not have found out my riddle."
[19]And the Spirit of the Lord came mightily upon him, and he went down to Ash'kelon and killed

---

ˣ Gk Vg: Heb and working.
ˢ Heb wonders, while Manoah and his wife looked on.
ᵗ Gk Syr: Heb seventh.
13:24: Lk 2:40.

thirty men of the town, and took their spoil and gave the festal garments to those who had told the riddle. In hot anger he went back to his father's house. [20]And Samson's wife was given to his companion, who had been his best man.

Samson Defeats the Philistines

15 After a while, at the time of wheat harvest, Samson went to visit his wife with a kid; and he said, "I will go in to my wife in the chamber." But her father would not allow him to go in. [2]And her father said, "I really thought that you utterly hated her; so I gave her to your companion. Is not her younger sister fairer than she? Please take her instead." [3]And Samson said to them, "This time I shall be blameless in regard to the Philis'tines, when I do them mischief." [4]So Samson went and caught three hundred foxes, and took torches; and he turned them tail to tail, and put a torch between each pair of tails. [5]And when he had set fire to the torches, he let the foxes go into the standing grain of the Philis'tines, and burned up the shocks and the standing grain, as well as the olive orchards. [6]Then the Philis'tines said, "Who has done this?" And they said, "Samson, the son-in-law of the Timnite, because he has taken his wife and given her to his companion." And the Philistines came up, and burned her and her father with fire. [7]And Samson said to them, "If this is what you do, I swear I will be avenged upon you, and after that I will quit." [8]And he struck them hip and thigh with great slaughter; and he went down and stayed in the cleft of the rock of E'tam.

9 Then the Philis'tines came up and encamped in Judah, and made a raid on Lehi. [10]And the men of Judah said, "Why have you come up against us?" They said, "We have come up to bind Samson, to do to him as he did to us." [11]Then three thousand men of Judah went down to the cleft of the rock of E'tam, and said to Samson, "Do you not know that the Philis'tines are rulers over us? What then is this that you have done to us?" And he said to them, "As they did to me, so have I done to them." [12]And they said to him, "We have come down to bind you, that we may give you into the hands of the Philis'tines." And Samson said to them, "Swear to me that you will not fall upon me yourselves." [13]They said to him, "No; we will only bind you and give you into their hands; we will not kill you." So they bound him with two new ropes, and brought him up from the rock.

14 When he came to Lehi, the Philis'tines came shouting to meet him; and the Spirit of the Lord came mightily upon him, and the ropes which were on his arms became as flax that has caught fire, and his bonds melted off his hands. [15]And he found a fresh jawbone of a donkey, and put out his hand and seized it, and with it he slew a thousand men. [16]And Samson said,

"With the jawbone of a donkey,
  heaps upon heaps,
with the jawbone of a donkey
  have I slain a thousand men."

[17]When he had finished speaking, he threw away the jawbone out of his hand; and that place was called Ra'math-le'hi. [u]

18 And he was very thirsty, and he called on the Lord and said, "You have granted this great deliverance by the hand of your servant; and shall I now die of thirst, and fall into the hands of the uncircumcised?" [19]And God split open the hollow place that is at Lehi, and there came water from it; and when he drank, his spirit returned, and he revived. Therefore the name of it was called En-hakkor'e; [v] it is at Lehi to this day. [20]And he judged Israel in the days of the Philis'tines twenty years.

Samson and Delilah

16 Samson went to Gaza, and there he saw a harlot, and he went in to her. [2]The Gazites were told, "Samson has come here," and they surrounded the place and lay in wait for him all night at the gate of the city. They kept quiet all night, saying, "Let us wait till the light of the morning; then we will kill him." [3]But Samson lay till midnight, and at midnight he arose and took hold of the doors of the gate of the city and the two posts, and pulled them up, bar and all, and put them on his shoulders and carried them to the top of the hill that is before He'bron.

4 After this he loved a woman in the valley of Sorek, whose name was Deli'lah. [5]And the lords of the Philis'tines came to her and said to her, "Entice him, and see wherein his great strength lies, and by what means we may overpower him, that we may bind him to subdue him; and we will each give you eleven hundred pieces of silver." [6]And Deli'lah said to Samson, "Please tell me wherein your great strength lies, and how you might be bound, that one could subdue you." [7]And Samson said to her, "If they bind me with seven fresh bowstrings which have not been dried, then I shall become weak, and be like any other man." [8]Then the lords of the Philis'tines brought her seven fresh bowstrings which had not been dried, and she bound him with them. [9]Now she had men lying in wait in an inner chamber. And she said to him, "The Philis'tines are upon you, Samson!" But he snapped the bowstrings, as a tow line snaps when it touches the fire. So the secret of his strength was not known.

10 And Deli'lah said to Samson, "Behold, you have mocked me, and told me lies; please tell me how you might be bound." [11]And he said to her, "If they bind me with new ropes that have not been used, then I shall become weak, and be like

---

[u] That is *The hill of the jawbone.*
[v] That is *The spring of him who called.*

any other man." ¹²So Deli'lah took new ropes and bound him with them, and said to him, "The Philis'tines are upon you, Samson!" And the men lying in wait were in an inner chamber. But he snapped the ropes off his arms like a thread.

13 And Deli'lah said to Samson, "Until now you have mocked me, and told me lies; tell me how you might be bound." And he said to her, "If you weave the seven locks of my head with the web and make it tight with the pin, then I shall become weak, and be like any other man." ¹⁴So while he slept, Deli'lah took the seven locks of his head and wove them into the web.ʷ And she made them tight with the pin, and said to him, "The Philis'tines are upon you, Samson!" But he awoke from his sleep, and pulled away the pin, the loom, and the web.

15 And she said to him, "How can you say, 'I love you,' when your heart is not with me? You have mocked me these three times, and you have not told me wherein your great strength lies." ¹⁶And when she pressed him hard with her words day after day, and urged him, his soul was vexed to death. ¹⁷And he told her all his mind, and said to her, "A razor has never come upon my head; for I have been a Naz'irite to God from my mother's womb. If I be shaved, then my strength will leave me, and I shall become weak, and be like any other man."

18 When Deli'lah saw that he had told her all his mind, she sent and called the lords of the Philis'tines, saying, "Come up this once, for he has told me all his mind." Then the lords of the Philistines came up to her, and brought the money in their hands. ¹⁹She made him sleep upon her knees; and she called a man, and had him shave off the seven locks of his head. Then she began to torment him, and his strength left him. ²⁰And she said, "The Philis'tines are upon you, Samson!" And he awoke from his sleep, and said, "I will go out as at other times, and shake myself free." And he did not know that the LORD had left him. ²¹And the Philis'tines seized him and gouged out his eyes, and brought him down to Gaza, and bound him with bronze fetters; and he ground at the mill in the prison. ²²But the hair of his head began to grow again after it had been shaved.

Samson's Death

23 Now the lords of the Philis'tines gathered to offer a great sacrifice to Da'gon their god, and to rejoice; for they said, "Our god has given Samson our enemy into our hand." ²⁴And when the people saw him, they praised their god; for they said, "Our god has given our enemy into our hand, the ravager of our country, who has slain many of us." ²⁵And when their hearts were merry, they said, "Call Samson, that he may make sport for us." So they called Samson out of the prison, and he made sport before them. They made him stand between the pillars; ²⁶and Samson said to the lad who held him by the hand, "Let me feel the pillars on which the house rests, that I may lean against them." ²⁷Now the house was full of men and women; all the lords of the Philis'tines were there, and on the roof there were about three thousand men and women, who looked on while Samson made sport.

28 Then Samson called to the LORD and said, "O Lord GOD, remember me, I beg you, and strengthen me, I beg you, only this once, O God, that I may be avenged upon the Philis'tines for one of my two eyes." ²⁹And Samson grasped the two middle pillars upon which the house rested, and he leaned his weight upon them, his right hand on the one and his left hand on the other. ³⁰And Samson said, "Let me die with the Philis'tines." Then he bowed with all his might; and the house fell upon the lords and upon all the people that were in it. So the dead whom he slew at his death were more than those whom he had slain during his life. ³¹Then his brothers and all his family came down and took him and brought him up and buried him between Zorah and Esh'taol in the tomb of Mano'ah his father. He had judged Israel twenty years.

Micah and the Levite

17 * There was a man of the hill country of E'phraim, whose name was Micah. ²And he said to his mother, "The eleven hundred pieces of silver which were taken from you, about which you uttered a curse, and also spoke it in my ears, behold, the silver is with me; I took it." And his mother said, "Blessed be my son by the LORD." ³And he restored the eleven hundred pieces of silver to his mother; and his mother said, "I consecrate the silver to the LORD from my hand for my son, to make a graven image and a molten image; now therefore I will restore it to you." ⁴So when he restored the money to his mother, his mother took two hundred pieces of silver, and gave it to the silversmith, who made it into a graven image and a molten image; and it was in the house of Micah. ⁵And the man Micah had a shrine, and he made an ephod and teraphim, and installed one of his sons, who became his priest. ⁶In those days there was no king in Israel; every man did what was right in his own eyes.

7 Now there was a young man of Bethlehem in Judah, of the family of Judah, who was a Levite; and he sojourned there. ⁸And the man departed from the town of Bethlehem in Judah, to live where he could find a place; and as he journeyed, he came to the hill country of E'phraim to the house of Micah. ⁹And Micah said to him, "From

---

ʷ Compare Gk: Heb lacks *and make it tight . . . into the web.*
* 17–21: Extracts from tribal tradition which give a dark picture of the times.

where do you come?" And he said to him, "I am a Levite of Bethlehem in Judah, and I am going to sojourn where I may find a place." [10]And Micah said to him, "Stay with me, and be to me a father and a priest, and I will give you ten pieces of silver a year, and a suit of apparel, and your living."[w2] [11]And the Levite was content to dwell with the man; and the young man became to him like one of his sons. [12]And Micah installed the Levite, and the young man became his priest, and was in the house of Micah. [13]Then Micah said, "Now I know that the LORD will prosper me, because I have a Levite as priest."

Micah and the Migration of Dan

18 In those days there was no king in Israel. And in those days the tribe of the Da'nites was seeking for itself an inheritance to dwell in; for until then no inheritance among the tribes of Israel had fallen to them. [2]So the Da'nites sent five able men from the whole number of their tribe, from Zorah and from Esh'ta-ol, to spy out the land and to explore it; and they said to them, "Go and explore the land." And they came to the hill country of E'phraim, to the house of Micah, and lodged there. [3]When they were by the house of Micah, they recognized the voice of the young Levite; and they turned aside and said to him, "Who brought you here? What are you doing in this place? What is your business here?" [4]And he said to them, "Thus and thus has Micah dealt with me: he has hired me, and I have become his priest." [5]And they said to him, "Inquire of God, we beg you, that we may know whether the journey on which we are setting out will succeed." [6]And the priest said to them, "Go in peace. The journey on which you go is under the eye of the LORD."

7 Then the five men departed, and came to La'ish, and saw the people who were there, how they dwelt in security, after the manner of the Sido'nians, quiet and unsuspecting, lacking[x] nothing that is in the earth, and possessing wealth, and how they were far from the Sidonians and had no dealings with any one. [8]And when they came to their brethren at Zorah and Esh'ta-ol, their brethren said to them, "What do you report?" [9]They said, "Arise, and let us go up against them; for we have seen the land, and behold, it is very fertile. And will you do nothing? Do not be slow to go, and enter in and possess the land. [10]When you go, you will come to an unsuspecting people. The land is broad; yes, God has given it into your hands, a place where there is no lack of anything that is in the earth."

11 And six hundred men of the tribe of Dan, armed with weapons of war, set forth from Zorah and Esh'ta-ol, [12]and went up and encamped at Kir'iath-je'arim in Judah. On this account that place is called Ma'haneh-dan[y] to this day; behold,

it is west of Kiriath-jearim. [13]And they passed on from there to the hill country of E'phraim, and came to the house of Micah.

14 Then the five men who had gone to spy out the country of La'ish said to their brethren, "Do you know that in these houses there are an ephod, teraphim, a graven image, and a molten image? Now therefore consider what you will do." [15]And they turned aside there, and came to the house of the young Levite, at the home of Micah, and asked him of his welfare. [16]Now the six hundred men of the Da'nites, armed with their weapons of war, stood by the entrance of the gate; [17]and the five men who had gone to spy out the land went up, and entered and took the graven image, the ephod, the teraphim, and the molten image, while the priest stood by the entrance of the gate with the six hundred men armed with weapons of war. [18]And when these went into Micah's house and took the graven image, the ephod, the teraphim, and the molten image, the priest said to them, "What are you doing?" [19]And they said to him, "Keep quiet, put your hand upon your mouth, and come with us, and be to us a father and a priest. Is it better for you to be priest to the house of one man, or to be priest to a tribe and family in Israel?" [20]And the priest's heart was glad; he took the ephod, and the teraphim, and the graven image, and went in the midst of the people.

21 So they turned and departed, putting the little ones and the cattle and the goods in front of them. [22]When they were a good way from the home of Micah, the men who were in the houses near Micah's house were called out, and they overtook the Da'nites. [23]And they shouted to the Da'nites, who turned round and said to Micah, "What ails you that you come with such a company?" [24]And he said, "You take my gods which I made, and the priest, and go away, and what have I left? How then do you ask me, 'What ails you?'" [25]And the Da'nites said to him, "Do not let your voice be heard among us, lest angry fellows fall upon you, and you lose your life with the lives of your household." [26]Then the Da'nites went their way; and when Micah saw that they were too strong for him, he turned and went back to his home.

The Danites Settle in Laish

27 And taking what Micah had made, and the priest who belonged to him, the Da'nites came to La'ish, to a people quiet and unsuspecting, and struck them with the edge of the sword, and burned the city with fire. [28]And there was no deliverer because it was far from Si'don, and they had no dealings with any one. It was in the valley

---

[w2] Heb *living, and the Levite went.*

[x] Cn Compare 18:10. The Hebrew text is uncertain.

[y] That is *Camp of Dan.*

18:7: Judg 18:27, 28.

which belongs to Beth-re′hob. And they rebuilt the city, and dwelt in it. [29]And they named the city Dan, after the name of Dan their ancestor, who was born to Israel; but the name of the city was La′ish at the first. [30]And the Da′nites set up the graven image for themselves; and Jonathan the son of Gershom, son of Moses, [z] and his sons were priests to the tribe of the Da′nites until the day of the captivity of the land. [31]So they set up Micah's graven image which he made, as long as the house of God was at Shiloh.

The Levite's Concubine

19 In those days, when there was no king in Israel, a certain Levite was sojourning in the remote parts of the hill country of E′phraim, who took to himself a concubine from Bethlehem in Judah. [2]And his concubine became angry with [a] him, and she went away from him to her father's house at Bethlehem in Judah, and was there some four months. [3]Then her husband arose and went after her, to speak kindly to her and bring her back. He had with him his servant and a couple of donkeys. And he came [b] to her father's house; and when the girl's father saw him, he came with joy to meet him. [4]And his father-in-law, the girl's father, made him stay, and he remained with him three days; so they ate and drank, and lodged there. [5]And on the fourth day they arose early in the morning, and he prepared to go; but the girl's father said to his son-in-law, "Strengthen your heart with a morsel of bread, and after that you may go." [6]So the two men sat and ate and drank together; and the girl's father said to the man, "Be pleased to spend the night, and let your heart be merry." [7]And when the man rose up to go, his father-in-law urged him, till he lodged there again. [8]And on the fifth day he arose early in the morning to depart; and the girl's father said, "Strengthen your heart, and tarry until the day declines." So they ate, both of them. [9]And when the man and his concubine and his servant rose up to depart, his father-in-law, the girl's father, said to him, "Behold, now the day has waned toward evening; please tarry all night. Behold, the day draws to its close; lodge here and let your heart be merry; and tomorrow you shall arise early in the morning for your journey, and go home."

[10] But the man would not spend the night; he rose up and departed, and arrived opposite Je′bus (that is, Jerusalem). He had with him a couple of saddled donkeys, and his concubine was with him. [11]When they were near Je′bus, the day was far spent, and the servant said to his master, "Come now, let us turn aside to this city of the Jeb′usites, and spend the night in it." [12]And his master said to him, "We will not turn aside into the city of foreigners, who do not belong to the sons of Israel; but we will pass on to Gib′e-ah." [13]And he

said to his servant, "Come and let us draw near to one of these places, and spend the night at Gib′e-ah or at Ra′mah." [14]So they passed on and went their way; and the sun went down on them near Gib′e-ah, which belongs to Benjamin, [15]and they turned aside there, to go in and spend the night at Gib′e-ah. And he went in and sat down in the open square of the city; for no man took them into his house to spend the night.

[16] And behold, an old man was coming from his work in the field at evening; the man was from the hill country of E′phraim, and he was sojourning in Gib′e-ah; the men of the place were Benjaminites. [17]And he lifted up his eyes, and saw the wayfarer in the open square of the city; and the old man said, "Where are you going? and from where do you come?" [18]And he said to him, "We are passing from Bethlehem in Judah to the remote parts of the hill country of E′phraim, from which I come. I went to Bethlehem in Judah; and I am going to my home; [c] and nobody takes me into his house. [19]We have straw and food for our donkeys, with bread and wine for me and your maidservant and the young man with your servants; there is no lack of anything." [20]And the old man said, "Peace be to you; I will care for all your wants; only, do not spend the night in the square." [21]So he brought him into his house, and fed the donkeys; and they washed their feet, and ate and drank.

The Crime of the Benjaminites of Gibe-ah

[22] As they were making their hearts merry, behold, the men of the city, base fellows, surrounded the house, beating on the door; and they said to the old man, the master of the house, "Bring out the man who came into your house, that we may know him." [23]And the man, the master of the house, went out to them and said to them, "No, my brethren, do not act so wickedly; seeing that this man has come into my house, do not do this vile thing. [24]Behold, here are my virgin daughter and his concubine; let me bring them out now. Ravish them and do with them what seems good to you; but against this man do not do so vile a thing." [25]But the men would not listen to him. So the man seized his concubine, and put her out to them; and they knew her, and abused her all night until the morning. And as the dawn began to break, they let her go. [26]And as morning appeared, the woman came and fell down at the door of the man's house where her master was, till it was light.

[27] And her master rose up in the morning, and when he opened the doors of the house and went out to go on his way, behold, there was his concu-

[z] Another reading is *Manasseh*.
[a] Gk Old Latin: Heb *played the harlot against*.
[b] Gk: Heb *she brought him*.
[c] Gk Compare 19:29. Heb *to the house of the* Lord.

bine lying at the door of the house, with her hands on the threshold. 28He said to her, "Get up, let us be going." But there was no answer. Then he put her upon the donkey; and the man rose up and went away to his home. 29And when he entered his house, he took a knife, and laying hold of his concubine he divided her, limb by limb, into twelve pieces, and sent her throughout all the territory of Israel. 30And all who saw it said, "Such a thing has never happened or been seen from the day that the sons of Israel came up out of the land of Egypt until this day; consider it, take counsel, and speak."

The Tribes of Israel Attack the Benjaminites

20 Then all the sons of Israel came out, from Dan to Be′er-she′ba, including the land of Gilead, and the congregation assembled as one man to the Lord at Mizpah. 2And the chiefs of all the people, of all the tribes of Israel, presented themselves in the assembly of the people of God, four hundred thousand men on foot that drew the sword. 3(Now the Benjaminites heard that the sons of Israel had gone up to Mizpah.) And the sons of Israel said, "Tell us, how was this wickedness brought to pass?" 4And the Levite, the husband of the woman who was murdered, answered and said, "I came to Gib′e-ah that belongs to Benjamin, I and my concubine, to spend the night. 5And the men of Gib′e-ah rose against me, and surrounded the house by night; they meant to kill me, and they ravished my concubine, and she is dead. 6And I took my concubine and cut her in pieces, and sent her throughout all the country of the inheritance of Israel; for they have committed abomination and wantonness in Israel. 7Behold, you sons of Israel, all of you, give your advice and counsel here."

8 And all the people arose as one man, saying, "None of us will go to his tent, and none of us will return to his house. 9But now this is what we will do to Gib′e-ah: we will go up against it by lot, 10and we will take ten men of a hundred throughout all the tribes of Israel, and a hundred of a thousand, and a thousand of ten thousand, to bring provisions for the people, that when they come they may repay Gib′e-ah of Benjamin, for all the wanton crime which they have committed in Israel." 11So all the men of Israel gathered against the city, united as one man.

12 And the tribes of Israel sent men through all the tribe of Benjamin, saying, "What wickedness is this that has taken place among you? 13Now therefore give up the men, the base fellows in Gib′e-ah, that we may put them to death, and put away evil from Israel." But the Benjaminites would not listen to the voice of their brethren, the sons of Israel. 14And the Benjaminites came together out of the cities to Gib′e-ah, to go out to battle against the sons of Israel. 15And the Benjaminites mustered out of their cities on that day twenty-six thousand men that drew the sword, besides the inhabitants of Gib′e-ah, who mustered seven hundred picked men. 16Among all these were seven hundred picked men who were left-handed; every one could sling a stone at a hair, and not miss. 17And the men of Israel, apart from Benjamin, mustered four hundred thousand men that drew sword; all these were men of war.

18 The sons of Israel arose and went up to Bethel, and inquired of God, "Which of us shall go up first to battle against the Benjaminites?" And the Lord said, "Judah shall go up first."

19 Then the sons of Israel rose in the morning, and encamped against Gib′e-ah. 20And the men of Israel went out to battle against Benjamin; and the men of Israel drew up the battle line against them at Gib′e-ah. 21The Benjaminites came out of Gib′e-ah, and struck down on that day twenty-two thousand men of the Israelites. 22But the people, the men of Israel, took courage, and again formed the battle line in the same place where they had formed it on the first day. 23And the sons of Israel went up and wept before the Lord until the evening; and they inquired of the Lord, "Shall we again draw near to battle against our brethren the Benjaminites?" And the Lord said, "Go up against them."

24 So the sons of Israel came near against the Benjaminites the second day. 25And Benjamin went against them out of Gib′e-ah the second day, and struck down eighteen thousand men of the sons of Israel; all these were men who drew the sword. 26Then all the sons of Israel, the whole army, went up and came to Bethel and wept; they sat there before the Lord, and fasted that day until evening, and offered burnt offerings and peace offerings before the Lord. 27And the sons of Israel inquired of the Lord (for the ark of the covenant of God was there in those days, 28and Phin′ehas the son of Elea′zar, son of Aaron, ministered before it in those days), saying, "Shall we yet again go out to battle against our brethren the Benjaminites, or shall we cease?" And the Lord said, "Go up; for tomorrow I will give them into your hand."

29 So Israel set men in ambush round about Gib′e-ah. 30And the sons of Israel went up against the Benjaminites on the third day, and set themselves in array against Gib′e-ah, as at other times. 31And the Benjaminites went out against the people, and were drawn away from the city; and as at other times they began to strike and kill some of the people, in the highways, one of which goes up to Bethel and the other to Gib′e-ah, and in the open country, about thirty men of Israel. 32And the Benjaminites said, "They are routed before us, as at the first." But the men of Israel said, "Let us flee, and draw them away from the

city to the highways." [33]And all the men of Israel rose up out of their place, and set themselves in array at Ba'al-ta'mar; and the men of Israel who were in ambush rushed out of their place west[d] of Ge'ba. [34]And there came against Gib'e-ah ten thousand picked men out of all Israel, and the battle was hard; but the Benjaminites did not know that disaster was close upon them. [35]And the LORD defeated Benjamin before Israel; and the men of Israel destroyed twenty-five thousand one hundred men of Benjamin that day; all these were men who drew the sword. [36]So the Benjaminites saw that they were defeated.

The men of Israel gave ground to Benjamin, because they trusted to the men in ambush whom they had set against Gib'e-ah. [37]And the men in ambush made haste and rushed upon Gib'e-ah; the men in ambush moved out and struck the whole city with the edge of the sword. [38]Now the appointed signal between the men of Israel and the men in ambush was that when they made a great cloud of smoke rise up out of the city [39]the men of Israel should turn in battle. Now Benjamin had begun to strike and kill about thirty men of Israel; they said, "Surely they are struck down before us, as in the first battle." [40]But when the signal began to rise out of the city in a column of smoke, the Benjaminites looked behind them; and behold, the whole city went up in smoke to heaven. [41]Then the men of Israel turned, and the men of Benjamin were dismayed, for they saw that disaster was close upon them. [42]Therefore they turned their backs before the men of Israel in the direction of the wilderness; but the battle overtook them, and those who came out of the cities destroyed them in the midst of them. [43]Cutting down[e] the Benjaminites, they pursued them and trod them down from No'hah[f] as far as opposite Gib'e-ah on the east. [44]Eighteen thousand men of Benjamin fell, all of them men of valor. [45]And they turned and fled toward the wilderness to the rock of Rimmon; five thousand men of them were cut down in the highways, and they were pursued hard to Gi'dom, and two thousand men of them were slain. [46]So all who fell that day of Benjamin were twenty-five thousand men that drew the sword, all of them men of valor. [47]But six hundred men turned and fled toward the wilderness to the rock of Rimmon, and abode at the rock of Rimmon four months. [48]And the men of Israel turned back against the Benjaminites, and struck them with the edge of the sword, men and beasts and all that they found. And all the towns which they found they set on fire.

The Benjaminites Saved from Extinction

21 Now the men of Israel had sworn at Mizpah, "No one of us shall give his daughter in marriage to Benjamin." [2]And the people came to Bethel, and sat there till evening before God, and they lifted up their voices and wept bitterly. [3]And they said, "O LORD, the God of Israel, why has this come to pass in Israel, that there should be today one tribe lacking in Israel?" [4]And the next day the people rose early, and built there an altar, and offered burnt offerings and peace offerings. [5]And the sons of Israel said, "Which of all the tribes of Israel did not come up in the assembly to the LORD?" For they had taken a great oath concerning him who did not come up to the LORD to Mizpah, saying, "He shall be put to death." [6]And the sons of Israel had compassion for Benjamin their brother, and said, "One tribe is cut off from Israel this day. [7]What shall we do for wives for those who are left, since we have sworn by the LORD that we will not give them any of our daughters for wives?"

8 And they said, "What one is there of the tribes of Israel that did not come up to the LORD to Mizpah?" And behold, no one had come to the camp from Ja'besh-gil'ead, to the assembly. [9]For when the people were mustered, behold, not one of the inhabitants of Ja'besh-gil'ead was there. [10]So the congregation sent twelve thousand of their bravest men there, and commanded them, "Go and strike the inhabitants of Ja'besh-gil'ead with the edge of the sword; also the women and the little ones. [11]This is what you shall do; every male and every woman that has lain with a male you shall utterly destroy." [12]And they found among the inhabitants of Ja'besh-gil'ead four hundred young virgins who had not known man by lying with him; and they brought them to the camp at Shiloh, which is in the land of Canaan.

13 Then the whole congregation sent word to the Benjaminites who were at the rock of Rimmon, and proclaimed peace to them. [14]And Benjamin returned at that time; and they gave them the women whom they had saved alive of the women of Ja'besh-gil'ead; but they did not suffice for them. [15]And the people had compassion on Benjamin because the LORD had made a breach in the tribes of Israel.

16 Then the elders of the congregation said, "What shall we do for wives for those who are left, since the women are destroyed out of Benjamin?" [17]And they said, "There must be an inheritance for the survivors of Benjamin, that a tribe be not blotted out from Israel. [18]Yet we cannot give them wives cf our daughters." For the sons of Israel had sworn, "Cursed be he who gives a wife to Benjamin." [19]So they said, "Behold, there is the yearly feast of the LORD at Shiloh, which is north of Bethel, on the east of the highway that goes up from Bethel to

---

[d] Gk Vg: Heb *in the plain.*
[e] Gk: Heb *surrounding.*
[f] Gk: Heb *(at their) resting place.*

She'chem, and south of Lebo'nah." ²⁰And they commanded the Benjaminites, saying, "Go and lie in wait in the vineyards, ²¹and watch; if the daughters of Shiloh come out to dance in the dances, then come out of the vineyards and seize each man his wife from the daughters of Shiloh, and go to the land of Benjamin. ²²And when their fathers or their brothers come to complain to us, we will say to them, 'Grant them graciously to us; because we did not take for each man of them his wife in battle, neither did you give them to them, else you would now be guilty.'" ²³And the Benjaminites did so, and took their wives, according to their number, from the dancers whom they carried off; then they went and returned to their inheritance, and rebuilt the towns, and dwelt in them. ²⁴And the sons of Israel departed from there at that time, every man to his tribe and family, and they went out from there every man to his inheritance.

25 In those days there was no king in Israel; every man did what was right in his own eyes.

THE BOOK OF
RUTH

Elimelech's Family Goes to Moab

1 In the days when the judges ruled there was a famine in the land, and a certain man of Bethlehem in Judah went to sojourn in the country of Moab, he and his wife and his two sons. ²The name of the man was Elim'elech and the name of his wife Na'omi, and the names of his two sons were Mahlon and Chil'ion; they were Eph'rathites from Bethlehem in Judah. They went into the country of Moab and remained there. ³But Elim'elech, the husband of Na'omi, died, and she was left with her two sons. ⁴These took Moabite wives; the name of the one was Orpah and the name of the other Ruth. They lived there about ten years; ⁵and both Mahlon and Chil'ion died, so that the woman was bereft of her two sons and her husband.

Naomi and Her Moabite Daughters-in-law

6 Then she started with her daughters-in-law to return from the country of Moab, for she had heard in the country of Moab that the Lord had visited his people and given them food. ⁷So she set out from the place where she was, with her two daughters-in-law, and they went on the way to return to the land of Judah. ⁸But Na'omi said to her two daughters-in-law, "Go, return each of you to her mother's house. May the Lord deal kindly with you, as you have dealt with the dead and with me. ⁹The Lord grant that you may find a home, each of you in the house of her husband!" Then she kissed them, and they lifted up their voices and wept. ¹⁰And they said to her, "No, we will return with you to your people." ¹¹But Na'omi said, "Turn back, my daughters, why will you go with me? Have I yet sons in my womb that they may become your husbands? ¹²Turn back, my daughters, go your way, for I am too old to have a husband. If I should say I have hope, even if I should have a husband this night and should bear sons, ¹³would you therefore wait till they were grown? Would you therefore refrain from marrying? No, my daughters, for it is exceedingly bitter to me for your sake that the hand of the Lord has gone forth against me." ¹⁴Then they lifted up their voices and wept again; and Orpah kissed her mother-in-law, but Ruth clung to her.

15 And she said, "See, your sister-in-law has gone back to her people and to her gods; return after your sister-in-law." ¹⁶But Ruth said, "Entreat me not to leave you or to return from following

you; for where you go I will go, and where you lodge I will lodge; your people shall be my people, and your God my God; ¹⁷where you die I will die, and there will I be buried. May the Lord do so to me and more also if even death parts me from you." ¹⁸And when Na'omi saw that she was determined to go with her, she said no more.

19 So the two of them went on until they came to Bethlehem. And when they came to Bethlehem, the whole town was stirred because of them; and the women said, "Is this Na'omi?" ²⁰She said to them, "Do not call me Na'omi, ᵃ call me Mara, ᵇ for the Almighty has dealt very bitterly with me. ²¹I went away full, and the Lord has brought me back empty. Why call me Na'omi, when the Lord has afflicted ᶜ me and the Almighty has brought calamity upon me?"

22 So Na'omi returned, and Ruth the Moabitess her daughter-in-law with her, who returned from the country of Moab. And they came to Bethlehem at the beginning of barley harvest.

Ruth Meets Boaz

2 Now Na'omi had a kinsman of her husband's, a man of wealth, of the family of Elim'elech, whose name was Boaz. ²And Ruth the Moabitess said to Na'omi, "Let me go to the field, and glean among the ears of grain after him in whose sight I shall find favor." And she said to her, "Go, my daughter." ³So she set forth and went and gleaned in the field after the reapers; and she happened to come to the part of the field belonging to Boaz, who was of the family of Elim'elech. ⁴And behold, Boaz came from Bethlehem; and he said to the reapers, "The Lord be with you!" And they answered, "The Lord bless you." ⁵Then Boaz said to his servant who was in charge of the reapers, "Whose maiden is this?" ⁶And the servant who was in charge of the reapers answered, "It is the Moabite maiden, who came back with Na'omi from the country of Moab. ⁷She said, 'Please, let

---

This charming tale of family life in the countryside of Bethlehem during the period of the judges is imbued with a deeply religious spirit. It is a story of family devotion and of piety toward one's ancestors. The book has significance for the ancestry of David and the Messiah. Though Jewish in feeling, it is not narrowly so; indeed, Boaz goes beyond what is strictly required by the law and, though the book insists that Israel's faith must remain uncontaminated, yet it also says it must be made available to all. The call of the Gentiles is foreseen. There is no certainty about the date of the book. It was probably written during the period of the kingship, though some think it was composed after the Exile.
ᵃ That is *Pleasant.*
ᵇ That is *Bitter.*
ᶜ Gk Syr Vg: Heb *testified against.*

me glean and gather among the sheaves after the reapers.' So she came, and she has continued from early morning until now, without resting even for a moment." [d]

8 Then Boaz said to Ruth, "Now, listen, my daughter, do not go to glean in another field or leave this one, but keep close to my maidens. [9]Let your eyes be upon the field which they are reaping, and go after them. Have I not charged the young men not to molest you? And when you are thirsty, go to the vessels and drink what the young men have drawn." [10]Then she fell on her face, bowing to the ground, and said to him, "Why have I found favor in your eyes, that you should take notice of me, when I am a foreigner?" [11]But Boaz answered her, "All that you have done for your mother-in-law since the death of your husband has been fully told me, and how you left your father and mother and your native land and came to a people that you did not know before. [12]The LORD recompense you for what you have done, and a full reward be given you by the LORD, the God of Israel, under whose wings you have come to take refuge!" [13]Then she said, "You are most gracious to me, my lord, for you have comforted me and spoken kindly to your maidservant, though I am not one of your maidservants."

14 And at mealtime Boaz said to her, "Come here, and eat some bread, and dip your morsel in the wine." So she sat beside the reapers, and he passed to her parched grain; and she ate until she was satisfied, and she had some left over. [15]When she rose to glean, Boaz instructed his young men, saying, "Let her glean even among the sheaves, and do not reproach her. [16]And also pull out some from the bundles for her, and leave it for her to glean, and do not rebuke her."

17 So she gleaned in the field until evening; then she beat out what she had gleaned, and it was about an ephah of barley. [18]And she took it up and went into the city; she showed her mother-in-law what she had gleaned, and she also brought out and gave her what food she had left over after being satisfied. [19]And her mother-in-law said to her, "Where did you glean today? And where have you worked? Blessed be the man who took notice of you." So she told her mother-in-law with whom she had worked, and said, "The name of the man with whom I worked today is Boaz." [20]And Na'omi said to her daughter-in-law, "Blessed be he by the LORD, whose kindness has not forsaken the living or the dead!" Na'omi also said to her, "The man is a relative of ours, one of our nearest kin." [21]And Ruth the Moabitess said, "Besides, he said to me, 'You shall keep close by my servants, till they have finished all my harvest.'" [22]And Na'omi said to Ruth, her daughter-in-law, "It is well, my daughter, that you go out with his maidens, lest in an-

other field you be molested." [23]So she kept close to the maidens of Boaz, gleaning until the end of the barley and wheat harvests; and she lived with her mother-in-law.

Ruth and Boaz at the Threshing Floor

3 Then Na'omi her mother-in-law said to her, "My daughter, should I not seek a home for you, that it may be well with you? [2]Now is not Boaz our kinsman, with whose maidens you were? See, he is winnowing barley tonight at the threshing floor. [3]Wash therefore and anoint yourself, and put on your best clothes and go down to the threshing floor; but do not make yourself known to the man until he has finished eating and drinking. [4]But when he lies down, observe the place where he lies; then, go and uncover his feet and lie down; and he will tell you what to do." [5]And she replied, "All that you say I will do."

6 So she went down to the threshing floor and did just as her mother-in-law had told her. [7]And when Boaz had eaten and drunk, and his heart was merry, he went to lie down at the end of the heap of grain. Then she came softly, and uncovered his feet, and lay down. [8]At midnight the man was startled, and turned over, and behold, a woman lay at his feet! [9]He said, "Who are you?" And she answered, "I am Ruth, your maidservant; spread your garment over your maidservant, for you are next of kin." [10]And he said, "May you be blessed by the LORD, my daughter; you have made this last kindness greater than the first, in that you have not gone after young men, whether poor or rich. [11]And now, my daughter, do not fear, I will do for you all that you ask, for all my fellow townsmen know that you are a woman of worth. [12]And now it is true that I am a near kinsman, yet there is a kinsman nearer than I. [13]Remain this night, and in the morning, if he will do the part of the next of kin for you, well; let him do it; but if he is not willing to do the part of the next of kin for you, then, as the LORD lives, I will do the part of the next of kin for you. Lie down until the morning."

14 So she lay at his feet until the morning, but arose before one could recognize another; and he said, "Let it not be known that the woman came to the threshing floor." [15]And he said, "Bring the mantle you are wearing and hold it out." So she held it, and he measured out six measures of barley, and laid it upon her; then she went into the city. [16]And when she came to her mother-in-law, she said, "How did you fare, my daughter?" Then she told her all that the man had done for her, [17]saying, "These six measures of barley he gave to me, for he said, 'You must not go back empty-handed to your mother-in-law.'" [18]She replied, "Wait, my daughter, until you learn how the

---

[d] Compare Gk Vg: the meaning of the Hebrew text is uncertain.

matter turns out, for the man will not rest, but will settle the matter today."

The Marriage of Boaz and Ruth

4 And Boaz went up to the gate and sat down there; and behold, the next of kin, of whom Boaz had spoken, came by. So Boaz said, "Turn aside, friend; sit down here"; and he turned aside and sat down. [2]And he took ten men of the elders of the city, and said, "Sit down here"; so they sat down. [3]Then he said to the next of kin, "Na'omi, who has come back from the country of Moab, is selling the parcel of land which belonged to our kinsman Elim'elech. [4]So I thought I would tell you of it, and say, Buy it in the presence of those sitting here, and in the presence of the elders of my people. If you will redeem it, redeem it; but if you will not, tell me, that I may know, for there is no one besides you to redeem it, and I come after you." And he said, "I will redeem it." [5]Then Boaz said, "The day you buy the field from the hand of Na'omi, you are also buying Ruth • the Moabitess, the widow of the dead, in order to restore the name of the dead to his inheritance." [6]Then the next of kin said, "I cannot redeem it for myself, lest I impair my own inheritance. Take my right of redemption yourself, for I cannot redeem it."

7 Now this was the custom in former times in Israel concerning redeeming and exchanging: to confirm a transaction, the one drew off his sandal and gave it to the other, and this was the manner of attesting in Israel. [8]So when the next of kin said to Boaz, "Buy it for yourself," he drew off his sandal. [9]Then Boaz said to the elders and all the people, "You are witnesses this day that I have bought from the hand of Na'omi all that belonged to Elim'elech and all that belonged to Chil'ion and to Mahlon. [10]Also Ruth the Moabitess, the widow of Mahlon, I have bought to be my wife, to

perpetuate the name of the dead in his inheritance, that the name of the dead may not be cut off from among his brethren and from the gate of his native place; you are witnesses this day." [11]Then all the people who were at the gate, and the elders, said, "We are witnesses. May the LORD make the woman, who is coming into your house, like Rachel and Leah, who together built up the house of Israel. May you prosper in Eph'rathah and be renowned in Bethlehem; [12]and may your house be like the house of Per'ez, whom Ta'mar bore to Judah, because of the children that the LORD will give you by this young woman."

The Genealogy of David

13 So Boaz took Ruth and she became his wife; and he went in to her, and the LORD gave her conception, and she bore a son. [14]Then the women said to Na'omi, "Blessed be the LORD, who has not left you this day without next of kin; and may his name be renowned in Israel! [15]He shall be to you a restorer of life and a nourisher of your old age; for your daughter-in-law who loves you, who is more to you than seven sons, has borne him." [16]Then Na'omi took the child and laid him in her bosom, and became his nurse. [17]And the women of the neighborhood gave him a name, saying, "A son has been born to Na'omi." They named him O'bed; he was the father of Jesse, the father of David.

18 Now these are the descendants of Per'ez: Perez was the father of Hezron, [19]Hezron of Ram, Ram of Ammin'adab, [20]Ammin'adab of Nahshon, Nahshon of Salmon, [21]Salmon of Boaz, Boaz of O'bed, [22]O'bed of Jesse, and Jesse of David.

• Old Latin Vg: Heb *of Naomi and from Ruth.*
4:7: Deut 25:8–10.

THE FIRST BOOK OF

SAMUEL

Samuel's Birth and Dedication

1 There was a certain man of Ramatha'im-zo'phim of the hill country of E'phraim, whose name was Elka'nah the son of Jero'ham, son of Eli'hu, son of To'hu, son of Zuph, an E'phraimite. [2]He had two wives; the name of the one was Hannah, and the name of the other Penin'nah. And Peninnah had children, but Hannah had no children.

3 Now this man used to go up year by year from his city to worship and to sacrifice to the Lord of hosts at Shiloh, * where the two sons of Eli, Hoph'ni and Phin'ehas, were priests of the Lord. [4]On the day when Elka'nah sacrificed, he would give portions to Penin'nah his wife and to all her sons and daughters; [5]and, although [a] he loved Hannah, he would give Hannah only one portion, because the Lord had closed her womb. [6]And her rival used to provoke her sorely, to irritate her, because the Lord had closed her womb. [7]So it went on year by year; as often as she went up to the house of the Lord, she used to provoke her. Therefore Hannah wept and would not eat. [8]And Elka'nah, her husband, said to her, "Hannah, why do you weep? And why do you not eat? And why is your heart sad? Am I not more to you than ten sons?"

9 After they had eaten and drunk in Shiloh, Hannah rose. Now Eli the priest was sitting on the seat beside the doorpost of the temple of the Lord. [10]She was deeply distressed and prayed to the Lord, and wept bitterly. [11]And she vowed a vow and said, "O Lord of hosts, if you will indeed look on the affliction of your maidservant, and remember me, and not forget your maidservant, but will give to your maidservant a son, then I will give him to the Lord all the days of his life, and no razor shall touch his head."

12 As she continued praying before the Lord, Eli observed her mouth. [13]Hannah was speaking in her heart; only her lips moved, and her voice was not heard; therefore Eli took her to be a drunken woman. [14]And Eli said to her, "How long will you be drunken? Put away your wine from you." [15]But Hannah answered, "No, my lord, I am a woman sorely troubled; I have drunk neither wine nor strong drink, but I have been pouring out my soul before the Lord. [16]Do not regard your maidservant as a base woman, for all along I have been speaking out of my great anxiety and vexa-tion." [17]Then Eli answered, "Go in peace, and the God of Israel grant your petition which you have made to him." [18]And she said, "Let your maidservant find favor in your eyes." Then the woman went her way and ate, and her countenance was no longer sad.

19 They rose early in the morning and worshiped before the Lord; then they went back to their house at Ra'mah. And Elka'nah knew Hannah his wife, and the Lord remembered her; [20]and in due time Hannah conceived and bore a son, and she called his name Samuel, for she said, "I have asked him of the Lord."

21 And the man Elka'nah and all his house went up to offer to the Lord the yearly sacrifice, and to pay his vow. [22]But Hannah did not go up, for she said to her husband, "As soon as the child is weaned, I will bring him, that he may appear in the presence of the Lord, and abide there for ever." [23]Elka'nah her husband said to her, "Do what seems best to you, wait until you have weaned him; only, may the Lord establish his word." So the woman remained and nursed her son, until she weaned him. [24]And when she had weaned him, she took him up with her, along with a three-year-old bull, [b] an ephah of flour, and a skin of wine; and she brought him to the house of the Lord at Shiloh; and the child was young. [25]Then they slew the bull, and they brought the child to Eli. [26]And she said, "Oh, my lord! As you live, my lord, I am the woman who was standing here in your presence, praying to the Lord. [27]For this child I prayed; and the Lord has granted me my petition which I made to him. [28]Therefore I have lent him to the Lord; as long as he lives, he is lent to the Lord."

And they [x] worshiped the Lord there.

The First and Second Books of Samuel (the First and Second Books of Kings): Samuel was traditionally supposed to have written these books—hence the title. The Latin Vulgate, following the Greek tradition, links these books with 1 and 2 Kings, calling them 1–4 Kings (Greek, 1–4 Kingdoms). 1 and 2 Samuel cover the early period of the monarchy and are, in fact, composed of two main traditions; this at times makes the sequence of events difficult to follow. The narrative makes plain the difficulty of centralizing the government of the tribes. David's character and achievement are well brought out, and there is special emphasis on the Messianic importance of both. Yet at the end the signs of possible schism are already manifest. The books were probably written during the period of the divided monarchy.

[a] Gk: Heb obscure.
[b] Gk Syr: Heb three bulls.
[x] Heb he.
* 1:3, Shiloh: At this time, the central sanctuary of the tribes and the residence of the ark, the visible assurance of the presence of Yahweh, Lord of the hosts of Israel.

Hannah's Prayer

2 Hannah also prayed and said, *
"My heart exults in the LORD;
my strength is exalted in the LORD.
My mouth derides my enemies,
because I rejoice in your salvation.

2 "There is none holy like the LORD,
there is none besides you;
there is no rock like our God.
3 Talk no more so very proudly,
let not arrogance come from your mouth;
for the LORD is a God of knowledge,
and by him actions are weighed.
4 The bows of the mighty are broken,
but the feeble gird on strength.
5 Those who were full have hired themselves out
for bread,
but those who were hungry have ceased to
hunger.
The barren has borne seven,
but she who has many children is forlorn.
6 The LORD kills and brings to life;
he brings down to Sheol and raises up.
7 The LORD makes poor and makes rich;
he brings low, he also exalts.
8 He raises up the poor from the dust;
he lifts the needy from the dung heap,
to make them sit with princes
and inherit a seat of honor.
For the pillars of the earth are the LORD's,
and on them he has set the world.

9 "He will guard the feet of his faithful ones;
but the wicked shall be cut off in darkness;
for not by might shall a man prevail.
10 The adversaries of the LORD shall be broken to
pieces;
against them he will thunder in heaven.
The LORD will judge the ends of the earth;
he will give strength to his king,
and exalt the power of his anointed."

Eli's Wicked Sons

11 Then Elka′nah went home to Ra′mah. And
the boy ministered to the LORD, in the presence of
Eli the priest.

12 Now the sons of Eli were worthless men;
they had no regard for the LORD. 13 The custom of
the priests with the people was that when any
man offered sacrifice, the priest's servant would
come, while the meat was boiling, with a three-
pronged fork in his hand, 14 and he would thrust it
into the pan, or kettle, or caldron, or pot; all that
the fork brought up the priest would take for
himself. c So they did at Shiloh to all the Israelites
who came there. 15 Moreover, before the fat was
burned, the priest's servant would come and say
to the man who was sacrificing, "Give meat for
the priest to roast; for he will not accept boiled

meat from you, but raw." 16 And if the man said to
him, "Let them burn the fat first, and then take as
much as you wish," he would say, "No, you must
give it now; and if not, I will take it by force."
17 Thus the sin of the young men was very great
in the sight of the LORD; for the men treated the
offering of the LORD with contempt.

The Boy Samuel

18 Samuel was ministering before the LORD, a
boy girded with a linen ephod. † 19 And his mother
used to make for him a little robe and take it to
him each year, when she went up with her husband to offer the yearly sacrifice. 20 Then Eli would
bless Elka′nah and his wife, and say, "The LORD
give you children by this woman for the loan
which she lent to d the LORD"; so then they would
return to their home.

21 And the LORD visited Hannah, and she con-
ceived and bore three sons and two daughters.
And the boy Samuel grew in the presence of the
LORD.

Eli Tries to Correct His Sons

22 Now Eli was very old, and he heard all that
his sons were doing to all Israel, and how they lay
with the women who served at the entrance to the
tent of meeting. 23 And he said to them, "Why do
you do such things? For I hear of your evil dealings from all the people. 24 No, my sons; it is no
good report that I hear the people of the LORD
spreading abroad. 25 If a man sins against a
man, God will mediate for him; but if a man sins
against the LORD, who can intercede for him?" But
they would not listen to the voice of their father;
for it was the will of the LORD to slay them.

Samuel's Virtues

26 Now the boy Samuel continued to grow both
in stature and in favor with the LORD and with
men.

A Prophecy against Eli's Household

27 And there came a man of God to Eli, and
said to him, "Thus the LORD has said, 'I revealed e
myself to the house of your father when they
were in Egypt subject to the house of Pharaoh.
28 And I chose him out of all the tribes of Israel to
be my priest, to go up to my altar, to burn incense,
to wear an ephod before me; and I gave to the
house of your father all my offerings by fire from
the sons of Israel. 29 Why then look with greedy
eye at f my sacrifices and my offerings which I

---

c Gk Syr Vg: Heb *with it.*
d Or *for the petition which she asked of.*
e Gk Tg: Heb *Did I reveal.*
f Or *treat with scorn.* Gk: Heb *kick at.*
2:1–10: Lk 1:46–55.
2:26: Lk 2:52.
* 2:1–10: This song, though certainly touched up at a later period (e.g.,
the reference to a king in verse 10), is meant to express Hannah's senti-
ments. It has profoundly influenced the Magnificat.
† 2:18, *ephod:* The ephod was either a distinctive priestly garment as
here, or a means of divination used by the priest, possibly a container for
the sacred lots; cf. 2:28.

commanded, and honor your sons above me by fattening yourselves upon the choicest parts of every offering of my people Israel?' [30]Therefore the Lord the God of Israel declares: 'I promised that your house and the house of your father should go in and out before me for ever'; but now the Lord declares: 'Far be it from me; for those who honor me I will honor, and those who despise me shall be lightly esteemed. [31]Behold, the days are coming, when I will cut off your strength and the strength of your father's house, so that there will not be an old man in your house. [32]Then in distress you will look with envious eye on all the prosperity which shall be bestowed upon Israel; and there shall not be an old man in your house for ever. [33]The man of you whom I shall not cut off from my altar shall be spared to weep out his [g] eyes and grieve his [g] heart; and all the increase of your house shall die by the sword of men. [h] [34]And this which shall befall your two sons, Hoph′ni and Phin′ehas, shall be the sign to you: both of them shall die on the same day. [35]And I will raise up for myself a faithful priest, who shall do according to what is in my heart and in my mind; and I will build him a sure house, and he shall go in and out before my anointed for ever. [36]And every one who is left in your house shall come to implore him for a piece of silver or a loaf of bread, and shall say, "Put me, I beg you, in one of the priest's places, that I may eat a morsel of bread.'"

The Lord Calls Samuel

3 * Now the boy Samuel was ministering to the Lord under Eli. And the word of the Lord was rare in those days; there was no frequent vision.

2 At that time Eli, whose eyesight had begun to grow dim, so that he could not see, was lying down in his own place; [3]the lamp of God had not yet gone out, and Samuel was lying down within the temple of the Lord, where the ark of God was. [4]Then the Lord called, "Samuel! Samuel!" [i] and he said, "Here I am!" [5]and ran to Eli, and said, "Here I am, for you called me." But he said, "I did not call; lie down again." So he went and lay down. [6]And the Lord called again, "Samuel!" And Samuel arose and went to Eli, and said, "Here I am, for you called me." But he said, "I did not call, my son; lie down again." [7]Now Samuel did not yet know the Lord, and the word of the Lord had not yet been revealed to him. [8]And the Lord called Samuel again the third time. And he arose and went to Eli, and said, "Here I am, for you called me." Then Eli perceived that the Lord was calling the boy. [9]Therefore Eli said to Samuel, "Go, lie down; and if he calls you, you shall say, 'Speak, Lord, for your servant hears.'" So Samuel went and lay down in his place.

10 And the Lord came and stood forth, calling as at other times, "Samuel! Samuel!" And Samuel said, "Speak, for your servant hears." [11]Then the Lord said to Samuel, "Behold, I am about to do a thing in Israel, at which the two ears of every one that hears it will tingle. [12]On that day I will fulfil against Eli all that I have spoken concerning his house, from beginning to end. [13]And I tell him that I am about to punish his house for ever, for the iniquity which he knew, because his sons were blaspheming God, [j] and he did not restrain them. [14]Therefore I swear to the house of Eli that the iniquity of Eli's house shall not be expiated by sacrifice or offering for ever."

15 Samuel lay until morning; then he opened the doors of the house of the Lord. And Samuel was afraid to tell the vision to Eli. [16]But Eli called Samuel and said, "Samuel, my son." And he said, "Here I am." [17]And Eli said, "What was it that he told you? Do not hide it from me. May God do so to you and more also, if you hide anything from me of all that he told you." [18]So Samuel told him everything and hid nothing from him. And he said, "It is the Lord; let him do what seems good to him."

Samuel's Prophecy and the Capture of the Ark of God

19 And Samuel grew, and the Lord was with him and let none of his words fall to the ground. [20]And all Israel from Dan to Be′er-she′ba knew that Samuel was established as a prophet of the Lord. [21]And the Lord appeared again at Shiloh, for the Lord revealed himself to Samuel at Shiloh by the word of the Lord. [1]And the word of Samuel came to all Israel.

4 † Now Israel went out to battle against the Philis′tines; they encamped at Ebenezer, and the Philistines encamped at A′phek. [2]The Philis′tines drew up in line against Israel, and when the battle spread, Israel was defeated by the Philistines, who slew about four thousand men on the field of battle. [3]And when the troops came to the camp, the elders of Israel said, "Why has the Lord put us to rout today before the Philis′tines? Let us bring the ark of the covenant of the Lord here from Shiloh, that he may come among us and save us from the power of our enemies." [4]So the people sent to Shiloh, and brought from there the ark of the covenant of the Lord of hosts, who is enthroned on the cherubim; and the two sons of Eli, Hoph′ni and Phin′ehas, were there with the ark of the covenant of God.

---

[g] Gk: Heb *your*.
[h] Gk: Heb *die as men*.
[i] Gk See 3:10: Heb *the Lord called Samuel*.
[j] Another reading is *for themselves*.
* 3:1: This account of the prophetic vocation of Samuel (cf. Is 6) is meant to begin a new chapter in the spiritual history of Israel.
† 4:1: Here begins a new phase in the epic struggle against the Philistines, which the editor has skilfully woven into the story of the ark and of Samuel.

5 When the ark of the covenant of the LORD came into the camp, all Israel gave a mighty shout, so that the earth resounded. ⁶And when the Philis′tines heard the noise of the shouting, they said, "What does this great shouting in the camp of the Hebrews mean?" And when they learned that the ark of the LORD had come to the camp, ⁷the Philis′tines were afraid; for they said, "A god has come into the camp." And they said, "Woe to us! For nothing like this has happened before. ⁸Woe to us! Who can deliver us from the power of these mighty gods? These are the gods who struck the Egyptians with every sort of plague in the wilderness. ⁹Take courage, and acquit yourselves like men, O Philis′tines, lest you become slaves to the Hebrews as they have been to you; acquit yourselves like men and fight."

10 So the Philis′tines fought, and Israel was defeated, and they fled, every man to his home; and there was a very great slaughter, for there fell of Israel thirty thousand foot soldiers. ¹¹And the ark of God was captured; and the two sons of Eli, Hoph′ni and Phin′ehas, were slain.

Death of Eli

12 A man of Benjamin ran from the battle line, and came to Shiloh the same day, with his clothes torn and with earth upon his head. ¹³When he arrived, Eli was sitting upon his seat by the road watching, for his heart trembled for the ark of God. And when the man came into the city and told the news, all the city cried out. ¹⁴When Eli heard the sound of the outcry, he said, "What is this uproar?" Then the man hastened and came and told Eli. ¹⁵Now Eli was ninety-eight years old and his eyes were set, so that he could not see. ¹⁶And the man said to Eli, "I am he who has come from the battle; I fled from the battle today." And he said, "How did it go, my son?" ¹⁷He who brought the tidings answered and said, "Israel has fled before the Philis′tines, and there has also been a great slaughter among the people; your two sons also, Hoph′ni and Phin′ehas, are dead, and the ark of God has been captured." ¹⁸When he mentioned the ark of God, Eli fell over backward from his seat by the side of the gate; and his neck was broken and he died, for he was an old man, and heavy. He had judged Israel forty years.

19 Now his daughter-in-law, the wife of Phin′ehas, was with child, about to give birth. And when she heard the tidings that the ark of God was captured, and that her father-in-law and her husband were dead, she bowed and gave birth; for her pains came upon her. ²⁰And about the time of her death the women attending her said to her, "Fear not, for you have borne a son." But she did not answer or give heed. ²¹And she named the child Ich′abod, * saying, "The glory has departed from Israel!" because the ark of God had been captured and because of her father-in-law

and her husband. ²²And she said, "The glory departed from Israel, for the ark of God has been captured."

The Philistines and the Ark

5 When the Philis′tines captured the ark of God, they carried it from Ebenezer to Ash′dod; ²then the Philis′tines took the ark of God and brought it into the house of Da′gon and set it up beside Dagon. ³And when the people of Ash′dod rose early the next day, behold, Da′gon had fallen face downward on the ground before the ark of the LORD. So they took Dagon and put him back in his place. ⁴But when they rose early on the next morning, behold, Da′gon had fallen face downward on the ground before the ark of the LORD, and the head of Dagon and both his hands were lying cut off upon the threshold; only the trunk of Dagon was left to him. ⁵This is why the priests of Da′gon and all who enter the house of Dagon do not tread on the threshold of Dagon in Ash′dod to this day.

6 The hand of the LORD was heavy upon the people of Ash′dod, and he terrified and afflicted them with tumors, both Ashdod and its territory. ⁷And when the men of Ash′dod saw how things were, they said, "The ark of the God of Israel must not remain with us; for his hand is heavy upon us and upon Da′gon our god." ⁸So they sent and gathered together all the lords of the Philis′tines, and said, "What shall we do with the ark of the God of Israel?" They answered, "Let the ark of the God of Israel be brought around to Gath." So they brought the ark of the God of Israel there. ⁹But after they had brought it around, the hand of the LORD was against the city, causing a very great panic, and he afflicted the men of the city, both young and old, so that tumors broke out upon them. ¹⁰So they sent the ark of God to Ek′ron. But when the ark of God came to Ekron, the people of Ekron cried out, "They have brought around to us the ark of the God of Israel to slay us and our people." ¹¹They sent therefore and gathered together all the lords of the Philis′tines, and said, "Send away the ark of the God of Israel, and let it return to its own place, that it may not slay us and our people." For there was a deathly panic throughout the whole city. The hand of God was very heavy there; ¹²the men who did not die were stricken with tumors, and the cry of the city went up to heaven.

The Ark Returned to Israel

6 The ark of the LORD was in the country of the Philis′tines seven months. ²And the Philis′tines called for the priests and the diviners and said, "What shall we do with the ark of the LORD?

---

* 4:21, *Ichabod:* The name means "The Glory is not"; i.e., the glory of the Lord enthroned over the ark has departed. Then followed the years during which the sanctuary of Shiloh was desolate and of which Jeremiah long afterward was acutely conscious; cf. Jer 7:12, 14; 26:6.

Tell us with what we shall send it to its place." ³They said, "If you send away the ark of the God of Israel, do not send it empty, but by all means return him a guilt offering. Then you will be healed, and it will be known to you why his hand does not turn away from you." ⁴And they said, "What is the guilt offering that we shall return to him?" They answered, "Five golden tumors and five golden mice, according to the number of the lords of the Philis'tines; for the same plague was upon all of you and upon your lords. ⁵So you must make images of your tumors and images of your mice that ravage the land, and give glory to the God of Israel; perhaps he will lighten his hand from off you and your gods and your land. ⁶Why should you harden your hearts as the Egyptians and Pharaoh hardened their hearts? After he had made sport of them, did not they let the people go, and they departed? ⁷Now then, take and prepare a new cart and two milch cows upon which there has never come a yoke, and yoke the cows to the cart, but take their calves home, away from them. ⁸And take the ark of the Lord and place it on the cart, and put in a box at its side the figures of gold, which you are returning to him as a guilt offering. Then send it off, and let it go its way. ⁹And watch; if it goes up on the way to its own land, to Beth-she'mesh, then it is he who has done us this great harm; but if not, then we shall know that it is not his hand that struck us, it happened to us by chance."

10 The men did so, and took two milch cows and yoked them to the cart, and shut up their calves at home. ¹¹And they put the ark of the Lord on the cart, and the box with the golden mice and the images of their tumors. ¹²And the cows went straight in the direction of Beth-she'mesh along one highway, lowing as they went; they turned neither to the right nor to the left, and the lords of the Philis'tines went after them as far as the border of Beth-shemesh. ¹³Now the people of Beth-she'mesh were reaping their wheat harvest in the valley; and when they lifted up their eyes and saw the ark, they rejoiced to see it. ¹⁴The cart came into the field of Joshua of Beth-she'mesh, and stopped there. A great stone was there; and they split up the wood of the cart and offered the cows as a burnt offering to the Lord. ¹⁵And the Levites took down the ark of the Lord and the box that was beside it, in which were the golden figures, and set them upon the great stone; and the men of Beth-she'mesh offered burnt offerings and sacrificed sacrifices on that day to the Lord. ¹⁶And when the five lords of the Philis'tines saw it, they returned that day to Ek'ron.

17 These are the golden tumors, which the Philis'tines returned as a guilt offering to the Lord: one for Ash'dod, one for Gaza, one for Ash'kelon, one for Gath, one for Ek'ron; ¹⁸also the golden

mice, according to the number of all the cities of the Philis'tines belonging to the five lords, both fortified cities and unwalled villages. The great stone, beside which they set down the ark of the Lord, is a witness to this day in the field of Joshua of Beth-she'mesh.

The Ark at Kiriath-jearim

19 And he slew some of the men of Beth-she'mesh, because they looked into the ark of the Lord; he slew seventy men of them, ᵏ and the people mourned because the Lord had made a great slaughter among the people. ²⁰Then the men of Beth-she'mesh said, "Who is able to stand before the Lord, this holy God? And to whom shall he go up away from us?" ²¹So they sent messengers to the inhabitants of Kir'iath-je'arim, saying, "The Philis'tines have returned the ark of the Lord. Come down and take it up to you."

7 ¹And the men of Kir'iath-je'arim came and took up the ark of the Lord, and brought it to the house of Abin'adab on the hill; and they consecrated his son, Elea'zar, to have charge of the ark of the Lord. ²From the day that the ark was lodged at Kir'iath-je'arim, a long time passed, some twenty years, and all the house of Israel lamented after the Lord. *

Samuel as Judge of Israel

3 Then Samuel said to all the house of Israel, "If you are returning to the Lord with all your heart, then put away the foreign gods and the Ash'taroth from among you, and direct your heart to the Lord, and serve him only, and he will deliver you out of the hand of the Philis'tines." ⁴Israel put away the Ba'als and the Ash'taroth, and they served the Lord only.

5 Then Samuel said, "Gather all Israel at Mizpah, and I will pray to the Lord for you." ⁶So they gathered at Mizpah, and drew water and poured it out before the Lord, and fasted on that day, and said there, "We have sinned against the Lord." And Samuel judged the sons of Israel at Mizpah. ⁷Now when the Philis'tines heard that the sons of Israel had gathered at Mizpah, the lords of the Philistines went up against Israel. And when the sons of Israel heard of it they were afraid of the Philistines. ⁸And the sons of Israel said to Samuel, "Do not cease to cry to the Lord our God for us, that he may save us from the hand of the Philis'tines." ⁹So Samuel took a suckling lamb and offered it as a whole burnt offering to the Lord; and Samuel cried to the Lord for Israel, and the Lord answered him. ¹⁰As Samuel was offering up the burnt offering, the Philis'tines drew near to attack Israel; but the Lord thundered with a mighty voice that day against the Philistines and threw them into confusion; and they were routed

---

ᵏ Cn: Heb *of the people seventy men, fifty thousand men.*
* 7:2: The story of the ark, which comes from a special source, is continued in 2 Sam 6.

before Israel. [11]And the men of Israel went out of Mizpah and pursued the Philis′tines, and struck them, as far as below Beth-car.

12 Then Samuel took a stone and set it up between Mizpah and Jesha′nah,[1] and called its name Ebenezer;[m] for he said, "Hitherto the Lord has helped us." [13]So the Philis′tines were subdued and did not again enter the territory of Israel. And the hand of the Lord was against the Philistines all the days of Samuel. [14]The cities which the Philis′tines had taken from Israel were restored to Israel, from Ek′ron to Gath; and Israel rescued their territory from the hand of the Philistines. There was peace also between Israel and the Am′orites.

15 Samuel judged Israel all the days of his life. [16]And he went on a circuit year by year to Bethel, Gilgal, and Mizpah; and he judged Israel in all these places. [17]Then he would come back to Ra′mah, for his home was there, and there also he administered justice to Israel. And he built there an altar to the Lord.

Israel Asks for a King

8 When Samuel became old, he made his sons judges over Israel. [2]The name of his firstborn son was Joel, and the name of his second, Abi′jah; they were judges in Be′er-she′ba. [3]Yet his sons did not walk in his ways, but turned aside after gain; they took bribes and perverted justice.

4 Then all the elders of Israel gathered together and came to Samuel at Ra′mah, [5]and said to him, "Behold, you are old and your sons do not walk in your ways; now appoint for us a king to govern us like all the nations." [6]But the thing displeased Samuel when they said, "Give us a king to govern us." And Samuel prayed to the Lord. [7]And the Lord said to Samuel, "Listen to the voice of the people in all that they say to you; for they have not rejected you, but they have rejected me from being king over them. [8]According to all the deeds which they have done to me,[n] from the day I brought them up out of Egypt even to this day, forsaking me and serving other gods, so they are also doing to you. [9]Now then, listen to their voice; only, you shall solemnly warn them, and show them the ways of the king who shall reign over them."

10 So Samuel told all the words of the Lord to the people who were asking a king from him.[*] [11]He said, "These will be the ways of the king who will reign over you: he will take your sons and appoint them to his chariots and to be his horsemen, and to run before his chariots; [12]and he will appoint for himself commanders of thousands and commanders of fifties, and some to plow his ground and to reap his harvest, and to make his implements of war and the equipment of his chariots. [13]He will take your daughters to be perfumers and cooks and bakers. [14]He will

take the best of your fields and vineyards and olive orchards and give them to his servants. [15]He will take the tenth of your grain and of your vineyards and give it to his officers and to his servants. [16]He will take your menservants and maidservants, and the best of your cattle[o] and your donkeys, and put them to his work. [17]He will take the tenth of your flocks, and you shall be his slaves. [18]And in that day you will cry out because of your king, whom you have chosen for yourselves; but the Lord will not answer you in that day."

Israel's Demand Granted

19 But the people refused to listen to the voice of Samuel; and they said, "No! but we will have a king over us, [20]that we also may be like all the nations, and that our king may govern us and go out before us and fight our battles." [21]And when Samuel had heard all the words of the people, he repeated them in the ears of the Lord. [22]And the Lord said to Samuel, "Listen to their voice, and make them a king." Samuel then said to the men of Israel, "Go every man to his city."

Saul Chosen to Be King

9 There was a man of Benjamin whose name was Kish, the son of Abi′el, son of Ze′ror, son of Beco′rath, son of Aphi′ah, a Benjaminite, a man of wealth; [2]and he had a son whose name was Saul, a handsome young man. There was not a man among the sons of Israel more handsome than he; from his shoulders upward he was taller than any of the people.

3 Now the donkeys of Kish, Saul's father, were lost. So Kish said to Saul his son, "Take one of the servants with you, and arise, go and look for the donkeys." [4]And they[p] passed through the hill country of E′phraim and passed through the land of Shal′ishah, but they did not find them. And they passed through the land of Sha′alim, but they were not there. Then they passed through the land of Benjamin, but did not find them.

5 When they came to the land of Zuph, Saul said to his servant who was with him, "Come, let us go back, lest my father cease to care about the donkeys and become anxious about us." [6]But he said to him, "Behold, there is a man of God in this city, and he is a man that is held in honor; all that he says comes true. Let us go there; perhaps he can tell us about the journey on which we have set out." [7]Then Saul said to his servant, "But if we go, what can we bring the man? For the bread in our

[1] Gk Syr: Heb Shen.
[m] That is Stone of help.
[n] Gk: Heb lacks to me.
[o] Gk: Heb young men.
[p] Gk Vg: Heb he.
[*] 8:10ff: Choosing a king. Two accounts are discernible—a monarchist and an antimonarchist. In the absence of a central sanctuary and in an atmosphere of defeat, one section of the people demanded a king to re-establish their fortunes; the others preferred to leave it to God to raise up leaders when necessary, as in the days of the judges.

sacks is gone, and there is no present to bring to the man of God. What have we?" [8]The servant answered Saul again, "Here, I have with me the fourth part of a shekel of silver, and I will give it to the man of God, to tell us our way." [9](Formerly in Israel, when a man went to inquire of God, he said, "Come, let us go to the seer"; for he who is now called a prophet was formerly called a seer.) [10]And Saul said to his servant, "Well said; come, let us go." So they went to the city where the man of God was.

11 As they went up the hill to the city, they met young maidens coming out to draw water, and said to them, "Is the seer here?" [12]They answered, "He is; behold, he is just ahead of you. Make haste; he has come just now to the city, because the people have a sacrifice today on the high place. [13]As soon as you enter the city, you will find him, before he goes up to the high place * to eat; for the people will not eat till he comes, since he must bless the sacrifice; afterward those eat who are invited. Now go up, for you will meet him immediately." [14]So they went up to the city. As they were entering the city, they saw Samuel coming out toward them on his way up to the high place.

15 Now the day before Saul came, the LORD had revealed to Samuel: [16]"Tomorrow about this time I will send to you a man from the land of Benjamin, and you shall anoint him to be prince over my people Israel. He shall save my people from the hand of the Philis'tines; for I have seen the affliction of [q] my people, because their cry has come to me." [17]When Samuel saw Saul, the LORD told him, "Here is the man of whom I spoke to you! He it is who shall rule over my people." [18]Then Saul approached Samuel in the gate, and said, "Tell me where is the house of the seer?" [19]Samuel answered Saul, "I am the seer; go up before me to the high place, for today you shall eat with me, and in the morning I will let you go and will tell you all that is on your mind. [20]As for your donkeys that were lost three days ago, do not set your mind on them, for they have been found. And for whom is all that is desirable in Israel? Is it not for you and for all your father's house?" [21]Saul answered, "Am I not a Benjaminite, from the least of the tribes of Israel? And is not my family the humblest of all the families of the tribe of Benjamin? Why then have you spoken to me in this way?"

22 Then Samuel took Saul and his servant and brought them into the hall and gave them a place at the head of those who had been invited, who were about thirty persons. [23]And Samuel said to the cook, "Bring the portion I gave you, of which I said to you, 'Put it aside.'" [24]So the cook took up the leg and the upper portion [r] and set them before Saul; and Samuel said, "See, what was kept is set before you. Eat; because it was kept for you

until the hour appointed, that you might eat with the guests." [s]

So Saul ate with Samuel that day. [25]And when they came down from the high place into the city, a bed was spread for Saul [t] upon the roof, and he lay down to sleep. [26]Then at the break of dawn [u] Samuel called to Saul upon the roof, "Up, that I may send you on your way." So Saul arose, and both he and Samuel went out into the street.

Samuel Anoints Saul

27 As they were going down to the outskirts of the city, Samuel said to Saul, "Tell the servant to pass on before us, and when he has passed on stop here yourself for a while, that I may make known to you the word of God."

10 Then Samuel took a vial of oil and poured it on his head, and kissed him and said, "Has not the LORD anointed you to be prince over his people Israel? And you shall reign over the people of the LORD and you will save them from the hand of their enemies round about. And this shall be the sign to you that the LORD has anointed you to be prince [w] over his heritage. [2]When you depart from me today you will meet two men by Rachel's tomb in the territory of Benjamin at Zelzah, and they will say to you, 'The donkeys which you went to seek are found, and now your father has ceased to care about the donkeys and is anxious about you, saying, "What shall I do about my son?"' [3]Then you shall go on from there further and come to the oak of Ta'bor; three men going up to God at Bethel will meet you there, one carrying three kids, another carrying three loaves of bread, and another carrying a skin of wine. [4]And they will greet you and give you two loaves of bread, which you shall accept from their hand. [5]After that you shall come to Gib'eath-elo'him, [x] where there is a garrison of the Philis'tines; and there, as you come to the city, you will meet a band of prophets † coming down from the high place with harp, tambourine, flute, and lyre before them, prophesying. [6]Then the spirit of the LORD will come mightily upon you, and you shall prophesy with them and be turned into another man. [7]Now when these signs meet you, do whatever your hand finds to do, for God is with you. [8]And you shall go down before

---

[q] Heb lacks *the affliction of.*
[r] Heb obscure.
[s] Cn: Heb *saying, I have invited the people.*
[t] Gk: Heb *and he spoke with Saul.*
[u] Gk: Heb *and they arose early and at break of dawn.*
[w] Gk: Heb lacks *over his people Israel? And you shall . . . to be prince.*
[x] Or *the hill of God.*
* 9:13, *high place:* It was customary in early Israel to worship God on raised platforms or hilltops, as the Canaanites did their gods. Later such practices were forbidden as leading to idolatry, and worship was allowed only in Jerusalem; cf. Deut 12:2ff.
† 10:5, *prophets:* An inferior kind of prophet who flourished for a time in Israel. They were quite different from the writing prophets, in that they cultivated states of ecstasy and even used musical instruments for the purpose.

me to Gilgal; and behold, I am coming to you to offer burnt offerings and to sacrifice peace offerings. Seven days you shall wait, until I come to you and show you what you shall do."

Saul Prophesies

9 When he turned his back to leave Samuel, God gave him another heart; and all these signs came to pass that day. [10]When they came to Gib'e-ah, [z] behold, a band of prophets met him; and the spirit of God came mightily upon him, and he prophesied among them. [11]And when all who knew him before saw how he prophesied with the prophets, the people said to one another, "What has come over the son of Kish? Is Saul also among the prophets?" [12]And a man of the place answered, "And who is their father?" Therefore it became a proverb, "Is Saul also among the prophets?" [13]When he had finished prophesying, he came to the high place.

14 Saul's uncle said to him and to his servant, "Where did you go?" And he said, "To seek the donkeys; and when we saw they were not to be found, we went to Samuel." [15]And Saul's uncle said, "Please, tell me what Samuel said to you." [16]And Saul said to his uncle, "He told us plainly that the donkeys had been found." But about the matter of the kingdom, of which Samuel had spoken, he did not tell him anything.

Saul Proclaimed King

17 Now Samuel called the people together to the LORD at Mizpah; [18]and he said to the sons of Israel, "Thus says the LORD, the God of Israel, 'I brought up Israel out of Egypt, and I delivered you from the hand of the Egyptians and from the hand of all the kingdoms that were oppressing you.' [19]But you have this day rejected your God, who saves you from all your calamities and your distresses; and you have said, 'No! but set a king over us.' Now therefore present yourselves before the LORD by your tribes and by your thousands."

20 Then Samuel brought all the tribes of Israel near, and the tribe of Benjamin was taken by lot. [21]He brought the tribe of Benjamin near by its families, and the family of the Ma'trites was taken by lot; finally he brought the family of the Matrites near man by man, [a] and Saul the son of Kish was taken by lot. But when they sought him, he could not be found. [22]So they inquired again of the LORD, "Did the man come here?" [b] and the LORD said, "Behold, he has hidden himself among the baggage." [23]Then they ran and fetched him from there; and when he stood among the people, he was taller than any of the people from his shoulders upward. [24]And Samuel said to all the people, "Do you see him whom the LORD has chosen? There is none like him among all the people." And all the people shouted, "Long live the king!"

25 Then Samuel told the people the rights and duties of the kingship; and he wrote them in a book and laid it up before the LORD. Then Samuel sent all the people away, each one to his home. [26]Saul also went to his home at Gib'e-ah, and with him went men of valor whose hearts God had touched. [27]But some worthless fellows said, "How can this man save us?" And they despised him, and brought him no present. But he held his peace.

Saul Defeats the Ammonite

11 Then Na'hash the Am'monite went up and besieged Ja'besh-gil'ead; and all the men of Ja'besh said to Nahash, "Make a treaty with us, and we will serve you." [2]But Na'hash the Am'monite said to them, "On this condition I will make a treaty with you, that I gouge out all your right eyes, and thus put disgrace upon all Israel." [3]The elders of Ja'besh said to him, "Give us seven days respite that we may send messengers through all the territory of Israel. Then, if there is no one to save us, we will give ourselves up to you." [4]When the messengers came to Gib'e-ah of Saul, they reported the matter in the hearing of the people; and all the people wept aloud.

5 Now Saul was coming from the field behind the oxen; and Saul said, "What ails the people, that they are weeping?" So they told him the tidings of the men of Ja'besh. [6]And the spirit of God came mightily upon Saul when he heard these words, and his anger was greatly kindled. [7]He took a yoke of oxen, and cut them in pieces and sent them throughout all the territory of Israel by the hand of messengers, saying, "Whoever does not come out after Saul and Samuel, so shall it be done to his oxen!" Then the dread of the LORD fell upon the people, and they came out as one man. [8]When he mustered them at Be'zek, the men of Israel were three hundred thousand, and the men of Judah thirty thousand.* [9]And they said to the messengers who had come, "Thus shall you say to the men of Ja'besh-gil'ead: 'Tomorrow, by the time the sun is hot, you shall have deliverance.'" When the messengers came and told the men of Ja'besh, they were glad. [10]Therefore the men of Ja'besh said, "Tomorrow we will give ourselves up to you, and you may do to us whatever seems good to you." [11]And the next day Saul put the people in three companies; and they came into the midst of the camp in the morning watch, and cut down the Am'monites until the heat of the day; and those who survived were scattered, so that no two of them were left together.

12 Then the people said to Samuel, "Who is it that said, 'Shall Saul reign over us?' Bring the men, that we may put them to death." [13]But Saul

---

[z] Or the hill.
[a] Gk: Heb lacks finally . . . man by man.
[b] Gk: Heb Is there yet a man to come here?
10:11–12: 19:23, 24.
* **11:8:** These figures are probably a later insertion.

said, "Not a man shall be put to death this day, for today the Lord has wrought deliverance in Israel." [14]Then Samuel said to the people, "Come, let us go to Gilgal and there renew the kingdom." [15]So all the people went to Gilgal, and there they made Saul king before the Lord in Gilgal. There they sacrificed peace offerings before the Lord, and there Saul and all the men of Israel rejoiced greatly.

Samuel's Farewell Address

12 And Samuel said to all Israel, "Behold, I have listened to your voice in all that you have said to me, and have made a king over you. [2]And now, behold, the king walks before you; and I am old and gray, and behold, my sons are with you; and I have walked before you from my youth until this day. [3]Here I am; testify against me before the Lord and before his anointed. Whose ox have I taken? Or whose donkey have I taken? Or whom have I defrauded? Whom have I oppressed? Or from whose hand have I taken a bribe to blind my eyes with it? Testify against me [c] and I will restore it to you." [4]They said, "You have not defrauded us or oppressed us or taken anything from any man's hand." [5]And he said to them, "The Lord is witness against you, and his anointed is witness this day, that you have not found anything in my hand." And they said, "He is witness."

[6] And Samuel said to the people, "The Lord is witness, [d] who appointed Moses and Aaron and brought your fathers up out of the land of Egypt. [7]Now therefore stand still, that I may plead with you before the Lord concerning all the saving deeds of the Lord which he performed for you and for your fathers. [8]When Jacob went into Egypt and the Egyptians oppressed them, [e] then your fathers cried to the Lord and the Lord sent Moses and Aaron, who brought forth your fathers out of Egypt, and made them dwell in this place. [9]But they forgot the Lord their God; and he sold them into the hand of Sis'era, commander of the army of Ja'bin king of [f] Ha'zor, and into the hand of the Philis'tines, and into the hand of the king of Moab; and they fought against them. [10]And they cried to the Lord, and said, 'We have sinned, because we have forsaken the Lord, and have served the Ba'als and the Ash'taroth; but now deliver us out of the hand of our enemies, and we will serve you.' [11]And the Lord sent Jerubba'al * and Barak, [g] and Jephthah, and Samuel, and delivered you out of the hand of your enemies on every side; and you dwelt in safety. [12]And when you saw that Na'hash the king of the Am'monites came against you, you said to me, 'No, but a king shall reign over us,' when the Lord your God was your king. [13]And now behold the king whom you have chosen, for whom you have asked; behold, the Lord has set a king over you. [14]If you will fear the Lord and serve

him and listen to his voice and not rebel against the commandment of the Lord, and if both you and the king who reigns over you will follow the Lord your God, it will be well; [15]but if you will not listen to the voice of the Lord, but rebel against the commandment of the Lord, then the hand of the Lord will be against you and your king. [h] [16]Now therefore stand still and see this great thing, which the Lord will do before your eyes. [17]Is it not wheat harvest today? I will call upon the Lord, that he may send thunder and rain; and you shall know and see that your wickedness is great, which you have done in the sight of the Lord, in asking for yourselves a king." [18]So Samuel called upon the Lord, and the Lord sent thunder and rain that day; and all the people greatly feared the Lord and Samuel.

[19] And all the people said to Samuel, "Pray for your servants to the Lord your God, that we may not die; for we have added to all our sins this evil, to ask for ourselves a king." [20]And Samuel said to the people, "Fear not; you have done all this evil, yet do not turn aside from following the Lord, but serve the Lord with all your heart; [21]and do not turn aside after [i] vain things which cannot profit or save, for they are vain. [22]For the Lord will not cast away his people, for his great name's sake, because it has pleased the Lord to make you a people for himself. [23]Moreover as for me, far be it from me that I should sin against the Lord by ceasing to pray for you; and I will instruct you in the good and the right way. [24]Only fear the Lord, and serve him faithfully with all your heart; for consider what great things he has done for you. [25]But if you still do wickedly, you shall be swept away, both you and your king." †

Saul's Unlawful Sacrifice

13 Saul was . . . [j] years old when he began to reign; and he reigned . . . and two [k] ‡ years over Israel.

[2] Saul chose three thousand men of Israel; two thousand were with Saul in Mich'mash and the hill country of Bethel, and a thousand were with Jonathan in Gib'e-ah of Benjamin; the rest of the people he sent home, every man to his tent. [3]Jonathan defeated the garrison of the Philis'tines which was at Ge'ba; and the Philistines heard of it. And Saul blew the trumpet throughout all the

---

[c] Gk: Heb lacks *Testify against me.*
[d] Gk: Heb lacks *is witness.*
[e] Gk: Heb lacks *and the Egyptians oppressed them.*
[f] Gk: Heb lacks *Jabin king of.*
[g] Gk Syr: Heb *Bedan.*
[h] Gk: Heb *fathers.*
[i] Gk Syr Tg Vg: Heb *because after.*
[j] The number is lacking in Heb.
[k] *Two* is not the entire number. Something has dropped out.
* 12:11, *Jerubbaal:* i.e., Gideon.
† 12:20–25: Samuel here summarizes the antimonarchist attitude; cf. Josh 24.
‡ 13:1: Acts 13:21 says Saul reigned forty years; but so did David (2 Sam 5:5). These must be round numbers, to indicate a fairly long rule.

land, saying, "Let the Hebrews hear." [4]And all Israel heard it said that Saul had defeated the garrison of the Philis'tines, and also that Israel had become odious to the Philistines. And the people were called out to join Saul at Gilgal.

5 And the Philis'tines mustered to fight with Israel, thirty thousand chariots, and six thousand horsemen, and troops like the sand on the seashore in multitude; they came up and encamped in Mich'mash, to the east of Beth-a'ven. [6]When the men of Israel saw that they were in straits (for the people were hard pressed), the people hid themselves in caves and in holes and in rocks and in tombs and in cisterns, [7]or crossed the fords of the Jordan[1] to the land of Gad and Gilead. Saul was still at Gilgal, and all the people followed him trembling.

8 He waited seven days, the time appointed by Samuel; but Samuel did not come to Gilgal, and the people were scattering from him. [9]So Saul said, "Bring the burnt offering here to me, and the peace offerings." And he offered the burnt offering. [10]As soon as he had finished offering the burnt offering, behold, Samuel came; and Saul went out to meet him and salute him. [11]Samuel said, "What have you done?" And Saul said, "When I saw that the people were scattering from me, and that you did not come within the days appointed, and that the Philis'tines had mustered at Mich'mash, [12]I said, 'Now the Philis'tines will come down upon me at Gilgal and I have not entreated the favor of the LORD'; so I forced myself, and offered the burnt offering." [13]And Samuel said to Saul, "You have done foolishly; you have not kept the commandment of the LORD your God, which he commanded you; for now the LORD would have established your kingdom over Israel for ever. [14]But now your kingdom shall not continue; the LORD has sought out a man after his own heart; and the LORD has appointed him to be prince over his people, because you have not kept what the LORD commanded you." [15]And Samuel arose, and went up from Gilgal to Gib'e-ah of Benjamin.

And Saul numbered the people who were present with him, about six hundred men. [16]And Saul, and Jonathan his son, and the people who were present with them, stayed in Ge'ba of Benjamin; but the Philis'tines encamped in Mich'mash. [17]And raiders came out of the camp of the Philis'tines in three companies; one company turned toward Oph'rah, to the land of Shual, [18]another company turned toward Beth-ho'ron, and another company turned toward the border that looks down upon the valley of Zebo'im toward the wilderness.

Preparations for Battle

19 Now there was no smith to be found throughout all the land of Israel; for the Philis'tines said, "Lest the Hebrews make themselves swords or spears"; [20]but every one of the Israelites went down to the Philis'tines to sharpen his plowshare, his mattock, his axe, or his sickle;[m] [21]and the charge was a pim for the plowshares and for the mattocks, and a third of a shekel for sharpening the axes and for setting the goads.[n] [22]So on the day of the battle there was neither sword nor spear found in the hand of any of the people with Saul and Jonathan; but Saul and Jonathan his son had them. [23]And the garrison of the Philis'tines went out to the pass of Mich'mash.

Jonathan Surprises the Philistines

14 One day Jonathan the son of Saul said to the young man who bore his armor, "Come, let us go over to the Philis'tine garrison on yonder side." But he did not tell his father. [2]Saul was staying in the outskirts of Gib'e-ah under the pomegranate tree which is at Migron; the people who were with him were about six hundred men, [3]and Ahi'jah the son of Ahi'tub, Ich'abod's brother, son of Phin'ehas, son of Eli, the priest of the LORD in Shiloh, wearing an ephod. And the people did not know that Jonathan had gone. [4]In the pass,[o] by which Jonathan sought to go over to the Philis'tine garrison, there was a rocky crag on the one side and a rocky crag on the other side; the name of the one was Bozez, and the name of the other Se'neh. [5]The one crag rose on the north in front of Mich'mash, and the other on the south in front of Ge'ba.

6 And Jonathan said to the young man who bore his armor, "Come, let us go over to the garrison of these uncircumcised; it may be that the LORD will work for us; for nothing can hinder the LORD from saving by many or by few." [7]And his armor-bearer said to him, "Do all that your mind inclines to;[p] behold, I am with you, as is your mind so is mine."[q] [8]Then said Jonathan, "Behold, we will cross over to the men, and we will show ourselves to them. [9]If they say to us, 'Wait until we come to you,' then we will stand still in our place, and we will not go up to them. [10]But if they say, 'Come up to us,' then we will go up; for the LORD has given them into our hand. And this shall be the sign to us." [11]So both of them showed themselves to the garrison of the Philis'tines; and the Philistines said, "Look, Hebrews are coming out of the holes where they have hid themselves." [12]And the men of the garrison hailed Jonathan and his armor-bearer, and said, "Come up to us, and we will show you a thing." And Jonathan said to his armor-bearer, "Come up after me; for the

---

[1] Cn: Heb *Hebrews crossed the Jordan.*
[m] Gk: Heb *plowshare.*
[n] The Heb of this verse is obscure.
[o] Heb *between the passes.*
[p] Gk: Heb *Do all that is in your mind. Turn.*
[q] Gk: Heb lacks *so is mine.*
13:14: Acts 13:22.

LORD has given them into the hand of Israel." [13]Then Jonathan climbed up on his hands and feet, and his armor-bearer after him. And they fell before Jonathan, and his armor-bearer killed them after him; [14]and that first slaughter, which Jonathan and his armor-bearer made, was of about twenty men within as it were half a furrow's length in an acre [x] of land. [15]And there was a panic in the camp, in the field, and among all the people; the garrison and even the raiders trembled; the earth quaked; and it became a very great panic.

16 And the watchmen of Saul in Gib'e-ah of Benjamin looked; and behold, the multitude was surging here and there. [s] [17]Then Saul said to the people who were with him, "Number and see who has gone from us." And when they had numbered, behold, Jonathan and his armor-bearer were not there. [18]And Saul said to Ahi'jah, "Bring the ark of God here." For the ark of God went at that time with the sons of Israel. [19]And while Saul was talking to the priest, the tumult in the camp of the Philis'tines increased more and more; and Saul said to the priest, "Withdraw your hand." [20]Then Saul and all the people who were with him rallied and went into the battle; and behold, every man's sword was against his fellow, and there was very great confusion. [21]Now the Hebrews who had been with the Philis'tines before that time and who had gone up with them into the camp, even they also turned to be with [t] the Israelites who were with Saul and Jonathan. [22]Likewise, when all the men of Israel who had hid themselves in the hill country of E'phraim heard that the Philis'tines were fleeing, they too followed hard after them in the battle. [23]So the LORD delivered Israel that day; and the battle passed beyond Beth-a'ven.

Saul's Rash Oath

24 And the men of Israel were distressed that day; for Saul laid an oath on the people, saying, "Cursed be the man who eats food until it is evening and I am avenged on my enemies." So none of the people tasted food. [25]And all the people [u] came into the forest; and there was honey on the ground. [26]And when the people entered the forest, behold, the honey was dropping, but no man put his hand to his mouth; for the people feared the oath. [27]But Jonathan had not heard his father charge the people with the oath; so he put forth the tip of the staff that was in his hand, and dipped it in the honeycomb, and put his hand to his mouth; and his eyes became bright. [28]Then one of the people said, "Your father strictly charged the people with an oath, saying, 'Cursed be the man who eats food this day.'" And the people were faint. [29]Then Jonathan said, "My father has troubled the land; see how my eyes have become bright, because I tasted a little of this honey. [30]How much better if the people had eaten freely today of the spoil of their enemies which they found; for now the slaughter among the Philis'tines has not been great."

31 They struck down the Philis'tines that day from Mich'mash to Ai'jalon. And the people were very faint; [32]the people flew upon the spoil, and took sheep and oxen and calves, and slew them on the ground; and the people ate them with the blood. [33]Then they told Saul, "Behold, the people are sinning against the LORD, by eating with the blood." And he said, "You have dealt treacherously; roll a great stone to me here." [v] [34]And Saul said, "Disperse yourselves among the people, and say to them, 'Let every man bring his ox or his sheep, and slay them here, and eat; and do not sin against the LORD by eating with the blood.'" So every one of the people brought his ox with him that night, and slew them there. [35]And Saul built an altar to the LORD; it was the first altar that he built to the LORD.

The People Ransom Jonathan

36 Then Saul said, "Let us go down after the Philis'tines by night and despoil them until the morning light; let us not leave a man of them." And they said, "Do whatever seems good to you." But the priest said, "Let us draw near here to God." [37]And Saul inquired of God, "Shall I go down after the Philis'tines? Will you give them into the hand of Israel?" But he did not answer him that day. [38]And Saul said, "Come here, all you leaders of the people; and know and see how this sin has arisen today. [39]For as the LORD lives who saves Israel, though it be in Jonathan my son, he shall surely die." But there was not a man among all the people that answered him. [40]Then he said to all Israel, "You shall be on one side, and I and Jonathan my son will be on the other side." And the people said to Saul, "Do what seems good to you." [41]Therefore Saul said, "O LORD God of Israel, why have you not answered your servant this day? If this guilt is in me or in Jonathan my son, O LORD, God of Israel, give U'rim; but if this guilt is in your people Israel, [w] give Thummim." And Jonathan and Saul were taken, but the people escaped. [42]Then Saul said, "Cast the lot between me and my son Jonathan." And Jonathan was taken. [*]

43 Then Saul said to Jonathan, "Tell me what you have done." And Jonathan told him, "I tasted a little honey with the tip of the staff that was in my hand; here I am, I will die." [44]And Saul said, "God do so to me and more also; you shall surely die, Jonathan." [45]Then the people said to Saul,

---

[x] Heb yoke.
[s] Gk: Heb they went and there.
[t] Gk Syr Vg Tg: Heb round about, they also, to be with.
[u] Heb land.
[v] Gk: Heb this day.
[w] Vg Compare Gk: Heb Saul said to the LORD, the God of Israel.
[*] 14:38–42: This passage shows how the sacred lots were cast to find out God's will.

"Shall Jonathan die, who has wrought this great victory in Israel? Far from it! As the LORD lives, there shall not one hair of his head fall to the ground; for he has wrought with God this day." So the people ransomed Jonathan, that he did not die. [46]Then Saul went up from pursuing the Philis'tines; and the Philistines went to their own place.

Saul's Continuing Wars

47 When Saul had taken the kingship over Israel, he fought against all his enemies on every side, against Moab, against the Am'monites, against E'dom, against the kings of Zobah, and against the Philis'tines; wherever he turned he put them to the worse. [48]And he did valiantly, and struck the Amal'ekites, and delivered Israel out of the hands of those who plundered them.

49 Now the sons of Saul were Jonathan, Ishvi, and Mal''chishu'a; and the names of his two daughters were these: the name of the first-born was Merab, and the name of the younger Michal; [50]and the name of Saul's wife was Ahin'o-am the daughter of Ahim'a-az. And the name of the commander of his army was Abner the son of Ner, Saul's uncle; [51]Kish was the father of Saul, and Ner the father of Abner was the son of Abi'el.

52 There was hard fighting against the Philis'tines all the days of Saul; and when Saul saw any strong man, or any valiant man, he attached him to himself.

Saul Defeats the Amalekites but Disobeys

15 And Samuel said to Saul, "The LORD sent me to anoint you king over his people Israel; now therefore listen to the words of the LORD. [2]Thus says the LORD of hosts, 'I will punish what Am'alek did to Israel in opposing them on the way, when they came up out of Egypt. [3]Now go and strike Am'alek, and utterly destroy all that they have; do not spare them, but kill both man and woman, infant and suckling, ox and sheep, camel and donkey.'"

4 So Saul summoned the people, and numbered them in Tela'im, two hundred thousand men on foot, and ten thousand men of Judah. [5]And Saul came to the city of Am'alek, and lay in wait in the valley. [6]And Saul said to the Kenites, "Go, depart, go down from among the Amal'ekites, lest I destroy you with them; for you showed kindness to all the people of Israel when they came up out of Egypt." So the Kenites departed from among the Amalekites. [7]And Saul defeated the Amal'ekites, from Hav'ilah as far as Shur, which is east of Egypt. [8]And he took A'gag the king of the Amal'ekites alive, and utterly destroyed all the people with the edge of the sword. [9]But Saul and the people spared A'gag, and the best of the sheep and of the oxen and of the fatlings, and the lambs, and all that was good, and would not utterly destroy them; all that was despised and worthless they utterly destroyed.

The Lord Rejects Saul for His Disobedience

10 The word of the LORD came to Samuel: [11]"I repent that I have made Saul king; for he has turned back from following me, and has not performed my commandments." And Samuel was angry; and he cried to the LORD all night. [12]And Samuel rose early to meet Saul in the morning; and it was told Samuel, "Saul came to Carmel, and behold, he set up a monument for himself and turned, and passed on, and went down to Gilgal." [13]And Samuel came to Saul, and Saul said to him, "Blessed be you to the LORD; I have performed the commandment of the LORD." [14]And Samuel said, "What then is this bleating of the sheep in my ears, and the lowing of the oxen which I hear?" [15]Saul said, "They have brought them from the Amal'ekites; for the people spared the best of the sheep and of the oxen, to sacrifice to the LORD your God; and the rest we have utterly destroyed." [16]Then Samuel said to Saul, "Stop! I will tell you what the LORD said to me this night." And he said to him, "Say on."

17 And Samuel said, "Though you are little in your own eyes, are you not the head of the tribes of Israel? The LORD anointed you king over Israel. [18]And the LORD sent you on a mission, and said, 'Go, utterly destroy the sinners, the Amal'ekites, and fight against them until they are consumed.' [19]Why then did you not obey the voice of the LORD? Why did you swoop on the spoil, and do what was evil in the sight of the LORD?" [20]And Saul said to Samuel, "I have obeyed the voice of the LORD, I have gone on the mission on which the LORD sent me, I have brought A'gag the king of Am'alek, and I have utterly destroyed the Amal'ekites. [21]But the people took of the spoil, sheep and oxen, the best of the things devoted to destruction, to sacrifice to the LORD your God in Gilgal." [22]And Samuel said,

"Has the LORD as great delight in burnt
    offerings and sacrifices,
  as in obeying the voice of the LORD?
Behold, to obey is better than sacrifice,
  and to listen than the fat of rams.
[23]For rebellion is as the sin of divination,
  and stubbornness is as iniquity and
    idolatry.
Because you have rejected the word of the
  LORD,
  he has also rejected you from being king." *

24 And Saul said to Samuel, "I have sinned; for I have transgressed the commandment of the LORD and your words, because I feared the people

---

14:49: 31:2; 1 Chron 10:2.
15:22: Mk 12:33.
* 15:22–23: Samuel does not condemn sacrifices but says obedience is better.

and obeyed their voice. [25]Now therefore, I beg, pardon my sin, and return with me, that I may worship the LORD." [26]And Samuel said to Saul, "I will not return with you; for you have rejected the word of the LORD, and the LORD has rejected you from being king over Israel." [27]As Samuel turned to go away, Saul laid hold upon the skirt of his robe, and it tore. [28]And Samuel said to him, "The LORD has torn the kingdom of Israel from you this day, and has given it to a neighbor of yours, who is better than you. [29]And also the Glory of Israel will not lie or repent; for he is not a man, that he should repent." [30]Then he said, "I have sinned; yet honor me now before the elders of my people and before Israel, and return with me, that I may worship the LORD your God." [31]So Samuel turned back after Saul; and Saul worshiped the LORD.

32 Then Samuel said, "Bring here to me A'gag the king of the Amal'ekites." And Agag came to him cheerfully. Agag said, "Surely the bitterness of death is past." [33]And Samuel said, "As your sword has made women childless, so shall your mother be childless among women." And Samuel hewed A'gag in pieces before the LORD in Gilgal.

34 Then Samuel went to Ra'mah; and Saul went up to his house in Gib'e-ah of Saul. [35]And Samuel did not see Saul again until the day of his death, but Samuel grieved over Saul. And the LORD repented that he had made Saul king over Israel.

David Anointed as King

16 The LORD said to Samuel, "How long will you grieve over Saul, seeing I have rejected him from being king over Israel? Fill your horn with oil, and go; I will send you to Jesse the Bethlehemite, for I have provided for myself a king among his sons." [2]And Samuel said, "How can I go? If Saul hears it, he will kill me." And the LORD said, "Take a heifer with you, and say, 'I have come to sacrifice to the LORD.' [3]And invite Jesse to the sacrifice, and I will show you what you shall do; and you shall anoint for me him whom I name to you." [4]Samuel did what the LORD commanded, and came to Bethlehem. The elders of the city came to meet him trembling, and said, "Do you come peaceably?" [5]And he said, "Peaceably; I have come to sacrifice to the LORD; consecrate yourselves, and come with me to the sacrifice." And he consecrated Jesse and his sons, and invited them to the sacrifice.

6 When they came, he looked on Eli'ab and thought, "Surely the LORD's anointed is before him." [7]But the LORD said to Samuel, "Do not look on his appearance or on the height of his stature, because I have rejected him; for the LORD sees not as man sees; man looks on the outward appearance, but the LORD looks on the heart." [8]Then Jesse called Abin'adab, and made him pass before

Samuel. And he said, "Neither has the LORD chosen this one." [9]Then Jesse made Shammah pass by. And he said, "Neither has the LORD chosen this one." [10]And Jesse made seven of his sons pass before Samuel. And Samuel said to Jesse, "The LORD has not chosen these." [11]And Samuel said to Jesse, "Are all your sons here?" And he said, "There remains yet the youngest, but behold, he is keeping the sheep." And Samuel said to Jesse, "Send and fetch him; for we will not sit down till he comes here." [12]And he sent, and brought him in. Now he was ruddy, and had beautiful eyes, and was handsome. And the LORD said, "Arise, anoint him; for this is he." [13]Then Samuel took the horn of oil, and anointed him in the midst of his brothers; and the Spirit of the LORD came mightily upon David from that day forward. And Samuel rose up, and went to Ra'mah.

David Plays the Lyre for Saul

14 Now the Spirit of the LORD departed from Saul, and an evil spirit from the LORD tormented him. [15]And Saul's servants said to him, "Behold now, an evil spirit from God is tormenting you. [16]Let our lord now command your servants, who are before you, to seek out a man who is skilful in playing the lyre; and when the evil spirit from God is upon you, he will play it, and you will be well." [17]So Saul said to his servants, "Provide for me a man who can play well, and bring him to me." [18]One of the young men answered, "Behold, I have seen a son of Jesse the Bethlehemite, who is skilful in playing, a man of valor, a man of war, prudent in speech, and a man of good presence; and the LORD is with him." [19]Therefore Saul sent messengers to Jesse, and said, "Send me David your son, who is with the sheep." [20]And Jesse took a donkey laden with bread, and a skin of wine and a kid, and sent them by David his son to Saul. [21]And David came to Saul, and entered his service. And Saul loved him greatly, and he became his armor-bearer. [22]And Saul sent to Jesse, saying, "Let David remain in my service, for he has found favor in my sight." [23]And whenever the evil spirit from God was upon Saul, David took the lyre and played it with his hand; so Saul was refreshed, and was well, and the evil spirit departed from him.

David and Goliath

17 Now the Philis'tines gathered their armies for battle; and they were gathered at Socoh, which belongs to Judah, and encamped between Socoh and Aze'kah, in E'phes-dam'mim. [2]And Saul and the men of Israel were gathered, and encamped in the valley of E'lah, and drew up in line of battle against the Philis'tines. [3]And the Philis'tines stood on the mountain on the one side, and Israel stood on the mountain on the other side, with a valley between them. [4]And there came out from the camp of the Philis'tines a

champion named Goliath, of Gath, whose height was six cubits and a span. ⁵He had a helmet of bronze on his head, and he was armed with a coat of mail, and the weight of the coat was five thousand shekels of bronze. ⁶And he had greaves of bronze upon his legs, and a javelin of bronze slung between his shoulders. ⁷And the shaft of his spear was like a weaver's beam, and his spear's head weighed six hundred shekels of iron; and his shield-bearer went before him. ⁸He stood and shouted to the ranks of Israel, "Why have you come out to draw up for battle? Am I not a Philis'tine, and are you not servants of Saul? Choose a man for yourselves, and let him come down to me. ⁹If he is able to fight with me and kill me, then we will be your servants; but if I prevail against him and kill him, then you shall be our servants and serve us." ¹⁰And the Philis'tine said, "I defy the ranks of Israel this day; give me a man, that we may fight together." ¹¹When Saul and all Israel heard these words of the Philis'tine, they were dismayed and greatly afraid.

12 Now David was the son of an Eph'rathite of Bethlehem in Judah, named Jesse, who had eight sons. In the days of Saul the man was already old and advanced in years. * ¹³The three eldest sons of Jesse had followed Saul to the battle; and the names of his three sons who went to the battle were Eli'ab the first-born, and next to him Abin'-adab, and the third Shammah. ¹⁴David was the youngest; the three eldest followed Saul, ¹⁵but David went back and forth from Saul to feed his father's sheep at Bethlehem. ¹⁶For forty days the Philis'tine came forward and took his stand, morning and evening.

17 And Jesse said to David his son, "Take for your brothers an ephah of this parched grain, and these ten loaves, and carry them quickly to the camp to your brothers; ¹⁸also take these ten cheeses to the commander of their thousand. See how your brothers fare, and bring some token from them."

19 Now Saul, and they, and all the men of Israel, were in the valley of E'lah, fighting with the Philis'tines. ²⁰And David rose early in the morning, and left the sheep with a keeper, and took the provisions, and went, as Jesse had commanded him; and he came to the encampment as the host was going forth to the battle line, shouting the war cry. ²¹And Israel and the Philis'tines drew up for battle, army against army. ²²And David left the things in charge of the keeper of the baggage, and ran to the ranks, and went and greeted his brothers. ²³As he talked with them, behold, the champion, the Philis'tine of Gath, Goliath by name, came up out of the ranks of the Philistines, and spoke the same words as before. And David heard him.

24 All the men of Israel, when they saw the man, fled from him, and were much afraid. ²⁵And the men of Israel said, "Have you seen this man who has come up? Surely he has come up to defy Israel; and the man who kills him, the king will enrich with great riches, and will give him his daughter, and make his father's house free in Israel." ²⁶And David said to the men who stood by him, "What shall be done for the man who kills this Philis'tine, and takes away the reproach from Israel? For who is this uncircumcised Philistine, that he should defy the armies of the living God?" ²⁷And the people answered him in the same way, "So shall it be done to the man who kills him."

28 Now Eli'ab his eldest brother heard when he spoke to the men; and Eliab's anger was kindled against David, and he said, "Why have you come down? And with whom have you left those few sheep in the wilderness? I know your presumption, and the evil of your heart; for you have come down to see the battle." ²⁹And David said, "What have I done now? Was it not but a word?" ³⁰And he turned away from him toward another, and spoke in the same way; and the people answered him again as before.

31 When the words which David spoke were heard, they repeated them before Saul; and he sent for him. ³²And David said to Saul, "Let no man's heart fail because of him; your servant will go and fight with this Philis'tine." ³³And Saul said to David, "You are not able to go against this Philis'tine to fight with him; for you are but a youth, and he has been a man of war from his youth." ³⁴But David said to Saul, "Your servant used to keep sheep for his father; and when there came a lion, or a bear, and took a lamb from the flock, ³⁵I went after him and struck him and delivered it out of his mouth; and if he arose against me, I caught him by his beard, and struck him and killed him. ³⁶Your servant has killed both lions and bears; and this uncircumcised Philis'tine shall be like one of them, seeing he has defied the armies of the living God." ³⁷And David said, "The Lord who delivered me from the paw of the lion and from the paw of the bear, will deliver me from the hand of this Philis'tine." And Saul said to David, "Go, and the Lord be with you!" ³⁸Then Saul clothed David with his armor; he put a helmet of bronze on his head, and clothed him with a coat of mail. ³⁹And David belted on his sword over his armor, and he tried in vain to go, for he was not used to them. Then David said to Saul, "I cannot go with these; for I am not used to them." And David put them off. ⁴⁰Then he took his staff in his hand, and chose five smooth stones from the brook, and put them in his shepherd's bag or

* Gk Syr: Heb *among men.*

214

wallet; his sling was in his hand, and he drew near to the Philis'tine.

41 And the Philis'tine came on and drew near to David, with his shield-bearer in front of him. ⁴²And when the Philis'tine looked, and saw David, he disdained him; for he was but a youth, ruddy and comely in appearance. ⁴³And the Philis'tine said to David, "Am I a dog, that you come to me with sticks?" And the Philistine cursed David by his gods. ⁴⁴The Philis'tine said to David, "Come to me, and I will give your flesh to the birds of the air and to the beasts of the field." ⁴⁵Then David said to the Philis'tine, "You come to me with a sword and with a spear and with a javelin; but I come to you in the name of the LORD of hosts, the God of the armies of Israel, whom you have defied. ⁴⁶This day the LORD will deliver you into my hand, and I will strike you down, and cut off your head; and I will give the dead bodies of the host of the Philis'tines this day to the birds of the air and to the wild beasts of the earth; that all the earth may know that there is a God in Israel, ⁴⁷and that all this assembly may know that the LORD saves not with sword and spear; for the battle is the LORD's and he will give you into our hand."

48 When the Philis'tine arose and came and drew near to meet David, David ran quickly toward the battle line to meet the Philistine. ⁴⁹And David put his hand in his bag and took out a stone, and slung it, and struck the Philis'tine on his forehead; the stone sank into his forehead, and he fell on his face to the ground.

50 So David prevailed over the Philis'tine with a sling and with a stone, and struck the Philistine, and killed him; there was no sword in the hand of David. ⁵¹Then David ran and stood over the Philis'tine, and took his sword and drew it out of its sheath, and killed him, and cut off his head with it. When the Philistines saw that their champion was dead, they fled. ⁵²And the men of Israel and Judah rose with a shout and pursued the Philis'tines as far as Gath^y and the gates of Ek'ron, so that the wounded Philistines fell on the way from Sha-ara'im as far as Gath and Ekron. ⁵³And the Israelites came back from chasing the Philis'tines, and they plundered their camp. ⁵⁴And David took the head of the Philis'tine and brought it to Jerusalem; but he put his armor in his tent.

55 When Saul saw David go forth against the Philis'tine, he said to Abner, the commander of the army, "Abner, whose son is this youth?" And Abner said, "As your soul lives, O king, I cannot tell." ⁵⁶And the king said, "Inquire whose son the stripling is." ⁵⁷And as David returned from the slaughter of the Philis'tine, Abner took him, and brought him before Saul with the head of the Philistine in his hand. ⁵⁸And Saul said to him, "Whose son are you, young man?" And David

answered, "I am the son of your servant Jesse the Bethlehemite."

Jonathan's Covenant with David

18 When he had finished speaking to Saul, the soul of Jonathan was knit to the soul of David, and Jonathan loved him as his own soul. ²And Saul took him that day, and would not let him return to his father's house. ³Then Jonathan made a covenant with David, because he loved him as his own soul. ⁴And Jonathan stripped himself of the robe that was upon him, and gave it to David, and his armor, and even his sword and his bow and his belt. ⁵And David went out and was successful wherever Saul sent him; so that Saul set him over the men of war. And this was good in the sight of all the people and also in the sight of Saul's servants.

6 As they were coming home, when David returned from slaying the Philis'tine, the women came out of all the cities of Israel, singing and dancing, to meet King Saul, with timbrels, with songs of joy, and with instruments ^z of music. ⁷And the women sang to one another as they made merry,

"Saul has slain his thousands,
    and David his ten thousands."

⁸And Saul was very angry, and this saying displeased him; he said, "They have ascribed to David ten thousands, and to me they have ascribed thousands; and what more can he have but the kingdom?" ⁹And Saul eyed David from that day on.

Saul Tries to Kill David

10 And the next day an evil spirit from God rushed upon Saul, and he raved within his house, while David was playing the lyre, as he did day by day. Saul had his spear in his hand; ¹¹and Saul cast the spear, for he thought, "I will pin David to the wall." But David evaded him twice.

12 Saul was afraid of David, because the LORD was with him but had departed from Saul. ¹³So Saul removed him from his presence, and made him a commander of a thousand; and he went out and came in before the people. ¹⁴And David had success in all his undertakings; for the LORD was with him. ¹⁵And when Saul saw that he had great success, he stood in awe of him. ¹⁶But all Israel and Judah loved David; for he went out and came in before them.

David Marries Michal

17 Then Saul said to David, "Here is my elder daughter Merab; I will give her to you for a wife; only be valiant for me and fight the LORD's battles." For Saul thought, "Let not my hand be upon him, but let the hand of the Philis'tines be upon him." ¹⁸And David said to Saul, "Who am I,

---

^y Gk: Heb *Gai.*
^z Or *triangles,* or *three-stringed instruments.*
18:7: 21:11; 29:5.

and who are my kinsfolk, my father's family in Israel, that I should be son-in-law to the king?" ¹⁹But at the time when Merab, Saul's daughter, should have been given to David, she was given to A′dri-el the Meho′lathite for a wife.

20 Now Saul's daughter Michal loved David; and they told Saul, and the thing pleased him. ²¹Saul thought, "Let me give her to him, that she may be a snare for him, and that the hand of the Philis′tines may be against him." Therefore Saul said to David a second time, ᵃ "You shall now be my son-in-law." ²²And Saul commanded his servants, "Speak to David in private and say, 'Behold, the king has delight in you, and all his servants love you; now then become the king's son-in-law.' " ²³And Saul's servants spoke those words in the ears of David. And David said, "Does it seem to you a little thing to become the king's son-in-law, seeing that I am a poor man and of no repute?" ²⁴And the servants of Saul told him, "Thus and so did David speak." ²⁵Then Saul said, "Thus shall you say to David, 'The king desires no marriage present * except a hundred foreskins of the Philis′tines, that he may be avenged of the king's enemies.' " Now Saul thought to make David fall by the hand of the Philistines. ²⁶And when his servants told David these words, it pleased David well to be the king's son-in-law. Before the time had expired, ²⁷David arose and went, along with his men, and killed two hundred of the Philis′tines; and David brought their foreskins, which were given in full number to the king, that he might become the king's son-in-law. And Saul gave him his daughter Michal for a wife. ²⁸But when Saul saw and knew that the Lord was with David, and that all Israel ᵇ loved him, ²⁹Saul was still more afraid of David. So Saul was David's enemy continually.

30 Then the princes of the Philis′tines came out to battle, and as often as they came out David had more success than all the servants of Saul; so that his name was highly esteemed.

Jonathan Intercedes for David

19 And Saul spoke to Jonathan his son and to all his servants, that they should kill David. But Jonathan, Saul's son, delighted much in David. ²And Jonathan told David, "Saul my father seeks to kill you; therefore take heed to yourself in the morning, stay in a secret place and hide yourself; ³and I will go out and stand beside my father in the field where you are, and I will speak to my father about you; and if I learn anything I will tell you." ⁴And Jonathan spoke well of David to Saul his father, and said to him, "Let not the king sin against his servant David; because he has not sinned against you, and because his deeds have been of good service to you; ⁵for he took his life in his hand and he slew the Philis′tine, and the Lord wrought a great victory

for all Israel. You saw it, and rejoiced; why then will you sin against innocent blood by killing David without cause?" ⁶And Saul listened to the voice of Jonathan; Saul swore, "As the Lord lives, he shall not be put to death." ⁷And Jonathan called David, and Jonathan showed him all these things. And Jonathan brought David to Saul, and he was in his presence as before.

Michal Helps David Escape from Saul

8 And there was war again; and David went out and fought with the Philis′tines, and made a great slaughter among them, so that they fled before him. ⁹Then an evil spirit from the Lord came upon Saul, as he sat in his house with his spear in his hand; and David was playing the lyre. ¹⁰And Saul sought to pin David to the wall with the spear; but he eluded Saul, so that he struck the spear into the wall. And David fled, and escaped.

11 That night Saul ˣ sent messengers to David's house to watch him, that he might kill him in the morning. But Michal, David's wife, told him, "If you do not save your life tonight, tomorrow you will be killed." ¹²So Michal let David down through the window; and he fled away and escaped. ¹³Michal took an image ᶜ and laid it on the bed and put a pillow ᵈ of goats' hair at its head, and covered it with the clothes. ¹⁴And when Saul sent messengers to take David, she said, "He is sick." ¹⁵Then Saul sent the messengers to see David, saying, "Bring him up to me in the bed, that I may kill him." ¹⁶And when the messengers came in, behold, the image ᶜ was in the bed, with the pillow ᵈ of goats' hair at its head. ¹⁷Saul said to Michal, "Why have you deceived me thus, and let my enemy go, so that he has escaped?" And Michal answered Saul, "He said to me, 'Let me go; why should I kill you?' "

David Joins Samuel in Ramah

18 Now David fled and escaped, and he came to Samuel at Ra′mah, and told him all that Saul had done to him. And he and Samuel went and dwelt at Naioth. ¹⁹And it was told Saul, "Behold, David is at Naioth in Ra′mah." ²⁰Then Saul sent messengers to take David; and when they saw the company of the prophets prophesying, and Samuel standing as head over them, the Spirit of God came upon the messengers of Saul, and they also prophesied. ²¹When it was told Saul, he sent other messengers, and they also prophesied. And Saul sent messengers again the third time, and they also prophesied. ²²Then he himself went to Ra′mah, and came to the great well that is in Secu; and he asked, "Where are Samuel and

ᵃ Heb by two.
ᵇ Gk: Heb Michal, Saul's daughter.
ˣ Gk Old Latin: Heb escaped that night. ¹¹And Saul.
ᶜ Heb teraphim.
ᵈ The meaning of the Hebrew word is uncertain.
* 18:25, marriage present: The usual payment for a bride.

David?" And one said, "Behold, they are at Naioth in Ra′mah." ²³And he went from ᶠ there to Naioth in Ra′mah; and the Spirit of God came upon him also, and as he went he prophesied, until he came to Naioth in Ramah. ²⁴And he too stripped off his clothes, and he too prophesied before Samuel, and lay naked all that day and all that night. Hence it is said, "Is Saul also among the prophets?" *

The Friendship of David and Jonathan

20 Then David fled from Naioth in Ra′mah, and came and said before Jonathan, "What have I done? What is my guilt? And what is my sin before your father, that he seeks my life?" ²And he said to him, "Far from it! You shall not die. Behold, my father does nothing either great or small without disclosing it to me; and why should my father hide this from me? It is not so." ³But David replied, ᵍ "Your father knows well that I have found favor in your eyes; and he thinks, 'Let not Jonathan know this, lest he be grieved.' But truly, as the LORD lives and as your soul lives, there is but a step between me and death." ⁴Then said Jonathan to David, "Whatever you say, I will do for you." ⁵David said to Jonathan, "Behold, tomorrow is the new moon, and I should not fail to sit at table with the king; but let me go, that I may hide myself in the field till the third day at evening. ⁶If your father misses me at all, then say, 'David earnestly asked leave of me to run to Bethlehem his city; for there is a yearly sacrifice there for all the family.' ⁷If he says, 'Good!' it will be well with your servant; but if he is angry, then know that evil is determined by him. ⁸Therefore deal kindly with your servant, for you have brought your servant into a sacred covenant ʰ with you. But if there is guilt in me, slay me yourself; for why should you bring me to your father?" ⁹And Jonathan said, "Far be it from you! If I knew that it was determined by my father that evil should come upon you, would I not tell you?" ¹⁰Then said David to Jonathan, "Who will tell me if your father answers you roughly?" ¹¹And Jonathan said to David, "Come, let us go out into the field." So they both went out into the field.

12 And Jonathan said to David, "The LORD, the God of Israel, be witness! ⁱ When I have sounded my father, about this time tomorrow, or the third day, behold, if he is well disposed toward David, shall I not then send and disclose it to you? ¹³But should it please my father to do you harm, the LORD do so to Jonathan, and more also, if I do not disclose it to you, and send you away, that you may go in safety. May the LORD be with you, as he has been with my father. ¹⁴If I am still alive, show me the loyal love of the LORD, that I may not die; ʲ ¹⁵and do not cut off your loyalty from my house for ever. When the LORD cuts off every one of the

enemies of David from the face of the earth, ¹⁶let not the name of Jonathan be cut off from the house of David. ᵏ And may the LORD take vengeance on David's enemies." ¹⁷And Jonathan made David swear again by his love for him; for he loved him as he loved his own soul.

18 Then Jonathan said to him, "Tomorrow is the new moon; and you will be missed, because your seat will be empty. ¹⁹And on the third day you will be greatly missed; ˡ then go to the place where you hid yourself when the matter was in hand, and remain beside yonder stone heap. ᵐ ²⁰And I will shoot three arrows to the side of it, as though I shot at a mark. ²¹And behold, I will send the lad, saying, 'Go, find the arrows.' If I say to the lad, 'Look, the arrows are on this side of you, take them,' then you are to come, for, as the LORD lives, it is safe for you and there is no danger. ²²But if I say to the youth, 'Look, the arrows are beyond you,' then go; for the LORD has sent you away. ²³And as for the matter of which you and I have spoken, behold, the LORD is between you and me for ever."

24 So David hid himself in the field; and when the new moon came, the king sat down to eat food. ²⁵The king sat upon his seat, as at other times, upon the seat by the wall; Jonathan sat opposite, ⁿ and Abner sat by Saul's side, but David's place was empty.

26 Yet Saul did not say anything that day; for he thought, "Something has befallen him; he is not clean, surely he is not clean." ²⁷But on the second day, the next day after the new moon, David's place was empty. And Saul said to Jonathan his son, "Why has not the son of Jesse come to the meal, either yesterday or today?" ²⁸Jonathan answered Saul, "David earnestly asked leave of me to go to Bethlehem; ²⁹he said, 'Let me go; for our family holds a sacrifice in the city, and my brother has commanded me to be there. So now, if I have found favor in your eyes, let me get away, and see my brothers.' For this reason he has not come to the king's table."

30 Then Saul's anger was kindled against Jonathan, and he said to him, "You son of a perverse, rebellious woman, do I not know that you have chosen the son of Jesse to your own shame, and to the shame of your mother's nakedness? ³¹For as long as the son of Jesse lives upon the

---

ᶠ Gk: Heb lacks *from*.
ᵍ Gk: Heb *swore again*.
ʰ Heb *a covenant of the* LORD.
ⁱ Heb lacks *be witness*.
ʲ Heb uncertain.
ᵏ Gk: Heb *earth, and Jonathan made a covenant with the house of David*.
ˡ Gk: Heb *go down quickly*.
ᵐ Gk: Heb *the stone Ezel*.
ⁿ Cn See Gk: Heb *stood up*.
19:23, 24: 10, 11, 12.
* 19:20–24: cf. 10:5.

earth, neither you nor your kingdom shall be established. Therefore send and fetch him to me, for he shall surely die." ³²Then Jonathan answered Saul his father, "Why should he be put to death? What has he done?" ³³But Saul cast his spear at him to strike him; so Jonathan knew that his father was determined to put David to death. ³⁴And Jonathan rose from the table in fierce anger and ate no food the second day of the month, for he was grieved for David, because his father had disgraced him.

35 In the morning Jonathan went out into the field to the appointment with David, and with him a little lad. ³⁶And he said to his lad, "Run and find the arrows which I shoot." As the lad ran, he shot an arrow beyond him. ³⁷And when the lad came to the place of the arrow which Jonathan had shot, Jonathan called after the lad and said, "Is not the arrow beyond you?" ³⁸And Jonathan called after the lad, "Hurry, make haste, stay not." So Jonathan's lad gathered up the arrows, and came to his master. ³⁹But the lad knew nothing; only Jonathan and David knew the matter. ⁴⁰And Jonathan gave his weapons to his lad, and said to him, "Go and carry them to the city." ⁴¹And as soon as the lad had gone, David rose from beside the stone heap ° and fell on his face to the ground, and bowed three times; and they kissed one another, and wept with one another, until David recovered himself. ᴾ ⁴²Then Jonathan said to David, "Go in peace, forasmuch as we have sworn both of us in the name of the LORD, saying, 'The LORD shall be between me and you, and between my descendants and your descendants, for ever.' " And he rose and departed; and Jonathan went into the city. �q

David and the Holy Bread

21 ˣ Then came David to Nob to Ahim′elech the priest; and Ahimelech came to meet David trembling, and said to him, "Why are you alone, and no one with you?" ²And David said to Ahim′elech the priest, "The king has charged me with a matter, and said to me, 'Let no one know anything of the matter about which I send you, and with which I have charged you.' I have made an appointment with the young men for such and such a place. ³Now then, what have you at hand? Give me five loaves of bread, or whatever is here." ⁴And the priest answered David, "I have no common bread at hand, but there is holy bread; if only the young men have kept themselves from women." ⁵And David answered the priest, "Of a truth women have been kept from us as always when I go on an expedition; the vessels of the young men are holy, even when it is a common journey; how much more today will their vessels be holy?" ⁶So the priest gave him the holy bread; for there was no bread there but the bread of the Presence, which is removed from before the LORD,

to be replaced by hot bread on the day it is taken away.

7 Now a certain man of the servants of Saul was there that day, detained before the LORD; his name was Do′eg the E′domite, the chief of Saul's herdsmen.

8 And David said to Ahim′elech, "And have you not here a spear or a sword at hand? For I have brought neither my sword nor my weapons with me, because the king's business required haste." ⁹And the priest said, "The sword of Goliath the Philis′tine, whom you killed in the valley of E′lah, behold, it is here wrapped in a cloth behind the ephod; if you will take that, take it, for there is none but that here." And David said, "There is none like that; give it to me."

David Flees to Gath

10 And David rose and fled that day from Saul, and went to A′chish the king of Gath. ¹¹And the servants of A′chish said to him, "Is not this David the king of the land? Did they not sing to one another of him in dances,

'Saul has slain his thousands,
and David his ten thousands'?"

¹²And David took these words to heart, and was much afraid of A′chish the king of Gath. ¹³So he changed his behavior before them, and feigned himself mad in their hands, and made marks on the doors of the gate, and let his spittle run down his beard. ¹⁴Then said A′chish to his servants, "Behold, you see the man is mad; why then have you brought him to me? ¹⁵Do I lack madmen, that you have brought this fellow to play the madman in my presence? Shall this fellow come into my house?"

David and His Followers at Adullam

22 David departed from there and escaped to the cave of Adul′lam; and when his brothers and all his father's house heard it, they went down there to him. ²And every one who was in distress, and every one who was in debt, and every one who was discontented, gathered to him; and he became captain over them. And there were with him about four hundred men.

3 And David went from there to Mizpeh of Moab; and he said to the king of Moab, "Please let my father and my mother stay ˢ with you, till I know what God will do for me." ⁴And he left them with the king of Moab, and they stayed with him all the time that David was in the stronghold. ⁵Then the prophet Gad said to David, "Do not remain in the stronghold; depart, and go into the land of Judah." So David departed, and went into the forest of He′reth.

° Gk: Heb *from beside the south.*
ᴾ Or *exceeded.*
q This sentence is 21:1 in Heb.
ˣ Ch 21:2 in Heb.
ˢ Syr Vg: Heb *come out.*
21:11: 18:7; 29:5.

Saul Slaughters the Priests at Nob

6 Now Saul heard that David was discovered, and the men who were with him. Saul was sitting at Gib′e-ah, under the tamarisk tree on the height, with his spear in his hand, and all his servants were standing about him. 7And Saul said to his servants who stood about him, "Hear now, you Benjaminites; will the son of Jesse give every one of you fields and vineyards, will he make you all commanders of thousands and commanders of hundreds, 8that all of you have conspired against me? No one discloses to me when my son makes a league with the son of Jesse, none of you is sorry for me or discloses to me that my son has stirred up my servant against me, to lie in wait, as at this day." 9Then answered Do′eg the E′domite, who stood by the servants of Saul, "I saw the son of Jesse coming to Nob, to Ahim′elech the son of Ahi′tub, 10and he inquired of the LORD for him, and gave him provisions, and gave him the sword of Goliath the Philis′tine."

11 Then the king sent to summon Ahim′elech the priest, the son of Ahi′tub, and all his father's house, the priests who were at Nob; and all of them came to the king. 12And Saul said, "Hear now, son of Ahi′tub." And he answered, "Here I am, my lord." 13And Saul said to him, "Why have you conspired against me, you and the son of Jesse, in that you have given him bread and a sword, and have inquired of God for him, so that he has risen against me, to lie in wait, as at this day?" 14Then Ahim′elech answered the king, "And who among all your servants is so faithful as David, who is the king's son-in-law, and captain over t your bodyguard, and honored in your house? 15Is today the first time that I have inquired of God for him? No! Let not the king impute anything to his servant or to all the house of my father; for your servant has known nothing of all this, much or little." 16And the king said, "You shall surely die, Ahim′elech, you and all your father's house." 17And the king said to the guard who stood about him, "Turn and kill the priests of the LORD; because their hand also is with David, and they knew that he fled, and did not disclose it to me." But the servants of the king would not put forth their hand to fall upon the priests of the LORD. 18Then the king said to Do′eg, "You turn and fall upon the priests." And Doeg the E′domite turned and fell upon the priests, and he killed on that day eighty-five persons who wore the linen ephod. 19And Nob, the city of the priests, he put to the sword; both men and women, children and sucklings, oxen, donkeys and sheep, he put to the sword.

20 But one of the sons of Ahim′elech the son of Ahi′tub, named Abi′athar, escaped and fled after David. 21And Abi′athar told David that Saul had killed the priests of the LORD. 22And David said to

Abi′athar, "I knew on that day, when Do′eg the E′domite was there, that he would surely tell Saul. I have occasioned the death of all the persons of your father's house. 23Stay with me, fear not; for he that seeks my life seeks your life; with me you shall be in safekeeping."

David Saves the City of Keilah

23 Now they told David, "Behold, the Philis′tines are fighting against Kei′lah, and are robbing the threshing floors." 2Therefore David inquired of the LORD, "Shall I go and attack these Philis′tines?" And the LORD said to David, "Go and attack the Philistines and save Kei′lah." 3But David's men said to him, "Behold, we are afraid here in Judah; how much more then if we go to Kei′lah against the armies of the Philis′tines?" 4Then David inquired of the LORD again. And the LORD answered him, "Arise, go down to Kei′lah; for I will give the Philis′tines into your hand." 5And David and his men went to Kei′lah, and fought with the Philis′tines, and brought away their cattle, and made a great slaughter among them. So David delivered the inhabitants of Keilah.

6 When Abi′athar the son of Ahim′elech fled to David to Kei′lah, he came down with an ephod in his hand. 7Now it was told Saul that David had come to Kei′lah. And Saul said, "God has given him into my hand; for he has shut himself in by entering a town that has gates and bars." 8And Saul summoned all the people to war, to go down to Kei′lah, to besiege David and his men. 9David knew that Saul was plotting evil against him; and he said to Abi′athar the priest, "Bring the ephod here." 10Then said David, "O LORD, the God of Israel, your servant has surely heard that Saul seeks to come to Kei′lah, to destroy the city on my account. 11Will the men of Kei′lah surrender me into his hand? Will Saul come down, as your servant has heard? O LORD, the God of Israel, I beg you, tell your servant." And the LORD said, "He will come down." 12Then said David, "Will the men of Kei′lah surrender me and my men into the hand of Saul?" And the LORD said, "They will surrender you." 13Then David and his men, who were about six hundred, arose and departed from Kei′lah, and they went wherever they could go. When Saul was told that David had escaped from Keilah, he gave up the expedition. 14And David remained in the strongholds in the wilderness, in the hill country of the wilderness of Ziph. And Saul sought him every day, but God did not give him into his hand.

David Eludes Saul in the Wilderness

15 And David was afraid because u Saul had come out to seek his life. David was in the

---

t Gk Tg: Heb and has turned aside to.
u Or saw that.

wilderness of Ziph at Horesh. ¹⁶And Jonathan, Saul's son, rose, and went to David at Horesh, and strengthened his hand in God. ¹⁷And he said to him, "Fear not; for the hand of Saul my father shall not find you; you shall be king over Israel, and I shall be next to you; Saul my father also knows this." ¹⁸And the two of them made a covenant before the Lord; David remained at Horesh, and Jonathan went home.

19 Then the Ziphites went up to Saul at Gib′e-ah, saying, "Does not David hide among us in the strongholds at Horesh, on the hill of Hachi′lah, which is south of Jeshi′mon? ²⁰Now come down, O king, according to all your heart's desire to come down; and our part shall be to surrender him into the king's hand." ²¹And Saul said, "May you be blessed by the Lord; for you have had compassion on me. ²²Go, make yet more sure; know and see the place where his haunt is, and who has seen him there; for it is told me that he is very cunning. ²³See therefore, and take note of all the lurking places where he hides, and come back to me with sure information. Then I will go with you; and if he is in the land, I will search him out among all the thousands of Judah." ²⁴And they arose, and went to Ziph ahead of Saul.

Now David and his men were in the wilderness of Maon, in the Ar′abah to the south of Jeshi′mon. ²⁵And Saul and his men went to seek him. And David was told; therefore he went down to the rock which is ᵛ in the wilderness of Maon. And when Saul heard that, he pursued after David in the wilderness of Maon. ²⁶Saul went on one side of the mountain, and David and his men on the other side of the mountain; and David was making haste to get away from Saul, as Saul and his men were closing in upon David and his men to capture them, ²⁷when a messenger came to Saul, saying, "Make haste and come; for the Philis′tines have made a raid upon the land." ²⁸So Saul returned from pursuing after David, and went against the Philis′-tines; therefore that place was called the Rock of Escape. ²⁹ᵂ And David went up from there, and dwelt in the strongholds of En-ge′di.

David Spares Saul's Life

24 When Saul returned from following the Philis′tines, he was told, "Behold, David is in the wilderness of En-ge′di." ²Then Saul took three thousand chosen men out of all Israel, and went to seek David and his men in front of the Wildgoats' Rocks. ³And he came to the sheepfolds by the way, where there was a cave; and Saul went in to relieve himself. Now David and his men were sitting in the innermost parts of the cave. ⁴And the men of David said to him, "Here is the day of which the Lord said to you, 'Behold, I will give your enemy into your hand, and you shall do to him as it shall seem good to you.'" Then David arose and stealthily cut off the skirt

of Saul's robe. ⁵And afterward David's heart struck him, because he had cut off Saul's skirt. ⁶He said to his men, "The Lord forbid that I should do this thing to my lord, the Lord's anointed, to put forth my hand against him, seeing he is the Lord's anointed." ⁷So David persuaded his men with these words, and did not permit them to attack Saul. And Saul rose up and left the cave, and went upon his way.

8 Afterward David also arose, and went out of the cave, and called after Saul, "My lord the king!" And when Saul looked behind him, David bowed with his face to the earth, and did obeisance. ⁹And David said to Saul, "Why do you listen to the words of men who say, 'Behold, David seeks your hurt'? ¹⁰Behold, this day your eyes have seen how the Lord gave you today into my hand in the cave; and some bade me kill you, but I ˣ spared you. I said, 'I will not put forth my hand against my lord; for he is the Lord's anointed.' ¹¹See, my father, see the skirt of your robe in my hand; for by the fact that I cut off the skirt of your robe, and did not kill you, you may know and see that there is no wrong or treason in my hands. I have not sinned against you, though you hunt my life to take it. ¹²May the Lord judge between me and you, may the Lord avenge me upon you; but my hand shall not be against you. ¹³As the proverb of the ancients says, 'Out of the wicked comes forth wickedness'; but my hand shall not be against you. ¹⁴After whom has the king of Israel come out? After whom do you pursue? After a dead dog! After a flea! ¹⁵May the Lord therefore be judge, and give sentence between me and you, and see to it, and plead my cause, and deliver me from your hand."

16 When David had finished speaking these words to Saul, Saul said, "Is this your voice, my son David?" And Saul lifted up his voice and wept. ¹⁷He said to David, "You are more righteous than I; for you have repaid me good, whereas I have repaid you evil. ¹⁸And you have declared this day how you have dealt well with me, in that you did not kill me when the Lord put me into your hands. ¹⁹For if a man finds his enemy, will he let him go away safe? So may the Lord reward you with good for what you have done to me this day. ²⁰And now, behold, I know that you shall surely be king, and that the kingdom of Israel shall be established in your hand. ²¹Swear to me therefore by the Lord that you will not cut off my descendants after me, and that you will not destroy my name out of my father's house." ²²And David swore this to Saul. Then Saul went home; but David and his men went up to the stronghold.

ᵛ Gk: Heb and dwelt.
ᵂ Ch 24:1 in Heb.
ˣ Gk Syr Tg: Heb you.
24:1–22: 26:1–25.

Death of Samuel

25 Now Samuel died; and all Israel assembled and mourned for him, and they buried him in his house at Ra′mah.

David and Abigail

Then David rose and went down to the wilderness of Par′an. [2]And there was a man in Maon, whose business was in Carmel. The man was very rich; he had three thousand sheep and a thousand goats. He was shearing his sheep in Carmel. [3]Now the name of the man was Nabal, and the name of his wife Ab′igail. The woman was of good understanding and beautiful, but the man was churlish and ill-behaved; he was a Ca′lebite. [4]David heard in the wilderness that Nabal was shearing his sheep. [5]So David sent ten young men; and David said to the young men, "Go up to Carmel, and go to Nabal, and greet him in my name. [6]And thus you shall salute him: 'Peace be to you, and peace be to your house, and peace be to all that you have. [7]I hear that you have shearers; now your shepherds have been with us, and we did them no harm, and they missed nothing, all the time they were in Carmel. [8]Ask your young men, and they will tell you. Therefore let my young men find favor in your eyes; for we come on a feast day. Please, give whatever you have at hand to your servants and to your son David.' "

9 When David's young men came, they said all this to Nabal in the name of David; and then they waited. [10]And Nabal answered David's servants, "Who is David? Who is the son of Jesse? There are many servants nowadays who are breaking away from their masters. [11]Shall I take my bread and my water and my meat that I have killed for my shearers, and give it to men who come from I do not know where?" [12]So David's young men turned away, and came back and told him all this. [13]And David said to his men, "Every man belt on his sword!" And every man of them belted on his sword; David also belted on his sword; and about four hundred men went up after David, while two hundred remained with the baggage.

14 But one of the young men told Ab′igail, Nabal's wife, "Behold, David sent messengers out of the wilderness to salute our master; and he railed at them. [15]Yet the men were very good to us, and we suffered no harm, and we did not miss anything when we were in the fields, as long as we went with them; [16]they were a wall to us both by night and by day, all the while we were with them keeping the sheep. [17]Now therefore know this and consider what you should do; for evil is determined against our master and against all his house, and he is so ill-natured that one cannot speak to him."

18 Then Ab′igail made haste, and took two hundred loaves, and two skins of wine, and five sheep ready dressed, and five measures of parched grain, and a hundred clusters of raisins, and two hundred cakes of figs, and laid them on donkeys. [19]And she said to her young men, "Go on before me; behold, I come after you." But she did not tell her husband Nabal. [20]And as she rode on the donkey, and came down under cover of the mountain, behold, David and his men came down toward her; and she met them. [21]Now David had said, "Surely in vain have I guarded all that this fellow has in the wilderness, so that nothing was missed of all that belonged to him; and he has returned me evil for good. [22]God do so to David[y] and more also, if by morning I leave so much as one male of all who belong to him."

23 When Ab′igail saw David, she made haste, and alighted from the donkey, and fell before David on her face, and bowed to the ground. [24]She fell at his feet and said, "Upon me alone, my lord, be the guilt; please let your handmaid speak in your hearing, and hear the words of your handmaid. [25]Let not my lord regard this ill-natured fellow, Nabal; for as his name is, so is he; Nabal[z] is his name, and folly is with him; but I your handmaid did not see the young men of my lord, whom you sent. [26]Now then, my lord, as the LORD lives, and as your soul lives, seeing the LORD has restrained you from bloodguilt, and from taking vengeance with your own hand, now then let your enemies and those who seek to do evil to my lord be as Nabal. [27]And now let this present which your servant has brought to my lord be given to the young men who follow my lord. [28]Please forgive the trespass of your handmaid; for the LORD will certainly make my lord a sure house, because my lord is fighting the battles of the LORD; and evil shall not be found in you so long as you live. [29]If men rise up to pursue you and to seek your life, the life of my lord shall be bound in the bundle of the living in the care of the LORD your God; and the lives of your enemies he shall sling out as from the hollow of a sling. [30]And when the LORD has done to my lord according to all the good that he has spoken concerning you, and has appointed you prince over Israel, [31]my lord shall have no cause of grief, or pangs of conscience, for having shed blood without cause or for my lord taking vengeance himself. And when the LORD has dealt well with my lord, then remember your handmaid."

32 And David said to Ab′igail, "Blessed be the LORD, the God of Israel, who sent you this day to meet me! [33]Blessed be your discretion, and blessed be you, who have kept me this day from bloodguilt and from avenging myself with my own hand! [34]For as surely as the LORD the God of Israel lives,

---

[y] Gk Compare Syr: Heb *the enemies of David*.
[z] That is *fool*.

who has restrained me from hurting you, unless you had made haste and come to meet me, truly by morning there had not been left to Nabal so much as one male." ³⁵Then David received from her hand what she had brought him; and he said to her, "Go up in peace to your house; see, I have listened to your voice, and I have granted your petition."

36 And Ab′igail came to Nabal; and behold, he was holding a feast in his house, like the feast of a king. And Nabal's heart was merry within him, for he was very drunk; so she told him nothing at all until the morning light. ³⁷And in the morning, when the wine had gone out of Nabal, his wife told him these things, and his heart died within him, and he became as a stone. ³⁸And about ten days later the LORD struck Nabal; and he died.

39 When David heard that Nabal was dead, he said, "Blessed be the LORD who has avenged the insult I received at the hand of Nabal, and has kept back his servant from evil; the LORD has returned the evil-doing of Nabal upon his own head." Then David sent and wooed Ab′igail, to make her his wife. ⁴⁰And when the servants of David came to Ab′igail at Carmel, they said to her, "David has sent us to you to take you to him as his wife." ⁴¹And she rose and bowed with her face to the ground, and said, "Behold, your handmaid is a servant to wash the feet of the servants of my lord." ⁴²And Ab′igail made haste and rose and mounted on a donkey, and her five maidens attended her; she went after the messengers of David, and became his wife.

Ahino-am of Jezreel

43 David also took Ahin′o-am of Jezre′el; and both of them became his wives. ⁴⁴Saul had given Michal his daughter, David's wife, to Palti the son of La′ish, who was of Gallim.

David Again Spares Saul's Life

26 Then the Ziphites came to Saul at Gib′e-ah, saying, "Is not David hiding himself on the hill of Hachi′lah, which is on the east of Jeshi′mon?" ²So Saul arose and went down to the wilderness of Ziph, with three thousand chosen men of Israel, to seek David in the wilderness of Ziph. ³And Saul encamped on the hill of Hachi′lah, which is beside the road on the east of Jeshi′mon. But David remained in the wilderness; and when he saw that Saul came after him into the wilderness, ⁴David sent out spies, and learned of a certainty that Saul had come. ⁵Then David rose and came to the place where Saul had encamped; and David saw the place where Saul lay, with Abner the son of Ner, the commander of his army; Saul was lying within the encampment, while the army was encamped around him.

6 Then David said to Ahim′elech the Hittite, and to Jo′ab's brother Abi′shai the son of Zeru′iah, "Who will go down with me into the camp to Saul?" And Abishai said, "I will go down with you." ⁷So David and Abi′shai went to the army by night; and there lay Saul sleeping within the encampment, with his spear stuck in the ground at his head; and Abner and the army lay around him. ⁸Then said Abi′shai to David, "God has given your enemy into your hand this day; now therefore let me pin him to the earth with one stroke of the spear, and I will not strike him twice." ⁹But David said to Abi′shai, "Do not destroy him; for who can put forth his hand against the LORD's anointed, and be guiltless?" ¹⁰And David said, "As the LORD lives, the LORD will strike him; or his day shall come to die; or he shall go down into battle and perish. ¹¹The LORD forbid that I should put forth my hand against the LORD's anointed; but take now the spear that is at his head, and the jar of water, and let us go." ¹²So David took the spear and the jar of water from Saul's head; and they went away. No man saw it, or knew it, nor did any awake; for they were all asleep, because a deep sleep from the LORD had fallen upon them.

13 Then David went over to the other side, and stood afar off on the top of the mountain, with a great space between them; ¹⁴and David called to the army, and to Abner the son of Ner, saying, "Will you not answer, Abner?" Then Abner answered, "Who are you that calls to the king?" ¹⁵And David said to Abner, "Are you not a man? Who is like you in Israel? Why then have you not kept watch over your lord the king? For one of the people came in to destroy the king your lord. ¹⁶This thing that you have done is not good. As the LORD lives, you deserve to die, because you have not kept watch over your lord, the LORD's anointed. And now see where the king's spear is, and the jar of water that was at his head."

17 Saul recognized David's voice, and said, "Is this your voice, my son David?" And David said, "It is my voice, my lord, O king." ¹⁸And he said, "Why does my lord pursue after his servant? For what have I done? What guilt is on my hands? ¹⁹Now therefore let my lord the king hear the words of his servant. If it is the LORD who has stirred you up against me, may he accept an offering; but if it is men, may they be cursed before the LORD, for they have driven me out this day that I should have no share in the heritage of the LORD, saying, 'Go, serve other gods.' * ²⁰Now therefore, let not my blood fall to the earth away from the presence of the LORD; for the king of Israel has come out to seek my life, ᵃ like one who hunts a partridge in the mountains."

21 Then Saul said, "I have done wrong; return, my son David, for I will no more do you harm,

---

ᵃ Gk: Heb *a flea* (as in 24:14).
26:1–25: 24:1–22.
* 26:19, *Go, serve other gods:* They did not consider the possibility of worshiping Yahweh, the God of Israel, in a foreign land.

because my life was precious in your eyes this day; behold, I have played the fool, and have erred exceedingly." ²²And David made answer, "Here is the spear, O king! Let one of the young men come over and fetch it. ²³The Lord rewards every man for his righteousness and his faithfulness; for the Lord gave you into my hand today, and I would not put forth my hand against the Lord's anointed. ²⁴Behold, as your life was precious this day in my sight, so may my life be precious in the sight of the Lord, and may he deliver me out of all tribulation." ²⁵Then Saul said to David, "Blessed be you, my son David! You will do many things and will succeed in them." So David went his way, and Saul returned to his place.

David Goes to King Achish in Gath

27 And David said in his heart, "I shall now perish one day by the hand of Saul; there is nothing better for me than that I should escape to the land of the Philis'tines; then Saul will despair of seeking me any longer within the borders of Israel, and I shall escape out of his hand." ²So David arose and went over, he and the six hundred men who were with him, to A'chish the son of Ma'och, king of Gath. ³And David dwelt with A'chish at Gath, he and his men, every man with his household, and David with his two wives, Ahin'o-am of Jezre'el, and Ab'igail of Carmel, Nabal's widow. ⁴And when it was told Saul that David had fled to Gath, he sought for him no more.

5 Then David said to A'chish, "If I have found favor in your eyes, let a place be given me in one of the country towns, that I may dwell there; for why should your servant dwell in the royal city with you?" ⁶So that day A'chish gave him Zik'lag; therefore Zik'lag has belonged to the kings of Judah to this day. ⁷And the number of the days that David dwelt in the country of the Philis'tines was a year and four months.

8 Now David and his men went up, and made raids upon the Gesh'urites, the Girzites, and the Amal'ekites; for these were the inhabitants of the land from of old, as far as Shur, to the land of Egypt. ⁹And David struck the land, and left neither man nor woman alive, but took away the sheep, the oxen, the donkeys, the camels, and the garments, and came back to A'chish. ¹⁰When A'chish asked, "Against whom^b have you made a raid today?" David would say, "Against the Neg'eb of Judah," or "Against the Negeb of the Jerah'-meelites," or, "Against the Negeb of the Kenites." ¹¹And David saved neither man nor woman alive, to bring tidings to Gath, thinking, "Lest they should tell about us, and say, 'So David has done.'" Such was his custom all the while he dwelt in the country of the Philis'tines. ¹²And A'chish trusted David, thinking, "He has made himself utterly abhorred by his people Israel; therefore he shall be my servant always."

28 In those days the Philis'tines gathered their forces for war, to fight against Israel. And A'chish said to David, "Understand that you and your men are to go out with me in the army." ²David said to A'chish, "Very well, you shall know what your servant can do." And Achish said to David, "Very well, I will make you my bodyguard for life."

Saul Consults a Medium at En-dor

3 Now Samuel had died, and all Israel had mourned for him and buried him in Ra'mah, his own city. And Saul had put the mediums and the wizards out of the land. ⁴The Philis'tines assembled, and came and encamped at Shu'nem; and Saul gathered all Israel, and they encamped at Gilbo'a. ⁵When Saul saw the army of the Philis'tines, he was afraid, and his heart trembled greatly. ⁶And when Saul inquired of the Lord, the Lord did not answer him, either by dreams, or by U'rim, or by prophets. ⁷Then Saul said to his servants, "Seek out for me a woman who is a medium, that I may go to her and inquire of her." And his servants said to him, "Behold, there is a medium at En-dor."

8 So Saul disguised himself and put on other garments, and went, he and two men with him; and they came to the woman by night. And he said, "Divine for me by a spirit, and bring up for me whomever I shall name to you." ⁹The woman said to him, "Surely you know what Saul has done, how he has cut off the mediums and the wizards from the land. Why then are you laying a snare for my life to bring about my death?" ¹⁰But Saul swore to her by the Lord, "As the Lord lives, no punishment shall come upon you for this thing." ¹¹Then the woman said, "Whom shall I bring up for you?" He said, "Bring up Samuel for me." ¹²When the woman saw Samuel, she cried out with a loud voice; and the woman said to Saul, "Why have you deceived me? You are Saul." ¹³The king said to her, "Have no fear; what do you see?" And the woman said to Saul, "I see a god coming up out of the earth." ¹⁴He said to her, "What is his appearance?" And she said, "An old man is coming up; and he is wrapped in a robe." And Saul knew that it was Samuel, and he bowed with his face to the ground, and did obeisance.

15 Then Samuel said to Saul, "Why have you disturbed me by bringing me up?" Saul answered, "I am in great distress; for the Philis'tines are warring against me, and God has turned away from me and answers me no more, either by prophets or by dreams; therefore I have summoned you to tell me what I shall do." ¹⁶And Samuel said, "Why then do you ask me, since the Lord has turned from you and become your

^b Gk Vg: Heb lacks *whom*.

enemy? [17]The LORD has done to you as he spoke by me; for the LORD has torn the kingdom out of your hand, and given it to your neighbor, David. [18]Because you did not obey the voice of the LORD, and did not carry out his fierce wrath against Am′alek, therefore the LORD has done this thing to you this day. [19]Moreover the LORD will give Israel also with you into the hand of the Philis′tines; and tomorrow you and your sons shall be with me; the LORD will give the army of Israel also into the hand of the Philistines.”

20 Then Saul fell at once full length upon the ground, filled with fear because of the words of Samuel; and there was no strength in him, for he had eaten nothing all day and all night. [21]And the woman came to Saul, and when she saw that he was terrified, she said to him, “Behold, your handmaid has listened to you; I have taken my life in my hand, and have listened to what you have said to me. [22]Now therefore, you also listen to your handmaid; let me set a morsel of bread before you; and eat, that you may have strength when you go on your way.” [23]He refused, and said, “I will not eat.” But his servants, together with the woman, urged him; and he listened to their words. So he arose from the earth, and sat upon the bed. [24]Now the woman had a fatted calf in the house, and she quickly killed it, and she took flour, and kneaded it and baked unleavened bread of it, [25]and she put it before Saul and his servants; and they ate. Then they rose and went away that night.

The Philistines Reject David

29 Now the Philis′tines gathered all their forces at A′phek; and the Israelites were encamped by the fountain which is in Jezre′el. [2]As the lords of the Philis′tines were passing on by hundreds and by thousands, and David and his men were passing on in the rear with A′chish, [3]the commanders of the Philis′tines said, “What are these Hebrews doing here?” And A′chish said to the commanders of the Philistines, “Is not this David, the servant of Saul, king of Israel, who has been with me now for days and years, and since he deserted to me I have found no fault in him to this day.” [4]But the commanders of the Philis′tines were angry with him; and the commanders of the Philistines said to him, “Send the man back, that he may return to the place to which you have assigned him; he shall not go down with us to battle, lest in the battle he become an adversary to us. For how could this fellow reconcile himself to his lord? Would it not be with the heads of the men here? [5]Is not this David, of whom they sing to one another in dances,

‘Saul has slain his thousands,
and David his ten thousands’?”

6 Then A′chish called David and said to him, “As the LORD lives, you have been honest, and to me it seems right that you should march out and in with me in the campaign; for I have found nothing wrong in you from the day of your coming to me to this day. Nevertheless the lords do not approve of you. [7]So go back now; and go peaceably, that you may not displease the lords of the Philis′tines.” [8]And David said to A′chish, “But what have I done? What have you found in your servant from the day I entered your service until now, that I may not go and fight against the enemies of my lord the king?” [9]And A′chish made answer to David, “I know that you are as blameless in my sight as an angel of God; nevertheless the commanders of the Philis′tines have said, ‘He shall not go up with us to the battle.’ [10]Now then rise early in the morning with the servants of your lord who came with you; and start early in the morning, and depart as soon as you have light.” [11]So David set out with his men early in the morning, to return to the land of the Philis′tines. But the Philistines went up to Jezre′el.

David Avenges the Destruction of Ziklag

30 Now when David and his men came to Zik′lag on the third day, the Amal′ekites had made a raid upon the Neg′eb and upon Ziklag. They had overcome Ziklag, and burned it with fire, [2]and taken captive the women and all [c] who were in it, both small and great; they killed no one, but carried them off, and went their way. [3]And when David and his men came to the city, they found it burned with fire, and their wives and sons and daughters taken captive. [4]Then David and the people who were with him raised their voices and wept, until they had no more strength to weep. [5]David's two wives also had been taken captive, Ahin′o-am of Jezre′el, and Ab′igail the widow of Nabal of Carmel. [6]And David was greatly distressed; for the people spoke of stoning him, because all the people were bitter in soul, each for his sons and daughters. But David strengthened himself in the LORD his God.

7 And David said to Abi′athar the priest, the son of Ahim′elech, “Bring me the ephod.” So Abiathar brought the ephod to David. [8]And David inquired of the LORD, “Shall I pursue after this band? Shall I overtake them?” He answered him, “Pursue; for you shall surely overtake and shall surely rescue.” [9]So David set out, and the six hundred men who were with him, and they came to the brook Be′sor, where those stayed who were left behind. [10]But David went on with the pursuit, he and four hundred men; two hundred stayed

---

[c] Gk: Heb lacks and all.
29:5: 18:7; 21:11.

behind, who were too exhausted to cross the brook Be′sor.

11 They found an Egyptian in the open country, and brought him to David; and they gave him bread and he ate, they gave him water to drink, [12]and they gave him a piece of a cake of figs and two clusters of raisins. And when he had eaten, his spirit revived; for he had not eaten bread or drunk water for three days and three nights. [13]And David said to him, "To whom do you belong? And where are you from?" He said, "I am a young man of Egypt, servant to an Amal′ekite; and my master left me behind because I fell sick three days ago. [14]We had made a raid upon the Neg′eb of the Cher′ethites and upon that which belongs to Judah and upon the Negeb of Caleb; and we burned Zik′lag with fire." [15]And David said to him, "Will you take me down to this band?" And he said, "Swear to me by God, that you will not kill me, or deliver me into the hands of my master, and I will take you down to this band."

16 And when he had taken him down, behold, they were spread abroad over all the land, eating and drinking and dancing, because of all the great spoil they had taken from the land of the Philis′tines and from the land of Judah. [17]And David struck them from twilight until the evening of the next day; and not a man of them escaped, except four hundred young men, who mounted camels and fled. [18]David recovered all that the Amal′ekites had taken; and David rescued his two wives. [19]Nothing was missing, whether small or great, sons or daughters, spoil or anything that had been taken; David brought back all. [20]David also captured all the flocks and herds; and the people drove those cattle before him, [d] and said, "This is David's spoil."

21 Then David came to the two hundred men, who had been too exhausted to follow David, and who had been left at the brook Be′sor; and they went out to meet David and to meet the people who were with him; and when David drew near to the people he saluted them. [22]Then all the wicked and base fellows among the men who had gone with David said, "Because they did not go with us, we will not give them any of the spoil which we have recovered, except that each man may lead away his wife and children, and depart." [23]But David said, "You shall not do so, my brothers, with what the LORD has given us; he has preserved us and given into our hand the band that came against us. [24]Who would listen to you in this matter? For as his share is who goes down into the battle, so shall his share be who stays by the baggage; they shall share alike." [25]And from

that day forward he made it a statute and an ordinance for Israel to this day.

26 When David came to Zik′lag, he sent part of the spoil to his friends, the elders of Judah, saying, "Here is a present for you from the spoil of the enemies of the LORD"; [27]it was for those in Bethel, in Ra′moth of the Neg′eb, in Jat′tir, [28]in Aro′er, in Siphmoth, in Eshtemo′a, [29]in Racal, in the cities of the Jerah′meelites, in the cities of the Kenites, [30]in Hormah, in Borash′an, in A′thach, [31]in He′bron, for all the places where David and his men had roamed.

The Death of Saul and His Sons

31 Now the Philis′tines fought against Israel; and the men of Israel fled before the Philistines, and fell slain on Mount Gilbo′a. [2]And the Philis′tines overtook Saul and his sons; and the Philistines slew Jonathan and Abin′adab and Mal″chishu′a, the sons of Saul. [3]The battle pressed hard upon Saul, and the archers found him; and he was badly wounded by the archers. [4]Then Saul said to his armor-bearer, "Draw your sword, and thrust me through with it, lest these uncircumcised come and thrust me through, and make sport of me." But his armor-bearer would not; for he feared greatly. Therefore Saul took his own sword, and fell upon it. [5]And when his armor-bearer saw that Saul was dead, he also fell upon his sword, and died with him. [6]Thus Saul died, and his three sons, and his armor-bearer, and all his men, on the same day together. [7]And when the men of Israel who were on the other side of the valley and those beyond the Jordan saw that the men of Israel had fled and that Saul and his sons were dead, they forsook their cities and fled; and the Philis′tines came and dwelt in them.

8 On the next day, when the Philis′tines came to strip the slain, they found Saul and his three sons fallen on Mount Gilbo′a. [9]And they cut off his head, and stripped off his armor, and sent messengers throughout the land of the Philis′tines, to carry the good news to their idols [e] and to the people. [10]They put his armor in the temple of Ash′taroth; and they fastened his body to the wall of Beth-shan. [11]But when the inhabitants of Ja′besh-gil′ead heard what the Philis′tines had done to Saul, [12]all the valiant men arose, and went all night, and took the body of Saul and the bodies of his sons from the wall of Beth-shan; and they came to Ja′besh and burnt them there. [13]And they took their bones and buried them under the tamarisk tree in Ja′besh, and fasted seven days.

---

[d] Cn: Heb *they drove before those cattle.*
[e] Gk Compare 1 Chron 10:9: Heb *to the house of their idols.*
31:1–13: 2 Sam 1:6–10; 1 Chron 10:1–12.

THE SECOND BOOK OF

SAMUEL

David Mourns Saul and Jonathan

1 After the death of Saul, when David had returned from the slaughter of the Amal′e-kites, David remained two days in Zik′lag; ²and on the third day, behold, a man came from Saul's camp, with his clothes torn and earth upon his head. And when he came to David, he fell to the ground and did obeisance. ³David said to him, "Where do you come from?" And he said to him, "I have escaped from the camp of Israel." ⁴And David said to him, "How did it go? Tell me." And he answered, "The people have fled from the battle, and many of the people also have fallen and are dead; and Saul and his son Jonathan are also dead." ⁵Then David said to the young man who told him, "How do you know that Saul and his son Jonathan are dead?" ⁶And the young man who told him said, "By chance I happened to be on Mount Gilbo′a; and there was Saul leaning upon his spear; and behold, the chariots and the horsemen were close upon him. ⁷And when he looked behind him, he saw me, and called to me. And I answered, 'Here I am.' ⁸And he said to me, 'Who are you?' I answered him, 'I am an Amal′e-kite.' ⁹And he said to me, 'Stand beside me and slay me; for anguish has seized me, and yet my life still lingers.' ¹⁰So I stood beside him, and slew him, because I was sure that he could not live after he had fallen; and I took the crown which was on his head and the armlet which was on his arm, and I have brought them here to my lord."

11 Then David took hold of his clothes, and tore them; and so did all the men who were with him; ¹²and they mourned and wept and fasted until evening for Saul and for Jonathan his son and for the people of the LORD and for the house of Israel, because they had fallen by the sword. ¹³And David said to the young man who told him, "Where do you come from?" And he answered, "I am the son of a sojourner, an Amal′e-kite." ¹⁴David said to him, "How is it you were not afraid to put forth your hand to destroy the LORD's anointed?" ¹⁵Then David called one of the young men and said, "Go, fall upon him." And he struck him so that he died. ¹⁶And David said to him, "Your blood be upon your head; for your own mouth has testified against you, saying, 'I have slain the LORD's anointed.'"

David's Lamentation

17 And David lamented with this lamentation over Saul and Jonathan his son, ¹⁸and he said it [a] should be taught to the people of Judah; behold, it is written in the Book of Jashar. [b] He said:
¹⁹ "Your glory, O Israel, is slain upon your high
        places!
      How are the mighty fallen!
²⁰Tell it not in Gath,
      publish it not in the streets of Ash′kelon;
   lest the daughters of the Philis′tines rejoice,
      lest the daughters of the uncircumcised
        exult.

²¹"You mountains of Gilbo′a,
      let there be no dew or rain upon you,
      nor upsurging of the deep! [c]
   For there the shield of the mighty was defiled,
      the shield of Saul, not anointed with oil.

²²"From the blood of the slain,
      from the fat of the mighty,
   the bow of Jonathan turned not back,
      and the sword of Saul returned not empty.

²³"Saul and Jonathan, beloved and lovely!
      In life and in death they were not divided;
   they were swifter than eagles,
      they were stronger than lions.

²⁴"You daughters of Israel, weep over Saul,
      who clothed you daintily in scarlet,
      who put ornaments of gold upon your
        apparel.

²⁵"How are the mighty fallen
      in the midst of the battle!

   "Jonathan lies slain upon your high places.
²⁶   I am distressed for you, my brother
        Jonathan;
   very pleasant have you been to me;
      your love to me was wonderful,
      passing the love of women. *

²⁷"How are the mighty fallen,
      and the weapons of war perished!"

---

a Gk: Heb *the Bow.*
b Or *The upright.*
c Cn: Heb *fields of offerings.*
1:6–10: 1 Sam 31:1–13; 1 Chron 10:1–12.
* 1:26: Vulgate adds, "As the mother loves her only son, so did I love you."

David Anointed King of Judah

2 After this David inquired of the Lord, "Shall I go up into any of the cities of Judah?" And the Lord said to him, "Go up." David said, "To which shall I go up?" And he said, "To He'bron." ²So David went up there, and his two wives also, Ahin'o-am of Jezre'el, and Ab'igail the widow of Nabal of Carmel. ³And David brought up his men who were with him, every one with his household; and they dwelt in the towns of He'bron. ⁴And the men of Judah came, and there they anointed David king over the house of Judah.

When they told David, "It was the men of Ja'besh-gil'ead who buried Saul," ⁵David sent messengers to the men of Ja'besh-gil'ead, and said to them, "May you be blessed by the Lord, because you showed this loyalty to Saul your lord, and buried him! ⁶Now may the Lord show mercy and faithfulness to you! And I will do good to you because you have done this thing. ⁷Now therefore let your hands be strong, and be valiant; for Saul your lord is dead, and the house of Judah has anointed me king over them."

Ish-bosheth Made King of Israel

8 Now Abner the son of Ner, commander of Saul's army, had taken Ish-bo'sheth * the son of Saul, and brought him over to Ma"hana'im; ⁹and he made him king over Gilead and the Ash'urites and Jezre'el and E'phraim and Benjamin and all Israel. ¹⁰Ish-bo'sheth, Saul's son, was forty years old when he began to reign over Israel, and he reigned two years. But the house of Judah followed David. ¹¹And the time that David was king in He'bron over the house of Judah was seven years and six months.

The Battle of Gibeon

12 Abner the son of Ner, and the servants of Ish-bo'sheth the son of Saul, went out from Ma"hana'im to Gib'eon. ¹³And Jo'ab the son of Zeru'iah, and the servants of David, went out and met them at the pool of Gib'eon; and they sat down, the one on the one side of the pool, and the other on the other side of the pool. ¹⁴And Abner said to Jo'ab, "Let the young men arise and play † before us." And Joab said, "Let them arise." ¹⁵Then they arose and passed over by number, twelve for Benjamin and Ish-bo'sheth the son of Saul, and twelve of the servants of David. ¹⁶And each caught his opponent by the head, and thrust his sword in his opponent's side; so they fell down together. Therefore that place was called Hel'kath-hazzu'rim, ᵈ which is at Gib'eon. ¹⁷And the battle was very fierce that day; and Abner and the men of Israel were beaten before the servants of David.

18 And the three sons of Zeru'iah were there, Jo'ab, Abi'shai, and As'ahel. Now Asahel was as swift of foot as a wild gazelle; ¹⁹and As'ahel pursued Abner, and as he went he turned neither to the right hand nor to the left from following Abner. ²⁰Then Abner looked behind him and said, "Is it you, As'ahel?" And he answered, "It is I." ²¹Abner said to him, "Turn aside to your right hand or to your left, and seize one of the young men, and take his spoil." But As'ahel would not turn aside from following him. ²²And Abner said again to As'ahel, "Turn aside from following me; why should I strike you to the ground? How then could I lift up my face to your brother Jo'ab?" ²³But he refused to turn aside; therefore Abner struck him in the belly with the butt of his spear, so that the spear came out at his back; and he fell there, and died where he was. And all who came to the place where As'ahel had fallen and died, stood still.

24 But Jo'ab and Abi'shai pursued Abner; and as the sun was going down they came to the hill of Ammah, which lies before Giah on the way to the wilderness of Gib'eon. ²⁵And the Benjaminites gathered themselves together behind Abner, and became one band, and took their stand on the top of a hill. ²⁶Then Abner called to Jo'ab, "Shall the sword devour for ever? Do you not know that the end will be bitter? How long will it be before you bid your people turn from the pursuit of their brethren?" ²⁷And Jo'ab said, "As God lives, if you had not spoken, surely the men would have given up the pursuit of their brethren in the morning." ²⁸So Jo'ab blew the trumpet; and all the men stopped, and pursued Israel no more, nor did they fight any more.

29 And Abner and his men went all that night through the Ar'abah; they crossed the Jordan, and marching the whole forenoon they came to Ma"hana'im. ³⁰Jo'ab returned from the pursuit of Abner; and when he had gathered all the people together, there were missing of David's servants nineteen men besides As'ahel. ³¹But the servants of David had slain of Benjamin three hundred and sixty of Abner's men. ³²And they took up As'ahel, and buried him in the tomb of his father, which was at Bethlehem. And Jo'ab and his men marched all night, and the day broke upon them at He'bron.

Abner Defects to David

3 There was a long war between the house of Saul and the house of David; and David grew stronger and stronger, while the house of Saul became weaker and weaker.

2 And sons were born to David at He'bron: his first-born was Amnon, of Ahin'o-am of Jezre'el;

ᵈ That is *the field of sword-edges.*
3:2-5: 1 Chron 3:1–4.
* 2:8, *Ish-bosheth:* "Man of shame." The name was really Ish-baal, "Man or servant of Baal," but the writer could not bring himself to pronounce so profane a name, especially as it belonged to an Israelite; cf. 1 Chron 8:33; 9:39, where the name is given as Esh-baal.
† 2:14, *play:* He meant "do battle." The idea was to settle the matter by a fight between two select groups of soldiers.

³and his second, Chil'e-ab, of Ab'igail the widow of Nabal of Carmel; and the third, Ab'salom the son of Ma'acah the daughter of Talmai king of Ge'shur; ⁴and the fourth, Adoni'jah the son of Haggith; and the fifth, Shephati'ah the son of Abi'tal; ⁵and the sixth, Ith're-am of Eglah, David's wife. These were born to David in He'bron.

6 While there was war between the house of Saul and the house of David, Abner was making himself strong in the house of Saul. ⁷Now Saul had a concubine, whose name was Rizpah, the daughter of Ai'ah; and Ish-bo'sheth said to Abner, "Why have you gone in to my father's concubine?" ⁸Then Abner was very angry over the words of Ish-bo'sheth, and said, "Am I a dog's head of Judah? This day I keep showing loyalty to the house of Saul your father, to his brothers, and to his friends, and have not given you into the hand of David; and yet you charge me today with a fault concerning a woman. ⁹God do so to Abner and more also, if I do not accomplish for David what the Lᴏʀᴅ has sworn to him, ¹⁰to transfer the kingdom from the house of Saul, and set up the throne of David over Israel and over Judah, from Dan to Be'er-she'ba." ¹¹And Ish-bo'sheth could not answer Abner another word, because he feared him.

12 And Abner sent messengers to David at He'bron, ● saying, "To whom does the land belong? Make your covenant with me, and behold, my hand shall be with you to bring over all Israel to you." ¹³And he said, "Good; I will make a covenant with you; but one thing I require of you; that is, you shall not see my face, unless you first bring Michal, Saul's daughter, when you come to see my face." ¹⁴Then David sent messengers to Ish-bo'sheth Saul's son, saying, "Give me my wife Michal, whom I betrothed at the price of a hundred foreskins of the Philis'tines." ¹⁵And Ish-bo'sheth sent, and took her from her husband Pal'ti-el the son of La'ish. ¹⁶But her husband went with her, weeping after her all the way to Bahu'rim. Then Abner said to him, "Go, return"; and he returned.

17 And Abner conferred with the elders of Israel, saying, "For some time past you have been seeking David as king over you. ¹⁸Now then bring it about; for the Lᴏʀᴅ has promised David, saying, 'By the hand of my servant David I will save my people Israel from the hand of the Philis'tines, and from the hand of all their enemies.'" ¹⁹Abner also spoke to Benjamin; and then Abner went to tell David at He'bron all that Israel and the whole house of Benjamin thought good to do.

20 When Abner came with twenty men to David at He'bron, David made a feast for Abner and the men who were with him. ²¹And Abner said to David, "I will arise and go, and will gather all Israel to my lord the king, that they may make a covenant with you, and that you may reign over all that your heart desires." So David sent Abner away; and he went in peace.

Abner Is Killed by Joab

22 Just then the servants of David arrived with Jo'ab from a raid, bringing much spoil with them. But Abner was not with David at He'bron, for he had sent him away, and he had gone in peace. ²³When Jo'ab and all the army that was with him came, it was told Joab, "Abner the son of Ner came to the king, and he has let him go, and he has gone in peace." ²⁴Then Jo'ab went to the king and said, "What have you done? Behold, Abner came to you; why is it that you have sent him away, so that he is gone? ²⁵You know that Abner the son of Ner came to deceive you, and to know your going out and your coming in, and to know all that you are doing."

26 When Jo'ab came out from David's presence, he sent messengers after Abner, and they brought him back from the cistern of Sirah; but David did not know about it. ²⁷And when Abner returned to He'bron, Jo'ab took him aside into the midst of the gate to speak with him privately, and there he struck him in the belly, so that he died, for the blood of As'ahel his brother. ²⁸Afterward, when David heard of it, he said, "I and my kingdom are for ever guiltless before the Lᴏʀᴅ for the blood of Abner the son of Ner. ²⁹May it fall upon the head of Jo'ab, and upon all his father's house; and may the house of Joab never be without one who has a discharge, or who is leprous, or who holds a spindle, or who is slain by the sword, or who lacks bread!" ³⁰So Jo'ab and Abi'shai his brother slew Abner, because he had killed their brother As'ahel in the battle at Gib'eon.

31 Then David said to Jo'ab and to all the people who were with him, "Tear your clothes, and put on sackcloth, and mourn before Abner." And King David followed the bier. ³²They buried Abner at He'bron; and the king lifted up his voice and wept at the grave of Abner; and all the people wept. ³³And the king lamented for Abner, saying,

"Should Abner die as a fool dies?
³⁴Your hands were not bound,
    your feet were not fettered;
as one falls before the wicked
    you have fallen."

And all the people wept again over him. ³⁵Then all the people came to persuade David to eat bread while it was yet day; but David swore, saying, "God do so to me and more also, if I taste bread or anything else till the sun goes down!" ³⁶And all the people took notice of it, and it pleased them; as everything that the king did pleased all the people. ³⁷So all the people and all

---

● Gk: Heb *where he was.*

Israel understood that day that it had not been the king's will to slay Abner the son of Ner. [38]And the king said to his servants, "Do you not know that a prince and a great man has fallen this day in Israel? [39]And I am this day weak, though anointed king; these men the sons of Zeru'iah are too hard for me. The LORD repay the evildoer according to his wickedness!"

Ish-bosheth Is Assassinated

4 When Ish-bo'sheth, Saul's son, heard that Abner had died at He'bron, his courage failed, and all Israel was dismayed. [2]Now Saul's son had two men who were captains of raiding bands; the name of the one was Ba'anah, and the name of the other Re'chab, sons of Rimmon a man of Benjamin from Be-er'oth (for Be-eroth also is reckoned to Benjamin; [3]the Be-er'othites fled to Gitta'im, and have been sojourners there to this day).

4 Jonathan, the son of Saul, had a son who was crippled in his feet. He was five years old when the news about Saul and Jonathan came from Jezre'el; and his nurse took him up, and fled; and, as she fled in her haste, he fell, and became lame. And his name was Mephib'osheth.

5 Now the sons of Rimmon the Be-er'othite, Re'chab and Ba'anah, set out, and about the heat of the day they came to the house of Ish-bo'sheth, as he was taking his noonday rest. [6]And behold, the doorkeeper of the house had been cleaning wheat, but she grew drowsy and slept; so Re'chab and Ba'anah his brother slipped in. [f] [7]When they came into the house, as he lay on his bed in his bedchamber, they struck him, and slew him, and beheaded him. They took his head, and went by the way of the Ar'abah all night, [8]and brought the head of Ish-bo'sheth to David at He'bron. And they said to the king, "Here is the head of Ish-bosheth, the son of Saul, your enemy, who sought your life; the LORD has avenged my lord the king this day on Saul and on his offspring." [9]But David answered Re'chab and Ba'anah his brother, the sons of Rimmon the Be-er'othite, "As the LORD lives, who has redeemed my life out of every adversity, [10]when one told me, 'Behold, Saul is dead,' and thought he was bringing good news, I seized him and slew him at Zik'lag, which was the reward I gave him for his news. [11]How much more, when wicked men have slain a righteous man in his own house upon his bed, shall I not now require his blood at your hand, and destroy you from the earth?" [12]And David commanded his young men, and they killed them, and cut off their hands and feet, and hanged them beside the pool at He'bron. But they took the head of Ish-bo'sheth, and buried it in the tomb of Abner at Hebron.

David Anointed King of All Israel

5 * Then all the tribes of Israel came to David at He'bron, and said, "Behold, we are your bone and flesh. [2]In times past, when Saul was king over us, it was you that led out and brought in Israel; and the LORD said to you, 'You shall be shepherd of my people Israel, and you shall be prince over Israel.'" [3]So all the elders of Israel came to the king at He'bron; and King David made a covenant with them at Hebron before the LORD, and they anointed David king over Israel. [4]David was thirty years old when he began to reign, and he reigned forty years. [5]At He'bron he reigned over Judah seven years and six months; and at Jerusalem he reigned over all Israel and Judah thirty-three years.

Jerusalem Is Made Capital of the Kingdom

6 And the king and his men went to Jerusalem against the Jeb'usites, the inhabitants of the land, who said to David, "You will not come in here, but the blind and the lame † will ward you off"—thinking, "David cannot come in here." [7]Nevertheless David took the stronghold of Zion, that is, the city of David. [8]And David said on that day, "Whoever would strike the Jeb'usites, let him get up the water shaft to attack the lame and the blind, who are hated by David's soul." Therefore it is said, "The blind and the lame shall not come into the house." [9]And David dwelt in the stronghold, and called it the city of David. And David built the city round about from the Millo inward. [10]And David became greater and greater, for the LORD, the God of hosts, was with him.

11 And Hiram king of Tyre sent messengers to David, and cedar trees, also carpenters and masons who built David a house. [12]And David perceived that the LORD had established him king over Israel, and that he had exalted his kingdom for the sake of his people Israel.

13 And David took more concubines and wives from Jerusalem, after he came from He'bron; and more sons and daughters were born to David. [14]And these are the names of those who were born to him in Jerusalem: Sham'mu-a, Shobab, Nathan, Solomon, [15]Ib'har, Eli'shu-a, Ne'pheg, Japhi'a, [16]Elish'ama, Eli'ada, and Eliph'elet.

Philistine Attack Repulsed

17 When the Philis'tines heard that David had been anointed king over Israel, all the Philistines went up in search of David; but David heard of it

---

f Gk: Heb [6]*And they came here into the middle of the house fetching wheat; and they struck him in the belly; and Rechab and Baanah his brother escaped.*
5:1-3: 1 Chron 11:1-3.
5:4, 5: 1 Chron 3:4.
5:6-10: 1 Chron 11:4-9.
5:11-12: 1 Chron 14:1, 2.
5:14-16: 1 Chron 3:5-8; 14:3-7.
5:17-21: 1 Chron 14:8-12.
***** 5:1: The two chapters 5-6 represent the climax of David's career with the establishment of Jerusalem as the political and religious center of Israel.
† 5:6, *the blind and the lame:* The meaning is, that the place was so strong that it could be defended even by the blind and the lame. But David took it by a stratagem, his men climbing secretly up a shaft from the spring Gihon. The place was ideal for a capital city.

and went down to the stronghold. [18]Now the Philis'tines had come and spread out in the valley of Reph'aim. [19]And David inquired of the LORD, "Shall I go up against the Philis'tines? Will you give them into my hand?" And the LORD said to David, "Go up; for I will certainly give the Philistines into your hand." [20]And David came to Ba'al-pera'zim, and David defeated them there; and he said, "The LORD has broken through[g] my enemies before me, like a bursting flood." Therefore the name of that place is called Ba'al-pera'zim.[h] [21]And the Philis'tines left their idols there, and David and his men carried them away.

22 And the Philis'tines came up yet again, and spread out in the valley of Reph'aim. [23]And when David inquired of the LORD, he said, "You shall not go up; go around to their rear, and come upon them opposite the balsam trees. [24]And when you hear the sound of marching in the tops of the balsam trees, then bestir yourself; for then the LORD has gone out before you to strike the army of the Philis'tines." [25]And David did as the LORD commanded him, and struck the Philis'tines from Ge'ba to Gezer.

David Brings the Ark to Jerusalem

6 David again gathered all the chosen men of Israel, thirty thousand. [2]And David arose and went with all the people who were with him from Ba'ale-ju'dah, to bring up from there the ark of God, which is called by the name of the LORD of hosts who sits enthroned on the cherubim. [3]And they carried the ark of God upon a new cart, and brought it out of the house of Abin'adab which was on the hill; and Uzzah and Ahi'o,[i] the sons of Abinadab, were driving the new cart[j] [4]with the ark of God; and Ahi'o[i] went before the ark. [5]And David and all the house of Israel were making merry before the LORD with all their might, with songs[k] and lyres and harps and tambourines and castanets and cymbals.

6 And when they came to the threshing floor of Nacon, Uzzah put out his hand to the ark of God and took hold of it, for the oxen stumbled. [7]And the anger of the LORD was kindled against Uzzah; and God struck him there because he put forth his hand to the ark;[l] and he died there beside the ark of God. [8]And David was angry because the LORD had broken forth upon Uzzah; and that place is called Per'ez-uz'zah,[m] to this day. [9]And David was afraid of the LORD that day; and he said, "How can the ark of the LORD come to me?" [10]So David was not willing to take the ark of the LORD into the city of David; but David took it aside to the house of O'bed-e'dom the Gittite. [11]And the ark of the LORD remained in the house of O'bed-e'dom the Gittite three months; and the LORD blessed Obed-edom and all his household.

12 And it was told King David, "The LORD has blessed the household of O'bed-e'dom and all that belongs to him, because of the ark of God." So David went and brought up the ark of God from the house of Obed-edom to the city of David with rejoicing; [13]and when those who bore the ark of the LORD had gone six paces, he sacrificed an ox and a fatling. [14]And David danced before the LORD with all his might; and David was belted with a linen ephod. [15]So David and all the house of Israel brought up the ark of the LORD with shouting, and with the sound of the horn.

16 As the ark of the LORD came into the city of David, Michal the daughter of Saul looked out of the window, and saw King David leaping and dancing before the LORD; and she despised him in her heart. [17]And they brought in the ark of the LORD, and set it in its place, inside the tent which David had pitched for it; and David offered burnt offerings and peace offerings before the LORD. [18]And when David had finished offering the burnt offerings and the peace offerings, he blessed the people in the name of the LORD of hosts, [19]and distributed among all the people, the whole multitude of Israel, both men and women, to each a cake of bread, a portion of meat,[n] and a cake of raisins. Then all the people departed, each to his house.

20 And David returned to bless his household. But Michal the daughter of Saul came out to meet David, and said, "How the king of Israel honored himself today, uncovering himself today before the eyes of his servants' maids, as one of the vulgar fellows shamelessly uncovers himself!" [21]And David said to Michal, "It was before the LORD, who chose me above your father, and above all his house, to appoint me as prince over Israel, the people of the LORD—and I will make merry before the LORD. [22]I will make myself yet more contemptible than this, and I will be abased in your[o] eyes; but by the maids of whom you have spoken, by them I shall be held in honor." [23]And Michal the daughter of Saul had no child to the day of her death.

God's Promise to David

7 Now when the king dwelt in his house, and the LORD had given him rest from all his enemies round about, [2]the king said to Nathan the prophet, "See now, I dwell in a house of cedar, but the ark of God dwells in a tent." [3]And Nathan

---

[g] Heb paraz.
[h] That is Lord of breaking through.
[i] Or and his brother.
[j] Compare Gk: Heb the new cart, and brought it out of the house of Abinadab which was on the hill.
[k] Gk 1 Chron 13:8: Heb fir-trees.
[l] 1 Chron 13:10: Heb uncertain.
[m] That is The breaking forth upon Uzzah.
[n] Vg: Heb uncertain.
[o] Gk: Heb my.
5:22-25: 1 Chron 14:13-16.
6:1-11: 1 Chron 13:1-14.
6:12-19: 1 Chron 15:1—16:3.
7:1-29: 1 Chron 17:1-27.

said to the king, "Go, do all that is in your heart; for the Lord is with you."

4 But that same night the word of the Lord came to Nathan, [5]"Go and tell my servant David, 'Thus says the Lord: Would you build me a house to dwell in? [6]I have not dwelt in a house since the day I brought up the sons of Israel from Egypt to this day, but I have been moving about in a tent for my dwelling. [7]In all places where I have moved with all the sons of Israel, did I speak a word with any of the judges[p] of Israel, whom I commanded to shepherd my people Israel, saying, "Why have you not built me a house of cedar?"' [8]Now therefore thus you shall say to my servant David, 'Thus says the Lord of hosts, I took you from the pasture, from following the sheep, that you should be prince over my people Israel; [9]and I have been with you wherever you went, and have cut off all your enemies from before you; and I will make for you a great name, like the name of the great ones of the earth. [10]And I will appoint a place for my people Israel, and will plant them, that they may dwell in their own place, and be disturbed no more; and violent men shall afflict them no more, as formerly, [11]from the time that I appointed judges over my people Israel; and I will give you rest from all your enemies. Moreover the Lord declares to you that the Lord will make you a house. [12]When your days are fulfilled and you lie down with your fathers, I will raise up your offspring after you, who shall come forth from your body, and I will establish his kingdom. [13]He shall build a house for my name, and I will establish the throne of his kingdom for ever. [14]I will be his father, and he shall be my son. When he commits iniquity, I will chasten him with the rod of men, with the stripes of the sons of men; [15]but I will not take[q] my merciful love from him, as I took it from Saul, whom I put away from before you. [16]And your house and your kingdom shall be made sure for ever before me; your throne shall be established for ever.'" [17]In accordance with all these words, and in accordance with all this vision, Nathan spoke to David.

David's Prayer

18 Then King David went in and sat before the Lord, and said, "Who am I, O Lord God, and what is my house, that you have brought me thus far? [19]And yet this was a small thing in your eyes, O Lord God; you have spoken also of your servant's house for a great while to come, and have shown me future generations,[r] O Lord God! [20]And what more can David say to you? For you know your servant, O Lord God! [21]Because of your promise, and according to your own heart, you have wrought all this greatness, to make your servant know it. [22]Therefore you are great, O Lord God; for there is none like you, and there is no God besides you, according to all that we have

heard with our ears. [23]What other[s] nation on earth is like your people Israel, whom God went to redeem to be his people, making himself a name, and doing for them[t] great and terrible things, by driving out[u] before his people a nation and its gods?[v] [24]And you established for yourself your people Israel to be your people for ever; and you, O Lord, became their God. [25]And now, O Lord God, confirm for ever the word which you have spoken concerning your servant and concerning his house, and do as you have spoken; [26]and your name will be magnified for ever, saying, 'The Lord of hosts is God over Israel,' and the house of your servant David will be established before you. [27]For you, O Lord of hosts, the God of Israel, have made this revelation to your servant, saying, 'I will build you a house'; therefore your servant has found courage to pray this prayer to you. [28]And now, O Lord God, you are God, and your words are true, and you have promised this good thing to your servant; [29]now therefore may it please you to bless the house of your servant, that it may continue for ever before you; for you, O Lord God, have spoken, and with your blessing shall the house of your servant be blessed for ever." *

David's Wars

8 After this David defeated the Philis'tines and subdued them, and David took Meth'eg-am'mah out of the hand of the Philistines.

2 And he defeated Moab, and measured them with a line, making them lie down on the ground; two lines he measured to be put to death, and one full line to be spared. And the Moabites became servants to David and brought tribute.

3 David also defeated Hadade'zer the son of Re'hob, king of Zobah, as he went to restore his power at the river Euphrates. [4]And David took from him a thousand and seven hundred horsemen, and twenty thousand foot soldiers; and David hamstrung all the chariot horses, but left enough for a hundred chariots. [5]And when the Syrians of Damascus came to help Hadade'zer king of Zobah, David slew twenty-two thousand men of the Syrians. [6]Then David put garrisons in Ar'am of Damascus; and the Syrians became servants to David and brought tribute. And the Lord gave victory to David wherever he went. [7]And David took the shields of gold which were

---

p 1 Chron 17:6: Heb *tribes.*
q Gk Syr Vg 1 Chron 17:13: Heb *shall not depart.*
r Cn: Heb *this is the law for man.*
s Gk: Heb *one.*
t Heb *you.*
u Gk 1 Chron 17:21: Heb *for your land.*
v Heb *before your people, whom you redeemed for yourself from Egypt, nations and its gods.*
7:14: Heb 1:5.
8:1–14: 1 Chron 18:1–13.
* 7:1–29: The point of this prophecy is the establishment of David's dynasty. Hence God says he will build David a house (verse 11). David thanks him suitably in a formal prayer (verses 18–29).

carried by the servants of Hadade'zer, and brought them to Jerusalem. [8]And from Betah and from Bero'thai, cities of Hadade'zer, King David took very much bronze.

9 When To'i king of Ha'math heard that David had defeated the whole army of Hadade'zer, [10]To'i sent his son Jo'ram to King David, to greet him, and to congratulate him because he had fought against Hadade'zer and defeated him; for Hadadezer had often been at war with Toi. And Joram brought with him articles of silver, of gold, and of bronze; [11]these also King David dedicated to the LORD, together with the silver and gold which he dedicated from all the nations he subdued, [12]from E'dom, Moab, the Am'monites, the Philis'tines, Am'alek, and from the spoil of Hadade'zer the son of Re'hob, king of Zobah.

13 And David won a name for himself. When he returned, he slew eighteen thousand E'domites[w] in the Valley of Salt. [14]And he put garrisons in E'dom; throughout all Edom he put garrisons, and all the E'domites became David's servants. And the LORD gave victory to David wherever he went.

David's Officers

15 So David reigned over all Israel; and David administered justice and equity to all his people. [16]And Jo'ab the son of Zeru'iah was over the army; and Jehosh'aphat the son of Ahi'lud was recorder; [17]and Zad'ok the son of Ahi'tub and Ahim'elech the son of Abi'athar were priests; and Serai'ah was secretary; [18]and Bena'iah the son of Jehoi'ada was over[x] the Cher'ethites and the Pel'ethites; and David's sons were priests.

David's Kindness to Mephibosheth

9 [*] And David said, "Is there still any one left of the house of Saul, that I may show him kindness for Jonathan's sake?" [2]Now there was a servant of the house of Saul whose name was Zi'ba, and they called him to David; and the king said to him, "Are you Ziba?" And he said, "Your servant is he." [3]And the king said, "Is there not still some one of the house of Saul, that I may show the kindness of God to him?" Zi'ba said to the king, "There is still a son of Jonathan; he is crippled in his feet." [4]The king said to him, "Where is he?" And Zi'ba said to the king, "He is in the house of Ma'chir the son of Am'miel, at Lo-de'bar." [5]Then King David sent and brought him from the house of Ma'chir the son of Am'miel, at Lo-de'bar. [6]And Mephib'osheth the son of Jonathan, son of Saul, came to David, and fell on his face and did obeisance. And David said, "Mephibosheth!" And he answered, "Behold, your servant." [7]And David said to him, "Do not fear; for I will show you kindness for the sake of your father Jonathan, and I will restore to you all the land of Saul your father; and you shall eat at my table always." [8]And he did obeisance, and said,

"What is your servant, that you should look upon a dead dog such as I?"

9 Then the king called Zi'ba, Saul's servant, and said to him, "All that belonged to Saul and to all his house I have given to your master's son. [10]And you and your sons and your servants shall till the land for him, and shall bring in the produce, that your master's son may have bread to eat; but Mephib'osheth your master's son shall always eat at my table." Now Zi'ba had fifteen sons and twenty servants. [11]Then Zi'ba said to the king, "According to all that my lord the king commands his servant, so will your servant do." So Mephib'osheth ate at David's[y] table, like one of the king's sons. [12]And Mephib'osheth had a young son, whose name was Mica. And all who dwelt in Zi'ba's house became Mephib'osheth's servants. [13]So Mephib'osheth dwelt in Jerusalem; for he ate always at the king's table. Now he was lame in both his feet.

The Ammonites and Syrians Are Defeated

10 After this the king of the Am'monites died, and Ha'nun his son reigned in his stead. [2]And David said, "I will deal loyally with Ha'nun the son of Na'hash, as his father dealt loyally with me." So David sent by his servants to console him concerning his father. And David's servants came into the land of the Am'monites. [3]But the princes of the Am'monites said to Ha'nun their lord, "Do you think, because David has sent comforters to you, that he is honoring your father? Has not David sent his servants to you to search the city, and to spy it out, and to overthrow it?" [4]So Ha'nun took David's servants, and shaved off half the beard of each, and cut off their garments in the middle, at their hips, and sent them away. [5]When it was told David, he sent to meet them, for the men were greatly ashamed. And the king said, "Remain at Jericho until your beards have grown, and then return."

6 When the Am'monites saw that they had become odious to David, the Ammonites sent and hired the Syrians of Beth-re'hob, and the Syrians of Zobah, twenty thousand foot soldiers, and the king of Ma'acah with a thousand men, and the men of Tob, twelve thousand men. [7]And when David heard of it, he sent Jo'ab and all the host of the mighty men. [8]And the Am'monites came out and drew up in battle array at the entrance of the gate; and the Syrians of Zobah and of Re'hob, and

---

[w] Gk: Heb *returned from striking eighteen thousand Syrians.*
[x] Syr Tg Vg 20:23; 1 Chron 18:17: Heb lacks *was over.*
[y] Gk: Heb *my.*
8:15–18: 2 Sam 20:23–26; 1 Chron 18:14–17.
10:1–19: 1 Chron 19:1–19.
[*] **9:1:** 2 Sam 9—1 Kings 2 (except 2 Sam 21–24) is the account of the struggle for the succession to David's throne. It goes back to the early monarchy and is probably the oldest continuous prose narrative in the Old Testament.

the men of Tob and Ma′acah, were by themselves in the open country.

9 When Jo′ab saw that the battle was set against him both in front and in the rear, he chose some of the picked men of Israel, and arrayed them against the Syrians; [10]the rest of his men he put in the charge of Abi′shai his brother, and he arrayed them against the Am′monites. [11]And he said, "If the Syrians are too strong for me, then you shall help me; but if the Am′monites are too strong for you, then I will come and help you. [12]Be of good courage, and let us play the man for our people, and for the cities of our God; and may the LORD do what seems good to him." [13]So Jo′ab and the people who were with him drew near to battle against the Syrians; and they fled before him. [14]And when the Am′monites saw that the Syrians fled, they likewise fled before Abi′shai, and entered the city. Then Jo′ab returned from fighting against the Ammonites, and came to Jerusalem.

15 But when the Syrians saw that they had been defeated by Israel, they gathered themselves together. [16]And Hadade′zer sent, and brought out the Syrians who were beyond the Euphra′tes; [z] and they came to He′lam, with Shobach the commander of the army of Hadadezer at their head. [17]And when it was told David, he gathered all Israel together, and crossed the Jordan, and came to He′lam. And the Syrians arrayed themselves against David, and fought with him. [18]And the Syrians fled before Israel; and David slew of the Syrians the men of seven hundred chariots, and forty thousand horsemen, and wounded Shobach the commander of their army, so that he died there. [19]And when all the kings who were servants of Hadade′zer saw that they had been defeated by Israel, they made peace with Israel, and became subject to them. So the Syrians feared to help the Am′monites any more.

David Commits Adultery with Bathsheba

11 * In the spring of the year, the time when kings go forth to battle, David sent Jo′ab, and his servants with him, and all Israel; and they ravaged the Am′monites, and besieged Rabbah. But David remained at Jerusalem.

2 It happened, late one afternoon, when David arose from his couch and was walking upon the roof of the king's house, that he saw from the roof a woman bathing; and the woman was very beautiful. [3]And David sent and inquired about the woman. And one said, "Is not this Bathshe′ba, the daughter of Eli′am, the wife of Uri′ah the Hittite?" [4]So David sent messengers, and took her; and she came to him, and he lay with her. (Now she was purifying herself from her uncleanness.) Then she returned to her house. [5]And the woman conceived; and she sent and told David, "I am with child."

6 So David sent word to Jo′ab, "Send me Uri′ah the Hittite." And Joab sent Uriah to David. [7]When Uri′ah came to him, David asked how Jo′ab was doing, and how the people fared, and how the war prospered. [8]Then David said to Uri′ah, "Go down to your house, and wash your feet." And Uriah went out of the king's house, and there followed him a present from the king. [9]But Uri′ah slept at the door of the king's house with all the servants of his lord, and did not go down to his house. [10]When they told David, "Uri′ah did not go down to his house," David said to Uriah, "Have you not come from a journey? Why did you not go down to your house?" [11]Uri′ah said to David, "The ark and Israel and Judah dwell in booths; and my lord Jo′ab and the servants of my lord are camping in the open field; shall I then go to my house, to eat and to drink, and to lie with my wife? † As you live, and as your soul lives, I will not do this thing." [12]Then David said to Uri′ah, "Remain here today also, and tomorrow I will let you depart." So Uriah remained in Jerusalem that day, and the next. [13]And David invited him, and he ate in his presence and drank, so that he made him drunk; and in the evening he went out to lie on his couch with the servants of his lord, but he did not go down to his house.

David Has Uriah Killed

14 In the morning David wrote a letter to Jo′ab, and sent it by the hand of Uri′ah. [15]In the letter he wrote, "Set Uri′ah in the forefront of the hardest fighting, and then draw back from him, that he may be struck down, and die." [16]And as Jo′ab was besieging the city, he assigned Uri′ah to the place where he knew there were valiant men. [17]And the men of the city came out and fought with Jo′ab; and some of the servants of David among the people fell. Uri′ah the Hittite was slain also. [18]Then Jo′ab sent and told David all the news about the fighting; [19]and he instructed the messenger, "When you have finished telling all the news about the fighting to the king, [20]then, if the king's anger rises, and if he says to you, 'Why did you go so near the city to fight? Did you not know that they would shoot from the wall? [21]Who killed Abim′elech the son of Jerub′besheth? Did not a woman cast an upper millstone upon him from the wall, so that he died at The′bez? Why did you go so near the wall?' then you shall say, 'Your servant Uri′ah the Hittite is dead also.'"

22 So the messenger went, and came and told David all that Jo′ab had sent him to tell. [23]The

---

z Heb *river.*

11:1: 1 Chron 20:1.

* 11:1: The story of David's double crime shows how he, too, unlike other contemporary monarchs, was under the divine law, not above it, and how God draws good from evil, since it was Bathsheba's son who would succeed David.

† 11:11: It was a religious law that soldiers should remain continent in time of war; cf. 1 Sam 21:4–5.

messenger said to David, "The men gained an advantage over us, and came out against us in the field; but we drove them back to the entrance of the gate. ²⁴Then the archers shot at your servants from the wall; some of the king's servants are dead; and your servant Uri′ah the Hittite is dead also." ²⁵David said to the messenger, "Thus shall you say to Jo′ab, 'Do not let this matter trouble you, for the sword devours now one and now another; strengthen your attack upon the city, and overthrow it.' And encourage him."

26 When the wife of Uri′ah heard that Uriah her husband was dead, she made lamentation for her husband. ²⁷And when the mourning was over, David sent and brought her to his house, and she became his wife, and bore him a son. But the thing that David had done displeased the LORD.

Nathan Condemns David, and God Punishes Him

12 And the LORD sent Nathan to David. He came to him, and said to him, "There were two men in a certain city, the one rich and the other poor. ²The rich man had very many flocks and herds; ³but the poor man had nothing but one little ewe lamb, which he had bought. And he brought it up, and it grew up with him and with his children; it used to eat of his morsel, and drink from his cup, and lie in his bosom, and it was like a daughter to him. ⁴Now there came a traveler to the rich man, and he was unwilling to take one of his own flock or herd to prepare for the wayfarer who had come to him, but he took the poor man's lamb, and prepared it for the man who had come to him." ⁵Then David's anger was greatly kindled against the man; and he said to Nathan, "As the LORD lives, the man who has done this deserves to die; ⁶and he shall restore the lamb fourfold, because he did this thing, and because he had no pity."

7 Nathan said to David, "You are the man. Thus says the LORD, the God of Israel, 'I anointed you king over Israel, and I delivered you out of the hand of Saul; ⁸and I gave you your master's house, and your master's wives into your bosom, and gave you the house of Israel and of Judah; and if this were too little, I would add to you as much more. ⁹Why have you despised the word of the LORD, to do what is evil in his sight? You have struck down Uri′ah the Hittite with the sword, and have taken his wife to be your wife, and have slain him with the sword of the Am′monites. ¹⁰Now therefore the sword shall never depart from your house, because you have despised me, and have taken the wife of Uri′ah the Hittite to be your wife.' ¹¹Thus says the LORD, 'Behold, I will raise up evil against you out of your own house; and I will take your wives before your eyes, and give them to your neighbor, and he shall lie with your wives in the sight of this sun. ¹²For you did it

secretly; but I will do this thing before all Israel, and before the sun.'" ¹³David said to Nathan, "I have sinned against the LORD." And Nathan said to David, "The LORD also has put away your sin; you shall not die. ¹⁴Nevertheless, because by this deed you have utterly scorned the LORD, ^a the child that is born to you shall die." ¹⁵Then Nathan went to his house.

And the LORD struck the child that Uri′ah's wife bore to David, and it became sick. ¹⁶David therefore besought God for the child; and David fasted, and went in and lay all night upon the ground. ¹⁷And the elders of his house stood beside him, to raise him from the ground; but he would not, nor did he eat food with them. ¹⁸On the seventh day the child died. And the servants of David feared to tell him that the child was dead; for they said, "Behold, while the child was yet alive, we spoke to him, and he did not listen to us; how then can we say to him the child is dead? He may do himself some harm." ¹⁹But when David saw that his servants were whispering together, David perceived that the child was dead; and David said to his servants, "Is the child dead?" They said, "He is dead." ²⁰Then David arose from the earth, and washed, and anointed himself, and changed his clothes; and he went into the house of the LORD, and worshiped; he then went to his own house; and when he asked, they set food before him, and he ate. ²¹Then his servants said to him, "What is this thing that you have done? You fasted and wept for the child while it was alive; but when the child died, you arose and ate food." ²²He said, "While the child was still alive, I fasted and wept; for I said, 'Who knows whether the LORD will be gracious to me, that the child may live?' ²³But now he is dead; why should I fast? Can I bring him back again? I shall go to him, but he will not return to me."

Solomon Is Born

24 Then David comforted his wife, Bathshe′ba, and went in to her, and lay with her; and she bore a son, and he called his name Solomon. And the LORD loved him, ²⁵and sent a message by Nathan the prophet; so he called his name Jedidi′ah, ^b because of the LORD.

The Ammonites Crushed

26 Now Jo′ab fought against Rabbah of the Am′monites, and took the royal city. ²⁷And Jo′ab sent messengers to David, and said, "I have fought against Rabbah; moreover, I have taken the city of waters. ²⁸Now, then, gather the rest of the people together, and encamp against the city, and take it; lest I take the city, and it be called by my name." ²⁹So David gathered all the people together and went to Rabbah, and fought against it and took it.

---

^a Heb *the enemies of the* LORD.
^b That is *beloved of the* LORD.
12:26–31: 1 Chron 20:1–3.

³⁰And he took the crown of their king^c from his head; the weight of it was a talent of gold, and in it was a precious stone; and it was placed on David's head. And he brought forth the spoil of the city, a very great amount. ³¹And he brought forth the people who were in it, and set them to labor with saws and iron picks and iron axes, and made them toil at ^d the brick-kilns; and thus he did to all the cities of the Am'monites. Then David and all the people returned to Jerusalem.

Amnon Defiles Tamar

13 * Now Ab'salom, David's son, had a beautiful sister, whose name was Ta'mar; and after a time Amnon, David's son, loved her. ²And Amnon was so tormented that he made himself ill because of his sister Ta'mar; for she was a virgin, and it seemed impossible to Amnon to do anything to her. ³But Amnon had a friend, whose name was Jon'adab, the son of Shim'e-ah, David's brother; and Jonadab was a very crafty man. ⁴And he said to him, "O son of the king, why are you so haggard morning after morning? Will you not tell me?" Amnon said to him, "I love Ta'mar, my brother Ab'salom's sister." ⁵Jon'adab said to him, "Lie down on your bed, and pretend to be ill; and when your father comes to see you, say to him, 'Let my sister Ta'mar come and give me bread to eat, and prepare the food in my sight, that I may see it, and eat it from her hand.'" ⁶So Amnon lay down, and pretended to be ill; and when the king came to see him, Amnon said to the king, "Please let my sister Ta'mar come and make a couple of cakes in my sight, that I may eat from her hand."

7 Then David sent home to Ta'mar, saying, "Go to your brother Amnon's house, and prepare food for him." ⁸So Ta'mar went to her brother Amnon's house, where he was lying down. And she took dough, and kneaded it, and made cakes in his sight, and baked the cakes. ⁹And she took the pan and emptied it out before him, but he refused to eat. And Amnon said, "Send out every one from me." So every one went out from him. ¹⁰Then Amnon said to Ta'mar, "Bring the food into the chamber, that I may eat from your hand." And Tamar took the cakes she had made, and brought them into the chamber to Amnon her brother. ¹¹But when she brought them near him to eat, he took hold of her, and said to her, "Come, lie with me, my sister." ¹²She answered him, "No, my brother, do not force me; for such a thing is not done in Israel; do not do this wanton folly. ¹³As for me, where could I carry my shame? And as for you, you would be as one of the wanton fools in Israel. Now therefore, I beg you, speak to the king; for he will not withhold me from you." ¹⁴But he would not listen to her; and being stronger than she, he forced her, and lay with her.

15 Then Amnon hated her with very great hatred; so that the hatred with which he hated her was greater than the love with which he had loved her. And Amnon said to her, "Arise, be gone." ¹⁶But she said to him, "No, my brother; for this wrong in sending me away is greater than the other which you did to me." ^e But he would not listen to her. ¹⁷He called the young man who served him and said, "Put this woman out of my presence, and bolt the door after her." ¹⁸Now she was wearing a long robe with sleeves; for thus were the virgin daughters of the king clad of old. ^f So his servant put her out, and bolted the door after her. ¹⁹And Ta'mar put ashes on her head, and tore the long robe which she wore; and she laid her hand on her head, and went away, crying aloud as she went.

20 And her brother Ab'salom said to her, "Has Amnon your brother been with you? Now hold your peace, my sister; he is your brother; do not take this to heart." So Ta'mar dwelt, a desolate woman, in her brother Absalom's house. ²¹When King David heard of all these things, he was very angry. ²²But Ab'salom spoke to Amnon neither good nor bad; for Absalom hated Amnon, because he had forced his sister Ta'mar.

Absalom Avenges His Sister

23 After two full years Ab'salom had sheep-shearers at Ba'al-ha'zor, which is near E'phraim, and Absalom invited all the king's sons. ²⁴And Ab'salom came to the king, and said, "Behold, your servant has sheepshearers; please let the king and his servants go with your servant." ²⁵But the king said to Ab'salom, "No, my son, let us not all go, lest we be burdensome to you." He pressed him, but he would not go but gave him his blessing. ²⁶Then Ab'salom said, "If not, please let my brother Amnon go with us." And the king said to him, "Why should he go with you?" ²⁷But Ab'salom pressed him until he let Amnon and all the king's sons go with him. ²⁸Then Ab'salom commanded his servants, "Mark when Amnon's heart is merry with wine, and when I say to you, 'Strike Amnon,' then kill him. Fear not; have I not commanded you? Be courageous and be valiant." ²⁹So the servants of Ab'salom did to Amnon as Absalom had commanded. Then all the king's sons arose, and each mounted his mule and fled.

30 While they were on the way, tidings came to David, "Ab'salom has slain all the king's sons, and not one of them is left." ³¹Then the king arose, and tore his garments, and lay on the earth; and all his servants who were standing by tore their

---

^c Or *Milcom* See Zeph 1:5.
^d Cn: Heb *pass through.*
^e Cn Compare Gk Vg: Heb *No, for this great wrong in sending me away is (worse) than the other which you did to me.*
^f Cn: Heb *clad in robes.*
* 13:1: The first signs of dissension become visible.

garments. [32]But Jon'adab the son of Shim'e-ah, David's brother, said, "Let not my lord suppose that they have killed all the young men the king's sons, for Amnon alone is dead, for by the command of Ab'salom this has been determined from the day he forced his sister Ta'mar. [33]Now therefore let not my lord the king so take it to heart as to suppose that all the king's sons are dead; for Amnon alone is dead."

34 But Ab'salom fled. And the young man who kept the watch lifted up his eyes, and looked, and behold, many people were coming from the Horona'im road [g] by the side of the mountain. [35]And Jon'adab said to the king, "Behold, the king's sons have come; as your servant said, so it has come about." [36]And as soon as he had finished speaking, behold, the king's sons came, and lifted up their voice and wept; and the king also and all his servants wept very bitterly.

Absalom Flees

37 But Ab'salom fled, and went to Talmai the son of Ammi'hud, king of Ge'shur. And David mourned for his son day after day. [38]So Ab'salom fled, and went to Ge'shur, and was there three years. [39]And the spirit [h] of the king longed to go forth to Ab'salom; for he was comforted about Amnon, seeing he was dead.

David Is Persuaded to Bring Absalom Back

14 Now Jo'ab the son of Zeru'iah perceived that the king's heart went out to Ab'salom. [2]And Jo'ab sent to Teko'a, and fetched from there a wise woman, and said to her, "Pretend to be a mourner, and put on mourning garments; do not anoint yourself with oil, but behave like a woman who has been mourning many days for the dead; [3]and go to the king, and speak thus to him." So Jo'ab put the words in her mouth.

4 When the woman of Teko'a came to the king, she fell on her face to the ground, and did obeisance, and said, "Help, O king." [5]And the king said to her, "What is your trouble?" She answered, "Alas, I am a widow; my husband is dead. [6]And your handmaid had two sons, and they quarreled with one another in the field; there was no one to part them, and one struck the other and killed him. [7]And now the whole family has risen against your handmaid, and they say, 'Give up the man who struck his brother, that we may kill him for the life of his brother whom he slew'; and so they would destroy the heir also. Thus they would quench my coal which is left, and leave to my husband neither name nor remnant upon the face of the earth."

8 Then the king said to the woman, "Go to your house, and I will give orders concerning you." [9]And the woman of Teko'a said to the king, "On me be the guilt, my lord the king, and on my father's house; let the king and his throne be guiltless." [10]The king said, "If any one says anything to you, bring him to me, and he shall never touch you again." [11]Then she said, "Please let the king invoke the Lord your God, that the avenger of blood slay no more, and my son be not destroyed." He said, "As the Lord lives, not one hair of your son shall fall to the ground."

12 Then the woman said, "Please let your handmaid speak a word to my lord the king." He said, "Speak." [13]And the woman said, "Why then have you planned such a thing against the people of God? For in giving this decision the king convicts himself, inasmuch as the king does not bring his banished one home again. [14]We must all die, we are like water spilt on the ground, which cannot be gathered up again; but God will not take away the life of him who devises [i] means not to keep his banished one an outcast. [15]Now I have come to say this to my lord the king because the people have made me afraid; and your handmaid thought, 'I will speak to the king; it may be that the king will perform the request of his servant. [16]For the king will hear, and deliver his servant from the hand of the man who would destroy me and my son together from the heritage of God.' [17]And your handmaid thought, 'The word of my lord the king will set me at rest'; for my lord the king is like the angel of God to discern good and evil. The Lord your God be with you!"

18 Then the king answered the woman, "Do not hide from me anything I ask you." And the woman said, "Let my lord the king speak." [19]The king said, "Is the hand of Jo'ab with you in all this?" The woman answered and said, "As surely as you live, my lord the king, one cannot turn to the right hand or to the left from anything that my lord the king has said. It was your servant Joab who bade me; it was he who put all these words in the mouth of your handmaid. [20]In order to change the course of affairs your servant Jo'ab did this. But my lord has wisdom like the wisdom of the angel of God to know all things that are on the earth."

21 Then the king said to Jo'ab, "Behold now, I grant this; go, bring back the young man Ab'salom." [22]And Jo'ab fell on his face to the ground, and did obeisance, and blessed the king; and Joab said, "Today your servant knows that I have found favor in your sight, my lord the king, in that the king has granted the request of his servant." [23]So Jo'ab arose and went to Ge'shur, and brought Ab'salom to Jerusalem. [24]And the king said, "Let him dwell apart in his own house; he is not to come into my presence." So Ab'salom dwelt apart in his own house, and did not come into the king's presence.

---

[g] Cn Compare Gk: Heb *the road behind him*.
[h] Gk: Heb *David*.
[i] Cn: Heb *and he devises*.

25 Now in all Israel there was no one so much to be praised for his beauty as Ab'salom; from the sole of his foot to the crown of his head there was no blemish in him. ²⁶And when he cut the hair of his head (for at the end of every year he used to cut it; when it was heavy on him, he cut it), he weighed the hair of his head, two hundred shekels by the king's weight. ²⁷There were born to Ab'salom three sons, and one daughter whose name was Ta'mar; she was a beautiful woman.

David Forgives Absalom

28 So Ab'salom dwelt two full years in Jerusalem, without coming into the king's presence. ²⁹Then Ab'salom sent for Jo'ab, to send him to the king; but Joab would not come to him. And he sent a second time, but Joab would not come. ³⁰Then he said to his servants, "See, Jo'ab's field is next to mine, and he has barley there; go and set it on fire." So Ab'salom's servants set the field on fire. ³¹Then Jo'ab arose and went to Ab'salom at his house, and said to him, "Why have your servants set my field on fire?" ³²Ab'salom answered Jo'ab, "Behold, I sent word to you, 'Come here, that I may send you to the king, to ask, "Why have I come from Ge'shur? It would be better for me to be there still." Now therefore let me go into the presence of the king; and if there is guilt in me, let him kill me.' " ³³Then Jo'ab went to the king, and told him; and he summoned Ab'salom. So he came to the king, and bowed himself on his face to the ground before the king; and the king kissed Absalom.

Absalom Usurps the Throne

15 After this Ab'salom got himself a chariot and horses, and fifty men to run before him. ²And Ab'salom used to rise early and stand beside the way of the gate; and when any man had a suit to come before the king for judgment, Absalom would call to him, and say, "From what city are you?" And when he said, "Your servant is of such and such a tribe in Israel," ³Ab'salom would say to him, "See, your claims are good and right; but there is no man deputed by the king to hear you." ⁴Ab'salom said moreover, "Oh that I were judge in the land! Then every man with a suit or cause might come to me, and I would give him justice." ⁵And whenever a man came near to do obeisance to him, he would put out his hand, and take hold of him, and kiss him. ⁶Thus Ab'salom did to all of Israel who came to the king for judgment; so Absalom stole the hearts of the men of Israel.

7 And at the end of four ^j years Ab'salom said to the king, "Please let me go and pay my vow, which I have vowed to the LORD, in He'bron. ⁸For your servant vowed a vow while I dwelt at Ge'shur in Ar'am, saying, 'If the LORD will indeed bring me back to Jerusalem, then I will offer worship to the LORD.' " ⁹The king said to him, "Go in

peace." So he arose, and went to He'bron. ¹⁰But Ab'salom sent secret messengers throughout all the tribes of Israel, saying, "As soon as you hear the sound of the trumpet, then say, 'Ab'salom is king at He'bron!' " ¹¹With Ab'salom went two hundred men from Jerusalem who were invited guests, and they went in their simplicity, and knew nothing. ¹²And while Ab'salom was offering the sacrifices, he sent for ^k Ahith'ophel the Gi'lonite, David's counselor, from his city Gi'loh. And the conspiracy grew strong, and the people with Absalom kept increasing.

David Flees from Jerusalem

13 And a messenger came to David, saying, "The hearts of the men of Israel have gone after Ab'salom." ¹⁴Then David said to all his servants who were with him at Jerusalem, "Arise, and let us flee; or else there will be no escape for us from Ab'salom; go in haste, lest he overtake us quickly, and bring down evil upon us, and strike the city with the edge of the sword." ¹⁵And the king's servants said to the king, "Behold, your servants are ready to do whatever my lord the king decides." ¹⁶So the king went forth, and all his household after him. And the king left ten concubines to keep the house. ¹⁷And the king went forth, and all the people after him; and they halted at the last house. ¹⁸And all his servants passed by him; and all the Cher'ethites, and all the Pel'ethites, and all the six hundred Gittites who had followed him from Gath, passed on before the king.

19 Then the king said to Ittai the Gittite, "Why do you also go with us? Go back, and stay with the king; for you are a foreigner, and also an exile from ^l your home. ²⁰You came only yesterday, and shall I today make you wander about with us, seeing I go I know not where? Go back, and take your brethren with you; and may the LORD show ^m mercy and faithfulness to you." ²¹But Ittai answered the king, "As the LORD lives, and as my lord the king lives, wherever my lord the king shall be, whether for death or for life, there also will your servant be." ²²And David said to Ittai, "Go then, pass on." So Ittai the Gittite passed on, with all his men and all the little ones who were with him. ²³And all the country wept aloud as all the people passed by, and the king crossed the brook Kidron, and all the people passed on toward the wilderness.

24 And Abi'athar came up, and behold, Za'dok came also, with all the Levites, bearing the ark of the covenant of God; and they set down the ark of God, until the people had all passed out of the city. ²⁵Then the king said to Za'dok, "Carry the ark of God back into the city. If I find favor in

---

^j Gk Syr: Heb *forty.*
^k Or *sent.*
^l Gk Syr Vg: Heb *to.*
^m Gk: Heb lacks *may the LORD show.*

the eyes of the LORD, he will bring me back and let me see both it and his habitation; [26]but if he says, 'I have no pleasure in you,' behold, here I am, let him do to me what seems good to him." [27]The king also said to Za'dok the priest, "Look, [n] go back to the city in peace, you and Abi'athar, [o] with your two sons, Ahim'a-az your son, and Jonathan the son of Abiathar. [28]See, I will wait at the fords of the wilderness, until word comes from you to inform me." [29]So Za'dok and Abi'athar carried the ark of God back to Jerusalem; and they remained there.

30 But David went up the ascent of the Mount of Olives, weeping as he went, barefoot and with his head covered; and all the people who were with him covered their heads, and they went up, weeping as they went. [31]And it was told David, "Ahith'ophel is among the conspirators with Ab'salom." And David said, "O LORD, I pray you, turn the counsel of Ahithophel into foolishness."

Hushai Becomes David's Spy

32 When David came to the summit, where God was worshiped, behold, Hu'shai the Ar'chite came to meet him with his coat torn and earth upon his head. [33]David said to him, "If you go on with me, you will be a burden to me. [34]But if you return to the city, and say to Ab'salom, 'I will be your servant, O king; as I have been your father's servant in time past, so now I will be your servant,' then you will defeat for me the counsel of Ahith'ophel. [35]Are not Za'dok and Abi'athar the priests with you there? So whatever you hear from the king's house, tell it to Zadok and Abiathar the priests. [36]Behold, their two sons are with them there, Ahim'a-az, Za'dok's son, and Jonathan, Abi'athar's son; and by them you shall send to me everything you hear." [37]So Hu'shai, David's friend, came into the city, just as Ab'salom was entering Jerusalem.

David Meets Ziba

16 When David had passed a little beyond the summit, Zi'ba the servant of Mephib'-osheth met him, with a couple of donkeys saddled, bearing two hundred loaves of bread, a hundred bunches of raisins, a hundred of summer fruits, and a skin of wine. [2]And the king said to Zi'ba, "Why have you brought these?" Ziba answered, "The donkeys are for the king's household to ride on, the bread and summer fruit for the young men to eat, and the wine for those who faint in the wilderness to drink." [3]And the king said, "And where is your master's son?" Zi'ba said to the king, "Behold, he remains in Jerusalem; for he said, 'Today the house of Israel will give me back the kingdom of my father.'" [4]Then the king said to Zi'ba, "Behold, all that belonged to Mephib'osheth is now yours." And Ziba said, "I do obeisance; let me ever find favor in your sight, my lord the king."

Shime-i Curses David

5 When King David came to Bahu'rim, there came out a man of the family of the house of Saul, whose name was Shim'e-i, the son of Gera; and as he came he cursed continually. [6]And he threw stones at David, and at all the servants of King David; and all the people and all the mighty men were on his right hand and on his left. [7]And Shim'e-i said as he cursed, "Begone, begone, you man of blood, you worthless fellow! [8]The LORD has avenged upon you all the blood of the house of Saul, in whose place you have reigned; and the LORD has given the kingdom into the hand of your son Ab'salom. See, your ruin is on you; for you are a man of blood."

9 Then Abi'shai the son of Zeru'iah said to the king, "Why should this dead dog curse my lord the king? Let me go over and take off his head." [10]But the king said, "What have I to do with you, you sons of Zeru'iah? If he is cursing because the LORD has said to him, 'Curse David,' who then shall say, 'Why have you done so?'" [11]And David said to Abi'shai and to all his servants, "Behold, my own son seeks my life; how much more now may this Benjaminite! Let him alone, and let him curse; for the LORD has bidden him. [12]It may be that the LORD will look upon my affliction, [p] and that the LORD will repay me with good for this cursing of me today." [13]So David and his men went on the road, while Shim'e-i went along on the hillside opposite him and cursed as he went, and threw stones at him and flung dust. [14]And the king, and all the people who were with him, arrived weary at the Jordan; [q] and there he refreshed himself.

The Counsel of Ahithophel

15 Now Ab'salom and all the people, the men of Israel, came to Jerusalem, and Ahith'ophel with him. [16]And when Hu'shai the Ar'chite, David's friend, came to Ab'salom, Hushai said to Absalom, "Long live the king! Long live the king!" [17]And Ab'salom said to Hu'shai, "Is this your loyalty to your friend? Why did you not go with your friend?" [18]And Hu'shai said to Ab'salom, "No; for whom the LORD and this people and all the men of Israel have chosen, his I will be, and with him I will remain. [19]And again, whom should I serve? Should it not be his son? As I have served your father, so I will serve you."

20 Then Ab'salom said to Ahith'ophel, "Give your counsel; what shall we do?" [21]Ahith'ophel said to Ab'salom, "Go in to your father's concubines, whom he has left to keep the house; and all Israel will hear that you have made yourself odious to your father, and the hands of all who are

---

[n] Gk: Heb *Are you a seer* or *Do you see?*
[o] Cn: Heb lacks *and Abiathar.*
[p] Gk Vg: Heb *iniquity.*
[q] Gk: Heb lacks *at the Jordan.*

with you will be strengthened." ²²So they pitched a tent for Ab'salom upon the roof; and Absalom went in to his father's concubines in the sight of all Israel. * ²³Now in those days the counsel which Ahith'ophel gave was as if one consulted the oracle ^r of God; so was all the counsel of Ahithophel esteemed, both by David and by Ab'salom.

17 Moreover Ahith'ophel said to Ab'salom, "Let me choose twelve thousand men, and I will set out and pursue David tonight. ²I will come upon him while he is weary and discouraged, and throw him into a panic; and all the people who are with him will flee. I will strike down the king only, ³and I will bring all the people back to you as a bride comes home to her husband. You seek the life of only one man, ^s and all the people will be at peace." ⁴And the advice pleased Ab'salom and all the elders of Israel.

The Counsel of Hushai

5 Then Ab'salom said, "Call Hu'shai the Ar'chite also, and let us hear what he has to say." ⁶And when Hu'shai came to Ab'salom, Absalom said to him, "Thus has Ahith'ophel spoken; shall we do as he advises? If not, you speak." ⁷Then Hu'shai said to Ab'salom, "This time the counsel which Ahith'ophel has given is not good." ⁸Hu'shai said moreover, "You know that your father and his men are mighty men, and that they are enraged, like a bear robbed of her cubs in the field. Besides, your father is expert in war; he will not spend the night with the people. ⁹Behold, even now he has hidden himself in one of the pits, or in some other place. And when some of the people fall ^t at the first attack, whoever hears it will say, 'There has been a slaughter among the people who follow Ab'salom.' ¹⁰Then even the valiant man, whose heart is like the heart of a lion, will utterly melt with fear; for all Israel knows that your father is a mighty man, and that those who are with him are valiant men. ¹¹But my counsel is that all Israel be gathered to you, from Dan to Be'er-she'ba, as the sand by the sea for multitude, and that you go to battle in person. ¹²So we shall come upon him in some place where he is to be found, and we shall light upon him as the dew falls on the ground; and of him and all the men with him not one will be left. ¹³If he withdraws into a city, then all Israel will bring ropes to that city, and we shall drag it into the valley, until not even a pebble is to be found there." ¹⁴And Ab'salom and all the men of Israel said, "The counsel of Hu'shai the Ar'chite is better than the counsel of Ahith'ophel." For the LORD had ordained to defeat the good counsel of Ahithophel, so that the LORD might bring evil upon Ab'salom.

Hushai Warns David to Escape

15 Then Hu'shai said to Za'dok and Abi'athar the priests, "Thus and so did Ahith'ophel counsel

Ab'salom and the elders of Israel; and thus and so have I counseled. ¹⁶Now therefore send quickly and tell David, 'Do not lodge tonight at the fords of the wilderness, but by all means pass over; lest the king and all the people who are with him be swallowed up.'" ¹⁷Now Jonathan and Ahim'a-az were waiting at En-ro'gel; a maidservant used to go and tell them, and they would go and tell King David; for they must not be seen entering the city. ¹⁸But a lad saw them, and told Ab'salom; so both of them went away quickly, and came to the house of a man at Bahu'rim, who had a well in his courtyard; and they went down into it. ¹⁹And the woman took and spread a covering over the well's mouth, and scattered grain upon it; and nothing was known of it. ²⁰When Ab'salom's servants came to the woman at the house, they said, "Where are Ahim'a-az and Jonathan?" And the woman said to them, "They have gone over the brook ^u of water." And when they had sought and could not find them, they returned to Jerusalem.

21 After they had gone, the men came up out of the well, and went and told King David. They said to David, "Arise, and go quickly over the water; for thus and so has Ahith'ophel counseled against you." ²²Then David arose, and all the people who were with him, and they crossed the Jordan; by daybreak not one was left who had not crossed the Jordan.

23 When Ahith'ophel saw that his counsel was not followed, he saddled his donkey, and went off home to his own city. And he set his house in order, and hanged himself; and he died, and was buried in the tomb of his father.

24 Then David came to Ma"hana'im. And Ab'salom crossed the Jordan with all the men of Israel. ²⁵Now Ab'salom had set Ama'sa over the army instead of Jo'ab. Amasa was the son of a man named Ithra the Ish'maelite, ^v who had married Ab'igail the daughter of Na'hash, sister of Zeru'iah, Jo'ab's mother. ²⁶And Israel and Ab'salom encamped in the land of Gilead.

27 When David came to Ma"hana'im, Shobi the son of Na'hash from Rabbah of the Am'monites, and Ma'chir the son of Am'mi-el from Lo-de'bar, and Barzil'lai the Gileadite from Ro'gelim, ²⁸brought beds, basins, and earthen vessels, wheat, barley, meal, parched grain, beans and lentils, ^w ²⁹honey and curds and sheep and cheese from the herd, for David and the people with him to eat; for they said, "The

^r Heb *word.*
^s Gk: Heb *like the return of the whole (is) the man whom you seek.*
^t Or *when he falls upon them.*
^u The meaning of the Hebrew word is uncertain.
^v 1 Chron 2:17: Heb *Israelite.*
^w Heb *lentils and parched grain.*
* 16:22: Absalom's action meant that he was supplanting his father in the kingship; cf. 3:7; 12:8.

people are hungry and weary and thirsty in the wilderness."

The Defeat and Death of Absalom

18 Then David mustered the men who were with him, and set over them commanders of thousands and commanders of hundreds. [2]And David sent forth the army, one third under the command of Jo′ab, one third under the command of Abi′shai the son of Zeru′iah, Joab's brother, and one third under the command of Ittai the Gittite. And the king said to the men, "I myself will also go out with you." [3]But the men said, "You shall not go out. For if we flee, they will not care about us. If half of us die, they will not care about us. But you are worth ten thousand of us; [x] therefore it is better that you send us help from the city." [4]The king said to them, "Whatever seems best to you I will do." So the king stood at the side of the gate, while all the army marched out by hundreds and by thousands. [5]And the king ordered Jo′ab and Abi′shai and Ittai, "Deal gently for my sake with the young man Ab′salom." And all the people heard when the king gave orders to all the commanders about Absalom.

6 So the army went out into the field against Israel; and the battle was fought in the forest of E′phraim. [7]And the men of Israel were defeated there by the servants of David, and the slaughter there was great on that day, twenty thousand men. [8]The battle spread over the face of all the country; and the forest devoured more people that day than the sword.

9 And Ab′salom chanced to meet the servants of David. Absalom was riding upon his mule, and the mule went under the thick branches of a great oak, and his head caught fast in the oak, and he was left hanging [y] between heaven and earth, while the mule that was under him went on. [10]And a certain man saw it, and told Jo′ab, "Behold, I saw Ab′salom hanging in an oak." [11]Jo′ab said to the man who told him, "What, you saw him! Why then did you not strike him there to the ground? I would have been glad to give you ten pieces of silver and a belt." [12]But the man said to Jo′ab, "Even if I felt in my hand the weight of a thousand pieces of silver, I would not put forth my hand against the king's son; for in our hearing the king commanded you and Abi′shai and Ittai, 'For my sake protect the young man Ab′salom.' [13]On the other hand, if I had dealt treacherously against his life [z] (and there is nothing hidden from the king), then you yourself would have stood aloof." [14]Jo′ab said, "I will not waste time like this with you." And he took three darts in his hand, and thrust them into the heart of Ab′salom, while he was still alive in the oak. [15]And ten young men, Jo′ab's armor-bearers, surrounded Ab′salom and struck him, and killed him.

16 Then Jo′ab blew the trumpet, and the troops came back from pursuing Israel; for Joab restrained them. [17]And they took Ab′salom, and threw him into a great pit in the forest, and raised over him a very great heap of stones; and all Israel fled every one to his own home. [18]Now Ab′salom in his lifetime had taken and set up for himself the pillar which is in the King's Valley, for he said, "I have no son to keep my name in remembrance"; he called the pillar after his own name, and it is called Absalom's monument to this day.

David Hears Tidings

19 Then said Ahim′a-az the son of Za′dok, "Let me run, and carry tidings to the king that the LORD has delivered him from the power of his enemies." [20]And Jo′ab said to him, "You are not to carry tidings today; you may carry tidings another day, but today you shall carry no tidings, because the king's son is dead." [21]Then Jo′ab said to the Cushite, "Go, tell the king what you have seen." The Cushite bowed before Jo′ab, and ran. [22]Then Ahim′a-az the son of Za′dok said again to Jo′ab, "Come what may, let me also run after the Cushite." And Jo′ab said, "Why will you run, my son, seeing that you will have no reward for the tidings?" [23]"Come what may," he said, "I will run." So he said to him, "Run." Then Ahim′a-az ran by the way of the plain, and outran the Cushite.

24 Now David was sitting between the two gates; and the watchman went up to the roof of the gate by the wall, and when he lifted up his eyes and looked, he saw a man running alone. [25]And the watchman called out and told the king. And the king said, "If he is alone, there are tidings in his mouth." And he came apace, and drew near. [26]And the watchman saw another man running; and the watchman called to the gate and said, "See, another man running alone!" The king said, "He also brings tidings." [27]And the watchman said, "I think the running of the foremost is like the running of Ahim′a-az the son of Za′dok." And the king said, "He is a good man, and comes with good tidings."

28 Then Ahim′a-az cried out to the king, "All is well." And he bowed before the king with his face to the earth, and said, "Blessed be the LORD your God, who has delivered up the men who raised their hand against my lord the king." [29]And the king said, "Is it well with the young man Ab′salom?" Ahim′a-az answered, "When Jo′ab sent your servant, [b] I saw a great tumult, but I do not know what it was." [30]And the king said, "Turn aside, and stand here." So he turned aside, and stood still.

---

[x] Gk Vg Symmachus: Heb *for now there are ten thousand such as we.*
[y] Gk Syr Tg: Heb *was put.*
[z] Another reading is *at the risk of my life.*
[b] Heb *the king's servant, your servant.*

31 And behold, the Cushite came; and the Cushite said, "Good tidings for my lord the king! For the LORD has delivered you this day from the power of all who rose up against you." [32]The king said to the Cushite, "Is it well with the young man Ab'salom?" And the Cushite answered, "May the enemies of my lord the king, and all who rise up against you for evil, be like that young man." [33] [c] And the king was deeply moved, and went up to the chamber over the gate, and wept; and as he went, he said, "O my son Ab'salom, my son, my son Absalom! Would I had died instead of you, O Absalom, my son, my son!"

David Mourns for Absalom

19 It was told Jo'ab, "Behold, the king is weeping and mourning for Ab'salom." [2]So the victory that day was turned into mourning for all the people; for the people heard that day, "The king is grieving for his son." [3]And the people stole into the city that day as people steal in who are ashamed when they flee in battle. [4]The king covered his face, and the king cried with a loud voice, "O my son Ab'salom, O Absalom, my son, my son!" [5]Then Jo'ab came into the house to the king, and said, "You have today covered with shame the faces of all your servants, who have this day saved your life, and the lives of your sons and your daughters, and the lives of your wives and your concubines, [6]because you love those who hate you and hate those who love you. For you have made it clear today that commanders and servants are nothing to you; for today I perceive that if Ab'salom were alive and all of us were dead today, then you would be pleased. [7]Now therefore arise, go out and speak kindly to your servants; for I swear by the LORD, if you do not go, not a man will stay with you this night; and this will be worse for you than all the evil that has come upon you from your youth until now." [8]Then the king arose, and took his seat in the gate. And the people were all told, "Behold, the king is sitting in the gate"; and all the people came before the king.

Now Israel had fled every man to his own home. [9]And all the people were at strife throughout all the tribes of Israel, saying, "The king delivered us from the hand of our enemies, and saved us from the hand of the Philis'tines; and now he has fled out of the land from Ab'salom. [10]But Ab'salom, whom we anointed over us, is dead in battle. Now therefore why do you say nothing about bringing the king back?"

David Is Recalled

11 And King David sent this message to Za'dok and Abi'athar the priests, "Say to the elders of Judah, 'Why should you be the last to bring the king back to his house, when the word of all Israel has come to the king? [d] [12]You are my

kinsmen, you are my bone and my flesh; why then should you be the last to bring back the king?' [13]And say to Ama'sa, 'Are you not my bone and my flesh? God do so to me, and more also, if you are not commander of my army henceforth in place of Jo'ab.'" [14]And he swayed the heart of all the men of Judah as one man; so that they sent word to the king, "Return, both you and all your servants." [15]So the king came back to the Jordan; and Judah came to Gilgal to meet the king and to bring the king over the Jordan.

Shime-i Meets David and Is Forgiven

16 And Shim'e-i the son of Gera, the Benjaminite, from Bahu'rim, made haste to come down with the men of Judah to meet King David; [17]and with him were a thousand men from Benjamin. And Zi'ba the servant of the house of Saul, with his fifteen sons and his twenty servants, rushed down to the Jordan before the king, [18]and they crossed the ford [e] to bring over the king's household, and to do his pleasure. And Shim'e-i the son of Gera fell down before the king, as he was about to cross the Jordan, [19]and said to the king, "Let not my lord hold me guilty or remember how your servant did wrong on the day my lord the king left Jerusalem; let not the king bear it in mind. [20]For your servant knows that I have sinned; therefore, behold, I have come this day, the first of all the house of Joseph to come down to meet my lord the king." [21]Abi'shai the son of Zeru'iah answered, "Shall not Shim'e-i be put to death for this, because he cursed the LORD's anointed?" [22]But David said, "What have I to do with you, you sons of Zeru'iah, that you should this day be as an adversary to me? Shall any one be put to death in Israel this day? For do I not know that I am this day king over Israel?" [23]And the king said to Shim'e-i, "You shall not die." And the king gave him his oath.

David and Mephibosheth Meet

24 And Mephib'osheth the son of Saul came down to meet the king; he had neither dressed his feet, nor trimmed his beard, nor washed his clothes, from the day the king departed until the day he came back in safety. [25]And when he came from [f] Jerusalem to meet the king, the king said to him, "Why did you not go with me, Mephib'osheth?" [26]He answered, "My lord, O king, my servant deceived me; for your servant said to him, 'Saddle a donkey for me, [g] that I may ride upon it and go with the king.' For your servant is lame. [27]He has slandered your servant to my lord the king. But my lord the king is like the angel of God; do therefore what seems good to you. [28]For

---

[c] Ch 19:1 in Heb.
[d] Gk: Heb to the king, to his house.
[e] Cn: Heb the ford crossed.
[f] Heb to.
[g] Gk Syr Vg: Heb said, I will saddle a donkey for myself.

all my father's house were but men doomed to death before my lord the king; but you set your servant among those who eat at your table. What further right have I, then, to cry to the king?" [29]And the king said to him, "Why speak any more of your affairs? I have decided: you and Zi′ba shall divide the land." [30]And Mephib′osheth said to the king, "Oh, let him take it all, since my lord the king has come safely home."

David Blesses Barzillai

31 Now Barzil′lai the Gileadite had come down from Ro′gelim; and he went on with the king to the Jordan, to escort him over the Jordan. [32]Barzil′lai was a very aged man, eighty years old; and he had provided the king with food while he stayed at Ma″hana′im; for he was a very wealthy man. [33]And the king said to Barzil′lai, "Come over with me, and I will provide for you with me in Jerusalem." [34]But Barzil′lai said to the king, "How many years have I still to live, that I should go up with the king to Jerusalem? [35]I am this day eighty years old; can I discern what is pleasant and what is not? Can your servant taste what he eats or what he drinks? Can I still listen to the voice of singing men and singing women? Why then should your servant be an added burden to my lord the king? [36]Your servant will go a little way over the Jordan with the king. Why should the king recompense me with such a reward? [37]Please let your servant return, that I may die in my own city, near the grave of my father and my mother. But here is your servant Chimham; let him go over with my lord the king; and do for him whatever seems good to you." [38]And the king answered, "Chimham shall go over with me, and I will do for him whatever seems good to you; and all that you desire of me I will do for you." [39]Then all the people went over the Jordan, and the king went over; and the king kissed Barzil′lai and blessed him, and he returned to his own home. [40]The king went on to Gilgal, and Chimham went on with him; all the people of Judah, and also half the sons of Israel, brought the king on his way.

Dissension between Israel and Judah

41 Then all the men of Israel came to the king, and said to the king, "Why have our brethren the men of Judah stolen you away, and brought the king and his household over the Jordan, and all David's men with him?" [42]All the men of Judah answered the men of Israel, "Because the king is near of kin to us. Why then are you angry over this matter? Have we eaten at all at the king's expense? Or has he given us any gift?" [43]And the men of Israel answered the men of Judah, "We have ten shares in the king, and in David also we have more than you. Why then did you despise us? Were we not the first to speak of bringing back our king?" But the words of the men of Judah were fiercer than the words of the men of Israel.

The Rebellion of Sheba

20 Now there happened to be there a worthless fellow, whose name was Sheba, the son of Bichri, a Benjaminite; and he blew the trumpet, and said,

"We have no portion in David,
and we have no inheritance in the son of Jesse;
every man to his tents, O Israel!"

[2]So all the men of Israel withdrew from David, and followed Sheba the son of Bichri; but the men of Judah followed their king steadfastly from the Jordan to Jerusalem.

3 And David came to his house at Jerusalem; and the king took the ten concubines whom he had left to care for the house, and put them in a house under guard, and provided for them, but did not go in to them. So they were shut up until the day of their death, living as if in widowhood.

4 Then the king said to Ama′sa, "Call the men of Judah together to me within three days, and be here yourself." [5]So Ama′sa went to summon Judah; but he delayed beyond the set time which had been appointed him. [6]And David said to Abi′shai, "Now Sheba the son of Bichri will do us more harm than Ab′salom; take your lord's servants and pursue him, lest he get himself fortified cities, and cause us trouble." [h] [7]And there went out after Abi′shai, Jo′ab [i] and the Cher′ethites and the Pel′ethites, and all the mighty men; they went out from Jerusalem to pursue Sheba the son of Bichri. [8]When they were at the great stone which is in Gib′eon, Ama′sa came to meet them. Now Jo′ab was wearing a soldier's garment, and over it was a belt with a sword in its sheath fastened upon his loins, and as he went forward it fell out. [9]And Jo′ab said to Ama′sa, "Is it well with you, my brother?" And Joab took Amasa by the beard with his right hand to kiss him. [10]But Ama′sa did not observe the sword which was in Jo′ab's hand; so Joab struck him with it in the body, and shed his bowels to the ground, without striking a second blow; and he died.*

Then Joab and Abi′shai his brother pursued Sheba the son of Bichri. [11]And one of Jo′ab's men took his stand by Ama′sa, and said, "Whoever favors Joab, and whoever is for David, let him follow Joab." [12]And Ama′sa lay wallowing in his blood in the highway. And any one who came by, seeing him, stopped; [j] and when the man saw that all the people stopped, he carried Amasa out of the highway into the field, and threw a garment over him. [13]When he was taken out of the

---

h Tg: Heb *snatch away our eyes.*
i Cn Compare Gk: Heb *after him Joab's men.*
j This clause is transposed from the end of the verse.
* 20:10: Thus did Joab remove his last rival and remain in power till David's death, in spite of the king's dislike of him.

highway, all the people went on after Jo'ab to pursue Sheba the son of Bichri.

14 And Sheba passed through all the tribes of Israel to Abel of Beth-ma'acah;[k] and all the Bichrites[1] assembled, and followed him in. [15]And all the men who were with Jo'ab came and besieged him in Abel of Beth-ma'acah; they cast up a mound against the city, and it stood against the rampart; and they were battering the wall, to throw it down. [16]Then a wise woman called from the city, "Hear! Hear! Tell Jo'ab, 'Come here, that I may speak to you.'" [17]And he came near her; and the woman said, "Are you Jo'ab?" He answered, "I am." Then she said to him, "Listen to the words of your maidservant." And he answered, "I am listening." [18]Then she said, "They were wont to say in old time, 'Let them but ask counsel at Abel'; and so they settled a matter. [19]I am one of those who are peaceable and faithful in Israel; you seek to destroy a city which is a mother in Israel; why will you swallow up the heritage of the Lord?" [20]Jo'ab answered, "Far be it from me, far be it, that I should swallow up or destroy! [21]That is not true. But a man of the hill country of E'phraim, called Sheba the son of Bichri, has lifted up his hand against King David; give up him alone, and I will withdraw from the city." And the woman said to Jo'ab, "Behold, his head shall be thrown to you over the wall." [22]Then the woman went to all the people in her wisdom. And they cut off the head of Sheba the son of Bichri, and threw it out to Jo'ab. So he blew the trumpet, and they dispersed from the city, every man to his home. And Joab returned to Jerusalem to the king.

23 Now Jo'ab was in command of all the army of Israel; and Bena'iah the son of Jehoi'ada was in command of the Cher'ethites and the Pel'ethites; [24]and Ador'am was in charge of the forced labor; and Jehosh'aphat the son of Ahi'lud was the recorder; [25]and Sheva was secretary; and Za'dok and Abi'athar were priests; [26]and Ira the Ja'irite was also David's priest.

David Avenges the Gibeonites

21 Now there was a famine in the days of David for three years, year after year; and David sought the face of the Lord. And the Lord said, "There is bloodguilt on Saul and on his house, because he put the Gib'eonites to death." [2]So the king called the Gib'eonites.[m] Now the Gibeonites were not of the sons of Israel, but of the remnant of the Am'orites; although the sons of Israel had sworn to spare them, Saul had sought to slay them in his zeal for the sons of Israel and Judah. [3]And David said to the Gib'eonites, "What shall I do for you? And how shall I make expiation, that you may bless the heritage of the Lord?" [4]The Gib'eonites said to him, "It is not a matter of silver or gold between us and Saul or his house;

neither is it for us to put any man to death in Israel." And he said, "What do you say that I shall do for you?" [5]They said to the king, "The man who consumed us and planned to destroy us, so that we should have no place in all the territory of Israel, [6]let seven of his sons be given to us, so that we may hang them up before the Lord at Gib'eon on the mountain of the Lord."[n] And the king said, "I will give them."

7 But the king spared Mephib'osheth, the son of Saul's son Jonathan, because of the oath of the Lord which was between them, between David and Jonathan the son of Saul. [8]The king took the two sons of Rizpah the daughter of Ai'ah, whom she bore to Saul, Armo'ni and Mephib'osheth; and the five sons of Merab[o] the daughter of Saul, whom she bore to A'dri-el the son of Barzil'lai the Meho'lathite; [9]and he gave them into the hands of the Gib'eonites, and they hanged them on the mountain before the Lord, and the seven of them perished together. They were put to death in the first days of harvest, at the beginning of barley harvest.

10 Then Rizpah the daughter of Ai'ah took sackcloth, and spread it for herself on the rock, from the beginning of harvest until rain fell upon them from the heavens; and she did not allow the birds of the air to come upon them by day, or the beasts of the field by night. [11]When David was told what Rizpah the daughter of Ai'ah, the concubine of Saul, had done, [12]David went and took the bones of Saul and the bones of his son Jonathan from the men of Ja'besh-gil'ead, who had stolen them from the public square of Beth-shan, where the Philis'tines had hanged them, on the day the Philistines killed Saul on Gilbo'a; [13]and he brought up from there the bones of Saul and the bones of his son Jonathan; and they gathered the bones of those who were hanged. [14]And they buried the bones of Saul and his son Jonathan in the land of Benjamin in Ze'la, in the tomb of Kish his father; and they did all that the king commanded. And after that God heeded supplications for the land.

Wars with the Philistines

15 The Philis'tines had war again with Israel, and David went down together with his servants, and they fought against the Philistines; and David grew weary. [16]And Ish'bi-be'nob, one of the descendants of the giants, whose spear weighed three hundred shekels of bronze, and who was armed with a new sword, thought to kill David. [17]But Abi'shai the son of Zeru'iah came to his aid,

---

[k] With 20:15: Heb and Beth-maacah.
[1] Heb Berites.
[m] Heb the Gibeonites and said to them.
[n] Cn Compare Gk and 21:9: Heb at Gibeah of Saul, the chosen of the Lord.
[o] Two Hebrew Mss Gk: Heb Michal.
20:23–26: 8:15–18; 1 Chron 18:14–17.

and attacked the Philis'tine and killed him. Then David's men adjured him, "You shall no more go out with us to battle, lest you quench the lamp of Israel."

18 After this there was again war with the Philis'tines at Gob; then Sib'becai the Hu'shathite slew Saph, who was one of the descendants of the giants. ¹⁹And there was again war with the Philis'tines at Gob; and Elha'nan the son of Ja'are-or'egim, the Bethlehemite, slew Goliath the Gittite, the shaft of whose spear was like a weaver's beam. ²⁰And there was again war at Gath, where there was a man of great stature, who had six fingers on each hand, and six toes on each foot, twenty-four in number; and he also was descended from the giants. ²¹And when he taunted Israel, Jonathan the son of Shim'e-i, David's brother, slew him. ²²These four were descended from the giants in Gath; and they fell by the hand of David and by the hand of his servants.

David's Song of Thanksgiving

22 And David spoke to the LORD the words of this song on the day when the LORD delivered him from the hand of all his enemies, and from the hand of Saul. ²He said,*
"The LORD is my rock, and my fortress, and my deliverer,
³ my ᴾ God, my rock, in whom I take refuge,
my shield and the horn of my salvation,
my stronghold and my refuge,
my savior; you save me from violence.
⁴I call upon the LORD, who is worthy to be praised,
and I am saved from my enemies.

⁵ "For the waves of death encompassed me,
the torrents of perdition assailed me;
⁶the cords of Sheol entangled me,
the snares of death confronted me.

⁷ "In my distress I called upon the LORD;
to my God I called.
From his temple he heard my voice,
and my cry came to his ears.

⁸ "Then the earth reeled and rocked;
the foundations of the heavens trembled
and quaked, because he was angry.
⁹Smoke went up from his nostrils,
and devouring fire from his mouth;
glowing coals flamed forth from him.
¹⁰He bowed the heavens, and came down;
thick darkness was under his feet.
¹¹He rode on a cherub, and flew;
he was seen upon the wings of the wind.
¹²He made darkness around him
his canopy, thick clouds, a gathering of water.

¹³Out of the brightness before him
coals of fire flamed forth.
¹⁴The LORD thundered from heaven,
and the Most High uttered his voice.
¹⁵And he sent out arrows, and scattered them;
lightning, and routed them.
¹⁶Then the channels of the sea were seen,
the foundations of the world were laid bare,
at the rebuke of the LORD,
at the blast of the breath of his nostrils.

¹⁷ "He reached from on high, he took me,
he drew me out of many waters.
¹⁸He delivered me from my strong enemy,
from those who hated me;
for they were too mighty for me.
¹⁹They came upon me in the day of my calamity;
but the LORD was my stay.
²⁰He brought me forth into a broad place;
he delivered me, because he delighted in me.

²¹ "The LORD rewarded me according to my righteousness;
according to the cleanness of my hands he recompensed me.
²²For I have kept the ways of the LORD,
and have not wickedly departed from my God.
²³For all his ordinances were before me,
and from his statutes I did not turn aside.
²⁴I was blameless before him,
and I kept myself from guilt.
²⁵Therefore the LORD has recompensed me
according to my righteousness,
according to my cleanness in his sight.

²⁶ "With the loyal you show yourself loyal;
with the blameless man you show yourself blameless;
²⁷with the pure you show yourself pure,
and with the crooked you show yourself perverse.
²⁸You deliver a humble people,
but your eyes are upon the haughty to bring them down.
²⁹Yes, you are my lamp, O LORD,
and my God lightens my darkness.
³⁰Yes, by you I can crush a troop,
and by my God I can leap over a wall.
³¹This God—his way is perfect;
the promise of the LORD proves true;
he is a shield for all those who take refuge in him.

ᴾ Gk Ps 18:2: Heb lacks *my.*
21:18-22: 1 Chron 20:4–8.
22:2-51: Ps 18:2–50.
* 22:2-51: This song, probably inserted later, is very similar to Psalm 18.

³²"For who is God, but the Lᴏʀᴅ?
   And who is a rock, except our God?
³³This God is my strong refuge,
   and has made ˣ my ˢ way safe.
³⁴He made my ˢ feet like deer's feet,
   and set me secure on the heights.
³⁵He trains my hands for war,
   so that my arms can bend a bow of
      bronze.
³⁶You have given me the shield of your
      salvation,
   and your help ᵗ made me great.
³⁷You gave a wide place for my steps under me,
   and my feet ᵘ did not slip;
³⁸I pursued my enemies and destroyed them,
   and did not turn back until they were
      consumed.
³⁹I consumed them; I thrust them through, so
      that they did not rise;
   they fell under my feet.
⁴⁰For you girded me with strength for the
      battle;
   you made my assailants sink under me.
⁴¹You made my enemies turn their backs
      to me,
   those who hated me, and I destroyed them.
⁴²They looked, but there was none to save;
   they cried to the Lᴏʀᴅ, but he did not
      answer them.
⁴³I beat them fine as the dust of the earth,
   I crushed them and stamped them down
      like the mire of the streets.

⁴⁴"You delivered me from strife with the
      peoples; ᵛ
   you kept me as the head of the nations;
   people whom I had not known served me.
⁴⁵Foreigners came cringing to me;
   as soon as they heard of me, they obeyed
      me.
⁴⁶Foreigners lost heart,
   and came trembling ʷ out of their
      fastnesses.

⁴⁷"The Lᴏʀᴅ lives; and blessed be my rock,
   and exalted be my God, the rock of my
      salvation,
⁴⁸the God who gave me vengeance
   and brought down peoples under me,
⁴⁹who brought me out from my enemies;
   you exalted me above my adversaries,
   you delivered me from men of violence.

⁵⁰"For this I will extol you, O Lᴏʀᴅ, among the
      nations,
   and sing praises to your name.
⁵¹Great triumphs he gives ˣ to his king,
   and shows mercy to his anointed,
   to David, and his descendants for ever."

Last Words of David

23 Now these are the last words of David:
   The oracle of David, the son of Jesse,
   the oracle of the man who was raised on
      high,
the anointed of the God of Jacob,
   the sweet psalmist of Israel: ʸ

²"The Spirit of the Lᴏʀᴅ speaks by me,
   his word is upon my tongue.
³The God of Israel has spoken,
   the Rock of Israel has said to me:
When one rules justly over men,
   ruling in the fear of God,
⁴he dawns on them like the morning light,
   like the sun shining forth upon a cloudless
      morning,
   like rain ᶻ that makes grass to sprout from
      the earth.
⁵Yes, does not my house stand so with God?
   For he has made with me an everlasting
      covenant,
   ordered in all things and secure.
For will he not cause to prosper
   all my help and my desire?
⁶But godless men ᵃ are all like thorns that are
      thrown away;
   for they cannot be taken with the hand;
⁷but the man who touches them
   arms himself with iron and the shaft of a
      spear,
   and they are utterly consumed with fire." ᵇ

David's Mighty Men

8 These are the names of the mighty men whom David had: Jo'sheb-basshe'beth a Tah-che'monite; he was chief of the three; ᶜ he wielded his spear ᵈ against eight hundred whom he slew at one time.

9 And next to him among the three mighty men was Elea'zar the son of Dodo, son of Aho'hi. He was with David when they defied the Phi·lis'tines who were gathered there for battle, and the men of Israel withdrew. ¹⁰He rose and struck down the Philis'tines until his hand was weary, and his hand clung to the sword; and the Lᴏʀᴅ wrought a great victory that day; and the men returned after him only to strip the slain.

11 And next to him was Shammah, the son of

ˣ Ps 18:32: Heb *set free.*
ˢ Another reading is *his.*
ᵗ Or *gentleness.*
ᵘ Heb *ankles.*
ᵛ Gk: Heb *from strife with my people.*
ʷ Ps 18:45: Heb *armed themselves.*
ˣ Another reading is *He is a tower of salvation.*
ʸ Or *the favorite of the songs of Israel.*
ᶻ Heb *from rain.*
ᵃ Heb *worthlessness.*
ᵇ Heb *fire in the sitting.*
ᶜ Or *captains.*
ᵈ 1 Chron 11:11: Heb obscure.
22:50: Rom 15:9.
23:8-39: 1 Chron 11:10–41.

Agee the Har'arite. The Philis'tines gathered together at Lehi, where there was a plot of ground full of lentils; and the men fled from the Philistines. [12]But he took his stand in the midst of the plot, and defended it, and slew the Philis'tines; and the Lord wrought a great victory.

13 And three of the thirty chief men went down, and came about harvest time to David at the cave of Adul'lam, when a band of Philis'tines was encamped in the valley of Reph'aim. [14]David was then in the stronghold; and the garrison of the Philis'tines was then at Bethlehem. [15]And David said longingly, "O that some one would give me water to drink from the well of Bethlehem which is by the gate!" [16]Then the three mighty men broke through the camp of the Philis'tines, and drew water out of the well of Bethlehem which was by the gate, and took and brought it to David. But he would not drink of it; he poured it out to the Lord, [17]and said, "Far be it from me, O Lord, that I should do this. Shall I drink the blood of the men who went at the risk of their lives?" Therefore he would not drink it. These things did the three mighty men.

18 Now Abi'shai, the brother of Jo'ab, the son of Zeru'iah, was chief of the thirty. [e] And he wielded his spear against three hundred men and slew them, and won a name beside the three. [19]He was the most renowned of the thirty, [f] and became their commander; but he did not attain to the three.

20 And Bena'iah the son of Jehoi'ada was a valiant man [g] of Kab'zeel, a doer of great deeds; he struck two Ariels [h] of Moab. He also went down and slew a lion in a pit on a day when snow had fallen. [21]And he slew an Egyptian, a handsome man. The Egyptian had a spear in his hand; but Bena'iah went down to him with a staff, and snatched the spear out of the Egyptian's hand, and slew him with his own spear. [22]These things did Bena'iah the son of Jehoi'ada, and won a name beside the three mighty men. [23]He was renowned among the thirty, but he did not attain to the three. And David set him over his bodyguard.

24 As'ahel the brother of Jo'ab was one of the thirty; Elha'nan the son of Dodo of Bethlehem, [25]Shammah of Harod, Eli'ka of Harod, [26]He'lez the Paltite, Ira the son of Ikkesh of Teko'a, [27]Abie'zer, of An'athoth, Mebun'nai the Hu'shathite, [28]Zalmon the Aho'hite, Ma'harai of Netoph'ah, [29]He'leb the son of Ba'anah of Netoph'ah, Ittai the son of Ribai of Gib'e-ah of the Benjaminites, [30]Bena'iah of Pir'athon, Hiddai of the brooks of Ga'ash, [31]A'bi-al'bon the Ar'bathite, Az'maveth of Bahu'rim, [32]Eli'ahba of Sha-al'bon, the sons of Jashen, Jonathan, [33]Shammah the Har'arite, Ahi'am the son of Sharar the Hararite, [34]Eliph'elet the son of Ahas'bai of Ma'acah, Eli'am the son of Ahith'ophel of Gilo, [35]Hezro [i] of Carmel, Pa'arai the Arbite, [36]I'gal the son of Nathan of Zobah, Ba'ni

the Gadite, [37]Zelek the Am'monite, Na'harai of Be-er'oth, the armor-bearer of Jo'ab the son of Zeru'iah, [38]Ira the Ithrite, Ga'reb the Ithrite, [39]Uri'ah the Hittite: thirty-seven in all.

David Takes a Census

24 Again the anger of the Lord was kindled against Israel, and he incited David against them, saying, "Go, number Israel and Judah." * [2]So the king said to Jo'ab and the commanders of the army, [j] who were with him, "Go through all the tribes of Israel, from Dan to Be'er-she'ba, and number the people, that I may know the number of the people." [3]But Jo'ab said to the king, "May the Lord your God add to the people a hundred times as many as they are, while the eyes of my lord the king still see it; but why does my lord the king delight in this thing?" [4]But the king's word prevailed against Jo'ab and the commanders of the army. So Joab and the commanders of the army went out from the presence of the king to number the people of Israel. [5]They crossed the Jordan, and began from Aro'er, [k] and from the city that is in the middle of the valley, toward Gad and on to Ja'zer. [6]Then they came to Gilead, and to Ka'desh in the land of the Hittites; [l] and they came to Dan, and from Dan [m] they went around to Si'don, [7]and came to the fortress of Tyre and to all the cities of the Hi'vites and Canaanites; and they went out to the Neg'eb of Judah at Be'er-she'ba. [8]So when they had gone through all the land, they came to Jerusalem at the end of nine months and twenty days. [9]And Jo'ab gave the sum of the numbering of the people to the king: in Israel there were eight hundred thousand valiant men who drew the sword, and the men of Judah were five hundred thousand.

Judgment on David's Sin

10 But David's heart struck him after he had numbered the people. And David said to the Lord, "I have sinned greatly in what I have done. But now, O Lord, I pray you, take away the iniquity of your servant; for I have done very foolishly." [11]And when David arose in the morning, the word of the Lord came to the prophet Gad, David's seer, saying, [12]"Go and say to David, 'Thus says the Lord, Three things I offer [n] you; choose one of them, that I may do it to you.'" [13]So

---

[e] Two Hebrew Mss Syr: MT *three.*
[f] 1 Chron 11:25: Heb *Was he he the most renowned of the three?*
[g] Another reading is *the son of Ish-hai.*
[h] Gk: *sons of Ariel.* Heb lacks *sons of.*
[i] Another reading is *Hezrai.*
[j] 1 Chron 21:2 Gk: Heb *to Joab the commander of the army.*
[k] Gk: Heb *encamped in Aroer.*
[l] Gk: Heb *to the land of Tahtim-hodshi.*
[m] Cn Compare Gk: Heb *they came to Dan-jaan and.*
[n] Or *hold over.*
24:1-25: 1 Chron 21:1–27.
* 24:1: God is here said to command the census, presumably on the general grounds of ascribing the king's policies to him, but in verse 10 David says he has sinned thereby, and in 1 Chron 21:1 the census is ascribed to Satan as an infringement of God's prerogatives.

Gad came to David and told him, and said to him, "Shall three° years of famine come to you in your land? Or will you flee three months before your foes while they pursue you? Or shall there be three days' pestilence in your land? Now consider, and decide what answer I shall return to him who sent me." [14]Then David said to Gad, "I am in great distress; let us fall into the hand of the LORD, for his mercy is great; but let me not fall into the hand of man."

15 So the LORD sent a pestilence upon Israel from the morning until the appointed time; and there died of the people from Dan to Be'er-she'ba seventy thousand men. [16]And when the angel stretched forth his hand toward Jerusalem to destroy it, the LORD repented of the evil, and said to the angel who was working destruction among the people, "It is enough; now stay your hand." And the angel of the LORD was by the threshing floor of Arau'nah the Jeb'usite. [17]Then David spoke to the LORD when he saw the angel who was striking down the people, and said, "Behold, I have sinned, and I have done wickedly; but these sheep, what have they done? Let your hand, I pray you, be against me and against my father's house."

David's Altar on the Threshing Floor

18 And Gad came that day to David, and said to him, "Go up, rear an altar to the LORD on the threshing floor of Arau'nah the Jeb'usite." [19]So David went up at Gad's word, as the LORD commanded. [20]And when Arau'nah looked down, he saw the king and his servants coming on toward him; and Araunah went forth, and did obeisance to the king with his face to the ground. [21]And Arau'nah said, "Why has my lord the king come to his servant?" David said, "To buy the threshing floor of you, in order to build an altar to the LORD, that the plague may be averted from the people." [22]Then Arau'nah said to David, "Let my lord the king take and offer up what seems good to him; here are the oxen for the burnt offering, and the threshing sledges and the yokes of the oxen for the wood. [23]All this, O king, Arau'nah gives to the king." And Araunah said to the king, "The LORD your God accept you." [24]But the king said to Arau'nah, "No, but I will buy it of you for a price; I will not offer burnt offerings to the LORD my God which cost me nothing." So David bought the threshing floor and the oxen for fifty shekels of silver. [25]And David built there an altar to the LORD, and offered burnt offerings and peace offerings. So the LORD heeded supplications for the land, and the plague was averted from Israel.

° 1 Chron 21:12 Gk: Heb *seven.*

THE FIRST BOOK OF THE

KINGS

The Struggle for Succession to the Throne

1 * Now King David was old and advanced in years; and although they covered him with clothes, he could not get warm. ²Therefore his servants said to him, "Let a young maiden be sought for my lord the king, and let her wait upon the king, and be his nurse; let her lie in your bosom, that my lord the king may be warm." ³So they sought for a beautiful maiden throughout all the territory of Israel, and found Ab'ishag the Shu'nammite, and brought her to the king. ⁴The maiden was very beautiful; and she became the king's nurse and ministered to him; but the king knew her not.

5 Now Adoni'jah the son of Haggith exalted himself, saying, "I will be king";† and he prepared for himself chariots and horsemen, and fifty men to run before him. ⁶His father had never at any time displeased him by asking, "Why have you done thus and so?" He was also a very handsome man; and he was born next after Ab'salom. ⁷He conferred with Jo'ab the son of Zeru'iah and with Abi'athar the priest; and they followed Adoni'jah and helped him. ⁸But Za'dok the priest, and Bena'iah the son of Jehoi'ada, and Nathan the prophet, and Shim'e-i, and Re'i, and David's mighty men were not with Adoni'jah.

9 Adoni'jah sacrificed sheep, oxen, and fatlings by the Serpent's Stone, which is beside En-ro'gel, and he invited all his brothers, the king's sons, and all the royal officials of Judah, ¹⁰but he did not invite Nathan the prophet or Bena'iah or the mighty men or Solomon his brother.

11 Then Nathan said to Bathshe'ba the mother of Solomon, "Have you not heard that Adoni'jah the son of Haggith has become king and David our lord does not know it? ¹²Now therefore come, let me give you counsel, that you may save your own life and the life of your son Solomon. ¹³Go in at once to King David, and say to him, 'Did you not, my lord the king, swear to your maidservant, saying, "Solomon your son shall reign after me, and he shall sit upon my throne"? Why then is Adoni'jah king?' ¹⁴Then while you are still speaking with the king, I also will come in after you and confirm your words."

15 So Bathshe'ba went to the king into his chamber (now the king was very old, and Ab'ishag the Shu'nammite was ministering to the king). ¹⁶Bathshe'ba bowed and did obeisance to the king, and the king said, "What do you desire?" ¹⁷She said to him, "My lord, you swore to your maidservant by the LORD your God, saying, 'Solomon your son shall reign after me, and he shall sit upon my throne.' ¹⁸And now, behold, Adoni'jah is king, although you, my lord the king, do not know it. ¹⁹He has sacrificed oxen, fatlings, and sheep in abundance, and has invited all the sons of the king, Abi'athar the priest, and Jo'ab the commander of the army; but Solomon your servant he has not invited. ²⁰And now, my lord the king, the eyes of all Israel are upon you, to tell them who shall sit on the throne of my lord the king after him. ²¹Otherwise it will come to pass, when my lord the king sleeps with his fathers, that I and my son Solomon will be counted offenders."

22 While she was still speaking with the king, Nathan the prophet came in. ²³And they told the king, "Here is Nathan the prophet." And when he came in before the king, he bowed before the king, with his face to the ground. ²⁴And Nathan said, "My lord the king, have you said, 'Adoni'jah shall reign after me, and he shall sit upon my throne'? ²⁵For he has gone down this day, and has sacrificed oxen, fatlings, and sheep in abundance, and has invited all the king's sons, Jo'ab the commander[a] of the army, and Abi'athar the priest; and behold, they are eating and drinking before him, and saying, 'Long live King Adoni'jah!' ²⁶But me, your servant, and Za'dok the priest, and Bena'iah the son of Jehoi'ada, and your servant Solomon, he has not invited. ²⁷Has this thing been brought about by my lord the king and you have not told your servants who should sit on the throne of my lord the king after him?"

Solomon Is Made King

28 Then King David answered, "Call Bathshe'ba to me." So she came into the king's presence, and stood before the king. ²⁹And the king swore, saying, "As the LORD lives, who has redeemed my soul out of every adversity, ³⁰as I

The First and Second Books of the Kings (the Third and Fourth Books of the Kings): the period covered in these books extends from the death of David to after the fall of Jerusalem in the year 586 B.C. The main theme is the steady decline of Israel dragged down by the monarchy, and her punishment by God for the worship of false gods, introduced by Solomon and actively promoted by many of his successors, especially in the northern kingdom.
ᵃ Gk: Heb *commanders*.
* 1:1: The story continues from 2 Sam 20:26.
† 1:5: There was as yet no natural right of succession and David had already given the right to Solomon, a younger son; cf. verse 13.

248

swore to you by the Lord, the God of Israel, saying, 'Solomon your son shall reign after me, and he shall sit upon my throne in my stead'; even so will I do this day." [31]Then Bathshe′ba bowed with her face to the ground, and did obeisance to the king, and said, "May my lord King David live for ever!"

32 King David said, "Call to me Za′dok the priest, Nathan the prophet, and Bena′iah the son of Jehoi′ada." So they came before the king. [33]And the king said to them, "Take with you the servants of your lord, and cause Solomon my son to ride on my own mule, and bring him down to Gi′hon; [34]and let Za′dok the priest and Nathan the prophet there anoint him king over Israel; then blow the trumpet, and say, 'Long live King Solomon!' [35]You shall then come up after him, and he shall come and sit upon my throne; for he shall be king in my stead; and I have appointed him to be ruler over Israel and over Judah." [36]And Bena′iah the son of Jehoi′ada answered the king, "Amen! May the Lord, the God of my lord the king, say so. [37]As the Lord has been with my lord the king, even so may he be with Solomon, and make his throne greater than the throne of my lord King David."

38 So Za′dok the priest, Nathan the prophet, and Bena′iah the son of Jehoi′ada, and the Cher′ethites and the Pel′ethites, went down and caused Solomon to ride on King David's mule, and brought him to Gi′hon. [39]There Za′dok the priest took the horn of oil from the tent, and anointed Solomon. Then they blew the trumpet; and all the people said, "Long live King Solomon!" [40]And all the people went up after him, playing on pipes, and rejoicing with great joy, so that the earth was split by their noise.

41 Adoni′jah and all the guests who were with him heard it as they finished feasting. And when Jo′ab heard the sound of the trumpet, he said, "What does this uproar in the city mean?" [42]While he was still speaking, behold, Jonathan the son of Abi′athar the priest came; and Adoni′jah said, "Come in, for you are a worthy man and bring good news." [43]Jonathan answered Adoni′jah, "No, for our lord King David has made Solomon king; [44]and the king has sent with him Za′dok the priest, Nathan the prophet, and Bena′iah the son of Jehoi′ada, and the Cher′ethites and the Pel′ethites; and they have caused him to ride on the king's mule; [45]and Za′dok the priest and Nathan the prophet have anointed him king at Gi′hon; and they have gone up from there rejoicing, so that the city is in an uproar. This is the noise that you have heard. [46]Solomon sits upon the royal throne. [47]Moreover the king's servants came to congratulate our lord King David, saying, 'Your God make the name of Solomon more famous than yours, and make his throne greater

than your throne.' And the king bowed himself upon the bed. [48]And the king also said, 'Blessed be the Lord, the God of Israel, who has granted one of my offspring[b] to sit on my throne this day, my own eyes seeing it.'"

49 Then all the guests of Adoni′jah trembled, and rose, and each went his own way. [50]And Adoni′jah feared Solomon; and he arose, and went, and caught hold of the horns of the altar. [51]And it was told Solomon, "Behold, Adoni′jah fears King Solomon; for behold, he has laid hold of the horns of the altar, saying, 'Let King Solomon swear to me first that he will not slay his servant with the sword.'" [52]And Solomon said, "If he prove to be a worthy man, not one of his hairs shall fall to the earth; but if wickedness is found in him, he shall die." [53]So King Solomon sent, and they brought him down from the altar. And he came and did obeisance to King Solomon; and Solomon said to him, "Go to your house."

David's Instructions to Solomon

2 When David's time to die drew near, he charged Solomon his son, saying, [2]"I am about to go the way of all the earth. Be strong, and show yourself a man, [3]and keep the charge of the Lord your God, walking in his ways and keeping his statutes, his commandments, his ordinances, and his testimonies, as it is written in the law of Moses, that you may prosper in all that you do and wherever you turn; [4]that the Lord may establish his word which he spoke concerning me, saying, 'If your sons take heed to their way, to walk before me in faithfulness with all their heart and with all their soul, there shall not fail you a man on the throne of Israel.'

5 "Moreover you know also what Jo′ab the son of Zeru′iah did to me, how he dealt with the two commanders of the armies of Israel, Abner the son of Ner, and Ama′sa the son of Je′ther, whom he murdered, avenging[c] in time of peace blood which had been shed in war, and putting innocent blood[d] upon the belt about my[e] loins, and upon the sandals on my[e] feet. [6]Act therefore according to your wisdom, but do not let his gray head go down to Sheol in peace. [7]But deal loyally with the sons of Barzil′lai the Gileadite, and let them be among those who eat at your table; for with such loyalty they met me when I fled from Ab′salom your brother. [8]And there is also with you Shim′e-i the son of Gera, the Benjaminite from Bahu′rim, who cursed me with a grievous curse on the day when I went to Ma″hana′im; but when he came down to meet me at the Jordan, I swore to him by the Lord, saying, 'I will not put you to death with the sword.' [9]Now therefore hold him not guiltless,

[b] Gk: Heb one.
[c] Gk: Heb placing.
[d] Gk: Heb blood of war.
[e] Gk: Heb his.

for you are a wise man; you will know what you ought to do to him, and you shall bring his gray head down with blood to Sheol."

Death and Burial of David

10 Then David slept with his fathers, and was buried in the city of David. [11]And the time that David reigned over Israel was forty years; he reigned seven years in He′bron, and thirty-three years in Jerusalem. [12]So Solomon sat upon the throne of David his father; and his kingdom was firmly established.

Adonijah's Intrigue

13 Then Adoni′jah the son of Haggith came to Bathshe′ba the mother of Solomon. And she said, "Do you come peaceably?" He said, "Peaceably." [14]Then he said, "I have something to say to you." She said, "Say on." [15]He said, "You know that the kingdom was mine, and that all Israel fully expected me to reign; however the kingdom has turned about and become my brother's, for it was his from the Lord. [16]And now I have one request to make of you; do not refuse me." She said to him, "Say on." [17]And he said, "Please ask King Solomon—he will not refuse you—to give me Ab′ishag the Shu′nammite as my wife." [18]Bathshe′ba said, "Very well; I will speak for you to the king."

19 So Bathshe′ba went to King Solomon, to speak to him on behalf of Adoni′jah. And the king rose to meet her, and bowed down to her; then he sat on his throne, and had a seat brought for the king's mother; and she sat on his right. [20]Then she said, "I have one small request to make of you; do not refuse me." And the king said to her, "Make your request, my mother; for I will not refuse you." [21]She said, "Let Ab′ishag the Shu′nammite be given to Adoni′jah your brother as his wife." [22]King Solomon answered his mother, "And why do you ask Ab′ishag the Shu′nammite for Adoni′jah? Ask for him the kingdom also; for he is my elder brother, and on his side are Abi′athar ᶠ the priest and Jo′ab the son of Zeru′iah." [23]Then King Solomon swore by the Lord, saying, "God do so to me and more also if this word does not cost Adoni′jah his life! [24]Now therefore as the Lord lives, who has established me, and placed me on the throne of David my father, and who has made me a house, as he promised, Adoni′jah shall be put to death this day." [25]So King Solomon sent Bena′iah the son of Jehoi′ada; and he struck him down, and he died.

Solomon Consolidates His Reign

26 And to Abi′athar the priest the king said, "Go to An′athoth, to your estate; for you deserve death. But I will not at this time put you to death, because you bore the ark of the Lord God before David my father, and because you shared in all the affliction of my father." [27]So Solomon expelled Abi′athar from being priest to the Lord, thus ful-

filling the word of the Lord which he had spoken concerning the house of Eli in Shi′loh.

28 When the news came to Jo′ab—for Joab had supported Adoni′jah although he had not supported Ab′salom—Joab fled to the tent of the Lord and caught hold of the horns of the altar. [29]And when it was told King Solomon, "Jo′ab has fled to the tent of the Lord, and behold, he is beside the altar," Solomon sent Bena′iah the son of Jehoi′ada, saying, "Go, strike him down." [30]So Bena′iah came to the tent of the Lord, and said to him, "The king commands, 'Come forth.'" But he said, "No, I will die here." Then Benaiah brought the king word again, saying, "Thus said Jo′ab, and thus he answered me." [31]The king replied to him, "Do as he has said, strike him down and bury him; and thus take away from me and from my father's house the guilt for the blood which Jo′ab shed without cause. [32]The Lord will bring back his bloody deeds upon his own head, because, without the knowledge of my father David, he attacked and slew with the sword two men more righteous and better than himself, Abner the son of Ner, commander of the army of Israel, and Ama′sa the son of Je′ther, commander of the army of Judah. [33]So shall their blood come back upon the head of Jo′ab and upon the head of his descendants for ever; but to David, and to his descendants, and to his house, and to his throne, there shall be peace from the Lord for evermore." [34]Then Bena′iah the son of Jehoi′ada went up, and struck him down and killed him; and he was buried in his own house in the wilderness. [35]The king put Bena′iah the son of Jehoi′ada over the army in place of Jo′ab, and the king put Za′dok the priest in the place of Abi′athar.

36 Then the king sent and summoned Shim′e-i, and said to him, "Build yourself a house in Jerusalem, and dwell there, and do not go forth from there to any place whatever. [37]For on the day you go forth, and cross the brook Kidron, know for certain that you shall die; your blood shall be upon your own head." [38]And Shim′e-i said to the king, "What you say is good; as my lord the king has said, so will your servant do." So Shime-i dwelt in Jerusalem many days.

39 But it happened at the end of three years that two of Shim′e-i's slaves ran away to A′chish, son of Ma′acah, king of Gath. And when it was told Shime-i, "Behold, your slaves are in Gath," [40]Shim′e-i arose and saddled a donkey, and went to Gath to A′chish, to seek his slaves; Shime-i went and brought his slaves from Gath. [41]And when Solomon was told that Shim′e-i had gone from Jerusalem to Gath and returned, [42]the king sent and summoned Shim′e-i, and said to him, "Did I

ᶠ Gk Syr Vg: Heb *and for him and for Abiathar*.
2:12: 1 Chron 29:23.

not make you swear by the LORD, and solemnly admonish you, saying, 'Know for certain that on the day you go forth and go to any place whatever, you shall die'? And you said to me, 'What you say is good; I obey.' ⁴³Why then have you not kept your oath to the LORD and the commandment with which I charged you?" ⁴⁴The king also said to Shim'e-i, "You know in your own heart all the evil that you did to David my father; so the LORD will bring back your evil upon your own head. ⁴⁵But King Solomon shall be blessed, and the throne of David shall be established before the LORD for ever." ⁴⁶Then the king commanded Bena'iah the son of Jehoi'ada; and he went out and struck him down, and he died.

So the kingdom was established in the hand of Solomon.

Solomon Prays for Wisdom

3 * Solomon made a marriage alliance with Pharaoh king of Egypt; he took Pharaoh's daughter, and brought her into the city of David, until he had finished building his own house and the house of the LORD and the wall around Jerusalem. ²The people were sacrificing at the high places, however, because no house had yet been built for the name of the LORD.

3 Solomon loved the LORD, walking in the statutes of David his father; only, he sacrificed and burnt incense at the high places. ⁴And the king went to Gib'eon to sacrifice there, for that was the great high place; Solomon used to offer a thousand burnt offerings upon that altar. ⁵At Gib'eon the LORD appeared to Solomon in a dream † by night; and God said, "Ask what I shall give you." ⁶And Solomon said, "You have shown great and merciful love to your servant David my father, because he walked before you in faithfulness, in righteousness, and in uprightness of heart toward you; and you have kept for him this great and merciful love, and have given him a son to sit on his throne this day. ⁷And now, O LORD my God, you have made your servant king in place of David my father, although I am but a little child; I do not know how to go out or come in. ⁸And your servant is in the midst of your people whom you have chosen, a great people, that cannot be numbered or counted for multitude. ⁹Give your servant therefore an understanding mind to govern your people, that I may discern between good and evil; for who is able to govern this great people of yours?"

10 It pleased the LORD that Solomon had asked this. ¹¹And God said to him, "Because you have asked this, and have not asked for yourself long life or riches or the life of your enemies, but have asked for yourself understanding to discern what is right, ¹²behold, I now do according to your word. Behold, I give you a wise and discerning mind, so that none like you has been before you and none like you shall arise after you. ¹³I give you also

what you have not asked, both riches and honor, so that no other king shall compare with you, all your days. ¹⁴And if you will walk in my ways, keeping my statutes and my commandments, as your father David walked, then I will lengthen your days."

15 And Solomon awoke, and behold, it was a dream. Then he came to Jerusalem, and stood before the ark of the covenant of the LORD, and offered up burnt offerings and peace offerings, and made a feast for all his servants.

Solomon's Wisdom in Judgment

16 Then two harlots came to the king, and stood before him. ¹⁷The one woman said, "Oh, my lord, this woman and I dwell in the same house; and I gave birth to a child while she was in the house. ¹⁸Then on the third day after I was delivered, this woman also gave birth; and we were alone; there was no one else with us in the house, only we two were in the house. ¹⁹And this woman's son died in the night, because she lay on it. ²⁰And she arose at midnight, and took my son from beside me, while your maidservant slept, and laid it in her bosom, and laid her dead son in my bosom. ²¹When I rose in the morning to nurse my child, behold, it was dead; but when I looked at it closely in the morning, behold, it was not the child that I had borne." ²²But the other woman said, "No, the living child is mine, and the dead child is yours." The first said, "No, the dead child is yours, and the living child is mine." Thus they spoke before the king.

23 Then the king said, "The one says, 'This is my son that is alive, and your son is dead'; and the other says, 'No; but your son is dead, and my son is the living one.'" ²⁴And the king said, "Bring me a sword." So a sword was brought before the king. ²⁵And the king said, "Divide the living child in two, and give half to the one, and half to the other." ²⁶Then the woman whose son was alive said to the king, because her heart yearned for her son, "Oh, my lord, give her the living child, and by no means slay it." But the other said, "It shall be neither mine nor yours; divide it." ²⁷Then the king answered and said, "Give the living child to the first woman, and by no means slay it; she is its mother." ²⁸And all Israel heard of the judgment which the king had rendered; and they stood in awe of the king, because they perceived that the wisdom of God was in him, to render justice.

Solomon's High Officials

4 King Solomon was king over all Israel, ²and these were his high officials: Azari'ah the son of Za'dok was the priest; ³Elihor'eph and

---

3:4–15: 2 Chron 1:3–13.
* 3:1: Chapters 3–11 give the history of Solomon. The *Pharaoh* of 3:1 and 9:16 (?) was of the twenty-first dynasty, possibly Psusennes II.
† 3:5, *a dream:* A common means of divine communication, especially before the age of the prophets.

Ahi′jah the sons of Shi′sha were secretaries; Jehosh′aphat the son of Ahi′lud was recorder; [4]Bena′iah the son of Jehoi′ada was in command of the army; Za′dok and Abi′athar were priests; [5]Azari′ah the son of Nathan was over the officers; Zabud the son of Nathan was priest and king's friend; [6]Ahi′shar was in charge of the palace; and Adoni′ram the son of Abda was in charge of the forced labor.

7 Solomon had twelve officers over all Israel, who provided food for the king and his household; each man had to make provision for one month in the year. [8]These were their names: Ben-hur, in the hill country of E′phraim; [9]Ben-de′ker, in Makaz, Sha-al′bim, Beth-she′mesh, and E′lonbeth-ha′nan; [10]Ben-he′sed, in Arub′both (to him belonged Socoh and all the land of He′pher); [11]Ben-abin′adab, in all Na′phath-dor (he had Ta′phath the daughter of Solomon as his wife); [12]Ba′ana the son of Ahi′lud, in Ta′anach, Megid′do, and all Beth-she′an which is beside Zar′ethan below Jezre′el, and from Beth-shean to A′bel-meho′lah, as far as the other side of Jok′meam; [13]Ben-ge′ber, in Ra′moth-gil′ead (he had the villages of Ja′ir the son of Manas′seh, which are in Gilead, and he had the region of Argob, which is in Bashan, sixty great cities with walls and bronze bars); [14]Ahin′adab the son of Iddo, in Ma″hana′im; [15]Ahi′ma-az, in Naph′tali (he had taken Bas′emath the daughter of Solomon as his wife); [16]Ba′ana the son of Hu′shai, in Asher and Bea′loth; [17]Jehosh′aphat the son of Paru′ah, in Is′sachar; [18]Shim′e-i the son of E′la, in Benjamin; [19]Geber the son of U′ri, in the land of Gilead, the country of Si′hon king of the Am′orites and of Og king of Bashan. And there was one officer in the land of Judah.

20 Judah and Israel were as many as the sand by the sea; they ate and drank and were happy. [21] [g] Solomon ruled over all the kingdoms from the Euphrates to the land of the Philis′tines and to the border of Egypt; they brought tribute and served Solomon all the days of his life.

22 Solomon's provision for one day was thirty cors of fine flour, and sixty cors of meal, [23]ten fat oxen, and twenty pasture-fed cattle, a hundred sheep, besides deer, gazelles, roebucks, and fatted fowl. [24]For he had dominion over all the region west of the Euphra′tes from Tiphsah to Gaza, over all the kings west of the Euphrates; and he had peace on all sides round about him. [25]And Judah and Israel dwelt in safety, from Dan even to Be′er-she′ba, every man under his vine and under his fig tree, all the days of Solomon. [26]Solomon also had forty thousand stalls of horses for his chariots, and twelve thousand horsemen. [27]And those officers supplied provisions for King Solomon, and for all who came to King Solomon's table, each one in his month; they let nothing be lacking. [28]Barley also and straw

for the horses and swift steeds they brought to the place where it was required, each according to his charge.

Fame of Solomon's Wisdom

29 And God gave Solomon wisdom and understanding beyond measure, and largeness of mind like the sand on the seashore, [30]so that Solomon's wisdom surpassed the wisdom of all the people of the east, and all the wisdom of Egypt. [31]For he was wiser than all other men, wiser than Ethan the Ez′rahite, and He′man, Calcol, and Darda, the sons of Mahol; and his fame was in all the nations round about. [32]He also uttered three thousand proverbs; * and his songs were a thousand and five. [33]He spoke of trees, from the cedar that is in Lebanon to the hyssop that grows out of the wall; he spoke also of beasts, and of birds, and of reptiles, and of fish. [34]And men came from all peoples to hear the wisdom of Solomon, and from all the kings of the earth, who had heard of his wisdom.

Preparations and Materials for the Temple

5 [h] Now Hiram king of Tyre sent his servants to Solomon, when he heard that they had anointed him king in place of his father; for Hiram always loved David. [2]And Solomon sent word to Hiram, [3]"You know that David my father could not build a house for the name of the LORD his God because of the warfare with which his enemies surrounded him, until the LORD put them under the soles of his feet. [4]But now the LORD my God has given me rest on every side; there is neither adversary nor misfortune. [5]And so I purpose to build a house for the name of the LORD my God, as the LORD said to David my father, 'Your son, whom I will set upon your throne in your place, shall build the house for my name.' [6]Now therefore command that cedars of Lebanon be cut for me; and my servants will join your servants, and I will pay you for your servants such wages as you set; for you know that there is no one among us who knows how to cut timber like the Sido′nians."

7 When Hiram heard the words of Solomon, he rejoiced greatly, and said, "Blessed be the LORD this day, who has given to David a wise son to be over this great people." [8]And Hiram sent to Solomon, saying, "I have heard the message which you have sent to me; I am ready to do all you desire in the matter of cedar and cypress timber. [9]My servants shall bring it down to the sea from Lebanon; and I will make it into rafts to go by sea to the place you direct, and I will have them

---

[g] Ch 5:1 in Heb.
[h] Ch 5:15 in Heb.
5:2–11: 2 Chron 2:3–16.
5:5: 2 Chron 2:1.
* **4:32,** *proverbs:* Doubtless some of those of the book of Proverbs are to be ascribed to Solomon. The book of Wisdom however (called in Greek The Wisdom of Solomon), is ascribed to him only because of his reputation for wisdom. It was actually written in the first century B.C.

broken up there, and you shall receive it; and you shall meet my wishes by providing food for my household." [10]So Hiram supplied Solomon with all the timber of cedar and cypress that he desired, [11]while Solomon gave Hiram twenty thousand cors of wheat as food for his household, and twenty thousand[i] cors of beaten oil. Solomon gave this to Hiram year by year. [12]And the LORD gave Solomon wisdom, as he promised him; and there was peace between Hiram and Solomon; and the two of them made a treaty.

[13] King Solomon raised a levy of forced labor out of all Israel; and the levy numbered thirty thousand men. [14]And he sent them to Lebanon, ten thousand a month in relays; they would be a month in Lebanon and two months at home; Adoni′ram was in charge of the levy. [15]Solomon also had seventy thousand burden-bearers and eighty thousand hewers of stone in the hill country, [16]besides Solomon's three thousand three hundred chief officers who were over the work, who had charge of the people who carried on the work. [17]At the king's command, they quarried out great, costly stones in order to lay the foundation of the house with dressed stones. [18]So Solomon's builders and Hiram's builders and the men of Ge′bal did the hewing and prepared the timber and the stone to build the house.

Solomon Builds the Temple

6 In the four hundred and eightieth year after the sons of Israel came out of the land of Egypt, in the fourth year of Solomon's reign over Israel, in the month of Ziv, which is the second month, he began to build the house of the LORD. * [2]The house which King Solomon built for the LORD was sixty cubits long, twenty cubits wide, and thirty cubits high. [3]The vestibule in front of the nave of the house was twenty cubits long, equal to the width of the house, and ten cubits deep in front of the house. [4]And he made for the house windows with recessed frames. [5]He also built a structure against the wall of the house, running round the walls of the house, both the nave and the inner sanctuary; and he made side chambers all around. [6]The lowest story[j] was five cubits broad, the middle one was six cubits broad, and the third was seven cubits broad; for around the outside of the house he made offsets on the wall in order that the supporting beams should not be inserted into the walls of the house.

[7] When the house was built, it was with stone prepared at the quarry; so that neither hammer nor axe nor any tool of iron was heard in the temple, while it was being built.

[8] The entrance for the lowest[k] story was on the south side of the house; and one went up by stairs to the middle story, and from the middle story to the third. [9]So he built the house, and finished it; and he made the ceiling of the house of beams and planks of cedar. [10]He built the structure against the whole house, each story[l] five cubits high, and it was joined to the house with timbers of cedar.

[11] Now the word of the LORD came to Solomon, [12]"Concerning this house which you are building, if you will walk in my statutes and obey my ordinances and keep all my commandments and walk in them, then I will establish my word with you, which I spoke to David your father. [13]And I will dwell among the children of Israel, and will not forsake my people Israel."

[14] So Solomon built the house, and finished it. [15]He lined the walls of the house on the inside with boards of cedar; from the floor of the house to the rafters[m] of the ceiling, he covered them on the inside with wood; and he covered the floor of the house with boards of cypress. [16]He built twenty cubits of the rear of the house with boards of cedar from the floor to the rafters,[m] and he built this within as an inner sanctuary, as the most holy place. [17]The house, that is, the nave in front of the inner sanctuary, was forty cubits long. [18]The cedar within the house was carved in the form of gourds and open flowers; all was cedar, no stone was seen. [19]The inner sanctuary he prepared in the innermost part of the house, to set there the ark of the covenant of the LORD. [20]The inner sanctuary[n] was twenty cubits long, twenty cubits wide, and twenty cubits high; and he overlaid it with pure gold. He also made[o] an altar of cedar. [21]And Solomon overlaid the inside of the house with pure gold, and he drew chains of gold across, in front of the inner sanctuary, and overlaid it with gold. [22]And he overlaid the whole house with gold, until all the house was finished. Also the whole altar that belonged to the inner sanctuary he overlaid with gold.

Furnishings of the Temple

[23] In the inner sanctuary he made two cherubim of olivewood, each ten cubits high. [24]Five cubits was the length of one wing of the cherub, and five cubits the length of the other wing of the cherub; it was ten cubits from the tip of one wing to the tip of the other. [25]The other cherub also measured ten cubits; both cherubim had the same measure and the same form. [26]The height of one cherub was ten cubits, and so was that of the other cherub. [27]He put the cherubim in the

---

[i] Gk: Heb *twenty.*
[j] Gk: Heb *structure.*
[k] Gk Tg: Heb *middle.*
[l] Heb lacks *each story.*
[m] Gk: Heb *walls.*
[n] Vg: Heb *and before the inner sanctuary.*
[o] Gk: Heb *covered.*

5:15, 16: 2 Chron 2:2, 18.
6:1–28: 2 Chron 3:1–13; Acts 7:47.
* **6:1:** The temple was built on the high ground to the north of Ophel, David's city.

innermost part of the house; and the wings of the cherubim were spread out so that a wing of one touched the one wall, and a wing of the other cherub touched the other wall; their other wings touched each other in the middle of the house. [28]And he overlaid the cherubim with gold.

29 He carved all the walls of the house round about with carved figures of cherubim and palm trees and open flowers, in the inner and outer rooms. [30]The floor of the house he overlaid with gold in the inner and outer rooms.

31 For the entrance to the inner sanctuary he made doors of olivewood; the lintel and the doorposts formed a pentagon. [p] [32]He covered the two doors of olivewood with carvings of cherubim, palm trees, and open flowers; he overlaid them with gold, and spread gold upon the cherubim and upon the palm trees.

33 So also he made for the entrance to the nave doorposts of olivewood, in the form of a square, [34]and two doors of cypress wood; the two leaves of the one door were folding, and the two leaves of the other door were folding. [35]On them he carved cherubim and palm trees and open flowers; and he overlaid them with gold evenly applied upon the carved work. [36]He built the inner court with three courses of hewn stone and one course of cedar beams.

37 In the fourth year the foundation of the house of the LORD was laid, in the month of Ziv. [38]And in the eleventh year, in the month of Bul, which is the eighth month, the house was finished in all its parts, and according to all its specifications. He was seven years in building it.

Solomon's House and Other Buildings

7 Solomon was building his own house thirteen years, and he finished his entire house.

2 He built the House of the Forest of Lebanon; its length was a hundred cubits, and its breadth fifty cubits, and its height thirty cubits, and it was built upon three [q] rows of cedar pillars, with cedar beams upon the pillars. [3]And it was covered with cedar above the chambers that were upon the forty-five pillars, fifteen in each row. [4]There were window frames in three rows, and window opposite window in three tiers. [5]All the doorways and windows [r] had square frames, and window was opposite window in three tiers.

6 And he made the Hall of Pillars; its length was fifty cubits, and its breadth thirty cubits; there was a porch in front with pillars, and a canopy before them.

7 And he made the Hall of the Throne where he was to pronounce judgment, even the Hall of Judgment; it was finished with cedar from floor to rafters. [s]

8 His own house where he was to dwell, in the other court back of the hall, was of like workmanship. Solomon also made a house like this

hall for Pharaoh's daughter whom he had taken in marriage.

9 All these were made of costly stones, hewn according to measure, sawed with saws, back and front, even from the foundation to the coping, and from the court of the house of the LORD [t] to the great court. [10]The foundation was of costly stones, huge stones, stones of eight and ten cubits. [11]And above were costly stones, hewn according to measurement, and cedar. [12]The great court had three courses of hewn stone round about, and a course of cedar beams; so had the inner court of the house of the LORD, and the vestibule of the house.

Works of Hiram the Bronzeworker

13 And King Solomon sent and brought Hiram from Tyre. [14]He was the son of a widow of the tribe of Naph'tali, and his father was a man of Tyre, a worker in bronze; and he was full of wisdom, understanding, and skill, for making any work in bronze. He came to King Solomon, and did all his work.

15 He cast two pillars of bronze. Eighteen cubits was the height of one pillar, and a line of twelve cubits measured its circumference; it was hollow, and its thickness was four fingers; the second pillar was the same. [u] [16]He also made two capitals of molten bronze, to set upon the tops of the pillars; the height of the one capital was five cubits, and the height of the other capital was five cubits. [17]Then he made two [v] nets of checker work with wreaths of chain work for the capitals upon the tops of the pillars; a net [w] for the one capital, and a net [w] for the other capital. [18]Likewise he made pomegranates; [x] in two rows round about upon the one network, to cover the capital that was upon the top of the pillar; and he did the same with the other capital. [19]Now the capitals that were upon the tops of the pillars in the vestibule were of lily-work, four cubits. [20]The capitals were upon the two pillars and also above the rounded projection which was beside the network; there were two hundred pomegranates, in two rows round about; and so with the other capital. [21]He set up the pillars at the vestibule of the temple; he set up the pillar on the south and called its name Ja'chin; and he set up the pillar on the north and called its name Boaz. [22]And upon the tops of the pillars was lily-work. Thus the work of the pillars was finished.

---

[p] Heb obscure.
[q] Gk: Heb *four*.
[r] Gk: Heb *posts*.
[s] Syr Vg: Heb *floor*.
[t] With 7:12: Heb *from the outside*.
[u] Tg Syr Compare Gk and Jer 52:21: Heb *and a line of twelve cubits measured the circumference of the second pillar*.
[v] Gk: Heb lacks *he made two*.
[w] Gk: Heb *seven*.
[x] With 2 Mss Compare Gk: Heb *pillars*.
7:15–21: 2 Chron 3:15–17.

23 Then he made the molten sea; it was round, ten cubits from brim to brim, and five cubits high, and a line of thirty cubits measured its circumference. ²⁴Under its brim were gourds, for thirty ʸ cubits, compassing the sea round about; the gourds were in two rows, cast with it when it was cast. ²⁵It stood upon twelve oxen, three facing north, three facing west, three facing south, and three facing east; the sea was set upon them, and all their posterior parts were inward. ²⁶Its thickness was a handbreadth; and its brim was made like the brim of a cup, like the flower of a lily; it held two thousand baths.

27 He also made the ten stands of bronze; each stand was four cubits long, four cubits wide, and three cubits high. ²⁸This was the construction of the stands: they had panels, and the panels were set in the frames ²⁹and on the panels that were set in the frames were lions, oxen, and cherubim. Upon the frames, both above and below the lions and oxen, there were wreaths of beveled work. ³⁰Moreover each stand had four bronze wheels and axles of bronze; and at the four corners were supports for a laver. The supports were cast, with wreaths at the side of each. ³¹Its opening was within a crown which projected upward one cubit; its opening was round, as a pedestal is made, a cubit and a half deep. At its opening there were carvings; and its panels were square, not round. ³²And the four wheels were underneath the panels; the axles of the wheels were of one piece with the stands; and the height of a wheel was a cubit and a half. ³³The wheels were made like a chariot wheel; their axles, their rims, their spokes, and their hubs, were all cast. ³⁴There were four supports at the four corners of each stand; the supports were of one piece with the stands. ³⁵And on the top of the stand there was a round band half a cubit high; and on the top of the stand its stays and its panels were of one piece with it. ³⁶And on the surfaces of its stays and on its panels, he carved cherubim, lions, and palm trees, according to the space of each, with wreaths round about. ³⁷After this manner he made the ten stands; all of them were cast alike, of the same measure and the same form.

38 And he made ten lavers of bronze; each laver held forty baths, each laver measured four cubits, and there was a laver for each of the ten stands. ³⁹And he set the stands, five on the south side of the house, and five on the north side of the house; and he set the sea at the southeast corner of the house.

40 Hiram also made the pots, the shovels, and the basins. So Hiram finished all the work that he did for King Solomon on the house of the LORD: ⁴¹the two pillars, the two bowls of the capitals that were on the tops of the pillars, and the two networks to cover the two bowls of the capitals that were on the tops of the pillars; ⁴²and the four hundred pomegranates for the two networks, two rows of pomegranates for each network, to cover the two bowls of the capitals that were upon the pillars; ⁴³the ten stands, and the ten lavers upon the stands; ⁴⁴and the one sea, and the twelve oxen underneath the sea.

45 Now the pots, the shovels, and the basins, all these vessels in the house of the LORD, which Hiram made for King Solomon, were of burnished bronze. ⁴⁶In the plain of the Jordan the king cast them, in the clay ground between Succoth and Zar′ethan. ⁴⁷And Solomon left all the vessels unweighed, because there were so many of them; the weight of the bronze was not found out.

48 So Solomon made all the vessels that were in the house of the LORD: the golden altar, the golden table for the bread of the Presence, ⁴⁹the lampstands of pure gold, five on the south side and five on the north, before the inner sanctuary; the flowers, the lamps, and the tongs, of gold; ⁵⁰the cups, snuffers, basins, dishes for incense, and firepans, of pure gold; and the sockets of gold, for the doors of the innermost part of the house, the most holy place, and for the doors of the nave of the temple.

51 Thus all the work that King Solomon did on the house of the LORD was finished. And Solomon brought in the things which David his father had dedicated, the silver, the gold, and the vessels, and stored them in the treasuries of the house of the LORD.

Dedication of the Temple

8 Then Solomon assembled the elders of Israel and all the heads of the tribes, the leaders of the fathers' houses of the sons of Israel, before King Solomon in Jerusalem, to bring up the ark of the covenant of the LORD out of the city of David, which is Zion. ²And all the men of Israel assembled to King Solomon at the feast in the month Eth′a-nim, which is the seventh month. ³And all the elders of Israel came, and the priests took up the ark. ⁴And they brought up the ark of the LORD, the tent of meeting, and all the holy vessels that were in the tent; the priests and the Levites brought them up. ⁵And King Solomon and all the congregation of Israel, who had assembled before him, were with him before the ark, sacrificing so many sheep and oxen that they could not be counted or numbered. ⁶Then the priests brought the ark of the covenant of the LORD to its place, in the inner sanctuary of the house, in the most holy place, underneath the wings of the cherubim. ⁷For the cherubim spread out their wings over the place of the ark, so that the cherubim made a covering

---

ʸ Heb *ten*.
7:23-26: 2 Chron 4:2-5.
7:38-51: 2 Chron 4:6, 5:1.
8:1-6: Rev 11:19.

above the ark and its poles. [8]And the poles were so long that the ends of the poles were seen from the holy place before the inner sanctuary; but they could not be seen from outside; and they are there to this day. [9]There was nothing in the ark except the two tables of stone which Moses put there at Horeb, where the Lord made a covenant with the sons of Israel, when they came out of the land of Egypt. [10]And when the priests came out of the holy place, a cloud * filled the house of the Lord, [11]so that the priests could not stand to minister because of the cloud; for the glory of the Lord filled the house of the Lord.

Solomon's Speech

12 Then Solomon said,

"The Lord has set the sun in the heavens,
but [z] has said that he would dwell in thick
darkness.
[13]I have built you an exalted house,
a place for you to dwell in for ever."

[14]Then the king faced about, and blessed all the assembly of Israel, while all the assembly of Israel stood. [15]And he said, "Blessed be the Lord, the God of Israel, who with his hand has fulfilled what he promised with his mouth to David my father, saying, [16]'Since the day that I brought my people Israel out of Egypt, I chose no city in all the tribes of Israel in which to build a house, that my name might be there; but I chose David to be over my people Israel.' [17]Now it was in the heart of David my father to build a house for the name of the Lord, the God of Israel. [18]But the Lord said to David my father, 'Whereas it was in your heart to build a house for my name, you did well that it was in your heart; [19]nevertheless you shall not build the house, but your son who shall be born to you shall build the house for my name.' [20]Now the Lord has fulfilled his promise which he made; for I have risen in the place of David my father, and sit on the throne of Israel, as the Lord promised, and I have built the house for the name of the Lord, the God of Israel. [21]And there I have provided a place for the ark, in which is the covenant of the Lord which he made with our fathers, when he brought them out of the land of Egypt."

Solomon's Prayer of Dedication

22 Then Solomon stood before the altar of the Lord in the presence of all the assembly of Israel, and spread forth his hands toward heaven; [23]and said, † "O Lord, God of Israel, there is no God like you, in heaven above or on earth beneath, keeping covenant and showing mercy to your servants who walk before you with all their heart; [24]who have kept with your servant David my father what you declared to him; yes, you spoke with your mouth, and with your hand have fulfilled it this day. [25]Now therefore, O Lord, God of Israel, keep with your servant David my father what you have promised him, saying,

'There shall never fail you a man before me to sit upon the throne of Israel, if only your sons take heed to their way, to walk before me as you have walked before me.' [26]Now therefore, O God of Israel, let your word be confirmed, which you have spoken to your servant David my father.

27 "But will God indeed dwell on the earth? Behold, heaven and the highest heaven cannot contain you; how much less this house which I have built! ‡ [28]Yet have regard to the prayer of your servant and to his supplication, O Lord my God, listening to the cry and to the prayer which your servant prays before you this day; [29]that your eyes may be open night and day toward this house, the place of which you have said, 'My name shall be there,' that you may listen to the prayer which your servant offers toward this place. [30]And hear the supplication of your servant and of your people Israel, when they pray toward this place; yes, hear in heaven your dwelling place; and when you hear, forgive.

31 "If a man sins against his neighbor and is made to take an oath, and comes and swears his oath before your altar in this house, [32]then hear in heaven, and act, and judge your servants, condemning the guilty by bringing his conduct upon his own head, and vindicating the righteous by rewarding him according to his righteousness.

33 "When your people Israel are defeated before the enemy because they have sinned against you, if they turn again to you, and acknowledge your name, and pray and make supplication to you in this house; [34]then hear in heaven, and forgive the sin of your people Israel, and bring them again to the land which you gave to their fathers.

35 "When heaven is shut up and there is no rain because they have sinned against you, if they pray toward this place, and acknowledge your name, and turn from their sin, when you afflict them, [36]then hear in heaven, and forgive the sin of your servants, your people Israel, when you teach them the good way in which they should walk; and grant rain upon your land, which you have given to your people as an inheritance.

37 "If there is famine in the land, if there is pestilence or blight or mildew or locust or caterpillar; if their enemy besieges them in any [a] of their cities; whatever plague, whatever sickness there is; [38]whatever prayer, whatever supplication is made by any man or by all your people Israel, each knowing the affliction of his own heart and

---

[z] Gk: Heb lacks *has set the sun in the heavens, but.*
[a] Gk Syr: Heb *the land.*

8:10, 11: 2 Chron 5:13, 14; Rev 15:8.
8:12–50: 2 Chron 6:1–39.
* 8:10, *cloud:* The visible sign of the presence of Yahweh taking possession of his sanctuary; later called the shekinah by the rabbis.
† 8:23–53: This eloquent prayer admirably sums up the relation of God to his people.
‡ 8:27: A reminder that Yahweh was very different from the gods of other nations, who dwelt in their temples.

stretching out his hands toward this house; [39]then hear in heaven your dwelling place, and forgive, and act, and render to each whose heart you know, according to all his ways (for you, you only, know the hearts of all the children of men); [40]that they may fear you all the days that they live in the land which you gave to our fathers.

41 "Likewise when a foreigner, who is not of your people Israel, comes from a far country for your name's sake [42](for they shall hear of your great name, and your mighty hand, and of your outstretched arm), when he comes and prays toward this house, [43]hear in heaven your dwelling place, and do according to all for which the foreigner calls to you; in order that all the peoples of the earth may know your name and fear you, as do your people Israel, and that they may know that this house which I have built is called by your name.

44 "If your people go out to battle against their enemy, by whatever way you shall send them, and they pray to the LORD toward the city which you have chosen and the house which I have built for your name, [45]then hear in heaven their prayer and their supplication, and maintain their cause.

46 "If they sin against you—for there is no man who does not sin—and you are angry with them, and give them to an enemy, so that they are carried away captive to the land of the enemy, far off or near; [47]yet if they lay it to heart in the land to which they have been carried captive, and repent, and make supplication to you in the land of their captors, saying, 'We have sinned, and have acted perversely and wickedly'; [48]if they repent with all their mind and with all their heart in the land of their enemies, who carried them captive, and pray to you toward their land, which you gave to their fathers, the city which you have chosen, and the house which I have built for your name; [49]then hear in heaven your dwelling place their prayer and their supplication, and maintain their cause [50]and forgive your people who have sinned against you, and all their transgressions which they have committed against you; and grant them compassion in the sight of those who carried them captive, that they may have compassion on them [51](for they are your people, and your heritage, which you brought out of Egypt, from the midst of the iron furnace). [52]Let your eyes be open to the supplication of your servant, and to the supplication of your people Israel, giving ear to them whenever they call to you. [53]For you separated them from among all the peoples of the earth, to be your heritage, as you declared through Moses, your servant, when you brought our fathers out of Egypt, O Lord GOD."

Solomon Blesses the Assembly

54 Now as Solomon finished offering all this prayer and supplication to the LORD, he arose from before the altar of the LORD, where he had knelt with hands outstretched toward heaven; [55]and he stood, and blessed all the assembly of Israel with a loud voice, saying, [56]"Blessed be the LORD who has given rest to his people Israel, according to all that he promised; not one word has failed of all his good promise, which he uttered by Moses his servant. [57]The LORD our God be with us, as he was with our fathers; may he not leave us or forsake us; [58]that he may incline our hearts to him, to walk in all his ways, and to keep his commandments, his statutes, and his ordinances, which he commanded our fathers. [59]Let these words of mine, wherewith I have made supplication before the LORD, be near to the LORD our God day and night, and may he maintain the cause of his servant, and the cause of his people Israel, as each day requires; [60]that all the peoples of the earth may know that the LORD is God; there is no other. [61]Let your heart therefore be wholly true to the LORD our God, walking in his statutes and keeping his commandments, as at this day."

Solomon Offers Sacrifices

62 Then the king, and all Israel with him, offered sacrifice before the LORD. [63]Solomon offered as peace offerings to the LORD twenty-two thousand oxen and a hundred and twenty thousand sheep. So the king and all the sons of Israel dedicated the house of the LORD. [64]The same day the king consecrated the middle of the court that was before the house of the LORD; for there he offered the burnt offering and the cereal offering and the fat pieces of the peace offerings, because the bronze altar that was before the LORD was too small to receive the burnt offering and the cereal offering and the fat pieces of the peace offerings.

65 So Solomon held the feast at that time, and all Israel with him, a great assembly, from the entrance of Ha'math to the Brook of Egypt, before the LORD our God, seven days. [b] [66]On the eighth day he sent the people away; and they blessed the king, and went to their homes joyful and glad of heart for all the goodness that the LORD had shown to David his servant and to Israel his people.

The Lord's Second Appearance to Solomon

9 When Solomon had finished building the house of the LORD and the king's house and all that Solomon desired to build, [2]the LORD appeared to Solomon a second time, as he had appeared to him at Gib'eon. [3]And the LORD said to him, * "I have heard your prayer and your supplication, which you have made before me; I have consecrated this house which you have built, and

---

[b] Gk: Heb *seven days and seven days, fourteen days.*
8:62–66: 2 Chron 7:4–10.
9:1–9: 2 Chron 7:11–22.
* 9:3–9: God's response to Solomon's prayer.

put my name there for ever; my eyes and my heart will be there for all time. [4]And as for you, if you will walk before me, as David your father walked, with integrity of heart and uprightness, doing according to all that I have commanded you, and keeping my statutes and my ordinances, [5]then I will establish your royal throne over Israel for ever, as I promised David your father, saying, 'There shall not fail you a man upon the throne of Israel.' [6]But if you turn aside from following me, you or your children, and do not keep my commandments and my statutes which I have set before you, but go and serve other gods and worship them, [7]then I will cut off Israel from the land which I have given them; and the house which I have consecrated for my name I will cast out of my sight; and Israel will become a proverb and a byword among all peoples. [8]And this house will become a heap of ruins; [c] every one passing by it will be astonished, and will hiss; and they will say, 'Why has the LORD done thus to this land and to this house?' [9]Then they will say, 'Because they forsook the LORD their God who brought their fathers out of the land of Egypt, and laid hold on other gods, and worshiped them and served them; therefore the LORD has brought all this evil upon them.'"

10 At the end of twenty years, in which Solomon had built the two houses, the house of the LORD and the king's house, [11]and Hiram king of Tyre had supplied Solomon with cedar and cypress timber and gold, as much as he desired, King Solomon gave to Hiram twenty cities in the land of Galilee. [12]But when Hiram came from Tyre to see the cities which Solomon had given him, they did not please him. [13]Therefore he said, "What kind of cities are these which you have given me, my brother?" So they are called the land of Ca'bul to this day. [14]Hiram had sent to the king one hundred and twenty talents of gold.

Other Works of Solomon

15 And this is the account of the forced labor which King Solomon levied to build the house of the LORD and his own house and the Millo and the wall of Jerusalem and Ha'zor and Megid'do and Gezer [16](Pharaoh king of Egypt had gone up and captured Gezer and burnt it with fire, and had slain the Canaanites who dwelt in the city, and had given it as dowry to his daughter, Solomon's wife; [17]so Solomon rebuilt Gezer) and Lower Beth-ho'ron [18]and Ba'alath and Ta'mar in the wilderness, in the land of Judah, [d] [19]and all the storecities that Solomon had, and the cities for his chariots, and the cities for his horsemen, and whatever Solomon desired to build in Jerusalem, in Lebanon, and in all the land of his dominion. [20]All the people who were left of the Am'orites, the Hittites, the Per'izzites, the Hi'vites, and the Jeb'usites, who were not of the sons of Israel—

[21]their descendants who were left after them in the land, whom the sons of Israel were unable to destroy utterly—these Solomon made a forced levy of slaves, and so they are to this day. [22]But of the sons of Israel Solomon made no slaves; they were the soldiers, they were his officials, his commanders, his captains, his chariot commanders and his horsemen.

23 These were the chief officers who were over Solomon's work: five hundred and fifty, who had charge of the people who carried on the work.

24 But Pharaoh's daughter went up from the city of David to her own house which Solomon had built for her; then he built the Millo.

25 Three times a year Solomon used to offer up burnt offerings and peace offerings upon the altar which he built to the LORD, burning incense [e] before the LORD. So he finished the house.

Solomon's Fleet

26 King Solomon built a fleet of ships at E'zion-ge'ber, which is near E'loth on the shore of the Red Sea, in the land of E'dom. [27]And Hiram sent with the fleet his servants, seamen who were familiar with the sea, together with the servants of Solomon; [28]and they went to O'phir, and brought from there gold, to the amount of four hundred and twenty talents; and they brought it to King Solomon.

Visit of the Queen of Sheba

10 Now when the queen of Sheba [*] heard of the fame of Solomon concerning the name of the LORD, she came to test him with hard questions. [2]She came to Jerusalem with a very great retinue, with camels bearing spices, and very much gold, and precious stones; and when she came to Solomon, she told him all that was on her mind. [3]And Solomon answered all her questions; there was nothing hidden from the king which he could not explain to her. [4]And when the queen of Sheba had seen all the wisdom of Solomon, the house that he had built, [5]the food of his table, the seating of his officials, and the attendance of his servants, their clothing, his cupbearers, and his burnt offerings which he offered at the house of the LORD, there was no more spirit in her.

6 And she said to the king, "The report was true which I heard in my own land of your affairs and of your wisdom, [7]but I did not believe the reports until I came and my own eyes had seen it; and behold, the half was not told me; your wisdom and prosperity surpass the report which I heard. [8]Happy are your wives! [f] Happy are these your servants, who continually stand before you

---

[c] Syr Old Latin: Heb *high*.
[d] Heb lacks *of Judah.*
[e] Gk: Heb *burning incense with it which.*
[f] Gk Syr: Heb *men*.
9:10–28: 2 Chron 8:8–18.
10:1–29: 2 Chron 9:1–28.
[*] 10:1, *Sheba:* A kingdom in southwestern Arabia.

and hear your wisdom! ⁹Blessed be the Lord your God, who has delighted in you and set you on the throne of Israel! Because the Lord loved Israel for ever, he has made you king, that you may execute justice and righteousness." ¹⁰Then she gave the king a hundred and twenty talents of gold, and a very great quantity of spices, and precious stones; never again came such an abundance of spices as these which the queen of Sheba gave to King Solomon.

11 Moreover the fleet of Hiram, which brought gold from O'phir, brought from Ophir a very great amount of almug wood and precious stones. ¹²And the king made of the almug wood supports for the house of the Lord, and for the king's house, lyres also and harps for the singers; no such almug wood has come or been seen, to this day.

13 And King Solomon gave to the queen of Sheba all that she desired, whatever she asked besides what was given her by the bounty of King Solomon. So she turned and went back to her own land, with her servants.

14 Now the weight of gold that came to Solomon in one year was six hundred and sixty-six talents of gold, ¹⁵besides that which came from the traders and from the traffic of the merchants, and from all the kings of Arabia and from the governors of the land. ¹⁶King Solomon made two hundred large shields of beaten gold; six hundred shekels of gold went into each shield. ¹⁷And he made three hundred shields of beaten gold; three minas of gold went into each shield; and the king put them in the House of the Forest of Lebanon. ¹⁸The king also made a great ivory throne, and overlaid it with the finest gold. ¹⁹The throne had six steps, and at the back of the throne was a calf's head, and on each side of the seat were arm rests and two lions standing beside the arm rests, ²⁰while twelve lions stood there, one on each end of a step on the six steps. The like of it was never made in any kingdom. ²¹All King Solomon's drinking vessels were of gold, and all the vessels of the House of the Forest of Lebanon were of pure gold; none were of silver, it was not considered as anything in the days of Solomon. ²²For the king had a fleet of ships of Tar'shish at sea with the fleet of Hiram. Once every three years the fleet of ships of Tarshish* used to come bringing gold, silver, ivory, apes, and peacocks. ᵍ

23 Thus King Solomon excelled all the kings of the earth in riches and in wisdom. ²⁴And the whole earth sought the presence of Solomon to hear his wisdom, which God had put into his mind. ²⁵Every one of them brought his present, articles of silver and gold, garments, myrrh, spices, horses, and mules, so much year by year.

26 And Solomon gathered together chariots and horsemen; he had fourteen hundred chariots and twelve thousand horsemen, whom he sta-

tioned in the chariot cities and with the king in Jerusalem. ²⁷And the king made silver as common in Jerusalem as stone, and he made cedar as plentiful as the sycamore of the Shephe'lah. ²⁸And Solomon's import of horses was from Egypt and Ku'e, and the king's traders received them from Kue at a price. ²⁹A chariot could be imported from Egypt for six hundred shekels of silver, and a horse for a hundred and fifty; and so through the king's traders they were exported to all the kings of the Hittites and the kings of Syria.

Solomon's Errors

11 † Now King Solomon loved many foreign women: the daughter of Pharaoh, and Moabite, Am'monite, E'domite, Sido'nian, and Hittite women, ²from the nations concerning which the Lord had said to the sons of Israel, "You shall not enter into marriage with them, neither shall they with you, for surely they will turn away your heart after their gods"; Solomon clung to these in love. ³He had seven hundred wives, princesses, and three hundred concubines; and his wives turned away his heart. ⁴For when Solomon was old his wives turned away his heart after other gods; and his heart was not wholly true to the Lord his God, as was the heart of David his father. ⁵For Solomon went after Ash'toreth the goddess of the Sido'nians, and after Milcom the abomination of the Am'monites. ⁶So Solomon did what was evil in the sight of the Lord, and did not wholly follow the Lord, as David his father had done. ⁷Then Solomon built a high place for Che'mosh the abomination of Moab, and for Mo'lech the abomination of the Am'monites, on the mountain east of Jerusalem. ⁸And so he did for all his foreign wives, who burned incense and sacrificed to their gods.

9 And the Lord was angry with Solomon, because his heart had turned away from the Lord, the God of Israel, who had appeared to him twice, ¹⁰and had commanded him concerning this thing, that he should not go after other gods; but he did not keep what the Lord commanded. ¹¹Therefore the Lord said to Solomon, "Since this has been your mind and you have not kept my covenant and my statutes which I have commanded you, I will surely tear the kingdom from you and will give it to your servant. ¹²Yet for the sake of David your father I will not do it in your days, but I will tear it out of the hand of your son. ¹³However I will not tear away all the kingdom; but I will give one tribe to your son, for the sake of David my

---

ᵍ Or *baboons.*
* 10:22, *ships of Tarshish:* i.e., ships that could sail to Tarshish (usually located in Spain). The word then came to be applied to ocean-going vessels.
† 11:1–8: This account of Solomon's moral decline stresses the connection between apostasy and sexual excess—a theme often met with in the Old Testament.

servant and for the sake of Jerusalem which I have chosen."

Adversaries of Solomon

14 * And the LORD raised up an adversary against Solomon, Ha'dad the E'domite; he was of the royal house in E'dom. [15]For when David was in E'dom, and Jo'ab the commander of the army went up to bury the slain, he slew every male in Edom [16](for Jo'ab and all Israel remained there six months, until he had cut off every male in E'dom); [17]but Ha'dad fled to Egypt, together with certain E'domites of his father's servants, Hadad being yet a little child. [18]They set out from Mid'ian and came to Par'an, and took men with them from Paran and came to Egypt, to Pharaoh king of Egypt, who gave him a house, and assigned him an allowance of food, and gave him land. [19]And Ha'dad found great favor in the sight of Pharaoh, so that he gave him in marriage the sister of his own wife, the sister of Tah'penes the queen. [20]And the sister of Tah'penes bore him Genu'bath his son, whom Tahpenes weaned in Pharaoh's house; and Genubath was in Pharaoh's house among the sons of Pharaoh. [21]But when Ha'dad heard in Egypt that David slept with his fathers and that Jo'ab the commander of the army was dead, Hadad said to Pharaoh, "Let me depart, that I may go to my own country." [22]But Pharaoh said to him, "What have you lacked with me that you are now seeking to go to your own country?" And he said to him, "Only let me go."

23 God also raised up as an adversary to him, Re'zon the son of Eli'ada, who had fled from his master Ha'dad-e'zer king of Zobah. [24]And he gathered men about him and became leader of a marauding band, after the slaughter by David; and they went to Damascus, and dwelt there, and made him king in Damascus. [25]He was an adversary of Israel all the days of Solomon, doing mischief as Ha'dad did; and he abhorred Israel, and reigned over Syria.

Jeroboam's Rebellion

26 Jerobo'am the son of Ne'bat, an E'phraimite of Zer'edah, a servant of Solomon, whose mother's name was Zeru'ah, a widow, also lifted up his hand against the king. [27]And this was the reason why he lifted up his hand against the king. Solomon built the Millo, and closed up the breach of the city of David his father. [28]The man Jerobo'am was very able, and when Solomon saw that the young man was industrious he gave him charge over all the forced labor of the house of Joseph. [29]And at that time, when Jerobo'am went out of Jerusalem, the prophet Ahi'jah the Shi'lonite found him on the road. Now Ahijah had clad himself with a new garment; and the two of them were alone in the open country. [30]Then Ahi'jah laid hold of the new garment that was on him, and tore it into twelve pieces. [31]And he said to Jerobo'am, "Take for your-

self ten pieces; for thus says the LORD, the God of Israel, 'Behold, I am about to tear the kingdom from the hand of Solomon, and will give you ten tribes [32](but he shall have one tribe, for the sake of my servant David and for the sake of Jerusalem, the city which I have chosen out of all the tribes of Israel), [33]because he has [h] forsaken me, and worshiped Ash'toreth the goddess of the Sido'nians, Che'mosh the god of Moab, and Milcom the god of the Am'monites, and has [h] not walked in my ways, doing what is right in my sight and keeping my statutes and my ordinances, as David his father did. [34]Nevertheless I will not take the whole kingdom out of his hand; but I will make him ruler all the days of his life, for the sake of David my servant whom I chose, who kept my commandments and my statutes; [35]but I will take the kingdom out of his son's hand, and will give it to you, ten tribes. [36]Yet to his son I will give one tribe, that David my servant may always have a lamp before me in Jerusalem, the city where I have chosen to put my name. [37]And I will take you, and you shall reign over all that your soul desires, and you shall be king over Israel. [38]And if you will listen to all that I command you, and will walk in my ways, and do what is right in my eyes by keeping my statutes and my commandments, as David my servant did, I will be with you, and will build you a sure house, as I built for David, and I will give Israel to you. [39]And I will for this afflict the descendants of David, but not for ever.' " [40]Solomon sought therefore to kill Jerobo'am; but Jeroboam arose, and fled into Egypt, to Shi'shak king of Egypt, and was in Egypt until the death of Solomon.

Death of Solomon

41 Now the rest of the acts of Solomon, and all that he did, and his wisdom, are they not written in the book of the acts of Solomon? [42]And the time that Solomon reigned in Jerusalem over all Israel was forty years. [43]And Solomon slept with his fathers, and was buried in the city of David his father; and Rehobo'am his son reigned in his stead.

The Northern Tribes Secede

12 Rehobo'am went to She'chem,† for all Israel had come to Shechem to make him king. [2]And when Jerobo'am the son of Ne'bat heard of it (for he was still in Egypt, whither he had fled from King Solomon), then Jeroboam returned from [i] Egypt. [3]And they sent and called

---

[h] Gk Syr Vg: Heb *they have*.
[i] Gk Vg Compare 2 Chron 10:2: Heb *dwelt in*.
11:42-43: 2 Chron 9:30, 31.
12:1-19: 2 Chron 10:1-19.
* 11:14: Because of Solomon's idolatry, God raised up enemies, to the south (Edom), to the north (Damascus), and within the kingdom (Jeroboam).
† 12:1, *Shechem* was the old religious center of the northern tribes. The alliance between these and Judah was never very strong, even during the united monarchy.

him; and Jerobo'am and all the assembly of Israel came and said to Rehobo'am, [4] "Your father made our yoke heavy. Now therefore lighten the hard service of your father and his heavy yoke upon us, and we will serve you." [5]He said to them, "Depart for three days, then come again to me." So the people went away.

6 Then King Rehobo'am took counsel with the old men, who had stood before Solomon his father while he was yet alive, saying, "How do you advise me to answer this people?" [7]And they said to him, "If you will be a servant to this people today and serve them, and speak good words to them when you answer them, then they will be your servants for ever." [8]But he forsook the counsel which the old men gave him, and took counsel with the young men who had grown up with him and stood before him. [9]And he said to them, "What do you advise that we answer this people who have said to me, 'Lighten the yoke that your father put upon us'?" [10]And the young men who had grown up with him said to him, "Thus shall you speak to this people who said to you, 'Your father made our yoke heavy, but please lighten it for us'; thus shall you say to them, 'My little finger is thicker than my father's loins. [11]And now, whereas my father laid upon you a heavy yoke, I will add to your yoke. My father chastised you with whips, but I will chastise you with scorpions.'"

12 So Jerobo'am and all the people came to Rehobo'am the third day, as the king said, "Come to me again the third day." [13]And the king answered the people harshly, and forsaking the counsel which the old men had given him, [14]he spoke to them according to the counsel of the young men, saying, "My father made your yoke heavy, but I will add to your yoke; my father chastised you with whips, but I will chastise you with scorpions." [15]So the king did not listen to the people; for it was a turn of affairs brought about by the Lord that he might fulfil his word, which the Lord spoke by Ahi'jah the Shi'lonite to Jerobo'am the son of Ne'bat.

Jeroboam Reigns over Israel

16 And when all Israel saw that the king did not listen to them, the people answered the king, "What portion have we in David?

We have no inheritance in the son of Jesse.

To your tents, O Israel!

Look now to your own house, David."

So Israel departed to their tents. [17]But Rehobo'am reigned over the sons of Israel who dwelt in the cities of Judah. [18]Then King Rehobo'am sent Ador'am, who was taskmaster over the forced labor, and all Israel stoned him to death with stones. And King Rehoboam made haste to mount his chariot, to flee to Jerusalem. [19]So Israel has been in rebellion against the house of David to this day. [20]And when all Israel heard that

Jerobo'am had returned, they sent and called him to the assembly and made him king over all Israel. There was none that followed the house of David, but the tribe of Judah only.

21 When Rehobo'am came to Jerusalem, he assembled all the house of Judah, and the tribe of Benjamin, a hundred and eighty thousand chosen warriors, to fight against the house of Israel, to restore the kingdom to Rehoboam the son of Solomon. [22]But the word of God came to Shemai'ah the man of God: [23] "Say to Rehobo'am the son of Solomon, king of Judah, and to all the house of Judah and Benjamin, and to the rest of the people, [24]'Thus says the Lord, You shall not go up or fight against your kinsmen the sons of Israel. Return every man to his home, for this thing is from me.'" So they listened to the word of the Lord, and went home again, according to the word of the Lord.

Jeroboam's Golden Calves

25 Then Jerobo'am built She'chem in the hill country of E'phraim, and dwelt there; and he went out from there and built Penu'el. [26]And Jerobo'am said in his heart, "Now the kingdom will turn back to the house of David; [27]if this people go up to offer sacrifices in the house of the Lord at Jerusalem, then the heart of this people will turn again to their lord, to Rehobo'am king of Judah, and they will kill me and return to Rehoboam king of Judah." [28]So the king took counsel, and made two calves of gold. And he said to the people, "You have gone up to Jerusalem long enough. Behold your gods, * O Israel, who brought you up out of the land of Egypt." [29]And he set one in Bethel, and the other he put in Dan. [30]And this thing became a sin, for the people went to the one at Bethel and to the other as far as Dan.[j] [31]He also made houses on high places, and appointed priests from among all the people, who were not of the Levites. [32]And Jerobo'am appointed a feast on the fifteenth day of the eighth month like the feast that was in Judah, and he offered sacrifices upon the altar; so he did in Bethel, sacrificing to the calves that he had made. And he placed in Bethel the priests of the high places that he had made. [33]He went up to the altar which he had made in Bethel on the fifteenth day in the eighth month, in the month which he had devised of his own heart; and he ordained a feast for the sons of Israel, and went up to the altar to burn incense.

---

[j] Gk: Heb *went to the one as far as Dan.*
12:22–24: 2 Chron 11:1–4.
* **12:28**, *Behold your gods*: Jeroboam seems to have had no intention of introducing false gods. These were to be images of Yahweh. But in doing this he debased the whole idea of true worship and made it more like pagan religion, to which it was bound to lead in the end; cf. 16:31. Judah, with all its advantages of temple and dynasty, was no better at this time, but reforms were instituted at intervals.

A Man of God from Judah

13 And behold, a man of God came out of Judah by the word of the Lord to Bethel. Jerobo'am was standing by the altar to burn incense. [2]And the man cried against the altar by the word of the Lord, and said, "O altar, altar, thus says the Lord: 'Behold, a son shall be born to the house of David, Josi'ah by name; and he shall sacrifice upon you the priests of the high places who burn incense upon you, and men's bones shall be burned upon you.'" [3]And he gave a sign the same day, saying, "This is the sign that the Lord has spoken: 'Behold, the altar shall be torn down, and the ashes that are upon it shall be poured out.'" [4]And when the king heard the saying of the man of God, which he cried against the altar at Bethel, Jerobo'am stretched out his hand from the altar, saying, "Lay hold of him." And his hand, which he stretched out against him, dried up, so that he could not draw it back to himself. [5]The altar also was torn down, and the ashes poured out from the altar, according to the sign which the man of God had given by the word of the Lord. [6]And the king said to the man of God, "Entreat now the favor of the Lord your God, and pray for me, that my hand may be restored to me." And the man of God entreated the Lord; and the king's hand was restored to him, and became as it was before. [7]And the king said to the man of God, "Come home with me, and refresh yourself, and I will give you a reward." [8]And the man of God said to the king, "If you give me half your house, I will not go in with you. And I will not eat bread or drink water in this place; [9]for so was it commanded me by the word of the Lord, saying, 'You shall neither eat bread, nor drink water, nor return by the way that you came.'" [10]So he went another way, and did not return by the way that he came to Bethel.

11 Now there dwelt an old prophet in Bethel. And his sons [k] came and told him all that the man of God had done that day in Bethel; the words also which he had spoken to the king, they told to their father. [12]And their father said to them, "Which way did he go?" And his sons showed him the way which the man of God who came from Judah had gone. [13]And he said to his sons, "Saddle the donkey for me." So they saddled the donkey for him and he mounted it. [14]And he went after the man of God, and found him sitting under an oak; and he said to him, "Are you the man of God who came from Judah?" And he said, "I am." [15]Then he said to him, "Come home with me and eat bread." [16]And he said, "I may not return with you, or go in with you; neither will I eat bread nor drink water with you in this place; [17]for it was said to me by the word of the Lord, 'You shall neither eat bread nor drink water there, nor return by the way that you came.'" [18]And he said to

him, "I also am a prophet as you are, and an angel spoke to me by the word of the Lord, saying, 'Bring him back with you into your house that he may eat bread and drink water.'" But he lied to him. [19]So he went back with him, and ate bread in his house, and drank water.

20 And as they sat at the table, the word of the Lord came to the prophet who had brought him back; [21]and he cried to the man of God who came from Judah, "Thus says the Lord, 'Because you have disobeyed the word of the Lord, and have not kept the commandment which the Lord your God commanded you, [22]but have come back, and have eaten bread and drunk water in the place of which he said to you, "Eat no bread, and drink no water"; your body shall not come to the tomb of your fathers.'" [23]And after he had eaten bread and drunk, he saddled the donkey for the prophet whom he had brought back. [24]And as he went away a lion met him on the road and killed him. And his body was thrown in the road, and the donkey stood beside it; the lion also stood beside the body. [25]And behold, men passed by, and saw the body thrown in the road, and the lion standing by the body. And they came and told it in the city where the old prophet dwelt.

26 And when the prophet who had brought him back from the way heard of it, he said, "It is the man of God, who disobeyed the word of the Lord; therefore the Lord has given him to the lion, which has torn him and slain him, according to the word which the Lord spoke to him." [27]And he said to his sons, "Saddle the donkey for me." And they saddled it. [28]And he went and found his body thrown in the road, and the donkey and the lion standing beside the body. The lion had not eaten the body or torn the donkey. [29]And the prophet took up the body of the man of God and laid it upon the donkey, and brought it back to the city, [1] to mourn and to bury him. [30]And he laid the body in his own grave; and they mourned over him, saying, "Alas, my brother!" [31]And after he had buried him, he said to his sons, "When I die, bury me in the grave in which the man of God is buried; lay my bones beside his bones. [32]For the saying which he cried by the word of the Lord against the altar in Bethel, and against all the houses of the high places which are in the cities of Samar'ia, shall surely come to pass."

33 After this incident Jerobo'am did not turn from his evil way, but made priests for the high places again from among all the people; any who would, he consecrated to be priests of the high places. [34]And this thing became sin to the house of Jerobo'am, so as to cut it off and to destroy it from the face of the earth.

---

[k] Gk Syr Vg: Heb *son*.
[1] Gk: Heb *he came to the city of the old prophet.*

Judgment on the House of Jeroboam

14 At that time Abi'jah the son of Jerobo'am fell sick. [2]And Jerobo'am said to his wife, "Arise, and disguise yourself, that it be not known that you are the wife of Jeroboam, and go to Shiloh; behold, Ahi'jah the prophet is there, who said of me that I should be king over this people. [3]Take with you ten loaves, some cakes, and a jar of honey, and go to him; he will tell you what shall happen to the child."

4 Jerobo'am's wife did so; she arose, and went to Shiloh, and came to the house of Ahi'jah. Now Ahijah could not see, for his eyes were dim because of his age. [5]And the LORD said to Ahi'jah, "Behold, the wife of Jerobo'am is coming to inquire of you concerning her son; for he is sick. Thus and thus shall you say to her."

When she came, she pretended to be another woman. [6]But when Ahi'jah heard the sound of her feet, as she came in at the door, he said, "Come in, wife of Jerobo'am; why do you pretend to be another? For I am charged with heavy tidings for you. [7]Go, tell Jerobo'am, 'Thus says the LORD, the God of Israel: "Because I exalted you from among the people, and made you leader over my people Israel, [8]and tore the kingdom away from the house of David and gave it to you; and yet you have not been like my servant David, who kept my commandments, and followed me with all his heart, doing only that which was right in my eyes, [9]but you have done evil above all that were before you and have gone and made for yourself other gods, and molten images, provoking me to anger, and have cast me behind your back; [10]therefore behold, I will bring evil upon the house of Jerobo'am, and will cut off from Jeroboam every male, both bond and free in Israel, and will utterly consume the house of Jeroboam, as a man burns up dung until it is all gone. [11]Any one belonging to Jerobo'am who dies in the city the dogs shall eat; and any one who dies in the open country the birds of the air shall eat; for the LORD has spoken it." ' [12]Arise therefore, go to your house. When your feet enter the city, the child shall die. [13]And all Israel shall mourn for him, and bury him; for he only of Jerobo'am shall come to the grave, because in him there is found something pleasing to the LORD, the God of Israel, in the house of Jeroboam. [14]Moreover the LORD will raise up for himself a king over Israel, who shall cut off the house of Jerobo'am today. And henceforth **m** [15]the LORD will strike Israel, as a reed is shaken in the water, and root up Israel out of this good land which he gave to their fathers, and scatter them beyond the Euphrates, because they have made their Ashe'rim, provoking the LORD to anger. [16]And he will give Israel up because of the sins of Jerobo'am, which he sinned and which he made Israel to sin."

Death of Jeroboam

17 Then Jerobo'am's wife arose, and departed, and came to Tirzah. And as she came to the threshold of the house, the child died. [18]And all Israel buried him and mourned for him, according to the word of the LORD, which he spoke by his servant Ahi'jah the prophet. [19]Now the rest of the acts of Jerobo'am, how he warred and how he reigned, behold, they are written in the Book of the Chronicles of the Kings of Israel. [20]And the time that Jerobo'am reigned was twenty-two years; and he slept with his fathers, and Na'dab his son reigned in his stead.

Rehoboam Reigns over Judah

21 Now Rehobo'am the son of Solomon reigned in Judah. Rehoboam was forty-one years old when he began to reign, and he reigned seventeen years in Jerusalem, the city which the LORD had chosen out of all the tribes of Israel, to put his name there. His mother's name was Na'amah the Am'monitess. [22]And Judah did what was evil in the sight of the LORD, and they provoked him to jealousy with their sins which they committed, more than all that their fathers had done. [23]For they also built for themselves high places, and pillars, and Ashe'rim on every high hill and under every green tree; [24]and there were also male cult prostitutes in the land. They did according to all the abominations of the nations which the LORD drove out before the sons of Israel.

25 In the fifth year of King Rehobo'am, Shi'shak king of Egypt came up against Jerusalem; [26]he took away the treasures of the house of the LORD and the treasures of the king's house; he took away everything. He also took away all the shields of gold which Solomon had made; [27]and King Rehobo'am made in their stead shields of bronze, and committed them to the hands of the officers of the guard, who kept the door of the king's house. [28]And as often as the king went into the house of the LORD, the guard bore them and brought them back to the guardroom.

29 Now the rest of the acts of Rehobo'am, and all that he did, are they not written in the Book of the Chronicles of the Kings of Judah? [30]And there was war between Rehobo'am and Jerobo'am continually. [31]And Rehobo'am slept with his fathers and was buried with his fathers in the city of David. His mother's name was Na'amah the Am'monitess. And Abi'jam his son reigned in his stead.

Abijam Reigns over Judah

15 Now in the eighteenth year of King Jerobo'am the son of Ne'bat, Abi'jam began to reign over Judah. [2]He reigned for three years in Jerusalem. His mother's name was Ma'acah the

m Heb obscure.
14:25-31: 2 Chron 12:1-16.
15:1, 2, 7: 2 Chron 13:1, 2.

daughter of Abish'alom. [3]And he walked in all the sins which his father did before him; and his heart was not wholly true to the LORD his God, as the heart of David his father. [4]Nevertheless for David's sake the LORD his God gave him a lamp in Jerusalem, setting up his son after him, and establishing Jerusalem; [5]because David did what was right in the eyes of the LORD, and did not turn aside from anything that he commanded him all the days of his life, except in the matter of Uri'ah the Hittite. [6]Now there was war between Reho-bo'am and Jerobo'am all the days of his life. [7]The rest of the acts of Abi'jam, and all that he did, are they not written in the Book of the Chronicles of the Kings of Judah? And there was war between Abijam and Jerobo'am. [8]And Abi'jam slept with his fathers; and they buried him in the city of David. And Asa his son reigned in his stead.

Asa Reigns over Judah

9 In the twentieth year of Jerobo'am king of Israel Asa began to reign over Judah, [10]and he reigned forty-one years in Jerusalem. His mother's name was Ma'acah the daughter of Abish'alom. [11]And Asa did what was right in the eyes of the LORD, as David his father had done. [12]He put away the male cult prostitutes out of the land, and removed all the idols that his fathers had made. [13]He also removed Ma'acah his mother from being queen mother because she had an abominable image made for Ashe'rah; and Asa cut down her image and burned it at the brook Kidron. [14]But the high places were not taken away. Nevertheless the heart of Asa was wholly true to the LORD all his days. [15]And he brought into the house of the LORD the votive gifts of his father and his own votive gifts, silver, and gold, and vessels.

War between Asa and Baasha

16 And there was war between Asa and Ba'asha king of Israel all their days. [17]Ba'asha king of Israel went up against Judah, and built Ra'mah, that he might permit no one to go out or come in to Asa king of Judah. [18]Then Asa took all the silver and the gold that were left in the treasures of the house of the LORD and the treasures of the king's house, and gave them into the hands of his servants; and King Asa sent them to Ben-ha'dad the son of Tabrim'mon, the son of He'zi-on, king of Syria, who dwelt in Damascus, saying, [19]"Let there be a league between me and you, as between my father and your father: behold, I am sending to you a present of silver and gold; go, break your league with Ba'asha king of Israel, that he may withdraw from me." [20]And Ben-ha'dad listened to King Asa, and sent the commanders of his armies against the cities of Israel, and conquered I'jon, Dan, A'bel-beth-ma'acah, and all Chin'neroth, with all the land of Naph'tali. [21]And when Ba'asha heard of it, he stopped building Ra'mah, and he dwelt in Tir-

zah. [22]Then King Asa made a proclamation to all Judah, none was exempt, and they carried away the stones of Ra'mah and its timber, with which Ba'asha had been building; and with them King Asa built Ge'ba of Benjamin and Mizpah. [23]Now the rest of all the acts of Asa, all his might, and all that he did, and the cities which he built, are they not written in the Book of the Chronicles of the Kings of Judah? But in his old age he was diseased in his feet. [24]And Asa slept with his fathers, and was buried with his fathers in the city of David his father; and Jehosh'aphat his son reigned in his stead.

Nadab Reigns over Israel

25 Nadab the son of Jerobo'am began to reign over Israel in the second year of Asa king of Judah; and he reigned over Israel two years. [26]He did what was evil in the sight of the LORD, and walked in the way of his father, and in his sin which he made Israel to sin.

27 Ba'asha the son of Ahi'jah, of the house of Is'sachar, conspired against him; and Baasha struck him down at Gib'bethon, which belonged to the Philis'tines; for Na'dab and all Israel were laying siege to Gibbethon. [28]So Ba'asha killed him in the third year of Asa king of Judah, and reigned in his stead. [29]And as soon as he was king, he killed all the house of Jerobo'am; he left to the house of Jeroboam not one that breathed, until he had destroyed it, according to the word of the LORD which he spoke by his servant Ahi'jah the Shi'lonite; [30]it was for the sins of Jerobo'am which he sinned and which he made Israel to sin, and because of the anger to which he provoked the LORD, the God of Israel.

31 Now the rest of the acts of Na'dab, and all that he did, are they not written in the Book of the Chronicles of the Kings of Israel? [32]And there was war between Asa and Ba'asha king of Israel all their days.

Baasha Reigns over Israel

33 In the third year of Asa king of Judah, Ba'asha the son of Ahi'jah began to reign over all Israel at Tirzah, and reigned twenty-four years. [34]He did what was evil in the sight of the LORD, and walked in the way of Jerobo'am and in his sin which he made Israel to sin.

16 And the word of the LORD came to Je'hu the son of Hana'ni against Ba'asha, saying, [2]"Since I exalted you out of the dust and made you leader over my people Israel, and you have walked in the way of Jerobo'am, and have made my people Israel to sin, provoking me to anger with their sins, [3]behold, I will utterly sweep away Ba'asha and his house, and I will make

15:8–12: 2 Chron 14:1–5.
15:13–22: 2 Chron 15:16—16:6.
15:23, 24: 2 Chron 16:12–14.
15:24: 2 Chron 17:1.

your house like the house of Jerobo'am the son of Ne'bat. [4]Any one belonging to Ba'asha who dies in the city the dogs shall eat; and any one of his who dies in the field the birds of the air shall eat."

5 Now the rest of the acts of Ba'asha, and what he did, and his might, are they not written in the Book of the Chronicles of the Kings of Israel? [6]And Ba'asha slept with his fathers, and was buried at Tirzah; and E'lah his son reigned in his stead. [7]Moreover the word of the LORD came by the prophet Je'hu the son of Hana'ni against Ba'asha and his house, both because of all the evil that he did in the sight of the LORD, provoking him to anger with the work of his hands, in being like the house of Jerobo'am, and also because he destroyed it.

Elah Reigns over Israel

8 In the twenty-sixth year of Asa king of Judah, E'lah the son of Ba'asha began to reign over Israel in Tirzah, and he reigned two years. [9]But his servant Zimri, commander of half his chariots, conspired against him. When he was at Tirzah, drinking himself drunk in the house of Arza, who was over the household in Tirzah, [10]Zimri came in and struck him down and killed him, in the twenty-seventh year of Asa king of Judah, and reigned in his stead.

11 When he began to reign, as soon as he had seated himself on his throne, he killed all the house of Ba'asha; he did not leave him a single male of his kinsmen or his friends. [12]Thus Zimri destroyed all the house of Ba'asha, according to the word of the LORD, which he spoke against Baasha by Je'hu the prophet, [13]for all the sins of Ba'asha and the sins of E'lah his son which they sinned, and which they made Israel to sin, provoking the LORD God of Israel to anger with their idols. [14]Now the rest of the acts of E'lah, and all that he did, are they not written in the Book of the Chronicles of the Kings of Israel?

The Conspiracy and Death of Zimri

15 In the twenty-seventh year of Asa king of Judah, Zimri reigned seven days in Tirzah. Now the troops were encamped against Gib'bethon, which belonged to the Philis'tines, [16]and the troops who were encamped heard it said, "Zimri has conspired, and he has killed the king"; therefore all Israel made Omri, the commander of the army, king over Israel that day in the camp. [17]So Omri went up from Gib'bethon, and all Israel with him, and they besieged Tirzah. [18]And when Zimri saw that the city was taken, he went into the citadel of the king's house, and burned the king's house over him with fire, and died, [19]because of his sins which he committed, doing evil in the sight of the LORD, walking in the way of Jerobo'am, and for his sin which he committed, making Israel to sin. [20]Now the rest of the acts of Zimri, and the conspiracy which he made, are they not written in the Book of the Chronicles of the Kings of Israel?

Omri Reigns over Israel and Builds Samaria

21 Then the sons of Israel were divided into two parts; half of the people followed Tibni the son of Ginath, to make him king, and half followed Omri. [22]But the people who followed Omri overcame the people who followed Tibni the son of Ginath; so Tibni died, and Omri became king. [23]In the thirty-first year of Asa king of Judah, Omri began to reign over Israel, and reigned for twelve years; six years he reigned in Tirzah. [24]He bought the hill of Samar'ia * from She'mer for two talents of silver; and he fortified the hill, and called the name of the city which he built, Samaria, after the name of Shemer, the owner of the hill.

25 Omri did what was evil in the sight of the LORD, and did more evil than all who were before him. [26]For he walked in all the way of Jerobo'am the son of Ne'bat, and in the sins which he made Israel to sin, provoking the LORD, the God of Israel, to anger by their idols. [27]Now the rest of the acts of Omri which he did, and the might that he showed, are they not written in the Book of the Chronicles of the Kings of Israel? [28]And Omri slept with his fathers, and was buried in Samar'ia; and A'hab his son reigned in his stead.

Ahab Reigns over Israel and Does Evil

29 In the thirty-eighth year of Asa king of Judah, A'hab the son of Omri began to reign over Israel, and Ahab the son of Omri reigned over Israel in Samar'ia twenty-two years. [30]And A'hab the son of Omri did evil in the sight of the LORD more than all that were before him. [31]And as if it had been a light thing for him to walk in the sins of Jerobo'am the son of Ne'bat, he took for his wife Jez'ebel the daughter of Ethba'al king of the Sido'nians, and went and served Ba'al, and worshiped him. [32]He erected an altar for Ba'al in the house of Baal, which he built in Samar'ia. [33]And A'hab made an Ashe'rah. Ahab did more to provoke the LORD, the God of Israel, to anger than all the kings of Israel who were before him. [34]In his days Hiel of Bethel built Jericho; he laid its foundation at the cost of Abi'ram his first-born, and set up its gates at the cost of his youngest son Segub, according to the word of the LORD, which he spoke by Joshua the son of Nun.

Elijah's Prophecy of a Drought

17 Now Eli'jah the Tishbite, of Tishbe[n] in Gilead, said to A'hab, "As the LORD the God of Israel lives, before whom I stand, there

---

[n] Gk: Heb of the settlers.
16:34: Josh 6:26.
17:1: Rev 11:6.
* 16:24, *hill of Samaria:* One of the most splendid sites in the Middle East for a capital city. But even so, the northern kingdom never achieved stability.

shall be neither dew nor rain these years, except by my word." * ²And the word of the LORD came to him, ³"Depart from here and turn eastward, and hide yourself by the brook Cherith, that is east of the Jordan. ⁴You shall drink from the brook, and I have commanded the ravens to feed you there." ⁵So he went and did according to the word of the LORD; he went and dwelt by the brook Cherith that is east of the Jordan. ⁶And the ravens brought him bread and meat in the morning, and bread and meat in the evening; and he drank from the brook. ⁷And after a while the brook dried up, because there was no rain in the land.

The Widow of Zarephath

8 Then the word of the LORD came to him. ⁹"Arise, go to Zar′ephath, which belongs to Si′don, and dwell there. Behold, I have commanded a widow there to feed you." ¹⁰So he arose and went to Zar′ephath; and when he came to the gate of the city, behold, a widow was there gathering sticks; and he called to her and said, "Bring me a little water in a vessel, that I may drink." ¹¹And as she was going to bring it, he called to her and said, "Bring me a morsel of bread in your hand." ¹²And she said, "As the LORD your God lives, I have nothing baked, only a handful of meal in a jar, and a little oil in a pitcher; and now, I am gathering a couple of sticks, that I may go in and prepare it for myself and my son, that we may eat it, and die." ¹³And Eli′jah said to her, "Fear not; go and do as you have said; but first make me a little cake of it and bring it to me, and afterward make for yourself and your son. ¹⁴For thus says the LORD the God of Israel, 'The jar of meal shall not be spent, and the pitcher of oil shall not fail, until the day that the LORD sends rain upon the earth.'" ¹⁵And she went and did as Eli′jah said; and she, and he, and her household ate for many days. ¹⁶The jar of meal was not spent, neither did the pitcher of oil fail, according to the word of the LORD which he spoke by Eli′jah.

Elijah Revives the Widow's Son

17 After this the son of the woman, the mistress of the house, became ill; and his illness was so severe that there was no breath left in him. ¹⁸And she said to Eli′jah, "What have you against me, O man of God? You have come to me to bring my sin to remembrance, and to cause the death of my son!" ¹⁹And he said to her, "Give me your son." And he took him from her bosom, and carried him up into the upper chamber, where he lodged, and laid him upon his own bed. ²⁰And he cried to the LORD, "O LORD my God, have you brought calamity even upon the widow with whom I sojourn, by slaying her son?" ²¹Then he stretched himself upon the child three times, and cried to the LORD, "O LORD my God, let this child's soul come into him again." ²²And the LORD listened to the voice of Eli′jah; and the soul of the child came into him

again, and he revived. ²³And Eli′jah took the child, and brought him down from the upper chamber into the house, and delivered him to his mother; and Elijah said, "See, your son lives." ²⁴And the woman said to Eli′jah, "Now I know that you are a man of God, and that the word of the LORD in your mouth is truth."

Elijah's Message to Ahab

18 After many days the word of the LORD came to Eli′jah, in the third year, saying, "Go, show yourself to A′hab; and I will send rain upon the earth." ²So Eli′jah went to show himself to A′hab. Now the famine was severe in Samar′ia. ³And A′hab called Obadi′ah, who was over the household. (Now Obadiah revered the LORD greatly; ⁴and when Jez′ebel cut off the prophets of the LORD, Obadi′ah took a hundred prophets and hid them by fifties in a cave, and fed them with bread and water.) ⁵And A′hab said to Obadi′ah, "Go through the land to all the springs of water and to all the valleys; perhaps we may find grass and save the horses and mules alive, and not lose some of the animals." ⁶So they divided the land between them to pass through it; A′hab went in one direction by himself, and Obadi′ah went in another direction by himself.

7 And as Obadi′ah was on the way, behold, Eli′jah met him; and Obadiah recognized him, and fell on his face, and said, "Is it you, my lord Elijah?" ⁸And he answered him, "It is I. Go, tell your lord, 'Behold, Eli′jah is here.'" ⁹And he said, "Wherein have I sinned, that you would give your servant into the hand of A′hab, to kill me? ¹⁰As the LORD your God lives, there is no nation or kingdom whither my lord has not sent to seek you; and when they would say, 'He is not here,' he would take an oath of the kingdom or nation, that they had not found you. ¹¹And now you say, 'Go, tell your lord, "Behold, Eli′jah is here."' ¹²And as soon as I have gone from you, the Spirit of the LORD will carry you I know not where; and so, when I come and tell A′hab and he cannot find you, he will kill me, although I your servant have revered the LORD from my youth. ¹³Has it not been told my lord what I did when Jez′ebel killed the prophets of the LORD, how I hid a hundred men of the LORD's prophets by fifties in a cave, and fed them with bread and water? ¹⁴And now you say, 'Go, tell your lord, "Behold, Eli′jah is here"'; and he will kill me." ¹⁵And Eli′jah said, "As the LORD of hosts lives, before whom I stand, I will surely show myself to him today." ¹⁶So Obadi′ah went to meet A′hab, and told him; and Ahab went to meet Eli′jah.

17:8–16: Lk 4:25, 26.
17:18: Mt 8:29; Mk 1:24; Jn 2:4.
* 17:1: With this description of the drought begins the prophetic career of Elijah, the great opponent of the nature religion that flourished in the northern kingdom and that Ahab and his Phoenician wife, Jezebel, were so active in promoting.

17 When A'hab saw Eli'jah, Ahab said to him, "Is it you, you troubler of Israel?" ¹⁸And he answered, "I have not troubled Israel; but you have, and your father's house, because you have forsaken the commandments of the Lord and followed the Ba'als. ¹⁹Now therefore send and gather all Israel to me at Mount Carmel, and the four hundred and fifty prophets of Ba'al * and the four hundred prophets of Ashe'rah, who eat at Jez'ebel's table."

Elijah Triumphs over the Prophets of Baal

20 So A'hab sent to all the sons of Israel, and gathered the prophets together at Mount Carmel. ²¹And Eli'jah came near to all the people, and said, "How long will you go limping with two different opinions? If the Lord is God, follow him; but if Ba'al, then follow him." And the people did not answer him a word. ²²Then Eli'jah said to the people, "I, even I only, am left a prophet of the Lord; but Ba'al's prophets are four hundred and fifty men. ²³Let two bulls be given to us; and let them choose one bull for themselves, and cut it in pieces and lay it on the wood, but put no fire to it; and I will prepare the other bull and lay it on the wood, and put no fire to it. ²⁴And you call on the name of your god and I will call on the name of the Lord; and the God who answers by fire, he is God." And all the people answered, "It is well spoken." ²⁵Then Eli'jah said to the prophets of Ba'al, "Choose for yourselves one bull and prepare it first, for you are many; and call on the name of your god, but put no fire to it." ²⁶And they took the bull which was given them, and they prepared it, and called on the name of Ba'al from morning until noon, saying, "O Baal, answer us!" But there was no voice, and no one answered. And they limped about the altar which they had made. ²⁷And at noon Eli'jah mocked them, saying, "Cry aloud, for he is a god; either he is musing, or he has gone aside, or he is on a journey, or perhaps he is asleep and must be awakened." ²⁸And they cried aloud, and cut themselves after their custom with swords and lances, until the blood gushed out upon them. ²⁹And as midday passed, they raved on until the time of the offering of the oblation, but there was no voice; no one answered, no one heeded.

30 Then Eli'jah said to all the people, "Come near to me"; and all the people came near to him. And he repaired the altar of the Lord that had been thrown down; ³¹Eli'jah took twelve stones, according to the number of the tribes of the sons of Jacob, to whom the word of the Lord came, saying, "Israel shall be your name"; ³²and with the stones he built an altar in the name of the Lord. And he made a trench about the altar, as great as would contain two measures of seed. ³³And he put the wood in order, and cut the bull in pieces and laid it on the wood. And he said, "Fill four jars with water, and pour it on the burnt offering, and on the wood." ³⁴And he said, "Do it a second time"; and they did it a second time. And he said, "Do it a third time"; and they did it a third time. ³⁵And the water ran round about the altar, and filled the trench also with water.

36 And at the time of the offering of the oblation, Eli'jah the prophet came near and said, "O Lord, God of Abraham, Isaac, and Israel, let it be known this day that you are God in Israel, and that I am your servant, and that I have done all these things at your word. ³⁷Answer me, O Lord, answer me, that this people may know that you, O Lord, are God, and that you have turned their hearts back." ³⁸Then the fire of the Lord fell, and consumed the burnt offering, and the wood, and the stones, and the dust, and licked up the water that was in the trench. ³⁹And when all the people saw it, they fell on their faces; and they said, "The Lord, he is God; the Lord, he is God." ⁴⁰And Eli'jah said to them, "Seize the prophets of Ba'al; let not one of them escape." And they seized them; and Elijah brought them down to the brook Ki'shon, and killed them there.

The Drought Ends

41 And Eli'jah said to A'hab, "Go up, eat and drink; for there is a sound of the rushing of rain." ⁴²So A'hab went up to eat and to drink. And Eli'jah went up to the top of Carmel; and he bowed himself down upon the earth, and put his face between his knees. ⁴³And he said to his servant, "Go up now, look toward the sea." And he went up and looked, and said, "There is nothing." And he said, "Go again seven times." ⁴⁴And at the seventh time he said, "Behold, a little cloud like a man's hand is rising out of the sea." And he said, "Go up, say to A'hab, 'Prepare your chariot and go down, lest the rain stop you.'" ⁴⁵And in a little while the heavens grew black with clouds and wind, and there was a great rain. And A'hab rode and went to Jezre'el. ⁴⁶And the hand of the Lord was on Eli'jah; and he girded up his loins and ran before A'hab to the entrance of Jezre'el.

Elijah Flees from Jezebel

19 A'hab told Jez'ebel all that Eli'jah had done, and how he had slain all the prophets with the sword. ²Then Jez'ebel sent a messenger to Eli'jah, saying, "So may the gods do to me, and more also, if I do not make your life as the life of one of them by this time tomorrow." ³Then he was afraid, and he arose and went for his life, and came to Be'er-she'ba, which belongs to Judah, and left his servant there.

4 But he himself went a day's journey into the wilderness, and came and sat down under a broom tree; and he asked that he might die, saying, "It is

* 18:19, *prophets of Baal:* These had been brought from Phoenicia by Jezebel.

267

enough; now, O Lᴏʀᴅ, take away my life; for I am no better than my fathers." ⁵And he lay down and slept under a broom tree; and behold, an angel touched him, and said to him, "Arise and eat." ⁶And he looked, and behold, there was at his head a cake baked on hot stones and a jar of water. And he ate and drank, and lay down again. ⁷And the angel of the Lᴏʀᴅ came again a second time, and touched him, and said, "Arise and eat, else the journey will be too great for you." ⁸And he arose, and ate and drank, and walked in the strength of that food forty days and forty nights to Horeb * the mount of God.

Elijah Meets God at Mount Horeb

9 And there he came to a cave, and lodged there; and behold, the word of the Lᴏʀᴅ came to him, and he said to him, "What are you doing here, Eli′jah?" ¹⁰He said, "I have been very jealous for the Lᴏʀᴅ, the God of hosts; for the sons of Israel have forsaken your covenant, thrown down your altars, and slain your prophets with the sword; and I, even I only, am left; and they seek my life, to take it away." ¹¹And he said, "Go forth, and stand upon the mount before the Lᴏʀᴅ." And behold, the Lᴏʀᴅ passed by, and a great and strong wind tore the mountains, and broke in pieces the rocks before the Lᴏʀᴅ, but the Lᴏʀᴅ was not in the wind; and after the wind an earthquake, but the Lᴏʀᴅ was not in the earthquake; ¹²and after the earthquake a fire, but the Lᴏʀᴅ was not in the fire; and after the fire a still small voice. ¹³And when Eli′jah heard it, he wrapped his face in his mantle and went out and stood at the entrance of the cave. And behold, there came a voice to him, and said, "What are you doing here, Eli′jah?" ¹⁴He said, "I have been very jealous for the Lᴏʀᴅ, the God of hosts; for the sons of Israel have forsaken your covenant, thrown down your altars, and slain your prophets with the sword; and I, even I only, am left; and they seek my life, to take it away." ¹⁵And the Lᴏʀᴅ said to him, "Go, return on your way to the wilderness of Damascus; and when you arrive, you shall anoint Haz′ael to be king over Syria; ¹⁶and Je′hu the son of Nimshi you shall anoint to be king over Israel; and Eli′sha the son of Sha′phat of A′bel-meho′lah you shall anoint to be prophet in your place. ¹⁷And him who escapes from the sword of Haz′ael shall Je′hu slay; and him who escapes from the sword of Jehu shall Eli′sha slay. ¹⁸Yet I will leave seven thousand in Israel, all the knees that have not bowed to Ba′al, and every mouth that has not kissed him."

Elisha Becomes Elijah's Disciple

19 So he departed from there, and found Eli′-sha the son of Sha′phat, who was plowing, with twelve yoke of oxen before him, and he was with the twelfth. Eli′jah passed by him and cast his mantle upon him. ²⁰And he left the oxen, and ran after Eli′jah, and said, "Let me kiss my father and my mother, and then I will follow you." And he said to him, "Go back again; for what have I done to you?" ²¹And he returned from following him, and took the yoke of oxen, and slew them, and boiled their flesh with the yokes of the oxen, and gave it to the people, and they ate. Then he arose and went after Eli′jah, and ministered to him.

Ahab's Wars with the Syrians

20 Ben-ha′dad the king of Syria gathered all his army together; thirty-two kings were with him, and horses and chariots; and he went up and besieged Samar′ia, and fought against it. ²And he sent messengers into the city to A′hab king of Israel, and said to him, "Thus says Ben-ha′dad: ³ 'Your silver and your gold are mine; your fairest wives and children also are mine.' " ⁴And the king of Israel answered, "As you say, my lord, O king, I am yours, and all that I have." ⁵The messengers came again, and said, "Thus says Ben-ha′dad: 'I sent to you, saying, "Deliver to me your silver and your gold, your wives and your children"; ⁶nevertheless I will send my servants to you tomorrow about this time, and they shall search your house and the houses of your servants, and lay hands on whatever pleases them, ° and take it away.' "

7 Then the king of Israel called all the elders of the land, and said, "Mark, now, and see how this man is seeking trouble; for he sent to me for my wives and my children, and for my silver and my gold, and I did not refuse him." ⁸And all the elders and all the people said to him, "Do not heed or consent." ⁹So he said to the messengers of Ben-ha′dad, "Tell my lord the king, 'All that you first demanded of your servant I will do; but this thing I cannot do.' " And the messengers departed and brought him word again. ¹⁰Ben-ha′dad sent to him and said, "The gods do so to me, and more also, if the dust of Samar′ia shall suffice for handfuls for all the people who follow me." ¹¹And the king of Israel answered, "Tell him, 'Let not him that belts on his armor boast himself as he that puts it off.' " ¹²When Ben-ha′dad heard this message as he was drinking with the kings in the booths, he said to his men, "Take your positions." And they took their positions against the city.

A Prophet Speaks to Ahab

13 And behold, a prophet came near to A′hab king of Israel and said, "Thus says the Lᴏʀᴅ, Have you seen all this great multitude? Behold, I will give it into your hand this day; and you shall know that I am the Lᴏʀᴅ." ¹⁴And A′hab said, "By whom?" He said, "Thus says the Lᴏʀᴅ, By the

---

° Gk Syr Vg: Heb *you.*
19:10: Rom 11:2, 3.
19:18: Rom 11:4.
* 19:8, *Horeb:* i.e., Mount Sinai, where the law was given to Moses and God made a covenant with his people.

servants of the governors of the districts." Then he said, "Who shall begin the battle?" He answered, "You." ¹⁵Then he mustered the servants of the governors of the districts, and they were two hundred and thirty-two; and after them he mustered all the sons of Israel, seven thousand.

The Syrians Are Defeated

16 And they went out at noon, while Ben-ha′dad was drinking himself drunk in the booths, he and the thirty-two kings who helped him. ¹⁷The servants of the governors of the districts went out first. And Ben-ha′dad sent out scouts, and they reported to him, "Men are coming out from Samar′ia." ¹⁸He said, "If they have come out for peace, take them alive; or if they have come out for war, take them alive."

19 So these went out of the city, the servants of the governors of the districts, and the army which followed them. ²⁰And each killed his man; the Syrians fled and Israel pursued them, but Ben-ha′dad king of Syria escaped on a horse with horsemen. ²¹And the king of Israel went out, and captured ᵖ the horses and chariots, and killed the Syrians with a great slaughter.

22 Then the prophet came near to the king of Israel, and said to him, "Come, strengthen yourself, and consider well what you have to do; for in the spring the king of Syria will come up against you."

23 And the servants of the king of Syria said to him, "Their gods are gods of the hills, and so they were stronger than we; but let us fight against them in the plain, and surely we shall be stronger than they. ²⁴And do this: remove the kings, each from his post, and put commanders in their places; ²⁵and muster an army like the army that you have lost, horse for horse, and chariot for chariot; then we will fight against them in the plain, and surely we shall be stronger than they." And he listened to their voice, and did so.

26 In the spring Ben-ha′dad mustered the Syrians, and went up to A′phek, to fight against Israel. ²⁷And the sons of Israel were mustered, and were provisioned, and went against them; the sons of Israel encamped before them like two little flocks of goats, but the Syrians filled the country. ²⁸And a man of God came near and said to the king of Israel, "Thus says the LORD, 'Because the Syrians have said, "The LORD is a god of the hills but he is not a god of the valleys," therefore I will give all this great multitude into your hand, and you shall know that I am the LORD.'" ²⁹And they encamped opposite one another seven days. Then on the seventh day the battle was joined; and the sons of Israel struck a hundred thousand Syrian foot soldiers in one day. ³⁰And the rest fled into the city of A′phek; and the wall fell upon twenty-seven thousand men that were left.

Ben-ha′dad also fled, and entered an inner chamber in the city. ³¹And his servants said to him, "Behold now, we have heard that the kings of the house of Israel are merciful kings; let us put sackcloth on our loins and ropes upon our heads, and go out to the king of Israel; perhaps he will spare your life." ³²So they belted sackcloth on their loins, and put ropes on their heads, and went to the king of Israel and said, "Your servant Ben-ha′dad says, 'Please, let me live.'" And he said, "Does he still live? He is my brother." ³³Now the men were watching for an omen, and they quickly took it up from him and said, "Yes, your brother Ben-ha′dad." Then he said, "Go and bring him." Then Ben-hadad came forth to him; and he caused him to come up into the chariot. ³⁴And Ben-ha′dad said to him, "The cities which my father took from your father I will restore; and you may establish bazaars for yourself in Damascus, as my father did in Samar′ia." And A′hab said, "I will let you go on these terms." So he made a covenant with him and let him go.

A Prophet Condemns Ahab

35 And a certain man of the sons of the prophets said to his fellow at the command of the LORD, "Strike me, I beg you." But the man refused to strike him. ³⁶Then he said to him, "Because you have not obeyed the voice of the LORD, behold, as soon as you have gone from me, a lion shall kill you." And as soon as he had departed from him, a lion met him and killed him. ³⁷Then he found another man, and said, "Strike me, I beg you." And the man struck him, hitting and wounding him. ³⁸So the prophet departed, and waited for the king by the way, disguising himself with a bandage over his eyes. ³⁹And as the king passed, he cried to the king and said, "Your servant went out into the midst of the battle; and behold, a soldier turned and brought a man to me, and said, 'Keep this man; if by any means he be missing, your life shall be for his life, or else you shall pay a talent of silver.' ⁴⁰And as your servant was busy here and there, he was gone." The king of Israel said to him, "So shall your judgment be; you yourself have decided it." ⁴¹Then he made haste to take the bandage away from his eyes; and the king of Israel recognized him as one of the prophets. ⁴²And he said to him, "Thus says the LORD, 'Because you have let go out of your hand the man whom I had devoted to destruction, therefore your life shall go for his life, and your people for his people.'" ⁴³And the king of Israel went to his house resentful and sullen, and came to Samar′ia.

Naboth's Vineyard

21 Now Naboth the Jezre′elite had a vineyard in Jezre′el, beside the palace of A′hab

ᵖ Gk: Heb *struck.*

king of Samar′ia. [2]And after this A′hab said to Naboth, "Give me your vineyard, that I may have it for a vegetable garden, because it is near my house; and I will give you a better vineyard for it; or, if it seems good to you, I will give you its value in money." [3]But Naboth said to A′hab, "The Lord forbid that I should give you the inheritance of my fathers." [4]And A′hab went into his house vexed and sullen because of what Naboth the Jezre′elite had said to him; for he had said, "I will not give you the inheritance of my fathers." And he lay down on his bed, and turned away his face, and would eat no food.

5 But Jez′ebel his wife came to him, and said to him, "Why is your spirit so vexed that you eat no food?" [6]And he said to her, "Because I spoke to Naboth the Jezre′elite, and said to him, 'Give me your vineyard for money; or else, if it please you, I will give you another vineyard for it'; and he answered, 'I will not give you my vineyard.' " [7]And Jez′ebel his wife said to him, "Do you now govern Israel? Arise, and eat bread, and let your heart be cheerful; I will give you the vineyard of Naboth the Jezre′elite."

8 So she wrote letters in A′hab's name and sealed them with his seal, and she sent the letters to the elders and the nobles who dwelt with Naboth in his city. [9]And she wrote in the letters, "Proclaim a fast, and set Naboth on high among the people; [10]and set two * base fellows opposite him, and let them bring a charge against him, saying, 'You have cursed God and the king.' Then take him out, and stone him to death." [11]And the men of his city, the elders and the nobles who dwelt in his city, did as Jez′ebel had sent word to them. As it was written in the letters which she had sent to them, [12]they proclaimed a fast, and set Naboth on high among the people. [13]And the two base fellows came in and sat opposite him; and the base fellows brought a charge against Naboth, in the presence of the people, saying, "Naboth cursed God and the king." So they took him outside the city, and stoned him to death with stones. [14]Then they sent to Jez′ebel, saying, "Naboth has been stoned; he is dead."

15 As soon as Jez′ebel heard that Naboth had been stoned and was dead, Jezebel said to A′hab, "Arise, take possession of the vineyard of Naboth the Jezre′elite, which he refused to give you for money; for Naboth is not alive, but dead." [16]And as soon as A′hab heard that Naboth was dead, Ahab arose to go down to the vineyard of Naboth the Jezre′elite, to take possession of it.

Elijah Pronounces God's Sentence

17 Then the word of the Lord came to Eli′jah the Tishbite, saying, [18]"Arise, go down to meet A′hab king of Israel, who is in Samar′ia; behold, he is in the vineyard of Naboth, where he has gone to take possession. [19]And you shall say to him,

'Thus says the Lord, "Have you killed, and also taken possession?" ' And you shall say to him, 'Thus says the Lord: "In the place where dogs licked up the blood of Naboth shall dogs lick your own blood." ' "

20 A′hab said to Eli′jah, "Have you found me, O my enemy?" He answered, "I have found you, because you have sold yourself to do what is evil in the sight of the Lord. [21]Behold, I will bring evil upon you; I will utterly sweep you away, and will cut off from A′hab every male, bond or free, in Israel; [22]and I will make your house like the house of Jerobo′am the son of Ne′bat, and like the house of Ba′asha the son of Ahi′jah, for the anger to which you have provoked me, and because you have made Israel to sin. [23]And of Jez′ebel the Lord also said, 'The dogs shall eat Jezebel within the bounds of Jezre′el.' [24]Any one belonging to A′hab who dies in the city the dogs shall eat; and any one of his who dies in the open country the birds of the air shall eat."

25 (There was none who sold himself to do what was evil in the sight of the Lord like A′hab, whom Jez′ebel his wife incited. [26]He did very abominably in going after idols, as the Am′orites had done, whom the Lord cast out before the sons of Israel.)

27 And when A′hab heard those words, he tore his clothes, and put sackcloth upon his flesh, and fasted and lay in sackcloth, and went about dejectedly. [28]And the word of the Lord came to Eli′jah the Tishbite, saying, [29] "Have you seen how Ahab has humbled himself before me? Because he has humbled himself before me, I will not bring the evil in his days; but in his son's days I will bring the evil upon his house." †

Judah and Israel Join to Fight the Syrians

22 For three years Syria and Israel continued without war. [2]But in the third year Jehosh′-aphat the king of Judah came down to the king of Israel. [3]And the king of Israel said to his servants, "Do you know that Ra′moth-gil′ead belongs to us, and we keep quiet and do not take it out of the hand of the king of Syria?" [4]And he said to Jehosh′aphat, "Will you go with me to battle at Ra′moth-gil′ead?" And Jehoshaphat said to the king of Israel, "I am as you are, my people as your people, my horses as your horses."

5 And Jehosh′aphat said to the king of Israel, "Inquire first for the word of the Lord." [6]Then the king of Israel gathered the prophets together, about four hundred men, and said to them, "Shall I go to

---

21:19: 2 Kings 9:26.
21:23: 2 Kings 9:36.
22:1–35: 2 Chron 18:1–34.
* 21:10: Two witnesses were required for a legal charge involving the death penalty; cf. Susanna and the elders; cf. Num 35:30; Deut 19:15; Dan 13:40; Mt 18:16.
† 21:29: God has mercy on the repentant king, as before in the case of David. But he does not say here that the dynasty will be preserved.

battle against Ra'moth-gil'ead, or shall I forbear?" And they said, "Go up; for the Lord will give it into the hand of the king." ⁷But Jehosh'aphat said, "Is there not here another prophet of the LORD of whom we may inquire?" ⁸And the king of Israel said to Jehosh'aphat, "There is yet one man by whom we may inquire of the LORD, Micai'ah the son of Imlah; but I hate him, for he never prophesies good concerning me, but evil." And Jehosh'aphat said, "Let not the king say so." ⁹Then the king of Israel summoned an officer and said, "Bring quickly Micai'ah the son of Imlah." ¹⁰Now the king of Israel and Jehosh'aphat the king of Judah were sitting on their thrones, wearing their robes, at the threshing floor at the entrance of the gate of Samar'ia; and all the prophets were prophesying before them. ¹¹And Zedeki'ah the son of Chena'anah made for himself horns of iron, and said, "Thus says the LORD, 'With these you shall push the Syrians until they are destroyed.'" ¹²And all the prophets prophesied so, and said, "Go up to Ra'moth-gil'ead and triumph; the LORD will give it into the hand of the king."

Micaiah's Prophecy

13 And the messenger who went to summon Micai'ah said to him, "Behold, the words of the prophets with one accord are favorable to the king; let your word be like the word of one of them, and speak favorably." ¹⁴But Micai'ah said, "As the LORD lives, what the LORD says to me, that I will speak." ¹⁵And when he had come to the king, the king said to him, "Micai'ah, shall we go to Ra'moth-gil'ead to battle, or shall we forbear?" And he answered him, "Go up and triumph; the LORD will give it into the hand of the king." ¹⁶But the king said to him, "How many times shall I adjure you that you speak to me nothing but the truth in the name of the LORD?" ¹⁷And he said, "I saw all Israel scattered upon the mountains, as sheep that have no shepherd; and the LORD said, 'These have no master; let each return to his home in peace.'" ¹⁸And the king of Israel said to Jehosh'aphat, "Did I not tell you that he would not prophesy good concerning me, but evil?" ¹⁹And Micai'ah said, "Therefore hear the word of the LORD: I saw the LORD sitting on his throne, and all the host of heaven standing beside him on his right hand and on his left; ²⁰and the LORD said, 'Who will entice A'hab, that he may go up and fall at Ra'moth-gil'ead?' And one said one thing, and another said another. ²¹Then a spirit came forward and stood before the LORD, saying, 'I will entice him.' ²²And the LORD said to him, 'By what means?' And he said, 'I will go forth, and will be a lying spirit in the mouth of all his prophets.' And he said, 'You are to entice him, and you shall succeed; go forth and do so.' ²³Now therefore behold, the LORD has put a lying spirit in the mouth of all these your prophets; the LORD has spoken evil concerning you."

24 Then Zedeki'ah the son of Chena'anah came near and struck Micai'ah on the cheek, and said, "How did the Spirit of the LORD go from me to speak to you?" ²⁵And Micai'ah said, "Behold, you shall see on that day when you go into an inner chamber to hide yourself." ²⁶And the king of Israel said, "Seize Micai'ah, and take him back to A'mon the governor of the city and to Jo'ash the king's son; ²⁷and say, 'Thus says the king, "Put this fellow in prison, and feed him with scant fare of bread and water, until I come in peace."'" ²⁸And Micai'ah said, "If you return in peace, the LORD has not spoken by me." And he said, "Hear, all you peoples!"

Defeat and Death of Ahab

29 So the king of Israel and Jehosh'aphat the king of Judah went up to Ra'moth-gil'ead. ³⁰And the king of Israel said to Jehosh'aphat, "I will disguise myself and go into battle, but you wear your robes." And the king of Israel disguised himself and went into battle. ³¹Now the king of Syria had commanded the thirty-two captains of his chariots, "Fight with neither small nor great, but only with the king of Israel." ³²And when the captains of the chariots saw Jehosh'aphat, they said, "It is surely the king of Israel." So they turned to fight against him; and Jehoshaphat cried out. ³³And when the captains of the chariots saw that it was not the king of Israel, they turned back from pursuing him. ³⁴But a certain man drew his bow by chance, and struck the king of Israel between the scale armor and the breastplate; therefore he said to the driver of his chariot, "Turn about, and carry me out of the battle, for I am wounded." ³⁵And the battle grew hot that day, and the king was propped up in his chariot facing the Syrians, until at evening he died; and the blood of the wound flowed into the bottom of the chariot. ³⁶And about sunset a cry went through the army, "Every man to his city, and every man to his country!"

37 So the king died, and was brought to Samar'ia; and they buried the king in Samaria. ³⁸And they washed the chariot by the pool of Samar'ia, and the dogs licked up his blood, and the harlots washed themselves in it, according to the word of the LORD which he had spoken. ³⁹Now the rest of the acts of A'hab, and all that he did, and the ivory house which he built, and all the cities that he built, are they not written in the Book of the Chronicles of the Kings of Israel? ⁴⁰So A'hab slept with his fathers; and Ahazi'ah his son reigned in his stead.

Jehoshaphat Reigns over Judah

41 Jehosh'aphat the son of Asa began to reign over Judah in the fourth year of A'hab king of Israel. ⁴²Jehosh'aphat was thirty-five years old

22:17: Mt 9:36.
22:41–43: 2 Chron 20:31–33.

when he began to reign, and he reigned twenty-five years in Jerusalem. His mother's name was Azu'bah the daughter of Shilhi. ⁴³He walked in all the way of Asa his father; he did not turn aside from it, doing what was right in the sight of the LORD; yet the high places were not taken away, and the people still sacrificed and burned incense on the high places. ⁴⁴Jehosh'aphat also made peace with the king of Israel.

45 Now the rest of the acts of Jehosh'aphat, and his might that he showed, and how he warred, are they not written in the Book of the Chronicles of the Kings of Judah? ⁴⁶And the remnant of the male cult prostitutes who remained in the days of his father Asa, he exterminated from the land.

47 There was no king in E'dom; a deputy was king. ⁴⁸Jehosh'aphat made ships of Tar'shish to go to O'phir for gold; but they did not go, for the ships were wrecked at E'zion-ge'ber. ⁴⁹Then Aha-zi'ah the son of A'hab said to Jehosh'aphat, "Let my servants go with your servants in the ships," but Jehoshaphat was not willing. ⁵⁰And Jehosh'a-phat slept with his fathers, and was buried with his fathers in the city of David his father; and Jeho'ram his son reigned in his stead.

Ahaziah Reigns over Israel

51 Ahazi'ah the son of A'hab began to reign over Israel in Samar'ia in the seventeenth year of Jehosh'aphat king of Judah, and he reigned two years over Israel. ⁵²He did what was evil in the sight of the LORD, and walked in the way of his father, and in the way of his mother, and in the way of Jerobo'am the son of Ne'bat, who made Israel to sin. ⁵³He served Ba'al and wor-shiped him, and provoked the LORD, the God of Israel, to anger in every way that his father had done.

22:48, 49: 2 Chron 20:35–37.
22:50: 2 Chron 21:1.

THE SECOND BOOK OF THE

KINGS

Elijah Denounces Ahaziah

1 After the death of A'hab, Moab rebelled against Israel.

2 Now Ahazi'ah fell through the lattice in his upper chamber in Samar'ia, and lay sick; so he sent messengers, telling them, "Go, inquire of Ba'al-ze'bub, the god of Ek'ron, whether I shall recover from this sickness." ³But the angel of the LORD said to Eli'jah the Tishbite, "Arise, go up to meet the messengers of the king of Samar'ia, and say to them, 'Is it because there is no God in Israel that you are going to inquire of Ba'al-ze'bub, the god of Ek'ron?' ⁴Now therefore thus says the LORD, 'You shall not come down from the bed to which you have gone, but you shall surely die.'" So Eli'jah went.

5 The messengers returned to the king, and he said to them, "Why have you returned?" ⁶And they said to him, "There came a man to meet us, and said to us, 'Go back to the king who sent you, and say to him, Thus says the LORD, Is it because there is no God in Israel that you are sending to inquire of Ba'al-ze'bub, the god of Ek'ron? Therefore you shall not come down from the bed to which you have gone, but shall surely die.'" ⁷He said to them, "What kind of man was he who came to meet you and told you these things?" ⁸They answered him, "He wore a garment of haircloth, with a belt of leather about his loins." And he said, "It is Eli'jah the Tishbite."

9 Then the king sent to him a captain of fifty men with his fifty. He went up to Eli'jah, who was sitting on the top of a hill, and said to him, "O man of God, the king says, 'Come down.'" ¹⁰But Eli'jah answered the captain of fifty, "If I am a man of God, let fire come down from heaven and consume you and your fifty." Then fire came down from heaven, and consumed him and his fifty.

11 Again the king sent to him another captain of fifty men with his fifty. And he went up ᵃ and said to him, "O man of God, this is the king's order, 'Come down quickly!'" ¹²But Eli'jah answered them, "If I am a man of God, let fire come down from heaven and consume you and your fifty." Then the fire of God came down from heaven and consumed him and his fifty.

13 Again the king sent the captain of a third fifty with his fifty. And the third captain of fifty went up, and came and fell on his knees before Eli'jah, and entreated him, "O man of God, I beg you, let my life, and the life of these fifty servants of yours, be precious in your sight. ¹⁴Behold, fire came down from heaven, and consumed the two former captains of fifty men with their fifties; but now let my life be precious in your sight." ¹⁵Then the angel of the LORD said to Eli'jah, "Go down with him; do not be afraid of him." So he arose and went down with him to the king, ¹⁶and said to him, "Thus says the LORD, 'Because you have sent messengers to inquire of Ba'al-ze'bub, the god of Ek'ron—is it because there is no God in Israel to inquire of his word?—therefore you shall not come down from the bed to which you have gone, but you shall surely die.'"

Death of Ahaziah

17 So he died according to the word of the LORD which Eli'jah had spoken. Jeho'ram, his brother, ᵇ became king in his stead in the second year of Jehoram the son of Jehosh'aphat, king of Judah, because Ahazi'ah had no son. ¹⁸Now the rest of the acts of Ahazi'ah which he did, are they not written in the Book of the Chronicles of the Kings of Israel?

Elijah Is Taken Up to Heaven

2 Now when the LORD was about to take Eli'jah up to heaven by a whirlwind, Elijah and Eli'sha were on their way from Gilgal. ²And Eli'jah said to Eli'sha, "Tarry here, I beg you; for the LORD has sent me as far as Bethel." But Elisha said, "As the LORD lives, and as you yourself live, I will not leave you." So they went down to Bethel. ³And the sons of the prophets who were in Bethel came out to Eli'sha, and said to him, "Do you know that today the LORD will take away your master from over you?" And he said, "Yes, I know it; hold your peace."

4 Eli'jah said to him, "Eli'sha, tarry here, I beg you; for the LORD has sent me to Jericho." But he said, "As the LORD lives, and as you yourself live, I will not leave you." So they came to Jericho. ⁵The sons of the prophets who were at Jericho drew near to Eli'sha, and said to him, "Do you know that today the LORD will take away your master from over you?" And he answered, "Yes, I know it; hold your peace."

6 Then Eli'jah said to him, "Tarry here, I beg you; for the LORD has sent me to the Jordan." But

---

ᵃ Gk Compare verses 9, 13: Heb *answered*.
ᵇ Gk Syr: Heb lacks *his brother*.
1:10–12: Lk 9:54; Rev 11:5; 20:9.

he said, "As the LORD lives, and as you yourself live, I will not leave you." So the two of them went on. ⁷Fifty men of the sons of the prophets also went, and stood at some distance from them, as they both were standing by the Jordan. ⁸Then Eli'jah took his coat, and rolled it up, and struck the water, and the water was parted to the one side and to the other, till the two of them could go over on dry ground.

Elisha Succeeds Elijah

9 When they had crossed, Eli'jah said to Eli'sha, "Ask what I shall do for you, before I am taken from you." And Elisha said, "I beg you, let me inherit a double share * of your spirit." ¹⁰And he said, "You have asked a hard thing; yet, if you see me as I am being taken from you, it shall be so for you; but if you do not see me, it shall not be so." ¹¹And as they still went on and talked, behold, a chariot of fire and horses of fire separated the two of them. And Eli'jah went up by a whirlwind into heaven. ¹²And Eli'sha saw it and he cried, "My father, my father! the chariots of Israel and its horsemen!" And he saw him no more.

Then he took hold of his own clothes and tore them in two pieces. ¹³And he took up the coat of Eli'jah that had fallen from him, and went back and stood on the bank of the Jordan. ¹⁴Then he took the coat of Eli'jah that had fallen from him, and struck the water, saying, "Where is the LORD, the God of Elijah?" And when he had struck the water, the water was parted to the one side and to the other; and Eli'sha went over.

15 Now when the sons of the prophets who were at Jericho saw him over against them, they said, "The spirit of Eli'jah rests on Eli'sha." And they came to meet him, and bowed to the ground before him. ¹⁶And they said to him, "Behold now, there are with your servants fifty strong men; please, let them go, and seek your master; it may be that the Spirit of the LORD has caught him up and cast him upon some mountain or into some valley." And he said, "You shall not send." ¹⁷But when they urged him till he was ashamed, he said, "Send." They sent therefore fifty men; and for three days they sought him but did not find him. ¹⁸And they came back to him, while he tarried at Jericho, and he said to them, "Did I not say to you, Do not go?"

Elisha Performs Miracles

19 Now the men of the city said to Eli'sha, "Behold, the situation of this city is pleasant, as my lord sees; but the water is bad, and the land is unfruitful." ²⁰He said, "Bring me a new bowl, and put salt in it." So they brought it to him. ²¹Then he went to the spring of water and threw salt in it, and said, "Thus says the LORD, I have made this water wholesome; henceforth neither death nor miscarriage shall come from it." ²²So the water

has been wholesome to this day, according to the word which Eli'sha spoke.

23 He went up from there to Bethel; and while he was going up on the way, some small boys came out of the city and jeered at him, saying, "Go up, you baldhead! Go up, you baldhead!" ²⁴And he turned around, and when he saw them, he cursed them in the name of the LORD. And two she-bears came out of the woods and tore forty-two of the boys. ²⁵From there he went on to Mount Carmel, and thence he returned to Samar'ia.

Jehoram Reigns over Israel

3 In the eighteenth year of Jehosh'aphat king of Judah, Jeho'ram the son of A'hab became king over Israel in Samar'ia, and he reigned twelve years. ²He did what was evil in the sight of the LORD, though not like his father and mother, for he put away the pillar of Ba'al which his father had made. ³Nevertheless he clung to the sin of Jerobo'am the son of Ne'bat, which he made Israel to sin; he did not depart from it.

War with Moab

4 † Now Me'sha king of Moab was a sheep breeder; and he had to deliver annually ᶜ to the king of Israel a hundred thousand lambs, and the wool of a hundred thousand rams. ⁵But when A'hab died, the king of Moab rebelled against the king of Israel. ⁶So King Jeho'ram marched out of Samar'ia at that time and mustered all Israel. ⁷And he went and sent word to Jehosh'aphat king of Judah, "The king of Moab has rebelled against me; will you go with me to battle against Moab?" And he said, "I will go; I am as you are, my people as your people, my horses as your horses." ⁸Then he said, "By which way shall we march?" Jeho'ram answered, "By the way of the wilderness of E'dom."

9 So the king of Israel went with the king of Judah and the king of E'dom. And when they had made a circuitous march of seven days, there was no water for the army or for the beasts which followed them. ¹⁰Then the king of Israel said, "Alas! The LORD has called these three kings to give them into the hand of Moab." ¹¹And Jehosh'-aphat said, "Is there no prophet of the LORD here, through whom we may inquire of the LORD?" Then one of the king of Israel's servants answered, "Eli'sha the son of Sha'phat is here, who poured water on the hands of Eli'jah." ¹²And Jehosh'aphat said, "The word of the LORD is with him." So the king of Israel and Jehoshaphat and the king of E'dom went down to him.

ᶜ Tg: Heb lacks *annually*.

2:11: Rev 11:12.

* 2:9, *a double share:* The eldest son inherited a double share of his father's property; cf. Deut 21:17. Elisha regarded himself as the son and so asked for Elijah's spirit as his inheritance.

† 3:4–27: The Moabite Stone, or Stele of Mesha, in the Louvre, found in Trans-Jordan in 1868, describes the liberation of Moab from Israel, but understandably is silent about its subjection.

13 And Eli'sha said to the king of Israel, "What have I to do with you? Go to the prophets of your father and the prophets of your mother." But the king of Israel said to him, "No; it is the LORD who has called these three kings to give them into the hand of Moab." ¹⁴And Eli'sha said, "As the LORD of hosts lives, whom I serve, were it not that I have regard for Jehosh'aphat the king of Judah, I would neither look at you, nor see you. ¹⁵But now bring me a minstrel." And when the minstrel played, the power of the LORD came upon him. ¹⁶And he said, "Thus says the LORD, 'I will make this dry stream-bed full of pools.' ¹⁷For thus says the LORD, 'You shall not see wind or rain, but that stream-bed shall be filled with water, so that you shall drink, you, your cattle, and your beasts.' ¹⁸This is a light thing in the sight of the LORD; he will also give the Moabites into your hand, ¹⁹and you shall conquer every fortified city, and every choice city, and shall fell every good tree, and stop up all springs of water, and ruin every good piece of land with stones." ²⁰The next morning, about the time of offering the sacrifice, behold, water came from the direction of E'dom, till the country was filled with water.

21 When all the Moabites heard that the kings had come up to fight against them, all who were able to put on armor, from the youngest to the oldest, were called out, and were drawn up at the frontier. ²²And when they rose early in the morning, and the sun shone upon the water, the Moabites saw the water opposite them as red as blood. ²³And they said, "This is blood; the kings have surely fought together, and slain one another. Now then, Moab, to the spoil!" ²⁴But when they came to the camp of Israel, the Israelites rose and attacked the Moabites, till they fled before them; and they went forward, slaughtering the Moabites as they went. ᵈ ²⁵And they overthrew the cities, and on every good piece of land every man threw a stone, until it was covered; they stopped every spring of water, and felled all the good trees; till only its stones were left in Kir-har'-eseth, and the slingers surrounded and conquered it. ²⁶When the king of Moab saw that the battle was going against him, he took with him seven hundred swordsmen to break through, opposite the king of E'dom; but they could not. ²⁷Then he took his eldest son who was to reign in his stead, and offered him for a burnt offering upon the wall. And there came great wrath upon Israel; and they withdrew from him and returned to their own land.

Elisha and the Widow's Jar of Oil

4 Now the wife of one of the sons of the prophets cried to Eli'sha, "Your servant my husband is dead; and you know that your servant feared the LORD, but the creditor has come to take my two children to be his slaves." ²And Eli'sha said to her, "What shall I do for you? Tell me; what have you in the house?" And she said, "Your maidservant has nothing in the house, except a jar of oil." ³Then he said, "Go outside, borrow vessels of all your neighbors, empty vessels and not too few. ⁴Then go in, and shut the door upon yourself and your sons, and pour into all these vessels; and when one is full, set it aside." ⁵So she went from him and shut the door upon herself and her sons; and as she poured they brought the vessels to her. ⁶When the vessels were full, she said to her son, "Bring me another vessel." And he said to her, "There is not another." Then the oil stopped flowing. ⁷She came and told the man of God, and he said, "Go, sell the oil and pay your debts, and you and your sons can live on the rest."

Elisha and the Shunammite Couple

8 One day Eli'sha went on to Shu'nem, where a wealthy woman lived, who urged him to eat some food. So whenever he passed that way, he would turn in there to eat food. ⁹And she said to her husband, "Behold now, I perceive that this is a holy man of God, who is continually passing our way. ¹⁰Let us make a small roof chamber with walls, and put there for him a bed, a table, a chair, and a lamp, so that whenever he comes to us, he can go in there."

11 One day he came there, and he turned into the chamber and rested there. ¹²And he said to Geha'zi his servant, "Call this Shu'nammite." When he had called her, she stood before him. ¹³And he said to him, "Say now to her, See, you have taken all this trouble for us; what is to be done for you? Would you have a word spoken on your behalf to the king or to the commander of the army?" She answered, "I dwell among my own people." ¹⁴And he said, "What then is to be done for her?" Geha'zi answered, "Well, she has no son, and her husband is old." ¹⁵He said, "Call her." And when he had called her, she stood in the doorway. ¹⁶And he said, "At this season, when the time comes round, you shall embrace a son." And she said, "No, my lord, O man of God; do not lie to your maidservant." ¹⁷But the woman conceived, and she bore a son about that time the following spring, as Eli'sha had said to her.

Elisha Restores the Shunammite's Son

18 When the child had grown, he went out one day to his father among the reapers. ¹⁹And he said to his father, "Oh, my head, my head!" The father said to his servant, "Carry him to his mother." ²⁰And when he had lifted him, and brought him to his mother, the child sat on her lap till noon, and then he died. ²¹And she went up and laid him on the bed of the man of God, and shut the door upon him, and went out. ²²Then she called to her husband, and said, "Send me one of the servants

---

ᵈ Gk: Heb uncertain.

and one of the donkeys, that I may quickly go to the man of God, and come back again." ²³And he said, "Why will you go to him today? It is neither new moon nor sabbath." She said, "It will be well." ²⁴Then she saddled the donkey, and she said to her servant, "Urge the beast on; do not slacken the pace for me unless I tell you." ²⁵So she set out, and came to the man of God at Mount Carmel.

When the man of God saw her coming, he said to Geha'zi his servant, "Look, yonder is the Shu'-nammite; ²⁶run at once to meet her, and say to her, Is it well with you? Is it well with your husband? Is it well with the child?" And she answered, "It is well." ²⁷And when she came to the mountain to the man of God, she caught hold of his feet. And Geha'zi came to thrust her away. But the man of God said, "Let her alone, for she is in bitter distress; and the Lord has hidden it from me, and has not told me." ²⁸Then she said, "Did I ask my lord for a son? Did I not say, Do not deceive me?" ²⁹He said to Geha'zi, "Gird up your loins, and take my staff in your hand, and go. If you meet any one, do not salute him; and if any one salutes you, do not reply; and lay my staff upon the face of the child." ³⁰Then the mother of the child said, "As the Lord lives, and as you yourself live, I will not leave you." So he arose and followed her. ³¹Geha'zi went on ahead and laid the staff upon the face of the child, but there was no sound or sign of life. Therefore he returned to meet him, and told him, "The child has not awaked."

32 When Eli'sha came into the house, he saw the child lying dead on his bed. ³³So he went in and shut the door upon the two of them, and prayed to the Lord. ³⁴Then he went up and lay upon the child, putting his mouth upon his mouth, his eyes upon his eyes, and his hands upon his hands; and as he stretched himself upon him, the flesh of the child became warm. ³⁵Then he got up again, and walked once back and forth in the house, and went up, and stretched himself upon him; the child sneezed seven times, and the child opened his eyes. ³⁶Then he summoned Geha'zi and said, "Call this Shu'nammite." So he called her. And when she came to him, he said, "Take up your son." ³⁷She came and fell at his feet, bowing to the ground; then she took up her son and went out.

Elisha Purifies the Pot of Pottage

38 And Eli'sha came again to Gilgal when there was a famine in the land. And as the sons of the prophets were sitting before him, he said to his servant, "Put on the great pot, and boil pottage for the sons of the prophets." ³⁹One of them went out into the field to gather herbs, and found a wild vine and gathered from it his lap full of wild gourds, and came and cut them up into the pot of pottage, not knowing what they were. ⁴⁰And they poured out for the men to eat. But while they were eating of the pottage, they cried out, "O man of God, there is death in the pot!" And they could not eat it. ⁴¹He said, "Then bring meal." And he threw it into the pot, and said, "Pour out for the men, that they may eat." And there was no harm in the pot.

Elisha Feeds a Hundred Men

42 A man came from Ba'al-shal'ishah, bringing the man of God bread of the first fruits, twenty loaves of barley, and fresh ears of grain in his sack. And Eli'sha said, "Give to the men, that they may eat." ⁴³But his servant said, "How am I to set this before a hundred men?" So he repeated, "Give them to the men, that they may eat, for thus says the Lord, 'They shall eat and have some left.'" ⁴⁴So he set it before them. And they ate, and had some left, according to the word of the Lord.

Naaman Is Cured of Leprosy

5 Na'aman, commander of the army of the king of Syria, was a great man with his master and in high favor, because by him the Lord had given victory to Syria. He was a mighty man of valor, but he was a leper. ²Now the Syrians on one of their raids had carried off a little maid from the land of Israel, and she waited on Na'aman's wife. ³She said to her mistress, "Would that my lord were with the prophet who is in Samar'ia! He would cure him of his leprosy." ⁴So Na'aman went in and told his lord, "Thus and so spoke the maiden from the land of Israel." ⁵And the king of Syria said, "Go now, and I will send a letter to the king of Israel."

So he went, taking with him ten talents of silver, six thousand shekels of gold, and ten festal garments. ⁶And he brought the letter to the king of Israel, which read, "When this letter reaches you, know that I have sent to you Na'aman my servant, that you may cure him of his leprosy." ⁷And when the king of Israel read the letter, he tore his clothes and said, "Am I God, to kill and to make alive, that this man sends word to me to cure a man of his leprosy? Only consider, and see how he is seeking a quarrel with me."

8 But when Eli'sha the man of God heard that the king of Israel had torn his clothes, he sent to the king, saying, "Why have you torn your clothes? Let him come now to me, that he may know that there is a prophet in Israel." ⁹So Na'aman came with his horses and chariots, and halted at the door of Eli'sha's house. ¹⁰And Eli'sha sent a messenger to him, saying, "Go and wash in the Jordan seven times, and your flesh shall be restored, and you shall be clean." ¹¹But Na'aman was angry, and went away, saying, "Behold, I thought that he would surely come out to me, and stand, and call on the name of the Lord his God,

4:33: Mt 6:6.

and wave his hand over the place, and cure the leper. [12]Are not Aba'na [e] and Pharpar, the rivers of Damascus, better than all the waters of Israel? Could I not wash in them, and be clean?" So he turned and went away in a rage. [13]But his servants came near and said to him, "My father, if the prophet had commanded you to do some great thing, would you not have done it? How much rather, then, when he says to you, 'Wash, and be clean'?" [14]So he went down and dipped himself seven times in the Jordan, according to the word of the man of God; and his flesh was restored like the flesh of a little child, and he was clean.

15 Then he returned to the man of God, he and all his company, and he came and stood before him; and he said, "Behold, I know that there is no God in all the earth but in Israel; [*] so accept now a present from your servant." [16]But he said, "As the LORD lives, whom I serve, I will receive none." And he urged him to take it, but he refused. [17]Then Na'aman said, "If not, I beg you, let there be given to your servant two mules' burden of earth; for henceforth your servant will not offer burnt offering or sacrifice to any god but the LORD. [18]In this matter may the LORD pardon your servant: when my master goes into the house of Rimmon to worship there, leaning on my arm, and I bow myself in the house of Rimmon, when I bow myself in the house of Rimmon, the LORD pardon your servant in this matter." [19]He said to him, "Go in peace."

But when Na'aman had gone from him a short distance, [20]Geha'zi, the servant of Eli'sha the man of God, said, "See, my master has spared this Na'aman the Syrian, in not accepting from his hand what he brought. As the LORD lives, I will run after him, and get something from him." [21]So Geha'zi followed Na'aman. And when Naaman saw some one running after him, he alighted from the chariot to meet him, and said, "Is all well?" [22]And he said, "All is well. My master has sent me to say, 'There have just now come to me from the hill country of E'phraim two young men of the sons of the prophets; please, give them a talent of silver and two festal garments.' " [23]And Na'aman said, "Be pleased to accept two talents." And he urged him, and tied up two talents of silver in two bags, with two festal garments, and laid them upon two of his servants; and they carried them before Geha'zi. [24]And when he came to the hill, he took them from their hand, and put them in the house; and he sent the men away, and they departed. [25]He went in, and stood before his master, and Eli'sha said to him, "Where have you been, Geha'zi?" And he said, "Your servant went nowhere." [26]But he said to him, "Did I not go with you in spirit when the man turned from his chariot to meet you? Was it a time to accept money and garments, olive orchards and vineyards,

sheep and oxen, menservants and maidservants? [27]Therefore the leprosy of Na'aman shall cling to you, and to your descendants for ever." So he went out from his presence a leper, as white as snow.

The Miracle of the Axe Head

6 Now the sons of the prophets said to Eli'sha, "See, the place where we dwell under your charge is too small for us. [2]Let us go to the Jordan and each of us get there a log, and let us make a place for us to dwell there." And he answered, "Go." [3]Then one of them said, "Be pleased to go with your servants." And he answered, "I will go." [4]So he went with them. And when they came to the Jordan, they cut down trees. [5]But as one was felling a log, his axe head fell into the water; and he cried out, "Alas, my master! It was borrowed." [6]Then the man of God said, "Where did it fall?" When he showed him the place, he cut off a stick, and threw it in there, and made the iron float. [7]And he said, "Take it up." So he reached out his hand and took it.

A Syrian Attack Is Thwarted

8 Once when the king of Syria was warring against Israel, he took counsel with his servants, saying, "At such and such a place shall be my camp." [9]But the man of God sent word to the king of Israel, "Beware that you do not pass this place, for the Syrians are going down there." [10]And the king of Israel sent to the place of which the man of God told him. Thus he used to warn him, so that he saved himself there more than once or twice.

11 And the mind of the king of Syria was greatly troubled because of this incident; and he called his servants and said to them, "Will you not show me who of us is for the king of Israel?" [12]And one of his servants said, "None, my lord, O king; but Eli'sha, the prophet who is in Israel, tells the king of Israel the words that you speak in your bedchamber." [13]And he said, "Go and see where he is, that I may send and seize him." It was told him, "Behold, he is in Do'than." [14]So he sent there horses and chariots and a great army; and they came by night, and surrounded the city.

15 When the servant of the man of God rose early in the morning and went out, behold, an army with horses and chariots was round about the city. And the servant said, "Alas, my master! What shall we do?" [16]He said, "Fear not, for those who are with us are more than those who are with them." [17]Then Eli'sha prayed, and said, "O LORD, I beg you, open his eyes that he may see." So the LORD opened the eyes of the young man, and he saw; and behold, the mountain was full of horses

---

[e] Another reading is *Amana.*
[*] 5:15: A forthright monotheism that not even an Israelite could improve on. However, Naaman realized that Yahweh had a special relation to Israel; cf. verse 17.

and chariots of fire round about Eli'sha. ¹⁸And when the Syrians came down against him, Eli'sha prayed to the LORD, and said, "Strike this people, I pray you, with blindness." So he struck them with blindness in accordance with the prayer of Elisha. ¹⁹And Eli'sha said to them, "This is not the way, and this is not the city; follow me, and I will bring you to the man whom you seek." And he led them to Samar'ia.

20 As soon as they entered Samar'ia, Eli'sha said, "O LORD, open the eyes of these men, that they may see." So the LORD opened their eyes, and they saw; and behold, they were in the midst of Samaria. ²¹When the king of Israel saw them he said to Eli'sha, "My father, shall I slay them? Shall I slay them?" ²²He answered, "You shall not slay them. Would you slay those whom you have taken captive with your sword and with your bow? Set bread and water before them, that they may eat and drink and go to their master." ²³So he prepared for them a great feast; and when they had eaten and drunk, he sent them away, and they went to their master. And the Syrians came no more on raids into the land of Israel.

Ben-hadad's Siege of Samaria

24 Afterward Ben-ha'dad king of Syria mustered his entire army, and went up, and besieged Samar'ia. ²⁵And there was a great famine in Samar'ia, as they besieged it, until a donkey's head was sold for eighty shekels of silver, and the fourth part of a kab of dove's dung for five shekels of silver. ²⁶Now as the king of Israel was passing by upon the wall, a woman cried out to him, saying, "Help, my lord, O king!" ²⁷And he said, "If the LORD will not help you, how shall I help you? From the threshing floor, or from the wine press?" ²⁸And the king asked her, "What is your trouble?" She answered, "This woman said to me, 'Give your son, that we may eat him today, and we will eat my son tomorrow.' ²⁹So we boiled my son, and ate him. And on the next day I said to her, 'Give your son, that we may eat him'; but she has hidden her son." ³⁰When the king heard the words of the woman he tore his clothes— now he was passing by upon the wall—and the people looked, and behold, he had sackcloth beneath upon his body—³¹and he said, "May God do so to me, and more also, if the head of Eli'sha the son of Sha'phat remains on his shoulders today."

32 Eli'sha was sitting in his house, and the elders were sitting with him. Now the king had dispatched a man from his presence; but before the messenger arrived Elisha said to the elders, "Do you see how this murderer has sent to take off my head? Look, when the messenger comes, shut the door, and hold the door fast against him. Is not the sound of his master's feet behind him?" ³³And while he was still speaking with them, the

king ᶠ came down to him and said, "This trouble is from the LORD! Why should I wait for the LORD any longer?" ¹But Eli'sha said, "Hear the word of the LORD: thus says the LORD, Tomorrow about this time a measure of fine meal shall be sold for a shekel, and two measures of barley for a shekel, at the gate of Samar'ia." ²Then the captain on whose hand the king leaned said to the man of God, "If the LORD himself should make windows in heaven, could this thing be?" But he said, "You shall see it with your own eyes, but you shall not eat of it."

The Syrians Flee

3 Now there were four men who were lepers at the entrance to the gate; and they said to one another, "Why do we sit here till we die? ⁴If we say, 'Let us enter the city,' the famine is in the city, and we shall die there; and if we sit here, we die also. So now come, let us go over to the camp of the Syrians; if they spare our lives we shall live, and if they kill us we shall but die." ⁵So they arose at twilight to go to the camp of the Syrians; but when they came to the edge of the camp of the Syrians, behold, there was no one there. ⁶For the Lord had made the army of the Syrians hear the sound of chariots, and of horses, the sound of a great army, so that they said to one another, "Behold, the king of Israel has hired against us the kings of the Hittites and the kings of Egypt to come upon us." ⁷So they fled away in the twilight and forsook their tents, their horses, and their donkeys, leaving the camp as it was, and fled for their lives. ⁸And when these lepers came to the edge of the camp, they went into a tent, and ate and drank, and they carried off silver and gold and clothing, and went and hid them; then they came back, and entered another tent, and carried off things from it, and went and hid them.

9 Then they said to one another, "We are not doing right. This day is a day of good news; if we are silent and wait until the morning light, punishment will overtake us; now therefore come, let us go and tell the king's household." ¹⁰So they came and called to the gatekeepers of the city, and told them, "We came to the camp of the Syrians, and behold, there was no one to be seen or heard there, nothing but the horses tied, and the donkeys tied, and the tents as they were." ¹¹Then the gatekeepers called out, and it was told within the king's household. ¹²And the king rose in the night, and said to his servants, "I will tell you what the Syrians have prepared against us. They know that we are hungry; therefore they have gone out of the camp to hide themselves in the open country, thinking, 'When they come out of the city, we shall take them alive and get into the

---

ᶠ See 7:2: Heb *messenger*.

city.' " ¹³And one of his servants said, "Let some men take five of the remaining horses, seeing that those who are left here will fare like the whole multitude of Israel that have already perished; let us send and see." ¹⁴So they took two mounted men, and the king sent them after the army of the Syrians, saying, "Go and see." ¹⁵So they went after them as far as the Jordan; and, behold, all the way was littered with garments and equipment which the Syrians had thrown away in their haste. And the messengers returned, and told the king.

16 Then the people went out, and plundered the camp of the Syrians. So a measure of fine meal was sold for a shekel, and two measures of barley for a shekel, according to the word of the LORD. ¹⁷Now the king had appointed the captain on whose hand he leaned to have charge of the gate; and the people trod upon him in the gate, so that he died, as the man of God had said when the king came down to him. ¹⁸For when the man of God had said to the king, "Two measures of barley shall be sold for a shekel, and a measure of fine meal for a shekel, about this time tomorrow in the gate of Samar'ia," ¹⁹the captain had answered the man of God, "If the LORD himself should make windows in heaven, could such a thing be?" And he had said, "You shall see it with your own eyes, but you shall not eat of it." ²⁰And so it happened to him, for the people trod upon him in the gate and he died.

The Shunammite Woman's Land Restored

8 Now Eli'sha had said to the woman whose son he had restored to life, "Arise, and depart with your household, and sojourn wherever you can; for the LORD has called for a famine, and it will come upon the land for seven years." ²So the woman arose, and did according to the word of the man of God; she went with her household and sojourned in the land of the Philis'tines seven years. ³And at the end of the seven years, when the woman returned from the land of the Philis'tines, she went forth to appeal to the king for her house and her land. ⁴Now the king was talking with Geha'zi the servant of the man of God, saying, "Tell me all the great things that Eli'sha has done." ⁵And while he was telling the king how Eli'sha had restored the dead to life, behold, the woman whose son he had restored to life appealed to the king for her house and her land. And Geha'zi said, "My lord, O king, here is the woman, and here is her son whom Elisha restored to life." ⁶And when the king asked the woman, she told him. So the king appointed an official for her, saying, "Restore all that was hers, together with all the produce of the fields from the day that she left the land until now."

The Death of Ben-hadad

7 Now Eli'sha came to Damascus. Ben-ha'dad the king of Syria was sick; and when it was told him, "The man of God has come here," ⁸the king said to Haz'ael, "Take a present with you and go to meet the man of God, and inquire of the LORD through him, saying, 'Shall I recover from this sickness?' " ⁹So Haz'ael went to meet him, and took a present with him, all kinds of goods of Damascus, forty camel loads. When he came and stood before him, he said, "Your son Ben-ha'dad king of Syria has sent me to you, saying, 'Shall I recover from this sickness?' " ¹⁰And Eli'sha said to him, "Go, say to him, 'You shall certainly recover'; but the LORD has shown me that he shall certainly die." ¹¹And he fixed his gaze and stared at him, until he was ashamed. And the man of God wept. ¹²And Haz'ael said, "Why does my lord weep?" He answered, "Because I know the evil that you will do to the sons of Israel; you will set on fire their fortresses, and you will slay their young men with the sword, and dash in pieces their little ones, and rip up their women with child." ¹³And Haz'ael said, "What is your servant, who is but a dog, that he should do this great thing?" Eli'sha answered, "The LORD has shown me that you are to be king over Syria." ¹⁴Then he departed from Eli'sha, and came to his master, who said to him, "What did Elisha say to you?" And he answered, "He told me that you would certainly recover." ¹⁵But the next day he took the coverlet and dipped it in water and spread it over his face, till he died. And Haz'ael became king in his stead.

Jehoram Reigns over Judah

16 In the fifth year of Jo'ram the son of A'hab, king of Israel, ᵍ Jeho'ram the son of Jehosh'aphat, king of Judah, began to reign. ¹⁷He was thirty-two years old when he became king, and he reigned eight years in Jerusalem. ¹⁸And he walked in the way of the kings of Israel, as the house of A'hab had done, for the daughter of Ahab was his wife. And he did what was evil in the sight of the LORD. ¹⁹Yet the LORD would not destroy Judah, for the sake of David his servant, since he promised to give a lamp to him and to his sons for ever.

20 In his days E'dom revolted from the rule of Judah, and set up a king of their own. ²¹Then Jo'ram passed over to Za'ir with all his chariots, and rose by night, and he and his chariot commanders struck the E'domites who had surrounded him; but his army fled home. ²²So E'dom revolted from the rule of Judah to this day. Then Libnah revolted at the same time. ²³Now the rest of the acts of Jo'ram, and all that he did, are they not written in the Book of the Chronicles of the Kings of Judah? ²⁴So Jo'ram slept with his fathers, and was buried with his fathers in the city of David; and Ahazi'ah his son reigned in his stead.

ᵍ Gk Syr: Heb *Israel, Jehoshaphat being king of Judah.*
8:17–24: 2 Chron 21:5–10, 20.
8:24–29: 2 Chron 22:1–6.

Ahaziah Reigns over Judah

25 In the twelfth year of Jo'ram the son of A'hab, king of Israel, Ahazi'ah the son of Jeho'ram, king of Judah, began to reign. 26Ahazi'ah was twenty-two years old when he began to reign, and he reigned one year in Jerusalem. His mother's name was Athali'ah; she was a granddaughter of Omri king of Israel. 27He also walked in the way of the house of A'hab, and did what was evil in the sight of the LORD, as the house of Ahab had done, for he was son-in-law to the house of Ahab.

28 He went with Jo'ram the son of A'hab to make war against Haz'ael king of Syria at Ra'mothgil'ead, where the Syrians wounded Joram. 29And King Jo'ram returned to be healed in Jezre'el of the wounds which the Syrians had given him at Ra'mah, when he fought against Haz'ael king of Syria. And Ahazi'ah the son of Jeho'ram king of Judah went down to see Joram the son of A'hab in Jezre'el, because he was sick.

Anointing of Jehu

9 Then Eli'sha the prophet called one of the sons of the prophets and said to him, "Gird up your loins, and take this flask of oil in your hand, and go to Ra'moth-gil'ead. 2And when you arrive, look there for Je'hu the son of Jehosh'aphat, son of Nimshi; and go in and bid him rise from among his fellows, and lead him to an inner chamber. 3Then take the flask of oil, and pour it on his head, and say, 'Thus says the LORD, I anoint you king over Israel.' Then open the door and flee; do not tarry."

4 So the young man, the prophet,h went to Ra'moth-gil'ead. 5And when he came, behold, the commanders of the army were in council; and he said, "I have an errand to you, O commander." And Je'hu said, "To which of us all?" And he said, "To you, O commander." 6So he arose, and went into the house; and the young man poured the oil on his head, saying to him, "Thus says the LORD the God of Israel, I anoint you king over the people of the LORD, over Israel. 7And you shall strike down the house of A'hab your master, that I may avenge on Jez'ebel the blood of my servants the prophets, and the blood of all the servants of the LORD. 8For the whole house of A'hab shall perish; and I will cut off from Ahab every male, bond or free, in Israel. 9And I will make the house of A'hab like the house of Jerobo'am the son of Ne'bat, and like the house of Ba'asha the son of Ahi'jah. 10And the dogs shall eat Jez'ebel in the territory of Jezre'el, and none shall bury her." Then he opened the door, and fled.

11 When Je'hu came out to the servants of his master, they said to him, "Is all well? Why did this mad fellow come to you?" And he said to them, "You know the fellow and his talk." 12And they said, "That is not true; tell us now." And he said, "Thus and so he spoke to me, saying, 'Thus says the LORD, I anoint you king over Israel.'" 13Then in haste every man of them took his garment, and put it under him on the barei steps, and they blew the trumpet, and proclaimed, "Je'hu is king."

Joram of Israel Killed

14 Thus Je'hu the son of Jehosh'aphat the son of Nimshi conspired against Jo'ram. (Now Joram with all Israel had been on guard at Ra'mothgil'ead against Haz'ael king of Syria; 15but King Jo'ram had returned to be healed in Jezre'el of the wounds which the Syrians had given him, when he fought with Haz'ael king of Syria.) So Je'hu said, "If this is your mind, then let no one slip out of the city to go and tell the news in Jezreel." 16Then Je'hu mounted his chariot, and went to Jezre'el, for Jo'ram lay there. And Ahazi'ah king of Judah had come down to visit Joram.

17 Now the watchman was standing on the tower in Jezre'el, and he spied the company of Je'hu as he came, and said, "I see a company." And Jo'ram said, "Take a horseman, and send to meet them, and let him say, 'Is it peace?'" 18So a man on horseback went to meet him, and said, "Thus says the king, 'Is it peace?'" And Je'hu said, "What have you to do with peace? Turn round and ride behind me." And the watchman reported, saying, "The messenger reached them, but he is not coming back." 19Then he sent out a second horseman, who came to them, and said, "Thus the king has said, 'Is it peace?'" And Je'hu answered, "What have you to do with peace? Turn round and ride behind me." 20Again the watchman reported, "He reached them, but he is not coming back. And the driving is like the driving of Je'hu the son of Nimshi; for he drives furiously."

21 Jo'ram said, "Make ready." And they made ready his chariot. Then Joram king of Israel and Ahazi'ah king of Judah set out, each in his chariot, and went to meet Je'hu, and met him at the property of Naboth the Jezre'elite. 22And when Jo'ram saw Je'hu, he said, "Is it peace, Jehu?" He answered, "What peace can there be, so long as the harlotries and the sorceries of your mother Jez'ebel are so many?" 23Then Jo'ram reined about and fled, saying to Ahazi'ah, "Treachery, O Ahaziah!" 24And Je'hu drew his bow with his full strength, and shot Jo'ram between the shoulders, so that the arrow pierced his heart, and he sank in his chariot.* 25Je'hu said to Bidkar his aide, "Take him up, and cast him on the plot of ground belonging to Naboth the Jezre'elite; for remember, when you and I rode side by side behind A'hab

---

h Gk Syr: Heb *the young man, the young man, the prophet.*
i The meaning of the Hebrew word is uncertain.
9:1—10:36; 2 Chron 22:7–9.
9:25: 1 Kings 21:19.
* 9:24: So was the sin of Ahab visited upon his son, according to the word of the Lord; cf. 1 Kings 21:29.

his father, how the Lord uttered this oracle against him: 26'As surely as I saw yesterday the blood of Naboth and the blood of his sons—says the Lord—I will repay you on this plot of ground.' Now therefore take him up and cast him on the plot of ground, in accordance with the word of the Lord."

Ahaziah of Judah Killed

27 When Ahazi'ah the king of Judah saw this, he fled in the direction of Beth-hag'gan. And Je'hu pursued him, and said, "Shoot him also"; and they shot him [j] in the chariot at the ascent of Gur, which is by Ib'leam. And he fled to Megid'do, and died there. 28His servants carried him in a chariot to Jerusalem, and buried him in his tomb with his fathers in the city of David.

29 In the eleventh year of Jo'ram the son of A'hab, Ahazi'ah began to reign over Judah.

Jezebel's Violent Death

30 When Je'hu came to Jezre'el, Jez'ebel heard of it; and she painted her eyes, and adorned her head, and looked out of the window. 31And as Je'hu entered the gate, she said, "Is it peace, you Zimri, murderer of your master?" 32And he lifted up his face to the window, and said, "Who is on my side? Who?" Two or three eunuchs looked out at him. 33He said, "Throw her down." So they threw her down; and some of her blood spattered on the wall and on the horses, and they trampled on her. 34Then he went in and ate and drank; and he said, "See now to this cursed woman, and bury her; for she is a king's daughter." 35But when they went to bury her, they found no more of her than the skull and the feet and the palms of her hands. 36When they came back and told him, he said, "This is the word of the Lord, which he spoke by his servant Eli'jah the Tishbite, 'In the territory of Jezre'el the dogs shall eat the flesh of Jez'ebel; 37and the corpse of Jez'ebel shall be as dung upon the face of the field in the territory of Jezre'el, so that no one can say, This is Jezebel.'"

Massacre of Ahab's Descendants

10 Now A'hab had seventy sons in Samar'ia. So Je'hu wrote letters, and sent them to Samar'ia, to the rulers of the city, [k] to the elders, and to the guardians of the sons of Ahab, saying, 2"Now then, as soon as this letter comes to you, seeing your master's sons are with you, and there are with you chariots and horses, fortified cities also, and weapons, 3select the best and fittest of your master's sons and set him on his father's throne, and fight for your master's house." 4But they were exceedingly afraid, and said, "Behold, the two kings could not stand before him; how then can we stand?" 5So he who was over the palace, and he who was over the city, together with the elders and the guardians, sent to Je'hu, saying, "We are your servants, and we will do all that you bid us. We will not make

any one king; do whatever is good in your eyes." 6Then he wrote to them a second letter, saying, "If you are on my side, and if you are ready to obey me, take the heads of your master's sons, and come to me at Jezre'el tomorrow at this time." Now the king's sons, seventy persons, were with the great men of the city, who were bringing them up. 7And when the letter came to them, they took the king's sons, and slew them, seventy persons, and put their heads in baskets, and sent them to him at Jezre'el. 8When the messenger came and told him, "They have brought the heads of the king's sons," he said, "Lay them in two heaps at the entrance of the gate until the morning." 9Then in the morning, when he went out, he stood, and said to all the people, "You are innocent. It was I who conspired against my master, and slew him; but who struck down all these? 10Know then that there shall fall to the earth nothing of the word of the Lord, which the Lord spoke concerning the house of A'hab; for the Lord has done what he said by his servant Eli'jah." 11So Je'hu slew all that remained of the house of A'hab in Jezre'el, all his great men, and his familiar friends, and his priests, until he left him none remaining.

12 Then he set out and went to Samar'ia. On the way, when he was at Beth-ek'ed of the Shepherds, 13Je'hu met the kinsmen of Ahazi'ah king of Judah, and he said, "Who are you?" And they answered, "We are the kinsmen of Ahazi'ah, and we came down to visit the royal princes and the sons of the queen mother." 14He said, "Take them alive." And they took them alive, and slew them at the pit of Beth-ek'ed, forty-two persons, and he spared none of them.

15 And when he departed from there, he met Jehon'adab the son of Re'chab coming to meet him; and he greeted him, and said to him, "Is your heart true to my heart as mine is to yours?" [l] And Jehonadab answered, "It is." Je'hu said, [m] "If it is, give me your hand." So he gave him his hand. And Jehu took him up with him into the chariot. 16And he said, "Come with me, and see my zeal for the Lord." So he [n] had him ride in his chariot. 17And when he came to Samar'ia, he slew all that remained to A'hab in Samaria, till he had wiped them out, according to the word of the Lord which he spoke to Eli'jah.

Jehu Slaughters the Worshipers of Baal

18 Then Je'hu assembled all the people, and said to them, "A'hab served Ba'al a little; but Jehu will serve him much. 19Now therefore call to me

---

[j] Syr Vg Compare Gk: Heb lacks *and they shot him.*
[k] Gk Vg: Heb *Jezreel.*
[l] Gk: Heb *Is it right with your heart, as my heart is with your heart?*
[m] Gk: Heb lacks *Jehu said.*
[n] Gk Syr Tg: Heb *they.*
9:36: 1 Kings 21:23.

all the prophets of Ba′al, all his worshipers and all his priests; let none be missing, for I have a great sacrifice to offer to Baal; whoever is missing shall not live." But Je′hu did it with cunning in order to destroy the worshipers of Ba′al. [20]And Je′hu ordered, "Sanctify a solemn assembly for Ba′al." So they proclaimed it. [21]And Je′hu sent throughout all Israel; and all the worshipers of Ba′al came, so that there was not a man left who did not come. And they entered the house of Baal, and the house of Baal was filled from one end to the other. [22]He said to him who was in charge of the wardrobe, "Bring out the vestments for all the worshipers of Ba′al." So he brought out the vestments for them. [23]Then Je′hu went into the house of Ba′al with Jehon′adab the son of Re′chab; and he said to the worshipers of Baal, "Search, and see that there is no servant of the Lord here among you, but only the worshipers of Baal." [24]Then he° went in to offer sacrifices and burnt offerings.

Now Je′hu had stationed eighty men outside, and said, "The man who allows any of those whom I give into your hands to escape shall forfeit his life." [25]So as soon as he had made an end of offering the burnt offering, Je′hu said to the guard and to the officers, "Go in and slay them; let not a man escape." So when they put them to the sword, the guard and the officers cast them out and went into the inner roomᵖ of the house of Ba′al [26]and they brought out the pillar that was in the house of Ba′al, and burned it. [27]And they demolished the pillar of Ba′al, and demolished the house of Baal, and made it a latrine to this day.

28 Thus Je′hu wiped out Ba′al from Israel. [29]But Je′hu did not turn aside from the sins of Jerobo′am the son of Ne′bat, which he made Israel to sin, the golden calves that were in Bethel, and in Dan. [30]And the Lord said to Je′hu, "Because you have done well in carrying out what is right in my eyes, and have done to the house of A′hab according to all that was in my heart, your sons of the fourth generation shall sit on the throne of Israel." [31]But Je′hu was not careful to walk in the law of the Lord the God of Israel with all his heart; he did not turn from the sins of Jerobo′am, which he made Israel to sin.

Death of Jehu

32 In those days the Lord began to cut off parts of Israel. Haz′ael defeated them throughout the territory of Israel: [33]from the Jordan eastward, all the land of Gilead, the Gadites, and the Reubenites, and the Manas′sites, from Aro′er, which is by the valley of the Arnon, that is, Gilead and Bashan. [34]Now the rest of the acts of Je′hu, and all that he did, and all his might, are they not written in the Book of the Chronicles of the Kings of Israel? [35]So Je′hu slept with his fathers, and they buried him in Samar′ia. And Jeho′ahaz his

son reigned in his stead. [36]The time that Je′hu reigned over Israel in Samar′ia was twenty-eight years.

Athaliah Reigns over Judah

11 Now when Athali′ah the mother of Aha-zi′ah saw that her son was dead, she arose and destroyed all the royal family. [2]But Jehosh′-eba, the daughter of King Jo′ram, sister of Aha-zi′ah, took Jo′ash the son of Ahaziah, and stole him away from among the king's sons who were about to be slain, and she put �q him and his nurse in a bedchamber. Thus she ʳ hid him from Atha-li′ah, so that he was not slain; [3]and he remained with her six years, hid in the house of the Lord, while Athali′ah reigned over the land.

Jehoiada Anoints the Child Joash

4 But in the seventh year Jehoi′ada sent and brought the captains of the Cari′tes and of the guards, and had them come to him in the house of the Lord; and he made a covenant with them and put them under oath in the house of the Lord, and he showed them the king's son. [5]And he commanded them, "This is the thing that you shall do: one third of you, those who come off duty on the sabbath and guard the king's house [6](another third being at the gate Sur and a third at the gate behind the guards), shall guard the palace; [7]and the two divisions of you, which come on duty in force on the sabbath and guard the house of the Lord,ˢ [8]shall surround the king, each with his weapons in his hand; and whoever approaches the ranks is to be slain. Be with the king when he goes out and when he comes in."

9 The captains did according to all that Jehoi′-ada the priest commanded, and each brought his men who were to go off duty on the sabbath, with those who were to come on duty on the sabbath, and came to Jehoiada the priest. [10]And the priest delivered to the captains the spears and shields that had been King David's, which were in the house of the Lord; [11]and the guards stood, every man with his weapons in his hand, from the south side of the house to the north side of the house, around the altar and the house.ᵗ [12]Then he brought out the king's son, and put the crown upon him, and gave him the covenant; and they proclaimed him king, and anointed him; and they clapped their hands, and said, "Long live the king!"

Death of Athaliah

13 When Athali′ah heard the noise of the guard and of the people, she went into the house of the Lord to the people; [14]and when she looked,

---

° Gk Compare verse 25: Heb *they.*
ᵖ Cn: Heb *city.*
�q With 2 Chron 22:11: Heb lacks *and she put.*
ʳ Gk Syr Vg Compare 2 Chron 22:11: Heb *they.*
ˢ Heb *the Lord to the king.*
ᵗ Heb *the house to the king.*
11:1–20: 2 Chron 22:10—23:21.

there was the king standing by the pillar, according to the custom, and the captains and the trumpeters beside the king, and all the people of the land rejoicing and blowing trumpets. And Athali'ah tore her clothes, and cried, "Treason! Treason!" [15]Then Jehoi'ada the priest commanded the captains who were set over the army, "Bring her out between the ranks; and slay with the sword any one who follows her." For the priest said, "Let her not be slain in the house of the LORD." [16]So they laid hands on her; and she went through the horses' entrance to the king's house, and there she was slain.

17 And Jehoi'ada made a covenant between the LORD and the king and people, that they should be the LORD's people; and also between the king and the people. [18]Then all the people of the land went to the house of Ba'al, and tore it down; his altars and his images they broke in pieces, and they slew Mattan the priest of Baal before the altars. And the priest posted watchmen over the house of the LORD. [19]And he took the captains, the Cari'tes, the guards, and all the people of the land; and they brought the king down from the house of the LORD, marching through the gate of the guards to the king's house. And he took his seat on the throne of the kings. [20]So all the people of the land rejoiced; and the city was quiet after Athali'ah had been slain with the sword at the king's house.

Reign of Jehoash and the Repair of the Temple

21 [u] Jeho'ash was seven years old when he began to reign.

12 In the seventh year of Je'hu Jeho'ash began to reign, and he reigned forty years in Jerusalem. His mother's name was Zib'iah of Be'er-she'ba. [2]And Jeho'ash did what was right in the eyes of the LORD all his days, because Jehoi'ada the priest instructed him. [3]Nevertheless the high places were not taken away; the people continued to sacrifice and burn incense on the high places.

4 Jeho'ash said to the priests, "All the money of the holy things which is brought into the house of the LORD, the money for which each man is assessed—the money from the assessment of persons—and the money which a man's heart prompts him to bring into the house of the LORD, [5]let the priests take, each from his acquaintance; and let them repair the house wherever any need of repairs is discovered." [6]But by the twenty-third year of King Jeho'ash the priests had made no repairs on the house. [7]Therefore King Jeho'ash summoned Jehoi'ada the priest and the other priests and said to them, "Why are you not repairing the house? Now therefore take no more money from your acquaintances, but hand it over for the repair of the house." [8]So the priests agreed that they should take no more money from the people, and that they should not repair the house.

9 Then Jehoi'ada the priest took a chest, and bored a hole in the lid of it, and set it beside the altar on the right side as one entered the house of the LORD; and the priests who guarded the threshold put in it all the money that was brought into the house of the LORD. [10]And whenever they saw that there was much money in the chest, the king's secretary and the high priest came up and they counted and tied up in bags the money that was found in the house of the LORD. [11]Then they would give the money that was weighed out into the hands of the workmen who had the oversight of the house of the LORD; and they paid it out to the carpenters and the builders who worked upon the house of the LORD, [12]and to the masons and the stonecutters, as well as to buy timber and quarried stone for making repairs on the house of the LORD, and for any outlay upon the repairs of the house. [13]But there were not made for the house of the LORD basins of silver, snuffers, bowls, trumpets, or any vessels of gold, or of silver, from the money that was brought into the house of the LORD, [14]for that was given to the workmen who were repairing the house of the LORD with it. [15]And they did not ask an accounting from the men into whose hand they delivered the money to pay out to the workmen; for they dealt honestly. [16]The money from the guilt offerings and the money from the sin offerings was not brought into the house of the LORD; it belonged to the priests.

Hazael of Syria Threatens Jerusalem

17 At that time Haz'ael king of Syria went up and fought against Gath, and took it. But when Hazael set his face to go up against Jerusalem, [18]Jeho'ash king of Judah took all the votive gifts that Jehosh'aphat and Jeho'ram and Ahazi'ah, his fathers, the kings of Judah, had dedicated, and his own votive gifts, and all the gold that was found in the treasuries of the house of the LORD and of the king's house, and sent these to Haz'ael king of Syria. Then Hazael went away from Jerusalem.

Death of Joash

19 Now the rest of the acts of Jo'ash, and all that he did, are they not written in the Book of the Chronicles of the Kings of Judah? [20]His servants arose and made a conspiracy, and slew Jo'ash in the house of Millo, on the way that goes down to Silla. [21]It was Jo'zacar the son of Shim'eath and Jeho'zabad the son of Shomer, his servants, who struck him down, so that he died. And they buried him with his fathers in the city of David, and Amazi'ah his son reigned in his stead.

---

[u] Ch 12:1 in Heb.
11:21–12:14: 2 Chron 24:1–14.
12:17–21: 2 Chron 24:23–26.

Jehoahaz Reigns over Israel

13 In the twenty-third year of Jo'ash the son of Ahazi'ah, king of Judah, Jeho'ahaz the son of Je'hu began to reign over Israel in Samar'ia, and he reigned seventeen years. [2]He did what was evil in the sight of the LORD, and followed the sins of Jerobo'am the son of Ne'bat, which he made Israel to sin; he did not depart from them. [3]And the anger of the LORD was kindled against Israel, and he gave them continually into the hand of Haz'ael king of Syria and into the hand of Ben-ha'dad the son of Hazael. [4]Then Jeho'ahaz besought the LORD, and the LORD listened to him; for he saw the oppression of Israel, how the king of Syria oppressed them. [5](Therefore the LORD gave Israel a savior, so that they escaped from the hand of the Syrians; and the sons of Israel dwelt in their homes as formerly. [6]Nevertheless they did not depart from the sins of the house of Jerobo'am, which he made Israel to sin, but walked ᵛ in them; and the Ashe'rah also remained in Samar'ia.) [7]For there was not left to Jeho'ahaz an army of more than fifty horsemen and ten chariots and ten thousand footmen; for the king of Syria had destroyed them and made them like the dust at threshing. [8]Now the rest of the acts of Jeho'ahaz and all that he did, and his might, are they not written in the Book of the Chronicles of the Kings of Israel? [9]So Jeho'ahaz slept with his fathers, and they buried him in Samar'ia; and Jo'ash his son reigned in his stead.

Jehoash Reigns over Israel

10 In the thirty-seventh year of Jo'ash king of Judah Jeho'ash the son of Jeho'ahaz began to reign over Israel in Samar'ia, and he reigned sixteen years. [11]He also did what was evil in the sight of the LORD; he did not depart from all the sins of Jerobo'am the son of Ne'bat, which he made Israel to sin, but he walked in them. [12]Now the rest of the acts of Jo'ash, and all that he did, and the might with which he fought against Amazi'ah king of Judah, are they not written in the Book of the Chronicles of the Kings of Israel? [13]So Jo'ash slept with his fathers, and Jerobo'am sat upon his throne; and Joash was buried in Samar'ia with the kings of Israel.

Death of Elisha

14 Now when Eli'sha had fallen sick with the illness of which he was to die, Jo'ash king of Israel went down to him, and wept before him, crying, "My father, my father! The chariots of Israel and its horsemen!" [15]And Eli'sha said to him, "Take a bow and arrows"; so he took a bow and arrows. [16]Then he said to the king of Israel, "Draw the bow"; and he drew it. And Eli'sha laid his hands upon the king's hands. [17]And he said, "Open the window eastward"; and he opened it. Then Eli'sha said, "Shoot"; and he shot. And he said, "The LORD's arrow of victory, the arrow of victory over Syria! For you shall fight the Syrians in A'phek until you have made an end of them." [18]And he said, "Take the arrows"; and he took them. And he said to the king of Israel, "Strike the ground with them"; and he struck three times, and stopped. [19]Then the man of God was angry with him, and said, "You should have struck five or six times; then you would have struck down Syria until you had made an end of it, but now you will strike down Syria only three times."

20 So Eli'sha died, and they buried him. Now bands of Moabites used to invade the land in the spring of the year. [21]And as a man was being buried, behold, a marauding band was seen and the man was cast into the grave of Eli'sha; and as soon as the man touched the bones of Elisha, he revived, and stood on his feet.

Israel Recaptures Its Cities from Syria

22 Now Haz'ael king of Syria oppressed Israel all the days of Jeho'ahaz. [23]But the LORD was gracious to them and had compassion on them, and he turned toward them, because of his covenant with Abraham, Isaac, and Jacob, and would not destroy them; nor has he cast them from his presence until now.

24 When Haz'ael king of Syria died, Ben-ha'dad his son became king in his stead. [25]Then Jeho'ash the son of Jeho'ahaz took again from Ben-ha'dad the son of Haz'ael the cities which he had taken from Jehoahaz his father in war. Three times Jo'ash defeated him and recovered the cities of Israel.

Amaziah Reigns over Judah

14 In the second year of Jo'ash the son of Jo'ahaz, king of Israel, Amazi'ah the son of Joash, king of Judah, began to reign. [2]He was twenty-five years old when he began to reign, and he reigned twenty-nine years in Jerusalem. His mother's name was Je'ho-ad'din of Jerusalem. [3]And he did what was right in the eyes of the LORD, yet not like David his father; he did in all things as Jo'ash his father had done. [4]But the high places were not removed; the people still sacrificed and burned incense on the high places. [5]And as soon as the royal power was firmly in his hand he killed his servants who had slain the king his father. [6]But he did not put to death the children of the murderers; according to what is written in the book of the law of Moses, where the LORD commanded, "The fathers shall not be put to death for the children, or the children be put to death for the fathers; but every man shall die for his own sin."

7 He killed ten thousand E'domites in the Valley of Salt and took Se'la by storm, and called it Jok'the-el, which is its name to this day.

ᵛ Gk Syr Tg Vg: Heb *he walked.*
14:2–6: 2 Chron 25:1–4.
14:7: 2 Chron 25:11.

8 Then Amazi'ah sent messengers to Jeho'ash the son of Jeho'ahaz, son of Je'hu, king of Israel, saying, "Come, let us look one another in the face." [9]And Jeho'ash king of Israel sent word to Amazi'ah king of Judah, "A thistle in Lebanon sent to a cedar in Lebanon, saying, 'Give your daughter to my son for a wife'; and a wild beast of Lebanon passed by and trampled down the thistle. [10]You have indeed struck down E'dom, and your heart has lifted you up. Be content with your glory, and stay at home; for why should you provoke trouble so that you fall, you and Judah with you?"

11 But Amazi'ah would not listen. So Jeho'ash king of Israel went up, and he and Amaziah king of Judah faced one another in battle at Beth-she'mesh, which belongs to Judah. [12]And Judah was defeated by Israel, and every man fled to his home. [13]And Jeho'ash king of Israel captured Amazi'ah king of Judah, the son of Jehoash, son of Ahazi'ah, at Beth-she'mesh, and came to Jerusalem, and broke down the wall of Jerusalem for four hundred cubits, from the E'phraim Gate to the Corner Gate. [14]And he seized all the gold and silver, and all the vessels that were found in the house of the Lord and in the treasuries of the king's house, also hostages, and he returned to Samar'ia.

15 Now the rest of the acts of Jeho'ash which he did, and his might, and how he fought with Amazi'ah king of Judah, are they not written in the Book of the Chronicles of the Kings of Israel? [16]And Jeho'ash slept with his fathers, and was buried in Samar'ia with the kings of Israel; and Jerobo'am his son reigned in his stead.

17 Amazi'ah the son of Jo'ash, king of Judah, lived fifteen years after the death of Jeho'ash son of Jeho'ahaz, king of Israel. [18]Now the rest of the deeds of Amazi'ah, are they not written in the Book of the Chronicles of the Kings of Judah? [19]And they made a conspiracy against him in Jerusalem, and he fled to La'chish. But they sent after him to Lachish, and slew him there. [20]And they brought him upon horses; and he was buried in Jerusalem with his fathers in the city of David. [21]And all the people of Judah took Azari'ah, * who was sixteen years old, and made him king instead of his father Amazi'ah. [22]He built E'lath and restored it to Judah, after the king slept with his fathers.

Jeroboam II Reigns over Israel

23 In the fifteenth year of Amazi'ah the son of Jo'ash, king of Judah, Jerobo'am the son of Joash, king of Israel, began to reign in Samar'ia, and he reigned forty-one years. [24]And he did what was evil in the sight of the Lord; he did not depart from all the sins of Jerobo'am the son of Ne'bat, which he made Israel to sin. [25]He restored the border of Israel from the entrance of Ha'math as far as the Sea of the Ar'abah, according to the word of the Lord, the God of Israel, which he spoke by his servant Jonah the son of Amit'tai, the prophet, who was from Gath-he'pher. [26]For the Lord saw that the affliction of Israel was very bitter, for there was none left, bond or free, and there was none to help Israel. [27]But the Lord had not said that he would blot out the name of Israel from under heaven, so he saved them by the hand of Jerobo'am the son of Jo'ash.

28 Now the rest of the acts of Jerobo'am, and all that he did, and his might, how he fought, and how he recovered for Israel Damascus and Ha'math, which had belonged to Judah, are they not written in the Book of the Chronicles of the Kings of Israel? [29]And Jerobo'am slept with his fathers, the kings of Israel, and Zechari'ah his son reigned in his stead.

Azariah Reigns over Judah

15 In the twenty-seventh year of Jerobo'am king of Israel Azari'ah the son of Amazi'ah, king of Judah, began to reign. [2]He was sixteen years old when he began to reign, and he reigned fifty-two years in Jerusalem. His mother's name was Jecoli'ah of Jerusalem. [3]And he did what was right in the eyes of the Lord, according to all that his father Amazi'ah had done. [4]Nevertheless the high places were not taken away; the people still sacrificed and burned incense on the high places. [5]And the Lord struck the king, so that he was a leper to the day of his death, and he dwelt in a separate house. And Jo'tham the king's son was over the household, governing the people of the land. [6]Now the rest of the acts of Azari'ah, and all that he did, are they not written in the Book of the Chronicles of the Kings of Judah? [7]And Azari'ah slept with his fathers, and they buried him with his fathers in the city of David, and Jo'tham his son reigned in his stead.

Zechariah Reigns over Israel

8 In the thirty-eighth year of Azari'ah king of Judah Zechari'ah the son of Jerobo'am reigned over Israel in Samar'ia six months. [9]And he did what was evil in the sight of the Lord, as his fathers had done. He did not depart from the sins of Jerobo'am the son of Ne'bat, which he made Israel to sin. [10]Shallum the son of Ja'besh conspired against him, and struck him down at Ib'leam, [w] and killed him, and reigned in his stead. [11]Now the rest of the deeds of Zechari'ah, behold, they are written in the Book of the Chronicles of the Kings of Israel. [12](This was the promise of the Lord which he gave to Je'hu, "Your sons shall sit

---

[w] Gk Compare 9:27: Heb *before the people.*
14:8–14: 2 Chron 25:17–24.
14:17–20: 2 Chron 25:25–28.
14:21, 22: 2 Chron 26:1, 2.
15:2, 3: 2 Chron 26:3, 4.
15:5–7: 2 Chron 26:20–23.
* 14:21, *Azariah:* Otherwise known as Uzziah; cf. 15:13; 2 Chron 26:1–23.

upon the throne of Israel to the fourth generation." And so it came to pass.)

Shallum Reigns over Israel

13 Shallum the son of Ja′besh began to reign in
the thirty-ninth year of Uzzi′ah king of Judah,
and he reigned one month in Samar′ia. [14]Then
Men′ahem the son of Gadi came up from Tirzah
and came to Samar′ia, and he struck down
Shallum the son of Ja′besh in Samaria and slew
him, and reigned in his stead. [15]Now the rest of
the deeds of Shallum, and the conspiracy which
he made, behold, they are written in the Book of
the Chronicles of the Kings of Israel. [16]At that
time Men′ahem sacked Tap′pu-ah * and all who
were in it and its territory from Tirzah on; because they did not open it to him, therefore he
sacked it, and he ripped up all the women in it
who were with child.

Menahem Reigns over Israel

17 In the thirty-ninth year of Azari′ah king of
Judah Men′ahem the son of Gadi began to reign
over Israel, and he reigned ten years in Samar′ia.
[18]And he did what was evil in the sight of the
Lord; he did not depart all his days from all
the sins of Jerobo′am the son of Ne′bat, which he
made Israel to sin. [19]Pul the king of Assyria came
against the land; and Men′ahem gave Pul * a
thousand talents of silver, that he might help him
to confirm his hold of the royal power. [20]Men′a-
hem exacted the money from Israel, that is, from
all the wealthy men, fifty shekels of silver from
every man, to give to the king of Assyria. So the
king of Assyria turned back, and did not stay
there in the land. [21]Now the rest of the deeds
of Men′ahem, and all that he did, are they not
written in the Book of the Chronicles of the
Kings of Israel? [22]And Men′ahem slept with his
fathers, and Pekahi′ah his son reigned in his
stead.

Pekahiah Reigns over Israel

23 In the fiftieth year of Azari′ah king of Judah
Pekahi′ah the son of Men′ahem began to reign
over Israel in Samar′ia, and he reigned two years.
[24]And he did what was evil in the sight of the
Lord; he did not turn away from the sins of
Jerobo′am the son of Ne′bat, which he made Israel
to sin. [25]And Pe′kah the son of Remali′ah, his
captain, conspired against him with fifty men of
the Gileadites, and slew him in Samar′ia, in the
citadel of the king's house; [y] he slew him, and
reigned in his stead. [26]Now the rest of the deeds
of Pekahi′ah, and all that he did, behold, they are
written in the Book of the Chronicles of the Kings
of Israel.

Pekah Reigns over Israel

27 In the fifty-second year of Azari′ah king of
Judah Pe′kah the son of Remali′ah began to reign
over Israel in Samar′ia, and he reigned twenty
years. [28]And he did what was evil in the sight of

the Lord; he did not depart from the sins of
Jerobo′am the son of Ne′bat, which he made Israel
to sin.

29 In the days of Pe′kah king of Israel Tig′lath-
pile′ser king of Assyria came and captured I′jon,
A′bel-beth-ma′acah, Jano′ah, Ke′desh, Ha′zor,
Gilead, and Galilee, all the land of Naph′tali; and
he carried the people captive to Assyria. [30]Then
Hoshe′a the son of E′lah made a conspiracy
against Pe′kah the son of Remali′ah, and struck
him down, and slew him, and reigned in his stead,
in the twentieth year of Jo′tham the son of Uzzi′ah.
[31]Now the rest of the acts of Pe′kah, and all that
he did, behold, they are written in the Book of the
Chronicles of the Kings of Israel.

Jotham Reigns over Judah

32 In the second year of Pe′kah the son of
Remali′ah, king of Israel, Jo′tham the son of
Uzzi′ah, king of Judah, began to reign. [33]He was
twenty-five years old when he began to reign, and
he reigned sixteen years in Jerusalem. His
mother's name was Jeru′sha the daughter of
Za′dok. [34]And he did what was right in the eyes of
the Lord, according to all that his father Uzzi′ah
had done. [35]Nevertheless the high places were not
removed; the people still sacrificed and burned
incense on the high places. He built the upper gate
of the house of the Lord. [36]Now the rest of the acts
of Jotham, and all that he did, are they not written
in the Book of the Chronicles of the Kings of
Judah? [37]In those days the Lord began to send
Re′zin the king of Syria and Pe′kah the son of
Remali′ah against Judah. [38]Jo′tham slept with his
fathers, and was buried with his fathers in the
city of David his father; and A′haz his son reigned
in his stead.

Ahaz Reigns over Judah

16 In the seventeenth year of Pe′kah the son
of Remali′ah, A′haz the son of Jo′tham,
king of Judah, began to reign. [2]Ahaz was twenty
years old when he began to reign, and he reigned
sixteen years in Jerusalem. And he did not do
what was right in the eyes of the Lord his God,
as his father David had done, [3]but he walked in
the way of the kings of Israel. He even burned
his son as an offering, [z] according to the abominable practices of the nations whom the Lord
drove out before the people of Israel. † [4]And he
sacrificed and burned incense on the high places,
and on the hills, and under every green tree.

5 Then Re′zin king of Syria and Pe′kah the
son of Remali′ah, king of Israel, came up to wage

---

x Compare Gk: Heb *Tiphsah.*
y Heb adds *Argob and Arieh,* which probably belong to the list of places
in verse 29.
z Or *made his son to pass through the fire.*
15:33–35: 2 Chron 27:1–3.
15:38: 2 Chron 27:9.
16:2–4: 2 Chron 28:1–4.
* 15:19, *Pul:* i.e., Tiglath-pileser III; cf. verse 29.
† 16:3: Human sacrifice to Moloch was practiced in Phoenicia.

war on Jerusalem, and they besieged A'haz but could not conquer him. [6]At that time [a] the king of E'dom [b] recovered E'lath for Edom, [b] and drove the men of Judah from Elath; and the E'domites came to Elath, where they dwell to this day. [7]So A'haz sent messengers to Tig'lath-pile'ser king of Assyria, saying, "I am your servant and your son. Come up, and rescue me from the hand of the king of Syria and from the hand of the king of Israel, who are attacking me." [8]A'haz also took the silver and gold that was found in the house of the Lord and in the treasures of the king's house, and sent a present to the king of Assyria. [9]And the king of Assyria listened to him; the king of Assyria marched up against Damascus, and took it, carrying its people captive to Kir, and he killed Re'zin.

10 When King A'haz went to Damascus to meet Tig'lath-pile'ser king of Assyria, he saw the altar that was at Damascus. And King Ahaz sent to Uri'ah the priest a model of the altar, and its pattern, exact in all its details. [11]And Uri'ah the priest built the altar; in accordance with all that King A'haz had sent from Damascus, so Uriah the priest made it, before King Ahaz arrived from Damascus. [12]And when the king came from Damascus, the king viewed the altar. Then the king drew near to the altar, and went up on it, [13]and burned his burnt offering and his cereal offering, and poured his drink offering, and threw the blood of his peace offerings upon the altar. [14]And the bronze altar which was before the Lord he removed from the front of the house, from the place between his altar and the house of the Lord, and put it on the north side of his altar. [15]And King A'haz commanded Uri'ah the priest, saying, "Upon the great altar burn the morning burnt offering, and the evening cereal offering, and the king's burnt offering, and his cereal offering, with the burnt offering of all the people of the land, and their cereal offering, and their drink offering; and throw upon it all the blood of the burnt offering, and all the blood of the sacrifice; but the bronze altar shall be for me to inquire by." [16]Uri'ah the priest did all this, as King A'haz commanded.

17 And King A'haz cut off the frames of the stands, and removed the laver from them, and he took down the sea from off the bronze oxen that were under it, and put it upon a pediment of stone. [18]And the covered way for the sabbath which had been built inside the palace, and the outer entrance for the king he removed from [c] the house of the Lord, because of the king of Assyria. [19]Now the rest of the acts of A'haz which he did, are they not written in the Book of the Chronicles of the Kings of Judah? [20]And A'haz slept with his fathers, and was buried with his fathers in the city of David; and Hezeki'ah his son reigned in his stead.

Hoshea Reigns over Israel

17 In the twelfth year of A'haz king of Judah Hoshe'a the son of E'lah began to reign in Samar'ia over Israel, and he reigned nine years. [2]And he did what was evil in the sight of the Lord, yet not as the kings of Israel who were before him. [3]Against him came up Shalmane'ser king of Assyria; and Hoshe'a became his vassal, and paid him tribute. [4]But the king of Assyria found treachery in Hoshe'a; for he had sent messengers to So, king of Egypt, and offered no tribute to the king of Assyria, as he had done year by year; therefore the king of Assyria shut him up, and bound him in prison. [5]Then the king of Assyria invaded all the land and came to Samar'ia, and for three years he besieged it. [6]In the ninth year of Hoshe'a the king of Assyria captured Samar'ia, and he carried the Israelites away to Assyria, and placed them in Ha'lah, and on the Ha'bor, the river of Gozan, and in the cities of the Medes.

Sins of Israel Lead to Deportation

7 And this was so, because the sons of Israel had sinned against the Lord their God, who had brought them up out of the land of Egypt from under the hand of Pharaoh king of Egypt, and had feared other gods [8]and walked in the customs of the nations whom the Lord drove out before the sons of Israel, and in the customs which the kings of Israel had introduced. [d] [9]And the sons of Israel did secretly against the Lord their God things that were not right. They built for themselves high places at all their towns, from watchtower to fortified city; [10]they set up for themselves pillars and Ashe'rim on every high hill and under every green tree; [11]and there they burned incense on all the high places, as the nations did whom the Lord carried away before them. And they did wicked things, provoking the Lord to anger, [12]and they served idols, of which the Lord had said to them, "You shall not do this." [13]Yet the Lord warned Israel and Judah by every prophet and every seer, saying, "Turn from your evil ways and keep my commandments and my statutes, in accordance with all the law which I commanded your fathers, and which I sent to you by my servants the prophets." [14]But they would not listen, but were stubborn, as their fathers had been, who did not believe in the Lord their God. [15]They despised his statutes, and his covenant that he made with their fathers, and the warnings which he gave them. They went after false idols, and became false, and they followed the nations that were round about them, concerning whom the

---

[a] Heb At that time Rezin.
[b] Heb Aram (Syria).
[c] Cn: Heb turned to.
[d] Heb obscure.
16:20: 2 Chron 28:27.

LORD had commanded them that they should not do like them. [16]And they forsook all the commandments of the LORD their God, and made for themselves molten images of two calves; and they made an Ashe′rah, and worshiped all the host of heaven, and served Ba′al. [17]And they burned their sons and their daughters as offerings, [e] and used divination and sorcery, and sold themselves to do evil in the sight of the LORD, provoking him to anger. [18]Therefore the LORD was very angry with Israel, and removed them out of his sight; none was left but the tribe of Judah only. [*]

[19] Judah also did not keep the commandments of the LORD their God, but walked in the customs which Israel had introduced. [20]And the LORD rejected all the descendants of Israel, and afflicted them, and gave them into the hand of spoilers, until he had cast them out of his sight.

[21] When he had torn Israel from the house of David they made Jerobo′am the son of Ne′bat king. And Jeroboam drove Israel from following the LORD and made them commit great sin. [22]The sons of Israel walked in all the sins which Jerobo′am did; they did not depart from them, [23]until the LORD removed Israel out of his sight, as he had spoken by all his servants the prophets. So Israel was exiled from their own land to Assyria until this day.

Assyria Resettles Samaria

[24] †And the king of Assyria brought people from Babylon, Cu′thah, Avva, Ha′math, and Sepharva′im, and placed them in the cities of Samar′ia instead of the sons of Israel; and they took possession of Samaria, and dwelt in its cities. [25]And at the beginning of their dwelling there, they did not fear the LORD; therefore the LORD sent lions among them, which killed some of them. [26]So the king of Assyria was told, "The nations which you have carried away and placed in the cities of Samar′ia do not know the law of the god of the land; therefore he has sent lions among them, and behold, they are killing them, because they do not know the law of the god of the land." [27]Then the king of Assyria commanded, "Send there one of the priests whom you carried away from there; and let. him [f] go and dwell there, and teach them the law of the god of the land." [28]So one of the priests whom they had carried away from Samar′ia came and dwelt in Bethel, and taught them how they should fear the LORD.

[29] But every nation still made gods of its own, and put them in the shrines of the high places which the Samar′itans had made, every nation in the cities in which they dwelt; [30]the men of Babylon made Suc′coth-be′noth, the men of Cuth made Ner′gal, the men of Ha′math made Ashi′ma, [31]and the Avvites made Nibhaz and Tartak; and the Sephar′vites burned their children in the fire to Adram′melech and Anam′melech, the gods of Sepharva′im. [32]They also feared the LORD, and appointed from among themselves all sorts of people as priests of the high places, who sacrificed for them in the shrines of the high places. [33]So they feared the LORD but also served their own gods, after the manner of the nations from among whom they had been carried away. [34]To this day they do according to the former manner.

They do not fear the LORD, and they do not follow the statutes or the ordinances or the law or the commandment which the LORD commanded the children of Jacob, whom he named Israel. [35]The LORD made a covenant with them, and commanded them, "You shall not fear other gods or bow yourselves to them or serve them or sacrifice to them; [36]but you shall fear the LORD, who brought you out of the land of Egypt with great power and with an outstretched arm; you shall bow yourselves to him, and to him you shall sacrifice. [37]And the statutes and the ordinances and the law and the commandment which he wrote for you, you shall always be careful to do. You shall not fear other gods, [38]and you shall not forget the covenant that I have made with you. You shall not fear other gods, [39]but you shall fear the LORD your God, and he will deliver you out of the hand of all your enemies." [40]However they would not listen, but they did according to their former manner.

[41] So these nations feared the LORD, and also served their graven images; their children likewise, and their children's children—as their fathers did, so they do to this day.

Hezekiah Reigns over Judah

18 In the third year of Hoshe′a son of E′lah, king of Israel, Hezeki′ah the son of A′haz, king of Judah, began to reign. [2]He was twenty-five years old when he began to reign, and he reigned twenty-nine years in Jerusalem. His mother's name was Abi the daughter of Zechari′ah. [3]And he did what was right in the eyes of the LORD, according to all that David his father had done. [4]He removed the high places, and broke the pillars, and cut down the Ashe′rah. And he broke in pieces the bronze serpent that Moses had made, for until those days the sons of Israel had burned incense to it; it was called Nehush′tan. [5]He trusted in the LORD the God of Israel; so that there was none like him among all the kings of Judah after him, nor among those who were before him. [6]For he held fast to the LORD; he did not depart from following him, but kept the commandments which the LORD commanded Moses.

---

[e] Or made their sons and their daughters pass through the fire.
[f] Syr Vg: Heb them.
18:1–3: 2 Chron 29:1, 2.
[*] 17:7–18: A full explanation of how Israel had sinned and was punished accordingly.
† 17:24–41: Origin of the Samaritans, written by an orthodox Jew.

[7]And the Lord was with him; wherever he went forth, he prospered. He rebelled against the king of Assyria, and would not serve him. [8]He struck the Philis′tines as far as Gaza and its territory, from watchtower to fortified city.

9 In the fourth year of King Hezeki′ah, which was the seventh year of Hoshe′a son of E′lah, king of Israel, Shalmane′ser king of Assyria came up against Samar′ia and besieged it [10]and at the end of three years he took it. In the sixth year of Hezeki′ah, which was the ninth year of Hoshe′a king of Israel, Samar′ia was taken. [11]The king of Assyria carried the Israelites away to Assyria, and put them in Ha′lah, and on the Ha′bor, the river of Gozan, and in the cities of the Medes, [12]because they did not obey the voice of the Lord their God but transgressed his covenant, even all that Moses the servant of the Lord commanded; they neither listened nor obeyed.

Sennacherib Invades Judah

13 In the fourteenth year of King Hezeki′ah Sennach′erib king of Assyria came up against all the fortified cities of Judah and took them. [14]And Hezeki′ah king of Judah sent to the king of Assyria at La′chish, saying, "I have done wrong; withdraw from me; whatever you impose on me I will bear." And the king of Assyria required of Hezekiah king of Judah three hundred talents of silver and thirty talents of gold. [15]And Hezeki′ah gave him all the silver that was found in the house of the Lord, and in the treasuries of the king's house. [16]At that time Hezeki′ah stripped the gold from the doors of the temple of the Lord, and from the doorposts which Hezekiah king of Judah had overlaid and gave it to the king of Assyria. [17]And the king of Assyria sent the Tartan, the Rab′saris, and the Rab′shakeh with a great army from La′chish to King Hezeki′ah at Jerusalem. And they went up and came to Jerusalem. When they arrived, they came and stood by the conduit of the upper pool, which is on the highway to the Fuller's Field. [18]And when they called for the king, there came out to them Eli′akim the son of Hilki′ah, who was over the household, and Shebnah the secretary, and Jo′ah the son of A′saph, the recorder.

19 And the Rab′shakeh said to them, "Say to Hezeki′ah, 'Thus says the great king, the king of Assyria: On what do you rest this confidence of yours? [20]Do you think that mere words are strategy and power for war? On whom do you now rely, that you have rebelled against me? [21]Behold, you are relying now on Egypt, that broken reed of a staff, which will pierce the hand of any man who leans on it. Such is Pharaoh king of Egypt to all who rely on him. [22]But if you say to me, "We rely on the Lord our God," is it not he whose high places and altars Hezeki′ah has removed, saying to Judah and to Jerusalem, "You shall worship before this altar in Jerusalem"? [23]Come now, make a wager with my master the king of Assyria: I will give you two thousand horses, if you are able on your part to set riders upon them. [24]How then can you repulse a single captain among the least of my master's servants, when you rely on Egypt for chariots and for horsemen? [25]Moreover, is it without the Lord that I have come up against this place to destroy it? The Lord said to me, Go up against this land, and destroy it.'"

26 Then Eli′akim the son of Hilki′ah, and Shebnah, and Jo′ah, said to the Rab′shakeh, "Please, speak to your servants in the Arama′ic language, for we understand it; do not speak to us in the language of Judah within the hearing of the people who are on the wall." [27]But the Rab′shakeh said to them, "Has my master sent me to speak these words to your master and to you, and not to the men sitting on the wall, who are doomed with you to eat their own dung and to drink their own urine?"

28 Then the Rab′shakeh stood and called out in a loud voice in the language of Judah: "Hear the word of the great king, the king of Assyria! [29]Thus says the king: 'Do not let Hezeki′ah deceive you, for he will not be able to deliver you out of my hand. [30]Do not let Hezeki′ah make you to rely on the Lord by saying, The Lord will surely deliver us, and this city will not be given into the hand of the king of Assyria.' [31]Do not listen to Hezeki′ah; for thus says the king of Assyria: 'Make your peace with me and come out to me; then every one of you will eat of his own vine, and every one of his own fig tree, and every one of you will drink the water of his own cistern; [32]until I come and take you away to a land like your own land, a land of grain and wine, a land of bread and vineyards, a land of olive trees and honey, that you may live, and not die. And do not listen to Hezeki′ah when he misleads you by saying, The Lord will deliver us. [33]Has any of the gods of the nations ever delivered his land out of the hand of the king of Assyria? [34]Where are the gods of Ha′math and Arpad? Where are the gods of Sepharva′im, He′na, and Ivvah? Have they delivered Samar′ia out of my hand? [35]Who among all the gods of the countries have delivered their countries out of my hand, that the Lord should deliver Jerusalem out of my hand?'"

36 But the people were silent and answered him not a word, for the king's command was, "Do not answer him." [37]Then Eli′akim the son of Hilki′ah, who was over the household, and Shebna the secretary, and Jo′ah the son of A′saph, the recorder, came to Hezeki′ah with their clothes torn, and told him the words of the Rab′shakeh.

18:13–19:35: 2 Chron 32:1–21; Is 36:1–37:38.

Hezekiah Consults Isaiah

19 When King Hezeki'ah heard it, he tore his clothes, and covered himself with sackcloth, and went into the house of the LORD. ²And he sent Eli'akim, who was over the household, and Shebna the secretary, and the senior priests, covered with sackcloth, to the prophet Isai'ah the son of A'moz. ³They said to him, "Thus says Hezeki'ah, This day is a day of distress, of rebuke, and of disgrace; children have come to the birth, and there is no strength to bring them forth. ⁴It may be that the LORD your God heard all the words of the Rab'shakeh, whom his master the king of Assyria has sent to mock the living God, and will rebuke the words which the LORD your God has heard; therefore lift up your prayer for the remnant that is left." ⁵When the servants of King Hezeki'ah came to Isai'ah, ⁶Isai'ah said to them, "Say to your master, 'Thus says the LORD: Do not be afraid because of the words that you have heard, with which the servants of the king of Assyria have reviled me. ⁷Behold, I will put a spirit in him, so that he shall hear a rumor and return to his own land; and I will cause him to fall by the sword in his own land.'"

Sennacherib's Mockery

8 The Rab'shakeh returned, and found the king of Assyria fighting against Libnah; for he heard that the king had left La'chish. ⁹And when the king heard concerning Tirha'kah king of Ethiopia, "Behold, he has set out to fight against you," he sent messengers again to Hezeki'ah, saying, ¹⁰"Thus shall you speak to Hezeki'ah king of Judah: 'Do not let your God on whom you rely deceive you by promising that Jerusalem will not be given into the hand of the king of Assyria. ¹¹Behold, you have heard what the kings of Assyria have done to all lands, destroying them utterly. And shall you be delivered? ¹²Have the gods of the nations delivered them, the nations which my fathers destroyed, Gozan, Haran, Rezeph, and the people of Eden who were in Tel-as'sar? ¹³Where is the king of Ha'math, the king of Arpad, the king of the city of Sepharva'im, the king of He'na, or the king of Ivvah?'"

Hezekiah's Prayer

14 Hezeki'ah received the letter from the hand of the messengers, and read it; and Hezekiah went up to the house of the LORD, and spread it before the LORD. ¹⁵And Hezeki'ah prayed before the LORD, and said: "O LORD the God of Israel, who are enthroned above the cherubim, you are the God, you alone, of all the kingdoms of the earth; you have made heaven and earth. ¹⁶Incline your ear, O LORD, and hear; open your eyes, O LORD, and see; and hear the words of Sennach'erib, which he has sent to mock the living God. ¹⁷Of a truth, O LORD, the kings of Assyria

have laid waste the nations and their lands, ¹⁸and have cast their gods into the fire; for they were no gods, but the work of men's hands, wood and stone; therefore they were destroyed. ¹⁹So now, O LORD our God, save us, I beg you, from his hand, that all the kingdoms of the earth may know that you, O LORD, are God alone."

20 Then Isai'ah the son of A'moz sent to Hezeki'ah, saying, "Thus says the LORD, the God of Israel: Your prayer to me about Sennach'erib king of Assyria I have heard. ²¹This is the word that the LORD has spoken concerning him:

"She despises you, she scorns you—
　the virgin daughter of Zion;
she wags her head behind you—
　the daughter of Jerusalem.

²²"Whom have you mocked and reviled?
　Against whom have you raised your voice
and haughtily lifted your eyes?
　Against the Holy One of Israel!
²³By your messengers you have mocked the
　LORD,
　and you have said, 'With my many
　　chariots
I have gone up the heights of the mountains,
　to the far recesses of Lebanon;
I felled its tallest cedars,
　its choicest cypresses;
I entered its farthest retreat,
　its densest forest.
²⁴I dug wells
　and drank foreign waters,
and I dried up with the sole of my foot
　all the streams of Egypt.'

²⁵"Have you not heard
　that I determined it long ago?
I planned from days of old
　what now I bring to pass,
that you should turn fortified cities
　into heaps of ruins,
²⁶while their inhabitants, shorn of strength,
　are dismayed and confounded,
and have become like plants of the field,
　and like tender grass,
like grass on the housetops;
　blighted before it is grown?

²⁷"But I know your sitting down
　and your going out and coming in,
　and your raging against me.
²⁸Because you have raged against me
　and your arrogance has come into my
　　ears,
I will put my hook in your nose
　and my bit in your mouth,
and I will turn you back on the way
　by which you came.

29 "And this shall be the sign for you: this year you shall eat what grows of itself, and in the second year what springs of the same; then in the third year sow, and reap, and plant vineyards, and eat their fruit. ³⁰And the surviving remnant of the house of Judah shall again take root downward, and bear fruit upward; ³¹for out of Jerusalem shall go forth a remnant, and out of Mount Zion a band of survivors. The zeal of the LORD will do this.

32 "Therefore thus says the LORD concerning the king of Assyria, He shall not come into this city or shoot an arrow there, or come before it with a shield or cast up a siege mound against it. ³³By the way that he came, by the same he shall return, and he shall not come into this city, says the LORD. ³⁴For I will defend this city to save it, for my own sake and for the sake of my servant David."

Sennacherib's Defeat and Death

35 And that night the angel of the LORD went forth, and slew a hundred and eighty-five thousand in the camp of the Assyrians;* and when men arose early in the morning, behold, these were all dead bodies. ³⁶Then Sennach'erib king of Assyria departed, and went home, and dwelt at Nin'eveh. ³⁷And as he was worshiping in the house of Nisroch his god, Adram'melech and Share'zer, his sons, slew him with the sword, and escaped into the land of Ar'arat. And Esarhad'don his son reigned in his stead.

Hezekiah's Illness

20 In those days Hezeki'ah became sick and was at the point of death. And Isai'ah the prophet the son of A'moz came to him, and said to him, "Thus says the LORD, 'Set your house in order; for you shall die, you shall not recover.'" ²Then Hezeki'ah turned his face to the wall, and prayed to the LORD, saying, ³"Remember now, O LORD, I beg you, how I have walked before you in faithfulness and with a whole heart, and have done what is good in your sight." And Hezeki'ah wept bitterly. ⁴And before Isai'ah had gone out of the middle court, the word of the LORD came to him: ⁵"Turn back, and say to Hezeki'ah the prince of my people, Thus says the LORD, the God of David your father: I have heard your prayer, I have seen your tears; behold, I will heal you; on the third day you shall go up to the house of the LORD. ⁶And I will add fifteen years to your life. I will deliver you and this city out of the hand of the king of Assyria, and I will defend this city for my own sake and for my servant David's sake." ⁷And Isai'ah said, "Bring a cake of figs. And let them take and lay it on the boil, that he may recover."

8 And Hezeki'ah said to Isai'ah, "What shall be the sign that the LORD will heal me, and that I shall go up to the house of the LORD on the third day?" ⁹And Isai'ah said, "This is the sign to you

from the LORD, that the LORD will do the thing that he has promised: shall the shadow go forward ten steps, or go back ten steps?" ¹⁰And Hezeki'ah answered, "It is an easy thing for the shadow to lengthen ten steps; rather let the shadow go back ten steps." ¹¹And Isai'ah the prophet cried to the LORD; and he brought the shadow back ten steps, by which the sun ᵍ had declined on the dial of A'haz.

Envoys from Babylon

12 At that time Mer'odach-bal'adan the son of Bal'adan, king of Babylon, sent envoys with letters and a present to Hezeki'ah; for he heard that Hezekiah had been sick. ¹³And Hezeki'ah welcomed them, and he showed them all his treasure house, the silver, the gold, the spices, the precious oil, his armory, all that was found in his storehouses; there was nothing in his house or in all his realm that Hezekiah did not show them. ¹⁴Then Isai'ah the prophet came to King Hezeki'ah, and said to him, "What did these men say? And from where did they come to you?" And Hezekiah said, "They have come from a far country, from Babylon." ¹⁵He said, "What have they seen in your house?" And Hezeki'ah answered, "They have seen all that is in my house; there is nothing in my storehouses that I did not show them."

16 Then Isai'ah said to Hezeki'ah, "Hear the word of the LORD: ¹⁷Behold, the days are coming, when all that is in your house, and that which your fathers have stored up till this day, shall be carried to Babylon; nothing shall be left, says the LORD. ¹⁸And some of your own sons, who are born to you, shall be taken away; and they shall be eunuchs in the palace of the king of Babylon." ¹⁹Then said Hezeki'ah to Isai'ah, "The word of the LORD which you have spoken is good." For he thought, "Why not, if there will be peace and security in my days?"

Death of Hezekiah

20 The rest of the deeds of Hezeki'ah, and all his might, and how he made the pool and the conduit and brought water into the city, are they not written in the Book of the Chronicles of the Kings of Judah? ²¹And Hezeki'ah slept with his fathers; and Manas'seh his son reigned in his stead.

Manasseh Reigns over Judah

21 Manas'seh was twelve years old when he began to reign, and he reigned fifty-five years in Jerusalem. His mother's name was Heph'zibah. ²And he did what was evil in the sight of the LORD, according to the abominable practices of the nations whom the LORD drove out

---

ᵍ Syr See Is 38:8 and Tg: Heb lacks *the sun*.
20:1-21: 2 Chron 32:24–33; Is 38:1—39:8.
21:1-9: 2 Chron 33:1–9.
* 19:35: It is usually supposed that the Assyrians were struck by a virulent disease.

before the people of Israel. [3]For he rebuilt the high places which Hezeki'ah his father had destroyed; and he erected altars for Ba'al, and made an Ashe'rah, as A'hab king of Israel had done, and worshiped all the host of heaven, and served them. [4]And he built altars in the house of the LORD, of which the LORD had said, "In Jerusalem will I put my name." [5]And he built altars for all the host of heaven in the two courts of the house of the LORD. [6]And he burned his son as an offering, and practiced soothsaying and augury, and dealt with mediums and with wizards. He did much evil in the sight of the LORD, provoking him to anger. [7]And the graven image of Ashe'rah that he had made he set in the house of which the LORD said to David and to Solomon his son, "In this house, and in Jerusalem, which I have chosen out of all the tribes of Israel, I will put my name for ever; [8]and I will not cause the feet of Israel to wander any more out of the land which I gave to their fathers, if only they will be careful to do according to all that I have commanded them, and according to all the law that my servant Moses commanded them." [9]But they did not listen, and Manas'seh seduced them to do more evil than the nations had done whom the LORD destroyed before the sons of Israel.

10 And the LORD said by his servants the prophets, [11]"Because Manas'seh king of Judah has committed these abominations, and has done things more wicked than all that the Am'orites did, who were before him, and has made Judah also to sin with his idols; [12]therefore thus says the LORD, the God of Israel, Behold, I am bringing upon Jerusalem and Judah such evil that the ears of every one who hears of it will tingle. [13]And I will stretch over Jerusalem the measuring line of Samar'ia, and the plummet of the house of A'hab; and I will wipe Jerusalem as one wipes a dish, wiping it and turning it upside down. [14]And I will cast off the remnant of my heritage, and give them into the hand of their enemies, and they shall become a prey and a spoil to all their enemies, [15]because they have done what is evil in my sight and have provoked me to anger, since the day their fathers came out of Egypt, even to this day."

16 Moreover Manas'seh shed very much innocent blood, till he had filled Jerusalem from one end to another, besides the sin which he made Judah to sin so that they did what was evil in the sight of the LORD.

17 Now the rest of the acts of Manas'seh, and all that he did, and the sin that he committed, are they not written in the Book of the Chronicles of the Kings of Judah? [18]And Manas'seh slept with his fathers, and was buried in the garden of his house, in the garden of Uzza; and A'mon his son reigned in his stead.

Amon Reigns over Judah

19 A'mon was twenty-two years old when he began to reign, and he reigned two years in Jerusalem. His mother's name was Meshul'lemeth the daughter of Haruz of Jotbah. [20]And he did what was evil in the sight of the LORD, as Manas'seh his father had done. [21]He walked in all the way in which his father walked, and served the idols that his father served, and worshiped them; [22]he forsook the LORD, the God of his fathers, and did not walk in the way of the LORD. [23]And the servants of A'mon conspired against him, and killed the king in his house. [24]But the people of the land slew all those who had conspired against King A'mon, and the people of the land made Josi'ah his son king in his stead. [25]Now the rest of the acts of A'mon which he did, are they not written in the Book of the Chronicles of the Kings of Judah? [26]And he was buried in his tomb in the garden of Uzza; and Josi'ah his son reigned in his stead.

Josiah Reigns over Judah

22 Josi'ah was eight years old when he began to reign, and he reigned thirty-one years in Jerusalem. His mother's name was Jedi'dah the daughter of Adai'ah of Bozkath. [2]And he did what was right in the eyes of the LORD, and walked in all the way of David his father, and he did not turn aside to the right hand or to the left.

Hilkiah Finds the Book of the Law

3 In the eighteenth year of King Josi'ah, the king sent Sha'phan the son of Azali'ah, son of Meshul'lam, the secretary, to the house of the LORD, saying, [4]"Go up to Hilki'ah the high priest, that he may reckon the amount of the money which has been brought into the house of the LORD, which the keepers of the threshold have collected from the people; [5]and let it be given into the hand of the workmen who have the oversight of the house of the LORD; and let them give it to the workmen who are at the house of the LORD, repairing the house, [6]that is, to the carpenters, and to the builders, and to the masons, as well as for buying timber and quarried stone to repair the house. [7]But no accounting shall be asked from them for the money which is delivered into their hand, for they deal honestly."

8 And Hilki'ah the high priest said to Sha'phan the secretary, "I have found the book of the law * in the house of the LORD." And Hilkiah gave the book to Shaphan, and he read it. [9]And Sha'phan

---

21:18: 2 Chron 33:20.
21:19–24: 2 Chron 33:21–25.
22:1, 2: 2 Chron 34:1, 2.
22:3–7: 2 Chron 34:8–12.
* 22:8, *book of the law:* Probably Deuteronomy. In Deut 12–26 may be seen details of Josiah's reform, especially as regards the centralization of worship. The book must have been hidden or lost during the reign of the wicked Manasseh.

the secretary came to the king, and reported to the king, "Your servants have emptied out the money that was found in the house, and have delivered it into the hand of the workmen who have the oversight of the house of the LORD." [10]Then Sha′phan the secretary told the king, "Hilki′ah the priest has given me a book." And Shaphan read it before the king.

Josiah Hears the Law and Is Penitent

[11] And when the king heard the words of the book of the law, he tore his clothes. [12]And the king commanded Hilki′ah the priest, and Ahi′kam the son of Sha′phan, and Achbor the son of Micai′ah, and Shaphan the secretary, and Asai′ah the king's servant, saying, [13]"Go, inquire of the LORD for me, and for the people, and for all Judah, concerning the words of this book that has been found; for great is the wrath of the LORD that is kindled against us, because our fathers have not obeyed the words of this book, to do according to all that is written concerning us."

[14] So Hilki′ah the priest, and Ahi′kam, and Achbor, and Sha′phan, and Asai′ah went to Huldah the prophetess, the wife of Shallum the son of Tikvah, son of Harhas, keeper of the wardrobe (now she dwelt in Jerusalem in the Second Quarter); and they talked with her. [15]And she said to them, "Thus says the LORD, the God of Israel: 'Tell the man who sent you to me, [16]Thus says the LORD, Behold, I will bring evil upon this place and upon its inhabitants, all the words of the book which the king of Judah has read. [17]Because they have forsaken me and have burned incense to other gods, that they might provoke me to anger with all the work of their hands, therefore my wrath will be kindled against this place, and it will not be quenched. [18]But as to the king of Judah, who sent you to inquire of the LORD, thus shall you say to him, Thus says the LORD, the God of Israel: Regarding the words which you have heard, [19]because your heart was penitent, and you humbled yourself before the LORD, when you heard how I spoke against this place, and against its inhabitants, that they should become a desolation and a curse, and you have torn your clothes and wept before me, I also have heard you, says the LORD. [20]Therefore, behold, I will gather you to your fathers, and you shall be gathered to your grave in peace, and your eyes shall not see all the evil which I will bring upon this place.'" And they brought back word to the king.

Josiah's Reforms

23 Then the king sent, and all the elders of Judah and Jerusalem were gathered to him. [2]And the king went up to the house of the LORD, and with him all the men of Judah and all the inhabitants of Jerusalem, and the priests and the prophets, all the people, both small and great;

and he read in their hearing all the words of the book of the covenant which had been found in the house of the LORD. [3]And the king stood by the pillar and made a covenant before the LORD, to walk after the LORD and to keep his commandments and his covenants and his statutes, with all his heart and all his soul, to perform the words of this covenant that were written in this book; and all the people joined in the covenant.

[4] And the king commanded Hilki′ah, the high priest, and the priests of the second order, and the keepers of the threshold, to bring out of the temple of the LORD all the vessels made for Ba′al, for Ashe′rah, and for all the host of heaven; he burned them outside Jerusalem in the fields of the Kidron, and carried their ashes to Bethel. [5]And he deposed the idolatrous priests whom the kings of Judah had ordained to burn incense in the high places at the cities of Judah and round about Jerusalem; those also who burned incense to Ba′al, to the sun, and the moon, and the constellations, and all the host of the heavens. [6]And he brought out the Ashe′rah from the house of the LORD, outside Jerusalem, to the brook Kidron, and burned it at the brook Kidron, and beat it to dust and cast the dust of it upon the graves of the common people. [7]And he broke down the houses of the male cult prostitutes which were in the house of the LORD, where the women wove hangings for the Ashe′rah. [8]And he brought all the priests out of the cities of Judah, and defiled the high places where the priests had burned incense, from Ge′ba to Be′er-she′ba; and he broke down the high places of the gates that were at the entrance of the gate of Joshua the governor of the city, which were on one's left at the gate of the city. [9]However, the priests of the high places did not come up to the altar of the LORD in Jerusalem, but they ate unleavened bread among their brethren. [10]And he defiled To′pheth, which is in the valley of the sons of Hin′nom, that no one might burn his son or his daughter as an offering to Mo′lech. [11]And he removed the horses that the kings of Judah had dedicated to the sun, at the entrance to the house of the LORD, by the chamber of Na′than-me′lech the chamberlain, which was in the precincts; [h] and he burned the chariots of the sun with fire. [12]And the altars on the roof of the upper chamber of A′haz, which the kings of Judah had made, and the altars which Manas′seh had made in the two courts of the house of the LORD, he pulled down and broke in pieces, [i] and cast the dust of them into the brook Kidron. [13]And the king defiled the high places that were east of Jerusalem, to the south of the mount of corruption, which Solomon the

---

[h] The meaning of the Hebrew word is uncertain.
[i] Heb *pieces from there.*
23:4-20: 2 Chron 34:3–7.

king of Israel had built for Ash'toreth the abomination of the Sido'nians, and for Che'mosh the abomination of Moab, and for Milcom the abomination of the Am'monites. [14]And he broke in pieces the pillars, and cut down the Ashe'rim, and filled their places with the bones of men.

15 Moreover the altar at Bethel, the high place erected by Jerobo'am the son of Ne'bat, who made Israel to sin, that altar with the high place he pulled down and he broke in pieces its stones, [j] crushing them to dust; also he burned the Ashe'rah. [16]And as Josi'ah turned, he saw the tombs there on the mount; and he sent and took the bones out of the tombs, and burned them upon the altar, and defiled it, according to the word of the LORD which the man of God proclaimed, who had predicted these things. [17]Then he said, "What is yonder monument that I see?" And the men of the city told him, "It is the tomb of the man of God who came from Judah and predicted these things which you have done against the altar at Bethel." [18]And he said, "Let him be; let no man move his bones." So they let his bones alone, with the bones of the prophet who came out of Samar'ia. [19]And all the shrines also of the high places that were in the cities of Samar'ia, which kings of Israel had made, provoking the LORD to anger, Josi'ah removed; he did to them according to all that he had done at Bethel. [20]And he slew all the priests of the high places who were there, upon the altars, and burned the bones of men upon them. Then he returned to Jerusalem.

The Passover Is Celebrated

21 And the king commanded all the people, "Keep the Passover to the LORD your God, as it is written in this book of the covenant." [22]For no such Passover had been kept since the days of the judges who judged Israel, or during all the days of the kings of Israel or of the kings of Judah; [23]but in the eighteenth year of King Josi'ah this Passover was kept to the LORD in Jerusalem.

24 Moreover Josi'ah put away the mediums and the wizards and the teraphim and the idols and all the abominations that were seen in the land of Judah and in Jerusalem, that he might establish the words of the law which were written in the book that Hilki'ah the priest found in the house of the LORD. [25]Before him there was no king like him, who turned to the LORD with all his heart and with all his soul and with all his might, according to all the law of Moses; nor did any like him arise after him.

26 Still the LORD did not turn from the fierceness of his great wrath, by which his anger was kindled against Judah, because of all the provocations with which Manas'seh had provoked him. [27]And the LORD said, "I will remove Judah also out of my sight, as I have removed Israel, and I will cast off this city which I have chosen, Jerusalem, and the house of which I said, My name shall be there."

Josiah Dies in Battle

28 Now the rest of the acts of Josi'ah, and all that he did, are they not written in the Book of the Chronicles of the Kings of Judah? [29]In his days Pharaoh Neco king of Egypt went up to the king of Assyria to the river Euphra'tes. King Josi'ah went to meet him; and Pharaoh Neco slew him at Megid'do, when he saw him. [30]And his servants carried him dead in a chariot from Megid'do, and brought him to Jerusalem, and buried him in his own tomb. And the people of the land took Jeho'ahaz the son of Josi'ah, and anointed him, and made him king in his father's stead.

31 Jeho'ahaz was twenty-three years old when he began to reign, and he reigned three months in Jerusalem. His mother's name was Hamu'tal the daughter of Jeremi'ah of Libnah. [32]And he did what was evil in the sight of the LORD, according to all that his fathers had done. [33]And Pharaoh Neco put him in bonds at Riblah in the land of Ha'math, that he might not reign in Jerusalem, and laid upon the land a tribute of a hundred talents of silver and a talent of gold. [34]And Pharaoh Ne'co made Eli'akim the son of Josi'ah king in the place of Josiah his father, and changed his name to Jehoi'akim. But he took Jeho'ahaz away; and he came to Egypt, and died there. [35]And Jehoi'akim gave the silver and the gold to Pharaoh, but he taxed the land to give the money according to the command of Pharaoh. He exacted the silver and the gold of the people of the land, from every one according to his assessment, to give it to Pharaoh Neco.

Jehoiakim Reigns over Judah

36 Jehoi'akim was twenty-five years old when he began to reign, and he reigned eleven years in Jerusalem. His mother's name was Zebi'dah the daughter of Pedai'ah of Ru'mah. [37]And he did what was evil in the sight of the LORD, according to all that his fathers had done.

Judah Overrun by Enemies

24 In his days Nebuchadnez'zar king of Babylon came up, and Jehoi'akim became his servant three years; then he turned and rebelled against him. [2]And the LORD sent against him bands of the Chalde'ans, and bands of the Syrians, and bands of the Moabites, and bands of the Am'monites, and sent them against Judah to destroy it, according to the word of the LORD which he spoke by his servants the prophets. [3]Surely this came upon Judah at the command of the LORD, to remove them out of his sight, for the

---

[j] Gk: Heb *he burned the high place.*
23:21–23: 2 Chron 35:1–19.
23:30–34: 2 Chron 36:1–4.
23:36–24:6: 2 Chron 36:5–8.

sins of Manas'seh, according to all that he had done, [4]and also for the innocent blood that he had shed; for he filled Jerusalem with innocent blood, and the LORD would not pardon. [5]Now the rest of the deeds of Jehoi'akim, and all that he did, are they not written in the Book of the Chronicles of the Kings of Judah? [6]So Jehoi'akim slept with his fathers, and Jehoi'achin his son reigned in his stead. [7]And the king of Egypt did not come again out of his land, for the king of Babylon had taken all that belonged to the king of Egypt from the Brook of Egypt to the river Euphrates.

Reign and Captivity of Jehoiachin

8 Jehoi'achin was eighteen years old when he became king, and he reigned three months in Jerusalem. His mother's name was Nehush'ta the daughter of Elna'than of Jerusalem. [9]And he did what was evil in the sight of the LORD, according to all that his father had done.

Babylon Conquers Jerusalem

10 At that time the servants of Nebuchad-nez'zar king of Babylon came up to Jerusalem, and the city was besieged. [11]And Nebuchad-nez'zar king of Babylon came to the city, while his servants were besieging it; [12]and Jehoi'achin the king of Judah gave himself up to the king of Babylon, himself, and his mother, and his ser-vants, and his princes, and his palace officials. The king of Babylon took him prisoner in the eighth year of his reign, [13]and carried off all the treasures of the house of the LORD, and the trea-sures of the king's house, and cut in pieces all the vessels of gold in the temple of the LORD, which Solomon king of Israel had made, as the LORD had foretold. [14]He carried away all Jerusalem, and all the princes, and all the mighty men of valor, ten thousand captives, and all the craftsmen and the smiths; none remained, except the poorest people of the land. [15]And he carried away Jehoi'a-chin to Babylon; the king's mother, the king's wives, his officials, and the chief men of the land, he took into captivity from Jerusalem to Babylon. [16]And the king of Babylon brought captive to Babylon all the men of valor, seven thousand, and the craftsmen and the smiths, one thousand, all of them strong and fit for war. [17]And the king of Babylon made Mattani'ah, Jehoi'achin's uncle, king in his stead, and changed his name to Zedeki'ah.

Zedekiah Reigns over Judah

18 Zedeki'ah was twenty-one years old when he became king, and he reigned eleven years in Jerusalem. His mother's name was Hamu'tal the daughter of Jeremi'ah of Libnah. [19]And he did what was evil in the sight of the LORD, according to all that Jehoi'akim had done. [20]For because of the anger of the LORD it came to the point in Jerusalem and Judah that he cast them out from his presence.

And Zedeki'ah rebelled against the king of Babylon. [1]And in the ninth year of his reign, in the tenth month, on the tenth day of the month, Nebuchadnez'zar king of Babylon came with all his army against Jerusalem, and laid siege to it; and they built siegeworks against it round about. [2]So the city was besieged till the eleventh year of King Zedeki'ah. [3]On the ninth day of the fourth month the famine was so severe in the city that there was no food for the people of the land. [4]Then a breach was made in the city; the king with all the men of war fled [k] by night by the way of the gate between the two walls, by the king's garden, though the Chalde'ans were around the city. And they went in the direction of the Ar'abah. [5]But the army of the Chalde'ans pur-sued the king, and overtook him in the plains of Jericho; and all his army was scattered from him. [6]Then they captured the king, and brought him up to the king of Babylon at Rib'lah, who passed sentence upon him. [7]They slew the sons of Zede-ki'ah before his eyes, and put out the eyes of Zedekiah, and bound him in fetters, and took him to Babylon.

The Babylonian Exile

8 In the fifth month, on the seventh day of the month—which was the nineteenth year of King Nebuchadnez'zar, king of Babylon—Nebu"za-rad'an, the captain of the bodyguard, a servant of the king of Babylon, came to Jerusalem. [9]And he burned the house of the LORD, and the king's house and all the houses of Jerusalem; every great house he burned down. [10]And all the army of the Chal-de'ans, who were with the captain of the guard, broke down the walls around Jerusalem. [11]And the rest of the people who were left in the city and the deserters who had deserted to the king of Babylon, together with the rest of the multitude, Nebu"zarad'an the captain of the guard carried into exile. [12]But the captain of the guard left some of the poorest of the land to be vinedressers and plowmen.

13 And the pillars of bronze that were in the house of the LORD, and the stands and the bronze sea that were in the house of the LORD, the Chal-de'ans broke in pieces, and carried the bronze to Babylon. [14]And they took away the pots, and the shovels, and the snuffers, and the dishes for in-cense and all the vessels of bronze used in the temple service, [15]the firepans also, and the bowls. What was of gold the captain of the guard took away as gold, and what was of silver, as silver. [16]As for the two pillars, the one sea, and the stands, which Solomon had made for the house of the LORD, the bronze of all these vessels was be-yond weight. [17]The height of the one pillar was

---

[k] Gk Compare Jer 39:4; 52:7: Heb lacks *the king* and *fled*.
24:8–17: 2 Chron 36:9–10.
24:18—25:21: 2 Chron 36:11–21; Jer 52:1–27.

eighteen cubits, and upon it was a capital of bronze; the height of the capital was three cubits; a network and pomegranates, all of bronze, were upon the capital round about. And the second pillar had the like, with the network.

18 And the captain of the guard took Serai'ah the chief priest, and Zephani'ah the second priest, and the three keepers of the threshold; [19]and from the city he took an officer who had been in command of the men of war, and five men of the king's council who were found in the city; and the secretary of the commander of the army who mustered the people of the land; and sixty men of the people of the land who were found in the city. [20]And Nebu"zarad'an the captain of the guard took them, and brought them to the king of Babylon at Riblah. [21]And the king of Babylon struck them, and put them to death at Riblah in the land of Ha'math. So Judah was taken into exile out of its land.

Gedaliah Made Governor of Judah

22 And over the people who remained in the land of Judah, whom Nebuchadnez'zar king of Babylon had left, he appointed Gedali'ah the son of Ahi'kam, son of Sha'phan, governor. [23]Now when all the captains of the forces in the open country [1] and their men heard that the king of Babylon had appointed Gedali'ah governor, they came with their men to Gedaliah at Mizpah, namely, Ish'mael the son of Nethani'ah, and Joha'nan the son of Kare'ah, and Serai'ah the son of Tan'humeth the Netoph'athite, and Ja-azani'ah the son of the Ma-ac'athite. [24]And Gedali'ah swore to them and their men, saying, "Do not be afraid because of the Chalde'an officials; dwell in the land, and serve the king of Babylon, and it shall be well with you." [25]But in the seventh month, Ish'mael the son of Nethani'ah, son of Elish'ama, of the royal family, came with ten men, and attacked and killed Gedali'ah and the Jews and the Chalde'ans who were with him at Mizpah. [26]Then all the people, both small and great, and the captains of the forces arose, and went to Egypt; for they were afraid of the Chalde'ans.

Jehoiachin Is Freed by Evil-merodach

27 And in the thirty-seventh year of the exile of Jehoi'achin king of Judah, in the twelfth month, on the twenty-seventh day of the month, E'vilmer'odach king of Babylon, in the year that he began to reign, graciously freed Jehoi'achin king of Judah from prison; [28]and he spoke kindly to him, and gave him a seat above the seats of the kings who were with him in Babylon. [29]So Jehoi'achin put off his prison garments. And every day of his life he dined regularly at the king's table; [30]and for his allowance, a regular allowance was given him by the king, every day a portion, as long as he lived.

---

[1] With Jer 40:7: Heb lacks *in the open country.*
25:22-26: Jer 40:7—43:7.
25:27-30: Jer 52:31-34.

THE FIRST BOOK OF THE

CHRONICLES

From Adam to Abraham

1 *Adam, Seth, E'nosh; ²Ke'nan, Ma-hal'alel, Jar'ed; ³E'noch, Methu'selah, La'mech; ⁴Noah, Shem, Ham, and Ja'pheth.

5 The sons of Ja'pheth: Gomer, Ma'gog, Ma'dai, Ja'van, Tu'bal, Me'shech, and Ti'ras. ⁶The sons of Gomer: Ash'kenaz, Di'phath, and Togar'mah. ⁷The sons of Ja'van: Eli'shah, Tar'shish, Kittim, and Ro'danim.

8 The sons of Ham: Cush, Egypt, Put, and Canaan. ⁹The sons of Cush: Seba, Hav'ilah, Sabta, Ra'ama, and Sab'teca. The sons of Ra'amah: Sheba and De'dan. ¹⁰Cush was the father of Nimrod; he began to be a mighty one in the earth.

11 Egypt was the father of Lu'dim, An'amim, Leha'bim, Naph'tuhim, ¹²Pathru'sim, Caslu'him (from whom came the Philis'tines), and Caph'torim.

13 Canaan was the father of Si'don his firstborn, and Heth, ¹⁴and the Jeb'usites, the Am'orites, the Gir'gashites, ¹⁵the Hi'vites, the Arkites, the Si'nites, ¹⁶the Ar'vadites, the Zem'arites, and the Ha'mathites.

17 The sons of Shem: E'lam, Asshur, Arpach'shad, Lud, Ar'am, Uz, Hul, Ge'ther, and Me'shech. ¹⁸Arpach'shad was the father of She'lah; and Shelah was the father of E'ber. ¹⁹To E'ber were born two sons: the name of the one was Pe'leg (for in his days the earth was divided), and the name of his brother Joktan. ²⁰Joktan was the father of Almo'dad, She'leph, Ha''zarma'veth, Je'rah, ²¹Hador'am, U'zal, Diklah, ²²E'bal, Abim'ael, Sheba, ²³O'phir, Hav'ilah, and Jo'bab; all these were the sons of Joktan.

24 Shem, Arpach'shad, She'lah; ²⁵E'ber, Pe'leg, Re'u; ²⁶Se'rug, Na'hor, Te'rah; ²⁷Abram, that is, Abraham.

Descendants of Abraham

28 The sons of Abraham: Isaac and Ish'mael. ²⁹These are their genealogies: the first-born of Ish'mael, Neba'ioth; and Ke'dar, Ad'beel, Mibsam, ³⁰Mishma, Du'mah, Massa, Ha'dad, Te'ma, ³¹Je'tur, Naphish, and Ked'emah. These are the sons of Ish'mael. ³²The sons of Ketu'rah, Abraham's concubine: she bore Zimran, Jok'shan, Me'dan, Mid'ian, Ishbak, and Shuah. The sons of Jokshan: Sheba and De'dan. ³³The sons of Mid'ian: E'phah, E'pher, Ha'noch, Abi'da, and Elda'ah. All these were the descendants of Ketu'rah.

34 Abraham was the father of Isaac. The sons of Isaac: Esau and Israel. ³⁵The sons of Esau: Eli'phaz, Reu'el, Je'ush, Ja'lam, and Ko'rah. ³⁶The sons of Eli'phaz: Te'man, Omar, Zephi, Ga'tam, Ke'naz, Timna, and Am'alek. ³⁷The sons of Reu'el: Na'hath, Ze'rah, Shammah, and Mizzah.

38 The sons of Se'ir: Lo'tan, Sho'bal, Zib'eon, An'ah, Di'shon, E'zer, and Di'shan. ³⁹The sons of Lo'tan: Ho'ri and Homam; and Lotan's sister was Timna. ⁴⁰The sons of Sho'bal: Al'ian, Man'ahath, E'bal, She'phi, and O'nam. The sons of Zib'eon: Ai'ah and An'ah. ⁴¹The sons of An'ah: Di'shon. The sons of Dishon: Hamran, Eshban, Ithran, and Che'ran. ⁴²The sons of E'zer: Bilhan, Za'avan, and Ja'akan. The sons of Di'shan: Uz and A'ran.

43 These are the kings who reigned in the land of E'dom before any king reigned over the Israelites: Be'la the son of Beor, the name of whose city was Din'habah. ⁴⁴When Be'la died, Jobab the son of Ze'rah of Bozrah reigned in his stead. ⁴⁵When Jobab died, Hu'sham of the land of the Te'manites reigned in his stead. ⁴⁶When Hu'sham died, Ha'dad the son of Be'dad, who defeated Mid'ian in the country of Moab, reigned in his stead; and the name of his city was A'vith. ⁴⁷When Ha'dad died, Samlah of Masre'kah reigned in his stead. ⁴⁸When Samlah died, Sha'ul of Reho'both on the Euphra'tes reigned in his stead. ⁴⁹When Sha'ul died, Ba'al-ha'nan, the son of Achbor, reigned in his stead. ⁵⁰When Ba'al-ha'nan died, Ha'dad reigned in his stead; and the name of his city was Pa'i, and his wife's name Mehet'abel the daughter of Ma'tred, the daughter of Me'zahab. ⁵¹And Ha'dad died.

The chiefs of E'dom were: chiefs Timna, Al'iah, Je'theth, ⁵²Oholiba'mah, E'lah, Pi'non, ⁵³Ke'naz, Te'man, Mibzar, ⁵⁴Mag'di-el, and I'ram; these are the chiefs of E'dom.

The First and Second Books of the Chronicles (the First and Second Paralipomenon): These books, written after the Exile, give a second account of the period of the kingship. Composed as they were during a time of religious revival, they aim at giving a more religious history of the period than is available in Samuel and Kings. The author's interest is mainly in Judah and in the worship in the temple. The kingdom of David is idealized and some developments that took place later are here situated in his reign.
1:1-53: Gen 5; 10; 11; 25; 36.
* 1:1: Much space is given to genealogies in Chronicles. Postexilic Judaism was greatly interested in these in its efforts to preserve the race.

Sons of Israel and Descendants of Judah

2 These are the sons of Israel: Reuben, Simeon, Levi, Judah, Is'sachar, Zeb'ulun, ²Dan, Joseph, Benjamin, Naph'tali, Gad, and Ash'er. ³The sons of Judah: Er, O'nan, and She'lah; these three Bath-shu'a the Canaanitess bore to him. Now Er, Judah's first-born, was wicked in the sight of the LORD, and he slew him. ⁴His daughter-in-law Ta'mar also bore him Per'ez and Ze'rah. Judah had five sons in all.

5 The sons of Per'ez: Hezron and Ha'mul. ⁶The sons of Ze'rah: Zimri, Ethan, He'man, Calcol, and Dara, five in all. ⁷The sons of Carmi: A'char, the troubler of Israel, who transgressed in the matter of the devoted thing; ⁸and Ethan's son was Azari'ah.

9 The sons of Hezron, that were born to him: Jerah'meel, Ram, and Chelu'bai. ¹⁰Ram was the father of Ammin'adab, and Amminadab was the father of Nahshon, prince of the sons of Judah. ¹¹Nahshon was the father of Salma, Salma of Boaz, ¹²Boaz of O'bed, Obed of Jesse. ¹³Jesse was the father of Eli'ab his first-born, Abin'adab the second, Shim'e-a the third, ¹⁴Nethan'el the fourth, Raddai the fifth, ¹⁵Ozem the sixth, David the seventh; ¹⁶and their sisters were Zeru'iah and Ab'i-gail. The sons of Zeruiah: Abi'shai, Jo'ab, and As'ahel, three. ¹⁷Ab'igail bore Ama'sa, and the father of Amasa was Je'ther the Ish'maelite.

18 Caleb the son of Hezron had children by his wife Azu'bah, and by Jer'ioth; and these were her sons: Jesher, Shobab, and Ardon. ¹⁹When Azu'bah died, Caleb married Eph'rath, who bore him Hur. ²⁰Hur was the father of U'ri, and Uri was the father of Bez'alel.

21 Afterward Hezron went in to the daughter of Ma'chir the father of Gilead, whom he married when he was sixty years old; and she bore him Segub; ²²and Segub was the father of Ja'ir, who had twenty-three cities in the land of Gilead. ²³But Ge'shur and Ar'am took from them Hav'voth-ja'ir, Ke'nath and its villages, sixty towns. All these were descendants of Ma'chir, the father of Gilead. ²⁴After the death of Hezron, Caleb went in to Eph'rathah, ᵃ the wife of Hezron his father, and she bore him Ash'hur, the father of Teko'a.

25 The sons of Jerah'meel, the first-born of Hezron: Ram, his first-born, Bunah, Oren, Ozem, and Ahi'jah. ²⁶Jerah'meel also had another wife, whose name was At'arah; she was the mother of O'nam. ²⁷The sons of Ram, the first-born of Jerah'meel: Ma'az, Ja'min, and E'ker. ²⁸The sons of O'nam: Shammai and Jada. The sons of Shammai: Na'dab and Abi'shur. ²⁹The name of Abi'-shur's wife was Ab'ihail, and she bore him Ahban and Molid. ³⁰The sons of Na'dab: Se'led and Ap'pa-im; and Seled died childless. ³¹The sons of Ap'pa-im: Ishi. The sons of Ishi: Sheshan. The sons of Sheshan: Ahlai. ³²The sons of Jada, Sham-mai's brother: Je'ther and Jonathan; and Jether died childless. ³³The sons of Jonathan: Pe'leth and Zaza. These were the descendants of Jerah'meel. ³⁴Now Sheshan had no sons, only daughters; but Sheshan had an Egyptian slave, whose name was Jarha. ³⁵So Sheshan gave his daughter in marriage to Jarha his slave; and she bore him Attai. ³⁶Attai was the father of Nathan, and Nathan of Zabad. ³⁷Zabad was the father of Ephlal, and Ephlal of O'bed. ³⁸O'bed was the father of Je'hu, and Jehu of Azari'ah. ³⁹Azari'ah was the father of He'lez, and Helez of E'le-a'sah. ⁴⁰Ele-a'sah was the father of Sismai, and Sismai of Shallum. ⁴¹Shallum was the father of Jekami'ah, and Jekamiah of Elish'ama.

42 The sons of Caleb the brother of Jerah'meel: Mare'shah ᵇ his first-born, who was the father of Ziph. The sons of Mareshah: He'bron. ᶜ ⁴³The sons of He'bron: Ko'rah, Tap'pu-ah, Re'kem, and Shema. ⁴⁴Shema was the father of Raham, the father of Jor'ke-am; and Re'kem was the father of Shammai. ⁴⁵The son of Shammai: Maon; and Maon was the father of Beth-zur. ⁴⁶E'phah also, Caleb's concubine, bore Haran, Moza, and Gazez; and Haran was the father of Gazez. ⁴⁷The sons of Jahdai: Re'gem, Jo'tham, Geshan, Pe'let, E'phah, and Sha'aph. ⁴⁸Ma'acah, Caleb's concubine, bore Sheber and Tir'hanah. ⁴⁹She also bore Sha'aph the father of Madman'nah, Sheva the father of Machbe'nah and the father of Gib'e-a; and the daughter of Caleb was Achsah. ⁵⁰These were the descendants of Caleb.

The sons ᵈ of Hur the first-born of Eph'rathah: Sho'bal the father of Kir'iath-je'arim, ⁵¹Salma, the father of Bethlehem, and Hareph the father of Beth-ga'der. ⁵²Sho'bal the father of Kir'iath-je'arim had other sons: Haro'eh, half of the Menu'-hoth. ⁵³And the families of Kir'iath-je'arim: the Ithrites, the Puthites, the Shu'mathites, and the Mish'raites; from these came the Zorathites and the Esh'taolites. ⁵⁴The sons of Salma: Bethlehem, the Netoph'athites, At'roth-beth-jo'ab, and half of the Man"aha'thites, the Zorites. ⁵⁵The families also of the scribes that dwelt at Ja'bez: the Ti'rathites, the Shim'e-athites, and the Su'cathites. These are the Kenites who came from Hammath, the father of the house of Re'chab.

Descendants of David and Solomon

3 These are the sons of David that were born to him in He'bron: the first-born Amnon, by Ahin'o-am the Jezre'elitess; the second Daniel, by Ab'igail the Car'melitess, ²the third Ab'salom,

---

ᵃ Gk Vg: Heb in Caleb Ephrathah.
ᵇ Gk: Heb Mesha.
ᶜ Heb the father of Hebron.
ᵈ Gk Vg: Heb son.
2:1–2: Gen 35:23–26.
2:3–4: Gen 38:3–7, 29–30; Num 26:19, 20.
2:5: Gen 46:12; Num 26:21.
2:6–8: Josh 7:1; 1 Kings 4:31.
3:1–9: 2 Sam 3:2–5; 5:14–16; 1 Chron 14:3–6.

whose mother was Ma′acah, the daughter of Talmai, king of Ge′shur; the fourth Adoni′jah, whose mother was Haggith; ³the fifth Shepha-ti′ah, by Abi′tal; the sixth Ith′re-am, by his wife Eglah; ⁴six were born to him in He′bron, where he reigned for seven years and six months. And he reigned thirty-three years in Jerusalem. ⁵These were born to him in Jerusalem: Shim′e-a, Sho′bab, Nathan, and Solomon, four by Bath-shu′a, the daughter of Am′mi-el; ⁶then Ibhar, Elish′ama, Eliph′elet, ⁷No′gah, Ne′pheg, Japhi′a, ⁸Elish′ama, Eli′ada, and Eliph′elet, nine. ⁹All these were David's sons, besides the sons of the concubines; and Ta′mar was their sister.

10 The descendants of Solomon: Rehobo′am, Abi′jah his son, Asa his son, Jehosh′aphat his son, ¹¹Jo′ram his son, Ahazi′ah his son, Jo′ash his son, ¹²Amazi′ah his son, Azari′ah his son, Jo′tham his son, ¹³A′haz his son, Hezeki′ah his son, Manas′seh his son, ¹⁴A′mon his son, Josi′ah his son. ¹⁵The sons of Josi′ah: Joha′nan the first-born, the second Jehoi′akim, the third Zedeki′ah, the fourth Shallum. ¹⁶The descendants of Jehoi′akim: Jeconi′ah his son, Zedeki′ah his son; ¹⁷and the sons of Jeconi′ah, the captive: She-al′ti-el his son, ¹⁸Malchi′ram, Pedai′ah, Shenaz′zar, Jekami′ah, Hosh′ama, and Nedabi′ah; ¹⁹and the sons of Pedai′ah: Zerub′babel and Shim′e-i; and the sons of Zerubbabel: Meshul′lam and Hanani′ah, and Shelo′mith was their sister; ²⁰and Hashu′bah, O′hel, Berechi′ah, Hasadi′ah, and Ju′shab-he′sed, five. ²¹The sons of Hanani′ah: Pelati′ah and Jesha′iah, his son ᵉ Rephai′ah, his son ᵉ Arnan, his son ᵉ Obadi′ah, his son ᵉ Shecani′ah. ²²The sons of Shecani′ah: Shemai′ah. And the sons of Shemaiah: Hattush, I′gal, Bari′ah, Neari′ah, and Sha′phat, six. ²³The sons of Neari′ah: El′i-o-e′nai, Hizki′aj, and Azri′kam, three. ²⁴The sons of El′i-o-e′nai: Hod″avi′ah, Eli′ashib, Pelai′ah, Akkub, Joha′nan, Delai′ah, and Ana′ni, seven.

Descendants of Judah

4 The sons of Judah: Per′ez, Hezron, Carmi, Hur, and Sho′bal. ²Re-ai′ah the son of Sho′bal was the father of Jahath, and Jahath was the father of Ahu′mai and Lahad. These were the families of the Zo′rathites. ³These were the sons ᶠ of E′tam: Jezre′el, Ishma, and Idbash; and the name of their sister was Hazzelelpo′ni, ⁴and Penu′el was the father of Gedor, and E′zer the father of Hu′shah. These were the sons of Hur, the first-born of Eph′rathah, the father of Bethlehem. ⁵Ash′hur, the father of Teko′a, had two wives, He′lah and Na′arah; ⁶Na′arah bore him Ahuz′zam, He′pher, Te′meni, and Ha-a-hash′tari. These were the sons of Naarah. ⁷The sons of He′lah: Ze′reth, Izhar, and Ethnan. ⁸Koz was the father of A′nub, Zobe′bah, and the families of Ahar′hel the son of Harum. ⁹Ja′bez was more honorable than his brothers; and his mother called his name Jabez,

saying, "Because I bore him in pain." ¹⁰Ja′bez called on the God of Israel, saying, "Oh that you would bless me and enlarge my border, and that your hand might be with me, and that you would keep me from harm so that it might not hurt me!" And God granted what he asked. ¹¹Che′lub, the brother of Shu′hah, was the father of Me′hir, who was the father of Eshton. ¹²Eshton was the father of Bethra′pha, Pase′ah, and Tehin′nah the father of Irna′hash. These are the men of Re′cah. ¹³The sons of Ke′naz: Oth′ni-el and Serai′ah; and the sons of Othni-el: Ha′thath and Meo′nothai. ᵍ ¹⁴Meo′nothai was the father of Oph′rah; and Serai′ah was the father of Jo′ab the father of Ge-har′ashim, ʰ so-called because they were crafts-men. ¹⁵The sons of Caleb the son of Jephun′neh: Iru, E′lah, and Na′am; and the sons of Elah: Ke′naz. ¹⁶The sons of Jehal′lelel: Ziph, Ziphah, Tir′i-a, and As′arel. ¹⁷The sons of Ezrah: Je′ther, Me′red, E′pher, and Ja′lon. These are the sons of Bith′i-ah, the daughter of Pharaoh, whom Mered married; ⁱ and she conceived and bore ʲ Miriam, Sham′mai, and Ish′bah, the father of Eshtemo′a. ¹⁸And his Jewish wife bore Je′red the father of Gedor, He′ber the father of Soco, and Jeku′thiel the father of Zano′ah. ¹⁹The sons of the wife of Hodi′ah, the sister of Na′ham, were the fathers of Kei′lah the Garmite and Eshtemo′a the Ma-ac′athite. ²⁰The sons of Shimon: Amnon, Rinnah, Ben-ha′nan, and Ti′lon. The sons of Ishi: Zoheth and Ben-zo′heth. ²¹The sons of She′lah the son of Judah: Er the father of Lecah, La′adah the father of Mare′shah, and the families of the house of linen workers at Beth-ashbe′a; ²²and Jokim, and the men of Coze′ba, and Jo′ash, and Saraph, who ruled in Moab and returned to Lehem ᵏ (now the records ˡ are ancient). ²³These were the potters and inhabitants of Neta′im and Gede′rah; they dwelt there with the king for his work.

Descendants of Simeon

24 The sons of Simeon: Nem′u-el, Ja′min, Ja′rib, Ze′rah, Sha′ul; ²⁵Shallum was his son, Mib′sam his son, Mishma his son. ²⁶The sons of Mishma: Ham′mu-el his son, Zaccur his son, Shim′e-i his son. ²⁷Shim′e-i had sixteen sons and six daughters; but his brothers had not many children, nor did all their family multiply like the men of Judah. ²⁸They dwelt in Be′er-she′ba, Mo′ladah, Ha′zar-shu′al, ²⁹Bilhah, E′zem, To′lad, ³⁰Bethu′el, Hormah, Zik′lag, ³¹Beth-mar′caboth,

ᵉ Gk Compare Syr Vg: Heb *sons of*.
ᶠ Gk Compare Vg: Heb *father*.
ᵍ Gk Vg: Heb lacks *Meonothai*.
ʰ That is *Valley of craftsmen*.
ⁱ The clause: *These are . . . married* is transposed from verse 18.
ʲ Heb lacks *and bore*.
ᵏ Vg Compare Gk: Heb *and Jashubi-lahem*.
ˡ Or *matters*.
3:4: 2 Sam 5:4, 5.
4:24: Gen 46:10; Ex 6:15; Num 26:12, 13.
4:28–33: Josh 19:2–8.

Ha'zar-su'sim, Beth-bir'i, and Sha-ara'im. These were their cities until David reigned. [32]And their villages were E'tam, A'in, Rimmon, Tochen, and A'shan, five cities, [33]along with all their villages which were round about these cities as far as Ba'al. These were their settlements, and they kept a genealogical record.

[34] Mesho'bab, Jamlech, Joshah the son of Amazi'ah, [35]Joel, Je'hu the son of Joshibi'ah, son of Serai'ah, son of As'i-el, [36]Eli-o-e'nai, Ja''ako'-bah, Jeshohai'ah, Asai'ah, Ad'i-el, Jesim'i-el, Bena'iah, [37]Ziza the son of Shi'phi, son of Allon, son of Jedai'ah, son of Shimri, son of Shemai'ah— [38]these mentioned by name were princes in their families, and their fathers' houses increased greatly. [39]They journeyed to the entrance of Gedor, to the east side of the valley, to seek pasture for their flocks, [40]where they found rich, good pasture, and the land was very broad, quiet, and peaceful; for the former inhabitants there belonged to Ham. [41]These, registered by name, came in the days of Hezeki'ah, king of Judah, and destroyed their tents and the Me-u'nim who were found there, and exterminated them to this day, and settled in their place, because there was pasture there for their flocks. [42]And some of them, five hundred men of the Simeonites, went to Mount Se'ir, having as their leaders Pelati'ah, Ne-ari'ah, Rephai'ah, and Uz'ziel, the sons of Ishi; [43]and they destroyed the remnant of the Amal'e-kites that had escaped, and they have dwelt there to this day.

Descendants of Reuben

5 The sons of Reuben the first-born of Israel (for he was the first-born; but because he polluted his father's couch, his birthright was given to the sons of Joseph the son of Israel, so that he is not enrolled in the genealogy according to the birthright; [2]though Judah became strong among his brothers and a prince was from him, yet the birthright belonged to Joseph), [3]the sons of Reuben, the first-born of Israel: Ha'noch, Pallu, Hezron, and Carmi. [4]The sons of Joel: Shemai'ah his son, Gog his son, Shim'e-i his son, [5]Micah his son, Re-ai'ah his son, Ba'al his son, [6]Beer'ah his son, whom Til'gath-pilne'ser king of Assyria carried away into exile; he was a chieftain of the Reubenites. [7]And his kinsmen by their families, when the genealogy of their generations was reckoned: the chief, Je-i'el, and Zechari'ah, [8]and Be'la the son of A'zaz, son of She'ma, son of Joel, who dwelt in Aro'er, as far as Nebo and Ba'al-me'on. [9]He also dwelt to the east as far as the entrance of the desert this side of the Euphrates, because their cattle had multiplied in the land of Gilead. [10]And in the days of Saul they made war on the Hag'rites, who fell by their hand; and they dwelt in their tents throughout all the region east of Gilead.

Descendants of Gad

[11] The sons of Gad dwelt over against them in the land of Bashan as far as Sal'ecah: [12]Joel the chief, Sha'pham the second, Ja'nai, and Sha'phat in Bashan. [13]And their kinsmen according to their fathers' houses: Michael, Meshul'lam, Sheba, Jo'rai, Ja'can, Zia, and E'ber, seven. [14]These were the sons of Ab'ihail the son of Huri, son of Jaro'ah, son of Gilead, son of Michael, son of Jeshish'ai, son of Jahdo, son of Buz; [15]A'hi the son of Ab'di-el, son of Gu'ni, was chief in their fathers' houses; [16]and they dwelt in Gilead, in Bashan and in its towns, and in all the pasture lands of Sharon to their limits. [17]All of these were enrolled by genealogies in the days of Jo'tham king of Judah, and in the days of Jerobo'am king of Israel.

[18] The Reubenites, the Gadites, and the half-tribe of Manas'seh had valiant men, who carried shield and sword, and drew the bow, expert in war, forty-four thousand seven hundred and sixty, ready for service. [19]They made war upon the Hag'rites, Je'tur, Na'phish, and No'dab; [20]and when they received help against them, the Hag'-rites and all who were with them were given into their hands, for they cried to God in the battle, and he granted their entreaty because they trusted in him. [21]They carried off their livestock: fifty thousand of their camels, two hundred and fifty thousand sheep, two thousand donkeys, and a hundred thousand men alive. [22]For many fell slain, because the war was of God. And they dwelt in their place until the exile.

The Half-tribe of Manasseh

[23] The members of the half-tribe of Manas'seh dwelt in the land; they were very numerous from Ba'shan to Ba'al-her'mon, Se'nir, and Mount Hermon. [24]These were the heads of their fathers' houses: E'pher,[m] Ishi, Eli'el, Az'ri-el, Jeremi'ah, Hod''avi'ah, and Jah'di-el, mighty warriors, famous men, heads of their fathers' houses. [25]But they transgressed against the God of their fathers, and played the harlot after the gods of the peoples of the land, whom God had destroyed before them. [26]So the God of Israel stirred up the spirit of Pul king of Assyria, the spirit of Til'gath-pilne'ser king of Assyria, and he carried them away, namely, the Reubenites, the Gadites, and the half-tribe of Manas'seh, and brought them to Ha'lah, Ha'bor, Hara, and the river Gozan, to this day.

Descendants of Levi

6 [n] The sons of Levi: Gershom, Ko'hath, and Merar'i. [2]The sons of Ko'hath: Amram, Izhar, Heb'ron, and Uz'ziel. [3]The children of Amram: Aaron, Moses, and Miriam. The sons of Aaron:

[m] Gk Vg: Heb and Epher.
[n] Ch 5:27 in Heb.
5:1-26: Gen 46:9; Num 26:5, 6.
6:1-15: Gen 46:11; Ex 6:16-20; Num 3:2.

Na'dab, Abi'hu, Elea'zar, and Ith'amar. ⁴Elea'zar was the father of Phin'ehas, Phinehas of Abishu'a, ⁵Abishu'a of Bukki, Bukki of Uzzi, ⁶Uzzi of Zerahi'ah, Zerahiah of Mera'ioth, ⁷Mera'ioth of Amari'ah, Amariah of Ahi'tub, ⁸Ahi'tub of Za'dok, Zadok of Ahim'a-az, ⁹Ahim'a-az of Azari'ah, Azariah of Joha'nan, ¹⁰and Joha'nan of Azari'ah (it was he who served as priest in the house that Solomon built in Jerusalem). ¹¹Azari'ah was the father of Amari'ah, Amariah of Ahi'tub, ¹²Ahi'tub of Za'dok, Zadok of Shallum, ¹³Shallum of Hilki'ah, Hilkiah of Azari'ah, ¹⁴Azariah of Serai'ah, Seraiah of Jehoz'adak; ¹⁵and Jehoz'adak went into exile when the Lord sent Judah and Jerusalem into exile by the hand of Nebuchadnez'zar.

16° The sons of Levi: Gershom, Ko'hath, and Merar'i. ¹⁷And these are the names of the sons of Gershom: Libni and Shim'e-i. ¹⁸The sons of Ko'hath: Amram, Izhar, He'bron, and Uz'ziel. ¹⁹The sons of Merar'i: Mah'li and Mu'shi. These are the families of the Levites according to their fathers. ²⁰Of Gershom: Libni his son, Jahath his son, Zimmah his son, ²¹Jo'ah his son, Iddo his son, Ze'rah his son, Je-ath'erai his son. ²²The sons of Ko'hath: Ammin'adab his son, Ko'rah his son, Assir his son, ²³Elka'nah his son, Ebi'asaph his son, Assir his son, ²⁴Ta'hath his son, Uri'el his son, Uzzi'ah his son, and Sha'ul his son. ²⁵The sons of Elka'nah: Ama'sai and Ahi'moth, ²⁶Elka'nah his son, Zo'phai his son, Na'hath his son, ²⁷Eli'ab his son, Jero'ham his son, Elka'nah his son. ²⁸The sons of Samuel: Joelᵖ his first-born, the second Abi'jah. ᑫ ²⁹The sons of Merar'i: Mah'li, Libni his son, Shim'e-i his son, Uzzah his son, ³⁰Shim'e-a his son, Haggi'ah his son, and Asai'ah his son.

Musicians Appointed by David

31 These are the men whom David put in charge of the service of song in the house of the Lord, after the ark rested there. ³²They ministered with song before the tabernacle of the tent of meeting, until Solomon had built the house of the Lord in Jerusalem; and they performed their service in due order. ³³These are the men who served and their sons. Of the sons of the Ko'hathites: He'man the singer the son of Joel, son of Samuel, ³⁴son of Elka'nah, son of Jero'ham, son of Eli'el, son of To'ah, ³⁵son of Zuph, son of Elka'nah, son of Mahath, son of Ama'sai, ³⁶son of Elka'nah, son of Joel, son of Azari'ah, son of Zephani'ah, ³⁷son of Ta'hath, son of Assir, son of Ebi'asaph, son of Ko'rah, ³⁸son of Izhar, son of Ko'hath, son of Levi, son of Israel; ³⁹and his brother A'saph, who stood on his right hand, namely, Asaph the son of Berechi'ah, son of Shim'e-a, ⁴⁰son of Michael, son of Ba-ase'iah, son of Malchi'jah, ⁴¹son of Ethni, son of Ze'rah, son of Adai'ah, ⁴²son of Ethan, son of Zimmah, son of Shim'e-i, ⁴³son of Jahath, son of Gershom, son of Levi. ⁴⁴On the left hand were their brethren the sons of Merar'i: Ethan the son of Kishi, son of Abdi, son of Mal'luch, ⁴⁵son of Hashabi'ah, son of Amazi'ah, son of Hilki'ah, ⁴⁶son of Amzi, son of Ba'ni, son of She'mer, ⁴⁷son of Mah'li, son of Mu'shi, son of Merar'i, son of Levi; ⁴⁸and their brethren the Levites were appointed for all the service of the tabernacle of the house of God.

49 But Aaron and his sons made offerings upon the altar of burnt offering and upon the altar of incense for all the work of the most holy place, and to make atonement for Israel, according to all that Moses the servant of God had commanded. ⁵⁰These are the sons of Aaron: Elea'zar his son, Phin'ehas his son, Abishu'a his son, ⁵¹Bukki his son, Uzzi his son, Zerahi'ah his son, ⁵²Mera'ioth his son, Amari'ah his son, Ahi'tub his son, ⁵³Za'dok his son, Ahim'a-az his son.

Settlements of the Levites

54 These are their dwelling places according to their settlements within their borders: to the sons of Aaron of the families of Ko'hathites, for theirs was the lot, ⁵⁵to them they gave He'bron in the land of Judah and its surrounding pasture lands, ⁵⁶but the fields of the city and its villages they gave to Caleb the son of Jephun'neh. ⁵⁷To the sons of Aaron they gave the cities of refuge: He'bron, Libnah with its pasture lands, Jat'tir, Eshtemo'a with its pasture lands, ⁵⁸Hilen with its pasture lands, De'bir with its pasture lands, ⁵⁹A'shan with its pasture lands, and Bethshe'mesh with its pasture lands; ⁶⁰and from the tribe of Benjamin, Ge'ba with its pasture lands, Al'emeth with its pasture lands, and An'athoth with its pasture lands. All their cities throughout their families were thirteen.

61 To the rest of the Ko'hathites were given by lot out of the family of the tribe, out of the half-tribe, the half of Manas'seh, ten cities. ⁶²To the Ger'shomites according to their families were allotted thirteen cities out of the tribes of Is'sachar, Asher, Naph'tali, and Manas'seh in Bashan. ⁶³To the Merar'ites according to their families were allotted twelve cities out of the tribes of Reuben, Gad, and Zeb'ulun. ⁶⁴So the sons of Israel gave the Levites the cities with their pasture lands. ⁶⁵They also gave them by lot out of the tribes of Judah, Simeon, and Benjamin these cities which are mentioned by name.

66 And some of the families of the sons of Ko'hath had cities of their territory out of the tribe of E'phraim. ⁶⁷They were given the cities of

---

° Ch 6:1 in Heb.
ᵖ Gk Syr Compare verse 33 and 1 Sam 8:2: Heb lacks *Joel*.
ᑫ Heb *and Abijah*.
6:16–53: Ex 6:16–24.
6:54–81: Josh 21:1–42.

refuge: She'chem with its pasture lands in the hill country of E'phraim, Gezer with its pasture lands, [68]Jok'me-am with its pasture lands, Beth-ho'ron with its pasture lands, [69]Ai'jalon with its pasture lands, Gath-rim'mon with its pasture lands, [70]and out of the half-tribe of Manas'seh, A'ner with its pasture lands, and Bil'e-am with its pasture lands, for the rest of the families of the Ko'hathites.

71 To the Ger'shomites were given out of the half-tribe of Manas'seh: Golan in Bashan with its pasture lands and Ash'taroth with its pasture lands; [72]and out of the tribe of Is'sachar: Ke'desh with its pasture lands, Dab'erath with its pasture lands, [73]Ra'moth with its pasture lands, and A'nem with its pasture lands; [74]out of the tribe of Asher: Mashal with its pasture lands, Abdon with its pasture lands, [75]Hukok with its pasture lands, and Re'hob with its pasture lands; [76]and out of the tribe of Naph'tali: Ke'desh in Galilee with its pasture lands, Ham'mon with its pasture lands, and Kir"iatha'im with its pasture lands. [77]To the rest of the Merar'ites were allotted out of the tribe of Zeb'ulun: Rim'mono with its pasture lands, Ta'bor with its pasture lands, [78]and beyond the Jordan at Jericho, on the east side of the Jordan, out of the tribe of Reuben: Bezer in the steppe with its pasture lands, Jah'zah with its pasture lands, [79]Ked'emoth with its pasture lands, and Meph'a-ath with its pasture lands; [80]and out of the tribe of Gad: Ra'moth in Gilead with its pasture lands, Ma"hana'im with its pasture lands, [81]Hesh'bon with its pasture lands, and Ja'zer with its pasture lands.

Descendants of Issachar

7 The sons [x] of Is'sachar: To'la, Puah, Jash'ub, and Shim'ron, four. [2]The sons of To'la: Uzzi, Rephai'ah, Je'ri-el, Jahmai, Ibsam, and Shemu'el, heads of their fathers' houses, namely of Tola, mighty warriors of their generations, their number in the days of David being twenty-two thousand six hundred. [3]The sons of Uzzi: Izrahi'ah. And the sons of Izrahiah: Michael, Obadi'ah, Joel, and Isshi'ah, five, all of them chief men; [4]and along with them, by their generations, according to their fathers' houses, were units of the army for war, thirty-six thousand, for they had many wives and sons. [5]Their kinsmen belonging to all the families of Is'sachar were in all eighty-seven thousand mighty warriors, enrolled by genealogy.

Descendants of Benjamin

6 The sons of Benjamin: Be'la, Be'cher, and Jedi'a-el, three. [7]The sons of Be'la: Ezbon, Uzzi, Uz'ziel, Jer'imoth, and Iri, five, heads of fathers' houses, mighty warriors; and their enrollment by genealogies was twenty-two thousand and thirty-four. [8]The sons of Be'cher: Zemi'rah, Jo'ash, Elie'zer, El'i-o-e'nai, Omri, Jer'emoth, Abi'jah,

An'athoth, and Al'emeth. All these were the sons of Becher; [9]and their enrollment by genealogies, according to their generations, as heads of their fathers' houses, mighty warriors, was twenty thousand two hundred. [10]The sons of Jedi'a-el: Bilhan. And the sons of Bilhan: Je'ush, Benjamin, E'hud, Chena'anah, Zethan, Tar'shish, and Ahish'ahar. [11]All these were the sons of Jedi'a-el according to the heads of their fathers' houses, mighty warriors, seventeen thousand and two hundred, ready for service in war. [12]And Shuppim and Huppim were the sons of Ir, Hu'shim the sons of A'her.

Descendants of Naphtali

13 The sons of Naph'tali: Jah'zi-el, Gu'ni, Je'zer, and Shallum, the offspring of Bilhah.

Descendants of Manasseh

14 The sons of Manas'seh: As'ri-el, whom his Arame'an concubine bore; she bore Ma'chir the father of Gilead. [15]And Ma'chir took a wife for Huppim and for Shuppim. The name of his sister was Ma'acah. And the name of the second was Zeloph'ehad; and Zelophehad had daughters. [16]And Ma'acah the wife of Ma'chir bore a son, and she called his name Peresh; and the name of his brother was Sheresh; and his sons were Ulam and Rakem. [17]The sons of Ulam: Be'dan. These were the sons of Gilead the son of Ma'chir, son of Manas'seh. [18]And his sister Hammo'lecheth bore Ish'hod, Abie'zer, and Mahlah. [19]The sons of Shemi'da were Ahi'an, She'chem, Likhi, and Ani'am.

Descendants of Ephraim

20 The sons of E'phraim: Shuthe'lah, and Be'red his son, Ta'hath his son, Ele-a'dah his son, Tahath his son, [21]Zabad his son, Shuthe'lah his son, and E'zer and E'le-ad, whom the men of Gath who were born in the land slew, because they came down to raid their cattle. [22]And E'phraim their father mourned many days, and his brothers came to comfort him. [23]And E'phraim went in to his wife, and she conceived and bore a son; and he called his name Beri'ah, because evil had befallen his house. [24]His daughter was She'erah, who built both Lower and Upper Beth-ho'ron, and Uz'zen-she'erah. [25]Rephah was his son, Resheph his son, Te'lah his son, Ta'han his son, [26]Ladan his son, Ammi'hud his son, Elish'-ama his son, [27]Nun his son, Joshua his son. [28]Their possessions and settlements were Bethel and its towns, and eastward Na'aran, and westward Gezer and its towns, She'chem and its towns, and Ayyah and its towns; [29]also along the borders of the Manas'sites, Beth-she'an and its towns, Ta'anach and its towns, Megid'do and its towns, Dor and its towns. In these dwelt the sons of Joseph the son of Israel.

---

[x] Syr Compare Vg: Heb *and to the sons*.

Descendants of Asher

30 The sons of Asher: Imnah, Ishvah, Ishvi, Beri'ah, and their sister Se'rah. [31]The sons of Beri'ah: He'ber and Mal'chi-el, who was the father of Bir'zaith. [32]He'ber was the father of Japhlet, Shomer, Ho'tham, and their sister Shua. [33]The sons of Japhlet: Pasach, Bimhal, and Ashvath. These are the sons of Japhlet. [34]The sons of She'mer his brother: Rohgah, Jehub'bah, and Ar'am. [35]The sons of He'lem his brother: Zo'phah, Imna, Shelesh, and A'mal. [36]The sons of Zo'phah: Su'ah, Har'nepher, Shual, Beri, Imrah, [37]Bezer, Hod, Shamma, Shilshah, Ithran, and Be-e'ra. [38]The sons of Je'ther: Jephun'neh, Pispa, and Ar'a. [39]The sons of Ulla: A'rah, Han'niel, and Rizi'a. [40]All of these were men of Asher, heads of fathers' houses, approved, mighty warriors, chief of the princes. Their number enrolled by genealogies, for service in war, was twenty-six thousand men.

Descendants of Benjamin in Detail

8 Benjamin was the father of Be'la his first-born, Ash'bel the second, A'harah the third, [2]No'hah the fourth, and Ra'pha the fifth. [3]And Be'la had sons: Addar, Gera, Abi'hud, [4]Abishu'a, Na'aman, Aho'ah, [5]Gera, Shephu'phan, and Hu'ram. [6]These are the sons of E'hud (they were heads of fathers' houses of the inhabitants of Ge'ba, and they were carried into exile to Mana'-hath): [7]Na'aman, [s] Ahi'jah, and Gera, that is, Heglam, [t] who was the father of Uzza and Ahi'hud. [8]And Sha"hara'im had sons in the country of Moab after he had sent away Hu'shim and Ba'ara his wives. [9]He had sons by Hodesh his wife: Jo'bab, Zib'ia, Me'sha, Malcam, [10]Je'uz, Sachi'a, and Mirmah. These were his sons, heads of fathers' houses. [11]He also had sons by Hu'shim: Abi'tub and Elpa'al. [12]The sons of Elpa'al: E'ber, Misham, and She'med, who built Ono and Lod with its towns, [13]and Beri'ah and She'ma (they were heads of fathers' houses of the inhabitants of Ai'jalon, who put to flight the inhabitants of Gath); [14]and Ahi'o, Shashak, and Jer'emoth. [15]Zebadi'ah, Ar'ad, E'der, [16]Michael, Ishpah, and Joha were sons of Beri'ah. [17]Zebadi'ah, Meshul'lam, Hizki, He'ber, [18]Ish'merai, Izli'ah, and Jo'bab were the sons of Elpa'al. [19]Ja'kim, Zich'ri, Zabdi, [20]E'li-e'nai, Zil'le-thai, Eli'el, [21]Adai'ah, Bera'iah, and Shimrath were the sons of Shim'e-i. [22]Ishpan, E'ber, Eli'el, [23]Abdon, Zich'ri, Ha'nan, [24]Hanani'ah, E'lam, Anthothi'jah, [25]Iphde'iah, and Penu'el were the sons of Shashak. [26]Sham'sherai, Shehari'ah, Athali'ah, [27]Ja-areshi'ah, Eli'jah, and Zich'ri were the sons of Jero'ham. [28]These were the heads of fathers' houses, according to their generations, chief men. These dwelt in Jerusalem.

[29]Je-i'el [u] the father of Gib'eon dwelt in Gibeon, and the name of his wife was Ma'acah.

[30]His first-born son: Abdon, then Zur, Kish, Ba'al, Na'dab, [31]Gedor, Ahi'o, Zecher, [32]and Mikloth (he was the father of Shim'e-ah). Now these also dwelt opposite their kinsmen in Jerusalem, with their kinsmen. [33]Ner was the father of Kish, Kish of Saul, Saul of Jonathan, Mal"chishu'a, Abin'adab, and Eshba'al; [34]and the son of Jonathan was Mer'ib-ba'al; and Merib-baal was the father of Micah. [35]The sons of Micah: Pithon, Melech, Tare'a, and A'haz. [36]A'haz was the father of Jeho'-addah; and Jehoaddah was the father of Al'emeth, Az'maveth, and Zimri; Zimri was the father of Moza. [37]Moza was the father of Bin'e-a; Ra'phah was his son, El-e-a'sah his son, A'zel his son. [38]A'zel had six sons, and these are their names: Azri'kam, Bo'cheru, Ish'mael, Sheari'ah, Oba-di'ah, and Ha'nan. All these were the sons of Azel. [39]The sons of E'shek his brother: Ulam his first-born, Je'ush the second, and Eliph'elet the third. [40]The sons of Ulam were men who were mighty warriors, bowmen, having many sons and grandsons, one hundred and fifty. All these were Benjaminites.

9 So all Israel was enrolled by genealogies; and these are written in the Book of the Kings of Israel. And Judah was taken into exile in Babylon because of their unfaithfulness. [2]Now the first to dwell again in their possessions in their cities were Israel, the priests, the Levites, and the temple servants. [3]And some of the people of Judah, Benjamin, E'phraim, and Manas'seh dwelt in Jerusalem: [4]Uthai the son of Ammi'hud, son of Omri, son of Imri, son of Ba'ni, from the sons of Per'ez the son of Judah. [5]And of the Shi'lonites: Asai'ah the first-born, and his sons. [6]Of the sons of Ze'rah: Jeu'el and their kinsmen, six hundred and ninety. [7]Of the Benjaminites: Sallu the son of Meshul'lam, son of Hod"avi'ah, son of Hassenu'ah, [8]Ibne'iah the son of Jero'ham, E'lah the son of Uzzi, son of Michri, and Meshul'lam the son of Shephati'ah, son of Reu'el, son of Ibni'jah; [9]and their kinsmen according to their generations, nine hundred and fifty-six. All these were heads of fathers' houses according to their fathers' houses.

Priestly Families

10 Of the priests: Jedai'ah, Jehoi'arib, Ja'chin, [11]and Azari'ah the son of Hilki'ah, son of Meshul'lam, son of Za'dok, son of Mera'ioth, son of Ahi'tub, the chief officer of the house of God; [12]and Adai'ah the son of Jero'ham, son of Pash-hur, son of Malchi'jah, and Ma'asai the son of Ad'i-el, son of Jah'zerah, son of Meshul'lam, son of Meshil'lemith, son of Immer; [13]besides

---

[s] Heb *and Naaman.*
[t] Or *he carried them into exile.*
[u] Compare 9:35: Heb lacks *Jeiel.*
9:1, 2: Ezra 2:70; Neh 7:73; 11:3.
9:3–17: Neh 11:4–19.

their kinsmen, heads of their fathers' houses, one thousand seven hundred and sixty, very able men for the work of the service of the house of God.

Levitical Families

14 Of the Levites: Shemai'ah the son of Hasshub, son of Azri'kam, son of Hashabi'ah, of the sons of Merar'i; [15]and Bakbak'kar, He'resh, Ga'lal, and Mattani'ah the son of Mica, son of Zich'ri, son of A'saph; [16]and Obadi'ah the son of Shemai'ah, son of Galal, son of Jedu'thun, and Berechi'ah the son of Asa, son of Elka'nah, who dwelt in the villages of the Netoph'athites.

17 The gatekeepers were: Shallum, Akkub, Talmon, Ahi'man, and their kinsmen (Shallum being the chief), [18]stationed hitherto in the king's gate on the east side. These were the gatekeepers of the camp of the Levites. [19]Shallum the son of Ko're, son of Ebi'asaph, son of Ko'rah, and his kinsmen of his fathers' house, the Ko'rahites, were in charge of the work of the service, keepers of the thresholds of the tent, as their fathers had been in charge of the camp of the LORD, keepers of the entrance. [20]And Phin'ehas the son of Elea'zar was the ruler over them in time past; the LORD was with him. [21]Zechari'ah the son of Meshelemi'ah was gatekeeper at the entrance of the tent of meeting. [22]All these, who were chosen as gatekeepers at the thresholds, were two hundred and twelve. They were enrolled by genealogies in their villages. David and Samuel the seer established them in their office of trust. [23]So they and their sons were in charge of the gates of the house of the LORD, that is, the house of the tent, as guards. [24]The gatekeepers were on the four sides, east, west, north, and south; [25]and their kinsmen who were in their villages were obliged to come in every seven days, from time to time, to be with these; [26]for the four chief gatekeepers, who were Levites, were in charge of the chambers and the treasures of the house of God. [27]And they lodged round about the house of God; for upon them lay the duty of watching, and they had charge of opening it every morning.

28 Some of them had charge of the utensils of service, for they were required to count them when they were brought in and taken out. [29]Others of them were appointed over the furniture, and over all the holy utensils, also over the fine flour, the wine, the oil, the incense, and the spices. [30]Others, of the sons of the priests, prepared the mixing of the spices, [31]and Mattithi'ah, one of the Levites, the first-born of Shallum the Ko'rahite, was in charge of making the flat cakes. [32]Also some of their kinsmen of the Ko'hathites had charge of the showbread, to prepare it every sabbath.

33 Now these are the singers, the heads of fathers' houses of the Levites, dwelling in the chambers of the temple free from other service, for they were on duty day and night. [34]These were heads of fathers' houses of the Levites, according to their generations, leaders, who lived in Jerusalem.

The Family of Saul

35 In Gib'eon dwelt the father of Gibeon, Je-i'el, and the name of his wife was Ma'acah, [36]and his first-born son Abdon, then Zur, Kish, Ba'al, Ner, Na'dab, [37]Gedor, Ahi'o, Zechari'ah, and Mikloth; [38]and Mikloth was the father of Shim'e-am; and these also dwelt opposite their kinsmen in Jerusalem, with their kinsmen. [39]Ner was the father of Kish, Kish of Saul, Saul of Jonathan, Mal"chishu'a, Abin'adab, and Eshba'al; [40]and the son of Jonathan was Mer'ib-ba'al; and Merib-baal was the father of Micah. [41]The sons of Micah: Pithon, Melech, Tah're-a, and A'haz;[v] [42]and A'haz was the father of Jarah, and Jarah of Al'emeth, Az'maveth, and Zimri; and Zimri was the father of Moza. [43]Moza was the father of Bin'e-a; and Rephai'ah was his son, Ele-a'sah his son, A'zel his son. [44]A'zel had six sons and these are their names: Azri'kam, Bo'cheru, Ish'mael, Sheari'ah, Obadi'ah, and Ha'nan; these were the sons of Azel.

The Death of Saul and His Sons

10 Now the Philis'tines fought against Israel; and the men of Israel fled before the Philis'tines, and fell slain on Mount Gilbo'a. [2]And the Philis'tines overtook Saul and his sons; and the Philistines slew Jonathan and Abin'adab and Mal"chishu'a, the sons of Saul. [3]The battle pressed hard upon Saul, and the archers found him; and he was wounded by the archers. [4]Then Saul said to his armor-bearer, "Draw your sword, and thrust me through with it, lest these uncircumcised come and make sport of me." But his armor-bearer would not; for he feared greatly. Therefore Saul took his own sword, and fell upon it. [5]And when his armor-bearer saw that Saul was dead, he also fell upon his sword, and died. [6]Thus Saul died; he and his three sons and all his house died together. [7]And when all the men of Israel who were in the valley saw that the army[w] had fled and that Saul and his sons were dead, they forsook their cities and fled; and the Philis'tines came and dwelt in them.

8 The next day, when the Philis'tines came to strip the slain, they found Saul and his sons fallen on Mount Gilbo'a. [9]And they stripped him and took his head and his armor, and sent messengers throughout the land of the Philis'tines, to carry the good news to their idols and to the people. [10]And they put his armor in the temple of their gods, and fastened his head in the temple of Da'gon. [11]But when all Ja'besh-gil'ead heard all

---

[v] Compare 8:35: Heb lacks *and Ahaz.*
[w] Heb *they.*
10:1–12: 1 Sam 31:1–13.

that the Philis′tines had done to Saul, ¹²all the valiant men arose, and took away the body of Saul and the bodies of his sons, and brought them to Ja′besh. And they buried their bones under the oak in Jabesh, and fasted seven days.

13 So Saul died for his unfaithfulness; he was unfaithful to the Lᴏʀᴅ in that he did not keep the command of the Lᴏʀᴅ, and also consulted a medium, seeking guidance, ¹⁴and did not seek guidance from the Lᴏʀᴅ. Therefore the Lᴏʀᴅ slew him, and turned the kingdom over to David the son of Jesse.

David Anointed King of All Israel

11 Then all Israel gathered together to David at He′bron, and said, "Behold, we are your bone and flesh. ²In times past, even when Saul was king, it was you that led out and brought in Israel; and the Lᴏʀᴅ your God said to you, 'You shall be shepherd of my people Israel, and you shall be prince over my people Israel.' " ³So all the elders of Israel came to the king at He′bron; and David made a covenant with them at Hebron before the Lᴏʀᴅ, and they anointed David king over Israel, according to the word of the Lᴏʀᴅ by Samuel.

David's Army Captures Jerusalem

4 And David and all Israel went to Jerusalem, that is Je′bus, where the Jeb′usites were, the inhabitants of the land. ⁵The inhabitants of Je′bus said to David, "You will not come in here." Nevertheless David took the stronghold of Zion, that is, the city of David. ⁶David said, "Whoever shall strike the Jeb′usites first shall be chief and commander." And Jo′ab the son of Zeru′iah went up first, so he became chief. ⁷And David dwelt in the stronghold; therefore it was called the city of David. ⁸And he built the city round about from the Millo in complete circuit; and Jo′ab repaired the rest of the city. ⁹And David became greater and greater, for the Lᴏʀᴅ of hosts was with him.

David's Mighty Men and Their Exploits

10 Now these are the chiefs of David's mighty men, who gave him strong support in his kingdom, together with all Israel, to make him king, according to the word of the Lᴏʀᴅ concerning Israel. ¹¹This is an account of David's mighty men: Jasho′be-am, a Hach′monite, was chief of the three;ˣ he wielded his spear against three hundred whom he slew at one time.

12 And next to him among the three mighty men was Elea′zar the son of Dodo, the Aho′hite. ¹³He was with David at Pas-dam′mim when the Philis′tines were gathered there for battle. There was a plot of ground full of barley, and the men fled from the Philistines. ¹⁴But heʸ took hisʸ stand in the midst of the plot, and defended it, and slew the Philis′tines; and the Lᴏʀᴅ saved them by a great victory.

15 Three of the thirty chief men went down to the rock to David at the cave of Adul′lam, when the army of Philis′tines was encamped in the valley of Reph′aim. ¹⁶David was then in the stronghold; and the garrison of the Philis′tines was then at Bethlehem. ¹⁷And David said longingly, "O that some one would give me water to drink from the well of Bethlehem which is by the gate!" ¹⁸Then the three mighty men broke through the camp of the Philis′tines, and drew water out of the well of Bethlehem which was by the gate, and took and brought it to David. But David would not drink of it; he poured it out to the Lᴏʀᴅ, ¹⁹and said, "Far be it from me before my God that I should do this. Shall I drink the lifeblood of these men? For at the risk of their lives they brought it." Therefore he would not drink it. These things did the three mighty men.

20 Now Abi′shai, the brother of Jo′ab, was chief of the thirty.ᶻ And he wielded his spear against three hundred men and slew them, and won a name beside the three. ²¹He was the most renownedᵃ of the thirty,ᶻ and became their commander; but he did not attain to the three.

22 And Bena′iah the son of Jehoi′ada was a valiant manᵇ of Kab′zeel, a doer of great deeds; he struck two Arielsᶜ of Moab. He also went down and slew a lion in a pit on a day when snow had fallen. ²³And he slew an Egyptian, a man of great stature, five cubits tall. The Egyptian had in his hand a spear like a weaver's beam; but Bena′iah went down to him with a staff, and snatched the spear out of the Egyptian's hand, and slew him with his own spear. ²⁴These things did Bena′iah the son of Jehoi′ada, and won a name beside the three mighty men. ²⁵He was renowned among the thirty, but he did not attain to the three. And David set him over his bodyguard.

26 The mighty men of the armies were As′ahel the brother of Jo′ab, Elha′nan the son of Dodo of Bethlehem, ²⁷Shammoth of Harod,ᵈ He′lez the Pel′onite, ²⁸Ira the son of Ikkesh of Teko′a, Abie′zer of An′athoth, ²⁹Sib′becai the Hu′shathite, Ilai the Aho′hite, ³⁰Ma′harai of Netoph′ah, He′led the son of Ba′anah of Netophah, ³¹Ithai the son of Ri′bai of Gib′e-ah of the Benjaminites, Bena′iah of Pir′athon, ³²Hurai of the brooks of Ga′ash, Abi′el the Ar′bathite, ³³Az′maveth of Baha′rum, Eli′ahba of Sha-al′bon, ³⁴Hashemᵉ the Gi′zonite, Jonathan the son of Sha′gee the Har′arite, ³⁵Ahi′am the son of Sachar the Har′arite, Eli′phal the son of Ur,

---

ˣ Compare 2 Sam 23:8: Heb *thirty* or *captains.*
ʸ Compare 2 Sam 23:12: Heb *they … their.*
ᶻ Syr: Heb *three.*
ᵃ Compare 2 Sam 23:19: Heb *more renowned among the two.*
ᵇ Syr: Heb *the son of a valiant man.*
ᶜ Gk: *sons of Ariel.* Heb lacks *sons of.*
ᵈ Compare 2 Sam 23:25: Heb *the Harorite.*
ᵉ Compare Gk and 2 Sam 23:32: Heb *the sons of Hashem.*
11:1-3: 2 Sam 5:1-3.
11:4-9: 2 Sam 5:6-10.
11:10-41: 2 Sam 23:8-39.

³⁶He'pher the Meche'rathite, Ahi'jah the Pel'onite, ³⁷Hezro of Carmel, Na'arai the son of Ezbai, ³⁸Joel the brother of Nathan, Mibhar the son of Hagri, ³⁹Zelek the Am'monite, Na'harai of Be-er'oth, the armor-bearer of Jo'ab the son of Zeru'iah, ⁴⁰Ira the Ithrite, Ga'reb the Ithrite, ⁴¹Uri'ah the Hittite, Zabad the son of Ahlai, ⁴²Ad'ina the son of Shiza the Reubenite, a leader of the Reubenites, and thirty with him, ⁴³Ha'nan the son of Ma'acah, and Josh'aphat the Mithnite, ⁴⁴Uzzi'a the Ash'terathite, Shama and Je-i'el the sons of Ho'tham the Aro'erite, ⁴⁵Jedi'a-el the son of Shimri, and Joha his brother, the Ti'zite, ⁴⁶Eli'el the Ma'havite, and Jer'ibai, and Joshavi'ah, the sons of El'na-am, and Ithmah the Moabite, ⁴⁷Eli'el, and O'bed, and Ja-asi'el the Mezo'baite.

David's Followers in the Wilderness

12 Now these are the men who came to David at Zik'lag, while he could not move about freely because of Saul the son of Kish; and they were among the mighty men who helped him in war. ²They were bowmen, and could shoot arrows and sling stones with either the right or the left hand; they were Benjaminites, Saul's kinsmen. ³The chief was Ahie'zer, then Jo'ash, both sons of Shema'ah of Gib'e-ah; also Je'zi-el and Pe'let the sons of Az'maveth; Ber'acah, Je'hu of An'athoth, ⁴Ishma'iah of Gib'eon, a mighty man among the thirty and a leader over the thirty; Jeremi'ah, ^f Jaha'ziel, Joha'nan, Joz'abad of Gede'-rah, ⁵Elu'zai, ^g Jer'imoth, Beali'ah, Shemari'ah, Shephati'ah the Har'uphite; ⁶Elka'nah, Isshi'ah, Az'arel, Jo-e'zer, and Jasho'be-am, the Ko'rahites; ⁷and Jo-e'lah and Zebadi'ah, the sons of Jero'ham of Gedor.

⁸ From the Gadites there went over to David at the stronghold in the wilderness mighty and experienced warriors, expert with shield and spear, whose faces were like the faces of lions, and who were swift as gazelles upon the mountains: ⁹E'zer the chief, Obadi'ah second, Eli'ab third, ¹⁰Mishman'nah fourth, Jeremi'ah fifth, ¹¹Attai sixth, Eli'el seventh, ¹²Joha'nan eighth, Elza'bad ninth, ¹³Jeremi'ah tenth, Mach'bannai eleventh. ¹⁴These Gadites were officers of the army, the lesser over a hundred and the greater over a thousand. ¹⁵These are the men who crossed the Jordan in the first month, when it was overflowing all its banks, and put to flight all those in the valleys, to the east and to the west.

¹⁶ And some of the men of Benjamin and Judah came to the stronghold to David. ¹⁷David went out to meet them and said to them, "If you have come to me in friendship to help me, my heart will be knit to you; but if to betray me to my adversaries, although there is no wrong in my hands, then may the God of our fathers see and rebuke you." ¹⁸Then the Spirit came upon Ama'sai, chief of the thirty, and he said,

"We are yours, O David;
and with you, O son of Jesse!
Peace, peace to you,
and peace to your helpers!
For your God helps you."

Then David received them, and made them officers of his troops.

¹⁹ Some of the men of Manas'seh deserted to David when he came with the Philis'tines for the battle against Saul. (Yet he did not help them, for the rulers of the Philistines took counsel and sent him away, saying, "At peril to our heads he will desert to his master Saul.") ²⁰As he went to Zik'lag these men of Manas'seh deserted to him: Adnah, Joz'abad, Jedi'a-el, Michael, Jozabad, Eli'hu, and Zil'lethai, chiefs of thousands in Manasseh. ²¹They helped David against the band of raiders; ^h for they were all mighty men of valor, and were commanders in the army. ²²For from day to day men kept coming to David to help him, until there was a great army, like an army of God.

David's Army at Hebron

²³ These are the numbers of the divisions of the armed troops, who came to David in He'bron, to turn the kingdom of Saul over to him, according to the word of the LORD. ²⁴The men of Judah bearing shield and spear were six thousand eight hundred armed troops. ²⁵Of the Simeonites, mighty men of valor for war, seven thousand one hundred. ²⁶Of the Levites four thousand six hundred. ²⁷The prince Jehoi'ada, of the house of Aaron, and with him three thousand seven hundred. ²⁸Za'dok, a young man mighty in valor, and twenty-two commanders from his own father's house. ²⁹Of the Benjaminites, the kinsmen of Saul, three thousand, of whom the majority had hitherto kept their allegiance to the house of Saul. ³⁰Of the E'phraimites twenty thousand eight hundred, mighty men of valor, famous men in their fathers' houses. ³¹Of the half-tribe of Manas'seh eighteen thousand, who were expressly named to come and make David king. ³²Of Is'sachar men who had understanding of the times, to know what Israel ought to do, two hundred chiefs, and all their kinsmen under their command. ³³Of Zeb'ulun fifty thousand seasoned troops, equipped for battle with all the weapons of war, to help David ⁱ with singleness of purpose. ³⁴Of Naph'tali a thousand commanders with whom were thirty-seven thousand men armed with shield and spear. ³⁵Of the Danites twenty-eight thousand six hundred men equipped for battle. ³⁶Of Asher forty thousand seasoned troops ready for battle. ³⁷Of the Reubenites and Gadites and

---

^f Heb verse 5.
^g Heb verse 6.
^h Or as officers of his troops.
ⁱ Gk: Heb lacks David.

the half-tribe of Manas'seh from beyond the Jordan, one hundred and twenty thousand men armed with all the weapons of war.

38 All these, men of war, arrayed in battle order, came to He'bron with full intent to make David king over all Israel; likewise all the rest of Israel were of a single mind to make David king. ³⁹And they were there with David for three days, eating and drinking, for their brethren had made preparation for them. ⁴⁰And also their neighbors, from as far as Is'sachar and Zeb'ulun and Naph'tali, came bringing food on donkeys and on camels and on mules and on oxen, abundant provisions of meal, cakes of figs, clusters of raisins, and wine and oil, oxen and sheep, for there was joy in Israel.

The Ark Brought from Kiriath-jearim

13 David consulted with the commanders of thousands and of hundreds, with every leader. ²And David said to all the assembly of Israel, "If it seems good to you, and if it is the will of the LORD our God, let us send abroad to our brethren who remain in all the land of Israel, and with them to the priests and Levites in the cities that have pasture lands, that they may come together to us. ³Then let us bring again the ark of our God to us; for we neglected it in the days of Saul." ⁴All the assembly agreed to do so, for the thing was right in the eyes of all the people.

5 So David assembled all Israel from the Shihor of Egypt to the entrance of Ha'math, to bring the ark of God from Kir'iath-je'arim. ⁶And David and all Israel went up to Ba'alah, that is, to Kir'iath-je'arim which belongs to Judah, to bring up from there the ark of God, which is called by the name of the LORD who sits enthroned above the cherubim. ⁷And they carried the ark of God upon a new cart, from the house of Abin'adab, and Uzzah and Ahi'o ʲ were driving the cart. ⁸And David and all Israel were making merry before God with all their might, with song and lyres and harps and tambourines and cymbals and trumpets.

9 And when they came to the threshing floor of Chidon, Uzzah put out his hand to hold the ark, for the oxen stumbled. ¹⁰And the anger of the LORD was kindled against Uzzah; and he struck him because he put forth his hand to the ark; and he died there before God. ¹¹And David was angry because the LORD had broken forth upon Uzzah; and that place is called Pe'rez-uzza ᵏ to this day. ¹²And David was afraid of God that day; and he said, "How can I bring the ark of God home to me?" ¹³So David did not take the ark home into the city of David, but took it aside to the house of O'bed-e'dom the Gittite. ¹⁴And the ark of God remained with the household of O'bed-e'dom in his house three months; and the LORD blessed the household of Obed-edom and all that he had.

David Established in Jerusalem

14 And Hiram king of Tyre sent messengers to David, and cedar trees, also masons and carpenters to build a house for him. ²And David perceived that the LORD had established him king over Israel, and that his kingdom was highly exalted for the sake of his people Israel.

3 And David took more wives in Jerusalem, and David begot more sons and daughters. ⁴These are the names of the children whom he had in Jerusalem: Sham'mu-a, Sho'bab, Nathan, Solomon, ⁵Ibhar, Eli'shu-a, El'pelet, ⁶No'gah, Ne'pheg, Japhi'a, ⁷Elish'ama, Beeli'ada, and Eliph'elet.

Defeat of the Philistines

8 When the Philis'tines heard that David had been anointed king over all Israel, all the Philistines went up in search of David; and David heard of it and went out against them. ⁹Now the Philis'tines had come and made a raid in the valley of Reph'aim. ¹⁰And David inquired of God, "Shall I go up against the Philis'tines? Will you give them into my hand?" And the LORD said to him, "Go up, and I will give them into your hand." ¹¹And he went up to Ba'al-pera'zim, and David defeated them there; and David said, "God has broken through ¹ my enemies by my hand, like a bursting flood." Therefore the name of that place is called Baal-perazim. ᵐ ¹²And they left their gods there, and David gave command, and they were burned.

13 And the Philis'tines yet again made a raid in the valley. ¹⁴And when David again inquired of God, God said to him, "You shall not go up after them; go around and come upon them opposite the balsam trees. ¹⁵And when you hear the sound of marching in the tops of the balsam trees, then go out to battle; for God has gone out before you to strike the army of the Philis'tines." ¹⁶And David did as God commanded him, and they struck the Philis'tine army from Gib'eon to Gezer. ¹⁷And the fame of David went out into all lands, and the LORD brought the fear of him upon all nations.

The Ark Brought to Jerusalem

15 David built houses for himself in the city of David; and he prepared a place for the ark of God, and pitched a tent for it. ²Then David said, "No one but the Levites may carry the ark of God, for the LORD chose them to carry the ark of the LORD and to minister to him for ever." ³And David assembled all Israel at Jerusalem, to bring

---

ʲ Or *and his brother.*
ᵏ That is *The breaking forth upon Uzzah.*
ˡ Heb *paraz.*
ᵐ That is *Lord of breaking through.*
13:1–14: 2 Sam 6:1–11.
14:1, 2: 2 Sam 5:11, 12.
14:3–7: 3:5–8; 2 Sam 5:14–16.
14:8–12: 2 Sam 5:17–21.
14:13–16: 2 Sam 5:22–25.
15:1–16:3: 2 Sam 6:12–19.

up the ark of the Lord to its place, which he had prepared for it. [4]And David gathered together the sons of Aaron and the Levites: [5]of the sons of Ko'hath, Uri'el the chief, with a hundred and twenty of his brethren; [6]of the sons of Merar'i, Asai'ah the chief, with two hundred and twenty of his brethren; [7]of the sons of Gershom, Joel the chief, with a hundred and thirty of his brethren; [8]of the sons of Eliza'phan, Shemai'ah the chief, with two hundred of his brethren; [9]of the sons of He'bron, Eli'el the chief, with eighty of his brethren; [10]of the sons of Uz'ziel, Ammin'adab the chief, with a hundred and twelve of his brethren. [11]Then David summoned the priests Za'dok and Abi'athar, and the Levites Uri'el, Asai'ah, Joel, Shemai'ah, Eli'el, and Ammin'adab, [12]and said to them, "You are the heads of the fathers' houses of the Levites; sanctify yourselves, you and your brethren, so that you may bring up the ark of the Lord, the God of Israel, to the place that I have prepared for it. [13]Because you did not carry it the first time,[n] the Lord our God broke forth upon us, because we did not care for it in the way that is ordained." [14]So the priests and the Levites sanctified themselves to bring up the ark of the Lord, the God of Israel. [15]And the Levites carried the ark of God upon their shoulders with the poles, as Moses had commanded according to the word of the Lord.

[16] David also commanded the chiefs of the Levites to appoint their brethren as the singers who should play loudly on musical instruments, on harps and lyres and cymbals, to raise sounds of joy. [17]So the Levites appointed He'man the son of Joel; and of his brethren A'saph the son of Berechi'ah; and of the sons of Merar'i, their brethren, Ethan the son of Kusha'iah; [18]and with them their brethren of the second order, Zechari'ah, Ja-a'ziel, Shemir'amoth, Jehi'el, Unni, Eli'ab, Bena'iah, Ma''asei'ah, Mattithi'ah, Eliph'elehu, and Mikne'iah, and the gatekeepers O'bed-e'dom and Je-i'el. [19]The singers, He'man, A'saph, and Ethan, were to sound bronze cymbals; [20]Zechari'ah, A'zi-el, Shemir'amoth, Jehi'el, Unni, Eli'ab, Ma''asei'ah, and Bena'iah were to play harps according to Al'amoth; [21]but Mattithi'ah, Eliph'elehu, Mikne'iah, O'bed-e'dom, Je-i'el, and Azazi'ah were to lead with lyres according to the Shem'inith. [22]Chenani'ah, leader of the Levites in music, should direct the music, for he understood it. [23]Berechi'ah and Elka'nah were to be gatekeepers for the ark. [24]Shebani'ah, Josh'aphat, Nethan'el, Ama'sai, Zechari'ah, Bena'iah, and Elie'zer, the priests, should blow the trumpets before the ark of God. O'bed-e'dom and Jehi'ah also were to be gatekeepers for the ark.

[25] So David and the elders of Israel, and the commanders of thousands, went to bring up the ark of the covenant of the Lord from the house of O'bed-e'dom with rejoicing. [26]And because God helped the Levites who were carrying the ark of the covenant of the Lord, they sacrificed seven bulls and seven rams. [27]David was clothed with a robe of fine linen, as also were all the Levites who were carrying the ark, and the singers, and Chenani'ah the leader of the music of the singers; and David wore a linen ephod. [28]So all Israel brought up the ark of the covenant of the Lord with shouting, to the sound of the horn, trumpets, and cymbals, and made loud music on harps and lyres.

[29] And as the ark of the covenant of the Lord came to the city of David, Michal the daughter of Saul looked out of the window, and saw King David dancing and making merry; and she despised him in her heart.

The Ark Placed in a Tent

16 And they brought in the ark of God, and set it inside the tent which David had pitched for it; and they offered burnt offerings and peace offerings before God. [2]And when David had finished offering the burnt offerings and the peace offerings, he blessed the people in the name of the Lord, [3]and distributed to all Israel, both men and women, to each a loaf of bread, a portion of meat,[o] and a cake of raisins.

[4] Moreover he appointed certain of the Levites as ministers before the ark of the Lord, to invoke, to thank, and to praise the Lord, the God of Israel. [5]A'saph was the chief, and second to him were Zechari'ah, Je-i'el, Shemir'amoth, Jehi'el, Mattithi'ah, Eli'ab, Bena'iah, O'bed-e'dom, and Je-iel, who were to play harps and lyres; Asaph was to sound the cymbals, [6]and Bena'iah and Jaha'ziel the priests were to blow trumpets continually, before the ark of the covenant of God.

David's Song of Thanksgiving

[7] Then on that day David first appointed that thanksgiving be sung to the Lord by A'saph and his brethren.

[8]O give thanks to the Lord, call on his name,
   make known his deeds among the peoples!
[9]Sing to him, sing praises to him,
   tell of all his wonderful works!
[10]Glory in his holy name;
   let the hearts of those who seek the Lord rejoice!
[11]Seek the Lord and his strength,
   seek his presence continually!
[12]Remember the wonderful works that he has done,
   the wonders he wrought, the judgments he uttered,
[13]O offspring of Abraham his servant,
   sons of Jacob, his chosen ones!

---

[n] The meaning of the Hebrew word is uncertain.
[o] Compare Gk Syr Vg: Heb uncertain.
16:8–22: Ps 105:1–15.

¹⁴He is the Lord our God;
  his judgments are in all the earth.
¹⁵He is mindful of his covenant for ever,
  of the word that he commanded, for a
    thousand generations,
¹⁶the covenant which he made with Abraham,
  his sworn promise to Isaac,
¹⁷which he confirmed as a statute to Jacob,
  as an everlasting covenant to Israel,
¹⁸saying, "To you I will give the land of Canaan,
  as your portion for an inheritance."

¹⁹When they were few in number,
  and of little account, and sojourners in it,
²⁰wandering from nation to nation,
  from one kingdom to another people,
²¹he allowed no one to oppress them;
  he rebuked kings on their account,
²²saying, "Touch not my anointed ones,
  do my prophets no harm!"

²³Sing to the Lord, all the earth!
  Tell of his salvation from day to day.
²⁴Declare his glory among the nations,
  his marvelous works among all the peoples!
²⁵For great is the Lord, and greatly to be praised,
  and he is to be held in awe above all gods.
²⁶For all the gods of the peoples are idols;
  but the Lord made the heavens.
²⁷Honor and majesty are before him;
  strength and joy are in his place.

²⁸Ascribe to the Lord, O families of the peoples,
  ascribe to the Lord glory and strength!
²⁹Ascribe to the Lord the glory due his name;
  bring an offering, and come before him!
  Worship the Lord in holy attire;
³⁰ tremble before him, all the earth;
  yes, the world stands firm, never to be
    moved.
³¹Let the heavens be glad, and let the earth rejoice,
  and let them say among the nations, "The
    Lord reigns!"
³²Let the sea roar, and all that fills it,
  let the field exult, and everything in it!
³³Then shall the trees of the wood sing for joy
  before the Lord, for he comes to judge the
    earth.
³⁴O give thanks to the Lord, for he is good;
  for his mercy endures for ever!

³⁵Say also:
  "Deliver us, O God of our salvation,
  and gather and save us from among the
    nations,
  that we may give thanks to your holy name,
  and glory in your praise.
³⁶Blessed be the Lord, the God of Israel,
  from everlasting to everlasting!"

Then all the people said "Amen!" and praised the
Lord.

Regular Worship Maintained

37 So David left A'saph and his brethren there
before the ark of the covenant of the Lord to
minister continually before the ark as each day
required, ³⁸and also O'bed-e'dom and his ᴾ sixty-
eight brethren; while Obed-edom, the son of
Jedu'thun, and Hosah were to be gatekeepers.
³⁹And he left Za'dok the priest and his brethren
the priests before the tabernacle of the Lord in
the high place that was at Gib'eon, ⁴⁰to offer burnt
offerings to the Lord upon the altar of burnt offering continually morning and evening, according to all that is written in the law of the Lord
which he commanded Israel. ⁴¹With them were
He'man and Jedu'thun, and the rest of those chosen and expressly named to give thanks to the
Lord, for his mercy endures for ever. ⁴²He'man
and Jedu'thun had trumpets and cymbals for the
music and instruments for sacred song. The sons
of Jeduthun were appointed to the gate.

43 Then all the people departed each to his
house, and David went home to bless his household.

God's Covenant with David

17 Now when David dwelt in his house, David
said to Nathan the prophet, "Behold, I
dwell in a house of cedar, but the ark of the
covenant of the Lord is under a tent." ²And
Nathan said to David, "Do all that is in your heart,
for God is with you."

3 But that same night the word of the Lord
came to Nathan, ⁴"Go and tell my servant David,
'Thus says the Lord: You shall not build me a
house to dwell in. ⁵For I have not dwelt in a house
since the day I led up Israel to this day, but I have
gone from tent to tent and from dwelling to dwelling. ⁶In all places where I have moved with all
Israel, did I speak a word with any of the judges
of Israel, whom I commanded to shepherd my
people, saying, "Why have you not built me a
house of cedar?"' ⁷Now therefore thus shall you
say to my servant David, 'Thus says the Lord of
hosts, I took you from the pasture, from following
the sheep, that you should be prince over my
people Israel; ⁸and I have been with you wherever
you went, and have cut off all your enemies from
before you; and I will make for you a name, like
the name of the great ones of the earth. ⁹And I
will appoint a place for my people Israel, and will
plant them, that they may dwell in their own place,
and be disturbed no more; and violent men shall
waste them no more, as formerly, ¹⁰from the time

ᴾ Heb *their.*
16:23-33: Ps 96:1-13.
16:34: Ps 106:1.
16:35-36: Ps 106:47, 48.
17:1-27: 2 Sam 7:1-29.

that I appointed judges over my people Israel; and I will subdue all your enemies. Moreover I declare to you that the Lord will build you a house. [11]When your days are fulfilled to go to be with your fathers, I will raise up your offspring after you, one of your own sons, and I will establish his kingdom. [12]He shall build a house for me, and I will establish his throne for ever. [13]I will be his father, and he shall be my son; I will not take my merciful love from him, as I took it from him who was before you, [14]but I will confirm him in my house and in my kingdom for ever and his throne shall be established for ever.'" [15]In accordance with all these words, and in accordance with all this vision, Nathan spoke to David.

David's Prayer

16 Then King David went in and sat before the Lord, and said, "Who am I, O Lord God, and what is my house, that you have brought me thus far? [17]And this was a small thing in your eyes, O God; you have also spoken of your servant's house for a great while to come, and have shown me future generations, [q] O Lord God! [18]And what more can David say to you for honoring your servant? For you know your servant. [19]For your servant's sake, O Lord, and according to your own heart, you have wrought all this greatness, in making known all these great things. [20]There is none like you, O Lord, and there is no God besides you, according to all that we have heard with our ears. [21]What other [r] nation on earth is like your people Israel, whom God went to redeem to be his people, making for yourself a name for great and terrible things, in driving out nations before your people whom you redeemed from Egypt? [22]And you made your people Israel to be your people for ever; and you, O Lord, became their God. [23]And now, O Lord, let the word which you have spoken concerning your servant and concerning his house be established for ever, and do as you have spoken; [24]and your name will be established and magnified for ever, saying, 'The Lord of hosts, the God of Israel, is Israel's God,' and the house of your servant David will be established before you. [25]For you, my God, have revealed to your servant that you will build a house for him; therefore your servant has found courage to pray before you. [26]And now, O Lord, you are God, and you have promised this good thing to your servant; [27]now therefore may it please you to bless the house of your servant, that it may continue for ever before you; for what you, O Lord, have blessed is blessed for ever."

David's Kingdom Established and Extended

18 After this David defeated the Philis'tines and subdued them, and he took Gath and its villages out of the hand of the Philistines.

2 And he defeated Moab, and the Moabites became servants to David and brought tribute.

3 David also defeated Hadade'zer king of Zobah, toward Ha'math, as he went to set up his monument [s] at the river Euphrates. [4]And David took from him a thousand chariots, seven thousand horsemen, and twenty thousand foot soldiers; and David hamstrung all the chariot horses, but left enough for a hundred chariots. [5]And when the Syrians of Damascus came to help Hadade'zer king of Zobah, David slew twenty-two thousand men of the Syrians. [6]Then David put garrisons [t] in Syria of Damascus; and the Syrians became servants to David, and brought tribute. And the Lord gave victory to David wherever he went. [7]And David took the shields of gold which were carried by the servants of Hadade'zer, and brought them to Jerusalem. [8]And from Tibhath and from Cun, cities of Hadade'zer, David took very much bronze; with it Solomon made the bronze sea and the pillars and the vessels of bronze.

9 When To'u king of Ha'math heard that David had defeated the whole army of Hadade'zer, king of Zobah, [10]he sent his son Hador'am to King David, to greet him, and to congratulate him because he had fought against Hadade'zer and defeated him; for Hadadezer had often been at war with To'u. And he sent all sorts of articles of gold, of silver, and of bronze; [11]these also King David dedicated to the Lord, together with the silver and gold which he had carried off from all the nations, from E'dom, Moab, the Am'monites, the Philis'tines, and Am'alek.

David's Just Administration

12 And Abi'shai, the son of Zeru'iah, slew eighteen thousand E'domites in the Valley of Salt. [13]And he put garrisons in E'dom; and all the E'domites became David's servants. And the Lord gave victory to David wherever he went.

14 So David reigned over all Israel; and he administered justice and equity to all his people. [15]And Jo'ab the son of Zeru'iah was over the army; and Jehosh'aphat the son of Ahi'lud was recorder; [16]and Za'dok the son of Ahi'tub and Ahim'elech the son of Abi'athar were priests; and Shavsha was secretary; [17]and Bena'iah the son of Jehoi'ada was over the Cher'ethites and the Pel'ethites; and David's sons were the chief officials in the service of the king.

Defeat of the Ammonites and Syrians

19 Now after this Na'hash the king of the Am'monites died, and his son reigned in his stead. [2]And David said, "I will deal loyally with Ha'nun the son of Na'hash, for his father

---

[q] Cn: Heb uncertain.
[r] Gk Vg: Heb one.
[s] Heb hand.
[t] Gk Vg 2 Sam 8:6 Compare Syr: Heb lacks garrisons.
18:1–13: 2 Sam 8:1–14.
18:14–17: 2 Sam 8:15–18.
19:1–19: 2 Sam 10:1–19.

dealt loyally with me." So David sent messengers to console him concerning his father. And David's servants came to Ha′nun in the land of the Am′monites, to console him. ³But the princes of the Am′monites said to Ha′nun, "Do you think, because David has sent comforters to you, that he is honoring your father? Have not his servants come to you to search and to overthrow and to spy out the land?" ⁴So Ha′nun took David's servants, and shaved them, and cut off their garments in the middle, at their hips, and sent them away; ⁵and they departed. When David was told concerning the men, he sent to meet them, for the men were greatly ashamed. And the king said, "Remain at Jericho until your beards have grown, and then return."

6 When the Am′monites saw that they had made themselves odious to David, Ha′nun and the Ammonites sent a thousand talents of silver to hire chariots and horsemen from Mesopota′mia, from Ar′am-ma′acah, and from Zobah. ⁷They hired thirty-two thousand chariots and the king of Ma′acah with his army, who came and encamped before Med′eba. And the Am′monites were mustered from their cities and came to battle. ⁸When David heard of it, he sent Jo′ab and all the army of the mighty men. ⁹And the Am′monites came out and drew up in battle array at the entrance of the city, and the kings who had come were by themselves in the open country.

10 When Jo′ab saw that the battle was set against him both in front and in the rear, he chose some of the picked men of Israel, and arrayed them against the Syrians; ¹¹the rest of his men he put in the charge of Abi′shai his brother, and they were arrayed against the Am′monites. ¹²And he said, "If the Syrians are too strong for me, then you shall help me; but if the Am′monites are too strong for you, then I will help you. ¹³Be of good courage, and let us play the man for our people, and for the cities of our God; and may the Lord do what seems good to him." ¹⁴So Jo′ab and the people who were with him drew near before the Syrians for battle; and they fled before him. ¹⁵And when the Am′monites saw that the Syrians fled, they likewise fled before Abi′shai, Jo′ab's brother, and entered the city. Then Joab came to Jerusalem.

16 But when the Syrians saw that they had been defeated by Israel, they sent messengers and brought out the Syrians who were beyond the Euphra′tes, with Shophach the commander of the army of Hadade′zer at their head. ¹⁷And when it was told David, he gathered all Israel together, and crossed the Jordan, and came to them, and drew up his forces against them. And when David set the battle in array against the Syrians, they fought with him. ¹⁸And the Syrians fled before Israel; and David slew of the Syrians the men of

seven thousand chariots, and forty thousand foot soldiers, and killed also Shophach the commander of their army. ¹⁹And when the servants of Hadade′zer saw that they had been defeated by Israel, they made peace with David, and became subject to him. So the Syrians were not willing to help the Am′monites any more.

The Siege and Capture of Rabbah

20 In the spring of the year, the time when kings go forth to battle, Jo′ab led out the army, and ravaged the country of the Am′monites, and came and besieged Rabbah. But David remained at Jerusalem. And Jo′ab struck Rabbah, and overthrew it. ²And David took the crown of their king ᵘ from his head; he found that it weighed a talent of gold, and in it was a precious stone; and it was placed on David's head. And he brought forth the spoil of the city, a very great amount. ³And he brought forth the people who were in it, and set them to labor ᵛ with saws and iron picks and axes; ᵂ and thus David did to all the cities of the Am′monites. Then David and all the people returned to Jerusalem.

War with the Philistines

4 And after this there arose war with the Philis′tines at Gezer; then Sib′becai the Hu′shathite slew Sippai, who was one of the descendants of the giants; and the Philistines were subdued. ⁵And there was again war with the Philis′tines; and Elha′nan the son of Ja′ir slew Lahmi the brother of Goliath the Gittite, the shaft of whose spear was like a weaver's beam. ⁶And there was again war at Gath, where there was a man of great stature, who had six fingers on each hand, and six toes on each foot, twenty-four in number; and he also was descended from the giants. ⁷And when he taunted Israel, Jonathan the son of Shim′e-a, David's brother, slew him. ⁸These were descended from the giants in Gath; and they fell by the hand of David and by the hand of his servants.

The Census and the Pestilence

21 * Satan stood up against Israel, and incited David to number Israel. ²So David said to Jo′ab and the commanders of the army, "Go, number Israel, from Be′er-she′ba to Dan, and bring me a report, that I may know their number." ³But Jo′ab said, "May the Lord add to his people a hundred times as many as they are! Are they not,

---

ᵘ Or *Milcom* See 1 Kings 11:5.
ᵛ Compare 2 Sam 12:31: Heb *he sawed*.
ᵂ Compare 2 Sam 12:31: Heb *saws*.
20:1: 2 Sam 11:1.
20:1–3: 2 Sam 12:26–31.
20:4–8: 2 Sam 21:18–22.
21:1–27: 2 Sam 24:1–25.
* 21—29: In these chapters the Chronicler enlarges on the organization of divine worship and of the clergy charged with carrying it out. He records the erection of a (permanent) altar to Yahweh on the site of the future temple and even describes David's preparation for the temple construction.

my lord the king, all of them my lord's servants? Why then should my lord require this? Why should he bring guilt upon Israel?" [4]But the king's word prevailed against Jo'ab. So Joab departed and went throughout all Israel, and came back to Jerusalem. [5]And Jo'ab gave the sum of the numbering of the people to David. In all Israel there were one million one hundred thousand men who drew the sword, and in Judah four hundred and seventy thousand who drew the sword. [6]But he did not include Levi and Benjamin in the numbering, for the king's command was abhorrent to Jo'ab.

7 But God was displeased with this thing, and he struck Israel. [8]And David said to God, "I have sinned greatly in that I have done this thing. But now, I pray you, take away the iniquity of your servant; for I have done very foolishly." [9]And the Lord spoke to Gad, David's seer, saying, [10]"Go and say to David, 'Thus says the Lord, Three things I offer you; choose one of them, that I may do it to you.'" [11]So Gad came to David and said to him, "Thus says the Lord, 'Take which you will: [12]either three years of famine; or three months of devastation by your foes, while the sword of your enemies overtakes you; or else three days of the sword of the Lord, pestilence upon the land, and the angel of the Lord destroying throughout all the territory of Israel.' Now decide what answer I shall return to him who sent me." [13]Then David said to Gad, "I am in great distress; let me fall into the hand of the Lord, for his mercy is very great; but let me not fall into the hand of man."

14 So the Lord sent a pestilence upon Israel; and there fell seventy thousand men of Israel. [15]And God sent the angel to Jerusalem to destroy it; but when he was about to destroy it, the Lord saw, and he repented of the evil; and he said to the destroying angel, "It is enough; now stay your hand." And the angel of the Lord was standing by the threshing floor of Ornan the Jeb'usite. [16]And David lifted his eyes and saw the angel of the Lord standing between earth and heaven, and in his hand a drawn sword stretched out over Jerusalem. Then David and the elders, clothed in sackcloth, fell upon their faces. [17]And David said to God, "Was it not I who gave command to number the people? It is I who have sinned and done very wickedly. But these sheep, what have they done? Let your hand, I pray you, O Lord my God, be against me and against my father's house; but let not the plague be upon your people."

David's Altar and Sacrifice

18 Then the angel of the Lord commanded Gad to say to David that David should go up and raise an altar to the Lord on the threshing floor of Ornan the Jeb'usite. [19]So David went up at Gad's word, which he had spoken in the name of the Lord. [20]Now Ornan was threshing wheat; he

turned and saw the angel, and his four sons who were with him hid themselves. [21]As David came to Ornan, Ornan looked and saw David and went forth from the threshing floor, and did obeisance to David with his face to the ground. [22]And David said to Ornan, "Give me the site of the threshing floor that I may build on it an altar to the Lord— give it to me at its full price—that the plague may be averted from the people." [23]Then Ornan said to David, "Take it; and let my lord the king do what seems good to him; see, I give the oxen for burnt offerings, and the threshing sledges for the wood, and the wheat for a cereal offering. I give it all." [24]But King David said to Ornan, "No, but I will buy it for the full price; I will not take for the Lord what is yours, nor offer burnt offerings which cost me nothing." [25]So David paid Ornan six hundred shekels of gold by weight for the site. [26]And David built there an altar to the Lord and presented burnt offerings and peace offerings, and called upon the Lord, and he answered him with fire from heaven upon the altar of burnt offering. [27]Then the Lord commanded the angel; and he put his sword back into its sheath.

The Site for the Temple Chosen

28 At that time, when David saw that the Lord had answered him at the threshing floor of Ornan the Jeb'usite, he made his sacrifices there. [29]For the tabernacle of the Lord, which Moses had made in the wilderness, and the altar of burnt offering were at that time in the high place at Gib'eon; [30]but David could not go before it to inquire of God, for he was afraid of the sword of 22 the angel of the Lord. [1]Then David said, "Here shall be the house of the Lord God and here the altar of burnt offering for Israel."

David's Preparations for the Temple

2 David commanded to gather together the aliens who were in the land of Israel, and he set stonecutters to prepare dressed stones for building the house of God. [3]David also provided great stores of iron for nails for the doors of the gates and for clamps, as well as bronze in quantities beyond weighing, [4]and cedar timbers without number; for the Sido'nians and Ty'rians brought great quantities of cedar to David. [5]For David said, "Solomon my son is young and inexperienced, and the house that is to be built for the Lord must be exceedingly magnificent, of fame and glory throughout all lands; I will therefore make preparation for it." So David provided materials in great quantity before his death.

David's Charge to Solomon and the Leaders of Israel

6 Then he called for Solomon his son, and charged him to build a house for the Lord, the God of Israel. [7]David said to Solomon, "My son, I had it in my heart to build a house to the name of the Lord my God. [8]But the word of the Lord came

to me, saying, 'You have shed much blood and have waged great wars; you shall not build a house to my name, because you have shed so much blood before me upon the earth. [9]Behold, a son shall be born to you; he shall be a man of peace. I will give him peace from all his enemies round about; for his name shall be Solomon, and I will give peace and quiet to Israel in his days. [10]He shall build a house for my name. He shall be my son, and I will be his father, and I will establish his royal throne in Israel for ever.' [11]Now, my son, the Lord be with you, so that you may succeed in building the house of the Lord your God, as he has spoken concerning you. [12]Only, may the Lord grant you discretion and understanding, that when he gives you charge over Israel you may keep the law of the Lord your God. [13]Then you will prosper if you are careful to observe the statutes and the ordinances which the Lord commanded Moses for Israel. Be strong, and of good courage. Fear not; be not dismayed. [14]With great pains I have provided for the house of the Lord a hundred thousand talents of gold, a million talents of silver, and bronze and iron beyond weighing, for there is so much of it; timber and stone too I have provided. To these you must add. [15]You have an abundance of workmen: stonecutters, masons, carpenters, and all kinds of craftsmen without number, skilled in working [16]gold, silver, bronze, and iron. Arise and be doing! The Lord be with you!"

17 David also commanded all the leaders of Israel to help Solomon his son, saying, [18]"Is not the Lord your God with you? And has he not given you peace on every side? For he has delivered the inhabitants of the land into my hand; and the land is subdued before the Lord and his people. [19]Now set your mind and heart to seek the Lord your God. Arise and build the sanctuary of the Lord God, so that the ark of the covenant of the Lord and the holy vessels of God may be brought into a house built for the name of the Lord."

Families of the Levites and Their Duties

23 When David was old and full of days, he made Solomon his son king over Israel.

2 David assembled all the leaders of Israel and the priests and the Levites. [3]The Levites, thirty years old and upward, were numbered, and the total was thirty-eight thousand men. [4]"Twenty-four thousand of these," David said, "shall have charge of the work in the house of the Lord, six thousand shall be officers and judges, [5]four thousand gatekeepers, and four thousand shall offer praises to the Lord with the instruments which I have made for praise." [6]And David organized them in divisions corresponding to the sons of Levi: Gershom, Ko'hath, and Merar'i.

7 The sons of Gershom* were Ladan and Shim'e-i. [8]The sons of Ladan: Jehi'el the chief,

and Zetham, and Joel, three. [9]The sons of Shim'e-i: Shelo'moth, Ha'zi-el, and Haran, three. These were the heads of the fathers' houses of Ladan. [10]And the sons of Shim'e-i: Jahath, Zina, and Je'ush, and Beri'ah. These four were the sons of Shim'e-i. [11]Jahath was the chief, and Zizah the second; but Je'ush and Beri'ah had not many sons, therefore they became a father's house in one reckoning.

12 The sons of Ko'hath: Amram, Izhar, He'bron, and Uz'ziel, four. [13]The sons of Amram: Aaron and Moses. Aaron was set apart to consecrate the most holy things, that he and his sons for ever should burn incense before the Lord, and minister to him and pronounce blessings in his name for ever. [14]But the sons of Moses the man of God were named among the tribe of Levi. [15]The sons of Moses: Gershom and Elie'zer. [16]The sons of Gershom: Shebu'el the chief. [17]The sons of Elie'zer: Rehabi'ah the chief; Eliezer had no other sons, but the sons of Rehabiah were very many. [18]The sons of Izhar: Shelo'mith the chief. [19]The sons of He'bron: Jeri'ah the chief, Amari'ah the second, Jaha'ziel the third, and Jekame'am the fourth. [20]The sons of Uz'ziel: Micah the chief and Isshi'ah the second.

21 The sons of Merar'i: Mah'li and Mu'shi. The sons of Mahli: Elea'zar and Kish. [22]Elea'zar died having no sons, but only daughters; their kinsmen, the sons of Kish, married them. [23]The sons of Mu'shi: Mah'li, E'der, and Jer'emoth, three.

24 These were the sons of Levi by their fathers' houses, the heads of fathers' houses as they were registered according to the number of the names of the individuals from twenty years old and upward who were to do the work for the service of the house of the Lord. [25]For David said, "The Lord, the God of Israel, has given peace to his people; and he dwells in Jerusalem for ever. [26]And so the Levites no longer need to carry the tabernacle or any of the things for its service"— [27]for by the last words of David these were the number of the Levites from twenty years old and upward— [28]"but their duty shall be to assist the sons of Aaron for the service of the house of the Lord, having the care of the courts and the chambers, the cleansing of all that is holy, and any work for the service of the house of God; [29]to assist also with the showbread, the flour for the cereal offering, the wafers of unleavened bread, the baked offering, the offering mixed with oil, and all measures of quantity or size. [30]And they shall stand every morning, thanking and praising the Lord, and likewise at evening, [31]and whenever burnt offerings are offered to the Lord on sabbaths, new moons, and feast days, according to the number required of them, continually before the Lord. [32]Thus they shall keep charge of

---

* Vg Compare Gk Syr: Heb *to the Gershonite*.

the tent of meeting and the sanctuary, and shall attend the sons of Aaron, their brethren, for the service of the house of the LORD."

The Divisions of the Sons of Aaron

24 The divisions of the sons of Aaron were these. The sons of Aaron: Na′dab, Abi′hu, Elea′zar, and Ith′amar. [2]But Na′dab and Abi′hu died before their father, and had no children, so Elea′zar and Ith′amar became the priests. [3]With the help of Za′dok of the sons of Elea′zar, and Ahim′elech of the sons of Ith′amar,* David organized them according to the appointed duties in their service. [4]Since more chief men were found among the sons of Elea′zar than among the sons of Ith′amar, they organized them under sixteen heads of fathers' houses of the sons of Eleazar, and eight of the sons of Ithamar. [5]They organized them by lot, all alike, for there were officers of the sanctuary and officers of God among both the sons of Elea′zar and the sons of Ith′amar. [6]And the scribe Shemai′ah the son of Nethan′el, a Levite, recorded them in the presence of the king, and the princes, and Za′dok the priest, and Ahim′elech the son of Abi′athar, and the heads of the fathers' houses of the priests and of the Levites; one father's house being chosen for Elea′zar and one chosen for Ith′amar.

7 The first lot fell to Jehoi′arib, the second to Jedai′ah, [8]the third to Harim, the fourth to Se-o′rim, [9]the fifth to Malchi′jah, the sixth to Mi′jamin, [10]the seventh to Hakkoz, the eighth to Abi′jah, [11]the ninth to Jesh′ua, the tenth to Shecani′ah, [12]the eleventh to Eli′ashib, the twelfth to Ja′kim, [13]the thirteenth to Huppah, the fourteenth to Jesheb′e-ab, [14]the fifteenth to Bilgah, the sixteenth to Immer, [15]the seventeenth to He′zir, the eighteenth to Hap′pizzez, [16]the nineteenth to Pethahi′ah, the twentieth to Jehez′kel, [17]the twenty-first to Ja′chin, the twenty-second to Gamul, [18]the twenty-third to Delai′ah, the twenty-fourth to Ma-azi′ah. [19]These had as their appointed duty in their service to come into the house of the LORD according to the procedure established for them by Aaron their father, as the LORD God of Israel had commanded him.

Other Levites

20 And of the rest of the sons of Levi: of the sons of Amram, Shu′ba-el; of the sons of Shuba-el, Jehde′iah. [21]Of Rehabi′ah: of the sons of Rehabiah, Isshi′ah the chief. [22]Of the Iz′harites, Shelo′moth; of the sons of Shelomoth, Jahath. [23]The sons of He′bron:ʸ Jeri′ah the chief,ᶻ Ama-ri′ah the second, Jahazi′el the third, Jekame′am the fourth. [24]The sons of Uz′ziel, Micah; of the sons of Micah, Sha′mir. [25]The brother of Micah, Isshi′ah; of the sons of Isshiah, Zechari′ah. [26]The sons of Merar′i: Mah′li and Mu′shi. The sons of Ja-azi′ah: Beno. [27]The sons of Merar′i: of Ja-azi′ah, Beno, Shoham, Zaccur, and Ibri. [28]Of Mah′li:

Elea′zar, who had no sons. [29]Of Kish, the sons of Kish: Jerah′meel. [30]The sons of Mu′shi: Mah′li, E′der, and Jer′imoth. These were the sons of the Levites according to their fathers' houses. [31]These also, the head of each father's house and his younger brother alike, cast lots, just as their brethren the sons of Aaron, in the presence of King David, Za′dok, Ahim′elech, and the heads of fathers' houses of the priests and of the Levites.

The Temple Musicians

25 David and the chiefs of the service also set apart for the service certain of the sons of A′saph, and of He′man, and of Jedu′thun, who should prophesy with lyres, with harps, and with cymbals. The list of those who did the work and of their duties was: [2]Of the sons of A′saph: Zaccur, Joseph, Nethani′ah, and Asha-re′lah, sons of Asaph, under the direction of Asaph, who prophesied under the direction of the king. [3]Of Jedu′thun, the sons of Jeduthun: Geda-li′ah, Zeri, Jeshai′ah, Shim′e-i,ᵃ Hashabi′ah, and Mattithi′ah, six, under the direction of their father Jeduthun, who prophesied with the lyre in thanksgiving and praise to the LORD. [4]Of He′man, the sons of Heman: Bukki′ah, Mattani′ah, Uz′ziel, Shebu′el, and Jer′imoth, Hanani′ah, Hana′ni, Eli′athah, Giddal′ti, and Romam′ti-e′zer, Josh-bekash′ah, Mallo′thi, Hothir, Maha′zi-oth. [5]All these were the sons of He′man the king's seer, according to the promise of God to exalt him; for God had given Heman fourteen sons and three daughters. [6]They were all under the direction of their father in the music in the house of the LORD with cymbals, harps, and lyres for the service of the house of God. A′saph, Jedu′thun, and He′man were under the order of the king. [7]The number of them along with their brethren, who were trained in singing to the LORD, all who were skilful, was two hundred and eighty-eight. [8]And they cast lots for their duties, small and great, teacher and pupil alike.

9 The first lot fell for A′saph to Joseph; the second to Gedali′ah, to him and his brethren and his sons, twelve; [10]the third to Zaccur, his sons and his brethren, twelve; [11]the fourth to Izri, his sons and his brethren, twelve; [12]the fifth to Nethani′ah, his sons and his brethren, twelve; [13]the sixth to Bukki′ah, his sons and his brethren, twelve; [14]the seventh to Jeshare′lah, his sons and his brethren, twelve; [15]the eighth to Jesha′iah, his sons and his brethren, twelve; [16]the ninth to Mattani′ah, his sons and his brethren, twelve; [17]the tenth to Shim′e-i, his sons and his brethren,

---

ʸ See 23:19: Heb lacks *Hebron.*
ᶻ See 23:19: Heb lacks *the chief.*
ᵃ One Ms: Gk: Heb lacks *Shime-i.*
* 24:3: There were two chief priests in the time of David, namely, Zadok and Abiathar, descended from Eleazar and Ithamar respectively; cf. 1 Sam 22:20; 2 Sam 15:24. Later, in the time of Solomon, Zadok became sole high priest.

twelve; [18]the eleventh to Az′arel, his sons and his brethren, twelve; [19]the twelfth to Hashabi′ah, his sons and his brethren, twelve; [20]to the thirteenth, Shu′ba-el, his sons and his brethren, twelve; [21]to the fourteenth, Mattithi′ah, his sons and his brethren, twelve; [22]to the fifteenth, to Jer′emoth, his sons and his brethren, twelve; [23]to the sixteenth, to Hanani′ah, his sons and his brethren, twelve; [24]to the seventeenth, to Joshbekash′ah, his sons and his brethren, twelve; [25]to the eighteenth, to Hana′ni, his sons and his brethren, twelve; [26]to the nineteenth, to Mallo′thi, his sons and his brethren, twelve; [27]to the twentieth, to Eli′athah, his sons and his brethren, twelve; [28]to the twenty-first, to Hothir, his sons and his brethren, twelve; [29]to the twenty-second, to Giddal′ti, his sons and his brethren, twelve; [30]to the twenty-third, to Maha′zi-oth, his sons and his brethren, twelve; [31]to the twenty-fourth, to Romam′ti-e′zer, his sons and his brethren, twelve.

The Divisions of the Gatekeepers

26 As for the divisions of the gatekeepers: of the Ko′rahites, Meshelemi′ah the son of Ko′re, of the sons of A′saph. [2]And Meshelemi′ah had sons: Zechari′ah the first-born, Jedi′a-el the second, Zebadi′ah the third, Jath′ni-el the fourth, [3]E′lam the fifth, Je′ho-ha′nan the sixth, El′ie-ho-e′nai the seventh. [4]And O′bed-e′dom had sons: Shemai′ah the first-born, Jeho′zabad the second, Jo′ah the third, Sachar the fourth, Nethan′el the fifth, [5]Am′mi-el the sixth, Is′sachar the seventh, Pe-ul′lethai the eighth; for God blessed him. [6]Also to his son Shemai′ah were sons born who were rulers in their fathers′ houses, for they were men of great ability. [7]The sons of Shemai′ah: Othni, Reph′a-el, O′bed, and Elza′bad, whose brethren were able men, Eli′hu and Semachi′ah. [8]All these were of the sons of O′bed-e′dom with their sons and brethren, able men qualified for the service; sixty-two of Obed-edom. [9]And Meshelemi′ah had sons and brethren, able men, eighteen. [10]And Ho′sah, of the sons of Merar′i, had sons: Shimri the chief (for though he was not the first-born, his father made him chief), [11]Hilki′ah the second, Tebali′ah the third, Zechari′ah the fourth: all the sons and brethren of Ho′sah were thirteen.

12 These divisions of the gatekeepers, corresponding to their chief men, had duties, just as their brethren did, ministering in the house of the LORD; [13]and they cast lots by fathers′ houses, small and great alike, for their gates. [14]The lot for the east fell to Shelemi′ah. They cast lots also for his son Zechari′ah, a shrewd counselor, and his lot came out for the north. [15]O′bed-e′dom′s came out for the south, and to his sons was allotted the storehouse. [16]For Shuppim and Ho′sah it came out for the west, at the gate of Shal′lecheth on the road that goes up. Watch corresponded to watch. [17]On the east there were six each day, [b] on the

north four each day, on the south four each day, as well as two and two at the storehouse; [18]and for the parbar [c] on the west there were four at the road and two at the parbar. [19]These were the divisions of the gatekeepers among the Ko′rahites and the sons of Merar′i.

The Treasurers, Officers, and Judges

20 And of the Levites, Ahi′jah had charge of the treasuries of the house of God and the treasuries of the dedicated gifts. [21]The sons of Ladan, the sons of the Ger′shonites belonging to Ladan, the heads of the fathers′ houses belonging to Ladan the Gershonite: Jehi′eli. [d]

22 The sons of Jehi′eli, Zetham and Joel his brother, were in charge of the treasuries of the house of the LORD. [23]Of the Am′ramites, the Iz′harites, the He′bronites, and the Uz′zielites— [24]and Shebu′el the son of Gershom, son of Moses, was chief officer in charge of the treasuries. [25]His brethren: from Elie′zer were his son Rehabi′ah, and his son Jeshai′ah, and his son Jo′ram, and his son Zich′ri, and his son Shelo′moth. [26]This Shelo′moth and his brethren were in charge of all the treasuries of the dedicated gifts which David the king, and the heads of the fathers′ houses, and the officers of the thousands and the hundreds, and the commanders of the army, had dedicated. [27]From spoil won in battles they dedicated gifts for the maintenance of the house of the LORD. [28]Also all that Samuel the seer, and Saul the son of Kish, and Abner the son of Ner, and Jo′ab the son of Zeru′iah had dedicated—all dedicated gifts were in the care of Shelo′moth [e] and his brethren.

29 Of the Iz′harites, Chenani′ah and his sons were appointed to outside duties for Israel, as officers and judges. [30]Of the He′bronites, Hashabi′ah and his brethren, one thousand seven hundred men of ability, had the oversight of Israel westward of the Jordan for all the work of the LORD and for the service of the king. [31]Of the He′bronites, Jeri′jah was chief of the Hebronites of whatever genealogy or fathers′ houses. (In the fortieth year of David′s reign search was made and men of great ability among them were found at Ja′zer in Gilead.) [32]King David appointed him and his brethren, two thousand seven hundred men of ability, heads of fathers′ houses, to have the oversight of the Reubenites, the Gadites, and the half-tribe of the Manas′sites for everything pertaining to God and for the affairs of the king.

The Military Divisions

27 This is the list of the people of Israel, the heads of fathers′ houses, the commanders of thousands and hundreds, and their officers who served the king in all matters concerning the

---

[b] Gk: Heb *Levites.*
[c] The meaning of the word *parbar* is unknown.
[d] The Hebrew text of verse 21 is confused.
[e] Heb *Shelomith.*

divisions that came and went, month after month throughout the year, each division numbering twenty-four thousand:

2 Jasho'beam the son of Zab'diel was in charge of the first division in the first month; in his division were twenty-four thousand. ³He was a descendant of Per'ez, and was chief of all the commanders of the army for the first month. ⁴Dodai the Aho'hite *f* was in charge of the division of the second month; in his division were twenty-four thousand. ⁵The third commander, for the third month, was Bena'iah, the son of Jehoi'ada the priest, as chief; in his division were twenty-four thousand. ⁶This is the Bena'iah who was a mighty man of the thirty and in command of the thirty; Ammiz'abad his son was in charge of his division. *g* ⁷As'ahel the brother of Jo'ab was fourth, for the fourth month, and his son Zebadi'ah after him; in his division were twenty-four thousand. ⁸The fifth commander, for the fifth month, was Shamhuth, the Iz'rahite; in his division were twenty-four thousand. ⁹Sixth, for the sixth month, was Ira, the son of Ikkesh the Teko'ite; in his division were twenty-four thousand. ¹⁰Seventh, for the seventh month, was He'lez the Pel'onite, of the sons of E'phraim; in his division were twenty-four thousand. ¹¹Eighth, for the eighth month, was Sib'becai the Hu'shathite, of the Ze'rahites; in his division were twenty-four thousand. ¹²Ninth, for the ninth month, was Abie'zer of An'athoth, a Benjaminite; in his division were twenty-four thousand. ¹³Tenth, for the tenth month, was Ma'harai of Netoph'ah, of the Ze'rahites; in his division were twenty-four thousand. ¹⁴Eleventh, for the eleventh month, was Bena'iah of Pir'athon, of the sons of E'phraim; in his division were twenty-four thousand. ¹⁵Twelfth, for the twelfth month, was Heldai the Netoph'athite, of Oth'ni-el; in his division were twenty-four thousand.

Leaders of the Tribes

16 Over the tribes of Israel, for the Reubenites Elie'zer the son of Zich'ri was chief officer; for the Simeonites, Shephati'ah the son of Ma'acah; ¹⁷for Levi, Hashabi'ah the son of Kemu'el; for Aaron, Za'dok; ¹⁸for Judah, Eli'hu, one of David's brothers; for Is'sachar, Omri the son of Michael; ¹⁹for Zeb'ulun, Ishma'iah the son of Obadi'ah; for Naph'tali, Jer'emoth the son of Az'ri-el; ²⁰for the E'phraimites, Hoshe'a the son of Azazi'ah; for the half-tribe of Manas'seh, Joel the son of Pedai'ah; ²¹for the half-tribe of Manas'seh in Gilead, Iddo the son of Zechari'ah; for Benjamin, Ja-asi'el the son of Abner; ²²for Dan, Az'arel the son of Jero'ham. These were the leaders of the tribes of Israel. ²³David did not number those below twenty years of age, for the LORD had promised to make Israel as many as the stars of heaven. ²⁴Jo'ab the son of Zeru'iah began to number, but did not finish; yet wrath came upon Israel for this, and the number was not entered in the chronicles of King David.

Stewards and Counselors

25 Over the king's treasuries was Az'maveth the son of Ad'i-el; and over the treasuries in the country, in the cities, in the villages and in the towers, was Jonathan the son of Uzzi'ah; ²⁶and over those who did the work of the field for tilling the soil was Ezri the son of Che'lub; ²⁷and over the vineyards was Shim'e-i the Ra'mathite; and over the produce of the vineyards for the wine cellars was Zabdi the Shiphmite. ²⁸Over the olive and sycamore trees in the Shephe'lah was Ba'alha'nan the Gede'rite; and over the stores of oil was Jo'ash. ²⁹Over the herds that pastured in Sharon was Shitrai the Sharonite; over the herds in the valleys was Sha'phat the son of Ad'lai. ³⁰Over the camels was Obil the Ish'maelite; and over the she-donkeys was Jehde'iah the Meron'othite. Over the flocks was Jaziz the Hag'rite. ³¹All these were stewards of King David's property.

32 Jonathan, David's uncle, was a counselor, being a man of understanding and a scribe; he and Jehi'el the son of Hach'moni attended the king's sons. ³³Ahith'ophel was the king's counselor, and Hu'shai the Ar'chite was the king's friend. ³⁴Ahith'ophel was succeeded by Jehoi'ada the son of Bena'iah, and Abi'athar. Jo'ab was commander of the king's army.

Solomon Instructed to Build the Temple

28 David assembled at Jerusalem all the officials of Israel, the officials of the tribes, the officers of the divisions that served the king, the commanders of thousands, the commanders of hundreds, the stewards of all the property and cattle of the king and his sons, together with the palace officials, the mighty men, and all the seasoned warriors. ²Then King David rose to his feet and said: "Hear me, my brethren and my people. I had it in my heart to build a house of rest for the ark of the covenant of the LORD, and for the footstool of our God; and I made preparations for building. ³But God said to me, 'You may not build a house for my name, for you are a warrior and have shed blood.' ⁴Yet the LORD God of Israel chose me from all my father's house to be king over Israel for ever; for he chose Judah as leader, and in the house of Judah my father's house, and among my father's sons he took pleasure in me to make me king over all Israel. ⁵And of all my sons (for the LORD has given me many sons) he has chosen Solomon my son to sit upon the throne of the kingdom of the LORD over Israel. ⁶He said to me, 'It is Solomon your son who shall build my house and my courts, for I have chosen him to be my son, and I will be his father. ⁷I will establish

f Gk: Heb *Ahohite and his division and Mikloth the chief officer.*
g Gk Vg: Heb *was his division.*

his kingdom for ever if he continues resolute in keeping my commandments and my ordinances, as he is today.' ⁸Now therefore in the sight of all Israel, the assembly of the Lord, and in the hearing of our God, observe and seek out all the commandments of the Lord your God; that you may possess this good land, and leave it for an inheritance to your children after you for ever.

9 "And you, Solomon my son, know the God of your father, and serve him with a whole heart and with a willing mind; for the Lord searches all hearts, and understands every plan and thought. If you seek him, he will be found by you; but if you forsake him, he will cast you off for ever. ¹⁰Take heed now, for the Lord has chosen you to build a house for the sanctuary; be strong, and do it."

11 Then David gave Solomon his son the plan of the vestibule of the temple, and of its houses, its treasuries, its upper rooms, and its inner chambers, and of the room for the mercy seat; ¹²and the plan of all that he had in mind for the courts of the house of the Lord, all the surrounding chambers, the treasuries of the house of God, and the treasuries for dedicated gifts; ¹³for the divisions of the priests and of the Levites, and all the work of the service in the house of the Lord; for all the vessels for the service in the house of the Lord, ¹⁴the weight of gold for all golden vessels for each service, the weight of silver vessels for each service, ¹⁵the weight of the golden lampstands and their lamps, the weight of gold for each lampstand and its lamps, the weight of silver for a lampstand and its lamps, according to the use of each lampstand in the service, ¹⁶the weight of gold for each table for the showbread, the silver for the silver tables, ¹⁷and pure gold for the forks, the basins, and the cups; for the golden bowls and the weight of each; for the silver bowls and the weight of each; ¹⁸for the altar of incense made of refined gold, and its weight; also his plan for the golden chariot of the cherubim that spread their wings and covered the ark of the covenant of the Lord. ¹⁹All this he made clear by the writing from the hand of the Lord concerning it, ʰ all the work to be done according to the plan.

20 Then David said to Solomon his son, "Be strong and of good courage, and do it. Fear not, be not dismayed; for the Lord God, even my God, is with you. He will not fail you or forsake you, until all the work for the service of the house of the Lord is finished. ²¹And behold the divisions of the priests and the Levites for all the service of the house of God; and with you in all the work will be every willing man who has skill for any kind of service; also the officers and all the people will be wholly at your command."

Provisions for Building the Temple

29 And David the king said to all the assembly, "Solomon my son, whom alone God has chosen, is young and inexperienced, and the work is great; for the palace will not be for man but for the Lord God. ²So I have provided for the house of my God, so far as I was able, the gold for the things of gold, the silver for the things of silver, and the bronze for the things of bronze, the iron for the things of iron, and wood for the things of wood, besides great quantities of onyx and stones for setting, antimony, colored stones, all sorts of precious stones, and marble. ³Moreover, in addition to all that I have provided for the holy house, I have a treasure of my own of gold and silver, and because of my devotion to the house of my God I give it to the house of my God: ⁴three thousand talents of gold, of the gold of Ophir, and seven thousand talents of refined silver, for overlaying the walls of the house, ⁵and for all the work to be done by craftsmen, gold for the things of gold and silver for the things of silver. Who then will offer willingly, consecrating himself today to the Lord?"

6 Then the heads of fathers' houses made their freewill offerings, as did also the leaders of the tribes, the commanders of thousands and of hundreds, and the officers over the king's work. ⁷They gave for the service of the house of God five thousand talents and ten thousand darics of gold, ten thousand talents of silver, eighteen thousand talents of bronze, and a hundred thousand talents of iron. ⁸And whoever had precious stones gave them to the treasury of the house of the Lord, in the care of Jehi'el the Ger'shonite. ⁹Then the people rejoiced because these had given willingly, for with a whole heart they had offered freely to the Lord; David the king also rejoiced greatly.

David's Prayer of Praise

10 Therefore David blessed the Lord in the presence of all the assembly; and David said: "Blessed are you, O Lord, the God of Israel our father, for ever and ever. ¹¹Yours, O Lord, is the greatness, and the power, and the glory, and the victory, and the majesty; for all that is in the heavens and in the earth is yours; yours is the kingdom, O Lord, and you are exalted as head above all. ¹²Both riches and honor come from you, and you rule over all. In your hand are power and might; and in your hand it is to make great and to give strength to all. ¹³And now we thank you, our God, and praise your glorious name.

14 "But who am I, and what is my people, that we should be able thus to offer willingly? For all things come from you, and of your own have we given you. ¹⁵For we are strangers before you, and sojourners, as all our fathers were; our days on the earth are like a shadow, and there is no abiding. ⁱ ¹⁶O Lord our God, all this abundance that we have provided for building you a house

---

ʰ Cn: Heb *upon me.*

for your holy name comes from your hand and is all your own. [17]I know, my God, that you try the heart, and have pleasure in uprightness; in the uprightness of my heart I have freely offered all these things, and now I have seen your people, who are present here, offering freely and joyously to you. [18]O Lord, the God of Abraham, Isaac, and Israel, our fathers, keep for ever such purposes and thoughts in the hearts of your people, and direct their hearts toward you. [19]Grant to Solomon my son that with a whole heart he may keep your commandments, your covenants, and your statutes, performing all, and that he may build the palace for which I have made provision."

The People Offer Sacrifice
and Anoint Solomon

20 Then David said to all the assembly, "Bless the Lord your God." And all the assembly blessed the Lord, the God of their fathers, and bowed their heads, and worshiped the Lord, and did obeisance to the king. [21]And they performed sacrifices to the Lord, and on the next day offered burnt offerings to the Lord, a thousand bulls, a thousand rams, and a thousand lambs, with their drink offerings, and sacrifices in abundance for all Israel; [22]and they ate and drank before the Lord on that day with great gladness.

And they made Solomon the son of David king the second time, and they anointed him as prince

for the Lord, and Za'dok as priest. [23]Then Solomon sat on the throne of the Lord as king instead of David his father; and he prospered, and all Israel obeyed him. [24]All the leaders and the mighty men, and also all the sons of King David, pledged their allegiance to King Solomon. [25]And the Lord gave Solomon great repute in the sight of all Israel, and bestowed upon him such royal majesty as had not been on any king before him in Israel.

Summary of David's Reign

26 Thus David the son of Jesse reigned over all Israel. [27]The time that he reigned over Israel was forty years; he reigned seven years in He'bron, and thirty-three years in Jerusalem. [28]Then he died in a good old age, full of days, riches, and honor; and Solomon his son reigned in his stead. [29]Now the acts of King David, from first to last, are written in the Chronicles of Samuel the seer, and in the Chronicles of Nathan the prophet, and in the Chronicles of Gad the seer, [30]with accounts of all his rule and his might and of the circumstances that came upon him and upon Israel, and upon all the kingdoms of the countries.

---

[1] Gk Vg: Heb *hope*.
29:23: 1 Kings 2:12.

THE SECOND BOOK OF THE
CHRONICLES

Solomon Requests Wisdom

1 Solomon the son of David established himself in his kingdom, and the LORD his God was with him and made him exceedingly great.* 2 Solomon spoke to all Israel, to the commanders of thousands and of hundreds, to the judges, and to all the leaders in all Israel, the heads of fathers' houses. ³And Solomon, and all the assembly with him, went to the high place that was at Gib′eon; for the tent of meeting of God, which Moses the servant of the LORD had made in the wilderness, was there. ⁴(But David had brought up the ark of God from Kir′iath-je′arim to the place that David had prepared for it, for he had pitched a tent for it in Jerusalem.) ⁵Moreover the bronze altar that Bez′alel the son of U′ri, son of Hur, had made, was there before the tabernacle of the LORD. And Solomon and the assembly sought the LORD. ⁶And Solomon went up there to the bronze altar before the LORD, which was at the tent of meeting, and offered a thousand burnt offerings upon it.

7 In that night God appeared to Solomon, and said to him, "Ask what I shall give you." ⁸And Solomon said to God, "You have shown great and merciful love to David my father, and have made me king in his stead. ⁹O LORD God, let your promise to David my father be now fulfilled, for you have made me king over a people as many as the dust of the earth. ¹⁰Give me now wisdom and knowledge to go out and come in before this people, for who can rule this your people, that is so great?" ¹¹God answered Solomon, "Because this was in your heart, and you have not asked possessions, wealth, honor, or the life of those who hate you, and have not even asked long life, but have asked wisdom and knowledge for yourself that you may rule my people over whom I have made you king, ¹²wisdom and knowledge are granted to you. I will also give you riches, possessions, and honor, such as none of the kings had who were before you, and none after you shall have the like." ¹³So Solomon came from ᵃ the high place at Gib′eon, from before the tent of meeting, to Jerusalem. And he reigned over Israel.

Solomon's Acquisitions

14 Solomon gathered together chariots and horsemen; he had fourteen hundred chariots and twelve thousand horsemen, whom he stationed in the chariot cities and with the king in Jerusalem. ¹⁵And the king made silver and gold as common in Jerusalem as stone, and he made cedar as plentiful as the sycamore of the Shephe′lah. ¹⁶And Solomon's import of horses was from Egypt and Ku′e, and the king's traders received them from Kue for a price. ¹⁷They imported a chariot from Egypt for six hundred shekels of silver, and a horse for a hundred and fifty; likewise through them these were exported to all the kings of the Hittites and the kings of Syria.

Preparations for Building the Temple

2 ᵇ Now Solomon purposed to build a temple for the name of the LORD, and a royal palace for himself. ² ᶜ And Solomon assigned seventy thousand men to bear burdens and eighty thousand to quarry in the hill country, and three thousand six hundred to oversee them. ³And Solomon sent word to Hu′ram the king of Tyre: "As you dealt with David my father and sent him cedar to build himself a house to dwell in, so deal with me. ⁴Behold, I am about to build a house for the name of the LORD my God and dedicate it to him for the burning of incense of sweet spices before him, and for the continual offering of the showbread, and for burnt offerings morning and evening, on the sabbaths and the new moons and the appointed feasts of the LORD our God, as ordained for ever for Israel. ⁵The house which I am to build will be great, for our God is greater than all gods. ⁶But who is able to build him a house, since heaven, even highest heaven, cannot contain him? Who am I to build a house for him, except as a place to burn incense before him? ⁷So now send me a man skilled to work in gold, silver, bronze, and iron, and in purple, crimson, and blue fabrics, trained also in engraving, to be with the skilled workers who are with me in Judah and Jerusalem, whom David my father provided. ⁸Send me also cedar, cypress, and algum timber from Lebanon,

---

ᵃ Gk Vg: Heb *to.*
ᵇ Ch 1:18 in Heb.
ᶜ Ch 2:1 in Heb.
1:3–13: 1 Kings 3:4–15.
1:14–17: 1 Kings 10:26–29.
2:1: 1 Kings 5:5.
2:2: 2:18; 1 Kings 5:15, 16.
2:3–16: 1 Kings 5:2–11.
* **1:1:** The Chronicler makes no mention of the rival claims of Adonijah and of his being put to death by Solomon; cf. 1 Kings 2:13–25. He concentrates on the favorable aspects of the reign and enlarges on the wisdom Solomon received from God.

for I know that your servants know how to cut timber in Lebanon. And my servants will be with your servants, [9]to prepare timber for me in abundance, for the house I am to build will be great and wonderful. [10]I will give for your servants, the hewers who cut timber, twenty thousand cors of crushed wheat, twenty thousand cors of barley, twenty thousand baths of wine, and twenty thousand baths of oil."

Huram Agrees to Help Solomon

11 Then Hu'ram the king of Tyre answered in a letter which he sent to Solomon, "Because the LORD loves his people he has made you king over them." [12]Hu'ram also said, "Blessed be the LORD God of Israel, who made heaven and earth, who has given King David a wise son, endued with discretion and understanding, who will build a temple for the LORD, and a royal palace for himself.

13 "Now I have sent a skilled man, endued with understanding, Hu'ram-a'bi, [14]the son of a woman of the daughters of Dan, and his father was a man of Tyre. He is trained to work in gold, silver, bronze, iron, stone, and wood, and in purple, blue, and crimson fabrics and fine linen, and to do all sorts of engraving and execute any design that may be assigned him, with your craftsmen, the craftsmen of my lord, David your father. [15]Now therefore the wheat and barley, oil and wine, of which my lord has spoken, let him send to his servants; [16]and we will cut whatever timber you need from Lebanon, and bring it to you in rafts by sea to Joppa, so that you may take it up to Jerusalem."

Census of the Aliens

17 Then Solomon took a census of all the aliens who were in the land of Israel, after the census of them which David his father had taken; and there were found a hundred and fifty-three thousand six hundred. [18]Seventy thousand of them he assigned to bear burdens, eighty thousand to quarry in the hill country, and three thousand six hundred as overseers to make the people work.

Solomon Builds the Temple

3 Then Solomon began to build the house of the LORD in Jerusalem on Mount Mori'ah, where the LORD had appeared to David his father, at the place that David had appointed, on the threshing floor of Ornan the Jeb'usite. [2]He began to build in the second month of the fourth year of his reign. [3]These are Solomon's measurements [d] for building the house of God: the length, in cubits of the old standard, was sixty cubits, and the breadth twenty cubits. [4]The vestibule in front of the nave of the house was twenty cubits long, equal to the width of the house; [e] and its height was a hundred and twenty cubits. He overlaid it on the inside with pure gold. [5]The nave he lined with cypress, and covered it with fine gold, and

made palms and chains on it. [6]He adorned the house with settings of precious stones. The gold was gold of Parva'im. [7]So he lined the house with gold—its beams, its thresholds, its walls, and its doors; and he carved cherubim on the walls.

8 And he made the most holy place; its length, corresponding to the breadth of the house, was twenty cubits, and its breadth was twenty cubits; he overlaid it with six hundred talents of fine gold. [9]The weight of the nails was one shekel [f] to fifty shekels of gold. And he overlaid the upper chambers with gold.

10 In the most holy place he made two cherubim of wood [g] and overlaid [h] them with gold. [11]The wings of the cherubim together extended twenty cubits: one wing of the one, of five cubits, touched the wall of the house, and its other wing, of five cubits, touched the wing of the other cherub; [12]and of this cherub, one wing, of five cubits, touched the wall of the house, and the other wing, also of five cubits, was joined to the wing of the first cherub. [13]The wings of these cherubim extended twenty cubits; the cherubim [i] stood on their feet, facing the nave. [14]And he made the veil of blue and purple and crimson fabrics and fine linen, and worked cherubim on it.

15 In front of the house he made two pillars thirty-five cubits high, with a capital of five cubits on the top of each. [16]He made chains like a necklace [j] and put them on the tops of the pillars; and he made a hundred pomegranates, and put them on the chains. [17]He set up the pillars in front of the temple, one on the south, the other on the north; that on the south he called Ja'chin, and that on the north Boaz.

Furnishings of the Temple

4 He made an altar of bronze, twenty cubits long, and twenty cubits wide, and ten cubits high. [2]Then he made the molten sea; it was round, ten cubits from brim to brim, and five cubits high, and a line of thirty cubits measured its circumference. [3]Under it were figures of gourds, [k] for thirty [l] cubits, compassing the sea round about; the gourds [k] were in two rows, cast with it when it was cast. [4]It stood upon twelve oxen, three facing north, three facing west, three facing south, and three facing east; the sea was set upon them, and all their posterior parts were inward. [5]Its thickness was a handbreadth; and its brim was made

---

[d] Syr: Heb *foundations.*
[e] 1 Kings 6:3: Heb uncertain.
[f] Compare Gk: Heb lacks *one shekel.*
[g] Gk: Heb uncertain.
[h] Heb *they overlaid.*
[i] Heb *they.*
[j] Cn: Heb *in the inner sanctuary.*
[k] 1 Kings 7:24: Heb *oxen.*
[l] Compare verse 2: Heb *ten.*
3:1–13: 1 Kings 6:1–28.
3:15–17: 1 Kings 7:15–21.
4:2–5: 1 Kings 7:23–26.

like the brim of a cup, like the flower of a lily; it held over three thousand baths. ⁶He also made ten lavers in which to wash, and set five on the south side, and five on the north. In these they were to rinse off what was used for the burnt offering, and the sea was for the priests to wash in.

7 And he made ten golden lampstands as prescribed, and set them in the temple, five on the south side and five on the north. ⁸He also made ten tables, and placed them in the temple, five on the south side and five on the north. And he made a hundred basins of gold. ⁹He made the court of the priests, and the great court, and doors for the court, and overlaid their doors with bronze; ¹⁰and he set the sea at the southeast corner of the house.

11 Hu′ram also made the pots, the shovels, and the basins. So Huram finished the work that he did for King Solomon on the house of God: ¹²the two pillars, the bowls, and the two capitals on the top of the pillars; and the two networks to cover the two bowls of the capitals that were on the top of the pillars; ¹³and the four hundred pomegranates for the two networks, two rows of pomegranates for each network, to cover the two bowls of the capitals that were upon the pillars. ¹⁴He made the stands also, and the lavers upon the stands, ¹⁵and the one sea, and the twelve oxen underneath it. ¹⁶The pots, the shovels, the forks, and all the equipment for these Hu′ram-a′bi made of burnished bronze for King Solomon for the house of the LORD. ¹⁷In the plain of the Jordan the king cast them, in the clay ground between Succoth and Zer′edah. ¹⁸Solomon made all these things in great quantities, so that the weight of the bronze was not ascertained.

19 So Solomon made all the things that were in the house of God: the golden altar, the tables for the bread of the Presence, ²⁰the lampstands and their lamps of pure gold to burn before the inner sanctuary, as prescribed; ²¹the flowers, the lamps, and the tongs, of purest gold; ²²the snuffers, basins, dishes for incense, and firepans, of pure gold; and the sockets ᵐ of the temple, for the inner doors to the most holy place and for the doors of the nave of the temple were of gold.

5 Thus all the work that Solomon did for the house of the LORD was finished. And Solomon brought in the things which David his father had dedicated, and stored the silver, the gold, and all the vessels in the treasuries of the house of God.

The Ark of the Covenant Brought into the Temple

2 Then Solomon assembled the elders of Israel and all the heads of the tribes, the leaders of the fathers' houses of the sons of Israel, in Jerusalem, to bring up the ark of the covenant of the LORD out of the city of David, which is Zion. ³And all the men of Israel assembled before the king at the

feast which is in the seventh month. ⁴And all the elders of Israel came, and the Levites took up the ark. ⁵And they brought up the ark, the tent of meeting, and all the holy vessels that were in the tent; the priests and the Levites brought them up. ⁶And King Solomon and all the congregation of Israel, who had assembled before him, were before the ark, sacrificing so many sheep and oxen that they could not be counted or numbered. ⁷So the priests brought the ark of the covenant of the LORD to its place, in the inner sanctuary of the house, in the most holy place, underneath the wings of the cherubim. ⁸For the cherubim spread out their wings over the place of the ark, so that the cherubim made a covering above the ark and its poles. ⁹And the poles were so long that the ends of the poles were seen from the holy place before the inner sanctuary; but they could not be seen from outside; and they are there to this day. ¹⁰There was nothing in the ark except the two tables which Moses put there at Horeb, where the LORD made a covenant with the sons of Israel, when they came out of Egypt. ¹¹Now when the priests came out of the holy place (for all the priests who were present had sanctified themselves, without regard to their divisions; ¹²and all the Levitical singers, A′saph, He′man, and Jedu′thun, their sons and kinsmen, arrayed in fine linen, with cymbals, harps, and lyres, stood east of the altar with a hundred and twenty priests who were trumpeters; ¹³and it was the duty of the trumpeters and singers to make themselves heard in unison in praise and thanksgiving to the LORD), and when the song was raised, with trumpets and cymbals and other musical instruments, in praise to the LORD,

"For he is good,
for his mercy endures for ever,"

the house, the house of the LORD, was filled with a cloud, ¹⁴so that the priests could not stand to minister because of the cloud; for the glory of the LORD filled the house of God.

Dedication of the Temple

6 Then Solomon said,
"The LORD has said that he would dwell in thick darkness.
²I have built you an exalted house,
a place for you to dwell in for ever."

³Then the king faced about, and blessed all the assembly of Israel, while all the assembly of Israel stood. ⁴And he said, "Blessed be the LORD, the God of Israel, who with his hand has fulfilled what he promised with his mouth to David my father, saying, ⁵'Since the day that I brought my people out of the land of Egypt, I chose no city in all the tribes of Israel in which to build a house,

ᵐ 1 Kings 7:50: Heb *the door of the house.*
4:6—5:1: 1 Kings 7:38–51.
5:13, 14: 1 Kings 8:10–11.
6:1–39: 1 Kings 8:12–50.

that my name might be there, and I chose no man as prince over my people Israel; [6]but I have chosen Jerusalem that my name may be there and I have chosen David to be over my people Israel.' [7]Now it was in the heart of David my father to build a house for the name of the Lord, the God of Israel. [8]But the Lord said to David my father, 'Whereas it was in your heart to build a house for my name, you did well that it was in your heart; [9]nevertheless you shall not build the house, but your son who shall be born to you shall build the house for my name.' [10]Now the Lord has fulfilled his promise which he made; for I have risen in the place of David my father, and sit on the throne of Israel, as the Lord promised, and I have built the house for the name of the Lord, the God of Israel. [11]And there I have set the ark, in which is the covenant of the Lord which he made with the sons of Israel."

Solomon's Prayer of Dedication

12 Then Solomon stood before the altar of the Lord in the presence of all the assembly of Israel, and spread forth his hands. [13]Solomon had made a bronze platform five cubits long, five cubits wide, and three cubits high, and had set it in the court; and he stood upon it. Then he knelt upon his knees in the presence of all the assembly of Israel, and spread forth his hands toward heaven; [14]and said, "O Lord, God of Israel, there is no God like you, in heaven or on earth, keeping covenant and showing mercy to your servants who walk before you with all their heart; [15]who have kept with your servant David my father what you declared to him; yes, you spoke with your mouth, and with your hand have fulfilled it this day. [16]Now therefore, O Lord, God of Israel, keep with your servant David my father what you have promised him, saying, 'There shall never fail you a man before me to sit upon the throne of Israel, if only your sons take heed to their way, to walk in my law as you have walked before me.' [17]Now therefore, O Lord, God of Israel, let your word be confirmed, which you have spoken to your servant David.

18 "But will God dwell indeed with man on the earth? Behold, heaven and the highest heaven cannot contain you; how much less this house which I have built! [19]Yet have regard to the prayer of your servant and to his supplication, O Lord my God, listening to the cry and to the prayer which your servant prays before you; [20]that your eyes may be open day and night toward this house, the place where you have promised to set your name, that you may listen to the prayer which your servant offers toward this place. [21]And listen to the supplications of your servant and of your people Israel, when they pray toward this place; yes, hear from heaven * your dwelling place; and when you hear, forgive.

22 "If a man sins against his neighbor and is made to take an oath, and comes and swears his oath before your altar in this house, [23]then hear from heaven, and act, and judge your servants, repaying the guilty by bringing his conduct upon his own head, and vindicating the righteous by rewarding him according to his righteousness.

24 "If your people Israel are defeated before the enemy because they have sinned against you, when they turn again and acknowledge your name, and pray and make supplication to you in this house, [25]then hear from heaven, and forgive the sin of your people Israel, and bring them again to the land which you gave to them and to their fathers.

26 "When heaven is shut up and there is no rain because they have sinned against you, if they pray toward this place, and acknowledge your name, and turn from their sin, when you afflict them, [27]then hear in heaven, and forgive the sin of your servants, your people Israel, when you teach them the good way[n] in which they should walk; and grant rain upon your land, which you have given to your people as an inheritance.

28 "If there is famine in the land, if there is pestilence or blight or mildew or locust or caterpillar; if their enemies besiege them in any of their cities; whatever plague, whatever sickness there is; [29]whatever prayer, whatever supplication is made by any man or by all your people Israel, each knowing his own affliction, and his own sorrow and stretching out his hands toward this house; [30]then hear from heaven your dwelling place, and forgive, and render to each whose heart you know, according to all his ways (for you, you only, know the hearts of the children of men); [31]that they may fear you and walk in your ways all the days that they live in the land which you gave to our fathers.

32 "Likewise when a foreigner, who is not of your people Israel, comes from a far country for the sake of your great name, and your mighty hand, and your outstretched arm, when he comes and prays toward this house, [33]hear from heaven your dwelling place, and do according to all for which the foreigner calls to you; in order that all the peoples of the earth may know your name and fear you, as do your people Israel, and that they may know that this house which I have built is called by your name.

34 "If your people go out to battle against their enemies, by whatever way you shall send them, and they pray to you toward this city which you have chosen and the house which I have built for your name, [35]then hear from

---

[n] Gk Syr Vg: Heb *toward the good way.*

* 6;21, *hear from heaven:* This phrase recurs like a refrain throughout this prayer, which seems to have been given a liturgical form.

heaven their prayer and their supplication, and maintain their cause.

36 "If they sin against you—for there is no man who does not sin—and you are angry with them, and give them to an enemy, so that they are carried away captive to a land far or near; [37]yet if they lay it to heart in the land to which they have been carried captive, and repent, and make supplication to you in the land of their captivity, saying, 'We have sinned, and have acted perversely and wickedly'; [38]if they repent with all their mind and with all their heart in the land of their captivity, to which they were carried captive, and pray toward their land, which you gave to their fathers, the city which you have chosen, and the house which I have built for your name, [39]then hear from heaven your dwelling place their prayer and their supplications, and maintain their cause and forgive your people who have sinned against you. [40]Now, O my God, let your eyes be open and your ears attentive to a prayer of this place.

[41]"And now arise, O Lord God, and go to your
    resting place,
  you and the ark of your might.
Let your priests, O Lord God, be clothed with
    salvation,
  and let your saints rejoice in your goodness.
[42]O Lord God, do not turn away the face of your
    anointed one!
  Remember your merciful love for David
    your servant."

The Consecration of the Temple

7 When Solomon had ended his prayer, fire came down * from heaven and consumed the burnt offering and the sacrifices, and the glory of the Lord filled the temple. [2]And the priests could not enter the house of the Lord, because the glory of the Lord filled the Lord's house. [3]When all the children of Israel saw the fire come down and the glory of the Lord upon the temple, they bowed down with their faces to the earth on the pavement, and worshiped and gave thanks to the Lord, saying,

"For he is good,
  for his mercy endures for ever."

4 Then the king and all the people offered sacrifice before the Lord. [5]King Solomon offered as a sacrifice twenty-two thousand oxen and a hundred and twenty thousand sheep. So the king and all the people dedicated the house of God. [6]The priests stood at their posts; the Levites also, with the instruments for music to the Lord which King David had made for giving thanks to the Lord—for his mercy endures for ever—whenever David offered praises by their ministry; opposite them the priests sounded trumpets; and all Israel stood.

7 And Solomon consecrated the middle of the court that was before the house of the Lord; for there he offered the burnt offering and the fat of the peace offerings, because the bronze altar Solomon had made could not hold the burnt offering and the cereal offering and the fat.

8 At that time Solomon held the feast for seven days, and all Israel with him, a very great congregation, from the entrance of Ha′math to the Brook of Egypt. [9]And on the eighth day they held a solemn assembly; for they had kept the dedication of the altar seven days and the feast seven days. [10]On the twenty-third day of the seventh month he sent the people away to their homes, joyful and glad of heart for the goodness that the Lord had shown to David and to Solomon and to Israel his people.

The Lord's Second Appearance to Solomon

11 Thus Solomon finished the house of the Lord and the king's house; all that Solomon had planned to do in the house of the Lord and in his own house he successfully accomplished. [12]Then the Lord appeared to Solomon in the night and said to him: "I have heard your prayer, and have chosen this place for myself as a house of sacrifice. [13]When I shut up the heavens so that there is no rain, or command the locust to devour the land, or send pestilence among my people, [14]if my people who are called by my name humble themselves, and pray and seek my face, and turn from their wicked ways, then I will hear from heaven, and will forgive their sin and heal their land. [15]Now my eyes will be open and my ears attentive to the prayer that is made in this place. [16]For now I have chosen and consecrated this house that my name may be there for ever; my eyes and my heart will be there for all time. [17]And as for you, if you walk before me, as David your father walked, doing according to all that I have commanded you and keeping my statutes and my ordinances, [18]then I will establish your royal throne, as I covenanted with David your father, saying, 'There shall not fail you a man to rule Israel.'

19 "But if you° turn aside and forsake my statutes and my commandments which I have set before you, and go and serve other gods and worship them, [20]then I will pluck youᴾ up from the land which I have given you;ᴾ and this house, which I have consecrated for my name, I will cast out of my sight, and will make it a proverb and a byword among all peoples. [21]And at this house, which is exalted, every one passing by will be astonished, and say, 'Why has the Lord done thus to this land and to this house?' [22]Then they will

---

° The word *you* is plural here.
ᴾ Heb *them.*
6:41–42: Ps 132:8–10.
7:4–10: 1 Kings 8:62–66.
7:11–22: 1 Kings 9:1–9.
* 7:1, *fire came down:* As it did for Elijah's sacrifice; cf. 1 Kings 18:38.

say, 'Because they forsook the LORD the God of their fathers who brought them out of the land of Egypt, and laid hold on other gods, and worshiped them and served them; therefore he has brought all this evil upon them.'"

Solomon Builds Many Cities

8 At the end of twenty years, in which Solomon had built the house of the LORD and his own house, [2]Solomon rebuilt the cities which Hu'ram had given to him, and settled the sons of Israel in them.

3 And Solomon went to Ha'math-zo'bah, and took it. [4]He built Tadmor in the wilderness and all the store-cities which he built in Ha'math. [5]He also built Upper Beth-ho'ron and Lower Beth-horon, fortified cities with walls, gates, and bars, [6]and Ba'alath, and all the store-cities that Solomon had, and all the cities for his chariots, and the cities for his horsemen, and whatever Solomon desired to build in Jerusalem, in Lebanon, and in all the land of his dominion. [7]All the people who were left of the Hittites, the Am'orites, the Per'izzites, the Hi'vites, and the Jeb'usites, who were not of Israel, [8]from their descendants who were left after them in the land, whom the sons of Israel had not destroyed—these Solomon made a forced levy and so they are to this day. [9]But of the sons of Israel Solomon made no slaves for his work; they were soldiers, and his officers, the commanders of his chariots, and his horsemen. [10]And these were the chief officers of King Solomon, two hundred and fifty, who exercised authority over the people.

11 Solomon brought Pharaoh's daughter up from the city of David to the house which he had built for her, for he said, "My wife shall not live in the house of David king of Israel, for the places to which the ark of the LORD has come are holy."

12 Then Solomon offered up burnt offerings to the LORD upon the altar of the LORD which he had built before the vestibule, [13]as the duty of each day required, offering according to the commandment of Moses for the sabbaths, the new moons, and the three annual feasts—the feast of unleavened bread, the feast of weeks, and the feast of tabernacles. [14]According to the ordinance of David his father, he appointed the divisions of the priests for their service, and the Levites for their offices of praise and ministry before the priests as the duty of each day required, and the gatekeepers in their divisions for the several gates; for so David the man of God had commanded. [15]And they did not turn aside from what the king had commanded the priests and Levites concerning any matter and concerning the treasuries.

16 Thus was accomplished all the work of Solomon from [q] the day the foundation of the house of the LORD was laid until it was finished. So the house of the LORD was completed.

17 Then Solomon went to E'zion-ge'ber and E'loth on the shore of the sea, in the land of E'dom. [18]And Hu'ram sent him by his servants ships and servants familiar with the sea, and they went to O'phir together with the servants of Solomon, and fetched from there four hundred and fifty talents of gold and brought it to King Solomon.

The Visit of the Queen of Sheba

9 Now when the queen of Sheba heard of the fame of Solomon she came to Jerusalem to test him with hard questions, having a very great retinue and camels bearing spices and very much gold and precious stones. When she came to Solomon, she told him all that was on her mind. [2]And Solomon answered all her questions; there was nothing hidden from Solomon which he could not explain to her. [3]And when the queen of Sheba had seen the wisdom of Solomon, the house that he had built, [4]the food of his table, the seating of his officials, and the attendance of his servants, and their clothing, his cupbearers, and their clothing, and his burnt offerings which he offered at the house of the LORD, there was no more spirit in her.

5 And she said to the king, "The report was true which I heard in my own land of your affairs and of your wisdom, [6]but I did not believe the [r] reports until I came and my own eyes had seen it; and behold, half the greatness of your wisdom was not told me; you surpass the report which I heard. [7]Happy are your wives! [s] Happy are these your servants, who continually stand before you and hear your wisdom! [8]Blessed be the LORD your God, who has delighted in you and set you on his throne as king for the LORD your God! Because your God loved Israel and would establish them for ever, he has made you king over them, that you may execute justice and righteousness." [9]Then she gave the king a hundred and twenty talents of gold, and a very great quantity of spices, and precious stones: there were no spices such as those which the queen of Sheba gave to King Solomon.

10 Moreover the servants of Hu'ram and the servants of Solomon, who brought gold from O'phir, brought algum wood and precious stones. [11]And the king made of the algum wood steps [t] for the house of the LORD and for the king's house, lyres also and harps for the singers; there never was seen the like of them before in the land of Judah.

12 And King Solomon gave to the queen of Sheba all that she desired, whatever she asked

---

[q] Gk Syr Vg: Heb *to.*
[r] Heb *their.*
[s] Gk Compare 1 Kings 10:8: Heb *men.*
[t] Gk Vg: The meaning of the Hebrew word is uncertain.
8:1–18: 1 Kings 9:10–28.
9:1–28: 1 Kings 10:1–29.

besides what she had brought to the king. So she turned and went back to her own land, with her servants.

Solomon's Wealth and Wisdom

13 Now the weight of gold that came to Solomon in one year was six hundred and sixty-six talents of gold, [14]besides that which the traders and merchants brought; and all the kings of Arabia and the governors of the land brought gold and silver to Solomon. [15]King Solomon made two hundred large shields of beaten gold; six hundred shekels of beaten gold went into each shield. [16]And he made three hundred shields of beaten gold; three hundred shekels of gold went into each shield; and the king put them in the House of the Forest of Lebanon. [17]The king also made a great ivory throne, and overlaid it with pure gold. [18]The throne had six steps and a footstool of gold, which were attached to the throne, and on each side of the seat were arm rests and two lions standing beside the arm rests, [19]while twelve lions stood there, one on each end of a step on the six steps. The like of it was never made in any kingdom. [20]All King Solomon's drinking vessels were of gold, and all the vessels of the House of the Forest of Lebanon were of pure gold; silver was not considered as anything in the days of Solomon. [21]For the king's ships went to Tar′shish with the servants of Hu′ram; once every three years the ships of Tarshish used to come bringing gold, silver, ivory, apes, and peacocks.*

22 Thus King Solomon excelled all the kings of the earth in riches and in wisdom. [23]And all the kings of the earth sought the presence of Solomon to hear his wisdom, which God had put into his mind. [24]Every one of them brought his present, articles of silver and of gold, garments, myrrh, spices, horses, and mules, so much year by year. [25]And Solomon had four thousand stalls for horses and chariots, and twelve thousand horsemen, whom he stationed in the chariot cities and with the king in Jerusalem. [26]And he ruled over all the kings from the Euphrates to the land of the Philis′tines, and to the border of Egypt. [27]And the king made silver as common in Jerusalem as stone, and cedar as plentiful as the sycamore of the Shephe′lah. [28]And horses were imported for Solomon from Egypt and from all lands.

The Death of Solomon

29 Now the rest of the acts of Solomon, from first to last, are they not written in the history of Nathan the prophet, and in the prophecy of Ahi′jah the Shi′lonite, and in the visions of Iddo the seer concerning Jerobo′am the son of Ne′bat? [30]Solomon reigned in Jerusalem over all Israel forty years. [31]And Solomon slept with his fathers, and was buried in the city of David his father; and Rehobo′am his son reigned in his stead.*

The Revolt against Rehoboam

10 Rehobo′am went to She′chem, for all Israel had come to Shechem to make him king. [2]And when Jerobo′am the son of Ne′bat heard of it (for he was in Egypt, whither he had fled from King Solomon), then Jeroboam returned from Egypt. [3]And they sent and called him; and Jerobo′am and all Israel came and said to Rehobo′am, [4]"Your father made our yoke heavy. Now therefore lighten the hard service of your father and his heavy yoke upon us, and we will serve you." [5]He said to them, "Come to me again in three days." So the people went away.

6 Then King Rehobo′am took counsel with the old men, who had stood before Solomon his father while he was yet alive, saying, "How do you advise me to answer this people?" [7]And they said to him, "If you will be kind to this people and please them, and speak good words to them, then they will be your servants for ever." [8]But he forsook the counsel which the old men gave him, and took counsel with the young men who had grown up with him and stood before him. [9]And he said to them, "What do you advise that we answer this people who have said to me, 'Lighten the yoke that your father put upon us'?" [10]And the young men who had grown up with him said to him, "Thus shall you speak to the people who said to you, 'Your father made our yoke heavy, but please lighten it for us'; thus shall you say to them, 'My little finger is thicker than my father's loins. [11]And now, whereas my father laid upon you a heavy yoke, I will add to your yoke. My father chastised you with whips, but I will chastise you with scorpions.'"

12 So Jerobo′am and all the people came to Rehobo′am the third day, as the king said, "Come to me again the third day." [13]And the king answered them harshly, and forsaking the counsel of the old men, [14]King Rehobo′am spoke to them according to the counsel of the young men, saying, "My father made your yoke heavy, but I will add to it; my father chastised you with whips, but I will chastise you with scorpions." [15]So the king did not listen to the people; for it was a turn of affairs brought about by God that the Lord might fulfil his word, which he spoke by Ahi′jah the Shi′lonite to Jerobo′am the son of Ne′bat.

16 And when all Israel saw that the king did not listen to them, the people answered the king,

"What portion have we in David?
We have no inheritance in the son of Jesse.
Each of you to your tents, O Israel!
Look now to your own house, David."

---

* Or *baboons.*
9:30, 31: 1 Kings 11:42–48.
10:1–19: 1 Kings 12:1–19.
* 9:31: One might have expected something to be said on Solomon's decline in morals, but it is passed over in silence. By contrast, the similar failings of his son Rehoboam are underlined; cf. chapters 11–12.

So all Israel departed to their tents. [17]But Rehobo'am reigned over the sons of Israel who dwelt in the cities of Judah. [18]Then King Rehobo'am sent Hador'am, who was taskmaster over the forced labor, and the sons of Israel stoned him to death with stones. And King Rehoboam made haste to mount his chariot, to flee to Jerusalem. [19]So Israel has been in rebellion against the house of David to this day.

Judah and Benjamin Fortified

11 When Rehobo'am came to Jerusalem, he assembled the house of Judah, and Benjamin, a hundred and eighty thousand chosen warriors, to fight against Israel, to restore the kingdom to Rehoboam. [2]But the word of the LORD came to Shemai'ah the man of God: [3]"Say to Rehobo'am the son of Solomon king of Judah, and to all Israel in Judah and Benjamin, [4]'Thus says the LORD, You shall not go up or fight against your brethren. Return every man to his home, for this thing is from me.'" So they listened to the word of the LORD, and returned and did not go against Jerobo'am.

[5] Rehobo'am dwelt in Jerusalem, and he built cities for defense in Judah. [6]He built Bethlehem, E'tam, Teko'a, [7]Beth-zur, Soco, Adul'lam, [8]Gath, Mare'shah, Ziph, [9]Adora'im, La'chish, Aze'kah, [10]Zorah, Ai'jalon, and He'bron, fortified cities which are in Judah and in Benjamin. [11]He made the fortresses strong, and put commanders in them, and stores of food, oil, and wine. [12]And he put shields and spears in all the cities, and made them very strong. So he held Judah and Benjamin.

Priests and Levites Support Rehoboam

[13] And the priests and the Levites that were in all Israel presented themselves to him from all places where they lived. [14]For the Levites left their common lands and their holdings and came to Judah and Jerusalem, because Jerobo'am and his sons cast them out from serving as priests of the LORD, [15]and he appointed his own priests for the high places, and for the satyrs, and for the calves which he had made. [16]And those who had set their hearts to seek the LORD God of Israel came after them from all the tribes of Israel to Jerusalem to sacrifice to the LORD, the God of their fathers. [17]They strengthened the kingdom of Judah, and for three years they made Rehobo'am the son of Solomon secure, for they walked for three years in the way of David and Solomon.

The Wives of Rehoboam

[18] Rehobo'am took as wife Ma'halath the daughter of Jer'imoth the son of David, and of Ab'ihail the daughter of Eli'ab the son of Jesse; [19]and she bore him sons, Je'ush, Shemari'ah, and Zaham. [20]After her he took Ma'acah the daughter of Ab'salom, who bore him Abi'jah, Attai, Ziza, and Shelo'mith. [21]Rehobo'am loved Ma'acah the daughter of Ab'salom above all his wives and concubines (he took eighteen wives and sixty concubines, and had twenty-eight sons and sixty daughters); [22]and Rehobo'am appointed Abi'jah the son of Ma'acah as chief prince among his brothers, for he intended to make him king. [23]And he dealt wisely, and distributed some of his sons through all the districts of Judah and Benjamin, in all the fortified cities; and he gave them abundant provisions, and procured wives for them. [u]

Egypt Attacks Judah

12 When the rule of Rehobo'am was established and was strong, he forsook the law of the LORD, and all Israel with him. [2]In the fifth year of King Rehobo'am, because they had been unfaithful to the LORD, Shishak king of Egypt came up against Jerusalem [3]with twelve hundred chariots and sixty thousand horsemen. And the people were without number who came with him from Egypt—Libyans, Suk'kiim, and Ethiopians. [4]And he took the fortified cities of Judah and came as far as Jerusalem. [5]Then Shemai'ah the prophet came to Rehobo'am and to the princes of Judah, who had gathered at Jerusalem because of Shishak, and said to them, "Thus says the LORD, 'You abandoned me, so I have abandoned you to the hand of Shishak.'" [6]Then the princes of Israel and the king humbled themselves and said, "The LORD is righteous." [7]When the LORD saw that they humbled themselves, the word of the LORD came to Shemai'ah: "They have humbled themselves; I will not destroy them, but I will grant them some deliverance, and my wrath shall not be poured out upon Jerusalem by the hand of Shishak. [8]Nevertheless they shall be servants to him, that they may know my service and the service of the kingdoms of the countries."

[9] So Shishak king of Egypt came up against Jerusalem; he took away the treasures of the house of the LORD and the treasures of the king's house; he took away everything. He also took away the shields of gold which Solomon had made; [10]and King Rehobo'am made in their stead shields of bronze, and committed them to the hands of the officers of the guard, who kept the door of the king's house. [11]And as often as the king went into the house of the LORD, the guard came and bore them, and brought them back to the guardroom. [12]And when he humbled himself the wrath of the LORD turned from him, so as not to make a complete destruction; moreover, conditions were good in Judah.

The Death of Rehoboam

[13] So King Rehobo'am established himself in Jerusalem and reigned. Rehoboam was forty-one years old when he began to reign, and he reigned seventeen years in Jerusalem, the city which the

---

u Cn: Heb *sought a multitude of wives.*
11:1–4: 1 Kings 12:22–24.
12:1–16: 1 Kings 14:25–31.

LORD had chosen out of all the tribes of Israel to put his name there. His mother's name was Na'amah the Am'monitess. [14]And he did evil, for he did not set his heart to seek the LORD.

15 Now the acts of Rehobo'am, from first to last, are they not written in the chronicles of Shemai'ah the prophet and of Iddo the seer?[v] There were continual wars between Rehobo'am and Jerobo'am. [16]And Rehobo'am slept with his fathers, and was buried in the city of David; and Abi'jah his son reigned in his stead.

Abijah's Reign over Judah

13 In the eighteenth year of King Jerobo'am Abi'jah began to reign over Judah. [2]He reigned for three years in Jerusalem. His mother's name was Micai'ah the daughter of U'riel of Gib'e-ah.

Now there was war between Abi'jah and Jerobo'am. [3]Abi'jah went out to battle having an army of valiant men of war, four hundred thousand picked men; and Jerobo'am drew up his line of battle against him with eight hundred thousand picked mighty warriors. [4]Then Abi'jah stood up on Mount Zemara'im which is in the hill country of E'phraim, and said, "Hear me, O Jerobo'am and all Israel! [5]Ought you not to know that the LORD God of Israel gave the kingship over Israel for ever to David and his sons by a covenant of salt? [6]Yet Jerobo'am the son of Ne'bat, a servant of Solomon the son of David, rose up and rebelled against his lord; [7]and certain worthless scoundrels gathered about him and defied Rehobo'am the son of Solomon, when Rehoboam was young and irresolute and could not withstand them.

8 "And now you think to withstand the kingdom of the LORD in the hand of the sons of David, because you are a great multitude and have with you the golden calves which Jerobo'am made you for gods. [9]Have you not driven out the priests of the LORD, the sons of Aaron, and the Levites, and made priests for yourselves like the peoples of other lands? Whoever comes to consecrate himself with a young bull or seven rams becomes a priest of what are no gods. [10]But as for us, the LORD is our God, and we have not forsaken him. We have priests ministering to the LORD who are sons of Aaron, and Levites for their service. [11]They offer to the LORD every morning and every evening burnt offerings and incense of sweet spices, set out the showbread on the table of pure gold, and care for the golden lampstand that its lamps may burn every evening; for we keep the charge of the LORD our God, but you have forsaken him. [12]Behold, God is with us at our head, and his priests with their battle trumpets to sound the call to battle against you. O sons of Israel, do not fight against the LORD, the God of your fathers; for you cannot succeed."

13 Jerobo'am had sent an ambush around to come on them from behind; thus his troops[w] were in front of Judah, and the ambush was behind them. [14]And when Judah looked, behold, the battle was before and behind them; and they cried to the LORD, and the priests blew the trumpets. [15]Then the men of Judah raised the battle shout. And when the men of Judah shouted, God defeated Jerobo'am and all Israel before Abi'jah and Judah. [16]The men of Israel fled before Judah, and God gave them into their hand. [17]Abi'jah and his people slew them with a great slaughter; so there fell slain of Israel five hundred thousand picked men. [18]Thus the men of Israel were subdued at that time, and the men of Judah prevailed, because they relied upon the LORD, the God of their fathers. [19]And Abi'jah pursued Jerobo'am, and took cities from him, Bethel with its villages and Jesha'nah with its villages and E'phron[x] with its villages. [20]Jerobo'am did not recover his power in the days of Abi'jah; and the LORD struck him, and he died. [21]But Abi'jah grew mighty. And he took fourteen wives, and had twenty-two sons and sixteen daughters. [22]The rest of the acts of Abi'jah, his ways and his sayings, are written in the story of the prophet Iddo.

Asa's Good Reign over Judah

14 [y]So Abi'jah slept with his fathers, and they buried him in the city of David; and Asa his son reigned in his stead. In his days the land had rest for ten years. [2][z]And Asa did what was good and right in the eyes of the LORD his God. [3]He took away the foreign altars and the high places, and broke down the pillars and hewed down the Ashe'rim, [4]and commanded Judah to seek the LORD, the God of their fathers, and to keep the law and the commandment. [5]He also took out of all the cities of Judah the high places and the incense altars. And the kingdom had rest under him. [6]He built fortified cities in Judah, for the land had rest. He had no war in those years, for the LORD gave him peace. [7]And he said to Judah, "Let us build these cities, and surround them with walls and towers, gates and bars; the land is still ours, because we have sought the LORD our God; we have sought him, and he has given us peace on every side." So they built and prospered. [8]And Asa had an army of three hundred thousand from Judah, armed with bucklers and spears, and two hundred and eighty thousand men from Benjamin, that carried shields and drew bows; all these were mighty men of valor.

---

[v] Heb seer, to enroll oneself.
[w] Heb they.
[x] Another reading is Ephrain.
[y] Ch 13:23 in Heb.
[z] Ch 14:1 in Heb.
13:1, 2: 1 Kings 15:1, 2, 7.
14:1–5: 1 Kings 15:8–12.

Judah Defeats the Ethiopians

9 Ze'rah the Ethiopian came out against them with an army of a million men and three hundred chariots, and came as far as Mare'shah. ¹⁰And Asa went out to meet him, and they drew up their lines of battle in the valley of Zeph'athah at Mare'shah. ¹¹And Asa cried to the LORD his God, "O LORD, there is none like you to help, between the mighty and the weak. Help us, O LORD our God, for we rely on you, and in your name we have come against this multitude. O LORD, you are our God; let man not prevail against you." ¹²So the LORD defeated the Ethiopians before Asa and before Judah, and the Ethiopians fled. ¹³Asa and the people that were with him pursued them as far as Ge'rar, and the Ethiopians fell until none remained alive; for they were broken before the LORD and his army. The men of Judah ᵃ carried away very much booty. ¹⁴And they struck all the cities round about Ge'rar, for the fear of the LORD was upon them. They plundered all the cities, for there was much plunder in them. ¹⁵And they struck the tents of those who had cattle, ᵇ and carried away sheep in abundance and camels. Then they returned to Jerusalem.

Azariah's Prophecy

15 The Spirit of God came upon Azari'ah the son of O'ded, ²and he went out to meet Asa, and said to him, "Hear me, Asa, and all Judah and Benjamin: The LORD is with you, while you are with him. If you seek him, he will be found by you, but if you forsake him, he will forsake you. ³For a long time Israel was without the true God, and without a teaching priest, and without law; ⁴but when in their distress they turned to the LORD, the God of Israel, and sought him, he was found by them. ⁵In those times there was no peace to him who went out or to him who came in, for great disturbances afflicted all the inhabitants of the lands. ⁶They were broken in pieces, nation against nation and city against city, for God troubled them with every sort of distress. ⁷But you, take courage! Do not let your hands be weak, for your work shall be rewarded."

Asa Has Idols Removed

8 When Asa heard these words, the prophecy of Azari'ah the son of O'ded,ᶜ he took courage, and put away the abominable idols from all the land of Judah and Benjamin and from the cities which he had taken in the hill country of E'phraim, and he repaired the altar of the LORD that was in front of the vestibule of the house of the LORD. ᵈ ⁹And he gathered all Judah and Benjamin, and those from E'phraim, Manas'seh, and Simeon who were sojourning with them, for great numbers had deserted to him from Israel when they saw that the LORD his God was with him. ¹⁰They were gathered at Jerusalem in the third month of the fifteenth year of the reign of Asa.

¹¹They sacrificed to the LORD on that day, from the spoil which they had brought, seven hundred oxen and seven thousand sheep. ¹²And they entered into a covenant to seek the LORD, the God of their fathers, with all their heart and with all their soul; ¹³and that whoever would not seek the LORD, the God of Israel, should be put to death, whether young or old, man or woman. ¹⁴They took oath to the LORD with a loud voice, and with shouting, and with trumpets, and with horns. ¹⁵And all Judah rejoiced over the oath; for they had sworn with all their heart, and had sought him with their whole desire, and he was found by them, and the LORD gave them rest round about.

16 Even Ma'acah, his mother, King Asa removed from being queen mother because she had made an abominable image for Ashe'rah. Asa cut down her image, crushed it, and burned it at the brook Kidron. ¹⁷But the high places were not taken out of Israel. Nevertheless the heart of Asa was blameless all his days. ¹⁸And he brought into the house of God the votive gifts of his father and his own votive gifts, silver, and gold, and vessels. ¹⁹And there was no more war until the thirty-fifth year of the reign of Asa.

Alliance with Syria Condemned

16 In the thirty-sixth year of the reign of Asa, Ba'asha king of Israel went up against Judah, and built Ra'mah, that he might permit no one to go out or come in to Asa king of Judah. ²Then Asa took silver and gold from the treasures of the house of the LORD and the king's house, and sent them to Ben-ha'dad king of Syria, who dwelt in Damascus, saying, ³"Let there be a league between me and you, as between my father and your father; behold, I am sending to you silver and gold; go, break your league with Ba'asha king of Israel, that he may withdraw from me." ⁴And Ben-ha'dad listened to King Asa, and sent the commanders of his armies against the cities of Israel, and they conquered I'jon, Dan, A'bel-ma'im, and all the store-cities of Naph'tali. ⁵And when Ba'asha heard of it, he stopped building Ra'mah, and let his work cease. ⁶Then King Asa took all Judah, and they carried away the stones of Ra'mah and its timber, with which Ba'asha had been building, and with them he built Ge'ba and Mizpah.

7 At that time Hana'ni the seer came to Asa king of Judah, and said to him, "Because you relied on the king of Syria, and did not rely on the LORD your God, the army of the king of Syria has escaped you. ⁸Were not the Ethiopians and the Libyans a huge army with exceedingly many

---

ᵃ Heb *they*.
ᵇ Heb obscure.
ᶜ Compare Syr Vg: Heb *the prophecy, Oded the prophet.*
ᵈ Heb *the vestibule of the* LORD.
15:16—16:6: 1 Kings 15:13–22.

chariots and horsemen? Yet because you relied on the LORD, he gave them into your hand. ⁹For the eyes of the LORD move back and forth throughout the whole earth, to show his might in behalf of those whose heart is blameless toward him. You have done foolishly in this; for from now on you will have wars." ¹⁰Then Asa was angry with the seer, and put him in the stocks, in prison, for he was in a rage with him because of this. And Asa inflicted cruelties upon some of the people at the same time.

Asa's Disease and Death

11 The acts of Asa, from first to last, are written in the Book of the Kings of Judah and Israel. ¹²In the thirty-ninth year of his reign Asa was diseased in his feet, and his disease became severe; yet even in his disease he did not seek the LORD, but sought help from physicians. ¹³And Asa slept with his fathers, dying in the forty-first year of his reign. ¹⁴They buried him in the tomb which he had hewn out for himself in the city of David. They laid him on a bier which had been filled with various kinds of spices prepared by the perfumer's art; and they made a very great fire in his honor.

Jehoshaphat's Reign

17 Jehosh'aphat his son reigned in his stead, and strengthened himself against Israel. ²He placed forces in all the fortified cities of Judah, and set garrisons in the land of Judah, and in the cities of E'phraim which Asa his father had taken. ³The LORD was with Jehosh'aphat, because he walked in the earlier ways of his father; • he did not seek the Ba'als, ⁴but sought the God of his father and walked in his commandments, and not according to the ways of Israel. ⁵Therefore the LORD established the kingdom in his hand; and all Judah brought tribute to Jehosh'aphat; and he had great riches and honor. ⁶His heart was courageous in the ways of the LORD; and furthermore he took the high places and the Ashe'rim out of Judah.

7 In the third year of his reign he sent his princes, Ben-ha'il, Obadi'ah, Zechari'ah, Nethan'el, and Micai'ah, to teach in the cities of Judah; ⁸and with them the Levites, Shemai'ah, Nethani'ah, Zebadi'ah, As'ahel, Shemi'ramoth, Jehon'athan, Adoni'jah, Tobi'jah, and Tobadoni'jah; and with these Levites, the priests Elish'ama and Jeho'ram. ⁹And they taught in Judah, having the book of the law of the LORD with them; they went about through all the cities of Judah and taught among the people.

10 And the fear of the LORD fell upon all the kingdoms of the lands that were round about Judah, and they made no war against Jehosh'aphat. ¹¹Some of the Philis'tines brought Jehosh'aphat presents, and silver for tribute; and the Arabs also brought him seven thousand seven hundred

rams and seven thousand seven hundred he-goats. ¹²And Jehosh'aphat grew steadily greater. He built in Judah fortresses and store-cities, ¹³and he had great stores in the cities of Judah. He had soldiers, mighty men of valor, in Jerusalem. ¹⁴This was the muster of them by fathers' houses: Of Judah, the commanders of thousands: Adnah the commander, with three hundred thousand mighty men of valor, ¹⁵and next to him Je'ho-ha'nan the commander, with two hundred and eighty thousand, ¹⁶and next to him Amasi'ah the son of Zich'ri, a volunteer for the service of the LORD, with two hundred thousand mighty men of valor. ¹⁷Of Benjamin: Eli'ada, a mighty man of valor, with two hundred thousand men armed with bow and shield, ¹⁸and next to him Jeho'zabad with a hundred and eighty thousand armed for war. ¹⁹These were in the service of the king, besides those whom the king had placed in the fortified cities throughout all Judah.

Jehoshaphat's Alliance with Ahab

18 Now Jehosh'aphat had great riches and honor; and he made a marriage alliance with A'hab. ²After some years he went down to A'hab in Samar'ia. And Ahab killed an abundance of sheep and oxen for him and for the people who were with him, and induced him to go up against Ra'moth-gil'ead. ³A'hab king of Israel said to Jehosh'aphat king of Judah, "Will you go with me to Ra'moth-gil'ead?" He answered him, "I am as you are, my people as your people. We will be with you in the war."

4 And Jehosh'aphat said to the king of Israel, "Inquire first for the word of the LORD." ⁵Then the king of Israel gathered the prophets together, four hundred men, and said to them, "Shall we go to battle against Ra'moth-gil'ead, or shall I forbear?" And they said, "Go up; for God will give it into the hand of the king." ⁶But Jehosh'aphat said, "Is there not here another prophet of the LORD of whom we may inquire?" ⁷And the king of Israel said to Jehosh'aphat, "There is yet one man by whom we may inquire of the LORD, Micai'ah the son of Imlah; but I hate him, for he never prophesies good concerning me, but always evil." And Jehoshaphat said, "Let not the king say so." ⁸Then the king of Israel summoned an officer and said, "Bring quickly Micai'ah the son of Imlah." ⁹Now the king of Israel and Jehosh'aphat the king of Judah were sitting on their thrones, attired in their robes; and they were sitting at the threshing floor at the entrance of the gate of Samar'ia; and all the prophets were prophesying before them. ¹⁰And Zedeki'ah the son of Chena'anah made for himself horns of iron, and said, "Thus says the LORD,

---

• Another reading is *his father David.*
16:12–14: 1 Kings 15:23, 24.
17:1: 1 Kings 15:24.
18:1–34: 1 Kings 22:1–35.

'With these you shall push the Syrians until they are destroyed.'" [11]And all the prophets prophesied so, and said, "Go up to Ra'moth-gil'ead and triumph; the LORD will give it into the hand of the king."

Micaiah's Prophecy of Defeat

12 And the messenger who went to summon Micai'ah said to him, "Behold, the words of the prophets * with one accord are favorable to the king; let your word be like the word of one of them, and speak favorably." [13]But Micai'ah said, "As the LORD lives, what my God says, that I will speak." [14]And when he had come to the king, the king said to him, "Micai'ah, shall we go to Ra'moth-gil'ead to battle, or shall I forbear?" And he answered, "Go up and triumph; they will be given into your hand." [15]But the king said to him, "How many times shall I adjure you that you speak to me nothing but the truth in the name of the LORD?" [16]And he said, "I saw all Israel scattered upon the mountains, as sheep that have no shepherd; and the LORD said, 'These have no master; let each return to his home in peace.'" [17]And the king of Israel said to Jehosh'aphat, "Did I not tell you that he would not prophesy good concerning me, but evil?" [18]And Micai'ah said, "Therefore hear the word of the LORD: I saw the LORD sitting on his throne, and all the host of heaven standing on his right hand and on his left; [19]and the LORD said, 'Who will entice A'hab the king of Israel, that he may go up and fall at Ra'moth-gil'ead?' And one said one thing, and another said another. [20]Then a spirit came forward and stood before the LORD, saying, 'I will entice him.' And the LORD said to him, 'By what means?' [21]And he said, 'I will go forth, and will be a lying spirit in the mouth of all his prophets.' And he said, 'You are to entice him, and you shall succeed; go forth and do so.' [22]Now therefore behold, the LORD has put a lying spirit in the mouth of these your prophets; the LORD has spoken evil concerning you."

23 Then Zedeki'ah the son of Chena'anah came near and struck Micai'ah on the cheek, and said, "Which way did the Spirit of the LORD go from me to speak to you?" [24]And Micai'ah said, "Behold, you shall see on that day when you go into an inner chamber to hide yourself." [25]And the king of Israel said, "Seize Micai'ah, and take him back to A'mon the governor of the city and to Jo'ash the king's son; [26]and say, 'Thus says the king, Put this fellow in prison, and feed him with scant fare of bread and water, until I return in peace.'" [27]And Micai'ah said, "If you return in peace, the LORD has not spoken by me." And he said, "Hear, all you peoples!"

The Death of Ahab

28 So the king of Israel and Jehosh'aphat the king of Judah went up to Ra'moth-gil'ead. [29]And the king of Israel said to Jehosh'aphat, "I will disguise myself and go into battle, but you wear your robes." And the king of Israel disguised himself; and they went into battle. [30]Now the king of Syria had commanded the captains of his chariots, "Fight with neither small nor great, but only with the king of Israel." [31]And when the captains of the chariots saw Jehosh'aphat, they said, "It is the king of Israel." So they turned to fight against him; and Jehoshaphat cried out, and the LORD helped him. God drew them away from him, [32]for when the captains of the chariots saw that it was not the king of Israel, they turned back from pursuing him. [33]But a certain man drew his bow and unknowingly struck the king of Israel between the scale armor and the breastplate; therefore he said to the driver of his chariot, "Turn about, and carry me out of the battle, for I am wounded." [34]And the battle grew hot that day, and the king of Israel propped himself up in his chariot facing the Syrians until evening; then at sunset he died.

The Reforms of Jehoshaphat

19 Jehosh'aphat the king of Judah returned in safety to his house in Jerusalem. [2]But Je'hu the son of Hana'ni the seer went out to meet him, and said to King Jehosh'aphat, "Should you help the wicked and love those who hate the LORD? Because of this, wrath has gone out against you from the LORD. [3]Nevertheless some good is found in you, for you destroyed the Ashe'rahs out of the land, and have set your heart to seek God."

4 Jehosh'aphat dwelt at Jerusalem; and he went out again among the people, from Be'er-she'ba to the hill country of E'phraim, and brought them back to the LORD, the God of their fathers. [5]He appointed judges in the land in all the fortified cities of Judah, city by city, [6]and said to the judges, "Consider what you do, for you judge not for man but for the LORD; he is with you in giving judgment. [7]Now then, let the fear of the LORD be upon you; take heed what you do, for there is no perversion of justice with the LORD our God, or partiality, or taking bribes."

8 Moreover in Jerusalem Jehosh'aphat appointed certain Levites and priests and heads of families of Israel, to give judgment for the LORD and to decide disputed cases. They had their seat at Jerusalem. [9]And he charged them: "Thus you shall do in the fear of the LORD, in faithfulness, and with your whole heart: [10]whenever a case comes to you from your brethren who live in their cities, concerning bloodshed, law or commandment, statutes or ordinances, then you shall

---

* 18:12, *prophets:* Jeremiah says that false prophets usually proclaim what their hearers want them to say: "every one deals falsely . . . saying, 'Peace, peace,' when there is no peace" (Jer 6:13–14). It will be noticed that the Chronicler omits a large part of 2 Kings which is concerned with the northern kingdom. Elijah, for example, is mentioned only once, in 21:12.

instruct them, that they may not incur guilt before the LORD and wrath may not come upon you and your brethren. Thus you shall do, and you will not incur guilt. ¹¹And behold, Amari′ah the chief priest is over you in all matters of the LORD; and Zebadi′ah the son of Ish′mael, the governor of the house of Judah, in all the king's matters; and the Levites will serve you as officers. Deal courageously, and may the LORD be with the upright!"

Invasion from the East

20 After this the Moabites and Am′monites, and with them some of the Me-u′nites, ᶠ came against Jehosh′aphat for battle. ²Some men came and told Jehosh′aphat, "A great multitude is coming against you from E′dom, ᵍ from beyond the sea; and, behold, they are in Haz′azon-ta′mar" (that is, En-ge′di). ³Then Jehosh′aphat feared, and set himself to seek the LORD, and proclaimed a fast throughout all Judah. ⁴And Judah assembled to seek help from the LORD; from all the cities of Judah they came to seek the LORD.

Jehoshaphat's Prayer and Victory

5 And Jehosh′aphat stood in the assembly of Judah and Jerusalem, in the house of the LORD, before the new court, ⁶and said, "O LORD, God of our fathers, are you not God in heaven? Do you not rule over all the kingdoms of the nations? In your hand are power and might, so that none is able to withstand you. ⁷Did you not, O our God, drive out the inhabitants of this land before your people Israel, and give it for ever to the descendants of Abraham your friend? ⁸And they have dwelt in it, and have built you in it a sanctuary for your name, saying, ⁹'If evil comes upon us, the sword, judgment, ʰ or pestilence, or famine, we will stand before this house, and before you, for your name is in this house, and cry to you in our affliction, and you will hear and save.' ¹⁰And now behold, the men of Ammon and Moab and Mount Se′ir, whom you would not let Israel invade when they came from the land of Egypt, and whom they avoided and did not destroy— ¹¹behold, they reward us by coming to drive us out of your possession, which you have given us to inherit. ¹²O our God, will you not execute judgment upon them? For we are powerless against this great multitude that is coming against us. We do not know what to do, but our eyes are upon you."

13 Meanwhile all the men of Judah stood before the LORD, with their little ones, their wives, and their children. ¹⁴And the Spirit of the LORD came upon Jahazi′el the son of Zechari′ah, son of Bena′iah, son of Je-i′el, son of Mattani′ah, a Levite of the sons of A′saph, in the midst of the assembly. ¹⁵And he said, "Listen, all Judah and inhabitants of Jerusalem, and King Jehosh′aphat: Thus says the LORD to you, 'Fear not, and be not dismayed at this great multitude; for the battle

is not yours but God's. ¹⁶Tomorrow go down against them; behold, they will come up by the ascent of Ziz; you will find them at the end of the valley, east of the wilderness of Jeru′el. ¹⁷You will not need to fight in this battle; take your position, stand still, and see the victory of the LORD on your behalf, O Judah and Jerusalem.' Fear not, and be not dismayed; tomorrow go out against them, and the LORD will be with you."

18 Then Jehosh′aphat bowed his head with his face to the ground, and all Judah and the inhabitants of Jerusalem fell down before the LORD, worshiping the LORD. ¹⁹And the Levites, of the Ko′hathites and the Ko′rahites, stood up to praise the LORD, the God of Israel, with a very loud voice.

20 And they rose early in the morning and went out into the wilderness of Teko′a; and as they went out, Jehosh′aphat stood and said, "Hear me, Judah and inhabitants of Jerusalem! Believe in the LORD your God, and you will be established; believe his prophets, and you will succeed." ²¹And when he had taken counsel with the people, he appointed those who were to sing to the LORD and praise him in holy splendor, as they went before the army, and say,

"Give thanks to the LORD,
    for his mercy endures for ever."

²²And when they began to sing and praise, the LORD set an ambush against the men of Ammon, Moab, and Mount Se′ir, who had come against Judah, so that they were routed. ²³For the men of Ammon and Moab rose against the inhabitants of Mount Se′ir, destroying them utterly, and when they had made an end of the inhabitants of Seir, they all helped to destroy one another.

24 When Judah came to the watchtower of the wilderness, they looked toward the multitude; and behold, they were dead bodies lying on the ground; none had escaped. ²⁵When Jehosh′aphat and his people came to take the spoil from them, they found cattle ⁱ in great numbers, goods, clothing, and precious things, which they took for themselves until they could carry no more. They were three days in taking the spoil, it was so much. ²⁶On the fourth day they assembled in the Valley of Bera′cah, ʲ for there they blessed the LORD; therefore the name of that place has been called the Valley of Beracah to this day. ²⁷Then they returned, every man of Judah and Jerusalem, and Jehosh′aphat at their head, returning to Jerusalem with joy, for the LORD had made them rejoice over their enemies. ²⁸They came to Jerusalem, with harps and lyres and trumpets, to the

---

ᶠ Compare 26:7: Heb *Ammonites.*
ᵍ One Ms: Heb *Aram* (Syria).
ʰ Or *the sword of judgment.*
ⁱ Gk: Heb *among them.*
ʲ That is *Blessing.*
20:7: Jas 2:23.

house of the Lord. ²⁹And the fear of God came on all the kingdoms of the countries when they heard that the Lord had fought against the enemies of Israel. ³⁰So the realm of Jehosh'aphat was quiet, for his God gave him rest round about.

The End of Jehoshaphat's Reign over Judah

31 Thus Jehosh'aphat reigned over Judah. He was thirty-five years old when he began to reign, and he reigned twenty-five years in Jerusalem. His mother's name was Azu'bah the daughter of Shilhi. ³²He walked in the way of Asa his father and did not turn aside from it; he did what was right in the sight of the Lord. ³³The high places, however, were not taken away; the people had not yet set their hearts upon the God of their fathers.

34 Now the rest of the acts of Jehosh'aphat, from first to last, are written in the chronicles of Je'hu the son of Hana'ni, which are recorded in the Book of the Kings of Israel.

35 After this Jehosh'aphat king of Judah joined with Ahazi'ah king of Israel, who did wickedly. ³⁶He joined him in building ships to go to Tar'-shish, and they built the ships in E'zion-ge'ber. ³⁷Then Elie'zer the son of Dodav'ahu of Mare'shah prophesied against Jehosh'aphat, saying, "Because you have joined with Ahazi'ah, the Lord will destroy what you have made." And the ships were wrecked and were not able to go to Tar'shish.

Jehoram's Reign over Judah

21 Jehosh'aphat slept with his fathers, and was buried with his fathers in the city of David; and Jeho'ram his son reigned in his stead. ²He had brothers, the sons of Jehosh'aphat: Aza-ri'ah, Jehi'el, Zechari'ah, Azariah, Michael, and Shephati'ah; all these were the sons of Jehosha-phat king of Judah. ³Their father gave them great gifts, of silver, gold, and valuable possessions, together with fortified cities in Judah; but he gave the kingdom to Jeho'ram, because he was the first-born. ⁴When Jeho'ram had ascended the throne of his father and was established, he slew all his brothers with the sword, and also some of the princes of Israel. ⁵Jeho'ram was thirty-two years old when he became king, and he reigned eight years in Jerusalem. ⁶And he walked in the way of the kings of Israel, as the house of A'hab had done; for the daughter of Ahab was his wife. And he did what was evil in the sight of the Lord. ⁷Yet the Lord would not destroy the house of David, because of the covenant which he had made with David, and since he had promised to give a lamp to him and to his sons for ever.

The Revolt of Edom

8 In his days E'dom revolted from the rule of Judah, and set up a king of their own. ⁹Then Jeho'ram passed over with his commanders and all his chariots, and he rose by night and struck

the E'domites who had surrounded him and his chariot commanders. ¹⁰So E'dom revolted from the rule of Judah to this day. At that time Libnah also revolted from his rule, because he had for-saken the Lord, the God of his fathers.

Elijah's Letter of Warning

11 Moreover he made high places in the hill country of Judah, and led the inhabitants of Jerusalem into unfaithfulness, and made Judah go astray. ¹²And a letter came to him from Eli'jah the prophet, saying, "Thus says the Lord, the God of David your father, 'Because you have not walked in the ways of Jehosh'aphat your father, or in the ways of Asa king of Judah, ¹³but have walked in the way of the kings of Israel, and have led Judah and the inhabitants of Jerusalem into unfaithful-ness, as the house of A'hab led Israel into unfaith-fulness, and also you have killed your brothers, of your father's house, who were better than your-self; ¹⁴behold, the Lord will bring a great plague on your people, your children, your wives, and all your possessions, ¹⁵and you yourself will have a severe sickness with a disease of your bowels, until your bowels come out because of the dis-ease, day by day.'"

16 And the Lord stirred up against Jeho'ram the anger of the Philis'tines and of the Arabs who are near the Ethiopians; ¹⁷and they came up against Judah, and invaded it, and carried away all the possessions they found that belonged to the king's house, and also his sons and his wives, so that no son was left to him except Jeho'ahaz, his youngest son.

Disease and Death of Jehoram

18 And after all this the Lord struck him in his bowels with an incurable disease. ¹⁹In course of time, at the end of two years, his bowels came out because of the disease, and he died in great agony. His people made no fire in his honor, like the fires made for his fathers. ²⁰He was thirty-two years old when he began to reign, and he reigned eight years in Jerusalem; and he departed with no one's regret. They buried him in the city of David, but not in the tombs of the kings.

Ahaziah's Reign over Judah

22 And the inhabitants of Jerusalem made Ahazi'ah his youngest son king in his stead; for the band of men that came with the Arabs to the camp had slain all the older sons. So Ahaziah the son of Jeho'ram king of Judah reigned. ²Ahazi'ah was forty-two years old when he began to reign, and he reigned one year in Jerusalem. His mother's name was Athali'ah, the granddaughter of Omri. ³He also walked in the

---

20:31–33: 1 Kings 22:41–43.
20:35–37: 1 Kings 22:48, 49.
21:1: 1 Kings 22:50.
21:5–10: 2 Kings 8:17–22.
21:20: 2 Kings 8:17, 24.
22:1–6: 2 Kings 8:24–29.

ways of the house of A'hab, for his mother was his counselor in doing wickedly. ⁴He did what was evil in the sight of the LORD, as the house of A'hab had done; for after the death of his father they were his counselors, to his undoing. ⁵He even followed their counsel, and went with Jeho'ram the son of A'hab king of Israel to make war against Haz'ael king of Syria at Ra'moth-gil'ead. And the Syrians wounded Jo'ram, ⁶and he returned to be healed in Jezre'el of the wounds which he had received at Ra'mah, when he fought against Haz'ael king of Syria. And Ahazi'ah the son of Jeho'ram king of Judah went down to see Jo'ram the son of A'hab in Jezreel, because he was sick.

The Downfall of Ahaziah

7 But it was ordained by God that the downfall of Ahazi'ah should come about through his going to visit Jo'ram. For when he came there he went out with Jeho'ram to meet Je'hu the son of Nimshi, whom the LORD had anointed to destroy the house of A'hab. ⁸And when Je'hu was executing judgment upon the house of A'hab, he met the princes of Judah and the sons of Ahazi'ah's brothers, who attended Ahaziah, and he killed them. ⁹He searched for Ahazi'ah, and he was captured while hiding in Samar'ia, and he was brought to Je'hu and put to death. They buried him, for they said, "He is the grandson of Jehosh'-aphat, who sought the LORD with all his heart." And the house of Ahaziah had no one able to rule the kingdom.

Athaliah Seizes the Throne

10 Now when Athali'ah the mother of Ahazi'ah saw that her son was dead, she arose and destroyed all the royal family of the house of Judah. ¹¹But Je'ho-shab'e-ath, the daughter of the king, took Jo'ash the son of Ahazi'ah, and stole him away from among the king's sons who were about to be slain, and she put him and his nurse in a bedchamber. Thus Jeho-shabe-ath, the daughter of King Jeho'ram and wife of Jehoi'ada the priest, because she was a sister of Ahaziah, hid him from Athali'ah, so that she did not slay him; ¹²and he remained with them six years, hid in the house of God, while Athali'ah reigned over the land.

23 But in the seventh year Jehoi'ada took courage, and entered into a compact with the commanders of hundreds, Azari'ah the son of Jero'ham, Ish'mael the son of Je'ho-ha'nan, Azariah the son of O'bed, Ma-asei'ah the son of Adai'ah, and Elisha'phat the son of Zich'ri. ²And they went about through Judah and gathered the Levites from all the cities of Judah, and the heads of fathers' houses of Israel, and they came to Jerusalem. ³And all the assembly made a covenant with the king in the house of God. And Jehoi'ada ¹ said to them, "Behold, the king's son! Let him reign, as the LORD spoke concerning the

sons of David. ⁴This is the thing that you shall do: of you priests and Levites who come off duty on the sabbath, one third shall be gatekeepers, ⁵and one third shall be at the king's house and one third at the Gate of the Foundation; and all the people shall be in the courts of the house of the LORD. ⁶Let no one enter the house of the LORD except the priests and ministering Levites; they may enter, for they are holy, but all the people shall keep the charge of the LORD. ⁷The Levites shall surround the king, each with his weapons in his hand; and whoever enters the house shall be slain. Be with the king when he comes in, and when he goes out."

Joash Crowned King of Judah

8 The Levites and all Judah did according to all that Jehoi'ada the priest commanded. They each brought his men, who were to go off duty on the sabbath, with those who were to come on duty on the sabbath; for Jehoiada the priest did not dismiss the divisions. ⁹And Jehoi'ada the priest delivered to the captains the spears and the large and small shields that had been King David's, which were in the house of God; ¹⁰and he set all the people as a guard for the king, every man with his weapon in his hand, from the south side of the house to the north side of the house, around the altar and the house. ¹¹Then he brought out the king's son, and put the crown upon him, and gave him the covenant; and they proclaimed him king, and Jehoi'ada and his sons anointed him, and they said, "Long live the king."

Athaliah Slain

12 When Athali'ah heard the noise of the people running and praising the king, she went into the house of the LORD to the people; ¹³and when she looked, there was the king standing by his pillar at the entrance, and the captains and the trumpeters beside the king, and all the people of the land rejoicing and blowing trumpets, and the singers with their musical instruments leading in the celebration. And Athali'ah tore her clothes, and cried, "Treason! Treason!" ¹⁴Then Jehoi'ada the priest brought out the captains who were set over the army, saying to them, "Bring her out between the ranks; any one who follows her is to be slain with the sword." For the priest said, "Do not slay her in the house of the LORD." ¹⁵So they laid hands on her; and she went into the entrance of the horse gate of the king's house and they slew her there.

Jehoiada's Covenant

16 And Jehoi'ada made a covenant between himself and all the people and the king that they should be the LORD's people. ¹⁷Then all the people went to the house of Ba'al, and tore it down; his

---

¹ Heb *he.*
22:7-9: 2 Kings 9:1—10:36.
22:10—23:21: 2 Kings 11:1–20.

altars and his images they broke in pieces, and they slew Mattan the priest of Baal before the altars. [18]And Jehoi'ada posted watchmen for the house of the LORD under the direction of the Levitical priests and the Levites whom David had organized to be in charge of the house of the LORD, to offer burnt offerings to the LORD, as it is written in the law of Moses, with rejoicing and with singing, according to the order of David. [19]He stationed the gatekeepers at the gates of the house of the LORD so that no one should enter who was in any way unclean. [20]And he took the captains, the nobles, the governors of the people, and all the people of the land; and they brought the king down from the house of the LORD, marching through the upper gate to the king's house. And they set the king upon the royal throne. [21]So all the people of the land rejoiced; and the city was quiet, after Athali'ah had been slain with the sword.

Joash Restores the Temple

24 Jo'ash was seven years old when he began to reign, and he reigned forty years in Jerusalem; his mother's name was Zib'iah of Be'er-she'ba. [2]And Jo'ash did what was right in the eyes of the LORD all the days of Jehoi'ada the priest. [3]Jehoi'ada got for him two wives, and he had sons and daughters.

4 After this Jo'ash decided to restore the house of the LORD. [5]And he gathered the priests and the Levites, and said to them, "Go out to the cities of Judah, and gather from all Israel money to repair the house of your God from year to year; and see that you hasten the matter." But the Levites did not hasten it. [6]So the king summoned Jehoi'ada the chief, and said to him, "Why have you not required the Levites to bring in from Judah and Jerusalem the tax levied by Moses, the servant of the LORD, on[m] the congregation of Israel for the tent of covenant?" [7]For the sons of Athali'ah, that wicked woman, had broken into the house of God; and had also used all the dedicated things of the house of the LORD for the Ba'als.

8 So the king commanded, and they made a chest, and set it outside the gate of the house of the LORD. [9]And proclamation was made throughout Judah and Jerusalem, to bring in for the LORD the tax that Moses the servant of God laid upon Israel in the wilderness. [10]And all the princes and all the people rejoiced and brought their tax and dropped it into the chest until they had finished. [11]And whenever the chest was brought to the king's officers by the Levites, when they saw that there was much money in it, the king's secretary and the officer of the chief priest would come and empty the chest and take it and return it to its place. Thus they did day after day, and collected money in abundance. [12]And the king and Jehoi'ada gave it to those who had charge of the work

of the house of the LORD, and they hired masons and carpenters to restore the house of the LORD, and also workers in iron and bronze to repair the house of the LORD. [13]So those who were engaged in the work labored, and the repairing went forward in their hands, and they restored the house of God to its proper condition and strengthened it. [14]And when they had finished, they brought the rest of the money before the king and Jehoi'ada, and with it were made utensils for the house of the LORD, both for the service and for the burnt offerings, and dishes for incense, and vessels of gold and silver. And they offered burnt offerings in the house of the LORD continually all the days of Jehoiada.

15 But Jehoi'ada grew old and full of days, and died; he was a hundred and thirty years old at his death. [16]And they buried him in the city of David among the kings, because he had done good in Israel, and toward God and his house.

Apostasy of Joash

17 Now after the death of Jehoi'ada the princes of Judah came and did obeisance to the king; then the king listened to them. [18]And they forsook the house of the LORD, the God of their fathers, and served the Ashe'rim and the idols. And wrath came upon Judah and Jerusalem for this their guilt. [19]Yet he sent prophets among them to bring them back to the LORD; these testified against them, but they would not give heed.

20 Then the Spirit of God took possession of[n] Zechari'ah the son of Jehoi'ada the priest; and he stood above the people, and said to them, "Thus says God, 'Why do you transgress the commandments of the LORD, so that you cannot prosper? Because you have forsaken the LORD, he has forsaken you.'" [21]But they conspired against him, and by command of the king they stoned him with stones in the court of the house of the LORD. [22]Thus Jo'ash the king did not remember the kindness which Jehoi'ada, Zechari'ah's father, had shown him, but killed his son. And when he was dying, he said, "May the LORD see and avenge!"

Death of Joash

23 At the end of the year the army of the Syrians came up against Jo'ash. They came to Judah and Jerusalem, and destroyed all the princes of the people from among the people, and sent all their spoil to the king of Damascus. [24]Though the army of the Syrians had come with few men, the LORD delivered into their hand a very great army, because they had forsaken the LORD, the God of their fathers. Thus they executed judgment on Jo'ash.

[m] Compare Vg: Heb *and.*
[n] Heb *clothed itself with.*
24:1-14: 2 Kings 11:21—12:14.
24:23-26: 2 Kings 12:17, 18, 20, 21.

25 When they had departed from him, leaving him severely wounded, his servants conspired against him because of the blood of the son ° of Jehoi′ada the priest, and slew him on his bed. So he died; and they buried him in the city of David, but they did not bury him in the tombs of the kings. 26Those who conspired against him were Zabad the son of Shim′e-ath the Am′monitess, and Jeho′zabad the son of Shimrith the Moabitess. 27Accounts of his sons, and of the many oracles against him, and of the rebuilding ᴾ of the house of God are written in the Commentary on the Book of the Kings. And Amazi′ah his son reigned in his stead.

Amaziah's Reign over Judah

25 Amazi′ah was twenty-five years old when he began to reign, and he reigned twenty-nine years in Jerusalem. His mother's name was Je′ho-ad′dan of Jerusalem. 2And he did what was right in the eyes of the Lord, yet not with a blameless heart. 3And as soon as the royal power was firmly in his hand he killed his servants who had slain the king his father. 4But he did not put their children to death, according to what is written in the law, in the book of Moses, where the Lord commanded, "The fathers shall not be put to death for the children, or the children be put to death for the fathers; but every man shall die for his own sin."

Slaughter of the Edomites

5 Then Amazi′ah assembled the men of Judah, and set them by fathers' houses under commanders of thousands and of hundreds for all Judah and Benjamin. He mustered those twenty years old and upward, and found that they were three hundred thousand picked men, fit for war, able to handle spear and shield. 6He hired also a hundred thousand mighty men of valor from Israel for a hundred talents of silver. 7But a man of God came to him and said, "O king, do not let the army of Israel go with you, for the Lord is not with Israel, with all these E′phraimites. 8But if you suppose that in this way you will be strong for war, �q God will cast you down before the enemy; for God has power to help or to cast down." 9And Amazi′ah said to the man of God, "But what shall we do about the hundred talents which I have given to the army of Israel?" The man of God answered, "The Lord is able to give you much more than this." 10Then Amazi′ah discharged the army that had come to him from E′phraim, to go home again. And they became very angry with Judah, and returned home in fierce anger. 11But Amazi′ah took courage, and led out his people, and went to the Valley of Salt and struck ten thousand men of Se′ir. 12The men of Judah captured another ten thousand alive, and took them to the top of a rock and threw them down from the top of the rock; and they were all dashed to pieces. 13But the men of the army whom Amazi′ah sent back, not letting them go with him to battle, fell upon the cities of Judah, from Samar′ia to Beth-ho′ron, and killed three thousand people in them, and took much spoil.

14 After Amazi′ah came from the slaughter of the E′domites, he brought the gods of the men of Se′ir, and set them up as his gods, and worshiped them, making offerings to them. 15Therefore the Lord was angry with Amazi′ah and sent to him a prophet, who said to him, "Why have you resorted to the gods of a people, which did not deliver their own people from your hand?" 16But as he was speaking the king said to him, "Have we made you a royal counselor? Stop! Why should you be put to death?" So the prophet stopped, but said, "I know that God has determined to destroy you, because you have done this and have not listened to my counsel."

Israel Defeats Judah

17 Then Amazi′ah king of Judah took counsel and sent to Jo′ash the son of Jeho′ahaz, son of Je′hu, king of Israel, saying, "Come, let us look one another in the face." 18And Jo′ash the king of Israel sent word to Amazi′ah king of Judah, "A thistle on Lebanon sent to a cedar on Lebanon, saying, 'Give your daughter to my son for a wife'; and a wild beast of Lebanon passed by and trampled down the thistle. 19You say, 'See, I have struck Edom,' and your heart has lifted you up in boastfulness. But now stay at home; why should you provoke trouble so that you fall, you and Judah with you?"

20 But Amazi′ah would not listen; for it was of God, in order that he might give them into the hand of their enemies, because they had sought the gods of E′dom. 21So Jo′ash king of Israel went up; and he and Amazi′ah king of Judah faced one another in battle at Beth-she′mesh, which belongs to Judah. 22And Judah was defeated by Israel, and every man fled to his home. 23And Jo′ash king of Israel captured Amazi′ah king of Judah, the son of Joash, son of Ahazi′ah, at Beth-she′mesh, and brought him to Jerusalem, and broke down the wall of Jerusalem for four hundred cubits, from the E′phraim Gate to the Corner Gate. 24And he seized all the gold and silver, and all the vessels that were found in the house of God, and O′bed-e′dom with them; he seized also the treasuries of the king's house, and hostages, and he returned to Samar′ia.

Death of Amaziah

25 Amazi′ah the son of Jo′ash king of Judah lived fifteen years after the death of Joash the son

---

° Gk Vg: Heb *sons*.
ᴾ Heb *founding*.
q Gk: Heb *But if you go, act, be strong for the battle*.
25:1–4: 2 Kings 14:2–6.
25:11: 2 Kings 14:7.
25:17-20, 21-24: 2 Kings 14:8–14.
25:25-28: 2 Kings 14:17–20.

of Jeho'ahaz, king of Israel. ²⁶Now the rest of the deeds of Amazi'ah, from first to last, are they not written in the Book of the Kings of Judah and Israel? ²⁷From the time when he turned away from the LORD they made a conspiracy against him in Jerusalem, and he fled to La'chish. But they sent after him to Lachish, and slew him there. ²⁸And they brought him upon horses; and he was buried with his fathers in the city of David.

Uzziah's Reign over Judah

26 And all the people of Judah took Uzzi'ah, who was sixteen years old, and made him king instead of his father Amazi'ah. ²He built E'loth and restored it to Judah, after the king slept with his fathers. ³Uzzi'ah was sixteen years old when he began to reign, and he reigned fifty-two years in Jerusalem. His mother's name was Jecoli'ah of Jerusalem. ⁴And he did what was right in the eyes of the LORD, according to all that his father Amazi'ah had done. ⁵He set himself to seek God in the days of Zechari'ah, who instructed him in the fear of God; and as long as he sought the LORD, God made him prosper.

6 He went out and made war against the Philis'tines, and broke down the wall of Gath and the wall of Jabneh and the wall of Ash'dod; and he built cities in the territory of Ashdod and elsewhere among the Philistines. ⁷God helped him against the Philis'tines, and against the Arabs that dwelt in Gurba'al, and against the Me-u'nites. ⁸The Am'monites paid tribute to Uzzi'ah, and his fame spread even to the border of Egypt, for he became very strong. ⁹Moreover Uzzi'ah built towers in Jerusalem at the Corner Gate and at the Valley Gate and at the Angle, and fortified them. ¹⁰And he built towers in the wilderness, and hewed out many cisterns, for he had large herds, both in the Shephe'lah and in the plain, and he had farmers and vinedressers in the hills and in the fertile lands, for he loved the soil. ¹¹Moreover Uzzi'ah had an army of soldiers, fit for war, in divisions according to the numbers in the muster made by Je-i'el the secretary and Ma-asei'ah the officer, under the direction of Hanani'ah, one of the king's commanders. ¹²The whole number of the heads of fathers' houses of mighty men of valor was two thousand six hundred. ¹³Under their command was an army of three hundred and seven thousand five hundred, who could make war with mighty power, to help the king against the enemy. ¹⁴And Uzzi'ah prepared for all the army shields, spears, helmets, coats of mail, bows, and stones for slinging. ¹⁵In Jerusalem he made engines, invented by skilful men, to be on the towers and the corners, to shoot arrows and great stones. And his fame spread far, for he was marvelously helped, till he was strong.

Pride and Apostasy

16 But when he was strong he grew proud, to his destruction. For he was false to the LORD his God, and entered the temple of the LORD to burn incense on the altar of incense. ¹⁷But Azari'ah the priest went in after him, with eighty priests of the LORD who were men of valor; ¹⁸and they withstood King Uzzi'ah, and said to him, "It is not for you, Uzziah, to burn incense to the LORD, but for the priests the sons of Aaron, who are consecrated to burn incense. Go out of the sanctuary; for you have done wrong, and it will bring you no honor from the LORD God." ¹⁹Then Uzzi'ah was angry. Now he had a censer in his hand to burn incense, and when he became angry with the priests leprosy broke out on his forehead, in the presence of the priests in the house of the LORD, by the altar of incense. ²⁰And Azari'ah the chief priest, and all the priests, looked at him, and behold, he was leprous in his forehead! And they thrust him out quickly, and he himself hastened to go out, because the LORD had struck him down. ²¹And King Uzzi'ah was a leper to the day of his death, and being a leper dwelt in a separate house, for he was excluded from the house of the LORD. And Jo'tham his son was over the king's household, governing the people of the land.

22 Now the rest of the acts of Uzzi'ah, from first to last, Isai'ah the prophet the son of A'moz wrote. ²³And Uzzi'ah slept with his fathers, and they buried him with his fathers in the burial field which belonged to the kings, for they said, "He is a leper." And Jo'tham his son reigned in his stead.

Jotham's Reign over Judah

27 Jo'tham was twenty-five years old when he began to reign, and he reigned sixteen years in Jerusalem. His mother's name was Jeru'shah the daughter of Za'dok. ²And he did what was right in the eyes of the LORD according to all that his father Uzzi'ah had done—only he did not invade the temple of the LORD. But the people still followed corrupt practices. ³He built the upper gate of the house of the LORD, and did much building on the wall of O'phel. ⁴Moreover he built cities in the hill country of Judah, and forts and towers on the wooded hills. ⁵He fought with the king of the Am'monites and prevailed against them. And the Ammonites gave him that year a hundred talents of silver, and ten thousand cors of wheat and ten thousand of barley. The Ammonites paid him the same amount in the second and the third years. ⁶So Jo'tham became mighty, because he ordered his ways before the LORD his God. ⁷Now the rest of the acts of Jo'tham, and all his wars, and his ways, behold,

26:1-4: 2 Kings 14:21, 22; 15:2, 3.
26:20-23: 2 Kings 15:5-7.
27:1-3: 2 Kings 15:33-35.

they are written in the Book of the Kings of Israel and Judah. [8]He was twenty-five years old when he began to reign, and he reigned sixteen years in Jerusalem. [9]And Jo'tham slept with his fathers, and they buried him in the city of David; and A'haz his son reigned in his stead.

Ahaz's Reign over Judah

28 A'haz was twenty years old when he began to reign, and he reigned sixteen years in Jerusalem. And he did not do what was right in the eyes of the LORD, like his father David, [2]but walked in the ways of the kings of Israel. He even made molten images for the Ba'als; [3]and he burned incense in the valley of the son of Hinnom, and burned his sons as an offering, according to the abominable practices of the nations whom the LORD drove out before the sons of Israel. [4]And he sacrificed and burned incense on the high places, and on the hills, and under every green tree.

Syria and Israel Defeat Judah

5 Therefore the LORD his God gave him into the hand of the king of Syria, who defeated him and took captive a great number of his people and brought them to Damascus. He was also given into the hand of the king of Israel, who defeated him with great slaughter. [6]For Pe'kah the son of Remali'ah slew a hundred and twenty thousand in Judah in one day, all of them men of valor, because they had forsaken the LORD, the God of their fathers. [7]And Zich'ri, a mighty man of E'phraim, slew Ma-asei'ah the king's son and Azri'kam the commander of the palace and Elka'nah the next in authority to the king.

The Prophet Oded Intercedes

8 The men of Israel took captive two hundred thousand of their kinsfolk, women, sons, and daughters; they also took much spoil from them and brought the spoil to Samar'ia. [9]But a prophet of the LORD was there, whose name was O'ded; and he went out to meet the army that came to Samar'ia, and said to them, "Behold, because the LORD, the God of your fathers, was angry with Judah, he gave them into your hand, but you have slain them in a rage which has reached up to heaven. [10]And now you intend to subjugate the people of Judah and Jerusalem, male and female, as your slaves. Have you not sins of your own against the LORD your God? [11]Now hear me, and send back the captives from your kinsfolk whom you have taken, for the fierce wrath of the LORD is upon you." [12]Certain chiefs also of the men of E'phraim, Azari'ah the son of Joha'nan, Berechi'ah the son of Meshil'lemoth, Jehizki'ah the son of Shallum, and Ama'sa the son of Hadlai, stood up against those who were coming from the war, [13]and said to them, "You shall not bring the captives in here, for you propose to bring upon us guilt against the LORD in addition to our present

sins and guilt. For our guilt is already great, and there is fierce wrath against Israel." [14]So the armed men left the captives and the spoil before the princes and all the assembly. [15]And the men who have been mentioned by name rose and took the captives, and with the spoil they clothed all that were naked among them; they clothed them, gave them sandals, provided them with food and drink, and anointed them; and carrying all the feeble among them on donkeys, they brought them to their kinsfolk at Jericho, the city of palm trees. Then they returned to Samar'ia.

16 At that time King A'haz sent to the king [r] of Assyria for help. [17]For the E'domites had again invaded and defeated Judah, and carried away captives. [18]And the Philis'tines had made raids on the cities in the Shephe'lah and the Neg'eb of Judah, and had taken Beth-she'mesh, Ai'jalon, Gede'roth, Soco with its villages, Timnah with its villages, and Gimzo with its villages; and they settled there. [19]For the LORD brought Judah low because of A'haz king of Israel, for he had dealt wantonly in Judah and had been faithless to the LORD. [20]So Til'gath-pilne'ser king of Assyria came against him, and afflicted him instead of strengthening him. [21]For A'haz took from the house of the LORD and the house of the king and of the princes, and gave tribute to the king of Assyria; but it did not help him.

Apostasy and Death of Ahaz

22 In the time of his distress he became yet more faithless to the LORD—this same King A'haz. [23]For he sacrificed to the gods of Damascus which had defeated him, and said, "Because the gods of the kings of Syria helped them, I will sacrifice to them that they may help me." But they were the ruin of him, and of all Israel. [24]And A'haz gathered together the vessels of the house of God and cut in pieces the vessels of the house of God, and he shut up the doors of the house of the LORD; and he made himself altars in every corner of Jerusalem. [25]In every city of Judah he made high places to burn incense to other gods, provoking to anger the LORD, the God of his fathers. [26]Now the rest of his acts and all his ways, from first to last, behold, they are written in the Book of the Kings of Judah and Israel. [27]And A'haz slept with his fathers, and they buried him in the city, in Jerusalem, for they did not bring him into the tombs of the kings of Israel. And Hezeki'ah his son reigned in his stead.

Hezekiah's Reign over Judah

29 Hezeki'ah began to reign when he was twenty-five years old, and he reigned

r Gk Syr Vg Compare 2 Kings 16:7: Heb *kings*.
27:9: 2 Kings 15:38.
28:1-4: 2 Kings 16:2-4.
28:27: 2 Kings 16:20.
29:1, 2: 2 Kings 18:1-3.

twenty-nine years in Jerusalem. His mother's name was Abi'jah the daughter of Zechari'ah. ²And he did what was right in the eyes of the LORD, according to all that David his father had done.

The Temple Is Cleansed

3 In the first year of his reign, in the first month, he opened the doors of the house of the LORD, and repaired them. ⁴He brought in the priests and the Levites, and assembled them in the square on the east, ⁵and said to them, "Hear me, Levites! Now sanctify yourselves, and sanctify the house of the LORD, the God of your fathers, and carry out the filth from the holy place. ⁶For our fathers have been unfaithful and have done what was evil in the sight of the LORD our God; they have forsaken him, and have turned away their faces from the habitation of the LORD, and turned their backs. ⁷They also shut the doors of the vestibule and put out the lamps, and have not burned incense or offered burnt offerings in the holy place to the God of Israel. ⁸Therefore the wrath of the LORD came on Judah and Jerusalem, and he has made them an object of horror, of astonishment, and of hissing, as you see with your own eyes. ⁹For behold, our fathers have fallen by the sword and our sons and our daughters and our wives are in captivity for this. ¹⁰Now it is in my heart to make a covenant with the LORD, the God of Israel, that his fierce anger may turn away from us. ¹¹My sons, do not now be negligent, for the LORD has chosen you to stand in his presence, to minister to him, and to be his ministers and burn incense to him."

12 Then the Levites arose, Mahath the son of Ama'sai, and Joel the son of Azari'ah, of the sons of the Ko'hathites; and of the sons of Merar'i, Kish the son of Abdi, and Azariah the son of Jehal'lelel; and of the Ger'shonites, Jo'ah the son of Zimmah, and Eden the son of Joah; ¹³and of the sons of Eliza'phan, Shimri and Jeu'el; and of the sons of A'saph, Zechari'ah and Mattani'ah; ¹⁴and of the sons of He'man, Jehu'el and Shim'e-i; and of the sons of Jedu'thun, Shemai'ah and Uz'ziel. ¹⁵They gathered their brethren, and sanctified themselves, and went in as the king had commanded, by the words of the LORD, to cleanse the house of the LORD. ¹⁶The priests went into the inner part of the house of the LORD to cleanse it, and they brought out all the uncleanness that they found in the temple of the LORD into the court of the house of the LORD; and the Levites took it and carried it out to the brook Kidron. ¹⁷They began to sanctify on the first day of the first month, and on the eighth day of the month they came to the vestibule of the LORD; then for eight days they sanctified the house of the LORD, and on the sixteenth day of the first month they finished. ¹⁸Then they went in to Hezeki'ah the king and said, "We have cleansed all the house of the LORD, the altar of burnt offering and all its utensils, and the table for the showbread and all its utensils. ¹⁹All the utensils which King A'haz discarded in his reign when he was faithless, we have made ready and sanctified; and behold, they are before the altar of the LORD."

Hezekiah Restores Temple Worship

20 Then Hezeki'ah the king rose early and gathered the officials of the city, and went up to the house of the LORD. ²¹And they brought seven bulls, seven rams, seven lambs, and seven he-goats for a sin offering for the kingdom and for the sanctuary and for Judah. And he commanded the priests the sons of Aaron to offer them on the altar of the LORD. ²²So they killed the bulls, and the priests received the blood and threw it against the altar; and they killed the rams and their blood was thrown against the altar; and they killed the lambs and their blood was thrown against the altar. ²³Then the he-goats for the sin offering were brought to the king and the assembly, and they laid their hands upon them, ²⁴and the priests killed them and made a sin offering with their blood on the altar, to make atonement for all Israel. For the king commanded that the burnt offering and the sin offering should be made for all Israel.

25 And he stationed the Levites in the house of the LORD with cymbals, harps, and lyres, according to the commandment of David and of Gad the king's seer and of Nathan the prophet; for the commandment was from the LORD through his prophets. ²⁶The Levites stood with the instruments of David, and the priests with the trumpets. ²⁷Then Hezeki'ah commanded that the burnt offering be offered on the altar. And when the burnt offering began, the song to the LORD began also, and the trumpets, accompanied by the instruments of David king of Israel. ²⁸The whole assembly worshiped, and the singers sang, and the trumpeters sounded; all this continued until the burnt offering was finished. ²⁹When the offering was finished, the king and all who were present with him bowed themselves and worshiped. ³⁰And Hezeki'ah the king and the princes commanded the Levites to sing praises to the LORD with the words of David and of A'saph the seer. And they sang praises with gladness, and they bowed down and worshiped.

31 Then Hezeki'ah said, "You have now consecrated yourselves to the LORD; come near, bring sacrifices and thank offerings to the house of the LORD." And the assembly brought sacrifices and thank offerings; and all who were of a willing heart brought burnt offerings. ³²The number of the burnt offerings which the assembly brought was seventy bulls, a hundred rams, and two hundred lambs; all these were for a burnt offering to the LORD. ³³And the consecrated offerings were six hundred bulls and three thousand sheep.

34But the priests were too few and could not flay all the burnt offerings, so until other priests had sanctified themselves their brethren the Levites helped them, until the work was finished—for the Levites were more upright in heart than the priests in sanctifying themselves. 35Besides the great number of burnt offerings there was the fat of the peace offerings, and there were the libations for the burnt offerings. Thus the service of the house of the Lord was restored. 36And Hezeki′ah and all the people rejoiced because of what God had done for the people; for the thing came about suddenly.

Keeping the Feast of the Passover

30 Hezeki′ah sent to all Israel and Judah, and wrote letters also to E′phraim and Manas′seh, that they should come to the house of the Lord at Jerusalem, to keep the Passover * to the Lord the God of Israel. 2For the king and his princes and all the assembly in Jerusalem had taken counsel to keep the Passover in the second month—3for they could not keep it in its time because the priests had not sanctified themselves in sufficient number, nor had the people assembled in Jerusalem—4and the plan seemed right to the king and all the assembly. 5So they decreed to make a proclamation throughout all Israel, from Be′er-she′ba to Dan, that the people should come and keep the Passover to the Lord the God of Israel, at Jerusalem; for they had not kept it in great numbers as prescribed. 6So couriers went throughout all Israel and Judah with letters from the king and his princes, as the king had commanded, saying, "O people of Israel, return to the Lord, the God of Abraham, Isaac, and Israel, that he may turn again to the remnant of you who have escaped from the hand of the kings of Assyria. 7Do not be like your fathers and your brethren, who were faithless to the Lord God of their fathers, so that he made them a desolation, as you see. 8Do not now be stiff-necked as your fathers were, but yield yourselves to the Lord, and come to his sanctuary, which he has sanctified for ever, and serve the Lord your God, that his fierce anger may turn away from you. 9For if you return to the Lord, your brethren and your children will find compassion with their captors, and return to this land. For the Lord your God is gracious and merciful, and will not turn away his face from you, if you return to him."

10 So the couriers went from city to city through the country of E′phraim and Manas′seh, and as far as Zeb′ulun; but they laughed them to scorn, and mocked them. 11Only a few men of Asher, of Manas′seh, and of Zeb′ulun humbled themselves and came to Jerusalem. 12The hand of God was also upon Judah to give them one heart to do what the king and the princes commanded by the word of the Lord.

13 And many people came together in Jerusalem to keep the feast of unleavened bread in the second month, a very great assembly. 14They set to work and removed the altars that were in Jerusalem, and all the altars for burning incense they took away and threw into the Kidron valley. 15And they killed the Passover lamb on the fourteenth day of the second month. And the priests and the Levites were put to shame, so that they sanctified themselves, and brought burnt offerings into the house of the Lord. 16They took their accustomed posts according to the law of Moses the man of God; the priests sprinkled the blood which they received from the hand of the Levites. 17For there were many in the assembly who had not sanctified themselves; therefore the Levites had to kill the Passover lamb for every one who was not clean, to make it holy to the Lord. 18For a multitude of the people, many of them from E′phraim, Manas′seh, Is′sachar, and Zeb′ulun, had not cleansed themselves, yet they ate the Passover otherwise than as prescribed. For Hezeki′ah had prayed for them, saying, "The good Lord pardon every one 19who sets his heart to seek God, the Lord the God of his fathers, even though not according to the sanctuary's rules of cleanness." 20And the Lord heard Hezeki′ah, and healed the people. 21And the sons of Israel that were present at Jerusalem kept the feast of unleavened bread seven days with great gladness; and the Levites and the priests praised the Lord day by day, singing with all their might ᵃ to the Lord. 22And Hezeki′ah spoke encouragingly to all the Levites who showed good skill in the service of the Lord. So the people ate the food of the festival for seven days, sacrificing peace offerings and giving thanks to the Lord the God of their fathers.

23 Then the whole assembly agreed together to keep the feast for another seven days; so they kept it for another seven days with gladness. 24For Hezeki′ah king of Judah gave the assembly a thousand bulls and seven thousand sheep for offerings, and the princes gave the assembly a thousand bulls and ten thousand sheep. And the priests sanctified themselves in great numbers. 25The whole assembly of Judah, and the priests and the Levites, and the whole assembly that came out of Israel, and the sojourners who came out of the land of Israel, and the sojourners who dwelt in Judah, rejoiced. 26So there was great joy in Jerusalem, for since the time of Solomon the son of David king of Israel there had been nothing like this in Jerusalem. 27Then the priests and the Levites arose and blessed the people, and their

---

ᵃ Compare 1 Chron 13:8: Heb *with instruments of might.*
* 30:1, *Passover:* This Passover is not mentioned in Kings. The celebration inspired the people to go out and destroy the illegal high places and altars.

voice was heard, and their prayer came to his holy habitation in heaven.

Pagan Shrines Destroyed

31 Now when all this was finished, all Israel who were present went out to the cities of Judah and broke in pieces the pillars and hewed down the Ashe'rim and broke down the high places and the altars throughout all Judah and Benjamin, and in E'phraim and Manas'seh, until they had destroyed them all. Then all the sons of Israel returned to their cities, every man to his possession.

2 And Hezeki'ah appointed the divisions of the priests and of the Levites, division by division, each according to his service, the priests and the Levites, for burnt offerings and peace offerings, to minister in the gates of the camp of the LORD and to give thanks and praise. ³The contribution of the king from his own possessions was for the burnt offerings: the burnt offerings of morning and evening, and the burnt offerings for the sabbaths, the new moons, and the appointed feasts, as it is written in the law of the LORD. ⁴And he commanded the people who lived in Jerusalem to give the portion due to the priests and the Levites, that they might give themselves to the law of the LORD. ⁵As soon as the command was spread abroad, the sons of Israel gave in abundance the first fruits of grain, wine, oil, honey, and of all the produce of the field; and they brought in abundantly the tithe of everything. ⁶And the sons of Israel and Judah who lived in the cities of Judah also brought in the tithe of cattle and sheep, and the dedicated things ᵗ which had been consecrated to the LORD their God, and laid them in heaps. ⁷In the third month they began to pile up the heaps, and finished them in the seventh month. ⁸When Hezeki'ah and the princes came and saw the heaps, they blessed the LORD and his people Israel. ⁹And Hezeki'ah questioned the priests and the Levites about the heaps. ¹⁰Azari'ah the chief priest, who was of the house of Za'dok, answered him, "Since they began to bring the contributions into the house of the LORD we have eaten and had enough and have plenty left; for the LORD has blessed his people, so that we have this great store left."

Reorganization of the Priests and Levites

11 Then Hezeki'ah commanded them to prepare chambers in the house of the LORD; and they prepared them. ¹²And they faithfully brought in the contributions, the tithes and the dedicated things. The chief officer in charge of them was Conani'ah the Levite, with Shim'e-i his brother as second; ¹³while Jehi'el, Azazi'ah, Na'hath, As'ahel, Jer'imoth, Joz'abad, Eli'el, Ismachi'ah, Mahath, and Bena'iah were overseers assisting Conani'ah and Shim'e-i his brother, by the appointment of Hezeki'ah the king and Azari'ah the chief officer

of the house of God. ¹⁴And Ko're the son of Imnah the Levite, keeper of the east gate, was over the freewill offerings to God, to apportion the contribution reserved for the LORD and the most holy offerings. ¹⁵Eden, Mini'amin, Jesh'ua, Shemai'ah, Amari'ah, and Shecani'ah were faithfully assisting him in the cities of the priests, to distribute the portions to their brethren, old and young alike, by divisions, ¹⁶except those enrolled by genealogy, males from three years old and upwards, all who entered the house of the LORD as the duty of each day required, for their service according to their offices, by their divisions. ¹⁷The enrollment of the priests was according to their fathers' houses; that of the Levites from twenty years old and upwards was according to their offices, by their divisions. ¹⁸The priests were enrolled with all their little children, their wives, their sons, and their daughters, the whole multitude; for they were faithful in keeping themselves holy. ¹⁹And for the sons of Aaron, the priests, who were in the fields of common land belonging to their cities, there were men in the several cities who were designated by name to distribute portions to every male among the priests and to every one among the Levites who was enrolled.

20 Thus Hezeki'ah did throughout all Judah; and he did what was good and right and faithful before the LORD his God. ²¹And every work that he undertook in the service of the house of God and in accordance with the law and the commandments, seeking his God, he did with all his heart, and prospered.

Invasion of Sennacherib, King of Assyria

32 After these things and these acts of faithfulness Sennach'erib king of Assyria came and invaded Judah and encamped against the fortified cities, thinking to win them for himself. ²And when Hezeki'ah saw that Sennach'erib had come and intended to fight against Jerusalem, ³he planned with his officers and his mighty men to stop the water of the springs that were outside the city; and they helped him. ⁴A great many people were gathered, and they stopped all the springs and the brook that flowed through the land, saying, "Why should the kings of Assyria come and find much water?" ⁵He set to work resolutely and built up all the wall that was broken down, and raised towers upon it, ᵘ and outside it he built another wall; and he strengthened the Millo in the city of David. He also made weapons and shields in abundance. ⁶And he set combat commanders over the people, and gathered them together to him in the square at the gate of the city and spoke encouragingly to them, saying, ⁷"Be strong and of good courage. Do not be afraid

---

ᵗ Heb *the tithe of the dedicated things.*
ᵘ Vg: Heb *and raised upon the towers.*
32:1: 2 Kings 18:13.

or dismayed before the king of Assyria and all the horde that is with him; for there is one greater with us than with him. [8]With him is an arm of flesh; but with us is the LORD our God, to help us and to fight our battles." And the people took confidence from the words of Hezeki'ah king of Judah.

9 After this Sennach'erib king of Assyria, who was besieging La'chish with all his forces, sent his servants to Jerusalem to Hezeki'ah king of Judah and to all the people of Judah that were in Jerusalem, saying, [10]"Thus says Sennach'erib king of Assyria, 'On what are you relying, that you stand siege in Jerusalem? [11]Is not Hezeki'ah misleading you, that he may give you over to die by famine and by thirst, when he tells you, "The LORD our God will deliver us from the hand of the king of Assyria"? [12]Has not this same Hezeki'ah taken away his high places and his altars and commanded Judah and Jerusalem, "Before one altar you shall worship, and upon it you shall burn your sacrifices"? [13]Do you not know what I and my fathers have done to all the peoples of other lands? Were the gods of the nations of those lands at all able to deliver their lands out of my hand? [14]Who among all the gods of those nations which my fathers utterly destroyed was able to deliver his people from my hand, that your God should be able to deliver you from my hand? [15]Now therefore do not let Hezeki'ah deceive you or mislead you in this fashion, and do not believe him, for no god of any nation or kingdom has been able to deliver his people from my hand or from the hand of my fathers. How much less will your God deliver you out of my hand!'"

16 And his servants said still more against the Lord GOD and against his servant Hezeki'ah. [17]And he wrote letters to cast contempt on the LORD the God of Israel and to speak against him, saying, "Like the gods of the nations of the lands who have not delivered their people from my hands, so the God of Hezeki'ah will not deliver his people from my hand." [18]And they shouted it with a loud voice in the language of Judah to the people of Jerusalem who were upon the wall, to frighten and terrify them, in order that they might take the city. [19]And they spoke of the God of Jerusalem as they spoke of the gods of the peoples of the earth, which are the work of men's hands.

Sennacherib's Defeat and Death

20 Then Hezeki'ah the king and Isai'ah the prophet, the son of A'moz, prayed because of this and cried to heaven. [21]And the LORD sent an angel, who cut off all the mighty warriors and commanders and officers in the camp of the king of Assyria. So he returned with shame of face to his own land. And when he came into the house of his god, some of his own sons struck him down there with the sword. [22]So the LORD saved Hezeki'ah and the inhabitants of Jerusalem from the hand of Sennach'erib king of Assyria and from the hand of all his enemies; and he gave them rest on every side. [23]And many brought gifts to the LORD to Jerusalem and precious things to Hezeki'ah king of Judah, so that he was exalted in the sight of all nations from that time onward.

Hezekiah's Sickness

24 In those days Hezeki'ah became sick and was at the point of death, and he prayed to the LORD; and he answered him and gave him a sign. [25]But Hezeki'ah did not make return according to the benefit done to him, for his heart was proud. Therefore wrath came upon him and Judah and Jerusalem. [26]But Hezeki'ah humbled himself for the pride of his heart, both he and the inhabitants of Jerusalem, so that the wrath of the LORD did not come upon them in the days of Hezekiah.

Hezekiah's Prosperity and Good Deeds

27 And Hezeki'ah had very great riches and honor; and he made for himself treasuries for silver, for gold, for precious stones, for spices, for shields, and for all kinds of costly vessels; [28]storehouses also for the yield of grain, wine, and oil; and stalls for all kinds of cattle, and sheepfolds. [29]He likewise provided cities for himself, and flocks and herds in abundance; for God had given him very great possessions. [30]This same Hezeki'ah closed the upper outlet of the waters of Gi'hon and directed them down to the west side of the city of David. And Hezekiah prospered in all his works. [31]And so in the matter of the envoys of the princes of Babylon, who had been sent to him to inquire about the sign that had been done in the land, God left him to himself, in order to try him and to know all that was in his heart.

32 Now the rest of the acts of Hezeki'ah, and his good deeds, behold, they are written in the vision of Isaiah the prophet the son of A'moz, in the Book of the Kings of Judah and Israel. [33]And Hezeki'ah slept with his fathers, and they buried him in the ascent of the tombs of the sons of David; and all Judah and the inhabitants of Jerusalem did him honor at his death. And Manas'seh his son reigned in his stead.

Manasseh's Evil Reign over Judah

33 Manas'seh was twelve years old when he began to reign, and he reigned fifty-five years in Jerusalem. [2]He did what was evil in the sight of the LORD, according to the abominable practices of the nations whom the LORD drove out before the sons of Israel. [3]For he rebuilt the high places which his father Hezeki'ah had broken down, and erected altars to the Ba'als, and made Ashe'rahs, and worshiped all the host of heaven, and served them. [4]And he built altars in the house

---

32:9-21: 2 Kings 18:17—19:37.
32:24-33: 2 Kings 20:1-21.
33:1-9: 2 Kings 21:1-9.

of the LORD, of which the LORD had said, "In Jerusalem shall my name be for ever." [5]And he built altars for all the host of heaven in the two courts of the house of the LORD. [6]And he burned his sons as an offering in the valley of the son of Hinnom, and practiced soothsaying and augury and sorcery, and dealt with mediums and with wizards. He did much evil in the sight of the LORD, provoking him to anger. [7]And the image of the idol which he had made he set in the house of God, of which God said to David and to Solomon his son, "In this house, and in Jerusalem, which I have chosen out of all the tribes of Israel, I will put my name for ever; [8]and I will no more remove the foot of Israel from the land which I appointed for your fathers, if only they will be careful to do all that I have commanded them, all the law, the statutes, and the ordinances given through Moses." [9]Manas'seh seduced Judah and the inhabitants of Jerusalem, so that they did more evil than the nations whom the LORD destroyed before the sons of Israel.

Manasseh Restored after Repentance

10 The LORD spoke to Manas'seh and to his people, but they gave no heed. [11]Therefore the LORD brought upon them the commanders of the army of the king of Assyria, who took Manas'seh with hooks and bound him with fetters of bronze and brought him to Babylon. [*] [12]And when he was in distress he entreated the favor of the LORD his God and humbled himself greatly before the God of his fathers. [13]He prayed to him, and God received his entreaty and heard his supplication and brought him again to Jerusalem into his kingdom. Then Manas'seh knew that the LORD was God.

14 Afterwards he built an outer wall for the city of David west of Gi'hon, in the valley, and for the entrance into the Fish Gate, and carried it round O'phel, and raised it to a very great height; he also put commanders of the army in all the fortified cities in Judah. [15]And he took away the foreign gods and the idol from the house of the LORD, and all the altars that he had built on the mountain of the house of the LORD and in Jerusalem, and he threw them outside of the city. [16]He also restored the altar of the LORD and offered upon it sacrifices of peace offerings and of thanksgiving; and he commanded Judah to serve the LORD the God of Israel. [17]Nevertheless the people still sacrificed at the high places, but only to the LORD their God.

Death of Manasseh

18 Now the rest of the acts of Manas'seh, and his prayer[†] to his God, and the words of the seers who spoke to him in the name of the LORD the God of Israel, behold, they are in the Chronicles of the Kings of Israel. [19]And his prayer, and how God received his entreaty, and all his sin and his faithlessness, and the sites on which he built high places and set up the Ashe'rim and the im-

ages, before he humbled himself, behold, they are written in the Chronicles of the Seers. [▼] [20]So Manas'seh slept with his fathers, and they buried him in his house; and A'mon his son reigned in his stead.

Amon's Reign and Death

21 A'mon was twenty-two years old when he began to reign, and he reigned two years in Jerusalem. [22]He did what was evil in the sight of the LORD, as Manas'seh his father had done. A'mon sacrificed to all the images that Manasseh his father had made, and served them. [23]And he did not humble himself before the LORD, as Manas'seh his father had humbled himself, but this A'mon incurred guilt more and more. [24]And his servants conspired against him and killed him in his house. [25]But the people of the land slew all those who had conspired against King A'mon; and the people of the land made Josi'ah his son king in his stead.

Josiah's Reign over Judah

34 Josi'ah was eight years old when he began to reign, and he reigned thirty-one years in Jerusalem. [2]He did what was right in the eyes of the LORD, and walked in the ways of David his father; and he did not turn aside to the right or to the left. [3]For in the eighth year of his reign, while he was yet a boy, he began to seek the God of David his father; and in the twelfth year he began to purge Judah and Jerusalem of the high places, the Ashe'rim, and the graven and the molten images. [4]And they broke down the altars of the Ba'als in his presence; and he hewed down the incense altars which stood above them; and he broke in pieces the Ashe'rim and the graven and the molten images, and he made dust of them and strewed it over the graves of those who had sacrificed to them. [5]He also burned the bones of the priests on their altars, and purged Judah and Jerusalem. [6]And in the cities of Manas'seh, E'phraim, and Simeon, and as far as Naph'tali, in their ruins [w] round about, [7]he broke down the altars, and beat the Ashe'rim and the images into powder, and hewed down all the incense altars throughout all the land of Israel. Then he returned to Jerusalem.

The Book of the Law Is Found

8 Now in the eighteenth year of his reign, when he had purged the land and the house, he sent

---

[▼] One Ms: Gk: Heb *of Hozai.*
[w] Heb uncertain.
33:20: 2 Kings 21:18.
33:21–25: 2 Kings 21:19–24.
34:1, 2: 2 Kings 22:1, 2.
34:3–7: 2 Kings 23:4–20.
34:8–12: 2 Kings 22:3–7.
[*] 33:11: There is no record of this captivity of Manasseh in Babylon or of his subsequent repentance, either in 2 Kings or in the Assyrian records, though he is known from the latter to have been a vassal of Assyria.
[†] 33:18, *prayer:* An apocryphal prayer of Manasseh is usually printed at the end of editions of the Vulgate Bible.

Sha'phan the son of Azali'ah, and Ma-asei'ah the governor of the city, and Jo'ah the son of Jo'ahaz, the recorder, to repair the house of the LORD his God. 9They came to Hilki'ah the high priest and delivered the money that had been brought into the house of God, which the Levites, the keepers of the threshold, had collected from Manas'seh and E'phraim and from all the remnant of Israel and from all Judah and Benjamin and from the inhabitants of Jerusalem. 10They delivered it to the workmen who had the oversight of the house of the LORD; and the workmen who were working in the house of the LORD gave it for repairing and restoring the house. 11They gave it to the carpenters and the builders to buy quarried stone, and timber for binders and beams for the buildings which the kings of Judah had let go to ruin. 12And the men did the work faithfully. Over them were set Jahath and Obadi'ah the Levites, of the sons of Merar'i, and Zechari'ah and Meshul'lam, of the sons of the Ko'hathites, to have oversight. The Levites, all who were skilful with instruments of music, 13were over the burden-bearers and directed all who did work in every kind of service; and some of the Levites were scribes, and officials, and gatekeepers.

14 While they were bringing out the money that had been brought into the house of the LORD, Hilki'ah the priest found the book of the law of the LORD given through Moses. 15Then Hilki'ah said to Sha'phan the secretary, "I have found the book of the law in the house of the LORD"; and Hilkiah gave the book to Shaphan. 16Sha'phan brought the book to the king, and further reported to the king, "All that was committed to your servants they are doing. 17They have emptied out the money that was found in the house of the LORD and have delivered it into the hand of the overseers and the workmen." 18Then Sha'phan the secretary told the king, "Hilki'ah the priest has given me a book." And Shaphan read it before the king.

19 When the king heard the words of the law he tore his clothes. 20And the king commanded Hilki'ah, Ahi'kam the son of Sha'phan, Abdon the son of Micah, Shaphan the secretary, and Asai'ah the king's servant, saying, 21"Go, inquire of the LORD for me and for those who are left in Israel and in Judah, concerning the words of the book that has been found; for great is the wrath of the LORD that is poured out on us, because our fathers have not kept the word of the LORD, to do according to all that is written in this book."

The Prophetess Huldah Consulted

22 So Hilki'ah and those whom the king had sent× went to Huldah the prophetess, the wife of Shallum the son of Tokhath, son of Hasrah, keeper of the wardrobe (now she dwelt in Jerusalem in the Second Quarter) and spoke to her to that effect. 23And she said to them, "Thus says the LORD, the God of Israel: 'Tell the man who sent you to me, 24Thus says the LORD, Behold, I will bring evil upon this place and upon its inhabitants, all the curses that are written in the book which was read before the king of Judah. 25Because they have forsaken me and have burned incense to other gods, that they might provoke me to anger with all the works of their hands, therefore my wrath will be poured out upon this place and will not be quenched. 26But to the king of Judah, who sent you to inquire of the LORD, thus shall you say to him, Thus says the LORD, the God of Israel: Regarding the words which you have heard, 27because your heart was penitent and you humbled yourself before God when you heard his words against this place and its inhabitants, and you have humbled yourself before me, and have torn your clothes and wept before me, I also have heard you, says the LORD. 28Behold, I will gather you to your fathers, and you shall be gathered to your grave in peace, and your eyes shall not see all the evil which I will bring upon this place and its inhabitants.'" And they brought back word to the king.

The Covenant Renewed

29 Then the king sent and gathered together all the elders of Judah and Jerusalem. 30And the king went up to the house of the LORD, with all the men of Judah and the inhabitants of Jerusalem and the priests and the Levites, all the people both great and small; and he read in their hearing all the words of the book of the covenant which had been found in the house of the LORD. 31And the king stood in his place and made a covenant before the LORD, to walk after the LORD and to keep his commandments and his covenants and his statutes, with all his heart and all his soul, to perform the words of the covenant that were written in this book. 32Then he made all who were present in Jerusalem and in Benjamin stand to it. And the inhabitants of Jerusalem did according to the covenant of God, the God of their fathers. 33And Josi'ah took away all the abominations from all the territory that belonged to the sons of Israel, and made all who were in Israel serve the LORD their God. All his days they did not turn away from following the LORD the God of their fathers.

Celebration of the Passover

35 Josi'ah kept a Passover to the LORD in Jerusalem; and they killed the Passover lamb on the fourteenth day of the first month. 2He appointed the priests to their offices and encouraged them in the service of the house of the LORD. 3And he said to the Levites who taught all Israel and who were holy to the LORD, "Put the

---

× Syr Vg: Heb lacks *had sent*.
35:1–19: 2 Kings 23:21–23.

343

holy ark in the house which Solomon the son of David, king of Israel, built; you need no longer carry it upon your shoulders. Now serve the LORD your God and his people Israel. ⁴Prepare yourselves according to your fathers' houses by your divisions, following the directions of David king of Israel and the directions of Solomon his son. ⁵And stand in the holy place according to the groupings of the fathers' houses of your brethren the lay people, and let there be for each a part of a father's house of the Levites. ʸ ⁶And kill the Passover lamb, and sanctify yourselves, and prepare for your brethren, to do according to the word of the LORD by Moses."

7 Then Josi'ah contributed to the lay people, as Passover offerings for all that were present, lambs and kids from the flock to the number of thirty thousand, and three thousand bulls; these were from the king's possessions. ⁸And his princes contributed willingly to the people, to the priests, and to the Levites. Hilki'ah, Zechari'ah, and Jehi'el, the chief officers of the house of God, gave to the priests for the Passover offerings two thousand six hundred lambs and kids and three hundred bulls. ⁹Conani'ah also, and Shemai'ah and Nethan'el his brothers, and Hashabi'ah and Je-i'el and Joz'abad, the chiefs of the Levites, gave to the Levites for the Passover offerings five thousand lambs and kids and five hundred bulls.

10 When the service had been prepared for, the priests stood in their place, and the Levites in their divisions according to the king's command. ¹¹And they killed the Passover lamb, and the priests sprinkled the blood which they received from them while the Levites flayed the victims. ¹²And they set aside the burnt offerings that they might distribute them according to the groupings of the fathers' houses of the lay people, to offer to the LORD, as it is written in the book of Moses. And so they did with the bulls. ¹³And they roasted the Passover lamb with fire according to the ordinance; and they boiled the holy offerings in pots, in caldrons, and in pans, and carried them quickly to all the lay people. ¹⁴And afterward they prepared for themselves and for the priests, because the priests the sons of Aaron were busied in offering the burnt offerings and the fat parts until night; so the Levites prepared for themselves and for the priests the sons of Aaron. ¹⁵The singers, the sons of A'saph, were in their place according to the command of David, and Asaph, and He'man, and Jedu'thun the king's seer; and the gatekeepers were at each gate; they did not need to depart from their service, for their brethren the Levites prepared for them.

16 So all the service of the LORD was prepared that day, to keep the Passover and to offer burnt offerings on the altar of the LORD, according to the command of King Josi'ah. ¹⁷And the sons of Israel who were present kept the Passover at that time, and the feast of unleavened bread seven days. ¹⁸No Passover like it had been kept in Israel since the days of Samuel the prophet; none of the kings of Israel had kept such a Passover as .was kept by Josi'ah, and the priests and the Levites, and all Judah and Israel who were present, and the inhabitants of Jerusalem. ¹⁹In the eighteenth year of the reign of Josi'ah this Passover was kept.

Defeat by Pharaoh Neco and the Death of Josiah

20 After all this, when Josi'ah had prepared the temple, Neco king of Egypt went up to fight at Car'chemish on the Euphrates and Josiah went out against him. ²¹But he sent envoys to him, saying, "What have we to do with each other, king of Judah? I am not coming against you this day, but against the house with which I am at war; and God has commanded me to make haste. Cease opposing God, who is with me, lest he destroy you." ²²Nevertheless Josi'ah would not turn away from him, but disguised himself in order to fight with him. He did not listen to the words of Neco from the mouth of God, but joined battle in the plain of Megid'do. ²³And the archers shot King Josi'ah; and the king said to his servants, "Take me away, for I am badly wounded." ²⁴So his servants took him out of the chariot and carried him in his second chariot and brought him to Jerusalem. And he died, and was buried in the tombs of his fathers. All Judah and Jerusalem mourned for Josi'ah. ²⁵Jeremi'ah also uttered a lament for Josi'ah; and all the singing men and singing women have spoken of Josiah in their laments to this day. They made these an ordinance in Israel; behold, they are written in the Laments. ²⁶Now the rest of the acts of Josi'ah, and his good deeds according to what is written in the law of the LORD, ²⁷and his acts, first and last, behold, they are written in the Book of the Kings of Israel and Judah.

Jehoahaz's Reign over Judah

36 The people of the land took Jeho'ahaz the son of Josi'ah and made him king in his father's stead in Jerusalem. ²Jeho'ahaz was twenty-three years old when he began to reign; and he reigned three months in Jerusalem. ³Then the king of Egypt deposed him in Jerusalem and laid upon the land a tribute of a hundred talents of silver and a talent of gold. ⁴And the king of Egypt made Eli'akim his brother king over Judah and Jerusalem, and changed his name to Jehoi'akim; but Neco took Jeho'ahaz his brother and carried him to Egypt.

ʸ Heb obscure.
36:1–4: 2 Kings 23:30–34.

The Reign and Captivity of Jehoiakim

5 Jehoi'akim was twenty-five years old when he began to reign, and he reigned eleven years in Jerusalem. He did what was evil in the sight of the Lord his God. [6]Against him came up Nebuchadnez'zar king of Babylon, and bound him in fetters to take him to Babylon. [7]Nebuchadnez'zar also carried part of the vessels of the house of the Lord to Babylon and put them in his palace in Babylon. [8]Now the rest of the acts of Jehoi'akim, and the abominations which he did, and what was found against him, behold, they are written in the Book of the Kings of Israel and Judah; and Jehoi'achin his son reigned in his stead.

The Reign and Captivity of Jehoiachin

9 Jehoi'achin was eight years old when he began to reign, and he reigned three months and ten days in Jerusalem. He did what was evil in the sight of the Lord. [10]In the spring of the year King Nebuchadnez'zar sent and brought him to Babylon, with the precious vessels of the house of the Lord, and made his brother Zedeki'ah king over Judah and Jerusalem.

Zedekiah's Reign over Judah

11 Zedeki'ah was twenty-one years old when he began to reign, and he reigned eleven years in Jerusalem. [12]He did what was evil in the sight of the Lord his God. He did not humble himself before Jeremi'ah the prophet, who spoke from the mouth of the Lord. [13]He also rebelled against King Nebuchadnez'zar, who had made him swear by God; he stiffened his neck and hardened his heart against turning to the Lord, the God of Israel. [14]All the leading priests and the people likewise were exceedingly unfaithful, following all the abominations of the nations; and they polluted the house of the Lord which he had hallowed in Jerusalem.

The Fall of Jerusalem

15 The Lord, the God of their fathers, sent persistently to them by his messengers, because he had compassion on his people and on his dwelling place; [16]but they kept mocking the messengers of God, despising his words, and scoffing at his prophets, till the wrath of the Lord rose against his people, till there was no remedy.

17 Therefore he brought up against them the king of the Chalde'ans, who slew their young men with the sword in the house of their sanctuary, and had no compassion on young man or virgin, old man or aged; he gave them all into his hand. [18]And all the vessels of the house of God, great and small, and the treasures of the house of the Lord, and the treasures of the king and of his princes, all these he brought to Babylon. [19]And they burned the house of God, and broke down the wall of Jerusalem, and burned all its palaces with fire, and destroyed all its precious vessels. [20]He took into exile in Babylon those who had escaped from the sword, and they became servants to him and to his sons until the establishment of the kingdom of Persia, [21]to fulfil the word of the Lord by the mouth of Jeremi'ah, until the land had enjoyed its sabbaths. All the days that it lay desolate it kept sabbath, to fulfil seventy years.

Cyrus Proclaims Liberty for the Exiles

22 Now in the first year of Cyrus king of Persia, that the word of the Lord by the mouth of Jeremi'ah might be accomplished, the Lord stirred up the spirit of Cyrus king of Persia so that he made a proclamation throughout all his kingdom and also put it in writing: [23]"Thus says Cyrus king of Persia, 'The Lord, the God of heaven, has given me all the kingdoms of the earth, and he has charged me to build him a house at Jerusalem, which is in Judah. Whoever is among you of all his people, may the Lord his God be with him. Let him go up.'"

36:5-8: 2 Kings 23:36—24:6.
36:9-10: 2 Kings 24:8-17.
36:11-21: 2 Kings 24:18—25:21.
36:22, 23: Ezra 1:1-3.

THE BOOK OF

EZRA

The End of the Babylonian Captivity

1 In the first year of Cyrus king of Persia, that the word of the Lord by the mouth of Jeremi'ah might be accomplished, the Lord stirred up the spirit of Cyrus king of Persia so that he made a proclamation throughout all his kingdom and also put it in writing:

2 "Thus says Cyrus king of Persia:* The Lord, the God of heaven, has given me all the kingdoms of the earth, and he has charged me to build him a house at Jerusalem, which is in Judah. ³Whoever is among you of all his people, may his God be with him, and let him go up to Jerusalem, which is in Judah, and rebuild the house of the Lord, the God of Israel—he is the God who is in Jerusalem; ⁴and let each survivor, in whatever place he sojourns, be assisted by the men of his place with silver and gold, with goods and with beasts, besides freewill offerings for the house of God which is in Jerusalem."

5 Then rose up the heads of the fathers' houses of Judah and Benjamin, and the priests and the Levites, every one whose spirit God had stirred to go up to rebuild the house of the Lord which is in Jerusalem; ⁶and all who were about them aided them with vessels of silver, with gold, with goods, with beasts, and with costly wares, besides all that was freely offered. ⁷Cyrus the king also brought out the vessels of the house of the Lord which Nebuchadnez'zar had carried away from Jerusalem and placed in the house of his gods. ⁸Cyrus king of Persia brought these out in charge of Mith'redath the treasurer, who counted them out to Shesh-baz'zar the prince of Judah. ⁹And this was the number of them: a thousand ᵃ basins of gold, a thousand basins of silver, twenty-nine censers, ¹⁰thirty bowls of gold, two thousand ᵇ four hundred and ten bowls of silver, and a thousand other vessels; ¹¹all the vessels of gold and of silver were five thousand four hundred and sixty-nine. ᶜ All these did Shesh-baz'zar bring up, when the exiles were brought up from Babylonia to Jerusalem.

List of Returned Exiles

2 Now these were the people of the province who came up out of the captivity of those exiles whom Nebuchadnez'zar the king of Babylon had carried captive to Babylonia; they returned to Jerusalem and Judah, each to his own town. ²They came with Zerub'babel, Jesh'ua,

Nehemi'ah, Serai'ah, Re-elai'ah, Mor'decai, Bilshan, Mispar, Bigvai, Re'hum, and Ba'anah.

The number of the men of the sons of Israel: ³the sons of Parosh, two thousand one hundred and seventy-two. ⁴The sons of Shephati'ah, three hundred and seventy-two. ⁵The sons of A'rah, seven hundred and seventy-five. ⁶The sons of Pa'hath-mo'ab, namely the sons of Jesh'ua and Jo'ab, two thousand eight hundred and twelve. ⁷The sons of E'lam, one thousand two hundred and fifty-four. ⁸The sons of Zattu, nine hundred and forty-five. ⁹The sons of Zaccai, seven hundred and sixty. ¹⁰The sons of Ba'ni, six hundred and forty-two. ¹¹The sons of Bebai, six hundred and twenty-three. ¹²The sons of Azgad, one thousand two hundred and twenty-two. ¹³The sons of Adoni'kam, six hundred and sixty-six. ¹⁴The sons of Bigvai, two thousand and fifty-six. ¹⁵The sons of A'din, four hundred and fifty-four. ¹⁶The sons of A'ter, namely of Hezeki'ah, ninety-eight. ¹⁷The sons of Bezai, three hundred and twenty-three. ¹⁸The sons of Jo'rah, one hundred and twelve. ¹⁹The sons of Hashum, two hundred and twenty-three. ²⁰The sons of Gibbar, ninety-five. ²¹The sons of Bethlehem, one hundred and twenty-three. ²²The men of Netoph'ah, fifty-six. ²³The men of An'athoth, one hundred and twenty-eight. ²⁴The sons of Az'maveth, forty-two. ²⁵The sons of Kir"iathar'im, Chephi'rah, and Be-er'oth, seven hundred and forty-three. ²⁶The sons of Ra'mah and Ge'ba, six hundred and twenty-one. ²⁷The men of Michmas, one hundred and twenty-two. ²⁸The men of Bethel and Ai, two hundred and twenty-three. ²⁹The sons of Nebo, fifty-two. ³⁰The sons of Magbish, one hundred and fifty-six. ³¹The sons of the other E'lam, one thousand two hundred

The Books of Ezra and Nehemiah (The First and Second Books of Esdras): These two books were originally one and were written probably by the same author as Chronicles. They deal with the century following the return from the Exile, but it is by no means a complete history that they give. The author's main purpose is to describe the religious and political reorganization after the return, and to underline the workings of God's providence. There is some uncertainty as to the chronology and order of the events described. Two main sources, the memoirs of Ezra and those of Nehemiah, are here intermingled.

ᵃ 1 Esdras 2:13: Heb *thirty*.
ᵇ 1 Esdras 2:13: Heb *of a second sort*.
ᶜ 1 Esdras 2:14: Heb *five thousand four hundred*.
1:1–3: 5:13; 6:3; 2 Chron 36:22, 23.
2:1–70: Neh 7:6–73.
* 1:2: The Persians, unlike the Babylonians, pursued a very liberal policy in matters of religion.

and fifty-four. [32]The sons of Harim, three hundred and twenty. [33]The sons of Lod, Ha'did, and Ono, seven hundred and twenty-five. [34]The sons of Jericho, three hundred and forty-five. [35]The sons of Sena'ah, three thousand six hundred and thirty.

36 The priests: the sons of Jedai'ah, of the house of Jesh'ua, nine hundred and seventy-three. [37]The sons of Immer, one thousand and fifty-two. [38]The sons of Pashhur, one thousand two hundred and forty-seven. [39]The sons of Harim, one thousand and seventeen.

40 The Levites: the sons of Jesh'ua and Kad'mi-el, of the sons of Hod"avi'ah, seventy-four. [41]The singers: the sons of A'saph, one hundred and twenty-eight. [42]The sons of the gatekeepers: the sons of Shallum, the sons of A'ter, the sons of Talmon, the sons of Akkub, the sons of Hati'ta, and the sons of Shobai, in all one hundred and thirty-nine.

43 The temple servants:[d] the sons of Ziha, the sons of Hasu'pha, the sons of Tabba'oth, [44]the sons of Keros, the sons of Si'aha, the sons of Padon, [45]the sons of Leba'nah, the sons of Hag'abah, the sons of Akkub, [46]the sons of Hagab, the sons of Shamlai, the sons of Ha'nan, [47]the sons of Giddel, the sons of Gahar, the sons of Re-ai'ah, [48]the sons of Re'zin, the sons of Neko'da, the sons of Gazzam, [49]the sons of Uzza, the sons of Pase'ah, the sons of Besai, [50]the sons of Asnah, the sons of Me-u'nim, the sons of Nephi'sim, [51]the sons of Bakbuk, the sons of Haku'pha, the sons of Harhur, [52]the sons of Bazluth, the sons of Mehi'da, the sons of Harsha, [53]the sons of Barkos, the sons of Sis'era, the sons of Te'mah, [54]the sons of Nezi'ah, and the sons of Hati'pha.

55 The sons of Solomon's servants: the sons of Sotai, the sons of Hasso'phereth, the sons of Peru'da, [56]the sons of Ja'alah, the sons of Darkon, the sons of Giddel, [57]the sons of Shephati'ah, the sons of Hattil, the sons of Po'chereth-hazzeba'im, and the sons of A'mi.

58 All the temple servants[d] and the sons of Solomon's servants were three hundred and ninety-two.

59 The following were those who came up from Tel-me'lah, Tel-har'sha, Cherub, Addan, and Immer, though they could not prove their fathers' houses or their descent, whether they belonged to Israel: [60]the sons of Delai'ah, the sons of Tobi'ah, and the sons of Neko'da, six hundred and fifty-two. [61]Also, of the sons of the priests: the sons of Habai'ah, the sons of Hakkoz, and the sons of Barzil'lai (who had taken a wife from the daughters of Barzillai the Gileadite, and was called by their name). [62]These sought their registration among those enrolled in the genealogies, but they were not found there, and so they were excluded from the priesthood as unclean; [63]the governor

told them that they were not to partake of the most holy food, until there should be a priest to consult U'rim and Thummim.

64 The whole assembly together was forty-two thousand three hundred and sixty, [65]besides their menservants and maidservants, of whom there were seven thousand three hundred and thirty-seven; and they had two hundred male and female singers. [66]Their horses were seven hundred and thirty-six, their mules were two hundred and forty-five, [67]their camels were four hundred and thirty-five, and their donkeys were six thousand seven hundred and twenty.

68 Some of the heads of families, when they came to the house of the LORD which is in Jerusalem, made freewill offerings for the house of God, to erect it on its site; [69]according to their ability they gave to the treasury of the work sixty-one thousand darics of gold, five thousand minas of silver, and one hundred priests' garments.

70 The priests, the Levites, and some of the people lived in Jerusalem and its vicinity;[e] and the singers, the gatekeepers, and the temple servants lived in their towns, and all Israel in their towns.

Worship Restored at Jerusalem

3 When the seventh month came, and the sons of Israel were in the towns, the people gathered as one man to Jerusalem. [2]Then arose Jesh'ua the son of Jo'zadak, with his fellow priests, and Zerub'babel the son of She-al'ti-el with his kinsmen, and they built the altar of the God of Israel, to offer burnt offerings upon it, as it is written in the law of Moses the man of God. [3]They set the altar in its place, for fear was upon them because of the peoples of the lands, and they offered burnt offerings upon it to the LORD, burnt offerings morning and evening. [4]And they kept the feast of booths, as it is written, and offered the daily burnt offerings by number according to the ordinance, as each day required, [5]and after that the continual burnt offerings, the offerings at the new moon and at all the appointed feasts of the LORD, and the offerings of every one who made a freewill offering to the LORD. [6]From the first day of the seventh month they began to offer burnt offerings to the LORD. But the foundation of the temple of the LORD was not yet laid. [7]So they gave money to the masons and the carpenters, and food, drink, and oil to the Sido'nians and the Tyr'ians to bring cedar trees from Lebanon to the sea, to Joppa, according to the grant which they had from Cyrus king of Persia.

Foundation of the Temple Laid

8 Now in the second year of their coming to the house of God at Jerusalem, in the second month,

---

[d] Heb *nethinim.*

[e] 1 Esdras 5:46: Heb lacks *lived in Jerusalem and its vicinity.*

Zerub'babel the son of She-al'ti-el and Jesh'ua the son of Jo'zadak made a beginning, together with the rest of their brethren, the priests and the Levites and all who had come to Jerusalem from the captivity. They appointed the Levites, from twenty years old and upward, to have the oversight of the work of the house of the LORD. [9]And Jesh'ua with his sons and his kinsmen, and Kad'mi-el and his sons, the sons of Judah, together took the oversight of the workmen in the house of God, along with the sons of Hen'adad and the Levites, their sons and kinsmen.

10 And when the builders laid the foundation of the temple of the LORD, the priests in their vestments came forward with trumpets, and the Levites, the sons of A'saph, with cymbals, to praise the LORD, according to the directions of David king of Israel; [11]and they sang responsively, praising and giving thanks to the LORD,

"For he is good,
  for his mercy endures for ever toward Israel."
And all the people shouted with a great shout, when they praised the LORD, because the foundation of the house of the LORD was laid. [12]But many of the priests and Levites and heads of fathers' houses, old men who had seen the first house, wept with a loud voice when they saw the foundation of this house being laid, though many shouted aloud for joy; [13]so that the people could not distinguish the sound of the joyful shout from the sound of the people's weeping, for the people shouted with a great shout, and the sound was heard afar.

Resistance to Rebuilding the Temple

4 Now when the adversaries of Judah and Benjamin heard that the returned exiles were building a temple to the LORD, the God of Israel, [2]they approached Zerub'babel and the heads of fathers' houses and said to them, "Let us build with you; for we worship your God as you do, and we have been sacrificing to him ever since the days of E'sar-had'don king of Assyria who brought us here." [3]But Zerub'babel, Jesh'ua, and the rest of the heads of fathers' houses in Israel said to them, "You have nothing to do with us in building a house to our God; but we alone will build to the LORD, the God of Israel, as King Cyrus the king of Persia has commanded us."

4 Then the people of the land discouraged the people of Judah, and made them afraid to build, * [5]and hired counselors against them to frustrate their purpose, all the days of Cyrus king of Persia, even until the reign of Dari'us king of Persia.

Letters of Protest against Rebuilding

6 And in the reign of Ahas'u-e'rus, in the beginning of his reign, they wrote an accusation against the inhabitants of Judah and Jerusalem.

7 And in the days of Ar-ta-xerx'es, Bishlam and Mith'redath and Ta'be-el and the rest of their associates wrote to Ar-ta-xerxes king of Persia; the letter was written in Arama'ic and translated. [f] [8]Re'hum the commander and Shimshai the scribe wrote a letter against Jerusalem to Ar-ta-xerx'es the king as follows—[9]then wrote Re'hum the commander, Shimshai the scribe, and the rest of their associates, the judges, the governors, the officials, the Persians, the men of E'rech, the Babylonians, the men of Susa, that is, the E'lamites, [10]and the rest of the nations whom the great and noble Osnap'par deported and settled in the cities of Samar'ia and in the rest of the province Beyond the River, and now [11]this is a copy of the letter that they sent—"To Ar-ta-xerx'es the king: Your servants, the men of the province Beyond the River, send greeting. And now [12]be it known to the king that the Jews who came up from you to us have gone to Jerusalem. They are rebuilding that rebellious and wicked city; they are finishing the walls and repairing the foundations. [13]Now be it known to the king that, if this city is rebuilt and the walls finished, they will not pay tribute, custom, or toll, and the royal revenue will be impaired. [14]Now because we eat the salt of the palace and it is not fitting for us to witness the king's dishonor, therefore we send and inform the king, [15]in order that search may be made in the book of the records of your fathers. You will find in the book of the records and learn that this city is a rebellious city, hurtful to kings and provinces, and that sedition was stirred up in it from of old. That was why this city was laid waste. [16]We make known to the king that, if this city is rebuilt and its walls finished, you will then have no possession in the province Beyond the River."

Rebuilding of Jerusalem Forced to Halt

17 The king sent an answer: "To Re'hum the commander and Shimshai the scribe and the rest of their associates who live in Samar'ia and in the rest of the province Beyond the River, greeting. And now [18]the letter which you sent to us has been plainly read before me. [19]And I made a decree, and search has been made, and it has been found that this city from of old has risen against kings, and that rebellion and sedition have been made in it. [20]And mighty kings have been over Jerusalem, who ruled over the whole province Beyond the River, to whom tribute, custom, and toll were paid. [21]Therefore make a decree that these men be made to cease, and that this city be not rebuilt, until a decree is made by me. [22]And take care not to be slack in this matter; why should damage grow to the hurt of the king?"

---

[f] Heb adds in Aramaic, indicating that 4:8—6:18 is in Aramaic. Another interpretation is *The letter was written in the Aramaic script and set forth in the Aramaic language.*
* 4:4: Understandably, the people who had occupied the land in the absence of the exiles now resented their return and, especially, the building of the temple.

23 Then, when the copy of King Ar-ta-xerx'es' letter was read before Re'hum and Shimshai the scribe and their associates, they went in haste to the Jews at Jerusalem and by force and power made them cease. [24]Then the work on the house of God which is in Jerusalem stopped; and it ceased until the second year of the reign of Dari'us king of Persia.

Restoration of the Temple Resumed

5 * Now the prophets, Hag'gai and Zechari'ah the son of Iddo, prophesied to the Jews who were in Judah and Jerusalem, in the name of the God of Israel who was over them. [2]Then Zerub'-babel the son of She-al'ti-el and Jesh'ua the son of Jo'zadak arose and began to rebuild the house of God which is in Jerusalem; and with them were the prophets of God, helping them.

3 At the same time Tat'tenai the governor of the province Beyond the River and She'thar-boz'enai and their associates came to them and spoke to them thus, "Who gave you a decree to build this house and to finish this structure?" [4]They [g] also asked them this, "What are the names of the men who are building this building?" [5]But the eye of their God was upon the elders of the Jews, and they did not stop them till a report should reach Dari'us and then answer be returned by letter concerning it.

6 The copy of the letter which Tat'tenai the governor of the province Beyond the River and She'thar-boz'enai and his associates the governors who were in the province Beyond the River sent to Dari'us the king; [7]they sent him a report, in which was written as follows: "To Dari'us the king, all peace. [8]Be it known to the king that we went to the province of Judah, to the house of the great God. It is being built with huge stones, and timber is laid in the walls; this work goes on diligently and prospers in their hands. [9]Then we asked those elders and spoke to them thus, 'Who gave you a decree to build this house and to finish this structure?' [10]We also asked them their names, for your information, that we might write down the names of the men at their head. [11]And this was their reply to us: 'We are the servants of the God of heaven and earth, and we are rebuilding the house that was built many years ago, which a great king of Israel built and finished. [12]But because our fathers had angered the God of heaven, he gave them into the hand of Nebuchadnez'zar king of Babylon, the Chalde'an, who destroyed this house and carried away the people to Babylonia. [13]However in the first year of Cyrus king of Babylon, Cyrus the king made a decree that this house of God should be rebuilt. [14]And the gold and silver vessels of the house of God, which Nebuchadnez'zar had taken out of the temple that was in Jerusalem and brought into the temple of Babylon, these Cyrus the king took out of the temple

of Babylon, and they were delivered to one whose name was Shesh-baz'zar, whom he had made governor; [15]and he said to him, "Take these vessels, go and put them in the temple which is in Jerusalem, and let the house of God be rebuilt on its site." [16]Then this Shesh-baz'zar came and laid the foundations of the house of God which is in Jerusalem; and from that time until now it has been in building, and it is not yet finished.' [17]Therefore, if it seem good to the king, let search be made in the royal archives there in Babylon, to see whether a decree was issued by Cyrus the king for the rebuilding of this house of God in Jerusalem. And let the king send us his pleasure in this matter."

The Decree of Darius

6 Then Dari'us the king made a decree, and search was made in Babylonia, in the house of the archives where the documents were stored. [2]And in Ecbat'ana, the capital which is in the province of Med'ia, a scroll was found on which this was written: "A record. [3]In the first year of Cyrus the king, Cyrus the king issued a decree: Concerning the house of God at Jerusalem, let the house be rebuilt, the place where sacrifices are offered and burnt offerings are brought; its height shall be sixty cubits and its breadth sixty cubits, [4]with three courses of great stones and one course of timber; let the cost be paid from the royal treasury. [5]And also let the gold and silver vessels of the house of God, which Nebuchadnez'zar took out of the temple that is in Jerusalem and brought to Babylon, be restored and brought back to the temple which is in Jerusalem, each to its place; you shall put them in the house of God.

6 "Now therefore, Tat'tenai, governor of the province Beyond the River, She'thar-boz'enai, and your associates the governors who are in the province Beyond the River, keep away; [7]let the work on this house of God alone; let the governor of the Jews and the elders of the Jews rebuild this house of God on its site. [8]Moreover I make a decree regarding what you shall do for these elders of the Jews for the rebuilding of this house of God; the cost is to be paid to these men in full and without delay from the royal revenue, the tribute of the province from Beyond the River. [9]And whatever is needed—young bulls, rams, or sheep for burnt offerings to the God of heaven, wheat, salt, wine, or oil, as the priests at Jerusalem require—let that be given to them day by day without fail, [10]that they may offer pleasing sacrifices to the God of heaven, and pray for the life of the king and his sons. [11]Also I make a decree that if

---

[g] Gk Syr: Aramaic We.
5:1: Hag 1:1; Zech 1:1.
5:13: 1:1; 6:3.
6:3: 1:1; 5:13.
* 5:1: Building is resumed nearly twenty years later, and the temple is completed in four years (515 B.C.)—but it was a mere shadow of Solomon's temple; cf. 3:12.

any one alters this edict, a beam shall be pulled out of his house, and he shall be impaled upon it, and his house shall be made a dunghill. [12]May the God who has caused his name to dwell there overthrow any king or people that shall put forth a hand to alter this, or to destroy this house of God which is in Jerusalem. I Dari′us make a decree; let it be done with all diligence."

Completion and Dedication of the Temple

13 Then, according to the word sent by Dari′us the king, Tat′tenai, the governor of the province Beyond the River, She′thar-boz′enai, and their associates did with all diligence what Darius the king had ordered. [14]And the elders of the Jews built and prospered, through the prophesying of Hag′gai the prophet and Zechari′ah the son of Iddo. They finished their building by command of the God of Israel and by decree of Cyrus and Dari′us and Ar-ta-xerx′es king of Persia; [15]and this house was finished on the third day of the month of Adar′, in the sixth year of the reign of Dari′us the king.

16 And the sons of Israel, the priests and the Levites, and the rest of the returned exiles, celebrated the dedication of this house of God with joy. [17]They offered at the dedication of this house of God one hundred bulls, two hundred rams, four hundred lambs, and as a sin offering for all Israel twelve he-goats, according to the number of the tribes of Israel. [18]And they set the priests in their divisions and the Levites in their courses, for the service of God at Jerusalem, as it is written in the book of Moses.

The Passover Is Celebrated

19 On the fourteenth day of the first month the returned exiles kept the Passover. [20]For the priests and the Levites had purified themselves together; all of them were clean. So they killed the Passover lamb for all the returned exiles, for their fellow priests, and for themselves; [21]it was eaten by the sons of Israel who had returned from exile, and also by every one who had joined them and separated himself from the pollutions of the peoples of the land to worship the LORD, the God of Israel. [22]And they kept the feast of unleavened bread seven days with joy; for the LORD had made them joyful, and had turned the heart of the king of Assyria to them, so that he aided them in the work of the house of God, the God of Israel.

The Arrival and Work of Ezra

7 * Now after this, in the reign of Ar-ta-xerx′es king of Persia, Ezra the son of Serai′ah, son of Azari′ah, son of Hilki′ah, [2]son of Shallum, son of Za′dok, son of Ahi′tub, [3]son of Amari′ah, son of Azari′ah, son of Mera′ioth, [4]son of Zerahi′ah, son of Uzzi, son of Bukki, [5]son of Abishu′a, son of Phin′ehas, son of Elea′zar, son of Aaron the chief priest—[6]this Ezra went up from Babylonia. He was

a scribe skilled in the law of Moses which the LORD the God of Israel had given; and the king granted him all that he asked, for the hand of the LORD his God was upon him.

7 And there went up also to Jerusalem, in the seventh year of Ar-ta-xerx′es the king, some of the sons of Israel, and some of the priests and Levites, the singers and gatekeepers, and the temple servants. [8]And he came to Jerusalem in the fifth month, which was in the seventh year of the king; [9]for on the first day of the first month he began [h] to go up from Babylonia, and on the first day of the fifth month he came to Jerusalem, for the good hand of his God was upon him. [10]For Ezra had set his heart to study the law of the LORD, and to do it, and to teach his statutes and ordinances in Israel.

The Letter of Ar-ta-xerxes to Ezra

11 This is a copy of the letter which King Ar-ta-xerx′es gave to Ezra the priest, the scribe, learned in matters of the commandments of the LORD and his statutes for Israel: [12] "Ar-ta-xerx′es, king of kings, to Ezra the priest, the scribe of the law of the God of heaven. [x] And now [13]I make a decree that any one of the sons of Israel or their priests or Levites in my kingdom, who freely offers to go to Jerusalem, may go with you. [14]For you are sent by the king and his seven counselors to make inquiries about Judah and Jerusalem according to the law of your God, which is in your hand, [15]and also to convey the silver and gold which the king and his counselors have freely offered to the God of Israel, whose dwelling is in Jerusalem, [16]with all the silver and gold which you shall find in the whole province of Babylonia, and with the freewill offerings of the people and the priests, vowed willingly for the house of their God which is in Jerusalem. [17]With this money, then, you shall with all diligence buy bulls, rams, and lambs, with their cereal offerings and their drink offerings, and you shall offer them upon the altar of the house of your God which is in Jerusalem. [18]Whatever seems good to you and your brethren to do with the rest of the silver and gold, you may do, according to the will of your God. [19]The vessels that have been given you for the service of the house of your God, you shall deliver before the God of Jerusalem. [20]And whatever else is required for the house of your God, which you have occasion to provide, you may provide it out of the king's treasury.

21 "And I, Ar-ta-xerx′es the king, make a decree to all the treasurers in the province Beyond

---

[h] Vg See Syr: Heb *that was the foundation of the going up.*
[x] Aramaic adds a word of uncertain meaning.
* 7:1: Fifty-seven years later, i.e., about 458 B.C., according to one view, Ezra the scribe came with other exiles from Babylonia to carry out a much-needed reform. The total number in this group was some 6,000 or 8,000 persons. Many commentators place Ezra's coming in the reign of Ar-ta-xerxes II, 398 B.C., and hence after Nehemiah.

the River: Whatever Ezra the priest, the scribe of the law of the God of heaven, requires of you, be it done with all diligence, [22]up to a hundred talents of silver, a hundred cors of wheat, a hundred baths of wine, a hundred baths of oil, and salt without prescribing how much. [23]Whatever is commanded by the God of heaven, let it be done in full for the house of the God of heaven, lest his wrath be against the realm of the king and his sons. [24]We also notify you that it shall not be lawful to impose tribute, custom, or toll upon any one of the priests, the Levites, the singers, the doorkeepers, the temple servants, or other servants of this house of God.

25 "And you, Ezra, according to the wisdom of your God which is in your hand, appoint magistrates and judges who may judge all the people in the province Beyond the River, all such as know the laws of your God; and those who do not know them, you shall teach. [26]Whoever will not obey the law of your God and the law of the king, let judgment be strictly executed upon him, whether for death or for banishment or for confiscation of his goods or for imprisonment."

27 Blessed be the LORD, the God of our fathers, who put such a thing as this into the heart of the king, to beautify the house of the LORD which is in Jerusalem, [28]and who extended to me his merciful love before the king and his counselors, and before all the king's mighty officers. I took courage, for the hand of the LORD my God was upon me, and I gathered leading men from Israel to go up with me.

Heads of Families Who Returned with Ezra

8 These are the heads of their fathers' houses, and this is the genealogy of those who went up with me from Babylonia, in the reign of Ar-ta-xerx'es the king: [2]Of the sons of Phin'ehas, Gershom. Of the sons of Ith'amar, Daniel. Of the sons of David, Hattush, [3]of the sons of Shecani'ah. Of the sons of Pa'rosh, Zechari'ah, with whom were registered one hundred and fifty men. [4]Of the sons of Pa'hath-mo'ab, El'ie-ho-e'nai the son of Zera-hi'ah, and with him two hundred men. [5]Of the sons of Zattu, [1] Shecani'ah the son of Jaha'ziel, and with him three hundred men. [6]Of the sons of A'din, E'bed the son of Jonathan, and with him fifty men. [7]Of the sons of E'lam, Jeshai'ah son of Athali'ah, and with him seventy men. [8]Of the sons of Shephati'ah, Zebadi'ah the son of Michael, and with him eighty men. [9]Of the sons of Jo'ab, Obadi'ah the son of Jehi'el, and with him two hundred and eighteen men. [10]Of the sons of Ba'ni, [j] Shelo'mith the son of Josiphi'ah, and with him a hundred and sixty men. [11]Of the sons of Bebai, Zechari'ah, the son of Bebai, and with him twenty-eight men. [12]Of the sons of Azgad, Joha'nan the son of Hak'katan, and with him a hundred and ten men. [13]Of the sons of Adoni'kam,

those who came later, their names being Eliph'e-let, Jeu'el, and Shemai'ah, and with them sixty men. [14]Of the sons of Bigvai, Uthai and Zaccur, and with them seventy men.

Ministers for the Temple

15 I gathered them to the river that runs to Aha'va, and there we encamped three days. As I reviewed the people and the priests, I found there none of the sons of Levi. [16]Then I sent for Elie'zer, Ar'iel, Shemai'ah, Elna'than, Jarib, Elnathan, Nathan, Zechari'ah, and Meshul'lam, leading men, and for Joi'arib and Elnathan, who were men of insight, [17]and sent them to Iddo, the leading man at the place Casiphi'a, telling them what to say to Iddo and his brethren the temple servants[k] at the place Casiphia, namely, to send us ministers for the house of our God. [18]And by the good hand of our God upon us, they brought us a man of discretion, of the sons of Mah'li the son of Levi, son of Israel, namely, Sherebi'ah with his sons and kinsmen, eighteen; [19]also Hashabi'ah and with him Jeshai'ah of the sons of Merar'i, with his kinsmen and their sons, twenty; [20]besides two hundred and twenty of the temple servants, whom David and his officials had set apart to attend the Levites. These were all mentioned by name.

Fasting and Prayer for Protection

21 Then I proclaimed a fast there, at the river Aha'va, that we might humble ourselves before our God, to seek from him a straight way for ourselves, our children, and all our goods. [22]For I was ashamed to ask the king for a band of soldiers and horsemen to protect us against the enemy on our way; since we had told the king, "The hand of our God is for good upon all that seek him, and the power of his wrath is against all that forsake him." [23]So we fasted and besought our God for this, and he listened to our entreaty.

Gifts for the Temple

24 Then I set apart twelve of the leading priests: Sherebi'ah, Hashabi'ah, and ten of their kinsmen with them. [25]And I weighed out to them the silver and the gold and the vessels, the offering for the house of our God which the king and his counselors and his lords and all Israel there present had offered; [26]I weighed out into their hand six hundred and fifty talents of silver, and silver vessels worth a hundred talents, and a hundred talents of gold, [27]twenty bowls of gold worth a thousand darics, and two vessels of fine bright bronze as precious as gold. [28]And I said to them, "You are holy to the LORD, and the vessels are holy; and the silver and the gold are a freewill offering to the LORD, the God of your fathers. [29]Guard them and keep them until you weigh them before the chief priests and the Levites and the

---

[1] Gk 1 Esdras 8:32: Heb lacks *of Zattu.*
[j] Gk 1 Esdras 8:36: Heb lacks *Bani.*
[k] Heb *nethinim.*

heads of fathers' houses in Israel at Jerusalem, within the chambers of the house of the LORD." [30]So the priests and the Levites took over the weight of the silver and the gold and the vessels, to bring them to Jerusalem, to the house of our God.

The Return to Jerusalem

31 Then we departed from the river Aha'va on the twelfth day of the first month, to go to Jerusalem; the hand of our God was upon us, and he delivered us from the hand of the enemy and from ambushes by the way. [32]We came to Jerusalem, and there we remained three days. [33]On the fourth day, within the house of our God, the silver and the gold and the vessels were weighed into the hands of Mer'emoth the priest, son of Uri'ah, and with him was Elea'zar the son of Phin'ehas, and with them were the Levites, Joz'abad the son of Jesh'ua and No-adi'ah the son of Bin'nui. [34]The whole was counted and weighed, and the weight of everything was recorded.

35 At that time those who had come from captivity, the returned exiles, offered burnt offerings to the God of Israel, twelve bulls for all Israel, ninety-six rams, seventy-seven lambs, and as a sin offering twelve he-goats; all this was a burnt offering to the LORD. [36]They also delivered the king's commissions to the king's satraps and to the governors of the province Beyond the River; and they aided the people and the house of God.

Denunciation of Intermarriage;
Ezra's Prayer

9 *After these things had been done, the officials approached me and said, "The sons of Israel and the priests and the Levites have not separated themselves from the peoples of the lands with their abominations, from the Canaanites, the Hittites, the Per'izzites, the Jeb'usites, the Am'monites, the Moabites, the Egyptians, and the Am'orites. [2]For they have taken some of their daughters to be wives for themselves and for their sons; so that the holy race has mixed itself with the peoples of the lands. And in this faithlessness the hand of the officials and chief men has been foremost." [3]When I heard this, I tore my garments and my mantle, and pulled hair from my head and beard, and sat appalled. [4]Then all who trembled at the words of the God of Israel, because of the faithlessness of the returned exiles, gathered round me while I sat appalled until the evening sacrifice. [5]And at the evening sacrifice I rose from my fasting, with my garments and my mantle torn, and fell upon my knees and spread out my hands to the LORD my God, [6]saying:

"O my God, I am ashamed and blush to lift my face to you, my God, for our iniquities have risen higher than our heads, and our guilt has mounted up to the heavens. [7]From the days of our fathers to this day we have been in great guilt; and for

our iniquities we, our kings, and our priests have been given into the hand of the kings of the lands, to the sword, to captivity, to plundering, and to utter shame, as at this day. [8]But now for a brief moment favor has been shown by the LORD our God, to leave us a remnant, and to give us a secure hold [1] within his holy place, that our God may brighten our eyes and grant us a little reviving in our bondage. [9]For we are bondmen; yet our God has not forsaken us in our bondage, but has extended to us his mercy before the kings of Persia, to grant us some reviving to set up the house of our God, to repair its ruins, and to give us protection [m] in Judea and Jerusalem.

10 "And now, O our God, what shall we say after this? For we have forsaken your commandments, [11]which you commanded by your servants the prophets, saying, 'The land which you are entering, to take possession of it, is a land unclean with the pollutions of the peoples of the lands, with their abominations which have filled it from end to end with their uncleanness. [12]Therefore give not your daughters to their sons, neither take their daughters for your sons, and never seek their peace or prosperity, that you may be strong, and eat the good of the land, and leave it for an inheritance to your children for ever.' [13]And after all that has come upon us for our evil deeds and for our great guilt, seeing that you, our God, have punished us less than our iniquities deserved and have given us such a remnant as this, [14]shall we break your commandments again and intermarry with the peoples who practice these abominations? Would you not be angry with us till you would consume us, so that there should be no remnant, nor any to escape? [15]O LORD the God of Israel, you are just, for we are left a remnant that has escaped, as at this day. Behold, we are before you in our guilt, for none can stand before you because of this."

The People's Response

10 While Ezra prayed and made confession, weeping and casting himself down before the house of God, a very great assembly of men, women, and children, gathered to him out of Israel; for the people wept bitterly. [2]And Shecani'ah the son of Jehi'el, of the sons of E'lam, addressed Ezra: "We have broken faith with our God and have married foreign women from the peoples of the land, but even now there is hope for Israel in spite of this. [3]Therefore let us make a covenant with our God to put away all these wives and their children, according to the counsel of my lord and of those who tremble at the command-

---

[1] Heb *nail* or *tent-pin*.
[m] Heb *a wall*.
* 9–10: Mixed marriages. Experience had shown that marriage with women of other races involved serious risk of idolatry; cf. Solomon, 1 Kings 11:1–8.

ment of our God; and let it be done according to the law. [4]Arise, for it is your task, and we are with you; be strong and do it." [5]Then Ezra arose and made the leading priests and Levites and all Israel take oath that they would do as had been said. So they took the oath.

Separation from Foreign Wives and Children

6 Then Ezra withdrew from before the house of God, and went to the chamber of Je'ho-ha'nan the son of Eli'ashib, where he spent the night, [n] neither eating bread nor drinking water; for he was mourning over the faithlessness of the exiles. [7]And a proclamation was made throughout Judah and Jerusalem to all the returned exiles that they should assemble at Jerusalem, [8]and that if any one did not come within three days, by order of the officials and the elders all his property should be forfeited, and he himself banned from the congregation of the exiles.

9 Then all the men of Judah and Benjamin assembled at Jerusalem within the three days; it was the ninth month, on the twentieth day of the month. And all the people sat in the open square before the house of God, trembling because of this matter and because of the heavy rain. [10]And Ezra the priest stood up and said to them, "You have trespassed and married foreign women, and so increased the guilt of Israel. [11]Now then make confession to the LORD the God of your fathers, and do his will; separate yourselves from the peoples of the land and from the foreign wives." [12]Then all the assembly answered with a loud voice, "It is so; we must do as you have said. [13]But the people are many, and it is a time of heavy rain; we cannot stand in the open. Nor is this a work for one day or for two; for we have greatly transgressed in this matter. [14]Let our officials stand for the whole assembly; let all in our cities who have taken foreign wives come at appointed times, and with them the elders and judges of every city, till the fierce wrath of our God over this matter be averted from us." [15]Only Jonathan the son of As'ahel and Jahzei'ah the son of Tikvah opposed this, and Meshul'lum and Shab'bethai the Levite supported them.

16 Then the returned exiles did so. Ezra the priest selected men, [o] heads of fathers' houses, according to their fathers' houses, each of them designated by name. On the first day of the tenth month they sat down to examine the matter; [17]and

by the first day of the first month they had come to the end of all the men who had married foreign women.

18 Of the sons of the priests who had married foreign women were found Ma-asei'ah, Elie'zer, Ja'rib, and Gedali'ah, of the sons of Jesh'ua the son of Jo'zadak and his brethren. [19]They pledged themselves to put away their wives, and their guilt offering was a ram of the flock for their guilt. [20]Of the sons of Immer: Hana'ni and Zebadi'ah. [21]Of the sons of Harim: Ma-asei'ah, Eli'jah, Shemai'ah, Jehi'el, and Uzzi'ah. [22]Of the sons of Pashhur: El'i-o-e'nai, Ma-asei'ah, Ish'mael, Nethan'el, Joz'abad, and Ela'sah.

23 Of the Levites: Joz'abad, Shim'e-i, Kelai'ah (that is, Keli'ta), Peth'a-hi'ah, Judah, and Elie'zer. [24]Of the singers: Eli'ashib. Of the gatekeepers: Shallum, Telem, and U'ri.

25 And of Israel: of the sons of Pa'rosh: Rami'ah, Izzi'ah, Malchi'jah, Mi'jamin, Elea'zar, Hashabi'ah, [p] and Bena'iah. [26]Of the sons of E'lam: Mattani'ah, Zechari'ah, Jehi'el, Abdi, Jer'emoth, and Eli'jah. [27]Of the sons of Zattu: El'i-o-e'nai, Eli'ashib, Mattani'ah, Jer'emoth, Zabad, and Azi'za. [28]Of the sons of Bebai were Je'ho-ha'nan, Hanani'ah, Zabbai, and Athlai. [29]Of the sons of Ba'ni were Meshul'lam, Malluch, Adai'ah, Jash'ub, She'al, and Jer'emoth. [30]Of the sons of Pa'hathmo'ab: Adna, Chelal, Bena'iah, Ma-asei'ah, Mattani'ah, Bez'alel, Bin'nui, and Manas'seh. [31]Of the sons of Harim: Elie'zer, Isshi'jah, Malchi'jah, Shemai'ah, Shim'e-on, [32]Benjamin, Malluch, and Shemari'ah. [33]Of the sons of Hashum: Matte'nai, Mattat'tah, Zabad, Eliph'elet, Jer'emai, Manas'seh, and Shim'e-i. [34]Of the sons of Ba'ni: Ma-ada'i, Amram, U'el, [35]Bena'iah, Bedei'ah, Chel'uhi, [36]Vani'ah, Mer'emoth, Eli'ashib, [37]Mattani'ah, Matte'nai, Jaa'su. [38]Of the sons of Bin'nui: [q] Shim'e-i, [39]Shelemi'ah, Nathan, Adai'ah, [40]Machnad'ebai, Shashai, Sharai, [41]Az'arel, Shelemi'ah, Shemari'ah, [42]Shallum, Amari'ah, and Joseph. [43]Of the sons of Nebo: Je-i'el, Mattithi'ah, Zabad, Zebi'na, Jaddai, Joel, and Bena'iah. [44]All these had married foreign women, and they put them away with their children. [r]

---

[n] 1 Esdras 9:2: Heb where he went.
[o] 1 Esdras 9:16 Syr: Heb and there were selected Ezra, etc.
[p] 1 Esdras 9:26 Gk: Heb Malchijah.
[q] Gk: Heb Bani, Binnui.
[r] 1 Esdras 9:36: Heb obscure.

THE BOOK OF

NEHEMIAH

Nehemiah's Prayers

1 The words of Nehemi′ah the son of Hacali′ah.
Now it happened in the month of Chis′lev,
in the twentieth year, as I was in Susa the capital,
²that Hana′ni, one of my brethren, came with certain men out of Judah; and I asked them concerning the Jews that survived, who had escaped exile,
and concerning Jerusalem. ³And they said to me,
"The survivors there in the province who escaped
exile are in great trouble and shame; the wall of
Jerusalem is broken down, and its gates are destroyed by fire."

4 When I heard these words I sat down and
wept, and mourned for days; and I continued
fasting and praying before the God of heaven.
⁵And I said, "O LORD God of heaven, the great
and terrible God who keeps covenant and merciful love with those who love him and keep his
commandments; ⁶let your ear be attentive, and
your eyes open, to hear the prayer of your servant which I now pray before you day and night
for the sons of Israel your servants, confessing
the sins of the sons of Israel, which we have
sinned against you. Yes, I and my father's house
have sinned. ⁷We have acted very corruptly
against you, and have not kept the commandments, the statutes, and the ordinances which
you commanded your servant Moses. ⁸Remember
the word which you commanded your servant
Moses, saying, 'If you are unfaithful, I will scatter you among the peoples; ⁹but if you return to
me and keep my commandments and do them,
though your dispersed be under the farthest
skies, I will gather them from there and bring
them to the place which I have chosen, to make
my name dwell there.' ¹⁰They are your servants
and your people, whom you have redeemed by
your great power and by your strong hand. ¹¹O
Lord, let your ear be attentive to the prayer of
your servant, and to the prayer of your servants
who delight to fear your name; and give success
to your servant today, and grant him mercy in
the sight of this man."

Now I was cupbearer to the king.

2 In the month of Ni′san, in the twentieth year
of King Ar-ta-xerx′es, when wine was before
him, I took up the wine and gave it to the king.
Now I had not been sad in his presence. ²And the
king said to me, "Why is your face sad, seeing
you are not sick? This is nothing else but sadness

of the heart." Then I was very much afraid. ³I
said to the king, "Let the king live for ever! Why
should not my face be sad, when the city, the
place of my fathers' sepulchres, lies waste, and
its gates have been destroyed by fire?" ⁴Then the
king said to me, "For what do you make request?"
So I prayed to the God of heaven. ⁵And I said to
the king, "If it pleases the king, and if your servant has found favor in your sight, that you send
me to Judah, to the city of my fathers' sepulchres,
that I may rebuild it." ⁶And the king said to me
(the queen sitting beside him), "How long will
you be gone, and when will you return?" So it
pleased the king to send me; and I set him a time.
⁷And I said to the king, "If it pleases the king, let
letters be given me to the governors of the province Beyond the River, that they may let me pass
through until I come to Judah; ⁸and a letter to
A′saph, the keeper of the king's forest, that he
may give me timber to make beams for the gates
of the fortress of the temple, and for the wall of
the city, and for the house which I shall occupy."
And the king granted me what I asked, for the
good hand of my God was upon me.

Nehemiah Sent to Judah

9 Then I came to the governors of the province
Beyond the River, and gave them the king's letters. Now the king had sent with me officers of
the army and horsemen. ¹⁰But when Sanbal′lat
the Hor′onite and Tobi′ah the servant, the Am′-
monite, heard this, it displeased them greatly that
some one had come to seek the welfare of the
children of Israel.

Nehemiah's Inspection of the Walls

11 So I came to Jerusalem and was there three
days. ¹²Then I arose in the night, I and a few men
with me; and I told no one what my God had
put into my heart to do for Jerusalem. There was
no beast with me but the beast on which I rode.
¹³I went out by night by the Valley Gate to the
Jackal's Well and to the Dung Gate, and I inspected the walls of Jerusalem which were broken down and its gates which had been destroyed
by fire. ¹⁴Then I went on to the Fountain Gate and
to the King's Pool; but there was no place for the

Some years after the arrival of Ezra (cf. Ezra 7), Nehemiah had himself
appointed governor of Jerusalem by the Persian king and came to that
city to build up its walls (445 B.C.). As before, the project was opposed
by the surrounding peoples (cf. chapters 4 and 6), but this time the work
was not interrupted.

beast that was under me to pass. [15]Then I went up in the night by the valley and inspected the wall; and I turned back and entered by the Valley Gate, and so returned. [16]And the officials did not know where I had gone or what I was doing; and I had not yet told the Jews, the priests, the nobles, the officials, and the rest that were to do the work.

Decision to Restore the Walls

[17] Then I said to them, "You see the trouble we are in, how Jerusalem lies in ruins with its gates burned. Come, let us build the wall of Jerusalem, that we may no longer suffer disgrace." [18]And I told them of the hand of my God which had been upon me for good, and also of the words which the king had spoken to me. And they said, "Let us rise up and build." So they strengthened their hands for the good work. [19]But when Sanbal'lat the Hor'onite and Tobi'ah the servant, the Am'monite, and Geshem the Arab heard of it, they derided us and despised us and said, "What is this thing that you are doing? Are you rebelling against the king?" [20]Then I replied to them, "The God of heaven will make us prosper, and we his servants will arise and build; but you have no portion or right or memorial in Jerusalem."

Organization of the Work

3 Then Eli'ashib the high priest rose up with his brethren the priests and they built the Sheep Gate. They consecrated it and set its doors; they consecrated it as far as the Tower of the Hundred, as far as the Tower of Hanan'el. [2]And next to him the men of Jericho built. And next to them [a] Zaccur the son of Imri built.

[3] And the sons of Hassena'ah built the Fish Gate; they laid its beams and set its doors, its bolts, and its bars. [4]And next to them Mer'emoth the son of Uri'ah, son of Hakkoz repaired. And next to them Meshul'lam the son of Berechi'ah, son of Meshez'abel repaired. And next to them Za'dok the son of Ba'ana repaired. [5]And next to them the Teko'ites repaired; but their nobles did not put their necks to the work of their Lord. [b]

[6] And Joi'ada the son of Pase'ah and Meshul'lam the son of Besodei'ah repaired the Old Gate; they laid its beams and set its doors, its bolts, and its bars. [7]And next to them repaired Melati'ah the Gib'eonite and Ja'don the Meron'othite, the men of Gib'eon and of Mizpah, who were under the jurisdiction of the governor of the province Beyond the River. [8]Next to them Uzziel the son of Harhai'ah, goldsmiths, repaired. Next to him Hanani'ah, one of the perfumers, repaired; and they restored [c] Jerusalem as far as the Broad Wall. [9]Next to them Rephai'ah the son of Hur, ruler of half the district of Jerusalem, repaired. [10]Next to them Jedai'a the son of Haru'maph repaired opposite his house; and next to him Hattush the son of Hashabnei'ah repaired. [11]Malchi'jah the son of

Harim and Hasshub the son of Pa'hath-mo'ab repaired another section and the Tower of the Ovens. [12]Next to him Shallum the son of Hallo'hesh, ruler of half the district of [d] Jerusalem, repaired, he and his daughters.

13 Ha'nun and the inhabitants of Zano'ah repaired the Valley Gate; they rebuilt it and set its doors, its bolts, and its bars, and repaired a thousand cubits of the wall, as far as the Dung Gate.

14 Malchi'jah the son of Re'chab, ruler of the district of [d] Beth-hacche'rem, repaired the Dung Gate; he rebuilt it and set its doors, its bolts, and its bars.

15 And Shallum the son of Colho'zeh, ruler of the district of [d] Mizpah, repaired the Fountain Gate; he rebuilt it and covered it and set its doors, its bolts, and its bars; and he built the wall of the Pool of She'lah of the king's garden, as far as the stairs that go down from the City of David. [16]After him Nehemi'ah the son of Azbuk, ruler of half the district of [d] Beth-zur, repaired to a point opposite the sepulchres of David, to the artificial pool, and to the house of the mighty men. [17]After him the Levites repaired: Re'hum the son of Ba'ni; next to him Hashabi'ah, ruler of half the district of [d] Kei'lah, repaired for his district. [18]After him their brethren repaired: Bavvai the son of Hen'adad, ruler of half the district of [d] Kei'lah; [19]next to him E'zer the son of Jeshu'a, ruler of Mizpah, repaired another section opposite the ascent to the armory at the Angle. [20]After him Baruch the son of Zabbai repaired another section from the Angle to the door of the house of Eli'ashib the high priest. [21]After him Mer'emoth the son of Uri'ah, son of Hakkoz repaired another section from the door of the house of Eli'ashib to the end of the house of Eliashib. [22]After him the priests, the men of the Plain, repaired. [23]After them Benjamin and Hasshub repaired opposite their house. After them Azari'ah the son of Ma-asei'ah, son of Anani'ah repaired beside his own house. [24]After him Bin'nui the son of Hen'adad repaired another section, from the house of Azari'ah to the Angle [25]and to the corner. Pa'lal the son of U'zai repaired opposite the Angle and the tower projecting from the upper house of the king at the court of the guard. After him Pedai'ah the son of Pa'rosh [26]and the temple servants living [e] on O'phel repaired to a point opposite the Water Gate on the east and the projecting tower. [27]After him the Teko'ites repaired another section opposite the great projecting tower as far as the wall of O'phel.

---

[a] Heb *him.*
[b] Or *lords.*
[c] Or *abandoned.*
[d] Or *foreman of half the portion assigned to.*
[e] Cn: Heb *were living.*

28 Above the Horse Gate the priests repaired, each one opposite his own house. [29]After them Za'dok the son of Immer repaired opposite his own house. After him Shemai'ah the son of Sheca-ni'ah, the keeper of the East Gate, repaired. [30]After him Hanani'ah the son of Shelemi'ah and Ha'nun the sixth son of Za'laph repaired another section. After him Meshul'lam the son of Bere-chi'ah repaired opposite his chamber. [31]After him Malchi'jah, one of the goldsmiths, repaired as far as the house of the temple servants and of the merchants, opposite the Muster Gate, f and to the upper chamber of the corner. [32]And between the upper chamber of the corner and the Sheep Gate the goldsmiths and the merchants repaired.

Hostile Plots Frustrated

4 g Now when Sanbal'lat heard that we were building the wall, he was angry and greatly enraged, and he ridiculed the Jews. [2]And he said in the presence of his brethren and of the army of Samar'ia, "What are these feeble Jews doing? Will they restore things? Will they sacrifice? Will they finish up in a day? Will they revive the stones out of the heaps of rubbish, and burned ones at that?" [3]Tobi'ah the Am'monite was by him, and he said, "Yes, what they are building—if a fox goes up on it he will break down their stone wall!" [4]Hear, O our God, for we are despised; turn back their taunt upon their own heads, and give them up to be plundered in a land where they are captives. [5]Do not cover their guilt, and let not their sin be blotted out from your sight; for they have provoked you to anger before the builders.

6 So we built the wall; and all the wall was joined together to half its height. For the people had a mind to work.

7 h But when Sanbal'lat and Tobi'ah and the Arabs and the Am'monites and the Ash'dodites heard that the repairing of the walls of Jerusalem was going forward and that the breaches were beginning to be closed, they were very angry, [8]and they all plotted together to come and fight against Jerusalem and to cause confusion in it. [9]And we prayed to our God, and set a guard as a protection against them day and night.

10 But Judah said, "The strength of the burden-bearers is failing, and there is much rubbish; we are not able to work on the wall." [11]And our enemies said, "They will not know or see till we come into the midst of them and kill them and stop the work." [12]When the Jews who lived by them came they said to us ten times, "From all the places where they live i they will come up against us." j [13]So in the lowest parts of the space behind the wall, in open places, I stationed the people according to their families, with their swords, their spears, and their bows. [14]And I looked, and arose, and said to the nobles and to the officials and to the rest of the people, "Do not be afraid of them.

Remember the Lord, who is great and terrible, and fight for your brethren, your sons, your daughters, your wives, and your homes."

15 When our enemies heard that it was known to us and that God had frustrated their plan, we all returned to the wall, each to his work. [16]From that day on, half of my servants worked on construction, and half held the spears, shields, bows, and coats of mail; and the leaders stood behind all the house of Judah, [17]who were building on the wall. Those who carried burdens were laden in such a way that each with one hand labored on the work and with the other held his weapon. [18]And each of the builders had his sword belted at his side while he built. The man who sounded the trumpet was beside me. [19]And I said to the nobles and to the officials and to the rest of the people, "The work is great and widely spread, and we are separated on the wall, far from one another. [20]In the place where you hear the sound of the trumpet, rally to us there. Our God will fight for us."

21 So we labored at the work, and half of them held the spears from the break of dawn till the stars came out. [22]I also said to the people at that time, "Let every man and his servant pass the night within Jerusalem, that they may be a guard for us by night and may labor by day." [23]So neither I nor my brethren nor my servants nor the men of the guard who followed me, none of us took off our clothes; each kept his weapon in his hand. k

Nehemiah Deals with Oppression

5 Now there arose a great outcry of the people and of their wives against their Jewish brethren. [2]For there were those who said, "With our sons and our daughters, we are many; let us get grain, that we may eat and keep alive." [3]There were also those who said, "We are mortgaging our fields, our vineyards, and our houses to get grain because of the famine." [4]And there were those who said, "We have borrowed money for the king's tax upon our fields and our vineyards. [5]Now our flesh is as the flesh of our brethren, our children are as their children; yet we are forcing our sons and our daughters to be slaves, and some of our daughters have already been enslaved; but it is not in our power to help it, for other men have our fields and our vineyards."

6 I was very angry when I heard their outcry and these words. [7]I took counsel with myself, and I brought charges against the nobles and the officials. I said to them, "You are exacting interest,

---

f Or Hammiphkad Gate.
g Ch 3:33 in Heb.
h Ch 4:1 in Heb.
i Cn: Heb you return.
j Compare Gk Syr: Heb uncertain.
k Cn: Heb each his weapon the water.

each from his brother." And I held a great assembly against them, [8]and said to them, "We, as far as we are able, have bought back our Jewish brethren who have been sold to the nations; but you even sell your brethren that they may be sold to us!" They were silent, and could not find a word to say. [9]So I said, "The thing that you are doing is not good. Ought you not to walk in the fear of our God to prevent the taunts of the nations our enemies? [10]Moreover I and my brethren and my servants are lending them money and grain. Let us leave off this interest. [11]Return to them this very day their fields, their vineyards, their olive orchards, and their houses, and the hundredth of money, grain, wine, and oil which you have been exacting of them." [12]Then they said, "We will restore these and require nothing from them. We will do as you say." And I called the priests, and took an oath of them to do as they had promised. [13]I also shook out my garment and said, "So may God shake out every man from his house and from his labor who does not perform this promise. So may he be shaken out and emptied." And all the assembly said "Amen" and praised the LORD. And the people did as they had promised.

The Generosity of Nehemiah

14 Moreover from the time that I was appointed to be their governor in the land of Judah, from the twentieth year to the thirty-second year of Ar-ta-xerx'es the king, twelve years, neither I nor my brethren ate the food allowance of the governor. [15]The former governors who were before me laid heavy burdens upon the people, and took from them food and wine, besides forty shekels of silver. Even their servants lorded it over the people. But I did not do so, because of the fear of God. [16]I also held to the work on this wall, and acquired no land; and all my servants were gathered there for the work. [17]Moreover there were at my table a hundred and fifty men, Jews and officials, besides those who came to us from the nations which were about us. [18]Now that which was prepared for one day was one ox and six choice sheep; fowls likewise were prepared for me, and every ten days skins of wine in abundance; yet with all this I did not demand the food allowance of the governor, because the servitude was heavy upon this people. [19]Remember for my good, O my God, all that I have done for this people.

Enemy Plots Avoided

6 Now when it was reported to Sanbal'lat and Tobi'ah and to Geshem the Arab and to the rest of our enemies that I had built the wall and that there was no breach left in it (although up to that time I had not set up the doors in the gates), [2]Sanbal'lat and Geshem sent to me, saying, "Come and let us meet together in one of the villages in the plain of Ono." But they intended to do me harm. [3]And I sent messengers to them, saying, "I am doing a great work and I cannot come down. Why should the work stop while I leave it and come down to you?" [4]And they sent to me four times in this way and I answered them in the same manner. [5]In the same way Sanbal'lat for the fifth time sent his servant to me with an open letter in his hand. [6]In it was written, "It is reported among the nations, and Geshem [1] also says it, that you and the Jews intend to rebel; that is why you are building the wall; and you wish to become their king, according to this report. [7]And you have also set up prophets to proclaim concerning you in Jerusalem, 'There is a king in Judah.' And now it will be reported to the king according to these words. So now come, and let us take counsel together." [8]Then I sent to him, saying, "No such things as you say have been done, for you are inventing them out of your own mind." [9]For they all wanted to frighten us, thinking, "Their hands will drop from the work, and it will not be done." But now, O God, strengthen my hands.

10 Now when I went into the house of She-mai'ah the son of Delai'ah, son of Mehet'abel, who was shut up, he said, "Let us meet together in the house of God, within the temple, and let us close the doors of the temple; for they are coming to kill you, at night they are coming to kill you." [11]But I said, "Should such a man as I flee? And what man such as I could go into the temple and live? [m] I will not go in." [12]And I understood, and saw that God had not sent him, but he had pronounced the prophecy against me because Tobi'ah and Sanbal'lat had hired him. [13]For this purpose he was hired, that I should be afraid and act in this way and sin, and so they could give me an evil name, in order to taunt me. [14]Remember Tobi'ah and Sanbal'lat, O my God, according to these things that they did, and also the prophetess No-adi'ah and the rest of the prophets who wanted to make me afraid.

The Wall Completed

15 So the wall was finished on the twenty-fifth day of the month E'lul, in fifty-two days. [16]And when all our enemies heard of it, all the nations round about us were afraid [n] and fell greatly in their own esteem; for they perceived that this work had been accomplished with the help of our God. [17]Moreover in those days the nobles of Judah sent many letters to Tobi'ah, and Tobiah's letters came to them. [18]For many in Judah were bound by oath to him, because he was the son-in-law of Shecani'ah the son of A'rah; and his son Je'ho-ha'nan had taken the daughter of Meshul'lam the son of Berechi'ah as his wife. [19]Also they spoke of

---

[1] Heb Gashmu.
[m] Or would go into the temple to save his life.
[n] Another reading is saw.

his good deeds in my presence, and reported my words to him. And Tobi'ah sent letters to make me afraid.

7 Now when the wall had been built and I had set up the doors, and the gatekeepers, the singers, and the Levites had been appointed, [2]I gave my brother Hana'ni and Hanani'ah the governor of the castle charge over Jerusalem, for he was a more faithful and God-fearing man than many. [3]And I said to them, "Let not the gates of Jerusalem be opened until the sun is hot; and while they are still standing guard° let them shut and bar the doors. Appoint guards from among the inhabitants of Jerusalem, each to his station and each opposite his own house." [4]The city was wide and large, but the people within it were few and no houses had been built.

Lists of Returned Exiles

5 Then God put it into my mind to assemble the nobles and the officials and the people to be enrolled by genealogy. And I found the book of the genealogy of those who came up at the first, and I found written in it:

6 These were the people of the province who came up out of the captivity of those exiles whom Nebuchadnez'zar the king of Babylon had carried into exile; they returned to Jerusalem and Judah, each to his town. [7]They came with Zerub'babel, Jesh'ua, Nehemi'ah, Azari'ah, Raami'ah, Naham'ani, Mor'decai, Bilshan, Mis'pereth, Bigvai, Nehum, Ba'anah.

The number of the men of the sons of Israel: [8]the sons of Pa'rosh, two thousand a hundred and seventy-two. [9]The sons of Shephati'ah, three hundred and seventy-two. [10]The sons of A'rah, six hundred and fifty-two. [11]The sons of Pa'hath-mo'ab, namely the sons of Jesh'ua and Jo'ab, two thousand eight hundred and eighteen. [12]The sons of E'lam, a thousand two hundred and fifty-four. [13]The sons of Zattu, eight hundred and forty-five. [14]The sons of Zaccai, seven hundred and sixty. [15]The sons of Bin'nui, six hundred and forty-eight. [16]The sons of Bebai, six hundred and twenty-eight. [17]The sons of Azgad, two thousand three hundred and twenty-two. [18]The sons of Adoni'kam, six hundred and sixty-seven. [19]The sons of Bigvai, two thousand and sixty-seven. [20]The sons of A'din, six hundred and fifty-five. [21]The sons of A'ter, namely of Hezeki'ah, ninety-eight. [22]The sons of Hashum, three hundred and twenty-eight. [23]The sons of Bezai, three hundred and twenty-four. [24]The sons of Hariph, a hundred and twelve. [25]The sons of Gib'eon, ninety-five. [26]The men of Bethlehem and Netoph'ah, a hundred and eighty-eight. [27]The men of An'athoth, a hundred and twenty-eight. [28]The men of Beth-az'maveth, forty-two. [29]The men of Kir'iath-je'arim, Chephi'rah, and Be-er'oth, seven hundred and forty-three. [30]The men of Ra'mah and Ge'ba,

six hundred and twenty-one. [31]The men of Michmas, a hundred and twenty-two. [32]The men of Bethel and Ai, a hundred and twenty-three. [33]The men of the other Nebo, fifty-two. [34]The sons of the other E'lam, a thousand two hundred and fifty-four. [35]The sons of Harim, three hundred and twenty. [36]The sons of Jericho, three hundred and forty-five. [37]The sons of Lod, Hadid, and Ono, seven hundred and twenty-one. [38]The sons of Sena'ah, three thousand nine hundred and thirty.

39 The priests: the sons of Jedai'ah, namely the house of Jesh'ua, nine hundred and seventy-three. [40]The sons of Immer, a thousand and fifty-two. [41]The sons of Pashhur, a thousand two hundred and forty-seven. [42]The sons of Harim, a thousand and seventeen.

43 The Levites: the sons of Jesh'ua, namely of Kad'mi-el of the sons of Ho'devah, seventy-four. [44]The singers: the sons of A'saph, a hundred and forty-eight. [45]The gatekeepers: the sons of Shallum, the sons of A'ter, the sons of Talmon, the sons of Akkub, the sons of Hati'ta, the sons of Shobai, a hundred and thirty-eight.

46 The temple servants:ᴾ the sons of Ziha, the sons of Hasu'pha, the sons of Tabba'oth, [47]the sons of Keros, the sons of Sia, the sons of Pa'don, [48]the sons of Leba'na, the sons of Hag'aba, the sons of Shalmai, [49]the sons of Ha'nan, the sons of Giddel, the sons of Ga'har, [50]the sons of Re-ai'ah, the sons of Re'zin, the sons of Neko'da, [51]the sons of Gazzam, the sons of Uzza, the sons of Pase'ah, [52]the sons of Besai, the sons of Me-u'nim, the sons of Nephush'esim, [53]the sons of Bakbuk, the sons of Haku'pha, the sons of Harhur, [54]the sons of Bazlith, the sons of Mehi'da, the sons of Harsha, [55]the sons of Barkos, the sons of Sis'era, the sons of Te'mah, [56]the sons of Nezi'ah, the sons of Hati'pha.

57 The sons of Solomon's servants: the sons of Sotai, the sons of So'phereth, the sons of Peri'da, [58]the sons of Ja'ala, the sons of Darkon, the sons of Giddel, [59]the sons of Shephati'ah, the sons of Hattil, the sons of Po'chereth-hazzeba'im, the sons of A'mon.

60 All the temple servants and the sons of Solomon's servants were three hundred and ninety-two.

61 The following were those who came up from Tel-me'lah, Tel-har'sha, Cherub, Addon, and Immer, but they could not prove their fathers' houses nor their descent, whether they belonged to Israel: [62]the sons of Delai'ah, the sons of Tobi'ah, the sons of Neko'da, six hundred and forty-two. [63]Also, of the priests: the sons of Hobai'ah, the sons of Hakkoz, the sons of Barzil'lai (who had

---

° Heb obscure.
ᴾ Heb nethinim.
7:6–73: Ezra 2:1–70.

taken a wife of the daughters of Barzillai the Gileadite and was called by their name). [64]These sought their registration among those enrolled in the genealogies, but it was not found there, so they were excluded from the priesthood as unclean; [65]the governor told them that they were not to partake of the most holy food, until a priest with U'rim and Thummim should arise.

66 The whole assembly together was forty-two thousand three hundred and sixty, [67]besides their menservants and maidservants, of whom there were seven thousand three hundred and thirty-seven; and they had two hundred and forty-five singers, male and female. [68]Their horses were seven hundred and thirty-six, their mules two hundred and forty-five, [q] [69]their camels four hundred and thirty-five, and their donkeys six thousand seven hundred and twenty.

70 Now some of the heads of fathers' houses gave to the work. The governor gave to the treasury a thousand darics of gold, fifty basins, five hundred and thirty priests' garments. [71]And some of the heads of fathers' houses gave into the treasury of the work twenty thousand darics of gold and two thousand two hundred minas of silver. [72]And what the rest of the people gave was twenty thousand darics of gold, two thousand minas of silver, and sixty-seven priests' garments.

Ezra Opens the Book of the Law

73 So the priests, the Levites, the gatekeepers, the singers, some of the people, the temple servants, and all Israel, lived in their towns.

And when the seventh month had come, the
8 children of Israel were in their towns. * [1]And all the people gathered as one man into the square before the Water Gate; and they told Ezra the scribe to bring the book of the law of Moses which the LORD had given to Israel. [2]And Ezra the priest brought the law before the assembly, both men and women and all who could hear with understanding, on the first day of the seventh month. [3]And he read from it facing the square before the Water Gate from early morning until midday, in the presence of the men and the women and those who could understand; and the ears of all the people were attentive to the book of the law. [4]And Ezra the scribe stood on a wooden pulpit which they had made for the purpose; and beside him stood Mattithi'ah, Shema, Anai'ah, Uri'ah, Hilki'ah, and Ma-asei'ah on his right hand; and Pedai'ah, Mish'a-el, Malchi'jah, Hashum, Hash-bad'danah, Zechari'ah, and Meshul'lam on his left hand. [5]And Ezra opened the book in the sight of all the people, for he was above all the people; and when he opened it all the people stood. [6]And Ezra blessed the LORD, the great God; and all the people answered, "Amen, Amen," lifting up their hands; and they bowed their heads and worshiped the LORD with their faces to the ground. [7]Also Jesh'ua, Ba'ni, Sherebi'ah, Ja'min, Akkub, Shab'bethai, Hodi'ah, Ma-asei'ah, Keli'ta, Azari'ah, Jo'zabad, Ha'nan, Pelai'ah, the Levites, [r] helped the people to understand the law, while the people remained in their places. [8]And they read from the book, from the law of God, clearly; [s] and they gave the sense, so that the people understood the reading. †

9 And Nehemi'ah, who was the governor, and Ezra the priest and scribe, and the Levites who taught the people said to all the people, "This day is holy to the LORD your God; do not mourn or weep." For all the people wept when they heard the words of the law. [10]Then he said to them, "Go your way, eat the fat and drink sweet wine and send portions to him for whom nothing is prepared; for this day is holy to our Lord; and do not be grieved, for the joy of the LORD is your strength." [11]So the Levites stilled all the people, saying, "Be quiet, for this day is holy; do not be grieved." [12]And all the people went their way to eat and drink and to send portions and to make great rejoicing, because they had understood the words that were declared to them.

The Feast of Booths Celebrated

13 On the second day the heads of fathers' houses of all the people, with the priests and the Levites, came together to Ezra the scribe in order to study the words of the law. [14]And they found it written in the law that the LORD had commanded by Moses that the sons of Israel should dwell in booths during the feast of the seventh month, [15]and that they should publish and proclaim in all their towns and in Jerusalem, "Go out to the hills and bring branches of olive, wild olive, myrtle, palm, and other leafy trees to make booths, as it is written." [16]So the people went out and brought them and made booths for themselves, each on his roof, and in their courts and in the courts of the house of God, and in the square at the Water Gate and in the square at the Gate of E'phraim. [17]And all the assembly of those who had returned from the captivity made booths and dwelt in the booths; for from the days of Jesh'ua the son of Nun to that day the sons of Israel had not done so. And there was very great rejoicing. [18]And day by day, from the first day to the last day, he read from the book of the law of God. They kept the feast seven days; and on the eighth day there was a solemn assembly, according to the ordinance.

---

q Ezra 2:66 and the margins of some Hebrew Mss: Heb lacks *their horses . . . forty-five*.
r 1 Esdras 9:48 Vg: Heb *and the Levites*.
s Or *with interpretation*.
* 8–10: As it was only thirteen years since the reform of Ezra, some scholars think that this passage belongs to the book of Ezra.
† 8:8: The book was of course written in Hebrew, but the people, since their sojourn in Babylonia, now spoke Aramaic, and it had to be translated for them into that tongue.

Public Confession and Worship

9 Now on the twenty-fourth day of this month the sons of Israel were assembled with fasting and in sackcloth, and with earth upon their heads. [2]And the Israelites separated themselves from all foreigners, and stood and confessed their sins and the iniquities of their fathers. [3]And they stood up in their place and read from the book of the law of the LORD their God for a fourth of the day; for another fourth of it they made confession and worshiped the LORD their God. [4]Upon the stairs of the Levites stood Jesh'ua, Ba'ni, Kad'mi-el, Shebani'ah, Bunni, Sherebi'ah, Bani, and Chena'ni; and they cried with a loud voice to the LORD their God. [5]Then the Levites, Jesh'ua, Kad'mi-el, Ba'ni, Hashabnei'ah, Sherebi'ah, Hodi'ah, Shebani'ah, and Pethahi'ah, said, "Stand up and bless the LORD your God from everlasting to everlasting. Blessed be your glorious name which is exalted above all blessing and praise."

Ezra's Prayer to God

6 And Ezra said: [t] "You are the LORD, you alone; you have made heaven, the heaven of heavens, with all their host, the earth and all that is on it, the seas and all that is in them; and you preserve all of them; and the host of heaven worships you. [7]You are the LORD, the God who chose Abram and brought him forth out of Ur of the Chalde'ans and gave him the name Abraham; [8]and you found his heart faithful before you, and made with him the covenant to give to his descendants the land of the Canaanite, the Hittite, the Am'orite, the Per'izzite, the Jeb'usite, and the Gir'gashite; and you have fulfilled your promise, for you are righteous.

9 "And you saw the affliction of our fathers in Egypt and heard their cry at the Red Sea, [10]and performed signs and wonders against Pharaoh and all his servants and all the people of his land, for you knew that they acted insolently against our fathers; and you got yourself a name, as it is to this day. [11]And you divided the sea before them, so that they went through the midst of the sea on dry land; and you cast their pursuers into the depths, as a stone into mighty waters. [12]By a pillar of cloud you led them in the day, and by a pillar of fire in the night to light for them the way in which they should go. [13]You came down upon Mount Sinai, and spoke with them from heaven and gave them right ordinances and true laws, good statutes and commandments, [14]and you made known to them your holy sabbath and commanded them commandments and statutes and a law by Moses your servant. [15]You gave them bread from heaven for their hunger and brought forth water for them from the rock for their thirst, and you told them to go in to possess the land which you had sworn to give them.

16 "But they and our fathers acted presumptuously and stiffened their neck and did not obey your commandments; [17]they refused to obey, and were not mindful of the wonders which you performed among them; but they stiffened their neck and appointed a leader to return to their bondage in Egypt. But you are a God ready to forgive, gracious and merciful, slow to anger and abounding in mercy, and did not forsake them. [18]Even when they had made for themselves a molten calf and said, 'This is your God who brought you up out of Egypt,' and had committed great blasphemies, [19]you in your great mercies did not forsake them in the wilderness; the pillar of cloud which led them in the way did not depart from them by day, nor the pillar of fire by night which lighted for them the way by which they should go. [20]You gave your good Spirit to instruct them, and did not withhold your manna from their mouth, and gave them water for their thirst. [21]Forty years you sustained them in the wilderness, and they lacked nothing; their clothes did not wear out and their feet did not swell. [22]And you gave them kingdoms and peoples, and allotted to them every corner; so they took possession of the land of Si'hon king of Heshbon and the land of Og king of Bashan. [23]You multiplied their descendants as the stars of heaven, and you brought them into the land which you had told their fathers to enter and possess. [24]So the descendants went in and possessed the land, and you subdued before them the inhabitants of the land, the Canaanites, and gave them into their hands, with their kings and the peoples of the land, that they might do with them as they would. [25]And they captured fortified cities and a rich land, and took possession of houses full of all good things, cisterns hewn out, vineyards, olive orchards and fruit trees in abundance; so they ate, and were filled and became fat, and delighted themselves in your great goodness.

26 "Nevertheless they were disobedient and rebelled against you and cast your law behind their back and killed your prophets, who had warned them in order to turn them back to you, and they committed great blasphemies. [27]Therefore you gave them into the hand of their enemies, who made them suffer; and in the time of their suffering they cried to you and you heard them from heaven; and according to your great mercies you gave them saviors who saved them from the hand of their enemies. [28]But after they had rest they did evil again before you, and you abandoned them to the hand of their enemies, so that they had dominion over them; yet when they turned and cried to you, you heard from heaven, and many times you delivered them according to your mercies. [29]And you warned them in order to turn them

---

[t] Gk: Heb lacks *and Ezra said.*

back to your law. Yet they acted presumptuously and did not obey your commandments, but sinned against your ordinances, by the observance of which a man shall live, and turned a stubborn shoulder and stiffened their neck and would not obey. [30]Many years you bore with them, and warned them by your Spirit through your prophets; yet they would not give ear. Therefore you gave them into the hand of the peoples of the lands. [31]Nevertheless in your great mercies you did not make an end of them or forsake them; for you are a gracious and merciful God.

32 "Now therefore, our God, the great and mighty and awesome God, who keep covenant and mercy, let not all the hardship seem little to you that has come upon us, upon our kings, our princes, our priests, our prophets, our fathers, and all your people, since the time of the kings of Assyria until this day. [33]Yet you have been just in all that has come upon us, for you have dealt faithfully and we have acted wickedly; [34]our kings, our princes, our priests, and our fathers have not kept your law or heeded your commandments and your warnings which you gave them. [35]They did not serve you in their kingdom, and in your great goodness which you gave them, and in the large and rich land which you set before them; and they did not turn from their wicked works. [36]Behold, we are slaves this day; in the land that you gave to our fathers to enjoy its fruit and its good gifts, behold, we are slaves. [37]And its rich yield goes to the kings whom you have set over us because of our sins; they have power also over our bodies and over our cattle at their pleasure, and we are in great distress."

The Signing of the Covenant

38[u] Because of all this we make a firm covenant and write it, and our princes, our Levites, and our priests set their seal to it.

10

[v] Those who set their seal are Nehemi′ah the governor, the son of Hacali′ah, Zede-ki′ah, [2]Serai′ah, Azari′ah, Jeremi′ah, [3]Pashhur, Amari′ah, Malchi′jah, [4]Hattush, Shebani′ah, Mal-luch, [5]Harim, Mer′emoth, Obadi′ah, [6]Daniel, Gin′nethon, Baruch, [7]Meshul′lam, Abi′jah, Mi′ja-min, [8]Ma-azi′ah, Bilgai, Shemai′ah; these are the priests. [9]And the Levites: Jesh′ua the son of Aza-ni′ah, Bin′nui of the sons of Hen′adad, Kad′mi-el; [10]and their brethren, Shebani′ah, Hodi′ah, Keli′ta, Pelai′ah, Hanan, [11]Mica, Re′hob, Hashabi′ah, [12]Zaccur, Sherebi′ah, Shebani′ah, [13]Hodi′ah, Ba′ni, Beni′nu. [14]The chiefs of the people: Pa′rosh, Pa′hath-mo′ab, E′lam, Zattu, Ba′ni, [15]Bunni, Azgad, Bebai, [16]Adoni′jah, Bigvai, A′din, [17]A′ter, Hezeki′ah, Azzur, [18]Hodi′ah, Hashum, Bezai, [19]Hariph, An′athoth, Nebai, [20]Mag′piash, Meshul′-am, He′zir, [21]Meshez′abel, Za′dok, Jad′du-a, [22]Pelati′ah, Hanan, Anai′ah, [23]Hoshe′a, Hanani′ah, Hasshub, [24]Hallo′hesh, Pilha, Shobek, [25]Re′hum,

Hashab′nah, Ma-asei′ah, [26]Ahi′ah, Ha′nan, A′nan, [27]Malluch, Harim, Ba′anah.

Summary of the Covenant

28 The rest of the people, the priests, the Levites, the gatekeepers, the singers, the temple servants, and all who have separated themselves from the peoples of the lands to the law of God, their wives, their sons, their daughters, all who have knowledge and understanding, [29]join with their brethren, their nobles, and enter into a curse and an oath to walk in God's law which was given by Moses the servant of God, and to observe and do all the commandments of the Lord our Lord and his ordinances and his statutes. [30]We will not give our daughters to the peoples of the land or take their daughters for our sons; [31]and if the peoples of the land bring in wares or any grain on the sabbath day to sell, we will not buy from them on the sabbath or on a holy day; and we will forego the crops of the seventh year and the exaction of every debt.

32 We also lay upon ourselves the obligation to charge ourselves yearly with the third part of a shekel for the service of the house of our God: [33]for the showbread, the continual cereal offering, the continual burnt offering, the sabbaths, the new moons, the appointed feasts, the holy things, and the sin offerings to make atonement for Israel, and for all the work of the house of our God. [34]We have likewise cast lots, the priests, the Levites, and the people, for the wood offering, to bring it into the house of our God, according to our fathers' houses, at times appointed, year by year, to burn upon the altar of the Lord our God, as it is written in the law. [35]We obligate ourselves to bring the first fruits of our ground and the first fruits of all fruit of every tree, year by year, to the house of the Lord; [36]also to bring to the house of our God, to the priests who minister in the house of our God, the first-born of our sons and of our cattle, as it is written in the law, and the firstlings of our herds and of our flocks; [37]and to bring the first of our coarse meal, and our contributions, the fruit of every tree, the wine and the oil, to the priests, to the chambers of the house of our God; and to bring to the Levites the tithes from our ground, for it is the Levites who collect the tithes in all our rural towns. [38]And the priest, the son of Aaron, shall be with the Levites when the Levites receive the tithes; and the Levites shall bring up the tithe of the tithes to the house of our God, to the chambers, to the storehouse. [39]For the sons of Israel and the sons of Levi shall bring the contribution of grain, wine, and oil to the chambers, where are the vessels of the sanctuary, and the priests that minister, and the gatekeepers and the singers. We will not neglect the house of our God.

---

u Ch 10:1 in Heb.
v Ch 10:2 in Heb.

The Inhabitants of Jerusalem

11 Now the leaders of the people lived in Jerusalem; and the rest of the people cast lots to bring one out of ten to live in Jerusalem the holy city, while nine tenths remained in the other towns. [2]And the people blessed all the men who willingly offered to live in Jerusalem.

3 These are the chiefs of the province who lived in Jerusalem; but in the towns of Judah every one lived on his property in their towns: Israel, the priests, the Levites, the temple servants, and the descendants of Solomon's servants. [4]And in Jerusalem lived certain of the sons of Judah and of the sons of Benjamin. Of the sons of Judah: Athai'ah the son of Uzzi'ah, son of Zechari'ah, son of Amari'ah, son of Shephati'ah, son of Mahal'alel, of the sons of Per'ez; [5]and Ma-asei'ah the son of Baruch, son of Col-ho'zeh, son of Hazai'ah, son of Adai'ah, son of Joi'arib, son of Zechari'ah, son of the Shilon'ite. [6]All the sons of Per'ez who lived in Jerusalem were four hundred and sixty-eight valiant men.

7 And these are the sons of Benjamin: Sallu the son of Meshul'lam, son of Jo'ed, son of Pedai'ah, son of Kolai'ah, son of Ma-asei'ah, son of I'thi-el, son of Jeshai'ah. [8]And after him Gabba'i, Sallai, nine hundred and twenty-eight. [9]Joel the son of Zich'ri was their overseer; and Judah the son of Hassenu'ah was second over the city.

10 Of the priests: Jedai'ah the son of Joi'arib, Ja'chin, [11]Serai'ah the son of Hilki'ah, son of Meshul'lam, son of Za'dok, son of Mera'ioth, son of Ahi'tub, ruler of the house of God, [12]and their brethren who did the work of the house, eight hundred and twenty-two; and Adai'ah the son of Jero'ham, son of Pelali'ah, son of Amzi, son of Zechari'ah, son of Pashhur, son of Malchi'jah, [13]and his brethren, heads of fathers' houses, two hundred and forty-two; and Amash'sai, the son of Az'arel, son of Ahzai, son of Meshil'lemoth, son of Immer, [14]and their brethren, mighty men of valor, a hundred and twenty-eight; their overseer was Zab'diel the son of Haggedo'lim.

15 And of the Levites: Shemai'ah the son of Hasshub, son of Azri'kam, son of Hashabi'ah, son of Bunni; [16]and Shab'bethai and Jo'zabad, of the chiefs of the Levites, who were over the outside work of the house of God; [17]and Mattani'ah the son of Mica, son of Zabdi, son of A'saph, who was the leader to begin the thanksgiving in prayer, and Bakbuki'ah, the second among his brethren; and Abda the son of Sham'mu-a, son of Galal, son of Jedu'thun. [18]All the Levites in the holy city were two hundred and eighty-four.

19 The gatekeepers, Akkub, Talmon and their brethren, who kept watch at the gates, were a hundred and seventy-two. [20]And the rest of Israel, and of the priests and the Levites, were in all the towns of Judah, every one in his inheritance. [21]But the temple servants lived on O'phel; and Ziha and Gishpa were over the temple servants.

22 The overseer of the Levites in Jerusalem was Uzzi the son of Ba'ni, son of Hashabi'ah, son of Mattani'ah, son of Mica, of the sons of A'saph, the singers, over the work of the house of God. [23]For there was a command from the king concerning them, and a settled provision for the singers, as every day required. [24]And Pethahi'ah the son of Meshez'abel, of the sons of Ze'rah the son of Judah, was at the king's hand in all matters concerning the people.

Villages outside Jerusalem

25 And as for the villages, with their fields, some of the people of Judah lived in Kir'iath-ar'ba and its villages, and in Di'bon and its villages, and in Jekab'zeel and its villages, [26]and in Jesh'ua and in Mo'ladah and Beth-pel'et, [27]in Ha'zar-shu'al, in Be'er-she'ba and its villages, [28]in Zik'lag, in Meco'nah and its villages, [29]in En-rim'mon, in Zo'rah, in Jarmuth, [30]Zano'ah, Adul'lam, and their villages, La'chish and its fields, and Aze'kah and its villages. So they encamped from Be'er-she'ba to the valley of Hinnom. [31]The people of Benjamin also lived from Ge'ba onward, at Michmash, Aija, Bethel and its villages, [32]An'athoth, Nob, Anani'ah, [33]Ha'zor, Ra'mah, Git'taim, [34]Hadid, Zebo'im, Nebal'lat, [35]Lod, and Ono, the valley of craftsmen. [36]And certain divisions of the Levites in Judah were joined to Benjamin.

Lists of Priests and Levites

12 These are the priests and the Levites who came up with Zerub'babel the son of She-al'tiel, and Jesh'ua: Serai'ah, Jeremi'ah, Ezra, [2]Amari'ah, Malluch, Hattush, [3]Shecani'ah, Re'hum, Mer'emoth, [4]Iddo, Gin'nethoi, Abi'jah, [5]Mi'jamin, Ma-adi'ah, Bilgah, [6]Shemai'ah, Joi'arib, Jedai'ah, [7]Sallu, A'mok, Hilki'ah, Jedai'ah. These were the chiefs of the priests and of their brethren in the days of Jesh'ua.

8 And the Levites: Jesh'ua, Bin'nui, Kad'mi-el, Sherebi'ah, Judah, and Mattani'ah, who with his brethren was in charge of the songs of thanksgiving. [9]And Bakbuki'ah and Unno their brethren stood opposite them in the service. [10]And Jesh'ua was the father of Joi'akim, Joiakim the father of Eli'ashib, Eliashib the father of Joi'ada, [11]Joi'ada the father of Jonathan, and Jonathan the father of Jad'du-a.

12 And in the days of Joi'akim were priests, heads of fathers' houses: of Serai'ah, Merai'ah; of Jeremi'ah, Hanani'ah; [13]of Ezra, Meshul'lam; of Amari'ah, Jeho-ha'nan; [14]of Mal'luchi, Jonathan; of Shebani'ah, Joseph; [15]of Harim, Adna; of Mera'ioth, Helkai; [16]of Iddo, Zechari'ah; of Gin'nethon, Meshul'lam; [17]of Abi'jah, Zich'ri; of Mini'amin, of Moadi'ah, Piltai; [18]of Bilgah,

11:3-22: 1 Chron 9:2-34.

Sham′mu-a; of Shemai′ah, Jehon′athan; [19]of Joi′a-rib, Matte′nai; of Jedai′ah, Uzzi, [20]of Sallai, Kallai; of A′mok, E′ber; [21]of Hilki′ah, Hashabi′ah; of Jedai′ah, Nethan′el.

22 As for the Levites, in the days of Eli′ashib, Joi′ada, Joha′nan, and Jad′du-a, there were re-corded the heads of fathers' houses; also the priests until the reign of Dari′us the Persian. [23]The sons of Levi, heads of fathers' houses, were writ-ten in the Book of the Chronicles until the days of Joha′nan the son of Eli′ashib. [24]And the chiefs of the Levites: Hashabi′ah, Sherebi′ah, and Jesh′ua the son of Kad′mi-el, with their brethren over against them, to praise and to give thanks, ac-cording to the commandment of David the man of God, watch corresponding to watch. [25]Matta-ni′ah, Bakbuki′ah, Obadi′ah, Meshul′lam, Talmon, and Akkub were gatekeepers standing guard at the storehouses of the gates. [26]These were in the days of Joi′akim the son of Jesh′ua son of Jo′zadak, and in the days of Nehemi′ah the governor and of Ezra the priest the scribe.

Dedication of the Wall of Jerusalem

27 And at the dedication of the wall of Jerusa-lem they sought the Levites in all their places, to bring them to Jerusalem to celebrate the dedica-tion with gladness, with thanksgivings and with singing, with cymbals, harps, and lyres. [28]And the sons of the singers gathered together from the circuit round Jerusalem and from the villages of the Netoph′athites; [29]also from Beth-gil′gal and from the region of Ge′ba and Az′maveth; for the singers had built for themselves villages around Jerusalem. [30]And the priests and the Levites puri-fied themselves; and they purified the people and the gates and the wall.

31 Then I brought up the princes of Judah upon the wall, and appointed two great compa-nies which gave thanks and went in procession. One went to the right upon the wall to the Dung Gate; [32]and after them went Hoshai′ah and half of the princes of Judah, [33]and Azari′ah, Ezra, Meshul′lam, [34]Judah, Benjamin, Shemai′ah, and Jeremi′ah, [35]and certain of the priests' sons with trumpets: Zechari′ah the son of Jonathan, son of Shemai′ah, son of Mattani′ah, son of Micai′ah, son of Zaccur, son of A′saph, [36]and his kinsmen, Shemai′ah, Az′arel, Mil′alai, Gil′alai, Ma′ai, Nethan′el, Judah, and Hana′ni, with the musical instruments of David the man of God; and Ezra the scribe went before them. [37]At the Fountain Gate they went up straight before them by the stairs of the city of David, at the ascent of the wall, above the house of David, to the Water Gate on the east.

38 The other company of those who gave thanks went to the left, and I followed them with half of the people, upon the wall, above the Tower of the Ovens, to the Broad Wall, [39]and above the

Gate of E′phraim, and by the Old Gate, and by the Fish Gate and the Tower of Hanan′el and the Tower of the Hundred, to the Sheep Gate; and they came to a halt at the Gate of the Guard. [40]So both companies of those who gave thanks stood in the house of God, and I and half of the officials with me; [41]and the priests Eli′akim, Ma-asei′ah, Mini′amin, Micai′ah, El′i-o-e′nai, Zechari′ah, and Hanani′ah, with trumpets; [42]and Ma-asei′ah, Shemai′ah, Elea′zar, Uzzi, Je′ho-ha′nan, Mal-chi′jah, E′lam, and E′zer. And the singers sang with Jezrahi′ah as their leader. [43]And they offered great sacrifices that day and rejoiced, for God had made them rejoice with great joy; the women and children also rejoiced. And the joy of Jerusalem was heard afar off.

Appointments to Temple Responsibilities

44 On that day men were appointed over the chambers for the stores, the contributions, the first fruits, and the tithes, to gather into them the portions required by the law for the priests and for the Levites according to the fields of the towns; for Judah rejoiced over the priests and the Levites who ministered. [45]And they performed the service of their God and the service of puri-fication, as did the singers and the gatekeepers, according to the command of David and his son Solomon. [46]For in the days of David and A′saph of old there was a chief of the singers, and there were songs of praise and thanksgiving to God. [47]And all Israel in the days of Zerub′babel and in the days of Nehemi′ah gave the daily portions for the singers and the gatekeepers; and they set apart that which was for the Levites; and the Levites set apart that which was for the sons of Aaron.

Foreigners Separated from Israel

13 On that day they read from the book of Moses in the hearing of the people; and in it was found written that no Am′monite or Moabite should ever enter the assembly of God; [2]for they did not meet the children of Israel with bread and water, but hired Balaam against them to curse them—yet our God turned the curse into a blessing. [3]When the people heard the law, they separated from Israel all those of foreign descent.

Reforms of Nehemiah

4 Now before this, Eli′ashib the priest, who was appointed over the chambers of the house of our God, and who was connected with Tobi′ah, [5]prepared for Tobi′ah a large chamber where they had previously put the cereal offering, the frank-incense, the vessels, and the tithes of grain, wine, and oil, which were given by command-ment to the Levites, singers, and gatekeepers, and the contributions for the priests. [6]While this was taking place I was not in Jerusalem, for in

13:1: Deut 23:3–5.

the thirty-second year of Ar-ta-xerx'es king of Babylon I went to the king. And after some time I asked leave of the king ⁷and came to Jerusalem, and I then discovered the evil that Eli'ashib had done for Tobi'ah, preparing for him a chamber in the courts of the house of God. ⁸And I was very angry, and I threw all the household furniture of Tobi'ah out of the chamber. ⁹Then I gave orders and they cleansed the chambers; and I brought back there the vessels of the house of God, with the cereal offering and the frankincense.

10 I also found out that the portions of the Levites had not been given to them; so that the Levites and the singers, who did the work, had fled each to his field. ¹¹So I remonstrated with the officials and said, "Why is the house of God forsaken?" And I gathered them together and set them in their stations. ¹²Then all Judah brought the tithe of the grain, wine, and oil into the storehouses. ¹³And I appointed as treasurers over the storehouses Shelemi'ah the priest, Za'dok the scribe, and Pedai'ah of the Levites, and as their assistant Ha'nan the son of Zaccur, son of Matta-ni'ah, for they were counted faithful; and their duty was to distribute to their brethren. ¹⁴Remember me, O my God, concerning this, and wipe not out my good deeds that I have done for the house of my God and for his service.

Sabbath Reforms Begun

15 In those days I saw in Judah men treading wine presses on the sabbath, and bringing in heaps of grain and loading them on donkeys; and also wine, grapes, figs, and all kinds of burdens, which they brought into Jerusalem on the sabbath day; and I warned them on the day when they sold food. ¹⁶Men of Tyre also, who lived in the city, brought in fish and all kinds of wares and sold them on the sabbath to the people of Judah, and in Jerusalem. ¹⁷Then I remonstrated with the nobles of Judah and said to them, "What is this evil thing which you are doing, profaning the sabbath day? ¹⁸Did not your fathers act in this way, and did not our God bring all this evil on us and on this city? Yet you bring more wrath upon Israel by profaning the sabbath."

19 When it began to be dark at the gates of Jerusalem before the sabbath, I commanded that the doors should be shut and gave orders that they should not be opened until after the sabbath. And I set some of my servants over the gates, that no burden might be brought in on the sabbath day. ²⁰Then the merchants and sellers of all kinds of wares lodged outside Jerusalem once or twice. ²¹But I warned them and said to them, "Why do you lodge before the wall? If you do so again I will lay hands on you." From that time on they did not come in on the sabbath. ²²And I commanded the Levites that they should purify themselves and come and guard the gates, to keep the sabbath day holy. Remember this also in my favor, O my God, and spare me according to the greatness of your mercy.

Intermarriage Condemned

23 In those days also I saw the Jews who had married women of Ash'dod, Ammon, and Moab; ²⁴and half of their children spoke the language of Ash'dod, and they could not speak the language of Judah, but the language of each people. ²⁵And I contended with them and cursed them and beat some of them and pulled out their hair; and I made them take oath in the name of God, saying, "You shall not give your daughters to their sons, or take their daughters for your sons or for yourselves. ²⁶Did not Solomon king of Israel sin on account of such women? Among the many nations there was no king like him, and he was beloved by his God, and God made him king over all Israel; nevertheless foreign women made even him to sin. ²⁷Shall we then listen to you and do all this great evil and act treacherously against our God by marrying foreign women?"

28 And one of the sons of Jehoi'ada, the son of Eli'ashib the high priest, was the son-in-law of Sanbal'lat the Hor'onite; therefore I chased him from me. ²⁹Remember them, O my God, because they have defiled the priesthood and the covenant of the priesthood and the Levites.

30 Thus I cleansed them from everything foreign, and I established the duties of the priests and Levites, each in his work; ³¹and I provided for the wood offering, at appointed times, and for the first fruits. Remember me, O my God, for good.

THE BOOK OF

TOBIT

1 The book of the acts [a] of Tobit the son of
Tobi′el, son of Anan′iel, son of Adu′el, son of
Gab′ael, of the descendants of As′i-el and the tribe
of Naph′tali, [2] who in the days of Shalmane′ser, [b]
king of the Assyrians, was taken into captivity
from Thisbe, which is to the south of Ke′desh
Naph′tali in Galilee above Asher.

Tobit's Youth and Virtuous Life

3 I, Tobit, walked in the ways of truth and
righteousness all the days of my life, and I performed many acts of charity to my brethren and
countrymen who went with me into the land of
the Assyrians, to Nin′eveh. [4] Now when I was in
my own country, in the land of Israel, while I was
still a young man, the whole tribe of Naph′tali my
forefather deserted the house of Jerusalem. This
was the place which had been chosen from among
all the tribes of Israel, where all the tribes should
sacrifice and where the temple of the dwelling of
the Most High was consecrated and established
for all generations for ever.

5 All the tribes that joined in apostasy used to
sacrifice to the calf [c] Ba′al, and so did the house of
Naph′tali my forefather. [6] But I alone went often to
Jerusalem for the feasts, as it is ordained for all
Israel by an everlasting decree. Taking the first
fruits and the tithes of my produce and the first
shearings, I would give these to the priests, the
sons of Aaron, at the altar. [7] Of all my produce I
would give a tenth to the sons of Levi who ministered at Jerusalem; a second tenth I would sell,
and I would go and spend the proceeds each year
at Jerusalem; [8] the third tenth I would give to those
to whom it was my duty, as Deborah my father's
mother had commanded me, for I was left an
orphan by my father. [9] When I became a man I
married Anna, a member of our family, and by
her I became the father of Tobi′as.

Tobit Taken Captive to Nineveh

10 Now when I was carried away captive to
Nin′eveh, all my brethren and my relatives ate the
food of the Gentiles; [11] but I kept myself from
eating it, [12] because I remembered God with all my
heart. [13] Then the Most High gave me favor and
good appearance in the sight of Shalmane′ser, [b]
and I was his buyer of provisions. [14] So I used to
go into Med′ia, and once at Ra′ges in Med′ia I left
ten talents of silver in trust with Gab′ael, the
brother of Ga′brias. [15] But when Shalmane′ser [b]
died, Sennach′erib his son reigned in his place;

and under him the highways were unsafe, so that
I could no longer go into Med′ia.

Courage in Burying the Dead

16 In the days of Shalmane′ser [b] I performed
many acts of charity to my brethren. [17] I would
give my bread to the hungry and my clothing to
the naked; and if I saw any one of my people
dead and thrown out behind the wall of Nin′eveh,
I would bury him. [18] And if Sennach′erib the king
put to death any who came fleeing from Judea, I
buried them secretly. For in his anger he put many
to death. When the bodies were sought by the
king, they were not found. [19] Then one of the men
of Nin′eveh went and informed the king about
me, that I was burying them; so I hid myself.
When I learned that I was being searched for, to
be put to death, I left home in fear. [20] Then all my
property was confiscated and nothing was left to
me except my wife Anna and my son Tobi′as.

21 But not fifty [d] days passed before two of
Sennach′erib's [e] sons killed him, and they fled to
the mountains of Ar′arat. Then E′sar-had′don, [f]
his son, reigned in his place; and he appointed

The Books of Tobit, Judith and Esther
These three books appear together in the Greek Bible, usually after the
historical books. The complete Aramaic original of Tobit and the Hebrew
of Judith have not survived, and neither book was included in the Jewish
canon at the end of the first century A.D. Existing as they did in the Greek
Bible, they would have been used and recognized as Scripture by the first
Christians. The Greek "Additions to Esther" were probably written two
centuries after the Hebrew text. They were composed in Egypt and they
exhibit a strictly Jewish doctrine. All three books have a literary form
somewhat strange to the Western mind. They are, in effect, religious tales
with the appearance of an historical narrative. They may have an historical basis, but the persons, places, events and dates are woven into the
narrative in such a way as to have little resemblance to the actual historical record as we know it from other sources. It would seem, therefore, that
the writers are intending, not to write history as we understand that term,
but to use historical material to impart a religious message.

The Book of Tobit (The Book of Tobias)
The author relates the story of a family living among a pagan people yet
trusting fully in God in spite of difficulties. Belief in one God is stressed;
marriage between Jews is likewise emphasized and angels figure promi-
nently in the narrative. The book has much to say, too, about the need for
good works. It was written after the Exile at some time during the Persian
period, though the story may be a good deal older than that. It shows
signs of dependence on earlier writings such as the Story of Ahikar, a
sixth-century work from Babylon. It also bears a likeness to Genesis in
certain points, e.g., to his last injunctions to the family, the important role
of angels, the son's search for a wife, and the care given to burial of the
dead. It is interesting to note that fragments of the Hebrew and Aramaic
texts have been found at Qumran, which favor the longer text of Codex
Sinaiticus, the Old Latin and the Vulgate.

a Gk words.
b Gk Enemessarus.
c Other authorities read heifer.
d Other authorities read fifty-five.
e Gk his.
f Gk Sacherdonus.

Ahi'kar, the son of my brother An'ael, over all the accounts of his kingdom and over the entire administration. [22]Ahi'kar interceded for me, and I returned to Nin'eveh. Now Ahikar was cupbearer, keeper of the signet, and in charge of administration of the accounts, for E'sar-had'don [f] had appointed him second to himself. [g] He was my nephew.

2 When I arrived home and my wife Anna and my son Tobi'as were restored to me, at the feast of Pentecost, which is the sacred festival of the seven weeks, a good dinner was prepared for me and I sat down to eat. [2]Upon seeing the abundance of food I said to my son, "Go and bring whatever poor man of our brethren you may find among the exiles in Nineveh, who is mindful of the Lord, and he shall eat together with me. I will wait for you until you come back." [3]So Tobias went out to look for some poor person of our people. When he came back, he said, "Father!" And I replied, "Here I am, my child." And he went on to say, "Look, Father, one of our own people has been murdered and thrown into the market place, and now he lies there strangled." [4]So before I tasted anything I sprang up and removed the body [h] to a place of shelter until sunset when I might bury it. [5]And when I returned I washed myself and ate my food in sorrow. [6]Then I remembered the prophecy of Amos, how he said against Bethel,

"Your feasts shall be turned into mourning,
  and all your songs into lamentation."
And I wept.

Tobit Becomes Blind

7 When the sun had set I went and dug a grave and buried the body. [h] [8]And my neighbors laughed at me and said, "He is still not afraid; he has already been hunted down to be put to death for doing this, and he ran away, yet here he is burying the dead again!" [9]On the same night after I, Tobit, returned from burying the dead, I went into my courtyard and slept by the wall of the courtyard, and my face was uncovered because of the heat. [10]I did not know that there were sparrows on the wall and their fresh droppings fell into my open eyes and white films formed on my eyes. I went to physicians to be healed, but the more they treated me with ointments, the more my vision was obscured by the white films, until I became completely blind. For four years I remained unable to see. All my kindred were sorry for me, and Ahi'kar took care of me for two years until he [i] went to El'yma'is.

Tobit's Wife Earns Their Livelihood

11 Then my wife Anna earned money at women's work. [12]She used to send the product to the owners, and they paid her wages. One day, the seventh of Dystrus, when she cut off a piece she had woven and sent it to the owners, they paid her full wages and they also gave her a kid. [13]When she returned to me it began to bleat. So I called her and said to her, "Where did you get the kid? It is not stolen, is it? Return it to the owners; for it is not right to eat what is stolen." [14]And she said, "It was given to me as a gift in addition to my wages." But I did not believe her, and told her to return it to the owners; and I blushed for her. Then she replied to me, "Where are your charities and your righteous deeds? You seem to know everything!"

Tobit's Prayer

3 Then in my grief I wept, and I prayed in anguish, saying, [2]"Righteous are you, O Lord; all your deeds are just and all your ways are mercy and truth, and you render true and righteous judgment for ever. [3]And now, O Lord, remember me and look favorably upon me; do not punish me for my sins and for my unwitting offenses and those which my fathers committed before you. [4]For we disobeyed your commandments, and you gave us over to plunder, captivity, and death; you made us the talk, the byword, and an object of reproach in all the nations among which you have dispersed us. [5]And now your many judgments are true in exacting penalty from me for my sins and those of my fathers, because we did not keep your commandments. For we did not walk in truth before you. [6]And now deal with me according to your pleasure; command my spirit to be taken up, that I may be released from the face of the earth and become dust. For it is better for me to die than to live, because I have heard false reproaches, and great is the sorrow within me. Command that I now be released from my distress; release me to go to the eternal abode; and do not, O Lord, turn your face away from me. For it is better for me to die than to see so much distress in my life and listen to such insults."

Sarah Falsely Accused

7 On the same day, at Ecbat'ana in Med'ia, it also happened that Sarah, the daughter of Rag'uel, was reproached by her father's maids, [8]because she had been given to seven husbands, and the evil demon As"mode'us had slain each of them before he had been with her as his wife. So the maids [j] said to her, "You are the one who kills your husbands! See, you already have had seven and have had no benefit from [k] any of them. [9]Why do you beat us? Because your husbands are dead? Go with them! May we never see a son or daughter of yours!"

---

[f] Gk Sacherdonus.
[g] Or a second time.
[h] Gk him.
[i] Other authorities read I.
[j] Gk they.
[k] Other authorities read have not borne the name of.

Sarah's Prayer for Death

10 On that day she was deeply grieved in spirit and wept. When she had gone up to her father's upper room, she intended to hang herself. But she thought it over and said, "Never shall they reproach my father, saying to him, 'You only had one beloved daughter but she hanged herself because of her distress.' And I shall bring his old age down in sorrow to the grave.[1] It is better for me not to hang myself, but to pray the Lord that I may die and not listen to these reproaches any more." [11]At that same time, with hands outstretched toward the window, she prayed and said, "Blessed are you, O Lord, merciful God, and blessed is your holy and honored name for ever. May all your works praise you for ever. [12]And now, O Lord, I have turned my eyes and my face toward you. [13]Command that I be released from the earth and that I hear reproach no more. [14]You know, O Lord, that I am innocent of any sin with man, [15]and that I did not stain my name or the name of my father in the land of my captivity. I am my father's only child, and he has no child to be his heir, no near kinsman or kinsman's[m] son for whom I should keep myself as wife. Already seven husbands of mine are dead. Why should I live? But if it be not pleasing to you to take my life, command that respect be shown to me and pity be taken upon me, and that I hear reproach no more."

An Answer to Prayer

16 At that very moment the prayer of both was heard in the presence of the glory of the great God. [17]And Ra'phael[n] was sent to heal the two of them: to scale away the white films of Tobit's eyes; to give Sarah the daughter of Rag'uel in marriage to Tobi'as the son of Tobit, and to bind As''mode'us the evil demon, because Tobias was entitled to possess her. At that very moment Tobit returned and entered his house and Sarah the daughter of Raguel came down from her upper room.

Tobit Gives Instructions to His Son

4 On that day Tobit remembered the money which he had left in trust with Gab'ael at Ra'ges in Med'ia, and he said to himself: [2]"I have asked for death. Why do I not call my son Tobi'as so that I may explain to him about the money[o] before I die?" [3]So he called him and said, "My son, when I die, bury me, and do not neglect your mother. Honor her all the days of your life; do what is pleasing to her, and do not grieve her. [4]Remember, my son, that she faced many dangers for you while you were yet unborn. When she dies, bury her beside me in the same grave.

5 "Remember the Lord our God all your days, my son, and refuse to sin or to transgress his commandments. Live uprightly all the days of your life, and do not walk in the ways of wrong-doing. [6]For if you do what is true, your ways will prosper through your deeds. [7]Give alms from your possessions to all who live uprightly, and do not let your eye begrudge the gift when you make it. Do not turn your face away from any poor man, and the face of God will not be turned away from you. [8]If you have many possessions, make your gift from them in proportion; if few, do not be afraid to give according to the little you have. [9]So you will be laying up a good treasure for yourself against the day of necessity. [10]For charity* delivers from death and keeps you from entering the darkness; [11]and for all who practice it charity is an excellent offering in the presence of the Most High.

12 "Beware, my son, of all immorality.† First of all take a wife from among the descendants of your fathers and do not marry a foreign woman, who is not of your father's tribe; for we are the sons of the prophets. Remember, my son, that Noah, Abraham, Isaac, and Jacob, our fathers of old, all took wives from among their brethren. They were blessed in their children, and their posterity will inherit the land. [13]So now, my son, love your brethren, and in your heart do not disdain your brethren and the sons and daughters of your people by refusing to take a wife for yourself from among them. For in pride there is ruin and great confusion; and in shiftlessness there is loss and great want, because shiftlessness is the mother of famine. [14]Do not hold over till the next day the wages of any man who works for you, but pay him at once; and if you serve God you will receive payment.

"Watch yourself, my son, in everything you do, and be disciplined in all your conduct. [15]And what you hate, do not do to any one. Do not drink wine to excess or let drunkenness go with you on your way. [16]Give of your bread to the hungry, and of your clothing to the naked. Give all your surplus to charity, and do not let your eye begrudge the gift when you make it. [17]Place your bread ‡ on the grave of the righteous, but give none to sinners. [18]Seek advice from every wise man, and do not despise any useful counsel. [19]Bless the Lord God on every occasion; ask him that your ways may be made straight and that all your paths and plans may prosper. For none of the nations has understanding; but the Lord himself gives all good things, and according to his will he humbles whomever he wishes.

---

[1] Gk to Hades.
[m] Gk his.
[n] Other authorities read the great Raphael. And he.
[o] Other authorities omit about the money.
* 4:10, charity: i.e., almsgiving; cf. also verses 11 and 16.
† 4:12, immorality: i.e., impurity, fornication.
‡ 4:17, place your bread: The Greek verb means literally "pour out." The Latin, with its "your bread and your wine," preserves better the original text, cf. the Story of Ahikar: "Pour out your wine on the graves of the righteous and drink it not with evil men."

"So, my son, remember my commands, and do not let them be blotted out of your mind. [20]And now let me explain to you about the ten talents of silver which I left in trust with Gab'ael the son of Ga'brias at Ra'ges in Med'ia. [21]Do not be afraid, my son, because we have become poor. You have great wealth if you fear God and refrain from every sin and do what is pleasing in his sight."

The Angel Raphael

5 Then Tobi'as answered him, "Father, I will do everything that you have commanded me; [2]but how can I obtain the money when I do not know the man?" [3]Then Tobit gave him the receipt, and said to him, "Find a man to go with you and I will pay him wages as long as I live; and go and get the money." [4]So he went to look for a man; and he found Ra'phael, who was an angel, [5]but Tobi'as[p] did not know it. Tobias[p] said to him, "Can you go with me to Ra'ges in Med'ia? Are you acquainted with that region?" [6]The angel replied, "I will go with you; I am familiar with the way, and I have stayed with our brother Gab'ael." [7]Then Tobi'as said to him, "Wait for me, and I shall tell my father." [8]And he said to him, "Go, and do not delay." So he went in and said to his father, "I have found some one to go with me." He said, "Call him to me, so that I may learn to what tribe he belongs, and whether he is a reliable man to go with you."

9 So Tobi'as[p] invited him in; he entered and they greeted each other. [10]Then Tobit said to him, "My brother, to what tribe and family do you belong? Tell me." [11]But he answered, "Are you looking for a tribe and a family or for a man whom you will pay to go with your son?" And Tobit said to him, "I should like to know, my brother, your people and your name." [12]He replied, "I am Azari'as the son of the great Anani'as, one of your relatives." [13]Then Tobit said to him, "You are welcome, my brother. Do not be angry with me because I tried to learn your tribe and family. You are a relative of mine, of a good and noble lineage. For I used to know Anani'as and Ja'than, the sons of the great Shemai'ah, when we went together to Jerusalem to worship and offered the first-born of our flocks and the tithes of our produce. They did not go astray in the error of our brethren. My brother, you come of good stock. [14]But tell me, what wages am I to pay you—a drachma a day, and expenses for yourself as for my son? [15]And besides, I will add to your wages if you both return safe and sound." So they agreed to these terms.

16 Then he said to Tobi'as, "Get ready for the journey, and good success to you both." So his son made the preparations for the journey. And his father said to him, "Go with this man; God who dwells in heaven will prosper your way, and may his angel attend you." So they both went out and departed, and the young man's dog was with them.

17 But Anna,[q] his mother, began to weep, and said to Tobit, "Why have you sent our child away? Is he not the staff of our hands as he goes in and out before us? [18]Do not add money to money, but consider it rubbish as compared to our child. [19]For the life that is given to us by the Lord is enough for us." [20]And Tobit said to her, "Do not worry, my sister; he will return safe and sound, and your eyes will see him. [21]For a good angel will go with him; his journey will be successful, and he will come back safe and sound." [22]So she stopped weeping.

A Miraculous Fish

6 Now as they proceeded on their way they came at evening to the Tigris river and camped there. [2]Then the young man went down to wash himself. A fish leaped up from the river and would have swallowed the young man; [3]and the angel said to him, "Catch the fish." So the young man seized the fish and threw it up on the land. [4]Then the angel said to him, "Cut open the fish and take the heart and liver and gall and put them away safely." [5]So the young man did as the angel told him; and they roasted and ate the fish.

And they both continued on their way until they came near to Ecbat'ana.[r] [6]Then the young man said to the angel, "Brother Azari'as, of what use is the liver and heart and gall of the fish?" [7]He replied, "As for the heart and liver, if a demon or evil spirit gives trouble to any one, you make a smoke from these before the man or woman, and that person will never be troubled again. [8]And as for the gall, anoint with it a man who has white films in his eyes, and he will be cured."

Raphael's Instructions

9 When he entered Med'ia and was already approaching Ecbat'ana, [10]Ra'phael said to the young man, "Brother Tobi'as!" "Here I am," he answered. Then Raphael said to him, "We must stay this night in the home of Ra'guel. He is your relative, and he has a daughter named Sarah. He has no male heir and no daughter except Sarah only, and you, as next of kin to her, have before all other men a hereditary claim on her. [11]Also, it is right for you to inherit her father's possessions. [12]Moreover, the girl is sensible, brave, and very beautiful, and her father is a good man."

13 Then the young man said to the angel, "Brother Azari'as, I have heard that the girl has been given to seven husbands and that each died in the bridal chamber. [14]Now I am the only son my father has, and I am afraid that if I go in I will die as those before me did, for a demon is in love with her, and he harms no one except those who

---

[p] Gk he.
[q] Other authorities omit Anna.
[r] Other authorities read Rages.

approach her. So now I fear that I may die and bring the lives of my father and mother to the grave in sorrow on my account. And they have no other son to bury them."

15 But the angel said to him, "Do you not remember the words with which your father commanded you to take a wife from among your own people? Now listen to me, brother, for she will become your wife; and do not worry about the demon, for this very night she will be given to you in marriage. [16]When you enter the bridal chamber, you shall take live ashes of incense and lay upon them some of the heart and liver of the fish so as to make a smoke. [17]Then the demon will smell it and flee away, and will never again return. And when you approach her, rise up, both of you, and cry out to the merciful God, and he will save you and have mercy on you. Do not be afraid, for she was destined for you from eternity. You will save her, and she will go with you, and I suppose that you will have children by her." When Tobi′as heard these things, he fell in love with her and yearned deeply for her.

Arrival at Raguel's Home; and a Marriage Contract

7 Now when they reached Ecbat′ana, Tobi′as said to him, "Brother Azari′ah, take me straight to our brother Rag′uel." So he took him to the house of Raguel, and they found Raguel sitting beside the courtyard door. They greeted him first, and he replied, "Joyous greetings, brothers; welcome and good health!" Then he brought them into his house. [2]Then Rag′uel said to his wife Edna, "How much the young man resembles my cousin Tobit!" [3]And Rag′uel asked them, "Where are you from, brethren?" They answered him, "We belong to the sons of Naph′tali, who are captives in Nin′eveh." [4]So he said to them, "Do you know our brother Tobit?" And they said, "Yes, we do." And he asked them, "Is he in good health?" [5]They replied, "He is alive and in good health." And Tobi′as said, "He is my father." [6]Then Rag′uel sprang up and kissed him and wept. [7]And he blessed him and exclaimed, "Son of that good and noble man!" When he heard that Tobit had lost his sight, he was stricken with grief and wept. [8]And his wife Edna and his daughter Sarah wept.

9 Then Rag′uel killed a ram from the flock and received them very warmly. When they had bathed and washed themselves and had reclined to dine, Tobi′as said to Ra′phael, "Brother Azari′as, ask Raguel to give me my kinswoman Sarah." [10]But Rag′uel overheard it and said to Tobi′as, "Eat, drink, and be merry; for no one except you, brother, has the right to marry my daughter Sarah. Likewise, I am not at liberty to give her to any other man than yourself, because you are my nearest relative. [11]But let me explain the true situation to

you. I have given my daughter to seven men of our kinsmen, and when each came to her he died in the night. But for the present, my child, eat and drink, and the Lord will act on behalf of you both." But Tobi′as said, "I will eat nothing here unless you make a binding agreement with me." [12]So Rag′uel said, "I will do so. She is given to you in accordance with the decree in the book of Moses, and it has been decreed from heaven that she be given to you. Take your kinswoman; from now on you are her brother and she is your sister. She is given to you from today and for ever. May the Lord of heaven, my child, guide and prosper you both this night and grant you mercy and peace." [13]Then he called his daughter Sarah, and taking her by the hand he gave her to Tobi′as to be his wife, saying, "Here she is; take her to be your wife in accordance with the law and the decree written in the book of Moses. Take her and bring her safely to your father. And may the God of heaven prosper your journey with his peace." [14]Then he called her mother and told her to bring writing material; and he wrote out a copy of the marriage contract, to the effect that he gave her to him as wife according to the law of Moses. [15]Then they began to eat and drink.

16 And Rag′uel called his wife Edna and said to her, "Sister, make up the other room, and take her into it." [17]So she did as he said, and took her there; and the girl[s] began to weep. But the mother[s] comforted her daughter in her tears, and said to her, [18]"Be brave, my child; the Lord of heaven and earth grant you joy[t] in place of this sorrow of yours. Be brave, my daughter."

Tobias Routs the Demon and Prays with Sarah

8 When they had finished eating and drinking, they wanted to retire; so they took the young man and brought him into the bedroom. [2]As he went he remembered the words of Ra′phael, and he took the live ashes of incense and put the heart and liver of the fish upon them and made a smoke. [3]And when the demon smelled the odor he fled to the remotest parts of Egypt, and the angel bound him. [4]When the door was shut and the two were alone, Tobi′as got up from the bed and said, "Sister, get up, and let us pray and implore our Lord that he grant us mercy and safety." [5]And they began to say,

"Blessed are you, O God of our fathers,
 and blessed be your holy and glorious name
  for ever.
 Let the heavens and all your creatures bless
  you.
[6]You made Adam and gave him Eve his wife
 as a helper and support.
 From them the race of mankind has sprung.

---

[s] Gk she.
[t] Other authorities read favor.

You said, 'It is not good that the man should be alone;

let us make a helper for him like himself.'
[7]And now, O Lord, I am not taking this sister of mine because of lust, but with sincerity. Grant that I may find mercy and may grow old together with her." [8]And they both said, "Amen, amen." [9]Then they both went to sleep for the night.

But Rag'uel arose and went and dug a grave, [10]with the thought, "Perhaps he too will die." [11]Then Rag'uel went into his house [12]and said to his wife Edna, "Send one of the maids to see whether he is alive; and if he is not, let us bury him without any one knowing about it." [13]So the maid opened the door and went in, and found them both asleep. [14]And she came out and told them that he was alive. [15]Then Rag'uel blessed God and said,

"Blessed are you, O God, with every pure and
   holy blessing.
Let your saints and all your creatures bless
   you;
let all your angels and your chosen people
   bless you for ever.
[16]Blessed are you, because you have made me
   glad.
It has not happened to me as I expected;
but you have treated us according to your
   great mercy.
[17]Blessed are you, because you have had
   compassion on two only children.
Show them mercy, O Lord;
and bring their lives to fulfilment in health
   and happiness and mercy."
[18]Then he ordered his servants to fill in the grave.

The Wedding Feast

19 After this he gave a wedding feast for them which lasted fourteen days. [20]And before the days of the feast were over, Rag'uel declared by oath to Tobi'as [u] that he should not leave until the fourteen days of the wedding feast were ended, [21]that then he should take half of Rag'uel's [v] property and return in safety to his father, and that the rest would be his "when my wife and I die."

The Money Recovered from Gabael

9 Then Tobi'as called Ra'phael and said to him, [2]"Brother Azari'as, take a servant and two camels with you and go to Gab'ael at Ra'ges in Med'ia and get the money for me; and bring him to the wedding feast. [3]For Rag'uel has sworn that I should not leave; [4]but my father is counting the days, and if I delay long he will be greatly distressed." [5]So Ra'phael made the journey and stayed overnight with Gab'ael. He gave him the receipt, and Gabael [w] brought out the money bags with their seals intact and gave them to him. [6]In the morning they both got up early and came to the wedding feast. And Gab'ael blessed Tobi'as and his wife. [x]

Tobias and Sarah Journey Home
to Tobit and Anna

10 Now his father Tobit was counting each day, and when the days for the journey had expired and they did not arrive, [2]he said, "Is it possible that he has been detained? [y] Or is it possible that Gab'ael has died and there is no one to give him the money?" [3]And he was greatly distressed. [4]And his wife said to him, "The lad has perished; his long delay proves it." Then she began to mourn for him, and said, [5]"Am I not distressed, my child, that I let you go, you who are the light of my eyes?" [6]But Tobit said to her, "Be still and stop worrying; he is well." [7]And she answered him, "Be still and stop deceiving me; my child has perished." And she went out every day to the road by which they had left; she ate nothing in the daytime, and throughout the nights she never stopped mourning for her son Tobi'as, until the fourteen days of the wedding feast had expired which Rag'uel had sworn that he should spend there.

At that time Tobias said to Raguel, "Send me back, for my father and mother have given up hope of ever seeing me again." [8]But his father-in-law said to him, "Stay with me, and I will send messengers to your father, and they will inform him how things are with you." [9]Tobi'as replied, "No, send me back to my father." [10]So Rag'uel arose and gave him his wife Sarah and half of his property in slaves, cattle, and money. [11]And when he had blessed them he sent them away, saying, "The God of heaven will prosper you, my children, before I die." [12]He said also to his daughter, "Honor your father-in-law and your mother-in-law; they are now your parents. Let me hear a good report of you." And he kissed her. And Edna said to Tobi'as, "The Lord of heaven bring you back safely, dear brother, and grant me to see your children by my daughter Sarah, that I may rejoice before the Lord. See, I am entrusting my daughter to you; do nothing to grieve her."

The Return

11 After this Tobi'as went on his way, praising God because he had made his journey a success. And he blessed Rag'uel and his wife Edna.

So he continued on his way until they came near to Nin'eveh. [2]Then Ra'phael said to Tobi'as, "Are you not aware, brother, of how you left your father? [3]Let us run ahead of your wife and prepare the house. [4]And take the gall of the fish with you." So they went their way, and the dog went along behind them.

---

[u] Gk *him.*
[v] Gk *his.*
[w] Gk *he.*
[x] Cn: Gk *And Tobias blessed his wife.*
[y] One Gk Ms Lat: Gk *they are put to shame* or *they are disappointed.*

5 Now Anna sat looking intently down the road for her son. [6]And she caught sight of him coming, and said to his father, "Behold, your son is coming, and so is the man who went with him!"

Tobit's Sight Restored

7 Ra'phael said to Tobi'as, before they approached his father, "I know that his eyes will be opened. [8]Smear the gall of the fish on his eyes, and the medicine will cause the white films to fall away. And your father will regain his sight and see the light."

9 Then Anna ran to meet them, and embraced her son, and said to him, "I have seen you, my child; now I am ready to die." And she wept. [10]Tobit got up, and came stumbling out through the courtyard door. But his son ran to him [11]with the gall of the fish in his hand, and holding him firmly, he blew into his eyes, saying, "Take courage, Father." [12]With this he applied the medicine on his eyes. [13]Next, with both his hands, he peeled off the white films from the corners of his eyes. [14]Then he saw his son and embraced him, and he wept and said, "Here I see my son, the light of my eyes!" Then he said, "Blessed be God, and blessed be his great name, and blessed be all his holy angels. May his holy name be blessed throughout all the ages. [15]Though he afflicted me, he has had mercy on me. Now I see my son Tobi'as!"

16 And his son went in rejoicing, and he reported to his father the great things that had happened to him in Med'ia. Then Tobit went out to meet his daughter-in-law at the gate of Nin'eveh, rejoicing and praising God. Those who saw him as he went were amazed because he could see. [17]And Tobit gave thanks before them that God had been merciful to him. When Tobit came near to Sarah his daughter-in-law, he blessed her, saying, "Welcome, daughter! Blessed is God who has brought you to us, and blessed are your father and your mother." So there was rejoicing among all his brethren in Nin'eveh. [18]Ahi'kar and his nephew Na'dab [z] came, [19]and Tobi'as' marriage was celebrated for seven days with great festivity.

Raphael's Wages

12 Tobit then called his son Tobi'as and said to him, "My son, see to the wages of the man who went with you; and he must also be given more." [2]He replied, "Father, it would do me no harm to give him half of what I have brought back. [3]For he has led me back to you safely, he cured my wife, he obtained the money for me, and he also healed you." [4]The old man said, "He deserves it." [5]So he called the angel and said to him, "Take for your wages half of all that you two have brought back, and farewell."

Raphael's Exhortation

6 Then the angel [a] called the two of them privately and said to them: "Praise God and give thanks to him; exalt him and give thanks to him

in the presence of all the living for what he has done for you. It is good to praise God and to exalt his name, worthily declaring the works of God, and with fitting honor to acknowledge him. Do not be slow to give him thanks. [7]It is good to guard the secret of a king, but gloriously to reveal the works of God, and with fitting honor to acknowledge him. Do good, and evil will not overtake you. [8]Prayer is good when accompanied by fasting, almsgiving, and righteousness. A little with righteousness is better than much with wrongdoing. It is better to give alms than to treasure up gold. [9]For almsgiving delivers from death, and it will purge away every sin. Those who perform deeds of charity* and of righteousness will have fulness of life; [10]but those who commit sin are the enemies of their own lives.

Raphael Reveals His Identity

11 "I will now declare the whole truth to you and I will not conceal anything from you. I have said, 'It is good to guard the secret of a king, but gloriously to reveal the works of God.' [12]And so, when you and your daughter-in-law Sarah prayed, I brought a reminder of your prayer before the Holy One; and when you buried the dead, I was likewise present with you. [13]When you did not hesitate to rise and leave your dinner in order to go and lay out the dead, I was sent to test you. [14]So now God sent me to heal you and your daughter-in-law Sarah. [15]I am Ra'phael, one of the seven holy angels who present the prayers of the saints and enter into the presence of the glory of the Lord."

16 They were both alarmed; and they fell upon their faces, for they were afraid. [17]But he said to them, "Do not be afraid; you will be safe. But praise God for ever. [18]For I did not come as a favor on my part, but by the will of our God. Therefore praise him for ever. [19]All these days I merely appeared to you and did not eat or drink, but you were seeing a vision. [20]And now bless the Lord upon the earth and give thanks to God, for I am ascending to him who sent me. Write in a book everything that has happened to you." [21]Then they stood up; but they saw him no more. [22]So they confessed the great and wonderful works of God, and acknowledged that the angel of the Lord had appeared to them.

Tobit's Prayer of Thanksgiving

13 Then Tobit wrote a prayer of rejoicing, and said:
"Blessed is God who lives for ever,
    and blessed is his kingdom.
[2]For he afflicts, and he shows mercy;
    he leads down to Hades, and brings up again,
    and there is no one who can escape his hand.

---

[z] Other authorities read *Nasbas*.
[a] Gk *he.*
* 12:9, *charity:* See note on 4:10.

³Acknowledge him before the nations, O sons of
Israel;
  for he has scattered us among them.
⁴Make his greatness known there,
  and exalt him in the presence of all the
  living;
because he is our Lord and God,
  he is our Father for ever.
⁵He will afflict us for our iniquities;
  and again he will show mercy,
and will gather us from all the nations
  among whom you ^b have been scattered.
⁶If you turn to him with all your heart and with
  all your soul,
  to do what is true before him,
then he will turn to you
  and will not hide his face from you.
But see what he will do with you;
  give thanks to him with your full voice.
Praise the Lord of righteousness,
  and exalt the King of the ages.
I give him thanks in the land of my captivity,
  and I show his power and majesty to a
  nation of sinners.
Turn back, you sinners, and do right before him;
  who knows if he will accept you and have
  mercy on you?
⁷I exalt my God;
  my soul exalts the King of heaven,
  and will rejoice in his majesty.
⁸Bless the Lord, all you his chosen ones,
  all of you, praise his glory.
Celebrate days of joy, and give thanks to him.
⁹O Jerusalem, the holy city,
  he will afflict you for the deeds of your
  sons,
  but again he will show mercy to the sons of
  the righteous.
¹⁰Give thanks worthily to the Lord,
  and praise the King of the ages,
  that his tent may be raised for you again
  with joy.
May he cheer those within you who are
  captives,
  and love those within you who are
  distressed,
  to all generations for ever.
¹¹Many nations will come from afar to the name
  of the Lord God,
  bearing gifts in their hands, gifts for the
  King of heaven.
Generations of generations will give you joyful
  praise.
¹²Cursed are all who hate you;
  blessed for ever will be all who love you.
¹³Rejoice and be glad for the sons of the
  righteous;
  for they will be gathered together,
  and will praise the Lord of the righteous.

¹⁴How blessed are those who love you!
  They will rejoice in your peace.
Blessed are those who grieved over all your
  afflictions;
  for they will rejoice for you upon seeing all
  your glory,
  and they will be made glad for ever.
¹⁵Let my soul praise God the great King.
¹⁶For Jerusalem will be built with sapphires and
  emeralds,
  her ^c walls with precious stones,
  and her towers and battlements with pure
  gold.
¹⁷The streets of Jerusalem will be paved ^d with
  beryl and ruby and stones of O'phir;
¹⁸ all her lanes will cry 'Hallelujah!' and will
  give praise,
  saying, 'Blessed is God, who has exalted
  you for ever.'"

Tobit's Final Counsel and Death

14 Here Tobit ended his words of praise. ²He
was fifty-eight years old when he lost his
sight, and after eight years he regained it. He
gave alms, and he continued to fear the Lord God
and to praise him. ³When he had grown very old
he called his son and grandsons, and said to him,
"My son, take your sons; behold, I have grown
old and am about to depart this life. ⁴Go to
Med'ia, my son, for I fully believe what Jonah the
prophet said about Nin'eveh, that it will be overthrown. But in Media there will be peace for a
time. Our brethren will be scattered over the
earth from the good land, and Jerusalem will be
desolate. The house of God in it will be burned
down and will be in ruins for a time. ⁵But God
will again have mercy on them, and bring them
back into their land; and they will rebuild the
house of God,^e though it will not be like the
former one until the times of the age are completed. After this they will return from the places
of their captivity, and will rebuild Jerusalem in
splendor. And the house of God will be rebuilt
there with a glorious building for all generations
for ever, just as the prophets said of it. ⁶Then all
the Gentiles will turn to fear the Lord God in
truth, and will bury their idols. ⁷All the Gentiles
will praise the Lord, and his people will give
thanks to God, and the Lord will exalt his people.
And all who love the Lord God in truth and
righteousness will rejoice, showing mercy to our
brethren.

8 "So now, my son, leave Nin'eveh, because
what the prophet Jonah said will surely happen.
⁹But keep the law and the commandments, and be
merciful and just, so that it may be well with you.

---

^b Other authorities read *we*.
^c Gk *your*.
^d Or *inlaid*.
^e Gk *house*.

¹⁰Bury me properly, and your mother with me. And do not live in Nin'eveh any longer. See, my son, what Na'dab ᶠ did to Ahi'kar who had reared him, how he brought him from light into darkness, and with what he repaid him. But Ahikar was saved, and the other received repayment as he himself went down into the darkness. Ahikar ᵍ gave alms and escaped the deathtrap which Nadab ʰ had set for him; but Nadab ᶠ fell into the trap and perished. ¹¹So now, my children, consider what almsgiving accomplishes and how righteousness delivers." As he said this he died in his bed. He was a hundred and fifty-eight years old; and Tobi'as ʰ gave him a magnificent funeral. ¹²And when Anna died he buried her with his father.

Then Tobi'as returned with his wife and his sons to Ecbat'ana, to Rag'uel his father-in-law. ¹³He grew old with honor, and he gave his father-in-law and mother-in-law magnificent funerals. He inherited their property and that of his father Tobit. ¹⁴He died in Ecbat'ana of Med'ia at the age of a hundred and twenty-seven years. ¹⁵But before he died he heard of the destruction of Nin'eveh, which Nebuchadnez'zar and Ahas'uerus had captured. Before his death he rejoiced over Nineveh.

ᶠ Other authorities read *Aman*.
ᵍ Other authorities read *Manasses*.
ʰ Gk *he*.

THE BOOK OF

JUDITH

Arphaxad Fortifies Ecbatana

1 In the twelfth year of the reign of Nebuchad-nez′zar, who ruled over the Assyrians in the great city of Nin′eveh, in the days of Arpha′xad, who ruled over the Medes in Ecbat′ana—²he is the king who built walls about Ecbat′ana with hewn stones three cubits thick and six cubits long; he made the walls seventy cubits high and fifty cubits wide; ³at the gates he built towers a hundred cubits high and sixty cubits wide at the foundations; ⁴and he made its gates, which were seventy cubits high and forty cubits wide, so that his armies could march out in force and his infantry form their ranks—⁵it was in those days that King Nebuchadnez′zar made war against King Arpha′xad in the great plain which is on the borders of Ragae. ⁶He was joined by all the people of the hill country and all those who lived along the Euphrates and the Tigris and the Hydas′pes and in the plain where Ar′ioch ruled the El″y-mae′ans. Many nations joined the forces of the Chalde′ans.

Nebuchadnezzar's Orders Disregarded

7 Then Nebuchadnez′zar king of the Assyrians sent to all who lived in Persia and to all who lived in the west, those who lived in Cili′cia and Damascus and Lebanon and An″ti-leb′anon and all who lived along the seacoast, ⁸and those among the nations of Carmel and Gilead, and Upper Galilee and the great Plain of Esdrae′lon, ⁹and all who were in Samar′ia and its surrounding towns, and beyond the Jordan as far as Jerusalem and Beth′any and Chelous and Ka′desh and the river of Egypt, and Tah′panhes and Ra-am′ses and the whole land of Go′shen, ¹⁰even beyond Tanis and Memphis, and all who lived in Egypt as far as the borders of Ethiopia. ¹¹But all who lived in the whole region disregarded the orders of Nebuchadnez′zar king of the Assyrians, and refused to join him in the war; for they were not afraid of him, but looked upon him as only one man,ᵃ and they sent back his messengers empty-handed and shamefaced.

Arphaxad Is Defeated

12 Then Nebuchadnez′zar was very angry with this whole region, and swore by his throne and kingdom that he would surely take revenge on the whole territory of Cili′cia and Damascus and Syria, that he would kill by the sword all the inhabitants of the land of Moab, and the people of Ammon, and all Jude′a, and every one in Egypt, as far as the coasts of the two seas. ¹³In the seventeenth year he led his forces against King Arpha′xad, and defeated him in battle, and overthrew the whole army of Arphaxad, and all his cavalry and all his chariots. ¹⁴Thus he took possession of his cities, and came to Ecbat′ana, captured its towers, plundered its markets, and turned its beauty into shame. ¹⁵He captured Arpha′xad in the mountains of Ragae and struck him down with hunting spears; and he utterly destroyed him, to this day. ¹⁶Then he returned with them to Nin′eveh, he and all his combined forces, a vast body of troops; and there he and his forces rested and feasted for one hundred and twenty days.

Revenge against the West

2 In the eighteenth year, on the twenty-second day of the first month, there was talk in the palace of Nebuchadnez′zar king of the Assyrians about carrying out his revenge on the whole region, just as he said. ²He called together all his officers and all his nobles and set forth to them his secret plan and recounted fully, with his own lips, all the wickedness of the region;ᵇ ³and it was decided that every one who had not obeyed his command should be destroyed. ⁴When he had finished setting forth his plan, Nebuchadnez′zar king of the Assyrians called Hol″ofer′nes, the chief general of his army, second only to himself, and said to him,

5 "Thus says the Great King, the lord of the whole earth: When you leave my presence, take with you men confident in their strength, to the number of one hundred and twenty thousand foot soldiers and twelve thousand cavalry. ⁶Go and attack the whole west country, because they disobeyed my orders. ⁷Tell them to prepare earth and water, for I am coming against them in my anger, and will cover the whole face of the earth with the

---

This is an account of the routing of an army and the freeing of the people of God through a stratagem devised and carried out by a woman (cf. Esther). The story is strongly nationalist in sentiment, especially the victory song in chapter 16. The writer stresses that Judith's strength comes from God in response to her trust in him, and because she faithfully keeps all the prescriptions of the law. The Greek version of the book (the basis of this translation) was made from a Hebrew original, now lost. The Latin version was made from an Aramaic text, almost a paraphrase, which is not now extant and which apparently omitted about a fifth of the book.
ᵃ Or *a man*.
ᵇ The meaning of the Greek of the last clause of this verse is uncertain.

feet of my armies, and will hand them over to be plundered by my troops,[c] [8]till their wounded shall fill their valleys, and every brook and river shall be filled with their dead, and overflow; [9]and I will lead them away captive to the ends of the whole earth. [10]You shall go and seize all their territory for me in advance. They will yield themselves to you, and you shall hold them for me till the day of their punishment. [11]But if they refuse, your eye shall not spare and you shall hand them over to slaughter and plunder throughout your whole region. [12]For as I live, and by the power of my kingdom, what I have spoken my hand will execute. [13]And you—take care not to transgress any of your sovereign's commands, but be sure to carry them out just as I have ordered you; and do not delay about it."

Campaign of Holofernes

14 So Hol"ofer'nes left the presence of his master, and called together all the commanders, generals, and officers of the Assyrian army, [15]and mustered the picked troops by divisions as his lord had ordered him to do, one hundred and twenty thousand of them, together with twelve thousand archers on horseback, [16]and he organized them as a great army is marshaled for a campaign. [17]He collected a vast number of camels and donkeys and mules for transport, and innumerable sheep and oxen and goats for provision; [18]also plenty of food for every man, and a huge amount of gold and silver from the royal palace. [19]So he set out with his whole army, to go ahead of King Nebuchadnez'zar and to cover the whole face of the earth to the west with their chariots and horsemen and picked troops of infantry. [20]Along with them went a mixed crowd like a swarm of locusts, like the dust of the earth—a multitude that could not be counted.

21 They marched for three days from Nin'eveh to the plain of Bec'tileth, and camped opposite Bectileth near the mountain which is to the north of Upper Cili'cia. [22]From there Hol"ofer'nes[d] took his whole army, his infantry, cavalry, and chariots, and went up into the hill country [23]and ravaged Put and Lud, and plundered all the people of Rassis and the Ish'maelites who lived along the desert, south of the country of the Chel'leans. [24]Then he followed[e] the Euphrates and passed through Mesopota'mia and destroyed all the hilltop cities along the brook Abron, as far as the sea. [25]He also seized the territory of Cili'cia, and killed every one who resisted him, and came to the southern borders of Ja'pheth, fronting toward Arabia. [26]He surrounded all the Mid'ianites, and burned their tents and plundered their sheepfolds. [27]Then he went down into the plain of Damascus during the wheat harvest, and burned all their fields and destroyed their flocks and herds and sacked their cities and ravaged their lands and

put to death all their young men with the edge of the sword.

28 So fear and terror of him fell upon all the people who lived along the seacoast, at Si'don and Tyre, and those who lived in Sur and Oci'na and all who lived in Jam'nia. Those who lived in Azo'tus and Asca'lon feared him exceedingly.

Entreaties for Peace

3 So they sent messengers to sue for peace, and said, [2] "Behold, we the servants of Nebuchadnez'zar, the Great King, lie prostrate before you. Do with us whatever you will. [3]Behold, our buildings, and all our land, and all our wheat fields, and our flocks and herds, and all our sheepfolds with their tents, lie before you; do with them whatever you please. [4]Our cities also and their inhabitants are your slaves; come and deal with them in any way that seems good to you."

5 The men came to Hol"ofer'nes and told him all this. [6]Then he went down to the seacoast with his army and stationed garrisons in the hilltop cities and took picked men from them as his allies. [7]And these people and all in the country round about welcomed him with garlands and dances and tambourines. [8]And he demolished all their shrines[f] and cut down their sacred groves; for it had been given to him to destroy all the gods of the land, so that all nations should worship Nebuchadnez'zar only, and all their tongues and tribes should call upon him as god.

9 Then he came to the edge of Esdrae'lon, near Do'than, fronting the great ridge of Jude'a; [10]here he camped between Ge'ba and Scythop'olis, and remained for a whole month in order to assemble all the supplies for his army.

Judea Prepares for Defense

4 By this time the people of Israel living in Judea heard of everything that Hol"ofer'nes, the general of Nebuchadnez'zar the king of the Assyrians, had done to the nations, and how he had plundered and destroyed all their temples; [2]they were therefore very greatly terrified at his approach, and were alarmed both for Jerusalem and for the temple of the Lord their God. [3]For they had only recently returned from the captivity, and all the people of Jude'a were newly gathered together, and the sacred vessels and the altar and the temple had been consecrated after their profanation. [4]So they sent to every district of Samar'ia, and to Kona and Beth-ho'ron and Bel'main and Jericho and to Choba and Aeso'ra and the valley of Salem, [5]and immediately seized all the high hilltops and fortified the villages on them and stored up food in preparation for war—since their fields had recently been harvested. [6]And

---

[c] Gk them.
[d] Gk he.
[e] Or crossed.
[f] Syr: Gk borders.

Jo'akim, the high priest, who was in Jerusalem at that time, wrote to the people of Beth"uli'a and Bet"omestha'im, which faces Esdrae'lon opposite the plain near Do'than, [7]ordering them to seize the passes up into the hills, since by them Jude'a could be invaded, and it was easy to stop any who tried to enter, for the approach was narrow, only wide enough for two men at the most.

Israel's Prayer and Penance

8 So the Israelites did as Jo'akim the high priest and the senate of the whole people of Israel, in session at Jerusalem, had given order. [9]And every man of Israel cried out to God with great fervor, and they humbled themselves with much fasting. [10]They and their wives and their children and their cattle and every resident alien and hired laborer and purchased slave—they all clothed themselves with sackcloth. [11]And all the men and women of Israel, and their children, living at Jerusalem, prostrated themselves before the temple and put ashes on their heads and spread out their sackcloth before the Lord. [12]They even surrounded the altar with sackcloth and cried out in unison, praying earnestly to the God of Israel not to give up their infants as prey and their wives as booty, and the cities they had inherited to be destroyed, and the sanctuary to be profaned and desecrated to the malicious joy of the Gentiles. [13]So the Lord heard their prayers and looked upon their affliction; for the people fasted many days throughout Jude'a and in Jerusalem before the sanctuary of the Lord Almighty. [14]And Jo'akim the high priest and all the priests who stood before the Lord and ministered to the Lord, with their loins clothed with sackcloth, offered the continual burnt offerings and the vows and freewill offerings of the people. [15]With ashes upon their turbans, they cried out to the Lord with all their might to look with favor upon the whole house of Israel.

Holofernes' Council against the Israelites

5 When Hol"ofer'nes, the general of the Assyrian army, heard that the people of Israel had prepared for war and had closed the passes in the hills and had fortified all the high hilltops and set up barricades in the plains, [2]he was very angry. So he called together all the princes of Moab and the commanders of Ammon and all the governors of the coastland, [3]and said to them, "Tell me, you Canaanites, what people is this that lives in the hill country? What cities do they inhabit? How large is their army, and in what does their power or strength consist? Who rules over them as king, leading their army? [4]And why have they alone, of all who live in the west, refused to come out and meet me?"

Achior's Report

5 Then A'chior, the leader of all the Am'monites, said to him, "Let my lord now hear a word from the mouth of your servant, and I will tell you the truth about this people that dwells in the nearby mountain district. No falsehood shall come from your servant's mouth. [6]This people is descended from the Chalde'ans. [7]At one time they lived in Mesopota'mia, because they would not follow the gods of their fathers who were in Chaldea. [8]For they had left the ways of their ancestors, and they worshiped the God of heaven, the God they had come to know; hence they drove them out from the presence of their gods; and they fled to Mesopota'mia, and lived there for a long time. [9]Then their God commanded them to leave the place where they were living and go to the land of Canaan. There they settled, and prospered, with much gold and silver and very many cattle. [10]When a famine spread over Canaan they went down to Egypt and lived there as long as they had food; and there they became a great multitude—so great that they could not be counted. [11]So the king of Egypt became hostile to them; he took advantage of them and set them to making bricks, and humbled them and made slaves of them. [12]Then they cried out to their God, and he afflicted the whole land of Egypt with incurable plagues; and so the Egyptians drove them out of their sight. [13]Then God dried up the Red Sea before them, [14]and he led them by the way of Sinai and Ka'desh-bar'nea, and drove out all the people of the wilderness. [15]So they lived in the land of the Am'orites, and by their might destroyed all the inhabitants of Heshbon; and crossing over the Jordan they took possession of all the hill country. [16]And they drove out before them the Canaanites and the Per'izzites and the Jeb'usites and the She'chemites and all the Ger'gesites, and lived there a long time. [17]As long as they did not sin against their God they prospered, for the God who hates iniquity is with them. [18]But when they departed from the way which he had appointed for them, they were utterly defeated in many battles and were led away captive to a foreign country; the temple of their God was razed to the ground, and their cities were captured by their enemies. [19]But now they have returned to their God, and have come back from the places to which they were scattered, and have occupied Jerusalem, where their sanctuary is, and have settled in the hill country, because it was uninhabited. [20]Now therefore, my master and lord, if there is any unwitting error in this people and they sin against their God and we find out their offense, then we will go up and defeat them. [21]But if there is no transgression in their nation, then let my lord pass them by; for their Lord will defend them, and their God will protect them, and we shall be put to shame before the whole world."

22 When A'chior had finished saying this, all the men standing around the tent began to com-

plain; Hol"ofer'nes' officers and all the men from the seacoast and from Moab insisted that he must be put to death. [23] "For," they said, "we will not be afraid of the Israelites; they are a people with no strength or power for making war. [24]Therefore let us go up, Lord Hol"ofer'nes, and they will be devoured by your vast army."

Achior Handed over to the Israelites

6 When the disturbance made by the men outside the council died down, Hol"ofer'nes, the commander of the Assyrian army, said to A'chior and all the Moabites in the presence of all the foreign contingents:

2 "And who are you, A'chior, and you hirelings of E'phraim, to prophesy among us as you have done today and tell us not to make war against the people of Israel because their God will defend them? Who is God except Nebuchadnez'zar? [3]He will send his forces and will destroy them from the face of the earth, and their God will not deliver them—we the king's [f] servants will destroy them as one man. They cannot resist the might of our cavalry. [4]We will burn them up, [g] and their mountains will be drunk with their blood, and their fields will be full of their dead. They [h] cannot withstand us, but will utterly perish. So says King Nebuchadnez'zar, the lord of the whole earth. For he has spoken; none of his words shall be in vain.

5 "But you, A'chior, you Am'monite hireling, who have said these words on the day of your iniquity, you shall not see my face again from this day until I take revenge on this race that came out of Egypt. [6]Then the sword of my army and the spear [i] of my servants shall pierce your sides, and you shall fall among their wounded, when I return. [7]Now my slaves are going to take you back into the hill country and put you in one of the cities beside the passes, [8]and you will not die until you perish along with them. [9]If you really hope in your heart that they will not be taken, do not look downcast! I have spoken and none of my words shall fail."

10 Then Hol"ofer'nes ordered his slaves, who waited on him in his tent, to seize A'chior and take him to Beth"uli'a and hand him over to the men of Israel. [11]So the slaves took him and led him out of the camp into the plain, and from the plain they went up into the hill country and came to the springs below Beth"uli'a. [12]When the men of the city saw them, [j] they caught up their weapons and ran out of the city to the top of the hill, and all the slingers kept them from coming up by casting stones at them. [13]However, they got under the shelter of the hill and they bound A'chior and left him lying at the foot of the hill, and returned to their master.

14 Then the men of Israel came down from their city and found him; and they untied him and

brought him into Beth"uli'a and placed him before the magistrates of their city, [15]who in those days were Uzzi'ah the son of Micah, of the tribe of Simeon, and Chabris the son of Gotho'niel, and Charmis the son of Melchi'el. [16]They called together all the elders of the city, and all their young men and their women ran to the assembly; and they set A'chior in the midst of all their people, and Uzzi'ah asked him what had happened. [17]He answered and told them what had taken place at the council of Hol"ofer'nes, and all that he had said in the presence of the Assyrian leaders, and all that Holofernes had said so boastfully against the house of Israel. [18]Then the people fell down and worshiped God, and cried out to him, and said,

19 "O Lord God of heaven, behold their arrogance, and have pity on the humiliation of our people, and look this day upon the faces of those who are consecrated to you."

20 Then they consoled A'chior, and praised him greatly. [21]And Uzzi'ah took him from the assembly to his own house and gave a banquet for the elders; and all that night they called on the God of Israel for help.

The Campaign against Bethulia

7 The next day Hol"ofer'nes ordered his whole army, and all the allies who had joined him, to break camp and move against Beth"uli'a, and to seize the passes up into the hill country and make war on the Israelites. [2]So all their warriors moved their camp that day; their force of men of war was one hundred and seventy thousand infantry and twelve thousand cavalry, together with the baggage and the foot soldiers handling it, a very great multitude. [3]They encamped in the valley near Beth"uli'a, beside the spring, and they spread out in breadth over Do'than as far as Balba'im and in length from Bethulia to Cy'amon, which faces Esdrae'lon.

4 When the Israelites saw their vast numbers they were greatly terrified, and every one said to his neighbor, "These men will now lick up the face of the whole land; neither the high mountains nor the valleys nor the hills will bear their weight." [5]Then each man took up his weapons, and when they had kindled fires on their towers they remained on guard all that night.

6 On the second day Hol"ofer'nes led out all his cavalry in full view of the Israelites in Beth"uli'a, [7]and examined the approaches to the city, and visited the springs that supplied their water, and seized them and set guards of soldiers over them, and then returned to his army.

---

[f] Gk *his*.
[g] Other authorities add *with it*.
[h] Gk *The track of their feet*.
[i] Lat Syr: Gk *people*.
[j] Other authorities add *on the top of the hill*.

8 Then all the chieftains of the people of Esau and all the leaders of the Moabites and the commanders of the coastland came to him and said, ⁹"Let our lord hear a word, lest his army be defeated. ¹⁰For these people, the Israelites, do not rely on their spears but on the height of the mountains where they live, for it is not easy to reach the tops of their mountains. ¹¹Therefore, my lord, do not fight against them in battle array, and not a man of your army will fall. ¹²Remain in your camp, and keep all the men in your forces with you; only let your servants take possession of the spring of water that flows from the foot of the mountain—¹³for this is where all the people of Beth"uli'a get their water. So thirst will destroy them, and they will give up their city. We and our people will go up to the tops of the nearby mountains and camp there to keep watch that not a man gets out of the city. ¹⁴They and their wives and children will waste away with famine, and before the sword reaches them they will be strewn about in the streets where they live. ¹⁵So you will pay them back with evil, because they rebelled and did not receive you peaceably."

16 These words pleased Hol"ofer'nes and all his servants, and he gave orders to do as they had said. ¹⁷So the army of the Am'monites moved forward, together with five thousand Assyrians, and they encamped in the valley and seized the water supply and the springs of the Israelites. ¹⁸And the sons of Esau and the sons of Ammon went up and encamped in the hill country opposite Do'than; and they sent some of their men toward the south and the east, toward Ac'raba, which is near Chu'si beside the brook Moch'mur. The rest of the Assyrian army encamped in the plain, and covered the whole face of the land, and their tents and supply trains spread out in great number, and they formed a vast multitude.

The Distress of the Israelites

19 The people of Israel cried out to the Lord their God, for their courage failed, because all their enemies had surrounded them and there was no way of escape from them. ²⁰The whole Assyrian army, their infantry, chariots, and cavalry, surrounded them for thirty-four days, until all the vessels of water belonging to every inhabitant of Beth"uli'a were empty; ²¹their cisterns were going dry, and they did not have enough water to drink their fill for a single day, because it was measured out to them to drink. ²²Their children lost heart, and the women and young men fainted from thirst and fell down in the streets of the city and in the passages through the gates; there was no strength left in them any longer.

23 Then all the people, the young men, the women, and the children, gathered about Uzzi'ah and the rulers of the city and cried out with a loud voice, and said before all the elders, ²⁴"God be judge between you and us! For you have done us a great injury in not making peace with the Assyrians. ²⁵For now we have no one to help us; God has sold us into their hands, to strew us on the ground before them with thirst and utter destruction. ²⁶Now call them in and surrender the whole city to the army of Hol"ofer'nes and to all his forces, to be plundered. ²⁷For it would be better for us to be captured by them; ᵏ for we will be slaves, but our lives will be spared, and we shall not witness the death of our infants before our eyes, or see our wives and children draw their last breath. ²⁸We call to witness against you heaven and earth and our God, the Lord of our fathers, who punishes us according to our sins and the sins of our fathers. Let him not do this day the things which we have described!"

29 Then great and general lamentation arose throughout the assembly, and they cried out to the Lord God with a loud voice. ³⁰And Uzzi'ah said to them, "Have courage, my brothers! Let us hold out for five more days; by that time the Lord our God will restore to us his mercy, for he will not forsake us utterly. ³¹But if these days pass by, and no help comes for us, I will do what you say."

32 Then he dismissed the people to their various posts, and they went up on the walls and towers of their city. The women and children he sent home. And they were greatly depressed in the city.

The Character of Judith

8 At that time Judith heard about these things: she was the daughter of Merar'i the son of Ox, son of Joseph, son of O'ziel, son of Elki'ah, son of Anani'as, son of Gideon, son of Raph'aim, son of Ahi'tub, son of Eli'jah, son of Hilki'ah, son of Eliab, son of Nathan'a-el, son of Sala'miel, son of Sara'sadai, son of Israel.* ²Her husband Manas'seh, who belonged to her tribe and family, had died during the barley harvest. ³For as he stood overseeing the men who were binding sheaves in the field, he was overcome by the burning heat, and took to his bed and died in Beth"uli'a his city. So they buried him with his fathers in the field between Do'than and Bal'amon. ⁴Judith had lived at home as a widow for three years and four months. ⁵She set up a tent for herself on the roof of her house, and belted sackcloth about her loins and wore the garments of her widowhood. ⁶She fasted all the days of her widowhood, except the day before the sabbath and the sabbath itself, the day before the new moon and the day of the new moon, and the feasts and days of rejoicing of the house of Israel. ⁷She was beautiful in appearance, and had a very lovely face; she was prudent of heart, discerning in judgment, and quite virtuous.

ᵏ Other authorities add *than to die of thirst.*
* 8:1: The names in this genealogy differ in the various texts and versions.

Her husband Manas'seh, the son of Joseph, the son of Ahi'tub, the son of Melchis, the son of E'liab, the son of Nathan'a-el, the son of Sara'-sadai, the son of Simeon, had left her gold and silver, and men and women slaves, and cattle, and fields; and she maintained this estate. [8]No one spoke ill of her, for she feared God with great devotion.

Judith Rebukes the Elders

9 When Judith heard the wicked words spoken by the people against the ruler, because they were faint for lack of water, and when she heard all that Uzziah said to them, and how he promised them under oath to surrender the city to the Assyrians after five days, [10]she sent her maid, who was in charge of all she possessed, to summon [1] Chabris and Charmis, the elders of her city. [11]They came to her, and she said to them,

"Listen to me, rulers of the people of Beth"uli'a! What you have said to the people today is not right; you have even sworn and pronounced this oath between God and you, promising to surrender the city to our enemies unless the Lord turns and helps us within so many days. [12]Who are you, that have put God to the test this day, and are setting yourselves up in the place of [m] God among the sons of men? [13]You are putting the Lord Almighty to the test—but you will never know anything! [14]You cannot plumb the depths of the human heart, nor find out what a man is thinking; how do you expect to search out God, who made all these things, and find out his mind or comprehend his thought? No, my brethren, do not provoke the Lord our God to anger. [15]For if he does not choose to help us within these five days, he has power to protect us within any time he pleases, or even to destroy us in the presence of our enemies. [16]Do not try to bind the purposes of the Lord our God; for God is not like man, to be threatened, nor like a human being, to be won over by pleading. [17]Therefore, while we wait for his deliverance, let us call upon him to help us, and he will hear our voice, if it pleases him.

18 "For never in our generation, nor in these present days, has there been any tribe or family or people or city of ours which worshiped gods made with hands, as was done in days gone by— [19]and that was why our fathers were handed over to the sword, and to be plundered, and so they suffered a great catastrophe before our enemies. [20]But we know no other god but him, and therefore we hope that he will not disdain us or any of our nation. [21]For if we are captured all Jude'a will be captured and our sanctuary will be plundered; and he will exact of us [n] the penalty for its desecration. [22]And the slaughter of our brethren and the captivity of the land and the desolation of our inheritance—all this he will bring upon our heads among the Gentiles, wherever we serve as slaves;

and we shall be an offense and a reproach in the eyes of those who acquire us. [23]For our slavery will not bring us into favor, but the Lord our God will turn it to dishonor.

24 "Now therefore, brethren, let us set an example to our brethren, for their lives depend upon us, and the sanctuary and the temple and the altar rest upon us. [25]In spite of everything let us give thanks to the Lord our God, who is putting us to the test as he did our forefathers. [26]Remember what he did with Abraham, and how he tested Isaac, and what happened to Jacob in Mesopota'mia in Syria, while he was keeping the sheep of La'ban, his mother's brother. [27]For he has not tried us with fire, as he did them, to search their hearts, nor has he taken revenge upon us; but the Lord scourges those who draw near to him, in order to admonish them."

28 Then Uzzi'ah said to her, "All that you have said has been spoken out of a true heart, and there is no one who can deny your words. [29]Today is not the first time your wisdom has been shown, but from the beginning of your life all the people have recognized your understanding, for your heart's disposition is right. [30]But the people were very thirsty, and they compelled us to do for them what we have promised, and made us take an oath which we cannot break. [31]So pray for us, since you are a devout woman, and the Lord will send us rain to fill our cisterns and we will no longer be faint."

32 Judith said to them, "Listen to me. I am about to do a thing which will go down through all generations of our descendants. [33]Stand at the city gate tonight, and I will go out with my maid; and within the days after which you have promised to surrender the city to our enemies, the Lord will deliver Israel by my hand. [34]Only, do not try to find out what I plan; for I will not tell you until I have finished what I am about to do."

35 Uzzi'ah and the rulers said to her, "Go in peace, and may the Lord God go before you, to take revenge upon our enemies." [36]So they returned from the tent and went to their posts.

The Prayer of Judith

9 Then Judith fell upon her face, and put ashes on her head, and uncovered the sackcloth she was wearing; and at the very time when that evening's incense was being offered in the house of God in Jerusalem, Judith cried out to the Lord with a loud voice, and said,

2 "O Lord God of my father Simeon, to whom you gave a sword to take revenge on the strangers who had loosed the girdle [o] of a virgin to defile her, and uncovered her thigh to put her to shame,

---

[1] Some authorities add *Uzziah and* (see verses 28 and 35).
[m] Or *above*.
[n] Gk *our blood*.
[o] Cn: Gk *womb*.

and polluted her womb to disgrace her; for you have said, 'It shall not be done'—yet they did it. [3]So you gave up their rulers to be slain, and their bed, which was ashamed of the deceit they had practiced, to be stained with blood, and you struck down slaves along with princes, and princes on their thrones; [4]and you gave their wives for a prey and their daughters to captivity, and all their booty to be divided among your beloved sons, who were zealous for you, and abhorred the pollution of their blood, and called on you for help—O God, my God, hear me also, a widow.

5 "For you have done these things and those that went before and those that followed; you have designed the things that are now, and those that are to come. Yes, the things you intended came to pass, [6]and the things you willed presented themselves and said, 'Behold, we are here'; for all your ways are prepared in advance, and your judgment is with foreknowledge.

7 "Behold now, the Assyrians are increased in their might; they are exalted, with their horses and riders; they glory in the strength of their foot soldiers; they trust in shield and spear, in bow and sling, and know not that you are the Lord who crushes wars; the Lord is your name. [8]Break their strength by your might, and bring down their power in your anger; for they intend to defile your sanctuary, and to pollute the tabernacle where your glorious name rests, and to cast down the horn of your altar with the sword. [9]Behold their pride, and send your wrath upon their heads; give to me, a widow, the strength to do what I plan. [10]By the deceit of my lips strike down the slave with the prince and the prince with his servant; crush their arrogance by the hand of a woman.

11 "For your power depends not upon numbers, nor your might upon men of strength; for you are God of the lowly, helper of the oppressed, upholder of the weak, protector of the forlorn, savior of those without hope. [12]Hear, O hear me, God of my father, God of the inheritance of Israel, Lord of heaven and earth, Creator of the waters, King of all your creation, hear my prayer! [13]Make my deceitful words to be their wound and stripe, for they have planned cruel things against your covenant, and against your consecrated house, and against the top of Zion, and against the house possessed by your children. [14]And cause your whole nation and every tribe to know and understand that you are God, the God of all power and might, and that there is no other who protects the people of Israel but you alone!"

Judith Prepares to Go to Holofernes

10 When Judith[p] had ceased crying out to the God of Israel, and had ended all these words, [2]she rose from where she lay prostrate and called her maid and went down into the house

where she lived on sabbaths and on her feast days; [3]and she removed the sackcloth which she had been wearing, and took off her widow's garments, and bathed her body with water, and anointed herself with precious ointment, and combed her hair and put on a tiara, and arrayed herself in her most festive apparel, which she used to wear while her husband Manas'seh was living. [4]And she put sandals on her feet, and put on her anklets and bracelets and rings, and her earrings and all her ornaments,* and made herself very beautiful, to entice the eyes of all men who might see her. [5]And she gave her maid a bottle of wine and a flask of oil, and filled a bag with parched grain and a cake of dried fruit and fine bread; and she wrapped up all her vessels and gave them to her to carry.

6 Then they went out to the city gate of Beth"uli'a, and found Uzzi'ah standing there with the elders of the city, Chabris and Charmis. [7]When they saw her, and noted how her face was altered and her clothing changed, they greatly admired her beauty, and said to her, [8]"May the God of our fathers grant you favor and fulfil your plans, that the people of Israel may glory and Jerusalem may be exalted." And she worshiped God.

9 Then she said to them, "Order the gate of the city to be opened for me, and I will go out and accomplish the things about which you spoke with me." So they ordered the young men to open the gate for her, as she had said. [10]When they had done this, Judith went out, she and her maid with her; and the men of the city watched her until she had gone down the mountain and passed through the valley and they could no longer see her.

Judith Is Captured

11 The women[q] went straight on through the valley; and an Assyrian patrol met her [12]and took her into custody, and asked her, "To what people do you belong, and where are you coming from, and where are you going?" She replied, "I am a daughter of the Hebrews, but I am fleeing from them, for they are about to be handed over to you to be devoured. [13]I am on my way to the presence of Hol"ofer'nes the commander of your army, to give him a true report; and I will show him a way by which he can go and capture all the hill country without losing one of his men, captured or slain."

14 When the men heard her words, and observed her face—she was in their eyes marvelously beautiful—they said to her, [15]"You have saved your life by hurrying down to the presence

---

[p] Gk *she.*

[q] Gk *They.*

* 10:4: The remainder of this verse reads in the Vulgate (verse 4): "[4]And the Lord also gave her more beauty: because all this dressing–up did not proceed from sensuality, but from virtue: and therefore the Lord increased this her beauty, so that she appeared to all men's eyes incomparably lovely."

of our lord. Go at once to his tent; some of us will escort you and hand you over to him. [16]And when you stand before him, do not be afraid in your heart, but tell him just what you have said, and he will treat you well."

17 They chose from their number a hundred men to accompany her and her maid, and they brought them to the tent of Hol″ofer′nes. [18]There was great excitement in the whole camp, for her arrival was reported from tent to tent, and they came and stood around her as she waited outside the tent of Hol″ofer′nes while they told him about her. [19]And they marveled at her beauty, and admired the Israelites, judging them by her, and every one said to his neighbor, "Who can despise these people, who have women like this among them? Surely not a man of them had better be left alive, for if we let them go they will be able to ensnare the whole world!"

Judith Is Brought before Holofernes

20 Then Hol″ofer′nes' companions and all his servants came out and led her into the tent. [21]Hol″ofer′nes was resting on his bed, under a canopy which was woven with purple and gold and emeralds and precious stones. [22]When they told him of her he came forward to the front of the tent, with silver lamps carried before him. [23]And when Judith came into the presence of Hol″ofer′nes *ʳ* and his servants, they all marveled at the beauty of her face; and she prostrated herself and made obeisance to him, and his slaves raised her up.

11 Then Hol″ofer′nes said to her, "Take courage, woman, and do not be afraid in your heart, for I have never hurt any one who chose to serve Nebuchadnez′zar, the king of all the earth. [2]And even now, if your people who live in the hill country had not slighted me, I would never have lifted my spear against them; but they have brought all this on themselves. [3]And now tell me why you have fled from them and have come over to us—since you have come to safety. [4]Have courage; you will live, tonight and from now on. No one will hurt you, but all will treat you well, as they do the servants of my lord King Nebuchadnez′zar."

Judith Deceives Holofernes

5 Judith replied to him, "Accept the words of your servant, and let your maidservant speak in your presence, and I will tell nothing false to my lord this night. [6]And if you follow out the words of your maidservant, God will accomplish something through you, and my lord will not fail to achieve his purposes. [7]Nebuchadnez′zar the king of the whole earth lives, and as his power endures, who had sent you to direct every living soul, not only do men serve him because of you, but also the beasts of the field and the cattle and the birds of the air will live by your power under

Nebuchadnezzar and all his house. [8]For we have heard of your wisdom and skill, and it is reported throughout the whole world that you are the one good man in the whole kingdom, thoroughly informed and marvelous in military strategy.

9 "Now as for the things A′chior said in your council, we have heard his words, for the men of Beth″uli′a spared him and he told them all he had said to you. [10]Therefore, my lord and master, do not disregard what he said, but keep it in your mind, for it is true: our nation cannot be punished, nor can the sword prevail against them, unless they sin against their God.

11 "And now, in order that my lord may not be defeated and his purpose frustrated, death will fall upon them, for a sin has overtaken them by which they are about to provoke their God to anger when they do what is wrong. [12]Since their food supply is exhausted and their water has almost given out, they have planned to kill their cattle and have determined to use all that God by his laws has forbidden them to eat. [13]They have decided to consume the first fruits of the grain and the tithes of the wine and oil, which they had consecrated and set aside for the priests who minister in the presence of our God at Jerusalem—although it is not lawful for any of the people so much as to touch these things with their hands. [14]They have sent men to Jerusalem, because even the people living there have been doing this, to bring back to them permission from the senate. [15]When the word reaches them and they proceed to do this, on that day they will be handed over to you to be destroyed.

16 "Therefore, when I, your servant, learned all this, I fled from them; and God has sent me to accomplish with you things that will astonish the whole world, as many as shall hear about them. [17]For your servant is religious, and serves the God of heaven day and night; therefore, my lord, I will remain with you, and every night your servant will go out into the valley, and I will pray to God and he will tell me when they have committed their sins. [18]And I will come and tell you, and then you shall go out with your whole army, and not one of them will withstand you. [19]Then I will lead you through the middle of Jude′a, till you come to Jerusalem; and I will set your throne *ˢ* in the midst of it; and you will lead them like sheep that have no shepherd, and not a dog will so much as open its mouth to growl at you. For this has been told me, by my foreknowledge; it was announced to me, and I was sent to tell you."

20 Her words pleased Hol″ofer′nes and all his servants, and they marveled at her wisdom and said, [21]"There is not such a woman from one end

---

ʳ Gk him.
ˢ Or chariot.

of the earth to the other, either for beauty of face or wisdom of speech!" ²²And Hol"ofer'nes said to her, "God has done well to send you before the people, to lend strength to our hands and to bring destruction upon those who have slighted my lord. ²³You are not only beautiful in appearance, but wise in speech; and if you do as you have said, your God shall be my God, and you shall live in the house of King Nebuchadnez'zar and be renowned throughout the whole world."

Judith as a Guest of Holofernes

12 Then he commanded them to bring her in where his silver dishes were kept, and ordered them to set a table for her with some of his own food and to serve her with his own wine. ²But Judith said, "I cannot eat it, lest it be an offense; but I will be provided from the things I have brought with me." ³Hol"ofer'nes said to her, "If your supply runs out, where can we get more like it for you? For none of your people is here with us." ⁴Judith replied, "As your soul lives, my lord, your servant will not use up the things I have with me before the Lord carries out by my hand what he has determined to do."

5 Then the servants of Hol"ofer'nes brought her into the tent, and she slept until midnight. Along toward the morning watch she arose ⁶and sent to Hol"ofer'nes and said, "Let my lord now command that your servant be permitted to go out and pray." ⁷So Hol"ofer'nes commanded his guards not to hinder her. And she remained in the camp for three days, and went out each night to the valley of Beth"uli'a, and bathed at the spring in the camp. ^{t 8}When she came up from the spring she prayed the Lord God of Israel to direct her way for the raising up of her people. ⁹So she returned clean and stayed in the tent until she ate her food toward evening.

Judith Attends Holofernes' Banquet

10 On the fourth day Hol"ofer'nes held a banquet for his slaves only, and did not invite any of his officers. ¹¹And he said to Bago'as, the eunuch who had charge of all his personal affairs, "Go now and persuade the Hebrew woman who is in your care to join us and eat and drink with us. ¹²For it will be a disgrace if we let such a woman go without enjoying her company, for if we do not embrace her she will laugh at us." ¹³So Bago'as went out from the presence of Hol"ofer'nes, and approached her and said, "This beautiful maid-servant will please come to my lord and be honored in his presence, and drink wine and be merry with us, and become today like one of the daughters of the Assyrians who serve in the house of Nebuchadnez'zar." ¹⁴And Judith said, "Who am I, to refuse my lord? Surely whatever pleases him I will do at once, and it will be a joy to me until the day of my death!" ¹⁵So she got up and arrayed herself in all her woman's finery, and her maid

went and spread on the ground for her before Hol"ofer'nes the soft fleeces which she had received from Bago'as for her daily use, so that she might recline on them when she ate.

16 Then Judith came in and lay down, and Hol"ofer'nes' heart was ravished with her and he was moved with great desire to possess her; for he had been waiting for an opportunity to deceive her, ever since the day he first saw her. ¹⁷So Hol"ofer'nes said to her, "Drink now, and be merry with us!" ¹⁸Judith said, "I will drink now, my lord, because my life means more to me today than in all the days since I was born." ¹⁹Then she took and ate and drank before him what her maid had prepared. ²⁰And Hol"ofer'nes was greatly pleased with her, and drank a great quantity of wine, much more than he had ever drunk in any one day since he was born.

Judith Beheads Holofernes

13 When evening came, his slaves quickly withdrew, and Bago'as closed the tent from outside and shut out the attendants from his master's presence; and they went to bed, for they all were weary because the banquet had lasted long. ²So Judith was left alone in the tent, with Hol"ofer'nes stretched out on his bed, for he was overcome with wine.

3 Now Judith had told her maid to stand outside the bedchamber and to wait for her to come out, as she did every day; for she said she would be going out for her prayers. And she had said the same thing to Bago'as. ⁴So every one went out, and no one, either small or great, was left in the bedchamber. Then Judith, standing beside his bed, said in her heart, "O Lord God of all might, look in this hour upon the work of my hands for the exaltation of Jerusalem. ⁵For now is the time to help your inheritance, and to carry out my undertaking for the destruction of the enemies who have risen up against us."

6 She went up to the post at the end of the bed, above Hol"ofer'nes' head, and took down his sword that hung there. ⁷She came close to his bed and took hold of the hair of his head, and said, "Give me strength this day, O Lord God of Israel!" ⁸And she struck his neck twice with all her might, and severed his head from his body. ⁹Then she tumbled his body off the bed and pulled down the canopy from the posts; after a moment she went out, and gave Hol"ofer'nes' head to her maid, ¹⁰who placed it in her food bag.

Then the two of them went out together, as they were accustomed to go for prayer; and they passed through the camp and circled around the valley and went up the mountain to Beth"uli'a and came to its gates. ¹¹Judith called out from afar to the watchmen at the gates, "Open, open the

---

^t Other authorities omit *in the camp.*

gate! God, our God, is still with us, to show his power in Israel, and his strength against our enemies, even as he has done this day!"

Judith Returns to Her People

12 When the men of her city heard her voice, they hurried down to the city gate and called together the elders of the city. [13]They all ran together, both small and great, for it was unbelievable that she had returned; they opened the gate and admitted them, and they kindled a fire for light, and gathered around them. [14]Then she said to them with a loud voice, "Praise God, O praise him! Praise God, who has not withdrawn his mercy from the house of Israel, but has destroyed our enemies by my hand this very night!"

15 Then she took the head out of the bag and showed it to them, and said, "See, here is the head of Hol"ofer'nes, the commander of the Assyrian army, and here is the canopy beneath which he lay in his drunken stupor. The Lord has struck him down by the hand of a woman. [16]As the Lord lives, who has protected me in the way I went, it was my face that tricked him to his destruction, and yet he committed no act of sin with me, to defile and shame me."

17 All the people were greatly astonished, and bowed down and worshiped God, and said with one accord, "Blessed are you, our God, who have brought into contempt this day the enemies of your people."

18 And Uzzi'ah said to her, "O daughter, you are blessed by the Most High God above all women on earth; and blessed be the Lord God, who created the heavens and the earth, who has guided you to strike the head of the leader of our enemies. [19]Your hope will never depart from the hearts of men, as they remember the power of God. [20]May God grant this to be a perpetual honor to you, and may he visit you with blessings, because you did not spare your own life when our nation was brought low, but have avenged our ruin, walking in the straight path before our God." And all the people said, "So be it, so be it!" *

Judith's Counsel

14 Then Judith said to them, "Listen to me, my brethren, and take this head and hang it upon the parapet of your wall. [2]And as soon as morning comes and the sun rises, let every valiant man take his weapons and go out of the city, and set a captain over them, as if you were going down to the plain against the Assyrian outpost; only do not go down. [3]Then they will seize their arms and go into the camp and rouse the officers of the Assyrian army; and they will rush into the tent of Hol"ofer'nes, and will not find him. Then fear will come over them, and they will flee before you, [4]and you and all who live within the borders of Israel shall pursue them and cut them down as they flee. [5]But before you do all this, bring A'chior

the Am'monite to me, and let him see and recognize the man who despised the house of Israel and sent him to us as if to his death."

6 So they summoned A'chior from the house of Uzzi'ah. And when he came and saw the head of Hol"ofer'nes in the hand of one of the men at the gathering of the people, he fell down on his face and his spirit failed him. [7]And when they raised him up he fell at Judith's feet, and knelt before her, and said, "Blessed are you in every tent of Judah! In every nation those who hear your name will be alarmed. [8]Now tell me what you have done during these days."

Then Judith described to him in the presence of the people all that she had done, from the day she left until the moment of her speaking to them. [9]And when she had finished, the people raised a great shout and made a joyful noise in their city. [10]And when A'chior saw all that the God of Israel had done, he believed firmly in God, and was circumcised, and joined the house of Israel, remaining so to this day.

Holofernes' Death Is Discovered

11 As soon as it was dawn they hung the head of Hol"ofer'nes on the wall, and every man took his weapons, and they went out in companies to the passes in the mountains. [12]And when the Assyrians saw them they sent word to their commanders, and they went to the generals and the captains and to all their officers. [13]So they came to Hol"ofer'nes' tent and said to the steward in charge of all his personal affairs, "Wake up our lord, for the slaves have been so bold as to come down against us to give battle in order to be destroyed completely."

14 So Bago'as went in and knocked at the door of the tent, for he supposed that he was sleeping with Judith. [15]But when no one answered, he opened it and went into the bedchamber and found him thrown down on the platform dead, with his head cut off and missing. [16]And he cried out with a loud voice and wept and groaned and shouted, and tore his garments. [17]Then he went to the tent where Judith had stayed, and when he did not find her he rushed out to the people and shouted, [18]"The slaves have tricked us! One Hebrew woman has brought disgrace upon the house of King Nebuchadnez'zar! For look, here is

---

* 13:20: Vulgate adds (verses 27-31): "[27]And Achior being called for came, and Judith said to him: The God of Israel, to whom you gave testimony, that he revenge himself of his enemies, he has cut off the head of all the unbelievers this night by my hand. [28]And that you may find that it is so, behold the head of Holofernes, who in the contempt of his pride despised the God of Israel, and threatened you with death, saying: When the people of Israel shall be taken, I will command your sides to be pierced with a sword. [29]Then Achior, seeing the head of Holofernes, being seized with a great fear he fell on his face upon the earth, and his soul swooned away. [30]But after he had recovered his spirits, he fell down at her feet, and reverenced her, and said: [31]Blessed are you by your God in every tabernacle of Jacob, for in every nation which shall hear your name, the God of Israel shall be magnified on occasion of you."

Hol"ofer'nes lying on the ground, and his head is not on him!"

19 When the leaders of the Assyrian army heard this, they tore their tunics and were greatly dismayed, and their loud cries and shouts arose in the midst of the camp.

The Assyrian Army Flees

15 When the men in the tents heard it, they were amazed at what had happened. [2]Fear and trembling came over them, so that they did not wait for one another, but with one impulse all rushed out and fled by every path across the plain and through the hill country. [3]Those who had camped in the hills around Beth"uli'a also took to flight. Then the men of Israel, every one that was a soldier, rushed out upon them. [4]And Uzz'iah sent men to Bet"omastha'im and Bebai and Choba and Ko'la, and to all the frontiers of Israel, to tell what had taken place and to urge all to rush out upon their enemies to destroy them. [5]And when the Israelites heard it, with one accord they fell upon the enemy, [u] and cut them down as far as Cho'ba. Those in Jerusalem and all the hill country also came, for they were told what had happened in the camp of the enemy; and those in Gilead and in Galilee outflanked them with great slaughter, even beyond Damascus and its borders. [6]The rest of the people of Beth"uli'a fell upon the Assyrian camp and plundered it, and were greatly enriched. [7]And the Israelites, when they returned from the slaughter, took possession of what remained, and the villages and towns in the hill country and in the plain got a great amount of booty, for there was a vast quantity of it.

The Israelites Celebrate

8 Then Jo'akim the high priest, and the senate of the people of Israel who lived at Jerusalem, came to witness the good things which the Lord had done for Israel, and to see Judith and to greet her. [9]And when they met her they all blessed her with one accord and said to her, "You are the exaltation of Jerusalem,* you are the great glory of Israel, you are the great pride of our nation! [10]You have done all this singlehanded; you have done great good to Israel, and God is well pleased with it. May the Almighty Lord bless you for ever!" And all the people said, "So be it!"

11 So all the people plundered the camp for thirty days. They gave Judith the tent of Hol"ofer'nes and all his silver dishes and his beds and his bowls and all his furniture; and she took them and loaded her mule and hitched up her carts and piled the things on them.

12 Then all the women of Israel gathered to see her, and blessed her, and some of them performed a dance for her; and she took branches in her hands and gave them to the women who were with her; [13]and they crowned themselves with olive wreaths, she and those who were with her;

and she went before all the people in the dance, leading all the women, while all the men of Israel followed, bearing their arms and wearing garlands and with songs on their lips.

The Song of Praise of Judith

16 Then Judith began this thanksgiving before all Israel, and all the people loudly sang this song of praise. [2]And Judith said,

Begin a song to my God with tambourines,
  sing to my Lord with cymbals.
Raise to him a new psalm; [v]
  exalt him, and call upon his name.
[3]For God is the Lord who crushes wars;
  for he has delivered me out of the hands of
    my pursuers,
  and brought me to his camp, in the midst of
    the people.

[4]The Assyrian came down from the mountains
  of the north;
  he came with myriads of his warriors;
  their multitude blocked up the valleys,
  their cavalry covered the hills.
[5]He boasted that he would burn up my
    territory,
  and kill my young men with the sword,
and dash my infants to the ground
  and seize my children as prey,
  and take my virgins as booty.

[6]But the Lord Almighty has foiled them
  by the hand of a woman.
[7]For their mighty one did not fall by the hands
  of the young men,
  nor did the sons of the Titans strike him,
  nor did tall giants set upon him;
but Judith the daughter of Merar'i undid him
  with the beauty of her countenance.

[8]For she took off her widow's mourning
  to exalt the oppressed in Israel.
She anointed her face with ointment
  and fastened her hair with a tiara
  and put on a linen gown to deceive him.
[9]Her sandal ravished his eyes,
  her beauty captivated his mind,
  and the sword severed his neck.
[10]The Persians trembled at her boldness,
  the Medes were daunted at her daring.

[11]Then my oppressed people shouted for joy;
  my weak people shouted [w] and the enemy [x]
    trembled;

---

[u] Gk *them.*
[v] Other authorities read *a psalm and praise.*
[w] Other authorities read *feared.*
[x] Gk *they.*
*15:9, *You are the exaltation of Jerusalem:* This passage is included in the office for feasts of the Blessed Virgin Mary, e.g., the little chapter for None on the Assumption, 15 August.

they lifted up their voices, and the enemy *
    were turned back.
[12]The sons of maidservants have pierced them
    through;
    they were wounded like the children of
        fugitives,
    they perished before the army of my Lord.

[13]I will sing to my God a new song:
    O Lord, you are great and glorious,
        wonderful in strength, invincible.
[14]Let all your creatures serve you,
    for you spoke, and they were made.
    You sent forth your Spirit, ʸ and it formed
        them;
    there is none that can resist your voice.
[15]For the mountains shall be shaken to their
        foundations with the waters;
    at your presence the rocks shall melt like
        wax,
    but to those who fear you
        you will continue to show mercy.
[16]For every sacrifice as a fragrant offering is a
        small thing,
    and all fat for burnt offerings to you is a
        very little thing,
    but he who fears the Lord shall be great for
        ever.

[17]Woe to the nations that rise up against my
        people!
    The Lord Almighty will take vengeance on
        them in the day of judgment;
    fire and worms he will give to their flesh;
        they shall weep in pain for ever.

18 When they arrived at Jerusalem they worshiped God. As soon as the people were purified, they offered their burnt offerings, their freewill offerings, and their gifts. [19]Judith also dedicated to God all the vessels of Hol"ofer'nes, which the people had given her; and the canopy which she took for herself from his bedchamber she gave as a votive offering to the Lord. [20]So the people continued feasting in Jerusalem before the sanctuary for three months, and Judith remained with them.

The Renown and Death of Judith

21 After this every one returned home to his own inheritance, and Judith went to Beth"uli'a, and remained on her estate, and was honored in her time throughout the whole country. [22]Many desired to marry her, but she remained a widow all the days of her life after Manas'seh her husband died and was gathered to his people. [23]She became more and more famous, and grew old in her husband's house, until she was one hundred and five years old. She set her maid free. She died in Beth"uli'a, and they buried her in the cave of her husband Manas'seh, [24]and the house of Israel mourned for her seven days. Before she died she distributed her property to all those who were next of kin to her husband Manas'seh, and to her own nearest kindred. [25]And no one ever again spread terror among the people of Israel in the days of Judith, or for a long time after her death.*

ˣ Gk *they*.
ʸ Or *breath*.
* 16:25: Vulgate adds (verse 31): " [31]But the day of the festivity of this victory is received by the Hebrews in the number of holy days, and is religiously observed by the Jews from that time until this day."

THE BOOK OF
ESTHER

Mordecai's Dream

11 *[2]In the second year of the reign of Artaxerxes the Great, on the first day of Nisan, Mordecai the son of Jair, son of Shimei, son of Kish, of the tribe of Benjamin, had a dream. [3]He was a Jew, dwelling in the city of Susa, a great man, serving in the court of the king. [4]He was one of the captives whom Nebuchadnezzar king of Babylon had brought from Jerusalem with Jeconiah king of Judea. And this was his dream:*

5 Behold, noise [a] and confusion, thunders and earthquake, tumult upon the earth! [6]And behold, two great dragons came forward, both ready to fight, and they roared terribly. [7]And at their roaring every nation prepared for war, to fight against the nation of the righteous. [8]And behold, a day of darkness and gloom, tribulation and distress, affliction and great tumult upon the earth! [9]And the whole righteous nation was troubled; they feared the evils that threatened them, and were ready to perish. [10]Then they cried to God; and from their cry, as though from a tiny spring, there came a great river, with abundant water; [11]light came, and the sun rose, and the lowly were exalted and consumed those held in honor.

12 Mordecai saw in this dream what God had determined to do, and after he awoke he had it on his mind and sought all day to understand it in every detail.

Mordecai Discovers a Plot against the King

12 *Now Mordecai took his rest in the courtyard with Gabatha and Tharra, the two eunuchs of the king who kept watch in the courtyard. [2]He overheard their conversation and inquired into their purposes, and learned that they were preparing to lay hands upon Artaxerxes the king; and he informed the king concerning them. [3]Then the king examined the two eunuchs, and when they confessed they were led to execution. [4]The king made a permanent record of these things, and Mordecai wrote an account of them. [5]And the king ordered Mordecai to serve in the court and rewarded him for these things. [6]But Haman, the son of Hammedatha, a Bougaean, was in great honor with the king, and he sought to injure Mordecai and his people because of the two eunuchs of the king.*

King Ahasuerus Deposes Queen Vashti

1 In the days of Ahas′u-e′rus, the Ahasu-erus who reigned from India to Ethiopia over one hundred and twenty-seven provinces, [2]in those days when King Ahas′u-e′rus sat on his royal throne in Susa the capital, [3]in the third year of his reign he gave a banquet for all his princes and servants, the army chiefs [a] of Persia and Med′ia and the nobles and governors of the provinces being before him, [4]while he showed the riches of his royal glory and the splendor and pomp of his majesty for many days, a hundred and eighty days. [5]And when these days were completed, the king gave for all the people present in Susa the capital, both great and small, a banquet lasting for seven days, in the court of the garden of the king's palace. [6]There were white cotton curtains and blue hangings caught up with cords of fine linen and purple to silver rings [b] and marble pillars, and also couches of gold and silver on a mosaic pavement of porphyry, marble, mother-of-pearl and precious stones. [7]Drinks were served in golden goblets, goblets of different kinds, and the royal wine was lavished according to the bounty of the king. [8]And drinking was according to the law, no one was compelled; for the king had given orders to all the officials of his palace to do as every man desired. [9]Queen Vashti also gave a banquet for the women in the palace which belonged to King Ahas′u-e′rus.

10 On the seventh day, when the heart of the king was merry with wine, he commanded Mehu′man, Biztha, Harbo′na, Bigtha and Abagtha, Ze′thar and Car′kas, the seven eunuchs who served King Ahas′u-e′rus as chamberlains, [11]to bring Queen Vashti before the king with her royal

---

Set in the Persian capital Susa, this story relates how God saved his people from the hands of an enemy, this time in a foreign country. As in the book of Judith, the deliverance is brought about through the instrumentality of a woman. The book gives details for the keeping of the feast of Purim in memory of this deliverance.

[a] Or *voices.*

[a] Heb *the army.*

[b] Or *rods.*

* 11:2: The disarrangement of the chapter and verse order is due to the insertion of the deuterocanonical portions in their logical place in the story of Esther, as narrated in the Greek version from which they are taken. They are printed in italics to enable the reader to recognize them at once.

In the old Vulgate these portions were placed by Jerome immediately after the Hebrew text of Esther, regardless of their logical position, because he himself did not regard them as canonical. Hence they came to be numbered 10:4—16:24. It has been thought best to leave the chapter and verse numbering unchanged in the present edition.

crown, in order to show the peoples and the princes her beauty; for she was fair to behold. [12]But Queen Vashti refused to come at the king's command conveyed by the eunuchs. At this the king was enraged, and his anger burned within him.

13 Then the king said to the wise men who knew the times—for this was the king's procedure toward all who were versed in law and judgment, [14]the men next to him being Carshe'na, She'thar, Adma'tha, Tar'shish, Me'res, Marse'na, and Memu'can, the seven princes of Persia and Med'ia, who saw the king's face, and sat first in the kingdom—: [15]"According to the law, what is to be done to Queen Vashti, because she has not performed the command of King Ahas'u-e'rus conveyed by the eunuchs?" [16]Then Memu'can said in presence of the king and the princes, "Not only to the king has Queen Vashti done wrong, but also to all the princes and all the peoples who are in all the provinces of King Ahas'u-e'rus. [17]For this deed of the queen will be made known to all women, causing them to look with contempt upon their husbands, since they will say, 'King Ahas'u-e'rus commanded Queen Vashti to be brought before him, and she did not come.' [18]This very day the ladies of Persia and Med'ia who have heard of the queen's behavior will be telling it to all the king's princes, and there will be contempt and wrath in plenty. [19]If it please the king, let a royal order go forth from him, and let it be written among the laws of the Persians and the Medes so that it may not be altered, that Vashti is to come no more before King Ahas'u-e'rus; and let the king give her royal position to another who is better than she. [20]So when the decree made by the king is proclaimed throughout all his kingdom, vast as it is, all women will give honor to their husbands, high and low." [21]This advice pleased the king and the princes, and the king did as Memu'can proposed; [22]he sent letters to all the royal provinces, to every province in its own script and to every people in its own language, that every man be lord in his own house and speak according to the language of his people.

Esther Is Chosen as Queen

2 After these things, when the anger of King Ahas'u-e'rus had abated, he remembered Vashti and what she had done and what had been decreed against her. [2]Then the king's servants who attended him said, "Let beautiful young virgins be sought out for the king. [3]And let the king appoint officers in all the provinces of his kingdom to gather all the beautiful young virgins to the harem in Susa the capital, under custody of Hegai the king's eunuch who is in charge of the women; let their ointments be given them. [4]And let the maiden who pleases the king be queen

instead of Vashti." This pleased the king, and he did so.

5 Now there was a Jew in Susa the capital whose name was Mor'decai, the son of Ja'ir, son of Shim'e-i, son of Kish, a Benjaminite, [6]who had been carried away from Jerusalem among the captives carried away with Jeconi'ah king of Judah, whom Nebuchadnez'zar king of Babylon had carried away. [7]He had brought up Hadas'sah, that is Esther, the daughter of his uncle, for she had neither father nor mother; the maiden was beautiful and lovely, and when her father and her mother died, Mor'decai adopted her as his own daughter. [8]So when the king's order and his edict were proclaimed, and when many maidens were gathered in Susa the capital in custody of Hegai, Esther also was taken into the king's palace and put in custody of Hegai who had charge of the women. [9]And the maiden pleased him and won his favor; and he quickly provided her with her ointments and her portion of food, and with seven chosen maids from the king's palace, and advanced her and her maids to the best place in the harem. [10]Esther had not made known her people or kindred, for Mor'decai had charged her not to make it known. [11]And every day Mor'decai walked in front of the court of the harem, to learn how Esther was and how she fared.

12 Now when the turn came for each maiden to go in to King Ahas'u-e'rus, after being twelve months under the regulations for the women, since this was the regular period of their beautifying, six months with oil of myrrh and six months with spices and ointments for women— [13]when the maiden went in to the king in this way she was given whatever she desired to take with her from the harem to the king's palace. [14]In the evening she went, and in the morning she came back to the second harem in custody of Shaash'gaz the king's eunuch who was in charge of the concubines; she did not go in to the king again, unless the king delighted in her and she was summoned by name.

15 When the turn came for Esther the daughter of Ab'ihail the uncle of Mor'decai, who had adopted her as his own daughter, to go in to the king, she asked for nothing except what Hegai the king's eunuch, who had charge of the women, advised. Now Esther found favor in the eyes of all who saw her. [16]And when Esther was taken to King Ahas'u-e'rus into his royal palace in the tenth month, which is the month of Te'beth, in the seventh year of his reign, [17]the king loved Esther more than all the women, and she found grace and favor in his sight more than all the virgins, so that he set the royal crown on her head and made her queen instead of Vashti. [18]Then the king gave a great banquet to all his princes and servants; it was Esther's banquet. He also granted a

remission of taxes[c] to the provinces, and gave gifts with royal liberality.

Mordecai Discovers a Plot

19 When the virgins were gathered together the second time, Mor'decai was sitting at the king's gate. [20]Now Esther had not made known her kindred or her people, as Mor'decai had charged her; for Esther obeyed Mordecai just as when she was brought up by him. [21]And in those days, as Mor'decai was sitting at the king's gate, Bigthan and Te'resh, two of the king's eunuchs, who guarded the threshold, became angry and sought to lay hands on King Ahas'u-e'rus. [22]And this came to the knowledge of Mor'decai, and he told it to Queen Esther, and Esther told the king in the name of Mordecai. [23]When the affair was investigated and found to be so, the men were both hanged on the gallows. And it was recorded in the Book of the Chronicles in the presence of the king.

Haman Seeks to Destroy the Jews

3 After these things King Ahas'u-e'rus promoted Ha'man the Ag'agite, the son of Hammeda'tha, and advanced him and set his seat above all the princes who were with him. [2]And all the king's servants who were at the king's gate bowed down and did obeisance to Ha'man; for the king had so commanded concerning him. But Mor'decai did not bow down or do obeisance. [3]Then the king's servants who were at the king's gate said to Mor'decai, "Why do you transgress the king's command?" [4]And when they spoke to him day after day and he would not listen to them, they told Ha'man, in order to see whether Mor'decai's words would avail; for he had told them that he was a Jew. [5]And when Ha'man saw that Mor'decai did not bow down or do obeisance to him, Ha'man was filled with fury. [6]But he disdained to lay hands on Mor'decai alone. So, as they had made known to him the people of Mordecai, Ha'man sought to destroy all the Jews, the people of Mordecai, throughout the whole kingdom of Ahas'u-e'rus.

7 In the first month, which is the month of Ni'san, in the twelfth year of King Ahas'u-e'rus, they cast Pur, that is the lot, before Ha'man day after day; and they cast it month after month till the twelfth month, which is the month of Adar'. [8]Then Ha'man said to King Ahas'u-e'rus, "There is a certain people scattered abroad and dispersed among the peoples in all the provinces of your kingdom; their laws are different from those of every other people, and they do not keep the king's laws, so that it is not for the king's profit to tolerate them. [9]If it please the king, let it be decreed that they be destroyed, and I will pay ten thousand talents of silver into the hands of those who have charge of the king's business, that they may put it into the king's treasuries." [10]So the king

took his signet ring from his hand and gave it to Ha'man the Ag'agite, the son of Hammeda'tha, the enemy of the Jews. [11]And the king said to Ha'man, "The money is given to you, the people also, to do with them as it seems good to you."

12 Then the king's secretaries were summoned on the thirteenth day of the first month, and an edict, according to all that Ha'man commanded, was written to the king's satraps and to the governors over all the provinces and to the princes of all the peoples, to every province in its own script and every people in its own language; it was written in the name of King Ahas'u-e'rus and sealed with the king's ring. [13]Letters were sent by couriers to all the king's provinces, to destroy, to slay, and to annihilate all Jews, young and old, women and children, in one day, the thirteenth day of the twelfth month, which is the month of Adar', and to plunder their goods.

The King's Letter

13 *This is a copy of the letter: "The Great King, Artaxerxes, to the rulers of the hundred and twenty-seven provinces from India to Ethiopia and to the governors under them, writes thus:*

2 "Having become ruler of many nations and master of the whole world, not elated with presumption of authority but always acting reasonably and with kindness, I have determined to settle the lives of my subjects in lasting tranquillity and, in order to make my kingdom peaceable and open to travel throughout all its extent, to re-establish the peace which all men desire.

3 "When I asked my counselors how this might be accomplished, Haman, who excels among us in sound judgment, and is distinguished for his unchanging good will and steadfast fidelity, and has attained the second place in the kingdom, [4]pointed out to us that among all the nations in the world there is scattered a certain hostile people, who have laws contrary to those of every nation and continually disregard the ordinances of the kings, so that the unifying of the kingdom which we honorably intend cannot be brought about. [5]We understand that this people, and it alone, stands constantly in opposition to all men, perversely following a strange manner of life and laws, and is ill-disposed to our government, doing all the harm they can so that our kingdom may not attain stability.

6 "Therefore we have decreed that those indicated to you in the letters of Haman, who is in charge of affairs and is our second father, shall all, with their wives and children, be utterly destroyed by the sword of their enemies, without pity or mercy, on the fourteenth day of the twelfth month, Adar, of this present year, [7]so that those

---

[c] Or *a holiday.*

who have long been and are now hostile may in one day go down in violence to Hades, and leave our government completely secure and untroubled hereafter."

[14]A copy of the document was to be issued as a decree in every province by proclamation to all the peoples to be ready for that day. [15]The couriers went in haste by order of the king, and the decree was issued in Susa the capital. And the king and Ha'man sat down to drink; but the city of Susa was perplexed.

Esther Agrees to Help the Jews

4 When Mor'decai learned all that had been done, Mordecai tore his clothes and put on sackcloth and ashes, and went out into the midst of the city, wailing with a loud and bitter cry; [2]he went up to the entrance of the king's gate, for no one might enter the king's gate clothed with sackcloth. [3]And in every province, wherever the king's command and his decree came, there was great mourning among the Jews, with fasting and weeping and lamenting, and most of them lay in sackcloth and ashes.

4 When Esther's maids and her eunuchs came and told her, the queen was deeply distressed; she sent garments to clothe Mor'decai, so that he might take off his sackcloth, but he would not accept them. [5]Then Esther called for Ha'thach, one of the king's eunuchs, who had been appointed to attend her, and ordered him to go to Mor'decai to learn what this was and why it was. [6]Ha'thach went out to Mor'decai in the open square of the city in front of the king's gate, [7]and Mor'decai told him all that had happened to him, and the exact sum of money that Ha'man had promised to pay into the king's treasuries for the destruction of the Jews. [8]Mor'decai also gave him a copy of the written decree issued in Susa for their destruction, that he might show it to Esther and explain it to her and charge her to go to the king to make supplication to him and entreat him for her people, *"Remembering the days of your lowliness, when you were cared for by me, because Haman, who is next to the king, spoke against us for our destruction. Beseech the Lord and speak to the king concerning us and deliver us from death."* [9]And Ha'thach went and told Esther what Mor'decai had said. [10]Then Esther spoke to Ha'thach and gave him a message for Mor'decai, saying, [11]"All the king's servants and the people of the king's provinces know that if any man or woman goes to the king inside the inner court without being called, there is but one law; all alike are to be put to death, except the one to whom the king holds out the golden scepter that he may live. And I have not been called to come in to the king these thirty days." [12]And they told Mor'decai what Esther had said. [13]Then Mor'decai told them to return answer to Esther, "Think not that in the king's palace you will escape any more than all the other Jews. [14]For if you keep silence at such a time as this, relief and deliverance will rise for the Jews from another quarter, but you and your father's house will perish. And who knows whether you have not come to the kingdom for such a time as this?" [15]Then Esther told them to reply to Mor'decai, [16]"Go, gather all the Jews to be found in Susa, and hold a fast on my behalf, and neither eat nor drink for three days, night or day. I and my maids will also fast as you do. Then I will go to the king, though it is against the law; and if I perish, I perish." [17]Mor'decai then went away and did everything as Esther had ordered him.

Mordecai's Prayer

[13] 8 *Then Mordecai* [b] *prayed to the Lord, and said: "O God of Abraham, God of Isaac, God of Jacob, blessed are you:*

9 *"O Lord, Lord, King who rule over all things, for the universe is in your power and there is no one who can oppose you if it is your will to save Israel.* [10]*For you have made heaven and earth and every wonderful thing under heaven,* [11]*and you are Lord of all, and there is no one who can resist you.* [12]*You know all things;* [13]*you know, O Lord, that I would have been willing to kiss the soles of Haman's feet to save Israel!* [14]*But I did not do this, lest I set the glory of man above the glory of God; I will not bow down to any one but you, O Lord, my God.* [15]*And now, O Lord God and King, God of Abraham, God of Isaac, and God of Jacob, spare your people; for the eyes of our foes are upon us* [c] *to annihilate us, and they desire to destroy your inheritance.* [16]*Do not neglect your portion, which you redeemed for yourself out of the land of Egypt.* [17]*Hear my prayer, and have mercy upon your inheritance; turn our mourning into feasting, that we may live and sing praise to your name, O Lord; do not destroy the mouth of those who praise you."*

18 *And all Israel cried out mightily, for their death was before their eyes.*

Esther's Prayer

14 *And Esther the queen, seized with deathly anxiety, fled to the Lord;* [2]*she took off her splendid apparel and put on the garments of distress and mourning, and instead of costly perfumes she covered her head with ashes and dung, and she utterly humbled her body, and every part that she loved to adorn she covered with her tangled hair.* [3]*And she lay on the earth together with all her maidservants, from morning until evening, and said: "God of Abraham, God of Isaac, and God of Jacob, blessed are you; help me, who am alone and have no helper but you,* [4]*for my danger is in my hand.* [5]*Ever since I was born I*

---

[b] Gk *he.*
[c] Gk *for they are looking upon us.*

have heard in the tribe of my family that you, O Lord, took Israel out of all the nations, and our fathers from among all their ancestors, for an everlasting inheritance, and that you did for them all that you promised. [6]And now we have sinned before you, and you have given us into the hands of our enemies, [7]because we glorified their gods. You are righteous, O Lord! [8]And now they are not satisfied that we are in bitter slavery, but they have covenanted with their idols [9]to abolish what your mouth has ordained and to destroy your inheritance, to stop the mouths of those who praise you and to quench your altar and the glory of your house, [10]to open the mouths of the nations for the praise of vain idols, and to magnify for ever a mortal king. [11]O Lord, do not surrender your scepter to what has no being; and do not let them mock at our downfall; but turn their plan against themselves, and make an example of the man who began this against us. I have heard from the books of my ancestors that you liberate all those who are pleasing to you, O Lord, until the very end. And now, assist me, who am all alone, and have no one but you, O Lord, my God. Come to my aid, for I am an orphan. [12]Remember, O Lord; make yourself known in this time of our affliction, and give me courage, O King of the gods and Master of all dominion! [13]Put eloquent speech in my mouth before the lion, and turn his heart to hate the man who is fighting against us, so that there may be an end of him and those who agree with him. [14]But save us from the hand of our enemies; turn our mourning into gladness and our affliction into well-being. [15]You have knowledge of all things; and you know that I hate the splendor of the wicked and abhor the bed of the uncircumcised and of any alien. [16]You know my necessity—that I abhor the sign of my proud position, which is upon my head on the days when I appear in public. I abhor it like a menstruous rag, and I do not wear it on the days when I am at leisure. [17]And your servant has not eaten at Haman's table, and I have not honored the king's feast or drunk the wine of the libations. [18]Your servant has had no joy since the day that I was brought here until now, except in you, O Lord God of Abraham. [19]O God, whose might is over all, hear the voice of the despairing, and save us from the hands of evildoers. And save me from my fear!"

Esther's Invitation to the King and Haman

15 [*] On the third day, when she ended her prayer, she took off the garments in which she had worshiped, and clothed herself in splendid attire. [2]Then, majestically adorned, after invoking the aid of the all-seeing God and Savior, she took her two maids with her, [3]leaning daintily on one, [4]while the other followed carrying her train. [5]She was radiant with perfect beauty, and she looked happy, as if beloved, but her heart was frozen with fear. [6]When she had gone through all the doors, she stood before the king. He was seated on his royal throne, clothed in the full array of his majesty, all covered with gold and precious stones. And he was most terrifying.

7 Lifting his face, flushed with splendor, he looked at her in fierce anger. And the queen faltered, and turned pale and faint, and collapsed upon the head of the maid who went before her. [8]Then God changed the spirit of the king to gentleness, and in alarm he sprang from his throne and took her in his arms until she came to herself. And he comforted her with soothing words, and said to her, [9]"What is it, Esther? I am your brother. Take courage; [10]you shall not die, for our law applies only to the people. [d] Come near."

11 Then he raised the golden scepter and touched it to her neck; [12]and he embraced her, and said, "Speak to me." [13]And she said to him, "I saw you, my lord, like an angel of God, and my heart was shaken with fear at your glory. [14]For you are wonderful, my lord, and your countenance is full of grace." [15]But as she was speaking, she fell fainting. [16]And the king was agitated, and all his servants sought to comfort her.

[5] [3] And the king said to her, "What is it, Queen Esther? What is your request? It shall be given you, even to the half of my kingdom." [4]And Esther said, "If it please the king, let the king and Ha'man come this day to a dinner that I have prepared for the king." [5]Then said the king, "Bring Ha'man quickly, that we may do as Esther desires." So the king and Ha'man came to the dinner that Esther had prepared. [6]And as they were drinking wine, the king said to Esther, "What is your petition? It shall be granted you. And what is your request? Even to the half of my kingdom, it shall be fulfilled." [7]But Esther said, "My petition and my request is: [8]If I have found favor in the sight of the king, and if it please the king to grant my petition and fulfil my request, let the king and Ha'man come tomorrow [d] to the dinner which I will prepare for them, and tomorrow I will do as the king has said."

Haman Plans to Have Mordecai Hanged

9 And Ha'man went out that day joyful and glad of heart. But when Haman saw Mor'decai in the king's gate, that he neither rose nor trembled before him, he was filled with wrath against

[d] The meaning of the Greek text of this clause is obscure.
[d] Gk: Heb lacks *tomorrow*.
5:3, 6: Mk 6:23.
[*] 15:1–16: This deuterocanonical passage is a later expansion of the Hebrew text 5:1–2, which is as follows: "On the third day Esther put on her royal robes and stood in the inner court of the king's palace, opposite the king's hall. The king was sitting on his royal throne inside the palace opposite the entrance to the palace; [2]and when the king saw Queen Esther standing in the court, she found favor in his sight and he held out to Esther the golden scepter that was in his hand. Then Esther approached and touched the top of the scepter." Greek and Hebrew rejoin at verse 3.

Mordecai. [10]Nevertheless Ha'man restrained himself, and went home; and he sent and fetched his friends and his wife Ze'resh. [11]And Ha'man recounted to them the splendor of his riches, the number of his sons, all the promotions with which the king had honored him, and how he had advanced him above the princes and the servants of the king. [12]And Ha'man added, "Even Queen Esther let no one come with the king to the banquet she prepared but myself. And tomorrow also I am invited by her together with the king. [13]Yet all this does me no good, so long as I see Mor'decai the Jew sitting at the king's gate." [14]Then his wife Ze'resh and all his friends said to him, "Let a gallows fifty cubits high be made, and in the morning tell the king to have Mor'decai hanged upon it; then go merrily with the king to the dinner." This counsel pleased Ha'man, and he had the gallows made.

The King Honors Mordecai

6 On that night the king could not sleep; and he gave orders to bring the book of memorable deeds, the chronicles, and they were read before the king. [2]And it was found written how Mor'decai had told about Big'thana and Te'resh, two of the king's eunuchs, who guarded the threshold, and who had sought to lay hands upon King Ahas'u-e'rus. [3]And the king said, "What honor or dignity has been bestowed on Mor'decai for this?" The king's servants who attended him said, "Nothing has been done for him." [4]And the king said, "Who is in the court?" Now Ha'man had just entered the outer court of the king's palace to speak to the king about having Mor'decai hanged on the gallows that he had prepared for him. [5]So the king's servants told him, "Ha'man is there, standing in the court." And the king said, "Let him come in." [6]So Ha'man came in, and the king said to him, "What shall be done to the man whom the king delights to honor?" And Haman said to himself, "Whom would the king delight to honor more than me?" [7]And Ha'man said to the king, "For the man whom the king delights to honor, [8]let royal robes be brought, which the king has worn, and the horse which the king has ridden, and on whose head a royal crown is set; [9]and let the robes and the horse be handed over to one of the king's most noble princes; let him • clothe the man whom the king delights to honor, and let him • conduct the man on horseback through the open square of the city, proclaiming before him: 'Thus shall it be done to the man whom the king delights to honor.'" [10]Then the king said to Ha'man, "Make haste, take the robes and the horse, as you have said, and do so to Mor'decai the Jew who sits at the king's gate. Leave out nothing that you have mentioned." [11]So Ha'man took the robes and the horse, and he clothed Mor'decai and made him ride through the open square of the city, proclaiming, "Thus shall it be done to the man whom the king delights to honor."

12 Then Mor'decai returned to the king's gate. But Ha'man hurried to his house, mourning and with his head covered. [13]And Ha'man told his wife Ze'resh and all his friends everything that had befallen him. Then his wise men and his wife Zeresh said to him, "If Mor'decai, before whom you have begun to fall, is of the Jewish people, you will not prevail against him but will surely fall before him."

Haman's Downfall and Mordecai's Advancement

14 While they were yet talking with him, the king's eunuchs arrived and brought Ha'man in haste to the banquet that Esther had prepared.

7 So the king and Ha'man went in to feast with Queen Esther. [2]And on the second day, as they were drinking wine, the king again said to Esther, "What is your petition, Queen Esther? It shall be granted you. And what is your request? Even to the half of my kingdom, it shall be fulfilled." [3]Then Queen Esther answered, "If I have found favor in your sight, O king, and if it please the king, let my life be given me at my petition, and my people at my request. [4]For we are sold, I and my people, to be destroyed, to be slain, and to be annihilated. If we had been sold merely as slaves, men and women, I would have held my peace; for our affliction is not to be compared with the loss to the king." [5]Then King Ahas'u-e'rus said to Queen Esther, "Who is he, and where is he, that would presume to do this?" [6]And Esther said, "A foe and enemy! This wicked Ha'man!" Then Ha'man was in terror before the king and the queen. [7]And the king rose from the feast in wrath and went into the palace garden; but Ha'man stayed to beg his life from Queen Esther, for he saw that evil was determined against him by the king. [8]And the king returned from the palace garden to the place where they were drinking wine, as Ha'man was falling on the couch where Esther was; and the king said, "Will he even assault the queen in my presence, in my own house?" As the words left the mouth of the king, they covered Haman's face. [9]Then said Harbo'na, one of the eunuchs in attendance on the king, "Moreover, the gallows which Ha'man has prepared for Mor'decai, whose word saved the king, is standing in Haman's house, fifty cubits high." [10]And the king said, "Hang him on that." So they hanged Ha'man on the gallows which he had prepared for Mor'decai. Then the anger of the king abated.

• Heb *them*.
7:2: Mk 6:23.

8 On that day King Ahas'u-e'rus gave to Queen Esther the house of Ha'man, the enemy of the Jews. And Mor'decai came before the king, for Esther had told what he was to her; ²and the king took off his signet ring, which he had taken from Ha'man, and gave it to Mor'decai. And Esther set Mordecai over the house of Haman.

Esther Saves the Jews

3 Then Esther spoke again to the king; she fell at his feet and besought him with tears to avert the evil design of Ha'man the Ag'agite and the plot which he had devised against the Jews. ⁴And the king held out the golden scepter to Esther, ⁵and Esther rose and stood before the king. And she said, "If it please the king, and if I have found favor in his sight, and if the thing seem right before the king, and I be pleasing in his eyes, let an order be written to revoke the letters devised by Ha'man the Ag'agite, the son of Hammeda'tha, which he wrote to destroy the Jews who are in all the provinces of the king. ⁶For how can I endure to see the calamity that is coming to my people? Or how can I endure to see the destruction of my kindred?" ⁷Then King Ahas'u-e'rus said to Queen Esther and to Mor'decai the Jew, "Behold, I have given Esther the house of Ha'man, and they have hanged him on the gallows, because he would lay hands on the Jews. ⁸And you may write as you please with regard to the Jews, in the name of the king, and seal it with the king's ring; for an edict written in the name of the king and sealed with the king's ring cannot be revoked."

9 The king's secretaries were summoned at that time, in the third month, which is the month of Si'van, on the twenty-third day; and an edict was written according to all that Mor'decai commanded concerning the Jews to the satraps and the governors and the princes of the provinces from India to Ethiopia, a hundred and twenty-seven provinces, to every province in its own script and to every people in its own language, and also to the Jews in their script and their language. ¹⁰The writing was in the name of King Ahas'u-e'rus and sealed with the king's ring, and letters were sent by mounted couriers riding on swift horses that were used in the king's service, bred from the royal stud. ¹¹By these the king allowed the Jews who were in every city to gather and defend their lives, to destroy, to slay, and to annihilate any armed force of any people or province that might attack them, with their children and women, and to plunder their goods, ¹²upon one day throughout all the provinces of King Ahas'u-e'rus, on the thirteenth day of the twelfth month, which is the month of Adar'.

The King's Edict

16 *The following is a copy of this letter: "The Great King, Artaxerxes, to the rul-*ers of the provinces from India to Ethiopia, one hundred and twenty-seven satrapies, and to those who are loyal to our government, greeting.*

2 *"The more often they are honored by the too great kindness of their benefactors, the more proud do many men become.* ³*They not only seek to injure our subjects, but in their inability to stand prosperity they even undertake to scheme against their own benefactors.* ⁴*They not only take away thankfulness from among men, but, carried away by the boasts of those who know nothing of goodness, they suppose that they will escape the evil-hating justice of God, who always sees everything.* ⁵*And often many of those who are set in places of authority have been made in part responsible for the shedding of innocent blood, and have been involved in irremediable calamities, by the persuasion of friends who have been entrusted with the administration of public affairs,* ⁶*when these men by the false trickery of their evil natures beguile the sincere good will of their sovereigns.*

7 *"What has been wickedly accomplished through the pestilent behavior of those who exercise authority unworthily, can be seen not so much from the more ancient records which we hand on as from investigation of matters close at hand.* ⁸*For the future we will take care to render our kingdom quiet and peaceable for all men,* ⁹*by changing our methods and always judging what comes before our eyes with more equitable consideration.* ¹⁰*For Haman, the son of Hammedatha, a Macedonian (really an alien to the Persian blood, and quite devoid of our kindliness), having become our guest,* ¹¹*so far enjoyed the good will that we have for every nation that he was called our father and was continually bowed down to by all as the person second to the royal throne.* ¹²*But, unable to restrain his arrogance, he undertook to deprive us of our kingdom and our life,* ¹³*and with intricate craft and deceit asked for the destruction of Mordecai, our savior and perpetual benefactor, and of Esther, the blameless partner of our kingdom, together with their whole nation.* ¹⁴*He thought that in this way he would find us undefended and would transfer the kingdom of the Persians to the Macedonians.*

15 *"But we find that the Jews, who were consigned to annihilation by this thrice accursed man, are not evildoers but are governed by most righteous laws* ¹⁶*and are sons of the Most High, the most mighty living God, who has directed the kingdom both for us and for our fathers in the most excellent order.*

17 *"You will therefore do well not to put in execution the letters sent by Haman the son of Hammedatha,* ¹⁸*because the man himself who did these things has been hanged at the gate of Susa, with all his household. For God, who rules over all*

things, has speedily inflicted on him the punishment he deserved.

19 *"Therefore post a copy of this letter publicly in every place, and permit the Jews to live under their own laws.* [20]*And give them reinforcements, so that on the thirteenth day of the twelfth month, Adar, on that very day they may defend themselves against those who attack them at the time of their affliction.* [21]*For God, who rules over all things, has made this day to be a joy to his chosen people instead of a day of destruction for them.*

22 *"Therefore you shall observe this with all good cheer as a notable day among your commemorative festivals,* [23]*so that both now and hereafter it may mean salvation for us and the loyal Persians, but that for those who plot against us it may be a reminder of destruction.*

24 *"Every city and country, without exception, which does not act accordingly, shall be destroyed in wrath with spear and fire. It shall be made not only impassable for men, but also most hateful for all time to beasts and birds."*

[13]A copy of what was written was to be issued as a decree in every province, and by proclamation to all peoples, and the Jews were to be ready on that day to avenge themselves upon their enemies. [14]So the couriers, mounted on their swift horses that were used in the king's service, rode out in haste, urged by the king's command; and the decree was issued in Susa the capital.

15 Then Mor'decai went out from the presence of the king in royal robes of blue and white, with a great golden crown and a mantle of fine linen and purple, while the city of Susa shouted and rejoiced. [16]The Jews had light and gladness and joy and honor. [17]And in every province and in every city, wherever the king's command and his edict came, there was gladness and joy among the Jews, a feast and a holiday. And many from the peoples of the country declared themselves Jews, for the fear of the Jews had fallen upon them.

The Destruction of the Enemies of the Jews

9 Now in the twelfth month, which is the month of Adar', on the thirteenth day of the same, when the king's command and edict were about to be executed, on the very day when the enemies of the Jews hoped to get the mastery over them, but which had been changed to a day when the Jews should get the mastery over their foes, [2]the Jews gathered in their cities throughout all the provinces of King Ahas'u-e'rus to lay hands on such as sought their hurt. And no one could make a stand against them, for the fear of them had fallen upon all peoples. [3]All the princes of the provinces and the satraps and the governors and the royal officials also helped the Jews, for the fear of Mor'decai had fallen upon them. [4]For Mor'decai was

great in the king's house, and his fame spread throughout all the provinces; for the man Mordecai grew more and more powerful. [5]So the Jews struck all their enemies with the sword, slaughtering, and destroying them, and did as they pleased to those who hated them. [6]In Susa the capital itself the Jews slew and destroyed five hundred men, [7]and also slew Par-shan-da'tha and Dalphon and Aspa'tha [8]and Pora'tha and Ada'lia and Arida'tha [9]and Parmash'ta and Ar'isai and Ar'idai and Vaiza'tha, [10]the ten sons of Ha'man the son of Hammeda'tha, the enemy of the Jews; but they laid no hand on the plunder.

11 That very day the number of those slain in Susa the capital was reported to the king. [12]And the king said to Queen Esther, "In Susa the capital the Jews have slain five hundred men and also the ten sons of Ha'man. What then have they done in the rest of the king's provinces! Now what is your petition? It shall be granted you. And what further is your request? It shall be fulfilled." [13]And Esther said, "If it please the king, let the Jews who are in Susa be allowed tomorrow also to do according to this day's edict. And let the ten sons of Ha'man be hanged on the gallows." [14]So the king commanded this to be done; a decree was issued in Susa, and the ten sons of Ha'man were hanged. [15]The Jews who were in Susa gathered also on the fourteenth day of the month of Adar' and they slew three hundred men in Susa; but they laid no hands on the plunder.

The Feast of Purim Inaugurated

16 Now the other Jews who were in the king's provinces also gathered to defend their lives, and got relief from their enemies, and slew seventy-five thousand of those who hated them; but they laid no hands on the plunder. [17]This was on the thirteenth day of the month of Adar', and on the fourteenth day they rested and made that a day of feasting and gladness. [18]But the Jews who were in Susa gathered on the thirteenth day and on the fourteenth, and rested on the fifteenth day, making that a day of feasting and gladness. [19]Therefore the Jews of the villages, who live in the open towns, hold the fourteenth day of the month of Adar' as a day for gladness and feasting and holiday-making, and a day on which they send choice portions to one another.

20 And Mor'decai recorded these things, and sent letters to all the Jews who were in all the provinces of King Ahas'u-e'rus, both near and far, [21]enjoining them that they should keep the fourteenth day of the month Adar' and also the fifteenth day of the same, year by year, [22]as the days on which the Jews got relief from their enemies, and as the month that had been turned for them from sorrow into gladness and from mourning into a holiday; that they should make them days of feasting and gladness, days for

sending choice portions to one another and gifts to the poor.

23 So the Jews undertook to do as they had begun, and as Mor'decai had written to them. [24]For Ha'man the Ag'agite, the son of Hammeda'tha, the enemy of all the Jews, had plotted against the Jews to destroy them, and had cast Pur, that is the lot, to crush and destroy them; [25]but when Esther came before the king, he gave orders in writing that his wicked plot which he had devised against the Jews should come upon his own head, and that he and his sons should be hanged on the gallows. [26]Therefore they called these days Purim, after the term Pur. And therefore, because of all that was written in this letter, and of what they had faced in this matter, and of what had befallen them, [27]the Jews ordained and took it upon themselves and their descendants and all who joined them, that without fail they would keep these two days according to what was written and at the time appointed every year, [28]that these days should be remembered and kept throughout every generation, in every family, province, and city, and that these days of Purim should never fall into disuse among the Jews, nor should the commemoration of these days cease among their descendants.

29 Then Queen Esther, the daughter of Ab'ihail, and Mor'decai the Jew gave full written authority, confirming this second letter about Purim. [30]Letters were sent to all the Jews, to the hundred and twenty-seven provinces of the kingdom of Ahas'u-e'rus, in words of peace and truth, [31]that these days of Purim should be observed at their appointed seasons, as Mor'decai the Jew and Queen Esther enjoined upon the Jews, and as they had laid down for themselves and for their descendants, with regard to their fasts and their lamenting. [32]The command of Queen Esther fixed these practices of Purim, and it was recorded in writing.

Mordecai's Dream Fulfilled

10 King Ahas'u-e'rus laid tribute on the land and on the coastlands of the sea. [2]And all the acts of his power and might, and the full account of the high honor of Mor'decai, to which the king advanced him, are they not written in the Book of the Chronicles of the kings of Med'ia and Persia? [3]For Mor'decai the Jew was next in rank to King Ahas'u-e'rus, and he was great among the Jews and popular with the multitude of his brethren, for he sought the welfare of his people and spoke peace to all his people.

10 [4] *And Mordecai said, "These things have come from God. [5]For I remember the dream that I had concerning these matters, and none of them has failed to be fulfilled. [6]The tiny spring which became a river, and there was light and the sun and abundant water—the river is Esther, whom the king married and made queen. [7]The two dragons are Haman and myself. [8]The nations are those that gathered to destroy the name of the Jews. [9]And my nation, this is Israel, who cried out to God and were saved. The Lord has saved his people; the Lord has delivered us from all these evils; God has done great signs and wonders, which have not occurred among the nations. [10]For this purpose he made two lots, one for the people of God and one for all the nations. [11]And these two lots came to the hour and moment and day of decision before God and among all the nations. [12]And God remembered his people and vindicated his inheritance. [13]So they will observe these days in the month of Adar, on the fourteenth and fifteenth of that month, with an assembly and joy and gladness before God, from generation to generation for ever among his people Israel."*

Postscript

11 [1]*In the fourth year of the reign of Ptolemy and Cleopatra, Dositheus, who said that he was a priest and a Levite, ᵉ and Ptolemy his son brought to Egypt ᶠ the preceeding Letter of Purim, which they said was genuine and had been translated by Lysimachus the son of Ptolemy, one of the residents of Jerusalem.*

ᵉ Or *priest, and Levitas.*
ᶠ Cn: Gk *brought in.*

THE BOOK OF

JOB

Job and His Family

1 There was a man in the land of Uz, whose name was Job; and that man was blameless and upright, one who feared God, and turned away from evil. [2]There were born to him seven sons and three daughters. [3]He had seven thousand sheep, three thousand camels, five hundred yoke of oxen, and five hundred she-donkeys, and very many servants; so that this man was the greatest of all the people of the east. [4]His sons used to go and hold a feast in the house of each on his day; and they would send and invite their three sisters to eat and drink with them. [5]And when the days of the feast had run their course, Job would send and sanctify them, and he would rise early in the morning and offer burnt offerings according to the number of them all; for Job said, "It may be that my sons have sinned, and cursed God in their hearts." Thus Job did continually.

Satan Is Allowed to Tempt Job

6 Now there was a day when the sons of God came to present themselves before the Lord, and Satan [a] also came among them. [7]The Lord said to Satan, "From where have you come?" Satan answered the Lord, "From going back and forth on the earth, and from walking up and down on it." [8]And the Lord said to Satan, "Have you considered my servant Job, that there is none like him on the earth, a blameless and upright man, who fears God and turns away from evil?" [9]Then Satan answered the Lord, "Does Job fear God for nothing? [10]Have you not put a hedge about him and his house and all that he has, on every side? You have blessed the work of his hands, and his possessions have increased in the land. [11]But put forth your hand now, and touch all that he has, and he will curse you to your face." [12]And the Lord said to Satan, "Behold, all that he has is in your power; only upon himself do not put forth your hand." So Satan went forth from the presence of the Lord.

Job Loses His Property and Children

13 Now there was a day when his sons and daughters were eating and drinking wine in their eldest brother's house; [14]and there came a messenger to Job, and said, "The oxen were plowing and the donkeys feeding beside them; [15]and the Sabe'ans fell upon them and took them, and slew the servants with the edge of the sword; and I alone have escaped to tell you." [16]While he was

yet speaking, there came another, and said, "The fire of God fell from heaven and burned up the sheep and the servants, and consumed them; and I alone have escaped to tell you." [17]While he was yet speaking, there came another, and said, "The Chalde'ans formed three companies, and made a raid upon the camels and took them, and slew the servants with the edge of the sword; and I alone have escaped to tell you." [18]While he was yet speaking, there came another, and said, "Your sons and daughters were eating and drinking wine in their eldest brother's house; [19]and behold, a great wind came across the wilderness, and struck the four corners of the house, and it fell upon the young people, and they are dead; and I alone have escaped to tell you."

20 Then Job arose, and tore his robe, and shaved his head, and fell upon the ground, and worshiped. [21]And he said, "Naked I came from my mother's womb, and naked shall I return; the Lord gave, and the Lord has taken away; blessed be the name of the Lord."

22 In all this Job did not sin or charge God with wrong.

Job Is Afflicted with Sores

2 Again there was a day when the sons of God came to present themselves before the Lord, and Satan also came among them to present himself before the Lord. [2]And the Lord said to Satan, "From where have you come?" Satan answered the Lord, "From going back and forth on the earth, and from walking up and down on it." [3]And

---

This book is one of the most interesting among the texts that make up the Wisdom literature of the Old Testament. It deals with a profound subject: the problem of the suffering of good men; and is written almost entirely in poetry. It is probably postexilic and its author is unknown.

The problem is clear enough. Material rewards and punishments are promised respectively for the observance or transgression of God's law; cf. Lev 26; Deut 28. We see the application of this, in Judges and Kings, to the people of Israel. This is collective responsibility; and sometimes, of course, the good have to suffer because of the bad. But when it is a case of individual responsibility, as in Job, why should the good man suffer? Various solutions are proposed but none that satisfies entirely. As yet there is no clear belief in the afterlife with its rewards and punishments; still less is there anything approaching the revelation of the New Testament as exemplified in Christ's life. Job knows he is innocent though suffering. Is God therefore unjust? He rejects the suggestion and submits himself to God's power and mercy without receiving a final answer. In the end he is reinstated in his former state of affluence.

The speeches of Elihu (chapters 32–37) are a later insertion. These chapters can be removed without causing any break in the narrative. Elihu is not mentioned elsewhere in the book, nor does Job appear to take any notice of what he has said. The insertion seems to have been made in order to stress the value of suffering in bringing a man back to God.
[a] Heb *the adversary*.

the Lord said to Satan, "Have you considered my servant Job, that there is none like him on the earth, a blameless and upright man, who fears God and turns away from evil? He still holds fast his integrity, although you moved me against him, to destroy him without cause." [4]Then Satan answered the Lord, "Skin for skin! All that a man has he will give for his life. [5]But put forth your hand now, and touch his bone and his flesh, and he will curse you to your face." [6]And the Lord said to Satan, "Behold, he is in your power; only spare his life."

7 So Satan went forth from the presence of the Lord, and afflicted Job with loathsome sores from the sole of his foot to the crown of his head. [8]And he took a potsherd with which to scrape himself, and sat among the ashes.

9 Then his wife said to him, "Do you still hold fast your integrity? Curse God, and die." [10]But he said to her, "You speak as one of the foolish women would speak. Shall we receive good at the hand of God, and shall we not receive evil?" In all this Job did not sin with his lips.

Job's Three Friends

11 Now when Job's three friends heard of all this evil that had come upon him, they came each from his own place, Eli′phaz the Te′manite, Bildad the Shuhite, and Zo′phar the Na′amathite. They made an appointment together to come to condole with him and comfort him. [12]And when they saw him from afar, they did not recognize him; and they raised their voices and wept; and they tore their robes and sprinkled dust upon their heads toward heaven. [13]And they sat with him on the ground seven days and seven nights, and no one spoke a word to him, for they saw that his suffering was very great.

Job Curses the Day of His Birth

3 After this Job opened his mouth and cursed the day of his birth.
[02]And Job said:
[03]"Let the day perish wherein I was born,
and the night which said,
'A man-child is conceived.'
[4]Let that day be darkness!
May God above not seek it,
nor light shine upon it.
[5]Let gloom and deep darkness claim it.
Let clouds dwell upon it;
let the blackness of the day terrify it.
[6]That night—let thick darkness seize it!
let it not rejoice among the days of the year,
let it not come into the number of the months.
[7]Yes, let that night be barren;
let no joyful cry be heard [b] in it.
[8]Let those curse it who curse the day,
who are skilled to rouse up Levi′athan.

[9]Let the stars of its dawn be dark;
let it hope for light, but have none,
nor see the eyelids of the morning;
[10]because it did not shut the doors of my mother's womb,
nor hide trouble from my eyes.

[11] "Why did I not die at birth,
come forth from the womb and expire?
[12]Why did the knees receive me?
Or why the breasts, that I should suck?
[13]For then I should have lain down and been quiet;
I should have slept; then I should have been at rest,
[14]with kings and counselors of the earth
who rebuilt ruins for themselves,
[15]or with princes who had gold,
who filled their houses with silver.
[16]Or why was I not as a hidden untimely birth,
as infants that never see the light?
[17]There the wicked cease from troubling,
and there the weary are at rest.
[18]There the prisoners are at ease together;
they hear not the voice of the taskmaster.
[19]The small and the great are there,
and the slave is free from his master.

[20] "Why is light given to him who is in misery,
and life to the bitter in soul,
[21]who long for death, but it comes not,
and dig for it more than for hidden treasures;
[22]who rejoice exceedingly,
and are glad, when they find the grave?
[23]Why is light given to a man whose way is hidden,
whom God has hedged in?
[24]For my sighing comes as [c] my bread,
and my groanings are poured out like water.
[25]For the thing that I fear comes upon me,
and what I dread befalls me.
[26]I am not at ease, nor am I quiet;
I have no rest; but trouble comes."

Eliphaz Speaks: Suffering Is a Result of Sin

4 Then Eli′phaz the Te′manite answered:
[2] "If one ventures a word with you, will you be offended?
Yet who can keep from speaking?
[3]Behold, you have instructed many,
and you have strengthened the weak hands.
[4]Your words have upheld him who was stumbling,
and you have made firm the feeble knees.

---

[b] Heb come.
[c] Heb before.
3:3–19: Jer 20:14–18.

⁵But now it has come to you, and you are
impatient;
it touches you, and you are dismayed.
⁶Is not your fear of God your confidence,
and the integrity of your ways your hope?

⁷ "Think now, who that was innocent ever
perished?
Or where were the upright cut off?
⁸As I have seen, those who plow iniquity
and sow trouble reap the same.
⁹By the breath of God they perish,
and by the blast of his anger they are
consumed.
¹⁰The roar of the lion, the voice of the fierce lion,
the teeth of the young lions, are broken.
¹¹The strong lion perishes for lack of prey,
and the whelps of the lioness are scattered.

¹² "Now a word was brought to me stealthily,
my ear received the whisper of it.
¹³Amid thoughts from visions of the night,
when deep sleep falls on men,
¹⁴dread came upon me, and trembling,
which made all my bones shake.
¹⁵A spirit glided past my face;
the hair of my flesh stood up.
¹⁶It stood still,
but I could not discern its appearance.
A form was before my eyes;
there was silence, then I heard a voice:
¹⁷"Can mortal man be righteous before ᵈ God?
Can a man be pure before ᵈ his Maker?
¹⁸Even in his servants he puts no trust,
and his angels he charges with error;
¹⁹how much more those who dwell in houses of
clay,
whose foundation is in the dust,
who are crushed before the moth.
²⁰Between morning and evening they are
destroyed;
they perish for ever without any regarding
it.
²¹If their tent-cord is plucked up within them,
do they not die, and that without wisdom?'

5 "Call now; is there any one who will answer
you?
To which of the holy ones will you turn?
²Surely vexation kills the fool,
and jealousy slays the simple.
³I have seen the fool taking root,
but suddenly I cursed his dwelling.
⁴His sons are far from safety,
they are crushed in the gate,
and there is no one to deliver them.
⁵His harvest the hungry eat,
and he takes it even out of thorns; ᵉ
and the thirsty ᶠ pant after his ᵍ wealth.

⁶For affliction does not come from the dust,
nor does trouble sprout from the ground;
⁷but man is born to trouble
as the sparks fly upward.

⁸ "As for me, I would seek God,
and to God would I commit my cause;
⁹who does great things and unsearchable,
marvelous things without number:
¹⁰he gives rain upon the earth
and sends waters upon the fields;
¹¹he sets on high those who are lowly,
and those who mourn are lifted to safety.
¹²He frustrates the devices of the crafty,
so that their hands achieve no success.
¹³He takes the wise in their own craftiness;
and the schemes of the wily are brought to
a quick end.
¹⁴They meet with darkness in the daytime,
and grope at noonday as in the night.
¹⁵But he saves the fatherless from their mouth, ʰ
the needy from the hand of the mighty.
¹⁶So the poor have hope,
and injustice shuts her mouth.

¹⁷ "Behold, happy is the man whom God
reproves;
therefore despise not the chastening of the
Almighty.
¹⁸For he wounds, but he binds up;
he strikes, but his hands heal.
¹⁹He will deliver you from six troubles;
in seven there shall no evil touch you.
²⁰In famine he will redeem you from death,
and in war from the power of the sword.
²¹You shall be hidden from the scourge of the
tongue,
and shall not fear destruction when it
comes.
²²At destruction and famine you shall laugh,
and shall not fear the beasts of the earth.
²³For you shall be in league with the stones of
the field,
and the beasts of the field shall be at peace
with you.
²⁴You shall know that your tent is safe,
and you shall inspect your fold and miss
nothing.
²⁵You shall know also that your descendants
shall be many,
and your offspring as the grass of the earth.
²⁶You shall come to your grave in ripe old age,
as a shock of grain comes up to the
threshing floor in its season.

ᵈ Or *more than.*
ᵉ Heb obscure.
ᶠ Aquila Symmachus Syr Vg: Heb *snare.*
ᵍ Heb *their.*
ʰ Cn: Heb uncertain.
5:12–13: 1 Cor 3:19.

²⁷Behold, this we have searched out; it is true.
  Hear, and know it for your good." [i]

Job Replies to Eliphaz

6 Then Job answered:
  ² "O that my vexation were weighed,
    and all my calamity laid in the balances!
³For then it would be heavier than the sand of
      the sea;
  therefore my words have been rash.
⁴For the arrows of the Almighty are in me;
  my spirit drinks their poison;
  the terrors of God are arrayed against me.
⁵Does the wild donkey bray when he has grass,
  or the ox low over his fodder?
⁶Can that which is tasteless be eaten without
      salt,
  or is there any taste in the slime of the
      purslane? [j]
⁷My appetite refuses to touch them;
  they are as food that is loathsome to me. [k]

⁸ "O that I might have my request,
  and that God would grant my desire;
⁹that it would please God to crush me,
  that he would let loose his hand and cut me
      off!
¹⁰This would be my consolation;
  I would even exult [l] in pain unsparing;
  for I have not denied the words of the Holy
      One.
¹¹What is my strength, that I should wait?
  And what is my end, that I should be
      patient?
¹²Is my strength the strength of stones,
  or is my flesh bronze?
¹³In truth I have no help in me,
  and any resource is driven from me.

¹⁴ "He who withholds [m] kindness from a friend
  forsakes the fear of the Almighty.
¹⁵My brethren are treacherous as a torrent-bed,
  as freshets that pass away,
¹⁶which are dark with ice,
  and where the snow hides itself.
¹⁷In time of heat they disappear;
  when it is hot, they vanish from their
      place.
¹⁸The caravans turn aside from their course;
  they go up into the waste, and perish.
¹⁹The caravans of Te′ma look,
  the travelers of Sheba hope.
²⁰They are disappointed because they were
      confident;
  they come there and are confounded.
²¹Such you have now become to me; [n]
  you see my calamity, and are afraid.
²²Have I said, 'Make me a gift'?
  Or, 'From your wealth offer a bribe for
      me'?

²³Or, 'Deliver me from the adversary's hand'?
  Or, 'Ransom me from the hand of
      oppressors'?

²⁴ "Teach me, and I will be silent;
  make me understand how I have erred.
²⁵How forceful are honest words!
  But what does reproof from you reprove?
²⁶Do you think that you can reprove words,
  when the speech of a despairing man is
      wind?
²⁷You would even cast lots over the fatherless,
  and bargain over your friend.

²⁸ "But now, be pleased to look at me;
  for I will not lie to your face.
²⁹Turn, I beg, let no wrong be done.
  Turn now, my vindication is at stake.
³⁰Is there any wrong on my tongue?
  Cannot my taste discern calamity?

Job Speaks of His Sufferings

7 "Has not man a hard service upon earth,
    and are not his days like the days of a
      hireling?
²Like a slave who longs for the shadow,
  and like a hireling who looks for his wages,
³so I am allotted months of emptiness,
  and nights of misery are apportioned
      to me.
⁴When I lie down I say, 'When shall I arise?'
  But the night is long,
  and I am full of tossing till the dawn.
⁵My flesh is clothed with worms and dirt;
  my skin hardens, then breaks out afresh.
⁶My days are swifter than a weaver's shuttle,
  and come to their end without hope.

⁷ "Remember that my life is a breath;
  my eye will never again see good.
⁸The eye of him who sees me will behold me no
      more;
  while your eyes are upon me, I shall be
      gone.
⁹As the cloud fades and vanishes,
  so he who goes down to Sheol does not
      come up;
¹⁰he returns no more to his house,
  nor does his place know him any more.

¹¹ "Therefore I will not restrain my mouth;
  I will speak in the anguish of my spirit;
  I will complain in the bitterness of my soul.
¹²Am I the sea, or a sea monster,
  that you set a guard over me?

---

[i] Heb *for yourself.*
[j] The meaning of the Hebrew word is uncertain.
[k] Heb obscure.
[l] The meaning of the Hebrew word is uncertain.
[m] Syr Vg Compare Tg: Heb obscure.
[n] Cn Compare Gk Syr: Heb obscure.

¹³When I say, 'My bed will comfort me,
  my couch will ease my complaint,'
¹⁴then you scare me with dreams
  and terrify me with visions,
¹⁵so that I would choose strangling
  and death rather than my bones.
¹⁶I loathe my life; I would not live for ever.
  Let me alone, for my days are a breath.
¹⁷What is man, that you make so much of him,
  and that you set your mind upon him,
¹⁸visit him every morning,
  and test him every moment?
¹⁹How long will you not look away from me,
  nor let me alone till I swallow my spittle?
²⁰If I sin, what do I do to you, you watcher of
    men?
  Why have you made me your mark?
  Why have I become a burden to you?
²¹Why do you not pardon my transgression
  and take away my iniquity?
  For now I shall lie in the earth;
  you will seek me, but I shall not be."

Bildad Speaks: God Is Just

8 Then Bildad the Shuhite answered:
  ² "How long will you say these things,
  and the words of your mouth be a great
    wind?
³Does God pervert justice?
  Or does the Almighty pervert the right?
⁴If your children have sinned against him,
  he has delivered them into the power of
    their transgression.
⁵If you will seek God
  and make supplication to the Almighty,
⁶if you are pure and upright,
  surely then he will rouse himself for you
  and reward you with a rightful habitation.
⁷And though your beginning was small,
  your latter days will be very great.

⁸ "For inquire, I beg you, of bygone ages,
  and consider what the fathers have found;
⁹for we are but of yesterday, and know nothing,
  for our days on earth are a shadow.
¹⁰Will they not teach you, and tell you,
  and utter words out of their
    understanding?

¹¹ "Can papyrus grow where there is no marsh?
  Can reeds flourish where there is no water?
¹²While yet in flower and not cut down,
  they wither before any other plant.
¹³Such are the paths of all who forget God;
  the hope of the godless man shall perish.
¹⁴His confidence breaks in sunder,
  and his trust is a spider's web. °
¹⁵He leans against his house, but it does not
    stand;
  he lays hold of it, but it does not endure.

¹⁶He thrives before the sun,
  and his shoots spread over his garden.
¹⁷His roots twine about the stone-heap;
  he lives among the rocks. ᴾ
¹⁸If he is destroyed from his place,
  then it will deny him, saying, 'I have never
    seen you.'
¹⁹Behold, this is the joy of his way;
  and out of the earth others will spring.

²⁰ "Behold, God will not reject a blameless man,
  nor take the hand of evildoers.
²¹He will yet fill your mouth with laughter,
  and your lips with shouting.
²²Those who hate you will be clothed with shame,
  and the tent of the wicked will be no
    more."

Job Replies to Bildad

9 Then Job answered:
  ² "Truly I know that it is so:
  But how can a man be just before God?
³If one wished to contend with him,
  one could not answer him once in a
    thousand times.
⁴He is wise in heart, and mighty in strength
  —who has hardened himself against him,
    and succeeded?—
⁵he who removes mountains, and they know it
    not,
  when he overturns them in his anger;
⁶who shakes the earth out of its place,
  and its pillars tremble;
⁷who commands the sun, and it does not rise;
  who seals up the stars;
⁸who alone stretched out the heavens,
  and trampled the waves of the sea; �q
⁹who made the Bear and Ori'on,
  the Plei'ades and the chambers of the south;
¹⁰who does great things beyond understanding,
  and marvelous things without number.
¹¹Behold, he passes by me, and I see him not;
  he moves on, but I do not perceive him.
¹²Behold, he snatches away; who can hinder him?
  Who will say to him, 'What are you doing?'

¹³ "God will not turn back his anger;
  beneath him bowed the helpers of Ra'hab.
¹⁴How then can I answer him,
  choosing my words with him?
¹⁵Though I am innocent, I cannot answer him;
  I must appeal for mercy to my accuser. ʳ
¹⁶If I summoned him and he answered me,
  I would not believe that he was listening to
    my voice.

° Heb *house.*
ᴾ Gk Vg: Heb uncertain.
q Or *trampled the back of the sea dragon.*
ʳ Or *for my right.*
7:17: Ps 8:4.

¹⁷For he crushes me with a tempest,
  and multiplies my wounds without cause;
¹⁸he will not let me get my breath,
  but fills me with bitterness.
¹⁹If it is a contest of strength, behold him!
  If it is a matter of justice, who can summon
    him? ˢ
²⁰Though I am innocent, my own mouth would
    condemn me;
  though I am blameless, he would prove me
    perverse.
²¹I am blameless; I regard not myself;
  I loathe my life.
²²It is all one; therefore I say,
  he destroys both the blameless and the
    wicked.
²³When disaster brings sudden death,
  he mocks at the calamity ᵗ of the innocent.
²⁴The earth is given into the hand of the wicked;
  he covers the faces of its judges—
  if it is not he, who then is it?

²⁵ "My days are swifter than a runner;
  they flee away, they see no good.
²⁶They go by like skiffs of reed,
  like an eagle swooping on the prey.
²⁷If I say, 'I will forget my complaint,
  I will put off my sad countenance, and be of
    good cheer,'
²⁸I become afraid of all my suffering,
  for I know you will not hold me innocent.
²⁹I shall be condemned;
  why then do I labor in vain?
³⁰If I wash myself with snow,
  and cleanse my hands with lye,
³¹yet you will plunge me into a pit,
  and my own clothes will abhor me.
³²For he is not a man, as I am, that I might
    answer him,
  that we should come to trial together.
³³There is no ᵘ umpire between us,
  who might lay his hand upon us both.
³⁴Let him take his rod away from me,
  and let not dread of him terrify me.
³⁵Then I would speak without fear of him,
  for I am not so in myself.

Job Says He Loathes His Life

10 "I loathe my life;
  I will give free utterance to my complaint;
  I will speak in the bitterness of my soul.
²I will say to God, Do not condemn me;
  let me know why you contend against me.
³Does it seem good to you to oppress,
  to despise the work of your hands
  and favor the designs of the wicked?
⁴Do you have eyes of flesh?
  Do you see as man sees?
⁵Are your days as the days of man,
  or your years as man's years,

⁶that you seek out my iniquity
  and search for my sin,
⁷although you know that I am not guilty,
  and there is none to deliver out of your
    hand?
⁸Your hands fashioned and made me;
  and now you turn about and destroy me. ᵛ
⁹Remember that you have made me of clay; ʷ
  and will you turn me to dust again?
¹⁰Did you not pour me out like milk
  and curdle me like cheese?
¹¹You clothed me with skin and flesh,
  and knit me together with bones and
    sinews.
¹²You have granted me life and mercy;
  and your care has preserved my spirit.
¹³Yet these things you hid in your heart;
  I know that this was your purpose.
¹⁴If I sin, you mark me,
  and do not acquit me of my iniquity.
¹⁵If I am wicked, woe to me!
  If I am righteous, I cannot lift up my head,
  for I am filled with disgrace
  and look upon my affliction.
¹⁶And if I lift myself up, ˣ you hunt me like a
    lion,
  and again work wonders against me;
¹⁷you renew your witnesses against me,
  and increase your vexation toward me;
  you bring fresh hosts against me. ʸ

¹⁸ "Why did you bring me forth from the
    womb?
  Would that I had died before any eye had
    seen me,
¹⁹and were as though I had not been,
  carried from the womb to the grave.
²⁰Are not the days of my life few? ᶻ
  Let me alone, that I may find a little
    comfort ᵃ
²¹before I go from where I shall not return,
  to the land of gloom and deep darkness,
²²the land of gloom ᵇ and chaos,
  where light is as darkness."

Zophar Speaks: Job's Guilt Deserves Punishment

11 Then Zo′phar the Na′amathite answered:
  ² "Should a multitude of words go
    unanswered,
  and a man full of talk be vindicated?

ˢ Compare Gk: Heb *me*. The text of the verse is uncertain.
ᵗ The meaning of the Hebrew word is uncertain.
ᵘ Another reading is *Would that there were.*
ᵛ Cn Compare Gk Syr: Heb *made me together round about and you destroy me.*
ʷ Gk: Heb *like clay.*
ˣ Syr: Heb *he lifts himself up.*
ʸ Cn Compare Gk: Heb *changes and a host are with me.*
ᶻ Cn Compare Gk Syr: Heb *Are not my days few? Let him cease.*
ᵃ Heb *brighten up.*
ᵇ Heb *gloom as darkness, deep darkness.*

³Should your babble silence men,
  and when you mock, shall no one shame
    you?
⁴For you say, 'My doctrine is pure,
  and I am clean in God's eyes.'
⁵But oh, that God would speak,
  and open his lips to you,
⁶and that he would tell you the secrets of
    wisdom!
  For he is manifold in understanding. ᶜ
  Know then that God exacts of you less than
    your guilt deserves.

⁷ "Can you find out the deep things of God?
  Can you find out the limit of the Almighty?
⁸It is higher than heaven ᵈ—what can you do?
  Deeper than Sheol—what can you know?
⁹Its measure is longer than the earth,
  and broader than the sea.
¹⁰If he passes through, and imprisons,
  and calls to judgment, who can hinder him?
¹¹For he knows worthless men;
  when he sees iniquity, will he not consider it?
¹²But a stupid man will get understanding,
  when a wild donkey's colt is born a man.

¹³ "If you set your heart aright,
  you will stretch out your hands toward him.
¹⁴If iniquity is in your hand, put it far away,
  and let not wickedness dwell in your tents.
¹⁵Surely then you will lift up your face without
    blemish;
  you will be secure, and will not fear.
¹⁶You will forget your misery;
  you will remember it as waters that have
    passed away.
¹⁷And your life will be brighter than the
    noonday;
  its darkness will be like the morning.
¹⁸And you will have confidence, because there is
    hope;
  you will be protected ᵉ and take your rest in
    safety.
¹⁹You will lie down, and none will make you
    afraid;
  many will entreat your favor.
²⁰But the eyes of the wicked will fail;
  all way of escape will be lost to them,
  and their hope is to breathe their last."

Job Replies to Zophar

12 Then Job answered:
  ² "No doubt you are the people,
  and wisdom will die with you.
³But I have understanding as well as you;
  I am not inferior to you.
  Who does not know such things as these?
⁴I am a laughingstock to my friends;
  I, who called upon God and he answered
    me,

a just and blameless man, am a
    laughingstock.
⁵In the thought of one who is at ease there is
    contempt for misfortune;
  it is ready for those whose feet slip.
⁶The tents of robbers are at peace,
  and those who provoke God are secure,
  who bring their god in their hand. ᶠ

⁷ "But ask the beasts, and they will teach you;
  the birds of the air, and they will tell you;
⁸or the plants of the earth, ᵍ and they will teach
    you;
  and the fish of the sea will declare to you.
⁹Who among all these does not know
  that the hand of the LORD has done this?
¹⁰In his hand is the life of every living thing
  and the breath of all mankind.
¹¹Does not the ear try words
  as the palate tastes food?
¹²Wisdom is with the aged,
  and understanding in length of days.

¹³ "With God ʰ are wisdom and might;
  he has counsel and understanding.
¹⁴If he tears down, none can rebuild;
  if he shuts a man in, none can open.
¹⁵If he withholds the waters, they dry up;
  if he sends them out, they overwhelm the
    land.
¹⁶With him are strength and wisdom;
  the deceived and the deceiver are his.
¹⁷He leads counselors away stripped,
  and judges he makes fools.
¹⁸He looses the bonds of kings,
  and binds a waistcloth on their loins.
¹⁹He leads priests away stripped,
  and overthrows the mighty.
²⁰He deprives of speech those who are trusted,
  and takes away the discernment of the
    elders.
²¹He pours contempt on princes,
  and looses the belt of the strong.
²²He uncovers the deeps out of darkness,
  and brings deep darkness to light.
²³He makes nations great, and he destroys them:
  he enlarges nations, and leads them away.
²⁴He takes away understanding from the chiefs
    of the people of the earth,
  and makes them wander in a pathless
    waste.
²⁵They grope in the dark without light;
  and he makes them stagger like a drunken
    man.

ᶜ Heb obscure.
ᵈ Heb *The heights of heaven.*
ᵉ Or *you will look around.*
ᶠ Hebrew uncertain.
ᵍ Or *speak to the earth.*
ʰ Heb *him.*

13

"Behold, my eye has seen all this,
my ear has heard and understood it.
[2]What you know, I also know;
I am not inferior to you.
[3]But I would speak to the Almighty,
and I desire to argue my case with God.
[4]As for you, you whitewash with lies;
worthless physicians are you all.
[5]Oh, that you would keep silent,
and it would be your wisdom!
[6]Hear now my reasoning,
and listen to the pleadings of my lips.
[7]Will you speak falsely for God,
and speak deceitfully for him?
[8]Will you show partiality toward him,
will you plead the case for God?
[9]Will it be well with you when he searches you
out?
Or can you deceive him, as one deceives a
man?
[10]He will surely rebuke you
if in secret you show partiality.
[11]Will not his majesty terrify you,
and the dread of him fall upon you?
[12]Your maxims are proverbs of ashes,
your defenses are defenses of clay.

[13]"Let me have silence, and I will speak,
and let come on me what may.
[14]I will take [i] my flesh in my teeth,
and put my life in my hand.
[15]Behold, he will slay me; I have no hope;
yet I will defend my ways to his face.
[16]This will be my salvation,
that a godless man shall not come before
him.
[17]Listen carefully to my words,
and let my declaration be in your ears.
[18]Behold, I have prepared my case;
I know that I shall be vindicated.
[19]Who is there that will contend with me?
For then I would be silent and die.
[20]Only grant two things to me,
then I will not hide myself from your
face:
[21]withdraw your hand far from me,
and let not dread of you terrify me.
[22]Then call, and I will answer;
or let me speak, and do reply to me.
[23]How many are my iniquities and my sins?
Make me know my transgression and my
sin.
[24]Why do you hide your face,
and count me as your enemy?
[25]Will you frighten a driven leaf
and pursue dry chaff?
[26]For you write bitter things against me,
and make me inherit the iniquities of my
youth.

[27]You put my feet in the stocks,
and watch all my paths;
you set a bound to the soles of my feet.
[28]Man [j] wastes away like a rotten thing,
like a garment that is moth-eaten.

The Frailty of Man

14

"Man that is born of a woman is of few
days, and full of trouble.
[2]He comes forth like a flower, and withers;
he flees like a shadow, and continues not.
[3]And do you open your eyes upon such a one
and bring him [k] into judgment with you?
[4]Who can bring a clean thing out of an
unclean?
There is not one.
[5]Since his days are determined,
and the number of his months is with you,
and you have appointed his bounds that he
cannot pass,
[6]look away from him, and desist, [l]
that he may enjoy, like a hireling, his day.

[7]"For there is hope for a tree,
if it be cut down, that it will sprout again,
and that its shoots will not cease.
[8]Though its root grow old in the earth,
and its stump die in the ground,
[9]yet at the scent of water it will bud
and put forth branches like a young plant.
[10]But man dies, and is laid low;
man breathes his last, and where is he?
[11]As waters fail from a lake,
and a river wastes away and dries up,
[12]so man lies down and rises not again;
till the heavens are no more he will not
awake,
or be roused out of his sleep.
[13]Oh, that you would hide me in Sheol,
that you would conceal me until your wrath
be past,
that you would appoint me a set time, and
remember me!
[14]If a man die, shall he live again?
All the days of my service I would wait,
till my release should come.
[15]You would call, and I would answer you;
you would long for the work of your
hands.
[16]For then you would number my steps,
you would not keep watch over my sin;
[17]my transgression would be sealed up in a bag,
and you would cover over my iniquity.

[18]"But the mountain falls and crumbles away,
and the rock is removed from its place;

---

[i] Gk: Heb *Why should I take?*
[j] Heb *He.*
[k] Gk Syr Vg: Heb *me.*
[l] Cn: Heb *that he may desist.*

¹⁹the waters wear away the stones;
the torrents wash away the soil of the
earth;
so you destroy the hope of man.
²⁰You prevail for ever against him, and he
passes;
you change his countenance, and send him
away.
²¹His sons come to honor, and he does not know
it;
they are brought low, and he perceives it
not.
²²He feels only the pain of his own body,
and he mourns only for himself."

Eliphaz Rebukes Job

15 Then Eli'phaz the Te'manite answered:
²"Should a wise man answer with windy
knowledge,
and fill himself with the east wind?
³Should he argue in unprofitable talk,
or in words with which he can do no good?
⁴But you are doing away with the fear of God,
and hindering meditation before God.
⁵For your iniquity teaches your mouth,
and you choose the tongue of the crafty.
⁶Your own mouth condemns you, and not I;
your own lips testify against you.

⁷"Are you the first man that was born?
Or were you brought forth before the hills?
⁸Have you listened in the council of God?
And do you limit wisdom to yourself?
⁹What do you know that we do not know?
What do you understand that is not clear to
us?
¹⁰Both the gray-haired and the aged are among
us,
older than your father.
¹¹Are the consolations of God too small for you,
or the word that deals gently with you?
¹²Why does your heart carry you away,
and why do your eyes flash,
¹³that you turn your spirit against God,
and let such words go out of your mouth?
¹⁴What is man, that he can be clean?
Or he who is born of a woman, that he can
be righteous?
¹⁵Behold, God puts no trust in his holy ones,
and the heavens are not clean in his sight;
¹⁶how much less one who is abominable and
corrupt,
a man who drinks iniquity like water!

¹⁷"I will show you, hear me;
and what I have seen I will declare
¹⁸(what wise men have told,
and their fathers have not hidden,
¹⁹to whom alone the land was given,
and no stranger passed among them).

²⁰The wicked man writhes in pain all his days,
through all the years that are laid up for the
ruthless.
²¹Terrifying sounds are in his ears;
in prosperity the destroyer will come upon
him.
²²He does not believe that he will return out of
darkness,
and he is destined for the sword.
²³He wanders abroad for bread, saying, 'Where is
it?'
He knows that a day of darkness is ready at
his hand;
²⁴distress and anguish terrify him;
they prevail against him, like a king
prepared for battle.
²⁵Because he has stretched forth his hand
against God,
and bids defiance to the Almighty,
²⁶running stubbornly against him
with a thick-bossed shield;
²⁷because he has covered his face with his fat,
and gathered fat upon his loins,
²⁸and has lived in desolate cities,
in houses which no man should inhabit,
which were destined to become heaps of
ruins;
²⁹he will not be rich, and his wealth will not
endure,
nor will he strike root in the earth;^m
³⁰he will not escape from darkness;
the flame will dry up his shoots,
and his blossomⁿ will be swept away^o by
the wind.
³¹Let him not trust in emptiness, deceiving
himself;
for emptiness will be his recompense.
³²It will be paid in full before his time,
and his branch will not be green.
³³He will shake off his unripe grape, like the
vine,
and cast off his blossom, like the olive tree.
³⁴For the company of the godless is barren,
and fire consumes the tents of bribery.
³⁵They conceive mischief and bring forth evil
and their heart prepares deceit."

Job Reaffirms His Innocence

16 Then Job answered:
²"I have heard many such things;
miserable comforters are you all.
³Shall windy words have an end?
Or what provokes you that you answer?
⁴I also could speak as you do,
if you were in my place;
I could join words together against you,
and shake my head at you.

---

^m Vg: Heb obscure.
ⁿ Gk: Heb *mouth*.
^o Cn: Heb *will depart*.

⁵I could strengthen you with my mouth,
and the solace of my lips would assuage
your pain.

⁶ "If I speak, my pain is not assuaged,
and if I forbear, how much of it leaves me?
⁷Surely now God has worn me out;
he has ᵖ made desolate all my company.
⁸And he has ᵖ shriveled me up,
which is a witness against me;
and my leanness has risen up against me,
it testifies to my face.
⁹He has torn me in his wrath, and hated me;
he has gnashed his teeth at me;
my adversary sharpens his eyes against
me.
¹⁰Men have gaped at me with their mouth,
they have struck me insolently upon the
cheek,
they mass themselves together against me.
¹¹God gives me up to the ungodly,
and casts me into the hands of the wicked.
¹²I was at ease, and he broke me asunder;
he seized me by the neck and dashed me to
pieces;
he set me up as his target,
¹³   his archers surround me.
He slashes open my kidneys, and does not
spare;
he pours out my gall on the ground.
¹⁴He breaks me with breach upon breach;
he runs upon me like a warrior.
¹⁵I have sewn sackcloth upon my skin,
and have laid my strength in the dust.
¹⁶My face is red with weeping,
and on my eyelids is deep darkness;
¹⁷although there is no violence in my hands,
and my prayer is pure.

¹⁸ "O earth, cover not my blood,
and let my cry find no resting place.
¹⁹Even now, behold, my witness is in heaven,
and he that vouches for me is on high.
²⁰My friends scorn me;
my eye pours out tears to God,
²¹that he would maintain the right of a man with
God,
like ᑫ that of a man with his neighbor.
²²For when a few years have come
I shall go the way from where I shall not
return.

Job Prays for Relief

17 My spirit is broken, my days are extinct,
the grave is ready for me.
²Surely there are mockers about me,
and my eye dwells on their provocation.

³ "Lay down a pledge for me with yourself;
who is there that will give surety for me?

⁴Since you have closed their minds to
understanding,
therefore you will not let them triumph.
⁵He who informs against his friends to get a
share of their property,
the eyes of his children will fail.

⁶ "He has made me a byword of the peoples,
and I am one before whom men spit.
⁷My eye has grown dim from grief,
and all my members are like a shadow.
⁸Upright men are appalled at this,
and the innocent stirs himself up against
the godless.
⁹Yet the righteous holds to his way,
and he that has clean hands grows stronger
and stronger.
¹⁰But you, come on again, all of you,
and I shall not find a wise man among you.
¹¹My days are past, my plans are broken off,
the desires of my heart.
¹²They make night into day;
'The light,' they say, 'is near to the
darkness.' ᴿ
¹³If I look for Sheol as my house,
if I spread my couch in darkness,
¹⁴if I say to the pit, 'You are my father,'
and to the worm, 'My mother,' or 'My
sister,'
¹⁵where then is my hope?
Who will see my hope?
¹⁶Will it go down to the bars of Sheol?
Shall we descend together into the dust?"

Bildad Speaks: God Punishes
the Wicked

18 Then Bildad the Shuhite answered:
² "How long will you hunt for words?
Consider, and then we will speak.
³Why are we counted as cattle?
Why are we stupid in your sight?
⁴You who tear yourself in your anger,
shall the earth be forsaken for you,
or the rock be removed out of its place?

⁵ "Yes, the light of the wicked is put out,
and the flame of his fire does not shine.
⁶The light is dark in his tent,
and his lamp above him is put out.
⁷His strong steps are shortened
and his own schemes throw him down.
⁸For he is cast into a net by his own feet,
and he walks on a pitfall.
⁹A trap seizes him by the heel,
a snare lays hold of him.
¹⁰A rope is hid for him in the ground,
a trap for him in the path.

ᵖ Heb *you have.*
ᑫ Syr Vg Tg: Heb *and.*
ᴿ Heb obscure.

¹¹Terrors frighten him on every side,
 and chase him at his heels.
¹²His strength is hunger-bitten,
 and calamity is ready for his stumbling.
¹³By disease his skin is consumed, ˢ
 the first-born of death consumes his limbs.
¹⁴He is torn from the tent in which he trusted,
 and is brought to the king of terrors.
¹⁵In his tent dwells that which is none of his;
 brimstone is scattered upon his habitation.
¹⁶His roots dry up beneath,
 and his branches wither above.
¹⁷His memory perishes from the earth,
 and he has no name in the street.
¹⁸He is thrust from light into darkness,
 and driven out of the world.
¹⁹He has no offspring or descendant among his
 people,
 and no survivor where he used to live.
²⁰They of the west are appalled at his day,
 and horror seizes them of the east.
²¹Surely such are the dwellings of the ungodly,
 such is the place of him who knows not
 God."

Job Answers: I Know That
My Redeemer Lives

19 Then Job answered:
 ² "How long will you torment me,
 and break me in pieces with words?
³These ten times you have cast reproach upon
 me;
 are you not ashamed to wrong me?
⁴And even if it be true that I have erred,
 my error remains with myself.
⁵If indeed you magnify yourselves against me,
 and make my humiliation an argument
 against me,
⁶know then that God has put me in the wrong,
 and closed his net about me.
⁷Behold, I cry out, 'Violence!' but I am not
 answered;
 I call aloud, but there is no justice.
⁸He has walled up my way, so that I cannot
 pass,
 and he has set darkness upon my paths.
⁹He has stripped from me my glory,
 and taken the crown from my head.
¹⁰He breaks me down on every side, and I am
 gone,
 and my hope has he pulled up like a tree.
¹¹He has kindled his wrath against me,
 and counts me as his adversary.
¹²His troops come on together;
 they have cast up siegeworks ᵗ against me,
 and encamp round about my tent.

¹³ "He has put my brethren far from me,
 and my acquaintances are wholly estranged
 from me.

¹⁴My kinsfolk and my close friends have failed
 me;
¹⁵ the guests in my house have forgotten me;
 my maidservants count me as a stranger;
 I have become an alien in their eyes.
¹⁶I call to my servant, but he gives me no answer;
 I must beseech him with my mouth.
¹⁷I am repulsive to my wife,
 loathsome to the sons of my own mother.
¹⁸Even young children despise me;
 when I rise they talk against me.
¹⁹All my intimate friends abhor me,
 and those whom I loved have turned against
 me.
²⁰My bones cling to my skin and to my flesh,
 and I have escaped by the skin of my teeth.
²¹Have pity on me, have pity on me, O you my
 friends,
 for the hand of God has touched me!
²²Why do you, like God, pursue me?
 Why are you not satisfied with my flesh?

²³ "Oh, that my words were written!
 Oh, that they were inscribed in a book!
²⁴Oh, that with an iron pen and lead
 they were graven in the rock for ever!
²⁵For I know that my Redeemer ᵘ lives,
 and at last he will stand upon the earth; ᵛ
²⁶and after my skin has been thus destroyed,
 then from ʷ my flesh I shall see God, ˣ
²⁷whom I shall see on my side, ʸ
 and my eyes shall behold, and not another.
 My heart faints within me!
²⁸If you say, 'How we will pursue him!'
 and, 'The root of the matter is found in
 him';
²⁹be afraid of the sword,
 for wrath brings the punishment of the
 sword,
 that you may know there is a judgment."

Zophar Speaks: Wickedness
Receives Retribution

20 Then Zo′phar the Na′amathite answered:
 ² "Therefore my thoughts answer me,
 because of my haste within me.
³I hear censure which insults me,
 and out of my understanding a spirit
 answers me.
⁴Do you not know this from of old,
 since man was placed upon earth,
⁵that the exulting of the wicked is short,
 and the joy of the godless but for a
 moment?

ˢ Cn: Heb *it consumes the limbs of his skin.*
ᵗ Heb *their way.*
ᵘ Or *Vindicator.*
ᵛ Or *dust.*
ʷ Or *without.*
ˣ The meaning of this verse is uncertain.
ʸ Or *for myself.*

⁶Though his height mount up to the heavens,
  and his head reach to the clouds,
⁷he will perish for ever like his own dung;
  those who have seen him will say, 'Where is
  he?'
⁸He will fly away like a dream, and not be
  found;
  he will be chased away like a vision of the
  night.
⁹The eye which saw him will see him no more,
  nor will his place any more behold him.
¹⁰His children will seek the favor of the poor,
  and his hands will give back his wealth.
¹¹His bones are full of youthful vigor,
  but it will lie down with him in the dust.

¹²"Though wickedness is sweet in his mouth,
  though he hides it under his tongue,
¹³though he is loath to let it go,
  and holds it in his mouth,
¹⁴yet his food is turned in his stomach;
  it is the gall of asps within him.
¹⁵He swallows down riches and vomits them up
  again;
  God casts them out of his belly.
¹⁶He will suck the poison of asps;
  the tongue of a viper will kill him.
¹⁷He will not look upon the rivers,
  the streams flowing with honey and
  curds.
¹⁸He will give back the fruit of his toil,
  and will not swallow it down;
from the profit of his trading
  he will get no enjoyment.
¹⁹For he has crushed and abandoned the poor,
  he has seized a house which he did not
  build.

²⁰ "Because his greed knew no rest,
  he will not save anything in which he
  delights.
²¹There was nothing left after he had eaten;
  therefore his prosperity will not endure.
²²In the fulness of his sufficiency he will be in
  straits;
  all the force of misery will come upon him.
²³To fill his belly to the full
  God ᶻ will send his fierce anger into him,
  and rain it upon him as his food. ᵃ
²⁴He will flee from an iron weapon;
  a bronze arrow will strike him through.
²⁵It is drawn forth and comes out of his body,
  the glittering point comes out of his gall;
  terrors come upon him.
²⁶Utter darkness is laid up for his treasures;
  a fire not blown upon will devour him;
  what is left in his tent will be consumed.
²⁷The heavens will reveal his iniquity,
  and the earth will rise up against him.

²⁸The possessions of his house will be carried
  away,
  dragged off in the day of God's ᵇ wrath.
²⁹This is the wicked man's portion from God,
  the heritage decreed for him by God."

Job Replies: The Wicked Often Prosper

21 Then Job answered:
  ² "Listen carefully to my words,
  and let this be your consolation.
³Bear with me, and I will speak,
  and after I have spoken, mock on.
⁴As for me, is my complaint against man?
  Why should I not be impatient?
⁵Look at me, and be appalled,
  and lay your hand upon your mouth.
⁶When I think of it I am dismayed,
  and shuddering seizes my flesh.
⁷Why do the wicked live,
  reach old age, and grow mighty in power?
⁸Their children are established in their
  presence,
  and their offspring before their eyes.
⁹Their houses are safe from fear,
  and no rod of God is upon them.
¹⁰Their bull breeds without fail;
  their cow calves, and does not cast her calf.
¹¹They send forth their little ones like a flock,
  and their children dance.
¹²They sing to the tambourine and the lyre,
  and rejoice to the sound of the pipe.
¹³They spend their days in prosperity,
  and in peace they go down to Sheol.
¹⁴They say to God, 'Depart from us!
  We do not desire the knowledge of your
  ways.
¹⁵What is the Almighty, that we should serve
  him?
  And what profit do we get if we pray to
  him?'
¹⁶Behold, is not their prosperity in their hand?
  The counsel of the wicked is far from me.

¹⁷ " How often is it that the lamp of the wicked is
  put out?
  That their calamity comes upon them?
  That God ᶜ distributes pains in his anger?
¹⁸That they are like straw before the wind,
  and like chaff that the storm carries away?
¹⁹You say, 'God stores up their iniquity for their
  sons.'
  Let him recompense it to themselves, that
  they may know it.
²⁰Let their own eyes see their destruction,
  and let them drink of the wrath of the
  Almighty.

ᶻ Heb *he.*
ᵃ Cn: Heb *in his flesh.*
ᵇ Heb *his.*
ᶜ Heb *he.*

²¹For what do they care for their houses after
them,
when the number of their months is cut off?
²²Will any teach God knowledge,
seeing that he judges those that are on
high?
²³One dies in full prosperity,
being wholly at ease and secure,
²⁴his body ᵈ full of fat
and the marrow of his bones moist.
²⁵Another dies in bitterness of soul,
never having tasted of good.
²⁶They lie down alike in the dust,
and the worms cover them.

²⁷ "Behold, I know your thoughts,
and your schemes to wrong me.
²⁸For you say, 'Where is the house of the prince?
Where is the tent in which the wicked
dwelt?'
²⁹Have you not asked those who travel the roads,
and do you not accept their testimony
³⁰that the wicked man is spared in the day of
calamity,
that he is rescued in the day of wrath?
³¹Who declares his way to his face,
and who repays him for what he has done?
³²When he is borne to the grave,
watch is kept over his tomb.
³³The clods of the valley are sweet to him;
all men follow after him,
and those who go before him are
innumerable.
³⁴How then will you comfort me with empty
nothings?
There is nothing left of your answers but
falsehood."

Eliphaz Speaks: Job's Wickedness
Must Be Great

22 Then Eli′phaz the Te′manite answered:
² "Can a man be profitable to God?
Surely he who is wise is profitable to
himself.
³Is it any pleasure to the Almighty if you are
righteous,
or is it gain to him if you make your ways
blameless?
⁴Is it for your fear of him that he reproves you,
and enters into judgment with you?
⁵Is not your wickedness great?
There is no end to your iniquities.
⁶For you have exacted pledges of your brothers
for nothing,
and stripped the naked of their clothing.
⁷You have given no water to the weary to drink,
and you have withheld bread from the
hungry.
⁸The man with power possessed the land,
and the favored man dwelt in it.

⁹You have sent widows away empty,
and the arms of the fatherless were
crushed.
¹⁰Therefore snares are round about you,
and sudden terror overwhelms you;
¹¹your light is darkened, so that ᵉ you cannot
see,
and a flood of water covers you.

¹² "Is not God high in the heavens?
See the highest stars, how lofty they are!
¹³Therefore you say, 'What does God know?
Can he judge through the deep darkness?
¹⁴Thick clouds enwrap him, so that he does not
see,
and he walks on the vault of heaven.'
¹⁵Will you keep to the old way
which wicked men have trod?
¹⁶They were snatched away before their time;
their foundation was washed away.
¹⁷They said to God, 'Depart from us,'
and 'What can the Almighty do to us?' ᶠ
¹⁸Yet he filled their houses with good things—
but the counsel of the wicked is far from
me.
¹⁹The righteous see it and are glad;
the innocent laugh them to scorn,
²⁰saying, 'Surely our adversaries are cut off,
and what they left the fire has consumed.'

²¹ "Agree with God, and be at peace;
thereby good will come to you.
²²Receive instruction from his mouth,
and lay up his words in your heart.
²³If you return to the Almighty and humble
yourself, ᵍ
if you remove unrighteousness far from
your tents,
²⁴if you lay gold in the dust,
and gold of O′phir among the stones of the
torrent bed,
²⁵and if the Almighty is your gold,
and your precious silver;
²⁶then you will delight yourself in the Almighty,
and lift up your face to God.
²⁷You will make your prayer to him, and he will
hear you;
and you will pay your vows.
²⁸You will decide on a matter, and it will be
established for you,
and light will shine on your ways.
²⁹For God abases the proud, ʰ
but he saves the lowly.

ᵈ The meaning of the Hebrew word is uncertain.
ᵉ Cn Compare Gk: Heb *or darkness.*
ᶠ Gk Syr: Heb *them.*
ᵍ Gk: Heb *you will be built up.*
ʰ Cn: Heb *when they abased you said, Proud.*
22:2, 3: 35:6–8.

[30]He delivers the innocent man; [i]
you will be delivered through the cleanness
of your hands."

Job Replies: I Am Hemmed In

23 Then Job answered:
[2] "Today also my complaint is bitter, [j]
his [k] hand is heavy in spite of my groaning.
[3]Oh, that I knew where I might find him,
that I might come even to his seat!
[4]I would lay my case before him
and fill my mouth with arguments.
[5]I would learn what he would answer me,
and understand what he would say to me.
[6]Would he contend with me in the greatness of
his power?
No; he would give heed to me.
[7]There an upright man could reason with him,
and I should be acquitted for ever by my
judge.

[8] "Behold, I go forward, but he is not there;
and backward, but I cannot perceive him;
[9]on the left hand I seek him, [l] but I cannot
behold him;
I [m] turn to the right hand, but I cannot see
him.
[10]But he knows the way that I take;
when he has tried me, I shall come forth as
gold.
[11]My foot has held fast to his steps;
I have kept his way and have not turned
aside.
[12]I have not departed from the commandment of
his lips;
I have treasured in [n] my bosom the words
of his mouth.
[13]But he is unchangeable and who can turn him?
What he desires, that he does.
[14]For he will complete what he appoints for me;
and many such things are in his mind.
[15]Therefore I am terrified at his presence;
when I consider, I am in dread of him.
[16]God has made my heart faint;
the Almighty has terrified me;
[17]for I am [o] hemmed in by darkness,
and thick darkness covers my face. [p]

Job Complains of Violence

24 "Why are not times of judgment kept by
the Almighty,
and why do those who know him never see
his days?
[2]Men remove landmarks;
they seize flocks and pasture them.
[3]They drive away the donkey of the fatherless;
they take the widow's ox for a pledge.
[4]They thrust the poor off the road;
the poor of the earth all hide themselves.
[5]Behold, like wild donkeys in the desert
they go forth to their toil,

seeking prey in the wilderness
as food [q] for their children.
[6]They gather their [r] fodder in the field
and they glean the vineyard of the wicked
man.
[7]They lie all night naked, without clothing,
and have no covering in the cold.
[8]They are wet with the rain of the mountains,
and cling to the rock for want of shelter.
[9](There are those who snatch the fatherless
child from the breast,
and take in pledge the infant of the poor.)
[10]They go about naked, without clothing;
hungry, they carry the sheaves;
[11]among the olive rows of the wicked [s] they
make oil;
they tread the wine presses, but suffer
thirst.
[12]From out of the city the dying groan,
and the soul of the wounded cries for help;
yet God pays no attention to their prayer.

[13] "There are those who rebel against the light,
who are not acquainted with its ways,
and do not stay in its paths.
[14]The murderer rises in the dark, [t]
that he may kill the poor and needy;
and in the night he is as a thief.
[15]The eye of the adulterer also waits for the
twilight,
saying, 'No eye will see me';
and he disguises his face.
[16]In the dark they dig through houses;
by day they shut themselves up;
they do not know the light.
[17]For deep darkness is morning to all of them;
for they are friends with the terrors of deep
darkness.

[18] "You say, 'They are swiftly carried away upon
the face of the waters;
their portion is cursed in the land;
no treader turns toward their vineyards.
[19]Drought and heat snatch away the snow waters;
so does Sheol those who have sinned.
[20]The squares of the town [u] forget them;
their name [v] is no longer remembered;
so wickedness is broken like a tree.'

---

[i] Gk Syr Vg: Heb *him that is not innocent.*
[j] Syr Vg Tg: Heb *rebellious.*
[k] Gk Syr: Heb *my.*
[l] Compare Syr: Heb *on the left hand when he works.*
[m] Syr Vg: Heb *he.*
[n] Gk Vg: Heb *from.*
[o] With one Ms: Heb *am not.*
[p] Vg: Heb *from my face.*
[q] Heb *food to him.*
[r] Heb *his.*
[s] Heb *their olive rows.*
[t] Cn: Heb *at the light,*
[u] Cn: Heb obscure.
[v] Cn: Heb *a worm.*

21 "They feed on the barren childless woman,
  and do no good to the widow.
22 Yet God [w] prolongs the life of the mighty by his
    power;
  they rise up when they despair of life.
23 He gives them security, and they are supported;
  and his eyes are upon their ways.
24 They are exalted a little while, and then are
    gone;
  they wither and fade like the mallow; [x]
  they are cut off like the heads of grain.
25 If it is not so, who will prove me a liar,
  and show that there is nothing in what I
    say?"

Bildad Speaks: How Can Man Be Righteous?

25 Then Bildad the Shuhite answered:
  2 "Dominion and fear are with God; [y]
  he makes peace in his high heaven.
3 Is there any number to his armies?
  Upon whom does his light not arise?
4 How then can man be righteous before God?
  How can he who is born of woman be
    clean?
5 Behold, even the moon is not bright
  and the stars are not clean in his sight;
6 how much less man, who is a maggot,
  and the son of man, who is a worm!"

Job Speaks of God's Power

26 Then Job answered:
  2 "How you have helped him who has no
    power!
  How you have saved the arm that has no
    strength!
3 How you have counseled him who has no
    wisdom,
  and plentifully declared sound knowledge!
4 With whose help have you uttered words,
  and whose spirit has come forth from you?
5 The shades below tremble,
  the waters and their inhabitants.
6 Sheol is naked before God,
  and Abad'don has no covering.
7 He stretches out the north over the void,
  and hangs the earth upon nothing.
8 He binds up the waters in his thick clouds,
  and the cloud is not torn under them.
9 He covers the face of the moon, [z]
  and spreads over it his cloud.
10 He has described a circle upon the face of the
    waters
  at the boundary between light and
    darkness.
11 The pillars of heaven tremble,
  and are astounded at his rebuke.
12 By his power he stilled the sea;
  by his understanding he struck Ra'hab.
13 By his wind the heavens were made fair;
  his hand pierced the fleeing serpent.

14 Behold, these are but the outskirts of his ways;
  and how small a whisper do we hear of him!
  But the thunder of his power who can
    understand?"

Job Maintains His Integrity

27 And Job again took up his discourse, and
  said:
2 "As God lives, who has taken away my right,
  and the Almighty, who has made my soul
    bitter;
3 as long as my breath is in me,
  and the spirit of God is in my nostrils;
4 my lips will not speak falsehood,
  and my tongue will not utter deceit.
5 Far be it from me to say that you are right;
  till I die I will not put away my integrity
    from me.
6 I hold fast my righteousness, and will not let it
    go;
  my heart does not reproach me for any of
    my days.

7 "Let my enemy be as the wicked,
  and let him that rises up against me be as
    the unrighteous.
8 For what is the hope of the godless when God
    cuts him off,
  when God takes away his life?
9 Will God hear his cry,
  when trouble comes upon him?
10 Will he take delight in the Almighty?
  Will he call upon God at all times?
11 I will teach you concerning the hand of God;
  what is with the Almighty I will not
    conceal.
12 Behold, all of you have seen it yourselves;
  why then have you become altogether vain?

13 "This is the portion of a wicked man with
    God,
  and the heritage which oppressors receive
    from the Almighty:
14 If his children are multiplied, it is for the
    sword;
  and his offspring have not enough to eat.
15 Those who survive him the pestilence buries,
  and their widows make no lamentation.
16 Though he heap up silver like dust,
  and pile up clothing like clay;
17 he may pile it up, but the just will wear it,
  and the innocent will divide the silver.
18 The house which he builds is like a spider's
    web, [a]
  like a booth which a watchman makes.

---

[w] Heb *he.*
[x] Gk: Heb *all.*
[y] Heb *him.*
[z] Or *his throne.*
[a] Cn Compare Gk Syr: Heb *He builds his house like the moth.*

[19]He goes to bed rich, but will do so no more;[b]
he opens his eyes, and his wealth is gone.
[20]Terrors overtake him like a flood;
in the night a whirlwind carries him off.
[21]The east wind lifts him up and he is gone;
it sweeps him out of his place.
[22]It[c] hurls at him without pity;
he flees from its[d] power in headlong flight.
[23]It[c] claps its[d] hands at him,
and hisses at him from its[d] place.

Where Shall Wisdom Be Found?

28 "Surely there is a mine for silver,
and a place for gold which they refine.
[2]Iron is taken out of the earth,
and copper is smelted from the ore.
[3]Men put an end to darkness,
and search out to the farthest bound
the ore in gloom and deep darkness.
[4]They open shafts in a valley away from where
men live;
they are forgotten by travelers,
they hang afar from men, they swing back
and forth.
[5]As for the earth, out of it comes bread;
but underneath it is turned up as by fire.
[6]Its stones are the place of sapphires,[e]
and it has dust of gold.

[7]"That path no bird of prey knows,
and the falcon's eye has not seen it.
[8]The proud beasts have not trodden it;
the lion has not passed over it.

[9]"Man puts his hand to the flinty rock,
and overturns mountains by the roots.
[10]He cuts out channels in the rocks,
and his eye sees every precious thing.
[11]He binds up the streams so that they do not
trickle,
and the thing that is hidden he brings forth
to light.

[12]"But where shall wisdom be found?
And where is the place of understanding?
[13]Man does not know the way to it,[f]
and it is not found in the land of the
living.
[14]The deep says, 'It is not in me,'
and the sea says, 'It is not with me.'
[15]It cannot be gotten for gold,
and silver cannot be weighed as its price.
[16]It cannot be valued in the gold of O'phir,
in precious onyx or sapphire.[g]
[17]Gold and glass cannot equal it,
nor can it be exchanged for jewels of fine
gold.
[18]No mention shall be made of coral or of
crystal;
the price of wisdom is above pearls.

[19]The topaz of Ethiopia cannot compare with it,
nor can it be valued in pure gold.

[20]"From where does wisdom come?
And where is the place of understanding?
[21]It is hidden from the eyes of all living,
and concealed from the birds of the air.
[22]Abad'don and Death say,
'We have heard a rumor of it with our ears.'

[23]"God understands the way to it,
and he knows its place.
[24]For he looks to the ends of the earth,
and sees everything under the heavens.
[25]When he gave to the wind its weight,
and meted out the waters by measure;
[26]when he made a decree for the rain,
and a way for the lightning of the thunder;
[27]then he saw it and declared it;
he established it, and searched it out.
[28]And he said to man,
'Behold, the fear of the Lord, that is wisdom;
and to depart from evil is understanding.'"

Job Recalls Past Happiness

29 And Job again took up his discourse, and
said:
[2]"Oh, that I were as in the months of old,
as in the days when God watched over me;
[3]when his lamp shone upon my head,
and by his light I walked through darkness;
[4]as I was in my autumn days,
when the friendship of God was upon my
tent;
[5]when the Almighty was yet with me,
when my children were about me;
[6]when my steps were washed with milk,
and the rock poured out for me streams of oil!
[7]When I went out to the gate of the city,
when I prepared my seat in the square,
[8]the young men saw me and withdrew,
and the aged rose and stood;
[9]the princes refrained from talking,
and laid their hand on their mouth;
[10]the voice of the nobles was hushed,
and their tongue cleaved to the roof of their
mouth.
[11]When the ear heard, it called me blessed,
and when the eye saw, it approved;
[12]because I delivered the poor who cried,
and the fatherless who had none to help
him.
[13]The blessing of him who was about to perish
came upon me,
and I caused the widow's heart to sing for joy.

---

[b] Gk Compare Syr: Heb *shall not be gathered.*
[c] Or *he* (that is God).
[d] Or *his.*
[e] Or *lapis lazuli.*
[f] Gk: Heb *its price.*
[g] Or *lapis lazuli.*

¹⁴I put on righteousness, and it clothed me;
    my justice was like a robe and a turban.
¹⁵I was eyes to the blind,
    and feet to the lame.
¹⁶I was a father to the poor,
    and I searched out the cause of him whom I
      did not know.
¹⁷I broke the fangs of the unrighteous,
    and made him drop his prey from his teeth.
¹⁸Then I thought, 'I shall die in my nest,
    and I shall multiply my days as the sand,
¹⁹my roots spread out to the waters,
    with the dew all night on my branches,
²⁰my glory fresh with me,
    and my bow ever new in my hand.'

²¹"Men listened to me, and waited,
    and kept silence for my counsel.
²²After I spoke they did not speak again,
    and my word dropped upon them.
²³They waited for me as for the rain;
    and they opened their mouths as for the
      spring rain.
²⁴I smiled on them when they had no confidence;
    and the light of my countenance they did
      not cast down.
²⁵I chose their way, and sat as chief,
    and I dwelt like a king among his troops,
    like one who comforts mourners.

Job Speaks of His Present Suffering

30 "But now they make sport of me,
    men who are younger than I,
whose fathers I would have disdained
    to set with the dogs of my flock.
²What could I gain from the strength of their
      hands,
    men whose vigor is gone?
³Through want and hard hunger
    they gnaw the dry and desolate ground; ^h
⁴they pick mallow and the leaves of bushes,
    and to warm themselves the roots of the
      broom.
⁵They are driven out from among men;
    they shout after them as after a thief.
⁶In the gullies of the torrents they must dwell,
    in holes of the earth and of the rocks.
⁷Among the bushes they bray;
    under the nettles they huddle together.
⁸A senseless, a disreputable brood,
    they have been whipped out of the land.

⁹"And now I have become their song,
    I am a byword to them.
¹⁰They abhor me, they keep aloof from me;
    they do not hesitate to spit at the sight of
      me.
¹¹Because God has loosed my cord and humbled
      me,
    they have cast off restraint in my presence.

¹²On my right hand the rabble rise,
    they drive me ⁱ forth,
    they cast up against me their ways of
      destruction.
¹³They break up my path,
    they promote my calamity;
    no one restrains ^j them.
¹⁴As through ^k a wide breach they come;
    amid the crash they roll on.
¹⁵Terrors are turned upon me;
    my honor is pursued as by the wind,
    and my prosperity has passed away like a
      cloud.

¹⁶ "And now my soul is poured out within me;
    days of affliction have taken hold of me.
¹⁷The night racks my bones,
    and the pain that gnaws me takes no rest.
¹⁸With violence it seizes my garment; ^l
    it binds me about like the collar of my tunic.
¹⁹God has cast me into the mire,
    and I have become like dust and ashes.
²⁰I cry to you and you do not answer me;
    I stand, and you do not ^m heed me.
²¹You have turned cruel to me;
    with the might of your hand you persecute
      me.
²²You lift me up on the wind, you make me ride
      on it,
    and you toss me about in the roar of the
      storm.
²³Yes, I know that you will bring me to death,
    and to the house appointed for all living.

²⁴ "Yet does not one in a heap of ruins stretch out
      his hand,
    and in his disaster cry for help? ⁿ
²⁵Did not I weep for him whose day was hard?
    Was not my soul grieved for the poor?
²⁶But when I looked for good, evil came;
    and when I waited for light, darkness came.
²⁷My heart is in turmoil, and is never still;
    days of affliction come to meet me.
²⁸I go about blackened, but not by the sun;
    I stand up in the assembly, and cry for
      help.
²⁹I am a brother of jackals,
    and a companion of ostriches.
³⁰My skin turns black and falls from me,
    and my bones burn with heat.
³¹My lyre is turned to mourning,
    and my pipe to the voice of those who
      weep.

---

^h Heb *ground yesterday waste.*
ⁱ Heb *my feet.*
^j Cn: Heb *helps.*
^k Cn: Heb *like.*
^l Gk: Heb *my garment is disfigured.*
^m One Heb Ms and Vg: Heb lacks *not.*
ⁿ Cn: Heb obscure.

Job Asserts His Integrity

31 "I have made a covenant with my eyes;
how then could I look upon a virgin?

[2] What would be my portion from God above,
and my heritage from the Almighty on
high?

[3] Does not calamity befall the unrighteous,
and disaster the workers of iniquity?

[4] Does not he see my ways,
and number all my steps?

[5] "If I have walked with falsehood,
and my foot has hastened to deceit;

[6] (Let me be weighed in a just balance,
and let God know my integrity!)

[7] if my step has turned aside from the way,
and my heart has gone after my eyes,
and if any spot has clung to my hands;

[8] then let me sow, and another eat;
and let what grows for me be rooted out.

[9] "If my heart has been enticed to a woman,
and I have lain in wait at my neighbor's
door;

[10] then let my wife grind for another,
and let others bow down upon her.

[11] For that would be a heinous crime;
that would be an iniquity to be punished by
the judges;

[12] for that would be a fire which consumes unto
Abad′don,
and it would burn to the root all my
increase.

[13] "If I have rejected the cause of my manservant
or my maidservant,
when they brought a complaint against me;

[14] what then shall I do when God rises up?
When he makes inquiry, what shall I
answer him?

[15] Did not he who made me in the womb make him?
And did not one fashion us in the womb?

[16] "If I have withheld anything that the poor
desired,
or have caused the eyes of the widow to fail,

[17] or have eaten my morsel alone,
and the fatherless has not eaten of it

[18] (for from his youth I reared him as a father,
and from his mother's womb I guided
him °);

[19] if I have seen any one perish for lack of
clothing,
or a poor man without covering;

[20] if his loins have not blessed me,
and if he was not warmed with the fleece of
my sheep;

[21] if I have raised my hand against the fatherless,
because I saw help in the gate;

[22] then let my shoulder blade fall from my
shoulder,
and let my arm be broken from its socket.

[23] For I was in terror of calamity from God,
and I could not have faced his majesty.

[24] "If I have made gold my trust,
or called fine gold my confidence;

[25] if I have rejoiced because my wealth was
great,
or because my hand had gotten much;

[26] if I have looked at the sun ᴾ when it shone,
or the moon moving in splendor,

[27] and my heart has been secretly enticed,
and my mouth has kissed my hand;

[28] this also would be an iniquity to be punished
by the judges,
for I should have been false to God above.

[29] "If I have rejoiced at the ruin of him that hated
me,
or exulted when evil overtook him

[30] (I have not let my mouth sin
by asking for his life with a curse);

[31] if the men of my tent have not said,
'Who is there that has not been filled with
his meat?'

[32] (the sojourner has not lodged in the street;
I have opened my doors to the wayfarer);

[33] if I have concealed my transgressions from
men, �q
by hiding my iniquity in my bosom,

[34] because I stood in great fear of the multitude,
and the contempt of families terrified me,
so that I kept silence, and did not go out of
doors—

[35] Oh, that I had one to hear me!
(Here is my signature! let the Almighty
answer me!)
Oh, that I had the indictment written by my
adversary!

[36] Surely I would carry it on my shoulder;
I would bind it on me as a crown;

[37] I would give him an account of all my steps;
like a prince I would approach him.

[38] "If my land has cried out against me,
and its furrows have wept together;

[39] if I have eaten its yield without payment,
and caused the death of its owners;

[40] let thorns grow instead of wheat,
and foul weeds instead of barley."

The words of Job are ended.

° Cn: Heb *for from my youth he grew up to me as a father, and from my
mother's womb I guided her.*
ᴾ Heb *the light.*
q Heb *like men* or *like Adam.*

Young Elihu Rebukes Job's Friends

32 So these three men ceased to answer Job, because he was righteous in his own eyes. [2]Then Eli'hu the son of Bar'achel the Buzite, of the family of Ram, became angry. He was angry at Job because he justified himself rather than God; [3]he was angry also at Job's three friends because they had found no answer, although they had declared Job to be in the wrong. [4]Now Eli'hu had waited to speak to Job because they were older than he. [5]And when Eli'hu saw that there was no answer in the mouths of these three men, he became angry.

6 And Eli'hu the son of Bar'achel the Buzite answered:
"I am young in years,
  and you are aged;
therefore I was timid and afraid
  to declare my opinion to you.
[7]I said, 'Let days speak,
  and many years teach wisdom.'
[8]But it is the spirit in a man,
  the breath of the Almighty, that makes him understand.
[9]It is not the old [r] that are wise,
  nor the aged that understand what is right.
[10]Therefore I say, 'Listen to me;
  let me also declare my opinion.'

[11] "Behold, I waited for your words.
  I listened for your wise sayings,
  while you searched out what to say.
[12]I gave you my attention,
  and, behold, there was none that confuted Job,
  or that answered his words, among you.
[13]Beware lest you say, 'We have found wisdom;
  God may vanquish him, not man.'
[14]He has not directed his words against me,
  and I will not answer him with your speeches.

[15] "They are discomfited, they answer no more;
  they have not a word to say.
[16]And shall I wait, because they do not speak,
  because they stand there, and answer no more?
[17]I also will give my answer;
  I also will declare my opinion.
[18]For I am full of words,
  the spirit within me constrains me.
[19]Behold, my heart is like wine that has no vent;
  like new wineskins, it is ready to burst.
[20]I must speak, that I may find relief;
  I must open my lips and answer.
[21]I will not show partiality to any person
  or use flattery toward any man.
[22]For I do not know how to flatter,
  else would my Maker soon put an end to me.

Elihu Addresses Job

33 "But now, hear my speech, O Job,
  and listen to all my words.
[2]Behold, I open my mouth;
  the tongue in my mouth speaks.
[3]My words declare the uprightness of my heart,
  and what my lips know they speak sincerely.
[4]The spirit of God has made me,
  and the breath of the Almighty gives me life.
[5]Answer me, if you can;
  set your words in order before me; take your stand.
[6]Behold, I am toward God as you are;
  I too was formed from a piece of clay.
[7]Behold, no fear of me need terrify you;
  my pressure will not be heavy upon you.

[8] "Surely, you have spoken in my hearing,
  and I have heard the sound of your words.
[9]You say, 'I am clean, without transgression;
  I am pure, and there is no iniquity in me.
[10]Behold, he finds occasions against me,
  he counts me as his enemy;
[11]he puts my feet in the stocks,
  and watches all my paths.'

[12] "Behold, in this you are not right. I will answer you.
  God is greater than man.
[13]Why do you contend against him,
  saying, 'He will answer none of my [s] words'?
[14]For God speaks in one way,
  and in two, though man does not perceive it.
[15]In a dream, in a vision of the night,
  when deep sleep falls upon men,
  while they slumber on their beds,
[16]then he opens the ears of men,
  and terrifies them with warnings,
[17]that he may turn man aside from his deed,
  and cut off [t] pride from man;
[18]he keeps back his soul from the Pit,
  his life from perishing by the sword.

[19] "Man is also chastened with pain upon his bed,
  and with continual strife in his bones;
[20]so that his life loathes bread,
  and his appetite dainty food.
[21]His flesh is so wasted away that it cannot be seen;
  and his bones which were not seen stick out.

---

[r] Gk Syr Vg: Heb many.
[s] Compare Gk: Heb his.
[t] Cn: Heb hide.

²²His soul draws near the Pit,
and his life to those who bring death.
²³If there be for him an angel,
a mediator, one of the thousand,
to declare to man what is right for him;
²⁴and he is gracious to him, and says,
'Deliver him from going down into the Pit,
I have found a ransom;
²⁵let his flesh become fresh with youth;
let him return to the days of his youthful
vigor';
²⁶then man prays to God, and he accepts him,
he comes into his presence with joy.
He recounts ᵘ to men his salvation,
²⁷ and he sings before men, and says:
'I sinned and perverted what was right,
and it was not repaid to me.
²⁸He has redeemed my soul from going down
into the Pit,
and my life shall see the light.'

²⁹"Behold, God does all these things,
twice, three times, with a man,
³⁰to bring back his soul from the Pit,
that he may see the light of life. ᵛ
³¹Give heed, O Job, listen to me;
be silent, and I will speak.
³²If you have anything to say, answer me;
speak, for I desire to justify you.
³³If not, listen to me;
be silent, and I will teach you wisdom."

Elihu Proclaims God's Justice

34 Then Eli'hu said:
² "Hear my words, you wise men,
and give ear to me, you who know;
³for the ear tests words
as the palate tastes food.
⁴Let us choose what is right;
let us determine among ourselves what is
good.
⁵For Job has said, 'I am innocent,
and God has taken away my right;
⁶in spite of my right I am counted a liar;
my wound is incurable, though I am
without transgression.'
⁷What man is like Job,
who drinks up scoffing like water,
⁸who goes in company with evildoers
and walks with wicked men?
⁹For he has said, 'It profits a man nothing
that he should take delight in God.'

¹⁰ "Therefore, hear me, you men of understanding,
far be it from God that he should do
wickedness,
and from the Almighty that he should do
wrong.
¹¹For according to the work of a man he will
repay him,

and according to his ways he will make it
befall him.
¹²Of a truth, God will not do wickedly,
and the Almighty will not pervert justice.
¹³Who gave him charge over the earth
and who laid on him ʷ the whole world?
¹⁴If he should take back his spirit ˣ to himself,
and gather to himself his breath,
¹⁵all flesh would perish together,
and man would return to dust.

¹⁶ "If you have understanding, hear this;
listen to what I say.
¹⁷Shall one who hates justice govern?
Will you condemn him who is righteous and
mighty,
¹⁸who says to a king, 'Worthless one,'
and to nobles, 'Wicked man';
¹⁹who shows no partiality to princes,
nor regards the rich more than the poor,
for they are all the work of his hands?
²⁰In a moment they die;
at midnight the people are shaken and pass
away,
and the mighty are taken away by no
human hand.

²¹ "For his eyes are upon the ways of a man,
and he sees all his steps.
²²There is no gloom or deep darkness
where evildoers may hide themselves.
²³For he has not appointed a time ʸ for any man
to go before God in judgment.
²⁴He shatters the mighty without investigation,
and sets others in their place.
²⁵Thus, knowing their works,
he overturns them in the night, and they are
crushed.
²⁶He strikes them for their wickedness
in the sight of men,
²⁷because they turned aside from following him,
and had no regard for any of his ways,
²⁸so that they caused the cry of the poor to come
to him,
and he heard the cry of the afflicted—
²⁹When he is quiet, who can condemn?
When he hides his face, who can behold
him,
whether it be a nation or a man? —
³⁰that a godless man should not reign,
that he should not ensnare the people.

³¹ "For has any one said to God,
'I have borne chastisement; I will not offend
any more;

ᵘ Cn: Heb *returns*.
ᵛ Syr: Heb *to be lighted with the light of life*.
ʷ Heb lacks *on him*.
ˣ Heb *his heart his spirit*.
ʸ Cn: Heb *yet*.

³²teach me what I do not see;
  if I have done iniquity, I will do it no
    more'?
³³Will he then make repayment to suit you,
  because you reject it?
 For you must choose, and not I;
  therefore declare what you know. ᶻ
³⁴Men of understanding will say to me,
  and the wise man who hears me will say:
³⁵'Job speaks without knowledge,
  his words are without insight.'
³⁶Would that Job were judged to the end,
  because he answers like wicked men.
³⁷For he adds rebellion to his sin;
  he claps his hands among us,
  and multiplies his words against God."

Elihu Condemns Self-righteousness

35 And Eli′hu said:
 ²"Do you think this to be just?
 Do you say, 'It is my right before God,'
³that you ask, 'What advantage have I?
  How am I better off than if I had sinned?'
⁴I will answer you
  and your friends with you.
⁵Look at the heavens, and see;
  and behold the clouds, which are higher
    than you.
⁶If you have sinned, what do you accomplish
    against him?
  And if your transgressions are multiplied,
    what do you do to him?
⁷If you are righteous, what do you give to him;
  or what does he receive from your hand?
⁸Your wickedness concerns a man like yourself,
  and your righteousness a son of man.

⁹"Because of the multitude of oppressions
    people cry out;
  they call for help because of the arm of the
    mighty.
¹⁰But none says, 'Where is God my Maker,
  who gives songs in the night,
¹¹who teaches us more than the beasts of the
    earth,
  and makes us wiser than the birds of the
    air?'
¹²There they cry out, but he does not answer,
  because of the pride of evil men.
¹³Surely God does not hear an empty cry,
  nor does the Almighty regard it.
¹⁴How much less when you say that you do not
    see him,
  that the case is before him, and you are
    waiting for him!
¹⁵And now, because his anger does not punish,
  and he does not greatly heed
    transgression, ᵃ
¹⁶Job opens his mouth in empty talk,
  he multiplies words without knowledge."

Elihu Speaks on God's Behalf

36 And Eli′hu continued, and said:
 ²"Bear with me a little, and I will show
    you,
  for I have yet something to say on God's
    behalf.
³I will fetch my knowledge from afar,
  and ascribe righteousness to my Maker.
⁴For truly my words are not false;
  one who is perfect in knowledge is with you.

⁵"Behold, God is mighty, and does not despise
    any;
  he is mighty in strength of understanding.
⁶He does not keep the wicked alive,
  but gives the afflicted their right.
⁷He does not withdraw his eyes from the
    righteous,
  but with kings upon the throne
  he sets them for ever, and they are exalted.
⁸And if they are bound in fetters
  and caught in the cords of affliction,
⁹then he declares to them their work
  and their transgressions, that they are
    behaving arrogantly.
¹⁰He opens their ears to instruction,
  and commands that they return from
    iniquity.
¹¹If they listen and serve him,
  they complete their days in prosperity,
  and their years in pleasantness.
¹²But if they do not listen, they perish by the
    sword,
  and die without knowledge.

¹³"The godless in heart cherish anger;
  they do not cry for help when he binds
    them.
¹⁴They die in youth,
  and their life ends in shame. ᵇ
¹⁵He delivers the afflicted by their affliction,
  and opens their ear by adversity.
¹⁶He also allured you out of distress
  into a broad place where there was no
    cramping,
  and what was set on your table was full of
    rich food.

¹⁷"But you are full of the judgment on the
    wicked;
  judgment and justice seize you.
¹⁸Beware lest wrath entice you into scoffing;
  and let not the greatness of the ransom
    turn you aside.

ᶻ The Hebrew of verses 29–33 is obscure.
ᵃ Theodotion Symmachus Compare Vg: The meaning of the Hebrew word is uncertain.
ᵇ Heb *among the cult prostitutes.*
35:6–8: 22:2–3.

^{19}Will your cry avail to keep you from distress,
    or all the force of your strength?
^{20}Do not long for the night,
    when peoples are cut off in their place.
^{21}Take heed, do not turn to iniquity,
    for this you have chosen rather than
       affliction.
^{22}Behold, God is exalted in his power;
    who is a teacher like him?
^{23}Who has prescribed for him his way,
    or who can say, 'You have done wrong'?

^{24} "Remember to extol his work,
    of which men have sung.
^{25}All men have looked on it;
    man beholds it from afar.
^{26}Behold, God is great, and we know him not;
    the number of his years is unsearchable.
^{27}For he draws up the drops of water,
    he ^{c} distils his mist in rain
^{28}which the skies pour down,
    and drop upon man abundantly.
^{29}Can any one understand the spreading of the
      clouds,
    the thunderings of his pavilion?
^{30}Behold, he scatters his lightning about him,
    and covers the roots of the sea.
^{31}For by these he judges peoples;
    he gives food in abundance.
^{32}He covers his hands with the lightning,
    and commands it to strike the mark.
^{33}Its crashing declares concerning him,
    who is jealous with anger against iniquity.

The Greatness of God

37 "At this also my heart trembles,
    and leaps out of its place.
^{2}Listen to the thunder of his voice
    and the rumbling that comes from his
      mouth.
^{3}Under the whole heaven he lets it go,
    and his lightning to the corners of the
      earth.
^{4}After it his voice roars;
    he thunders with his majestic voice
    and he does not restrain the bolts of
      lightning ^{d} when his voice is heard.
^{5}God thunders wondrously with his voice;
    he does great things which we cannot
      comprehend.
^{6}For to the snow he says, 'Fall on the earth';
    and to the shower and the rain, ^{e} 'Be strong.'
^{7}He seals up the hand of every man,
    that all men may know his work. ^{f}
^{8}Then the beasts go into their lairs,
    and remain in their dens.
^{9}From its chamber comes the whirlwind,
    and cold from the scattering winds.
^{10}By the breath of God ice is given,
    and the broad waters are frozen fast.

^{11}He loads the thick cloud with moisture;
    the clouds scatter his lightning.
^{12}They turn round and round by his guidance,
    to accomplish all that he commands them
    on the face of the habitable world.
^{13}Whether for correction, or for his land,
    or for love, he causes it to happen.

^{14} "Hear this, O Job;
    stop and consider the wondrous works of
      God.
^{15}Do you know how God lays his command upon
      them,
    and causes the lightning of his cloud to
      shine?
^{16}Do you know the balancings of the clouds,
    the wondrous works of him who is perfect
      in knowledge,
^{17}you whose garments are hot
    when the earth is still because of the south
      wind?
^{18}Can you, like him, spread out the skies,
    hard as a molten mirror?
^{19}Teach us what we shall say to him;
    we cannot draw up our case because of
      darkness.
^{20}Shall it be told him that I would speak?
    Did a man ever wish that he would be
      swallowed up?

^{21} "And now men cannot look on the light
    when it is bright in the skies,
    when the wind has passed and cleared
      them.
^{22}Out of the north comes golden splendor;
    God is clothed with awesome majesty.
^{23}The Almighty—we cannot find him;
    he is great in power and justice,
    and abundant righteousness he will not
      violate.
^{24}Therefore men fear him;
    he does not regard any who are wise in their
      own conceit."

The Lord Answers Job

38 Then the LORD answered Job out of the
    whirlwind:
^{2} "Who is this that darkens counsel by words
    without knowledge?
^{3}Gird up your loins like a man,
    I will question you, and you shall declare to
      me.

^{4} "Where were you when I laid the foundation of
    the earth?
    Tell me, if you have understanding.

---

^{c} Cn: Heb *they distil.*
^{d} Heb *them.*
^{e} Cn Compare Syr: Heb *shower of rain and shower of rains.*
^{f} Vg Compare Syr Tg: Heb *that all men whom he has made may know it.*

⁵Who determined its measurements—surely
  you know!
  Or who stretched the line upon it?
⁶On what were its bases sunk,
  or who laid its cornerstone,
⁷when the morning stars sang together,
  and all the sons of God shouted for joy?

⁸"Or who shut in the sea with doors,
  when it burst forth from the womb;
⁹when I made clouds its garment,
  and thick darkness its swaddling band;
¹⁰and prescribed bounds for it,
  and set bars and doors,
¹¹and said, 'Thus far shall you come, and no
  farther,
  and here shall your proud waves be stayed'?

¹²"Have you commanded the morning since your
  days began,
  and caused the dawn to know its place,
¹³that it might take hold of the skirts of the
  earth,
  and the wicked be shaken out of it?
¹⁴It is changed like clay under the seal,
  and it is dyed ᵍ like a garment.
¹⁵From the wicked their light is withheld,
  and their uplifted arm is broken.

¹⁶"Have you entered into the springs of the sea,
  or walked in the recesses of the deep?
¹⁷Have the gates of death been revealed to you,
  or have you seen the gates of deep
  darkness?
¹⁸Have you comprehended the expanse of the
  earth?
  Declare, if you know all this.

¹⁹"Where is the way to the dwelling of light,
  and where is the place of darkness,
²⁰that you may take it to its territory
  and that you may discern the paths to its
  home?
²¹You know, for you were born then,
  and the number of your days is great!

²²"Have you entered the storehouses of the
  snow,
  or have you seen the storehouses of the hail,
²³which I have reserved for the time of trouble,
  for the day of battle and war?
²⁴What is the way to the place where the light is
  distributed,
  or where the east wind is scattered upon the
  earth?

²⁵"Who has cleft a channel for the torrents of
  rain,
  and a way for the thunderbolt,

²⁶to bring rain on a land where no man is,
  on the desert in which there is no man;
²⁷to satisfy the waste and desolate land,
  and to make the ground put forth grass?

²⁸"Has the rain a father,
  or who has begotten the drops of dew?
²⁹From whose womb did the ice come forth,
  and who has given birth to the hoarfrost of
  heaven?
³⁰The waters become hard like stone,
  and the face of the deep is frozen.

³¹"Can you bind the chains of the Plei'ades,
  or loose the cords of Ori'on?
³²Can you lead forth the Maz'zaroth in their
  season,
  or can you guide the Bear with its
  children?
³³Do you know the ordinances of the heavens?
  Can you establish their rule on the earth?

³⁴"Can you lift up your voice to the clouds,
  that a flood of waters may cover you?
³⁵Can you send forth bolts of lightning, that they
  may go
  and say to you, 'Here we are'?
³⁶Who has put wisdom in the clouds, ʰ
  or given understanding to the mists? ʰ
³⁷Who can number the clouds by wisdom?
  Or who can tilt the waterskins of the
  heavens,
³⁸when the dust runs into a mass
  and the clods cling tightly together?

³⁹"Can you hunt the prey for the lion,
  or satisfy the appetite of the young lions,
⁴⁰when they crouch in their dens,
  or lie in wait in their hiding places?
⁴¹Who provides for the raven its prey,
  when its young ones cry to God,
  and wander about for lack of food?

The Lord Questions Job

39 "Do you know when the mountain goats
  bring forth?
  Do you observe the deer bringing forth their
  young?
²Can you number the months that they fulfil,
  and do you know the time when they bring
  forth,
³when they crouch, bring forth their offspring,
  and are delivered of their young?
⁴Their young ones become strong, they grow up
  in the open;
  they go forth, and do not return to them.

ᵍ Cn: Heb *they stand forth.*
ʰ The meaning of the Hebrew word is uncertain.
38:10: Jer 5:22.

5 "Who has let the wild donkey go free?
   Who has loosed the bonds of the swift
      donkey,
6 to whom I have given the steppe for his home,
   and the salt land for his dwelling place?
7 He scorns the tumult of the city;
   he hears not the shouts of the driver.
8 He ranges the mountains as his pasture,
   and he searches after every green thing.

9 "Is the wild ox willing to serve you?
   Will he spend the night at your crib?
10 Can you bind him in the furrow with ropes,
   or will he harrow the valleys after you?
11 Will you depend on him because his strength is
      great,
   and will you leave to him your labor?
12 Do you have faith in him that he will return,
   and bring your grain to your threshing
      floor? [i]

13 "The wings of the ostrich wave proudly;
   but are they the pinions and plumage of
      love? [j]
14 For she leaves her eggs to the earth,
   and lets them be warmed on the ground,
15 forgetting that a foot may crush them,
   and that the wild beast may trample them.
16 She deals cruelly with her young, as if they
      were not hers;
   though her labor be in vain, yet she has no
      fear;
17 because God has made her forget wisdom,
   and given her no share in understanding.
18 When she rouses herself to flee, [k]
   she laughs at the horse and his rider.

19 "Do you give the horse his might?
   Do you clothe his neck with strength? [l]
20 Do you make him leap like the locust?
   His majestic snorting is terrible.
21 He paws [m] in the valley, and exults in his
      strength;
   he goes out to meet the weapons.
22 He laughs at fear, and is not dismayed;
   he does not turn back from the sword.
23 Upon him rattle the quiver,
   the flashing spear and the javelin.
24 With fierceness and rage he swallows the
      ground;
   he cannot stand still at the sound of the
      trumpet.
25 When the trumpet sounds, he says 'Aha!'
   He smells the battle from afar,
   the thunder of the captains, and the
      shouting.

26 "Is it by your wisdom that the hawk soars,
   and spreads his wings toward the south?

27 Is it at your command that the eagle mounts up
   and makes his nest on high?
28 On the rock he dwells and makes his home
   in the fastness of the rocky crag.
29 From there he spies out the prey;
   his eyes behold it afar off.
30 His young ones suck up blood;
   and where the slain are, there is he."

Dialogue: God Challenges Job

40 And the LORD said to Job:
2 "Shall a faultfinder contend with the
      Almighty?
   He who argues with God, let him answer
      it."

3 Then Job answered the LORD:
4 "Behold, I am of small account; what shall I
      answer you?
   I lay my hand on my mouth.
5 I have spoken once, and I will not answer;
   twice, but I will proceed no further."

6 Then the LORD answered Job out of the whirlwind:
7 "Gird up your loins like a man;
   I will question you, and you declare to me.
8 Will you even put me in the wrong?
   Will you condemn me that you may be
      justified?
9 Have you an arm like God,
   and can you thunder with a voice like his?

10 "Deck yourself with majesty and dignity;
   clothe yourself with glory and splendor.
11 Pour forth the overflowings of your anger,
   and look on every one that is proud, and
      abase him.
12 Look on every one that is proud, and bring him
      low;
   and tread down the wicked where they
      stand.
13 Hide them all in the dust together;
   bind their faces in the world below. [n]
14 Then will I also acknowledge to you,
   that your own right hand can give you
      victory.

15 "Behold, Be'hemoth, [o]
   which I made as I made you;
   he eats grass like an ox.
16 Behold, his strength in his loins,
   and his power in the muscles of his belly.
17 He makes his tail stiff like a cedar;
   the sinews of his thighs are knit together.

---

[i] Heb *your grain and your threshing floor.*
[j] Heb obscure.
[k] Heb obscure.
[l] Tg: The meaning of the Hebrew word is obscure.
[m] Gk Syr Vg: Heb *they dig.*
[n] Heb *hidden place.*
[o] Or *the hippopotamus.*

¹⁸His bones are tubes of bronze,
  his limbs like bars of iron.

¹⁹"He is the first of the works ^p of God;
  let him who made him bring near his sword!
²⁰For the mountains yield food for him
  where all the wild beasts play.
²¹Under the lotus plants he lies,
  in the hiding place of the reeds and in the
    marsh.
²²For his shade the lotus trees cover him;
  the willows of the brook surround him.
²³Behold, if the river is turbulent he is not
    frightened;
  he is confident though Jordan rushes
    against his mouth.
²⁴Can one take him with hooks, ^q
  or pierce his nose with a snare?

41 ^r"Can you draw out Levi'athan ^s with a
    fishhook,
  or press down his tongue with a cord?
²Can you put a rope in his nose,
  or pierce his jaw with a hook?
³Will he make many supplications to you?
  Will he speak to you soft words?
⁴Will he make a covenant with you
  to take him for your servant for ever?
⁵Will you play with him as with a bird,
  or will you put him on leash for your
    maidens?
⁶Will traders bargain over him?
  Will they divide him up among the
    merchants?
⁷Can you fill his skin with harpoons,
  or his head with fishing spears?
⁸Lay hands on him;
  think of the battle; you will not do it
    again!
⁹ ^t Behold, the hope of a man is disappointed;
  he is laid low even at the sight of him.
¹⁰No one is so fierce that he dares to stir him up.
  Who then is he that can stand before me?
¹¹Who has given to me, ^u that I should repay
    him?
  Whatever is under the whole heaven is
    mine.

¹²"I will not keep silence concerning his limbs,
  or his mighty strength, or his large frame.
¹³Who can strip off his outer garment?
  Who can penetrate his double coat of
    mail? ^v
¹⁴Who can open the doors of his face?
  Round about his teeth is terror.
¹⁵His back ^w is made of rows of shields,
  shut up closely as with a seal.
¹⁶One is so near to another
  that no air can come between them.

¹⁷They are joined one to another;
  they clasp each other and cannot be
    separated.
¹⁸His sneezings flash forth light,
  and his eyes are like the eyelids of the dawn.
¹⁹Out of his mouth go flaming torches;
  sparks of fire leap forth.
²⁰Out of his nostrils comes forth smoke,
  as from a boiling pot and burning rushes.
²¹His breath kindles coals,
  and a flame comes forth from his mouth.
²²In his neck abides strength,
  and terror dances before him.
²³The folds of his flesh cling together,
  firmly cast upon him and immovable.
²⁴His heart is hard as a stone,
  hard as the nether millstone.
²⁵When he raises himself up the mighty ^x are
    afraid;
  at the crashing they are beside themselves.
²⁶Though the sword reaches him, it does not
    avail;
  nor the spear, the dart, or the javelin.
²⁷He counts iron as straw,
  and bronze as rotten wood.
²⁸The arrow cannot make him flee;
  for him slingstones are turned to stubble.
²⁹Clubs are counted as stubble;
  he laughs at the rattle of javelins.
³⁰His underparts are like sharp potsherds;
  he spreads himself like a threshing sledge
    on the mire.
³¹He makes the deep boil like a pot;
  he makes the sea like a pot of ointment.
³²Behind him he leaves a shining wake;
  one would think the deep to be hoary.
³³Upon earth there is not his like,
  a creature without fear.
³⁴He beholds everything that is high;
  he is king over all the sons of pride."

Job Is Humbled and Repents

42 Then Job answered the LORD:
  ²"I know that you can do all things,
  and that no purpose of yours can be
    thwarted.
³'Who is this that hides counsel without
    knowledge?'
  Therefore I have uttered what I did not
    understand,
  things too wonderful for me, which I did not
    know.

---

^p Heb *ways.*
^q Cn: Heb *in his eyes.*
^r Ch 40:25 in Heb.
^s Or *the crocodile.*
^t Ch 41:1 in Heb.
^u The meaning of the Hebrew is uncertain.
^v Gk: Heb *bridle.*
^w Cn Compare Gk Vg: Heb *pride.*
^x Or *gods.*
41:11: Rom 11.35.

⁴"Hear, and I will speak;
    I will question you, and you declare to me."
⁵I had heard of you by the hearing of the ear,
    but now my eye sees you;
⁶therefore I despise myself,
    and repent in dust and ashes."

Job's Friends Are Humiliated

7 After the Lord had spoken these words to Job, the Lord said to Eli′phaz the Te′manite: "My wrath is kindled against you and against your two friends; for you have not spoken of me what is right, as my servant Job has. ⁸Now therefore take seven bulls and seven rams, and go to my servant Job, and offer up for yourselves a burnt offering; and my servant Job shall pray for you, for I will accept his prayer not to deal with you according to your folly; for you have not spoken of me what is right, as my servant Job has." ⁹So Eli′phaz the Te′manite and Bildad the Shuhite and Zo′phar the Na′amathite went and did what the Lord had told them; and the Lord accepted Job's prayer.

Job's Fortunes Are Restored Twofold

10 And the Lord restored the fortunes of Job, when he had prayed for his friends; and the Lord gave Job twice as much as he had before. ¹¹Then came to him all his brothers and sisters and all who had known him before, and ate bread with him in his house; and they showed him sympathy and comforted him for all the evil that the Lord had brought upon him; and each of them gave him a piece of money ʸ and a ring of gold. ¹²And the Lord blessed the latter days of Job more than his beginning; and he had fourteen thousand sheep, six thousand camels, a thousand yoke of oxen, and a thousand she-donkeys. ¹³He had also seven sons and three daughters. ¹⁴And he called the name of the first Jemi′mah; and the name of the second Kezi′ah; and the name of the third Ker′en-hap′puch. ¹⁵And in all the land there were no women so fair as Job's daughters; and their father gave them inheritance among their brothers. ¹⁶And after this Job lived a hundred and forty years, and saw his sons, and his sons' sons, four generations. ¹⁷And Job died, an old man, and full of days.

ʸ Heb qesitah.

THE BOOK OF
THE PSALMS

BOOK I

The Two Ways

1 Blessed is the man
who walks not in the counsel of the
wicked,
nor stands in the way of sinners,
nor sits in the seat of scoffers;
²but his delight is in the law of the LORD,
and on his law he meditates day and night.
³He is like a tree
planted by streams of water,
that yields its fruit in its season,
and its leaf does not wither.
In all that he does, he prospers.

⁴The wicked are not so,
but are like chaff which the wind drives
away.
⁵Therefore the wicked will not stand in the
judgment,
nor sinners in the congregation of the
righteous;
⁶for the LORD knows the way of the righteous,
but the way of the wicked will perish.

God's Promise to His Anointed

2 * Why do the nations conspire
and the peoples plot in vain?
²The kings of the earth set themselves,
and the rulers take counsel together,
against the LORD and his anointed, saying,
³"Let us burst their bonds asunder,
and cast their cords from us."

⁴He who sits in the heavens laughs;
the LORD has them in derision.
⁵Then he will speak to them in his wrath,
and terrify them in his fury, saying,
⁶"I have set my king
on Zion, my holy mountain."

⁷I will tell of the decree of the LORD:
He said to me, "You are my son,
today I have begotten you.
⁸Ask of me, and I will make the nations your
heritage,
and the ends of the earth your possession.
⁹You shall break them with a rod of iron,
and dash them in pieces like a potter's
vessel."

¹⁰Now therefore, O kings, be wise;
be warned, O rulers of the earth.
¹¹Serve the LORD with fear,
with trembling ¹²rejoice, ᵃ
lest he be angry, and you perish in the way;
for his wrath is quickly kindled.

Blessed are all who take refuge in him.

Trust in God under Adversity

A Psalm of David, when he fled from Absalom his son.

3 O LORD, how many are my foes!
Many are rising against me;
²many are saying of me,
there is no help for him in God. *Selah*
³But you, O LORD, are a shield about me,
my glory, and the lifter of my head.
⁴I cry aloud to the LORD,
and he answers me from his holy mountain.
Selah

⁵I lie down and sleep;
I wake again, for the LORD sustains me.
⁶I am not afraid of ten thousands of people
who have set themselves against me round
about.

⁷Arise, O LORD!
Deliver me, O my God!
For you strike all my enemies on the cheek,
you break the teeth of the wicked.

The Psalter consists of 150 psalms or sacred hymns. In it we find poetical compositions of different kinds—hymns of praise, prayers for specific liturgical occasions, lamentations both of the individual and the nation, among others. There are psalms that express the deepest emotions of the human heart. They were used in, and many of them composed for, the temple worship. Some of them date back to King David, others were written after the Exile. Their composition thus covers a long period. They were gradually brought together in small collections and finally edited in one large collection arranged in five books. This became the hymnbook of the Second Temple.

The Christian Church took over the Psalter and used it following the example of Jesus himself. The Psalms have always been used extensively in the liturgy and in the daily office of the priest. In the early Church lay people became familiar with them, as St. Jerome tells us.

The numbering of the Psalms used here is that of the Hebrew Bible, which is, of course, followed in the Revised Standard Version. It varies somewhat from the Greek, which is followed by the Latin Vulgate and vernacular versions based on it. This alternative numbering is given in brackets. Psalms 9 and 10 in the Hebrew form Psalm 9 in the Vulgate. Psalms 114 and 115 in the Hebrew are counted as Psalm 113 in the Vulgate.

ᵃ Cn: *kiss his feet.* The Hebrew of 11b and 12a is uncertain.
1:1–3: Jer 17:7–8.
2:1–2: Acts 4:25–26.
2:7: Mt 3:17; Acts 13:33; Heb 1:5; 5:5; 2 Pet 1:17.
2:8–9: Rev 2:26; 12:5; 19:15.
*** 2:** Together with Ps 110 a royal, Messianic psalm, often applied to Jesus as Messiah in the New Testament.

[8]Deliverance belongs to the LORD;
  your blessing be upon your people! *Selah*

Confident Plea for Deliverance from Enemies
To the choirmaster: with stringed instruments.
A Psalm of David.

4 Answer me when I call, O God of my
  right!
    You have given me room when I was in
      distress.
    Be gracious to me, and hear my prayer.

[2]O sons of men, how long will you be dull of
    heart?
    How long will you love vain words, and
      seek after lies? *Selah*
[3]But know that the LORD has set apart the godly
    for himself;
    the LORD hears when I call to him.

[4]Be angry, but sin not;
    commune with your own hearts on your
      beds, and be silent. *Selah*
[5]Offer right sacrifices,
    and put your trust in the LORD.

[6]There are many who say, "O that we might see
    some good!
    Lift up the light of your countenance upon
      us, O LORD!"
[7]You have put more joy in my heart
    than they have when their grain and wine
      abound.

[8]In peace I will both lie down and sleep;
    for you alone, O LORD, make me dwell in
      safety.

Trust in God for Deliverance from Enemies
To the choirmaster: for the flutes.
A Psalm of David.

5 Give ear to my words, O LORD;
  give heed to my groaning.
[2]Listen to the sound of my cry,
    my King and my God,
    for to you do I pray.
[3]O LORD, in the morning you hear my voice;
    in the morning I prepare a sacrifice for you,
      and watch.

[4]For you are not a God who delights in
    wickedness;
    evil may not sojourn with you.
[5]The boastful may not stand before your eyes;
    you hate all evildoers.
[6]You destroy those who speak lies;
    the LORD abhors bloodthirsty and deceitful
      men.

[7]But I through the abundance of your merciful
    love
    will enter your house,

I will worship toward your holy temple
  in the fear of you.
[8]Lead me, O LORD, in your righteousness
    because of my enemies;
    make your way straight before me.

[9]For there is no truth in their mouth;
    their heart is destruction,
    their throat is an open sepulchre,
    they flatter with their tongue.
[10]Make them bear their guilt, O God;
    let them fall by their own counsels;
    because of their many transgressions cast
      them out,
    for they have rebelled against you.

[11]But let all who take refuge in you rejoice,
    let them ever sing for joy;
    and do defend them,
    that those who love your name may exult in
      you.
[12]For you bless the righteous, O LORD;
    you cover him with favor as with a shield.

Prayer for Recovery from Grave Illness
To the choirmaster: with stringed instruments;
according to The Sheminith.
A Psalm of David.

6 O LORD, rebuke me not in your anger,
  nor chasten me in your wrath.
[2]Have mercy on me, O LORD, for I am
    languishing;
    O LORD, heal me, for my bones are troubled.
[3]My soul also is sorely troubled.
    But you, O LORD—how long?

[4]Turn, O Lord, save my life;
    deliver me for the sake of your merciful
      love.
[5]For in death there is no remembrance of you;
    in Sheol who can give you praise?

[6]I am weary with my moaning;
    every night I flood my bed with tears;
    I drench my couch with my weeping.
[7]My eye wastes away because of grief,
    it grows weak because of all my foes.

[8]Depart from me, all you workers of evil;
    for the LORD has heard the sound of my
      weeping.
[9]The LORD has heard my supplication;
    the LORD accepts my prayer.
[10]All my enemies shall be ashamed and sorely
    troubled;
    they shall turn back, and be put to shame in
      a moment.

4:4: Eph 4:26.
5:9: Rom 3:13.
6:8: Mt 7:23; Lk 13:27.

Plea for Help against Persecution

A Shiggaion of David, which he sang to the Lord concerning Cush a Benjaminite.

7 O Lord my God, in you I take refuge;
  save me from all my pursuers, and deliver me,
[2] lest like a lion they rend me,
  dragging me away, with none to rescue.

[3] O Lord my God, if I have done this,
  if there is wrong in my hands,
[4] if I have repaid my friend with evil
  or plundered my enemy without cause,
[5] let the enemy pursue me and overtake me,
  and let him trample my life to the ground,
  and lay my soul in the dust.   *Selah*

[6] Arise, O Lord, in your anger,
  lift yourself up against the fury of my enemies;
  awake, O my God;[b] you have appointed a judgment.
[7] Let the assembly of the peoples be gathered about you;
  and over it take your seat[c] on high.
[8] The Lord judges the peoples;
  judge me, O Lord, according to my righteousness
  and according to the integrity that is in me.

[9] O let the evil of the wicked come to an end,
  but establish the righteous,
  you who try the minds and hearts,
  O righteous God.
[10] My shield is with God,
  who saves the upright in heart.
[11] God is a righteous judge,
  and a God who has indignation every day.

[12] If a man[d] does not repent, God[d] will whet his sword;
  he has bent and strung his bow;
[13] he has prepared his deadly weapons,
  making his arrows fiery shafts.
[14] Behold, the wicked man conceives evil,
  and is pregnant with mischief,
  and brings forth lies.
[15] He makes a pit, digging it out,
  and falls into the hole which he has made.
[16] His mischief returns upon his own head,
  and on his own skull his violence descends.

[17] I will give to the Lord the thanks due to his righteousness,
  and I will sing praise to the name of the Lord, the Most High.

Divine Majesty and Human Dignity

*To the choirmaster: according to The Gittith.
A Psalm of David.*

8 * O Lord, our Lord,
  how majestic is your name in all the earth!

You whose glory above the heavens is chanted
[2]   by the mouth of babies and infants,
  you have founded a bulwark because of your foes,
  to still the enemy and the avenger.

[3] When I look at your heavens, the work of your fingers,
  the moon and the stars which you have established;
[4] what is man that you are mindful of him,
  and the son of man that you care for him?

[5] Yet you have made him little less than the angels,
  and you have crowned him with glory and honor.
[6] You have given him dominion over the works of your hands;
  you have put all things under his feet,
[7] all sheep and oxen,
  and also the beasts of the field,
[8] the birds of the air, and the fish of the sea,
  whatever passes along the paths of the sea.

[9] O Lord, our Lord,
  how majestic is your name in all the earth!

God's Power and Justice

*To the choirmaster: according to Muth-labben.
A Psalm of David.*

9 I will give thanks to the Lord with my whole heart;
  I will tell of all your wonderful deeds.
[2] I will be glad and exult in you,
  I will sing praise to your name, O Most High.

[3] When my enemies turned back,
  they stumbled and perished before you.
[4] For you have maintained my just cause;
  you have sat on the throne giving righteous judgment.

[5] You have rebuked the nations, you have destroyed the wicked;
  you have blotted out their name for ever and ever.

---

b Or *for me.*
c Cn: Heb *return.*
d Heb *he.*
7:9: Rev 2:23.
8:2: Mt 21:16.
8:4–6: Job 7:17–18; Ps 144:3; Heb 2:6–8.
8:6: 1 Cor 15:27; Eph 1:22.
* 8: A magnificent hymn to the glory of God as seen in creation and reflected in man.

⁶The enemies have vanished in everlasting
  ruins;
    their cities you have rooted out;
    the very memory of them has perished.

⁷But the LORD sits enthroned for ever,
    he has established his throne for judgment;
⁸and he judges the world with righteousness,
    he judges the peoples with equity.

⁹The LORD is a stronghold for the oppressed,
    a stronghold in times of trouble.
¹⁰And those who know your name put their trust
  in you,
    for you, O LORD, have not forsaken those who
    seek you.

¹¹Sing praises to the LORD, who dwells in Zion!
    Tell among the peoples his deeds!
¹²For he who avenges blood is mindful of them;
    he does not forget the cry of the poor.

¹³Be gracious to me, O LORD!
    Behold what I suffer from those who hate
    me,
    O you who lift me up from the gates of
    death,
¹⁴that I may recount all your praises,
    that in the gates of the daughter of Zion
    I may rejoice in your deliverance.

¹⁵The nations have sunk in the pit which they
  made;
    in the net which they hid has their own foot
    been caught.
¹⁶The LORD has made himself known, he has
  executed judgment;
    the wicked are snared in the work of their
    own hands.   *Higgaion. Selah*

¹⁷The wicked shall depart to Sheol,
    all the nations that forget God.

¹⁸For the needy shall not always be forgotten,
    and the hope of the poor shall not perish for
    ever.

¹⁹Arise, O LORD! Let not man prevail;
    let the nations be judged before you!
²⁰Put them in fear, O LORD!
    Let the nations know that they are but men!
                                        Selah

Prayer for Deliverance from Enemies

10 Why do you stand afar off, O LORD?
      Why do you hide yourself in times of
    trouble?
²In arrogance the wicked hotly pursue the poor;
    let them be caught in the schemes which
    they have devised.

³For the wicked boasts of the desires of his
  heart,

and the man greedy for gain curses and
    renounces the LORD.
⁴In the pride of his countenance the wicked
  does not seek him;
    all his thoughts are, "There is no God."

⁵His ways prosper at all times;
    your judgments are on high, out of his
    sight;
    as for all his foes, he puffs at them.
⁶He thinks in his heart, "I shall not be moved;
    throughout all generations I shall not meet
    adversity."

⁷His mouth is filled with cursing and deceit and
  oppression;
    under his tongue are mischief and iniquity.
⁸He sits in ambush in the villages;
    in hiding places he murders the innocent.

  His eyes stealthily watch for the hapless,
⁹   he lurks in secret like a lion in his den;
    he lurks that he may seize the poor,
    he seizes the poor when he draws him into
    his net.

¹⁰The hapless is crushed, sinks down,
    and falls by his might.
¹¹He thinks in his heart, "God has forgotten,
    he has hidden his face, he will never see it."

¹²Arise, O LORD; O God, lift up your hand;
    forget not the poor.
¹³Why does the wicked renounce God,
    and say in his heart, "You will not call to
    account"?

¹⁴You see; yes, you note trouble and vexation,
    that you may take it into your hands;
    the hapless commits himself to you;
    you have been the helper of the fatherless.

¹⁵Break the arm of the wicked and evildoer;
    seek out his wickedness till you find none.
¹⁶The LORD is king for ever and ever;
    the nations shall perish from his land.

¹⁷O LORD, you will hear the desire of the meek;
    you will strengthen their heart, you will
    incline your ear
¹⁸to do justice to the fatherless and the
  oppressed,
    so that man who is of the earth may strike
    terror no more.

Song of Trust in God
To the choirmaster. Of David.

11 [10] In the LORD I take refuge;
            how can you say to me,
      "Flee like a bird to the mountains; •

• Gk Syr Jerome Tg: Heb flee to your mountain, O bird.
9:8: Acts 17:31.
10:7: Rom 3:14.

² for behold, the wicked bend the bow,
they have fitted their arrow to the string,
to shoot in the dark at the upright in heart;
³ if the foundations are destroyed,
what can the righteous do?"

⁴ The Lord is in his holy temple,
the Lord's throne is in heaven;
his eyes behold, his eyelids test, the children
of men.
⁵ The Lord tests the righteous and the wicked,
and his soul hates him that loves violence.
⁶ On the wicked he will rain coals of fire and
brimstone;
a scorching wind shall be the portion of
their cup.
⁷ For the Lord is righteous, he loves righteous
deeds;
the upright shall behold his face.

Plea for Help in Evil Times
To the choirmaster: according to The Sheminith.
A Psalm of David.

12 [11] Help, Lord; for there is no longer
any one that is godly;
for the faithful have vanished from among
the sons of men.
² Every one utters lies to his neighbor;
with flattering lips and a double heart they
speak.

³ May the Lord cut off all flattering lips,
the tongue that makes great boasts,
⁴ those who say, "With our tongue we will
prevail,
our lips are with us; who is our master?"

⁵ "Because the poor are despoiled, because the
needy groan,
I will now arise," says the Lord;
"I will place him in the safety for which he
longs."
⁶ The promises of the Lord are promises that are
pure,
silver refined in a furnace on the ground,
purified seven times.

⁷ Do, O Lord, protect us,
guard us for ever from this generation.
⁸ On every side the wicked prowl,
as vileness is exalted among the sons of
men.

Prayer for Deliverance from Enemies
To the choirmaster.
A Psalm of David.

13 [12] How long, O Lord? Will you forget
me for ever?
How long will you hide your face from me?
² How long must I bear pain ᶠ in my soul,
and have sorrow in my heart all the day?

How long shall my enemy be exalted over me?

³ Consider and answer me, O Lord my God;
lighten my eyes, lest I sleep the sleep of
death;
⁴ lest my enemy say, "I have prevailed over him";
lest my foes rejoice because I am shaken.

⁵ But I have trusted in your merciful love;
my heart shall rejoice in your salvation.
⁶ I will sing to the Lord,
because he has dealt bountifully with me.

Denunciation of Godlessness
To the choirmaster.
Of David.

14 [13] The fool says in his heart, "There
is no God."
They are corrupt, they do abominable deeds,
there is none that does good.

² The Lord looks down from heaven upon the
children of men,
to see if there are any that act wisely,
that seek after God.

³ They have all gone astray, they are all alike
corrupt;
there is none that does good,
no, not one.

⁴ Have they no knowledge, all the evildoers
who eat up my people as they eat bread,
and do not call upon the Lord?

⁵ There they shall be in great terror,
for God is with the generation of the
righteous.
⁶ You would confound the plans of the poor,
but the Lord is his refuge.

⁷ O that deliverance for Israel would come out of
Zion!
When the Lord restores the fortunes of his
people,
Jacob shall rejoice, Israel shall be glad.

Who Shall Abide in God's Sanctuary?
A Psalm of David.

15 [14] O Lord, who shall sojourn in your
tent?
Who shall dwell on your holy mountain?

² He who walks blamelessly, and does what is
right,
and speaks truth from his heart;
³ who does not slander with his tongue,
and does no evil to his friend,
nor takes up a reproach against his
neighbor;

ᶠ Syr: Heb *hold counsels.*
14:1-3: Rom 3:10–12.
14:1-7: Ps 53:1–6.

⁴in whose eyes a reprobate is despised,
  but who honors those who fear the Lord;
who swears to his own hurt and does not
  change;
⁵who does not put out his money at interest,
  and does not take a bribe against the
  innocent.

He who does these things shall never be
  moved.

Song of Trust and Security in God
A Miktam of David.

16 [15] Preserve me, O God, for in you I
  take refuge.
² I say to the Lord, "You are my Lord;
I have no good apart from you." ᵍ

³As for the saints in the land, they are the
  noble,
  in whom is all my delight.

⁴Those who choose another god multiply their
  sorrows; ʰ
  their libations of blood I will not pour out
  or take their names upon my lips.

⁵The Lord is my chosen portion and my cup;
  you hold my lot.
⁶The lines have fallen for me in pleasant
  places;
  yes, I have a goodly heritage.

⁷I bless the Lord who gives me counsel;
  in the night also my heart instructs me.
⁸I keep the Lord always before me;
  because he is at my right hand, I shall not
  be moved.

⁹Therefore my heart is glad, and my soul
  rejoices;
  my body also dwells secure.
¹⁰For you do not give me up to Sheol,
  or let your godly one see the Pit.

¹¹You show me the path of life;
  in your presence there is fulness of joy,
  in your right hand are pleasures for
  evermore.

Prayer for Deliverance from Persecutors
A Prayer of David.

17 [16] Hear a just cause, O Lord;
  attend to my cry!
Give ear to my prayer from lips free of
  deceit!
²From you let my vindication come!
Let your eyes see the right!

³If you try my heart, if you visit me by night,
  if you test me, you will find no wickedness
  in me;
  my mouth does not transgress.

⁴With regard to the works of men, by the word
  of your lips
  I have avoided the ways of the violent.
⁵My steps have held fast to your paths,
  my feet have not slipped.

⁶I call upon you, for you will answer me,
  O God;
  incline your ear to me, hear my words.
⁷Wondrously show your mercies,
  O savior of those who seek refuge
  from their adversaries at your right hand.

⁸Keep me as the apple of the eye;
  hide me in the shadow of your wings,
⁹from the wicked who despoil me,
  my deadly enemies who surround me.

¹⁰They close their hearts to pity;
  with their mouths they speak arrogantly.
¹¹They track me down; now they surround me;
  they set their eyes to cast me to the ground.
¹²They are like a lion eager to tear,
  as a young lion lurking in ambush.

¹³Arise, O Lord! confront them, overthrow them!
  Deliver my life from the wicked by your
  sword,
¹⁴from men by your hand, O Lord,
  from men whose portion in life is of the
  world.
May their belly be filled with what you have
  stored up for them;
  may their children have more than enough;
  may they leave something over to their
  babies.

¹⁵As for me, I shall behold your face in
  righteousness;
  when I awake, I shall be satisfied with
  beholding your form.

Royal Thanksgiving for Victory
To the choirmaster.

A Psalm of David the servant of the Lord,
who addressed the words of this song to the Lord
on the day when the Lord delivered him
from the hand of all his enemies,
and from the hand of Saul.
He said:

18 [17] * I love you, O Lord, my strength.
²The Lord is my rock, and my
  fortress, and my deliverer,
  my God, my rock, in whom I take refuge,
  my shield, and the horn of my salvation, my
  stronghold.

ᵍ Jerome Tg: The meaning of the Hebrew is uncertain.
ʰ Cn: The meaning of the Hebrew is uncertain.
16:8-11: Acts 2:25-28, 31.
16:10: Acts 13:35.
18:1-50: 2 Sam 22:2-51.
* 18: A slightly different form of this psalm is found in 2 Sam 22.

³I call upon the Lord, who is worthy to be
praised,
and I am saved from my enemies.

⁴The cords of death encompassed me,
the torrents of perdition assailed me;
⁵the cords of Sheol entangled me,
the snares of death confronted me.

⁶In my distress I called upon the Lord;
to my God I cried for help.
From his temple he heard my voice,
and my cry to him reached his ears.

⁷Then the earth reeled and rocked;
the foundations also of the mountains
trembled
and quaked, because he was angry.
⁸Smoke went up from his nostrils,
and devouring fire from his mouth;
glowing coals flamed forth from him.
⁹He bowed the heavens, and came down;
thick darkness was under his feet.
¹⁰He rode on a cherub, and flew;
he came swiftly upon the wings of the
wind.
¹¹He made darkness his covering around him,
his canopy thick clouds dark with water.
¹²Out of the brightness before him
there broke through his clouds
hailstones and coals of fire.
¹³The Lord also thundered in the heavens,
and the Most High uttered his voice,
hailstones and coals of fire.
¹⁴And he sent out his arrows, and scattered
them;
he flashed forth lightnings, and routed
them.
¹⁵Then the channels of the sea were seen,
and the foundations of the world were laid
bare,
at your rebuke, O Lord,
at the blast of the breath of your nostrils.

¹⁶He reached from on high, he took me,
he drew me out of many waters.
¹⁷He delivered me from my strong enemy,
and from those who hated me;
for they were too mighty for me.
¹⁸They came upon me in the day of my calamity;
but the Lord was my stay.
¹⁹He brought me forth into a broad place;
he delivered me, because he delighted in me.

²⁰The Lord rewarded me according to my
righteousness;
according to the cleanness of my hands he
recompensed me.
²¹For I have kept the ways of the Lord,
and have not wickedly departed from my
God.

²²For all his ordinances were before me,
and his statutes I did not put away from me.
²³I was blameless before him,
and I kept myself from guilt.
²⁴Therefore the Lord has recompensed me
according to my righteousness,
according to the cleanness of my hands in
his sight.

²⁵With the loyal you show yourself loyal;
with the blameless man you show yourself
blameless;
²⁶with the pure you show yourself pure;
and with the crooked you show yourself
perverse.
²⁷For you deliver a humble people;
but the haughty eyes you bring down.
²⁸Yes, you light my lamp;
the Lord my God lightens my darkness.
²⁹Yes, by you I can crush a troop;
and by my God I can leap over a wall.
³⁰This God—his way is perfect;
the promise of the Lord proves true;
he is a shield for all those who take refuge
in him.

³¹For who is God, but the Lord?
And who is a rock, except our God?—
³²the God who girded me with strength,
and made my way safe.
³³He made my feet like deer's feet,
and set me secure on the heights.
³⁴He trains my hands for war,
so that my arms can bend a bow of bronze.
³⁵You have given me the shield of your salvation,
and your right hand supported me,
and your help ⁱ made me great.
³⁶You gave a wide place for my steps under me,
and my feet did not slip.
³⁷I pursued my enemies and overtook them;
and did not turn back till they were
consumed.
³⁸I thrust them through, so that they were not
able to rise;
they fell under my feet.
³⁹For you girded me with strength for the battle;
you made my assailants sink under me.
⁴⁰You made my enemies turn their backs to me,
and those who hated me I destroyed.
⁴¹They cried for help, but there was none to save,
they cried to the Lord, but he did not
answer them.
⁴²I beat them fine as dust before the wind;
I cast them out like the mire of the streets.

⁴³You delivered me from strife with the peoples; ʲ
you made me the head of the nations;
people whom I had not known served me.

ⁱ Or *gentleness.*
ʲ Gk Tg: Heb *people.*

427

⁴⁴As soon as they heard of me they obeyed me;
  foreigners came cringing to me.
⁴⁵Foreigners lost heart,
  and came trembling out of their
    strongholds.
⁴⁶The LORD lives; and blessed be my rock,
  and exalted be the God of my salvation,
⁴⁷the God who gave me vengeance
  and subdued peoples under me;
⁴⁸who delivered me from my enemies;
  yes, you exalted me above my adversaries;
    you delivered me from men of violence.

⁴⁹For this I will extol you, O LORD, among the
    nations,
  and sing praises to your name.
⁵⁰Great triumphs he gives to his king,
  and shows mercy to his anointed,
    to David and his descendants for ever.

God's Glory in Creation and the Law
To the choirmaster.
A Psalm of David.

19 [18] The heavens are telling the glory
      of God;
  and the firmament proclaims his handiwork.
²Day to day pours forth speech,
  and night to night declares knowledge.
³There is no speech, nor are there words;
  their voice is not heard;
⁴yet their voice ᵏ goes out through all the earth,
  and their words to the end of the world.

In them he has set a tent for the sun,
⁵which comes forth like a bridegroom leaving his
    chamber,
  and like a strong man runs its course with
    joy.
⁶Its rising is from the end of the heavens,
  and its circuit to the end of them;
  and there is nothing hidden from its heat.

⁷The law of the LORD is perfect,
  reviving the soul;
  the testimony of the LORD is sure,
    making wise the simple;
⁸the precepts of the LORD are right,
  rejoicing the heart;
  the commandment of the LORD is pure,
    enlightening the eyes;
⁹the fear of the LORD is clean,
  enduring for ever;
  the ordinances of the LORD are true,
    and righteous altogether.
¹⁰More to be desired are they than gold,
  even much fine gold;
  sweeter also than honey
    and drippings of the honeycomb.

¹¹Moreover by them is your servant warned;
  in keeping them there is great reward.

¹²But who can discern his errors?
  Clear me from hidden faults.
¹³Keep back your servant also from
    presumptuous sins;
  let them not have dominion over me!
Then I shall be blameless,
  and innocent of great transgression.

¹⁴Let the words of my mouth and the meditation
    of my heart
  be acceptable in your sight,
    O LORD, my rock and my redeemer.

Prayer for Victory
To the choirmaster.
A Psalm of David.

20 [19] The LORD answer you in the day
      of trouble!
  The name of the God of Jacob protect you!
²May he send you help from the sanctuary,
  and give you support from Zion!
³May he remember all your offerings,
  and regard with favor your burnt sacrifices!
                                      Selah

⁴May he grant you your heart's desire,
  and fulfil all your plans!
⁵May we shout for joy over your victory,
  and in the name of our God set up our
    banners!
  May the LORD fulfil all your petitions!

⁶Now I know that the LORD will help his
    anointed;
  he will answer him from his holy heaven
  with mighty victories by his right hand.
⁷Some boast of chariots, and some of horses;
  but we boast of the name of the LORD our
    God.
⁸They will collapse and fall;
  but we shall rise and stand upright.

⁹Give victory to the king, O LORD;
  answer us when we call. ¹

Thanksgiving for Victory
To the choirmaster.
A Psalm of David.

21 [20] In your strength the king rejoices,
      O LORD;
  and in your help how greatly he exults!
²You have given him his heart's desire,
  and have not withheld the request of his
    lips.   *Selah*
³For you meet him with goodly blessings;
  you set a crown of fine gold upon his
    head.

ᵏ Gk Jerome Compare Syr: Heb *line.*
¹ Gk: Heb *give victory, O LORD, let the King answer us when we call.*
18:49: Rom 15:9.
19:4: Rom 10:18.

⁴He asked life of you; you gave it to him,
    length of days for ever and ever.
⁵His glory is great through your help;
    splendor and majesty you bestow upon him.
⁶Yes, you make him most blessed for ever;
    you make him glad with the joy of your
    face.
⁷For the king trusts in the Lord;
    and through the steadfast love of the Most
    High he shall not be moved.

⁸Your hand will find out all your enemies;
    your right hand will find out those who hate
    you.
⁹You will make them as a blazing oven
    when you appear.
The Lord will swallow them up in his wrath;
    and fire will consume them.
¹⁰You will destroy their offspring from the earth,
    and their children from among the sons of
    men.
¹¹If they plan evil against you,
    if they devise mischief, they will not
    succeed.
¹²For you will put them to flight;
    you will aim at their faces with your bows.

¹³Be exalted, O Lord, in your strength!
    We will sing and praise your power.

Plea for Deliverance from Suffering and Hostility

To the choirmaster: according to The Hind of the Dawn.
A Psalm of David.

22 [21]   * My God, my God, why have you
    forsaken me?
Why are you so far from helping me, from
    the words of my groaning?
²O my God, I cry by day, but you do not answer;
    and by night, but find no rest.

³Yet you are holy,
    enthroned on the praises of Israel.
⁴In you our fathers trusted;
    they trusted, and you delivered them.
⁵To you they cried, and were saved;
    in you they trusted, and were not
    disappointed.

⁶But I am a worm, and no man;
    scorned by men, and despised by the
    people.
⁷All who see me mock at me,
    they make mouths at me, they wag their
    heads;
⁸"He committed his cause to the Lord; let him
    deliver him,
    let him rescue him, for he delights in him!"

⁹Yet you are he who took me from the womb;
    you kept me safe upon my mother's breasts.

¹⁰Upon you was I cast from my birth,
    and since my mother bore me you have been
    my God.
¹¹Be not far from me,
    for trouble is near
    and there is none to help.

¹²Many bulls encompass me,
    strong bulls of Bashan surround me;
¹³they open wide their mouths at me,
    like a ravening and roaring lion.

¹⁴I am poured out like water,
    and all my bones are out of joint;
my heart is like wax,
    it is melted within my breast;
¹⁵my strength is dried up like a potsherd,
    and my tongue cleaves to my jaws;
    you lay me in the dust of death.

¹⁶Yes, dogs are round about me;
    a company of evildoers encircle me;
    they have pierced ᵐ my hands and feet—
¹⁷I can count all my bones—
    they stare and gloat over me;
¹⁸they divide my garments among them,
    and for my clothing they cast lots.

¹⁹But you, O Lord, be not far off!
    O my help, hasten to my aid!
²⁰Deliver my soul from the sword,
    my life ⁿ from the power of the dog!
²¹Save me from the mouth of the lion,
    my afflicted soul ᵒ from the horns of the
    wild oxen!

²²I will tell of your name to my brethren;
    in the midst of the congregation I will
    praise you:
²³You who fear the Lord, praise him!
    all you sons of Jacob, glorify him,
    and stand in awe of him, all you sons of
    Israel!
²⁴For he has not despised or abhorred
    the affliction of the afflicted;
and he has not hidden his face from him,
    but has heard, when he cried to him.

²⁵From you comes my praise in the great
    congregation;
    my vows I will pay before those who fear
    him.
²⁶The afflicted ᵖ shall eat and be satisfied;
    those who seek him shall praise the Lord!
    May your hearts live for ever!

ᵐ Gk Syr Jerome: Heb *like a lion.*
ⁿ Heb *my only one.*
ᵒ Gk Syr: Heb *you have answered me.*
ᵖ Or *poor.*
22:1: Mt 27:46; Mk 15:34.
22:7–8: Mt 27:39, 43; Mk 15:29; Lk 23:35.
22:18: Mt 27:35; Mk 15:24; Lk 23:34; Jn 19:24.
22:22: Heb 2:12.
* 22: This lamentation of the righteous man in his sufferings has profoundly influenced the Gospel passion story. See especially Mt 27:46.

²⁷All the ends of the earth shall remember
    and turn to the Lᴏʀᴅ;
and all the families of the nations
    shall worship before him. �q
²⁸For dominion belongs to the Lᴏʀᴅ,
    and he rules over the nations.

²⁹Yes, to him ʳ shall all the proud of the earth
    bow down;
before him shall bow all who go down to the
    dust,
    and he who cannot keep himself alive.
³⁰Posterity shall serve him;
    men shall tell of the Lord to the coming
    generation,
³¹and proclaim his deliverance to a people yet
    unborn,
    that he has wrought it.

The Divine Shepherd
A Psalm of David.

23 **[22]**   The Lᴏʀᴅ is my shepherd, I shall
              not want;
²   he makes me lie down in green pastures.
He leads me beside still waters; ˢ
³   he restores my soul. ᵗ
He leads me in paths of righteousness ᵘ
    for his name's sake.

⁴Even though I walk through the valley of the
    shadow of death,ᵛ
    I fear no evil;
for you are with me;
    your rod and your staff,
    they comfort me.

⁵You prepare a table before me
    in the presence of my enemies;
you anoint my head with oil,
    my cup overflows.
⁶Surely ʷ goodness and mercy ˣ shall follow me
    all the days of my life;
and I shall dwell in the house of the Lᴏʀᴅ
    for ever. ʸ

Entrance into the Temple
A Psalm of David.

24 **[23]**   The earth is the Lᴏʀᴅ's and the
              fulness thereof,
    the world and those who dwell therein;
²for he has founded it upon the seas,
    and established it upon the rivers.

³Who shall ascend the hill of the Lᴏʀᴅ?
    And who shall stand in his holy place?
⁴He who has clean hands and a pure heart,
    who does not lift up his soul to what is false,
    and does not swear deceitfully.
⁵He will receive blessing from the Lᴏʀᴅ,
    and vindication from the God of his
    salvation.

⁶Such is the generation of those who seek him,
    who seek the face of the God of Jacob. ᶻ
                             Selah

⁷Lift up your heads, O gates!
    and be lifted up, O ancient doors!
    that the King of glory may come in.
⁸Who is the King of glory?
    The Lᴏʀᴅ, strong and mighty,
    the Lᴏʀᴅ, mighty in battle!
⁹Lift up your heads, O gates!
    and be lifted up,ᵃ O ancient doors!
    that the King of glory may come in.
¹⁰Who is this King of glory?
    The Lᴏʀᴅ of hosts,
    he is the King of glory!   *Selah*

Prayer for Guidance and for Deliverance
A Psalm of David.

25 **[24]**   To you, O Lᴏʀᴅ, I lift up my soul.
           ²O my God, in you I trust,
    let me not be put to shame;
    let not my enemies exult over me.
³Yes, let none that wait for you be put to
    shame;
    let them be ashamed who are wantonly
    treacherous.

⁴Make me to know your ways, O Lᴏʀᴅ;
    teach me your paths.
⁵Lead me in your truth, and teach me,
    for you are the God of my salvation;
    for you I wait all the day long.

⁶Be mindful of your compassion, O Lᴏʀᴅ, and
    of your merciful love,
    for they have been from of old.
⁷Remember not the sins of my youth, or my
    transgressions;
according to your mercy remember me,
    for your goodness' sake, O Lᴏʀᴅ!

⁸Good and upright is the Lᴏʀᴅ;
    therefore he instructs sinners in the way.
⁹He leads the humble in what is right,
    and teaches the humble his way.
¹⁰All the paths of the Lᴏʀᴅ are mercy and
    faithfulness,
    for those who keep his covenant and his
    testimonies.

---

q Gk Syr Jerome: Heb *you.*
ʳ Cn: Heb *they have eaten and.*
ˢ Heb *the waters of rest.*
ᵗ Or *life.*
ᵘ Or *right paths.*
ᵛ Or *the valley of deep darkness.*
ʷ Or *Only.*
ˣ Or *kindness.*
ʸ Or *as long as I live.*
ᶻ Gk Syr: Heb *your face, O Jacob.*
ᵃ Gk Syr Jerome Tg Compare verse 7: Heb *lift up.*
23:2: Rev 7:17.
24:1: 1 Cor 10:26.
24:4: Mt 5:8.

¹¹For your name's sake, O LORD,
     pardon my guilt, for it is great.
¹²Who is the man that fears the LORD?
     Him will he instruct in the way that he
       should choose.
¹³He himself shall abide in prosperity,
     and his children shall possess the land.
¹⁴The friendship of the LORD is for those who
       fear him,
     and he makes known to them his covenant.
¹⁵My eyes are ever toward the LORD,
     for he will pluck my feet out of the net.

¹⁶Turn to me, and be gracious to me;
     for I am lonely and afflicted.
¹⁷Relieve the troubles of my heart,
     and bring me ᵇ out of my distresses.
¹⁸Consider my affliction and my trouble,
     and forgive all my sins.

¹⁹Consider how many are my foes,
     and with what violent hatred they hate me.
²⁰Oh, guard my life, and deliver me;
     let me not be put to shame, for I take refuge
       in you.
²¹May integrity and uprightness preserve me,
     for I wait for you.

²²Redeem Israel, O God,
     out of all his troubles.

Plea for Justice; and Declaration of Righteousness
A Psalm of David.

26 [25] Vindicate me, O LORD,
     for I have walked in my integrity,
   and I have trusted in the LORD without
       wavering.
²Prove me, O LORD, and try me;
     test my heart and my mind.
³For your mercy is before my eyes,
     and I walk in faithfulness to you. ᶜ

⁴I do not sit with false men,
     nor do I consort with dissemblers;
⁵I hate the company of evildoers,
     and I will not sit with the wicked.

⁶I wash my hands in innocence,
     and go about your altar, O LORD,
⁷singing aloud a song of thanksgiving,
     and telling all your wondrous deeds.

⁸O LORD, I love the habitation of your house,
     and the place where your glory dwells.
⁹Sweep me not away with sinners,
     nor my life with bloodthirsty men,
¹⁰men in whose hands are evil devices,
     and whose right hands are full of bribes.

¹¹But as for me, I walk in my integrity;
     redeem me, and have mercy on me.

¹²My foot stands on level ground;
     in the great congregation I will bless the
       LORD.

Triumphant Song of Confidence
A Psalm of David.

27 [26] The LORD is my light and my
     salvation;
   whom shall I fear?
   The LORD is the stronghold ᵈ of my life;
     of whom shall I be afraid?

²When evildoers assail me,
     to devour my flesh, ᵉ
   my adversaries and foes,
     they shall stumble and fall.

³Though a host encamp against me,
     my heart shall not fear;
   though war arise against me,
     yet I will be confident.

⁴One thing have I asked of the LORD,
     that will I seek after;
   that I may dwell in the house of the LORD
     all the days of my life,
   to behold the beauty of the LORD,
     and to inquire in his temple.

⁵For he will hide me in his shelter
     in the day of trouble;
   he will conceal me under the cover of his tent,
     he will set me high upon a rock.

⁶And now my head shall be lifted up
     above my enemies round about me;
   and I will offer in his tent
     sacrifices with shouts of joy;
   I will sing and make melody to the LORD.

⁷Hear, O LORD, when I cry aloud,
     be gracious to me and answer me!
⁸You have said, "Seek my face."
     My heart says to you,
   "Your face, LORD, do I seek."
⁹   Hide not your face from me.

Turn not your servant away in anger,
     you who have been my help.
   Cast me not off, forsake me not,
     O God of my salvation!
¹⁰For my father and my mother have forsaken
       me,
     but the LORD will take me up.

¹¹Teach me your way, O LORD;
     and lead me on a level path
       because of my enemies.

ᵇ Or *The troubles of my heart are enlarged; bring me.*
ᶜ Or *in your faithfulness.*
ᵈ Or *refuge.*
ᵉ Or *uttering slanders against me.*

¹²Give me not up to the will of my adversaries;
   for false witnesses have risen against me,
   and they breathe out violence.

¹³I believe that I shall see the goodness of the
   LORD
   in the land of the living!
¹⁴Wait for the LORD;
   be strong, and let your heart take courage;
   yes, wait for the LORD!

Prayer for Help; and Thanksgiving for It
A Psalm of David.

28 [27] To you, O LORD, I call;
   my rock, be not deaf to me,
lest, if you be silent to me,
   I become like those who go down to the Pit.
²Hear the voice of my supplication,
   as I cry to you for help,
as I lift up my hands
   toward your most holy sanctuary. ᶠ

³Take me not off with the wicked,
   with those who are workers of evil,
who speak peace with their neighbors,
   while mischief is in their hearts.
⁴Repay them according to their work,
   and according to the evil of their deeds;
repay them according to the work of their
   hands;
   render them their due reward.
⁵Because they do not regard the works of the
   LORD,
   or the work of his hands,
he will break them down and build them up no
   more.

⁶Blessed be the LORD!
   for he has heard the voice of my
   supplications.
⁷The LORD is my strength and my shield;
   in him my heart trusts;
so I am helped, and my heart exults,
   and with my song I give thanks to him.

⁸The LORD is the strength of his people,
   he is the saving refuge of his anointed.
⁹O save your people, and bless your heritage;
   be their shepherd, and carry them for ever.

The Voice of God in a Great Storm
A Psalm of David.

29 [28] Ascribe to the LORD, O sons of
   God, ᵍ
   ascribe to the LORD glory and strength.
²Ascribe to the LORD the glory of his name;
   worship the LORD in holy attire.

³The voice of the LORD is upon the waters;
   the God of glory thunders,
   the LORD, upon many waters.

⁴The voice of the LORD is powerful,
   the voice of the LORD is full of majesty.

⁵The voice of the LORD breaks the cedars,
   the LORD breaks the cedars of Lebanon.
⁶He makes Lebanon to skip like a calf,
   and Sir'ion like a young wild ox.
⁷The voice of the LORD flashes forth flames of
   fire.
⁸The voice of the LORD shakes the wilderness,
   the LORD shakes the wilderness of Kadesh.
⁹The voice of the LORD makes the oaks to
   whirl, ʰ
   and strips the forests bare;
   and in his temple all cry, "Glory!"

¹⁰The LORD sits enthroned over the flood;
   the LORD sits enthroned as king for ever.
¹¹May the LORD give strength to his people!
   May the LORD bless his people with peace!

Thanksgiving for Recovery from Grave Illness
A Psalm of David.
A Song at the dedication of the Temple.

30 [29] I will extol you, O LORD, for you
   have drawn me up,
   and have not let my foes rejoice over me.
²O LORD my God, I cried to you for help,
   and you have healed me.
³O LORD, you have brought up my soul from
   Sheol,
   restored me to life from among those gone
   down to the Pit. ⁱ

⁴Sing praises to the LORD, O you his saints,
   and give thanks to his holy name.
⁵For his anger is but for a moment,
   and his favor is for a lifetime.
Weeping may last for the night,
   but joy comes with the morning.

⁶As for me, I said in my prosperity,
   "I shall never be moved."
⁷By your favor, O LORD,
   you had established me as a strong
   mountain;
you hid your face,
   I was dismayed.

⁸To you, O LORD, I cried;
   and to the LORD I made supplication:
⁹"What profit is there in my death,
   if I go down to the Pit?
Will the dust praise you?
   Will it tell of your faithfulness?
¹⁰Hear, O LORD, and be gracious to me!
   O LORD, be my helper!"

ᶠ Heb *your innermost sanctuary.*
ᵍ Or *heavenly beings.*
ʰ Or *makes the deer bring forth young.*
ⁱ Or *that I should not go down to the Pit.*

¹¹You have turned my mourning into dancing;
  you have loosed my sackcloth
  and clothed me with gladness,
¹²that my soul ʲ may praise you and not be silent.
  O Lᴏʀᴅ my God, I will give thanks to you
   for ever.

Prayer and Praise for Deliverance
from Enemies
To the choirmaster.
A Psalm of David.

31 [30]
In you, O Lᴏʀᴅ, I seek refuge;
  let me never be put to shame;
in your righteousness deliver me!
²Incline your ear to me,
  rescue me speedily!
 Be a rock of refuge for me,
  a strong fortress to save me!

³Yes, you are my rock and my fortress;
  for your name's sake lead me and guide me,
⁴take me out of the net which is hidden for me,
  for you are my refuge.
⁵Into your hand I commit my spirit;
  you have redeemed me, O Lᴏʀᴅ, faithful
   God.

⁶You hate ᵏ those who pay regard to vain idols;
  but I trust in the Lᴏʀᴅ.
⁷I will rejoice and be glad for your merciful love,
  because you have seen my lowliness,
  you have taken heed of my adversities,
⁸and have not delivered me into the hand of the
   enemy;
  you have set my feet in a broad place.

⁹Be gracious to me, O Lᴏʀᴅ, for I am in distress;
  my eye is wasted from grief,
  my soul and my body also.
¹⁰For my life is spent with sorrow,
  and my years with sighing;
 my strength fails because of my misery, ˡ
  and my bones waste away.

¹¹I am the scorn of all my adversaries,
  a horror ᵐ to my neighbors,
  an object of dread to my acquaintances;
   those who see me in the street flee from me.
¹²I have passed out of mind like one who is
   dead;
  I have become like a broken vessel.
¹³Yes, I hear the whispering of many—
   terror on every side!—
  as they scheme together against me,
  as they plot to take my life.

¹⁴But I trust in you, O Lᴏʀᴅ,
  I say, "You are my God."
¹⁵My times are in your hand;
  deliver me from the hand of my enemies
  and persecutors!

¹⁶Let your face shine on your servant;
  save me in your merciful love!
¹⁷Let me not be put to shame, O Lᴏʀᴅ,
  for I call on you;
 let the wicked be put to shame,
  let them go dumbfounded to Sheol.
¹⁸Let the lying lips be silent,
  which speak insolently against the
   righteous
  in pride and contempt.

¹⁹O how abundant is your goodness,
  which you have laid up for those who fear
   you,
 and wrought for those who take refuge in you,
  in the sight of the sons of men!
²⁰In the shelter of your presence you hide them
   from the plots of men;
  you hold them safe under your shelter
   from the strife of tongues.

²¹Blessed be the Lᴏʀᴅ,
  for he has wondrously shown me his
   merciful love
  when I was beset as in a besieged city.
²²I had said in my alarm,
  "I am driven far ⁿ from your sight."
 But you heard my supplications,
  when I cried to you for help.

²³Love the Lᴏʀᴅ, all you his saints!
  The Lᴏʀᴅ preserves the faithful,
  but abundantly repays him who acts
   haughtily.
²⁴Be strong, and let your heart take courage,
  all you who wait for the Lᴏʀᴅ!

The Joy of Forgiveness
A Psalm of David.
A Maskil.

32 [31]
Blessed is he whose transgression
  is forgiven,
whose sin is covered.
²Blessed is the man to whom the Lᴏʀᴅ imputes
  no iniquity,
  and in whose spirit there is no deceit.

³When I declared not my sin, my body wasted
   away
  through my groaning all day long.
⁴For day and night your hand was heavy upon
   me;
  my strength was dried up ° as by the heat
   of summer.   *Selah*

ʲ Heb *that glory.*
ᵏ With one Heb Ms Gk Syr Jerome: Heb *I hate.*
ˡ Gk Syr: Heb *iniquity.*
ᵐ Cn: Heb *exceedingly.*
ⁿ Another reading is *cut off.*
° Heb obscure.
31:5: Lk 23:46.
31:13: Jer 6:25; 20:3, 10; 46:5; 49:29.
32:1–2: Rom 4:7–8.

5I acknowledged my sin to you,
   and I did not hide my iniquity;
I said, "I will confess my transgressions to the
      LORD";
   then you forgave the guilt of my sin.   *Selah*

6Therefore let every one who is godly
   offer prayer to you;
at a time of distress, P in the rush of great
      waters,
   they shall not reach him.
7You are a hiding place for me,
   you preserve me from trouble;
   you surround me with deliverance. q   *Selah*

8I will instruct you and teach you
   the way you should go;
   I will counsel you with my eye upon you.
9Be not like a horse or a mule, without
      understanding,
   which must be curbed with bit and bridle,
   else it will not keep with you.

10Many are the pangs of the wicked;
   but steadfast love surrounds him who
      trusts in the LORD.
11Be glad in the LORD, and rejoice, O righteous,
   and shout for joy, all you upright in heart!

The Greatness and Goodness of God

33 [32]   Rejoice in the LORD, O you
            righteous!
   Praise befits the upright.
2Praise the LORD with the lyre,
   make melody to him with the harp of ten
      strings!
3Sing to him a new song,
   play skillfully on the strings, with loud
      shouts.

4For the word of the LORD is upright;
   and all his work is done in faithfulness.
5He loves righteousness and justice;
   the earth is full of the mercy of the LORD.

6By the word of the LORD the heavens were
      made,
   and all their host by the breath of his
      mouth.
7He gathered the waters of the sea as in a
      bottle;
   he put the deeps in storehouses.

8Let all the earth fear the LORD,
   let all the inhabitants of the world stand in
      awe of him!
9For he spoke, and it came to be;
   he commanded, and it stood forth.

10The LORD brings the counsel of the nations to
      nought;
   [he fr]ustrates the plans of the peoples.

11The counsel of the LORD stands for ever,
   the thoughts of his heart to all generations.
12Blessed is the nation whose God is the LORD,
   the people whom he has chosen as his
      heritage!

13The LORD looks down from heaven,
   he sees all the sons of men;
14from where he sits enthroned he looks forth
   on all the inhabitants of the earth,
15he who fashions the hearts of them all,
   and observes all their deeds.
16A king is not saved by his great army;
   a warrior is not delivered by his great
      strength.
17The war horse is a vain hope for victory,
   and by its great might it cannot save.

18Behold, the eye of the LORD is on those who
      fear him,
   on those who hope in his merciful love,
19that he may deliver their soul from death,
   and keep them alive in famine.

20Our soul waits for the LORD;
   he is our help and shield.
21Yes, our heart is glad in him,
   because we trust in his holy name.
22Let your mercy, O LORD, be upon us,
   even as we hope in you.

Praise for Deliverance from Trouble

A Psalm of David,
when he feigned madness before Abimelech,
so that he drove him out, and he went away.

34 [33]   I will bless the LORD at all times;
            his praise shall continually be in
   my mouth.
2My soul makes its boast in the LORD;
   let the humble hear and be glad.
3O magnify the LORD with me,
   and let us exalt his name together!

4I sought the LORD, and he answered me,
   and delivered me from all my fears.
5Look to him, and be radiant;
   so your r faces shall never be ashamed.
6This poor man cried, and the LORD heard him,
   and saved him out of all his troubles.
7The angel of the LORD encamps
   around those who fear him, and delivers
      them.

8O taste and see that the LORD is good!
   Blessed is the man who takes refuge in
      him!
9O fear the LORD, you his saints,
   for those who fear him have no want!

P Cn: Heb *at a time of finding only.*
q Cn: Heb *shouts of deliverance.*
r Gk Syr Jerome: Heb *their.*
34:8: 1 Pet 2:3.

¹⁰The young lions suffer want and hunger;
but those who seek the LORD lack no good
thing.

¹¹Come, O sons, listen to me,
I will teach you the fear of the LORD.
¹²What man is there who desires life,
and covets many days, that he may enjoy
good?
¹³Keep your tongue from evil,
and your lips from speaking deceit.
¹⁴Depart from evil, and do good;
seek peace, and pursue it.

¹⁵The eyes of the LORD are toward the
righteous,
and his ears toward their cry.
¹⁶The face of the LORD is against evildoers,
to cut off the remembrance of them from
the earth.
¹⁷When the righteous cry for help, the LORD
hears,
and delivers them out of all their troubles.
¹⁸The LORD is near to the brokenhearted,
and saves the crushed in spirit.

¹⁹Many are the afflictions of the righteous;
but the LORD delivers him out of them all.
²⁰He keeps all his bones;
not one of them is broken.
²¹Evil shall slay the wicked;
and those who hate the righteous will be
condemned.
²²The LORD redeems the life of his servants;
none of those who take refuge in him will
be condemned.

Prayer for Deliverance from Enemies
A Psalm of David.

35 [34] Contend, O LORD, with those who
contend with me;
fight against those who fight against me!
²Take hold of shield and buckler,
and rise for my help!
³Draw the spear and javelin
against my pursuers!
Say to my soul,
"I am your deliverance!"

⁴Let them be put to shame and dishonor
who seek after my life!
Let them be turned back and confounded
who devise evil against me!
⁵Let them be like chaff before the wind,
with the angel of the LORD driving them on!
⁶Let their way be dark and slippery,
with the angel of the LORD pursuing them!

⁷For without cause they hid their net for me;
without cause they dug a pit ˢ for my life.
⁸Let ruin come upon them unawares!

And let the net which they hid ensnare them;
let them fall therein to ruin!

⁹Then my soul shall rejoice in the LORD,
exulting in his deliverance.
¹⁰All my bones shall say,
"O LORD, who is like you,
you who deliver the weak
from him who is too strong for him,
the weak and needy from him who despoils
him?"

¹¹Malicious witnesses rise up;
they ask me of things that I do not know.
¹²They repay me evil for good;
my soul is forlorn.
¹³But I, when they were sick—
I wore sackcloth,
I afflicted myself with fasting.
I prayed with head bowed ᵗ on my bosom,
¹⁴ as though I grieved for my friend or my
brother;
I went about as one who laments his mother,
bowed down and in mourning.

¹⁵But at my stumbling they gathered in glee,
they gathered together against me;
cripples whom I did not know
slandered me without ceasing;
¹⁶they impiously mocked more and more, ᵘ
gnashing at me with their teeth.

¹⁷How long, O LORD, will you look on?
Rescue me from their ravages,
my life from the lions!
¹⁸Then I will thank you in the great
congregation;
in the mighty throng I will praise you.

¹⁹Let not those rejoice over me
who are wrongfully my foes,
and let not those wink the eye
who hate me without cause.
²⁰For they do not speak peace,
but against those who are quiet in the land
they conceive words of deceit.
²¹They open wide their mouths against me;
they say, "Aha, Aha!
our eyes have seen it!"

²²You have seen, O LORD; be not silent!
O Lord, be not far from me!
²³Bestir yourself, and awake for my right,
for my cause, my God and my Lord!
²⁴Vindicate me, O LORD, my God, according to
your righteousness;
and let them not rejoice over me!

ˢ The word *pit* is transposed from the preceding line.
ᵗ Or *My prayer turned back.*
ᵘ Cn Compare Gk: Heb *like the profanest of mockers of a cake.*
34:12–16: 1 Pet 3:10–12.
35:19: Ps 69:4; Jn 15:25.

25Let them not say to themselves,
"Aha, we have our heart's desire!"
Let them not say, "We have swallowed him
up."

26Let them be put to shame and confusion
altogether
who rejoice at my calamity!
Let them be clothed with shame and dishonor
who magnify themselves against me!

27Let those who desire my vindication
shout for joy and be glad,
and say evermore,
"Great is the LORD,
who delights in the welfare of his
servant!"

28Then my tongue shall tell of your
righteousness
and of your praise all the day long.

Human Wickedness and Divine Goodness
To the choirmaster.
A Psalm of David, the servant of the LORD.

36 [35] Transgression speaks to the
wicked deep in his heart;
there is no fear of God
before his eyes.

2For he flatters himself in his own eyes
that his iniquity cannot be found out and
hated.

3The words of his mouth are mischief and
deceit;
he has ceased to act wisely and do good.

4He plots mischief while on his bed;
he sets himself in a way that is not good;
he spurns not evil.

5Your mercy, O LORD, extends to the heavens,
your faithfulness to the clouds.

6Your righteousness is like the mountains of
God,
your judgments are like the great deep;
man and beast you save, O LORD.

7How precious is your mercy, O God!
The children of men take refuge in the
shadow of your wings.

8They feast on the abundance of your house,
and you give them drink from the river of
your delights.

9For with you is the fountain of life;
in your light do we see light.

10O continue your steadfast love to those who
know you,
and your salvation to the upright of heart!

11Let not the foot of arrogance come upon me,
nor the hand of the wicked drive me away.

12There the evildoers lie prostrate,
they are thrust down, unable to rise.

Exhortation to Patience and Trust
A Psalm of David.

37 [36] Do not fret because of the wicked,
be not envious of wrongdoers!

2For they will soon fade like the grass,
and wither like the green herb.

3Trust in the LORD, and do good;
so you will dwell in the land, and be
nourished in safety.

4Take delight in the LORD,
and he will give you the desires of your
heart.

5Commit your way to the LORD;
trust in him, and he will act.

6He will bring forth your vindication as the
light,
and your right as the noonday.

7Be still before the LORD, and wait patiently for
him;
do not fret over him who prospers in his
way,
over the man who carries out evil devices!

8Refrain from anger, and forsake wrath!
Do not fret; it tends only to evil.

9For the wicked shall be cut off;
but those who wait for the LORD shall
possess the land.

10Yet a little while, and the wicked will be no
more;
though you look well at his place, he will
not be there.

11But the meek shall possess the land,
and delight themselves in abundant
prosperity.

12The wicked plots against the righteous,
and gnashes his teeth at him;

13but the LORD laughs at the wicked,
for he sees that his day is coming.

14The wicked draw the sword and bend their
bows,
to bring down the poor and needy,
to slay those who walk uprightly;

15their sword shall enter their own heart,
and their bows shall be broken.

16Better is a little that the righteous has
than the abundance of many wicked.

17For the arms of the wicked shall be broken;
but the LORD upholds the righteous.

18The LORD knows the days of the blameless,
and their heritage will abide for ever;

19they are not put to shame in evil times,
in the days of famine they have abundance.

36:1: Rom 3:18.
37:11: Mt 5:5.

²⁰But the wicked perish;
    the enemies of the Lord are like the glory of
      the pastures,
    they vanish—like smoke they vanish
      away.

²¹The wicked borrows, and cannot pay back,
    but the righteous is generous and gives;
²²for those blessed by the Lord shall possess the
      land,
    but those cursed by him shall be cut off.

²³The steps of a man are from the Lord,
    and he establishes him in whose way he
      delights;
²⁴though he fall, he shall not be cast headlong,
    for the Lord is the stay of his hand.

²⁵I have been young, and now am old;
    yet I have not seen the righteous forsaken
    or his children begging bread.
²⁶He is ever giving liberally and lending,
    and his children become a blessing.

²⁷Depart from evil, and do good;
    so shall you abide for ever.
²⁸For the Lord loves justice;
    he will not forsake his saints.

The righteous shall be preserved for ever,
    but the children of the wicked shall be cut
      off.
²⁹The righteous shall possess the land,
    and dwell upon it for ever.

³⁰The mouth of the righteous utters wisdom,
    and his tongue speaks justice.
³¹The law of his God is in his heart;
    his steps do not slip.

³²The wicked watches the righteous,
    and seeks to slay him.
³³The Lord will not abandon him to his power,
    or let him be condemned when he is brought
      to trial.

³⁴Wait for the Lord, and keep to his way,
    and he will exalt you to possess the land;
    you will look on the destruction of the
      wicked.

³⁵I have seen a wicked man overbearing,
    and towering like a cedar of Lebanon. ᵛ
³⁶Again I ʷ passed by, and, behold, he was no
      more;
    though I sought him, he could not be
      found.

³⁷Mark the blameless man, and behold the
      upright,
    for there is posterity for the man of peace.
³⁸But transgressors shall be altogether
      destroyed;
    the posterity of the wicked shall be cut off.

³⁹The salvation of the righteous is from the
    Lord;
    he is their refuge in the time of trouble.
⁴⁰The Lord helps them and delivers them;
    he delivers them from the wicked, and saves
      them,
    because they take refuge in him.

A Penitent Sufferer's Plea for Healing

A Psalm of David, for the memorial offering.

38 [37] O Lord, rebuke me not in your
         anger,
    nor chasten me in your wrath!
²For your arrows have sunk into me,
    and your hand has come down on me.

³There is no soundness in my flesh
    because of your indignation;
there is no health in my bones
    because of my sin.
⁴For my iniquities have gone over my head;
    they weigh like a burden too heavy for me.

⁵My wounds grow foul and fester
    because of my foolishness,
⁶I am utterly bowed down and prostrate;
    all the day I go about mourning.
⁷For my loins are filled with burning,
    and there is no soundness in my flesh.
⁸I am utterly spent and crushed;
    I groan because of the tumult of my heart.

⁹Lord, all my longing is known to you,
    my sighing is not hidden from you.
¹⁰My heart throbs, my strength fails me;
    and the light of my eyes—it also has gone
      from me.
¹¹My friends and companions stand aloof from
      my plague,
    and my kinsmen stand afar off.

¹²Those who seek my life lay their snares,
    those who seek my hurt speak of ruin,
    and meditate treachery all the day long.

¹³But I am like a deaf man, I do not hear,
    like a mute man who does not open his
      mouth.
¹⁴Yes, I am like a man who does not hear,
    and in whose mouth are no rebukes.

¹⁵But for you, O Lord, do I wait;
    it is you, O Lord my God, who will answer.
¹⁶For I pray, "Only let them not rejoice over me,
    who boast against me when my foot slips!"

¹⁷For I am ready to fall,
    and my pain is ever with me.
¹⁸I confess my iniquity,
    I am sorry for my sin.

ᵛ Gk: Heb obscure.
ʷ Gk Syr Jerome: Heb *he.*

¹⁹Those who are my foes without cause ˣ are
  mighty,
  and many are those who hate me wrongfully.
²⁰Those who render me evil for good
  are my adversaries because I follow after
    good.

²¹Do not forsake me, O Lᴏʀᴅ!
  O my God, be not far from me!
²²Make haste to help me,
  O Lord, my salvation!

Prayer for Wisdom and Forgiveness
To the choirmaster: to Jeduthun.
A Psalm of David.

39 [38] I said, "I will guard my ways,
     that I may not sin with my
tongue;
  I will bridle ʸ my mouth,
  so long as the wicked are in my presence."

²I was mute and silent,
  I held my peace to no avail;
my distress grew worse,
³ my heart became hot within me.
  As I mused, the fire burned;
  then I spoke with my tongue:

⁴"Lᴏʀᴅ, let me know my end,
  and what is the measure of my days;
  let me know how fleeting my life is!
⁵Behold, you have made my days a few
    handbreadths,
  and my lifetime is as nothing in your sight.
  Surely every man stands as a mere breath!
                                    Selah
⁶ Surely man goes about as a shadow!
  Surely for nought are they in turmoil;
    man heaps up, and knows not who will
      gather!

⁷"And now, Lord, for what do I wait?
  My hope is in you.
⁸Deliver me from all my transgressions.
  Make me not the scorn of the fool!
⁹I am silent, I do not open my mouth;
  for it is you who have done it.
¹⁰Remove your stroke from me;
  I am spent by the blows ᶻ of your hand.
¹¹When you chasten man
    with rebukes for sin,
  you consume like a moth what is dear to him;
    surely every man is a mere breath!   *Selah*

¹²"Hear my prayer, O Lᴏʀᴅ,
  and give ear to my cry;
  hold not your peace at my tears!
  For I am your passing guest,
    a sojourner, like all my fathers.
¹³Look away from me, that I may know gladness,
  before I depart and be no more!"

Thanksgiving for Deliverance; and Prayer for Help
To the choirmaster.
A Psalm of David.

40 [39] I waited patiently for the Lᴏʀᴅ;
      he inclined to me and heard my
cry.
²He drew me up from the desolate pit, ᵃ
  out of the miry bog,
  and set my feet upon a rock,
    making my steps secure.
³He put a new song in my mouth,
  a song of praise to our God.
Many will see and fear,
  and put their trust in the Lᴏʀᴅ.

⁴Blessed is the man who makes
  the Lᴏʀᴅ his trust,
who does not turn to the proud,
  to those who go astray after false gods!
⁵You have multiplied, O Lᴏʀᴅ my God,
  your wondrous deeds and your thoughts
    toward us;
  none can compare with you!
Were I to proclaim and tell of them,
  they would be more than can be numbered.

⁶Sacrifice and offering you do not desire;
  but you have given me an open ear. ᵇ
Burnt offering and sin offering
  you have not required.
⁷Then I said, "Behold, I come;
  in the roll of the book it is written of me;
⁸I delight to do your will, O my God;
  your law is within my heart."

⁹I have told the glad news of deliverance
  in the great congregation;
behold, I have not restrained my lips,
  as you know, O Lᴏʀᴅ.
¹⁰I have not hidden your saving help within my
    heart,
  I have spoken of your faithfulness and your
    salvation;
I have not concealed your mercy and your
    faithfulness
  from the great congregation.

¹¹Do not, O Lᴏʀᴅ, withhold
  your compassion from me,
  let your mercy and your faithfulness
    ever preserve me!
¹²For evils have encompassed me
    without number;
  my iniquities have overtaken me,
    till I cannot see;

ˣ Cn: Heb *living.*
ʸ Heb *muzzle.*
ᶻ Heb *hostility.*
ᵃ Cn: Heb *pit of tumult.*
ᵇ Heb *ears you have dug for me.*
40:6–8: Heb 10:5–9.

they are more than the hairs of my head;
my heart fails me.

¹³Be pleased, O Lord, to deliver me!
O Lord, make haste to help me!
¹⁴Let them be put to shame and confusion
altogether
who seek to snatch away my life;
let them be turned back and brought to
dishonor
who desire my hurt!
¹⁵Let them be appalled because of their shame
who say to me, "Aha, Aha!"

¹⁶But may all who seek you
rejoice and be glad in you;
may those who love your salvation
say continually, "Great is the Lord!"
¹⁷As for me, I am poor and needy;
but the Lord takes thought for me.
You are my help and my deliverer;
do not delay, O my God!

Assurance of God's Help; and a Plea for Healing
To the choirmaster.
A Psalm of David.

41 [40] Blessed is he who considers the
poor! ᶜ
The Lord delivers him in the day of
trouble;
²the Lord protects him and keeps him alive;
he is called blessed in the land;
you do not give him up to the will of his
enemies.
³The Lord sustains him on his sickbed;
in his illness you heal all his infirmities. ᵈ

⁴As for me, I said, "O Lord, be gracious to me;
heal me, for I have sinned against you!"
⁵My enemies say of me in malice:
"When will he die, and his name perish?"
⁶And when one comes to see me, he utters
empty words,
while his heart gathers mischief;
when he goes out, he tells it abroad.
⁷All who hate me whisper together about me;
they imagine the worst for me.
⁸They say, "A deadly thing has fastened upon
him;
he will not rise again from where he lies."
⁹Even my bosom friend in whom I trusted,
who ate of my bread, has lifted his heel
against me.
¹⁰But you, O Lord, be gracious to me,
and raise me up, that I may repay them!

¹¹By this I know that you are pleased with me,
in that my enemy has not triumphed over
me.

¹²But you have upheld me because of my
integrity,
and set me in your presence for ever.

¹³Blessed be the Lord, the God of Israel,
from everlasting to everlasting!
Amen and Amen.

BOOK II

Longing for God and His Help in Distress
To the choirmaster.
A Maskil of the Sons of Korah.

42 [41] * As a deer longs
for flowing streams,
so longs my soul
for you, O God.
²My soul thirsts for God,
for the living God.
When shall I come and behold
the face of God?
³My tears have been my food
day and night,
while men say to me continually,
"Where is your God?"

⁴These things I remember,
as I pour out my soul:
how I went with the throng,
and led them in procession to the house of
God,
with glad shouts and songs of thanksgiving,
a multitude keeping festival.
⁵Why are you cast down, O my soul,
and why are you disquieted within me?
Hope in God; for I shall again praise him,
my savior ⁶and my God.

My soul is cast down within me,
therefore I remember you
from the land of Jordan and of Hermon,
from Mount Mizar.
⁷Deep calls to deep
at the thunder of your cataracts;
all your waves and your billows
have gone over me.
⁸By day the Lord commands his steadfast love;
and at night his song is with me,
a prayer to the God of my life.

⁹I say to God, my rock:
"Why have you forgotten me?
Why do I go mourning
because of the oppression of the enemy?"

ᶜ Or weak.
ᵈ Heb you change all his bed.
40:13–17: Ps 70:1–5.
41:9: Jn 13:18.
* 42: This and the following psalm were originally one, as can be seen
from the refrain repeated three times.

439

¹⁰As with a deadly wound in my body,
    my adversaries taunt me,
while they say to me continually,
    "Where is your God?"

¹¹Why are you cast down, O my soul,
    and why are you disquieted within me?
Hope in God; for I shall again praise him,
    my help and my God.

Prayer to God in Time of Trouble

43 [42] Vindicate me, O God, and defend
    my cause
against an ungodly people;
from deceitful and unjust men
    deliver me!
²For you are the God in whom I take refuge;
    why have you cast me off?
Why do I go mourning
    because of the oppression of the enemy?

³Oh, send out your light and your truth;
    let them lead me,
let them bring me to your holy hill
    and to your dwelling!
⁴Then I will go to the altar of God,
    to God my exceeding joy;
and I will praise you with the lyre,
    O God, my God.

⁵Why are you cast down, O my soul,
    and why are you disquieted within me?
Hope in God; for I shall again praise him,
    my savior and my God.

National Lament and Prayer for Help

To the choirmaster.
A Maskil of the Sons of Korah.

44 [43] We have heard with our ears, O
    God,
our fathers have told us,
what deeds you performed in their days,
    in the days of old:

²you with your own hand drove out the
    nations,
    but you planted them;
you afflicted the peoples,
    but you set them free;
³for not by their own sword did they win the
    land,
    nor did their own arm give them victory;
but your right hand, and your arm,
    and the light of your countenance;
    for you delighted in them.

⁴You are my King and my God,
    who ordain ᵉ victories for Jacob.
⁵Through you we push down our foes;
    through your name we tread down our
    assailants.

⁶For not in my bow do I trust,
    nor can my sword save me.
⁷But you have saved us from our foes,
    and have put to confusion those who hate
    us.
⁸In God we have boasted continually,
    and we will give thanks to your name for
    ever.   *Selah*

⁹Yet you have cast us off and abased us,
    and have not gone out with our armies.
¹⁰You have made us turn back from the foe;
    and our enemies have gotten spoil.
¹¹You have made us like sheep for slaughter,
    and have scattered us among the nations.
¹²You have sold your people for a trifle,
    demanding no high price for them.

¹³You have made us the taunt of our neighbors,
    the derision and scorn of those about us.
¹⁴You have made us a byword among the
    nations,
    a laughingstock ᶠ among the peoples.
¹⁵All day long my disgrace is before me,
    and shame has covered my face,
¹⁶at the words of the taunters and revilers,
    at the sight of the enemy and the avenger.

¹⁷All this has come upon us,
    though we have not forgotten you,
    or been false to your covenant.
¹⁸Our heart has not turned back,
    nor have our steps departed from your
    way,
¹⁹that you should have broken us in the place of
    jackals,
    and covered us with deep darkness.

²⁰If we had forgotten the name of our God,
    or spread forth our hands to a strange
    god,
²¹would not God discover this?
    For he knows the secrets of the heart.
²²No, for your sake we are slain all the day
    long,
    and accounted as sheep for the slaughter.

²³Rouse yourself! Why do you sleep, O Lord?
    Awake! Do not cast us off for ever!
²⁴Why do you hide your face?
    Why do you forget our affliction and
    oppression?
²⁵For our soul is bowed down to the dust;
    our body clings to the ground.
²⁶Rise up, come to our help!
    Deliver us for the sake of your merciful
    love!

ᵉ Gk Syr: Heb *You are my King, O God; ordain.*
ᶠ Heb *a shaking of the head.*
44:22: Rom 8:36.

Ode for a Royal Wedding

To the choirmaster: according to Lilies.
A Maskil of the Sons of Korah; a love song.

45 [44] My heart overflows with a goodly theme;
I address my verses to the king;
my tongue is like the pen of a ready scribe.

²You are the fairest of the sons of men;
grace is poured upon your lips;
therefore God has blessed you for ever.
³Gird your sword upon your thigh, O mighty one,
in your glory and majesty!

⁴In your majesty ride forth victoriously
for the cause of truth and to defend ᵍ the right;
let your right hand teach you dread deeds!
⁵Your arrows are sharp
in the heart of the king's enemies;
the peoples fall under you.

⁶Your divine throne ʰ endures for ever and ever.
Your royal scepter is a scepter of equity;
⁷ you love righteousness and hate wickedness.
Therefore God, your God, has anointed you
with the oil of gladness above your fellows;
⁸ your robes are all fragrant with myrrh and aloes and cassia.
From ivory palaces stringed instruments make you glad;
⁹ daughters of kings are among your ladies of honor;
at your right hand stands the queen in gold of Ophir.

¹⁰Hear, O daughter, consider, and incline your ear;
forget your people and your father's house;
¹¹ and the king will desire your beauty.
Since he is your lord, bow to him;
¹² the people ⁱ of Tyre will court your favor with gifts,
the richest of the people ¹³with all kinds of wealth.

The daughter of the king is decked in her chamber with gold-woven robes; ʲ
¹⁴ in many-colored robes she is led to the king,
with her virgin companions, her escort,ᵏ in her train.

¹⁵With joy and gladness they are led along
as they enter the palace of the king.

¹⁶Instead of your fathers shall be your sons;
you will make them princes in all the earth.

¹⁷I will cause your name to be celebrated in all generations;
therefore the peoples will praise you for ever and ever.

God's Defense of His City and People

To the choirmaster.
A Psalm of the Sons of Korah.
According to Alamoth.
A Song.

46 [45] God is our refuge and strength,
a very present ¹ help in trouble.
²Therefore we will not fear though the earth should change,
though the mountains shake in the heart of the sea;
³though its waters roar and foam,
though the mountains tremble with its tumult. *Selah*

⁴There is a river whose streams make glad the city of God,
the holy habitation of the Most High.
⁵God is in the midst of her, she shall not be moved;
God will help her when morning dawns.
⁶The nations rage, the kingdoms totter;
he utters his voice, the earth melts.
⁷The LORD of hosts is with us;
the God of Jacob is our refuge. ᵐ *Selah*

⁸Come, behold the works of the LORD,
how he has wrought desolations in the earth.
⁹He makes wars cease to the end of the earth;
he breaks the bow, and shatters the spear,
he burns the chariots with fire!
¹⁰"Be still, and know that I am God.
I am exalted among the nations,
I am exalted in the earth!"
¹¹The LORD of hosts is with us;
the God of Jacob is our refuge. ᵐ *Selah*

God's Rule over the Nations

To the choirmaster.
A Psalm of the Sons of Korah.

47 [46] Clap your hands, all peoples!
Shout to God with loud songs of joy!
²For the LORD, the Most High, is awesome,
a great king over all the earth.
³He subdued peoples under us,
and nations under our feet.

ᵍ Cn: Heb *and the meekness of.*
ʰ Or *Your throne is a throne of God,* or *Your throne, O God.*
¹ Heb *daughter.*
ʲ Or *people. All glorious is the princess within, gold embroidery is her clothing.*
ᵏ Heb *those brought to you.*
ˡ Or *well proved.*
ᵐ Or *fortress.*
45:6–7: Heb 1:8–9.

⁴He chose our heritage for us,
the pride of Jacob whom he loves.   *Selah*

⁵God has gone up with a shout,
the LORD with the sound of a trumpet.
⁶Sing praises to God, sing praises!
Sing praises to our King, sing praises!
⁷For God is the king of all the earth;
sing praises with a psalm! ⁿ

⁸God reigns over the nations;
God sits on his holy throne.
⁹The princes of the peoples gather
as the people of the God of Abraham.
For the shields of the earth belong to God;
he is highly exalted!

The Glory and Strength of Zion
A Song.
A Psalm of the Sons of Korah.

48 [47] Great is the LORD and greatly to be
praised
in the city of our God!
His holy mountain, ²beautiful in elevation,
is the joy of all the earth,
Mount Zion, in the far north,
the city of the great King.
³Within her citadels God
has shown himself a sure defense.

⁴For behold, the kings assembled,
they came on together.
⁵As soon as they saw it, they were astounded,
they were in panic, they took to flight;
⁶trembling took hold of them there,
anguish as of a woman with labor pains.
⁷By the east wind you shattered
the ships of Tarshish.
⁸As we have heard, so have we seen
in the city of the LORD of hosts,
in the city of our God,
which God establishes for ever.   *Selah*

⁹We have thought on your mercy, O God,
in the midst of your temple.
¹⁰As your name, O God,
so your praise reaches to the ends of the
earth.
Your right hand is filled with victory;
¹¹ let Mount Zion be glad!
Let the daughters of Judah rejoice
because of your judgments!

¹²Walk about Zion, go round about her,
number her towers,
¹³consider well her ramparts,
go through her citadels;
that you may tell the next generation
¹⁴ that this is God,
our God for ever and ever.
He will be our guide for ever.

The Folly of Trust in Riches
To the choirmaster.
A Psalm of the Sons of Korah.

49 [48] Hear this, all peoples!
Give ear, all inhabitants of the
world,
²both low and high,
rich and poor together!
³My mouth shall speak wisdom;
the meditation of my heart shall be
understanding.
⁴I will incline my ear to a proverb;
I will solve my riddle to the music of the
lyre.

⁵Why should I fear in times of trouble,
when the iniquity of my persecutors
surrounds me,
⁶men who trust in their wealth
and boast of the abundance of their riches?
⁷Truly no man can ransom himself, ^o
or give to God the price of his life,
⁸for the ransom of his ^p life is costly,
and can never suffice,
⁹that he should continue to live on for ever,
and never see the Pit.

¹⁰Yes, he shall see that even the wise die,
the fool and the stupid alike must perish
and leave their wealth to others.
¹¹Their graves ^q are their homes for ever,
their dwelling places to all generations,
though they named lands their own.
¹²Man cannot abide in his pomp,
he is like the beasts that perish.

¹³This is the fate of those who have foolish
confidence,
the end of those ^r who are pleased with
their portion.   *Selah*
¹⁴Like sheep they are appointed for Sheol;
Death shall be their shepherd;
straight to the grave they descend, ^s
and their form shall waste away;
Sheol shall be their home.^t
¹⁵But God will ransom my soul from the power
of Sheol,
for he will receive me.   *Selah*

¹⁶Be not afraid when one becomes rich,
when the glory ^u of his house increases.
¹⁷For when he dies he will carry nothing away;
his glory ^u will not go down after him.

ⁿ Heb *Maskil.*
^o Another reading is *no man can ransom his brother.*
^p Gk: Heb *their.*
^q Gk Syr Compare Tg: Heb *their inward* (thought).
^r Tg: Heb *after them.*
^s Cn: Heb *the upright shall have dominion over them in the morning.*
^t Heb uncertain.
^u Or *wealth.*
48:2: Mt 5:35.

¹⁸Though, while he lives, he counts himself
happy,
and though a man gets praise when he does
well for himself,
¹⁹he will go to the generation of his fathers,
who will never more see the light.
²⁰Man cannot abide in his pomp,
he is like the beasts that perish.

The Acceptable Sacrifice
A Psalm of Asaph.

50 [49] The Mighty One, God the Lord,
speaks and summons the earth
from the rising of the sun to its setting.
²Out of Zion, the perfection of beauty,
God shines forth.

³Our God comes, he does not keep silence,
before him is a devouring fire,
round about him a mighty tempest.
⁴He calls to the heavens above
and to the earth, that he may judge his
people:
⁵"Gather to me my faithful ones,
who made a covenant with me by
sacrifice!"
⁶The heavens declare his righteousness,
for God himself is judge!   *Selah*

⁷"Hear, O my people, and I will speak,
O Israel, I will testify against you.
I am God, your God.
⁸I do not reprove you for your sacrifices;
your burnt offerings are continually before
me.
⁹I will accept no bull from your house,
nor he-goat from your folds.
¹⁰For every beast of the forest is mine,
the cattle on a thousand hills.
¹¹I know all the birds of the air, ᵛ
and all that moves in the field is mine.

¹²"If I were hungry, I would not tell you;
for the world and all that is in it is mine.
¹³Do I eat the flesh of bulls,
or drink the blood of goats?
¹⁴Offer to God a sacrifice of thanksgiving, ʷ
and pay your vows to the Most High;
¹⁵and call upon me in the day of trouble;
I will deliver you, and you shall glorify me."

¹⁶But to the wicked God says:
"What right have you to recite my statutes,
or take my covenant on your lips?
¹⁷For you hate discipline,
and you cast my words behind you.
¹⁸If you see a thief, you are a friend of his;
and you keep company with adulterers.
¹⁹"You give your mouth free rein for evil,
and your tongue frames deceit.

²⁰You sit and speak against your brother;
you slander your own mother's son.
²¹These things you have done and I have been
silent;
you thought that I was one like yourself.
But now I rebuke you, and lay the charge
before you.

²²"Mark this, then, you who forget God,
lest I tear, and there be none to deliver!
²³He who brings thanksgiving as his sacrifice
honors me;
to him who orders his way aright
I will show the salvation of God!"

Prayer for Cleansing and Pardon
To the choirmaster.
A Psalm of David, when Nathan the prophet came to him,
after he had gone in to Bathsheba.

51 [50] * Have mercy on me, O God,
according to your merciful love;
according to your abundant mercy blot out
my transgressions.
²Wash me thoroughly from my iniquity,
and cleanse me from my sin!

³For I know my transgressions,
and my sin is ever before me.
⁴Against you, you only, have I sinned,
and done that which is evil in your sight,
so that you are justified in your sentence
and blameless in your judgment.
⁵Behold, I was brought forth in iniquity,
and in sin did my mother conceive me.

⁶Behold, you desire truth in the inward being;
therefore teach me wisdom in my secret
heart.
⁷Purge me with hyssop, and I shall be clean;
wash me, and I shall be whiter than snow.
⁸Make me hear ˣ joy and gladness;
let the bones which you have broken
rejoice.
⁹Hide your face from my sins,
and blot out all my iniquities.

¹⁰Create in me a clean heart, O God,
and put a new and right ʸ spirit within me.
¹¹Cast me not away from your presence,
and take not your holy Spirit from me.
¹²Restore to me the joy of your salvation,
and uphold me with a willing spirit.

¹³Then I will teach transgressors your ways,
and sinners will return to you.

ᵛ Gk Syr Tg: Heb *mountains.*
ʷ Or *make thanksgiving your sacrifice to God.*
ˣ Syr *Fill me with.*
ʸ Or *steadfast.*
51:4: Rom 3:4.
* 51: This psalm, known as the "Miserere," is the one most used in the
Liturgy of the Hours to express repentance for sin.

¹⁴Deliver me from bloodguilt,ᶻ O God,
   O God of my salvation,
   and my tongue will sing aloud of your
      deliverance.

¹⁵O Lord, open my lips,
   and my mouth shall show forth your
      praise.

¹⁶For you take no delight in sacrifice;
   were I to give a burnt offering, you would
      not be pleased.

¹⁷The sacrifice acceptable to Godᵃ is a broken
      spirit;
   a broken and contrite heart, O God, you will
      not despise.

¹⁸Do good to Zion in your good pleasure;
   rebuild the walls of Jerusalem,

¹⁹then will you delight in right sacrifices,
   in burnt offerings and whole burnt
      offerings;
   then bulls will be offered on your altar.

Judgment on the Deceitful

To the choirmaster.
A Maskil of David, when Doeg, the Edomite,
came and told Saul,
"David has come to the house of Ahimelech."

52 [51] Why do you boast, O mighty
      man,
   of mischief done against the
      godly?ᵇ
All the day ²you are plotting destruction.
Your tongue is like a sharp razor,
   you worker of treachery.

³You love evil more than good,
   and lying more than speaking the truth.
                                          Selah

⁴You love all words that devour,
   O deceitful tongue.

⁵But God will break you down for ever;
   he will snatch and tear you from your
      tent;
   he will uproot you from the land of the
      living.   *Selah*

⁶The righteous shall see, and fear,
   and shall laugh at him, saying,

⁷"See the man who would not make God his
      refuge,
   but trusted in the abundance of his riches,
   and sought refuge in his wealth!"ᶜ

⁸But I am like a green olive tree
   in the house of God.
I trust in the mercy of God
   for ever and ever.

⁹I will thank you for ever,
   because you have done it.
I will proclaimᵈ your name, for it is good,
   in the presence of the godly.

Denunciation of Godlessness

To the choirmaster: according to Mahalath.
A Maskil of David.

53 [52] The fool says in his heart,
      "There is no God."
They are corrupt, doing abominable iniquity;
   there is none that does good.

²God looks down from heaven
   upon the sons of men
to see if there are any that are wise,
   that seek after God.

³They have all fallen away;
   they are all alike depraved;
there is none that does good,
   no, not one.

⁴Have those who work evil no understanding,
   who eat up my people as they eat bread,
   and do not call upon God?

⁵There they are, in great terror,
   in terror such as has not been!
For God will scatter the bones of the
      ungodly;ᵉ
   they will be put to shame,ᶠ for God has
      rejected them.

⁶O that deliverance for Israel would come from
      Zion!
When God restores the fortunes of his
      people,
Jacob will rejoice and Israel be glad.

Prayer for Vindication

To the choirmaster: with stringed instruments.
A Maskil of David, when the Ziphites went and told Saul,
"David is in hiding among us."

54 [53] Save me, O God, by your name,
      and vindicate me by your might.
²Hear my prayer, O God;
   give ear to the words of my mouth.

³For insolent menᵍ have risen against me,
   ruthless men seek my life;
   they do not set God before them.   *Selah*

⁴Behold, God is my helper;
   the Lord is the upholderʰ of my life.

⁵He will repay my enemies with evil;
   in your faithfulness put an end to them.

ᶻ Or *death*.
ᵃ Or *My sacrifice, O God*.
ᵇ Cn Compare Syr: Heb *the kindness of God*.
ᶜ Syr Tg: Heb *his destruction*.
ᵈ Cn: Heb *wait for*.
ᵉ Cn Compare Gk Syr: Heb *him who encamps against you*.
ᶠ Gk: Heb *you will put to shame*.
ᵍ Another reading is *strangers*.
ʰ Gk Syr Jerome: Heb *of* or *with those who uphold*.
53:1-3: Rom 3:10-12.
53:1-6: Ps 14:1-7.

⁶With a freewill offering I will sacrifice to you;
  I will give thanks to your name, O LORD, for
    it is good.
⁷For you have delivered me from every trouble,
  and my eye has looked in triumph on my
    enemies.

Complaint about a Friend's Treachery

To the choirmaster: with stringed instruments.
A Maskil of David.

55 [54] Give ear to my prayer, O God;
  and hide not yourself from my
  supplication!
²Attend to me, and answer me;
  I am overcome by my trouble.
I am distraught ³by the noise of the enemy,
  because of the oppression of the wicked.
For they bring ⁱ trouble upon me,
  and in anger they cherish enmity against
    me.

⁴My heart is in anguish within me,
  the terrors of death have fallen upon me.
⁵Fear and trembling come upon me,
  and horror overwhelms me.
⁶And I say, "O that I had wings like a dove!
  I would fly away and be at rest;
⁷yes, I would wander afar,
  I would lodge in the wilderness,   *Selah*
⁸I would wait for him who saves me
  from the raging wind and tempest."

⁹Destroy their plans, ʲ O Lord, confuse their
    tongues;
  for I see violence and strife in the city.
¹⁰Day and night they go around it
  on its walls;
  and mischief and trouble are within it,
¹¹ ruin is in its midst;
  oppression and fraud
    do not depart from its market place.

¹²It is not an enemy who taunts me—
    then I could bear it;
  it is not an adversary who deals insolently with
    me—
    then I could hide from him.
¹³But it is you, my equal,
  my companion, my familiar friend.
¹⁴We used to hold sweet converse together;
  within God's house we walked in fellowship.
¹⁵Let death ᵏ come upon them;
  let them go down to Sheol alive;
  let them go away in terror into their
    graves. ˡ

¹⁶But I call upon God;
  and the LORD will save me.
¹⁷Evening and morning and at noon
  I utter my complaint and moan,
  and he will hear my voice.

¹⁸He will deliver my soul in safety
  from the battle that I wage,
  for many are arrayed against me.
¹⁹God will give ear, and humble them,
  he who is enthroned from of old;
  because they keep no law, ᵐ
  and do not fear God.   *Selah*

²⁰My companion stretched out his hand against
    his friends,
  he violated his covenant.
²¹His speech was smoother than butter,
  yet war was in his heart;
  his words were softer than oil,
  yet they were drawn swords.

²²Cast your burden ⁿ on the LORD,
  and he will sustain you;
  he will never permit
    the righteous to be moved.

²³But you, O God, will cast them down
  into the lowest pit;
  men of blood and treachery
    shall not live out half their days.
But I will trust in you.

Trust in God under Persecution

To the choirmaster:
according to The Dove on Far-off Terebinths.

A Miktam of David, when the Philistines
seized him in Gath.

56 [55] Have mercy on me, O God, for men
    trample upon me;
  all day long foes oppress me;
²my enemies trample upon me all day long,
  for many fight against me proudly.
³When I am afraid,
  I put my trust in you.
⁴In God, whose word I praise,
  in God I trust without a fear.
  What can flesh do to me?

⁵All day long they seek to injure my cause;
  all their thoughts are against me for evil.
⁶They band themselves together, they lurk,
  they watch my steps.
  As they have waited for my life,
⁷ so recompense ° them for their crime;
  in wrath cast down the peoples, O God!

⁸You have kept count of my tossings;
  put my tears in your bottle!
  Are they not in your book?

ⁱ Cn Compare Gk: Heb *they cause to totter.*
ʲ Tg: Heb lacks *their plans.*
ᵏ Or *desolations.*
ˡ Cn: Heb *evils are in their habitation, in their midst.*
ᵐ Or *do not change.*
ⁿ Or *what he has given you.*
° Cn: Heb *deliver.*
55:22: 1 Pet 5:7.

⁹Then my enemies will be turned back
  in the day when I call.
    This I know, that ᴾ God is for me.
¹⁰In God, whose word I praise,
  in the Lᴏʀᴅ, whose word I praise,
¹¹in God I trust without a fear.
    What can man do to me?

¹²My vows to you I must perform, O God;
  I will render thank offerings to you.
¹³For you have delivered my soul from death,
  yes, my feet from falling,
    that I may walk before God
      in the light of life.

Praise and Assurance
under Persecution

To the choirmaster: according to Do Not Destroy.
A Miktam of David, when he fled from Saul, in the cave.

57 [56] Be merciful to me, O God, be
      merciful to me,
  for in you my soul takes refuge;
  in the shadow of your wings I will take
    refuge,
      till the storms of destruction pass by.
²I cry to God Most High,
  to God who fulfils his purpose for me.
³He will send from heaven and save me,
  he will put to shame those who trample
    upon me.   *Selah*
  God will send forth his mercy and his
    faithfulness!

⁴I lie in the midst of lions
  that greedily devour �q the sons of men;
  their teeth are spears and arrows,
    their tongues sharp swords.

⁵Be exalted, O God, above the heavens!
  Let your glory be over all the earth!

⁶They set a net for my steps;
  my soul was bowed down.
  They dug a pit in my way,
    but they have fallen into it themselves.
                          Selah

⁷My heart is steadfast, O God,
  my heart is steadfast!
  I will sing and make melody!
⁸ Awake, my soul!
  Awake, O harp and lyre!
    I will awake the dawn!
⁹I will give thanks to you, O Lord, among the
    peoples;
    I will sing praises to you among the
      nations.
¹⁰For your mercy is great to the heavens,
  your faithfulness to the clouds.

¹¹Be exalted, O God, above the heavens!
  Let your glory be over all the earth!

Prayer for Vengeance

To the choirmaster: according to Do Not Destroy.
A Miktam of David.

58 [57] Do you indeed decree what is
      right, you gods? ˢ
  Do you judge the sons of men uprightly?
²No, in your hearts you devise wrongs;
  your hands deal out violence on earth.

³The wicked go astray from the womb,
  they err from their birth, speaking lies.
⁴They have venom like the venom of a serpent,
  like the deaf adder that stops its ear,
⁵so that it does not hear the voice of charmers
  or of the cunning enchanter.

⁶O God, break the teeth in their mouths;
  tear out the fangs of the young lions, O
    Lᴏʀᴅ!
⁷Let them vanish like water that runs away;
  like grass let them be trodden down and
    wither.ᵗ
⁸Let them be like the snail which dissolves into
    slime,
    like the untimely birth that never sees the
      sun.
⁹Sooner than your pots can feel the heat of
    thorns,
    whether green or ablaze, may he sweep
      them away!

¹⁰The righteous will rejoice when he sees the
    vengeance;
  he will bathe his feet in the blood of the
    wicked.
¹¹Men will say, "Surely there is a reward for the
    righteous;
  surely there is a God who judges on earth."

Prayer for Deliverance from Enemies

To the choirmaster: according to Do Not Destroy.
A Miktam of David, when Saul sent men
  to watch his house in order to kill him.

59 [58] Deliver me from my enemies, O my
      God,
  protect me from those who rise up against
    me,
²deliver me from those who work evil,
  and save me from bloodthirsty men.

³For behold, they lie in wait for my life;
  fierce men band themselves against me.
  For no transgression or sin of mine, O Lᴏʀᴅ,
⁴ for no fault of mine, they run and make
    ready.

ᴾ Or *because.*
q Cn: Heb *are aflame.*
ˢ Or *mighty lords.*
ᵗ Cn: Heb uncertain.
57:7–11: Ps 108:1–5.

Rouse yourself, come to my help, and see!
5   You, Lord God of hosts, are God of Israel.
Awake to punish all the nations;
    spare none of those who treacherously plot
      evil.   *Selah*

6Each evening they come back,
  howling like dogs
  and prowling about the city.
7There they are, bellowing with their mouths,
  and snarling with ᵘ their lips—
    for "Who," they think, "will hear us?"

8But you, O Lord, laugh at them;
  you hold all the nations in derision.
9O my Strength, I will sing praises to you; ᵛ
  for you, O God, are my fortress.
10My God in his mercy will meet me;
  my God will let me look in triumph on my
    enemies.

11Slay them not, lest my people forget;
  make them totter by your power, and bring
    them down,
  O Lord, our shield!
12For the sin of their mouths, the words of their
    lips,
  let them be trapped in their pride.
  For the cursing and lies which they utter,
13   consume them in wrath,
  consume them till they are no more,
  that men may know that God rules over Jacob
  to the ends of the earth.   *Selah*

14Each evening they come back,
  howling like dogs
  and prowling about the city.
15They roam about for food,
  and growl if they do not get their fill.

16But I will sing of your might;
  I will sing aloud of your mercy in the
    morning.
  For you have been to me a fortress
  and a refuge in the day of my distress.
17O my Strength, I will sing praises to you,
  for you, O God, are my fortress,
  the God who shows me mercy.

Prayer for National Victory after Defeat

To the choirmaster: according to Shushan Eduth.

A Miktam of David; for instruction; when he
strove with Aram-naharaim and with Aram-zobah,
and when Joab on his return killed twelve thousand of
Edom in the Valley of Salt.

60 [59]   O God, you have rejected us,
          broken our defenses;
  you have been angry; oh, restore us.
2You have made the land to quake, you have torn
    it open;
  repair its breaches, for it totters.

3You have made your people suffer hard things;
  you have given us wine to drink that made
    us reel.

4You have set up a banner for those who fear
    you,
  to rally to it from the bow. ᵂ   *Selah*
5That your beloved may be delivered,
  give victory by your right hand and
    answer us!

6God has spoken in his sanctuary: ˣ
  "With exultation I will divide up Shechem
  and portion out the Vale of Succoth.
7Gilead is mine; Manas'seh is mine;
  E'phraim is my helmet;
  Judah is my scepter.
8Moab is my washbasin;
  upon Edom I cast my shoe;
  over Philistia I shout in triumph."

9Who will bring me to the fortified city?
  Who will lead me to Edom?
10Have you not rejected us, O God?
  You do not go forth, O God, with our
    armies.
11O grant us help against the foe,
  for vain is the help of man!
12With God we shall do valiantly;
  it is he who will tread down our foes.

Assurance of God's Protection

To the choirmaster: with stringed instruments.
A Psalm of David.

61 [60]   Hear my cry, O God,
          listen to my prayer;
2from the end of the earth I call to you,
  when my heart is faint.

Lead me
  to the rock that is higher than I;
3for you are my refuge,
  a strong tower against the enemy.

4Let me dwell in your tent for ever!
  Oh, to be safe under the shelter of your
    wings!   *Selah*
5For you, O God, have heard my vows,
  you have given me the heritage of those
    who fear your name.

6Prolong the life of the king;
  may his years endure to all generations!
7May he be enthroned for ever before God;
  bid steadfast love and faithfulness watch
    over him!

ᵘ Cn: Heb *swords in.*
ᵛ Syr: Heb *I will watch for you.*
ᵂ Gk Syr Jerome: Heb *truth.*
ˣ Or *by his holiness.*
60:5–12: Ps 108:6–13.

8So will I ever sing praises to your name,
  as I pay my vows day after day.

Song of Trust in God Alone
To the choirmaster: according to Jeduthun.
A Psalm of David.

62 [61] For God alone my soul waits in
              silence;
  from him comes my salvation.
2He only is my rock and my salvation,
  my fortress; I shall not be greatly moved.

3How long will you set upon a man
  to shatter him, all of you,
  like a leaning wall, a tottering fence?
4They only plan to thrust him down from his
  eminence.
  They take pleasure in falsehood.
They bless with their mouths,
  but inwardly they curse.   *Selah*

5For God alone my soul waits in silence,
  for my hope is from him.
6He only is my rock and my salvation,
  my fortress; I shall not be shaken.
7On God rests my deliverance and my honor;
  my mighty rock, my refuge is God.

8Trust in him at all times, O people;
  pour out your heart before him;
God is a refuge for us.   *Selah*

9Men of low estate are but a breath,
  men of high estate are a delusion;
in the balances they go up;
  they are together lighter than a breath.
10Put no confidence in extortion,
  set no vain hopes on robbery;
  if riches increase, set not your heart on
    them.

11Once God has spoken;
  twice have I heard this:
that power belongs to God;
12   and that to you, O Lord, belongs steadfast
      love.
For you repay a man
  according to his work.

Comfort and Assurance in God's Presence
A Psalm of David, when he was in
the Wilderness of Judah.

63 [62] O God, you are my God, I seek you,
              my soul thirsts for you;
my flesh faints for you,
  as in a dry and weary land where no water
    is.
2So I have looked upon you in the sanctuary,
  beholding your power and glory.
3Because your merciful love is better than life,
  my lips will praise you.

4So I will bless you as long as I live;
  I will lift up my hands and call on your
    name.

5My soul is feasted as with marrow and fat,
  and my mouth praises you with joyful lips,
6when I think of you upon my bed,
  and meditate on you in the watches of the
    night;
7for you have been my help,
  and in the shadow of your wings I sing for
    joy.
8My soul clings to you;
  your right hand upholds me.

9But those who seek to destroy my life
  shall go down into the depths of the earth;
10they shall be given over to the power of the
    sword,
  they shall be prey for jackals.
11But the king shall rejoice in God;
  all who swear by him shall glory;
  for the mouths of liars will be stopped.

Prayer for Protection from Enemies
To the choirmaster.
A Psalm of David.

64 [63] Hear my voice, O God, in my
              complaint;
  preserve my life from dread of the enemy,
2hide me from the secret plots of the wicked,
  from the scheming of evildoers,
3who whet their tongues like swords,
  who aim bitter words like arrows,
4shooting from ambush at the blameless,
  shooting at him suddenly and without fear.
5They hold fast to their evil purpose;
  they talk of laying snares secretly,
thinking, "Who can see us? y
6   Who can search out our crimes? z
We have thought out a cunningly conceived
    plot."
  For the inward mind and heart of a man are
    deep!

7But God will shoot his arrow at them;
  they will be wounded suddenly.
8Because of their tongue he will bring them to
    ruin; a
  all who see them will wag their heads.
9Then all men will fear;
  they will tell what God has wrought,
  and ponder what he has done.

10Let the righteous rejoice in the Lord,
  and take refuge in him!
Let all the upright in heart glory!

---

y Syr: Heb *them.*
z Cn: Heb *they search out crimes.*
a Cn: Heb *They will bring him to ruin, their tongue being against them.*
62:12: Jer 17:10; Rev 2:23; 22:12.

Thanksgiving for Earth's Bounty
To the choirmaster. A Psalm of David. A Song.

65 [64] Praise is due to you,
O God, in Zion;
and to you shall vows be performed in
Jerusalem,
2 O you who hear prayer!
To you shall all flesh come
3 on account of sins.
When our transgressions prevail over us, [b]
you forgive them.
4 Blessed is he whom you choose and bring near,
to dwell in your courts!
We shall be satisfied with the goodness of your
house,
your holy temple!

5 By dread deeds you answer us with deliverance,
O God of our salvation,
who are the hope of all the ends of the earth,
and of the farthest seas;
6 who by your strength have established the
mountains,
being girded with might;
7 who still the roaring of the seas,
the roaring of their waves,
the tumult of the peoples;
8 so that those who dwell at earth's farthest
bounds
are afraid at your signs;
you make the outgoings of the morning and
the evening
to shout for joy.

9 You visit the earth and water it,
you greatly enrich it;
the river of God is full of water;
you provide their grain,
for so you have prepared it.
10 You water its furrows abundantly,
settling its ridges,
softening it with showers,
and blessing its growth.
11 You crown the year with your bounty;
the tracks of your chariot overflow with
richness.
12 The pastures of the wilderness drip,
the hills gird themselves with joy,
13 the meadows clothe themselves with flocks,
the valleys deck themselves with grain,
they shout and sing together for joy.

Praise for God's Goodness to Israel
To the choirmaster. A Song. A Psalm.

66 [65] Make a joyful noise to God, all the
earth;
2 sing the glory of his name;
give to him glorious praise!

3 Say to God, "How awesome are your deeds!
So great is your power that your enemies
cringe before you.
4 All the earth worships you;
they sing praises to you,
sing praises to your name." *Selah*

5 Come and see what God has done:
he is awesome in his deeds among men.
6 He turned the sea into dry land;
men passed through the river on foot.
There did we rejoice in him,
7 who rules by his might for ever,
whose eyes keep watch on the nations—
let not the rebellious exalt
themselves. *Selah*

8 Bless our God, O peoples,
let the sound of his praise be heard,
9 who has kept us among the living,
and has not let our feet slip.
10 For you, O God, have tested us;
you have tried us as silver is tried.
11 You brought us into the net;
you laid affliction on our backs;
12 you let men ride over our heads;
we went through fire and through water;
yet you have brought us forth to a spacious
place. [c]

13 I will come into your house with burnt offerings;
I will pay you my vows,
14 that which my lips uttered
and my mouth promised when I was in
trouble.
15 I will offer to you burnt offerings of fatlings,
with the smoke of the sacrifice of rams;
I will make an offering of bulls and
goats. *Selah*

16 Come and hear, all you who fear God,
and I will tell what he has done for me.
17 I cried aloud to him,
and he was extolled with my tongue.
18 If I had cherished iniquity in my heart,
the Lord would not have listened.
19 But truly God has listened;
he has given heed to the voice of my prayer.
20 Blessed be God,
because he has not rejected my prayer
or removed his merciful love from me!

The Nations Called to Praise God
To the choirmaster: with stringed instruments.
A Psalm. A Song.

67 [66] May God be gracious to us and
bless us
and make his face to shine upon us, *Selah*

---
[b] Gk: Heb *me.*
[c] Cn Compare Gk Syr Jerome Tg: Heb *saturation.*

²that your way may be known upon earth,
  your saving power among all nations.
³Let the peoples praise you, O God;
  let all the peoples praise you!

⁴Let the nations be glad and sing for joy,
  for you judge the peoples with equity
  and guide the nations upon earth.   *Selah*
⁵Let the peoples praise you, O God;
  let all the peoples praise you!

⁶The earth has yielded its increase;
  God, our God, has blessed us.
⁷God has blessed us;
  let all the ends of the earth fear him!

Praise and Thanksgiving
To the choirmaster.
A Psalm of David.
A Song.

68 [67]   * Let God arise, let his enemies be
  scattered;
  let those who hate him flee before him!
²As smoke is driven away, so drive them away;
  as wax melts before fire,
  let the wicked perish before God!
³But let the righteous be joyful;
  let them exult before God;
  let them be jubilant with joy!

⁴Sing to God, sing praises to his name;
  lift up a song to him who rides upon the
  clouds; ᵈ
  his name is the Lᴏʀᴅ, exult before him!

⁵Father of the fatherless and protector of
  widows
  is God in his holy habitation.
⁶God gives the desolate a home to dwell in;
  he leads out the prisoners to prosperity;
  but the rebellious dwell in a parched land.

⁷O God, when you went forth before your
  people,
  when you marched through the wilderness,
                                        Selah
⁸the earth quaked, the heavens poured down
  rain,
  at the presence of God;
  yon Sinai quaked at the presence of God,
  the God of Israel.

⁹Rain in abundance, O God, you showered
  abroad;
  you restored your heritage as it languished;
¹⁰your flock found a dwelling in it;
  in your goodness, O God, you provided for
  the needy.

¹¹The Lord gives the command;
  great is the host of those who bore the
  tidings:

¹² "The kings of the armies, they flee, they
  flee!"
The women at home divide the spoil,
¹³   though they stay among the sheepfolds—
  the wings of a dove covered with silver,
  its pinions with green gold.
¹⁴When the Almighty scattered kings there,
  snow fell on Zalmon.

¹⁵O mighty mountain, mountain of Bashan;
  O many-peaked mountain, mountain of
  Bashan!
¹⁶Why do you look with envy, O many-peaked
  mountain,
  at the mount which God desired for his
  abode,
  yes, where the Lᴏʀᴅ will dwell for ever?

¹⁷With mighty chariotry, twice ten thousand,
  thousands upon thousands,
  the Lord came from Sinai into the holy
  place. ᵉ
¹⁸You ascended the high mount,
  leading captives in your train,
  and receiving gifts among men,
even among the rebellious, that the Lᴏʀᴅ God
  may dwell there.

¹⁹Blessed be the Lord,
  who daily bears us up;
  God is our salvation.   *Selah*
²⁰Our God is a God of salvation;
  and to Gᴏᴅ, the Lord, belongs escape from
  death.

²¹But God will shatter the heads of his enemies,
  the hairy crown of him who walks in his
  guilty ways.
²²The Lord said,
  "I will bring them back from Bashan,
  I will bring them back from the depths of
  the sea,
²³that you may bathe ᶠ your feet in blood,
  that the tongues of your dogs may have
  their portion from the foe."

²⁴Your solemn processions are seen, ᵍ O God,
  the processions of my God, my King, into
  the sanctuary—
²⁵the singers in front, the minstrels last,
  between them maidens playing timbrels:
²⁶"Bless God in the great congregation,
  the Lᴏʀᴅ, O you who are of Israel's
  fountain!"

ᵈ Or *cast up a highway for him who rides through the deserts.*
ᵉ Cn: Heb *The Lord among them Sinai in the holy place.*
ᶠ Gk Syr Tg: Heb *shatter.*
ᵍ Or *have been seen.*
68:18: Eph 4:8.
* 68: This is one of the most ancient compositions in the Psalter and has
been influenced by Canaanite motifs and representations.

²⁷There is Benjamin, the least of them, in the
lead,
  the princes of Judah in their throng,
  the princes of Zeb'ulun, the princes of
    Naph'tali.

²⁸Summon your might, O God;
  show your strength, O God, you who have
    wrought for us.
²⁹Because of your temple at Jerusalem
  kings bear gifts to you.
³⁰Rebuke the beasts that dwell among the
  reeds,
  the herd of bulls with the calves of the
    peoples.
  Trample ʰ under foot those who lust after
    tribute;
  scatter the peoples who delight in war. ⁱ
³¹Let bronze be brought from Egypt;
  let Ethiopia hasten to stretch out her hands
    to God.

³²Sing to God, O kingdoms of the earth;
  sing praises to the Lord,   *Selah*
³³to him who rides in the heavens, the ancient
  heavens;
  behold, he sends forth his voice, his mighty
    voice.
³⁴Ascribe power to God,
  whose majesty is over Israel,
  and his power is in the skies.
³⁵Awesome is God in his ʲ sanctuary,
  the God of Israel,
  he gives power and strength to his people.

Blessed be God!

Prayer for Deliverance from Persecution

To the choirmaster: according to Lilies.
A Psalm of David.

69 [68]   Save me, O God!
        For the waters have come up to
  my neck.
²I sink in deep mire,
  where there is no foothold;
I have come into deep waters,
  and the flood sweeps over me.
³I am weary with my crying;
  my throat is parched.
My eyes grow dim
  with waiting for my God.

⁴More in number than the hairs of my head
  are those who hate me without cause;
mighty are those who would destroy me,
  those who attack me with lies.
What I did not steal
  must I now restore?
⁵O God, you know my folly;
  the wrongs I have done are not hidden from
    you.

⁶Let not those who hope in you be put to shame
  through me,
  O Lord God of hosts;
  let not those who seek you be brought to
    dishonor through me,
  O God of Israel.
⁷For it is for your sake that I have borne
  reproach,
  that shame has covered my face.
⁸I have become a stranger to my brethren,
  an alien to my mother's sons.

⁹For zeal for your house has consumed me,
  and the insults of those who insult you have
    fallen on me.
¹⁰When I humbled ᵏ my soul with fasting,
  it became my reproach.
¹¹When I made sackcloth my clothing,
  I became a byword to them.
¹²I am the talk of those who sit in the gate,
  and the drunkards make songs about me.

¹³But as for me, my prayer is to you, O Lord.
  At an acceptable time, O God,
  in the abundance of your mercy answer
    me.
With your faithful help ¹⁴rescue me
  from sinking in the mire;
  let me be delivered from my enemies
  and from the deep waters.
¹⁵Let not the flood sweep over me,
  or the deep swallow me up,
  or the pit close its mouth over me.

¹⁶Answer me, O Lord, for your merciful love is
  good;
  according to your abundant compassion,
    turn to me.
¹⁷Hide not your face from your servant;
  for I am in distress, make haste to answer
    me.
¹⁸Draw near to me, redeem me,
  set me free because of my enemies!

¹⁹You know my reproach,
  and my shame and my dishonor;
  my foes are all known to you.
²⁰Insults have broken my heart,
  so that I am in despair.
I looked for pity, but there was none;
  and for comforters, but I found none.
²¹They gave me gall for food,
  and for my thirst they gave me vinegar to
    drink.

ʰ Cn: Heb *trampling.*
ⁱ The Hebrew of verse 30 is obscure.
ʲ Gk: Heb *from your.*
ᵏ Gk Syr: Heb *I wept with fasting my soul* or *I made my soul mourn with
fasting.*
69:4: Ps 35:19; Jn 15:25.
69:9: Jn 2:17; Rom 15:3.
69:21: Mt 27:34,48; Mk 15:36; Lk 23:36; Jn 19:29.

²²Let their own table before them become a
snare;
let their sacrificial feasts ¹ be a trap.
²³Let their eyes be darkened, so that they cannot
see;
and make their loins tremble continually.
²⁴Pour out your indignation upon them,
and let your burning anger overtake them.
²⁵May their camp be a desolation,
let no one dwell in their tents.
²⁶For they persecute him whom you have struck
down,
and him ᵐ whom you have wounded, they
afflict still more. ⁿ
²⁷Add to them punishment upon punishment;
may they have no acquittal from you.
²⁸Let them be blotted out of the book of the
living;
let them not be enrolled among the
righteous.

²⁹But I am afflicted and in pain;
let your salvation, O God, set me on high!

³⁰I will praise the name of God with a song;
I will magnify him with thanksgiving.
³¹This will please the LORD more than an ox
or a bull with horns and hoofs.
³²Let the humble see it and be glad;
you who seek God, let your hearts revive.
³³For the LORD hears the needy,
and does not despise his own that are in
bonds.

³⁴Let heaven and earth praise him,
the seas and everything that moves therein.
³⁵For God will save Zion
and rebuild the cities of Judah;
and his servants shall dwell ° there and possess
it;
³⁶ the children of his servants shall inherit it,
and those who love his name shall dwell
in it.

Prayer for Deliverance from Enemies
To the choirmaster.
A Psalm of David, for the memorial offering.

70 [69]
Be pleased, O God, to deliver me!
O LORD, make haste to help me!
²Let them be put to shame and confusion
who seek my life!
Let them be turned back and brought to
dishonor
who desire my harm!
³Let them be appalled because of their shame
who say, "Aha, Aha!"

⁴May all who seek you
rejoice and be glad in you!
May those who love your salvation
say evermore, "God is great!"

⁵But I am poor and needy;
hasten to me, O God!
You are my help and my deliverer;
O LORD, do not delay!

Prayer for Lifelong Protection and Help

71 [70]
In you, O LORD, I take refuge;
let me never be put to shame!
²In your righteousness deliver me and rescue me;
incline your ear to me, and save me!
³Be to me a rock of refuge,
a strong fortress, ᵖ to save me,
for you are my rock and my fortress.

⁴Rescue me, O my God, from the hand of the
wicked,
from the grasp of the unjust and cruel man.
⁵For you, O Lord, are my hope,
my trust, O LORD, from my youth.
⁶Upon you I have leaned from my birth;
from my mother's womb, you have been my
strength.
My praise is continually of you.

⁷I have been as a portent to many;
but you are my strong refuge.
⁸My mouth is filled with your praise,
and with your glory all the day.
⁹Do not cast me off in the time of old age;
forsake me not when my strength is spent.
¹⁰For my enemies speak concerning me,
those who watch for my life consult
together,
¹¹and say, "God has forsaken him;
pursue and seize him,
for there is none to deliver him."

¹²O God, be not far from me;
O my God, make haste to help me!
¹³May my accusers be put to shame and
consumed;
with scorn and disgrace may they be
covered
who seek my harm.
¹⁴But I will hope continually,
and will praise you yet more and more.
¹⁵My mouth will tell of your righteous acts,
of your deeds of salvation all the day,
for their number is past my knowledge.
¹⁶With the mighty deeds of the Lord GOD I will
come,
I will praise your righteousness, yours alone.

---

¹ Tg: Heb *for security.*
ᵐ One Ms Tg Compare Syr: Heb *those.*
ⁿ Gk Syr: Heb *recount the pain of.*
° Syr: Heb *and they shall dwell.*
ᵖ Gk Compare 31:3: Heb *to come continually you have commanded.*
69:22–23: Rom 11:9–10.
69:24: Rev 16:1.
69:25: Acts 1:20.
69:28: Rev 3:5; 13:8; 17:8; 20:12, 15; 21:27.
70:1–5: Ps 40:13–17.

[17]O God, from my youth you have taught me,
and I still proclaim your wondrous deeds.
[18]So even to old age and gray hairs,
O God, do not forsake me,
till I proclaim your might
to all the generations to come. [q]
Your power [19]and your righteousness, O God,
reach the high heavens.

You who have done great things,
O God, who is like you?
[20]You who have made me see many sore troubles
will revive me again;
from the depths of the earth
you will bring me up again.
[21]You will increase my honor,
and comfort me again.

[22]I will also praise you with the harp
for your faithfulness, O my God;
I will sing praises to you with the lyre,
O Holy One of Israel.
[23]My lips will shout for joy,
when I sing praises to you;
my soul also, which you have rescued.
[24]And my tongue will talk of your righteous help
all the day long,
for they have been put to shame and disgraced
who sought to do me harm.

Prayer for Guidance and Support for the King
A Psalm of Solomon.

72 [71]
Give the king your justice, O God,
and your righteousness to the
royal son!
[2]May he judge your people with righteousness,
and your poor with justice!
[3]Let the mountains bear prosperity for the
people,
and the hills, in righteousness!
[4]May he defend the cause of the poor of the
people,
give deliverance to the needy,
and crush the oppressor!

[5]May he live [r] while the sun endures,
and as long as the moon, throughout all
generations!
[6]May he be like rain that falls on the mown
grass,
like showers that water the earth!
[7]In his days may righteousness flourish,
and peace abound, till the moon be no
more!

[8]May he have dominion from sea to sea,
and from the River to the ends of the
earth!
[9]May his foes [s] bow down before him,
and his enemies lick the dust!

[10]May the kings of Tarshish and of the isles
render him tribute,
may the kings of Sheba and Seba bring gifts!
[11]May all kings fall down before him,
all nations serve him!

[12]For he delivers the needy when he calls,
the poor and him who has no helper.
[13]He has pity on the weak and the needy,
and saves the lives of the needy.
[14]From oppression and violence he redeems their
souls;
and precious is their blood in his sight.

[15]Long may he live,
may gold of Sheba be given to him!
May prayer be made for him continually,
and blessings invoked for him all the day!
[16]May there be abundance of grain in the land;
on the tops of the mountains may it wave;
may its fruit be like Lebanon;
and may men blossom forth from the cities
like the grass of the field!
[17]May his name endure for ever,
his fame continue as long as the sun!
May men bless themselves by him,
all nations call him blessed!

[18]Blessed be the LORD, the God of Israel,
who alone does wondrous things.
[19]Blessed be his glorious name for ever;
may his glory fill the whole earth! Amen
and Amen!

[20]The prayers of David, the son of Jesse, are
ended.

BOOK III

Plea for Relief from Oppressors
A Psalm of Asaph.

73 [72]
Truly God is good to the upright,
to those who are pure in heart.[t]
[2]But as for me, my feet had almost stumbled,
my steps had well nigh slipped.
[3]For I was envious of the arrogant,
when I saw the prosperity of the wicked.

[4]For they have no pangs;
their bodies are sound and sleek.
[5]They are not in trouble as other men are;
they are not stricken like other men.
[6]Therefore pride is their necklace;
violence covers them as a garment.
[7]Their eyes swell out with fatness,
their hearts overflow with follies.

---

[q] Gk Compare Syr: Heb *to a generation, to all that come.*
[r] Gk: Heb *may they fear you.*
[s] Cn: Heb *those who dwell in the wilderness.*
[t] Or *Truly God is good to Israel, to those who are pure in heart.*

⁸They scoff and speak with malice;
    loftily they threaten oppression.
⁹They set their mouths against the heavens,
    and their tongue struts through the earth.

¹⁰Therefore the people turn and praise them; ᵘ
    and find no fault in them.ᵛ
¹¹And they say, "How can God know?
    Is there knowledge in the Most High?"
¹²Behold, these are the wicked;
    always at ease, they increase in riches.
¹³All in vain have I kept my heart clean
    and washed my hands in innocence.
¹⁴For all the day long I have been stricken,
    and chastened every morning.

¹⁵If I had said, "I will speak thus,"
    I would have been untrue to the generation
      of your children.
¹⁶But when I thought how to understand this,
    it seemed to me a wearisome task,
¹⁷until I went into the sanctuary of God;
    then I perceived their end.
¹⁸Truly you set them in slippery places;
    you make them fall to ruin.
¹⁹How they are destroyed in a moment,
    swept away utterly by terrors!
²⁰They are ʷ like a dream when one awakes,
    on awaking you despise their phantoms.

²¹When my soul was embittered,
    when I was pricked in heart,
²²I was stupid and ignorant,
    I was like a beast toward you.
²³Nevertheless I am continually with you;
    you hold my right hand.
²⁴You guide me with your counsel,
    and afterward you will receive me to glory. ˣ
²⁵Whom have I in heaven but you?
    And there is nothing upon earth that I
      desire besides you.
²⁶My flesh and my heart may fail,
    but God is the strength ʸ of my heart and
      my portion for ever.

²⁷For behold, those who are far from you shall
      perish;
    you put an end to those who are false to
      you.
²⁸But for me it is good to be near God;
    I have made the Lord God my refuge,
    that I may tell of all your works.

Plea for Help in Time of National Humiliation
A Maskil of Asaph.

74 [73]   O God, why do you cast us off for
      ever?
    Why does your anger smoke against the
      sheep of your pasture?
²Remember your congregation, which you have
    gotten of old,

which you have redeemed to be the tribe of
    your heritage!
Remember Mount Zion, where you have
    dwelt.
³Direct your steps to the perpetual ruins;
    the enemy has destroyed everything in the
      sanctuary!

⁴Your foes have roared in the midst of your holy
      place;
    they set up their own signs for signs.
⁵At the upper entrance they hacked
    the wooden trellis with axes. ᶻ
⁶And then all its carved wood
    they broke down with hatchets and
      hammers.
⁷They set your sanctuary on fire;
    to the ground they desecrated the dwelling
      place of your name.
⁸They said to themselves, "We will utterly
      subdue them";
    they burned all the meeting places of God
      in the land.

⁹We do not see our signs;
    there is no longer any prophet,
    and there is none among us who knows how
      long.
¹⁰How long, O God, is the foe to scoff?
    Is the enemy to revile your name for ever?
¹¹Why do you hold back your hand,
    why do you keep your right hand in ᵃ your
      bosom?

¹²Yet God my King is from of old,
    working salvation in the midst of the earth.
¹³You divided the sea by your might;
    you broke the heads of the dragons on the
      waters.
¹⁴You crushed the heads of Leviathan,
    you gave him as food ᵇ for the creatures of
      the wilderness.
¹⁵You cut open springs and brooks;
    you dried up ever-flowing streams.
¹⁶Yours is the day, yours also the night;
    you have established the luminaries and the
      sun.
¹⁷You have fixed all the bounds of the earth;
    you have made summer and winter.

¹⁸Remember this, O Lord, how the enemy
      scoffs,
    and an impious people reviles your name.

ᵘ Cn: Heb *his people return hither.*
ᵛ Cn: Heb *abundant waters are drained by them.*
ʷ Cn: Heb *Lord.*
ˣ Or *honor.*
ʸ Heb *rock.*
ᶻ Cn Compare Gk Syr: Heb uncertain.
ᵃ Cn: Heb *consume your right hand from.*
ᵇ Heb *food for the people.*

[19]Do not deliver the soul of your dove to the wild
    beasts;
  do not forget the souls of your poor for ever.

[20]Have regard for your [c] covenant;
  for the dark places of the land are full of
    the habitations of violence.
[21]Let not the humble be put to shame;
  let the poor and needy praise your name.

[22]Arise, O God, plead your cause;
  remember how the impious scoff at you all
    the day!
[23]Do not forget the clamor of your foes,
  the uproar of your adversaries which goes
    up continually!

Thanksgiving for God's Wondrous Deeds

To the choirmaster: according to Do Not Destroy.
A Psalm of Asaph. A Song.

75 [74] We give thanks to you, O God; we
    give thanks;
  we call on your name and recount [d] your
    wondrous deeds.

[2]At the set time which I appoint
  I will judge with equity.
[3]When the earth totters, and all its inhabitants,
  it is I who keep steady its pillars. *Selah*
[4]I say to the boastful, "Do not boast,"
  and to the wicked, "Do not lift up your horn;
[5]do not lift up your horn on high,
  or speak with insolent neck."

[6]For not from the east or from the west
  and not from the wilderness comes lifting
    up;
[7]but it is God who executes judgment,
  putting down one and lifting up another.
[8]For in the hand of the Lord there is a cup,
  with foaming wine, well mixed;
  and he will pour a draught from it,
  and all the wicked of the earth
    shall drain it down to the dregs.

[9]But I will rejoice [e] for ever,
  I will sing praises to the God of Jacob.
[10]All the horns of the wicked he [f] will cut off,
  but the horns of the righteous shall be
    exalted.

Israel's God—Judge of All the Earth

To the choirmaster: with stringed instruments.
A Psalm of Asaph. A Song.

76 [75] In Judah God is known,
    his name is great in Israel.
[2]His abode has been established in Salem,
  his dwelling place in Zion.
[3]There he broke the flashing arrows,
  the shield, the sword, and the weapons of
    war. *Selah*

[4]Glorious are you, more majestic
  than the everlasting mountains. [g]
[5]The stouthearted were stripped of their spoil;
  they sank into sleep;
 all the men of war
  were unable to use their hands.
[6]At your rebuke, O God of Jacob,
  both rider and horse lay stunned.

[7]But you, you are awesome!
  Who can stand before you
  when once your anger is roused?
[8]From the heavens you pronounced judgment;
  the earth feared and was still,
[9]when God arose to establish judgment
  to save all the oppressed of the earth. *Selah*

[10]Surely the wrath of men shall praise you;
  the residue of wrath you will bind around
    you.
[11]Make your vows to the Lord your God, and
    perform them;
  let all around him bring gifts
  to him who is to be feared,
[12]who cuts off the spirit of princes,
  who is awesome to the kings of the earth.

God's Mighty Deeds Recalled

To the choirmaster: according to Jeduthun.
A Psalm of Asaph.

77 [76] I cry aloud to God,
    aloud to God, that he may hear
  me.
[2]In the day of my trouble I seek the Lord;
  in the night my hand is stretched out
    without wearying;
  my soul refuses to be comforted.

[3]I think of God, and I moan;
  I meditate, and my spirit faints. *Selah*
[4]You keep my eyelids from closing;
  I am so troubled that I cannot speak.
[5]I consider the days of old,
  I remember the years long ago.
[6]I commune [h] with my heart in the night;
  I meditate and search my spirit: [i]
[7]"Will the Lord spurn for ever,
  and never again be favorable?
[8]Has his steadfast love for ever ceased?
  Are his promises at an end for all time?
[9]Has God forgotten to be gracious?
  Has he in anger shut up his compassion?"
    Selah

---

[c] Gk Syr: Heb *the.*
[d] Syr Compare Gk: Heb *and near is your name. They recount.*
[e] Gk: Heb *declare.*
[f] Heb *I.*
[g] Gk: Heb *the mountains of prey.*
[h] Gk Syr: Heb *my music.*
[i] Syr Jerome: Heb *my spirit searches.*

[10]And I say, "It is my grief
  that the right hand of the Most High has
    changed."

[11]I will call to mind the deeds of the Lord;
  yes, I will remember your wonders of old.
[12]I will meditate on all your work,
  and muse on your mighty deeds.
[13]Your way, O God, is holy.
  What god is great like our God?
[14]You are the God who works wonders,
  who have manifested your might among the
    peoples.
[15]With your arm you redeemed your people,
  the sons of Jacob and Joseph.   *Selah*

[16]When the waters saw you, O God,
  when the waters saw you, they were afraid,
  yes, the deep trembled.
[17]The clouds poured out water;
  the skies gave forth thunder;
  your arrows flashed on every side.
[18]The crash of your thunder was in the
    whirlwind;
  your lightnings lighted up the world;
  the earth trembled and shook.
[19]Your way was through the sea,
  your path through the great waters;
  yet your footprints were unseen.
[20]You led your people like a flock
  by the hand of Moses and Aaron.

God's Goodness and Israel's Ingratitude
A Maskil of Asaph.

78 [77]

Give ear, O my people, to my
  teaching;
  incline your ears to the words of my mouth!
[2]I will open my mouth in a parable;
  I will utter dark sayings from of old,
[3]things that we have heard and known,
  that our fathers have told us.
[4]We will not hide them from their children,
  but tell to the coming generation
the glorious deeds of the Lord, and his might,
  and the wonders which he has wrought.

[5]He established a testimony in Jacob,
  and appointed a law in Israel,
which he commanded our fathers
  to teach to their children;
[6]that the next generation might know them,
  the children yet unborn,
and arise and tell them to their children,
[7] so that they should set their hope in God,
  and not forget the works of God,
  but keep his commandments;
[8]and that they should not be like their fathers,
  a stubborn and rebellious generation,
a generation whose heart was not steadfast,
  whose spirit was not faithful to God.

[9]The E'phraimites, armed with [j] the bow,
  turned back on the day of battle.
[10]They did not keep God's covenant,
  but refused to walk according to his law.
[11]They forgot what he had done,
  and the miracles that he had shown them.
[12]In the sight of their fathers he wrought
    marvels
  in the land of Egypt, in the fields of Zo'an.
[13]He divided the sea and let them pass through it,
  and made the waters stand like a heap.
[14]In the daytime he led them with a cloud,
  and all the night with a fiery light.
[15]He cleft rocks in the wilderness,
  and gave them drink abundantly as from
    the deep.
[16]He made streams come out of the rock,
  and caused waters to flow down like rivers.

[17]Yet they sinned still more against him,
  rebelling against the Most High in the
    desert.
[18]They tested God in their heart
  by demanding the food they craved.
[19]They spoke against God, saying,
  "Can God spread a table in the wilderness?
[20]He struck the rock so that water gushed out
  and streams overflowed.
  Can he also give bread,
  or provide meat for his people?"

[21]Therefore, when the Lord heard, he was full of
    wrath;
  a fire was kindled against Jacob,
  his anger mounted against Israel;
[22]because they had no faith in God,
  and did not trust his saving power.
[23]Yet he commanded the skies above,
  and opened the doors of heaven;
[24]and he rained down upon them manna to eat,
  and gave them the bread of heaven.
[25]Man ate of the bread of the angels;
  he sent them food in abundance.
[26]He caused the east wind to blow in the heavens,
  and by his power he led out the south wind;
[27]he rained flesh upon them like dust,
  winged birds like the sand of the seas;
[28]he let them fall in the midst of their camp,
  all around their habitations.
[29]And they ate and were well filled,
  for he gave them what they craved.
[30]But before they had sated their craving,
  while the food was still in their mouths,
[31]the anger of God rose against them
  and he slew the strongest of them,
  and laid low the picked men of Israel.

---

[j] Heb *armed with shooting.*
78:2: Mt 13:35.
78:24: Jn 6:31.

³²In spite of all this they still sinned;
  despite his wonders they did not believe.
³³So he made their days vanish like a breath,
  and their years in terror.
³⁴When he slew them, they sought for him;
  they repented and sought God earnestly.
³⁵They remembered that God was their rock,
  the Most High God their redeemer.
³⁶But they flattered him with their mouths;
  they lied to him with their tongues.
³⁷Their heart was not steadfast toward him;
  they were not true to his covenant.
³⁸Yet he, being compassionate,
  forgave their iniquity,
  and did not destroy them;
 he restrained his anger often,
  and did not stir up all his wrath.
³⁹He remembered that they were but flesh,
  a wind that passes and comes not again.
⁴⁰How often they rebelled against him in the
    wilderness
  and grieved him in the desert!
⁴¹They tested him again and again,
  and provoked the Holy One of Israel.
⁴²They did not keep in mind his power,
  or the day when he redeemed them from the
    foe;
⁴³when he wrought his signs in Egypt,
  and his miracles in the fields of Zo′an.
⁴⁴He turned their rivers to blood,
  so that they could not drink of their
    streams.
⁴⁵He sent among them swarms of flies, which
    devoured them,
  and frogs, which destroyed them.
⁴⁶He gave their crops to the caterpillar,
  and the fruit of their labor to the locust.
⁴⁷He destroyed their vines with hail,
  and their sycamores with frost.
⁴⁸He gave over their cattle to the hail,
  and their flocks to thunderbolts.
⁴⁹He let loose on them his fierce anger,
  wrath, indignation, and distress,
  a company of destroying angels.
⁵⁰He made a path for his anger;
  he did not spare them from death,
  but gave their lives over to the plague.
⁵¹He struck all the first-born in Egypt,
  the first issue of their strength in the tents
    of Ham.
⁵²Then he led forth his people like sheep,
  and guided them in the wilderness like a
    flock.
⁵³He led them in safety, so that they were not
    afraid;
  but the sea overwhelmed their enemies.
⁵⁴And he brought them to his holy land,
  to the mountain which his right hand had
    won.

⁵⁵He drove out nations before them;
  he apportioned them for a possession
  and settled the tribes of Israel in their tents.
⁵⁶Yet they tested and rebelled against the Most
    High God,
  and did not observe his decrees,
⁵⁷but turned away and acted treacherously like
    their fathers;
  they twisted like a deceitful bow.
⁵⁸For they provoked him to anger with their high
    places;
  they moved him to jealousy with their
    graven images.
⁵⁹When God heard, he was full of wrath,
  and he utterly rejected Israel.
⁶⁰He forsook his dwelling at Shiloh,
  the tent where he dwelt among men,
⁶¹and delivered his power to captivity,
  his glory to the hand of the foe.
⁶²He gave his people over to the sword,
  and vented his wrath on his heritage.
⁶³Fire devoured their young men,
  and their maidens had no marriage song.
⁶⁴Their priests fell by the sword,
  and their widows made no lamentation.
⁶⁵Then the Lord awoke as from sleep,
  like a strong man shouting because of
    wine.
⁶⁶And he put his adversaries to rout;
  he put them to everlasting shame.

⁶⁷He rejected the tent of Joseph,
  he did not choose the tribe of E′phraim;
⁶⁸but he chose the tribe of Judah,
  Mount Zion, which he loves.
⁶⁹He built his sanctuary like the high heavens,
  like the earth, which he has founded for
    ever.
⁷⁰He chose David his servant,
  and took him from the sheepfolds;
⁷¹from tending the ewes that had young he
    brought him
  to be the shepherd of Jacob his people,
  of Israel his inheritance.
⁷²With upright heart he tended them,
  and guided them with skilful hand.

Plea for Mercy for Jerusalem
A Psalm of Asaph.

79 [78] O God, the heathen have come into
    your inheritance;
  they have defiled your holy temple;
  they have laid Jerusalem in ruins.
²They have given the bodies of your servants
  to the birds of the air for food,
  the flesh of your saints to the beasts of the
    earth.

78:37: Acts 8.21.

³They have poured out their blood like water
   round about Jerusalem,
   and there was none to bury them.
⁴We have become a taunt to our neighbors,
   mocked and derided by those round about
      us.

⁵How long, O LORD? Will you be angry for ever?
   Will your jealous wrath burn like fire?
⁶Pour out your anger on the nations that do not
      know you,
   and on the kingdoms
      that do not call on your name!
⁷For they have devoured Jacob,
   and laid waste his habitation.

⁸Do not remember against us the iniquities of
      our forefathers;
   let your compassion come speedily to meet
      us,
   for we are brought very low.
⁹Help us, O God of our salvation,
   for the glory of your name;
deliver us, and forgive our sins,
   for your name's sake!
¹⁰Why should the nations say,
   "Where is their God?"
Let the avenging of the outpoured blood of
      your servants
   be known among the nations before our
      eyes!

¹¹Let the groans of the prisoners come before
      you;
   according to your great power preserve
      those doomed to die!
¹²Return sevenfold into the bosom of our
      neighbors
   the taunts with which they have taunted
      you, O Lord!
¹³Then we your people, the flock of your
      pasture,
   will give thanks to you for ever;
   from generation to generation we will
      recount your praise.

Prayer for Israel's Restoration

To the choirmaster: according to Lilies.
A Testimony of Asaph.
A Psalm.

80 [79]

Give ear, O Shepherd of Israel,
   you who lead Joseph like a flock!
You who are enthroned upon the cherubim,
   shine forth
²   before Ephraim and Benjamin and
      Manas'seh!
Stir up your might,
   and come to save us!

³Restore us, O God;
   let your face shine, that we may be saved!

⁴O LORD God of hosts,
   how long will you be angry with your
      people's prayers?
⁵You have fed them with the bread of tears,
   and given them tears to drink in full
      measure.
⁶You make us the scorn ᵏ of our neighbors;
   and our enemies laugh among themselves.

⁷Restore us, O God of hosts;
   let your face shine, that we may be saved!

⁸You brought a vine out of Egypt;
   you drove out the nations and planted it.
⁹You cleared the ground for it;
   it took deep root and filled the land.
¹⁰The mountains were covered with its shade,
   the mighty cedars with its branches;
¹¹it sent out its branches to the sea,
   and its shoots to the River.
¹²Why then have you broken down its walls,
   so that all who pass along the way pluck its
      fruit?
¹³The boar from the forest ravages it,
   and all that move in the field feed on it.

¹⁴Turn again, O God of hosts!
   Look down from heaven, and see;
have regard for this vine,
¹⁵   the stock which your right hand planted. ¹
¹⁶They have burned it with fire, they have cut it
      down;
   may they perish at the rebuke of your
      countenance!
¹⁷But let your hand be upon the man of your
      right hand,
   the son of man whom you have made
      strong for yourself!
¹⁸Then we will never turn back from you;
   give us life, and we will call on your
      name!

¹⁹Restore us, O LORD God of hosts!
   let your face shine, that we may be saved!

God's Appeal to Stubborn Israel

To the choirmaster: according to The Gittith.
A Psalm of Asaph.

81 [80]

Sing aloud to God our strength;
   shout for joy to the God of
Jacob!
²Raise a song, sound the timbrel,
   the sweet lyre with the harp.
³Blow the trumpet at the new moon,
   at the full moon, on our feast day.
⁴For it is a statute for Israel,
   an ordinance of the God of Jacob.

ᵏ Syr: Heb *strife.*
¹ Heb *planted and upon the son whom you have reared for yourself.*

⁵He made it a decree in Joseph,
when he went out over ᵐ the land of Egypt.

I hear a voice I had not known:
⁶"I relieved your ⁿ shoulder of the burden;
your ⁿ hands were freed from the basket.
⁷In distress you called, and I delivered you;
I answered you in the secret place of
thunder;
I tested you at the waters of Mer′ibah.
Selah
⁸Hear, O my people, while I admonish you!
O Israel, if you would but listen to me!
⁹There shall be no strange god among you;
you shall not bow down to a foreign god.
¹⁰I am the LORD your God,
who brought you up out of the land of
Egypt.
Open your mouth wide, and I will fill it.

¹¹"But my people did not listen to my voice;
Israel would have none of me.
¹²So I gave them over to their stubborn hearts,
to follow their own counsels.
¹³O that my people would listen to me,
that Israel would walk in my ways!
¹⁴I would soon subdue their enemies,
and turn my hand against their foes.
¹⁵Those who hate the LORD would cringe toward
him,
and their fate would last for ever.
¹⁶I would feed you ° with the finest of the wheat,
and with honey from the rock I would
satisfy you."

A Plea for Justice
A Psalm of Asaph.

82 [81] God has taken his place in the
divine council;
in the midst of the angels he holds
judgment:
²"How long will you judge unjustly
and show partiality to the wicked? *Selah*
³Give justice to the weak and the fatherless;
maintain the right of the afflicted and the
destitute.
⁴Rescue the weak and the needy;
deliver them from the hand of the wicked."

⁵They have neither knowledge nor
understanding,
they walk about in darkness;
all the foundations of the earth are shaken.

⁶I say, "You are gods,
sons of the Most High, all of you;
⁷nevertheless, you shall die like men,
and fall like any prince." ᵖ

⁸Arise, O God, judge the earth;
for to you belong all the nations!

Prayer for Judgment on Israel's Foes
A Song.
A Psalm of Asaph.

83 [82] O God, do not keep silence;
do not hold your peace or be still,
O God!
²For behold, your enemies are in tumult;
those who hate you have raised their heads.
³They lay crafty plans against your people;
they consult together against your protected
ones.
⁴They say, "Come, let us wipe them out as a
nation;
let the name of Israel be remembered no
more!"
⁵Yes, they conspire with one accord;
against you they make a covenant—
⁶the tents of Edom and the Ish′maelites,
Moab and the Hagrites,
⁷Gebal and Ammon and Am′alek,
Philistia with the inhabitants of Tyre;
⁸Assyria also has joined them;
they are the strong arm of the children of
Lot. *Selah*

⁹Do to them as you did to Mid′ian,
as to Sis′era and Jabin at the river Kishon,
¹⁰who were destroyed at En-dor,
who became dung for the ground.
¹¹Make their nobles like Oreb and Zeeb,
all their princes like Zebah and Zalmun′na,
¹²who said, "Let us take possession for ourselves
of the pastures of God."

¹³O my God, make them like whirling dust,�q
like chaff before the wind.
¹⁴As fire consumes the forest,
as the flame sets the mountains ablaze,
¹⁵so you pursue them with your tempest
and terrify them with your hurricane!
¹⁶Fill their faces with shame,
that they may seek your name, O LORD.
¹⁷Let them be put to shame and dismayed for
ever;
let them perish in disgrace.
¹⁸Let them know that you alone,
whose name is the LORD,
are the Most High over all the earth.

The Joy of Worship in the Temple
To the choirmaster: according to The Gittith.
A Psalm of the Sons of Korah.

84 [83] How lovely is your dwelling place,
O LORD of hosts!

ᵐ Or *against*.
ⁿ Heb *his*.
° Cn Compare verse 16b: Heb *he would feed him*.
ᵖ Or *fall as one man, O princes*.
q Or *a tumbleweed*.
82:6: Jn 10.34.

459

²My soul longs, yes, faints
　　for the courts of the Lord;
　my heart and flesh sing for joy
　　to the living God.

³Even the sparrow finds a home,
　　and the swallow a nest for herself,
　　where she may lay her young,
　at your altars, O Lord of hosts,
　　my King and my God.
⁴Blessed are those who dwell in your house,
　　ever singing your praise!　　　　　*Selah*

⁵Blessed are the men whose strength is in you,
　　in whose heart are the highways to Zion.ᵡ
⁶As they go through the valley of Baca
　　they make it a place of springs;
　　the early rain also covers it with pools.
⁷They go from strength to strength;
　　the God of gods will be seen in Zion.

⁸O Lord God of hosts, hear my prayer;
　　give ear, O God of Jacob!　　　　*Selah*
⁹Behold our shield, O God;
　　look upon the face of your anointed!

¹⁰For a day in your courts is better
　　than a thousand elsewhere.
　I would rather be a doorkeeper in the house of
　　my God
　　than dwell in the tents of wickedness.
¹¹For the Lord God is a sun and shield;
　　he bestows favor and honor.
　No good thing does the Lord withhold
　　from those who walk uprightly.
¹²O Lord of hosts,
　　blessed is the man who trusts in you!

Prayer for the Restoration of God's Favor
To the choirmaster.
A Psalm of the Sons of Korah.

85 [84] Lord, you were favorable to your
　　land;
　you brought back the captives of Jacob.
²You forgave the iniquity of your people;
　　you pardoned all their sin.　　　　*Selah*
³You withdrew all your wrath;
　　you turned from your hot anger.

⁴Restore us again, O God of our salvation,
　　and put away your indignation toward us!
⁵Will you be angry with us for ever?
　　Will you prolong your anger to all
　　generations?
⁶Will you not revive us again,
　　that your people may rejoice in you?
⁷Show us your merciful love, O Lord,
　　and grant us your salvation.

⁸Let me hear what God the Lord will speak,
　　for he will speak peace to his people,

to his saints, to those who turn to him in
　　their hearts. ˢ
⁹Surely his salvation is at hand for those who
　　fear him,
　　that glory may dwell in our land.
¹⁰Mercy and faithfulness will meet;
　　righteousness and peace will kiss each
　　other.
¹¹Faithfulness will spring up from the ground,
　　and righteousness will look down from
　　heaven.
¹²Yes, the Lord will give what is good,
　　and our land will yield its increase.
¹³Righteousness will go before him,
　　and make his footsteps a way.

Supplication for Help against Enemies
A Prayer of David.

86 [85] Incline your ear, O Lord, and
　　answer me,
　for I am poor and needy.
²Preserve my life, for I am godly;
　　save your servant who trusts in you.
　You are my God; ³have mercy on me, O Lord,
　　for to you do I cry all the day.
⁴Gladden the soul of your servant,
　　for to you, O Lord, do I lift up my soul.
⁵For you, O Lord, are good and forgiving,
　　abounding in mercy to all who call on you.
⁶Give ear, O Lord, to my prayer;
　　listen to my cry of supplication.
⁷In the day of my trouble I call on you,
　　for you do answer me.

⁸There is none like you among the gods,
　　O Lord,
　　nor are there any works like yours.
⁹All the nations you have made shall come
　　and bow down before you, O Lord,
　　and shall glorify your name.
¹⁰For you are great and do wondrous things,
　　you alone are God.
¹¹Teach me your way, O Lord,
　　that I may walk in your truth;
　　unite my heart to fear your name.
¹²I give thanks to you, O Lord my God, with my
　　whole heart,
　　and I will glorify your name for ever.
¹³For great is your merciful love toward me;
　　you have delivered my soul from the depths
　　of Sheol.

¹⁴O God, insolent men have risen up against me;
　　a band of ruthless men seek my life,
　　and they do not set you before them.
¹⁵But you, O Lord, are a God merciful and
　　gracious,

ᵡ Heb lacks *to Zion.*
ˢ Gk: Heb *but let them not turn back to folly.*

slow to anger and abounding in mercy and
faithfulness.
[16]Turn to me and take pity on me;
give your strength to your servant,
and save the son of your handmaid.
[17]Show me a sign of your favor,
that those who hate me may see and be put
to shame
because you, LORD, have helped me and
comforted me.

The Joy of Living in Zion
A Psalm of the Sons of Korah.
A Song.

87 [86]
On the holy mount stands the city
he founded;
[2] the LORD loves the gates of Zion
more than all the dwelling places of Jacob.
[3]Glorious things are spoken of you,
O city of God.   *Selah*

[4]Among those who know me I mention Rahab
and Babylon;
behold, Philis'tia and Tyre, with Ethiopia—
"This one was born there," they say.
[5]And of Zion it shall be said,
"This one and that one were born in her";
for the Most High himself will establish her.
[6]The LORD records as he registers the peoples,
"This one was born there."   *Selah*

[7]Singers and dancers alike say,
"All my springs are in you."

Prayer for Help in Despondency
A Song. A Psalm of the Sons of Korah.
To the choirmaster: according to Mahalath Leannoth.
A Maskil of Heman the Ezrahite.

88 [87]
O LORD, my God, I call for help [t]
by day;
I cry out in the night before you.
[2]Let my prayer come before you,
incline your ear to my cry!

[3]For my soul is full of troubles,
and my life draws near to Sheol.
[4]I am reckoned among those who go down to
the Pit;
I am a man who has no strength,
[5]like one forsaken among the dead,
like the slain that lie in the grave,
like those whom you remember no more,
for they are cut off from your hand.
[6]You have put me in the depths of the Pit,
in the regions dark and deep.
[7]Your wrath lies heavy upon me,
and you overwhelm me with all your
waves.   *Selah*
[8]You have caused my companions to shun me;
you have made me a thing of horror to them.

I am shut in so that I cannot escape;
[9] my eye grows dim through sorrow.
Every day I call upon you, O LORD;
I spread out my hands to you.
[10]Do you work wonders for the dead?
Do the shades rise up to praise you?   *Selah*
[11]Is your mercy declared in the grave,
or your faithfulness in Abad'don?
[12]Are your wonders known in the darkness,
or your saving help in the land of
forgetfulness?

[13]But I, O LORD, cry to you;
in the morning my prayer comes before you.
[14]O LORD, why do you cast me off?
Why do you hide your face from me?
[15]Afflicted and close to death from my youth,
I suffer your terrors; I am helpless. [u]
[16]Your wrath has swept over me;
your dread assaults destroy me.
[17]They surround me like a flood all day long;
they close in upon me together.
[18]You have caused loved one and friend to shun
me;
my companions are in darkness.

God's Covenant with David
A Maskil of Ethan the Ezrahite.

89 [88]
I will sing of your mercies,
O LORD,[v] for ever;
with my mouth I will proclaim your
faithfulness to all generations.
[2]For your merciful love was established for ever,
your faithfulness is firm as the heavens.
[3]You have said, "I have made a covenant with
my chosen one,
I have sworn to David my servant:
[4]'I will establish your descendants for ever,
and build your throne for all generations.'"
Selah

[5]Let the heavens praise your wonders, O LORD,
your faithfulness in the assembly of the
holy ones!
[6]For who in the skies can be compared to the
LORD?
Who among the heavenly beings [w] is like the
LORD,
[7]a God feared in the council of the holy ones,
great and awesome [x] above all that are
round about him?
[8]O LORD God of hosts,
who is mighty as you are, O LORD,
with your faithfulness round about you?

---

[t] Cn: Heb *O LORD, God of my salvation*.
[u] The meaning of the Hebrew word is uncertain.
[v] Gk: Heb *the merciful love of the* LORD.
[w] Or *sons of gods*.
[x] Gk Syr: Heb *greatly awesome*.
89:3-4: Ps 132:11; Acts 2:30.

⁹You rule the raging of the sea;
  when its waves rise, you still them.
¹⁰You crushed Rahab like a carcass,
  you scattered your enemies with your
    mighty arm.
¹¹The heavens are yours, the earth also is yours;
  the world and all that is in it, you have
    founded them.
¹²The north and the south, you have created
    them;
  Tabor and Hermon joyously praise your
    name.
¹³You have a mighty arm;
  strong is your hand, high your right hand.
¹⁴Righteousness and justice are the foundation of
    your throne;
  steadfast love and faithfulness go before
    you.
¹⁵Blessed are the people who know the festal
    shout,
  who walk, O Lord, in the light of your
    countenance,
¹⁶who exult in your name all the day,
  and extol ʸ your righteousness.
¹⁷For you are the glory of their strength;
  by your favor our horn is exalted.
¹⁸For our shield belongs to the Lord,
  our king to the Holy One of Israel.

¹⁹Of old you spoke in a vision
  to your faithful one, and said:
"I have set the crown ᶻ upon one who is mighty,
  I have exalted one chosen from the people.
²⁰I have found David, my servant;
  with my holy oil I have anointed him;
²¹so that my hand shall ever abide with him,
  my arm also shall strengthen him.
²²The enemy shall not outwit him,
  the wicked shall not humble him.
²³I will crush his foes before him
  and strike down those who hate him.
²⁴My faithfulness and my mercy shall be with
    him,
  and in my name shall his horn be exalted.
²⁵I will set his hand on the sea
  and his right hand on the rivers.
²⁶He shall cry to me, 'You are my Father,
  my God, and the Rock of my salvation.'
²⁷And I will make him the first-born,
  the highest of the kings of the earth.
²⁸My merciful love I will keep for him for ever,
  and my covenant will stand firm for him.
²⁹I will establish his line for ever
  and his throne as the days of the heavens.
³⁰If his children forsake my law
  and do not walk according to my
    ordinances,
³¹if they violate my statutes
  and do not keep my commandments,

³²then I will punish their transgression with the
    rod
  and their iniquity with scourges;
³³but I will not remove from him my merciful love,
  or be false to my faithfulness.
³⁴I will not violate my covenant,
  or alter the word that went forth from my
    lips.
³⁵Once for all I have sworn by my holiness;
  I will not lie to David.
³⁶His line shall endure for ever,
  his throne as long as the sun before me.
³⁷Like the moon it shall be established for ever;
  it shall stand firm while the skies
    endure." ᵃ   *Selah*

³⁸But now you have cast off and rejected,
  you are full of wrath against your anointed.
³⁹You have renounced the covenant with your
    servant;
  you have defiled his crown in the dust.
⁴⁰You have breached all his walls;
  you have laid his strongholds in ruins.
⁴¹All that pass by despoil him;
  he has become the scorn of his neighbors.
⁴²You have exalted the right hand of his foes;
  you have made all his enemies rejoice.
⁴³Yes, you have turned back the edge of his
    sword,
  and you have not made him stand in battle.
⁴⁴You have removed the scepter from his hand,ᵇ
  and cast his throne to the ground.
⁴⁵You have cut short the days of his youth;
  you have covered him with shame.   *Selah*

⁴⁶How long, O Lord? Will you hide yourself for
    ever?
  How long will your wrath burn like fire?
⁴⁷Remember, O Lord,ᶜ what the measure of life
    is,
  for what vanity you have created all the
    sons of men!
⁴⁸What man can live and never see death?
  Who can deliver his soul from the power of
    Sheol?   *Selah*

⁴⁹Lord, where is your steadfast love of old,
  which by your faithfulness you swore to
    David?
⁵⁰Remember, O Lord, how your servant is
    scorned;
  how I bear in my bosom the insults ᵈ of the
    peoples,

ʸ Cn: Heb *are exalted in.*
ᶻ Cn: Heb *help.*
ᵃ Cn: Heb *the witness in the skies is sure.*
ᵇ Cn: Heb *removed his cleanness.*
ᶜ Cn: Heb *I.*
ᵈ Cn: Heb *all of many.*
89:20: Acts 13:22.
89:27: Rev 1:5.
89:37: Rev 1:5; 3:14.

⁵¹with which your enemies taunt, O LORD,
with which they mock the footsteps of your anointed.

⁵² Blessed be the LORD for ever! Amen and Amen.

BOOK IV

God's Eternity and Human Frailty
A Prayer of Moses, the man of God.

90 [89]

LORD, you have been our dwelling place ᵉ
in all generations.
²Before the mountains were brought forth,
or ever you had formed the earth and the world,
from everlasting to everlasting you are God.

³You turn man back to the dust,
and say, "Turn back, O children of men!"
⁴For a thousand years in your sight
are but as yesterday when it is past,
or as a watch in the night.

⁵You sweep men away; they are like a dream,
like grass which is renewed in the morning:
⁶in the morning it flourishes and is renewed;
in the evening it fades and withers.

⁷For we are consumed by your anger;
by your wrath we are overwhelmed.
⁸You have set our iniquities before you,
our secret sins in the light of your countenance.

⁹For all our days pass away under your wrath,
our years come to an end ᶠ like a sigh.
¹⁰The years of our life are threescore and ten,
or even by reason of strength fourscore;
yet their span ᵍ is but toil and trouble;
they are soon gone, and we fly away.

¹¹Who considers the power of your anger,
and your wrath according to the fear of you?
¹²So teach us to number our days
that we may get a heart of wisdom.

¹³Return, O LORD! How long?
Have pity on your servants!
¹⁴Satisfy us in the morning with your mercy,
that we may rejoice and be glad all our days.

¹⁵Make us glad as many days as you have afflicted us,
and as many years as we have seen evil.
¹⁶Let your work be manifest to your servants,
and your glorious power to their children.

¹⁷Let the favor of the Lord our God be upon us,
and establish the work of our hands upon us,
yes, establish the work of our hands.

Assurance of God's Protection

91 [90]

He who dwells in the shelter of the Most High,
who abides in the shadow of the Almighty,
²will say to the LORD, "My refuge and my fortress;
my God, in whom I trust."
³For he will deliver you from the snare of the fowler
and from the deadly pestilence;
⁴he will cover you with his pinions,
and under his wings you will find refuge;
his faithfulness is a shield and buckler.
⁵You will not fear the terror of the night,
nor the arrow that flies by day,
⁶nor the pestilence that stalks in darkness,
nor the destruction that wastes at noonday.

⁷A thousand may fall at your side,
ten thousand at your right hand;
but it will not come near you.
⁸You will only look with your eyes
and see the recompense of the wicked.

⁹Because you have made the LORD your refuge, ʰ
the Most High your habitation,
¹⁰no evil shall befall you,
no scourge come near your tent.

¹¹For he will give his angels charge of you
to guard you in all your ways.
¹²On their hands they will bear you up,
lest you dash your foot against a stone.
¹³You will tread on the lion and the adder,
the young lion and the serpent you will trample under foot.

¹⁴Because he clings to me in love, I will deliver him;
I will protect him, because he knows my name.
¹⁵When he calls to me, I will answer him;
I will be with him in trouble,
I will rescue him and honor him.
¹⁶With long life I will satisfy him,
and show him my salvation.

ᵉ Another reading is *refuge.*
ᶠ Syr: Heb *we bring our years to an end.*
ᵍ Cn Compare Gk Syr Jerome Tg: Heb *pride.*
ʰ Cn: Heb *Because you,* LORD, *are my refuge; you have made.*
90:4: 2 Pet 3:8.
91:11-12: Mt 4:6; Lk 4:10–11.
91:13: Lk 10:19.

Thanksgiving for Vindication
A Psalm.
A Song for the Sabbath.

92 [91]
It is good to give thanks to the LORD,
   to sing praises to your name, O Most High;
[2]to declare your merciful love in the morning,
   and your faithfulness by night,
[3]to the music of the lute and the harp,
   to the melody of the lyre.
[4]For you, O LORD, have made me glad by your work;
   at the works of your hands I sing for joy.

[5]How great are your works, O LORD!
   Your thoughts are very deep!
[6]The dull man cannot know,
   the stupid cannot understand this:
[7]that, though the wicked sprout like grass
   and all evildoers flourish,
   they are doomed to destruction for ever,
[8]   but you, O LORD, are on high for ever.
[9]For, behold, your enemies, O LORD,
   for, behold, your enemies shall perish;
   all evildoers shall be scattered.

[10]But you have exalted my horn like that of the wild ox;
   you have poured over me [i] fresh oil.
[11]My eyes have seen the downfall of my enemies,
   my ears have heard the doom of my evil assailants.

[12]The righteous flourish like the palm tree,
   and grow like a cedar in Lebanon.
[13]They are planted in the house of the LORD,
   they flourish in the courts of our God.
[14]They still bring forth fruit in old age,
   they are ever full of sap and green,
[15]to show that the LORD is upright;
   he is my rock, and there is no unrighteousness in him.

The Majesty of God's Rule

93 [92]
* The LORD reigns; he is robed in majesty;
   the LORD is robed, he is girded with strength.
Yes, the world is established; it shall never be moved;
[2]   your throne is established from of old;
   you are from everlasting.

[3]The floods have lifted up, O LORD,
   the floods have lifted up their voice,
   the floods lift up their roaring.
[4]Mightier than the thunders of many waters,
   mightier than the waves [j] of the sea,
   the LORD on high is mighty!

[5]Your decrees are very sure;

holiness befits your house,
   O LORD, for evermore.

God the Avenger of the Righteous

94 [93]
O LORD, you God of vengeance,
   you God of vengeance, shine forth!
[2]Rise up, O judge of the earth;
   render to the proud their deserts!
[3]O LORD, how long shall the wicked,
   how long shall the wicked exult?

[4]They pour out their arrogant words,
   they boast, all the evildoers.
[5]They crush your people, O LORD,
   and afflict your heritage.
[6]They slay the widow and the sojourner,
   and murder the fatherless;
[7]and they say, "The LORD does not see;
   the God of Jacob does not perceive."

[8]Understand, O dullest of the people!
   Fools, when will you be wise?
[9]He who planted the ear, does he not hear?
   He who formed the eye, does he not see?
[10]He who chastens the nations, does he not chastise?
   He who teaches men knowledge,
[11]   the LORD, knows the thoughts of man,
   that they are but a breath.

[12]Blessed is the man whom you chasten, O LORD,
   and whom you teach out of your law
[13]to give him respite from days of trouble,
   until a pit is dug for the wicked.
[14]For the LORD will not forsake his people;
   he will not abandon his heritage;
[15]for justice will return to the righteous,
   and all the upright in heart will follow it.

[16]Who rises up for me against the wicked?
   Who stands up for me against evildoers?
[17]If the LORD had not been my help,
   my soul would soon have dwelt in the land of silence.
[18]When I thought, "My foot slips,"
   your mercy, O LORD, held me up.
[19]When the cares of my heart are many,
   your consolations cheer my soul.
[20]Can wicked rulers be allied with you,
   who frame mischief by statute?
[21]They band together against the life of the righteous,
   and condemn the innocent to death.
[22]But the LORD has become my stronghold,
   and my God the rock of my refuge.

---

[i] Syr: Heb uncertain.
[j] Cn: Heb *mighty the waves*.
94:11: 1 Cor 3:20.
* 93: The first of several psalms which represent Yahweh as enthroned in heaven.

[23]He will bring back on them their iniquity
and wipe them out for their wickedness;
the Lord our God will wipe them out.

A Call to Worship and Obedience

95 [94] O come, let us sing to the Lord;
let us make a joyful noise to the
rock of our salvation!
[2]Let us come into his presence with
thanksgiving;
let us make a joyful noise to him with songs
of praise!
[3]For the Lord is a great God,
and a great King above all gods.
[4]In his hand are the depths of the earth;
the heights of the mountains are his also.
[5]The sea is his, for he made it;
for his hands formed the dry land.

[6]O come, let us worship and bow down,
let us kneel before the Lord, our Maker!
[7]For he is our God,
and we are the people of his pasture,
and the sheep of his hand.

O that today you would listen to his voice!
[8]   Harden not your hearts, as at Mer′ibah,
as on the day at Massah in the wilderness,
[9]when your fathers tested me,
and put me to the proof, though they had
seen my work.
[10]For forty years I was wearied of that
generation
and said, "They are a people who err in
heart,
and they do not regard my ways."
[11]Therefore I swore in my anger
that they should not enter my rest.

Praise to God Who Comes in Judgment

96 [95] O sing to the Lord a new song;
sing to the Lord, all the earth!
[2]Sing to the Lord, bless his name;
tell of his salvation from day to day.
[3]Declare his glory among the nations,
his marvelous works among all the
peoples!
[4]For great is the Lord, and greatly to be praised;
he is to be feared above all gods.
[5]For all the gods of the peoples are idols;
but the Lord made the heavens.
[6]Honor and majesty are before him;
strength and beauty are in his sanctuary.

[7]Ascribe to the Lord, O families of the peoples,
ascribe to the Lord glory and strength!
[8]Ascribe to the Lord the glory due his name;
bring an offering, and come into his courts!
[9]Worship the Lord in holy attire;
tremble before him, all the earth!

[10]Say among the nations, "The Lord reigns!
Yes, the world is established, it shall never
be moved;
he will judge the peoples with equity."
[11]Let the heavens be glad, and let the earth
rejoice;
let the sea roar, and all that fills it;
[12]   let the field exult, and everything in it!
Then shall all the trees of the wood sing for
joy
[13]   before the Lord, for he comes,
for he comes to judge the earth.
He will judge the world with righteousness,
and the peoples with his truth.

The Glory of God's Reign

97 [96] The Lord reigns; let the earth
rejoice;
let the many islands be glad!
[2]Clouds and thick darkness are round about
him;
righteousness and justice are the foundation
of his throne.
[3]Fire goes before him,
and burns up his adversaries round about.
[4]His lightnings lighten the world;
the earth sees and trembles.
[5]The mountains melt like wax before the Lord,
before the Lord of all the earth.

[6]The heavens proclaim his righteousness;
and all the peoples behold his glory.
[7]All worshipers of images are put to shame,
who make their boast in worthless idols;
let all his angels bow down before him.
[8]Zion hears and is glad,
and the daughters of Judah rejoice,
because of your judgments, O God.
[9]For you, O Lord, are most high over all the
earth;
you are exalted far above all gods.

[10]The Lord loves those who hate evil; [k]
he preserves the lives of his saints;
he delivers them from the hand of the
wicked.
[11]Light dawns [1] for the righteous,
and joy for the upright in heart.
[12]Rejoice in the Lord, O you righteous,
and give thanks to his holy name!

Praise the Judge of the World
A Psalm.

98 [97] O sing to the Lord a new song,
for he has done marvelous things!

---

k Cn: Heb *You who love the* Lord *hate evil.*
1 Gk Syr Jerome: Heb *is sown.*
95:7–11: Heb 3:7–11; 4:3–11.
96:1–13: 1 Chron 16:23–33.
97:7: Heb 1:6.

His right hand and his holy arm
    have gotten him victory.
2The Lord has made known his victory,
    he has revealed his vindication in the sight
        of the nations.
3He has remembered his mercy and faithfulness
    to the house of Israel.
All the ends of the earth have seen
    the victory of our God.

4Make a joyful noise to the Lord, all the earth;
    break forth into joyous song and sing
        praises!
5Sing praises to the Lord with the lyre,
    with the lyre and the sound of melody!
6With trumpets and the sound of the horn
    make a joyful noise before the King, the
        Lord!

7Let the sea roar, and all that fills it;
    the world and those who dwell in it!
8Let the floods clap their hands;
    let the hills sing for joy together
9before the Lord, for he comes
    to judge the earth.
He will judge the world with righteousness,
    and the peoples with equity.

Praise to God for His Holiness

99 [98]
The Lord reigns; let the peoples
    tremble!
He sits enthroned upon the cherubim; let the
    earth quake!
2The Lord is great in Zion;
    he is exalted over all the peoples.
3Let them praise your great and awesome
    name!
    Holy is he!

4Mighty King,m lover of justice,
    you have established equity;
you have executed justice
    and righteousness in Jacob.
5Extol the Lord our God;
    worship at his footstool!
    Holy is he!

6Moses and Aaron were among his priests,
    Samuel also was among those who called on
        his name.
    They cried to the Lord, and he answered
        them.
7He spoke to them in the pillar of cloud;
    they kept his testimonies,
    and the statutes that he gave them.

8O Lord our God, you answered them;
    you were a forgiving God to them,
    but an avenger of their wrongdoings.
9Extol the Lord our God,
    and worship at his holy mountain;
    for the Lord our God is holy!

All Lands Summoned to Praise God
A Psalm for the thank offering.

100 [99]
Make a joyful noise to the
    Lord, all the lands!n
2 Serve the Lord with gladness!
Come into his presence with singing!

3Know that the Lord is God!
    It is he that made us, and we are his;o
    we are his people, and the sheep of his
        pasture.

4Enter his gates with thanksgiving,
    and his courts with praise!
    Give thanks to him, bless his name!

5For the Lord is good;
    his mercy endures for ever,
    and his faithfulness to all generations.

A Sovereign's Pledge of Integrity and Justice
A Psalm of David.

101 [100]
I will sing of mercy and of
    justice;
to you, O Lord, I will sing.
2I will give heed to the way that is blameless.
    Oh, when will you come to me?

I will walk with integrity of heart
    within my house;
3I will not set before my eyes
    anything that is base.

I hate the work of those who fall away;
    it shall not cling to me.

4Perverseness of heart shall be far from me;
    I will know nothing of evil.

5Him who slanders his neighbor secretly
    I will destroy.
The man of haughty looks and arrogant heart
    I will not endure.

6I will look with favor on the faithful in the
    land,
    that they may dwell with me;
he who walks in the way that is blameless
    shall minister to me.

7No man who practices deceit
    shall dwell in my house;
no man who utters lies
    shall continue in my presence.

8Morning by morning I will destroy
    all the wicked in the land,
cutting off all the evildoers
    from the city of the Lord.

---

m Cn: Heb *and the king's strength.*
n Heb *land* or *earth.*
o Another reading is *and not we ourselves.*

Prayer to the Eternal King for Help

A prayer of one afflicted, when he is faint and pours out his complaint before the Lord.

102 [101] Hear my prayer, O Lord;
let my cry come to you!
²Do not hide your face from me
in the day of my distress!
Incline your ear to me;
answer me speedily in the day when I call!

³For my days pass away like smoke,
and my bones burn like a furnace.
⁴My heart is struck down like grass, and
withered;
I forget to eat my bread.
⁵Because of my loud groaning
my bones cling to my flesh.
⁶I am like a vulture ᵖ of the wilderness,
like an owl of the waste places;
⁷I lie awake,
I am like a lonely bird on the housetop.
⁸All the day my enemies taunt me,
those who deride me use my name for a
curse.
⁹For I eat ashes like bread,
and mingle tears with my drink,
¹⁰because of your indignation and anger;
for you have taken me up and thrown me
away.
¹¹My days are like an evening shadow;
I wither away like grass.

¹²But you, O Lord, are enthroned for ever;
your name endures to all generations.
¹³You will arise and have pity on Zion;
it is the time to favor her;
the appointed time has come.
¹⁴For your servants hold her stones dear,
and have pity on her dust.
¹⁵The nations will fear the name of the Lord,
and all the kings of the earth your glory.
¹⁶For the Lord will build up Zion,
he will appear in his glory;
¹⁷he will regard the prayer of the destitute,
and will not despise their supplication.

¹⁸Let this be recorded for a generation to come,
so that a people yet unborn may praise the
Lord:
¹⁹that he looked down from his holy height,
from heaven the Lord looked at the earth,
²⁰to hear the groans of the prisoners,
to set free those who were doomed to die;
²¹that men may declare in Zion the name of the
Lord,
and in Jerusalem his praise,
²²when peoples gather together,
and kingdoms, to worship the Lord.

²³He has broken my strength in mid-course;
he has shortened my days.

²⁴"O my God," I say, "do not take me from here
in the midst of my days,
you whose years endure
throughout all generations!"
²⁵Of old you laid the foundation of the earth,
and the heavens are the work of your
hands.
²⁶They will perish, but you endure;
they will all wear out like a garment.
You change them like clothing, and they pass
away;
²⁷ but you are the same, and your years have
no end.
²⁸The children of your servants shall dwell
secure;
their posterity shall be established before
you.

Thanksgiving for God's Goodness

A Psalm of David.

103 [102] Bless the Lord, O my soul;
and all that is within me,
bless his holy name!
²Bless the Lord, O my soul,
and forget not all his benefits,
³who forgives all your iniquity,
who heals all your diseases,
⁴who redeems your life from the Pit,
who crowns you with mercy and
compassion,
⁵who satisfies you with good as long as you
live �q
so that your youth is renewed like the
eagle's.

⁶The Lord works vindication
and justice for all who are oppressed.
⁷He made known his ways to Moses,
his acts to the people of Israel.
⁸The Lord is merciful and gracious,
slow to anger and abounding in mercy.
⁹He will not always chide,
nor will he keep his anger for ever.
¹⁰He does not deal with us according to our sins,
nor repay us according to our iniquities.
¹¹For as the heavens are high above the earth,
so great is his mercy toward those who fear
him;
¹²as far as the east is from the west,
so far does he remove our transgressions
from us.
¹³As a father pities his children,
so the Lord pities those who fear him.
¹⁴For he knows our frame;
he remembers that we are dust.

ᵖ The meaning of the Hebrew word is uncertain.
q Heb uncertain.
102:25-27: Heb 1:10-12.
103:8 Jas 5:11.

¹⁵As for man, his days are like grass;
  he flourishes like a flower of the field;
¹⁶for the wind passes over it, and it is gone,
  and its place knows it no more.
¹⁷But the mercy of the LORD is from everlasting
   to everlasting
  upon those who fear him,
  and his righteousness to children's children,
¹⁸to those who keep his covenant
  and remember to do his commandments.

¹⁹The LORD has established his throne in the
   heavens,
  and his kingdom rules over all.
²⁰Bless the LORD, O you his angels,
  you mighty ones who do his word,
  hearkening to the voice of his word!
²¹Bless the LORD, all his hosts,
  his ministers that do his will!
²²Bless the LORD, all his works,
  in all places of his dominion.
  Bless the LORD, O my soul!

God the Creator and Provider

104 [103]

* Bless the LORD, O my soul!
  O LORD my God, you are
very great!
You are clothed with honor and majesty,
² who cover yourself with light as with a
   garment,
who have stretched out the heavens like a
   tent,
³ who have laid the beams of your chambers
   on the waters,
who make the clouds your chariot,
  who ride on the wings of the wind,
⁴who make the winds your messengers,
  fire and flame your ministers.

⁵You set the earth on its foundations,
  so that it should never be shaken.
⁶You covered it with the deep as with a
   garment;
  the waters stood above the mountains.
⁷At your rebuke they fled;
  at the sound of your thunder they took to
   flight.
⁸The mountains rose, the valleys sank down
  to the place which you appointed for them.
⁹You set a bound which they should not pass,
  so that they might not again cover the
   earth.

¹⁰You make springs gush forth in the valleys;
  they flow between the hills,
¹¹they give drink to every beast of the field;
  the wild donkeys quench their thirst.
¹²By them the birds of the air have their
   habitation;
  they sing among the branches.

¹³From your lofty abode you water the
   mountains;
  the earth is satisfied with the fruit of your
   work.
¹⁴You cause the grass to grow for the cattle,
  and plants for man to cultivate, ⁿ
that he may bring forth food from the earth,
¹⁵ and wine to gladden the heart of man,
  oil to make his face shine,
  and bread to strengthen man's heart.
¹⁶The trees of the LORD are watered abundantly,
  the cedars of Lebanon which he planted.
¹⁷In them the birds build their nests;
  the stork has her home in the fir trees.
¹⁸The high mountains are for the wild goats;
  the rocks are a refuge for the badgers.
¹⁹You have made the moon to mark the seasons;
  the sun knows its time for setting.
²⁰You make darkness, and it is night,
  when all the beasts of the forest creep forth.
²¹The young lions roar for their prey,
  seeking their food from God.
²²When the sun rises, they get them away
  and lie down in their dens.
²³Man goes forth to his work
  and to his labor until the evening.

²⁴O LORD, how manifold are your works!
  In wisdom you have made them all;
  the earth is full of your creatures.
²⁵Yonder is the sea, great and wide,
  which teems with things innumerable,
  living things both small and great.
²⁶There go the ships,
  and Leviathan which you formed to sport
   in it.

²⁷These all look to you,
  to give them their food in due season.
²⁸When you give to them, they gather it up;
  when you open your hand, they are filled
   with good things.
²⁹When you hide your face, they are dismayed;
  when you take away their spirit, they die
   and return to their dust.
³⁰When you send forth your Spirit,ˢ they are
   created;
  and you renew the face of the earth.

³¹May the glory of the LORD endure for ever,
  may the LORD rejoice in his works,
³²who looks on the earth and it trembles,
  who touches the mountains and they
   smoke!

ⁿ Or *fodder for the animals that serve man.*
ˢ Or *breath.*
103:17: Lk 1:50.
104:4: Heb 1:7.
104:12: Mt 13:32; Mk 4:32; Lk 13:19.
* 104: A magnificent hymn of creation, it should be compared with Gen 1. It is remarkably similar to an Egyptian hymn to Aten, the sun god.

³³I will sing to the Lᴏʀᴅ as long as I live;
  I will sing praise to my God while I have
    being.
³⁴May my meditation be pleasing to him,
  for I rejoice in the Lᴏʀᴅ.
³⁵Let sinners be consumed from the earth,
  and let the wicked be no more!
  Bless the Lᴏʀᴅ, O my soul!
  Praise the Lᴏʀᴅ!

God's Faithfulness to Israel

105 [104]
O give thanks to the Lᴏʀᴅ,
  call on his name,
    make known his deeds among the peoples!
²Sing to him, sing praises to him,
  tell of all his wonderful works!
³Glory in his holy name;
  let the hearts of those who seek the Lᴏʀᴅ
    rejoice!
⁴Seek the Lᴏʀᴅ and his strength,
  seek his presence continually!
⁵Remember the wonderful works that he has
    done,
  his miracles, and the judgments he uttered,
⁶O offspring of Abraham his servant,
  sons of Jacob, his chosen ones!

⁷He is the Lᴏʀᴅ our God;
  his judgments are in all the earth.
⁸He is mindful of his covenant for ever,
  of the word that he commanded, for a
    thousand generations,
⁹the covenant which he made with Abraham,
  his sworn promise to Isaac,
¹⁰which he confirmed to Jacob as a statute,
  to Israel as an everlasting covenant,
¹¹saying, "To you I will give the land of Canaan
  as your portion for an inheritance."

¹²When they were few in number,
  of little account, and sojourners in it,
¹³wandering from nation to nation,
  from one kingdom to another people,
¹⁴he allowed no one to oppress them;
  he rebuked kings on their account,
¹⁵saying, "Touch not my anointed ones,
  do my prophets no harm!"

¹⁶When he summoned a famine on the land,
  and broke every staff of bread,
¹⁷he had sent a man ahead of them,
  Joseph, who was sold as a slave.
¹⁸His feet were hurt with shackles,
  his neck was put in a collar of iron;
¹⁹until what he had said came to pass
  the word of the Lᴏʀᴅ tested him.
²⁰The king sent and released him,
  the ruler of the peoples set him free;
²¹he made him lord of his house,
  and ruler of all his possessions,

²²to instruct ᵗ his princes at his pleasure,
  and to teach his elders wisdom.
²³Then Israel came to Egypt;
  Jacob sojourned in the land of Ham.
²⁴And the Lᴏʀᴅ made his people very fruitful,
  and made them stronger than their foes.
²⁵He turned their hearts to hate his people,
  to deal craftily with his servants.

²⁶He sent Moses his servant,
  and Aaron whom he had chosen.
²⁷They wrought his signs among them,
  and miracles in the land of Ham.
²⁸He sent darkness, and made the land dark;
  they rebelled ᵘ against his words.
²⁹He turned their waters into blood,
  and caused their fish to die.
³⁰Their land swarmed with frogs,
  even in the chambers of their kings.
³¹He spoke, and there came swarms of flies,
  and gnats throughout their country.
³²He gave them hail for rain,
  and lightning that flashed through their
    land.
³³He struck their vines and fig trees,
  and shattered the trees of their country.
³⁴He spoke, and the locusts came,
  and young locusts without number;
³⁵which devoured all the vegetation in their land,
  and ate up the fruit of their ground.
³⁶He struck all the first-born in their land,
  the first issue of all their strength.

³⁷Then he led forth Israel with silver and gold,
  and there was none among his tribes who
    stumbled.
³⁸Egypt was glad when they departed,
  for dread of them had fallen upon it.
³⁹He spread a cloud for a covering,
  and fire to give light by night.
⁴⁰They asked, and he brought quails,
  and gave them bread from heaven in
    abundance.
⁴¹He opened the rock, and water gushed forth;
  it flowed through the desert like a river.
⁴²For he remembered his holy promise,
  and Abraham his servant.

⁴³So he led forth his people with joy,
  his chosen ones with singing.
⁴⁴And he gave them the lands of the nations;
  and they took possession of the fruit of the
    peoples' toil,
⁴⁵to the end that they should keep his statutes,
  and observe his laws.
  Praise the Lᴏʀᴅ!

ᵗ Gk Syr Jerome: Heb *to bind.*
ᵘ Cn Compare Gk Syr: Heb *they did not rebel.*
105:1–15: 1 Chron 16:8–22.
105:8–9: Lk 1:72–73.

A Confession of Israel's Sins

106 [105]
Praise the LORD!
O give thanks to the LORD, for
he is good;
for his mercy endures for ever!
²Who can utter the mighty doings of the LORD,
or show forth all his praise?
³Blessed are they who observe justice,
who do righteousness at all times!

⁴Remember me, O LORD, when you show favor
to your people;
help me when you deliver them;
⁵that I may see the prosperity of your chosen
ones,
that I may rejoice in the gladness of your
nation,
that I may glory with your heritage.

⁶Both we and our fathers have sinned;
we have committed iniquity, we have done
wickedly.
⁷Our fathers, when they were in Egypt,
did not consider your wonderful works;
they did not remember the abundance of your
mercy,
but rebelled against the Most High ᵛ at the
Red Sea.
⁸Yet he saved them for his name's sake,
that he might make known his mighty
power.
⁹He rebuked the Red Sea, and it became dry;
and he led them through the deep as
through a desert.
¹⁰So he saved them from the hand of the foe,
and delivered them from the power of the
enemy.
¹¹And the waters covered their adversaries;
not one of them was left.
¹²Then they believed his words;
they sang his praise.

¹³But they soon forgot his works;
they did not wait for his counsel.
¹⁴But they had a wanton craving in the
wilderness,
and put God to the test in the desert;
¹⁵he gave them what they asked,
but sent a wasting disease among them.

¹⁶When men in the camp were jealous of Moses
and Aaron, the holy one of the LORD,
¹⁷the earth opened and swallowed up Dathan,
and covered the company of Abi′ram.
¹⁸Fire also broke out in their company;
the flame burned up the wicked.

¹⁹They made a calf in Horeb
and worshiped a molten image.
²⁰They exchanged the glory of God
for the image of an ox that eats grass.

²¹They forgot God, their Savior,
who had done great things in Egypt,
²²wondrous works in the land of Ham,
and awesome things by the Red Sea.
²³Therefore he said he would destroy them—
had not Moses, his chosen one,
stood in the breach before him,
to turn away his wrath from destroying
them.

²⁴Then they despised the pleasant land,
having no faith in his promise.
²⁵They murmured in their tents,
and did not obey the voice of the LORD.
²⁶Therefore he raised his hand and swore to
them
that he would make them fall in the
wilderness,
²⁷and would disperse ᵂ their descendants among
the nations,
scattering them over the lands.

²⁸Then they attached themselves to the Ba′al of
Peor,
and ate sacrifices offered to the dead;
²⁹they provoked the LORD to anger with their
doings,
and a plague broke out among them.
³⁰Then Phin′ehas stood up and interposed,
and the plague was stayed.
³¹And that has been reckoned to him as
righteousness
from generation to generation for ever.

³²They angered him at the waters of Mer′ibah,
and it went ill with Moses on their account;
³³for they made his spirit bitter,
and he spoke words that were rash.

³⁴They did not destroy the peoples,
as the LORD commanded them,
³⁵but they mingled with the nations
and learned to do as they did.
³⁶They served their idols,
which became a snare to them.
³⁷They sacrificed their sons
and their daughters to the demons;
³⁸they poured out innocent blood,
the blood of their sons and daughters,
whom they sacrificed to the idols of Canaan;
and the land was polluted with blood.
³⁹Thus they became unclean by their acts,
and played the harlot in their doings.

⁴⁰Then the anger of the LORD was kindled
against his people,
and he abhorred his heritage;

ᵛ Cn Compare 78:17, 56: Heb *at the sea.*
ᵂ Syr Compare Ezek 20:23: Heb *cause to fall.*
106:1: 1 Chron 16:34.
106:47–48: 1 Chron 16:35–36.

⁴¹he gave them into the hand of the nations,
  so that those who hated them ruled over
    them.
⁴²Their enemies oppressed them,
  and they were brought into subjection
    under their power.
⁴³Many times he delivered them,
  but they were rebellious in their purposes,
  and were brought low through their
    iniquity.
⁴⁴Nevertheless he regarded their distress,
  when he heard their cry.
⁴⁵He remembered for their sake his covenant,
  and relented according to the abundance of
    his mercy.
⁴⁶He caused them to be pitied
  by all those who held them captive.

⁴⁷Save us, O Lord our God,
  and gather us from among the nations,
  that we may give thanks to your holy name
  and glory in your praise.

⁴⁸Blessed be the Lord, the God of Israel,
  from everlasting to everlasting!
  And let all the people say, "Amen!"
    Praise the Lord!

BOOK V

Thanksgiving for Deliverance from Many Troubles

107 [106] O give thanks to the Lord, for
  he is good;
  for his mercy endures for ever!
²Let the redeemed of the Lord say so,
  whom he has redeemed from trouble
³and gathered in from the lands,
  from the east and from the west,
  from the north and from the south.

⁴Some wandered in desert wastes,
  finding no way to a city to dwell in;
⁵hungry and thirsty,
  their soul fainted within them.
⁶Then they cried to the Lord in their trouble,
  and he delivered them from their distress;
⁷he led them by a straight way,
  till they reached a city to dwell in.
⁸Let them thank the Lord for his merciful love,
  for his wonderful works to the sons of men!
⁹For he satisfies him who is thirsty,
  and the hungry he fills with good things.

¹⁰Some sat in darkness and in gloom,
  prisoners in affliction and in irons,
¹¹for they had rebelled against the words of
    God,
  and spurned the counsel of the Most High.

¹²Their hearts were bowed down with hard labor;
  they fell down, with none to help.
¹³Then they cried to the Lord in their trouble,
  and he delivered them from their distress;
¹⁴he brought them out of darkness and gloom,
  and broke their bonds asunder.
¹⁵Let them thank the Lord for his steadfast love,
  for his wonderful works to the sons of men!
¹⁶For he shatters the doors of bronze,
  and cuts in two the bars of iron.

¹⁷Some were sick * through their sinful ways,
  and because of their iniquities suffered
    affliction;
¹⁸they loathed any kind of food,
  and they drew near to the gates of death.
¹⁹Then they cried to the Lord in their trouble,
  and he delivered them from their distress;
²⁰he sent forth his word, and healed them,
  and delivered them from destruction.
²¹Let them thank the Lord for his steadfast love,
  for his wonderful works to the sons of men!
²²And let them offer sacrifices of thanksgiving,
  and tell of his deeds in songs of joy!

²³Some went down to the sea in ships,
  doing business on the great waters;
²⁴they saw the deeds of the Lord,
  his wondrous works in the deep.
²⁵For he commanded, and raised the stormy
    wind,
  which lifted up the waves of the sea.
²⁶They mounted up to heaven, they went down to
    the depths;
  their courage melted away in their evil
    plight;
²⁷they reeled and staggered like drunken men,
  and were at their wits' end.
²⁸Then they cried to the Lord in their trouble,
  and he delivered them from their distress;
²⁹he made the storm be still,
  and the waves of the sea were hushed.
³⁰Then they were glad because they had quiet,
  and he brought them to their desired haven.
³¹Let them thank the Lord for his merciful love,
  for his wonderful works to the sons of men!
³²Let them extol him in the congregation of the
    people,
  and praise him in the assembly of the
    elders.

³³He turns rivers into a desert,
  springs of water into thirsty ground,
³⁴a fruitful land into a salty waste,
  because of the wickedness of its
    inhabitants.
³⁵He turns a desert into pools of water,
  a parched land into springs of water.

---

* Cn: Heb *fools.*

³⁶And there he lets the hungry dwell,
   and they establish a city to live in;
³⁷they sow fields, and plant vineyards,
   and get a fruitful yield.
³⁸By his blessing they multiply greatly;
   and he does not let their cattle decrease.

³⁹When they are diminished and brought low
   through oppression, trouble, and sorrow,
⁴⁰he pours contempt upon princes
   and makes them wander in trackless
      wastes;
⁴¹but he raises up the needy out of affliction,
   and makes their families like flocks.
⁴²The upright see it and are glad;
   and all wickedness stops its mouth.
⁴³Whoever is wise, let him give heed to these
      things;
   let men consider the steadfast love of the
      LORD.

Praise and Prayer for Victory
A Song.
A Psalm of David.

108 [107]
My heart is steadfast, O God,
   my heart is steadfast!
I will sing and make melody!
   Awake, my soul!
²Awake, O harp and lyre!
   I will awake the dawn!
³I will give thanks to you, O LORD, among the
      peoples,
   I will sing praises to you among the nations.
⁴For your steadfast love is great above the
      heavens,
   your faithfulness reaches to the clouds.

⁵Be exalted, O God, above the heavens!
   Let your glory be over all the earth!
⁶That your beloved may be delivered,
   give help by your right hand, and answer me!

⁷God has promised in his sanctuary:ʸ
   "With exultation I will divide up She'chem,
      and portion out the Vale of Succoth.
⁸Gilead is mine; Manas'seh is mine;
   E'phraim is my helmet;
      Judah my scepter.
⁹Moab is my washbasin;
   upon Edom I cast my shoe;
      over Philistia I shout in triumph."

¹⁰Who will bring me to the fortified city?
   Who will lead me to Edom?
¹¹Have you not rejected us, O God?
   You do not go forth, O God, with our
      armies.
¹²O grant us help against the foe,
   for vain is the help of man!
¹³With God we shall do valiantly;
   it is he who will tread down our foes.

Prayer for Vindication and Vengeance
To the choirmaster.
A Psalm of David.

109 [108]
Be not silent, O God of my
   praise!
²For wicked and deceitful mouths are opened
      against me,
   speaking against me with lying tongues.
³They beset me with words of hate,
   and attack me without cause.
⁴In return for my love they accuse me,
   even as I make prayer for them.ᶻ
⁵So they reward me evil for good,
   and hatred for my love.

⁶Appoint a wicked man against him;
   let an accuser bring him to trial. ᵃ
⁷When he is tried, let him come forth guilty;
   let his prayer be counted as sin!
⁸May his days be few;
   may another seize his goods!
⁹May his children be fatherless,
   and his wife a widow!
¹⁰May his children wander about and beg;
   may they be driven out of ᵇ the ruins they
      inhabit!
¹¹May the creditor seize all that he has;
   may strangers plunder the fruits of his toil!
¹²Let there be none to extend kindness to him,
   nor any to pity his fatherless children!
¹³May his posterity be cut off;
   may his name be blotted out in the second
      generation!
¹⁴May the iniquity of his fathers be remembered
      before the LORD,
   and let not the sin of his mother be blotted
      out!
¹⁵Let them be before the LORD continually;
   and may hisᶜ memory be cut off from the
      earth!
¹⁶For he did not remember to show kindness,
   but pursued the poor and needy
      and the brokenhearted to their death.
¹⁷He loved to curse; let curses come on him!
   He did not like blessing; may it be far from
      him!
¹⁸He clothed himself with cursing as his coat,
   may it soak into his body like water,
      like oil into his bones!
¹⁹May it be like a garment which he wraps round
      him,
   like a belt with which he daily girds himself!

ʸ Or by his holiness.
ᶻ Syr: Heb I prayer.
ᵃ Heb stand at his right hand.
ᵇ Gk: Heb and seek.
ᶜ Gk: Heb their.
108:1-5: Ps 57:7–11.
108:6-13: Ps 60:5–12.
109:8: Acts 1:20.

[20]May this be the reward of my accusers from
the Lord,
of those who speak evil against my life!
[21]But you, O God my Lord,
deal on my behalf for your name's sake;
because your mercy is good, deliver me!
[22]For I am poor and needy,
and my heart is stricken within me.
[23]I am gone, like a shadow at evening;
I am shaken off like a locust.
[24]My knees are weak through fasting;
my body has become gaunt.
[25]I am an object of scorn to my accusers;
when they see me, they wag their heads.

[26]Help me, O Lord my God!
Save me according to your merciful love!
[27]Let them know that this is your hand;
you, O Lord, have done it!
[28]Let them curse, but do bless!
Let my assailants be put to shame;[d] may
your servant be glad!
[29]May my accusers be clothed with dishonor;
may they be wrapped in their own shame as
in a mantle!

[30]With my mouth I will give great thanks to the
Lord;
I will praise him in the midst of the throng.
[31]For he stands at the right hand of the needy,
to save him from those who condemn him to
death.

Assurance of Victory for God's Priest-King
A Psalm of David.

110 [109]
[*] The Lord says to my lord:
"Sit at my right hand,
till I make your enemies your footstool."

[2]The Lord sends forth from Zion
your mighty scepter.
Rule in the midst of your foes!
[3]Yours is dominion
on the day you lead your host
in holy splendor.[e]
From the womb of the morning
I begot you.[f]
[4]The Lord has sworn
and will not change his mind,
"You are a priest for ever
according to the order of Melchiz'edek."

[5]The Lord is at your right hand;
he will shatter kings on the day of his
wrath.
[6]He will execute judgment among the nations,
filling them with corpses;
he will shatter chiefs[g]
over the wide earth.
[7]He will drink from the brook by the way;
therefore he will lift up his head.

Praise for God's Wonderful Works

111 [110]
Praise the Lord!
I will give thanks to the Lord
with my whole heart,
in the company of the upright, in the
congregation.
[2]Great are the works of the Lord,
studied by all who have pleasure in them.
[3]Full of honor and majesty is his work,
and his righteousness endures for ever.
[4]He has caused his wonderful works to be
remembered;
the Lord is gracious and merciful.
[5]He provides food for those who fear him;
he is ever mindful of his covenant.
[6]He has shown his people the power of his
works,
in giving them the heritage of the nations.
[7]The works of his hands are faithful and just;
all his precepts are trustworthy,
[8]they are established for ever and ever,
to be performed with faithfulness and
uprightness.
[9]He sent redemption to his people;
he has commanded his covenant for ever.
Holy and awesome is his name!
[10]The fear of the Lord is the beginning of
wisdom;
a good understanding have all those who
practice it.
His praise endures for ever!

Blessings of the Righteous

112 [111]
Praise the Lord!
Blessed is the man who fears
the Lord,
who greatly delights in his commandments!
[2]His descendants will be mighty in the land;
the generation of the upright will be
blessed.
[3]Wealth and riches are in his house;
and his righteousness endures for ever.
[4]Light rises in the darkness for the upright;
the Lord[h] is gracious, merciful, and
righteous.
[5]It is well with the man who deals generously
and lends,
who conducts his affairs with justice.
[6]For the righteous will never be moved;
he will be remembered for ever.

---

[d] Gk: Heb they have arisen and have been put to shame.
[e] Other readings are in holy array or upon the holy mountain.
[f] Heb the dew of your youth.
[g] Or the head.
[h] Gk: Heb lacks the Lord.
109:25: Mt 27:39; Mk 15:29.
110:1: Mt 22:44; 26:64; Mk 12:36; 14:62; 16:19; Lk 20:42–43; 22:69; Acts
2:34; 1 Cor 15:25; Eph 1:20; Col 3:1; Heb 1:3, 13; 10:12–13; 12:2.
110:4: Heb 5:6, 10; 6:20; 7:11, 15, 21.
* 110: See note on Ps 2.

⁷He is not afraid of evil tidings;
   his heart is firm, trusting in the Lord.
⁸His heart is steady, he will not be afraid,
   until he sees his desire on his adversaries.
⁹He has distributed freely, he has given to the
      poor;
   his righteousness endures for ever;
   his horn is exalted in honor.
¹⁰The wicked man sees it and is angry;
   he gnashes his teeth and melts away;
   the desire of the wicked man comes to
      nought.

God the Helper of the Needy

113 [112] Praise the Lord!
   Praise, O servants of the
   Lord,
   praise the name of the Lord!

²Blessed be the name of the Lord
   from this time forth and for evermore!
³From the rising of the sun to its setting
   the name of the Lord is to be praised!
⁴The Lord is high above all nations,
   and his glory above the heavens!

⁵Who is like the Lord our God,
   who is seated on high,
⁶who looks far down
   upon the heavens and the earth?
⁷He raises the poor from the dust,
   and lifts the needy from the ash heap,
⁸to make them sit with princes,
   with the princes of his people.
⁹He gives the barren woman a home,
   making her the joyous mother of children.
   Praise the Lord!

God's Wonders at the Exodus

114 [113] When Israel went forth from
   Egypt,
   the house of Jacob from a people of strange
      language,
²Judah became his sanctuary,
   Israel his dominion.

³The sea looked and fled,
   Jordan turned back.
⁴The mountains skipped like rams,
   the hills like lambs.

⁵What ails you, O sea, that you flee?
   O Jordan, that you turn back?
⁶O mountains, that you skip like rams?
   O hills, like lambs?

⁷Tremble, O earth, at the presence of the
      Lord,
   at the presence of the God of Jacob,
⁸who turns the rock into a pool of water,
   the flint into a spring of water.

The Impotence of Idols and the Greatness of God

115 Not to us, O Lord, not to us,
   but to your name give glory,
   for the sake of your mercy and your
      faithfulness!
²Why should the nations say,
   "Where is their God?"

³Our God is in the heavens;
   he does whatever he pleases.
⁴Their idols are silver and gold,
   the work of men's hands.
⁵They have mouths, but do not speak;
   eyes, but do not see.
⁶They have ears, but do not hear;
   noses, but do not smell.
⁷They have hands, but do not feel;
   feet, but do not walk;
   and they do not make a sound in their
      throat.
⁸Those who make them are like them;
   so are all who trust in them.

⁹O Israel, trust in the Lord!
   He is their help and their shield.
¹⁰O house of Aaron, put your trust in the Lord!
   He is their help and their shield.
¹¹You who fear the Lord, trust in the Lord!
   He is their help and their shield.

¹²The Lord has been mindful of us; he will bless
      us;
   he will bless the house of Israel;
   he will bless the house of Aaron;
¹³he will bless those who fear the Lord,
   both small and great.

¹⁴May the Lord give you increase,
   you and your children!
¹⁵May you be blessed by the Lord,
   who made heaven and earth!

¹⁶The heavens are the Lord's heavens,
   but the earth he has given to the sons of
      men.
¹⁷The dead do not praise the Lord,
   nor do any that go down into silence.
¹⁸But we will bless the Lord
   from this time forth and for evermore.
   Praise the Lord!

Thanksgiving for Recovery from Illness

116 [114] I love the Lord, because he
   has heard
   my voice and my supplications.
²Because he inclined his ear to me,
   therefore I will call on him as long as I live.

112:9: 2 Cor 9:9.
115:4–8: Ps 135:15–18.
115:13: Rev 11:18; 19:5.

³The snares of death encompassed me;
    the pangs of Sheol laid hold on me;
    I suffered distress and anguish.
⁴Then I called on the name of the Lord:
    "O Lord, I beg you, save my life!"

⁵Gracious is the Lord, and righteous;
    our God is merciful.
⁶The Lord preserves the simple;
    when I was brought low, he saved me.
⁷Return, O my soul, to your rest;
    for the Lord has dealt bountifully with
      you.

⁸For you have delivered my soul from death,
    my eyes from tears,
    my feet from stumbling;
⁹I walk before the Lord
    in the land of the living.
[115] ¹⁰I kept my faith, even when I said,
    "I am greatly afflicted";
¹¹I said in my consternation,
    "Men are all a vain hope."

¹²What shall I render to the Lord
    for all his bounty to me?
¹³I will lift up the chalice of salvation
    and call on the name of the Lord,
¹⁴I will pay my vows to the Lord
    in the presence of all his people.
¹⁵Precious in the sight of the Lord
    is the death of his saints.
¹⁶O Lord, I am your servant;
    I am your servant, the son of your
      handmaid.
    You have loosed my bonds.
¹⁷I will offer to you the sacrifice of thanksgiving
    and call on the name of the Lord.
¹⁸I will pay my vows to the Lord
    in the presence of all his people,
¹⁹in the courts of the house of the Lord,
    in your midst, O Jerusalem.
    Praise the Lord!

Universal Call to Worship

117 [116] Praise the Lord, all nations!
    Extol him, all peoples!
²For great is his mercy toward us;
    and the faithfulness of the Lord endures
      for ever.
    Praise the Lord!

A Song of Victory

118 [117] O give thanks to the Lord, for
    he is good;
    his mercy endures for ever!

²Let Israel say,
    "His mercy endures for ever."
³Let the house of Aaron say,
    "His mercy endures for ever."

⁴Let those who fear the Lord say,
    "His mercy endures for ever."

⁵Out of my distress I called on the Lord;
    the Lord answered me and set me free.
⁶With the Lord on my side I do not fear.
    What can man do to me?
⁷The Lord is on my side to help me;
    I shall look in triumph on those who hate
      me.
⁸It is better to take refuge in the Lord
    than to put confidence in man.
⁹It is better to take refuge in the Lord
    than to put confidence in princes.

¹⁰All nations surrounded me;
    in the name of the Lord I cut them off!
¹¹They surrounded me, surrounded me on every
      side;
    in the name of the Lord I cut them off!
¹²They surrounded me like bees,
    they blazed ⁱ like a fire of thorns;
    in the name of the Lord I cut them off!
¹³I was pushed hard, ʲ so that I was falling,
    but the Lord helped me.
¹⁴The Lord is my strength and my song;
    he has become my salvation.

¹⁵Listen, glad songs of victory
    in the tents of the righteous:
    "The right hand of the Lord does valiantly!
¹⁶   The right hand of the Lord is exalted;
    the right hand of the Lord does valiantly!"
¹⁷I shall not die, but I shall live,
    and recount the deeds of the Lord.
¹⁸The Lord has chastened me sorely,
    but he has not given me over to death.

¹⁹Open to me the gates of righteousness,
    that I may enter through them
    and give thanks to the Lord.

²⁰This is the gate of the Lord;
    the righteous shall enter through it.

²¹I thank you that you have answered me
    and have become my salvation.
²²The stone which the builders rejected
    has become the cornerstone.
²³This is the Lord's doing;
    it is marvelous in our eyes.
²⁴This is the day which the Lord has made;
    let us rejoice and be glad in it.
²⁵Save us, we beg you, O Lord!
    O Lord, we beg you, give us success!

ⁱ Gk: Heb *were extinguished.*
ʲ Gk Syr Jerome: Heb *you pushed me hard.*
116:10: 2 Cor 4:13.
117:1: Rom 15:11.
118:6: Heb 13:6.
118:22–23: Mt 21:42; Mk 12:10–11; Lk 20:17; Acts 4:11; 1 Pet 2:7.
118:25–26: Mt 21:9; 23:39; Mk 11:9–10; Lk 13:35; 19:38; Jn 12:13.

²⁶Blessed be he who enters in the name of the
    Lord!
    We bless you from the house of the Lord.
²⁷The Lord is God,
    and he has given us light.
Bind the festal procession with branches,
    up to the horns of the altar!

²⁸You are my God, and I will give thanks to you;
    you are my God, I will extol you.

²⁹O give thanks to the Lord, for he is good;
    for his mercy endures for ever!

The Glories of God's Law

119 [118] * Blessed are those whose
    way is blameless,
who walk in the law of the Lord!
²Blessed are those who keep his testimonies,
    who seek him with their whole heart,
³who also do no wrong,
    but walk in his ways!
⁴You have commanded your precepts
    to be kept diligently.
⁵O that my ways may be steadfast
    in keeping your statutes!
⁶Then I shall not be put to shame,
    having my eyes fixed on all your
      commandments.
⁷I will praise you with an upright heart,
    when I learn your righteous ordinances.
⁸I will observe your statutes;
    O forsake me not utterly!

⁹How can a young man keep his way pure?
    By guarding it according to your word.
¹⁰With my whole heart I seek you;
    let me not wander from your
      commandments!
¹¹I have laid up your word in my heart,
    that I might not sin against you.
¹²Blessed are you, O Lord;
    teach me your statutes!
¹³With my lips I declare
    all the ordinances of your mouth.
¹⁴In the way of your testimonies I delight
    as much as in all riches.
¹⁵I will meditate on your precepts,
    and fix my eyes on your ways.
¹⁶I will delight in your statutes;
    I will not forget your word.

¹⁷Deal bountifully with your servant,
    that I may live and observe your word.
¹⁸Open my eyes, that I may behold
    wondrous things out of your law.
¹⁹I am a sojourner on earth;
    hide not your commandments from me!
²⁰My soul is consumed with longing
    for your ordinances at all times.

²¹You rebuke the insolent, accursed ones,
    who wander from your commandments;
²²take away from me their scorn and contempt,
    for I have kept your testimonies.
²³Even though princes sit plotting against me,
    your servant will meditate on your
      statutes.
²⁴Your testimonies are my delight,
    they are my counselors.

²⁵My soul clings to the dust;
    revive me according to your word!
²⁶When I told of my ways, you answered me;
    teach me your statutes!
²⁷Make me understand the way of your precepts,
    and I will meditate on your wondrous
      works.
²⁸My soul melts away for sorrow;
    strengthen me according to your word!
²⁹Put false ways far from me;
    and graciously teach me your law!
³⁰I have chosen the way of faithfulness,
    I set your ordinances before me.
³¹I cling to your testimonies, O Lord;
    let me not be put to shame!
³²I will run in the way of your commandments
    when you enlarge my understanding!

³³Teach me, O Lord, the way of your statutes;
    and I will keep it to the end.
³⁴Give me understanding, that I may keep your
    law
    and observe it with my whole heart.
³⁵Lead me in the path of your commandments,
    for I delight in it.
³⁶Incline my heart to your testimonies,
    and not to gain!
³⁷Turn my eyes from looking at vanities;
    and give me life in your ways.
³⁸Confirm to your servant your promise,
    which is for those who fear you.
³⁹Turn away the reproach which I dread;
    for your ordinances are good.
⁴⁰Behold, I long for your precepts;
    in your righteousness give me life!

⁴¹Let your mercy come to me, O Lord,
    your salvation according to your promise;
⁴²then shall I have an answer for those who taunt
    me,
    for I trust in your word.
⁴³And take not the word of truth utterly out of
    my mouth,
    for my hope is in your ordinances.
⁴⁴I will keep your law continually,
    for ever and ever;
⁴⁵and I shall walk at liberty,
    for I have sought your precepts.

* 119: This great hymn of praise for the Torah, the law of God, is typical of the best Jewish piety after the Exile.

⁴⁶I will also speak of your testimonies before
 kings,
 and shall not be put to shame;
⁴⁷for I find my delight in your commandments,
 which I love.
⁴⁸I revere your commandments, which I love,
 and I will meditate on your statutes.

⁴⁹Remember your word to your servant,
 in which you have made me hope.
⁵⁰This is my comfort in my affliction
 that your promise gives me life.
⁵¹Godless men utterly deride me,
 but I do not turn away from your law.
⁵²When I think of your ordinances from of old,
 I take comfort, O Lord.
⁵³Hot indignation seizes me because of the
 wicked,
 who forsake your law.
⁵⁴Your statutes have been my songs
 in the house of my pilgrimage.
⁵⁵I remember your name in the night, O Lord,
 and keep your law.
⁵⁶This blessing has fallen to me,
 that I have kept your precepts.

⁵⁷The Lord is my portion;
 I promise to keep your words.
⁵⁸I entreat your favor with all my heart;
 be gracious to me according to your
 promise.
⁵⁹When I think of your ways,
 I turn my feet to your testimonies;
⁶⁰I hasten and do not delay
 to keep your commandments.
⁶¹Though the cords of the wicked ensnare me,
 I do not forget your law.
⁶²At midnight I rise to praise you,
 because of your righteous ordinances.
⁶³I am a companion of all who fear you,
 of those who keep your precepts.
⁶⁴The earth, O Lord, is full of your steadfast
 love;
 teach me your statutes!

⁶⁵You have dealt well with your servant,
 O Lord, according to your word.
⁶⁶Teach me good judgment and knowledge,
 for I believe in your commandments.
⁶⁷Before I was afflicted I went astray;
 but now I keep your word.
⁶⁸You are good and do good;
 teach me your statutes.
⁶⁹The godless besmear me with lies,
 but with my whole heart I keep your
 precepts;
⁷⁰their heart is gross like fat,
 but I delight in your law.
⁷¹It is good for me that I was afflicted,
 that I might learn your statutes.

⁷²The law of your mouth is better to me
 than thousands of gold and silver pieces.

⁷³Your hands have made and fashioned me;
 give me understanding that I may learn
 your commandments.
⁷⁴Those who fear you shall see me and rejoice,
 because I have hoped in your word.
⁷⁵I know, O Lord, that your judgments are right,
 and that in faithfulness you have afflicted
 me.
⁷⁶Let your mercy be ready to comfort me
 according to your promise to your servant.
⁷⁷Let your compassion come to me, that I may
 live;
 for your law is my delight.
⁷⁸Let the godless be put to shame,
 because they have subverted me with
 guile;
 as for me, I will meditate on your precepts.
⁷⁹Let those who fear you turn to me,
 that they may know your testimonies.
⁸⁰May my heart be blameless in your statutes,
 that I may not be put to shame!

⁸¹My soul languishes for your salvation;
 I hope in your word.
⁸²My eyes fail with watching for your promise;
 I ask, "When will you comfort me?"
⁸³For I have become like a wineskin in the
 smoke,
 yet I have not forgotten your statutes.
⁸⁴How long must your servant endure?
 When will you judge those who persecute
 me?
⁸⁵Godless men have dug pitfalls for me,
 men who do not conform to your law.
⁸⁶All your commandments are sure;
 they persecute me with falsehood; help me!
⁸⁷They have almost made an end of me on earth;
 but I have not forsaken your precepts.
⁸⁸In your mercy spare my life,
 that I may keep the testimonies of your
 mouth.

⁸⁹For ever, O Lord, your word
 is firmly fixed in the heavens.
⁹⁰Your faithfulness endures to all generations;
 you have established the earth, and it
 stands fast.
⁹¹By your appointment they stand this day;
 for all things are your servants.
⁹²If your law had not been my delight,
 I should have perished in my affliction.
⁹³I will never forget your precepts;
 for by them you have given me life.
⁹⁴I am yours, save me;
 for I have sought your precepts.
⁹⁵The wicked lie in wait to destroy me;
 but I consider your testimonies.

⁹⁶I have seen a limit to all perfection,
    but your commandment is exceedingly
        broad.

⁹⁷Oh, how I love your law!
    It is my meditation all the day.
⁹⁸Your commandment makes me wiser than my
        enemies,
    for it is ever with me.
⁹⁹I have more understanding than all my
        teachers,
    for your testimonies are my meditation.
¹⁰⁰I understand more than the aged,
    for I keep your precepts.
¹⁰¹I hold back my feet from every evil way,
    in order to keep your word.
¹⁰²I do not turn aside from your ordinances,
    for you have taught me.
¹⁰³How sweet are your words to my taste,
    sweeter than honey to my mouth!
¹⁰⁴Through your precepts I get understanding;
    therefore I hate every false way.

¹⁰⁵Your word is a lamp to my feet
    and a light to my path.
¹⁰⁶I have sworn an oath and confirmed it,
    to observe your righteous ordinances.
¹⁰⁷I am sorely afflicted;
    give me life, O LORD, according to your word!
¹⁰⁸Accept my offerings of praise, O LORD,
    and teach me your ordinances.
¹⁰⁹I hold my life in my hand continually,
    but I do not forget your law.
¹¹⁰The wicked have laid a snare for me,
    but I do not stray from your precepts.
¹¹¹Your testimonies are my heritage for ever;
    yes, they are the joy of my heart.
¹¹²I incline my heart to perform your statutes
    for ever, to the end.

¹¹³I hate double-minded men,
    but I love your law.
¹¹⁴You are my hiding place and my shield;
    I hope in your word.
¹¹⁵Depart from me, you evildoers,
    that I may keep the commandments of my
        God.
¹¹⁶Uphold me according to your promise, that I
        may live,
    and let me not be put to shame in my
        hope!
¹¹⁷Hold me up, that I may be safe
    and have regard for your statutes
        continually!
¹¹⁸You spurn all who go astray from your
        statutes;
    yes, their cunning is in vain.
¹¹⁹All the wicked of the earth you count as
        dross;
    therefore I love your testimonies.

¹²⁰My flesh trembles for fear of you,
    and I am afraid of your judgments.

¹²¹I have done what is just and right;
    do not leave me to my oppressors.
¹²²Be surety for your servant for good;
    let not the godless oppress me.
¹²³My eyes fail with watching for your salvation,
    and for the fulfilment of your righteous
        promise.
¹²⁴Deal with your servant according to your
        steadfast love,
    and teach me your statutes.
¹²⁵I am your servant; give me understanding,
    that I may know your testimonies!
¹²⁶It is time for the LORD to act,
    for your law has been broken.
¹²⁷Therefore I love your commandments
    above gold, above fine gold.
¹²⁸Therefore I direct my steps by all your
        precepts; ᵏ
    I hate every false way.

¹²⁹Your testimonies are wonderful;
    therefore my soul keeps them.
¹³⁰The unfolding of your words gives light;
    it imparts understanding to the simple.
¹³¹With open mouth I pant,
    because I long for your commandments.
¹³²Turn to me and be gracious to me,
    as you always do toward those who love
        your name.
¹³³Keep steady my steps according to your
        promise,
    and let no iniquity get dominion over me.
¹³⁴Redeem me from man's oppression,
    that I may keep your precepts.
¹³⁵Make your face shine upon your servant,
    and teach me your statutes.
¹³⁶My eyes shed streams of tears,
    because men do not keep your law.

¹³⁷You are righteous, O LORD,
    and right are your judgments.
¹³⁸You have appointed your testimonies in
        righteousness
    and in all faithfulness.
¹³⁹My zeal consumes me,
    because my foes forget your words.
¹⁴⁰Your promise is well tried,
    and your servant loves it.
¹⁴¹I am small and despised,
    yet I do not forget your precepts.
¹⁴²Your righteousness is righteous for ever,
    and your law is true.
¹⁴³Trouble and anguish have come upon me,
    but your commandments are my delight.
¹⁴⁴Your testimonies are righteous for ever;
    give me understanding that I may live.

ᵏ Gk Jerome: Heb uncertain.

145With my whole heart I cry; answer me, O LORD!
  I will keep your statutes.
146I cry to you; save me,
  that I may observe your testimonies.
147I rise before dawn and cry for help;
  I hope in your words.
148My eyes are awake before the watches of the
    night,
  that I may meditate upon your promise.
149Hear my voice in your steadfast love;
  O LORD, in your justice preserve my life.
150They draw near who persecute me with evil
    purpose;
  they are far from your law.
151But you are near, O LORD,
  and all your commandments are true.
152Long have I known from your testimonies
  that you have founded them for ever.

153Look on my affliction and deliver me,
  for I do not forget your law.
154Plead my cause and redeem me;
  give me life according to your promise!
155Salvation is far from the wicked,
  for they do not seek your statutes.
156Great is your mercy, O LORD;
  give me life according to your justice.
157Many are my persecutors and my adversaries,
  but I do not swerve from your testimonies.
158I look at the faithless with disgust,
  because they do not keep your commands.
159Consider how I love your precepts!
  Preserve my life according to your steadfast
    love.
160The sum of your word is truth;
  and every one of your righteous ordinances
    endures for ever.

161Princes persecute me without cause,
  but my heart stands in awe of your words.
162I rejoice at your word
  like one who finds great spoil.
163I hate and abhor falsehood,
  but I love your law.
164Seven times a day I praise you
  for your righteous ordinances.
165Great peace have those who love your law;
  nothing can make them stumble.
166I hope for your salvation, O LORD,
  and I do your commandments.
167My soul keeps your testimonies;
  I love them exceedingly.
168I keep your precepts and testimonies,
  for all my ways are before you.

169Let my cry come before you, O LORD;
  give me understanding according to your
    word!
170Let my supplication come before you;
  deliver me according to your word.

171My lips will pour forth praise
  that you teach me your statutes.
172My tongue will sing of your word,
  for all your commandments are right.
173Let your hand be ready to help me,
  for I have chosen your precepts.
174I long for your salvation, O LORD,
  and your law is my delight.
175Let my soul live, that I may praise you,
  and let your ordinances help me.
176I have gone astray like a lost sheep; seek your
    servant,
  for I do not forget your commandments.

Prayer for Deliverance from Slanderers
A Song of Ascents.

120 [119] * In my distress I cry to the
    LORD,
  that he may answer me:
2"Deliver me, O LORD,
  from lying lips,
  from a deceitful tongue."

3What shall be given to you?
  And what more shall be done to you,
  you deceitful tongue?
4A warrior's sharp arrows,
  with glowing coals of the broom tree!

5Woe is me, that I sojourn in Meshech,
  that I dwell among the tents of Kedar!
6Too long have I had my dwelling
  among those who hate peace.
7I am for peace;
  but when I speak,
  they are for war!

Assurance of God's Protection
A Song of Ascents.

121 [120] I lift up my eyes to the hills.
    From where does my help
  come?
2My help comes from the LORD,
  who made heaven and earth.

3He will not let your foot be moved,
  he who keeps you will not slumber.
4Behold, he who keeps Israel
  will neither slumber nor sleep.

5The LORD is your keeper;
  the LORD is your shade
  on your right hand.
6The sun shall not strike you by day,
  nor the moon by night.

7The LORD will keep you from all evil;
  he will keep your life.

---

* 120: The first of the "Songs of Ascents," or "Gradual Psalms," that is,
those that were recited or sung during the journey to Jerusalem on the
occasion of the great pilgrim feasts.

⁸The LORD will keep
    your going out and your coming in
    from this time forth and for evermore.

Song of Praise; and a Prayer for Jerusalem
A Song of Ascents.
Of David.

122 [121]
I was glad when they said to me,
  "Let us go to the house of the LORD!"
²Our feet have been standing
  within your gates, O Jerusalem!

³Jerusalem, built as a city
  which is bound firmly together,
⁴to which the tribes go up,
  the tribes of the LORD,
as was decreed for Israel,
  to give thanks to the name of the LORD.
⁵There thrones for judgment were set,
  the thrones of the house of David.

⁶Pray for the peace of Jerusalem!
  "May they prosper who love you!
⁷Peace be within your walls,
  and security within your towers!"
⁸For my brethren and companions' sake
  I will say, "Peace be within you!"
⁹For the sake of the house of the LORD our God,
  I will seek your good.

Supplication for Mercy
A Song of Ascents.

123 [122]
To you I lift up my eyes,
  O you who are enthroned in the heavens!
²Behold, as the eyes of servants
  look to the hand of their master,
as the eyes of a maid
  to the hand of her mistress,
so our eyes look to the LORD our God,
  till he have mercy upon us.

³Have mercy upon us, O LORD, have mercy upon us,
  for we have had more than enough of contempt.
⁴Too long our soul has been sated
  with the scorn of those who are at ease,
  the contempt of the proud.

Thanksgiving for Israel's Deliverance
A Song of Ascents.
Of David.

124 [123]
If it had not been the LORD who was on our side,
  let Israel now say—
²if it had not been the LORD who was on our side,
  when men rose up against us,

³then they would have swallowed us up alive,
  when their anger was kindled against us;
⁴then the flood would have swept us away,
  the torrent would have gone over us;
⁵then over us would have gone
  the raging waters.

⁶Blessed be the LORD,
  who has not given us
  as prey to their teeth!
⁷We have escaped as a bird
  from the snare of the fowlers;
the snare is broken,
  and we have escaped!

⁸Our help is in the name of the LORD,
  who made heaven and earth.

The Security of God's People
A Song of Ascents.

125 [124]
Those who trust in the LORD
  are like Mount Zion,
which cannot be moved, but abides for ever.
²As the mountains are round about Jerusalem,
  so the LORD is round about his people,
  from this time forth and for evermore.
³For the scepter of wickedness shall not rest
  upon the land allotted to the righteous,
lest the righteous put forth
  their hands to do wrong.
⁴Do good, O LORD, to those who are good,
  and to those who are upright in their hearts!
⁵But those who turn aside upon their crooked ways
  the LORD will lead away with evildoers!
  Peace be in Israel!

A Harvest of Joy
A Song of Ascents.

126 [125]
When the LORD restored the fortunes of Zion, [1]
  we were like those who dream.
²Then our mouth was filled with laughter,
  and our tongue with shouts of joy;
then they said among the nations,
  "The LORD has done great things for them."
³The LORD has done great things for us;
  we are glad.

⁴Restore our fortunes, O LORD,
  like the watercourses in the Neg'eb!
⁵May those who sow in tears
  reap with shouts of joy!
⁶He that goes forth weeping,
  bearing the seed for sowing,
shall come home with shouts of joy,
  bringing his sheaves with him.

---

[1] Or *brought back those who returned to Zion.*

God's Blessings in the Home
A Song of Ascents.
Of Solomon.

127 [126] Unless the Lᴏʀᴅ builds the house,
those who build it labor in vain.
Unless the Lᴏʀᴅ watches over the city,
the watchman stays awake in vain.
²It is in vain that you rise up early
and go late to rest,
eating the bread of anxious toil;
for ᵐ he gives to his beloved sleep.

³Behold, sons are a heritage from the Lᴏʀᴅ,
the fruit of the womb a reward.
⁴Like arrows in the hand of a warrior
are the sons of one's youth.
⁵Happy is the man who has
his quiver full of them!
He shall not be put to shame
when he speaks with his enemies in the gate.

The Happy Home of the Faithful
A Song of Ascents.

128 [127] Blessed is every one who fears the Lᴏʀᴅ,
who walks in his ways!
²You shall eat the fruit of the labor of your
hands;
you shall be happy, and it shall be well with
you.

³Your wife will be like a fruitful vine
within your house;
your children will be like olive shoots
around your table.
⁴Behold, thus shall the man be blessed
who fears the Lᴏʀᴅ.

⁵The Lᴏʀᴅ bless you from Zion!
May you see the prosperity of Jerusalem
all the days of your life!
⁶May you see your children's children!
Peace be upon Israel!

Prayer for the Downfall of Israel's Enemies
A Song of Ascents.

129 [128] "Sorely have they afflicted me from my youth,"
let Israel now say—
²"Sorely have they afflicted me from my youth,
yet they have not prevailed against me.
³The plowers plowed upon my back;
they made long their furrows."
⁴The Lᴏʀᴅ is righteous;
he has cut the cords of the wicked.
⁵May all who hate Zion
be put to shame and turned backward!
⁶Let them be like the grass on the housetops,
which withers before it grows up,

⁷with which the reaper does not fill his hand
or the binder of sheaves his arms,
⁸while those who pass by do not say,
"The blessing of the Lᴏʀᴅ be upon you!
We bless you in the name of the Lᴏʀᴅ!"

Waiting for Divine Redemption
A Song of Ascents.

130 [129] Out of the depths I cry to you, O Lᴏʀᴅ!
² Lord, hear my voice!
Let your ears be attentive
to the voice of my supplications!

³If you, O Lᴏʀᴅ, should mark iniquities,
Lord, who could stand?
⁴But there is forgiveness with you,
that you may be feared.

⁵I wait for the Lᴏʀᴅ, my soul waits,
and in his word I hope;
⁶my soul waits for the Lᴏʀᴅ
more than watchmen for the morning,
more than watchmen for the morning.

⁷O Israel, hope in the Lᴏʀᴅ!
For with the Lᴏʀᴅ there is mercy,
and with him is plenteous redemption.
⁸And he will redeem Israel
from all his iniquities.

Song of Quiet Trust
A Song of Ascents.
Of David.

131 [130] O Lᴏʀᴅ, my heart is not lifted up,
my eyes are not raised too high;
I do not occupy myself with things
too great and too marvelous for me.
²But I have calmed and quieted my soul,
like a child quieted at its mother's breast;
like a child that is quieted is my soul.

³O Israel, hope in the Lᴏʀᴅ
from this time forth and for evermore.

The Eternal Dwelling of God in Zion
A Song of Ascents.

132 [131] Remember, O Lᴏʀᴅ, in David's favor,
his humility;
²how he swore to the Lᴏʀᴅ
and vowed to the Mighty One of Jacob,
³"I will not enter my house
or get into my bed;
⁴I will not give sleep to my eyes
or slumber to my eyelids,

ᵐ Another reading is *so.*
130:3: Ps 143:2; Rom 3:20; Gal 2:16.

⁵until I find a place for the Lord,
a dwelling place for the Mighty One of
Jacob."

⁶Behold, we heard of it in Eph'rathah,
we found it in the fields of Ja'ar.
⁷"Let us go to his dwelling place;
let us worship at his footstool!"

⁸Arise, O Lord, and go to your resting place,
you and the ark of your might.
⁹Let your priests be clothed with righteousness,
and let your saints shout for joy.
¹⁰For your servant David's sake
do not turn away the face of your anointed
one.

¹¹The Lord swore to David a sure oath
from which he will not turn back:
"One of the sons of your body
I will set on your throne.
¹²If your sons keep my covenant
and my testimonies which I shall teach them,
their sons also for ever
shall sit upon your throne."

¹³For the Lord has chosen Zion;
he has desired it for his habitation:
¹⁴"This is my resting place for ever;
here I will dwell, for I have desired it.
¹⁵I will abundantly bless her provisions;
I will satisfy her poor with bread.
¹⁶Her priests I will clothe with salvation,
and her saints will shout for joy.
¹⁷There I will make a horn to sprout for David;
I have prepared a lamp for my anointed.
¹⁸His enemies I will clothe with shame,
but upon himself his crown will shed its
luster."

The Blessedness of Unity
A Song of Ascents.

133 [132] Behold, how good and
pleasant it is
when brothers dwell in unity!
²It is like the precious oil upon the head,
running down upon the beard,
upon the beard of Aaron,
running down on the collar of his robes!
³It is like the dew of Hermon,
which falls on the mountains of Zion!
For there the Lord has commanded the
blessing,
life for evermore.

Praise in the Night
A Song of Ascents.

134 [133] Come, bless the Lord,
all you servants of the Lord,
who stand by night in the house of the
Lord!

²Lift up your hands to the holy place,
and bless the Lord!

³May the Lord bless you from Zion,
he who made heaven and earth!

Praise for God's Goodness and Might

135 [134] Praise the Lord!
Praise the name of the Lord,
give praise, O servants of the Lord,
²you that stand in the house of the Lord,
in the courts of the house of our God!
³Praise the Lord, for the Lord is good;
sing to his name, for he is gracious!
⁴For the Lord has chosen Jacob for himself,
Israel as his own possession.

⁵For I know that the Lord is great,
and that our Lord is above all gods.
⁶Whatever the Lord pleases he does,
in heaven and on earth,
in the seas and all deeps.
⁷He it is who makes the clouds rise at the end of
the earth,
who makes lightnings for the rain
and brings forth the wind from his
storehouses.

⁸He it was who struck the first-born of Egypt,
both of man and of beast;
⁹who in your midst, O Egypt,
sent signs and wonders
against Pharaoh and all his servants;
¹⁰who struck many nations
and slew mighty kings,
¹¹Sihon, king of the Amorites,
and Og, king of Bashan,
and all the kingdoms of Canaan,
¹²and gave their land as a heritage,
a heritage to his people Israel.

¹³Your name, O Lord, endures for ever,
your renown, O Lord, throughout all ages.
¹⁴For the Lord will vindicate his people,
and have compassion on his servants.

¹⁵The idols of the nations are silver and gold,
the work of men's hands.
¹⁶They have mouths, but they speak not,
they have eyes, but they see not,
¹⁷they have ears, but they hear not,
nor is there any breath in their mouths.
¹⁸Like them be those who make them!—
yes, every one who trusts in them!

¹⁹O house of Israel, bless the Lord!
O house of Aaron, bless the Lord!
²⁰O house of Levi, bless the Lord!
You that fear the Lord, bless the Lord!

132:11: Ps 89:3–4; Acts 2:30.
135:14: Heb 10:30.
135:15–18: Ps 115:4–8.

²¹Blessed be the Lord from Zion,
   he who dwells in Jerusalem!
   Praise the Lord!

God's Work in Creation and in History

136 [135]
O give thanks to the Lord, for
he is good,
   for his mercy endures for ever.
²O give thanks to the God of gods,
   for his mercy endures for ever.
³O give thanks to the Lord of lords,
   for his mercy endures for ever;

⁴to him who alone does great wonders,
   for his mercy endures for ever;
⁵to him who by understanding made the
      heavens,
   for his mercy endures for ever;
⁶to him who spread out the earth upon the
      waters,
   for his mercy endures for ever;
⁷to him who made the great lights,
   for his mercy endures for ever;
⁸the sun to rule over the day,
   for his mercy endures for ever;
⁹the moon and stars to rule over the night,
   for his mercy endures for ever;

¹⁰to him who struck the first-born of Egypt,
   for his mercy endures for ever;
¹¹and brought Israel out from among them,
   for his mercy endures for ever;
¹²with a strong hand and an outstretched arm,
   for his mercy endures for ever;
¹³to him who divided the Red Sea in two,
   for his mercy endures for ever;
¹⁴and made Israel pass through the midst of it,
   for his mercy endures for ever;
¹⁵but overthrew Pharaoh and his host in the Red
      Sea,
   for his mercy endures for ever;
¹⁶to him who led his people through the
      wilderness,
   for his mercy endures for ever;
¹⁷to him who struck great kings,
   for his mercy endures for ever;
¹⁸and slew famous kings,
   for his mercy endures for ever;
¹⁹Sihon, king of the Amorites,
   for his mercy endures for ever;
²⁰and Og, king of Bashan,
   for his mercy endures for ever;
²¹and gave their land as a heritage,
   for his mercy endures for ever;
²²a heritage to Israel his servant,
   for his mercy endures for ever.

²³It is he who remembered us in our low estate,
   for his mercy endures for ever;

²⁴and rescued us from our foes,
   for his mercy endures for ever;
²⁵he who gives food to all flesh,
   for his mercy endures for ever.

²⁶O give thanks to the God of heaven,
   for his mercy endures for ever.

Lament over the Destruction of Jerusalem

137 [136]
* By the waters ° of Babylon,
   there we sat down and
wept,
   when we remembered Zion.
²On the willows ᴾ there
   we hung up our lyres.
³For there our captors
   required of us songs,
and our tormentors, mirth, saying,
   "Sing us one of the songs of Zion!"

⁴How shall we sing the Lord's song
   in a foreign land?
⁵If I forget you, O Jerusalem,
   let my right hand wither!
⁶Let my tongue cleave to the roof of my
      mouth,
   if I do not remember you,
   if I do not set Jerusalem
      above my highest joy!

⁷Remember, O Lord, against the E'domites
   the day of Jerusalem,
how they said, "Raze it, raze it!
   Down to its foundations!"

⁸O daughter of Babylon, you devastator! �q
   Happy shall he be who repays you
   with what you have done to us!
⁹Happy shall he be who takes your little ones
   and dashes them against the rock!

Thanksgiving and Praise
A Psalm of David.

138 [137]
I give you thanks, O Lord,
   with my whole heart;
before the angels I sing your praise;
²I bow down toward your holy temple
   and give thanks to your name for your
      mercy and your faithfulness;
for you have exalted above everything
   your name and your word. ʳ
³On the day I called, you answered me,
   my strength of soul you increased. ˢ

° Heb streams.
ᴾ Or poplars.
q Or you who are devastated.
ʳ Cn: Heb you have exalted your word above all your name.
ˢ Syr Compare Gk Tg: Heb you made me arrogant in my soul with
strength.
* 137: This psalm breathes the spirit of sadness and homesickness of the
Israelite in exile in Babylon.

⁴All the kings of the earth shall praise you, O
　　Lord,
　for they have heard the words of your
　　mouth;
⁵and they shall sing of the ways of the Lord,
　for great is the glory of the Lord.
⁶For though the Lord is high, he regards the
　　lowly;
　but the haughty he knows from afar.

⁷Though I walk in the midst of trouble,
　you preserve my life;
　you stretch out your hand against the wrath of
　　my enemies,
　and your right hand delivers me.
⁸The Lord will fulfil his purpose for me;
　your mercy, O Lord, endures for ever.
　Do not forsake the work of your hands.

The Inescapable God
To the choirmaster.
A Psalm of David.

139 [138] O Lord, you have searched
　　　　　　me and known me!
²You know when I sit down and when I rise up;
　you discern my thoughts from afar.
³You search out my path and my lying down,
　and are acquainted with all my ways.
⁴Even before a word is on my tongue,
　behold, O Lord, you know it altogether.
⁵You beset me behind and before,
　and lay your hand upon me.
⁶Such knowledge is too wonderful for me;
　it is high, I cannot attain it.

⁷Where shall I go from your Spirit?
　Or where shall I flee from your presence?
⁸If I ascend to heaven, you are there!
　If I make my bed in Sheol, you are there!
⁹If I take the wings of the morning
　and dwell in the uttermost parts of the sea,
¹⁰even there your hand shall lead me,
　and your right hand shall hold me.
¹¹If I say, "Let only darkness cover me,
　and the light about me be night,"
¹²even the darkness is not dark to you,
　the night is bright as the day;
　for darkness is as light with you.

¹³For you formed my inward parts,
　you knitted me together in my mother's
　　womb.
¹⁴I praise you, for I am wondrously made.ᵗ
　Wonderful are your works!
　You know me right well;
¹⁵　my frame was not hidden from you,
　when I was being made in secret,
　　intricately wrought in the depths of the
　　earth.

¹⁶Your eyes beheld my unformed substance;
　in your book were written, every one of
　　them,
　the days that were formed for me,
　when as yet there was none of them.
¹⁷How precious to me are your thoughts, O God!
　How vast is the sum of them!
¹⁸If I would count them, they are more than the
　　sand.
　When I awake, I am still with you.ᵘ

¹⁹O that you would slay the wicked, O God,
　and that men of blood would depart from
　　me,
²⁰men who maliciously defy you,
　who lift themselves up against you for
　　evil!ᵛ
²¹Do I not hate them that hate you, O Lord?
　And do I not loathe them that rise up
　　against you?
²²I hate them with perfect hatred;
　I count them my enemies.
²³Search me, O God, and know my heart!
　Try me and know my thoughts!
²⁴And see if there be any wickedᵂ way in me,
　and lead me in the way everlasting!ˣ

Prayer for Deliverance from Enemies
To the choirmaster.
A Psalm of David.

140 [139] Deliver me, O Lord, from evil
　　　　　　men;
　preserve me from violent men,
²who plan evil things in their heart,
　and stir up wars continually.
³They make their tongue sharp as a serpent's,
　and under their lips is the poison of vipers.
　　　　　　　　　　　　　　Selah

⁴Guard me, O Lord, from the hands of the
　　wicked;
　preserve me from violent men,
　who have planned to trip up my feet.
⁵Arrogant men have hidden a trap for me,
　and with cords they have spread a net,ʸ
　by the wayside they have set snares for me.
　　　　　　　　　　　　　　Selah

⁶I say to the Lord, You are my God;
　give ear to the voice of my supplications, O
　　Lord!
⁷O Lord, my Lord, my strong deliverer,
　you have covered my head in the day of
　　battle.

ᵗ Or *you are awesome and wonderful.*
ᵘ Or *were I to come to the end I would still be with you.*
ᵛ Cn: Heb uncertain.
ᵂ Heb *hurtful.*
ˣ Or *the ancient way.* Compare Jer 6:16.
ʸ Or *they have spread cords as a net.*
140:3: Rom 3:13.

⁸Grant not, O Lᴏʀᴅ, the desires of the wicked;
  do not further his evil plot!　　　　*Selah*

⁹Those who surround me lift up their head,ᶻ
  let the mischief of their lips overwhelm
    them!
¹⁰Let burning coals fall upon them!
  Let them be cast into pits, no more to rise!
¹¹Let not the slanderer be established in the
    land;
  let evil hunt down the violent man
    speedily!

¹²I know that the Lᴏʀᴅ maintains the cause of the
    afflicted,
  and executes justice for the needy.
¹³Surely the righteous shall give thanks to your
    name;
  the upright shall dwell in your presence.

Prayer for Preservation from Evil
A Psalm of David.

141 [140]
I call upon you, O Lᴏʀᴅ; make
haste to me!
  Give ear to my voice, when I call to you!
²Let my prayer be counted as incense before
    you,
  and the lifting up of my hands as an
    evening sacrifice!

³Set a guard over my mouth, O Lᴏʀᴅ,
  keep watch over the door of my lips!
⁴Incline not my heart to any evil,
  to busy myself with wicked deeds
in company with men who work iniquity;
  and let me not eat of their dainties!

⁵Let a good man strike or rebuke me in
    kindness,
  but let the oil of the wicked never anoint
    my head;ᵃ
  for my prayer is continually ᵇ against their
    wicked deeds.
⁶When they are given over to those who shall
    condemn them,
  then they shall learn that the word of the
    Lᴏʀᴅ is true.
⁷As a rock which one cleaves and shatters on
    the land,
  so shall their bones be strewn at the mouth
    of Sheol. ᶜ

⁸But my eyes are toward you, O Lᴏʀᴅ God;
  in you I seek refuge; leave me not
    defenseless!
⁹Keep me from the trap which they have laid for
    me,
  and from the snares of evildoers!
¹⁰Let the wicked together fall into their own
    nets,
  while I escape.

Prayer for Deliverance from Persecutors
A Maskil of David, when he was in the cave.
A Prayer.

142 [141]
I cry with my voice to the
Lᴏʀᴅ,
  with my voice I make supplication to the
    Lᴏʀᴅ,
²I pour out my complaint before him,
  I tell my trouble before him.
³When my spirit is faint,
  you know my way!

In the path where I walk
  they have hidden a trap for me.
⁴I look to the right and watch,ᵈ
  but there is none who takes notice of me;
no refuge remains to me,
  no man cares for me.

⁵I cry to you, O Lᴏʀᴅ;
  I say, You are my refuge,
  my portion in the land of the living.
⁶Give heed to my cry;
  for I am brought very low!

Deliver me from my persecutors;
  for they are too strong for me!
⁷Bring me out of prison,
  that I may give thanks to your name!
The righteous will surround me;
  for you will deal bountifully with me.

Prayer for Deliverance from Enemies
A Psalm of David.

143 [142]
Hear my prayer, O Lᴏʀᴅ; give
ear to my supplications!
In your faithfulness answer me, in your
    righteousness!
²Enter not into judgment with your servant;
  for no man living is righteous before you.

³For the enemy has pursued me;
  he has crushed my life to the ground;
  he has made me sit in darkness like those
    long dead.
⁴Therefore my spirit faints within me;
  my heart within me is appalled.

⁵I remember the days of old,
  I meditate on all that you have done;
  I muse on what your hands have wrought.
⁶I stretch out my hands to you;
  my soul thirsts for you like a parched land.
　　　　Selah

ᶻ Cn Compare Gk: Heb *those who surround me are uplifted in head.*
ᵃ Gk: Heb obscure.
ᵇ Cn: Heb *for continually and my prayer.*
ᶜ The Hebrew of verses 5–7 is obscure.
ᵈ Or *Look to the right and watch.*
141:2: Rev 5:8; 8:3–4.
143:2: Ps 130:3; Rom 3:20; Gal 2:16.

⁷Make haste to answer me, O LORD!
　My spirit fails!
　Hide not your face from me,
　　lest I be like those who go down to the Pit.
⁸Let me hear in the morning of your merciful
　　love,
　　for in you I put my trust.
　Teach me the way I should go,
　　for to you I lift up my soul.

⁹Deliver me, O LORD, from my enemies!
　I have fled to you for refuge! ᵉ
¹⁰Teach me to do your will,
　　for you are my God!
　Let your good spirit lead me
　　on a level path!

¹¹For your name's sake, O LORD, preserve my life!
　In your righteousness bring me out of
　　trouble!
¹²And in your steadfast love cut off my enemies,
　　and destroy all my adversaries,
　　for I am your servant.

Prayer for National Deliverance and Security

A Psalm of David.

144 [143] Blessed be the LORD, my rock,
　who trains my hands for war,
and my fingers for battle;
²my mercy ᶠ and my fortress,
　my stronghold and my deliverer,
my shield and he in whom I take refuge,
　who subdues my people under me. ᵍ

³O LORD, what is man that you regard him,
　or the son of man that you think of him?
⁴Man is like a breath,
　his days are like a passing shadow.

⁵Bow your heavens, O LORD, and come down!
　Touch the mountains that they smoke!
⁶Flash forth the lightning and scatter them,
　send out your arrows and rout them!
⁷Stretch forth your hand from on high,
　rescue me and deliver me from the many
　　waters,
　from the hand of aliens,
⁸whose mouths speak lies,
　and whose right hand is a right hand of
　　falsehood.

⁹I will sing a new song to you, O God;
　upon a ten-stringed harp I will play to you,
¹⁰who give victory to kings,
　who rescue David your ʰ servant from the
　　cruel sword.
¹¹Rescue me from the cruel sword,
　and deliver me from the hand of aliens,
whose mouths speak lies,
　and whose right hand is a right hand of
　　falsehood.

¹²May our sons in their youth
　be like plants full grown,
our daughters like corner pillars
　cut for the structure of a palace;
¹³may our garners be full,
　providing all manner of store;
may our sheep bring forth thousands
　and ten thousands in our fields;
¹⁴may our cattle be heavy with young,
　suffering no mischance or failure in bearing;
may there be no cry of distress in our streets!
¹⁵Happy the people to whom such blessings fall!
　Happy the people whose God is the LORD!

The Greatness and the Goodness of God

A Song of Praise.
Of David.

145 [144] I will extol you, my God and
　King,
and bless your name for ever and ever.
²Every day I will bless you,
　and praise your name for ever and ever.
³Great is the LORD, and greatly to be praised,
　and his greatness is unsearchable.

⁴One generation shall laud your works to
　another,
　and shall declare your mighty acts.
⁵On the glorious splendor of your majesty,
　and on your wondrous works, I will
　　meditate.
⁶Men shall proclaim the might of your awesome
　　acts,
　and I will declare your greatness.
⁷They shall pour forth the fame of your
　　abundant goodness,
　and shall sing aloud of your righteousness.

⁸The LORD is gracious and merciful,
　slow to anger and abounding in mercy.
⁹The LORD is good to all,
　and his compassion is over all that he has
　　made.

¹⁰All your works shall give thanks to you,
　O LORD,
　and all your saints shall bless you!
¹¹They shall speak of the glory of your
　　kingdom,
　and tell of your power,
¹²to make known to the sons of men your ʰ
　　mighty deeds,
　and the glorious splendor of your ʰ
　　kingdom.
¹³Your kingdom is an everlasting kingdom,
　and your dominion endures throughout all
　　generations.

ᵉ One Heb Ms Gk: Heb *to you I have hidden.*
ᶠ With 18:2 2 Sam 22:2: Heb *my merciful love* or *my rock.*
ᵍ Another reading is *the peoples under him.*
ʰ Heb *his.*

The LORD is faithful in all his words,
and gracious in all his deeds. [1]
[14]The LORD upholds all who are falling,
and raises up all who are bowed down.
[15]The eyes of all look to you,
and you give them their food in due season.
[16]You open your hand,
you satisfy the desire of every living
thing.
[17]The LORD is just in all his ways,
and kind in all his doings.
[18]The LORD is near to all who call upon him,
to all who call upon him in truth.
[19]He fulfils the desire of all who fear him,
he also hears their cry, and saves them.
[20]The LORD preserves all who love him;
but all the wicked he will destroy.

[21]My mouth will speak the praise of the LORD,
and let all flesh bless his holy name for ever
and ever.

Praise for God's Help

146 [145] Praise the LORD!
Praise the LORD, O my soul!
[2]I will praise the LORD as long as I live;
I will sing praises to my God while I have
being.

[3]Put not your trust in princes,
in a son of man, in whom there is no help.
[4]When his breath departs he returns to his
earth;
on that very day his plans perish.

[5]Happy is he whose help is the God of Jacob,
whose hope is in the LORD his God,
[6]who made heaven and earth,
the sea, and all that is in them;
who keeps faith for ever;
[7] who executes justice for the oppressed;
who gives food to the hungry.

The LORD sets the prisoners free;
[8] the LORD opens the eyes of the blind.
The LORD lifts up those who are bowed down;
the LORD loves the righteous.
[9]The LORD watches over the sojourners,
he upholds the widow and the fatherless;
but the way of the wicked he brings to
ruin.

[10]The LORD will reign for ever,
your God, O Zion, to all generations.
Praise the LORD!

Praise for God's Care for Jerusalem

147 [146] Praise the LORD!
For it is good to sing praises
to our God;
for he is gracious, and a song of praise is
seemly.

[2]The LORD builds up Jerusalem;
he gathers the outcasts of Israel.
[3]He heals the brokenhearted,
and binds up their wounds.
[4]He determines the number of the stars,
he gives to all of them their names.
[5]Great is our LORD, and abundant in power;
his understanding is beyond measure.
[6]The LORD lifts up the downtrodden,
he casts the wicked to the ground.

[7]Sing to the LORD with thanksgiving;
make melody to our God upon the lyre!
[8]He covers the heavens with clouds,
he prepares rain for the earth,
he makes grass grow upon the hills.
[9]He gives to the beasts their food,
and to the young ravens which cry.
[10]His delight is not in the strength of the horse,
nor his pleasure in the legs of a man;
[11]but the LORD takes pleasure in those who fear
him,
in those who hope in his steadfast love.

[147] [12]Praise the LORD, O Jerusalem!
Praise your God, O Zion!
[13]For he strengthens the bars of your gates;
he blesses your sons within you.
[14]He makes peace in your borders;
he fills you with the finest of the wheat.
[15]He sends forth his command to the earth;
his word runs swiftly.
[16]He gives snow like wool;
he scatters hoarfrost like ashes.
[17]He casts forth his ice like morsels;
who can stand before his cold?
[18]He sends forth his word, and melts them;
he makes his wind blow, and the waters
flow.
[19]He declares his word to Jacob,
his statutes and ordinances to Israel.
[20]He has not dealt thus with any other nation;
they do not know his ordinances.
Praise the LORD!

Praise for God's Universal Glory

148 Praise the LORD!
Praise the LORD from the heavens,
praise him in the heights!
[2]Praise him, all his angels,
praise him, all his host!

[3]Praise him, sun and moon,
praise him, all you shining stars!
[4]Praise him, you highest heavens,
and you waters above the heavens!

[5]Let them praise the name of the LORD!
For he commanded and they were created.

---

[1] These two lines are supplied by one Hebrew Ms, Gk, and Syr.

⁶And he established them for ever and ever;
he fixed their bounds which cannot be
passed. ʲ

⁷Praise the LORD from the earth,
you sea monsters and all deeps,
⁸fire and hail, snow and frost,
stormy wind fulfilling his command!

⁹Mountains and all hills,
fruit trees and all cedars!
¹⁰Beasts and all cattle,
creeping things and flying birds!

¹¹Kings of the earth and all peoples,
princes and all rulers of the earth!
¹²Young men and maidens together,
old men and children!

¹³Let them praise the name of the LORD,
for his name alone is exalted;
his glory is above earth and heaven.
¹⁴He has raised up a horn for his people,
praise for all his saints,
for the people of Israel who are near to him.
Praise the LORD!

Praise for God's Goodness to Israel

149 Praise the LORD!
Sing to the LORD a new song,
his praise in the assembly of the faithful!
²Let Israel be glad in his Maker,
let the sons of Zion rejoice in their King!
³Let them praise his name with dancing,
making melody to him with timbrel and
lyre!

⁴For the LORD takes pleasure in his people;
he adorns the humble with victory.
⁵Let the faithful exult in glory;
let them sing for joy on their couches.
⁶Let the high praises of God be in their throats
and two-edged swords in their hands,
⁷to wreak vengeance on the nations
and chastisement on the peoples,
⁸to bind their kings with chains
and their nobles with fetters of iron,
⁹to execute on them the judgment written!
This is glory for all his faithful ones.
Praise the LORD!

Praise for God's Surpassing Greatness

150 * Praise the LORD!
Praise God in his sanctuary;
praise him in his mighty firmament!
²Praise him for his mighty deeds;
praise him according to his exceeding
greatness!

³Praise him with trumpet sound;
praise him with lute and harp!
⁴Praise him with timbrel and dance;
praise him with strings and pipe!
⁵Praise him with sounding cymbals;
praise him with loud clashing cymbals!
⁶Let everything that breathes praise the LORD!
Praise the LORD!

ʲ Or *he set a law which cannot pass away.*
* 150: This exclamation of praise serves as the epilogue to the Psalter.

THE BOOK OF

THE PROVERBS

The Call of Wisdom

1 The proverbs of Solomon, son of David, king of Israel:

2That men may know wisdom and instruction,
  understand words of insight,
3receive instruction in wise dealing,
  righteousness, justice, and equity;
4that prudence may be given to the simple,
  knowledge and discretion to the youth—
5the wise man also may hear and increase in learning,
  and the man of understanding acquire skill,
6to understand a proverb and a figure,
  the words of the wise and their riddles.

7The fear of the LORD is the beginning of knowledge;
  fools despise wisdom and instruction.

8Hear, my son, your father's instruction,
  and reject not your mother's teaching;
9for they are a fair garland for your head,
  and pendants for your neck.
10My son, if sinners entice you,
  do not consent.
11If they say, "Come with us, let us lie in wait for blood,
  let us wantonly ambush the innocent;
12like Sheol let us swallow them alive
  and whole, like those who go down to the Pit;
13we shall find all precious goods,
  we shall fill our houses with spoil;
14throw in your lot among us,
  we will all have one purse"—
15my son, do not walk in the way with them,
  hold back your foot from their paths;
16for their feet run to evil,
  and they make haste to shed blood.
17For in vain is a net spread
  in the sight of any bird;
18but these men lie in wait for their own blood,
  they set an ambush for their own lives.
19Such are the ways of all who get gain by violence;
  it takes away the life of its possessors.
20Wisdom cries aloud in the street;
  in the markets she raises her voice;

21on the top of the walls a she cries out;
  at the entrance of the city gates she speaks:
22"How long, O simple ones, will you love being simple?
  How long will scoffers delight in their scoffing
  and fools hate knowledge?
23Give heed b to my reproof;
  behold, I will pour out my thoughts c to you;
  I will make my words known to you.
24Because I have called and you refused to listen,
  have stretched out my hand and no one has heeded,
25and you have ignored all my counsel
  and would have none of my reproof,
26I also will laugh at your calamity;
  I will mock when panic strikes you,
27when panic strikes you like a storm,
  and your calamity comes like a whirlwind,
  when distress and anguish come upon you.
28Then they will call upon me, but I will not answer;
  they will seek me diligently but will not find me.
29Because they hated knowledge
  and did not choose the fear of the LORD,
30would have none of my counsel,
  and despised all my reproof,
31therefore they shall eat the fruit of their way
  and be sated with their own devices.
32For the simple are killed by their turning away,
  and the complacence of fools destroys them;
33but he who listens to me will dwell secure
  and will be at ease, without dread of evil."

The proverb or saying (*mashal*) was a typical form of expression in a society that depended to a large extent on oral tradition. Each saying expressed some important truth in pithy and memorable form. The proverbs contained in this book were, of course, regarded as divinely inspired teaching and had a correspondingly weighty authority. The book contains a number of collections of proverbs, two of which are ascribed to Solomon (10:1—22:16 and 25:1—29:27), but it is not likely that all the proverbs in these collections are in fact attributable to Solomon. It is probable that 10:1—22:16 forms the original nucleus of the book.

The general subject of the proverbs is the art of right living. Some points are dealt with in detail, for example, wisdom and folly, justice and injustice, and so on. They are not simply maxims of natural wisdom but presuppose a background of revealed religion and inculcate its principles. Religion is in fact regarded as the basis of all morality. The book was finally edited and put together after the Exile.

a Heb uncertain.
b Heb *Turn.*
c Heb *spirit.*
1:20, 21: 8:1–3.

The Treasure of Wisdom

2 My son, if you receive my words
   and treasure up my commandments with
   you,
[2]making your ear attentive to wisdom
   and inclining your heart to understanding;
[3]yes, if you cry out for insight
   and raise your voice for understanding,
[4]if you seek it like silver
   and search for it as for hidden treasures;
[5]then you will understand the fear of the LORD
   and find the knowledge of God.
[6]For the LORD gives wisdom;
   from his mouth come knowledge and
   understanding;
[7]he stores up sound wisdom for the upright;
   he is a shield to those who walk in
   integrity,
[8]guarding the paths of justice
   and preserving the way of his saints.
[9]Then you will understand righteousness and
   justice
   and equity, every good path;
[10]for wisdom will come into your heart,
   and knowledge will be pleasant to your
   soul;
[11]discretion will watch over you;
   understanding will guard you;
[12]delivering you from the way of evil,
   from men of perverted speech,
[13]who forsake the paths of uprightness
   to walk in the ways of darkness,
[14]who rejoice in doing evil
   and delight in the perverseness of evil;
[15]men whose paths are crooked,
   and who are devious in their ways.

[16]You will be saved from the loose [d] woman,
   from the adventuress [e] with her smooth
   words,
[17]who forsakes the companion of her youth
   and forgets the covenant of her God;
[18]for her house sinks down to death,
   and her paths to the shades;
[19]none who go to her come back
   nor do they regain the paths of life.

[20]So you will walk in the way of good men
   and keep to the paths of the righteous.
[21]For the upright will inhabit the land,
   and men of integrity will remain in it;
[22]but the wicked will be cut off from the land,
   and the treacherous will be rooted out of it.

Exhortation to Be Wise and to Honor God

3 My son, do not forget my teaching,
   but let your heart keep my
   commandments;
[2]for length of days and years of life
   and abundant welfare will they give you.

[3]Let not loyalty and faithfulness forsake you;
   bind them about your neck,
   write them on the tablet of your heart.
[4]So you will find favor and good repute [f]
   in the sight of God and man.

[5]Trust in the LORD with all your heart,
   and do not rely on your own insight.
[6]In all your ways acknowledge him,
   and he will make straight your paths.
[7]Be not wise in your own eyes;
   fear the LORD, and turn away from evil.
[8]It will be healing to your flesh [g]
   and refreshment [h] to your bones.

[9]Honor the LORD with your substance
   and with the first fruits of all your produce;
[10]then your barns will be filled with plenty,
   and your vats will be bursting with wine.

[11]My son, do not despise the LORD's discipline
   or be weary of his reproof,
[12]for the LORD reproves him whom he loves,
   as a father the son in whom he delights.

[13]Happy is the man who finds wisdom,
   and the man who gets understanding,
[14]for the gain from it is better than gain from
   silver
   and its profit better than gold.
[15]She is more precious than jewels,
   and nothing you desire can compare with
   her.
[16]Long life is in her right hand;
   in her left hand are riches and honor.
[17]Her ways are ways of pleasantness,
   and all her paths are peace.
[18]She is a tree of life to those who lay hold of
   her;
   those who hold her fast are called happy.

[19]The LORD by wisdom founded the earth;
   by understanding he established the
   heavens;
[20]by his knowledge the deeps broke forth,
   and the clouds drop down the dew.

[21]My son, keep sound wisdom and discretion;
   let them not escape from your sight, [i]
[22]and they will be life for your soul
   and adornment for your neck.

---

[d] Heb *strange.*
[e] Heb *foreign woman.*
[f] Cn: Heb *understanding.*
[g] Heb *navel.*
[h] Or *medicine.*
[i] Reversing the order of the clauses.
3:4: Rom 12:17.
3:7: Rom 12:16.
3:11, 12: Heb 12:5, 6.

[23]Then you will walk on your way securely
  and your foot will not stumble.
[24]If you sit down,[j] you will not be afraid;
  when you lie down, your sleep will be
  sweet.
[25]Do not be afraid of sudden panic,
  or of the ruin [k] of the wicked, when it
  comes;
[26]for the LORD will be your confidence
  and will keep your foot from being caught.
[27]Do not withhold good from those to whom it [l]
  is due,
  when it is in your power to do it.

[28]Do not say to your neighbor, "Go, and come
  again,
  tomorrow I will give it"—when you have it
  with you.
[29]Do not plan evil against your neighbor
  who dwells trustingly beside you.
[30]Do not contend with a man for no reason,
  when he has done you no harm.
[31]Do not envy a man of violence
  and do not choose any of his ways;
[32]for the perverse man is an abomination to the
  LORD,
  but the upright are in his confidence.
[33]The LORD's curse is on the house of the wicked,
  but he blesses the abode of the righteous.
[34]Toward the scorners he is scornful,
  but to the humble he shows favor.
[35]The wise will inherit honor,
  but fools get [m] disgrace.

A Father's Advice

4 Hear, O sons, a father's instruction,
  and be attentive, that you may gain [n]
  insight;
[2]for I give you good precepts:
  do not forsake my teaching.
[3]When I was a son with my father,
  tender, the only one in the sight of my
  mother,
[4]he taught me, and said to me,
  "Let your heart hold fast my words;
  keep my commandments, and live;
[5]do not forget, and do not turn away from the
  words of my mouth.
  Get wisdom; get insight.[o]
[6]Do not forsake her, and she will keep you;
  love her, and she will guard you.
[7]The beginning of wisdom is this: Get wisdom,
  and whatever you get, get insight.
[8]Prize her highly, [p] and she will exalt you;
  she will honor you if you embrace her.
[9]She will place on your head a fair garland;
  she will bestow on you a beautiful crown."

[10]Hear, my son, and accept my words,
  that the years of your life may be many.

[11]I have taught you the way of wisdom;
  I have led you in the paths of uprightness.
[12]When you walk, your step will not be
  hampered;
  and if you run, you will not stumble.
[13]Keep hold of instruction, do not let go;
  guard her, for she is your life.
[14]Do not enter the path of the wicked,
  and do not walk in the way of evil men.
[15]Avoid it; do not go on it;
  turn away from it and pass on.
[16]For they cannot sleep unless they have done
  wrong;
  they are robbed of sleep unless they have
  made someone stumble.
[17]For they eat the bread of wickedness
  and drink the wine of violence.
[18]But the path of the righteous is like the light of
  dawn,
  which shines brighter and brighter until full
  day.
[19]The way of the wicked is like deep darkness;
  they do not know over what they stumble.

[20]My son, be attentive to my words;
  incline your ear to my sayings.
[21]Let them not escape from your sight;
  keep them within your heart.
[22]For they are life to him who finds them,
  and healing to all his flesh.
[23]Keep your heart with all vigilance;
  for from it flow the springs of life.
[24]Put away from you crooked speech,
  and put devious talk far from you.
[25]Let your eyes look directly forward,
  and your gaze be straight before you.
[26]Take heed to [q] the path of your feet,
  then all your ways will be sure.
[27]Do not swerve to the right or to the left;
  turn your foot away from evil.

Warning against Loose Women

5 My son, be attentive to my wisdom,
  incline your ear to my understanding;
[2]that you may keep discretion,
  and your lips may guard knowledge.
[3]For the lips of a loose woman drip honey,
  and her speech [r] is smoother than oil;
[4]but in the end she is bitter as wormwood,
  sharp as a two-edged sword.

---

[j] Gk: Heb *lie down.*
[k] Heb *storm.*
[l] Heb *Do not withhold good from its owners.*
[m] Cn: Heb *exalt.*
[n] Heb *know.*
[o] Reversing the order of the lines.
[p] The meaning of the Hebrew is uncertain.
[q] The meaning of the Hebrew word is uncertain.
[r] Heb *palate.*
3:34 (Gk): Jas 4:6; 1 Pet 5:5.
4:26 (Gk): Heb 12:13.

⁵Her feet go down to death;
 her steps follow the path to ᵃ Sheol;
⁶she does not take heed to ᵗ the path of life;
 her ways wander, and she does not know it.

⁷And now, O sons, listen to me,
 and do not depart from the words of my
  mouth.
⁸Keep your way far from her,
 and do not go near the door of her house;
⁹lest you give your honor to others
 and your years to the merciless;
¹⁰lest strangers take their fill of your strength,ᵘ
 and your labors go to the house of an alien;
¹¹and at the end of your life you groan,
 when your flesh and body are consumed,
¹²and you say, "How I hated discipline,
 and my heart despised reproof!
¹³I did not listen to the voice of my teachers
 or incline my ear to my instructors.
¹⁴I was at the point of utter ruin
 in the assembled congregation."

¹⁵Drink water from your own cistern,
 flowing water from your own well.
¹⁶Should your springs be scattered abroad,
 streams of water in the streets?
¹⁷Let them be for yourself alone,
 and not for strangers with you.
¹⁸Let your fountain be blessed,
 and rejoice in the wife of your youth,
¹⁹ a lovely deer, a graceful doe.
 Let her affection fill you at all times with
  delight,
 be infatuated always with her love.
²⁰Why should you be infatuated, my son, with a
  loose woman
 and embrace the bosom of an adventuress?
²¹For a man's ways are before the eyes of the
  LORD,
 and he watches ᵛ all his paths.
²²The iniquities of the wicked ensnare him,
 and he is caught in the toils of his sin.
²³He dies for lack of discipline,
 and because of his great folly he is lost.

Practical Admonitions and Warnings

6 My son, if you have become surety for your
 neighbor,
 have given your pledge for a stranger;
²if you are snared in the utterance of your lips,ʷ
 caught in the words of your mouth;
³then do this, my son, and save yourself,
 for you have come into your neighbor's
  power:
 go, hasten,ˣ and importune your neighbor.
⁴Give your eyes no sleep
 and your eyelids no slumber;
⁵save yourself like a gazelle from the hunter, ʸ
 like a bird from the hand of the fowler.

⁶Go to the ant, O sluggard;
 consider her ways, and be wise.
⁷Without having any chief,
 officer or ruler,
⁸she prepares her food in summer,
 and gathers her sustenance in harvest.
⁹How long will you lie there, O sluggard?
 When will you arise from your sleep?
¹⁰A little sleep, a little slumber,
 a little folding of the hands to rest,
¹¹and poverty will come upon you like a
  vagabond,
 and want like an armed man.

¹²A worthless person, a wicked man,
 goes about with crooked speech,
¹³winks with his eyes, scrapes ᶻ with his feet,
 points with his finger,
¹⁴with perverted heart devises evil,
 continually sowing discord;
¹⁵therefore calamity will come upon him
  suddenly;
 in a moment he will be broken beyond
  healing.

¹⁶There are six things which the LORD hates,
 seven which are an abomination to him:
¹⁷haughty eyes, a lying tongue,
 and hands that shed innocent blood,
¹⁸a heart that devises wicked plans,
 feet that make haste to run to evil,
¹⁹a false witness who breathes out lies,
 and a man who sows discord among
  brothers.

²⁰My son, keep your father's commandment,
 and forsake not your mother's teaching.
²¹Bind them upon your heart always;
 tie them about your neck.
²²When you walk, they ᵃ will lead you;
 when you lie down, they ᵃ will watch over
  you;
 and when you awake, they ᵃ will talk with
  you.
²³For the commandment is a lamp and the
  teaching a light,
 and the reproofs of discipline are the way
  of life,
²⁴to preserve you from the evil woman,
 from the smooth tongue of the
  adventuress.

ᵃ Heb lay hold of.
ᵗ The meaning of the Hebrew word is uncertain.
ᵘ Or wealth.
ᵛ The meaning of the Hebrew word is uncertain.
ʷ Cn Compare Gk Syr: Heb the words of your mouth.
ˣ Or humble yourself.
ʸ Cn: Heb hand.
ᶻ Or taps.
ᵃ Heb it.

²⁵Do not desire her beauty in your heart,
and do not let her capture you with her
eyelashes;
²⁶for a harlot may be hired for a loaf of bread,^b
but an adulteress ^c stalks a man's very life.
²⁷Can a man carry fire in his bosom
and his clothes not be burned?
²⁸Or can one walk upon hot coals
and his feet not be scorched?
²⁹So is he who goes in to his neighbor's wife;
none who touches her will go unpunished.
³⁰Men do not despise ^d a thief if he steals
to satisfy his appetite when he is hungry.
³¹And if he is caught, he will pay sevenfold;
he will give all the goods of his house.
³²He who commits adultery has no sense;
he who does it destroys himself.
³³Wounds and dishonor will he get,
and his disgrace will not be wiped away.
³⁴For jealousy makes a man furious,
and he will not spare when he takes
revenge.
³⁵He will accept no compensation,
nor be appeased though you multiply gifts.

False Attractions of Adultery

7 My son, keep my words
and treasure up my commandments with
you;
²keep my commandments and live,
keep my teachings as the apple of your eye;
³bind them on your fingers,
write them on the tablet of your heart.
⁴Say to wisdom, "You are my sister,"
and call insight your intimate friend;
⁵to preserve you from the loose woman,
from the adventuress with her smooth
words.

⁶For at the window of my house
I have looked out through my lattice,
⁷and I have seen among the simple,
I have perceived among the youths,
a young man without sense,
⁸passing along the street near her corner,
taking the road to her house
⁹in the twilight, in the evening,
at the time of night and darkness.

¹⁰And behold, a woman meets him,
dressed as a harlot, wily of heart.^e
¹¹She is loud and wayward,
her feet do not stay at home;
¹²now in the street, now in the market,
and at every corner she lies in wait.
¹³She seizes him and kisses him,
and with impudent face she says to him:
¹⁴"I had to offer sacrifices,
and today I have paid my vows;
¹⁵so now I have come out to meet you,

to seek you eagerly, and I have found you.
¹⁶I have decked my couch with coverings,
colored spreads of Egyptian linen;
¹⁷I have perfumed my bed with myrrh,
aloes, and cinnamon.
¹⁸Come, let us take our fill of love till morning;
let us delight ourselves with love.
¹⁹For my husband is not at home;
he has gone on a long journey;
²⁰he took a bag of money with him;
at full moon he will come home."

²¹With much seductive speech she persuades
him;
with her smooth talk she compels him.
²²All at once he follows her,
as an ox goes to the slaughter,
or as a stag is caught fast ^f
²³ till an arrow pierces its entrails;
as a bird rushes into a snare;
he does not know that it will cost him his
life.

²⁴And now, O sons, listen to me,
and be attentive to the words of my mouth.
²⁵Let not your heart turn aside to her ways,
do not stray into her paths;
²⁶for many a victim has she laid low;
yes, all her slain are a mighty host.
²⁷Her house is the way to Sheol,
going down to the chambers of death.

Eternity of Wisdom

8 Does not wisdom call,
does not understanding raise her voice?
²On the heights beside the way,
in the paths she takes her stand;
³beside the gates in front of the town,
at the entrance of the portals she cries
aloud:
⁴"To you, O men, I call,
and my cry is to the sons of men.
⁵O simple ones, learn prudence;
O foolish men, pay attention.
⁶Hear, for I will speak noble things,
and from my lips will come what is right;
⁷for my mouth will utter truth;
wickedness is an abomination to my lips.
⁸All the words of my mouth are righteous;
there is nothing twisted or crooked in them.
⁹They are all straight to him who understands
and right to those who find knowledge.
¹⁰Take my instruction instead of silver,
and knowledge rather than choice gold;

---

^b Cn Compare Gk Syr Vg Tg: Heb *for because of a harlot to a piece of bread.*
^c Heb *a man's wife.*
^d Or *Do not men despise . . . ?*
^e The meaning of the Hebrew is uncertain.
^f Cn Compare Gk: Heb uncertain.
8:1–3: 1:20, 21.

[11]for wisdom is better than jewels,
and all that you may desire cannot compare
with her.
[12]I, wisdom, dwell in prudence, [g]
and I find knowledge and discretion.
[13]The fear of the LORD is hatred of evil.
Pride and arrogance and the way of evil
and perverted speech I hate.
[14]I have counsel and sound wisdom,
I have insight, I have strength.
[15]By me kings reign,
and rulers decree what is just;
[16]by me princes rule,
and nobles govern [h] the earth.
[17]I love those who love me,
and those who seek me diligently find me.
[18]Riches and honor are with me,
enduring wealth and prosperity.
[19]My fruit is better than gold, even fine gold,
and my yield than choice silver.
[20]I walk in the way of righteousness,
in the paths of justice,
[21]endowing with wealth those who love me,
and filling their treasuries.

[22]The LORD created me at the beginning of his
work,[i]
the first of his acts of old.
[23]Ages ago I was set up,
at the first, before the beginning of the
earth.
[24]When there were no depths I was brought
forth,
when there were no springs abounding with
water.
[25]Before the mountains had been shaped,
before the hills, I was brought forth;
[26]before he had made the earth with its fields, [j]
or the first of the dust [j] of the world.
[27]When he established the heavens, I was there,
when he drew a circle on the face of the
deep,
[28]when he made firm the skies above,
when he established [j] the fountains of the
deep,
[29]when he assigned to the sea its limit,
so that the waters might not transgress his
command,
when he marked out the foundations of the
earth,
[30]   then I was beside him, like a master
workman;[l]
and I was daily his [m] delight,
rejoicing before him always,
[31]rejoicing in his inhabited world
and delighting in the sons of men.

[32]And now, my sons, listen to me:
happy are those who keep my ways.

[33]Hear instruction and be wise,
and do not neglect it.
[34]Happy is the man who listens to me,
watching daily at my gates,
waiting beside my doors.
[35]For he who finds me finds life
and obtains favor from the LORD;
[36]but he who misses me injures himself;
all who hate me love death."

The Feast of Wisdom; and General Maxims

9 Wisdom has built her house,
she has set up [n] her seven pillars.
[2]She has slaughtered her beasts, she has mixed
her wine,
she has also set her table.
[3]She has sent out her maids to call
from the highest places in the town,
[4]"Whoever is simple, let him turn in here!"
To him who is without sense she says,
[5]"Come, eat of my bread
and drink of the wine I have mixed.
[6]Leave simpleness,[o] and live,
and walk in the way of insight."

[7]He who corrects a scoffer gets himself abuse,
and he who reproves a wicked man incurs
injury.
[8]Do not reprove a scoffer, or he will hate you;
reprove a wise man, and he will love you.
[9]Give instruction [p] to a wise man, and he will be
still wiser;
teach a righteous man and he will increase
in learning.
[10]The fear of the LORD is the beginning of
wisdom,
and the knowledge of the Holy One is
insight.
[11]For by me your days will be multiplied,
and years will be added to your life.
[12]If you are wise, you are wise for yourself;
if you scoff, you alone will bear it.

[13]A foolish woman is noisy;
she is wanton [q] and knows no shame.[r]
[14]She sits at the door of her house,
she takes a seat on the high places of the
town,
[15]calling to those who pass by,
who are going straight on their way,

---

[g] Heb obscure.
[h] Gk: Heb *all the governors of.*
[i] Heb *way.*
[j] The meaning of the Hebrew is uncertain.
[l] Another reading is *little child.*
[m] Gk: Heb lacks *his.*
[n] Gk Syr Tg: Heb *hewn.*
[o] Gk Syr Vg Tg: Heb *simple ones.*
[p] Heb lacks *instruction.*
[q] Cn Compare Syr Vg: The meaning of the Hebrew is uncertain.
[r] Gk Syr: The meaning of the Hebrew is uncertain.

¹⁶"Whoever is simple, let him turn in here!"
  And to him who is without sense she says,
¹⁷"Stolen water is sweet,
  and bread eaten in secret is pleasant."
¹⁸But he does not know that the dead ^s are there,
  that her guests are in the depths of Sheol.

Wise Sayings of Solomon

10 The proverbs of Solomon.

A wise son makes a glad father,
  but a foolish son is a sorrow to his mother.
²Treasures gained by wickedness do not profit,
  but righteousness delivers from death.
³The Lord does not let the righteous go hungry,
  but he thwarts the craving of the wicked.
⁴A slack hand causes poverty,
  but the hand of the diligent makes rich.
⁵A son who gathers in summer is prudent,
  but a son who sleeps in harvest brings
  shame.
⁶Blessings are on the head of the righteous,
  but the mouth of the wicked conceals
  violence.
⁷The memory of the righteous is a blessing,
  but the name of the wicked will rot.
⁸The wise of heart will heed commandments,
  but a prating fool will come to ruin.
⁹He who walks in integrity walks securely,
  but he who perverts his ways will be found
  out.
¹⁰He who winks the eye causes trouble,
  but he who boldly reproves makes peace.^t
¹¹The mouth of the righteous is a fountain of
  life,
  but the mouth of the wicked conceals
  violence.
¹²Hatred stirs up strife,
  but love covers all offenses.
¹³On the lips of him who has understanding
  wisdom is found,
  but a rod is for the back of him who lacks
  sense.
¹⁴Wise men lay up knowledge,
  but the babbling of a fool brings ruin near.
¹⁵A rich man's wealth is his strong city;
  the poverty of the poor is their ruin.
¹⁶The wage of the righteous leads to life,
  the gain of the wicked to sin.
¹⁷He who heeds instruction is on the path to life,
  but he who rejects reproof goes astray.
¹⁸He who conceals hatred has lying lips,
  and he who utters slander is a fool.
¹⁹When words are many, transgression is not
  lacking,
  but he who restrains his lips is prudent.
²⁰The tongue of the righteous is choice silver;
  the mind of the wicked is of little worth.
²¹The lips of the righteous feed many,
  but fools die for lack of sense.

²²The blessing of the Lord makes rich,
  and he adds no sorrow with it.^u
²³It is like sport to a fool to do wrong,
  but wise conduct is pleasure to a man of
  understanding.
²⁴What the wicked dreads will come upon him,
  but the desire of the righteous will be
  granted.
²⁵When the tempest passes, the wicked is no
  more,
  but the righteous is established for ever.
²⁶Like vinegar to the teeth, and smoke to the
  eyes,
  so is the sluggard to those who send him.
²⁷The fear of the Lord prolongs life,
  but the years of the wicked will be short.
²⁸The hope of the righteous ends in gladness,
  but the expectation of the wicked comes to
  nothing.
²⁹The Lord is a stronghold to him whose way is
  upright,
  but destruction to evildoers.
³⁰The righteous will never be removed,
  but the wicked will not dwell in the land.
³¹The mouth of the righteous brings forth
  wisdom,
  but the perverse tongue will be cut off.
³²The lips of the righteous know what is
  acceptable,
  but the mouth of the wicked, what is
  perverse.

11 A false balance is an abomination to the Lord,
  but a just weight is his delight.
²When pride comes, then comes disgrace;
  but with the humble is wisdom.
³The integrity of the upright guides them,
  but the crookedness of the treacherous
  destroys them.
⁴Riches do not profit in the day of wrath,
  but righteousness delivers from death.
⁵The righteousness of the blameless keeps his
  way straight,
  but the wicked falls by his own
  wickedness.
⁶The righteousness of the upright delivers
  them,
  but the treacherous are taken captive by
  their lust.
⁷When the wicked dies, his hope perishes,
  and the expectation of the godless comes to
  nothing.
⁸The righteous is delivered from trouble,
  and the wicked gets into it instead.

---

^s Heb *shades.*
^t Gk: Heb *but a prating fool will come to ruin.*
^u Or *and toil adds nothing to it.*
10:12: Jas 5:20; 1 Pet 4:8.

⁹With his mouth the godless man would destroy
his neighbor,
but by knowledge the righteous are
delivered.
¹⁰When it goes well with the righteous, the city
rejoices;
and when the wicked perish there are
shouts of gladness.
¹¹By the blessing of the upright a city is exalted,
but it is overthrown by the mouth of the
wicked.
¹²He who belittles his neighbor lacks sense,
but a man of understanding remains
silent.
¹³He who goes about as a talebearer reveals
secrets,
but he who is trustworthy in spirit keeps a
thing hidden.
¹⁴Where there is no guidance, a people falls;
but in an abundance of counselors there is
safety.
¹⁵He who gives surety for a stranger will smart
for it,
but he who hates suretyship is secure.
¹⁶A gracious woman gets honor,
and violent men get riches.
¹⁷A man who is kind benefits himself,
but a cruel man hurts himself.
¹⁸A wicked man earns deceptive wages,
but one who sows righteousness gets a sure
reward.
¹⁹He who is steadfast in righteousness will live,
but he who pursues evil will die.
²⁰Men of perverse mind are an abomination to
the LORD,
but those of blameless ways are his
delight.
²¹Be assured, an evil man will not go
unpunished,
but those who are righteous will be
delivered.
²²Like a gold ring in a swine's snout
is a beautiful woman without discretion.
²³The desire of the righteous ends only in good;
the expectation of the wicked in wrath.
²⁴One man gives freely, yet grows all the richer;
another withholds what he should give, and
only suffers want.
²⁵A liberal man will be enriched,
and one who waters will himself be
watered.
²⁶The people curse him who holds back grain,
but a blessing is on the head of him who
sells it.
²⁷He who diligently seeks good seeks favor,
but evil comes to him who searches for it.
²⁸He who trusts in his riches will wither,ᵛ
but the righteous will flourish like a green
leaf.

²⁹He who troubles his household will inherit
wind,
and the fool will be servant to the wise.
³⁰The fruit of the righteous is a tree of life,
but lawlessnessʷ takes away lives.
³¹If the righteous is repaid on earth,
how much more the wicked and the sinner!

12

Whoever loves discipline loves
knowledge,
but he who hates reproof is stupid.
²A good man obtains favor from the LORD,
but a man of evil devices he condemns.
³A man is not established by wickedness,
but the root of the righteous will never be
moved.
⁴A good wife is the crown of her husband,
but she who brings shame is like rottenness
in his bones.
⁵The thoughts of the righteous are just;
the counsels of the wicked are treacherous.
⁶The words of the wicked lie in wait for blood,
but the mouth of the upright delivers men.
⁷The wicked are overthrown and are no more,
but the house of the righteous will stand.
⁸A man is commended according to his good
sense,
but one of perverse mind is despised.
⁹Better is a man of humble standing who works
for himself
than one who plays the great man but lacks
bread.
¹⁰A righteous man has regard for the life of his
beast,
but the mercy of the wicked is cruel.
¹¹He who tills his land will have plenty of
bread,
but he who follows worthless pursuits has
no sense.
¹²The strong tower of the wicked comes to ruin,
but the root of the righteous stands firm.ˣ
¹³An evil man is ensnared by the transgression
of his lips,
but the righteous escapes from trouble.
¹⁴From the fruit of his words a man is satisfied
with good,
and the work of a man's hand comes back
to him.
¹⁵The way of a fool is right in his own eyes,
but a wise man listens to advice.
¹⁶The vexation of a fool is known at once,
but the prudent man ignores an insult.
¹⁷He who speaks the truth gives honest
evidence,
but a false witness utters deceit.

ᵛ Cn: Heb *fall.*
ʷ Cn Compare Gk Syr: Heb *a wise man.*
ˣ Cn: The Hebrew of verse 12 is obscure.
11:31 (Gk): 1 Pet 4:18.

¹⁸There is one whose rash words are like sword
thrusts,
but the tongue of the wise brings healing.
¹⁹Truthful lips endure for ever,
but a lying tongue is but for a moment.
²⁰Deceit is in the heart of those who devise
evil,
but those who plan good have joy.
²¹No ill befalls the righteous,
but the wicked are filled with trouble.
²²Lying lips are an abomination to the LORD,
but those who act faithfully are his delight.
²³A prudent man conceals his knowledge,
but fools ʸ proclaim their folly.
²⁴The hand of the diligent will rule,
while the slothful will be put to forced labor.
²⁵Anxiety in a man's heart weighs him down,
but a good word makes him glad.
²⁶A righteous man turns away from evil,ᶻ
but the way of the wicked leads them
astray.
²⁷A slothful man will not catch his prey,ᵃ
but the diligent man will get precious
wealth.ᵇ
²⁸In the path of righteousness is life,
but the way of error leads to death.ᶜ

13 A wise son hears his father's instruction,
but a scoffer does not listen to rebuke.
²From the fruit of his mouth a good man eats
good,
but the desire of the treacherous is for
violence.
³He who guards his mouth preserves his life;
he who opens wide his lips comes to ruin.
⁴The soul of the sluggard craves, and gets
nothing,
while the soul of the diligent is richly
supplied.
⁵A righteous man hates falsehood,
but a wicked man acts shamefully and
disgracefully.
⁶Righteousness guards him whose way is
upright,
but sin overthrows the wicked.
⁷One man pretends to be rich, yet has nothing;
another pretends to be poor, yet has great
wealth.
⁸The ransom of a man's life is his wealth,
but a poor man has no means of
redemption.ᵈ
⁹The light of the righteous rejoices,
but the lamp of the wicked will be put out.
¹⁰By insolence the heedless make strife,
but with those who take advice is wisdom.
¹¹Wealth hastily gotten ᵉ will dwindle,
but he who gathers little by little will
increase it.
¹²Hope deferred makes the heart sick,
but a desire fulfilled is a tree of life.

¹³He who despises the word brings destruction
on himself,
but he who respects the commandment will
be rewarded.
¹⁴The teaching of the wise is a fountain of life,
that one may avoid the snares of death.
¹⁵Good sense wins favor,
but the way of the faithless is their ruin. ᶠ
¹⁶In everything a prudent man acts with
knowledge,
but a fool flaunts his folly.
¹⁷A bad messenger plunges men into trouble,
but a faithful envoy brings healing.
¹⁸Poverty and disgrace come to him who ignores
instruction,
but he who heeds reproof is honored.
¹⁹A desire fulfilled is sweet to the soul;
but to turn away from evil is an
abomination to fools.
²⁰He who walks with wise men becomes wise,
but the companion of fools will suffer harm.
²¹Misfortune pursues sinners,
but prosperity rewards the righteous.
²²A good man leaves an inheritance to his
children's children,
but the sinner's wealth is laid up for the
righteous.
²³The fallow ground of the poor yields much
food,
but it is swept away through injustice.
²⁴He who spares the rod hates his son,
but he who loves him is diligent to
discipline him.
²⁵The righteous has enough to satisfy his
appetite,
but the belly of the wicked suffers want.

14 Wisdom ᵍ builds her house,
but folly with her own hands tears it
down.
²He who walks in uprightness fears the LORD,
but he who is devious in his ways despises
him.
³The talk of a fool is a rod for his back,ʰ
but the lips of the wise will preserve them.
⁴Where there are no oxen, there is no ⁱ grain;
but abundant crops come by the strength of
the ox.
⁵A faithful witness does not lie,
but a false witness breathes out lies.

ʸ Heb *the heart of fools.*
ᶻ Cn: The meaning of the Hebrew is uncertain.
ᵃ Cn Compare Gk Syr: The meaning of the Hebrew is uncertain.
ᵇ Cn: The meaning of the Hebrew is uncertain.
ᶜ Cn: The meaning of the Hebrew is uncertain.
ᵈ Cn: Heb *does not hear rebuke.*
ᵉ Gk Vg: Heb *from vanity.*
ᶠ Cn Compare Gk Syr Vg Tg: Heb *is enduring.*
ᵍ Heb *Wisdom of women.*
ʰ Cn: Heb *a rod of pride.*
ⁱ Heb *a manger of.*

[6]A scoffer seeks wisdom in vain,
  but knowledge is easy for a man of
    understanding.
[7]Leave the presence of a fool,
  for there you do not meet words of
    knowledge.
[8]The wisdom of a prudent man is to discern his
    way,
  but the folly of fools is deceiving.
[9]God scorns the wicked, [j]
  but the upright enjoy his favor.
[10]The heart knows its own bitterness,
  and no stranger shares its joy.
[11]The house of the wicked will be destroyed,
  but the tent of the upright will flourish.
[12]There is a way which seems right to a man,
  but its end is the way to death.[k]
[13]Even in laughter the heart is sad,
  and the end of joy is grief.
[14]A perverse man will be filled with the fruit of
    his ways,
  and a good man with the fruit of his
    deeds.[1]
[15]The simple believes everything,
  but the prudent looks where he is going.
[16]A wise man is cautious and turns away from
    evil,
  but a fool throws off restraint and is
    careless.
[17]A man of quick temper acts foolishly,
  but a man of discretion is patient.[m]
[18]The simple acquire folly,
  but the prudent are crowned with
    knowledge.
[19]The evil bow down before the good,
  the wicked at the gates of the righteous.
[20]The poor is disliked even by his neighbor,
  but the rich has many friends.
[21]He who despises his neighbor is a sinner,
  but happy is he who is kind to the poor.
[22]Do they not err that devise evil?
  Those who devise good meet loyalty and
    faithfulness.
[23]In all toil there is profit,
  but mere talk tends only to want.
[24]The crown of the wise is their wisdom,[n]
  but folly is the garland[o] of fools.
[25]A truthful witness saves lives,
  but one who utters lies is a betrayer.
[26]In the fear of the LORD one has strong
    confidence,
  and his children will have a refuge.
[27]The fear of the LORD is a fountain of life,
  that one may avoid the snares of death.
[28]In a multitude of people is the glory of a king,
  but without people a prince is ruined.
[29]He who is slow to anger has great
    understanding,
  but he who has a hasty temper exalts folly.

[30]A tranquil mind gives life to the flesh,
  but passion makes the bones rot.
[31]He who oppresses a poor man insults his
    Maker,
  but he who is kind to the needy honors him.
[32]The wicked is overthrown through his evil-
    doing,
  but the righteous finds refuge through his
    integrity. [p]
[33]Wisdom abides in the mind of a man of
    understanding,
  but it is not [q] known in the heart of fools.
[34]Righteousness exalts a nation,
  but sin is a reproach to any people.
[35]A servant who deals wisely has the king's
    favor,
  but his wrath falls on one who acts
    shamefully.

15 A soft answer turns away wrath,
  but a harsh word stirs up anger.
[2]The tongue of the wise dispenses
    knowledge, [r]
  but the mouths of fools pour out folly.
[3]The eyes of the LORD are in every place,
  keeping watch on the evil and the good.
[4]A gentle tongue is a tree of life,
  but perverseness in it breaks the spirit.
[5]A fool despises his father's instruction,
  but he who heeds admonition is prudent.
[6]In the house of the righteous there is much
    treasure,
  but trouble befalls the income of the
    wicked.
[7]The lips of the wise spread knowledge;
  not so the minds of fools.
[8]The sacrifice of the wicked is an abomination
    to the LORD,
  but the prayer of the upright is his delight.
[9]The way of the wicked is an abomination to
    the LORD,
  but he loves him who pursues
    righteousness.
[10]There is severe discipline for him who forsakes
    the way;
  he who hates reproof will die.
[11]Sheol and Abad'don lie open before the LORD,
  how much more the hearts of men!
[12]A scoffer does not like to be reproved;
  he will not go to the wise.
[13]A glad heart makes a cheerful countenance,
  but by sorrow of heart the spirit is broken.

---

[j] Cn: Heb obscure.
[k] Heb *ways of death.*
[1] Cn: Heb *from upon him.*
[m] Gk: Heb *is hated.*
[n] Cn Compare Gk: Heb *riches.*
[o] Cn: Heb *folly.*
[p] Gk Syr: Heb *in his death.*
[q] Gk Syr: Heb lacks *not.*
[r] Cn: Heb *makes knowledge good.*

¹⁴The mind of him who has understanding seeks
   knowledge,
   but the mouths of fools feed on folly.
¹⁵All the days of the afflicted are evil,
   but a cheerful heart has a continual feast.
¹⁶Better is a little with the fear of the Lord
   than great treasure and trouble with it.
¹⁷Better is a dinner of herbs where love is
   than a fatted ox and hatred with it.
¹⁸A hot-tempered man stirs up strife,
   but he who is slow to anger quiets
   contention.
¹⁹The way of a sluggard is overgrown with
   thorns,
   but the path of the upright is a level
   highway.
²⁰A wise son makes a glad father,
   but a foolish man despises his mother.
²¹Folly is a joy to him who has no sense,
   but a man of understanding walks aright.
²²Without counsel plans go wrong,
   but with many advisers they succeed.
²³To make an apt answer is a joy to a man,
   and a word in season, how good it is!
²⁴The wise man's path leads upward to life,
   that he may avoid Sheol beneath.
²⁵The Lord tears down the house of the proud,
   but maintains the widow's boundaries.
²⁶The thoughts of the wicked are an abomination
   to the Lord,
   the words of the pure are pleasing to him. ˢ
²⁷He who is greedy for unjust gain makes trouble
   for his household,
   but he who hates bribes will live.
²⁸The mind of the righteous ponders how to
   answer,
   but the mouth of the wicked pours out evil
   things.
²⁹The Lord is far from the wicked,
   but he hears the prayer of the righteous.
³⁰The light of the eyes rejoices the heart,
   and good news refreshes ᵗ the bones.
³¹He whose ear heeds wholesome admonition
   will abide among the wise.
³²He who ignores instruction despises himself,
   but he who heeds admonition gains
   understanding.
³³The fear of the Lord is instruction in wisdom,
   and humility goes before honor.

Solomon's Proverbs on Life and Conduct

16 The plans of the mind belong to man,
   but the answer of the tongue is from
   the Lord.
²All the ways of a man are pure in his own eyes,
   but the Lord weighs the spirit.
³Commit your work to the Lord,
   and your plans will be established.
⁴The Lord has made everything for its purpose,
   even the wicked for the day of trouble.

⁵Every one who is arrogant is an abomination to
   the Lord;
   be assured, he will not go unpunished.
⁶By loyalty and faithfulness iniquity is atoned
   for,
   and by the fear of the Lord a man avoids
   evil.
⁷When a man's ways please the Lord,
   he makes even his enemies to be at peace
   with him.
⁸Better is a little with righteousness
   than great revenues with injustice.
⁹A man's mind plans his way,
   but the Lord directs his steps.
¹⁰Inspired decisions are on the lips of a king;
   his mouth does not sin in judgment.
¹¹A just balance and scales are the Lord's;
   all the weights in the bag are his work.
¹²It is an abomination to kings to do evil,
   for the throne is established by
   righteousness.
¹³Righteous lips are the delight of a king,
   and he loves him who speaks what is
   right.
¹⁴A king's wrath is a messenger of death,
   and a wise man will appease it.
¹⁵In the light of a king's face there is life,
   and his favor is like the clouds that bring
   the spring rain.
¹⁶To get wisdom is better ᵘ than gold;
   to get understanding is to be chosen rather
   than silver.
¹⁷The highway of the upright turns aside from
   evil;
   he who guards his way preserves his life.
¹⁸Pride goes before destruction,
   and a haughty spirit before a fall.
¹⁹It is better to be of a lowly spirit with the poor
   than to divide the spoil with the proud.
²⁰He who gives heed to the word will prosper,
   and happy is he who trusts in the Lord.
²¹The wise of heart is called a man of
   discernment,
   and pleasant speech increases
   persuasiveness.
²²Wisdom is a fountain of life to him who has it,
   but folly is the chastisement of fools.
²³The mind of the wise makes his speech
   judicious,
   and adds persuasiveness to his lips.
²⁴Pleasant words are like a honeycomb,
   sweetness to the soul and health to the
   body.
²⁵There is a way which seems right to a man,
   but its end is the way to death. ᵛ

ˢ Cn Compare Gk: Heb *pleasant words are pure.*
ᵗ Heb *makes fat.*
ᵘ Gk Syr Vg Tg: Heb *how much better.*
ᵛ Heb *ways of death.*

²⁶A worker's appetite works for him;
    his mouth urges him on.
²⁷A worthless man plots evil,
    and his speech is like a scorching fire.
²⁸A perverse man spreads strife,
    and a whisperer separates close friends.
²⁹A man of violence entices his neighbor
    and leads him in a way that is not good.
³⁰He who winks his eyes plans ^w perverse
    things,
    he who compresses his lips brings evil to
    pass.
³¹A hoary head is a crown of glory;
    it is gained in a righteous life.
³²He who is slow to anger is better than the
    mighty,
    and he who rules his spirit than he who
    takes a city.
³³The lot is cast into the lap,
    but the decision is wholly from the LORD.

17 Better is a dry morsel with quiet
    than a house full of feasting with
    strife.
²A slave who deals wisely will rule over a son
    who acts shamefully,
    and will share the inheritance as one of the
    brothers.
³The crucible is for silver, and the furnace is for
    gold,
    and the LORD tries hearts.
⁴An evildoer listens to wicked lips;
    and a liar gives heed to a mischievous
    tongue.
⁵He who mocks the poor insults his Maker;
    he who is glad at calamity will not go
    unpunished.
⁶Grandchildren are the crown of the aged,
    and the glory of sons is their fathers.
⁷Fine speech is not becoming to a fool;
    still less is false speech to a prince.
⁸A bribe is like a magic stone in the eyes of him
    who gives it;
    wherever he turns he prospers.
⁹He who forgives an offense seeks love,
    but he who repeats a matter alienates a
    friend.
¹⁰A rebuke goes deeper into a man of
    understanding
    than a hundred blows into a fool.
¹¹An evil man seeks only rebellion,
    and a cruel messenger will be sent against
    him.
¹²Let a man meet a she-bear robbed of her cubs,
    rather than a fool in his folly.
¹³If a man returns evil for good,
    evil will not depart from his house.
¹⁴The beginning of strife is like letting out
    water;
    so quit before the quarrel breaks out.

¹⁵He who justifies the wicked and he who
    condemns the righteous
    are both alike an abomination to the LORD.
¹⁶Why should a fool have a price in his hand to
    buy wisdom,
    when he has no mind?
¹⁷A friend loves at all times,
    and a brother is born for adversity.
¹⁸A man without sense gives a pledge,
    and becomes surety in the presence of his
    neighbor.
¹⁹He who loves transgression loves strife;
    he who makes his door high seeks
    destruction.
²⁰A man of crooked mind does not prosper,
    and one with a perverse tongue falls into
    calamity.
²¹A stupid son is a grief to a father;
    and the father of a fool has no joy.
²²A cheerful heart is a good medicine,
    but a downcast spirit dries up the bones.
²³A wicked man accepts a bribe from the bosom
    to pervert the ways of justice.
²⁴A man of understanding sets his face toward
    wisdom,
    but the eyes of a fool are on the ends of the
    earth.
²⁵A foolish son is a grief to his father
    and bitterness to her who bore him.
²⁶To impose a fine on a righteous man is not
    good;
    to flog noble men is wrong.
²⁷He who restrains his words has knowledge,
    and he who has a cool spirit is a man of
    understanding.
²⁸Even a fool who keeps silent is considered
    wise;
    when he closes his lips, he is deemed
    intelligent.

18 He who is estranged ^x seeks pretexts ^y
    to break out against all sound judgment.
²A fool takes no pleasure in understanding,
    but only in expressing his opinion.
³When wickedness comes, contempt comes
    also;
    and with dishonor comes disgrace.
⁴The words of a man's mouth are deep waters;
    the fountain of wisdom is a gushing
    stream.
⁵It is not good to be partial to a wicked man,
    or to deprive a righteous man of justice.
⁶A fool's lips bring strife,
    and his mouth invites a flogging.
⁷A fool's mouth is his ruin,
    and his lips are a snare to himself.

---

^w Gk Syr Vg Tg: Heb *to plan*.
^x Heb *separated*.
^y Gk Vg: Heb *desire*.

[8]The words of a whisperer are like delicious morsels;
  they go down into the inner parts of the body.

[9]He who is slack in his work
  is a brother to him who destroys.

[10]The name of the LORD is a strong tower;
  the righteous man runs into it and is safe.

[11]A rich man's wealth is his strong city,
  and like a high wall protecting him.[z]

[12]Before destruction a man's heart is haughty,
  but humility goes before honor.

[13]If one gives answer before he hears,
  it is his folly and shame.

[14]A man's spirit will endure sickness;
  but a broken spirit who can bear?

[15]An intelligent mind acquires knowledge,
  and the ear of the wise seeks knowledge.

[16]A man's gift makes room for him
  and brings him before great men.

[17]He who states his case first seems right,
  until the other comes and examines him.

[18]The lot puts an end to disputes
  and decides between powerful contenders.

[19]A brother helped is like a strong city,[a]
  but quarreling is like the bars of a castle.

[20]From the fruit of his mouth a man is satisfied;
  he is satisfied by the yield of his lips.

[21]Death and life are in the power of the tongue,
  and those who love it will eat its fruits.

[22]He who finds a wife finds a good thing,
  and obtains favor from the LORD.

[23]The poor use entreaties,
  but the rich answer roughly.

[24]There are[b] friends who pretend to be friends,[c]
  but there is a friend who sticks closer than a brother.

19

Better is a poor man who walks in his integrity
  than a man who is perverse in speech, and is a fool.

[2]It is not good for a man to be without knowledge,
  and he who makes haste with his feet misses his way.

[3]When a man's folly brings his way to ruin,
  his heart rages against the LORD.

[4]Wealth brings many new friends,
  but a poor man is deserted by his friend.

[5]A false witness will not go unpunished,
  and he who utters lies will not escape.

[6]Many seek the favor of a generous man,
  and every one is a friend to a man who gives gifts.

[7]All a poor man's brothers hate him;
  how much more do his friends go far from him!

He pursues them with words, but does not have them.[d]

[8]He who gets wisdom loves himself;
  he who keeps understanding will prosper.

[9]A false witness will not go unpunished,
  and he who utters lies will perish.

[10]It is not fitting for a fool to live in luxury,
  much less for a slave to rule over princes.

[11]Good sense makes a man slow to anger,
  and it is his glory to overlook an offense.

[12]A king's wrath is like the growling of a lion,
  but his favor is like dew upon the grass.

[13]A foolish son is ruin to his father,
  and a wife's quarreling is a continual dripping of rain.

[14]House and wealth are inherited from fathers,
  but a prudent wife is from the LORD.

[15]Slothfulness casts into a deep sleep,
  and an idle person will suffer hunger.

[16]He who keeps the commandment keeps his life;
  he who despises the word[e] will die.

[17]He who is kind to the poor lends to the LORD,
  and he will repay him for his deed.

[18]Discipline your son while there is hope;
  do not set your heart on his destruction.

[19]A man of great wrath will pay the penalty;
  for if you deliver him, you will only have to do it again.[f]

[20]Listen to advice and accept instruction,
  that you may gain wisdom for the future.

[21]Many are the plans in the mind of a man,
  but it is the purpose of the LORD that will be established.

[22]What is desired in a man is loyalty,
  and a poor man is better than a liar.

[23]The fear of the LORD leads to life;
  and he who has it rests satisfied;
  he will not be visited by harm.

[24]The sluggard buries his hand in the dish,
  and will not even bring it back to his mouth.

[25]Strike a scoffer, and the simple will learn prudence;
  reprove a man of understanding, and he will gain knowledge.

[26]He who does violence to his father and chases away his mother
  is a son who causes shame and brings reproach.

[27]Cease, my son, to hear instruction
  only to stray from the words of knowledge.

[28]A worthless witness mocks at justice,
  and the mouth of the wicked devours iniquity.

---

[z] Or in his imagination.
[a] Gk Syr Vg Tg: The meaning of the Hebrew is uncertain.
[b] Syr Tg: Heb A man of.
[c] Cn Compare Syr Vg Tg: Heb to be broken.
[d] Heb uncertain.
[e] Cn Compare 13:13: Heb his ways.
[f] Heb obscure.

²⁹Condemnation is ready for scoffers,
and flogging for the backs of fools.

20
Wine is a mocker, strong drink a brawler;
and whoever is led astray by it is not
wise.

²The dread wrath of a king is like the growling
of a lion;
he who provokes him to anger forfeits his
life.

³It is an honor for a man to keep aloof from
strife;
but every fool will be quarreling.

⁴The sluggard does not plow in the autumn;
he will seek at harvest and have nothing.

⁵The purpose in a man's mind is like deep
water,
but a man of understanding will draw it
out.

⁶Many a man proclaims his own loyalty,
but a faithful man who can find?

⁷A righteous man who walks in his integrity—
blessed are his sons after him!

⁸A king who sits on the throne of judgment
winnows all evil with his eyes.

⁹Who can say, "I have made my heart clean;
I am pure from my sin"?

¹⁰Diverse weights and diverse measures
are both alike an abomination to the Lord.

¹¹Even a child makes himself known by his
acts,
whether what he does is pure and right.

¹²The hearing ear and the seeing eye,
the Lord has made them both.

¹³Love not sleep, lest you come to poverty;
open your eyes, and you will have plenty of
bread.

¹⁴"It is bad, it is bad," says the buyer;
but when he goes away, then he boasts.

¹⁵There is gold, and abundance of costly stones;
but the lips of knowledge are a precious
jewel.

¹⁶Take a man's garment when he has given
surety for a stranger,
and hold him in pledge when he gives
surety for foreigners.

¹⁷Bread gained by deceit is sweet to a man,
but afterward his mouth will be full of
gravel.

¹⁸Plans are established by counsel;
by wise guidance wage war.

¹⁹He who goes about gossiping reveals secrets;
therefore do not associate with one who
speaks foolishly.

²⁰If one curses his father or his mother,
his lamp will be put out in utter darkness.

²¹An inheritance gotten hastily in the beginning
will in the end not be blessed.

²²Do not say, "I will repay evil";
wait for the Lord, and he will help you.

²³Diverse weights are an abomination to the Lord,
and false scales are not good.

²⁴A man's steps are ordered by the Lord;
how then can man understand his way?

²⁵It is a snare for a man to say rashly, "It is holy,"
and to reflect only after making his vows.

²⁶A wise king winnows the wicked,
and drives the wheel over them.

²⁷The spirit of man is the lamp of the Lord,
searching all his innermost parts.

²⁸Loyalty and faithfulness preserve the king
and his throne is upheld by righteousness. ᵍ

²⁹The glory of young men is their strength,
but the beauty of old men is their gray
hair.

³⁰Blows that wound cleanse away evil;
strokes make clean the innermost parts.

21
The king's heart is a stream of water in
the hand of the Lord;
he turns it wherever he will.

²Every way of a man is right in his own eyes,
but the Lord weighs the heart.

³To do righteousness and justice
is more acceptable to the Lord than
sacrifice.

⁴Haughty eyes and a proud heart,
the lamp of the wicked, are sin.

⁵The plans of the diligent lead surely to
abundance,
but every one who is hasty comes only to
want.

⁶The getting of treasures by a lying tongue
is a fleeting vapor and a snare of death.

⁷The violence of the wicked will sweep them
away,
because they refuse to do what is just.

⁸The way of the guilty is crooked,
but the conduct of the pure is right.

⁹It is better to live in a corner of the housetop
than in a house shared with a contentious
woman.

¹⁰The soul of the wicked desires evil;
his neighbor finds no mercy in his eyes.

¹¹When a scoffer is punished, the simple becomes
wise;
when a wise man is instructed, he gains
knowledge.

¹²The righteous observes the house of the
wicked;
the wicked are cast down to ruin.

¹³He who closes his ear to the cry of the poor
will himself cry out and not be heard.

¹⁴A gift in secret averts anger;
and a bribe in the bosom, strong wrath.

¹⁵When justice is done, it is a joy to the
righteous,
but dismay to evildoers.

ᵍ Gk: Heb *loyalty.*

¹⁶A man who wanders from the way of
  understanding
  will rest in the assembly of the dead.
¹⁷He who loves pleasure will be a poor man;
  he who loves wine and oil will not be rich.
¹⁸The wicked is a ransom for the righteous,
  and the faithless for the upright.
¹⁹It is better to live in a desert land
  than with a contentious and fretful woman.
²⁰Precious treasure remains ^h in a wise man's
  dwelling,
  but a foolish man devours it.
²¹He who pursues righteousness and kindness
  will find life ⁱ and honor.
²²A wise man scales the city of the mighty
  and brings down the stronghold in which
  they trust.
²³He who keeps his mouth and his tongue
  keeps himself out of trouble.
²⁴"Scoffer" is the name of the proud, haughty
  man
  who acts with arrogant pride.
²⁵The desire of the sluggard kills him
  for his hands refuse to labor.
²⁶All day long the wicked covets, ^j
  but the righteous gives and does not hold
  back.
²⁷The sacrifice of the wicked is an abomination;
  how much more when he brings it with evil
  intent.
²⁸A false witness will perish,
  but the word of a man who hears will
  endure.
²⁹A wicked man puts on a bold face,
  but an upright man considers ^k his ways.
³⁰No wisdom, no understanding, no counsel,
  can avail against the LORD.
³¹The horse is made ready for the day of battle,
  but the victory belongs to the LORD.

22 A good name is to be chosen rather than
  great riches,
  and favor is better than silver or gold.
²The rich and the poor meet together;
  the LORD is the maker of them all.
³A prudent man sees danger and hides
  himself;
  but the simple go on, and suffer for it.
⁴The reward for humility and fear of the LORD
  is riches and honor and life.
⁵Thorns and snares are in the way of the
  perverse;
  he who guards himself will keep far from
  them.
⁶Train up a child in the way he should go,
  and when he is old he will not depart from it.
⁷The rich rules over the poor,
  and the borrower is the slave of the lender.
⁸He who sows injustice will reap calamity,
  and the rod of his fury will fail.

⁹He who has a bountiful eye will be blessed,
  for he shares his bread with the poor.
¹⁰Drive out a scoffer, and strife will go out,
  and quarreling and abuse will cease.
¹¹He who loves purity of heart,
  and whose speech is gracious, will have the
  king as his friend.
¹²The eyes of the LORD keep watch over
  knowledge,
  but he overthrows the words of the
  faithless.
¹³The sluggard says, "There is a lion outside!
  I shall be slain in the streets!"
¹⁴The mouth of a loose woman is a deep pit;
  he with whom the LORD is angry will fall
  into it.
¹⁵Folly is bound up in the heart of a child,
  but the rod of discipline drives it far from
  him.
¹⁶He who oppresses the poor to increase his own
  wealth,
  or gives to the rich, will only come to want.

Sayings of the Wise
¹⁷Incline your ear, and hear the words of the
  wise,
  and apply your mind to my knowledge;
¹⁸for it will be pleasant if you keep them within
  you,
  if all of them are ready on your lips.
¹⁹That your trust may be in the LORD,
  I have made them known to you today, even
  to you.

²⁰Have I not written for you thirty sayings
  of admonition and knowledge,
²¹to show you what is right and true,
  that you may give a true answer to those
  who sent you?

²²Do not rob the poor, because he is poor,
  or crush the afflicted at the gate;
²³for the LORD will plead their cause
  and despoil of life those who despoil them.
²⁴Make no friendship with a man given to anger,
  nor go with a wrathful man,
²⁵lest you learn his ways
  and entangle yourself in a snare.
²⁶Be not one of those who give pledges,
  who become surety for debts.
²⁷If you have nothing with which to pay,
  why should your bed be taken from under
  you?
²⁸Remove not the ancient landmark
  which your fathers have set.

^h Gk: Heb *and oil.*
ⁱ Gk: Heb *life and righteousness.*
^j Gk: Heb *all day long he covets covetously.*
^k Another reading is *establishes.*
22:8 (Gk): 1 Cor 9.7.

[29]Do you see a man skilful in his work?
he will stand before kings;
he will not stand before obscure men.

Precepts and Warnings

23 When you sit down to eat with a ruler,
observe carefully what [1] is before you;
[2]and put a knife to your throat
if you are a man given to appetite.
[3]Do not desire his delicacies,
for they are deceptive food.
[4]Do not toil to acquire wealth;
be wise enough to desist.
[5]When your eyes light upon it, it is gone;
for suddenly it takes to itself wings,
flying like an eagle toward heaven.
[6]Do not eat the bread of a man who is stingy;
do not desire his delicacies;
[7]for he is like one who is inwardly reckoning.[m]
"Eat and drink!" he says to you;
but his heart is not with you.
[8]You will vomit up the morsels which you have
eaten,
and waste your pleasant words.
[9]Do not speak in the hearing of a fool,
for he will despise the wisdom of your
words.
[10]Do not remove an ancient landmark
or enter the fields of the fatherless;
[11]for their Redeemer is strong;
he will plead their cause against you.
[12]Apply your mind to instruction
and your ear to words of knowledge.
[13]Do not withhold discipline from a child;
if you beat him with a rod, he will not die.
[14]If you beat him with the rod
you will save his life from Sheol.
[15]My son, if your heart is wise,
my heart too will be glad.
[16]My soul will rejoice
when your lips speak what is right.
[17]Let not your heart envy sinners,
but continue in the fear of the Lord all the
day.
[18]Surely there is a future,
and your hope will not be cut off.

[19]Hear, my son, and be wise,
and direct your mind in the way.
[20]Be not among winebibbers,
or among gluttonous eaters of meat;
[21]for the drunkard and the glutton will come to
poverty,
and drowsiness will clothe a man with rags.

[22]Listen to your father who begot you,
and do not despise your mother when she is
old.
[23]Buy truth, and do not sell it;
buy wisdom, instruction, and understanding.

[24]The father of the righteous will greatly
rejoice;
he who begets a wise son will be glad in
him.
[25]Let your father and mother be glad,
let her who bore you rejoice.
[26]My son, give me your heart,
and let your eyes observe [n] my ways.
[27]For a harlot is a deep pit;
an adventuress is a narrow well.
[28]She lies in wait like a robber
and increases the faithless among men.

[29]Who has woe? Who has sorrow?
Who has strife? Who has complaining?
Who has wounds without cause? Who has
redness of eyes?
[30]Those who tarry long over wine,
those who go to try mixed wine.
[31]Do not look at wine when it is red,
when it sparkles in the cup
and goes down smoothly.
[32]At the last it bites like a serpent,
and stings like an adder.
[33]Your eyes will see strange things,
and your mind utter perverse things.
[34]You will be like one who lies down in the midst
of the sea,
like one who lies on the top of a mast. [o]
[35]"They struck me," you will say, [p] "but I was
not hurt;
they beat me, but I did not feel it.
When shall I awake?
I will seek another drink."

24 Be not envious of evil men,
nor desire to be with them;
[2]for their minds devise violence,
and their lips talk of mischief.

[3]By wisdom a house is built,
and by understanding it is established;
[4]by knowledge the rooms are filled
with all precious and pleasant riches.
[5]A wise man is mightier than a strong man, [q]
and a man of knowledge than he who has
strength;
[6]for by wise guidance you can wage your war,
and in abundance of counselors there is
victory.
[7]Wisdom is too high for a fool;
in the gate he does not open his mouth.

---

[1] Or *who.*
[m] Heb obscure.
[n] Another reading is *delight in.*
[o] Heb obscure.
[p] Gk Syr Vg Tg: Heb lacks *you will say.*
[q] Gk Compare Syr Tg: Heb *is in strength.*

[8]He who plans to do evil
　　will be called a mischief-maker.
[9]The devising of folly is sin,
　　and the scoffer is an abomination to men.

[10]If you faint in the day of adversity,
　　your strength is small.
[11]Rescue those who are being taken away to
　　death;
　　hold back those who are stumbling to the
　　slaughter.
[12]If you say, "Behold, we did not know this,"
　　does not he who weighs the heart perceive
　　it?
　Does not he who keeps watch over your soul
　　know it,
　　and will he not repay man according to his
　　work?

[13]My son, eat honey, for it is good,
　　and the drippings of the honeycomb are
　　sweet to your taste.
[14]Know that wisdom is such to your soul;
　　if you find it, there will be a future,
　　and your hope will not be cut off.

[15]Lie not in wait as a wicked man against the
　　dwelling of the righteous;
　　do not violence to his home;
[16]for a righteous man falls seven times, and rises
　　again;
　　but the wicked are overthrown by calamity.

[17]Do not rejoice when your enemy falls,
　　and let not your heart be glad when he
　　stumbles;
[18]lest the LORD see it, and be displeased,
　　and turn away his anger from him.

[19]Fret not yourself because of evildoers,
　　and be not envious of the wicked;
[20]for the evil man has no future;
　　the lamp of the wicked will be put out.

[21]My son, fear the LORD and the king,
　　and do not disobey either of them;[r]
[22]for disaster from them will rise suddenly,
　　and who knows the ruin that will come from
　　them both?

[23]　These also are sayings of the wise.

　Partiality in judging is not good.
[24]He who says to the wicked, "You are innocent,"
　　will be cursed by peoples, abhorred by
　　nations;
[25]but those who rebuke the wicked will have
　　delight,
　　and a good blessing will be upon them.

[26]He who gives a right answer
　　kisses the lips.

[27]Prepare your work outside,
　　get everything ready for you in the field;
　　and after that build your house.

[28]Be not a witness against your neighbor without
　　cause,
　　and do not deceive with your lips.
[29]Do not say, "I will do to him as he has done to
　　me;
　　I will pay the man back for what he has
　　done."

[30]I passed by the field of a sluggard,
　　by the vineyard of a man without sense;
[31]and behold, it was all overgrown with thorns;
　　the ground was covered with nettles,
　　and its stone wall was broken down.
[32]Then I saw and considered it;
　　I looked and received instruction.
[33]A little sleep, a little slumber,
　　a little folding of the hands to rest,
[34]and poverty will come upon you like a robber,
　　and want like an armed man.

Further Wise Sayings of Solomon

25 These also are proverbs of Solomon
　　which the men of Hezeki′ah king of Judah
copied.

[2]It is the glory of God to conceal things,
　　but the glory of kings is to search things
　　out.
[3]As the heavens for height, and the earth for
　　depth,
　　so the mind of kings is unsearchable.
[4]Take away the dross from the silver,
　　and the smith has material for a vessel;
[5]take away the wicked from the presence of the
　　king,
　　and his throne will be established in
　　righteousness.
[6]Do not put yourself forward in the king's
　　presence
　　or stand in the place of the great;
[7]for it is better to be told, "Come up here,"
　　than to be put lower in the presence of the
　　prince.

　What your eyes have seen
[8]　do not hastily bring into court;
　for [s] what will you do in the end,
　　when your neighbor puts you to shame?
[9]Argue your case with your neighbor himself,
　　and do not disclose another's secret;

---

[r] Gk: Heb *do not associate with those who change.*
[s] Cn: Heb *lest.*

¹⁰lest he who hears you bring shame upon you,
 and your ill repute have no end.

¹¹A word fitly spoken
 is like apples of gold in a setting of silver.
¹²Like a gold ring or an ornament of gold
 is a wise reprover to a listening ear.
¹³Like the cold of snow in the time of harvest
 is a faithful messenger to those who send
 him,
 he refreshes the spirit of his masters.
¹⁴Like clouds and wind without rain
 is a man who boasts of a gift he does not
 give.

¹⁵With patience a ruler may be persuaded,
 and a soft tongue will break a bone.
¹⁶If you have found honey, eat only enough for
 you,
 lest you be sated with it and vomit it.
¹⁷Let your foot be seldom in your neighbor's
 house,
 lest he become weary of you and hate you.
¹⁸A man who bears false witness against his
 neighbor
 is like a war club, or a sword, or a sharp
 arrow.
¹⁹Trust in a faithless man in time of trouble
 is like a bad tooth or a foot that slips.
²⁰He who sings songs to a heavy heart
 is like one who takes off a garment on a
 cold day,
 and like vinegar on a wound. ^t
²¹If your enemy is hungry, give him bread to
 eat;
 and if he is thirsty, give him water to
 drink;
²²for you will heap coals of fire on his head,
 and the LORD will reward you.
²³The north wind brings forth rain;
 and a backbiting tongue, angry looks.
²⁴It is better to live in a corner of the housetop
 than in a house shared with a contentious
 woman.
²⁵Like cold water to a thirsty soul,
 so is good news from a far country.
²⁶Like a muddied spring or a polluted fountain
 is a righteous man who gives way before
 the wicked.
²⁷It is not good to eat much honey,
 so be sparing of complimentary words. ^u
²⁸A man without self-control
 is like a city broken into and left without
 walls.

26

 Like snow in summer or rain in harvest,
 so honor is not fitting for a fool.
²Like a sparrow in its flitting, like a swallow in
 its flying,
 a curse that is causeless does not alight.

³A whip for the horse, a bridle for the donkey,
 and a rod for the back of fools.
⁴Answer not a fool according to his folly,
 lest you be like him yourself.
⁵Answer a fool according to his folly,
 lest he be wise in his own eyes.
⁶He who sends a message by the hand of a fool
 cuts off his own feet and drinks violence.
⁷Like a lame man's legs, which hang useless,
 is a proverb in the mouth of fools.
⁸Like one who binds the stone in the sling
 is he who gives honor to a fool.
⁹Like a thorn that goes up into the hand of a
 drunkard
 is a proverb in the mouth of fools.
¹⁰Like an archer who wounds everybody
 is he who hires a passing fool or drunkard. ^v
¹¹Like a dog that returns to his vomit
 is a fool who repeats his folly.
¹²Do you see a man who is wise in his own eyes?
 There is more hope for a fool than for him.
¹³The sluggard says, "There is a lion in the road!
 There is a lion in the streets!"
¹⁴As a door turns on its hinges,
 so does a sluggard on his bed.
¹⁵The sluggard buries his hand in the dish;
 it wears him out to bring it back to his
 mouth.
¹⁶The sluggard is wiser in his own eyes
 than seven men who can answer discreetly.
¹⁷He who meddles in a quarrel not his own
 is like one who takes a passing dog by the
 ears.
¹⁸Like a madman who throws firebrands,
 arrows, and death,
¹⁹is the man who deceives his neighbor
 and says, "I am only joking!"
²⁰For lack of wood the fire goes out;
 and where there is no whisperer, quarreling
 ceases.
²¹As charcoal to hot embers and wood to fire,
 so is a quarrelsome man for kindling strife.
²²The words of a whisperer are like delicious
 morsels;
 they go down into the inner parts of the
 body.
²³Like the glaze ^w covering an earthen vessel
 are smooth ^x lips with an evil heart.
²⁴He who hates, dissembles with his lips
 and harbors deceit in his heart;
²⁵when he speaks graciously, believe him not,
 for there are seven abominations in his
 heart;

---

^t Gk: Heb *lye.*
^u Cn Compare Gk Syr Tg: Heb *searching out their glory is glory.*
^v The Hebrew text of this verse is uncertain.
^w Cn: Heb *silver of dross.*
^x Gk: Heb *burning.*
25:21, 22: Rom 12:20.
26:11: 2 Pet 2:22.

[26] though his hatred be covered with guile,
   his wickedness will be exposed in the
     assembly.
[27] He who digs a pit will fall into it,
   and a stone will come back upon him who
     starts it rolling.
[28] A lying tongue hates its victims,
   and a flattering mouth works ruin.

27 Do not boast about tomorrow,
      for you do not know what a day may
       bring forth.
[2] Let another praise you, and not your own
     mouth;
   a stranger, and not your own lips.
[3] A stone is heavy, and sand is weighty,
   but a fool's provocation is heavier than
     both.
[4] Wrath is cruel, anger is overwhelming;
   but who can stand before jealousy?
[5] Better is open rebuke
   than hidden love.
[6] Faithful are the wounds of a friend;
   profuse are the kisses of an enemy.
[7] He who is sated loathes honey,
   but to one who is hungry everything bitter
     is sweet.
[8] Like a bird that strays from its nest,
   is a man who strays from his home.
[9] Oil and perfume make the heart glad,
   but the soul is torn by trouble. [y]
[10] Your friend, and your father's friend, do not
     forsake;
   and do not go to your brother's house in the
     day of your calamity.
   Better is a neighbor who is near
     than a brother who is far away.
[11] Be wise, my son, and make my heart glad,
   that I may answer him who reproaches me.
[12] A prudent man sees danger and hides
     himself;
   but the simple go on, and suffer for it.
[13] Take a man's garment when he has given
     surety for a stranger,
   and hold him in pledge when he gives
     surety for foreigners. [z]
[14] He who blesses his neighbor with a loud voice,
   rising early in the morning,
   will be counted as cursing.
[15] A continual dripping on a rainy day
   and a contentious woman are alike;
[16] to restrain her is to restrain the wind [a]
   or to grasp oil in one's right hand.
[17] Iron sharpens iron,
   and one man sharpens another.
[18] He who tends a fig tree will eat its fruit,
   and he who guards his master will be
     honored.
[19] As in water face answers to face,
   so the mind of man reflects the man.

[20] Sheol and Abad'don are never satisfied,
   and never satisfied are the eyes of man.
[21] The crucible is for silver, and the furnace is for
     gold,
   and a man is judged by his praise.
[22] Crush a fool in a mortar with a pestle
     along with crushed grain,
   yet his folly will not depart from him.

[23] Know well the condition of your flocks,
   and give attention to your herds;
[24] for riches do not last for ever;
   and does a crown endure to all generations?
[25] When the grass is gone, and the new growth
     appears,
   and the herbage of the mountains is
     gathered,
[26] the lambs will provide your clothing,
   and the goats the price of a field;
[27] there will be enough goats' milk for your food,
   for the food of your household
   and maintenance for your maidens.

The Wicked and the Righteous Contrasted

28 The wicked flee when no one pursues,
      but the righteous are bold as a lion.
[2] When a land transgresses
     it has many rulers;
   but with men of understanding and knowledge
     its stability will long continue.
[3] A poor man who oppresses the poor
   is a beating rain that leaves no food.
[4] Those who forsake the law praise the wicked,
   but those who keep the law strive against
     them.
[5] Evil men do not understand justice,
   but those who seek the LORD understand it
     completely.
[6] Better is a poor man who walks in his integrity
   than a rich man who is perverse in his
     ways.
[7] He who keeps the law is a wise son,
   but a companion of gluttons shames his
     father.
[8] He who augments his wealth by interest and
     increase
   gathers it for him who is kind to the poor.
[9] If one turns away his ear from hearing the
     law,
   even his prayer is an abomination.
[10] He who misleads the upright into an evil way
   will fall into his own pit;
   but the blameless will have an excellent
     inheritance.
[11] A rich man is wise in his own eyes,
   but a poor man who has understanding will
     find him out.

---

[y] Gk: Heb *the sweetness of his friend from hearty counsel.*
[z] Vg and 20:16: Heb *a foreign woman.*
[a] Heb obscure.

¹²When the righteous triumph, there is great
  glory;
  but when the wicked rise, men hide
  themselves.
¹³He who conceals his transgressions will not
  prosper,
  but he who confesses and forsakes them
  will obtain mercy.
¹⁴Blessed is the man who fears the Lord always;
  but he who hardens his heart will fall into
  calamity.
¹⁵Like a roaring lion or a charging bear
  is a wicked ruler over a poor people.
¹⁶A ruler who lacks understanding is a cruel
  oppressor;
  but he who hates unjust gain will prolong
  his days.
¹⁷If a man is burdened with the blood of another,
  let him be a fugitive until death;
  let no one help him.
¹⁸He who walks in integrity will be delivered,
  but he who is perverse in his ways will fall
  into a pit. ᵇ
¹⁹He who tills his land will have plenty of bread,
  but he who follows worthless pursuits will
  have plenty of poverty.
²⁰A faithful man will abound with blessings,
  but he who hastens to be rich will not go
  unpunished.
²¹To show partiality is not good;
  but for a piece of bread a man will do
  wrong.
²²A miserly man hastens after wealth,
  and does not know that want will come
  upon him.
²³He who rebukes a man will afterward find
  more favor
  than he who flatters with his tongue.
²⁴He who robs his father or his mother
  and says, "That is no transgression,"
  is the companion of a man who destroys.
²⁵A greedy man stirs up strife,
  but he who trusts in the Lord will be
  enriched.
²⁶He who trusts in his own mind is a fool;
  but he who walks in wisdom will be
  delivered.
²⁷He who gives to the poor will not want,
  but he who hides his eyes will get many a
  curse.
²⁸When the wicked rise, men hide themselves,
  but when they perish, the righteous
  increase.

29 He who is often reproved, yet stiffens his
  neck,
  will suddenly be broken beyond healing.
²When the righteous are in authority, the people
  rejoice;
  but when the wicked rule, the people groan.

³He who loves wisdom makes his father glad,
  but one who keeps company with harlots
  squanders his substance.
⁴By justice a king gives stability to the land,
  but one who exacts gifts ruins it.
⁵A man who flatters his neighbor
  spreads a net for his feet.
⁶An evil man is ensnared in his transgression,
  but a righteous man sings and rejoices.
⁷A righteous man knows the rights of the poor;
  a wicked man does not understand such
  knowledge.
⁸Scoffers set a city aflame,
  but wise men turn away wrath.
⁹If a wise man has an argument with a fool,
  the fool only rages and laughs, and there is
  no quiet.
¹⁰Bloodthirsty men hate one who is blameless,
  and the wicked ᶜ seek his life.
¹¹A fool gives full vent to his anger,
  but a wise man quietly holds it back.
¹²If a ruler listens to falsehood,
  all his officials will be wicked.
¹³The poor man and the oppressor meet
  together;
  the Lord gives light to the eyes of both.
¹⁴If a king judges the poor with equity
  his throne will be established for ever.
¹⁵The rod and reproof give wisdom,
  but a child left to himself brings shame to
  his mother.
¹⁶When the wicked are in authority,
  transgression increases;
  but the righteous will look upon their
  downfall.
¹⁷Discipline your son, and he will give you rest;
  he will give delight to your heart.
¹⁸Where there is no prophecy the people cast off
  restraint,
  but blessed is he who keeps the law.
¹⁹By mere words a servant is not disciplined,
  for though he understands, he will not give
  heed.
²⁰Do you see a man who is hasty in his words?
  There is more hope for a fool than for him.
²¹He who pampers his servant from childhood,
  will in the end find him his heir. ᵈ
²²A man of wrath stirs up strife,
  and a man given to anger causes much
  transgression.
²³A man's pride will bring him low,
  but he who is lowly in spirit will obtain
  honor.
²⁴The partner of a thief hates his own life;
  he hears the curse, but discloses nothing.

ᵇ Syr: Heb *in one.*
ᶜ Cn: Heb *upright.*
ᵈ The meaning of the Hebrew word is uncertain.

²⁵The fear of man lays a snare,
  but he who trusts in the Lord is safe.
²⁶Many seek the favor of a ruler,
  but from the Lord a man gets justice.
²⁷An unjust man is an abomination to the
    righteous,
  but he whose way is straight is an
    abomination to the wicked.

Sayings of Agur

30 The words of Agur son of Ja'keh of
    Mas'sa. ᵉ

The man says to Ith'iel,
  to Ithiel and U'cal: ᶠ
²Surely I am too stupid to be a man.
  I have not the understanding of a man.
³I have not learned wisdom,
  nor have I knowledge of the Holy One.
⁴Who has ascended to heaven and come down?
  Who has gathered the wind in his fists?
Who has wrapped up the waters in a garment?
  Who has established all the ends of the
    earth?
What is his name, and what is his son's name?
  Surely you know!

⁵Every word of God proves true;
  he is a shield to those who take refuge in
    him.
⁶Do not add to his words,
  lest he rebuke you, and you be found a liar.

⁷Two things I ask of you;
  deny them not to me before I die:
⁸Remove far from me falsehood and lying;
  give me neither poverty nor riches;
  feed me with the food that is needful for
    me,
⁹lest I be full, and deny you,
  and say, "Who is the Lord?"
  or lest I be poor, and steal,
  and profane the name of my God.

¹⁰Do not slander a servant to his master,
  lest he curse you, and you be held guilty.

¹¹There are those who curse their fathers
  and do not bless their mothers.
¹²There are those who are pure in their own eyes
  but are not cleansed of their filth.
¹³There are those—how lofty are their eyes,
  how high their eyelids lift!
¹⁴There are those whose teeth are swords,
  whose teeth are knives,
  to devour the poor from off the earth,
  the needy from among men.

¹⁵The leech ᵍ has two daughters;
  "Give, give," they cry.

Three things are never satisfied;
  four never say, "Enough":
¹⁶Sheol, the barren womb,
  the earth ever thirsty for water,
  and the fire which never says, "Enough." ʰ

¹⁷The eye that mocks a father
  and scorns to obey a mother
will be picked out by the ravens of the valley
  and eaten by the vultures.

¹⁸Three things are too wonderful for me;
  four I do not understand:
¹⁹the way of an eagle in the sky,
  the way of a serpent on a rock,
  the way of a ship on the high seas,
  and the way of a man with a maiden.

²⁰This is the way of an adulteress:
  she eats, and wipes her mouth,
  and says, "I have done no wrong."

²¹Under three things the earth trembles;
  under four it cannot bear up:
²²a slave when he becomes king,
  and a fool when he is filled with food;
²³an unloved woman when she gets a husband,
  and a maid when she succeeds her mistress.

²⁴Four things on earth are small,
  but they are exceedingly wise:
²⁵the ants are a people not strong,
  yet they provide their food in the summer;
²⁶the badgers are a people not mighty,
  yet they make their homes in the rocks;
²⁷the locusts have no king,
  yet all of them march in rank;
²⁸the lizard you can take in your hands,
  yet it is in kings' palaces.

²⁹Three things are stately in their tread;
  four are stately in their stride:
³⁰the lion, which is mightiest among beasts
  and does not turn back before any;
³¹the strutting cock, ⁱ the he-goat,
  and a king striding before ʲ his people.

³²If you have been foolish, exalting yourself,
  or if you have been devising evil,
  put your hand on your mouth.
³³For pressing milk produces curds,
  pressing the nose produces blood,
  and pressing anger produces strife.

ᵉ Or *the oracle.*
ᶠ The Hebrew of this verse is obscure.
ᵍ The meaning of the Hebrew word is uncertain.
ʰ Heb obscure.
ⁱ Gk Syr Tg Compare Vg: Heb obscure.
ʲ The meaning of the Hebrew is uncertain.

Sayings of Lemuel's Mother;
Praise of a Good Wife

31 The words of Lem'uel, king of Massa,[k]
which his mother taught him:

²What, my son? What, son of my womb?
What, son of my vows?
³Give not your strength to women,
your ways to those who destroy kings.
⁴It is not for kings, O Lem'uel,
it is not for kings to drink wine,
or for rulers to desire [l] strong drink;
⁵lest they drink and forget what has been
decreed,
and pervert the rights of all the afflicted.
⁶Give strong drink to him who is perishing,
and wine to those in bitter distress;
⁷let them drink and forget their poverty,
and remember their misery no more.
⁸Open your mouth for the mute,
for the rights of all who are left desolate. [m]
⁹Open your mouth, judge righteously,
maintain the rights of the poor and needy.

¹⁰Who can find a good wife?
She is far more precious than jewels.
¹¹The heart of her husband trusts in her,
and he will have no lack of gain.
¹²She does him good, and not harm,
all the days of her life.
¹³She seeks wool and flax,
and works with willing hands.
¹⁴She is like the ships of the merchant,
she brings her food from afar.
¹⁵She rises while it is yet night
and provides food for her household
and tasks for her maidens.
¹⁶She considers a field and buys it;
with the fruit of her hands she plants a
vineyard.

¹⁷She clothes her loins with strength
and makes her arms strong.
¹⁸She perceives that her merchandise is
profitable.
Her lamp does not go out at night.
¹⁹She puts her hands to the distaff,
and her hands hold the spindle.
²⁰She opens her hand to the poor,
and reaches out her hands to the needy.
²¹She is not afraid of snow for her household,
for all her household are clothed in scarlet.
²²She makes herself coverings;
her clothing is fine linen and purple.
²³Her husband is known in the gates,
when he sits among the elders of the land.
²⁴She makes linen garments and sells them;
she delivers sashes to the merchant.
²⁵Strength and dignity are her clothing,
and she laughs at the time to come.
²⁶She opens her mouth with wisdom,
and the teaching of kindness is on her
tongue.
²⁷She looks well to the ways of her household,
and does not eat the bread of idleness.
²⁸Her children rise up and call her blessed;
her husband also, and he praises her:
²⁹"Many women have done excellently,
but you surpass them all."
³⁰Charm is deceitful, and beauty is vain,
but a woman who fears the LORD is to be
praised.
³¹Give her of the fruit of her hands,
and let her works praise her in the gates.

---

[k] Or *King Lemuel, the oracle.*
[l] Cn: Heb *where.*
[m] Heb *are sons of passing away.*

THE BOOK OF
ECCLESIASTES

All Is Vanity

1 The words of the Preacher,[a] the son of David,
king in Jerusalem.
[2] Vanity of vanities, says the Preacher,
vanity of vanities! All is vanity.
[3] What does man gain by all the toil
at which he toils under the sun?
[4] A generation goes, and a generation comes,
but the earth remains for ever.
[5] The sun rises and the sun goes down,
and hastens to the place where it rises.
[6] The wind blows to the south,
and goes round to the north;
round and round goes the wind,
and on its circuits the wind returns.
[7] All streams run to the sea,
but the sea is not full;
to the place where the streams flow,
there they flow again.
[8] All things are full of weariness;
a man cannot utter it;
the eye is not satisfied with seeing,
nor the ear filled with hearing.
[9] What has been is what will be,
and what has been done is what will be
done;
and there is nothing new under the sun.
[10] Is there a thing of which it is said,
"See, this is new"?
It has been already,
in the ages before us.
[11] There is no remembrance of former things,
nor will there be any remembrance
of later things yet to happen
among those who come after.

Vanity in Seeking Wisdom

12 I the Preacher have been king over Israel
in Jerusalem. [13] And I applied my mind to seek
and to search out by wisdom all that is done
under heaven; it is an unhappy business that God
has given to the sons of men to be busy with.
[14] I have seen everything that is done under the
sun; and behold, all is vanity and a striving after
wind.[b]
[15] What is crooked cannot be made straight,
and what is lacking cannot be numbered.

16 I said to myself, "I have acquired great wisdom, surpassing all who were over Jerusalem before me; and my mind has had great experience
of wisdom and knowledge." [17] And I applied my
mind to know wisdom and to know madness and

folly. I perceived that this also is but a striving
after wind.
[18] For in much wisdom is much vexation,
and he who increases knowledge increases
sorrow.

Vanity in Self-indulgence

2 I said to myself, "Come now, I will make a
test of pleasure; enjoy yourself." But behold,
this also was vanity. [2] I said of laughter, "It is
mad," and of pleasure, "What use is it?" [3] I
searched with my mind how to cheer my body
with wine—my mind still guiding me with wisdom—and how to lay hold on folly, till I might see
what was good for the sons of men to do under
heaven during the few days of their life. [4] I made
great works; I built houses and planted vineyards
for myself; [5] I made myself gardens and parks,
and planted in them all kinds of fruit trees. [6] I
made myself pools from which to water the forest of growing trees. [7] I bought male and female
slaves, and had slaves who were born in my
house; I had also great possessions of herds and
flocks, more than any who had been before me in
Jerusalem. [8] I also gathered for myself silver and
gold and the treasure of kings and provinces; I
got singers, both men and women, and many
concubines, [c] man's delight.

9 So I became great and surpassed all who
were before me in Jerusalem; also my wisdom
remained with me. [10] And whatever my eyes desired I did not keep from them; I kept my heart
from no pleasure, for my heart found pleasure
in all my toil, and this was my reward for all
my toil. [11] Then I considered all that my hands
had done and the toil I had spent in doing it,
and behold, all was vanity and a striving after

The name is the Greek rendering of the Hebrew, Qoheleth, which means
"one who convenes or speaks in an assembly." Hence the name: the
Preacher. By a literary device the book is ascribed to Solomon, but in
fact it was written after the Exile, probably in the third century B.C.
There is no knowledge in the book of any idea of rewards and punishments after this life, thus much the same problem is met with here as in
the book of Job. Why do the good suffer and the wicked flourish? Belief
and experience do not harmonize. Ecclesiastes has to insist on God's
goodness and power and providence even though experience seems at
times to show the contrary. He has no solution to offer other than faith
in God and trust that he will, in his own way and time, punish and
reward good; cf. 3:17; 8:12–13. He constantly emphasizes the vanity of
created things, which can never satisfy the heart of man. Thus he gives
us something more than an unsolved problem and stimulates faith and
trust in God in spite of appearances which might influence us to the
contrary.
[a] Heb *Qoheleth*.
[b] Or *a feeding on wind*. See Hos 12:1.
[c] The meaning of the Hebrew word is uncertain.

wind, and there was nothing to be gained under the sun.

Vanity of Folly and Toil

12 So I turned to consider wisdom and madness and folly; for what can the man do who comes after the king? Only what he has already done. [13]Then I saw that wisdom excels folly as light excels darkness. [14]The wise man has his eyes in his head, but the fool walks in darkness; and yet I perceived that one fate comes to all of them. [15]Then I said to myself, "What befalls the fool will befall me also; why then have I been so very wise?" And I said to myself that this also is vanity. [16]For of the wise man as of the fool there is no enduring remembrance, seeing that in the days to come all will have been long forgotten. How the wise man dies just like the fool! [17]So I hated life, because what is done under the sun was grievous to me; for all is vanity and a striving after wind.

18 I hated all my toil in which I had toiled under the sun, seeing that I must leave it to the man who will come after me; [19]and who knows whether he will be a wise man or a fool? Yet he will be master of all for which I toiled and used my wisdom under the sun. This also is vanity. [20]So I turned about and gave my heart up to despair over all the toil of my labors under the sun, [21]because sometimes a man who has toiled with wisdom and knowledge and skill must leave all to be enjoyed by a man who did not toil for it. This also is vanity and a great evil. [22]What has a man from all the toil and strain with which he toils beneath the sun? [23]For all his days are full of pain, and his work is a vexation; even in the night his mind does not rest. This also is vanity.

24 There is nothing better for a man than that he should eat and drink and find enjoyment in his toil. This also, I saw, is from the hand of God; [25]for apart from him [a] who can eat or who can have enjoyment? [26]For to the man who pleases him God gives wisdom and knowledge and joy; but to the sinner he gives the work of gathering and heaping, only to give to one who pleases God. This also is vanity and a striving after wind.

Everything Has a Season

3 For everything there is a season, and a time for every matter under heaven:
[2]a time to be born, and a time to die;
a time to plant, and a time to pluck up what is planted;
[3]a time to kill, and a time to heal;
a time to break down, and a time to build up;
[4]a time to weep, and a time to laugh;
a time to mourn, and a time to dance;
[5]a time to cast away stones, and a time to gather stones together;
a time to embrace, and a time to refrain from embracing;
[6]a time to seek, and a time to lose;

a time to keep, and a time to cast away;
[7]a time to tear, and a time to sew;
a time to keep silence, and a time to speak;
[8]a time to love, and a time to hate;
a time for war, and a time for peace.
[9]What gain has the worker from his toil?

God-given Tasks

10 I have seen the business that God has given to the sons of men to be busy with. [11]He has made everything beautiful in its time; also he has put eternity into man's mind, yet so that he cannot find out what God has done from the beginning to the end. [12]I know that there is nothing better for them than to be happy and enjoy themselves as long as they live; [13]also that it is God's gift to man that every one should eat and drink and take pleasure in all his toil. [14]I know that whatever God does endures for ever; nothing can be added to it, nor anything taken from it; God has made it so, in order that men should fear before him. [15]That which is, already has been; that which is to be, already has been; and God seeks what has been driven away.

Judgment and the Future Belong to God

16 Moreover I saw under the sun that in the place of justice, even there was wickedness, and in the place of righteousness, even there was wickedness. [17]I said in my heart, God will judge the righteous and the wicked, for he has appointed a time for every matter, and for every work. [18]I said in my heart with regard to the sons of men that God is testing them to show them that they are but beasts. [19]For the fate of the sons of men and the fate of beasts is the same; as one dies, so dies the other. They all have the same breath, and man has no advantage over the beasts; for all is vanity. [20]All go to one place; all are from the dust, and all turn to dust again. [21]Who knows whether the spirit of man goes upward and the spirit of the beast goes down to the earth? [22]So I saw that there is nothing better than that a man should enjoy his work, for that is his lot; who can bring him to see what will be after him?

Injustice of Life

4 Again I saw all the oppressions that are practiced under the sun. And behold, the tears of the oppressed, and they had no one to comfort them! On the side of their oppressors there was power, and there was no one to comfort them. [2]And I thought the dead who are already dead more fortunate than the living who are still alive; [3]but better than both is he who has not yet been, and has not seen the evil deeds that are done under the sun.

4 Then I saw that all toil and all skill in work come from a man's envy of his neighbor. This also is vanity and a striving after wind.

---

[a] Gk Syr: Heb *apart from me.*

5 The fool folds his hands, and eats his own flesh.

6 Better is a handful of quietness than two hands full of toil and a striving after wind.

7 Again, I saw vanity under the sun: [8]a person who has no one, either son or brother, yet there is no end to all his toil, and his eyes are never satisfied with riches, so that he never asks, "For whom am I toiling and depriving myself of pleasure?" This also is vanity and an unhappy business.

Value of Friendship

9 Two are better than one, because they have a good reward for their toil. [10]For if they fall, one will lift up his fellow; but woe to him who is alone when he falls and has not another to lift him up. [11]Again, if two lie together, they are warm; but how can one be warm alone? [12]And though a man might prevail against one who is alone, two will withstand him. A threefold cord is not quickly broken.

13 Better is a poor and wise youth than an old and foolish king, who will no longer take advice, [14]even though he had gone from prison to the throne or in his own kingdom had been born poor. [15]I saw all the living who move about under the sun, as well as that [f] youth, who was to stand in his place; [16]there was no end of all the people; he was over all of them. Yet those who come later will not rejoice in him. Surely this also is vanity and a striving after wind.

Reverence, Humility, Enjoyment

5 [g] Guard your steps when you go to the house of God; to draw near to listen is better than to offer the sacrifice of fools; for they do not know that they are doing evil. [2] [h] Be not rash with your mouth, nor let your heart be hasty to utter a word before God, for God is in heaven, and you upon earth; therefore let your words be few.

3 For a dream comes with much business, and a fool's voice with many words.

4 When you vow a vow to God, do not delay paying it; for he has no pleasure in fools. Pay what you vow. [5]It is better that you should not vow than that you should vow and not pay. [6]Let not your mouth lead you into sin, and do not say before the messenger [i] that it was a mistake; why should God be angry at your voice, and destroy the work of your hands?

7 For when dreams increase, empty words grow many: [j] but you must fear God.

8 If you see in a province the poor oppressed and justice and right violently taken away, do not be amazed at the matter; for the high official is watched by a higher, and there are yet higher ones over them. [9]But in all, a king is an advantage to a land with cultivated fields. [k]

10 He who loves money will not be satisfied with money; nor he who loves wealth, with gain: this also is vanity.

11 When goods increase, they increase who eat them; and what gain has their owner but to see them with his eyes?

12 Sweet is the sleep of a laborer, whether he eats little or much; but the surfeit of the rich will not let him sleep.

13 There is a grievous evil which I have seen under the sun: riches were kept by their owner to his hurt, [14]and those riches were lost in a bad venture; and he is father of a son, but he has nothing in his hand. [15]As he came from his mother's womb he shall go again, naked as he came, and shall take nothing for his toil, which he may carry away in his hand. [16]This also is a grievous evil: just as he came, so shall he go; and what gain has he that he toiled for the wind, [17]and spent all his days in darkness and grief,[1] in much vexation and sickness and resentment?

18 Behold, what I have seen to be good and to be fitting is to eat and drink and find enjoyment in all the toil with which one toils under the sun the few days of his life which God has given him, for this is his lot. [19]Every man also to whom God has given wealth and possessions and power to enjoy them, and to accept his lot and find enjoyment in his toil—this is the gift of God. [20]For he will not much remember the days of his life because God keeps him occupied with joy in his heart.

Frustration of Desires

6 There is an evil which I have seen under the sun, and it lies heavy upon men: [2]a man to whom God gives wealth, possessions, and honor, so that he lacks nothing of all that he desires, yet God does not give him power to enjoy them, but a stranger enjoys them; this is vanity; it is a sore affliction. [3]If a man begets a hundred children, and lives many years, so that the days of his years are many, but he does not enjoy life's good things, and also has no burial, I say that an untimely birth is better off than he. [4]For it comes into vanity and goes into darkness, and in darkness its name is covered; [5]moreover it has not seen the sun or known anything; yet it finds rest rather than he. [6]Even though he should live a thousand years twice told, yet enjoy no good—do not all go to the one place?

7 All the toil of man is for his mouth, yet his appetite is not satisfied. [8]For what advantage has the wise man over the fool? And what does the poor man have who knows how to conduct himself before the living? [9]Better is the sight of the

---

[f] Heb *the second.*
[g] Ch 4:17 in Heb.
[h] Ch 5:1 in Heb.
[i] Or *angel.*
[j] Or *For in a multitude of dreams there is futility, and ruin in a flood of words.*
[k] Or *The profit of the land is among all of them; a cultivated field has a king.*
[1] Gk: Heb *all his days also he eats in darkness.*

eyes than the wandering of desire; this also is vanity and a striving after wind.

10 Whatever has come to be has already been named, and it is known what man is, and that he is not able to dispute with one stronger than he. [11]The more words, the more vanity, and what is man the better? [12]For who knows what is good for man while he lives the few days of his vain life, which he passes like a shadow? For who can tell man what will be after him under the sun?

Wisdom and Folly Compared

7 A good name is better than precious ointment;
and the day of death, than the day of birth.
[2]It is better to go to the house of mourning
than to go to the house of feasting;
for this is the end of all men,
and the living will lay it to heart.
[3]Sorrow is better than laughter,
for by sadness of countenance the heart is made glad.
[4]The heart of the wise is in the house of mourning;
but the heart of fools is in the house of mirth.
[5]It is better for a man to hear the rebuke of the wise
than to hear the song of fools.
[6]For as the crackling of thorns under a pot,
so is the laughter of the fools;
this also is vanity.
[7]Surely oppression makes the wise man foolish,
and a bribe corrupts the mind.
[8]Better is the end of a thing than its beginning;
and the patient in spirit is better than the proud in spirit.
[9]Be not quick to anger,
for anger lodges in the bosom of fools.
[10]Say not, "Why were the former days better than these?"
For it is not from wisdom that you ask this.
[11]Wisdom is good with an inheritance,
an advantage to those who see the sun.
[12]For the protection of wisdom is like the protection of money;
and the advantage of knowledge is that wisdom preserves the life of him who has it.
[13]Consider the work of God;
who can make straight what he has made crooked?

14 In the day of prosperity be joyful, and in the day of adversity consider; God has made the one as well as the other, so that man may not find out anything that will be after him.

Inequalities of Life

15 In my vain life I have seen everything; there is a righteous man who perishes in his righteousness, and there is a wicked man who prolongs his life in his evil-doing. [16]Be not righteous overmuch, and do not make yourself overwise; why should you destroy yourself? [17]Be not wicked overmuch, neither be a fool; why should you die before your time? [18]It is good that you should take hold of this, and from that withhold not your hand; for he who fears God shall come forth from them all.

19 Wisdom gives strength to the wise man more than ten rulers that are in a city.

20 Surely there is not a righteous man on earth who does good and never sins.

21 Do not give heed to all the things that men say, lest you hear your servant cursing you; [22]your heart knows that many times you have yourself cursed others.

23 All this I have tested by wisdom; I said, "I will be wise"; but it was far from me. [24]That which is, is far off, and deep, very deep; who can find it out? [25]I turned my mind to know and to search out and to seek wisdom and the sum of things, and to know the wickedness of folly and the foolishness which is madness. [26]And I found more bitter than death the woman whose heart is snares and nets, and whose hands are fetters; he who pleases God escapes her, but the sinner is taken by her. [27]Behold, this is what I found, says the Preacher, adding one thing to another to find the sum, [28]which my mind has sought repeatedly, but I have not found. One man among a thousand I found, but a woman among all these I have not found. [29]Behold, this alone I found, that God made man upright, but they have sought out many devices.

Obedience to Rulers

8 Who is like the wise man?
And who knows the interpretation of a thing?
A man's wisdom makes his face shine,
and the hardness of his countenance is changed.

2 Keep [m] the king's command, and because of your sacred oath be not dismayed; [3]go from his presence, do not delay when the matter is unpleasant, for he does whatever he pleases. [4]For the word of the king is supreme, and who may say to him, "What are you doing?" [5]He who obeys a command will meet no harm, and the mind of a wise man will know the time and way. [6]For every matter has its time and way, although man's trouble lies heavy upon him. [7]For he does not know what is to be, for who can tell him how it will be? [8]No man has power to retain the spirit, or authority over the day of death; there is no discharge from war, nor will wickedness deliver those who are given to it. [9]All this I observed while applying my mind to all that is done under the sun, while man lords it over man to his hurt.

---

[m] Heb inserts an *I.*

God's Ways Are Inscrutable

10 Then I saw the wicked buried; they used to go in and out of the holy place, and were praised in the city where they had done such things. This also is vanity. [11]Because sentence against an evil deed is not executed speedily, the heart of the sons of men is fully set to do evil. [12]Though a sinner does evil a hundred times and prolongs his life, yet I know that it will be well with those who fear God, because they fear before him; [13]but it will not be well with the wicked, neither will he prolong his days like a shadow, because he does not fear before God.

14 There is a vanity which takes place on earth, that there are righteous men to whom it happens according to the deeds of the wicked, and there are wicked men to whom it happens according to the deeds of the righteous. I said that this also is vanity. [15]And I commend enjoyment, for man has no good thing under the sun but to eat and drink and enjoy himself, for this will go with him in his toil through the days of life which God gives him under the sun.

16 When I applied my mind to know wisdom, and to see the business that is done on earth, how neither day nor night one's eyes see sleep; [17]then I saw all the work of God, that man cannot find out the work that is done under the sun. However much man may toil in seeking, he will not find it out; even though a wise man claims to know, he cannot find it out.

Acceptance of Life As It Comes

9 But all this I laid to heart, examining it all, how the righteous and the wise and their deeds are in the hand of God; whether it is love or hate man does not know. Everything before them is vanity, [n] [2]since one fate comes to all, to the righteous and the wicked, to the good and the evil, [o] to the clean and the unclean, to him who sacrifices and him who does not sacrifice. As is the good man, so is the sinner; and he who swears is as he who shuns an oath. [3]This is an evil in all that is done under the sun, that one fate comes to all; also the hearts of men are full of evil, and madness is in their hearts while they live, and after that they go to the dead. [4]But he who is joined with all the living has hope, for a living dog is better than a dead lion. [5]For the living know that they will die, but the dead know nothing, and they have no more reward; but the memory of them is lost. [6]Their love and their hate and their envy have already perished, and they have no more for ever any share in all that is done under the sun.

7 Go, eat your bread with enjoyment, and drink your wine with a merry heart; for God has already approved what you do.

8 Let your garments be always white; let not oil be lacking on your head.

9 Enjoy life with the wife whom you love, all the days of your vain life which he has given you under the sun, because that is your portion in life and in your toil at which you toil under the sun. [10]Whatever your hand finds to do, do it with your might; for there is no work or thought or knowledge or wisdom in Sheol, to which you are going.

11 Again I saw that under the sun the race is not to the swift, nor the battle to the strong, nor bread to the wise, nor riches to the intelligent, nor favor to the men of skill; but time and chance happen to them all. [12]For man does not know his time. Like fish which are taken in an evil net, and like birds which are caught in a snare, so the sons of men are snared at an evil time, when it suddenly falls upon them.

Wisdom Superior to Folly

13 I have also seen this example of wisdom under the sun, and it seemed great to me. [14]There was a little city with few men in it; and a great king came against it and besieged it, building great siegeworks against it. [15]But there was found in it a poor wise man, and he by his wisdom delivered the city. Yet no one remembered that poor man. [16]But I say that wisdom is better than might, though the poor man's wisdom is despised, and his words are not heeded.

17 The words of the wise heard in quiet are better than the shouting of a ruler among fools. [18]Wisdom is better than weapons of war, but one sinner destroys much good.

Observations of Wisdom

10 Dead flies make the perfumer's ointment
   give off an evil odor;
 so a little folly outweighs wisdom and
   honor.
[2]A wise man's heart inclines him toward the
   right,
 but a fool's heart toward the left.
[3]Even when the fool walks on the road, he lacks
   sense,
 and he says to every one that he is a fool.
[4]If the anger of the ruler rises against you, do
   not leave your place,
 for deference will make amends for great
   offenses.

5 There is an evil which I have seen under the sun, as it were an error proceeding from the ruler: [6]folly is set in many high places, and the rich sit in a low place. [7]I have seen slaves on horses, and princes walking on foot like slaves.
[8]He who digs a pit will fall into it;
 and a serpent will bite him who breaks
   through a wall.
[9]He who quarries stones is hurt by them;
 and he who splits logs is endangered by
   them.

---

[n] Syr Compare Gk: Heb *Everything before them is everything.*
[o] Gk Syr Vg: Heb lacks *and the evil.*

[10]If the iron is blunt, and one does not whet the
  edge,
he must put forth more strength;
  but wisdom helps one to succeed.
[11]If the serpent bites before it is charmed,
  there is no advantage in a charmer.

[12]The words of a wise man's mouth win him
  favor,
  but the lips of a fool consume him.
[13]The beginning of the words of his mouth is
  foolishness,
  and the end of his talk is wicked madness.
[14]A fool multiplies words,
  though no man knows what is to be,
  and who can tell him what will be after
    him?
[15]The toil of a fool wearies him,
  so that he does not know the way to the city.

[16]Woe to you, O land, when your king is a child,
  and your princes feast in the morning!
[17]Happy are you, O land, when your king is the
    son of free men,
  and your princes feast at the proper time,
  for strength, and not for drunkenness!
[18]Through sloth the roof sinks in,
  and through indolence the house leaks.
[19]Bread is made for laughter,
  and wine gladdens life,
  and money answers everything.
[20]Even in your thought, do not curse the king,
  nor in your bedchamber curse the rich;
for a bird of the air will carry your voice,
  or some winged creature tell the matter.

The Value of Diligence

11 Cast your bread upon the waters,
  for you will find it after many days.
[2]Give a portion to seven, or even to eight,
  for you know not what evil may happen on
    earth.
[3]If the clouds are full of rain,
  they empty themselves on the earth;
and if a tree falls to the south or to the north,
  in the place where the tree falls, there it will
    lie.
[4]He who observes the wind will not sow;
  and he who regards the clouds will not reap.
5 As you do not know how the spirit comes to
the bones in the womb [p] of a woman with child,
so you do not know the work of God who makes
everything.
6 In the morning sow your seed, and at evening
withhold not your hand; for you do not know
which will prosper, this or that, or whether both
alike will be good.

Youth and Old Age

7 Light is sweet, and it is pleasant for the eyes
to behold the sun.

8 For if a man lives many years, let him rejoice
in them all; but let him remember that the days of
darkness will be many. All that comes is vanity.
9 Rejoice, O young man, in your youth, and let
your heart cheer you in the days of your youth;
walk in the ways of your heart and the sight of
your eyes. But know that for all these things God
will bring you into judgment.
10 Remove vexation from your mind, and put
away pain from your body; for youth and the
dawn of life are vanity.

Advice to the Young

12 Remember also your Creator in the days
  of your youth, before the evil days come,
and the years draw nigh, when you will say, "I
have no pleasure in them"; [2]before the sun and the
light and the moon and the stars are darkened
and the clouds return after the rain; [3]in the day
when the keepers of the house tremble, and the
strong men are bent, and the grinders cease because they are few, and those that look through
the windows are dimmed, [4]and the doors on the
street are shut; when the sound of the grinding is
low, and one rises up at the voice of a bird, and all
the daughters of song are brought low; [5]they are
afraid also of what is high, and terrors are in the
way; the almond tree blossoms, the grasshopper
drags itself along [q] and desire fails; because
man goes to his eternal home, and the mourners
go about the streets; [6]before the silver cord is
snapped,[r] or the golden bowl is broken, or the
pitcher is broken at the fountain, or the wheel
broken at the cistern, [7]and the dust returns to the
earth as it was, and the spirit returns to God who
gave it. [8]Vanity of vanities, says the Preacher; all
is vanity.

Epilogue

9 Besides being wise, the Preacher also taught
the people knowledge, weighing and studying
and arranging proverbs with great care. [10]The
Preacher sought to find pleasing words, and uprightly he wrote words of truth.
11 The sayings of the wise are like goads, and
like nails firmly fixed are the collected sayings
which are given by one Shepherd. [12]My son, beware of anything beyond these. Of making many
books there is no end, and much study is a weariness of the flesh.
13 The end of the matter; all has been heard.
Fear God, and keep his commandments; for this is
the whole duty of man. [s] [14]For God will bring
every deed into judgment, with [t] every secret
thing, whether good or evil.

---

[p] Or *As you do not know the way of the wind, or how the bones grow in
the womb.*
[q] Or *is a burden.*
[r] Syr Vg Compare Gk: Heb *is removed.*
[s] Or *the duty of all men.*
[t] Or *into the judgment on.*

THE
SONG OF SOLOMON

Song of the Bride and Her Companions

1 The Song of Songs, which is Solomon's.

[2]O that you [a] would kiss me with the kisses of
    your [b] mouth!
For your love is better than wine,
[3]   your anointing oils are fragrant,
your name is oil poured out;
    therefore the maidens love you.
[4]Draw me after you, let us make haste.
    The king has brought me into his chambers.
We will exult and rejoice in you;
    we will extol your love more than wine;
    rightly do they love you.

[5]I am very dark, but comely,
    O daughters of Jerusalem,
like the tents of Ke′dar,
    like the curtains of Solomon.
[6]Do not gaze at me because I am swarthy,
    because the sun has scorched me.
My mother's sons were angry with me,
    they made me keeper of the vineyards;
    but, my own vineyard I have not kept!
[7]Tell me, you whom my soul loves,
    where you pasture your flock,
    where you make it lie down at noon;
for why should I be like one who wanders [c]
    beside the flocks of your companions?

[8]If you do not know,
    O fairest among women,
follow in the tracks of the flock,
    and pasture your kids
    beside the shepherds' tents.

[9]I compare you, my love,
    to a mare of Pharaoh's chariots.
[10]Your cheeks are comely with ornaments,
    your neck with strings of jewels.
[11]We will make you ornaments of gold,
    studded with silver.

[12]While the king was on his couch,
    my nard gave forth its fragrance.
[13]My beloved is to me a bag of myrrh,
    that lies between my breasts.
[14]My beloved is to me a cluster of henna
    blossoms
    in the vineyards of En-ge′di.

[15]Behold, you are beautiful, my love;
    behold, you are beautiful;
    your eyes are doves.
[16]Behold, you are beautiful, my beloved,
    truly lovely.
Our couch is green;
[17]   the beams of our house are cedar,
    our rafters [d] are pine.

A Springtime Canticle

2 I am a rose [e] of Sharon,
    a lily of the valleys.

[2]As a lily among brambles,
    so is my love among maidens.

[3]As an apple tree among the trees of the wood,
    so is my beloved among young men.
With great delight I sat in his shadow,
    and his fruit was sweet to my taste.
[4]He brought me to the banqueting house,
    and his banner over me was love.
[5]Sustain me with raisins,
    refresh me with apples;
    for I am sick with love.
[6]O that his left hand were under my head,
    and that his right hand embraced me!

The full title is "The Song of Songs Which Is Solomon's." But, as in the
case of other books, it is ascribed to him because of his fame. It is a love
song or collection of love songs written probably in the fifth century B.C.
The Jews had some doubts as to its canonical character but finally included it in their canon of Scripture, and it has always been accepted by
the Christian Church as inspired and canonical.

   The interpretations of the book have been of great variety. For our
purpose we may summarize them thus: (1) It is purely allegorical. For the
Jews it represented the relationship between God and his chosen people
Israel, which is often in the Old Testament described under the figure of a
marriage. The Christian Fathers, of course, saw it as an allegory of Christ
and his Church, describing the mystic union between the two; cf. Eph
5:21–33. (2) Others hold it to be a poem describing human love between
bride and groom without seeking to identify actual historical persons.
The writer's purpose was to extol married love and the sanctity of the
marriage bond as instituted and blessed by God. There is support in the
Old Testament for this view, e.g., in Proverbs and Sirach. (3) Others
again, while admitting the above literal sense of the book, say that it is to
be taken in the typical sense of the union of God with Israel, and of the
union of Christ with his Church.

   Catholics tend to adopt the first or third of these positions. Either way,
the interpretation can be developed to include the relations between God
and the individual soul, as is done by mystical writers, e.g., St. John of the
Cross. The Song of Solomon is extensively used in the liturgy, particu-
larly on feasts of the Blessed Virgin Mary and of Holy Women.

   Although this is the one book of the Bible where God is never mentioned by name, its presence in the Bible indicates the sanctity of human
love.
[a] Heb *he.*
[b] Heb *his.*
[c] Gk Syr Vg: Heb *is veiled.*
[d] The meaning of the Hebrew word is uncertain.
[e] Heb *crocus.*

⁷I adjure you, O daughters of Jerusalem,
    by the gazelles or the deer of the field,
that you stir not up nor awaken love
    until it please.

⁸The voice of my beloved!
    Behold, he comes,
leaping upon the mountains,
    bounding over the hills.
⁹My beloved is like a gazelle,
    or a young stag.
Behold, there he stands
    behind our wall,
gazing in at the windows,
    looking through the lattice.
¹⁰My beloved speaks and says to me:
    "Arise, my love, my dove, my fair one,
    and come away;
¹¹for behold, the winter is past,
    the rain is over and gone.
¹²The flowers appear on the earth,
    the time of pruning has come,
and the voice of the turtledove
    is heard in our land.
¹³The fig tree puts forth its figs,
    and the vines are in blossom;
    they give forth fragrance.
Arise, my love, my fair one,
    and come away.
¹⁴O my dove, in the clefts of the rock,
    in the covert of the cliff,
let me see your face,
    let me hear your voice,
for your voice is sweet,
    and your face is comely.
¹⁵Catch us the foxes,
    the little foxes,
that spoil the vineyards,
    for our vineyards are in blossom."

¹⁶My beloved is mine and I am his,
    he pastures his flock among the lilies.
¹⁷Until the day breathes
    and the shadows flee,
turn, my beloved, be like a gazelle,
    or a young stag upon rugged ᶠ mountains.

Love Seeking the Bridegroom

3 Upon my bed by night
    I sought him whom my soul loves;
I sought him, but found him not;
    I called him, but he gave no answer. ᵍ
²"I will rise now and go about the city,
    in the streets and in the squares;
I will seek him whom my soul loves."
    I sought him, but found him not.
³The watchmen found me,
    as they went about in the city.
"Have you seen him whom my soul loves?"
⁴Scarcely had I passed them,
    when I found him whom my soul loves.

I held him, and would not let him go
    until I had brought him into my mother's
      house,
    and into the chamber of her that conceived
      me.
⁵I adjure you, O daughters of Jerusalem,
    by the gazelles or the deer of the field,
that you stir not up nor awaken love until it
    please.

⁶What is that coming up from the wilderness,
    like a column of smoke,
perfumed with myrrh and frankincense,
    with all the fragrant powders of the
      merchant?
⁷Behold, it is the litter of Solomon!
    About it are sixty mighty men
    of the mighty men of Israel,
⁸all belted with swords
    and expert in war,
each with his sword at his thigh,
    against alarms by night.
⁹King Solomon made himself a palanquin
    from the wood of Lebanon.
¹⁰He made its posts of silver,
    its back of gold, its seat of purple;
it was lovingly wrought within ʰ
    by the daughters of Jerusalem.
¹¹Go forth, O daughters of Zion,
    and behold King Solomon,
with the crown with which his mother crowned
      him
    on the day of his wedding,
    on the day of the gladness of his heart.

The Bride's Beauty Extolled

4 Behold, you are beautiful, my love,
    behold, you are beautiful!
Your eyes are doves
    behind your veil.
Your hair is like a flock of goats,
    moving down the slopes of Gilead.
²Your teeth are like a flock of shorn ewes
    that have come up from the washing,
all of which bear twins,
    and not one among them is bereaved.
³Your lips are like a scarlet thread,
    and your mouth is lovely.
Your cheeks are like halves of a pomegranate
    behind your veil.
⁴Your neck is like the tower of David,
    built for an arsenal, ⁱ
whereon hang a thousand bucklers,
    all of them shields of warriors.
⁵Your two breasts are like two fawns,
    twins of a gazelle,
    that feed among the lilies.

ᶠ The meaning of the Hebrew word is unknown.
ᵍ Gk: Heb lacks this line.
ʰ The meaning of the Hebrew is uncertain.
ⁱ The meaning of the Hebrew word is uncertain.

⁶Until the day breathes
 and the shadows flee,
 I will hasten to the mountain of myrrh
 and the hill of frankincense.
⁷You are all fair, my love;
 there is no flaw in you.
⁸Come with me from Lebanon, my bride;
 come with me from Lebanon.
 Depart ^j from the peak of Ama′na,
 from the peak of Se′nir and Hermon,
 from the dens of lions,
 from the mountains of leopards.

⁹You have ravished my heart, my sister, my
 bride,
 you have ravished my heart with a glance
 of your eyes,
 with one jewel of your necklace.
¹⁰How sweet is your love, my sister, my bride!
 how much better is your love than wine,
 and the fragrance of your oils than any
 spice!
¹¹Your lips distil nectar, my bride;
 honey and milk are under your tongue;
 the scent of your garments is like the scent
 of Lebanon.
¹²A garden locked is my sister, my bride,
 a garden locked, a fountain sealed.
¹³Your shoots are an orchard of pomegranates
 with all choicest fruits,
 henna with nard,
¹⁴nard and saffron, calamus and cinnamon,
 with all trees of frankincense,
 myrrh and aloes,
 with all chief spices—
¹⁵a garden fountain, a well of living water,
 and flowing streams from Lebanon.

¹⁶Awake, O north wind,
 and come, O south wind!
 Blow upon my garden,
 let its fragrance be wafted abroad.
 Let my beloved come to his garden,
 and eat its choicest fruits.

The Groom's Song of Love; and the Torment of Separation

5 I come to my garden, my sister, my bride,
 I gather my myrrh with my spice,
 I eat my honeycomb with my honey,
 I drink my wine with my milk.

 Eat, O friends, and drink:
 drink deeply, O lovers!
²I slept, but my heart was awake.
 Hark! my beloved is knocking.
 "Open to me, my sister, my love,
 my dove, my perfect one;
 for my head is wet with dew,
 my locks with the drops of the night."

³I had put off my garment,
 how could I put it on?
 I had bathed my feet,
 how could I soil them?
⁴My beloved put his hand to the latch,
 and my heart was thrilled within me.
⁵I arose to open to my beloved,
 and my hands dripped with myrrh,
 my fingers with liquid myrrh,
 upon the handles of the bolt.
⁶I opened to my beloved,
 but my beloved had turned and gone.
 My soul failed me when he spoke.
 I sought him, but found him not;
 I called him, but he gave no answer.
⁷The watchmen found me,
 as they went about in the city;
 they beat me, they wounded me,
 they took away my mantle,
 those watchmen of the walls.
⁸I adjure you, O daughters of Jerusalem,
 if you find my beloved,
 that you tell him
 I am sick with love.

⁹What is your beloved more than another
 beloved,
 O fairest among women?
 What is your beloved more than another
 beloved,
 that you thus adjure us?

¹⁰My beloved is all radiant and ruddy,
 distinguished among ten thousand.
¹¹His head is the finest gold;
 his locks are wavy,
 black as a raven.
¹²His eyes are like doves
 beside springs of water,
 bathed in milk,
 fitly set.^k
¹³His cheeks are like beds of spices,
 yielding fragrance.
 His lips are lilies,
 distilling liquid myrrh.
¹⁴His arms are rounded gold,
 set with jewels.
 His body is ivory work,^l
 encrusted with sapphires.^m
¹⁵His legs are alabaster columns,
 set upon bases of gold.
 His appearance is like Lebanon,
 choice as the cedars.
¹⁶His speech is most sweet,
 and he is altogether desirable.

---

^j Or Look.
^k The meaning of the Hebrew is uncertain.
^l The meaning of the Hebrew word is uncertain.
^m Heb lapis lazuli.

This is my beloved and this is my friend,
    O daughters of Jerusalem.

Colloquy of the Friends and the Bride;
the Bridegroom's Praise of the Bride

6 Where has your beloved gone,
    O fairest among women?
Where has your beloved turned,
    that we may seek him with you?

[2]My beloved has gone down to his garden,
    to the beds of spices,
to pasture his flock in the gardens,
    and to gather lilies.
[3]I am my beloved's and my beloved is mine;
    he pastures his flock among the lilies.

[4]You are beautiful as Tirzah, my love,
    comely as Jerusalem,
    terrible as an army with banners.
[5]Turn away your eyes from me,
    for they disturb me——
Your hair is like a flock of goats,
    moving down the slopes of Gilead.
[6]Your teeth are like a flock of ewes,
    that have come up from the washing,
all of them bear twins,
    not one among them is bereaved.
[7]Your cheeks are like halves of a pomegranate
    behind your veil.
[8]There are sixty queens and eighty concubines,
    and maidens without number.
[9]My dove, my perfect one, is only one,
    the darling of her mother,
    flawless to her that bore her.
The maidens saw her and called her happy;
    the queens and concubines also, and they
    praised her.
[10]"Who is this that looks forth like the dawn,
    fair as the moon, bright as the sun,
    terrible as an army with banners?"

[11]I went down to the nut orchard,
    to look at the blossoms of the valley,
to see whether the vines had budded,
    whether the pomegranates were in bloom.
[12]Before I was aware, my fancy set me
    in a chariot beside my prince.[n]

[13] [o]Return, return, O Shu'lammite,
    return, return, that we may look upon you.

Why should you look upon the Shulammite,
    as upon a dance before two armies?[p]

Colloquy of the Bride and the Groom

7 How graceful are your feet in sandals,
    O queenly maiden!
Your rounded thighs are like jewels,
    the work of a master hand.
[2]Your navel is a rounded bowl
    that never lacks mixed wine.

Your belly is a heap of wheat,
    encircled with lilies.
[3]Your two breasts are like two fawns,
    twins of a gazelle.
[4]Your neck is like an ivory tower.
Your eyes are pools in Hesh'bon,
    by the gate of Bath-rab'bim.
Your nose is like a tower of Lebanon,
    overlooking Damascus.
[5]Your head crowns you like Car'mel,
    and your flowing locks are like purple;
    a king is held captive in the tresses. [q]

[6]How fair and pleasant you are,
    O loved one, delectable maiden! [r]
[7]You are stately [s] as a palm tree,
    and your breasts are like its clusters.
[8]I say I will climb the palm tree
    and lay hold of its branches.
Oh, may your breasts be like clusters of the
    vine,
    and the scent of your breath like apples,
[9]and your kisses [t] like the best wine
    that goes down [u] smoothly,
    gliding over lips and teeth. [v]

[10]I am my beloved's,
    and his desire is for me.
[11]Come, my beloved,
    let us go forth into the fields,
    and lodge in the villages;
[12]let us go out early to the vineyards,
    and see whether the vines have budded,
whether the grape blossoms have opened
    and the pomegranates are in bloom.
There I will give you my love.
[13]The mandrakes give forth fragrance,
    and over our doors are all choice fruits,
new as well as old,
    which I have laid up for you, O my beloved.

Metaphors of Love

8 O that you were like a brother to me,
    that nursed at my mother's breast!
If I met you outside, I would kiss you,
    and none would despise me.
[2]I would lead you and bring you
    into the house of my mother,
    and into the chamber of her that conceived
    me. [w]
I would give you spiced wine to drink,
    the juice of my pomegranates.

---

[n] Cn: The meaning of the Hebrew is uncertain.
[o] Ch 7:1 in Heb.
[p] Or *dance of Mahanaim.*
[q] The meaning of the Hebrew word is uncertain.
[r] Syr: Heb *in delights.*
[s] Heb *This your stature is.*
[t] Heb *palate.*
[u] Heb *down for my lover.*
[v] Gk Syr Vg: Heb *lips of sleepers.*
[w] Gk Syr: Heb *mother; she* (or *you*) *will teach me.*

³O that his left hand were under my head,
and that his right hand embraced me!
⁴I adjure you, O daughters of Jerusalem,
that you stir not up nor awaken love
until it please.

⁵Who is that coming up from the wilderness,
leaning upon her beloved?

Under the apple tree I awakened you.
There your mother was in travail with you,
there she who bore you was in travail.

⁶Set me as a seal upon your heart,
as a seal upon your arm;
for love is strong as death,
jealousy is cruel as the grave.
Its flashes are flashes of fire,
a most vehement flame.
⁷Many waters cannot quench love,
neither can floods drown it.
If a man offered for love
all the wealth of his house,
it would be utterly scorned.

⁸We have a little sister,
and she has no breasts.
What shall we do for our sister,
on the day when she is spoken for?

⁹If she is a wall,
we will build upon her a battlement of
silver;
but if she is a door,
we will enclose her with boards of cedar.
¹⁰I was a wall,
and my breasts were like towers;
then I was in his eyes
as one who brings ˣ peace.

¹¹Solomon had a vineyard at Ba′al-ha′mon;
he let out the vineyard to keepers;
each one was to bring for its fruit a
thousand pieces of silver.
¹²My vineyard, my very own, is for myself;
you, O Solomon, may have the thousand,
and the keepers of the fruit two hundred.
¹³O you who dwell in the gardens,
my companions are listening for your voice;
let me hear it.

¹⁴Make haste, my beloved,
and be like a gazelle
or a young stag
upon the mountains of spices.

ˣ Or *finds*.

THE
WISDOM OF SOLOMON

Exhortation to Uprightness and Avoidance of Evil

1 Love righteousness, you rulers of the earth,
  think of the Lord with uprightness,
and seek him with sincerity of heart;
[2]because he is found by those who do not put
  him to the test,
and manifests himself to those who do not
  distrust him.
[3]For perverse thoughts separate men from God,
and when his power is tested, it convicts the
  foolish;
[4]because wisdom will not enter a deceitful soul,
nor dwell in a body enslaved to sin.
[5]For a holy and disciplined spirit * will flee from
  deceit,
and will rise and depart from foolish thoughts,
and will be ashamed at the approach of
  unrighteousness.

[6]For wisdom is a kindly spirit
and will not free a blasphemer from the guilt of
  his words;
because God is witness of his inmost feelings,
and a true observer of his heart, and a hearer
  of his tongue.
[7]Because the Spirit of the Lord has filled the
  world,
and that which holds all things together knows
  what is said;
[8]therefore no one who utters unrighteous things
  will escape notice,
and justice, when it punishes, will not pass him
  by.
[9]For inquiry will be made into the counsels of
  an ungodly man,
and a report of his words will come to the
  Lord,
to convict him of his lawless deeds;
[10]because a jealous ear hears all things,
and the sound of murmurings does not go
  unheard.
[11]Beware then of useless murmuring,
and keep your tongue from slander;
because no secret word is without result, [a]
and a lying mouth destroys the soul.

[12]Do not invite death by the error of your life,
  nor bring on destruction by the works of your
  hands;

[13]because God did not make death, and
he does not delight in the death of the living.
[14]For he created all things that they might exist,
and the creatures [b] of the world are
  wholesome,
and there is no destructive poison in them;
and the dominion [c] of Hades is not on earth.
[15]For righteousness is immortal.

[16]But ungodly men by their words and deeds
  summoned death; [d]
considering him a friend, they pined away,
and they made a covenant with him,
because they are fit to belong to his party.

2 For they reasoned unsoundly, saying to
  themselves,
"Short and sorrowful is our life,
and there is no remedy when a man comes to
  his end,
and no one has been known to return from
  Hades.
[2]Because we were born by mere chance,
and hereafter we shall be as though we had
  never been;
because the breath in our nostrils is smoke,
and reason is a spark kindled by the beating of
  our hearts.
[3]When it is extinguished, the body will turn to
  ashes,
and the spirit will dissolve like empty air.
[4]Our name will be forgotten in time,
and no one will remember our works;
our life will pass away like the traces of a
  cloud,

The book describes the part that Wisdom plays in the life and destiny of
men and how we should acquire it, says much about the divine Wisdom,
and, in the latter part of the book, relates how the chosen people were
guided thereby throughout their history. At times the book proclaims
truths not exactly in harmony with beliefs then current, e.g., that suffering is not necessarily the consequence of sin. The book was written in
Greek, probably in the first century B.C. Its author is unknown. It is
ascribed to Solomon according to a widespread practice of the time of
adopting the name of a famous man in antiquity to "father" one's work.
Thus David was known to have written psalms and hence many subsequent psalms were ascribed to him. Moses enacted laws and thus many
subsequent laws were ascribed to him which at best could be said to be
only indirectly connected with the great lawgiver. So here, Solomon was
the "wise man"—and hence it was natural to attribute the book to him.
 [a] Or *will go unpunished.*
 [b] Or *the generative forces.*
 [c] Or *palace.*
 [d] Gk *him.*
 * 1:5, a *holy and disciplined spirit:* Literally, "a holy spirit of discipline."
Verse 6 seems to suggest here a personification of the Holy Spirit; cf. also
verse 7: *the Spirit of the Lord.*

and be scattered like mist
that is chased by the rays of the sun
and overcome by its heat.
⁵For our allotted time is the passing of a
shadow,
and there is no return from our death,
because it is sealed up and no one turns back.

⁶"Come, therefore, let us enjoy the good things
that exist,
and make use of the creation to the full as in
youth.
⁷Let us take our fill of costly wine and perfumes,
and let no flower of spring pass by us.
⁸Let us crown ourselves with rosebuds before
they wither.
⁹Let none of us fail to share in our revelry,
everywhere let us leave signs of enjoyment,
because this is our portion, and this our lot.
¹⁰Let us oppress the righteous poor man;
let us not spare the widow
nor regard the gray hairs of the aged.
¹¹But let our might be our law of right,
for what is weak proves itself to be useless.

¹²"Let us lie in wait for the righteous man,
because he is inconvenient to us and opposes
our actions;
he reproaches us for sins against the law,
and accuses us of sins against our training.
¹³He professes to have knowledge of God,
and calls himself a child ᵉ of the Lord.
¹⁴He became to us a reproof of our thoughts;
¹⁵the very sight of him is a burden to us,
because his manner of life is unlike that of
others,
and his ways are strange.
¹⁶We are considered by him as something base,
and he avoids our ways as unclean;
he calls the last end of the righteous happy,
and boasts that God is his father.
¹⁷Let us see if his words are true,
and let us test what will happen at the end of
his life;
¹⁸for if the righteous man is God's son, he will
help him,
and will deliver him from the hand of his
adversaries.
¹⁹Let us test him with insult and torture,
that we may find out how gentle he is,
and make trial of his forbearance.
²⁰Let us condemn him to a shameful death,
for, according to what he says, he will be
protected."

²¹Thus they reasoned, but they were led astray,
for their wickedness blinded them,
²²and they did not know the secret purposes of
God,

nor hope for the wages of holiness,
nor discern the prize for blameless souls;
²³for God created man for incorruption,
and made him in the image of his own
eternity, ᶠ
²⁴but through the devil's envy death entered the
world,
and those who belong to his party experience it.

**The Destiny of the Righteous
Contrasted to the Ungodly**

3 But the souls of the righteous are in the hand
of God,
and no torment will ever touch them.
²In the eyes of the foolish they seemed to have
died,
and their departure was thought to be an
affliction,
³and their going from us to be their destruction;
but they are at peace.
⁴For though in the sight of men they were
punished,
their hope is full of immortality.
⁵Having been disciplined a little, they will
receive great good,
because God tested them and found them
worthy of himself;
⁶like gold in the furnace he tried them,
and like a sacrificial burnt offering he accepted
them.
⁷In the time of their visitation they will shine
forth,
and will run like sparks through the stubble.
⁸They will govern nations and rule over
peoples,
and the Lord will reign over them for ever.
⁹Those who trust in him will understand truth,
and the faithful will abide with him in love,
because grace and mercy are upon his elect,
and he watches over his holy ones. ᵍ
¹⁰But the ungodly will be punished as their
reasoning deserves,
who disregarded the righteous man ʰ and
rebelled against the Lord;
¹¹for whoever despises wisdom and instruction is
miserable.
Their hope is vain, their labors are
unprofitable,
and their works are useless.
¹²Their wives are foolish, and their children evil;
¹³their offspring are accursed.
For blessed is the barren woman who is
undefiled,
who has not entered into a sinful union;
she will have fruit when God examines souls.

ᵉ Or *servant*.
ᶠ Other ancient authorities read *nature*.
ᵍ The text of this line is uncertain, and it is omitted here by some
ancient authorities. Compare 4:15.
ʰ Or *what is right*.

¹⁴Blessed also is the eunuch whose hands have
    done no lawless deed,
and who has not devised wicked things against
    the Lord;
for special favor will be shown him for his
    faithfulness,
and a place of great delight in the temple of
    the Lord.
¹⁵For the fruit of good labors is renowned,
and the root of understanding does not fail.
¹⁶But children of adulterers will not come to
    maturity,
and the offspring of an unlawful union will
    perish.
¹⁷Even if they live long they will be held of no
    account,
and finally their old age will be without honor.
¹⁸If they die young, they will have no hope
and no consolation in the day of decision.
¹⁹For the end of an unrighteous generation is
    grievous.

The Reward of the Righteous

4 Better than this is childlessness with virtue,
    for in the memory of virtue ʲ is immortality,
because it is known both by God and by men.
²When it is present, men imitate ʲ it,
and they long for it when it has gone;
and throughout all time it marches crowned in
    triumph,
victor in the contest for prizes that are undefiled.
³But the prolific brood of the ungodly will be of
    no use,
and none of their illegitimate seedlings will
    strike a deep root
or take a firm hold.
⁴For even if they put forth boughs for a while,
standing insecurely they will be shaken by the
    wind,
and by the violence of the winds they will be
    uprooted.
⁵The branches will be broken off before they
    come to maturity,
and their fruit will be useless,
not ripe enough to eat, and good for nothing.
⁶For children born of unlawful unions
are witnesses of evil against their parents
    when God examines them.ᵏ

⁷But the righteous man, though he die early, will
    be at rest.
⁸For old age is not honored for length of time,
nor measured by number of years;
⁹but understanding is gray hair for men,
and a blameless life is ripe old age.

¹⁰There was one who pleased God and was loved
    by him,
and while living among sinners he was taken
    up.

¹¹He was caught up lest evil change his
    understanding
or guile deceive his soul.
¹²For the fascination of wickedness obscures
    what is good,
and roving desire perverts the innocent mind.
¹³Being perfected in a short time, he fulfilled long
    years;
¹⁴for his soul was pleasing to the Lord,
therefore he took him quickly from the midst
    of wickedness.
¹⁵Yet the peoples saw and did not understand,
nor take such a thing to heart,
that God's grace and mercy are with his elect,
and he watches over his holy ones.

¹⁶The righteous man who has died will condemn
    the ungodly who are living,
and youth that is quickly perfected ˡ will
    condemn the prolonged old age of the
    unrighteous man.
¹⁷For they will see the end of the wise man,
and will not understand what the Lord
    purposed for him,
and for what he kept him safe.
¹⁸They will see, and will have contempt for him,
but the Lord will laugh them to scorn.
After this they will become dishonored
    corpses,
and an outrage among the dead for ever;
¹⁹because he will dash them speechless to the
    ground,
and shake them from the foundations;
they will be left utterly dry and barren,
and they will suffer anguish,
and the memory of them will perish.

²⁰They will come with dread when their sins are
    reckoned up,
and their lawless deeds will convict them to
    their face.

5 Then the righteous man will stand with
    great confidence
in the presence of those who have afflicted him,
and those who make light of his labors.
²When they see him, they will be shaken with
    dreadful fear,
and they will be amazed at his unexpected
    salvation.
³They will speak to one another in repentance,
and in anguish of spirit they will groan, and
    say,
⁴"This is the man whom we once held in
    derision
and made a byword of reproach—we fools!

ⁱ Gk it.
ʲ Other ancient authorities read honor.
ᵏ Gk at their examination.
ˡ Or ended.

We thought that his life was madness
and that his end was without honor.
⁵Why has he been numbered among the sons of
God?
And why is his lot among the saints?
⁶So it was we who strayed from the way of
truth,
and the light of righteousness did not shine on
us,
and the sun did not rise upon us.
⁷We took our fill of the paths of lawlessness
and destruction,
and we journeyed through trackless deserts,
but the way of the Lord we have not known.
⁸What has our arrogance profited us?
And what good has our boasted wealth
brought us?
⁹"All those things have vanished like a shadow,
and like a rumor that passes by;
¹⁰like a ship that sails through the billowy
water,
and when it has passed no trace can be found,
nor track of its keel in the waves;
¹¹or as, when a bird flies through the air,
no evidence of its passage is found;
the light air, lashed by the beat of its pinions
and pierced by the force of its rushing flight,
is traversed by the movement of its wings,
and afterward no sign of its coming is found
there;
¹²or as, when an arrow is shot at a target,
the air, thus divided, comes together at once,
so that no one knows its pathway.
¹³So we also, as soon as we were born, ceased to
be,
and we had no sign of virtue to show,
but were consumed in our wickedness." *
¹⁴Because the hope of the ungodly man is like
chaff ᵐ carried by the wind,
and like a light hoarfrost ⁿ driven away by a
storm;
it is dispersed like smoke before the wind,
and it passes like the remembrance of a guest
who stays but a day.

¹⁵But the righteous live for ever,
and their reward is with the Lord;
the Most High takes care of them.
¹⁶Therefore they will receive a glorious crown
and a beautiful diadem from the hand of the
Lord,
because with his right hand he will cover them,
and with his arm he will shield them.
¹⁷The Lord ° will take his zeal as his whole
armor,
and will arm all creation to repel ᵖ his enemies;
¹⁸he will put on righteousness as a breastplate,
and wear impartial justice as a helmet;
¹⁹he will take holiness as an invincible shield,

²⁰and sharpen stern wrath for a sword,
and creation will join with him to fight against
the madmen.
²¹Shafts of lightning will fly with true aim,
and will leap to the target as from a well-drawn
bow of clouds,
²²and hailstones full of wrath will be hurled as
from a catapult;
the water of the sea will rage against them,
and rivers will relentlessly overwhelm them;
²³a mighty wind will rise against them,
and like a tempest it will winnow them away.
Lawlessness will lay waste the whole earth,
and evil-doing will overturn the thrones of
rulers.

Admonition to Rulers

6 Listen therefore, O kings, and understand;
learn, O judges of the ends of the earth.
²Give ear, you that rule over multitudes,
and boast of many nations.
³For your dominion was given you from the
Lord,
and your sovereignty from the Most High,
who will search out your works and inquire
into your plans.
⁴Because as servants of his kingdom you did
not rule rightly,
nor keep the law,
nor walk according to the purpose of God,
⁵he will come upon you terribly and swiftly,
because severe judgment falls on those in high
places.
⁶For the lowliest man may be pardoned in
mercy,
but mighty men will be mightily tested. †
⁷For the Lord of all will not stand in awe of any
one,
nor show deference to greatness;
because he himself made both small and
great,
and he takes thought for all alike.
⁸But a strict inquiry is in store for the mighty.
⁹To you then, O monarchs, my words are
directed,
that you may learn wisdom and not
transgress.
¹⁰For they will be made holy who observe holy
things in holiness,
and those who have been taught them will find
a defense.
¹¹Therefore set your desire on my words;
long for them, and you will be instructed.

ᵐ Or *dust.*
ⁿ Other authorities read *spider's web.*
° Gk *He.*
ᵖ Or *punish.*
* 5:13: Vulgate adds (verse 14): "¹⁴Such things as these the sinners said
in hell."
† 6:6, *tested:* The meaning seems rather to be "tormented" and to refer to
punishment.

¹²Wisdom is radiant and unfading,
and she is easily discerned by those who love
her,
and is found by those who seek her.
¹³She hastens to make herself known to those
who desire her.
¹⁴He who rises early to seek her will have no
difficulty,
for he will find her sitting at his gates.
¹⁵To fix one's thought on her is perfect
understanding,
and he who is vigilant on her account will soon
be free from care,
¹⁶because she goes about seeking those worthy
of her,
and she graciously appears to them in their
paths,
and meets them in every thought.

¹⁷The beginning of wisdom �q is the most sincere
desire for instruction,
and concern for instruction is love of her,
¹⁸and love of her is the keeping of her laws,
and giving heed to her laws is assurance of
immortality,
¹⁹and immortality brings one near to God;
²⁰so the desire for wisdom leads to a kingdom.

²¹Therefore if you delight in thrones and
scepters, O monarchs over the peoples,
honor wisdom, that you may reign for ever.
²²I will tell you what wisdom is and how she
came to be,
and I will hide no secrets from you,
but I will trace her course from the beginning
of creation,
and make knowledge of her clear,
and I will not pass by the truth;
²³neither will I travel in the company of sickly
envy,
for envy ʳ does not associate with wisdom.
²⁴A multitude of wise men is the salvation of the
world,
and a sensible king is the stability of his
people.
²⁵Therefore be instructed by my words,
and you will profit.

Solomon's Prayer for and Love of Wisdom

7 I also am mortal, like all men,
a descendant of the first-formed child of
earth;
and in the womb of a mother I was molded into
flesh,
²within the period of ten months, compacted
with blood,
from the seed of a man and the pleasure of
marriage.
³And when I was born, I began to breathe the
common air,

and fell upon the kindred earth,
and my first sound was a cry, like that of all.
⁴I was nursed with care in swaddling cloths.
⁵For no king has had a different beginning of
existence;
⁶there is for all mankind one entrance into life,
and a common departure.

⁷Therefore I prayed, and understanding was
given me;
I called upon God, and the spirit of wisdom
came to me.
⁸I preferred her to scepters and thrones,
and I accounted wealth as nothing in
comparison with her.
⁹Neither did I liken to her any priceless gem,
because all gold is but a little sand in her sight,
and silver will be accounted as clay before her.
¹⁰I loved her more than health and beauty,
and I chose to have her rather than light,
because her radiance never ceases.
¹¹All good things came to me along with her,
and in her hands uncounted wealth.
¹²I rejoiced in them all, because wisdom leads
them;
but I did not know that she was their mother.
¹³I learned without guile and I impart without
grudging;
I do not hide her wealth,
¹⁴for it is an unfailing treasure for men;
those who get it obtain friendship with God,
commended for the gifts that come from
instruction.
¹⁵May God grant that I speak with judgment
and have thoughts worthy of what I have
received,
for he is the guide even of wisdom
and the corrector of the wise.
¹⁶For both we and our words are in his hand,
as are all understanding and skill in crafts.
¹⁷For it is he who gave me unerring knowledge
of what exists,
to know the structure of the world and the
activity of the elements;
¹⁸the beginning and end and middle of times,
the alternations of the solstices and the
changes of the seasons,
¹⁹the cycles of the year and the constellations of
the stars,
²⁰the natures of animals and the tempers of wild
beasts,
the powers of spirits ˢ and the reasonings of
men,
the varieties of plants and the virtues of roots;
²¹I learned both what is secret and what is
manifest,

�q Gk Her beginning.
ʳ Gk this.
ˢ Or winds.

²²for wisdom, the fashioner of all things, taught
    me.

For in her there is a spirit that is intelligent,
    holy,
unique, manifold, subtle,
mobile, clear, unpolluted,
distinct, invulnerable, loving the good, keen,
irresistible, ²³beneficent, humane,
steadfast, sure, free from anxiety,
all-powerful, overseeing all,
and penetrating through all spirits
that are intelligent and pure and most subtle.
²⁴For wisdom is more mobile than any motion;
    because of her pureness she pervades and
        penetrates all things.
²⁵For she is a breath of the power of God,
    and a pure emanation of the glory of the
        Almighty;
    therefore nothing defiled gains entrance into
        her.
²⁶For she is a reflection of eternal light,
    a spotless mirror of the working of God,
    and an image of his goodness.
²⁷Though she is but one, she can do all things,
    and while remaining in herself, she renews all
        things;
    in every generation she passes into holy souls
    and makes them friends of God, and
        prophets;
²⁸for God loves nothing so much as the man who
    lives with wisdom.
²⁹For she is more beautiful than the sun,
    and excels every constellation of the stars.
    Compared with the light she is found to be
        superior,
³⁰for it is succeeded by the night,
    but against wisdom evil does not prevail.

8 She reaches mightily from one end of the
    earth to the other,
    and she orders all things well.

²I loved her and sought her from my youth,
    and I desired to take her for my bride,
    and I became enamored of her beauty.
³She glorifies her noble birth by living with
    God,
    and the Lord of all loves her.
⁴For she is an initiate in the knowledge of God,
    and an associate in his works.
⁵If riches are a desirable possession in life,
    what is richer than wisdom who effects all
        things?
⁶And if understanding is effective,
    who more than she is fashioner of what
        exists?
⁷And if any one loves righteousness,
    her labors are virtues;
    for she teaches self-control and prudence,

justice and courage;
nothing in life is more profitable for men than
    these.
⁸And if any one longs for wide experience,
    she knows the things of old, and infers the
        things to come;
    she understands turns of speech and the
        solutions of riddles;
    she has foreknowledge of signs and wonders
    and of the outcome of seasons and times.
⁹Therefore I determined to take her to live with
    me,
    knowing that she would give me good counsel
    and encouragement in cares and grief.
¹⁰Because of her I shall have glory among the
    multitudes
    and honor in the presence of the elders, though
        I am young.
¹¹I shall be found keen in judgment,
    and in the sight of rulers I shall be admired.
¹²When I am silent they will wait for me,
    and when I speak they will give heed;
    and when I speak at greater length
    they will put their hands on their mouths.
¹³Because of her I shall have immortality,
    and leave an everlasting remembrance to those
        who come after me.
¹⁴I shall govern peoples,
    and nations will be subject to me;
¹⁵dread monarchs will be afraid of me when they
        hear of me;
    among the people I shall show myself capable,
    and courageous in war.
¹⁶When I enter my house, I shall find rest with
        her,
    for companionship with her has no bitterness,
    and life with her has no pain, but gladness and
        joy.
¹⁷When I considered these things inwardly,
    and thought upon them in my mind,
    that in kinship with wisdom there is
        immortality,
¹⁸and in friendship with her, pure delight,
    and in the labors of her hands, unfailing
        wealth,
    and in the experience of her company,
        understanding,
    and renown in sharing her words,
    I went about seeking how to get her for myself.
¹⁹As a child I was by nature well endowed,
    and a good soul fell to my lot;
²⁰or rather, being good, I entered an undefiled
        body.
²¹But I perceived that I would not possess
        wisdom unless God gave her to me—
    and it was a mark of insight to know whose
        gift she was—
    so I appealed to the Lord and implored him,
    and with my whole heart I said:

The Prayer of Solomon

9 "O God of my fathers and Lord of mercy,
who have made all things by your word,
[2]and by your wisdom have formed man,
to have dominion over the creatures you have
made,
[3]and rule the world in holiness and
righteousness,
and pronounce judgment in uprightness of
soul,
[4]give me the wisdom that sits by your throne,
and do not reject me from among your
servants.
[5]For I am your slave and the son of your
maidservant,
a man who is weak and short-lived,
with little understanding of judgment and
laws;
[6]for even if one is perfect among the sons of
men,
yet without the wisdom that comes from you he
will be regarded as nothing.
[7]You have chosen me to be king of your people
and to be judge over your sons and daughters.
[8]You have given command to build a temple on
your holy mountain,
and an altar in the city of your habitation,
a copy of the holy tent which you prepared
from the beginning.
[9]With you is wisdom, who knows your works
and was present when you made the world,
and who understands what is pleasing in your
sight
and what is right according to your
commandments.
[10]Send her forth from the holy heavens,
and from the throne of your glory send her,
that she may be with me and toil,
and that I may learn what is pleasing to you.
[11]For she knows and understands all things,
and she will guide me wisely in my actions
and guard me with her glory.
[12]Then my works will be acceptable,
and I shall judge your people justly,
and shall be worthy of the throne [t] of my
father.
[13]For what man can learn the counsel of God?
Or who can discern what the Lord wills?
[14]For the reasoning of mortals is worthless,
and our designs are likely to fail,
[15]for a perishable body weighs down the soul,
and this earthy tent burdens the thoughtful [u]
mind.
[16]We can hardly guess at what is on earth,
and what is at hand we find with labor;
but who has traced out what is in the heavens?
[17]Who has learned your counsel, unless you have
given wisdom
and sent your holy Spirit from on high?

[18]And thus the paths of those on earth were set
right,
and men were taught what pleases you,
and were saved by wisdom."

The Deeds of Wisdom

10 Wisdom [v] protected the first-formed
father of the world,
when he alone had been created;
she delivered him from his transgression,
[2]and gave him strength to rule all things.
[3]But when an unrighteous man departed from
her in his anger,
he perished because in rage he slew his brother.
[4]When the earth was flooded because of him,
wisdom again saved it,
steering the righteous man by a paltry piece of
wood.
[5]Wisdom [w] also, when the nations in wicked
agreement had been confounded,
recognized the righteous man and preserved
him blameless before God,
and kept him strong in the face of his
compassion for his child.
[6]Wisdom [w] rescued a righteous man when the
ungodly were perishing;
he escaped the fire that descended on the Five
Cities. [x]
[7]Evidence of their wickedness still remains:
a continually smoking wasteland,
plants bearing fruit that does not ripen,
and a pillar of salt standing as a monument to
an unbelieving soul.
[8]For because they passed wisdom by,
they not only were hindered from recognizing
the good,
but also left for mankind a reminder of their
folly,
so that their failures could never go unnoticed.

[9]Wisdom rescued from troubles those who
served her.
[10]When a righteous man fled from his brother's
wrath,
she guided him on straight paths;
she showed him the kingdom of God,
and gave him knowledge of angels; [y]
she prospered him in his labors,
and increased the fruit of his toil.
[11]When his oppressors were covetous,
she stood by him and made him rich.
[12]She protected him from his enemies,
and kept him safe from those who lay in wait
for him;

---

[t] Gk *thrones.*
[u] Or *anxious.*
[v] Gk *She.*
[w] Gk *She.*
[x] Or *Pentapolis.*
[y] Or *of holy things.*

in his arduous contest she gave him the victory,
so that he might learn that godliness is more
    powerful than anything.

[13]When a righteous man was sold, wisdom [z] did
    not desert him,
but delivered him from sin.
She descended with him into the dungeon,
[14]and when he was in prison she did not leave
    him,
until she brought him the scepter of a kingdom
and authority over his masters.
Those who accused him she showed to be false,
and she gave him everlasting honor.

[15]A holy people and blameless race
    wisdom [a] delivered from a nation of oppressors.
[16]She entered the soul of a servant of the Lord,
    and withstood dread kings with wonders and
        signs.
[17]She gave to holy men the reward of their
        labors;
she guided them along a marvelous way,
and became a shelter to them by day,
and a starry flame through the night.
[18]She brought them over the Red Sea,
    and led them through deep waters;
[19]but she drowned their enemies,
    and cast them up from the depth of the sea.
[20]Therefore the righteous plundered the
        ungodly;
they sang hymns, O Lord, to your holy name,
and praised with one accord your defending
        hand,
[21]because wisdom opened the mouth of the mute,
and made the tongues of infants speak clearly.

11 Wisdom [a] prospered their works by the
    hand of a holy prophet.
[2]They journeyed through an uninhabited
    wilderness,
and pitched their tents in untrodden places.
[3]They withstood their enemies and fought off
    their foes.
[4]When they thirsted they called upon you,
and water was given them out of flinty rock,
and slaking of thirst from hard stone.
[5]For through the very things by which their
        enemies were punished,
they themselves received benefit in their need.
[6]Instead of the fountain of an ever-flowing
        river,
stirred up and defiled with blood
[7]in rebuke for the decree to slay the infants,
you gave them abundant water unexpectedly,
[8]showing by their thirst at that time
how you punished their enemies.
[9]For when they were tried, though they were
    being disciplined in mercy,

they learned how the ungodly were tormented
    when judged in wrath.
[10]For you tested them as a father does in
    warning,
but you examined the ungodly [b] as a stern king
    does in condemnation.
[11]Whether absent or present, they were equally
    distressed,
[12]for a twofold grief possessed them,
and a groaning at the memory of what had
    occurred.
[13]For when they heard that through their own
    punishments
the righteous [c] had received benefit, they
    perceived it was the Lord's doing.
[14]For though they had mockingly rejected him
    who long before had been cast out and
    exposed,
at the end of the events they marveled at him,
for their thirst was not like that of the
    righteous.

[15]In return for their foolish and wicked thoughts,
    which led them astray to worship irrational
        serpents and worthless animals,
you sent upon them a multitude of irrational
        creatures to punish them,
[16]that they might learn that one is punished by
    the very things by which he sins.
[17]For your all-powerful hand,
which created the world out of formless
        matter,
did not lack the means to send upon them a
    multitude of bears, or bold lions,
[18]or newly created unknown beasts full of rage,
or such as breathe out fiery breath,
or belch forth a thick pall of smoke,
or flash terrible sparks from their eyes;
[19]not only could their damage exterminate men,[d]
but the mere sight of them could kill by fright.
[20]Even apart from these, men [e] could fall at a
    single breath
when pursued by justice
and scattered by the breath of your power.
But you have arranged all things by measure
    and number and weight.

[21]For it is always in your power to show great
    strength,
and who can withstand the might of your arm?
[22]Because the whole world before you is like a
    speck that tips the scales,
and like a drop of morning dew that falls upon
    the ground.

---

[z] Gk *she.*
[a] Gk *she.*
[b] Gk *those.*
[c] Gk *they.*
[d] Gk *them.*
[e] Gk *they.*

²³But you are merciful to all, for you can do all things,
and you overlook men's sins, that they may repent.
²⁴For you love all things that exist,
and you loathe none of the things which you have made,
for you would not have made anything if you had hated it.
²⁵How would anything have endured if you had not willed it?
Or how would anything not called forth by you have been preserved?
²⁶You spare all things, for they are yours, O Lord who love the living. *

12 For your immortal spirit is in all things.
²Therefore you correct little by little those who trespass,
and remind and warn them of the things wherein they sin,
that they may be freed from wickedness and put their trust in you, O Lord.

³Those who dwelt of old in your holy land
⁴you hated for their detestable practices,
their works of sorcery and unholy rites,
⁵their merciless slaughter ᶠ of children,
and their sacrificial feasting on human flesh and blood.
These initiates from the midst of a heathen cult, ᵍ
⁶these parents who murder helpless lives,
you wanted to destroy by the hands of our fathers,
⁷that the land most precious of all to you
might receive a worthy colony of the servants ʰ of God.
⁸But even these you spared, since they were but men,
and sent wasps ⁱ as forerunners of your army,
to destroy them little by little,
⁹though you were not unable to give the ungodly into the hands of the righteous in battle,
or to destroy them at one blow by dread wild beasts or your stern word.
¹⁰But judging them little by little you gave them a chance to repent,
though you were not unaware that their origin ʲ was evil
and their wickedness inborn,
and that their way of thinking would never change.
¹¹For they were an accursed race from the beginning,
and it was not through fear of any one that you left them unpunished for their sins.

¹²For who will say, "What have you done?"
Or who will resist your judgment?

Who will accuse you for the destruction of nations which you made?
Or who will come before you to plead as an advocate for unrighteous men?
¹³For neither is there any god besides you, whose care is for all men, ᵏ
to whom you should prove that you have not judged unjustly;
¹⁴nor can any king or monarch confront you about those whom you have punished.
¹⁵You are righteous and rule all things righteously,
deeming it alien to your power
to condemn him who does not deserve to be punished.
¹⁶For your strength is the source of righteousness,
and your sovereignty over all causes you to spare all.
¹⁷For you show your strength when men doubt the completeness of your power,
and rebuke any insolence among those who know it. ˡ
¹⁸You who are sovereign in strength judge with mildness,
and with great forbearance you govern us;
for you have power to act whenever you choose.

¹⁹Through such works you have taught your people
that the righteous man must be kind,
and you have filled your sons with good hope,
because you give repentance for sins.
²⁰For if you punished with such great care and indulgence ᵐ
the enemies of your servants ⁿ and those deserving of death,
granting them time and opportunity to give up their wickedness,
²¹with what strictness you have judged your sons,
to whose fathers you gave oaths and covenants full of good promises!
²²So while chastening us you scourge our enemies ten thousand times more,
so that we may meditate upon your goodness when we judge,
and when we are judged we may expect mercy.

ᶠ Cn: Gk *slaughterers*.
ᵍ The Greek text of this line is uncertain.
ʰ Or *children*.
ⁱ Or *hornets*.
ʲ Or *nature*.
ᵏ Or *all things*.
ˡ The Greek text of this line is uncertain.
ᵐ Some ancient authorities omit *and indulgence*; others read *and entreaty*.
ⁿ Or *children*.
* 11:26, *Lord who love the living*: Vulgate has "souls" for "living." The Greek word could mean either.

23Therefore those who in folly of life lived
     unrighteously
you tormented through their own
     abominations.
24For they went far astray on the paths of error,
accepting as gods those animals which even
     their enemies ° despised;
they were deceived like foolish infants.
25Therefore, as to thoughtless children,
you sent your judgment to mock them.
26But those who have not heeded the warning of
     light rebukes
will experience the deserved judgment of God.
27For when in their suffering they became
     incensed
at those creatures which they had thought to be
     gods, being punished by means of them,
they saw and recognized as the true God him
     whom they had before refused to know.
Therefore the utmost condemnation came upon
     them.

The Foolishness of Idolatry

13 For all men who were ignorant of God
     were foolish by nature;
and they were unable from the good things that
     are seen to know him who exists,
nor did they recognize the craftsman while
     paying heed to his works;
2but they supposed that either fire or wind or
     swift air,
or the circle of the stars, or turbulent water,
or the luminaries of heaven were the gods that
     rule the world.
3If through delight in the beauty of these things
     men ᴾ assumed them to be gods,
let them know how much better than these is
     their Lord,
for the author of beauty created them.
4And if men ᴾ were amazed at their power and
     working,
let them perceive from them
how much more powerful is he who formed
     them.
5For from the greatness and beauty of created
     things
comes a corresponding perception of their
     Creator.
6Yet these men are little to be blamed,
for perhaps they go astray
while seeking God and desiring to find him.
7For as they live among his works they keep
     searching,
and they trust in what they see, because the
     things that are seen are beautiful.
8Yet again, not even they are to be excused;
9for if they had the power to know so much
that they could investigate the world,
how did they fail to find sooner the Lord of
     these things?

10But miserable, with their hopes set on dead
     things, are the men
who give the name "gods" to the works of
     men's hands,
gold and silver fashioned with skill,
and likenesses of animals,
or a useless stone, the work of an ancient hand.
11A skilled woodcutter may saw down a tree
     easy to handle
and skilfully strip off all its bark,
and then with pleasing workmanship
make a useful vessel that serves life's needs,
12and burn the castoff pieces of his work
to prepare his food, and eat his fill.
13But a castoff piece from among them, useful
     for nothing,
a stick crooked and full of knots,
he takes and carves with care in his leisure,
and shapes it with skill gained in idleness; ᑫ
he forms it like the image of a man,
14or makes it like some worthless animal,
giving it a coat of red paint and coloring its
     surface red
and covering every blemish in it with paint;
15then he makes for it a niche that befits it,
and sets it in the wall, and fastens it there with
     iron.
16So he takes thought for it, that it may not fall,
because he knows that it cannot help itself,
for it is only an image and has need of help.
17When he prays about possessions and his
     marriage and children,
he is not ashamed to address a lifeless thing.
18For health he appeals to a thing that is weak;
for life he prays to a thing that is dead;
for aid he entreats a thing that is utterly
     inexperienced;
for a prosperous journey, a thing that cannot
     take a step;
19for money-making and work and success with
     his hands
he asks strength of a thing whose hands have
     no strength.

14 Again, one preparing to sail and about to
     voyage over raging waves
calls upon a piece of wood more fragile than
     the ship which carries him.
2For it was desire for gain that planned that
     vessel,
and wisdom was the craftsman who built it;
3but it is your providence, O Father, that steers
     its course,
because you have given it a path in the sea,
and a safe way through the waves,
4showing that you can save from every danger,

° Gk *they.*
ᴾ Gk *they.*
ᑫ Other authorities read *with intelligent skill.*

so that even if a man lacks skill, he may put to
sea.

⁵It is your will that works of your wisdom
should not be without effect;
therefore men trust their lives even to the
smallest piece of wood,
and passing through the billows on a raft they
come safely to land.

⁶For even in the beginning, when arrogant
giants were perishing,
the hope of the world took refuge on a raft,
and guided by your hand left to the world the
seed of a new generation.

⁷For blessed is the wood by which righteousness
comes.

⁸But the idol made with hands is accursed, and
so is he who made it;
because he did the work, and the perishable
thing was named a god.

⁹For equally hateful to God are the ungodly man
and his ungodliness,

¹⁰for what was done will be punished together
with him who did it.

¹¹Therefore there will be a visitation also upon
the heathen idols,
because, though part of what God created,
they became an abomination,
and became traps for the souls of men
and a snare to the feet of the foolish.

¹²For the idea of making idols was the beginning
of fornication,
and the invention of them was the corruption
of life,

¹³for neither have they existed from the
beginning
nor will they exist for ever.

¹⁴For through the vanity of men they entered the
world,
and therefore their speedy end has been
planned.

¹⁵For a father, consumed with grief at an
untimely bereavement,
made an image of his child, who had been
suddenly taken from him;
and he now honored as a god what was once a
dead human being,
and handed on to his dependents secret rites
and initiations.

¹⁶Then the ungodly custom, grown strong with
time, was kept as a law,
and at the command of monarchs graven
images were worshiped.

¹⁷When men could not honor monarchs ʳ in their
presence, since they lived at a distance,
they imagined their appearance far away,
and made a visible image of the king whom
they honored,

so that by their zeal they might flatter the
absent one as though present.

¹⁸Then the ambition of the craftsman impelled
even those who did not know the king to
intensify their worship.

¹⁹For he, perhaps wishing to please his ruler,
skilfully forced the likeness to take more
beautiful form,

²⁰and the multitude, attracted by the charm of
his work,
now regarded as an object of worship the one
whom shortly before they had honored as
a man.

²¹And this became a hidden trap for mankind,
because men, in bondage to misfortune or to
royal authority,
bestowed on objects of stone or wood the name
that ought not to be shared.

²²Afterward it was not enough for them to err
about the knowledge of God,
but they live in great strife due to ignorance,
and they call such great evils peace.

²³For whether they kill children in their
initiations, or celebrate secret mysteries,
or hold frenzied revels with strange customs,

²⁴they no longer keep either their lives or their
marriages pure,
but they either treacherously kill one another,
or grieve one another by adultery,

²⁵and all is a raging riot of blood and murder,
theft and deceit, corruption, faithlessness,
tumult, perjury,

²⁶confusion over what is good, forgetfulness of
favors,
pollution of souls, sex perversion,
disorder in marriage, adultery, and debauchery.

²⁷For the worship of idols not to be named
is the beginning and cause and end of every
evil.

²⁸For their worshipers ˢ either rave in exultation,
or prophesy lies,
or live unrighteously, or readily commit
perjury;

²⁹for because they trust in lifeless idols
they swear wicked oaths and expect to suffer
no harm.

³⁰But just penalties will overtake them on two
counts:
because they thought wickedly of God in
devoting themselves to idols,
and because in deceit they swore unrighteously
through contempt for holiness.

³¹For it is not the power of the things by which
men swear, ᵗ

ʳ GK them.
ˢ GK they.
ᵗ Or of the oaths men swear.

but the just penalty for those who sin,
that always pursues the transgression of the
  unrighteous.

True Worship of God Contrasted to Idols

15 But you, our God, are kind and true,
  patient, and ruling all things [u] in mercy.
[2]For even if we sin we are yours, knowing your
  power;
but we will not sin, because we know that we
  are considered yours.
[3]For to know you is complete righteousness,
and to know your power is the root of
  immortality.
[4]For neither has the evil intent of human art
  misled us,
nor the fruitless toil of painters,
a figure stained with varied colors,
[5]whose appearance arouses yearning in fools,
so that they desire [v] the lifeless form of a dead
  image.
[6]Lovers of evil things and fit for such objects of
  hope [w]
are those who either make or desire or worship
  them.

[7]For when a potter kneads the soft earth
and laboriously molds each vessel for our
  service,
he fashions out of the same clay
both the vessels that serve clean uses
and those for contrary uses, making all in like
  manner;
but which shall be the use of each of these
the worker in clay decides.
[8]With misspent toil, he forms a futile god from
  the same clay—
this man who was made of earth a short time
  before
and after a little while goes to the earth from
  which he was taken,
when he is required to return the soul that was
  lent him.
[9]But he is not concerned that he is destined to
  die
or that his life is brief,
but he competes with workers in gold and
  silver,
and imitates workers in copper;
and he counts it his glory that he molds
  counterfeit gods.
[10]His heart is ashes, his hope is cheaper than
  dirt,
and his life is of less worth than clay,
[11]because he failed to know the one who formed
  him
and inspired him with an active soul
and breathed into him a living spirit.
[12]But he [x] considered our existence an idle game,
and life a festival held for profit,

for he says one must get money however one
  can, even by base means.
[13]For this man, more than all others, knows that
  he sins
when he makes from earthy matter fragile
  vessels and graven images.

[14]But most foolish, and more miserable than an
  infant,
are all the enemies who oppressed your people.
[15]For they thought that all their heathen idols
  were gods,
though these have neither the use of their eyes
  to see with,
nor nostrils with which to draw breath,
nor ears with which to hear,
nor fingers to feel with,
and their feet are of no use for walking.
[16]For a man made them,
and one whose spirit is borrowed formed them;
for no man can form a god which is like
  himself.
[17]He is mortal, and what he makes with lawless
  hands is dead,
for he is better than the objects he worships,
since [y] he has life, but they never have.

[18]The enemies of your people [z] worship even the
  most hateful animals,
which are worse than all others, when judged
  by their lack of intelligence;
[19]and even as animals they are not so beautiful in
  appearance that one would desire them,
but they have escaped both the praise of God
  and his blessing.

16 Therefore those men were deservedly
  punished through such creatures,
and were tormented by a multitude of
  animals.
[2]Instead of this punishment you showed
  kindness to your people,
and you prepared quails to eat,
a delicacy to satisfy the desire of appetite;
[3]in order that those men, when they desired
  food,
might lose the least remnant of appetite [a]
because of the odious creatures sent to them,
while your people,[b] after suffering want a short
  time,
might partake of delicacies.
[4]For it was necessary that upon those
  oppressors inexorable want should come,

---

[u] Or *ruling the universe.*
[v] Gk *and he desires.*
[w] Gk *such hopes.*
[x] Other authorities read *they.*
[y] Other authorities read *of which.*
[z] Gk *They.*
[a] Gk *loathe the necessary appetite.*
[b] Gk *they.*

while to these it was merely shown how their
enemies were being tormented.

[5]For when the terrible rage of wild beasts came
upon your people [c]
and they were being destroyed by the bites of
writhing serpents,
your wrath did not continue to the end;
[6]they were troubled for a little while as a
warning,
and received a token of deliverance to remind
them of your law's command.
[7]For he who turned toward it was saved, not by
what he saw,
but by you, the Savior of all.
[8]And by this also you convinced our enemies
that it is you who deliver from every evil.
[9]For they were killed by the bites of locusts and
flies,
and no healing was found for them,
because they deserved to be punished by such
things;
[10]but your sons were not conquered even by the
teeth of venomous serpents,
for your mercy came to their help and healed
them.
[11]To remind them of your oracles they were
bitten,
and then were quickly delivered,
lest they should fall into deep forgetfulness
and become unresponsive [d] to your kindness.
[12]For neither herb nor poultice cured them,
but it was your word, O Lord, which heals all
men.
[13]For you have power over life and death;
you lead men down to the gates of Hades and
back again.
[14]A man in his wickedness kills another,
but he cannot bring back the departed spirit,
nor set free the imprisoned soul.
[15]To escape from your hand is impossible;
[16]for the ungodly, refusing to know you,
were scourged by the strength of your arm,
pursued by unusual rains and hail and
relentless storms,
and utterly consumed by fire.
[17]For—most incredible of all—in the water,
which quenches all things,
the fire had still greater effect,
for the universe defends the righteous.
[18]At one time the flame was restrained,
so that it might not consume the creatures sent
against the ungodly,
but that seeing this they might know
that they were being pursued by the judgment
of God;
[19]and at another time even in the midst of water
it burned more intensely than fire,
to destroy the crops of the unrighteous land.

[20]Instead of these things you gave your people
the food of angels,
and without their toil you supplied them from
heaven with bread ready to eat,
providing every pleasure and suited to every
taste.
[21]For your sustenance manifested your sweetness
toward your children;
and the bread, ministering [e] to the desire of the
one who took it,
was changed to suit every one's liking.
[22]Snow and ice withstood fire without melting,
so that they might know that the crops of their
enemies
were being destroyed by the fire that blazed in
the hail
and flashed in the showers of rain;
[23]whereas the fire,[f] in order that the righteous
might be fed,
even forgot its native power.
[24]For creation, serving you who have made it,
exerts itself to punish the unrighteous,
and in kindness relaxes on behalf of those who
trust in you.
[25]Therefore at that time also, changed into all
forms,
it served your all-nourishing bounty,
according to the desire of those who had
need, [g]
[26]so that your sons, whom you loved, O Lord,
might learn
that it is not the production of crops that feeds
man,
but that your word preserves those who trust
in you.
[27]For what was not destroyed by fire
was melted when simply warmed by a fleeting
ray of the sun,
[28]to make it known that one must rise before the
sun to give you thanks,
and must pray to you at the dawning of the
light;
[29]for the hope of an ungrateful man will melt
like wintry frost,
and flow away like waste water.

The Plague of Darkness and Death

17 Great are your judgments and hard to
describe;
therefore uninstructed souls have gone astray.
[2]For when lawless men supposed that they held
the holy nation in their power,
they themselves lay as captives of darkness
and prisoners of long night,

---

[c] Gk them.
[d] The meaning of the Greek is obscure.
[e] Gk and it, ministering.
[f] Gk this.
[g] Or who made supplication.

shut in under their roofs, exiles from eternal
providence.
[3]For thinking that in their secret sins they were
unobserved
behind a dark curtain of forgetfulness,
they were scattered, terribly [h] alarmed,
and appalled by specters.
[4]For not even the inner chamber that held them
protected them from fear,
but terrifying sounds rang out around them,
and dismal phantoms with gloomy faces
appeared.
[5]And no power of fire was able to give light,
nor did the brilliant flames of the stars
avail to illumine that hateful night.
[6]Nothing was shining through to them
except a dreadful, self-kindled fire,
and in terror they deemed the things which
they saw
to be worse than that unseen appearance.
[7]The delusions of their magic art lay humbled,
and their boasted wisdom was scornfully
rebuked.
[8]For those who promised to drive off the fears
and disorders of a sick soul
were sick themselves with ridiculous fear.
[9]For even if nothing disturbing frightened them,
yet, scared by the passing of beasts and the
hissing of serpents,
[10]they perished in trembling fear,
refusing to look even at the air, though it
nowhere could be avoided.
[11]For wickedness is a cowardly thing, condemned
by its own testimony; [i]
distressed by conscience, it has always
exaggerated [j] the difficulties.
[12]For fear is nothing but surrender of the helps
that come from reason;
[13]and the inner expectation of help, being weak,
prefers ignorance of what causes the torment.
[14]But throughout the night, which was really
powerless,
and which beset them from the recesses of
powerless Hades,
they all slept the same sleep,
[15]and now were driven by monstrous specters,
and now were paralyzed by their souls'
surrender,
for sudden and unexpected fear overwhelmed
them.
[16]And whoever was there fell down,
and thus was kept shut up in a prison not made
of iron;
[17]for whether he was a farmer or a shepherd
or a workman who toiled in the wilderness,
he was seized, and endured the inescapable
fate;
for with one chain of darkness they all were
bound.

[18]Whether there came a whistling wind,
or a melodious sound of birds in wide-
spreading branches,
or the rhythm of violently rushing water,
[19]or the harsh crash of rocks hurled down,
or the unseen running of leaping animals,
or the sound of the most savage roaring
beasts,
or an echo thrown back from a hollow of the
mountains,
it paralyzed them with terror.
[20]For the whole world was illumined with
brilliant light,
and was engaged in unhindered work,
[21]while over those men alone heavy night was
spread,
an image of the darkness that was destined to
receive them;
but still heavier than darkness were they to
themselves.

18

But for your holy ones there was very
great light.
Their enemies [k] heard their voices but did not
see their forms,
and counted them happy for not having
suffered,
[2]and were thankful that your holy ones, [k]
though previously wronged, were doing
them no injury;
and they begged their pardon for having been
at variance with them. [l]
[3]Therefore you provided a flaming pillar of fire
as a guide for your people's [m] unknown journey,
and a harmless sun for their glorious
wandering.
[4]For their enemies [n] deserved to be deprived of
light and imprisoned in darkness,
those who had kept your sons imprisoned,
through whom the imperishable light of the
law was to be given to the world.
[5]When they had resolved to kill the infants of
your holy ones,
and one child had been exposed and rescued,
in punishment you took away a multitude of
their children;
and you destroyed them all together by a
mighty flood.
[6]That night was made known beforehand to our
fathers,
so that they might rejoice in sure knowledge of
the oaths in which they trusted.

---

[h] Or, with other authorities, *unobserved, they were darkened behind a
dark curtain of forgetfulness, terribly.*
[i] The Greek text of this line is uncertain and probably corrupt.
[j] Other ancient authorities read *anticipated.*
[k] Gk *they.*
[l] The meaning of the Greek of this line is uncertain.
[m] Gk *their.*
[n] Gk *those men.*

7The deliverance of the righteous and the
destruction of their enemies
were expected by your people.
8For by the same means by which you punished
our enemies
you called us to yourself and glorified us.
9For in secret the holy children of good men
offered sacrifices,
and with one accord agreed to the divine law,
that the saints would share alike the same
things,
both blessings and dangers;
and already they were singing the praises of
the fathers. °
10But the discordant cry of their enemies echoed
back,
and their piteous lament for their children was
spread abroad.
11The slave was punished with the same penalty
as the master,
and the common man suffered the same loss as
the king;
12and they all together, by the one form of death,
had corpses too many to count.
For the living were not sufficient even to bury
them,
since in one instant their most valued children
had been destroyed.
13For though they had disbelieved everything
because of their magic arts,
yet, when their first-born were destroyed, they
acknowledged your people to be God's
son.
14For while gentle silence enveloped all things,
and night in its swift course was now half gone,
15your all-powerful word leaped from heaven,
from the royal throne,
into the midst of the land that was doomed,
a stern warrior 16carrying the sharp sword of
your authentic command,
and stood and filled all things with death,
and touched heaven while standing on the
earth.
17Then at once apparitions in dreadful dreams
greatly troubled them,
and unexpected fears assailed them;
18and one here and another there, hurled down
half dead,
made known why they were dying;
19for the dreams which disturbed them
forewarned them of this,
so that they might not perish without knowing
why they suffered.

20The experience of death touched also the
righteous,
and a plague came upon the multitude in the
desert,
but the wrath did not long continue.

21For a blameless man was quick to act as their
champion;
he brought forward the shield of his ministry,
prayer and propitiation by incense;
he withstood the anger and put an end to the
disaster,
showing that he was your servant.
22He conquered the wrath ᵖ not by strength of
body,
and not by force of arms,
but by his word he subdued the punisher,
appealing to the oaths and covenants given to
our fathers.
23For when the dead had already fallen on one
another in heaps,
he intervened and held back the wrath,
and cut off its way to the living.
24For upon his long robe the whole world was
depicted,
and the glories of the fathers were engraved on
the four rows of stones,
and your majesty on the diadem upon his head.
25To these the destroyer yielded, these he �q
feared;
for merely to test the wrath was enough.

God's Continuing Help for His People

19 But the ungodly were assailed to the end
by pitiless anger,
for God ʳ knew in advance even their future
actions,
2that, though they themselves had permitted ˢ
your people to depart
and hastily sent them forth,
they would change their minds and pursue
them.
3For while they were still busy at mourning,
and were lamenting at the graves of their
dead,
they reached another foolish decision,
and pursued as fugitives those whom they had
begged and compelled to depart.
4For the fate they deserved drew them on to this
end,
and made them forget what had happened,
in order that they might fill up the punishment
which their torments still lacked,
5and that your people might experience ᵗ an
incredible journey,
but they themselves might meet a strange
death.

6For the whole creation in its nature was
fashioned anew,

° Other authorities read dangers, the fathers already leading the songs of
praise.
ᵖ Cn: Gk multitude.
q Other authorities read they.
ʳ Gk he.
ˢ Other authorities read had changed their minds to permit.
ᵗ Other authorities read accomplish.

complying with your commands,
that your children [u] might be kept unharmed.
[7]The cloud was seen overshadowing the camp,
and dry land emerging where water had stood
before,
an unhindered way out of the Red Sea,
and a grassy plain out of the raging waves,
[8]where those protected by your hand passed
through as one nation,
after gazing on marvelous wonders.
[9]For they ranged like horses,
and leaped like lambs,
praising you, O Lord, who delivered them.
[10]For they still recalled the events of their
sojourn,
how instead of producing animals the earth
brought forth gnats,
and instead of fish the river spewed out vast
numbers of frogs.
[11]Afterward they saw also a new kind [v] of birds,
when desire led them to ask for luxurious
food;
[12]for, to give them relief, quails came up from the
sea.

[13]The punishments did not come upon the
sinners
without prior signs in the violence of thunder,
for they justly suffered because of their wicked
acts;
for they practiced a more bitter hatred of
strangers.
[14]Others had refused to receive strangers when
they came to them,
but these made slaves of guests who were their
benefactors.
[15]And not only so, but punishment of some sort
will come upon the former
for their hostile reception of the strangers;

[16]but the latter, after receiving them with festal
celebrations,
afflicted with terrible sufferings
those who had already shared the same rights.
[17]They were stricken also with loss of sight—
just as were those at the door of the righteous
man—
when, surrounded by yawning darkness,
each tried to find the way through his own
door.

[18]For the elements changed [w] places with one
another,
as on a harp the notes vary the nature of the
rhythm,
while each note remains the same. [x]
This may be clearly inferred from the sight of
what took place.
[19]For land animals were transformed into water
creatures,
and creatures that swim moved over to the
land.
[20]Fire even in water retained its normal power,
and water forgot its fire-quenching nature.
[21]Flames, on the contrary, failed to consume
the flesh of perishable creatures that walked
among them,
nor did they melt [y] the crystalline, easily
melted kind of heavenly food.

[22]For in everything, O Lord, you have exalted
and glorified your people;
and you have not neglected to help them at all
times and in all places.

---

[u] Or *servants*.
[v] Or *production*.
[w] Gk *changing*.
[x] The meaning of this verse is uncertain.
[y] Cn: Gk *nor could be melted*.

THE BOOK OF

SIRACH

The Prologue

Whereas many great teachings have been given to us through the law and the prophets and the others that followed them, on account of which we should praise Israel for instruction and wisdom; and since it is necessary not only that the readers themselves should acquire understanding but also that those who love learning should be able to help the outsiders by both speaking and writing, my grandfather Jesus, after devoting himself especially to the reading of the law and the prophets and the other books of our fathers, and after acquiring considerable proficiency in them, was himself also led to write something pertaining to instruction and wisdom, in order that, by becoming conversant with this also, those who love learning should make even greater progress in living according to the law.

You are urged therefore to read with good will and attention, and to be indulgent [a] in cases where, despite our diligent labor in translating, we may seem to have rendered some phrases imperfectly. For what was originally expressed in Hebrew does not have exactly the same sense when translated into another language. Not only this work, but even the law itself, the prophecies, and the rest of the books differ not a little as originally expressed.

When I came to Egypt in the thirty-eighth year of the reign of Euer'getes and stayed for some time, I found opportunity for no little instruction. [b] It seemed highly necessary that I should myself devote some pains and labor to the translation of the following book, using in that period of time great watchfulness and skill in order to complete and publish the book for those living abroad who wished to gain learning, being prepared in character to live according to the law.

In Praise of Wisdom

1 All wisdom comes from the Lord
and is with him for ever.
[2] The sand of the sea, the drops of rain,
and the days of eternity—who can count them?
[3] The height of heaven, the breadth of the earth,
the abyss, and wisdom—who can search them out?
[4] Wisdom was created before all things,
and prudent understanding from eternity. [c]

[5] The source of wisdom is God's word in the highest heaven,
and her ways are the eternal commandments.
[6] The root of wisdom—to whom has it been revealed?
Her clever devices—who knows them? [d]
[7] The knowledge of wisdom—to whom was it manifested?
And her abundant experience—who has understood it?
[8] There is One who is wise, the Creator of all,
the King greatly to be feared, sitting upon his throne, and ruling as God.
[9] The Lord himself created wisdom [e] in the holy spirit;
he saw her and apportioned her,
he poured her out upon all his works.
[10] She dwells with all flesh according to his gift,
and he supplied her to those who love him.

[11] The fear of the Lord is glory and exultation,
and gladness and a crown of rejoicing.
[12] The fear of the Lord delights the heart,
and gives gladness and joy and long life.

The Book of Sirach (Ecclesiasticus) belongs to the Wisdom literature and was written by Ben Sira, a "sage of Israel," in the early second century B.C. It was originally composed in Hebrew, as we learn from the Prologue, and translated into Greek some fifty years later by his grandson. During these fifty years there had been a violent persecution of the Jews by the Seleucid kings in order to force them to adopt Greek religion and culture. The beginnings of this were already apparent in the time of Ben Sira, and it was to counteract such influences that his book was written. It is full of traditional Jewish wisdom and morals; indeed, full of worldly wisdom and written by one with wide experience of life. He re-emphasizes the traditional truths, but manages to do this in an interesting way and sometimes even from a new angle, e.g., his words on death (40:2; 41:2).

Sirach was included in the Greek Bible but not in the later Jewish canon. The Hebrew text was known to Jerome but later disappeared and was rediscovered, though not complete, only at the end of the nineteenth century in Cairo. Further fragments have been found recently in Palestine.

The Church accepted the book as canonical, but it was the Greek text she accepted. The name Ecclesiasticus was given to it in its Old Latin version—a name which appears to date from the time of St. Cyprian. St. Jerome did not translate the book or revise the Old Latin, so the text is substantially as he found it. It is a version made from the Greek, but a Greek text notably different from the one we use, chiefly in the quantity of additional material. However, these additions do not add anything substantially new to the book except, perhaps, the spirit in which they are written. The version has been described as "a Pharisaic recension of the original work of Ben Sira."

[a] Or *Please read therefore with good will and attention, and be indulgent.*
[b] Other authorities read *a copy affording no little instruction.*
[c] Other authorities omit verse 5.
[d] Other authorities omit verse 7.
[e] Gk *her.*

¹³With him who fears the Lord it will go well at
the end;
on the day of his death he will be blessed.

¹⁴To fear the Lord is the beginning of wisdom;
she is created with the faithful in the womb.
¹⁵She made ᶠ among men an eternal foundation,
and among their descendants she will be
trusted.
¹⁶To fear the Lord is wisdom's full measure;
she satisfies ᵍ men with her fruits;
¹⁷she fills their whole house with desirable
goods,
and their storehouses with her produce.
¹⁸The fear of the Lord is the crown of wisdom,
making peace and perfect health to
flourish.
¹⁹He saw her and apportioned her;
he rained down knowledge and discerning
comprehension,
and he exalted the glory of those who held
her fast.
²⁰To fear the Lord is the root of wisdom,
and her branches are long life. ʰ

²²Unrighteous anger cannot be justified,
for a man's anger tips the scale to his ruin.
²³A patient man will endure until the right
moment,
and then joy will burst forth for him.
²⁴He will hide his words until the right moment,
and the lips of many will tell of his good
sense.
²⁵In the treasuries of wisdom are wise sayings,
but godliness is an abomination to a
sinner.
²⁶If you desire wisdom, keep the
commandments,
and the Lord will supply it for you.
²⁷For the fear of the Lord is wisdom and
instruction,
and he delights in fidelity and meekness.
²⁸Do not disobey the fear of the Lord;
do not approach him with a divided mind.
²⁹Be not a hypocrite in men's sight, ⁱ
and keep watch over your lips.
³⁰Do not exalt yourself lest you fall,
and thus bring dishonor upon yourself.
The Lord will reveal your secrets
and cast you down in the midst of the
congregation,
because you did not come in the fear of the
Lord,
and your heart was full of deceit.

Duties toward God

2 My son, if you come forward to serve the
Lord,
remain in justice and in fear,
and prepare yourself for temptation. ʲ

²Set your heart right and be steadfast,
incline your ear, and receive words of
understanding,
and do not be hasty in time of calamity.
³Await God's patience, cling to him and do not
depart,
that you may be wise in all your ways.
⁴Accept whatever is brought upon you,
and endure it in sorrow;
in changes that humble you be patient.
⁵For gold and silver are tested in the fire,
and acceptable men in the furnace of
humiliation.
⁶Trust in God, and he will help you;
hope in him, and he will make your ways
straight.
Stay in fear of him, and grow old in him.

⁷You who fear the Lord, wait for his mercy;
and turn not aside, lest you fall.
⁸You who fear the Lord, trust in him,
and your reward will not fail;
⁹you who fear the Lord, hope for good things,
for everlasting joy and mercy.
You who fear the Lord, love him,
and your hearts will be made radiant.
¹⁰Consider the ancient generations and see:
who ever trusted in the Lord and was put to
shame?
Or who ever persevered in his commandments ᵏ
and was forsaken?
Or who ever called upon him and was
overlooked?
¹¹For the Lord is compassionate and merciful;
he forgives sins and saves in time of
affliction,
and he is the shield of all who seek him in
truth.

¹²Woe to timid hearts and to slack hands,
and to the sinner who walks along two
ways!
¹³Woe to the faint heart, for it has no trust!
Therefore it will not be sheltered.
¹⁴Woe to you who have lost your endurance!
What will you do when the Lord punishes
you?
¹⁵Those who fear the Lord will not disobey his
words,
and those who love him will keep his ways.
¹⁶Those who fear the Lord will seek his approval,
and those who love him will be filled with
the law.

ᶠ Gk *made as nest.*
ᵍ Gk *intoxicates.*
ʰ Other authorities add as verse 21, *The fear of the Lord drives away
sins; and where it abides, it will turn away all anger.*
ⁱ Syr: Gk *in the mouths of men.*
ʲ Or *trials.*
ᵏ Or *the fear of the Lord.*

[17]Those who fear the Lord will prepare their
   hearts,
   and will humble themselves before him.
[18]Let us fall[1] into the hands of the Lord,
   but not into the hands of men;
   for as his majesty is,
   so also is his mercy.

Duties toward Parents and Others

3 Listen to me your father, O children;
   and act accordingly, that you may be kept
   in safety.
[2]For the Lord honored the father above the
   children,
   and he confirmed the right of the mother
   over her sons.
[3]Whoever honors his father atones for sins,
   and preserves himself from them.
   When he prays, he is heard;
[4]   and whoever glorifies his mother is like one
   who lays up treasure.
[5]Whoever honors his father will be gladdened
   by his own children,
   and when he prays he will be heard.
[6]Whoever glorifies his father will have long
   life,
   and whoever obeys the Lord will refresh his
   mother;
[7]   he will serve his parents as his masters.[m]
[8]Honor your father by word and deed,
   that a blessing from him may come upon
   you.
[9]For a father's blessing strengthens the houses
   of the children,
   but a mother's curse uproots their
   foundations.

[10]Do not glorify yourself by dishonoring your
   father,
   for your father's dishonor is no glory to you.
[11]For a man's glory comes from honoring his
   father,
   and it is a disgrace for children not to
   respect their mother.
[12]O son, help your father in his old age,
   and do not grieve him as long as he lives;
[13]even if he is lacking in understanding, show
   forbearance;
   and do not despise him all the days of his
   life.
[14]For kindness to a father will not be forgotten,
   and against your sins it will be credited to
   you
   —a house raised in justice to you.
[15]in the day of your affliction it will be
   remembered in your favor;
   as frost in fair weather, your sins will melt
   away.
[16]Whoever forsakes his father is like a
   blasphemer,

and whoever angers his mother is cursed by
   the Lord.

[17]My son, perform your tasks in meekness;
   then you will be loved more than a giver of
   gifts.
[18]The greater you are, the more you must humble
   yourself;
   so you will find favor with God.[n]
[19]There are many who are noble and renowned,
   but it is to the humble that he reveals his
   mysteries.
[20]For great is the might of the Lord;
   he is glorified by the humble.
[21]Seek not what is too difficult for you,
   nor investigate what is beyond your power.
[22]Reflect upon what has been assigned to you,
   and do not be curious about many of his
   works,
   for you do not need to see with your eyes
   what is hidden.
[23]Do not meddle in what is beyond your tasks,
   for matters too great for human
   understanding have been shown you.
[24]For their hasty judgment has led many astray,
   and wrong opinion has caused their
   thoughts to slip.[o]
[26]A stubborn mind will be afflicted at the end,
   and whoever loves danger will perish by it.
[27]A stubborn mind will be burdened by troubles,
   and the sinner will heap sin upon sin.
[28]The affliction of the proud has no healing,
   for a plant of wickedness has taken root in
   them,
   though it will not be perceived.
[29]The mind of the wise man will ponder the
   words of the wise,
   and an attentive ear is the wise man's
   desire.
[30]Water extinguishes a blazing fire:
   so almsgiving atones for sin.
[31]Whoever repays favors gives thought to the
   future;
   at the moment of his falling he will find
   support.

Precepts for Everyday Life

4 My son, deprive not the poor of his living,
   and do not keep needy eyes waiting.
[2]Do not grieve the one who is hungry,
   nor anger a man in want.
[3]Do not add to the troubles of an angry mind,
   nor delay your gift to a beggar.

---

[1] Gk *We shall fall.*
[m] In other authorities this line is preceded by *Whoever fears the Lord will honor his father.*
[n] Other authorities omit verse 19.
[o] Other authorities add as verse 25, *If you have no eyes you will be without light; if you lack knowledge do not profess to have it.*

⁴Do not reject an afflicted suppliant,
    nor turn your face away from the poor.
⁵Do not avert your eye from the needy,
    nor give a man occasion to curse you;
⁶for if in bitterness of soul he calls down a
        curse upon you,
    his Creator will hear his prayer.

⁷Make yourself beloved in the congregation;
    bow your head low to a great man.
⁸Incline your ear to the poor,
    and answer him peaceably and gently.
⁹Deliver him who is wronged from the hand of
        the wrongdoer;
    and do not be fainthearted in judging a
        case.
¹⁰Be like a father to orphans,
    and instead of a husband to their mother;
you will then be like a son of the Most High,
    and he will love you more than does your
        mother.

¹¹Wisdom breathes life into her sons
    and gives help to those who seek her.
¹²Whoever loves her loves life,
    and those who seek her early
    will win the Lord's good favor.
¹³Whoever holds her fast will obtain glory,
    and the Lord will bless the place she ᵖ
        enters.
¹⁴Those who serve her will minister to the Holy
        One; ᵍ
    the Lord loves those who love her.
¹⁵He who obeys her will judge the nations,
    and whoever gives heed to her will dwell
        secure.
¹⁶If he has faith in her he will obtain her;
    and his descendants will remain in
        possession of her.
¹⁷For she will walk with him in disguise,
    and at first she will put him to the test;
    she will bring fear and cowardice upon him,
    and will torment him by her discipline
    until he holds her in his thoughts,
    and she trusts him.
¹⁸Then she will come straight back to him and
        strengthen him,
    she will gladden him and will reveal her
        secrets to him,
    and store up for him knowledge
    and the discernment of what is right.
¹⁹But if he goes astray she will forsake him,
    and give him over into the hands of his foe.

²⁰Observe the right time, and beware of evil; ʳ
    and do not bring shame on yourself.
²¹For there is a shame which brings sin,
    and there is a shame which is glory and
        favor.

²²Do not show partiality, to your own harm,
    or deference, to your downfall.
²³Do not refrain from speaking at the crucial
        time, ˢ
    and do not hide your wisdom. ᵗ
²⁴For wisdom is known through speech,
    and education through the words of the
        tongue.
²⁵Never speak against the truth,
    but be mindful of your ignorance.
²⁶Do not be ashamed to confess your sins,
    and do not try to stop the current of a
        river.
²⁷Do not subject yourself to a foolish fellow,
    nor show partiality to a ruler.
²⁸Strive even to death for the truth
    and the Lord God will fight for you.

²⁹Do not be reckless in your speech,
    or sluggish and remiss in your deeds.
³⁰Do not be like a lion in your home,
    nor be a faultfinder with your servants.
³¹Let not your hand be extended to receive,
    but withdrawn when it is time to repay.

5 Do not set your heart on your wealth,
    nor say, "I have enough."
²Do not follow your inclination and strength,
    walking according to the desires of your
        heart.
³Do not say, "Who will have power over me?"
    or "Who will bring me down because of my
        deeds?"
    for God will surely punish you.

⁴Do not say, "I sinned, and what happened to
        me?"
    for the Most High is slow to anger.
⁵Do not be so confident of atonement
    that you add sin to sin.
⁶Do not say, "His mercy is great,
    he will forgive ᵘ the multitude of my sins,"
    for both mercy and wrath are with him,
    and his anger rests on sinners.
⁷Do not delay to turn to the Lord,
    nor postpone it from day to day;
    for suddenly the wrath of the Lord will go
        forth,
    and at the time of punishment you will
        perish.

⁸Do not depend on dishonest wealth,
    for it will not benefit you in the day of
        calamity.

ᵖ Or *he.*
ᵍ Or *at the holy place.*
ʳ Or *an evil man.*
ˢ Cn: Gk *at a time of salvation.*
ᵗ So some Gk Mss and Heb Syr Vg: other Gk Mss omit *and do not hide your wisdom.*
ᵘ Heb: Gk *he* (or *it*) *will atone for.*

⁹Do not winnow with every wind,
nor follow every path:
the double-tongued sinner does that.
¹⁰Be steadfast in your understanding,
and let your speech be consistent.
¹¹Be quick to hear,
and be deliberate in answering.
¹²If you have understanding, answer your
neighbor;
but if not, put your hand on your mouth.
¹³Glory and dishonor come from speaking,
and a man's tongue is his downfall.

¹⁴Do not be called a slanderer,
and do not lie in ambush with your tongue;
for shame comes to the thief,
and severe condemnation to the double-
tongued.
¹⁵In great or small matters do not act amiss,
and do not become an enemy instead of a
friend;

6 for a bad name incurs shame and reproach:
so fares the double-tongued sinner.

²Do not exalt yourself through your soul's
counsel,
lest your soul be torn in pieces like a bull. ᵛ
³You will devour your leaves and destroy your
fruit,
and will be left like a withered tree.
⁴An evil soul will destroy him who has it,
and make him the laughingstock of his
enemies.

⁵A pleasant voice multiplies friends and softens
enemies,
and a gracious tongue multiplies courtesies.
⁶Let those that are at peace with you be many,
but let your advisers be one in a thousand.
⁷When you gain a friend, gain him through
testing,
and do not trust him hastily.
⁸For there is a friend who is such at his own
convenience,
but will not stand by you in your day of
trouble.
⁹And there is a friend who changes into an
enemy,
and will disclose a quarrel to your disgrace.
¹⁰And there is a friend who is a table companion,
but will not stand by you in your day of
trouble.
¹¹In prosperity he will make himself your equal,
and be bold with your servants;
¹²but if you are brought low he will turn against
you,
and will hide himself from your presence.
¹³Keep yourself far from your enemies,
and be on guard toward your friends.

¹⁴A faithful friend is a sturdy shelter:
he that has found one has found a treasure.
¹⁵There is nothing so precious as a faithful
friend,
and no scales can measure his excellence.
¹⁶A faithful friend is an elixir of life;
and those who fear the Lord will find him.
¹⁷Whoever fears the Lord directs his friendship
aright,
for as he is, so is his neighbor also.

¹⁸My son, from your youth up choose instruction,
and until you are old you will keep finding
wisdom.
¹⁹Come to her like one who plows and sows,
and wait for her good harvest.
For in her service you will toil a little while,
and soon you will eat of her produce.
²⁰She seems very harsh to the uninstructed;
a weakling will not remain with her.
²¹She will weigh him down like a heavy testing
stone,
and he will not be slow to cast her off.
²²For wisdom is like her name,
and is not manifest to many.

²³Listen, my son, and accept my judgment;
do not reject my counsel.
²⁴Put your feet into her chains,
and your neck into her collar.
²⁵Put your shoulder under her and carry her,
and do not fret under her bonds.
²⁶Come to her with all your soul,
and keep her ways with all your might.
²⁷Search out and seek, and she will become
known to you;
and when you get hold of her, do not let her
go.
²⁸For at last you will find the rest she gives,
and she will be changed into joy for you.
²⁹Then her chains will become for you a strong
protection,
and her collar a glorious robe.
³⁰Her yoke ᵂ is a golden ornament,
and her bonds are a cord of blue.
³¹You will wear her like a glorious robe,
and put her on like a crown of gladness.

³²If you are willing, my son, you will be taught,
and if you apply yourself you will become
clever.
³³If you love to listen you will gain knowledge,
and if you incline your ear you will become
wise.
³⁴Stand in the assembly of the elders.
Who is wise? Cling to him.

ᵛ The meaning of the Greek of this verse is obscure.
ᵂ Heb: Gk *Upon her.*

³⁵Be ready to listen to every ˣ narrative,
    and do not let wise proverbs escape you.
³⁶If you see an intelligent man, visit him early;
    let your foot wear out his doorstep.
³⁷Reflect on the statutes of the Lord,
    and meditate at all times on his
    commandments.
  It is he who will give insight to ʸ your mind,
    and your desire for wisdom will be granted.

Advice for Right Conduct

7 Do no evil, and evil will never befall you.
  ²Stay away from wrong, and it will turn
    away from you.
³My son, do not sow the furrows of injustice,
    and you will not reap a sevenfold crop.

⁴Do not seek from the Lord the highest office,
    nor the seat of honor from the king.
⁵Do not assert your righteousness before the
    Lord,
    nor display your wisdom before the king.
⁶Do not seek to become a judge,
    lest you be unable to remove iniquity,
  lest you be partial to a powerful man,
    and thus put a blot on your integrity.
⁷Do not offend against the public,
    and do not disgrace yourself among the
    people.

⁸Do not commit a sin twice;
    even for one you will not go unpunished.
⁹Do not say, "He will consider the multitude of
    my gifts,
    and when I make an offering to the Most
    High God he will accept it."
¹⁰Do not be fainthearted in your prayer,
    nor neglect to give alms.

¹¹Do not ridicule a man who is bitter in soul,
    for there is One who abases and exalts.
¹²Do not devise ᶻ a lie against your brother,
    nor do the like to a friend.
¹³Refuse to utter any lie,
    for the habit of lying serves no good.
¹⁴Do not prattle in the assembly of the elders,
    nor repeat yourself in your prayer.

¹⁵Do not hate toilsome labor,
    or farm work, which were created by the
    Most High.
¹⁶Do not count yourself among the crowd of
    sinners;
    remember that wrath does not delay.
¹⁷Humble yourself greatly,
    for the punishment of the ungodly is fire
    and worms. ᵃ

¹⁸Do not exchange a friend for money,
    or a real brother for the gold of Ophir.

¹⁹Do not deprive yourself of a wise and good
    wife,
    for her charm is worth more than gold.
²⁰Do not abuse a servant who performs his work
    faithfully,
    or a hired laborer who devotes himself to
    you.
²¹Let your soul love ᵇ an intelligent servant;
    do not withhold from him his freedom.

²²Do you have cattle? Look after them;
    if they are profitable to you, keep them.
²³Do you have children? Discipline them,
    and make them obedient ᶜ from their youth.
²⁴Do you have daughters? Be concerned for their
    chastity, ᵈ
    and do not show yourself too indulgent
    with them.
²⁵Give a daughter in marriage; you will have
    finished a great task.
  But give her to a man of understanding.

²⁶If you have a wife who pleases you, ᵉ do not
    cast her out;
    but do not trust yourself to one whom you
    detest.
²⁷With all your heart honor your father,
    and do not forget the birth pangs of your
    mother.
²⁸Remember that through your parents ᶠ you
    were born;
    and what can you give back to them that
    equals their gift to you?

²⁹With all your soul fear the Lord,
    and honor his priests.
³⁰With all your might love your Maker,
    and do not forsake his ministers.
³¹Fear the Lord and honor the priest,
    and give him his portion, as is commanded
    you:
  the first fruits, the guilt offering, the gift of the
    shoulders,
    the sacrifice of sanctification, and the first
    fruits of the holy things.

³²Stretch forth your hand to the poor,
    so that your blessing may be complete.
³³Give graciously to all the living,
    and withhold not kindness from the dead.
³⁴Do not fail those who weep,
    but mourn with those who mourn.

ˣ Heb: Greek adds *divine.*
ʸ Heb: Gk *will confirm.*
ᶻ Heb: Gk *plow.*
ᵃ The Hebrew text reads *for the expectation of man is worms.*
ᵇ The Hebrew text reads *Love like yourself.*
ᶜ Gk *bend their necks.*
ᵈ Gk *body.*
ᵉ Heb Syr omit *who pleases you.*
ᶠ Gk *them.*

³⁵Do not shrink from visiting a sick man,
because for such deeds you will be loved.
³⁶In all you do, remember the end of your life,
and then you will never sin.

Prudence

8 Do not contend with a powerful man,
lest you fall into his hands.
²Do not quarrel with a rich man,
lest his resources outweigh yours;
for gold has ruined many,
and has perverted the minds of kings.
³Do not argue with a chatterer,
nor heap wood on his fire.

⁴Do not jest with an ill-bred person,
lest your ancestors be disgraced.
⁵Do not reproach a man who is turning away
from sin;
remember that we all deserve punishment.
⁶Do not disdain a man when he is old,
for some of us are growing old.
⁷Do not rejoice over any one's death;
remember that we all must die.
⁸Do not slight the discourse of the sages,
but busy yourself with their maxims;
because from them you will gain instruction
and learn how to serve great men.
⁹Do not disregard the discourse of the aged,
for they themselves learned from their
fathers;
because from them you will gain
understanding
and learn how to give an answer in time of
need.

¹⁰Do not kindle the coals of a sinner,
lest you be burned in his flaming fire.
¹¹Do not get up and leave an insolent fellow,
lest he lie in ambush against your words.
¹²Do not lend to a man who is stronger than
you;
but if you do lend anything, be as one who
has lost it.
¹³Do not give surety beyond your means,
but if you give surety, be concerned as one
who must pay.

¹⁴Do not go to law against a judge,
for the decision will favor him because of
his standing.
¹⁵Do not travel on the road with a foolhardy
fellow,
lest he be burdensome to you;
for he will act as he pleases,
and through his folly you will perish with
him.
¹⁶Do not fight with a wrathful man,
and do not cross the wilderness with him;
because blood is as nothing in his sight,

and where no help is at hand, he will strike
you down.
¹⁷Do not consult with a fool,
for he will not be able to keep a secret.
¹⁸In the presence of a stranger do nothing that is
to be kept secret,
for you do not know what he will divulge. ^g
¹⁹Do not reveal your thoughts to every one,
lest you drive away your good luck. ^h

On Conduct toward Others

9 Do not be jealous of the wife of your bosom,
and do not teach her an evil lesson to your
own hurt.
²Do not give yourself to a woman
so that she gains mastery over your
strength.
³Do not go to meet a loose woman,
lest you fall into her snares.
⁴Do not associate with a woman singer,
lest you be caught in her intrigues.
⁵Do not look intently at a virgin,
lest you stumble and incur penalties for her.
⁶Do not give yourself to harlots
lest you lose your inheritance.
⁷Do not look around in the streets of a city,
nor wander about in its deserted sections.
⁸Turn away your eyes from a shapely woman,
and do not look intently at beauty
belonging to another;
many have been misled by a woman's beauty,
and by it passion is kindled like a fire.
⁹Never dine with another man's wife,
nor revel with her at wine;
lest your heart turn aside to her,
and in blood ⁱ you be plunged into
destruction.

¹⁰Forsake not an old friend,
for a new one does not compare with him.
A new friend is like new wine;
when it has aged you will drink it with
pleasure.

¹¹Do not envy the honors of a sinner,
for you do not know what his end will be.
¹²Do not delight in what pleases the ungodly;
remember that they will not be held
guiltless as long as they live.

¹³Keep far from a man who has the power to kill,
and you will not be worried by the fear of
death.
But if you approach him, make no misstep,
lest he rob you of your life.
Know that you are walking in the midst of
snares,

---

^g Or *it will bring forth.*
^h Heb: Gk *let him not return a favor to you.*
ⁱ Heb: Gk *by your spirit.*

and that you are going about on the city battlements.

¹⁴As much as you can, aim to know your neighbors,
and consult with the wise.
¹⁵Let your conversation be with men of understanding,
and let all your discussion be about the law of the Most High.
¹⁶Let righteous men be your dinner companions,
and let your glorying be in the fear of the Lord.
¹⁷A work will be praised for the skill of the craftsmen;
so a people's leader is proved wise by his words.
¹⁸A babbler is feared in his city,
and the man who is reckless in speech will be hated.

10

¹A wise magistrate will educate his people,
and the rule of an understanding man will be well ordered.
²Like the magistrate of the people, so are his officials;
and like the ruler of the city, so are all its inhabitants.
³An undisciplined king will ruin his people,
but a city will grow through the understanding of its rulers.
⁴The government of the earth is in the hands of the Lord,
and over it he will raise up the right man for the time.
⁵The success of a man is in the hands of the Lord,
and he confers his honor upon the person of the scribe. ^j

⁶Do not be angry with your neighbor for any injury,
and do not attempt anything by acts of insolence.
⁷Arrogance is hateful before the Lord and before men,
and injustice is outrageous to both.
⁸Sovereignty passes from nation to nation
on account of injustice and insolence and wealth.
⁹How can he who is dust and ashes be proud?
for even in life his bowels decay. ^k
¹⁰A long illness baffles the physician; ^l
the king of today will die tomorrow.
¹¹For when a man is dead,
he will inherit creeping things, and wild beasts, and worms.
¹²The beginning of man's pride is to depart from the Lord;

his heart has forsaken his Maker.
¹³For the beginning of pride is sin,
and the man who clings to it pours out abominations.
Therefore the Lord brought upon them extraordinary afflictions,
and destroyed them utterly.
¹⁴The Lord has cast down the thrones of rulers,
and has seated the lowly in their place.
¹⁵The Lord has plucked up the roots of the nations, ^m
and has planted the humble in their place.
¹⁶The Lord has overthrown the lands of the nations,
and has destroyed them to the foundations of the earth.
¹⁷He has removed some of them and destroyed them,
and has extinguished the memory of them from the earth.
¹⁸Pride was not created for men,
nor fierce anger for those born of women.

¹⁹What race is worthy of honor? The human race.
What race is worthy of honor? Those who fear the Lord.
What race is unworthy of honor? The human race.
What race is unworthy of honor? Those who transgress the commandments.
²⁰Among brothers their leader is worthy of honor,
and those who fear the Lord are worthy of honor in his eyes. ⁿ
²²The rich, and the eminent, and the poor—
their glory is the fear of the Lord.
²³It is not right to despise an intelligent poor man,
nor is it proper to honor a sinful man.
²⁴The nobleman, and the judge, and the ruler will be honored,
but none of them is greater than the man who fears the Lord.
²⁵Free men will be at the service of a wise servant,
and a man of understanding will not grumble.
²⁶Do not make a display of your wisdom when you do your work,
nor glorify yourself at a time when you are in want.

---

^j Or *the official.*
^k Heb: Greek is obscure.
^l Heb Vg: Greek is uncertain.
^m Some authorities read *proud nations.*
ⁿ Other authorities add as verse 21, *The fear of the Lord is the beginning of acceptance; obduracy and pride are the beginning of rejection.*

²⁷Better is a man who works and has an
    abundance of everything,
    than one who goes about boasting, but lacks
      bread.
²⁸My son, glorify yourself with humility,
    and ascribe to yourself honor according to
      your worth.
²⁹Who will justify the man that sins against
    himself?
    And who will honor the man that dishonors
      his own life?
³⁰A poor man is honored for his knowledge,
    while a rich man is honored for his wealth.
³¹A man honored in poverty, how much more in
    wealth!
    And a man dishonored in wealth, how much
      more in poverty!

11

The wisdom of a humble man will lift up
his head,
    and will seat him among the great.

²Do not praise a man for his good looks,
    nor loathe a man because of his
      appearance.
³The bee is small among flying creatures,
    but her product is the best of sweet things.
⁴Do not boast about wearing fine clothes,
    nor exalt yourself in the day that you are
      honored;
    for the works of the Lord are wonderful,
    and his works are concealed from men.
⁵Many kings have had to sit on the ground,
    but one who was never thought of has
      worn a crown.
⁶Many rulers have been greatly disgraced,
    and illustrious men have been handed over
      to others.

⁷Do not find fault before you investigate;
    first consider, and then reprove.
⁸Do not answer before you have heard,
    nor interrupt a speaker in the midst of his
      words.
⁹Do not argue about a matter which does not
    concern you,
    nor sit with sinners when they judge a case.

¹⁰My son, do not busy yourself with many
    matters;
    if you multiply activities you will not go
      unpunished,
    and if you pursue you will not overtake,
    and by fleeing you will not escape.
¹¹There is a man who works, and toils, and
    presses on,
    but is so much the more in want.
¹²There is another who is slow and needs help,
    who lacks strength and abounds in
      poverty;

but the eyes of the Lord look upon him for his
    good;
    he lifts him out of his low estate
¹³and raises up his head,
    so that many are amazed at him.

¹⁴Good things and bad, life and death,
    poverty and wealth, come from the Lord. ^o
¹⁷The gift of the Lord endures for those who are
    godly,
    and what he approves will have lasting
      success.
¹⁸There is a man who is rich through his
    diligence and self-denial,
    and this is the reward allotted to him:
¹⁹when he says, "I have found rest,
    and now I shall enjoy ^p my goods!"
    he does not know how much time will pass
    until he leaves them to others and dies.
²⁰Stand by your covenant ^q and attend to it,
    and grow old in your work.

²¹Do not wonder at the works of a sinner,
    but trust in the Lord and keep at your toil;
    for it is easy in the sight of the Lord
    to enrich a poor man quickly and
      suddenly.
²²The blessing of the Lord is ^r the reward of the
    godly,
    and quickly God causes his blessing to
      flourish.
²³Do not say, "What do I need,
    and what prosperity could be mine in the
      future?"
²⁴Do not say, "I have enough,
    and what calamity could happen to me in
      the future?"
²⁵In the day of prosperity, adversity is
    forgotten,
    and in the day of adversity, prosperity is
      not remembered.
²⁶For it is easy in the sight of the Lord
    to reward a man on the day of death
    according to his conduct.
²⁷The misery of an hour makes one forget
    luxury,
    and at the close of a man's life his deeds
      will be revealed.
²⁸Call no one happy before his death;
    a man will be known through his children.

²⁹Do not bring every man into your home,
    for many are the wiles of the crafty.

---

^o Other authorities add as verses 15 and 16, ¹⁵*Wisdom, understanding,
and knowledge of the law come from the Lord; affection and the ways of
good works come from him.* ¹⁶*Error and darkness were created with
sinners; evil will grow old with those who take pride in malice.*
^p Gk *eat of.*
^q Heb *task.*
^r Gk *is in.*

³⁰Like a decoy partridge in a cage, so is the mind
of a proud man,
and like a spy he observes your weakness; ˢ
³¹for he lies in wait, turning good into evil,
and to worthy actions he will attach blame.
³²From a spark of fire come many burning coals,
and a sinner lies in wait to shed blood.
³³Beware of a scoundrel, for he devises evil,
lest he give you a lasting blemish.
³⁴Receive a stranger into your home and he will
upset you with commotion,
and will estrange you from your family.

Friends and Enemies

12 If you do a kindness, know to whom you
do it,
and you will be thanked for your good
deeds.
²Do good to a godly man, and you will be
repaid—
if not by him, certainly by the Most High.
³No good will come to the man who persists in
evil
or to him who does not give alms.
⁴Give to the godly man, but do not help the
sinner.
5   Do good to the humble, but do not give to
the ungodly;
hold back his bread, and do not give it to him,
lest by means of it he subdue you;
for you will receive twice as much evil
for all the good which you do to him.
⁶For the Most High also hates sinners
and will inflict punishment on the ungodly. ᵗ
⁷Give to the good man, but do not help the
sinner.

⁸A friend will not be known ᵘ in prosperity,
nor will an enemy be hidden in adversity.
⁹A man's enemies are grieved when he prospers,
and in his adversity even his friend will
separate from him.
¹⁰Never trust your enemy,
for like the rusting of copper, so is his
wickedness.
¹¹Even if he humbles himself and goes about
cringing,
watch yourself, and be on your guard
against him;
and you will be to him like one who has
polished a mirror,
and you will know that it was not
hopelessly tarnished.
¹²Do not put him next to you,
lest he overthrow you and take your place;
do not have him sit at your right,
lest he try to take your seat of honor,
and at last you will realize the truth of my
words,
and be stung by what I have said.

¹³Who will pity a snake charmer bitten by a
serpent,
or any who go near wild beasts?
¹⁴So no one will pity a man who associates with a
sinner
and becomes involved in his sins.
¹⁵He will stay with you for a time,
but if you falter, he will not stand by you.

¹⁶An enemy will speak sweetly with his lips,
but in his mind he will plan to throw you
into a pit;
an enemy will weep with his eyes,
but if he finds an opportunity his thirst for
blood will be insatiable.
¹⁷If calamity befalls you, you will find him there
ahead of you;
and while pretending to help you, he will
trip you by the heel;
¹⁸he will shake his head, and clap his hands,
and whisper much, and change his
expression.

Responsible Use of Riches

13 Whoever touches pitch will be defiled,
and whoever associates with a proud
man will become like him.
²Do not lift a weight beyond your strength,
nor associate with a man mightier and
richer than you.
How can the clay pot associate with the iron
kettle?
The pot will strike against it, and will itself
be broken.
³A rich man does wrong, and he even adds
reproaches;
a poor man suffers wrong, and he must add
apologies.
⁴A rich man ᵛ will exploit you if you can be of
use to him,
but if you are in need he will forsake you.
⁵If you own something, he will live with you;
he will drain your resources and he will not
care.
⁶When he needs you he will deceive you,
he will smile at you and give you hope.
He will speak to you kindly and say, "What do
you need?"
⁷He will shame you with his foods,
until he has drained you two or three
times;
and finally he will deride you.
Should he see you afterwards, he will forsake
you,
and shake his head at you.

ˢ Heb: Gk *downfall*.
ᵗ Other authorities add *and he is keeping them for the mighty day of
their punishment*.
ᵘ Other authorities read *punished*.
ᵛ Gk *He*.

⁸Take care not to be led astray,
   and not to be humiliated in your feasting. ʷ
⁹When a powerful man invites you, be reserved;
   and he will invite you the more often.
¹⁰Do not push forward, lest you be repulsed;
   and do not remain at a distance, lest you be
      forgotten.
¹¹Do not try to treat him as an equal,
   nor trust his abundance of words;
for he will test you through much talk,
   and while he smiles he will be examining
      you.
¹²Cruel is he who does not keep words to himself;
   he will not hesitate to injure or to imprison.
¹³Keep words to yourself and be very watchful,
   for you are walking about with your own
      downfall. ˣ

¹⁵Every creature loves its like,
   and every person his neighbor;
¹⁶all living beings associate by species,
   and a man clings to one like himself.
¹⁷What fellowship has a wolf with a lamb?
   No more has a sinner with a godly man.
¹⁸What peace is there between a hyena and a
      dog?
   And what peace between a rich man and a
      poor man?
¹⁹Wild donkeys in the wilderness are the prey of
      lions;
   likewise the poor are pastures for the rich.
²⁰Humility is an abomination to a proud man;
   likewise a poor man is an abomination to a
      rich one.

²¹When a rich man totters, he is steadied by
      friends,
   but when a humble man falls, he is even
      pushed away by friends.
²²If a rich man slips, his helpers are many;
   he speaks unseemly words, and they justify
      him.
If a humble man slips, they even reproach him;
   he speaks sensibly, and receives no
      attention.
²³When the rich man speaks all are silent,
   and they extol to the clouds what he says.
When the poor man speaks they say, "Who is
      this fellow?"
   And should he stumble, they even push him
      down.
²⁴Riches are good if they are free from sin,
   and poverty is evil in the opinion of the
      ungodly.
²⁵A man's heart changes his countenance,
   either for good or for evil. ʸ
²⁶The mark of a happy heart is a cheerful face,
   but to devise proverbs requires painful
      thinking.

14 Blessed is the man who does not blunder
      with his lips
   and need not suffer grief for sin.
²Blessed is he whose heart does not condemn
      him,
   and who has not given up his hope.

³Riches are not seemly for a stingy man;
   and of what use is property to an envious
      man?
⁴Whoever accumulates by depriving himself,
      accumulates for others;
   and others will live in luxury on his goods.
⁵If a man is mean to himself, to whom will he be
      generous?
   He will not enjoy his own riches.
⁶No one is meaner than the man who is
      grudging to himself,
   and this is the retribution for his baseness;
⁷even if he does good, he does it unintentionally,
   and betrays his baseness in the end.
⁸Evil is the man with a grudging eye;
   he averts his face and disregards people.
⁹A greedy man's eye is not satisfied with a
      portion,
   and mean injustice withers the soul.
¹⁰A stingy man's eye begrudges bread,
   and it is lacking at his table.

¹¹My son, treat yourself well, according to your
      means,
   and present worthy offerings to the Lord.
¹²Remember that death will not delay,
   and the decree ᶻ of Hades has not been
      shown to you.
¹³Do good to a friend before you die,
   and reach out and give to him as much as
      you can.
¹⁴Do not deprive yourself of a happy day;
   let not your share of desired good pass by
      you.
¹⁵Will you not leave the fruit of your labors to
      another,
   and what you acquired by toil to be divided
      by lot?
¹⁶Give, and take, and beguile yourself,
   because in Hades one cannot look for
      luxury.
¹⁷All living beings become old like a garment,
   for the decree ᵃ from of old is, "You must
      surely die!"
¹⁸Like flourishing leaves on a spreading tree
   which sheds some and puts forth others,

ʷ Other authorities read *folly.*
ˣ Other authorities add *When you hear these things in your sleep, wake
up!* ¹⁴*During all your life love the Lord, and call on him for your
salvation.*
ʸ Other authorities add *and a glad heart makes a cheerful countenance.*
ᶻ Gk *covenant.*
ᵃ Gk *covenant.*

so are the generations of flesh and blood:
    one dies and another is born.
¹⁹Every product decays and ceases to exist,
    and the man who made it will pass away
      with it.

²⁰Blessed is the man who meditates on ᵇ wisdom
    and who reasons intelligently.
²¹He who reflects in his mind on her ways
    will also ponder her secrets.
²²Pursue wisdom ᶜ like a hunter,
    and lie in wait on her paths.
²³He who peers through her windows
    will also listen at her doors;
²⁴he who encamps near her house
    will also fasten his tent peg to her walls;
²⁵he will pitch his tent near her,
    and will lodge in an excellent lodging
      place;
²⁶he will place his children under her shelter,
    and will camp under her boughs;
²⁷he will be sheltered by her from the heat,
    and will dwell in the midst of her glory.

Freedom of Choice and Its Consequences

15 The man who fears the Lord will do this,
    and he who holds to the law will obtain
      wisdom. ᵈ
²She will come to meet him like a mother,
    and like the wife of his youth she will
      welcome him.
³She will feed him with the bread of
      understanding,
    and give him the water of wisdom to drink.
⁴He will lean on her and will not fall,
    and he will rely on her and will not be put to
      shame.
⁵She will exalt him above his neighbors,
    and will open his mouth in the midst of the
      assembly;
she will fill him with a spirit of wisdom and
      understanding,
    and clothe him with a robe of glory.
⁶He will find gladness and a crown of rejoicing,
    and will acquire an everlasting name.
⁷Foolish men will not obtain her,
    and sinful men will not see her.
⁸She is far from men of pride,
    and liars will never think of her.

⁹A hymn of praise is not fitting on the lips of a
      sinner,
    for it has not been sent from the Lord.
¹⁰For a hymn of praise should be uttered in
      wisdom,
    and the Lord will prosper it.
¹¹Do not say, "Because of the Lord I left the right
      way";
    for he ᵉ will not do what he hates.

¹²Do not say, "It was he who led me astray";
    for he has no need of a sinful man.
¹³The Lord hates all abominations,
    and they are not loved by those who fear
      him.
¹⁴It was he who created man in the beginning,
    and he left him in the power of his own
      inclination.
¹⁵If you will, you can keep the commandments,
    they will save you;
    if you trust in God, you too shall live.
¹⁶He has placed before you fire and water:
    stretch out your hand for whichever you
      wish.
¹⁷Before a man ᶠ are life and death, good and
      evil,
    and whichever he chooses will be given to
      him.
¹⁸For great is the wisdom of the Lord;
    he is mighty in power and sees everything.
¹⁹The eyes of the Lord are on those who fear
      him,
    and he knows every deed of man.
²⁰He has not commanded any one to be ungodly,
    and he has not given any one permission to
      sin.

16 Do not desire a multitude of useless
    children,
    nor rejoice in ungodly sons.
²If they multiply, do not rejoice in them,
    unless the fear of the Lord is in them.
³Do not trust in their survival,
    and do not rely on their multitude;
  for one is better than a thousand, ᵍ
    and to die childless is better than to have
      ungodly children.
⁴For through one man of understanding a city
      will be filled with people,
    but through a tribe of lawless men it will be
      made desolate.
⁵Many such things my eye has seen,
    and my ear has heard things more striking
      than these.

⁶In an assembly of sinners a fire will be kindled,
    and in a disobedient nation wrath was
      kindled.
⁷He was not propitiated for the ancient giants
    who revolted in their might.
⁸He did not spare the neighbors of Lot,
    whom he loathed on account of their
      insolence.

ᵇ Other authorities read *dies in*.
ᶜ Gk *her*.
ᵈ Gk *her*.
ᵉ Heb: Gk *you*.
ᶠ Gk *men*.
ᵍ The text of this line is uncertain.

⁹He showed no pity for a nation devoted to
  destruction,
  for those destroyed in their sins;
¹⁰nor for the six hundred thousand men on foot,
  who rebelliously assembled in their
  stubbornness.
¹¹Even if there is only one stiffnecked person,
  it will be a wonder if he remains
  unpunished.
  For mercy and wrath are with the Lord; ʰ
  he is mighty to forgive, and he pours out
  wrath.
¹²As great as his mercy, so great is also his
  reproof;
  he judges a man according to his deeds.
¹³The sinner will not escape with his plunder,
  and the patience of the godly will not be
  frustrated.
¹⁴He will make room for every act of mercy;
  every one will receive in accordance with
  his deeds. ⁱ

¹⁷Do not say, "I shall be hidden from the Lord,
  and who from on high will remember me?
  Among so many people I shall not be known,
  for what is my soul in the boundless
  creation?
¹⁸Behold, heaven and the highest heaven,
  the abyss and the earth, will tremble at his
  visitation.
¹⁹The mountains also and the foundations of the
  earth
  shake with trembling when he looks upon
  them.
²⁰And no mind will reflect on this.
  Who will ponder his ways?
²¹Like a tempest which no man can see,
  so most of his works are concealed.
²²Who will announce his acts of justice?
  Or who will await them? For the covenant is
  far off."
²³This is what one devoid of understanding
  thinks;
  a senseless and misguided man thinks
  foolishly.

²⁴Listen to me, my son, and acquire knowledge,
  and pay close attention to my words.
²⁵I will impart instruction by weight,
  and declare knowledge accurately.

²⁶The works of the Lord have existed from the
  beginning by his creation, ʲ
  and when he made them, he determined
  their divisions.
²⁷He arranged his works in an eternal order,
  and their dominion ᵏ for all ˡ generations;
they neither hunger nor grow weary,
  and they do not cease from their labors.

²⁸They do not crowd one another aside,
  and they will never disobey his word.
²⁹After this the Lord looked upon the earth,
  and filled it with his good things;
³⁰with all kinds of living beings he covered its
  surface,
  and to it they return.

Wisdom concerning God's Gifts to Men

17 The Lord created man out of earth,
  and made him into his own image;
²he turned him back into earth again,
  but clothed him in strength like his own. ᵒ
³He gave to men ᵐ few days, a limited time,
  but granted them authority over the things
  upon the earth. ⁿ
⁴He placed the fear of them ᵖ in all flesh,
  and granted them dominion over beasts and
  birds. �q
⁶He made for them ʳ discretion, with a tongue
  and eyes and ears;
  he gave them a mind for thinking,
  and filled them with the discipline of
  discernment.
⁷He created in them the knowledge of the
  spirit;
  he filled their hearts with understanding,
  and showed them good and evil.
⁸He placed the fear of him into their hearts,
  showing them the majesty of his works. ˢ
⁹He made them glory in his wondrous deeds,
10 that they might praise his holy name,
  to proclaim the grandeur of his works.
¹¹He bestowed knowledge upon them,
  and allotted to them the law of life.
¹²He established with them an eternal covenant,
  and showed them his justice and his
  judgments.
¹³Their eyes saw his glorious majesty,
  and their ears heard the glory of his voice.
¹⁴And he said to them, "Beware of all
  unrighteousness." ᵗ
  And he gave commandment to each of them
  concerning his neighbor.

ʰ Gk *him.*
ⁱ Other authorities add ¹⁵*The Lord hardened Pharaoh so that he did not know him; in order that his works might be known under heaven.* ¹⁶*His mercy is manifest to the whole of creation, and he divided his light and darkness with a plumb line.*
ʲ Heb: Gk *judgment.*
ᵏ Or *elements.*
ˡ Gk *their.*
ᵐ Gk *them.*
ⁿ Gk *it.*
ᵒ Cn: Gk *proper to them.*
ᵖ Syr: Gk *him.*
q Other authorities add ⁵*They obtained the use of the five operations of the Lord; as sixth he distributed to them the gift of mind, and as seventh reason, the interpreter of his operations.*
ʳ Syr: Gk *Inclination and.*
ˢ Other authorities add ⁹*and he gave them to boast of his marvels for ever.*
ᵗ Or *every unrighteous man.*

¹⁵Their ways are always before him,
  they will not be hidden from his eyes. ᵘ
¹⁷He appointed a ruler for every nation,
  but Israel is the Lord's own portion. ᵛ
¹⁹All their works are as the sun before him,
  and his eyes are continually upon their
  ways.
²⁰Their iniquities are not hidden from him,
  and all their sins are before the Lord. ʷ
²²A man's almsgiving is like a signet with the
  Lord, ˣ
  and he will keep a person's kindness like the
  apple of his eye.
²³Afterward he will arise and repay them,
  and he will bring their recompense on their
  heads.
²⁴Yet to those who repent he grants a return,
  and he encourages those whose endurance
  is failing,
  and he has appointed to them the lot of
  truth.

²⁵Turn to the Lord and forsake your sins;
  pray in his presence and lessen your
  offenses.
²⁶Return to the Most High and turn away from
  iniquity, ʸ
  and hate abominations intensely.
Know the justice and the judgments of God,
  and stand firm the lot that is set before you,
  in prayer to God, the Almighty.
²⁷Who will sing praises to the Most High in
  Hades,
  as do those who are alive and give thanks?
Tarry not in the waywardness of the ungodly,
  and give thanks before death.
²⁸From the dead, as from one who does not exist,
  thanksgiving has ceased;
  he who is alive and well sings the Lord's
  praises.
²⁹How great is the mercy of the Lord,
  and his forgiveness for those who turn to
  him!
³⁰For all things cannot be in men, ᶻ
  since a son of man is not immortal.
³¹What is brighter than the sun? Yet its light
  fails. ᵃ
So flesh and blood devise evil.
³²He marshals the host of the height of heaven;
  but all men are dust and ashes.

God and Man

18 He who lives for ever created the whole
  universe;
² the Lord alone will be declared righteous. ᵇ
⁴To none has he given power to proclaim his
  works;
  and who can search out his mighty deeds?
⁵Who can measure his majestic power?
  And who can fully recount his mercies?

⁶It is not possible to diminish or increase them,
  nor is it possible to trace the wonders of the
  Lord.
⁷When a man has finished, he is just beginning,
  and when he stops, he will be at a loss.
⁸What is man, and of what use is he?
  What is his good and what is his evil?
⁹The number of a man's days is great if he
  reaches a hundred years.
¹⁰Like a drop of water from the sea and a grain ᶜ
  of sand
  so are a few years in the day of eternity.
¹¹Therefore the Lord is patient with them
  and pours out his mercy upon them.
¹²He sees and recognizes that their end will be
  evil;
  therefore he grants them forgiveness in
  abundance.
¹³The compassion of man is for his neighbor,
  but the compassion of the Lord is for all
  living beings.
He rebukes and trains and teaches them,
  and turns them back, as a shepherd his
  flock.
¹⁴He has compassion on those who accept his
  discipline
  and who are eager for his judgments.

¹⁵My son, do not mix reproach with your good
  deeds,
  nor cause grief by your words when you
  present a gift.
¹⁶Does not the dew assuage the scorching heat?
  So a word is better than a gift.
¹⁷Indeed, does not a word surpass a good gift?
  Both are to be found in a gracious man.
¹⁸A fool is ungracious and abusive,
  and the gift of a grudging man makes the
  eyes dim.

¹⁹Before you speak, learn,
  and before you fall ill, take care of your
  health.
²⁰Before judgment, examine yourself,
  and in the hour of visitation you will find
  forgiveness.

ᵘ Other authorities add ¹⁶*Their ways from youth tend toward evil, and they are unable to make for themselves hearts of flesh in place of their stony hearts.* ¹⁷*For in the division of the nations of the whole earth.*
ᵛ Other authorities add ¹⁸*whom, being his first-born, he brings up with discipline, and allotting to him the light of his love, he does not neglect him.*
ʷ Other authorities add ²¹*But the Lord, who is gracious and knows his creatures, has neither left nor abandoned them, but spared them.*
ˣ Gk *him.*
ʸ Other authorities add *for he will lead you out of darkness to the light of health.*
ᶻ The Greek text of this line is uncertain.
ᵃ Or *suffers eclipse.*
ᵇ Other authorities add *and there is no other beside him;* ³*he steers the world with the span of his hand, and all things obey his will; for he is king of all things, by his power separating among them the holy things from the profane.*
ᶜ Gk *pebble.*

²¹Before falling ill, humble yourself,
  and when you are on the point of sinning,
    turn back.
²²Let nothing hinder you from paying a vow
    promptly,
  and do not wait until death to be released
    from it.
²³Before making a vow,ᵈ prepare yourself;
  and do not be like a man who tempts the
    Lord.
²⁴Think of his wrath on the day of death,
  and of the moment of vengeance when he
    turns away his face.
²⁵In the time of plenty think of the time of
    hunger;
  in the days of wealth think of poverty and
    need.
²⁶From morning to evening conditions change,
  and all things move swiftly before the Lord.

²⁷A wise man is cautious in everything,
  and in days of sin he guards against
    wrongdoing.
²⁸Every intelligent man knows wisdom,
  and he praises the one who finds her.
²⁹Those who understand sayings become skilled
    themselves,
  and pour forth apt proverbs.

³⁰Do not follow your base desires,
  but restrain your appetites.
³¹If you allow your soul to take pleasure in base
    desire,
  it will make you the laughingstock of your
    enemies.
³²Do not revel in great luxury,
  lest you become impoverished by its
    expense.
³³Do not become a beggar by feasting with
    borrowed money,
  when you have nothing in your purse.

True Wisdom Contrasted to Cleverness and Evil

19 A workman who is a drunkard will not
  become rich;
  he who despises small things will fail little
    by little.
²Wine and women lead intelligent men astray,
  and the man who consorts with harlots is
    very reckless.
³Decay and worms will inherit him,
  and the reckless soul will be snatched away.

⁴One who trusts others too quickly is
    lightminded,
  and one who sins does wrong to himself.
⁵One who rejoices in wickednessᵉ will be
    condemned,ᶠ
⁶and for one who hates gossip evil is lessened.

⁷Never repeat a conversation,
  and you will lose nothing at all.
⁸With friend or foe do not report it,
  and unless it would be a sin for you, do not
    disclose it;
⁹for some one has heard you and watched you,
  and when the time comes he will hate you.
¹⁰Have you heard a word? Let it die with you.
  Be brave! It will not make you burst!
¹¹With such a word a fool will suffer pangs
  like a woman in labor with a child.
¹²Like an arrow stuck in the flesh of the thigh,
  so is a word inside a fool.

¹³Question a friend, perhaps he did not do it;
  but if he did anything, so that he may do it
    no more.
¹⁴Question a neighbor, perhaps he did not say it;
  but if he said it, so that he may not say it
    again.
¹⁵Question a friend, for often it is slander;
  so do not believe everything you hear.
¹⁶A person may make a slip without intending it.
  Who has never sinned with his tongue?
¹⁷Question your neighbor before you threaten
    him;
  and let the law of the Most High take its
    course.ᵍ

²⁰All wisdom is the fear of the Lord,
  and in all wisdom there is the fulfilment of
    the law.ʰ
²²But the knowledge of wickedness is not
    wisdom,
  nor is there prudence where sinners take
    counsel.
²³There is a cleverness which is abominable,
  but there is a fool who merely lacks
    wisdom.
²⁴Better is the God-fearing man who lacks
    intelligence,
  than the highly prudent man who
    transgresses the law.
²⁵There is a cleverness which is scrupulous but
    unjust,
  and there are people who distort kindness
    to gain a verdict.
²⁶There is a rascal bowed down in mourning,ⁱ
  but inwardly he is full of deceit.

ᵈ Or *offering a prayer.*
ᵉ Other authorities read *heart.*
ᶠ Other authorities add *but he who withstands pleasures crowns his
life.* ⁶*He who controls his tongue will live without strife,.*
ᵍ Other authorities add *and do not be angry.* ¹⁸*The fear of the Lord is
the beginning of acceptance, and wisdom obtains his love.* ¹⁹*The
knowledge of the Lord's commandments is life-giving discipline; and
those who do what is pleasing to him enjoy the fruit of the tree of
immortality.*
ʰ Other authorities add *and the knowledge of his omnipotence.* ²¹*When a
servant says to his master, "I will not act as you wish," even if later he
does it, he angers the one who supports him.*
ⁱ Gk *blackness.*

²⁷He hides his face and pretends not to hear;
  but where no one notices, he will forestall
    you.
²⁸And if by lack of strength he is prevented from
    sinning,
  he will do evil when he finds an
    opportunity.
²⁹A man is known by his appearance,
  and a sensible man is known by his face,
    when you meet him.
³⁰A man's attire and open-mouthed laughter,
  and a man's manner of walking, show what
    he is.

On Silence and Speech

20 There is a reproof which is not timely;
  and there is a man who keeps silent but
    is wise.
²How much better it is to reprove than to stay
    angry!
  And the one who confesses his fault will be
    kept from loss. ʲ
⁴Like a eunuch's desire to violate a maiden
  is a man who executes judgments by
    violence.
⁵There is one who by keeping silent is found
    wise,
  while another is detested for being too
    talkative.
⁶There is one who keeps silent because he has
    no answer,
  while another keeps silent because he
    knows when to speak.
⁷A wise man will be silent until the right
    moment,
  but a braggart and fool goes beyond the
    right moment.
⁸Whoever uses too many words will be loathed,
  and whoever usurps the right to speak will
    be hated.

⁹There may be good fortune for a man in
    adversity,
  and a windfall may result in a loss.
¹⁰There is a gift that profits you nothing,
  and there is a gift that brings a double
    return.
¹¹There are losses because of glory,
  and there are men who have raised their
    heads from humble circumstances.
¹²There is a man who buys much for a little,
  but pays for it seven times over.

¹³The wise man makes himself beloved through
    his words,
  but the courtesies of fools are wasted.
¹⁴A fool's gift will profit you nothing,
  for he has many eyes instead of one.
¹⁵He gives little and upbraids much,
  he opens his mouth like a herald;

today he lends and tomorrow he asks it
    back;
  such a one is a hateful man.
¹⁶A fool will say, "I have no friend,
  and there is no gratitude for my good deeds;
    those who eat my bread speak unkindly."
¹⁷How many will ridicule him, and how often!

¹⁸A slip on the pavement is better than a slip of
    the tongue;
  so the downfall of the wicked will occur
    speedily.
¹⁹An ungracious man is like a story told at the
    wrong time,
  which is continually on the lips of the
    ignorant.
²⁰A proverb from a fool's lips will be rejected,
  for he does not tell it at its proper time.

²¹A man may be prevented from sinning by his
    poverty,
  so when he rests he feels no remorse.
²²A man may lose his life through shame,
  or lose it because of his foolish look.
²³A man may for shame make promises to a
    friend,
  and needlessly make him an enemy.

²⁴A lie is an ugly blot on a man;
  it is continually on the lips of the ignorant.
²⁵A thief is preferable to a habitual liar,
  but the lot of both is ruin.
²⁶The disposition of a liar brings disgrace,
  and his shame is ever with him.

²⁷He who speaks wisely will advance himself,
  and a sensible man will please great men.
²⁸Whoever cultivates the soil will heap up his
    harvest,
  and whoever pleases great men will atone
    for injustice.
²⁹Presents and gifts blind the eyes of the wise;
  like a muzzle on the mouth they avert
    reproofs.
³⁰Hidden wisdom and unseen treasure,
  what advantage is there in either of them?
³¹Better is the man who hides his folly
  than the man who hides his wisdom. ᵏ

Various Sins and Foolishness

21 Have you sinned, my son? Do so no more,
  but pray about your former sins.
²Flee from sin as from a snake;
  for if you approach sin, it will bite you.
  Its teeth are lion's teeth,
    and destroy the souls of men.

ʲ Other authorities add ³*How good it is to show repentance when you are
reproved, for so you will escape deliberate sin!*
ᵏ Other authorities add ³²*Unwearied patience in seeking the Lord is
better than a masterless charioteer of one's own life.*

³All lawlessness is like a two-edged sword;
 there is no healing for its wound.

⁴Terror and violence will lay waste riches;
 thus the house of the proud will be laid
  waste.
⁵The prayer of a poor man goes from his lips to
  the ears of God, ¹
 and his judgment comes speedily.
⁶Whoever hates reproof walks in the steps of
  the sinner,
 but he that fears the Lord will repent in his
  heart.
⁷He who is mighty in speech is known from
  afar;
 but the sensible man, when he slips, is
  aware of it.

⁸A man who builds his house with other
  people's money
 is like one who gathers stones for his burial
  mound. ᵐ
⁹An assembly of the wicked is like tow gathered
  together,
 and their end is a flame of fire.
¹⁰The way of sinners is smoothly paved with
  stones,
 but at its end is the pit of Hades.

¹¹Whoever keeps the law controls his thoughts,
 and wisdom is the fulfilment of the fear of
  the Lord.
¹²He who is not clever cannot be taught,
 but there is a cleverness which increases
  bitterness.
¹³The knowledge of a wise man will increase like
  a flood,
 and his counsel like a flowing spring.
¹⁴The mind of a fool is like a broken jar;
 it will hold no knowledge.

¹⁵When a man of understanding hears a wise
  saying,
 he will praise it and add to it;
when a reveler hears it, he dislikes it
 and casts it behind his back.
¹⁶A fool's narration is like a burden on a
  journey,
 but delight will be found in the speech of
  the intelligent.
¹⁷The utterance of a sensible man will be sought
  in the assembly,
 and they will ponder his words in their
  minds.

¹⁸Like a house that has vanished, so is wisdom to
  a fool;
 and the knowledge of the ignorant is
  unexamined talk.

¹⁹To a senseless man education is chains on his
  feet,
 and like manacles on his right hand.
²⁰A fool raises his voice when he laughs,
 but a clever man smiles quietly.
²¹To a sensible man education is like a golden
  ornament,
 and like a bracelet on the right arm.

²²The foot of a fool rushes into a house,
 but a man of experience stands respectfully
  before it.
²³A boor peers into the house from the door,
 but a cultivated man remains outside.
²⁴It is ill-mannered for a man to listen at a door,
 and a discreet man is grieved by the
  disgrace.
²⁵The lips of strangers will speak of these
  things, ⁿ
 but the words of the prudent will be
  weighed in the balance.
²⁶The mind of fools is in their mouth,
 but the mouth of wise men is in ° their
  mind.
²⁷When an ungodly man curses his adversary, ᵖ
 he curses his own soul.
²⁸A whisperer defiles his own soul
 and is hated in his neighborhood.

On Wisdom, Folly, and Self-Control

22 The indolent may be compared to a filthy
  stone,
 and every one hisses at his disgrace.
²The indolent may be compared to the filth of
  dunghills;
 any one that picks it up will shake it off his
  hand.

³It is a disgrace to be the father of an
  undisciplined son,
 and the birth of a daughter is a loss.
⁴A sensible daughter obtains her husband,
 but one who acts shamefully brings grief to
  her father.
⁵An impudent daughter disgraces father and
  husband,
 and will be despised by both.
⁶Like music in mourning is a tale told at the
  wrong time,
 but chastising and discipline are wisdom at
  all times.

⁷He who teaches a fool is like one who glues
  potsherds together,
 or who rouses a sleeper from deep slumber.

---

¹ Gk *his ears.*
ᵐ Other authorities read *for the winter.*
ⁿ The Greek text of this line is uncertain.
° Other authorities omit *in.*
ᵖ Or *curses Satan.*

⁸He who tells a story to a fool tells it to a
  drowsy man;
  and at the end he will say, "What is it?" ᵖ
¹¹Weep for the dead, for he lacks the light;
  and weep for the fool, for he lacks
    intelligence;
weep less bitterly for the dead, for he has
    attained rest;
  but the life of the fool is worse than death.
¹²Mourning for the dead lasts seven days,
  but for a fool or an ungodly man it lasts all
    his life.

¹³Do not talk much with a foolish man,
  and do not visit an unintelligent man;
guard yourself from him to escape trouble,
  and you will not be soiled when he shakes
    himself off;
avoid him and you will find rest,
  and you will never be wearied by his
    madness.
¹⁴What is heavier than lead?
  And what is its name except "Fool"?
¹⁵Sand, salt, and a piece of iron
  are easier to bear than a stupid man.

¹⁶A wooden beam firmly bonded into a building
  will not be torn loose by an earthquake;
so the mind firmly fixed on a reasonable
    counsel
  will not be afraid in a crisis.
¹⁷A mind settled on an intelligent thought
  is like the stucco decoration on the wall of a
    colonnade. ʳ
¹⁸Fences set on a high place
  will not stand firm against the wind;
so a timid heart with a fool's purpose
  will not stand firm against any fear.

¹⁹A man who pricks an eye will make tears fall,
  and one who pricks the heart makes it show
    feeling.
²⁰One who throws a stone at birds scares them
    away,
  and one who reviles a friend will break off
    the friendship.
²¹Even if you have drawn your sword against a
    friend,
  do not despair, for a renewal of friendship
    is possible.
²²If you have opened your mouth against your
    friend,
  do not worry, for reconciliation is possible;
but as for reviling, arrogance, disclosure of
    secrets, or a treacherous blow—
  in these cases any friend will flee.

²³Gain the trust of your neighbor in his poverty,
  that you may rejoice with him in his
    prosperity;

stand by him in time of affliction,
  that you may share with him in his
    inheritance. ˢ
²⁴The vapor and smoke of the furnace precede
    the fire;
  so insults precede bloodshed.
²⁵I will not be ashamed to protect a friend,
  and I will not hide from him;
²⁶but if some harm should happen to me because
    of him,
  whoever hears of it will beware of him.

²⁷O that a guard were set over my mouth,
  and a seal of prudence upon my lips,
that it may keep me from falling,
  so that my tongue may not destroy me! ᵗ

23 O Lord, Father and Ruler of my life,
   do not abandon me to their counsel,
   and let me not fall because of them!
²O that whips were set over my thoughts,
  and the discipline of wisdom over my
    mind! ᵘ
That they may not spare me in my errors,
  and that it may not pass by my ᵛ sins;
³in order that my mistakes may not be
    multiplied,
  and my sins may not abound;
then I will not fall before my adversaries,
  and my enemy will not rejoice over me.
⁴O Lord, Father and God of my life,
  do not give me haughty eyes,
⁵ and remove from me evil desire.
⁶Let neither gluttony nor lust overcome me,
  and do not surrender me to a shameless
    soul.

⁷Listen, my children, to instruction concerning
    speech;
  the one who observes it will never be
    caught.
⁸The sinner is overtaken through his lips,
  the reviler and the arrogant are tripped by
    them.
⁹Do not accustom your mouth to oaths,
  and do not habitually utter the name of the
    Holy One;
¹⁰for as a servant who is continually examined
    under torture
  will not lack bruises,
so also the man who always swears and utters
    the Name
  will not be cleansed from sin.

ᵖ Other authorities add ⁹*Children who are brought up in a good life,
conceal the lowly birth of their parents.* ¹⁰*Children who are disdainfully
and boorishly haughty stain the nobility of their kindred.*
ʳ Or *on a smooth wall.*
ˢ Other authorities add *For one should not always despise restricted
circumstances, nor admire a rich man who is stupid.*
ᵗ Or *Who will set a guard . . . destroy me?*
ᵘ Or *Who will set whips . . . my mind?*
ᵛ Gk *their.*

¹¹A man who swears many oaths will be filled
  with iniquity,
   and the scourge will not leave his house;
if he offends, his sin remains on him,
   and if he disregards it, he sins doubly;
if he has sworn needlessly, he will not be
  justified,
   for his house will be filled with calamities.

¹²There is an utterance which is comparable to
  death; ʷ
   may it never be found in the inheritance of
   Jacob!
For all these errors will be far from the godly,
   and they will not wallow in sins.
¹³Do not accustom your mouth to lewd vulgarity,
   for it involves sinful speech.
¹⁴Remember your father and mother
   when ˣ you sit among great men;
lest you be forgetful in their presence,
   and be deemed a fool on account of your
   habits;
then you will wish that you had never been
  born,
   and you will curse the day of your birth.
¹⁵A man accustomed to using insulting words
   will never become disciplined all his days.

¹⁶Two sorts of men multiply sins,
   and a third incurs wrath.
The soul heated like a burning fire
   will not be quenched until it is consumed;
a man who commits fornication with his near
   of kin ʸ
   will never cease until the fire burns him up.
¹⁷To a fornicator all bread tastes sweet;
   he will never cease until he dies.
¹⁸A man who breaks his marriage vows
   says to himself, "Who sees me?
Darkness surrounds me, and the walls hide me,
   and no one sees me. Why should I fear?
The Most High will not take notice of my
   sins."
¹⁹His fear is confined to the eyes of men,
   and he does not realize that the eyes of the
   Lord
   are ten thousand times brighter than the
   sun;
they look upon all the ways of men,
   and perceive even the hidden places.
²⁰Before the universe was created, it was known
   to him;
   so it was also after it was finished.
²¹This man will be punished in the streets of the
   city,
   and where he least suspects it, he will be
   seized.
²²So it is with a woman who leaves her husband
   and provides an heir by a stranger.

²³For first of all, she has disobeyed the law of
   the Most High;
second, she has committed an offense
   against her husband;
and third, she has committed adultery through
   harlotry
   and brought forth children by another man.
²⁴She herself will be brought before the
   assembly,
   and punishment will fall on her children.
²⁵Her children will not take root,
   and her branches will not bear fruit.
²⁶She will leave her memory for a curse,
   and her disgrace will not be blotted out.
²⁷Those who survive her will recognize
   that nothing is better than the fear of the
   Lord,
and nothing sweeter than to heed the
   commandments of the Lord. ᶻ

The Praise of Wisdom

24 Wisdom will praise herself and is
   honored in God,
   and will glory in the midst of her people. ᵃ
²In the assembly of the Most High she will open
   her mouth,
   and in the presence of his host she will
   glory.
In the midst of her people she is exalted;
   in holy fulness she is admired.
In the multitude of the chosen she finds praise,
   and among the blessed she is blessed,
   saying:
³"I came forth from the mouth of the Most
   High,
   the first-born before all creatures.
I ordained that an unfailing light
   should arise in the heavens,
   and I covered the earth like a mist.
⁴I dwelt in high places,
   and my throne was in a pillar of cloud.
⁵Alone I have made the circuit of the vault of
   heaven
   and have walked in the depths of the
   abyss.
⁶In the waves of the sea, in the whole earth,
   and in every people and nation I have gotten
   a possession.
⁷Among all these I sought a resting place;
   I sought in whose territory I might lodge.

⁸"Then the Creator of all things gave me a
   commandment,
   and the one who created me assigned a
   place for my tent.

ʷ Other authorities read *clothed about with death.*
ˣ Gk *for.*
ʸ Gk *in the body of his flesh.*
ᶻ Other authorities add ²⁸*It is a great honor to follow God, and to be
received by him is long life.*
ᵃ Or *will glorify herself in the midst of the people.*

And he said, 'Make your dwelling in Jacob,
   and in Israel receive your inheritance,
   and among my chosen put down your
      roots.'
[9]From eternity, in the beginning, he created me,
   and for eternity I shall not cease to exist.
[10]In the holy tabernacle I ministered before him,
   and so I was established in Zion.
[11]In the beloved city likewise he gave me a
      resting place,
   and in Jerusalem was my dominion.
[12]So I took root in an honored people,
   in the portion of the Lord, who is their
      inheritance,
   and my abode was in the full assembly of
      the saints.

[13]"I grew tall like a cedar in Lebanon,
   and like a cypress on the heights of
      Hermon.
[14]I grew tall like a palm tree in En-ge'di, [b]
   and like rose plants in Jericho;
   like a beautiful olive tree in the field,
   and like a plane tree I grew tall.
[15]Like cassia and camel's thorn I gave forth the
      aroma of spices,
   and like choice myrrh I spread a pleasant
      odor,
   like galbanum, onycha, and stacte,
   and like the fragrance of frankincense in
      the tabernacle.
[16]Like a terebinth I spread out my branches,
   and my branches are glorious and graceful.
[17]Like a vine I caused loveliness to bud,
   and my blossoms became glorious and
      abundant fruit. [c]

[19]"Come to me, you who desire me,
   and eat your fill of my produce.
[20]For my teaching is sweeter than honey,
   and my inheritance sweeter than the
      honeycomb,
   and my remembrance lasts throughout all
      generations.
[21]Those who eat me will hunger for more,
   and those who drink me will thirst for
      more.
[22]Whoever obeys me will not be put to shame,
   and those who work with my help will not
      sin."

[23]All this is the book of the covenant of the Most
      High God,
   the law which Moses commanded us
   as an inheritance for the congregations of
      Jacob. [d]
[25]It fills men with wisdom, like the Pi'shon,
   and like the Tigris at the time of the first
      fruits.

[26]It makes them full of understanding, like the
      Euphrates,
   and like the Jordan at harvest time.
[27]It makes instruction shine forth like light,
   like the Gi'hon at the time of vintage.
[28]Just as the first man did not know her perfectly,
   the last one has not fathomed her;
[29]for her thought is more abundant than the sea,
   and her counsel deeper than the great
      abyss.

[30]I went forth like a canal from a river
   and like a water channel into a garden.
[31]I said, "I will water my orchard
   and drench my garden plot";
   and behold, my canal became a river,
   and my river became a sea.
[32]I will again make instruction shine forth like
      the dawn,
   and I will make it shine afar;
[33]I will again pour out teaching like prophecy,
   and leave it to all future generations.
[34]Observe that I have not labored for myself
      alone,
   but for all who seek instruction. [e]

The Good and the Evil in Daily Life

25 My soul takes pleasure in three things,
   and they are beautiful in the sight of the
   Lord and of men: [f]
agreement between brothers, friendship between
      neighbors,
   and a wife and husband who live in
      harmony.
[2]My soul hates three kinds of men,
   and I am greatly offended at their life:
   a beggar who is proud, a rich man who is a liar,
   and an adulterous old man who lacks good
      sense.

[3]You have gathered nothing in your youth;
   how then can you find anything in your old
      age?
[4]What an attractive thing is judgment in gray-
      haired men,
   and for the aged to possess good counsel!
[5]How attractive is wisdom in the aged,
   and understanding and counsel in
      honorable men!
[6]Rich experience is the crown of the aged,
   and their boast is the fear of the Lord.

---

[b] Other authorities read *on the beaches.*
[c] Other authorities add [18]*I am the mother of beautiful love, of fear, of knowledge, and of holy hope; being eternal, I therefore am given to all my children, to those who are named by him.*
[d] Other authorities add [24]*"Do not cease to be strong in the Lord, cleave to him so that he may strengthen you; the Lord Almighty alone is God, and besides him there is no savior."*
[e] Gk *it.*
[f] Syr Vg: Gk *In three things I was beautified and I stood in beauty before the Lord and men.*

⁷With nine thoughts I have gladdened my
heart,
and a tenth I shall tell with my tongue:
a man rejoicing in his children;
a man who lives to see the downfall of his
foes;
⁸happy is he who lives with an intelligent wife,
and he who has not made a slip with his
tongue,
and he who has not served a man inferior to
himself;
⁹happy is he who has gained good sense,
and he who speaks to attentive listeners.
¹⁰How great is he who has gained wisdom!
But there is no one superior to him who
fears the Lord.
¹¹The fear of the Lord surpasses everything;
to whom shall be likened the one who holds
it fast? ᵍ

¹³Any wound, but not a wound of the heart!
Any wickedness, but not the wickedness of
a wife!
¹⁴Any attack, but not an attack from those who
hate!
And any vengeance, but not the vengeance
of enemies!
¹⁵There is no venom ʰ worse than a snake's
venom, ʰ
and no wrath worse than an enemy's
wrath.
¹⁶I would rather dwell with a lion and a dragon
than dwell with an evil wife.
¹⁷The wickedness of a wife changes her
appearance,
and darkens her face like that of a bear.
¹⁸Her husband takes his meals among the
neighbors,
and he cannot help sighing ⁱ bitterly.
¹⁹Any iniquity is insignificant compared to a
wife's iniquity;
may a sinner's lot befall her!
²⁰A sandy ascent for the feet of the aged—
such is a garrulous wife for a quiet
husband.
²¹Do not be ensnared by a woman's beauty,
and do not desire a woman for her
possessions. ʲ
²²There is wrath and impudence and great
disgrace
when a wife supports her husband.
²³A dejected mind, a gloomy face,
and a wounded heart are caused by an evil
wife.
Drooping hands and weak knees
are caused by the wife who does not make
her husband happy.
²⁴From a woman sin had its beginning,
and because of her we all die.

²⁵Allow no outlet to water,
and no boldness of speech in an evil wife.
²⁶If she does not go as you direct,
separate her from yourself.

26 Happy is the husband of a good wife;
the number of his days will be doubled.
²A loyal wife rejoices her husband,
and he will complete his years in peace.
³A good wife is a great blessing;
she will be granted among the blessings of
the man who fears the Lord.
⁴Whether rich or poor, his heart is glad,
and at all times his face is cheerful.

⁵Of three things my heart is afraid,
and of a fourth I am frightened: ᵏ
The slander of a city, the gathering of a mob,
and false accusation—all these are worse
than death.
⁶There is grief of heart and sorrow when a wife
is envious of a rival,
and a tongue-lashing makes it known
to all.
⁷An evil wife is an ox yoke which chafes;
taking hold of her is like grasping a
scorpion.
⁸There is great anger when a wife is drunken;
she will not hide her shame.
⁹A wife's harlotry shows in her lustful eyes,
and she is known by her eyelids.
¹⁰Keep strict watch over a headstrong daughter,
lest, when she finds liberty, she use it to her
hurt.
¹¹Be on guard against her impudent eye,
and do not wonder if she sins against you.
¹²As a thirsty wayfarer opens his mouth
and drinks from any water near him,
so will she sit in front of every post
and open her quiver to the arrow.

¹³A wife's charm delights her husband,
and her skill puts fat on his bones.
¹⁴A sensible and silent wife is a gift of the Lord,
and there is nothing so precious as a
disciplined soul.
¹⁵A modest wife adds charm to charm,
and no balance can weigh the value of a
chaste soul.
¹⁶Like the sun rising in the heights of the Lord,
so is the beauty of a good wife in her well-
ordered home.
¹⁷Like the shining lamp on the holy lampstand,
so is a beautiful face on a stately figure.

ᵍ Other authorities add ¹²*The fear of the Lord is the beginning of love
for him, and faith is the beginning of clinging to him.*
ʰ Cn: Gk *head.*
ⁱ Other authorities read *and listening he sighs.*
ʲ Heb Syr: Some Greek authorities read *for her beauty.*
ᵏ The Greek of this line is uncertain.

¹⁸Like pillars of gold on a base of silver,
    so are beautiful feet with a steadfast heart. ¹

²⁸At two things my heart is grieved,
    and because of a third anger comes over
        me:
  a warrior in want through poverty,
    and intelligent men who are treated
        contemptuously;
  a man who turns back from righteousness to
        sin—
    the Lord will prepare him for the sword!

²⁹A merchant can hardly keep from wrongdoing,
    and a tradesman will not be declared
        innocent of sin.

27 Many have committed sin for a trifle,ᵐ
    and whoever seeks to get rich will avert
        his eyes.

²As a stake is driven firmly into a fissure
        between stones,
    so sin is wedged in between selling and
        buying.

³If a man is not steadfast and zealous in the
        fear of the Lord,
    his house will be quickly overthrown.

⁴When a sieve is shaken, the refuse remains;
    so a man's filth remains in his thoughts.

⁵The kiln tests the potter's vessels;
    so the test of just men is in tribulation.

⁶The fruit discloses the cultivation of a tree;
    so the expression of a thought discloses the
        cultivation of a man's mind.

⁷Do not praise a man before you hear him
        speak,
    for this is the test of men.

⁸If you pursue justice, you will attain it
    and wear it as a glorious robe.

⁹Birds flock with their kind;
    so truth returns to those who practice it.

¹⁰A lion lies in wait for prey;
    so does sin for the workers of iniquity.

¹¹The talk of the godly man is always wise,
    but the fool changes like the moon.

¹²Among stupid people watch for a chance to
        leave,
    but among thoughtful people stay on.

¹³The talk of fools is offensive,
    and their laughter is wantonly sinful.

¹⁴The talk of men given to swearing makes one's
        hair stand on end,
    and their quarrels make a man stop his ears.

¹⁵The strife of the proud leads to bloodshed,
    and their abuse is grievous to hear.

¹⁶Whoever betrays secrets destroys confidence,
    and he will never find a congenial friend.

¹⁷Love your friend and keep faith with him;
    but if you betray his secrets, do not run
        after him.

¹⁸For as a man destroys his enemy,
    so you have destroyed the friendship of
        your neighbor.

¹⁹And as you allow a bird to escape from your
        hand,
    so you have let your neighbor go, and will
        not catch him again.

²⁰Do not go after him, for he is too far off,
    and has escaped like a gazelle from a snare.

²¹For a wound may be bandaged,
    and there is reconciliation after abuse,
  but whoever has betrayed secrets is without
        hope.

²²Whoever winks his eye plans evil deeds,
    and no one can keep him from them.

²³In your presence his mouth is all sweetness,
    and he admires your words;
  but later he will twist his speech
    and with your own words he will give
        offense.

²⁴I have hated many things, but none to be
        compared to him;
    even the Lord will hate him.

²⁵Whoever throws a stone straight up throws it
        on his own head;
    and a treacherous blow opens up wounds.

²⁶He who digs a pit will fall into it,
    and he who sets a snare will be caught in it.

²⁷If a man does evil, it will roll back upon him,
    and he will not know where it came from.

²⁸Mockery and abuse issue from the proud man, ⁿ
    but vengeance lies in wait for him like a lion.

²⁹Those who rejoice in the fall of the godly will
        be caught in a snare,
    and pain will consume them before their
        death.

---

¹ Other authorities add verses 19–27:
  ¹⁹*My son, keep sound the bloom of your youth,*
      and do not give your strength to strangers.
  ²⁰*Seek a fertile field within the whole plain,*
      and sow it with your own seed, trusting in your fine stock.
  ²¹*So your offspring will survive*
      and, having confidence in their good descent, will grow great.
  ²²*A harlot is regarded as spittle,*
      and a married woman as a tower of death to her lovers.
  ²³*A godless wife is given as a portion to a lawless man,*
      but a pious wife is given to the man who fears the Lord.
  ²⁴*A shameless woman constantly acts disgracefully,*
      but a modest daughter will even be embarrassed before her
          husband.
  ²⁵*A headstrong wife is regarded as a dog,*
      but one who has a sense of shame will fear the Lord.
  ²⁶*A wife honoring her husband will seem wise to all,*
      but if she dishonors him in her pride she will be known to all as
          ungodly.
  Happy is the husband of a good wife;
      for the number of his years will be doubled.
  ²⁷*A loud-voiced and garrulous wife is regarded as a war trumpet for*
          putting the enemy to flight,
      and every person like this lives in the anarchy of war.
ᵐ One ancient authority reads *gain.*
ⁿ Other authorities read *proud men.*

³⁰Anger and wrath, these also are abominations,
    and the sinful man will possess them.

28 He that takes vengeance will suffer
    vengeance from the Lord,
    and he will firmly establish ° his sins.
²Forgive your neighbor the wrong he has done,
    and then your sins will be pardoned when
        you pray.
³Does a man harbor anger against another,
    and yet seek for healing from the Lord?
⁴Does he have no mercy toward a man like
        himself,
    and yet pray for his own sins?
⁵If he himself, being flesh, maintains wrath,
    will he then seek forgiveness from God?
    Who will make expiation for his sins?
⁶Remember the end of your life, and cease from
        enmity,
    remember destruction and death, and be
        true to the commandments.
⁷Remember the commandments, and do not be
        angry with your neighbor;
    remember the covenant of the Most High,
        and overlook ignorance.

⁸Refrain from strife, and you will lessen sins;
    for a man given to anger will kindle strife,
⁹and a sinful man will disturb friends
    and inject enmity among those who are at
        peace.
¹⁰In proportion to the fuel for the fire, so will be
        the burning,
    and in proportion to the obstinacy of strife
        will be the burning; ᵖ
in proportion to the strength of the man will be
        his anger,
    and in proportion to his wealth he will
        heighten his wrath.
¹¹A hasty quarrel kindles fire,
    and urgent strife sheds blood.
¹²If you blow on a spark, it will glow;
    if you spit on it, it will be put out;
    and both come out of your mouth.

¹³Curse the whisperer and deceiver,
    for he has destroyed many who were at
        peace.
¹⁴Slander ᑫ has shaken many,
    and scattered them from nation to nation,
    and destroyed strong cities,
    and overturned the houses of great men.
¹⁵Slander ᑫ has driven away courageous women,
    and deprived them of the fruit of their toil.
¹⁶Whoever pays heed to slander ᣴ will not find
        rest,
    nor will he settle down in peace.
¹⁷The blow of a whip raises a welt,
    but a blow of the tongue crushes the bones.
¹⁸Many have fallen by the edge of the sword,

but not so many as have fallen because of
        the tongue.
¹⁹Happy is the man who is protected from it,
    who has not been exposed to its anger,
who has not borne its yoke,
    and has not been bound with its chains;
²⁰for its yoke is a yoke of iron,
    and its chains are chains of bronze;
²¹its death is an evil death,
    and Hades is preferable to it.
²²It will not be master over the godly,
    and they will not be burned in its flame.
²³Those who forsake the Lord will fall into its
        power;
    it will burn among them and will not be put
        out.
It will be sent out against them like a lion;
    like a leopard it will mangle them.
²⁴See that you fence in your property with
        thorns,
    lock up your silver and gold,
²⁵make balances and scales for your words,
    and make a door and a bolt for your mouth.
²⁶Beware lest you err with your tongue, ˢ
    lest you fall before him who lies in wait.

On Lending and Borrowing,
Home, and Hospitality

29 He that shows mercy will lend to his
    neighbor,
    and he that strengthens him with his hand
        keeps the commandments.
²Lend to your neighbor in the time of his need;
    and in turn, repay your neighbor
        promptly.
³Confirm your word and keep faith with him,
    and on every occasion you will find what
        you need.
⁴Many persons regard a loan as a windfall,
    and cause trouble to those who help them.
⁵A man will kiss another's hands until he gets a
        loan,
    and will lower his voice in speaking of his
        neighbor's money;
but at the time for repayment he will delay,
    and will pay in words of unconcern,
    and will find fault with the time.
⁶If the lender ᵗ exerts pressure, he will hardly
        get back half,
    and will regard that as a windfall.
If he does not, the borrower ᵘ has robbed him
        of his money,
    and he has needlessly made him his
        enemy;

° Other authorities read *closely observe.*
ᵖ Other authorities place this line at the end of the verse, or omit it.
ᑫ Gk *a third tongue.*
ᣴ Gk *it.*
ˢ Gk *with it.*
ᵗ Gk *he.*
ᵘ Gk *he.*

he will repay him with curses and reproaches,
  and instead of glory will repay him with
    dishonor.
⁷Because of such wickedness, therefore, ⁿ many
  have refused to lend;
    they have been afraid of being defrauded
      needlessly.

⁸Nevertheless, be patient with a man in humble
  circumstances,
    and do not make him wait for your alms.
⁹Help a poor man for the commandment's sake,
  and because of his need do not send him
    away empty.
¹⁰Lose your silver for the sake of a brother or a
  friend,
    and do not let it rust under a stone and be
      lost.
¹¹Lay up your treasure according to the
  commandments of the Most High,
    and it will profit you more than gold.
¹²Store up almsgiving in your treasury,
  and it will rescue you from all affliction;
¹³more than a mighty shield and more than a
  heavy spear,
    it will fight on your behalf against your
      enemy.

¹⁴A good man will be surety for his neighbor,
  but a man who has lost his sense of shame
    will fail him.
¹⁵Do not forget all the kindness of your surety,
  for he has given his life for you.
¹⁶A sinner will overthrow the prosperity of his
  surety,
¹⁷ and one who does not feel grateful will
    abandon his rescuer.
¹⁸Being surety has ruined many men who were
  prosperous,
    and has shaken them like a wave of the sea;
  it has driven men of power into exile,
    and they have wandered among foreign
      nations.
¹⁹The sinner who has fallen into suretyship
  and pursues gain will fall into lawsuits.
²⁰Assist your neighbor according to your ability,
  but take heed to yourself lest you fall.

²¹The essentials for life are water and bread
  and clothing and a house to cover one's
    nakedness.
²²Better is the life of a poor man under the
  shelter of his roof
    than sumptuous food in another man's
      house.
²³Be content with little or much. ʷ
²⁴It is a miserable life to go from house to house,
  and where you are a stranger you may not
    open your mouth;

²⁵you will play the host and provide drink
  without being thanked,
    and besides this you will hear bitter words:
²⁶"Come here, stranger, prepare the table,
  and if you have anything at hand, let me
    have it to eat."
²⁷"Give place, stranger, to an honored person;
  my brother has come to stay with me; I need
    my house."
²⁸These things are hard to bear for a man who
  has feeling:
    scolding about lodging ˣ and the reproach
      of the moneylender.

Discipline of Children, Right Attitudes

30 He who loves his son will whip him often,
  in order that he may rejoice at the way
    he turns out.
²He who disciplines his son will profit by him,
  and will boast of him among acquaintances.
³He who teaches his son will make his enemies
  envious,
    and will glory in him in the presence of
      friends.
⁴The ʸ father may die, and yet he is not dead,
  for he has left behind him one like himself;
⁵while alive he saw and rejoiced,
  and when he died he was not grieved;
⁶he has left behind him an avenger against his
  enemies,
    and one to repay the kindness of his
      friends.

⁷He who spoils his son will bind up his wounds,
  and his feelings will be troubled at every
    cry.
⁸A horse that is untamed turns out to be
  stubborn,
    and a son unrestrained turns out to be
      wilful.
⁹Pamper a child, and he will frighten you;
  play with him, and he will give you grief.
¹⁰Do not laugh with him, lest you have sorrow
  with him,
    and in the end you will gnash your teeth.
¹¹Give him no authority in his youth,
  and do not ignore his errors.
¹²Bow down his neck in his youth, ᶻ
  and beat his sides while he is young,
    lest he become stubborn and disobey you,
      and you have sorrow of soul from him. ᵃ
¹³Discipline your son and take pains with him,
  that you may not be offended by his
    shamelessness.

ⁿ Other authorities read *It is not because of wickedness that.*
ʷ Other authorities add *and you will not hear reproach for your
sojourning.*
ˣ Or *from the household,* or (Syr) *from the host.*
ʸ Gk *His.*
ᶻ Other authorities omit this line and the preceding line.
ᵃ Other authorities omit this line.

[14]Better off is a poor man who is well and strong
  in constitution
    than a rich man who is severely afflicted in
    body.
[15]Health and soundness are better than all gold,
  and a robust body than countless riches.
[16]There is no wealth better than health of body,
  and there is no gladness above joy of heart.
[17]Death is better than a miserable life,
  and eternal rest [b] than chronic sickness.

[18]Good things poured out upon a mouth that is
  closed
    are like offerings of food placed upon a
    grave.
[19]Of what use to an idol is an offering of fruit?
  For it can neither eat nor smell.
So is he who is afflicted by the Lord;
[20]he sees with his eyes and groans,
    like a eunuch who embraces a maiden and
    groans.

[21]Do not give yourself over to sorrow,
  and do not afflict yourself deliberately.
[22]Gladness of heart is the life of man,
  and the rejoicing of a man is length of days.
[23]Delight your soul and comfort your heart,
  and remove sorrow far from you,
for sorrow has destroyed many,
  and there is no profit in it.
[24]Jealousy and anger shorten life,
  and anxiety brings on old age too soon.
[25]A man of cheerful and good heart
  will give heed to the food he eats.

Right Conduct

31 Wakefulness over wealth wastes away
  one's flesh,
    and anxiety about it removes sleep.
[2]Wakeful anxiety prevents slumber,
  and a severe illness carries off sleep. [c]
[3]The rich man toils as his wealth accumulates,
  and when he rests he fills himself with his
    dainties.
[4]The poor man toils as his livelihood
  diminishes,
    and when he rests he becomes needy.

[5]He who loves gold will not be justified,
  and he who pursues money will be led
    astray [d] by it.
[6]Many have come to ruin because of gold,
  and their destruction has met them face to
    face.
[7]It is a stumbling block to those who are
  devoted to it,
    and every fool will be taken captive by it.

[8]Blessed is the rich man who is found blameless,
  and who does not go after gold.

[9]Who is he? And we will call him blessed,
  for he has done wonderful things among his
    people.
[10]Who has been tested by it and been found
  perfect?
Let it be for him a ground for boasting.
Who has had the power to transgress and did
  not transgress,
    and to do evil and did not do it?
[11]His prosperity will be established,
  and the assembly will relate his acts of
    charity.

[12]Are you seated at the table of a great man? [e]
  Do not be greedy [f] at it,
    and do not say, "There is certainly much
    upon it!"
[13]Remember that a greedy [g] eye is a bad thing.
  What has been created more greedy [g] than
    the eye?
    Therefore it sheds tears from every face.
[14]Do not reach out your hand for everything you
  see,
    and do not crowd your neighbor [h] at the
    dish.
[15]Judge your neighbor's feelings by your own,
  and in every matter be thoughtful.
[16]Eat like a human being what is set before you,
  and do not chew greedily, lest you be hated.
[17]Be the first to stop eating, for the sake of good
  manners,
    and do not be insatiable, lest you give
    offense.
[18]If you are seated among many persons,
  do not reach out your hand before they do.

[19]How ample a little is for a well-disciplined
  man!
He does not breathe heavily upon his bed.
[20]Healthy sleep depends on moderate eating;
  he rises early, and feels fit. [i]
The distress of sleeplessness and of nausea
  and colic are with the glutton.
[21]If you are overstuffed with food,
  get up in the middle of the meal, and you
    will have relief.
[22]Listen to me, my son, and do not disregard me,
  and in the end you will appreciate my
    words.
In all your work be industrious,
  and no sickness will overtake you.

---

[b] Some authorities omit *eternal rest*.
[c] Other authorities read *sleep carries off a severe illness*.
[d] Heb Syr: Gk *will be filled*.
[e] Heb Syr: Gk *at a great table*.
[f] Gk *open your throat*.
[g] Gk *evil*.
[h] Gk *him*.
[i] Gk *his soul is with him*.

²³Men will praise the one who is liberal with food,
  and their testimony to his excellence is
    trustworthy.
²⁴The city will complain of the one who is
    miserly with food,
  and their testimony to his miserliness is
    accurate.

²⁵Do not aim to be valiant over wine,
  for wine has destroyed many.
²⁶Fire and water prove ʲ the temper of steel,
  so wine tests hearts in the strife of the
    proud.
²⁷Wine is like life to men,
  if you drink it in moderation.
What is life to a man who is without wine?
  It has been created to make men glad.
²⁸Wine drunk in season and temperately
  is rejoicing of heart and gladness of soul.
²⁹Wine drunk to excess is bitterness of soul,
  with provocation and stumbling.
³⁰Drunkenness increases the anger of a fool to
    his injury,
  reducing his strength and adding wounds.

³¹Do not reprove your neighbor at a banquet of
    wine,
  and do not despise him in his merrymaking;
speak no word of reproach to him,
  and do not afflict him by making demands
    of him.

32 If they make you master of the feast, do
    not exalt yourself;
  be among them as one of them;
take good care of them and then be seated;
² when you have fulfilled your duties, take
    your place,
that you may be merry on their account
  and receive a wreath for your excellent
    leadership.

³Speak, you who are older, for it is fitting that
    you should,
  but with accurate knowledge, and do not
    interrupt the music.
⁴Where there is entertainment, do not pour out
    talk;
  do not display your cleverness out of
    season.
⁵A ruby seal in a setting of gold
  is a concert of music at a banquet of wine.
⁶A seal of emerald in a rich setting of gold
  is the melody of music with good wine.

⁷Speak, young man, if there is need of you,
  but no more than twice, and only if asked.
⁸Speak concisely, say much in few words;
  be as one who knows and yet holds his
    tongue.

⁹Among the great do not act as their equal;
  and when another is speaking, do not
    babble.

¹⁰Lightning speeds before the thunder,
  and approval precedes a modest man.
¹¹Leave in good time and do not be the last;
  go home quickly and do not linger.
¹²Amuse yourself there, and do what you have in
    mind,
  but do not sin through proud speech.
¹³And for these things bless him who made you
  and satisfies you with his good gifts.

¹⁴He who fears the Lord will accept his
    discipline,
  and those who rise early to seek him ᵏ will
    find favor.
¹⁵He who seeks the law will be filled with it,
  but the hypocrite will stumble at it.
¹⁶Those who fear the Lord will form true
    judgments,
  and like a light they will kindle righteous
    deeds.
¹⁷A sinful man will shun reproof,
  and will find a decision according to his
    liking.

¹⁸A man of judgment will not overlook an idea,
  and an insolent ¹ and proud man will not
    cower in fear. ᵐ
¹⁹Do nothing without deliberation;
  and when you have acted, do not regret it.
²⁰Do not go on a path full of hazards,
  and do not stumble over stony ground.
²¹Do not be overconfident on a smooth ⁿ way,
²² and give good heed to your paths. ᵒ
²³Guard ᵖ yourself in every act,
  for this is the keeping of the commandments.

²⁴He who believes the law gives heed to the
    commandments,
  and he who trusts the Lord will not suffer
    loss.

Practical Advice

33 No evil will befall the man who fears the
    Lord,
  but in trial he will deliver him again and
    again.
²A wise man will not hate the law,
  but he who is hypocritical about it is like a
    boat in a storm.

ʲ Gk *The furnace by dipping proves.*
ᵏ Other authorities omit *to seek him.*
¹ Heb: Gk *alien.*
ᵐ The meaning of this line is uncertain. Other authorities add the
phrases *and after acting, with him, without deliberation.*
ⁿ Or an *unexplored.*
ᵒ Syr Vg: Gk *and beware of your children.*
ᵖ Heb Syr: Gk *Trust.*

³A man of understanding will trust in the law;
  for him the law is as dependable as an
    inquiry by means of Urim.

⁴Prepare what to say, and thus you will be heard;
  bind together your instruction, and make
    your answer.
⁵The heart of a fool is like a cart wheel,
  and his thoughts like a turning axle.
⁶A stallion is like a mocking friend;
  he neighs under every one who sits on him.

⁷Why is any day better than another,
  when all the daylight in the year is from the
    sun?
⁸By the Lord's decision they were distinguished,
  and he appointed the different seasons and
    feasts;
⁹some of them he exalted and hallowed,
  and some of them he made ordinary days.
¹⁰All men are from the ground,
  and Adam was created of the dust.
¹¹In the fulness of his knowledge the Lord
    distinguished them
  and appointed their different ways;
¹²some of them he blessed and exalted,
  and some of them he made holy and
    brought near to himself;
  but some of them he cursed and brought low,
    and he turned them out of their place.
¹³As clay in the hand of the potter—
  for all his ways are as he pleases—
so men are in the hand of him who made them,
  to give them as he decides.

¹⁴Good is the opposite of evil,
  and life the opposite of death;
so the sinner is the opposite of the godly.
¹⁵Look upon all the works of the Most High;
  they likewise are in pairs, one the opposite
    of the other.
¹⁶I was the last on watch;
  I was like one who gleans after the grape-
    gatherers;
by the blessing of the Lord I excelled,
  and like a grape-gatherer I filled my wine
    press.
¹⁷Consider that I have not labored for myself
    alone,
  but for all who seek instruction.
¹⁸Hear me, you who are great among the people,
  and you leaders of the congregation, listen.

¹⁹To son or wife, to brother or friend,
  do not give power over yourself, as long as
    you live;
and do not give your property to another,
  lest you change your mind and must ask
    for it.

²⁰While you are still alive and have breath in you,
  do not let any one take your place.
²¹For it is better that your children should ask
    from you
  than that you should look to the hand of
    your sons.
²²Excel in all that you do;
  bring no stain upon your honor.
²³At the time when you end the days of your life,
  in the hour of death, distribute your
    inheritance.

²⁴Fodder and a stick and burdens for a donkey;
  bread and discipline and work for a
    servant.
²⁵Set your slave to work, and you will find rest;
  leave his hands idle, and he will seek
    liberty.
²⁶Yoke and thong will bow the neck,
  and for a wicked servant there are racks
    and tortures.
²⁷Put him to work, that he may not be idle,
  for idleness teaches much evil.
²⁸Set him to work, as is fitting for him,
  and if he does not obey, make his chains
    heavy.
²⁹Do not act immoderately toward anybody,
  and do nothing without discretion.

³⁰If you have a servant, let him be as yourself,
  because you have bought him with blood.
³¹If you have a servant, treat him as a brother,
  for as your own soul you will need him.
If you ill-treat him, and he leaves and runs
    away,
  which way will you go to seek him?

Fear of the Lord, Sacrifices, Justice, and Prayer

34 A man of no understanding has vain and
    false hopes,
  and dreams give wings to fools.
²As one who catches at a shadow and pursues
    the wind,
  so is he who gives heed to dreams.
³The vision of dreams is this against that,
  the likeness of a face confronting a face.
⁴From an unclean thing what will be made
    clean?
  And from something false what will be
    true?
⁵Divinations and omens and dreams are folly,
  and like a woman with labor pains the mind
    has fancies.
⁶Unless they are sent from the Most High as a
    visitation,
  do not give your mind to them.
⁷For dreams have deceived many,
  and those who put their hope in them have
    failed.

[8]Without such deceptions the law will be
fulfilled,
and wisdom is made perfect in truthful
lips.

[9]An educated [q] man knows many things,
and one with much experience will speak
with understanding.
[10]He that is inexperienced knows few things,
but he that has traveled acquires much
cleverness.
[11]I have seen many things in my travels,
and I understand more than I can express.
[12]I have often been in danger of death,
but have escaped because of these
experiences.

[13]The spirit of those who fear the Lord will live,
for their hope is in him who saves them.
[14]He who fears the Lord will not be timid,
nor play the coward, for he is his hope.
[15]Blessed is the soul of the man who fears the
Lord!
To whom does he look? And who is his
support?
[16]The eyes of the Lord are upon those who love
him,
a mighty protection and strong support,
a shelter from the hot wind and a shade from
noonday sun,
a guard against stumbling and a defense
against falling.
[17]He lifts up the soul and gives light to the eyes;
he grants healing, life, and blessing.

[18]If one sacrifices from what has been
wrongfully obtained, the offering is
blemished; [r]
the gifts [s] of the lawless are not acceptable.
[19]The Most High is not pleased with the offerings
of the ungodly;
and he is not propitiated for sins by a
multitude of sacrifices.
[20]Like one who kills a son before his father's
eyes
is the man who offers a sacrifice from the
property of the poor.
[21]The bread of the needy is the life of the poor;
whoever deprives them of it is a man of
blood.
[22]To take away a neighbor's living is to murder
him;
to deprive an employee of his wages is to
shed blood.

[23]When one builds and another tears down,
what do they gain but toil?
[24]When one prays and another curses,
to whose voice will the Lord listen?

[25]If a man washes after touching a dead body,
and touches it again,
what has he gained by his washing?
[26]So if a man fasts for his sins,
and goes again and does the same things,
who will listen to his prayer?
And what has he gained by humbling
himself?

The Law and Sacrifice—Divine Justice

35 He who keeps the law makes many
offerings;
he who heeds the commandments sacrifices
a peace offering.
[2]He who returns a kindness offers fine flour,
and he who gives alms sacrifices a thank
offering.
[3]To keep from wickedness is pleasing to the
Lord,
and to forsake unrighteousness is
atonement.
[4]Do not appear before the Lord empty-handed,
[5] for all these things are to be done because
of the commandment.
[6]The offering of a righteous man anoints the
altar,
and its pleasing odor rises before the Most
High.
[7]The sacrifice of a righteous man is acceptable,
and the memory of it will not be forgotten.
[8]Glorify the Lord generously,
and do not stint the first fruits of your
hands.
[9]With every gift show a cheerful face,
and dedicate your tithe with gladness.
[10]Give to the Most High as he has given,
and as generously as your hand has found.
[11]For the Lord is the one who repays,
and he will repay you sevenfold.

[12]Do not offer him a bribe, for he will not
accept it;
and do not trust to an unrighteous sacrifice;
for the Lord is the judge,
and with him is no partiality.
[13]He will not show partiality in the case of a
poor man;
and he will listen to the prayer of one who
is wronged.
[14]He will not ignore the supplication of the
fatherless,
nor the widow when she pours out her
story.
[15]Do not the tears of the widow run down her
cheek
as she cries out against him who has caused
them to fall?

---

[q] Other authorities read *A traveled.*
[r] Other authorities read *is made in mockery.*
[s] Other authorities read *mockeries.*

[16]He whose service is pleasing to the Lord will be
accepted,
and his prayer will reach to the clouds.
[17]The prayer of the humble pierces the clouds,
and he will not be consoled until it reaches
the Lord; [t]
he will not desist until the Most High visits him,
and the just judge executes judgment.
[18]And the Lord will not delay,
neither will he be patient with them,
till he crushes the loins of the unmerciful
and repays vengeance on the nations;
till he takes away the multitude of the insolent,
and breaks the scepters of the unrighteous;
[19]till he repays man according to his deeds,
and the works of men according to their
devices;
till he judges the case of his people
and makes them rejoice in his mercy.
[20]Mercy is as welcome when he afflicts them
as clouds of rain in the time of drought.

A Prayer for God's People; Wise Sayings

36 Have mercy upon us, O Lord, the God of
all, and look upon us,
and show us the light of your mercy;
[2] send fear of you upon the nations.
[3]Lift up your hand against foreign nations
and let them see your might.
[4]As in us you have been sanctified before them,
so in them may you be magnified before us;
[5]and let them know you, as we have known
that there is no God but you, O Lord.
[6]Show signs anew, and work further wonders;
make your hand and your right arm
glorious.
[7]Rouse your anger and pour out your wrath;
destroy the adversary and wipe out the
enemy.
[8]Hasten the day, and remember the appointed
time, [u]
and let people recount your mighty deeds.
[9]Let him who survives be consumed in the fiery
wrath,
and may those who harm your people meet
destruction.
[10]Crush the heads of the rulers of the enemy,
who say, "There is no one but ourselves."
[11]Gather all the tribes of Jacob,
and give [v] them their inheritance, as at the
beginning.
[12]Have mercy, O Lord, upon the people called by
your name,
upon Israel, whom you have likened to a [w]
first-born son.
[13]Have pity on the city of your sanctuary, [x]
Jerusalem, the place of your rest.
[14]Fill Zion with the celebration of your wondrous
deeds,
and your temple [y] with your glory.

[15]Bear witness to those whom you created in the
beginning,
and fulfil the prophecies spoken in your
name.
[16]Reward those who wait for you,
and let your prophets be found trustworthy.
[17]Listen, O Lord, to the prayer of your servants,
according to the blessing of Aaron for your
people,
and direct us in the way of righteousness,
and all who are on the earth will know
that you are the Lord, the God of the ages.

[18]The stomach will take any food,
yet one food is better than another.
[19]As the palate tastes the kinds of game,
so an intelligent mind detects false words.
[20]A perverse mind will cause grief,
but a man of experience will pay him back.
[21]A woman will accept any man,
but one daughter is better than another.
[22]A woman's beauty gladdens the countenance,
and surpasses every human desire.
[23]If kindness and humility mark her speech,
her husband is not like other men.
[24]He who acquires a wife gets his best
possession, [z]
a helper fit for him and a pillar of support. [a]
[25]Where there is no fence, the property will be
plundered;
and where there is no wife, a man will
wander about and sigh.
[26]For who will trust a nimble robber
that skips from city to city?
So who will trust a man that has no home,
and lodges wherever night finds him?

Concerning Good Council, Reason, and Moderation

37 Every friend will say, "I too am a friend";
but some friends are friends only in
name.
[2]Is it not a grief to the death
when a companion and friend turns to
enmity?
[3]O evil imagination, why were you formed
to cover the land with deceit?
[4]Some companions rejoice in the happiness of a
friend,
but in time of trouble are against him.
[5]Some companions help a friend for their
stomachs' sake,
and in the face of battle take up the shield.

---

[t] Or *until the Lord draws near.*
[u] Other authorities read *remember your oath.*
[v] Other authorities read *I gave.*
[w] Other authorities read *have named your.*
[x] Or *on your holy city.*
[y] Heb Syr: Gk Vg *people.*
[z] Heb: Gk *enters upon a possession.*
[a] Heb: Gk *rest.*

⁶Do not forget a friend in your heart,
and be not unmindful of him in your wealth.

⁷Every counselor praises counsel,
but some give counsel in their own interest.
⁸Be wary of a counselor,
and learn first what is his interest—
for he will take thought for himself—
lest he cast the lot against you
⁹   and tell you, "Your way is good,"
and then stand aloof to see what will
happen to you.
¹⁰Do not consult with one who looks at you
suspiciously;
hide your counsel from those who are
jealous of you.
¹¹Do not consult with a woman about her rival
or with a coward about war,
with a merchant about barter
or with a buyer about selling,
with a grudging man about gratitude
or with a merciless man about kindness,
with an idler about any work
or with a man hired for a year about
completing his work,
with a lazy servant about a big task—
pay no attention to these in any matter of
counsel.
¹²But stay constantly with a godly man
whom you know to be a keeper of the
commandments,
whose soul is in accord with your soul,
and who will sorrow with you if you fail.
¹³And establish the counsel of your own heart,
for no one is more faithful to you than it is.
¹⁴For a man's soul sometimes keeps him better
informed
than seven watchmen sitting high on a
watchtower.
¹⁵And besides all this pray to the Most High
that he may direct your way in truth.

¹⁶Reason is the beginning of every work,
and counsel precedes every undertaking.
¹⁷As a clue to changes of heart
¹⁸   four turns of fortune appear,
good and evil, life and death;
and it is the tongue that continually rules
them.
¹⁹A man may be shrewd and the teacher of
many,
and yet be unprofitable to himself.
²⁰A man skilled in words may be hated;
he will be destitute of all food,
²¹for grace was not given him by the Lord,
since he is lacking in all wisdom.
²²A man may be wise to his own advantage,
and the fruits of his understanding may be
trustworthy on his lips.

²³A wise man will instruct his own people,
and the fruits of his understanding will be
trustworthy.
²⁴A wise man will have praise heaped upon him,
and all who see him will call him happy.
²⁵The life of a man is numbered by days,
but the days of Israel are without number.
²⁶He who is wise among his people will inherit
confidence, ᵇ
and his name will live for ever.

²⁷My son, test your soul while you live;
see what is bad for it and do not give it
that.
²⁸For not everything is good for every one,
and not every person enjoys everything.
²⁹Do not have an insatiable appetite for any
luxury,
and do not give yourself up to food;
³⁰for overeating brings sickness,
and gluttony leads to nausea.
³¹Many have died of gluttony,
but he who is careful to avoid it prolongs
his life.

Concerning Physicians, Tradesmen, and Craftsmen

38 Honor the physician with the honor due
him, ᶜ according to your need of him,
for the Lord created him;
²for healing comes from the Most High,
and he will receive a gift from the king.
³The skill of the physician lifts up his head,
and in the presence of great men he is
admired.
⁴The Lord created medicines from the earth,
and a sensible man will not despise them.
⁵Was not water made sweet with a tree
in order that his ᵈ power might be known?
⁶And he gave skill to men
that he ᵉ might be glorified in his marvelous
works.
⁷By them he heals and takes away pain;
⁸   the pharmacist makes of them a compound.
His works will never be finished;
and from him health ᶠ is upon the face of
the earth.

⁹My son, when you are sick do not be negligent,
but pray to the Lord, and he will heal you.
¹⁰Give up your faults and direct your hands
aright,
and cleanse your heart from all sin.
¹¹Offer a sweet-smelling sacrifice, and a
memorial portion of fine flour,

ᵇ Other authorities read *honor*.
ᶜ Other authorities omit *with the honor due him*.
ᵈ Or *its*.
ᵉ Or *they*.
ᶠ Or *peace*.

and pour oil on your offering, as much as
you can afford. g

12And give the physician his place, for the Lord
created him;
let him not leave you, for there is need of
him.

13There is a time when success lies in the hands
of physicians, h

14 for they too will pray to the Lord
that he should grant them success in
diagnosis i
and in healing, for the sake of preserving
life.

15He who sins before his Maker,
may he fall into the care j of a physician.

16My son, let your tears fall for the dead,
and as one who is suffering grievously
begin the lament.
Lay out his body with the honor due him,
and do not neglect his burial.

17Let your weeping be bitter and your wailing
fervent;
observe the mourning according to his
merit,
for one day, or two, to avoid criticism;
then be comforted for your sorrow.

18For sorrow results in death,
and sorrow of heart saps one's strength.

19In calamity sorrow continues,
and the life of the poor man weighs down
his heart.

20Do not give your heart to sorrow;
drive it away, remembering the end of life.

21Do not forget, there is no coming back;
you do the dead k no good, and you injure
yourself.

22"Remember my doom, for yours is like it:
yesterday it was mine, and today it is
yours."

23When the dead is at rest, let his remembrance
cease,
and be comforted for him when his spirit
has departed.

24The wisdom of the scribe depends on the
opportunity of leisure;
and he who has little business may become
wise.

25How can he become wise who handles the plow,
and who glories in the shaft of a goad,
who drives oxen and is occupied with their
work,
and whose talk is about l bulls?

26He sets his heart on plowing furrows,
and he is careful about fodder for the
heifers.

27So too is every craftsman and master workman
who labors by night as well as by day;

those who cut the signets of seals,
each is diligent in making a great variety;
he sets his heart on painting a lifelike image,
and he is careful to finish his work.

28So too is the smith sitting by the anvil,
intent upon his handiwork in iron;
the breath of the fire melts his flesh,
and he wastes away in m the heat of the
furnace;
he inclines his ear to the sound of the
hammer, n
and his eyes are on the pattern of the
object.
He sets his heart on finishing his handiwork,
and he is careful to complete its decoration.

29So too is the potter sitting at his work
and turning the wheel with his feet;
he is always deeply concerned over his work,
and all his output is by number.

30He moulds the clay with his arm
and makes it pliable with his feet;
he sets his heart to finish the glazing,
and he is careful to clean the furnace.

31All these rely upon their hands,
and each is skilful in his own work.

32Without them a city cannot be established,
and men can neither sojourn nor live there.

33Yet they are not sought out for the council of
the people,
nor do they attain eminence in the public
assembly.
They do not sit in the judge's seat,
nor do they understand the sentence of
judgment;
they cannot expound discipline or judgment,
and they are not found using proverbs.

34But they keep stable the fabric of the world,
and their prayer is in the practice of their
trade.

The Student of the Law;
and Praise of God

39 On the other hand he who devotes himself
to the study of the law of the Most High
will seek out the wisdom of all the ancients,
and will be concerned with prophecies;

2he will preserve the discourse of notable men
and penetrate the subtleties of parables;

3he will seek out the hidden meanings of
proverbs
and be at home with the obscurities of
parables.

g Heb: Vulgate omits *as much as you can afford*; Greek is obscure.
h Gk *in their hands*.
i Heb: Gk *rest*.
j Gk *hands*.
k Gk *him*.
l Or *among*.
m Cn Compare Syr: Gk *contends with*.
n Cn: Gk *the sound of the hammer renews his ear*.

[4]He will serve among great men
and appear before rulers;
he will travel through the lands of foreign
nations,
for he tests the good and the evil among
men.
[5]He will set his heart to rise early
to seek the Lord who made him,
and will make supplication before the Most
High;
he will open his mouth in prayer
and make supplication for his sins.

[6]If the great Lord is willing,
he will be filled with the spirit of
understanding;
he will pour forth words ° of wisdom
and give thanks to the Lord in prayer.
[7]He will direct his counsel and knowledge
rightly,
and meditate on his secrets.
[8]He will reveal instruction in his teaching,
and will glory in the law of the Lord's
covenant.
[9]Many will praise his understanding,
and it will never be blotted out;
his memory will not disappear,
and his name will live through all
generations.
[10]Nations will declare his wisdom,
and the congregation will proclaim his
praise;
[11]if he lives long, he will leave a name greater
than a thousand,
and if he goes to rest, it is enough ᴾ for him.

[12]I have yet more to say, which I have thought
upon,
and I am filled, like the moon at the full.
[13]Listen to me, O you holy sons,
and bud like a rose growing by a stream of
water;
[14]send forth fragrance like frankincense,
and put forth blossoms like a lily.
Scatter the fragrance, and sing a hymn of
praise;
bless the Lord for all his works;
[15]ascribe majesty to his name
and give thanks to him with praise,
with songs on your lips, and with lyres;
and this you shall say in thanksgiving:
[16]"All things are the works of the Lord, for they
are very good,
and whatever he commands will be done in
his time."

[17]No one can say, "What is this?" " Why is that?"
for in God's ᑫ time all things will be sought
after.

At his word the waters stood in a heap,
and the reservoirs of water at the word of
his mouth.
[18]At his command whatever pleases him is done,
and none can limit his saving power.
[19]The works of all flesh are before him,
and nothing can be hid from his eyes.
[20]From everlasting to everlasting he beholds
them,
and nothing is marvelous to him.
[21]No one can say, "What is this?" " Why is that?"
for everything has been created for its use.

[22]His blessing covers the dry land like a river,
and drenches it like a flood.
[23]The nations will incur his wrath,
just as he turns fresh water into salt.
[24]To the holy his ways are straight,
just as they are obstacles to the wicked.
[25]From the beginning good things were created
for good people,
just as evil things for sinners.
[26]Basic to all the needs of man's life
are water and fire and iron and salt
and wheat flour and milk and honey,
the blood of the grape, and oil and clothing.
[27]All these are for good to the godly,
just as they turn into evils for sinners.

[28]There are winds that have been created for
vengeance,
and in their anger they scourge heavily;
in the time of consummation they will pour out
their strength
and calm the anger of their Maker.
[29]Fire and hail and famine and pestilence,
all these have been created for vengeance;
[30]the teeth of wild beasts, and scorpions and
vipers,
and the sword that punishes the ungodly
with destruction;
[31]they will rejoice in his commands,
and be made ready on earth for their
service,
and when their times come they will not
transgress his word.

[32]Therefore from the beginning I have been
convinced,
and have thought this out and left it in
writing:
[33]The works of the Lord are all good,
and he will supply every need in its hour.
[34]And no one can say, "This is worse than that,"
for all things will prove good in their
season.

° Other authorities read *his words*.
ᴾ Cn: the meaning of Greek is uncertain.
ᑫ Gk *his*.

[35]So now sing praise with all your heart and
voice,
and bless the name of the Lord.

Human Wretchedness and Joys of Life

40 Much labor was created for every man,
and a heavy yoke is upon the sons of
Adam,
from the day they come forth from their
mother's womb
till the day they return to [r] the mother of
all.
[2]Their perplexities and fear of heart—
their anxious thought is the day of death,
[3]from the man who sits on a splendid throne
to the one who is humbled in dust and
ashes,
[4]from the man who wears purple and a crown
to the one who is clothed in burlap;
[5]there is anger and envy and trouble and unrest,
and fear of death, and fury and strife.
And when one rests upon his bed,
his sleep at night confuses his mind.
[6]He gets little or no rest,
and afterward in his sleep, as though he
were on watch,
he is troubled by the visions of his mind
like one who has escaped from the battle-
front;
[7]at the moment of his rescue he wakes up,
and wonders that his fear came to nothing.
[8]With all flesh, both man and beast,
and upon sinners seven times more,
[9]are death and bloodshed and strife and sword,
calamities, famine and affliction and plague.
[10]All these were created for the wicked,
and on their account the flood came.
[11]All things that are from the earth turn back to
the earth,
and what is from the waters returns to the
sea.

[12]All bribery and injustice will be blotted out,
but good faith will stand for ever.
[13]The wealth of the unjust will dry up like a
torrent,
and crash like a loud clap of thunder in a
rain.
[14]A generous man will be made glad;
likewise transgressors will utterly fail.
[15]The children of the ungodly will not put forth
many branches;
they are unhealthy roots upon sheer rock.
[16]The reeds by any water or river bank
will be plucked up before any grass.
[17]Kindness is like a garden of blessings,
and almsgiving endures for ever.

[18]Life is sweet for the self-reliant and the
worker, [s]

but he who finds treasure is better off than
both.
[19]Children and the building of a city establish a
man's name,
but a blameless wife is accounted better
than both.
[20]Wine and music gladden the heart,
but the love of wisdom is better than both.
[21]The flute and the harp make pleasant melody,
but a pleasant voice is better than both.
[22]The eye desires grace and beauty,
but the green shoots of grain more than
both.
[23]A friend or a companion never meets one
amiss,
but a wife with her husband is better than
both.
[24]Brothers and help are for a time of trouble,
but almsgiving rescues better than both.
[25]Gold and silver make the foot stand sure,
but good counsel is esteemed more than
both.
[26]Riches and strength lift up the heart,
but the fear of the Lord is better than both.
There is no loss in the fear of the Lord,
and with it there is no need to seek for help.
[27]The fear of the Lord is like a garden of
blessing,
and covers a man [t] better than any glory.

[28]My son, do not lead the life of a beggar;
it is better to die than to beg.
[29]When a man looks to the table of another,
his existence cannot be considered as life.
He pollutes himself with another man's food,
but a man who is intelligent and well
instructed guards against that.
[30]In the mouth of the shameless begging is
sweet,
but in his stomach a fire is kindled.

A Series of Contrasts

41 O death, how bitter is the reminder of you
to one who lives at peace among his
possessions,
to a man without distractions, who is
prosperous in everything,
and who still has the vigor to enjoy his food!
[2]O death, how welcome is your sentence
to one who is in need and is failing in
strength,
very old and distracted over everything;
to one who is contrary, and has lost his
patience!
[3]Do not fear the sentence of death;
remember your former days and the end of
life;

---

[r] Other authorities read *are buried in.*
[s] Cn: Gk *self-reliant worker.*
[t] Gk *him.*

this is the decree from the Lord for all flesh,
4   and how can you reject the good pleasure of
     the Most High?
Whether life is for ten or a hundred or a
     thousand years,
     there is no inquiry about it in Hades.

5The children of sinners are abominable
     children,
   and they frequent the haunts of the
     ungodly.
6The inheritance of the children of sinners will
     perish,
   and on their posterity will be a perpetual
     reproach.
7Children will blame an ungodly father,
   for they suffer reproach because of him.
8Woe to you, ungodly men,
   who have forsaken the law of the Most
     High God!
9When you are born, you are born to a curse;
   and when you die, a curse is your lot.
10Whatever is from the dust returns to dust;
   so the ungodly go from curse to
     destruction.

11The mourning of men is about their bodies,
   but the evil name of sinners will be blotted
     out.
12Have regard for your name, since it will remain
     for you
   longer than a thousand great stores of gold.
13The days of a good life are numbered,
   but a good name endures for ever.

14My children, observe instruction and be at
     peace;
   hidden wisdom and unseen treasure,
     what advantage is there in either of them?
15Better is the man who hides his folly
   than the man who hides his wisdom.
16Therefore show respect for my words:
For it is not good to retain every kind of
     shame,
   and not everything is confidently esteemed
     by every one.

17Be ashamed of immorality, before your father
     or mother;
   and of a lie, before a prince or a ruler;
18of a transgression, before a judge or
     magistrate;
   and of iniquity, before a congregation or the
     people;
of unjust dealing, before your partner or
     friend;
19   and of theft, in the place where you live.
Be ashamed before the truth of God and his
     covenant.

Be ashamed of selfish behavior at meals,ᵘ
   of surliness in receiving and giving,
20   and of silence, before those who greet you;
   of looking at a woman who is a harlot,
21   and of rejecting the appeal of a kinsman;
   of taking away some one's portion or gift,
   and of gazing at another man's wife;
22of meddling with his maidservant—
   and do not approach her bed;
of abusive words, before friends—
   and do not upbraid after making a gift;
23of repeating and telling what you hear,
   and of revealing secrets.
Then you will show proper shame,
   and will find favor with every man.

42 Of the following things do not be
     ashamed,
     and do not let partiality lead you to sin:
2of the law of the Most High and his covenant,
   and of rendering judgment to acquit the
     ungodly;
3of keeping accounts with a partner or with
     traveling companions,
   and of dividing the inheritance of friends;
4of accuracy with scales and weights,
   and of acquiring much or little;
5of profit from dealing with merchants,
   and of much discipline of children,
   and of whipping a wicked servant
     severely.ᵛ
6Where there is an evil wife, a seal is a good
     thing;
   and where there are many hands, lock
     things up.
7Whatever you deal out, let it be by number and
     weight,
   and make a record of all that you give out
     or take in.
8Do not be ashamed to instruct the stupid or
     foolish
   or the aged man who quarrels with the
     young.
Then you will be truly instructed,
   and will be approved before all men.

9A daughter keeps her father secretly wakeful,
   and worry over her robs him of sleep;
when she is young, lest she not marry,
   or if married, lest she be hated;
10while a virgin, lest she be defiled
   or become pregnant in her father's house;
or having a husband, lest she prove unfaithful,
   or, though married, lest she be barren.
11Keep strict watch over a headstrong daughter,
   lest she make you a laughingstock to your
     enemies,

ᵘ Gk *of fixing the elbow on the bread.*
ᵛ Gk *making the side of a wicked servant bleed.*

a byword in the city and notorious[w] among the people,
and put you to shame before the great multitude.

¹²Do not look upon any one for beauty,
and do not sit in the midst of women;
¹³for from garments comes the moth,
and from a woman comes woman's wickedness.
¹⁴Better is the wickedness of a man than a woman who does good;
and it is a woman who brings shame and disgrace.

¹⁵I will now call to mind the works of the Lord,
and will declare what I have seen.
By the words of the Lord his works are done,
and in his will, justice is carried out.
¹⁶The sun looks down on everything with its light,
and the work of the Lord is full of his glory.
¹⁷The Lord has not enabled his holy ones
to recount all his marvelous works,
which the Lord the Almighty has established
that the universe may stand firm in his glory.
¹⁸He searches out the abyss, and the hearts of men,[x]
and considers their crafty devices.
For the Most High knows all that may be known,
and he looks into the signs[y] of the age.
¹⁹He declares what has been and what is to be,
and he reveals the tracks of hidden things.
²⁰No thought escapes him,
and not one word is hidden from him.
²¹He has ordained the splendors of his wisdom,
and he is from everlasting and to everlasting.
Nothing can be added or taken away,
and he needs no one to be his counselor.
²²How greatly to be desired are all his works,
and how sparkling they are to see![z]
²³All these things live and remain for ever
for every need, and are all obedient.
²⁴All things are twofold, one opposite the other,
and he has made nothing incomplete.
²⁵One confirms the good things of the other,
and who can have enough of beholding his glory?

God's Greatness in Creation

43 The pride of the heavenly heights is the clear firmament,
the appearance of heaven in a spectacle of glory.
²The sun, when it appears, making proclamation as it goes forth,

is a marvelous instrument, the work of the Most High.
³At noon it parches the land;
and who can withstand its burning heat?
⁴A man tending[a] a furnace works in burning heat,
but the sun burns the mountains three times as much;
it breathes out fiery vapors,
and with bright beams it blinds the eyes.
⁵Great is the Lord who made it;
and at his command it hastens on its course.

⁶He made the moon also, to serve in its season[b]
to mark the times and to be an everlasting sign.
⁷From the moon comes the sign for feast days,
a light that wanes when it has reached the full.
⁸The month is named for the moon,
increasing marvelously in its phases,
an instrument of the hosts on high
shining forth in the firmament of heaven.

⁹The glory of the stars is the beauty of heaven,
a gleaming array in the heights of the Lord.
¹⁰At the command of the Holy One they stand as ordered,
they never relax in their watches.
¹¹Look upon the rainbow, and praise him who made it,
exceedingly beautiful in its brightness.
¹²It encircles the heaven with its glorious arc;
the hands of the Most High have stretched it out.

¹³By his command he sends the driving snow
and speeds the lightning of his judgment.
¹⁴Therefore the storehouses are opened,
and the clouds fly forth like birds.
¹⁵In his majesty he amasses the clouds,
and the hailstones are broken in pieces.
¹⁶At his appearing the mountains are shaken;
at his will the south wind blows.
¹⁷The voice of his thunder rebukes the earth;
so do the tempest from the north and the whirlwind.
He scatters the snow like birds flying down,
and its descent is like locusts alighting.
¹⁸The eye marvels at the beauty of its whiteness,
and the mind is amazed at its falling.
¹⁹He pours the hoarfrost upon the earth like salt,
and when it freezes, it becomes pointed thorns.

---

[w] Gk *called out*.
[x] Gk *and the heart*.
[y] Gk *sign*.
[z] The Greek of this line is uncertain.
[a] Other authorities read *blowing*.
[b] The Greek text of this line is uncertain.

20The cold north wind blows,
  and ice freezes over the water;
it rests upon every pool of water,
  and the water puts it on like a breastplate.
21He consumes the mountains and burns up the
    wilderness,
  and withers the tender grass like fire.
22A mist quickly heals all things;
  when the dew appears, it refreshes from the
    heat.

23By his counsel he stilled the great deep
  and planted islands in it.
24Those who sail the sea tell of its dangers,
  and we marvel at what we hear.
25For in it are strange and marvelous works,
  all kinds of living things, and huge
    creatures of the sea.
26Because of him his messenger finds the way,
  and by his word all things hold together.

27Though we speak much we cannot reach the
    end,
  and the sum of our words is: "He is the all."
28Where shall we find strength to praise him?
  For he is greater than all his works.
29Terrible is the Lord and very great,
  and marvelous is his power.
30When you praise the Lord, exalt him as much
    as you can;
  for he will surpass even that.
When you exalt him, put forth all your
    strength,
  and do not grow weary, for you cannot
    praise him enough.
31Who has seen him and can describe him?
  Or who can extol him as he is?
32Many things greater than these lie hidden,
  for we have seen but few of his works.
33For the Lord has made all things,
  and to the godly he has granted wisdom.

Praise of Our Fathers

44 Let us now praise famous men,
  and our fathers in their generations.
2The Lord apportioned to them c great glory,
  his majesty from the beginning.
3There were those who ruled in their
    kingdoms,
  and were men renowned for their power,
giving counsel by their understanding,
  and proclaiming prophecies;
4leaders of the people in their deliberations
  and in understanding of learning for the
    people,
  wise in their words of instruction;
5those who composed musical tunes,
  and set forth verses in writing;
6rich men furnished with resources,
  living peaceably in their habitations—

7all these were honored in their generations,
  and were the glory of their times.
8There are some of them who have left a name,
  so that men declare their praise.
9And there are some who have no memorial,
  who have perished as though they had not
    lived;
they have become as though they had not been
    born,
  and so have their children after them.
10But these were men of mercy,
  whose righteous deeds have not been
    forgotten;
11their prosperity will remain with their
    descendants,
  and their inheritance to their children's
    children. d
12Their descendants stand by the covenants;
  their children also, for their sake.
13Their posterity will continue for ever,
  and their glory will not be blotted out.
14Their bodies were buried in peace,
  and their name lives to all generations.
15Peoples will declare their wisdom,
  and the congregation proclaims their praise.

16E'noch pleased the Lord, and was taken up;
  he was an example of repentance to all
    generations.

17Noah was found perfect and righteous;
  in the time of wrath he was taken in
    exchange;
therefore a remnant was left to the earth
  when the flood came.
18Everlasting covenants were made with him
  that all flesh should not be blotted out by a
    flood.

19Abraham was the great father of a multitude
    of nations,
  and no one has been found like him in
    glory;
20he kept the law of the Most High,
  and was taken into covenant with him;
he established the covenant in his flesh,
  and when he was tested he was found
    faithful.
21Therefore the Lord e assured him by an oath
  that the nations would be blessed through
    his posterity;
that he would multiply him like the dust of the
    earth,
  and exalt his posterity like the stars,
and cause them to inherit from sea to sea
  and from the River to the ends of the earth.

---

c Heb: Gk created.
d Heb Compare Vg Syr: The Greek of this verse is uncertain.
e Gk he.

²²To Isaac also he gave the same assurance
 for the sake of Abraham his father.

²³The blessing of all men and the covenant
 he made to rest upon the head of Jacob;
he acknowledged him with his blessings,
 and gave him his inheritance; ^f
he determined his portions,
 and distributed them among twelve
  tribes.

45 From his descendants the Lord ^g brought
 forth a man of mercy,
 who found favor in the sight of all flesh
and was beloved by God and man,
 Moses, whose memory is blessed.
²He made him equal in glory to the holy ones,
 and made him great in the fears of his
  enemies.
³By his words he caused signs to cease;
 the Lord ^g glorified him in the presence of
  kings.
He gave him commands for his people,
 and showed him part of his glory.
⁴He sanctified him through faithfulness and
  meekness;
 he chose him out of all mankind.
⁵He made him hear his voice,
 and led him into the thick darkness,
and gave him the commandments face to face,
 the law of life and knowledge,
to teach Jacob the covenant,
 and Israel his judgments.

⁶He exalted Aaron, the brother of Moses, ^h
 a holy man like him, of the tribe of Levi.
⁷He made an everlasting covenant with him,
 and gave him the priesthood of the people.
He blessed him with splendid vestments,
 and put a glorious robe upon him.
⁸He clothed him with superb perfection,
 and strengthened him with the symbols of
  authority,
 the linen breeches, the long robe, and the
  ephod.
⁹And he encircled him with pomegranates,
 with very many golden bells round about,
to send forth a sound as he walked,
 to make their ringing heard in the temple
 as a reminder to the sons of his people;
¹⁰with a holy garment, of gold and blue
 and purple, the work of an embroiderer;
with the oracle of judgment, U'rim and
  Thummim;
¹¹ with twisted scarlet, the work of a
  craftsman;
with precious stones engraved like signets,
 in a setting of gold, the work of a jeweler,
for a reminder, in engraved letters,

according to the number of the tribes of
 Israel;
¹²with a gold crown upon his turban,
 inscribed like a signet with "Holiness,"
a distinction to be prized, the work of an
  expert,
 the delight of the eyes, richly adorned.
¹³Before his time there never were such beautiful
  things.
 No outsider ever put them on,
but only his sons
 and his descendants perpetually.
¹⁴His sacrifices shall be wholly burned
 twice every day continually.
¹⁵Moses ordained him,
 and anointed him with holy oil;
it was an everlasting covenant for him
 and for his descendants all the days of
  heaven,
to minister to the Lord ⁱ and serve as priest
 and bless his people in his name.
¹⁶He chose him out of all the living
 to offer sacrifice to the Lord,
incense and a pleasing odor as a memorial
  portion,
 to make atonement for the people. ^j
¹⁷In his commandments he gave him
 authority in statutes and ^k judgments,
to teach Jacob the testimonies,
 and to enlighten Israel with his law.
¹⁸Outsiders conspired against him,
 and envied him in the wilderness,
Da'than and Abi'ram and their men
 and the company of Ko'rah, in wrath and
  anger.
¹⁹The Lord saw it and was not pleased,
 and in the wrath of his anger they were
  destroyed;
he wrought wonders against them
 to consume them in flaming fire.
²⁰He added glory to Aaron
 and gave him a heritage;
he allotted to him the first of the first fruits,
 he prepared bread of first fruits in
  abundance;
²¹for they eat the sacrifices to the Lord,
 which he gave to him and his descendants.
²²But in the land of the people he has no
  inheritance,
 and he has no portion among the people;
for the Lord ^l himself is his ^m portion and
  inheritance.

---

^f Heb: Gk *by inheritance.*
^g Gk *he.*
^h Gk *him.*
ⁱ Gk *him.*
^j Other authorities read *your people.*
^k Heb: Gk *in covenants of.*
^l Gk *he.*
^m Other authorities read *your.*

²³Phin'ehas the son of Elea'zar is the third in
  glory,
    for he was zealous in the fear of the Lord,
  and stood fast, when the people turned away,
    in the ready goodness of his soul,
    and made atonement for Israel.
²⁴Therefore a covenant of peace was established
    with him,
    that he should be leader of the sanctuary
      and of his people,
  that he and his descendants should have
    the dignity of the priesthood for ever.
²⁵A covenant was also established with David,
    the son of Jesse, of the tribe of Judah:
  the heritage of the king is from son to son only;
    so the heritage of Aaron is for his
      descendants.
²⁶May the Lord ⁿ grant you wisdom in your heart
    to judge his people in righteousness,
  so that their prosperity may not vanish,
    and that their glory may endure throughout
      their generations. ᵒ

46 Joshua the son of Nun was mighty in
  war,
    and was the successor of Moses in
      prophesying.
  He became, in accordance with his name,
    a great savior of God's ᵖ elect,
  to take vengeance on the enemies that rose
    against them,
    so that he might give Israel its inheritance.
²How glorious he was when he lifted his hands
    and stretched out his sword against the
      cities!
³Who before him ever stood so firm?
    For he waged the wars of the Lord.
⁴Was not the sun held back by his hand?
    And did not one day become as long as two?
⁵He called upon the Most High, the Mighty One,
    when enemies pressed him on every side,
⁶and the great Lord answered him
    with hailstones of mighty power.
  He hurled down war upon that nation,
    and at the descent of Beth-ho'ron ᵠ he
      destroyed those who resisted,
  so that the nations might know his armament,
    that he was fighting in the sight of the
      Lord;
    for he wholly followed the Mighty One.
⁷And in the days of Moses he did a loyal deed,
    he and Caleb the son of Jephun'neh:
    they withstood the congregation, ʳ
    restrained the people from sin,
    and stilled their wicked murmuring.
⁸And these two alone were preserved
    out of six hundred thousand people on foot,
  to bring them into their inheritance,
    into a land flowing with milk and honey.

⁹And the Lord gave Caleb strength,
    which remained with him to old age,
  so that he went up to the hill country,
    and his children obtained it for an
      inheritance;
¹⁰so that all the sons of Israel might see
    that it is good to follow the Lord.

¹¹The judges also, with their respective names,
    those whose hearts did not fall into idolatry
  and who did not turn away from the Lord—
    may their memory be blessed!
¹²May their bones revive from where they lie,
    and may the name of those who have been
      honored
    live again in their sons!

¹³Samuel, beloved by his Lord,
    a prophet of the Lord, established the
      kingdom
    and anointed rulers over his people.
¹⁴By the law of the Lord he judged the
    congregation,
    and the Lord watched over Jacob.
¹⁵By his faithfulness he was proved to be a
    prophet,
    and by his words he became known as a
      trustworthy seer.
¹⁶He called upon the Lord, the Mighty One,
    when his enemies pressed him on every
      side,
    and he offered in sacrifice a sucking lamb.
¹⁷Then the Lord thundered from heaven,
    and made his voice heard with a mighty
      sound;
¹⁸and he wiped out the leaders of the people of
    Tyre
    and all the rulers of the Philis'tines.
¹⁹Before the time of his eternal sleep,
    Samuel ˢ called men to witness before the
      Lord and his anointed:
  "I have not taken any one's property,
    not so much as a pair of shoes."
  And no man accused him.
²⁰Even after he had fallen asleep he prophesied
    and revealed to the king his death,
  and lifted up his voice out of the earth in
    prophecy,
    to blot out the wickedness of the people.

47 And after him Nathan rose up
  to prophesy in the days of David.
²As the fat is selected from the peace offering,
    so David was selected from the sons of
      Israel.

ⁿ Gk *he.*
ᵒ The Greek of this line is obscure.
ᵖ Gk *his.*
ᵠ Compare Joshua 10:11: Greek lacks *of Beth-horon.*
ʳ Other authorities read *the enemy.*
ˢ Gk *he.*

³He played with lions as with young goats,
  and with bears as with lambs of the flock.
⁴In his youth did he not kill a giant,
  and take away reproach from the people,
when he lifted his hand with a stone in the
    sling
  and struck down the boasting of Goliath?
⁵For he appealed to the Lord, the Most High,
  and he gave him strength in his right hand
to slay a man mighty in war,
  to exalt the power ᵗ of his people.
⁶So they glorified him for his ten thousands,
  and praised him for the blessings of the
    Lord,
  when the glorious diadem was bestowed
    upon him.
⁷For he wiped out his enemies on every side,
  and annihilated his adversaries the
    Philis'tines;
  he crushed their power ᵗ even to this day.
⁸In all that he did he gave thanks
  to the Holy One, the Most High, with
    ascriptions of glory;
  he sang praise with all his heart,
    and he loved his Maker.
⁹He placed singers before the altar,
  to make sweet melody with their voices.
¹⁰He gave beauty to the feasts,
  and arranged their times throughout the
    year, ᵘ
  while they praised God's ᵛ holy name,
    and the sanctuary resounded from early
      morning.
¹¹The Lord took away his sins,
  and exalted his power ʷ for ever;
he gave him the covenant of kings
  and a throne of glory in Israel.

¹²After him rose up a wise son
  who fared amply ˣ because of him;
¹³Solomon reigned in days of peace,
  and God gave him rest on every side,
that he might build a house for his name
  and prepare a sanctuary to stand for
    ever.
¹⁴How wise you became in your youth!
  You overflowed like a river with
    understanding.
¹⁵Your soul covered the earth,
  and you filled it with parables and riddles.
¹⁶Your name reached to far-off islands,
  and you were loved for your peace.
¹⁷For your songs and proverbs and parables,
  and for your interpretations, the countries
    marveled at you.
¹⁸In the name of the Lord God,
  who is called the God of Israel,
you gathered gold like tin
  and amassed silver like lead.

¹⁹But you laid your loins beside women,
  and through your body you were brought
    into subjection.
²⁰You put stain upon your honor,
  and defiled your posterity,
so that you brought wrath upon your children
  and they were grieved ʸ at your folly,
²¹so that the sovereignty was divided
  and a disobedient kingdom arose out of
    E'phraim.
²²But the Lord will never give up his mercy,
  nor cause any of his works to perish;
he will never blot out the descendants of his
    chosen one,
  nor destroy the posterity of him who loved
    him;
so he gave a remnant to Jacob,
  and to David a root of his stock.

²³Solomon rested with his fathers,
  and left behind him one of his sons,
ample in ᶻ folly and lacking in understanding,
  Rehobo'am, whose policy caused the people
    to revolt.
Also Jerobo'am the son of Ne'bat, who caused
    Israel to sin
  and gave to E'phraim a sinful way.
²⁴Their sins became exceedingly many,
  so as to remove them from their land.
²⁵For they sought out every sort of wickedness,
  till vengeance came upon them.

48 Then the prophet Eli'jah arose like a
      fire,
  and his word burned like a torch.
²He brought a famine upon them,
  and by his zeal he made them few in
    number.
³By the word of the Lord he shut up the
    heavens,
  and also three times brought down fire.
⁴How glorious you were, O Eli'jah, in your
    wondrous deeds!
  And who has the right to boast which you
    have?
⁵You who raised a corpse from death
  and from Hades, by the word of the Most
    High;
⁶who brought kings down to destruction,
  and famous men from their beds,
  and easily destroyed their dominion;
⁷who heard rebuke at Sinai
  and judgments of vengeance at Horeb;

ᵗ Gk horn.
ᵘ Gk to completion.
ᵛ Gk his.
ʷ Gk horn.
ˣ Gk lived in a broad place.
ʸ Other authorities read I was grieved.
ᶻ Heb (with a play on the name Rehoboam) Syr: Gk the people's.

[8]who anointed kings to inflict retribution,
   and prophets to succeed you. [a]
[9]You who were taken up by a whirlwind of fire,
   in a chariot with horses of fire;
[10]you who are ready [b] at the appointed time, it is
      written,
   to calm the wrath of God before it breaks
      out in fury,
   to turn the heart of the father to the son,
      and to restore the tribes of Jacob.
[11]Blessed are those who saw you,
   and those who have fallen asleep [c] in your
      love;
   for we also shall surely live,
      but our name, after death, will not be such. [d]

[12]It was Eli'jah who was covered by the
      whirlwind,
   and Eli'sha was filled with his spirit;
   in all his days he did not tremble before any
      ruler,
   and no one brought him into subjection.
[13]Nothing was too hard for him,
   and when he was dead his body
      prophesied.
[14]As in his life he did wonders,
   so in death his deeds were marvelous.

[15]For all this the people did not repent,
   and they did not forsake their sins,
   till they were carried away captive from their
      land
   and were scattered over all the earth;
   the people were left very few in number,
      but with rulers from the house of David.
[16]Some of them did what was pleasing to God, [e]
   but others multiplied sins.

[17]Hezeki'ah fortified his city,
   and brought water into the midst of it;
   he tunneled the sheer rock with iron
   and built pools for water.
[18]In his days Sennach'erib came up,
   and sent the Rab'shakeh; [f]
   he lifted up his hand against Zion
   and made great boasts in his arrogance.
[19]Then their hearts were shaken and their hands
      trembled,
   and they were in anguish, like women with
      labor pains.
[20]But they called upon the Lord who is merciful,
   spreading forth their hands toward him;
   and the Holy One quickly heard them from
      heaven,
   and delivered them by the hand of Isaiah.
[21]The Lord [g] struck the camp of the Assyrians,
   and his angel wiped them out.
[22]For Hezeki'ah did what was pleasing to the
      Lord,

and he held strongly to the ways of David
   his father,
which Isai'ah the prophet commanded,
   who was great and faithful in his vision.
[23]In his days the sun went backward,
   and he lengthened the life of the king.
[24]By the spirit of might he saw the last things,
   and comforted those who mourned in Zion.
[25]He revealed what was to occur to the end of
      time,
   and the hidden things before they came to
      pass.

49 The memory of Josi'ah is like a blending
   of incense
   prepared by the art of the perfumer;
   it is sweet as honey to every mouth,
   and like music at a banquet of wine.
[2]He was led aright in converting the people,
   and took away the abominations of iniquity.
[3]He set his heart upon the Lord;
   in the days of wicked men he strengthened
      godliness.

[4]Except David and Hezeki'ah and Josi'ah
   they all sinned greatly,
   for they forsook the law of the Most High;
      the kings of Judah came to an end;
[5]for they gave their power to others,
   and their glory to a foreign nation,
[6]who set fire to the chosen city of the sanctuary,
   and made her streets desolate,
   according to the word [h] of Jeremi'ah.
[7]For they had afflicted him;
   yet he had been consecrated in the womb as
      prophet,
   to pluck up and afflict and destroy,
   and likewise to build and to plant.

[8]It was Ezek'iel who saw the vision of glory
   which God [i] showed him above the chariot
      of the cherubim.
[9]For God [i] remembered his enemies with storm,
   and did good to those who directed their
      ways rightly. [j]

[10]May the bones of the twelve prophets
   revive from where they lie,
   for they comforted the people of Jacob
   and delivered them with confident hope.

---

[a] Heb: Gk *him*.
[b] Heb: Gk *are for reproofs*.
[c] Other authorities read *who have died*.
[d] The text and meaning of this verse are uncertain.
[e] Greek lacks *to God*.
[f] Other authorities add *and departed*.
[g] Gk *He*.
[h] Gk *by the hand*.
[i] Gk *he*.
[j] The text and meaning of this verse are uncertain.

¹¹How shall we magnify Zerub'babel?
He was like a signet on the right hand,
¹² and so was Jesh'ua the son of Jo'zadak;
in their days they built the house
and raised a temple ᵏ holy to the Lord,
prepared for everlasting glory.
¹³The memory of Nehemi'ah also is lasting;
he raised for us the walls that had fallen,
and set up the gates and bars
and rebuilt our ruined houses.

¹⁴No one like E'noch has been created on earth,
for he was taken up from the earth.
¹⁵And no man like Joseph ¹ has been born,
and his bones are cared for.
¹⁶Shem and Seth were honored among men,
and Adam above every living being in the
creation.

Simon Son of Onias;
a Benediction, and an Epilogue

50 The leader of his brethren and the pride
of his people ᵐ
was Simon the high priest, son of Oni'as,
who in his life repaired the house,
and in his time fortified the temple.
²He laid the foundations for the high double
walls, ⁿ
the high retaining walls for the temple
enclosure.
³In his days a cistern for water was quarried
out, ᵒ
a reservoir like the sea in circumference.
⁴He considered how to save his people from
ruin,
and fortified the city to withstand a seige.
⁵How glorious he was when the people gathered
round him
as he came out of the inner sanctuary! ᵖ
⁶Like the morning star among the clouds,
like the moon when it is full;
⁷like the sun shining upon the temple of the
Most High,
and like the rainbow gleaming in glorious
clouds;
⁸like roses in the days of the first fruits,
like lilies by a spring of water,
like a green shoot on Lebanon �q on a
summer day;
⁹like fire and incense in the censer,
like a vessel of hammered gold
adorned with all kinds of precious stones;
¹⁰like an olive tree putting forth its fruit,
and like a cypress towering in the clouds.
¹¹When he put on his glorious robe
and clothed himself with superb
perfection
and went up to the holy altar,
he made the court of the sanctuary
glorious.

¹²And when he received the portions from the
hands of the priests,
as he stood by the hearth of the altar
with a garland of brethren around him,
he was like a young cedar on Lebanon;
and they surrounded him like the trunks of
palm trees,
¹³ all the sons of Aaron in their splendor
with the Lord's offering in their hands,
before the whole congregation of Israel.
¹⁴Finishing the service at the altars,
and arranging the offering to the Most High,
the Almighty,
¹⁵he reached out his hand to the cup
and poured a libation of the blood of the
grape;
he poured it out at the foot of the altar,
a pleasing odor to the Most High, the King
of all.
¹⁶Then the sons of Aaron shouted,
they sounded the trumpets of hammered
work,
they made a great noise to be heard
for remembrance before the Most High.
¹⁷Then all the people together made haste
and fell to the ground upon their faces
to worship their Lord,
the Almighty, God Most High.
¹⁸And the singers praised him with their voices
in sweet and full-toned melody. ʳ
¹⁹And the people besought the Lord Most High
in prayer before him who is merciful,
till the order of worship of the Lord was
ended;
so they completed his service.
²⁰Then Simon ˢ came down, and lifted up his
hands
over the whole congregation of the sons of
Israel,
to pronounce the blessing of the Lord with his
lips,
and to glory in his name;
²¹and they bowed down in worship a second
time,
to receive the blessing from the Most High.

²²And now bless the God of all,
who in every way does great things;
who exalts our days from birth,
and deals with us according to his mercy.

ᵏ Other authorities read *people.*
¹ Heb Syr: Greek adds *the leader of his brothers, the support of the
people.*
ᵐ Heb Syr: Greek lacks this line. Compare 49:15.
ⁿ The meaning of this phrase is obscure.
ᵒ Cn Compare Heb: Gk *was diminished.*
ᵖ Gk *the house of the veil.*
q Or *a sprig of frankincense.*
ʳ Other authorities read *in sweet melody throughout the house.*
ˢ Gk *he.*

23May he give us t gladness of heart,
and grant that peace may be in our days in
Israel,
as in the days of old,
24that Israel may believe that the God of mercy is
with us
to deliver us in our u days!

25With two nations my soul is vexed,
and the third is no nation:
26Those who live on Mount Se'ir, v and the
Philis'tines,
and the foolish people that dwell in
She'chem.

27Instruction in understanding and knowledge
I have written in this book,
Jesus the son of Si'rach, son of Elea'zar, w of
Jerusalem,
who out of his heart poured forth wisdom.
28Blessed is he who concerns himself with these
things,
and he who lays them to heart will become
wise.
29For if he does them, he will be strong for all
things,
for the light of the Lord is his path.

The Search for Wisdom

51 I will give thanks to you, O Lord and
King,
and will praise you as God my Savior.
I give thanks to your name,
2   for you have been my protector and helper
and have delivered my body from destruction
and from the snare of a slanderous tongue,
from lips that utter lies.
Before those who stood by
you were my helper, 3and delivered me,
in the greatness of your mercy and of your
name,
from the gnashings of teeth about to devour
me, x
from the hand of those who sought my
life,
from the many afflictions that I endured,
4from choking fire on every side
and from the midst of fire which I did not
kindle,
5from the depths of the belly of Hades,
from an unclean tongue and lying words—
6   the slander of an unrighteous tongue to the
king.
My soul drew near to death,
and my life was very near to Hades
beneath.
7They surrounded me on every side,
and there was no one to help me;
I looked for the assistance of men,
and there was none.

8Then I remembered your mercy, O Lord,
and your work from of old,
that you deliver those who wait for you
and save them from the hand of their
enemies.
9And I sent up my supplication from the earth,
and prayed for deliverance from death.
10I appealed to the Lord, the Father of my lord,
not to forsake me in the days of affliction,
at the time when there is no help against the
proud.
11I will praise your name continually,
and will sing praise with thanksgiving.
My prayer was heard,
12   for you saved me from destruction
and rescued me from an evil plight.
Therefore I will give thanks to you and praise
you,
and I will bless the name of the Lord.

13While I was still young, before I went on my
travels,
I sought wisdom openly in my prayer.
14Before the temple I asked for her,
and I will search for her to the last.
15From blossom to y ripening grape
my heart delighted in her;
my foot entered upon the straight path;
from my youth I followed her steps.
16I inclined my ear a little and received her,
and I found for myself much instruction.
17I made progress therein;
to him who gives wisdom I will give glory.
18For I resolved to live according to wisdom, z
and I was zealous for the good;
and I shall never be put to shame.
19My soul grappled with wisdom, z
and in my conduct I was strict; a
I spread out my hands to the heavens,
and lamented my ignorance of her.
20I directed my soul to her,
and through purification I found her.
I gained understanding b with her from the
first,
therefore I will not be forsaken.
21My heart was stirred to seek her,
therefore I have gained a good possession.
22The Lord gave me a tongue as my reward,
and I will praise him with it.

23Draw near to me, you who are untaught,
and lodge in my school.

---

t Other authorities read *you.*
u Other authorities read *his.*
v Heb Vg: Gk *on the mountain of Samaria.*
w The text of this line is uncertain.
x Cn Compare Vg: Gk *when I was about to be devoured.*
y Other authorities read *As from.*
z Gk *her.*
a The Greek text of this line is uncertain.
b Gk *heart.*

²⁴Why do you say you are lacking in these
things, ᶜ
and why are your souls very thirsty?
²⁵I opened my mouth and said,
Get these things ᵈ for yourselves without
money.
²⁶Put your neck under the yoke,
and let your souls receive instruction;
it is to be found close by.
²⁷See with your eyes that I have labored little
and found for myself much rest.

²⁸Get instruction with a large sum of silver,
and you will gain by it much gold.
²⁹May your soul rejoice in his mercy,
and may you not be put to shame when you
praise him.
³⁰Do your work before the appointed time,
and in God's ᵉ time he will give you your
reward.

ᶜ Cn Compare Heb Syr: The Greek text of this line is uncertain.
ᵈ Greek lacks these things.
ᵉ Gk his.

THE BOOK OF THE PROPHET

ISAIAH

The Sinfulness of Judah

1 The vision of Isaiah the son of A'moz, which he saw concerning Judah and Jerusalem in the days of Uzzi'ah, Jo'tham, A'haz, and Hezeki'ah, kings of Judah.

[2] Hear, O heavens, and give ear, O earth;
  for the LORD has spoken:
"Sons have I reared and brought up,
  but they have rebelled against me.
[3] The ox knows its owner,
  and the donkey its master's crib;
but Israel does not know,
  my people does not understand."

[4] Ah, sinful nation,
  a people laden with iniquity,
offspring of evildoers,
  sons who deal corruptly!
They have forsaken the LORD,
  they have despised the Holy One of Israel,
  they are utterly estranged.

[5] Why will you still be struck down,
  that you continue to rebel?
The whole head is sick,
  and the whole heart faint.
[6] From the sole of the foot even to the head,
  there is no soundness in it,
but bruises and sores
  and bleeding wounds;
they are not pressed out, or bound up,
  or softened with oil.

[7] Your country lies desolate,
  your cities are burned with fire;
in your very presence
  strangers devour your land;
  it is desolate, as overthrown by strangers.
[8] And the daughter of Zion is left
  like a booth in a vineyard,
like a lodge in a cucumber field,
  like a besieged city.

[9] If the LORD of hosts
  had not left us a few survivors,
we should have been like Sodom,
  and become like Gomor'rah.

[10] Hear the word of the LORD,
  you rulers of Sodom!
Give ear to the teaching of our God,
  you people of Gomor'rah!
[11] "What to me is the multitude of your
      sacrifices?
  says the LORD;
I have had enough of burnt offerings of rams
  and the fat of fed beasts;
I do not delight in the blood of bulls,
  or of lambs, or of he-goats.

The Books of Prophecy
In ancient times there were prophets of many different religions, men who claimed to speak in the name of their gods; and not infrequently they existed in large groups. Thus Elijah had to confront no less than 450 prophets of Baal on the occasion of the contest on Mount Carmel (1 Kings 18). There were similar groups of prophets who spoke in the name of Yahweh. These prophets experienced ecstasies and trances often induced by the playing of music (2 Kings 10:5), and seem to have been organized into communities (2 Kings 2:3–18).

The prophets, however, whom we know by name and whose actions are recorded in the Bible, were very different from these and their influence on Israel was much more profound. So far from their seeking prophecy as a profession, it was imposed on them by God and they could not refuse (Jer 1:9; Amos 3:8). So far from their trying by fair words to please their hearers, they often had to announce approaching disaster as punishment for sin. Not only their words, their whole life was given up to the ministry, and they had to lead a life of great penance and sacrifice often ending in violent death. The prophet received an inner, wordless message, which he was then compelled to communicate, sometimes in lyric poetry, sometimes in prose, often making use of parables, allegories, and symbolic actions. When disaster had fallen on the nation, then the role of the prophet changed from one of threat to one of consolation (Is 40ff.). It was in such times as these that many Messianic prophecies were uttered, foretelling the coming of God's kingdom in "the last days" heralded by God's anointed or "messiah." The character and mission of Christ are vividly portrayed in Isaiah and even his sufferings are described, though it does not follow that those who first heard the prophecies understood all that was being said. Many prophecies were fully understood only when they came to pass.

The Book of Isaiah
Isaiah, the greatest of all the prophets, lived at a critical time in Israel's history. The very existence of the people was threatened by the king of Assyria in the latter part of the eighth century B.C. The well-known and beautiful Immanuel prophecies (chapters 6–12) were uttered on occasions of great national danger when Judah was ruled by an unworthy king—Ahaz. Under his successor, Hezekiah, a good and prudent king, Isaiah, who was himself of noble birth, occupied a position of influence in promoting religious reform, and many of his prophecies are to be ascribed to this period. He was by now a national figure with a large following. He appears last of all in the great crisis of 701 B.C. when, as he had promised, Jerusalem was saved from destruction by the Assyrians.

His prophecies are distinguished both for their poetical quality and for the elevation of their thought. The monotheism of Isaiah is declared in eloquent terms. Likewise, his Messianic predictions attain a clarity that has induced some to give him the title of "evangelist." The second part of the book (chapters 40–55), quite different from the first and perhaps even more sublime, is generally held now not to be by Isaiah himself but by a later prophet writing at the time of the Exile, doubtless a member of the Isaian school and following in his tradition. These chapters are remarkable for the words of comfort and encouragement they contain and perhaps even more for the remarkable "Servant Songs," prophecies about the Messiah to come, foretelling his sufferings. The remaining chapters (56–66) contain a varied selection of prophecies of different dates.
1:9: Rom 9:29.

¹²"When you come to appear before me,
who requires of you
this trampling of my courts?
¹³Bring no more vain offerings;
incense is an abomination to me.
New moon and sabbath and the calling of
assemblies—
I cannot endure iniquity and solemn
assembly.
¹⁴Your new moons and your appointed feasts
my soul hates;
they have become a burden to me,
I am weary of bearing them.
¹⁵When you spread forth your hands,
I will hide my eyes from you;
even though you make many prayers,
I will not listen;
your hands are full of blood.
¹⁶Wash yourselves; make yourselves clean;
remove the evil of your doings
from before my eyes;
cease to do evil,
¹⁷   learn to do good;
seek justice,
correct oppression;
defend the fatherless,
plead for the widow.

¹⁸"Come now, let us reason together,
says the LORD:
though your sins are like scarlet,
they shall be as white as snow;
though they are red like crimson,
they shall become like wool.
¹⁹If you are willing and obedient,
you shall eat the good of the land;
²⁰but if you refuse and rebel,
you shall be devoured by the sword;
for the mouth of the LORD has spoken."
²¹How the faithful city
has become a harlot,
she that was full of justice!
Righteousness lodged in her,
but now murderers.
²²Your silver has become dross,
your wine mixed with water.
²³Your princes are rebels
and companions of thieves.
Every one loves a bribe
and runs after gifts.
They do not defend the fatherless,
and the widow's cause does not come to
them.

²⁴Therefore the Lord says,
the LORD of hosts,
the Mighty One of Israel:
"Ah, I will vent my wrath on my enemies,
and avenge myself on my foes.

²⁵I will turn my hand against you
and will smelt away your dross as with lye
and remove all your alloy.
²⁶And I will restore your judges as at the first,
and your counselors as at the beginning.
Afterward you shall be called the city of
righteousness,
the faithful city."

²⁷Zion shall be redeemed by justice,
and those in her who repent, by
righteousness.
²⁸But rebels and sinners shall be destroyed
together,
and those who forsake the LORD shall be
consumed.
²⁹For you shall be ashamed of the oaks
in which you delighted;
and you shall blush for the gardens
which you have chosen.
³⁰For you shall be like an oak
whose leaf withers,
and like a garden without water.
³¹And the strong shall become tow,
and his work a spark,
and both of them shall burn together,
with none to quench them.

The Lord's Universal Reign

2 The word which Isai′ah the son of A′moz
saw concerning Judah and Jerusalem.
²It shall come to pass in the latter days
that the mountain of the house of the LORD
shall be established as the highest of the
mountains,
and shall be raised above the hills;
and all the nations shall flow to it,
³   and many peoples shall come, and say:
"Come, let us go up to the mountain of the
LORD,
to the house of the God of Jacob;
that he may teach us his ways
and that we may walk in his paths."
For out of Zion shall go forth the law,
and the word of the LORD from
Jerusalem.
⁴He shall judge between the nations,
and shall decide for many peoples;
and they shall beat their swords into
plowshares,
and their spears into pruning hooks;
nation shall not lift up sword against nation,
neither shall they learn war any more. *

⁵O house of Jacob,
come, let us walk
in the light of the LORD.

2:2–4: Mic 4:1–3.
* 2:2–4: Note the universalism of this prophecy.

⁶For you have rejected your people,
  the house of Jacob,
because they are full of diviners ᵃ from the east
  and of soothsayers like the Philis′tines,
  and they strike hands with foreigners.
⁷Their land is filled with silver and gold,
  and there is no end to their treasures;
  their land is filled with horses,
  and there is no end to their chariots.
⁸Their land is filled with idols;
  they bow down to the work of their hands,
  to what their own fingers have made.
⁹So man is humbled,
  and men are brought low—
  forgive them not!
¹⁰Enter into the rock,
  and hide in the dust
from before the terror of the LORD,
  and from the glory of his majesty.
¹¹The haughty looks of man shall be brought
  low,
  and the pride of men shall be humbled;
and the LORD alone will be exalted in that day.

¹²For the LORD of hosts has a day
  against all that is proud and lofty,
  against all that is lifted up and high; ᵇ
¹³against all the cedars of Lebanon,
  lofty and lifted up;
  and against all the oaks of Bashan;
¹⁴against all the high mountains,
  and against all the lofty hills;
¹⁵against every high tower,
  and against every fortified wall;
¹⁶against all the ships of Tar′shish,
  and against all the beautiful craft.
¹⁷And the haughtiness of man shall be humbled,
  and the pride of men shall be brought low;
  and the LORD alone will be exalted in that
  day.
¹⁸And the idols shall utterly pass away.
¹⁹And men shall enter the caves of the rocks
  and the holes of the ground,
from before the terror of the LORD,
  and from the glory of his majesty,
  when he rises to terrify the earth.

²⁰In that day men will cast forth
  their idols of silver and their idols of gold,
which they made for themselves to worship,
  to the moles and to the bats,
²¹to enter the caverns of the rocks and the clefts
  of the cliffs,
from before the terror of the LORD,
  and from the glory of his majesty,
  when he rises to terrify the earth.
²²Turn away from man
  in whose nostrils is breath,
  for of what account is he?

The Lord's Judgment

3 For behold, the Lord, the LORD of hosts,
  is taking away from Jerusalem and from
    Judah
stay and staff,
  the whole stay of bread,
  and the whole stay of water;
²the mighty man and the soldier,
  the judge and the prophet,
  the diviner and the elder,
³the captain of fifty
  and the man of rank,
the counselor and the skilful magician
  and the expert in charms.
⁴And I will make boys their princes,
  and infants shall rule over them.
⁵And the people will oppress one another,
  every man his fellow
  and every man his neighbor;
the youth will be insolent to the elder,
  and the base fellow to the honorable.

⁶When a man takes hold of his brother
  in the house of his father, saying:
"You have a mantle;
  you shall be our leader,
and this heap of ruins
  shall be under your rule";
⁷in that day he will speak out, saying:
"I will not be a healer;
  in my house there is neither bread nor
    mantle;
you shall not make me
  leader of the people."
⁸For Jerusalem has stumbled,
  and Judah has fallen;
because their speech and their deeds are
  against the LORD,
  defying his glorious presence.

⁹Their partiality witnesses against them;
  they proclaim their sin like Sodom,
  they do not hide it.
Woe to them!
  For they have brought evil upon
    themselves.
¹⁰Tell the righteous that it shall be well with
  them,
  for they shall eat the fruit of their deeds.
¹¹Woe to the wicked! It shall be ill with him,
  for what his hands have done shall be done
    to him.
¹²My people—children are their oppressors,
  and women rule over them.
O my people, your leaders mislead you,
  and confuse the course of your paths.

ᵃ Cn: Heb lacks *of diviners.*
ᵇ Cn Compare Gk: Heb *low.*

¹³The Lord has taken his place to contend,
 he stands to judge his people. ᵈ
¹⁴The Lord enters into judgment
 with the elders and princes of his people:
"It is you who have devoured the vineyard,
 the spoil of the poor is in your houses.
¹⁵What do you mean by crushing my people,
 by grinding the face of the poor?" says the
 Lord God of hosts.

¹⁶The Lord said:
Because the daughters of Zion are haughty
 and walk with outstretched necks,
 glancing wantonly with their eyes,
mincing along as they go,
 tinkling with their feet;
¹⁷the Lord will strike with a scab
 the heads of the daughters of Zion,
 and the Lord will lay bare their secret parts.

18 In that day the Lord will take away the
finery of the anklets, the headbands, and the crescents; ¹⁹the pendants, the bracelets, and the scarfs;
²⁰the headdresses, the armlets, the sashes, the perfume boxes, and the amulets; ²¹the signet rings
and nose rings; ²²the festal robes, the mantles, the
cloaks, and the handbags; ²³the garments of
gauze, the linen garments, the turbans, and the
veils.
²⁴Instead of perfume there will be rottenness;
 and instead of a belt, a rope;
and instead of well-set hair, baldness;
 and instead of a rich robe, a putting on of
 sackcloth;
 instead of beauty, shame. ᵉ
²⁵Your men shall fall by the sword
 and your mighty men in battle.
²⁶And her gates shall lament and mourn;
 ravaged, she shall sit upon the ground.

4 And seven women shall take hold of one man
in that day, saying, "We will eat our own
bread and wear our own clothes, only let us be
called by your name; take away our reproach."

2 In that day the branch of the Lord shall be
beautiful and glorious, and the fruit of the land
shall be the pride and glory of the survivors of
Israel. ³And he who is left in Zion and remains in
Jerusalem will be called holy, every one who has
been recorded for life in Jerusalem, ⁴when the
Lord shall have washed away the filth of the
daughters of Zion and cleansed the bloodstains
of Jerusalem from its midst by a spirit of judgment and by a spirit of burning. ⁵Then the Lord
will create over the whole site of Mount Zion and
over her assemblies a cloud by day, and smoke
and the shining of a flaming fire by night; for
over all the glory there will be a canopy and a
pavilion. ⁶It will be for a shade by day from the

heat, and for a refuge and a shelter from the storm
and rain.

The Parable of the Vineyard

5 * Let me sing for my beloved
 a love song concerning his vineyard:
My beloved had a vineyard
 on a very fertile hill.
²He dug it and cleared it of stones,
 and planted it with choice vines;
he built a watchtower in the midst of it,
 and hewed out a wine vat in it;
and he looked for it to yield grapes,
 but it yielded wild grapes.

³And now, O inhabitants of Jerusalem
 and men of Judah,
judge, I beg you, between me
 and my vineyard.
⁴What more was there to do for my vineyard,
 that I have not done in it?
When I looked for it to yield grapes,
 why did it yield wild grapes?

⁵And now I will tell you
 what I will do to my vineyard.
I will remove its hedge,
 and it shall be devoured;
I will break down its wall,
 and it shall be trampled down.
⁶I will make it a waste;
 it shall not be pruned or hoed,
 and briers and thorns shall grow up;
I will also command the clouds
 that they rain no rain upon it.

⁷For the vineyard of the Lord of hosts
 is the house of Israel,
and the men of Judah
 are his pleasant planting;
and he looked for justice,
 but behold, bloodshed;
for righteousness,
 but behold, a cry!

⁸Woe to those who join house to house,
 who add field to field,
until there is no more room,
 and you are made to dwell alone
 in the midst of the land.
⁹The Lord of hosts has sworn in my hearing:
"Surely many houses shall be desolate,
 large and beautiful houses, without
 inhabitant.

ᵈ Gk Syr: Heb *judge peoples.*
ᵉ One ancient Ms: Heb lacks *shame.*
4:2: Jer 23:5; 33:15; Zech 3:8; 6:12.
5:1–7: Mt 21:33–46; Mk 12:1–12; Lk 20:9–19.
* 5:1–7: This moving allegory may be compared with similar passages in
the New Testament, e.g., Mt 21:33–41; Jn 15:1–2.

¹⁰For ten acres of vineyard shall yield but one
    bath,
  and a homer of seed shall yield but an
    ephah."

¹¹Woe to those who rise early in the morning,
  that they may run after strong drink,
who linger late into the evening
  till wine inflames them!
¹²They have lyre and harp,
  timbrel and flute and wine at their feasts;
but they do not regard the deeds of the Lord,
  or see the work of his hands.

¹³Therefore my people go into exile for want of
    knowledge;
  their honored men are dying of hunger,
    and their multitude is parched with thirst.
¹⁴Therefore Sheol has enlarged its appetite
  and opened its mouth beyond measure,
and the nobility of Jerusalem *f* and her
    multitude go down,
  her throng and he who exults in her.
¹⁵Man is bowed down, and men are brought
    low,
  and the eyes of the haughty are humbled.
¹⁶But the Lord of hosts is exalted in justice,
  and the Holy God shows himself holy in
    righteousness.
¹⁷Then shall the lambs graze as in their pasture,
  fatlings and kids *g* shall feed among the
    ruins.

¹⁸Woe to those who draw iniquity with cords of
    falsehood,
  who draw sin as with cart ropes,
¹⁹who say: "Let him make haste,
  let him speed his work
  that we may see it;
let the purpose of the Holy One of Israel draw
    near,
  and let it come, that we may know it!"
²⁰Woe to those who call evil good and good evil,
who put darkness for light
  and light for darkness,
who put bitter for sweet
  and sweet for bitter!
²¹Woe to those who are wise in their own eyes,
  and shrewd in their own sight!
²²Woe to those who are heroes at drinking wine,
  and valiant men in mixing strong drink,
²³who acquit the guilty for a bribe,
  and deprive the innocent of his right!

²⁴Therefore, as the tongue of fire devours the
    stubble,
  and as dry grass sinks down in the flame,
so their root will be as rottenness,
  and their blossom go up like dust;

for they have rejected the law of the Lord of
    hosts,
  and have despised the word of the Holy One
    of Israel.
²⁵Therefore the anger of the Lord was kindled
    against his people,
  and he stretched out his hand against them
    and struck them,
  and the mountains quaked;
and their corpses were as refuse
  in the midst of the streets.
For all this his anger is not turned away
  and his hand is stretched out still.

²⁶He will raise a signal for a nation afar off,
  and whistle for it from the ends of the
    earth;
and behold, swiftly, speedily it comes!
²⁷None is weary, none stumbles,
  none slumbers or sleeps,
not a waistcloth is loose,
  not a sandal-thong broken;
²⁸their arrows are sharp,
  all their bows bent,
their horses' hoofs seem like flint,
  and their wheels like the whirlwind.
²⁹Their roaring is like a lion,
  like young lions they roar;
they growl and seize their prey,
  they carry it off, and none can rescue.
³⁰They will growl over it on that day,
  like the roaring of the sea.
And if one look to the land,
  behold, darkness and distress;
and the light is darkened by its clouds.

A Vision of the Lord in the Temple

6 * In the year that King Uzzi′ah died I saw the
Lord sitting upon a throne, high and lifted
up; and his train filled the temple. ²Above him
stood the seraphim; each had six wings: with
two he covered his face, and with two he covered
his feet, and with two he flew. ³And one called to
another and said:
"Holy, holy, holy is the Lord of hosts;
  the whole earth is full of his glory."
⁴And the foundations of the thresholds shook
at the voice of him who called, and the house was
filled with smoke. ⁵And I said: "Woe is me! For I
am lost; for I am a man of unclean lips, and I
dwell in the midst of a people of unclean lips; for
my eyes have seen the King, the Lord of hosts!"
  6 Then flew one of the seraphim to me, having
in his hand a burning coal which he had taken

---

f Heb *her nobility.*
g Cn Compare Gk: Heb *aliens.*
6:3: Rev 4:8.
6:4: Rev 15:8.
* 6:1–13: This vision stresses the solemnity of the prophet's calling. The
"*Holy, holy, holy*" is fittingly included in the Mass. The vision also serves
to introduce the Immanuel prophecies.

with tongs from the altar. [7]And he touched my mouth, and said: "Behold, this has touched your lips; your guilt is taken away, and your sin forgiven." [8]And I heard the voice of the Lord saying, "Whom shall I send, and who will go for us?" Then I said, "Here am I! Send me." [9]And he said, "Go, and say to this people:

'Hear and hear, but do not understand;
see and see, but do not perceive.'
[10]Make the heart of this people fat,
and their ears heavy,
and shut their eyes;
lest they see with their eyes,
and hear with their ears,
and understand with their hearts,
and turn and be healed."
[11]Then I said, "How long, O Lord?"
And he said:
"Until cities lie waste
without inhabitant,
and houses without men,
and the land is utterly desolate,
[12]and the LORD removes men far away,
and the forsaken places are many in the
midst of the land.
[13]And though a tenth remain in it,
it will be burned again,
like a terebinth or an oak,
whose stump remains standing
when it is felled."
The holy seed is its stump.

Isaiah Reassures King Ahaz

7 In the days of A′haz the son of Jo′tham, son of Uzzi′ah, king of Judah, Re′zin the king of Syria and Pe′kah the son of Remali′ah the king of Israel came up to Jerusalem to wage war against it, but they could not conquer it. [2]When the house of David was told, "Syria is in league with E′phraim," his heart and the heart of his people shook as the trees of the forest shake before the wind.

3 And the LORD said to Isai′ah, "Go forth to meet A′haz, you and She′arjash′ub[h] your son, at the end of the conduit of the upper pool on the highway to the Fuller's Field, [4]and say to him, 'Take heed, be quiet, do not fear, and do not let your heart be faint because of these two smoldering stumps of firebrands, at the fierce anger of Re′zin and Syria and the son of Remali′ah. [5]Because Syria, with E′phraim and the son of Remali′ah, has devised evil against you, saying, [6]"Let us go up against Judah and terrify it, and let us conquer it for ourselves, and set up the son of Ta′be-el as king in the midst of it," [7]thus says the Lord GOD:

It shall not stand,
and it shall not come to pass.
[8]For the head of Syria is Damascus,
and the head of Damascus is Re′zin.

(Within sixty-five years E′phraim will be broken to pieces so that it will no longer be a people.)
[9]And the head of E′phraim is Samar′ia,
and the head of Samaria is the son of
Remali′ah.
If you will not believe,
surely you shall not be established.'"

The Sign of Immanuel

10 Again the LORD spoke to A′haz, [11]"Ask a sign of the LORD your God; let it be deep as Sheol or high as heaven." [12]But A′haz said, "I will not ask, and I will not put the LORD to the test." [13]And he said, "Hear then, O house of David! Is it too little for you to weary men, that you weary my God also? [14]Therefore the Lord himself will give you a sign. Behold, a virgin [i] * shall conceive and bear [j] a son, and shall call his name Imman′u-el.[k] [15]He shall eat curds and honey when he knows how to refuse the evil and choose the good. [16]For before the child knows how to refuse the evil and choose the good, the land before whose two kings you are in dread will be deserted. [17]The LORD will bring upon you and upon your people and upon your father's house such days as have not come since the day that E′phraim departed from Judah—the king of Assyria."

18 In that day the LORD will whistle for the fly which is at the sources of the streams of Egypt, and for the bee which is in the land of Assyria. [19]And they will all come and settle in the steep ravines, and in the clefts of the rocks, and on all the thornbushes, and on all the pastures.

20 In that day the Lord will shave with a razor which is hired beyond the River—with the king of Assyria—the head and the hair of the feet, and it will sweep away the beard also.

21 In that day a man will keep alive a young cow and two sheep; [22]and because of the abundance of milk which they give, he will eat curds; for every one that is left in the land will eat curds and honey.

23 In that day every place where there used to be a thousand vines, worth a thousand shekels of silver, will become briers and thorns. [24]With bow and arrows men will come there, for all the land will be briers and thorns; [25]and as for all the hills which used to be hoed with a hoe, you will not come there for fear of briers and thorns; but they will become a place where cattle are let loose and where sheep tread.

---

[h] That is *A remnant shall return.*
[i] Or *young woman.*
[j] Or *is with child and shall bear.*
[k] That is *God is with us.*
6:9–10: Mt 13:14–15; Mk 4:12; Lk 8:10; Jn 12:39–41; Acts 28:26–27.
7:14: Mt 1:23.
* 7:14, *virgin or young woman:* The Hebrew word *'almah* is not explicit. The Greek translates this as *parthenos,* "virgin," and may be regarded as a witness to later Jewish tradition as to the meaning of the prophecy. The virginal conception is, of course, unequivocally stated in the Gospel where this prophecy is quoted (Mt 1:23; cf. also Lk 1:35).

Isaiah's Son a Sign of Assyrian Invasion

8 Then the LORD said to me, "Take a large tablet and write upon it in common characters, 'Belonging to Ma'her-shal'al-hash"-baz.'"[1] [2]And I got reliable witnesses, Uri'ah the priest and Zechari'ah the son of Jeberechi'ah, to attest for me. [3]And I went to the prophetess, and she conceived and bore a son. Then the LORD said to me, "Call his name Ma'her-shal'al-hash"-baz; [4]for before the child knows how to cry 'My father' or 'My mother,' the wealth of Damascus and the spoil of Samar'ia will be carried away before the king of Assyria."

5 The LORD spoke to me again: [6]"Because this people have refused the waters of Shilo'ah that flow gently, and melt in fear before[m] Re'zin and the son of Remali'ah; [7]therefore, behold, the Lord is bringing up against them the waters of the River, mighty and many, the king of Assyria and all his glory; and it will rise over all its channels and go over all its banks; [8]and it will sweep on into Judah, it will overflow and pass on, reaching even to the neck; and its outspread wings will fill the breadth of your land, O Imman'u-el."

[9]Be broken, you peoples, and be dismayed;
give ear, all you far countries;
gird yourselves and be dismayed;
gird yourselves and be dismayed.
[10]Take counsel together, but it will come to
nought;
speak a word, but it will not stand,
for God is with us.[x]

11 For the LORD spoke thus to me with his strong hand upon me, and warned me not to walk in the way of this people, saying: [12]"Do not call conspiracy all that this people call conspiracy, and do not fear what they fear, nor be in dread. [13]But the LORD of hosts, him you shall regard as holy; let him be your fear, and let him be your dread. [14]And he will become a sanctuary, and a stone of offense, and a rock of stumbling to both houses of Israel, a trap and a snare to the inhabitants of Jerusalem. [15]And many shall stumble thereon; they shall fall and be broken; they shall be snared and taken."

Disciples of Isaiah

16 Bind up the testimony, seal the teaching among my disciples. [17]I will wait for the LORD, who is hiding his face from the house of Jacob, and I will hope in him. [18]Behold, I and the children whom the LORD has given me are signs and portents in Israel from the LORD of hosts, who dwells on Mount Zion. [19]And when they say to you, "Consult the mediums and the wizards who chirp and mutter," should not a people consult their God? Should they consult the dead on behalf of the living? [20]To the teaching and to the testimony! Surely for this word which they speak there is no

dawn. [21]They will pass through the land,[n] greatly distressed and hungry; and when they are hungry, they will be enraged and will curse[o] their king and their God, and turn their faces upward; [22]and they will look to the earth, but behold, distress and darkness, the gloom of anguish; and they will be thrust into thick darkness.

The Righteous Reign

9[p] But there will be no gloom for her that was in anguish. In the former time he brought into contempt the land of Zeb'ulun and the land of Naph'tali, but in the latter time he will make glorious the way of the sea, the land beyond the Jordan, Galilee of the nations.
[2][q] The people who walked in darkness
have seen a great light;
those who dwelt in a land of deep darkness,
on them has light shined.
[3]You have multiplied the nation,
you have increased its joy;
they rejoice before you
as with joy at the harvest,
as men rejoice when they divide the spoil.
[4]For the yoke of his burden,
and the staff for his shoulder,
the rod of his oppressor,
you have broken as on the day of Mid'ian.
[5]For every boot of the tramping warrior in
battle tumult
and every garment rolled in blood
will be burned as fuel for the fire.
[6]For to us a child is born,
to us a son is given;
and the government will be upon his shoulder,
and his name will be called
"Wonderful Counselor, Mighty God,
Everlasting Father, Prince of Peace."[*]
[7]Of the increase of his government and of
peace
there will be no end,
upon the throne of David, and over his
kingdom,
to establish it, and to uphold it
with justice and with righteousness
from this time forth and for evermore.
The zeal of the LORD of hosts will do this.

[8]The Lord has sent a word against Jacob,
and it will light upon Israel;

---

[1] That is *The spoil speeds, the prey hastes.*
[m] Cn: Heb *rejoices in.*
[x] Heb *immanu el.*
[n] Heb *it.*
[o] Or *curse by.*
[p] Ch 8:23 in Heb.
[q] Ch 9:1 in Heb.
8:12–13: 1 Pet 3:14–15.
8:14: Rom 9:32–33; 1 Pet 2:8.
8:17–18: Heb 2:13.
9:1–2: Mt 4:15–16; Lk 1:79.
[*] 9:6: Passage selected for the Introit of the Mass of Christmas Day, showing that the Church regards these words as being fulfilled in Jesus Christ.

⁹and all the people will know,
    E'phraim and the inhabitants of Samar'ia,
    who say in pride and in arrogance of heart:
¹⁰"The bricks have fallen,
    but we will build with dressed stones;
  the sycamores have been cut down,
    but we will put cedars in their place."
¹¹So the LORD raises adversaries ʳ against them,
    and stirs up their enemies.
¹²The Syrians on the east and the Philis'tines on
      the west
  devour Israel with open mouth.
  For all this his anger is not turned away
    and his hand is stretched out still.

¹³The people did not turn to him who struck
      them,
    nor seek the LORD of hosts.
¹⁴So the LORD cut off from Israel head and tail,
    palm branch and reed in one day—
¹⁵the elder and honored man is the head,
    and the prophet who teaches lies is the tail;
¹⁶for those who lead this people lead them
      astray,
    and those who are led by them are
      swallowed up.
¹⁷Therefore the Lord does not rejoice over their
      young men,
  and has no compassion on their fatherless and
      widows;
  for every one is godless and an evildoer,
    and every mouth speaks folly.
  For all this his anger is not turned away
    and his hand is stretched out still.

¹⁸For wickedness burns like a fire,
    it consumes briers and thorns;
  it kindles the thickets of the forest,
    and they roll upward in a column of smoke.
¹⁹Through the wrath of the LORD of hosts
    the land is burned,
  and the people are like fuel for the fire;
    no man spares his brother.
²⁰They snatch on the right, but are still hungry,
    and they devour on the left, but are not
      satisfied;
  each devours his neighbor's ᵃ flesh,
²¹Manas'seh E'phraim, and Ephraim Manasseh,
    and together they are against Judah.
  For all this his anger is not turned away
    and his hand is stretched out still.

Judgment on the Oppressors

10 Woe to those who decree iniquitous
      decrees,
    and the writers who keep writing
      oppression,
²to turn aside the needy from justice
    and to rob the poor of my people of their
      right,

that widows may be their spoil,
    and that they may make the fatherless their
      prey!
³What will you do on the day of punishment,
    in the storm which will come from afar?
  To whom will you flee for help,
    and where will you leave your wealth?
⁴Nothing remains but to crouch among the
      prisoners
    or fall among the slain.
  For all this his anger is not turned away
    and his hand is stretched out still.

⁵Ah, Assyria, the rod of my anger,
    the staff of my fury!ᵗ
⁶Against a godless nation I send him,
    and against the people of my wrath I
      command him,
  to take spoil and seize plunder,
    and to tread them down like the mire of the
      streets.
⁷But he does not so intend,
    and his mind does not so think;
  but it is in his mind to destroy,
    and to cut off nations not a few;
⁸for he says:
  "Are not my commanders all kings?
⁹Is not Calno like Car'chemish?
    Is not Ha'math like Arpad?
    Is not Samar'ia like Damascus?
¹⁰As my hand has reached to the kingdoms of
      the idols
    whose graven images were greater than
      those of Jerusalem and Samar'ia,
¹¹shall I not do to Jerusalem and her idols
    as I have done to Samar'ia and her images?"

12 When the Lord has finished all his work on
Mount Zion and on Jerusalem heᵘ will punish the
arrogant boasting of the king of Assyria and his
haughty pride. ¹³For he says:
  "By the strength of my hand I have done it,
    and by my wisdom, for I have
      understanding;
  I have removed the boundaries of peoples,
    and have plundered their treasures;
    like a bull I have brought down those who
      sat on thrones.
¹⁴My hand has found like a nest
    the wealth of the peoples;
  and as men gather eggs that have been
      forsaken
    so I have gathered all the earth;
  and there was none that moved a wing,
    or opened the mouth, or chirped."

ʳ Cn: Heb *the adversaries of Rezin*.
ᵃ Tg Compare Gk: Heb *the flesh of his arm*.
ᵗ Heb *a staff it is in their hand my fury*.
ᵘ Heb *I*.
10:5–34: Nahum; Zeph 2:13–15.

¹⁵Shall the axe vaunt itself over him who hews
  with it,
  or the saw magnify itself against him who
    wields it?
As if a rod should wield him who lifts it,
  or as if a staff should lift him who is not
    wood!
¹⁶Therefore the Lord, the LORD of hosts,
  will send wasting sickness among his stout
    warriors,
and under his glory a burning will be kindled,
  like the burning of fire.
¹⁷The light of Israel will become a fire,
  and his Holy One a flame;
and it will burn and devour
  his thorns and briers in one day.
¹⁸The glory of his forest and of his fruitful land
  the LORD will destroy, both soul and body,
  and it will be as when a sick man wastes
    away.
¹⁹The remnant of the trees of his forest will be
  so few
  that a child can write them down.

The Repentant Remnant of Israel

20 In that day the remnant of Israel and the
survivors of the house of Jacob will no more lean
upon him that struck them, but will lean upon the
LORD, the Holy One of Israel, in truth. ²¹A remnant
will return, the remnant of Jacob, to the mighty
God. ²²For though your people Israel be as the
sand of the sea, only a remnant of them will return. Destruction is decreed, overflowing with
righteousness. ²³For the Lord, the LORD of hosts,
will make a full end, as decreed, in the midst of all
the earth.

24 Therefore thus says the Lord, the LORD of
hosts: "O my people, who dwell in Zion, be not
afraid of the Assyrians when they strike with the
rod and lift up their staff against you as the Egyptians did. ²⁵For in a very little while my indignation will come to an end, and my anger will be
directed to their destruction. ²⁶And the LORD of
hosts will wield against them a scourge, as when
he struck Mid′ian at the rock of Or′eb; and his
rod will be over the sea, and he will lift it as he did
in Egypt. ²⁷And in that day his burden will depart
from your shoulder, and his yoke will be destroyed
from your neck."

He has gone up from Rimmon,ᵛ
²⁸ he has come to Ai′ath;
he has passed through Migron,
  at Mich′mash he stores his baggage;
²⁹they have crossed over the pass,
  at Ge′ba they lodge for the night;
Ra′mah trembles,
  Gib′eah of Saul has fled.
³⁰Cry aloud, O daughter of Gallim!
  Listen, O La′ishah!

Answer her, O An′athoth!
³¹Madme′nah is in flight,
  the inhabitants of Gebim flee for safety.
³²This very day he will halt at Nob,
  he will shake his fist
  at the mount of the daughter of Zion,
    the hill of Jerusalem.

³³Behold, the Lord, the LORD of hosts
  will lop the boughs with terrifying power;
  the great in height will be hewn down,
    and the lofty will be brought low.
³⁴He will cut down the thickets of the forest with
  an axe,
  and Lebanon with its majestic treesʷ will
    fall.

The Shoot from the Stump of Jesse
and the Peaceful Kingdom

11 * There shall come forth a shoot from the
    stump of Jesse,
  and a branch shall grow out of his roots.
²And the Spirit of the LORD shall rest upon him,
  the spirit of wisdom and understanding,
  the spirit of counsel and might,
  the spirit of knowledge and the fear of the
    LORD. †
³And his delight shall be in the fear of the
  LORD.

He shall not judge by what his eyes see,
  or decide by what his ears hear;
⁴but with righteousness he shall judge the poor,
  and decide with equity for the meek of the
    earth;
and he shall strike the earth with the rod of his
  mouth,
  and with the breath of his lips he shall slay
    the wicked.
⁵Righteousness shall be the belt of his waist,
  and faithfulness the belt of his loins.

⁶The wolf shall dwell with the lamb,
  and the leopard shall lie down with the kid,
and the calf and the lion and the fatling
  together,
  and a little child shall lead them.
⁷The cow and the bear shall feed;
  their young shall lie down together;
  and the lion shall eat straw like the ox.

ᵛ Cn: Heb *and his yoke from your neck, and a yoke will be destroyed*
because of fatness.
ʷ Cn Compare Gk Vg: Heb *with a majestic one.*
10:22–23: Rom 9:27–28.
11:1: Is 11:10; Rom 15:12.
11:2: 1 Pet 4:14.
11:5: Eph 6:14.
11:6–9: Is 65:25; Hab 2:14.
* 11:1–3: cf. 61:1–2 and Lk 4:18–19.
† 11:2: The enumeration of the "gifts of the Holy Spirit" is taken from
this passage.

[8]The sucking child shall play over the hole of
the asp,
and the weaned child shall put his hand on
the adder's den.
[9]They shall not hurt or destroy
in all my holy mountain;
for the earth shall be full of the knowledge of
the LORD
as the waters cover the sea.

10 In that day the root of Jesse shall stand as
an ensign to the peoples; him shall the nations
seek, and his dwellings shall be glorious.

11 In that day the Lord will extend his hand
yet a second time to recover the remnant which is
left of his people, from Assyria, from Egypt, from
Path'ros, from Ethiopia, from E'lam, from Shi'nar,
from Ha'math, and from the islands of the sea.
[12]He will raise an ensign for the nations,
and will assemble the outcasts of Israel,
and gather the dispersed of Judah
from the four corners of the earth.
[13]The jealousy of E'phraim shall depart,
and those who harass Judah shall be cut off;
Ephraim shall not be jealous of Judah,
and Judah shall not harass Ephraim.
[14]But they shall swoop down upon the shoulder
of the Philis'tines in the west,
and together they shall plunder the people
of the east.
They shall put forth their hand against E'dom
and Moab,
and the Am'monites shall obey them.
[15]And the LORD will utterly destroy
the tongue of the sea of Egypt;
and will wave his hand over the River
with his scorching wind,
and strike it into seven channels
that men may cross dryshod.
[16]And there will be a highway from Assyria
for the remnant which is left of his people,
as there was for Israel
when they came up from the land of Egypt.

Thanksgiving and Praise

12 You will say in that day:
"I will give thanks to you, O LORD,
for though you were angry with me,
your anger turned away,
and you did comfort me.

[2]"Behold, God is my salvation;
I will trust, and will not be afraid;
for the LORD GOD is my strength and my song,
and he has become my salvation."

3 With joy you will draw water from the wells
of salvation. [4]And you will say in that day:
"Give thanks to the LORD,
call upon his name;

make known his deeds among the nations,
proclaim that his name is exalted.

[5]"Sing praises to the LORD, for he has done
gloriously;
let this be known * in all the earth.
[6]Shout, and sing for joy, O inhabitant of Zion,
for great in your midst is the Holy One of
Israel."

An Oracle concerning Babylon

13 The oracle concerning Babylon which
Isai'ah the son of A'moz saw.
[2]On a bare hill raise a signal,
cry aloud to them;
wave the hand for them to enter
the gates of the nobles.
[3]I myself have commanded my consecrated
ones,
have summoned my mighty men to execute
my anger,
my proudly exulting ones.

[4]Listen, a tumult on the mountains
as of a great multitude!
Listen, an uproar of kingdoms,
of nations gathering together!
The LORD of hosts is mustering
a host for battle.
[5]They come from a distant land,
from the end of the heavens,
the LORD and the weapons of his indignation,
to destroy the whole earth.

[6]Wail, for the day of the LORD is near;
as destruction from the Almighty it will
come!
[7]Therefore all hands will be feeble,
and every man's heart will melt,
[8] and they will be dismayed.
Pangs and agony will seize them;
they will be in anguish like a woman with
labor pains.
They will look aghast at one another;
their faces will be aflame.

[9]Behold, the day of the LORD comes,
cruel, with wrath and fierce anger,
to make the earth a desolation
and to destroy its sinners from it.
[10]For the stars of the heavens and their
constellations
will not give their light;
the sun will be dark at its rising
and the moon will not shed its light.

---

* Or *this is made known.*
11:10: Is 11:1; Rom 15:12.
13:1–14:23: Is 47; Jer 50–51; Hab 1–2.
13:10: Mt 24:29; Mk 13:24; Rev 6:12; 8:12.

¹¹I will punish the world for its evil,
and the wicked for their iniquity;
I will put an end to the pride of the arrogant,
and lay low the haughtiness of the
ruthless.
¹²I will make men more rare than fine gold,
and mankind than the gold of O'phir.
¹³Therefore I will make the heavens tremble,
and the earth will be shaken out of its
place,
at the wrath of the LORD of hosts
in the day of his fierce anger.
¹⁴And like a hunted gazelle,
or like sheep with none to gather them,
every man will turn to his own people,
and every man will flee to his own land.
¹⁵Whoever is found will be thrust through,
and whoever is caught will fall by the
sword.
¹⁶Their infants will be dashed in pieces
before their eyes;
their houses will be plundered
and their wives ravished.

¹⁷Behold, I am stirring up the Medes against
them,
who have no regard for silver
and do not delight in gold.
¹⁸Their bows will slaughter the young men;
they will have no mercy on the fruit of the
womb;
their eyes will not pity children.
¹⁹And Babylon, the glory of kingdoms,
the splendor and pride of the Chalde'ans,
will be like Sodom and Gomor'rah
when God overthrew them.
²⁰It will never be inhabited
or dwelt in for all generations;
no Arab will pitch his tent there,
no shepherds will make their flocks lie
down there.
²¹But wild beasts will lie down there,
and its houses will be full of howling
creatures;
there ostriches will dwell,
and there satyrs will dance.
²²Hyenas will cry in its towers,
and jackals in the pleasant palaces;
its time is close at hand
and its days will not be prolonged.

Restoration of Israel

14 The LORD will have compassion on Jacob
and will again choose Israel, and will set
them in their own land, and strangers will join
them and will cling to the house of Jacob. ²And
the peoples will take them and bring them to
their place, and the house of Israel will possess
them in the LORD's land as male and female
slaves; they will take captive those who were

their captors, and rule over those who oppressed
them.

3 When the LORD has given you rest from your
pain and turmoil and the hard service with which
you were made to serve, ⁴you will take up this
taunt against the king of Babylon:
"How the oppressor has ceased,
the insolent fury ^y ceased!
⁵The LORD has broken the staff of the wicked,
the scepter of rulers,
⁶that struck the peoples in wrath
with unceasing blows,
that ruled the nations in anger
with unrelenting persecution.
⁷The whole earth is at rest and quiet;
they break forth into singing.
⁸The cypresses rejoice at you,
the cedars of Lebanon, saying,
'Since you were laid low,
no hewer comes up against us.'
⁹Sheol beneath is stirred up
to meet you when you come,
it rouses the shades to greet you,
all who were leaders of the earth;
it raises from their thrones
all who were kings of the nations.
¹⁰All of them will speak
and say to you:
'You too have become as weak as we!
You have become like us!'
¹¹Your pomp is brought down to Sheol,
the sound of your harps;
maggots are the bed beneath you,
and worms are your covering.

¹²"How you are fallen from heaven,
O Day Star, son of Dawn!
How you are cut down to the ground,
you who laid the nations low!
¹³You said in your heart,
'I will ascend to heaven;
above the stars of God
I will set my throne on high;
I will sit on the mount of assembly
in the far north;
¹⁴I will ascend above the heights of the clouds,
I will make myself like the Most High.'
¹⁵But you are brought down to Sheol,
to the depths of the Pit.
¹⁶Those who see you will stare at you,
and ponder over you:
'Is this the man who made the earth tremble,
who shook kingdoms,
¹⁷who made the world like a desert
and overthrew its cities,
who did not let his prisoners go home?'

---

^y One ancient Ms Compare Gk Syr Vg: The meaning of the Hebrew
word is uncertain.
13:21: Rev 18:2.

¹⁸All the kings of the nations lie in glory,
    each in his own tomb;
¹⁹but you are cast out, away from your sepulchre,
    like a loathed untimely birth,^z
clothed with the slain, those pierced by the sword,
    who go down to the stones of the Pit,
    like a dead body trodden under foot.
²⁰You will not be joined with them in burial,
    because you have destroyed your land,
    you have slain your people.

"May the descendants of evildoers
    nevermore be named!
²¹Prepare slaughter for his sons
    because of the guilt of their fathers,
lest they rise and possess the earth,
    and fill the face of the world with cities."

22 "I will rise up against them," says the LORD
of hosts, "and will cut off from Babylon name and
remnant, offspring and posterity, says the LORD.
²³And I will make it a possession of the hedgehog,
and pools of water, and I will sweep it with the
broom of destruction, says the LORD of hosts."

²⁴The LORD of hosts has sworn:
"As I have planned,
    so shall it be,
and as I have purposed,
    so shall it stand,
²⁵that I will break the Assyrian in my land,
    and upon my mountains trample him under
        foot;
and his yoke shall depart from them,
    and his burden from their shoulder."
²⁶This is the purpose that is purposed
    concerning the whole earth;
and this is the hand that is stretched out
    over all the nations.
²⁷For the LORD of hosts has purposed,
    and who will annul it?
His hand is stretched out,
    and who will turn it back?

²⁸In the year that King A'haz died came this
    oracle:
²⁹"Rejoice not, O Philis'tia, all of you,
    that the rod which struck you is broken,
for from the serpent's root will come forth an
        adder,
    and its fruit will be a flying serpent.
³⁰And the first-born of the poor will feed,
    and the needy lie down in safety;
but I will kill your root with famine,
    and your remnant I^a will slay.
³¹Wail, O gate; cry, O city;
    melt in fear, O Philis'tia, all of you!
For smoke comes out of the north,
    and there is no straggler in his ranks."

³²What will one answer the messengers of the
    nation?
"The LORD has founded Zion,
    and in her the afflicted of his people find
        refuge."

An Oracle concerning Moab

15 An oracle concerning Moab.
    Because Ar is laid waste in a night
Moab is undone;
because Kir is laid waste in a night
    Moab is undone.
²The daughter of Di'bon^b has gone up
    to the high places to weep;
over Nebo and over Med'eba
    Moab wails.
On every head is baldness,
    every beard is shorn;
³in the streets they put on sackcloth;
    on the housetops and in the squares
    every one wails and melts in tears.
⁴Heshbon and E''lea'leh cry out,
    their voice is heard as far as Ja'haz;
therefore the armed men of Moab cry aloud;
    his soul trembles.
⁵My heart cries out for Moab;
    his fugitives flee to Zoar,
    to Eg'lath-shelish'iyah.
For at the ascent of Lu'hith
    they go up weeping;
on the road to Horona'im
    they raise a cry of destruction;
⁶the waters of Nimrim
    are a desolation;
the grass is withered, the new growth fails,
    the verdure is no more.
⁷Therefore the abundance they have gained
    and what they have laid up
they carry away
    over the Brook of the Willows.
⁸For a cry has gone
    round the land of Moab;
the wailing reaches to Egla'im,
    the wailing reaches to Be'er-e'lim.
⁹For the waters of Di'bon^c are full of blood;
    yet I will bring upon Dibon^c even more,
a lion for those of Moab who escape,
    for the remnant of the land.

16 They have sent lambs
    to the ruler of the land,
from Se'la, by way of the desert,
    to the mount of the daughter of Zion.

---

^z Cn Compare Tg Symmachus: Heb *a loathed branch.*
^a One ancient Ms Vg: Heb *he.*
^b Cn: Heb *the house and Dibon.*
^c One ancient Ms Vg Compare Syr: Heb *Dimon.*
14:29–31: Jer 47; Ezek 25:15–17; Joel 3:4–8; Amos 1:6–8; Zeph 2:4–
7; Zech 9:5–7.
15–16: Is 25:10–12; Jer 48; Ezek 25:8–11; Amos 2:1–3; Zeph 2:8–11.

²Like fluttering birds,
    like scattered nestlings,
so are the daughters of Moab
    at the fords of the Arnon.
³"Give counsel,
    grant justice;
make your shade like night
    at the height of noon;
hide the outcasts,
    betray not the fugitive;
⁴let the outcasts of Moab
    sojourn among you;
be a refuge to them
    from the destroyer.
When the oppressor is no more,
    and destruction has ceased,
and he who tramples under foot
    has vanished from the land,
⁵then a throne will be established in steadfast
    love
    and on it will sit in faithfulness
    in the tent of David
one who judges and seeks justice
    and is swift to do righteousness."

⁶We have heard of the pride of Moab,
    how proud he was;
of his arrogance, his pride, and his insolence—
    his boasts are false.
⁷Therefore let Moab wail,
    let every one wail for Moab.
Mourn, utterly stricken,
    for the raisin-cakes of Kir′-har′eseth.

⁸For the fields of Heshbon languish,
    and the vine of Sibmah;
the lords of the nations
    have struck down its branches,
which reached to Ja′zer
    and strayed to the desert;
its shoots spread abroad
    and passed over the sea.
⁹Therefore I weep with the weeping of Ja′zer
    for the vine of Sibmah;
I drench you with my tears,
    O Heshbon and E″lea′leh;
for upon your fruit and your harvest
    the battle shout has fallen.
¹⁰And joy and gladness are taken away
    from the fruitful field;
and in the vineyards no songs are sung,
    no shouts are raised;
no treader treads out wine in the presses;
    the vintage shout is hushed. ᵈ
¹¹Therefore my soul moans like a lyre for Moab,
    and my heart for Kirhe′res.

12 And when Moab presents himself, when he
wearies himself upon the high place, when he
comes to his sanctuary to pray, he will not prevail.

13 This is the word which the LORD spoke concerning Moab in the past. ¹⁴But now the LORD
says, "In three years, like the years of a hireling,
the glory of Moab will be brought into contempt,
in spite of all his great multitude, and those who
survive will be very few and feeble."

An Oracle concerning Damascus

17 An oracle concerning Damascus.
    Behold, Damascus will cease to be a city,
    and will become a heap of ruins.
²Her cities will be deserted for ever; ᵉ
    they will be for flocks,
    which will lie down, and none will make
        them afraid.
³The fortress will disappear from E′phraim,
    and the kingdom from Damascus;
and the remnant of Syria will be
    like the glory of the children of Israel, says
    the LORD of hosts.

⁴And in that day
    the glory of Jacob will be brought low,
    and the fat of his flesh will grow lean.
⁵And it shall be as when the reaper gathers
    standing grain
    and his arm harvests the ears,
and as when one gleans the ears of grain
    in the Valley of Reph′aim.
⁶Gleanings will be left in it,
    as when an olive tree is beaten—
two or three berries
    in the top of the highest bough,
four or five
    on the branches of a fruit tree,
        says the LORD God of Israel.

7 In that day men will regard their Maker, and
their eyes will look to the Holy One of Israel; ⁸they
will not have regard for the altars, the work of
their hands, and they will not look to what their
own fingers have made, either the Ashe′rim or the
altars of incense.

9 In that day their strong cities will be like
the deserted places of the Hi′vites and the Am′o-
rites, ᶠ which they deserted because of the children of Israel, and there will be desolation.

¹⁰For you have forgotten the God of your salvation,
    and have not remembered the Rock of your
        refuge;
therefore, though you plant pleasant plants
    and set out slips of an alien god,
¹¹though you make them grow on the day that
    you plant them,
    and make them blossom in the morning that
    you sow;

ᵈ Gk: Heb *I have hushed.*
ᵉ Cn Compare Gk: Heb *the cities of Aroer are deserted.*
ᶠ Cn Compare Gk: Heb *the wood and the highest bough.*
17:1–3: Jer 49:23–27; Amos 1:3–5; Zech 9:1.

yet the harvest will flee away
   in a day of grief and incurable pain.

[12]Ah, the thunder of many peoples,
   they thunder like the thundering of the sea!
Ah, the roar of nations,
   they roar like the roaring of mighty waters!
[13]The nations roar like the roaring of many
   waters,
   but he will rebuke them, and they will flee
     far away,
chased like chaff on the mountains before the
   wind
   and whirling dust before the storm.
[14]At evening time, behold, terror!
   Before morning, they are no more!
This is the portion of those who despoil us,
   and the lot of those who plunder us.

18

Ah, land of whirring wings
   which is beyond the rivers of Ethiopia;
[2]which sends ambassadors by the Nile,
   in vessels of papyrus upon the waters!
Go, you swift messengers,
   to a nation, tall and smooth,
to a people feared near and far,
   a nation mighty and conquering,
   whose land the rivers divide.

[3]All you inhabitants of the world,
   you who dwell on the earth,
when a signal is raised on the mountains,
   look!
   When a trumpet is blown, hear!
[4]For thus the Lord said to me:
"I will quietly look from my dwelling
   like clear heat in sunshine,
   like a cloud of dew in the heat of harvest."
[5]For before the harvest, when the blossom is
   over,
   and the flower becomes a ripening grape,
he will cut off the shoots with pruning hooks,
   and the spreading branches he will hew
     away.
[6]They shall all of them be left
   to the birds of prey of the mountains
   and to the beasts of the earth.
And the birds of prey will summer upon them,
   and all the beasts of the earth will winter
     upon them.

7 At that time gifts will be brought to the Lord
of hosts
   from a people tall and smooth,
   from a people feared near and far,
   a nation mighty and conquering,
   whose land the rivers divide,
to Mount Zion, the place of the name of the Lord
of hosts.

An Oracle concerning Egypt

19

An oracle concerning Egypt.
   Behold, the Lord is riding on a swift
   cloud
   and comes to Egypt;
and the idols of Egypt will tremble at his
   presence,
   and the heart of the Egyptians will melt
     within them.
[2]And I will stir up Egyptians against
   Egyptians,
   and they will fight, every man against his
     brother
   and every man against his neighbor,
   city against city, kingdom against kingdom;
[3]and the spirit of the Egyptians within them
   will be emptied out,
   and I will confound their plans;
and they will consult the idols and the
   sorcerers,
   and the mediums and the wizards;
[4]and I will give over the Egyptians
   into the hand of a hard master;
and a fierce king will rule over them,
   says the Lord, the Lord of hosts.

[5]And the waters of the Nile will be dried up,
   and the river will be parched and dry;
[6]and its canals will become foul,
   and the branches of Egypt's Nile will
     diminish and dry up,
   reeds and rushes will rot away.
[7]There will be bare places by the Nile,
   on the brink of the Nile,
and all that is sown by the Nile will dry up,
   be driven away, and be no more.
[8]The fishermen will mourn and lament,
   all who cast hook in the Nile;
and they will languish
   who spread nets upon the water.
[9]The workers in combed flax will be in despair,
   and the weavers of white cotton.
[10]Those who are the pillars of the land will be
   crushed,
   and all who work for hire will be grieved.

[11]The princes of Zoan are utterly foolish;
   the wise counselors of Pharaoh give stupid
     counsel.
How can you say to Pharaoh,
   "I am a son of the wise,
   a son of ancient kings"?
[12]Where then are your wise men?
   Let them tell you and make known
   what the Lord of hosts has purposed
     against Egypt.

18: Zeph 2:12.
19: Jer 46; Ezek 29–32; Zech 14:18–19.

¹³The princes of Zoan have become fools,
and the princes of Memphis are deluded;
those who are the cornerstones of her tribes
have led Egypt astray.
¹⁴The LORD has mingled within her a spirit of
confusion;
and they have made Egypt stagger in all her
doings
as a drunken man staggers in his vomit.
¹⁵And there will be nothing for Egypt
which head or tail, palm branch or reed,
may do.

16 In that day the Egyptians will be like
women, and tremble with fear before the hand
which the LORD of hosts shakes over them. ¹⁷And
the land of Judah will become a terror to the
Egyptians; every one to whom it is mentioned
will fear because of the purpose which the LORD
of hosts has purposed against them.

18 In that day there will be five cities in the
land of Egypt which speak the language of
Canaan and swear allegiance to the LORD of hosts.
One of these will be called the City of the Sun.

19 In that day there will be an altar to the LORD
in the midst of the land of Egypt, and a pillar to
the LORD at its border. ²⁰It will be a sign and a
witness to the LORD of hosts in the land of Egypt;
when they cry to the LORD because of oppressors
he will send them a savior, and will defend and
deliver them. ²¹And the LORD will make himself
known to the Egyptians; and the Egyptians will
know the LORD in that day and worship with sacrifice and burnt offering, and they will make vows
to the LORD and perform them. ²²And the LORD
will strike Egypt, striking and healing, and they
will return to the LORD, and he will heed their
supplications and heal them.

23 In that day there will be a highway from
Egypt to Assyria, and the Assyrian will come
into Egypt, and the Egyptian into Assyria, and
the Egyptians will worship with the Assyrians.

24 In that day Israel will be the third with
Egypt and Assyria, a blessing in the midst of the
earth, ²⁵whom the LORD of hosts has blessed, saying, "Blessed be Egypt my people, and Assyria
the work of my hands, and Israel my heritage."

The Conquest of Egypt and Ethiopia

20 In the year that the commander in chief,
who was sent by Sargon the king of
Assyria, came to Ash'dod and fought against it
and took it,—²at that time the LORD had spoken by
Isai'ah the son of A'moz, saying, "Go, and loose
the sackcloth from your loins and take off your
shoes from your feet," and he had done so, walking naked and barefoot—³the LORD said, "As my
servant Isai'ah has walked naked and barefoot for
three years as a sign and a portent against Egypt
and Ethiopia, ⁴so shall the king of Assyria lead

away the Egyptians captives and the Ethiopians
exiles, both the young and old, naked and barefoot, with buttocks uncovered, to the shame of
Egypt. ⁵Then they shall be dismayed and confounded because of Ethiopia their hope and of
Egypt their boast. ⁶And the inhabitants of this
coastland will say in that day, 'Behold, this is what
has happened to those in whom we hoped and to
whom we fled for help to be delivered from the
king of Assyria! And we, how shall we escape?' "

Oracles concerning Babylon, Edom, and Arabia

21 The oracle concerning the wilderness of
the sea.
As whirlwinds in the Neg'eb sweep on,
it comes from the desert,
from a terrible land.
²A stern vision is told to me;
the plunderer plunders,
and the destroyer destroys.
Go up, O E'lam,
lay siege, O Med'ia;
all the sighing she has caused
I bring to an end.
³Therefore my loins are filled with anguish;
pangs have seized me,
like the pangs of a woman with labor pains;
I am bowed down so that I cannot hear,
I am dismayed so that I cannot see.
⁴My mind reels, horror has appalled me;
the twilight I longed for
has been turned for me into trembling.
⁵They prepare the table,
they spread the rugs,
they eat, they drink.
Arise, O princes,
oil the shield!
⁶For thus the Lord said to me:
"Go, set a watchman,
let him announce what he sees.
⁷When he sees riders, horsemen in pairs,
riders on donkeys, riders on camels,
let him listen diligently,
very diligently."
⁸Then he who saw ᵍ cried:
"Upon a watchtower I stand, O LORD,
continually by day,
and at my post I am stationed whole nights.
⁹And, behold, here come riders,
horsemen in pairs!"
And he answered,
"Fallen, fallen is Babylon;
and all the images of her gods
he has shattered to the ground."
¹⁰O my threshed and winnowed one,
what I have heard from the LORD of hosts,
the God of Israel, I announce to you.

ᵍ One ancient Ms: Heb *a lion.*

[11]The oracle concerning Du'mah.

One is calling to me from Se'ir,
"Watchman, what of the night?
Watchman, what of the night?"
[12]The watchman says:
"Morning comes, and also the night.
If you will inquire, inquire;
come back again."

[13]The oracle concerning Arabia.

In the thickets in Arabia you will lodge,
O caravans of De'danites.
[14]To the thirsty bring water,
meet the fugitive with bread,
O inhabitants of the land of Te'ma.
[15]For they have fled from the swords,
from the drawn sword,
from the bent bow,
and from the press of battle.

16 For thus the Lord said to me, "Within a year, according to the years of a hireling, all the glory of Ke'dar will come to an end; [17]and the remainder of the archers of the mighty men of the sons of Ke'dar will be few; for the LORD, the God of Israel, has spoken."

An Oracle concerning the Valley of Vision

22 The oracle concerning the valley of vision.

What do you mean that you have gone up,
all of you, to the housetops,
[2]you who are full of shoutings,
tumultuous city, exultant town?
Your slain are not slain with the sword
or dead in battle.
[3]All your rulers have fled together,
without the bow they were captured.
All of you who were found were captured,
though they had fled far away. [h]
[4]Therefore I said:
"Look away from me,
let me weep bitter tears;
do not labor to comfort me
for the destruction of the daughter of my
people."

[5]For the Lord GOD of hosts has a day
of tumult and trampling and confusion
in the valley of vision,
a battering down of walls
and a shouting to the mountains.
[6]And E'lam bore the quiver
with chariots and horsemen, [i]
and Kir uncovered the shield.
[7]Your choicest valleys were full of chariots,
and the horsemen took their stand at the
gates.
[8]He has taken away the covering of Judah.

In that day you looked to the weapons of the House of the Forest, [9]and you saw that the breaches of the city of David were many, and you collected the waters of the lower pool, [10]and you counted the houses of Jerusalem, and you broke down the houses to fortify the wall. [11]You made a reservoir between the two walls for the water of the old pool. But you did not look to him who did it, or have regard for him who planned it long ago.

[12]In that day the Lord GOD of hosts
called to weeping and mourning,
to baldness and putting on of sackcloth;
[13]and behold, joy and gladness,
slaying oxen and killing sheep,
eating flesh and drinking wine.
"Let us eat and drink,
for tomorrow we die."
[14]The LORD of hosts has revealed himself in my
ears:
"Surely this iniquity will not be forgiven you
till you die,"
says the Lord GOD of hosts.

Denunciation of Self-Seeking Officials

15 Thus says the Lord GOD of hosts, "Come, go to this steward, to Shebna, who is over the household, and say to him: [16]What have you to do here and whom have you here, that you have hewn here a tomb for yourself, you who hew a tomb on the height, and carve a habitation for yourself in the rock? [17]Behold, the LORD will hurl you away violently, O you strong man. He will seize firm hold on you, [18]and whirl you round and round, and throw you like a ball into a wide land; there you shall die, and there shall be your splendid chariots, you shame of your master's house. [19]I will thrust you from your office, and you will be cast down from your station. [20]In that day I will call my servant Eli'akim the son of Hilki'ah, [21]and I will clothe him with your robe, and will bind your belt on him, and will commit your authority to his hand; and he shall be a father to the inhabitants of Jerusalem and to the house of Judah. [22]And I will place on his shoulder the key of the house of David; he shall open, and none shall shut; and he shall shut, and none shall open. [23]And I will fasten him like a peg in a sure place, and he will become a throne of honor to his father's house. [24]And they will hang on him the whole weight of his father's house, the offspring and issue, every small vessel, from the cups to all the flagons. [25]In that day, says the LORD of hosts, the peg that was fastened in a sure place will give way; and it will be cut down and fall, and the burden that was upon it will be cut off, for the LORD has spoken."

---

[h] Gk Syr Vg: Heb *from far away.*
[i] The Hebrew of this line is obscure.
22:22: Rev 3:7.

An Oracle concerning Tyre

23 The oracle concerning Tyre.

Wail, O ships of Tar'shish,
for Tyre is laid waste, without house or
haven!
From the land of Cyprus
it is revealed to them.
²Be still, O inhabitants of the coast,
O merchants of Si'don;
your messengers passed over the sea ʲ
³ and were on many waters;
your revenue was the grain of Shihor,
the harvest of the Nile;
you were the merchant of the nations.
⁴Be ashamed, O Si'don, for the sea has spoken,
the stronghold of the sea, saying:
"I have neither endured labor pains nor given
birth,
I have neither reared young men nor
brought up virgins."
⁵When the report comes to Egypt,
they will be in anguish over the report
about Tyre.
⁶Pass over to Tar'shish,
wail, O inhabitants of the coast!
⁷Is this your exultant city
whose origin is from days of old,
whose feet carried her
to settle afar?
⁸Who has purposed this
against Tyre, the bestower of crowns,
whose merchants were princes,
whose traders were the honored of the
earth?
⁹The LORD of hosts has purposed it,
to defile the pride of all glory,
to dishonor all the honored of the earth.
¹⁰Overflow your land like the Nile,
O daughter of Tar'shish;
there is no restraint any more.
¹¹He has stretched out his hand over the sea,
he has shaken the kingdoms;
the LORD has given command concerning
Canaan
to destroy its strongholds.
¹²And he said:
"You will no more exult,
O oppressed virgin daughter of Si'don;
arise, pass over to Cyprus,
even there you will have no rest."

13 Behold the land of the Chalde'ans! This is
the people; it was not Assyria. They destined Tyre
for wild beasts. They erected their siege towers,
they razed her palaces, they made her a ruin.ᵏ
¹⁴Wail, O ships of Tar'shish,
for your stronghold is laid waste.
¹⁵In that day Tyre will be forgotten for seventy
years, like the days of one king. At the end of

seventy years, it will happen to Tyre as in the
song of the harlot:
¹⁶"Take a harp,
go about the city,
O forgotten harlot!
Make sweet melody,
sing many songs,
that you may be remembered."
¹⁷At the end of seventy years, the LORD will visit
Tyre, and she will return to her hire, and will play
the harlot with all the kingdoms of the world
upon the face of the earth. ¹⁸Her merchandise and
her hire will be dedicated to the LORD; it will not
be stored or hoarded, but her merchandise will
supply abundant food and fine clothing for those
who dwell before the LORD.

Impending Judgment on the Earth

24 Behold, the LORD will lay waste the earth
and make it desolate,
and he will twist its surface and scatter its
inhabitants.
²And it shall be, as with the people, so with the
priest;
as with the slave, so with his master;
as with the maid, so with her mistress;
as with the buyer, so with the seller;
as with the lender, so with the borrower;
as with the creditor, so with the debtor.
³The earth shall be utterly laid waste and
utterly despoiled;
for the LORD has spoken this word.
⁴The earth mourns and withers,
the world languishes and withers;
the heavens languish together with the earth.
⁵The earth lies polluted
under its inhabitants;
for they have transgressed the laws,
violated the statutes,
broken the everlasting covenant.
⁶Therefore a curse devours the earth,
and its inhabitants suffer for their guilt;
therefore the inhabitants of the earth are
scorched,
and few men are left.
⁷The wine mourns,
the vine languishes,
all the merry-hearted sigh.
⁸The mirth of the timbrels is stilled,
the noise of the jubilant has ceased,
the mirth of the lyre is stilled.
⁹No more do they drink wine with singing;
strong drink is bitter to those who drink it.
¹⁰The city of chaos is broken down,
every house is shut up so that none can
enter.

ʲ One ancient Ms: Heb *who passed over the sea, they replenished you.*
ᵏ The Hebrew of this verse is obscure.
23: Ezek 26:1—28:19; Joel 3:4–8; Amos 1:9–10; Zech 9:3–4.
23:17: Rev 17:2.
24:8: Rev 18:22.

¹¹There is an outcry in the streets for lack of
  wine;
    all joy has reached its eventide;
    the gladness of the earth is banished.
¹²Desolation is left in the city,
    the gates are battered into ruins.
¹³For thus it shall be in the midst of the earth
    among the nations,
  as when an olive tree is beaten,
    as at the gleaning when the vintage is done.

¹⁴They lift up their voices, they sing for joy;
    over the majesty of the LORD they shout
      from the west.
¹⁵Therefore in the east give glory to the LORD;
    in the islands of the sea, to the name of the
      LORD, the God of Israel.
¹⁶From the ends of the earth we hear songs of
    praise,
    of glory to the Righteous One.
But I say, "I pine away,
  I pine away. Woe is me!
For the treacherous deal treacherously,
    the treacherous deal very treacherously."
¹⁷Terror, and the pit, and the snare are upon you,
    O inhabitant of the earth!
¹⁸He who flees at the sound of the terror
    shall fall into the pit;
  and he who climbs out of the pit shall be
    caught in the snare.
For the windows of heaven are opened,
    and the foundations of the earth tremble.
¹⁹The earth is utterly broken,
    the earth is torn apart,
    the earth is violently shaken.
²⁰The earth staggers like a drunken man,
    it sways like a hut;
  its transgression lies heavy upon it,
    and it falls, and will not rise again.

²¹On that day the LORD will punish
    the host of heaven, in heaven,
    and the kings of the earth, on the earth.
²²They will be gathered together
    as prisoners in a pit;
  they will be shut up in a prison,
    and after many days they will be punished.
²³Then the moon will be confounded,
    and the sun ashamed;
  for the LORD of hosts will reign
    on Mount Zion and in Jerusalem
  and before his elders he will manifest his glory.

Praise for Deliverance from Oppression

25 O LORD, you are my God;
    I will exalt you, I will praise your name;
  for you have done wonderful things,
    plans formed of old, faithful and sure.
²For you have made the city a heap,
    the fortified city a ruin;

the palace of strangers is a city no more,
    it will never be rebuilt.
³Therefore strong peoples will glorify you;
    cities of ruthless nations will fear you.
⁴For you have been a stronghold to the poor,
    a stronghold to the needy in his distress,
    a shelter from the storm and a shade from
      the heat;
  for the blast of the ruthless is like a storm
    against a wall,
⁵ like heat in a dry place.
You subdue the noise of the strangers;
    as heat by the shade of a cloud,
    so the song of the ruthless is stilled.

6 On this mountain the LORD of hosts will
make for all peoples a feast of fat things, a feast
of choice wines—of fat things full of marrow, of
choice wines well refined. ⁷And he will destroy on
this mountain the covering that is cast over all
peoples, the veil that is spread over all nations.
⁸He will swallow up death for ever, and the Lord
GOD will wipe away tears from all faces, and the
reproach of his people he will take away from all
the earth, for the LORD has spoken.

9 It will be said on that day, "Behold, this is our
God; we have waited for him, that he might save
us. This is the LORD; we have waited for him; let
us be glad and rejoice in his salvation."

10 For the hand of the LORD will rest on this
mountain, and Moab shall be trodden down in his
place, as straw is trodden down in a dung-pit.
¹¹And he will spread out his hands in the midst of
it as a swimmer spreads his hands out to swim;
but the LORD will lay low his pride together with
the skill¹ of his hands. ¹²And the high fortifications of his walls he will bring down, lay low, and
cast to the ground, even to the dust.

Judah's Song of Praise to God

26 In that day this song will be sung in the
    land of Judah:
  "We have a strong city;
    he sets up salvation
      as walls and bulwarks.
²Open the gates,
    that the righteous nation which keeps faith
      may enter in.
³You keep him in perfect peace,
    whose mind is stayed on you,
    because he trusts in you.
⁴Trust in the LORD for ever,
    for the LORD GOD
    is an everlasting rock.
⁵For he has brought low
    the inhabitants of the height,
    the lofty city.

---

¹ The meaning of the Hebrew word is uncertain.
25:8: 1 Cor 15:54; Rev 7:17; 21:4.
25:10–12: Is 15–16; Jer 48; Ezek 25:8–11; Amos 2:1–3; Zeph 2:8–11.

He lays it low, lays it low to the ground,
    casts it to the dust.
[6]The foot tramples it,
    the feet of the poor,
    the steps of the needy."

[7]The way of the righteous is level;
    you[m] make smooth the path of the
      righteous.
[8]In the path of your judgments,
    O Lord, we wait for you;
    your memorial name
      is the desire of our soul.
[9]My soul yearns for you in the night,
    my spirit within me earnestly seeks you.
For when your judgments are in the earth,
    the inhabitants of the world learn
      righteousness.
[10]If favor is shown to the wicked,
    he does not learn righteousness;
in the land of uprightness he deals perversely
    and does not see the majesty of the Lord.
[11]O Lord, your hand is lifted up,
    but they see it not.
Let them see your zeal for your people, and be
      ashamed.
    Let the fire for your adversaries consume
      them.
[12]O Lord, you will ordain peace for us,
    you have wrought for us all our works.
[13]O Lord our God,
    other lords besides you have ruled over us,
    but your name alone we acknowledge.
[14]They are dead, they will not live;
    they are shades, they will not arise;
to that end you have visited them with
      destruction
    and wiped out all remembrance of them.
[15]But you have increased the nation, O Lord,
    you have increased the nation; you are
      glorified;
    you have enlarged all the borders of the
      land.

[16]O Lord, in distress they sought you,
    they poured out a prayer[n]
    when your chastening was upon them.
[17]Like a woman with child,
    who writhes and cries out in her pangs,
    when she is near her time,
so were we because of you, O Lord;
[18]   we were with child, we writhed,
    but we gave birth only to wind.
We have wrought no deliverance in the earth,
    and the inhabitants of the world have not
      fallen.
[19]Your dead shall live, their bodies[o] shall rise.
    O dwellers in the dust, awake and sing for
      joy!

For your dew is a dew of light,
    and on the land of the shades you will let it
      fall.

[20]Come, my people, enter your chambers,
    and shut your doors behind you;
hide yourselves for a little while
    until the wrath is past.
[21]For behold, the Lord is coming forth out of his
      place
    to punish the inhabitants of the earth for
      their iniquity,
and the earth will disclose the blood shed upon
      her,
    and will no more cover her slain.

Israel's Expiation

27 In that day the Lord with his hard and
great and strong sword will punish Levi'a-
than the fleeing serpent, Leviathan the twisting
serpent, and he will slay the dragon that is in
the sea.

[2]In that day:
"A pleasant vineyard, sing of it!
[3]   I, the Lord, am its keeper;
    every moment I water it.
Lest any one harm it,
    I guard it night and day;
[4]   I have no wrath.
Would that I had thorns and briers to battle!
    I would set out against them,
    I would burn them up together.
[5]Or let them lay hold of my protection,
    let them make peace with me,
    let them make peace with me."

[6]In days to come[q] Jacob shall take root,
    Israel shall blossom and put forth shoots,
    and fill the whole world with fruit.

[7]Has he struck them down as he struck those
      who struck them?
    Or have they been slain as their slayers
      were slain?
[8]Measure by measure,[r] by exile you contended
      with them;
he removed them with his fierce blast in the
      day of the east wind.
[9]Therefore by this the guilt of Jacob will be
      expiated,
    and this will be the full fruit of the removal
      of his sin:
when he makes all the stones of the altars
    like chalkstones crushed to pieces,
    no Ashe'rim or incense altars will remain
      standing.

---

[m] Cn Compare Gk: Heb *thou (that art) upright.*
[n] Heb uncertain.
[o] Cn Compare Syr Tg: Heb *my body.*
[q] Heb *Those to come.*
[r] Compare Syr Vg Tg: The meaning of the Hebrew word is unknown.

¹⁰For the fortified city is solitary,
a habitation deserted and forsaken, like the
wilderness;
there the calf grazes,
there he lies down, and strips its branches.
¹¹When its boughs are dry, they are broken;
women come and make a fire of them.
For this is a people without discernment;
therefore he who made them will not have
compassion on them,
he that formed them will show them no
favor.

¹²In that day from the river Euphra′tes to the
Brook of Egypt the LORD will thresh out the grain,
and you will be gathered one by one, O people of
Israel. ¹³And in that day a great trumpet will be
blown, and those who were lost in the land of
Assyria and those who were driven out to the
land of Egypt will come and worship the LORD on
the holy mountain at Jerusalem.

Warning to Jerusalem

28 Woe to the proud crown of the drunkards
of E′phraim,
and to the fading flower of its glorious
beauty,
which is on the head of the rich valley of
those overcome with wine!
²Behold, the Lord has one who is mighty and
strong;
like a storm of hail, a destroying tempest,
like a storm of mighty, overflowing waters,
he will cast down to the earth with violence.
³The proud crown of the drunkards of
E′phraim
will be trodden under foot;
⁴and the fading flower of its glorious beauty,
which is on the head of the rich valley,
will be like a first-ripe fig before the summer:
when a man sees it, he eats it up
as soon as it is in his hand.

⁵In that day the LORD of hosts will be a crown
of glory,
and a diadem of beauty, to the remnant of
his people;
⁶and a spirit of justice to him who sits in
judgment,
and strength to those who turn back the
battle at the gate.

⁷These also reel with wine
and stagger with strong drink;
the priest and the prophet reel with strong
drink,
they are confused with wine,
they stagger with strong drink;
they err in vision,
they stumble in giving judgment.

⁸For all tables are full of vomit,
no place is without filthiness.

⁹"Whom will he teach knowledge,
and to whom will he explain the message?
Those who are weaned from the milk,
those taken from the breast?
¹⁰For it is precept upon precept, precept upon
precept,
line upon line, line upon line,
here a little, there a little."

¹¹No, but by men of strange lips
and with an alien tongue
the LORD will speak to this people,
¹²   to whom he has said,
"This is rest;
give rest to the weary;
and this is repose";
yet they would not hear.
¹³Therefore the word of the LORD will be to them
precept upon precept, precept upon precept,
line upon line, line upon line,
here a little, there a little;
that they may go, and fall backward,
and be broken, and snared, and taken.

¹⁴Therefore hear the word of the LORD, you
scoffers,
who rule this people in Jerusalem!
¹⁵Because you have said, "We have made a
covenant with death,
and with Sheol we have an agreement;
when the overwhelming scourge passes
through
it will not come to us;
for we have made lies our refuge,
and in falsehood we have taken shelter";
¹⁶therefore thus says the Lord GOD,
"Behold, I am laying in Zion for a foundation
a stone, a tested stone,
a precious cornerstone, of a sure
foundation:
'He who believes will not be in haste.'
¹⁷And I will make justice the line,
and righteousness the plummet;
and hail will sweep away the refuge of lies,
and waters will overwhelm the shelter."
¹⁸Then your covenant with death will be
annulled,
and your agreement with Sheol will not
stand;
when the overwhelming scourge passes
through
you will be beaten down by it.

27:13: Mt 24:31; 1 Cor 15:52; 1 Thess 4:16.
28:11-12: 1 Cor 14:21.
28:12: Mt 11:29.
28:16: Rom 9:33; 10:11; 1 Pet 2:4–6.

¹⁹As often as it passes through it will take you;
    for morning by morning it will pass
        through,
    by day and by night;
  and it will be sheer terror to understand the
      message.
²⁰For the bed is too short to stretch oneself on it,
    and the covering too narrow to wrap
      oneself in it.
²¹For the Lord will rise up as on Mount Pera′zim,
    he will rage as in the valley of Gib′eon;
  to do his deed—strange is his deed!
    and to work his work—alien is his work!
²²Now therefore do not scoff,
    lest your bonds be made strong;
  for I have heard a decree of destruction
    from the Lord God of hosts upon the whole
      land.

²³Give ear, and hear my voice;
    listen, and hear my speech.
²⁴Does he who plows for sowing plow
      continually?
    does he continually open and harrow his
      ground?
²⁵When he has leveled its surface,
    does he not scatter dill, sow cummin,
  and put in wheat in rows
    and barley in its proper place,
    and spelt as the border?
²⁶For he is instructed rightly;
    his God teaches him.

²⁷Dill is not threshed with a threshing sledge,
    nor is a cart wheel rolled over cummin;
  but dill is beaten out with a stick,
    and cummin with a rod.
²⁸Does one crush bread grain?
    No, he does not thresh it for ever;
  when he drives his cart wheel over it
    with his horses, he does not crush it.
²⁹This also comes from the Lord of hosts;
    he is wonderful in counsel,
    and excellent in wisdom.

The Siege of Jerusalem

29 Ho Ar′iel, Ariel,
    the city where David encamped!
Add year to year;
    let the feasts run their round.
²Yet I will distress Ar′iel,
    and there shall be moaning and
      lamentation,
  and she shall be to me like an Ariel.
³And I will encamp against you round about,
    and will besiege you with towers
    and I will raise siegeworks against you.
⁴Then deep from the earth you shall speak,
    from low in the dust your words shall
      come;

your voice shall come from the ground like the
    voice of a ghost,
    and your speech shall whisper out of the
      dust.

⁵But the multitude of your foes ˢ shall be like
    small dust,
    and the multitude of the ruthless like
      passing chaff.
And in an instant, suddenly,
⁶ you will be visited by the Lord of hosts
with thunder and with earthquake and great
    noise,
    with whirlwind and tempest, and the flame
      of a devouring fire.
⁷And the multitude of all the nations that fight
    against Ar′iel,
    all that fight against her and her stronghold
      and distress her,
    shall be like a dream, a vision of the night.
⁸As when a hungry man dreams he is eating
    and awakes with his hunger not satisfied,
  or as when a thirsty man dreams he is drinking
    and awakes faint, with his thirst not
      quenched,
  so shall the multitude of all the nations be
    that fight against Mount Zion.

⁹Stupefy yourselves and be in a stupor,
    blind yourselves and be blind!
Be drunk, but not with wine;
    stagger, but not with strong drink!
¹⁰For the Lord has poured out upon you
    a spirit of deep sleep,
  and has closed your eyes, the prophets,
    and covered your heads, the seers.

11 And the vision of all this has become to you like the words of a book that is sealed. When men give it to one who can read, saying, "Read this," he says, "I cannot, for it is sealed." ¹²And when they give the book to one who cannot read, saying, "Read this," he says, "I cannot read."

¹³And the Lord said:
"Because this people draw near with their
    mouth
    and honor me with their lips,
    while their hearts are far from me,
  and their fear of me is a commandment of men
    learned by rote;
¹⁴therefore, behold, I will again
    do marvelous things with this people,
    wonderful and marvelous;
  and the wisdom of their wise men shall perish,
    and the discernment of their discerning
      men shall be hidden."

ˢ Cn: Heb *strangers*.
29:13: Mt 15:8–9; Mk 7:6–7.
29:14: 1 Cor 1:19.

[15]Woe to those who hide deep from the LORD
    their counsel,
  whose deeds are in the dark,
  and who say, "Who sees us? Who knows
    us?"
[16]You turn things upside down!
  Shall the potter be regarded as the clay;
that the thing made should say of its maker,
  "He did not make me";
or the thing formed say of him who formed it,
  "He has no understanding"?

[17]Is it not yet a very little while
  until Lebanon shall be turned into a fruitful
    field,
  and the fruitful field shall be regarded as a
    forest?
[18]In that day the deaf shall hear the words of a
    book,
  and out of their gloom and darkness
  the eyes of the blind shall see.
[19]The meek shall obtain fresh joy in the LORD,
  and the poor among men shall exult in the
    Holy One of Israel.
[20]For the ruthless shall come to nothing and the
    scoffer cease,
  and all who watch to do evil shall be cut off,
[21]who by a word make a man out to be an
    offender,
  and lay a snare for him who reproves in the
    gate,
  and with an empty plea turn aside him who
    is in the right.

Hope for the Future

22 Therefore thus says the LORD, who redeemed Abraham, concerning the house of Jacob:
"Jacob shall no more be ashamed,
  no more shall his face grow pale.
[23]For when he sees his children,
  the work of my hands, in his midst,
  they will sanctify my name;
they will sanctify the Holy One of Jacob,
  and will stand in awe of the God of Israel.
[24]And those who err in spirit will come to
    understanding,
  and those who murmur will accept
    instruction."

A Rebellious People

30 "Woe to the rebellious children," says the
    LORD,
  "who carry out a plan, but not mine;
and who make a league, but not of my spirit,
  that they may add sin to sin;
[2]who set out to go down to Egypt,
  without asking for my counsel,
to take refuge in the protection of Pharaoh,
  and to seek shelter in the shadow of Egypt!
[3]Therefore the protection of Pharaoh shall turn
  to your shame,

and the shelter in the shadow of Egypt to
  your humiliation.
[4]For though his officials are at Zoan
  and his envoys reach Han'es,
[5]every one comes to shame
  through a people that cannot profit them,
that brings neither help nor profit,
  but shame and disgrace."

[6]An oracle on the beasts of the Neg'eb.
Through a land of trouble and anguish,
  from where come the lioness and the lion,
  the viper and the flying serpent,
they carry their riches on the backs of
    donkeys,
  and their treasures on the humps of camels,
  to a people that cannot profit them.
[7]For Egypt's help is worthless and empty,
  therefore I have called her
  "Ra'hab who sits still."

[8]And now, go, write it before them on a tablet,
  and inscribe it in a book,
that it may be for the time to come as a witness
  for ever.
[9]For they are a rebellious people,
  lying sons,
sons who will not hear
  the instruction of the LORD;
[10]who say to the seers, "See not";
  and to the prophets, "Prophesy not to us
    what is right;
speak to us smooth things,
  prophesy illusions,
[11]leave the way, turn aside from the path,
  let us hear no more of the Holy One of
    Israel."
[12]Therefore thus says the Holy One of Israel,
  "Because you despise this word,
    and trust in oppression and perverseness,
    and rely on them;
[13]therefore this iniquity shall be to you
  like a break in a high wall, bulging out, and
    about to collapse,
  whose crash comes suddenly, in an instant;
[14]and its breaking is like that of a potter's vessel
  which is smashed so ruthlessly
that among its fragments not a shard is found
  with which to take fire from the hearth,
  or to dip up water out of the cistern."

[15]For thus said the Lord GOD, the Holy One of
    Israel,
  "In returning and rest you shall be saved;
  in quietness and in trust shall be your
    strength."

29:16: Is 45:9; Rom 9:20.
29:18-19: Mt 11:5.

And you would not, [16]but you said,
"No! We will speed upon horses,"
    therefore you shall speed away;
and, "We will ride upon swift steeds,"
    therefore your pursuers shall be swift.
[17]A thousand shall flee at the threat of one,
    at the threat of five you shall flee,
till you are left
    like a flagstaff on the top of a mountain,
    like a signal on a hill.

[18]Therefore the Lord waits to be gracious to you;
    therefore he exalts himself to show mercy
        to you.
For the Lord is a God of justice;
    blessed are all those who wait for him.

God's Promise to Zion

19 Yes, O people in Zion who dwell at Jerusalem; you shall weep no more. He will surely be gracious to you at the sound of your cry; when he hears it, he will answer you. [20]And though the Lord give you the bread of adversity and the water of affliction, yet your Teacher will not hide himself any more, but your eyes shall see your Teacher. [21]And your ears shall hear a word behind you, saying, "This is the way, walk in it," when you turn to the right or when you turn to the left. [22]Then you will defile your silver-covered graven images and your gold-plated molten images. You will scatter them as unclean things; you will say to them, "Begone!"

23 And he will give rain for the seed with which you sow the ground, and grain, the produce of the ground, which will be rich and plenteous. In that day your flock will be given pasture, and the lamb will graze in open fields; [24]and the oxen and the donkeys that till the ground will eat salted food, which has been winnowed with shovel and fork. [25]And upon every lofty mountain and every high hill there will be brooks running with water, in the day of the great slaughter, when the towers fall. [26]Moreover the light of the moon will be as the light of the sun, and the light of the sun will be sevenfold, as the light of seven days, in the day when the Lord binds up the hurt of his people, and heals the wounds inflicted by his blow.

[27]Behold, the name of the Lord comes from far,
    burning with his anger, and in thick rising
        smoke;
his lips are full of indignation,
    and his tongue is like a devouring fire;
[28]his breath is like an overflowing stream
    that reaches up to the neck;
to sift the nations with the sieve of
        destruction,
    and to place on the jaws of the peoples a
        bridle that leads astray.

Judgment on Assyria

29 You shall have a song as in the night when a holy feast is kept; and gladness of heart, as when one sets out to the sound of the flute to go to the mountain of the Lord, to the Rock of Israel. [30]And the Lord will cause his majestic voice to be heard and the descending blow of his arm to be seen, in furious anger and a flame of devouring fire, with a cloudburst and tempest and hailstones. [31]The Assyrians will be terror-stricken at the voice of the Lord, when he strikes with his rod. [32]And every stroke of the staff of punishment which the Lord lays upon them will be to the sound of timbrels and lyres; battling with brandished arm he will fight with them. [33]For a burning place [t] has long been prepared; yes, for the king [u] it is made ready, its pyre made deep and wide, with fire and wood in abundance; the breath of the Lord, like a stream of brimstone, kindles it.

Help from Egypt Is Futile

31 Woe to those who go down to Egypt for
    help
  and rely on horses,
who trust in chariots because they are many
    and in horsemen because they are very
        strong,
but do not look to the Holy One of Israel
    or consult the Lord!
[2]And yet he is wise and brings disaster,
    he does not call back his words,
but will arise against the house of the
       evildoers,
    and against the helpers of those who work
       iniquity.
[3]The Egyptians are men, and not God;
    and their horses are flesh, and not spirit.
When the Lord stretches out his hand,
    the helper will stumble, and he who is
       helped will fall,
    and they will all perish together.

[4]For thus the Lord said to me,
As a lion or a young lion growls over his prey,
    and when a band of shepherds is called
       forth against him
is not terrified by their shouting
    or daunted at their noise,
so the Lord of hosts will come down
    to fight upon Mount Zion and upon its hill.
[5]Like birds hovering, so the Lord of hosts
    will protect Jerusalem;
he will protect and deliver it,
    he will spare and rescue it.

6 Turn to him from whom you [v] have deeply revolted, O people of Israel. [7]For in that day every

---

[t] Or *Topheth.*
[u] Or *Molech.*
[v] Heb *they.*

one shall cast away his idols of silver and his idols of gold, which your hands have sinfully made for you.

⁸"And the Assyrian shall fall by a sword, not of man;
and a sword, not of man, shall devour him;
and he shall flee from the sword,
and his young men shall be put to forced labor.
⁹His rock shall pass away in terror,
and his officers desert the standard in panic,"
says the LORD, whose fire is in Zion,
and whose furnace is in Jerusalem.

A Reign of Righteousness and Justice

32 Behold, a king will reign in righteousness,
and princes will rule in justice.
²Each will be like a hiding place from the wind,
a covert from the tempest,
like streams of water in a dry place,
like the shade of a great rock in a weary land.
³Then the eyes of those who see will not be closed,
and the ears of those who hear will listen.
⁴The mind of the rash will have good judgment,
and the tongue of the stammerers will speak readily and distinctly.
⁵The fool will no more be called noble,
nor the knave said to be honorable.
⁶For the fool speaks folly,
and his mind plots iniquity:
to practice ungodliness,
to utter error concerning the LORD,
to leave the craving of the hungry unsatisfied,
and to deprive the thirsty of drink.
⁷The knaveries of the knave are evil;
he devises wicked devices
to ruin the poor with lying words,
even when the plea of the needy is right.
⁸But he who is noble devises noble things,
and by noble things he stands.

⁹Rise up, you women who are at ease, hear my voice;
you complacent daughters, give ear to my speech.
¹⁰In little more than a year
you will shudder, you complacent women;
for the vintage will fail,
the fruit harvest will not come.
¹¹Tremble, you women who are at ease,
shudder, you complacent ones;
strip, and make yourselves bare,
and put sackcloth upon your loins.
¹²Beat upon your breasts for the pleasant fields,
for the fruitful vine,
¹³for the soil of my people
growing up in thorns and briers;

yes, for all the joyous houses
in the joyful city.
¹⁴For the palace will be forsaken,
the populous city deserted;
the hill and the watchtower
will become dens for ever,
a joy of wild donkeys,
a pasture of flocks;
¹⁵until the Spirit is poured upon us from on high,
and the wilderness becomes a fruitful field,
and the fruitful field is deemed a forest.
¹⁶Then justice will dwell in the wilderness,
and righteousness abide in the fruitful field.
¹⁷And the effect of righteousness will be peace,
and the result of righteousness, quietness and trust for ever.
¹⁸My people will abide in a peaceful habitation,
in secure dwellings, and in quiet resting places.
¹⁹And the forest will utterly go down,ʷ
and the city will be utterly laid low.
²⁰Happy are you who sow beside all waters,
who let the feet of the ox and the donkey range free.

A Prophecy of Deliverance: The Lord, the Majestic King

33 Woe to you, destroyer,
who yourself have not been destroyed;
you treacherous one,
with whom none has dealt treacherously!
When you have ceased to destroy,
you will be destroyed;
and when you have made an end of dealing treacherously,
you will be dealt with treacherously.

²O LORD, be gracious to us; we wait for you.
Be our arm every morning,
our salvation in the time of trouble.
³At the thunderous noise peoples flee,
at the lifting up of yourself nations are scattered;
⁴and spoil is gathered as the caterpillar gathers;
as locusts leap, men leap upon it.

⁵The LORD is exalted, for he dwells on high;
he will fill Zion with justice and righteousness;
⁶and he will be the stability of your times,
abundance of salvation, wisdom, and knowledge;
the fear of the LORD is his treasure.

⁷Behold, the valiant onesʸ cry without;
the envoys of peace weep bitterly.

ʷ Cn: Heb *And it will hail when the forest comes down.*
ʸ The meaning of the Hebrew word is uncertain.

[8]The highways lie waste,
the wayfaring man ceases.
Covenants are broken,
witnesses [z] are despised,
there is no regard for man.
[9]The land mourns and languishes;
Lebanon is confounded and withers away;
Sharon is like a desert;
and Bashan and Carmel shake off their
leaves.

[10]"Now I will arise," says the LORD,
"now I will lift myself up;
now I will be exalted.
[11]You conceive chaff, you bring forth stubble;
your breath is a fire that will consume you.
[12]And the peoples will be as if burned to lime,
like thorns cut down, that are burned in the
fire."

[13]Hear, you who are far off, what I have done;
and you who are near, acknowledge my
might.
[14]The sinners in Zion are afraid;
trembling has seized the godless:
"Who among us can dwell with the devouring
fire?
Who among us can dwell with everlasting
burnings?"
[15]He who walks righteously and speaks
uprightly,
who despises the gain of oppressions,
who shakes his hands, lest they hold a bribe,
who stops his ears from hearing of
bloodshed
and shuts his eyes from looking upon evil,
[16]he will dwell on the heights;
his place of defense will be the fortresses of
rocks;
his bread will be given him, his water will
be sure.

[17]Your eyes will see the king in his beauty;
they will behold a land that stretches afar.
[18]Your mind will muse on the terror:
"Where is he who counted, where is he who
weighed the tribute?
Where is he who counted the towers?"
[19]You will see no more the insolent people,
the people of an obscure speech which you
cannot comprehend,
stammering in a tongue which you cannot
understand.
[20]Look upon Zion, the city of our appointed
feasts!
Your eyes will see Jerusalem,
a quiet habitation, an immovable tent,
whose stakes will never be plucked up,
nor will any of its cords be broken.

[21]But there the LORD in majesty will be for us
a place of broad rivers and streams,
where no galley with oars can go,
nor stately ship can pass.
[22]For the LORD is our judge, the LORD is our ruler,
the LORD is our king; he will save us.

[23]Your tackle hangs loose;
it cannot hold the mast firm in its place,
or keep the sail spread out.

Then prey and spoil in abundance will be
divided;
even the lame will take the prey.
[24]And no inhabitant will say, "I am sick";
the people who dwell there will be forgiven
their iniquity.

The Wrath of the Lord

34 Draw near, O nations, to hear,
and listen, O peoples!
Let the earth listen, and all that fills it;
the world, and all that comes from it.
[2]For the LORD is enraged against all the nations,
and furious against all their host,
he has doomed them, has given them over
for slaughter.
[3]Their slain shall be cast out,
and the stench of their corpses shall rise;
the mountains shall flow with their blood.
[4]All the host of heaven shall rot away,
and the skies roll up like a scroll.
All their host shall fall,
as leaves fall from the vine,
like leaves falling from the fig tree.

[5]For my sword has drunk its fill in the heavens;
behold, it descends for judgment upon
E'dom,
upon the people I have doomed.
[6]The LORD has a sword; it is sated with blood,
it is gorged with fat,
with the blood of lambs and goats,
with the fat of the kidneys of rams.
For the LORD has a sacrifice in Bozrah,
a great slaughter in the land of E'dom.
[7]Wild oxen shall fall with them,
and young steers with the mighty bulls.
Their land shall be soaked with blood,
and their soil made rich with fat.

[8]For the LORD has a day of vengeance,
a year of recompense for the cause of Zion.
[9]And the streams of E'dom [a] shall be turned
into pitch,

[z] One ancient Ms: Heb *cities*.
[a] Heb *her streams*.
34: Is 63:1–6; Jer 49:7–22; Ezek 25:12–14; 35; Amos 1:11–12; Obad; Mal 1:2–5.
34:4: Rev 6:13–14.
34:9–10: Rev 19:3.

and her soil into brimstone;
    her land shall become burning pitch.
[10]Night and day it shall not be quenched;
    its smoke shall go up for ever.
From generation to generation it shall lie
        waste;
    none shall pass through it for ever and ever.
[11]But the hawk and the porcupine shall possess
        it,
    the owl and the raven shall dwell in it.
He shall stretch the line of confusion over it,
    and the plummet of chaos over [b] its nobles.
[12]They shall name it No Kingdom There,
    and all its princes shall be nothing.

[13]Thorns shall grow over its strongholds,
    nettles and thistles in its fortresses.
It shall be the haunt of jackals,
    an abode for ostriches.
[14]And wild beasts shall meet with hyenas,
    the satyr shall cry to his fellow;
yes, there shall the night creature alight,
    and find for herself a resting place.

[15]There shall the owl nest and lay
    and hatch and gather her young in her
        shadow;
yes, there shall the kites be gathered,
    each one with her mate.
[16]Seek and read from the book of the LORD:
    Not one of these shall be missing;
    none shall be without her mate.
For the mouth of the LORD has commanded,
    and his Spirit has gathered them.
[17]He has cast the lot for them,
    his hand has portioned it out to them with
        the line;
they shall possess it for ever,
    from generation to generation they shall
        dwell in it.

The Lord Will Come to Save

35 The wilderness and the dry land shall be
    glad,
    the desert shall rejoice and blossom;
like the lily [2]it shall blossom abundantly,
    and rejoice with joy and singing.
The glory of Lebanon shall be given to it,
    the majesty of Car'mel and Sharon.
They shall see the glory of the LORD,
    the majesty of our God.

[3]Strengthen the weak hands,
    and make firm the feeble knees.
[4]Say to those who are of a fearful heart,
    "Be strong, fear not!
Behold, your God
    will come with vengeance,
with the recompense of God.
    He will come and save you."

[5]Then the eyes of the blind shall be opened,
    and the ears of the deaf unstopped;
[6]then shall the lame man leap like a deer,
    and the tongue of the mute sing for joy.
For waters shall break forth in the wilderness,
    and streams in the desert;
[7]the burning sand shall become a pool,
    and the thirsty ground springs of water;
the haunt of jackals shall become a swamp, [c]
    the grass shall become reeds and rushes.

[8]And a highway shall be there,
    and it shall be called the Holy Way;
the unclean shall not pass over it, [d]
    and fools shall not err therein.
[9]No lion shall be there,
    nor shall any ravenous beast come up on it;
they shall not be found there,
    but the redeemed shall walk there.
[10]And the ransomed of the LORD shall return,
    and come to Zion with singing;
everlasting joy shall be upon their heads;
    they shall obtain joy and gladness,
    and sorrow and sighing shall flee away.

Sennacherib Threatens Jerusalem

36 In the fourteenth year of King Hezeki'ah,
    Sennach'erib king of Assyria came up
against all the fortified cities of Judah and took
them. [2]And the king of Assyria sent the Rab'-
shakeh from La'chish to King Hezeki'ah at Jerusalem, with a great army. And he stood by the
conduit of the upper pool on the highway to the
Fuller's Field. [3]And there came out to him Eli'a-
kim the son of Hilki'ah, who was over the household, and Shebna the secretary, and Jo'ah the son
of A'saph, the recorder.

4 And the Rab'shakeh said to them, "Say to
Hezeki'ah, 'Thus says the great king, the king of
Assyria: On what do you rest this confidence of
yours? [5]Do you think that mere words are strategy and power for war? On whom do you now
rely, that you have rebelled against me? [6]Behold,
you are relying on Egypt, that broken reed of a
staff, which will pierce the hand of any man who
leans on it. Such is Pharaoh king of Egypt to all
who rely on him. [7]But if you say to me, "We rely
on the LORD our God," is it not he whose high
places and altars Hezeki'ah has removed, saying
to Judah and to Jerusalem, "You shall worship
before this altar"? [8]Come now, make a wager with
my master the king of Assyria: I will give you
two thousand horses, if you are able on your part
to set riders upon them. [9]How then can you repulse a single captain among the least of my

---

[b] Heb lacks *over.*
[c] Cn: Heb *in the haunt of jackals is her resting place.*
[d] Heb *it and he is for them a wayfarer.*
35:3: Heb 12:12.
35:5–6: Mt 11:5; Lk 7:22.
36:1–38:8, 21–22: 2 Kings 18:13—20:11; 2 Chron 32:1–24.

master's servants, when you rely on Egypt for chariots and for horsemen? ¹⁰Moreover, is it without the LORD that I have come up against this land to destroy it? The LORD said to me, Go up against this land, and destroy it.' "

11 Then Eli'akim, Shebna, and Jo'ah said to the Rab'shakeh, "Please, speak to your servants in Arama'ic, for we understand it; do not speak to us in the language of Judah within the hearing of the people who are on the wall." ¹²But the Rab'shakeh said, "Has my master sent me to speak these words to your master and to you, and not to the men sitting on the wall, who are doomed with you to eat their own dung and drink their own urine?"

13 Then the Rab'shakeh stood and called out in a loud voice in the language of Judah: "Hear the words of the great king, the king of Assyria! ¹⁴Thus says the king: 'Do not let Hezeki'ah deceive you, for he will not be able to deliver you. ¹⁵Do not let Hezeki'ah make you rely on the LORD by saying, "The LORD will surely deliver us; this city will not be given into the hand of the king of Assyria." ¹⁶Do not listen to Hezeki'ah; for thus says the king of Assyria: Make your peace with me and come out to me; then every one of you will eat of his own vine, and every one of his own fig tree, and every one of you will drink the water of his own cistern; ¹⁷until I come and take you away to a land like your own land, a land of grain and wine, a land of bread and vineyards. ¹⁸Beware lest Hezeki'ah mislead you by saying, "The LORD will deliver us." Has any of the gods of the nations delivered his land out of the hand of the king of Assyria? ¹⁹Where are the gods of Ha'math and Arpad? Where are the gods of Sepharva'im? Have they delivered Samar'ia out of my hand? ²⁰Who among all the gods of these countries have delivered their countries out of my hand, that the LORD should deliver Jerusalem out of my hand?' "

21 But they were silent and answered him not a word, for the king's command was, "Do not answer him." ²²Then Eli'akim the son of Hilki'ah, who was over the household, and Sheb'na the secretary, and Jo'ah the son of A'saph, the recorder, came to Hezeki'ah with their clothes torn, and told him the words of the Rab'shakeh.

Hezekiah Consults Isaiah

37 When King Hezeki'ah heard it, he tore his clothes, and covered himself with sackcloth, and went into the house of the LORD. ²And he sent Eli'akim, who was over the household, and Shebna the secretary, and the senior priests, clothed with sackcloth, to the prophet Isai'ah the son of A'moz. ³They said to him, "Thus says Hezeki'ah, 'This day is a day of distress, of rebuke, and of disgrace; children have come to the birth, and there is no strength to bring them forth.

⁴It may be that the LORD your God heard the words of the Rab'shakeh, whom his master the king of Assyria has sent to mock the living God, and will rebuke the words which the LORD your God has heard; therefore lift up your prayer for the remnant that is left.' "

5 When the servants of King Hezeki'ah came to Isai'ah, ⁶Isai'ah said to them, "Say to your master, 'Thus says the LORD: Do not be afraid because of the words that you have heard, with which the servants of the king of Assyria have reviled me. ⁷Behold, I will put a spirit in him, so that he shall hear a rumor, and return to his own land; and I will make him fall by the sword in his own land.' "

8 The Rab'shakeh returned, and found the king of Assyria fighting against Libnah; for he had heard that the king had left La'chish. ⁹Now the king heard concerning Tirha'kah king of Ethiopia, "He has set out to fight against you." And when he heard it, he sent messengers to Hezeki'ah, saying, ¹⁰"Thus shall you speak to Hezeki'ah king of Judah: 'Do not let your God on whom you rely deceive you by promising that Jerusalem will not be given into the hand of the king of Assyria. ¹¹Behold, you have heard what the kings of Assyria have done to all lands, destroying them utterly. And shall you be delivered? ¹²Have the gods of the nations delivered them, the nations which my fathers destroyed, Gozan, Haran, Rezeph, and the people of Eden who were in Telas'sar? ¹³Where is the king of Ha'math, the king of Arpad, the king of the city of Sepharva'im, the king of He'na, or the king of Ivvah?' "

Hezekiah's Prayer

14 Hezeki'ah received the letter from the hand of the messengers, and read it; and Hezekiah went up to the house of the LORD, and spread it before the LORD. ¹⁵And Hezeki'ah prayed to the LORD: ¹⁶ "O LORD of hosts, God of Israel, who are enthroned above the cherubim, you are the God, you alone, of all the kingdoms of the earth; you have made heaven and earth. ¹⁷Incline your ear, O LORD, and hear; open your eyes, O LORD, and see; and hear all the words of Sennach'erib, which he has sent to mock the living God. ¹⁸Of a truth, O LORD, the kings of Assyria have laid waste all the nations and their lands, ¹⁹and have cast their gods into the fire; for they were no gods, but the work of men's hands, wood and stone; therefore they were destroyed. ²⁰So now, O LORD our God, save us from his hand, that all the kingdoms of the earth may know that you alone are the LORD."

21 Then Isai'ah the son of A'moz sent to Hezeki'ah, saying, "Thus says the LORD, the God of Israel: Because you have prayed to me concerning Sennach'erib king of Assyria, ²²this is the word that the LORD has spoken concerning him:

'She despises you, she scorns you—
    the virgin daughter of Zion;
she wags her head behind you—
    the daughter of Jerusalem.

²³'Whom have you mocked and reviled?
    Against whom have you raised your voice
and haughtily lifted your eyes?
    Against the Holy One of Israel!
²⁴By your servants you have mocked the Lord,
    and you have said, With my many chariots
I have gone up the heights of the mountains,
    to the far recesses of Lebanon;
I felled its tallest cedars,
    its choicest cypresses;
I came to its remotest height,
    its densest forest.
²⁵I dug wells
    and drank waters,
and I dried up with the sole of my foot
    all the streams of Egypt.

²⁶'Have you not heard
    that I determined it long ago?
I planned from days of old
    what now I bring to pass,
that you should make fortified cities
    crash into heaps of ruins,
²⁷while their inhabitants, shorn of strength,
    are dismayed and confounded,
and have become like plants of the field
    and like tender grass,
like grass on the housetops,
    blighted ^e before it is grown.

²⁸'I know your sitting down
    and your going out and coming in,
    and your raging against me.
²⁹Because you have raged against me
    and your arrogance has come to my ears,
I will put my hook in your nose
    and my bit in your mouth,
and I will turn you back on the way
    by which you came.'

30 "And this shall be the sign for you: this year eat what grows of itself, and in the second year what springs of the same; then in the third year sow and reap, and plant vineyards, and eat their fruit. ³¹And the surviving remnant of the house of Judah shall again take root downward, and bear fruit upward; ³²for out of Jerusalem shall go forth a remnant, and out of Mount Zion a band of survivors. The zeal of the Lord of hosts will accomplish this.

33 "Therefore thus says the Lord concerning the king of Assyria: He shall not come into this city, or shoot an arrow there, or come before it with a shield, or cast up a siege mound against it.

³⁴By the way that he came, by the same he shall return, and he shall not come into this city, says the Lord. ³⁵For I will defend this city to save it, for my own sake and for the sake of my servant David."

Sennacherib's Defeat and Death

36 And the angel of the Lord went forth, and slew a hundred and eighty-five thousand in the camp of the Assyrians; and when men arose early in the morning, behold, these were all dead bodies. ³⁷Then Sennach'erib king of Assyria departed, and went home and dwelt at Nin'eveh. ³⁸And as he was worshiping in the house of Nis'-roch his god, Adram'melech and Share'zer, his sons, slew him with the sword, and escaped into the land of Ar'arat. And E'sar-had'don his son reigned in his stead.

Hezekiah's Sickness

38 In those days Hezeki'ah became sick and was at the point of death. And Isai'ah the prophet the son of A'moz came to him, and said to him, "Thus says the Lord: Set your house in order; for you shall die, you shall not recover." ²Then Hezeki'ah turned his face to the wall, and prayed to the Lord, ³and said, "Remember now, O Lord, I beseech you, how I have walked before you in faithfulness and with a whole heart, and have done what is good in your sight." And Hezeki'ah wept bitterly. ⁴Then the word of the Lord came to Isai'ah: ⁵"Go and say to Hezeki'ah, Thus says the Lord, the God of David your father: I have heard your prayer, I have seen your tears; behold, I will add fifteen years to your life. ⁶I will deliver you and this city out of the hand of the king of Assyria, and defend this city.

7 "This is the sign to you from the Lord, that the Lord will do this thing that he has promised: ⁸Behold, I will make the shadow cast by the declining sun on the dial of A'haz turn back ten steps." So the sun turned back on the dial the ten steps by which it had declined. ^f

9 A writing of Hezeki'ah king of Judah, after he had been sick and had recovered from his sickness:
¹⁰I said, In the noontide of my days
    I must depart;
I am consigned to the gates of Sheol
    for the rest of my years.
¹¹I said, I shall not see the Lord
    in the land of the living;
I shall look upon man no more
    among the inhabitants of the world.
¹²My dwelling is plucked up and removed from
    me
    like a shepherd's tent;

---

^e With 2 Kings 19:26: Heb *field.*
^f The Hebrew of this verse is obscure.

like a weaver I have rolled up my life;
    he cuts me off from the loom;
from day to night you bring me to an end; ^g
¹³ I cry for help ^h until morning;
like a lion he breaks all my bones;
    from day to night you bring me to an end. ^g

¹⁴Like a swallow or a crane ⁱ I clamor,
    I moan like a dove.
My eyes are weary with looking upward.
O Lord, I am oppressed; be my security!
¹⁵But what can I say? For he has spoken to me,
    and he himself has done it.
All my sleep has fled ^j
    because of the bitterness of my soul.

¹⁶O Lord, by these things men live,
    and in all these is the life of my spirit.^k
    Oh, restore me to health and make me live!
¹⁷Behold, it was for my welfare
    that I had great bitterness;
but you have held back ^l my life
    from the pit of destruction,
for you have cast all my sins behind your back.
¹⁸For Sheol cannot thank you,
    death cannot praise you;
those who go down to the pit cannot hope
    for your faithfulness.
¹⁹The living, the living, he thanks you,
    as I do this day;
the father makes known to the children
    your faithfulness.

²⁰The Lord will save me,
    and we will sing to stringed instruments^m
all the days of our life,
    at the house of the Lord.

²¹Now Isai′ah had said, "Let them take a cake of figs, and apply it to the boil, that he may recover." ²²Hezeki′ah also had said, "What is the sign that I shall go up to the house of the Lord?"

Envoys from Babylon Welcomed

39 At that time Mer′odach-bal′adan the son of Bal′adan, king of Babylon, sent envoys with letters and a present to Hezeki′ah, for he heard that he had been sick and had recovered. ²And Hezeki′ah welcomed them; and he showed them his treasure house, the silver, the gold, the spices, the precious oil, his whole armory, all that was found in his storehouses. There was nothing in his house or in all his realm that Hezekiah did not show them. ³Then Isai′ah the prophet came to King Hezeki′ah, and said to him, "What did these men say? And from where did they come to you?" Hezeki′ah said, "They have come to me from a far country, from Babylon." ⁴He said, "What have they seen in your house?" Hezeki′ah answered, "They have seen all that is in my house; there is

nothing in my storehouses that I did not show them."

5 Then Isai′ah said to Hezeki′ah, "Hear the word of the Lord of hosts: ⁶Behold, the days are coming, when all that is in your house, and that which your fathers have stored up till this day, shall be carried to Babylon; nothing shall be left, says the Lord. ⁷And some of your own sons, who are born to you, shall be taken away; and they shall be eunuchs in the palace of the king of Babylon." ⁸Then said Hezeki′ah to Isai′ah, "The word of the Lord which you have spoken is good." For he thought, "There will be peace and security in my days."

God Comforts His People

40 [*] Comfort, comfort my people, says your God.
²Speak tenderly to Jerusalem,
    and cry to her
that her warfare ⁿ is ended,
    that her iniquity is pardoned,
that she has received from the Lord's hand
    double for all her sins.

³A voice cries:
"In the wilderness prepare the way of the
    Lord,
    make straight in the desert a highway for
    our God.
⁴Every valley shall be lifted up,
    and every mountain and hill be made low;
the uneven ground shall become level,
    and the rough places a plain.
⁵And the glory of the Lord shall be revealed,
    and all flesh shall see it together,
for the mouth of the Lord has spoken."

⁶A voice says, "Cry!"
    And I said, "What shall I cry?"
All flesh is grass,
    and all its beauty is like the flower of the
    field.
⁷The grass withers, the flower fades,
    when the breath of the Lord blows upon it;
    surely the people is grass.
⁸The grass withers, the flower fades;
    but the word of our God will stand for ever.

---

^g Heb uncertain.
^h Cn: Heb obscure.
ⁱ Heb uncertain.
^j Cn Compare Syr: Heb *I will walk slowly all my years.*
^k Heb uncertain.
^l Cn Compare Gk Vg: Heb *loved.*
^m Heb *my stringed instruments.*
ⁿ Or *time of service.*
39:1–8: 2 Kings 20:12–19; 2 Chron 32:31.
40:3: Mt 3:3; Mk 1:3; Lk 3:4; Jn 1:23.
40:4–5: Lk 3:5–6.
40:6–8: 1 Pet 1:24–25.
[*] 40:1: Here begins the "Book of the Consolation of Israel," as it has been beautifully called. It was written to comfort and console the people in their exile in Babylonia.

⁹Get you up to a high mountain,
  O Zion, herald of good tidings; °
lift up your voice with strength,
  O Jerusalem, herald of good tidings, ᴾ
  lift it up, fear not;
say to the cities of Judah,
  "Behold your God!"
¹⁰Behold, the Lord GOD comes with might,
  and his arm rules for him;
behold, his reward is with him,
  and his recompense before him.
¹¹He will feed his flock like a shepherd,
  he will gather the lambs in his arms,
he will carry them in his bosom,
  and gently lead those that are with young.

¹²Who has measured the waters in the hollow of
    his hand
  and marked off the heavens with a span,
enclosed the dust of the earth in a measure
  and weighed the mountains in scales
  and the hills in a balance?
¹³Who has directed the Spirit of the LORD,
  or as his counselor has instructed him?
¹⁴Whom did he consult for his enlightenment,
  and who taught him the path of justice,
and taught him knowledge,
  and showed him the way of understanding?
¹⁵Behold, the nations are like a drop from a
    bucket,
  and are accounted as the dust on the scales;
behold, he takes up the isles like fine dust.
¹⁶Lebanon would not suffice for fuel,
  nor are its beasts enough for a burnt
    offering.
¹⁷All the nations are as nothing before him,
  they are accounted by him as less than
    nothing and emptiness.

¹⁸To whom then will you liken God,
  or what likeness compare with him?
¹⁹The idol! a workman casts it,
  and a goldsmith overlays it with gold,
  and casts for it silver chains.
²⁰He who is impoverished �q chooses for an
    offering
  wood that will not rot;
he seeks out a skilful craftsman
  to set up an image that will not move.

²¹Have you not known? Have you not heard?
  Has it not been told you from the
    beginning?
Have you not understood from the
    foundations of the earth?
²²It is he who sits above the circle of the earth,
  and its inhabitants are like grasshoppers;
who stretches out the heavens like a curtain,
  and spreads them like a tent to dwell in;

²³who brings princes to nought,
  and makes the rulers of the earth as
    nothing.

²⁴Scarcely are they planted, scarcely sown,
  scarcely has their stem taken root in the
    earth,
when he blows upon them, and they wither,
  and the tempest carries them off like
    stubble.

²⁵To whom then will you compare me,
  that I should be like him?
  says the Holy One.
²⁶Lift up your eyes on high and see:
  who created these?
He who brings out their host by number,
  calling them all by name;
by the greatness of his might,
  and because he is strong in power
  not one is missing.

²⁷Why do you say, O Jacob,
  and speak, O Israel,
"My way is hidden from the LORD,
  and my right is disregarded by my God"?
²⁸Have you not known? Have you not heard?
  The LORD is the everlasting God,
  the Creator of the ends of the earth.
He does not faint or grow weary,
  his understanding is unsearchable.
²⁹He gives power to the faint,
  and to him who has no might he increases
    strength.
³⁰Even youths shall faint and be weary,
  and young men shall fall exhausted;
³¹but they who wait for the LORD shall renew
    their strength,
  they shall mount up with wings like eagles,
they shall run and not be weary,
  they shall walk and not faint.

Israel Assured of God's Help

41 Listen to me in silence, O islands;
  let the peoples renew their strength;
let them approach, then let them speak;
  let us together draw near for judgment.

²Who stirred up one from the east
  whom victory meets at every step?
He gives up nations before him,
  so that he tramples kings under foot;
he makes them like dust with his sword,
  like driven stubble with his bow.

° Or O herald of good tidings to Zion.
ᴾ Or O herald of good tidings to Jerusalem.
q Heb uncertain.
40:9: Is 52:7; Nah 1:15; Acts 10:36; Rom 10:15.
40:10: Rev 22:7, 12.
40:13: Rom 11:34; 1 Cor 2:16.

³He pursues them and passes on safely,
  by paths his feet have not trod.
⁴Who has performed and done this,
  calling the generations from the
    beginning?
I, the LORD, the first,
  and with the last; I am He.
⁵The islands have seen and are afraid,
  the ends of the earth tremble;
  they have drawn near and come.
⁶Every one helps his neighbor,
  and says to his brother, "Take courage!"
⁷The craftsman encourages the goldsmith,
  and he who smooths with the hammer him
    who strikes the anvil,
  saying of the soldering, "It is good";
  and they fasten it with nails so that it
    cannot be moved.

⁸But you, Israel, my servant,
  Jacob, whom I have chosen,
  the offspring of Abraham, my friend;
⁹you whom I took from the ends of the earth,
  and called from its farthest corners,
  saying to you, "You are my servant,
    I have chosen you and not cast you off";
¹⁰fear not, for I am with you,
  be not dismayed, for I am your God;
I will strengthen you, I will help you,
  I will uphold you with my victorious right
    hand.

¹¹Behold, all who are incensed against you
  shall be put to shame and confounded;
  those who strive against you
    shall be as nothing and shall perish.
¹²You shall seek those who contend with you,
  but you shall not find them;
  those who war against you
    shall be as nothing at all.
¹³For I, the LORD your God,
  hold your right hand;
  it is I who say to you, "Fear not,
    I will help you."

¹⁴Fear not, you worm Jacob,
  you men of Israel!
I will help you, says the LORD;
  your Redeemer is the Holy One of Israel.
¹⁵Behold, I will make of you a threshing sledge,
  new, sharp, and having teeth;
  you shall thresh the mountains and crush
    them,
  and you shall make the hills like chaff;
¹⁶you shall winnow them and the wind shall
    carry them away,
  and the tempest shall scatter them.
And you shall rejoice in the LORD;
  in the Holy One of Israel you shall glory.

¹⁷When the poor and needy seek water,
  and there is none,
  and their tongue is parched with thirst,
I the LORD will answer them,
  I the God of Israel will not forsake them.
¹⁸I will open rivers on the bare heights,
  and fountains in the midst of the valleys;
I will make the wilderness a pool of water,
  and the dry land springs of water.
¹⁹I will put in the wilderness the cedar,
  the acacia, the myrtle, and the olive;
I will set in the desert the cypress,
  the plane and the pine together;
²⁰that men may see and know,
  may consider and understand together,
  that the hand of the LORD has done this,
    the Holy One of Israel has created it.

²¹Set forth your case, says the LORD;
  bring your proofs, says the King of Jacob.
²²Let them bring them, and tell us
  what is to happen.
Tell us the former things, what they are,
  that we may consider them,
  that we may know their outcome;
  or declare to us the things to come.
²³Tell us what is to come hereafter,
  that we may know that you are gods;
do good, or do harm,
  that we may be dismayed and terrified.
²⁴Behold, you are nothing,
  and your work is nought;
  an abomination is he who chooses you.

²⁵I stirred up one from the north, and he has
    come,
  from the rising of the sun, and he shall call
    on my name;
he shall trample ᶠ on rulers as on mortar,
  as the potter treads clay.
²⁶Who declared it from the beginning, that we
    might know,
  and beforetime, that we might say, "He is
    right"?
There was none who declared it, none who
    proclaimed,
  none who heard your words.
²⁷I first have declared it to Zion,ᵍ
  and I give to Jerusalem a herald of good
    tidings.
²⁸But when I look there is no one;
  among these there is no counselor
  who, when I ask, gives an answer.

ᶠ Cn: Heb *come.*
ᵍ Cn: Heb *first to Zion, Behold, behold them.*
41:8: Jas 2:23.
41:8–9: Lk 1:54; Heb 2:16.
41:10: Acts 18:10.

²⁹Behold, they are all a delusion;
    their works are nothing;
    their molten images are empty wind.

The Lord's Servant; and Israel's Disobedience

42 * Behold my servant, whom I uphold,
    my chosen, in whom my soul
    delights;
I have put my Spirit upon him,
    he will bring forth justice to the nations.
²He will not cry or lift up his voice,
    or make it heard in the street;
³a bruised reed he will not break,
    and a dimly burning wick he will not
    quench;
    he will faithfully bring forth justice.
⁴He will not fail ᵗ or be discouraged ᵘ
    till he has established justice in the earth;
    and the islands wait for his law.

⁵Thus says God, the Lᴏʀᴅ,
    who created the heavens and stretched them
    out,
    who spread forth the earth and what comes
    from it,
who gives breath to the people upon it
    and spirit to those who walk in it:
⁶"I am the Lᴏʀᴅ, I have called you in
    righteousness,
    I have taken you by the hand and kept
    you;
I have given you as a covenant to the people,
    a light to the nations,
⁷   to open the eyes that are blind,
to bring out the prisoners from the dungeon,
    from the prison those who sit in darkness.
⁸I am the Lᴏʀᴅ, that is my name;
    my glory I give to no other,
    nor my praise to graven images.
⁹Behold, the former things have come to pass,
    and new things I now declare;
before they spring forth
    I tell you of them."

¹⁰Sing to the Lᴏʀᴅ a new song,
    his praise from the end of the earth!
Let the sea roar ᵛ and all that fills it,
    the islands and their inhabitants.
¹¹Let the desert and its cities lift up their voice,
    the villages that Ke′dar inhabits;
let the inhabitants of Se′la sing for joy,
    let them shout from the top of the
    mountains.
¹²Let them give glory to the Lᴏʀᴅ,
    and declare his praise in the islands.
¹³The Lᴏʀᴅ goes forth like a mighty man,
    like a man of war he stirs up his fury;
he cries out, he shouts aloud,
    he shows himself mighty against his foes.

¹⁴For a long time I have held my peace,
    I have kept still and restrained myself;
now I will cry out like a woman with labor
    pains,
    I will gasp and pant.
¹⁵I will lay waste mountains and hills,
    and dry up all their herbage;
I will turn the rivers into islands,
    and dry up the pools.
¹⁶And I will lead the blind
    in a way that they know not,
in paths that they have not known
    I will guide them.
I will turn the darkness before them into light,
    the rough places into level ground.
These are the things I will do,
    and I will not forsake them.
¹⁷They shall be turned back and utterly put to
    shame,
    who trust in graven images,
who say to molten images,
    "You are our gods."

¹⁸Hear, you deaf;
    and look, you blind, that you may see!
¹⁹Who is blind but my servant,
    or deaf as my messenger whom I send?
Who is blind as my dedicated one,
    or blind as the servant of the Lᴏʀᴅ?
²⁰He sees ʷ many things, but does not observe
    them;
    his ears are open, but he does not hear.
²¹The Lᴏʀᴅ was pleased, for his righteousness'
    sake,
    to magnify his law and make it glorious.
²²But this is a people robbed and plundered,
    they are all of them trapped in holes
    and hidden in prisons;
they have become a prey with none to rescue,
    a spoil with none to say, "Restore!"
²³Who among you will give ear to this,
    will attend and listen for the time to come?
²⁴Who gave up Jacob to the spoiler,
    and Israel to the robbers?
Was it not the Lᴏʀᴅ, against whom we have
    sinned,
    in whose ways they would not walk,
    and whose law they would not obey?
²⁵So he poured upon him the heat of his anger
    and the might of battle;

ᵗ Or *burn dimly.*
ᵘ Or *bruised.*
ᵛ Cn Compare Ps 96:11; 98:7: Heb *Those who go down to the sea.*
ʷ Heb *you see.*
42:1–4: Mt 12:18–21.
42:5: Acts 17:24–25.
42:6: Is 49:6; Lk 2:32; Acts 13:47; 26:23.
42:7, 16: Acts 26:18.
* 42:1–4: The "Servant of Yahweh" is here introduced. This and three other prophecies (49:1–6; 50:4–9; 52:13—53:12) depict the Messiah in a new light, giving details of his meekness and suffering.

it set him on fire round about, but he did not
  understand;
    it burned him, but he did not take it to heart.

The Lord Is Redeemer of Israel

43 But now thus says the Lord, he who
    created you, O Jacob,
  he who formed you, O Israel:
"Fear not, for I have redeemed you;
  I have called you by name, you are mine.
²When you pass through the waters I will be
  with you;
    and through the rivers, they shall not
      overwhelm you;
  when you walk through fire you shall not be
    burned,
    and the flame shall not consume you.
³For I am the Lord your God,
  the Holy One of Israel, your Savior.
I give Egypt as your ransom,
  Ethiopia and Seba in exchange for you.
⁴Because you are precious in my eyes,
  and honored, and I love you,
I give men in return for you,
  peoples in exchange for your life.
⁵Fear not, for I am with you;
  I will bring your offspring from the east,
  and from the west I will gather you;
⁶I will say to the north, Give up,
  and to the south, Do not withhold;
bring my sons from afar
  and my daughters from the end of the
    earth,
⁷every one who is called by my name,
  whom I created for my glory,
  whom I formed and made."

⁸Bring forth the people who are blind, yet have
  eyes,
  who are deaf, yet have ears!
⁹Let all the nations gather together,
  and let the peoples assemble.
Who among them can declare this,
  and show us the former things?
Let them bring their witnesses to justify them,
  and let them hear and say, It is true.
¹⁰"You are my witnesses," says the Lord,
  "and my servant whom I have chosen,
that you may know and believe me
  and understand that I am He.
Before me no god was formed,
  nor shall there be any after me.
¹¹I, I am the Lord,
  and besides me there is no savior.
¹²I declared and saved and proclaimed,
  when there was no strange god among you;
  and you are my witnesses," says the Lord.
¹³"I am God, and also henceforth I am He;
  there is none who can deliver from my hand;
  I work and who can hinder it?"

¹⁴Thus says the Lord,
  your Redeemer, the Holy One of Israel:
"For your sake I will send to Babylon
  and break down all the bars,
  and the shouting of the Chalde'ans will be
    turned to lamentations. *
¹⁵I am the Lord, your Holy One,
  the Creator of Israel, your King."
¹⁶Thus says the Lord,
  who makes a way in the sea,
  a path in the mighty waters,
¹⁷who brings forth chariot and horse,
  army and warrior;
they lie down, they cannot rise,
  they are extinguished, quenched like a
    wick:
¹⁸"Remember not the former things,
  nor consider the things of old.
¹⁹Behold, I am doing a new thing;
  now it springs forth, do you not perceive
    it?
I will make a way in the wilderness and rivers
  in the desert.
²⁰The wild beasts will honor me,
  the jackals and the ostriches;
for I give water in the wilderness,
  rivers in the desert,
to give drink to my chosen people,
²¹ the people whom I formed for myself
that they might declare my praise.

²²"Yet you did not call upon me, O Jacob;
  but you have been weary of me, O Israel!
²³You have not brought me your sheep for burnt
  offerings,
  or honored me with your sacrifices.
I have not burdened you with offerings,
  or wearied you with frankincense.
²⁴You have not bought me sweet cane with
  money,
  or satisfied me with the fat of your
    sacrifices.
But you have burdened me with your sins,
  you have wearied me with your iniquities.

²⁵"I, I am He
  who blots out your transgressions for my
    own sake,
  and I will not remember your sins.
²⁶Put me in remembrance, let us argue
  together;
  set forth your case, that you may be proved
    right.
²⁷Your first father sinned,
  and your mediators transgressed against
    me.

---

* Heb obscure.
43:5: Acts 18:10.

28Therefore I profaned the princes of the
sanctuary,
  I delivered Jacob to utter destruction
  and Israel to reviling.

God's Blessing on Israel

44 "But now hear, O Jacob my servant,
  Israel whom I have chosen!
2Thus says the LORD who made you,
  who formed you from the womb and will
  help you:
Fear not, O Jacob my servant,
  Jesh'urun whom I have chosen.
3For I will pour water on the thirsty land,
  and streams on the dry ground;
I will pour my Spirit upon your descendants,
  and my blessing on your offspring.
4They shall spring up like grass amid waters,y
  like willows by flowing streams.
5This one will say, 'I am the LORD's,'
  another will call himself by the name of
  Jacob,
and another will write on his hand, 'The
  LORD's,'
  and surname himself by the name of
  Israel."

6Thus says the LORD, the King of Israel
  and his Redeemer, the LORD of hosts:
"I am the first and I am the last;
  besides me there is no god.
7Who is like me? Let him proclaim it,
  let him declare and set it forth before me.
Who has announced from of old the things to
  come?z
  Let them tell usa what is yet to be.
8Fear not, nor be afraid;
  have I not told you from of old and declared
  it?
  And you are my witnesses!
Is there a God besides me?
  There is no Rock; I know not any."

The Folly of Idol Worship

9 All who make idols are nothing, and the
things they delight in do not profit; their witnesses neither see nor know, that they may be put
to shame. 10Who fashions a god or casts an image,
that is profitable for nothing? 11Behold, all his
fellows shall be put to shame, and the craftsmen
are but men; let them all assemble, let them stand
forth, they shall be terrified, they shall be put to
shame together.

12 The ironsmith fashions itb and works it
over the coals; he shapes it with hammers, and
forges it with his strong arm; he becomes hungry
and his strength fails, he drinks no water and
is faint. 13The carpenter stretches a line, he marks
it out with a pencil; he fashions it with planes,
and marks it with a compass; he shapes it into
the figure of a man, with the beauty of a man, to

dwell in a house. 14He cuts down cedars; or he
chooses a holm tree or an oak and lets it grow
strong among the trees of the forest; he plants a
cedar and the rain nourishes it. 15Then it becomes
fuel for a man; he takes a part of it and warms
himself, he kindles a fire and bakes bread; also he
makes a god and worships it, he makes it a
graven image and falls down before it. 16Half of
it he burns in the fire; over the half he eats flesh,
he roasts meat and is satisfied; also he warms
himself and says, "Aha, I am warm, I have seen
the fire!" 17And the rest of it he makes into a god,
his idol; and falls down to it and worships it;
he prays to it and says, "Deliver me, for you are
my god!"

Israel Is Not Forgotten

18 They know not, nor do they discern; for he
has shut their eyes, so that they cannot see, and
their minds, so that they cannot understand. 19No
one considers, nor is there knowledge or discernment to say, "Half of it I burned in the fire, I also
baked bread on its coals, I roasted flesh and have
eaten; and shall I make the residue of it an abomination? Shall I fall down before a block of wood?"
20He feeds on ashes; a deluded mind has led him
astray, and he cannot deliver himself or say, "Is
there not a lie in my right hand?"

21Remember these things, O Jacob,
  and Israel, for you are my servant;
I formed you, you are my servant;
  O Israel, you will not be forgotten by me.
22I have swept away your transgressions like a
  cloud,
  and your sins like mist;
return to me, for I have redeemed you.

23Sing, O heavens, for the LORD has done it;
  shout, O depths of the earth;
break forth into singing, O mountains,
  O forest, and every tree in it!
For the LORD has redeemed Jacob,
  and will be glorified in Israel.

24Thus says the LORD, your Redeemer,
  who formed you from the womb:
"I am the LORD, who made all things,
  who stretched out the heavens alone,
  who spread out the earth—Who was with
  me?c—
25who frustrates the omens of liars,
  and makes fools of diviners;

---

y Gk Compare Tg: Heb *They shall spring up in among grass.*
z Cn: Heb *from my placing an eternal people and things to come.*
a Tg: Heb *them.*
b Cn: Heb *an axe.*
c Another reading is *who spread out the earth by myself.*
44:6: Is 48:12; Rev 1:17; 2:8; 22:13.
44:23: Jer 51:48; Rev 12:12; 18:20.
44:25: 1 Cor 1:20.

who turns wise men back,
  and makes their knowledge foolish;
[26]who confirms the word of his servant,
  and performs the counsel of his
    messengers;
who says of Jerusalem, 'She shall be inhabited,'
  and of the cities of Judah, 'They shall be
    built,
  and I will raise up their ruins';
[27]who says to the deep, 'Be dry,
  I will dry up your rivers';
[28]who says of Cyrus, 'He is my shepherd,
  and he shall fulfil all my purpose';
saying of Jerusalem, 'She shall be built,'
  and of the temple, 'Your foundation shall be
    laid.'"

Cyrus, God's Instrument

45 Thus says the LORD to his anointed, to
  Cyrus,
  whose right hand I have grasped,
to subdue nations before him
  and uncover the loins of kings,
to open doors before him
  that gates may not be closed:
[2]"I will go before you
  and level the mountains,[d]
I will break in pieces the doors of bronze
  and cut asunder the bars of iron,
[3]I will give you the treasures of darkness
  and the hoards in secret places,
that you may know that it is I, the LORD,
  the God of Israel, who call you by your
    name.
[4]For the sake of my servant Jacob,
  and Israel my chosen,
I call you by your name,
  I surname you, though you do not know
    me.
[5]I am the LORD, and there is no other,
  besides me there is no God;
I clothe you, though you do not know me,
[6]that men may know, from the rising of the sun
  and from the west, that there is none
    besides me;
I am the LORD, and there is no other.
[7]I form light and create darkness,
  I make well-being and create woe,
I am the LORD, who do all these things.

[8]"Shower, O heavens, from above,
  and let the skies rain down righteousness;
let the earth open, that salvation may sprout
    forth, [e]
  and let it cause righteousness to spring up
    also;
I the LORD have created it.

[9]"Woe to him who strives with his Maker,
  an earthen vessel with the potter! [f]

Does the clay say to him who fashions it, 'What
    are you making?'
  or 'Your work has no handles'?
[10]Woe to him who says to a father, 'What are you
    begetting?'
  or to a woman, 'With what are you suffering
    labor pains?' "
[11]Thus says the LORD,
  the Holy One of Israel, and his Maker:
"Will you question me [g] about my children,
  or command me concerning the work of my
    hands?
[12]I made the earth,
  and created man upon it;
it was my hands that stretched out the
    heavens,
  and I commanded all their host.
[13]I have aroused him in righteousness,
  and I will make straight all his ways;
he shall build my city
  and set my exiles free,
not for price or reward,"
  says the LORD of hosts.

[14]Thus says the LORD:
"The wealth of Egypt and the merchandise of
    Ethiopia,
  and the Sabe'ans, men of stature,
shall come over to you and be yours,
  they shall follow you;
  they shall come over in chains and bow
    down to you.
They will make supplication to you, saying:
  'God is with you only, and there is no other,
    no god besides him.' "
[15]Truly, you are a God who hide yourself,
  O God of Israel, the Savior.
[16]All of them are put to shame and confounded,
  the makers of idols go in confusion
    together.
[17]But Israel is saved by the LORD
  with everlasting salvation;
you shall not be put to shame or confounded
  to all eternity.

[18]For thus says the LORD,
  who created the heavens
    (he is God!),
who formed the earth and made it
    (he established it;
he did not create it a chaos,
  he formed it to be inhabited!):
"I am the LORD, and there is no other.

---

[d] One ancient Ms Gk: Heb *the swellings.*
[e] One ancient Ms: Heb *that they may bring forth salvation.*
[f] Cn: Heb *potsherds* or *potters.*
[g] Cn: Heb *Ask me of things to come.*
45:9: Is 29:16; Rom 9:20.
45:14: 1 Cor 14:25
45:17: Heb 5:9.

¹⁹I did not speak in secret,
  in a land of darkness;
I did not say to the offspring of Jacob,
  'Seek me in chaos.'
I the Lord speak the truth,
  I declare what is right.

²⁰"Assemble yourselves and come,
  draw near together,
  you survivors of the nations!
They have no knowledge
  who carry about their wooden idols,
and keep on praying to a god
  that cannot save.
²¹Declare and present your case;
  let them take counsel together!
Who told this long ago?
  Who declared it of old?
Was it not I, the Lord?
  And there is no other god besides me,
a righteous God and a Savior;
  there is none besides me.

²²"Turn to me and be saved,
  all the ends of the earth!
For I am God, and there is no other.
²³By myself I have sworn,
  from my mouth has gone forth in
    righteousness
  a word that shall not return:
'To me every knee shall bow,
  every tongue shall swear.'

²⁴"Only in the Lord, it shall be said of me,
  are righteousness and strength;
to him shall come and be ashamed,
  all who were incensed against him.
²⁵In the Lord all the offspring of Israel
  shall triumph and glory."

Idols Cannot Save

46 Bel bows down, Nebo stoops,
  their idols are on beasts and cattle;
these things you carry are loaded
  as burdens on weary beasts.
²They stoop, they bow down together,
  they cannot save the burden,
but themselves go into captivity.

³"Listen to me, O house of Jacob,
  all the remnant of the house of Israel,
who have been borne by me from your birth,
  carried from the womb;
⁴even to your old age I am He,
  and to gray hairs I will carry you.
I have made, and I will bear;
  I will carry and will save.

⁵"To whom will you liken me and make me
    equal,
  and compare me, that we may be alike?

⁶Those who lavish gold from the purse,
  and weigh out silver in the scales,
hire a goldsmith, and he makes it into a god;
  then they fall down and worship!
⁷They lift it upon their shoulders, they carry it,
  they set it in its place, and it stands there;
  it cannot move from its place.
If one cries to it, it does not answer
  or save him from his trouble.

⁸"Remember this and consider,
  recall it to mind, you transgressors,
⁹ remember the former things of old;
for I am God, and there is no other;
  I am God, and there is none like me,
¹⁰declaring the end from the beginning
  and from ancient times things not yet done,
saying, 'My counsel shall stand,
  and I will accomplish all my purpose,'
¹¹calling a bird of prey from the east,
  the man of my counsel from a far country.
I have spoken, and I will bring it to pass;
  I have planned, and I will do it.

¹²"Listen to me, you stubborn of heart,
  you who are far from deliverance:
¹³I bring near my deliverance, it is not far off,
  and my salvation will not tarry;
I will put salvation in Zion,
  for Israel my glory."

The Humiliation of Babylon

47 Come down and sit in the dust,
  O virgin daughter of Babylon;
sit on the ground without a throne,
  O daughter of the Chalde′ans!
For you shall no more be called
  tender and delicate.
²Take the millstones and grind meal,
  put off your veil,
strip off your robe, uncover your legs,
  pass through the rivers.
³Your nakedness shall be uncovered,
  and your shame shall be seen.
I will take vengeance,
  and I will spare no man.
⁴Our Redeemer—the Lord of hosts is his
    name—
  is the Holy One of Israel.

⁵Sit in silence, and go into darkness,
  O daughter of the Chalde′ans;
for you shall no more be called
  the mistress of kingdoms.
⁶I was angry with my people,
  I profaned my heritage;

45:21: Acts 15:18.
45:23: Rom 14:11; Phil 2:10–11.
47: Is 13:1–14:23; Jer 50–51; Hab 1–2.

I gave them into your hand,
  you showed them no mercy;
on the aged you made your yoke
  exceedingly heavy.
[7]You said, "I shall be mistress for ever,"
  so that you did not lay these things to heart
  or remember their end.

[8]Now therefore hear this, you lover of pleasures,
  who sit securely,
who say in your heart,
  "I am, and there is no one besides me;
I shall not sit as a widow
  or know the loss of children":
[9]These two things shall come to you
  in a moment, in one day;
the loss of children and widowhood
  shall come upon you in full measure,
in spite of your many sorceries
  and the great power of your enchantments.

[10]You felt secure in your wickedness,
  you said, "No one sees me";
your wisdom and your knowledge
  led you astray,
and you said in your heart,
  "I am, and there is no one besides me."
[11]But evil shall come upon you,
  for which you cannot atone;
disaster shall fall upon you,
  which you will not be able to expiate;
and ruin shall come on you suddenly,
  of which you know nothing.

[12]Stand fast in your enchantments
  and your many sorceries,
  with which you have labored from your
    youth;
perhaps you may be able to succeed,
  perhaps you may inspire terror.
[13]You are wearied with your many counsels;
  let them stand forth and save you,
those who divide the heavens,
  who gaze at the stars,
who at the new moons predict
  what [h] shall befall you.

[14]Behold, they are like stubble,
  the fire consumes them;
they cannot deliver themselves
  from the power of the flame.
No coal for warming oneself is this,
  no fire to sit before!
[15]Such to you are those with whom you have
    labored,
  who have trafficked with you from your
    youth;
they wander about each in his own direction;
  there is no one to save you.

Israel's Unfaithfulness to God
the Creator and Redeemer

48 Hear this, O house of Jacob,
  who are called by the name of Israel,
and who came forth from the loins [i] of
    Judah;
who swear by the name of the LORD,
  and confess the God of Israel,
  but not in truth or right.
[2]For they call themselves after the holy city,
  and stay themselves on the God of Israel;
  the LORD of hosts is his name.

[3]"The former things I declared of old,
  they went forth from my mouth and I made
    them known;
  then suddenly I did them and they came to
    pass.
[4]Because I know that you are obstinate,
  and your neck is an iron sinew
  and your forehead brass,
[5]I declared them to you from of old,
  before they came to pass I announced them
    to you,
lest you should say, 'My idol did them,
  my graven image and my molten image
  commanded them.'

[6]"You have heard; now see all this;
  and will you not declare it?
From this time forth I make you hear new
    things,
  hidden things which you have not known.
[7]They are created now, not long ago;
  before today you have never heard of them,
  lest you should say, 'Behold, I knew them.'
[8]You have never heard, you have never known,
  from of old your ear has not been opened.
For I knew that you would deal very
    treacherously,
  and that from birth you were called a rebel.

[9]"For my name's sake I defer my anger,
  for the sake of my praise I restrain it for you,
  that I may not cut you off.
[10]Behold, I have refined you, but not like [j] silver;
  I have tried you in the furnace of affliction.
[11]For my own sake, for my own sake, I do it,
  for how should my name [k] be profaned?
  My glory I will not give to another.

[12]"Listen to me, O Jacob,
  and Israel, whom I called!

---

[h] Gk Syr Compare Vg: Heb *from what*.
[i] Cn: Heb *waters*.
[j] Cn: Heb *with*.
[k] Gk Old Latin: Heb lacks *my name*.
47:8: Rev 18:7.
47:9: Rev 18:8.
48:12: Is 44:6; Rev 1:17; 2:8; 22:13.

I am He, I am the first,
and I am the last.
¹³My hand laid the foundation of the earth,
and my right hand spread out the heavens;
when I call to them,
they stand forth together.

¹⁴"Assemble, all of you, and hear!
Who among them has declared these
things?
The Lord loves him;
he shall perform his purpose on Babylon,
and his arm shall be against the Chalde′ans.
¹⁵I, even I, have spoken and called him,
I have brought him, and he will prosper in
his way.
¹⁶Draw near to me, hear this:
from the beginning I have not spoken in
secret,
from the time it came to be I have been
there."
And now the Lord God has sent me and his
Spirit.

¹⁷Thus says the Lord,
your Redeemer, the Holy One of Israel:
"I am the Lord your God, who teaches you
to profit,
who leads you in the way you should go.
¹⁸O that you had listened to my commandments!
Then your peace would have been like a
river,
and your righteousness like the waves of
the sea;
¹⁹your offspring would have been like the sand,
and your descendants like its grains;
their name would never be cut off
or destroyed from before me."

²⁰Go forth from Babylon, flee from Chalde′a,
declare this with a shout of joy, proclaim it,
send it forth to the end of the earth;
say, "The Lord has redeemed his servant
Jacob!"
²¹They thirsted not when he led them through
the deserts;
he made water flow for them from the rock;
he cleft the rock and the water gushed out.
²²"There is no peace," says the Lord, "for the
wicked."

The Servant's Mission

49 Listen to me, O islands,
and pay attention, you peoples from
afar.
The Lord called me from the womb,
from the body of my mother he named my
name.
²He made my mouth like a sharp sword,
in the shadow of his hand he hid me;

he made me a polished arrow,
in his quiver he hid me away.
³And he said to me, "You are my servant,
Israel, in whom I will be glorified."
⁴But I said, "I have labored in vain,
I have spent my strength for nothing and
vanity;
yet surely my right is with the Lord,
and my recompense with my God."

⁵And now the Lord says,
who formed me from the womb to be his
servant,
to bring Jacob back to him,
and that Israel might be gathered to him,
for I am honored in the eyes of the Lord,
and my God has become my strength—
⁶he says:
"It is too light a thing that you should be my
servant
to raise up the tribes of Jacob
and to restore the preserved of Israel;
I will give you as a light to the nations,
that my salvation may reach to the end of
the earth."

⁷Thus says the Lord,
the Redeemer of Israel and his Holy One,
to one deeply despised, abhorred by the
nations,
the servant of rulers:
"Kings shall see and arise;
princes, and they shall prostrate
themselves;
because of the Lord, who is faithful,
the Holy One of Israel, who has chosen
you."

⁸Thus says the Lord:
"In a time of favor I have answered you,
in a day of salvation I have helped you;
I have kept you and given you
as a covenant to the people,
to establish the land,
to apportion the desolate heritages;
⁹saying to the prisoners, 'Come forth,'
to those who are in darkness, 'Appear.'
They shall feed along the ways,
on all bare heights shall be their pasture;
¹⁰they shall not hunger or thirst,
neither scorching wind nor sun shall strike
them,
for he who has pity on them will lead them,
and by springs of water will guide them.

49:1: Jer 1:5; Gal 1:15.
49:4: Phil 2:16.
49:6: Is 42:6; Lk 2:32; Acts 13:47; 26:23.
49:8: 2 Cor 6:2.
49:10: Rev 7:16.

[11]And I will make all my mountains a way,
  and my highways shall be raised up.
[12]Behold, these shall come from afar,
  and behold, these from the north and from
    the west,
  and these from the land of Sye′ne." [1]
[13]Sing for joy, O heavens, and exult, O earth;
  break forth, O mountains, into singing!
For the LORD has comforted his people,
  and will have compassion on his afflicted.

[14]But Zion said, "The LORD has forsaken me,
  my Lord has forgotten me."
[15]"Can a woman forget her sucking child,
  that she should have no compassion on the
    son of her womb?
Even these may forget,
  yet I will not forget you.
[16]Behold, I have graven you on the palms of my
    hands;
  your walls are continually before me.
[17]Your builders outstrip your destroyers,
  and those who laid you waste go forth from
    you.
[18]Lift up your eyes round about and see;
  they all gather, they come to you.
As I live, says the LORD,
  you shall put them all on as an ornament,
  you shall bind them on as a bride does.

[19]"Surely your waste and your desolate places
  and your devastated land—
surely now you will be too narrow for your
    inhabitants,
  and those who swallowed you up will be far
    away.
[20]The children born in the time of your
    bereavement
  will yet say in your ears:
'The place is too narrow for me;
  make room for me to dwell in.'
[21]Then you will say in your heart:
'Who has borne me these?
I was bereaved and barren,
  exiled and put away,
  but who has brought up these?
Behold, I was left alone;
  from where then have these come?'"

[22]Thus says the Lord GOD:
"Behold, I will lift up my hand to the nations,
  and raise my signal to the peoples;
and they shall bring your sons in their bosom,
  and your daughters shall be carried on their
    shoulders.
[23]Kings shall be your foster fathers,
  and their queens your nursing mothers.
With their faces to the ground they shall bow
    down to you, and lick the dust of your
    feet.

Then you will know that I am the LORD;
  those who wait for me shall not be put to
    shame."

[24]Can the prey be taken from the mighty,
  or the captives of a tyrant [m] be rescued?
[25]Surely, thus says the LORD:
"Even the captives of the mighty shall be
    taken,
  and the prey of the tyrant be rescued,
for I will contend with those who contend with
    you,
  and I will save your children.
[26]I will make your oppressors eat their own flesh,
  and they shall be drunk with their own
    blood as with wine.
Then all flesh shall know
  that I am the LORD your Savior,
  and your Redeemer, the Mighty One of
    Jacob."

The Sufferings of the Servant

50 Thus says the LORD:
"Where is your mother's bill of divorce,
  with which I put her away?
Or which of my creditors is it
  to whom I have sold you?
Behold, for your iniquities you were sold,
  and for your transgressions your mother
    was put away.
[2]Why, when I came, was there no man?
  When I called, was there no one to answer?
Is my hand shortened, that it cannot redeem?
  Or have I no power to deliver?
Behold, by my rebuke I dry up the sea,
  I make the rivers a desert;
their fish stink for lack of water,
  and die of thirst.
[3]I clothe the heavens with blackness,
  and make sackcloth their covering."

[4]The Lord GOD has given me
  the tongue of those who are taught,
that I may know how to sustain with a word
  him that is weary.
Morning by morning he wakens,
  he wakens my ear
to hear as those who are taught.
[5]The Lord GOD has opened my ear,
  and I was not rebellious,
  I turned not backward.
[6]I gave my back to those who struck me,
  and my cheeks to those who pulled out the
    beard;
I hid not my face
  from shame and spitting.

---

[1] Cn: Heb *Sinim.*
[m] One ancient Ms Syr Vg: Heb *righteous man.*
49:13: Is 44:23; Jer 51:48; Rev 12:12; 18:20.

[7]For the Lord God helps me;
    therefore I have not been confounded;
therefore I have set my face like a flint,
    and I know that I shall not be put to shame;
[8] he who vindicates me is near.
Who will contend with me?
    Let us stand up together.
Who is my adversary?
    Let him come near to me.
[9]Behold, the Lord God helps me;
    who will declare me guilty?
Behold, all of them will wear out like a
    garment;
    the moth will eat them up.

[10]Who among you fears the Lord
    and obeys the voice of his servant,
who walks in darkness
    and has no light,
yet trusts in the name of the Lord
    and relies upon his God?
[11]Behold, all you who kindle a fire,
    who set brands alight. [n]
Walk by the light of your fire,
    and by the brands which you have
      kindled!
This shall you have from my hand:
    you shall lie down in torment.

The Lord Will Comfort Zion

51 "Listen to me, you who pursue deliverance,
    you who seek the Lord;
look to the rock from which you were hewn,
    and to the quarry from which you were dug.
[2]Look to Abraham your father
    and to Sarah who bore you;
for when he was but one I called him,
    and I blessed him and made him many.
[3]For the Lord will comfort Zion:
    he will comfort all her waste places,
and will make her wilderness like Eden,
    her desert like the garden of the Lord;
joy and gladness will be found in her,
    thanksgiving and the voice of song.

[4]"Listen to me, my people,
    and give ear to me, my nation;
for a law will go forth from me,
    and my justice for a light to the peoples.
[5]My deliverance draws near speedily,
    my salvation has gone forth,
    and my arms will rule the peoples;
the islands wait for me,
    and for my arm they hope.
[6]Lift up your eyes to the heavens,
    and look at the earth beneath;
for the heavens will vanish like smoke,
    the earth will wear out like a garment,
    and they who dwell in it will die like
      gnats; [o]

but my salvation will be for ever,
    and my deliverance will never be ended.

[7]"Listen to me, you who know righteousness,
    the people in whose heart is my law;
fear not the reproach of men,
    and be not dismayed at their revilings.
[8]For the moth will eat them up like a garment,
    and the worm will eat them like wool;
but my deliverance will be for ever,
    and my salvation to all generations."

[9]Awake, awake, put on strength,
    O arm of the Lord;
awake, as in days of old,
    the generations of long ago.
Was it not you who cut Ra′hab in pieces,
    who pierced the dragon?
[10]Was it not you who dried up the sea,
    the waters of the great deep;
who made the depths of the sea a way
    for the redeemed to pass over?
[11]And the ransomed of the Lord shall return,
    and come to Zion with singing;
everlasting joy shall be upon their heads;
    they shall obtain joy and gladness,
    and sorrow and sighing shall flee away.

[12]"I, I am he who comforts you;
    who are you that you are afraid of man who
      dies,
    of the son of man who is made like grass,
[13]and have forgotten the Lord, your Maker,
    who stretched out the heavens
    and laid the foundations of the earth,
and fear continually all the day
    because of the fury of the oppressor,
when he sets himself to destroy?
    And where is the fury of the oppressor?
[14]He who is bowed down shall speedily be
      released;
    he shall not die and go down to the Pit,
    neither shall his bread fail.
[15]For I am the Lord your God,
    who stirs up the sea so that its waves
      roar—
    the Lord of hosts is his name.
[16]And I have put my words in your mouth,
    and hid you in the shadow of my hand,
stretching out [p] the heavens
    and laying the foundations of the earth,
    and saying to Zion, 'You are my people.' "

[17]Rouse yourself, rouse yourself,
    stand up, O Jerusalem,

---

[n] Syr: Heb *gird yourselves with brands*.
[o] Or *in like manner*.
[p] Syr: Heb *plant*.
50:8-9: Rom 8:33; Heb 1:11.
51:6: Heb 1:11.

you who have drunk at the hand of the LORD
    the cup of his wrath,
who have drunk to the dregs
    the bowl of staggering.
18There is none to guide her
    among all the sons she has borne;
there is none to take her by the hand
    among all the sons she has brought up.
19These two things have befallen you—
    who will condole with you?—
devastation and destruction, famine and
    sword;
    who will comfort you? �q
20Your sons have fainted,
    they lie at the head of every street
    like an antelope in a net;
they are full of the wrath of the LORD,
    the rebuke of your God.

21Therefore hear this, you who are afflicted,
    who are drunk, but not with wine:
22Thus says your Lord, the LORD,
    your God who pleads the cause of his
    people:
"Behold, I have taken from your hand
    the cup of staggering;
the bowl of my wrath
    you shall drink no more;
23and I will put it into the hand of your
    tormentors,
    who have said to you,
'Bow down, that we may pass over';
and you have made your back like the
    ground
    and like the street for them to pass over."

Awake to Good Tidings of Redemption

52 Awake, awake,
    put on your strength, O Zion;
put on your beautiful garments,
    O Jerusalem, the holy city;
for there shall no more come into you
    the uncircumcised and the unclean.
2Shake yourself from the dust, arise,
    O captive ʳ Jerusalem;
loose the bonds from your neck,
    O captive daughter of Zion.

3 For thus says the LORD: "You were sold for nothing, and you shall be redeemed without money. 4For thus says the Lord GOD: My people went down at the first into Egypt to sojourn there, and the Assyrian oppressed them for nothing. 5Now therefore what have I here, says the LORD, seeing that my people are taken away for nothing? Their rulers wail, says the LORD, and continually all the day my name is despised. 6Therefore my people shall know my name; therefore in that day they shall know that it is I who speak; here am I."

7How beautiful upon the mountains
    are the feet of him who brings good
    tidings,
who publishes peace, who brings good tidings
    of good,
who publishes salvation,
    who says to Zion, "Your God reigns."
8Listen, your watchmen lift up their voice,
    together they sing for joy;
for eye to eye they see
    the return of the LORD to Zion.
9Break forth together into singing,
    you waste places of Jerusalem;
for the LORD has comforted his people,
    he has redeemed Jerusalem.
10The LORD has bared his holy arm
    before the eyes of all the nations;
and all the ends of the earth shall see
    the salvation of our God.

11Depart, depart, go out from there,
    touch no unclean thing;
go out from the midst of her, purify
    yourselves,
    you who bear the vessels of the LORD.
12For you shall not go out in haste,
    and you shall not go in flight,
for the LORD will go before you,
    and the God of Israel will be your rear
    guard.

13Behold, my servant shall prosper,
    he shall be exalted and lifted up,
    and shall be very high.
14As many were astonished at him ˢ —
    his appearance was so marred, beyond
      human semblance,
    and his form beyond that of the sons of
      men—
15so shall he startle ᵗ many nations;
    kings shall shut their mouths because of
      him;
for that which has not been told them they
    shall see,
    and that which they have not heard they
      shall understand.

The Lord's Suffering Servant

53 Who has believed what we have heard?
    And to whom has the arm of the LORD
    been revealed?

�q One ancient Ms Gk Syr Vg: Heb *how may I comfort you.*
ʳ Cn: Heb *sit.*
ˢ Syr Tg: Heb *you.*
ᵗ The meaning of the Hebrew word is uncertain.
52:1: Rev 21:27.
52:5: Rom 2:24.
52:7: Acts 10:36; Rom 10:15; Eph 6:15.
52:10: Lk 2:30; 3:6.
52:11: 2 Cor 6:17.
52:15: Rom 15:21.
53:1: Jn 12:38; Rom 10:16.

²For he grew up before him like a young plant,
  and like a root out of dry ground;
he had no form or comeliness that we should
    look at him,
  and no beauty that we should desire him.
³He was despised and rejected ᵘ by men;
  a man of sorrows, ᵛ and acquainted with
    grief; ʷ
and as one from whom men hide their faces
  he was despised, and we esteemed him not.

⁴Surely he has borne our griefs ˣ
  and carried our sorrows; ʸ
yet we esteemed him stricken,
  struck down by God, and afflicted.
⁵But he was wounded for our transgressions,
  he was bruised for our iniquities;
upon him was the chastisement that made us
    whole,
  and with his stripes we are healed.
⁶All we like sheep have gone astray;
  we have turned every one to his own way;
and the LORD has laid on him
  the iniquity of us all. *

⁷He was oppressed, and he was afflicted,
  yet he opened not his mouth;
like a lamb that is led to the slaughter,
  and like a sheep that before its shearers is
    silent,
  so he opened not his mouth.
⁸By oppression and judgment he was taken
    away;
  and as for his generation, who considered
that he was cut off out of the land of the
    living,
  stricken for the transgression of my
    people?
⁹And they made his grave with the wicked
  and with a rich man in his death,
although he had done no violence,
  and there was no deceit in his mouth.

¹⁰Yet it was the will of the LORD to bruise him;
  he has put him to grief; ᶻ
when he makes himself ᵃ an offering for sin,
  he shall see his offspring, he shall prolong
    his days;
the will of the LORD shall prosper in his hand;
¹¹ he shall see the fruit of the travail of his
    soul and be satisfied;
by his knowledge shall the righteous one, my
    servant,
  make many to be accounted righteous;
  and he shall bear their iniquities.
¹²Therefore I will divide him a portion with the
    great,
  and he shall divide the spoil with the
    strong;

because he poured out his soul to death,
  and was numbered with the transgressors;
yet he bore the sin of many,
  and made intercession for the transgressors.

Mercy and Comfort Offered

54 "Sing, O barren one, who did not bear;
  break forth into singing and cry
    aloud,
you who have not had labor pains!
For the children of the desolate one will be
    more
  than the children of her that is married,
  says the LORD.
²Enlarge the place of your tent,
  and let the curtains of your habitations be
    stretched out;
hold not back, lengthen your cords
  and strengthen your stakes.
³For you will spread abroad to the right and to
    the left,
  and your descendants will possess the
    nations
  and will people the desolate cities.

⁴"Fear not, for you will not be ashamed;
  be not confounded, for you will not be put to
    shame;
for you will forget the shame of your youth,
  and the reproach of your widowhood you
    will remember no more.
⁵For your Maker is your husband,
  the LORD of hosts is his name;
and the Holy One of Israel is your Redeemer,
  the God of the whole earth he is called.
⁶For the LORD has called you
  like a wife forsaken and grieved in spirit,
like a wife of youth when she is cast off,
  says your God.
⁷For a brief moment I forsook you,
  but with great compassion I will gather
    you.
⁸In overflowing wrath for a moment
  I hid my face from you,
but with everlasting mercy I will have
    compassion on you,
  says the LORD, your Redeemer.

ᵘ Or forsaken.
ᵛ Or pains.
ʷ Or sickness.
ˣ Or sicknesses.
ʸ Or pains.
ᶻ Heb made him sick.
ᵃ Vg: Heb thou makest his soul.
53:4: Mt 8:17.
53:5–6: 1 Pet 2:24–25.
53:7–8: Acts 8:32–33.
53:9: 1 Pet 2:22.
53:12: Lk 22:37.
54:1: Gal 4:27.
* 53:4–6: The doctrine of vicarious atonement is the unique characteristic of this prophecy. We find it in the New Testament in all its fulness.

[9]"For this is like the days of Noah to me:
as I swore that the waters of Noah
should no more go over the earth,
so I have sworn that I will not be angry with
you
and will not rebuke you.
[10]For the mountains may depart
and the hills be removed,
but my mercy shall not depart from you,
and my covenant of peace shall not be
removed,
says the LORD, who has compassion on you.

[11]"O afflicted one, storm-tossed, and not
comforted,
behold, I will set your stones in antimony,
and lay your foundations with sapphires. [b]
[12]I will make your pinnacles of agate,
your gates of carbuncles,
and all your wall of precious stones.
[13]All your sons shall be taught by the LORD,
and great shall be the prosperity of your
sons.
[14]In righteousness you shall be established;
you shall be far from oppression, for you
shall not fear;
and from terror, for it shall not come near
you.
[15]If any one stirs up strife,
it is not from me;
whoever stirs up strife with you
shall fall because of you.
[16]Behold, I have created the smith
who blows the fire of coals,
and produces a weapon for its purpose.
I have also created the ravager to destroy;
[17] no weapon that is fashioned against you
shall prosper,
and you shall confute every tongue that
rises against you in judgment.
This is the heritage of the servants of the
LORD
and their vindication from me, says the
LORD."

An Invitation to Abundant Life

55

"Ho, every one who thirsts,
come to the waters;
and he who has no money,
come, buy and eat!
Come, buy wine and milk
without money and without price.
[2]Why do you spend your money for that which
is not bread,
and your labor for that which does not
satisfy?
Listen diligently to me, and eat what is good,
and delight yourselves in rich food.
[3]Incline your ear, and come to me;
hear, that your soul may live;

and I will make with you an everlasting
covenant,
my steadfast, merciful love for David.
[4]Behold, I made him a witness to the peoples,
a leader and commander for the peoples.
[5]Behold, you shall call nations that you know
not,
and nations that knew you not shall run to
you,
because of the LORD your God, and of the Holy
One of Israel,
for he has glorified you.

[6]"Seek the LORD while he may be found,
call upon him while he is near;
[7]let the wicked forsake his way,
and the unrighteous man his thoughts;
let him return to the LORD, that he may have
mercy on him,
and to our God, for he will abundantly
pardon.
[8]For my thoughts are not your thoughts,
neither are your ways my ways, says the
LORD.
[9]For as the heavens are higher than the earth,
so are my ways higher than your ways
and my thoughts than your thoughts.

[10]"For as the rain and the snow come down from
heaven,
and do not return there but water the earth,
making it bring forth and sprout,
giving seed to the sower and bread to the
eater,
[11]so shall my word be that goes forth from my
mouth;
it shall not return to me empty,
but it shall accomplish that which I intend,
and prosper in the thing for which I sent it.

[12]"For you shall go out in joy,
and be led forth in peace;
the mountains and the hills before you
shall break forth into singing,
and all the trees of the field shall clap their
hands.
[13]Instead of the thorn shall come up the
cypress;
instead of the brier shall come up the
myrtle;
and it shall be to the LORD for a memorial,
for an everlasting sign which shall not be
cut off."

[b] Or lapis lazuli.
54:11-12: Rev 21:19.
54:13: Jn 6:45.
55:1: Rev 21:6; 22:17.
55:3: Acts 13:34; Heb 13:20.
55:10: 2 Cor 9:10.

Rewards of Righteousness

56 * Thus says the LORD:
"Keep justice, and do righteousness,
for soon my salvation will come,
and my deliverance be revealed.
[2]Blessed is the man who does this,
and the son of man who holds it fast,
who keeps the sabbath, not profaning it,
and keeps his hand from doing any evil."

[3]Let not the foreigner who has joined himself to
the LORD say,
"The LORD will surely separate me from his
people";
and let not the eunuch say,
"Behold, I am a dry tree."
[4]For thus says the LORD:
"To the eunuchs who keep my sabbaths,
who choose the things that please me
and hold fast my covenant,
[5]I will give in my house and within my walls
a monument and a name
better than sons and daughters;
I will give them an everlasting name
which shall not be cut off.

[6]"And the foreigners who join themselves to the
LORD,
to minister to him, to love the name of the
LORD,
and to be his servants,
every one who keeps the sabbath, and does not
profane it,
and holds fast my covenant—
[7]these I will bring to my holy mountain,
and make them joyful in my house of
prayer;
their burnt offerings and their sacrifices
will be accepted on my altar;
for my house shall be called a house of prayer
for all peoples.
[8]Thus says the Lord GOD,
who gathers the outcasts of Israel,
I will gather yet others to him
besides those already gathered." [c]

[9]All you beasts of the field, come to devour—
all you beasts in the forest.
[10]His watchmen are blind,
they are all without knowledge;
they are all mute dogs,
they cannot bark;
dreaming, lying down,
loving to slumber.
[11]The dogs have a mighty appetite;
they never have enough.
The shepherds also have no understanding;
they have all turned to their own way,
each to his own gain, one and all.

[12]"Come," they say, "let us [d] get wine,
let us fill ourselves with strong drink;
and tomorrow will be like this day,
great beyond measure."

Idolatry Condemned

57 The righteous man perishes,
and no one lays it to heart;
devout men are taken away,
while no one understands.
For the righteous man is taken away from
calamity,
[2] he enters into peace;
they rest in their beds
who walk in their uprightness.
[3]But you, draw near to here,
sons of the sorceress,
offspring of the adulterer and the harlot.
[4]Of whom are you making sport?
Against whom do you open your mouth
wide
and put out your tongue?
Are you not children of transgression,
the offspring of deceit,
[5]you who burn with lust among the oaks,
under every green tree;
who slay your children in the valleys,
under the clefts of the rocks?
[6]Among the smooth stones of the valley is your
portion;
they, they, are your lot;
to them you have poured out a drink offering,
you have brought a cereal offering.
Shall I be appeased for these things?
[7]Upon a high and lofty mountain
you have set your bed,
and from there you went up to offer
sacrifice.
[8]Behind the door and the doorpost
you have set up your symbol;
for, deserting me, you have uncovered your
bed,
you have gone up to it,
you have made it wide;
and you have made a bargain for yourself with
them,
you have loved their bed,
you have looked on nakedness. [e]
[9]You journeyed to Mo'lech [f] with oil
and multiplied your perfumes;
you sent your envoys far off,
and sent down even to Sheol.
[10]You were wearied with the length of your way,
but you did not say, "It is hopeless";

---

[c] Heb *his gathered ones.*
[d] One ancient Ms Syr Vg Tg: Heb *me.*
[e] The meaning of the Hebrew is uncertain.
[f] Or *the king.*
56:7: Mt 21:13; Mk 11:17; Lk 19:46.
* 56 to the end: These prophecies were probably uttered in the difficult
days of the return from exile, about the year 538 B.C.

you found new life for your strength,
and so you were not faint.

[11]Whom did you dread and fear,
so that you lied,
and did not remember me,
did not give me a thought?
Have I not held my peace, even for a long time,
and so you do not fear me?
[12]I will tell of your righteousness and your doings,
but they will not help you.
[13]When you cry out, let your collection of idols deliver you!
The wind will carry them off,
a breath will take them away.
But he who takes refuge in me shall possess the land,
and shall inherit my holy mountain.

[14]And it shall be said,
"Build up, build up, prepare the way,
remove every obstruction from my people's way."
[15]For thus says the high and lofty One
who inhabits eternity, whose name is Holy:
"I dwell in the high and holy place,
and also with him who is of a contrite and humble spirit,
to revive the spirit of the humble,
and to revive the heart of the contrite.
[16]For I will not contend for ever,
nor will I always be angry;
for from me proceeds the spirit,
and I have made the breath of life.
[17]Because of the iniquity of his covetousness I was angry,
I struck him, I hid my face and was angry;
but he went on backsliding in the way of his own heart.
[18]I have seen his ways, but I will heal him;
I will lead him and repay him with comfort,
creating for his mourners the fruit of the lips.
[19]Peace, peace, to the far and to the near, says the LORD;
and I will heal him.
[20]But the wicked are like the tossing sea;
for it cannot rest,
and its waters toss up mire and dirt.
[21]There is no peace, says my God, for the wicked."

True and False Fasting and Worship

58 "Cry aloud, spare not,
lift up your voice like a trumpet;
declare to my people their transgression,
to the house of Jacob their sins.
[2]Yet they seek me daily,
and delight to know my ways,

as if they were a nation that did righteousness
and did not forsake the ordinance of their God;
they ask of me righteous judgments,
they delight to draw near to God.
[3]'Why have we fasted, and you see it not?
Why have we humbled ourselves, and you take no knowledge of it?'
Behold, in the day of your fast you seek your own pleasure,[g]
and oppress all your workers.
[4]Behold, you fast only to quarrel and to fight
and to hit with wicked fist.
Fasting like yours this day
will not make your voice to be heard on high.
[5]Is such the fast that I choose,
a day for a man to humble himself?
Is it to bow down his head like a rush,
and to spread sackcloth and ashes under him?
Will you call this a fast,
and a day acceptable to the LORD?

[6]"Is not this the fast that I choose:
to loose the bonds of wickedness,
to undo the thongs of the yoke,
to let the oppressed go free,
and to break every yoke?
[7]Is it not to share your bread with the hungry,
and bring the homeless poor into your house;
when you see the naked, to cover him,
and not to hide yourself from your own flesh?
[8]Then shall your light break forth like the dawn,
and your healing shall spring up speedily;
your righteousness shall go before you,
the glory of the LORD shall be your rear guard.
[9]Then you shall call, and the LORD will answer;
you shall cry, and he will say, Here I am.

"If you take away from the midst of you the yoke,
the pointing of the finger, and speaking wickedness,
[10]if you pour yourself out for the hungry
and satisfy the desire of the afflicted,
then shall your light rise in the darkness
and your gloom be as the noonday.
[11]And the LORD will guide you continually,
and satisfy your desire with good things,[h]
and make your bones strong;

---

[g] Or *pursue your own business.*
[h] The meaning of the Hebrew word is uncertain.
57:15: Mt 5:3.
57:19: Acts 2:39; Eph 2:13, 17.
58:6: Acts 8:23.

and you shall be like a watered garden,
 like a spring of water,
 whose waters do not fail.
¹²And your ancient ruins shall be rebuilt;
 you shall raise up the foundations of many
  generations;
you shall be called the repairer of the breach,
 the restorer of streets to dwell in.

¹³"If you turn back your foot from the sabbath,
 from doing your pleasure ¹ on my holy day,
and call the sabbath a delight
 and the holy day of the LORD honorable;
if you honor it, not going your own ways,
 or seeking your own pleasure, ³ or talking
  idly;
¹⁴then you shall take delight in the LORD,
 and I will make you ride upon the heights
  of the earth;
I will feed you with the heritage of Jacob your
 father,
 for the mouth of the LORD has spoken."

Injustice and Oppression to Be Punished

59 Behold, the LORD's hand is not shortened,
 that it cannot save,
 or his ear dull, that it cannot hear;
²but your iniquities have made a separation
 between you and your God,
and your sins have hidden his face from you
 so that he does not hear.
³For your hands are defiled with blood
 and your fingers with iniquity;
your lips have spoken lies,
 your tongue mutters wickedness.
⁴No one enters suit justly,
 no one goes to law honestly;
they rely on empty pleas, they speak lies,
 they conceive mischief and bring forth
  iniquity.
⁵They hatch adders' eggs,
 they weave the spider's web;
he who eats their eggs dies,
 and from one which is crushed a viper is
  hatched.
⁶Their webs will not serve as clothing;
 men will not cover themselves with what
  they make.
Their works are works of iniquity,
 and deeds of violence are in their hands.
⁷Their feet run to evil,
 and they make haste to shed innocent
  blood;
their thoughts are thoughts of iniquity,
 desolation and destruction are in their
  highways.
⁸The way of peace they know not,
 and there is no justice in their paths;
they have made their roads crooked,
 no one who goes in them knows peace.

⁹Therefore justice is far from us,
 and righteousness does not overtake us;
we look for light, and behold, darkness,
 and for brightness, but we walk in gloom.
¹⁰We grope for the wall like the blind,
 we grope like those who have no eyes;
we stumble at noon as in the twilight,
 among those in full vigor we are like dead
  men.
¹¹We all growl like bears,
 we moan and moan like doves;
we look for justice, but there is none;
 for salvation, but it is far from us.
¹²For our transgressions are multiplied before you,
 and our sins testify against us;
for our transgressions are with us,
 and we know our iniquities:
¹³transgressing, and denying the LORD,
 and turning away from following our God,
speaking oppression and revolt,
 conceiving and uttering from the heart lying
  words.
¹⁴Justice is turned back,
 and righteousness stands afar off;
for truth has fallen in the public squares,
 and uprightness cannot enter.
¹⁵Truth is lacking,
 and he who departs from evil makes
  himself a prey.

The LORD saw it, and it displeased him
 that there was no justice.
¹⁶He saw that there was no man,
 and wondered that there was no one to
  intervene;
then his own arm brought him victory,
 and his righteousness upheld him.
¹⁷He put on righteousness as a breastplate,
 and a helmet of salvation upon his head;
he put on garments of vengeance for clothing,
 and wrapped himself in fury as a mantle.
¹⁸According to their deeds, so will he repay,
 wrath to his adversaries, repayment to his
  enemies;
to the islands he will render repayment.
¹⁹So they shall fear the name of the LORD from
 the west,
 and his glory from the rising of the sun;
for he will come like a rushing stream,
 which the wind of the LORD drives.

²⁰ "And he will come to Zion as Redeemer,
 to those in Jacob who turn from
  transgression, says the LORD.

---

¹ Or *business*.
³ Or *pursuing your own business*.
59:7–8: Rom 3:15–17.
59:17: Eph 6:14, 17; 1 Thess 5:8.
59:19: Mt 8:11; Lk 13:29.
59:20–21: Rom 11:26–27.

[21] "And as for me, this is my covenant with them, says the LORD: my spirit which is upon you, and my words which I have put in your mouth, shall not depart out of your mouth, or out of the mouth of your children, or out of the mouth of your children's children, says the LORD, from this time forth and for evermore."

The Lord Will Come as a Light and Will Gather His People

60 Arise, shine; for your light has come, and the glory of the LORD has risen upon you.
[2] For behold, darkness shall cover the earth, and thick darkness the peoples;
but the LORD will arise upon you, and his glory will be seen upon you.
[3] And nations shall walk by your light, and kings in the brightness of your rising.

[4] Lift up your eyes round about, and see; they all gather together, they come to you;
your sons shall come from far, and your daughters shall be carried in the arms.
[5] Then you shall see and be radiant, your heart shall thrill and rejoice;[k]
because the abundance of the sea shall be turned to you, the wealth of the nations shall come to you.
[6] A multitude of camels shall cover you, the young camels of Mid'ian and E'phah;
all those from Sheba shall come.
They shall bring gold and frankincense, and shall proclaim the praise of the LORD.
[7] All the flocks of Ke'dar shall be gathered to you,
the rams of Nebai'oth shall minister to you;
they shall come up with acceptance on my altar,
and I will glorify my glorious house.

[8] Who are these that fly like a cloud, and like doves to their windows?
[9] For the islands shall wait for me, the ships of Tar'shish first,
to bring your sons from far, their silver and gold with them,
for the name of the LORD your God, and for the Holy One of Israel,
because he has glorified you.

[10] Foreigners shall build up your walls, and their kings shall minister to you;
for in my wrath I struck you, but in my favor I have had mercy on you.
[11] Your gates shall be open continually; day and night they shall not be shut;

that men may bring to you the wealth of the nations,
with their kings led in procession.
[12] For the nation and kingdom that will not serve you shall perish;
those nations shall be utterly laid waste.
[13] The glory of Lebanon shall come to you, the cypress, the plane, and the pine,
to beautify the place of my sanctuary; and I will make the place of my feet glorious.
[14] The sons of those who oppressed you shall come bending low to you;
and all who despised you shall bow down at your feet;
they shall call you the City of the LORD, the Zion of the Holy One of Israel.

[15] Whereas you have been forsaken and hated, with no one passing through,
I will make you majestic for ever, a joy from age to age.
[16] You shall suck the milk of nations, you shall suck the breast of kings;
and you shall know that I, the LORD, am your Savior
and your Redeemer, the Mighty One of Jacob.

[17] Instead of bronze I will bring gold, and instead of iron I will bring silver;
instead of wood, bronze, instead of stones, iron.
I will make your overseers peace and your taskmasters righteousness.
[18] Violence shall no more be heard in your land, devastation or destruction within your borders;
you shall call your walls Salvation, and your gates Praise.

[19] The sun shall no longer be your light by day,
nor for brightness shall the moon give light to you by night;[1]
but the LORD will be your everlasting light, and your God will be your glory.
[20] Your sun shall no more go down, nor your moon withdraw itself;
for the LORD will be your everlasting light, and your days of mourning shall be ended.
[21] Your people shall all be righteous; they shall possess the land for ever,

---

[k] Heb be enlarged.
[1] One ancient Ms Gk Old Latin Tg: Heb lacks by night.
60:6: Mt 2:11.
60:11: Rev 21:25–26.
60:14: Rev 3:9.
60:19: Rev 21:23; 22:5.

the shoot of my planting, the work of my hands,
that I might be glorified.
[22]The least one shall become a clan,
and the smallest one a mighty nation;
I am the LORD;
in its time I will hasten it.

Good Tidings for the Afflicted

61 * The Spirit of the Lord GOD is upon me,
because the LORD has anointed me
to bring good tidings to the afflicted;[m]
he has sent me to bind up the
brokenhearted,
to proclaim liberty to the captives,
and the opening of the prison[n] to those
who are bound;
[2]to proclaim the year of the LORD's favor,
and the day of vengeance of our God;
to comfort all who mourn;
[3]to grant to those who mourn in Zion—
to give them a garland instead of ashes,
the oil of gladness instead of mourning,
the mantle of praise instead of a faint
spirit;
that they may be called oaks of righteousness,
the planting of the LORD, that he may be
glorified.
[4]They shall build up the ancient ruins,
they shall raise up the former devastations;
they shall repair the ruined cities,
the devastations of many generations.

[5]Aliens shall stand and feed your flocks,
foreigners shall be your plowmen and
vinedressers;
[6]but you shall be called the priests of the LORD,
men shall speak of you as the ministers of
our God;
you shall eat the wealth of the nations,
and in their riches you shall glory.
[7]Instead of your shame you shall have a double
portion,
instead of dishonor you[o] shall rejoice in
your[p] lot;
therefore in your[p] land you[o] shall possess a
double portion;
yours[q] shall be everlasting joy.

[8]For I the LORD love justice,
I hate robbery and wrong;[r]
I will faithfully give them their recompense,
and I will make an everlasting covenant
with them.
[9]Their descendants shall be known among the
nations,
and their offspring in the midst of the
peoples;
all who see them shall acknowledge them,
that they are a people whom the LORD has
blessed.

[10]I will greatly rejoice in the LORD,
my soul shall exult in my God;
for he has clothed me with the garments of
salvation,
he has covered me with the robe of
righteousness,
as a bridegroom decks himself with a garland,
and as a bride adorns herself with her
jewels.
[11]For as the earth brings forth its shoots,
and as a garden causes what is sown in it to
spring up,
so the Lord GOD will cause righteousness and
praise
to spring forth before all the nations.

The Vindication and Salvation of Zion

62 For Zion's sake I will not keep silent,
and for Jerusalem's sake I will not rest,
until her vindication goes forth as brightness,
and her salvation as a burning torch.
[2]The nations shall see your vindication,
and all the kings your glory;
and you shall be called by a new name
which the mouth of the LORD will give.
[3]You shall be a crown of beauty in the hand of
the LORD,
and a royal diadem in the hand of your God.
[4]You shall no more be termed Forsaken,[s]
and your land shall no more be termed
Desolate;[t]
but you shall be called My delight is in her,[u]
and your land Married;[v]
for the LORD delights in you,
and your land shall be married.
[5]For as a young man marries a virgin,
so shall your sons marry you,
and as the bridegroom rejoices over the bride,
so shall your God rejoice over you.

[6]Upon your walls, O Jerusalem,
I have set watchmen;
all the day and all the night
they shall never be silent.
You who put the LORD in remembrance,
take no rest,
[7]and give him no rest
until he establishes Jerusalem
and makes it a praise in the earth.

---

[m] Or *poor.*
[n] Or *the opening of the eyes:* Heb *the opening.*
[o] Heb *they.*
[p] Heb *their.*
[q] Heb *theirs.*
[r] Or *robbery with a burnt offering.*
[s] Heb *Azubah.*
[t] Heb *Shemamah.*
[u] Heb *Hephzibah.*
[v] Heb *Beulah.*
61:1–2: Mt 11:5; Lk 4:18–19; 7:22.
61:6: Ex 19:6; 1 Pet 2:5; Rev 1:6; 5:10; 20:6.
62:2: Rev 2:17.
* 61:1–4: cf. Lk 4:18–19.

⁸The Lᴏʀᴅ has sworn by his right hand
  and by his mighty arm:
"I will not again give your grain
  to be food for your enemies,
and foreigners shall not drink your wine
  for which you have labored;
⁹but those who garner it shall eat it
  and praise the Lᴏʀᴅ,
and those who gather it shall drink it
  in the courts of my sanctuary."

¹⁰Go through, go through the gates,
  prepare the way for the people;
build up, build up the highway,
  clear it of stones,
  lift up an ensign over the peoples.
¹¹Behold, the Lᴏʀᴅ has proclaimed
  to the end of the earth:
Say to the daughter of Zion,
  "Behold, your salvation comes;
behold, his reward is with him,
  and his recompense before him."
¹²And they shall be called The holy people,
  The redeemed of the Lᴏʀᴅ;
and you shall be called Sought out,
  a city not forsaken.

Vengeance on Enemies; God's Mercy Recounted and Sought

63 Who is this that comes from E′dom,
  in crimsoned garments from Bozrah,
he that is glorious in his apparel,
  marching in the greatness of his strength?

"It is I, announcing vindication,
  mighty to save."

²Why is your apparel red,
  and your garments like his who treads in
    the wine press?

³"I have trodden the wine press alone,
  and from the peoples no one was with me;
I trod them in my anger
  and trampled them in my wrath;
their lifeblood is sprinkled upon my garments,
  and I have stained all my clothing.
⁴For the day of vengeance was in my heart,
  and my year of redemption ʷ has come.
⁵I looked, but there was no one to help;
  I was appalled, but there was no one to
    uphold;
so my own arm brought me victory,
  and my wrath upheld me.
⁶I trod down the peoples in my anger,
  I made them drunk in my wrath,
  and I poured out their lifeblood on the earth."

⁷I will recount the merciful love of the Lᴏʀᴅ,
  the praises of the Lᴏʀᴅ,
according to all that the Lᴏʀᴅ has granted us,
  and the great goodness to the house of
    Israel
which he has granted them according to his
  mercy,
  according to the abundance of his steadfast
    love.
⁸For he said, Surely they are my people,
  sons who will not deal falsely;
  and he became their Savior.
⁹In all their affliction he was afflicted, ˣ
  and the angel of his presence saved them;
in his love and in his pity he redeemed them;
  he lifted them up and carried them all the
    days of old.

¹⁰But they rebelled
  and grieved his holy Spirit;
therefore he turned to be their enemy,
  and himself fought against them.
¹¹Then he remembered the days of old,
  of Moses his servant.
Where is he who brought up out of the sea
  the shepherds of his flock?
Where is he who put in the midst of them
  his holy Spirit,
¹²who caused his glorious arm
  to go at the right hand of Moses,
who divided the waters before them
  to make for himself an everlasting name,
13 who led them through the depths?
Like a horse in the desert,
  they did not stumble.
¹⁴Like cattle that go down into the valley,
  the Spirit of the Lᴏʀᴅ gave them rest.
So you led your people,
  to make for yourself a glorious name.

¹⁵Look down from heaven and see,
  from your holy and glorious habitation.
Where are your zeal and your might?
  The yearning of your heart and your
    compassion
  are withheld from me.
¹⁶For you are our Father,
  though Abraham does not know us
  and Israel does not acknowledge us;
you, O Lᴏʀᴅ, are our Father,
  our Redeemer from of old is your name.
¹⁷O Lᴏʀᴅ, why do you make us err from your
    ways
  and harden our heart, so that we fear you
    not?

ʷ Or *the year of my redeemed.*
ˣ Another reading is *he did not afflict.*
63:1–6: Is 34; Jer 49:7–22; Ezek 25:12–14; 35; Amos 1:11–12; Obad; Mal 1:2–5.
63:3: Rev 19:15.
63:11: Heb 13:20.

Return for the sake of your servants,
the tribes of your heritage.
[18]Your holy people possessed your sanctuary a
little while;
our adversaries have trodden it down.
[19]We have become like those over whom you
have never ruled,
like those who are not called by your name.

Prayer for Mercy

64 O that you would tear the heavens and
come down,
that the mountains might quake at your
presence—
[2]y as when fire kindles brushwood
and the fire causes water to boil—
to make your name known to your
adversaries,
and that the nations might tremble at your
presence!
[3]When you did terrible things which we looked
not for,
you came down, the mountains quaked at
your presence.
[4]From of old no one has heard
or perceived by the ear,
no eye has seen a God besides you,
who works for those who wait for him.
[5]You meet him that joyfully works
righteousness,
those that remember you in your ways.
Behold, you were angry, and we sinned;
in our sins we have been a long time, and
shall we be saved? z
[6]We have all become like one who is unclean,
and all our righteous deeds are like a
polluted garment.
We all fade like a leaf,
and our iniquities, like the wind, take us
away.
[7]There is no one that calls upon your name,
that bestirs himself to take hold of you;
for you have hidden your face from us,
and have delivered a us into the hand of our
iniquities.

[8]Yet, O Lord, you are our Father;
we are the clay, and you are our potter;
we are all the work of your hand.
[9]Be not exceedingly angry, O Lord,
and remember not iniquity for ever.
Behold, consider, we are all your people.
[10]Your holy cities have become a wilderness,
Zion has become a wilderness,
Jerusalem a desolation.
[11]Our holy and beautiful house,
where our fathers praised you,
has been burned by fire,
and all our pleasant places have become
ruins.

[12]Will you restrain yourself at these things, O
Lord?
Will you keep silent, and afflict us sorely?

The Righteousness of God's Judgment

65 I was ready to be sought by those who
did not ask for me;
I was ready to be found by those who did
not seek me.
I said, "Here am I, here am I,"
to a nation that did not call on my name.
[2]I spread out my hands all the day
to a rebellious people,
who walk in a way that is not good,
following their own devices;
[3]a people who provoke me
to my face continually,
sacrificing in gardens
and burning incense upon bricks;
[4]who sit in tombs,
and spend the night in secret places;
who eat swine's flesh,
and broth of abominable things is in their
vessels;
[5]who say, "Keep to yourself,
do not come near me, for I am set apart
from you."
These are a smoke in my nostrils,
a fire that burns all the day.
[6]Behold, it is written before me:
"I will not keep silent, but I will repay,
yes, I will repay into their bosom
[7]   their b iniquities and their b fathers'
iniquities together,

says the Lord;
because they burned incense upon the
mountains
and reviled me upon the hills,
I will measure into their bosom
payment for their former doings."

[8]Thus says the Lord:
"As the wine is found in the cluster,
and they say, 'Do not destroy it,
for there is a blessing in it,'
so I will do for my servants' sake,
and not destroy them all.
[9]I will bring forth descendants from Jacob,
and from Judah inheritors of my mountains;
my chosen shall inherit it,
and my servants shall dwell there.
[10]Sharon shall become a pasture for flocks,
and the Valley of A'chor a place for herds
to lie down,
for my people who have sought me.

y Ch 64:1 in Heb.
z Hebrew obscure.
a Gk Syr Old Latin Tg: Heb *melted.*
b Gk Syr: Heb *your.*
64:4: 1 Cor 2:9.
65:1-2: Rom 10:20–21.

¹¹But you who forsake the LORD,
who forget my holy mountain,
who set a table for Fortune
and fill cups of mixed wine for Destiny;
¹²I will destine you to the sword,
and all of you shall bow down to the
slaughter;
because, when I called, you did not answer,
when I spoke, you did not listen,
but you did what was evil in my eyes,
and chose what I did not delight in."

¹³Therefore thus says the Lord GOD:
"Behold, my servants shall eat,
but you shall be hungry;
behold, my servants shall drink,
but you shall be thirsty;
behold, my servants shall rejoice,
but you shall be put to shame;
¹⁴behold, my servants shall sing for gladness of
heart,
but you shall cry out for pain of heart,
and shall wail for anguish of spirit.
¹⁵You shall leave your name to my chosen for a
curse,
and the Lord GOD will slay you;
but his servants he will call by a different
name.
¹⁶So that he who blesses himself in the land
shall bless himself by the God of truth,
and he who takes an oath in the land
shall swear by the God of truth;
because the former troubles are forgotten
and are hidden from my eyes.

¹⁷"For behold, I create new heavens
and a new earth;
and the former things shall not be remembered
or come into mind.
¹⁸But be glad and rejoice for ever
in that which I create;
for behold, I create Jerusalem a rejoicing,
and her people a joy.
¹⁹I will rejoice in Jerusalem,
and be glad in my people;
no more shall be heard in it the sound of
weeping
and the cry of distress.
²⁰No more shall there be in it
an infant that lives but a few days,
or an old man who does not fill out his days,
for the child shall die a hundred years old,
and the sinner a hundred years old shall be
accursed.
²¹They shall build houses and inhabit them;
they shall plant vineyards and eat their
fruit.
²²They shall not build and another inhabit;
they shall not plant and another eat;

for like the days of a tree shall the days of my
people be,
and my chosen shall long enjoy the work of
their hands.
²³They shall not labor in vain,
or bear children for calamity; ᶜ
for they shall be the offspring of the blessed of
the LORD,
and their children with them.
²⁴Before they call I will answer,
while they are yet speaking I will hear.
²⁵The wolf and the lamb shall feed together,
the lion shall eat straw like the ox;
and dust shall be the serpent's food.
They shall not hurt or destroy
in all my holy mountain,
                    says the LORD."

The Judgment of God

66 Thus says the LORD:
Heaven is my throne
and the earth is my footstool;
what is the house which you would build for
me,
and what is the place of my rest?
²All these things my hand has made,
and so all these things are mine, ᵈ
                    says the LORD.
But this is the man to whom I will look,
he that is humble and contrite in spirit,
and trembles at my word.

³"He who slaughters an ox is like him who kills
a man;
he who sacrifices a lamb, like him who
breaks a dog's neck;
he who presents a cereal offering, like him who
offers swine's blood;
he who makes a memorial offering of
frankincense, like him who blesses an
idol.
These have chosen their own ways,
and their soul delights in their
abominations;
⁴I also will choose affliction for them,
and bring their fears upon them;
because, when I called, no one answered,
when I spoke they did not listen;
but they did what was evil in my eyes,
and chose that in which I did not delight."
⁵Hear the word of the LORD,
you who tremble at his word:
"Your brethren who hate you
and cast you out for my name's sake

ᶜ Or *sudden terror.*
ᵈ Gk Syr: Heb *came to be.*
65:17: Is 66:22; 2 Pet 3:13; Rev 21:1.
65:25: Is 11:6–9.
66:1–2: Mt 5:34; Acts 7:49–50.

have said, 'Let the LORD be glorified,
　that we may see your joy';
but it is they who shall be put to shame.

6"Listen, an uproar from the city!
　A voice from the temple!
The voice of the LORD,
　rendering recompense to his enemies!

7"Before she was in labor
　she gave birth;
before her pain came upon her
　she was delivered of a son.
8Who has heard such a thing?
　Who has seen such things?
Shall a land be born in one day?
　Shall a nation be brought forth in one
　　moment?
For as soon as Zion was in labor
　she brought forth her sons.
9Shall I bring to the birth and not cause to bring
　　forth?
　says the LORD;
shall I, who cause to bring forth, shut the
　　womb?
　says your God.

10"Rejoice with Jerusalem, and be glad for her,
　all you who love her;
rejoice with her in joy,
　all you who mourn over her;
11that you may suck and be satisfied
　with her consoling breasts;
that you may drink deeply with delight
　from the abundance of her glory."

12For thus says the LORD:
"Behold, I will extend prosperity to her like a
　　river,
　and the wealth of the nations like an
　　overflowing stream;
and you shall suck, you shall be carried upon
　　her hip,
　and fondled upon her knees.
13As one whom his mother comforts,
　so I will comfort you;
　you shall be comforted in Jerusalem.
14You shall see, and your heart shall rejoice;
　your bones shall flourish like the grass;
and it shall be known that the hand of the
　　LORD is with his servants,
　and his indignation is against his enemies.

15"For behold, the LORD will come in fire,
　and his chariots like the stormwind,
to render his anger in fury,
　and his rebuke with flames of fire.
16For by fire will the LORD execute judgment,
　and by his sword, upon all flesh;
　and those slain by the LORD shall be many.

17 "Those who sanctify and purify themselves
to go into the gardens, following one in the midst,
eating swine's flesh and the abomination and
mice, shall come to an end together, says the LORD.

The New Heavens and New Earth

18 "For I know e their works and their thoughts,
and I am f coming to gather all nations and
tongues; and they shall come and shall see my
glory, 19and I will set a sign among them. And
from them I will send survivors to the nations, to
Tar′shish, Put, g and Lud, who draw the bow, to
Tu′bal and Ja′van, to the islands afar off, that have
not heard my fame or seen my glory; and they
shall declare my glory among the nations. 20And
they shall bring all your brethren from all the nations as an offering to the LORD, upon horses, and
in chariots, and in litters, and upon mules, and
upon dromedaries, to my holy mountain Jerusalem, says the LORD, just as the sons of Israel bring
their cereal offering in a clean vessel to the house
of the LORD. 21And some of them also I will take
for priests and for Levites, says the LORD.

22 "For as the new heavens and the new earth
　which I will make
shall remain before me, says the LORD;
　so shall your descendants and your name
　　remain.
23From new moon to new moon,
　and from sabbath to sabbath,
all flesh shall come to worship before me,
　says the LORD.

24 "And they shall go forth and look on the
dead bodies of the men that have rebelled against
me; for their worm shall not die, their fire shall
not be quenched, and they shall be an abhorrence
to all flesh."

---

e Gk Syr: Heb lacks *know*.
f Gk Syr Vg Tg: Heb *it is*.
g Gk: Heb *Pul*.
66:6: Rev 16:1, 17.
66:7: Rev 12:5.
66:22: Is 65:17; 2 Pet 3:13; Rev 21:1.
66:24: Mk 9:48.

THE BOOK OF

JEREMIAH

Introduction

1 The words of Jeremi'ah, the son of Hilki'ah, of the priests who were in An'athoth in the land of Benjamin, ²to whom the word of the LORD came in the days of Josi'ah the son of A'mon, king of Judah, in the thirteenth year of his reign. ³It came also in the days of Jehoi'akim the son of Josi'ah, king of Judah, and until the end of the eleventh year of Zedeki'ah, the son of Josiah, king of Judah, until the captivity of Jerusalem in the fifth month.

Jeremiah's Call and Commission

4 Now the word of the LORD came to me saying,
⁵"Before I formed you in the womb I knew you,
 and before you were born I consecrated you;
I appointed you a prophet to the nations."
⁶Then I said, "Ah, Lord GOD! Behold, I do not know how to speak, for I am only a youth." * ⁷But the LORD said to me,
"Do not say, 'I am only a youth';
for to all to whom I send you you shall go,
 and whatever I command you you shall speak.
⁸Be not afraid of them,
 for I am with you to deliver you,
                       says the LORD."
⁹Then the LORD put forth his hand and touched my mouth; and the LORD said to me,
"Behold, I have put my words in your mouth.
¹⁰See, I have set you this day over nations and
            over kingdoms,
to pluck up and to break down,
to destroy and to overthrow,
to build and to plant."

11 And the word of the LORD came to me, saying, "Jeremi'ah, what do you see?" And I said, "I see a rod of almond." ᵃ ¹²Then the LORD said to me, "You have seen well, for I am watching ᵇ over my word to perform it."

13 The word of the LORD came to me a second time, saying, "What do you see?" And I said, "I see a boiling pot, facing away from the north." ¹⁴Then the LORD said to me, "Out of the north evil shall break forth upon all the inhabitants of the land. ¹⁵For, behold, I am calling all the tribes of the kingdoms of the north, says the LORD; and they shall come and every one shall set his throne at the entrance of the gates of Jerusalem, against all its walls round about, and against all the cities of Judah. ¹⁶And I will utter my judgments against

them, for all their wickedness in forsaking me; they have burned incense to other gods, and worshiped the works of their own hands. ¹⁷But you, gird up your loins; arise, and say to them everything that I command you. Do not be dismayed by them, lest I dismay you before them. ¹⁸And I, behold, I make you this day a fortified city, an iron pillar, and bronze walls, against the whole land, against the kings of Judah, its princes, its priests, and the people of the land. ¹⁹They will fight against you; but they shall not prevail against you, for I am with you, says the LORD, to deliver you."

Israel's Apostasy

2 The word of the LORD came to me, saying, ²"Go and proclaim in the hearing of Jerusalem, Thus says the LORD,
I remember the devotion of your youth,
 your love as a bride,
how you followed me in the wilderness,
 in a land not sown.
³Israel was holy to the LORD,
 the first fruits of his harvest.
All who ate of it became guilty;
 evil came upon them,
                       says the LORD."

4 Hear the word of the LORD, O house of Jacob, and all the families of the house of Israel. ⁵Thus says the LORD:

Jeremiah, sometimes called a prophet of doom, lived at the most tragic period of Israel's history, during which Jerusalem was destroyed by Nebuchadrezzar and the people were carried off into captivity. He was of a priestly family and he makes it clear in his book that he obeyed God's call to prophesy most reluctantly. It was his task, under the circumstances, to preach repentance and prophesy destruction if repentance was not forthcoming. But his words fell on deaf ears. In so far as the people heard at all, it was only to resent what he said and make him suffer for it. As the prophet was of a specially sensitive and affectionate nature, his sufferings were all the more acute.

He did not always prophesy doom. Thus in 31:31–34, he foretells the new covenant in terms that remind us of passages in the prophet Isaiah. His words may not have had much effect during his lifetime but after his death his influence was considerable, as was the case with other prophets also; cf. Mt 23:29–30. Not all the prophecies in the book are from Jeremiah himself but some have been inserted later. An important feature of the book is the quantity of biographical material, which tells us a great deal about the prophet.

ᵃ Heb *shaqed*.
ᵇ Heb *shoqed*.
1:5: Is 49:1; Gal 1:15.
1:8: Is 43:5; Acts 18:9–10.
1:10: Rev 10:11.
* **1:6:** Typically, Jeremiah is reluctant to accept an office for which he feels himself ill suited, and which, he foresees, can bring nothing but suffering and disappointment.

"What wrong did your fathers find in me
   that they went far from me,
and went after worthlessness, and became
   worthless?
[6]They did not say, 'Where is the LORD
   who brought us up from the land of Egypt,
who led us in the wilderness,
   in a land of deserts and pits,
   in a land of drought and deep darkness,
   in a land that none passes through,
   where no man dwells?'
[7]And I brought you into a plentiful land
   to enjoy its fruits and its good things.
But when you came in you defiled my land,
   and made my heritage an abomination.
[8]The priests did not say, 'Where is the LORD?'
   Those who handle the law did not know
   me;
the rulers [c] transgressed against me;
   the prophets prophesied by Ba'al,
   and went after things that do not profit.

[9]"Therefore I still contend with you,
             says the LORD,
   and with your children's children I will
   contend.
[10]For cross to the coasts of Cyprus and see,
   or send to Kedar and examine with care;
   see if there has been such a thing.
[11]Has a nation changed its gods,
   even though they are no gods?
But my people have changed their glory
   for that which does not profit.
[12]Be appalled, O heavens, at this,
   be shocked, be utterly desolate,
             says the LORD,
[13]for my people have committed two evils:
   they have forsaken me,
the fountain of living waters,
   and hewed out cisterns for themselves,
broken cisterns,
   that can hold no water.

[14]"Is Israel a slave? Is he a homeborn servant?
   Why then has he become a prey?
[15]The lions have roared against him,
   they have roared loudly.
They have made his land a waste;
   his cities are in ruins, without inhabitant.
[16]Moreover, the men of Memphis and
   Tah'panhes
   have broken the crown of your head.
[17]Have you not brought this upon yourself
   by forsaking the LORD your God,
   when he led you in the way?
[18]And now what do you gain by going to Egypt,
   to drink the waters of the Nile?
Or what do you gain by going to Assyria,
   to drink the waters of the Euphra'tes?

[19]Your wickedness will chasten you,
   and your apostasy will reprove you.
Know and see that it is evil and bitter
   for you to forsake the LORD your God;
the fear of me is not in you,
             says the Lord GOD of hosts.

[20]"For long ago you broke your yoke
   and burst your bonds;
   and you said, 'I will not serve.'
Yes, upon every high hill
   and under every green tree
   you bowed down as a harlot.
[21]Yet I planted you a choice vine,
   wholly of pure seed.
How then have you turned degenerate
   and become a wild vine?
[22]Though you wash yourself with lye
   and use much soap,
   the stain of your guilt is still before me,
             says the Lord GOD.
[23]How can you say, 'I am not defiled,
   I have not gone after the Ba'als'?
Look at your way in the valley;
   know what you have done—
a restive young camel interlacing her tracks,
[24]   a wild donkey used to the wilderness,
in her heat sniffing the wind!
   Who can restrain her lust?
None who seek her need weary themselves;
   in her month they will find her.
[25]Keep your feet from going unshod
   and your throat from thirst.
But you said, 'It is hopeless,
   for I have loved strangers,
   and after them I will go.'

[26]"As a thief is shamed when caught,
   so the house of Israel shall be shamed:
they, their kings, their princes,
   their priests, and their prophets,
[27]who say to a tree, 'You are my father,'
   and to a stone, 'You gave me birth.'
For they have turned their back to me,
   and not their face.
But in the time of their trouble they say,
   'Arise and save us!'
[28]But where are your gods
   that you made for yourself?
Let them arise, if they can save you,
   in your time of trouble;
for as many as your cities
   are your gods, O Judah.

[29]"Why do you complain against me?
   You have all rebelled against me,
             says the LORD.

---

[c] Heb *shepherds.*

³⁰In vain have I struck down your children,
  they took no correction;
your own sword devoured your prophets
  like a ravening lion.
³¹And you, O generation, heed the word of the
  LORD.
Have I been a wilderness to Israel,
  or a land of thick darkness?
Why then do my people say, 'We are free,
  we will come no more to you'?
³²Can a maiden forget her ornaments,
  or a bride her attire?
Yet my people have forgotten me
  days without number.
³³"How well you direct your course
  to seek lovers!
So that even to wicked women
  you have taught your ways.
³⁴Also on your skirts is found
  the lifeblood of guiltless poor;
you did not find them breaking in.
  Yet in spite of all these things
³⁵you say, 'I am innocent;
  surely his anger has turned from me.'
Behold, I will bring you to judgment
  for saying, 'I have not sinned.'
³⁶How lightly you gad about,
  changing your way!
You shall be put to shame by Egypt
  as you were put to shame by Assyria.
³⁷From it too you will come away
  with your hands upon your head,
for the LORD has rejected those in whom you
  trust,
  and you will not prosper by them.

Unfaithful Israel

3 "If ᵈ a man divorces his wife
  and she goes from him
and becomes another man's wife,
  will he return to her?
Would not that land be greatly polluted?
You have played the harlot with many lovers;
  and would you return to me?
                              says the LORD.
²Lift up your eyes to the bare heights, and see!
  Where have you not been lain with?
By the waysides you have sat awaiting lovers
  like an Arab in the wilderness.
You have polluted the land
  with your vile harlotry.
³Therefore the showers have been withheld,
  and the spring rain has not come;
yet you have a harlot's brow,
  you refuse to be ashamed.
⁴Have you not just now called to me,
  'My father, you are the friend of my
  youth—
⁵will he be angry for ever,
  will he be indignant to the end?'

Behold, you have spoken,
  but you have done all the evil that you
  could."

A Call to Repentance

6 The LORD said to me in the days of King
Josi'ah: "Have you seen what she did, that faithless one, Israel, how she went up on every high
hill and under every green tree, and there played
the harlot? ⁷And I thought, 'After she has done all
this she will return to me'; but she did not return,
and her false sister Judah saw it. ⁸She saw that
for all the adulteries of that faithless one, Israel,
I had sent her away with a decree of divorce; yet
her false sister Judah did not fear, but she too
went and played the harlot. ⁹Because harlotry
was so light to her, she polluted the land, committing adultery with stone and tree. ¹⁰Yet for all
this her false sister Judah did not return to me
with her whole heart, but in pretense, says the
LORD."

11 And the LORD said to me, "Faithless Israel
has shown herself less guilty than false Judah.
¹²Go, and proclaim these words toward the north,
and say,
'Return, faithless Israel,
                              says the LORD.
I will not look on you in anger,
  for I am merciful,
                              says the LORD;
I will not be angry for ever.
¹³Only acknowledge your guilt,
  that you rebelled against the LORD your God
and scattered your favors among strangers
  under every green tree,
  and that you have not obeyed my voice,
                              says the LORD.
¹⁴Return, O faithless children,
                              says the LORD;
  for I am your master;
I will take you, one from a city and two from a
  family,
  and I will bring you to Zion.
15 "'And I will give you shepherds after my
own heart, who will feed you with knowledge and
understanding. ¹⁶And when you have multiplied
and increased in the land, in those days, says the
LORD, they shall no more say, "The ark of the
covenant of the LORD." It shall not come to mind,
or be remembered, or missed; it shall not be made
again. * ¹⁷At that time Jerusalem shall be called
the throne of the LORD, and all nations shall gather
to it, to the presence of the LORD in Jerusalem, and
they shall no more stubbornly follow their own
evil heart. ¹⁸In those days the house of Judah
shall join the house of Israel, and together they

ᵈ Gk Syr: Heb *Saying, If*.
* 3:16: The ark must have been destroyed at the same time as the temple
in 586 B.C. In the Messianic times the presence of the Lord will not be
restricted to the ark of the covenant; cf. Rev 21:22.

shall come from the land of the north to the land
that I gave your fathers for a heritage.
¹⁹" 'I thought
how I would set you among my sons,
and give you a pleasant land,
a heritage most beauteous of all nations.
And I thought you would call me, My Father,
and would not turn from following me.
²⁰Surely, as a faithless wife leaves her husband,
so have you been faithless to me, O house
of Israel,

says the LORD.' "

²¹A voice on the bare heights is heard,
the weeping and pleading of Israel's sons,
because they have perverted their way,
they have forgotten the LORD their God.
²²"Return, O faithless sons,
I will heal your faithlessness."
"Behold, we come to you;
for you are the LORD our God.
²³Truly the hills are a delusion,
the orgies on the mountains.
Truly in the LORD our God
is the salvation of Israel.
24 "But from our youth the shameful thing has
devoured all for which our fathers labored, their
flocks and their herds, their sons and their daughters. ²⁵Let us lie down in our shame, and let our
dishonor cover us; for we have sinned against the
LORD our God, we and our fathers, from our youth
even to this day; and we have not obeyed the voice
of the LORD our God."

4 "If you return, O Israel,
says the LORD,
to me you should return.
If you remove your abominations from my
presence,
and do not waver,
²and if you swear, 'As the LORD lives,'
in truth, in justice, and in uprightness,
then nations shall bless themselves in him,
and in him shall they glory."
3 For thus says the LORD to the men of Judah
and to the inhabitants of Jerusalem:
"Break up your fallow ground,
and sow not among thorns.
⁴Circumcise yourselves to the LORD,
remove the foreskin of your hearts,
O men of Judah and inhabitants of Jerusalem;
lest my wrath go forth like fire,
and burn with none to quench it,
because of the evil of your doings."

Judah Threatened with Invasion

5 Declare in Judah, and proclaim in Jerusalem,
and say,
"Blow the trumpet through the land;
cry aloud and say,

'Assemble, and let us go
into the fortified cities!'
⁶Raise a standard toward Zion,
flee for safety, stay not,
for I bring evil from the north,
and great destruction.
⁷A lion has gone up from his thicket,
a destroyer of nations has set out;
he has gone forth from his place
to make your land a waste;
your cities will be ruins
without inhabitant.
⁸For this clothe yourself with sackcloth,
lament and wail;
for the fierce anger of the LORD
has not turned back from us."

9 "In that day, says the LORD, courage shall fail
both king and princes; the priests shall be appalled and the prophets astounded." ¹⁰Then I said,
"Ah, Lord GOD, surely you have utterly deceived
this people and Jerusalem, saying, 'It shall be well
with you'; whereas the sword has reached their
very life."

11 At that time it will be said to this people
and to Jerusalem, "A hot wind from the bare
heights in the desert toward the daughter of my
people, not to winnow or cleanse, ¹²a wind too full
for this comes for me. Now it is I who speak in
judgment upon them."
¹³Behold, he comes up like clouds,
his chariots like the whirlwind;
his horses are swifter than eagles—
woe to us, for we are ruined!
¹⁴O Jerusalem, wash your heart from
wickedness,
that you may be saved.
How long shall your evil thoughts
lodge within you?
¹⁵For a voice declares from Dan
and proclaims evil from Mount E'phraim.
¹⁶Warn the nations that he is coming;
announce to Jerusalem,
"Besiegers come from a distant land;
they shout against the cities of Judah.
¹⁷Like keepers of a field they are against her
round about,
because she has rebelled against me,
says the LORD.
¹⁸Your ways and your doings
have brought this upon you.
This is your doom, and it is bitter;
it has reached your very heart."

¹⁹My anguish, my anguish! I writhe in pain!
Oh, the walls of my heart!
My heart is beating wildly;
I cannot keep silent;

for I hear the sound of the trumpet,
the alarm of war.
²⁰Disaster follows hard on disaster;
the whole land is laid waste.
Suddenly my tents are destroyed,
my curtains in a moment.
²¹How long must I see the standard,
and hear the sound of the trumpet?
²²"For my people are foolish,
they know me not;
they are stupid children,
they have no understanding.
They are skilled in doing evil,
but how to do good they know not."

²³I looked on the earth, and behold, it was waste
and void;
and to the heavens, and they had no light.
²⁴I looked on the mountains, and behold, they
were quaking,
and all the hills moved back and forth.
²⁵I looked, and behold, there was no man,
and all the birds of the air had fled.
²⁶I looked, and behold, the fruitful land was a
desert,
and all its cities were laid in ruins
before the Lord, before his fierce anger.
27 For thus says the Lord, "The whole land
shall be a desolation; yet I will not make a full end.
²⁸For this the earth shall mourn,
and the heavens above be black,
for I have spoken, I have planned;
I have not relented nor will I turn back."

²⁹At the noise of horseman and archer
every city takes to flight;
they enter thickets; they climb among rocks;
all the cities are forsaken,
and no man dwells in them.
³⁰And you, O desolate one,
what do you mean that you dress in scarlet,
that you deck yourself with ornaments of
gold,
that you enlarge your eyes with paint?
In vain you beautify yourself.
Your lovers despise you;
they seek your life.
³¹For I heard a cry as of a woman with labor
pains,
anguish as of one bringing forth her first
child,
the cry of the daughter of Zion gasping for
breath,
stretching out her hands,
"Woe me! I am fainting before murderers."

The Godlessness of Jerusalem

5 Run back and forth through the streets of
Jerusalem,
look and take note!

Search her squares to see
if you can find a man,
one who does justice
and seeks truth;
that I may pardon her.
²Though they say, "As the Lord lives,"
yet they swear falsely.
³O Lord, do not your eyes look for truth?
You have struck them down,
but they felt no anguish;
you have consumed them,
but they refused to take correction.
They have made their faces harder than rock;
they have refused to repent.

⁴Then I said, "These are only the poor,
they have no sense;
for they do not know the way of the Lord,
the law of their God.
⁵I will go to the great,
and will speak to them;
for they know the way of the Lord,
the law of their God."
But they all alike had broken the yoke,
they had burst the bonds.

⁶Therefore a lion from the forest shall slay
them,
a wolf from the desert shall destroy them.
A leopard is watching against their cities,
every one who goes out of them shall be
torn in pieces;
because their transgressions are many,
their apostasies are great.

⁷"How can I pardon you?
Your children have forsaken me,
and have sworn by those who are no gods.
When I fed them to the full,
they committed adultery
and trooped to the houses of harlots.
⁸They were well-fed lusty stallions,
each neighing for his neighbor's wife.
⁹Shall I not punish them for these things?
says the Lord;
and shall I not avenge myself
on a nation such as this?

¹⁰"Go up through her vine-rows and destroy,
but make not a full end;
strip away her branches,
for they are not the Lord's.
¹¹For the house of Israel and the house of Judah
have been utterly faithless to me,
says the Lord.
¹²They have spoken falsely of the Lord,
and have said, 'He will do nothing;
no evil will come upon us,
nor shall we see sword or famine.

¹³The prophets will become wind;
and the word is not in them.
Thus shall it be done to them!'"

¹⁴Therefore thus says the LORD, the God of hosts:
"Because they ^e have spoken this word,
behold, I am making my words in your mouth
a fire,
and this people wood, and the fire shall
devour them.
¹⁵Behold, I am bringing upon you
a nation from afar, O house of Israel,
says the LORD.

It is an enduring nation,
it is an ancient nation,
a nation whose language you do not know,
nor can you understand what they say.
¹⁶Their quiver is like an open tomb,
they are all mighty men.
¹⁷They shall eat up your harvest and your food;
they shall eat up your sons and your
daughters;
they shall eat up your flocks and your herds;
they shall eat up your vines and your fig
trees;
your fortified cities in which you trust
they shall destroy with the sword."

18 "But even in those days, says the LORD, I
will not make a full end of you. ¹⁹And when your
people say, 'Why has the LORD our God done all
these things to us?' you shall say to them, 'As you
have forsaken me and served foreign gods in your
land, so you shall serve strangers in a land that is
not yours.'"

²⁰Declare this in the house of Jacob,
proclaim it in Judah:
²¹"Hear this, O foolish and senseless people,
who have eyes, but see not,
who have ears, but hear not.
²²Do you not fear me? says the LORD;
Do you not tremble before me?
I placed the sand as the bound for the sea,
a perpetual barrier which it cannot pass;
though the waves toss, they cannot prevail,
though they roar, they cannot pass over it.
²³But this people has a stubborn and rebellious
heart;
they have turned aside and gone away.
²⁴They do not say in their hearts,
'Let us fear the LORD our God,
who gives the rain in its season,
the autumn rain and the spring rain,
and keeps for us
the weeks appointed for the harvest.'
²⁵Your iniquities have turned these away,
and your sins have kept good from you.
²⁶For wicked men are found among my people;
they lurk like fowlers lying in wait. ^f

They set a trap;
they catch men.
²⁷Like a basket full of birds,
their houses are full of treachery;
therefore they have become great and rich,
²⁸ they have grown fat and sleek.
They know no bounds in deeds of wickedness;
they judge not with justice
the cause of the fatherless, to make it prosper,
and they do not defend the rights of the
needy.
²⁹Shall I not punish them for these things?
says the LORD,
and shall I not avenge myself
on a nation such as this?"

³⁰An appalling and horrible thing
has happened in the land:
³¹the prophets prophesy falsely,
and the priests rule at their direction;
my people love to have it so,
but what will you do when the end comes?

A Warning to Judah

6 Flee for safety, O people of Benjamin,
from the midst of Jerusalem!
Blow the trumpet in Teko'a,
and raise a signal on Beth"-hacche'rem;
for evil looms out of the north,
and great destruction.
²The comely and delicately bred I will destroy,
the daughter of Zion.
³Shepherds with their flocks shall come against
her;
they shall pitch their tents around her,
they shall pasture, each in his place.
⁴"Prepare war against her;
up, and let us attack at noon!"
"Woe to us, for the day declines,
for the shadows of evening lengthen!"
⁵"Up, and let us attack by night,
and destroy her palaces!"

⁶For thus says the LORD of hosts:
"Hew down her trees;
cast up a siege mound against Jerusalem.
This is the city which must be punished;
there is nothing but oppression within her.
⁷As a well keeps its water fresh,
so she keeps fresh her wickedness;
violence and destruction are heard within her;
sickness and wounds are ever before me.
⁸Be warned, O Jerusalem,
lest I be alienated from you;
lest I make you a desolation,
an uninhabited land."

^e Heb you.
^f Heb uncertain.
5:21: Is 6:9–10; Mt 13:10–15; Mk 8:17–18.

[9]Thus says the LORD of hosts:
"Glean [g] thoroughly as a vine
  the remnant of Israel;
like a grape-gatherer pass your hand again
  over its branches."
[10]To whom shall I speak and give warning,
  that they may hear?
Behold, their ears are closed, [h]
  they cannot listen;
behold, the word of the LORD is to them an
  object of scorn,
they take no pleasure in it.
[11]Therefore I am full of the wrath of the LORD;
  I am weary of holding it in.
"Pour it out upon the children in the street,
  and upon the gatherings of young men,
    also;
both husband and wife shall be taken,
  the old folk and the very aged.
[12]Their houses shall be turned over to others,
  their fields and wives together;
for I will stretch out my hand
  against the inhabitants of the land,"
                              says the LORD.
[13]"For from the least to the greatest of them,
  every one is greedy for unjust gain;
and from prophet to priest,
  every one deals falsely.
[14]They have healed the wound of my people
    lightly,
  saying, 'Peace, peace,'
  when there is no peace.
[15]Were they ashamed when they committed
    abomination?
No, they were not at all ashamed;
  they did not know how to blush.
Therefore they shall fall among those who fall;
  at the time that I punish them, they shall be
    overthrown,"
                              says the LORD.

[16]Thus says the LORD:
"Stand by the roads, and look,
  and ask for the ancient paths,
where the good way is; and walk in it,
  and find rest for your souls.
But they said, 'We will not walk in it.'
[17]I set watchmen over you, saying,
  'Give heed to the sound of the trumpet!'
But they said, 'We will not give heed.'
[18]Therefore hear, O nations,
  and know, O congregation, what will
    happen to them.
[19]Hear, O earth; behold, I am bringing evil upon
    this people,
  the fruit of their devices,
because they have not given heed to my
    words;
  and as for my law, they have rejected it.

[20]To what purpose does frankincense come to me
  from Sheba,
  or sweet cane from a distant land?
Your burnt offerings are not acceptable,
  nor your sacrifices pleasing to me.
[21]Therefore thus says the LORD:
'Behold, I will lay before this people
  stumbling blocks against which they shall
    stumble;
fathers and sons together,
  neighbor and friend shall perish.'"

[22]Thus says the LORD:
"Behold, a people is coming from the north
    country,
  a great nation is stirring from the farthest
    parts of the earth.
[23]They lay hold on bow and spear,
  they are cruel and have no mercy,
  the sound of them is like the roaring sea;
they ride upon horses,
  set in array as a man for battle,
  against you, O daughter of Zion!"
[24]We have heard the report of it,
  our hands fall helpless;
anguish has taken hold of us,
  pain as of a woman with labor pains.
[25]Go not forth into the field,
  nor walk on the road;
for the enemy has a sword,
  terror is on every side.
[26]O daughter of my people, put on sackcloth,
  and roll in ashes;
make mourning as for an only son,
  most bitter lamentation;
for suddenly the destroyer
  will come upon us.
[27]"I have made you an assayer and tester among
    my people,
  that you may know and assay their ways.
[28]They are all stubbornly rebellious,
  going about with slanders;
they are bronze and iron,
  all of them act corruptly.
[29]The bellows blow fiercely,
  the lead is consumed by the fire;
in vain the refining goes on,
  for the wicked are not removed.
[30]Refuse silver they are called,
  for the LORD has rejected them."

Impending Punishment of Judah

7 The word that came to Jeremi′ah from the
LORD: [2]"Stand in the gate of the LORD's house,
and proclaim there this word, and say, Hear the
word of the LORD, all you men of Judah who enter

---

[g] Cn: Heb *they shall glean.*
[h] Heb *uncircumcised.*
6:16: Mt 11:29.
6:25: Jer 20:3, 10; 46:5; 49:29; Ps 31:13.

these gates to worship the LORD. [3]Thus says the LORD of hosts, the God of Israel, Amend your ways and your doings, and I will let you dwell in this place. [4]Do not trust in these deceptive words: 'This is the temple of the LORD, the temple of the LORD, the temple of the LORD.' *

5 "For if you truly amend your ways and your doings, if you truly execute justice one with another, [6]if you do not oppress the alien, the fatherless or the widow, or shed innocent blood in this place, and if you do not go after other gods to your own hurt, [7]then I will let you dwell in this place, in the land that I gave of old to your fathers for ever.

8 "Behold, you trust in deceptive words to no avail. [9]Will you steal, murder, commit adultery, swear falsely, burn incense to Ba'al, and go after other gods that you have not known, [10]and then come and stand before me in this house, which is called by my name, and say, 'We are delivered!'— only to go on doing all these abominations? [11]Has this house, which is called by my name, become a den of robbers in your eyes? Behold, I myself have seen it, says the LORD. [12]Go now to my place that was in Shiloh, where I made my name dwell at first, and see what I did to it for the wickedness of my people Israel. [13]And now, because you have done all these things, says the LORD, and when I spoke to you persistently you did not listen, and when I called you, you did not answer, [14]therefore I will do to the house which is called by my name, and in which you trust, and to the place which I gave to you and to your fathers, as I did to Shiloh. [15]And I will cast you out of my sight, as I cast out all your kinsmen, all the offspring of E'phraim.

The People's Disobedience

16 "As for you, do not pray for this people, or lift up cry or prayer for them, and do not intercede with me, for I do not hear you. [17]Do you not see what they are doing in the cities of Judah and in the streets of Jerusalem? [18]The children gather wood, the fathers kindle fire, and the women knead dough, to make cakes for the queen of heaven; and they pour out drink offerings to other gods, to provoke me to anger. [19]Is it I whom they provoke? says the LORD. Is it not themselves, to their own confusion? [20]Therefore thus says the Lord GOD: Behold, my anger and my wrath will be poured out on this place, upon man and beast, upon the trees of the field and the fruit of the ground; it will burn and not be quenched."

21 Thus says the LORD of hosts, the God of Israel: "Add your burnt offerings to your sacrifices, and eat the flesh. [22]For in the day that I brought them out of the land of Egypt, I did not speak to your fathers or command them concerning burnt offerings and sacrifices. [23]But this command I gave them, 'Obey my voice, and I will be your God, and you shall be my people; and walk in all the way that I command you, that it may be well with you.' [24]But they did not obey or incline their ear, but walked in their own counsels and the stubbornness of their evil hearts, and went backward and not forward. [25]From the day that your fathers came out of the land of Egypt to this day, I have persistently sent all my servants the prophets to them, day after day; [26]yet they did not listen to me, or incline their ear, but stiffened their neck. They did worse than their fathers.

27 "So you shall speak all these words to them, but they will not listen to you. You shall call to them, but they will not answer you. [28]And you shall say to them, 'This is the nation that did not obey the voice of the LORD their God, and did not accept discipline; truth has perished; it is cut off from their lips.'

[29]Cut off your hair and cast it away;
    raise a lamentation on the bare heights,
for the LORD has rejected and forsaken
    the generation of his wrath.'

30 "For the sons of Judah have done evil in my sight, says the LORD; they have set their abominations in the house which is called by my name, to defile it. [31]And they have built the high place [i] of To'pheth, which is in the valley of the son of Hin'nom, to burn their sons and their daughters in the fire; which I did not command, nor did it come into my mind. [32]Therefore, behold, the days are coming, says the LORD, when it will no more be called To'pheth, or the valley of the son of Hinnom, but the valley of Slaughter: for they will bury in Topheth, because there is no room elsewhere. [33]And the dead bodies of this people will be food for the birds of the air, and for the beasts of the earth; and none will frighten them away. [34]And I will make to cease from the cities of Judah and from the streets of Jerusalem the voice of mirth and the voice of gladness, the voice of the bridegroom and the voice of the bride; for the land shall become a waste.

A Lament for Judah

8 "At that time, says the LORD, the bones of the kings of Judah, the bones of its princes, the bones of the priests, the bones of the prophets, and the bones of the inhabitants of Jerusalem shall be brought out of their tombs; [2]and they shall be spread before the sun and the moon and all the host of heaven, which they have loved and served, which they have gone after, and which they have sought and worshiped; and they shall not be gathered or buried; they shall be as dung on the surface of the ground. [3]Death shall be preferred to life by all the remnant that remains

---

[i] Gk Tg: Heb *high places*.
7:11: Mt 21:13; Mk 11:17; Lk 19:46.
7:34: Rev 18:23.
* 7:4: Trust in the temple's presence without true service of God and observance of his commands is vain, just as earlier a similar trust in the presence of the ark was fruitless without moral observance; 1 Sam 4:3.

of this evil family in all the places where I have driven them, says the Lord of hosts.

4"You shall say to them, Thus says the Lord:

When men fall, do they not rise again?
 If one turns away, does he not return?
5Why then has this people turned away
 in perpetual backsliding?
They hold fast to deceit,
 they refuse to return.
6I have given heed and listened,
 but they have not spoken rightly;
no man repents of his wickedness,
 saying, 'What have I done?'
Every one turns to his own course,
 like a horse plunging headlong into battle.
7Even the stork in the heavens
 knows her times;
and the turtledove, swallow, and crane j
 keep the time of their coming;
but my people know not
 the ordinance of the Lord. *

8"How can you say, 'We are wise,
 and the law of the Lord is with us'?
But, behold, the false pen of the scribes
 has made it into a lie.
9The wise men shall be put to shame,
 they shall be dismayed and taken;
behold, they have rejected the word of the
 Lord,
 and what wisdom is in them?
10Therefore I will give their wives to others
 and their fields to conquerors,
because from the least to the greatest
 every one is greedy for unjust gain;
from prophet to priest
 every one deals falsely.
11They have healed the wound of my people
 lightly,
 saying, 'Peace, peace,'
 when there is no peace.
12Were they ashamed when they committed
 abomination?
 No, they were not at all ashamed;
 they did not know how to blush.
Therefore they shall fall among the fallen;
 when I punish them, they shall be
 overthrown,

says the Lord.

13When I would gather them, says the Lord,
 there are no grapes on the vine,
 nor figs on the fig tree;
even the leaves are withered,
 and what I gave them has passed away
 from them." k

14Why do we sit still?
Gather together, let us go into the fortified cities
 and perish there;

for the Lord our God has doomed us to perish,
 and has given us poisoned water to drink,
because we have sinned against the Lord.
15We looked for peace, but no good came,
 for a time of healing, but behold, terror.

16"The snorting of their horses is heard from
 Dan;
at the sound of the neighing of their
 stallions
 the whole land quakes.
They come and devour the land and all that
 fills it,
 the city and those who dwell in it.
17For behold, I am sending among you serpents,
 adders which cannot be charmed,
 and they shall bite you,"

says the Lord.

18My grief is beyond healing, l
 my heart is sick within me.
19Listen, the cry of the daughter of my people
 from the length and breadth of the land:
"Is the Lord not in Zion?
 Is her King not in her?"
"Why have they provoked me to anger with
 their graven images,
 and with their foreign idols?"
20"The harvest is past, the summer is ended,
 and we are not saved."
21For the wound of the daughter of my people
 my heart is wounded,
 I mourn, and dismay has taken hold on me.

22Is there no balm in Gilead?
 Is there no physician there?
Why then has the health of the daughter of my
 people
 not been restored?

9 m O that my head were waters,
 and my eyes a fountain of tears,
that I might weep day and night
 for the slain of the daughter of my people!
2 n O that I had in the desert
 a wayfarers' lodging place,
that I might leave my people
 and go away from them!
For they are all adulterers,
 a company of treacherous men.
3They bend their tongue like a bow;
 falsehood and not truth has grown strong o
 in the land;

---

j The meaning of the Hebrew word is uncertain.
k Heb uncertain.
l Cn Compare Gk: Heb uncertain.
m Ch 8:23 in Heb.
n Ch 9:1 in Heb.
o Gk: Heb and not for truth they have grown strong.
* 8:7: cf. Is 1:3.

for they proceed from evil to evil,
and they do not know me, says the LORD.

[4]Let every one beware of his neighbor,
and put no trust in any brother;
for every brother is a supplanter,
and every neighbor goes about as a
slanderer.
[5]Every one deceives his neighbor,
and no one speaks the truth;
they have taught their tongue to speak lies;
they commit iniquity and are too weary to
repent. [p]
[6]Heaping oppression upon oppression, and
deceit upon deceit,
they refuse to know me, says the LORD.

[7]Therefore thus says the LORD of hosts:
"Behold, I will refine them and test them,
for what else can I do, because of my
people?
[8]Their tongue is a deadly arrow;
it speaks deceitfully;
with his mouth each speaks peaceably to his
neighbor,
but in his heart he plans an ambush for
him.
[9]Shall I not punish them for these things? says
the LORD;
and shall I not avenge myself
on a nation such as this?

[10]"Take up [q] weeping and wailing for the
mountains,
and a lamentation for the pastures of the
wilderness,
because they are laid waste so that no one
passes through,
and the lowing of cattle is not heard;
both the birds of the air and the beasts
have fled and are gone.
[11]I will make Jerusalem a heap of ruins,
a lair of jackals;
and I will make the cities of Judah a desolation,
without inhabitant."

[12] Who is the man so wise that he can understand this? To whom has the mouth of the LORD spoken, that he may declare it? Why is the land ruined and laid waste like a wilderness, so that no one passes through? [13]And the LORD says: "Because they have forsaken my law which I set before them, and have not obeyed my voice, or walked in accord with it, [14]but have stubbornly followed their own hearts and have gone after the Ba'als, as their fathers taught them. [15]Therefore thus says the LORD of hosts, the God of Israel: Behold, I will feed this people with wormwood, and give them poisonous water to drink. [16]I will

scatter them among the nations whom neither they nor their fathers have known; and I will send the sword after them, until I have consumed them."

[17]Thus says the LORD of hosts:
"Consider, and call for the mourning women to
come;
send for the skilful women to come;
[18]let them make haste and raise a wailing over
us,
that our eyes may run down with tears,
and our eyelids gush with water.
[19]For a sound of wailing is heard from Zion:
'How we are ruined!
We are utterly shamed,
because we have left the land,
because they have cast down our
dwellings.'"

[20]Hear, O women, the word of the LORD,
and let your ear receive the word of his
mouth;
teach to your daughters a lament,
and each to her neighbor a dirge.
[21]For death has come up into our windows,
it has entered our palaces,
cutting off the children from the streets
and the young men from the squares.
[22]Speak, "Thus says the LORD:
'The dead bodies of men shall fall
like dung upon the open field,
like sheaves after the reaper,
and none shall gather them.'"

23 Thus says the LORD: "Let not the wise man glory in his wisdom, let not the mighty man glory in his might, let not the rich man glory in his riches; [24]but let him who glories glory in this, that he understands and knows me, that I am the LORD who practice steadfast love, justice, and righteousness in the earth; for in these things I delight, says the LORD." [*]

25 "Behold, the days are coming, says the LORD, when I will punish all those who are circumcised but yet uncircumcised— [26]Egypt, Judah, E'dom, the sons of Ammon, Moab, and all who dwell in the desert that cut the corners of their hair; for all these nations are uncircumcised, and all the house of Israel is uncircumcised in heart."

Idolatry Has Brought Ruin on Israel

10 Hear the word which the LORD speaks to you, O house of Israel. [2]Thus says the LORD:

---

[p] Cn Compare Gk: Heb *your dwelling.*
[q] Gk Syr: Heb *I will take up.*
9:24: 1 Cor 1:31; 2 Cor 10:17.
9:26: Acts 7:51.
[*] 9:23–24: The basis of true religion.

"Learn not the way of the nations,
  nor be dismayed at the signs of the heavens
  because the nations are dismayed at them,
³for the customs of the peoples are false.
A tree from the forest is cut down,
  and worked with an axe by the hands of a
    craftsman.
⁴Men deck it with silver and gold;
  they fasten it with hammer and nails
  so that it cannot move.
⁵Their idols ʳ are like scarecrows in a cucumber
    field,
  and they cannot speak;
they have to be carried,
  for they cannot walk.
Be not afraid of them,
  for they cannot do evil,
  neither is it in them to do good."

⁶There is none like you, O LORD;
  you are great, and your name is great in
    might.
⁷Who would not fear you, O King of the
    nations?
  For this is your due;
for among all the wise ones of the nations
  and in all their kingdoms
  there is none like you.
⁸They are both stupid and foolish;
  the instruction of idols is but wood!
⁹Beaten silver is brought from Tar'shish,
  and gold from U'phaz.
They are the work of the craftsman and of the
    hands of the goldsmith;
  their clothing is violet and purple;
  they are all the work of skilled men.
¹⁰But the LORD is the true God;
  he is the living God and the everlasting
    King.
At his wrath the earth quakes,
  and the nations cannot endure his
    indignation.

11 Thus shall you say to them: "The gods who
did not make the heavens and the earth shall
perish from the earth and from under the
heavens." ˢ

¹²It is he who made the earth by his power,
  who established the world by his wisdom,
  and by his understanding stretched out the
    heavens.
¹³When he utters his voice there is a tumult of
    waters in the heavens,
  and he makes the mist rise from the ends of
    the earth.
He makes lightning for the rain,
  and he brings forth the wind from his
    storehouses.

¹⁴Every man is stupid and without knowledge;
  every goldsmith is put to shame by his idols;
  for his images are false,
  and there is no breath in them.
¹⁵They are worthless, a work of delusion;
  at the time of their punishment they shall
    perish.
¹⁶Not like these is he who is the portion of Jacob,
  for he is the one who formed all things,
  and Israel is the tribe of his inheritance;
  the LORD of hosts is his name.

¹⁷Gather up your bundle from the ground,
  O you who dwell under siege!
¹⁸For thus says the LORD:
"Behold, I am slinging out the inhabitants of
    the land
    at this time,
  and I will bring distress on them,
  that they may feel it."

¹⁹Woe is me because of my hurt!
  My wound is grievous.
But I said, "Truly this is an affliction,
  and I must bear it."
²⁰My tent is destroyed,
  and all my cords are broken;
my children have gone from me,
  and they are not;
there is no one to spread my tent again,
  and to set up my curtains.
²¹For the shepherds are stupid,
  and do not inquire of the LORD;
therefore they have not prospered,
  and all their flock is scattered.

²²Listen, a rumor! Behold, it comes!—
  a great commotion out of the north country
to make the cities of Judah a desolation,
  a lair of jackals.

²³I know, O LORD, that the way of man is not in
    himself,
  that it is not in man who walks to direct his
    steps.
²⁴Correct me, O LORD, but in just measure;
  not in your anger, lest you bring me to
    nothing.

²⁵Pour out your wrath upon the nations that
    know you not,
  and upon the peoples that call not on your
    name;
for they have devoured Jacob;
  they have devoured him and consumed him,
  and have laid waste his habitation.

ʳ Heb *They.*
ˢ This verse is in Aramaic.
10:25: 1 Thess 4:5; Rev 16:1.

Israel and Judah Have Broken the Covenant

11 The word that came to Jeremi'ah from the LORD: [2]"Hear the words of this covenant, and speak to the men of Judah and the inhabitants of Jerusalem. [3]You shall say to them, Thus says the LORD, the God of Israel: Cursed be the man who does not heed the words of this covenant [4]which I commanded your fathers when I brought them out of the land of Egypt, from the iron furnace, saying, Listen to my voice, and do all that I command you. So shall you be my people, and I will be your God, [5]that I may perform the oath which I swore to your fathers, to give them a land flowing with milk and honey, as at this day." Then I answered, "So be it, LORD."

[6] And the LORD said to me, "Proclaim all these words in the cities of Judah, and in the streets of Jerusalem: Hear the words of this covenant and do them. [7]For I solemnly warned your fathers when I brought them up out of the land of Egypt, warning them persistently, even to this day, saying, Obey my voice. [8]Yet they did not obey or incline their ear, but every one walked in the stubbornness of his evil heart. Therefore I brought upon them all the words of this covenant, which I commanded them to do, but they did not."

[9] Again the LORD said to me, "There is revolt among the men of Judah and the inhabitants of Jerusalem. [10]They have turned back to the iniquities of their forefathers, who refused to hear my words; they have gone after other gods to serve them; the house of Israel and the house of Judah have broken my covenant which I made with their fathers. [11]Therefore, thus says the LORD, Behold, I am bringing evil upon them which they cannot escape; though they cry to me, I will not listen to them. [12]Then the cities of Judah and the inhabitants of Jerusalem will go and cry to the gods to whom they burn incense, but they cannot save them in the time of their trouble. [13]For your gods have become as many as your cities, O Judah; and as many as the streets of Jerusalem are the altars you have set up to shame, altars to burn incense to Ba'al.

[14] "Therefore do not pray for this people, or lift up a cry or prayer on their behalf, for I will not listen when they call to me in the time of their trouble. [15]What right has my beloved in my house, when she has done vile deeds? Can vows [t] and sacrificial flesh avert your doom? Can you then exult? [16]The LORD once called you, 'A green olive tree, fair with excellent fruit'; but with the roar of a great tempest he will set fire to it, and its branches will be consumed. [17]The LORD of hosts, who planted you, has pronounced evil against you, because of the evil which the house of Israel and the house of Judah have done, provoking me to anger by burning incense to Ba'al."

[18]The LORD made it known to me and I knew; then you showed me their evil deeds. [19]But I was like a gentle lamb led to the slaughter. I did not know it was against me they devised schemes, saying, "Let us destroy the tree with its fruit, let us cut him off from the land of the living, that his name be remembered no more." [20]But, O LORD of hosts, who judge righteously, who test the heart and the mind, let me see your vengeance upon them, for to you have I committed my cause.

[21] Therefore thus says the LORD concerning the men of An'athoth, who seek your life, and say, "Do not prophesy in the name of the LORD, or you will die by our hand"— [22]therefore thus says the LORD of hosts: "Behold, I will punish them; the young men shall die by the sword; their sons and their daughters shall die by famine; [23]and none of them shall be left. For I will bring evil upon the men of An'athoth, the year of their punishment."

Jeremiah Complains to God

12 Righteous are you, O LORD, when I complain to you; yet I would plead my case before you. Why does the way of the wicked prosper? Why do all who are treacherous thrive? [2]You plant them, and they take root; they grow and bring forth fruit; you are near in their mouth and far from their heart. [3]But you, O LORD, know me; you see me, and test my mind toward you. Pull them out like sheep for the slaughter, and set them apart for the day of slaughter. [4]How long will the land mourn, and the grass of every field wither? For the wickedness of those who dwell in it the beasts and the birds are swept away, because men said, "He will not see our latter end."

[5]"If you have raced with men on foot, and they have wearied you, how will you compete with horses? And if in a safe land you fall down, how will you do in the jungle of the Jordan? [6]For even your brothers and the house of your father, even they have dealt treacherously with you; they are in full cry after you; believe them not, though they speak fair words to you."

---

[t] Gk: Heb *many.*

⁷"I have forsaken my house,
  I have abandoned my heritage;
 I have given the beloved of my soul
   into the hands of her enemies.
⁸My heritage has become to me
   like a lion in the forest,
 she has lifted up her voice against me;
   therefore I hate her.
⁹Is my heritage to me like a speckled bird of prey?
   Are the birds of prey against her round
     about?
 Go, assemble all the wild beasts;
   bring them to devour.
¹⁰Many shepherds have destroyed my vineyard,
   they have trampled down my portion,
 they have made my pleasant portion
   a desolate wilderness.
¹¹They have made it a desolation;
   desolate, it mourns to me.
 The whole land is made desolate,
   but no man lays it to heart.
¹²Upon all the bare heights in the desert
   destroyers have come;
 for the sword of the Lord devours
   from one end of the land to the other;
   no flesh has peace.
¹³They have sown wheat and have reaped
     thorns,
   they have tired themselves out but profit
     nothing.
 They shall be ashamed of their ᵘ harvests
   because of the fierce anger of the Lord."

The Lord's Answer

14 Thus says the Lord concerning all my evil
neighbors who touch the heritage which I have
given my people Israel to inherit: "Behold, I will
pluck them up from their land, and I will pluck up
the house of Judah from among them. ¹⁵And after
I have plucked them up, I will again have compassion on them, and I will bring them again each to
his heritage and each to his land. ¹⁶And it shall
come to pass, if they will diligently learn the
ways of my people, to swear by my name, 'As the
Lord lives,' even as they taught my people to
swear by Ba'al, then they shall be built up in the
midst of my people. ¹⁷But if any nation will not
listen, then I will utterly pluck it up and destroy it,
says the Lord."

The Linen Waistcloth

13 * Thus said the Lord to me, "Go and buy a
linen waistcloth, and put it on your loins,
and do not dip it in water." ²So I bought a waistcloth according to the word of the Lord, and put
it on my loins. ³And the word of the Lord came to
me a second time, ⁴"Take the waistcloth which
you have bought, which is upon your loins, and
arise, go to the Euphra'tes, and hide it there in a
cleft of the rock." ⁵So I went, and hid it by the
Euphra'tes, as the Lord commanded me. ⁶And

after many days the Lord said to me, "Arise, go to
the Euphra'tes, and take from there the waistcloth
which I commanded you to hide there." ⁷Then I
went to the Euphra'tes, and dug, and I took the
waistcloth from the place where I had hidden it.
And behold, the waistcloth was spoiled; it was
good for nothing.

8 Then the word of the Lord came to me:
⁹"Thus says the Lord: Even so will I spoil the
pride of Judah and the great pride of Jerusalem.
¹⁰This evil people, who refuse to hear my words,
who stubbornly follow their own heart and have
gone after other gods to serve them and worship
them, shall be like this waistcloth, which is good
for nothing. ¹¹For as the waistcloth clings to the
loins of a man, so I made the whole house of Israel
and the whole house of Judah cling to me, says the
Lord, that they might be for me a people, a name,
a praise, and a glory, but they would not listen.

The Jars Filled with Wine

12 "You shall speak to them this word: 'Thus
says the Lord, the God of Israel, "Every jar shall
be filled with wine." ' And they will say to you, 'Do
we not indeed know that every jar will be filled
with wine?' ¹³Then you shall say to them, 'Thus
says the Lord: Behold, I will fill with drunkenness
all the inhabitants of this land: the kings who sit
on David's throne, the priests, the prophets, and
all the inhabitants of Jerusalem. ¹⁴And I will dash
them one against another, fathers and sons together, says the Lord. I will not pity or spare or
have compassion, that I should not destroy them.' "

¹⁵Hear and give ear; be not proud,
   for the Lord has spoken.
¹⁶Give glory to the Lord your God
   before he brings darkness,
 before your feet stumble
   on the twilight mountains,
 and while you look for light
   he turns it into gloom
   and makes it deep darkness.
¹⁷But if you will not listen,
   my soul will weep in secret for your pride;
 my eyes will weep bitterly and run down with
     tears,
   because the Lord's flock has been taken
     captive.

¹⁸Say to the king and the queen mother:
   "Take a lowly seat,
 for your beautiful crown
   has come down from your head." ᵛ
¹⁹The cities of the Neg'eb are shut up,
   with none to open them;

ᵘ Heb *your.*
ᵛ Gk Syr Vg: Heb obscure.
* 13:1–11: Note here and elsewhere the use of symbolic action throughout Jeremiah's ministry.

all Judah is taken into exile,
  wholly taken into exile.

20"Lift up your eyes and see
  those who come from the north.
Where is the flock that was given you,
  your beautiful flock?
21What will you say when they set as head over
    you
  those whom you yourself have taught
  to be friends to you?
Will not pangs take hold of you,
  like those of a woman with labor pains?
22And if you say in your heart,
  'Why have these things come upon me?'
it is for the greatness of your iniquity
  that your skirts are lifted up,
  and you suffer violence.
23Can the Ethiopian change his skin
  or the leopard his spots?
Then also you can do good
  who are accustomed to do evil.
24I will scatter you w like chaff
  driven by the wind from the desert.
25This is your lot,
  the portion I have measured out to you, says
    the Lord,
because you have forgotten me
  and trusted in lies.
26I myself will lift up your skirts over your
    face,
  and your shame will be seen.
27I have seen your abominations,
  your adulteries and neighings, your lewd
    harlotries,
  on the hills in the field.
Woe to you, O Jerusalem!
  How long will it be
  before you are made clean?"

The Great Drought

14 The word of the Lord which came to
Jeremi'ah concerning the drought:

2"Judah mourns
  and her gates languish;
her people lament on the ground,
  and the cry of Jerusalem goes up.
3Her nobles send their servants for water;
  they come to the cisterns,
they find no water,
  they return with their vessels empty;
they are ashamed and confounded
  and cover their heads.
4Because of the ground which is dismayed,
  since there is no rain on the land,
the farmers are ashamed,
  they cover their heads.
5Even the deer in the field forsakes her
    newborn fawn
  because there is no grass.

6The wild donkeys stand on the bare heights,
  they pant for air like jackals;
their eyes fail
  because there is no herbage.

7"Though our iniquities testify against us,
  act, O Lord, for your name's sake;
for our backslidings are many,
  we have sinned against you.
8O you hope of Israel,
  its savior in time of trouble,
why should you be like a stranger in the land,
  like a wayfarer who turns aside to linger for
    a night?
9Why should you be like a man confused,
  like a mighty man who cannot save?
Yet you, O Lord, are in the midst of us,
  and we are called by your name;
  leave us not."

10Thus says the Lord concerning this people:
"They have loved to wander thus,
  they have not restrained their feet;
therefore the Lord does not accept them,
  now he will remember their iniquity
  and punish their sins."

11 The Lord said to me: "Do not pray for the
welfare of this people. 12Though they fast, I will
not hear their cry, and though they offer burnt
offering and cereal offering, I will not accept them;
but I will consume them by the sword, by famine,
and by pestilence."

Denunciation of Lying Prophets;
and a Prayer for Mercy

13 Then I said: "Ah, Lord God, behold, the
prophets say to them, 'You shall not see the sword,
nor shall you have famine, but I will give you assured peace in this place.'" 14And the Lord said to
me: "The prophets are prophesying lies in my name;
I did not send them, nor did I command them or
speak to them. They are prophesying to you a lying vision, worthless divination, and the deceit of
their own minds. 15Therefore thus says the Lord
concerning the prophets who prophesy in my name
although I did not send them, and who say, 'Sword
and famine shall not come on this land': By sword
and famine those prophets shall be consumed.
16And the people to whom they prophesy shall be
cast out in the streets of Jerusalem, victims of famine and sword, with none to bury them—them,
their wives, their sons, and their daughters. For I
will pour out their wickedness upon them.

17"You shall say to them this word:
  'Let my eyes run down with tears night and day,
    and let them not cease,

---

w Heb them.
14:12: Rev 6:8.

for the virgin daughter of my people is struck
    down with a great wound,
    with a very grievous blow.
[18]If I go out into the field,
    behold, those slain by the sword!
And if I enter the city,
    behold, the diseases of famine!
For both prophet and priest ply their trade
    through the land,
    and have no knowledge.'"

[19]Have you utterly rejected Judah?
    Does your soul loathe Zion?
Why have you struck us down
    so that there is no healing for us?
We looked for peace, but no good came;
    for a time of healing, but behold, terror.
[20]We acknowledge our wickedness, O LORD,
    and the iniquity of our fathers,
    for we have sinned against you.
[21]Do not spurn us, for your name's sake;
    do not dishonor your glorious throne;
    remember and do not break your covenant
      with us.
[22]Are there any among the false gods of the
    nations that can bring rain?
Or can the heavens give showers?
Are you not he, O LORD our God?
    We set our hope on you,
    for you do all these things.

Anguish and Terror Foretold

15 Then the LORD said to me, "Though Moses and Samuel stood before me, yet my heart would not turn toward this people. Send them out of my sight, and let them go! [2]And when they ask you, 'Where shall we go?' you shall say to them, 'Thus says the LORD:

"Those who are for pestilence, to pestilence,
    and those who are for the sword, to the
      sword;
those who are for famine, to famine,
    and those who are for captivity, to
      captivity."'

[3]"I will appoint over them four kinds of destroyers, says the LORD: the sword to slay, the dogs to tear, and the birds of the air and the beasts of the earth to devour and destroy. [4]And I will make them a horror to all the kingdoms of the earth because of what Manas'seh the son of Hezeki'ah, king of Judah, did in Jerusalem.

[5]"Who will have pity on you, O Jerusalem,
    or who will bemoan you?
Who will turn aside
    to ask about your welfare?
[6]You have rejected me, says the LORD,
    you keep going backward;
so I have stretched out my hand against you
    and destroyed you;—

I am weary of relenting.
[7]I have winnowed them with a winnowing fork
    in the gates of the land;
I have bereaved them, I have destroyed my
    people;
    they did not turn from their ways.
[8]I have made their widows more in number
    than the sand of the seas;
I have brought against the mothers of young
    men
    a destroyer at noonday;
I have made anguish and terror
    fall upon them suddenly.
[9]She who bore seven has languished;
    she has swooned away;
her sun went down while it was yet day;
    she has been shamed and disgraced.
And the rest of them I will give to the sword
    before their enemies,
          says the LORD."

Jeremiah Pleads Again and Is Reassured

10 Woe is me, my mother, that you bore me, a man of strife and contention to the whole land! I have not lent, nor have I borrowed, yet all of them curse me. [11]So let it be, O LORD,* if I have not entreated y you for their good, if I have not pleaded with you on behalf of the enemy in the time of trouble and in the time of distress! [12]Can one break iron, iron from the north, and bronze?

[13]"Your wealth and your treasures I will give as spoil, without price, for all your sins, throughout all your territory. [14]I will make you serve your enemies in a land which you do not know, for in my anger a fire is kindled which shall burn for ever."

[15]O LORD, you know;
    remember me and visit me,
    and take vengeance for me on my
      persecutors.
In your forbearance take me not away;
    know that for your sake I bear reproach.
[16]Your words were found, and I ate them,
    and your words became to me a joy
    and the delight of my heart;
for I am called by your name,
    O LORD, God of hosts.
[17]I did not sit in the company of merrymakers,
    nor did I rejoice;
I sat alone, because your hand was upon me,
    for you had filled me with indignation.
[18]Why is my pain unceasing,
    my wound incurable,
    refusing to be healed?
Will you be to me like a deceitful brook,
    like waters that fail?

---

* Gk Old Latin: Heb *the LORD said.*
y Cn: Heb obscure.
15:2: Rev 13:10.

[19]Therefore thus says the LORD:
"If you return, I will restore you,
    and you shall stand before me.
If you utter what is precious, and not what is
        worthless,
    you shall be as my mouth.
They shall turn to you,
    but you shall not turn to them.
[20]And I will make you to this people
    a fortified wall of bronze;
they will fight against you,
    but they shall not prevail over you,
for I am with you
    to save you and deliver you, says the LORD.
[21]I will deliver you out of the hand of the
        wicked,
    and redeem you from the grasp of the
        ruthless."

Jeremiah's Celibacy and Message

16 The word of the LORD came to me: [2]"You shall not take a wife, nor shall you have sons or daughters in this place. [3]For thus says the LORD concerning the sons and daughters who are born in this place, and concerning the mothers who bore them and the fathers who begot them in this land: [4]They shall die of deadly diseases. They shall not be lamented, nor shall they be buried; they shall be as dung on the surface of the ground. They shall perish by the sword and by famine, and their dead bodies shall be food for the birds of the air and for the beasts of the earth.

5 "For thus says the LORD: Do not enter the house of mourning, or go to lament, or bemoan them; for I have taken away my peace from this people, says the LORD, my steadfast love and mercy. [6]Both great and small shall die in this land; they shall not be buried, and no one shall lament for them or cut himself or make himself bald for them. [7]No one shall break bread for the mourner, to comfort him for the dead; nor shall any one give him the cup of consolation to drink for his father or his mother. [8]You shall not go into the house of feasting to sit with them, to eat and drink. [9]For thus says the LORD of hosts, the God of Israel: Behold, I will make to cease from this place, before your eyes and in your days, the voice of mirth and the voice of gladness, the voice of the bridegroom and the voice of the bride.

10 "And when you tell this people all these words, and they say to you, 'Why has the LORD pronounced all this great evil against us? What is our iniquity? What is the sin that we have committed against the LORD our God?' [11]then you shall say to them: 'Because your fathers have forsaken me, says the LORD, and have gone after other gods and have served and worshiped them, and have forsaken me and have not kept my law, [12]and because you have done worse than your fathers,

for behold, every one of you follows his stubborn evil will, refusing to listen to me; [13]therefore I will hurl you out of this land into a land which neither you nor your fathers have known, and there you shall serve other gods day and night, for I will show you no favor.'

God Will Restore Israel

14 "Therefore, behold, the days are coming, says the LORD, when it shall no longer be said, 'As the LORD lives who brought up the sons of Israel out of the land of Egypt,' [15]but 'As the LORD lives who brought up the sons of Israel out of the north country and out of all the countries where he had driven them.' For I will bring them back to their own land which I gave to their fathers.

16 "Behold, I am sending for many fishers, says the LORD, and they shall catch them; and afterwards I will send for many hunters, and they shall hunt them from every mountain and every hill, and out of the clefts of the rocks. [17]For my eyes are upon all their ways; they are not hidden from me, nor is their iniquity concealed from my eyes. [18]And [z] I will doubly recompense their iniquity and their sin, because they have polluted my land with the carcasses of their detestable idols, and have filled my inheritance with their abominations."

[19]O LORD, my strength and my stronghold,
    my refuge in the day of trouble,
to you shall the nations come
    from the ends of the earth and say:
"Our fathers have inherited nothing but lies,
    worthless things in which there is no profit.
[20]Can man make for himself gods?
    Such are no gods!"

21 "Therefore, behold, I will make them know, this once I will make them know my power and my might, and they shall know that my name is the LORD."

Judah's Sin and Shame

17 "The sin of Judah is written with a pen of iron; with a point of diamond it is engraved on the tablet of their heart, and on the horns of their altars, [2]while their children remember their altars and their Ashe'rim, beside every green tree, and on the high hills, [3]on the mountains in the open country. Your wealth and all your treasures I will give for spoil as the price of your sin [a] throughout all your territory. [4]You shall loosen your hand [b] from your heritage which I gave to you, and I will make you serve your enemies in a land which you do not know, for in my anger a fire is kindled which shall burn for ever."

---

[z] Gk: Heb *And first.*
[a] Cn: Heb *your high places for sin.*
[b] Cn: Heb *and in you.*
16:9: Jer 7:34; 25:10; Rev 18:23.

⁵Thus says the Lord:
"Cursed is the man who trusts in man
  and makes flesh his arm,
  whose heart turns away from the Lord.
⁶He is like a shrub in the desert,
  and shall not see any good come.
He shall dwell in the parched places of the
    wilderness,
  in an uninhabited salt land.

⁷"Blessed is the man who trusts in the Lord,
  whose trust is the Lord.
⁸He is like a tree planted by water,
  that sends out its roots by the stream,
and does not fear when heat comes,
  for its leaves remain green,
and is not anxious in the year of drought,
  for it does not cease to bear fruit."

⁹The heart is deceitful above all things,
  and desperately corrupt;
  who can understand it?
¹⁰"I the Lord search the mind
  and test the heart,
to give to every man according to his ways,
  according to the fruit of his doings."

¹¹Like the partridge that gathers a brood which
    she did not hatch,
  so is he who gets riches but not by right;
in the midst of his days they will leave him,
  and at his end he will be a fool.

¹²A glorious throne set on high from the
    beginning
  is the place of our sanctuary.
¹³O Lord, the hope of Israel,
  all who forsake you shall be put to shame;
those who turn away from you ᶜ shall be
    written in the earth,
  for they have forsaken the Lord, the
    fountain of living water.

¹⁴Heal me, O Lord, and I shall be healed;
  save me, and I shall be saved;
  for you are my praise.
¹⁵Behold, they say to me,
  "Where is the word of the Lord?
  Let it come!"
¹⁶I have not pressed you to send evil,
  nor have I desired the day of disaster,
  you know;
that which came out of my lips
  was before your face.
¹⁷Be not a terror to me;
  you are my refuge in the day of evil.
¹⁸Let those be put to shame who persecute me,
  but let me not be put to shame;

let them be dismayed,
  but let me not be dismayed;
bring upon them the day of evil;
  destroy them with double destruction!

19 Thus said the Lord to me: "Go and stand in the Benjamin ᵈ Gate, by which the kings of Judah enter and by which they go out, and in all the gates of Jerusalem, ²⁰and say: 'Hear the word of the Lord, you kings of Judah, and all Judah, and all the inhabitants of Jerusalem, who enter by these gates. ²¹Thus says the Lord: Take heed for the sake of your lives, and do not bear a burden on the sabbath day or bring it in by the gates of Jerusalem. ²²And do not carry a burden out of your houses on the sabbath or do any work, but keep the sabbath day holy, as I commanded your fathers. ²³Yet they did not listen or incline their ear, but stiffened their neck, that they might not hear and receive instruction.

24 "'But if you listen to me, says the Lord, and bring in no burden by the gates of this city on the sabbath day, but keep the sabbath day holy and do no work on it, ²⁵then there shall enter by the gates of this city kings ᵉ who sit on the throne of David, riding in chariots and on horses, they and their princes, the men of Judah and the inhabitants of Jerusalem; and this city shall be inhabited for ever. ²⁶And people shall come from the cities of Judah and the places round about Jerusalem, from the land of Benjamin, from the Shephe'lah, from the hill country, and from the Neg'eb, bringing burnt offerings and sacrifices, cereal offerings and frankincense, and bringing thank offerings to the house of the Lord. ²⁷But if you do not listen to me, to keep the sabbath day holy, and not to bear a burden and enter by the gates of Jerusalem on the sabbath day, then I will kindle a fire in its gates, and it shall devour the palaces of Jerusalem and shall not be quenched.'"

The Potter and the Clay

18 The word that came to Jeremi'ah from the Lord: ²"Arise, and go down to the potter's house, and there I will let you hear my words." ³So I went down to the potter's house, and there he was working at his wheel. ⁴And the vessel he was making of clay was spoiled in the potter's hand, and he reworked it into another vessel, as it seemed good to the potter to do.

5 Then the word of the Lord came to me: ⁶"O house of Israel, can I not do with you as this potter has done? says the Lord. Behold, like the clay in the potter's hand, so are you in my hand, O house of Israel. ⁷If at any time I declare

---
ᶜ Heb me.
ᵈ Cn: Heb sons of people.
ᵉ Cn: Heb kings and princes.
17:7–8: Ps 1:1–3.
17:10: Ps 62:12; Rev 2:23; 22:12.

concerning a nation or a kingdom, that I will pluck up and break down and destroy it, [8]and if that nation, concerning which I have spoken, turns from its evil, I will repent of the evil that I intended to do to it. [9]And if at any time I declare concerning a nation or a kingdom that I will build and plant it, [10]and if it does evil in my sight, not listening to my voice, then I will repent of the good which I had intended to do to it. [11]Now, therefore, say to the men of Judah and the inhabitants of Jerusalem: 'Thus says the LORD, Behold, I am shaping evil against you and devising a plan against you. Return, every one from his evil way, and amend your ways and your doings.'

Israel's Stubborn Idolatry

12 "But they say, 'That is in vain! We will follow our own plans, and everyone will act according to the stubbornness of his evil heart.'

[13]"Therefore thus says the LORD:
Ask among the nations,
    who has heard the like of this?
The virgin Israel
    has done a very horrible thing.
[14]Does the snow of Lebanon leave
    the crags of Sir'ion? [f]
Do the mountain [g] waters run dry, [h]
    the cold flowing streams?
[15]But my people have forgotten me,
    they burn incense to false gods;
they have stumbled [i] in their ways,
    in the ancient roads,
and have gone into bypaths,
    not the highway,
[16]making their land a horror,
    a thing to be hissed at for ever.
Every one who passes by it is horrified
    and shakes his head.
[17]Like the east wind I will scatter them
    before the enemy.
I will show them my back, not my face,
    in the day of their calamity."

Plots against Jeremiah

18 Then they said, "Come, let us make plots against Jeremi'ah, for the law shall not perish from the priest, nor counsel from the wise, nor the word from the prophet. Come, let us strike him with the tongue, and let us not heed any of his words."

[19]Give heed to me, O LORD,
    and listen to my plea. [j]
[20]Is evil a recompense for good?
    Yet they have dug a pit for my life.
Remember how I stood before you
    to speak good for them,
    to turn away your wrath from them.
[21]Therefore deliver up their children to famine;
    give them over to the power of the sword,

let their wives become childless and widowed.
May their men meet death by pestilence,
    their youths be slain by the sword in battle.
[22]May a cry be heard from their houses,
    when you bring the marauder suddenly
        upon them!
For they have dug a pit to take me,
    and laid snares for my feet.
[23]Yet, you, O LORD, know
    all their plotting to slay me.
Forgive not their iniquity,
    nor blot out their sin from your sight.
Let them be overthrown before you;
    deal with them in the time of your anger.

The Broken Earthen Flask

19 Thus said the LORD, "Go, buy a potter's earthen flask, and take some of the elders of the people and some of the senior priests, [2]and go out to the valley of the son of Hinnom at the entry of the Potsherd Gate, and proclaim there the words that I tell you. [3]You shall say, 'Hear the word of the LORD, O kings of Judah and inhabitants of Jerusalem. Thus says the LORD of hosts, the God of Israel, Behold, I am bringing such evil upon this place that the ears of every one who hears of it will tingle. [4]Because the people have forsaken me, and have profaned this place by burning incense in it to other gods whom neither they nor their fathers nor the kings of Judah have known; and because they have filled this place with the blood of innocents, [5]and have built the high places of Ba'al to burn their sons in the fire as burnt offerings to Baal, which I did not command or decree, nor did it come into my mind; [6]therefore, behold, days are coming, says the LORD, when this place shall no more be called To'pheth, or the valley of the son of Hinnom, but the valley of Slaughter. [7]And in this place I will make void the plans of Judah and Jerusalem, and will cause their people to fall by the sword before their enemies, and by the hand of those who seek their life. I will give their dead bodies for food to the birds of the air and to the beasts of the earth. [8]And I will make this city a horror, a thing to be hissed at; every one who passes by it will be horrified and will hiss because of all its disasters. [9]And I will make them eat the flesh of their sons and their daughters, and every one shall eat the flesh of his neighbor in the siege and in the distress, with which their enemies and those who seek their life afflict them.'

10 "Then you shall break the flask in the sight of the men who go with you, [11]and shall say to

---

[f] Cn: Heb *the field*.
[g] Cn: Heb *foreign*.
[h] Cn: Heb *Are . . . plucked up?*
[i] Gk Syr Vg: Heb *they made them stumble*.
[j] Gk Compare Syr Tg: Heb *my adversaries*.
18:6: Rom 9:21.

them, 'Thus says the LORD of hosts: So will I break this people and this city, as one breaks a potter's vessel, so that it can never be mended. Men shall bury in To'pheth because there will be no place else to bury. ¹²Thus will I do to this place, says the LORD, and to its inhabitants, making this city like To'pheth. ¹³The houses of Jerusalem and the houses of the kings of Judah—all the houses upon whose roofs incense has been burned to all the host of heaven, and drink offerings have been poured out to other gods—shall be defiled like the place of To'pheth.' "

14 Then Jeremi'ah came from To'pheth, where the LORD had sent him to prophesy, and he stood in the court of the LORD's house, and said to all the people: ¹⁵"Thus says the LORD of hosts, the God of Israel, Behold, I am bringing upon this city and upon all its towns all the evil that I have pronounced against it, because they have stiffened their neck, refusing to hear my words."

Jeremiah Is Persecuted by Pashhur and Complains to God

20 Now Pashhur the priest, the son of Im'mer, who was chief officer in the house of the LORD, heard Jeremi'ah prophesying these things. ²Then Pashhur beat Jeremi'ah the prophet, and put him in the stocks that were in the upper Benjamin Gate of the house of the LORD. ³On the next day, when Pashhur released Jeremi'ah from the stocks, Jeremi'ah said to him, "The LORD does not call your name Pashhur, but Terror on every side. ⁴For thus says the LORD: Behold, I will make you a terror to yourself and to all your friends. They shall fall by the sword of their enemies while you look on. And I will give all Judah into the hand of the king of Babylon; he shall carry them captive to Babylon, and shall slay them with the sword. ⁵Moreover, I will give all the wealth of the city, all its gains, all its prized belongings, and all the treasures of the kings of Judah into the hand of their enemies, who shall plunder them, and seize them, and carry them to Babylon. ⁶And you, Pashhur, and all who dwell in your house, shall go into captivity; to Babylon you shall go; and there you shall die, and there you shall be buried, you and all your friends, to whom you have prophesied falsely."

⁷O LORD, you have deceived me,
    and I was deceived;
you are stronger than I,
    and you have prevailed.
I have become a laughingstock all the day;
    every one mocks me.
⁸For whenever I speak, I cry out,
    I shout, "Violence and destruction!"
For the word of the LORD has become for me
    a reproach and derision all day long.

⁹If I say, "I will not mention him,
    or speak any more in his name,"
there is in my heart as it were a burning fire
    shut up in my bones,
and I am weary with holding it in,
    and I cannot.
¹⁰For I hear many whispering.
    Terror is on every side!
"Denounce him! Let us denounce him!"
    say all my familiar friends,
    watching for my fall.
"Perhaps he will be deceived,
    then we can overcome him,
    and take our revenge on him."
¹¹But the LORD is with me as a dread warrior;
    therefore my persecutors will stumble,
    they will not overcome me.
They will be greatly shamed,
    for they will not succeed.
Their eternal dishonor
    will never be forgotten.
¹²O LORD of hosts, who test the righteous,
    who see the heart and the mind,
let me see your vengeance upon them,
    for to you have I committed my cause.

¹³Sing to the LORD;
    praise the LORD!
For he has delivered the life of the needy
    from the hand of evildoers.

¹⁴Cursed be the day
    on which I was born!
The day when my mother bore me,
    let it not be blessed!
¹⁵Cursed be the man
    who brought the news to my father,
"A son is born to you,"
    making him very glad.
¹⁶Let that man be like the cities
    which the LORD overthrew without pity;
let him hear a cry in the morning
    and an alarm at noon,
¹⁷because he did not kill me in the womb;
    so my mother would have been my grave,
    and her womb for ever great.
¹⁸Why did I come forth from the womb
    to see toil and sorrow,
    and spend my days in shame?

The Fall of Jerusalem

21 This is the word which came to Jeremi'ah from the LORD, when King Zedeki'ah sent to him Pashhur the son of Malchi'ah and Zephani'ah the priest, the son of Ma-asei'ah, saying, ²"Inquire of the LORD for us, for Nebuchadrez'zar king of Babylon is making war against us;

19:13: Acts 7:42.
20:3, 10: Jer 6:25; 46:5; 49:29; Ps 31:13.
20:14–18: Job 3:3–13.

perhaps the LORD will deal with us according to all his wonderful deeds, and will make him withdraw from us."

3 Then Jeremi'ah said to them: [4]"Thus you shall say to Zedeki'ah, 'Thus says the LORD, the God of Israel: Behold, I will turn back the weapons of war which are in your hands and with which you are fighting against the king of Babylon and against the Chalde'ans who are besieging you outside the walls; and I will bring them together into the midst of this city. [5]I myself will fight against you with outstretched hand and strong arm, in anger, and in fury, and in great wrath. [6]And I will strike the inhabitants of this city, both man and beast; they shall die of a great pestilence. [7]Afterward, says the LORD, I will give Zedeki'ah king of Judah, and his servants, and the people in this city who survive the pestilence, sword, and famine, into the hand of Nebuchadrez'zar king of Babylon and into the hand of their enemies, into the hand of those who seek their lives. He shall strike them with the edge of the sword; he shall not pity them, or spare them, or have compassion.'

8 "And to this people you shall say: 'Thus says the LORD: Behold, I set before you the way of life and the way of death. [9]He who stays in this city shall die by the sword, by famine, and by pestilence; but he who goes out and surrenders to the Chalde'ans who are besieging you shall live and shall have his life as a prize of war. [10]For I have set my face against this city for evil and not for good, says the LORD: it shall be given into the hand of the king of Babylon, and he shall burn it with fire.'

Message to the King of Judah

11 "And to the house of the king of Judah say, 'Hear the word of the LORD, [12]O house of David! Thus says the LORD:

" 'Execute justice in the morning,
    and deliver from the hand of the oppressor
    him who has been robbed,
lest my wrath go forth like fire,
    and burn with none to quench it,
    because of your evil doings.' "

[13]"Behold, I am against you, O inhabitant of the valley,
O rock of the plain,
                        says the LORD;
you who say, 'Who shall come down
    against us,
    or who shall enter our habitations?'
[14]I will punish you according to the fruit of your doings,
                        says the LORD;
    I will kindle a fire in her forest,
    and it shall devour all that is round about her."

Exhortation to Repentance

22 Thus says the LORD: "Go down to the house of the king of Judah, and speak there this word, [2]and say, 'Hear the word of the LORD, O King of Judah, who sit on the throne of David, you, and your servants, and your people who enter these gates. [3]Thus says the LORD: Do justice and righteousness, and deliver from the hand of the oppressor him who has been robbed. And do no wrong or violence to the alien, the fatherless, and the widow, nor shed innocent blood in this place. [4]For if you will indeed obey this word, then there shall enter the gates of this house kings who sit on the throne of David, riding in chariots and on horses, they, and their servants, and their people. [5]But if you will not heed these words, I swear by myself, says the LORD, that this house shall become a desolation. [6]For thus says the LORD concerning the house of the king of Judah:

" 'You are as Gilead to me,
    as the summit of Lebanon,
yet surely I will make you a desert,
    an uninhabited city. [k]
[7]I will prepare destroyers against you,
    each with his weapons;
and they shall cut down your choicest cedars,
    and cast them into the fire.

8 " 'And many nations will pass by this city, and every man will say to his neighbor, "Why has the LORD dealt thus with this great city?" [9]And they will answer, "Because they forsook the covenant of the LORD their God, and worshiped other gods and served them." ' "

[10]Weep not for him who is dead,
    nor bemoan him;
but weep bitterly for him who goes away,
    for he shall return no more
    to see his native land.

Message to the Sons of Josiah

11 For thus says the LORD concerning Shallum the son of Josi'ah, king of Judah, who reigned instead of Josiah his father, and who went away from this place: "He shall return here no more, [12]but in the place where they have carried him captive, there shall he die, and he shall never see this land again."

[13]"Woe to him who builds his house by unrighteousness,
    and his upper rooms by injustice;
who makes his neighbor serve him for nothing,
    and does not give him his wages;
[14]who says, 'I will build myself a great house
    with spacious upper rooms,'

---

[k] Cn: Heb cities.
22:5: Mt 23:38; Lk 13:35.

and cuts out windows for it,
  paneling it with cedar,
  and painting it with vermilion.
[15]Do you think you are a king
  because you compete in cedar?
Did not your father eat and drink
  and do justice and righteousness?
Then it was well with him.
[16]He judged the cause of the poor and needy;
  then it was well.
Is not this to know me?
  says the LORD.
[17]But you have eyes and heart
  only for your dishonest gain,
for shedding innocent blood,
  and for practicing oppression and
  violence."
[18]Therefore thus says the LORD concerning
  Jehoi'akim the son of Josi'ah, king of
  Judah:
"They shall not lament for him, saying,
  'Ah my brother!' or 'Ah sister!'
They shall not lament for him, saying,
  'Ah lord!' or 'Ah his majesty!'
[19]With the burial of a donkey he shall be buried,
  dragged and cast forth beyond the gates of
  Jerusalem."

[20]"Go up to Lebanon, and cry out,
  and lift up your voice in Bashan;
cry from Ab'arim,
  for all your lovers are destroyed.
[21]I spoke to you in your prosperity,
  but you said, 'I will not listen.'
This has been your way from your youth,
  that you have not obeyed my voice.
[22]The wind shall shepherd all your shepherds,
  and your lovers shall go into captivity;
then you will be ashamed and confounded
  because of all your wickedness.
[23]O inhabitant of Lebanon,
  nested among the cedars,
how you will groan [1] when pangs come upon
  you,
  pain as of a woman with labor pains!"

Message concerning Coniah the Son of Jehoiakim

24 "As I live, says the LORD, though Coni'ah the son of Jehoi'akim, king of Judah, were the signet ring on my right hand, yet I would tear you off [25]and give you into the hand of those who seek your life, into the hand of those of whom you are afraid, even into the hand of Nebuchadrez'zar king of Babylon and into the hand of the Chalde'ans. [26]I will hurl you and the mother who bore you into another country, where you were not born, and there you shall die. [27]But to the land to which they will long to return, there they shall not return."

[28]Is this man Coni'ah a despised, broken pot,
  a vessel no one cares for?
Why are he and his children hurled and cast
  into a land which they do not know?
[29]O land, land, land,
  hear the word of the LORD!
[30]Thus says the LORD:
"Write this man down as childless,
  a man who shall not succeed in his days;
for none of his offspring shall succeed
  in sitting on the throne of David,
  and ruling again in Judah."

A Remnant to Be Restored after Exile

23 "Woe to the shepherds who destroy and scatter the sheep of my pasture!" says the LORD. [2]Therefore thus says the LORD, the God of Israel, concerning the shepherds who care for my people: "You have scattered my flock, and have driven them away, and you have not attended to them. Behold, I will attend to you for your evil doings, says the LORD. [3]Then I will gather the remnant of my flock out of all the countries where I have driven them, and I will bring them back to their fold, and they shall be fruitful and multiply. [4]I will set shepherds over them who will care for them, and they shall fear no more, nor be dismayed, neither shall any be missing, says the LORD.

The Righteous Branch

5 "Behold, the days are coming, says the LORD, when I will raise up for David a righteous Branch, and he shall reign as king and deal wisely, and shall execute justice and righteousness in the land. [6]In his days Judah will be saved, and Israel will dwell securely. And this is the name by which he will be called: 'The LORD is our righteousness.'

7 "Therefore, behold, the days are coming, says the LORD, when men shall no longer say, 'As the LORD lives who brought up the sons of Israel out of the land of Egypt,' [8]but 'As the LORD lives who brought up and led the descendants of the house of Israel out of the north country and out of all the countries where he[m] had driven them.' Then they shall dwell in their own land."

False Prophets Denounced

9 Concerning the prophets:
My heart is broken within me,
  all my bones shake;
I am like a drunken man,
  like a man overcome by wine,
because of the LORD
  and because of his holy words.
[10]For the land is full of adulterers;
  because of the curse the land mourns,
  and the pastures of the wilderness are
  dried up.

---

[1] Gk Vg Syr: Heb be pitied.
[m] Gk: Heb I.
23:5: Jer 33:15; Is 4:2; Zech 3:8; 6:12.

Their course is evil,
and their might is not right.
[11]"Both prophet and priest are ungodly;
even in my house I have found their
wickedness,
says the LORD.
[12]Therefore their way shall be to them
like slippery paths in the darkness,
into which they shall be driven and fall;
for I will bring evil upon them
in the year of their punishment,
says the LORD.
[13]In the prophets of Samar′ia
I saw an unsavory thing:
they prophesied by Ba′al
and led my people Israel astray.
[14]But in the prophets of Jerusalem
I have seen a horrible thing:
they commit adultery and walk in lies;
they strengthen the hands of evildoers,
so that no one turns from his wickedness;
all of them have become like Sodom to me,
and its inhabitants like Gomor′rah."
[15]Therefore thus says the LORD of hosts concerning the prophets:
"Behold, I will feed them with wormwood,
and give them poisoned water to drink;
for from the prophets of Jerusalem
ungodliness has gone forth into all the
land."

16 Thus says the LORD of hosts: "Do not listen to the words of the prophets who prophesy to you, filling you with vain hopes; they speak visions of their own minds, not from the mouth of the LORD. [17]They say continually to those who despise the word of the LORD, 'It shall be well with you'; and to every one who stubbornly follows his own heart, they say, 'No evil shall come upon you.'"

[18]For who among them has stood in the council
of the LORD
to perceive and to hear his word,
or who has given heed to his word and
listened?
[19]Behold, the storm of the LORD!
Wrath has gone forth,
a whirling tempest;
it will burst upon the head of the wicked.
[20]The anger of the LORD will not turn back
until he has executed and accomplished
the intents of his mind.
In the latter days you will understand it clearly.

[21]"I did not send the prophets,
yet they ran;
I did not speak to them,
yet they prophesied.

[22]But if they had stood in my council,
then they would have proclaimed my words
to my people,
and they would have turned them from their
evil way,
and from the evil of their doings.

23 "Am I a God at hand, says the LORD, and not a God afar off? [24]Can a man hide himself in secret places so that I cannot see him? says the LORD. Do I not fill heaven and earth? says the LORD. [25]I have heard what the prophets have said who prophesy lies in my name, saying, 'I have dreamed, I have dreamed!' [26]How long shall there be lies[n] in the heart of the prophets who prophesy lies, and who prophesy the deceit of their own heart, [27]who think to make my people forget my name by their dreams which they tell one another, even as their fathers forgot my name for Ba′al? [28]Let the prophet who has a dream tell the dream, but let him who has my word speak my word faithfully. What has straw in common with wheat? says the LORD. [29]Is not my word like fire, says the LORD, and like a hammer which breaks the rock in pieces? [30]Therefore, behold, I am against the prophets, says the LORD, who steal my words from one another. [31]Behold, I am against the prophets, says the LORD, who use their tongues and say, 'Says the LORD.' [32]Behold, I am against those who prophesy lying dreams, says the LORD, and who tell them and lead my people astray by their lies and their recklessness, when I did not send them or charge them; so they do not profit this people at all, says the LORD.

33 "When one of this people, or a prophet, or a priest asks you, 'What is the burden of the LORD?' you shall say to them, 'You are the burden,[o] and I will cast you off, says the LORD.' [34]And as for the prophet, priest, or one of the people who says, 'The burden of the LORD,' I will punish that man and his household. [35]Thus shall you say, every one to his neighbor and every one to his brother, 'What has the LORD answered?' or 'What has the LORD spoken?' [36]But 'the burden of the LORD' you shall mention no more, for the burden is every man's own word, and you pervert the words of the living God, the LORD of hosts, our God. [37]Thus you shall say to the prophet, 'What has the LORD answered you?' or 'What has the LORD spoken?' [38]But if you say, 'The burden of the LORD,' thus says the LORD, 'Because you have said these words, "The burden of the LORD," when I sent to you, saying, "You shall not say, 'The burden of the LORD,'"' [39]therefore, behold, I will surely lift you up and cast you away from my presence, you and the city which I gave to

---

[n] Cn Compare Syr: Heb obscure.
[o] Gk Vg: Heb What burden.

you and your fathers. [40]And I will bring upon you everlasting reproach and perpetual shame, which shall not be forgotten.'"

Two Baskets: Good and Bad Figs

24 After Nebuchadrez'zar king of Babylon had taken into exile from Jerusalem Jeconi'ah the son of Jehoi'akim, king of Judah, together with the princes of Judah, the craftsmen, and the smiths, and had brought them to Babylon, the LORD showed me this vision: Behold, two baskets of figs placed before the temple of the LORD. [2]One basket had very good figs, like first-ripe figs, but the other basket had very bad figs, so bad that they could not be eaten. [3]And the LORD said to me, "What do you see, Jeremi'ah?" I said, "Figs, the good figs very good, and the bad figs very bad, so bad that they cannot be eaten."

[4] Then the word of the LORD came to me: [5]"Thus says the LORD, the God of Israel: Like these good figs, so I will regard as good the exiles from Judah, whom I have sent away from this place to the land of the Chalde'ans. [6]I will set my eyes upon them for good, and I will bring them back to this land. I will build them up, and not tear them down; I will plant them, and not uproot them. [7]I will give them a heart to know that I am the LORD; and they shall be my people and I will be their God, for they shall return to me with their whole heart.

[8]"But thus says the LORD: Like the bad figs which are so bad they cannot be eaten, so will I treat Zedeki'ah the king of Judah, his princes, the remnant of Jerusalem who remain in this land, and those who dwell in the land of Egypt. [9]I will make them a horror [p] to all the kingdoms of the earth, to be a reproach, a byword, a taunt, and a curse in all the places where I shall drive them. [10]And I will send sword, famine, and pestilence upon them, until they shall be utterly destroyed from the land which I gave to them and their fathers."

The Babylonian Captivity Foretold

25 The word that came to Jeremi'ah concerning all the people of Judah, in the fourth year of Jehoi'akim the son of Josi'ah, king of Judah (that was the first year of Nebuchadrez'zar king of Babylon), [2]which Jeremi'ah the prophet spoke to all the people of Judah and all the inhabitants of Jerusalem: [3]"For twenty-three years, from the thirteenth year of Josi'ah the son of A'mon, king of Judah, to this day, the word of the LORD has come to me, and I have spoken persistently to you, but you have not listened. [4]You have neither listened nor inclined your ears to hear, although the LORD persistently sent to you all his servants the prophets, [5]saying, 'Turn now, every one of you, from his evil way and wrong doings, and dwell upon the land which the LORD has given to you and your fathers from of old and for ever;

[6]do not go after other gods to serve and worship them, or provoke me to anger with the work of your hands. Then I will do you no harm.' [7]Yet you have not listened to me, says the LORD, that you might provoke me to anger with the work of your hands to your own harm.

[8] "Therefore thus says the LORD of hosts: Because you have not obeyed my words, [9]behold, I will send for all the tribes of the north, says the LORD, and for Nebuchadrez'zar the king of Babylon, my servant, and I will bring them against this land and its inhabitants, and against all these nations round about; I will utterly destroy them, and make them a horror, a hissing, and an everlasting reproach. [q] [10]Moreover, I will banish from them the voice of mirth and the voice of gladness, the voice of the bridegroom and the voice of the bride, the grinding of the millstones and the light of the lamp. [11]This whole land shall become a ruin and a waste, and these nations shall serve the king of Babylon seventy years. [12]Then after seventy years are completed, I will punish the king of Babylon and that nation, the land of the Chalde'ans, for their iniquity, says the LORD, making the land an everlasting waste. [13]I will bring upon that land all the words which I have uttered against it, everything written in this book, which Jeremi'ah prophesied against all the nations. [14]For many nations and great kings shall make slaves even of them; and I will recompense them according to their deeds and the work of their hands."

The Cup of the Lord's Wrath

[15] Thus the LORD, the God of Israel, said to me: "Take from my hand this cup of the wine of wrath, and make all the nations to whom I send you drink it. [16]They shall drink and stagger and be crazed because of the sword which I am sending among them."

[17] So I took the cup from the LORD's hand, and made all the nations to whom the Lord sent me drink it: [18]Jerusalem and the cities of Judah, its kings and princes, to make them a desolation and a waste, a hissing and a curse, as at this day; [19]Pharaoh king of Egypt, his servants, his princes, all his people, [20]and all the foreign folk among them; all the kings of the land of Uz and all the kings of the land of the Philis'tines (Ash'kelon, Gaza, Ek'ron, and the remnant of Ash'dod); [21]E'dom, Moab, and the sons of Ammon; [22]all the kings of Tyre, all the kings of Sidon, and the kings of the islands across the sea; [23]De'dan, Te'ma, Buz, and all who cut the corners of their hair; [24]all the kings of Arabia and all the kings of the mixed tribes that dwell in

---

[p] Compare Gk: Heb *horror for evil.*
[q] Gk Compare Syr: Heb *desolations.*
25:10: Jer 7:34; 16:9; Rev 18:23.
25:15: Jer 51:7; Rev 14:8, 10; 16:19; 17:4; 18:3.

the desert; 25all the kings of Zimri, all the kings of E'lam, and all the kings of Med'ia; 26all the kings of the north, far and near, one after another, and all the kingdoms of the world which are on the face of the earth. And after them the king of Babylon ᵉ shall drink.

27 "Then you shall say to them, 'Thus says the Lord of hosts, the God of Israel: Drink, be drunk and vomit, fall and rise no more, because of the sword which I am sending among you.'

28 "And if they refuse to accept the cup from your hand to drink, then you shall say to them, 'Thus says the Lord of hosts: You must drink! 29For behold, I begin to work evil at the city which is called by my name, and shall you go unpunished? You shall not go unpunished, for I am summoning a sword against all the inhabitants of the earth, says the Lord of hosts.'

30 "You, therefore, shall prophesy against them all these words, and say to them:

'The Lord will roar from on high,
    and from his holy habitation utter his voice;
he will roar mightily against his fold,
    and shout, like those who tread grapes,
    against all the inhabitants of the earth.
31The clamor will resound to the ends of the earth,
    for the Lord has an indictment against the nations;
he is entering into judgment with all flesh,
    and the wicked he will put to the sword,
                        says the Lord.'

32"Thus says the Lord of hosts:
Behold, evil is going forth
    from nation to nation,
and a great tempest is stirring
    from the farthest parts of the earth!

33 "And those slain by the Lord on that day shall extend from one end of the earth to the other. They shall not be lamented, or gathered, or buried; they shall be dung on the surface of the ground. 34"Wail, you shepherds, and cry,
    and roll in ashes, you lords of the flock,
for the days of your slaughter and dispersion have come,
    and you shall fall like choice rams. ˢ
35No refuge will remain for the shepherds,
    nor escape for the lords of the flock.
36Listen, the cry of the shepherds,
    and the wail of the lords of the flock!
For the Lord is despoiling their pasture,
37and the peaceful folds are devastated,
    because of the fierce anger of the Lord.
38Like a lion he has left his den,
    for their land has become a waste
because of the sword of the oppressor,
    and because of his fierce anger."

Jeremiah Threatened with Death

26 In the beginning of the reign of Jehoi'akim the son of Josi'ah, king of Judah, this word came from the Lord, 2"Thus says the Lord: Stand in the court of the Lord's house, and speak to all the cities of Judah which come to worship in the house of the Lord all the words that I command you to speak to them; do not hold back a word. 3It may be they will listen, and every one turn from his evil way, that I may repent of the evil which I intend to do to them because of their evil doings. 4You shall say to them, 'Thus says the Lord: If you will not listen to me, to walk in my law which I have set before you, 5and to heed the words of my servants the prophets whom I send to you urgently, though you have not heeded, 6then I will make this house like Shiloh, and I will make this city a curse for all the nations of the earth.'"

7 The priests and the prophets and all the people heard Jeremi'ah speaking these words in the house of the Lord. 8And when Jeremi'ah had finished speaking all that the Lord had commanded him to speak to all the people, then the priests and the prophets and all the people laid hold of him, saying, "You shall die! 9Why have you prophesied in the name of the Lord, saying, 'This house shall be like Shiloh, and this city shall be desolate, without inhabitant'?" And all the people gathered about Jeremi'ah in the house of the Lord.

10 When the princes of Judah heard these things, they came up from the king's house to the house of the Lord and took their seat in the entry of the New Gate of the house of the Lord. 11Then the priests and the prophets said to the princes and to all the people, "This man deserves the sentence of death, because he has prophesied against this city, as you have heard with your own ears."

12 Then Jeremi'ah spoke to all the princes and all the people, saying, "The Lord sent me to prophesy against this house and this city all the words you have heard. 13Now therefore amend your ways and your doings, and obey the voice of the Lord your God, and the Lord will repent of the evil which he has pronounced against you. 14But as for me, behold, I am in your hands. Do with me as seems good and right to you. 15Only know for certain that if you put me to death, you will bring innocent blood upon yourselves and upon this city and its inhabitants, for in truth the Lord sent me to you to speak all these words in your ears."

16 Then the princes and all the people said to the priests and the prophets, "This man does not deserve the sentence of death, for he has spoken

---

ᵉ Heb *Sheshach*, a cipher for Babylon.
ˢ Gk: Heb *a choice vessel.*

to us in the name of the LORD our God." [17]And certain of the elders of the land arose and spoke to all the assembled people, saying, [18]"Micah of Mo'resheth prophesied in the days of Hezeki'ah king of Judah, and said to all the people of Judah: 'Thus says the LORD of hosts,

Zion shall be plowed as a field;
    Jerusalem shall become a heap of ruins,
    and the mountain of the house a wooded
        height.'

[19]Did Hezeki'ah king of Judah and all Judah put him to death? Did he not fear the LORD and entreat the favor of the LORD, and did not the LORD repent of the evil which he had pronounced against them? But we are about to bring great evil upon ourselves."

20 There was another man who prophesied in the name of the LORD, Uri'ah the son of She-mai'ah from Kir'iath-je'arim. He prophesied against this city and against this land in words like those of Jeremi'ah. [21]And when King Jehoi'a-kim, with all his warriors and all the princes, heard his words, the king sought to put him to death; but when Uri'ah heard of it, he was afraid and fled and escaped to Egypt. [22]Then King Jehoi'akim sent to Egypt certain men, Elna'than the son of Achbor and others with him, [23]and they fetched Uri'ah from Egypt and brought him to King Jehoi'akim, who slew him with the sword and cast his dead body into the burial place of the common people.

[24]But the hand of Ahi'kam the son of Sha'phan was with Jeremi'ah so that he was not given over to the people to be put to death.

The Sign of the Thongs and Yoke-bars

27 In the beginning of the reign of Zede-ki'ah[u] the son of Josi'ah, king of Judah, this word came to Jeremi'ah from the LORD. [2]Thus the LORD said to me: "Make yourself thongs and yoke-bars, and put them on your neck. [3]Send word[v] to the king of E'dom, the king of Moab, the king of the sons of Ammon, the king of Tyre, and the king of Si'don by the hand of the envoys who have come to Jerusalem to Zedeki'ah king of Judah. [4]Give them this charge for their masters: 'Thus says the LORD of hosts, the God of Israel: This is what you shall say to your masters: [5]"It is I who by my great power and my outstretched arm have made the earth, with the men and animals that are on the earth, and I give it to whomever it seems right to me. [6]Now I have given all these lands into the hand of Nebuchadnez'zar, the king of Babylon, my servant, and I have given him also the beasts of the field to serve him. [7]All the nations shall serve him and his son and his grandson, until the time of his own land comes; then many nations and great kings shall make him their slave.

8 "'"But if any nation or kingdom will not serve this Nebuchadnez'zar king of Babylon, and put its neck under the yoke of the king of Babylon, I will punish that nation with the sword, with famine, and with pestilence, says the LORD, until I have consumed it by his hand. [9]So do not listen to your prophets, your diviners, your dreamers,[w] your soothsayers, or your sorcerers, who are saying to you, 'You shall not serve the king of Babylon.' [10]For it is a lie which they are prophesying to you, with the result that you will be removed far from your land, and I will drive you out, and you will perish. [11]But any nation which will bring its neck under the yoke of the king of Babylon and serve him, I will leave on its own land, to till it and dwell there, says the LORD."'"

12 To Zedeki'ah king of Judah I spoke in like manner: "Bring your necks under the yoke of the king of Babylon, and serve him and his people, and live. [13]Why will you and your people die by the sword, by famine, and by pestilence, as the LORD has spoken concerning any nation which will not serve the king of Babylon? [14]Do not listen to the words of the prophets who are saying to you, 'You shall not serve the king of Babylon,' for it is a lie which they are prophesying to you. [15]I have not sent them, says the LORD, but they are prophesying falsely in my name, with the result that I will drive you out and you will perish, you and the prophets who are prophesying to you."

16 Then I spoke to the priests and to all this people, saying, "Thus says the LORD: Do not listen to the words of your prophets who are prophesying to you, saying, 'Behold, the vessels of the LORD's house will now shortly be brought back from Babylon,' for it is a lie which they are prophesying to you. [17]Do not listen to them; serve the king of Babylon and live. Why should this city become a desolation? [18]If they are prophets, and if the word of the LORD is with them, then let them intercede with the LORD of hosts, that the vessels which are left in the house of the LORD, in the house of the king of Judah, and in Jerusalem may not go to Babylon. [19]For thus says the LORD of hosts concerning the pillars, the sea, the stands, and the rest of the vessels which are left in this city, [20]which Nebuchadnez'zar king of Babylon did not take away, when he took into exile from Jerusalem to Babylon Jeconi'ah the son of Jehoi'a-kim, king of Judah, and all the nobles of Judah and Jerusalem— [21]thus says the LORD of hosts, the God of Israel, concerning the vessels which are left in the house of the LORD, in the house of the king of Judah, and in Jerusalem: [22]They shall be carried to Babylon and remain there until the day when I give attention to them, says the LORD.

---

u Another reading is *Jehoiakim*.
v Cn: Heb *send them*.
w Gk Syr Vg: Heb *dreams*.

Then I will bring them back and restore them to this place."

Hananiah's False Prophecy

28 In that same year, at the beginning of the reign of Zedeki'ah king of Judah, in the fifth month of the fourth year, Hanani'ah the son of Azzur, the prophet from Gib'eon, spoke to me in the house of the LORD, in the presence of the priests and all the people, saying, ²"Thus says the LORD of hosts, the God of Israel: I have broken the yoke of the king of Babylon. ³Within two years I will bring back to this place all the vessels of the LORD's house, which Nebuchadnez'zar king of Babylon took away from this place and carried to Babylon. ⁴I will also bring back to this place Jeconi'ah the son of Jehoi'akim, king of Judah, and all the exiles from Judah who went to Babylon, says the LORD, for I will break the yoke of the king of Babylon."

5 Then the prophet Jeremi'ah spoke to Hanani'ah the prophet in the presence of the priests and all the people who were standing in the house of the LORD; ⁶and the prophet Jeremi'ah said, "Amen! May the LORD do so; may the LORD make the words which you have prophesied come true, and bring back to this place from Babylon the vessels of the house of the LORD, and all the exiles. ⁷Yet hear now this word which I speak in your hearing and in the hearing of all the people. ⁸The prophets who preceded you and me from ancient times prophesied war, famine, and pestilence against many countries and great kingdoms. ⁹As for the prophet who prophesies peace, when the word of that prophet comes to pass, then it will be known that the LORD has truly sent the prophet."

10 Then the prophet Hanani'ah took the yoke-bars from the neck of Jeremi'ah the prophet, and broke them. ¹¹And Hanani'ah spoke in the presence of all the people, saying, "Thus says the LORD: Even so will I break the yoke of Nebuchadnez'zar king of Babylon from the neck of all the nations within two years." But Jeremi'ah the prophet went his way.

12 Sometime after the prophet Hanani'ah had broken the yoke-bars from off the neck of Jeremi'ah the prophet, the word of the LORD came to Jeremi'ah: ¹³"Go, tell Hanani'ah, 'Thus says the LORD: You have broken wooden bars, but I* will make in their place bars of iron. ¹⁴For thus says the LORD of hosts, the God of Israel: I have put upon the neck of all these nations an iron yoke of servitude to Nebuchadnez'zar king of Babylon, and they shall serve him, for I have given to him even the beasts of the field.'" ¹⁵And Jeremi'ah the prophet said to the prophet Hanani'ah, "Listen, Hananiah, the LORD has not sent you, and you have made this people trust in a lie. ¹⁶Therefore thus says the LORD: 'Behold, I will remove you

from the face of the earth. This very year you shall die, because you have uttered rebellion against the LORD.'"

17 In that same year, in the seventh month, the prophet Hanani'ah died.

Jeremiah's Letters to the Exiles in Babylon

29 These are the words of the letter which Jeremi'ah the prophet sent from Jerusalem to the elders ʸ of the exiles, and to the priests, the prophets, and all the people, whom Nebuchadnez'zar had taken into exile from Jerusalem to Babylon. ²This was after King Jeconi'ah, and the queen mother, the eunuchs, the princes of Judah and Jerusalem, the craftsmen, and the smiths had departed from Jerusalem. ³The letter was sent by the hand of Ela'sah the son of Sha'phan and Gemari'ah the son of Hilki'ah, whom Zedeki'ah king of Judah sent to Babylon to Nebuchadnez'zar king of Babylon. It said: ⁴"Thus says the LORD of hosts, the God of Israel, to all the exiles whom I have sent into exile from Jerusalem to Babylon: ⁵Build houses and live in them; plant gardens and eat their produce. ⁶Take wives and have sons and daughters; take wives for your sons, and give your daughters in marriage, that they may bear sons and daughters; multiply there, and do not decrease. ⁷But seek the welfare of the city where I have sent you into exile, and pray to the LORD on its behalf, for in its welfare you will find your welfare. ⁸For thus says the LORD of hosts, the God of Israel: Do not let your prophets and your diviners who are among you deceive you, and do not listen to the dreams which they dream, ᶻ ⁹for it is a lie which they are prophesying to you in my name; I did not send them, says the LORD.

10 "For thus says the LORD: When seventy years are completed for Babylon, I will visit you, and I will fulfil to you my promise and bring you back to this place. ¹¹For I know the plans I have for you, says the LORD, plans for welfare and not for evil, to give you a future and a hope. ¹²Then you will call upon me and come and pray to me, and I will hear you. ¹³You will seek me and find me; when you seek me with all your heart, ¹⁴I will be found by you, says the LORD, and I will restore your fortunes and gather you from all the nations and all the places where I have driven you, says the LORD, and I will bring you back to the place from which I sent you into exile.

15 "Because you have said, 'The LORD has raised up prophets for us in Babylon,'— ¹⁶Thus says the LORD concerning the king who sits on the throne of David, and concerning all the people who dwell in this city, your kinsmen who did not go out with you into exile: ¹⁷Thus says the LORD

---

* Gk: Heb *you*.
ʸ Gk: Heb *the rest of the elders*.
ᶻ Cn: Heb *your dreams which you cause to dream*.

of hosts, Behold, I am sending on them sword, famine, and pestilence, and I will make them like vile figs which are so bad they cannot be eaten. [18]I will pursue them with sword, famine, and pestilence, and will make them a horror to all the kingdoms of the earth, to be a curse, a terror, a hissing, and a reproach among all the nations where I have driven them, [19]because they did not heed my words, says the LORD, which I persistently sent to you by my servants the prophets, but you would not listen, says the LORD.'— [20]Hear the word of the LORD, all you exiles whom I sent away from Jerusalem to Babylon: [21]Thus says the LORD of hosts, the God of Israel, concerning A'hab the son of Kolai'ah and Zedeki'ah the son of Ma-asei'ah, who are prophesying a lie to you in my name: Behold, I will deliver them into the hand of Nebuchadrez'zar king of Babylon, and he shall slay them before your eyes. [22]Because of them this curse shall be used by all the exiles from Judah in Babylon: "The LORD make you like Zedeki'ah and A'hab, whom the king of Babylon roasted in the fire," [23]because they have committed folly in Israel, they have committed adultery with their neighbors' wives, and they have spoken in my name lying words which I did not command them. I am the one who knows, and I am witness, says the LORD.'"

24 To Shemai'ah of Nehel'am you shall say: [25]"Thus says the LORD of hosts, the God of Israel: You have sent letters in your name to all the people who are in Jerusalem, and to Zephani'ah the son of Ma-asei'ah the priest, and to all the priests, saying, [26]'The LORD has made you priest instead of Jehoi'ada the priest, to have charge in the house of the LORD over every madman who prophesies, to put him in the stocks and collar. [27]Now why have you not rebuked Jeremi'ah of An'athoth who is prophesying to you? [28]For he has sent to us in Babylon, saying, "Your exile will be long; build houses and live in them, and plant gardens and eat their produce."'"

29 Zephani'ah the priest read this letter in the hearing of Jeremi'ah the prophet. [30]Then the word of the LORD came to Jeremi'ah: [31]"Send to all the exiles, saying, 'Thus says the LORD concerning Shemai'ah of Nehel'am: Because Shemaiah has prophesied to you when I did not send him, and has made you trust in a lie, [32]therefore thus says the LORD: Behold, I will punish Shemai'ah of Nehel'am and his descendants; he shall not have any one living among this people to see [a] the good that I will do to my people, says the LORD, for he has talked rebellion against the LORD.'"

Hope for the Restoration of Israel

30 The word that came to Jeremi'ah from the LORD: [2]"Thus says the LORD, the God of Israel: Write in a book all the words that I have spoken to you. [3]For behold, days are coming, says the LORD, when I will restore the fortunes of my people, Israel and Judah, says the LORD, and I will bring them back to the land which I gave to their fathers, and they shall take possession of it."

4 These are the words which the LORD spoke concerning Israel and Judah:
[5]"Thus says the LORD:
We have heard a cry of panic,
  of terror, and no peace.
[6]Ask now, and see,
  can a man bear a child?
Why then do I see every man
  with his hands on his loins like a woman in
    labor?
  Why has every face turned pale?
[7]Alas! that day is so great
    there is none like it;
  it is a time of distress for Jacob;
    yet he shall be saved out of it.

8 "And it shall come to pass in that day, says the LORD of hosts, that I will break the yoke from off their [b] neck, and I will burst their [b] bonds, and strangers shall no more make servants of them. [c] * [9]But they shall serve the LORD their God and David their king, whom I will raise up for them.

[10]"Then fear not, O Jacob my servant, says the
    LORD,
  nor be dismayed, O Israel;
for behold, I will save you from afar,
  and your offspring from the land of their
    captivity.
Jacob shall return and have quiet and ease,
  and none shall make him afraid.
[11]For I am with you to save you,
                    says the LORD;
I will make a full end of all the nations
  among whom I scattered you,
  but of you I will not make a full end.
I will chasten you in just measure,
  and I will by no means leave you
    unpunished.

[12]"For thus says the LORD:
Your hurt is incurable,
  and your wound is grievous.
[13]There is none to uphold your cause,
  no medicine for your wound,
  no healing for you.
[14]All your lovers have forgotten you;
  they care nothing for you;
for I have dealt you the blow of an enemy,
  the punishment of a merciless foe,

---

[a] Gk: Heb *and he shall not see.*
[b] Gk Old Latin: Heb *your.*
[c] Heb *make a servant of him.*
* 30:8: The new covenant and the restoration.

because your guilt is great,
    because your sins are flagrant.
¹⁵Why do you cry out over your hurt?
    Your pain is incurable.
Because your guilt is great,
    because your sins are flagrant,
    I have done these things to you.
¹⁶Therefore all who devour you shall be
        devoured,
    and all your foes, every one of them, shall
        go into captivity;
those who despoil you shall become a spoil,
    and all who prey on you I will make a prey.
¹⁷For I will restore health to you,
    and your wounds I will heal,
                                    says the Lord,
because they have called you an outcast:
    'It is Zion, for whom no one cares!'

¹⁸"Thus says the Lord:
Behold, I will restore the fortunes of the tents
        of Jacob,
    and have compassion on his dwellings;
the city shall be rebuilt upon its mound,
    and the palace shall stand where it used to
        be.
¹⁹Out of them shall come songs of thanksgiving,
    and the voices of those who make merry.
I will multiply them, and they shall not be few;
    I will make them honored, and they shall
        not be small.
²⁰Their children shall be as they were of old,
    and their congregation shall be established
        before me;
    and I will punish all who oppress them.
²¹Their prince shall be one of themselves,
    their ruler shall come forth from their
        midst;
I will make him draw near, and he shall
        approach me,
    for who would dare of himself to approach
        me?
                                    says the Lord.
²²And you shall be my people,
    and I will be your God."
²³Behold the storm of the Lord!
    Wrath has gone forth,
a whirling tempest;
    it will burst upon the head of the wicked.
²⁴The fierce anger of the Lord will not turn back
    until he has executed and accomplished
    the intents of his mind.
In the latter days you will understand this.

31 "At that time, says the Lord, I will be the
        God of all the families of Israel, and they
shall be my people."
²Thus says the Lord:
    "The people who survived the sword
        found grace in the wilderness;

when Israel sought for rest,
³   the Lord appeared to him ᵈ from afar.
I have loved you with an everlasting love;
    therefore I have continued my faithfulness
        to you.
⁴Again I will build you, and you shall be built,
    O virgin Israel!
Again you shall adorn yourself with timbrels,
    and shall go forth in the dance of the
        merrymakers.
⁵Again you shall plant vineyards
    upon the mountains of Samar'ia;
the planters shall plant,
    and shall enjoy the fruit.
⁶For there shall be a day when watchmen will
        call
    in the hill country of E'phraim:
'Arise, and let us go up to Zion,
    to the Lord our God.'"

⁷For thus says the Lord:
"Sing aloud with gladness for Jacob,
    and raise shouts for the chief of the
        nations;
proclaim, give praise, and say,
    'The Lord has saved his people,
    the remnant of Israel.'
⁸Behold, I will bring them from the north
        country,
    and gather them from the farthest parts of
        the earth,
among them the blind and the lame,
    the woman with child and her who has
        labor pains, together;
a great company, they shall return here.
⁹With weeping they shall come,
    and with consolations ᵉ I will lead them
        back,
I will make them walk by brooks of water,
    in a straight path in which they shall not
        stumble;
for I am a father to Israel,
    and E'phraim is my first-born.

¹⁰"Hear the word of the Lord, O nations,
    and declare it in the islands afar off;
say, 'He who scattered Israel will gather him,
    and will keep him as a shepherd keeps his
        flock.'
¹¹For the Lord has ransomed Jacob,
    and has redeemed him from hands too
        strong for him.
¹²They shall come and sing aloud on the height
        of Zion,
    and they shall be radiant over the goodness
        of the Lord,

ᵈ Gk: Heb me.
ᵉ Gk Compare Vg Tg: Heb supplications.

over the grain, the wine, and the oil,
and over the young of the flock and the
herd;
their life shall be like a watered garden,
and they shall languish no more.
[13]Then shall the maidens rejoice in the dance,
and the young men and the old shall be
merry.
I will turn their mourning into joy,
I will comfort them, and give them gladness
for sorrow.
[14]I will feast the soul of the priests with
abundance,
and my people shall be satisfied with my
goodness,
says the Lord."

[15]Thus says the Lord:
"A voice is heard in Ra′mah,
lamentation and bitter weeping.
Rachel is weeping for her children;
she refuses to be comforted for her children,
because they are not." *

[16]Thus says the Lord:
"Keep your voice from weeping,
and your eyes from tears;
for your work shall be rewarded, says the Lord,
and they shall come back from the land of
the enemy.
[17]There is hope for your future,
says the Lord,
and your children shall come back to their
own country.
[18]I have heard E′phraim bemoaning,
'You have chastened me, and I was chastened,
like an untrained calf;
bring me back that I may be restored,
for you are the Lord my God.
[19]For after I had turned away I repented;
and after I was instructed, I struck my thigh;
I was ashamed, and I was confounded,
because I bore the disgrace of my youth.'
[20]Is E′phraim my dear son?
Is he my darling child?
For as often as I speak against him,
I do remember him still.
Therefore my heart yearns for him;
I will surely have mercy on him,
says the Lord.

[21]"Set up waymarks for yourself,
make yourself guideposts;
consider well the highway,
the road by which you went.
Return, O virgin Israel,
return to these your cities.
[22]How long will you waver,
O faithless daughter?

For the Lord has created a new thing on the
earth:
a woman protects a man."

23 Thus says the Lord of hosts, the God of Israel: "Once more they shall use these words in the land of Judah and in its cities, when I restore their fortunes:
'The Lord bless you, O habitation of
righteousness,
O holy hill!'
[24]And Judah and all its cities shall dwell there together, and the farmers and those who wander [f] with their flocks. [25]For I will satisfy the weary soul, and every languishing soul I will replenish."
26 Thereupon I awoke and looked, and my sleep was pleasant to me.

Individual Responsibility for Conduct
27 "Behold, the days are coming, says the Lord, when I will sow the house of Israel and the house of Judah with the seed of man and the seed of beast. [28]And it shall come to pass that as I have watched over them to pluck up and break down, to overthrow, destroy, and bring evil, so I will watch over them to build and to plant, says the Lord. [29]In those days they shall no longer say:
'The fathers have eaten sour grapes,
and the children's teeth are set on edge.'
[30]But every one shall die for his own sin; each man who eats sour grapes, his teeth shall be set on edge.

A New Covenant Promised
31 † "Behold, the days are coming, says the Lord, when I will make a new covenant with the house of Israel and the house of Judah, [32]not like the covenant which I made with their fathers when I took them by the hand to bring them out of the land of Egypt, my covenant which they broke, and I showed myself their Master, says the Lord. [33]But this is the covenant which I will make with the house of Israel after those days, says the Lord: I will put my law within them, and I will write it upon their hearts; and I will be their God, and they shall be my people. [34]And no longer shall each man teach his neighbor and each his brother, saying, 'Know the Lord,' for they shall all know me, from the least of them to the greatest, says the Lord; for I will forgive their iniquity, and I will remember their sin no more."

[35]Thus says the Lord,
who gives the sun for light by day
and the fixed order of the moon and the
stars for light by night,

---
[f] Cn Compare Syr Vg Tg: Heb *and they shall wander.*
31:15: Mt 2:18.
31:31: Lk 22:20; 1 Cor 11:25.
31:31–34: Jer 32:38–40; Heb 8:8–12; 10:16–17.
* 31:15: Quoted by Matthew and applied to the Holy Innocents (Mt 2:18).
† 31:31–34: The new covenant; cf. Mt 26:28.

who stirs up the sea so that its waves roar—
the LORD of hosts is his name:
[36]"If this fixed order departs
from before me, says the LORD,
then shall the descendants of Israel cease
from being a nation before me for ever."

[37]Thus says the LORD:
"If the heavens above can be measured,
and the foundations of the earth below can
be explored,
then I will cast off all the descendants of Israel
for all that they have done,
says the LORD."

The City Will Be Rebuilt

38 "Behold, the days are coming, says the LORD,
when the city shall be rebuilt for the LORD from
the tower of Hanan'el to the Corner Gate. [39]And
the measuring line shall go out farther, straight to
the hill Ga'reb, and shall then turn to Goah. [40]The
whole valley of the dead bodies and the ashes,
and all the fields as far as the brook Kid'ron, to
the corner of the Horse Gate toward the east, shall
be sacred to the LORD. It shall not be uprooted or
overthrown any more for ever."

Jeremiah Buys a Field at Anathoth

32 The word that came to Jeremi'ah from the
LORD in the tenth year of Zedeki'ah king
of Judah, which was the eighteenth year of Nebuchadrez'zar. [2]At that time the army of the king of
Babylon was besieging Jerusalem, and Jeremi'ah
the prophet was shut up in the court of the guard
which was in the palace of the king of Judah.
[3]For Zedeki'ah king of Judah had imprisoned him,
saying, "Why do you prophesy and say, 'Thus
says the LORD: Behold, I am giving this city into
the hand of the king of Babylon, and he shall
take it; [4]Zedeki'ah king of Judah shall not escape
out of the hand of the Chalde'ans, but shall surely
be given into the hand of the king of Babylon,
and shall speak with him face to face and see him
eye to eye; [5]and he shall take Zedeki'ah to
Babylon, and there he shall remain until I visit
him, says the LORD; though you fight against the
Chalde'ans, you shall not succeed'?"

6 Jeremi'ah said, "The word of the LORD came
to me: [7]Behold, Han'amel the son of Shallum your
uncle will come to you and say, 'Buy my field
which is at An'athoth, for the right of redemption
by purchase is yours.' [8]Then Han'amel my cousin
came to me in the court of the guard, in accordance with the word of the LORD, and said to me,
'Buy my field which is at An'athoth in the land of
Benjamin, for the right of possession and redemption is yours; buy it for yourself.' Then I knew
that this was the word of the LORD.

9 "And I bought the field at An'athoth from
Han'amel my cousin, and weighed out the money
to him, seventeen shekels of silver. [10]I signed the
deed, sealed it, got witnesses, and weighed the
money on scales. [11]Then I took the sealed deed of
purchase, containing the terms and conditions,
and the open copy; [12]and I gave the deed of purchase to Baruch the son of Neri'ah son of Mah'-
seiah, in the presence of Han'amel my cousin, in
the presence of the witnesses who signed the deed
of purchase, and in the presence of all the Jews
who were sitting in the court of the guard. [13]I
charged Baruch in their presence, saying, [14]"Thus
says the LORD of hosts, the God of Israel: Take
these deeds, both this sealed deed of purchase
and this open deed, and put them in an earthenware vessel, that they may last for a long time.
[15]For thus says the LORD of hosts, the God of
Israel: Houses and fields and vineyards shall
again be bought in this land.'

God's Assurance of the People's Return

16 "After I had given the deed of purchase to
Baruch the son of Neri'ah, I prayed to the LORD,
saying: [17]'Ah Lord GOD! It is you who have made
the heavens and the earth by your great power
and by your outstretched arm! Nothing is too hard
for you, [18]who show mercy to thousands, but repay the guilt of fathers to their children after
them, O great and mighty God whose name is the
LORD of hosts, [19]great in counsel and mighty in
deed; whose eyes are open to all the ways of men,
rewarding every man according to his ways and
according to the fruit of his doings; [20]who have
shown signs and wonders in the land of Egypt,
and to this day in Israel and among all mankind,
and have made you a name, as at this day. [21]You
brought your people Israel out of the land of
Egypt with signs and wonders, with a strong
hand and outstretched arm, and with great terror;
[22]and you gave them this land, which you swore
to their fathers to give them, a land flowing with
milk and honey; [23]and they entered and took possession of it. But they did not obey your voice or
walk in your law; they did nothing of all you
commanded them to do. Therefore you have made
all this evil come upon them. [24]Behold, the siege
mounds have come up to the city to take it, and
because of sword and famine and pestilence the
city is given into the hands of the Chalde'ans who
are fighting against it. What you spoke has come
to pass, and behold, you see it. [25]Yet you, O Lord
GOD, have said to me, "Buy the field for money
and get witnesses"—though the city is given into
the hands of the Chalde'ans.'"

26 The word of the LORD came to Jeremi'ah:
[27]"Behold, I am the LORD, the God of all flesh; is
anything too hard for me? [28]Therefore, thus says
the LORD: Behold, I am giving this city into the
hands of the Chalde'ans and into the hand of
Nebuchadrez'zar king of Babylon, and he shall
take it. [29]The Chalde'ans who are fighting against
this city shall come and set this city on fire, and

burn it, with the houses on whose roofs incense has been offered to Ba′al and drink offerings have been poured out to other gods, to provoke me to anger. ³⁰For the sons of Israel and the sons of Judah have done nothing but evil in my sight from their youth; the sons of Israel have done nothing but provoke me to anger by the work of their hands, says the LORD. ³¹This city has aroused my anger and wrath, from the day it was built to this day, so that I will remove it from my sight ³²because of all the evil of the sons of Israel and the sons of Judah which they did to provoke me to anger—their kings and their princes, their priests and their prophets, the men of Judah and the inhabitants of Jerusalem. ³³They have turned to me their back and not their face; and though I have taught them persistently they have not listened to receive instruction. ³⁴They set up their abominations in the house which is called by my name, to defile it. ³⁵They built the high places of Ba′al in the valley of the son of Hinnom, to offer up their sons and daughters to Mo′lech, though I did not command them, nor did it enter into my mind, that they should do this abomination, to cause Judah to sin.

36 "Now therefore thus says the LORD, the God of Israel, concerning this city of which you say, 'It is given into the hand of the king of Babylon by sword, by famine, and by pestilence': ³⁷Behold, I will gather them from all the countries to which I drove them in my anger and my wrath and in great indignation; I will bring them back to this place, and I will make them dwell in safety. ³⁸And they shall be my people, and I will be their God. ³⁹I will give them one heart and one way, that they may fear me for ever, for their own good and the good of their children after them. ⁴⁰I will make with them an everlasting covenant, that I will not turn away from doing good to them; and I will put the fear of me in their hearts, that they may not turn from me. ⁴¹I will rejoice in doing them good, and I will plant them in this land in faithfulness, with all my heart and all my soul.

42 "For thus says the LORD: Just as I have brought all this great evil upon this people, so I will bring upon them all the good that I promise them. ⁴³Fields shall be bought in this land of which you are saying, It is a desolation, without man or beast; it is given into the hands of the Chalde′ans. ⁴⁴Fields shall be bought for money, and deeds shall be signed and sealed and witnessed, in the land of Benjamin, in the places about Jerusalem, and in the cities of Judah, in the cities of the hill country, in the cities of the Shephe′lah, and in the cities of the Neg′eb; for I will restore their fortunes, says the LORD."

Healing after Punishment

33 The word of the LORD came to Jeremi′ah a second time, while he was still shut up in the court of the guard: ²"Thus says the LORD who made the earth, ᵍ the LORD who formed it to establish it—the LORD is his name: ³Call to me and I will answer you, and will tell you great and hidden things which you have not known. ⁴For thus says the LORD, the God of Israel, concerning the houses of this city and the houses of the kings of Judah which were torn down to make a defense against the siege mounds and before the sword: ʰ ⁵The Chalde′ans are coming in to fight ⁱ and to fill them with the dead bodies of men whom I shall strike in my anger and my wrath, for I have hidden my face from this city because of all their wickedness. ⁶Behold, I will bring to it health and healing, and I will heal them and reveal to them abundance ʲ of prosperity and security. ⁷I will restore the fortunes of Judah and the fortunes of Israel, and rebuild them as they were at first. ⁸I will cleanse them from all the guilt of their sin against me, and I will forgive all the guilt of their sin and rebellion against me. ⁹And this city ᵏ shall be to me a name of joy, a praise and a glory before all the nations of the earth who shall hear of all the good that I do for them; they shall fear and tremble because of all the good and all the prosperity I provide for it.

10 "Thus says the LORD: In this place of which you say, 'It is a waste without man or beast,' in the cities of Judah and the streets of Jerusalem that are desolate, without man or inhabitant or beast, there shall be heard again ¹¹the voice of mirth and the voice of gladness, the voice of the bridegroom and the voice of the bride, the voices of those who sing, as they bring thank offerings to the house of the LORD:

'Give thanks to the LORD of hosts,
  for the LORD is good,
  for his mercy endures for ever!'

For I will restore the fortunes of the land as at first, says the LORD.

12 "Thus says the LORD of hosts: In this place which is waste, without man or beast, and in all of its cities, there shall again be habitations of shepherds resting their flocks. ¹³In the cities of the hill country, in the cities of the Shephe′lah, and in the cities of the Neg′eb, in the land of Benjamin, the places about Jerusalem, and in the cities of Judah, flocks shall again pass under the hands of the one who counts them, says the LORD.

14 "Behold, the days are coming, says the LORD, when I will fulfil the promise I made to the house of Israel and the house of Judah. ¹⁵In those days and at that time I will cause a righteous Branch to

---

ᵍ Gk: Heb *it*.
ʰ Heb obscure.
ⁱ Cn: Heb *They are coming in to fight against the Chaldeans.*
ʲ Heb uncertain.
ᵏ Heb *and it.*
32:38–40: Jer 31:31–34.
33:15: Jer 23:5; Is 4:2; Zech 3:8; 6:12.

spring forth for David; * and he shall execute justice and righteousness in the land. [16]In those days Judah will be saved and Jerusalem will dwell securely. And this is the name by which it will be called: 'The Lord is our righteousness.'

17 "For thus says the Lord: David shall never lack a man to sit on the throne of the house of Israel, [18]and the Levitical priests shall never lack a man in my presence to offer burnt offerings, to burn cereal offerings, and to make sacrifices for ever."

19 The word of the Lord came to Jeremi'ah: [20]"Thus says the Lord: If you can break my covenant with the day and my covenant with the night, so that day and night will not come at their appointed time, [21]then also my covenant with David my servant may be broken, so that he shall not have a son to reign on his throne, and my covenant with the Levitical priests my ministers. [22]As the host of heaven cannot be numbered and the sands of the sea cannot be measured, so I will multiply the descendants of David my servant, and the Levitical priests who minister to me."

23 The word of the Lord came to Jeremi'ah: [24]"Have you not observed what these people are saying, 'The Lord has rejected the two families which he chose'? Thus they have despised my people so that they are no longer a nation in their sight. [25]Thus says the Lord: If I have not established my covenant with day and night and the ordinances of heaven and earth, [26]then I will reject the descendants of Jacob and David my servant and will not choose one of his descendants to rule over the seed of Abraham, Isaac, and Jacob. For I will restore their fortunes, and will have mercy upon them."

Death in Captivity Predicted for Zedekiah

34 The word which came to Jeremi'ah from the Lord, when Nebuchadrez'zar king of Babylon and all his army and all the kingdoms of the earth under his dominion and all the peoples were fighting against Jerusalem and all of its cities: [2]"Thus says the Lord, the God of Israel: Go and speak to Zedeki'ah king of Judah and say to him, 'Thus says the Lord: Behold, I am giving this city into the hand of the king of Babylon, and he shall burn it with fire. [3]You shall not escape from his hand, but shall surely be captured and delivered into his hand; you shall see the king of Babylon eye to eye and speak with him face to face; and you shall go to Babylon.' [4]Yet hear the word of the Lord, O Zedeki'ah king of Judah! Thus says the Lord concerning you: 'You shall not die by the sword. [5]You shall die in peace. And as spices were burned for your fathers, the former kings who were before you, so men shall burn spices for you and lament for you, saying, "Alas, lord!"' For I have spoken the word, says the Lord."

6 Then Jeremi'ah the prophet spoke all these words to Zedeki'ah king of Judah, in Jerusalem, [7]when the army of the king of Babylon was fighting against Jerusalem and against all the cities of Judah that were left, La'chish and Aze'kah; for these were the only fortified cities of Judah that remained.

Treatment of Hebrew Slaves

8 The word which came to Jeremi'ah from the Lord, after King Zedeki'ah had made a covenant with all the people in Jerusalem to make a proclamation of liberty to them, [9]that every one should set free his Hebrew slaves, male and female, so that no one should enslave a Jew, his brother. [10]And they obeyed, all the princes and all the people who had entered into the covenant that every one would set free his slave, male or female, so that they would not be enslaved again; they obeyed and set them free. [11]But afterward they turned around and took back the male and female slaves they had set free, and brought them into subjection as slaves. [12]The word of the Lord came to Jeremi'ah from the Lord: [13]"Thus says the Lord, the God of Israel: I made a covenant with your fathers when I brought them out of the land of Egypt, out of the house of bondage, saying, [14]At the end of six[1] years each of you must set free the fellow Hebrew who has been sold to you and has served you six years; you must set him free from your service.' But your fathers did not listen to me or incline their ears to me. [15]You recently repented and did what was right in my eyes by proclaiming liberty, each to his neighbor, and you made a covenant before me in the house which is called by my name; [16]but then you turned around and profaned my name when each of you took back his male and female slaves, whom you had set free according to their desire, and you brought them into subjection to be your slaves. [17]Therefore, thus says the Lord: You have not obeyed me by proclaiming liberty, every one to his brother and to his neighbor; behold, I proclaim to you liberty to the sword, to pestilence, and to famine, says the Lord. I will make you a horror to all the kingdoms of the earth. [18]And the men who transgressed my covenant and did not keep the terms of the covenant which they made before me, I will make like[m] the calf which they cut in two and passed between its parts— [19]the princes of Judah, the princes of Jerusalem, the eunuchs, the priests, and all the people of the land who passed between the parts of the calf; [20]and I will give them into the hand of their enemies and into the hand of those who seek their lives. Their dead bodies shall be food for the birds of the air and the

---

[1] Gk: Heb *seven*.
[m] Cn: Heb lacks *like*.
* 33:15: cf. Is 11:1: "a shoot from the stump of Jesse."

beasts of the earth. [21]And Zedeki'ah king of Judah, and his princes I will give into the hand of their enemies and into the hand of those who seek their lives, into the hand of the army of the king of Babylon which has withdrawn from you. [22]Behold, I will command, says the LORD, and will bring them back to this city; and they will fight against it, and take it, and burn it with fire. I will make the cities of Judah a desolation without inhabitant."

The Rechabites Commended

35 [*] The word which came to Jeremi'ah from the LORD in the days of Jehoi'akim the son of Josi'ah, king of Judah: [2]"Go to the house of the Re'chabites, and speak with them, and bring them to the house of the LORD, into one of the chambers; then offer them wine to drink." [3]So I took Ja-azani'ah the son of Jeremi'ah, son of Ha"bazzini'ah, and his brothers, and all his sons, and the whole house of the Re'chabites. [4]I brought them to the house of the LORD into the chamber of the sons of Ha'nan the son of Igdali'ah, the man of God, which was near the chamber of the princes, above the chamber of Ma-asei'ah the son of Shallum, keeper of the threshold. [5]Then I set before the Re'chabites pitchers full of wine, and cups; and I said to them, "Drink wine." [6]But they answered, "We will drink no wine, for Jon'adab the son of Re'chab, our father, commanded us, 'You shall not drink wine, neither you nor your sons for ever; [7]you shall not build a house; you shall not sow seed; you shall not plant or have a vineyard; but you shall live in tents all your days, that you may live many days in the land where you sojourn.' [8]We have obeyed the voice of Jon'adab the son of Re'chab, our father, in all that he commanded us, to drink no wine all our days, ourselves, our wives, our sons, or our daughters, [9]and not to build houses to dwell in. We have no vineyard or field or seed; [10]but we have lived in tents, and have obeyed and done all that Jon'adab our father commanded us. [11]But when Nebuchadrez'zar king of Babylon came up against the land, we said, 'Come, and let us go to Jerusalem for fear of the army of the Chalde'ans and the army of the Syrians.' So we are living in Jerusalem."

[12] Then the word of the LORD came to Jeremi'ah: [13]"Thus says the LORD of hosts, the God of Israel: Go and say to the men of Judah and the inhabitants of Jerusalem, Will you not receive instruction and listen to my words? says the LORD. [14]The command which Jon'adab the son of Re'chab gave to his sons, to drink no wine, has been kept; and they drink none to this day, for they have obeyed their father's command. I have spoken to you persistently, but you have not listened to me. [15]I have sent to you all my servants the prophets, sending them persistently, saying, 'Turn now every one of you from his evil way, and amend your doings, and do not go after other gods to serve them, and then you shall dwell in the land which I gave to you and your fathers.' But you did not incline your ear or listen to me. [16]The sons of Jon'adab the son of Re'chab have kept the command which their father gave them, but this people has not obeyed me. [17]Therefore, thus says the LORD, the God of hosts, the God of Israel: Behold, I am bringing on Judah and all the inhabitants of Jerusalem all the evil that I have pronounced against them; because I have spoken to them and they have not listened, I have called to them and they have not answered."

[18] But to the house of the Re'chabites Jeremi'ah said, "Thus says the LORD of hosts, the God of Israel: Because you have obeyed the command of Jon'adab your father, and kept all his precepts, and done all that he commanded you, [19]therefore thus says the LORD of hosts, the God of Israel: Jon'adab the son of Re'chab shall never lack a man to stand before me."

The Scroll Is Read

36 In the fourth year of Jehoi'akim the son of Josi'ah, king of Judah, this word came to Jeremi'ah from the LORD: [2]"Take a scroll and write on it all the words that I have spoken to you against Israel and Judah and all the nations, from the day I spoke to you, from the days of Josi'ah until today. [3]It may be that the house of Judah will hear all the evil which I intend to do to them, so that every one may turn from his evil way, and that I may forgive their iniquity and their sin."

[4] Then Jeremi'ah called Baruch the son of Neri'ah, and Baruch wrote upon a scroll at the dictation of Jeremi'ah all the words of the LORD which he had spoken to him. [5]And Jeremi'ah ordered Baruch, saying, "I am debarred from going to the house of the LORD; [6]so you are to go, and on a fast day in the hearing of all the people in the LORD's house you shall read the words of the LORD from the scroll which you have written at my dictation. You shall read them also in the hearing of all the men of Judah who come out of their cities. [7]It may be that their supplication will come before the LORD, and that every one will turn from his evil way, for great is the anger and wrath that the LORD has pronounced against this people." [8]And Baruch the son of Neri'ah did all that Jeremi'ah the prophet ordered him about reading from the scroll the words of the LORD in the LORD's house.

[9] In the fifth year of Jehoi'akim the son of Josi'ah, king of Judah, in the ninth month, all the people in Jerusalem and all the people who came

---

* 35: This chapter is our chief source of information about the little-known sect of Rechabites; cf. 2 Kings 10:15–16, 23. They obeyed what they felt to be a call to serve God in the wilderness and desert places. The ancient nomad life during the Exodus was always looked back to as the time of the greatest fidelity to God.

from the cities of Judah to Jerusalem proclaimed a fast before the LORD. [10]Then, in the hearing of all the people, Baruch read the words of Jeremi'ah from the scroll, in the house of the LORD, in the chamber of Gemari'ah the son of Sha'phan the secretary, which was in the upper court, at the entry of the New Gate of the LORD's house.

11 When Micai'ah the son of Gemari'ah, son of Sha'phan, heard all the words of the LORD from the scroll, [12]he went down to the king's house, into the secretary's chamber; and all the princes were sitting there: Elish'ama the secretary, Delai'ah the son of Shemai'ah, Elna'than the son of Achbor, Gemari'ah the son of Sha'phan, Zedeki'ah the son of Hanani'ah, and all the princes. [13]And Micai'ah told them all the words that he had heard, when Baruch read the scroll in the hearing of the people. [14]Then all the princes sent Jehu'di the son of Nethani'ah, son of Shelemi'ah, son of Cu'shi, to say to Baruch, "Take in your hand the scroll that you read in the hearing of the people, and come." So Baruch the son of Neri'ah took the scroll in his hand and came to them. [15]And they said to him, "Sit down and read it." So Baruch read it to them. [16]When they heard all the words, they turned one to another in fear; and they said to Baruch, "We must report all these words to the king." [17]Then they asked Baruch, "Tell us, how did you write all these words? Was it at his dictation?" [18]Baruch answered them, "He dictated all these words to me, while I wrote them with ink on the scroll." [19]Then the princes said to Baruch, "Go and hide, you and Jeremi'ah, and let no one know where you are."

King Jehoiakim Burns the Scroll

20 So they went into the court to the king, having put the scroll in the chamber of Elish'ama the secretary; and they reported all the words to the king. [21]Then the king sent Jehu'di to get the scroll, and he took it from the chamber of Elish'ama the secretary; and Jehudi read it to the king and all the princes who stood beside the king. [22]It was the ninth month, and the king was sitting in the winter house and there was a fire burning in the brazier before him. [23]As Jehu'di read three or four columns, the king would cut them off with a penknife and throw them into the fire in the brazier, until the entire scroll was consumed in the fire that was in the brazier. [24]Yet neither the king, nor any of his servants who heard all these words, was afraid, nor did they tear their garments. [25]Even when Elna'than and Delai'ah and Gemari'ah urged the king not to burn the scroll, he would not listen to them. [26]And the king commanded Jerah'meel the king's son and Serai'ah the son of Az'ri-el and Shelemi'ah the son of Abde'el to seize Baruch the secretary and Jeremi'ah the prophet, but the LORD hid them.

Jeremiah Dictates Another Scroll

27 Now, after the king had burned the scroll with the words which Baruch wrote at Jeremi'ah's dictation, the word of the LORD came to Jeremiah: [28]"Take another scroll and write on it all the former words that were in the first scroll, which Jehoi'akim the king of Judah has burned. [29]And concerning Jehoi'akim king of Judah you shall say, 'Thus says the LORD, You have burned this scroll, saying, "Why have you written in it that the king of Babylon will certainly come and destroy this land, and will cut off from it man and beast?" [30]Therefore thus says the LORD concerning Jehoi'akim king of Judah, He shall have none to sit upon the throne of David, and his dead body shall be cast out to the heat by day and the frost by night. [31]And I will punish him and his offspring and his servants for their iniquity; I will bring upon them, and upon the inhabitants of Jerusalem, and upon the men of Judah, all the evil that I have pronounced against them, but they would not hear.' "

32 Then Jeremi'ah took another scroll and gave it to Baruch the scribe, the son of Neri'ah, who wrote on it at the dictation of Jeremi'ah all the words of the scroll which Jehoi'akim king of Judah had burned in the fire; and many similar words were added to them.

Zedekiah Asks Jeremiah's Prayers

37 Zedeki'ah the son of Josi'ah, whom Nebuchadrez'zar king of Babylon made king in the land of Judah, reigned instead of Coni'ah the son of Jehoi'akim. [2]But neither he nor his servants nor the people of the land listened to the words of the LORD which he spoke through Jeremi'ah the prophet.

3 King Zedeki'ah sent Jehu'cal the son of Shelemi'ah, and Zephani'ah the priest, the son of Ma-asei'ah, to Jeremi'ah the prophet, saying, "Pray for us to the LORD our God." [4]Now Jeremi'ah was still going in and out among the people, for he had not yet been put in prison. [5]The army of Pharaoh had come out of Egypt; and when the Chalde'ans who were besieging Jerusalem heard news of them, they withdrew from Jerusalem.

6 Then the word of the LORD came to Jeremi'ah the prophet: [7]"Thus says the LORD, God of Israel: Thus shall you say to the king of Judah who sent you to me to inquire of me, 'Behold, Pharaoh's army which came to help you is about to return to Egypt, to its own land. [8]And the Chalde'ans shall come back and fight against this city; they shall take it and burn it with fire. [9]Thus says the LORD, Do not deceive yourselves, saying, "The Chalde'ans will surely stay away from us," for they will not stay away. [10]For even if you should defeat the whole army of Chalde'ans who are fighting against you, and there remained of them only wounded men,

every man in his tent, they would rise up and burn this city with fire.' "

Jeremiah Is Imprisoned

11 Now when the Chalde'an army had withdrawn from Jerusalem at the approach of Pharaoh's army, [12]Jeremi'ah set out from Jerusalem to go to the land of Benjamin to receive his portion [n] there among the people. [13]When he was at the Benjamin Gate, a sentry there named Iri'jah the son of Shelemi'ah, son of Hanani'ah, seized Jeremi'ah the prophet, saying, "You are deserting to the Chalde'ans." [14]And Jeremi'ah said, "It is false; I am not deserting to the Chalde'ans." But Iri'jah would not listen to him, and seized Jeremiah and brought him to the princes. [15]And the princes were enraged at Jeremi'ah, and they beat him and imprisoned him in the house of Jonathan the secretary, for it had been made a prison.

16 When Jeremi'ah had come to the dungeon cells, and remained there many days, [17]King Zedeki'ah sent for him, and received him. The king questioned him secretly in his house, and said, "Is there any word from the Lord?" Jeremi'ah said, "There is." Then he said, "You shall be delivered into the hand of the king of Babylon." [18]Jeremi'ah also said to King Zedeki'ah, "What wrong have I done to you or your servants or this people, that you have put me in prison? [19]Where are your prophets who prophesied to you, saying, 'The king of Babylon will not come against you and against this land'? [20]Now hear, I beg you, O my lord the king: let my humble plea come before you, and do not send me back to the house of Jonathan the secretary, lest I die there." [21]So King Zedeki'ah gave orders, and they committed Jeremi'ah to the court of the guard; and a loaf of bread was given him daily from the bakers' street, until all the bread of the city was gone. So Jeremiah remained in the court of the guard.

Jeremiah in the Cistern

38 Now Shephati'ah the son of Mattan, Gedali'ah the son of Pashhur, Ju'cal the son of Shelemi'ah, and Pashhur the son of Malchi'ah heard the words that Jeremi'ah was saying to all the people, [2]"Thus says the Lord, He who stays in this city shall die by the sword, by famine, and by pestilence; but he who goes out to the Chalde'ans shall live; he shall have his life as a prize of war, and live. [3]Thus says the Lord, This city shall surely be given into the hand of the army of the king of Babylon and be taken." [4]Then the princes said to the king, "Let this man be put to death, for he is weakening the hands of the soldiers who are left in this city, and the hands of all the people, by speaking such words to them. For this man is not seeking the welfare of this people, but their harm." [5]King Zedeki'ah said, "Behold, he is in your hands; for the king can do nothing against you." [6]So they took Jeremi'ah and

cast him into the cistern of Malchi'ah, the king's son, which was in the court of the guard, letting Jeremiah down by ropes. And there was no water in the cistern, but only mire, and Jeremiah sank in the mire.

Ebed-melech rescues Jeremiah

7 When E'bed-mel'ech the Ethiopian, a eunuch, who was in the king's house, heard that they had put Jeremi'ah into the cistern—the king was sitting in the Benjamin Gate— [8]E'bed-mel'ech went from the king's house and said to the king, [9]"My lord the king, these men have done evil in all that they did to Jeremi'ah the prophet by casting him into the cistern; and he will die there of hunger, for there is no bread left in the city." [10]Then the king commanded E'bed-mel'ech, the Ethiopian, "Take three men with you from here, and lift Jeremi'ah the prophet out of the cistern before he dies." [11]So E'bed-mel'ech took the men with him and went to the house of the king, to a wardrobe of [o] the storehouse, and took from there old rags and worn-out clothes, which he let down to Jeremi'ah in the cistern by ropes. [12]Then E'bed-mel'ech the Ethiopian said to Jeremi'ah, "Put the rags and clothes between your armpits and the ropes." Jeremi'ah did so. [13]Then they drew Jeremi'ah up with ropes and lifted him out of the cistern. And Jeremiah remained in the court of the guard.

14 King Zedeki'ah sent for Jeremi'ah the prophet and received him at the third entrance of the temple of the Lord. The king said to Jeremi'ah, "I will ask you a question; hide nothing from me." [15]Jeremi'ah said to Zedeki'ah, "If I tell you, will you not be sure to put me to death? And if I give you counsel, you will not listen to me." [16]Then King Zedeki'ah swore secretly to Jeremi'ah, "As the Lord lives, who made our souls, I will not put you to death or deliver you into the hand of these men who seek your life."

17 Then Jeremi'ah said to Zedeki'ah, "Thus says the Lord, the God of hosts, the God of Israel, If you will surrender to the princes of the king of Babylon, then your life shall be spared, and this city shall not be burned with fire, and you and your house shall live. [18]But if you do not surrender to the princes of the king of Babylon, then this city shall be given into the hand of the Chalde'ans, and they shall burn it with fire, and you shall not escape from their hand." [19]King Zedeki'ah said to Jeremi'ah, "I am afraid of the Jews who have deserted to the Chalde'ans, lest I be handed over to them and they abuse me." [20]Jeremi'ah said, "You shall not be given to them. Obey now the voice of the Lord in what I say to you, and it shall be well with you, and your life shall be

---

[n] Heb obscure.
[o] Cn: Heb to under.

spared. [21]But if you refuse to surrender, this is the vision which the LORD has shown to me: [22]Behold, all the women left in the house of the king of Judah were being led out to the princes of the king of Babylon and were saying,

'Your trusted friends have deceived you
and prevailed against you;
now that your feet are sunk in the mire,
they turn away from you.'

[23]All your wives and your sons shall be led out to the Chalde'ans, and you yourself shall not escape from their hand, but shall be seized by the king of Babylon; and this city shall be burned with fire."

24 Then Zedeki'ah said to Jeremi'ah, "Let no one know of these words and you shall not die. [25]If the princes hear that I have spoken with you and come to you and say to you, 'Tell us what you said to the king and what the king said to you; hide nothing from us and we will not put you to death,' [26]then you shall say to them, 'I made a humble plea to the king that he would not send me back to the house of Jonathan to die there.'" [27]Then all the princes came to Jeremi'ah and asked him, and he answered them as the king had instructed him. So they left off speaking with him, for the conversation had not been overheard. [28]And Jeremi'ah remained in the court of the guard until the day that Jerusalem was taken.

The Fall of Jerusalem

39 In the ninth year of Zedeki'ah king of Judah, in the tenth month, Nebuchadrez'zar king of Babylon and all his army came against Jerusalem and besieged it; [2]in the eleventh year of Zedeki'ah, in the fourth month, on the ninth day of the month, a breach was made in the city. [3]When Jerusalem was taken,[p] all the princes of the king of Babylon came and sat in the middle gate: Ner'gal-share'zer, Sam'gar-ne'bo, Sar'sechim the Rab'saris, Nergal-sharezer the Rabmag, with all the rest of the officers of the king of Babylon. [4]When Zedeki'ah king of Judah and all the soldiers saw them, they fled, going out of the city at night by way of the king's garden through the gate between the two walls; and they went toward the Ar'abah. [5]But the army of the Chalde'ans pursued them, and overtook Zedeki'ah in the plains of Jericho; and when they had taken him, they brought him up to Nebuchadrez'zar king of Babylon, at Riblah, in the land of Ha'math; and he passed sentence upon him. [6]The king of Babylon slew the sons of Zedeki'ah at Riblah before his eyes; and the king of Babylon slew all the nobles of Judah. [7]He put out the eyes of Zedeki'ah, and bound him in chains to take him to Babylon. [8]The Chalde'ans burned the king's house and the house of the people, and broke down the walls of Jerusalem. [9]Then Nebu'zarad'an, the captain of the guard, carried into exile to Babylon the rest of the people who were left in the city, those who had deserted to him, and the people who remained. [10]Nebu'zarad'an, the captain of the guard, left in the land of Judah some of the poor people who owned nothing, and gave them vineyards and fields at the same time.

Jeremiah Is Sent to Ebed-melech

11 Nebuchadrez'zar king of Babylon gave command concerning Jeremi'ah through Nebu'zarad'an, the captain of the guard, saying, [12]"Take him, look after him well and do him no harm, but deal with him as he tells you." [13]So Nebu'zarad'an the captain of the guard, Nebushaz'ban the Rab'saris, Ner'gal-share'zer the Rabmag, and all the chief officers of the king of Babylon [14]sent and took Jeremi'ah from the court of the guard. They entrusted him to Gedali'ah the son of Ahi'kam, son of Sha'phan, that he should take him home. So he dwelt among the people.

15 The word of the LORD came to Jeremi'ah while he was shut up in the court of the guard: [16]"Go, and say to E'bed-mel'ech the Ethiopian, 'Thus says the LORD of hosts, the God of Israel: Behold, I will fulfil my words against this city for evil and not for good, and they shall be accomplished before you on that day. [17]But I will deliver you on that day, says the LORD, and you shall not be given into the hand of the men of whom you are afraid. [18]For I will surely save you, and you shall not fall by the sword; but you shall have your life as a prize of war, because you have put your trust in me, says the LORD.'"

Jeremiah with Gedaliah the Governor

40 The word that came to Jeremi'ah from the LORD after Nebu'zarad'an the captain of the guard had let him go from Ra'mah, when he took him bound in chains along with all the captives of Jerusalem and Judah who were being exiled to Babylon. [2]The captain of the guard took Jeremi'ah and said to him, "The LORD your God pronounced this evil against this place; [3]the LORD has brought it about, and has done as he said. Because you sinned against the LORD, and did not obey his voice, this thing has come upon you. [4]Now, behold, I release you today from the chains on your hands. If it seems good to you to come with me to Babylon, come, and I will look after you well; but if it seems wrong to you to come with me to Babylon, do not come. See, the whole land is before you; go wherever you think it good and right to go. [5]If you remain,[q] then return to Gedali'ah the son of Ahi'kam, son of Sha'phan, whom the king of Babylon appointed governor of the cities of Judah, and dwell with him among the people; or go wherever you think it right to

---

[p] This clause has been transposed from the end of Chapter 38.
[q] Syr: Heb obscure.

go." So the captain of the guard gave him an allowance of food and a present, and let him go. [6]Then Jeremi'ah went to Gedali'ah the son of Ahi'kam, at Mizpah, and dwelt with him among the people who were left in the land.

7 When all the captains of the forces in the open country and their men heard that the king of Babylon had appointed Gedali'ah the son of Ahi'kam governor in the land, and had committed to him men, women, and children, those of the poorest of the land who had not been taken into exile to Babylon, [8]they went to Gedali'ah at Mizpah—Ish'mael the son of Nethani'ah, Joha'-nan the son of Kare'ah, Serai'ah the son of Tan'humeth, the sons of E'phai the Netoph'athite, Jezani'ah the son of the Ma-ac'athite, they and their men. [9]Gedali'ah the son of Ahi'kam, son of Sha'phan, swore to them and their men, saying, "Do not be afraid to serve the Chalde'ans. Dwell in the land, and serve the king of Babylon, and it shall be well with you. [10]As for me, I will dwell at Mizpah, to stand for you before the Chalde'ans who will come to us; but as for you, gather wine and summer fruits and oil, and store them in your vessels, and dwell in your cities that you have taken." [11]Likewise, when all the Jews who were in Moab and among the Am'monites and in E'dom and in other lands heard that the king of Babylon had left a remnant in Judah and had appointed Gedali'ah the son of Ahi'kam, son of Sha'phan, as governor over them, [12]then all the Jews returned from all the places to which they had been driven and came to the land of Judah, to Gedali'ah at Mizpah; and they gathered wine and summer fruits in great abundance.

13 Now Joha'nan the son of Kare'ah and all the leaders of the forces in the open country came to Gedali'ah at Mizpah [14]and said to him, "Do you know that Ba'alis the king of the Am'monites has sent Ish'mael the son of Nethani'ah to take your life?" But Gedali'ah the son of Ahi'kam would not believe them. [15]Then Joha'nan the son of Kare'ah spoke secretly to Gedali'ah at Mizpah, "Let me go and slay Ish'mael the son of Nethani'ah, and no one will know it. Why should he take your life, so that all the Jews who are gathered about you would be scattered, and the remnant of Judah would perish?" [16]But Gedali'ah the son of Ahi'kam said to Joha'nan the son of Kare'ah, "You shall not do this thing, for you are speaking falsely of Ish'mael."

Insurrection against Gedaliah

41 In the seventh month, Ish'mael the son of Nethani'ah, son of Elish'ama, of the royal family, one of the chief officers of the king, came with ten men to Gedali'ah the son of Ahi'kam, at Mizpah. As they ate bread together there at Mizpah, [2]Ish'mael the son of Nethani'ah and the ten men with him rose up and struck down

Gedali'ah the son of Ahi'kam, son of Sha'phan, with the sword, and killed him, whom the king of Babylon had appointed governor in the land. [3]Ish'mael also slew all the Jews who were with Gedali'ah at Mizpah, and the Chalde'an soldiers who happened to be there.

4 On the day after the murder of Gedali'ah, before any one knew of it, [5]eighty men arrived from She'chem and Shiloh and Samar'ia, with their beards shaved and their clothes torn, and their bodies gashed, bringing cereal offerings and incense to present at the temple of the LORD. [6]And Ish'mael the son of Nethani'ah came out from Mizpah to meet them, weeping as he came. As he met them, he said to them, "Come in to Gedali'ah the son of Ahi'kam." [7]When they came into the city, Ish'mael the son of Nethani'ah and the men with him slew them, and cast them into a cistern. [8]But there were ten men among them who said to Ish'mael, "Do not kill us, for we have stores of wheat, barley, oil, and honey hidden in the fields." So he refrained and did not kill them with their companions.

9 Now the cistern into which Ish'mael cast all the bodies of the men whom he had slain was the large cistern ͬ which King Asa had made for defense against Ba'asha king of Israel; Ishmael the son of Nethani'ah filled it with the slain. [10]Then Ish'mael took captive all the rest of the people who were in Mizpah, the king's daughters and all the people who were left at Mizpah whom Nebu'zarad'an, the captain of the guard, had committed to Gedali'ah the son of Ahi'kam. Ish'mael the son of Nethani'ah took them captive and set out to cross over to the Am'monites.

Johanan and Ishmael

11 But when Joha'nan the son of Kare'ah and all the leaders of the forces with him heard of all the evil which Ish'mael the son of Nethani'ah had done, [12]they took all their men and went to fight against Ish'mael the son of Nethani'ah. They came upon him at the great pool which is in Gib'eon. [13]And when all the people who were with Ish'mael saw Joha'nan the son of Kare'ah and all the leaders of the forces with him, they rejoiced. [14]So all the people whom Ish'mael had carried away captive from Mizpah turned about and came back, and went to Joha'nan the son of Kare'ah. [15]But Ish'mael the son of Nethani'ah escaped from Joha'nan with eight men, and went to the Am'monites. [16]Then Joha'nan the son of Kare'ah and all the leaders of the forces with him took all the rest of the people whom Ish'mael the son of Nethani'ah had carried away captive ˢ from Mizpah after he had slain Gedali'ah the son of Ahi'kam—soldiers, women, children, and

---

ͬ Gk: Heb he had slain by the hand of Gedaliah.
ˢ Cn: Heb whom he recovered from Ishmael.

eunuchs, whom Johanan brought back from Gib'eon. [17]And they went and stayed at Ge'ruth Chimham near Bethlehem, intending to go to Egypt [18]because of the Chalde'ans; for they were afraid of them, because Ish'mael the son of Netha-ni'ah had slain Gedali'ah the son of Ahi'kam, whom the king of Babylon had made governor over the land.

Jeremiah Advises Survivors Not to Go to Egypt

42 Then all the commanders of the forces, and Joha'nan the son of Kare'ah and Azari'ah [t] the son of Hoshai'ah, and all the people from the least to the greatest, came near [2]and said to Jeremi'ah the prophet, "Let our supplication come before you, and pray to the LORD your God for us, for all this remnant (for we are left but a few of many, as your eyes see us), [3]that the LORD your God may show us the way we should go, and the thing that we should do." [4]Jeremi'ah the prophet said to them, "I have heard you; behold, I will pray to the LORD your God according to your request, and whatever the LORD answers you I will tell you; I will keep nothing back from you." [5]Then they said to Jeremi'ah, "May the LORD be a true and faithful witness against us if we do not act according to all the word with which the LORD your God sends you to us. [6]Whether it is good or evil, we will obey the voice of the LORD our God to whom we are sending you, that it may be well with us when we obey the voice of the LORD our God."

7 At the end of ten days the word of the LORD came to Jeremi'ah. [8]Then he summoned Joha'nan the son of Kare'ah and all the commanders of the forces who were with him, and all the people from the least to the greatest, [9]and said to them, "Thus says the LORD, the God of Israel, to whom you sent me to present your supplication before him: [10]If you will remain in this land, then I will build you up and not pull you down; I will plant you, and not pluck you up; for I repent of the evil which I did to you. [11]Do not fear the king of Babylon, of whom you are afraid; do not fear him, says the LORD, for I am with you, to save you and to deliver you from his hand. [12]I will grant you mercy, that he may have mercy on you and let you remain in your own land. [13]But if you say, 'We will not remain in this land,' disobeying the voice of the LORD your God [14]and saying, 'No, we will go to the land of Egypt, where we shall not see war, or hear the sound of the trumpet, or be hungry for bread, and we will dwell there,' [15]then hear the word of the LORD, O remnant of Judah. Thus says the LORD of hosts, the God of Israel: If you set your faces to enter Egypt and go to live there, [16]then the sword which you fear shall overtake you there in the land of Egypt; and the famine of which you are afraid shall follow hard after you to Egypt; and there you shall die. [17]All the men who set their faces to go to Egypt to live there shall die by the sword, by famine, and by pestilence; they shall have no remnant or survivor from the evil which I will bring upon them.

18 "For thus says the LORD of hosts, the God of Israel: As my anger and my wrath were poured out on the inhabitants of Jerusalem, so my wrath will be poured out on you when you go to Egypt. You shall become an execration, a horror, a curse, and a taunt. You shall see this place no more. [19]The LORD has said to you, O remnant of Judah, 'Do not go to Egypt.' Know for a certainty that I have warned you this day [20]that you have gone astray at the cost of your lives. For you sent me to the LORD your God, saying, 'Pray for us to the LORD our God, and whatever the LORD our God says declare to us and we will do it.' [21]And I have this day declared it to you, but you have not obeyed the voice of the LORD your God in anything that he sent me to tell you. [22]Now therefore know for a certainty that you shall die by the sword, by famine, and by pestilence in the place where you desire to go to live."

Jeremiah Warns of Judgment

43 When Jeremi'ah finished speaking to all the people all these words of the LORD their God, with which the LORD their God had sent him to them, [2]Azari'ah the son of Hoshai'ah and Joha'nan the son of Kare'ah and all the insolent men said to Jeremi'ah, "You are telling a lie. The LORD our God did not send you to say, 'Do not go to Egypt to live there'; [3]but Baruch the son of Neri'ah has set you against us, to deliver us into the hand of the Chalde'ans, that they may kill us or take us into exile in Babylon." [4]So Joha'nan the son of Kare'ah and all the commanders of the forces and all the people did not obey the voice of the LORD, to remain in the land of Judah. [5]But Joha'nan the son of Kare'ah and all the commanders of the forces took all the remnant of Judah who had returned to live in the land of Judah from all the nations to which they had been driven— [6]the men, the women, the children, the princesses, and every person whom Nebu'zarad'an the captain of the guard had left with Gedali'ah the son of Ahi'kam, son of Sha'phan; also Jeremi'ah the prophet and Baruch the son of Neri'ah. [7]And they came into the land of Egypt, for they did not obey the voice of the LORD. And they arrived at Tah'panhes.

8 Then the word of the LORD came to Jeremi'ah in Tah'panhes: [9]"Take in your hands large stones, and hide them in the mortar in the pavement which is at the entrance to Pharaoh's palace in Tah'panhes, in the sight of the men of Judah, [10]and say to them, 'Thus says the LORD of hosts,

---

[t] Gk: Heb Jezaniah.

the God of Israel: Behold, I will send and take Nebuchadrez′zar the king of Babylon, my servant, and he [u] will set his throne above these stones which I have hid, and he will spread his royal canopy over them. [11]He shall come and strike the land of Egypt, giving to the pestilence those who are doomed to the pestilence, to captivity those who are doomed to captivity, and to the sword those who are doomed to the sword. [12]He [v] shall kindle a fire in the temples of the gods of Egypt; and he shall burn them and carry them away captive; and he shall clean the land of Egypt, as a shepherd cleans his cloak of vermin; and he shall go away from there in peace. [13]He shall break the obelisks of He″liop′olis which is in the land of Egypt; and the temples of the gods of Egypt he shall burn with fire.' ″

Denunciation of Idolatry in Egypt

44 The word that came to Jeremi′ah concerning all the Jews that dwelt in the land of Egypt, at Migdol, at Tah′panhes, at Memphis, and in the land of Path′ros, [2]"Thus says the LORD of hosts, the God of Israel: You have seen all the evil that I brought upon Jerusalem and upon all the cities of Judah. Behold, this day they are a desolation, and no one dwells in them, [3]because of the wickedness which they committed, provoking me to anger, in that they went to burn incense and serve other gods that they knew not, neither they, nor you, nor your fathers. [4]Yet I persistently sent to you all my servants the prophets, saying, 'Oh, do not do this abominable thing that I hate!' [5]But they did not listen or incline their ear, to turn from their wickedness and burn no incense to other gods. [6]Therefore my wrath and my anger were poured forth and kindled in the cities of Judah and in the streets of Jerusalem; and they became a waste and a desolation, as at this day. [7]And now thus says the LORD God of hosts, the God of Israel: Why do you commit this great evil against yourselves, to cut off from you man and woman, infant and child, from the midst of Judah, leaving you no remnant? [8]Why do you provoke me to anger with the works of your hands, burning incense to other gods in the land of Egypt where you have come to live, that you may be cut off and become a curse and a taunt among all the nations of the earth? [9]Have you forgotten the wickedness of your fathers, the wickedness of the kings of Judah, the wickedness of their [w] wives, your own wickedness, and the wickedness of your wives, which they committed in the land of Judah and in the streets of Jerusalem? [10]They have not humbled themselves even to this day, nor have they feared, nor walked in my law and my statutes which I set before you and before your fathers.

[11] "Therefore thus says the LORD of hosts, the God of Israel: Behold, I will set my face against you for evil, to cut off all Judah. [12]I will take the remnant of Judah who have set their faces to come to the land of Egypt to live, and they shall all be consumed; in the land of Egypt they shall fall; by the sword and by famine they shall be consumed; from the least to the greatest, they shall die by the sword and by famine; and they shall become an execration, a horror, a curse, and a taunt. [13]I will punish those who dwell in the land of Egypt, as I have punished Jerusalem, with the sword, with famine, and with pestilence, [14]so that none of the remnant of Judah who have come to live in the land of Egypt shall escape or survive or return to the land of Judah, to which they desire to return to dwell there; for they shall not return, except some fugitives."

15 Then all the men who knew that their wives had offered incense to other gods, and all the women who stood by, a great assembly, all the people who dwelt in Path′ros in the land of Egypt, answered Jeremi′ah: [16]"As for the word which you have spoken to us in the name of the LORD, we will not listen to you. [17]But we will do everything that we have vowed, burn incense to the queen of heaven and pour out libations to her, as we did, both we and our fathers, our kings and our princes, in the cities of Judah and in the streets of Jerusalem; for then we had plenty of food, and prospered, and saw no evil. [18]But since we left off burning incense to the queen of heaven and pouring out libations to her, we have lacked everything and have been consumed by the sword and by famine." [19]And the women said, [x] "When we burned incense to the queen of heaven and poured out libations to her, was it without our husbands' approval that we made cakes for her bearing her image and poured out libations to her?"

20 Then Jeremi′ah said to all the people, men and women, all the people who had given him this answer: [21]"As for the incense that you burned in the cities of Judah and in the streets of Jerusalem, you and your fathers, your kings and your princes, and the people of the land, did not the LORD remember it? [y] Did it not come into his mind? [22]The LORD could no longer bear your evil doings and the abominations which you committed; therefore your land has become a desolation and a waste and a curse, without inhabitant, as it is this day. [23]It is because you burned incense, and because you sinned against the LORD and did not obey the voice of the LORD or walk in his law and in his statutes and in his testimonies, that this evil has befallen you, as at this day."

---

[u] Gk Syr: Heb *I*.
[v] Gk Syr Vg: Heb *I*.
[w] Heb *his*.
[x] Compare Syr: Heb lacks *And the women said*.
[y] Syr: Heb *them*.

24 Jeremi'ah said to all the people and all the women, "Hear the word of the LORD, all you of Judah who are in the land of Egypt, 25Thus says the LORD of hosts, the God of Israel: You and your wives have declared with your mouths, and have fulfilled it with your hands, saying, 'We will surely perform our vows that we have made, to burn incense to the queen of heaven and to pour out libations to her.' Then confirm your vows and perform your vows! 26Therefore hear the word of the LORD, all you of Judah who dwell in the land of Egypt: Behold, I have sworn by my great name, says the LORD, that my name shall no more be invoked by the mouth of any man of Judah in all the land of Egypt, saying, 'As the Lord GOD lives.' 27Behold, I am watching over them for evil and not for good; all the men of Judah who are in the land of Egypt shall be consumed by the sword and by famine, until there is an end of them. 28And those who escape the sword shall return from the land of Egypt to the land of Judah, few in number; and all the remnant of Judah, who came to the land of Egypt to live, shall know whose word will stand, mine or theirs. 29This shall be the sign to you, says the LORD, that I will punish you in this place, in order that you may know that my words will surely stand against you for evil: 30Thus says the LORD, Behold, I will give Pharaoh Hoph'ra king of Egypt into the hand of his enemies and into the hand of those who seek his life, as I gave Zedeki'ah king of Judah into the hand of Nebuchadrez'zar king of Babylon, who was his enemy and sought his life."

A Word of Comfort to Baruch

45 The word that Jeremi'ah the prophet spoke to Baruch the son of Neri'ah, when he wrote these words in a book at the dictation of Jeremiah, in the fourth year of Jehoi'akim the son of Josi'ah, king of Judah: 2"Thus says the LORD, the God of Israel, to you, O Baruch: 3You said, 'Woe is me! for the LORD has added sorrow to my pain; I am weary with my groaning, and I find no rest.' 4Thus shall you say to him, Thus says the LORD: Behold, what I have built I am breaking down, and what I have planted I am plucking up—that is, the whole land. 5And do you seek great things for yourself? Seek them not; for behold, I am bringing evil upon all flesh, says the LORD; but I will give you your life as a prize of war in all places to which you may go."

Judgment against Egypt

46 The word of the LORD which came to Jeremi'ah the prophet concerning the nations.

2 About Egypt. Concerning the army of Pharaoh Neco, king of Egypt, which was by the river Euphra'tes at Car'chemish and which Nebuchadrez'zar king of Babylon defeated in the fourth year of Jehoi'akim the son of Josi'ah, king of Judah:

3"Prepare buckler and shield,
  and advance for battle!
4Harness the horses;
  mount, O horsemen!
Take your stations with your helmets,
  polish your spears,
  put on your coats of mail!
5Why have I seen it?
They are dismayed
  and have turned backward.
Their warriors are beaten down,
  and have fled in haste;
they look not back—
  terror on every side!
                    says the LORD.

6The swift cannot flee away,
  nor the warrior escape;
in the north by the river Euphra'tes
  they have stumbled and fallen.

7"Who is this, rising like the Nile,
  like rivers whose waters surge?
8Egypt rises like the Nile,
  like rivers whose waters surge.
He said, I will rise, I will cover the earth,
  I will destroy cities and their inhabitants.
9Advance, O horses,
  and rage, O chariots!
Let the warriors go forth:
  men of Ethiopia and Put who handle the
    shield,
  men of Lud, skilled in handling the bow.
10That day is the day of the Lord GOD of hosts,
  a day of vengeance,
  to avenge himself on his foes.
The sword shall devour and be sated,
  and drink its fill of their blood.
For the Lord GOD of hosts holds a sacrifice
  in the north country by the river Euphra'tes.
11Go up to Gilead, and take balm,
  O virgin daughter of Egypt!
In vain you have used many medicines;
  there is no healing for you.
12The nations have heard of your shame,
  and the earth is full of your cry;
for warrior has stumbled against warrior;
  they have both fallen together."

13 The word which the LORD spoke to Jeremi'ah the prophet about the coming of Nebuchadrez'zar king of Babylon to strike the land of Egypt:

14"Declare in Egypt, and proclaim in Migdol;
  proclaim in Memphis and Tah'panhes;

46: Is 19; Ezek 29–32; Zech 14:18–19.
46:5: Jer 6:25; 20:3, 10; 49:29; Ps 31:13.

Say, 'Stand ready and be prepared,
    for the sword shall devour round about you.'
[15]Why has A′pis fled? [z]
    Why did not your bull stand?
      Because the LORD thrust him down.
[16]Your multitude stumbled [a] and fell,
    and they said one to another,
Arise, and let us go back to our own people
    and to the land of our birth,
      because of the sword of the oppressor.'
[17]Call the name of Pharaoh, king of Egypt,
    'Noisy one who lets the hour go by.'

[18]"As I live, says the King,
    whose name is the LORD of hosts,
like Ta′bor among the mountains,
    and like Carmel by the sea, shall one come.
[19]Prepare yourselves baggage for exile,
    O inhabitants of Egypt!
For Memphis shall become a waste,
    a ruin, without inhabitant.

[20]"A beautiful heifer is Egypt,
    but a gadfly from the north has come upon
      her.
[21]Even her hired soldiers in her midst
    are like fatted calves;
yes, they have turned and fled together,
    they did not stand;
for the day of their calamity has come upon
    them,
      the time of their punishment.

[22]"She makes a sound like a serpent gliding
    away;
    for her enemies march in force,
and come against her with axes,
    like those who fell trees.
[23]They shall cut down her forest,

                      says the LORD,
    though it is impenetrable,
because they are more numerous than locusts;
    they are without number.
[24]The daughter of Egypt shall be put to shame,
    she shall be delivered into the hand of a
      people from the north."

25 The LORD of hosts, the God of Israel, said: "Behold, I am bringing punishment upon A′mon of Thebes, and Pharaoh, and Egypt and her gods and her kings, upon Pharaoh and those who trust in him. [26]I will deliver them into the hand of those who seek their life, into the hand of Nebuchad-rez′zar king of Babylon and his officers. Afterward Egypt shall be inhabited as in the days of old, says the LORD.

[27]"But fear not, O Jacob my servant,
    nor be dismayed, O Israel;

for behold, I will save you from afar,
    and your offspring from the land of their
      captivity.
Jacob shall return and have quiet and ease,
    and none shall make him afraid.
[28]Fear not, O Jacob my servant,

                      says the LORD,
    for I am with you.
I will make a full end of all the nations
    to which I have driven you,
    but of you I will not make a full end.
I will chasten you in just measure,
    and I will by no means leave you
      unpunished."

Judgment against the Philistines

47 The word of the LORD that came to Jeremi′ah the prophet concerning the Philis′tines, before Pharaoh struck Gaza.
[2]"Thus says the LORD:
Behold, waters are rising out of the north,
    and shall become an overflowing torrent;
they shall overflow the land and all that fills it,
    the city and those who dwell in it.
Men shall cry out,
    and every inhabitant of the land shall wail.
[3]At the noise of the stamping of the hoofs of
      his stallions,
    at the rushing of his chariots, at the
      rumbling of their wheels,
the fathers look not back to their children,
    so feeble are their hands,
[4]because of the day that is coming to destroy
    all the Philis′tines,
to cut off from Tyre and Si′don
    every helper that remains.
For the LORD is destroying the Philistines,
    the remnant of the coastland of Caphtor.
[5]Baldness has come upon Gaza,
    Ash′kelon has perished.
O remnant of the An′akim, [b]
    how long will you gash yourselves?
[6]Ah, sword of the LORD!
    How long till you are quiet?
Put yourself into your scabbard,
    rest and be still!
[7]How can it [c] be quiet,
    when the LORD has given it a charge?
Against Ash′kelon and against the seashore
    he has appointed it."

Judgment against Moab

48 Concerning Moab.
Thus says the LORD of hosts, the God of Israel:

---

[z] Gk: Heb *Why was it swept away.*
[a] Gk: Heb *He made many stumble.*
[b] Gk: Heb *their valley.*
[c] Gk Vg: Heb *you.*
47: Is 14:29–31; Ezek 25:15–17; Amos 1:6–8; Zeph 2:4–7; Zech 9:5–7.
48: Is 15–16; 25:10–12; Ezek 25:8–11; Amos 2:1–3; Zeph 2:8–11.

"Woe to Nebo, for it is laid waste!
    Kir"iatha'im is put to shame, it is taken;
the fortress is put to shame and broken down;
2   the renown of Moab is no more.
In Heshbon they planned evil against her:
    'Come, let us cut her off from being a
        nation!'
You also, O Madmen, shall be brought to
      silence;
    the sword shall pursue you.

3"Listen! a cry from Horona'im,
    'Desolation and great destruction!'
4Moab is destroyed;
    a cry is heard as far as Zoar. d
5For at the ascent of Lu'hith
    they go up weeping; e
for at the descent of Horona'im
    they have heard the cry f of destruction.
6Flee! Save yourselves!
    Be like a wild donkey g in the desert!
7For, because you trusted in your strongholds h
      and your treasures,
    you also shall be taken;
and Che'mosh shall go forth into exile,
    with his priests and his princes.
8The destroyer shall come upon every city,
    and no city shall escape;
the valley shall perish,
    and the plain shall be destroyed,
    as the LORD has spoken.

9"Give wings to Moab,
    for she would fly away;
her cities shall become a desolation,
    with no inhabitant in them.

10 "Cursed is he who does the work of the
LORD with slackness; and cursed is he who keeps
back his sword from bloodshed.

11"Moab has been at ease from his youth
    and has settled on his dregs;
he has not been emptied from vessel to
      vessel,
    nor has he gone into exile;
so his taste remains in him,
    and his scent is not changed.
12 "Therefore, behold, the days are coming,
says the LORD, when I shall send to him tilters
who will tilt him, and empty his vessels, and break
his i jars in pieces. 13Then Moab shall be ashamed
of Che'mosh, as the house of Israel was ashamed
of Bethel, their confidence.

14"How do you say, 'We are heroes
    and mighty men of war'?
15The destroyer of Moab and his cities has
    come up,

and the choicest of his young men have
    gone down to slaughter,
    says the King, whose name is the LORD of
      hosts.
16The calamity of Moab is near at hand
    and his affliction hastens apace.
17Bemoan him, all you who are round about
      him,
    and all who know his name;
    say, 'How the mighty scepter is broken,
    the glorious staff.'

18"Come down from your glory,
    and sit on the parched ground,
    O inhabitant of Di'bon!
For the destroyer of Moab has come up against
      you;
    he has destroyed your strongholds.
19Stand by the way and watch,
    O inhabitant of Aro'er!
Ask him who flees and her who escapes;
    say, 'What has happened?'
20Moab is put to shame, for it is broken;
    wail and cry!
Tell it by the Arnon,
    that Moab is laid waste.

21 "Judgment has come upon the tableland,
upon Ho'lon, and Jah'zah, and Meph'a-ath, 22and
Di'bon, and Nebo, and Beth"-diblatha'im, 23and
Kir"iatha'im, and Beth-ga'mul, and Beth-me'on,
24and Ker'ioth, and Bozrah, and all the cities of
the land of Moab, far and near. 25The horn of
Moab is cut off, and his arm is broken, says the
LORD.

26 "Make him drunk, because he magnified
himself against the LORD; so that Moab shall wallow in his vomit, and he too shall be held in derision. 27Was not Israel a derision to you? Was he
found among thieves, that whenever you spoke of
him you wagged your head?

28"Leave the cities, and dwell in the rock,
    O inhabitants of Moab!
Be like the dove that nests
    in the sides of the mouth of a gorge.
29We have heard of the pride of Moab—
    he is very proud—
of his loftiness, his pride, and his arrogance,
    and the haughtiness of his heart.
30I know his insolence, says the LORD;
    his boasts are false,
    his deeds are false.

---

d Gk: Heb her little ones.
e Cn: Heb weeping goes up with weeping.
f Gk Compare Is 15:5: Heb the distress of the cry.
g Gk Aquila: Heb like Aroer.
h Gk: Heb works.
i Gk Aquila: Heb their.

³¹Therefore I wail for Moab;
  I cry out for all Moab;
  for the men of Kir-he′res I mourn.
³²More than for Ja′zer I weep for you,
  O vine of Sibmah!
Your branches passed over the sea,
  reached as far as Jazer, ʲ
upon your summer fruits and your vintage
  the destroyer has fallen.
³³Gladness and joy have been taken away
  from the fruitful land of Moab;
I have made the wine cease from the wine
  presses;
  no one treads them with shouts of joy;
  the shouting is not the shout of joy.

34 "Heshbon and Ele-a′leh cry out; ᵏ as far as
Ja′haz they utter their voice, from Zoar to Horo-
na′im and Eg′lath-shelish′iyah. For the waters of
Nimrim also have become desolate. ³⁵And I will
bring to an end in Moab, says the LORD, him who
offers sacrifice in the high place and burns incense to his god. ³⁶Therefore my heart moans for
Moab like a flute, and my heart moans like a flute
for the men of Kir-he′res; therefore the riches they
gained have perished.

37 "For every head is shaved and every beard
cut off; upon all the hands are gashes, and on
the loins is sackcloth. ³⁸On all the housetops of
Moab and in the squares there is nothing but
lamentation; for I have broken Moab like a vessel
for which no one cares, says the LORD. ³⁹How it is
broken! How they wail! How Moab has turned his
back in shame! So Moab has become a derision
and a horror to all that are round about
him."

⁴⁰For thus says the LORD:
"Behold, one shall fly swiftly like an eagle,
  and spread his wings against Moab;
⁴¹the cities shall be taken
  and the strongholds seized.
The heart of the warriors of Moab shall be in
    that day
  like the heart of a woman with her labor
    pains;
⁴²Moab shall be destroyed and be no longer a
    people,
  because he magnified himself against the
    LORD.
⁴³Terror, pit, and snare
  are before you, O inhabitant of Moab!
                        says the LORD.
⁴⁴He who flees from the terror
  shall fall into the pit,
and he who climbs out of the pit
  shall be caught in the snare.
For I will bring these things ˡ upon Moab
  in the year of their punishment,
                        says the LORD.

⁴⁵"In the shadow of Heshbon
  fugitives stop without strength;
for a fire has gone forth from Heshbon,
  a flame from the house of Si′hon;
it has destroyed the forehead of Moab,
  the crown of the sons of tumult.
⁴⁶Woe to you, O Moab!
  The people of Che′mosh is undone;
for your sons have been taken captive,
  and your daughters into captivity.
⁴⁷Yet I will restore the fortunes of Moab
  in the latter days, says the LORD."
Thus far is the judgment on Moab.

Judgment against the Ammonites

49

Concerning the Am′monites.
Thus says the LORD:
"Has Israel no sons?
  Has he no heir?
Why then has Milcom dispossessed Gad,
  and his people settled in its cities?
²Therefore, behold, the days are coming,
  says the LORD,
when I will cause the battle cry to be heard
  against Rabbah of the Am′monites;
it shall become a desolate mound,
  and its villages shall be burned with fire;
then Israel shall dispossess those who
    dispossessed him,
  says the LORD.

³"Wail, O Heshbon, for Ai is laid waste!
  Cry, O daughters of Rabbah!
Clothe yourselves with sackcloth,
  lament, and run to and fro among the
    hedges!
For Milcom shall go into exile,
  with his priests and his princes.
⁴Why do you boast of your valleys, ᵐ
  O faithless daughter,
who trusted in her treasures, saying,
  'Who will come against me?'
⁵Behold, I will bring terror upon you,
  says the Lord GOD of hosts,
  from all who are round about you,
and you shall be driven out, every man straight
    before him,
  with none to gather the fugitives.

6 But afterward I will restore the fortunes of
the Am′monites, says the LORD."

Judgment against Edom

7 Concerning E′dom.
Thus says the LORD of hosts:

ʲ Cn: Heb *the sea of Jazer.*
ᵏ Cn: Heb *From the cry of Heshbon to Elealeh.*
ˡ Gk Syr: Heb *to her.*
ᵐ Heb *valleys, your valley flows.*
49:1–6: Ezek 21:28–32; 25:1–7; Amos 1:13–15; Zeph 2:8–11.
49:7–22: Is 34; 63:1–6; Ezek 25:12–14; 35; Amos 1:11–12; Obad;
Mal 1:2–5.

"Is wisdom no more in Te'man?
　Has counsel perished from the prudent?
　Has their wisdom vanished?
[8]Flee, turn back, dwell in the depths,
　O inhabitants of De'dan!
For I will bring the calamity of Esau upon
　him,
　the time when I punish him.
[9]If grape-gatherers came to you,
　would they not leave gleanings?
If thieves came by night,
　would they not destroy only enough for
　　themselves?
[10]But I have stripped Esau bare,
　I have uncovered his hiding places,
　and he is not able to conceal himself.
His children are destroyed, and his brothers,
　and his neighbors; and he is no more.
[11]Leave your fatherless children, I will keep them
　alive;
　and let your widows trust in me."

12 For thus says the LORD: "If those who did not deserve to drink the cup must drink it, will you go unpunished? You shall not go unpunished, but you must drink. [13]For I have sworn by myself, says the LORD, that Bozrah shall become a horror, a taunt, a waste, and a curse; and all her cities shall be perpetual wastes."

[14]I have heard tidings from the LORD,
　and a messenger has been sent among the
　　nations:
"Gather yourselves together and come against
　her,
　and rise up for battle!"
[15]For behold, I will make you small among the
　nations,
　despised among men.
[16]The horror you inspire has deceived you,
　and the pride of your heart,
you who live in the clefts of the rock,[n]
　who hold the height of the hill.
Though you make your nest as high as the
　eagle's,
　I will bring you down from there,
　　　　　　　　　　　　　　says the LORD.

17 "E'dom shall become a horror; every one who passes by it will be horrified and will hiss because of all its disasters. [18]As when Sodom and Gomor'rah and their neighbor cities were overthrown, says the LORD, no man shall dwell there, no man shall sojourn in her. [19]Behold, like a lion coming up from the jungle of the Jordan against a strong sheepfold, I will suddenly make them[o] run away from her; and I will appoint over her whomever I choose. For who is like me? Who will summon me? What shepherd can stand before me? [20]Therefore hear the plan which the LORD has made against E'dom and the purposes which he has formed against the inhabitants of Te'man:

Even the little ones of the flock shall be dragged away; surely their fold shall be appalled at their fate. [21]At the sound of their fall the earth shall tremble; the sound of their cry shall be heard at the Red Sea. [22]Behold, one shall mount up and fly swiftly like an eagle, and spread his wings against Bozrah, and the heart of the warriors of E'dom shall be in that day like the heart of a woman with her labor pains."

Judgment against Damascus

23 Concerning Damascus.
"Ha'math and Arpad are confounded,
　for they have heard evil tidings;
they melt in fear, they are troubled like the sea[p]
　which cannot be quiet.
[24]Damascus has become feeble, she turned to
　flee,
　and panic seized her;
anguish and sorrows have taken hold of her,
　as of a woman with labor pains.
[25]How the famous city is forsaken,[q]
　the joyful city![r]
[26]Therefore her young men shall fall in her
　squares,
　and all her soldiers shall be destroyed in
　　that day,
　　　　　　　　　　says the LORD of hosts.
[27]And I will kindle a fire in the wall of
　Damascus,
　and it shall devour the strongholds of
　　Benha'dad."

Judgment against Kedar and Hazor

28 Concerning Ke'dar and the kingdoms of Ha'zor which Nebuchadrez'zar king of Babylon struck.

Thus says the LORD:
"Rise up, advance against Kedar!
　Destroy the people of the east!
[29]Their tents and their flocks shall be taken,
　their curtains and all their goods;
their camels shall be borne away from them,
　and men shall cry to them: 'Terror on every
　　side!'
[30]Flee, wander far away, dwell in the depths,
　O inhabitants of Ha'zor!
　　　　　　　　　　　　　　says the LORD.
For Nebuchadrez'zar king of Babylon
　has made a plan against you,
　and formed a purpose against you.

[31]"Rise up, advance against a nation at ease,
　that dwells securely,
　　　　　　　　　　　　　　says the LORD,

---

[n] Or Sela.
[o] Gk Syr: Heb him.
[p] Cn: Heb there is trouble in the sea.
[q] vg: Heb not forsaken.
[r] Syr Vg Tg: Heb city of my joy.
49:23–27: Is 17:1–3; Amos 1:3–5; Zech 9:1.
49:29: Jer 6:25; 20:3, 10; 46:5; Ps 31:13.

that has no gates or bars,
    that dwells alone.
[32]Their camels shall become booty,
    their herds of cattle a spoil.
I will scatter to every wind
    those who cut the corners of their hair,
and I will bring their calamity
    from every side of them,
                    says the Lord.
[33]Ha'zor shall become a haunt of jackals,
    an everlasting waste;
  no man shall dwell there,
    no man shall sojourn in her."

Judgment against Elam

34 The word of the Lord that came to Jeremi'ah the prophet concerning E'lam, in the beginning of the reign of Zedeki'ah king of Judah.

35 Thus says the Lord of hosts: "Behold, I will break the bow of E'lam, the mainstay of their might; [36]and I will bring upon E'lam the four winds from the four quarters of heaven; and I will scatter them to all those winds, and there shall be no nation to which those driven out of Elam shall not come. [37]I will terrify E'lam before their enemies, and before those who seek their life; I will bring evil upon them, my fierce anger, says the Lord. I will send the sword after them, until I have consumed them; [38]and I will set my throne in E'lam, and destroy their king and princes, says the Lord.

39 "But in the latter days I will restore the fortunes of E'lam, says the Lord."

Judgment against Babylon

50 The word which the Lord spoke concerning Babylon, concerning the land of the Chalde'ans, by Jeremi'ah the prophet:
[2]"Declare among the nations and proclaim,
  set up a banner and proclaim,
  conceal it not, and say:
'Babylon is taken,
  Bel is put to shame,
  Mer'odach is dismayed.
Her images are put to shame,
  her idols are dismayed.'

3 "For out of the north a nation has come up against her, which shall make her land a desolation, and none shall dwell in it; both man and beast shall flee away.

4 "In those days and in that time, says the Lord, the people of Israel and the people of Judah shall come together, weeping as they come; and they shall seek the Lord their God. [5]They shall ask the way to Zion, with faces turned toward it, saying, 'Come, let us join ourselves to the Lord in an everlasting covenant which will never be forgotten.'

6 "My people have been lost sheep; their shepherds have led them astray, turning them away on the mountains; from mountain to hill they have gone, they have forgotten their fold. [7]All who found them have devoured them, and their enemies have said, 'We are not guilty, for they have sinned against the Lord, their true habitation, the Lord, the hope of their fathers.'

8 "Flee from the midst of Babylon, and go out of the land of the Chalde'ans, and be as he-goats before the flock. [9]For behold, I am stirring up and bringing against Babylon a company of great nations, from the north country; and they shall array themselves against her; from there she shall be taken. Their arrows are like a skilled warrior who does not return empty-handed. [10]Chalde'a shall be plundered; all who plunder her shall be sated, says the Lord.

[11]"Though you rejoice, though you exult,
  O plunderers of my heritage,
though you are wanton as a heifer at grass,
  and neigh like stallions,
[12]your mother shall be utterly shamed,
  and she who bore you shall be disgraced.
Behold, she shall be the last of the nations,
  a wilderness dry and desert.
[13]Because of the wrath of the Lord she shall not
    be inhabited,
  but shall be an utter desolation;
every one who passes by Babylon shall be
    appalled,
  and hiss because of all her wounds.
[14]Set yourselves in array against Babylon round
    about,
  all you that bend the bow;
shoot at her, spare no arrows,
  for she has sinned against the Lord.
[15]Raise a shout against her round about,
  she has surrendered;
her bulwarks have fallen,
  her walls are thrown down.
For this is the vengeance of the Lord:
  take vengeance on her,
  do to her as she has done.
[16]Cut off from Babylon the sower,
    and the one who handles the sickle in time
    of harvest;
because of the sword of the oppressor,
    every one shall turn to his own people,
  and every one shall flee to his own land.

17 "Israel is a hunted sheep driven away by lions. First the king of Assyria devoured him, and now at last Nebuchadrez'zar king of Babylon has gnawed his bones. [18]Therefore, thus says the Lord of hosts, the God of Israel: Behold, I am bringing

---

50–51: Is 13:1–14:23; 47; Hab 1–2.
50:8: Jer 51:6, 9, 45; 2 Cor 6:17; Rev 18:4.

punishment on the king of Babylon and his land, as I punished the king of Assyria. [19]I will restore Israel to his pasture, and he shall feed on Car'mel and in Ba'shan, and his desire shall be satisfied on the hills of E'phraim and in Gilead. [20]In those days and in that time, says the LORD, iniquity shall be sought in Israel, and there shall be none; and sin in Judah, and none shall be found; for I will pardon those whom I leave as a remnant.

[21]"Go up against the land of Meratha'im, [a]
  and against the inhabitants of Pe'kod. [t]
Slay, and utterly destroy after them, says the
    LORD,
  and do all that I have commanded you.
[22]The noise of battle is in the land,
  and great destruction!
[23]How the hammer of the whole earth
  is cut down and broken!
How Babylon has become
  a horror among the nations!
[24]I set a snare for you and you were taken, O
    Babylon,
  and you did not know it;
you were found and caught,
  because you strove against the LORD.
[25]The LORD has opened his armory,
  and brought out the weapons of his wrath,
for the Lord GOD of hosts has a work to do
  in the land of the Chalde'ans.
[26]Come against her from every quarter;
  open her granaries;
pile her up like heaps of grain, and destroy her
    utterly;
  let nothing be left of her.
[27]Slay all her bulls,
  let them go down to the slaughter.
Woe to them, for their day has come,
  the time of their punishment.

28 "Listen! they flee and escape from the land of Babylon, to declare in Zion the vengeance of the LORD our God, vengeance for his temple.

29 "Summon archers against Babylon, all those who bend the bow. Encamp round about her; let no one escape. Repay her according to her deeds, do to her according to all that she has done; for she has proudly defied the LORD, the Holy One of Israel. [30]Therefore her young men shall fall in her squares, and all her soldiers shall be destroyed on that day, says the LORD.

[31]"Behold, I am against you, O proud one,
  says the Lord GOD of hosts;
for your day has come,
  the time when I will punish you.
[32]The proud one shall stumble and fall,
  with none to raise him up,

and I will kindle a fire in his cities,
  and it will devour all that is round about
    him.

33 "Thus says the LORD of hosts: The people of Israel are oppressed, and the people of Judah with them; all who took them captive have held them fast, they refuse to let them go. [34]Their Redeemer is strong; the LORD of hosts is his name. He will surely plead their cause, that he may give rest to the earth, but unrest to the inhabitants of Babylon.

[35]"A sword upon the Chalde'ans, says the LORD,
  and upon the inhabitants of Babylon,
  and upon her princes and her wise men!
[36]A sword upon the diviners,
  that they may become fools!
A sword upon her warriors,
  that they may be destroyed!
[37]A sword upon her horses and upon her
    chariots,
  and upon all the foreign troops in her midst,
  that they may become women!
A sword upon all her treasures,
  that they may be plundered!
[38]A drought upon her waters,
  that they may be dried up!
For it is a land of images,
  and they are mad over idols.

39 "Therefore wild beasts shall dwell with hyenas in Babylon, and ostriches shall dwell in her; she shall be peopled no more for ever, nor inhabited for all generations. [40]As when God overthrew Sodom and Gomor'rah and their neighbor cities, says the LORD, so no man shall dwell there, and no son of man shall sojourn in her.

[41]"Behold, a people comes from the north;
  a mighty nation and many kings
  are stirring from the farthest parts of the
    earth.
[42]They lay hold of bow and spear;
  they are cruel, and have no mercy.
The sound of them is like the roaring of the
    sea;
  they ride upon horses,
clothed as a man for battle
  against you, O daughter of Babylon!

[43]"The king of Babylon heard the report of
    them,
  and his hands fell helpless;
anguish seized him,
  pain as of a woman in labor.

---

[a] Or Double Rebellion.
[t] Or Punishment.

44 "Behold, like a lion coming up from the jungle of the Jordan against a strong sheepfold, I will suddenly make them run away from her; and I will appoint over her whomever I choose. For who is like me? Who will summon me? What shepherd can stand before me? 45Therefore hear the plan which the LORD has made against Babylon, and the purposes which he has formed against the land of the Chalde′ans: Surely the little ones of their flock shall be dragged away; surely their fold shall be appalled at their fate. 46At the sound of the capture of Babylon the earth shall tremble, and her cry shall be heard among the nations."

51 Thus says the LORD:
Behold, I will stir up the spirit of a
    destroyer against Babylon,
  against the inhabitants of Chalde′a; ᵘ
2and I will send to Babylon winnowers,
  and they shall winnow her,
and they shall empty her land,
  when they come against her from every side
    on the day of trouble.
3Let not the archer bend his bow,
  and let him not stand up in his coat of mail.
Spare not her young men;
  utterly destroy all her host.
4They shall fall down slain in the land of the
    Chalde′ans,
  and wounded in her streets.
5For Israel and Judah have not been forsaken
  by their God, the LORD of hosts;
but the land of the Chalde′ans ᵛ is full of guilt
  against the Holy One of Israel.

6"Flee from the midst of Babylon,
  let every man save his life!
Be not cut off in her punishment,
  for this is the time of the LORD's
    vengeance,
  the repayment he is rendering her.
7Babylon was a golden cup in the LORD's hand,
  making all the earth drunken;
the nations drank of her wine,
  therefore the nations went mad.
8Suddenly Babylon has fallen and been broken;
  wail for her!
Take balm for her pain;
  perhaps she may be healed.
9We would have healed Babylon,
  but she was not healed.
Forsake her, and let us go
  each to his own country;
for her judgment has reached up to heaven
  and has been lifted up even to the skies.
10The LORD has brought forth our vindication;
  come, let us declare in Zion
  the work of the LORD our God.

11"Sharpen the arrows!
  Take up the shields!
The LORD has stirred up the spirit of the kings of the Medes, because his purpose concerning Babylon is to destroy it, for that is the vengeance of the LORD, the vengeance for his temple.
12Set up a standard against the walls of Babylon;
  make the watch strong;
set up watchmen;
  prepare the ambushes;
for the LORD has both planned and done
  what he spoke concerning the inhabitants
    of Babylon.
13O you who dwell by many waters,
  rich in treasures,
your end has come,
  the thread of your life is cut.
14The LORD of hosts has sworn by himself:
Surely I will fill you with men, as many as
    locusts,
  and they shall raise the shout of victory
    over you.

15"It is he who made the earth by his power,
  who established the world by his wisdom,
and by his understanding
  stretched out the heavens.
16When he utters his voice there is a tumult of
    waters in the heavens,
  and he makes the mist rise from the ends of
    the earth.
He makes lightning for the rain,
  and he brings forth the wind from his
    storehouses.
17Every man is stupid and without knowledge;
  every goldsmith is put to shame by his
    idols;
for his images are false,
  and there is no breath in them.
18They are worthless, a work of delusion;
  at the time of their punishment they shall
    perish.
19Not like these is he who is the portion of Jacob,
  for he is the one who formed all things,
and Israel is the tribe of his inheritance;
  the LORD of hosts is his name.

20"You are my hammer and weapon of war:
with you I break nations in pieces;
  with you I destroy kingdoms;
21with you I break in pieces the horse and his
    rider;
  with you I break in pieces the chariot and
    the charioteer;

ᵘ Heb *Leb-qamai*, a cipher for Chaldea.
ᵛ Heb *their land*.
51:6, 9, 45: Jer 50:8; 2 Cor 6:17; Rev 18:4.
51:7–8: Jer 25:15; Rev 14:8, 10; 16:19; 17:4; 18:3.
51:13: Rev 17:1.

22with you I break in pieces man and woman;
    with you I break in pieces the old man and
        the youth;
with you I break in pieces the young man and
    the maiden;
23 with you I break in pieces the shepherd and
    his flock;
with you I break in pieces the farmer and his
    team;
    with you I break in pieces governors and
        commanders.

The Doom of Babylon

24 "I will repay Babylon and all the inhabitants of Chalde′a before your very eyes for all the
evil that they have done in Zion, says the Lord.

25"Behold, I am against you, O destroying
    mountain,
                      says the Lord,
  which destroys the whole earth;
I will stretch out my hand against you,
  and roll you down from the crags,
  and make you a burnt mountain.
26No stone shall be taken from you for a corner
  and no stone for a foundation,
but you shall be a perpetual waste,
  says the Lord.

27"Set up a standard on the earth,
  blow the trumpet among the nations;
prepare the nations for war against her,
  summon against her the kingdoms,
    Ar′arat, Minni, and Ash′kenaz;
appoint a marshal against her,
  bring up horses like bristling locusts.
28Prepare the nations for war against her,
  the kings of the Medes, with their
    governors and deputies,
  and every land under their dominion.
29The land trembles and writhes in pain,
  for the Lord's purposes against Babylon
    stand,
to make the land of Babylon a desolation,
  without inhabitant.
30The warriors of Babylon have ceased fighting,
  they remain in their strongholds;
their strength has failed,
  they have become women;
her dwellings are on fire,
  her bars are broken.
31One runner runs to meet another,
  and one messenger to meet another,
to tell the king of Babylon
  that his city is taken on every side;
32the fords have been seized,
  the bulwarks are burned with fire,
  and the soldiers are in panic.
33For thus says the Lord of hosts, the God of
  Israel:

The daughter of Babylon is like a threshing
  floor
  at the time when it is trodden;
yet a little while
  and the time of her harvest will come."

34"Nebuchadrez′zar the king of Babylon has
  devoured me,
  he has crushed me;
he has made me an empty vessel,
  he has swallowed me like a monster;
he has filled his belly with my delicacies,
  he has rinsed me out.
35The violence done to me and to my kinsmen be
  upon Babylon,"
  let the inhabitant of Zion say.
"My blood be upon the inhabitants of
  Chalde′a,"
  let Jerusalem say.
36Therefore thus says the Lord:
"Behold, I will plead your cause
  and take vengeance for you.
I will dry up her sea
  and make her fountain dry;
37and Babylon shall become a heap of ruins,
  the haunt of jackals,
a horror and a hissing,
  without inhabitant.

38"They shall roar together like lions;
  they shall growl like lions' whelps.
39While they are inflamed I will prepare them a
  feast
  and make them drunk, till they swoon
    away w
and sleep a perpetual sleep
  and not wake, says the Lord.
40I will bring them down like lambs to the
  slaughter,
  like rams and he-goats.

41"How Babylon x is taken,
  the praise of the whole earth seized!
How Babylon has become
  a horror among the nations!
42The sea has come up on Babylon;
  she is covered with its tumultuous waves.
43Her cities have become a horror,
  a land of drought and a desert,
a land in which no one dwells,
  and through which no son of man passes.
44And I will punish Bel in Babylon,
  and take out of his mouth what he has
    swallowed.
The nations shall no longer flow to him;
  the wall of Babylon has fallen.

---

w Gk Vg: Heb *rejoice*.
x Heb *Sheshach*, a cipher for Babylon.

45"Go out of the midst of her, my people!
Let every man save his life
from the fierce anger of the Lord!
46Let not your heart faint, and be not fearful
at the report heard in the land,
when a report comes in one year
and afterward a report in another year,
and violence is in the land,
and ruler is against ruler.

47"Therefore, behold, the days are coming
when I will punish the images of Babylon;
her whole land shall be put to shame,
and all her slain shall fall in the midst of her.
48Then the heavens and the earth,
and all that is in them,
shall sing for joy over Babylon;
for the destroyers shall come against them
out of the north,
says the Lord.
49Babylon must fall for the slain of Israel,
as for Babylon have fallen the slain of all
the earth.

50"You that have escaped from the sword,
go, stand not still!
Remember the Lord from afar,
and let Jerusalem come into your mind:
51'We are put to shame, for we have heard
reproach;
dishonor has covered our face,
for aliens have come
into the holy places of the Lord's house.'

52"Therefore, behold, the days are coming, says
the Lord,
when I will execute judgment upon her
images,
and through all her land
the wounded shall groan.
53Though Babylon should mount up to heaven,
and though she should fortify her strong
height,
yet destroyers would come from me upon her,
says the Lord.

54"Listen! a cry from Babylon!
The noise of great destruction from the
land of the Chalde'ans!
55For the Lord is laying Babylon waste,
and stilling her mighty voice.
Their waves roar like many waters,
the noise of their voice is raised;
56for a destroyer has come upon her,
upon Babylon;
her warriors are taken,
their bows are broken in pieces;
for the Lord is a God of recompense,
he will surely repay.

57I will make drunk her princes and her wise
men,
her governors, her commanders, and her
warriors;
they shall sleep a perpetual sleep and not
wake,
says the King, whose name is the Lord of
hosts.
58"Thus says the Lord of hosts:
The broad wall of Babylon
shall be leveled to the ground
and her high gates
shall be burned with fire.
The peoples labor for nothing,
and the nations weary themselves only for
fire."

Jeremiah's Command to Seraiah

59 The word which Jeremi'ah the prophet commanded Serai'ah the son of Neri'ah, son of Mahsei'ah, when he went with Zedeki'ah king of Judah to Babylon, in the fourth year of his reign. Seraiah was the quartermaster. 60Jeremi'ah wrote in a book all the evil that should come upon Babylon, all these words that are written concerning Babylon. 61And Jeremi'ah said to Serai'ah: "When you come to Babylon, see that you read all these words, 62and say, 'O Lord, you have said concerning this place that you will cut it off, so that nothing shall dwell in it, neither man nor beast, and it shall be desolate for ever.' 63When you finish reading this book, bind a stone to it, and cast it into the midst of the Euphra'tes, 64and say, 'Thus shall Babylon sink, to rise no more, because of the evil that I am bringing upon her.'" *y*

Thus far are the words of Jeremi'ah.

Zedekiah Is Captured

52 * Zedeki'ah was twenty-one years old when he became king; and he reigned eleven years in Jerusalem. His mother's name was Hamu'tal the daughter of Jeremi'ah of Libnah. 2And he did what was evil in the sight of the Lord, according to all that Jehoi'akim had done. 3Surely because of the anger of the Lord things came to such a pass in Jerusalem and Judah that he cast them out from his presence.

And Zedeki'ah rebelled against the king of Babylon. 4And in the ninth year of his reign, in the tenth month, on the tenth day of the month, Nebuchadrez'zar king of Babylon came with all his army against Jerusalem, and they laid siege to it and built siegeworks against it round about. 5So the city was besieged till the eleventh year of

---

y Gk: Heb *upon her. And they shall weary themselves.*
51:48: Is 44:23; Rev 12:12; 18:20.
51:63–64: Rev 18:21.
52: 2 Kings 24:18—25:30; 2 Chron 36:11–13.
* 52: Historical supplement which recapitulates and enlarges on 2 Kings 24:18—25:30. Cf. Is 36–39, which was added in the same way.

King Zedeki'ah. [6]On the ninth day of the fourth month the famine was so severe in the city, that there was no food for the people of the land. [7]Then a breach was made in the city; and all the men of war fled and went out from the city by night by the way of a gate between the two walls, by the king's garden, while the Chalde'ans were round about the city. And they went in the direction of the Ar'abah. [8]But the army of the Chalde'ans pursued the king, and overtook Zedeki'ah in the plains of Jericho; and all his army was scattered from him. [9]Then they captured the king, and brought him up to the king of Babylon at Riblah in the land of Ha'math, and he passed sentence upon him. [10]The king of Babylon slew the sons of Zedeki'ah before his eyes, and also slew all the princes of Judah at Riblah. [11]He put out the eyes of Zedeki'ah, and bound him in chains, and the king of Babylon took him to Babylon, and put him in prison till the day of his death.

Jerusalem Is Plundered and Burned

12 In the fifth month, on the tenth day of the month—which was the nineteenth year of King Nebuchadrez'zar, king of Babylon—Nebu'zarad'an the captain of the bodyguard who served the king of Babylon, entered Jerusalem. [13]And he burned the house of the LORD, and the king's house and all the houses of Jerusalem; every great house he burned down. [14]And all the army of the Chalde'ans, who were with the captain of the guard, broke down all the walls round about Jerusalem. [15]And Nebu'zarad'an the captain of the guard carried away captive some of the poorest of the people and the rest of the people who were left in the city and the deserters who had deserted to the king of Babylon, together with the rest of the artisans. [16]But Nebu'zarad'an the captain of the guard left some of the poorest of the land to be vinedressers and plowmen.

17 And the pillars of bronze that were in the house of the LORD, and the stands and the bronze sea that were in the house of the LORD, the Chalde'ans broke in pieces, and carried all the bronze to Babylon. [18]And they took away the pots, and the shovels, and the snuffers, and the basins, and the dishes for incense, and all the vessels of bronze used in the temple service; [19]also the small bowls, and the firepans, and the basins, and the pots, and the lampstands, and the dishes for incense, and the bowls for libation. What was of gold the captain of the guard took away as gold, and what was of silver, as silver. [20]As for the two pillars, the one sea, the twelve bronze bulls which were under the sea, [z] and the stands, which Solomon the king had made for the house of the

LORD, the bronze of all these things was beyond weight. [21]As for the pillars, the height of the one pillar was eighteen cubits, its circumference was twelve cubits, and its thickness was four fingers, and it was hollow. [22]Upon it was a capital of bronze; the height of the one capital was five cubits; a network and pomegranates, all of bronze, were upon the capital round about. And the second pillar had the like, with pomegranates. [23]There were ninety-six pomegranates on the sides; all the pomegranates were a hundred upon the network round about.

24 And the captain of the guard took Serai'ah the chief priest, and Zephani'ah the second priest, and the three keepers of the threshold; [25]and from the city he took an officer who had been in command of the men of war, and seven men of the king's council, who were found in the city; and the secretary of the commander of the army who mustered the people of the land; and sixty men of the people of the land, who were found in the midst of the city. [26]And Nebu'zarad'an the captain of the guard took them, and brought them to the king of Babylon at Riblah. [27]And the king of Babylon struck them, and put them to death at Riblah in the land of Ha'math. So Judah was carried captive out of its land.

The Captives Taken to Babylon

28 This is the number of the people whom Nebuchadrez'zar carried away captive: in the seventh year, three thousand and twenty-three Jews; [29]in the eighteenth year of Nebuchadrez'zar he carried away captive from Jerusalem eight hundred and thirty-two persons; [30]in the twenty-third year of Nebuchadrez'zar, Nebu'zarad'an the captain of the guard carried away captive of the Jews seven hundred and forty-five persons; all the persons were four thousand and six hundred.

Jehoiachin Favored in Captivity

31 And in the thirty-seventh year of the captivity of Jehoi'achin king of Judah, in the twelfth month, on the twenty-fifth day of the month, E'vil-mer'odach king of Babylon, in the year that he became king, lifted up the head of Jehoiachin king of Judah and brought him out of prison; [32]and he spoke kindly to him, and gave him a seat above the seats of the kings who were with him in Babylon. [33]So Jehoi'achin put off his prison garments. And every day of his life he dined regularly at the king's table; [34]as for his allowance, a regular allowance was given him by the king according to his daily need, until the day of his death as long as he lived.

---

[z] Heb lacks *the sea.*

THE LAMENTATIONS
OF JEREMIAH

The Deserted City

1 How lonely sits the city
  that was full of people!
How like a widow has she become,
  she that was great among the nations!
She that was a princess among the cities
  has become a vassal.

²She weeps bitterly in the night,
  tears on her cheeks;
among all her lovers
  she has none to comfort her;
all her friends have dealt treacherously with
    her,
  they have become her enemies.

³Judah has gone into exile because of affliction
  and hard servitude;
she dwells now among the nations,
  but finds no resting place;
her pursuers have all overtaken her
  in the midst of her distress.

⁴The roads to Zion mourn,
  for none come to the appointed feasts;
all her gates are desolate,
  her priests groan;
her maidens have been dragged away, ᵃ
  and she herself suffers bitterly.

⁵Her foes have become the head,
  her enemies prosper,
because the Lᴏʀᴅ has made her suffer
  for the multitude of her transgressions;
her children have gone away,
  captives before the foe.

⁶From the daughter of Zion has departed
  all her majesty.
Her princes have become like deer
  that find no pasture;
they fled without strength
  before the pursuer.

⁷Jerusalem remembers
  in the days of her affliction and bitterness ᵇ
all the precious things
  that were hers from days of old.
When her people fell into the hand of the foe,
  and there was none to help her,

the foe gloated over her,
  mocking at her downfall.

⁸Jerusalem sinned grievously,
  therefore she became filthy;
all who honored her despise her,
  for they have seen her nakedness;
yes, she herself groans,
  and turns her face away.

⁹Her uncleanness was in her skirts;
  she took no thought of her doom;
therefore her fall is terrible,
  she has no comforter.
"O Lᴏʀᴅ, behold my affliction,
  for the enemy has triumphed!"

¹⁰The enemy has stretched out his hands
  over all her precious things;
yes, she has seen the nations
  invade her sanctuary,
those whom you forbade
  to enter your congregation.

¹¹All her people groan
  as they search for bread;
they trade their treasures for food
  to revive their strength.
"Look, O Lᴏʀᴅ, and behold,
  for I am despised."

¹²"Is it nothing to you, ᶜ all you who pass by?
  Look and see
if there is any sorrow like my sorrow
  which was brought upon me,
which the Lᴏʀᴅ inflicted
  on the day of his fierce anger.

¹³"From on high he sent fire;
  into my bones ᵈ he made it descend;
he spread a net for my feet;
  he turned me back;

This book is traditionally ascribed to Jeremiah but is probably not all by
him. It seems rather to have been composed by more than one author,
though at about the same period of the siege and exile. The poems, written in the rhythm known as *qinah*, were probably composed for the liturgical services that continued to be held on the site of the temple.
ᵃ Gk Old Latin: Heb *afflicted*.
ᵇ Cn: Heb *wandering*.
ᶜ Heb uncertain.
ᵈ Gk: Heb *bones and*.

he has left me stunned,
    faint all the day long.

¹⁴"My transgressions were bound ^e into a
    yoke;
    by his hand they were fastened together;
they were set upon my neck;
    he caused my strength to fail;
the Lord gave me into the hands
    of those whom I cannot withstand.

¹⁵"The Lord flouted all my mighty men
    in the midst of me;
he summoned an assembly against me
    to crush my young men;
the Lord has trodden as in a wine press
    the virgin daughter of Judah.

¹⁶"For these things I weep;
    my eyes flow with tears;
for a comforter is far from me,
    one to revive my courage;
my children are desolate,
    for the enemy has prevailed."

¹⁷Zion stretches out her hands,
    but there is none to comfort her;
the Lord has commanded against Jacob
    that his neighbors should be his foes;
Jerusalem has become
    a filthy thing among them.

¹⁸"The Lord is in the right,
    for I have rebelled against his word;
but hear, all you peoples,
    and behold my suffering;
my maidens and my young men
    have gone into captivity.

¹⁹"I called to my lovers
    but they deceived me;
my priests and elders
    perished in the city,
while they sought food
    to revive their strength.

²⁰"Behold, O Lord, for I am in distress,
    my soul is in tumult,
my heart is wrung within me,
    because I have been very rebellious.
In the street the sword bereaves;
    in the house it is like death.

²¹"Hear ^f how I groan;
    there is none to comfort me.
All my enemies have heard of my trouble;
    they are glad that you have done it.
Bring ^g the day you have announced,
    and let them be as I am.

²²"Let all their evil-doing come before you;
    and deal with them
as you have dealt with me
    because of all my transgressions;
for my groans are many
    and my heart is faint."

God's Warnings Are Fulfilled

2 How the Lord in his anger
    has set the daughter of Zion under a cloud!
He has cast down from heaven to earth
    the splendor of Israel;
he has not remembered his footstool
    in the day of his anger.

²The Lord has destroyed without mercy
    all the habitations of Jacob;
in his wrath he has broken down
    the strongholds of the daughter of Judah;
he has brought down to the ground in dishonor
    the kingdom and its rulers.

³He has cut down in fierce anger
    all the might of Israel;
he has withdrawn from them his right hand
    in the face of the enemy;
he has burned like a flaming fire in Jacob,
    consuming all around.

⁴He has bent his bow like an enemy,
    with his right hand set like a foe;
and he has slain all the pride of our eyes
    in the tent of the daughter of Zion;
he has poured out his fury like fire.

⁵The Lord has become like an enemy,
    he has destroyed Israel;
he has destroyed all its palaces,
    laid in ruins its strongholds;
and he has multiplied in the daughter of Judah
    mourning and lamentation.

⁶He has broken down his booth like that of a
    garden,
    laid in ruins the place of his appointed
    feasts;
the Lord has brought to an end in Zion
    appointed feast and sabbath,
and in his fierce indignation has spurned
    king and priest.

⁷The Lord has scorned his altar,
    disowned his sanctuary;
he has delivered into the hand of the enemy
    the walls of her palaces;
a clamor was raised in the house of the Lord
    as on the day of an appointed feast.

^e Cn: Heb uncertain.
^f Gk Syr: Heb *they heard.*
^g Syr: Heb *you have brought.*

⁸The Lord determined to lay in ruins
the wall of the daughter of Zion;
he marked it off by the line;
he restrained not his hand from
destroying;
he caused rampart and wall to lament,
they languish together.

⁹Her gates have sunk into the ground;
he has ruined and broken her bars;
her king and princes are among the nations;
the law is no more,
and her prophets obtain
no vision from the Lord.

¹⁰The elders of the daughter of Zion
sit on the ground in silence;
they have cast dust on their heads
and put on sackcloth;
the maidens of Jerusalem
have bowed their heads to the ground.

¹¹My eyes are spent with weeping;
my soul is in tumult;
my heart is poured out in grief ʰ
because of the destruction of the daughter
of my people,
because infants and babies faint
in the streets of the city.

¹²They cry to their mothers,
"Where is bread and wine?"
as they faint like wounded men
in the streets of the city,
as their life is poured out
on their mothers' bosom.

¹³What can I say for you, to what compare you,
O daughter of Jerusalem?
What can I liken to you, that I may comfort
you,
O virgin daughter of Zion?
For vast as the sea is your ruin;
who can restore you?

¹⁴Your prophets have seen for you
false and deceptive visions;
they have not exposed your iniquity
to restore your fortunes,
but have seen for you oracles
false and misleading.

¹⁵All who pass along the way
clap their hands at you;
they hiss and wag their heads
at the daughter of Jerusalem;
"Is this the city which was called
the perfection of beauty,
the joy of all the earth?"

¹⁶All your enemies
rail against you;
they hiss, they gnash their teeth,
they cry: "We have destroyed her!
Ah, this is the day we longed for;
now we have it; we see it!"

¹⁷The Lord has done what he planned,
has carried out his threat;
as he ordained long ago,
he has demolished without pity;
he has made the enemy rejoice over you,
and exalted the might of your foes.

¹⁸Cry aloud ⁱ to the Lord!
O ʲ daughter of Zion!
Let tears stream down like a torrent
day and night!
Give yourself no rest,
your eyes no respite!

¹⁹Arise, cry out in the night,
at the beginning of the watches!
Pour out your heart like water
before the presence of the Lord!
Lift your hands to him
for the lives of your children,
who faint for hunger
at the head of every street.

²⁰Look, O Lord, and see!
With whom have you dealt thus?
Should women eat their offspring,
the children of their tender care?
Should priest and prophet be slain
in the sanctuary of the Lord?

²¹In the dust of the streets
lie the young and the old;
my maidens and my young men
have fallen by the sword;
in the day of your anger you have slain them,
slaughtering without mercy.

²²You invited as to the day of an appointed
feast
my terrors on every side;
and on the day of the anger of the Lord
none escaped or survived;
those whom I dandled and reared
my enemy destroyed.

God's Merciful Love Endures

3 I am the man who has seen affliction
under the rod of his wrath;
²he has driven and brought me
into darkness without any light;

ʰ Heb to the ground.
ⁱ Cn: Heb Their heart cried.
ʲ Cn: Heb O wall of.

³surely against me he turns his hand
again and again the whole day long.

⁴He has made my flesh and my skin waste away,
and broken my bones;
⁵he has besieged and enveloped me
with bitterness and tribulation;
⁶he has made me dwell in darkness
like the dead of long ago.

⁷He has walled me about so that I cannot escape;
he has put heavy chains on me;
⁸though I call and cry for help,
he shuts out my prayer;
⁹he has blocked my ways with hewn stones,
he has made my paths crooked.

¹⁰He is to me like a bear lying in wait,
like a lion in hiding;
¹¹he led me off my way and tore me to pieces;
he has made me desolate;
¹²he bent his bow and set me
as a mark for his arrow.

¹³He drove into my heart
the arrows of his quiver;
¹⁴I have become the laughingstock of all
peoples,
the burden of their songs all day long.
¹⁵He has filled me with bitterness,
he has sated me with wormwood.

¹⁶He has made my teeth grind on gravel,
and made me cower in ashes;
¹⁷my soul is bereft of peace,
I have forgotten what happiness is;
¹⁸so I say, "Gone is my glory,
and my expectation from the LORD."

¹⁹Remember my affliction and my bitterness,ᵏ
the wormwood and the gall!
²⁰My soul continually thinks of it
and is bowed down within me.
²¹But this I call to mind,
and therefore I have hope:

²²The steadfast love of the LORD never ceases,¹
his mercies never come to an end;
²³they are new every morning;
great is your faithfulness.
²⁴"The LORD is my portion," says my soul,
"therefore I will hope in him."

²⁵The LORD is good to those who wait for him,
to the soul that seeks him.
²⁶It is good that one should wait quietly
for the salvation of the LORD.
²⁷It is good for a man that he bear
the yoke in his youth.

²⁸Let him sit alone in silence
when he has laid it on him;
²⁹let him put his mouth in the dust—
there may yet be hope;
³⁰let him give his cheek to the one who strikes
him,
and be filled with insults.

³¹For the Lord will not
cast off for ever,
³²but, though he cause grief, he will have
compassion
according to the abundance of his steadfast
love;
³³for he does not willingly afflict
or grieve the sons of men.

³⁴To crush under foot
all the prisoners of the earth,
³⁵to turn aside the right of a man
in the presence of the Most High,
³⁶to subvert a man in his cause,
the Lord does not approve.

³⁷Who has commanded and it came to pass,
unless the Lord has ordained it?
³⁸Is it not from the mouth of the Most High
that good and evil come?
³⁹Why should a living man complain,
a man, about the punishment of his sins?

⁴⁰Let us test and examine our ways,
and return to the LORD!
⁴¹Let us lift up our hearts and hands
to God in heaven:
⁴²"We have transgressed and rebelled,
and you have not forgiven.

⁴³"You have wrapped yourself with anger and
pursued us,
slaying without pity;
⁴⁴you have wrapped yourself with a cloud
so that no prayer can pass through.
⁴⁵You have made us offscouring and refuse
among the peoples.

⁴⁶"All our enemies
rail against us;
⁴⁷panic and pitfall have come upon us,
devastation and destruction;
⁴⁸my eyes flow with rivers of tears
because of the destruction of the daughter
of my people.

⁴⁹"My eyes will flow without ceasing,
without respite,

ᵏ Cn: Heb *wandering*.
¹ Syr Tg: Heb *we are not cut off.*

⁵⁰until the LORD from heaven
  looks down and sees;
⁵¹my eyes cause me grief
  at the fate of all the maidens of my city.

⁵²"I have been hunted like a bird
  by those who were my enemies without
    cause;
⁵³they flung me alive into the pit
  and cast stones on me;
⁵⁴water closed over my head;
  I said, 'I am lost.'

⁵⁵"I called on your name, O LORD,
  from the depths of the pit;
⁵⁶you heard my plea, 'Do not close
  your ear to my cry for help!'ᵐ
⁵⁷You came near when I called on you;
  you said, 'Do not fear!'

⁵⁸"You have taken up my cause, O Lord,
  you have redeemed my life.
⁵⁹You have seen the wrong done to me, O LORD;
  do judge my cause.
⁶⁰You have seen all their vengeance,
  all their devices against me.

⁶¹"You have heard their taunts, O LORD,
  all their devices against me.
⁶²The lips and thoughts of my assailants
  are against me all the day long.
⁶³Behold their sitting and their rising;
  I am the burden of their songs.

⁶⁴"You will repay them, O LORD,
  according to the work of their hands.
⁶⁵You will give them dullness of heart;
  your curse will be on them.
⁶⁶You will pursue them in anger and destroy
    them
  from under your heavens, O LORD."ⁿ

The Punishment and Distress of Zion

4 How the gold has grown dim,
  how the pure gold is changed!
The holy stones lie scattered
  at the head of every street.

²The precious sons of Zion,
  worth their weight in fine gold,
how they are reckoned as earthen pots,
  the work of a potter's hands!

³Even the jackals give the breast
  and suckle their young,
but the daughter of my people has become
    cruel,
  like the ostriches in the wilderness.

⁴The tongue of the infant clings
  to the roof of its mouth for thirst;

the children beg for food,
  but no one gives to them.

⁵Those who feasted on dainties
  perish in the streets;
those who were brought up in purple
  lie on ash heaps.

⁶For the chastisementº of the daughter of my
    people has been greater
  than the punishmentᵖ of Sodom,
which was overthrown in a moment,
  no hand being laid on it.ᑫ

⁷Her princes were purer than snow,
  whiter than milk;
their bodies were more ruddy than coral,
  the beauty of their formˣ was like
    sapphire.ˢ

⁸Now their visage is blacker than soot,
  they are not recognized in the streets;
their skin has shriveled upon their bones,
  it has become as dry as wood.

⁹Happier were the victims of the sword
  than the victims of hunger,
who pined away, stricken
  by want of the fruits of the field.

¹⁰The hands of compassionate women
  have boiled their own children;
they became their food
  in the destruction of the daughter of my
    people.

¹¹The LORD gave full vent to his wrath,
  he poured out his hot anger;
and he kindled a fire in Zion,
  which consumed its foundations.

¹²The kings of the earth did not believe,
  or any of the inhabitants of the world,
that foe or enemy could enter
  the gates of Jerusalem.

¹³This was for the sins of her prophets
  and the iniquities of her priests,
who shed in the midst of her
  the blood of the righteous.

¹⁴They wandered, blind, through the streets,
  so defiled with blood

ᵐ Heb uncertain.
ⁿ Syr Compare Gk Vg: Heb the heavens of the LORD.
º Or iniquity.
ᵖ Or sin.
ᑫ Heb uncertain.
ˣ Heb uncertain.
ˢ Heb lapis lazuli.

that none could touch
    their garments.

15"Away! Unclean!" men cried at them;
    "Away! Away! Touch not!"
So they became fugitives and wanderers;
    men said among the nations,
    "They shall stay with us no longer."

16The Lord himself has scattered them,
    he will regard them no more;
no honor was shown to the priests,
    no favor to the elders.

17Our eyes failed, ever watching
    vainly for help;
in our watching t we watched
    for a nation which could not save.

18Men dogged our steps
    so that we could not walk in our streets;
our end drew near; our days were numbered;
    for our end had come.

19Our pursuers were swifter
    than the vultures in the heavens;
they chased us on the mountains,
    they lay in wait for us in the wilderness.

20The breath of our nostrils, the Lord's anointed,
    was taken in their pits,
he of whom we said, "Under his shadow
    we shall live among the nations."

21Rejoice and be glad, O daughter of E'dom,
    dweller in the land of Uz;
but to you also the cup shall pass;
    you shall become drunk and strip yourself
    bare.

22The punishment of your iniquity,
    O daughter of Zion, is accomplished,
he will keep you in exile no longer;
but your iniquity, O daughter of E'dom, he will
    punish,
he will uncover your sins.

A Prayer for Mercy

5 Remember, O Lord, what has befallen us;
    behold, and see our disgrace!

2Our inheritance has been turned over to
    strangers,
    our homes to aliens.
3We have become orphans, fatherless;
    our mothers are like widows.
4We must pay for the water we drink,
    the wood we get must be bought.
5With a yoke u on our necks we are hard driven;
    we are weary, we are given no rest.
6We have given the hand to Egypt,
    and to Assyria, to get bread enough.
7Our fathers sinned, and are no more;
    and we bear their iniquities.
8Slaves rule over us;
    there is none to deliver us from their hand.
9We get our bread at the peril of our lives,
    because of the sword in the wilderness.
10Our skin is hot as an oven
    with the burning heat of famine.
11Women are ravished in Zion,
    virgins in the towns of Judah.
12Princes are hung up by their hands;
    no respect is shown to the elders.
13Young men are compelled to grind at the mill;
    and boys stagger under loads of wood.
14The old men have quit the city gate,
    the young men their music.
15The joy of our hearts has ceased;
    our dancing has been turned to mourning.
16The crown has fallen from our head;
    woe to us, for we have sinned!
17For this our heart has become sick,
    for these things our eyes have grown dim,
18for Mount Zion which lies desolate;
    jackals prowl over it.

19But you, O Lord, reign for ever;
    your throne endures to all generations.
20Why do you forget us for ever,
    why do you so long forsake us?
21Restore us to yourself, O Lord, that we may be
    restored!
    Renew our days as of old!
22Or have you utterly rejected us?
    Are you exceedingly angry with us?

---

t Heb uncertain.
u Symmachus: Heb lacks *with a yoke.*

THE BOOK OF

BARUCH

Baruch and the Jews of Babylon

1 These are the words of the book which
Baruch the son of Nerai'ah, son of Mah'seiah,
son of Zedeki'ah, son of Hasadi'ah, son of Hilki'ah, wrote in Babylon, [2]in the fifth year, on the
seventh day of the month, at the time when the
Chalde'ans took Jerusalem and burned it with
fire. [3]And Baruch read the words of this book in
the hearing of Jeconi'ah the son of Jehoi'akim,
king of Judah, and in the hearing of all the people
who came to hear the book, [4]and in the hearing of
the mighty men and the princes, and in the hearing of the elders, and in the hearing of all the
people, small and great, all who dwelt in Babylon
by the river Sud.

5 Then they wept, and fasted, and prayed before the Lord; [6]and they collected money, each
giving what he could; [7]and they sent it to Jerusalem to Jehoi'akim the high priest, [a] the son of
Hilki'ah, son of Shallum, and to the priests, and to
all the people who were present with him in
Jerusalem. [8]At the same time, on the tenth day of
Si'van, Baruch [b] took the vessels of the house of
the Lord, which had been carried away from the
temple, to return them to the land of Judah—the
silver vessels which Zedeki'ah the son of Josi'ah,
king of Judah, had made, [9]after Nebuchadnez'zar
king of Babylon had carried away from Jerusalem
Jeconi'ah and the princes and the prisoners and
the mighty men and the people of the land, and
brought them to Babylon.

A Letter to Jerusalem

10 And they said: "Herewith we send you
money; so buy with the money burnt offerings
and sin offerings and incense, and prepare a cereal offering, and offer them upon the altar of the
Lord our God; [11]and pray for the life of Nebuchadnez'zar king of Babylon, and for the life of
Belshaz'zar his son, that their days on earth may
be like the days of heaven. [12]And the Lord will
give us strength, and he will give light to our eyes,
and we shall live under the protection [c] of Nebuchadnez'zar king of Babylon, and under the
protection [c] of Belshaz'zar his son, and we shall
serve them many days and find favor in their
sight. [13]And pray for us to the Lord our God, for
we have sinned against the Lord our God, and to
this day the anger of the Lord and his wrath have
not turned away from us. [14]And you shall read
this book which we are sending you, to make your
confession in the house of the Lord on the days of
the feasts and at appointed seasons.

Confession of Sins

15 "And you shall say: 'Righteousness belongs
to the Lord our God, but confusion of face, as at
this day, to us, to the men of Judah, to the inhabitants of Jerusalem, [16]and to our kings and our
princes and our priests and our prophets and our
fathers, [17]because we have sinned before the Lord,
[18]and have disobeyed him, and have not heeded
the voice of the Lord our God, to walk in the
statutes of the Lord which he set before us. [19]From
the day when the Lord brought our fathers out of
the land of Egypt until today, we have been disobedient to the Lord our God, and we have been
negligent, in not heeding his voice. [20]So to this
day there have clung to us the calamities and the
curse which the Lord declared through Moses his
servant at the time when he brought our fathers
out of the land of Egypt to give to us a land
flowing with milk and honey. [21]We did not heed
the voice of the Lord our God in all the words of
the prophets whom he sent to us, but we each
followed the intent of his own wicked heart by
serving other gods and doing what is evil in the
sight of the Lord our God.

2 "So the Lord confirmed his word, which he
spoke against us, and against our judges who
judged Israel, and against our kings and against
our princes and against the men of Israel and
Judah. [2]Under the whole heaven there has not
been done the like of what he has done in Jerusalem, in accordance with what is written in the law
of Moses, [3]that we should eat, one the flesh of his
son and another the flesh of his daughter. [4]And
he gave them into subjection to all the kingdoms
around us, to be a reproach and a desolation
among all the surrounding peoples, where the
Lord has scattered them. [5]They were brought low
and not raised up, because we sinned against the
Lord our God, in not heeding his voice.

This book, one of the deuterocanonical books, is not extant in Hebrew
and is placed here after Lamentations in the Latin Vulgate. It is said to
have been composed by Baruch at Babylon during the Exile, but in fact
the evidence indicates rather that some of it was composed about the
second or even first century B.C. The material may well have been composed at different periods, and the final editing have taken place toward
the time of Christ. The particular value of the book is that it gives an
insight into Jewish life in the Dispersion.

[a] Gk the priest.
[b] Gk he.
[c] Gk in the shadow.

6 " 'Righteousness belongs to the Lord our God, but confusion of face to us and our fathers, as at this day. [7]All those calamities with which the Lord threatened us have come upon us. [8]Yet we have not entreated the favor of the Lord by turning away, each of us, from the thoughts of his wicked heart. [9]And the Lord has kept the calamities ready, and the Lord has brought them upon us, for the Lord is righteous in all his works which he has commanded us to do. [10]Yet we have not obeyed his voice, to walk in the statutes of the Lord which he set before us.

Prayer for Deliverance

11 " 'And now, O Lord God of Israel, who brought your people out of the land of Egypt with a mighty hand and with signs and wonders and with great power and outstretched arm, and have made you a name, as at this day, [12]we have sinned, we have been ungodly, we have done wrong, O Lord our God, against all your ordinances. [13]Let your anger turn away from us, for we are left, few in number, among the nations where you have scattered us. [14]Hear, O Lord, our prayer and our supplication, and for your own sake deliver us, and grant us favor in the sight of those who have carried us into exile; [15]that all the earth may know that you are the Lord our God, for Israel and his descendants are called by your name. [16]O Lord, look down from your holy habitation, and consider us. Incline your ear, O Lord, and hear; [17]open your eyes, O Lord, and see; for the dead who are in Hades, whose spirit has been taken from their bodies, will not ascribe glory or justice to the Lord, [18]but the person that is greatly distressed, [d] that goes about bent over and feeble, and the eyes that are failing, and the person that hungers, will ascribe to you glory and righteousness, O Lord. [19]For it is not because of any righteous deeds of our fathers or our kings that we bring before you our prayer for mercy, O Lord our God. [20]For you have sent your anger and your wrath upon us, as you declared by your servants the prophets, saying: [21]"Thus says the Lord: Bend your shoulders and serve the king of Babylon, and you will remain in the land which I gave to your fathers. [22]But if you will not obey the voice of the Lord and will not serve the king of Babylon, [23]I will make to cease from the cities of Judah and from the region about Jerusalem the voice of mirth and the voice of gladness, the voice of the bridegroom and the voice of the bride, and the whole land will be a desolation without inhabitants."

24 " 'But we did not obey your voice, to serve the king of Babylon; and you have confirmed your words, which you spoke by your servants the prophets, that the bones of our kings and the bones of our fathers would be brought out of their graves; [e] [25]and behold, they have been cast out to the heat of day and the frost of night. They perished in great misery, by famine and sword and pestilence. [26]And the house which is called by your name you have made as it is today, because of the wickedness of the house of Israel and the house of Judah.

God's Covenant Recalled

27 " 'Yet you have dealt with us, O Lord our God, in all your kindness and in all your great compassion, [28]as you spoke by your servant Moses on the day when you commanded him to write your law in the presence of the people of Israel, saying, [29]"If you will not obey my voice, this very great multitude will surely turn into a small number among the nations, where I will scatter them. [30]For I know that they will not obey me, for they are a stiff-necked people. But in the land of their exile they will come to themselves, [31]and they will know that I am the Lord their God. I will give them a heart that obeys and ears that hear; [32]and they will praise me in the land of their exile, and will remember my name, [33]and will turn from their stubbornness and their wicked deeds; for they will remember the ways of their fathers, who sinned before the Lord. [34]I will bring them again into the land which I swore to give to their fathers, to Abraham and to Isaac and to Jacob, and they will rule over it; and I will increase them, and they will not be diminished. [35]I will make an everlasting covenant with them to be their God and they shall be my people; and I will never again remove my people Israel from the land which I have given them."

In Praise of Wisdom

3 " 'O Lord Almighty, God of Israel, the soul in anguish and the wearied spirit cry out to you. [2]Hear, O Lord, and have mercy, for we have sinned before you. [3]For you are enthroned for ever, and we are perishing for ever. [4]O Lord Almighty, God of Israel, hear now the prayer of the dead of Israel and of the sons of those who sinned before you, who did not heed the voice of the Lord their God, so that calamities have clung to us. [5]Remember not the iniquities of our fathers, but in this crisis remember your power and your name. [6]For you are the Lord our God, and you, O Lord, will we praise. [7]For you have put the fear of you in our hearts in order that we should call upon your name; and we will praise you in our exile, for we have put away from our hearts all the iniquity of our fathers who sinned before you. [8]Behold, we are today in our exile where you have scattered us, to be reproached and cursed and punished for all the iniquities of our fathers who forsook the Lord our God.' "

---

[d] The meaning of the Greek is uncertain.
[e] Gk their place.

⁹Hear the commandments of life, O Israel;
    give ear, and learn wisdom!
¹⁰Why is it, O Israel, why is it that you are in the
    land of your enemies,
    that you are growing old in a foreign
        country,
  that you are defiled with the dead,
¹¹   that you are counted among those in
    Hades?
¹²You have forsaken the fountain of wisdom.
¹³If you had walked in the way of God,
    you would be dwelling in peace for ever.
¹⁴Learn where there is wisdom,
    where there is strength,
    where there is understanding,
  that you may at the same time discern
    where there is length of days, and life,
    where there is light for the eyes, and peace.

¹⁵Who has found her place?
    And who has entered her storehouses?
¹⁶Where are the princes of the nations,
    and those who rule over the beasts on the
        earth;
¹⁷those who have sport with the birds of the air,
    and who hoard up silver and gold,
  in which men trust,
    and there is no end to their getting;
¹⁸those who scheme to get silver, and are
    anxious,
    whose labors are beyond measure?
¹⁹They have vanished and gone down to Hades,
    and others have arisen in their place.

²⁰Young men have seen the light of day,
    and have dwelt upon the earth;
  but they have not learned the way to
    knowledge,
    nor understood her paths,
    nor laid hold of her.
²¹Their sons have strayed far from her [f] way.
²²She has not been heard of in Canaan,
    nor seen in Te′man;
²³the sons of Hagar, who seek for understanding
    on the earth,
    the merchants of Merran and Te′man,
    the story-tellers and the seekers for
    understanding,
  have not learned the way to wisdom,
    nor given thought to her paths.

²⁴O Israel, how great is the house of God!
    And how vast the territory that he
    possesses!
²⁵It is great and has no bounds;
    it is high and immeasurable.
²⁶The giants were born there, who were famous
    of old,
    great in stature, expert in war.

²⁷God did not choose them,
    nor give them the way to knowledge;
²⁸so they perished because they had no wisdom,
    they perished through their folly.
²⁹Who has gone up into heaven, and taken her,
    and brought her down from the clouds?
³⁰Who has gone over the sea, and found her,
    and will buy her for pure gold?
³¹No one knows the way to her,
    or is concerned about the path to her.
³²But he who knows all things knows her,
    he found her by his understanding.
  He who prepared the earth for all time
    filled it with four-footed creatures;
³³he who sends forth the light, and it goes,
    called it, and it obeyed him in fear;
³⁴the stars shone in their watches, and were glad;
    he called them, and they said, "Here we
    are!"
  They shone with gladness for him who
    made them.
³⁵This is our God;
    no other can be compared to him!
³⁶He found the whole way to knowledge,
    and gave her to Jacob his servant
    and to Israel whom he loved.
³⁷Afterward she appeared upon earth and lived
    among men.

Encouragement for Israel

4 She is the book of the commandments of
    God,
  and the law that endures for ever.
  All who hold her fast will live,
    and those who forsake her will die.
²Turn, O Jacob, and take her;
    walk toward the shining of her light.
³Do not give your glory to another,
    or your advantages to an alien people.
⁴Happy are we, O Israel,
    for we know what is pleasing to God.

⁵Take courage, my people,
    O memorial of Israel!
⁶It was not for destruction
    that you were sold to the nations,
  but you were handed over to your enemies
    because you angered God.
⁷For you provoked him who made you,
    by sacrificing to demons and not to God.
⁸You forgot the everlasting God, who brought
    you up,
    and you grieved Jerusalem, who reared you.
⁹For she saw the wrath that came upon you from
    God,
  and she said:
  "Listen, you neighbors of Zion,
    God has brought great sorrow upon me;

---

[f] Other authorities read *their*

¹⁰for I have seen the captivity of my sons and
    daughters,
    which the Everlasting brought upon them.
¹¹With joy I nurtured them,
    but I sent them away with weeping and
    sorrow.
¹²Let no one rejoice over me, a widow
    and bereaved of many;
I was left desolate because of the sins of my
    children,
    because they turned away from the law of
    God.
¹³They had no regard for his statutes;
    they did not walk in the ways of God's
    commandments,
    nor tread the paths of discipline in his
    righteousness.
¹⁴Let the neighbors of Zion come;
    remember the capture of my sons and
    daughters,
    which the Everlasting brought upon them.
¹⁵For he brought against them a nation from afar,
    a shameless nation, of a strange language,
who had no respect for an old man,
    and had no pity for a child.
¹⁶They led away the widow's beloved sons,
    and bereaved the lonely woman of her
    daughters.

¹⁷"But I, how can I help you?
¹⁸For he who brought these calamities upon you
    will deliver you from the hand of your
    enemies.
¹⁹Go, my children, go;
    for I have been left desolate.
²⁰I have taken off the robe of peace
    and put on the sackcloth of my
    supplication;
    I will cry to the Everlasting all my days.

²¹"Take courage, my children, cry to God,
    and he will deliver you from the power and
    hand of the enemy.
²²For I have put my hope in the Everlasting to
    save you,
    and joy has come to me from the Holy One,
because of the mercy which soon will come to
    you
    from your everlasting Savior. ᵍ
²³For I sent you out with sorrow and weeping,
    but God will give you back to me with joy
    and gladness for ever.
²⁴For as the neighbors of Zion have now seen
    your capture,
    so they soon will see your salvation by God,
which will come to you with great glory
    and with the splendor of the Everlasting.
²⁵My children, endure with patience the wrath
    that has come upon you from God.

Your enemy has overtaken you,
    but you will soon see their destruction
    and will tread upon their necks.
²⁶My tender sons have traveled rough roads;
    they were taken away like a flock carried
    off by the enemy.

²⁷"Take courage, my children, and cry to God,
    for you will be remembered by him who
    brought this upon you.
²⁸For just as you planned to go astray from God,
    return with tenfold zeal to seek him.
²⁹For he who brought these calamities upon you
    will bring you everlasting joy with your
    salvation."

³⁰Take courage, O Jerusalem,
    for he who named you will comfort you.
³¹Wretched will be those who afflicted you
    and rejoiced at your fall.
³²Wretched will be the cities which your children
    served as slaves;
    wretched will be the city which received
    your sons.
³³For just as she rejoiced at your fall
    and was glad for your ruin,
    so she will be grieved at her own desolation.
³⁴And I will take away her pride in her great
    population,
    and her insolence will be turned to grief.
³⁵For fire will come upon her from the
    Everlasting for many days,
    and for a long time she will be inhabited by
    demons.

³⁶Look toward the east, O Jerusalem,
    and see the joy that is coming to you from
    God!
³⁷Behold, your sons are coming, whom you sent
    away;
    they are coming, gathered from east and
    west,
at the word of the Holy One,
    rejoicing in the glory of God.

Encouragement for Jerusalem

5 Take off the garment of your sorrow and
    affliction, O Jerusalem,
    and put on for ever the beauty of the glory
    from God.
²Put on the robe of the righteousness from God;
    put on your head the diadem of the glory of
    the Everlasting.
³For God will show your splendor everywhere
    under heaven.
⁴For your name will for ever be called by God,
    "Peace of righteousness and glory of
    godliness."

ᵍ Or from the Everlasting, your Savior.

[5]Arise, O Jerusalem, stand upon the height
  and look toward the east,
and see your children gathered from west and
    east,
  at the word of the Holy One,
  rejoicing that God has remembered them.
[6]For they went forth from you on foot,
  led away by their enemies;
but God will bring them back to you,
  carried in glory, as on a royal throne.
[7]For God has ordered that every high mountain
  and the everlasting hills be made low
  and the valleys filled up, to make level
    ground,
  so that Israel may walk safely in the glory
    of God.
[8]The woods and every fragrant tree
  have shaded Israel at God's command.
[9]For God will lead Israel with joy,
  in the light of his glory,
  with the mercy and righteousness that come
    from him.

A Letter of Jeremiah to the Captives

6[h] A copy of a letter which Jeremi'ah sent to those who were to be taken to Babylon as captives by the king of the Babylonians, to give them the message which God had commanded him.

2 Because of the sins which you have committed before God, you will be taken to Babylon as captives by Nebuchadnez'zar, king of the Babylonians. [3]Therefore when you have come to Babylon you will remain there for many years, for a long time, up to seven generations; after that I will bring you away from there in peace. [4]Now in Babylon you will see gods made of silver and gold and wood, which are carried on men's shoulders and inspire fear in the heathen. [5]So take care not to become at all like the foreigners or to let fear for these gods[i] possess you, when you see the multitude before and behind them worshiping them. [6]But say in your heart, "It is you, O Lord, whom we must worship." [7]For my angel is with you, and he is watching your lives.

The Futility of Idols and Idolatry

8 Their tongues are smoothed by the craftsman, and they themselves are overlaid with gold and silver; but they are false and cannot speak. [9]People[j] take gold and make crowns for the heads of their gods, as they would for a girl who loves ornaments; [10]and sometimes the priests secretly take gold and silver from their gods and spend it upon themselves, [11]and even give some of it to the harlots in the brothel. They deck their gods[k] out with garments like men—these gods of silver and gold and wood, [12]which cannot save themselves from rust and corrosion. When they have been dressed in purple robes, [13]their faces are wiped because of the dust from the temple, which is

thick upon them. [14]Like a local ruler the god[l] holds a scepter, though unable to destroy any one who offends it. [15]It has a dagger in its right hand, and has an axe; but it cannot save itself from war and robbers. [16]Therefore they evidently are not gods; so do not fear them.

17 For just as one's dish is useless when it is broken, so are the gods of the heathen,[m] when they have been set up in the temples. Their eyes are full of the dust raised by the feet of those who enter. [18]And just as the gates are shut on every side upon a man who has offended a king, as though he were sentenced to death, so the priests make their temples secure with doors and locks and bars, in order that they may not be plundered by robbers. [19]They light lamps, even more than they light for themselves, though their gods[n] can see none of them. [20]They are[o] just like a beam of the temple, but men say their hearts have melted, when worms from the earth devour them and their robes. They do not notice [21]when their faces have been blackened by the smoke of the temple. [22]Bats, swallows, and birds light on their bodies and heads; and so do cats. [23]From this you will know that they are not gods; so do not fear them.

24 As for the gold which they wear for beauty—they will not shine unless some one wipes off the rust; for even when they were being cast, they had no feeling. [25]They are bought at any cost, but there is no breath in them. [26]Having no feet, they are carried on men's shoulders, revealing to mankind their worthlessness. [27]And those who serve them are ashamed because through them these gods[n] are made to stand, lest they fall to the ground. If any one sets one of them upright, it cannot move of itself; and if it is tipped over, it cannot straighten itself; but gifts are placed before them just as before the dead. [28]The priests sell the sacrifices that are offered to these gods[p] and use the money; and likewise their wives preserve some with salt, but give none to the poor or helpless. [29]Sacrifices to them may be touched by women in menstruation or at childbirth. Since you know by these things that they are not gods, do not fear them.

30 For why should they be called gods? Women serve meals for gods of silver and gold and wood; [31]and in their temples the priests sit with their clothes torn, their heads and beards shaved, and

---

[h] The King James Version prints *The Epistle of Jeremy* as Chapter 6 of the book of Baruch, and the chapter and verse numbers are here retained.
[i] Gk *for them.*
[j] Gk *They.*
[k] Gk *them.*
[l] Gk *he.*
[m] Gk *of them.*
[n] Gk *they.*
[o] Gk *It is.*
[p] Gk *to them.*

their heads uncovered. ³²They howl and shout before their gods as some do at a funeral feast for a man who has died. ³³The priests take some of the clothing of their gods q to clothe their wives and children. ³⁴Whether one does evil to them or good, they will not be able to repay it. They cannot set up a king or depose one. ³⁵Likewise they are not able to give either wealth or money; if one makes a vow to them and does not keep it, they will not require it. ³⁶They cannot save a man from death or rescue the weak from the strong. ³⁷They cannot restore sight to a blind man; they cannot rescue a man who is in distress. ³⁸They cannot take pity on a widow or do good to an orphan. ³⁹These things that are made of wood and overlaid with gold and silver are like stones from the mountain, and those who serve them will be put to shame. ⁴⁰Why then must any one think that they are gods, or call them gods?

Besides, even the Chalde´ans themselves dishonor them; ⁴¹for when they see a mute man, who cannot speak, they bring him and pray Bel r that the man may speak, as though Bel s were able to understand. ⁴²Yet they themselves cannot perceive this and abandon them, for they have no sense. ⁴³And the women, with cords about them, sit along the passageways, burning bran for incense; and when one of them is led off by one of the passersby and is lain with, she derides the woman next to her, because she was not as attractive as herself and her cord was not broken. ⁴⁴Whatever is done for them is false. Why then must any one think that they are gods, or call them gods?

45 They are made by carpenters and goldsmiths; they can be nothing but what the craftsmen wish them to be. ⁴⁶The men that make them will certainly not live very long themselves; how then can the things that are made by them be gods? ⁴⁷They have left only lies and reproach for those who come after. ⁴⁸For when war or calamity comes upon them, the priests consult together as to where they can hide themselves and their gods. t ⁴⁹How then can one fail to see that these are not gods, for they cannot save themselves from war or calamity? ⁵⁰Since they are made of wood and overlaid with gold and silver, it will afterward be known that they are false. ⁵¹It will be manifest to all the nations and kings that they are not gods but the work of men's hands, and that there is no work of God in them. ⁵²Who then can fail to know that they are not gods? u

53 For they cannot set up a king over a country or give rain to men. ⁵⁴They cannot judge their own cause or deliver one who is wronged, for they have no power; they are like crows between heaven and earth. ⁵⁵When fire breaks out in a temple of wooden gods overlaid with gold or silver, their priests will flee and escape, but the gods v will be burned in two like beams. ⁵⁶Be-

sides, they can offer no resistance to a king or any enemies. Why then must any one admit or think that they are gods?

57 Gods made of wood and overlaid with silver and gold are not able to save themselves from thieves and robbers. ⁵⁸Strong men will strip them of their gold and silver and of the robes they wear, and go off with this booty, and they will not be able to help themselves. ⁵⁹So it is better to be a king who shows his courage, or a household utensil that serves its owner's need, than to be these false gods; better even the door of a house that protects its contents, than these false gods; better also a wooden pillar in a palace, than these false gods.

60 For sun and moon and stars, shining and sent forth for service, are obedient. ⁶¹So also the lightning, when it flashes, is widely seen; and the wind likewise blows in every land. ⁶²When God commands the clouds to go over the whole world, they carry out his command. ⁶³And the fire sent from above to consume mountains and woods does what it is ordered. But these idols w are not to be compared with them in appearance or power. ⁶⁴Therefore one must not think that they are gods nor call them gods, for they are not able either to decide a case or to do good to men. ⁶⁵Since you know then that they are not gods, do not fear them.

66 For they can neither curse nor bless kings; ⁶⁷they cannot show signs in the heavens and x among the nations, or shine like the sun or give light like the moon. ⁶⁸The wild beasts are better than they are, for they can flee to cover and help themselves. ⁶⁹So we have no evidence whatever that they are gods; therefore do not fear them.

70 Like a scarecrow in a cucumber bed, that guards nothing, so are their gods of wood, overlaid with gold and silver. ⁷¹In the same way, their gods of wood, overlaid with gold and silver, are like a thorn bush in a garden, on which every bird sits; or like a dead body cast out in the darkness. ⁷²By the purple and linen y that rot upon them you will know that they are not gods; and they will finally themselves be consumed, and be a reproach in the land. ⁷³Better therefore is a just man who has no idols, for he will be far from reproach.

---

q Gk them.
r Or they bring Bel and pray.
s Gk he.
t Gk them.
u The Greek text of this verse is uncertain.
v Gk they.
w Gk these things.
x Other ancient authorities omit and.
y Cn: Gk marble, Syr silk.

THE BOOK OF

EZEKIEL

The Vision of the Four Living Creatures

1 In the thirtieth year, in the fourth month, on the fifth day of the month, as I was among the exiles by the river Che′bar, the heavens were opened, and I saw visions of God. ²On the fifth day of the month (it was the fifth year of the exile of King Jehoi′achin), ³the word of the Lord came to Ezek′iel the priest, the son of Buzi, in the land of the Chalde′ans by the river Che′bar; and the hand of the Lord was upon him there.

4 As I looked, behold, a stormy wind came out of the north, and a great cloud, with brightness round about it, and fire flashing forth continually, and in the midst of the fire, as it were gleaming bronze. ⁵And from the midst of it came the likeness of four living creatures. * And this was their appearance: they had the form of men, ⁶but each had four faces, and each of them had four wings. ⁷Their legs were straight, and the soles of their feet were like the sole of a calf's foot; and they sparkled like burnished bronze. ⁸Under their wings on their four sides they had human hands. And the four had their faces and their wings thus: ⁹their wings touched one another; they went every one straight forward, without turning as they went. ¹⁰As for the likeness of their faces, each had the face of a man in front; ᵃ the four had the face of a lion on the right side, the four had the face of an ox on the left side, and the four had the face of an eagle at the back. ᵇ ¹¹Such were their faces. And their wings were spread out above; each creature had two wings, each of which touched the wing of another, while two covered their bodies. ¹²And each went straight forward; wherever the spirit would go, they went, without turning as they went. ¹³In the midst ᶜ of the living creatures there was something that looked like burning coals of fire, like torches moving back and forth among the living creatures; and the fire was bright, and out of the fire went forth lightning. ¹⁴And the living creatures darted back and forth, like a flash of lightning.

15 Now as I looked at the living creatures, I saw a wheel upon the earth beside the living creatures, one for each of the four of them. ᵈ ¹⁶As for the appearance of the wheels and their construction: their appearance was like the gleaming of a chrysolite; and the four had the same likeness, their construction being as it were a wheel within a wheel. ¹⁷When they went, they went in any of their four directions ᵉ without turning as they went. ¹⁸The four wheels had rims and they had spokes; ᶠ and their rims were full of eyes round about. ¹⁹And when the living creatures went, the wheels went beside them; and when the living creatures rose from the earth, the wheels rose. ²⁰Wherever the spirit would go, they went, and the wheels rose along with them; for the spirit of the living creatures was in the wheels. ²¹When those went, these went; and when those stood, these stood; and when those rose from the earth, the wheels rose along with them; for the spirit of the living creatures was in the wheels.

22 Over the heads of the living creatures there was the likeness of a firmament, shining like crystal, ᵍ spread out above their heads. ²³And under the firmament their wings were stretched out straight, one toward another; and each creature had two wings covering its body. † ²⁴And when they went, I heard the sound of their wings like the sound of many waters, like the thunder of the Almighty, a sound of tumult like the sound of a host; when they stood still, they let down their wings. ²⁵And there came a voice from above the firmament over their heads; when they stood still, they let down their wings.

The beginning of Ezekiel's ministry overlapped the end of that of Jeremiah and the prophet is concerned with the same evils. But his style and matter are very different. Ezekiel was a priest and mainly concerned with the temple worship and the observances of the law. His description of the future temple should be compared with that in Rev 21. Ezekiel performs a great variety of symbolic actions—as did Jeremiah on a smaller scale. Ezekiel's visions make one think of apocalyptic writing, e.g., Daniel and Revelation. He does not enlarge greatly on Messianic themes. He speaks of a new covenant (16:60) and, like Jeremiah, of personal responsibility (chapter 18). Above all, he insists on the need for interior renewal, and thus prepares the way for the teaching of Christ.

ᵃ Cn: Heb lacks *in front*.
ᵇ Cn: Heb lacks *at the back*.
ᶜ Gk Old Latin: Heb *And the likeness of*.
ᵈ Heb *of their faces*.
ᵉ Heb *on their four sides*.
ᶠ Cn: Heb uncertain.
ᵍ Gk: Heb *awesome crystal*.
1:1: Rev 19:11.
1:5, 18: Rev 4:6.
1:10: Rev 4:7.
1:13: Rev 4:5.
1:18: Ezek 10:12; Rev 4:8.
1:24: Ezek 43:2; Rev 1:15; 14:2; 19:6.
* 1:5, *four living creatures:* The description recalls the Assyrian *karibu* statues of animals with human heads guarding the palace at Nineveh. Here these creatures are pressed into the service of Yahweh. They are met again in Rev 4:6–8. The point of the vision is that Yahweh is not tied to Jerusalem and could follow his people into exile.
† 1:23: cf. the cherubim over the ark (Ex 25:20–22; 1 Sam 4:4).

The Glory of the Lord

26 And above the firmament over their heads there was the likeness of a throne, in appearance like sapphire;[h] and seated above the likeness of a throne was a likeness as it were of a human form. [27]And upward from what had the appearance of his loins I saw as it were gleaming bronze, like the appearance of fire enclosed round about; and downward from what had the appearance of his loins I saw as it were the appearance of fire, and there was brightness round about him.[i] [28]Like the appearance of the bow that is in the cloud on the day of rain, so was the appearance of the brightness round about.

Such was the appearance of the likeness of the glory of the LORD.[*] And when I saw it, I fell upon my face, and I heard the voice of one speaking.

2 And he said to me, "Son of man, stand upon your feet, and I will speak with you." [2]And when he spoke to me, the Spirit entered into me and set me upon my feet; and I heard him speaking to me. [3]And he said to me, "Son of man, I send you to the sons of Israel, to a nation[j] of rebels, who have rebelled against me; they and their fathers have transgressed against me to this very day. [4]The people also are impudent and stubborn: I send you to them; and you shall say to them, 'Thus says the Lord GOD.' [5]And whether they hear or refuse to hear (for they are a rebellious house) they will know that there has been a prophet among them. [6]And you, son of man, be not afraid of them, nor be afraid of their words, though briers and thorns are with you and you sit upon scorpions; be not afraid of their words, nor be dismayed at their looks, for they are a rebellious house. [7]And you shall speak my words to them, whether they hear or refuse to hear; for they are a rebellious house.

The Vision of the Scroll

8 "But you, son of man, hear what I say to you; be not rebellious like that rebellious house; open your mouth, and eat what I give you." [9]And when I looked, behold, a hand was stretched out to me, and behold, a written scroll was in it; [10]and he spread it before me; and it had writing on the front and on the back, and there were written on it words of lamentation and mourning and woe.

3 [1]And he said to me, "Son of man, eat what is offered to you; eat this scroll, and go, speak to the house of Israel." [2]So I opened my mouth, and he gave me the scroll to eat. [3]And he said to me, "Son of man, eat this scroll that I give you and fill your stomach with it." Then I ate it; and it was in my mouth as sweet as honey.

4 And he said to me, "Son of man, go, get you to the house of Israel, and speak with my words to them. [5]For you are not sent to a people of foreign speech and a hard language, but to the house of Israel— [6]not to many peoples of foreign speech and a hard language, whose words you cannot understand. Surely, if I sent you to such, they would listen to you. [7]But the house of Israel will not listen to you; for they are not willing to listen to me; because all the house of Israel are of a hard forehead and of a stubborn heart. [8]Behold, I have made your face hard against their faces, and your forehead hard against their foreheads. [9]Like adamant harder than flint have I made your forehead; fear them not, nor be dismayed at their looks, for they are a rebellious house." [10]Moreover he said to me, "Son of man, all my words that I shall speak to you receive in your heart, and hear with your ears. [11]And go, get you to the exiles, to your people, and say to them, 'Thus says the Lord GOD'; whether they hear or refuse to hear."

Ezekiel at the River Chebar

12 Then the Spirit lifted me up, and as the glory of the LORD arose[k] from its place, I heard behind me the sound of a great earthquake; [13]it was the sound of the wings of the living creatures as they touched one another, and the sound of the wheels beside them, that sounded like a great earthquake. [14]The Spirit lifted me up and took me away, and I went in bitterness in the heat of my spirit, the hand of the LORD being strong upon me; [15]and I came to the exiles at Tela′bib, who dwelt by the river Che′bar.[l] And I sat there overwhelmed among them seven days.

16 And at the end of seven days, the word of the LORD came to me: [17]"Son of man, I have made you a watchman for the house of Israel; whenever you hear a word from my mouth, you shall give them warning from me. [18]If I say to the wicked, 'You shall surely die,' and you give him no warning, nor speak to warn the wicked from his wicked way, in order to save his life, that wicked man shall die in his iniquity; but his blood I will require at your hand. [19]But if you warn the wicked, and he does not turn from his wickedness, or from his wicked way, he shall die in his iniquity; but you will have saved your life. [20]Again, if a righteous man turns from his righteousness and commits iniquity, and I lay a stumbling block before him, he shall die; because you have not warned him, he shall die for his sin, and his righteous deeds which he has done shall not be remembered; but his blood I will require at your hand. [21]Nevertheless if you warn the righteous man not to sin, and he does not sin, he shall surely live,

---

[h] Heb *lapis lazuli*.
[i] Or *it*.
[j] Syr: Heb *nations*.
[k] Cn: Heb *blessed be the glory of the* LORD.
[l] Heb *Chebar, and to where they dwelt*. Another reading is *Chebar, and I sat where they sat*.
1:26: Rev 1:13; 4:2.
2:8–3:3: Rev 5:1; 10:8–10.
3:16–21: Ezek 33:1–9.
[*] **1:28**, *the glory of the* LORD: The luminous cloud, or shekinah (Ex 24:16), that normally dwelt in the temple.

because he took warning; and you will have saved your life."

Ezekiel Bound and Silenced

22 And the hand of the Lord was there upon me; and he said to me, "Arise, go forth into the plain,[m] and there I will speak with you." 23So I arose and went forth into the plain;[m] and behold, the glory of the Lord stood there, like the glory which I had seen by the river Che'bar; and I fell on my face. 24But the Spirit entered into me, and set me upon my feet; and he spoke with me and said to me, "Go, shut yourself within your house. 25And you, O son of man, behold, cords will be placed upon you, and you shall be bound with them, so that you cannot go out among the people; 26and I will make your tongue cleave to the roof of your mouth, so that you shall be mute and unable to reprove them; for they are a rebellious house. 27But when I speak with you, I will open your mouth, and you shall say to them, 'Thus says the Lord God'; he that will hear, let him hear; and he that will refuse to hear, let him refuse; for they are a rebellious house.

A Brick: The Siege of Jerusalem Portrayed

4 "And you, O son of man, take a brick and lay it before you, and portray upon it a city, even Jerusalem; 2and put siegeworks against it, and build a siege wall against it, and cast up a mound against it; set camps also against it, and plant battering rams against it round about. 3And take an iron plate, and place it as an iron wall between you and the city; and set your face toward it, and let it be in a state of siege, and press the siege against it. This is a sign for the house of Israel.

4 "Then lie upon your left side, and I will lay the punishment of the house of Israel upon you;[n] for the number of the days that you lie upon it, you shall bear their punishment. 5For I assign to you a number of days, three hundred and ninety days, equal to the number of the years of their punishment; so long shall you bear the punishment of the house of Israel. 6And when you have completed these, you shall lie down a second time, but on your right side, and bear the punishment of the house of Judah; forty days I assign you, a day for each year. 7And you shall set your face toward the siege of Jerusalem, with your arm bared; and you shall prophesy against the city. 8And behold, I will put cords upon you, so that you cannot turn from one side to the other, till you have completed the days of your siege.

9 "And you, take wheat and barley, beans and lentils, millet and spelt, and put them into a single vessel, and make bread of them. During the number of days that you lie upon your side, three hundred and ninety days, you shall eat it. 10And the food which you eat shall be by weight, twenty shekels a day; once a day you shall eat it. 11And water you shall drink by measure, the sixth part

of a hin; once a day you shall drink. 12And you shall eat it as a barley cake, baking it in their sight on human dung." 13And the Lord said, "Thus shall the people of Israel eat their bread unclean, among the nations where I will drive them." 14Then I said, "Ah, Lord God! behold, I have never defiled myself; from my youth up till now I have never eaten what died of itself or was torn by beasts, nor has foul flesh come into my mouth." 15Then he said to me, "See, I will let you have cow's dung instead of human dung, on which you may prepare your bread." 16Moreover he said to me, "Son of man, behold, I will break the staff of bread in Jerusalem; they shall eat bread by weight and with fearfulness; and they shall drink water by measure and in dismay. 17I will do this that they may lack bread and water, and look at one another in dismay, and waste away under their punishment.

A Sharp Sword

5 "And you, O son of man, take a sharp sword; use it as a barber's razor and pass it over your head and your beard; then take balances for weighing, and divide the hair. 2A third part you shall burn in the fire in the midst of the city, when the days of the siege are completed; and a third part you shall take and strike with the sword round about the city; and a third part you shall scatter to the wind, and I will unsheathe the sword after them. 3And you shall take from these a small number, and bind them in the skirts of your robe. 4And of these again you shall take some, and cast them into the fire, and burn them in the fire; from there a fire will come forth into all the house of Israel. 5Thus says the Lord God: This is Jerusalem; I have set her in the center of the nations, with countries round about her. 6And she has wickedly rebelled against my ordinances[o] more than the nations, and against my statutes more than the countries round about her, by rejecting my ordinances and not walking in my statutes. 7Therefore thus says the Lord God: Because you are more turbulent than the nations that are round about you, and have not walked in my statutes or kept my ordinances, but have acted[p] according to the ordinances of the nations that are round about you; 8therefore thus says the Lord God: Behold, I, even I, am against you; and I will execute judgments in the midst of you in the sight of the nations. 9And because of all your abominations I will do with you what I have never yet done, and the like of which I will never do again. 10Therefore fathers shall eat their sons in the midst of you, and sons shall eat their fathers; and I will execute judgments on you, and any of you who

---

[m] Or valley.
[n] Cn: Heb you shall lay ... upon it.
[o] Or changed my ordinances into wickedness.
[p] Another reading is and have not acted.

survive I will scatter to all the winds. [11]Wherefore, as I live, says the Lord God, surely, because you have defiled my sanctuary with all your detestable things and with all your abominations, therefore I will cut you down; [q] my eye will not spare, and I will have no pity. [12]A third part of you shall die of pestilence and be consumed with famine in the midst of you; a third part shall fall by the sword round about you; and a third part I will scatter to all the winds and will unsheathe the sword after them.

[13] "Thus shall my anger spend itself, and I will vent my fury upon them and satisfy myself; and they shall know that I, the Lord, have spoken in my jealousy, when I spend my fury upon them. [14]Moreover I will make you a desolation and an object of reproach among the nations round about you and in the sight of all that pass by. [15]You shall be [r] a reproach and a taunt, a warning and a horror, to the nations round about you, when I execute judgments on you in anger and fury, and with furious chastisements—I, the Lord, have spoken— [16]when I loose against you [s] my deadly arrows of famine, arrows for destruction, which I will loose to destroy you, and when I bring more and more famine upon you, and break your staff of bread. [17]I will send famine and wild beasts against you, and they will rob you of your children; pestilence and blood shall pass through you; and I will bring the sword upon you. I, the Lord, have spoken."

Judgment against Idolatrous Israel

6 The word of the Lord came to me: [2]"Son of man, set your face toward the mountains of Israel, and prophesy against them, [3]and say, You mountains of Israel, hear the word of the Lord God! Thus says the Lord God to the mountains and the hills, to the ravines and the valleys: Behold, I, even I, will bring a sword upon you, and I will destroy your high places. [4]Your altars shall become desolate, and your incense altars shall be broken; and I will cast down your slain before your idols. [5]And I will lay the dead bodies of the people of Israel before their idols; and I will scatter your bones round about your altars. [6]Wherever you dwell your cities shall be waste and your high places ruined, so that your altars will be waste and ruined, [t] your idols broken and destroyed, your incense altars cut down, and your works wiped out. [7]And the slain shall fall in the midst of you, and you shall know that I am the Lord.

8 "Yet I will leave some of you alive. When you have among the nations some who escape the sword, and when you are scattered through the countries, [9]then those of you who escape will remember me among the nations where they are carried captive, when I have broken [u] their wanton heart which has departed from me, and blinded their eyes which turn wantonly after their idols; and they will be loathsome in their own sight for the evils which they have committed, for all their abominations. [10]And they shall know that I am the Lord; I have not said in vain that I would do this evil to them."

11 Thus says the Lord God: "Clap your hands, and stamp your foot, and say, Alas! because of all the evil abominations of the house of Israel; for they shall fall by the sword, by famine, and by pestilence. [12]He that is far off shall die of pestilence; and he that is near shall fall by the sword; and he that is left and is preserved shall die of famine. Thus I will spend my fury upon them. [13]And you shall know that I am the Lord, when their slain lie among their idols round about their altars, upon every high hill, on all the mountain tops, under every green tree, and under every leafy oak, wherever they offered pleasing odor to all their idols. [14]And I will stretch out my hand against them, and make the land desolate and waste, throughout all their habitations, from the wilderness to Riblah. [v] Then they will know that I am the Lord."

Impending Doom

7 The word of the Lord came to me: [2]"And you, O son of man, thus says the Lord God to the land of Israel: An end! The end has come upon the four corners of the land. [3]Now the end is upon you, and I will let loose my anger upon you, and will judge you according to your ways; and I will punish you for all your abominations. [4]And my eye will not spare you, nor will I have pity; but I will punish you for your ways, while your abominations are in your midst. Then you will know that I am the Lord.

5 "Thus says the Lord God: Disaster after disaster! Behold, it comes. [6]An end has come, the end has come; it has awakened against you. Behold, it comes. [7]Your doom [w] has come to you, O inhabitant of the land; the time has come, the day is near, a day of tumult, and not of joyful shouting upon the mountains. [8]Now I will soon pour out my wrath upon you, and spend my anger against you, and judge you according to your ways; and I will punish you for all your abominations. [9]And my eye will not spare, nor will I have pity; I will punish you according to your ways, while your abominations are in your midst. Then you will know that I am the Lord, who strike.

10 "Behold, the day! Behold, it comes! Your doom [w] has come, injustice [x] has blossomed, pride

---

[q] Another reading is *I will withdraw.*
[r] Gk Syr Vg Tg: Heb *And it shall be.*
[s] Heb *them.*
[t] Syr Vg Tg: Heb *and be made guilty.*
[u] Syr Vg Tg: Heb *I have been broken.*
[v] Another reading is *Diblah.*
[w] The meaning of the Hebrew word is uncertain.
[x] Or *the rod.*
6:9: Ezek 20:43; 36:31.
7:2: Rev 7:1; 20:8.

has budded. [11]Violence has grown up into a rod of wickedness; none of them shall remain, nor their abundance, nor their wealth; neither shall there be preeminence among them. [y] [12]The time has come, the day draws near. Let not the buyer rejoice, nor the seller mourn, for wrath [z] is upon all their multitude. [13]For the seller shall not return to what he has sold, while they live. For wrath is upon all their multitude; it shall not turn back; and because of his iniquity, none can maintain his life. [a]

14 "They have blown the trumpet and made all ready; but none goes to battle, for my wrath is upon all their multitude. [15]The sword is without, pestilence and famine are within; he that is in the field dies by the sword; and him that is in the city famine and pestilence devour. [16]And if any survivors escape, they will be on the mountains, like doves of the valleys, all of them moaning, every one over his iniquity. [17]All hands are feeble, and all knees weak as water. [18]They clothe themselves with sackcloth, and horror covers them; shame is upon all faces, and baldness on all their heads. [19]They cast their silver into the streets, and their gold is like an unclean thing; their silver and gold are not able to deliver them in the day of the wrath of the LORD; they cannot satisfy their hunger or fill their stomachs with it. For it was the stumbling block of their iniquity. [20]Their [b] beautiful ornament they used for vainglory, and they made their abominable images and their detestable things of it; therefore I will make it an unclean thing to them. [21]And I will give it into the hands of foreigners for a prey, and to the wicked of the earth for a spoil; and they shall profane it. [22]I will turn my face from them, that they may profane my precious [c] place; robbers shall enter and profane it, [23]and make a desolation. [d]

"Because the land is full of bloody crimes and the city is full of violence, [24]I will bring the worst of the nations to take possession of their houses; I will put an end to their proud might, and their holy places shall be profaned. [25]When anguish comes, they will seek peace, but there shall be none. [26]Disaster comes upon disaster, rumor follows rumor; they seek a vision from the prophet, but the law perishes from the priest, and counsel from the elders. [27]The king mourns, the prince is wrapped in despair, and the hands of the people of the land are palsied by terror. According to their way I will do to them, and according to their own judgments I will judge them; and they shall know that I am the LORD."

Vision of Abominations in the Temple

8 In the sixth year, in the sixth month, on the fifth day of the month, as I sat in my house, with the elders of Judah sitting before me, the hand of the Lord GOD fell there upon me. [2]Then I beheld a form that had the appearance of a man; [e]

below what appeared to be his loins it was fire, and above his loins it was like the appearance of brightness, like gleaming bronze. [3]He put forth the form of a hand, and took me by a lock of my head; and the Spirit lifted me up between earth and heaven, and brought me in visions of God to Jerusalem, to the entrance of the gateway of the inner court that faces north, where was the seat of the image of jealousy, which provokes to jealousy. [4]And behold, the glory of the God of Israel was there, like the vision that I saw in the plain.

5 Then he said to me, "Son of man, lift up your eyes now in the direction of the north." So I lifted up my eyes toward the north, and behold, north of the altar gate, in the entrance, was this image of jealousy. [6]And he said to me, "Son of man, do you see what they are doing, the great abominations that the house of Israel are committing here, to drive me far from my sanctuary? But you will see still greater abominations."

7 And he brought me to the door of the court; and when I looked, behold, there was a hole in the wall. [8]Then said he to me, "Son of man, dig in the wall"; and when I dug in the wall, behold, there was a door. [9]And he said to me, "Go in, and see the vile abominations that they are committing here." [10]So I went in and saw; and there, portrayed upon the wall round about, were all kinds of creeping things, and loathsome beasts, and all the idols of the house of Israel. [11]And before them stood seventy men of the elders of the house of Israel, with Ja-azani'ah the son of Sha'phan standing among them. Each had his censer in his hand, and the smoke of the cloud of incense went up. [12]Then he said to me, "Son of man, have you seen what the elders of the house of Israel are doing in the dark, every man in his room [f] of pictures? For they say, 'The LORD does not see us, the LORD has forsaken the land.'" [13]He said also to me, "You will see still greater abominations which they commit."

14 Then he brought me to the entrance of the north gate of the house of the LORD; and behold, there sat women weeping for Tammuz.* [15]Then he said to me, "Have you seen this, O son of man? You will see still greater abominations than these."

16 And he brought me into the inner court of the house of the LORD; and behold, at the door of the temple of the LORD, between the porch and the altar, were about twenty-five men, with their

y The Hebrew of verse 11 is uncertain.
z Cn: Heb *vision*.
a Heb obscure.
b Syr Symmachus: Heb *Its*.
c Or *secret*.
d Cn: Heb *make the chain*.
e Gk: Heb *fire*.
f Gk Syr Vg Tg: Heb *rooms*.

* 8:14, *weeping for Tammuz*: A vegetation god known as Adonis to the Phoenicians. He was supposed to die in the summer and come to life again in the spring. Women wept at the time of his departure to the underworld.

backs to the temple of the Lord, and their faces toward the east, worshiping the sun toward the east. [17]Then he said to me, "Have you seen this, O son of man? Is it too slight a thing for the house of Judah to commit the abominations which they commit here, that they should fill the land with violence, and provoke me further to anger? Behold, they put the branch to their nose. [18]Therefore I will deal in wrath; my eye will not spare, nor will I have pity; and though they cry in my ears with a loud voice, I will not hear them."

Vision of the Executioners

9 Then he cried in my ears with a loud voice, saying, "Draw near, you executioners of the city, each with his destroying weapon in his hand." [2]And behold, six men came from the direction of the upper gate, which faces north, every man with his weapon for slaughter in his hand, and with them was a man clothed in linen, with a writing case at his side. And they went in and stood beside the bronze altar.

3 Now the glory of the God of Israel had gone up from the cherubim on which it rested to the threshold of the house; and he called to the man clothed in linen, who had the writing case at his side. [4]And the Lord said to him, "Go through the city, through Jerusalem, and put a mark upon the foreheads of the men who sigh and groan over all the abominations that are committed in it." [5]And to the others he said in my hearing, "Pass through the city after him, and kill; your eye shall not spare, and you shall show no pity; [6]slay old men outright, young men and maidens, little children and women, but touch no one upon whom is the mark. And begin at my sanctuary." So they began with the elders who were before the house. [7]Then he said to them, "Defile the house, and fill the courts with the slain. Go forth." So they went forth, and killed in the city. [8]And while they were killing, and I was left alone, I fell upon my face, and cried, "Ah, Lord God! will you destroy all that remains of Israel in the outpouring of your wrath upon Jerusalem?"

9 Then he said to me, "The guilt of the house of Israel and Judah is exceedingly great; the land is full of blood, and the city full of injustice; for they say, 'The Lord has forsaken the land, and the Lord does not see.' [10]As for me, my eye will not spare, nor will I have pity, but I will repay their deeds upon their heads."

11 And behold, the man clothed in linen, with the writing case at his side, brought back word, saying, "I have done as you commanded me."

Divine Glory over the Cherubim

10 Then I looked, and behold, on the firmament that was over the heads of the cherubim there appeared above them something like a sapphire, in form resembling a throne. [2]And he said to the man clothed in linen, "Go in among the whirling wheels underneath the cherubim; fill your hands with burning coals from between the cherubim, and scatter them over the city."

And he went in before my eyes. [3]Now the cherubim were standing on the south side of the house, when the man went in; and a cloud filled the inner court. [4]And the glory of the Lord went up from the cherubim to the threshold of the house; and the house was filled with the cloud, and the court was full of the brightness of the glory of the Lord. [5]And the sound of the wings of the cherubim was heard as far as the outer court, like the voice of God Almighty when he speaks.

6 And when he commanded the man clothed in linen, "Take fire from between the whirling wheels, from between the cherubim," he went in and stood beside a wheel. [7]And a cherub stretched forth his hand from between the cherubim to the fire that was between the cherubim, and took some of it, and put it into the hands of the man clothed in linen, who took it and went out. [8]The cherubim appeared to have the form of a human hand under their wings.

9 And I looked, and behold, there were four wheels beside the cherubim, one beside each cherub; and the appearance of the wheels was like sparkling chrysolite. [10]And as for their appearance, the four had the same likeness, as if a wheel were within a wheel. [11]When they went, they went in any of their four directions [g] without turning as they went, but in whatever direction the front wheel faced the others followed without turning as they went. [12]And [h] their rims, and their spokes, [i] and the wheels were full of eyes round about—the wheels that the four of them had. [13]As for the wheels, they were called in my hearing the whirling wheels. [14]And every one had four faces: the first face was the face of the cherub, and the second face was the face of a man, and the third the face of a lion, and the fourth the face of an eagle.

15 And the cherubim mounted up. These were the living creatures that I saw by the river Che'-bar. [16]And when the cherubim went, the wheels went beside them; and when the cherubim lifted up their wings to mount up from the earth, the wheels did not turn from beside them. [17]When they stood still, these stood still, and when they mounted up, these mounted up with them; for the spirit of the living creatures [j] was in them.

18 Then the glory of the Lord went forth from the threshold of the house, and stood over the

[g] Heb *on their four sides.*
[h] Gk: Heb *And their whole body and.*
[i] Heb *spokes and their wings.*
[j] Or *of life.*
9:4, 6: 1 Pet 4:17; Rev 7:3; 9:4; 14:1.
10:1: Rev 4:2.
10:2: Rev 8:5.
10:12: Ezek 1:18; Rev 4:8.
10:14: Ezek 1:10; Rev 4:7.

cherubim. [19]And the cherubim lifted up their wings and mounted up from the earth in my sight as they went forth, with the wheels beside them; and they stood at the door of the east gate of the house of the Lord; and the glory of the God of Israel was over them.

20 These were the living creatures that I saw underneath the God of Israel by the river Che'-bar; and I knew that they were cherubim. [21]Each had four faces, and each four wings, and underneath their wings the semblance of human hands. [22]And as for the likeness of their faces, they were the very faces whose appearance I had seen by the river Che'bar. They went every one straight forward.

Judgment against the Wicked Counselors

11 The Spirit lifted me up, and brought me to the east gate of the house of the Lord, which faces east. And behold, at the door of the gateway there were twenty-five men; and I saw among them Ja-azani'ah the son of Azzur, and Pelati'ah the son of Bena'iah, princes of the people. [2]And he said to me, "Son of man, these are the men who devise iniquity and who give wicked counsel in this city; [3]who say, 'The time is not near [k] to build houses; this city is the caldron, and we are the flesh.' [4]Therefore prophesy against them, prophesy, O son of man."

5 And the Spirit of the Lord fell upon me, and he said to me, "Say, Thus says the Lord: So you think, O house of Israel; for I know the things that come into your mind. [6]You have multiplied your slain in this city, and have filled its streets with the slain. [7]Therefore thus says the Lord God: Your slain whom you have laid in the midst of it, they are the flesh, and this city is the caldron; but you shall be brought forth out of the midst of it. [8]You have feared the sword; and I will bring the sword upon you, says the Lord God. [9]And I will bring you forth out of the midst of it, and give you into the hands of foreigners, and execute judgments upon you. [10]You shall fall by the sword; I will judge you at the border of Israel; and you shall know that I am the Lord. [11]This city shall not be your caldron, nor shall you be the flesh in the midst of it; I will judge you at the border of Israel; [12]and you shall know that I am the Lord; for you have not walked in my statutes, nor executed my ordinances, but have acted according to the ordinances of the nations that are round about you."

13 And it came to pass, while I was prophesying, that Pelati'ah the son of Bena'iah died. Then I fell down upon my face, and cried with a loud voice, and said, "Ah, Lord God! will you make a full end of the remnant of Israel?"

God Will Restore Israel

14 And the word of the Lord came to me: [15]"Son of man, your brethren, even your brethren, your fellow exiles, [1] the whole house of Israel, all of them, are those of whom the inhabitants of Jerusalem have said, 'They have gone far from the Lord; to us this land is given for a possession.' [16]Therefore say, 'Thus says the Lord God: Though I removed them far off among the nations, and though I scattered them among the countries, yet I have been a sanctuary to them for a while [m] in the countries where they have gone.' [17]Therefore say, 'Thus says the Lord God: I will gather you from the peoples, and assemble you out of the countries where you have been scattered, and I will give you the land of Israel.' [18]And when they come there, they will remove from it all its detestable things and all its abominations. [19]And I will give them one [n] heart, and put a new spirit within them; I will take the stony heart out of their flesh and give them a heart of flesh, [20]that they may walk in my statutes and keep my ordinances and obey them; and they shall be my people, and I will be their God. [21]But as for those [o] whose heart goes after their detestable things and their abominations, I will repay their deeds upon their own heads, says the Lord God."

22 Then the cherubim lifted up their wings, with the wheels beside them; and the glory of the God of Israel was over them. [23]And the glory of the Lord went up from the midst of the city, and stood upon the mountain which is on the east side of the city. [24]And the Spirit lifted me up and brought me in the vision by the Spirit of God into Chalde'a, to the exiles. Then the vision that I had seen went up from me. [25]And I told the exiles all the things that the Lord had showed me.

Judah's Captivity Portrayed

12 The word of the Lord came to me: [2]"Son of man, you dwell in the midst of a rebellious house, who have eyes to see, but see not, who have ears to hear, but hear not; [3]for they are a rebellious house. Therefore, son of man, prepare for yourself an exile's baggage, and go into exile by day in their sight; you shall go like an exile from your place to another place in their sight. Perhaps they will understand, though [p] they are a rebellious house. [4]You shall bring out your baggage by day in their sight, as baggage for exile; and you shall go forth yourself at evening in their sight, as men do who must go into exile. [5]Dig through the wall in their sight, and go [q] out through it. [6]In their sight you shall lift the

---

[k] Or *Is not the time near . . . ?*

[1] Gk Syr: Heb *men of your kindred.*

[m] Or *in small measure.*

[n] Another reading is *a new.*

[o] Cn: Heb *To the heart of their detestable things and their abominations their heart goes.*

[p] Or *will see that.*

[q] Gk Syr Vg Tg: Heb *bring.*

11:19: Ezek 18:31; 36:26; 2 Cor 3:3.

12:2: Mk 8:18.

baggage upon your shoulder, and carry it out in the dark; you shall cover your face, that you may not see the land; for I have made you a sign for the house of Israel."

7 And I did as I was commanded. I brought out my baggage by day, as baggage for exile, and in the evening I dug through the wall with my own hands; I went forth in the dark, carrying my outfit upon my shoulder in their sight.

8 In the morning the word of the LORD came to me: [9]"Son of man, has not the house of Israel, the rebellious house, said to you, 'What are you doing?' [10]Say to them, 'Thus says the Lord GOD: This oracle concerns the prince in Jerusalem and all the house of Israel who are in it.' [r] [11]Say, 'I am a sign for you: as I have done, so shall it be done to them; they shall go into exile, into captivity.' [12]And the prince who is among them shall lift his baggage upon his shoulder in the dark, and shall go forth; he [s] shall dig through the wall and go [t] out through it; he shall cover his face, that he may not see the land with his eyes. [13]And I will spread my net over him, and he shall be taken in my snare; and I will bring him to Babylon in the land of the Chalde'ans, yet he shall not see it; and he shall die there. [14]And I will scatter toward every wind all who are round about him, his helpers [u] and all his troops; and I will unsheathe the sword after them. [15]And they shall know that I am the LORD, when I disperse them among the nations and scatter them through the countries. [16]But I will let a few of them escape from the sword, from famine and pestilence, that they may confess all their abominations among the nations where they go, and may know that I am the LORD."

Judgment Will Not Be Delayed

17 Moreover the word of the LORD came to me: [18]"Son of man, eat your bread with quaking, and drink water with trembling and with fearfulness; [19]and say of the people of the land, Thus says the Lord GOD concerning the inhabitants of Jerusalem in the land of Israel: They shall eat their bread with fearfulness, and drink water in dismay, because their land will be stripped of all it contains, on account of the violence of all those who dwell in it. [20]And the inhabited cities shall be laid waste, and the land shall become a desolation; and you shall know that I am the LORD."

21 And the word of the LORD came to me: [22]"Son of man, what is this proverb that you have about the land of Israel, saying, 'The days grow long, and every vision comes to nothing'? [23]Tell them therefore, 'Thus says the Lord GOD: I will put an end to this proverb, and they shall no more use it as a proverb in Israel.' But say to them, The days are at hand, and the fulfilment [v] of every vision. [24]For there shall be no more any false vision or flattering divination within the house of

Israel. [25]But I the LORD will speak the word which I will speak, and it will be performed. It will no longer be delayed, but in your days, O rebellious house, I will speak the word and perform it, says the Lord GOD."

26 Again the word of the LORD came to me: [27]"Son of man, behold, they of the house of Israel say, 'The vision that he sees is for many days hence, and he prophesies of times far off.' [28]Therefore say to them, Thus says the Lord GOD: None of my words will be delayed any longer, but the word which I speak will be performed, says the Lord GOD."

False Prophets Condemned

13 The word of the LORD came to me: [2]"Son of man, prophesy against the prophets of Israel, prophesy [w] and say to those who prophesy out of their own minds: 'Hear the word of the LORD!' [3]Thus says the Lord GOD, Woe to the foolish prophets who follow their own spirit, and have seen nothing! [4]Your prophets have been like foxes among ruins, O Israel. [5]You have not gone up into the breaches, or built up a wall for the house of Israel, that it might stand in battle in the day of the LORD. [6]They have spoken falsehood and divined a lie; they say, 'Says the LORD,' when the LORD has not sent them, and yet they expect him to fulfil their word. [7]Have you not seen a delusive vision, and uttered a lying divination, whenever you have said, 'Says the LORD,' although I have not spoken?"

8 Therefore thus says the Lord God: "Because you have uttered delusions and seen lies, therefore behold, I am against you, says the Lord GOD. [9]My hand will be against the prophets who see delusive visions and who give lying divinations; they shall not be in the council of my people, nor be enrolled in the register of the house of Israel, nor shall they enter the land of Israel; and you shall know that I am the Lord GOD. [10]Because, yes, because they have misled my people, saying, 'Peace,' when there is no peace; and because, when the people build a wall, these prophets daub it with whitewash; [11]say to those who daub it with whitewash that it shall fall! There will be a deluge of rain, [x] great hailstones will fall, and a stormy wind break out; [12]and when the wall falls, will it not be said to you, 'Where is the daubing with which you daubed it?' [13]Therefore thus says the Lord GOD: I will make a stormy wind break out in my wrath; and there shall be a deluge of rain in my anger, and great hailstones in wrath to destroy it. [14]And I will break down the wall that you

---

[r] Heb *in the midst of them.*
[s] Gk Syr: Heb *they.*
[t] Gk Syr Tg: Heb *bring.*
[u] Gk Syr Tg: Heb *his help.*
[v] Heb *word.*
[w] Gk: Heb *who prophesy.*
[x] Heb *rain and you.*

have daubed with whitewash, and bring it down to the ground, so that its foundation will be laid bare; when it falls, you shall perish in the midst of it; and you shall know that I am the LORD. ¹⁵Thus will I spend my wrath upon the wall, and upon those who have daubed it with whitewash; and I will say to you, The wall is no more, nor those who daubed it, ¹⁶the prophets of Israel who prophesied concerning Jerusalem and saw visions of peace for her, when there was no peace, says the Lord GOD.

17 "And you, son of man, set your face against the daughters of your people, who prophesy out of their own minds; prophesy against them ¹⁸and say, Thus says the Lord GOD: Woe to the women who sew magic bands upon all wrists, and make veils for the heads of persons of every stature, in the hunt for souls! Will you hunt down souls belonging to my people, and keep other souls alive for your profit? ¹⁹You have profaned me among my people for handfuls of barley and for pieces of bread, putting to death persons who should not die and keeping alive persons who should not live, by your lies to my people, who listen to lies.

20 "Wherefore thus says the Lord GOD: Behold, I am against your magic bands with which you hunt the souls,^y and I will tear them from your arms; and I will let the souls that you hunt go free^z like birds. ²¹Your veils also I will tear off, and deliver my people out of your hand, and they shall be no more in your hand as prey; and you shall know that I am the LORD. ²²Because you have disheartened the righteous falsely, although I have not disheartened him, and you have encouraged the wicked, that he should not turn from his wicked way to save his life; ²³therefore you shall no more see delusive visions nor practice divination; I will deliver my people out of your hand. Then you will know that I am the LORD."

Idolatry Condemned

14 Then came certain of the elders of Israel to me; and sat before me. ²And the word of the LORD came to me: ³"Son of man, these men have taken their idols into their hearts, and set the stumbling block of their iniquity before their faces; should I let myself be inquired of at all by them? ⁴Therefore speak to them, and say to them, Thus says the Lord GOD: Any man of the house of Israel who takes his idols into his heart and sets the stumbling block of his iniquity before his face, and yet comes to the prophet, I the LORD will answer him myself^a because of the multitude of his idols, ⁵that I may lay hold of the hearts of the house of Israel, who are all estranged from me through their idols.

6 "Therefore say to the house of Israel, Thus says the Lord GOD: Repent and turn away from your idols; and turn away your faces from all your abominations. ⁷For any one of the house of

Israel, or of the strangers that sojourn in Israel, who separates himself from me, taking his idols into his heart and putting the stumbling block of his iniquity before his face, and yet comes to a prophet to inquire for himself of me, I the LORD will answer him myself; ⁸and I will set my face against that man, I will make him a sign and a byword and cut him off from the midst of my people; and you shall know that I am the LORD. ⁹And if the prophet be deceived and speak a word, I, the LORD, have deceived that prophet, and I will stretch out my hand against him, and will destroy him from the midst of my people Israel. ¹⁰And they shall bear their punishment—the punishment of the prophet and the punishment of the inquirer shall be alike— ¹¹that the house of Israel may go no more astray from me, nor defile themselves any more with all their transgressions, but that they may be my people and I may be their God, says the Lord GOD."

12 * And the word of the LORD came to me: ¹³"Son of man, when a land sins against me by acting faithlessly, and I stretch out my hand against it, and break its staff of bread and send famine upon it, and cut off from it man and beast, ¹⁴even if these three men, Noah, Daniel,† and Job, were in it, they would deliver but their own lives by their righteousness, says the Lord GOD. ¹⁵If I cause wild beasts to pass through the land, and they ravage it, and it be made desolate, so that no man may pass through because of the beasts; ¹⁶even if these three men were in it, as I live, says the Lord GOD, they would deliver neither sons nor daughters; they alone would be delivered, but the land would be desolate. ¹⁷Or if I bring a sword upon that land, and say, Let a sword go through the land; and I cut off from it man and beast; ¹⁸though these three men were in it, as I live, says the Lord GOD, they would deliver neither sons nor daughters, but they alone would be delivered. ¹⁹Or if I send a pestilence into that land, and pour out my wrath upon it with blood, to cut off from it man and beast; ²⁰even if Noah, Daniel, and Job were in it, as I live, says the Lord GOD, they would deliver neither son nor daughter; they would deliver but their own lives by their righteousness.

21 "For thus says the Lord GOD: How much more when I send upon Jerusalem my four sore

---

^y Gk Syr: Heb *souls for birds.*
^z Cn: Heb *the souls.*
^a Cn Compare Tg: Heb uncertain.
14:21: Rev 6:8.
* **14:12–23:** The Lord stresses individual responsibility rather than collective responsibility. It had been taken for granted that some just men would have to suffer in a group or city with the guilty majority.
† **14:14,** *Daniel:* It is possible that this refers to Danel, an ancient Phoenician sage known to us from the Ras Shamra literature. It is unlikely that Ezekiel would have been speaking of Daniel the prophet as the other names in this passage are both of more ancient personages. Moreover, the spelling of the name in the book of Ezekiel is different from the spelling used in the book of Daniel.

acts of judgment, sword, famine, evil beasts, and pestilence, to cut off from it man and beast! [22]Yet, if there should be left in it any survivors to lead out sons and daughters, when they come forth to you, and you see their ways and their doings, you will be consoled for the evil that I have brought upon Jerusalem, for all that I have brought upon it. [23]They will console you, when you see their ways and their doings; and you shall know that I have not done without cause all that I have done in it, says the Lord God."

The Useless Vine

15 And the word of the Lord came to me: [2]"Son of man, how does the wood of the vine surpass any wood, the vine branch which is among the trees of the forest? [3]Is wood taken from it to make anything? Do men take a peg from it to hang any vessel on? [4]Behold, it is given to the fire for fuel; when the fire has consumed both ends of it, and the middle of it is charred, is it useful for anything? [5]Behold, when it was whole, it was used for nothing; how much less, when the fire has consumed it and it is charred, can it ever be used for anything! [6]Therefore thus says the Lord God: Like the wood of the vine among the trees of the forest, which I have given to the fire for fuel, so will I give up the inhabitants of Jerusalem. [7]And I will set my face against them; though they escape from the fire, the fire shall yet consume them; and you will know that I am the Lord, when I set my face against them. [8]And I will make the land desolate, because they have acted faithlessly, says the Lord God."

God's Unfaithful Bride

16 Again the word of the Lord came to me: [2]"Son of man, make known to Jerusalem her abominations, [3]and say, Thus says the Lord God to Jerusalem: Your origin and your birth are of the land of the Canaanites; your father was an Am'orite, and your mother a Hittite. [4]And as for your birth, on the day you were born your navel string was not cut, nor were you washed with water to cleanse you, nor rubbed with salt, nor swathed with bands. [5]No eye pitied you, to do any of these things to you out of compassion for you; but you were cast out on the open field, for you were abhorred, on the day that you were born.

6 "And when I passed by you, and saw you weltering in your blood, I said to you in your blood, 'Live, [7]and grow up[b] like a plant of the field.' And you grew up and became tall and arrived at full maidenhood;[c] your breasts were formed, and your hair had grown; yet you were naked and bare.

8 "When I passed by you again and looked upon you, behold, you were at the age for love; and I spread my skirt over you, and covered your nakedness: yes, I pledged myself to you and en-

tered into a covenant with you, says the Lord God, and you became mine. [9]Then I bathed you with water and washed off your blood from you, and anointed you with oil. [10]I clothed you also with embroidered cloth and shod you with leather, I wrapped you in fine linen and covered you with silk. [11]And I decked you with ornaments, and put bracelets on your arms, and a chain on your neck. [12]And I put a ring on your nose, and earrings in your ears, and a beautiful crown upon your head. [13]Thus you were decked with gold and silver; and your clothing was of fine linen, and silk, and embroidered cloth; you ate fine flour and honey and oil. You grew exceedingly beautiful, and came to regal estate. [14]And your renown went forth among the nations because of your beauty, for it was perfect through the splendor which I had bestowed upon you, says the Lord God.

15 "But you trusted in your beauty, and played the harlot because of your renown, and lavished your harlotries on any passer-by. [16]You took some of your garments, and made for yourself gaily decked shrines, and on them played the harlot; the like has never been, nor ever shall be. [17]You also took your fair jewels of my gold and of my silver, which I had given you, and made for yourself images of men, and with them played the harlot; [18]and you took your embroidered garments to cover them, and set my oil and my incense before them. [19]Also my bread which I gave you—I fed you with fine flour and oil and honey—you set before them for a pleasing odor, says the Lord God.[d] [20]And you took your sons and your daughters, whom you had borne to me, and these you sacrificed to them to be devoured. Were your harlotries so small a matter [21]that you slaughtered my children and delivered them up as an offering by fire to them? [22]And in all your abominations and your harlotries you did not remember the days of your youth, when you were naked and bare, weltering in your blood.

23 "And after all your wickedness (woe, woe to you! says the Lord God), [24]you built yourself a vaulted chamber, and made yourself a lofty place in every square; [25]at the head of every street you built your lofty place and prostituted your beauty, offering yourself to any passer-by, and multiplying your harlotry. [26]You also played the harlot with the Egyptians, your lustful neighbors, multiplying your harlotry, to provoke me to anger. [27]Behold, therefore, I stretched out my hand against you, and diminished your allotted portion, and delivered you to the greed of your enemies, the daughters of the Philis'tines, who were ashamed

---

[b] Gk Syr: Heb *I made you a myriad.*
[c] Cn: Heb *ornament of ornaments.*
[d] Syr: Heb *and it was, says the Lord God.*
16:3: Ezek 16:45.

their heads uncovered. [32]They howl and shout before their gods as some do at a funeral feast for a man who has died. [33]The priests take some of the clothing of their gods [q] to clothe their wives and children. [34]Whether one does evil to them or good, they will not be able to repay it. They cannot set up a king or depose one. [35]Likewise they are not able to give either wealth or money; if one makes a vow to them and does not keep it, they will not require it. [36]They cannot save a man from death or rescue the weak from the strong. [37]They cannot restore sight to a blind man; they cannot rescue a man who is in distress. [38]They cannot take pity on a widow or do good to an orphan. [39]These things that are made of wood and overlaid with gold and silver are like stones from the mountain, and those who serve them will be put to shame. [40]Why then must any one think that they are gods, or call them gods?

Besides, even the Chalde'ans themselves dishonor them; [41]for when they see a mute man, who cannot speak, they bring him and pray Bel [r] that the man may speak, as though Bel [s] were able to understand. [42]Yet they themselves cannot perceive this and abandon them, for they have no sense. [43]And the women, with cords about them, sit along the passageways, burning bran for incense; and when one of them is led off by one of the passersby and is lain with, she derides the woman next to her, because she was not as attractive as herself and her cord was not broken. [44]Whatever is done for them is false. Why then must any one think that they are gods, or call them gods?

45 They are made by carpenters and goldsmiths; they can be nothing but what the craftsmen wish them to be. [46]The men that make them will certainly not live very long themselves; how then can the things that are made by them be gods? [47]They have left only lies and reproach for those who come after. [48]For when war or calamity comes upon them, the priests consult together as to where they can hide themselves and their gods. [t] [49]How then can one fail to see that these are not gods, for they cannot save themselves from war or calamity? [50]Since they are made of wood and overlaid with gold and silver, it will afterward be known that they are false. [51]It will be manifest to all the nations and kings that they are not gods but the work of men's hands, and that there is no work of God in them. [52]Who then can fail to know that they are not gods? [u]

53 For they cannot set up a king over a country or give rain to men. [54]They cannot judge their own cause or deliver one who is wronged, for they have no power; they are like crows between heaven and earth. [55]When fire breaks out in a temple of wooden gods overlaid with gold or silver, their priests will flee and escape, but the gods [v] will be burned in two like beams. [56]Be-

sides, they can offer no resistance to a king or any enemies. Why then must any one admit or think that they are gods?

57 Gods made of wood and overlaid with silver and gold are not able to save themselves from thieves and robbers. [58]Strong men will strip them of their gold and silver and of the robes they wear, and go off with this booty, and they will not be able to help themselves. [59]So it is better to be a king who shows his courage, or a household utensil that serves its owner's need, than to be these false gods; better even the door of a house that protects its contents, than these false gods; better also a wooden pillar in a palace, than these false gods.

60 For sun and moon and stars, shining and sent forth for service, are obedient. [61]So also the lightning, when it flashes, is widely seen; and the wind likewise blows in every land. [62]When God commands the clouds to go over the whole world, they carry out his command. [63]And the fire sent from above to consume mountains and woods does what it is ordered. But these idols [w] are not to be compared with them in appearance or power. [64]Therefore one must not think that they are gods nor call them gods, for they are not able either to decide a case or to do good to men. [65]Since you know then that they are not gods, do not fear them.

66 For they can neither curse nor bless kings; [67]they cannot show signs in the heavens and [x] among the nations, or shine like the sun or give light like the moon. [68]The wild beasts are better than they are, for they can flee to cover and help themselves. [69]So we have no evidence whatever that they are gods; therefore do not fear them.

70 Like a scarecrow in a cucumber bed, that guards nothing, so are their gods of wood, overlaid with gold and silver. [71]In the same way, their gods of wood, overlaid with gold and silver, are like a thorn bush in a garden, on which every bird sits; or like a dead body cast out in the darkness. [72]By the purple and linen [y] that rot upon them you will know that they are not gods; and they will finally themselves be consumed, and be a reproach in the land. [73]Better therefore is a just man who has no idols, for he will be far from reproach.

---

[q] Gk them.
[r] Or they bring Bel and pray.
[s] Gk he.
[t] Gk them.
[u] The Greek text of this verse is uncertain.
[v] Gk they.
[w] Gk these things.
[x] Other ancient authorities omit and.
[y] Cn: Gk marble, Syr silk.

THE BOOK OF

EZEKIEL

The Vision of the Four Living Creatures

1 In the thirtieth year, in the fourth month, on the fifth day of the month, as I was among the exiles by the river Che'bar, the heavens were opened, and I saw visions of God. ²On the fifth day of the month (it was the fifth year of the exile of King Jehoi'achin), ³the word of the LORD came to Ezek'iel the priest, the son of Buzi, in the land of the Chalde'ans by the river Che'bar; and the hand of the LORD was upon him there.

4 As I looked, behold, a stormy wind came out of the north, and a great cloud, with brightness round about it, and fire flashing forth continually, and in the midst of the fire, as it were gleaming bronze. ⁵And from the midst of it came the likeness of four living creatures. * And this was their appearance: they had the form of men, ⁶but each had four faces, and each of them had four wings. ⁷Their legs were straight, and the soles of their feet were like the sole of a calf's foot; and they sparkled like burnished bronze. ⁸Under their wings on their four sides they had human hands. And the four had their faces and their wings thus: ⁹their wings touched one another; they went every one straight forward, without turning as they went. ¹⁰As for the likeness of their faces, each had the face of a man in front; [a] the four had the face of a lion on the right side, the four had the face of an ox on the left side, and the four had the face of an eagle at the back. [b] ¹¹Such were their faces. And their wings were spread out above; each creature had two wings, each of which touched the wing of another, while two covered their bodies. ¹²And each went straight forward; wherever the spirit would go, they went, without turning as they went. ¹³In the midst [c] of the living creatures there was something that looked like burning coals of fire, like torches moving back and forth among the living creatures; and the fire was bright, and out of the fire went forth lightning. ¹⁴And the living creatures darted back and forth, like a flash of lightning.

15 Now as I looked at the living creatures, I saw a wheel upon the earth beside the living creatures, one for each of the four of them. [d] ¹⁶As for the appearance of the wheels and their construction: their appearance was like the gleaming of a chrysolite; and the four had the same likeness, their construction being as it were a wheel within a wheel. ¹⁷When they went, they went in any of their four directions [e] without turning as they went. ¹⁸The four wheels had rims and they had spokes; [f] and their rims were full of eyes round about. ¹⁹And when the living creatures went, the wheels went beside them; and when the living creatures rose from the earth, the wheels rose. ²⁰Wherever the spirit would go, they went, and the wheels rose along with them; for the spirit of the living creatures was in the wheels. ²¹When those went, these went; and when those stood, these stood; and when those rose from the earth, the wheels rose along with them; for the spirit of the living creatures was in the wheels.

22 Over the heads of the living creatures there was the likeness of a firmament, shining like crystal, [g] spread out above their heads. ²³And under the firmament their wings were stretched out straight, one toward another; and each creature had two wings covering its body. † ²⁴And when they went, I heard the sound of their wings like the sound of many waters, like the thunder of the Almighty, a sound of tumult like the sound of a host; when they stood still, they let down their wings. ²⁵And there came a voice from above the firmament over their heads; when they stood still, they let down their wings.

[a] Cn: Heb lacks *in front.*
[b] Cn: Heb lacks *at the back.*
[c] Gk Old Latin: Heb *And the likeness of.*
[d] Heb *of their faces.*
[e] Heb *on their four sides.*
[f] Cn: Heb uncertain.
[g] Gk: Heb *awesome crystal.*
1:1: Rev 19:11.
1:5, 18: Rev 4:6.
1:10: Rev 4:7.
1:13: Rev 4:5.
1:18: Ezek 10:12; Rev 4:8.
1:24: Ezek 43:2; Rev 1:15; 14:2; 19:6.
* 1:5, *four living creatures:* The description recalls the Assyrian *karibu*: statues of animals with human heads guarding the palace at Nineveh. Here these creatures are pressed into the service of Yahweh. They are met again in Rev 4:6–8. The point of the vision is that Yahweh is not tied to Jerusalem and could follow his people into exile.
† 1:23: cf. the cherubim over the ark (Ex 25:20–22; 1 Sam 4:4).

dream, and we will show the interpretation." [5]The king answered the Chalde'ans, "The word from me is sure: if you do not make known to me the dream and its interpretation, you shall be torn limb from limb, and your houses shall be laid in ruins. [6]But if you show the dream and its interpretation, you shall receive from me gifts and rewards and great honor. Therefore show me the dream and its interpretation." [7]They answered a second time, "Let the king tell his servants the dream, and we will show its interpretation." [8]The king answered, "I know with certainty that you are trying to gain time, because you see that the word from me is sure [9]that if you do not make the dream known to me, there is but one sentence for you. You have agreed to speak lying and corrupt words before me till the times change. Therefore tell me the dream, and I shall know that you can show me its interpretation." [10]The Chalde'ans answered the king, "There is not a man on earth who can meet the king's demand; for no great and powerful king has asked such a thing of any magician or enchanter or Chalde'an. [11]The thing that the king asks is difficult, and none can show it to the king except the gods, whose dwelling is not with flesh."

[12] Because of this the king was angry and very furious, and commanded that all the wise men of Babylon be destroyed. [13]So the decree went forth that the wise men were to be slain, and they sought Daniel and his companions, to slay them. [14]Then Daniel replied with prudence and discretion to Ar'ioch, the captain of the king's guard, who had gone out to slay the wise men of Babylon; [15]he said to Ar'ioch, the king's captain, "Why is the decree of the king so severe?" Then Arioch made the matter known to Daniel. [16]And Daniel went in and besought the king to appoint him a time, that he might show to the king the interpretation.

God Reveals Nebuchadnezzar's Dream

[17] Then Daniel went to his house and made the matter known to Hanani'ah, Mish'a-el, and Azari'ah, his companions, [18]and told them to seek mercy of the God of heaven concerning this mystery, so that Daniel and his companions might not perish with the rest of the wise men of Babylon. [19]Then the mystery was revealed to Daniel in a vision of the night. Then Daniel blessed the God of heaven. [20]Daniel said:

"Blessed be the name of God for ever and ever.
   to whom belong wisdom and might.
[21]He changes times and seasons;
   he removes kings and sets up kings;
he gives wisdom to the wise
   and knowledge to those who have
      understanding;
[22]he reveals deep and mysterious things;
   he knows what is in the darkness,
   and the light dwells with him.

[23]To you, O God of my fathers,
   I give thanks and praise,
for you have given me wisdom and strength,
   and have now made known to me what we
      asked of you,
   for you have made known to us the king's
      matter."

Daniel Interprets the Dream

[24] Therefore Daniel went in to Ar'ioch, whom the king had appointed to destroy the wise men of Babylon; he went and said thus to him, "Do not destroy the wise men of Babylon; bring me in before the king, and I will show the king the interpretation."

[25] Then Ar'ioch brought in Daniel before the king in haste, and said thus to him: "I have found among the exiles from Judah a man who can make known to the king the interpretation." [26]The king said to Daniel, whose name was Belteshaz'zar, "Are you able to make known to me the dream that I have seen and its interpretation?" [27]Daniel answered the king, "No wise men, enchanters, magicians, or astrologers can show to the king the mystery which the king has asked, [28]but there is a God in heaven who reveals mysteries, and he has made known to King Nebuchadnez'zar what will be in the latter days. Your dream and the visions of your head as you lay in bed are these: [29]To you, O king, as you lay in bed came thoughts of what would be hereafter, and he who reveals mysteries made known to you what is to be. [30]But as for me, not because of any wisdom that I have more than all the living has this mystery been revealed to me, but in order that the interpretation may be made known to the king, and that you may know the thoughts of your mind.

[31] "You saw, O king, and behold, a great image. This image, mighty and of exceeding brightness, stood before you, and its appearance was frightening. [32]The head of this image was of fine gold, its breast and arms of silver, its belly and thighs of bronze, [33]its legs of iron, its feet partly of iron and partly of clay. [34]As you looked, a stone was cut out by no human hand, and it struck the image on its feet of iron and clay, and broke them in pieces; [35]then the iron, the clay, the bronze, the silver, and the gold, all together were broken in pieces, and became like the chaff of the summer threshing floors; and the wind carried them away, so that not a trace of them could be found. But the stone that struck the image became a great mountain and filled the whole earth.

[36] "This was the dream; now we will tell the king its interpretation. [37]You, O king, the king of kings, to whom the God of heaven has given the kingdom, the power, and the might, and the glory, [38]and into whose hand he has given, wherever they dwell, the sons of men, the beasts of the field, and the birds of the air, making you rule

over them all—you are the head of gold. ³⁹After you shall arise another kingdom inferior to you, and yet a third kingdom of bronze, which shall rule over all the earth. ⁴⁰And there shall be a fourth kingdom, strong as iron, because iron breaks to pieces and shatters all things; and like iron which crushes, it shall break and crush all these. ⁴¹And as you saw the feet and toes partly of potter's clay and partly of iron, it shall be a divided kingdom; but some of the firmness of iron shall be in it, just as you saw iron mixed with the miry clay. ⁴²And as the toes of the feet were partly iron and partly clay, so the kingdom shall be partly strong and partly brittle. ⁴³As you saw the iron mixed with miry clay, so they will mix with one another in marriage, ᵇ but they will not hold together, just as iron does not mix with clay. ⁴⁴And in the days of those kings the God of heaven will set up a kingdom which shall never be destroyed, nor shall its sovereignty be left to another people. It shall break in pieces all these kingdoms and bring them to an end, and it shall stand for ever; ⁴⁵just as you saw that a stone was cut from a mountain by no human hand, and that it broke in pieces the iron, the bronze, the clay, the silver, and the gold. A great God has made known to the king what shall be hereafter. The dream is certain, and its interpretation sure."

Daniel and His Friends Promoted

46 Then King Nebuchadnez'zar fell upon his face, and did homage to Daniel, and commanded that an offering and incense be offered up to him. ⁴⁷The king said to Daniel, "Truly, your God is God of gods and Lord of kings, and a revealer of mysteries, for you have been able to reveal this mystery." ⁴⁸Then the king gave Daniel high honors and many great gifts, and made him ruler over the whole province of Babylon, and chief prefect over all the wise men of Babylon. ⁴⁹Daniel made request of the king, and he appointed Shad'rach, Me'shach, and Abed'nego over the affairs of the province of Babylon; but Daniel remained at the king's court.

The Golden Image

3 King Nebuchadnez'zar made an image of gold, whose height was sixty cubits and its breadth six cubits. He set it up on the plain of Dura, in the province of Babylon. ²Then King Nebuchadnez'zar sent to assemble the satraps, the prefects, and the governors, the counselors, the treasurers, the justices, the magistrates, and all the officials of the provinces to come to the dedication of the image which King Nebuchadnezzar had set up. ³Then the satraps, the prefects, and the governors, the counselors, the treasurers, the justices, the magistrates, and all the officials of the provinces, were assembled for the dedication of the image that King Nebuchadnez'zar had set up; and they stood before the image that

Nebuchadnezzar had set up. ⁴And the herald proclaimed aloud, "You are commanded, O peoples, nations, and languages, ⁵that when you hear the sound of the horn, pipe, lyre, trigon, harp, bagpipe, and every kind of music, you are to fall down and worship the golden image that King Nebuchadnez'zar has set up; ⁶and whoever does not fall down and worship shall immediately be cast into a burning fiery furnace." ⁷Therefore, as soon as all the peoples heard the sound of the horn, pipe, lyre, trigon, harp, bagpipe, and every kind of music, all the peoples, nations, and languages fell down and worshiped the golden image which King Nebuchadnez'zar had set up.

8 Therefore at that time certain Chalde'ans came forward and maliciously accused the Jews. ⁹They said to King Nebuchadnez'zar, "O king, live for ever! ¹⁰You, O king, have made a decree, that every man who hears the sound of the horn, pipe, lyre, trigon, harp, bagpipe, and every kind of music, shall fall down and worship the golden image; ¹¹and whoever does not fall down and worship shall be cast into a burning fiery furnace. ¹²There are certain Jews whom you have appointed over the affairs of the province of Babylon: Shad'rach, Me'shach, and Abed'nego. These men, O king, pay no heed to you; they do not serve your gods or worship the golden image which you have set up."

13 Then Nebuchadnez'zar in furious rage commanded that Shad'rach, Me'shach, and Abed'nego be brought. Then they brought these men before the king. ¹⁴Nebuchadnez'zar said to them, "Is it true, O Shad'rach, Me'shach, and Abed'nego, that you do not serve my gods or worship the golden image which I have set up? ¹⁵Now if you are ready when you hear the sound of the horn, pipe, lyre, trigon, harp, bagpipe, and every kind of music, to fall down and worship the image which I have made, well and good; but if you do not worship, you shall immediately be cast into a burning fiery furnace; and who is the god that will deliver you out of my hands?"

16 Shad'rach, Me'shach, and Abed'nego answered the king, "O Nebuchadnez'zar, we have no need to answer you in this matter. ¹⁷If it be so, our God whom we serve is able to deliver us from the burning fiery furnace; and he will deliver us out of your hand, O king. ᶜ ¹⁸But if not, be it known to you, O king, that we will not serve your gods or worship the golden image which you have set up."

The Fiery Furnace

19 Then Nebuchadnez'zar was full of fury, and the expression of his face was changed against Shad'rach, Me'shach, and Abed'nego. He ordered

---

ᵇ Aramaic by the seed of men.
ᶜ Or Behold, our God . . . king. Or If our God is able to deliver us, he will deliver us from the burning fiery furnace and out of your hand, O king.
2:44: Rev 11:15.
3:5, 6: Rev 13:15.

the furnace heated seven times more than it was accustomed to be heated. [20]And he ordered certain mighty men of his army to bind Shad'rach, Me'shach, and Abed'nego, and to cast them into the burning fiery furnace. [21]Then these men were bound in their mantles, [d] their tunics, [d] their hats, and their other garments, and they were cast into the burning fiery furnace. [22]Because the king's order was strict and the furnace very hot, the flame of the fire slew those men who took up Shad'rach, Me'shach, and Abed'nego. [23]And these three men, Shad'rach, Me'shach, and Abed'nego, fell bound into the burning fiery furnace. *

The Prayer of Azariah in the Furnace

1 *And they walked about in the midst of the flames, singing hymns to God and blessing the Lord.* [2]*Then Azariah stood and offered this prayer; in the midst of the fire he opened his mouth and said:*

[3]*"Blessed are you, O Lord, God of our fathers,*
  and worthy of praise;
  and your name is glorified for ever.
[4]*For you are just in all that you have done to us,*
  and all your works are true and your ways right,
  and all your judgments are truth.
[5]*You have executed true judgments in all that you have brought upon us*
  and upon Jerusalem, the holy city of our fathers,
  for in truth and justice you have brought all this upon us because of our sins.
[6]*For we have sinfully and lawlessly departed from you,*
  and have sinned in all things and have not obeyed your commandments;
[7]*we have not observed them or done them,*
  as you have commanded us that it might go well with us.
[8]*So all that you have brought upon us,*
  and all that you have done to us,
  you have done in true judgment.
[9]*You have given us into the hands of lawless enemies, most hateful rebels,*
  and to an unjust king, the most wicked in all the world.
[10]*And now we cannot open our mouths;*
  shame and disgrace have befallen your servants and worshipers.
[11]*For your name's sake do not give us up utterly,*
  and do not break your covenant,
[12] *and do not withdraw your mercy from us,*
  for the sake of Abraham your beloved
  and for the sake of Isaac your servant
  and Israel your holy one,
[13]*to whom you promised*
  to make their descendants as many as the stars of heaven
  and as the sand on the shore of the sea.

[14]*For we, O Lord, have become fewer than any nation,*
  and are brought low this day in all the world because of our sins.
[15]*And at this time there is no prince, or prophet, or leader,*
  no burnt offering, or sacrifice, or oblation, or incense,
  no place to make an offering before you or to find mercy.
[16]*Yet with a contrite heart and a humble spirit may we be accepted,*
  as though it were with burnt offerings of rams and bulls,
  and with tens of thousands of fat lambs;
[17] *such may our sacrifice be in your sight this day,*
  and may we wholly follow you,
  for there will be no shame for those who trust in you.
[18]*And now with all our heart we follow you,*
  we fear you and seek your face.
[19]*Do not put us to shame,*
  but deal with us in your forbearance and in your abundant mercy.
[20]*Deliver us in accordance with your marvelous works,*
  and give glory to your name, O Lord!
  Let all who do harm to your servants be put to shame;
[21]*let them be disgraced and deprived of all power and dominion,*
  and let their strength be broken.
[22]*Let them know that you are the Lord, the only God,*
  glorious over the whole world."

[23] *Now the king's servants who threw them in did not cease feeding the furnace fires with naphtha, pitch, tow, and brush.* [24]*And the flame streamed out above the furnace forty-nine cubits,* [25]*and it broke through and burned those of the Chaldeans whom it caught about the furnace.* [26]*But the angel of the Lord came down into the furnace to be with Azariah and his companions, and drove the fiery flame out of the furnace,* [27]*and made the midst of the furnace like a moist whistling wind, so that the fire did not touch them at all or hurt or trouble them.*

---

[d] The meaning of the Aramaic word is uncertain.
* 3:23: After this verse the section (sixty-eight verses) printed in italics is contained only in the Greek. It is here translated from Theodotion's version. Concordance of verse numberings:

RSV	Vulgate	RSV	Vulgate
1–28	24–51	36	59
29–30	52	37	58
31	53	38–45	60–67
32	55	46	68–69
33	54	47	71
34	56	48	72
35	57	49–50	70
		51–68	73–90

The Song of the Three Young Men

28 Then the three, as with one mouth, praised and glorified and blessed God in the furnace, saying:

29 "Blessed are you, O Lord, God of our fathers,
and to be praised and highly exalted for
ever;

30 And blessed is your glorious, holy name
and to be highly praised and highly exalted
for ever;

31 Blessed are you in the temple of your holy glory
and to be extolled and highly glorified for
ever.

32 Blessed are you, who sit upon cherubim and
look upon the deeps,
and to be praised and highly exalted for ever.

33 Blessed are you upon the throne of your
kingdom
and to be extolled and highly exalted for
ever.

34 Blessed are you in the firmament of heaven
and to be sung and glorified for ever.

35 "Bless the Lord, all works of the Lord,
sing praise to him and highly exalt him for
ever.

36 Bless the Lord, you heavens,
sing praise to him and highly exalt him for
ever.

37 Bless the Lord, you angels of the Lord,
sing praise to him and highly exalt him for
ever.

38 Bless the Lord, all waters above the heaven,
sing praise to him and highly exalt him for
ever.

39 Bless the Lord, all powers,
sing praise to him and highly exalt him for
ever.

40 Bless the Lord, sun and moon,
sing praise to him and highly exalt him for
ever.

41 Bless the Lord, stars of heaven,
sing praise to him and highly exalt him for
ever.

42 Bless the Lord, all rain and dew,
sing praise to him and highly exalt him for
ever.

43 Bless the Lord, all winds,
sing praise to him and highly exalt him for
ever.

44 Bless the Lord, fire and heat,
sing praise to him and highly exalt him for
ever.

45 Bless the Lord, winter cold and summer heat,
sing praise to him and highly exalt him for
ever.

46 Bless the Lord, dews and snows,
sing praise to him and highly exalt him for
ever.

47 Bless the Lord, nights and days,
sing praise to him and highly exalt him for
ever.

48 Bless the Lord, light and darkness,
sing praise to him and highly exalt him for
ever.

49 Bless the Lord, ice and cold,
sing praise to him and highly exalt him for
ever.

50 Bless the Lord, frosts and snows,
sing praise to him and highly exalt him for
ever.

51 Bless the Lord, lightnings and clouds,
sing praise to him and highly exalt him for
ever.

52 Let the earth bless the Lord;
let it sing praise to him and highly exalt him
for ever.

53 Bless the Lord, mountains and hills,
sing praise to him and highly exalt him for
ever.

54 Bless the Lord, all things that grow on the
earth,
sing praise to him and highly exalt him for
ever.

55 Bless the Lord, you springs,
sing praise to him and highly exalt him for
ever.

56 Bless the Lord, seas and rivers,
sing praise to him and highly exalt him for
ever.

57 Bless the Lord, you whales and all creatures
that move in the waters,
sing praise to him and highly exalt him for
ever.

58 Bless the Lord, all birds of the air,
sing praise to him and highly exalt him for
ever.

59 Bless the Lord, all beasts and cattle,
sing praise to him and highly exalt him for
ever.

60 Bless the Lord, you sons of men,
sing praise to him and highly exalt him for
ever.

61 Bless the Lord, O Israel,
sing praise to him and highly exalt him for
ever.

62 Bless the Lord, you priests of the Lord,
sing praise to him and highly exalt him for
ever.

63 Bless the Lord, you servants of the Lord,
sing praise to him and highly exalt him for
ever.

64 Bless the Lord, spirits and souls of the
righteous,
sing praise to him and highly exalt him for
ever.

65 Bless the Lord, you who are holy and humble in
heart,

*sing praise to him and highly exalt him for
ever.*
[66]*Bless the Lord, Hananiah, Azariah, and
Mishael,
sing praise to him and highly exalt him for
ever;
for he has rescued us from Hades and saved us
from the hand of death,
and delivered us from the midst of the
burning fiery furnace;
from the midst of the fire he has delivered
us.*
[67]*Give thanks to the Lord, for he is good,
for his mercy endures for ever.*
[68]*Bless him, all who worship the Lord, the God of
gods,
sing praise to him and give thanks to him,
for his mercy endures for ever."* *

24 Then King Nebuchadnez'zar was astonished and rose up in haste. He said to his counselors, "Did we not cast three men bound into the
fire?" They answered the king, "True, O king."
[25]He answered, "But I see four men loose, walking
in the midst of the fire, and they are not hurt; and
the appearance of the fourth is like a son of the
gods."

The Three Men Are Taken Out of the Furnace

26 Then Nebuchadnez'zar came near to the
door of the burning fiery furnace and said,
"Shad'rach, Me'shach, and Abed'nego, servants
of the Most High God, come forth, and come here!"
Then Shadrach, Meshach, and Abednego came
out from the fire. [27]And the satraps, the prefects,
the governors, and the king's counselors gathered
together and saw that the fire had not had any
power over the bodies of those men; the hair of
their heads was not singed, their mantles [d] were
not harmed, and no smell of fire had come upon
them. [28]Nebuchadnez'zar said, "Blessed be the
God of Shad'rach, Me'shach, and Abed'nego, who
has sent his angel and delivered his servants, who
trusted in him, and set at nothing the king's command, and yielded up their bodies rather than
serve and worship any god except their own God.
[29]Therefore I make a decree: Any people, nation,
or language that speaks anything against the God
of Shad'rach, Me'shach, and Abed'nego shall be
torn limb from limb, and their houses laid in ruins; for there is no other god who is able to deliver
in this way." [30]Then the king promoted Shad'rach,
Me'shach, and Abed'nego in the province of
Babylon.

Nebuchadnezzar's Second Dream

4 [e] [†] King Nebuchadnez'zar to all peoples,
nations, and languages, that dwell in all
the earth: Peace be multiplied to you! [2]It has
seemed good to me to show the signs and wonders that the Most High God has wrought
toward me.

[3]How great are his signs,
how mighty his wonders!
His kingdom is an everlasting kingdom,
and his dominion is from generation to
generation.

4 [f] I, Nebuchadnez'zar, was at ease in my house
and prospering in my palace. [5]I had a dream which
made me afraid; as I lay in bed the fancies and the
visions of my head alarmed me. [6]Therefore I made
a decree that all the wise men of Babylon should
be brought before me, that they might make known
to me the interpretation of the dream. [7]Then the
magicians, the enchanters, the Chalde'ans, and the
astrologers came in; and I told them the dream,
but they could not make known to me its interpretation. [8]At last Daniel came in before me—he who
was named Belteshaz'zar ‡ after the name of my
god, and in whom is the spirit of the holy gods [g]—
and I told him the dream, saying, [9]"O Belteshaz'zar,
chief of the magicians, because I know that the
spirit of the holy gods [g] is in you and that no
mystery is difficult for you, here is [h] the dream
which I saw; tell me its interpretation. [10]The visions of my head as I lay in bed were these: I saw,
and behold, a tree in the midst of the earth; and its
height was great. [11]The tree grew and became
strong, and its top reached to heaven, and it was
visible to the end of the whole earth. [12]Its leaves
were fair and its fruit abundant, and in it was food
for all. The beasts of the field found shade under
it, and the birds of the air dwelt in its branches,
and all flesh was fed from it.

13 "I saw in the visions of my head as I lay in
bed, and behold, a watcher, a holy one,** came
down from heaven. [14]He cried aloud and said thus,
'Hew down the tree and cut off its branches, strip
off its leaves and scatter its fruit; let the beasts
flee from under it and the birds from its branches.
[15]But leave the stump of its roots in the earth,
bound with a band of iron and bronze, amid the
tender grass of the field. Let him be wet with
the dew of heaven; let his lot be with the beasts in
the grass of the earth; [16]let his mind be changed
from a man's, and let a beast's mind be given to
him; and let seven times pass over him. [17]The

---

[d] The meaning of the Aramaic word is uncertain.
[e] Ch 3:31 in Aramaic.
[f] Ch 4:1 in Aramaic.
[g] Or *Spirit of the holy God.*
[h] Cn: Aramaic *visions of.*
4:12, 21: Ezek 17:23; 31:6; Mt 13:32; Mk 4:32; Lk 13:19.
* 3:68: The reader will notice that the roman figures used for the remaining verses of this chapter take up again the numbering of the
protocanonical text. Verses 24–30 are numbered 91–97 in the Greek and
Vulgate; they are written in Aramaic, not Hebrew.
† 4:1–3: These verses correspond to 3:31–33 in the Aramaic and to 3:98–
100 in the Greek and Vulgate. The chapter is considerably longer in the
Greek than in the Aramaic.
‡ 4:8, *Belteshazzar:* The name given to Daniel means "May Bel protect
his life."
** 4:13, *a watcher, a holy one:* An angel, so called because he is ever
watchful to serve God. In Ezek 1:18 the wheels representing angels are
said to be full of eyes.

sentence is by the decree of the watchers, the decision by the word of the holy ones, to the end that the living may know that the Most High rules the kingdom of men, and gives it to whom he will, and sets over it the lowliest of men.' [18]This dream I, King Nebuchadnez'zar, saw. And you, O Belteshaz'zar, declare the interpretation, because all the wise men of my kingdom are not able to make known to me the interpretation, but you are able, for the spirit of the holy gods [1] is in you."

Daniel Interprets the Second Dream

19 Then Daniel, whose name was Belteshaz'zar, was dismayed for a moment, and his thoughts alarmed him. The king said, "Belteshaz'zar, let not the dream or the interpretation alarm you." Belteshazzar answered, "My lord, may the dream be for those who hate you and its interpretation for your enemies! [20]The tree you saw, which grew and became strong, so that its top reached to heaven, and it was visible to the end of the whole earth; [21]whose leaves were fair and its fruit abundant, and in which was food for all; under which beasts of the field found shade, and in whose branches the birds of the air dwelt— [22]it is you, O king, who have grown and become strong. Your greatness has grown and reaches to heaven, and your dominion to the ends of the earth. [23]And whereas the king saw a watcher, a holy one, coming down from heaven and saying, 'Hew down the tree and destroy it, but leave the stump of its roots in the earth, bound with a band of iron and bronze, in the tender grass of the field; and let him be wet with the dew of heaven; and let his lot be with the beasts of the field, till seven times pass over him'; [24]this is the interpretation, O king: It is a decree of the Most High, which has come upon my lord the king, [25]that you shall be driven from among men, and your dwelling shall be with the beasts of the field; you shall be made to eat grass like an ox, and you shall be wet with the dew of heaven, and seven times shall pass over you, till you know that the Most High rules the kingdom of men, and gives it to whom he will. [26]And as it was commanded to leave the stump of the roots of the tree, your kingdom shall be sure for you from the time that you know that Heaven rules. [27]Therefore, O king, let my counsel be acceptable to you; break off your sins by practicing righteousness, and your iniquities by showing mercy to the oppressed, that there may perhaps be a lengthening of your tranquillity."

28 All this came upon King Nebuchadnez'zar. [29]At the end of twelve months he was walking on the roof of the royal palace of Babylon, [30]and the king said, "Is not this great Babylon, which I have built by my mighty power as a royal residence and for the glory of my majesty?" [31]While the words were still in the king's mouth, there fell a voice from heaven, "O King Nebuchadnez'zar, to you it is spoken: The kingdom has departed from you, [32]and you shall be driven from among men, and your dwelling shall be with the beasts of the field; and you shall be made to eat grass like an ox; and seven times shall pass over you, until you have learned that the Most High rules the kingdom of men and gives it to whom he will." [33]Immediately the word was fulfilled upon Nebuchadnez'zar. He was driven from among men, and ate grass like an ox, and his body was wet with the dew of heaven till his hair grew as long as eagles' feathers, and his nails were like birds' claws.

Nebuchadnezzar Praises God

34 At the end of the days I, Nebuchadnez'zar, lifted my eyes to heaven, and my reason returned to me, and I blessed the Most High, and praised and honored him who lives for ever;

for his dominion is an everlasting dominion,
  and his kingdom endures from generation
    to generation;
[35]all the inhabitants of the earth are accounted
    as nothing;
  and he does according to his will in the host
    of heaven
  and among the inhabitants of the earth;
and none can stay his hand
  or say to him, "What have you done?"
[36]At the same time my reason returned to me; and for the glory of my kingdom, my majesty and splendor returned to me. My counselors and my lords sought me, and I was established in my kingdom, and still more greatness was added to me. [37]Now I, Nebuchadnez'zar, praise and extol and honor the King of heaven; for all his works are right and his ways are just; and those who walk in pride he is able to abase.

Belshazzar's Feast

5 King Belshaz'zar * made a great feast for a thousand of his lords, and drank wine in front of the thousand.

2 Belshaz'zar, when he tasted the wine, commanded that the vessels of gold and of silver which Nebuchadnez'zar his father had taken out of the temple in Jerusalem be brought, that the king and his lords, his wives, and his concubines might drink from them. [3]Then they brought in the golden and silver vessels [j] which had been taken out of the temple, the house of God in Jerusalem; and the king and his lords, his wives, and his concubines drank from them. [4]They drank wine, and praised the gods of gold and silver, bronze, iron, wood, and stone.

The Handwriting on the Wall

5 Immediately the fingers of a man's hand appeared and wrote on the plaster of the wall of the

---

[1] Or *Spirit of the holy God.*
[j] Theodotion Vg: Aramaic *golden vessels.*
* 5:1, *Belshazzar.* He was the son of Nabonidus and was never in fact king.

king's palace, opposite the lampstand; and the king saw the hand as it wrote. ⁶Then the king's color changed, and his thoughts alarmed him; his limbs gave way, and his knees knocked together. ⁷The king cried aloud to bring in the enchanters, the Chalde′ans, and the astrologers. The king said to the wise men of Babylon, "Whoever reads this writing, and shows me its interpretation, shall be clothed with purple, and have a chain of gold about his neck, and shall be the third ruler in the kingdom." ⁸Then all the king's wise men came in, but they could not read the writing or make known to the king the interpretation. ⁹Then King Belshaz′zar was greatly alarmed, and his color changed; and his lords were perplexed.

10 The queen, because of the words of the king and his lords, came into the banqueting hall; and the queen said, "O king, live for ever! Let not your thoughts alarm you or your color change. ¹¹There is in your kingdom a man in whom is the spirit of the holy gods.ᵏ In the days of your father light and understanding and wisdom, like the wisdom of the gods, were found in him, and King Nebuchadnez′zar, your father, made him chief of the magicians, enchanters, Chalde′ans, and astrologers, ¹ ¹²because an excellent spirit, knowledge, and understanding to interpret dreams, explain riddles, and solve problems were found in this Daniel, whom the king named Belteshaz′zar. Now let Daniel be called, and he will show the interpretation."

Daniel Interprets the Writing on the Wall

13 Then Daniel was brought in before the king. The king said to Daniel, "You are that Daniel, one of the exiles of Judah, whom the king my father brought from Judah. ¹⁴I have heard of you that the spirit of the holy godsᵏ is in you, and that light and understanding and excellent wisdom are found in you. ¹⁵Now the wise men, the enchanters, have been brought in before me to read this writing and make known to me its interpretation; but they could not show the interpretation of the matter. ¹⁶But I have heard that you can give interpretations and solve problems. Now if you can read the writing and make known to me its interpretation, you shall be clothed with purple, and have a chain of gold about your neck, and shall be the third ruler in the kingdom.

17 Then Daniel answered before the king, "Let your gifts be for yourself, and give your rewards to another; nevertheless I will read the writing to the king and make known to him the interpretation. ¹⁸O king, the Most High God gave Nebuchadnez′zar your father kingship and greatness and glory and majesty; ¹⁹and because of the greatness that he gave him, all peoples, nations, and languages trembled and feared before him; whom he would he slew, and whom he would he kept alive; whom he would he raised up, and whom he would

he put down. ²⁰But when his heart was lifted up and his spirit was hardened so that he dealt proudly, he was deposed from his kingly throne, and his glory was taken from him; ²¹he was driven from among men, and his mind was made like that of a beast, and his dwelling was with the wild donkeys; he was fed grass like an ox, and his body was wet with the dew of heaven, until he knew that the Most High God rules the kingdom of men, and sets over it whom he will. ²²And you his son, Belshaz′zar, have not humbled your heart, though you knew all this, ²³but you have lifted up yourself against the Lord of heaven; and the vessels of his house have been brought in before you, and you and your lords, your wives, and your concubines have drunk wine from them; and you have praised the gods of silver and gold, of bronze, iron, wood, and stone, which do not see or hear or know, but the God in whose hand is your breath, and whose are all your ways, you have not honored.

24 "Then from his presence the hand was sent, and this writing was inscribed. ²⁵And this is the writing that was inscribed: MENE, MENE, TEKEL, and PARSIN. ²⁶This is the interpretation of the matter: MENE, God has numbered the days of your kingdom and brought it to an end; ²⁷TEKEL, you have been weighed in the balances and found wanting; ²⁸PERES, your kingdom is divided and given to the Medes and Persians."

29 Then Belshaz′zar commanded, and Daniel was clothed with purple, a chain of gold was put about his neck, and proclamation was made concerning him, that he should be the third ruler in the kingdom.

30 That very night Belshaz′zar the Chalde′an king was slain. ³¹And Dari′us the Mede* received the kingdom, being about sixty-two years old.

A Plot against Daniel

6 It pleased Dari′us to set over the kingdom a hundred and twenty satraps, to be throughout the whole kingdom; ²and over them three presidents, of whom Daniel was one, to whom these satraps should give account, so that the king might suffer no loss. ³Then this Daniel became distinguished above all the other presidents and satraps, because an excellent spirit was in him; and the king planned to set him over the whole kingdom. ⁴Then the presidents and the satraps sought to find a ground for complaint against Daniel with regard to the kingdom; but they could find no ground for complaint or any fault, because he was faithful, and no error or fault was found in him. ⁵Then these men said,

ᵏ Or *Spirit of the holy God.*
¹ Aramaic repeats *the king your father.*
* 5:31, *Dari′us the Mede:* Nothing is known in history of this person. The Persians, moreover, had already conquered the Medes before taking Babylon.

"We shall not find any ground for complaint against this Daniel unless we find it in connection with the law of his God."

6 Then these presidents and satraps came by agreement[m] to the king and said to him, "O King Dari′us, live for ever! [7]All the presidents of the kingdom, the prefects and the satraps, the counselors and the governors are agreed that the king should establish an ordinance and enforce an interdict, that whoever makes petition to any god or man for thirty days, except to you, O king, shall be cast into the den of lions. [8]Now, O king, establish the interdict and sign the document, so that it cannot be changed, according to the law of the Medes and the Persians, which cannot be revoked." [9]Therefore King Dari′us signed the document and interdict.

Daniel in the Den of Lions

10 When Daniel knew that the document had been signed, he went to his house where he had windows in his upper chamber open toward Jerusalem; and he got down upon his knees three times a day and prayed and gave thanks before his God, as he had done previously. [11]Then these men came by agreement[m] and found Daniel making petition and supplication before his God. [12]Then they came near and said before the king, concerning the interdict, "O king! Did you not sign an interdict, that any man who makes petition to any god or man within thirty days except to you, O king, shall be cast into the den of lions?" The king answered, "The thing stands fast, according to the law of the Medes and Persians, which cannot be revoked." [13]Then they answered before the king, "That Daniel, who is one of the exiles from Judah, pays no heed to you, O king, or the interdict you have signed, but makes his petition three times a day."

14 Then the king, when he heard these words, was much distressed, and set his mind to deliver Daniel; and he labored till the sun went down to rescue him. [15]Then these men came by agreement[m] to the king, and said to the king, "Know, O king, that it is a law of the Medes and Persians that no interdict or ordinance which the king establishes can be changed."

16 Then the king commanded, and Daniel was brought and cast into the den of lions. The king said to Daniel, "May your God, whom you serve continually, deliver you!" [17]And a stone was brought and laid upon the mouth of the den, and the king sealed it with his own signet and with the signet of his lords, that nothing might be changed concerning Daniel. [18]Then the king went to his palace, and spent the night fasting; no diversions were brought to him, and sleep fled from him.

God Saves Daniel from the Lions

19 Then, at break of day, the king arose and went in haste to the den of lions. [20]When he came near to the den where Daniel was, he cried out in a tone of anguish and said to Daniel, "O Daniel, servant of the living God, has your God, whom you serve continually, been able to deliver you from the lions?" [21]Then Daniel said to the king, "O king, live for ever! [22]My God sent his angel and shut the lions' mouths, and they have not hurt me, because I was found blameless before him; and also before you, O king, I have done no wrong." [23]Then the king was exceedingly glad, and commanded that Daniel be taken up out of the den. So Daniel was taken up out of the den, and no kind of hurt was found upon him, because he had trusted in his God. [24]And the king commanded, and those men who had accused Daniel were brought and cast into the den of lions—they, their children, and their wives; and before they reached the bottom of the den the lions overpowered them and broke all their bones in pieces.

25 Then King Dari′us wrote to all the peoples, nations, and languages that dwell in all the earth: "Peace be multiplied to you. [26]I make a decree, that in all my royal dominion men tremble and fear before the God of Daniel,

for he is the living God,
   enduring for ever;
his kingdom shall never be destroyed,
   and his dominion shall be to the end.
[27]He delivers and rescues,
   he works signs and wonders
in heaven and on earth,
he who has saved Daniel
   from the power of the lions."

28 So this Daniel prospered during the reign of Dari′us and the reign of Cyrus the Persian.

Visions of the Four Beasts and the Ancient of Days

7 In the first year of Belshaz′zar king of Babylon, Daniel had a dream and visions of his head as he lay in his bed. Then he wrote down the dream, and told the sum of the matter. [2]Daniel said, "I saw in my vision by night, and behold, the four winds of heaven were stirring up the great sea. [3]And four great beasts came up out of the sea, different from one another. [4]The first was like a lion and had eagles' wings. Then as I looked its wings were plucked off, and it was lifted up from the ground and made to stand upon two feet like a man; and the mind of a man was given to it. [5]And behold, another beast, a second one, like a bear. It was raised up on one side; it had three ribs in its mouth between its teeth; and it was told, 'Arise, devour much flesh.' [6]After this I looked, and behold, another, like a leopard, with

---

[m] Or *thronging.*
6:22: 2 Tim 4:17.
7:3: Rev 13:1.
7:3, 7, 21: Rev 11:7.
7:4-6: Rev 13:2.

four wings of a bird on its back; and the beast had four heads; and dominion was given to it. [7]After this I saw in the night visions, and behold, a fourth beast, terrifying and dreadful and exceedingly strong; and it had great iron teeth; it devoured and broke in pieces, and stamped the residue with its feet. It was different from all the beasts that were before it; and it had ten horns. [8]I considered the horns, and behold, there came up among them another horn, a little one,* before which three of the first horns were plucked up by the roots; and behold, in this horn were eyes like the eyes of a man, and a mouth speaking great things. [9]As I looked,

thrones were placed
    and one that was ancient of days took his
        seat;
his clothing was white as snow,
    and the hair of his head like pure wool;
his throne was fiery flames,
    its wheels were burning fire.
[10]A stream of fire issued
    and came forth from before him;
a thousand thousands served him,
    and ten thousand times ten thousand stood
        before him;
the court sat in judgment,
    and the books were opened.
[11]I looked then because of the sound of the great words which the horn was speaking. And as I looked, the beast was slain, and its body destroyed and given over to be burned with fire. [12]As for the rest of the beasts, their dominion was taken away, but their lives were prolonged for a season and a time. [13]I saw in the night visions,
and behold, with the clouds of heaven
    there came one like a son of man, †
and he came to the Ancient of Days
    and was presented before him.
[14]And to him was given dominion
    and glory and kingdom,
that all peoples, nations, and languages
    should serve him;
his dominion is an everlasting dominion,
    which shall not pass away,
and his kingdom one
    that shall not be destroyed.

Daniel's Visions Interpreted

15 "As for me, Daniel, my spirit within me was anxious and the visions of my head alarmed me. [16]I approached one of those who stood there and asked him the truth concerning all this. So he told me, and made known to me the interpretation of the things. [17]'These four great beasts are four kings who shall arise out of the earth. [18]But the saints of the Most High shall receive the kingdom, and possess the kingdom for ever, for ever and ever.'

19 "Then I desired to know the truth concern-

ing the fourth beast, which was different from all the rest, exceedingly terrifying, with its teeth of iron and claws of bronze; and which devoured and broke in pieces, and stamped the residue with its feet; [20]and concerning the ten horns that were on its head, and the other horn which came up and before which three of them fell, the horn which had eyes and a mouth that spoke great things, and which seemed greater than its fellows. [21]As I looked, this horn made war with the saints, and prevailed over them, [22]until the Ancient of Days came, and judgment was given for the saints of the Most High, and the time came when the saints received the kingdom.
[23]"Thus he said: 'As for the fourth beast,
    there shall be a fourth kingdom on earth,
        which shall be different from all the
            kingdoms,
    and it shall devour the whole earth,
        and trample it down, and break it to
            pieces.
[24]As for the ten horns,
    out of this kingdom
        ten kings shall arise,
        and another shall arise after them;
    he shall be different from the former ones,
        and shall put down three kings.
[25]He shall speak words against the Most High,
    and shall wear out the saints of the Most
        High,
    and shall think to change the times and the
        law;
and they shall be given into his hand
    for a time, two times, and half a time.
[26]But the court shall sit in judgment,
    and his dominion shall be taken away,
    to be consumed and destroyed to the end.
[27]And the kingdom and the dominion
    and the greatness of the kingdoms under
        the whole heaven
    shall be given to the people of the saints of
        the Most High;
their kingdom shall be an everlasting kingdom,
    and all dominions shall serve and obey
        them.'
28 "Here is the end of the matter. As for me, Daniel, my thoughts greatly alarmed me, and my color changed; but I kept the matter in my mind."

7:7: Rev 12:3; 13:1; 17:3.
7:8, 11: Rev 13:5.
7:9: Rev 1:14; 20:4, 11.
7:10: Rev 5:11; 20:12.
7:13–14: Mt 24:30; 26:64; Mk 13:26; 14:62; Lk 21:27; 22:69; Rev 1:7, 13; 14:14.
7:14, 18, 22, 27: Rev 11:15.
7:20, 24: Rev 17:12.
7:21: Rev 13:7.
7:25: Rev 12:14.
* 7:8, *another horn, a little one*: Antiochus Epiphanes, who originally was of no importance.
† 7:13, *a son of man*: The same title with which God addressed Ezekiel. Here it means someone who is more than human.

Vision of a Ram and a Goat

8 In the third year of the reign of King Belshaz'zar a vision appeared to me, Daniel, after that which appeared to me at the first. [2]And I saw in the vision; and when I saw, I was in Susa the capital, which is in the province of E'lam; and I saw in the vision, and I was at the river U'lai. [3]I raised my eyes and saw, and behold, a ram standing on the bank of the river. It had two horns; and both horns were high, but one was higher than the other, and the higher one came up last. [4]I saw the ram charging westward and northward and southward; no beast could stand before him, and there was no one who could rescue from his power; he did as he pleased and magnified himself.

5 As I was considering, behold, a he-goat came from the west across the face of the whole earth, without touching the ground; and the goat had a conspicuous horn between his eyes. [6]He came to the ram with the two horns, which I had seen standing on the bank of the river, and he ran at him in his mighty wrath. [7]I saw him come close to the ram, and he was enraged against him and struck the ram and broke his two horns; and the ram had no power to stand before him, but he cast him down to the ground and trampled upon him; and there was no one who could rescue the ram from his power. [8]Then the he-goat magnified himself exceedingly; but when he was strong, the great horn was broken, and instead of it there came up four conspicuous horns toward the four winds of heaven.

9 Out of one of them came forth a little horn, which grew exceedingly great toward the south, toward the east, and toward the glorious land. [10]It grew great, even to the host of heaven; and some of the host of the stars it cast down to the ground, and trampled upon them. [11]It magnified itself, even up to the Prince of the host; and the continual burnt offering was taken away from him, and the place of his sanctuary was overthrown. [12]And the host was given over to it together with the continual burnt offering through transgression; [n] and truth was cast down to the ground, and the horn acted and prospered. [13]Then I heard a holy one speaking; and another holy one said to the one that spoke, "For how long is the vision concerning the continual burnt offering, the transgression that makes desolate, and the giving over of the sanctuary and host to be trampled under foot?" [o] [14]And he said to him, [p] "For two thousand and three hundred evenings and mornings; then the sanctuary shall be restored to its rightful state."

Gabriel Interprets the Vision

15 When I, Daniel, had seen the vision, I sought to understand it; and behold, there stood before me one having the appearance of a man. [16]And I heard a man's voice between the banks of the U'lai, and it called, "Gabriel, make this man understand the vision." [17]So he came near where I stood; and when he came, I was frightened and fell upon my face. But he said to me, "Understand, O son of man, that the vision is for the time of the end."

18 As he was speaking to me, I fell into a deep sleep with my face to the ground; but he touched me and set me on my feet. [19]He said, "Behold, I will make known to you what shall be at the latter end of the indignation; for it pertains to the appointed time of the end. [20]As for the ram which you saw with the two horns, these are the kings of Me'dia and Persia. [21]And the he-goat [q] is the king of Greece; and the great horn between his eyes is the first king. [22]As for the horn that was broken, in place of which four others arose, four kingdoms shall arise from his [r] nation, but not with his power. [23]And at the latter end of their rule, when the transgressors have reached their full measure, a king of bold countenance, one who understands riddles, shall arise. [24]His power shall be great, [s] and he shall cause fearful destruction, and shall succeed in what he does, and destroy mighty men and the people of the saints. [25]By his cunning he shall make deceit prosper under his hand, and in his own mind he shall magnify himself. Without warning he shall destroy many; and he shall even rise up against the Prince of princes; but, by no human hand, he shall be broken. [26]The vision of the evenings and the mornings which has been told is true; but seal up the vision, for it pertains to many days hence."

27 And I, Daniel, was overcome and lay sick for some days; then I rose and went about the king's business; but I was appalled by the vision and did not understand it.

Daniel's Prayer for the People

9 In the first year of Dari'us the son of Ahas'uerus, by birth a Mede, who became king over the realm of the Chalde'ans— [2]in the first year of his reign, I, Daniel, perceived in the books the number of years which, according to the word of the LORD to Jeremi'ah the prophet, must pass before the end of the desolations of Jerusalem, namely, seventy years.

3 Then I turned my face to the Lord God, seeking him by prayer and supplications with fasting and sackcloth and ashes. [4]I prayed to the LORD my God and made confession, saying, "O Lord, the great and awesome God, who keeps covenant

---

[n] Heb obscure.
[o] Heb obscure.
[p] Theodotion Gk Syr Vg: Heb me.
[q] Or shaggy he-goat.
[r] Theodotion Gk Vg: Heb the.
[s] Theodotion and Beatty papyrus of Gk: Heb repeats but not with his power from verse 22.
8:10: Rev 12:4.
8:13: Lk 21:24.

and merciful love with those who love him and keep his commandments, [5]we have sinned and done wrong and acted wickedly and rebelled, turning aside from your commandments and ordinances; [6]we have not listened to your servants the prophets, who spoke in your name to our kings, our princes, and our fathers, and to all the people of the land. [7]To you, O Lord, belongs righteousness, but to us confusion of face, as at this day, to the men of Judah, to the inhabitants of Jerusalem, and to all Israel, those that are near and those that are far away, in all the lands to which you have driven them, because of the treachery which they have committed against you. [8]To us, O Lord, belongs confusion of face, to our kings, to our princes, and to our fathers, because we have sinned against you. [9]To the Lord our God belong mercy and forgiveness; because we have rebelled against him, [10]and have not obeyed the voice of the Lord our God by following his laws, which he set before us by his servants the prophets. [11]All Israel has transgressed your law and turned aside, refusing to obey your voice. And the curse and oath which are written in the law of Moses the servant of God have been poured out upon us, because we have sinned against him. [12]He has confirmed his words, which he spoke against us and against our rulers who ruled us, by bringing upon us a great calamity; for under the whole heaven there has not been done the like of what has been done against Jerusalem. [13]As it is written in the law of Moses, all this calamity has come upon us, yet we have not entreated the favor of the Lord our God, turning from our iniquities and giving heed to your truth. [14]Therefore the Lord has kept ready the calamity and has brought it upon us; for the Lord our God is righteous in all the works which he has done, and we have not obeyed his voice. [15]And now, O Lord our God, who brought your people out of the land of Egypt with a mighty hand, and have made you a name, as at this day, we have sinned, we have done wickedly. [16]O Lord, according to all your righteous acts, let your anger and your wrath turn away from your city Jerusalem, your holy hill; because for our sins, and for the iniquities of our fathers, Jerusalem and your people have become a byword among all who are round about us. [17]Now therefore, O our God, listen to the prayer of your servant and to his supplications, and for your own sake, O Lord, [t] cause your face to shine upon your sanctuary, which is desolate. [18]O my God, incline your ear and hear; open your eyes and behold our desolations, and the city which is called by your name; for we do not present our supplications before you on the ground of our righteousness, but on the ground of your great mercy. [19]O Lord, hear; O Lord, forgive; O Lord, give heed and act; delay not, for your own sake, O

my God, because your city and your people are called by your name."

The Seventy Weeks

20 While I was speaking and praying, confessing my sin and the sin of my people Israel, and presenting my supplication before the Lord my God for the holy hill of my God; [21]while I was speaking in prayer, the man Gabriel, whom I had seen in the vision at the first, came to me in swift flight at the time of the evening sacrifice. [22]He came [u] and he said to me, "O Daniel, I have now come out to give you wisdom and understanding. [23]At the beginning of your supplications a word went forth, and I have come to tell it to you, for you are greatly beloved; therefore consider the word and understand the vision.

24 * "Seventy weeks of years are decreed concerning your people and your holy city, to finish the transgression, to put an end to sin, and to atone for iniquity, to bring in everlasting righteousness, to seal both vision and prophet, and to anoint a most holy place. [v] [25]Know therefore and understand that from the going forth of the word to restore and build Jerusalem to the coming of an anointed one, a prince, there shall be seven weeks. Then for sixty-two weeks it shall be built again with squares and moat, but in a troubled time. [26]And after the sixty-two weeks, an anointed one shall be cut off, and shall have nothing; and the people of the prince who is to come shall destroy the city and the sanctuary. Its [w] end shall come with a flood, and to the end there shall be war; desolations are decreed. [27]And he shall make a strong covenant with many for one week; and for half of the week he shall cause sacrifice and offering to cease; and upon the wing of abominations shall come one who makes desolate, until the decreed end is poured out on the desolator."

Daniel's Vision "for Days Yet to Come"

10 [†] In the third year of Cyrus king of Persia a word was revealed to Daniel, who was named Belteshaz′zar. And the word was true, and it was a great conflict. And he understood the word and had understanding of the vision.

2 In those days I, Daniel, was mourning for three weeks. [3]I ate no delicacies, no meat or wine entered my mouth, nor did I anoint myself at all,

---

t Theodotion Vg Compare Syr: Heb *for the Lord's sake.*
u Gk Syr: Heb *made to understand.*
v Or *thing* or *one.*
w Or *his.*
9:27: Dan 11:31; 12:11; Mt 24:15; Mk 13:14.
* 9:24–27: Prophecy of the seventy weeks. The prophecy, made to encourage the Jews in time of persecution, looks to the future Messianic age in the time of the end; cf. 12:9. The seventy weeks are seventy seven-year periods, i.e., 490 years. But we can hardly take it as an exact historical period. Its immediate application seems to be to the period 170–163 B.C., i.e., from the beginning of the persecution of the Jews by Antiochus Epiphanes to the purification of the temple and the death of Antiochus.
† 10–12: Summary of the history of the Persian and Greek periods down to Antiochus Epiphanes and thence to the time of the end.

for the full three weeks. [4]On the twenty-fourth day of the first month, as I was standing on the bank of the great river, that is, the Tigris, [5]I lifted up my eyes and looked, and behold, a man clothed in linen, whose loins were belted with gold of U'phaz. [6]His body was like beryl, his face like the appearance of lightning, his eyes like flaming torches, his arms and legs like the gleam of burnished bronze, and the sound of his words like the noise of a multitude. [7]And I, Daniel, alone saw the vision, for the men who were with me did not see the vision, but a great trembling fell upon them, and they fled to hide themselves. [8]So I was left alone and saw this great vision, and no strength was left in me; my radiant appearance was fearfully changed, and I retained no strength. [9]Then I heard the sound of his words; and when I heard the sound of his words, I fell on my face in a deep sleep with my face to the ground.

10 And behold, a hand touched me and set me trembling on my hands and knees. [11]And he said to me, "O Daniel, man greatly beloved, give heed to the words that I speak to you, and stand upright, for now I have been sent to you." While he was speaking this word to me, I stood up trembling. [12]Then he said to me, "Fear not, Daniel, for from the first day that you set your mind to understand and humbled yourself before your God, your words have been heard, and I have come because of your words. [13]The prince of the kingdom of Persia withstood me twenty-one days; but Michael, one of the chief princes, came to help me, so I left him there with the prince of the kingdom of Persia[x] [14]and came to make you understand what is to befall your people in the latter days. For the vision is for days yet to come."

15 When he had spoken to me according to these words, I turned my face toward the ground and was speechless. [16]And behold, one in the likeness of the sons of men touched my lips; then I opened my mouth and spoke. I said to him who stood before me, "O my lord, by reason of the vision pains have come upon me, and I retain no strength. [17]How can my lord's servant talk with my lord? For now no strength remains in me, and no breath is left in me."

18 Again one having the appearance of a man touched me and strengthened me. [19]And he said, "O man greatly beloved, fear not, peace be with you; be strong and of good courage." And when he spoke to me, I was strengthened and said, "Let my lord speak, for you have strengthened me." [20]Then he said, "Do you know why I have come to you? But now I will return to fight against the prince of Persia; and when I am through with him, behold, the prince of Greece will come. [21]But I will tell you what is inscribed in the book of truth: there is none who contends by my side against these except Michael, your prince.

11 And as for me, in the first year of Dari'us the Mede, I stood up to confirm and strengthen him.

Coming Conflict of the Nations

2 "And now I will show you the truth. Behold, three more kings shall arise in Persia; and a fourth shall be far richer than all of them; and when he has become strong through his riches, he shall stir up all against the kingdom of Greece. [3]Then a mighty king shall arise, who shall rule with great dominion and do according to his will. [4]And when he has arisen, his kingdom shall be broken and divided toward the four winds of heaven, but not to his posterity, nor according to the dominion with which he ruled; for his kingdom shall be plucked up and go to others besides these.

5 "Then the king of the south shall be strong, but one of his princes shall be stronger than he and his dominion shall be a great dominion. [6]After some years they shall make an alliance, and the daughter of the king of the south shall come to the king of the north to make peace; but she shall not retain the strength of her arm, and he and his offspring shall not endure; but she shall be given up, and her attendants, her child, and he who got possession of[y] her.

7 "In those times a branch[z] from her roots shall arise in his place; he shall come against the army and enter the fortress of the king of the north, and he shall deal with them and shall prevail. [8]He shall also carry off to Egypt their gods with their molten images and with their precious vessels of silver and of gold; and for some years he shall refrain from attacking the king of the north. [9]Then the latter shall come into the realm of the king of the south but shall return into his own land.

10 "His sons shall wage war and assemble a multitude of great forces, which shall come on and overflow and pass through, and again shall carry the war as far as his fortress. [11]Then the king of the south, moved with anger, shall come out and fight with the king of the north; and he shall raise a great multitude, but it shall be given into his hand. [12]And when the multitude is taken, his heart shall be exalted, and he shall cast down tens of thousands, but he shall not prevail. [13]For the king of the north shall again raise a multitude, greater than the former; and after some years[a] he shall come on with a great army and abundant supplies.

14 "In those times many shall rise against the king of the south; and the men of violence among

---

[x] Theodotion Compare Gk: Heb *I was left there with the kings of Persia.*
[y] Or *supported.*
[z] Gk: Heb *from a branch.*
[a] Heb *at the end of the times years.*
10:5-6: Rev 1:13-14; 2:18.
10:13, 21: Rev 12:7.

your own people shall lift themselves up in order to fulfil the vision; but they shall fail. [15]Then the king of the north shall come and throw up siegeworks, and take a well-fortified city. And the forces of the south shall not stand, or even his picked troops, for there shall be no strength to stand. [16]But he who comes against him shall do according to his own will, and none shall stand before him; and he shall stand in the glorious land, and all of it shall be in his power. [17]He shall set his face to come with the strength of his whole kingdom, and he shall bring terms of peace [b] and perform them. He shall give him the daughter of women to destroy the kingdom; [c] but it shall not stand or be to his advantage. [18]Afterward he shall turn his face to the islands, and shall take many of them; but a commander shall put an end to his insolence; indeed [d] he shall turn his insolence back upon him. [19]Then he shall turn his face back toward the fortresses of his own land; but he shall stumble and fall, and shall not be found.

20 "Then shall arise in his place one who shall send an exactor of tribute through the glory of the kingdom; but within a few days he shall be broken, neither in anger nor in battle. [21]In his place shall arise a contemptible person to whom royal majesty has not been given; he shall come in without warning and obtain the kingdom by flatteries. [22]Armies shall be utterly swept away before him and broken, and the prince of the covenant also. [23]And from the time that an alliance is made with him he shall act deceitfully; and he shall become strong with a small people. [24]Without warning he shall come into the richest parts [e] of the province; and he shall do what neither his fathers nor his fathers' fathers have done, scattering among them plunder, spoil, and goods. He shall devise plans against strongholds, but only for a time. [25]And he shall stir up his power and his courage against the king of the south with a great army; and the king of the south shall wage war with an exceedingly great and mighty army; but he shall not stand, for plots shall be devised against him. [26]Even those who eat his rich food shall be his undoing; his army shall be swept away, and many shall fall down slain. [27]And as for the two kings, their minds shall be bent on mischief; they shall speak lies at the same table, but to no avail; for the end is yet to be at the time appointed. [28]And he shall return to his land with great substance, but his heart shall be set against the holy covenant. And he shall work his will, and return to his own land.

29 "At the time appointed he shall return and come into the south; but it shall not be this time as it was before. [30]For ships of Kittim shall come against him, and he shall be afraid and withdraw, and shall turn back and be enraged and take action against the holy covenant. He shall turn back and give heed to those who forsake the holy covenant. [31]Forces from him shall appear and profane the temple and fortress, and shall take away the continual burnt offering. And they shall set up the abomination that makes desolate. [32]He shall seduce with flattery those who violate the covenant; but the people who know their God shall stand firm and take action. [33]And those among the people who are wise shall make many understand, though they shall fall by sword and flame, by captivity and plunder, for some days. [34]When they fall, they shall receive a little help. And many shall join themselves to them with flattery; [35]and some of those who are wise shall fall, to refine and to cleanse them [f] and to make them white, until the time of the end, for it is yet for the time appointed.

36 "And the king shall do according to his will; he shall exalt himself and magnify himself above every god, and shall speak astonishing things against the God of gods. He shall prosper till the indignation is accomplished; for what is determined shall be done. [37]He shall give no heed to the gods of his fathers, or to the one beloved by women; he shall not give heed to any other god, for he shall magnify himself above all. [38]He shall honor the god of fortresses instead of these; a god whom his fathers did not know he shall honor with gold and silver, with precious stones and costly gifts. [39]He shall deal with the strongest fortresses by the help of a foreign god; those who acknowledge him he shall magnify with honor. He shall make them rulers over many and shall divide the land for a price.

The Time of the End

40 "At the time of the end the king of the south shall attack [g] him; but the king of the north shall rush upon him like a whirlwind, with chariots and horsemen, and with many ships; and he shall come into countries and shall overflow and pass through. [41]He shall come into the glorious land. And tens of thousands shall fall, but these shall be delivered out of his hand: E'dom and Moab and the main part of the Am'monites. [42]He shall stretch out his hand against the countries, and the land of Egypt shall not escape. [43]He shall become ruler of the treasures of gold and of silver, and all the precious things of Egypt; and the Libyans and the Ethiopians shall follow in his train. [44]But tidings from the east and the north shall alarm him, and he shall go forth with great fury to exterminate and utterly destroy many. [45]And he shall

---

[b] Gk: Heb *upright ones*.
[c] Heb *her* or *it*.
[d] Heb obscure.
[e] Or *among the richest men*.
[f] Gk: Heb *among them*.
[g] Heb *thrust at*.
11:31: Dan 9:27; 12:11; Mt 24:15; Mk 13:14.
11:36: Ezek 28:2; 2 Thess 2:4; Rev 13:5.

pitch his palatial tents between the sea and the glorious holy mountain; yet he shall come to his end, with none to help him.

The Resurrection of the Dead

12 "At that time shall arise Michael, the great prince who has charge of your people. And there shall be a time of trouble, such as never has been since there was a nation till that time; but at that time your people shall be delivered, every one whose name shall be found written in the book. [2]And many of those who sleep in the dust of the earth shall awake, some to everlasting life, and some to shame and everlasting contempt. [3]And those who are wise shall shine like the brightness of the firmament; and those who turn many to righteousness, like the stars for ever and ever. [4]But you, Daniel, shut up the words, and seal the book, until the time of the end. Many shall run back and forth, and knowledge shall increase."

5 Then I Daniel looked, and behold, two others stood, one on this bank of the stream and one on that bank of the stream. [6]And I [h] said to the man clothed in linen, who was above the waters of the stream, "How long shall it be till the end of these wonders?" [7]The man clothed in linen, who was above the waters of the stream, raised his right hand and his left hand toward heaven; and I heard him swear by him who lives for ever that it would be for a time, two times, and half a time; and that when the shattering of the power of the holy people comes to an end all these things would be accomplished. [8]I heard, but I did not understand. Then I said, "O my lord, what shall be the issue of these things?" [9]He said, "Go your way, Daniel, for the words are shut up and sealed until the time of the end. [10]Many shall purify themselves, and make themselves white, and be refined; but the wicked shall do wickedly; and none of the wicked shall understand; but those who are wise shall understand. [11]And from the time that the continual burnt offering is taken away, and the abomination that makes desolate is set up, there shall be a thousand two hundred and ninety days. [12]Blessed is he who waits and comes to the thousand three hundred and thirty-five days. [13]But go your way till the end; and you shall rest, and shall stand in your allotted place at the end of the days."

Two Elders' Lust for Susanna

13 [*] There was a man living in Babylon whose name was Jo′akim. [2]And he took a wife named Susanna, the daughter of Hilki′ah, a very beautiful woman and one who feared the Lord. [3]Her parents were righteous, and had taught their daughter according to the law of Moses. [4]Jo′akim was very rich, and had a spacious garden adjoining his house; and the Jews used to come to him because he was the most honored of them all.

5 In that year two elders from the people were appointed as judges. Concerning them the Lord had said: "Iniquity came forth from Babylon, from elders who were judges, who were supposed to govern the people." [6]These men were frequently at Jo′akim's house, and all who had suits at law came to them.

7 When the people departed at noon, Susanna would go into her husband's garden to walk. [8]The two elders used to see her every day, going in and walking about, and they began to desire her. [9]And they perverted their minds and turned away their eyes from looking to Heaven or remembering righteous judgments. [10]Both were overwhelmed with passion for her, but they did not tell each other of their distress, [11]for they were ashamed to disclose their lustful desire to possess her. [12]And they watched eagerly, day after day, to see her.

13 They said to each other, "Let us go home, for it is mealtime." [14]And when they went out, they parted from each other. But turning back, they met again; and when each pressed the other for the reason, they confessed their lust. And then together they arranged for a time when they could find her alone.

The Elders Attempt to Seduce Susanna

15 Once, while they were watching for an opportune day, she went in as before with only two maids, and wished to bathe in the garden, for it was very hot. [16]And no one was there except the two elders, who had hid themselves and were watching her. [17]She said to her maids, "Bring me oil and ointments, and shut the garden doors so that I may bathe." [18]They did as she said, shut the garden doors, and went out by the side doors to bring what they had been commanded; and they did not see the elders, because they were hidden.

19 When the maids had gone out, the two elders rose and ran to her, and said: [20]"Look, the garden doors are shut, no one sees us, and we are in love with you; so give your consent, and lie with us. [21]If you refuse, we will testify against you that a young man was with you, and this was why you sent your maids away."

22 Susanna sighed deeply, and said, "I am hemmed in on every side. For if I do this thing, it is death for me; and if I do not, I shall not escape your hands. [23]I choose not to do it and to fall

---

[h] Gk Vg: Heb *he.*
12:1: Mt 24:21; Mk 13:19; Rev 12:7; 16:18.
12:2: Mt 25:46.
12:3: Mt 13:43.
12:4: Rev 22:10.
12:7: Rev 4:9; 10:5; 12:14.
12:11: Dan 9:27; 11:31; Mt 24:15; Mk 13:14.
* **13:1:** The story of Susanna, here translated from the Greek of Theodotion, is accepted by the Catholic Church as canonical Scripture and placed among the deuterocanonical writings. It is prefixed to the book of Daniel in the Septuagint Greek, but in the Vulgate Latin it is placed here as chapter 13.

into your hands, rather than to sin in the sight of the Lord."

24 Then Susanna cried out with a loud voice, and the two elders shouted against her. [25]And one of them ran and opened the garden doors. [26]When the household servants heard the shouting in the garden, they rushed in at the side door to see what had happened to her. [27]And when the elders told their tale, the servants were greatly ashamed, for nothing like this had ever been said about Susanna.

The Elders Testify against Susanna

28 The next day, when the people gathered at the house of her husband Jo'akim, the two elders came, full of their wicked plot to have Susanna put to death. [29]They said before the people, "Send for Susanna, the daughter of Hilki'ah, who is the wife of Jo'akim." [30]So they sent for her. And she came, with her parents, her children, and all her kindred.

31 Now Susanna was a woman of great refinement, and beautiful in appearance. [32]As she was veiled, the wicked men ordered her to be unveiled, that they might feed upon her beauty. [33]But her family and friends and all who saw her wept.

34 Then the two elders stood up in the midst of the people, and laid their hands upon her head. [35]And she, weeping, looked up toward heaven, for her heart trusted in the Lord. [36]The elders said, "As we were walking in the garden alone, this woman came in with two maids, shut the garden doors, and dismissed the maids. [37]Then a young man, who had been hidden, came to her and lay with her. [38]We were in a corner of the garden, and when we saw this wickedness we ran to them. [39]We saw them embracing, but we could not hold the man, for he was too strong for us, and he opened the doors and dashed out. [40]So we seized this woman and asked her who the young man was, but she would not tell us. These things we testify."

41 The assembly believed them, because they were elders of the people and judges; and they condemned her to death.

42 Then Susanna cried out with a loud voice, and said, "O eternal God, who discern what is secret, who are aware of all things before they come to be, [43]you know that these men have borne false witness against me. And now I am to die! Yet I have done none of the things that they have wickedly invented against me!"

Daniel Rescues Susanna

44 The Lord heard her cry. [45]And as she was being led away to be put to death, God aroused the holy spirit of a young lad named Daniel; [46]and he cried with a loud voice, "I am innocent of the blood of this woman."

47 All the people turned to him, and said, "What is this that you have said?" [48]Taking his stand in the midst of them, he said, "Are you such fools, you sons of Israel? Have you condemned a daughter of Israel without examination and without learning the facts? [49]Return to the place of judgment. For these men have borne false witness against her."

50 Then all the people returned in haste. And the elders said to him, "Come, sit among us and inform us, for God has given you that right." [51]And Daniel said to them, "Separate them far from each other, and I will examine them."

52 When they were separated from each other, he summoned one of them and said to him, "You old relic of wicked days, your sins have now come home, which you have committed in the past, [53]pronouncing unjust judgments, condemning the innocent and letting the guilty go free, though the Lord said, 'Do not put to death an innocent and righteous person.' [54]Now then, if you really saw her, tell me this: Under what tree did you see them being intimate with each other?" He answered, "Under a mastic tree." [a] [55]And Daniel said, "Very well! You have lied against your own head, for the angel of God has received the sentence from God and will immediately cut [a] you in two."

56 Then he put him aside, and commanded them to bring the other. And he said to him, "You offspring of Canaan and not of Judah, beauty has deceived you and lust has perverted your heart. [57]This is how you both have been dealing with the daughters of Israel, and they were intimate with you through fear; but a daughter of Judah would not endure your wickedness. [58]Now then, tell me: Under what tree did you catch them being intimate with each other?" He answered, "Under an evergreen oak." [b] [59]And Daniel said to him, "Very well! You also have lied against your own head, for the angel of God is waiting with his sword to saw [b] you in two, that he may destroy you both."

60 Then all the assembly shouted loudly and blessed God, who saves those who hope in him. [61]And they rose against the two elders, for out of their own mouths Daniel had convicted them of bearing false witness; [62]and they did to them as they had wickedly planned to do to their neighbor; acting in accordance with the law of Moses, they put them to death. Thus innocent blood was saved that day.

63 And Hilki'ah and his wife praised God for their daughter Susanna, and so did Jo'akim her husband and all her kindred, because nothing shameful was found in her. [64]And from that day onward Daniel had a great reputation among the people.

---

[a] The Greek words for *mastic tree* and *cut* are so similar that the use of *cut* is ironic wordplay.
[b] The Greek words for *evergreen oak* and *saw* are so similar that the use of *saw* is ironic wordplay.

Daniel and the Priests of Bel

14 * When King Asty'ages was laid with his fathers, Cyrus the Persian received his kingdom. ²And Daniel was a companion of the king, and was the most honored of his friends.

3 Now the Babylonians had an idol called Bel, and every day they spent on it twelve bushels of fine flour and forty sheep and fifty gallons of wine. ⁴The king revered it and went every day to worship it. But Daniel worshiped his own God.

5 And the king said to him, "Why do you not worship Bel?" He answered, "Because I do not revere man-made idols, but the living God, who created heaven and earth and has dominion over all flesh."

6 The king said to him, "Do you not think that Bel is a living God? Do you not see how much he eats and drinks every day?" ⁷Then Daniel laughed, and said, "Do not be deceived, O king; for this is but clay inside and brass outside, and it never ate or drank anything."

8 Then the king was angry, and he called his priests and said to them, "If you do not tell me who is eating these provisions, you shall die. ⁹But if you prove that Bel is eating them, Daniel shall die, because he blasphemed against Bel." And Daniel said to the king, "Let it be done as you have said."

10 Now there were seventy priests of Bel, besides their wives and children. And the king went with Daniel into the temple of Bel. ¹¹And the priests of Bel said, "Behold, we are going outside; you yourself, O king, shall set forth the food and mix and place the wine, and shut the door and seal it with your signet. ¹²And when you return in the morning, if you do not find that Bel has eaten it all, we will die; or else Daniel will, who is telling lies about us." ¹³They were unconcerned, for beneath the table they had made a hidden entrance, through which they used to go in regularly and consume the provisions. ¹⁴When they had gone out, the king set forth the food for Bel. Then Daniel ordered his servants to bring ashes and they sifted them throughout the whole temple in the presence of the king alone. Then they went out, shut the door and sealed it with the king's signet, and departed. ¹⁵In the night the priests came with their wives and children, as they were accustomed to do, and ate and drank everything.

16 Early in the morning the king rose and came, and Daniel with him. ¹⁷And the king said, "Are the seals unbroken, Daniel?" He answered, "They are unbroken, O king." ¹⁸As soon as the doors were opened, the king looked at the table, and shouted in a loud voice, "You are great, O Bel; and with you there is no deceit, none at all."

19 Then Daniel laughed, and restrained the king from going in, and said, "Look at the floor, and notice whose footsteps these are." ²⁰The king said, "I see the footsteps of men and women and children."

21 Then the king was enraged, and he seized the priests and their wives and children; and they showed him the secret doors through which they were accustomed to enter and devour what was on the table. ²²Therefore the king put them to death, and gave Bel over to Daniel, who destroyed it and its temple.

Daniel Kills a Dragon

23 There was also a great dragon, which the Babylonians revered. ²⁴And the king said to Daniel, "You cannot deny that this is a living god; so worship him." ²⁵Daniel said, "I will worship the Lord my God, for he is the living God. ²⁶But if you, O king, will give me permission, I will slay the dragon without sword or club." The king said, "I give you permission."

27 Then Daniel took pitch, fat, and hair, and boiled them together and made cakes, which he fed to the dragon. The dragon ate them, and burst open. And Daniel said, "See what you have been worshiping!"

28 When the Babylonians heard it, they were very indignant and conspired against the king, saying, "The king has become a Jew; he has destroyed Bel, and slain the dragon, and slaughtered the priests." ²⁹Going to the king, they said, "Hand Daniel over to us, or else we will kill you and your household." ³⁰The king saw that they were pressing him hard, and under compulsion he handed Daniel over to them.

Daniel in the Lions' Den

31 They threw Daniel into the lions' den, and he was there for six days. ³²There were seven lions in the den, and every day they had been given two human bodies and two sheep; but these were not given to them now, so that they might devour Daniel.

33 Now the prophet Habak'kuk was in Jude'a. He had boiled pottage and had broken bread into a bowl, and was going into the field to take it to the reapers. ³⁴But the angel of the Lord said to Habak'kuk, "Take the dinner which you have to Babylon, to Daniel, in the lions' den." ³⁵Habak'kuk said, "Sir, I have never seen Babylon, and I know nothing about the den." ³⁶Then the angel of the Lord took him by the crown of his head, and lifted him by his hair and set him down in Babylon, right over the den, with the rushing sound of the wind itself.

37 Then Habak'kuk shouted, "Daniel, Daniel! Take the dinner which God has sent you." ³⁸And

---

* 14:1: Bel and the Dragon. These stories, here translated from the Greek of Theodotion, are added at the end of Daniel by both Greek and Vulgate. The latter treats the appendix as chapter 14, but attaches verse 1 to the preceding chapter as 13:65.

Daniel said, "You have remembered me, O God, and have not forsaken those who love you." [39]So Daniel arose and ate. And the angel of God immediately returned Habak′kuk to his own place.

40 On the seventh day the king came to mourn for Daniel. When he came to the den he looked in, and there sat Daniel. [41]And the king shouted with a loud voice, "You are great, O Lord God of Daniel, and there is no other besides you." [42]And he pulled Daniel [a] out, and threw into the den the men who had attempted his destruction, and they were devoured immediately before his eyes.

---

[a] Gk *him.*

THE BOOK OF

HOSEA

1 The word of the Lᴏʀᴅ that came to Hose'a the son of Bee'ri, in the days of Uzzi'ah, Jo'tham, A'haz, and Hezeki'ah, kings of Judah, and in the days of Jerobo'am the son of Jo'ash, king of Israel.

Hosea Marries a Harlot and Has Children

2 When the Lᴏʀᴅ first spoke through Hose'a, the Lᴏʀᴅ said to Hosea, "Go, take to yourself a wife of harlotry and have children of harlotry, for the land commits great harlotry by forsaking the Lᴏʀᴅ." ³So he went and took Gomer the daughter of Dibla'im, and she conceived and bore him a son.

4 And the Lᴏʀᴅ said to him, "Call his name Jezre'el; for yet a little while, and I will punish the house of Je'hu for the blood of Jezreel, and I will put an end to the kingdom of the house of Israel. ⁵And on that day, I will break the bow of Israel in the valley of Jezre'el."

6 She conceived again and bore a daughter. And the Lᴏʀᴅ said to him, "Call her name Not pitied, for I will no more have pity on the house of Israel, to forgive them at all. ⁷But I will have pity on the house of Judah, and I will deliver them by the Lᴏʀᴅ their God; I will not deliver them by bow, nor by sword, nor by war, nor by horses, nor by horsemen."

8 When she had weaned Not pitied, she conceived and bore a son. ⁹And the Lᴏʀᴅ said, "Call his name Not my people, for you are not my people and I am not your God." ᵃ

Israel's Restoration

10 ᵇ Yet the number of the people of Israel shall be like the sand of the sea, which can be neither measured nor numbered; and in the place where it was said to them, "You are not my people," it shall be said to them, "Sons of the living God." ¹¹And the people of Judah and the people of Israel shall be gathered together, and they shall appoint for themselves one head; and they shall go up from the land, for great shall be the day of Jezre'el.

Israel's Infidelity, Punishment, and Redemption

2 ᶜ Say to your brother, ᵈ "My people," and to your sister, ᵉ "She has obtained pity."
²"Plead with your mother, plead—
  for she is not my wife,
  and I am not her husband—
that she put away her harlotry from her face,
  and her adultery from between her
  breasts;
³lest I strip her naked
  and make her as in the day she was born,
and make her like a wilderness,
  and set her like a parched land,
  and slay her with thirst.
⁴Upon her children also I will have no pity,
  because they are children of harlotry.
⁵For their mother has played the harlot;
  she that conceived them has acted
  shamefully.
For she said, 'I will go after my lovers,
  who give me my bread and my water,
  my wool and my flax, my oil and my
  drink.'
⁶Therefore I will hedge up her ᶠ way with
  thorns;
  and I will build a wall against her,
  so that she cannot find her paths.
⁷She shall pursue her lovers,
  but not overtake them;
and she shall seek them,
  but shall not find them.
Then she shall say, 'I will go
  and return to my first husband,
  for it was better with me then than now.'

Hosea (Osee) preached and prophesied during the century—the eighth—that saw the decline and final destruction of the northern kingdom. It was a period of both moral and material dissolution, and it is this that gives his prophecy its peculiar characteristics. Hosea seems to take occasion of his own unhappy marriage to draw a parallel between it and the relationship between God and his unfaithful spouse Israel. He attacks passionately the moral evils and the injustice of the society in which he lives. Above all, he condemns the idolatry rampant everywhere, as well as the debased Yahweh worship. Israel will be punished, but after repentance the people will be welcomed back to their God.

ᵃ Heb I am not yours.
ᵇ Ch 2:1 in Heb.
ᶜ Ch 2:3 in Heb.
ᵈ Gk: Heb brothers.
ᵉ Gk Vg: Heb sisters.
ᶠ Gk Syr: Heb your.
1:6, 9: Hos 2:23; 1 Pet 2:10.
1:10: Rom 9:26.
2:1, 23: Rom 9:25; 1 Pet 2:10.

The Books of the Minor Prophets
These twelve are grouped together both in the Hebrew and in the Greek. The only reason for this seems to be that the books happen to be short. They are not "minor" in any other way; their religious value is great. They do not belong to any one historical period, and they range from Amos (eighth century B.C.) to Malachi, Joel, Obadiah, and Jonah (fifth to fourth century B.C.). They are here arranged according to their traditional order in the Hebrew, which is not the same as their historical order. The Latin Vulgate also follows the order of the Hebrew.

[8]And she did not know
    that it was I who gave her
    the grain, the wine, and the oil,
and who lavished upon her silver
    and gold which they used for Ba'al.
[9]Therefore I will take back
    my grain in its time,
    and my wine in its season;
and I will take away my wool and my flax,
    which were to cover her nakedness.
[10]Now I will uncover her lewdness
    in the sight of her lovers,
    and no one shall rescue her out of my hand.
[11]And I will put an end to all her mirth,
    her feasts, her new moons, her sabbaths,
    and all her appointed feasts.
[12]And I will lay waste her vines and her fig trees,
    of which she said,
'These are my hire,
    which my lovers have given me.'
I will make them a forest,
    and the beasts of the field shall devour them.
[13]And I will punish her for the feast days of the
    Ba'als
    when she burned incense to them
and decked herself with her ring and jewelry,
    and went after her lovers,
    and forgot me, says the LORD.

[14]"Therefore, behold, I will allure her,
    and bring her into the wilderness,
    and speak tenderly to her.
[15]And there I will give her her vineyards,
    and make the Valley of A'chor a door of
    hope.
And there she shall answer as in the days of
    her youth,
    as at the time when she came out of the
    land of Egypt.
16 "And in that day, says the LORD, you will
call me, 'My husband,' and no longer will you call
me, 'My Ba'al.' [17]For I will remove the names of
the Ba'als from her mouth, and they shall be mentioned by name no more. [18]And I will make for
you [g] a covenant on that day with the beasts of
the field, the birds of the air, and the creeping
things of the ground; and I will abolish [h] the bow,
the sword, and war from the land; and I will make
you lie down in safety. [19]And I will espouse you
for ever; I will espouse you in righteousness and
in justice, in steadfast love, and in mercy. [20]I will
espouse you in faithfulness; and you shall know
the LORD.
[21]"And in that day, says the LORD,
    I will answer the heavens
    and they shall answer the earth;
[22]and the earth shall answer the grain, the wine,
    and the oil,
    and they shall answer Jezre'el; [i]

[23]   and I will sow him [j] for myself in the land.
And I will have pity on Not pitied,
    and I will say to Not my people, 'You are my
    people';
    and he shall say 'You are my God.' "

The Lord's Love for His Unfaithful People

3 And the LORD said to me, "Go again, love a
woman who is beloved of a paramour and is
an adulteress; even as the LORD loves the people
of Israel, though they turn to other gods and love
cakes of raisins." [2]So I bought her for fifteen shekels of silver and a homer and a lethech of barley.
[3]And I said to her, "You must dwell as mine for
many days; you shall not play the harlot, or belong to another man; so will I also be to you." [4]For
the children of Israel shall dwell many days without king or prince, without sacrifice or pillar, without ephod or teraphim. [5]Afterward the children
of Israel shall return and seek the LORD their
God, and David their king; and they shall come in
fear to the LORD and to his goodness in the latter
days.

God Accuses Israel

4 Hear the word of the LORD, O people of
    Israel;
    for the LORD has a controversy with the
    inhabitants of the land.
There is no faithfulness or kindness,
    and no knowledge of God in the land;
[2]there is swearing, lying, killing, stealing, and
    committing adultery;
    they break all bounds and murder follows
    murder.
[3]Therefore the land mourns,
    and all who dwell in it languish,
and also the beasts of the field,
    and the birds of the air;
    and even the fish of the sea are taken
    away.

[4]Yet let no one contend,
    and let none accuse,
    for with you is my contention, O priest. [k]
[5]You shall stumble by day,
    the prophet also shall stumble with you by
    night;
    and I will destroy your mother.
[6]My people are destroyed for lack of
    knowledge;
    because you have rejected knowledge,
    I reject you from being a priest to me.
And since you have forgotten the law of your
    God,
    I also will forget your children.

[g] Heb them.
[h] Heb break.
[i] That is God sows.
[j] Cn: Heb her.
[k] Cn: Heb uncertain.

[7]The more they increased,
the more they sinned against me;
I will change their glory into shame.
[8]They feed on the sin of my people;
they are greedy for their iniquity.
[9]And it shall be like people, like priest;
I will punish them for their ways,
and repay them for their deeds.
[10]They shall eat, but not be satisfied;
they shall play the harlot, but not multiply;
because they have forsaken the LORD
to cherish harlotry.

[11]Wine and new wine
take away the understanding.
[12]My people inquire of a thing of wood,
and their staff gives them oracles.
For a spirit of harlotry has led them astray,
and they have left their God to play the
harlot.
[13]They sacrifice on the tops of the mountains,
and make offerings upon the hills,
under oak, poplar, and terebinth,
because their shade is good.

Therefore your daughters play the harlot,
and your brides commit adultery.
[14]I will not punish your daughters when they
play the harlot,
nor your brides when they commit adultery;
for the men themselves go aside with harlots,
and sacrifice with cult prostitutes,
and a people without understanding shall come
to ruin.

[15]Though you play the harlot, O Israel,
let not Judah become guilty.
Enter not into Gilgal,
nor go up to Beth-a′ven,
and swear not, "As the LORD lives."
[16]Like a stubborn heifer,
Israel is stubborn;
can the LORD now feed them
like a lamb in a broad pasture?

[17]E′phraim is joined to idols,
let him alone.
[18]A band [1] of drunkards, they give themselves to
harlotry;
they love shame more than their glory. [m]
[19]A wind has wrapped them [n] in its wings,
and they shall be ashamed because of their
altars. [o]

Impending Judgment on Israel and Judah;
and a Call to Repentance

5 Hear this, O priests!
Give heed, O house of Israel!
Listen, O house of the king!
For the judgment pertains to you;

for you have been a snare at Mizpah,
and a net spread upon Ta′bor.
[2]And they have made deep the pit of Shittim; [p]
but I will chastise all of them.

[3]I know E′phraim,
and Israel is not hidden from me;
for now, O Ephraim, you have played the
harlot,
Israel is defiled.
[4]Their deeds do not permit them
to return to their God.
For the spirit of harlotry is within them,
and they know not the LORD.
[5]The pride of Israel testifies to his face;
E′phraim [q] shall stumble in his guilt;
Judah also shall stumble with them.
[6]With their flocks and herds they shall go
to seek the LORD,
but they will not find him;
he has withdrawn from them.
[7]They have dealt faithlessly with the LORD;
for they have borne alien children.
Now the new moon shall devour them with
their fields.

[8]Blow the horn in Gib′e-ah,
the trumpet in Ra′mah.
Sound the alarm at Beth-a′ven;
tremble, [r] O Benjamin!
[9]E′phraim shall become a desolation
in the day of punishment;
among the tribes of Israel
I declare what is sure.
[10]The princes of Judah have become
like those who remove the landmark;
upon them I will pour out
my wrath like water.
[11]E′phraim is oppressed, crushed in judgment,
because he was determined to go after
vanity. [s]
[12]Therefore I am like a moth to E′phraim,
and like dry rot to the house of Judah.

[13]When E′phraim saw his sickness,
and Judah his wound,
then Ephraim went to Assyria,
and sent to the great king. [t]
But he is not able to cure you
or heal your wound.
[14]For I will be like a lion to E′phraim,
and like a young lion to the house of Judah.

---

[1] Cn: Heb uncertain.
[m] Cn Compare Gk: Heb of this line uncertain.
[n] Heb *her*.
[o] Gk Syr: Heb *sacrifices*.
[p] Cn: Heb uncertain.
[q] Heb *Israel and Ephraim*.
[r] Cn Compare Gk: Heb *after you*.
[s] Gk: Heb a *command*.
[t] Cn: Heb *a king that will contend*.

I, even I, will tear and go away,
    I will carry off, and none shall rescue.
[15]I will return again to my place,
    until they acknowledge their guilt and seek
        my face,
    and in their distress they seek me, saying,

6 "Come, let us return to the LORD;
    for he has torn, that he may heal us;
    he has stricken, and he will bind us up.
[2]After two days he will revive us;
    on the third day he will raise us up,
    that we may live before him.
[3]Let us know, let us press on to know the LORD;
    his going forth is sure as the dawn;
    he will come to us as the showers,
    as the spring rains that water the earth."
[4]What shall I do with you, O E'phraim?
    What shall I do with you, O Judah?
    Your love is like a morning cloud,
    like the dew that goes early away.
[5]Therefore I have hewn them by the prophets,
    I have slain them by the words of my
        mouth,
    and my judgment goes forth as the light.[u]

[6]For I desire mercy and not sacrifice,
    the knowledge of God, rather than burnt
        offerings.

[7]But at[v] Adam they transgressed the covenant;
    there they dealt faithlessly with me.
[8]Gilead is a city of evildoers,
    tracked with blood.
[9]As robbers lie in wait[w] for a man,
    so the priests are banded together;[x]
    they murder on the way to She'chem,
    yes, they commit villainy.
[10]In the house of Israel I have seen a horrible
        thing;
    E'phraim's harlotry is there, Israel is
        defiled.

[11]For you also, O Judah, a harvest is appointed.
    When I would restore the fortunes of my
        people,

7 [1]when I would heal Israel,
    the corruption of E'phraim is revealed,
    and the wicked deeds of Samar'ia;
    for they deal falsely,
    the thief breaks in,
    and the bandits raid without.
[2]But they do not consider
    that I remember all their evil works.
    Now their deeds encompass them,
    they are before my face.
[3]By their wickedness they make the king glad,
    and the princes by their treachery.
[4]They are all adulterers;
    they are like a heated oven,

whose baker ceases to stir the fire,
    from the kneading of the dough until it is
        leavened.
[5]On the day of our king the princes
    became sick with the heat of wine;
    he stretched out his hand with mockers.
[6]For like an oven their hearts burn[y] with
        intrigue;
    all night their anger smolders;
    in the morning it blazes like a flaming fire.
[7]All of them are hot as an oven,
    and they devour their rulers.
    All their kings have fallen;
    and none of them calls upon me.

[8]E'phraim mixes himself with the peoples;
    Ephraim is a cake not turned.
[9]Aliens devour his strength,
    and he knows it not;
    gray hairs are sprinkled upon him,
    and he knows it not.
[10]The pride of Israel witnesses against him;
    yet they do not return to the LORD their
        God,
    nor seek him, for all this.

[11]E'phraim is like a dove,
    silly and without sense,
    calling to Egypt, going to Assyria.
[12]As they go, I will spread over them my net;
    I will bring them down like birds of the air;
    I will chastise them for their wicked
        deeds.[z]
[13]Woe to them, for they have strayed from me!
    Destruction to them, for they have rebelled
        against me!
    I would redeem them,
    but they speak lies against me.

[14]They do not cry to me from the heart,
    but they wail upon their beds;
    for grain and wine they gash themselves,
    they rebel against me.
[15]Although I trained and strengthened their
        arms,
    yet they devise evil against me.
[16]They turn to Ba'al;[a]
    they are like a treacherous bow,
    their princes shall fall by the sword
    because of the insolence of their tongue.
    This shall be their derision in the land of
        Egypt.

---

[u] Gk Syr: Heb *your judgment goes forth.*
[v] Cn: Heb *like.*
[w] Cn: Heb uncertain.
[x] Syr: Heb *a company.*
[y] Gk Syr: Heb *brought near.*
[z] Cn: Heb *according to the report to their congregation.*
[a] Cn: Heb uncertain.
6:6: Mt 9:13; 12:7.

Israel's Apostasy

8 Set the trumpet to your lips,
    for [b] a vulture is over the house of the LORD,
because they have broken my covenant,
    and transgressed my law.
²To me they cry,
    My God, we Israel know you.
³Israel has spurned the good;
    the enemy shall pursue him.

⁴They made kings, but not through me.
    They set up princes, but without my
        knowledge.
With their silver and gold they made idols
    for their own destruction.
⁵I have [c] spurned your calf, O Samar′ia.
    My anger burns against them.
How long will it be
    till they are pure ⁶in Israel? [d]

A workman made it;
    it is not God.
The calf of Samar′ia
    shall be broken to pieces. [e]

⁷For they sow the wind,
    and they shall reap the whirlwind.
The standing grain has no heads,
    it shall yield no meal;
if it were to yield,
    aliens would devour it.
⁸Israel is swallowed up;
    already they are among the nations
    as a useless vessel.
⁹For they have gone up to Assyria,
    a wild donkey wandering alone;
    E′phraim has hired lovers.
¹⁰Though they hire allies among the nations,
    I will soon gather them up.
And they shall cease [f] for a little while
    from anointing [g] king and princes.

¹¹Because E′phraim has multiplied altars for
        sinning,
    they have become to him altars for sinning.
¹²Were I to write for him my laws by ten
        thousands,
    they would be regarded as a strange thing.
¹³They love sacrifice; [h]
    they sacrifice flesh and eat it;
    but the LORD has no delight in them.
Now he will remember their iniquity,
    and punish their sins;
    they shall return to Egypt.
¹⁴For Israel has forgotten his Maker,
    and built palaces;
and Judah has multiplied fortified cities;
    but I will send a fire upon his cities,
    and it shall devour his strongholds.

Punishment for Israel's Sin

9 Rejoice not, O Israel!
    Exult not [i] like the peoples;
for you have played the harlot, forsaking your
        God.
You have loved a harlot's hire
    upon all threshing floors.
²Threshing floor and winevat shall not feed
        them,
    and the new wine shall fail them.
³They shall not remain in the land of the LORD;
    but E′phraim shall return to Egypt,
    and they shall eat unclean food in Assyria.

⁴They shall not pour libations of wine to the
        LORD;
    and they shall not please him with their
        sacrifices.
Their bread [j] shall be like mourners' bread;
    all who eat of it shall be defiled;
for their bread shall be for their hunger only;
    it shall not come to the house of the LORD.

⁵What will you do on the day of appointed
        festival,
    and on the day of the feast of the LORD?
⁶For behold, they are going to Assyria; [k]
    Egypt shall gather them,
    Memphis shall bury them.
Nettles shall possess their precious things of
        silver;
    thorns shall be in their tents.

⁷The days of punishment have come,
    the days of recompense have come;
    Israel shall know it.
The prophet is a fool,
    the man of the spirit is mad,
because of your great iniquity
    and great hatred.
⁸The prophet is the watchman of E′phraim,
    the people of my God,
yet a fowler's snare is on all his ways,
    and hatred in the house of his God.
⁹They have deeply corrupted themselves
    as in the days of Gib′e-ah:
he will remember their iniquity,
    he will punish their sins.

---

[b] Cn: Heb *as*.
[c] Heb *He has*.
[d] Gk: Heb *for from Israel*.
[e] Or *shall go up in flames*.
[f] Gk: Heb *begin*.
[g] Gk: Heb *burden*.
[h] Cn: Heb uncertain.
[i] Gk: Heb *to exultation*.
[j] Cn: Heb *to them*.
[k] Cn: Heb *from destruction*.
8:14: Amos 1:4, 7, 10, 12, 14; 2:2, 5.
9:7: Lk 21:22.

[10]Like grapes in the wilderness,
 I found Israel.
Like the first fruit on the fig tree,
 in its first season,
 I saw your fathers.
But they came to Ba′al-pe′or,
 and consecrated themselves to Ba′al,[1]
 and became detestable like the thing they
 loved.
[11]E′phraim's glory shall fly away like a bird—
 no birth, no pregnancy, no conception!
[12]Even if they bring up children,
 I will bereave them till none is left.
Woe to them
 when I depart from them!
[13]E′phraim's sons, as I have seen, are destined for
 a prey;[m]
 Ephraim must lead forth his sons to
 slaughter.
[14]Give them, O Lord—
 what will you give?
Give them a miscarrying womb
 and dry breasts.

[15]Every evil of theirs is in Gilgal;
 there I began to hate them.
Because of the wickedness of their deeds
 I will drive them out of my house.
I will love them no more;
 all their princes are rebels.

[16]E′phraim is stricken,
 their root is dried up,
 they shall bear no fruit.
Even though they bring forth,
 I will slay their beloved children.
[17]My God will cast them off,
 because they have not listened to him;
 they shall be wanderers among the nations.

Israel's Sin and Captivity

10 Israel is a luxuriant vine
 that yields its fruit.
The more his fruit increased
 the more altars he built;
as his country improved
 he improved his pillars.
[2]Their heart is false;
 now they must bear their guilt.
The Lord[n] will break down their altars,
 and destroy their pillars.

[3]For now they will say:
 "We have no king,
for we fear not the Lord,
 and a king, what could he do for us?"
[4]They utter mere words;
 with empty oaths they make covenants;
so judgment springs up like poisonous weeds
 in the furrows of the field.

[5]The inhabitants of Samar′ia tremble
 for the calf[o] of Beth-a′ven.
Its people shall mourn for it,
 and its idolatrous priests shall wail[p]
 over it,
 over its glory which has departed from it.
[6]Yes, the thing itself shall be carried to Assyria,
 as tribute to the great king.[q]
E′phraim shall be put to shame,
 and Israel shall be ashamed of his idol.[r]

[7]Samar′ia's king shall perish,
 like a chip on the face of the waters.
[8]The high places of A′ven, the sin of Israel,
 shall be destroyed.
Thorn and thistle shall grow up
 on their altars;
and they shall say to the mountains, Cover us,
 and to the hills, Fall upon us.

[9]From the days of Gib′e-ah, you have sinned,
 O Israel;
 there they have continued.
Shall not war overtake them in Gibe-ah?
[10]I will come[s] against the wayward people to
 chastise them;
 and nations shall be gathered against them
 when they are chastised[t] for their double
 iniquity.

[11]E′phraim was a trained heifer
 that loved to thresh,
 and I spared her fair neck;
but I will put Ephraim to the yoke,
 Judah must plow,
 Jacob must harrow for himself.
[12]Sow for yourselves righteousness,
 reap the fruit[u] of mercy;
break up your fallow ground,
for it is the time to seek the Lord,
 that he may come and rain salvation upon
 you.

[13]You have plowed iniquity,
 you have reaped injustice,
 you have eaten the fruit of lies.
Because you have trusted in your chariots[v]
 and in the multitude of your warriors,

---

[1] Heb *shame.*
[m] Cn Compare Gk: Heb uncertain.
[n] Heb *he.*
[o] Gk Syr: Heb *calves.*
[p] Cn: Heb *exult.*
[q] Cn: Heb *a king that will contend.*
[r] Cn: Heb *counsel.*
[s] Cn Compare Gk: Heb *in my desire.*
[t] Gk: Heb *bound.*
[u] Gk: Heb *according to.*
[v] Gk: Heb *way.*
10:8: Lk 23:30; Rev 6:16.
10:12: 2 Cor 9:10.

14therefore the tumult of war shall arise among
  your people,
  and all your fortresses shall be destroyed,
as Shal'man destroyed Beth-ar'bel on the day
  of battle;
  mothers were dashed in pieces with their
  children.
15Thus it shall be done to you, O house of
  Israel, ʷ
  because of your great wickedness.
In the storm ˣ the king of Israel
  shall be utterly cut off.

God's Compassion Despite Israel's
Unfaithfulness

11 When Israel was a child, I loved him,
  and out of Egypt I called my son.
2The more I ʸ called them,
  the more they went from me; ᶻ
they kept sacrificing to the Ba'als,
  and burning incense to idols.

3Yet it was I who taught E'phraim to walk,
  I took them up in my ᵃ arms;
but they did not know that I healed them.
4I led them with cords of compassion, ᵇ
  with the bands of love,
and I became to them as one
  who raises an infant to his cheeks,
  and I bent down to them and fed them.

5They shall return to the land of Egypt,
  and Assyria shall be their king,
because they have refused to return to me.
6The sword shall rage against their cities,
  consume the bars of their gates,
  and devour them in their fortresses. ᶜ
7My people are bent on turning away from me; ᵈ
  so they are appointed to the yoke,
  and none shall remove it.

8How can I give you up, O E'phraim!
  How can I hand you over, O Israel!
How can I make you like Admah!
  How can I treat you like Zeboi'im!
My heart recoils within me,
  my compassion grows warm and tender.
9I will not execute my fierce anger,
  I will not again destroy E'phraim;
for I am God and not man,
  the Holy One in your midst,
  and I will not come to destroy. ᵉ

10They shall go after the LORD,
  he will roar like a lion;
yes, he will roar,
  and his sons shall come trembling from the
  west;
11they shall come trembling like birds from
  Egypt,

and like doves from the land of Assyria;
  and I will return them to their homes, says
  the LORD.
12 ᶠ E'phraim has encompassed me with lies,
  and the house of Israel with deceit;
but Judah is still known by ᵍ God,
  and is faithful to the Holy One.

The Long History of Israel's Rebellion

12 E'phraim herds the wind,
  and pursues the east wind all day
  long;
they multiply falsehood and violence;
  they make a bargain with Assyria,
  and oil is carried to Egypt.

2The LORD has an indictment against Judah,
  and will punish Jacob according to his
  ways,
  and repay him according to his deeds.
3In the womb he took his brother by the heel,
  and in his manhood he strove with God.
4He strove with the angel and prevailed,
  he wept and sought his favor.
He met God at Bethel,
  and there God spoke with him ʰ—
5the LORD the God of hosts,
  the LORD is his name:
6"So you, by the help of your God, return,
  hold fast to love and justice,
  and wait continually for your God."

7A trader, in whose hands are false balances,
  he loves to oppress.
8E'phraim has said, "Ah, but I am rich,
  I have gained wealth for myself";
but all his riches can never offset ⁱ
  the guilt he has incurred.
9I am the LORD your God
  from the land of Egypt;
I will again make you dwell in tents,
  as in the days of the appointed feast.

10I spoke to the prophets;
  it was I who multiplied visions,
  and through the prophets gave parables.
11If there is iniquity in Gilead
  they shall surely come to nothing;

ʷ Gk: Heb O Bethel.
ˣ Cn: Heb dawn.
ʸ Gk: Heb they.
ᶻ Gk: Heb them.
ᵃ Gk Syr Vg: Heb his.
ᵇ Heb man.
ᶜ Cn: Heb counsels.
ᵈ The meaning of the Hebrew is uncertain.
ᵉ Cn: Heb into the city.
ᶠ Ch 12:1 in Heb.
ᵍ Cn Compare Gk: Heb roams with.
ʰ Gk Syr: Heb us.
ⁱ Cn Compare Gk: Heb obscure.
11:1: Mt 2:15.
12:8: Rev 3:17.

if in Gilgal they sacrifice bulls,
  their altars also shall be like stone heaps
  on the furrows of the field.
[12](Jacob fled to the land of Ar′am,
  there Israel did service for a wife,
  and for a wife he herded sheep.)
[13]By a prophet the Lord brought Israel up from
    Egypt,
  and by a prophet he was preserved.
[14]E′phraim has given bitter provocation;
  so his Lord will leave his bloodguilt upon
    him,
  and will turn back upon him his reproaches.

God the Savior and Judge of Israel

13 When E′phraim spoke, men trembled;
  he was exalted in Israel;
  but he incurred guilt through Ba′al and
    died.
[2]And now they sin more and more,
  and make for themselves molten images,
  idols skilfully made of their silver,
  all of them the work of craftsmen.
  Sacrifice to these, they say.[j]
  Men kiss calves!
[3]Therefore they shall be like the morning mist
  or like the dew that goes early away,
  like the chaff that swirls from the threshing
    floor
  or like smoke from a window.

[4]I am the Lord your God
  from the land of Egypt;
  you know no God but me,
  and besides me there is no savior.
[5]It was I who knew you in the wilderness,
  in the land of drought;
[6]but when they had fed[k] to the full,
  they were filled, and their heart was lifted
    up;
  therefore they forgot me.
[7]So I will be to them like a lion,
  like a leopard I will lurk beside the way.
[8]I will fall upon them like a bear robbed of her
    cubs,
  I will tear open their breast,
  and there I will devour them like a lion,
  as a wild beast would tear them.

[9]I will destroy you, O Israel;
  who[l] can help you?
[10]Where[m] now is your king, to save you;
  where are all[n] your princes,[o] to defend
    you[p]—
  those of whom you said,
  "Give me a king and princes"?
[11]I have given you kings in my anger,
  and I have taken them away in my wrath.
[12]The iniquity of E′phraim is bound up,
  his sin is kept in store.

[13]The pangs of childbirth come for him,
  but he is an unwise son;
  for now he does not present himself
  at the mouth of the womb.

[14]Shall I ransom them from the power of Sheol?
  Shall I redeem them from Death?
  O Death, where[q] are your plagues?
  O Sheol, where[q] is your destruction?
  Compassion is hidden from my eyes.

[15]Though he may flourish as the reed plant,[r]
  the east wind, the wind of the Lord, shall
    come,
  rising from the wilderness;
  and his fountain shall dry up,
  his spring shall be parched;
  it shall strip his treasury
  of every precious thing.
[16] [s]Samar′ia shall bear her guilt,
  because she has rebelled against her God;
  they shall fall by the sword,
  their little ones shall be dashed in pieces,
  and their pregnant women ripped open.

A Plea for Repentance and a Promise

14 Return, O Israel, to the Lord your God,
  for you have stumbled because of your
    iniquity.
[2]Take with you words
  and return to the Lord;
  say to him,
  "Take away all iniquity;
  accept that which is good
  and we will render
  the fruit[t] of our lips.
[3]Assyria shall not save us,
  we will not ride upon horses;
  and we will say no more, 'Our God,'
  to the work of our hands.
  In you the orphan finds mercy."

[4]I will heal their faithlessness;
  I will love them freely,
  for my anger has turned from them.
[5]I will be as the dew to Israel;
  he shall blossom as the lily,
  he shall strike root as the poplar;[u]

---

[j] Gk: Heb *to these they say sacrifices of.*
[k] Cn: Heb *according to their pasture.*
[l] Gk Syr: Heb *for in me.*
[m] Gk Syr Vg: Heb *I will be.*
[n] Cn: Heb *in all.*
[o] Cn: Heb *cities.*
[p] Cn Compare Gk: Heb *and your judges.*
[q] Gk Syr: Heb *I will be.*
[r] Cn: Heb *among brothers.*
[s] Ch 14:1 in Heb.
[t] Gk Syr: Heb *bulls.*
[u] Cn: Heb *Lebanon.*
13:14: 1 Cor 15:55.
14:2: Heb 13:15.

⁶his shoots shall spread out;
  his beauty shall be like the olive,
  and his fragrance like Lebanon.
⁷They shall return and dwell beneath my ᵛ
    shadow,
  they shall flourish as a garden;ʷ
they shall blossom as the vine,
  their fragrance shall be like the wine of
    Lebanon.
⁸O E′phraim, what have I to do with idols?
  It is I who answer and look after you. ˣ
I am like an evergreen cypress,
  from me comes your fruit.

⁹Whoever is wise, let him understand these
    things;
  whoever is discerning, let him know them;
for the ways of the Lᴏʀᴅ are right,
  and the upright walk in them,
  but transgressors stumble in them.

ᵛ Heb *his.*
ʷ Cn: Heb *they shall grow grain.*
ˣ Heb *him.*
14:9: Acts 13:10.

THE BOOK OF

JOEL

Lament and Call to Repentance

1 The word of the LORD that came to Joel, the son of Pethu'el:

[2]Hear this, you aged men,
give ear, all inhabitants of the land!
Has such a thing happened in your days,
or in the days of your fathers?
[3]Tell your children of it,
and let your children tell their children,
and their children another generation.

[4]What the cutting locust left,
the swarming locust has eaten.
What the swarming locust left,
the hopping locust has eaten,
and what the hopping locust left,
the destroying locust has eaten.

[5]Awake, you drunkards, and weep;
and wail, all you drinkers of wine,
because of the sweet wine,
for it is cut off from your mouth.
[6]For a nation has come up against my land,
powerful and without number;
its teeth are lions' teeth,
and it has the fangs of a lioness.
[7]It has laid waste my vines,
and splintered my fig trees;
it has stripped off their bark and thrown it
down;
their branches are made white.
[8]Lament like a virgin clothed with sackcloth
for the bridegroom of her youth.
[9]The cereal offering and the drink offering are
cut off
from the house of the LORD.
The priests mourn,
the ministers of the LORD.
[10]The fields are laid waste,
the ground mourns;
because the grain is destroyed,
the wine fails,
the oil languishes.

[11]Be confounded, O tillers of the soil,
wail, O vinedressers,
for the wheat and the barley;
because the harvest of the field has
perished.

[12]The vine withers,
the fig tree languishes.
Pomegranate, palm, and apple,
all the trees of the field are withered;
and gladness fails
from the sons of men.

[13]Put on sackcloth and lament, O priests,
wail, O ministers of the altar.
Go in, pass the night in sackcloth,
O ministers of my God!
Because cereal offering and drink offering
are withheld from the house of your God.

[14]Sanctify a fast,
call a solemn assembly.
Gather the elders
and all the inhabitants of the land
to the house of the LORD your God;
and cry to the LORD.

[15]Alas for the day!
For the day of the LORD is near,
and as destruction from the Almighty it
comes.
[16]Is not the food cut off
before our eyes,
joy and gladness
from the house of our God?

[17]The seed shrivels under the clods, [a]
the storehouses are desolate;
the granaries are ruined
because the grain has failed.
[18]How the beasts groan!
The herds of cattle are perplexed
because there is no pasture for them;
even the flocks of sheep are dismayed.

[19]Unto you, O LORD, I cry.
For fire has devoured
the pastures of the wilderness,

Joel prophesied about four centuries later than Hosea, during the post-exilic period. He foretells a plague of locusts as punishment and speaks threateningly of the "day of the LORD"; but then at once declares the Lord to be merciful and kind to those who repent. Toward the end of chapter 2 the style becomes apocalyptic and he speaks of the outpouring of the Spirit upon the people in the Messianic age. This was fulfilled (Acts 2:16-21) at Pentecost.
[a] Heb uncertain.
1:6: Rev 9:8.

763

and flame has burned
all the trees of the field.
[20]Even the wild beasts cry to you
because the water brooks are dried up,
and fire has devoured
the pastures of the wilderness.

The Day of the Lord Is Coming

2 Blow the trumpet in Zion;
sound the alarm on my holy mountain!
Let all the inhabitants of the land tremble,
for the day of the LORD is coming, it is near,
[2]a day of darkness and gloom,
a day of clouds and thick darkness!
Like blackness there is spread upon the
mountains
a great and powerful people;
their like has never been from of old,
nor will be again after them
through the years of all generations.

[3]Fire devours before them,
and behind them a flame burns.
The land is like the garden of Eden before
them,
but after them a desolate wilderness,
and nothing escapes them.

[4]Their appearance is like the appearance of
horses,
and like war horses they run.
[5]As with the rumbling of chariots,
they leap on the tops of the mountains,
like the crackling of a flame of fire
devouring the stubble,
like a powerful army
drawn up for battle.

[6]Before them peoples are in anguish,
all faces grow pale.
[7]Like warriors they charge,
like soldiers they scale the wall.
They march each on his way,
they do not swerve[b] from their paths.
[8]They do not jostle one another,
each marches in his path;
they burst through the weapons
and are not halted.
[9]They leap upon the city,
they run upon the walls;
they climb up into the houses,
they enter through the windows like
a thief.

[10]The earth quakes before them,
the heavens tremble.
The sun and the moon are darkened,
and the stars withdraw their shining.
[11]The LORD utters his voice
before his army,

for his host is exceedingly great;
he that executes his word is powerful.
For the day of the LORD is great and very
awesome;
who can endure it?

[12]"Yet even now," says the LORD,
"return to me with all your heart,
with fasting, with weeping, and with
mourning;
[13]   and tear your hearts and not your
garments."
Return to the LORD, your God,
for he is gracious and merciful,
slow to anger, and abounding in mercy,
and repents of evil.
[14]Who knows whether he will not turn and
repent,
and leave a blessing behind him,
a cereal offering and a drink offering
for the LORD, your God?

[15]Blow the trumpet in Zion;
sanctify a fast;
call a solemn assembly;
[16]   gather the people.
Sanctify the congregation;
assemble the elders;
gather the children,
even nursing infants.
Let the bridegroom leave his room,
and the bride her chamber.

[17]Between the vestibule and the altar
let the priests, the ministers of the LORD,
weep
and say, "Spare your people, O LORD,
and make not your heritage a reproach,
a byword among the nations.
Why should they say among the peoples,
'Where is their God?'"

[18]Then the LORD became jealous for his land,
and had pity on his people.
[19]The LORD answered and said to his people,
"Behold, I am sending to you
grain, wine, and oil,
and you will be satisfied;
and I will no more make you
a reproach among the nations.

[20]"I will remove the northerner far from you,
and drive him into a parched and desolate
land,

---

[b] Gk Syr Vg: Heb *take a pledge.*
2:4–5: Rev 9:7, 9.
2:10: Rev 9:2.
2:11: Rev 6:17.

his front into the eastern sea,
and his rear into the western sea;
the stench and foul smell of him will rise,
for he has done great things.

21"Fear not, O land;
be glad and rejoice,
for the Lord has done great things!
22Fear not, you beasts of the field,
for the pastures of the wilderness are
green;
the tree bears its fruit,
the fig tree and vine give their full yield.

23"Be glad, O sons of Zion,
and rejoice in the Lord, your God;
for he has given the early rain for your
vindication,
he has poured down for you abundant rain,
the early and the latter rain, as before.

24"The threshing floors shall be full of grain,
the vats shall overflow with wine and oil.
25I will restore to you the years
which the swarming locust has eaten,
the hopper, the destroyer, and the cutter,
my great army, which I sent among you.

26"You shall eat in plenty and be satisfied,
and praise the name of the Lord your God,
who has dealt wondrously with you.
And my people shall never again be put to
shame.
27You shall know that I am in the midst of
Israel,
and that I, the Lord, am your God and there
is none else.
And my people shall never again be put to
shame.

28 c "And it shall come to pass afterward,
that I will pour out my spirit on all flesh;
your sons and your daughters shall prophesy,
your old men shall dream dreams,
and your young men shall see visions.
29Even upon the menservants and maidservants
in those days, I will pour out my spirit.

Portents in Heaven
and Judgment of the Nations

30 "And I will give signs in the heavens and on
the earth, blood and fire and columns of smoke.
31The sun shall be turned to darkness, and the
moon to blood, before the great and awesome day
of the Lord comes. 32And it shall come to pass
that all who call upon the name of the Lord shall
be delivered; for in Mount Zion and in Jerusalem
there shall be those who escape, as the Lord has
said, and among the survivors shall be those
whom the Lord calls.

3 d "For behold, in those days and at that time,
when I restore the fortunes of Judah and Jerusalem, 2I will gather all the nations and bring them
down to the valley of Jehosh'aphat, and I will enter into judgment with them there, on account of
my people and my heritage Israel, because they
have scattered them among the nations, and have
divided up my land, 3and have cast lots for my
people, and have given a boy for a harlot, and have
sold a girl for wine, and have drunk it.

4 "What are you to me, O Tyre and Si'don, and
all the regions of Philis'tia? Are you paying me
back for something? If you are paying me back, I
will repay your deed upon your own head swiftly
and speedily. 5For you have taken my silver and
my gold, and have carried my rich treasures into
your temples. e 6You have sold the people of Judah
and Jerusalem to the Greeks, removing them far
from their own border. 7But now I will stir them
up from the place to which you have sold them,
and I will repay your deed upon your own head. 8I
will sell your sons and your daughters into the
hand of the sons of Judah, and they will sell them
to the Sabe'ans, to a nation far off; for the Lord
has spoken."

9Proclaim this among the nations:
Prepare war,
stir up the mighty men.
Let all the men of war draw near,
let them come up.
10Beat your plowshares into swords,
and your pruning hooks into spears;
let the weak say, "I am a warrior."

11Hasten and come,
all you nations round about,
gather yourselves there.
Bring down your warriors, O Lord.
12Let the nations bestir themselves,
and come up to the valley of Jehosh'aphat;
for there I will sit to judge
all the nations round about.

13Put in the sickle,
for the harvest is ripe.
Go in, tread,
for the wine press is full.
The vats overflow,
for their wickedness is great.

---

c Ch 3:1 in Heb.
d Ch 4:1 in Heb.
e Or *palaces*.
2:28-32: Acts 2:17–21.
2:31: Rev 6:12.
2:32: Rom 10:13.
3:4-8: Is 23; Ezek 26:1–28:19; Amos 1:9–10; Zech 9:3–4; Ezek 28:20–26;
Zech 9:2; Is 14:29–31; Jer 47; Ezek 25:15–17; Amos 1:6–8; Zeph 2:4–7;
Zech 9:5–7.
3:10: Is 2:4; Mic 4:3.
3:13: Mk 4:29; Rev 14:15, 18, 19.

¹⁴Multitudes, multitudes,
    in the valley of decision!
  For the day of the Lord is near
    in the valley of decision.
¹⁵The sun and the moon are darkened,
    and the stars withdraw their shining.

¹⁶And the Lord roars from Zion,
    and utters his voice from Jerusalem,
    and the heavens and the earth shake.
  But the Lord is a refuge to his people,
    a stronghold to the people of Israel.

¹⁷"So you shall know that I am the Lord your
    God,
  who dwell in Zion, my holy mountain.
  And Jerusalem shall be holy
    and strangers shall never again pass
      through it.

¹⁸"And in that day
  the mountains shall drip sweet wine,
    and the hills shall flow with milk,

and all the stream beds of Judah
    shall flow with water;
and a fountain shall come forth from the house
    of the Lord
  and water the valley of Shittim.

¹⁹"Egypt shall become a desolation
    and E'dom a desolate wilderness,
  for the violence done to the people of Judah,
    because they have shed innocent blood in
      their land.
²⁰But Judah shall be inhabited for ever,
    and Jerusalem to all generations.
²¹I will avenge their blood, and I will not clear the
    guilty, ᵍ
    for the Lord dwells in Zion."

ᵍ Gk Syr: Heb *I will hold innocent their blood which I have not held innocent.*
3:16: Amos 1:2.
3:18: Ezek 47:1–12; Amos 9:13; Zech 14:8; Rev 22:1.

THE BOOK OF

AMOS

Judgment on Israel's Neighbors

1 The words of Amos, who was among the shepherds of Teko'a, which he saw concerning Israel in the days of Uzzi'ah king of Judah and in the days of Jerobo'am the son of Jo'ash, king of Israel, two years ^a before the earthquake. ²And he said:

"The LORD roars from Zion,
  and utters his voice from Jerusalem;
the pastures of the shepherds mourn,
  and the top of Carmel withers."

³Thus says the LORD:
"For three transgressions of Damascus,
  and for four, I will not revoke the
    punishment; ^b
because they have threshed Gilead
  with threshing sledges of iron.
⁴So I will send a fire upon the house of Haz'ael,
  and it shall devour the strongholds of
    Benha'dad.
⁵I will break the bar of Damascus,
  and cut off the inhabitants from the Valley
    of A'ven, ^c
and him that holds the scepter from
  Beth-e'den;
  and the people of Syria shall go into exile
    to Kir,"
                    says the LORD.

⁶Thus says the LORD:
"For three transgressions of Gaza,
  and for four, I will not revoke the
    punishment; ^b
because they carried into exile a whole people
  to deliver them up to E'dom.
⁷So I will send a fire upon the wall of Gaza,
  and it shall devour her strongholds.
⁸I will cut off the inhabitants from Ash'dod,
  and him that holds the scepter from
    Ash'kelon;
I will turn my hand against Ek'ron;
  and the remnant of the Philis'tines shall
    perish,"
                    says the Lord GOD.

⁹Thus says the LORD:
"For three transgressions of Tyre,
  and for four, I will not revoke the
    punishment; ^b

because they delivered up a whole people to
  E'dom,
and did not remember the covenant of
  brotherhood.
¹⁰So I will send a fire upon the wall of Tyre,
  and it shall devour her strongholds."

¹¹Thus says the LORD:
"For three transgressions of E'dom,
  and for four, I will not revoke the
    punishment; ^b
because he pursued his brother with the
  sword,
  and cast off all pity,
and his anger tore perpetually,
  and he kept his wrath ^d for ever.
¹²So I will send a fire upon Te'man,
  and it shall devour the strongholds of
    Bozrah."

¹³Thus says the LORD:
"For three transgressions of the Am'monites,
  and for four, I will not revoke the
    punishment; ^b
because they have ripped up women with child
  in Gilead,
  that they might enlarge their border.
¹⁴So I will kindle a fire in the wall of Rabbah,
  and it shall devour her strongholds,
with shouting in the day of battle,
  with a tempest in the day of the whirlwind;
¹⁵and their king shall go into exile,
  he and his princes together,"
                    says the LORD.

Amos was a shepherd of Judah called suddenly by God to denounce social corruption and injustice in the northern kingdom during the reign of Jeroboam II (eighth century B.C.). It was a time of great material luxury and worldly splendor, and the pastoral origins of the prophet contrasted strongly with the sophisticated decadence which, together with the people's infidelity, he denounced. He foretells the "day of the LORD," a time of punishment for men's sins, but holds out a hope of God's mercy to "the remnant of Joseph" (5:15). Some of the prophecies are probably of a later age.

^a Or *during two years.*
^b Heb *cause it to return.*
^c Or *On.*
^d Gk Syr Vg: Heb *his wrath kept.*
1:2: Joel 3:16.
1:3–5: Is 17:1–3; Jer 49:23–27; Zech 9:1.
1:6–8: Is 14:29–31; Jer 47; Ezek 25:15–17; Joel 3:4–8; Zeph 2:4–7; Zech 9:5–7.
1:9–10: Is 23; Ezek 26:1—28:19; Joel 3:4–8; Zech 9:3-4.
1:11–12: Is 34; 63:1–6; Jer 49:7–22; Ezek 25:12–14; 35; Obad; Mal 1:2–5.
1:13–15: Jer 49:1–6; Ezek 21:28–32; 25:1–7; Zeph 2:8–11.

Judgment on Israel, Judah, and the Nations

2 Thus says the LORD:
"For three transgressions of Moab,
and for four, I will not revoke the
punishment; [e]
because he burned to lime
the bones of the king of E′dom.
[2]So I will send a fire upon Moab,
and it shall devour the strongholds of
Ker′ioth,
and Moab shall die amid uproar,
amid shouting and the sound of the
trumpet;
[3]I will cut off the ruler from its midst,
and will slay all its princes with him,"
says the LORD.

[4]Thus says the LORD:
"For three transgressions of Judah,
and for four, I will not revoke the
punishment; [e]
because they have rejected the law of the LORD,
and have not kept his statutes,
but their lies have led them astray,
after which their fathers walked.
[5]So I will send a fire upon Judah,
and it shall devour the strongholds of
Jerusalem."

[6]Thus says the LORD:
"For three transgressions of Israel,
and for four, I will not revoke the
punishment; [e]
because they sell the righteous for silver,
and the needy for a pair of shoes—
[7]they that trample the head of the poor into the
dust of the earth,
and turn aside the way of the afflicted;
a man and his father go in to the same maiden,
so that my holy name is profaned;
[8]they lay themselves down beside every altar
upon garments taken in pledge;
and in the house of their God they drink
the wine of those who have been fined.

[9]"Yet I destroyed the Am′orite before them,
whose height was like the height of the
cedars,
and who was as strong as the oaks;
I destroyed his fruit above,
and his roots beneath.
[10]Also I brought you up out of the land of
Egypt,
and led you forty years in the wilderness,
to possess the land of the Am′orite.
[11]And I raised up some of your sons for
prophets,
and some of your young men for Naz′irites.

Is it not indeed so, O people of Israel?"
says the LORD.

[12]"But you made the Naz′irites drink wine,
and commanded the prophets,
saying, 'You shall not prophesy.'

[13]"Behold, I will press you down in your place,
as a cart full of sheaves presses down.
[14]Flight shall perish from the swift,
and the strong shall not retain his strength,
nor shall the mighty save his life;
[15]he who handles the bow shall not stand,
and he who is swift of foot shall not save
himself,
nor shall he who rides the horse save his
life;
[16]and he who is stout of heart among the mighty
shall flee away naked in that day,"
says the LORD.

Israel's Transgression and Punishment

3 Hear this word that the LORD has spoken
against you, O sons of Israel, against the
whole family which I brought up out of the land
of Egypt:
[2]"You only have I known
of all the families of the earth;
therefore I will punish you
for all your iniquities.

[3]"Do two walk together,
unless they have made an appointment?
[4]Does a lion roar in the forest,
when he has no prey?
Does a young lion cry out from his den,
if he has taken nothing?
[5]Does a bird fall in a snare on the earth,
when there is no trap for it?
Does a snare spring up from the ground,
when it has taken nothing?
[6]Is a trumpet blown in a city,
and the people are not afraid?
Does evil befall a city,
unless the LORD has done it?
[7]Surely the Lord GOD does nothing,
without revealing his secret
to his servants the prophets.
[8]The lion has roared;
who will not fear?
The Lord GOD has spoken;
who can but prophesy?"

[9]Proclaim to the strongholds in Assyria, [f]
and to the strongholds in the land of
Egypt,

---

[e] Heb *cause it to return.*
[f] Gk: Heb *Ashdod.*
2:1–3: Is 15–16; 25:10–12; Jer 48; Ezek 25:8–11; Zeph 2:8–11.
3:7: Rev 10:7.

and say, "Assemble yourselves upon the
   mountains of Samar'ia,
   and see the great tumults within her,
   and the oppressions in her midst."
10"They do not know how to do right," says the
   LORD,
   "those who store up violence and robbery in
   their strongholds."
11Therefore thus says the Lord GOD:
"An adversary shall surround the land,
   and bring down your defenses from you,
   and your strongholds shall be plundered."

12 Thus says the LORD: "As the shepherd rescues from the mouth of the lion two legs, or a
piece of an ear, so shall the people of Israel who
dwell in Samar'ia be rescued, with the corner of a
couch and part *g* of a bed."

13"Hear, and testify against the house of Jacob,"
   says the Lord GOD, the God of hosts,
14"that on the day I punish Israel for his
   transgressions,
   I will punish the altars of Bethel,
and the horns of the altar shall be cut off
   and fall to the ground.
15I will strike the winter house with the summer
   house;
   and the houses of ivory shall perish,
and the great houses *h* shall come to an end,"
                              says the LORD.

Punishments of Israel

4 "Hear this word, you cows of Bashan,
   who are in the mountain of Samar'ia,
who oppress the poor, who crush the needy,
   who say to their husbands, 'Bring, that we
   may drink!'
2The Lord GOD has sworn by his holiness
   that, behold, the days are coming upon you,
   when they shall take you away with hooks,
   even the last of you with fishhooks.
3And you shall go out through the breaches,
   every one straight before her;
   and you shall be cast forth into Har'mon,"
                              says the LORD.

4"Come to Bethel, and transgress;
   to Gilgal, and multiply transgression;
bring your sacrifices every morning,
   your tithes every three days;
5offer a sacrifice of thanksgiving of that which
   is leavened,
   and proclaim freewill offerings, publish
   them;
   for so you love to do, O people of Israel!"
                              says the Lord GOD.

6"I gave you cleanness of teeth in all your cities,
   and lack of bread in all your places,

yet you did not return to me,"
   says the LORD.

7"And I also withheld the rain from you
   when there were yet three months to the
   harvest;
I would send rain upon one city,
   and send no rain upon another city;
one field would be rained upon,
   and the field on which it did not rain
   withered;
8so two or three cities wandered to one city
   to drink water, and were not satisfied;
yet you did not return to me,"
                              says the LORD.

9"I struck you with blight and mildew;
   I laid waste *i* your gardens and your
   vineyards;
   your fig trees and your olive trees the locust
   devoured;
yet you did not return to me,"
                              says the LORD.

10"I sent among you a pestilence after the manner
   of Egypt;
I slew your young men with the sword;
I carried away your horses; *j*
   and I made the stench of your camp go up
   into your nostrils;
yet you did not return to me,"
                              says the LORD.

11"I overthrew some of you,
   as when God overthrew Sodom and
   Gomor'rah,
   and you were as a brand plucked out of the
   burning;
yet you did not return to me,"
                              says the LORD.

12"Therefore thus I will do to you, O Israel;
   because I will do this to you,
   prepare to meet your God, O Israel!"

13For behold, he who forms the mountains, and
   creates the wind,
   and declares to man what is his thought;
who makes the morning darkness,
   and treads on the heights of the earth—
the LORD, the God of hosts, is his name!

A Lamentation for Israel's Sins

5 Hear this word which I take up over you in
   lamentation, O house of Israel:

---

g The meaning of the Hebrew word is uncertain.
h Or *many houses.*
i Cn: Heb *the multitude of.*
j Heb *with the captivity of your horses.*

2"Fallen, no more to rise,
is the virgin Israel;
forsaken on her land,
with none to raise her up."

3For thus says the Lord GOD:
"The city that went forth a thousand
shall have a hundred left,
and that which went forth a hundred
shall have ten left
to the house of Israel."

4For thus says the LORD to the house of Israel:
"Seek me and live;
5   but do not seek Bethel,
and do not enter into Gilgal
or cross over to Be′er-she′ba;
for Gilgal shall surely go into exile,
and Bethel shall come to nothing."

6Seek the LORD and live,
lest he break out like fire in the house of
Joseph,
and it devour, with none to quench it for
Bethel,
7O you who turn justice to wormwood,
and cast down righteousness to the earth!

8He who made the Pleiades and Orion,
and turns deep darkness into the morning,
and darkens the day into night,
who calls for the waters of the sea,
and pours them out upon the surface of the
earth,
the LORD is his name,
9who makes destruction flash forth against the
strong,
so that destruction comes upon the
fortress.

10They hate him who reproves in the gate,
and they abhor him who speaks the truth.
11Therefore because you trample upon the poor
and take from him exactions of wheat,
you have built houses of hewn stone,
but you shall not dwell in them;
you have planted pleasant vineyards,
but you shall not drink their wine.
12For I know how many are your transgressions,
and how great are your sins—
you who afflict the righteous, who take a
bribe,
and turn aside the needy in the gate.
13Therefore he who is prudent will keep silent in
such a time;
for it is an evil time.

14Seek good, and not evil,
that you may live;

and so the LORD, the God of hosts, will be with
you,
as you have said.
15Hate evil, and love good,
and establish justice in the gate;
it may be that the LORD, the God of hosts,
will be gracious to the remnant of Joseph.

16Therefore thus says the LORD, the God of hosts,
the Lord:
"In all the squares there shall be wailing;
and in all the streets they shall say, 'Alas!
alas!'
They shall call the farmers to mourning
and to wailing those who are skilled in
lamentation,
17and in all vineyards there shall be wailing,
for I will pass through the midst of you,"
says the LORD.

18Woe to you who desire the day of the LORD!
Why would you have the day of the LORD?
It is darkness, and not light;
19   as if a man fled from a lion,
and a bear met him;
or went into the house and leaned with his
hand against the wall,
and a serpent bit him.
20Is not the day of the LORD darkness, and not
light,
and gloom with no brightness in it?

21"I hate, I despise your feasts,
and I take no delight in your solemn
assemblies.
22Even though you offer me your burnt offerings
and cereal offerings,
I will not accept them,
and the peace offerings of your fatted beasts
I will not look upon.
23Take away from me the noise of your songs;
to the melody of your harps I will not listen.
24But let justice roll down like waters,
and righteousness like an ever-flowing
stream.

25 "Did you bring to me sacrifices and offerings the forty years in the wilderness, O house of
Israel? 26You shall take up Sakkuth your king, and
Kai′wan your star-god, your images, k which you
made for yourselves; 27therefore I will take you
into exile beyond Damascus," says the LORD,
whose name is the God of hosts.

Punishment of Complacency and Pride

6 "Woe to those who are at ease in Zion,
and to those who feel secure on the
mountain of Samar′ia,

---

k Heb *your images, your star-god.*
5:25–27: Acts 7:42–43.

the notable men of the first of the nations,
to whom the house of Israel come!
²Pass over to Cal'neh, and see;
and from there go to Ha'math the great;
then go down to Gath of the Philis'tines.
Are they better than these kingdoms?
Or is their territory greater than your
territory,
³O you who put far away the evil day,
and bring near the seat of violence?

⁴"Woe to those who lie upon beds of ivory,
and stretch themselves upon their
couches,
and eat lambs from the flock,
and calves from the midst of the stall;
⁵who sing idle songs to the sound of the harp,
and like David invent for themselves
instruments of music;
⁶who drink wine in bowls,
and anoint themselves with the finest oils,
but are not grieved over the ruin of Joseph!
⁷Therefore they shall now be the first of those
to go into exile,
and the revelry of those who stretch
themselves shall pass away."

⁸The Lord God has sworn by himself
(says the Lord, the God of hosts):
"I abhor the pride of Jacob,
and hate his strongholds;
and I will deliver up the city and all that is
in it."

Oppression and Devastation to Come

9 And if ten men remain in one house, they
shall die. ¹⁰And when a man's kinsman, he who
burns him, ¹ shall take him up to bring the bones
out of the house, and shall say to him who is in
the innermost parts of the house, "Is there still
any one with you?" he shall say, "No"; and he shall
say, "Hush! We must not mention the name of the
Lord."

¹¹For behold, the Lord commands,
and the great house shall be struck down
into fragments,
and the little house into bits.
¹²Do horses run upon rocks?
Does one plow the sea with oxen?
But you have turned justice into poison
and the fruit of righteousness into
wormwood—
¹³you who rejoice in Lo-de'bar, ⁿ
who say, "Have we not by our own strength
taken Karna'im ° for ourselves?"
¹⁴"For behold, I will raise up against you a
nation,
O house of Israel," says the Lord, the God
of hosts;

"and they shall oppress you from the entrance
of Ha'math
to the Brook of the Ar'abah."

Locusts and Fire

7 Thus the Lord God showed me: behold, he
was forming locusts in the beginning of the
shooting up of the latter growth; and behold, it
was the latter growth after the king's mowings.
²When they had finished eating the grass of the
land, I said,
"O Lord God, forgive, I beg you!
How can Jacob stand?
He is so small!"
³The Lord repented concerning this;
"It shall not be," said the Lord.

4 Thus the Lord God showed me: behold, the
Lord God was calling for a judgment by fire, and
it devoured the great deep and was eating up the
land. ⁵Then I said,
"O Lord God, cease, I beg you!
How can Jacob stand?
He is so small!"
⁶The Lord repented concerning this;
"This also shall not be," said the Lord
God.

The Plumb Line

7 He showed me: behold, the Lord was standing beside a wall built with a plumb line, with a
plumb line in his hand. ⁸And the Lord said to me,
"Amos, what do you see?". And I said, "A plumb
line." Then the Lord said,
"Behold, I am setting a plumb line
in the midst of my people Israel;
I will never again pass by them;
⁹the high places of Isaac shall be made
desolate,
and the sanctuaries of Israel shall be laid
waste,
and I will rise against the house of
Jerobo'am with the sword."

Amaziah's Complaint

10 Then Amazi'ah the priest of Bethel sent to
Jerobo'am king of Israel, saying, "Amos has conspired against you in the midst of the house of
Israel; the land is not able to bear all his words.
¹¹For thus Amos has said,
'Jerobo'am shall die by the sword,
and Israel must go into exile away from his
land.'"
¹²And Amazi'ah said to Amos, "O seer, go, flee
away to the land of Judah, and eat bread there,
and prophesy there; ¹³but never again prophesy
at Bethel, for it is the king's sanctuary, and it is a
temple of the kingdom."

---

¹ Or who makes a burning for him.
ⁿ Or a thing of nought.
° Or horns.

Amos' Reply

14 Then Amos answered Amazi′ah, "I am no prophet, nor a prophet's son;[p] but I am a herdsman, and a dresser of sycamore trees, [15]and the LORD took me from following the flock, and the LORD said to me, 'Go, prophesy to my people Israel.'

[16]"Now therefore hear the word of the LORD.
You say, 'Do not prophesy against Israel,
and do not preach against the house of
Isaac.'

[17]Therefore thus says the LORD:
'Your wife shall be a harlot in the city,
and your sons and your daughters shall fall
by the sword,
and your land shall be parceled out by line;
you yourself shall die in an unclean land,
and Israel shall surely go into exile away
from its land.'"

The Basket of Summer Fruit

8 Thus the Lord GOD showed me: behold, a basket of summer fruit.[q] [2]And he said, "Amos, what do you see?" And I said, "A basket of summer fruit."[q] Then the LORD said to me, "The end[r] has come upon my people Israel;
I will never again pass by them.
[3]The songs of the temple[s] shall become
wailings in that day,"
says the Lord GOD;
"the dead bodies shall be many;
in every place they shall be cast out in
silence."[t]

[4]Hear this, you who trample upon the needy,
and bring the poor of the land to an end,
[5]saying, "When will the new moon be over,
that we may sell grain?
And the sabbath,
that we may offer wheat for sale,
that we may make the ephah small and the
shekel great,
and deal deceitfully with false balances,
[6]that we may buy the poor for silver
and the needy for a pair of sandals,
and sell the refuse of the wheat?"

[7]The LORD has sworn by the pride of Jacob:
"Surely I will never forget any of their deeds.
[8]Shall not the land tremble on this account,
and every one mourn who dwells in it,
and all of it rise like the Nile,
and be tossed about and sink again, like the
Nile of Egypt?"

[9]"And on that day," says the Lord GOD,
"I will make the sun go down at noon,
and darken the earth in broad daylight.
[10]I will turn your feasts into mourning,
and all your songs into lamentation;

I will bring sackcloth upon all loins,
and baldness on every head;
I will make it like the mourning for an only son,
and the end of it like a bitter day.

[11]"Behold, the days are coming," says the Lord
GOD,
"when I will send a famine on the land;
not a famine of bread, nor a thirst for water,
but of hearing the words of the LORD.
[12]They shall wander from sea to sea,
and from north to east;
they shall run back and forth, to seek the word
of the LORD,
but they shall not find it.
[13]"In that day the fair virgins and the young men
shall faint for thirst.
[14]Those who swear by Ash′imah of Samar′ia,
and say, 'As your god lives, O Dan,'
and, 'As the way of Be′er-she′ba lives,'
they shall fall, and never rise again."

Destruction, Captivity, and Restoration

9 I saw the LORD standing beside[u] the altar, and he said:
"Strike the capitals until the thresholds shake,
and shatter them on the heads of all the
people;[v]
and what are left of them I will slay with the
sword;
not one of them shall flee away,
not one of them shall escape.

[2]"Though they dig into Sheol,
from there shall my hand take them;
though they climb up to heaven,
from there I will bring them down.
[3]Though they hide themselves on the top of
Carmel,
from there I will search out and take them;
and though they hide from my sight at the
bottom of the sea,
there I will command the serpent, and it
shall bite them.
[4]And though they go into captivity before their
enemies,
there I will command the sword, and it shall
slay them;
and I will set my eyes upon them for evil and
not for good."

[5]The Lord, GOD of hosts,
he who touches the earth and it melts,
and all who dwell in it mourn,

---

[p] Or one of the sons of the prophets.
[q] Heb qayits.
[r] Heb qets.
[s] or palace.
[t] or be silent!.
[u] Or upon.
[v] Heb all of them.

and all of it rises like the Nile,
  and sinks again, like the Nile of Egypt;
⁶who builds his upper chambers in the heavens,
  and founds his vault upon the earth;
who calls for the waters of the sea,
    and pours them out upon the surface of the
      earth—
  the LORD is his name.

⁷"Are you not like the Ethiopians to me,
  O people of Israel?" says the LORD.
  "Did I not bring up Israel from the land of
      Egypt,
    and the Philis'tines from Caphtor and the
      Syrians from Kir?
⁸Behold, the eyes of the Lord GOD are upon the
    sinful kingdom,
  and I will destroy it from the surface of the
    ground;
  except that I will not utterly destroy the
    house of Jacob,"
                                 says the LORD.

⁹"For behold, I will command,
  and shake the house of Israel among all the
    nations
as one shakes with a sieve,
  but no pebble shall fall upon the earth.
¹⁰All the sinners of my people shall die by the
    sword,

who say, 'Evil shall not overtake or
  meet us.'

¹¹"In that day I will raise up
  the booth of David that is fallen
and repair its breaches,
  and raise up its ruins,
  and rebuild it as in the days of old;
¹²that they may possess the remnant of E'dom
  and all the nations who are called by my
    name,"
  says the LORD who does this.

¹³"Behold, the days are coming," says the LORD,
  "when the plowman shall overtake the
    reaper
  and the treader of grapes him who sows the
    seed;
the mountains shall drip sweet wine,
  and all the hills shall flow with it.
¹⁴I will restore the fortunes of my people Israel,
  and they shall rebuild the ruined cities and
    inhabit them;
they shall plant vineyards and drink their wine,
  and they shall make gardens and eat their
    fruit.
¹⁵I will plant them upon their land,
  and they shall never again be plucked up
  out of the land which I have given them,"
                         says the LORD your God.

THE BOOK OF

OBADIAH

Edom Will Be Brought Low and Israel Triumph

¹The vision of Obadi′ah.

Thus says the Lord God concerning E′dom:
We have heard tidings from the Lord,
  and a messenger has been sent among the
    nations:
"Rise up! let us rise against her for battle!"
²Behold, I will make you small among the
    nations,
  you shall be utterly despised.
³The pride of your heart has deceived you,
  you who live in the clefts of the rock, ᵃ
    whose dwelling is high,
who say in your heart,
  "Who will bring me down to the ground?"
⁴Though you soar aloft like the eagle,
  though your nest is set among the stars,
    from there I will bring you down,
                              says the Lord.

⁵If thieves came to you,
  if plunderers by night—
    how you have been destroyed!—
  would they not steal only enough for
    themselves?
If grape gatherers came to you,
  would they not leave gleanings?
⁶How Esau has been pillaged,
  his treasures sought out!
⁷All your allies have deceived you,
  they have driven you to the border;
your confederates have prevailed against you;
  your trusted friends have set a trap under
    you—
    there is no understanding of it.
⁸Will I not on that day, says the Lord,
  destroy the wise men out of E′dom,
    and understanding out of Mount Esau?
⁹And your mighty men shall be dismayed, O
    Te′man,
  so that every man from Mount Esau will be
    cut off by slaughter.
¹⁰For the violence done to your brother Jacob,
  shame shall cover you,
    and you shall be cut off for ever.
¹¹On the day that you stood aloof,
  on the day that strangers carried off his
    wealth,

and foreigners entered his gates
  and cast lots for Jerusalem,
    you were like one of them.
¹²But you should not have gloated over the day
    of your brother
  in the day of his misfortune;
you should not have rejoiced over the people of
    Judah
  in the day of their ruin;
you should not have boasted
  in the day of distress.
¹³You should not have entered the gate of my
    people
  in the day of his calamity;
you should not have gloated over his disaster
  in the day of his calamity;
you should not have looted his goods
  in the day of his calamity.
¹⁴You should not have stood at the parting of the
    ways
  to cut off his fugitives;
you should not have delivered up his survivors
  in the day of distress.
¹⁵For the day of the Lord is near upon all the
    nations.
As you have done, it shall be done to you,
  your deeds shall return on your own head.
¹⁶For as you have drunk upon my holy mountain,
  all the nations round about shall drink;
they shall drink, and stagger, ᵇ
  and shall be as though they had not been.
¹⁷But in Mount Zion there shall be those that
    escape,
  and it shall be holy;
and the house of Jacob shall possess their own
    possessions.
¹⁸The house of Jacob shall be a fire,
  and the house of Joseph a flame,
    and the house of Esau stubble;
they shall burn them and consume them,
  and there shall be no survivor to the house
    of Esau;
                    for the Lord has spoken.

The book of Obadiah (Abdias) is so short that it is difficult to be certain of
its date and character. It is a tirade against the people of Edom, who are
told not to exult over the misfortune of Jerusalem, for they shall be utterly
destroyed, while a remnant from Israel shall survive. It seems to apply to
the situation of the postexilic period when the surrounding nations, including Edom, had partly occupied the vacant territory of Judah.
ᵃ Or *Sela*.
ᵇ Cn: Heb *swallow*.

¹⁹Those of the Neg'eb shall possess Mount Esau,
  and those of the Shephe'lah the land of the
    Philis'tines;
they shall possess the land of E'phraim and
    the land of Samar'ia
  and Benjamin shall possess Gilead.
²⁰The exiles in Ha'lah ᶜ who are of the people of
    Israel
  shall possess ᵈ Phoeni'cia as far as
    Zar'ephath;

and the exiles of Jerusalem who are in
    Sephar'ad
  shall possess the cities of the Neg'eb.
²¹Saviors shall go up to Mount Zion
  to rule Mount Esau;
  and the kingdom shall be the LORD's.

ᶜ Cn: Heb *this army*.
ᵈ Cn: Heb *which*.
1–21: Is 34; 63:1–6; Jer 49:7–22; Ezek 25:12–14; 35; Amos 1:11–12; Mal
1:2–5.

THE BOOK OF

JONAH

Jonah Tries to Flee God

1 Now the word of the LORD came to Jonah the son of Amit'tai, saying, [2]"Arise, go to Nin'eveh, that great city, and cry against it; for their wickedness has come up before me." [3]But Jonah rose to flee to Tar'shish from the presence of the LORD. He went down to Joppa and found a ship going to Tarshish; so he paid the fare, and went on board, to go with them to Tarshish, away from the presence of the LORD.

4 But the LORD hurled a great wind upon the sea, and there was a mighty tempest on the sea, so that the ship threatened to break up. [5]Then the mariners were afraid, and each cried to his god; and they threw the wares that were in the ship into the sea, to lighten it for them. But Jonah had gone down into the inner part of the ship and had lain down, and was fast asleep. [6]So the captain came and said to him, "What do you mean, you sleeper? Arise, call upon your god! Perhaps the god will give a thought to us, that we do not perish."

7 And they said to one another, "Come, let us cast lots, that we may know on whose account this evil has come upon us." So they cast lots, and the lot fell upon Jonah. [8]Then they said to him, "Tell us on whose account this evil has come upon us. What is your occupation? And from where do you come? What is your country? And of what people are you?" [9]And he said to them, "I am a Hebrew; and I fear the LORD, the God of heaven, who made the sea and the dry land." [10]Then the men were exceedingly afraid, and said to him, "What is this that you have done!" For the men knew that he was fleeing from the presence of the LORD, because he had told them.

Jonah Is Thrown into the Sea and Swallowed

11 Then they said to him, "What shall we do to you, that the sea may quiet down for us?" For the sea grew more and more tempestuous. [12]He said to them, "Take me up and throw me into the sea; then the sea will quiet down for you; for I know it is because of me that this great tempest has come upon you." [13]Nevertheless the men rowed hard to bring the ship back to land, but they could not, for the sea grew more and more tempestuous against them. [14]Therefore they cried to the LORD, "We beg you, O LORD, let us not perish for this man's life, and lay not on us innocent blood; for you, O LORD, have done as it pleased you." [15]So they took up

Jonah and threw him into the sea; and the sea ceased from its raging. [16]Then the men feared the LORD exceedingly, and they offered a sacrifice to the LORD and made vows.

17 [a] And the LORD appointed a great fish to swallow up Jonah; and Jonah was in the belly of the fish three days and three nights.

Jonah's Prayer and Deliverance

2 Then Jonah prayed to the LORD his God from the belly of the fish, [2]saying,

"I called to the LORD, out of my distress,
 and he answered me;
out of the belly of Sheol I cried,
 and you heard my voice.
[3]For you cast me into the deep,
 into the heart of the seas,
 and the flood was round about me;
all your waves and your billows
 passed over me.
[4]Then I said, 'I am cast out
 from your presence;
how shall I again look
 upon your holy temple?'
[5]The waters closed in over me,
 the deep was round about me;
weeds were wrapped about my head
[6]   at the roots of the mountains.
I went down to the land
 whose bars closed upon me for ever;
yet you brought up my life from the Pit,
 O LORD my God.
[7]When my soul fainted within me,
 I remembered the LORD;
and my prayer came to you,
 into your holy temple.
[8]Those who pay regard to vain idols
 forsake their true loyalty.
[9]But I with the voice of thanksgiving
 will sacrifice to you;

The Book of Jonah (Jonas) is set in the reign of Jeroboam II (eighth century B.C.), but the book was probably written long after the Exile. This suggests that it is not meant to be taken historically, although the central figure, Jonah, is mentioned in 2 Kings 14:25 and appears to have been a well-known prophet of the time. In this story the writer, making use of many improbable details, teaches that God is merciful even in his punishments, if only his people will repent; and so far from being the God of Israel alone, he is prepared to extend his mercy to others, provided they possess or acquire the necessary dispositions of heart. Our Lord himself quotes the conversion of the Ninevites and the three days Jonah spent inside the great fish (Mt 12:38–41), but this is not a testimony to its historical character. He is concerned rather with its teaching.
[a] Ch 2:1 in Heb.
1:17: Mt 12:40.

what I have vowed I will pay.

Deliverance belongs to the Lord!" [10]And the Lord spoke to the fish, and it vomited out Jonah upon the dry land.

Nineveh Repents

3 Then the word of the Lord came to Jonah the second time, saying, [2]"Arise, go to Nin'eveh, that great city, and proclaim to it the message that I tell you." [3]So Jonah arose and went to Nin'eveh, according to the word of the Lord. Now Nineveh was an exceedingly great city, three days' journey in breadth. [4]Jonah began to go into the city, going a day's journey. And he cried, "Yet forty days, and Nin'eveh shall be overthrown!" [5]And the people of Nin'eveh believed God; they proclaimed a fast, and put on sackcloth, from the greatest of them to the least of them.

6 Then tidings reached the king of Nin'eveh, and he arose from his throne, removed his robe, and covered himself with sackcloth, and sat in ashes. [7]And he made proclamation and published through Nin'eveh, "By the decree of the king and his nobles: Let neither man nor beast, herd nor flock, taste anything; let them not feed, or drink water, [8]but let man and beast be covered with sackcloth, and let them cry mightily to God; yes, let every one turn from his evil way and from the violence which is in his hands. [9]Who knows, God may yet repent and turn from his fierce anger, so that we perish not?"

10 When God saw what they did, how they turned from their evil way, God repented of the evil which he had said he would do to them; and he did not do it.

Jonah's Anger

4 But it displeased Jonah exceedingly, and he was angry. [2]And he prayed to the Lord and said, "I pray you, Lord, is not this what I said when I was yet in my country? That is why I made haste to flee to Tar'shish; for I knew that you are a gracious God and merciful, slow to anger, and abounding in mercy, and that you repent of evil. [3]Therefore now, O Lord, take my life from me, I beg you, for it is better for me to die than to live." [4]And the Lord said, "Do you do well to be angry?" [5]Then Jonah went out of the city and sat to the east of the city, and made a booth for himself there. He sat under it in the shade, till he should see what would become of the city.

God Reproves Jonah

6 And the Lord God appointed a plant, [b] and made it come up over Jonah, that it might be a shade over his head, to save him from his discomfort. So Jonah was exceedingly glad because of the plant. [b] [7]But when dawn came up the next day, God appointed a worm which attacked the plant, [b] so that it withered. [8]When the sun rose, God appointed a sultry east wind, and the sun beat upon the head of Jonah so that he was faint; and he asked that he might die, and said, "It is better for me to die than to live." [9]But God said to Jonah, "Do you do well to be angry for the plant?" [b] And he said, "I do well to be angry, angry enough to die." [10]And the Lord said, "You pity the plant, [b] for which you did not labor, nor did you make it grow, which came into being in a night, and perished in a night. [11]And should not I pity Nin'eveh, that great city, in which there are more than a hundred and twenty thousand persons who do not know their right hand from their left, and also much cattle?"

---

[b] Heb *qiqayon*, probably *the castor oil plant*.
3:9: Joel 2:14.
4:2: Ex 34:6.

THE BOOK OF

MICAH

Prophecy concerning Samaria and Judah

1 The word of the LORD that came to Mi′cah of Mo′resheth in the days of Jo′tham, A′haz, and Hezeki′ah, kings of Judah, which he saw concerning Samar′ia and Jerusalem.

²Hear, you peoples, all of you;
 listen, O earth, and all that is in it;
and let the Lord GOD be a witness against you,
 the Lord from his holy temple.
³For behold, the LORD is coming forth out of his place,
 and will come down and tread upon the high places of the earth.
⁴And the mountains will melt under him
 and the valleys will be cleft,
like wax before the fire,
 like waters poured down a steep place.
⁵All this is for the transgression of Jacob
 and for the sins of the house of Israel.
What is the transgression of Jacob?
 Is it not Samar′ia?
And what is the sin of the house ᵃ of Judah?
 Is it not Jerusalem?
⁶Therefore I will make Samar′ia a heap in the open country,
 a place for planting vineyards;
and I will pour down her stones into the valley,
 and uncover her foundations.
⁷All her images shall be beaten to pieces,
 all her hires shall be burned with fire,
 and all her idols I will lay waste;
for from the hire of a harlot she gathered them,
 and to the hire of a harlot they shall return.

⁸For this I will lament and wail;
 I will go stripped and naked;
I will make lamentation like the jackals,
 and mourning like the ostriches.
⁹For her wound ᵇ is incurable;
 and it has come to Judah,
it has reached to the gate of my people,
 to Jerusalem.

¹⁰Tell it not in Gath,
 weep not at all;
in Beth″-le-aph′rah
 roll yourselves in the dust.
¹¹Pass on your way,
 inhabitants of Sha′phir,

in nakedness and shame;
the inhabitants of Za′anan
 do not come forth;
the wailing of Beth-e′zel
 shall take away from you its standing place.
¹²For the inhabitants of Ma′roth
 wait anxiously for good,
because evil has come down from the LORD
 to the gate of Jerusalem.
¹³Harness the steeds to the chariots,
 inhabitants of La′chish;
you were ᶜ the beginning of sin
 to the daughter of Zion,
for in you were found
 the transgressions of Israel.
¹⁴Therefore you shall give parting gifts
 to Mo′resheth-gath;
the houses of Ach′zib shall be a deceitful thing
 to the kings of Israel.
¹⁵I will again bring a conqueror upon you,
 inhabitants of Mare′shah;
the glory of Israel
 shall come to Adul′lam.
¹⁶Make yourselves bald and cut off your hair,
 for the children of your delight;
make yourselves as bald as the eagle,
 for they shall go from you into exile.

Evils of the People Denounced but a Remnant Will Be Gathered

2 Woe to those who devise wickedness
 and work evil upon their beds!
When the morning dawns, they perform it,
 because it is in the power of their hand.
²They covet fields, and seize them;
 and houses, and take them away;
they oppress a man and his house,
 a man and his inheritance.
³Therefore thus says the LORD:
Behold, against this family I am devising evil,
 from which you cannot remove your necks;

Micah lived and prophesied at about the same time as Isaiah, in the kingdom of Judah. Like his contemporaries, he denounces the evils of his age, which he contrasts dramatically with the requirements of God: "to do justice, and to love kindness, and to walk humbly" with God (6:8). He foretells God's punishments, even the fall of Jerusalem (3:12). At the same time he prophesies, like Isaiah, that a remnant shall be saved (chapters 4–5) and speaks of the Messiah to come (5:2).
ᵃ Gk Tg Compare Syr: Heb *what are the high places.*
ᵇ Gk Syr Vg: Heb *wounds.*
ᶜ Cn: Heb *it was.*
1:2: 1 Kings 22.28.

and you shall not walk haughtily,
  for it will be an evil time.
⁴In that day they shall take up a taunt song
    against you,
  and wail with bitter lamentation,
and say, "We are utterly ruined;
  he changes the portion of my people;
how he removes it from me!
  Among our captors ᵈ he divides our fields."
⁵Therefore you will have none to cast the line
    by lot
  in the assembly of the LORD.

⁶"Do not preach"—thus they preach—
  "one should not preach of such things;
  disgrace will not overtake us."
⁷Should this be said, O house of Jacob?
  Is the Spirit of the LORD impatient?
  Are these his doings?
Do not my words do good
  to him who walks uprightly?
⁸But you rise against my people ᵉ as an enemy;
  you strip the robe from the peaceful, ᶠ
from those who pass by trustingly
  with no thought of war.
⁹The women of my people you drive out
  from their pleasant houses;
from their young children you take away
  my glory for ever.
¹⁰Arise and go,
  for this is no place to rest;
because of uncleanness that destroys
  with a grievous destruction.
¹¹If a man should go about and utter wind and
    lies,
  saying, "I will preach to you of wine and
    strong drink,"
  he would be the preacher for this people!

¹²I will surely gather all of you, O Jacob,
  I will gather the remnant of Israel;
I will set them together
  like sheep in a fold,
like a flock in its pasture,
  a noisy multitude of men.
¹³He who opens the breach will go up before
    them;
  they will break through and pass the gate,
  going out by it.
Their king will pass on before them,
  the LORD at their head.

Evil Rulers and Prophets

3 And I said:
Hear, you heads of Jacob
  and rulers of the house of Israel!
Is it not for you to know justice?—
² you who hate the good and love the evil,
who tear the skin from off my people,
  and their flesh from off their bones;

³who eat the flesh of my people,
  and flay their skin from off them,
and break their bones in pieces,
  and chop them up like meat ᵍ in a kettle,
  like flesh in a caldron.

⁴Then they will cry to the LORD,
  but he will not answer them;
he will hide his face from them at that time,
  because they have made their deeds evil.

⁵Thus says the LORD concerning the prophets
  who lead my people astray,
who cry "Peace"
  when they have something to eat,
but declare war against him
  who puts nothing into their mouths.
⁶Therefore it shall be night to you, without
    vision,
  and darkness to you, without divination.
The sun shall go down upon the prophets,
  and the day shall be black over them;
⁷the seers shall be disgraced,
  and the diviners put to shame;
they shall all cover their lips,
  for there is no answer from God.
⁸But as for me, I am filled with power,
  with the Spirit of the LORD,
  and with justice and might,
to declare to Jacob his transgression
  and to Israel his sin.

⁹Hear this, you heads of the house of Jacob
  and rulers of the house of Israel,
who abhor justice
  and pervert all equity,
¹⁰who build Zion with blood
  and Jerusalem with wrong.
¹¹Its heads give judgment for a bribe,
  its priests teach for hire,
  its prophets divine for money;
yet they lean upon the LORD and say,
  "Is not the LORD in the midst of us?
  No evil shall come upon us."
¹²Therefore because of you
  Zion shall be plowed as a field;
Jerusalem shall become a heap of ruins,
  and the mountain of the house a wooded
    height.

Prophecy of Restoration of Zion

4 It shall come to pass in the latter days
  that the mountain of the house of the
  LORD

ᵈ Cn: Heb *the rebellious.*
ᵉ Cn: Heb *yesterday my people rose.*
ᶠ Cn: Heb *from before a garment.*
ᵍ Gk: Heb *as.*
4:1–3: Is 2:2–4.

shall be established as the highest of the
mountains,
and shall be raised up above the hills;
and peoples shall flow to it,
² and many nations shall come, and say:
"Come, let us go up to the mountain of the
LORD,
to the house of the God of Jacob;
that he may teach us his ways
and we may walk in his paths."
For out of Zion shall go forth the law,
and the word of the LORD from Jerusalem.
³He shall judge between many peoples,
and shall decide for strong nations
afar off;
and they shall beat their swords into
plowshares,
and their spears into pruning hooks;
nation shall not lift up sword against nation,
neither shall they learn war any more;
⁴but they shall sit every man under his vine and
under his fig tree,
and none shall make them afraid;
for the mouth of the LORD of hosts has
spoken.

⁵For all the peoples walk
each in the name of its god,
but we will walk in the name of the LORD our
God
for ever and ever.

⁶In that day, says the LORD,
I will assemble the lame
and gather those who have been driven away,
and those whom I have afflicted;
⁷and the lame I will make the remnant;
and those who were cast off, a strong
nation;
and the LORD will reign over them in Mount
Zion
from this time forth and for evermore.

⁸And you, O tower of the flock,
hill of the daughter of Zion,
to you shall it come,
the former dominion shall come,
the kingdom of the daughter of Jerusalem.

⁹Now why do you cry aloud?
Is there no king in you?
Has your counselor perished,
that pangs have seized you like a woman in
labor?
¹⁰Writhe and groan,ʰ O daughter of Zion,
like a woman with labor pains;
for now you shall go forth from the city
and dwell in the open country;
you shall go to Babylon.

There you shall be rescued,
there the LORD will redeem you
from the hand of your enemies.

¹¹Now many nations
are assembled against you,
saying, "Let her be profaned,
and let our eyes gaze upon Zion."
¹²But they do not know
the thoughts of the LORD,
they do not understand his plan,
that he has gathered them as sheaves to the
threshing floor.
¹³Arise and thresh,
O daughter of Zion,
for I will make your horn iron
and your hoofs bronze;
you shall beat in pieces many peoples,
and shallⁱ devote their gain to the LORD,
their wealth to the Lord of the whole earth.

A Ruler from Bethlehem

5 ʲ Now you are walled about with a wall;ᵏ
siege is laid against us;
with a rod they strike upon the cheek
the ruler of Israel.

² ¹ But you, O Bethlehem Eph′rathah,
who are little to be among the clans of
Judah,
from you shall come forth for me
one who is to be ruler in Israel,
whose origin is from of old,
from ancient days.
³Therefore he shall give them up until the time
when she who has labor pains has brought
forth;
then the rest of his brethren shall return
to the sons of Israel.
⁴And he shall stand and feed his flock in the
strength of the LORD,
in the majesty of the name of the LORD his
God.
And they shall dwell secure, for now he shall
be great
to the ends of the earth.

⁵And this shall be peace,
when the Assyrian comes into our land
and treads upon our soil,ᵐ
that we will raise against him seven shepherds
and eight princes of men;

ʰ Heb uncertain.
ⁱ Gk Syr Tg: Heb *I will.*
ʲ Ch 4:14 in Heb.
ᵏ Cn Compare Gk: Heb obscure.
ˡ Ch 5:1 in Heb.
ᵐ Gk: Heb *in our palaces.*
4:4: Zech 3:10.
5:2: Mt 2:6; Jn 7:42.

⁶they shall rule the land of Assyria with the
sword,
and the land of Nimrod with the drawn
sword; [n]
and they [o] shall deliver us from the Assyrian
when he comes into our land
and treads within our border.

⁷Then the remnant of Jacob shall be
in the midst of many peoples
like dew from the Lord,
like showers upon the grass,
which do not depend upon men
nor wait for the sons of men.
⁸And the remnant of Jacob shall be among the
nations,
in the midst of many peoples,
like a lion among the beasts of the forest,
like a young lion among the flocks of
sheep,
which, when it goes through, treads down
and tears in pieces, and there is none to
deliver.
⁹Your hand shall be lifted up over your
adversaries,
and all your enemies shall be cut off.

¹⁰And in that day, says the Lord,
I will cut off your horses from among you
and will destroy your chariots;
¹¹and I will cut off the cities of your land
and throw down all your strongholds;
¹²and I will cut off sorceries from your hand,
and you shall have no more soothsayers;
¹³and I will cut off your images
and your pillars from among you,
and you shall bow down no more
to the work of your hands;
¹⁴and I will root out your Ashe'rim from among
you
and destroy your cities.
¹⁵And in anger and wrath I will execute
vengeance
upon the nations that did not obey.

What the Lord Requires

6 Hear what the Lord says:
Arise, plead your case before the mountains,
and let the hills hear your voice.
²Hear, you mountains, the controversy of the
Lord,
and you enduring foundations of the earth;
for the Lord has a controversy with his people,
and he will contend with Israel.

³"O my people, what have I done to you?
In what have I wearied you? Answer me!
⁴For I brought you up from the land of Egypt,
and redeemed you from the house of
bondage;

and I sent before you Moses,
Aaron, and Miriam.
⁵O my people, remember what Balak king of
Moab devised,
and what Balaam the son of Beor answered
him,
and what happened from Shittim to Gilgal,
that you may know the saving acts of the
Lord."

⁶"With what shall I come before the Lord,
and bow myself before God on high?
Shall I come before him with burnt offerings,
with calves a year old?
⁷Will the Lord be pleased with thousands of
rams,
with ten thousands of rivers of oil?
Shall I give my first-born for my
transgression,
the fruit of my body for the sin of my
soul?"
⁸He has showed you, O man, what is good;
and what does the Lord require of you
but to do justice, and to love kindness, [p]
and to walk humbly with your God?

⁹The voice of the Lord cries to the city—
and it is sound wisdom to fear your name:
"Hear, O tribe and assembly of the city! [q]
¹⁰   Can I forget [r] the treasures of wickedness in
the house of the wicked,
and the scant measure that is accursed?
¹¹Shall I acquit the man with wicked scales
and with a bag of deceitful weights?
¹²Your [s] rich men are full of violence;
your [s] inhabitants speak lies,
and their tongue is deceitful in their mouth.
¹³Therefore I have begun [t] to strike you,
making you desolate because of your sins.
¹⁴You shall eat, but not be satisfied,
and there shall be hunger in your inward
parts;
you shall put away, but not save,
and what you save I will give to the sword.
¹⁵You shall sow, but not reap;
you shall tread olives, but not anoint
yourselves with oil;
you shall tread grapes, but not drink wine.
¹⁶For you have kept the statutes of Omri, [u]
and all the works of the house of A'hab;
and you have walked in their counsels;

---

[n] Cn: Heb *in its entrances.*
[o] Heb *he.*
[p] Or *steadfast love.*
[q] Cn Compare Gk: Heb *and who has appointed it yet.*
[r] Cn: Heb uncertain.
[s] Heb *whose.*
[t] Gk Syr Vg: Heb *have made sick.*
[u] Gk Syr Vg Tg: Heb *the statutes of Omri are kept.*

that I may make you a desolation, and your [v]
    inhabitants a hissing;
so you shall bear the scorn of the peoples." [w]

Corruption, Repentance, and God's Compassion and Love

7 Woe is me! For I have become
    as when the summer fruit has been
      gathered,
    as when the vintage has been gleaned:
there is no cluster to eat,
    no first-ripe fig which my soul desires.
[2]The godly man has perished from the earth,
    and there is none upright among men;
they all lie in wait for blood,
    and each hunts his brother with a net.
[3]Their hands are upon what is evil, to do it
      diligently;
    the prince and the judge ask for a bribe,
and the great man utters the evil desire of his
      soul;
    thus they weave it together.
[4]The best of them is like a brier,
    the most upright of them a thorn hedge.
The day of their [x] watchmen, of their [x]
      punishment, has come;
    now their confusion is at hand.
[5]Put no trust in a neighbor,
    have no confidence in a friend;
guard the doors of your mouth
    from her who lies in your bosom;
[6]for the son treats the father with contempt,
    the daughter rises up against her mother,
the daughter-in-law against her mother-in-law;
    a man's enemies are the men of his own
      house.
[7]But as for me, I will look to the LORD,
    I will wait for the God of my salvation;
    my God will hear me.

[8]Rejoice not over me, O my enemy;
    when I fall, I shall rise;
when I sit in darkness,
    the LORD will be a light to me.
[9]I will bear the indignation of the LORD
    because I have sinned against him,
until he pleads my cause
    and executes judgment for me.
He will bring me forth to the light;
    I shall behold his deliverance.
[10]Then my enemy will see,
    and shame will cover her who said to me,
    "Where is the LORD your God?"
My eyes will gloat over her;
    now she will be trodden down
    like the mire of the streets.

[11]A day for the building of your walls!
    In that day the boundary shall be far
      extended.
[12]In that day they will come to you,
    from Assyria to [y] Egypt,
  and from Egypt to the River,
    from sea to sea and from mountain to
      mountain.
[13]But the earth will be desolate
    because of its inhabitants,
    for the fruit of their doings.

[14]Shepherd your people with your staff,
    the flock of your inheritance,
who dwell alone in a forest
    in the midst of a garden land;
let them feed in Bashan and Gilead
    as in the days of old.

[15]As in the days when you came out of the land
    of Egypt
    I will show them [z] marvelous things.

[16]The nations shall see and be ashamed
    of all their might;
they shall lay their hands on their mouths;
    their ears shall be deaf;
[17]they shall lick the dust like a serpent,
    like the crawling things of the earth;
they shall come trembling out of their
      strongholds,
    they shall turn in dread to the LORD our
      God,
    and they shall fear because of you.

[18]Who is a God like you, pardoning iniquity
    and passing over transgression
    for the remnant of his inheritance?
He does not retain his anger for ever
    because he delights in mercy.
[19]He will again have compassion upon us,
    he will tread our iniquities under foot.
You will cast all our [a] sins
    into the depths of the sea.
[20]You will show faithfulness to Jacob
    and mercy to Abraham,
as you have sworn to our fathers
    from the days of old.

---

[v] Heb *its*.
[w] Gk: Heb *my people*.
[x] Heb *your*.
[y] Cn: Heb *and cities of*.
[z] Heb *him*.
[a] Gk Syr Vg Tg: Heb *their*.
7:6: Mt 10:21, 35, 36; Mk 13:12; Lk 12:53.
7:20: Lk 1:55.

THE BOOK OF
NAHUM

God's Wrath toward Nineveh and Peace for Judah

1 An oracle concerning Nin'eveh. The book of the vision of Na'hum of El'kosh. ²The LORD is a jealous God and avenging, the LORD is avenging and wrathful; the LORD takes vengeance on his adversaries and keeps wrath for his enemies. ³The LORD is slow to anger and of great might, and the LORD will by no means clear the guilty.

His way is in whirlwind and storm, and the clouds are the dust of his feet. ⁴He rebukes the sea and makes it dry, he dries up all the rivers; Bashan and Carmel wither, the bloom of Lebanon fades. ⁵The mountains quake before him, the hills melt; the earth is laid waste before him, the world and all that dwell therein.

⁶Who can stand before his indignation? Who can endure the heat of his anger? His wrath is poured out like fire, and the rocks are broken asunder by him. ⁷The LORD is good, a stronghold in the day of trouble; he knows those who take refuge in him. ⁸But with an overflowing flood he will make a full end of his adversaries, ᵃ and will pursue his enemies into darkness. ⁹What do you plot against the LORD? He will make a full end; he will not take vengeance ᵇ twice on his foes. ᶜ ¹⁰Like entangled thorns they are consumed, ᵈ like dry stubble. ¹¹Did one not ᵉ come out from you, who plotted evil against the LORD, and counseled villainy?

¹²Thus says the LORD, "Though they be strong and many, ᶠ they will be cut off and pass away. Though I have afflicted you, I will afflict you no more.

¹³And now I will break his yoke from off you and will burst your bonds asunder."

¹⁴The LORD has given commandment about you: "No more shall your name be perpetuated; from the house of your gods I will cut off the graven image and the molten image. I will make your grave, for you are vile."

¹⁵ ᵍ Behold, on the mountains the feet of him who brings good tidings, who proclaims peace! Keep your feasts, O Judah, fulfil your vows, for never again shall the wicked come against you, he is utterly cut off.

The Overthrow of Nineveh

2 The shatterer has come up against you. Man the ramparts; watch the road; gird your loins; collect all your strength.

²(For the LORD is restoring the majesty of Jacob as the majesty of Israel, for plunderers have stripped them and ruined their branches.)

³The shield of his mighty men is red, his soldiers are clothed in scarlet. The chariots flash like flame ʰ when mustered in array; the chargers ⁱ prance. ⁴The chariots rage in the streets, they rush back and forth through the squares;

The opening words of the Book of Nahum announce the central theme— the coming destruction of Nineveh, the great oppressor of God's people. The passion with which this lyric poetry is imbued is explained by the tyranny endured for so long by Israel. But the deliverance announced will not, unfortunately, be of long duration. The fall of Nineveh (612 B.C.) will be followed by the fall of Jerusalem, but that is not part of the prophet's message.

ᵃ Gk: Heb *her place.*
ᵇ Gk: Heb *rise up.*
ᶜ Cn: Heb *distress.*
ᵈ Heb *are consumed, drunken as with their drink.*
ᵉ Cn: Heb *fully.*
ᶠ Heb uncertain.
ᵍ Ch 2:1 in Heb.
ʰ Cn: The meaning of the Hebrew word is uncertain.
ⁱ Cn Compare Gk Syr: Heb *cypresses.*
1–3: Is 10:5–34; Zeph 2:12–15.
1:15: Is 40:9; 52:7; Acts 10:36; Rom 10:15.

they gleam like torches,
  they dart like lightning.
[5]The officers are summoned,
  they stumble as they go,
they hasten to the wall,
  the mantelet is set up.
[6]The river gates are opened,
  the palace is in dismay;
[7]its mistress [j] is stripped, she is carried off,
  her maidens lamenting,
moaning like doves,
  and beating their breasts.
[8]Nin'eveh is like a pool
  whose waters [k] run away.
"Halt! Halt!" they cry;
  but none turns back.
[9]Plunder the silver,
  plunder the gold!
There is no end of treasure,
  or wealth of every precious thing.
[10]Desolate! Desolation and ruin!
  Hearts faint and knees tremble,
anguish is on all loins,
  all faces grow pale!
[11]Where is the lions' den,
  the cave [l] of the young lions,
where the lion brought his prey,
  where his cubs were, with none to disturb?
[12]The lion tore enough for his whelps
  and strangled prey for his lionesses;
he filled his caves with prey
  and his dens with torn flesh.

Utter Ruin of the Evil City

13 Behold, I am against you, says the LORD of hosts, and I will burn your [m] chariots in smoke, and the sword shall devour your young lions; I will cut off your prey from the earth, and the voice of your messengers shall no more be heard.

3 Woe to the bloody city,
  all full of lies and booty—
  no end to the plunder!
[2]The crack of whip, and rumble of wheel,
  galloping horse and bounding chariot!
[3]Horsemen charging,
  flashing sword and glittering spear,
hosts of slain,
  heaps of corpses,
dead bodies without end—
  they stumble over the bodies!
[4]And all for the countless harlotries of the
    harlot,
  graceful and of deadly charms,
who betrays nations with her harlotries,
  and peoples with her charms.

[5]Behold, I am against you,
  says the LORD of hosts,
  and will lift up your skirts over your face;

and I will let nations look on your nakedness
  and kingdoms on your shame.
[6]I will throw filth at you
  and treat you with contempt,
  and make you an object of scorn.
[7]And all who look on you will shrink from you
    and say,
Wasted is Nin'eveh; who will moan over her?
  from where shall I seek comforters
    for her? [n]

[8]Are you better than Thebes [o]
  that sat by the Nile,
with water around her,
  her rampart a sea,
  and water her wall?
[9]Ethiopia was her strength,
  Egypt too, and that without limit;
  Put and the Libyans were her [p] helpers.

[10]Yet she was carried away,
  she went into captivity;
her little ones were dashed in pieces
  at the head of every street;
for her honored men lots were cast,
  and all her great men were bound in chains.
[11]You also will be drunken,
  you will be dazed;
you will seek
  a refuge from the enemy.
[12]All your fortresses are like fig trees
  with first-ripe figs—
if shaken they fall
  into the mouth of the eater.
[13]Behold, your troops
  are women in your midst.
The gates of your land
  are wide open to your foes;
  fire has devoured your bars.
[14]Draw water for the siege,
  strengthen your forts;
go into the clay,
  tread the mortar,
  take hold of the brick mold!
[15]There will the fire devour you,
  the sword will cut you off.
  It will devour you like the locust.

Multiply yourselves like the locust,
  multiply like the grasshopper!
[16]You increased your merchants
  more than the stars of the heavens.

---

[j] The meaning of the Hebrew is uncertain.
[k] Cn Compare Gk: Heb *from the days that she has become, and they.*
[l] Cn: Heb *pasture.*
[m] Heb *her.*
[n] Gk: Heb *you.*
[o] Heb *No-amon.*
[p] Gk: Heb *your.*

The locust spreads its wings and flies
   away.
[17]Your princes are like grasshoppers,
   your scribes �ۊ like clouds of locusts
settling on the fences
   in a day of cold—
when the sun rises, they fly away;
   no one knows where they are.

[18]Your shepherds are asleep,
   O king of Assyria;

your nobles slumber.
Your people are scattered on the mountains
   with none to gather them.
[19]There is no assuaging your hurt,
   your wound is grievous.
All who hear the news of you
   clap their hands over you.
For upon whom has not come
   your unceasing evil?

ᵠ Or *marshals.*

THE BOOK OF
HABAKKUK

The Prophet's Complaint

1 The oracle of God which Habak'kuk the prophet saw.

[2]O Lord, how long shall I cry for help,
and you will not hear?
Or cry to you "Violence!"
and you will not save?
[3]Why do you make me see wrongs
and look upon trouble?
Destruction and violence are before me;
strife and contention arise.
[4]So the law is slacked
and justice never goes forth.
For the wicked surround the righteous,
so justice goes forth perverted.
[5]Look among the nations, and see;
wonder and be astounded.
For I am doing a work in your days
that you would not believe if told.
[6]For behold, I am rousing the Chalde'ans,
that bitter and hasty nation,
who march through the breadth of the earth,
to seize habitations not their own.
[7]Dread and fearsome are they;
their justice and dignity proceed from
themselves.
[8]Their horses are swifter than leopards,
more fierce than the evening wolves;
their horsemen press proudly on.
Yes, their horsemen come from afar;
they fly like an eagle swift to devour.
[9]They all come for violence;
terror [a] of them goes before them.
They gather captives like sand.
[10]At kings they scoff,
and of rulers they make sport.
They laugh at every fortress,
for they heap up earth and take it.
[11]Then they sweep by like the wind and go on,
guilty men, whose own might is their god!

[12]Are you not from everlasting,
O Lord my God, my Holy One?
We shall not die.
O Lord, you have ordained them as a
judgment;
and you, O Rock, have established them for
chastisement.
[13]You who are of purer eyes than to behold evil
and cannot look on wrong,

why do you look on faithless men,
and are silent when the wicked swallows up
the man more righteous than he?
[14]For you make men like the fish of the sea,
like crawling things that have no ruler.
[15]He brings all of them up with a hook,
he drags them out with his net,
he gathers them in his seine;
so he rejoices and exults.
[16]Therefore he sacrifices to his net
and burns incense to his seine;
for by them he lives in luxury, [b]
and his food is rich.
[17]Is he then to keep on emptying his net,
and mercilessly slaying nations for ever?

God's Reply

2 I will take my stand to watch,
and station myself on the tower,
and look forth to see what he will say to me,
and what I will answer concerning my
complaint.
[2]And the Lord answered me:
"Write the vision;
make it plain upon tablets,
so he may run who reads it.
[3]For still the vision awaits its time;
it hastens to the end—it will not lie.
If it seem slow, wait for it;
it will surely come, it will not delay.
[4]Behold, he whose soul is not upright in him
shall fail, [c]
but the righteous shall live by his faith. [d]
[5]Moreover, wine is treacherous;
the arrogant man shall not abide. [e]

There is not much evidence for the date of the Book of Habakkuk (Habacuc), but it is likely that the prophet is speaking against the Chaldeans under Nebuchadnezzar, who destroyed Jerusalem in 586 B.C. The book starts with a dialogue between the prophet and God—the prophet complaining, and the Lord explaining and foretelling the coming destruction of the oppressor. All this took place probably before the fall of Jerusalem. Habakkuk has some originality; he asks God to explain his thought: for example, why does he punish his erring people by a nation more wicked than itself? And hence, why does wickedness seem to triumph? This is the problem found all through the Old Testament.

[a] Cn: Heb uncertain.
[b] Heb *his portion is fat.*
[c] Cn: Heb *is puffed up.*
[d] Or *faithfulness.*
[e] The Hebrew of these two lines is obscure.
1:2: Is 13:1–14:23; 47; Jer 50–51.
1:5: Acts 13:41.
1:6: Rev 20:9.
2:1: Is 21:8.
2:3: Heb 10:37.
2:4: Rom 1:17; Gal 3:11; Heb 10:38–39.

His greed is as wide as Sheol;
  like death he has never enough.
He gathers for himself all nations,
  and collects as his own all peoples."

⁶Shall not all these take up their taunt against
him, in scoffing derision of him, and say,
  "Woe to him who heaps up what is not his
    own—
    for how long?—
    and loads himself with pledges!"
⁷Will not your debtors suddenly arise,
  and those awake who will make you
    tremble?
  Then you will be booty for them.
⁸Because you have plundered many nations,
  all the remnant of the peoples shall plunder
    you,
for the blood of men and violence to the earth,
  to cities and all who dwell therein.

⁹Woe to him who gets evil gain for his house,
  to set his nest on high,
  to be safe from the reach of harm!
¹⁰You have devised shame to your house
  by cutting off many peoples;
  you have forfeited your life.
¹¹For the stone will cry out from the wall,
  and the beam from the woodwork respond.

¹²Woe to him who builds a town with blood,
  and founds a city on iniquity!
¹³Behold, is it not from the LORD of hosts
  that peoples labor only for fire,
  and nations weary themselves for nothing?
¹⁴For the earth will be filled
  w th the knowledge of the glory of the LORD,
  as the waters cover the sea.

¹⁵Woe to him who makes his neighbors drink
  of the cup of his wrath, ᶠ and makes them
    drunk,
  to gaze on their shame!
¹⁶You will be sated with contempt instead of
    glory.
  Drink, yourself, and stagger! ᵍ
The cup in the LORD's right hand
  will come around to you,
  and shame will come upon your glory!
¹⁷The violence done to Lebanon will overwhelm
    you;
  the destruction of the beasts will terrify
    you, ʰ
for the blood of men and violence to the earth,
  to cities and all who dwell therein.

¹⁸What profit is an idol
  when its maker has shaped it,
  a metal image, a teacher of lies?

For the workman trusts in his own creation
  when he makes dumb idols!
¹⁹Woe to him who says to a wooden thing,
    Awake;
  to a mute stone, Arise!
  Can this give revelation?
Behold, it is overlaid with gold and silver,
  and there is no breath at all in it.

²⁰But the LORD is in his holy temple;
  let all the earth keep silence before him.

Habakkuk's Prayer

3 A prayer of Habak′kuk the prophet, according to Shigion′oth.
²O LORD, I have heard the report of you,
  and your work, O LORD, I fear.
In the midst of the years renew it;
  in the midst of the years make it known;
  in wrath remember mercy.
³God came from Te′man,
  and the Holy One from Mount Par′an.
His glory covered the heavens,
  and the earth was full of his praise.   *Selah*
⁴His brightness was like the light,
  rays flashed from his hand;
  and there he veiled his power.
⁵Before him went pestilence,
  and plague followed close behind.
⁶He stood and measured the earth;
  he looked and shook the nations;
Then the eternal mountains were scattered,
  the everlasting hills sank low.
  His ways were as of old.
⁷I saw the tents of Cush′an in affliction;
  the curtains of the land of Mid′ian
    trembled.
⁸Was your wrath against the rivers, O LORD?
  Was your anger against the rivers,
  or your indignation against the sea,
when you rode upon your horses,
  upon your chariot of victory?
⁹You stripped the sheath from your bow,
  and put the arrows to the string. ⁱ   *Selah*
  You split the earth with rivers.
¹⁰The mountains saw you, and writhed;
  the raging waters swept on;
the deep gave forth its voice,
  it lifted its hands on high.
¹¹The sun and moon stood still in their
    habitation ʲ
  at the light of your arrows as they sped,
  at the flash of your glittering spear.

ᶠ Cn: Heb *joining to your wrath.*
ᵍ Cn Compare Gk Syr: Heb *be uncircumcised.*
ʰ Gk Syr: Heb *them.*
ⁱ Cn: Heb obscure.
ʲ Heb uncertain.
2:14: Is 11:9.
2:20: Zeph 1:7; Zech 2:13.

¹²You bestrode the earth in fury,
   you trampled the nations in anger.
¹³You went forth for the salvation of your
      people,
   for the salvation of your anointed.
   You crushed the head of the wicked, ᵏ
   laying him bare from thigh to neck. ˡ   *Selah*
¹⁴You pierced with your ᵐ shafts the head of his
      warriors, ⁿ
   who came like a whirlwind to scatter me,
   rejoicing as if to devour the poor in secret.
¹⁵You trampled the sea with your horses,
   the surging of mighty waters.
¹⁶I hear, and my body trembles,
   my lips quiver at the sound;
   rottenness enters into my bones,
   my steps totter ᵒ beneath me.
   I will quietly wait for the day of trouble
   to come upon people who invade us.

¹⁷Though the fig tree does not blossom,
   nor fruit be on the vines,
   the produce of the olive fail
      and the fields yield no food,
   the flock be cut off from the fold
      and there be no herd in the stalls,
¹⁸yet I will rejoice in the LORD,
   I will joy in the God of my salvation.
¹⁹GOD, the Lord, is my strength;
   he makes my feet like deer's feet,
   he makes me tread upon my high places.

To the choirmaster: with stringed ᵖ instruments.

ᵏ Cn: Heb *head from the house of the wicked.*
ˡ Heb obscure.
ᵐ Heb *his.*
ⁿ Vg Compare Gk Syr: Heb uncertain.
ᵒ Cn Compare Gk: Heb *I tremble because.*
ᵖ Heb *my stringed.*

THE BOOK OF

ZEPHANIAH

The Day of the Lord

1 The word of the LORD which came to
Zephani'ah the son of Cu'shi, son of Gedali'ah, son of Amari'ah, son of Hezeki'ah, in the
days of Josi'ah the son of A'mon, king of Judah.

2"I will utterly sweep away everything
    from the face of the earth," says the LORD.
3"I will sweep away man and beast;
    I will sweep away the birds of the air
    and the fish of the sea.
I will overthrow ª the wicked;
    I will cut off mankind
    from the face of the earth," says the LORD.
4"I will stretch out my hand against Judah,
    and against all the inhabitants of
        Jerusalem;
and I will cut off from this place the remnant
        of Ba'al
    and the name of the idolatrous priests; ᵇ
5those who bow down on the roofs
    to the host of the heavens;
those who bow down and swear to the LORD
    and yet swear by Milcom;
6those who have turned back from following the
        LORD,
    who do not seek the LORD or inquire
        of him."

7Be silent before the Lord GOD!
    For the day of the LORD is at hand;
the LORD has prepared a sacrifice
    and consecrated his guests.
8And on the day of the LORD's sacrifice—
    "I will punish the officials and the king's
        sons
    and all who clothe themselves in foreign
        attire.
9On that day I will punish
    every one who leaps over the threshold,
and those who fill their master's house
    with violence and fraud."

10"On that day," says the LORD,
    "a cry will be heard from the Fish Gate,
a wail from the Second Quarter,
    a loud crash from the hills.
11Wail, O inhabitants of the Mortar!
    For all the traders are no more;
    all who weigh out silver are cut off.

12At that time I will search Jerusalem with lamps,
    and I will punish the men
who are thickening on their dregs,
    those who say in their hearts,
'The LORD will not do good,
    nor will he do ill.'
13Their goods shall be plundered,
    and their houses laid waste.
Though they build houses,
    they shall not inhabit them;
though they plant vineyards,
    they shall not drink wine from them."

14The great day of the LORD is near,
    near and hastening fast;
the sound of the day of the LORD is bitter,
    the mighty man cries aloud there.
15A day of wrath is that day,
    a day of distress and anguish,
a day of ruin and devastation,
    a day of darkness and gloom,
a day of clouds and thick darkness,
16   a day of trumpet blast and battle cry
against the fortified cities
    and against the lofty battlements.

17I will bring distress on men,
    so that they shall walk like the blind,
    because they have sinned against the LORD;
their blood shall be poured out like dust,
    and their flesh like dung.
18Neither their silver nor their gold
    shall be able to deliver them
    on the day of the wrath of the LORD.
In the fire of his jealous wrath,
    all the earth shall be consumed;
for a full, yes, sudden end
    he will make of all the inhabitants of the
        earth.

Zephaniah (Sophonias) prophesied shortly before the religious reform of
Josiah, i.e., about the year 630 B.C., and he proclaims in clarion tones the
"day of the LORD," when his people will be crushed by their enemies
because of their sins; cf. Amos. The words of Zephaniah (1:15) remind
one of the *Dies irae*, which seems to have drawn its imagery from here.
The prophet foretells punishment not only for Judah but also for the
nations round about (2:4–15). Then, after more threats against Jerusalem
(3:1–8), he utters consolations (3:9–20): the people will be restored, but
chastened and humble. The reform of Josiah was too short-lived to affect
the results of these prophecies—the Exile and the return followed within
the century.
ª Cn: Heb *the stumbling blocks.*
ᵇ Compare Gk: Heb *idolatrous priests with the priests.*
1:7: Hab 2:20; Zech 2:13.

Judgment on Israel's Enemies

2 Come together and hold assembly,
O shameless nation,
[2] before you are driven away
like the drifting chaff, [c]
before there comes upon you
the fierce anger of the Lord,
before there comes upon you
the day of the wrath of the Lord.
[3] Seek the Lord, all you humble of the land,
who do his commands;
seek righteousness, seek humility;
perhaps you may be hidden
on the day of the wrath of the Lord.
[4] For Gaza shall be deserted,
and Ash'kelon shall become a desolation;
Ash'dod's people shall be driven out at noon,
and Ek'ron shall be uprooted.
[5] Woe to you inhabitants of the seacoast,
you nation of the Cher'ethites!
The word of the Lord is against you,
O Canaan, land of the Philis'tines;
and I will destroy you till no inhabitant is
left.
[6] And you, O seacoast, shall be pastures,
meadows for shepherds
and folds for flocks.
[7] The seacoast shall become the possession
of the remnant of the house of Judah,
on which they shall pasture,
and in the houses of Ash'kelon
they shall lie down at evening.
For the Lord their God will be mindful of them
and restore their fortunes.

[8] "I have heard the taunts of Moab
and the revilings of the Am'monites,
how they have taunted my people
and made boasts against their territory.
[9] Therefore, as I live," says the Lord of hosts,
the God of Israel,
"Moab shall become like Sodom,
and the Am'monites like Gomor'rah,
a land possessed by nettles and salt pits,
and a waste for ever.
The remnant of my people shall plunder them,
and the survivors of my nation shall
possess them."
[10] This shall be their lot in return for their pride,
because they scoffed and boasted
against the people of the Lord of hosts.
[11] The Lord will be terrifying against them;
yes, he will famish all the gods of the earth,
and to him shall bow down,
each in its place,
all the lands of the nations.

[12] You also, O Ethiopians,
shall be slain by my sword.

[13] And he will stretch out his hand against the
north,
and destroy Assyria;
and he will make Nin'eveh a desolation,
a dry waste like the desert.
[14] Herds shall lie down in the midst of her,
all the beasts of the field; [d]
the vulture [e] and the hedgehog
shall lodge in her capitals;
the owl [f] shall hoot in the window,
the raven [g] croak on the threshold;
for her cedar work will be laid bare.
[15] This is the exultant city
that dwelt secure,
that said to herself,
"I am and there is none else."
What a desolation she has become,
a lair for wild beasts!
Every one who passes by her
hisses and shakes his fist.

Wickedness of the Nations

3 Woe to her that is rebellious and defiled,
the oppressing city!
[2] She listens to no voice,
she accepts no correction.
She does not trust in the Lord,
she does not draw near to her God.

[3] Her officials within her
are roaring lions;
her judges are evening wolves
that leave nothing till the morning.
[4] Her prophets are wanton,
faithless men;
her priests profane what is sacred,
they do violence to the law.
[5] The Lord within her is righteous,
he does no wrong;
every morning he shows forth his justice,
each dawn he does not fail;
but the unjust knows no shame.

[6] "I have cut off nations;
their battlements are in ruins;
I have laid waste their streets
so that none walks in them;
their cities have been made desolate,
without a man, without an inhabitant.
[7] I said, 'Surely she will fear me,
she will accept correction;

---

[c] Cn Compare Gk Syr: Heb *before a decree is born; like chaff a day has passed away.*
[d] Tg Compare Gk: Heb *nation.*
[e] The meaning of the Hebrew word is uncertain.
[f] Cn: Heb *a voice.*
[g] Gk Vg: Heb *desolation.*
2:4–7: Is 14:29–31; Jer 47; Ezek 25:15–17; Joel 3:4–8; Amos 1:6–8; Zech 9:5–7.
2:8–11: Is 15–16; 25:10–12; Jer 48; Ezek 25:8–11; Amos 2:1–3.
2:12: Is 18.
2:13–15: Is 10:5–34; Nahum.

she will not lose sight [h]
of all that I have enjoined upon her.'
But all the more they were eager
to make all their deeds corrupt."

[8]"Therefore wait for me," says the LORD,
"for the day when I arise as a witness.
For my decision is to gather nations,
to assemble kingdoms,
to pour out upon them my indignation,
all the heat of my anger;
for in the fire of my jealous wrath
all the earth shall be consumed.

Restoration of Israel

[9]"Yes, at that time I will change the speech of
the peoples
to a pure speech,
that all of them may call on the name of the
LORD
and serve him with one accord.
[10]From beyond the rivers of Ethiopia
my suppliants, the daughter of my
dispersed ones,
shall bring my offering.

[11]"On that day you shall not be put to shame
because of the deeds by which you have
rebelled against me;
for then I will remove from your midst
your proudly exultant ones,
and you shall no longer be haughty
in my holy mountain.
[12]For I will leave in the midst of you
a people humble and lowly.
They shall seek refuge in the name of the LORD,
[13]   those who are left in Israel;
they shall do no wrong
and utter no lies,
nor shall there be found in their mouth
a deceitful tongue.

For they shall pasture and lie down,
and none shall make them afraid."

[14]Sing aloud, O daughter of Zion;
shout, O Israel!
Rejoice and exult with all your heart,
O daughter of Jerusalem!
[15]The LORD has taken away the judgments
against you,
he has cast out your enemies.
The King of Israel, the LORD, is in your midst;
you shall fear evil no more.
[16]On that day it shall be said to Jerusalem:
"Do not fear, O Zion;
let not your hands grow weak.
[17]The LORD, your God, is in your midst,
a warrior who gives victory;
he will rejoice over you with gladness,
he will renew you [i] in his love;
he will exult over you with loud singing
[18]as on a day of festival. [j]
"I will remove disaster [k] from you,
so that you will not bear reproach for it.
[19]Behold, at that time I will deal
with all your oppressors.
And I will save the lame
and gather the outcast,
and I will change their shame into praise
and renown in all the earth.
[20]At that time I will bring you home,
at the time when I gather you together;
yes, I will make you renowned and praised
among all the peoples of the earth,
when I restore your fortunes
before your eyes," says the LORD.

---

[h] Gk Syr: Heb *and her dwelling will not be cut off.*
[i] Gk Syr: Heb *he will be silent.*
[j] Gk Syr: Heb obscure.
[k] Cn: Heb *they were.*
3:13: Rev 14:5.

THE BOOK OF

HAGGAI

The Command to Rebuild the Temple

1 In the second year of Dari′us the king, in the sixth month, on the first day of the month, the word of the LORD came by Hag′gai the prophet to Zerub′babel the son of She-al′ti-el, governor of Judah, and to Joshua the son of Jehoz′adak, the high priest, [2]"Thus says the LORD of hosts: This people say the time has not yet come to rebuild the house of the LORD." [3]Then the word of the LORD came by Hag′gai the prophet, [4]"Is it a time for you yourselves to dwell in your paneled houses, while this house lies in ruins? [5]Now therefore thus says the LORD of hosts: Consider how you have fared. [6]You have sown much, and harvested little; you eat, but you never have enough; you drink, but you never have your fill; you clothe yourselves, but no one is warm; and he who earns wages earns wages to put them into a bag with holes.

7 "Thus says the LORD of hosts: Consider how you have fared. [8]Go up to the hills and bring wood and build the house, that I may take pleasure in it and that I may appear in my glory, says the LORD. [9]You have looked for much, and behold, it came to little; and when you brought it home, I blew it away. Why? says the LORD of hosts. Because of my house that lies in ruins, while you busy yourselves each with his own house. [10]Therefore the heavens above you have withheld the dew, and the earth has withheld its produce. [11]And I have called for a drought upon the land and the hills, upon the grain, the new wine, the oil, upon what the ground brings forth, upon men and cattle, and upon all their labors."

The People Obey

12 Then Zerub′babel the son of She-al′ti-el, and Joshua the son of Jehoz′adak, the high priest, with all the remnant of the people, obeyed the voice of the LORD their God, and the words of Hag′gai the prophet, as the LORD their God had sent him; and the people feared before the LORD. [13]Then Hag′gai, the messenger of the LORD, spoke to the people with the LORD's message, "I am with you, says the LORD." [14]And the LORD stirred up the spirit of Zerub′babel the son of She-al′ti-el, governor of Judah, and the spirit of Joshua the son of Jehoz′adak, the high priest, and the spirit of all the remnant of the people; and they came and worked on the house of the LORD of hosts, their God, [15]on the twenty-fourth day of the month, in the sixth month.

The Splendor of the Temple

2 In the second year of Dari′us the king, [1]in the seventh month, on the twenty-first day of the month, the word of the LORD came by Hag′gai the prophet, [2]"Speak now to Zerub′babel the son of She-al′ti-el, governor of Judah, and to Joshua the son of Jehoz′adak, the high priest, and to all the remnant of the people, and say, [3]'Who is left among you that saw this house in its former glory? How do you see it now? Is it not in your sight as nothing? [4]Yet now take courage, O Zerub′babel, says the LORD; take courage, O Joshua, son of Jehoz′adak, the high priest; take courage, all you people of the land, says the LORD; work, for I am with you, says the LORD of hosts, [5]according to the promise that I made you when you came out of Egypt. My Spirit abides among you; fear not. [6]For thus says the LORD of hosts: Once again, in a little while, I will shake the heavens and the earth and the sea and the dry land; [7]and I will shake all nations, so that the treasures of all nations shall come in, and I will fill this house with splendor, says the LORD of hosts. [8]The silver is mine, and the gold is mine, says the LORD of hosts. [9]The latter splendor of this house shall be greater than the former, says the LORD of hosts; and in this place I will give prosperity, says the LORD of hosts.'"

A Rebuke and a Promise

10 On the twenty-fourth day of the ninth month, in the second year of Dari′us, the word of the LORD came by Hag′gai the prophet, [11]"Thus says the LORD of hosts: Ask the priests to decide this question, [12]'If one carries holy flesh in the skirt of his garment, and touches with his skirt bread, or pottage, or wine, or oil, or any kind of food, does it become holy?'" The priests answered, "No." [13]Then said Hag′gai, "If one who is unclean by contact with a dead body touches any of these, does it become unclean?" The priests answered, "It does become unclean." [14]Then Hag′gai said, "So is it with this people, and with this nation before me, says the LORD; and so with

---

Haggai (Aggeus) is the first of the postexilic prophets and differs considerably from the earlier. No longer do we read threats of punishment for sin or words of consolation. The people need to be helped in their work of restoration and encouraged to persevere. Haggai first insists that the temple must be built before they think of anything else. This is to be the focal point of their life, as it was in the past, and they cannot hope for any prosperity without it. In spite of its humble appearance, the Spirit of God will rest upon it and the "latter splendor of this house shall be greater than the former, says the LORD of hosts" (2:9).
2:6: Heb 12:26

every work of their hands; and what they offer there is unclean. ¹⁵Please now, consider what will come to pass from this day onward. Before a stone was placed upon a stone in the temple of the Lord, ¹⁶how did you fare? ᵃ When one came to a heap of twenty measures, there were but ten; when one came to the winevat to draw fifty measures, there were but twenty. ¹⁷I struck you and all the products of your toil with blight and mildew and hail; yet you did not return to me, says the Lord. ¹⁸Consider from this day onward, from the twenty-fourth day of the ninth month. Since the day that the foundation of the Lord's temple was laid, consider: ¹⁹Is the seed yet in the barn? Do the vine, the fig tree, the pomegranate, and the olive tree still yield nothing? From this day on I will bless you."

God's Promise to Zerubbabel

20 The word of the Lord came a second time to Hag′gai on the twenty-fourth day of the month, ²¹"Speak to Zerub′babel, governor of Judah, saying, I am about to shake the heavens and the earth, ²²and to overthrow the throne of kingdoms; I am about to destroy the strength of the kingdoms of the nations, and overthrow the chariots and their riders; and the horses and their riders shall go down, every one by the sword of his fellow. ²³On that day, says the Lord of hosts, I will take you, O Zerub′babel my servant, the son of She-al′ti-el, says the Lord, and make you like a signet ring; for I have chosen you, says the Lord of hosts."

ᵃ Gk: Heb *since they were.*

THE BOOK OF
ZECHARIAH

Israel Urged to Repent

1 In the eighth month, in the second year of Dari′us, the word of the LORD came to Zechari′ah the son of Berechi′ah, son of Iddo, the prophet, saying, [2]"The LORD was very angry with your fathers. [3]Therefore say to them, Thus says the LORD of hosts: Return to me, says the LORD of hosts, and I will return to you, says the LORD of hosts. [4]Be not like your fathers, to whom the former prophets cried out, 'Thus says the LORD of hosts, Return from your evil ways and from your evil deeds.' But they did not hear or heed me, says the LORD. [5]Your fathers, where are they? And the prophets, do they live for ever? [6]But my words and my statutes, which I commanded my servants the prophets, did they not overtake your fathers? So they repented and said, As the LORD of hosts purposed to deal with us for our ways and deeds, so has he dealt with us."

First Vision: The Horsemen

[7] On the twenty-fourth day of the eleventh month which is the month of Shebat′, in the second year of Dari′us, the word of the LORD came to Zechari′ah the son of Berechi′ah, son of Iddo, the prophet; and Zechariah said, [8]"I saw in the night, and behold, a man riding upon a red horse! He was standing among the myrtle trees in the glen; and behind him were red, sorrel, and white horses. [9]Then I said, 'What are these, my lord?' The angel who talked with me said to me, 'I will show you what they are.' [10]So the man who was standing among the myrtle trees answered, 'These are they whom the LORD has sent to patrol the earth.' [11]And they answered the angel of the LORD who was standing among the myrtle trees, 'We have patrolled the earth, and behold, all the earth remains at rest.' [12]Then the angel of the LORD said, 'O LORD of hosts, how long will you have no mercy on Jerusalem and the cities of Judah, against which you have had indignation these seventy years?' [13]And the LORD answered gracious and comforting words to the angel who talked with me. [14]So the angel who talked with me said to me, 'Cry out, Thus says the LORD of hosts: I am exceedingly jealous for Jerusalem and for Zion. [15]And I am very angry with the nations that are at ease; for while I was only a little angry they furthered the disaster. [16]Therefore, thus says the LORD, I have returned to Jerusalem with compassion; my house shall be built in it, says the LORD

of hosts, and the measuring line shall be stretched out over Jerusalem. [17]Cry again, Thus says the LORD of hosts: My cities shall again overflow with prosperity, and the LORD will again comfort Zion and again choose Jerusalem.' "

Second Vision: Four Horns and Four Smiths

[18] [a] And I lifted my eyes and saw, and behold, four horns! [19]And I said to the angel who talked with me, "What are these?" And he answered me, "These are the horns which have scattered Judah, Israel, and Jerusalem." [20]Then the LORD showed me four smiths. [21]And I said, "What are these coming to do?" He answered, "These are the horns which scattered Judah, so that no man raised his head; and these have come to terrify them, to cast down the horns of the nations who lifted up their horns against the land of Judah to scatter it."

Third Vision: The Man with a Measuring Line

2 [b] And I lifted my eyes and saw, and behold, a man with a measuring line in his hand! [2]Then I said, "Where are you going?" And he said to me, "To measure Jerusalem, to see what is its breadth and what is its length." [3]And behold, the angel who talked with me came forward, and another angel came forward to meet him, [4]and said to him, "Run, say to that young man, 'Jerusalem shall be inhabited as villages without walls, because of the multitude of men and cattle in it. [5]For I will be to her a wall of fire round about, says the LORD, and I will be the glory within her.' "

[6] Ho! ho! Flee from the land of the north, says the LORD; for I have spread you abroad as the four winds of the heavens, says the LORD. [7]Ho! Escape to Zion, you who dwell with the daughter of Babylon. [8]For thus said the LORD of hosts, after his glory sent me to the nations who plundered you, for he who touches you touches the apple of his eye: [9]"Behold, I will shake my hand over them,

---

Zechariah (Zacharias) prophesied at the same time as Haggai, about 520 B.C. and, like him, exhorted the people to press on with the building of the temple, but he goes on to develop the plans for the national restoration. He speaks in terms of a Messianic era in which the priesthood is supreme but the royal prerogatives are possessed by "the Branch" (6:12), a Messianic term for Zerubbabel. Chapters 1–8 relate a series of visions and are apocalyptic in tone. The second part (chapters 9–14) is quite different, and consists of a collection of prophecies dating from the fourth century and edited later during the Greek period. These are chiefly noteworthy for the Messianic passages in them, especially 9:9, fulfilled on Palm Sunday, and 12:10: "when they look on him whom they have pierced, they shall mourn."

[a] Ch 2:1 in Heb.
[b] Ch 2:5 in Heb.

and they shall become plunder for those who served them. Then you will know that the Lord of hosts has sent me. [10]Sing and rejoice, O daughter of Zion; for behold, I come and I will dwell in the midst of you, says the Lord. [11]And many nations shall join themselves to the Lord in that day, and shall be my people; and I will dwell in the midst of you, and you shall know that the Lord of hosts has sent me to you. [12]And the Lord will inherit Judah as his portion in the holy land, and will again choose Jerusalem."

13 Be silent, all flesh, before the Lord; for he has roused himself from his holy dwelling.

Fourth Vision: Joshua and Satan

3 Then he showed me Joshua the high priest standing before the angel of the Lord, and Satan standing at his right hand to accuse him. [2]And the Lord said to Satan, "The Lord rebuke you, O Satan! The Lord who has chosen Jerusalem rebuke you! Is not this a brand plucked from the fire?" [3]Now Joshua was standing before the angel, clothed with filthy garments. [4]And the angel said to those who were standing before him, "Remove the filthy garments from him." And to him he said, "Behold, I have taken your iniquity away from you, and I will clothe you with rich apparel." [5]And I said, "Let them put a clean turban on his head." So they put a clean turban on his head and clothed him with garments; and the angel of the Lord was standing by.

6 And the angel of the Lord enjoined Joshua, [7]"Thus says the Lord of hosts: If you will walk in my ways and keep my charge, then you shall rule my house and have charge of my courts, and I will give you the right of access among those who are standing here. [8]Hear now, O Joshua the high priest, you and your friends who sit before you, for they are men of good omen: behold, I will bring my servant the Branch. [9]For behold, upon the stone which I have set before Joshua, upon a single stone with seven facets, I will engrave its inscription, says the Lord of hosts, and I will remove the guilt of this land in a single day. [10]In that day, says the Lord of hosts, every one of you will invite his neighbor under his vine and under his fig tree."

Fifth Vision: The Lampstand and Olive Trees

4 And the angel who talked with me came again, and waked me, like a man that is wakened out of his sleep. [2]And he said to me, "What do you see?" I said, "I see, and behold, a lampstand all of gold, with a bowl on the top of it, and seven lamps on it, with seven lips on each of the lamps which are on the top of it. [3]And there are two olive trees by it, one on the right of the bowl and the other on its left." [4]And I said to the angel who talked with me, "What are these, my lord?" [5]Then the angel who talked with me answered

me, "Do you not know what these are?" I said, "No, my lord." [6]Then he said to me, "This is the word of the Lord to Zerub'babel: Not by might, nor by power, but by my Spirit, says the Lord of hosts. [7]What are you, O great mountain? Before Zerub'babel you shall become a plain; and he shall bring forward the top stone amid shouts of 'Grace, grace to it!' " [8]Moreover the word of the Lord came to me, saying, [9]"The hands of Zerub'-babel have laid the foundation of this house; his hands shall also complete it. Then you will know that the Lord of hosts has sent me to you. [10]For whoever has despised the day of small things shall rejoice, and shall see the plummet in the hand of Zerub'babel.

"These seven are the eyes of the Lord, which range through the whole earth." [11]Then I said to him, "What are these two olive trees on the right and the left of the lampstand?" [12]And a second time I said to him, "What are these two branches of the olive trees, which are beside the two golden pipes from which the oil[c] is poured out?" [13]He said to me, "Do you not know what these are?" I said, "No, my lord." [14]Then he said, "These are the two anointed who stand by the Lord of the whole earth."

Sixth Vision: The Flying Scroll

5 Again I lifted my eyes and saw, and behold, a flying scroll! [2]And he said to me, "What do you see?" I answered, "I see a flying scroll; its length is twenty cubits, and its breadth ten cubits." [3]Then he said to me, "This is the curse that goes out over the face of the whole land; for every one who steals shall be cut off henceforth according to it, and every one who swears falsely shall be cut off henceforth according to it. [4]I will send it forth, says the Lord of hosts, and it shall enter the house of the thief, and the house of him who swears falsely by my name; and it shall abide in his house and consume it, both timber and stones."

Seventh Vision: The Woman in an Ephah

5 Then the angel who talked with me came forward and said to me, "Lift your eyes, and see what this is that goes forth." [6]And I said, "What is it?" He said, "This is the ephah that goes forth." And he said, "This is their iniquity[d] in all the land." [7]And behold, the leaden cover was lifted, and there was a woman sitting in the ephah! [8]And he said, "This is Wickedness." And he thrust her back into the ephah, and thrust down the leaden weight upon its mouth. [9]Then I lifted my eyes and

[c] Cn: Heb *gold.*
[d] Gk Compare Syr: Heb *eye.*
2:13: Hab 2:20; Zeph 1:7.
3:2: Jude 9.
3:8: Is 4:2; Jer 23:5; 33:15; Zech 6:12.
3:10: Mic 4:4.
4:3, 11–14: Rev 11:4.
4:10: Rev 5:6.

saw, and behold, two women coming forward! The wind was in their wings; they had wings like the wings of a stork, and they lifted up the ephah between earth and heaven. ¹⁰Then I said to the angel who talked with me, "Where are they taking the ephah?" ¹¹He said to me, "To the land of Shi'nar, to build a house for it; and when this is prepared, they will set the ephah down there on its base."

Eighth Vision: Four Chariots

6 And again I lifted my eyes and saw, and behold, four chariots came out from between two mountains; and the mountains were mountains of bronze. ²The first chariot had red horses, the second black horses, ³the third white horses, and the fourth chariot dappled gray ᵉ horses. ⁴Then I said to the angel who talked with me, "What are these, my lord?" ⁵And the angel answered me, "These are going forth to the four winds of heaven, after presenting themselves before the LORD of all the earth. ⁶The chariot with the black horses goes toward the north country, the white ones go toward the west country, ᶠ and the dappled ones go toward the south country." ⁷When the steeds came out, they were impatient to get off and patrol the earth. And he said, "Go, patrol the earth." So they patrolled the earth. ⁸Then he cried to me, "Behold, those who go toward the north country have set my Spirit at rest in the north country."

The Crown and the Branch

9 And the word of the LORD came to me: ¹⁰"Take from the exiles Hel'dai, Tobi'jah, and Jedai'ah, who have arrived from Babylon; and go the same day to the house of Josi'ah, the son of Zephani'ah. ¹¹Take from them silver and gold, and make a crown, ᵍ and set it upon the head of Joshua, the son of Jehoz'adak, the high priest; ¹²and say to him, 'Thus says the LORD of hosts, "Behold, the man whose name is the Branch: for he shall grow up in his place, and he shall build the temple of the LORD. ¹³It is he who shall build the temple of the LORD, and shall bear royal honor, and shall sit and rule upon his throne. And there shall be a priest by his throne, and peaceful understanding shall be between them both." ' ¹⁴And the crown ʰ shall be in the temple of the LORD as a reminder to Hel'dai, ⁱ Tobi'jah, Jedai'ah, and Josi'ah ʲ the son of Zephani'ah.

15 "And those who are far off shall come and help to build the temple of the LORD; and you shall know that the LORD of hosts has sent me to you. And this shall come to pass, if you will diligently obey the voice of the LORD your God."

Hypocritical Fasting Condemned

7 In the fourth year of King Dari'us, the word of the LORD came to Zechari'ah in the fourth day of the ninth month, which is Chis'lev. ²Now the people of Bethel had sent Share'zer and Reg'em-mel'ech and their men, to entreat the favor of the LORD, ³and to ask the priests of the house of the LORD of hosts and the prophets, "Should I mourn and fast in the fifth month, as I have done for so many years?" ⁴Then the word of the LORD of hosts came to me: ⁵"Say to all the people of the land and the priests, When you fasted and mourned in the fifth month and in the seventh, for these seventy years, was it for me that you fasted? ⁶And when you eat and when you drink, do you not eat for yourselves and drink for yourselves? ⁷When Jerusalem was inhabited and in prosperity, with her cities round about her, and the South and the lowland were inhabited, were not these the words which the LORD proclaimed by the former prophets?"

Punishment for Rejecting God's Commands

8 And the word of the LORD came to Zechari'ah, saying, ⁹"Thus says the LORD of hosts, Render true judgments, show kindness and mercy each to his brother, ¹⁰do not oppress the widow, the fatherless, the sojourner, or the poor; and let none of you devise evil against his brother in your heart." ¹¹But they refused to listen, and turned a stubborn shoulder, and stopped their ears that they might not hear. ¹²They made their hearts like adamant lest they should hear the law and the words which the LORD of hosts had sent by his Spirit through the former prophets. Therefore great wrath came from the LORD of hosts. ¹³"As I called, and they would not hear, so they called, and I would not hear," says the LORD of hosts, ¹⁴"and I scattered them with a whirlwind among all the nations which they had not known. Thus the land they left was desolate, so that no one went back and forth, and the pleasant land was made desolate."

God's Promise to Zion

8 And the word of the LORD of hosts came to me, saying, ²"Thus says the LORD of hosts: I am jealous for Zion with great jealousy, and I am jealous for her with great wrath. ³Thus says the LORD: I will return to Zion, and will dwell in the midst of Jerusalem, and Jerusalem shall be called the faithful city, and the mountain of the LORD of hosts, the holy mountain. ⁴Thus says the LORD of hosts: Old men and old women shall again sit in the streets of Jerusalem, each with staff in hand for very age. ⁵And the streets of the city shall be full of boys and girls playing in its streets. ⁶Thus says the LORD of hosts: If it is

---

ᵉ Compare Gk: The meaning of the Hebrew word is uncertain.
ᶠ Cn: Heb *after them.*
ᵍ Gk Mss: Heb *crowns.*
ʰ Gk: Heb *crowns.*
ⁱ With verse 10: Heb *Helem.*
ʲ With verse 10: Heb *Hen.*
6:1–3: Rev 6:2–8.
6:5: Rev 7:1.
6:12: Zech 3:8; Is 4:2; Jer 23:5; 33:15.

marvelous in the sight of the remnant of this people in these days, should it also be marvelous in my sight, says the LORD of hosts? [7]Thus says the LORD of hosts: Behold, I will save my people from the east country and from the west country; [8]and I will bring them to dwell in the midst of Jerusalem; and they shall be my people and I will be their God, in faithfulness and in righteousness."

9 Thus says the LORD of hosts: "Let your hands be strong, you who in these days have been hearing these words from the mouth of the prophets, since the day that the foundation of the house of the LORD of hosts was laid, that the temple might be built. [10]For before those days there was no wage for man or any wage for beast, neither was there any safety from the foe for him who went out or came in; for I set every man against his fellow. [11]But now I will not deal with the remnant of this people as in the former days, says the LORD of hosts. [12]For there shall be a sowing of peace; the vine shall yield its fruit, and the ground shall give its increase, and the heavens shall give their dew; and I will cause the remnant of this people to possess all these things. [13]And as you have been a byword of cursing among the nations, O house of Judah and house of Israel, so will I save you and you shall be a blessing. Fear not, but let your hands be strong."

14 For thus says the LORD of hosts: "As I planned to do evil to you, when your fathers provoked me to wrath, and I did not relent, says the LORD of hosts, [15]so again I have planned in these days to do good to Jerusalem and to the house of Judah; fear not. [16]These are the things that you shall do: Speak the truth to one another, render in your gates judgments that are true and make for peace, [17]do not devise evil in your hearts against one another, and love no false oath, for all these things I hate, says the LORD."

Joyful Fasting

18 And the word of the LORD of hosts came to me, saying, [19]"Thus says the LORD of hosts: The fast of the fourth month, and the fast of the fifth, and the fast of the seventh, and the fast of the tenth, shall be to the house of Judah seasons of joy and gladness, and cheerful feasts; therefore love truth and peace.

Many Peoples Will Be Drawn to Jerusalem

20 "Thus says the LORD of hosts: Peoples shall yet come, even the inhabitants of many cities; [21]the inhabitants of one city shall go to another, saying, 'Let us go at once to entreat the favor of the LORD, and to seek the LORD of hosts; I am going.' [22]Many peoples and strong nations shall come to seek the LORD of hosts in Jerusalem, and to entreat the favor of the LORD. [23]Thus says the LORD of hosts: In those days ten men from the nations of every tongue shall take hold of the robe of a Jew, saying, 'Let us go with you, for we have heard that God is with you.'"

Judgment on Israel's Enemies

9

An Oracle

The word of the LORD is against the land of Had'rach
and will rest upon Damascus.
For to the LORD belong the cities of Ar'am,[k]
even as all the tribes of Israel;
[2]Hamath also, which borders thereon,
Tyre and Si'don, though they are very wise.
[3]Tyre has built herself a rampart,
and heaped up silver like dust,
and gold like the dirt of the streets.
[4]But behold, the Lord will strip her of her possessions
and hurl her wealth into the sea,
and she shall be devoured by fire.

[5]Ash'kelon shall see it, and be afraid;
Gaza too, and shall writhe in anguish;
Ek'ron also, because its hopes are confounded.
The king shall perish from Gaza;
Ashkelon shall be uninhabited;
[6]a mongrel people shall dwell in Ash'dod;
and I will make an end of the pride of Philis'tia.
[7]I will take away its blood from its mouth,
and its abominations from between its teeth;
it too shall be a remnant for our God;
it shall be like a clan in Judah,
and Ek'ron shall be like the Jeb'usites.
[8]Then I will encamp at my house as a guard,
so that none shall march back and forth;
no oppressor shall again overrun them,
for now I see with my own eyes.

The Coming of Israel's King

[9]Rejoice greatly, O daughter of Zion!
Shout aloud, O daughter of Jerusalem!
Behold, your king comes to you;
triumphant and victorious is he,
humble and riding on a donkey,
on a colt the foal of a donkey.
[10]I will cut off the chariot from E'phraim
and the war horse from Jerusalem;
and the battle bow shall be cut off,
and he shall command peace to the nations;
his dominion shall be from sea to sea,
and from the River to the ends of the earth.

[11]As for you also, because of the blood of my covenant with you,

---

k Cn: Heb *the eye of Adam* (or *man*).
8:16: Eph 4:25.
9:9: Mt 21:5; Jn 12:15.

I will set your captives free from the
waterless pit.
[12]Return to your stronghold, O prisoners of hope;
today I declare that I will restore to you
double.
[13]For I have bent Judah as my bow;
I have made E'phraim its arrow.
I will brandish your sons, O Zion,
over your sons, O Greece,
and wield you like a warrior's sword.

[14]Then the LORD will appear over them,
and his arrow go forth like lightning;
the Lord GOD will sound the trumpet,
and march forth in the whirlwinds of the
south.
[15]The LORD of hosts will protect them,
and they shall devour and tread down the
slingers;[1]
and they shall drink their blood[m] like wine,
and be full like a bowl,
drenched like the corners of the altar.

[16]On that day the LORD their God will save them
for they are the flock of his people;
for like the jewels of a crown
they shall shine on his land.
[17]Yes, how good and how fair it shall be!
Grain shall make the young men flourish,
and new wine the maidens.

Restoration of Judah and Israel

10 Ask rain from the LORD
in the season of the spring rain,
from the LORD who makes the storm clouds,
who gives men showers of rain,
to every one the vegetation in the field.
[2]For the teraphim utter nonsense,
and the diviners see lies;
the dreamers tell false dreams,
and give empty consolation.
Therefore the people wander like sheep;
they are afflicted for want of a shepherd.

[3]"My anger is hot against the shepherds,
and I will punish the leaders;[n]
for the LORD of hosts cares for his flock, the
house of Judah,
and will make them like his proud steed in
battle.
[4]Out of them shall come the cornerstone,
out of them the tent peg,
out of them the battle bow,
out of them every ruler.
[5]Together they shall be like mighty men in
battle,
trampling the foe in the mud of the streets;
they shall fight because the LORD is with them,
and they shall confound the riders on
horses.

[6]"I will strengthen the house of Judah,
and I will save the house of Joseph.
I will bring them back because I have
compassion on them,
and they shall be as though I had not
rejected them;
for I am the LORD their God and I will
answer them.
[7]Then E'phraim shall become like a mighty
warrior,
and their hearts shall be glad as with wine.
Their children shall see it and rejoice,
their hearts shall exult in the LORD.

[8]"I will signal for them and gather them in,
for I have redeemed them,
and they shall be as many as of old.
[9]Though I scattered them among the nations,
yet in far countries they shall remember me,
and with their children they shall live and
return.
[10]I will bring them home from the land of Egypt,
and gather them from Assyria;
and I will bring them to the land of Gilead and
to Lebanon,
till there is no room for them.
[11]They shall pass through the sea of Egypt,[o]
and the waves of the sea shall be struck
down,
and all the depths of the Nile dried up.
The pride of Assyria shall be laid low,
and the scepter of Egypt shall depart.
[12]I will make them strong in the LORD
and they shall glory[p] in his name," says the
LORD.

11 Open your doors, O Lebanon,
that the fire may devour your cedars!
[2]Wail, O cypress, for the cedar has fallen,
for the glorious trees are ruined!
Wail, oaks of Ba'shan,
for the thick forest has been felled!
[3]Listen, the wail of the shepherds,
for their glory is despoiled!
Listen, the roar of the lions,
for the jungle of the Jordan is laid waste!

Two Kinds of Shepherd

4 Thus said the LORD my God: "Become shepherd of the flock doomed to slaughter. [5]Those who buy them slay them and go unpunished; and those who sell them say, 'Blessed be the LORD, I have become rich'; and their own shepherds have no pity on them. [6]For I will no longer have pity on the inhabitants of this land, says the LORD.

---

[1] Cn: Heb *the slingstones.*
[m] Gk: Heb *be turbulent.*
[n] Or *he-goats.*
[o] Cn: Heb *distress.*
[p] Gk: Heb *walk.*

Behold, I will cause men to fall each into the hand of his shepherd, and each into the hand of his king; and they shall crush the earth, and I will deliver none from their hand."

7 So I became the shepherd of the flock doomed to be slain for those who trafficked in the sheep. And I took two staffs; one I named Grace, the other I named Union. And I tended the sheep. [8]In one month I destroyed the three shepherds. But I became impatient with them, and they also detested me. [9]So I said, "I will not be your shepherd. What is to die, let it die; what is to be destroyed, let it be destroyed; and let those that are left devour the flesh of one another." [10]And I took my staff Grace, and I broke it, annulling the covenant which I had made with all the peoples. [11]So it was annulled on that day, and the traffickers in the sheep, who were watching me, knew that it was the word of the Lord. [12]Then I said to them, "If it seems right to you, give me my wages; but if not, keep them." And they weighed out as my wages thirty shekels of silver. [13]Then the Lord said to me, "Cast it into the treasury"[q]—the lordly price at which I was paid off by them. So I took the thirty shekels of silver and cast them into the treasury[q] in the house of the Lord. [14]Then I broke my second staff Union, annulling the brotherhood between Judah and Israel.

15 Then the Lord said to me, "Take once more the implements of a worthless shepherd. [16]For behold, I am raising up in the land a shepherd who does not care for the perishing, or seek the wandering,[r] or heal the maimed, or nourish the sound, but devours the flesh of the fat ones, tearing off even their hoofs.

[17]Woe to my worthless shepherd,
    who deserts the flock!
May the sword strike his arm
    and his right eye!
Let his arm be wholly withered,
    his right eye utterly blinded!"

Jerusalem's Victory

12

An Oracle

The word of the Lord concerning Israel: Thus says the Lord, who stretched out the heavens and founded the earth and formed the spirit of man within him: [2]"Behold, I am about to make Jerusalem a cup of reeling to all the peoples round about; it will be against Judah also in the siege against Jerusalem. [3]On that day I will make Jerusalem a heavy stone for all the peoples; all who lift it shall grievously hurt themselves. And all the nations of the earth will come together against it. [4]On that day, says the Lord, I will strike every horse with panic, and its rider with madness. But upon the house of Judah I will open my eyes, when I strike every horse of the peoples with blindness. [5]Then the clans of Judah shall say to themselves,

'The inhabitants of Jerusalem have strength through the Lord of hosts, their God.' [6]"On that day I will make the clans of Judah like a blazing pot in the midst of wood, like a flaming torch among sheaves; and they shall devour to the right and to the left all the peoples round about, while Jerusalem shall still be inhabited in its place, in Jerusalem.

7 "And the Lord will give victory to the tents of Judah first, that the glory of the house of David and the glory of the inhabitants of Jerusalem may not be exalted over that of Judah. [8]On that day the Lord will put a shield about the inhabitants of Jerusalem so that the feeblest among them on that day shall be like David, and the house of David shall be like God, like the angel of the Lord, at their head. [9]And on that day I will seek to destroy all the nations that come against Jerusalem.

Mourning for the Pierced One

10 "And I will pour out on the house of David and the inhabitants of Jerusalem a spirit of compassion and supplication, so that, when they look on him whom they have pierced, they shall mourn for him, as one mourns for an only child, and weep bitterly over him, as one weeps over a firstborn. [11]On that day the mourning in Jerusalem will be as great as the mourning for Ha'dadrim'mon in the plain of Megid'do. [12]The land shall mourn, each family by itself; the family of the house of David by itself, and their wives by themselves; the family of the house of Nathan by itself, and their wives by themselves; [13]the family of the house of Levi by itself, and their wives by themselves; the family of the Shime'ites by itself, and their wives by themselves; [14]and all the families that are left, each by itself, and their wives by themselves.

13

On that day there shall be a fountain opened for the house of David and the inhabitants of Jerusalem to cleanse them from sin and uncleanness.

The Wounded Prophet

2 "And on that day, says the Lord of hosts, I will cut off the names of the idols from the land, so that they shall be remembered no more; and also I will remove from the land the prophets and the unclean spirit. [3]And if any one again appears as a prophet, his father and mother who bore him will say to him, 'You shall not live, for you speak lies in the name of the Lord'; and his father and mother who bore him shall pierce him through when he prophesies. [4]On that day every prophet will be ashamed of his vision when he prophesies; he will not put on a hairy mantle in order to

---

[q] Syr: Heb *to the potter.*
[r] syr Compare Gk Vg: Heb *the youth.*
11:12-13: Mt 26:15; 27:9.
12:10: Jn 19:37.

deceive, [5]but he will say, 'I am no prophet, I am a tiller of the soil; for the land has been my possession[t] since my youth.' [6]And if one asks him, 'What are these wounds on your back?' he will say, 'The wounds I received in the house of my friends.'"

[7]"Awake, O sword, against my shepherd,
   against the man who stands next to me,"
                        says the LORD of hosts.
"Strike the shepherd, that the sheep may be
   scattered;
   I will turn my hand against the little ones.
[8]In the whole land, says the LORD,
   two thirds shall be cut off and perish,
   and one third shall be left alive.
[9]And I will put this third into the fire,
   and refine them as one refines silver,
   and test them as gold is tested.
They will call on my name,
   and I will answer them.
I will say, 'They are my people';
   and they will say, 'The LORD is my God.'"

The Day of the Lord Is Coming

14 Behold, a day of the LORD is coming, when the spoil taken from you will be divided in the midst of you. [2]For I will gather all the nations against Jerusalem to battle, and the city shall be taken and the houses plundered and the women ravished; half of the city shall go into exile, but the rest of the people shall not be cut off from the city. [3]Then the LORD will go forth and fight against those nations as when he fights on a day of battle. [4]On that day his feet shall stand on the Mount of Olives which lies before Jerusalem on the east; and the Mount of Olives shall be split in two from east to west by a very wide valley; so that one half of the Mount shall withdraw northward, and the other half southward. [5]And the valley of my mountains shall be stopped up, for the valley of the mountains shall touch the side of it; and you shall flee as you fled from the earth-quake in the days of Uzzi'ah king of Judah. Then the LORD your[u] God will come, and all the holy ones with him. [v]

6 On that day there shall be neither cold nor frost. [w] [7]And there shall be continuous day (it is known to the LORD), not day and not night, for at evening time there shall be light.

8 On that day living waters shall flow out from Jerusalem, half of them to the eastern sea and half of them to the western sea; it shall continue in summer as in winter.

9 And the LORD will become king over all the earth; on that day the LORD will be one and his name one.

[10]The whole land shall be turned into a plain from Ge'ba to Rimmon south of Jerusalem. But Jerusalem shall remain aloft upon its site from the Gate of Benjamin to the place of the former gate, to the Corner Gate, and from the Tower of Hanan'el to the king's wine presses. [11]And it shall be inhabited, for there shall be no more curse;[x] Jerusalem shall dwell in security.

12 And this shall be the plague with which the LORD will strike all the peoples that wage war against Jerusalem: their flesh shall rot while they are still on their feet, their eyes shall rot in their sockets, and their tongues shall rot in their mouths. [13]And on that day a great panic from the LORD shall fall on them, so that each will lay hold on the hand of his fellow, and the hand of the one will be raised against the hand of the other; [14]even Judah will fight against Jerusalem. And the wealth of all the nations round about shall be collected, gold, silver, and garments in great abundance. [15]And a plague like this plague shall fall on the horses, the mules, the camels, the don-keys, and whatever beasts may be in those camps.

Survivors of the Nations Will Come to Jerusalem

16 Then every one that survives of all the na-tions that have come against Jerusalem shall go up year after year to worship the King, the LORD of hosts, and to keep the feast of booths. [17]And if any of the families of the earth do not go up to Jerusalem to worship the King, the LORD of hosts, there will be no rain upon them. [18]And if the family of Egypt do not go up and present them-selves, then upon them shall[y] come the plague with which the LORD afflicts the nations that do not go up to keep the feast of booths. [19]This shall be the punishment to Egypt and the punishment to all the nations that do not go up to keep the feast of booths.

20 And on that day there shall be inscribed on the bells of the horses, "Holy to the LORD." And the pots in the house of the LORD shall be as the bowls before the altar; [21]and every pot in Jerusa-lem and Judah shall be sacred to the LORD of hosts, so that all who sacrifice may come and take of them and boil the flesh of the sacrifice in them. And there shall no longer be a trader in the house of the LORD of hosts on that day.

---

[t] Cn: Heb *for man has caused me to possess.*
[u] Heb *my.*
[v] Gk Syr Vg Tg: Heb *you.*
[w] Compare Gk Syr Vg Tg: Heb uncertain.
[x] Or *ban of utter destruction.*
[y] Gk Syr: Heb *shall not.*
13:7: Mt 26:31; Mk 14:27.
14:8: Ezek 47:1–12; Rev 22:1–2.
14:11: Rev 22:3.
14:18–19: Is 19; Jer 46; Ezek 29–32.

THE BOOK OF

MALACHI

Israel Preferred to Edom

1 The oracle of the word of the Lord to Israel by Mal'achi.[a]

2 "I have loved you," says the Lord. But you say, "How have you loved us?" "Is not Esau Jacob's brother?" says the Lord. "Yet I have loved Jacob [3]but I have hated Esau; I have laid waste his hill country and left his heritage to jackals of the desert." [4]If E'dom says, "We are shattered but we will rebuild the ruins," the Lord of hosts says, "They may build, but I will tear down, till they are called the wicked country, the people with whom the Lord is angry for ever." [5]Your own eyes shall see this, and you shall say, "Great is the Lord, beyond the border of Israel!"

Corruption of the Priesthood

6 "A son honors his father, and a servant his master. If then I am a father, where is my honor? And if I am a master, where is my fear? says the Lord of hosts to you, O priests, who despise my name. You say, 'How have we despised your name?' [7]By offering polluted food upon my altar. And you say, 'How have we polluted it?'[b] By thinking that the Lord's table may be despised. [8]When you offer blind animals in sacrifice, is that no evil? And when you offer those that are lame or sick, is that no evil? Present that to your governor; will he be pleased with you or show you favor? says the Lord of hosts. [9]And now entreat the favor of God, that he may be gracious to us. With such a gift from your hand, will he show favor to any of you? says the Lord of hosts. [10]Oh, that there were one among you who would shut the doors, that you might not kindle fire upon my altar in vain! I have no pleasure in you, says the Lord of hosts, and I will not accept an offering from your hand. [11] For from the rising of the sun to its setting my name is great among the nations, and in every place incense is offered to my name, and a pure offering; for my name is great among the nations, says the Lord of hosts. [12]But you profane it when you say that the Lord's table is polluted, and the food for it[c] may be despised. [13]'What a weariness this is,' you say, and you sniff at me,[d] says the Lord of hosts. You bring what has been taken by violence or is lame or sick, and this you bring as your offering! Shall I accept that from your hand? says the Lord. [14]Cursed be the cheat who has a male in his flock, and vows it, and yet sacrifices to the Lord what is blemished;

for I am a great King, says the Lord of hosts, and my name is feared among the nations.

2 "And now, O priests, this command is for you. [2]If you will not listen, if you will not lay it to heart to give glory to my name, says the Lord of hosts, then I will send the curse upon you and I will curse your blessings; indeed I have already cursed them, because you do not lay it to heart. [3]Behold, I will rebuke your offspring, and spread dung upon your faces, the dung of your offerings, and I will put you out of my presence.[e] [4]So shall you know that I have sent this command to you, that my covenant with Levi may hold, says the Lord of hosts. [5]My covenant with him was a covenant of life and peace, and I gave them to him, that he might fear; and he feared me, he stood in awe of my name. [6]True instruction[f] was in his mouth, and no wrong was found on his lips. He walked with me in peace and uprightness, and turned many from iniquity. [7]For the lips of a priest should guard knowledge, and men should seek instruction[f] from his mouth, for he is the messenger of the Lord of hosts. [8]But you have turned aside from the way; you have caused many to stumble by your instruction;[f] you have corrupted the covenant of Levi, says the Lord of hosts, [9]and so I make you despised and abased before all the people, inasmuch as you have not kept my ways but have shown partiality in your instruction."[f]

The Covenant Profaned by Judah

10 Have we not all one father? Has not one God created us? Why then are we faithless to one another, profaning the covenant of our fathers? [11] Judah has been faithless, and abomination has been committed in Israel and in Jerusalem; for Judah has profaned the sanctuary of the Lord,

---

The name Malachi (Malachias) merely means "my messenger," and the book is probably anonymous. Its contents suggest that the historical context is the period of Ezra and Nehemiah. The theme is the love of God for his people in spite of their backsliding. Both priests and people are guilty of not offering a clean sacrifice—and in 1:11 is the prophecy of the universal sacrifice, relating evidently to Messianic times. The prophet also denounces marriages with Gentiles and the practice of divorce. He goes on to proclaim the "day of the Lord," "great and terrible." Like many prophets, he does not distinguish between the first and second coming.

a Or *my messenger.*
b Gk: Heb *you.*
c Heb *its fruit, its food.*
d Another reading is *it.*
e Cn Compare Gk Syr: Heb *and he shall bear you to it.*
f Or *law.*
1:2-3: Rom 9:13.
1:2-5: Is 34; 63:1-6; Jer 49:7-22; Ezek 25:12-14; 35; Amos 1:11-12; Obad.

which he loves, and has married the daughter of a foreign god. [12]May the LORD cut off from the tents of Jacob, for the man who does this, any to witness [g] or answer, or to bring an offering to the LORD of hosts!

13 And this again you do. You cover the LORD's altar with tears, with weeping and groaning because he no longer regards the offering or accepts it with favor at your hand. [14]You ask, "Why does he not?" Because the LORD was witness to the covenant between you and the wife of your youth, to whom you have been faithless, though she is your companion and your wife by covenant. [15]Has not the one God made [h] and sustained for us the spirit of life? And what does he desire? [i] Godly offspring. So take heed to yourselves, and let none be faithless to the wife of his youth. [16]"For I hate [j] divorce, says the LORD the God of Israel, and covering one's garment with violence, says the LORD of hosts. So take heed to yourselves and do not be faithless."

17 You have wearied the LORD with your words. Yet you say, "How have we wearied him?" By saying, "Every one who does evil is good in the sight of the LORD, and he delights in them." Or by asking, "Where is the God of justice?"

The Coming Messenger

3 "Behold, I send my messenger to prepare the way before me, and the Lord whom you seek will suddenly come to his temple; the messenger of the covenant in whom you delight, behold, he is coming, says the LORD of hosts. [2]But who can endure the day of his coming, and who can stand when he appears?

"For he is like a refiner's fire and like fullers' soap; [3]he will sit as a refiner and purifier of silver, and he will purify the sons of Levi and refine them like gold and silver, till they present right offerings to the LORD. [4]Then the offering of Judah and Jerusalem will be pleasing to the LORD as in the days of old and as in former years.

5 "Then I will draw near to you for judgment; I will be a swift witness against the sorcerers, against the adulterers, against those who swear falsely, against those who oppress the hireling in his wages, the widow and the orphan, against those who thrust aside the sojourner, and do not fear me, says the LORD of hosts.

God Must Not Be Robbed

6 "For I the LORD do not change; therefore you, O sons of Jacob, are not consumed. [7]From the days of your fathers you have turned aside from my statutes and have not kept them. Return to me, and I will return to you, says the LORD of hosts. But you say, 'How shall we return?' [8]Will man rob God? Yet you are robbing me. But you say, 'How are we robbing you?' In your tithes and offerings. [9]You are cursed with a curse, for you are robbing me; the whole nation of you. [10]Bring the full tithes into the storehouse, that there may be food in my house; and thereby put me to the test, says the LORD of hosts, if I will not open the windows of heaven for you and pour down for you an overflowing blessing. [11]I will rebuke the devourer [k] for you, so that it will not destroy the fruits of your soil; and your vine in the field shall not fail to bear, says the LORD of hosts. [12]Then all nations will call you blessed, for you will be a land of delight, says the LORD of hosts.

13 "Your words have been stout against me, says the LORD. Yet you say, 'How have we spoken against you?' [14]You have said, 'It is vain to serve God. What is the good of our keeping his charge or of walking as in mourning before the LORD of hosts? [15]Henceforth we deem the arrogant blessed; evildoers not only prosper but when they put God to the test they escape.' "

The Reward of Those Who Fear the Lord

16 Then those who feared the LORD spoke with one another; the LORD heeded and heard them, and a book of remembrance was written before him of those who feared the LORD and thought on his name. [17]"They shall be mine, says the LORD of hosts, my special possession on the day when I act, and I will spare them as a man spares his son who serves him. [18]Then once more you shall distinguish between the righteous and the wicked, between one who serves God and one who does not serve him.

The Great Day of the Lord

4 [1] "For behold, the day comes, burning like an oven, when all the arrogant and all evildoers will be stubble; the day that comes shall burn them up, says the LORD of hosts, so that it will leave them neither root nor branch. [2]But for you who fear my name the sun of righteousness shall rise, with healing in its wings. You shall go forth leaping like calves from the stall. [3]And you shall tread down the wicked, for they will be ashes under the soles of your feet, on the day when I act, says the LORD of hosts.

4 "Remember the law of my servant Moses, the statutes and ordinances that I commanded him at Horeb for all Israel.

5 "Behold, I will send you Eli'jah the prophet before the great and awesome day of the LORD comes. [6]And he will turn the hearts of fathers to their children and the hearts of children to their fathers, lest I come and strike the land with a curse." [m]

---

[g] Cn Compare Gk: Heb *arouse*.
[h] Or *has he not made one?*
[i] Cn: Heb *and a remnant of spirit was his*.
[j] Cn: Heb *he hates*.
[k] Or *devouring locust*.
[l] Ch 4:1–6 are Ch 3:19–24 in the Hebrew.
[m] Or *ban of utter destruction*.
3:1: Mt 11:10; Mk 1:2; Lk 1:17, 76; 7:27.
3:2: Rev 6:17
4:5: Mt 17:11; Mk 9:12.
4:6: Lk 1:17.

THE FIRST BOOK OF THE
MACCABEES

Alexander the Great

1 After Alexander son of Philip, the Macedonian, who came from the land of Kittim, had defeated[a] Dari′us, king of the Persians and the Medes, he succeeded him as king. (He had previously become king of Greece.) [2]He fought many battles, conquered strongholds, and put to death the kings of the earth. [3]He advanced to the ends of the earth, and plundered many nations. When the earth became quiet before him, he was exalted, and his heart was lifted up. [4]He gathered a very strong army and ruled over countries, nations, and princes, and they became tributary to him.

5 After this he fell sick and perceived that he was dying. [6]So he summoned his most honored officers, who had been brought up with him from youth, and divided his kingdom among them while he was still alive. [7]And after Alexander had reigned twelve years, he died.

8 Then his officers began to rule, each in his own place. [9]They all put on crowns after his death, and so did their sons after them for many years; and they caused many evils on the earth.

Antiochus Epiphanes and Renegade Jews

10 From them came forth a sinful root, Anti′ochus Epiph′anes, son of Anti′ochus the king; he had been a hostage in Rome. He began to reign in the one hundred and thirty-seventh year of the kingdom of the Greeks.[b]

11 In those days lawless men came forth from Israel, and misled many, saying, "Let us go and make a covenant with the Gentiles round about us, for since we separated from them many evils have come upon us." [12]This proposal pleased them, [13]and some of the people eagerly went to the king. He authorized them to observe the ordinances of the Gentiles. [14]So they built a gymnasium in Jerusalem, according to Gentile custom, [15]and removed the marks of circumcision, and abandoned the holy covenant. They joined with the Gentiles and sold themselves to do evil.

Antiochus in Egypt

16 When Anti′ochus saw that his kingdom was established, he determined to become king of the land of Egypt, that he might reign over both kingdoms. [17]So he invaded Egypt with a strong force, with chariots and elephants and cavalry and with a large fleet. [18]He engaged Ptol′emy king of Egypt in battle, and Ptolemy turned and fled before him, and many were wounded and fell. [19]And they captured the fortified cities in the land of Egypt, and he plundered the land of Egypt.

Persecution of the Jews

20 After subduing Egypt, Anti′ochus returned in the one hundred and forty-third year.[c] He went up against Israel and came to Jerusalem with a strong force. [21]He arrogantly entered the sanctuary and took the golden altar, the lampstand for the light, and all its utensils. [22]He took also the table for the bread of the Presence, the cups for drink offerings, the bowls, the golden censers, the curtain, the crowns, and the gold decoration on the front of the temple; he stripped it all off. [23]He took the silver and the gold, and the costly vessels; he took also the hidden treasures which he found. [24]Taking them all, he departed to his own land.

He committed deeds of murder,
　and spoke with great arrogance.
[25]Israel mourned deeply in every community,
[26]　rulers and elders groaned,
maidens and young men became faint,
　the beauty of women faded.
[27]Every bridegroom took up the lament;
　she who sat in the bridal chamber was
　　mourning.
[28]Even the land shook for its inhabitants,
　and all the house of Jacob was clothed with
　　shame.

The First and Second Books of the Maccabees

1 Maccabees deals with the history of the Jews in Palestine during the forty years from the accession of the Syrian king Antiochus Epiphanes to the death of Simon in 134 B.C. It was a life–and–death struggle between the Jews and the Syrians who wanted to impose Greek religion and culture on them. The book recounts the heroic deeds of the three great leaders, Judas Maccabeus and his brothers Jonathan and Simon, who were in turn at the head of the Jewish people until death overtook them. It was written with a strong religious purpose, and the high point is reached with a description of the rededication of the temple. Originally written in Hebrew about the year 100 B.C. the book now exists only in a Greek translation.

2 Maccabees is quite different. It is not a continuation of 1 Maccabees but concentrates on the period of about fifteen years covered by 1 Maccabees, chapters 1–7. It aims at bringing out even more strongly the religious lessons of the time, and the story is written in a way that is more like a sermon than a history. The historical facts are arranged to suit the religious purpose of the book. Several passages in the work are well known in reference to particular doctrines, e.g., the resurrection of the body (7:9, 11; 14:46); rewards and punishments after death (6:26); prayers for the dead (12:42–45); the intercession of the saints (15:12–16).

---

a Greek adds *and he defeated.*
b 175 B.C.
c 169 B.C.

Occupation of Jerusalem

29 Two years later the king sent to the cities of Judah a chief collector of tribute, and he came to Jerusalem with a large force. [30]Deceitfully he spoke peaceable words to them, and they believed him; but he suddenly fell upon the city, dealt it a severe blow, and destroyed many people of Israel. [31]He plundered the city, burned it with fire, and tore down its houses and its surrounding walls. [32]And they took captive the women and children, and seized the cattle. [33]Then they fortified the city of David with a great strong wall and strong towers, and it became their citadel. [34]And they stationed there a sinful people, lawless men. These strengthened their position; [35]they stored up arms and food, and collecting the spoils of Jerusalem they stored them there, and became a great snare.
[36]It became an ambush against the sanctuary,
     an evil adversary of Israel continually.
[37]On every side of the sanctuary they shed
     innocent blood;
     they even defiled the sanctuary.
[38]Because of them the residents of Jerusalem
     fled;
     she became a dwelling of strangers;
she became strange to her offspring,
     and her children forsook her.
[39]Her sanctuary became desolate as a desert;
     her feasts were turned into mourning,
     her sabbaths into a reproach,
     her honor into contempt.
[40]Her dishonor now grew as great as her glory;
     her exaltation was turned into mourning.

Installation of Gentile Cults

41 Then the king wrote to his whole kingdom that all should be one people, [42]and that each should give up his customs. [43]All the Gentiles accepted the command of the king. Many even from Israel gladly adopted his religion; they sacrificed to idols and profaned the sabbath. [44]And the king sent letters by messengers to Jerusalem and the cities of Judah; he directed them to follow customs strange to the land, [45]to forbid burnt offerings and sacrifices and drink offerings in the sanctuary, to profane sabbaths and feasts, [46]to defile the sanctuary and the priests, [47]to build altars and sacred precincts and shrines for idols, to sacrifice swine and unclean animals, [48]and to leave their sons uncircumcised. They were to make themselves abominable by everything unclean and profane, [49]so that they should forget the law and change all the ordinances. [50]"And whoever does not obey the command of the king shall die."

51 In such words he wrote to his whole kingdom. And he appointed inspectors over all the people and commanded the cities of Judah to offer sacrifice, city by city. [52]Many of the people, every one who forsook the law, joined them, and they did evil in the land; [53]they drove Israel into hiding in every place of refuge they had.

54 Now on the fifteenth day of Chis'lev, in the one hundred and forty-fifth year, [d] they erected a desolating sacrilege upon the altar of burnt offering. They also built altars in the surrounding cities of Judah, [55]and burned incense at the doors of the houses and in the streets. [56]The books of the law which they found they tore to pieces and burned with fire. [57]Where the book of the covenant was found in the possession of any one, or if any one adhered to the law, the decree of the king condemned him to death. [58]They kept using violence against Israel, against those found month after month in the cities. [59]And on the twenty-fifth day of the month they offered sacrifice on the altar which was upon the altar of burnt offering. [60]According to the decree, they put to death the women who had their children circumcised, [61]and their families and those who circumcised them; and they hung the infants from their mothers' necks.

62 But many in Israel stood firm and were resolved in their hearts not to eat unclean food. [63]They chose to die rather than to be defiled by food or to profane the holy covenant; and they did die. [64]And very great wrath came upon Israel.

Mattathias and His Sons

2 In those days Mattathi'as the son of John, son of Simeon, a priest of the sons of Jo'arib, moved from Jerusalem and settled in Mo'dein. [2]He had five sons, John surnamed Gaddi, [3]Simon called Thassi, [4]Judas called Mac"cabe'us, [5]Eleazar called Av'aran, and Jonathan called Ap'phus. [6]He saw the blasphemies being committed in Judah and Jerusalem, [7]and said,
"Alas! Why was I born to see this,
     the ruin of my people, the ruin of the holy
         city,
and to dwell there when it was given over to
         the enemy,
     the sanctuary given over to aliens?
[8]Her temple has become like a man without
         honor; [e]
[9]   her glorious vessels have been carried into
         captivity.
Her infants have been killed in her streets,
     her youths by the sword of the foe.
[10]What nation has not inherited her palaces [f]
     and has not seized her spoils?
[11]All her adornment has been taken away;
     no longer free, she has become a slave.
[12]And behold, our holy place, our beauty,
     and our glory have been laid waste;
the Gentiles have profaned it.
[13]   Why should we live any longer?"

---

[d] 167 b.c.
[e] The text of this verse is uncertain.
[f] Other authorities read *has not had a part in her kingdom.*

14 And Mattathi'as and his sons tore their clothes, put on sackcloth, and mourned greatly.

Pagan Worship Refused

15 Then the king's officers who were enforcing the apostasy came to the city of Mo'dein to make them offer sacrifice. [16]Many from Israel came to them; and Mattathi'as and his sons were assembled. [17]Then the king's officers spoke to Mattathi'as as follows: "You are a leader, honored and great in this city, and supported by sons and brothers. [18]Now be the first to come and do what the king commands, as all the Gentiles and the men of Judah and those that are left in Jerusalem have done. Then you and your sons will be numbered among the friends of the king, and you and your sons will be honored with silver and gold and many gifts."

19 But Mattathi'as answered and said in a loud voice: "Even if all the nations that live under the rule of the king obey him, and have chosen to do his commandments, departing each one from the religion of his fathers, [20]yet I and my sons and my brothers will live by the covenant of our fathers. [21]Far be it from us to desert the law and the ordinances. [22]We will not obey the king's words by turning aside from our religion to the right hand or to the left."

23 When he had finished speaking these words, a Jew came forward in the sight of all to offer sacrifice upon the altar in Mo'dein, according to the king's command. [24]When Mattathi'as saw it, he burned with zeal and his heart was stirred. He gave vent to righteous anger; he ran and killed him upon the altar. [25]At the same time he killed the king's officer who was forcing them to sacrifice, and he tore down the altar. [26]Thus he burned with zeal for the law, as Phin'ehas did against Zimri the son of Sa'lu.

27 Then Mattathi'as cried out in the city with a loud voice, saying: "Let every one who is zealous for the law and supports the covenant come out with me!" [28]And he and his sons fled to the hills and left all that they had in the city.

29 Then many who were seeking righteousness and justice went down to the wilderness to dwell there, [30]they, their sons, their wives, and their cattle, because evils pressed heavily upon them. [31]And it was reported to the king's officers, and to the troops in Jerusalem the city of David, that men who had rejected the king's command had gone down to the hiding places in the wilderness. [32]Many pursued them, and overtook them; they encamped opposite them and prepared for battle against them on the sabbath day. [33]And they said to them, "Enough of this! Come out and do what the king commands, and you will live." [34]But they said, "We will not come out, nor will we do what the king commands and so profane the sabbath day." [35]Then the enemy [g] hastened to

attack them. [36]But they did not answer them or hurl a stone at them or block up their hiding places, [37]for they said, "Let us all die in our innocence; heaven and earth testify for us that you are killing us unjustly." [38]So they attacked them on the sabbath, and they died, with their wives and children and cattle, to the number of a thousand persons.

39 When Mattathi'as and his friends learned of it, they mourned for them deeply. [40]And each said to his neighbor: "If we all do as our brethren have done and refuse to fight with the Gentiles for our lives and for our ordinances, they will quickly destroy us from the earth." [41]So they made this decision that day: "Let us fight against every man who comes to attack us on the sabbath day; let us not all die as our brethren died in their hiding places."

Counterattack

42 Then there united with them a company of Hasid'eans, mighty warriors of Israel, every one who offered himself willingly for the law. [43]And all who became fugitives to escape their troubles joined them and reinforced them. [44]They organized an army, and struck down sinners in their anger and lawless men in their wrath; the survivors fled to the Gentiles for safety. [45]And Mattathi'as and his friends went about and tore down the altars; [46]they forcibly circumcised all the uncircumcised boys that they found within the borders of Israel. [47]They hunted down the arrogant men, and the work prospered in their hands. [48]They rescued the law out of the hands of the Gentiles and kings, and they never let the sinner gain the upper hand.

Last Words of Mattathias

49 Now the days drew near for Mattathi'as to die, and he said to his sons: "Arrogance and reproach have now become strong; it is a time of ruin and furious anger. [50]Now, my children, show zeal for the law, and give your lives for the covenant of our fathers.

51 "Remember the deeds of the fathers, which they did in their generations; and receive great honor and an everlasting name. [52]Was not Abraham found faithful when tested, and it was reckoned to him as righteousness? [53]Joseph in the time of his distress kept the commandment, and became lord of Egypt. [54]Phin'ehas our father, because he was deeply zealous, received the covenant of everlasting priesthood. [55]Joshua, because he fulfilled the command, became a judge in Israel. [56]Caleb, because he testified in the assembly, received an inheritance in the land. [57]David, because he was merciful, inherited the throne of the kingdom for ever. [58]Eli'jah because of great zeal for the law was taken up into heaven. [59]Hanani'ah,

[g] Gk they.

805

Azari′ah, and Mish′a-el believed and were saved from the flame. [60]Daniel because of his innocence was delivered from the mouth of the lions.

61 "And so observe, from generation to generation, that none who put their trust in him will lack strength. [62]Do not fear the words of a sinner, for his splendor will turn into dung and worms. [63]Today he will be exalted, but tomorrow he will not be found, because he has returned to the dust, and his plans will perish. [64]My children, be courageous and grow strong in the law, for by it you will gain honor.

65 "Now behold, I know that Simeon your brother is wise in counsel; always listen to him; he shall be your father. [66]Judas Mac″cabe′us has been a mighty warrior from his youth; he shall command the army for you and fight the battle against the peoples. [h] [67]You shall rally about you all who observe the law, and avenge the wrong done to your people. [68]Pay back the Gentiles in full, and heed what the law commands."

69 Then he blessed them, and was gathered to his fathers. [70]He died in the one hundred and forty-sixth year [i] and was buried in the tomb of his fathers at Mo′dein. And all Israel mourned for him with great lamentation.

Early Victories of Judas Maccabeus

3 Then Judas his son, who was called Mac″cabe′us, took command in his place. [2]All his brothers and all who had joined his father helped him; they gladly fought for Israel.
[3]He extended the glory of his people.

Like a giant he put on his breastplate;
he belted on his armor of war and waged
battles,
protecting the host by his sword.
[4]He was like a lion in his deeds,
like a lion's cub roaring for prey.
[5]He searched out and pursued the lawless;
he burned those who troubled his people.
[6]Lawless men shrank back for fear of him;
all the evildoers were confounded;
and deliverance prospered by his hand.
[7]He embittered many kings,
but he made Jacob glad by his deeds,
and his memory is blessed for ever.
[8]He went through the cities of Judah;
he destroyed the ungodly out of the land; [j]
thus he turned away wrath from Israel.
[9]He was renowned to the ends of the earth;
he gathered in those who were perishing.

10 But Apollo′nius gathered together Gentiles and a large force from Samar′ia to fight against Israel. [11]When Judas learned of it, he went out to meet him, and he defeated and killed him. Many were wounded and fell, and the rest fled. [12]Then they seized their spoils; and Judas took the sword of Apollo′nius, and used it in battle the rest of his life.

13 Now when Se′ron, the commander of the Syrian army, heard that Judas had gathered a large company, including a body of faithful men who stayed with him and went out to battle, [14]he said, "I will make a name for myself and win honor in the kingdom. I will make war on Judas and his companions, who scorn the king's command." [15]And again a strong army of ungodly men went up with him to help him, to take vengeance on the sons of Israel.

16 When he approached the ascent of Beth-ho′ron, Judas went out to meet him with a small company. [17]But when they saw the army coming to meet them, they said to Judas, "How can we, few as we are, fight against so great and strong a multitude? And we are faint, for we have eaten nothing today." [18]Judas replied, "It is easy for many to be hemmed in by few, for in the sight of Heaven there is no difference between saving by many or by few. [19]It is not on the size of the army that victory in battle depends, but strength comes from Heaven. [20]They come against us in great pride and lawlessness to destroy us and our wives and our children, and to despoil us; [21]but we fight for our lives and our laws. [22]He himself will crush them before us; as for you, do not be afraid of them."

23 When he finished speaking, he rushed suddenly against Se′ron and his army, and they were crushed before him. [24]They pursued them [k] down the descent of Beth-ho′ron to the plain; eight hundred of them fell, and the rest fled into the land of the Philis′tines. [25]Then Judas and his brothers began to be feared, and terror fell upon the Gentiles round about them. [26]His fame reached the king, and the Gentiles talked of the battles of Judas.

The Policy of Antiochus

27 When king Anti′ochus heard these reports, he was greatly angered; and he sent and gathered all the forces of his kingdom, a very strong army. [28]And he opened his coffers and gave a year's pay to his forces, and ordered them to be ready for any need. [29]Then he saw that the money in the treasury was exhausted, and that the revenues from the country were small because of the dissension and disaster which he had caused in the land by abolishing the laws that had existed from the earliest days. [30]He feared that he might not have such funds as he had before for his expenses and for the gifts which he used to give more lavishly than preceding kings. [31]He was greatly perplexed in mind, and determined to go to Persia and collect the revenues from those regions and raise a large fund.

32 He left Lys′ias, a distinguished man of royal lineage, in charge of the king's affairs from the

---

h Or of the people.
i 166 B.C.
j Gk it.
k Other authorities read him.

river Euphra'tes to the borders of Egypt. [33]Lys'ias was also to take care of Anti'ochus his son until he returned. [34]And he turned over to Lys'ias[l] half of his troops and the elephants, and gave him orders about all that he wanted done. As for the residents of Judea and Jerusalem, [35]Lys'ias was to send a force against them to wipe out and destroy the strength of Israel and the remnant of Jerusalem; he was to banish the memory of them from the place, [36]settle aliens in all their territory, and distribute their land. [37]Then the king took the remaining half of his troops and departed from Antioch his capital in the one hundred and forty-seventh year.[m] He crossed the Euphra'tes river and went through the upper provinces.

Preparations for Battle

38 Lys'ias chose Ptol'emy the son of Dorym'-enes, and Nica'nor and Gor'gias, mighty men among the friends of the king, [39]and sent with them forty thousand infantry and seven thousand cavalry to go into the land of Judah and destroy it, as the king had commanded. [40]So they departed with their entire force, and when they arrived they encamped near Emma'us in the plain. [41]When the traders of the region heard what was said of them, they took silver and gold in immense amounts, and shackles,[n] and went to the camp to get the sons of Israel for slaves. And forces from Syria and the land of the Philis'tines joined with them.

42 Now Judas and his brothers saw that misfortunes had increased and that the forces were encamped in their territory. They also learned what the king had commanded to do to the people to cause their final destruction. [43]But they said to one another, "Let us repair the destruction of our people, and fight for our people and the sanctuary." [44]And the congregation assembled to be ready for battle, and to pray and ask for mercy and compassion.

[45]Jerusalem was uninhabited like a wilderness;
  not one of her children went in or out.
The sanctuary was trampled down,
  and the sons of aliens held the citadel;
  it was a lodging place for the Gentiles.
Joy was taken from Jacob;
  the flute and the harp ceased to play.

46 So they assembled and went to Mizpah, opposite Jerusalem, because Israel formerly had a place of prayer in Mizpah. [47]They fasted that day, put on sackcloth and sprinkled ashes on their heads, and tore their clothes. [48]And they opened the book of the law to inquire into those matters about which the Gentiles were consulting the images of their idols. [49]They also brought the garments of the priesthood and the first fruits and the tithes, and they stirred up the Naz'irites who had completed their days; [50]and they cried aloud to Heaven, saying,

"What shall we do with these?
  Where shall we take them?
[51]Your sanctuary is trampled down and
    profaned,
  and your priests mourn in humiliation.
[52]And behold, the Gentiles are assembled against
    us to destroy us;
  you know what they plot against us.
[53]How will we be able to withstand them,
  if you do not help us?"

54 Then they sounded the trumpets and gave a loud shout. [55]After this Judas appointed leaders of the people, in charge of thousands and hundreds and fifties and tens. [56]And he said to those who were building houses, or were betrothed, or were planting vineyards, or were fainthearted, that each should return to his home, according to the law. [57]Then the army marched out and encamped to the south of Emma'us.

58 And Judas said, "Gird yourselves and be valiant. Be ready early in the morning to fight with these Gentiles who have assembled against us to destroy us and our sanctuary. [59]It is better for us to die in battle than to see the misfortunes of our nation and of the sanctuary. [60]But as his will in heaven may be, so he will do."

The Battle at Emmaus

4 Now Gor'gias took five thousand infantry and a thousand picked cavalry, and this division moved out by night [2]to fall upon the camp of the Jews and attack them suddenly. Men from the citadel were his guides. [3]But Judas heard of it, and he and his mighty men moved out to attack the king's force in Emma'us [4]while the division was still absent from the camp. [5]When Gor'gias entered the camp of Judas by night, he found no one there, so he looked for them in the hills, because he said, "These men are fleeing from us."

6 At daybreak Judas appeared in the plain with three thousand men, but they did not have armor and swords such as they desired. [7]And they saw the camp of the Gentiles, strong and fortified, with cavalry round about it; and these men were trained in war. [8]But Judas said to the men who were with him, "Do not fear their numbers or be afraid when they charge. [9]Remember how our fathers were saved at the Red Sea, when Pharaoh with his forces pursued them. [10]And now let us cry to Heaven, to see whether he will favor us and remember his covenant with our fathers and crush this army before us today. [11]Then all the Gentiles will know that there is one who redeems and saves Israel."

12 When the foreigners looked up and saw them coming against them, [13]they went forth from

---
[l] Gk him.
[m] 165 B.C.
[n] Syr: Gk slaves.

their camp to battle. Then the men with Judas blew their trumpets [14]and engaged in battle. The Gentiles were crushed and fled into the plain, [15]and all those in the rear fell by the sword. They pursued them to Gaza'ra, and to the plains of Idume'a, and to Azo'tus and Jam'nia; and three thousand of them fell. [16]Then Judas and his force turned back from pursuing them, [17]and he said to the people, "Do not be greedy for plunder, for there is a battle before us; [18]Gor'gias and his force are near us in the hills. But stand now against our enemies and fight them, and afterward seize the plunder boldly."

19 Just as Judas was finishing this speech, a detachment appeared, coming out of the hills. [20]They saw that their army° had been put to flight, and that the Jews° were burning the camp, for the smoke that was seen showed what had happened. [21]When they perceived this they were greatly frightened, and when they also saw the army of Judas drawn up in the plain for battle, [22]they all fled into the land of the Philis'tines. [23]Then Judas returned to plunder the camp, and they seized much gold and silver, and cloth dyed blue and sea purple, and great riches. [24]On their return they sang hymns and praises to Heaven, for he is good, for his mercy endures for ever. [25]Thus Israel had a great deliverance that day.

First Campaign of Lysias

26 Those of the foreigners who escaped went and reported to Lys'ias all that had happened. [27]When he heard it, he was perplexed and discouraged, for things had not happened to Israel as he had intended, nor had they turned out as the king had commanded him. [28]But the next year he mustered sixty thousand picked infantrymen and five thousand cavalry to subdue them. [29]They came into Idume'a and encamped at Beth-zur,* and Judas met them with ten thousand men.

30 When he saw that the army was strong, he prayed, saying, "Blessed are you, O Savior of Israel, who did crush the attack of the mighty warrior by the hand of your servant David, and did give the camp of the Philis'tines into the hands of Jonathan, the son of Saul, and of the man who carried his armor. [31]So do you hem in this army by the hand of your people Israel, and let them be ashamed of their troops and their cavalry. [32]Fill them with cowardice; melt the boldness of their strength; let them tremble in their destruction. [33]Strike them down with the sword of those who love you, and let all who know your name praise you with hymns."

34 Then both sides attacked, and there fell of the army of Lys'ias five thousand men; they fell in action.ᴾ [35]And when Lys'ias saw the rout of his troops and observed the boldness which inspired those of Judas, and how ready they were either to live or to die nobly, he de-

parted to Antioch and enlisted mercenaries, to invade Judea again with an even larger army.

Cleansing and Dedication of the Temple

36 Then said Judas and his brothers, "Behold, our enemies are crushed; let us go up to cleanse the sanctuary and dedicate it." [37]So all the army assembled and they went up to Mount Zion. [38]And they saw the sanctuary desolate, the altar profaned, and the gates burned. In the courts they saw bushes sprung up as in a thicket, or as on one of the mountains. They saw also the chambers of the priests in ruins. [39]Then they tore their clothes, and mourned with great lamentation, and sprinkled themselves with ashes. [40]They fell face down on the ground, and sounded the signal on the trumpets, and cried out to Heaven. [41]Then Judas detailed men to fight against those in the citadel until he had cleansed the sanctuary.

42 He chose blameless priests devoted to the law, [43]and they cleansed the sanctuary and removed the defiled stones to an unclean place. [44]They deliberated what to do about the altar of burnt offering, which had been profaned. [45]And they thought it best to tear it down, lest it bring reproach upon them, for the Gentiles had defiled it. So they tore down the altar, [46]and stored the stones in a convenient place on the temple hill until there should come a prophet to tell what to do with them. [47]Then they took unhewn�q stones, as the law directs, and built a new altar like the former one. [48]They also rebuilt the sanctuary and the interior of the temple, and consecrated the courts. [49]They made new holy vessels, and brought the lampstand, the altar of incense, and the table into the temple. [50]Then they burned incense on the altar and lighted the lamps on the lampstand, and these gave light in the temple. [51]They placed the bread on the table and hung up the curtains. Thus they finished all the work they had undertaken.

52 Early in the morning on the twenty-fifth day of the ninth month, which is the month of Chis'lev, in the one hundred and forty-eighth year,ᵉ [53]they rose and offered sacrifice, as the law directs, on the new altar of burnt offering which they had built. [54]At the very season and on the very day that the Gentiles had profaned it, it was dedicated with songs and harps and lutes and cymbals. [55]All the people fell on their faces and worshiped and blessed Heaven, who had prospered them. [56]So they celebrated the dedication of the altar for eight days, and offered burnt offerings with gladness; they offered a sacrifice of deliverance and praise. [57]They decorated the front of the temple with

---

° Gk *they.*
ᴾ Or *and some fell on the opposite side.*
�q Gk *whole.*
ᵉ 164 B.C.
* 4:29: Vulgate has "Judea" for *Idumea* and "Beth-horon" for *Beth-zur.*

golden crowns and small shields; they restored the gates and the chambers for the priests, and furnished them with doors. [58]There was very great gladness among the people, and the reproach of the Gentiles was removed.

59 Then Judas and his brothers and all the assembly of Israel determined that every year at that season the days of the dedication of the altar should be observed with gladness and joy for eight days, beginning with the twenty-fifth day of the month of Chis'lev.

60 At that time they fortified Mount Zion with high walls and strong towers round about, to keep the Gentiles from coming and trampling them down as they had done before. [61]And he stationed a garrison there to hold it. He also [s] fortified Bethzur, so that the people might have a stronghold that faced Idume'a.

Wars with Neighboring Peoples

5 When the Gentiles round about heard that the altar had been built and the sanctuary dedicated as it was before, they became very angry, [2]and they determined to destroy the descendants of Jacob who lived among them. So they began to kill and destroy among the people. [3]But Judas made war on the sons of Esau in Idume'a, at Ak"rabatte'ne, because they kept lying in wait for Israel. He dealt them a heavy blow and humbled them and despoiled them. [4]He also remembered the wickedness of the sons of Bae'an, who were a trap and a snare to the people and ambushed them on the highways. [5]They were shut up by him in their towers; and he encamped against them, vowed their complete destruction, and burned with fire their [t] towers and all who were in them. [6]Then he crossed over to attack the Am'monites, where he found a strong band and many people with Timothy as their leader. [7]He engaged in many battles with them and they were crushed before him; he struck them down. [8]He also took Ja'zer and its villages; then he returned to Judea.

Liberation of Galilean Jews

9 Now the Gentiles in Gilead gathered together against the Israelites who lived in their territory, and planned to destroy them. But they fled to the stronghold of Dath'ema, [10]and sent to Judas and his brothers a letter which said, "The Gentiles around us have gathered together against us to destroy us. [11]They are preparing to come and capture the stronghold to which we have fled, and Timothy is leading their forces. [12]Now then come and rescue us from their hands, for many of us have fallen, [13]and all our brethren who were in the land of Tob have been killed; the enemy [u] have captured their wives and children and goods, and have destroyed about a thousand men there."

14 While the letter was still being read, behold, other messengers, with their garments torn, came from Galilee and made a similar report; [15]they said that against them had gathered together men of Ptolema'is and Tyre and Si'don, and all Galilee of the Gentiles, [v] "to annihilate us." [16]When Judas and the people heard these messages, a great assembly was called to determine what they should do for their brethren who were in distress and were being attacked by enemies. [w] [17]Then Judas said to Simon his brother, "Choose your men and go and rescue your brethren in Galilee; I and Jonathan my brother will go to Gilead." [18]But he left Joseph, the son of Zechari'ah, and Azari'ah, a leader of the people, with the rest of the forces, in Judea to guard it; [19]and he gave them this command, "Take charge of this people, but do not engage in battle with the Gentiles until we return." [20]Then three thousand men were assigned to Simon to go to Galilee, and eight thousand to Judas for Gilead.

21 So Simon went to Galilee and fought many battles against the Gentiles, and the Gentiles were crushed before him. [22]He pursued them to the gate of Ptolema'is, and as many as three thousand of the Gentiles fell, and he despoiled them. [23]Then he took the Jews [x] of Galilee and Ar'batta, with their wives and children, and all they possessed, and led them to Judea with great rejoicing.

Judas and Jonathan in Gilead

24 Judas Mac"cabe'us and Jonathan his brother crossed the Jordan and went three days' journey into the wilderness. [25]They encountered the Nab"ate'ans, who met them peaceably and told them all that had happened to their brethren in Gilead: [26]"Many of them have been shut up in Bozrah and Bo'sor, in Al'ema and Chas'pho, Ma'ked and Carna'im"—all these cities were strong and large—[27]"and some have been shut up in the other cities of Gilead; the enemy [y] are getting ready to attack the strongholds tomorrow and take and destroy all these men in one day."

28 Then Judas and his army quickly turned back by the wilderness road to Bozrah; and he took the city, and killed every male by the edge of the sword; then he seized all its spoils and burned it with fire. [29]He departed from there at night, and they went all the way to the stronghold of Dath'ema. [z] [30]At dawn they looked up, and behold, a large company, that could not be counted, carrying ladders and engines of war to capture the stronghold, and attacking the Jews

---

[s] Greek adds *to hold it.*
[t] Gk *her.*
[u] Gk *they.*
[v] Gk *aliens.*
[w] Gk *them.*
[x] Gk *those.*
[y] Gk *they.*
[z] Greek lacks *of Dathema.* See verse 9.

within.[a] [31]So Judas saw that the battle had begun and that the cry of the city went up to Heaven with trumpets and loud shouts, [32]and he said to the men of his forces, "Fight today for your brethren!" [33]Then he came up behind them in three companies, who sounded their trumpets and cried aloud in prayer. [34]And when the army of Timothy realized that it was Mac"cabe'us, they fled before him, and he dealt them a heavy blow. As many as eight thousand of them fell that day.

35 Next he turned aside to Al'ema,[b] * and fought against it and took it; and he killed every male in it, plundered it, and burned it with fire. [36]From there he marched on and took Chas'pho, Ma'ked, and Bo'sor, and the other cities of Gilead.

37 After these things Timothy gathered another army and encamped opposite Ra'phon on the other side of the stream. [38]Judas sent men to spy out the camp, and they reported to him, "All the Gentiles around us have gathered to him; it is a very large force. [39]They also have hired Arabs to help them, and they are encamped across the stream, ready to come and fight against you." And Judas went to meet them.

40 Now as Judas and his army drew near to the stream of water, Timothy said to the officers of his forces, "If he crosses over to us first, we will not be able to resist him, for he will surely defeat us. [41]But if he shows fear and camps on the other side of the river, we will cross over to him and defeat him." [42]When Judas approached the stream of water, he stationed the scribes of the people at the stream and gave them this command, "Permit no man to encamp, but make them all enter the battle." [43]Then he crossed over against them first, and the whole army followed him. All the Gentiles were defeated before him, and they threw away their arms and fled into the sacred precincts at Carna'im. [44]But he took the city and burned the sacred precincts with fire, together with all who were in them. Thus Carna'im was conquered; they could stand before Judas no longer.

The Return to Jerusalem

45 Then Judas gathered together all the Israelites in Gilead, the small and the great, with their wives and children and goods, a very large company, to go to the land of Judah. [46]So they came to E'phron. This was a large and very strong city on the road, and they could not go round it to the right or to the left; they had to go through it. [47]But the men of the city shut them out and blocked up the gates with stones. [48]And Judas sent them this friendly message, "Let us pass through your land to get to our land. No one will do you harm; we will simply pass by on foot." But they refused to open to him. [49]Then Judas ordered proclamation to be made to the army that each should encamp where he was. [50]So the men of the forces encamped, and

he fought against the city all that day and all the night, and the city was delivered into his hands. [51]He destroyed every male by the edge of the sword, and razed and plundered the city. Then he passed through the city over the slain.

52 And they crossed the Jordan into the large plain before Beth-shan. [53]And Judas kept rallying the laggards and encouraging the people all the way till he came to the land of Judah. [54]So they went up to Mount Zion with gladness and joy, and offered burnt offerings, because not one of them had fallen before they returned in safety.

55 Now while Judas and Jonathan were in Gilead and Simon his brother was in Galilee before Ptolema'is, [56]Joseph, the son of Zechari'ah, and Azari'ah, the commanders of the forces, heard of their brave deeds and of the heroic war they had fought. [57]So they said, "Let us also make a name for ourselves; let us go and make war on the Gentiles around us." [58]And they issued orders to the men of the forces that were with them, and they marched against Jam'nia. [59]And Gor'gias and his men came out of the city to meet them in battle. [60]Then Joseph and Azari'ah were routed, and were pursued to the borders of Judea; as many as two thousand of the people of Israel fell that day. [61]Thus the people suffered a great rout because, thinking to do a brave deed, they did not listen to Judas and his brothers. [62]But they did not belong to the family of those men through whom deliverance was given to Israel.

63 The man Judas and his brothers were greatly honored in all Israel and among all the Gentiles, wherever their name was heard. [64]Men gathered to them and praised them.

Success at Hebron and Philistia

65 Then Judas and his brothers went forth and fought the sons of Esau in the land to the south. He struck He'bron and its villages and tore down its strongholds and burned its towers round about. [66]Then he marched off to go into the land of the Philis'tines, and passed through Mar'isa.[c] † [67]On that day some priests, who wished to do a brave deed, fell in battle, for they went out to battle unwisely. [68]But Judas turned aside to Azo'tus in the land of the Philis'tines; † he tore down their altars, and the graven images of their gods he burned with fire; he plundered the cities and returned to the land of Judah.

The Last Days of Antiochus Epiphanes

6 King Anti'ochus was going through the upper provinces when he heard that Elyma'is in Persia was a city famed for its wealth in silver

---

[a] Gk *and they were attacking them.*
[b] The name is uncertain.
[c] Other authorities read *Samaria.*
* 5:35: Vulgate reads "Maspha" (i.e., Mizpah) for *Alema;* cf. note b.
† 5:66, 68: Vulgate has "aliens" and "strangers" for *Philistines,* and "Samaria" for *Marisa;* cf. note c.

and gold. [2]Its temple was very rich, containing golden shields, breastplates, and weapons left there by Alexander, the son of Philip, the Macedonian king who first reigned over the Greeks. [3]So he came and tried to take the city and plunder it, but he could not, because his plan became known to the men of the city [4]and they withstood him in battle. So he fled and in great grief departed from there to return to Babylon.

[5] Then some one came to him in Persia and reported that the armies which had gone into the land of Judah had been routed; [6]that Lys'ias had gone first with a strong force, but had turned and fled before the Jews; [d] that the Jews [e] had grown strong from the arms, supplies, and abundant spoils which they had taken from the armies they had cut down; [7]that they had torn down the abomination which he had erected upon the altar in Jerusalem; and that they had surrounded the sanctuary with high walls as before, and also Beth-zur, his city.

[8] When the king heard this news, he was astounded and badly shaken. He took to his bed and became sick from grief, because things had not turned out for him as he had planned. [9]He lay there for many days, because deep grief continually gripped him, and he concluded that he was dying. [10]So he called all his friends and said to them, "Sleep departs from my eyes and I am downhearted with worry. [11]I said to myself, 'To what distress I have come! And into what a great flood I now am plunged! For I was kind and beloved in my power.' [12]But now I remember the evils I did in Jerusalem. I seized all her vessels of silver and gold; and I sent to destroy the inhabitants of Judah without good reason. [13]I know that it is because of this that these evils have come upon me; and behold, I am perishing of deep grief in a strange land."

[14] Then he called for Philip, one of his friends, and made him ruler over all his kingdom. [15]He gave him the crown and his robe and the signet, that he might guide Anti'ochus his son and bring him up to be king. [16]Thus Anti'ochus the king died there in the one hundred and forty-ninth year. [f] [17]And when Lys'ias learned that the king was dead, he set up Anti'ochus the king's [g] son to reign. Lysias [h] had brought him up as a boy, and he named him Eu'pator.

Renewed Attacks from Syria

[18] Now the men in the citadel kept hemming Israel in around the sanctuary. They were trying in every way to harm them and strengthen the Gentiles. [19]So Judas decided to destroy them, and assembled all the people to besiege them. [20]They gathered together and besieged the citadel [i] in the one hundred and fiftieth year; [j] and he built siege towers and other engines of war. [21]But some of the garrison escaped from the siege and some of

the ungodly Israelites joined them. [22]They went to the king and said, "How long will you fail to do justice and to avenge our brethren? [23]We were happy to serve your father, to live by what he said and to follow his commands. [24]For this reason the sons of our people besieged the citadel [k] and became hostile to us; moreover, they have put to death as many of us as they have caught, and they have seized our inheritances. [25]And not against us alone have they stretched out their hands, but also against all the lands on their borders. [26]And behold, today they have encamped against the citadel in Jerusalem to take it; they have fortified both the sanctuary and Beth-zur; [27]and unless you quickly prevent them, they will do still greater things, and you will not be able to stop them."

[28] The king was enraged when he heard this. He assembled all his friends, the commanders of his forces and those in authority. [l] [29]And mercenary forces came to him from other kingdoms and from islands of the seas. [30]The number of his forces was a hundred thousand foot soldiers, twenty thousand horsemen, and thirty-two elephants accustomed to war. [31]They came through Idume'a and encamped against Beth-zur, and for many days they fought and built engines of war; but the Jews [m] sallied out and burned these with fire, and fought manfully.

The Battle at Beth-zechariah

[32] Then Judas marched away from the citadel and encamped at Beth-zech"ari'ah, opposite the camp of the king. [33]Early in the morning the king rose and took his army by a forced march along the road to Beth-zech"ari'ah, and his troops made ready for battle and sounded their trumpets. [34]They showed the elephants the juice of grapes and mulberries, to arouse them for battle. [35]And they distributed the beasts among the phalanxes; with each elephant they stationed a thousand men armed with coats of mail, and with brass helmets on their heads; and five hundred picked horsemen were assigned to each beast. [36]These took their position beforehand wherever the beast was; wherever it went they went with it, and they never left it. [37]And upon the elephants [n] were wooden towers, strong and covered; they were fastened upon each beast by special harness, and upon each were four [o] armed men who fought from

---

[d] Gk them.
[e] Gk they.
[f] 163 B.C.
[g] Gk his.
[h] Gk He.
[i] Gk it.
[j] 162 B.C.
[k] The Greek text underlying the sons . . . the citadel is uncertain.
[l] Gk those over the reins.
[m] Gk they.
[n] Gk them.
[o] Cn: Some authorities read thirty; others thirty-two.

there, and also its Indian driver. [38]The rest of the horsemen were stationed on either side, on the two flanks of the army, to harass the enemy while being themselves protected by the phalanxes. [39]When the sun shone upon the shields of gold and brass, the hills were ablaze with them and gleamed like flaming torches.

40 Now a part of the king's army was spread out on the high hills, and some troops were on the plain, and they advanced steadily and in good order. [41]All who heard the noise made by their multitude, by the marching of the multitude and the clanking of their arms, trembled, for the army was very large and strong. [42]But Judas and his army advanced to the battle, and six hundred men of the king's army fell. [43]And Elea′zar, called Av′aran, saw that one of the beasts was equipped with royal armor. It was taller than all the others, and he supposed that the king was upon it. [44]So he gave his life to save his people and to win for himself an everlasting name. [45]He courageously ran into the midst of the phalanx to reach it; he killed men right and left, and they parted before him on both sides. [46]He got under the elephant, stabbed it from beneath, and killed it; but it fell to the ground upon him and there he died. [47]And when the Jews [p] saw the royal might and the fierce attack of the forces, they turned away in flight.

48 The soldiers of the king's army went up to Jerusalem against them, and the king encamped in Judea and at Mount Zion. [49]He made peace with the men of Beth-zur, and they evacuated the city, because they had no provisions there to withstand a siege, since it was a sabbatical year for the land. [50]So the king took Beth-zur and stationed a guard there to hold it. [51]Then he encamped before the sanctuary for many days. He set up siege towers, engines of war to throw fire and stones, machines to shoot arrows, and catapults. [52]The Jews [q] also made engines of war to match theirs, and fought for many days. [53]But they had no food in storage, [r] because it was the seventh year; those who found safety in Judea from the Gentiles had consumed the last of the stores. [54]Few men were left in the sanctuary, because famine had prevailed over the rest and they had been scattered, each to his own place.

Syria Offers Terms

55 Then Lys′ias heard that Philip, whom King Anti′ochus while still living had appointed to bring up Antiochus his son to be king, [56]had returned from Persia and Med′ia with the forces that had gone with the king, and that he was trying to seize control of the government. [57]So he quickly gave orders to depart, and said to the king, to the commanders of the forces, and to the men, "We daily grow weaker, our food supply is scant, the place against which we are fighting is strong, and the affairs of the kingdom press urgently upon us. [58]Now then let us come to terms with these men, and make peace with them and with all their nation, [59]and agree to let them live by their laws as they did before; for it was on account of their laws which we abolished that they became angry and did all these things."

60 The speech pleased the king and the commanders, and he sent to the Jews [s] an offer of peace, and they accepted it. [61]So the king and the commanders gave them their oath. On these conditions the Jews [t] evacuated the stronghold. [62]But when the king entered Mount Zion and saw what a strong fortress the place was, he broke the oath he had sworn and gave orders to tear down the wall all around. [63]Then he departed with haste and returned to Antioch. He found Philip in control of the city, but he fought against him, and took the city by force.

Expedition of Bacchides and Alcimun

7 In the one hundred and fifty-first year [u] Deme′trius the son of Seleu′cus set forth from Rome, sailed with a few men to a city by the sea, and there began to reign. [2]As he was entering the royal palace of his fathers, the army seized Anti′ochus and Lys′ias to bring them to him. [3]But when this act became known to him, he said, "Do not let me see their faces!" [4]So the army killed them, and Deme′trius took his seat upon the throne of his kingdom.

5 Then there came to him all the lawless and ungodly men of Israel; they were led by Al′cimus, who wanted to be high priest. [6]And they brought to the king this accusation against the people: "Judas and his brothers have destroyed all your friends, and have driven us out of our land. [7]Now then send a man whom you trust; let him go and see all the ruin which Judas [v] has brought upon us and upon the land of the king, and let him punish them and all who help them."

8 So the king chose Bacchi′des, one of the king's friends, governor of the province Beyond the River; he was a great man in the kingdom and was faithful to the king. [9]And he sent him, and with him the ungodly Al′cimus, whom he made high priest; and he commanded him to take vengeance on the sons of Israel. [10]So they marched away and came with a large force into the land of Judah; and he sent messengers to Judas and his brothers with peaceable but treacherous words. [11]But they paid no attention to their words, for they saw that they had come with a large force.

12 Then a group of scribes appeared in a body

[p] Gk they.
[q] Gk They.
[r] Other authorities read in the sanctuary.
[s] Gk them.
[t] Gk they.
[u] 161 B.C.
[v] Gk he.

before Al'cimus and Bacchi'des to ask for just terms. [13]The Hasid'eans were first among the sons of Israel to seek peace from them, [14]for they said, "A priest of the line of Aaron has come with the army, and he will not harm us." [15]And he spoke peaceable words to them and swore this oath to them, "We will not seek to injure you or your friends." [16]So they trusted him; but he seized sixty of them and killed them in one day, in accordance with the word which was written,

[17]"The flesh of your saints and their blood
　they poured out round about Jerusalem,
　and there was none to bury them."

[18]Then the fear and dread of them fell upon all the people, for they said, "There is no truth or justice in them, for they have violated the agreement and the oath which they swore."

19 Then Bacchi'des departed from Jerusalem and encamped in Beth-za'ith. And he sent and seized many of the men who had deserted to him,[w] and some of the people, and killed them and threw them into the great pit. [20]He placed Al'cimus in charge of the country and left with him a force to help him; then Bacchi'des went back to the king.

21 Al'cimus strove for the high priesthood, [22]and all who were troubling their people joined him. They gained control of the land of Judah and did great damage in Israel. [23]And Judas saw all the evil that Al'cimus and those with him had done among the sons of Israel; it was more than the Gentiles had done. [24]So Judas[x] went out into all the surrounding parts of Judea, and took vengeance on the men who had deserted, and he prevented those in the city[y] from going out into the country. [25]When Al'cimus saw that Judas and those with him had grown strong, and realized that he could not withstand them, he returned to the king and brought wicked charges against them.

Nicanor in Judea

26 Then the king sent Nica'nor, one of his honored princes, who hated and detested Israel, and he commanded him to destroy the people. [27]So Nica'nor came to Jerusalem with a large force, and treacherously sent to Judas and his brothers this peaceable message, [28]"Let there be no fighting between me and you; I shall come with a few men to see you face to face in peace." [29]So he came to Judas, and they greeted one another peaceably. But the enemy were ready to seize Judas. [30]It became known to Judas that Nica'nor[x] had come to him with treacherous intent, and he was afraid of him and would not meet him again. [31]When Nica'nor learned that his plan had been disclosed, he went out to meet Judas in battle near Caph"ar-sal'ama. [32]About five hundred men of the army of Nica'nor fell, and the rest[z] fled into the city of David.

Nicanor Threatens the Temple

33 After these events Nica'nor went up to Mount Zion. Some of the priests came out of the sanctuary, and some of the elders of the people, to greet him peaceably and to show him the burnt offering that was being offered for the king. [34]But he mocked them and derided them and defiled them and spoke arrogantly, [35]and in anger he swore this oath, "Unless Judas and his army are delivered into my hands this time, then if I return safely I will burn up this house." And he went out in great anger. [36]Then the priests went in and stood before the altar and the temple, and they wept and said,

[37]"You chose this house to be called by your name,
　and to be for your people a house of prayer and supplication.
[38]Take vengeance on this man and on his army,
　and let them fall by the sword;
remember their blasphemies,
　and let them live no longer."

The Death of Nicanor

39 Now Nica'nor went out from Jerusalem and encamped in Beth-ho'ron, and the Syrian army joined him. [40]And Judas encamped in Ad'asa with three thousand men. Then Judas prayed and said, [41]"When the messengers from the king spoke blasphemy, your angel went forth and struck down one hundred and eighty-five thousand of the Assyrians.[a] [42]So also crush this army before us today; let the rest learn that Nica'nor[b] has spoken wickedly against your sanctuary, and judge him according to this wickedness." [43]So the armies met in battle on the thirteenth day of the month of Adar'. The army of Nica'nor was crushed, and he himself was the first to fall in the battle. [44]When his army saw that Nica'nor had fallen, they threw down their arms and fled. [45]The Jews[c] pursued them a day's journey, from Ad'asa as far as Gaza'ra, and as they followed kept sounding the battle call on the trumpets. [46]And men came out of all the villages of Judea round about, and they outflanked the enemy[d] and drove them back to their pursuers,[e] so that they all fell by the sword; not even one of them was left. [47]Then the Jews[f] seized the spoils and the plunder, and they cut off Nica'nor's head and the right hand which he so arrogantly stretched out, and brought them and displayed

---

[w] Or *many of his men who had deserted.*
[x] Gk *he.*
[y] Gk *they were prevented.*
[z] Gk *they.*
[a] Gk *of them.*
[b] Gk *he.*
[c] Gk *They.*
[d] Gk *them.*
[e] Gk *these.*
[f] Gk *they.*

them just outside Jerusalem. [48]The people rejoiced greatly and celebrated that day as a day of great gladness. [49]And they decreed that this day should be celebrated each year on the thirteenth day of Adar'. [50]So the land of Judah had rest for a few days.

An Eulogy of the Romans

8 Now Judas heard of the fame of the Romans, that they were very strong and were well-disposed toward all who made an alliance with them, that they pledged friendship to those who came to them, [2]and that they were very strong. Men told him of their wars and of the brave deeds which they were doing among the Gauls, how they had defeated them and forced them to pay tribute, [3]and what they had done in the land of Spain to get control of the silver and gold mines there, [4]and how they had gained control of the whole region by their planning and patience, even though the place was far distant from them. They also subdued the kings who came against them from the ends of the earth, until they crushed them and inflicted great disaster upon them; the rest paid them tribute every year. [5]Philip, and Per'seus king of the Macedonians, [g] and the others who rose up against them, they crushed in battle and conquered. [6]They also defeated Anti'ochus the Great, king of Asia, who went to fight against them with a hundred and twenty elephants and with cavalry and chariots and a very large army. He was crushed by them; [7]they took him alive and decreed that he and those who should reign after him should pay a heavy tribute and give hostages and surrender some of their best provinces, [8]the country of India and Med'ia and Lyd'ia. These they took from him and gave to Eu'menes the king. [9]The Greeks planned to come and destroy them, [10]but this became known to them, and they sent a general against the Greeks [h] and attacked them. Many of them were wounded and fell, and the Romans [i] took captive their wives and children; they plundered them, conquered the land, tore down their strongholds, and enslaved them to this day. [11]The remaining kingdoms and islands, as many as ever opposed them, they destroyed and enslaved; [12]but with their friends and those who rely on them they have kept friendship. They have subdued kings far and near, and as many as have heard of their fame have feared them. [13]Those whom they wish to help and to make kings, they make kings, and those whom they wish they depose; and they have been greatly exalted. [14]Yet for all this not one of them has put on a crown or worn purple as a mark of pride, [15]but they have built for themselves a senate chamber, and every day three hundred and twenty senators constantly deliberate concerning the people, to govern them well. [16]They trust one man each year to

rule over them and to control all their land; they all heed the one man, and there is no envy or jealousy among them.

An Alliance with Rome

[17] So Judas chose Eupol'emus the son of John, son of Ac'cos, and Jason the son of Elea'zar, and sent them to Rome to establish friendship and alliance, [18]and to free themselves from the yoke; for they saw that the kingdom of the Greeks was completely enslaving Israel. [19]They went to Rome, a very long journey; and they entered the senate chamber and spoke as follows: [20]"Judas, who is also called Mac"cabe'us, and his brothers and the people of the Jews have sent us to you to establish alliance and peace with you, that we may be enrolled as your allies and friends." [21]The proposal pleased them, [22]and this is a copy of the letter which they wrote in reply, on bronze tablets, and sent to Jerusalem to remain with them there as a memorial of peace and alliance:

[23] "May all go well with the Romans and with the nation of the Jews at sea and on land for ever, and may sword and enemy be far from them. [24]If war comes first to Rome or to any of their allies in all their dominion, [25]the nation of the Jews shall act as their allies wholeheartedly, as the occasion may indicate to them. [26]And to the enemy who makes war they shall not give or supply grain, arms, money, or ships, as Rome has decided; and they shall keep their obligations without receiving any return. [27]In the same way, if war comes first to the nation of the Jews, the Romans shall willingly act as their allies, as the occasion may indicate to them. [28]And to the enemy allies shall be given no grain, arms, money, or ships, as Rome has decided; and they shall keep these obligations and do so without deceit. [29]Thus on these terms the Romans make a treaty with the Jewish people. [30]If after these terms are in effect both parties shall determine to add or delete anything, they shall do so at their discretion, and any addition or deletion that they may make shall be valid.

[31] "And concerning the wrongs which King Deme'trius is doing to them we have written to him as follows, 'Why have you made your yoke heavy upon our friends and allies the Jews? [32]If now they appeal again for help against you, we will defend their rights and fight you on sea and on land.'"

Bacchides Returns to Judea

9 When Deme'trius heard that Nica'nor and his army had fallen in battle, he sent Bacchi'des and Al'cimus into the land of Judah a second time, and with them the right wing of the army. [2]They went by the road which leads to

---

[g] Or *Kittim*.
[h] Gk *them*.
[i] Gk *they*.

Gilgal and encamped against Mes'aloth in Arbe'la, and they took it and killed many people. [3]In the first month of the one hundred and fifty-second year [j] they encamped against Jerusalem; [4]then they marched off and went to Bere'a with twenty thousand foot soldiers and two thousand cavalry.

5 Now Judas was encamped in El'asa, and with him were three thousand picked men. [6]When they saw the huge number of the enemy forces, they were greatly frightened, and many slipped away from the camp, until no more than eight hundred of them were left.

7 When Judas saw that his army had slipped away and the battle was imminent, he was crushed in spirit, for he had no time to assemble them. [8]He became faint, but he said to those who were left, "Let us rise and go up against our enemies. We may be able to fight them." [9]But they tried to dissuade him, saying, "We are not able. Let us rather save our own lives now, and let us come back with our brethren and fight them; we are too few." [10]But Judas said, "Far be it from us to do such a thing as to flee from them. If our time has come, let us die bravely for our brethren, and leave no cause to question our honor."

The Last Battle of Judas

11 Then the army of Bacchi'des [k] marched out from the camp and took its stand for the encounter. The cavalry was divided into two companies, and the slingers and the archers went ahead of the army, as did all the chief warriors. [12]Bacchi'des was on the right wing. Flanked by the two companies, the phalanx advanced to the sound of the trumpets; and the men with Judas also blew their trumpets. [13]The earth was shaken by the noise of the armies, and the battle raged from morning till evening.

14 Judas saw that Bacchi'des and the strength of his army were on the right; then all the stouthearted men went with him, [15]and they crushed the right wing, and he pursued them as far as Mount Azo'tus. [16]When those on the left wing saw that the right wing was crushed, they turned and followed close behind Judas and his men. [17]The battle became desperate, and many on both sides were wounded and fell. [18]Judas also fell, and the rest fled.

19 Then Jonathan and Simon took Judas their brother and buried him in the tomb of their fathers at Mo'dein, [20]and wept for him. And all Israel made great lamentation for him; they mourned many days and said,

[21]"How is the mighty fallen,
    the savior of Israel!"

[22]Now the rest of the acts of Judas, and his wars and the brave deeds that he did, and his greatness, have not been recorded, for they were very many.

Jonathan Succeeds Judas

23 After the death of Judas, the lawless emerged in all parts of Israel; all the doers of injustice appeared. [24]In those days a very great famine occurred, and the country deserted with them to the enemy. [25]And Bacchi'des chose the ungodly and put them in charge of the country. [26]They sought and searched for the friends of Judas, and brought them to Bacchi'des, and he took vengeance on them and made sport of them. [27]Thus there was great distress in Israel, such as had not been since the time that prophets ceased to appear among them.

28 Then all the friends of Judas assembled and said to Jonathan, [29]"Since the death of your brother Judas there has been no one like him to go against our enemies and Bacchi'des, and to deal with those of our nation who hate us. [30]So now we have chosen you today to take his place as our ruler and leader, to fight our battle." [31]And Jonathan at that time accepted the leadership and took the place of Judas his brother.

The Campaigns of Jonathan

32 When Bacchi'des learned of this, he tried to kill him. [33]But Jonathan and Simon his brother and all who were with him heard of it, and they fled into the wilderness of Teko'a and camped by the water of the pool of As'phar. [34]Bacchi'des found this out on the sabbath day, and he with all his army crossed the Jordan.

35 And Jonathan [l] sent his brother as leader of the multitude and begged the Nab"ate'ans, who were his friends, for permission to store with them the great amount of baggage which they had. [36]But the sons of Jam'bri from Med'eba came out and seized John and all that he had, and departed with it.

37 After these things it was reported to Jonathan and Simon his brother, "The sons of Jam'bri are celebrating a great wedding, and are conducting the bride, a daughter of one of the great nobles of Canaan, from Nad'abath * with a large escort." [38]And they remembered the blood of John their brother, and went up and hid under cover of the mountain. [39]They raised their eyes and looked, and saw a tumultuous procession with much baggage; and the bridegroom came out with his friends and his brothers to meet them with tambourines and musicians and many weapons. [40]Then they rushed upon them from the ambush and began killing them. Many were wounded and fell, and the rest fled to the mountain; and they took all their goods. [41]Thus the wedding was turned into mourning and the voice of their musicians into a funeral dirge. [42]And

---

[j] 160 B.C.
[k] Gk the army.
[l] Gk he.
* 9:37: Vulgate reads "Madaba" (i.e., Medeba, as in verse 36) for Nadabath.

when they had fully avenged the blood of their brother, they returned to the marshes of the Jordan.

43 When Bacchi'des heard of this, he came with a large force on the sabbath day to the banks of the Jordan. [44]And Jonathan said to those with him, "Let us rise up now and fight for our lives, for today things are not as they were before. [45]For look! the battle is in front of us and behind us; the water of the Jordan is on this side and on that, with marsh and thicket; there is no place to turn. [46]Cry out now to Heaven that you may be delivered from the hands of our enemies." [47]So the battle began, and Jonathan stretched out his hand to strike Bacchi'des, but he eluded him and went to the rear. [48]Then Jonathan and the men with him leaped into the Jordan and swam across to the other side, and the enemy [m] did not cross the Jordan to attack them. [49]And about one thousand of Bacchi'des' men fell that day.

Bacchides Builds Fortifications

50 Bacchi'des [n] then returned to Jerusalem and built strong cities in Judea: the fortress in Jericho, and Emma'us, and Beth-ho'ron, and Beth'el, and Tim'nath, and [o] Phar'athon, and Teph'on, with high walls and gates and bars. [51]And he placed garrisons in them to harass Israel. [52]He also fortified the city of Beth-zur, and Gaza'ra, and the citadel, and in them he put troops and stores of food. [53]And he took the sons of the leading men of the land as hostages and put them under guard in the citadel at Jerusalem.

54 In the one hundred and fifty-third year, [p] in the second month, Al'cimus gave orders to tear down the wall of the inner court of the sanctuary. He tore down the work of the prophets! [55]But he only began to tear it down, for at that time Al'cimus was stricken and his work was hindered; his mouth was stopped and he was paralyzed, so that he could no longer say a word or give commands concerning his house. [56]And Al'cimus died at that time in great agony. [57]When Bacchi'des saw that Al'cimus was dead, he returned to the king, and the land of Judah had rest for two years.

The End of the War

58 Then all the lawless plotted and said, "See! Jonathan and his men are living in quiet and confidence. So now let us bring Bacchi'des back, and he will capture them all in one night." [59]And they went and consulted with him. [60]He started to come with a large force, and secretly sent letters to all his allies in Judea, telling them to seize Jonathan and his men; but they were unable to do it, because their plan became known. [61]And Jonathan's men [q] seized about fifty of the men of the country who were leaders in this treachery, and killed them.

62 Then Jonathan with his men, and Simon, withdrew to Beth-ba'si in the wilderness; he rebuilt the parts of it that had been demolished, and they fortified it. [63]When Bacchi'des learned of this, he assembled all his forces, and sent orders to the men of Judea. [64]Then he came and encamped against Beth-ba'si; he fought against it for many days and made machines of war.

65 But Jonathan left Simon his brother in the city, while he went out into the country; and he went with only a few men. [66]He struck down Odomer'a and his brothers and the sons of Pha'siron in their tents. [67]Then he [r] began to attack and went into battle with his forces; and Simon and his men sallied out from the city and set fire to the machines of war. [68]They fought with Bacchi'des, and he was crushed by them. They distressed him greatly, for his plan and his expedition had been in vain. [69]So he was greatly enraged at the lawless men who had counseled him to come into the country, and he killed many of them. Then he decided to depart to his own land.

70 When Jonathan learned of this, he sent ambassadors to him to make peace with him and obtain release of the captives. [71]He agreed, and did as he said; and he swore to Jonathan [s] that he would not try to harm him as long as he lived. [72]He restored to him the captives whom he had formerly taken from the land of Judah; then he turned and departed to his own land, and came no more into their territory. [73]Thus the sword ceased from Israel. And Jonathan dwelt in Mich'mash. And Jonathan began to judge the people, and he destroyed the ungodly out of Israel.

Revolt of Alexander Epiphanes

10 In the one hundred and sixtieth year [t] Alexander Epiph'anes, the son of Anti'ochus, landed and occupied Ptolema'is. They welcomed him, and there he began to reign. [2]When Deme'trius the king heard of it, he assembled a very large army and marched out to meet him in battle. [3]And Deme'trius sent Jonathan a letter in peaceable words to honor him; [4]for he said, "Let us act first to make peace with him [u] before he makes peace with Alexander against us, [5]for he will remember all the wrongs which we did to him and to his brothers and his nation." [6]So Deme'trius [v] gave him authority to recruit troops, to equip them with arms, and to become his ally; and he commanded that the hostages in the citadel should be released to him.

---

[m] Gk *they.*
[n] Gk *He.*
[o] Some authorities omit *and.*
[p] 159 b.c.
[q] Gk *they.*
[r] Other authorities read *they.*
[s] Gk *him.*
[t] 152 b.c.
[u] Gk *them.*
[v] Gk *he.*

7 Then Jonathan came to Jerusalem and read the letter in the hearing of all the people and of the men in the citadel. [8]They were greatly alarmed when they heard that the king had given him authority to recruit troops. [9]But the men in the citadel released the hostages to Jonathan, and he returned them to their parents.

10 And Jonathan dwelt in Jerusalem and began to rebuild and restore the city. [11]He directed those who were doing the work to build the walls and encircle Mount Zion with squared stones, for better fortification; and they did so.

12 Then the foreigners who were in the strongholds that Bacchi'des had built fled; [13]each left his place and departed to his own land. [14]Only in Beth-zur did some remain who had forsaken the law and the commandments, for it served as a place of refuge.

15 Now Alexander the king heard of all the promises which Deme'trius had sent to Jonathan, and men told him of the battles that Jonathan[w] and his brothers had fought, of the brave deeds that they had done, and of the troubles that they had endured. [16]So he said, "Shall we find another such man? Come now, we will make him our friend and ally." [17]And he wrote a letter and sent it to him, in the following words:

Jonathan Becomes High Priest

18 "King Alexander to his brother Jonathan, greeting. [19]We have heard about you, that you are a mighty warrior and worthy to be our friend. [20]And so we have appointed you today to be the high priest of your nation; you are to be called the king's friend" (and he sent him a purple robe and a golden crown) "and you are to take our side and keep friendship with us."

Demetrius Writes to Jonathan

21 So Jonathan put on the holy garments in the seventh month of the one hundred and sixtieth year,[x] at the feast of tabernacles, and he recruited troops and equipped them with arms in abundance. [22]When Deme'trius heard of these things he was grieved and said, [23]"What is this that we have done? Alexander has gotten ahead of us in forming a friendship with the Jews to strengthen himself. [24]I also will write them words of encouragement and promise them honor and gifts, that I may have their help." [25]So he sent a message to them in the following words:

"King Deme'trius to the nation of the Jews, greeting. [26]Since you have kept your agreement with us and have continued your friendship with us, and have not sided with our enemies, we have heard of it and rejoiced. [27]And now continue still to keep faith with us, and we will repay you with good for what you do for us. [28]We will grant you many immunities and give you gifts.

29 "And now I free you and exempt all the Jews from payment of tribute and salt tax and crown levies, [30]and instead of collecting the third of the grain and the half of the fruit of the trees that I should receive, I release them from this day and henceforth. I will not collect them from the land of Judah or from the three districts added to it from Samar'ia and Galilee, from this day and for all time. [31]And let Jerusalem and her environs, her tithes and her revenues, be holy and free from tax. [32]I release also my control of the citadel in Jerusalem and give it to the high priest, that he may station in it men of his own choice to guard it. [33]And every one of the Jews taken as a captive from the land of Judah into any part of my kingdom, I set free without payment; and let all officials cancel also the taxes on their cattle.

34 "And all the feasts and sabbaths and new moons and appointed days, and the three days before a feast and the three after a feast—let them all be days of immunity and release for all the Jews who are in my kingdom. [35]No one shall have authority to exact anything from them or annoy any of them about any matter.

36 "Let Jews be enrolled in the king's forces to the number of thirty thousand men, and let the maintenance be given them that is due to all the forces of the king. [37]Let some of them be stationed in the great strongholds of the king, and let some of them be put in positions of trust in the kingdom. Let their officers and leaders be of their own number, and let them live by their own laws, just as the king has commanded in the land of Judah.

38 "As for the three districts that have been added to Judea from the country of Samar'ia, let them be so annexed to Judea that they are considered to be under one ruler and obey no other authority but the high priest. [39]Ptolema'is and the land adjoining it I have given as a gift to the sanctuary in Jerusalem, to meet the necessary expenses of the sanctuary. [40]I also grant fifteen thousand shekels of silver yearly out of the king's revenues from appropriate places. [41]And all the additional funds which the government officials have not paid as they did in the first years,[y] they shall give from now on for the service of the temple.[z] [42]Moreover, the five thousand shekels of silver which my officials[a] have received every year from the income of the services of the temple, this too is canceled, because it belongs to the priests who minister there. [43]And whoever takes refuge at the temple in Jerusalem, or in any of its precincts, because he owes money to the king or has any debt, let him be released and receive back all his property in my kingdom.

w Gk he.
x 152 b.c.
y The Greek text of this verse is uncertain.
z Gk house.
a Gk they.

44 "Let the cost of rebuilding and restoring the structures of the sanctuary be paid from the revenues of the king. [45]And let the cost of rebuilding the walls of Jerusalem and fortifying it round about, and the cost of rebuilding the walls in Judea, also be paid from the revenues of the king."

Death of Demetrius

46 When Jonathan and the people heard these words, they did not believe or accept them, because they remembered the great wrongs which Deme'trius [b] had done in Israel and how he had greatly oppressed them. [47]They favored Alexander, because he had been the first to speak peaceable words to them, and they remained his allies all his days.

48 Now Alexander the king assembled large forces and encamped opposite Deme'trius. [49]The two kings met in battle, and the army of Deme'trius fled, and Alexander [c] pursued him and defeated them. [50]He pressed the battle strongly until the sun set, and Deme'trius fell on that day.

Treaty of Ptolemy and Alexander

51 Then Alexander sent ambassadors to Ptol'emy king of Egypt with the following message: [52]"Since I have returned to my kingdom and have taken my seat on the throne of my fathers, and established my rule—for I crushed Deme'trius and gained control of our country; [53]I met him in battle, and he and his army were crushed by us, and we have taken our seat on the throne of his kingdom—[54]now therefore let us establish friendship with one another; give me now your daughter as my wife, and I will become your son-in-law, and will make gifts to you and to her in keeping with your position."

55 Ptol'emy the king replied and said, "Happy was the day on which you returned to the land of your fathers and took your seat on the throne of their kingdom. [56]And now I will do for you as you wrote, but meet me at Ptolema'is, so that we may see one another, and I will become your father-in-law, as you have said."

57 So Ptol'emy set out from Egypt, he and Cleopa'tra his daughter, and came to Ptolema'is in the one hundred and sixty-second year. [d] [58]Alexander the king met him, and Ptol'emy [e] gave him Cleopa'tra his daughter in marriage, and celebrated her wedding at Ptolema'is with great pomp, as kings do.

59 Then Alexander the king wrote to Jonathan to come to meet him. [60]So he went with pomp to Ptolema'is and met the two kings; he gave them and their friends silver and gold and many gifts, and found favor with them. [61]A group of pestilent men from Israel, lawless men, gathered together against him to accuse him; but the king paid no attention to them. [62]The king gave orders to take off Jonathan's garments and to clothe him in purple, and they did so. [63]The king also seated

him at his side; and he said to his officers, "Go forth with him into the middle of the city and proclaim that no one is to bring charges against him about any matter, and let no one annoy him for any reason." [64]And when his accusers saw the honor that was paid him, in accordance with the proclamation, and saw him clothed in purple, they all fled. [65]Thus the king honored him and enrolled him among his chief friends, and made him general and governor of the province. [66]And Jonathan returned to Jerusalem in peace and gladness.

Apollonius Is Defeated by Jonathan

67 In the one hundred and sixty-fifth year [f] Deme'trius the son of Demetrius came from Crete to the land of his fathers. [68]When Alexander the king heard of it, he was greatly grieved and returned to Antioch. [69]And Deme'trius appointed Apollo'nius the governor of Coe'le-syr'ia, and he assembled a large force and encamped against Jam'nia. Then he sent the following message to Jonathan the high priest:

70 "You are the only one to rise up against us, and I have become a laughingstock and reproach because of you. Why do you assume authority against us in the hill country? [71]If you now have confidence in your forces, come down to the plain to meet us, and let us match strength with each other there, for I have with me the power of the cities. [72]Ask and learn who I am and who the others are that are helping us. Men will tell you that you cannot stand before us, for your fathers were twice put to flight in their own land. [73]And now you will not be able to withstand my cavalry and such an army in the plain, where there is no stone or pebble, or place to flee."

74 When Jonathan heard the words of Apollo'nius, his spirit was aroused. He chose ten thousand men and set out from Jerusalem, and Simon his brother met him to help him. [75]He encamped before Joppa, but the men of the city closed its gates, for Apollo'nius had a garrison in Joppa. [76]So they fought against it, and the men of the city became afraid and opened the gates, and Jonathan gained possession of Joppa.

77 When Apollo'nius heard of it, he mustered three thousand cavalry and a large army, and went to Azo'tus as though he were going farther. At the same time he advanced into the plain, for he had a large troop of cavalry and put confidence in it. [78]Jonathan [g] pursued him to Azo'tus, and the armies engaged in battle. [79]Now Apollo'nius had secretly left a thousand cavalry behind them. [80]Jonathan learned that there was an ambush be-

---

b Gk *he*.
c Other authorities read *Alexander fled, and Demetrius*.
d 150 B.C.
e Gk *he*.
f 147 B.C.
g Gk *He*.

hind him, for they surrounded his army and shot arrows at his men from early morning till late afternoon. [81]But his men stood fast, as Jonathan commanded, and the enemy's [h] horses grew tired.

82 Then Simon brought forward his force and engaged the phalanx in battle (for the cavalry was exhausted); they were overwhelmed by him and fled, [83]and the cavalry was dispersed in the plain. They fled to Azo'tus and entered Beth-da'gon, the temple of their idol, for safety. [84]But Jonathan burned Azo'tus and the surrounding towns and plundered them; and the temple of Da'gon, and those who had taken refuge in it he burned with fire. [85]The number of those who fell by the sword, with those burned alive, came to eight thousand men.

86 Then Jonathan departed from there and encamped against Aska'lon, and the men of the city came out to meet him with great pomp. [87]And Jonathan and those with him returned to Jerusalem with much booty. [88]When Alexander the king heard of these things, he honored Jonathan still more; [89]and he sent to him a golden buckle, such as it is the custom to give to the kinsmen of kings. He also gave him Ek'ron and all its environs as his possession.

Ptolemy Invades Syria

11 Then the king of Egypt gathered great forces, like the sand by the seashore, and many ships; and he tried to get possession of Alexander's kingdom by trickery and add it to his own kingdom. [2]He set out for Syria with peaceable words, and the people of the cities opened their gates to him and went to meet him, for Alexander the king had commanded them to meet him, since he was Alexander's [i] father-in-law. [3]But when Ptol'emy entered the cities he stationed forces as a garrison in each city.

4 When he [j] approached Azo'tus, they showed him the temple of Da'gon burned down, and Azotus and its suburbs destroyed, and the corpses lying about, and the charred bodies of those whom Jonathan [k] had burned in the war, for they had piled them in heaps along his route. [5]They also told the king what Jonathan had done, to throw blame on him; but the king kept silent. [6]Jonathan met the king at Joppa with pomp, and they greeted one another and spent the night there. [7]And Jonathan went with the king as far as the river called Eleu'therus; then he returned to Jerusalem.

8 So King Ptol'emy gained control of the coastal cities as far as Seleu'cia by the sea, and he kept devising evil designs against Alexander. [9]He sent envoys to Deme'trius the king, saying, "Come, let us make a covenant with each other, and I will give you in marriage my daughter who was Alexander's wife, and you shall reign over your father's kingdom. [10]For I now regret that I gave him my daughter, for he has tried to kill me." [11]He threw blame on Alexander [l] because he coveted his kingdom. [12]So he took his daughter away from him and gave her to Deme'trius. He was estranged from Alexander, and their enmity became manifest.

13 Then Ptol'emy entered Antioch and put on the crown of Asia. Thus he put two crowns upon his head, the crown of Egypt and that of Asia. [14]Now Alexander the king was in Cili'cia at that time, because the people of that region were in revolt. [15]And Alexander heard of it and came against him in battle. Ptol'emy marched out and met him with a strong force, and put him to flight. [16]So Alexander fled into Arabia to find protection there, and King Ptol'emy was exalted. [17]And Zab'diel the Arab cut off the head of Alexander and sent it to Ptol'emy. [18]But King Ptol'emy died three days later, and his troops in the strongholds were killed by the inhabitants of the strongholds. [19]So Deme'trius became king in the one hundred and sixty-seventh year. [m]

Jonathan's Diplomacy

20 In those days Jonathan assembled the men of Judea to attack the citadel in Jerusalem, and he built many engines of war to use against it. [21]But certain lawless men who hated their nation went to the king and reported to him that Jonathan was besieging the citadel. [22]When he heard this he was angry, and as soon as he heard it he set out and came to Ptolema'is; and he wrote Jonathan not to continue the siege, but to meet him for a conference at Ptolemais as quickly as possible.

23 When Jonathan heard this, he gave orders to continue the siege; and he chose some of the elders of Israel and some of the priests, and put himself in danger, [24]for he went to the king at Ptolema'is, taking silver and gold and clothing and numerous other gifts. And he won his favor. [25]Although certain lawless men of his nation kept making complaints against him, [26]the king treated him as his predecessors had treated him; he exalted him in the presence of all his friends. [27]He confirmed him in the high priesthood and in as many other honors as he had formerly had, and made him to be regarded as one of his chief friends. [28]Then Jonathan asked the king to free Judea and the three districts of Samar'ia [n] from tribute, and promised him three hundred talents. [29]The king consented, and wrote a letter to Jonathan about all these things; its contents were as follows:

---

[h] Gk their.
[i] Gk his.
[j] Other ancient authorities read they.
[k] Gk he.
[l] Gk him.
[m] 145 B.C.
[n] Cn: Gk the three districts and Samaria.

30 "King Deme'trius to Jonathan his brother and to the nation of the Jews, greeting. [31]This copy of the letter which we wrote concerning you to Las'thenes our kinsman we have written to you also, so that you may know what it says. [32]'King Deme'trius to Las'thenes his father, greeting. [33]To the nation of the Jews, who are our friends and fulfil their obligations to us, we have determined to do good, because of the good will they show toward us. [34]We have confirmed as their possession both the territory of Judea and the three districts of Aphai'rema and Lydda and Rath'amin; the latter, with all the region bordering them, were added to Judea from Samar'ia. To all those who offer sacrifice in Jerusalem, we have granted release from ° the royal taxes which the king formerly received from them each year, from the crops of the land and the fruit of the trees. [35]And the other payments henceforth due to us of the tithes, and the taxes due to us, and the salt pits and the crown taxes due to us—from all these we shall grant them release. [36]And not one of these grants shall be canceled from this time forth for ever. [37]Now therefore take care to make a copy of this, and let it be given to Jonathan and put up in a conspicuous place on the holy mountain."

The Intrigue of Trypho

38 Now when Deme'trius the king saw that the land was quiet before him and that there was no opposition to him, he dismissed all his troops, each man to his own place, except the foreign troops which he had recruited from the islands of the nations. So all the troops who had served his fathers hated him. [39]Now Try'pho had formerly been one of Alexander's supporters. He saw that all the troops were murmuring against Deme'trius. So he went to Imal'kue the Arab, who was bringing up Anti'ochus, the young son of Alexander, [40]and insistently urged him to hand Anti'ochus ᴾ over to him, to become king in place of his father. He also reported to Imal'kue ᴾ what Deme'trius had done and told of the hatred which the troops of Demetrius had for him; and he stayed there many days.

41 Now Jonathan sent to Deme'trius the king the request that he remove the troops of the citadel from Jerusalem, and the troops in the strongholds; for they kept fighting against Israel. [42]And Deme'trius sent this message to Jonathan, "Not only will I do these things for you and your nation, but I will confer great honor on you and your nation, if I find an opportunity. [43]Now then you will do well to send me men who will help me, for all my troops have revolted." [44]So Jonathan sent three thousand stalwart men to him at Antioch, and when they came to the king, the king rejoiced at their arrival.

45 Then the men of the city assembled within the city, to the number of a hundred and twenty thousand, and they wanted to kill the king. [46]But the king fled into the palace. Then the men of the city seized the main streets of the city and began to fight. [47]So the king called the Jews to his aid, and they all rallied about him and then spread out through the city; and they killed on that day as many as a hundred thousand men. [48]They set fire to the city and seized much spoil on that day, and they saved the king. [49]When the men of the city saw that the Jews had gained control of the city as they pleased, their courage failed and they cried out to the king with this entreaty, [50]"Grant us peace, and make the Jews stop fighting against us and our city." [51]And they threw down their arms and made peace. So the Jews gained glory in the eyes of the king and of all the people in his kingdom, and they returned to Jerusalem with much spoil.

52 So Deme'trius the king sat on the throne of his kingdom, and the land was quiet before him. [53]But he broke his word about all that he had promised; and he became estranged from Jonathan and did not repay the favors which Jonathan �q had done him, but oppressed him greatly.

Trypho Seizes Power

54 After this Try'pho returned, and with him the young boy Anti'ochus who began to reign and put on the crown. [55]All the troops that Deme'trius had cast off gathered around him, and they fought against Demetrius, ʳ and he fled and was routed. [56]And Try'pho captured the elephants ˢ and gained control of Antioch. [57]Then the young Anti'ochus wrote to Jonathan, saying, "I confirm you in the high priesthood and set you over the four districts and make you one of the friends of the king." [58]And he sent him gold plate and a table service, and granted him the right to drink from gold cups and dress in purple and wear a gold buckle. [59]Simon his brother he made governor from the Ladder of Tyre to the borders of Egypt.

Campaigns of Jonathan and Simon

60 Then Jonathan set forth and traveled beyond the river and among the cities, and all the army of Syria gathered to him as allies. When he came to Aska'lon, the people of the city met him and paid him honor. [61]From there he departed to Gaza, but the men of Gaza shut him out. So he besieged it and burned its suburbs with fire and plundered them. [62]Then the people of Gaza pleaded with Jonathan, and he made peace with them, and took the sons of their rulers as hostages and sent them to Jerusalem. And he passed through the country as far as Damascus.

° Or *Samaria, for all those who offer sacrifice in Jerusalem, in place of.*
ᴾ Gk *him.*
�q Gk *he.*
ʳ Gk *him.*
ˢ Gk *beasts.*

63 Then Jonathan heard that the officers of Deme′trius had come to Ka′desh in Galilee with a large army, intending to remove him from office. [64]He went to meet them, but left his brother Simon in the country. [65]Simon encamped before Beth-zur and fought against it for many days and hemmed it in. [66]Then they asked him to grant them terms of peace, and he did so. He removed them from there, took possession of the city, and set a garrison over it.

67 Jonathan and his army encamped by the waters of Gennes′aret. Early in the morning they marched to the plain of Ha′zor, [68]and behold, the army of the foreigners met him in the plain; they had set an ambush against him in the mountains, but they themselves met him face to face. [69]Then the men in ambush emerged from their places and joined battle. [70]All the men with Jonathan fled; not one of them was left except Mattathi′as the son of Ab′salom and Judas the son of Chal′phi, commanders of the forces of the army. [71]Jonathan tore his garments and put dust on his head, and prayed. [72]Then he turned back to the battle against the enemy[t] and routed them, and they fled. [73]When his men who were fleeing saw this, they returned to him and joined him in the pursuit as far as Ka′desh, to their camp, and there they encamped. [74]As many as three thousand of the foreigners fell that day. And Jonathan returned to Jerusalem.

Alliances with Rome and Sparta

12 Now when Jonathan saw that the time was favorable for him, he chose men and sent them to Rome to confirm and renew the friendship with them. [2]He also sent letters to the same effect to the Spartans and to other places. [3]So they went to Rome and entered the senate chamber and said, "Jonathan the high priest and the Jewish nation have sent us to renew the former friendship and alliance with them." [4]And the Romans[u] gave them letters to the people in every place, asking them to provide for the envoys[v] safe conduct to the land of Judah.

5 This is a copy of the letter which Jonathan wrote to the Spartans: [6]"Jonathan the high priest, the senate of the nation, the priests, and the rest of the Jewish people to their brethren the Spartans, greeting. [7]Already in time past a letter was sent to Oni′as the high priest from A′rius,[w] who was king among you, stating that you are our brethren, as the appended copy shows. [8]Oni′as welcomed the envoy with honor, and received the letter, which contained a clear declaration of alliance and friendship. [9]Therefore, though we have no need of these things, since we have as encouragement the holy books which are in our hands, [10]we have undertaken to send to renew our brotherhood and friendship with you, so that we may not become estranged from you, for considerable

time has passed since you sent your letter to us. [11]We therefore remember you constantly on every occasion, both in our feasts and on other appropriate days, at the sacrifices which we offer and in our prayers, as it is right and proper to remember brethren. [12]And we rejoice in your glory. [13]But as for ourselves, many afflictions and many wars have encircled us; the kings round about us have waged war against us. [14]We were unwilling to annoy you and our other allies and friends with these wars, [15]for we have the help which comes from Heaven for our aid; and we were delivered from our enemies and our enemies were humbled. [16]We therefore have chosen Nume′nius the son of Anti′ochus and Antip′ater the son of Jason, and have sent them to Rome to renew our former friendship and alliance with them. [17]We have commanded them to go also to you and greet you and deliver to you this letter from us concerning the renewal of our brotherhood. [18]And now please send us a reply to this."

19 This is a copy of the letter which they sent to Oni′as: [20]"A′rius, king of the Spartans, to Oni′as the high priest, greeting. [21]It has been found in writing concerning the Spartans and the Jews that they are brethren and are of the family of Abraham. [22]And now that we have learned this, please write us concerning your welfare; [23]we on our part write to you that your cattle and your property belong to us, and ours belong to you. We therefore command that our envoys[x] report to you accordingly."

Further Campaigns of Jonathan and Simon

24 Now Jonathan heard that the commanders of Deme′trius had returned, with a larger force than before, to wage war against him. [25]So he marched away from Jerusalem and met them in the region of Ha′math, for he gave them no opportunity to invade his own country. [26]He sent spies to their camp, and they returned and reported to him that the enemy[y] were being drawn up in formation to fall upon the Jews[z] by night. [27]So when the sun set, Jonathan commanded his men to be alert and to keep their arms at hand so as to be ready all night for battle, and he stationed outposts around the camp. [28]When the enemy heard that Jonathan and his men were prepared for battle, they were afraid and were terrified at heart; so they kindled fires in their camp and withdrew.[a] [29]But Jonathan and his men did not know it until morning, for they saw the fires burning. [30]Then Jonathan pursued them, but he did

---

[t] Gk them.
[u] Gk they.
[v] Gk them.
[w] Vg Compare verse 20: Gk Darius.
[x] Gk they.
[y] Gk they.
[z] Gk them.
[a] Other ancient authorities omit and withdrew.

not overtake them, for they had crossed the Eleu'therus river. [31]So Jonathan turned aside against the Arabs who are called Zabade'ans and he crushed them and plundered them. [32]Then he broke camp and went to Damascus, and marched through all that region.

33 Simon also went forth and marched through the country as far as Aska'lon and the neighboring strongholds. He turned aside to Joppa and took it by surprise, [34]for he had heard that they were ready to hand over the stronghold to the men whom Deme'trius had sent. And he stationed a garrison there to guard it.

35 When Jonathan returned he convened the elders of the people and planned with them to build strongholds in Judea, [36]to build the walls of Jerusalem still higher, and to erect a high barrier between the citadel and the city to separate it from the city, in order to isolate it so that its garrison[b] could neither buy nor sell. [37]So they gathered together to build up the city; part of the wall on the valley to the east had fallen, and he repaired the section called Chaphen'atha. [38]And Simon built Ad'ida in the Shephe'lah; he fortified it and installed gates with bolts.

Trypho Captures Jonathan

39 Then Try'pho attempted to become king of Asia and put on the crown, and to raise his hand against Anti'ochus the king. [40]He feared that Jonathan might not permit him to do so, but might make war on him, so he kept seeking to seize and kill him, and he marched forth and came to Bethshan. [41]Jonathan went out to meet him with forty thousand picked fighting men, and he came to Beth-shan. [42]When Try'pho saw that he had come with a large army, he was afraid to raise his hand against him. [43]So he received him with honor and commended him to all his friends, and he gave him gifts and commanded his friends and his troops to obey him as they would himself. [44]Then he said to Jonathan, "Why have you wearied all these people when we are not at war? [45]Dismiss them now to their homes and choose for yourself a few men to stay with you, and come with me to Ptolema'is. I will hand it over to you as well as the other strongholds and the remaining troops and all the officials, and will turn round and go home. For that is why I am here."

46 Jonathan[c] trusted him and did as he said; he sent away the troops, and they returned to the land of Judah. [47]He kept with himself three thousand men, two thousand of whom he left in Galilee, while a thousand accompanied him. [48]But when Jonathan entered Ptolema'is, the men of Ptolemais closed the gates and seized him, and all who had entered with him they killed with the sword.

49 Then Try'pho sent troops and cavalry into Galilee and the Great Plain to destroy all Jonathan's soldiers. [50]But they realized that Jonathan[c] had been seized and had perished along with his men, and they encouraged one another and kept marching in close formation, ready for battle. [51]When their pursuers saw that they would fight for their lives, they turned back. [52]So they all reached the land of Judah safely, and they mourned for Jonathan and his companions and were in great fear; and all Israel mourned deeply. [53]And all the nations round about them tried to destroy them, for they said, "They have no leader or helper. Now therefore let us make war on them and blot out the memory of them from among men."

Simon Takes Command

13 Simon heard that Try'pho had assembled a large army to invade the land of Judah and destroy it, [2]and he saw that the people were trembling and fearful. So he went up to Jerusalem, and gathering the people together [3]he encouraged them, saying to them, "You yourselves know what great things I and my brothers and the house of my father have done for the laws and the sanctuary; you know also the wars and the difficulties which we have seen. [4]By reason of this all my brothers have perished for the sake of Israel, and I alone am left. [5]And now, far be it from me to spare my life in any time of distress, for I am not better than my brothers. [6]But I will avenge my nation and the sanctuary and your wives and children, for all the nations have gathered together out of hatred to destroy us."

7 The spirit of the people was rekindled when they heard these words, [8]and they answered in a loud voice, "You are our leader in place of Judas and Jonathan your brother. [9]Fight our battles, and all that you say to us we will do." [10]So he assembled all the warriors and hastened to complete the walls of Jerusalem, and he fortified it on every side. [11]He sent Jonathan the son of Ab'salom to Joppa, and with him a considerable army; he drove out its occupants and remained there.

Deceit and Treachery of Trypho

12 Then Try'pho departed from Ptolema'is with a large army to invade the land of Judah, and Jonathan was with him under guard. [13]And Simon encamped in Ad'ida, facing the plain. [14]Try'pho learned that Simon had risen up in place of Jonathan his brother, and that he was about to join battle with him, so he sent envoys to him and said, [15]"It is for the money that Jonathan your brother owed the royal treasury, in connection with the offices he held, that we are detaining him. [16]Send now a hundred talents of silver

---

[b] Gk *they*.
[c] Gk *he*.

and two of his sons as hostages, so that when released he will not revolt against us, and we will release him."

17 Simon knew that they were speaking deceitfully to him, but he sent to get the money and the sons, lest he arouse great hostility among the people, who might say, [18] "Because Simon [d] did not send him the money and the sons, he perished." [19]So he sent the sons and the hundred talents, but Try′pho [e] broke his word and did not release Jonathan.

20 After this Try′pho came to invade the country and destroy it, and he circled around by the way to Ado′ra. But Simon and his army kept marching along opposite him to every place he went. [21]Now the men in the citadel kept sending envoys to Try′pho urging him to come to them by way of the wilderness and to send them food. [22]So Try′pho got all his cavalry ready to go, but that night a very heavy snow fell, and he did not go because of the snow. He marched off and went into the land of Gilead. [23]When he approached Bas′kama, he killed Jonathan, and he was buried there. [24]Then Try′pho turned back and departed to his own land.

Jonathan's Tomb

25 And Simon sent and took the bones of Jonathan his brother, and buried him in Mo′dein, the city of his fathers. [26]All Israel bewailed him with great lamentation, and mourned for him many days. [27]And Simon built a monument over the tomb of his father and his brothers; he made it high that it might be seen, with polished stone at the front and back. [28]He also erected seven pyramids, opposite one another, for his father and mother and four brothers. [29]And for the pyramids [f] he devised an elaborate setting, erecting about them great columns, and upon the columns he put suits of armor for a permanent memorial, and beside the suits of armor carved ships, so that they could be seen by all who sail the sea. [30]This is the tomb which he built in Mo′dein; it remains to this day.

Judea Gains Independence

31 Try′pho dealt treacherously with the young king Anti′ochus; he killed him [32]and became king in his place, putting on the crown of Asia; and he brought great calamity upon the land. [33]But Simon built up the strongholds of Judea and walled them all around, with high towers and great walls and gates and bolts, and he stored food in the strongholds. [34]Simon also chose men and sent them to Deme′trius the king with a request to grant relief to the country, for all that Try′pho did was to plunder. [35]Deme′trius the king sent him a favorable reply to this request, and wrote him a letter as follows, [36]"King Deme′trius to Simon, the high priest and friend of kings, and to the elders and nation of the Jews, greeting.

[37]We have received the gold crown and the palm branch which you [g] sent, and we are ready to make a general peace with you and to write to our officials to grant you release from tribute. [38]All the grants that we have made to you remain valid, and let the strongholds that you have built be your possession. [39]We pardon any errors and offenses committed to this day, and cancel the crown tax which you owe; and whatever other tax has been collected in Jerusalem shall be collected no longer. [40]And if any of you are qualified to be enrolled in our bodyguard, [h] let them be enrolled, and let there be peace between us."

41 In the one hundred and seventieth year [i] the yoke of the Gentiles was removed from Israel, [42]and the people began to write in their documents and contracts, "In the first year of Simon the great high priest and commander and leader of the Jews."

The Capture of Gazara by Simon

43 In those days Simon [j] encamped against Gaza′ra [k] and surrounded it with troops. He made a siege engine, brought it up to the city, and battered and captured one tower. [44]The men in the siege engine leaped out into the city, and a great tumult arose in the city. [45]The men in the city, with their wives and children, went up on the wall with their clothes torn, and they cried out with a loud voice, asking Simon to make peace with them; [46]they said, "Do not treat us according to our wicked acts but according to your mercy." [47]So Simon reached an agreement with them and stopped fighting against them. But he expelled them from the city and cleansed the houses in which the idols were, and then entered it with hymns and praise. [48]He cast out of it all uncleanness, and settled in it men who observed the law. He also strengthened its fortifications and built in it a house for himself.

Simon Regains the Citadel

49 The men in the citadel at Jerusalem were prevented from going out to the country and back to buy and sell. So they were very hungry, and many of them perished from famine. [50]Then they cried to Simon to make peace with them, and he did so. But he expelled them from there and cleansed the citadel from its pollutions. [51]On the twenty-third day of the second month, in the one hundred and seventy-first year, [l] the Jews [m] entered it with praise and palm branches, and with harps and cymbals and stringed instruments, and

---

[d] Gk I.
[e] Gk he.
[f] Gk for these.
[g] The word you in verses 37–40 is plural.
[h] Or court.
[i] 142 B.C.
[j] Gk he.
[k] Cn: Gk Gaza.
[l] 141 B.C.
[m] Gk they.

with hymns and songs, because a great enemy had been crushed and removed from Israel. [52]And Simon [n] decreed that every year they should celebrate this day with rejoicing. He strengthened the fortifications of the temple hill alongside the citadel, and he and his men dwelt there. [53]And Simon saw that John his son had reached manhood, so he made him commander of all the forces, and he dwelt in Gaza′ra.

Capture of Demetrius;
and the Eulogy of Simon

14 In the one hundred and seventy-second year [o] Deme′trius the king assembled his forces and marched into Med′ia to secure help, so that he could make war against Try′pho. [2]When Ar′saces the king of Persia and Med′ia heard that Deme′trius had invaded his territory, he sent one of his commanders to take him alive. [3]And he went and defeated the army of Deme′trius, and seized him and took him to Ar′saces, who put him under guard.

[4]The land [p] had rest all the days of Simon.

He sought the good of his nation;
  his rule was pleasing to them,
    as was the honor shown him, all his days.
[5]To crown all his honors he took Joppa for a
    harbor,
  and opened a way to the isles of the sea.
[6]He extended the borders of his nation,
  and gained full control of the country.
[7]He gathered a host of captives;
  he ruled over Gaza′ra and Beth-zur and the
    citadel,
  and he removed its uncleanness from it;
  and there was none to oppose him.
[8]They tilled their land in peace;
  the ground gave its increase,
  and the trees of the plains their fruit.
[9]Old men sat in the streets;
  they all talked together of good things;
  and the youths donned the glories and
    garments of war.
[10]He supplied the cities with food,
  and furnished them with the means of
    defense,
  till his renown spread to the ends of the
    earth.
[11]He established peace in the land,
  and Israel rejoiced with great joy.
[12]Each man sat under his vine and his fig tree,
  and there was none to make them afraid.
[13]No one was left in the land to fight them,
  and the kings were crushed in those days.
[14]He strengthened all the humble of his people;
  he sought out the law,
  and did away with every lawless and
    wicked man.
[15]He made the sanctuary glorious,
  and added to the vessels of the sanctuary.

Diplomacy with Rome and Sparta

16 It was heard in Rome, and as far away as Sparta, that Jonathan had died, and they were deeply grieved. [17]When they heard that Simon his brother had become high priest in his place, and that he was ruling over the country and the cities in it, [18]they wrote to him on bronze tablets to renew with him the friendship and alliance which they had established with Judas and Jonathan his brothers. [19]And these were read before the assembly in Jerusalem.

20 This is a copy of the letter which the Spartans sent: "The rulers and the city of the Spartans to Simon the high priest and to the elders and the priests and the rest of the Jewish people, our brethren, greeting. [21]The envoys who were sent to our people have told us about your glory and honor, and we rejoiced at their coming. [22]And what they said we have recorded in our public decrees, as follows, 'Nume′nius the son of Anti′ochus and Antip′ater the son of Jason, envoys of the Jews, have come to us to renew their friendship with us. [23]It has pleased our people to receive these men with honor and to put a copy of their words in the public archives, so that the people of the Spartans may have a record of them. And they have sent a copy of this to Simon the high priest.'"

24 After this Simon sent Nume′nius to Rome with a large gold shield weighing a thousand minas, to confirm the alliance with the Romans. [q]

Official Honors for Simon

25 When the people heard these things they said, "How shall we thank Simon and his sons? [26]For he and his brothers and the house of his father have stood firm; they have fought and repulsed Israel's enemies and established its freedom." [27]So they made a record on bronze tablets and put it upon pillars on Mount Zion.

This is a copy of what they wrote: "On the eighteenth day of E′lul, in the one hundred and seventy-second year, [r] which is the third year of Simon the great high priest, [28]in Asar′amel, [s] in the great assembly of the priests and the people and the rulers of the nation and the elders of the country, the following was proclaimed to us:

29 "Since wars often occurred in the country, Simon the son of Mattathi′as, a priest of the sons [t] of Jo′arib, and his brothers, exposed themselves to danger and resisted the enemies of their nation, in order that their sanctuary and the law might be perserved; and they brought great glory

---

[n] Gk *he*.
[o] 140 B.C.
[p] Other authorities add *of Judah*.
[q] Gk *them*.
[r] 140 B.C.
[s] This word resembles the Hebrew words for *the court of the people of God* or *the prince of the people of God*.
[t] The Greek text of this phrase is uncertain.

to their nation. [30]Jonathan rallied the [u] nation, and became their high priest, and was gathered to his people. [31]And when their enemies decided to invade their country and lay hands on their sanctuary, [32]then Simon rose up and fought for his nation. He spent great sums of his own money; he armed the men of his nation's forces and paid them wages. [33]He fortified the cities of Judea, and Beth-zur on the borders of Judea, where formerly the arms of the enemy had been stored, and he placed there a garrison of Jews. [34]He also fortified Joppa, which is by the sea, and Gaza'ra, which is on the borders of Azo'tus, where the enemy formerly dwelt. He settled Jews there, and provided in those cities [v] whatever was necessary for their restoration.

35 "The people saw Simon's faithfulness [w] and the glory which he had resolved to win for his nation, and they made him their leader and high priest, because he had done all these things and because of the justice and loyalty which he had maintained toward his nation. He sought in every way to exalt his people. [36]And in his days things prospered in his hands, so that the Gentiles were put out of the [x] country, as were also the men in the city of David in Jerusalem, who had built themselves a citadel from which they used to sally forth and defile the environs of the sanctuary and do great damage to its purity. [37]He settled Jews in it, and fortified it for the safety of the country and of the city, and built the walls of Jerusalem higher.

38 "In view of these things King Deme'trius confirmed him in the high priesthood, [39]and he made him one of the king's [y] friends and paid him high honors. [40]For he had heard that the Jews were addressed by the Romans as friends and allies and brethren, and that the Romans [z] had received the envoys of Simon with honor.

41 "And [a] the Jews and their priests decided that Simon should be their leader and high priest for ever, until a trustworthy prophet should arise, [42]and that he should be governor over them and that he should take charge of the sanctuary and appoint men over its tasks and over the country and the weapons and the strongholds, and that he should take charge of the sanctuary, [43]and that he should be obeyed by all, and that all contracts in the country should be written in his name, and that he should be clothed in purple and wear gold.

44 "And none of the people or priests shall be permitted to nullify any of these decisions or to oppose what he says, or to convene an assembly in the country without his permission, or to be clothed in purple or put on a gold buckle. [45]Whoever acts contrary to these decisions or nullifies any of them shall be liable to punishment."

46 And all the people agreed to grant Simon

the right to act in accord with these decisions. [47]So Simon accepted and agreed to be high priest, to be commander and ethnarch of the Jews and priests, and to be protector of them all. [b] [48]And they gave orders to inscribe this decree upon bronze tablets, to put them up in a conspicuous place in the precincts of the sanctuary, [49]and to deposit copies of them in the treasury, so that Simon and his sons might have them.

Letter of Antiochus VII

15 Anti'ochus, the son of Deme'trius the king, sent a letter from the islands of the sea to Simon, the priest and ethnarch of the Jews, and to all the nation; [2]its contents were as follows: "King Anti'ochus to Simon the high priest and ethnarch and to the nation of the Jews, greeting. [3]Whereas certain pestilent men have gained control of the kingdom of our fathers, and I intend to lay claim to the kingdom so that I may restore it as it formerly was, and have recruited a host of mercenary troops and have equipped warships, [4]and intend to make a landing in the country so that I may proceed against those who have destroyed our country and those who have devastated many cities in my kingdom, [5]now therefore I confirm to you all the tax remissions that the kings before me have granted you, and release from all the other payments from which they have released you. [6]I permit you to mint your own coinage as money for your country, [7]and I grant freedom to Jerusalem and the sanctuary. All the weapons which you have prepared and the strongholds which you have built and now hold shall remain yours. [8]Every debt you owe to the royal treasury and any such future debts shall be canceled for you from now on and for all time. [9]When we gain control of our kingdom, we will bestow great honor upon you and your nation and the temple, so that your glory will become manifest in all the earth."

10 In the one hundred and seventy-fourth year [c] Anti'ochus set out and invaded the land of his fathers. All the troops rallied to him, so that there were few with Try'pho. [11]Anti'ochus pursued him, and he came in his flight to Dor, which is by the sea; [12]for he knew that troubles had converged upon him, and his troops had deserted him. [13]So Anti'ochus encamped against Dor, and with him were a hundred and twenty thousand warriors and eight thousand cavalry. [14]He surrounded the city, and the ships joined battle from

---

[u] Gk *their.*
[v] Gk *them.*
[w] Other authorities read *conduct.*
[x] Gk *their.*
[y] Gk *his.*
[z] Gk *they.*
[a] Gk *honor; and that.*
[b] Or *to preside over them all.*
[c] 138 B.C.

the sea; he pressed the city hard from land and sea, and permitted no one to leave or enter it.

Rome Supports the Jews

15 Then Nume'nius and his companions arrived from Rome, with letters to the kings and countries, in which the following was written: ¹⁶"Lucius, consul of the Romans, to King Ptol'emy, greeting. ¹⁷The envoys of the Jews have come to us as our friends and allies to renew our ancient friendship and alliance. They had been sent by Simon the high priest and by the people of the Jews, ¹⁸and have brought a gold shield weighing a thousand minas. ¹⁹We therefore have decided to write to the kings and countries that they should not seek their harm or make war against them and their cities and their country, or make alliance with those who war against them. ²⁰And it has seemed good to us to accept the shield from them. ²¹Therefore if any pestilent men have fled to you from their country, hand them over to Simon the high priest, that he may punish them according to their law."

22 The consul^d wrote the same thing to Deme'trius the king and to At'talus and A"riara'thes and Ar'saces, ²³and to all the countries, and to Samp'sames, ^e and to the Spartans, and to De'los, and to Myn'dos, and to Sic'yon, and to Ca'ria, and to Sa'mos, and to Pamphyl'ia, and to Ly'cia, and to Hal"icarnas'sus, and to Rhodes, and to Phase'lis, and to Cos, and to Si'de, and to Ar'adus and Gorty'na and Cni'dus and Cyprus and Cyre'ne. ²⁴They also sent a copy of these things to Simon the high priest.

Antiochus VII Threatens Simon

25 Anti'ochus the king besieged Dor anew, ^f continually throwing his forces against it and making engines of war; and he shut Try'pho up and kept him from going out or in. ²⁶And Simon sent to Anti'ochus^g two thousand picked men, to fight for him, and silver and gold and much military equipment. ²⁷But he refused to receive them, and he broke all the agreements he formerly had made with Simon, ^g and became estranged from him. ²⁸He sent to him Ath"eno'bius, one of his friends, to confer with him, saying, "You hold control of Joppa and Gaza'ra and the citadel in Jerusalem; they are cities of my kingdom. ²⁹You have devastated their territory, you have done great damage in the land, and you have taken possession of many places in my kingdom. ³⁰Now then, hand over the cities which you have seized and the tribute money of the places which you have conquered outside the borders of Judea; ³¹or else give me for them five hundred talents of silver, and for the destruction that you have caused and the tribute money of the cities, five hundred talents more. Otherwise we will come and conquer you."

32 So Ath"eno'bius the friend of the king came

to Jerusalem, and when he saw the splendor of Simon, and the sideboard with its gold and silver plate, and his great magnificence, he was amazed. He reported to him the words of the king, ³³but Simon gave him this reply: "We have neither taken foreign land nor seized foreign property, but only the inheritance of our fathers, which at one time had been unjustly taken by our enemies. ³⁴Now that we have the opportunity, we are firmly holding the inheritance of our fathers. ³⁵As for Joppa and Gaza'ra, which you demand, they were causing great damage among the people and to our land; for them we will give you a hundred talents." Ath"eno'bius ^h did not answer him a word, ³⁶but returned in wrath to the king and reported to him these words and the splendor of Simon and all that he had seen. And the king was greatly angered.

Victory over Cendebeus

37 Now Try'pho embarked on a ship and escaped to Orthosi'a. ³⁸Then the king made Cendebe'us commander-in-chief of the coastal country, and gave him troops of infantry and cavalry. ³⁹He commanded him to encamp against Judea, and commanded him to build up Ked'ron and fortify its gates, and to make war on the people; but the king pursued Try'pho. ⁴⁰So Cendebe'us came to Jam'nia and began to provoke the people and invade Judea and take the people captive and kill them. ⁴¹He built up Ked'ron and stationed there horsemen and troops, so that they might go out and make raids along the highways of Judea, as the king had ordered him.

16 John went up from Gaza'ra and reported to Simon his father what Cendebe'us had done. ²And Simon called in his two older sons Judas and John, and said to them: "I and my brothers and the house of my father have fought the wars of Israel from our youth until this day, and things have prospered in our hands so that we have delivered Israel many times. ³But now I have grown old, and you by His mercy are mature in years. Take my place and my brother's, and go out and fight for our nation, and may the help which comes from Heaven be with you."

4 So John ⁱ chose out of the country twenty thousand warriors and horsemen, and they marched against Cendebe'us and camped for the night in Mo'dein. ⁵Early in the morning they arose and marched into the plain, and behold, a large force of infantry and horsemen was coming to meet them; and a stream lay between them. ⁶Then he and his army lined up against them. And he

---

^d Gk *He.*
^e The name is uncertain.
^f Or *on the second day.*
^g Gk *him.*
^h Gk *He.*
ⁱ Other authorities read *he.*

saw that the soldiers were afraid to cross the stream, so he crossed over first; and when his men saw him, they crossed over after him. [7]Then he divided the army and placed the horsemen in the midst of the infantry, for the cavalry of the enemy were very numerous. [8]And they sounded the trumpets, and Cendebe′us and his army were put to flight, and many of them were wounded and fell; the rest fled into the stronghold. [9]At that time Judas the brother of John was wounded, but John pursued them until Cendebe′us *j* reached Ked′ron, which he had built. [10]They also fled into the towers that were in the fields of Azo′tus, and John *j* burned it with fire, and about two thousand of them fell. And he returned to Judea safely.

Murder of Simon and His Sons

11 Now Ptol′emy the son of Abu′bus had been appointed governor over the plain of Jericho, and he had much silver and gold, [12]for he was son-in-law of the high priest. [13]His heart was lifted up; he determined to get control of the country, and made treacherous plans against Simon and his sons, to do away with them. [14]Now Simon was visiting the cities of the country and attending to their needs, and he went down to Jericho with Mattathi′as and Judas his sons, in the one hundred and seventy-seventh year, *k* in the eleventh month, which is the month of Shebat′. [15]The son of Abu′bus received them treacherously in the little stronghold called Dok, which he had built; he gave them a great banquet, and hid men there.

[16]When Simon and his sons were drunk, Ptol′emy and his men rose up, took their weapons, and rushed in against Simon in the banquet hall, and they killed him and his two sons and some of his servants. [17]So he committed an act of great treachery and returned evil for good.

John Succeeds Simon

18 Then Ptol′emy wrote a report about these things and sent it to the king, asking him to send troops to aid him and to turn over to him the cities and the country. [19]He sent other men to Gaza′ra to do away with John; he sent letters to the captains asking them to come to him so that he might give them silver and gold and gifts; [20]and he sent other men to take possession of Jerusalem and the temple hill. [21]But some one ran ahead and reported to John at Gaza′ra that his father and brothers had perished, and that "he has sent men to kill you also." [22]When he heard this, he was greatly shocked; and he seized the men who came to destroy him and killed them, for he had found out that they were seeking to destroy him.

23 The rest of the acts of John and his wars and the brave deeds which he did, and the building of the walls which he built, and his achievements, [24]behold, they are written in the chronicles of his high priesthood, from the time that he became high priest after his father.

---

j Gk *he.*
k 134 B.C.

THE SECOND BOOK OF THE
MACCABEES

A Letter to the Jews in Egypt

1 The Jewish brethren in Jerusalem and those in the land of Judea,

To their Jewish brethren in Egypt,

Greeting, and good peace.

2 May God do good to you, and may he remember his covenant with Abraham and Isaac and Jacob, his faithful servants. [3]May he give you all a heart to worship him and to do his will with a strong heart and a willing spirit. [4]May he open your heart to his law and his commandments, and may he bring peace. [5]May he hear your prayers and be reconciled to you, and may he not forsake you in time of evil. [6]We are now praying for you here.

7 In the reign of Deme'trius, in the one hundred and sixty-ninth year, [a] we Jews wrote to you, in the critical distress which came upon us in those years after Jason and his company revolted from the holy land and the kingdom [8]and burned the gate and shed innocent blood. We begged the Lord and we were heard, and we offered sacrifice and cereal offering, and we lighted the lamps and we set out the loaves. [9]And now see that you keep the feast of booths in the month of Chis'lev, in the one hundred and eighty-eighth year. [b]

A Letter to Aristobulus

10 Those in Jerusalem and those in Judea and the senate and Judas,

To Aristob'ulus, who is of the family of the anointed priests, teacher of Ptol'emy the king, and to the Jews in Egypt,

Greeting, and good health.

11 Having been saved by God out of grave dangers we thank him greatly for taking our side against the king. [c] [12]For he drove out those who fought against the holy city. [13]For when the leader reached Persia with a force that seemed irresistible, they were cut to pieces in the temple of Nane'a by a deception employed by the priests of Nanea. [14]For under pretext of intending to marry her, Anti'ochus came to the place together with his friends, to secure most of its treasures as a dowry. [15]When the priests of the temple of Nane'a had set out the treasures and Anti'ochus had come with a few men inside the wall of the sacred precinct, they closed the temple as soon as he entered it. [16]Opening the secret door in the ceiling, they threw stones and struck down the leader and his men, and dismembered them and

cut off their heads and threw them to the people outside. [17]Blessed in every way be our God, who has brought judgment upon those who have behaved impiously.

Fire Consumes Nehemiah's Sacrifice

18 Since on the twenty-fifth day of Chis'lev we shall celebrate the purification of the temple, we thought it necessary to notify you, in order that you also may celebrate the feast of booths and the feast of the fire given when Nehemi'ah, who built the temple and the altar, offered sacrifices.

19 For when our fathers were being led captive to Persia, the pious priests of that time took some of the fire of the altar and secretly hid it in the hollow of a dry cistern, where they took such precautions that the place was unknown to any one. [20]But after many years had passed, when it pleased God, Nehemi'ah, having been commissioned by the king of Persia, sent the descendants of the priests who had hidden the fire to get it. And when they reported to us that they had not found fire but thick liquid, he ordered them to dip it out and bring it. [21]And when the materials for the sacrifices were presented, Nehemi'ah ordered the priests to sprinkle the liquid on the wood and what was laid upon it. [22]When this was done and some time had passed and the sun, which had been clouded over, shone out, a great fire blazed up, so that all marveled. [23]And while the sacrifice was being consumed, the priests offered prayer—the priests and every one. Jonathan led, and the rest responded, as did Nehemi'ah. [24]The prayer was to this effect:

"O Lord, Lord God, Creator of all things, who are awe-inspiring and strong and just and merciful, who alone are King and are kind, [25]who alone are bountiful, who alone are just and almighty and eternal, who rescue Israel from every evil, who chose the fathers and consecrated them, [26]accept this sacrifice on behalf of all your people Israel and preserve your portion and make it holy. [27]Gather together our scattered people, set free those who are slaves among the Gentiles, look upon those who are rejected and despised, and let the Gentiles know that you are our God. [28]Afflict those who oppress and are insolent with pride.

---

[a] 143 B.C.
[b] 124 B.C.
[c] Cn: Gk *as those who array themselves against a king.*

²⁹Plant your people in your holy place, as Moses said."

30 Then the priests sang the hymns. ³¹And when the materials of the sacrifice were consumed, Nehemi′ah ordered that the liquid that was left should be poured upon large stones. ³²When this was done, a flame blazed up; but when the light from the altar shone back, it went out. ³³When this matter became known, and it was reported to the king of the Persians that, in the place where the exiled priests had hidden the fire, the liquid had appeared with which Nehemi′ah and his associates had burned the materials of the sacrifice, ³⁴the king investigated the matter, and enclosed the place and made it sacred. ³⁵And with those persons whom the king favored he exchanged many excellent gifts. ³⁶Nehemi′ah and his associates called this "nephthar," which means purification, but by most people it is called naphtha.ᵈ

Jeremiah Hides the Tent, Ark, and Altar

2 One finds in the records that Jeremi′ah the prophet ordered those who were being deported to take some of the fire, as has been told, ²and that the prophet after giving them the law instructed those who were being deported not to forget the commandments of the Lord, nor to be led astray in their thoughts upon seeing the gold and silver statues and their adornment. ³And with other similar words he exhorted them that the law should not depart from their hearts.

4 It was also in the writing that the prophet, having received an oracle, ordered that the tent and the ark should follow with him, and that he went out to the mountain where Moses had gone up and had seen the inheritance of God. ⁵And Jeremi′ah came and found a cave, and he brought there the tent and the ark and the altar of incense, and he sealed up the entrance. ⁶Some of those who followed him came up to mark the way, but could not find it. ⁷When Jeremi′ah learned of it, he rebuked them and declared: "The place shall be unknown until God gathers his people together again and shows his mercy. ⁸And then the Lord will disclose these things, and the glory of the Lord and the cloud will appear, as they were shown in the case of Moses, and as Solomon asked that the place should be specially consecrated."

9 It was also made clear that being possessed of wisdom Solomonᵉ offered sacrifice for the dedication and completion of the temple. ¹⁰Just as Moses prayed to the Lord, and fire came down from heaven and devoured the sacrifices, so also Solomon prayed, and the fire came down and consumed the whole burnt offerings. ¹¹And Moses said, "They were consumed because the sin offering had not been eaten." ¹²Likewise Solomon also kept the eight days.

13 The same things are reported in the records

and in the memoirs of Nehemi′ah, and also that he founded a library and collected the books about the kings and prophets, and the writings of David, and letters of kings about votive offerings. ¹⁴In the same way Judas also collected all the books that had been lost on account of the war which had come upon us, and they are in our possession. ¹⁵So if you have need of them, send people to get them for you.

16 Since, therefore, we are about to celebrate the purification, we write to you. Will you therefore please keep the days? ¹⁷It is God who has saved all his people, and has returned the inheritance to all, and the kingship and priesthood and consecration, ¹⁸as he promised through the law. For we have hope in God that he will soon have mercy upon us and will gather us from everywhere under heaven into his holy place, for he has rescued us from great evils and has purified the place.

The Compiler's Preface

19 The story of Judas Mac″cabe′us and his brothers, and the purification of the great temple, and the dedication of the altar, ²⁰and further the wars against Anti′ochus Epiph′anes and his son Eu′pator, ²¹and the appearances which came from heaven to those who strove zealously on behalf of Judaism, so that though few in number they seized the whole land and pursued the barbarian hordes, ²²and recovered the temple famous throughout the world and freed the city and restored the laws that were about to be abolished, while the Lord with great kindness became gracious to them—²³all this, which has been set forth by Jason of Cyre′ne in five volumes, we shall attempt to condense into a single book. ²⁴For considering the flood of numbers involved and the difficulty there is for those who wish to enter upon the narratives of history because of the mass of material, ²⁵we have aimed to please those who wish to read, to make it easy for those who are inclined to memorize, and to profit all readers. ²⁶For us who have undertaken the toil of abbreviating, it is no light matter but calls for sweat and loss of sleep, ²⁷just as it is not easy for one who prepares a banquet and seeks the benefit of others. However, to secure the gratitude of many we will gladly endure the uncomfortable toil, ²⁸leaving the responsibility for exact details to the compiler, while devoting our effort to arriving at the outlines of the condensation. ²⁹For as the master builder of a new house must be concerned with the whole construction, while the one who undertakes its painting and decoration has to consider only what is suitable for its adornment, such in my judgment is the case with us. ³⁰It is the duty

---

ᵈ Gk *nephthai*.
ᵉ Gk *he*.

of the original historian to occupy the ground and to discuss matters from every side and to take trouble with details, [31]but the one who recasts the narrative should be allowed to strive for brevity of expression and to forego exhaustive treatment. [32]At this point therefore let us begin our narrative, adding only so much to what has already been said; for it is foolish to lengthen the preface while cutting short the history itself.

Arrival of Heliodorus in Jerusalem

3 While the holy city was inhabited in unbroken peace and the laws were very well observed because of the piety of the high priest Oni'as and his hatred of wickedness, [2]it came about that the kings themselves honored the place and glorified the temple with the finest presents, [3]so that even Seleu'cus, the king of Asia, defrayed from his own revenues all the expenses connected with the service of the sacrifices. [4]But a man named Simon, of the tribe of Benjamin, who had been made captain of the temple, had a disagreement with the high priest about the administration of the city market; [5]and when he could not prevail over Oni'as he went to Apollo'nius of Tarsus, [f] who at that time was governor of Coe'le-syr'ia and Phoeni'cia. [6]He reported to him that the treasury in Jerusalem was full of untold sums of money, so that the amount of the funds could not be reckoned, and that they did not belong to the account of the sacrifices, but that it was possible for them to fall under the control of the king. [7]When Apollo'nius met the king, he told him of the money about which he had been informed. The king [g] chose He"liodo'rus, who was in charge of his affairs, and sent him with commands to effect the removal of the aforesaid money. [8]He"liodo'rus at once set out on his journey, ostensibly to make a tour of inspection of the cities of Coe'le-syr'ia and Phoeni'cia, but in fact to carry out the king's purpose.

[9] When he had arrived at Jerusalem and had been kindly welcomed by the high priest of [h] the city, he told about the disclosure that had been made and stated why he had come, and he inquired whether this really was the situation. [10]The high priest explained that there were some deposits belonging to widows and orphans, [11]and also some money of Hyrca'nus, son of Tobi'as, a man of very prominent position, and that it totaled in all four hundred talents of silver and two hundred of gold. To such an extent the impious Simon had misrepresented the facts. [12]And he said that it was utterly impossible that wrong should be done to those people who had trusted in the holiness of the place and in the sanctity and inviolability of the temple which is honored throughout the whole world. [13]But He"liodo'rus, because of the king's commands which he had, said that this money must in any case be confiscated for the king's treasury. [14]So he set a day and went in to direct the inspection of these funds.

There was no little distress throughout the whole city. [15]The priests prostrated themselves before the altar in their priestly garments and called toward heaven upon him who had given the law about deposits, that he should keep them safe for those who had deposited them. [16]To see the appearance of the high priest was to be wounded at heart, for his face and the change in his color disclosed the anguish of his soul. [17]For terror and bodily trembling had come over the man, which plainly showed to those who looked at him the pain lodged in his heart. [18]People also hurried out of their houses in crowds to make a general supplication because the holy place was about to be brought into contempt. [19]Women, clothed with sackcloth under their breasts, thronged the streets. Some of the maidens who were kept indoors ran together to the gates, and some to the walls, while others peered out of the windows. [20]And holding up their hands to heaven, they all made entreaty. [21]There was something pitiable in the prostration of the whole populace and the anxiety of the high priest in his great anguish.

The Lord Protects His Temple

[22] While they were calling upon the Almighty Lord that he would keep what had been entrusted safe and secure for those who had entrusted it, [23]He"liodo'rus went on with what had been decided. [24]But when he arrived at the treasury with his bodyguard, then and there the Sovereign of spirits and of all authority caused so great a manifestation that all who had been so bold as to accompany him were astounded by the power of God, and became faint with terror. [25]For there appeared to them a magnificently caparisoned horse, with a rider of frightening mien, and it rushed furiously at He"liodo'rus and struck at him with its front hoofs. Its rider was seen to have armor and weapons of gold. [26]Two young men also appeared to him, remarkably strong, gloriously beautiful and splendidly dressed, who stood on each side of him and scourged him continuously, inflicting many blows on him. [27]When he suddenly fell to the ground and deep darkness came over him, his men took him up and put him on a stretcher [28]and carried him away, this man who had just entered the aforesaid treasury with a great retinue and all his bodyguard but was now unable to help himself; and they recognized clearly the sovereign power of God. [29]While he lay prostrate, speechless because of the divine intervention and deprived of any hope of recovery, [30]they praised

---

[f] Gk Apollonius son of Tharseas.
[g] Gk He.
[h] Some authorities read and.

the Lord who had acted marvelously for his own place. And the temple, which a little while before was full of fear and disturbance, was filled with joy and gladness, now that the Almighty Lord had appeared.

Onias Prays for Heliodorus

31 Quickly some of He"lio'do'rus' friends asked Oni'as to call upon the Most High and to grant life to one who was lying quite at his last breath. [32]And the high priest, fearing that the king might get the notion that some foul play had been perpetrated by the Jews with regard to He"lio'do'rus, offered sacrifice for the man's recovery. [33]While the high priest was making the offering of atonement, the same young men appeared again to He"lio'do'rus dressed in the same clothing, and they stood and said, "Be very grateful to Oni'as the high priest, since for his sake the Lord has granted you your life. [34]And see that you, who have been scourged by heaven, report to all men the majestic power of God." Having said this they vanished.

The Conversion of Heliodorus

35 Then He"lio'do'rus offered sacrifice to the Lord and made very great vows to the Savior of his life, and having bidden Oni'as farewell, he marched off with his forces to the king. [36]And he bore testimony to all men of the deeds of the supreme God, which he had seen with his own eyes. [37]When the king asked He"lio'do'rus what sort of person would be suitable to send on another mission to Jerusalem, he replied, [38]"If you have any enemy or plotter against your government, send him there, for you will get him back thoroughly scourged, if he escapes at all, for there certainly is about the place some power of God. [39]For he who has his dwelling in heaven watches over that place himself and brings it aid, and he strikes and destroys those who come to do it injury." [40]This was the outcome of the episode of He"lio'do'rus and the protection of the treasury.

Simon Accuses Onias

4 The previously mentioned Simon, who had informed about the money against[i] his own country, slandered Oni'as, saying that it was he who had incited He"lio'do'rus and had been the real cause of the misfortune. [2]He dared to designate as a plotter against the government the man who was the benefactor of the city, the protector of his fellow countrymen, and a zealot for the laws. [3]When his hatred progressed to such a degree that even murders were committed by one of Simon's approved agents, [4]Oni'as recognized that the rivalry was serious and that Apollo'nius, the son of Menes'theus[j] and governor of Coe'le-syr'ia and Phoeni'cia, was intensifying the malice of Simon. [5]So he betook himself to the king, not accusing his fellow citizens but having in view the welfare, both public and private, of all the

people. [6]For he saw that without the king's attention public affairs could not again reach a peaceful settlement, and that Simon would not stop his folly.

Jason's Reforms

7 When Seleu'cus died and Anti'ochus who was called Epiph'anes succeeded to the kingdom, Jason the brother of Oni'as obtained the high priesthood by corruption, [8]promising the king at an interview[k] three hundred and sixty talents of silver and, from another source of revenue, eighty talents. [9]In addition to this he promised to pay one hundred and fifty more if permission were given to establish by his authority a gymnasium and a body of youth for it, and to enroll the men of Jerusalem as citizens of Antioch. [10]When the king assented and Jason[l] came to office, he at once shifted his countrymen over to the Greek way of life. [11]He set aside the existing royal concessions to the Jews, secured through John the father of Eupol'emus, who went on the mission to establish friendship and alliance with the Romans; and he destroyed the lawful ways of living and introduced new customs contrary to the law. [12]For with alacrity he founded a gymnasium right under the citadel, and he induced the noblest of the young men[m] to wear the Greek hat. [13]There was such an extreme of Hellenization and increase in the adoption of foreign ways because of the surpassing wickedness of Jason, who was ungodly and no high priest, [14]that the priests were no longer intent upon their service at the altar. Despising the sanctuary and neglecting the sacrifices, they hastened to take part in the unlawful proceedings in the wrestling arena after the call to the discus, [15]disdaining the honors prized by their fathers and putting the highest value upon Greek forms of prestige. [16]For this reason heavy disaster overtook them, and those whose ways of living they admired and wished to imitate completely became their enemies and punished them. [17]For it is no light thing to show irreverence to the divine laws—a fact which later events will make clear.

Jason Introduces Greek Customs

18 When the quadrennial games were being held at Tyre and the king was present, [19]the vile Jason sent envoys, chosen as being An"tio'chian citizens from Jerusalem, to carry three hundred silver drachmas for the sacrifice to Hercules. Those who carried the money, however, thought best not to use it for sacrifice, because that was inappropriate, but to expend it for another purpose. [20]So this money was intended by the sender for the sacrifice to Hercules, but by the decision of

---

[i] Gk and.

[j] Vg Compare verse 21: Gk uncertain.

[k] Or by a petition.

[l] Gk he.

[m] Some authorities add subjecting them.

its carriers it was applied to the construction of triremes.

21 When Apollo'nius the son of Menes'theus was sent to Egypt for the coronation [n] of Phil'ome'tor as king, Anti'ochus learned that Philometor [o] had become hostile to his government, and he took measures for his own security. Therefore upon arriving at Joppa he proceeded to Jerusalem. [22]He was welcomed magnificently by Jason and the city, and ushered in with a blaze of torches and with shouts. Then he marched into Phoeni'cia.

Menelaus Becomes High Priest

23 After a period of three years Jason sent Menela'us, the brother of the previously mentioned Simon, to carry the money to the king and to complete the records of essential business. [24]But he, when presented to the king, extolled him with an air of authority, and secured the high priesthood for himself, outbidding Jason by three hundred talents of silver. [25]After receiving the king's orders he returned, possessing no qualification for the high priesthood, but having the hot temper of a cruel tyrant and the rage of a savage wild beast. [26]So Jason, who after supplanting his own brother was supplanted by another man, was driven as a fugitive into the land of Am'mon. [27]And Menela'us held the office, but he did not pay regularly any of the money promised to the king. [28]When Sos'tratus the captain of the citadel kept requesting payment, for the collection of the revenue was his responsibility, the two of them were summoned by the king on account of this issue. [29]Menela'us left his own brother Lysim'achus as deputy in the high priesthood, while Sos'tratus left Cra'tes, the commander of the Cyprian troops. *

The Murder of Onias;
and the Punishment of Andronicus

30 While such was the state of affairs, it happened that the people of Tarsus and of Mallus revolted because their cities had been given as a present to Anti'ochis, the king's concubine. [31]So the king went hastily to settle the trouble, leaving Andron'icus, a man of high rank, to act as his deputy. [32]But Menela'us, thinking he had obtained a suitable opportunity, stole some of the gold vessels of the temple and gave them to Andron'icus; other vessels, as it happened, he had sold to Tyre and the neighboring cities. [33]When Oni'as became fully aware of these acts he publicly exposed them, having first withdrawn to a place of sanctuary at Daphne near Antioch. [34]Therefore Menela'us, taking Andron'icus aside, urged him to kill Oni'as. Andronicus [p] came to Onias, and resorting to treachery offered him sworn pledges and gave them his right hand, and in spite of his suspicion persuaded Onias [q] to come out from the place of sanctuary; then, with no regard for jus-

tice, he immediately put him out of the way. [†] [35]For this reason not only Jews, but many also of other nations, were grieved and displeased at the unjust murder of the man. [36]When the king returned from the region of Cili'cia, the Jews in the city [r] appealed to him with regard to the unreasonable murder of Oni'as, and the Greeks shared their hatred of the crime. [37]Therefore Anti'ochus was grieved at heart and filled with pity, and wept because of the moderation and good conduct of the deceased; [38]and inflamed with anger, he immediately stripped off the purple robe from Andron'icus, tore off his garments, and led him about the whole city to that very place where he had committed the outrage against Oni'as, and there he dispatched the bloodthirsty fellow. The Lord thus repaid him with the punishment he deserved.

Unpopularity of Lysimachus and Menelaus

39 When many acts of sacrilege had been committed in the city by Lysim'achus with the connivance of Menela'us, and when report of them had spread abroad, the populace gathered against Lysimachus, because many of the gold vessels had already been stolen. [40]And since the crowds were becoming aroused and filled with anger, Lysim'achus armed about three thousand men and launched an unjust attack, under the leadership of a certain Aura'nus, [‡] a man advanced in years and no less advanced in folly. [41]But when the Jews [s] became aware of Lysim'achus' attack, some picked up stones, some blocks of wood, and others took handfuls of the ashes that were lying about, and threw them in wild confusion at Lysimachus and his men. [42]As a result, they wounded many of them, and killed some, and put them all to flight; and the temple robber himself they killed close by the treasury.

43 Charges were brought against Menela'us about this incident. [44]When the king came to Tyre, three men sent by the senate presented the case before him. [45]But Menela'us, already as good as beaten, promised a substantial bribe to Ptol'emy son of Dorym'enes to win over the king. [46]Therefore Ptol'emy, taking the king aside into a colonnade as if for refreshment, induced the king to change his mind. [47]Menela'us, the cause of all the evil, he acquitted of the charges against him, while he sentenced to death those unfortunate men, who would have been freed unconditioned if

---

[n] The exact meaning of the Greek word is uncertain.
[o] Gk *he.*
[p] Gk *He.*
[q] Gk *him.*
[r] Or *in each city.*
[s] Gk *they.*
* 4:29: Vulgate reads: "And Menelaus was removed from the priesthood, Lysimachus his brother succeeding: and Sostratus was made governor of the Cyprians."
† 4:34, *put him out of the way:* Vulgate has "slew him."
‡ 4:40, *Auranus:* Vulgate has "Tyrannus."

they had pleaded even before Scyth'ians. [48]And so those who had spoken for the city and the villages [t] and the holy vessels quickly suffered the unjust penalty. [49]Therefore even the Ty'rians, showing their hatred of the crime, provided magnificently for their funeral. [50]But Menela'us, because of the cupidity of those in power, remained in office, growing in wickedness, having become the chief plotter against his fellow citizens.

Jason Tries to Regain Control

5 About this time Anti'ochus made his second invasion of Egypt. [2]And it happened that over all the city, for almost forty days, there appeared golden-clad horsemen charging through the air, in companies fully armed with lances and drawn swords—[3]troops of horsemen drawn up, attacks and counterattacks made on this side and on that, brandishing of shields, massing of spears, hurling of missiles, the flash of golden trappings, and armor of all sorts. [4]Therefore all men prayed that the apparition might prove to have been a good omen.

5 When a false rumor arose that Anti'ochus was dead, Jason took no less than a thousand men and suddenly made an assault upon the city. When the troops upon the wall had been forced back and at last the city was being taken, Menela'us took refuge in the citadel. [6]But Jason kept relentlessly slaughtering his fellow citizens, not realizing that success at the cost of one's kindred is the greatest misfortune, but imagining that he was setting up trophies of victory over enemies and not over fellow countrymen. [7]He did not gain control of the government, however; and in the end got only disgrace from his conspiracy, and fled again into the country of the Am'monites. [8]Finally he met a miserable end. Accused [u] before Ar'etas the ruler of the Arabs, fleeing from city to city, pursued by all men, hated as a rebel against the laws, and abhorred as the executioner of his country and his fellow citizens, he was cast ashore in Egypt; [9]and he who had driven many from their own country into exile died in exile, having embarked to go to the Lac"edaemo'nians in hope of finding protection because of their kinship. [10]He who had cast out many to lie unburied had no one to mourn for him; he had no funeral of any sort and no place in the tomb of his fathers.

11 When news of what had happened reached the king, he took it to mean that Judea was in revolt. So, raging inwardly, he left Egypt and took the city by storm. [12]And he commanded his soldiers to cut down relentlessly every one they met and to slay those who went into the houses. [13]Then there was killing of young and old, destruction of boys, women, and children, and slaughter of virgins and infants. [14]Within the total of three days eighty thousand were destroyed, forty thousand

in hand-to-hand fighting; and as many were sold into slavery as were slain.

Pillage of the Temple

15 Not content with this, Anti'ochus [v] dared to enter the most holy temple in all the world, guided by Menela'us, who had become a traitor both to the laws and to his country. [16]He took the holy vessels with his polluted hands, and swept away with profane hands the votive offerings which other kings had made to enhance the glory and honor of the place. [17]Anti'ochus was elated in spirit, and did not perceive that the Lord was angered for a little while because of the sins of those who dwelt in the city, and that therefore he was disregarding the holy place. [18]But if it had not happened that they were involved in many sins, this man would have been scourged and turned back from his rash act as soon as he came forward, just as He"liodo'rus was, whom Seleu'cus the king sent to inspect the treasury. [19]But the Lord did not choose the nation for the sake of the holy place, but the place for the sake of the nation. [20]Therefore the place itself shared in the misfortunes that befell the nation and afterward participated in its benefits; and what was forsaken in the wrath of the Almighty was restored again in all its glory when the great Lord became reconciled.

21 So Anti'ochus carried off eighteen hundred talents from the temple, and hurried away to Antioch, thinking in his arrogance that he could sail on the land and walk on the sea, because his mind was elated. [22]And he left governors to afflict the people: at Jerusalem, Philip, by birth a Phryg'ian and in character more barbarous than the man who appointed him; [23]and at Ger'izim, Andron'icus; and besides these Menela'us, who lorded it over his fellow citizens worse than the others did. In his malice toward the Jewish citizens, [w] [24]Anti'ochus [x] sent Apollo'nius, the captain of the Mysians, with an army of twenty-two thousand, and commanded him to slay all the grown men and to sell the women and boys as slaves. [25]When this man arrived in Jerusalem, he pretended to be peaceably disposed and waited until the holy sabbath day; then, finding the Jews not at work, he ordered his men to parade under arms. [26]He put to the sword all those who came out to see them, then rushed into the city with his armed men and killed great numbers of people.

27 But Judas Mac"cabe'us, with about nine others, got away to the wilderness, and kept himself and his companions alive in the mountains as wild animals do; they continued to live on what

---

[t] Other authorities read *the people.*
[u] Cn: Gk *Imprisoned.*
[v] Gk *he.*
[w] Or *worse than the others did in his malice toward the Jewish citizens.*
[x] Gk *he.*

grew wild, so that they might not share in the defilement.

The Suppression of Judaism

6 Not long after this, the king sent an Athenian [y] senator [z] to compel the Jews to forsake the laws of their fathers and cease to live by the laws of God, [2]and also to pollute the temple in Jerusalem and call it the temple of Olympian Zeus, and to call the one in Ger'izim the temple of Zeus the Friend of Strangers, as did the people who dwelt in that place.

3 Harsh and utterly grievous was the onslaught of evil. [4]For the temple was filled with debauchery and reveling by the Gentiles, who dallied with harlots and had intercourse with women within the sacred precincts, and besides brought in things for sacrifice that were unfit. [5]The altar was covered with abominable offerings which were forbidden by the laws. [6]A man could neither keep the sabbath, nor observe the feasts of his fathers, nor so much as confess himself to be a Jew.

7 On the monthly celebration of the king's birthday, the Jews [a] were taken, under bitter constraint, to partake of the sacrifices; and when the feast of Diony'sus came, they were compelled to walk in the procession in honor of Dionysus, wearing wreaths of ivy. [8]At the suggestion of Ptol'emy a decree was issued to the neighboring Greek cities, that they should adopt the same policy toward the Jews and make them partake of the sacrifices, [9]and should slay those who did not choose to change over to Greek customs. One could see, therefore, the misery that had come upon them. [10]For example, two women were brought in for having circumcised their children. These women they publicly paraded about the city, with their babies hung at their breasts, then hurled them down headlong from the wall. [11]Others who had assembled in the caves near by, to observe the seventh day secretly, were betrayed to Philip and were all burned together, because their piety kept them from defending themselves, in view of their regard for that most holy day.

Providential Significance of the Persecution

12 Now I urge those who read this book not to be depressed by such calamities, but to recognize that these punishments were designed not to destroy but to discipline our people. [13]In fact, not to let the impious alone for long, but to punish them immediately, is a sign of great kindness. [14]For in the case of the other nations the Lord waits patiently to punish them until they have reached the full measure of their sins; but he does not deal in this way with us, [15]in order that he may not take vengeance on us afterward when our sins have reached their height. [16]Therefore he never withdraws his mercy from us. Though he disciplines us with calamities, he does not forsake his own

people. [17]Let what we have said serve as a reminder; we must go on briefly with the story.

The Martyrdom of Eleazar

18 Elea'zar, one of the scribes in high position, a man now advanced in age and of noble presence, was being forced to open his mouth to eat swine's flesh. [19]But he, welcoming death with honor rather than life with pollution, went up to the rack of his own accord, spitting out the flesh, [20]as men ought to go who have the courage to refuse things that it is not right to taste, even for the natural love of life.

21 Those who were in charge of that unlawful sacrifice took the man aside, because of their long acquaintance with him, and privately urged him to bring meat of his own providing, proper for him to use, and pretend that he was eating the flesh of the sacrificial meal which had been commanded by the king, [22]so that by doing this he might be saved from death, and be treated kindly on account of his old friendship with them. [23]But making a high resolve, worthy of his years and the dignity of his old age and the gray hairs which he had reached with distinction and his excellent life even from childhood, and moreover according to the holy God-given law, he declared himself quickly, telling them to send him to Hades.

24 "Such pretense is not worthy of our time of life," he said, "lest many of the young should suppose that Elea'zar in his ninetieth year has gone over to an alien religion, [25]and through my pretense, for the sake of living a brief moment longer, they should be led astray because of me, while I defile and disgrace my old age. [26]For even if for the present I should avoid the punishment of men, yet whether I live or die I shall not escape the hands of the Almighty. [27]Therefore, by manfully giving up my life now, I will show myself worthy of my old age [28]and leave to the young a noble example of how to die a good death willingly and nobly for the revered and holy laws."

When he had said this, he went [b] at once to the rack. [29]And those who a little before had acted toward him with good will now changed to ill will, because the words he had uttered were in their opinion sheer madness. [c] [30]When he was about to die under the blows, he groaned aloud and said: "It is clear to the Lord in his holy knowledge that, though I might have been saved from death, I am enduring terrible sufferings in my body under this beating, but in my soul I am glad to suffer these things because I fear him."

31 So in this way he died, leaving in his death

---

[y] Some authorities read *Antiochian*.
[z] Or *Geron an Athenian*.
[a] Gk *they*.
[b] Other authorities read *was dragged*.
[c] The Greek text of this verse is uncertain.

an example of nobility and a memorial of courage, not only to the young but to the great body of his nation.

The Martyrdom of the Seven Brothers

7 It happened also that seven brothers and their mother were arrested and were being compelled by the king, under torture with whips and cords, to partake of unlawful swine's flesh. ²One of them, acting as their spokesman, said, "What do you intend to ask and learn from us? For we are ready to die rather than transgress the laws of our fathers."

3 The king fell into a rage, and gave orders that pans and caldrons be heated. ⁴These were heated immediately, and he commanded that the tongue of their spokesman be cut out and that they scalp him and cut off his hands and feet, while the rest of the brothers and the mother looked on. ⁵When he was utterly helpless, the king ᵈ ordered them to take him to the fire, still breathing, and to fry him in a pan. The smoke from the pan spread widely, but the brothers ᵉ and their mother encouraged one another to die nobly, saying, ⁶"The Lord God is watching over us and in truth has compassion on us, as Moses declared in his song which bore witness against the people to their faces, when he said, 'And he will have compassion on his servants.'"

7 After the first brother had died in this way, they brought forward the second for their sport. They tore off the skin of his head with the hair, and asked him, "Will you eat rather than have your body punished limb by limb?" ⁸He replied in the language of his fathers, and said to them, "No." Therefore he in turn underwent tortures as the first brother had done. ⁹And when he was at his last breath, he said, "You accursed wretch, you dismiss us from this present life, but the King of the universe will raise us up to an everlasting renewal of life, * because we have died for his laws."

10 After him, the third was the victim of their sport. When it was demanded, he quickly put out his tongue and courageously stretched forth his hands, ¹¹and said nobly, "I got these from Heaven, and because of his laws I disdain them, and from him I hope to get them back again." ¹²As a result the king himself and those with him were astonished at the young man's spirit, for he regarded his sufferings as nothing.

13 When he too had died, they maltreated and tortured the fourth in the same way. ¹⁴And when he was near death, he said, "One cannot but choose to die at the hands of men and to cherish the hope that God gives of being raised again by him. But for you there will be no resurrection to life!"

15 Next they brought forward the fifth and maltreated him. ¹⁶But he looked at the king, ᶠ and said, "Because you have authority among men, mortal though you are, you do what you please. But do not think that God has forsaken our people. ¹⁷Keep on, and see how his mighty power will torture you and your descendants!"

18 After him they brought forward the sixth. And when he was about to die, he said, "Do not deceive yourself in vain. For we are suffering these things on our own account, because of our sins against our own God. Therefore ᵍ astounding things have happened. ¹⁹But do not think that you will go unpunished for having tried to fight against God!"

20 The mother was especially admirable and worthy of honorable memory. Though she saw her seven sons perish within a single day, she bore it with good courage because of her hope in the Lord. ²¹She encouraged each of them in the language of their fathers. Filled with a noble spirit, she fired her woman's reasoning with a man's courage, and said to them, ²²"I do not know how you came into being in my womb. It was not I who gave you life and breath, nor I who set in order the elements within each of you. ²³Therefore the Creator of the world, who shaped the beginning of man and devised the origin of all things, will in his mercy give life and breath back to you again, since you now forget yourselves for the sake of his laws."

24 Anti'ochus felt that he was being treated with contempt, and he was suspicious of her reproachful tone. The youngest brother being still alive, Antiochus ʰ not only appealed to him in words, but promised with oaths that he would make him rich and enviable if he would turn from the ways of his fathers, and that he would take him for his friend and entrust him with public affairs. ²⁵Since the young man would not listen to him at all, the king called the mother to him and urged her to advise the youth to save himself. ²⁶After much urging on his part, she undertook to persuade her son. ²⁷But, leaning close to him, she spoke in their native tongue as follows, deriding the cruel tyrant: "My son, have pity on me. I carried you nine months in my womb, and nursed you for three years, and have reared you and brought you up to this point in your life, and have taken care of you. ⁱ ²⁸I beg you, my child, to look at the heaven and the earth and see everything that is in them, and recognize that God did not make them out of things that

---

ᵈ Gk he.
ᵉ Gk they.
ᶠ Gk him.
ᵍ Lat: other authorities omit Therefore.
ʰ Gk he.
ⁱ Or have borne the burden of your education.
* 7:9, to an everlasting renewal of life: Vulgate has: "in the resurrection of eternal life."

existed.ʲ Thus also mankind comes into being. ²⁹Do not fear this butcher, but prove worthy of your brothers. Accept death, so that in God's mercy I may get you back again with your brothers."

30 While she was still speaking, the young man said, "What are youᵏ waiting for? I will not obey the king's command, but I obey the command of the law that was given to our fathers through Moses. ³¹But you,¹ who have contrived all sorts of evil against the Hebrews, will certainly not escape the hands of God. ³²For we are suffering because of our own sins. ³³And if our living Lord is angry for a little while, to rebuke and discipline us, he will again be reconciled with his own servants. ³⁴But you, unholy wretch, you most defiled of all men, do not be elated in vain and puffed up by uncertain hopes, when you raise your hand against the children of heaven. ³⁵You have not yet escaped the judgment of the almighty, all-seeing God. ³⁶For our brothers after enduring a brief suffering have drunkᵐ of everflowing life under God's covenant; but you, by the judgment of God, will receive just punishment for your arrogance. ³⁷I, like my brothers, give up body and life for the laws of our fathers, appealing to God to show mercy soon to our nation and by afflictions and plagues to make you confess that he alone is God, ³⁸and through me and my brothers to bring to an end the wrath of the Almighty which has justly fallen on our whole nation."

39 The king fell into a rage, and handled him worse than the others, being exasperated at his scorn. ⁴⁰So he died in his integrity, putting his whole trust in the Lord.

41 Last of all, the mother died, after her sons.

42 Let this be enough, then, about the eating of sacrifices and the extreme tortures.

The Revolt of Judas Maccabeus

8 But Judas, who was also called Mac"cabe'us, and his companions secretly entered the villages and summoned their kinsmen and enlisted those who had continued in the Jewish faith, and so they gathered about six thousand men. ²They begged the Lord to look upon the people who were oppressed by all, and to have pity on the temple which had been profaned by ungodly men, ³and to have mercy on the city which was being destroyed and about to be leveled to the ground, and to heed the blood that cried out to him, ⁴and to remember also the lawless destruction of the innocent babies and the blasphemies committed against his name, and to show his hatred of evil.

5 As soon as Mac"cabe'us got his army organized, the Gentiles could not withstand him, for the wrath of the Lord had turned to mercy. ⁶Coming without warning, he would set fire to towns and villages. He captured strategic positions and put to flight not a few of the enemy. ⁷He found the

nights most advantageous for such attacks. And talk of his valor spread everywhere.

8 When Philip saw that the man was gaining ground little by little, and that he was pushing ahead with more frequent successes, he wrote to Ptol'emy, the governor of Coe'le-syr'ia and Phoeni'cia, for aid to the king's government. ⁹And Ptol'emyⁿ promptly appointed Nica'nor the son of Patro'clus, one of the king's chief friends, and sent him, in command of no fewer than twenty thousand Gentiles of all nations, to wipe out the whole race of Judea. He associated with him Gor'gias, a general and a man of experience in military service. ¹⁰Nica'nor determined to make up for the king the tribute due to the Romans, two thousand talents, by selling the captured Jews into slavery. ¹¹And he immediately sent to the cities on the seacoast, inviting them to buy Jewish slaves and promising to hand over ninety slaves for a talent, not expecting the judgment from the Almighty that was about to overtake him.

Preparation for Battle

12 Word came to Judas concerning Nica'nor's invasion; and when he told his companions of the arrival of the army, ¹³those who were cowardly and distrustful of God's justice ran off and got away. ¹⁴Others sold all their remaining property, and at the same time begged the Lord to rescue those who had been sold by the ungodly Nica'nor before he ever met them, ¹⁵if not for their own sake, yet for the sake of the covenants made with their fathers, and because he had called them by his holy and glorious name. ¹⁶But Mac"cabe'us gathered his men together, to the number of six thousand, and exhorted them not to be frightened by the enemy and not to fear the great multitude of Gentiles who were wickedly coming against them, but to fight nobly, ¹⁷keeping before their eyes the lawless outrage which the Gentilesº had committed against the holy place, and the torture of the derided city, and besides, the overthrow of their ancestral way of life. ¹⁸"For they trust to arms and acts of daring," he said, "but we trust in the Almighty God, who is able with a single nod to strike down those who are coming against us and even the whole world."

19 Moreover, he told them of the times when help came to their ancestors; both the time of Sennach'erib, when one hundred and eighty-five thousand perished, ²⁰and the time of the battle with the Galatians that took place in Babylonia, when eight thousand in all went into the affair, with four thousand Macedonians; and when the

---

ʲ Or *God made them out of things that did not exist.*
ᵏ The Greek here for *you* is plural.
¹ The Greek here for *you* is singular.
ᵐ Cn: Gk *fallen.*
ⁿ Gk *he.*
º Gk *they.*

Macedonians were hard pressed, the eight thousand, by the help that came to them from heaven, destroyed one hundred and twenty thousand and took much booty.

Judas Defeats Nicanor

21 With these words he filled them with good courage and made them ready to die for their laws and their country; then he divided his army into four parts. ²²He appointed his brothers also, Simon and Joseph and Jonathan, each to command a division, putting fifteen hundred men under each. ²³Besides, he appointed Elea′zar to read aloud ᴾ from the holy book, and gave the watchword, "God's help"; then, leading the first division himself, he joined battle with Nica′nor.

24 With the Almighty as their ally, they slew more than nine thousand of the enemy, and wounded and disabled most of Nica′nor's army, and forced them all to flee. ²⁵They captured the money of those who had come to buy them as slaves. After pursuing them for some distance, they were obliged to return because the hour was late. ²⁶For it was the day before the sabbath, and for that reason they did not continue their pursuit. ²⁷And when they had collected the arms of the enemy and stripped them of their spoils, they kept the sabbath, giving great praise and thanks to the Lord, who had preserved them for that day and allotted it to them as the beginning of mercy. ²⁸After the sabbath they gave some of the spoils to those who had been tortured and to the widows and orphans, and distributed the rest among themselves and their children. ²⁹When they had done this, they made common supplication and begged the merciful Lord to be wholly reconciled with his servants.

30 In encounters with the forces of Timothy and Bacchi′des they killed more than twenty thousand of them and got possession of some exceedingly high strongholds, and they divided very much plunder, giving to those who had been tortured and to the orphans and widows, and also to the aged, shares equal to their own. ³¹Collecting the arms of the enemy, � they stored them all carefully in strategic places, and carried the rest of the spoils to Jerusalem. ³²They killed the commander of Timothy's forces, a most unholy man, and one who had greatly troubled the Jews. ³³While they were celebrating the victory in the city of their fathers, they burned those who had set fire to the sacred gates, Callis′thenes and some others, who had fled into one little house; so these received the proper recompense for their impiety. ˣ

34 The thrice-accursed Nica′nor, who had brought the thousand merchants to buy the Jews, ³⁵having been humbled with the help of the Lord by opponents whom he regarded as of the least account, took off his splendid uniform and made his way alone like a runaway slave across the country till he reached Antioch, having succeeded chiefly in the destruction of his own army! ³⁶Thus he who had undertaken to secure tribute for the Romans by the capture of the people of Jerusalem proclaimed that the Jews had a Defender, and that therefore the Jews were invulnerable, because they followed the laws ordained by him.

The Last Campaign of Antiochus Ephiphanes

9 About that time, as it happened, Anti′ochus had retreated in disorder from the region of Persia. ²For he had entered the city called Persep′olis, and attempted to rob the temples and control the city. Therefore the people rushed to the rescue with arms, and Anti′ochus and his men were defeated, ˢ with the result that Antiochus was put to flight by the inhabitants and beat a shameful retreat. ³While he was in Ecbat′ana, news came to him of what had happened to Nica′nor and the forces of Timothy. ⁴Transported with rage, he conceived the idea of turning upon the Jews the injury done by those who had put him to flight; so he ordered his charioteer to drive without stopping until he completed the journey. But the judgment of heaven rode with him! For in his arrogance he said, "When I get there I will make Jerusalem a cemetery of Jews."

5 But the all-seeing Lord, the God of Israel, struck him an incurable and unseen blow. As soon as he ceased speaking he was seized with a pain in his bowels for which there was no relief and with sharp internal tortures—⁶and that very justly, for he had tortured the bowels of others with many and strange inflictions. ⁷Yet he did not in any way stop his insolence, but was even more filled with arrogance, breathing fire in his rage against the Jews, and giving orders to hasten the journey. And so it came about that he fell out of his chariot as it was rushing along, and the fall was so hard as to torture every limb of his body. ⁸Thus he who had just been thinking that he could command the waves of the sea, in his superhuman arrogance, and imagining that he could weigh the high mountains in a balance, was brought down to earth and carried in a litter, making the power of God manifest to all. ⁹And so the ungodly man's body swarmed with worms, and while he was still living in anguish and pain, his flesh rotted away, and because of his stench the whole army felt revulsion at his decay. ¹⁰Because of his intolerable stench no one was able to carry the man who a little while before had thought that he could touch the stars of heaven. ¹¹Then it was that, broken in spirit, he began to lose much of his arrogance and to come to his senses under the

ᴾ The Greek text of this clause is uncertain.
ᑫ Gk *their arms*.
ˣ The Greek text of this verse is uncertain.
ˢ Gk *they were defeated*.

scourge of God, for he was tortured with pain every moment. [12]And when he could not endure his own stench, he uttered these words: "It is right to be subject to God, and no mortal should think that he is equal to God." [t]

Antiochus Makes a Promise to God

13 Then the abominable fellow made a vow to the Lord, who would no longer have mercy on him, stating [14]that the holy city, which he was hastening to level to the ground and to make a cemetery, he was now declaring to be free; [15]and the Jews, whom he had not considered worth burying but had planned to throw out with their children to the beasts, for the birds to pick, he would make, all of them, equal to citizens of Athens; [16]and the holy sanctuary, which he had formerly plundered, he would adorn with the finest offerings; and the holy vessels he would give back, all of them, many times over; and the expenses incurred for the sacrifices he would provide from his own revenues; [17]and in addition to all this he also would become a Jew and would visit every inhabited place to proclaim the power of God. [18]But when his sufferings did not in any way abate, for the judgment of God had justly come upon him, he gave up all hope for himself and wrote to the Jews the following letter, in the form of a supplication. This was its content:

Antiochus' Letter and Death

19 "To his worthy Jewish citizens, Anti'ochus their king and general sends hearty greetings and good wishes for their health and prosperity. [20]If you and your children are well and your affairs are as you wish, I am glad. As my hope is in heaven, [21]I remember with affection your esteem and good will. On my way back from the region of Persia I suffered an annoying illness, and I have deemed it necessary to take thought for the general security of all. [22]I do not despair of my condition, for I have good hope of recovering from my illness, [23]but I observed that my father, on the occasions when he made expeditions into the upper country, appointed his successor, [24]so that, if anything unexpected happened or any unwelcome news came, the people throughout the realm would not be troubled, for they would know to whom the government was left. [25]Moreover, I understand how the princes along the borders and the neighbors to my kingdom keep watching for opportunities and waiting to see what will happen. So I have appointed my son Anti'ochus to be king, whom I have often entrusted and commended to most of you when I hastened off to the upper provinces; and I have written to him what is written here. [26]I therefore urge and beg you to remember the public and private services rendered to you and to maintain your present good will, each of you, toward me and my son. [27]For I am sure that he will follow

my policy and will treat you with moderation and kindness."

28 So the murderer and blasphemer, having endured the more intense suffering, such as he had inflicted on others, came to the end of his life by a most pitiable fate, among the mountains in a strange land. [29]And Philip, one of his courtiers, took his body home; then, fearing the son of Anti'ochus, he betook himself to Ptol'emy Phil"ome'tor in Egypt.

The Purification of the Temple

10 Now Mac"cabe'us and his followers, the Lord leading them on, recovered the temple and the city; [2]and they tore down the altars which had been built in the public square by the foreigners, and also destroyed the sacred precincts. [3]They purified the sanctuary, and made another altar of sacrifice; then, striking fire out of flint, they offered sacrifices, after a lapse of two years, and they burned incense and lighted lamps and set out the bread of the Presence. [4]And when they had done this, they fell prostrate and begged the Lord that they might never again fall into such misfortunes, but that, if they should ever sin, they might be disciplined by him with forbearance and not be handed over to blasphemous and barbarous nations. [5]It happened that on the same day on which the sanctuary had been profaned by the foreigners, the purification of the sanctuary took place, that is, on the twenty-fifth day of the same month, which was Chis'lev. [6]And they celebrated it for eight days with rejoicing, in the manner of the feast of booths, remembering how not long before, during the feast of booths, they had been wandering in the mountains and caves like wild animals. [7]Therefore bearing ivy-wreathed wands and beautiful branches and also fronds of palm, they offered hymns of thanksgiving to him who had given success to the purifying of his own holy place. [8]They decreed by public ordinance and vote that the whole nation of the Jews should observe these days every year.

9 Such then was the end of Anti'ochus, who was called Epiph'anes.

10 Now we will tell what took place under Anti'ochus Eu'pator, who was the son of that ungodly man, and will give a brief summary of the principal calamities of the wars. [11]This man, when he succeeded to the kingdom, appointed one Lys'ias to have charge of the government and to be chief governor of Coe'le-syr'ia and Phoeni'cia. [12]Ptol'emy, who was called Ma'cron, took the lead in showing justice to the Jews because of the wrong that had been done to them, and attempted to maintain peaceful relations with them.

---

[t] Or *think thoughts proper only to God.*

[13]As a result he was accused before Eu'pator by the king's friends. He heard himself called a traitor at every turn, because he had abandoned Cyprus, which Phil''ome'tor had entrusted to him, and had gone over to Anti'ochus Epiph'anes. Unable to command the respect due his office,[u] he took poison and ended his life.

Campaign in Idumea

14 When Gor'gias became governor of the region, he maintained a force of mercenaries, and at every turn kept on warring against the Jews. [15]Besides this, the Idume'ans, who had control of important strongholds, were harassing the Jews; they received those who were banished from Jerusalem, and endeavored to keep up the war. [16]But Mac''cabe'us and his men, after making solemn supplication and begging God to fight on their side, rushed to the strongholds of the Idume'ans. [17]Attacking them vigorously, they gained possession of the places, and beat off all who fought upon the wall, and slew those whom they encountered, killing no fewer than twenty thousand.

18 When no less than nine thousand took refuge in two very strong towers well equipped to withstand a siege, [19]Mac''cabe'us left Simon and Joseph, and also Zacchae'us and his men, a force sufficient to besiege them; and he himself set off for places where he was more urgently needed. [20]But the men with Simon, who were money-hungry, were bribed by some of those who were in the towers, and on receiving seventy thousand drachmas let some of them slip away. [21]When word of what had happened came to Mac''cabe'us, he gathered the leaders of the people, and accused these men of having sold their brethren for money by setting their enemies free to fight against them. [22]Then he slew these men who had turned traitor, and immediately captured the two towers. [23]Having success at arms in everything he undertook, he destroyed more than twenty thousand in the two strongholds.

Judas Defeats Timothy

24 Now Timothy, who had been defeated by the Jews before, gathered a tremendous force of mercenaries and collected the cavalry from Asia in no small number. He came on, intending to take Judea by storm. [25]As he drew near, Mac''cabe'us and his men sprinkled dust upon their heads and put on sackcloth, in supplication to God. [26]Falling upon the steps before the altar, they begged him to be gracious to them and to be an enemy to their enemies and an adversary to their adversaries, as the law declares. [27]And rising from their prayer they took up their arms and advanced a considerable distance from the city; and when they came near to the enemy they halted. [28]Just as dawn was breaking, the two armies joined battle, the one having as pledge of success and victory not only their valor but their reliance upon the Lord, while the other made rage their leader in the fight.

29 When the battle became fierce, there appeared to the enemy from heaven five resplendent men on horses with golden bridles, and they were leading the Jews. [30]Surrounding Mac''cabe'us and protecting him with their own armor and weapons, they kept him from being wounded. And they showered arrows and thunderbolts upon the enemy, so that, confused and blinded, they were thrown into disorder and cut to pieces. [31]Twenty thousand five hundred were slaughtered, besides six hundred horsemen.

32 Timothy himself fled to a stronghold called Gaza'ra, especially well garrisoned, where Chae'reas was commander. [33]Then Mac''cabe'us and his men were glad, and they besieged the fort for four days. [34]The men within, relying on the strength of the place, blasphemed terribly and hurled out wicked words. [35]But at dawn of the fifth day, twenty young men in the army of Mac''cabe'us, fired with anger because of the blasphemies, bravely stormed the wall and with savage fury cut down every one they met. [36]Others who came up in the same way wheeled around against the defenders and set fire to the towers; they kindled fires and burned the blasphemers alive. Others broke open the gates and let in the rest of the force, and they occupied the city. [37]They killed Timothy, who was hidden in a cistern, and his brother Chae'reas, and Apol'loph'anes. [38]When they had accomplished these things, with hymns and thanksgivings they blessed the Lord who shows great kindness to Israel and gives them the victory.

Lysias Besieges Beth-zur

11 Very soon after this, Lys'ias, the king's guardian and kinsman, who was in charge of the government, being vexed at what had happened, [2]gathered about eighty thousand men and all his cavalry and came against the Jews. He intended to make the city a home for Greeks, [3]and to levy tribute on the temple as he did on the sacred places of the other nations, and to put up the high priesthood for sale every year. [4]He took no account whatever of the power of God, but was elated with his ten thousands of infantry, and his thousands of cavalry, and his eighty elephants. [5]Invading Judea, he approached Beth-zur, which was a fortified place about five leagues[v] from Jerusalem, and pressed it hard.

6 When Mac''cabe'us and his men got word that Lys'ias[w] was besieging the strongholds, they and all the people, with lamentations and tears, begged the Lord to send a good angel to save Israel. [7]Mac''cabe'us himself was the first to take

---

[u] Cn: The Greek text here is uncertain.
[v] About twenty miles. The text is uncertain here.
[w] Gk he.

up arms, and he urged the others to risk their lives with him to aid their brethren. Then they eagerly rushed off together. [8]And there, while they were still near Jerusalem, a horseman appeared at their head, clothed in white and brandishing weapons of gold. [9]And they all together praised the merciful God, and were strengthened in heart, ready to assail not only men but the wildest beasts or walls of iron. [10]They advanced in battle order, having their heavenly ally, for the Lord had mercy on them. [11]They hurled themselves like lions against the enemy, and slew eleven thousand of them and sixteen hundred horsemen, and forced all the rest to flee. [12]Most of them got away stripped and wounded, and Lys'ias himself escaped by disgraceful flight. [13]And as he was not without intelligence, he pondered over the defeat which had befallen him, and realized that the Hebrews were invincible because the mighty God fought on their side. So he sent to them [14]and persuaded them to settle everything on just terms, promising that he would persuade the king, constraining him to be their friend. [x] [15]Mac"cabe'us, having regard for the common good, agreed to all that Lys'ias urged. For the king granted every request in behalf of the Jews which Maccabeus delivered to Lysias in writing.

16 The letter written to the Jews by Lys'ias was to this effect:

"Lysias to the people of the Jews, greeting. [17]John and Ab'salom, who were sent by you, have delivered your signed communication and have asked about the matters indicated therein. [18]I have informed the king of everything that needed to be brought before him, and he has agreed to what was possible. [19]If you will maintain your good will toward the government, I will endeavor for the future to help promote your welfare. [20]And concerning these matters and their details, I have ordered these men and my representatives to confer with you. [21]Farewell. The one hundred and forty-eighth year, [y] Di"oscorin'thius twenty-fourth."

22 The king's letter ran thus:

"King Anti'ochus to his brother Lys'ias, greeting. [23]Now that our father has gone on to the gods, we desire that the subjects of the kingdom be undisturbed in caring for their own affairs. [24]We have heard that the Jews do not consent to our father's change to Greek customs but prefer their own way of living and ask that their own customs be allowed them. [25]Accordingly, since we choose that this nation also be free from disturbance, our decision is that their temple be restored to them and that they live according to the customs of their ancestors. [26]You will do well, therefore, to send word to them and give them pledges of friendship, so that they may know our

policy and be of good cheer and go on happily in the conduct of their own affairs."

27 To the nation the king's letter was as follows:

"King Anti'ochus to the senate of the Jews and to the other Jews, greeting. [28]If you are well, it is as we desire. We also are in good health. [29]Menela'us has informed us that you wish to return home and look after your own affairs. [30]Therefore those who go home by the thirtieth day of Xan'thicus will have our pledge of friendship and full permission [31]for the Jews to enjoy their own food and laws, just as formerly, and none of them shall be molested in any way for what he may have done in ignorance. [32]And I have also sent Menela'us to encourage you. [33]Farewell. The one hundred and forty-eighth year, [z] Xan'thicus fifteenth."

34 The Romans also sent them a letter, which read thus:

"Quint'us Mem'mius and Titus Ma'nius, envoys of the Romans, to the people of the Jews, greeting. [35]With regard to what Lys'ias the kinsman of the king has granted you, we also give consent. [36]But as to the matters which he decided are to be referred to the king, as soon as you have considered them, send some one promptly, so that we may make proposals appropriate for you. For we are on our way to Antioch. [37]Therefore make haste and send some men, so that we may have your judgment. [38]Farewell. The one hundred and forty-eighth year, [a] Xan'thicus fifteenth."

Incidents at Joppa and Jamnia

12 When this agreement had been reached, Lys'ias returned to the king, and the Jews went about their farming.

2 But some of the governors in various places, Timothy and Apollo'nius the son of Gennae'us, as well as Hi"eron'ymus and Dem'ophon, and in addition to these Nica'nor the governor of Cyprus, would not let them live quietly and in peace. [3]And some men of Joppa did so ungodly a deed as this: they invited the Jews who lived among them to embark, with their wives and children, on boats which they had provided, as though there were no ill will to the Jews; [b] [4]and this was done by public vote of the city. And when they accepted, because they wished to live peaceably and suspected nothing, the men of Joppa [c] took them out to sea and drowned them, not less than two hundred. [5]When Judas heard of the cruelty visited on his countrymen, he gave orders to his men [6]and, calling upon God the righteous Judge, attacked the murderers

---

[x] The Greek text here is corrupt.
[y] 164 B.C.
[z] 164 B.C.
[a] 164 B.C.
[b] Gk *them.*
[c] Gk *they.*

of his brethren. He set fire to the harbor by night, and burned the boats, and massacred those who had taken refuge there. [7]Then, because the city's gates were closed, he withdrew, intending to come again and root out the whole community of Joppa. [8]But learning that the men in Jam'nia meant in the same way to wipe out the Jews who were living among them, [9]he attacked the people of Jam'nia by night and set fire to the harbor and the fleet, so that the glow of the light was seen in Jerusalem, thirty miles [d] distant.

The Campaign in Gilead

10 When they had gone more than a mile [e] from there, on their march against Timothy, not less than five thousand Arabs with five hundred horsemen attacked them. [11]After a hard fight Judas and his men won the victory, by the help of God. The defeated nomads begged Judas to grant them pledges of friendship, promising to give him cattle and to help his people [f] in all other ways. [12]Judas, thinking that they might really be useful in many ways, agreed to make peace with them; and after receiving his pledges they departed to their tents.

13 He also attacked a certain city which was strongly fortified with earthworks [g] and walls, and inhabited by all sorts of Gentiles. Its name was Cas'pin. [14]And those who were within, relying on the strength of the walls and on their supply of provisions, behaved most insolently toward Judas and his men, railing at them and even blaspheming and saying unholy things. [15]But Judas and his men, calling upon the great Sovereign of the world, who without battering-rams or engines of war overthrew Jericho in the days of Joshua, rushed furiously upon the walls. [16]They took the city by the will of God, and slaughtered untold numbers, so that the adjoining lake, a quarter of a mile [h] wide, appeared to be running over with blood.

Judas Defeats Timothy's Army

17 When they had gone ninety-five miles [i] from there, they came to Cha'rax, to the Jews who are called Tou"bia'ni. [18]They did not find Timothy in that region, for he had by then departed from the region without accomplishing anything, though in one place he had left a very strong garrison. [19]Dosith'eus and Sosip'ater, who were captains under Mac"cabe'us, marched out and destroyed those whom Timothy had left in the stronghold, more than ten thousand men. [20]But Mac"cabe'us arranged his army in divisions, set men [j] in command of the divisions, and hastened after Timothy, who had with him a hundred and twenty thousand infantry and two thousand five hundred cavalry. [21]When Timothy learned of the approach of Judas, he sent off the women and the children and also the baggage to a place called Carna'im; for that place was hard to besiege and

difficult of access because of the narrowness of all the approaches. [22]But when Judas' first division appeared, terror and fear came over the enemy at the manifestation to them of him who sees all things; and they rushed off in flight and were swept on, this way and that, so that often they were injured by their own men and pierced by the points of their swords. [23]And Judas pressed the pursuit with the utmost vigor, putting the sinners to the sword, and destroyed as many as thirty thousand men.

24 Timothy himself fell into the hands of Dosith'eus and Sosip'ater and their men. With great guile he begged them to let him go in safety, because he held the parents of most of them and the brothers of some and no consideration would be shown them. [25]And when with many words he had confirmed his solemn promise to restore them unharmed, they let him go, for the sake of saving their brethren.

Judas Wins Other Victories

26 Then Judas [k] marched against Carna'im and the temple of Atar'gatis, and slaughtered twenty-five thousand people. [27]After the rout and destruction of these, he marched also against E'phron, a fortified city where Lys'ias dwelt with multitudes of people of all nationalities. [l] Stalwart young men took their stand before the walls and made a vigorous defense; and great stores of war engines and missiles were there. [28]But the Jews [m] called upon the Sovereign who with power shatters the might of his enemies, and they got the city into their hands, and killed as many as twenty-five thousand of those who were within it.

29 Setting out from there, they hastened to Scythop'olis, which is seventy-five miles [n] from Jerusalem. [30]But when the Jews who dwelt there bore witness to the good will which the people of Scythop'olis had shown them and their kind treatment of them in times of misfortune, [31]they thanked them and exhorted them to be well disposed to their race in the future also. Then they went up to Jerusalem, as the feast of weeks was close at hand.

Judas Defeats Gorgias

32 After the feast called Pentecost, they hastened against Gor'gias, the governor of Idume'a. [33]And he came out with three thousand infantry and four hundred cavalry. [34]When they joined battle, it happened that a few of the Jews fell.

---

[d] Gk *two hundred and forty stadia.*
[e] Gk *nine stadia.*
[f] Gk *them.*
[g] The Greek text here is uncertain.
[h] Gk *two stadia.*
[i] Gk *seven hundred and fifty stadia.*
[j] Gk *them.*
[k] Gk *he.*
[l] The Greek text of this sentence is uncertain.
[m] Gk *the.*
[n] Gk *six hundred stadia.*

35But a certain Dosith'eus, one of Bace'nor's men, who was on horseback and was a strong man, caught hold of Gor'gias, and grasping his cloak was dragging him off by main strength, wishing to take the accursed man alive, when one of the Thracian horsemen bore down upon him and cut off his arm; so Gorgias escaped and reached Mar'isa.

36 As Es'dris and his men had been fighting for a long time and were weary, Judas called upon the Lord to show himself their ally and leader in the battle. 37In the language of their fathers he raised the battle cry, with hymns; then he charged against Gor'gias' men when they were not expecting it, and put them to flight.

Prayers for Those Killed in Battle

38 Then Judas assembled his army and went to the city of Adul'lam. As the seventh day was coming on, they purified themselves according to the custom, and they kept the sabbath there.

39 On the next day, as by that time it had become necessary, Judas and his men went to take up the bodies of the fallen and to bring them back to lie with their kinsmen in the sepulchres of their fathers. 40Then under the tunic of every one of the dead they found sacred tokens of the idols of Jam'nia, which the law forbids the Jews to wear. And it became clear to all that this was why these men had fallen. 41So they all blessed the ways of the Lord, the righteous Judge, who reveals the things that are hidden; 42and they turned to prayer, begging that the sin which had been committed might be wholly blotted out. And the noble Judas exhorted the people to keep themselves free from sin, for they had seen with their own eyes what had happened because of the sin of those who had fallen. 43He also took up a collection, man by man, to the amount of two thousand drachmas of silver, and sent it to Jerusalem to provide for a sin offering. In doing this he acted very well and honorably, taking account of the resurrection. 44For if he were not expecting that those who had fallen would rise again, it would have been superfluous and foolish to pray for the dead. 45But if he was looking to the splendid reward that is laid up for those who fall asleep in godliness, it was a holy and pious thought. Therefore he made atonement for the dead, that they might be delivered from their sin.*

Menelaus I Put to Death

13 In the one hundred and forty-ninth year° word came to Judas and his men that Anti'ochus Eu'pator was coming with a great army against Judea, 2and with him Lys'ias, his guardian, who had charge of the government. Each of them had a Greek force of one hundred and ten thousand infantry, five thousand three hundred cavalry, twenty-two elephants, and three hundred chariots armed with scythes.

3 Menela'us also joined them and with utter hypocrisy urged Anti'ochus on, not for the sake of his country's welfare, but because he thought that he would be established in office. 4But the King of kings aroused the anger of Anti'ochus against the scoundrel; and when Lys'ias informed him that this man was to blame for all the trouble, he ordered them to take him to Beroe'a and to put him to death by the method which is the custom in that place. 5For there is a tower in that place, fifty cubits high, full of ashes, and it has a rim running around it which on all sides inclines precipitously into the ashes. 6There they all push to destruction any man guilty of sacrilege or notorious for other crimes. 7By such a fate it came about that Menela'us the lawbreaker died, without even burial in the earth. 8And this was eminently just; because he had committed many sins against the altar whose fire and ashes were holy, he met his death in ashes.

A Battle Near Modein

9 The king with barbarous arrogance was coming to show the Jews things far worse than those that had been doneᴾ in his father's time. 10But when Judas heard of this, he ordered the people to call upon the Lord day and night, now if ever to help those who were on the point of being deprived of the law and their country and the holy temple, 11and not to let the people who had just begun to revive fall into the hands of the blasphemous Gentiles. 12When they had all joined in the same petition and had begged the merciful Lord with weeping and fasting and lying prostrate for three days without ceasing, Judas exhorted them and ordered them to stand ready.

13 After consulting privately with the elders, he determined to march out and decide the matter by the help of God before the king's army could enter Judea and get possession of the city. 14So, committing the decision to the Creator of the world and exhorting his men to fight nobly to the death for the laws, temple, city, country, and commonwealth, he pitched his camp near Mo'dein. 15He gave his men the watchword, "God's victory," and with a picked force of the bravest young men, he attacked the king's pavilion at night and slew as many as two thousand men in the camp. He stabbed �q the leading elephant and its rider. 16In the end they filled the camp with terror and confusion and withdrew in triumph. 17This happened, just as day was dawning, because the Lord's help protected him.

° 163 B.C.
ᴾ Or *the worst of the things that had been done.*
q The Greek text here is uncertain.
* 12:45: Vulgate has (verses 45–46): "45And because he considered that they who had fallen asleep with godliness had great grace laid up for them. 46It is therefore a holy and wholesome thought to pray for the dead, that they may be loosed from sins."

Antiochus Makes a Treaty with the Jews

18 The king, having had a taste of the daring of the Jews, tried strategy in attacking their positions. ¹⁹He advanced against Beth-zur, a strong fortress of the Jews, was turned back, attacked again, ˣ and was defeated. ²⁰Judas sent in to the garrison whatever was necessary. ²¹But Rhod′ocus, a man from the ranks of the Jews, gave secret information to the enemy; he was sought for, caught, and put in prison. ²²The king negotiated a second time with the people in Beth-zur, gave pledges, received theirs, withdrew, attacked Judas and his men, was defeated; ²³he got word that Philip, who had been left in charge of the government, had revolted in Antioch; he was dismayed, called in the Jews, yielded and swore to observe all their rights, settled with them and offered sacrifice, honored the sanctuary and showed generosity to the holy place. ²⁴He received Mac″cabe′us, left Hegemon′ides as governor from Ptolema′is to Ge′rar, ²⁵and went to Ptolemais. The people of Ptolema′is were indignant over the treaty; in fact they were so angry that they wanted to annul its terms. ᵃ ²⁶Lys′ias took the public platform, made the best possible defense, convinced them, appeased them, gained their good will, and set out for Antioch. This is how the king's attack and withdrawal turned out.

Alcimus Speaks against Judas

14 Three years later, word came to Judas and his men that Deme′trius, the son of Seleu′cus, had sailed into the harbor of Trip′olis with a strong army and a fleet, ²and had taken possession of the country, having made away with Anti′ochus and his guardian Lys′ias.

3 Now a certain Al′cimus, who had formerly been high priest but had wilfully defiled himself in the times of separation, realized that there was no way for him to be safe or to have access again to the holy altar, ⁴and went to King Deme′trius in about the one hundred and fifty-first year, ᵗ presenting to him a crown of gold and a palm, and besides these some of the customary olive branches from the temple. During that day he kept quiet. ⁵But he found an opportunity that furthered his mad purpose when he was invited by Deme′trius to a meeting of the council and was asked about the disposition and intentions of the Jews. He answered:

6 "Those of the Jews who are called Hasid′eans, whose leader is Judas Mac″cabe′us, are keeping up war and stirring up sedition, and will not let the kingdom attain tranquillity. ⁷Therefore I have laid aside my ancestral glory—I mean the high priesthood—and have now come here, ⁸first because I am genuinely concerned for the interests of the king, and second because I have regard also for my fellow citizens. For through the

folly of those whom I have mentioned our whole nation is now in no small misfortune. ⁹Since you are acquainted, O king, with the details of this matter, deign to take thought for our country and our hard-pressed nation with the gracious kindness which you show to all. ¹⁰For as long as Judas lives, it is impossible for the government to find peace."

11 When he had said this, the rest of the king's friends, who were hostile to Judas, quickly inflamed Deme′trius still more. ¹²And he immediately chose Nica′nor, who had been in command of the elephants, appointed him governor of Judea, and sent him off ¹³with orders to kill Judas and scatter his men, and to set up Al′cimus as high priest of the greatest temple. ¹⁴And the Gentiles throughout Judea, who had fled before ᵘ Judas, flocked to join Nica′nor, thinking that the misfortunes and calamities of the Jews would mean prosperity for themselves.

Nicanor Makes Friends with Judas

15 When the Jews ᵛ heard of Nica′nor's coming and the gathering of the Gentiles, they sprinkled dust upon their heads and prayed to him who established his own people for ever and always upholds his own heritage by manifesting himself. ¹⁶At the command of the leader, they ʷ set out from there immediately and engaged them in battle at a village called Des′sau. ˣ ¹⁷Simon, the brother of Judas, had encountered Nica′nor, but had been temporarily ʸ checked because of the sudden consternation created by the enemy.

18 Nevertheless Nica′nor, hearing of the valor of Judas and his men and their courage in battle for their country, shrank from deciding the issue by bloodshed. ¹⁹Therefore he sent Pos″ido′nius and Theod′otus and Mattathi′as to give and receive pledges of friendship. ²⁰When the terms had been fully considered, and the leader had informed the people, and it had appeared that they were of one mind, they agreed to the covenant. ²¹And the leaders ᶻ set a day on which to meet by themselves. A chariot came forward from each army; seats of honor were set in place; ²²Judas posted armed men in readiness at key places to prevent sudden treachery on the part of the enemy; they held the proper conference.

23 Nica′nor stayed on in Jerusalem and did nothing out of the way, but dismissed the flocks of people that had gathered. ²⁴And he kept Judas

---

ˣ Or faltered.
ᵃ The Greek text of this clause is uncertain.
ᵗ 161 B.C.
ᵘ The Greek text is uncertain.
ᵛ Gk they.
ʷ Gk he.
ˣ The name is uncertain.
ʸ Other authorities read slowly.
ᶻ Gk they.

always in his presence; he was warmly attached to the man. ²⁵And he urged him to marry and have children; so he married, settled down, and shared the common life.

Nicanor Turns against Judas

26 But when Al′cimus noticed their good will for one another, he took the covenant that had been made and went to Deme′trius. He told him that Nica′nor was disloyal to the government, for he had appointed that conspirator against the kingdom, Judas, to be his successor. ²⁷The king became excited and, provoked by the false accusations of that depraved man, wrote to Nica′nor, stating that he was displeased with the covenant and commanding him to send Mac″cabe′us to Antioch as a prisoner without delay.

28 When this message came to Nica′nor, he was troubled and grieved that he had to annul their agreement when the man had done no wrong. ²⁹Since it was not possible to oppose the king, he watched for an opportunity to accomplish this by a stratagem. ³⁰But Mac″cabe′us, noticing that Nica′nor was more austere in his dealings with him and was meeting him more rudely than had been his custom, concluded that this austerity did not spring from the best motives. So he gathered not a few of his men, and went into hiding from Nicanor.

31 When the latter became aware that he had been cleverly outwitted by the man, he went to the great ᵃ and holy temple while the priests were offering the customary sacrifices, and commanded them to hand the man over. ³²And when they declared on oath that they did not know where the man was whom he sought, ³³he stretched out his right hand toward the sanctuary, and swore this oath: "If you do not hand Judas over to me as a prisoner, I will level this precinct of God to the ground and tear down the altar, and I will build here a splendid temple to Diony′sus."

34 Having said this, he went away. Then the priests stretched forth their hands toward heaven and called upon the constant Defender of our nation, in these words: ³⁵"O Lord of all, who have need of nothing, you were pleased that there be a temple for your habitation among us; ³⁶so now, O holy One, Lord of all holiness, keep undefiled for ever this house that has been so recently purified."

Razis Dies for His Country

37 A certain Ra′zis, one of the elders of Jerusalem, was denounced to Nica′nor as a man who loved his fellow citizens and was very well thought of and for his good will was called father of the Jews. ³⁸For in former times, when there was no mingling with the Gentiles, he had been accused of Judaism, and for Judaism he had with all zeal risked body and life. ³⁹Nica′nor, wishing to exhibit the enmity which he had for the Jews, sent

more than five hundred soldiers to arrest him; ⁴⁰for he thought that by arresting ᵇ him he would do them an injury. ⁴¹When the troops were about to capture the tower and were forcing the door of the courtyard, they ordered that fire be brought and the doors burned. Being surrounded, Ra′zis ᶜ fell upon his own sword, ⁴²preferring to die nobly rather than to fall into the hands of sinners and suffer outrages unworthy of his noble birth. ⁴³But in the heat of the struggle he did not hit exactly, and the crowd was now rushing in through the doors. He bravely ran up on the wall, and manfully threw himself down into the crowd. ⁴⁴But as they quickly drew back, a space opened and he fell in the middle of the empty space. ⁴⁵Still alive and aflame with anger, he rose, and though his blood gushed forth and his wounds were severe he ran through the crowd; and standing upon a steep rock, ⁴⁶with his blood now completely drained from him, he tore out his entrails, took them with both hands and hurled them at the crowd, calling upon the Lord of life and spirit to give them back to him again. This was the manner of his death.

Nicanor's Arrogance

15 When Nica′nor heard that Judas and his men were in the region of Samar′ia, he made plans to attack them with complete safety on the day of rest. ²And when the Jews who were compelled to follow him said, "Do not destroy so savagely and barbarously, but show respect for the day which he who sees all things has honored and hallowed above other days," ³the thrice-accursed wretch asked if there were a sovereign in heaven who had commanded the keeping of the sabbath day. ⁴And when they declared, "It is the living Lord himself, the Sovereign in heaven, who ordered us to observe the seventh day," ⁵he replied, "And I am a sovereign also, on earth, and I command you to take up arms and finish the king's business." Nevertheless, he did not succeed in carrying out his abominable design.

Judas Prepares the Jews for Battle

6 This Nica′nor in his utter boastfulness and arrogance had determined to erect a public monument of victory over Judas and his men. ⁷But Mac″cabe′us did not cease to trust with all confidence that he would get help from the Lord. ⁸And he exhorted his men not to fear the attack of the Gentiles, but to keep in mind the former times when help had come to them from heaven, and now to look for the victory which the Almighty would give them. ⁹Encouraging them from the law and the prophets, and reminding them also of the struggles they had won, he made them the more eager. ¹⁰And when he had aroused their

---

ᵃ Gk *greatest*.
ᵇ The Greek text here is uncertain.
ᶜ Gk *he*.

courage, he gave his orders, at the same time pointing out the perfidy of the Gentiles and their violation of oaths. [11]He armed each of them not so much with confidence in shields and spears as with the inspiration of brave words, and he cheered them all by relating a dream, a sort of vision, [d] which was worthy of belief.

12 What he saw was this: Oni'as, who had been high priest, a noble and good man, of modest bearing and gentle manner, one who spoke fittingly and had been trained from childhood in all that belongs to excellence, was praying with outstretched hands for the whole body of the Jews. [13]Then likewise a man appeared, distinguished by his gray hair and dignity, and of marvelous majesty and authority. [14]And Oni'as spoke, saying, "This is a man who loves the brethren and prays much for the people and the holy city, Jeremi'ah, the prophet of God." [15]Jeremi'ah stretched out his right hand and gave to Judas a golden sword, and as he gave it he addressed him thus: [16]"Take this holy sword, a gift from God, with which you will strike down your adversaries."

17 Encouraged by the words of Judas, so noble and so effective in arousing valor and awaking manliness in the souls of the young, they determined not to carry on a campaign but to attack bravely, and to decide the matter, by fighting hand to hand with all courage, because the city and the sanctuary and the temple were in danger. [18]Their concern for wives and children, and also for brethren and relatives, lay upon them less heavily; their greatest and first fear was for the consecrated sanctuary. [19]And those who had to remain in the city were in no little distress, being anxious over the encounter in the open country.

The Defeat and Death of Nicanor

20 When all were now looking forward to the coming decision, and the enemy was already close at hand with their army drawn up for battle, the elephants [e] strategically stationed and the cavalry deployed on the flanks, [21]Mac"cabe'us, perceiving the hosts that were before him and the varied supply of arms and the savagery of the elephants, [e] stretched out his hands toward heaven and called upon the Lord who works wonders; for he knew that it is not by arms, but as the Lord [f] decides, that he gains the victory for those who deserve it. [22]And he called upon him in these words: "O Lord, you sent your angel in the time of Hezeki'ah king of Judea, and he slew fully a hundred and eighty-five thousand in the camp of Sennach'erib. [23]So now, O Sovereign of the heavens, send a good angel to carry terror and trembling before us. [24]By the might of your arm may these blasphemers who come

against your holy people be struck down." With these words he ended his prayer.

25 Nica'nor and his men advanced with trumpets and battle songs; [26]and Judas and his men met the enemy in battle with invocation to God and prayers. [27]So, fighting with their hands and praying to God in their hearts, they laid low no less than thirty-five thousand men, and were greatly gladdened by God's manifestation.

28 When the action was over and they were returning with joy, they recognized Nica'nor, lying dead, in full armor. [29]Then there was shouting and tumult, and they blessed the Sovereign Lord in the language of their fathers. [30]And the man who was ever in body and soul the defender of his fellow citizens, the man who maintained his youthful good will toward his countrymen, ordered them to cut off Nica'nor's head and arm and carry them to Jerusalem. [31]And when he arrived there and had called his countrymen together and stationed the priests before the altar, he sent for those who were in the citadel. [32]He showed them the vile Nica'nor's head and that profane man's arm, which had been boastfully stretched out against the holy house of the Almighty; [33]and he cut out the tongue of the ungodly Nica'nor and said that he would give it piecemeal to the birds and hang up these rewards of his folly opposite the sanctuary. [34]And they all, looking to heaven, blessed the Lord who had manifested himself, saying, "Blessed is he who has kept his own place undefiled." [35]And he hung Nica'nor's head from the citadel, a clear and conspicuous sign to every one of the help of the Lord. [36]And they all decreed by public vote never to let this day go unobserved, but to celebrate the thirteenth day of the twelfth month—which is called Adar' in the Syrian language—the day before Mor'decai's day.

The Compiler's Epilogue

37 This, then, is how matters turned out with Nica'nor. And from that time the city has been in the possession of the Hebrews. So I too will here end my story. [38]If it is well told and to the point, that is what I myself desired; if it is poorly done and mediocre, that was the best I could do. [39]For just as it is harmful to drink wine alone, or, again, to drink water alone, while wine mixed with water is sweet and delicious and enhances one's enjoyment, so also the style of the story delights the ears of those who read the work. And here will be the end.

---

[d] The Greek text here is uncertain.
[e] Gk *beasts.*
[f] Gk *he.*

The
NEW TESTAMENT

OF OUR LORD AND SAVIOR
JESUS CHRIST

Revised Standard Version | *Second Catholic Edition*

TRANSLATED FROM THE GREEK
BEING THE VERSION SET FORTH A.D. 1611
REVISED A.D. 1881 AND A.D. 1901

COMPARED WITH THE MOST ANCIENT AUTHORITIES
AND REVISED A.D. 1946 AND 1966

THE ORIGINAL CATHOLIC EDITION OF THE RSV TRANSLATION
WAS PREPARED BY THE
CATHOLIC BIBLICAL ASSOCIATION OF GREAT BRITAIN

THIS EDITION WAS REVISED ACCORDING TO
LITURGIAM AUTHENTICAM, 2001

The Names and Order of the Books of

THE NEW TESTAMENT

	Page
Matthew	1
Mark	30
Luke	48
John	78
The Acts	100
Romans	126
1 Corinthians	138
2 Corinthians	150
Galatians	157
Ephesians	161
Philippians	165
Colossians	168
1 Thessalonians	171
2 Thessalonians	174

	Page
1 Timothy	176
2 Timothy	179
Titus	181
Philemon	183
Hebrews	184
James	193
1 Peter	196
2 Peter	199
1 John	201
2 John	204
3 John	205
Jude	206
Revelation of John (The Apocalypse)	207

THE NEW TESTAMENT

THE GOSPEL ACCORDING TO
MATTHEW

The Genealogy of Jesus Christ

1 The book of the genealogy of Jesus Christ, the son of David, the son of Abraham. *

2 Abraham was the father of Isaac, and Isaac the father of Jacob, and Jacob the father of Judah and his brothers, ³and Judah the father of Per'ez and Ze'rah by Ta'mar, and Perez the father of Hezron, and Hezron the father of Ram, ᵃ ⁴and Ram ᵃ the father of Ammin'adab, and Amminadab the father of Nahshon, and Nahshon the father of Salmon, ⁵and Salmon the father of Boaz by Ra'hab, and Boaz the father of O'bed by Ruth, and Obed the father of Jesse, ⁶and Jesse the father of David the king.

And David was the father of Solomon by the wife of Uri'ah, ⁷and Solomon the father of Reho-bo'am, and Rehoboam the father of Abi'jah, and Abijah the father of Asa, ᵇ ⁸and Asa ᵇ the father of Jehosh'aphat, and Jehoshaphat the father of Jo'ram, and Joram the father of Uzzi'ah, ⁹and Uzzi'ah the father of Jo'tham, and Jotham the father of A'haz, and Ahaz the father of Hezeki'ah, ¹⁰and Hezeki'ah the father of Manas'seh, and Manasseh the father of Amos, ᶜ and Amos ᶜ the father of Josi'ah, ¹¹and Josi'ah the father of Jecho-ni'ah and his brothers, at the time of the deportation to Babylon.

12 And after the deportation to Babylon: Jechoni'ah was the father of She-al'ti-el, ᵈ and She-alti-el ᵈ the father of Zerub'babel, ¹³and Zerub'-babel the father of Abi'ud, and Abiud the father of Eli'akim, and Eliakim the father of A'zor, ¹⁴and A'zor the father of Za'dok, and Zadok the father of A'chim, and Achim the father of Eli'ud, ¹⁵and Eli'ud the father of Elea'zar, and Eleazar the father of Matthan, and Matthan the father of Jacob, ¹⁶and Jacob the father of Joseph the husband of Mary, of whom Jesus was born, who is called Christ. †

17 So all the generations from Abraham to David were fourteen generations, and from David to the deportation to Babylon fourteen generations, and from the deportation to Babylon to the Christ fourteen generations.

The Birth of Jesus Christ

18 Now the birth of Jesus Christ ᶠ took place in this way. When his mother Mary had been betrothed to Joseph, before they came together she was found to be with child of the Holy Spirit; ¹⁹and her husband Joseph, being a just man and

unwilling to put her to shame, resolved to send her away quietly. ²⁰But as he considered this, behold, an angel of the Lord appeared to him in a dream, saying, "Joseph, son of David, do not fear to take Mary your wife, for that which is conceived in her is of the Holy Spirit; ²¹she will bear a son, and you shall call his name Jesus, for he will save his people from their sins." ²²All this took place to fulfil what the Lord had spoken by the prophet:

²³"Behold, a virgin shall conceive and bear a son,
   and his name shall be called Emmanuel"

(which means, God with us). ²⁴When Joseph woke from sleep, he did as the angel of the Lord commanded him; he took his wife, ²⁵but knew her not until she had borne a son; ‡ and he called his name Jesus.

The Visit of the Wise Men

2 Now when Jesus was born in Bethlehem of Judea in the days of Herod the king, behold, Wise Men from the East came to Jerusalem, saying, ²"Where is he who has been born king of the Jews? For we have seen his star in the East, and have come to worship him." ³When Herod the king heard this, he was troubled, and all Jerusalem with him; ⁴and assembling all the chief priests and scribes of the people, he inquired of them where the Christ was to be born. ⁵They told him, "In Bethlehem of Judea; for so it is written by the prophet:

⁶'And you, O Bethlehem, in the land of Judah,
   are by no means least among the rulers of
      Judah;

ᵃ Greek Aram.
ᵇ Greek Asaph.
ᶜ Other authorities read Amon.
ᵈ Greek Salathiel.
ᶠ Other ancient authorities read of the Christ.
1:1–17: Lk 3:23–38.
1:3–6: Ruth 4:18–22; 1 Chron 2:1–15.
1:11: 2 Kings 24:14; Jer 27:20.
1:18: Lk 1:26–38.
1:21: Lk 2:21; Jn 1:29; Acts 13:23.
1:23: Is 7:14.
2:1: Lk 2:4–7; 1:5.
2:2: Jer 23:5; Zech 9:9; Mk 15:2; Jn 1:49; Num 24:17.
2:5: Jn 7:42.
2:6: Mic 5:2.

* 1:1: The genealogy is given to show that Jesus had the descent required for Messiahship, i.e., from Abraham and, in particular, from David the King.

† 1:16: Joseph's, not Mary's, descent is given here, as the Jews did not usually reckon descent through the mother. Joseph was the legal and presumed father, and it was this fact that conferred rights of inheritance, in this case, the fulfilment of the Messianic promises.

‡ 1:25: This means only that Joseph had nothing to do with the conception of Jesus. It implies nothing as to what happened afterward.

for from you shall come a ruler
who will govern my people Israel.' "

7 Then Herod summoned the Wise Men secretly and ascertained from them what time the star appeared; [8]and he sent them to Bethlehem, saying, "Go and search diligently for the child, and when you have found him bring me word, that I too may come and worship him." [9]When they had heard the king they went their way; and behold, the star which they had seen in the East went before them, till it came to rest over the place where the child was. [10]When they saw the star, they rejoiced exceedingly with great joy; [11]and going into the house they saw the child with Mary his mother, and they fell down and worshiped him. Then, opening their treasures, they offered him gifts, gold and frankincense and myrrh. [12]And being warned in a dream not to return to Herod, they departed to their own country by another way.

The Escape to Egypt

13 Now when they had departed, behold, an angel of the Lord appeared to Joseph in a dream and said, "Rise, take the child and his mother, and flee to Egypt, and remain there till I tell you; for Herod is about to search for the child, to destroy him." [14]And he rose and took the child and his mother by night, and departed to Egypt, [15]and remained there until the death of Herod. This was to fulfil what the Lord had spoken by the prophet, "Out of Egypt have I called my son."

16 Then Herod, when he saw that he had been tricked by the Wise Men, was in a furious rage, and he sent and killed all the male children in Bethlehem and in all that region who were two years old or under, according to the time which he had ascertained from the Wise Men. [17]Then was fulfilled what was spoken by the prophet Jeremiah:

[18]"A voice was heard in Ra'mah,
wailing and loud lamentation,
Rachel weeping for her children;
she refused to be consoled,
because they were no more."

The Return from Egypt

19 But when Herod died, behold, an angel of the Lord appeared in a dream to Joseph in Egypt, saying, [20]"Rise, take the child and his mother, and go to the land of Israel, for those who sought the child's life are dead." [21]And he rose and took the child and his mother, and went to the land of Israel. [22]But when he heard that Archela'us reigned over Judea in place of his father Herod, he was afraid to go there, and being warned in a dream he withdrew to the district of Galilee. [23]And he went and dwelt in a city called Nazareth, that what was spoken by the prophets might be fulfilled. "He shall be called a Nazarene."

The Preaching of John the Baptist

3 In those days came John the Baptist, preaching in the wilderness of Judea, [2]"Repent, * for the kingdom of heaven is at hand." [3]For this is he who was spoken of by the prophet Isaiah when he said,

"The voice of one crying in the wilderness:
Prepare the way of the Lord,
make his paths straight."

[4]Now John wore a garment of camel's hair, and a leather belt around his waist; and his food was locusts and wild honey. [5]Then went out to him Jerusalem and all Judea and all the region about the Jordan, [6]and they were baptized by him in the river Jordan, confessing their sins. †

7 But when he saw many of the Pharisees and Sad'ducees coming for baptism, he said to them, "You brood of vipers! Who warned you to flee from the wrath to come? [8]Bear fruit that befits repentance, [9]and do not presume to say to yourselves, 'We have Abraham as our father'; for I tell you, God is able from these stones to raise up children to Abraham. [10]Even now the axe is laid to the root of the trees; every tree therefore that does not bear good fruit is cut down and thrown into the fire.

11 "I baptize you with water for repentance, but he who is coming after me is mightier than I, whose sandals I am not worthy to carry; he will baptize you with the Holy Spirit and with fire. [12]His winnowing fork is in his hand, and he will clear his threshing floor and gather his wheat into the granary, but the chaff he will burn with unquenchable fire."

The Baptism of Jesus

13 Then Jesus came from Galilee to the Jordan to John, to be baptized by him. [14]John would have prevented him, saying, "I need to be baptized by you, and do you come to me?" [15]But Jesus answered him, "Let it be so now; for thus it is fitting for us to fulfil all righteousness." Then he consented. ‡ [16]And when Jesus was baptized, he went up immediately from the water, and behold, the heavens were opened [g] and he saw the Spirit

---

[g] Other ancient authorities add *to him.*
2:11: Mt 1:18; 12:46.
2:12: Mt 2:22; Acts 10:22; Heb 11:7.
2:15: Hos 11:1; Ex 4:22.
2:18: Jer 31:15.
2:19: Mt 1:20; 2:13.
2:23: Lk 1:26; Is 11:1; Mk 1:24.
3:1–12: Mk 1:3–8; Lk 3:2–17; Jn 1:6–8, 19–28.
3:2: Mt 4:17; Dan 2:44; 4:17; Mt 10:7.
3:3: Is 40:3.
3:4: 2 Kings 1:8; Zech 13:4; Lev 11:22.
3:7: Mt 12:34; 23:33; 1 Thess 1:10.
3:9: Jn 8:33; Rom 4:16.
3:10: Mt 7:19.
3:12: Mt 13:30.
3:13–17: Mk 1:9–11; Lk 3:21–22; Jn 1:31–34.
* 3:2: *Repent* implies an internal change of heart.
† 3:6: Not a Christian baptism but a preparation for it.
‡ 3:15: Though without sin, Jesus wished to be baptized by John, as this was the final preparation for his mission as Messiah.

of God descending like a dove, and alighting on him; [17]and behold, a voice from heaven, saying, "This is my beloved Son, [h] with whom I am well pleased."

The Temptation of Jesus

4 Then Jesus was led up by the Spirit into the wilderness to be tempted by the devil. [2]And he fasted forty days and forty nights, and afterward he was hungry. [3]And the tempter came and said to him, "If you are the Son of God, command these stones to become loaves of bread." [4]But he answered, "It is written,

'Man shall not live by bread alone,
but by every word that proceeds from the
mouth of God.' "

[5]Then the devil took him to the holy city, and set him on the pinnacle of the temple, [6]and said to him, "If you are the Son of God, throw yourself down; for it is written,

'He will give his angels charge of you,'
and
'On their hands they will bear you up,
lest you strike your foot against a stone.' "

[7]Jesus said to him, "Again it is written, 'You shall not tempt the Lord your God.' " [8]Again, the devil took him to a very high mountain, and showed him all the kingdoms of the world and the glory of them; [9]and he said to him, "All these I will give you, if you will fall down and worship me." [10]Then Jesus said to him, "Begone, Satan! for it is written,

'You shall worship the Lord your God
and him only shall you serve.' "

[11]Then the devil left him, and behold, angels came and ministered to him.

Jesus Begins Preaching in Galilee

12 Now when he heard that John had been arrested, he withdrew into Galilee; [13]and leaving Nazareth he went and dwelt in Caper'na-um by the sea, in the territory of Zeb'ulun and Naph'tali, [14]that what was spoken by the prophet Isaiah might be fulfilled:

[15]"The land of Zeb'ulun and the land of
Naph'tali,
toward the sea, across the Jordan,
Galilee of the Gentiles—
[16]the people who sat in darkness
have seen a great light,
and for those who sat in the region and shadow
of death
light has dawned."

[17]From that time Jesus began to preach, saying, "Repent, for the kingdom of heaven is at hand."

Jesus Calls the First Disciples

18 As he walked by the Sea of Galilee, he saw two brothers, Simon who is called Peter and Andrew his brother, casting a net into the sea; for they were fishermen. [19]And he said to them, "Follow me, and I will make you fishers of men."

[20]Immediately they left their nets and followed him. [21]And going on from there he saw two other brothers, James the son of Zeb'edee and John his brother, in the boat with Zebedee their father, mending their nets, and he called them. [22]Immediately they left the boat and their father, and followed him.

Jesus Ministers to Crowds of people

23 And he went about all Galilee, teaching in their synagogues and preaching the gospel of the kingdom and healing every disease and every infirmity among the people. [24]So his fame spread throughout all Syria, and they brought him all the sick, those afflicted with various diseases and pains, demoniacs, epileptics, and paralytics, and he healed them. [25]And great crowds followed him from Galilee and the Decap'olis and Jerusalem and Judea and from beyond the Jordan.

The Beatitudes

5 Seeing the crowds, he went up on the mountain, and when he sat down his disciples came to him. [2]And he opened his mouth and taught them, saying:

3 "Blessed are the poor in spirit, for theirs is the kingdom of heaven.

4 "Blessed are those who mourn, for they shall be comforted.

5 "Blessed are the meek, for they shall inherit the earth.

6 "Blessed are those who hunger and thirst for righteousness, for they shall be satisfied.

7 "Blessed are the merciful, for they shall obtain mercy.

8 "Blessed are the pure in heart, for they shall see God.

9 "Blessed are the peacemakers, for they shall be called sons of God.

10 "Blessed are those who are persecuted for righteousness' sake, for theirs is the kingdom of heaven.

11 "Blessed are you when men revile you and persecute you and utter all kinds of evil against

---

[h] Or my Son, my (or the) Beloved.
3:17: Mt 12:18; 17:5; Mk 9:7; Lk 9:35; Ps 2:7; Is 42:1.
4:1–11: Mk 1:12–13; Lk 4:1–13; Heb 2:18; 4:15.
4:2: Ex 34:28; 1 Kings 19:8.
4:4: Deut 8:3.
4:5: Mt 27:53; Neh 11:1; Dan 9:24; Rev 21:10.
4:6: Ps 91:11–12.
4:7: Deut 6:16.
4:10: Deut 6:13; Mk 8:33.
4:11: Mt 26:53; Lk 22:43.
4:12: Mk 1:14; Lk 4:14; Mt 14:3; Jn 1:43.
4:13: Jn 2:12; Mk 1:21; Lk 4:23.
4:15: Is 9:1–2.
4:17: Mk 1:15; Mt 3:2; 10:7.
4:18–22: Mk 1:16–20; Lk 5:1–11; Jn 1:35–42.
4:23–25: Mk 1:39; Lk 4:15, 44; Mt 9:35; Mk 3:7–8; Lk 6:17.
5:1–12: Lk 6:17, 20–23; Mk 3:13; Jn 6:3.
5:3: Mk 10:14; Lk 22:29.
5:4: Is 61:2; Jn 16:20, Rev 7:17.
5:5: Ps 37:11.
5:6: Is 55:1–2; Jn 4:14; 6:48–51.
5:8: Ps 24:4; Heb 12:14; 1 Jn 3:2; Rev 22:4.
5:10: 1 Pet 3:14; 4:14.

you falsely on my account. [12]Rejoice and be glad, for your reward is great in heaven, for so men persecuted the prophets who were before you.

Salt and Light

13 "You are the salt of the earth; but if salt has lost its taste, how shall its saltiness be restored? It is no longer good for anything except to be thrown out and trodden under foot by men.

14 "You are the light of the world. A city set on a hill cannot be hidden. [15]Nor do men light a lamp and put it under a bushel, but on a stand, and it gives light to all in the house. [16]Let your light so shine before men, that they may see your good works and give glory to your Father who is in heaven.

The Fulfillment of the Law and the Prophets

17 "Do not think that I have come to abolish the law and the prophets; I have come not to abolish them but to fulfil them. * [18]For truly, I say to you, till heaven and earth pass away, not an iota, not a dot, will pass from the law until all is accomplished. [19]Whoever then relaxes one of the least of these commandments and teaches men so, shall be called least in the kingdom of heaven; but he who does them and teaches them shall be called great in the kingdom of heaven. [20]For I tell you, unless your righteousness exceeds that of the scribes and Pharisees, you will never enter the kingdom of heaven.

Concerning Anger

21 "You have heard that it was said to the men of old, 'You shall not kill; and whoever kills shall be liable to judgment.' [22]But I say to you that every one who is angry with his brother [i] shall be liable to judgment; whoever insults [j] his brother shall be liable to the council, and whoever says, 'You fool!' shall be liable to the hell [k] of fire. [23]So if you are offering your gift at the altar, and there remember that your brother has something against you, [24]leave your gift there before the altar and go; first be reconciled to your brother, and then come and offer your gift. [25]Make friends quickly with your accuser, while you are going with him to court, lest your accuser hand you over to the judge, and the judge to the guard, and you be put in prison; [26]truly, I say to you, you will never get out till you have paid the last penny.

Concerning Adultery

27 "You have heard that it was said, 'You shall not commit adultery.' [28]But I say to you that every one who looks at a woman lustfully has already committed adultery with her in his heart. [29]If your right eye causes you to sin, pluck it out and throw it away; it is better that you lose one of your members than that your whole body be thrown into hell. [k] [†] [30]And if your right hand causes you to sin, cut it off and throw it away; it is better that you lose one of your members than that your whole body go into hell. [k]

Concerning Divorce

31 "It was also said, 'Whoever divorces his wife, let him give her a certificate of divorce.' [32]But I say to you that every one who divorces his wife, except on the ground of unchastity, ‡ makes her an adulteress; and whoever marries a divorced woman commits adultery.

Concerning Swearing Oaths

33 "Again you have heard that it was said to the men of old, 'You shall not swear falsely, but shall perform to the Lord what you have sworn.' [34]But I say to you, Do not swear at all, either by heaven, for it is the throne of God, [35]or by the earth, for it is his footstool, or by Jerusalem, for it is the city of the great King. [36]And do not swear by your head, for you cannot make one hair white or black. [37]Let what you say be simply 'Yes' or 'No'; anything more than this comes from the Evil One. [1]

Concerning Retaliation

38 "You have heard that it was said, 'An eye for an eye and a tooth for a tooth.' [39]But I say to you, Do not resist one who is evil. But if any one strikes you on the right cheek, turn to him the other also; [40]and if any one would sue you and take your coat, let him have your cloak as well; [41]and if any one forces you to go one mile, go with him two miles. [42]Give to him who begs from you, and do not refuse him who would borrow from you.

Love for Enemies

43 "You have heard that it was said, 'You shall love your neighbor and hate your enemy.' [44]But I say to you, Love your enemies and pray for those who persecute you, [45]so that you may be sons of your Father who is in heaven; for he makes his

---

[i] Other ancient authorities insert *without cause.*
[j] Greek *says Raca to* (an obscure term of abuse).
[k] Greek *Gehenna.*
[1] Or *Evil.*
5:12: 2 Chron 36:16; Mt 23:37; Acts 7:52; 1 Thess 2:15; Jas 5:10.
5:13: Mk 9:49–50; Lk 14:34–35.
5:14: Eph 5:8; Phil 2:15; Jn 8:12.
5:15–16: Lk 11:33; Mk 4:21; 1 Pet 2:12.
5:18: Lk 16:17; Mk 13:31.
5:19: Jas 2:10.
5:21: Ex 20:13; Deut 5:17; 16:18.
5:25–26: Lk 12:57–59.
5:27: Ex 20:14; Deut 5:18.
5:29–30: Mk 9:43–48; Mt 18:8–9.
5:31–32: Lk 16:18; Mk 10:11–12; Mt 19:9; 1 Cor 7:10–11; Deut 24:1–4.
5:33–37: Mt 23:16–22; Jas 5:12; Lev 19:12; Num 30:2; Deut 23:21.
5:35: Is 66:1; Acts 7:49; Ps 48:2.
5:38: Ex 21:24; Lev 24:20; Deut 19:21.
5:39–42: Lk 6:29–30; 1 Cor 6:7; Rom 12:17; 1 Pet 2:19; 3:9; Prov 24:29.
5:43–48: Mt 6:27–28, 32–36; Lev 19:18; Prov 25:21–22.
* **5:17:** Jesus came to bring the old law to its natural fulfilment in the new, while discarding what had become obsolete; cf. Jn 4:21.
† **5:29:** An exaggeration to emphasize the need to avoid occasions of sin.
‡ **5:32,** *unchastity*: The Greek word used here appears to refer to marriages that were not legally marriages because they were either within the forbidden degrees of consanguinity (Lev 18:6–16) or contracted with a Gentile. The phrase *except on the ground of unchastity* does not occur in the parallel passage in Lk 16:18. See also Mt 19:9 (Mk 10:11–12), and especially 1 Cor 7:10–11, which shows that the prohibition is unconditional.

sun rise on the evil and on the good, and sends rain on the just and on the unjust. ⁴⁶For if you love those who love you, what reward have you? Do not even the tax collectors do the same? ⁴⁷And if you salute only your brethren, what more are you doing than others? Do not even the Gentiles do the same? ⁴⁸You, therefore, must be perfect, as your heavenly Father is perfect.

Concerning Almsgiving

6 "Beware of practicing your piety before men in order to be seen by them; for then you will have no reward from your Father who is in heaven.

2 "Thus, when you give alms, sound no trumpet before you, as the hypocrites do in the synagogues and in the streets, that they may be praised by men. Truly, I say to you, they have their reward. ³But when you give alms, do not let your left hand know what your right hand is doing, ⁴so that your alms may be in secret; and your Father who sees in secret will reward you.

Concerning Prayer

5 "And when you pray, you must not be like the hypocrites; for they love to stand and pray in the synagogues and at the street corners, that they may be seen by men. Truly, I say to you, they have their reward. ⁶But when you pray, go into your room and shut the door and pray to your Father who is in secret; and your Father who sees in secret will reward you. *

7 "And in praying do not heap up empty phrases as the Gentiles do; for they think that they will be heard for their many words. ⁸Do not be like them, for your Father knows what you need before you ask him. ⁹Pray then like this:

Our Father who art in heaven,
Hallowed be thy name.
¹⁰Thy kingdom come.
Thy will be done
On earth as it is in heaven.
¹¹Give us this day our daily bread; ᵐ
¹²And forgive us our trespasses
As we forgive those who trespass against us;
¹³And lead us not into temptation,
But deliver us from evil. ⁿ

¹⁴For if you forgive men their trespasses, your heavenly Father also will forgive you; ¹⁵but if you do not forgive men their trespasses, neither will your Father forgive your trespasses.

Concerning Fasting

16 "And when you fast, do not look dismal, like the hypocrites, for they disfigure their faces that their fasting may be seen by men. Truly, I say to you, they have their reward. ¹⁷But when you fast, anoint your head and wash your face, ¹⁸that your fasting may not be seen by men but by your Father who is in secret; and your Father who sees in secret will reward you.

Concerning Treasures

19 "Do not lay up for yourselves treasures on earth, where moth and rust ° consume and where thieves break in and steal, ²⁰but lay up for yourselves treasures in heaven, where neither moth nor rust ° consumes and where thieves do not break in and steal. ²¹For where your treasure is, there will your heart be also.

The Sound Eye

22 "The eye is the lamp of the body. So, if your eye is sound, your whole body will be full of light; ²³but if your eye is not sound, your whole body will be full of darkness. If then the light in you is darkness, how great is the darkness!

Serving Two Masters

24 "No one can serve two masters; for either he will hate the one and love the other, or he will be devoted to the one and despise the other. You cannot serve God and mammon. †

Do Not Be Anxious

25 "Therefore I tell you, do not be anxious about your life, what you shall eat or what you shall drink, nor about your body, what you shall put on. Is not life more than food, and the body more than clothing? ²⁶Look at the birds of the air: they neither sow nor reap nor gather into barns, and yet your heavenly Father feeds them. Are you not of more value than they? ²⁷And which of you by being anxious can add one cubit to his span of life? ᵖ ²⁸And why are you anxious about clothing? Consider the lilies of the field, how they grow; they neither toil nor spin; ²⁹yet I tell you, even Solomon in all his glory was not clothed like one of these. ³⁰But if God so clothes the grass of the field, which today is alive and tomorrow is thrown into the oven, will he not much more clothe you, O you of little faith? ³¹Therefore do not be anxious, saying, 'What shall we eat?' or 'What shall we drink?' or 'What shall we wear?' ³²For the Gentiles

---

ᵐ Or *our bread for the morrow.*
ⁿ Or *the evil one.* Other authorities, some ancient, add, in some form, *For thine is the kingdom and the power and the glory, for ever. Amen.*
° Or *worm.*
ᵖ Or *to his stature.*
5:48: Lev 19:2.
6:1: Mt 23:5.
6:4: Col 3:23–24.
6:5: Mk 11:25; Lk 18:10–14.
6:7: 1 Kings 18:25–29.
6:8: Mt 6:32; Lk 12:30.
6:9–13: Lk 11:2–4.
6:13: 2 Thess 3:3; Jn 17:15; Jas 1:13.
6:14–15: Mt 18:35; Mk 11:25; Eph 4:32; Col 3:13.
6:16: Is 58:5.
6:18: Mt 6:4, 6.
6:19–21: Lk 12:33–34; Mk 10:21; 1 Tim 6:17–19; Jas 5:1–3.
6:22–23: Lk 11:34–36; Mt 20:15; Mk 7:22.
6:24: Lk 16:13.
6:25–33: Lk 12:22–31; 10:41; 12:11; Phil 4:6; 1 Pet 5:7.
6:26: Mt 10:29.
6:27: Ps 39:5.
6:29: 1 Kings 10:4–7.
6:30: Mt 8:26; 14:31; 16:8.
* 6:6: This does not, of course, exclude public worship but ostentatious prayer.
† 6:24, *mammon:* i.e., riches.

seek all these things; and your heavenly Father knows that you need them all. [33]But seek first his kingdom and his righteousness, and all these things shall be yours as well.

34 "Therefore do not be anxious about tomorrow, for tomorrow will be anxious for itself. Let the day's own trouble be sufficient for the day.

Judging Others

7 "Judge not, that you be not judged. [2]For with the judgment you pronounce you will be judged, and the measure you give will be the measure you get. [3]Why do you see the speck that is in your brother's eye, but do not notice the log that is in your own eye? [4]Or how can you say to your brother, 'Let me take the speck out of your eye,' when there is the log in your own eye? [5]You hypocrite, first take the log out of your own eye, and then you will see clearly to take the speck out of your brother's eye.

Profaning the Holy

6 "Do not give dogs what is holy; and do not throw your pearls before swine, lest they trample them under foot and turn to attack you.

Ask, Seek, Knock

7 "Ask, and it will be given you; seek, and you will find; knock, and it will be opened to you. [8]For every one who asks receives, and he who seeks finds, and to him who knocks it will be opened. [9]Or what man of you, if his son asks him for bread, will give him a stone? [10]Or if he asks for a fish, will give him a serpent? [11]If you then, who are evil, know how to give good gifts to your children, how much more will your Father who is in heaven give good things to those who ask him! [12]So whatever you wish that men would do to you, do so to them; for this is the law and the prophets.

The Narrow Gate

13 "Enter by the narrow gate; for the gate is wide and the way is easy, [q] that leads to destruction, and those who enter by it are many. [14]For the gate is narrow and the way is hard, that leads to life, and those who find it are few.

False Prophets

15 "Beware of false prophets, who come to you in sheep's clothing but inwardly are ravenous wolves. [16]You will know them by their fruits. Are grapes gathered from thorns, or figs from thistles? [17]So, every sound tree bears good fruit, but the bad tree bears evil fruit. [18]A sound tree cannot bear evil fruit, nor can a bad tree bear good fruit. [19]Every tree that does not bear good fruit is cut down and thrown into the fire. [20]Thus you will know them by their fruits.

Concerning Self-Deception

21 "Not every one who says to me, 'Lord, Lord,' shall enter the kingdom of heaven, but he who does the will of my Father who is in heaven. [22]On that day many will say to me, 'Lord, Lord, did we not prophesy in your name, and cast out demons

in your name, and do many mighty works in your name?' [23]And then will I declare to them, 'I never knew you; depart from me, you evildoers.'

Hearers and Doers

24 "Every one then who hears these words of mine and does them will be like a wise man who built his house upon the rock; [25]and the rain fell, and the floods came, and the winds blew and beat upon that house, but it did not fall, because it had been founded on the rock. [26]And every one who hears these words of mine and does not do them will be like a foolish man who built his house upon the sand; [27]and the rain fell, and the floods came, and the winds blew and beat against that house, and it fell; and great was the fall of it."

28 And when Jesus finished these sayings, the crowds were astonished at his teaching, [29]for he taught them as one who had authority, and not as their scribes.

Jesus Cleanses a Leper

8 When he came down from the mountain, great crowds followed him; [2]and behold, a leper came to him and knelt before him, saying, "Lord, if you will, you can make me clean." [3]And he stretched out his hand and touched him, saying, "I will; be clean." And immediately his leprosy was cleansed. * [4]And Jesus said to him, "See that you say nothing to any one; but go, show yourself to the priest, and offer the gift that Moses commanded, for a proof to the people." [x]

Jesus Heals a Centurion's Servant

5 As he entered Caper'na-um, a centurion came forward to him, begging him [6]and saying, "Lord, my servant is lying paralyzed at home, in terrible distress." [7]And he said to him, "I will come and heal him." [8]But the centurion answered him, "Lord, I am not worthy to have you come under my roof; but only say the word, and my servant will be healed. [9]For I am a man under authority, with soldiers under me; and I say to one, 'Go,' and he goes, and to another, 'Come,' and he comes, and

---

[q] Other ancient authorities read *for the way is wide and easy.*
[x] Greek *to them.*
6:33: Mt 19:28; Mk 10:29–30; Lk 18:29–30.
7:1–2: Lk 6:37–38; Mk 4:24; Rom 2:1; 14:10.
7:3–5: Lk 6:41–42.
7:7–11: Lk 11:9–13; Mk 11:24; Jn 15:7; 16:23–24; Jas 4:3; 1 Jn 3:22; 5:14.
7:12: Lk 6:31.
7:13–14: Lk 13:23–24; Jer 21:8; Deut 30:19; Jn 14:6; 10:7.
7:15: Mt 24:11, 24; Ezek 22:27; 1 Jn 4:1; Jn 10:12.
7:16–20: Lk 6:43–44; Mt 12:33–35; Mt 3:10; Jas 3:12; Lk 13:7.
7:21: Lk 6:46.
7:22–23: Lk 13:26–27; Mt 25:12; Ps 6:8.
7:24–27: Lk 6:47–49; Jas 1:22–25.
7:28–29: Mk 1:22; Lk 4:32; Mt 11:1; 13:53; 19:1; 26:1.
8:2–4: Mk 1:40–44; Lk 5:12–14.
8:2: Mt 9:18; 15:25; 18:26; 20:20; Jn 9:38.
8:4: Mk 3:12; 5:43; 7:36; 8:30; 9:9; Lev 14:2.
8:5–13: Lk 7:1–10; Jn 4:46–53.
* **8:3:** The miracles of Jesus were never performed to amaze people and shock them into belief. They were worked with a view to a real strengthening of faith in the recipient or beholder, from whom the proper dispositions were required.

to my slave, 'Do this,' and he does it." [10]When Jesus heard him, he marveled, and said to those who followed him, "Truly, I say to you, not even **ᵍ** in Israel have I found such faith. [11]I tell you, many will come from east and west and sit at table with Abraham, Isaac, and Jacob in the kingdom of heaven, [12]while the sons of the kingdom will be thrown into the outer darkness; there men will weep and gnash their teeth." [13]And to the centurion Jesus said, "Go; let it be done for you as you have believed." And the servant was healed at that very moment.

Jesus Heals Many at Peter's House

14 And when Jesus entered Peter's house, he saw his mother-in-law lying sick with a fever; [15]he touched her hand, and the fever left her, and she rose and served him. [16]That evening they brought to him many who were possessed with demons; and he cast out the spirits with a word, and healed all who were sick. [17]This was to fulfil what was spoken by the prophet Isaiah, "He took our infirmities and bore our diseases."

Would-be Followers of Jesus

18 Now when Jesus saw great crowds around him, he gave orders to go over to the other side. [19]And a scribe came up and said to him, "Teacher, I will follow you wherever you go." [20]And Jesus said to him, "Foxes have holes, and birds of the air have nests; but the Son of man has nowhere to lay his head." [21]Another of the disciples said to him, "Lord, let me first go and bury my father." [22]But Jesus said to him, "Follow me, and leave the dead to bury their own dead."

Jesus Calms the Storm at Sea

23 And when he got into the boat, his disciples followed him. [24]And behold, there arose a great storm on the sea, so that the boat was being swamped by the waves; but he was asleep. [25]And they went and woke him, saying, "Save us, Lord; we are perishing." [26]And he said to them, "Why are you afraid, O men of little faith?" Then he rose and rebuked the winds and the sea; and there was a great calm. [27]And the men marveled, saying, "What sort of man is this, that even winds and sea obey him?"

Jesus Heals the Gadarene Demoniacs

28 And when he came to the other side, to the country of the Gad'arenes, **ᵗ** two demoniacs met him, coming out of the tombs, so fierce that no one could pass that way. [29]And behold, they cried out, "What have you to do with us, O Son of God? Have you come here to torment us before the time?" * [30]Now a herd of many swine was feeding at some distance from them. [31]And the demons begged him, "If you cast us out, send us away into the herd of swine." [32]And he said to them, "Go." So they came out and went into the swine; and behold, the whole herd rushed down the steep bank into the sea, and perished in the waters.

[33]The herdsmen fled, and going into the city they told everything, and what had happened to the demoniacs. [34]And behold, all the city came out to meet Jesus; and when they saw him, they begged him to leave their neighborhood.

Jesus Heals a Paralytic

9 And getting into a boat he crossed over and came to his own city. [2]And behold, they brought to him a paralytic, lying on his bed; and when Jesus saw their faith, he said to the paralytic, "Take heart, my son; your sins are forgiven." [3]And behold, some of the scribes said to themselves, "This man is blaspheming." [4]But Jesus, knowing **ᵘ** their thoughts, said, "Why do you think evil in your hearts? [5]For which is easier, to say, 'Your sins are forgiven,' or to say, 'Rise and walk'? [6]But that you may know that the Son of man has authority on earth to forgive sins"—he then said to the paralytic—"Rise, take up your bed and go home." [7]And he rose and went home. [8]When the crowds saw it, they were afraid, and they glorified God, who had given such authority to men.

The Call of Matthew

9 As Jesus passed on from there, he saw a man called Matthew sitting at the tax office; and he said to him, "Follow me." And he rose and followed him.

10 And as he sat at table **ᵛ** in the house, behold, many tax collectors and sinners came and sat down with Jesus and his disciples. [11]And when the Pharisees saw this, they said to his disciples, "Why does your teacher eat with tax collectors and sinners?" [12]But when he heard it, he said, "Those who are well have no need of a physician, but those who are sick. [13]Go and learn what this means, 'I desire mercy, and not sacrifice.' For I came not to call the righteous, but sinners."

The Question about Fasting

14 Then the disciples of John came to him, saying, "Why do we and the Pharisees fast, **ʷ** but your disciples do not fast?" [15]And Jesus said to them, "Can the wedding guests mourn as long as

---

ᵍ Other ancient authorities read *with no one*.
ᵗ Other ancient authorities read *Gergesenes*; some, *Gerasenes*.
ᵘ Other ancient authorities read *seeing*.
ᵛ Greek *reclined*.
ʷ Other ancient authorities add *much* or *often*.
8:11–12: Lk 13:28–29; Is 49:12; 59:19; Mal 1:11; Ps 107:3.
8:12: Mt 13:42, 50; 22;13; 24:51; 25:30; Lk 13:28.
8:14–16: Mk 1:29–34; Lk 4:38–41; Mt 4:23–24.
8:17: Is 53:4.
8:18–22: Lk 9:57–60; Mk 4:35; Lk 8:22.
8:22: Mt 9:9; Jn 1:43; 21:19.
8:23–27: Mk 4:36–41; Lk 8:22–25.
8:26: Mk 6:30; 14:31; 16:8.
8:28–34: Mk 5:1–17; Lk 8:26–37.
8:29: Judg 11:12; 2 Sam 16:10; Mk 1:24; Jn 2:4.
9:1–8: Mk 2:1–12, Lk 5:17–26.
9:2: Mt 9:22; Mk 6:50; 10:49; Jn 16:33; Acts 23:11; Lk 7:48.
9:9–13: Mk 2:13–17; Lk 5:27–32; 15:1–2; 7:34.
9:13: Hos 6:6; Mt 12:7; 1 Tim 1:15.
9:14–17: Mk 2:18–22; Lk 5:33–39; 18:12.
* **8:29,** *before the time*: Before the day of judgment the demons are permitted by God to tempt men and even to possess them.

the bridegroom is with them? The days will come, when the bridegroom is taken away from them, and then they will fast. [16]And no one puts a piece of unshrunk cloth on an old garment, for the patch tears away from the garment, and a worse tear is made. [17]Neither is new wine put into old wineskins; if it is, the skins burst, and the wine is spilled, and the skins are destroyed; but new wine is put into fresh wineskins, and so both are preserved."

A Girl Restored to Life and a Woman Healed

18 While he was thus speaking to them, behold, a ruler came in and knelt before him, saying, "My daughter has just died; but come and lay your hand on her, and she will live." [19]And Jesus rose and followed him, with his disciples. [20]And behold, a woman who had suffered from a hemorrhage for twelve years came up behind him and touched the fringe of his garment; [21]for she said to herself, "If I only touch his garment, I shall be made well." [22]Jesus turned, and seeing her he said, "Take heart, daughter; your faith has made you well." And instantly the woman was made well. [23]And when Jesus came to the ruler's house, and saw the flute players, and the crowd making a tumult, [24]he said, "Depart; for the girl is not dead but sleeping." And they laughed at him. [25]But when the crowd had been put outside, he went in and took her by the hand, and the girl arose. [26]And the report of this went through all that district.

Jesus Heals Two Blind Men

27 And as Jesus passed on from there, two blind men followed him, crying aloud, "Have mercy on us, Son of David." [28]When he entered the house, the blind men came to him; and Jesus said to them, "Do you believe that I am able to do this?" They said to him, "Yes, Lord." [29]Then he touched their eyes, saying, "According to your faith let it be done to you." [30]And their eyes were opened. And Jesus sternly charged them, "See that no one knows it." [31]But they went away and spread his fame through all that district.

Jesus Heals a Man Who Was Mute

32 As they were going away, behold, a mute demoniac was brought to him. [33]And when the demon had been cast out, the mute man spoke; and the crowds marveled, saying, "Never was anything like this seen in Israel." [34]But the Pharisees said, "He casts out demons by the prince of demons."

The Harvest Is Plentiful, the Laborers Are Few

35 And Jesus went about all the cities and villages, teaching in their synagogues and preaching the gospel of the kingdom, and healing every disease and every infirmity. [36]When he saw the crowds, he had compassion for them, because they were harassed and helpless, like sheep without a shepherd. [37]Then he said to his disciples, "The harvest is plentiful, but the laborers are few; [38]pray therefore the Lord of the harvest to send out laborers into his harvest."

The Twelve Disciples

10 And he called to him his twelve disciples and gave them authority over unclean spirits, to cast them out, and to heal every disease and every infirmity. [2]The names of the twelve apostles are these: first, Simon, who is called Peter, and Andrew his brother; James the son of Zeb'edee, and John his brother; [3]Philip and Bartholomew; Thomas and Matthew the tax collector; James the son of Alphae'us, and Thaddae'us;* [4]Simon the Cananaean, and Judas Iscariot, who betrayed him.

The Mission of the Twelve

5 These Twelve Jesus sent out, charging them, "Go nowhere among the Gentiles, and enter no town of the Samaritans,* [6]but go rather to the lost sheep of the house of Israel. [7]And preach as you go, saying, 'The kingdom of heaven is at hand.' [8]Heal the sick, raise the dead, cleanse lepers, cast out demons. You received without pay, give without pay. [9]Take no gold, nor silver, nor copper in your belts, [10]no bag for your journey, nor two tunics, nor sandals, nor a staff; for the laborer deserves his food. [11]And whatever town or village you enter, find out who is worthy in it, and stay with him until you depart. [12]As you enter the house, salute it. [13]And if the house is worthy, let your peace come upon it; but if it is not worthy, let your peace return to you. [14]And if any one will not receive you or listen to your words, shake off the dust from your feet as you leave that house or town. [15]Truly, I say to you, it shall be more tolerable on the day of judgment for the land of Sodom and Gomor'rah than for that town.

Coming Persecutions

16 "Behold, I send you out as sheep in the midst of wolves; so be wise as serpents and

---

* Other ancient authorities read *Lebbaeus* or *Labbaeus called Thaddaeus.*
9:18–26: Mk 5:21–43; Lk 8:40–56.
9:18: Mt 8:2; 15:25; 18:26; 20:20; Jn 9:38.
9:20: Num 15:38; Deut 22:12; Mt 14:36; Mk 3:10.
9:22: Mk 10:52; Lk 7:50; 17:19; Mt 15:28; 9:29.
9:27–31: Mt 20:29–34.
9:32–34: Lk 11:14–15; Mt 12:22–24; Mk 3:22; Jn 7:20.
9:35: Mt 4:23; Mk 6:6.
9:36: Mk 6:34; Mt 14:14; 15:32; Num 27:17; Zech 10:2.
9:37–38: Lk 10:2; Jn 4:35.
10:1–4: Mk 6:7; 3:16–19; Lk 9:1; 6:14–16; Acts 1:13.
10:5: Mk 9:52; Jn 4:9; Acts 8:5, 25.
10:6: Mt 15:24; 10:23.
10:7–8: Lk 9:2; 10:9–11; Mt 4:17.
10:10: 1 Cor 9:14; 1 Tim 5:18.
10:14: Acts 13:51.
10:15: Mt 11:24; Lk 10:12; Jude 7; 2 Pet 2:6.
10:16: Lk 10:3; Gen 3:1; Rom 16:19.
* 10:5: The gospel, the Messianic salvation, had first to be preached and offered to the chosen people, Israel. Later it would be offered to the Gentiles.

innocent as doves. [17]Beware of men; for they will deliver you up to councils, and flog you in their synagogues, [18]and you will be dragged before governors and kings for my sake, to bear testimony before them and the Gentiles. [19]When they deliver you up, do not be anxious about how you are to speak or what you are to say; for what you are to say will be given to you in that hour; [20]for it is not you who speak, but the Spirit of your Father speaking through you. [21]Brother will deliver up brother to death, and the father his child, and children will rise against parents and have them put to death; [22]and you will be hated by all for my name's sake. But he who endures to the end will be saved. [23]When they persecute you in one town, flee to the next; for truly, I say to you, you will not have gone through all the towns of Israel, before the Son of man comes.

24 "A disciple is not above his teacher, nor a servant [y] above his master; [25]it is enough for the disciple to be like his teacher, and the servant [y] like his master. If they have called the master of the house Be-el'zebul, how much more will they malign those of his household.

Whom to Fear

26 "So have no fear of them; for nothing is covered that will not be revealed, or hidden that will not be known. [27]What I tell you in the dark, utter in the light; and what you hear whispered, proclaim upon the housetops. [28]And do not fear those who kill the body but cannot kill the soul; rather fear him who can destroy both soul and body in hell. [z] [29]Are not two sparrows sold for a penny? And not one of them will fall to the ground without your Father's will. [30]But even the hairs of your head are all numbered. [31]Fear not, therefore; you are of more value than many sparrows. [32]So every one who acknowledges me before men, I also will acknowledge before my Father who is in heaven; [33]but whoever denies me before men, I also will deny before my Father who is in heaven.

Taking Up One's Cross

34 "Do not think that I have come to bring peace on earth; I have not come to bring peace, but a sword. [35]For I have come to set a man against his father, and a daughter against her mother, and a daughter-in-law against her mother-in-law; [36]and a man's foes will be those of his own household. [37]He who loves father or mother more than me is not worthy of me; and he who loves son or daughter more than me is not worthy of me; [38]and he who does not take his cross and follow me is not worthy of me. [39]He who finds his life will lose it, and he who loses his life for my sake will find it.

Rewards

40 "He who receives you receives me, and he who receives me receives him who sent me. [41]He who receives a prophet because he is a prophet

shall receive a prophet's reward, and he who receives a righteous man because he is a righteous man shall receive a righteous man's reward. [42]And whoever gives to one of these little ones even a cup of cold water because he is a disciple, truly, I say to you, he shall not lose his reward."

11 And when Jesus had finished instructing his twelve disciples, he went on from there to teach and preach in their cities.

Messengers from John the Baptist

2 Now when John heard in prison about the deeds of the Christ, he sent word by his disciples [3]and said to him, "Are you he who is to come, or shall we look for another?" * [4]And Jesus answered them, "Go and tell John what you hear and see: [5]the blind receive their sight and the lame walk, lepers are cleansed and the deaf hear, and the dead are raised up, and the poor have good news preached to them. [6]And blessed is he who takes no offense at me."

Jesus Praises John the Baptist

7 As they went away, Jesus began to speak to the crowds concerning John: "What did you go out into the wilderness to behold? A reed shaken by the wind? [8]Why then did you go out? To see a man [a] dressed in soft robes? Behold, those who wear soft robes are in kings' houses. [9]Why then did you go out? To see a prophet? [b] Yes, I tell you, and more than a prophet. [10]This is he of whom it is written,

'Behold, I send my messenger before your face,
    who shall prepare your way before you.'

[11]Truly, I say to you, among those born of women there has arisen no one greater than John the Baptist; yet he who is least in the kingdom of

---

[y] Or *slave.*
[z] Greek *Gehenna.*
[a] Or *What then did you go out to see? A man....*
[b] Other ancient authorities read *What then did you go out to see? A prophet?*

10:17–22: Mt 13:9–13; Lk 12:11–12; 21:12–19; Jn 16:2.
10:18: Acts 25:24–26.
10:20: Jn 16:7–11.
10:21: Mt 10:35–36; Lk 12:52–53.
10:22: Jn 15:18; Mt 24:9.
10:23: Mt 16:27; 1 Thess 4:17.
10:24: Lk 6:40; Jn 13:16; 15:20.
10:25: Mt 9:34; 12:24; Mk 3:22; Lk 11:15; 2 Kings 1:2.
10:26–33: Lk 12:2–9.
10:26: Mk 4:22; Lk 8:17; Eph 5:13.
10:28: Heb 10:31.
10:31: Mt 12:12.
10:32: Mk 8:38; Lk 9:26; Rev 3:5; 2 Tim 2:12.
10:34–36: Lk 12:51–53; Mt 10:21; Mk 13:12; Mic 7:6.
10:37–39: Lk 14:25–27; 17:33; 9:23–24; Mt 16:24–25; Mk 8:34–35; Jn 12:25.
10:40: Lk 10:16; Jn 13:20; Gal 4:14; Mk 9:37; Mt 18:5; Lk 9:48.
10:42: Mk 9:41; Mt 25:40.
11:1: Mt 7:28; 13:53; 19:1; 26:1.
11:2–19: Lk 7:18–35.
11:3: Mk 1:7–8; Hab 2:3; Jn 11:27.
11:5: Is 35:5–6; 61:1; Lk 4:18–19.
11:9: Mt 14:5; 21:26; Lk 1:76.
11:10: Mal 3:1; Mk 1:2.

* 11:3: The Baptist expected more obvious signs of the Messiah. By quoting the prophet Isaiah, Jesus showed that he was indeed inaugurating the Messianic kingdom—but by doing good rather than by glorious manifestations or sudden punishments.

heaven is greater than he. [12]From the days of John the Baptist until now the kingdom of heaven has suffered violence, [c] and men of violence take it by force. [13]For all the prophets and the law prophesied until John; [14]and if you are willing to accept it, he is Eli'jah who is to come. [15]He who has ears to hear, [d] let him hear.

16 "But to what shall I compare this generation? It is like children sitting in the market places and calling to their playmates,

[17]'We piped to you, and you did not dance;
  we wailed, and you did not mourn.'

[18]For John came neither eating nor drinking, and they say, 'He has a demon'; [19]the Son of man came eating and drinking, and they say, 'Behold, a glutton and a drunkard, a friend of tax collectors and sinners!' Yet wisdom is justified by her deeds." [e]

Jesus Upbraids the Unrepentant Cities

20 Then he began to upbraid the cities where most of his mighty works had been done, because they did not repent. [21]"Woe to you, Chora'zin! woe to you, Beth-sa'ida! for if the mighty works done in you had been done in Tyre and Si'don, they would have repented long ago in sackcloth and ashes. [22]But I tell you, it shall be more tolerable on the day of judgment for Tyre and Si'don than for you. [23]And you, Caper'na-um, will you be exalted to heaven? You shall be brought down to Hades. For if the mighty works done in you had been done in Sodom, it would have remained until this day. [24]But I tell you that it shall be more tolerable on the day of judgment for the land of Sodom than for you."

Jesus Thanks His Father

25 At that time Jesus declared, "I thank you, Father, Lord of heaven and earth, that you have hidden these things from the wise and understanding and revealed them to infants; [26]yes, Father, for such was your gracious will. [f] [27]All things have been delivered to me by my Father; and no one knows the Son except the Father, and no one knows the Father except the Son and any one to whom the Son chooses to reveal him. [*] [28]Come to me, all who labor and are heavy laden, and I will give you rest. [29]Take my yoke upon you, and learn from me; for I am gentle and lowly in heart, and you will find rest for your souls. [30]For my yoke is easy, and my burden is light."

Plucking Grain on the Sabbath

12 At that time Jesus went through the grainfields on the sabbath; his disciples were hungry, and they began to pluck heads of grain and to eat. [2]But when the Pharisees saw it, they said to him, "Look, your disciples are doing what is not lawful to do on the sabbath." [3]He said to them, "Have you not read what David did, when he was hungry, and those who were with him: [4]how he entered the house of God and ate the showbread, which it was not lawful for him

to eat nor for those who were with him, but only for the priests? [5]Or have you not read in the law how on the sabbath the priests in the temple profane the sabbath, and are guiltless? [6]I tell you, something greater than the temple is here. [7]And if you had known what this means, 'I desire mercy, and not sacrifice,' you would not have condemned the guiltless. [8]For the Son of man is lord of the sabbath."

The Man with a Withered Hand

9 And he went on from there, and entered their synagogue. [10]And behold, there was a man with a withered hand. And they asked him, "Is it lawful to heal on the sabbath?" so that they might accuse him. [11]He said to them, "What man of you, if he has one sheep and it falls into a pit on the sabbath, will not lay hold of it and lift it out? [12]Of how much more value is a man than a sheep! So it is lawful to do good on the sabbath." [13]Then he said to the man, "Stretch out your hand." And the man stretched it out, and it was restored, whole like the other. [14]But the Pharisees went out and took counsel against him, how to destroy him. †

God's Chosen Servant

15 Jesus, aware of this, withdrew from there. And many followed him, and he healed them all, [16]and ordered them not to make him known. [17]This was to fulfil what was spoken by the prophet Isaiah:

[18]"Behold, my servant whom I have chosen,
  my beloved with whom my soul is well
    pleased.
  I will put my Spirit upon him,
    and he shall proclaim justice to the Gentiles.
[19]He will not wrangle or cry aloud,
    nor will any one hear his voice in the streets;

---

[c] Or *has been coming violently.*
[d] Other ancient authorities omit *to hear.*
[e] Other ancient authorities read *children* (Luke 7:35).
[f] Or *so it was well-pleasing before you.*

11:12–13: Lk 16:16.
11:14: Mal 4:5; Mt 17:10–13; Jn 1:21; Lk 1:17.
11:15: Mt 13:9, 43; Mk 4:23; Rev 13:9; 2:7.
11:16–19: Lk 7:31–35.
11:20–24: Lk 10:13–15.
11:24: Mt 10:15; Lk 10:12.
11:25–27: Lk 10:21–22.
11:25: 1 Cor 1:26–29.
11:27: Jn 3:35; 5:20; 13:3; 7:29; 10:15; 17:25; Mt 28:18.
11:29: Jn 13:15; Phil 2:5; 1 Pet 2:21; Jer 6:16.
12:1–8: Mk 2:23–28; Lk 6:1–5.
12:1: Deut 23:25.
12:3: 1 Sam 21:1–6; Lev 24:9.
12:5: Num 28:9–10.
12:6: Mt 12:41–42; Lk 11:31–32.
12:7: Hos 6:6; Mt 9:13.
12:8: Jn 5:1–18; 7:19–24; 9:1–41.
12:9–14: Mk 3:1–6; Lk 6:6–11.
12:11: Lk 14:5.
12:12: Mt 10:31.
12:14: Mk 14:1; Jn 7:30; 8:59; 10:39; 11:53.
12:15–16: Mk 3:7–12; Lk 6:17–19.
12:18–21: Is 42:1–4.
[*] 11:27: This shows a profound relationship between the Son and the Father, far superior to adoptive sonship.
† 12:14: The Pharisees regarded healing as work and so forbade it on the sabbath.

[20]he will not break a bruised reed
  or quench a smoldering wick,
  till he brings justice to victory;
[21] and in his name will the Gentiles hope."

Jesus and Beelzebul

22 Then a blind and mute demoniac was brought to him, and he healed him, so that the mute man spoke and saw. [23]And all the people were amazed, and said, "Can this be the Son of David?" [24]But when the Pharisees heard it they said, "It is only by Be-el'zebul, * the prince of demons, that this man casts out demons." [25]Knowing their thoughts, he said to them, "Every kingdom divided against itself is laid waste, and no city or house divided against itself will stand; [26]and if Satan casts out Satan, he is divided against himself; how then will his kingdom stand? [27]And if I cast out demons by Be-el'zebul, by whom do your sons cast them out? Therefore they shall be your judges. [28]But if it is by the Spirit of God that I cast out demons, then the kingdom of God has come upon you. [29]Or how can one enter a strong man's house and plunder his goods, unless he first binds the strong man? Then indeed he may plunder his house. [30]He who is not with me is against me, and he who does not gather with me scatters. [31]Therefore I tell you, every sin and blasphemy will be forgiven men, but the blasphemy against the Spirit will not be forgiven. † [32]And whoever says a word against the Son of man will be forgiven; but whoever speaks against the Holy Spirit will not be forgiven, either in this age or in the age to come.

A Tree and Its Fruit

33 "Either make the tree good, and its fruit good; or make the tree bad, and its fruit bad; for the tree is known by its fruit. [34]You brood of vipers! how can you speak good things, when you are evil? For out of the abundance of the heart the mouth speaks. [35]The good man out of his good treasure brings forth good, and the evil man out of his evil treasure brings forth evil. [36]I tell you, on the day of judgment men will render account for every careless word they utter; [37]for by your words you will be justified, and by your words you will be condemned."

The Sign of Jonah

38 Then some of the scribes and Pharisees said to him, "Teacher, we wish to see a sign from you." [39]But he answered them, "An evil and adulterous generation seeks for a sign; but no sign shall be given to it except the sign of the prophet Jonah. [40]For as Jonah was three days and three nights in the belly of the whale, so will the Son of man be three days and three nights in the heart of the earth. [41]The men of Nin'eveh will arise at the judgment with this generation and condemn it; for they repented at the preaching of Jonah, and behold, something greater than Jonah is here.

[42]The queen of the South will arise at the judgment with this generation and condemn it; for she came from the ends of the earth to hear the wisdom of Solomon, and behold, something greater than Solomon is here.

The Return of the Unclean Spirit

43 "When the unclean spirit has gone out of a man, he passes through waterless places seeking rest, but he finds none. [44]Then he says, 'I will return to my house from which I came.' And when he comes he finds it empty, swept, and put in order. [45]Then he goes and brings with him seven other spirits more evil than himself, and they enter and dwell there; and the last state of that man becomes worse than the first. So shall it be also with this evil generation."

The True Kindred of Jesus

46 While he was still speaking to the people, behold, his mother and his brethren ‡ stood outside, asking to speak to him. ᵍ [48]But he replied to the man who told him, "Who is my mother, and who are my brethren?" § [49]And stretching out his hand toward his disciples, he said, "Here are my mother and my brethren! [50]For whoever does the will of my Father in heaven is my brother, and sister, and mother."

The Parable of the Sower

13 That same day Jesus went out of the house and sat beside the sea. [2]And great crowds gathered about him, so that he got into a boat and sat there; and the whole crowd stood on the beach. [3]And he told them many things in parables, saying: "A sower went out to sow. [4]And as he sowed, some seeds fell along the path, and the birds came and devoured them. [5]Other seeds fell on rocky ground, where they had not much soil, and immediately they sprang up, since they had no

---

ᵍ Other ancient authorities insert verse 47, *Some one told him, "Your mother and your brethren ‡ are standing outside, asking to speak to you"*.

12:22–29: Mk 3:22–27; Lk 11:14–22.
12:22: Mt 9:32–33.
12:24: Mt 9:34; 10:25; Jn 7:20; 8:52; 10:20.
12:30: Lk 11:23; Mk 9:40.
12:31–32: Mk 3:28–30; Lk 12:10.
12:33–35: Lk 6:43–45; Mt 7:16–20; Jas 3:11–12; Mt 15:18.
12:38–42: Lk 11:16, 29–32; Mk 8:11–12; Mt 16:1–4; Jn 2:18; 6:30; 1 Cor 1:22.
12:40: Jon 1:17.
12:41: Jon 3:5.
12:42: 1 Kings 10:1–10; 2 Chron 9:1–12.
12:43–45: Lk 11:24–26; 2 Pet 2:20.
12:46–50: Mk 3:31–35; Lk 8:19–21.
12:46: Jn 2:1–12; 19:25–27; 7:1–10; Mk 6:3; 1 Cor 9:5.
12:50: Jn 15:14.
13:1–9: Mk 4:1–9; Lk 8:4–8; 5:1–3.

* 12:24, *Beel-zebul*: Name of a Canaanite god meaning "the Prince-god." The Jews interpreted this name as "Prince of demons," because for them all false gods were demons. The form "Beel-zebub" is a contemptuous adaptation meaning "Lord of the flies."
† 12:31: To attribute to the devil the works of the Holy Spirit seems to imply a hardness of heart that precludes repentance.
‡ 12:46, *brethren*: The Greek word or its Semitic equivalent was used for varying degrees of blood relationship; cf. Gen 14:14; 29:12; Lev 10:4.
§ 12:48: Jesus puts the work of salvation before family relationships. It is not said, however, that he refused to see them.

depth of soil, [6]but when the sun rose they were scorched; and since they had no root they withered away. [7]Other seeds fell upon thorns, and the thorns grew up and choked them. [8]Other seeds fell on good soil and brought forth grain, some a hundredfold, some sixty, some thirty. [9]He who has ears, [h] let him hear."

The Purpose of the Parables

10 Then the disciples came and said to him, "Why do you speak to them in parables?" [11]And he answered them, "To you it has been given to know the secrets of the kingdom of heaven, but to them it has not been given. [12]For to him who has will more be given, and he will have abundance; but from him who has not, even what he has will be taken away. * [13]This is why I speak to them in parables, because seeing they do not see, and hearing they do not hear, nor do they understand. [14]With them indeed is fulfilled the prophecy of Isaiah which says:

'You shall indeed hear but never understand,
    and you shall indeed see but never perceive.
[15]For this people's heart has grown dull,
    and their ears are heavy of hearing,
    and their eyes they have closed,
lest they should perceive with their eyes,
    and hear with their ears,
and understand with their heart,
    and turn for me to heal them.'

[16]But blessed are your eyes, for they see, and your ears, for they hear. [17]Truly, I say to you, many prophets and righteous men longed to see what you see, and did not see it, and to hear what you hear, and did not hear it.

The Parable of the Sower Explained

18 "Hear then the parable of the sower. [19]When any one hears the word of the kingdom and does not understand it, the Evil One comes and snatches away what is sown in his heart; this is what was sown along the path. [20]As for what was sown on rocky ground, this is he who hears the word and immediately receives it with joy; [21]yet he has no root in himself, but endures for a while, and when tribulation or persecution arises on account of the word, immediately he falls away. [i] [22]As for what was sown among thorns, this is he who hears the word, but the cares of the world and the delight in riches choke the word, and it proves unfruitful. [23]As for what was sown on good soil, this is he who hears the word and understands it; he indeed bears fruit, and yields, in one case a hundredfold, in another sixty, and in another thirty."

The Parable of Weeds among the Wheat

24 Another parable he put before them, saying, "The kingdom of heaven may be compared to a man who sowed good seed in his field; [25]but while men were sleeping, his enemy came and sowed weeds among the wheat, and went away. [26]So when the plants came up and bore grain,

then the weeds appeared also. [27]And the servants [j] of the householder came and said to him, 'Sir, did you not sow good seed in your field? How then has it weeds?' [28]He said to them, 'An enemy has done this.' The servants [j] said to him, 'Then do you want us to go and gather them?' [29]But he said, 'No; lest in gathering the weeds you root up the wheat along with them. [30]Let both grow together until the harvest; and at harvest time I will tell the reapers, Gather the weeds first and bind them in bundles to be burned, but gather the wheat into my barn.' "

The Parable of the Mustard Seed

31 Another parable he put before them, saying, "The kingdom of heaven is like a grain of mustard seed which a man took and sowed in his field; [32]it is the smallest of all seeds, but when it has grown it is the greatest of shrubs and becomes a tree, so that the birds of the air come and make nests in its branches."

The Parable of the Leaven

33 He told them another parable. "The kingdom of heaven is like leaven which a woman took and hid in three measures of meal, till it was all leavened."

Why Jesus Speaks in Parables

34 All this Jesus said to the crowds in parables; indeed he said nothing to them without a parable. [35]This was to fulfil what was spoken by the prophet: [k]

"I will open my mouth in parables,
I will utter what has been hidden since the
    foundation of the world."

Jesus Explains the Parable of the Weeds

36 Then he left the crowds and went into the house. And his disciples came to him, saying, "Explain to us the parable of the weeds of the field." [37]He answered, "He who sows the good seed is the Son of man; [38]the field is the world, and the good seed means the sons of the kingdom; the weeds are the sons of the evil one, [39]and the enemy who sowed them is the devil; the harvest is the close of the age, and the reapers are angels. [40]Just as the weeds are gathered and burned with

---

[h] Other ancient authorities add here and in verse 43 to hear.
[i] Or stumbles.
[j] Or slaves.
[k] Other ancient authorities read the prophet Isaiah.
13:10-13: Mk 4:10–12; Lk 8:9–10.
13:12: Mk 4:25; Lk 8:18; Mt 25:29; Lk 19:26.
13:14-15: Is 6:9–10; Mk 8:18; Jn 12:39–41; Acts 28:26–27.
13:16-17: Lk 10:23–24; Jn 8:56; Heb 11:13; 1 Pet 1:10–12.
13:18-23: Mk 4:13–20; Lk 8:11–15.
13:22: Mt 19:23; 1 Tim 6:9–10, 17.
13:24-30: Mk 4:26–29.
13:31-32: Mk 4:30–32; Lk 13:18–19; Mt 17:20.
13:33: Lk 13:20–21; Gal 5:9; Gen 18:6.
13:34: Mk 4:33–34; Jn 10:6; 16:25.
13:35: Ps 78:2.
* 13:12: To those well-disposed Jews who have made good use of the old covenant will now be given the perfection of the new. On the other hand, from those who have rejected God's advances will now be taken away even that which they have, because the old covenant is passing away.

fire, so will it be at the close of the age. [41]The Son of man will send his angels, and they will gather out of his kingdom all causes of sin and all evildoers, [42]and throw them into the furnace of fire, where there will be weeping and gnashing of teeth. [43]Then the righteous will shine like the sun in the kingdom of their Father. He who has ears, let him hear.

Three Parables about the Kingdom

[44] "The kingdom of heaven is like treasure hidden in a field, which a man found and covered up; then in his joy he goes and sells all that he has and buys that field.

[45] "Again, the kingdom of heaven is like a merchant in search of fine pearls, [46]who, on finding one pearl of great value, went and sold all that he had and bought it.

[47] "Again, the kingdom of heaven is like a net which was thrown into the sea and gathered fish of every kind; [48]when it was full, men drew it ashore and sat down and sorted the good into vessels but threw away the bad. [49]So it will be at the close of the age. The angels will come out and separate the evil from the righteous, [50]and throw them into the furnace of fire, where there will be weeping and gnashing of teeth.

Treasures New and Old

[51] "Have you understood all this?" They said to him, "Yes." [52]And he said to them, "Therefore every scribe who has been trained for the kingdom of heaven is like a householder who brings out of his treasure what is new and what is old." *

The Rejection of Jesus at Nazareth

[53] And when Jesus had finished these parables, he went away from there, [54]and coming to his own country he taught them in their synagogue, so that they were astonished, and said, "Where did this man get this wisdom and these mighty works? [55]Is not this the carpenter's son? Is not his mother called Mary? And are not his brethren † James and Joseph and Simon and Judas? [56]And are not all his sisters with us? Where then did this man get all this?" [57]And they took offense at him. But Jesus said to them, "A prophet is not without honor except in his own country and in his own house." [58]And he did not do many mighty works there, because of their unbelief.

The Death of John the Baptist

14 At that time Herod the tetrarch heard about the fame of Jesus; [2]and he said to his servants, "This is John the Baptist; he has been raised from the dead; that is why these powers are at work in him." [3]For Herod had seized John and bound him and put him in prison, for the sake of Hero′di-as, his brother Philip's wife; [1] [4]because John said to him, "It is not lawful for you to have her." [5]And though he wanted to put him to death, he feared the people, because they held him to be a prophet. [6]But when Herod's birthday

came, the daughter of Hero′di-as danced before the company, and pleased Herod, [7]so that he promised with an oath to give her whatever she might ask. [8]Prompted by her mother, she said, "Give me the head of John the Baptist here on a platter." [9]And the king was sorry, but because of his oaths and his guests he commanded it to be given; [10]he sent and had John beheaded in the prison, [11]and his head was brought on a platter and given to the girl, and she brought it to her mother. [12]And his disciples came and took the body and buried it; and they went and told Jesus.

Feeding the Five Thousand

[13] Now when Jesus heard this, he withdrew from there in a boat to a lonely place apart. But when the crowds heard it, they followed him on foot from the towns. [14]As he went ashore he saw a great throng; and he had compassion on them, and healed their sick. [15]When it was evening, the disciples came to him and said, "This is a lonely place, and the day is now over; send the crowds away to go into the villages and buy food for themselves." [16]Jesus said, "They need not go away; you give them something to eat." [17]They said to him, "We have only five loaves here and two fish." [18]And he said, "Bring them here to me." [19]Then he ordered the crowds to sit down on the grass; and taking the five loaves and the two fish he looked up to heaven, and blessed, and broke and gave the loaves to the disciples, and the disciples gave them to the crowds. [20]And they all ate and were satisfied. And they took up twelve baskets full of the broken pieces left over. [21]And those who ate were about five thousand men, besides women and children.

Jesus Walks on the Sea

[22] Then he made the disciples get into the boat and go before him to the other side, while he dismissed the crowds. [23]And after he had dismissed the crowds, he went up into the hills by himself to pray. When evening came, he was there alone, [24]but the boat by this time was many furlongs distant from the land, [m] beaten by the waves; for the wind was against them. [25]And in the fourth

---

[1] Other ancient authorities read *his brother's wife*.
[m] Other ancient authorities read *was out on the sea*.
13:38: Jn 8:44; 1 Jn 3:10.
13:41: Mt 24:31.
13:42: Mt 13:50; 8:12; 22:13; 24:51; 25:30; Lk 13:28.
13:47-50: Mt 13:40–42.
13:53: Mt 7:28; 11:1; 19:1; 26:1.
13:54-58: Mk 6:1–6; Lk 4:16–30.
14:1-2: Mk 6:14–16; Lk 9:7–9; Mk 8:28.
14:3-4: Mk 6:17–18; Lk 3:19–20; Lev 18:16; 20:21.
14:5-12: Mk 6:19–29.
14:13-21: Mk 6:32–44; Lk 9:10–17; Jn 6:1–13; Mt 15:32–38.
14:19: Mk 14:22; Lk 24:30.
14:22-23: Mk 6:45–46; Jn 6:15–17.
14:24-33: Mk 6:47–52; Jn 6:16–21.
* 13:52: This is Matthew's ideal: that the learned Jew should become the disciple of Jesus and so add the riches of the new covenant to those of the old, which he already possesses; cf. verse 12.
† 13:55: See note on Mt 12:46.

watch of the night he came to them, walking on the sea. [26]But when the disciples saw him walking on the sea, they were terrified, saying, "It is a ghost!" And they cried out for fear. [27]But immediately he spoke to them, saying, "Take heart, it is I; have no fear."

28 And Peter answered him, "Lord, if it is you, bid me come to you on the water." [29]He said, "Come." So Peter got out of the boat and walked on the water and came to Jesus; [30]but when he saw the wind, [n] he was afraid, and beginning to sink he cried out, "Lord, save me." [31]Jesus immediately reached out his hand and caught him, saying to him, "O you of little faith, why did you doubt?" [32]And when they got into the boat, the wind ceased. [33]And those in the boat worshiped him, saying, "Truly you are the Son of God." *

Jesus Heals the Sick in Gennesaret

34 And when they had crossed over, they came to land at Gennes'aret. [35]And when the men of that place recognized him, they sent round to all that region and brought to him all that were sick, [36]and begged him that they might only touch the fringe of his garment; and as many as touched it were made well.

The Tradition of the Elders

15 Then Pharisees and scribes came to Jesus from Jerusalem and said, [2]"Why do your disciples transgress the tradition of the elders? For they do not wash their hands when they eat." [3]He answered them, "And why do you transgress the commandment of God for the sake of your tradition? [4]For God commanded, 'Honor your father and your mother,' and, 'He who speaks evil of father or mother, let him surely die.' [5]But you say, 'If any one tells his father or his mother, What you would have gained from me is given to God, [o] he need not honor his father.' [†] [6]So, for the sake of your tradition, you have made void the word [p] of God. [7]You hypocrites! Well did Isaiah prophesy of you, when he said:

[8]'This people honors me with their lips,
  but their heart is far from me;
[9]in vain do they worship me,
  teaching as doctrines the precepts of men.'"

Things That Defile a Man

10 And he called the people to him and said to them, "Hear and understand: [11]not what goes into the mouth defiles a man, but what comes out of the mouth, this defiles a man." [12]Then the disciples came and said to him, "Do you know that the Pharisees were offended when they heard this saying?" [13]He answered, "Every plant which my heavenly Father has not planted will be rooted up. [14]Let them alone; they are blind guides. And if a blind man leads a blind man, both will fall into a pit." [15]But Peter said to him, "Explain the parable to us." [16]And he said, "Are you also still without understanding? [17]Do you not see that

whatever goes into the mouth passes into the stomach, and so passes on? [q] [18]But what comes out of the mouth proceeds from the heart, and this defiles a man. [19]For out of the heart come evil thoughts, murder, adultery, fornication, theft, false witness, slander. [20]These are what defile a man; but to eat with unwashed hands does not defile a man."

The Canaanite Woman's Faith

21 And Jesus went away from there and withdrew to the district of Tyre and Si'don. [22]And behold, a Canaanite woman from that region came out and cried, "Have mercy on me, O Lord, Son of David; my daughter is severely possessed by a demon." [23]But he did not answer her a word. And his disciples came and begged him, saying, "Send her away, for she is crying after us." [24]He answered, "I was sent only to the lost sheep of the house of Israel." [‡] [25]But she came and knelt before him, saying, "Lord, help me." [26]And he answered, "It is not fair to take the children's bread and throw it to the dogs." [27]She said, "Yes, Lord, yet even the dogs eat the crumbs that fall from their masters' table." [28]Then Jesus answered her, "O woman, great is your faith! Let it be done for you as you desire." And her daughter was healed instantly.

Jesus Heals Many People

29 And Jesus went on from there and passed along the Sea of Galilee. And he went up on the mountain, and sat down there. [30]And great crowds came to him, bringing with them the lame, the maimed, the blind, the mute, and many others, and they put them at his feet, and he healed them, [31]so that the throng wondered, when they saw the mute speaking, the maimed whole, the lame walking, and the blind seeing; and they glorified the God of Israel.

---

[n] Other ancient authorities read *strong wind.*
[o] Or *an offering.*
[p] Other ancient authorities read *law.*
[q] Or *is evacuated.*
14:26: Lk 24:37.
14:29: Jn 21:7.
14:31: Mt 6:30; 8:26; 16:8.
14:33: Mt 28:9, 17.
14:34–36: Mk 6:53–56; Jn 6:22–26.
14:36: Mk 3:10; Num 15:38; Mt 9:20.
15:1–20: Mk 7:1–23.
15:4: Ex 20:12; Deut 5:16; Ex 21:17; Lev 20:9.
15:8–9: Is 29:13.
15:11: Acts 10:14–15; 1 Tim 4:3.
15:13: Is 60:21; Jn 15:2.
15:14: Lk 6:39; Mt 23:16, 24; Rom 2:19.
15:19: Gal 5:19–21; 1 Cor 6:9–10; Rom 14:14.
15:21–28: Mk 7:24–30.
15:24: Mt 10:6, 23.
15:25: Mt 8:2; 18:26; 20:20; Jn 9:38.
15:28: Mt 9:22, 28; Mk 10:52; Lk 7:50; 17:19.
15:29–31: Mk 7:31–37.
* 14:33: Their realization of his Godhead was the prelude to Peter's confession of faith at Caesarea Philippi (Mt 16:16).
† 15:5: By dedicating his property to God, i.e., to the temple, a man could avoid having to help his parents, without actually giving up what he had. The scribes held such a vow to be valid without necessarily approving it.
‡ 15:24: See note on Mt 10:5.

Feeding the Four Thousand

32 Then Jesus called his disciples to him and said, "I have compassion on the crowd, because they have been with me now three days, and have nothing to eat; and I am unwilling to send them away hungry, lest they faint on the way." ³³And the disciples said to him, "Where are we to get bread enough in the desert to feed so great a crowd?" ³⁴And Jesus said to them, "How many loaves have you?" They said, "Seven, and a few small fish." ³⁵And commanding the crowd to sit down on the ground, ³⁶he took the seven loaves and the fish, and having given thanks he broke them and gave them to the disciples, and the disciples gave them to the crowds. ³⁷And they all ate and were satisfied; and they took up seven baskets full of the broken pieces left over. ³⁸Those who ate were four thousand men, besides women and children. ³⁹And sending away the crowds, he got into the boat and went to the region of Mag'adan.

The Demand for a Sign

16 And the Pharisees and Sad'ducees came, and to test him they asked him to show them a sign from heaven. ²He answered them, ˣ "When it is evening, you say, 'It will be fair weather; for the sky is red.' ³And in the morning, 'It will be stormy today, for the sky is red and threatening.' You know how to interpret the appearance of the sky, but you cannot interpret the signs of the times. ⁴An evil and adulterous generation seeks for a sign, but no sign shall be given to it except the sign of Jonah." So he left them and departed.

The Leaven of the Pharisees and Sadducees

5 When the disciples reached the other side, they had forgotten to bring any bread. ⁶Jesus said to them, "Take heed and beware of the leaven of the Pharisees and Sad'ducees." ⁷And they discussed it among themselves, saying, "We brought no bread." ⁸But Jesus, aware of this, said, "O men of little faith, why do you discuss among yourselves the fact that you have no bread? ⁹Do you not yet perceive? Do you not remember the five loaves of the five thousand, and how many baskets you gathered? ¹⁰Or the seven loaves of the four thousand, and how many baskets you gathered? ¹¹How is it that you fail to perceive that I did not speak about bread? Beware of the leaven of the Pharisees and Sad'ducees." ¹²Then they understood that he did not tell them to beware of the leaven of bread, but of the teaching of the Pharisees and Sad'ducees.

Peter's Declaration That Jesus Is the Christ

13 Now when Jesus came into the district of Caesare'a Philip'pi, he asked his disciples, "Who do men say that the Son of man is?" ¹⁴And they said, "Some say John the Baptist, others say Eli'jah, and others Jeremiah or one of the proph-

ets." * ¹⁵He said to them, "But who do you say that I am?" ¹⁶Simon Peter replied, "You are the Christ, the Son of the living God." † ¹⁷And Jesus answered him, "Blessed are you, Simon Bar-Jona! For flesh and blood has not revealed this to you, but my Father who is in heaven. ¹⁸And I tell you, you are Peter, ˢ and on this rock ᵗ I will build my Church, and the gates of Hades ᵘ shall not prevail against it. ‡ ¹⁹I will give you the keys of the kingdom of heaven, § and whatever you bind on earth shall be bound in heaven, and whatever you loose on earth shall be loosed in heaven." ²⁰Then he strictly charged the disciples to tell no one that he was the Christ.

Jesus Foretells His Death and Resurrection

21 From that time Jesus began to show his disciples that he must go to Jerusalem and suffer many things from the elders and chief priests and scribes, and be killed, and on the third day be raised. ²²And Peter took him and began to rebuke him, saying, "God forbid, Lord! This shall never happen to you." ²³But he turned and said to Peter, "Get behind me, Satan! You are a hindrance ᵛ to me; for you are not on the side of God, but of men."

ˣ Other ancient authorities omit the following words to the end of verse 3.
ˢ Greek *Petros*.
ᵗ Greek *petra*.
ᵘ Or *the powers of death*.
ᵛ Greek *stumbling block*.
15:32–39: Mk 8:1–10; Mt 14:13–21.
15:32: Mt 9:36.
16:1–4: Mk 8:11–12; Lk 11:16, 29; 12:54–56; Mt 12:38–39; Jn 2:18; 6:30.
16:4: Jon 3:4–5.
16:5–12: Mk 8:13–21.
16:6: Lk 12:1.
16:8: Mt 6:30; 8:26; 14:31.
16:9: Mt 14:17–21.
16:10: Mt 15:34–38.
16:13–16: Mk 8:27–30; Lk 9:18–21.
16:14: Mt 14:2; Mk 6:15; Lk 9:7–8; Jn 1:21.
16:16: Jn 1:16; Jn 11:27; 1:49.
16:17: 1 Cor 15:50; Gal 1:16; Eph 6:12; Heb 2:14.
16:18: Jn 1:40–42; 21:15–17; 1 Cor 15:5.
16:19: Is 22:22; Rev 1:18; Mt 18:18; Jn 20:23.
16:20: Mt 8:4; Mk 3:12; 5:43; 7:36; 9:9.
16:21–28: Mk 8:31—9:1; Lk 9:22–27.
16:21: Mt 17:22–23; 20:17–19; Lk 17:25; Mt 17:12; 26:2.
16:23: Mt 4:10.
* 16:14: The title of prophet had a Messianic significance because the gift of prophecy, which had been extinct since Malachi, was expected to return at the beginning of the Messianic era, especially by an outpouring of the Spirit as foretold by the prophet Joel and as realized in Acts 2:16.
† 16:16: The context shows that Peter recognizes the sonship of Jesus as divine and not adoptive like ours. Mark and Luke in the parallel passages mention only the confession of the Messiahship.
‡ 16:18: The name "Peter" comes from the Greek word for "rock." Jesus makes him the foundation on which the church is to be built. The word "church" means "assembly" or "society" of believers. The Hebrew equivalent is used in the Old Testament to indicate the chosen people. In applying it to the church, Jesus shows it to be the Messianic community foretold by the prophets.
§ 16:19, *the kingdom of heaven*: Peter has the key to the gates of the city of God. This power is exercised through the church. "Binding" and "loosing" are rabbinic terms referring to excommunication, then later to forbidding or allowing something. Not only can Peter admit to the kingdom; he also has power to make authoritative decisions in matters of faith or morals.

The Cross and Self-Denial

24 Then Jesus told his disciples, "If any man would come after me, let him deny himself and take up his cross and follow me. [25]For whoever would save his life will lose it, and whoever loses his life for my sake will find it. [26]For what will it profit a man, if he gains the whole world and forfeits his life? * Or what shall a man give in return for his life? * [27]For the Son of man is to come with his angels in the glory of his Father, and then he will repay every man for what he has done. [28]Truly, I say to you, there are some standing here who will not taste death before they see the Son of man coming in his kingdom."

The Transfiguration

17 And after six days Jesus took with him Peter and James and John his brother, and led them up a high mountain apart. [2]And he was transfigured before them, and his face shone like the sun, and his garments became white as light. [3]And behold, there appeared to them Moses and Eli′jah, talking with him. [4]And Peter said to Jesus, "Lord, it is well that we are here; if you wish, I will make three booths here, one for you and one for Moses and one for Eli′jah." † [5]He was still speaking, when behold, a bright cloud overshadowed them, and a voice from the cloud said, "This is my beloved Son, [w] with whom I am well pleased; listen to him." [6]When the disciples heard this, they fell on their faces, and were filled with awe. [7]But Jesus came and touched them, saying, "Rise, and have no fear." [8]And when they lifted up their eyes, they saw no one but Jesus only.

9 And as they were coming down the mountain, Jesus commanded them, "Tell no one the vision, until the Son of man is raised from the dead." [10]And the disciples asked him, "Then why do the scribes say that first Eli′jah must come?" [11]He replied, "Eli′jah does come, and he is to restore all things; [12]but I tell you that Eli′jah has already come, and they did not know him, but did to him whatever they pleased. So also the Son of man will suffer at their hands." [13]Then the disciples understood that he was speaking to them of John the Baptist.

Jesus Cures an Epileptic Boy

14 And when they came to the crowd, a man came up to him and kneeling before him said, [15]"Lord, have mercy on my son, for he is an epileptic and he suffers terribly; for often he falls into the fire, and often into the water. [16]And I brought him to your disciples, and they could not heal him." [17]And Jesus answered, "O faithless and perverse generation, how long am I to be with you? How long am I to bear with you? Bring him here to me." [18]And Jesus rebuked him, and the demon came out of him, and the boy was cured instantly. [19]Then the disciples came to Jesus privately and said, "Why could we not cast it out?" [20]He said to them, "Because of your little faith. For truly, I say to you, if you have faith as a grain of mustard seed, you will say to this mountain, 'Move from here to there,' and it will move; and nothing will be impossible to you." [x]

Jesus Again Foretells His Death and Resurrection

22 As they were gathering [y] in Galilee, Jesus said to them, "The Son of man is to be delivered into the hands of men, [23]and they will kill him, and he will be raised on the third day." And they were greatly distressed.

Jesus and the Temple Tax

24 When they came to Caper′na-um, the collectors of the half-shekel tax went up to Peter and said, "Does not your teacher pay the tax?" [25]He said, "Yes." And when he came home, Jesus spoke to him first, saying, "What do you think, Simon? From whom do kings of the earth take toll or tribute? From their sons or from others?" [26]And when he said, "From others," Jesus said to him, "Then the sons are free. [27]However, not to give offense to them, go to the sea and cast a hook, and take the first fish that comes up, and when you open its mouth you will find a shekel; take that and give it to them for me and for yourself."

True Greatness

18 At that time the disciples came to Jesus, saying, "Who is the greatest in the kingdom of heaven?" [2]And calling to him a child, he put him in the midst of them, [3]and said, "Truly, I say to you, unless you turn and become like children, you will never enter the kingdom of heaven. [4]Whoever humbles himself like this child, he is the greatest in the kingdom of heaven.

---

[w] Or *my Son, my* (or *the*) *Beloved.*
[x] Other ancient authorities insert verse 21, *"But this kind never comes out except by prayer and fasting."*
[y] Other ancient authorities read *abode.*

16:24–26: Mt 10:38–39; Lk 14:27; 17:33; Jn 12:25.
16:27: Mt 10:33; Lk 12:9; 1 Jn 2:28; Rom 2:6; Rev 22:12.
16:28: Mk 10:23; 1 Cor 16:22; 1 Thess 4:15–18; Rev 1:7; Jas 5:7.
17:1–9: Mk 9:2–10; Lk 9:28–36; 2 Pet 1:17–18.
17:1: Mt 26:37; Mk 5:37; 13:3.
17:5: Mt 3:17; Is 42:1; Ps 2:7; Jn 12:28.
17:9: Mt 8:4; 16:20; Mk 3:12; 5:43; 7:36.
17:10–13: Mk 9:11–13; Mt 11:14; Mal 4:5.
17:12: Mt 16:21; 17:22; 20:17; 26:2; Lk 17:25.
17:14–18: Mk 9:14–27; Lk 9:37–43.
17:19–21: Mk 9:28–29.
17:20: Lk 17:6; Mt 21:21.; Mk 11:22–23; 1 Cor 13:2; Mk 9:23.
17:22–23: Mk 9:30–32; Lk 9:43–45; Mt 16:21; 20:17–19; 26:2.
17:24: Ex 30:13; 38:26.
17:25: Rom 13:7; Mt 22:17–21.
17:27: Mt 5:29; 18:6–9; Jn 6:61; 1 Cor 8:13.
18:1–5: Mk 9:33–37; Lk 9:46–48.
18:3: Mk 10:15; Lk 18:17; 1 Pet 2:2.

* 16:26, *life* (both times): A play on the word "life"—natural and supernatural; cf. Mk 8:35–36.
† 17:4: Peter thought the glorious Messianic kingdom had come. In fact, Jesus allowed this glimpse of his glory to strengthen them for the coming passion.

16

Temptations to Sin

5 "Whoever receives one such child in my name receives me; [6]but whoever causes one of these little ones who believe in me to sin, [z] it would be better for him to have a great millstone fastened round his neck and to be drowned in the depth of the sea.

7 "Woe to the world for temptations to sin! [a] For it is necessary that temptations come, but woe to the man by whom the temptation comes! [8]And if your hand or your foot causes you to sin, [z] cut it off and throw it from you; it is better for you to enter life maimed or lame than with two hands or two feet to be thrown into the eternal fire. [9]And if your eye causes you to sin, [z] pluck it out and throw it from you; it is better for you to enter life with one eye than with two eyes to be thrown into the hell [b] * of fire.

The Parable of the Lost Sheep

10 "See that you do not despise one of these little ones; for I tell you that in heaven their angels always behold the face of my Father who is in heaven. [c] [12]What do you think? If a man has a hundred sheep, and one of them has gone astray, does he not leave the ninety-nine on the hills and go in search of the one that went astray? [13]And if he finds it, truly, I say to you, he rejoices over it more than over the ninety-nine that never went astray. [14]So it is not the will of my [d] Father who is in heaven that one of these little ones should perish.

Binding and Loosing of Sins

15 "If your brother sins against you, go and tell him his fault, between you and him alone. If he listens to you, you have gained your brother. [16]But if he does not listen, take one or two others along with you, that every word may be confirmed by the evidence of two or three witnesses. [17]If he refuses to listen to them, tell it to the Church; and if he refuses to listen even to the Church, let him be to you as a Gentile and a tax collector. [18]Truly, I say to you, whatever you bind on earth shall be bound in heaven, and whatever you loose on earth shall be loosed in heaven. † [19]Again I say to you, if two of you agree on earth about anything they ask, it will be done for them by my Father in heaven. [20]For where two or three are gathered in my name, there am I in the midst of them."

Repeated Forgiveness

21 Then Peter came up and said to him, "Lord, how often shall my brother sin against me, and I forgive him? As many as seven times?" [22]Jesus said to him, "I do not say to you seven times, but seventy times seven. [e]

The Parable of the Unmerciful Servant

23 "Therefore the kingdom of heaven may be compared to a king who wished to settle accounts with his servants. [24]When he began the reckoning, one was brought to him who owed him ten thousand talents; [f] [25]and as he could not pay, his lord ordered him to be sold, with his wife and children and all that he had, and payment to be made. [26]So the servant fell on his knees, imploring him, 'Lord, have patience with me, and I will pay you everything.' [27]And out of pity for him the lord of that servant released him and forgave him the debt. [28]But that same servant, as he went out, came upon one of his fellow servants who owed him a hundred denarii; [g] and seizing him by the throat he said, 'Pay what you owe.' [29]So his fellow servant fell down and pleaded with him, 'Have patience with me, and I will pay you.' [30]He refused and went and put him in prison till he should pay the debt. [31]When his fellow servants saw what had taken place, they were greatly distressed, and they went and reported to their lord all that had taken place. [32]Then his lord summoned him and said to him, 'You wicked servant! I forgave you all that debt because you pleaded with me; [33]and should not you have had mercy on your fellow servant, as I had mercy on you?' [34]And in anger his lord delivered him to the jailers, [h] till he should pay all his debt. [35]So also my heavenly Father will do to every one of you, if you do not forgive your brother from your heart."

Teachings about Divorce

19 Now when Jesus had finished these sayings, he went away from Galilee and entered the region of Judea beyond the Jordan; [2]and large crowds followed him, and he healed them there.

3 And Pharisees came up to him and tested him by asking, "Is it lawful to divorce one's wife

---

[z] Greek *causes ... to stumble.*
[a] Greek *stumbling blocks.*
[b] Greek *Gehenna.*
[c] Other ancient authorities add verse 11, *For the Son of man came to save the lost.*
[d] Other ancient authorities read *your.*
[e] Or *seventy-seven times.*
[f] This talent was more than fifteen years' wages of a laborer.
[g] This denarius was a day's wage for a laborer.
[h] Greek *torturers.*

18:5: Mt 10:40; Lk 10:16; Jn 13:20.
18:6–9: Mk 9:42–48; Lk 17:1–2.
18:8–9: Mt 5:29–30; 17:27.
18:10: Acts 12:11.
18:11: Lk 19:10.
18:12–14: Lk 15:3–7.
18:15–17: Lk 17:3; 1 Cor 6:1–6; Gal 6:1; Jas 5:19–20; Lev 19:17; Deut 19:15.
18:18: Mt 16:19; Jn 20:23.
18:19–20: Mt 7:7; 21:22; Jas 1:5–7; 1 Jn 5:14; Jn 14:13.
18:21–22: Lk 17:4; Gen 4:24.
18:23: Mt 25:19.
18:25: Lk 7:42.
18:26: Mt 8:2.
18:35: Mt 6:14.
19:1: Mt 7:28; 11:1; 13:53; 26:1.
19:1–9: Mk 10:1–12.

* 18:9: Gehenna (see footnote b) was the name of a valley south of Jerusalem where human sacrifice had once been practiced; cf. 2 Chron 33:6. Later it became a cursed place and a refuse dump, and the name came to symbolize the Christian place of punishment.
† 18:18: To the other apostles is given a share in the authority given to Peter.

for any cause?" ⁴He answered, "Have you not read that he who made them from the beginning made them male and female, ⁵and said, 'For this reason a man shall leave his father and mother and be joined to his wife, and the two shall become one'? ⁱ ⁶So they are no longer two but one. ⁱ What therefore God has joined together, let no man put asunder." ⁷They said to him, "Why then did Moses command one to give a certificate of divorce, and to put her away?" ⁸He said to them, "For your hardness of heart Moses allowed you to divorce your wives, but from the beginning it was not so. ⁹And I say to you: whoever divorces his wife, except for unchastity, ʲ and marries another, commits adultery; and he who marries a divorced woman, commits adultery." ᵏ *

10 The disciples said to him, "If such is the case of a man with his wife, it is not expedient to marry." ¹¹But he said to them, "Not all men can receive this precept, but only those to whom it is given. ¹²For there are eunuchs who have been so from birth, and there are eunuchs who have been made eunuchs by men, and there are eunuchs who have made themselves eunuchs for the sake of the kingdom of heaven. He who is able to receive this, let him receive it." †

Jesus Blesses the Children

13 Then children were brought to him that he might lay his hands on them and pray. The disciples rebuked the people; ¹⁴but Jesus said, "Let the children come to me, and do not hinder them; for to such belongs the kingdom of heaven." ¹⁵And he laid his hands on them and went away.

The Rich Young Man

16 And behold, one came up to him, saying, "Teacher, what good deed must I do, to have eternal life?" ¹⁷And he said to him, "Why do you ask me about what is good? One there is who is good. If you would enter life, keep the commandments." ¹⁸He said to him, "Which?" And Jesus said, "You shall not kill, You shall not commit adultery, You shall not steal, You shall not bear false witness, ¹⁹Honor your father and mother, and, You shall love your neighbor as yourself." ²⁰The young man said to him, "All these I have observed; what do I still lack?" ²¹Jesus said to him, "If you would be perfect, go, sell what you possess and give to the poor, and you will have treasure in heaven; and come, follow me." ²²When the young man heard this he went away sorrowful; for he had great possessions.

23 And Jesus said to his disciples, "Truly, I say to you, it will be hard for a rich man to enter the kingdom of heaven. ²⁴Again I tell you, it is easier for a camel to go through the eye of a needle than for a rich man to enter the kingdom of God." ²⁵When the disciples heard this they were greatly astonished, saying, "Who then can be saved?" ²⁶But Jesus looked at them and said to them, "With

men this is impossible, but with God all things are possible." ²⁷Then Peter said in reply, "Behold, we have left everything and followed you. What then shall we have?" ²⁸Jesus said to them, "Truly, I say to you, in the new world, when the Son of man shall sit on his glorious throne, you who have followed me will also sit on twelve thrones, judging the twelve tribes of Israel. ²⁹And every one who has left houses or brothers or sisters or father or mother or children or lands, for my name's sake, will receive a hundredfold, ˡ and inherit eternal life. ³⁰But many that are first will be last, and the last first.

The Laborers in the Vineyard

20 "For the kingdom of heaven is like a householder who went out early in the morning to hire laborers for his vineyard. ²After agreeing with the laborers for a denarius ᵐ a day, he sent them into his vineyard. ³And going out about the third hour he saw others standing idle in the market place; ⁴and to them he said, 'You go into the vineyard too, and whatever is right I will give you.' So they went. ⁵Going out again about the sixth hour and the ninth hour, he did the same. ⁶And about the eleventh hour he went out and found others standing; and he said to them, 'Why do you stand here idle all day?' ⁷They said to him, 'Because no one has hired us.' He said to them, 'You go into the vineyard too.' ⁸And when evening came, the owner of the vineyard said to his steward, 'Call the laborers and pay them their wages, beginning with the last, up to the first.' ⁹And when those hired about the eleventh hour came, each of them received a denarius. ¹⁰Now when the first came, they thought they would receive more; but each of them also received a denarius. ¹¹And on receiving it they grumbled at the householder, ¹²saying, 'These last worked only

---

ⁱ Greek *one flesh.*
ʲ Other ancient authorities, after *unchastity,* read *makes her commit adultery.*
ᵏ Other ancient authorities omit *and he who marries a divorced woman, commits adultery.*
ˡ Other ancient authorities read *manifold.*
ᵐ The denarius was a day's wage for a laborer.
19:5: Gen 1:27; 2:24; Eph 5:31; 1 Cor 6:16.
19:7: Deut 24:1–4.
19:9: Mt 5:32; Lk 16:18; 1 Cor 7:10–13.
19:11: 1 Cor 7:7–9.
19:13–15: Mk 10:13–16; Lk 18:15–17; Mt 18:2–3; 1 Cor 14:20.
19:16–22: Mk 10:17–22; Lk 18:18–23.
19:16: Lk 10:25; Lev 18:5.
19:18: Ex 20:12–16; Deut 5:16–20; Rom 13:9; Jas 2:11.
19:19: Lev 19:18; Mt 22:39.
19:21: Lk 12:33; Acts 2:45; 4:34; Mt 6:20.
19:23–26: Mk 10:23–27; Lk 18:24–27.
19:26: Gen 18:14; Job 42:2.
19:27–30: Mk 10:28–31; Lk 18:28–30; Mt 4:18–22.
19:28: Lk 22:30; Mt 20:21; Rev 3:21.
19:30: Mt 20:16; Lk 13:30.
20:1: Mt 21:28, 33.
20:8: Lev 19:13; Deut 24:15.
* 19:9: This appears to refer to the case in Mt 5:32, though the Greek word for "except" is different.
† 19:11–12: Jesus means that a life of continence is to be chosen only by those who are called to it for the sake of the kingdom of God.

one hour, and you have made them equal to us who have borne the burden of the day and the scorching heat.' ¹³But he replied to one of them, 'Friend, I am doing you no wrong; did you not agree with me for a denarius? ¹⁴Take what belongs to you, and go; I choose to give to this last as I give to you. ¹⁵Am I not allowed to do what I choose with what belongs to me? Or do you begrudge my generosity?' ⁿ ¹⁶So the last will be first, and the first last."

A Third Time Jesus Foretells
His Death and Resurrection

17 And as Jesus was going up to Jerusalem, he took the twelve disciples aside, and on the way he said to them, ¹⁸"Behold, we are going up to Jerusalem; and the Son of man will be delivered to the chief priests and scribes, and they will condemn him to death, ¹⁹and deliver him to the Gentiles to be mocked and scourged and crucified, and he will be raised on the third day."

The Request of the Mother
of James and John

20 Then the mother of the sons of Zeb'edee came up to him, with her sons, and kneeling before him she asked him for something. ²¹And he said to her, "What do you want?" She said to him, "Command that these two sons of mine may sit, one at your right hand and one at your left, in your kingdom." ²²But Jesus answered, "You do not know what you are asking. Are you able to drink the chalice that I am to drink?" They said to him, "We are able." ²³He said to them, "You will drink my chalice, but to sit at my right hand and at my left is not mine to grant, but it is for those for whom it has been prepared by my Father." ²⁴And when the Ten heard it, they were indignant at the two brothers. ²⁵But Jesus called them to him and said, "You know that the rulers of the Gentiles lord it over them, and their great men exercise authority over them. ²⁶It shall not be so among you; but whoever would be great among you must be your servant, ²⁷and whoever would be first among you must be your slave; ²⁸even as the Son of man came not to be served but to serve, and to give his life as a ransom for many."

Jesus Heals Two Blind Men

29 And as they went out of Jericho, a great crowd followed him. ³⁰And behold, two blind men sitting by the roadside, when they heard that Jesus was passing by, cried out, ° "Have mercy on us, Son of David!" ³¹The crowd rebuked them, telling them to be silent; but they cried out the more, "Lord, have mercy on us, Son of David!" ³²And Jesus stopped and called them, saying, "What do you want me to do for you?" ³³They said to him, "Lord, let our eyes be opened." ³⁴And Jesus in pity touched their eyes, and immediately they received their sight and followed him.

Jesus' Entry into Jerusalem

21 And when they drew near to Jerusalem and came to Beth'phage, to the Mount of Olives, then Jesus sent two disciples, ²saying to them, "Go into the village opposite you, and immediately you will find a donkey tied, and a colt with her; untie them and bring them to me. ³If any one says anything to you, you shall say, 'The Lord has need of them,' and he will send them immediately." ⁴This took place to fulfil what was spoken by the prophet, saying,

⁵"Tell the daughter of Zion,
Behold, your king is coming to you,
humble, and mounted on a donkey,
and on a colt, the foal of a donkey."

⁶The disciples went and did as Jesus had directed them; ⁷they brought the donkey and the colt, and put their garments on them, and he sat on them. ⁸Most of the crowd spread their garments on the road, and others cut branches from the trees and spread them on the road. ⁹And the crowds that went before him and that followed him shouted, "Hosanna to the Son of David! Blessed is he who comes in the name of the Lord! Hosanna in the highest!" * ¹⁰And when he entered Jerusalem, all the city was stirred, saying, "Who is this?" ¹¹And the crowds said, "This is the prophet Jesus from Nazareth of Galilee."

Jesus Cleanses the Temple

12 And Jesus entered the temple of God ᵖ and drove out all who sold and bought in the temple, and he overturned the tables of the money-changers and the seats of those who sold pigeons. ¹³He said to them, "It is written, 'My house shall be called a house of prayer'; but you make it a den of robbers."

14 And the blind and the lame came to him in the temple, and he healed them. ¹⁵But when the chief priests and the scribes saw the wonderful

---

ⁿ Or *is your eye evil because I am good?*
° Other ancient authorities insert *Lord.*
ᵖ Other ancient authorities omit *of God.*
20:13: Mt 22:12; 26:50.
20:15: Mt 6:23; Mk 7:22; Deut 15:9.
20:16: Lk 13:30; Mt 19:30; Mk 10:31.
20:17-19: Mk 10:32-34; Lk 18:31-34; Mt 16:21; 17:12, 22-23; 26:2.
20:20-24: Mk 10:35-41.
20:20: Mt 8:2; 9:18; 15:25; 18:26; Jn 9:38.
20:21: Mt 19:28.
20:22: Mt 26:39; Jn 18:11.
20:23: Acts 12:2; Rev 1:9; Mt 13:11.
20:25-28: Mk 10:42-45; Lk 22:25-27.
20:26: Mt 23:11; Mk 9:35; Lk 9:48.
20:28: Mt 26:28; 1 Tim 2:5-6; Jn 13:15-16; Tit 2:14; 1 Pet 1:18.
20:29-34: Mk 10:46-52; Lk 18:35-43; Mt 9:27-31.
21:1-9: Mk 11:1-10; Lk 19:29-38; Jn 12:12-18.
21:5: Is 62:11; Zech 9:9.
21:8: 2 Kings 9:13.
21:9: Ps 118:26; Lk 2:14; Mt 21:15; 23:39.
21:11: Jn 6:14; 7:40; Acts 3:22; Mk 6:15; Lk 13:33.
21:12-13: Mk 11:15-17; Lk 19:45-46; Jn 2:13-17; Ex 30:13; Lev 1:14.
21:13: Is 56:7; Jer 7:11.
21:15: Lk 19:39; Mt 21:9.
* 21:9: The crowd openly recognizes Jesus as the Messiah and he allows it for the first time.

things that he did, and the children crying out in the temple, "Hosanna to the Son of David!" they were indignant; [16]and they said to him, "Do you hear what these are saying?" And Jesus said to them, "Yes; have you never read,

'Out of the mouths of babies and infants
    you have brought perfect praise'?"

[17]And leaving them, he went out of the city to Beth'any and lodged there.

Jesus Curses the Fig Tree

18 In the morning, as he was returning to the city, he was hungry. [19]And seeing a fig tree by the wayside he went to it, and found nothing on it but leaves only. And he said to it, "May no fruit ever come from you again!" And the fig tree withered at once. [20]When the disciples saw it they marveled, saying, "How did the fig tree wither at once?" [21]And Jesus answered them, "Truly, I say to you, if you have faith and never doubt, you will not only do what has been done to the fig tree, but even if you say to this mountain, 'Be taken up and cast into the sea,' it will be done. [22]And whatever you ask in prayer, you will receive, if you have faith."

The Authority of Jesus Questioned

23 And when he entered the temple, the chief priests and the elders of the people came up to him as he was teaching, and said, "By what authority are you doing these things, and who gave you this authority?" * [24]Jesus answered them, "I also will ask you a question; and if you tell me the answer, then I also will tell you by what authority I do these things. [25]The baptism of John, where was it from? From heaven or from men?" And they argued with one another, "If we say, 'From heaven,' he will say to us, 'Why then did you not believe him?' [26]But if we say, 'From men,' we are afraid of the multitude; for all hold that John was a prophet." [27]So they answered Jesus, "We do not know." And he said to them, "Neither will I tell you by what authority I do these things.

The Parable of the Two Sons

28 "What do you think? A man had two sons; and he went to the first and said, 'Son, go and work in the vineyard today.' [29]And he answered, 'I will not'; but afterward he repented and went. [30]And he went to the second and said the same; and he answered, 'I go, sir,' but did not go. [31]Which of the two did the will of his father?" They said, "The first." Jesus said to them, "Truly, I say to you, the tax collectors and the harlots go into the kingdom of God before you. [32]For John came to you in the way of righteousness, and you did not believe him, but the tax collectors and the harlots believed him; and even when you saw it, you did not afterward repent and believe him.

The Parable of the Wicked Tenants

33 "Hear another parable. † There was a householder who planted a vineyard, and set a hedge around it, and dug a wine press in it, and built a tower, and leased it to tenants, and went into another country. [34]When the season of fruit drew near, he sent his servants to the tenants, to get his fruit; [35]and the tenants took his servants and beat one, killed another, and stoned another. [36]Again he sent other servants, more than the first; and they did the same to them. [37]Afterward he sent his son to them, saying, 'They will respect my son.' [38]But when the tenants saw the son, they said to themselves, 'This is the heir; come, let us kill him and have his inheritance.' [39]And they took him and cast him out of the vineyard, and killed him. [40]When therefore the owner of the vineyard comes, what will he do to those tenants?" [41]They said to him, "He will put those wretches to a miserable death, and lease the vineyard to other tenants who will give him the fruits in their seasons."

The Stone Which the Builders Rejected

42 Jesus said to them, "Have you never read in the Scriptures:

'The very stone which the builders rejected
    has become the cornerstone;
this was the Lord's doing,
    and it is marvelous in our eyes'?

[43]Therefore I tell you, the kingdom of God will be taken away from you and given to a nation producing the fruits of it. [44]And he who falls on this stone will be broken to pieces; but when it falls on any one, it will crush him." �

45 When the chief priests and the Pharisees heard his parables, they perceived that he was speaking about them. [46]But when they tried to arrest him, they feared the multitudes, because they held him to be a prophet.

The Parable of the Marriage Feast

22 And again Jesus spoke to them in parables, saying, [2]"The kingdom of heaven may be compared to a king who gave a marriage feast for his son, [3]and sent his servants to call those who were invited to the marriage feast; but they would not come. [4]Again he sent other

---

ᵠ Other ancient authorities omit verse 44.

21:16: Ps 8:2.
21:17–19: Mk 11:11–14; Lk 13:6–9.
21:20–22: Mk 11:20–24.
21:21: Mt 17:20; Lk 17:6; 1 Cor 13:2; Jas 1:6.
21:22: Jn 14:13–14; 16:23.
21:23–27: Mk 11:27–33; Lk 20:1–8; Jn 2:18–22.
21:26: Mt 11:9; 14:5; Lk 1:76.
21:28: Mt 20:1; 21:33.
21:32: Lk 7:29–30.
21:33–46: Mk 12:1–12; Lk 20:9–19; Is 5:1–7.
21:34: Mt 22:3.
21:41: Mt 8:11; Acts 13:46; 18:6; 28:28.
21:42: Ps 118:22–23; Acts 4:11; 1 Pet 2:7.
22:1–10: Lk 14:16–24.
22:3: Mt 21:34.

* 21:23: They object to the assumption of authority implicit in the manner of his entry into the city and in his expulsion of the sellers from the temple.
† 21:33–44: This parable is really an allegory in which almost every detail represents something in God's dealings with Israel.

servants, saying, 'Tell those who are invited, Behold, I have made ready my dinner, my oxen and my fat calves are killed, and everything is ready; come to the marriage feast.' ⁵But they made light of it and went off, one to his farm, another to his business, ⁶while the rest seized his servants, treated them shamefully, and killed them. ⁷The king was angry, and he sent his troops and destroyed those murderers and burned their city. ⁸Then he said to his servants, 'The wedding is ready, but those invited were not worthy. ⁹Go therefore to the streets, and invite to the marriage feast as many as you find.' ¹⁰And those servants went out into the streets and gathered all whom they found, both bad and good; so the wedding hall was filled with guests.

11 "But when the king came in to look at the guests, he saw there a man who had no wedding garment; * ¹²and he said to him, 'Friend, how did you get in here without a wedding garment?' And he was speechless. ¹³Then the king said to the attendants, 'Bind him hand and foot, and cast him into the outer darkness, where there will be weeping and gnashing of teeth.' ¹⁴For many are called, but few are chosen."

The Question about Paying Taxes

15 Then the Pharisees went and took counsel how to entangle him in his talk. ¹⁶And they sent their disciples to him, along with the Hero'di-ans, saying, "Teacher, we know that you are true, and teach the way of God truthfully, and care for no man; for you do not regard the position of men. ¹⁷Tell us, then, what you think. Is it lawful to pay taxes to Caesar, or not?" ¹⁸But Jesus, aware of their malice, said, "Why put me to the test, you hypocrites? ¹⁹Show me the money for the tax." And they brought him a coin. ˣ ²⁰And Jesus said to them, "Whose likeness and inscription is this?" ²¹They said, "Caesar's." Then he said to them, "Render therefore to Caesar the things that are Caesar's, and to God the things that are God's." ²²When they heard it, they marveled; and they left him and went away.

The Question about Man's Resurrection

23 The same day Sad'ducees came to him, who say that there is no resurrection; and they asked him a question, ²⁴saying, "Teacher, Moses said, 'If a man dies, having no children, his brother must marry the widow, and raise up children for his brother.' ²⁵Now there were seven brothers among us; the first married, and died, and having no children left his wife to his brother. ²⁶So too the second and third, down to the seventh. ²⁷After them all, the woman died. ²⁸In the resurrection, therefore, to which of the seven will she be wife? For they all had her."

29 But Jesus answered them, "You are wrong, because you know neither the Scriptures nor the power of God. ³⁰For in the resurrection they nei-

ther marry nor are given in marriage, but are like angels ˢ in heaven. ³¹And as for the resurrection of the dead, have you not read what was said to you by God, ³²'I am the God of Abraham, and the God of Isaac, and the God of Jacob'? He is not God of the dead, but of the living." ³³And when the crowd heard it, they were astonished at his teaching.

The Greatest Commandment

34 But when the Pharisees heard that he had silenced the Sad'ducees, they came together. ³⁵And one of them, a lawyer, asked him a question, to test him. ³⁶"Teacher, which is the great commandment in the law?" ³⁷And he said to him, "You shall love the Lord your God with all your heart, and with all your soul, and with all your mind. ³⁸This is the great and first commandment. ³⁹And a second is like it, You shall love your neighbor as yourself. ⁴⁰On these two commandments depend all the law and the prophets."

A Question about the Christ

41 Now while the Pharisees were gathered together, Jesus asked them a question, ⁴²saying, "What do you think of the Christ? Whose son is he?" They said to him, "The son of David." ⁴³He said to them, "How is it then that David, inspired by the Spirit, ᵗ calls him Lord, saying,

⁴⁴'The Lord said to my Lord,
   Sit at my right hand,
   till I put your enemies under your feet'?

⁴⁵If David thus calls him Lord, how is he his son?" ⁴⁶And no one was able to answer him a word, nor from that day did any one dare to ask him any more questions.

Jesus Denounces the Hypocrisy of the Scribes and Pharisees

23 Then said Jesus to the crowds and to his disciples, ²"The scribes and the Pharisees sit on Moses' seat; ³so practice and observe whatever they tell you, but not what they do; for they preach, but do not practice. ⁴They bind heavy

---

ˣ Greek *a denarius*.
ˢ Other ancient authorities add *of God*.
ᵗ Or *David in the Spirit*.
22:10: Mt 13:47.
22:12: Mt 20:13; 26:50.
22:13: Mt 8:12; 13:42, 50; 24:51; 25:30; Lk 13:28.
22:15–22: Mk 12:13–17; Lk 20:20–26.
22:15: Mk 3:6; 8:15.
22:21: Rom 13:7.
22:23–33: Mk 12:18–27; Lk 20:27–38.
22:23: Acts 4:1–2; 23:6–10.
22:24: Deut 25:5.
22:32: Ex 3:6.
22:33: Mt 7:28.
22:34–40: Mk 12:28–34; Lk 20:39–40; 10:25–28.
22:35: Lk 7:30; 11:45; 14:3.
22:37: Deut 6:5.
22:39: Lev 19:18; Mt 19:19; Gal 5:14; Rom 13:9; Jas 2:8.
22:41–46: Mk 12:35–37; Lk 20:41–44.
22:44: Ps 110:1; Acts 2:34–35; Heb 1:13; 10:13.
22:46: Mk 12:34, Lk 20:40.
* **22:11:** The wedding garment represents the dispositions necessary for admission to the kingdom.

21

burdens, hard to bear, [u] and lay them on men's shoulders; but they themselves will not move them with their finger. [5]They do all their deeds to be seen by men; for they make their phylacteries * broad and their fringes long, [6]and they love the place of honor at feasts and the best seats in the synagogues, [7]and salutations in the market places, and being called rabbi by men. [8]But you are not to be called rabbi, for you have one teacher, and you are all brethren. [9]And call no man your father on earth, for you have one Father, who is in heaven. † [10]Neither be called masters, for you have one master, the Christ. [11]He who is greatest among you shall be your servant; [12]whoever exalts himself will be humbled, and whoever humbles himself will be exalted.

13 "But woe to you, scribes and Pharisees, hypocrites! because you shut the kingdom of heaven against men; for you neither enter yourselves, nor allow those who would enter to go in. [v] [15]Woe to you, scribes and Pharisees, hypocrites! for you traverse sea and land to make a single proselyte, and when he becomes a proselyte, you make him twice as much a child of hell [w] as yourselves.

16 "Woe to you, blind guides, who say, 'If any one swears by the temple, it is nothing; but if any one swears by the gold of the temple, he is bound by his oath.' [17]You blind fools! For which is greater, the gold or the temple that has made the gold sacred? [18]And you say, 'If any one swears by the altar, it is nothing; but if any one swears by the gift that is on the altar, he is bound by his oath.' [19]You blind men! For which is greater, the gift or the altar that makes the gift sacred? [20]So he who swears by the altar, swears by it and by everything on it; [21]and he who swears by the temple, swears by it and by him who dwells in it; [22]and he who swears by heaven, swears by the throne of God and by him who sits upon it.

23 "Woe to you, scribes and Pharisees, hypocrites! for you tithe mint and dill and cummin, and have neglected the weightier matters of the law, justice and mercy and faith; these you ought to have done, without neglecting the others. [24]You blind guides, straining out a gnat and swallowing a camel!

25 "Woe to you, scribes and Pharisees, hypocrites! for you cleanse the outside of the cup and of the plate, but inside they are full of extortion and rapacity. [26]You blind Pharisee! first cleanse the inside of the cup and of the plate, that the outside also may be clean.

27 "Woe to you, scribes and Pharisees, hypocrites! for you are like whitewashed tombs, which outwardly appear beautiful, but within they are full of dead men's bones and all uncleanness. [28]So you also outwardly appear righ-

teous to men, but within you are full of hypocrisy and iniquity.

29 "Woe to you, scribes and Pharisees, hypocrites! for you build the tombs of the prophets and adorn the monuments of the righteous, [30]saying, 'If we had lived in the days of our fathers, we would not have taken part with them in shedding the blood of the prophets.' [31]Thus you witness against yourselves, that you are sons of those who murdered the prophets. [32]Fill up, then, the measure of your fathers. [33]You serpents, you brood of vipers, how are you to escape being sentenced to hell? [w] [34]Therefore I send you prophets and wise men and scribes, some of whom you will kill and crucify, and some you will scourge in your synagogues and persecute from town to town, [35]that upon you may come all the righteous blood shed on earth, from the blood of innocent Abel to the blood of Zechari'ah the son of Barachi'ah, whom you murdered between the sanctuary and the altar. [36]Truly, I say to you, all this will come upon this generation.

The Lament over Jerusalem

37 "O Jerusalem, Jerusalem, killing the prophets and stoning those who are sent to you! How often would I have gathered your children together as a hen gathers her brood under her wings, and you would not! [38]Behold, your house is forsaken and desolate. * [39]For I tell you, you will not see me again, until you say, 'Blessed is he who comes in the name of the Lord.' "

---

[u] Other ancient authorities omit *hard to bear.*
[v] Other ancient authorities add here (or after verse 12) verse 14, *Woe to you, scribes and Pharisees, hypocrites! for you devour widows' houses and for a pretense you make long prayers; therefore you will receive the greater condemnation.*
[w] Greek *Gehenna.*
[x] Other ancient authorities omit *and desolate.*
23:4: Lk 11:46; Acts 15:10.
23:5: Mt 6:1; 5, 16; Ex 13:9; Deut 6:8; Mt 9:20.
23:6–7: Mk 12:38–39; Lk 20:46; 14:7–11; 11:43.
23:8: Jas 3:1.
23:11: Mt 20:26; Mk 9:35; 10:43; Lk 9:48; 22:26.
23:12: Lk 14:11; 18:14; Mt 18:4; 1 Pet 5:6.
23:13: Lk 11:52.
23:15: Acts 2:10; 6:5; 13:43.
23:16–22: Mt 5:33–37; 15:14.
23:17: Ex 30:29.
23:21: 1 Kings 8:13; Ps 26:8.
23:23–24: Lk 11:42; Lev 27:30; Mic 6:8.
23:25–26: Lk 11:39–41; Mk 7:4.
23:27–28: Lk 11:44; Acts 23:3; Ps 5:9.
23:29–32: Lk 11:47–48; Acts 7:51–53.
23:33: Mt 3:7; Lk 3:7.
23:34–36: Lk 11:49–51; 2 Chron 36:15–16.
23:34: Mt 10:17, 23.
23:35: Gen 4:8; Heb 11:4; Zech 1:1; 2 Chron 24:21.
23:36: Mt 10:23; 16:28; 24:34.
23:37–39: Lk 13:34–35.
23:38: 1 Kings 9:7; Jer 22:5.
23:39: Mt 21:9; Ps 118:26.
* 23:5, *phylacteries*: Little leather boxes containing, on a very small scroll, the principal words of the law; cf. Deut 6:4–9. Taking the command literally, they fastened these to their arms and their foreheads.
† 23:9: i.e., "Do not use the title without reference to God's universal fatherhood." He cannot mean that the title is never to be used by a son to his father.

The Destruction of the Temple Foretold

24 Jesus left the temple and was going away, when his disciples came to point out to him the buildings of the temple. * [2]But he answered them, "You see all these, do you not? Truly, I say to you, there will not be left here one stone upon another, that will not be thrown down."

Signs of Jesus' Coming and of the Close of the Age

3 As he sat on the Mount of Olives, the disciples came to him privately, saying, "Tell us, when will this be, and what will be the sign of your coming and of the close of the age?" [4]And Jesus answered them, "Take heed that no one leads you astray. [5]For many will come in my name, saying, 'I am the Christ,' and they will lead many astray. [6]And you will hear of wars and rumors of wars; see that you are not alarmed; for this must take place, but the end is not yet. [7]For nation will rise against nation, and kingdom against kingdom, and there will be famines and earthquakes in various places: [8]all this is but the beginning of the sufferings.

Persecutions Foretold

9 "Then they will deliver you up to tribulation, and put you to death; and you will be hated by all nations for my name's sake. [10]And then many will fall away,[y] and betray one another, and hate one another. [11]And many false prophets will arise and lead many astray. [12]And because wickedness is multiplied, most men's love will grow cold. [13]But he who endures to the end will be saved. [14]And this gospel of the kingdom will be preached throughout the whole world, as a testimony to all nations; and then the end will come.

The Desolating Sacrilege

15 "So when you see the desolating sacrilege spoken of by the prophet Daniel, standing in the holy place (let the reader understand), [16]then let those who are in Judea flee to the mountains; [17]let him who is on the housetop not go down to take what is in his house; [18]and let him who is in the field not turn back to get a coat. [19]And alas for those who are with child and for those who are nursing in those days! [20]Pray that your flight may not be in winter or on a sabbath. [21]For then there will be great tribulation, such as has not been from the beginning of the world until now, no, and never will be. [22]And if those days had not been shortened, no human being would be saved; but for the sake of the elect those days will be shortened. [23]Then if any one says to you, 'Behold, here is the Christ!' or 'There he is!' do not believe it. [24]For false Christs and false prophets will arise and show great signs and wonders, so as to lead astray, if possible, even the elect. [25]Behold, I have told you beforehand. [26]So, if they say to you, 'Behold, he is in the wilderness,' do not go out; if they say, 'Behold, he is in the inner rooms,' do not

believe it. [27]For as the lightning comes from the east and shines as far as the west, so will be the coming of the Son of man. [28]Wherever the body is, there the eagles[z] will be gathered together.

The Coming of the Son of Man

29 "Immediately after the tribulation of those days the sun will be darkened, and the moon will not give its light, and the stars will fall from heaven, and the powers of the heavens will be shaken; [30]then will appear the sign of the Son of man in heaven, and then all the tribes of the earth will mourn, and they will see the Son of man coming on the clouds of heaven with power and great glory; [31]and he will send out his angels with a loud trumpet call, and they will gather his elect from the four winds, from one end of heaven to the other.

The Lesson of the Fig Tree

32 "From the fig tree learn its lesson: as soon as its branch becomes tender and puts forth its leaves, you know that summer is near. [33]So also, when you see all these things, you know that he is near, at the very gates. [34]Truly, I say to you, this generation will not pass away till all these things take place. [35]Heaven and earth will pass away, but my words will not pass away.

The Necessity for Watchfulness

36 "But of that day and hour no one knows, not even the angels of heaven, nor the Son,[a] but the Father only. [37]As were the days of Noah, so will be the coming of the Son of man. [38]For as in those days before the flood they were eating and drinking, marrying and giving in marriage, until the day when Noah entered the ark, [39]and they did

---

y Or *stumble.*
z Or *vultures.*
a Other ancient authorities omit *nor the Son.*
24:1–35: Mk 13:1–31; Lk 21:1–33.
24:2: Mt 26:61; 27:39–40; Lk 19:44; Jn 2:19.
24:3: Lk 17:20; Mt 13:39, 40, 49; 28:20; 16:27.
24:5: Mt 24:11, 23–24; 1 Jn 2:18.
24:6–7: Rev 6:3–8, 12–17; Is 19:2.
24:9: Mt 10:17–18, 22; Jn 15:18; 16:2.
24:13: Mt 10:22; Rev 2:7.
24:14: Mt 28:19; Rom 10:18.
24:15: Dan 9:27; 11:31; 12:11.
24:17–18: Lk 17:31.
24:19: Lk 23:29.
24:21: Dan 12:1; Joel 2:2.
24:26–27: Lk 17:22–24; Rev 1:7.
24:28: Lk 17:37; Job 39:30.
24:29: Rev 8:12; Is 13:10; Ezek 32:7; Joel 2:10–11; Zeph 1:15.
24:30: Mt 16:27; Dan 7:13; Rev 1:7.
24:31: 1 Cor 15:52; 1 Thess 4:16; Is 27:13; Zech 9:14.
24:34: Mt 16:28.
24:35: Mt 5:18; Lk 16:17.
24:36: Acts 1:6–7.
24:37–39: Lk 17:26–27; Gen 6:5–8; 7:6–24.
* 24:1—25:46: The "Eschatological Discourse," as it is called, deals with the fall of Jerusalem and the end of the world. The two themes seem to be inextricably intermingled in the Gospel as we now have it, but it is possible that originally they were in separate discourses. However, the fusion of the two does bring out their connection. The one prefigures the other. Moreover, in the reverse direction, so to speak, the language used to describe the day of the Lord in Joel and elsewhere is here applied to the fall of Jerusalem, the details of which must therefore not be taken too literally (24:29).

not know until the flood came and swept them all away, so will be the coming of the Son of man. [40]Then two men will be in the field; one is taken and one is left. [41]Two women will be grinding at the mill; one is taken and one is left. [42]Watch therefore, for you do not know on what day your Lord is coming. [43]But know this, that if the householder had known in what part of the night the thief was coming, he would have watched and would not have let his house be broken into. [44]Therefore you also must be ready; for the Son of man is coming at an hour you do not expect.

The Faithful and the Unfaithful Servant

45 "Who then is the faithful and wise servant, whom his master has set over his household, to give them their food at the proper time? [46]Blessed is that servant whom his master when he comes will find so doing. [47]Truly, I say to you, he will set him over all his possessions. [48]But if that wicked servant says to himself, 'My master is delayed,' [49]and begins to beat his fellow servants, and eats and drinks with the drunken, [50]the master of that servant will come on a day when he does not expect him and at an hour he does not know, [51]and will punish [b] him, and put him with the hypocrites; there men will weep and gnash their teeth.

The Parable of the Wise and the Foolish Maidens

25 "Then the kingdom of heaven shall be compared to ten maidens who took their lamps and went to meet the bridegroom. [c] [2]Five of them were foolish, and five were wise. [3]For when the foolish took their lamps, they took no oil with them; [4]but the wise took flasks of oil with their lamps. [5]As the bridegroom was delayed, they all slumbered and slept. [6]But at midnight there was a cry, 'Behold, the bridegroom! Come out to meet him.' [7]Then all those maidens rose and trimmed their lamps. [8]And the foolish said to the wise, 'Give us some of your oil, for our lamps are going out.' [9]But the wise replied, 'Perhaps there will not be enough for us and for you; go rather to the dealers and buy for yourselves.' [10]And while they went to buy, the bridegroom came, and those who were ready went in with him to the marriage feast; and the door was shut. [11]Afterward the other maidens came also, saying, 'Lord, lord, open to us.' [12]But he replied, 'Truly, I say to you, I do not know you.' [13]Watch therefore, for you know neither the day nor the hour.

The Parable of the Talents

14 "For it will be as when a man going on a journey called his servants and entrusted to them his property; [15]to one he gave five talents, [d] to another two, to another one, to each according to his ability. Then he went away. [16]He who had received the five talents went at once and traded with them; and he made five talents more. [17]So

also, he who had the two talents made two talents more. [18]But he who had received the one talent went and dug in the ground and hid his master's money. [19]Now after a long time the master of those servants came and settled accounts with them. [20]And he who had received the five talents came forward, bringing five talents more, saying, 'Master, you delivered to me five talents; here I have made five talents more.' [21]His master said to him, 'Well done, good and faithful servant; you have been faithful over a little, I will set you over much; enter into the joy of your master.' [22]And he also who had the two talents came forward, saying, 'Master, you delivered to me two talents; here I have made two talents more.' [23]His master said to him, 'Well done, good and faithful servant; you have been faithful over a little, I will set you over much; enter into the joy of your master.' [24]He also who had received the one talent came forward, saying, 'Master, I knew you to be a hard man, reaping where you did not sow, and gathering where you did not winnow; [25]so I was afraid, and I went and hid your talent in the ground. Here you have what is yours.' [26]But his master answered him, 'You wicked and slothful servant! You knew that I reap where I have not sowed, and gather where I have not winnowed? [27]Then you ought to have invested my money with the bankers, and at my coming I should have received what was my own with interest. [28]So take the talent from him, and give it to him who has the ten talents. [29]For every one who has will more be given, and he will have abundance; but from him who has not, even what he has will be taken away. * [30]And cast the worthless servant into the outer darkness, where there will be weeping and gnashing of teeth.'

The Judgment of the Nations

31 "When the Son of man comes in his glory, and all the angels with him, then he will sit on his glorious throne. [32]Before him will be gathered all the nations, and he will separate them one from

---

[b] Or *cut him in pieces.*
[c] Other ancient authorities add *and the bride.*
[d] This talent was more than fifteen years' wages of a laborer.
24:40–41: Lk 17:34–35.
24:42: Mk 13:35; Lk 12:40; Mt 25:13.
24:43–51: Lk 12:39–46.
24:43: 1 Thess 5:2; Rev 3:3; 16:15; 2 Pet 3:10.
24:45: Mt 25:21, 23.
24:49: Lk 21:34.
24:51: Mt 8:12; 13:42, 50; 22:13; 25:30; Lk 13:28.
25:1: Lk 12:35–38; Mk 13:34.
25:2: Mt 7:24–27.
25:10: Rev 19:9.
25:11–12: Lk 13:25; Mt 7:21–23.
25:13: Mt 24:42; Mk 13:35; Lk 12:40.
25:14–30: Lk 19:12–28.
25:19: Mt 18:23.
25:21: Lk 16:10; Mt 24:45.
25:29: Mt 13:12; Mk 4:25; Lk 8:18.
25:30: Mt 8:12; 13:42, 50; 22:13; Lk 13:28.
25:31: Mt 16:27; 19:28.
25:32: Ezek 34:17.
* 25:29: See note on Mt 13:12.

another as a shepherd separates the sheep from the goats, [33]and he will place the sheep at his right hand, but the goats at the left. [34]Then the King will say to those at his right hand, 'Come, O blessed of my Father, inherit the kingdom prepared for you from the foundation of the world; [35]for I was hungry and you gave me food, I was thirsty and you gave me drink, I was a stranger and you welcomed me, [36]I was naked and you clothed me, I was sick and you visited me, I was in prison and you came to me.' [37]Then the righteous will answer him, 'Lord, when did we see you hungry and feed you, or thirsty and give you drink? [38]And when did we see you a stranger and welcome you, or naked and clothe you? [39]And when did we see you sick or in prison and visit you?' [40]And the King will answer them, 'Truly, I say to you, as you did it to one of the least of these my brethren, you did it to me.' [41]Then he will say to those at his left hand, 'Depart from me, you cursed, into the eternal fire prepared for the devil and his angels; [42]for I was hungry and you gave me no food, I was thirsty and you gave me no drink, [43]I was a stranger and you did not welcome me, naked and you did not clothe me, sick and in prison and you did not visit me.' [44]Then they also will answer, 'Lord, when did we see you hungry or thirsty or a stranger or naked or sick or in prison, and did not minister to you?' [45]Then he will answer them, 'Truly, I say to you, as you did it not to one of the least of these, you did it not to me.' [46]And they will go away into eternal punishment, but the righteous into eternal life."

The Conspiracy to Kill Jesus

26 When Jesus had finished all these sayings, he said to his disciples, [2]"You know that after two days the Passover is coming, and the Son of man will be delivered up to be crucified."

3 Then the chief priests and the elders of the people gathered in the palace of the high priest, who was called Cai'aphas, [4]and took counsel together in order to arrest Jesus by stealth and kill him. [5]But they said, "Not during the feast, lest there be a tumult among the people."

The Anointing at Bethany

6 Now when Jesus was at Beth'any in the house of Simon the leper, [7]a woman came up to him with an alabaster jar of very expensive ointment, and she poured it on his head, as he sat at table. [8]But when the disciples saw it, they were indignant, saying, "Why this waste? [9]For this ointment might have been sold for a large sum, and given to the poor." [10]But Jesus, aware of this, said to them, "Why do you trouble the woman? For she has done a beautiful thing to me. [11]For you always have the poor with you, but you will not always have me. [12]In pouring this ointment on my body she has done it to prepare me for burial. [13]Truly, I say to you, wherever this gospel is preached in the

whole world, what she has done will be told in memory of her."

Judas Agrees to Betray Jesus

14 Then one of the Twelve, who was called Judas Iscariot, went to the chief priests [15]and said, "What will you give me if I deliver him to you?" And they paid him thirty pieces of silver. [16]And from that moment he sought an opportunity to betray him.

The Passover with the Disciples

17 Now on the first day of Unleavened Bread the disciples came to Jesus, saying, "Where will you have us prepare for you to eat the Passover?" * [18]He said, "Go into the city to such a one, and say to him, 'The Teacher says, My time is at hand; I will keep the Passover at your house with my disciples.'" [19]And the disciples did as Jesus had directed them, and they prepared the Passover.

20 When it was evening, he sat at table with the twelve disciples; [21]and as they were eating, he said, "Truly, I say to you, one of you will betray me." [22]And they were very sorrowful, and began to say to him one after another, "Is it I, Lord?" [23]He answered, "He who has dipped his hand in the dish with me, will betray me. [24]The Son of man goes as it is written of him, but woe to that man by whom the Son of man is betrayed! It would have been better for that man if he had not been born." [25]Judas, who betrayed him, said, "Is it I, Master?" f He said to him, "You have said so."

The Institution of the Last Supper

26 Now as they were eating, † Jesus took bread, and blessed, and broke it, and gave it to the disciples and said, "Take, eat; this is my body." [27]And he took a chalice, and when he had given thanks he gave it to them, saying, "Drink of it, all

---

e Other authorities omit *disciples*.
f Or *Rabbi*.

25:34: Lk 12:32; Mt 5:3; Rev 13:8; 17:8.
25:35-36: Is 58:7; Jas 1:27; 2:15-16; Heb 13:2; 2 Tim 1:16.
25:40: Mt 10:42; Mk 9:41; Heb 6:10; Prov 19:17.
25:41: Mk 9:48; Lk 16:23; Rev 20:10.
25:46: Dan 12:2; Jn 5:29.
26:1: Mt 7:28; 11:1; l3:53; 19:1.
26:2-5: Mk 14:1-2; Lk 22:1-2; Jn 11:47-53.
26:6-13: Mk 14:3-9; Jn 12:1-8; Lk 7:36-38.
26:11: Deut 15:11.
26:12: Jn 19:40.
26:14-16: Mk 14:10-11; Lk 22:3-6.
26:15: Ex 21:32; Zech 11:12.
26:17-19: Mk 14:12-16; Lk 22:7-13.
26:18: Mt 26:45; Jn 7:6; 12:23; 13:1; 17:1.
26:19: Mt 21:6; Deut 16:5-8.
26:20-24: Mk 14:17-21; Lk 22:14, 21-23; Jn 13:21-30.
26:24: Ps 41:9; Lk 24:25; 1 Cor 15:3; Acts 17:2-3; Mt 18:7.
26:26-29: Mk 14:22-25; Lk 22:17-19; 1 Cor 10:16; 11:23-26; Mt 14:19; 15:36.
* 26:17: The passover supper was eaten this year on the Friday evening (Jn 18:28). Jesus must have anticipated the passover meal because he would be dead the following day and because the meal prefigured his death.
† 26:26: The details of the Eucharist are superimposed on the ritual of the passover.

of you; [28]for this is my blood of the [g] covenant, which is poured out for many for the forgiveness of sins. [29]I tell you I shall not drink again of this fruit of the vine until that day when I drink it new with you in my Father's kingdom."

Peter's Denial Foretold

30 And when they had sung a hymn, they went out to the Mount of Olives. [31]Then Jesus said to them, "You will all fall away because of me this night; for it is written, 'I will strike the shepherd, and the sheep of the flock will be scattered.' [32]But after I am raised up, I will go before you to Galilee." [33]Peter declared to him, "Though they all fall away because of you, I will never fall away." [34]Jesus said to him, "Truly, I say to you, this very night, before the cock crows, you will deny me three times." [35]Peter said to him, "Even if I must die with you, I will not deny you." And so said all the disciples.

Jesus Prays in Gethsemane

36 Then Jesus went with them to a place called Gethsem'ane, and he said to his disciples, "Sit here, while I go over there and pray." [37]And taking with him Peter and the two sons of Zeb'edee, he began to be sorrowful and troubled. [38]Then he said to them, "My soul is very sorrowful, even to death; remain here, and watch[h] with me." [39]And going a little farther he fell on his face and prayed, "My Father, if it be possible, let this chalice pass from me; nevertheless, not as I will, but as you will." [40]And he came to the disciples and found them sleeping; and he said to Peter, "So, could you not watch[h] with me one hour? [41]Watch[h] and pray that you may not enter into temptation; the spirit indeed is willing, but the flesh is weak." [42]Again, for the second time, he went away and prayed, "My Father, if this cannot pass unless I drink it, your will be done." [43]And again he came and found them sleeping, for their eyes were heavy. [44]So, leaving them again, he went away and prayed for the third time, saying the same words. [45]Then he came to the disciples and said to them, "Are you still sleeping and taking your rest? Behold, the hour is at hand, and the Son of man is betrayed into the hands of sinners. [46]Rise, let us be going; see, my betrayer is at hand."

The Betrayal and Arrest of Jesus

47 While he was still speaking, Judas came, one of the Twelve, and with him a great crowd with swords and clubs, from the chief priests and the elders of the people. [48]Now the betrayer had given them a sign, saying, "The one I shall kiss is the man; seize him." [49]And he came up to Jesus at once and said, "Hail, Master!"[i] And he kissed him. [50]Jesus said to him, "Friend, why are you here?"[j] Then they came up and laid hands on Jesus and seized him. [51]And behold, one of those who were with Jesus stretched out his hand and

drew his sword, and struck the slave of the high priest, and cut off his ear. * [52]Then Jesus said to him, "Put your sword back into its place; for all who take the sword will perish by the sword. [53]Do you think that I cannot appeal to my Father, and he will at once send me more than twelve legions of angels? [54]But how then should the Scriptures be fulfilled, that it must be so?" [55]At that hour Jesus said to the crowds, "Have you come out as against a robber, with swords and clubs to capture me? Day after day I sat in the temple teaching, and you did not seize me. [56]But all this has taken place, that the Scriptures of the prophets might be fulfilled." Then all the disciples deserted him and fled.

Jesus before the High Priest

57 Then those who had seized Jesus led him to Cai'aphas the high priest, where the scribes and the elders had gathered. [58]But Peter followed him at a distance, as far as the courtyard of the high priest, and going inside he sat with the guards to see the end. [59]Now the chief priests and the whole council sought false testimony against Jesus that they might put him to death, † [60]but they found none, though many false witnesses came forward. At last two came forward [61]and said, "This fellow said, 'I am able to destroy the temple of God, and to build it in three days.'" [62]And the high priest stood up and said, "Have you no answer to make? What is it that these men testify against you?" [63]But Jesus was silent. And the high priest said to him, "I adjure you by the living God, tell us if you are the Christ, the Son of God." ‡ [64]Jesus said to him, "You have said so. But I tell you, hereafter you will see the Son of man seated at the right hand of Power, and coming on the clouds of heaven." [65]Then the high priest tore his robes, and

---

[g] Other ancient authorities insert *new*.
[h] Or *keep awake*.
[i] Or *Rabbi*.
[j] Or *do that for which you have come*.
26:28: Heb 9:20; Mt 20:28; Mk 1:4; Ex 24:6–8.
26:30-35: Mk 14:26–31; Lk 22:33–34, 39; Jn 14:31; 18:1; 13:36–38.
26:31: Zech 13:7; Jn 16:32.
26:32: Mt 28:7, 10, 16.
26:36-46: Mk 14:32–42; Lk 22:40–46.
26:38: Jn 12:27; Heb 5:7–8.
26:39: Jn 18:11; Mt 20:22.
26:41: Mt 6:13; Lk 11:4.
26:42: Jn 4:34; 5:30; 6:38.
26:45: Mt 26:18; Jn 12:23; 13:1; 17:1.
26:47-56: Mk 14:43–50; Lk 22:47–53; Jn 18:2–11.
26:50: Mt 20:13; 22:12.
26:52: Gen 9:6; Rev 13:10.
26:55: Lk 19:47; Jn 18:19–21.
26:57-75: Mk 14:53–72; Lk 22:54–71; Jn 18:12–27.
26:61: Mt 24:2; 27:40; Acts 6:14; Jn 2:19.
26:63: Mt 27:11; Jn 18:33.
26:64: Mt 16:28; Dan 7:13; Ps 110:1.
26:65: Num 14:6; Acts 14:14; Lev 24:16.
* 26:51: It was Peter, as John in his later Gospel tells us (Jn 18:10), though Matthew is reluctant to say so.
† 26:59: They sought evidence against him and this was necessarily false.
‡ 26:64–65: For the first time Jesus speaks clearly of his own identity. Caiaphas evidently understands him to claim divinity.

said, "He has uttered blasphemy. Why do we still need witnesses? You have now heard his blasphemy. [66]What is your judgment?" They answered, "He deserves death." [67]Then they spat in his face, and struck him; and some slapped him, [68]saying, "Prophesy to us, you Christ! Who is it that struck you?"

Peter Denies Jesus

69 Now Peter was sitting outside in the courtyard. And a maid came up to him, and said, "You also were with Jesus the Galilean." [70]But he denied it before them all, saying, "I do not know what you mean." [71]And when he went out to the porch, another maid saw him, and she said to the bystanders, "This man was with Jesus of Nazareth." [72]And again he denied it with an oath, "I do not know the man." [73]After a little while the bystanders came up and said to Peter, "Certainly you are also one of them, for your accent betrays you." [74]Then he began to invoke a curse on himself and to swear, "I do not know the man." And immediately the cock crowed. [75]And Peter remembered the saying of Jesus, "Before the cock crows, you will deny me three times." And he went out and wept bitterly.

Jesus Brought before Pilate

27 When morning came, all the chief priests and the elders of the people took counsel against Jesus to put him to death; [2]and they bound him and led him away and delivered him to Pilate the governor.

Judas Hangs Himself

3 When Judas, his betrayer, saw that he was condemned, he repented and brought back the thirty pieces of silver to the chief priests and the elders, [4]saying, "I have sinned in betraying innocent blood." They said, "What is that to us? See to it yourself." [5]And throwing down the pieces of silver in the temple, he departed; and he went and hanged himself. [6]But the chief priests, taking the pieces of silver, said, "It is not lawful to put them into the treasury, since they are blood money." [7]So they took counsel, and bought with them the potter's field, to bury strangers in. [8]Therefore that field has been called the Field of Blood to this day. [9]Then was fulfilled what had been spoken by the prophet Jeremiah, saying, "And they took the thirty pieces of silver, the price of him on whom a price had been set by some of the sons of Israel, [10]and they gave them for the potter's field, as the Lord directed me."

Pilate Questions Jesus

11 Now Jesus stood before the governor; and the governor asked him, "Are you the King of the Jews?" Jesus said to him, "You have said so." [12]But when he was accused by the chief priests and elders, he made no answer. [13]Then Pilate said to him, "Do you not hear how many things they testify against you?" [14]But he gave him no answer,

not even to a single charge; so that the governor wondered greatly.

Barabbas or Jesus?

15 Now at the feast the governor was accustomed to release for the crowd any one prisoner whom they wanted. [16]And they had then a notorious prisoner, called Barab'bas.* [17]So when they had gathered, Pilate said to them, "Whom do you want me to release for you, Barab'bas* or Jesus who is called Christ?" [18]For he knew that it was out of envy that they had delivered him up. [19]Besides, while he was sitting on the judgment seat, his wife sent word to him, "Have nothing to do with that righteous man, for I have suffered much over him today in a dream." [20]Now the chief priests and the elders persuaded the people to ask for Barab'bas and destroy Jesus. [21]The governor again said to them, "Which of the two do you want me to release for you?" And they said, "Barab'bas." [22]Pilate said to them, "Then what shall I do with Jesus who is called Christ?" They all said, "Let him be crucified." [23]And he said, "Why, what evil has he done?" But they shouted all the more, "Let him be crucified."

Pilate Delivers Jesus to Be Crucified

24 So when Pilate saw that he was gaining nothing, but rather that a riot was beginning, he took water and washed his hands before the crowd, saying, "I am innocent of this righteous man's blood;[1] see to it yourselves." [25]And all the people answered, "His blood be on us and on our children!" [26]Then he released for them Barab'bas, and having scourged Jesus, delivered him to be crucified.

The Soldiers Mock Jesus

27 Then the soldiers of the governor took Jesus into the praetorium, and they gathered the whole battalion before him. [28]And they stripped him and put a scarlet robe upon him, [29]and plaiting a crown of thorns they put it on his head, and put a reed in his right hand. And kneeling before him they mocked him, saying, "Hail, King of the Jews!" [30]And they spat upon him, and took the reed and struck him on the head. [31]And when they had mocked him, they stripped him of the robe, and put his own clothes on him, and led him away to crucify him.

* Other ancient authorities read *Jesus Barabbas*.
[1] Other ancient authorities omit *righteous* or *man's*.
26:75: Mt 26:34.
27:1-2: Mk 15:1; Lk 23:1; Jn 18:28.
27:3-10: Acts 1:16–20.
27:3: Mt 26:15; Ex 21:32.
27:6: Deut 23:18.
27:9: Zech 11:12–13; Jer 32:6–15; 18:2–3.
27:11-26: Mk 15:2–15; Lk 23:3, 18–25; Jn 18:29–19:16.
27:14: Lk 23:9; Mt 26:62; Mk 14:60; 1 Tim 6:13.
27:19: Lk 23:4.
27:21: Acts 3:13–14.
27:24: Deut 21:6–9; Ps 26:6.
27:25: Acts 5:28; Josh 2:19.
27:27-31: Mk 15:16–20; Lk 23:2; Jn 19:2–3.

The Crucifixion of Jesus

32 As they were marching out, they came upon a man of Cyre'ne, Simon by name; this man they compelled to carry his cross. [33]And when they came to a place called Gol'gotha (which means the place of a skull), [34]they offered him wine to drink, mingled with gall; but when he tasted it, he would not drink it. [35]And when they had crucified him, they divided his garments among them by casting lots; [36]then they sat down and kept watch over him there. [37]And over his head they put the charge against him, which read, "This is Jesus the King of the Jews." [38]Then two robbers were crucified with him, one on the right and one on the left. [39]And those who passed by derided him, wagging their heads [40]and saying, "You who would destroy the temple and build it in three days, save yourself! If you are the Son of God, come down from the cross." [41]So also the chief priests, with the scribes and elders, mocked him, saying, [42]"He saved others; he cannot save himself. He is the King of Israel; let him come down now from the cross, and we will believe in him. [43]He trusts in God; let God deliver him now, if he desires him; for he said, 'I am the Son of God.'" [44]And the robbers who were crucified with him also reviled him in the same way.

The Death of Jesus

45 Now from the sixth hour there was darkness over all the land [m] until the ninth hour. [46]And about the ninth hour Jesus cried with a loud voice, "Eli, Eli, la'ma sabach-tha'ni?" that is, "My God, my God, why have you forsaken me?" [*] [47]And some of the bystanders hearing it said, "This man is calling Eli'jah." [48]And one of them at once ran and took a sponge, filled it with vinegar, and put it on a reed, and gave it to him to drink. [49]But the others said, "Wait, let us see whether Eli'jah will come to save him." [n] [50]And Jesus cried again with a loud voice and yielded up his spirit.

51 And behold, the curtain of the temple was torn in two, from top to bottom; and the earth shook, and the rocks were split; [52]the tombs also were opened, and many bodies of the saints who had fallen asleep were raised, [53]and coming out of the tombs after his resurrection they went into the holy city and appeared to many. [54]When the centurion and those who were with him, keeping watch over Jesus, saw the earthquake and what took place, they were filled with awe, and said, "Truly this was the Son [x] of God!"

55 There were also many women there, looking on from afar, who had followed Jesus from Galilee, ministering to him; [56]among whom were Mary Mag'dalene, and Mary the mother of James and Joseph, and the mother of the sons of Zeb'edee.

The Burial of Jesus

57 When it was evening, there came a rich man from Arimathe'a, named Joseph, who also was a disciple of Jesus. [58]He went to Pilate and asked for the body of Jesus. Then Pilate ordered it to be given to him. [59]And Joseph took the body, and wrapped it in a clean linen shroud, [60]and laid it in his own new tomb, which he had hewn in the rock; and he rolled a great stone to the door of the tomb, and departed. [61]Mary Mag'dalene and the other Mary were there, sitting opposite the tomb.

The Guard at the Tomb

62 Next day, that is, after the day of Preparation, the chief priests and the Pharisees gathered before Pilate [63]and said, "Sir, we remember how that impostor said, while he was still alive, 'After three days I will rise again.' [64]Therefore order the tomb to be made secure until the third day, lest his disciples go and steal him away, and tell the people, 'He has risen from the dead,' and the last fraud will be worse than the first." [65]Pilate said to them, "You have a guard [o] of soldiers; go, make it as secure as you can." [p] [66]So they went and made the tomb secure by sealing the stone and setting a guard. [†]

The Resurrection of Jesus

28 [‡] Now after the sabbath, toward the dawn of the first day of the week, Mary Mag'-dalene and the other Mary went to see the tomb. [2]And behold, there was a great earthquake; for an angel of the Lord descended from heaven and came and rolled back the stone, and sat upon it. [3]His appearance was like lightning, and his clothing white as snow. [4]And for fear of him the guards trembled and became like dead men. [5]But

---

[m] Or *earth.*
[n] Other ancient authorities insert *And another took a spear and pierced his side, and out came water and blood.*
[x] Or *a son.*
[o] Or *Take a guard.*
[p] Greek *know.*

27:32: Mk 15:21; Lk 23:26; Jn 19:17; Heb 13:12.
27:33–44: Mk 15:22–32; Lk 23:33–39; Jn 19:17–24.
27:35: Ps 22:18.
27:39: Ps 22:7–8; 109:25.
27:40: Mt 26:61; Acts 6:14; Jn 2:19.
27:45–56: Mk 15:33–41; Lk 23:44–54; Jn 19:28–30.
27:46: Ps 22:1.
27:48: Ps 69:21.
27:51: Heb 9:8; 10:19; Ex 26:31–35; Mt 28:2.
27:54: Mt 3:17; 17:5.
27:56: Lk 24:10.
27:57–61: Mk 15:42–47; Lk 23:50–56; Jn 19:38–42; Acts 13:29.
27:63: Mt 16:21; 17:23; 20:19.
27:66: Mt 27:60; 28:11–15.
28:1–8: Mk 16:1–8; Lk 24:1–9; Jn 20:1–2.
28:1: Lk 8:2; Mt 27:56.
28:2: Mt 27:51, 60.
28:4: Mt 27:62–66.
* 27:46: Jesus applies Psalm 22 (Vulgate 21) to himself.
† 27:66: The sealing and guarding only helped to make the subsequent resurrection more obvious.
‡ 28:1–20: The resurrection appearances. There are divergent traditions in the gospels, Galilean and Judean. Paul adds his own record (1 Cor 15). The accounts do not easily fit together, but this is surely evidence of their genuineness. There is no attempt to produce an artificial conformity.

the angel said to the women, "Do not be afraid; for I know that you seek Jesus who was crucified. [6]He is not here; for he has risen, as he said. Come, see the place where he ᑫ lay. [7]Then go quickly and tell his disciples that he has risen from the dead, and behold, he is going before you to Galilee; there you will see him. Behold, I have told you." [8]So they departed quickly from the tomb with fear and great joy, and ran to tell his disciples. [9]And behold, Jesus met them and said, "Hail!" And they came up and took hold of his feet and worshiped him. [10]Then Jesus said to them, "Do not be afraid; go and tell my brethren to go to Galilee, and there they will see me."

The Report of the Guard

11 While they were going, behold, some of the guard went into the city and told the chief priests all that had taken place. [12]And when they had assembled with the elders and taken counsel, they gave a sum of money to the soldiers [13]and said, "Tell people, 'His disciples came by night and stole him away while we were asleep.' [14]And if this comes to the governor's ears, we will satisfy

him and keep you out of trouble." [15]So they took the money and did as they were directed; and this story has been spread among the Jews to this day.

Jesus Commissions the Disciples

16 Now the eleven disciples went to Galilee, to the mountain to which Jesus had directed them. [17]And when they saw him they worshiped him; but some doubted. [18]And Jesus came and said to them, "All authority in heaven and on earth has been given to me. [19]Go therefore and make disciples of all nations, baptizing them in the name of the Father and of the Son and of the Holy Spirit, [20]teaching them to observe all that I have commanded you; and behold, I am with you always, to the close of the age."

ᑫ Other ancient authorities read *the Lord*.
28:7: Mt 26:32; 28:16; Jn 21:1–23.
28:9: Jn 20:14–18.
28:11: Mt 27:62–66.
28:16–17: 1 Cor 15:5; Jn 21:1–23.
28:18: Mt 11:27; Lk 10:22; Phil 2:9; Eph 1:20–22.
28:19: Lk 24:47; Acts 1:8.
28:20: Mt 13:39, 49; 24:3; 18:20; Acts 18:10.

MARK

The Preaching of John the Baptist

1 The beginning of the gospel of Jesus Christ, the Son of God. [a]

2 As it is written in Isaiah the prophet, [b]
"Behold, I send my messenger before your face,
who shall prepare your way;
[3]the voice of one crying in the wilderness:
Prepare the way of the Lord,
make his paths straight—"

[4]John the Baptist appeared [c] in the wilderness, preaching a baptism of repentance for the forgiveness of sins. [5]And there went out to him all the country of Judea, and all the people of Jerusalem; and they were baptized by him in the river Jordan, confessing their sins. [6]Now John was clothed with camel's hair, and had a leather belt around his waist, and ate locusts and wild honey. [7]And he preached, saying, "After me comes he who is mightier than I, the thong of whose sandals I am not worthy to stoop down and untie. [8]I have baptized you with water; but he will baptize you with the Holy Spirit."

The Baptism of Jesus

9 In those days Jesus came from Nazareth of Galilee and was baptized by John in the Jordan. [10]And when he came up out of the water, immediately he saw the heavens opened and the Spirit descending upon him like a dove; [11]and a voice came from heaven, "You are my beloved Son; [d] with you I am well pleased."

The Temptation of Jesus

12 The Spirit immediately drove him out into the wilderness. [13]And he was in the wilderness forty days, tempted by Satan; and he was with the wild beasts; and the angels ministered to him.

Jesus Preaches the Gospel in Galilee

14 Now after John was arrested, Jesus came into Galilee, preaching the gospel of God, [15]and saying, "The time is fulfilled, and the kingdom of God is at hand; repent, and believe in the gospel."

Jesus Calls the First Disciples

16 And passing along by the Sea of Galilee, he saw Simon and Andrew the brother of Simon casting a net in the sea; for they were fishermen. [17]And Jesus said to them, "Follow me and I will make you become fishers of men." [18]And immediately they left their nets and followed him. [19]And going on a little farther, he saw James the son of Zeb'edee and John his brother, who were in their boat mending the nets. [20]And immediately he called them; and they left their father Zeb'edee in the boat with the hired servants, and followed him.

The Man with an Unclean Spirit

21 And they went into Caper'na-um; and immediately on the sabbath he entered the synagogue and taught. [22]And they were astonished at his teaching, for he taught them as one who had authority, and not as the scribes. [23]And immediately there was in their synagogue a man with an unclean spirit; [24]and he cried out, "What have you to do with us, Jesus of Nazareth? Have you come to destroy us? I know who you are, the Holy One of God." [25]But Jesus rebuked him, saying, "Be silent, and come out of him!" [26]And the unclean spirit, convulsing him and crying with a loud voice, came out of him. [27]And they were all amazed, so that they questioned among themselves, saying, "What is this? A new teaching! With authority he commands even the unclean spirits, and they obey him." [28]And at once his fame spread everywhere throughout all the surrounding region of Galilee.

Healings at Simon's House

29 And immediately he [e] left the synagogue, and entered the house of Simon and Andrew, with James and John. [30]Now Simon's mother-in-law lay sick with a fever, and immediately they told him of her. [31]And he came and took her by the hand and lifted her up, and the fever left her; and she served them.

32 That evening, at sundown, they brought to him all who were sick or possessed with demons. [33]And the whole city was gathered together about

---

[a] Other ancient authorities omit *the Son of God*.
[b] Other ancient authorities read *in the prophets*.
[c] Other ancient authorities read *John was baptizing*.
[d] Or *my Son, my* (or *the*) *Beloved*.
[e] Other ancient authorities read *they*.
1:2–8: Mt 3:1–12; Lk 3:2–16; Jn 1:6, 15, 19–28.
1:2: Mal 3:1; Mt 11:10; Lk 7:27.
1:3: Is 40:3.
1:4: Acts 13:24.
1:9–11: Mt 3:13–17; Lk 3:21–22; Jn 1:29–34.
1:11: Ps 2:7; Is 42:1.
1:12–13: Mt 4:1–11; Lk 4:1–13.
1:14–15: Mt 4:12–17; Lk 4:14–15.
1:16–20: Mt 4:18–22; Lk 5:1–11; Jn 1:40–42.
1:21–22: Mt 7:28–29; Lk 4:31–32.
1:23–28: Lk 4:33–37.
1:24: Jn 6:69.
1:29–31: Mt 8:14–15; Lk 4:38–39.
1:32–34: Mt 8:16–17; Lk 4:40–41.

the door. [34]And he healed many who were sick with various diseases, and cast out many demons; and he would not permit the demons to speak, because they knew him. *

Jesus Preaches and Heals throughout Galilee

35 And in the morning, a great while before day, he rose and went out to a lonely place, and there he prayed. [36]And Simon and those who were with him followed him, [37]and they found him and said to him, "Every one is searching for you." [38]And he said to them, "Let us go on to the next towns, that I may preach there also; for that is why I came out." [39]And he went throughout all Galilee, preaching in their synagogues and casting out demons.

Jesus Cleanses a Leper

40 And a leper came to him begging him, and kneeling said to him, "If you will, you can make me clean." [41]Moved with pity, he stretched out his hand and touched him, and said to him, "I will; be clean." [42]And immediately the leprosy left him, and he was made clean. [43]And he sternly charged him, and sent him away at once, [44]and said to him, "See that you say nothing to any one; but go, show yourself to the priest, and offer for your cleansing what Moses commanded, for a proof to the people." [f] [45]But he went out and began to talk freely about it, and to spread the news, so that Jesus [g] could no longer openly enter a town, but was out in the country; and people came to him from every quarter.

Jesus Heals a Paralytic

2 And when he returned to Caper'na-um after some days, it was reported that he was at home. [2]And many were gathered together, so that there was no longer room for them, not even about the door; and he was preaching the word to them. [3]And they came, bringing to him a paralytic carried by four men. [4]And when they could not get near him because of the crowd, they removed the roof above him; and when they had made an opening, they let down the pallet on which the paralytic lay. [5]And when Jesus saw their faith, he said to the paralytic, "Child, your sins are forgiven." [6]Now some of the scribes were sitting there, questioning in their hearts, [7]"Why does this man speak like this? It is blasphemy! Who can forgive sins but God alone?" [8]And immediately Jesus, perceiving in his spirit that they questioned like this within themselves, said to them, "Why do you question like this in your hearts? [9]Which is easier, to say to the paralytic, 'Your sins are forgiven,' or to say, 'Rise, take up your pallet and walk'? [10]But that you may know that the Son of man has authority on earth to forgive sins"—he said to the paralytic—[11]"I say to you, rise, take up your pallet and go home." [12]And he rose, and immediately took up the pallet and went out before them all; so that they were all amazed and glorified God, saying, "We never saw anything like this!"

Jesus Calls Levi

13 He went out again beside the sea; and all the crowd gathered about him, and he taught them. [14]And as he passed on, he saw Levi † the son of Alphae'us sitting at the tax office, and he said to him, "Follow me." And he rose and followed him.

15 And as he sat at table in his house, many tax collectors and sinners were sitting with Jesus and his disciples; for there were many who followed him. [16]And the scribes of [h] the Pharisees, when they saw that he was eating with sinners and tax collectors, said to his disciples, "Why does he eat [i] with tax collectors and sinners?" [17]And when Jesus heard it, he said to them, "Those who are well have no need of a physician, but those who are sick; I came not to call the righteous, but sinners."

The Question about Fasting

18 Now John's disciples and the Pharisees were fasting; and people came and said to him, "Why do John's disciples and the disciples of the Pharisees fast, but your disciples do not fast?" [19]And Jesus said to them, "Can the wedding guests fast while the bridegroom is with them? As long as they have the bridegroom with them, they cannot fast. [20]The days will come, when the bridegroom is taken away from them, and then they will fast in that day. [21]No one sews a piece of unshrunk cloth on an old garment; if he does, the patch tears away from it, the new from the old, and a worse tear is made. [22]And no one puts new wine into old wineskins; if he does, the wine will burst the skins, and the wine is lost, and so are the skins; but new wine is for fresh skins." [j]

A Teaching about the Sabbath

23 One sabbath he was going through the grainfields; and as they made their way his disciples began to pluck heads of grain. [24]And the

---

[f] Greek to them.
[g] Greek he.
[h] Other ancient authorities read and.
[i] Other ancient authorities add and drink.
[j] Other ancient authorities omit but new wine is for fresh skins.
1:35–38: Lk 4:42–43.
1:39: Mt 4:23–25; Lk 4:44.
1:40–45: Mt 8:2–4; Lk 5:12–16.
1:44: Lev 13:49; 14:2–32.
2:3–12: Mt 9:2–8; Lk 5:18–26.
2:12: Mt 9:33.
2:14–17: Mt 9:9–13; Lk 5:27–32.
2:16: Acts 23:9.
2:18–22: Mt 9:14–17; Lk 5:33–38.
2:20: Lk 17:22.
2:23–28: Mt 12:1–8; Lk 6:1–5.
2:23: Deut 23:25.
* 1:34: Throughout his ministry Jesus forbade the demons and those he healed of their infirmities to reveal his identity as Messiah, because the people, with their ideas of a national leader to come, were only too prone to mistake his true mission.
† 2:14, *Levi:* Mark does not identify him with Matthew the apostle; cf. Mt 9:9.

Pharisees said to him, "Look, why are they doing what is not lawful on the sabbath?" [25]And he said to them, "Have you never read what David did, when he was in need and was hungry, he and those who were with him: [26]how he entered the house of God, when Abi'athar was high priest, and ate the showbread, which it is not lawful for any but the priests to eat, and also gave it to those who were with him?" [27]And he said to them, "The sabbath was made for man, not man for the sabbath; [28]so the Son of man is lord even of the sabbath."

The Man with a Withered Hand

3 Again he entered the synagogue, and a man was there who had a withered hand. [2]And they watched him, to see whether he would heal him on the sabbath, so that they might accuse him. [3]And he said to the man who had the withered hand, "Come here." [4]And he said to them, "Is it lawful on the sabbath to do good or to do harm, to save life or to kill?" But they were silent. [5]And he looked around at them with anger, grieved at their hardness of heart, and said to the man, "Stretch out your hand." He stretched it out, and his hand was restored. [6]The Pharisees went out, and immediately held counsel with the Hero'dians against him, how to destroy him.

A Multitude by the Sea

7 Jesus withdrew with his disciples to the sea, and a great multitude from Galilee followed; also from Judea [8]and Jerusalem and Idume'a and from beyond the Jordan and from about Tyre and Si'don a great multitude, hearing all that he did, came to him. [9]And he told his disciples to have a boat ready for him because of the crowd, lest they should crush him; [10]for he had healed many, so that all who had diseases pressed upon him to touch him. [11]And whenever the unclean spirits saw him, they fell down before him and cried out, "You are the Son of God." [12]And he strictly ordered them not to make him known.

Jesus Appoints the Twelve

13 And he went up on the mountain, and called to him those whom he desired; and they came to him. [14]And he appointed twelve,[k] to be with him, and to be sent out to preach [15]and have authority to cast out demons: [16]Simon whom he surnamed Peter; [17]James the son of Zeb'edee and John the brother of James, whom he surnamed Bo-aner'ges, that is, sons of thunder; [18]Andrew, and Philip, and Bartholomew, and Matthew, and Thomas, and James the son of Alphae'us, and Thaddae'us, and Simon the Cananaean, [19]and Judas Iscariot, who betrayed him.

Jesus and Beelzebul

Then he went home; [20]and the crowd came together again, so that they could not even eat. [21]And when his friends heard it, they went out to seize him, for they said, "He is beside himself."

[22]And the scribes who came down from Jerusalem said, "He is possessed by Be-el'zebul, and by the prince of demons he casts out the demons." [23]And he called them to him, and said to them in parables, "How can Satan cast out Satan? [24]If a kingdom is divided against itself, that kingdom cannot stand. [25]And if a house is divided against itself, that house will not be able to stand. [26]And if Satan has risen up against himself and is divided, he cannot stand, but is coming to an end. [27]But no one can enter a strong man's house and plunder his goods, unless he first binds the strong man; then indeed he may plunder his house.

28 "Truly, I say to you, all sins will be forgiven the sons of men, and whatever blasphemies they utter; [29]but whoever blasphemes against the Holy Spirit never has forgiveness, but is guilty of an eternal sin"——[30]for they had said, "He has an unclean spirit."

The True Kindred of Jesus

31 And his mother and his brethren * came; and standing outside they sent to him and called him. [32]And a crowd was sitting about him; and they said to him, "Your mother and your brethren[1] are outside, asking for you." [33]And he replied, "Who are my mother and my brethren?" [34]And looking around on those who sat about him, he said, "Here are my mother and my brethren! [35]Whoever does the will of God is my brother, and sister, and mother."

The Parable of the Sower

4 Again he began to teach beside the sea. And a very large crowd gathered about him; so that he got into a boat and sat in it on the sea; and the whole crowd was beside the sea on the land. [2]And he taught them many things in parables, and in his teaching he said to them: [3]"Listen! A sower went out to sow. [4]And as he sowed, some seed fell along the path, and the birds came and devoured it. [5]Other seed fell on rocky ground, where it had not much soil, and immediately it

---

[k] Other ancient authorities add *whom also he named apostles.*
[1] Other early authorities add *and your sisters.*
2:26: 1 Sam 21:1–6; 2 Sam 8:17.
2:27: Ex 23:12; Deut 5:14.
3:1–6: Mt 12:9–14; Lk 6:6–11.
3:2: Lk 11:54.
3:6: Mk 12:13.
3:7–12: Mt 4:24–25; 12:15–16; Lk 6:17–19.
3:8: Mt 11:21.
3:10: Mk 5:29, 34; 6:56.
3:12: Mk 1:45.
3:13: Mt 5:1; Lk 6:12.
3:14–15: Mt 10:1.
3:16–19: Mt 10:2–4; Lk 6:14–16; Acts 1:13.
3:19: Mk 2:1; 7:17.
3:20: Mk 6:31.
3:21: Mk 3:31–35; Jn 10:20.
3:22–27: Mt 12:24–29; Lk 11:15–22.
3:22: Mt 9:34; 10:25.
3:27: Is 49:24–25.
3:28–30: Mt 12:31–32; Lk 12:10.
3:31–35: Mt 12:46–50; Lk 8:19–21.
4:1–9: Mt 13:1–9; Lk 8:4–8.
* 3:31, *brethren:* See note on Mt 12:46.

sprang up, since it had no depth of soil; [6]and when the sun rose it was scorched, and since it had no root it withered away. [7]Other seed fell among thorns and the thorns grew up and choked it, and it yielded no grain. [8]And other seeds fell into good soil and brought forth grain, growing up and increasing and yielding thirtyfold and sixtyfold and a hundredfold." [9]And he said, "He who has ears to hear, let him hear."

Explanation of the Parable

10 And when he was alone, those who were about him with the Twelve asked him concerning the parables. [11]And he said to them, "To you has been given the secret of the kingdom of God, but for those outside everything is in parables; [12]so that * they may indeed see but not perceive, and may indeed hear but not understand; lest they should turn again, and be forgiven." [13]And he said to them, "Do you not understand this parable? How then will you understand all the parables? [14]The sower sows the word. [15]And these are the ones along the path, where the word is sown; when they hear, Satan immediately comes and takes away the word which is sown in them. [16]And these in like manner are the ones sown upon rocky ground, who, when they hear the word, immediately receive it with joy; [17]and they have no root in themselves, but endure for a while; then, when tribulation or persecution arises on account of the word, immediately they fall away.[m] [18]And others are the ones sown among thorns; they are those who hear the word, [19]but the cares of the world, and the delight in riches, and the desire for other things, enter in and choke the word, and it proves unfruitful. [20]But those that were sown upon the good soil are the ones who hear the word and accept it and bear fruit, thirtyfold and sixtyfold and a hundredfold."

A Lamp Is Not Hidden

21 And he said to them, "Is a lamp brought in to be put under a bushel, or under a bed, and not on a stand? [22]For there is nothing hidden, except to be made manifest; nor is anything secret, except to come to light. [23]If any man has ears to hear, let him hear." [24]And he said to them, "Take heed what you hear; the measure you give will be the measure you get, and still more will be given you. [25]For to him who has will more be given; and from him who has not, even what he has will be taken away."

A Parable about Seeds

26 And he said, "The kingdom of God is as if a man should scatter seed upon the ground, [27]and should sleep and rise night and day, and the seed should sprout and grow, he knows not how. [28]The earth produces of itself, first the blade, then the ear, then the full grain in the ear. [29]But when the grain is ripe, at once he puts in the sickle, because the harvest has come."

30 And he said, "With what can we compare the kingdom of God, or what parable shall we use for it? [31]It is like a grain of mustard seed, which, when sown upon the ground, is the smallest of all the seeds on earth; [32]yet when it is sown it grows up and becomes the greatest of all shrubs, and puts forth large branches, so that the birds of the air can make nests in its shade."

The Use of Parables

33 With many such parables he spoke the word to them, as they were able to hear it; [34]he did not speak to them without a parable, but privately to his own disciples he explained everything.

Jesus Calms a Storm on the Sea

35 On that day, when evening had come, he said to them, "Let us go across to the other side." [36]And leaving the crowd, they took him with them, just as he was, in the boat. And other boats were with him. [37]And a great storm of wind arose, and the waves beat into the boat, so that the boat was already filling. [38]But he was in the stern, asleep on the cushion; and they woke him and said to him, "Teacher, do you not care if we perish?" [39]And he awoke and rebuked the wind, and said to the sea, "Peace! Be still!" And the wind ceased, and there was a great calm. [40]He said to them, "Why are you afraid? Have you no faith?" [41]And they were filled with awe, and said to one another, "Who then is this, that even wind and sea obey him?"

Jesus Heals the Gerasene Demoniac

5 They came to the other side of the sea, to the country of the Ger′asenes.[n] [2]And when he had come out of the boat, there met him out of the tombs a man with an unclean spirit, [3]who lived among the tombs; and no one could bind him any more, even with a chain; [4]for he had often been bound with shackles and chains, but the chains he wrenched apart, and the shackles he broke in pieces; and no one had the strength to subdue him. [5]Night and day among the tombs and on the mountains he was always crying out, and bruising himself with stones. [6]And when he saw Jesus from afar, he ran and worshiped him;

---

[n] Other ancient authorities read Gergesenes, some Gadarenes.
4:10–12: Mt 13:10–15; Lk 8:9–10.
4:11: 1 Cor 5:12–13; Col 4:5; 1 Thess 4:12; 1 Tim 3:7.
4:12: Is 6:9–10.
4:13–20: Mt 13:18–23; Lk 8:11–15.
4:21: Mt 5:15; Lk 8:16; 11:33.
4:22: Mt 10:26; Lk 8:17; 12:2.
4:23: Mt 11:15; Mk 4:9.
4:24: Mt 7:2; Lk 6:38.
4:25: Mt 13:12; 25:29; Lk 8:18; 19:26.
4:26–29: Mt 13:24–30.
4:30–32: Mt 13:31–32; Lk 13:18–19.
4:34: Mt 13:34; Jn 16:25.
4:35–41: Mt 8:18, 23–27; Lk 8:22–25.
5:1–20: Mt 8:28–34; Lk 8:26–39.
* 4:12, so that . . . : One might rephrase this: "so that the Scripture might be fulfiled"; cf. Jn 18:32; 19:24, 28. It was not God's intention to prevent their understanding. Matthew avoids this difficulty by writing, "I speak to them in parables, because seeing they do not see" (Mt 13:13).

[7]and crying out with a loud voice, he said, "What have you to do with me, Jesus, Son of the Most High God? I adjure you by God, do not torment me." [8]For he had said to him, "Come out of the man, you unclean spirit!" [9]And Jesus ° asked him, "What is your name?" He replied, "My name is Legion; for we are many." [10]And he begged him eagerly not to send them out of the country. [11]Now a great herd of swine was feeding there on the hillside; [12]and they begged him, "Send us to the swine, let us enter them." [13]So he gave them leave. And the unclean spirits came out, and entered the swine; and the herd, numbering about two thousand, rushed down the steep bank into the sea, and were drowned in the sea.

14 The herdsmen fled, and told it in the city and in the country. And people came to see what it was that had happened. [15]And they came to Jesus, and saw the demoniac sitting there, clothed and in his right mind, the man who had had the legion; and they were afraid. [16]And those who had seen it told what had happened to the demoniac and to the swine. [17]And they began to beg Jesus ᴾ to depart from their neighborhood. [18]And as he was getting into the boat, the man who had been possessed with demons begged him that he might be with him. [19]But he refused, and said to him, "Go home to your friends, and tell them how much the Lord has done for you, and how he has had mercy on you." [20]And he went away and began to proclaim in the Decap′olis how much Jesus had done for him; and all men marveled.

A Girl Restored to Life and a Woman Healed

21 And when Jesus had crossed again in the boat to the other side, a great crowd gathered about him; and he was beside the sea. [22]Then came one of the rulers of the synagogue, Ja′irus by name; and seeing him, he fell at his feet, [23]and begged him, saying, "My little daughter is at the point of death. Come and lay your hands on her, so that she may be made well, and live." [24]And he went with him.

And a great crowd followed him and thronged about him. [25]And there was a woman who had had a flow of blood for twelve years, [26]and who had suffered much under many physicians, and had spent all that she had, and was no better but rather grew worse. [27]She had heard the reports about Jesus, and came up behind him in the crowd and touched his garment. [28]For she said, "If I touch even his garments, I shall be made well." [29]And immediately the hemorrhage ceased; and she felt in her body that she was healed of her disease. [30]And Jesus, perceiving in himself that power had gone forth from him, immediately turned about in the crowd, and said, "Who touched my garments?" [31]And his disciples said to him, "You see the crowd pressing around you, and yet you say, 'Who touched me?'" [32]And he

looked around to see who had done it. [33]But the woman, knowing what had been done to her, came in fear and trembling and fell down before him, and told him the whole truth. [34]And he said to her, "Daughter, your faith has made you well; go in peace, and be healed of your disease."

35 While he was still speaking, there came from the ruler's house some who said, "Your daughter is dead. Why trouble the Teacher any further?" [36]But ignoring ᑫ what they said, Jesus said to the ruler of the synagogue, "Do not fear, only believe." [37]And he allowed no one to follow him except Peter and James and John the brother of James. [38]When they came to the house of the ruler of the synagogue, he saw a tumult, and people weeping and wailing loudly. [39]And when he had entered, he said to them, "Why do you make a tumult and weep? The child is not dead but sleeping." [40]And they laughed at him. But he put them all outside, and took the child's father and mother and those who were with him, and went in where the child was. [41]Taking her by the hand he said to her, "Tal′itha cu′mi"; which means, "Little girl, I say to you, arise." [42]And immediately the girl got up and walked; for she was twelve years old. And immediately they were overcome with amazement. [43]And he strictly charged them that no one should know this, * and told them to give her something to eat.

The Rejection of Jesus at Nazareth

6 He went away from there and came to his own country; and his disciples followed him. [2]And on the sabbath he began to teach in the synagogue; and many who heard him were astonished, saying, "Where did this man get all this? What is the wisdom given to him? What mighty works are wrought by his hands! [3]Is not this the carpenter, the son of Mary and brother of James and Joses and Judas and Simon, and are not his sisters here with us?" And they took offense ᶠ at him. [4]And Jesus said to them, "A prophet is not without honor, except in his own country, and among his own kin, and in his own house." [5]And

---

° Greek *he*.
ᴾ Greek *him*.
ᑫ Or *overhearing*. Other ancient authorities read *hearing*.
ᶠ Or *stumbled*.
5:7: Acts 16:17; Heb 7:1; Mk 1:24.
5:20: Mk 7:31.
5:21–43: Mt 9:18–26; Lk 8:40–56.
5:22: Lk 13:14; Acts 13:15; 18:8, 17.
5:23: Mk 6:5; 7:32; 8:23; Acts 9:17; 28:8.
5:30: Lk 5:17.
5:34: Lk 7:50; Mk 10:52.
5:37: Mk 9:2; 13:3.
5:41: Lk 7:14; Acts 9:40.
5:43: Mk 1:43–44; 7:36.
6:1–6: Mt 13:53–58; Lk 4:16–30.
6:2: Mk 1:21; Mt 7:28.
6:3: Mt 11:6.
6:5: Mk 5:23; 7:32; 8:23.
* 5:43: Knowing their nationalistic views about the Messiah to come, Jesus wished to avoid a tumult.

he could do no mighty work there, except that he laid his hands upon a few sick people and healed them. [6]And he marveled because of their unbelief.

And he went about among the villages teaching.

The Mission of the Twelve

7 And he called to him the Twelve, and began to send them out two by two, and gave them authority over the unclean spirits. [8]He charged them to take nothing for their journey except a staff; no bread, no bag, no money in their belts; [9]but to wear sandals and not put on two tunics. [10]And he said to them, "Where you enter a house, stay there until you leave the place. [11]And if any place will not receive you and they refuse to hear you, when you leave, shake off the dust that is on your feet for a testimony against them." [12]So they went out and preached that men should repent. [13]And they cast out many demons, and anointed with oil many that were sick and healed them.

The Death of John the Baptist

14 King Herod heard of it; for Jesus'[s] name had become known. Some[t] said, "John the Baptist has been raised from the dead; that is why these powers are at work in him." [15]But others said, "It is Eli'jah." And others said, "It is a prophet, like one of the prophets of old." [16]But when Herod heard of it he said, "John, whom I beheaded, has been raised." [17]For Herod had sent and seized John, and bound him in prison for the sake of Hero'di-as, his brother Philip's wife; because he had married her. [18]For John said to Herod, "It is not lawful for you to have your brother's wife." [19]And Hero'di-as had a grudge against him, and wanted to kill him. But she could not, [20]for Herod feared John, knowing that he was a righteous and holy man, and kept him safe. When he heard him, he was much perplexed; and yet he heard him gladly. [21]But an opportunity came when Herod on his birthday gave a banquet for his courtiers and officers and the leading men of Galilee. [22]For when Hero'di-as' daughter came in and danced, she pleased Herod and his guests; and the king said to the girl, "Ask me for whatever you wish, and I will grant it." [23]And he vowed to her, "Whatever you ask me, I will give you, even half of my kingdom." [24]And she went out, and said to her mother, "What shall I ask?" And she said, "The head of John the Baptist." [25]And she came in immediately with haste to the king, and asked, saying, "I want you to give me at once the head of John the Baptist on a platter." [26]And the king was exceedingly sorry; but because of his oaths and his guests he did not want to break his word to her. [27]And immediately the king sent a soldier of the guard and gave orders to bring his head. He went and beheaded him in the prison, [28]and brought his head on a platter, and gave it to the girl; and the girl gave it to her mother. [29]When his disciples heard of it, they came and took his body, and laid it in a tomb.

Feeding the Five Thousand

30 The apostles returned to Jesus, and told him all that they had done and taught. [31]And he said to them, "Come away by yourselves to a lonely place, and rest a while." For many were coming and going, and they had no leisure even to eat. [32]And they went away in the boat to a lonely place by themselves. [33]Now many saw them going, and knew them, and they ran there on foot from all the towns, and got there ahead of them. [34]As he landed he saw a great throng, and he had compassion on them, because they were like sheep without a shepherd; and he began to teach them many things. [35]And when it grew late, his disciples came to him and said, "This is a lonely place, and the hour is now late; [36]send them away, to go into the country and villages round about and buy themselves something to eat." [37]But he answered them, "You give them something to eat." And they said to him, "Shall we go and buy two hundred denarii[u] worth of bread, and give it to them to eat?" [38]And he said to them, "How many loaves have you? Go and see." And when they had found out, they said, "Five, and two fish." [39]Then he commanded them all to sit down by companies upon the green grass. [40]So they sat down in groups, by hundreds and by fifties. [41]And taking the five loaves and the two fish he looked up to heaven, and blessed, and broke the loaves, and gave them to the disciples to set before the people; and he divided the two fish among them all. [42]And they all ate and were satisfied. [43]And they took up twelve baskets full of broken pieces and of the fish. [44]And those who ate the loaves were five thousand men.

Jesus Walks on the Sea

45 Immediately he made his disciples get into the boat and go before him to the other side, to Beth-sa'ida, while he dismissed the crowd. [46]And after he had taken leave of them, he went up on the mountain to pray. [47]And when evening came, the boat was out on the sea, and he was alone on

---

[s] Greek *his*.
[t] Other ancient authorities read *he*.
[u] The denarius was a day's wage for a laborer.
6:6: Mt 9:35.
6:7–11: Mt 10:1, 5, 7–11; Lk 9:1–5.
6:7: Lk 10:1.
6:11: Mt 10:14.
6:12–13: Mt 11:1; Lk 9:6.
6:13: Jas 5:14.
6:14–16: Mt 14:1–2; Lk 9:7–9; 9:19; Mt 21:11.
6:17–18: Mt 14:3–4; Lk 3:19–20.
6:19–29: Mt 14:5–12.
6:20: Mt 21:26.
6:23: Esther 5:3, 6.
6:30–31: Lk 9:10; Mk 3:20.
6:32–44: Mt 14:13–21; Lk 9:11–17; Jn 6:5–13; Mk 8:1–10; Mt 15:32–39.
6:34: Mt 9:36.
6:37: 2 Kings 4:42–44.
6:41: Mk 14:22; Lk 24:30–31.
6:45–52: Mt 14:22–33; Jn 6:15–21.

the land. [48]And he saw that they were distressed in rowing, for the wind was against them. And about the fourth watch of the night he came to them, walking on the sea. He meant to pass by them, [49]but when they saw him walking on the sea they thought it was a ghost, and cried out; [50]for they all saw him, and were terrified. But immediately he spoke to them and said, "Take heart, it is I; have no fear." [51]And he got into the boat with them and the wind ceased. And they were utterly astounded, [52]for they did not understand about the loaves, but their hearts were hardened.

Jesus Heals the Sick in Gennesaret

53 And when they had crossed over, they came to land at Gennes'aret, and moored to the shore. [54]And when they got out of the boat, immediately the people recognized him, [55]and ran about the whole neighborhood and began to bring sick people on their pallets to any place where they heard he was. [56]And wherever he came, in villages, cities, or country, they laid the sick in the market places, and begged him that they might touch even the fringe of his garment; and as many as touched it were made well.

The Tradition of the Elders

7 Now when the Pharisees gathered together to him, with some of the scribes, who had come from Jerusalem, [2]they saw that some of his disciples ate with hands defiled, that is, unwashed. [3](For the Pharisees, and all the Jews, do not eat unless they wash their hands, [v] observing the tradition of the elders; * [4]and when they come from the market place, they do not eat unless they purify [w] themselves; and there are many other traditions which they observe, the washing of cups and pots and vessels of bronze. [x]) [5]And the Pharisees and the scribes asked him, "Why do your disciples not live [y] according to the tradition of the elders, but eat with hands defiled?" [6]And he said to them, "Well did Isaiah prophesy of you hypocrites, as it is written,

'This people honors me with their lips,
  but their heart is far from me;
[7]in vain do they worship me,
  teaching as doctrines the precepts of men.'

[8]You leave the commandment of God, and hold fast the tradition of men."

9 And he said to them, "You have a fine way of rejecting the commandment of God, in order to keep your tradition! [10]For Moses said, 'Honor your father and your mother'; and, 'He who speaks evil of father or mother, let him surely die'; [11]but you say, 'If a man tells his father or his mother, What you would have gained from me is Corban' (that is, given to God) [z]—[12]then you no longer permit him to do anything for his father or his mother, [13]thus making void the word of God through your tradition which you hand on. And many such things you do."

14 And he called the people to him again, and said to them, "Hear me, all of you, and understand: [15]there is nothing outside a man which by going into him can defile him; but the things which come out of a man are what defile him." [a] [17]And when he had entered the house, and left the people, his disciples asked him about the parable. [18]And he said to them, "Then are you also without understanding? Do you not see that whatever goes into a man from outside cannot defile him, [19]since it enters, not his heart but his stomach, and so passes on?" [b] (Thus he declared all foods clean.) [20]And he said, "What comes out of a man is what defiles a man. [21]For from within, out of the heart of man, come evil thoughts, fornication, theft, murder, adultery, [22]coveting, wickedness, deceit, licentiousness, envy, slander, pride, foolishness. [23]All these evil things come from within, and they defile a man."

The Syrophoenician Woman's Faith

24 And from there he arose and went away to the region of Tyre and Sidon. [c] And he entered a house, and would not have any one know it; yet he could not be hidden. [25]But immediately a woman, whose little daughter was possessed by an unclean spirit, heard of him, and came and fell down at his feet. [26]Now the woman was a Greek, a Syrophoeni'cian by birth. And she begged him to cast the demon out of her daughter. [27]And he said to her, "Let the children first be fed, for it is not right to take the children's bread and throw it to the dogs." [28]But she answered him, "Yes, Lord; yet even the dogs under the table eat the children's crumbs." [29]And he said to her, "For this saying you may go your way; the demon has left your daughter." [30]And she went home, and found the child lying in bed, and the demon gone.

Jesus Cures a Deaf Man

31 Then he returned from the region of Tyre, and went through Sidon to the Sea of Galilee,

---

[v] One Greek word is of uncertain meaning and is not translated.
[w] Other ancient authorities read baptize.
[x] Other ancient authorities add and beds.
[y] Greek walk.
[z] Or an offering.
[a] Other ancient authorities add verse 16, "If any man has ears to hear, let him hear."
[b] Or is evacuated.
[c] Other ancient authorities omit and Sidon.

6:48: Mk 13:35.
6:50: Mt 9:2.
6:52: Mk 8:17.
6:53-56: Mt 14:34-36.
6:56: Mk 3:10; Mt 9:20.
7:1-15: Mt 15:1-11; Lk 11:38.
7:4: Mt 23:25; Lk 11:39.
7:5: Gal 1:14.
7:6-7: Is 29:13.
7:10: Ex 20:12; Deut 5:16; Ex 21:17; Lev 20:9.
7:17-23: Mt 15:15-20; Mk 4:10.
7:18-19: 1 Cor 10:25-27; Rom 14:14; Tit 1:15; Acts 10:15.
7:20-23: Rom 1:28-31; Gal 5:19-21.
7:22: Mt 6:23; 20:15.
7:24-30: Mt 15:21-28.
7:31-37: Mt 15:29-31.
* 7:3: Mark, writing for Gentiles, explains these Jewish customs.

through the region of the Decap'olis. ³²And they brought to him a man who was deaf and had an impediment in his speech; and they begged him to lay his hand upon him. ³³And taking him aside from the multitude privately, he put his fingers into his ears, and he spat and touched his tongue; ³⁴and looking up to heaven, he sighed, and said to him, "Eph'phatha," that is, "Be opened." ³⁵And his ears were opened, his tongue was released, and he spoke plainly. ³⁶And he charged them to tell no one; but the more he charged them, the more zealously they proclaimed it. ³⁷And they were astonished beyond measure, saying, "He has done all things well; he even makes the deaf hear and the mute speak."

Feeding the Four Thousand

8 In those days, when again a great crowd had gathered, and they had nothing to eat, he called his disciples to him, and said to them, ²"I have compassion on the crowd, because they have been with me now three days, and have nothing to eat; ³and if I send them away hungry to their homes, they will faint on the way; and some of them have come a long way." ⁴And his disciples answered him, "How can one feed these men with bread here in the desert?" ⁵And he asked them, "How many loaves have you?" They said, "Seven." ⁶And he commanded the crowd to sit down on the ground; and he took the seven loaves, and having given thanks he broke them and gave them to his disciples to set before the people; and they set them before the crowd. ⁷And they had a few small fish; and having blessed them, he commanded that these also should be set before them. ⁸And they ate, and were satisfied; and they took up the broken pieces left over, seven baskets full. ⁹And there were about four thousand people. ¹⁰And he sent them away; and immediately he got into the boat with his disciples, and went to the district of Dalmanu'tha. ᵈ

The Demand for a Sign

11 The Pharisees came and began to argue with him, seeking from him a sign from heaven, to test him. ¹²And he sighed deeply in his spirit, and said, "Why does this generation seek a sign? Truly, I say to you, no sign shall be given to this generation." ¹³And he left them, and getting into the boat again he departed to the other side.

The Leaven of the Pharisees and of Herod

14 Now they had forgotten to bring bread; and they had only one loaf with them in the boat. ¹⁵And he cautioned them, saying, "Take heed, beware of the leaven of the Pharisees and the leaven of Herod." ᵉ ¹⁶And they discussed it with one another, saying, "We have no bread." ¹⁷And being aware of it, Jesus said to them, "Why do you discuss the fact that you have no bread? Do you not yet perceive or understand? Are your hearts hardened? ¹⁸Having eyes do you not see, and hav-

ing ears do you not hear? And do you not remember? ¹⁹When I broke the five loaves for the five thousand, how many baskets full of broken pieces did you take up?" They said to him, "Twelve." ²⁰"And the seven for the four thousand, how many baskets full of broken pieces did you take up?" And they said to him, "Seven." ²¹And he said to them, "Do you not yet understand?"

Jesus Cures a Blind Man at Beth-saida

22 And they came to Beth-sa'ida. And some people brought to him a blind man, and begged him to touch him. ²³And he took the blind man by the hand, and led him out of the village; and when he had spit on his eyes and laid his hands upon him, he asked him, "Do you see anything?" ²⁴And he looked up and said, "I see men; but they look like trees, walking." ²⁵Then again he laid his hands upon his eyes; and he looked intently and was restored, and saw everything clearly. ²⁶And he sent him away to his home, saying, "Do not even enter the village."

Peter's Declaration That Jesus Is the Christ

27 And Jesus went on with his disciples, to the villages of Caesare'a Philip'pi; and on the way he asked his disciples, "Who do men say that I am?" ²⁸And they told him, "John the Baptist; and others say, Eli'jah; and others one of the prophets." ²⁹And he asked them, "But who do you say that I am?" Peter answered him, "You are the Christ." ³⁰And he charged them to tell no one about him.

Jesus Foretells His Death and Resurrection

31 And he began to teach them that the Son of man must suffer many things, and be rejected by the elders and the chief priests and the scribes, and be killed, and after three days rise again. ³²And he said this plainly. And Peter took him, and began to rebuke him. ³³But turning and seeing his disciples, he rebuked Peter, and said, "Get behind me, Satan! For you are not on the side of God, but of men."

34 And he called to him the multitude with his disciples, and said to them, "If any man would come after me, let him deny himself and take up

---

ᵈ Other ancient authorities read *Magadan* or *Magdala*.
ᵉ Other ancient authorities read *the Herodians*.

7:32: Mk 5:23.
7:33: Mk 8:23.
7:36: Mk 1:44; 5:43.
8:1-10: Mt 15:32–39; Mk 6:32–44; Mt 14:13–21; Lk 9:11–17; Jn 6:5–13.
8:11-12: Mt 16:1–4; 12:38–39; Lk 11:29.
8:13-21: Mt 16:4–12.
8:15: Lk 12:1; Mk 6:14; 12:13.
8:17: Mk 6:52; Jer 5:21; Is 6:9–10; Mt 13:10–15.
8:19: Mk 6:41–44.
8:20: Mk 8:1–10.
8:22-26: Mk 10:46–52; Jn 9:1–7.
8:22: Mk 6:45; Lk 9:10.
8:23: Mk 7:33; 5:23.
8:27-30: Mt 16:13–20; Lk 9:18–21; Jn 6:66–69.
8:28: Mk 6:14.
8:30: Mk 9:9; 1:34.
8:31–9:1: Mt 16:21–28; Lk 9:22–27.
8:33: Mt 4:10.
8:34: Mt 10:38; Lk 14:27.

his cross and follow me. [35]For whoever would save his life will lose it; and whoever loses his life for my sake and the gospel's will save it. [36]For what does it profit a man, to gain the whole world and forfeit his life? * [37]For what can a man give in return for his life? [38]For whoever is ashamed of me and of my words in this adulterous and sinful generation, of him will the Son of man also be ashamed, when he comes in the glory of his

9 Father with the holy angels." [1]And he said to them, "Truly, I say to you, there are some standing here who will not taste death before they see the kingdom of God come with power."

The Transfiguration

[2] And after six days Jesus took with him Peter and James and John, and led them up a high mountain apart by themselves; and he was transfigured before them, [3]and his garments became glistening, intensely white, as no fuller on earth could bleach them. [4]And there appeared to them Eli'jah with Moses; and they were talking to Jesus. [5]And Peter said to Jesus, "Master, [f] it is well that we are here; let us make three booths, one for you and one for Moses and one for Eli'jah." [6]For he did not know what to say, for they were exceedingly afraid. [7]And a cloud overshadowed them, and a voice came out of the cloud, "This is my beloved Son; [g] listen to him." [8]And suddenly looking around they no longer saw any one with them but Jesus only.

The Coming of Elijah

[9] And as they were coming down the mountain, he charged them to tell no one what they had seen, until the Son of man should have risen from the dead. [10]So they kept the matter to themselves, questioning what the rising from the dead meant. [11]And they asked him, "Why do the scribes say that first Eli'jah must come?" [12]And he said to them, "Eli'jah does come first to restore all things; and how is it written of the Son of man, that he should suffer many things and be treated with contempt? [13]But I tell you that Eli'jah has come, † and they did to him whatever they pleased, as it is written of him."

The Healing of a Boy with a Mute Spirit

[14] And when they came to the disciples, they saw a great crowd about them, and scribes arguing with them. [15]And immediately all the crowd, when they saw him, were greatly amazed, and ran up to him and greeted him. [16]And he asked them, "What are you discussing with them?" [17]And one of the crowd answered him, "Teacher, I brought my son to you, for he has a mute spirit; [18]and wherever it seizes him, it dashes him down; and he foams and grinds his teeth and becomes rigid; and I asked your disciples to cast it out, and they were not able." [19]And he answered them, "O faithless generation, how long am I to be with you?

How long am I to bear with you? Bring him to me." [20]And they brought the boy to him; and when the spirit saw him, immediately it convulsed the boy, and he fell on the ground and rolled about, foaming at the mouth. [21]And Jesus [h] asked his father, "How long has he had this?" And he said, "From childhood. [22]And it has often cast him into the fire and into the water, to destroy him; but if you can do anything, have pity on us and help us." [23]And Jesus said to him, "If you can! All things are possible to him who believes." [24]Immediately the father of the child cried out [i] and said, "I believe; help my unbelief!" [25]And when Jesus saw that a crowd came running together, he rebuked the unclean spirit, saying to it, "You mute and deaf spirit, I command you, come out of him, and never enter him again." [26]And after crying out and convulsing him terribly, it came out, and the boy was like a corpse; so that most of them said, "He is dead." [27]But Jesus took him by the hand and lifted him up, and he arose. [28]And when he had entered the house, his disciples asked him privately, "Why could we not cast it out?" [29]And he said to them, "This kind cannot be driven out by anything but prayer and fasting." [j]

Jesus Again Foretells His Death and Resurrection

[30] They went on from there and passed through Galilee. And he would not have any one know it; [31]for he was teaching his disciples, saying to them, "The Son of man will be delivered into the hands of men, and they will kill him; and when he is killed, after three days he will rise." [32]But they did not understand the saying, and they were afraid to ask him.

True Greatness

[33] And they came to Caper'na-um; and when he was in the house he asked them, "What were you discussing on the way?" [34]But they were silent; for on the way they had discussed with one

---

f Or *Rabbi.*
g Or *my Son, my* (or *the*) *Beloved.*
h Greek *he.*
i Other ancient authorities add *with tears.*
j Other ancient authorities omit *and fasting.*
8:35: Mt 10:39; Lk 17:33; Jn 12:25.
8:38: Mt 10:33; Lk 12:9.
9:1: Mk 13:30; Mt 10:23; Lk 22:18.
9:2-8: Mt 17:1-8; Lk 9:28-36.
9:2: Mk 5:37; 13:3.
9:3: Mt 28:3.
9:7: 2 Pet 1:17-18; Mt 3:17; Jn 12:28-29.
9:9-13: Mt 17:9-13; Lk 9:36.
9:9: Mk 8:30; 5:43; 7:36.
9:11: Mt 11:14.
9:12: Mk 8:31; 9:31; 10:33.
9:14-27: Mt 17:14-18; Lk 9:37-43.
9:23: Mt 17:20; Lk 17:6; Mk 11:22-24.
9:30-32: Mt 17:22-23; Lk 9:43-45.
9:31: Mk 8:31; 10:33.
9:32: Jn 12:16.
9:33-37: Mt 18:1-5; Lk 9:46-48.
9:34: Lk 22:24.
* 8:36, *life:* See note on Mt 16:26.
† 9:13, *Elijah has come:* i.e., in the person of the Baptist (Mt 11:14).

another who was the greatest. [35]And he sat down and called the Twelve and he said to them, "If any one would be first, he must be last of all and servant of all." [36]And he took a child, and put him in the midst of them; and taking him in his arms, he said to them, [37]"Whoever receives one such child in my name receives me; and whoever receives me, receives not me but him who sent me."

Another Exorcist

38 John said to him, "Teacher, we saw a man casting out demons in your name, [k] and we forbade him, because he was not following us." [39]But Jesus said, "Do not forbid him; for no one who does a mighty work in my name will be able soon after to speak evil of me. [40]For he that is not against us is for us. [41]For truly, I say to you, whoever gives you a cup of water to drink because you bear the name of Christ, will by no means lose his reward.

Temptations to Sin

42 "Whoever causes one of these little ones who believe in me to sin, [l] it would be better for him if a great millstone were hung round his neck and he were thrown into the sea. [43]And if your hand causes you to sin, [l] cut it off; it is better for you to enter life maimed than with two hands to go to hell, [m] to the unquenchable fire. [n] [45]And if your foot causes you to sin, [l] cut it off; it is better for you to enter life lame than with two feet to be thrown into hell. [m] [n] [47]And if your eye causes you to sin, [l] pluck it out; it is better for you to enter the kingdom of God with one eye than with two eyes to be thrown into hell, [m] [48]where their worm does not die, and the fire is not quenched. [49]For every one will be salted with fire. [o] [50]Salt is good; but if the salt has lost its saltiness, how will you season it? Have salt in yourselves, and be at peace with one another."

Teachings about Divorce

10 And he left there and went to the region of Judea and beyond the Jordan, and crowds gathered to him again; and again, as his custom was, he taught them.

2 And Pharisees came up and in order to test him asked, "Is it lawful for a man to divorce his wife?" [3]He answered them, "What did Moses command you?" [4]They said, "Moses allowed a man to write a certificate of divorce, and to put her away." [5]But Jesus said to them, "For your hardness of heart he wrote you this commandment. [6]But from the beginning of creation, 'God made them male and female.' [7]'For this reason a man shall leave his father and mother and be joined to his wife, [p] [8]and the two shall become one flesh.' [q] So they are no longer two but one flesh. [q] [9]What therefore God has joined together, let not man put asunder."

10 And in the house the disciples asked him again about this matter. [11]And he said to them, "Whoever divorces his wife and marries another, commits adultery against her; [12]and if she divorces her husband and marries another, she commits adultery."

Jesus Blesses the Children

13 And they were bringing children to him, that he might touch them; and the disciples rebuked them. [14]But when Jesus saw it he was indignant, and said to them, "Let the children come to me, do not hinder them; for to such belongs the kingdom of God. [15]Truly, I say to you, whoever does not receive the kingdom of God like a child shall not enter it." [16]And he took them in his arms and blessed them, laying his hands upon them.

The Rich Man

17 And as he was setting out on his journey, a man ran up and knelt before him, and asked him, "Good Teacher, what must I do to inherit eternal life?" [18]And Jesus said to him, "Why do you call me good? No one is good but God alone. [19]You know the commandments: 'Do not kill, Do not commit adultery, Do not steal, Do not bear false witness, Do not defraud, Honor your father and mother.' " [20]And he said to him, "Teacher, all these I have observed from my youth." [21]And Jesus looking upon him loved him, and said to him, "You lack one thing; go, sell what you have, and give to the poor, and you will have treasure in heaven; and come, follow me." [22]At that saying his countenance fell, and he went away sorrowful; for he had great possessions.

23 And Jesus looked around and said to his disciples, "How hard it will be for those who have riches to enter the kingdom of God!" [24]And the disciples were amazed at his words. * But Jesus

---

[k] Other ancient authorities add *who does not follow us.*
[l] Greek *stumble.*
[m] Greek *Gehenna.*
[n] Verses 44 and 46 (which are identical with verse 48) are omitted by the best ancient authorities.
[o] Other ancient authorities add *and every sacrifice will be salted with salt.*
[p] Other ancient authorities omit *and be joined to his wife.*
[q] Other ancient authorities read *one.*
9:35: Mk 10:43–44; Mt 20:26–27; 23:11; Lk 22:26.
9:36: Mk 10:16.
9:37: Mt 10:40; Lk 10:16; Jn 12:44; 13:20.
9:38–40: Lk 9:49–50; 11:23; Mt 12:30; Num 11:27–29.
9:41: Mt 10:42.
9:42–48: Mt 18:6–9; 5:29–30; Lk 17:1–2.
9:48: Is 66:24.
9:49–50: Mt 5:13; Lk 14:34–35.
9:50: Col 4:6; 1 Thess 5:13.
10:1–12: Mt 19:1–9.
10:1: Lk 9:51; Jn 10:40; 11:7.
10:4: Deut 24:1–4.
10:6: Gen 1:27; 5:2.
10:7–8: Gen 2:24.
10:11: Mt 5:32; Lk 16:18; 1 Cor 7:10–11; Rom 7:2–3.
10:13–16: Mt 19:13–15; 18:3; Lk 18:15–17.
10:16: Mk 9:36.
10:17–31: Mt 19:16–30; Lk 18:18–30.
10:17: Lk 10:25; Mk 1:40.
10:19: Ex 20:12–16; Deut 5:16–20.
10:21: Mt 6:20; Lk 12:33; Acts 2:45; 4:34–35.
* 10:24, *amazed at his words*: The Old Testament often records God's offers of material rewards for observance of his laws. This was because the future life was not yet revealed. It was therefore taken for granted, in spite of contrary evidence, that riches were a sign of God's favor.

said to them again, "Children, how hard it is for those who trust in riches ^z to enter the kingdom of God! ²⁵It is easier for a camel to go through the eye of a needle than for a rich man to enter the kingdom of God." ²⁶And they were exceedingly astonished, and said to him, ^a "Then who can be saved?" ²⁷Jesus looked at them and said, "With men it is impossible, but not with God; for all things are possible with God." ²⁸Peter began to say to him, "Behold, we have left everything and followed you." ²⁹Jesus said, "Truly, I say to you, there is no one who has left house or brothers or sisters or mother or father or children or lands, for my sake and for the gospel, ³⁰who will not receive a hundredfold now in this time, houses and brothers and sisters and mothers and children and lands, with persecutions, and in the age to come eternal life. * ³¹But many that are first will be last, and the last first."

A Third Time Jesus Foretells His Death and Resurrection

32 And they were on the road, going up to Jerusalem, and Jesus was walking ahead of them; and they were amazed, and those who followed were afraid. And taking the Twelve again, he began to tell them what was to happen to him, ³³saying, "Behold, we are going up to Jerusalem; and the Son of man will be delivered to the chief priests and the scribes, and they will condemn him to death, and deliver him to the Gentiles; ³⁴and they will mock him, and spit upon him, and scourge him, and kill him; and after three days he will rise."

The Request of James and John

35 And James and John, the sons of Zeb'edee, came forward to him, and said to him, "Teacher, we want you to do for us whatever we ask of you." ³⁶And he said to them, "What do you want me to do for you?" ³⁷And they said to him, "Grant us to sit, one at your right hand and one at your left, in your glory." ³⁸But Jesus said to them, "You do not know what you are asking. Are you able to drink the chalice that I drink, or to be baptized with the baptism with which I am baptized?" ³⁹And they said to him, "We are able." And Jesus said to them, "The chalice that I drink you will drink; and with the baptism with which I am baptized, you will be baptized; ⁴⁰but to sit at my right hand or at my left is not mine to grant, but it is for those for whom it has been prepared." ⁴¹And when the ten heard it, they began to be indignant at James and John. ⁴²And Jesus called them to him and said to them, "You know that those who are supposed to rule over the Gentiles lord it over them, and their great men exercise authority over them. ⁴³But it shall not be so among you; but whoever would be great among you must be your servant, ⁴⁴and whoever would be first among you must be slave of all. ⁴⁵For the Son of man also came not to be served but to serve, and to give his life as a ransom for many."

Bartimaeus Receives His Sight

46 And they came to Jericho; and as he was leaving Jericho with his disciples and a great multitude, Bartimae'us, a blind beggar, the son of Timae'us, was sitting by the roadside. ⁴⁷And when he heard that it was Jesus of Nazareth, he began to cry out and say, "Jesus, Son of David, have mercy on me!" ⁴⁸And many rebuked him, telling him to be silent; but he cried out all the more, "Son of David, have mercy on me!" ⁴⁹And Jesus stopped and said, "Call him." And they called the blind man, saying to him, "Take heart; rise, he is calling you." ⁵⁰And throwing off his cloak he sprang up and came to Jesus. ⁵¹And Jesus said to him, "What do you want me to do for you?" And the blind man said to him, "Master, ^t let me receive my sight." ⁵²And Jesus said to him, "Go your way; your faith has made you well." And immediately he received his sight and followed him on the way.

Jesus' Entry into Jerusalem

11 And when they drew near to Jerusalem, to Beth'phage and Beth'any, at the Mount of Olives, he sent two of his disciples, ²and said to them, "Go into the village opposite you, and immediately as you enter it you will find a colt tied, on which no one has ever sat; untie it and bring it. ³If any one says to you, 'Why are you doing this?' say, 'The Lord has need of it and will send it back here immediately.'" ⁴And they went away, and found a colt tied at the door out in the open street; and they untied it. ⁵And those who stood there said to them, "What are you doing, untying the colt?" ⁶And they told them what Jesus had said; and they let them go. ⁷And they brought the colt to Jesus, and threw their garments on it; and he sat upon it. ⁸And many spread their garments on the road, and others spread leafy branches which they had cut from the fields. ⁹And those who went

---

^z Other ancient authorities omit *for those who trust in riches*.
^a Other ancient authorities read *to one another*.
^t Or *Rabbi*.

10:28: Mk 1:16–20.
10:30: Mt 6:33.
10:31: Mt 20:16; Lk 13:30.
10:32–34: Mt 20:17–19; Lk 18:31–34.
10:33: Mk 8:31; 9:12; 9:33.
10:34: Mk 14:65; 15:19, 26–32.
10:35–45: Mt 20:20–28.
10:37: Mt 19:28; Lk 22:30.
10:38: Lk 12:50; Jn 18:11.
10:39: Acts 12:2; Rev 1:9.
10:42–45: Lk 22:25–27.
10:43: Mk 9:35.
10:45: 1 Tim 2:5–6.
10:46–52: Mt 20:29–34; Lk 18:35–43; Mk 8:22–26.
10:47: Mt 9:27.
10:52: Mt 9:22; Mk 5:34; Lk 7:50; 8:48; 17:19.
11:1–10: Mt 21:1–9; Lk 19:29–38.
11:4: Mk 14:16.
11:7–10: Jn 12:12–15.
11:9: Ps 118:26; Mt 21:15; 23:39.
* 10:30: Some of the reward will be given in this life.

before and those who followed cried out, "Hosanna! Blessed is he who comes in the name of the Lord! [10]Blessed is the kingdom of our father David that is coming! Hosanna in the highest!"

11 And he entered Jerusalem, and went into the temple; and when he had looked round at everything, as it was already late, he went out to Beth'any with the Twelve.

Jesus Curses the Fig Tree

12 On the following day, when they came from Beth'any, he was hungry. [13]And seeing in the distance a fig tree in leaf, he went to see if he could find anything on it. When he came to it, he found nothing but leaves, for it was not the season for figs. [14]And he said to it, "May no one ever eat fruit from you again." And his disciples heard it.

Jesus Cleanses the Temple

15 And they came to Jerusalem. And he entered the temple and began to drive out those who sold and those who bought in the temple, and he overturned the tables of the money-changers and the seats of those who sold pigeons; [16]and he would not allow any one to carry anything through the temple. [17]And he taught, and said to them, "Is it not written, 'My house shall be called a house of prayer for all the nations'? But you have made it a den of robbers." [18]And the chief priests and the scribes heard it and sought a way to destroy him; for they feared him, because all the multitude was astonished at his teaching. [19]And when evening came they [u] went out of the city.

The Lesson from the Withered Fig Tree

20 As they passed by in the morning, they saw the fig tree withered away to its roots. [21]And Peter remembered and said to him, "Master, [v] look! The fig tree which you cursed has withered." [22]And Jesus answered them, "Have faith in God. [23]Truly, I say to you, whoever says to this mountain, 'Be taken up and cast into the sea,' and does not doubt in his heart, but believes that what he says will come to pass, it will be done for him. [24]Therefore I tell you, whatever you ask in prayer, believe that you receive it, and you will. [25]And whenever you stand praying, forgive, if you have anything against any one; so that your Father also who is in heaven may forgive you your trespasses." [w]

Jesus' Authority Is Questioned

27 And they came again to Jerusalem. And as he was walking in the temple, the chief priests and the scribes and the elders came to him, [28]and they said to him, "By what authority are you doing these things, or who gave you this authority to do them?" [29]Jesus said to them, "I will ask you a question; answer me, and I will tell you by what authority I do these things. [30]Was the baptism of John from heaven or from men? Answer me." [31]And they argued with one another, "If we say, 'From heaven,' he will say, 'Why then did you not

believe him?' [32]But shall we say, 'From men'?"—they were afraid of the people, for all held that John was a real prophet. [33]So they answered Jesus, "We do not know." And Jesus said to them, "Neither will I tell you by what authority I do these things."

The Parable of the Wicked Tenants

12 And he began to speak to them in parables. "A man planted a vineyard, and set a hedge around it, and dug a pit for the wine press, and built a tower, and leased it to tenants, and went into another country. [2]When the time came, he sent a servant to the tenants, to get from them some of the fruit of the vineyard. [3]And they took him and beat him, and sent him away empty-handed. [4]Again he sent to them another servant, and they wounded him in the head, and treated him shamefully. [5]And he sent another, and him they killed; and so with many others, some they beat and some they killed. [6]He had still one other, a beloved son; finally he sent him to them, saying, 'They will respect my son.' [7]But those tenants said to one another, 'This is the heir; come, let us kill him, and the inheritance will be ours.' [8]And they took him and killed him, and cast him out of the vineyard. [9]What will the owner of the vineyard do? He will come and destroy the tenants, and give the vineyard to others. [10]Have you not read this Scripture:

'The very stone which the builders rejected
has become the cornerstone;
[11]this was the Lord's doing,
and it is marvelous in our eyes'?"

12 And they tried to arrest him, but feared the multitude, for they perceived that he had told the parable against them; so they left him and went away.

The Question about Paying Taxes

13 And they sent to him some of the Pharisees and some of the Hero'dians, to entrap him in his talk. [14]And they came and said to him, "Teacher, we know that you are true, and care for no man; for you do not regard the position of men, but truly teach the way of God. Is it lawful to pay taxes to Caesar, or not? [15]Should we pay them, or

[u] Other ancient authorities read he.
[v] Or Rabbi.
[w] Other ancient authorities add verse 26, *"But if you do not forgive, neither will your Father who is in heaven forgive your trespasses."*

11:11: Mt 21:10–11, 17.
11:12–14: Mt 21:18–19; Lk 13:6–9.
11:15–18: Mt 21:12–16; Lk 19:45–48; Jn 2:13–16.
11:17: Is 56:7; Jer 7:11.
11:19: Lk 21:37.
11:20–25: Mt 21:20–22; Mt 17:20; Lk 17:6.
11:24: Jn 14:13–14; 16:23; Mt 7:7–11.
11:25: Mt 6:14–15; 18:35.
11:27–33: Mt 21:23–27; Lk 20:1–8; Jn 2:18.
12:1–12: Mt 21:33–46; Lk 20:9–19; Is 5:1–7.
12:10–11: Ps 118:22–23; Acts 4:11; 1 Pet 2:7.
12:12: Mk 11:18.
12:13–17: Mt 22:15–22; Lk 20:20–26.
12:13: Mk 3:6; Lk 11:54.

should we not?" But knowing their hypocrisy, he said to them, "Why put me to the test? Bring me a coin, * and let me look at it." [16]And they brought one. And he said to them, "Whose likeness and inscription is this?" They said to him, "Caesar's." [17]Jesus said to them, "Render to Caesar the things that are Caesar's, and to God the things that are God's." And they were amazed at him.

The Question about Man's Resurrection

18 And Sad'ducees came to him, who say that there is no resurrection; and they asked him a question, saying, [19]"Teacher, Moses wrote for us that if a man's brother dies and leaves a wife, and leaves no child, the man ʸ must take the wife, and raise up children for his brother. [20]There were seven brothers; the first took a wife, and when he died left no children; [21]and the second took her, and died, leaving no children; and the third likewise; [22]and the seven left no children. Last of all the woman also died. [23]In the resurrection whose wife will she be? For the seven had her as wife."

24 Jesus said to them, "Is not this why you are wrong, that you know neither the Scriptures nor the power of God? [25]For when they rise from the dead, they neither marry nor are given in marriage, but are like angels in heaven. [26]And as for the dead being raised, have you not read in the book of Moses, in the passage about the bush, how God said to him, 'I am the God of Abraham, and the God of Isaac, and the God of Jacob'? [27]He is not God of the dead, but of the living; you are quite wrong."

The First Commandment

28 And one of the scribes came up and heard them disputing with one another, and seeing that he answered them well, asked him, "Which commandment is the first of all?" [29]Jesus answered, "The first is, 'Hear, O Israel: The Lord our God, the Lord is one; [30]and you shall love the Lord your God with all your heart, and with all your soul, and with all your mind, and with all your strength.' [31]The second is this, 'You shall love your neighbor as yourself.' There is no other commandment greater than these." [32]And the scribe said to him, "You are right, Teacher; you have truly said that he is one, and there is no other but he; [33]and to love him with all the heart, and with all the understanding, and with all the strength, and to love one's neighbor as oneself, is much more than all whole burnt offerings and sacrifices." [34]And when Jesus saw that he answered wisely, he said to him, "You are not far from the kingdom of God." And after that no one dared to ask him any question.

A Question about the Christ

35 And as Jesus taught in the temple, he said, "How can the scribes say that the Christ is the son of David? [36]David himself, inspired by ᶻ the Holy Spirit, declared,

'The Lord said to my Lord,
Sit at my right hand,
till I put your enemies under your feet.'

[37]David himself calls him Lord; so how is he his son?" And the great throng heard him gladly.

Jesus Denounces the Hypocrisy of the Scribes

38 And in his teaching he said, "Beware of the scribes, who like to go about in long robes, and to have salutations in the market places [39]and the best seats in the synagogues and the places of honor at feasts, [40]who devour widows' houses and for a pretense make long prayers. They will receive the greater condemnation."

The Widow's Offering

41 And he sat down opposite the treasury, and watched the multitude putting money into the treasury. Many rich people put in large sums. [42]And a poor widow came, and put in two copper coins, which make a penny. [43]And he called his disciples to him, and said to them, "Truly, I say to you, this poor widow has put in more than all those who are contributing to the treasury. [44]For they all contributed out of their abundance; but she out of her poverty has put in everything she had, her whole living."

The Destruction of the Temple Foretold

13 And as he came out of the temple, one of his disciples said to him, "Look, Teacher, what wonderful stones and what wonderful buildings!" [2]And Jesus said to him, "Do you see these great buildings? There will not be left here one stone upon another, that will not be thrown down."

3 And as he sat on the Mount of Olives opposite the temple, Peter and James and John and Andrew asked him privately, [4]"Tell us, when will this be, and what will be the sign when these things are all to be accomplished?" [5]And Jesus began to say to them, "Take heed that no one leads you astray. [6]Many will come in my name, saying, 'I am he!' and they will lead many astray. [7]And when you hear of wars and rumors of wars, do not be alarmed; this must take place,

---

ˣ Greek a denarius.
ʸ Greek his brother.
ᶻ Or himself, in.
12:17: Rom 13:7.
12:18–27: Mt 22:23–33; Lk 20:27–38.
12:19: Deut 25:5.
12:26: Ex 3:6.
12:28–34: Mt 22:34–40; Lk 20:39–40; 10:25–28.
12:29: Deut 6:4.
12:31: Lev 19:18; Rom 13:9; Gal 5:14; Jas 2:8.
12:33: 1 Sam 15:22; Hos 6:6; Mic 6:6–8; Mt 9:13.
12:35–37: Mt 22:41–46; Lk 20:41–44.
12:36: Ps 110:1; Acts 2:34–35; Heb 1:13.
12:38–40: Mt 23:5–7; Lk 20:46–47; Lk 11:43.
12:41–44: Lk 21:1–4; Jn 8:20.
13:1–37: Mt 24; Lk 21:5–36.
13:2: Lk 19:43–44; Mk 14:58; 15:29; Jn 2:19; Acts 6:14.
13:3: Mk 5:37; 9:2.
13:4: Lk 17:20.
13:6: Jn 8:24; 1 Jn 2:18.

but the end is not yet. [8]For nation will rise against nation, and kingdom against kingdom; there will be earthquakes in various places, there will be famines; this is but the beginning of the sufferings.

Persecutions Foretold

9 "But take heed to yourselves; for they will deliver you up to councils; and you will be beaten in synagogues; and you will stand before governors and kings for my sake, to bear testimony before them. [10]And the gospel must first be preached to all nations. [11]And when they bring you to trial and deliver you up, do not be anxious beforehand about what you are to say; but say whatever is given you in that hour, for it is not you who speak, but the Holy Spirit. [12]And brother will deliver up brother to death, and the father his child, and children will rise against parents and have them put to death; [13]and you will be hated by all for my name's sake. But he who endures to the end will be saved.

The Desolating Sacrilege

14 "But when you see the desolating sacrilege set up where it ought not to be (let the reader understand), then let those who are in Judea flee to the mountains; [15]let him who is on the housetop not go down, nor enter his house, to take anything away; [16]and let him who is in the field not turn back to get a coat. [17]And alas for those who are with child and for those who are nursing in those days! [18]Pray that it may not happen in winter. [19]For in those days there will be such tribulation as has not been from the beginning of the creation which God created until now, and never will be. [20]And if the Lord had not shortened the days, no human being would be saved; but for the sake of the elect, whom he chose, he shortened the days. [21]And then if any one says to you, 'Look, here is the Christ!' or 'Look, there he is!' do not believe it. [22]False Christs and false prophets will arise and show signs and wonders, to lead astray, if possible, the elect. [23]But take heed; I have told you all things beforehand.

The Coming of the Son of Man

24 "But in those days, after that tribulation, the sun will be darkened, and the moon will not give its light, [25]and the stars will be falling from heaven, and the powers in the heavens will be shaken. [26]And then they will see the Son of man coming in clouds with great power and glory. [27]And then he will send out the angels, and gather his elect from the four winds, from the ends of the earth to the ends of heaven.

The Lesson of the Fig Tree

28 "From the fig tree learn its lesson: as soon as its branch becomes tender and puts forth its leaves, you know that summer is near. [29]So also, when you see these things taking place, you know that he is near, at the very gates. [30]Truly, I say to you, this generation will not pass away before all these things take place. [31]Heaven and earth will pass away, but my words will not pass away.

The Necessity for Watchfulness

32 "But of that day or that hour no one knows, not even the angels in heaven, nor the Son, but only the Father. [33]Take heed, watch and pray; [a] for you do not know when the time will come. [34]It is like a man going on a journey, when he leaves home and puts his servants in charge, each with his work, and commands the doorkeeper to be on the watch. [35]Watch therefore—for you do not know when the master of the house will come, in the evening, or at midnight, or at cockcrow, or in the morning—[36]lest he come suddenly and find you asleep. [37]And what I say to you I say to all: Watch."

The Conspiracy to Kill Jesus

14 It was now two days before the Passover and the feast of Unleavened Bread. And the chief priests and the scribes were seeking how to arrest him by stealth, and kill him; [2]for they said, "Not during the feast, lest there be a tumult of the people."

The Anointing at Bethany

3 And while he was at Beth'any in the house of Simon the leper, as he sat at table, a woman came with an alabaster jar of ointment of pure nard, very costly, and she broke the jar and poured it over his head. [4]But there were some who said to themselves indignantly, "Why was the ointment thus wasted? [5]For this ointment might have been sold for more than three hundred denarii, [b] and given to the poor." And they reproached her. [6]But Jesus said, "Let her alone; why do you trouble her? She has done a beautiful thing to me. [7]For you always have the poor with you, and whenever you will, you can do good to them; but you will not always have me. [8]She has done what she could; she has anointed my body beforehand for burying. [9]And truly, I say to you, wherever the gospel is preached in the whole world, what she has done will be told in memory of her."

---

[a] Other ancient authorities omit *and pray.*
[b] The denarius was a day's wage for a laborer.
13:9-13: Mt 10:17–22.
13:11: Jn 14:26; 16:7–11; Lk 12:11–12.
13:13: Jn 15:21
13:14: Dan 9:27; 11:31; 12:11.
13:17: Lk 23:29.
13:22: Mt 7:15; Jn 4:48.
13:26: Mk 8:38; Mt 10:23; Dan 7:13.
13:30: Mk 9:1.
13:31: Mt 5:18; Lk 16:17.
13:32: Acts 1:7.
13:33: Eph 6:18; Col 4:2.
13:34: Mt 25:14.
13:35: Lk 12:35–40.
14:1-2: Mt 26:1–5; Lk 22:1–2; Jn 11:47–53.
14:3-9: Mt 26:6–13; Lk 7:36–38; Jn 12:1–8.
14:7: Deut 15:11.
14:8: Jn 19:40.

Judas Agrees to Betray Jesus

10 Then Judas Iscariot, who was one of the Twelve, went to the chief priests in order to betray him to them. [11]And when they heard it they were glad, and promised to give him money. And he sought an opportunity to betray him.

The Passover with the Disciples

12 And on the first day of Unleavened Bread, when they sacrificed the Passover lamb, his disciples said to him, "Where will you have us go and prepare for you to eat the Passover?" [13]And he sent two of his disciples, and said to them, "Go into the city, and a man carrying a jar of water will meet you; follow him,* [14]and wherever he enters, say to the householder, 'The Teacher says, Where is my guest room, where I am to eat the Passover with my disciples?' [15]And he will show you a large upper room furnished and ready; there prepare for us." [16]And the disciples set out and went to the city, and found it as he had told them; and they prepared the Passover.

17 And when it was evening he came with the Twelve. [18]And as they were at table eating, Jesus said, "Truly, I say to you, one of you will betray me, one who is eating with me." [19]They began to be sorrowful, and to say to him one after another, "Is it I?" [20]He said to them, "It is one of the Twelve, one who is dipping bread in the same dish with me. [21]For the Son of man goes as it is written of him, but woe to that man by whom the Son of man is betrayed! It would have been better for that man if he had not been born."

The Institution of the Last Supper

22 And as they were eating, he took bread, and blessed, and broke it, and gave it to them, and said, "Take; this is my body." [23]And he took a chalice, and when he had given thanks he gave it to them, and they all drank of it. [24]And he said to them, "This is my blood of the [c] covenant, which is poured out for many. [25]Truly, I say to you, I shall not drink again of the fruit of the vine until that day when I drink it new in the kingdom of God."

Peter's Denial Foretold

26 And when they had sung a hymn, they went out to the Mount of Olives. [27]And Jesus said to them, "You will all fall away; for it is written, 'I will strike the shepherd, and the sheep will be scattered.' [28]But after I am raised up, I will go before you to Galilee." [29]Peter said to him, "Even though they all fall away, I will not." [30]And Jesus said to him, "Truly, I say to you, this very night, before the cock crows twice, you will deny me three times." [31]But he said vehemently, "If I must die with you, I will not deny you." And they all said the same.

Jesus Prays in Gethsemane

32 And they went to a place which was called Gethsem'ane; and he said to his disciples, "Sit here, while I pray." [33]And he took with him Peter and James and John, and began to be greatly distressed and troubled. [34]And he said to them, "My soul is very sorrowful, even to death; remain here, and watch." [d] [35]And going a little farther, he fell on the ground and prayed that, if it were possible, the hour might pass from him. [36]And he said, "Abba, Father, all things are possible to you; remove this chalice from me; yet not what I will, but what you will." [37]And he came and found them sleeping, and he said to Peter, "Simon, are you asleep? Could you not watch [d] one hour? [38]Watch [d] and pray that you may not enter into temptation; the spirit indeed is willing, but the flesh is weak." [39]And again he went away and prayed, saying the same words. [40]And again he came and found them sleeping, for their eyes were very heavy; and they did not know what to answer him. [41]And he came the third time, and said to them, "Are you still sleeping and taking your rest? It is enough; the hour has come; the Son of man is betrayed into the hands of sinners. [42]Rise, let us be going; see, my betrayer is at hand."

The Betrayal and Arrest of Jesus

43 And immediately, while he was still speaking, Judas came, one of the Twelve, and with him a crowd with swords and clubs, from the chief priests and the scribes and the elders. [44]Now the betrayer had given them a sign, saying, "The one I shall kiss is the man; seize him and lead him away safely." [45]And when he came, he went up to him at once, and said, "Master!" [e] And he kissed him. [46]And they laid hands on him and seized him. [47]But one of those who stood by drew his sword, and struck the slave of the high priest and cut off his ear. [48]And Jesus said to them, "Have you come out as against a robber, with swords and clubs to capture me? [49]Day after day I was with you in the temple teaching, and you did not seize me. But let the Scriptures be fulfilled." [50]And they all deserted him and fled.

51 And a young man followed him, with nothing but a linen cloth about his body; and they

---

[c] Other ancient authorities insert new.
[d] Or keep awake.
[e] Or Rabbi.
14:10–11: Mt 26:14–16; Lk 22:3–6.
14:12–16: Mt 26:17–19; Lk 22:7–13.
14:17–21: Mt 26:20–25; Lk 22:14, 21–23; Jn 13:21–30; Ps 41:9.
14:22–25: Mt 26:26–29; Lk 22:17–19; 1 Cor 11:23–26.
14:22: Mk 6:41; 8:6; Lk 24:30.
14:23: 1 Cor 10:16.
14:24: Ex 24:8; Heb 9:20
14:26–31: Mt 26:30–35; Lk 22:39, 33–34.
14:27: Zech 13:7; Jn 16:32.
14:28: Mk 16:7.
14:30: Mk 14:66–72; Jn 13:36–38; 18:17–18, 25–27.
14:32–42: Mt 26:36–46; Lk 22:40–46; Heb 5:7–8.
14:34: Jn 12:27.
14:36: Rom 8:15; Gal 4:6; Mk 10:38; Jn 18:11.
14:38: Mt 6:13; Lk 11:4.
14:43–50: Mt 26:47–56; Lk 22:47–53; Jn 18:2–11.
14:49: Lk 19:47; Jn 18:19–21.
* 14:13: It was unusual for a man to carry water; it was a woman's task.

seized him, [52]but he left the linen cloth and ran away naked. *

Jesus before the Council

53 And they led Jesus to the high priest; and all the chief priests and the elders and the scribes were assembled. [54]And Peter had followed him at a distance, right into the courtyard of the high priest; and he was sitting with the guards, and warming himself at the fire. [55]Now the chief priests and the whole council sought testimony against Jesus to put him to death; but they found none. [56]For many bore false witness against him, and their witness did not agree. [57]And some stood up and bore false witness against him, saying, [58]"We heard him say, 'I will destroy this temple that is made with hands, and in three days I will build another, not made with hands.'" [59]Yet not even so did their testimony agree. [60]And the high priest stood up in their midst, and asked Jesus, "Have you no answer to make? What is it that these men testify against you?" [61]But he was silent and made no answer. Again the high priest asked him, "Are you the Christ, the Son of the Blessed?" [62]And Jesus said, "I am; and you will see the Son of man sitting at the right hand of Power, and coming with the clouds of heaven." [63]And the high priest tore his clothes, and said, "Why do we still need witnesses? [64]You have heard his blasphemy. What is your decision?" And they all condemned him as deserving death. [65]And some began to spit on him, and to cover his face, and to strike him, saying to him, "Prophesy!" And the guards received him with blows.

Peter Denies Jesus

66 And as Peter was below in the courtyard, one of the maids of the high priest came; [67]and seeing Peter warming himself, she looked at him, and said, "You also were with the Nazarene, Jesus." [68]But he denied it, saying, "I neither know nor understand what you mean." And he went out into the gateway. [f] [69]And the maid saw him, and began again to say to the bystanders, "This man is one of them." [70]But again he denied it. And after a little while again the bystanders said to Peter, "Certainly you are one of them; for you are a Galilean." [71]But he began to invoke a curse on himself and to swear, "I do not know this man of whom you speak." [72]And immediately the cock crowed a second time. And Peter remembered how Jesus had said to him, "Before the cock crows twice, you will deny me three times." And he broke down and wept.

Jesus before Pilate

15 And as soon as it was morning the chief priests, with the elders and scribes, and the whole council held a consultation; and they bound Jesus and led him away and delivered him to Pilate. [†] [2]And Pilate asked him, "Are you the King of the Jews?" And he answered him,

"You have said so." [3]And the chief priests accused him of many things. [4]And Pilate again asked him, "Have you no answer to make? See how many charges they bring against you." [5]But Jesus made no further answer, so that Pilate wondered.

Pilate Delivers Jesus to Be Crucified

6 Now at the feast he used to release for them one prisoner for whom they asked. [7]And among the rebels in prison, who had committed murder in the insurrection, there was a man called Barab'bas. [8]And the crowd came up and began to ask Pilate to do as he always did for them. [9]And he answered them, "Do you want me to release for you the King of the Jews?" [10]For he perceived that it was out of envy that the chief priests had delivered him up. [11]But the chief priests stirred up the crowd to have him release for them Barab'bas instead. [12]And Pilate again said to them, "Then what shall I do with the man whom you call the King of the Jews?" [13]And they cried out again, "Crucify him." [14]And Pilate said to them, "Why, what evil has he done?" But they shouted all the more, "Crucify him." [15]So Pilate, wishing to satisfy the crowd, released for them Barab'bas; and having scourged Jesus, he delivered him to be crucified.

The Soldiers Mock Jesus

16 And the soldiers led him away inside the palace (that is, the praetorium); and they called together the whole battalion. [17]And they clothed him in a purple cloak, and plaiting a crown of thorns they put it on him. [18]And they began to salute him, "Hail, King of the Jews!" [19]And they struck his head with a reed, and spat upon him, and they knelt down in homage to him. [20]And when they had mocked him, they stripped him of the purple cloak, and put his own clothes on him. And they led him out to crucify him.

The Crucifixion of Jesus

21 And they compelled a passer-by, Simon of Cyre'ne, who was coming in from the country, the father of Alexander and Rufus, to carry his cross. [22]And they brought him to the place called Gol'gotha (which means the place of a skull). [23]And they offered him wine mingled with myrrh; but

---

[f] Or fore-court. Other ancient authorities add and the cock crowed.
14:53–65: Mt 26:57–68; Lk 22:54–55, 63–71; Jn 18:12–24.
14:58: Mk 13:2; 15:29; Acts 6:14; Jn 2:19.
14:62: Dan 7:13; Mk 9:1; 13:26.
14:63: Acts 14:14; Num 14:6.
14:64: Lev 24:16.
14:66–72: Mt 26:69–75; Lk 22:56–62; Jn 18:16–18, 25–27; Mk 14:30.
15:1: Mt 27:1–2; Lk 23:1; Jn 18:28.
15:2–15: Mt 27:11–26; Lk 23:2–3, 18–25; Jn 18:29—19:16.
15:11: Acts 3:14.
15:16–20: Mt 27:27–31; Lk 23:11; Jn 19:2–3.
15:21: Mt 27:32; Lk 23:26; Rom 16:13.
15:22–32: Mt 27:33–44; Lk 23:33–39; Jn 19:17–24.
* 14:51–52: This young man is usually supposed to have been the evangelist himself.
† 15:1: The Jews could not execute Jesus without the Roman governor's permission.

he did not take it. ²⁴And they crucified him, and divided his garments among them, casting lots for them, to decide what each should take. ²⁵And it was the third hour, when they crucified him. ²⁶And the inscription of the charge against him read, "The King of the Jews." ²⁷And with him they crucified two robbers, one on his right and one on his left. ᵍ ²⁹And those who passed by derided him, shaking their heads, and saying, "Aha! You who would destroy the temple and build it in three days, ³⁰save yourself, and come down from the cross!" ³¹So also the chief priests mocked him to one another with the scribes, saying, "He saved others; he cannot save himself. ³²Let the Christ, the King of Israel, come down now from the cross, that we may see and believe." Those who were crucified with him also reviled him.

The Death of Jesus

33 And when the sixth hour had come, there was darkness over the whole land ʰ until the ninth hour. ³⁴And at the ninth hour Jesus cried with a loud voice, "E'lo-i, Elo-i, la'ma sabach-tha'ni?" which means, "My God, my God, why have you forsaken me?" ³⁵And some of the bystanders hearing it said, "Behold, he is calling Eli'jah." ³⁶And one ran and, filling a sponge full of vinegar, put it on a reed and gave it to him to drink, saying, "Wait, let us see whether Eli'jah will come to take him down." ³⁷And Jesus uttered a loud cry, and breathed his last. ³⁸And the curtain of the temple was torn in two, from top to bottom. ³⁹And when the centurion, who stood facing him, saw that he thus ⁱ breathed his last, he said, "Truly this man was the Son ˣ of God!"

40 There were also women looking on from afar, among whom were Mary Mag'dalene, and Mary the mother of James the younger * and of Joses, and Salo'me, ⁴¹who, when he was in Galilee, followed him, and ministered to him; and also many other women who came up with him to Jerusalem.

The Burial of Jesus

42 And when evening had come, since it was the day of Preparation, that is, the day before the sabbath, ⁴³Joseph of Arimathe'a, a respected member of the council, who was also himself looking for the kingdom of God, took courage and went to Pilate, and asked for the body of Jesus. ⁴⁴And Pilate wondered if he were already dead; and summoning the centurion, he asked him whether he was already dead. ʲ ⁴⁵And when he learned from the centurion that he was dead, he granted the body to Joseph. ⁴⁶And he bought a linen shroud, and taking him down, wrapped him in the linen shroud, and laid him in a tomb which had been hewn out of the rock; and he rolled a stone against the door of the tomb. ⁴⁷Mary Mag'dalene and Mary the mother of Joses saw where he was laid.

The Resurrection of Jesus

16 And when the sabbath was past, Mary Mag'dalene, and Mary the mother of James, and Salo'me, bought spices, so that they might go and anoint him. † ²And very early on the first day of the week they went to the tomb when the sun had risen. ³And they were saying to one another, "Who will roll away the stone for us from the door of the tomb?" ⁴And looking up, they saw that the stone was rolled back; for it was very large. ⁵And entering the tomb, they saw a young man sitting on the right side, dressed in a white robe; and they were amazed. ⁶And he said to them, "Do not be amazed; you seek Jesus of Nazareth, who was crucified. He has risen, he is not here; see the place where they laid him. ⁷But go, tell his disciples and Peter that he is going before you to Galilee; there you will see him, as he told you." ⁸And they went out and fled from the tomb; for trembling and astonishment had come upon them; and they said nothing to any one, for they were afraid.

Jesus Appears to Mary Magdalene

9 Now when he rose early on the first day of the week, he appeared first to Mary Magdalene, from whom he had cast out seven demons. ¹⁰She went and told those who had been with him, as they mourned and wept. ¹¹But when they heard that he was alive and had been seen by her, they would not believe it.

Jesus Appears to Two Disciples

12 After this he appeared in another form to two of them, as they were walking into the country. ¹³And they went back and told the rest, but they did not believe them.

Jesus Commissions the Disciples

14 Afterward he appeared to the Eleven themselves as they sat at table; and he upbraided them for their unbelief and hardness of heart, because they had not believed those who saw him after he had risen. ¹⁵And he said to them, "Go into all the

---

ᵍ Other ancient authorities insert verse 28, *And the Scripture was fulfilled which says, "He was reckoned with the transgressors."*
ʰ Or *earth.*
ⁱ Other ancient authorities insert *cried out and.*
ˣ Or *a son.*
ʲ Other ancient authorities read *whether he had been some time dead.*
15:24: Ps 22:18.
15:29: Mk 13:2; 14:58; Jn 2:19.
15:31: Mk 22:7–8.
15:33–41: Mt 27:45–56; Lk 23:44–49; Jn 19:28–30.
15:34: Ps 22:1.
15:36: Ps 69:21.
15:38: Heb 10:19–20.
15:39: Mk 1:11; 9:7.
15:40: Jn 19:25.
15:41: Lk 8:1–3.
15:42–47: Mt 27:57–61; Lk 23:50–56; Jn 19:38–42; Acts 13:29.
15:42: Deut 21:22–23.
16:1–8: Mt 28:1–8; Lk 24:1–10; Jn 20:1–2.
16:1: Lk 23:56; Jn 19:39.
16:7: Mk 14:28; Jn 21:1–23; Mt 28:7.
* 15:40, *the younger,* or "the Less."
† 16:1: There had been no time on the Friday to anoint him before the sabbath rest.

world and preach the gospel to the whole creation. [16]He who believes and is baptized will be saved; but he who does not believe will be condemned. [17]And these signs will accompany those who believe: in my name they will cast out demons; they will speak in new tongues; [18]they will pick up serpents, and if they drink any deadly thing, it will not hurt them; they will lay their hands on the sick, and they will recover."

The Ascension of Jesus

19 So then the Lord Jesus, after he had spoken to them, was taken up into heaven, and sat down at the right hand of God. [20]And they went forth and preached everywhere, while the Lord worked with them and confirmed the message by the signs that attended it. Amen. [k] [*]

---

[k] Other ancient authorities omit verses 9–20. Some ancient authorities conclude Mark instead with the following: *But they reported briefly to Peter and those with him all that they had been told. And after this, Jesus himself sent out by means of them, from east to west, the sacred and imperishable proclamation of eternal salvation.*

[*] 16:9–20: This passage is regarded as inspired and canonical Scripture even if not written by Mark. As it is missing from some important manuscripts, it is possible that Mark did not write it. On the other hand, he would hardly have left his Gospel unfinished at verse 8. Many think that the original ending was lost at a very early date and that this ending was composed at the end of the apostolic period to take its place.

THE GOSPEL ACCORDING TO

LUKE

Dedication to Theophilus

1 Inasmuch as many have undertaken to compile a narrative of the things which have been accomplished among us, ²just as they were delivered to us by those who from the beginning were eyewitnesses and ministers of the word, ³it seemed good to me also, having followed all things closely ᵃ for some time past, to write an orderly account for you, most excellent Theoph′i-lus, * ⁴that you may know the truth concerning the things of which you have been informed.

The Birth of John the Baptist Foretold

5 † In the days of Herod, king of Judea, there was a priest named Zechari′ah, ᵇ of the division of Abi′jah; and he had a wife of the daughters of Aaron, and her name was Elizabeth. ⁶And they were both righteous before God, walking in all the commandments and ordinances of the Lord blamelessly. ⁷But they had no child, because Elizabeth was barren, and both were advanced in years.

8 Now while he was serving as priest before God when his division was on duty, ⁹according to the custom of the priesthood, it fell to him by lot to enter the temple of the Lord and burn incense. ¹⁰And the whole multitude of the people were praying outside at the hour of incense. ¹¹And there appeared to him an angel of the Lord standing on the right side of the altar of incense. ¹²And Zechari′ah was troubled when he saw him, and fear fell upon him. ¹³But the angel said to him, "Do not be afraid, Zechari′ah, for your prayer is heard, and your wife Elizabeth will bear you a son, and you shall call his name John.
¹⁴And you will have joy and gladness,
    and many will rejoice at his birth;
¹⁵for he will be great before the Lord,
    and he shall drink no wine nor strong drink,
    and he will be filled with the Holy Spirit,
    even from his mother's womb.
¹⁶And he will turn many of the sons of Israel to
    the Lord their God,
¹⁷and he will go before him in the spirit and
    power of Eli′jah,
to turn the hearts of the fathers to the children,
    and the disobedient to the wisdom of the just,
to make ready for the Lord a people prepared."
¹⁸And Zechari′ah said to the angel, "How shall I know this? For I am an old man, and my wife is advanced in years." ¹⁹And the angel answered him, "I am Gabriel, who stand in the presence of

God; and I was sent to speak to you, and to bring you this good news. ²⁰And behold, you will be silent and unable to speak until the day that these things come to pass, because you did not believe my words, which will be fulfilled in their time." ²¹And the people were waiting for Zechari′ah, and they wondered at his delay in the temple. ²²And when he came out, he could not speak to them, and they perceived that he had seen a vision in the temple; and he made signs to them and remained mute. ²³And when his time of service was ended, he went to his home.

24 After these days his wife Elizabeth conceived, and for five months she hid herself, saying, ²⁵"Thus the Lord has done to me in the days when he looked on me, to take away my reproach among men."

The Birth of Jesus Foretold

26 In the sixth month the angel Gabriel was sent from God to a city of Galilee named Nazareth, ²⁷to a virgin betrothed to a man whose name was Joseph, of the house of David; and the virgin's name was Mary. ²⁸And he came to her and said, "Hail, full of grace, ᵇ² the Lord is with you!" ᶜ ²⁹But she was greatly troubled at the saying, and considered in her mind what sort of greeting this might be. ³⁰And the angel said to her, ‡ "Do not be afraid, Mary, for you have found favor with God. ³¹And behold, you will conceive in your womb and bear a son, and you shall call his name Jesus.

ᵃ Or *accurately.*
ᵇ Greek *Zacharias.*
ᵇ² Or *O favored one.*
ᶜ Other ancient authorities add *"Blessed are you among women!"*
1:2: 1 Jn 1:1; Acts 1:21; Heb 2:3.
1:3: Acts 1:1.
1:4: Jn 20:31.
1:5: Mt 2:1; 1 Chron 24:10; 2 Chron 31:2.
1:9: Ex 30:7.
1:11: Lk 2:9; Acts 5:19.
1:13: Lk 1:30, 60.
1:15: Num 6:3; Lk 7:33.
1:17: Mt 11:14; 17:13; Mal 4:5.
1:18: Lk 1:34.
1:19: Dan 8:16; 9:21; Mt 18:10.
1:25: Gen 30:23; Is 4:1.
1:30: Lk 1:13.
1:31: Lk 2:21; Mt 1:21.
* 1:3: Theophilus is again referred to in Acts 1:1, but nothing is known of him.
† 1:5—2:52: The "Infancy Gospel," as it is called, is written in a markedly Semitic style, which differs from that of the rest of the Gospel. It appears to be based on the reminiscences of Mary.
‡ 1:30: The words of the angel are drawn from Messianic passages in the Old Testament.

48

³²He will be great, and will be called the Son of
the Most High;
and the Lord God will give to him the throne of
his father David,
³³and he will reign over the house of Jacob for
ever;
and of his kingdom there will be no end."
³⁴And Mary said to the angel, "How can this be, *
since I have no husband?" ³⁵And the angel said
to her,

"The Holy Spirit will come upon you,
and the power of the Most High will
overshadow you;
therefore the child to be born ᵈ will be called
holy,
the Son of God.
³⁶And behold, your kinswoman Elizabeth in her
old age has also conceived a son; and this is the
sixth month with her who was called barren. ³⁷For
with God nothing will be impossible." ³⁸And Mary
said, "Behold, I am the handmaid of the Lord; let
it be to me according to your word." And the
angel departed from her.

Mary Visits Elizabeth; and
Mary's Song of Praise

39 In those days Mary arose and went with
haste into the hill country, to a city of Judah,
⁴⁰and she entered the house of Zechari'ah and
greeted Elizabeth. ⁴¹And when Elizabeth heard
the greeting of Mary, the child leaped in her
womb; and Elizabeth was filled with the Holy
Spirit ⁴²and she exclaimed with a loud cry,
"Blessed are you among women, and blessed is
the fruit of your womb! ⁴³And why is this granted
me, that the mother of my Lord should come to
me? ⁴⁴For behold, when the voice of your greeting
came to my ears, the child in my womb leaped for
joy. ⁴⁵And blessed is she who believed that there
would be ᵉ a fulfilment of what was spoken to her
from the Lord." ⁴⁶And Mary said,

"My soul magnifies the Lord,
⁴⁷and my spirit rejoices in God my Savior,
⁴⁸for he has regarded the low estate of his
handmaiden.
For behold, henceforth all generations will call
me blessed;
⁴⁹for he who is mighty has done great things for
me,
and holy is his name.
⁵⁰And his mercy is on those who fear him
from generation to generation.
⁵¹He has shown strength with his arm,
he has scattered the proud in the imagination
of their hearts,
⁵²he has put down the mighty from their
thrones,
and exalted those of low degree;
⁵³he has filled the hungry with good things,
and the rich he has sent empty away.

⁵⁴He has helped his servant Israel,
in remembrance of his mercy,
⁵⁵as he spoke to our fathers,
to Abraham and to his posterity for ever." †
⁵⁶And Mary remained with her about three
months, and returned to her home.

The Birth of John the Baptist

57 Now the time came for Elizabeth to be delivered, and she gave birth to a son. ⁵⁸And her neighbors and kinsfolk heard that the Lord had shown
great mercy to her, and they rejoiced with her.
⁵⁹And on the eighth day they came to circumcise
the child; and they would have named him
Zechari'ah after his father, ⁶⁰but his mother said,
"Not so; he shall be called John." ⁶¹And they said
to her, "None of your kindred is called by this
name." ⁶²And they made signs to his father, in-
quiring what he would have him called. ⁶³And he
asked for a writing tablet, and wrote, "His name is
John." And they all marveled. ⁶⁴And immediately
his mouth was opened and his tongue loosed, and
he spoke, blessing God. ⁶⁵And fear came on all
their neighbors. And all these things were talked
about through all the hill country of Judea; ⁶⁶and
all who heard them laid them up in their hearts,
saying, "What then will this child be?" For the
hand of the Lord was with him.

Zechariah's Prophecy

67 And his father Zechari'ah was filled with
the Holy Spirit, and prophesied, saying,
⁶⁸"Blessed be the Lord God of Israel,
for he has visited and redeemed his people,
⁶⁹and has raised up a horn of salvation ‡ for us
in the house of his servant David,
⁷⁰as he spoke by the mouth of his holy prophets
from of old,
⁷¹that we should be saved from our enemies,
and from the hand of all who hate us;
⁷²to perform the mercy promised to our fathers,
and to remember his holy covenant,
⁷³the oath which he swore to our father
Abraham, ⁷⁴to grant us
that we, being delivered from the hand of our
enemies,
might serve him without fear,

ᵈ Other ancient authorities add *of you.*
ᵉ Or *believed, for there will be.*
1:33: Mt 28:18; Dan 2:44.
1:34: Lk 1:18.
1:35: Mt 1:20.
1:37: Gen 18:14.
1:42: Lk 11:27–28.
1:46–55: 1 Sam 2:1–10.
1:47: 1 Tim 2:3; Tit 2:10; Jude 25.
1:55: Mic 7:20; Gen 17:7; 18:18; 22:17.
1:59: Lev 12:3; Gen 17:12.
1:63: Lk 1:13.
* 1:34: *How can this be:* alternate reading is *How will this be.*
† 1:46–55: The Magnificat is based on the Song of Hannah (1 Sam 2:1–10), and other Old Testament passages that describe God's favor toward Israel and especially toward the poor and lowly.
‡ 1:69, *a horn of salvation*: i.e., a mighty savior.

[75]in holiness and righteousness before him all the days of our life.

[76]And you, child, will be called the prophet of the Most High;

for you will go before the Lord to prepare his ways,

[77]to give knowledge of salvation to his people in the forgiveness of their sins,

[78]through the tender mercy of our God,

when the day shall dawn upon [f] us from on high

[79]to give light to those who sit in darkness and in the shadow of death,

to guide our feet into the way of peace."

[80]And the child grew and became strong in spirit, and he was in the wilderness till the day of his manifestation to Israel.

The Birth of Jesus

2 In those days a decree went out from Caesar Augustus that all the world should be enrolled. [2]This was the first enrollment, when Quirin'ius was governor of Syria. [3]And all went to be enrolled, each to his own city. [4]And Joseph also went up from Galilee, from the city of Nazareth, to Judea, to the city of David, which is called Bethlehem, because he was of the house and lineage of David, [5]to be enrolled with Mary his betrothed, who was with child. [6]And while they were there, the time came for her to be delivered. [7]And she gave birth to her first-born[*] son and wrapped him in swaddling cloths, and laid him in a manger, because there was no place for them in the inn.

The Shepherds and the Angels

8 And in that region there were shepherds out in the field, keeping watch over their flock by night. [9]And an angel of the Lord appeared to them, and the glory of the Lord shone around them, and they were filled with fear. [10]And the angel said to them, "Be not afraid; for behold, I bring you good news of a great joy which will come to all the people; [11]for to you is born this day in the city of David a Savior, who is Christ the Lord. [12]And this will be a sign for you: you will find a baby wrapped in swaddling cloths and lying in a manger." [13]And suddenly there was with the angel a multitude of the heavenly host praising God and saying,

[14]"Glory to God in the highest,

and on earth peace among men with whom he is pleased!" [g]

15 When the angels went away from them into heaven, the shepherds said to one another, "Let us go over to Bethlehem and see this thing that has happened, which the Lord has made known to us." [16]And they went with haste, and found Mary and Joseph, and the baby lying in a manger. [17]And when they saw it they made known the saying which had been told them concerning this child;

[18]and all who heard it wondered at what the shepherds told them. [19]But Mary kept all these things, pondering them in her heart. [20]And the shepherds returned, glorifying and praising God for all they had heard and seen, as it had been told them.

Jesus Is Circumcised and Named

21 And at the end of eight days, when he was circumcised, he was called Jesus, the name given by the angel before he was conceived in the womb.

Jesus Is Presented in the Temple

22 And when the time came for their purification according to the law of Moses, they brought him up to Jerusalem to present him to the Lord [23](as it is written in the law of the Lord, "Every male that opens the womb shall be called holy to the Lord") [24]and to offer a sacrifice according to what is said in the law of the Lord, "a pair of turtledoves, or two young pigeons." [25]Now there was a man in Jerusalem, whose name was Simeon, and this man was righteous and devout, looking for the consolation of Israel, and the Holy Spirit was upon him. [26]And it had been revealed to him by the Holy Spirit that he should not see death before he had seen the Lord's Christ. [27]And inspired by the Spirit [h] he came into the temple; and when the parents brought in the child Jesus, to do for him according to the custom of the law, [28]he took him up in his arms and blessed God and said,

[29]"Lord, now let your servant depart in peace, according to your word;

[30]for my eyes have seen your salvation

[31]which you have prepared in the presence of all peoples,

[32]a light for revelation to the Gentiles,

and for glory to your people Israel."

33 And his father and his mother marveled at what was said about him; [34]and Simeon blessed them and said to Mary his mother,

---

[f] Or *whereby the dayspring will visit.* Other ancient authorities read *since the dayspring has visited.*

[g] Other ancient authorities read *peace, good will among men.*

[h] Or *in the Spirit.*

1:76: Lk 7:26; Mal 4:5.
1:77: Mk 1:4.
1:78: Mal 4:2; Eph 5:14.
1:79: Is 9:2; Mt 4:16.
1:80: Lk 2:40; 2:52.
2:1: Lk 3:1.
2:4: Lk 1:27.
2:9: Lk 1:11; Acts 5:19.
2:11: Jn 4:42; Acts 5:31; Mt 16:16; Acts 2:36.
2:12: 1 Sam 2:34; 2 Kings 19:29; Is 7:14.
2:14: Lk 3:8; 3:22.
2:19: Lk 2:51.
2:21: Lk 1:59, 31; Mt 1:25.
2:22-24: Lev 12:2-8.
2:23: Ex 13:2, 12.
2:25: Lk 2:38; 23:51.
2:30: Is 52:10; Lk 3:6.
2:32: Is 42:6; 49:6; Acts 13:47; 26:23.

[*] 2:7, *first-born:* The term connotes possession of certain rights, privileges, and obligations; cf. Ex 13:1-2, 11-16. The word is used even in modern times without necessarily implying subsequent births.

"Behold, this child is set for the fall * and rising
of many in Israel,
and for a sign that is spoken against
[35](and a sword will pierce through your own soul
also),
that thoughts out of many hearts may be
revealed."

36 And there was a prophetess, Anna, the daughter of Phan'uel, of the tribe of Asher; she was of a great age, having lived with her husband seven years from her virginity, [37]and as a widow till she was eighty-four. She did not depart from the temple, worshiping with fasting and prayer night and day. [38]And coming up at that very hour she gave thanks to God, and spoke of him to all who were looking for the redemption of Jerusalem.

The Return to Nazareth

39 And when they had performed everything according to the law of the Lord, they returned into Galilee, to their own city, Nazareth. [40]And the child grew and became strong, filled with wisdom; and the favor of God was upon him.

The Boy Jesus in the Temple

41 Now his parents went to Jerusalem every year at the feast of the Passover. [42]And when he was twelve years old, they went up according to custom; [43]and when the feast was ended, as they were returning, the boy Jesus stayed behind in Jerusalem. His parents did not know it, [44]but supposing him to be in the company they went a day's journey, and they sought him among their kinsfolk and acquaintances; [45]and when they did not find him, they returned to Jerusalem, seeking him. [46]After three days they found him in the temple, sitting among the teachers, listening to them and asking them questions; [47]and all who heard him were amazed at his understanding and his answers. [48]And when they saw him they were astonished; and his mother said to him, "Son, why have you treated us so? Behold, your father and I have been looking for you anxiously." [49]And he said to them, "How is it that you sought me? Did you not know that I must be in my Father's house?" † [50]And they did not understand the saying which he spoke to them. [51]And he went down with them and came to Nazareth, and was obedient to them; and his mother kept all these things in her heart.

52 And Jesus increased in wisdom and in stature, [i] and in favor with God and man.

The Preaching of John the Baptist

3 In the fifteenth year of the reign of Tibe'rius Caesar, Pontius Pilate being governor of Judea, and Herod being tetrarch of Galilee, and his brother Philip tetrarch of the region of Iturae'a and Trachoni'tis, and Lysa'nias tetrarch of Abile'ne, [2]in the high-priesthood of Annas and Cai'aphas, ‡ the word of God came to John the

son of Zechari'ah in the wilderness; [3]and he went into all the region about the Jordan, preaching a baptism of repentance for the forgiveness of sins. [4]As it is written in the book of the words of Isaiah the prophet,
"The voice of one crying in the wilderness:
Prepare the way of the Lord,
make his paths straight.
[5]Every valley shall be filled,
and every mountain and hill shall be brought
low,
and the crooked shall be made straight,
and the rough ways shall be made smooth;
[6]and all flesh shall see the salvation of God."

7 He said therefore to the multitudes that came out to be baptized by him, "You brood of vipers! § Who warned you to flee from the wrath to come? [8]Bear fruits that befit repentance, and do not begin to say to yourselves, 'We have Abraham as our father'; for I tell you, God is able from these stones to raise up children to Abraham. [9]Even now the axe is laid to the root of the trees; every tree therefore that does not bear good fruit is cut down and thrown into the fire."

10 And the multitudes asked him, "What then shall we do?" [11]And he answered them, "He who has two coats, let him share with him who has none; and he who has food, let him do likewise." [12]Tax collectors also came to be baptized, and said to him, "Teacher, what shall we do?" [13]And he said to them, "Collect no more than is appointed you." [14]Soldiers also asked him, "And we, what shall we do?" And he said to them, "Rob no one by violence or by false accusation, and be content with your wages."

15 As the people were in expectation, and all men questioned in their hearts concerning John, whether perhaps he were the Christ, [16]John answered them all, "I baptize you with water; but he who is mightier than I is coming, the thong of

---

i Or years.
2:36: Acts 21:9; Josh 19:24; 1 Tim 5:9.
2:40: Judg 13:24; 1 Sam 2:26.
2:41: Deut 16:1–8; Ex 23:15.
2:48: Mk 3:31–35.
2:51: Lk 2:19.
2:52: Lk 1:80; 2:40.
3:1: Lk 23:1; 9:7; 13:31; 23:7.
3:2: Jn 18:13; Acts 4:6; Mt 26:3; Jn 11:49.
3:3–9: Mt 3:1–10; Mk 1:1–5; Jn 1:6, 23.
3:4–6: Is 40:3–5.
3:6: Lk 2:30.
3:7: Mt 12:34; 23:33.
3:8: Jn 8:33, 39.
3:9: Mt 7:19; Heb 6:7–8.
3:11: Lk 6:29.
3:15: Acts 13:25; Jn 1:19–22.
3:16–18: Mt 3:11–12; Mk 1:7–8; Jn 1:26–27, 33; Acts 1:5; 11:16; 19:4.
* 2:34, *for the fall*: i.e., in the sense that by rejecting his claims many would sin grievously.
† 2:49: Jesus stresses the priority of his duty to his Father, which involves a high degree of independence of earthly ties.
‡ 3:2: See note on Jn 18:13.
§ 3:7, *brood of vipers*: This epithet seems to have been directed mainly at the Pharisees; cf. Mt 3:7.

whose sandals I am not worthy to untie; he will baptize you with the Holy Spirit and with fire. [17]His winnowing fork is in his hand, to clear his threshing floor, and to gather the wheat into his granary, but the chaff he will burn with unquenchable fire."

18 So, with many other exhortations, he preached good news to the people. [19]But Herod the tetrarch, who had been reproved by him for Hero'di-as, his brother's wife, and for all the evil things that Herod had done, [20]added this to them all, that he shut up John in prison.

The Baptism of Jesus

21 Now when all the people were baptized, and when Jesus also had been baptized and was praying, the heaven was opened, [22]and the Holy Spirit descended upon him in bodily form, as a dove, and a voice came from heaven, "You are my beloved Son; [j] with you I am well pleased." [k]

The Ancestry of Jesus

23 Jesus, when he began his ministry, was about thirty years of age, being the son (as was supposed) of Joseph, [*] the son of He'li, [24]the son of Matthat, the son of Levi, the son of Melchi, the son of Jan'na-i, the son of Joseph, [25]the son of Mattathi'as, the son of Amos, the son of Na'hum, the son of Es'li, the son of Nag'ga-i, [26]the son of Ma'ath, the son of Mattathi'as, the son of Sem'e-in, the son of Jo'sech, the son of Jo'da, [27]the son of Jo-an'an, the son of Rhesa, the son of Zerub'-babel, the son of She-al'ti-el, [1] the son of Ne'ri, [28]the son of Melchi, the son of Addi, the son of Co'sam, the son of Elma'dam, the son of Er, [29]the son of Joshua, the son of Elie'zer, the son of Jo'rim, the son of Matthat, the son of Levi, [30]the son of Simeon, the son of Judah, the son of Joseph, the son of Jo'nam, the son of Eli'akim, [31]the son of Me'le-a, the son of Menna, the son of Mat'tatha, the son of Nathan, the son of David, [32]the son of Jesse, the son of O'bed, the son of Boaz, the son of Sa'la, the son of Nahshon, [33]the son of Ammin'adab, the son of Admin, the son of Arni, the son of Hezron, the son of Per'ez, the son of Judah, [34]the son of Jacob, the son of Isaac, the son of Abraham, the son of Te'rah, the son of Na'hor, [35]the son of Se'rug, the son of Re'u, the son of Pe'leg, the son of E'ber, the son of She'lah, [36]the son of Ca-i'nan, the son of Arpha'xad, the son of Shem, the son of Noah, the son of La'mech, [37]the son of Methu'selah, the son of E'noch, the son of Jar'ed, the son of Maha'lale"el, the son of Ca-i'nan, [38]the son of E'nos, the son of Seth, the son of Adam, the son of God.

The Temptation of Jesus

4 And Jesus, full of the Holy Spirit, returned from the Jordan, and was led by the Spirit [2]for forty days in the wilderness, tempted by the devil. And he ate nothing in those days; and when they were ended, he was hungry. [3]The devil said to him, "If you are the Son of God, command this stone to become bread." [4]And Jesus answered him, "It is written, 'Man shall not live by bread alone.' " [5]And the devil took him up, and showed him all the kingdoms of the world in a moment of time, [6]and said to him, "To you I will give all this authority and their glory; for it has been delivered to me, and I give it to whom I will. [7]If you, then, will worship me, it shall all be yours." [8]And Jesus answered him, "It is written,

'You shall worship the Lord your God,
    and him only shall you serve.' "

[9]And he took him to Jerusalem, and set him on the pinnacle of the temple, and said to him, "If you are the Son of God, throw yourself down from here; [10]for it is written,

'He will give his angels charge of you, to guard
    you,'

[11]and

'On their hands they will bear you up,
    lest you strike your foot against a stone.' "

[12]And Jesus answered him, "It is said, 'You shall not tempt the Lord your God.' " [13]And when the devil had ended every temptation, he departed from him until an opportune time.

Jesus Begins Preaching and Teaching in Galilee

14 And Jesus returned in the power of the Spirit into Galilee, and a report concerning him went out through all the surrounding country. [15]And he taught in their synagogues, being glorified by all.

The Rejection of Jesus at Nazareth

16 And he came to Nazareth, where he had been brought up; and he went to the synagogue, as was his custom, on the sabbath day. [†] And he stood up to read; [17]and there was given to him the book of the prophet Isaiah. He opened the book and found the place where it was written,

---

[j] Or *my Son, my* (or *the*) *Beloved.*
[k] Other ancient authorities read *today I have begotten you.*
[1] Greek *Salathiel.*
3:19–20: Mt 14:3–4; Mk 6:17–18.
3:21–22: Mt 3:13–17; Mk 1:9–11; Jn 1:29–34.
3:21: Lk 5:16; 6:12; 9:18; 9:28; 11:1; Mk 1:35.
3:22: Ps 2:7; Is 42:1; Lk 9:35; Acts 10:38; 2 Pet 1:17.
3:23–38: Mt 1:1–17; Gen 5:3–32; 11:10–26; Ruth 4:18–22; 1 Chron 1:1–4, 24–28; 2:1–15.
3:23: Jn 8:57; Lk 1:27.
4:1–13: Mt 4:1–11; Mk 1:12–13.
4:2: Deut 9:9; 1 Kings 19:8.
4:4: Deut 8:3.
4:6: 1 Jn 5:19.
4:8: Deut 6:13.
4:10–11: Ps 91:11–12.
4:12: Deut 6:16.
4:13: Lk 22:28.
4:14: Mt 4:12; Mk 1:14; Mt 9:26; Lk 4:37.
4:15: Mt 4:23; 9:35; 11:1.
4:16–30: Mt 13:53–58; Mk 6:1–6; Acts 13:14–16.
* 3:23: This genealogy is more universalist than that of Matthew. Like Matthew, however, it gives the genealogy of Joseph, though Mary may well have been of the family of David.
† 4:16–30: This account of the visit to the synagogue seems to be composed of the details of more than one visit. Luke is trying here to underline the contrast between Christ's offer of salvation and the people's refusal of it.

[18]"The Spirit of the Lord is upon me,
because he has anointed me to preach good
    news to the poor.
He has sent me to proclaim release to the
    captives
and recovering of sight to the blind,
to set at liberty those who are oppressed,
[19]to proclaim the acceptable year of the Lord."
[20]And he closed the book, and gave it back to the attendant, and sat down; and the eyes of all in the synagogue were fixed on him. [21]And he began to say to them, "Today this Scripture has been fulfilled in your hearing." [22]And all spoke well of him, and wondered at the gracious words which proceeded out of his mouth; and they said, "Is not this Joseph's son?" [23]And he said to them, "Doubtless you will quote to me this proverb, 'Physician, heal yourself; what we have heard you did at Caper'na-um, do here also in your own country.'" [24]And he said, "Truly, I say to you, no prophet is acceptable in his own country. [25]But in truth, I tell you, there were many widows in Israel in the days of Eli'jah, when the heaven was shut up three years and six months, when there came a great famine over all the land; [26]and Eli'jah was sent to none of them but only to Zar'ephath, in the land of Si'don, to a woman who was a widow. [27]And there were many lepers in Israel in the time of the prophet Eli'sha; and none of them was cleansed, but only Na'aman the Syrian." [28]When they heard this, all in the synagogue were filled with wrath. [29]And they rose up and put him out of the city, and led him to the brow of the hill on which their city was built, that they might throw him down headlong. [30]But passing through the midst of them he went away.

The Man with an Unclean Spirit

31 And he went down to Caper'na-um, a city of Galilee. And he was teaching them on the sabbath; [32]and they were astonished at his teaching, for his word was with authority. [33]And in the synagogue there was a man who had the spirit of an unclean demon; and he cried out with a loud voice, [34]"Ah![m] What have you to do with us, Jesus of Nazareth? Have you come to destroy us? I know who you are, the Holy One of God." [35]But Jesus rebuked him, saying, "Be silent, and come out of him!" And when the demon had thrown him down in their midst, he came out of him, having done him no harm. [36]And they were all amazed and said to one another, "What is this? For with authority and power he commands the unclean spirits, and they come out." [37]And reports of him went out into every place in the surrounding region.

Healings at Simon's House

38 And he arose and left the synagogue, and entered Simon's house. Now Simon's mother-in-law was ill with a high fever, and they asked him about her. [39]And he stood over her and rebuked the fever, and it left her; and immediately she rose and served them.

40 Now when the sun was setting, all those who had any that were sick with various diseases brought them to him; and he laid his hands on every one of them and healed them. [41]And demons also came out of many, crying, "You are the Son of God!" But he rebuked them, and would not allow them to speak, because they knew that he was the Christ.

Jesus Preaches in the Synagogues of Judea

42 And when it was day he departed and went into a lonely place. And the people sought him and came to him, and would have kept him from leaving them; [43]but he said to them, "I must preach the good news of the kingdom of God to the other cities also; for I was sent for this purpose." [44]And he was preaching in the synagogues of Judea.[n]

Jesus Calls the First Disciples

5 While the people pressed upon him to hear the word of God, he was standing by the lake of Gennes'aret. [2]And he saw two boats by the lake; but the fishermen had gone out of them and were washing their nets. [3]Getting into one of the boats, which was Simon's, he asked him to put out a little from the land. And he sat down and taught the people from the boat. [4]And when he had ceased speaking, he said to Simon, "Put out into the deep and let down your nets for a catch." [5]And Simon answered, "Master, we toiled all night and took nothing! But at your word I will let down the nets." [6]And when they had done this, they enclosed a great shoal of fish; and as their nets were breaking, [7]they beckoned to their partners in the other boat to come and help them. And they came and filled both the boats, so that they began to sink. [8]But when Simon Peter saw it, he fell down at Jesus' knees, saying, "Depart from me, for I am a sinful man, O Lord." [9]For he was astonished, and all that were with him, at the catch of fish which they had taken; [10]and so also were James and John, sons of Zeb'edee, who were partners with Simon. And Jesus said to Simon,

---

[m] Or let us alone.
[n] Other ancient authorities read Galilee.
4:18-19: Is 61:1-2.
4:22: Jn 6:42; 7:15.
4:23: Mk 1:21; 2:1; Jn 4:46.
4:24: Jn 4:44.
4:25: 1 Kings 17:1, 8-16; 18:1; Jas 5:17-18.
4:27: 2 Kings 5:1-14.
4:29: Acts 7:58; Num 15:35.
4:30: Jn 8:59; 10:39.
4:31-37: Mk 1:21-28.
4:32: Mt 7:28; 13:54; 22:33; Mk 11:18; Jn 7:46.
4:37: Lk 4:14; 5:15; Mt 9:26.
4:38-41: Mt 8:14-17; Mk 1:29-34.
4:42-43: Mk 1:35-38.
4:44: Mt 4:23; Mk 1:39; Mt 9:35.
5:1-11: Mt 4:18-22; Mk 1:16-20; Jn 1:40-42; 21:1-19.
5:3: Mt 13:1-2; Mk 4:1.
5:5: Lk 8:24, 45; 9:33, 49; 17:13.

"Do not be afraid; henceforth you will be catching men." [11]And when they had brought their boats to land, they left everything and followed him.

Jesus Cleanses a Leper

12 While he was in one of the cities, there came a man full of leprosy; and when he saw Jesus, he fell on his face and begged him, "Lord, if you will, you can make me clean." [13]And he stretched out his hand, and touched him, saying, "I will; be clean." And immediately the leprosy left him. [14]And he charged him to tell no one; but "go and show yourself to the priest, and make an offering for your cleansing, as Moses commanded, for a proof to the people." [o] [15]But so much the more the report went abroad concerning him; and great multitudes gathered to hear and to be healed of their infirmities. [16]But he withdrew to the wilderness and prayed.

Jesus Heals a Paralytic

17 On one of those days, as he was teaching, there were Pharisees and teachers of the law sitting by, who had come from every village of Galilee and Judea and from Jerusalem; and the power of the Lord was with him to heal. [p] [18]And behold, men were bringing on a bed a man who was paralyzed, and they sought to bring him in and lay him before Jesus; [q] [19]but finding no way to bring him in, because of the crowd, they went up on the roof and let him down with his bed through the tiles into their midst before Jesus. [20]And when he saw their faith he said, "Man, your sins are forgiven you." [21]And the scribes and the Pharisees began to question, saying, "Who is this that speaks blasphemies? Who can forgive sins but God only?" [22]When Jesus perceived their questionings, he answered them, "Why do you question in your hearts? [23]Which is easier, to say, 'Your sins are forgiven you,' or to say, 'Rise and walk'? [24]But that you may know that the Son of man has authority on earth to forgive sins"—he said to the man who was paralyzed—"I say to you, rise, take up your bed and go home." [25]And immediately he rose before them, and took up that on which he lay, and went home, glorifying God. [26]And amazement seized them all, and they glorified God and were filled with awe, saying, "We have seen strange things today."

Jesus Calls Levi

27 After this he went out, and saw a tax collector, named Levi, sitting at the tax office; and he said to him, "Follow me." [28]And he left everything, and rose and followed him.

29 And Levi made him a great feast in his house; and there was a large company of tax collectors and others sitting at table [r] with them. [30]And the Pharisees and their scribes murmured against his disciples, saying, "Why do you eat and drink with tax collectors and sinners?" [31]And Jesus answered them, "Those who are well have no need of a physician, but those who are sick; [32]I have not come to call the righteous, but sinners to repentance."

The Question about Fasting

33 And they said to him, "The disciples of John fast often and offer prayers, and so do the disciples of the Pharisees, but yours eat and drink." [34]And Jesus said to them, "Can you make wedding guests fast while the bridegroom is with them? [35]The days will come, when the bridegroom is taken away from them, and then they will fast in those days." [36]He told them a parable also: "No one tears a piece from a new garment and puts it upon an old garment; if he does, he will tear the new, and the piece from the new will not match the old. [37]And no one puts new wine into old wineskins; if he does, the new wine will burst the skins and it will be spilled, and the skins will be destroyed. [38]But new wine must be put into fresh wineskins. [39]And no one after drinking old wine desires new; for he says, 'The old is good.' " [s]

A Teaching about the Sabbath

6 On a sabbath, [t] while he was going through the grainfields, his disciples plucked and ate some heads of grain, rubbing them in their hands. [2]But some of the Pharisees said, "Why are you doing what is not lawful to do on the sabbath?" [3]And Jesus answered, "Have you not read what David did when he was hungry, he and those who were with him: [4]how he entered the house of God, and took and ate the showbread, which it is not lawful for any but the priests to eat, and also gave it to those with him?" [5]And he said to them, "The Son of man is lord of the sabbath."

The Man with a Withered Hand

6 On another sabbath, when he entered the synagogue and taught, a man was there whose right hand was withered. [7]And the scribes and the Pharisees watched him, to see whether he

---

[o] Greek *to them.*
[p] Other ancient authorities read *was present to heal them.*
[q] Greek *him.*
[r] Greek *reclining.*
[s] Other ancient authorities read *better.*
[t] Other ancient authorities read *On the second first sabbath* (on the second sabbath after the first).

5:12-16: Mt 8:1–4; Mk 1:40–45; Lk 17:11–19.
5:14: Lev 13:49; 14:2–32.
5:15: Lk 4:14, 37; Mt 9:26.
5:16: Lk 3:21; 6:12; 9:18, 28; 11:1.
5:17-26: Mt 9:1–8; Mk 2:1–12; Jn 5:1–9.
5:17: Mt 15:1; Mk 5:30; Lk 6:19.
5:20: Lk 7:48–49.
5:27-32: Mt 9:9–13; Mk 2:13–17.
5:30: Lk 15:1–2.
5:32: 1 Tim 1:15.
5:33-38: Mt 9:14–17; Mk 2:18–22.
5:33: Lk 7:18; 11:1; Jn 3:25–26.
5:35: Lk 9:22; 17:22.
6:1-5: Mt 12:1–8; Mk 2:23–28.
6:1: Deut 23:25.
6:2: Ex 20:10; 23:12; Deut 5:14.
6:3: 1 Sam 21:1–6.
6:4: Lev 24:9.
6:6-11: Mt 12:9–14; Mk 3:1–6.

would heal on the sabbath, so that they might find an accusation against him. [8]But he knew their thoughts, and he said to the man who had the withered hand, "Come and stand here." And he rose and stood there. [9]And Jesus said to them, "I ask you, is it lawful on the sabbath to do good or to do harm, to save life or to destroy it?" [10]And he looked around on them all, and said to him, "Stretch out your hand." And he did so, and his hand was restored. [11]But they were filled with fury and discussed with one another what they might do to Jesus.

Jesus Chooses the Twelve Disciples

12 In these days he went out to the hills to pray; and all night he continued in prayer to God. [13]And when it was day, he called his disciples, and chose from them twelve, whom he named apostles; [14]Simon, whom he named Peter, and Andrew his brother, and James and John, and Philip, and Bartholomew, [15]and Matthew, and Thomas, and James the son of Alphae'us, and Simon who was called the Zealot, [16]and Judas the son of James, and Judas Iscariot, who became a traitor.

Jesus Teaches and Heals

17 And he came down with them and stood on a level place, with a great crowd of his disciples and a great multitude of people from all Judea and Jerusalem and the seacoast of Tyre and Si'don, who came to hear him and to be healed of their diseases; [18]and those who were troubled with unclean spirits were cured. [19]And all the crowd sought to touch him, for power came forth from him and healed them all.

Blessings and Woes

20 And he lifted up his eyes on his disciples, and said: *

"Blessed are you poor, for yours is the kingdom of God.

21 "Blessed are you that hunger now, for you shall be satisfied.

"Blessed are you that weep now, for you shall laugh.

22 "Blessed are you when men hate you, and when they exclude you and revile you, and cast out your name as evil, on account of the Son of man! [23]Rejoice in that day, and leap for joy, for behold, your reward is great in heaven; for so their fathers did to the prophets.

24 "But woe to you that are rich, for you have received your consolation.

25 "Woe to you that are full now, for you shall hunger.

"Woe to you that laugh now, for you shall mourn and weep.

26 "Woe to you, when all men speak well of you, for so their fathers did to the false prophets.

Love for Enemies

27 "But I say to you that hear, Love your enemies, do good to those who hate you, [28]bless those who curse you, pray for those who abuse you. [29]To him who strikes you on the cheek, offer the other also; and from him who takes away your cloak do not withhold your coat as well. [30]Give to every one who begs from you; and of him who takes away your goods do not ask them again. [31]And as you wish that men would do to you, do so to them.

32 "If you love those who love you, what credit is that to you? For even sinners love those who love them. [33]And if you do good to those who do good to you, what credit is that to you? For even sinners do the same. [34]And if you lend to those from whom you hope to receive, what credit is that to you? Even sinners lend to sinners, to receive as much again. [35]But love your enemies, and do good, and lend, expecting nothing in return;[v] and your reward will be great, and you will be sons of the Most High; for he is kind to the ungrateful and the selfish. [36]Be merciful, even as your Father is merciful.

Judging Others

37 "Judge not, and you will not be judged; condemn not, and you will not be condemned; forgive, and you will be forgiven; [38]give, and it will be given to you; good measure, pressed down, shaken together, running over, will be put into your lap. For the measure you give will be the measure you get back."

39 He also told them a parable: "Can a blind man lead a blind man? Will they not both fall into a pit? [40]A disciple is not above his teacher, but every one when he is fully taught will be like his teacher. [41]Why do you see the speck that is in your brother's eye, but do not notice the log that is in your own eye? [42]Or how can you say to your brother, 'Brother, let me take out the speck that is in your eye,' when you yourself do not see the log that is in your own eye? You hypocrite, first take the log out of your own eye, and then you will see clearly to take out the speck that is in your brother's eye.

---

[v] Other ancient authorities read *despairing of no man.*

6:12-16: Mk 3:13–19; Mt 10:2–4; Acts 1:13.
6:12: Lk 3:21; 5:16; 9:18, 28; 11:1.
6:17-19: Mt 5:1–2; 4:24–25; Mk 3:7–12.
6:19: Mk 3:10; Mt 9:21; 14:36; Lk 5:17.
6:20-23: Mt 5:3–12.
6:22: 1 Pet 4:14; Jn 9:22; 16:2.
6:24-26: Lk 10:13–15; 11:38–52; 17:1; 21:23; 22:22.
6:24: Lk 16:25; Jas 5:1–5; Mt 6:2.
6:27-30: Mt 5:39–44; Rom 12:17; 1 Cor 6:7.
6:31: Mt 7:12.
6:32-36: Mt 5:44–48.
6:35: Mt 5:9.
6:37-38: Mt 7:1–2; Rom 2:1.
6:38: Mk 4:24; Acts 20:35.
6:39: Mt 15:14.
6:40: Mt 10:24–25; Jn 13:16; 15:20.
6:41-42: Mt 7:3–5.

* 6:20–49: Luke's discourse is shorter than that of Matthew because it does not contain Matthew's additional material collected from other occasions, or his details that would interest only Jews.

A Tree and Its Fruit

43 "For no good tree bears bad fruit, nor again does a bad tree bear good fruit; ⁴⁴for each tree is known by its own fruit. For figs are not gathered from thorns, nor are grapes picked from a bramble bush. ⁴⁵The good man out of the good treasure of his heart produces good, and the evil man out of his evil treasure produces evil; for out of the abundance of the heart his mouth speaks.

Hearers and Doers

46 "Why do you call me 'Lord, Lord,' and not do what I tell you? ⁴⁷Every one who comes to me and hears my words and does them, I will show you what he is like: ⁴⁸he is like a man building a house, who dug deep, and laid the foundation upon rock; and when a flood arose, the stream broke against that house, and could not shake it, because it had been well built. ^w ⁴⁹But he who hears and does not do them is like a man who built a house on the ground without a foundation; against which the stream broke, and immediately it fell, and the ruin of that house was great."

Jesus Heals a Centurion's Slave

7 After he had ended all his sayings in the hearing of the people he entered Caper'na-um. ²Now a centurion had a slave who was dear ^x to him, who was sick and at the point of death. ³When he heard of Jesus, he sent to him elders of the Jews, asking him to come and heal his slave. ⁴And when they came to Jesus, they begged him earnestly, saying, "He is worthy to have you do this for him, ⁵for he loves our nation, and he built us our synagogue." ⁶And Jesus went with them. When he was not far from the house, the centurion sent friends to him, saying to him, "Lord, do not trouble yourself, for I am not worthy to have you come under my roof; ⁷therefore I did not presume to come to you. But say the word, and let my servant be healed. ⁸For I am a man set under authority, with soldiers under me: and I say to one, 'Go,' and he goes; and to another, 'Come,' and he comes; and to my slave, 'Do this,' and he does it." ⁹When Jesus heard this he marveled at him, and turned and said to the multitude that followed him, "I tell you, not even in Israel have I found such faith." ¹⁰And when those who had been sent returned to the house, they found the slave well.

Jesus Raises a Widow's Son at Nain

11 Soon afterward ^y he went to a city called Na'in, and his disciples and a great crowd went with him. ¹²As he drew near to the gate of the city, behold, a man who had died was being carried out, the only son of his mother, and she was a widow; and a large crowd from the city was with her. ¹³And when the Lord saw her, he had compassion on her and said to her, "Do not weep." ¹⁴And he came and touched the bier, and the bearers stood still. And he said, "Young man, I say to you,

arise." ¹⁵And the dead man sat up, and began to speak. And he gave him to his mother. ¹⁶Fear seized them all; and they glorified God, saying, "A great prophet has arisen among us!" and "God has visited his people!" ¹⁷And this report concerning him spread through the whole of Judea and all the surrounding country.

Messengers from John the Baptist

18 The disciples of John told him of all these things. ¹⁹And John, calling to him two of his disciples, sent them to the Lord, saying, "Are you he who is to come, or shall we look for another?" ²⁰And when the men had come to him, they said, "John the Baptist has sent us to you, saying, 'Are you he who is to come, or shall we look for another?' " ²¹In that hour he cured many of diseases and plagues and evil spirits, and on many that were blind he bestowed sight. ²²And he answered them, "Go and tell John what you have seen and heard: the blind receive their sight, the lame walk, lepers are cleansed, and the deaf hear, the dead are raised up, the poor have good news preached to them. ²³And blessed is he who takes no offense at me."

24 When the messengers of John had gone, he began to speak to the crowds concerning John: "What did you go out into the wilderness to behold? A reed shaken by the wind? ²⁵What then did you go out to see? A man clothed in soft raiment? Behold, those who are gorgeously appareled and live in luxury are in kings' courts. ²⁶What then did you go out to see? A prophet? Yes, I tell you, and more than a prophet. ²⁷This is he of whom it is written,

'Behold, I send my messenger before your face,

who shall prepare your way before you.'

²⁸I tell you, among those born of women none is greater than John; yet he who is least in the kingdom of God is greater than he." [*] ²⁹(When they heard this all the people and the tax collectors justified God, having been baptized with the baptism of John; ³⁰but the Pharisees and the lawyers

^w Other ancient authorities read *founded upon the rock.*
^x Or *valuable.*
^y Other ancient authorities read *Next day.*
6:43–45: Mt 7:18–19; 12:33–35; Jas 3:11–12.
6:45: Mt 7:20.
6:46: Mt 7:21.
6:47–49: Mt 7:24–27; Jas 1:22–25.
7:1–10: Mt 8:5–10, 13; Jn 4:46–53.
7:5: Acts 10:2.
7:11–17: Mk 5:21–24, 35–43; Jn 11:1–44; 1 Kings 17:17–24; 2 Kings 4:32–37.
7:13: Lk 7:19; 10:1; 11:39; 12:42; 13:15; 17:5–6; 18:6; 19:8; 22:61; 24:3.
7:16: Lk 7:39; 24:19; Mt 21:11; Jn 6:14.
7:18–35: Mt 11:2–19.
7:21: Mt 4:23; Mk 3:10.
7:22: Is 29:18–19; 35:5–6; 61:1; Lk 4:18–19.
7:27: Mal 3:1; Mk 1:2.
7:29–30: Mt 21:32; Lk 3:12.
[*] 7:28: John, by virtue of his office, belonged to the old dispensation, the time of preparation for the kingdom. In terms of spiritual status, even the humbler members of the kingdom were superior to him.

rejected the purpose of God for themselves, not having been baptized by him.)

31 "To what then shall I compare the men of this generation, and what are they like? [32]They are like children sitting in the market place and calling to one another,

'We piped to you, and you did not dance;
we wailed, and you did not weep.'

[33]For John the Baptist has come eating no bread and drinking no wine; and you say, 'He has a demon.' [34]The Son of man has come eating and drinking; and you say, 'Behold, a glutton and a drunkard, a friend of tax collectors and sinners!' [35]Yet wisdom is justified by all her children."

A Sinful Woman Forgiven

36 One of the Pharisees asked him to eat with him, and he went into the Pharisee's house, and sat at table. [37]And behold, a woman of the city, who was a sinner, when she learned that he was sitting at table in the Pharisee's house, brought an alabaster flask of ointment, [38]and standing behind him at his feet, weeping, she began to wet his feet with her tears, and wiped them with the hair of her head, and kissed his feet, and anointed them with the ointment. [39]Now when the Pharisee who had invited him saw it, he said to himself, "If this man were a prophet, he would have known who and what sort of woman this is who is touching him, for she is a sinner." [40]And Jesus answering said to him, "Simon, I have something to say to you." And he answered, "What is it, Teacher?" [41]"A certain creditor had two debtors; one owed five hundred denarii, and the other fifty. [42]When they could not pay, he forgave them both. Now which of them will love him more?" [43]Simon answered, "The one, I suppose, to whom he forgave more." And he said to him, "You have judged rightly." [44]Then turning toward the woman he said to Simon, "Do you see this woman? I entered your house, you gave me no water for my feet, but she has wet my feet with her tears and wiped them with her hair. [45]You gave me no kiss, but from the time I came in she has not ceased to kiss my feet. [46]You did not anoint my head with oil, but she has anointed my feet with ointment. [47]Therefore I tell you, her sins, which are many, are forgiven, for she loved much; but he who is forgiven little, loves little." * [48]And he said to her, "Your sins are forgiven." [49]Then those who were at table with him began to say among themselves, "Who is this, who even forgives sins?" [50]And he said to the woman, "Your faith has saved you; go in peace."

Some Women Accompany Jesus

8 Soon afterward he went on through cities and villages, preaching and bringing the good news of the kingdom of God. And the Twelve were with him, [2]and also some women who had been healed of evil spirits and infirmities: Mary, called Mag′dalene, from whom seven demons had gone out, [3]and Jo-an′na, the wife of Chuza, Herod's steward, and Susanna, and many others, who provided for them ᶻ out of their means.

The Parable of the Sower

4 And when a great crowd came together and people from town after town came to him, he said in a parable: [5]"A sower went out to sow his seed; and as he sowed, some fell along the path, and was trodden under foot, and the birds of the air devoured it. [6]And some fell on the rock; and as it grew up, it withered away, because it had no moisture. [7]And some fell among thorns; and the thorns grew with it and choked it. [8]And some fell into good soil and grew, and yielded a hundredfold." As he said this, he called out, "He who has ears to hear, let him hear."

The Explanation of the Parable

9 And when his disciples asked him what this parable meant, [10]he said, "To you it has been given to know the secrets of the kingdom of God; but for others they are in parables, so that seeing they may not see, and hearing they may not understand. [11]Now the parable is this: The seed is the word of God. [12]The ones along the path are those who have heard; then the devil comes and takes away the word from their hearts, that they may not believe and be saved. [13]And the ones on the rock are those who, when they hear the word, receive it with joy; but these have no root, they believe for a while and in time of temptation fall away. [14]And as for what fell among the thorns, they are those who hear, but as they go on their way they are choked by the cares and riches and pleasures of life, and their fruit does not mature. [15]And as for that in the good soil, they are those who, hearing the word, hold it fast in an honest and good heart, and bring forth fruit with patience.

A Lamp Is Not Hidden

16 "No one after lighting a lamp covers it with a vessel, or puts it under a bed, but puts it on a

---

ᶻ Other ancient authorities read *him.*
7:33: Lk 1:15.
7:34: Lk 5:29; 15:1–2; 7:36–50.
7:36–50: Mt 26:6–13; Mk 14:3–9; Jn 12:1–8.
7:36: Lk 11:37; 14:1.
7:39: Lk 7:16; 24:19; Mt 21:11; Jn 6:14.
7:42: Mt 18:25.
7:43: Lk 10:28.
7:48: Mt 9:2; Mk 2:5; Lk 5:20.
7:50: Mt 9:22; Mk 5:34; Lk 8:48.
8:1–3: Lk 4:15; Mk 15:40–41; Mt 27:55–56; Lk 23:49.
8:4–8: Mt 13:1–9; Mk 4:1–9.
8:8: Mt 11:15.
8:9–10: Mt 13:10–13; Mk 4:10–12; Is 6:9–10; Jer 5:21; Ezek 12:2.
8:11–15: Mt 13:18–23; Mk 4:13–20.
8:11: 1 Thess 2:13; 1 Pet 1:23.
8:16: Mk 4:21; Mt 5:15; Lk 11:33.
* 7:47: The preceding parable suggests that she loved much because she had been forgiven much. Jesus now implies that her love is a sign rather than a cause of forgiveness, thus confirming the point of the parable.

stand, that those who enter may see the light. [17]For nothing is hidden that shall not be made manifest, nor anything secret that shall not be known and come to light. [18]Take heed then how you hear; for to him who has will more be given, and from him who has not, even what he thinks that he has will be taken away."

The True Kindred of Jesus

19 Then his mother and his brethren * came to him, but they could not reach him for the crowd. [20]And he was told, "Your mother and your brethren are standing outside, desiring to see you." [21]But he said to them, "My mother and my brethren are those who hear the word of God and do it."

Jesus Calms a Storm on the Sea

22 One day he got into a boat with his disciples, and he said to them, "Let us go across to the other side of the lake." So they set out, [23]and as they sailed he fell asleep. And a storm of wind came down on the lake, and they were filling with water, and were in danger. [24]And they went and woke him, saying, "Master, Master, we are perishing!" And he awoke and rebuked the wind and the raging waves; and they ceased, and there was a calm. [25]He said to them, "Where is your faith?" And they were afraid, and they marveled, saying to one another, "Who then is this, that he commands even wind and water, and they obey him?"

Jesus Heals the Gerasene Demoniac

26 Then they arrived at the country of the Ger'asenes, ᵃ which is opposite Galilee. [27]And as he stepped out on land, there met him a man from the city who had demons; for a long time he had worn no clothes, and he lived not in a house but among the tombs. [28]When he saw Jesus, he cried out and fell down before him, and said with a loud voice, "What have you to do with me, Jesus, Son of the Most High God? I beg you, do not torment me." [29]For he had commanded the unclean spirit to come out of the man. (For many a time it had seized him; he was kept under guard, and bound with chains and shackles, but he broke the bonds and was driven by the demon into the desert.) [30]Jesus then asked him, "What is your name?" And he said, "Legion"; for many demons had entered him. [31]And they begged him not to command them to depart into the abyss. [32]Now a large herd of swine was feeding there on the hillside; and they begged him to let them enter these. So he gave them leave. [33]Then the demons came out of the man and entered the swine, and the herd rushed down the steep bank into the lake and were drowned.

34 When the herdsmen saw what had happened, they fled, and told it in the city and in the country. [35]Then people went out to see what had happened, and they came to Jesus, and found the man from whom the demons had gone, sitting at the feet of Jesus, clothed and in his right mind; and they were afraid. [36]And those who had seen it told them how he who had been possessed with demons was healed. [37]Then all the people of the surrounding country of the Ger'asenes ᵃ asked him to depart from them; for they were seized with great fear; so he got into the boat and returned. [38]The man from whom the demons had gone begged that he might be with him; but he sent him away, saying, [39]"Return to your home, and declare how much God has done for you." And he went away, proclaiming throughout the whole city how much Jesus had done for him. †

A Girl Restored to Life and a Woman Healed

40 Now when Jesus returned, the crowd welcomed him, for they were all waiting for him. [41]And there came a man named Ja'irus, who was a ruler of the synagogue; and falling at Jesus' feet he begged him to come to his house, [42]for he had an only daughter, about twelve years of age, and she was dying.

As he went, the people pressed round him. [43]And a woman who had had a flow of blood for twelve years and had spent all her living upon physicians ᵇ and could not be healed by any one, [44]came up behind him, and touched the fringe of his garment; and immediately her flow of blood ceased. [45]And Jesus said, "Who was it that touched me?" When all denied it, Peter ᶜ said, "Master, the multitudes surround you and press upon you!" [46]But Jesus said, "Some one touched me; for I perceive that power has gone forth from me." [47]And when the woman saw that she was not hidden, she came trembling, and falling down before him declared in the presence of all the people why she had touched him, and how she had been immediately healed. [48]And he said to her, "Daughter, your faith has made you well; go in peace."

49 While he was still speaking, a man from the ruler's house came and said, "Your daughter is dead; do not trouble the Teacher any more." [50]But Jesus on hearing this answered him, "Do not fear; only believe, and she shall be well." [51]And when

---

ᵃ Other ancient authorities read *Gadarenes*, others *Gergesenes*.
ᵇ Other ancient authorities omit *and had spent all her living upon physicians*.
ᶜ Other ancient authorities add *and those who were with him*.
8:17: Mk 4:22–23; Mt 10:26–27; Lk 12:2–3; Eph 5:13.
8:18: Mk 4:24–25; Mt 13:12; 25:29; Lk 19:26.
8:19–21: Mt 12:46–50; Mk 3:31–35.
8:21: Lk 11:28; Jn 15:14.
8:22–25: Mt 8:23–27; Mk 4:35–41; 6:47–52; Jn 6:16–21.
8:24: Lk 5:5; 8:45; 9:33, 49; 17:13.
8:26–39: Mt 8:28–34; Mk 5:1–20.
8:28: Mk 1:24; Jn 2:4.
8:40–56: Mt 9:18–26; Mk 5:21–43.
8:45: Lk 8:24.
8:46: Lk 5:17; 6:19.
8:48: Mt 9:22; Lk 7:50; 17:19; 18:42.
* **8:19,** *brethren*: See note on Mt 12:46.
† 8:39: There was no reason for secrecy (to avoid popular disturbance) in a non-Jewish area.

he came to the house, he permitted no one to enter with him, except Peter and John and James, and the father and mother of the child. [52]And all were weeping and bewailing her; but he said, "Do not weep; for she is not dead but sleeping." [53]And they laughed at him, knowing that she was dead. [54]But taking her by the hand he called, saying, "Child, arise." [55]And her spirit returned, and she got up at once; and he directed that something should be given her to eat. [56]And her parents were amazed; but he charged them to tell no one what had happened.

The Mission of the Twelve

9 And he called the Twelve together and gave them power and authority over all demons and to cure diseases, [2]and he sent them out to preach the kingdom of God and to heal. [3]And he said to them, "Take nothing for your journey, no staff, nor bag, nor bread, nor money; and do not have two tunics. [4]And whatever house you enter, stay there, and from there depart. [5]And wherever they do not receive you, when you leave that town shake off the dust from your feet as a testimony against them." [6]And they departed and went through the villages, preaching the gospel and healing everywhere.

Herod's Perplexity

7 Now Herod the tetrarch heard of all that was done, and he was perplexed, because it was said by some that John had been raised from the dead, [8]by some that Eli'jah had appeared, and by others that one of the old prophets had risen. [9]Herod said, "John I beheaded; but who is this about whom I hear such things?" And he sought to see him.

Feeding the Five Thousand

10 On their return the apostles told him what they had done. And he took them and withdrew apart to a city called Beth-sa'ida. [11]When the crowds learned it, they followed him; and he welcomed them and spoke to them of the kingdom of God, and cured those who had need of healing. [12]Now the day began to wear away; and the Twelve came and said to him, "Send the crowd away, to go into the villages and country round about, to lodge and get provisions; for we are here in a lonely place." [13]But he said to them, "You give them something to eat." They said, "We have no more than five loaves and two fish—unless we are to go and buy food for all these people." [14]For there were about five thousand men. And he said to his disciples, "Make them sit down in companies, about fifty each." [15]And they did so, and made them all sit down. [16]And taking the five loaves and the two fish he looked up to heaven, and blessed and broke them, and gave them to the disciples to set before the crowd. [17]And all ate and were satisfied. And they took up what was left over, twelve baskets of broken pieces.

Peter's Declaration That Jesus Is the Christ

18 Now it happened that as he was praying alone the disciples were with him; and he asked them, "Who do the people say that I am?" [19]And they answered, "John the Baptist; but others say, Eli'jah; and others, that one of the old prophets has risen." [20]And he said to them, "But who do you say that I am?" And Peter answered, "The Christ of God." [21]But he charged and commanded them to tell this to no one, [22]saying, "The Son of man must suffer many things, and be rejected by the elders and chief priests and scribes, and be killed, and on the third day be raised."

Taking Up One's Cross

23 And he said to all, "If any man would come after me, let him deny himself and take up his cross daily and follow me. [24]For whoever would save his life will lose it; and whoever loses his life for my sake, he will save it. [25]For what does it profit a man if he gains the whole world and loses or forfeits himself? [26]For whoever is ashamed of me and of my words, of him will the Son of man be ashamed when he comes in his glory and the glory of the Father and of the holy angels. [27]But I tell you truly, there are some standing here who will not taste death before they see the kingdom of God."

The Transfiguration

28 Now about eight days after these sayings he took with him Peter and John and James, and went up on the mountain to pray. [29]And as he was praying, the appearance of his countenance was altered, and his clothing became dazzling white. [30]And behold, two men talked with him, Moses and Eli'jah, [31]who appeared in glory and spoke of his exodus, which he was to accomplish at Jerusalem. [32]Now Peter and those who were with him were heavy with sleep but kept awake, and they saw his glory and the two men who stood with him. [33]And as the men were parting from him, Peter said to Jesus, "Master, it is well that we are

---

8:56: Mt 8:4; Mk 3:12; 7:36; Lk 9:21.
9:1–6: Mt 10:1, 5, 7–11, 14; Mk 6:7–12; Lk 10:4–11.
9:5: Acts 13:51.
9:7–9: Mt 14:1–2; Mk 6:14–16; Lk 9:19.
9:9: Lk 23:8.
9:10: Mk 6:30–31; Lk 10:17; Jn 1:44.
9:11–17: Mt 14:13–21; Mk 6:32–44; Jn 6:1–14; Mk 8:4–10.
9:13: 2 Kings 4:42–44.
9:16: Lk 22:19; 24:30–31; Acts 2:42; 20:11; 27:35.
9:18–21: Mt 16:13–20; Mk 8:27–30; Jn 1:49; 11:27; 6:66–69.
9:18: Lk 3:21; 5:16; 6:12; 9:28; 11:1.
9:19: Lk 9:9; Mk 9:11–13.
9:22: Mt 16:21; Mk 8:31; Lk 9:43–45; 18:31–34; 17:25.
9:23–27: Mt 16:24–28; Mk 8:34–9:1.
9:24–25: Mt 10:38–39; Lk 14:27; 17:33; Jn 12:25.
9:26: Mt 10:33; Lk 12:9; 1 Jn 2:28.
9:27: Lk 22:18; Mt 10:23; 1 Thess 4:15–18; Jn 21:22.
9:28–36: Mt 17:1–8; Mk 9:2–8; 2 Pet 1:17–18.
9:28: Lk 8:51; 3:21; 5:16; 6:12; 9:18; 11:1.
9:30: Acts 1:9–11.
9:32: Jn 1:14.
9:33: Lk 5:5; 8:24, 45; 9:49; 17:13.

here; let us make three booths, one for you and one for Moses and one for Eli'jah"—not knowing what he said. ³⁴As he said this, a cloud came and overshadowed them; and they were afraid as they entered the cloud. ³⁵And a voice came out of the cloud, saying, "This is my Son, my Chosen; ᵈ listen to him!" ³⁶And when the voice had spoken, Jesus was found alone. And they kept silence and told no one in those days anything of what they had seen.

Jesus Heals a Boy with a Demon

37 On the next day, when they had come down from the mountain, a great crowd met him. ³⁸And behold, a man from the crowd cried, "Teacher, I beg you to look upon my son, for he is my only child; ³⁹and behold, a spirit seizes him, and he suddenly cries out; it convulses him till he foams, and shatters him, and will hardly leave him. ⁴⁰And I begged your disciples to cast it out, but they could not." ⁴¹Jesus answered, "O faithless and perverse generation, how long am I to be with you and bear with you? Bring your son here." ⁴²While he was coming, the demon tore him and convulsed him. But Jesus rebuked the unclean spirit, and healed the boy, and gave him back to his father. ⁴³And all were astonished at the majesty of God.

Jesus Again Foretells His Death

But while they were all marveling at everything he did, he said to his disciples, ⁴⁴"Let these words sink into your ears; for the Son of man is to be delivered into the hands of men." ⁴⁵But they did not understand this saying, and it was concealed from them, that they should not perceive it; and they were afraid to ask him about this saying.

True Greatness

46 And an argument arose among them as to which of them was the greatest. ⁴⁷But when Jesus perceived the thought of their hearts, he took a child and put him by his side, ⁴⁸and said to them, "Whoever receives this child in my name receives me, and whoever receives me receives him who sent me; for he who is least among you all is the one who is great."

Another Exorcist

49 John answered, "Master, we saw a man casting out demons in your name, and we forbade him, because he does not follow with us." ⁵⁰But Jesus said to him, "Do not forbid him; for he that is not against you is for you."

A Samaritan Village Refuses to Receive Jesus

51 When the days drew near for him to be received up, * he set his face to go to Jerusalem. † ⁵²And he sent messengers ahead of him, who went and entered a village of the Samaritans, to make ready for him; ⁵³but the people would not receive him, because his face was set toward Jerusalem. † ⁵⁴And when his disciples James and John saw it, they said, "Lord, do you want us to

bid fire come down from heaven and consume them?" ᵉ ⁵⁵But he turned and rebuked them. ᶠ ⁵⁶And they went on to another village.

Would-Be Followers of Jesus

57 As they were going along the road, a man said to him, "I will follow you wherever you go." ⁵⁸And Jesus said to him, "Foxes have holes, and birds of the air have nests; but the Son of man has nowhere to lay his head." ⁵⁹To another he said, "Follow me." But he said, "Lord, let me first go and bury my father." ⁶⁰But he said to him, "Leave the dead to bury their own dead; but as for you, go and proclaim the kingdom of God." ⁶¹Another said, "I will follow you, Lord; but let me first say farewell to those at my home." ⁶²Jesus said to him, "No one who puts his hand to the plow and looks back is fit for the kingdom of God."

The Mission of the Seventy

10 After this the Lord appointed seventy ᵍ others, and sent them on ahead of him, two by two, into every town and place where he himself was about to come. ²And he said to them, "The harvest is plentiful, but the laborers are few; pray therefore the Lord of the harvest to send out laborers into his harvest. ³Go your way; behold, I send you out as lambs in the midst of wolves. ⁴Carry no purse, no bag, no sandals; and salute no one on the road. ⁵Whatever house you enter, first say, 'Peace be to this house!' ⁶And if a son of peace is there, your peace shall rest upon him; but if not, it shall return to you. ⁷And remain in the same house, eating and drinking what they provide, for the laborer deserves his wages; do not go from house to house. ⁸Whenever you enter a town and they receive you, eat what is set before you; ⁹heal the sick in it and say to them, 'The kingdom

---

ᵈ Other ancient authorities read *my Beloved*.
ᵉ Other ancient authorities add *as Elijah did*.
ᶠ Other ancient authorities add *and he said, "You do not know what manner of spirit you are of; for the Son of man came not to destroy men's lives but to save them."*
ᵍ Other ancient authorities read *seventy-two*.
9:35: Lk 3:22; Jn 12:28–30.
9:36: Mt 17:9; Mk 9:9–10.
9:37-43: Mt 17:14–18; Mk 9:14–27.
9:43-45: Mt 17:22–23; Mk 9:30–32; Lk 9:22; 18:31–34; 17:25.
9:46-48: Mt 18:1–5; Mk 9:33–37.
9:48: Lk 10:16; Mt 10:40.
9:49-50: Mk 9:38–40; Lk 11:23.
9:49: Lk 5:5; 8:24, 45; 9:33; 17:13.
9:51-56: Mk 10:1; Lk 17:11; Jn 4:40–42.
9:52: Mt 10:5; Jn 4:4.
9:54: Mk 3:17; 2 Kings 1:9–16.
9:57-60: Mt 8:19–22.
9:61: 1 Kings 19:20; Phil 3:13.
10:1: Lk 9:1–2, 51–52; 7:13.
10:2: Mt 9:37–38; Jn 4:35.
10:3-12: Mt 10:7–16; Mk 6:8–11; Lk 9:2–5; 22:35–36.
10:5: 1 Sam 25:6.
10:7: 1 Cor 10:27; 9:14; 1 Tim 5:18; Deut 24:15.
9:51: Here begins the "Travel Narrative" of Luke, which continues up to the passion.
* **9:51:** *received up:* i.e., into heaven; cf. 2 Kings 2:9–11; Acts 1:2, 11. The term here includes his passion, death, resurrection, and ascension.
† **9:51, 53:** The Samaritans worshiped on Mount Gerizim, while orthodox Jews, of course, went to Jerusalem, and to Jerusalem only, for sacrifice.

of God has come near to you.' [10]But whenever you enter a town and they do not receive you, go into its streets and say, [11]'Even the dust of your town that clings to our feet, we wipe off against you; nevertheless know this, that the kingdom of God has come near.' [12]I tell you, it shall be more tolerable on that day for Sodom than for that town.

Woes to Unrepentant Cities

13 "Woe to you, Chora'zin! woe to you, Beth-sa'ida! for if the mighty works done in you had been done in Tyre and Si'don, they would have repented long ago, sitting in sackcloth and ashes. [14]But it shall be more tolerable in the judgment for Tyre and Si'don than for you. [15]And you, Caper'na-um, will you be exalted to heaven? You shall be brought down to Hades.

16 "He who hears you hears me, and he who rejects you rejects me, and he who rejects me rejects him who sent me."

The Return of the Seventy

17 The seventy [g] returned with joy, saying, "Lord, even the demons are subject to us in your name!" [18]And he said to them, "I saw Satan fall like lightning from heaven. * [19]Behold, I have given you authority to tread upon serpents and scorpions, and over all the power of the enemy; and nothing shall hurt you. [20]Nevertheless do not rejoice in this, that the spirits are subject to you; but rejoice that your names are written in heaven."

Jesus Rejoices and Thanks the Father

21 In that same hour he rejoiced in the Holy Spirit and said, "I thank you, Father, Lord of heaven and earth, that you have hidden these things from the wise and understanding and revealed them to infants; yes, Father, for such was your gracious will. [h] [22]All things have been delivered to me by my Father; and no one knows who the Son is except the Father, or who the Father is except the Son and any one to whom the Son chooses to reveal him."

23 Then turning to the disciples he said privately, "Blessed are the eyes which see what you see! [24]For I tell you that many prophets and kings desired to see what you see, and did not see it, and to hear what you hear, and did not hear it."

The Parable of the Good Samaritan

25 And behold, a lawyer stood up to put him to the test, saying, "Teacher, what shall I do to inherit eternal life?" [26]He said to him, "What is written in the law? What do you read there?" [27]And he answered, "You shall love the Lord your God with all your heart, and with all your soul, and with all your strength, and with all your mind; and your neighbor as yourself." [28]And he said to him, "You have answered right; do this, and you will live."

29 But he, desiring to justify himself, said to Jesus, "And who is my neighbor?" [30]Jesus replied, "A man was going down from Jerusalem to Jericho, and he fell among robbers, who stripped him and beat him, and departed, leaving him half dead. [31]Now by chance a priest was going down that road; and when he saw him he passed by on the other side. [32]So likewise a Levite, when he came to the place and saw him, passed by on the other side. [33]But a Samaritan, as he journeyed, came to where he was; and when he saw him, he had compassion, [34]and went to him and bound up his wounds, pouring on oil and wine; then he set him on his own beast and brought him to an inn, and took care of him. [35]And the next day he took out two denarii [i] and gave them to the innkeeper, saying, 'Take care of him; and whatever more you spend, I will repay you when I come back.' [36]Which of these three, do you think, proved neighbor to the man who fell among the robbers?" [37]He said, "The one who showed mercy on him." And Jesus said to him, "Go and do likewise."

Jesus Visits Martha and Mary

38 Now as they went on their way, he entered a village; and a woman named Martha received him into her house. [39]And she had a sister called Mary, who sat at the Lord's feet and listened to his teaching. [40]But Martha was distracted with much serving; and she went to him and said, "Lord, do you not care that my sister has left me to serve alone? Tell her then to help me." [41]But the Lord answered her, "Martha, Martha, you are anxious and troubled about many things; [42]one thing is needful. [j] Mary has chosen the good portion, which shall not be taken away from her."

The Lord's Prayer

11 He was praying in a certain place, and when he ceased, one of his disciples said to him, "Lord, teach us to pray, as John taught his disciples." [2]And he said to them, "When you pray, say:

"Father, hallowed be your name. Your kingdom come. [3]Give us each day our daily bread; [k] [4]and

---

[g] Other ancient authorities read seventy-two.
[h] Or so it was well-pleasing before you.
[i] The denarius was a day's wage for a laborer.
[j] Other ancient authorities read few things are needful, or only one.
[k] Or our bread for the morrow.
10:11: Acts 13:51.
10:12: Mt 11:24; Gen 19:24–28; Jude 7.
10:13–15: Mt 11:21–23; Lk 6:24–26.
10:16: Mt 10:40; 18:5; Mk 9:37; Lk 9:48; Jn 13:20; 12:48.
10:18: Rev 12:9; Jn 12:31.
10:20: Ex 32:32; Ps 69:28; Dan 12:1; Phil 4:3; Heb 12:23; Rev 3:5; 13:8; 21:27.
10:21–22: Mt 11:25–27.
10:21 1 Cor 1:26–29.
10:22: Mt 28:18; Jn 3:35; 13:3; 10:15; 17:25.
10:23–24: Mt 13:16–17; Jn 8:56; Heb 11:13; 1 Pet 1:10–12.
10:25–28: Mt 22:34–39; Mk 12:28–31.
10:25: Mk 10:17; Mt 19:16; Lk 18:18.
10:27: Deut 6:5; Lev 19:18; Rom 13:9; Gal 5:14; Jas 2:8.
10:28: Lk 20:39; Lev 18:5.
10:33: Lk 9:51–56; 17:11–19; Jn 4:4–42.
10:38–42: Jn 12:1–3; 11:1–45.
10:41: Lk 7:13.
11:1: Mk 1:35; Lk 3:21; 5:16; 6:12; 9:18, 28; 5:33; 7:18.
11:2–4: Mt 6:9–13.
* 10:18: Jesus refers to the fall of the angels (cf. Rev 12:9), while he speaks of his conquest of the forces of evil.

forgive us our sins, for we ourselves forgive every one who is indebted to us; and lead us not into temptation."

Perseverance in Prayer

5 And he said to them, "Which of you who has a friend will go to him at midnight and say to him, 'Friend, lend me three loaves; [6]for a friend of mine has arrived on a journey, and I have nothing to set before him'; [7]and he will answer from within, 'Do not bother me; the door is now shut, and my children are with me in bed; I cannot get up and give you anything'? [8]I tell you, though he will not get up and give him anything because he is his friend, yet because of his importunity he will rise and give him whatever he needs. [9]And I tell you, Ask, and it will be given you; seek, and you will find; knock, and it will be opened to you. [10]For every one who asks receives, and he who seeks finds, and to him who knocks it will be opened. [11]What father among you, if his son asks for [1] a fish, will instead of a fish give him a serpent; [12]or if he asks for an egg, will give him a scorpion? [13]If you then, who are evil, know how to give good gifts to your children, how much more will the heavenly Father give the Holy Spirit to those who ask him!"

Jesus and Be-elzebul

14 Now he was casting out a demon that was mute; when the demon had gone out, the mute man spoke, and the people marveled. [15]But some of them said, "He casts out demons by Be-el'zebul, the prince of demons"; [16]while others, to test him, sought from him a sign from heaven. [17]But he, knowing their thoughts, said to them, "Every kingdom divided against itself is laid waste, and house falls upon house. [18]And if Satan also is divided against himself, how will his kingdom stand? For you say that I cast out demons by Be-el'zebul. [19]And if I cast out demons by Be-el'zebul, by whom do your sons cast them out? Therefore they shall be your judges. [20]But if it is by the finger of God that I cast out demons, then the kingdom of God has come upon you. [21]When a strong man, fully armed, guards his own palace, his goods are in peace; [22]but when one stronger than he assails him and overcomes him, he takes away his armor in which he trusted, and divides his spoil. [23]He who is not with me is against me, and he who does not gather with me scatters.

The Return of the Unclean Spirit

24 "When the unclean spirit has gone out of a man, he passes through waterless places seeking rest; and finding none he says, 'I will return to my house from which I came.' [25]And when he comes he finds it swept and put in order. [26]Then he goes and brings seven other spirits more evil than himself, and they enter and dwell there; and the last state of that man becomes worse than the first."

True Blessedness

27 As he said this, a woman in the crowd raised her voice and said to him, "Blessed is the womb that bore you, and the breasts that you sucked!" [28]But he said, "Blessed rather are those who hear the word of God and keep it!"

The Sign of Jonah

29 When the crowds were increasing, he began to say, "This generation is an evil generation; it seeks a sign, but no sign shall be given to it except the sign of Jonah. [30]For as Jonah became a sign to the men of Nin'eveh, so will the Son of man be to this generation. [31]The queen of the South will arise at the judgment with the men of this generation and condemn them; for she came from the ends of the earth to hear the wisdom of Solomon, and behold, something greater than Solomon is here. [32]The men of Nin'eveh will arise at the judgment with this generation and condemn it; for they repented at the preaching of Jonah, and behold, something greater than Jonah is here.

The Light of the Body

33 "No one after lighting a lamp puts it in a cellar or under a bushel, but on a stand, that those who enter may see the light. [34]Your eye is the lamp of your body; when your eye is sound, your whole body is full of light; but when it is not sound, your body is full of darkness. [35]Therefore be careful lest the light in you be darkness. [36]If then your whole body is full of light, having no part dark, it will be wholly bright, as when a lamp with its rays gives you light."

Jesus Denounces the Hypocrisy of the Pharisees and Lawyers

37 While he was speaking, a Pharisee asked him to dine with him; so he went in and sat at table. [38]The Pharisee was astonished to see that he did not first wash before dinner. [39]And the Lord said to him, "Now you Pharisees cleanse the outside of the cup and of the dish, but inside

---

[1] Other ancient authorities insert *bread, will give him a stone; or if he asks for.*

11:4: Mk 11:25; Mt 18:35.
11:5-8: Lk 18:1-8.
11:9-13: Mt 7:7-11.
11:9: Mt 18:19; 21:22; Mk 11:24; Jas 1:5-8; 1 Jn 5:14-15; Jn 15:7; 16:23-24.
11:14-23: Mt 12:22-30; 10:25; Mk 3:23-27.
11:14-15: Mt 9:32-34.
11:16: Mt 12:38; 16:1; Mk 8:11; Jn 2:18; 6:30.
11:23: Lk 9:50.
11:24-26: Mt 12:43-45.
11:27: Lk 1:42; 23:29.
11:28: Lk 8:21; Jn 15:14.
11:29-32: Mt 12:39-42.
11:29: Mt 16:4; Mk 8:12; Lk 11:16; Jon 3:4-5.
11:31: 1 Kings 10:1-10; 2 Chron 9:1-12.
11:32: Mt 12:6.
11:33: Mt 5:15; Mk 4:21; Lk 8:16.
11:34-35: Mt 6:22-23.
11:37: Lk 7:36; 14:1.
11:38: Mk 7:1-5.
11:39-41: Mt 23:25-26.
11:39: Lk 7:13.

you are full of extortion and wickedness. [40]You fools! Did not he who made the outside make the inside also? [41]But give for alms those things which are within; and behold, everything is clean for you.

42 "But woe to you Pharisees! for you tithe mint and rue and every herb, and neglect justice and the love of God; these you ought to have done, without neglecting the others. [43]Woe to you Pharisees! for you love the best seat in the synagogues and salutations in the market places. [44]Woe to you! for you are like graves which are not seen, and men walk over them without knowing it."

45 One of the lawyers answered him, "Teacher, in saying this you reproach us also." [46]And he said, "Woe to you lawyers also! for you load men with burdens hard to bear, and you yourselves do not touch the burdens with one of your fingers. [47]Woe to you! for you build the tombs of the prophets whom your fathers killed. [48]So you are witnesses and consent to the deeds of your fathers; for they killed them, and you build their tombs. [49]Therefore also the Wisdom of God said, 'I will send them prophets and apostles, some of whom they will kill and persecute,' [50]that the blood of all the prophets, shed from the foundation of the world, may be required of this generation, [51]from the blood of Abel to the blood of Zechari'ah, who perished between the altar and the sanctuary. Yes, I tell you, it shall be required of this generation. [52]Woe to you lawyers! for you have taken away the key of knowledge; you did not enter yourselves, and you hindered those who were entering."

53 As he went away from there, the scribes and the Pharisees began to press him hard, and to provoke him to speak of many things, [54]lying in wait for him, to catch him in something he might say.

A Warning against Hypocrisy

12 In the meantime, when so many thousands of the multitude had gathered together that they trod upon one another, he began to say to his disciples first, "Beware of the leaven of the Pharisees, which is hypocrisy. [2]Nothing is covered up that will not be revealed, or hidden that will not be known. [3]Whatever you have said in the dark shall be heard in the light, and what you have whispered in private rooms shall be proclaimed upon the housetops.

Whom to Fear

4 "I tell you, my friends, do not fear those who kill the body, and after that have no more that they can do. [5]But I will warn you whom to fear: fear him who, after he has killed, has power to cast into hell; [m] yes, I tell you, fear him! [6]Are not five sparrows sold for two pennies? And not one of them is forgotten before God. [7]Why, even the

hairs of your head are all numbered. Fear not; you are of more value than many sparrows.

8 "And I tell you, every one who acknowledges me before men, the Son of man also will acknowledge before the angels of God; [9]but he who denies me before men will be denied before the angels of God. [10]And every one who speaks a word against the Son of man will be forgiven; but he who blasphemes against the Holy Spirit will not be forgiven. [11]And when they bring you before the synagogues and the rulers and the authorities, do not be anxious about how or what you are to answer or what you are to say; [12]for the Holy Spirit will teach you in that very hour what you ought to say."

The Parable of the Rich Fool

13 One of the multitude said to him, "Teacher, bid my brother divide the inheritance with me." [14]But he said to him, "Man, who made me a judge or divider over you?" [15]And he said to them, "Take heed, and beware of all covetousness; for a man's life does not consist in the abundance of his possessions." [16]And he told them a parable, saying, "The land of a rich man brought forth plentifully; [17]and he thought to himself, 'What shall I do, for I have nowhere to store my crops?' [18]And he said, 'I will do this: I will pull down my barns, and build larger ones; and there I will store all my grain and my goods. [19]And I will say to my soul, Soul, you have ample goods laid up for many years; take your ease, eat, drink, be merry.' [20]But God said to him, 'Fool! This night your soul is required of you; and the things you have prepared, whose will they be?' [21]So is he who lays up treasure for himself, and is not rich toward God."

Do Not Be Anxious

22 And he said to his disciples, "Therefore I tell you, do not be anxious about your life, what you shall eat, nor about your body, what you shall put on. [23]For life is more than food, and the body more than clothing. [24]Consider the ravens: they

---

m Greek *Gehenna.*
11:41: Tit 1:15; Mk 7:19.
11:42: Mt 23:23–24; Lev 27:30; Mic 6:8.
11:43: Mt 23:6–7; Mk 12:38–39; Lk 20:46.
11:44: Mt 23:27.
11:46: Mt 23:4.
11:47–48: Mt 23:29–32; Acts 7:51–53.
11:49–51: Mt 23:34–36.
11:49: 1 Cor 1:24; Col 2:3.
11:51: Gen 4:8; 2 Chron 24:20–21; Zech 1:1.
11:52: Mt 23:13.
11:53–54: Mk 12:13.
12:1: Mt 16:6; Mk 8:15.
12:2–3: Mt 10:26–27; Mk 4:22; Lk 8:17; Eph 5:13.
12:4: Jn 15:14–15.
12:4–9: Mt 10:28–33.
12:5: Heb 10:31.
12:7: Lk 21:18; Acts 27:34; Mt 12:12.
12:9: Mk 8:38; Lk 9:26; 2 Tim 2:12.
12:10: Mt 12:31–32; Mk 3:28–29.
12:11–12: Mt 10:19–20; Mk 13:11; Lk 21:14–15.
12:15: 1 Tim 6:6–10.
12:20: Jer 17:11; Job 27:8; Ps 39:6; Lk 12:33–34.
12:22–31: Mt 6:25–33.

neither sow nor reap, they have neither storehouse nor barn, and yet God feeds them. Of how much more value are you than the birds! [25]And which of you by being anxious can add a cubit to his span of life? [n] [26]If then you are not able to do as small a thing as that, why are you anxious about the rest? [27]Consider the lilies, how they grow; they neither toil nor spin; [o] yet I tell you, even Solomon in all his glory was not clothed like one of these. [28]But if God so clothes the grass which is alive in the field today and tomorrow is thrown into the oven, how much more will he clothe you, O men of little faith! [29]And do not seek what you are to eat and what you are to drink, nor be of anxious mind. [30]For all the nations of the world seek these things; and your Father knows that you need them. [31]Instead, seek his [p] kingdom, and these things shall be yours as well.

32 "Fear not, little flock, for it is your Father's good pleasure to give you the kingdom. [33]Sell your possessions, and give alms; provide yourselves with purses that do not grow old, with a treasure in the heavens that does not fail, where no thief approaches and no moth destroys. [34]For where your treasure is, there will your heart be also.

The Necessity of Watchfulness

35 "Let your loins be girded and your lamps burning, [36]and be like men who are waiting for their master to come home from the marriage feast, so that they may open to him at once when he comes and knocks. [37]Blessed are those servants whom the master finds awake when he comes; truly, I say to you, he will put on his apron and have them sit at table, and he will come and serve them. [38]If he comes in the second watch, or in the third, and finds them so, blessed are those servants! [39]But know this, that if the householder had known at what hour the thief was coming, he would have been awake and [q] would not have left his house to be broken into. [40]You also must be ready; for the Son of man is coming at an hour you do not expect."

The Faithful and the Unfaithful Servant

41 Peter said, "Lord, are you telling this parable for us or for all?" [42]And the Lord said, "Who then is the faithful and wise steward, whom his master will set over his household, to give them their portion of food at the proper time? [43]Blessed is that servant whom his master when he comes will find so doing. [44]Truly I tell you, he will set him over all his possessions. [45]But if that servant says to himself, 'My master is delayed in coming,' and begins to beat the menservants and the maidservants, and to eat and drink and get drunk, [46]the master of that servant will come on a day when he does not expect him and at an hour he does not know, and will punish [r] him, and put him with the unfaithful. [47]And that servant who knew his master's will, but did not make ready or act

according to his will, shall receive a severe beating. [48]But he who did not know, and did what deserved a beating, shall receive a light beating. Every one to whom much is given, of him will much be required; and of him to whom men commit much they will demand the more.

Jesus the Cause of Division

49 "I came to cast fire upon the earth; and would that it were already kindled! [50]I have a baptism to be baptized with; and how I am constrained until it is accomplished! [51]Do you think that I have come to give peace on earth? No, I tell you, but rather division; [52]for henceforth in one house there will be five divided, three against two and two against three; [53]they will be divided, father against son and son against father, mother against daughter and daughter against her mother, mother-in-law against her daughter-in-law and daughter-in-law against her mother-in-law."

Interpreting the Present Time

54 He also said to the multitudes, "When you see a cloud rising in the west, you say at once, 'A shower is coming'; and so it happens. [55]And when you see the south wind blowing, you say, 'There will be scorching heat'; and it happens. [56]You hypocrites! You know how to interpret the appearance of earth and sky; but why do you not know how to interpret the present time?

Settling with Your Accuser

57 "And why do you not judge for yourselves what is right? [58]As you go with your accuser before the magistrate, make an effort to settle with him on the way, lest he drag you to the judge, and the judge hand you over to the officer, and the officer put you in prison. [59]I tell you, you will never get out till you have paid the very last copper."

Repent or Perish

13 There were some present at that very time who told him of the Galileans whose blood Pilate had mingled with their sacrifices. [2]And he

---

[n] Or *to his stature.*
[o] Other ancient authorities read *Consider the lilies; they neither spin nor weave.*
[p] Other ancient authorities read *God's.*
[q] Other ancient authorities omit *would have been awake and.*
[r] Or *cut him in pieces.*
12:24: Lk 12:6–7.
12:27: 1 Kings 10:1–10.
12:30: Mt 6:8.
12:32: Jn 21:15–17.
12:33–34: Mt 6:19–21; Lk 18:22.
12:35: Eph 6:14; Mt 25:1–13; Mk 13:33–37.
12:37: Jn 13:3–5; Mt 24:42; Lk 21:36.
12:39–40: Mt 24:43–44; 1 Thess 5:2; Rev 3:3; 16:15; 2 Pet 3:10.
12:42–46: Mt 24:45–51.
12:42: Lk 7:13.
12:47–48: Deut 25:2–3; Num 15:29–30; Lk 8:18; 19:26.
12:49: Lk 22:15.
12:50: Mk 10:38–39; Jn 12:27.
12:51–53: Mt 10:34–36; Lk 21:16; Mic 7:6.
12:54–56: Mt 16:2–3.
12:57–59: Mt 5:25–26.
13:2: Jn 9:1–3.

answered them, "Do you think that these Galileans were worse sinners than all the other Galileans, because they suffered thus? [3]I tell you, No; but unless you repent you will all likewise perish. [4]Or those eighteen upon whom the tower in Silo'am fell and killed them, do you think that they were worse offenders than all the others who dwelt in Jerusalem? [5]I tell you, No; but unless you repent you will all likewise perish."

The Parable of the Barren Fig Tree

6 And he told this parable: "A man had a fig tree planted in his vineyard; and he came seeking fruit on it and found none. [7]And he said to the vinedresser, 'Behold, these three years I have come seeking fruit on this fig tree, and I find none. Cut it down; why should it use up the ground?' [8]And he answered him, 'Let it alone, sir, this year also, till I dig about it and put on manure. [9]And if it bears fruit next year, well and good; but if not, you can cut it down.'"

Jesus Heals a Crippled Woman

10 Now he was teaching in one of the synagogues on the sabbath. [11]And there was a woman who had had a spirit of infirmity for eighteen years; she was bent over and could not fully straighten herself. [12]And when Jesus saw her, he called her and said to her, "Woman, you are freed from your infirmity." [13]And he laid his hands upon her, and immediately she was made straight, and she praised God. [14]But the ruler of the synagogue, indignant because Jesus had healed on the sabbath, said to the people, "There are six days on which work ought to be done; come on those days and be healed, and not on the sabbath day." [15]Then the Lord answered him, "You hypocrites! Does not each of you on the sabbath untie his ox or his donkey from the manger, and lead it away to water it? [16]And ought not this woman, a daughter of Abraham whom Satan bound for eighteen years, be loosed from this bond on the sabbath day?" [17]As he said this, all his adversaries were put to shame; and all the people rejoiced at all the glorious things that were done by him.

The Parable of the Mustard Seed

18 He said therefore, "What is the kingdom of God like? And to what shall I compare it? [19]It is like a grain of mustard seed which a man took and sowed in his garden; and it grew and became a tree, and the birds of the air made nests in its branches."

The Parable of the Leaven

20 And again he said, "To what shall I compare the kingdom of God? [21]It is like leaven which a woman took and hid in three measures of meal, till it was all leavened."

The Narrow Door

22 He went on his way through towns and villages, teaching, and journeying toward Jerusalem. [23]And some one said to him, "Lord, will those who are saved be few?" And he said to them, [24]"Strive to enter by the narrow door; for many, I tell you, will seek to enter and will not be able. [25]When once the householder has risen up and shut the door, you will begin to stand outside and to knock at the door, saying, 'Lord, open to us.' He will answer you, 'I do not know where you come from.' [26]Then you will begin to say, 'We ate and drank in your presence, and you taught in our streets.' [27]But he will say, 'I tell you, I do not know where you come from; depart from me, all you workers of iniquity!' [28]There you will weep and gnash your teeth, when you see Abraham and Isaac and Jacob and all the prophets in the kingdom of God and you yourselves thrust out. [29]And men will come from east and west, and from north and south, and sit at table in the kingdom of God. [30]And behold, some are last who will be first, and some are first who will be last."

The Lament over Jerusalem

31 At that very hour some Pharisees came, and said to him, "Get away from here, for Herod wants to kill you." [32]And he said to them, "Go and tell that fox, 'Behold, I cast out demons and perform cures today and tomorrow, and the third day I finish my course. [33]Nevertheless I must go on my way today and tomorrow and the day following; for it cannot be that a prophet should perish away from Jerusalem.' [34]O Jerusalem, Jerusalem, killing the prophets and stoning those who are sent to you! How often would I have gathered your children together as a hen gathers her brood under her wings, and you would not! [35]Behold, your house is forsaken. And I tell you, you will not see me until you say, 'Blessed is he who comes in the name of the Lord!'"

Jesus Heals the Man with Dropsy on the Sabbath

14 One sabbath when he went to dine at the house of a ruler who belonged to the Pharisees, they were watching him. [2]And behold, there was a man before him who had dropsy. [3]And Jesus spoke to the lawyers and Pharisees, saying, "Is it lawful to heal on the sabbath, or not?" [4]But they were silent. Then he took him and

13:6-9: Mt 21:18-20; Mk 11:12-14, 20-21.
13:7: Mt 3:10; 7:19; Lk 3:9.
13:14: Ex 20:9-10; Lk 6:6-11; 14:1-6; Jn 5:1-18.
13:15: Lk 7:13; 14:5; Mt 12:11.
13:16: Lk 19:9.
13:18-19: Mt 13:31-32; Mk 4:30-32.
13:20-21: Mt 13:33.
13:22: Lk 9:51; 17:11; 18:31; 19:11.
13:23-24: Mt 7:13-14; Jn 10:7.
13:25: Mt 25:10-12.
13:26-27: Mt 7:21-23; 25:41; Lk 6:46.
13:28-29: Mt 8:11-12.
13:30: Mt 19:30; Mk 10:31.
13:32: Heb 2:10; 7:28.
13:34-35: Mt 23:37-39; Lk 19:41.
13:35: Jer 22:5; Ps 118:26; Lk 19:38.
14:1: Lk 7:36; 11:37; Mk 3:2.
14:3: Mt 12:10; Mk 3:4; Lk 6:9.

healed him, and let him go. [5]And he said to them, "Which of you, having a son [a] or an ox that has fallen into a well, will not immediately pull him out on a sabbath day?" [6]And they could not reply to this.

Humility and Hospitality

[7] Now he told a parable to those who were invited, when he marked how they chose the places of honor, saying to them, [8]"When you are invited by any one to a marriage feast, do not sit down in a place of honor, lest a more eminent man than you be invited by him; [9]and he who invited you both will come and say to you, 'Give place to this man,' and then you will begin with shame to take the lowest place. [10]But when you are invited, go and sit in the lowest place, so that when your host comes he may say to you, 'Friend, go up higher'; then you will be honored in the presence of all who sit at table with you. [11]For every one who exalts himself will be humbled, and he who humbles himself will be exalted."

[12] He said also to the man who had invited him, "When you give a dinner or a banquet, do not invite your friends or your brothers or your kinsmen or rich neighbors, lest they also invite you in return, and you be repaid. [13]But when you give a feast, invite the poor, the maimed, the lame, the blind, [14]and you will be blessed, because they cannot repay you. You will be repaid at the resurrection of the just."

The Parable of the Great Banquet

[15] When one of those who sat at table with him heard this, he said to him, "Blessed is he who shall eat bread in the kingdom of God!" [16]But he said to him, "A man once gave a great banquet, and invited many; [17]and at the time for the banquet he sent his servant to say to those who had been invited, 'Come; for all is now ready.' [18]But they all alike began to make excuses. The first said to him, 'I have bought a field, and I must go out and see it; please, have me excused.' [19]And another said, 'I have bought five yoke of oxen, and I go to examine them; please, have me excused.' [20]And another said, 'I have married a wife, and therefore I cannot come.' [21]So the servant came and reported this to his master. Then the householder in anger said to his servant, 'Go out quickly to the streets and lanes of the city, and bring in the poor and maimed and blind and lame.' [22]And the servant said, 'Sir, what you commanded has been done, and still there is room.' [23]And the master said to the servant, 'Go out to the highways and hedges, and compel people to come in, that my house may be filled. [24]For I tell you, none of those men who were invited shall taste my banquet.'"

The Cost of Discipleship

[25] Now great multitudes accompanied him; and he turned and said to them, [26]"If any one comes to me and does not hate his own father and mother and wife and children and brothers and sisters, yes, and even his own life, he cannot be my disciple. * [27]Whoever does not bear his own cross and come after me, cannot be my disciple. [28]For which of you, desiring to build a tower, does not first sit down and count the cost, whether he has enough to complete it? [29]Otherwise, when he has laid a foundation, and is not able to finish, all who see it begin to mock him, [30]saying, 'This man began to build, and was not able to finish.' [31]Or what king, going to encounter another king in war, will not sit down first and take counsel whether he is able with ten thousand to meet him who comes against him with twenty thousand? [32]And if not, while the other is yet a great way off, he sends an embassy and asks terms of peace. [33]So therefore, whoever of you does not renounce all that he has cannot be my disciple.

About Salt

[34] "Salt is good; but if salt has lost its taste, how shall its saltiness be restored? [35]It is fit neither for the land nor for the dunghill; men throw it away. He who has ears to hear, let him hear."

The Parable of the Lost Sheep

15 Now the tax collectors and sinners were all drawing near to hear him. [2]And the Pharisees and the scribes murmured, saying, "This man receives sinners and eats with them."

[3] So he told them this parable: [4]"What man of you, having a hundred sheep, if he has lost one of them, does not leave the ninety-nine in the wilderness, and go after the one which is lost, until he finds it? [5]And when he has found it, he lays it on his shoulders, rejoicing. [6]And when he comes home, he calls together his friends and his neighbors, saying to them, 'Rejoice with me, for I have found my sheep which was lost.' [7]Just so, I tell you, there will be more joy in heaven over one sinner who repents than over ninety-nine righteous persons who need no repentance.

The Parable of the Lost Coin

[8] "Or what woman, having ten silver coins, [t] if she loses one coin, does not light a lamp and

---

[a] Other ancient authorities read *a donkey*.
[t] The drachma, rendered here by *silver coin*, was about a day's wage for a laborer.
14:5: Mt 12:11; Lk 13:15.
14:8: Prov 25:6–7; Lk 11:43; 20:46.
14:11: Mt 23:12; Lk 18:14; Mt 18:4; 1 Pet 5:6.
14:12: Jas 2:2–4.
14:13: Lk 14:21.
14:15: Rev 19:9.
14:16–24: Mt 22:1–10.
14:20: Deut 24:5; 1 Cor 7:33.
14:21: Lk 14:13.
14:26–27: Mt 10:37–38.
14:27: Mt 16:24; Mk 8:34; Lk 9:23.
14:33: Lk 18:29–30; Phil 3:7.
14:34–35: Mt 5:13; Mk 9:49–50; Mt 11:15.
15:1–2: Lk 5:29–30; 19:7.
15:4–7: Mt 18:10–14.
15:7: Jas 5:20; Lk 19:10; 15:10.
* 14:26: Christ's disciples must be prepared to part from any one who prevents them from serving him.

sweep the house and seek diligently until she finds it? ⁹And when she has found it, she calls together her friends and neighbors, saying, 'Rejoice with me, for I have found the coin which I had lost.' ¹⁰Just so, I tell you, there is joy before the angels of God over one sinner who repents."

The Parable of the Prodigal and His Brother

11 And he said, "There was a man who had two sons; ¹²and the younger of them said to his father, 'Father, give me the share of property that falls to me.' And he divided his living between them. ¹³Not many days later, the younger son gathered all he had and took his journey into a far country, and there he squandered his property in loose living. ¹⁴And when he had spent everything, a great famine arose in that country, and he began to be in want. ¹⁵So he went and joined himself to one of the citizens of that country, who sent him into his fields to feed swine. ¹⁶And he would gladly have fed on ᵘ the pods that the swine ate; and no one gave him anything. ¹⁷But when he came to himself he said, 'How many of my father's hired servants have bread enough and to spare, but I perish here with hunger! ¹⁸I will arise and go to my father, and I will say to him, "Father, I have sinned against heaven and before you; ¹⁹I am no longer worthy to be called your son; treat me as one of your hired servants." ' ²⁰And he arose and came to his father. But while he was yet at a distance, his father saw him and had compassion, and ran and embraced him and kissed him. ²¹And the son said to him, 'Father, I have sinned against heaven and before you; I am no longer worthy to be called your son.' ᵛ ²²But the father said to his servants, 'Bring quickly the best robe, and put it on him; and put a ring on his hand, and shoes on his feet; ²³and bring the fatted calf and kill it, and let us eat and make merry; ²⁴for this my son was dead, and is alive again; he was lost, and is found.' And they began to make merry.

25 "Now his elder son was in the field; and as he came and drew near to the house, he heard music and dancing. ²⁶And he called one of the servants and asked what this meant. ²⁷And he said to him, 'Your brother has come, and your father has killed the fatted calf, because he has received him safe and sound.' ²⁸But he was angry and refused to go in. His father came out and entreated him, ²⁹but he answered his father, 'Behold, these many years I have served you, and I never disobeyed your command; yet you never gave me a kid, that I might make merry with my friends. ³⁰But when this son of yours came, who has devoured your living with harlots, you killed for him the fatted calf!' ³¹And he said to him, 'Son, you are always with me, and all that is mine is yours. ³²It was fitting to make merry and be glad, for this your brother was dead, and is alive; he was lost, and is found.' "

The Parable of the Dishonest Steward

16 He also said to the disciples, "There was a rich man who had a steward, and charges were brought to him that this man was wasting his goods. ²And he called him and said to him, 'What is this that I hear about you? Turn in the account of your stewardship, for you can no longer be steward.' ³And the steward said to himself, 'What shall I do, since my master is taking the stewardship away from me? I am not strong enough to dig, and I am ashamed to beg. ⁴I have decided what to do, so that people may receive me into their houses when I am put out of the stewardship.' ⁵So, summoning his master's debtors one by one, he said to the first, 'How much do you owe my master?' ⁶He said, 'A hundred measures of oil.' And he said to him, 'Take your bill, and sit down quickly and write fifty.' ⁷Then he said to another, 'And how much do you owe?' He said, 'A hundred measures of wheat.' He said to him, 'Take your bill, and write eighty.' ⁸The master commended the dishonest steward for his prudence; for the sons of this world ʷ are wiser in their own generation than the sons of light. * ⁹And I tell you, make friends for yourselves by means of unrighteous mammon, so that when it fails they may receive you into the eternal habitations.

10 "He who is faithful in a very little is faithful also in much; and he who is dishonest in a very little is dishonest also in much. ¹¹If then you have not been faithful in the unrighteous mammon, who will entrust to you the true riches? ¹²And if you have not been faithful in that which is another's, who will give you that which is your own? ¹³No servant can serve two masters; for either he will hate the one and love the other, or he will be devoted to the one and despise the other. You cannot serve God and mammon."

The Law and the Kingdom of God

14 The Pharisees, who were lovers of money, heard all this, and they scoffed at him. ¹⁵But he said to them, "You are those who justify yourselves before men, but God knows your hearts; for what is exalted among men is an abomination in the sight of God.

16 "The law and the prophets were until John; since then the good news of the kingdom of God

---

ᵘ Other ancient authorities read *filled his belly with.*
ᵛ Other ancient authorities add *treat me as one of your hired servants.*
ʷ Greek *age.*
15:11: Mt 21:28.
15:12: Deut 21:15–17.
15:22: Gen 41:42; Zech 3:4.
15:24: 1 Tim 5:6; Eph 2:1; Lk 9:60.
16:8: 1 Thess 5:5; Eph 5:8; Lk 20:34; Jn 12:36.
16:9: Lk 12:33; 18:22.
16:10: Mt 25:21; Lk 19:17.
16:13: Mt 6:24.
16:15: 1 Sam 16:7; Prov 21:2; Acts 1:24; Lk 10:29.
16:16: Mt 11:12–13.
* **16:8:** The master commended his foresight without approving what he actually did.

is preached, and every one enters it violently. [17]But it is easier for heaven and earth to pass away, than for one dot of the law to become void.

18 "Every one who divorces his wife and marries another commits adultery, and he who marries a woman divorced from her husband commits adultery.

The Rich Man and Lazarus

19 "There was a rich man, who was clothed in purple and fine linen and who feasted sumptuously every day. [20]And at his gate lay a poor man named Laz′arus, full of sores, [21]who desired to be fed with what fell from the rich man's table; moreover the dogs came and licked his sores. [22]The poor man died and was carried by the angels to Abraham's bosom. The rich man also died and was buried; [23]and in Hades, being in torment, he lifted up his eyes, and saw Abraham far off and Laz′arus in his bosom. [24]And he called out, 'Father Abraham, have mercy upon me, and send Laz′arus to dip the end of his finger in water and cool my tongue; for I am in anguish in this flame.' [25]But Abraham said, 'Son, remember that you in your lifetime received your good things, and Laz′arus in like manner evil things; but now he is comforted here, and you are in anguish. [26]And besides all this, between us and you a great chasm has been fixed, in order that those who would pass from here to you may not be able, and none may cross from there to us.' [27]And he said, 'Then I beg you, father, to send him to my father's house, [28]for I have five brothers, so that he may warn them, lest they also come into this place of torment.' [29]But Abraham said, 'They have Moses and the prophets; let them hear them.' [30]And he said, 'No, father Abraham; but if some one goes to them from the dead, they will repent.' [31]He said to him, 'If they do not hear Moses and the prophets, neither will they be convinced if some one should rise from the dead.'"

Some Sayings of Jesus

17 And he said to his disciples, "Temptations to sin[x] are sure to come; but woe to him by whom they come! [2]It would be better for him if a millstone were hung round his neck and he were cast into the sea, than that he should cause one of these little ones to sin. [y] [3]Take heed to yourselves; if your brother sins, rebuke him, and if he repents, forgive him; [4]and if he sins against you seven times in the day, and turns to you seven times, and says, 'I repent,' you must forgive him."

5 The apostles said to the Lord, "Increase our faith!" [6]And the Lord said, "If you had faith as a grain of mustard seed, you could say to this sycamine tree, 'Be rooted up, and be planted in the sea,' and it would obey you.

7 "Will any one of you, who has a servant plowing or keeping sheep, say to him when he has come in from the field, 'Come at once and sit down at table'? [8]Will he not rather say to him, 'Prepare supper for me, and put on your apron and serve me, till I eat and drink; and afterward you shall eat and drink'? [9]Does he thank the servant because he did what was commanded? [10]So you also, when you have done all that is commanded you, say, 'We are unworthy servants; we have only done what was our duty.'"

Jesus Cleanses Ten Lepers

11 On the way to Jerusalem he was passing along between Sama′ria and Galilee. [12]And as he entered a village, he was met by ten lepers, who stood at a distance [13]and lifted up their voices and said, "Jesus, Master, have mercy on us." [14]When he saw them he said to them, "Go and show yourselves to the priests." And as they went they were cleansed. [15]Then one of them, when he saw that he was healed, turned back, praising God with a loud voice; [16]and he fell on his face at Jesus' feet, giving him thanks. Now he was a Samaritan. [17]Then said Jesus, "Were not ten cleansed? Where are the nine? [18]Was no one found to return and give praise to God except this foreigner?" [19]And he said to him, "Rise and go your way; your faith has made you well."

The Coming of the Kingdom

20 Being asked by the Pharisees when the kingdom of God was coming, he answered them, "The kingdom of God is not coming with signs to be observed; [*] [21]nor will they say, 'Behold, here it is!' or 'There!' for behold, the kingdom of God is in your midst."[z]

22 And he said to the disciples, "The days are coming when you will desire to see one of the days of the Son of man, and you will not see it. [23]And they will say to you, 'Behold, there!' or 'Behold, here!' Do not go, do not follow them. [24]For as the lightning flashes and lights up the sky from one side to the other, so will the Son of man be in

[x] Greek *stumbling blocks*.
[y] Greek *stumble*.
[z] Or *within you*.
16:17: Mt 5:17–18; Lk 21:33.
16:18: Mt 5:31–32; 19:9; Mk 10:11–12; 1 Cor 7:10–11.
16:20: Jn 11:1–44; 12:1, 9.
16:22: Jn 13:23.
16:25: Lk 6:24.
16:29: Jn 5:45–47; Acts 15:21; Lk 4:17.
16:30: Lk 3:8; 19:9.
17:1–2: Mt 18:6–7; Mk 9:42; 1 Cor 8:12.
17:3–4: Mt 18:15, 21–22.
17:5–6: Mt 17:20, 21:21; Mk 11:22–23.
17:5: Lk 7:13.
17:8: Lk 12:37; Jn 13:3–5.
17:11: Lk 9:51; 13:22; 19:11.
17:12: Lev 13:45–46.
17:13: Lk 5:5; 8:24, 45; 9:33, 49.
17:14: Lk 5:14; Mt 8:4; Mk 1:44; Lev 14:2–32.
17:19: Mt 9:22; Mk 5:34; Lk 8:48; 18:42.
17:20: Lk 19:11; 21:7; Acts 1:6.
17:22: Mt 9:15; Mk 2:20; Lk 5:35.
17:23: Mt 24:23; Mk 13:21.
17:24: Mt 24:27; Rev 1:7.
* 17:20: At that time many persons were expecting to see the kingdom inaugurated with striking manifestations; cf. 19:11.

his day. [a] [25]But first he must suffer many things and be rejected by this generation. [26]As it was in the days of Noah, so will it be in the days of the Son of man. [27]They ate, they drank, they married, they were given in marriage, until the day when Noah entered the ark, and the flood came and destroyed them all. [28]Likewise as it was in the days of Lot—they ate, they drank, they bought, they sold, they planted, they built, [29]but on the day when Lot went out from Sodom, fire and brimstone rained from heaven and destroyed them all—[30]so will it be on the day when the Son of man is revealed. [31]On that day, let him who is on the housetop, with his goods in the house, not come down to take them away; and likewise let him who is in the field not turn back. [32]Remember Lot's wife. [33]Whoever seeks to gain his life will lose it, but whoever loses his life will preserve it. [34]I tell you, in that night there will be two men in one bed; one will be taken and the other left. [35]There will be two women grinding together; one will be taken and the other left." [b] [37]And they said to him, "Where, Lord?" He said to them, "Where the body is, there the eagles [c] will be gathered together."

The Parable of the Widow and the Unrighteous Judge

18 And he told them a parable, to the effect that they ought always to pray and not lose heart. [2]He said, "In a certain city there was a judge who neither feared God nor regarded man; [3]and there was a widow in that city who kept coming to him and saying, 'Vindicate me against my adversary.' [4]For a while he refused; but afterward he said to himself, 'Though I neither fear God nor regard man, [5]yet because this widow bothers me, I will vindicate her, or she will wear me out by her continual coming.' " [6]And the Lord said, "Hear what the unrighteous judge says. [7]And will not God vindicate his elect, who cry to him day and night? Will he delay long over them? [8]I tell you, he will vindicate them speedily. Nevertheless, when the Son of man comes, will he find faith on earth?"

The Parable of the Pharisees and the Tax Collector

9 He also told this parable to some who trusted in themselves that they were righteous and despised others: [10]"Two men went up into the temple to pray, one a Pharisee and the other a tax collector. [11]The Pharisee stood and prayed thus with himself, 'God, I thank you that I am not like other men, extortioners, unjust, adulterers, or even like this tax collector. [12]I fast twice a week, I give tithes of all that I get.' [13]But the tax collector, standing far off, would not even lift up his eyes to heaven, but beat his breast, saying, 'God, be merciful to me a sinner!' [14]I tell you, this man went down to his house justified rather than the other;

for every one who exalts himself will be humbled, but he who humbles himself will be exalted."

Jesus Blesses the Children

15 Now they were bringing even infants to him that he might touch them; and when the disciples saw it, they rebuked them. [16]But Jesus called them to him, saying, "Let the children come to me, and do not hinder them; for to such belongs the kingdom of God. [17]Truly, I say to you, whoever does not receive the kingdom of God like a child shall not enter it."

The Rich Ruler

18 And a ruler asked him, "Good Teacher, what shall I do to inherit eternal life?" [19]And Jesus said to him, "Why do you call me good? No one is good but God alone. [20]You know the commandments: 'Do not commit adultery, Do not kill, Do not steal, Do not bear false witness, Honor your father and mother.' " [21]And he said, "All these I have observed from my youth." [22]And when Jesus heard it, he said to him, "One thing you still lack. Sell all that you have and distribute to the poor, and you will have treasure in heaven; and come, follow me." [23]But when he heard this he became sad, for he was very rich. [24]Jesus looking at him said, "How hard it is for those who have riches to enter the kingdom of God! [25]For it is easier for a camel to go through the eye of a needle than for a rich man to enter the kingdom of God." [26]Those who heard it said, "Then who can be saved?" [27]But he said, "What is impossible with men is possible with God." [28]And Peter said, "Behold, we have left our homes and followed you." [29]And he said to them, "Truly, I say to you, there is no man who has left house or wife or brothers or parents or children, for the sake of the kingdom of God, [30]who will not receive manifold more in this time, and in the age to come eternal life."

---

[a] Other ancient authorities omit *in his day.*
[b] Other ancient authorities add verse 36, *"Two men will be in the field; one will be taken and the other left."*
[c] Or *vultures.*

17:25: Lk 9:22.
17:26–27: Mt 24:37–39; Gen 6:5–8; 7:6–24.
17:28–30: Gen 18:20–33; 19:24–25.
17:31: Mt 24:17–18; Mk 13:15–16; Lk 21:21.
17:32: Gen 19:26.
17:33: Mt 10:39; 16:25; Mk 8:35; Lk 9:24; Jn 12:25.
17:34–35: Mt 24:40–41.
17:37: Mt 24:28.
18:1–8: Lk 11:5–8.
18:6: Lk 7:13.
18:7: Rev 6:10; Mt 24:22; Rom 8:33; Col 3:12; 2 Tim 2:10.
18:11: Mt 6:5; Mk 11:25.
18:12: Lk 5:33; 11:42.
18:14: Mt 18:4; 23:12; Lk 14:11; 1 Pet 5:6.
18:15–17: Mt 19:13–15; 18:3; Mk 10:13–16.
18:18–23: Mt 19:16–22; Mk 10:17–22.
18:18: Lk 10:25.
18:20: Ex 20:12–16; Deut 5:16–20; Rom 13:9; Jas 2:11.
18:22: Lk 12:33; Acts 2:45; 4:32.
18:24–27: Mt 19:23–26; Mk 10:23–27.
18:27: Gen 18:14; Job 42:2; Jer 32:17; Lk 1:37.
18:28–30: Mt 19:27–30; Mk 10:28–31; Lk 5:1–11.

A Third Time Jesus Foretells His Death and Resurrection

31 And taking the Twelve, he said to them, "Behold, we are going up to Jerusalem, and everything that is written of the Son of man by the prophets will be accomplished. [32]For he will be delivered to the Gentiles, and will be mocked and shamefully treated and spit upon; [33]they will scourge him and kill him, and on the third day he will rise." [34]But they understood none of these things; this saying was hidden from them, and they did not grasp what was said.

Jesus Heals a Blind Beggar near Jericho

35 As he drew near to Jericho, a blind man was sitting by the roadside begging; [36]and hearing a multitude going by, he inquired what this meant. [37]They told him, "Jesus of Nazareth is passing by." [38]And he cried, "Jesus, Son of David, have mercy on me!" [39]And those who were in front rebuked him, telling him to be silent; but he cried out all the more, "Son of David, have mercy on me!" [40]And Jesus stopped, and commanded him to be brought to him; and when he came near, he asked him, [41]"What do you want me to do for you?" He said, "Lord, let me receive my sight." [42]And Jesus said to him, "Receive your sight; your faith has made you well." [43]And immediately he received his sight and followed him, glorifying God; and all the people, when they saw it, gave praise to God.

Jesus and Zacchaeus

19 He entered Jericho and was passing through. [2]And there was a man named Zacchae'us; he was a chief tax collector, and rich. [3]And he sought to see who Jesus was, but could not, on account of the crowd, because he was small of stature. [4]So he ran on ahead and climbed up into a sycamore tree to see him, for he was to pass that way. [5]And when Jesus came to the place, he looked up and said to him, "Zacchae'us, make haste and come down; for I must stay at your house today." [6]So he made haste and came down, and received him joyfully. [7]And when they saw it they all murmured, "He has gone in to be the guest of a man who is a sinner." [8]And Zacchae'us stood and said to the Lord, "Behold, Lord, the half of my goods I give to the poor; and if I have defrauded any one of anything, I restore it fourfold." [9]And Jesus said to him, "Today salvation has come to this house, since he also is a son of Abraham. [10]For the Son of man came to seek and to save the lost."

The Parable of the Ten Pounds

11 As they heard these things, he proceeded to tell a parable, because he was near to Jerusalem, and because they supposed that the kingdom of God was to appear immediately. [12]He said therefore, "A nobleman went into a far country to receive kingly power [d] and then return. [13]Calling ten of his servants, he gave them ten pounds, [e] and said to them, 'Trade with these till I come.' [14]But his citizens hated him and sent an embassy after him, saying, 'We do not want this man to reign over us.' [15]When he returned, having received the kingly power, [d] he commanded these servants, to whom he had given the money, to be called to him, that he might know what they had gained by trading. [16]The first came before him, saying, 'Lord, your pound has made ten pounds more.' [17]And he said to him, 'Well done, good servant! Because you have been faithful in a very little, you shall have authority over ten cities.' [18]And the second came, saying, 'Lord, your pound has made five pounds.' [19]And he said to him, 'And you are to be over five cities.' [20]Then another came, saying, 'Lord, here is your pound, which I kept laid away in a napkin; [21]for I was afraid of you, because you are a severe man; you take up what you did not lay down, and reap what you did not sow.' [22]He said to him, 'I will condemn you out of your own mouth, you wicked servant! You knew that I was a severe man, taking up what I did not lay down and reaping what I did not sow? [23]Why then did you not put my money into the bank, and at my coming I should have collected it with interest?' [24]And he said to those who stood by, 'Take the pound from him, and give it to him who has the ten pounds.' [25](And they said to him, 'Lord, he has ten pounds!') [26]'I tell you, that to every one who has will more be given; but from him who has not, even what he has will be taken away. [27]But as for these enemies of mine, who did not want me to reign over them, bring them here and slay them before me.' "

Jesus' Entry into Jerusalem

28 And when he had said this, he went on ahead, going up to Jerusalem. [29]When he drew near to Beth'phage and Beth'any, at the mount that is called Olivet, he sent two of the disciples, [30]saying, "Go into the village opposite, where on entering you will find a colt tied, on which no one has ever yet sat; untie it and bring it here. [31]If any one asks you, 'Why are you untying it?' you shall say this, 'The Lord has need of it.'" [32]So those

---

[d] Greek *a kingdom*.

[e] The mina, rendered here by *pound*, was about three months' wages for a laborer.

18:31–34: Mt 20:17–19; Mk 10:32–34; Lk 9:22, 44–45; 17:25.
18:35–43: Mt 20:29–34; Mk 10:46–52; Mt 9:27–31; Mk 8:22; Jn 9:1–7.
18:42: Mt 9:22; Mk 5:34; 10:52; Lk 7:50; 8:48; 17:19.
19:1: Mk 10:46.
19:7: Lk 5:29–30; 15:1–2.
19:8: Lk 7:13; 3:14; Ex 22:1; Lev 6:5; Num 5:6–7.
19:9: Lk 3:8; 13:16; Rom 4:16.
19:11: Lk 9:51; 13:22; 17:11; 18:31; 9:27.
19:12–28: Mt 25:14–30.
19:12: Mk 13:34.
19:17: Lk 16:10.
19:26: Mt 13:12; Mk 4:25; Lk 8:18.
19:28: Mk 10:32.
19:29–38: Mt 21:1–9; Mk 11:1–10; Jn 12:12–18.
19:32: Lk 22:13.

who were sent went away and found it as he had told them. ³³And as they were untying the colt, its owners said to them, "Why are you untying the colt?" ³⁴And they said, "The Lord has need of it." ³⁵And they brought it to Jesus, and throwing their garments on the colt they set Jesus upon it. ³⁶And as he rode along, they spread their garments on the road. ³⁷As he was now drawing near, at the descent of the Mount of Olives, the whole multitude of the disciples began to rejoice and praise God with a loud voice for all the mighty works that they had seen, ³⁸saying, "Blessed is the King who comes in the name of the Lord! Peace in heaven and glory in the highest!" ³⁹And some of the Pharisees in the multitude said to him, "Teacher, rebuke your disciples." ⁴⁰He answered, "I tell you, if these were silent, the very stones would cry out."

Jesus Weeps over Jerusalem

41 And when he drew near and saw the city he wept over it, ⁴²saying, "Would that even today you knew the things that make for peace! But now they are hidden from your eyes. ⁴³For the days shall come upon you, when your enemies will cast up a bank about you and surround you, and hem you in on every side, ⁴⁴and dash you to the ground, you and your children within you, and they will not leave one stone upon another in you; because you did not know the time of your visitation." *

Jesus Cleanses the Temple

45 And he entered the temple and began to drive out those who sold, ⁴⁶saying to them, "It is written, 'My house shall be a house of prayer'; but you have made it a den of robbers."

47 And he was teaching daily in the temple. The chief priests and the scribes and the principal men of the people sought to destroy him; ⁴⁸but they did not find anything they could do, for all the people hung upon his words.

The Authority of Jesus Questioned

20 One day, as he was teaching the people in the temple and preaching the gospel, the chief priests and the scribes with the elders came up ²and said to him, "Tell us by what authority you do these things, or who it is that gave you this authority." ³He answered them, "I also will ask you a question; now tell me, ⁴Was the baptism of John from heaven or from men?" ⁵And they discussed it with one another, saying, "If we say, 'From heaven,' he will say, 'Why did you not believe him?' ⁶But if we say, 'From men,' all the people will stone us; for they are convinced that John was a prophet." ⁷So they answered that they did not know where it was from. ⁸And Jesus said to them, "Neither will I tell you by what authority I do these things."

The Parable of the Wicked Tenants

9 And he began to tell the people this parable: "A man planted a vineyard, and leased it to ten-

ants, and went into another country for a long while. ¹⁰When the time came, he sent a servant to the tenants, that they should give him some of the fruit of the vineyard; but the tenants beat him, and sent him away empty-handed. ¹¹And he sent another servant; him also they beat and treated shamefully, and sent him away empty-handed. ¹²And he sent yet a third; this one they wounded and cast out. ¹³Then the owner of the vineyard said, 'What shall I do? I will send my beloved son; it may be they will respect him.' ¹⁴But when the tenants saw him, they said to themselves, 'This is the heir; let us kill him, that the inheritance may be ours.' ¹⁵And they cast him out of the vineyard and killed him. What then will the owner of the vineyard do to them? ¹⁶He will come and destroy those tenants, and give the vineyard to others." When they heard this, they said, "God forbid!" ¹⁷But he looked at them and said, "What then is this that is written:

'The very stone which the builders rejected
  has become the cornerstone'?

¹⁸Every one who falls on that stone will be broken to pieces; but when it falls on any one it will crush him."

The Question about Paying Taxes

19 The scribes and the chief priests tried to lay hands on him at that very hour, but they feared the people; for they perceived that he had told this parable against them. ²⁰So they watched him, and sent spies, who pretended to be sincere, that they might take hold of what he said, so as to deliver him up to the authority and jurisdiction of the governor. ²¹They asked him, "Teacher, we know that you speak and teach rightly, and show no partiality, but truly teach the way of God. ²²Is it lawful for us to give tribute to Caesar, or not?" ²³But he perceived their craftiness, and said to them, ²⁴"Show me a coin. ⁶ Whose likeness

---

ᶠ Greek *denarius*.
19:34: Lk 7:13.
19:36: 2 Kings 9:13.
19:38: Ps 118:26; Lk 13:35; 2:14.
19:39-40: Mt 21:15–16; Hab 2:11.
19:41: Lk 13:33–34.
19:43: Lk 21:21–24; 21:6; Is 29:3; Jer 6:6; Ezek 4:2.
19:44: 1 Pet 2:12.
19:45-46: Mt 21:12–13; Mk 11:15–17; Jn 2:13–17.
19:47-48: Mk 11:18; Lk 21:37; 22:53.
20:1-8: Mt 21:23–27; Mk 11:27–33.
20:2: Jn 2:18.
20:6: Mt 14:5; Lk 7:29.
20:9-19: Mt 21:33–46; Mk 12:1–12.
20:9: Is 5:1–7; Mt 25:14.
20:16: Acts 13:46; 18:6; 28:28.
20:17: Ps 118:22–23; Acts 4:11; 1 Pet 2:6–7.
20:18: Is 8:14–15.
20:19: Lk 19:47.
20:20-26: Mt 22:15–22; Mk 12:13–17.
20:21: Jn 3:2.
* 19:41–44: These moving words spoken over the city are full of scriptural allusions. Moreover, the details given could apply as well to the siege of 587 B.C. as to that of A.D. 70. It is not safe, therefore, to argue from this passage that the fall of the city had already taken place when Luke wrote his Gospel.

and inscription has it?" They said, "Caesar's." ²⁵He said to them, "Then render to Caesar the things that are Caesar's, and to God the things that are God's." ²⁶And they were not able in the presence of the people to catch him by what he said; but marveling at his answer they were silent.

The Question about Man's Resurrection

27 There came to him some Sad'ducees, those who say that there is no resurrection, ²⁸and they asked him a question, saying, "Teacher, Moses wrote for us that if a man's brother dies, having a wife but no children, the man ᵍ must take the wife and raise up children for his brother. ²⁹Now there were seven brothers; the first took a wife, and died without children; ³⁰and the second ³¹and the third took her, and likewise all seven left no children and died. ³²Afterward the woman also died. ³³In the resurrection, therefore, whose wife will the woman be? For the seven had her as wife."

34 And Jesus said to them, "The sons of this age marry and are given in marriage; ³⁵but those who are accounted worthy to attain to that age and to the resurrection from the dead neither marry nor are given in marriage, ³⁶for they cannot die any more, because they are equal to angels and are sons of God, being sons of the resurrection. ³⁷But that the dead are raised, even Moses showed, in the passage about the bush, where he calls the Lord the God of Abraham and the God of Isaac and the God of Jacob. * ³⁸Now he is not God of the dead, but of the living; for all live to him." ³⁹And some of the scribes answered, "Teacher, you have spoken well." ⁴⁰For they no longer dared to ask him any question.

A Question about the Messiah

41 But he said to them, "How can they say that the Christ is David's son? ⁴²For David himself says in the Book of Psalms,

'The Lord said to my Lord,
Sit at my right hand,

⁴³till I make your enemies a stool for your feet.'
⁴⁴David thus calls him Lord; so how is he his son?"

Jesus Denounces the Hypocrisy of the Scribes

45 And in the hearing of all the people he said to his disciples, ⁴⁶"Beware of the scribes, who like to go about in long robes, and love salutations in the market places and the best seats in the synagogues and the places of honor at feasts, ⁴⁷who devour widows' houses and for a pretense make long prayers. They will receive the greater condemnation."

The Widow's Offering

21 He looked up and saw the rich putting their gifts into the treasury; ²and he saw a poor widow put in two copper coins. ³And he said, "Truly I tell you, this poor widow has put in more than all of them; ⁴for they all contributed out of

their abundance, but she out of her poverty put in all the living that she had."

The Destruction of the Temple Foretold

5 And as some spoke of the temple, how it was adorned with noble stones and offerings, he said, ⁶"As for these things which you see, the days will come when there shall not be left here one stone upon another that will not be thrown down." ⁷And they asked him, "Teacher, when will this be, and what will be the sign when this is about to take place?" ⁸And he said, "Take heed that you are not led astray; for many will come in my name, saying, 'I am he!' and, 'The time is at hand!' Do not go after them. ⁹And when you hear of wars and tumults, do not be terrified; for this must first take place, but the end will not be at once."

Signs and Persecutions

10 Then he said to them, "Nation will rise against nation, and kingdom against kingdom; ¹¹there will be great earthquakes, and in various places famines and pestilences; and there will be terrors and great signs from heaven. ¹²But before all this they will lay their hands on you and persecute you, delivering you up to the synagogues and prisons, and you will be brought before kings and governors for my name's sake. ¹³This will be a time for you to bear testimony. ¹⁴Settle it therefore in your minds, not to meditate beforehand how to answer; ¹⁵for I will give you a mouth and wisdom, which none of your adversaries will be able to withstand or contradict. ¹⁶You will be delivered up even by parents and brothers and kinsmen and friends, and some of you they will put to death; ¹⁷you will be hated by all for my name's sake. ¹⁸But not a hair of your head will perish. ¹⁹By your endurance you will gain your lives.

The Destruction of Jerusalem Foretold

20 "But when you see Jerusalem surrounded by armies, then know that its desolation has come

---

ᵍ Greek *his brother.*
20:25: Rom 13:7; Lk 23:2.
20:27-38: Mt 22:23-33; Mk 12:18-27.
20:27: Acts 4:1-2; 23:6-10.
20:28: Deut 25:5.
20:37: Ex 3:6.
20:39: Mk 12:28.
20:40: Mk 12:34; Mt 22:46.
20:41-44: Mt 22:41-45; Mk 12:35-37; Ps 110:1.
20:45-47: Mk 12:38-40; Mt 23:6-7; Lk 11:43; 14:7-11.
21:1-4: Mk 12:41-44.
21:5-23: Mt 24:1-19; Mk 13:1-17.
21:6: Lk 19:43-44; Mk 14:58; 15:29; Acts 6:14.
21:7: Lk 12:20; Acts 1:6.
21:8: Lk 17:23; Mk 13:21; 1 Jn 2:18.
21:10: 2 Chron 15:6; Is 19:2.
21:12-17: Mt 10:17-21.
21:12: Acts 25:24; Jn 16:2.
21:13: Phil 1:12.
21:14-15: Lk 12:11-12.
21:16: Lk 12:52-53.
21:17: Mt 10:22; Jn 15:18-25.
21:18: Lk 12:7; Mt 10:30; Acts 27:34; 1 Sam 14:45.
21:19: Mt 10:22; Rev 2:7.
21:20-22: Lk 19:41-44; 23:28-31; 17:31.
* 20:37: As elsewhere (1 Cor 15:13-19), survival after death is linked with the resurrection of the body.

near. [21]Then let those who are in Judea flee to the mountains, and let those who are inside the city depart, and let not those who are out in the country enter it; [22]for these are days of vengeance, to fulfil all that is written. [23]Alas for those who are with child and for those who are nursing in those days! For great distress shall be upon the earth and wrath upon this people; [24]they will fall by the edge of the sword, and be led captive among all nations; and Jerusalem will be trodden down by the Gentiles, until the times of the Gentiles * are fulfilled.

The Coming of the Son of Man

25 "And there will be signs in sun and moon and stars, and upon the earth distress of nations in perplexity at the roaring of the sea and the waves, [26]men fainting with fear and with foreboding of what is coming on the world; for the powers of the heavens will be shaken. [27]And then they will see the Son of man coming in a cloud with power and great glory. [28]Now when these things begin to take place, look up and raise your heads, because your redemption is drawing near."

The Lesson of the Fig Tree

29 And he told them a parable: "Look at the fig tree, and all the trees; [30]as soon as they come out in leaf, you see for yourselves and know that the summer is already near. [31]So also, when you see these things taking place, you know that the kingdom of God is near. [32]Truly, I say to you, this generation will not pass away till all has taken place. [33]Heaven and earth will pass away, but my words will not pass away.

Exhortation to Watchfulness

34 "But take heed to yourselves lest your hearts be weighed down with dissipation and drunkenness and cares of this life, and that day come upon you suddenly like a snare; [35]for it will come upon all who dwell upon the face of the whole earth. [36]But watch at all times, praying that you may have strength to escape all these things that will take place, and to stand before the Son of man."

37 And every day he was teaching in the temple, but at night he went out and lodged on the mount called Olivet. [38]And early in the morning all the people came to him in the temple to hear him.

The Conspiracy to Kill Jesus

22 Now the feast of Unleavened Bread drew near, which is called the Passover. [2]And the chief priests and the scribes were seeking how to put him to death; for they feared the people.

3 Then Satan entered into Judas called Iscariot, who was of the number of the Twelve; [4]he went away and conferred with the chief priests and captains how he might betray him to them. [5]And they were glad, and engaged to give him money. [6]So he agreed, and sought an opportunity to betray him to them in the absence of the multitude.

The Preparation of the Passover

7 Then came the day of Unleavened Bread, on which the Passover lamb had to be sacrificed. [8]So Jesus [h] sent Peter and John, saying, "Go and prepare the Passover for us, that we may eat it." [9]They said to him, "Where will you have us prepare it?" [10]He said to them, "Behold, when you have entered the city, a man carrying a jar of water will meet you; follow him into the house which he enters, [11]and tell the householder, 'The Teacher says to you, Where is the guest room, where I am to eat the Passover with my disciples?' [12]And he will show you a large upper room furnished; there make ready." [13]And they went, and found it as he had told them; and they prepared the Passover.

Jesus Institutes the Eucharist

14 And when the hour came, he sat at table, and the apostles with him. [15]And he said to them, "I have earnestly desired to eat this Passover with you before I suffer; [16]for I tell you I shall not eat it [i] until it is fulfilled in the kingdom of God." [17]And he took a chalice, and when he had given thanks he said, "Take this, and divide it among yourselves; [18]for I tell you that from now on I shall not drink of the fruit of the vine until the kingdom of God comes." [19]And he took bread, and when he had given thanks he broke it and gave it to them, saying, "This is my body which is given for you. Do this in remembrance of me." [20]And likewise the chalice after supper, saying, "This chalice which is poured out for you is the new covenant in my blood." [j] [21]But behold the hand of

[h] Greek he.
[i] Other ancient authorities read never eat it again.
[j] Other ancient authorities omit which is given for you. Do this in remembrance of me." [20]And likewise the chalice after supper, saying, "This chalice which is poured out for you is the new covenant in my blood."

21:23: Lk 23:29.
21:24: Rom 11:25; Is 63:18; Dan 8:13; Rev 11:2.
21:25-27: Mt 24:29-30; Mk 13:24-26.
21:25: Rev 6:12-13; Is 13:10; Joel 2:10; Zeph 1:15.
21:27: Lk 9:27; Dan 7:13-14.
21:28: Lk 18:7-8.
21:29-33: Mt 24:32-35; Mk 13:28-31.
21:32: Lk 9:27.
21:33: Lk 16:17.
21:34: Lk 12:45; Mk 4:19; 1 Thess 5:6-7.
21:36: Mk 13:33.
21:37: Lk 19:47; Mk 11:19.
22:1-2: Mt 26:2-5; Mk 14:1-2; Jn 11:47-53.
22:3-6: Mt 26:14-16; Mk 14:10-11; Jn 13:2.
22:7-13: Mt 26:17-19; Mk 14:12-16.
22:7: Ex 12:18-20; Deut 16:5-8.
22:8: Acts 3:1; Lk 19:29.
22:14: Mt 26:20; Mk 14:17; Jn 13:17.
22:15: Lk 12:49-50.
22:16: Lk 14:15.
22:17: Mt 26:27; Mk 14:23; 1 Cor 10:16.
22:18: Mt 26:29; Mk 14:25.
22:19: Mt 26:26; Mk 14:22; 1 Cor 10:16; 11:23-26; Lk 9:16.

* 21:24, *the times of the Gentiles*: i.e., those during which the Gentiles will take the place of the unbelieving people of Israel. Evidently, therefore, the end of the world does not coincide with the fall of Jerusalem. St. Paul says that the Jews will be converted before the end (Rom 11:26).

him who betrays me is with me on the table. [22]For the Son of man goes as it has been determined; but woe to that man by whom he is betrayed!" [23]And they began to question one another, which of them it was that would do this.

The Dispute about Greatness

24 A dispute also arose among them, which of them was to be regarded as the greatest. [25]And he said to them, "The kings of the Gentiles exercise lordship over them; and those in authority over them are called benefactors. [26]But not so with you; rather let the greatest among you become as the youngest, and the leader as one who serves. [27]For which is the greater, one who sits at table, or one who serves? Is it not the one who sits at table? But I am among you as one who serves.

28 "You are those who have continued with me in my trials; [29]as my Father appointed a kingdom for me, so do I appoint for you [30]that you may eat and drink at my table in my kingdom, and sit on thrones judging the twelve tribes of Israel.

Peter's Denial Foretold

31 "Simon, Simon, behold, Satan demanded to have you,[k] that he might sift you[k] like wheat, [32]but I have prayed for you that your faith may not fail; and when you have turned again, strengthen your brethren." [33]And he said to him, "Lord, I am ready to go with you to prison and to death." [34]He said, "I tell you, Peter, the cock will not crow this day, until you three times deny that you know me."

Purse, Bag, and Sword

35 And he said to them, "When I sent you out with no purse or bag or sandals, did you lack anything?" They said, "Nothing." [36]He said to them, "But now, let him who has a purse take it, and likewise a bag. And let him who has no sword sell his cloak and buy one. [37]For I tell you that this Scripture must be fulfilled in me, 'And he was reckoned with transgressors'; for what is written about me has its fulfilment." [38]And they said, "Look, Lord, here are two swords." And he said to them, "It is enough."

Jesus Prays on the Mount of Olives

39 And he came out, and went, as was his custom, to the Mount of Olives; and the disciples followed him. [40]And when he came to the place he said to them, "Pray that you may not enter into temptation." [41]And he withdrew from them about a stone's throw, and knelt down and prayed, [42]"Father, if you are willing, remove this chalice from me; nevertheless not my will, but yours, be done." [43]And there appeared to him an angel from heaven, strengthening him. [44]And being in an agony he prayed more earnestly; and his sweat became like great drops of blood falling down upon the ground.[l] [45]And when he rose from prayer, he came to the disciples and found them sleeping for sorrow, [46]and he said to them, "Why do you sleep? Rise and pray that you may not enter into temptation."

The Betrayal and Arrest of Jesus

47 While he was still speaking, there came a crowd, and the man called Judas, one of the Twelve, was leading them. He drew near to Jesus to kiss him; [48]but Jesus said to him, "Judas, would you betray the Son of man with a kiss?" [49]And when those who were about him saw what would follow, they said, "Lord, shall we strike with the sword?" [50]And one of them struck the slave of the high priest and cut off his right ear. [51]But Jesus said, "No more of this!" And he touched his ear and healed him. [52]Then Jesus said to the chief priests and captains of the temple and elders, who had come out against him, * "Have you come out as against a robber, with swords and clubs? [53]When I was with you day after day in the temple, you did not lay hands on me. But this is your hour, and the power of darkness."

Peter Denies Jesus

54 Then they seized him and led him away, bringing him into the high priest's house. Peter followed at a distance; [55]and when they had kindled a fire in the middle of the courtyard and sat down together, Peter sat among them. [56]Then a maid, seeing him as he sat in the light and gazing at him, said, "This man also was with him." [57]But he denied it, saying, "Woman, I do not know him." [58]And a little later some one else saw him and said, "You also are one of them." But Peter said, "Man, I am not." [59]And after an interval of about an hour still another insisted, saying, "Certainly this man also was with him; for he is a Galilean." [60]But Peter said, "Man, I do not know what you are saying." And immediately, while he was still speaking, the cock crowed. [61]And the Lord turned and looked at Peter. And Peter remembered the

---

k The Greek word for *you* here is plural; in verse 32 it is singular.
l Other ancient authorities omit verses 43 and 44.
22:21-23: Mt 26:21-24; Mk 14:18-21; Ps 41:9; Jn 13:21-30.
22:24: Lk 9:46; Mk 9:34.
22:25-27: Mt 20:25-28; Mk 10:42-45; Jn 13:3-16.
22:26: Lk 9:48.
22:28-30: Mt 19:28.
22:28: Lk 4:13; Heb 2:18; 4:15.
22:29: Mk 14:24; Heb 9:20.
22:30: Mk 10:37; Rev 3:21; 20:4.
22:31: Job 1:6-12; Amos 9:9.
22:32: Jn 17:15; 21:15-17.
22:33-34: Mt 26:33-35; Mk 14:29-31; Jn 13:37-38.
22:35: Lk 10:4; Mt 10:9.
22:36: Lk 22:49-50.
22:37: Is 53:12.
22:39: Mt 26:30; Mk 14:26; Jn 18:1.
22:40-46: Mt 26:36-46; Mk 14:32-42; Heb 5:7-8.
22:40: Lk 11:4.
22:42: Mk 10:38; Jn 18:11; 5:30.
22:47-53: Mt 26:47-56; Mk 14:43-49; Jn 18:3-11.
22:49: Lk 22:38.
22:53: Lk 19:47.
22:54-55: Mt 26:57-58; Mk 14:53-54; Jn 18:12-16.
22:56-62: Mt 26:69-75; Mk 14:66-72; Jn 18:16-18, 25-27.
* 22:52: Matthew and Mark describe the arrest first, before Christ's words. Luke and John both put his address to the soldiers and officials before the arrest, doubtless to stress his command over events.

word of the Lord, how he had said to him, "Before the cock crows today, you will deny me three times." ⁶²And he went out and wept bitterly.

The Mocking and Beating of Jesus

63 Now the men who were holding Jesus mocked him and beat him; ⁶⁴they also blindfolded him and asked him, "Prophesy! Who is it that struck you?" ⁶⁵And they spoke many other words against him, reviling him.

Jesus before the Council

66 When day came, the assembly of the elders of the people gathered together, both chief priests and scribes; and they led him away to their council, and they said, ⁶⁷"If you are the Christ, tell us." But he said to them, "If I tell you, you will not believe; ⁶⁸and if I ask you, you will not answer. ⁶⁹But from now on the Son of man shall be seated at the right hand of the power of God." ⁷⁰And they all said, "Are you the Son of God, then?" And he said to them, "You say that I am." ⁷¹And they said, "What further testimony do we need? We have heard it ourselves from his own lips."

Jesus before Pilate

23 Then the whole company of them arose, and brought him before Pilate. ²And they began to accuse him, saying, "We found this man perverting our nation, and forbidding us to give tribute to Caesar, and saying that he himself is Christ a king." * ³And Pilate asked him, "Are you the King of the Jews?" And he answered him, "You have said so." ⁴And Pilate said to the chief priests and the multitudes, "I find no crime in this man." ⁵But they were urgent, saying, "He stirs up the people, teaching throughout all Judea, from Galilee even to this place."

Jesus before Herod

6 When Pilate heard this, he asked whether the man was a Galilean. ⁷And when he learned that he belonged to Herod's jurisdiction, he sent him over to Herod, who was himself in Jerusalem at that time. ⁸When Herod saw Jesus, he was very glad, for he had long desired to see him, because he had heard about him, and he was hoping to see some sign done by him. ⁹So he questioned him at some length; but he made no answer. ¹⁰The chief priests and the scribes stood by, vehemently accusing him. ¹¹And Herod with his soldiers treated him with contempt and mocked him; then, clothing him in gorgeous apparel, he sent him back to Pilate. ¹²And Herod and Pilate became friends with each other that very day, for before this they had been at enmity with each other.

Jesus Sentenced to Death

13 Pilate then called together the chief priests and the rulers and the people, ¹⁴and said to them, "You brought me this man as one who was perverting the people; and after examining him before you, behold, I did not find this man guilty of any of your charges against him; † ¹⁵neither did

Herod, for he sent him back to us. Behold, nothing deserving death has been done by him; ¹⁶I will therefore chastise him and release him." ^m

18 But they all cried out together, "Away with this man, and release to us Barab′bas"—¹⁹a man who had been thrown into prison for an insurrection started in the city, and for murder. ²⁰Pilate addressed them once more, desiring to release Jesus; ²¹but they shouted out, "Crucify, crucify him!" ²²A third time he said to them, "Why, what evil has he done? I have found in him no crime deserving death; I will therefore chastise him and release him." ²³But they were urgent, demanding with loud cries that he should be crucified. And their voices prevailed. ²⁴So Pilate gave sentence that their demand should be granted. ²⁵He released the man who had been thrown into prison for insurrection and murder, whom they asked for; but Jesus he delivered up to their will.

The Crucifixion of Jesus

26 And as they led him away, they seized one Simon of Cyre′ne, who was coming in from the country, and laid on him the cross, to carry it behind Jesus. ²⁷And there followed him a great multitude of the people, and of women who bewailed and lamented him. ²⁸But Jesus turning to them said, "Daughters of Jerusalem, do not weep for me, but weep for yourselves and for your children. ²⁹For behold, the days are coming when they will say, 'Blessed are the barren, and the wombs that never bore, and the breasts that never nursed!' ³⁰Then they will begin to say to the mountains, 'Fall on us'; and to the hills, 'Cover us.' ³¹For if they do this when the wood is green, what will happen when it is dry?" ‡

32 Two others also, who were criminals, were led away to be put to death with him. ³³And when they came to the place which is called The Skull, there they crucified him, and the criminals, one on

^m Here, or after verse 19, other ancient authorities add verse 17, *Now he was obliged to release one man to them at the festival.*
22:61: Lk 7:13; 22:34.
22:63–65: Mt 26:67–68; Mk 14:65; Jn 18:22–24.
22:66: Mt 26:57; Mk 14:53; Lk 22:54.
22:67–71: Mt 26:63–66; Mk 14:61–64; Jn 18:19–21.
22:70: Lk 23:3; Mt 27:11.
23:1: Mt 27:1–2; Mk 15:1; Jn 18:28.
23:2: Lk 20:25.
23:3: Mt 27:11–12; Mk 15:2–3; Jn 18:29–38; Lk 22:70.
23:4: Lk 23:14, 22, 41; Mt 27:24; Jn 19:4, 6; Acts 13:28.
23:8: Lk 9:9; Acts 4:27–28.
23:9: Mk 15:5.
23:11: Mk 15:17–19; Jn 19:2–3.
23:14: Lk 23:4, 22, 41.
23:16: Lk 23:22; Jn 19:12–14.
23:18–23: Mt 27:20–23; Mk 15:11–14; Acts 3:13–14; Jn 18:38–40; 19:14–15.
23:23–25: Mt 27:26; Mk 15:15.
23:26: Mt 27:32; Mk 15:21; Jn 19:17.
23:28–31: Lk 21:23–24; 19:41–44.
* 23:2: They purposely produce political charges, as these alone would interest Pilate.
† 23:14: Luke, writing for Gentiles, makes it clear that Pilate wanted to release Jesus.
‡ 23:31: One does not burn green wood. The meaning is that, if an innocent man is thus punished, what must the guilty (dry wood) expect?

the right and one on the left. [34]And Jesus said, "Father, forgive them; for they know not what they do." [n] And they cast lots to divide his garments. [35]And the people stood by, watching; but the rulers scoffed at him, saying, "He saved others; let him save himself, if he is the Christ of God, his Chosen One!" [36]The soldiers also mocked him, coming up and offering him vinegar, [37]and saying, "If you are the King of the Jews, save yourself!" [38]There was also an inscription over him, [o] "This is the King of the Jews."

39 One of the criminals who were hanged railed at him, saying, "Are you not the Christ? Save yourself and us!" [40]But the other rebuked him, saying, "Do you not fear God, since you are under the same sentence of condemnation? [41]And we indeed justly; for we are receiving the due reward of our deeds; but this man has done nothing wrong." [42]And he said, "Jesus, remember me when you come in your kingly power." [p] [43]And he said to him, "Truly, I say to you, today you will be with me in Paradise."

The Death of Jesus

44 It was now about the sixth hour, and there was darkness over the whole land [q] until the ninth hour, [45]while the sun's light failed; [r] and the curtain of the temple was torn in two. [46]Then Jesus, crying with a loud voice, said, "Father, into your hands I commit my spirit!" And having said this he breathed his last. [47]Now when the centurion saw what had taken place, he praised God, and said, "Certainly this man was innocent!" [48]And all the multitudes who assembled to see the sight, when they saw what had taken place, returned home beating their breasts. [49]And all his acquaintances and the women who had followed him from Galilee stood at a distance and saw these things.

The Burial of Jesus

50 Now there was a man named Joseph from the Jewish town of Arimathe′a. He was a member of the council, a good and righteous man, [51]who had not consented to their purpose and deed, and he was looking for the kingdom of God. [52]This man went to Pilate and asked for the body of Jesus. [53]Then he took it down and wrapped it in a linen shroud, and laid him in a rock-hewn tomb, where no one had ever yet been laid. [54]It was the day of Preparation, and the sabbath was beginning. [s] [55]The women who had come with him from Galilee followed, and saw the tomb, and how his body was laid; [56]then they returned, and prepared spices and ointments.

On the sabbath they rested according to the commandment.

The Resurrection of Jesus

24 But on the first day of the week, at early dawn, they went to the tomb, taking the spices which they had prepared. [2]And they found the stone rolled away from the tomb, [3]but when they went in they did not find the body. [t] [4]While they were perplexed about this, behold, two men stood by them in dazzling apparel; [5]and as they were frightened and bowed their faces to the ground, the men said to them, "Why do you seek the living among the dead? He is not here, but has risen. [u] [6]Remember how he told you, while he was still in Galilee, [7]that the Son of man must be delivered into the hands of sinful men, and be crucified, and on the third day rise." [8]And they remembered his words, [9]and returning from the tomb they told all this to the Eleven and to all the rest. [10]Now it was Mary Mag′dalene and Jo-an′na and Mary the mother of James and the other women with them who told this to the apostles; [11]but these words seemed to them an idle tale, and they did not believe them. [12]But Peter rose and ran to the tomb; stooping and looking in, he saw the linen cloths by themselves; and he went home wondering at what had happened. [v]

The Walk to Emmaus

13 That very day two of them were going to a village named Emma′us, about seven miles [w] from Jerusalem, [14]and talking with each other about all these things that had happened. [15]While they were talking and discussing together, Jesus himself drew near and went with them. [16]But their eyes were kept from recognizing him. [17]And he said to them, "What is this conversation which you are holding with each other as you walk?" And they stood still, looking sad. [18]Then one of them, named Cle′opas, answered him, "Are you the only visitor to Jerusalem who does not know the things that have happened there in these days?" [19]And he said to them, "What things?" And they said to him, "Concerning Jesus of Nazareth, who was a

[n] Other ancient authorities omit the sentence *And Jesus . . . what they do.*
[o] Other ancient authorities add *in letters of Greek and Latin and Hebrew.*
[p] Greek *kingdom.*
[q] Or *earth.*
[r] Or *the sun was eclipsed.* Other ancient authorities read *the sun was darkened.*
[s] Greek *was dawning.*
[t] Other ancient authorities add *of the Lord Jesus.*
[u] Other ancient authorities omit *He is not here, but has risen.*
[v] Other ancient authorities omit verse 12.
[w] Greek *sixty stadia;* some ancient authorities read *a hundred and sixty stadia.*
23:33–39: Mt 27:33–44; Mk 15:22–32; Jn 19:17–24.
23:34: Acts 7:60; Ps 22:18.
23:35: Lk 4:23.
23:36: Mk 15:23; Ps 69:21.
23:41: Lk 23:4, 14, 22.
23:43: 2 Cor 12:3; Rev 2:7.
23:44–49: Mt 27:45–56; Mk 15:33–41; Jn 19:25–30.
23:45: Ex 26:31–35; Heb 9:8; 10:19.
23:46: Ps 31:5.
23:49: Lk 8:1–3; 23:55–56; 24:10.
23:50–56: Mt 27:57–61; Mk 15:42–47; Jn 19:38–42; Acts 13:29.
23:56: Mk 16:1; Ex 12:16; 20:10.
24:1–9: Mt 28:1–8; Mk 16:1–7; Jn 20:1, 11–13.
24:6: Lk 9:22; 13:32–33.
24:10: Mk 16:1; Lk 8:1–3; Jn 20:2.
24:16: Jn 20:14; 21:4.

prophet mighty in deed and word before God and all the people, [20]and how our chief priests and rulers delivered him up to be condemned to death, and crucified him. [21]But we had hoped that he was the one to redeem Israel. Yes, and besides all this, it is now the third day since this happened. [22]Moreover, some women of our company amazed us. They were at the tomb early in the morning [23]and did not find his body; and they came back saying that they had even seen a vision of angels, who said that he was alive. [24]Some of those who were with us went to the tomb, and found it just as the women had said; but him they did not see." [25]And he said to them, "O foolish men, and slow of heart to believe all that the prophets have spoken! [26]Was it not necessary that the Christ should suffer these things and enter into his glory?" [27]And beginning with Moses and all the prophets, he interpreted to them in all the Scriptures the things concerning himself.

28 So they drew near to the village to which they were going. He appeared to be going further, [29]but they constrained him, saying, "Stay with us, for it is toward evening and the day is now far spent." So he went in to stay with them. [30]When he was at table with them, he took the bread and blessed and broke it, and gave it to them. [31]And their eyes were opened and they recognized him; and he vanished out of their sight. [32]They said to each other, "Did not our hearts burn within us while he talked to us on the road, while he opened to us the Scriptures?" [33]And they rose that same hour and returned to Jerusalem; and they found the Eleven gathered together and those who were with them, [34]who said, "The Lord has risen indeed, and has appeared to Simon!" [35]Then they told what had happened on the road, and how he was known to them in the breaking of the bread.

Jesus Appears to His Disciples

36 As they were saying this, Jesus himself stood among them, and said to them, "Peace to you." [x] [37]But they were startled and frightened, and supposed that they saw a spirit. [38]And he said to them, "Why are you troubled, and why do questionings rise in your hearts? [*] [39]See my hands and my feet, that it is I myself; handle me, and

see; for a spirit has not flesh and bones as you see that I have." [40]And when he had said this he showed them his hands and his feet. [y] [41]And while they still disbelieved for joy, and wondered, he said to them, "Have you anything here to eat?" [42]They gave him a piece of broiled fish, [43]and he took it and ate before them.

44 Then he said to them, "These are my words which I spoke to you, while I was still with you, that everything written about me in the law of Moses and the prophets and the psalms must be fulfilled." [45]Then he opened their minds to understand the Scriptures, [46]and said to them, "Thus it is written, that the Christ should suffer and on the third day rise from the dead, [47]and that repentance and forgiveness of sins should be preached in his name to all nations, [z] beginning from Jerusalem. [48]You are witnesses of these things. [49]And behold, I send the promise of my Father upon you; but stay in the city, until you are clothed with power from on high."

The Ascension of Jesus

50 Then he led them out as far as Beth′any, and lifting up his hands he blessed them. [51]While he blessed them, he parted from them, and was carried up into heaven. [a] [52]And they worshiped him, and [b] returned to Jerusalem with great joy, [53]and were continually in the temple blessing God.

---

[x] Other ancient authorities omit and said to them, "Peace to you."
[y] Other ancient authorities omit verse 40.
[z] Or nations. Beginning from Jerusalem you are witnesses.
[a] Other ancient authorities omit and was carried up into heaven.
[b] Other ancient authorities omit worshiped him, and.
24:19: Mt 21:11; Lk 7:16; 13:33; Acts 3:22.
24:24: Jn 20:3–10.
24:27: Lk 24:44–45; Acts 28:23; 1 Pet 1:11.
24:28: Mk 6:48.
24:30: Lk 9:16; 22:19.
24:34: 1 Cor 15:5.
24:36–43: Jn 20:19–20, 27; Jn 21:5, 9–13; 1 Cor 15:5; Acts 10:40–41.
24:39: 1 Jn 1:1.
24:44: Lk 24:26–27; Acts 28:23.
24:46: Hos 6:2; 1 Cor 15:3–4.
24:47: Acts 1:4–8; Mt 28:19.
24:49: Acts 2:1–4; Jn 14:26; 20:21–23.
24:51: Acts 1:9–11.
24:52–53: Acts 1:12–14.
* 24:38: Luke stresses this episode for the benefit of his Greek readers, for whom the resurrection of the body was both impossible and absurd; cf. Acts 17:32.

THE GOSPEL ACCORDING TO

JOHN

The Word Became Flesh

1 In the beginning was the Word, and the Word was with God, and the Word was God. * [2]He was in the beginning with God; [3]all things were made through him, and without him was not anything made that was made. [4]In him was life, [a] and the life was the light of men. [5]The light shines in the darkness, † and the darkness has not overcome it.

6 There was a man sent from God, whose name was John. [7]He came for testimony, to bear witness to the light, that all might believe through him. [8]He was not the light, but came to bear witness to the light.

9 The true light that enlightens every man was coming into the world. [10]He was in the world, and the world was made through him, yet the world knew him not. [11]He came to his own home, and his own people received him not. [12]But to all who received him, who believed in his name, he gave power to become children of God; [13]who were born, not of blood nor of the will of the flesh nor of the will of man, but of God.

14 And the Word became flesh and dwelt among us, full of grace and truth; we have beheld his glory, glory as of the only-begotten Son from the Father. [15](John bore witness to him, and cried, "This was he of whom I said, 'He who comes after me ranks before me, for he was before me.' ") [16]And from his fulness have we all received, grace upon grace. [17]For the law was given through Moses; grace and truth came through Jesus Christ. [18]No one has ever seen God; the only-begotten Son, [b] who is in the bosom of the Father, he has made him known.

The Testimony of John the Baptist

[19]And this is the testimony of John, when the Jews sent priests and Levites from Jerusalem to ask him, "Who are you?" [20]He confessed, he did not deny, but confessed, "I am not the Christ." [21]And they asked him, "What then? Are you Eli'jah?" He said, "I am not." "Are you the prophet?" And he answered, "No." [22]They said to him then, "Who are you? Let us have an answer for those who sent us. What do you say about yourself?" [23]He said, "I am the voice of one crying in the wilderness, 'Make straight the way of the Lord,' as the prophet Isaiah said."

24 Now they had been sent from the Pharisees. [25]They asked him, "Then why are you baptizing, if you are neither the Christ, nor Eli'jah, nor the prophet?" [26]John answered them, "I baptize with water; but among you stands one whom you do not know, [27]even he who comes after me, the thong of whose sandal I am not worthy to untie." [28]This took place in Beth'any beyond the Jordan, where John was baptizing.

The Lamb of God

29 The next day he saw Jesus coming toward him, and said, "Behold, the Lamb of God, who takes away the sin of the world! ‡ [30]This is he of whom I said, 'After me comes a man who ranks before me, for he was before me.' [31]I myself did not know him; but for this I came baptizing with water, that he might be revealed to Israel." [32]And John bore witness, "I saw the Spirit descend as a dove from heaven, and remain on him. [33]I myself did not know him; but he who sent me to baptize with water said to me, 'He on whom you see the Spirit descend and remain, this is he who baptizes with the Holy Spirit.' [34]And I have seen and have borne witness that this is the Son of God."

---

[a] Or *was not anything made. That which has been made was life in him.*
[b] Other ancient authorities read *God.*

1:1: Gen 1:1; 1 Jn 1:1; Rev 19:13; Jn 17:5.
1:3: Col 1:16; 1 Cor 8:6; Heb 1:2.
1:4: Jn 5:26; 11:25; 14:6.
1:5: Jn 9:5; 12:46.
1:6: Mk 1:4; Mt 3:1; Lk 3:3; Jn 1:19–23.
1:9: 1 Jn 2:8.
1:12: Gal 3:26; Jn 3:18; 1 Jn 5:13.
1:13: Jn 3:5; 1 Pet 1:23; Jas 1:18; 1 Jn 3:9.
1:14: Rom 1:3; Gal 4:4; Phil 2:7; 1 Tim 3:16; Heb 2:14; 1 Jn 4:2.
1:15: Jn 1:30.
1:16: Col 1:19; 2:9; Eph 1:23; Rom 5:21.
1:17: Jn 7:19.
1:18: Ex 33:20; Jn 6:26; 1 Jn 4:12; Jn 3:11.
1:19: Jn 1:6.
1:20: Jn 3:28.
1:21: Mt 11:14; 16:14; Mk 9:13; Mt 17:13; Deut 18:15, 18.
1:23: Is 40:3; Mk 1:3; Mt 3:3; Lk 3:4.
1:26–27: Mk 1:7–8; Mt 3:11; Lk 3:16.
1:28: Jn 3:26; 10:40.
1:29: Jn 1:36; Is 53:7; Acts 8:32; 1 Pet 1:19; Rev 5:6; 1 Jn 3:5.
1:30: Jn 1:15.
1:32: Mk 1:10; Mt 3:16; Lk 3:22.

* 1:1: John begins by giving his Gospel a theological background. By speaking at once of "the Word" he implies that his readers are familiar with the term. To Gentiles it indicated some form of divine revelation or self-expression. Jews would equate it with the divine Wisdom described in Proverbs, which already appears as something more than a divine quality and has some relationship with the visible world. In Sirach and Wisdom the idea is further developed. In the last-named book, Wisdom appears as a pre-existing person, taking part in the creation of the world and having a mission to reveal God to his creatures; cf. Wis 7:22—8:1.
† 1:5, *light ... darkness:* One of the familiar themes of the Gospel.
‡ 1:29: John applies to Jesus the Messianic prophecy of Isaiah 53:6–7, perhaps worded more explicitly by the evangelist in later years.

The First Disciples of Jesus

35 The next day again John was standing with two of his disciples; ³⁶and he looked at Jesus as he walked, and said, "Behold, the Lamb of God!" ³⁷The two disciples heard him say this, and they followed Jesus. ³⁸Jesus turned, and saw them following, and said to them, "What do you seek?" And they said to him, "Rabbi" (which means Teacher), "where are you staying?" ³⁹He said to them, "Come and see." They came and saw where he was staying; and they stayed with him that day, for it was about the tenth hour. ⁴⁰One of the two who heard John speak, and followed him, was Andrew, Simon Peter's brother. ⁴¹He first found his brother Simon, and said to him, "We have found the Messiah" (which means Christ). ⁴²He brought him to Jesus. Jesus looked at him, and said, "So you are Simon the son of John? You shall be called Ce′phas" (which means Peter ᶜ).

Jesus Calls Philip and Nathanael

43 The next day Jesus decided to go to Galilee. And he found Philip and said to him, "Follow me." ⁴⁴Now Philip was from Beth-sa′ida, the city of Andrew and Peter. ⁴⁵Philip found Nathan′a-el, and said to him, "We have found him of whom Moses in the law and also the prophets wrote, Jesus of Nazareth, the son of Joseph." ⁴⁶Nathan′a-el said to him, "Can anything good come out of Nazareth?" Philip said to him, "Come and see." ⁴⁷Jesus saw Nathan′a-el coming to him, and said of him, "Behold, an Israelite indeed, in whom is no guile!" ⁴⁸Nathan′a-el said to him, "How do you know me?" Jesus answered him, "Before Philip called you, when you were under the fig tree, I saw you." ⁴⁹Nathan′a-el answered him, "Rabbi, you are the Son of God! You are the King of Israel!" ⁵⁰Jesus answered him, "Because I said to you, I saw you under the fig tree, do you believe? You shall see greater things than these." ⁵¹And he said to him, "Truly, truly, I say to you, you will see heaven opened, and the angels of God ascending and descending upon the Son of man."

The Marriage at Cana

2 On the third day there was a marriage at Cana in Galilee, and the mother of Jesus was there; ²Jesus also was invited to the marriage, with his disciples. ³When the wine failed, the mother of Jesus said to him, "They have no wine." ⁴And Jesus said to her, "O woman, what have you to do with me? * My hour has not yet come." ⁵His mother said to the servants, "Do whatever he tells you." ⁶Now six stone jars were standing there, for the Jewish rites of purification, each holding twenty or thirty gallons. ⁷Jesus said to them, "Fill the jars with water." And they filled them up to the brim. ⁸He said to them, "Now draw some out, and take it to the steward of the feast." So they took it. ⁹When the steward of the feast tasted the water now become wine, and did not know where it came from (though the servants who had drawn the water knew), the steward of the feast called the bridegroom ¹⁰and said to him, "Every man serves the good wine first; and when men have drunk freely, then the poor wine; but you have kept the good wine until now." ¹¹This, the first of his signs, Jesus did at Cana in Galilee, and manifested his glory; and his disciples believed in him.

12 After this he went down to Caper′na-um, with his mother and his brethren † and his disciples; and there they stayed for a few days.

The Cleansing of the Temple

13 The Passover of the Jews was at hand, and Jesus went up to Jerusalem. ¹⁴In the temple he found those who were selling oxen and sheep and pigeons, and the money-changers at their business. ¹⁵And making a whip of cords, he drove them all, with the sheep and oxen, out of the temple; and he poured out the coins of the money-changers and overturned their tables. ¹⁶And he told those who sold the pigeons, "Take these things away; you shall not make my Father's house a house of trade." ¹⁷His disciples remembered that it was written, "Zeal for your house will consume me." ¹⁸The Jews then said to him, "What sign have you to show us for doing this?" ¹⁹Jesus answered them, "Destroy this temple, and in three days I will raise it up." ²⁰The Jews then said, "It has taken forty-six years to build this temple, and will you raise it up in three days?" ²¹But he spoke of the temple of his body. ²²When therefore he was raised from the dead, his disciples remembered that he had said this; and they believed the Scripture and the word which Jesus had spoken.

23 Now when he was in Jerusalem at the Passover feast, many believed in his name when they saw the signs which he did; ²⁴but Jesus did not

---

ᶜ From the word for *rock* in Aramaic and Greek, respectively.
1:35: Lk 7:18.
1:40–42: Mt 4:18–22; Mk 1:16–20; Lk 5:2–11.
1:41: Dan 9:25; Jn 4:25.
1:42: Jn 21:15–17; 1 Cor 15:5; Mt 16:18.
1:43: Mt 10:3; Jn 6:5; 12:21; 14:8.
1:45: Lk 24:27.
1:46: Jn 7:41; Mk 6:2.
1:49: Ps 2:7; Mk 15:32; Jn 12:13.
1:51: Lk 3:21; Gen 28:12.
2:1: Jn 4:46; 21:2.
2:3: Jn 19:26; Mk 3:31.
2:4: Mk 1:24; 5:7; Jn 7:6, 30; 8:20.
2:6: Mk 7:3; Jn 3:25.
2:11: Jn 2:23; 3:2; 4:54; 6:2.
2:12: Mt 4:13; Jn 7:3; Mk 3:31.
2:13: Jn 6:4; 11:55; Deut 16:1–6; Lk 2:41.
2:14–16: Mt 21:12–13; Mk 11:15–17; Lk 19:45–46.
2:16: Lk 2:49.
2:17: Ps 69:9.
2:18: Mk 11:28; Mt 21:23; Lk 20:2.
2:19: Mk 14:58; Acts 6:14.
2:21: 1 Cor 6:19; Jn 8:57.
2:22: Jn 12:16; 14:26.
* 2:4, *What have you to do with me?*: What is that to you or to me? While this expression always implies a divergence of view, the precise meaning is to be determined by the context, which here shows that it is not an unqualified refusal, still less a rebuke.
† 2:12, *brethren*: See note on Mt 12:46.

trust himself to them, [25]because he knew all men and needed no one to bear witness of man; for he himself knew what was in man.

Nicodemus Visits Jesus

3 Now there was a man of the Pharisees, named Nicode′mus, a ruler of the Jews. [2]This man came to Jesus [d] by night and said to him, "Rabbi, we know that you are a teacher come from God; for no one can do these signs that you do, unless God is with him." [3]Jesus answered him, "Truly, truly, I say to you, unless one is born anew, [e] he cannot see the kingdom of God." [4]Nicode′mus said to him, "How can a man be born when he is old? Can he enter a second time into his mother's womb and be born?" [5]Jesus answered, "Truly, truly, I say to you, unless one is born of water and the Spirit, he cannot enter the kingdom of God. [6]That which is born of the flesh is flesh, and that which is born of the Spirit is spirit. [f] [7]Do not marvel that I said to you, 'You must be born anew.' [e] [8]The wind [f] blows where it wills, and you hear the sound of it, but you do not know where it comes from or where it goes; so it is with every one who is born of the Spirit." [9]Nicode′mus said to him, "How can this be?" [10]Jesus answered him, "Are you a teacher of Israel, and yet you do not understand this? [11]Truly, truly, I say to you, we speak of what we know, and bear witness to what we have seen; but you do not receive our testimony. [12]If I have told you earthly things and you do not believe, how can you believe if I tell you heavenly things? [13]No one has ascended into heaven but he who descended from heaven, the Son of man. [g] [14]And as Moses lifted up the serpent in the wilderness, so must the Son of man be lifted up, [15]that whoever believes in him may have eternal life." [h]

16 For God so loved the world that he gave his only-begotten Son, that whoever believes in him should not perish but have eternal life. [17]For God sent the Son into the world, not to condemn the world, but that the world might be saved through him. [18]He who believes in him is not condemned; he who does not believe is condemned already, because he has not believed in the name of the only-begotten Son of God. [19]And this is the judgment, that the light has come into the world, and men loved darkness rather than light, because their deeds were evil. [20]For every one who does evil hates the light, and does not come to the light, lest his deeds should be exposed. [21]But he who does what is true comes to the light, that it may be clearly seen that his deeds have been wrought in God.

Jesus and John the Baptist

22 After this Jesus and his disciples went into the land of Judea; there he remained with them and baptized. * [23]John also was baptizing at Ae′non near Sa′lim, because there was much wa-

ter there; and people came and were baptized. [24]For John had not yet been put in prison. †

25 Now a discussion arose between John's disciples and a Jew over purifying. [26]And they came to John, and said to him, "Rabbi, he who was with you beyond the Jordan, to whom you bore witness, here he is, baptizing, and all are going to him." [27]John answered, "No one can receive anything except what is given him from heaven. [28]You yourselves bear me witness, that I said, I am not the Christ, but I have been sent before him. [29]He who has the bride is the bridegroom; the friend of the bridegroom, who stands and hears him, rejoices greatly at the bridegroom's voice; therefore this joy of mine is now full. [30]He must increase, but I must decrease." [i]

He Who Comes from Heaven

31 He who comes from above is above all; he who is of the earth belongs to the earth, and of the earth he speaks; he who comes from heaven is above all. [32]He bears witness to what he has seen and heard, yet no one receives his testimony; [33]he who receives his testimony sets his seal to this, that God is true. [34]For he whom God has sent utters the words of God, for it is not by measure that he gives the Spirit; [35]the Father loves the Son, and has given all things into his hand. [36]He who believes in the Son has eternal life; he who does not obey the Son shall not see life, but the wrath of God rests upon him.

Jesus and the Woman of Samaria

4 Now when the Lord knew that the Pharisees had heard that Jesus was making and baptizing more disciples than John [2](although Jesus him-

---

d Greek *him*.
e Or *from above*.
f The same Greek word means both *wind* and *spirit*.
g Other ancient authorities add *who is in heaven*.
h Some interpreters hold that the quotation continues through verse 21.
i Some interpreters hold that the quotation continues through verse 36.
2:25: Jn 1:47; 6:61; 13:11; Mk 2:8.
3:1: Jn 7:50; 19:39; Lk 23:13; Jn 7:26.
3:2: Jn 2:11; 7:31; 9:16; Acts 10:38.
3:3: Jn 1:13; 1 Pet 1:23; Jas 1:18; 1 Jn 3:9.
3:5: Ezek 36:25–27; Eph 5:26; Tit 3:5.
3:6: 1 Cor 15:50.
3:8: Ezek 37:9.
3:11: Jn 8:26; 1:18; 3:32.
3:13: Rom 10:6; Eph 4:9.
3:14: Num 21:9; Jn 8:28; 12:34.
3:16: Rom 5:8; 8:32; Eph 2:4; 1 Jn 4:9–10.
3:17: Jn 8:15; 12:47; Lk 19:10; 1 Jn 4:14.
3:19: Jn 1:4; 8:12; Eph 5:11, 13.
3:21: 1 Jn 1:6.
3:22: Jn 4:2.
3:24: Mk 1:14; 6:17–18.
3:26: Jn 1:7, 28.
3:27: 1 Cor 4:7.
3:28: Jn 1:20, 23.
3:29: Mk 2:19–20; Mt 25:1; Jn 15:11.
3:31: Jn 3:13; 8:23; 1 Jn 4:5.
3:32: Jn 3:11.
3:36: Jn 3:16; 5:24.
4:1: Jn 3:22.
* 3:22, *baptized*: A baptism like that of John. The time for baptism "in the Spirit" had not yet come.
† 3:24: From the other Gospels we learn that, after John was arrested, Jesus withdrew from Judea.

self did not baptize, but only his disciples), [3]he left Judea and departed again to Galilee. [4]He had to pass through Samar′ia. [5]So he came to a city of Samar′ia, called Sy′char, near the field that Jacob gave to his son Joseph. [6]Jacob's well was there, and so Jesus, wearied as he was with his journey, sat down beside the well. It was about the sixth hour.

[7] There came a woman of Samar′ia to draw water. Jesus said to her, "Give me a drink." [8]For his disciples had gone away into the city to buy food. [9]The Samaritan woman said to him, "How is it that you, a Jew, ask a drink of me, a woman of Samar′ia?" For Jews have no dealings with Samaritans. [10]Jesus answered her, "If you knew the gift of God, and who it is that is saying to you, 'Give me a drink,' you would have asked him and he would have given you living water." [11]The woman said to him, "Sir, you have nothing to draw with, and the well is deep; where do you get that living water? [12]Are you greater than our father Jacob, who gave us the well, and drank from it himself, and his sons, and his cattle?" [13]Jesus said to her, "Every one who drinks of this water will thirst again, [14]but whoever drinks of the water that I shall give him will never thirst; the water that I shall give him will become in him a spring of water welling up to eternal life." [15]The woman said to him, "Sir, give me this water, that I may not thirst, nor come here to draw."

[16] Jesus said to her, "Go, call your husband, and come here." [17]The woman answered him, "I have no husband." Jesus said to her, "You are right in saying, 'I have no husband'; [18]for you have had five husbands, and he whom you now have is not your husband; this you said truly." [19]The woman said to him, "Sir, I perceive that you are a prophet. [20]Our fathers worshiped on this mountain;* and you say that in Jerusalem is the place where men ought to worship." [21]Jesus said to her, "Woman, believe me, the hour is coming when neither on this mountain nor in Jerusalem will you worship the Father. [22]You worship what you do not know; we worship what we know, for salvation is from the Jews. [23]But the hour is coming, and now is, when the true worshipers will worship the Father in spirit and truth, for such the Father seeks to worship him. [24]God is spirit, and those who worship him must worship in spirit and truth." [25]The woman said to him, "I know that Messiah is coming (he who is called Christ); when he comes, he will show us all things." [26]Jesus said to her, "I who speak to you am he."

[27] Just then his disciples came. They marveled that he was talking with a woman, but none said, "What do you wish?" or, "Why are you talking with her?" [28]So the woman left her water jar, and went away into the city, and said to the people, [29]"Come, see a man who told me all that I ever did.

Can this be the Christ?" [30]They went out of the city and were coming to him.

[31] Meanwhile the disciples begged him, saying, "Rabbi, eat." [32]But he said to them, "I have food to eat of which you do not know." [33]So the disciples said to one another, "Has any one brought him food?" [34]Jesus said to them, "My food is to do the will of him who sent me, and to accomplish his work. [35]Do you not say, 'There are yet four months, then comes the harvest'? I tell you, lift up your eyes, and see how the fields are already white for harvest. [36]He who reaps receives wages, and gathers fruit for eternal life, so that sower and reaper may rejoice together. [37]For here the saying holds true, 'One sows and another reaps.' [38]I sent you to reap that for which you did not labor; others have labored, and you have entered into their labor."

[39] Many Samaritans from that city believed in him because of the woman's testimony, "He told me all that I ever did." [40]So when the Samaritans came to him, they asked him to stay with them; and he stayed there two days. [41]And many more believed because of his word. [42]They said to the woman, "It is no longer because of your words that we believe, for we have heard for ourselves, and we know that this is indeed the Savior of the world."

Jesus Departs for Galilee

[43] After the two days he departed to Galilee. [44]For Jesus himself testified that a prophet has no honor in his own country. [45]So when he came to Galilee, the Galileans welcomed him, having seen all that he had done in Jerusalem at the feast, for they too had gone to the feast.

Jesus Heals an Official's Son

[46] So he came again to Cana in Galilee, where he had made the water wine. And at Caper′na-um there was an official whose son was ill. [47]When he heard that Jesus had come from Judea to Galilee, he went and begged him to come down and heal his son, for he was at the point of death. [48]Jesus

4:4: Lk 9:52; 17:11.
4:5: Gen 33:19; 48:22; Josh 24:32.
4:9: Mt 10:5; Jn 8:48; Ezra 4:3–6.
4:10: Jn 7:37; Rev 21:6; 22:17.
4:14: Jn 6:35; 7:38.
4:15: Jn 6:34.
4:18: 2 Kings 17:24; Hos 2:7.
4:20: Deut 11:29; Josh 8:33; Lk 9:53.
4:21: Jn 5:25; 16:2, 32; Mal 1:11.
4:22: 2 Kings 17:28–41; Is 2:3; Rom 9:4.
4:24: Phil 3:3.
4:26: Jn 8:24.
4:29: Jn 7:26; Mt 12:23.
4:32: Mt 4:4.
4:34: Jn 5:30; 6:38; 17:4.
4:35: Lk 10:2; Mt 9:37.
4:37: Job 31:8; Mic 6:15.
4:42: 1 Jn 4:14; 2 Tim 1:10.
4:44: Mk 6:4; Mt 13:57.
4:46: Jn 2:1–11; Mt 8:5–10; Lk 7:2–10.
4:48: Dan 4:2; Mk 13:22; Acts 2:19; 4:30; Rom 15:19; Heb 2:4.
* 4:20, this mountain: Gerizim, on which the Samaritans worshiped.

therefore said to him, "Unless you see signs and wonders you will not believe." [49]The official said to him, "Sir, come down before my child dies." [50]Jesus said to him, "Go; your son will live." The man believed the word that Jesus spoke to him and went his way. [51]As he was going down, his servants met him and told him that his son was living. [52]So he asked them the hour when he began to mend, and they said to him, "Yesterday at the seventh hour the fever left him." [53]The father knew that was the hour when Jesus had said to him, "Your son will live"; and he himself believed, and all his household. [54]This was now the second sign that Jesus did when he had come from Judea to Galilee.

Jesus Heals on the Sabbath

5 After this there was a feast of the Jews, and Jesus went up to Jerusalem.

[2] Now there is in Jerusalem by the Sheep Gate a pool, in Hebrew called Beth-za′tha, [j] which has five porticoes. [3]In these lay a multitude of invalids, blind, lame, paralyzed. [k] [5]One man was there, who had been ill for thirty-eight years. [6]When Jesus saw him and knew that he had been lying there a long time, he said to him, "Do you want to be healed?" [7]The sick man answered him, "Sir, I have no man to put me into the pool when the water is troubled, and while I am going another steps down before me." [8]Jesus said to him, "Rise, take up your pallet, and walk." [9]And at once the man was healed, and he took up his pallet and walked.

Now that day was the sabbath. [10]So the Jews said to the man who was cured, "It is the sabbath, it is not lawful for you to carry your pallet." [11]But he answered them, "The man who healed me said to me, 'Take up your pallet, and walk.' " [12]They asked him, "Who is the man who said to you, 'Take up your pallet, and walk'?" [13]Now the man who had been healed did not know who it was, for Jesus had withdrawn, as there was a crowd in the place. [14]Afterward, Jesus found him in the temple, and said to him, "See, you are well! Sin no more, that nothing worse befall you." [15]The man went away and told the Jews that it was Jesus who had healed him. [16]And this was why the Jews persecuted Jesus, because he did this on the sabbath. [17]But Jesus answered them, "My Father is working still, and I am working." [18]This was why the Jews sought all the more to kill him, because he not only broke the sabbath * but also called God his Father, making himself equal with God.

The Authority of the Son

[19] Jesus said to them, "Truly, truly, I say to you, the Son can do nothing of his own accord, but only what he sees the Father doing; for whatever he does, that the Son does likewise. [20]For the Father loves the Son, and shows him all that he himself is doing; and greater works than these

will he show him, that you may marvel. [21]For as the Father raises the dead and gives them life, so also the Son gives life to whom he will. [22]The Father judges no one, but has given all judgment to the Son, [23]that all may honor the Son, even as they honor the Father. He who does not honor the Son does not honor the Father who sent him. [24]Truly, truly, I say to you, he who hears my word and believes him who sent me, has eternal life; he does not come into judgment, but has passed from death to life.

[25] "Truly, truly, I say to you, the hour is coming, and now is, when the dead will hear the voice of the Son of God, and those who hear will live. [26]For as the Father has life in himself, so he has granted the Son also to have life in himself, [27]and has given him authority to execute judgment, because he is the Son of man. [28]Do not marvel at this; for the hour is coming when all who are in the tombs will hear his voice [29]and come forth, those who have done good, to the resurrection of life, and those who have done evil, to the resurrection of judgment.

The Testimony to Jesus

[30] "I can do nothing on my own authority; as I hear, I judge; and my judgment is just, because I seek not my own will but the will of him who sent me. [31]If I bear witness to myself, my testimony is not true; [32]there is another who bears witness to me, and I know that the testimony which he bears to me is true. [33]You sent to John, and he has borne witness to the truth. [34]Not that the testimony which I receive is from man; but I say this that you may be saved. [35]He was a burning and shining lamp, and you were willing to rejoice for a while in his light. [36]But the testimony which I have is greater than that of John; for the works which the Father has granted me to accomplish, these very works which I am doing, bear me

---

[j] Other ancient authorities read *Bethesda*, others *Bethsaida*.
[k] Other ancient authorities insert, wholly or in part, *waiting for the moving of the water;* [4]*for an angel of the Lord went down at certain seasons into the pool, and troubled the water; whoever stepped in first after the troubling of the water was healed of whatever disease he had.*
4:53: Acts 11:14.
4:54: Jn 2:11.
5:2: Neh 3:1; 12:39.
5:8: Mk 2:11; Mt 9:6; Lk 5:24.
5:10: Neh 13:19; Jer 17:21; Jn:7:23; 9:16; Mk 2:24.
5:14: Mk 2:5.
5:17: Gen 2:3.
5:18: Jn 7:1; 10:33.
5:19: Jn 5:30; 8:28; 14:10.
5:20: Jn 14:12.
5:21: Rom 4:17; 8:11; Jn 11:25.
5:23: Lk 10:16; 1 Jn 2:23.
5:24: Jn 3:18.
5:25: Jn 4:21; 16:2, 32.
5:29: Dan 12:2; Acts 24:15; Jn 11:24; Mt 25:46; 1 Cor 15:52.
5:30: Jn 5:19; 8:16; 6:38.
5:31-37: Jn 8:14-18.
5:33: Jn 1:7, 19.
5:34: 1 Jn 5:9.
5:36: Jn 10:25; 14:11; 15:24; Mt 11:4.
* 5:18, *broke the sabbath*: i.e., broke the sabbath as interpreted by them; see note on Mt 12:14.

witness that the Father has sent me. [37]And the Father who sent me has himself borne witness to me. His voice you have never heard, his form you have never seen; [38]and you do not have his word abiding in you, for you do not believe him whom he has sent. [39]You search the Scriptures, because you think that in them you have eternal life; and it is they that bear witness to me; [40]yet you refuse to come to me that you may have life. [41]I do not receive glory from men. [42]But I know that you have not the love of God within you. [43]I have come in my Father's name, and you do not receive me; if another comes in his own name, him you will receive. [44]How can you believe, who receive glory from one another and do not seek the glory that comes from the only God? [45]Do not think that I shall accuse you to the Father; it is Moses who accuses you, on whom you set your hope. [46]If you believed Moses, you would believe me, for he wrote of me. [47]But if you do not believe his writings, how will you believe my words?"

Feeding the Five Thousand

6 After this Jesus went to the other side of the Sea of Galilee, which is the Sea of Tibe'ri-as. [2]And a multitude followed him, because they saw the signs which he did on those who were diseased. [3]Jesus went up into the hills, and there sat down with his disciples. [4]Now the Passover, the feast of the Jews, was at hand. [5]Lifting up his eyes, then, and seeing that a multitude was coming to him, Jesus said to Philip, "How are we to buy bread, so that these people may eat?" [6]This he said to test him, for he himself knew what he would do. [7]Philip answered him, "Two hundred denarii [1] would not buy enough bread for each of them to get a little." [8]One of his disciples, Andrew, Simon Peter's brother, said to him, [9]"There is a lad here who has five barley loaves and two fish; but what are they among so many?" [10]Jesus said, "Make the people sit down." Now there was much grass in the place; so the men sat down, in number about five thousand. [11]Jesus then took the loaves, and when he had given thanks, he distributed them to those who were seated; so also the fish, as much as they wanted. [12]And when they had eaten their fill, he told his disciples, "Gather up the fragments left over, that nothing may be lost." [13]So they gathered them up and filled twelve baskets with fragments from the five barley loaves, left by those who had eaten. [14]When the people saw the sign which he had done, they said, "This is indeed the prophet who is to come into the world!"

[15]Perceiving then that they were about to come and take him by force to make him king, Jesus withdrew again to the hills by himself.

Jesus Walks on the Sea

[16]When evening came, his disciples went down to the sea, [17]got into a boat, and started across the sea to Caper'na-um. It was now dark, and Jesus had not yet come to them. [18]The sea rose because a strong wind was blowing. [19]When they had rowed about three or four miles, [m] they saw Jesus walking on the sea and drawing near to the boat. They were frightened, [20]but he said to them, "It is I; do not be afraid." [21]Then they were glad to take him into the boat, and immediately the boat was at the land to which they were going.

The Bread from Heaven

22 On the next day the people who remained on the other side of the sea saw that there had been only one boat there, and that Jesus had not entered the boat with his disciples, but that his disciples had gone away alone. [23]However, boats from Tibe'ri-as came near the place where they ate the bread after the Lord had given thanks. [24]So when the people saw that Jesus was not there, nor his disciples, they themselves got into the boats and went to Caper'na-um, seeking Jesus.

25 When they found him on the other side of the sea, they said to him, "Rabbi, when did you come here?" [26]Jesus answered them, "Truly, truly, I say to you, you seek me, not because you saw signs, but because you ate your fill of the loaves. [27]Do not labor for the food which perishes, but for the food which endures to eternal life, which the Son of man will give to you; for on him has God the Father set his seal." [28]Then they said to him, "What must we do, to be doing the works of God?" [29]Jesus answered them, "This is the work of God, that you believe in him whom he has sent." [30]So they said to him, "Then what sign do you do, that we may see, and believe you? What work do you perform? [31]Our fathers ate the manna in the wilderness; as it is written, 'He gave them bread from heaven to eat.'" [32]Jesus then said to them, "Truly, truly, I say to you, it was not Moses who gave you the bread from heaven; my Father gives you the true bread from heaven. [33]For the bread of God is that which comes down from heaven, and gives life to the world." [34]They said to him, "Lord, give us this bread always."

---

[1] The denarius was a day's wage for a laborer.
[m] Greek *twenty-five or thirty stadia.*
5:39: Lk 24:27; Acts 13:27.
5:43: Mt 24:5.
5:45: Jn 9:28; Rom 2:17.
5:47: Lk 16:29, 31.
6:1–13: Mt 14:13–21; Mk 6:32–44; Lk 9:10–17.
6:5: Jn 1:43; 12:21.
6:8: Jn 1:40; 12:22.
6:9: Jn 21:9–13.
6:14: Mt 21:11.
6:15: Jn 6:3; 18:36.
6:16–21: Mt 14:22–27; Mk 6:45–51.
6:27: Is 55:2.
6:29: 1 Thess 1:3; 1 Jn 3:23.
6:30: Mt 12:38; Mk 8:11.
6:31: Ex 16:4, 15; Num 11:8; Neh 9:15; Ps 78:24; 105:40.
6:34: Jn 4:15; Mt 6:11.

35 Jesus said to them, "I am the bread of life; he who comes to me shall not hunger, and he who believes in me shall never thirst. [36]But I said to you that you have seen me and yet do not believe. [37]All that the Father gives me will come to me; and him who comes to me I will not cast out. [38]For I have come down from heaven, not to do my own will, but the will of him who sent me; [39]and this is the will of him who sent me, that I should lose nothing of all that he has given me, but raise it up at the last day. [40]For this is the will of my Father, that every one who sees the Son and believes in him should have eternal life; and I will raise him up at the last day."

41 The Jews then murmured at him, because he said, "I am the bread which came down from heaven." [42]They said, "Is not this Jesus, the son of Joseph, whose father and mother we know? How does he now say, 'I have come down from heaven'?" [43]Jesus answered them, "Do not murmur among yourselves. [44]No one can come to me unless the Father who sent me draws him; and I will raise him up at the last day. [45]It is written in the prophets, 'And they shall all be taught by God.' Every one who has heard and learned from the Father comes to me. [46]Not that any one has seen the Father except him who is from God; he has seen the Father. [47]Truly, truly, I say to you, he who believes has eternal life. [48]I am the bread of life. [49]Your fathers ate the manna in the wilderness, and they died. [50]This is the bread which comes down from heaven, that a man may eat of it and not die. [51]I am the living bread * which came down from heaven; if any one eats of this bread, he will live for ever; and the bread which I shall give for the life of the world is my flesh."

52 The Jews then disputed among themselves, saying, "How can this man give us his flesh to eat?" † [53]So Jesus said to them, "Truly, truly, I say to you, unless you eat the flesh of the Son of man and drink his blood, you have no life in you; [54]he who eats my flesh and drinks my blood has eternal life, and I will raise him up at the last day. [55]For my flesh is food indeed, and my blood is drink indeed. [56]He who eats my flesh and drinks my blood abides in me, and I in him. [57]As the living Father sent me, and I live because of the Father, so he who eats me will live because of me. [58]This is the bread which came down from heaven, not such as the fathers ate and died; he who eats this bread will live for ever." [59]This he said in the synagogue, as he taught at Caper'na-um.

The Words of Eternal Life

60 Many of his disciples, when they heard it, said, "This is a hard saying; who can listen to it?" [61]But Jesus, knowing in himself that his disciples murmured at it, said to them, "Do you take offense at this? [62]Then what if you were to see the Son of man ascending where he was before? ‡ [63]It is the Spirit that gives life, the flesh is of no avail; the words that I have spoken to you are Spirit and life. [64]But there are some of you that do not believe." For Jesus knew from the first who those were that did not believe, and who it was that would betray him. [65]And he said, "This is why I told you that no one can come to me unless it is granted him by the Father."

66 After this many of his disciples drew back and no longer walked with him. [67]Jesus said to the Twelve, "Will you also go away?" [68]Simon Peter answered him, "Lord, to whom shall we go? You have the words of eternal life; [69]and we have believed, and have come to know, that you are the Holy One of God." [70]Jesus answered them, "Did I not choose you, the Twelve, and one of you is a devil?" [71]He spoke of Judas the son of Simon Iscariot, for he, one of the Twelve, was to betray him.

The Unbelief of Jesus' Brethren

7 After this Jesus went about in Galilee; he would not go about in Judea, because the Jews [n] sought to kill him. [2]Now the Jews' feast of Tabernacles was at hand. [3]So his brethren § said to him, "Leave here and go to Judea, that your disciples may see the works you are doing. [4]For no man works in secret if he seeks to be known openly. If you do these things, show yourself to the world." [5]For even his brethren did not believe in him. [6]Jesus said to them, "My time has not yet come, but your time is always here. [7]The world cannot hate you, but it hates me because I testify of it that its works are evil. [8]Go to

[n] Or *Judeans*.
6:35: Jn 6:48–50; 4:14.
6:37: Jn 17:2.
6:38: Jn 4:34; 5:30.
6:39: Jn 17:12; 18:9.
6:40: Jn 5:29; 11:24; 6:54.
6:42: Lk 4:22; Jn 7:27.
6:44: Jer 31:3; Hos 11:4; Jn 12:32; 6:65.
6:45: 1 Thess 4:9; 1 Jn 2:27; Is 54:13.
6:46: Jn 1:18.
6:52: Jn 3:4; 4:9.
6:56: Jn 15:4; 1 Jn 3:24; 4:15.
6:58: Jn 6:41, 51.
6:59: Jn 6:25.
6:61: Mt 11:6.
6:62: Jn 3:13; 17:5.
6:63: 2 Cor 3:6; Jn 6:68.
6:64: Jn 2:25.
6:65: Jn 6:44; 3:27.
6:68–69: Mk 8:27–30.
6:70: Jn 15:16, 19.
6:71: Jn 13:2, 27; 17:12.
7:2: Lev 23:34; Deut 16:16.
7:3: Mk 3:21, 31; Mt 12:46.
7:6: Mt 26:18; Jn 2:4; 7:30.
7:7: Jn 15:18–21.

* 6:51: Jesus is the "living bread" both as Word of God (verses 32ff.) and as sacrificial victim for the salvation of man.
† 6:52: A natural question to ask. Jesus answers, not by explaining it away, but by reemphasizing the reality, though not, of course, in the crude sense implied in their question.
‡ 6:62: When Jesus ascends into heaven they will know that he spoke the truth.
§ 7:3, *brethren*: See note on Mt 12:46.

the feast yourselves; I am not° going up to this feast, for my time has not yet fully come." ⁹So saying, he remained in Galilee.

Jesus at the Feast of Tabernacles

10 But after his brethren had gone up to the feast, then he also went up, not publicly but in private. ¹¹The Jews were looking for him at the feast, and saying, "Where is he?" ¹²And there was much muttering about him among the people. While some said, "He is a good man," others said, "No, he is leading the people astray." ¹³Yet for fear of the Jews no one spoke openly of him.

14 About the middle of the feast Jesus went up into the temple and taught. ¹⁵The Jews marveled at it, saying, "How is it that this man has learning,ᴾ when he has never studied?" ¹⁶So Jesus answered them, "My teaching is not mine, but his who sent me; ¹⁷if any man's will is to do his will, he shall know whether the teaching is from God or whether I am speaking on my own authority. ¹⁸He who speaks on his own authority seeks his own glory; but he who seeks the glory of him who sent him is true, and in him there is no falsehood. ¹⁹Did not Moses give you the law? Yet none of you keeps the law. Why do you seek to kill me?" ²⁰The people answered, "You have a demon! Who is seeking to kill you?" ²¹Jesus answered them, "I did one deed, and you all marvel at it. ²²Moses gave you circumcision (not that it is from Moses, but from the fathers), and you circumcise a man upon the sabbath. ²³If on the sabbath a man receives circumcision, so that the law of Moses may not be broken, are you angry with me because on the sabbath I made a man's whole body well? ²⁴Do not judge by appearances, but judge with right judgment."

Is This the Christ?

25 Some of the people of Jerusalem therefore said, "Is not this the man whom they seek to kill? ²⁶And here he is, speaking openly, and they say nothing to him! Can it be that the authorities really know that this is the Christ? ²⁷Yet we know where this man comes from; and when the Christ appears, no one will know where he comes from." ²⁸So Jesus proclaimed, as he taught in the temple, "You know me, and you know where I come from? But I have not come of my own accord; he who sent me is true, and him you do not know. ²⁹I know him, for I come from him, and he sent me." ³⁰So they sought to arrest him; but no one laid hands on him, because his hour had not yet come. ³¹Yet many of the people believed in him; they said, "When the Christ appears, will he do more signs than this man has done?"

Officers Are Sent to Arrest Jesus

32 The Pharisees heard the crowd thus muttering about him, and the chief priests and Pharisees sent officers to arrest him. ³³Jesus then said, "I shall be with you a little longer, and then I go to him who sent me; ³⁴you will seek me and you will not find me; where I am you cannot come." ³⁵The Jews said to one another, "Where does this man intend to go that we shall not find him? Does he intend to go to the Dispersion among the Greeks and teach the Greeks? ³⁶What does he mean by saying, 'You will seek me and you will not find me,' and, 'Where I am you cannot come'?"

Rivers of Living Water

37 On the last day of the feast, the great day, Jesus stood up and proclaimed, "If any one thirst, let him come to me and drink. ³⁸He who believes in me, as �q the Scripture has said, 'Out of his heart shall flow rivers of living water.' " ³⁹Now this he said about the Spirit, which those who believed in him were to receive; for as yet the Spirit had not been given, because Jesus was not yet glorified.

Division among the People

40 When they heard these words, some of the people said, "This is really the prophet." ⁴¹Others said, "This is the Christ." But some said, "Is the Christ to come from Galilee? ⁴²Has not the Scripture said that the Christ is descended from David, and comes from Bethlehem, the village where David was?" ⁴³So there was a division among the people over him. ⁴⁴Some of them wanted to arrest him, but no one laid hands on him.

The Authorities and
the Woman Caught in Adultery

45 The officers then went back to the chief priests and Pharisees, who said to them, "Why did you not bring him?" ⁴⁶The officers answered, "No man ever spoke like this man!" ⁴⁷The Pharisees answered them, "Are you led astray, you also? ⁴⁸Have any of the authorities or of the Pharisees believed in him? ⁴⁹But this crowd, who do not know the law, are accursed." ⁵⁰Nicode′mus, who had gone to him before, and who was one of them, said to them, ⁵¹"Does our law judge a man

° Other ancient authorities add yet.
ᴾ Or this man knows his letters.
 q Or let him come to me, and let him who believes in me drink. As. . . .
7:12: Jn 7:40–43.
7:13: Jn 19:38; 20:19.
7:19: Jn 1:17.
7:20: Jn 8:48; 10:20; Mt 11:18; Mk 3:22.
7:21: Jn 5:2–9.
7:22: Lev 12:3; Gen 17:10; 21:4.
7:23: Mk 3:5; Lk 13:12; 14:4.
7:24: Jn 8:15; Is 11:3; Zech 7:9.
7:27: Jn 6:42; 7:41; 9:29.
7:28: Jn 8:42.
7:29: Jn 8:55; 17:25; Mt 11:27.
7:30: Jn 7:44; 10:39; Mk 12:12; Jn 8:20.
7:31: Jn 8:30; 10:42; 11:45.
7:33: Jn 8:21; 12:35; 13:33; 14:19; 16:16–19.
7:35: Jas 1:1; 1 Pet 1:1; Jn 12:20; Acts 11:20.
7:37: Lev 23:36; Jn 4:10, 14.
7:38: Is 44:3; 55:1; 58:11.
7:39: Jn 20:22; 12:23.
7:40: Jn 1:21; Mt 21:11.
7:42: Mic 5:2; Mt 1:1; Lk 2:4.
7:44: Jn 7:30; 10:39.
7:46: Mt 7:28.
7:50: Jn 3:1; 19:39.
7:51: Deut 17:6; Ex 23:1.

without first giving him a hearing and learning what he does?" [52]They replied, "Are you from Galilee too? Search and you will see that no prophet is to rise from Galilee." * [53]They went each to his

8 own house, [1]but Jesus went to the Mount of Olives. [2]Early in the morning he came again to the temple; all the people came to him, and he sat down and taught them. [3]The scribes and the Pharisees brought a woman who had been caught in adultery, and placing her in their midst [4]they said to him, "Teacher, this woman has been caught in the act of adultery. [5]Now in the law Moses commanded us to stone such. What do you say about her?" [6]This they said to test him, that they might have some charge to bring against him. Jesus bent down and wrote with his finger on the ground. [7]And as they continued to ask him, he stood up and said to them, "Let him who is without sin among you be the first to throw a stone at her." [8]And once more he bent down and wrote with his finger on the ground. [9]But when they heard it, they went away, one by one, beginning with the eldest, and Jesus was left alone with the woman standing before him. [10]Jesus looked up and said to her, "Woman, where are they? Has no one condemned you?" [11]She said, "No one, Lord." And Jesus said, "Neither do I condemn you; go, and do not sin again." [r]

Jesus and the Light of the World

12 Again Jesus spoke to them, saying, "I am the light of the world; he who follows me will not walk in darkness, but will have the light of life." [13]The Pharisees then said to him, "You are bearing witness to yourself; your testimony is not true." [14]Jesus answered, "Even if I do bear witness to myself, my testimony is true, for I know where I have come from and where I am going, but you do not know where I come from or where I am going. [15]You judge according to the flesh, I judge no one. [16]Yet even if I do judge, my judgment is true, for it is not I alone that judge, but I and he [s] who sent me. [17]In your law it is written that the testimony of two men is true; [18]I bear witness to myself, and the Father who sent me bears witness to me." [19]They said to him therefore, "Where is your Father?" Jesus answered, "You know neither me nor my Father; if you knew me, you would know my Father also." [20]These words he spoke in the treasury, as he taught in the temple; but no one arrested him, because his hour had not yet come.

Jesus Alludes to His Death

21 Again he said to them, "I go away, and you will seek me and die in your sin; [†] where I am going, you cannot come." [22]Then said the Jews, "Will he kill himself, since he says, 'Where I am going, you cannot come'?" [23]He said to them, "You are from below, I am from above; you are of this world, I am not of this world. [24]I told you that you

would die in your sins, for you will die in your sins unless you believe that I am he." [25]They said to him, "Who are you?" Jesus said to them, "Even what I have told you from the beginning. [t] [26]I have much to say about you and much to judge; but he who sent me is true, and I declare to the world what I have heard from him." [27]They did not understand that he spoke to them of the Father. [28]So Jesus said, "When you have lifted up the Son of man, then you will know that I am he, and that I do nothing on my own authority but speak thus as the Father taught me. [29]And he who sent me is with me; he has not left me alone, for I always do what is pleasing to him." [30]As he spoke thus, many believed in him.

True Disciples of Jesus

31 Jesus then said to the Jews who had believed in him, "If you continue in my word, you are truly my disciples, [32]and you will know the truth, and the truth will make you free." [33]They answered him, "We are descendants of Abraham, and have never been in bondage to any one. How is it that you say, 'You will be made free'?"

34 Jesus answered them, "Truly, truly, I say to you, every one who commits sin is a slave to sin. [35]The slave does not continue in the house for ever; the son continues for ever. [36]So if the Son makes you free, you will be free indeed. [37]I know that you are descendants of Abraham; yet you seek to kill me, because my word finds no place in you. [38]I speak of what I have seen with my Father, and you do what you have heard from your father."

Jesus and Abraham

39 They answered him, "Abraham is our father." Jesus said to them, "If you were Abraham's children, you would do what Abraham did, [40]but

---

[r] Some ancient authorities insert 7:53—8:11 either at the end of this Gospel or after Luke 21:38, with variations of the text. Others omit it altogether.
[s] Other ancient authorities read *the Father*.
[t] Or *Why do I talk to you at all?*
7:52: 2 Kings 14:25.
8:12: Jn 9:5; 12:35; 1.4.
8:13–18: Jn 5:31–39.
8:15: Jn 7:24; 3.17.
8:16: Jn 5:30.
8:17: Deut 19:15; Mt 18:16.
8:19: Jn 14:7.
8:20: Mk 12:41; Jn 7:30.
8:21–22: Jn 7:33–36.
8:23: Jn 3:31; 17:14; 1 Jn 4:5.
8:24: Jn 8:28; 4:26; 13:19; Mk 13:6.
8:28: Jn 3:14; 12:32.
8:30: Jn 7:31; 10:42; 11:45.
8:31: Jn 15:7; 2 Jn 9.
8:32: 2 Cor 3:17; Gal 5:1.
8:33: Mt 3:9; Gal 3:7.
8:34: Rom 6:16; 2 Pet 2:19.
8:35: Gen 21:10; Gal 4:30.
* 7:53—8:11: This passage, though absent from some of the most ancient manuscripts, is regarded as inspired and canonical by the Church. The style suggests that it is not by St. John, and that it belongs to the Synoptic tradition.
† 8:21, *die in your sin:* Theirs is that sin against the truth which is the sin against the Spirit; cf. Mt 12:31.

now you seek to kill me, a man who has told you the truth which I heard from God; this is not what Abraham did. [41]You do the works of your father." They said to him, "We were not born of fornication; we have one Father, even God." * [42]Jesus said to them, "If God were your Father, you would love me, for I proceeded and came forth from God; I came not of my own accord, but he sent me. [43]Why do you not understand what I say? It is because you cannot bear to hear my word. [44]You are of your father the devil, and your will is to do your father's desires. He was a murderer from the beginning, and has nothing to do with the truth, because there is no truth in him. When he lies, he speaks according to his own nature, for he is a liar and the father of lies. [45]But, because I tell the truth, you do not believe me. [46]Which of you convicts me of sin? If I tell the truth, why do you not believe me? [47]He who is of God hears the words of God; the reason why you do not hear them is that you are not of God."

48 The Jews answered him, "Are we not right in saying that you are a Samaritan and have a demon?" [49]Jesus answered, "I have not a demon; but I honor my Father, and you dishonor me. [50]Yet I do not seek my own glory; there is One who seeks it and he will be the judge. [51]Truly, truly, I say to you, if any one keeps my word, he will never see death." [52]The Jews said to him, "Now we know that you have a demon. Abraham died, as did the prophets; and you say, 'If any one keeps my word, he will never taste death.' [53]Are you greater than our father Abraham, who died? And the prophets died! Who do you claim to be?" [54]Jesus answered, "If I glorify myself, my glory is nothing; it is my Father who glorifies me, of whom you say that he is your God. [55]But you have not known him; I know him. If I said, I do not know him, I should be a liar like you; but I do know him and I keep his word. [56]Your father Abraham rejoiced that he was to see my day; he saw it † and was glad." [57]The Jews then said to him, "You are not yet fifty years old, and have you seen Abraham?" u [58]Jesus said to them, "Truly, truly, I say to you, before Abraham was, I am." ‡ [59]So they took up stones to throw at him; but Jesus hid himself, and went out of the temple.

Healing of the Blind Man

9 As he passed by, he saw a man blind from his birth. [2]And his disciples asked him, "Rabbi, who sinned, this man or his parents, that he was born blind?" [3]Jesus answered, "It was not that this man sinned, or his parents, but that the works of God might be made manifest in him.§ [4]We must work the works of him who sent me, while it is day; night comes, when no one can work. [5]As long as I am in the world, I am the light of the world." [6]As he said this, he spat on the ground and made clay of the spittle and

anointed the man's eyes with the clay, [7]saying to him, "Go, wash in the pool of Silo′am" (which means Sent). So he went and washed and came back seeing. [8]The neighbors and those who had seen him before as a beggar, said, "Is not this the man who used to sit and beg?" [9]Some said, "It is he"; others said, "No, but he is like him." He said, "I am the man." [10]They said to him, "Then how were your eyes opened?" [11]He answered, "The man called Jesus made clay and anointed my eyes and said to me, 'Go to Silo′am and wash'; so I went and washed and received my sight." [12]They said to him, "Where is he?" He said, "I do not know."

The Pharisees Investigate the Healing

13 They brought to the Pharisees the man who had formerly been blind. [14]Now it was a sabbath day when Jesus made the clay and opened his eyes. [15]The Pharisees again asked him how he had received his sight. And he said to them, "He put clay on my eyes, and I washed, and I see." [16]Some of the Pharisees said, "This man is not from God, for he does not keep the sabbath." But others said, "How can a man who is a sinner do such signs?" There was a division among them. [17]So they again said to the blind man, "What do you say about him, since he has opened your eyes?" He said, "He is a prophet."

18 The Jews did not believe that he had been blind and had received his sight, until they called the parents of the man who had received his sight, [19]and asked them, "Is this your son, who you say was born blind? How then does he now see?" [20]His parents answered, "We know that this is our son, and that he was born blind; [21]but how he now sees we do not know, nor do we know who opened his eyes. Ask him; he is of age, he will speak for himself." [22]His parents said this because they feared the Jews, for the Jews had already agreed that if any one should confess him to be Christ, he

---

u Other ancient authorities read *has Abraham seen you?*
8:41: Deut 32:6; Is 63:16; 64:8.
8:42: Jn 13:3; 16:28.
8:44: 1 Jn 3:8, 15; Gen 3:4; 1 Jn 2:4; Mt 12:34.
8:46: 1 Jn 3:5; Jn 18:37.
8:48: Jn 7:20; 10:20; 4:9.
8:53: Jn 4:12.
8:56: Mt 13:17; Heb 11:13.
8:57: Jn 2:20.
8:58: Jn 1:1; 17:5, 24.
8:59: Jn 10:31; 11:8.
9:2: Lk 13:2; Acts 28:4; Ezek 18:20; Ex 20:5.
9:3: Jn 11:4.
9:4: Jn 11:9; 12:35.
9:5: Jn 1:4; 8:12; 12:46.
9:6: Mk 7:33; 8:23.
9:7: Lk 13:4.
9:16: Mt 12:2; Jn 5:9; 7:43; 10:19.
9:22: Jn 7:13; 12:42; Lk 6:22.
* 8:41: They mean, "We are not idolaters," and protest their fidelity to God their Father; see notes on Rev 14:4 and 17:2.
† 8:56, *he saw it* either in prophetic vision while on earth or by some special privilege after death.
‡ 8:58: The present tense indicates Christ's eternal existence as God.
§ 9:3: Jesus explains in advance the purpose of the miracle.

was to be put out of the synagogue. ²³Therefore his parents said, "He is of age, ask him."

24 So for the second time they called the man who had been blind, and said to him, "Give God the praise; we know that this man is a sinner." ²⁵He answered, "Whether he is a sinner, I do not know; one thing I know, that though I was blind, now I see." ²⁶They said to him, "What did he do to you? How did he open your eyes?" ²⁷He answered them, "I have told you already, and you would not listen. Why do you want to hear it again? Do you too want to become his disciples?" ²⁸And they reviled him, saying, "You are his disciple, but we are disciples of Moses. ²⁹We know that God has spoken to Moses, but as for this man, we do not know where he comes from." ³⁰The man answered, "Why, this is a marvel! You do not know where he comes from, and yet he opened my eyes. ³¹We know that God does not listen to sinners, but if any one is a worshiper of God and does his will, God listens to him. ³²Never since the world began has it been heard that any one opened the eyes of a man born blind. ³³If this man were not from God, he could do nothing." ³⁴They answered him, "You were born in utter sin, and would you teach us?" And they cast him out.

Spiritual Blindness

35 Jesus heard that they had cast him out, and having found him he said, "Do you believe in the Son of man?" ᵛ ³⁶He answered, "And who is he, sir, that I may believe in him?" ³⁷Jesus said to him, "You have seen him, and it is he who speaks to you." ³⁸He said, "Lord, I believe"; and he worshiped him. ³⁹Jesus said, "For judgment I came into this world, that those who do not see may see, and that those who see may become blind." ⁴⁰Some of the Pharisees near him heard this, and they said to him, "Are we also blind?" ⁴¹Jesus said to them, "If you were blind, you would have no guilt; but now that you say, 'We see,' your guilt remains.

Jesus the Good Shepherd

10 "Truly, truly, I say to you, he who does not enter the sheepfold by the door but climbs in by another way, that man is a thief and a robber; ²but he who enters by the door is the shepherd of the sheep. ³To him the gatekeeper opens; the sheep hear his voice, and he calls his own sheep by name and leads them out. ⁴When he has brought out all his own, he goes before them, and the sheep follow him, for they know his voice. ⁵A stranger they will not follow, but they will flee from him, for they do not know the voice of strangers." ⁶This figure Jesus used with them, but they did not understand what he was saying to them.

7 So Jesus again said to them, "Truly, truly, I say to you, I am the door of the sheep. ⁸All who came before me are thieves and robbers; but the sheep did not heed them. ⁹I am the door; if any one enters by me, he will be saved, and will go in and out and find pasture. ¹⁰The thief comes only to steal and kill and destroy; I came that they may have life, and have it abundantly. ¹¹I am the good shepherd. The good shepherd lays down his life for the sheep. ¹²He who is a hireling and not a shepherd, whose own the sheep are not, sees the wolf coming and leaves the sheep and flees; and the wolf snatches them and scatters them. ¹³He flees because he is a hireling and cares nothing for the sheep. ¹⁴I am the good shepherd; * I know my own and my own know me, ¹⁵as the Father knows me and I know the Father; and I lay down my life for the sheep. ¹⁶And I have other sheep, that are not of this fold; I must bring them also, and they will heed my voice. So there shall be one flock, one shepherd. ¹⁷For this reason the Father loves me, because I lay down my life, that I may take it again. ¹⁸No one takes it from me, but I lay it down of my own accord. I have power to lay it down, and I have power to take it again; this charge I have received from my Father." †

19 There was again a division among the Jews because of these words. ²⁰Many of them said, "He has a demon, and he is mad; why listen to him?" ²¹Others said, "These are not the sayings of one who has a demon. Can a demon open the eyes of the blind?"

Jesus Is Rejected by the Jews

22 It was the feast of the Dedication at Jerusalem; ²³it was winter, and Jesus was walking in the temple, in the portico of Solomon. ²⁴So the Jews gathered round him and said to him, "How long will you keep us in suspense? If you are the Christ, tell us plainly." ²⁵Jesus answered them, "I told you, and you do not believe. The works that I do in my Father's name, they bear witness to me; ²⁶but you do not believe, because you do not belong to my sheep. ²⁷My sheep hear my voice, and I know them, and they follow me;

ᵛ Other ancient authorities read *the Son of God.*
9:28: Jn 5:45.
9:38: Mt 28:9.
9:39: Jn 5:27; 3:19; Mt 15:14.
9:41: Jn 15:22.
10:2: Mk 6:34.
10:6: Jn 16:25.
10:8: Jer 23:1; Ezek 34:2.
10:11: Is 40:11; Ezek 34:11–16; Heb 13:20; 1 Pet 5:4; Rev 7:17; 1 Jn 3:16; Jn 15:13.
10:15: Mt 11:27.
10:16: Is 56:8; Jn 11:52; 17:20; Eph 2:13–18; 1 Pet 2:25.
10:18: Jn 14:31; 15:10; Phil 2:8; Heb 5:8.
10:19: Jn 7:43; 9:16.
10:20: Jn 7:20; 8:48; Mt 11:18.
10:21: Jn 9:32; Ex 4:11.
10:23: Acts 3:11; 5:12.
10:25: Jn 5:36; 10:38.
10:26: Jn 8:47.
* 10:14, *the good shepherd:* The name has Messianic significance; cf. Ezek 34.
† 10:18: Throughout the Gospel, Jesus insists that he is master of his own life and no one takes it from him; cf. 18:6 (at his arrest); 19:11 (before Pilate); 19:30 (on the cross).

²⁸and I give them eternal life, and they shall never perish, and no one shall snatch them out of my hand. ²⁹My Father, who has given them to me,ʷ is greater than all, and no one is able to snatch them out of the Father's hand. ³⁰I and the Father are one."

31 The Jews took up stones again to stone him. ³²Jesus answered them, "I have shown you many good works from the Father; for which of these do you stone me?" ³³The Jews answered him, "We stone you for no good work but for blasphemy; because you, being a man, make yourself God." ³⁴Jesus answered them, "Is it not written in your law, 'I said, you are gods'? ³⁵If he called them gods to whom the word of God came (and Scripture cannot be nullified), ³⁶do you say of him whom the Father consecrated and sent into the world, 'You are blaspheming,' because I said, 'I am the Son of God'? ³⁷If I am not doing the works of my Father, then do not believe me; ³⁸but if I do them, even though you do not believe me, believe the works, that you may know and understand that the Father is in me and I am in the Father." ³⁹Again they tried to arrest him, but he escaped from their hands.

40 He went away again across the Jordan to the place where John at first baptized, and there he remained. ⁴¹And many came to him; and they said, "John did no sign, but everything that John said about this man was true." ⁴²And many believed in him there.

The Death of Lazarus

11 Now a certain man was ill, Laz′arus of Beth′any, the village of Mary and her sister Martha. ²It was Mary who anointed the Lord with ointment and wiped his feet with her hair, whose brother Laz′arus was ill. ³So the sisters sent to him, saying, "Lord, he whom you love is ill." ⁴But when Jesus heard it he said, "This illness is not unto death; it is for the glory of God, so that the Son of God may be glorified by means of it."

5 Now Jesus loved Martha and her sister and Laz′arus. ⁶So when he heard that he was ill, he stayed two days longer * in the place where he was. ⁷Then after this he said to the disciples, "Let us go into Judea again." ⁸The disciples said to him, "Rabbi, the Jews were but now seeking to stone you, and are you going there again?" ⁹Jesus answered, "Are there not twelve hours in the day? If any one walks in the day, he does not stumble, because he sees the light of this world. ¹⁰But if any one walks in the night, he stumbles, because the light is not in him." ¹¹Thus he spoke, and then he said to them, "Our friend Laz′arus has fallen asleep, but I go to awake him out of sleep." ¹²The disciples said to him, "Lord, if he has fallen asleep, he will recover." ¹³Now Jesus had spoken of his death, but they thought that he meant taking rest in sleep. ¹⁴Then Jesus told them plainly,

"Laz′arus is dead; ¹⁵and for your sake I am glad that I was not there, so that you may believe. But let us go to him." ¹⁶Thomas, called the Twin, said to his fellow disciples, "Let us also go, that we may die with him."

Jesus the Resurrection and the Life

17 Now when Jesus came, he found that Laz′arus ˣ had already been in the tomb four days. ¹⁸Beth′any was near Jerusalem, about two miles ʸ off, ¹⁹and many of the Jews had come to Martha and Mary to console them concerning their brother. ²⁰When Martha heard that Jesus was coming, she went and met him, while Mary sat in the house. ²¹Martha said to Jesus, "Lord, if you had been here, my brother would not have died. ²²And even now I know that whatever you ask from God, God will give you." ²³Jesus said to her, "Your brother will rise again." ²⁴Martha said to him, "I know that he will rise again in the resurrection at the last day." ²⁵Jesus said to her, "I am the resurrection and the life; ᶻ he who believes in me, though he die, yet shall he live, ²⁶and whoever lives and believes in me shall never die. Do you believe this?" ²⁷She said to him, "Yes, Lord; I believe that you are the Christ, the Son of God, he who is coming into the world."

Jesus Weeps

28 When she had said this, she went and called her sister Mary, saying quietly, "The Teacher is here and is calling for you." ²⁹And when she heard it, she rose quickly and went to him. ³⁰Now Jesus had not yet come to the village, but was still in the place where Martha had met him. ³¹When the Jews who were with her in the house, consoling her, saw Mary rise quickly and go out, they followed her, supposing that she was going to the tomb to weep there. ³²Then Mary, when she came where Jesus was and saw him, fell at his feet, saying to him, "Lord, if you had been here, my

---

ʷ Other ancient authorities read *What my Father has given to me.*
ˣ Greek *he.*
ʸ Greek *fifteen stadia.*
ᶻ Other ancient authorities omit *and the life.*
10:28: Jn 17:2; 1 Jn 2:25.
10:30: Jn 17:21.
10:31: Jn 8:59; 11:8.
10:33: Lev 24:16; Mk 14:64.
10:34: Jn 8:17; Ps 82:6.
10:39: Jn 7:30; 8:59; Lk 4:30.
10:40: Jn 1:28.
10:42: Jn 7:31; 11:45.
11:1: Mk 11:1; Lk 10:38.
11:2: Jn 12:3; Lk 7:38; Mk 14:3.
11:4: Jn 9:3.
11:8: Jn 8:59; 10:31.
11:9: Jn 9:4; 12:35; Lk 13:33.
11:11: Mk 5:39; Acts 7:60.
11:16: Mt 10:3; Jn 20:24–28.
11:19: Job 2:11.
11:24: Dan 12:2; Jn 5:28; Acts 24:15.
11:25: Jn 1:4; 5:26; Rev 1:18.
11:26: Jn 6:47; 8:51.
11:27: Mt 16:16.
11:32: Jn 11:22.
* 11:6, *stayed two days longer*. This is explained in verse 15.

brother would not have died." ³³When Jesus saw her weeping, and the Jews who came with her also weeping, he was deeply moved in spirit and troubled; ³⁴and he said, "Where have you laid him?" They said to him, "Lord, come and see." ³⁵Jesus wept. ³⁶So the Jews said, "See how he loved him!" ³⁷But some of them said, "Could not he who opened the eyes of the blind man have kept this man from dying?"

Jesus Raises Lazarus to Life

38 Then Jesus, deeply moved again, came to the tomb; it was a cave, and a stone lay upon it. ³⁹Jesus said, "Take away the stone." Martha, the sister of the dead man, said to him, "Lord, by this time there will be an odor, for he has been dead four days." ⁴⁰Jesus said to her, "Did I not tell you that if you would believe you would see the glory of God?" ⁴¹So they took away the stone. And Jesus lifted up his eyes and said, "Father, I thank you that you have heard me. ⁴²I knew that you always hear me, but I have said this on account of the people standing by, that they may believe that you sent me." ⁴³When he had said this, he cried with a loud voice, "Laz'arus, come out." ⁴⁴The dead man came out, his hands and feet bound with bandages, and his face wrapped with a cloth. Jesus said to them, "Unbind him, and let him go."

The Plot to Put Jesus to Death

45 Many of the Jews therefore, who had come with Mary and had seen what he did, believed in him; ⁴⁶but some of them went to the Pharisees and told them what Jesus had done. ⁴⁷So the chief priests and the Pharisees gathered the council, and said, "What are we to do? For this man performs many signs. ⁴⁸If we let him go on like this, every one will believe in him, and the Romans will come and destroy both our holy place ᵃ and our nation." ⁴⁹But one of them, Cai'aphas, who was high priest that year, said to them, "You know nothing at all; ⁵⁰you do not understand that it is expedient for you that one man should die for the people, and that the whole nation should not perish." * ⁵¹He did not say this of his own accord, but being high priest that year he prophesied that Jesus should die for the nation, ⁵²and not for the nation only, but to gather into one the children of God who are scattered abroad. ⁵³So from that day on they took counsel about how to put him to death.

54 Jesus therefore no longer went about openly among the Jews, but went from there to the country near the wilderness, to a town called E'phraim; and there he stayed with the disciples.

55 Now the Passover of the Jews was at hand, and many went up from the country to Jerusalem before the Passover, to purify themselves. ⁵⁶They were looking for Jesus and saying to one another as they stood in the temple, "What do you think?

That he will not come to the feast?" ⁵⁷Now the chief priests and the Pharisees had given orders that if any one knew where he was, he should let them know, so that they might arrest him.

Mary of Bethany Anoints Jesus

12 † Six days before the Passover, Jesus came to Beth'any, where Laz'arus was, whom Jesus had raised from the dead. ²There they made him a supper; Martha served, and Laz'arus was one of those at table with him. ³Mary took a pound of costly ointment of pure nard and anointed the feet of Jesus and wiped his feet with her hair; and the house was filled with the fragrance of the ointment. ⁴But Judas Iscariot, one of his disciples (he who was to betray him), said, ⁵"Why was this ointment not sold for three hundred denarii ᵇ and given to the poor?" ⁶This he said, not that he cared for the poor but because he was a thief, and as he had the money box he used to take what was put into it. ⁷Jesus said, "Let her alone, let her keep it for the day of my burial. ⁸The poor you always have with you, but you do not always have me."

The Plot to Put Lazarus to Death

9 When the great crowd of the Jews learned that he was there, they came, not only on account of Jesus but also to see Laz'arus, whom he had raised from the dead. ¹⁰So the chief priests planned to put Laz'arus also to death, ¹¹because on account of him many of the Jews were going away and believing in Jesus.

Jesus' Triumphal Entry into Jerusalem

12 The next day a great crowd who had come to the feast heard that Jesus was coming to Jerusalem. ¹³So they took branches of palm trees and went out to meet him, crying, "Hosanna! Blessed is he who comes in the name of the Lord, even the King of Israel!" ¹⁴And Jesus found a young donkey and sat upon it; as it is written,

---

ᵃ Greek *our place.*
ᵇ The denarius was a day's wage for a laborer.
11:35: Lk 19:41.
11:37: Jn 9:7.
11:38: Mt 27:60; Mk 15:46; Lk 24:2; Jn 20:1.
11:41: Jn 17:1; Mt 11:25.
11:42: Jn 12:30.
11:44: Jn 19:40; 20:7.
11:49: Mt 26:3.
11:52: Jn 10:16; 17:21.
11:55: Mt 26:1; Mk 14:1; Lk 22:1; Jn 13:1.
11:56: Jn 7:11.
12:1–8: Mt 26:6–13; Mk 14:3–9; Lk 7:37–38.
12:4: Jn 6:71; 13:26.
12:6: Lk 8:3.
12:7: Jn 19:40.
12:10: Mk 14:1.
12:12–15: Mt 21:4–9; Mk 11:7–10; Lk 19:35–38.
12:13: Ps 118:25; Jn 1:49.
* 11:50: Caiaphas agreed that, as Jesus was not (in their opinion) the Messiah, any popular insurrection now could end only in disaster; so it was better, he argued, to do away with him. He was unconscious of the deeper meaning of his words, namely that Jesus must die for the salvation of man.
† 12:1: Here begins the last week of Jesus' public life. This is described in great detail, as was the first week in chapter 1.

¹⁵"Fear not, daughter of Zion;
  behold, your king is coming,
  sitting on a donkey's colt!"
¹⁶His disciples did not understand this at first; but when Jesus was glorified, then they remembered that this had been written of him and had been done to him. ¹⁷The crowd that had been with him when he called Laz′arus out of the tomb and raised him from the dead bore witness. ¹⁸The reason why the crowd went to meet him was that they heard he had done this sign. ¹⁹The Pharisees then said to one another, "You see that you can do nothing; look, the world has gone after him."

Some Greeks Wish to See Jesus

20 Now among those who went up to worship at the feast were some Greeks. ²¹So these came to Philip, who was from Beth-sa′ida in Galilee, and said to him, "Sir, we wish to see Jesus." ²²Philip went and told Andrew; Andrew went with Philip and they told Jesus. ²³And Jesus answered them, "The hour has come for the Son of man to be glorified. ²⁴Truly, truly, I say to you, unless a grain of wheat falls into the earth and dies, it remains alone; but if it dies, it bears much fruit. ²⁵He who loves his life loses it, and he who hates his life in this world will keep it for eternal life. ²⁶If any one serves me, he must follow me; and where I am, there shall my servant be also; if any one serves me, the Father will honor him.

Jesus Speaks about His Death

27 "Now is my soul troubled. And what shall I say? 'Father, save me from this hour'? No, for this purpose I have come to this hour. ²⁸Father, glorify your name." Then a voice came from heaven, "I have glorified it, and I will glorify it again." ²⁹The crowd standing by heard it and said that it had thundered. Others said, "An angel has spoken to him." ³⁰Jesus answered, "This voice has come for your sake, not for mine. ³¹Now is the judgment of this world, now shall the ruler of this world be cast out; ³²and I, when I am lifted up * from the earth, will draw all men to myself." ³³He said this to show by what death he was to die. ³⁴The crowd answered him, "We have heard from the law that the Christ remains for ever. How can you say that the Son of man must be lifted up? Who is this Son of man?" ³⁵Jesus said to them, "The light is with you for a little longer. Walk while you have the light, lest the darkness overtake you; he who walks in the darkness does not know where he goes. ³⁶While you have the light, believe in the light, that you may become sons of light."

The Unbelief of the People

When Jesus had said this, he departed and hid himself from them. ³⁷Though he had done so many signs before them, yet they did not believe in him; ³⁸it was that the word spoken by the prophet Isaiah might be fulfilled:

"Lord, who has believed our report,
  and to whom has the arm of the Lord been
  revealed?"
³⁹Therefore they could not believe. For Isaiah again said,
⁴⁰"He has blinded their eyes and hardened their
  heart,
  lest they should see with their eyes and
  perceive with their heart,
  and turn for me to heal them."
⁴¹Isaiah said this because he saw his glory and spoke of him. ⁴²Nevertheless many even of the authorities believed in him, but for fear of the Pharisees they did not confess it, lest they should be put out of the synagogue: ⁴³for they loved the praise of men more than the praise of God.

Summary of Jesus' Teaching

44 And Jesus cried out and said, "He who believes in me, believes not in me but in him who sent me. ⁴⁵And he who sees me sees him who sent me. ⁴⁶I have come as light into the world, that whoever believes in me may not remain in darkness. ⁴⁷If any one hears my sayings and does not keep them, I do not judge him; for I did not come to judge the world but to save the world. ⁴⁸He who rejects me and does not receive my sayings has a judge; the word that I have spoken will be his judge on the last day. ⁴⁹For I have not spoken on my own authority; the Father who sent me has himself given me commandment what to say and what to speak. ⁵⁰And I know that his commandment is eternal life. What I say, therefore, I say as the Father has bidden me."

Jesus Washes the Disciples' Feet

13 † Now before the feast of the Passover, when Jesus knew that his hour had come to depart out of this world to the Father, having

---

12:15: Zech 9:9.
12:16: Mk 9:32; Jn 2:22.
12:20: Jn 7:35; Acts 11:20.
12:21: Jn 1:44; 6:5.
12:23: Jn 13:1; 17:1; Mk 14:35, 41.
12:24: 1 Cor 15:36.
12:25: Mt 10:39; Mk 8:35; Lk 9:24; 14:26.
12:27: Jn 11:33; Mt 26:38; Mk 14:34.
12:28: Mk 1:11; 9:7.
12:31: Jn 16:11; 2 Cor 4:4; Eph 2:2.
12:32: Jn 3:14; 8:28.
12:34: Ps 110:4; Is 9:7; Ezek 37:25; Dan 7:14.
12:35: Jn 7:33; 9:4; Eph 5:8; 1 Jn 2:11.
12:36: Lk 16:8; Jn 8:59.
12:38: Is 53:1; Rom 10:16.
12:40: Is 6:10; Mt 13:14.
12:41: Is 6:1; Lk 24:27.
12:42: Jn 9:22; Lk 6:22.
12:44: Mt 10:40; Jn 5:24.
12:45: Jn 14:9.
12:46: Jn 1:4; 8:12; 9:5.
12:47: Jn 3:17.
12:48: Mt 10:14–15.
13:1: Jn 11:55; 12:23; 16:28.

* 12:32, *lifted up*: i.e., on the cross; but the words also contain a reference to his going up into heaven. The two mysteries are inseparable.
† 13:1: John begins here to unfold the mystery of the love of Jesus for "his own." Note the solemn introduction to the "hour" of his passion and death.

loved his own who were in the world, he loved them to the end. ²And during supper, when the devil had already put it into the heart of Judas Iscariot, Simon's son, to betray him, ³Jesus, knowing that the Father had given all things into his hands, and that he had come from God and was going to God, ⁴rose from supper, laid aside his garments, and tied a towel around himself. ⁵Then he poured water into a basin, and began to wash the disciples' feet, and to wipe them with the towel that was tied around him. ⁶He came to Simon Peter; and Peter said to him, "Lord, do you wash my feet?" ⁷Jesus answered him, "What I am doing you do not know now, but afterward you will understand." ⁸Peter said to him, "You shall never wash my feet." Jesus answered him, "If I do not wash you, you have no part in me." ⁹Simon Peter said to him, "Lord, not my feet only but also my hands and my head!" ¹⁰Jesus said to him, "He who has bathed does not need to wash, except for his feet, ᶜ but he is clean all over; and you are clean, but not all of you." ¹¹For he knew who was to betray him; that was why he said, "You are not all clean."

12 When he had washed their feet, and taken his garments, and resumed his place, he said to them, "Do you know what I have done to you? ¹³You call me Teacher and Lord; and you are right, for so I am. ¹⁴If I then, your Lord and Teacher, have washed your feet, you also ought to wash one another's feet. ¹⁵For I have given you an example, that you also should do as I have done to you. ¹⁶Truly, truly, I say to you, a servant ᵈ is not greater than his master; nor is he who is sent greater than he who sent him. ¹⁷If you know these things, blessed are you if you do them. ¹⁸I am not speaking of you all; I know whom I have chosen; it is that the Scripture may be fulfilled, 'He who ate my bread has lifted his heel against me.' ¹⁹I tell you this now, before it takes place, that when it does take place you may believe that I am he. ²⁰Truly, truly, I say to you, he who receives any one whom I send receives me; and he who receives me receives him who sent me."

Jesus Foretells His Betrayal

21 When Jesus had thus spoken, he was troubled in spirit, and testified, "Truly, truly, I say to you, one of you will betray me." ²²The disciples looked at one another, uncertain of whom he spoke. ²³One of his disciples, whom Jesus loved, was lying close to the breast of Jesus; ²⁴so Simon Peter beckoned to him and said, "Tell us who it is of whom he speaks." ²⁵So lying thus, close to the breast of Jesus, he said to him, "Lord, who is it?" ²⁶Jesus answered, "It is he to whom I shall give this morsel when I have dipped it." So when he had dipped the morsel, he gave it to Judas, the son of Simon Iscariot. ²⁷Then after the morsel, Satan

entered into him. Jesus said to him, "What you are going to do, do quickly." ²⁸Now no one at the table knew why he said this to him. ²⁹Some thought that, because Judas had the money box, Jesus was telling him, "Buy what we need for the feast"; or, that he should give something to the poor. ³⁰So, after receiving the morsel, he immediately went out; and it was night.

The New Commandment

31 When he had gone out, Jesus said, "Now is the Son of man glorified, and in him God is glorified; ³²if God is glorified in him, God will also glorify him in himself, and glorify him at once. ³³Little children, yet a little while I am with you. You will seek me; and as I said to the Jews so now I say to you, 'Where I am going you cannot come.' ³⁴A new commandment* I give to you, that you love one another; even as I have loved you, that you also love one another. ³⁵By this all men will know that you are my disciples, if you have love for one another."

Jesus Foretells Peter's Denial

36 Simon Peter said to him, "Lord, where are you going?" Jesus answered, "Where I am going you cannot follow me now; but you shall follow afterward." ³⁷Peter said to him, "Lord, why can I not follow you now? I will lay down my life for you." ³⁸Jesus answered, "Will you lay down your life for me? Truly, truly, I say to you, the cock will not crow, till you have denied me three times.

Jesus the Way, the Truth, and the Life

14 "Let not your hearts be troubled; believe ᵉ in God, believe also in me. ²In my Father's house are many rooms; if it were not so, would I have told you that I go to prepare a place for you? ³And when I go and prepare a place for you, I will come again and will take you to myself, that where I am you may be also. ⁴And you know the

---

ᶜ Other ancient authorities omit *except for his feet.*
ᵈ Or *slave.*
ᵉ Or *you believe.*
13:2: Jn 6:71; Mk 14:10.
13:5: Lk 7:44; 22:27.
13:8: Deut 12:12; Jn 3:5; 9:7.
13:11: Jn 13:2.
13:15: 1 Pet 2:21.
13:16: Mt 10:24; Lk 6:40.
13:17: Lk 11:28; Jas 1:25.
13:18: Ps 41:9.
13:19: Jn 14:29; 8:28.
13:20: Mt 10:40; Lk 10:16.
13:21–26: Mt 26:21–25; Mk 14:18–21; Lk 22:21–23.
13:23: Jn 19:26; 20:2; 21:7, 20.
13:26: Jn 6:71.
13:29: Jn 12:6.
13:30: Lk 22:53.
13:31–32: Jn 17:1.
13:33: 1 Jn 2:1; Jn 7:33.
13:34: Jn 15:12, 17; 1 Jn 3:23; 2 Jn 5; Lev 19:18; 1 Thess 4:9; 1 Pet 1:22; Heb 13:1; Eph 5:2; 1 Jn 4:10.
13:36: Jn 21:18; 2 Pet 1:14.
13:37–38: Mt 26:33–35; Mk 14:29–31; Lk 22:33–34.
14:2: Jn 13:33.
* 13:34, *new commandment*: Jesus gives a new depth to the familiar commandment of the Old Testament. The standard now is, "as I have loved you."

way where I am going." **f** [5]Thomas said to him, "Lord, we do not know where you are going; how can we know the way?" [6]Jesus said to him, "I am the way, and the truth, and the life; no one comes to the Father, but by me. [7]If you had known me, you would have known my Father also; henceforth you know him and have seen him."

8 Philip said to him, "Lord, show us the Father, and we shall be satisfied." [9]Jesus said to him, "Have I been with you so long, and yet you do not know me, Philip? He who has seen me has seen the Father; how can you say, 'Show us the Father'? [10]Do you not believe that I am in the Father and the Father is in me? The words that I say to you I do not speak on my own authority; but the Father who dwells in me does his works. [11]Believe me that I am in the Father and the Father is in me; or else believe me for the sake of the works themselves.

12 "Truly, truly, I say to you, he who believes in me will also do the works that I do; and greater works than these will he do, because I go to the Father. [13]Whatever you ask in my name, I will do it, that the Father may be glorified in the Son; [14]if you ask **g** anything in my name, I will do it.

The Promise of the Holy Spirit

15 "If you love me, you will keep my commandments. [16]And I will ask the Father, and he will give you another Counselor, to be with you for ever, [17]even the Spirit of truth, whom the world cannot receive, because it neither sees him nor knows him; you know him, for he dwells with you, and will be in you.

18 "I will not leave you desolate; I will come to you. [19]Yet a little while, and the world will see me no more, but you will see me; because I live, you will live also. [20]In that day you will know that I am in my Father, and you in me, and I in you. [21]He who has my commandments and keeps them, he it is who loves me; and he who loves me will be loved by my Father, and I will love him and manifest myself to him." [22]Judas (not Iscariot) said to him, "Lord, how is it that you will manifest yourself to us, and not to the world?" [23]Jesus answered him, "If a man loves me, he will keep my word, and my Father will love him, and we will come to him and make our home with him. [24]He who does not love me does not keep my words; and the word which you hear is not mine but the Father's who sent me.

25 "These things I have spoken to you, while I am still with you. [26]But the Counselor, the Holy Spirit, whom the Father will send in my name, he will teach you all things, * and bring to your remembrance all that I have said to you. [27]Peace I leave with you; my peace I give to you; not as the world gives do I give to you. Let not your hearts be troubled, neither let them be afraid. [28]You heard me say to you, 'I go away, and I will come to you.'

If you loved me, you would have rejoiced, because I go to the Father; for the Father is greater than I. [29]And now I have told you before it takes place, so that when it does take place, you may believe. [30]I will no longer talk much with you, for the ruler of this world is coming. He has no power over me; [31]but I do as the Father has commanded me, so that the world may know that I love the Father. Rise, let us go from here.

Jesus the True Vine

15 "I am the true vine, and my Father is the vinedresser. [2]Every branch of mine that bears no fruit, he takes away, and every branch that does bear fruit he prunes, that it may bear more fruit. [3]You are already made clean by the word which I have spoken to you. [4]Abide in me, and I in you. As the branch cannot bear fruit by itself, unless it abides in the vine, neither can you, unless you abide in me. [5]I am the vine, you are the branches. He who abides in me, and I in him, he it is that bears much fruit, for apart from me you can do nothing. [6]If a man does not abide in me, he is cast forth as a branch and withers; and the branches are gathered, thrown into the fire and burned. [7]If you abide in me, and my words abide in you, ask whatever you will, and it shall be done for you. [8]By this my Father is glorified, that you bear much fruit, and so prove to be my disciples. [9]As the Father has loved me, so have I loved you; abide in my love. [10]If you keep my commandments, you will abide in my love, just as I have kept my Father's commandments and abide in his love. [11]These things I have spoken to you, that my joy may be in you, and that your joy may be full.

12 "This is my commandment, that you love one another as I have loved you. [13]Greater love has no man than this, that a man lay down his

---

f Other ancient authorities read *where I am going you know, and the way you know.*
g Other ancient authorities add *me.*
14:5: Jn 11:16.
14:6: Jn 10:9; 1:4, 14.
14:9: Jn 12:45.
14:11: Jn 10:38.
14:13: Mt 7:7; Jn 15:7, 16; 16:23; Jas 1:5.
14:15: Jn 15:10; 1 Jn 5:3; 2 Jn 6.
14:16: Jn 14:26; 15:26; 16:7; 1 Jn 2:1.
14:19: Jn 7:33.
14:22: Acts 1:13; 10:40–41.
14:23: 1 Jn 2:24; Rev 21:3.
14:27: Jn 16:33; Phil 4:7; Col 3:15; Jn 20:19.
14:29: Jn 13:19.
14:30: Jn 12:31.
14:31: Mk 14:42; Jn 18:1.
15:1: Is 5:1–7; Ezek 19:10; Mk 12:1–9; Mt 15:13; Rom 11:17.
15:3: Jn 13:10.
15:4: Jn 6:56; 1 Jn 2:6.
15:7: Jn 14:13; 16:23; Mt 7:7; Jas 1:5.
15:8: Mt 5:16.
15:10: Jn 14:15; 1 Jn 5:3.
15:12: Jn 13:34.
15:13: Rom 5:7; Jn 10:11.
* 14:26, *all things*: After Jesus has gone to his Father, the Holy Spirit will complete his revelation to the world.

life for his friends. [14]You are my friends if you do what I command you. [15]No longer do I call you servants, [h] for the servant [i] does not know what his master is doing; but I have called you friends, for all that I have heard from my Father I have made known to you. [16]You did not choose me, but I chose you and appointed you that you should go and bear fruit and that your fruit should abide; so that whatever you ask the Father in my name, he may give it to you. [17]This I command you, to love one another.

The World's Hatred

18 "If the world hates you, know that it has hated me before it hated you. * [19]If you were of the world, the world would love its own; but because you are not of the world, but I chose you out of the world, therefore the world hates you. [20]Remember the word that I said to you, 'A servant [i] is not greater than his master.' If they persecuted me, they will persecute you; if they kept my word, they will keep yours also. [21]But all this they will do to you on my account, because they do not know him who sent me. [22]If I had not come and spoken to them, they would not have sin; but now they have no excuse for their sin. [23]He who hates me hates my Father also. [24]If I had not done among them the works which no one else did, they would not have sin; but now they have seen and hated both me and my Father. [25]It is to fulfil the word that is written in their law, 'They hated me without a cause.' [26]But when the Counselor comes, whom I shall send to you from the Father, even the Spirit of truth, who proceeds from the Father, he will bear witness to me; [27]and you also are witnesses, because you have been with me from the beginning.

16 "I have said all this to you to keep you from falling away. [2]They will put you out of the synagogues; indeed, the hour is coming when whoever kills you will think he is offering service to God. [3]And they will do this because they have not known the Father, nor me. [4]But I have said these things to you, that when their hour comes you may remember that I told you of them.

The Work of the Spirit

"I did not say these things to you from the beginning, because I was with you. [5]But now I am going to him who sent me; yet none of you asks me, 'Where are you going?' [6]But because I have said these things to you, sorrow has filled your hearts. [7]Nevertheless I tell you the truth: it is to your advantage that I go away, for if I do not go away, the Counselor will not come to you; but if I go, I will send him to you. [8]And when he comes, he will convince the world of sin and of righteousness and of judgment: [9]of sin, because they do not believe in me; [10]of righteousness, because I go to the Father, and you will see me no more; †

[11]of judgment, because the ruler of this world is judged.

12 "I have yet many things to say to you, but you cannot bear them now. [13]When the Spirit of truth comes, he will guide you into all the truth; for he will not speak on his own authority, but whatever he hears he will speak, and he will declare to you the things that are to come. [14]He will glorify me, for he will take what is mine and declare it to you. [15]All that the Father has is mine; therefore I said that he will take what is mine and declare it to you.

Sorrow Will Turn into Joy

16 "A little while, and you will see me no more; again a little while, and you will see me." [17]Some of his disciples said to one another, "What is this that he says to us, 'A little while, and you will not see me, and again a little while, and you will see me'; and, 'because I go to the Father'?" [18]They said, "What does he mean by 'a little while'? We do not know what he means." [19]Jesus knew that they wanted to ask him; so he said to them, "Is this what you are asking yourselves, what I meant by saying, 'A little while, and you will not see me, and again a little while, and you will see me'? [20]Truly, truly, I say to you, you will weep and lament, but the world will rejoice; you will be sorrowful, but your sorrow will turn into joy. [21]When a woman is in labor, she has pain, because her hour has come; but when she is delivered of the child, she no longer remembers the anguish, for joy that a child [j] is born into the world. [22]So you have sorrow now, but I will see you again and your hearts will rejoice, and no one will take your joy from you. [23]In that day you will ask nothing of me. Truly, truly, I say to you, if you ask anything of the Father, he will give it to you in my name. [24]Until now you have asked nothing in my name; ask, and you will receive, that your joy may be full.

[h] Or *slaves.*
[i] Or *slave.*
[j] Greek *a human being.*
15:14: Lk 12:4.
15:16: Jn 6:70; 13:18; 14:13; 16:23.
15:18: Jn 7:7; 1 Jn 3:13; Mt 10:22; 24:9.
15:20: Jn 13:16; Mt 10:24; 1 Cor 4:12; Acts 4:17; 1 Pet 4:14; Rev 2:3.
15:22: Jn 9:41.
15:25: Ps 35:19; 69:4.
15:26: Jn 14:16, 26; 16:7; 1 Jn 2:1; 5:7.
15:27: Jn 19:35; 21:24; 1 Jn 4:14.
16:2: Jn 9:22; Acts 26:9–11; Is 66:5.
16:5: Jn 7:33; 14:5.
16:7: Jn 14:16, 26; 15:26.
16:9: Jn 15:22.
16:10: Acts 3:14; 7:52; 1 Pet 3:18.
16:11: Jn 12:31.
16:14: Jn 7:39.
16:16–24: Jn 14:18–24.
16:20: Jn 20:20.
16:21: Is 13:8; Hos 13:13; Mic 4:9; 1 Thess 5:3.
16:24: Jn 14:14; 15:11.
* 15:18: Jesus contrasts the love his disciples have with the hatred the world bears them.
† 16:10: Jesus is taken from them because they did not receive him.

Peace for the Disciples

25 "I have said this to you in figures; the hour is coming when I shall no longer speak to you in figures but tell you plainly of the Father. [26]In that day you will ask in my name; and I do not say to you that I shall ask the Father for you; [27]for the Father himself loves you, because you have loved me and have believed that I came from the Father. [28]I came from the Father and have come into the world; again, I am leaving the world and going to the Father."

29 His disciples said, "Ah, now you are speaking plainly, not in any figure! [30]Now we know that you know all things, and need none to question you; by this we believe that you came from God." [31]Jesus answered them, "Do you now believe? [32]The hour is coming, indeed it has come, when you will be scattered, every man to his home, and will leave me alone; yet I am not alone, for the Father is with me. [33]I have said this to you, that in me you may have peace. In the world you have tribulation; but be of good cheer, I have overcome the world."

Jesus Prays for the Church

17 When Jesus had spoken these words, he lifted up his eyes to heaven and said, * "Father, the hour has come; glorify your Son that the Son may glorify you, [2]since you have given him power over all flesh, to give eternal life to all whom you have given him. [3]And this is eternal life, that they know you the only true God, and Jesus Christ whom you have sent. [4]I glorified you on earth, having accomplished the work which you gave me to do; [5]and now, Father, glorify me in your own presence with the glory which I had with you before the world was made. †

6 "I have manifested your name to the men whom you gave me out of the world; they were yours, and you gave them to me, and they have kept your word. [7]Now they know that everything that you have given me is from you; [8]for I have given them the words which you gave me, and they have received them and know in truth that I came from you; and they have believed that you sent me. [9]I am praying for them; I am not praying for the world but for those whom you have given me, for they are yours; [10]all mine are yours, and yours are mine, and I am glorified in them. [11]And now I am no more in the world, but they are in the world, and I am coming to you. Holy Father, keep them in your name, which you have given me, that they may be one, even as we are one. [12]While I was with them, I kept them in your name, which you have given me; I have guarded them, and none of them is lost but the son of perdition, that the Scripture might be fulfilled. [13]But now I am coming to you; and these things I speak in the world, that they may have my joy fulfilled in themselves. [14]I have given them your word; and the

world has hated them because they are not of the world, even as I am not of the world. [15]I do not pray that you should take them out of the world, but that you should keep them from the evil one. ᵏ [16]They are not of the world, even as I am not of the world. [17]Sanctify them in the truth; your word is truth. [18]As you sent me into the world, so I have sent them into the world. [19]And for their sake I consecrate myself, that they also may be consecrated in truth.

20 "I do not pray for these only, but also for those who believe in me through their word, [21]that they may all be one; even as you, Father, are in me, and I in you, that they also may be in us, so that the world may believe that you have sent me. [22]The glory which you have given me I have given to them, that they may be one even as we are one, [23]I in them and you in me, that they may become perfectly one, so that the world may know that you have sent me and have loved them even as you have loved me. [24]Father, I desire that they also, whom you have given me, may be with me where I am, to behold my glory which you have given me in your love for me before the foundation of the world. [25]O righteous Father, the world has not known you, but I have known you; and these know that you have sent me. [26]I made known to them your name, and I will make it known, that the love with which you have loved me may be in them, and I in them."

The Arrest of Jesus

18 When Jesus had spoken these words, he went forth with his disciples across the Kidron valley, where there was a garden, which he and his disciples entered. [2]Now Judas, who betrayed him, also knew the place; for Jesus often met there with his disciples. [3]So Judas, procuring a band of soldiers and some officers from the chief priests and the Pharisees, went there with lanterns and torches and weapons. [4]Then Jesus, knowing all that was to befall him, came forward and said to them, "Whom do you seek?" [5]They answered him, "Jesus of Nazareth." Jesus said to them, "I am he." Judas, who betrayed him, was standing with them. [6]When he said to them, "I am he," they drew back and fell to the ground. [7]Again he asked them,

---

ᵏ Or from evil.
16:25: Jn 10:6; Mt 13:34.
16:32: Jn 4:23; Mk 14:27; Zech 13:7.
16:33: Jn 14:27; 15:18; Rom 8:37; 2 Cor 2:14; Rev 3:21.
17:1: Jn 11:41; 13:31.
17:5: Jn 1:1; 8:58; Phil 2:6.
17:9: Lk 22:32; Jn 14:16.
17:11: Phil 2:9; Rev 19:12; Rom 12:5; Gal 3:28; Jn 17:21.
17:12: Ps 41:9; Jn 6:70; 18:9.
17:14: Jn 15:19; 8:23.
17:21: Jn 10:38; 17:11.
17:24: Jn 1:14; 17:5; Mt 25:34.
18:1: Mt 26:30, 36; Mk 14:26, 32; Lk 22:39; 2 Sam 15:23.
18:3–11: Mt 26:47–56; Mk 14:43–50; Lk 22:47–53.
18:4: Jn 6:64; 13:1.
* 17:1–26: The priestly prayer of Jesus, before his sacrifice.
† 17:5 declares his pre-existence.

"Whom do you seek?" And they said, "Jesus of Nazareth." [8]Jesus answered, "I told you that I am he; so, if you seek me, let these men go." [9]This was to fulfil the word which he had spoken, "Of those whom you gave me I lost not one." [10]Then Simon Peter, having a sword, drew it and struck the high priest's slave and cut off his right ear. The slave's name was Malchus. [11]Jesus said to Peter, "Put your sword into its sheath; shall I not drink the chalice which the Father has given me?"

Jesus before the High Priest

12 So the band of soldiers and their captain and the officers of the Jews seized Jesus and bound him. [13]First they led him to Annas; for he was the father-in-law of Cai'aphas, who was high priest that year. * [14]It was Cai'aphas who had given counsel to the Jews that it was expedient that one man should die for the people.

Peter Denies Jesus

15 Simon Peter followed Jesus, and so did another disciple. As this disciple was known to the high priest, he entered the court of the high priest along with Jesus, [16]while Peter stood outside at the door. So the other disciple, who was known to the high priest, went out and spoke to the maid who kept the door, and brought Peter in. [17]The maid who kept the door said to Peter, "Are not you also one of this man's disciples?" He said, "I am not." [18]Now the servants [1] and officers had made a charcoal fire, because it was cold, and they were standing and warming themselves; Peter also was with them, standing and warming himself.

The High Priest Questions Jesus

19 The high priest then questioned Jesus about his disciples and his teaching. [20]Jesus answered him, "I have spoken openly to the world; I have always taught in synagogues and in the temple, where all Jews come together; I have said nothing secretly. [21]Why do you ask me? Ask those who have heard me, what I said to them; they know what I said." [22]When he had said this, one of the officers standing by struck Jesus with his hand, saying, "Is that how you answer the high priest?" [23]Jesus answered him, "If I have spoken wrongly, bear witness to the wrong; but if I have spoken rightly, why do you strike me?" [24]Annas then sent him bound to Cai'aphas the high priest.

Peter Denies Jesus Again

25 Now Simon Peter was standing and warming himself. They said to him, "Are not you also one of his disciples?" He denied it and said, "I am not." [26]One of the servants [1] of the high priest, a kinsman of the man whose ear Peter had cut off, asked, "Did I not see you in the garden with him?" [27]Peter again denied it; and at once the cock crowed.

Jesus before Pilate

28 Then they led Jesus from the house of Cai'aphas to the praetorium. It was early. They themselves did not enter the praetorium, so that they might not be defiled, but might eat the Passover. †
[29]So Pilate went out to them and said, "What accusation do you bring against this man?" ‡ [30]They answered him, "If this man were not an evildoer, we would not have handed him over." [31]Pilate said to them, "Take him yourselves and judge him by your own law." The Jews said to him, "It is not lawful for us to put any man to death." § [32]This was to fulfil the word which Jesus had spoken to show by what death he was to die.

Jesus Sentenced to Death

33 Pilate entered the praetorium again and called Jesus, and said to him, "Are you the King of the Jews?" [34]Jesus answered, "Do you say this of your own accord, or did others say it to you about me?" [35]Pilate answered, "Am I a Jew? Your own nation and the chief priests have handed you over to me; what have you done?" [36]Jesus answered, "My kingship is not of this world; if my kingship were of this world, my servants would fight, that I might not be handed over to the Jews; but my kingship is not from the world." [37]Pilate said to him, "So you are a king?" Jesus answered, "You say that I am a king. For this I was born, and for this I have come into the world, to bear witness to the truth. Every one who is of the truth hears my voice." [38]Pilate said to him, "What is truth?"

After he had said this, he went out to the Jews again, and told them, "I find no crime in him. [39]But you have a custom that I should release one man for you at the Passover; will you have me release for you the King of the Jews?" [40]They cried out again, "Not this man, but Barab'bas!" Now Barab'bas was a robber.

19 Then Pilate took Jesus and scourged him. [2]And the soldiers plaited a crown of thorns, and put it on his head, and clothed him in a purple robe; [3]they came up to him, saying, "Hail, King of the Jews!" and struck him with

---

[1] Or *slaves.*
18:9: Jn 17:12; 6:39.
18:11: Mk 10:38; 14:36.
18:12–13: Mt 26:57; Mk 14:53; Lk 22:54; 3:2.
18:14: Jn 11:49–51.
18:15–16: Mt 26:58; Mk 14:54; Lk 22:54.
18:17–18: Mt 26:69–72; Mk 14:66–69; Lk 22:56–58.
18:19–23: Mt 26:59–66; Mk 14:55–64; Lk 22:67–71.
18:23: Mt 5:39; Acts 23:2–5.
18:24: Jn 18:13; Lk 3:2.
18:25–27: Mt 26:73–75; Mk 14:70–72; Lk 22:59–62.
18:28: Jn 11:55; Mt 27:1–2; Mk 15:1; Lk 23:1.
18:29–38: Mt 27:11–14; Mk 15:2–5; Lk 23:2–3.
18:32: Jn 3:14; 12:32.
18:36: Jn 6:15; Mt 26:53.
18:37: Jn 3:32; 8:14, 47; 1 Jn 4:6.
18:38–40: Mt 27:15–26; Mk 15:6–15; Lk 23:18–19; Acts 3:14.
19:2–3: Mt 27:27–31; Mk 15:16–20; Lk 22:63–65; 23:11.
* 18:13: According to Jewish law the high-priesthood was for life. The Romans had deposed Annas, the legal holder, in A.D. 15, and appointed another in his place, but many Jews continued to recognize Annas.
† 18:28: They would have contracted a legal impurity by entering the house of a pagan.
‡ 18:29: See note on Lk 23:2.
§ 18:31: Crucifixion was a Roman, not a Jewish, punishment.

their hands. [4]Pilate went out again, and said to them, "Behold, I am bringing him out to you, that you may know that I find no crime in him." [5]So Jesus came out, wearing the crown of thorns and the purple robe. Pilate said to them, "Here is the man!" [6]When the chief priests and the officers saw him, they cried out, "Crucify him, crucify him!" Pilate said to them, "Take him yourselves and crucify him, for I find no crime in him." [7]The Jews answered him, "We have a law, and by that law he ought to die, because he has made himself the Son of God." * [8]When Pilate heard these words, he was even more afraid; [9]he entered the praetorium again and said to Jesus, "Where are you from?" † But Jesus gave no answer. [10]Pilate therefore said to him, "You will not speak to me? Do you not know that I have power to release you, and power to crucify you?" [11]Jesus answered him, "You would have no power over me unless it had been given you from above; therefore he who delivered me to you has the greater sin."

[12] Upon this Pilate sought to release him, but the Jews cried out, "If you release this man, you are not Caesar's friend; every one who makes himself a king sets himself against Caesar." [13]When Pilate heard these words, he brought Jesus out and sat down on the judgment seat at a place called The Pavement, and in Hebrew, Gab'batha. [14]Now it was the day of Preparation of the Passover; it was about the sixth hour. He said to the Jews, "Here is your King!" [15]They cried out, "Away with him, away with him, crucify him!" Pilate said to them, "Shall I crucify your King?" The chief priests answered, "We have no king but Caesar." [16]Then he handed him over to them to be crucified.

The Crucifixion

[17] So they took Jesus, and he went out, bearing his own cross, to the place called the place of a skull, which is called in Hebrew Gol'gotha. [18]There they crucified him, and with him two others, one on either side, and Jesus between them. [19]Pilate also wrote a title and put it on the cross; it read, "Jesus of Nazareth, the King of the Jews." [20]Many of the Jews read this title, for the place where Jesus was crucified was near the city; and it was written in Hebrew, in Latin, and in Greek. [21]The chief priests of the Jews then said to Pilate, "Do not write, 'The King of the Jews,' but, 'This man said, I am King of the Jews.'" [22]Pilate answered, "What I have written I have written."

[23] When the soldiers had crucified Jesus they took his garments and made four parts, one for each soldier; also his tunic. But the tunic was without seam, woven from top to bottom; [24]so they said to one another, "Let us not tear it, but cast lots for it to see whose it shall be." This was to fulfil the Scripture,

"They parted my garments among them,
and for my clothing they cast lots."

[25] So the soldiers did this. But standing by the cross of Jesus were his mother, and his mother's sister, Mary the wife of Clopas, and Mary Mag'dalene. [26]When Jesus saw his mother, and the disciple whom he loved standing near, he said to his mother, "Woman, behold, your son!" [27]Then he said to the disciple, "Behold, your mother!" And from that hour the disciple took her to his own home. ‡

[28] After this Jesus, knowing that all was now finished, said (to fulfil the Scripture), "I thirst." [29]A bowl full of vinegar stood there; so they put a sponge full of the vinegar on hyssop and held it to his mouth. [30]When Jesus had received the vinegar, he said, "It is finished"; and he bowed his head and gave up his spirit.

Jesus' Side Is Pierced

[31] Since it was the day of Preparation, in order to prevent the bodies from remaining on the cross on the sabbath (for that sabbath was a high day), the Jews asked Pilate that their legs might be broken, and that they might be taken away. [32]So the soldiers came and broke the legs of the first, and of the other who had been crucified with him; [33]but when they came to Jesus and saw that he was already dead, they did not break his legs. [34]But one of the soldiers pierced his side with a spear, and at once there came out blood and water. [35]He who saw it has borne witness—his testimony is true, and he knows that he tells the truth—that you also may believe. [36]For these things took place that the Scripture might be fulfilled, "Not a bone of him shall be broken." [37]And again another Scripture says, "They shall look on him whom they have pierced."

The Burial of Jesus

[38] After this Joseph of Arimathe'a, who was a disciple of Jesus, but secretly, for fear of the Jews, asked Pilate that he might take away the body of Jesus, and Pilate gave him leave. So he came and

19:4: Jn 18:38; 19:6; Lk 23:4.
19:7: Lev 24:16; Mk 14:61–64; Jn 5:18; 10:33.
19:11: Rom 13:1; Jn 18:28.
19:12: Lk 23:2.
19:14: Mk 15:42; Jn 19:31, 42; Mk 15:25, 33.
19:17–24: Mt 27:33–44; Mk 15:22–32; Lk 23:33–43.
19:24: Ex 28:32; Ps 22:18.
19:25: Mt 27:55–56; Mk 15:40–41; Lk 23:49; Jn 2:3; Mk 3:31; Lk 24:18; Jn 20:1, 18.
19:26: Jn 13:23; 20:2; 21:20.
19:28–30: Ps 69:21; Mt 27:45–50; Mk 15:33–37; Lk 23:44–46; Jn 17:4.
19:31: Deut 21:23; Ex 12:16.
19:34: 1 Jn 5:6–8.
19:35: Jn 15:27; 21:24.
19:36: Ex 12:46; Num 9:12; Ps 34:20.
19:37: Zech 12:10.
19:38–42: Mt 27:57–61; Mk 15:42–47; Lk 23:50–56.
* 19:7: At last, because of Pilate's reluctance, they produce the real charge.
† 19:8–9: Pilate is afraid and asks Jesus where he comes from—not his country, but his mysterious origins, as implied in the charge.
‡ 19:27, *took her to his own home*: Joseph must now have been dead.

took away his body. ³⁹Nicode′mus also, who had at first come to him by night, came bringing a mixture of myrrh and aloes, about a hundred pounds' weight. ⁴⁰They took the body of Jesus, and bound it in linen cloths with the spices, as is the burial custom of the Jews. ⁴¹Now in the place where he was crucified there was a garden, and in the garden a new tomb where no one had ever been laid. ⁴²So because of the Jewish day of Preparation, as the tomb was close at hand, they laid Jesus there.

The Resurrection of Jesus

20 Now on the first day of the week, Mary Mag′dalene came to the tomb early, while it was still dark, and saw that the stone had been taken away from the tomb. ²So she ran, and went to Simon Peter and the other disciple, the one whom Jesus loved, and said to them, "They have taken the Lord out of the tomb, and we do not know where they have laid him." ³Peter then came out with the other disciple, and they went toward the tomb. ⁴They both ran, but the other disciple outran Peter and reached the tomb first; ⁵and stooping to look in, he saw the linen cloths lying there, but he did not go in. ⁶Then Simon Peter came, following him, and went into the tomb; he saw the linen cloths lying, ⁷and the napkin, which had been on his head, not lying with the linen cloths but rolled up in a place by itself. ⁸Then the other disciple, who reached the tomb first, also went in, and he saw and believed; ⁹for as yet they did not know the Scripture, that he must rise from the dead. ¹⁰Then the disciples went back to their homes.

Jesus Appears to Mary Magdalene

11 But Mary stood weeping outside the tomb, and as she wept she stooped to look into the tomb; ¹²and she saw two angels in white, sitting where the body of Jesus had lain, one at the head and one at the feet. ¹³They said to her, "Woman, why are you weeping?" She said to them, "Because they have taken away my Lord, and I do not know where they have laid him." ¹⁴Saying this, she turned round and saw Jesus standing, but she did not know that it was Jesus. ¹⁵Jesus said to her, "Woman, why are you weeping? Whom do you seek?" Supposing him to be the gardener, she said to him, "Sir, if you have carried him away, tell me where you have laid him, and I will take him away." ¹⁶Jesus said to her, "Mary." She turned and said to him in Hebrew, "Rab-bo′ni!" (which means Teacher). ¹⁷Jesus said to her, "Do not hold me, for I have not yet ascended to the Father; but go to my brethren and say to them, I am ascending to my Father and your Father, to my God and your God." * ¹⁸Mary Mag′dalene went and said to the disciples, "I have seen the Lord"; and she told them that he had said these things to her.

Jesus Gives the Disciples the Power to Forgive Sins

19 On the evening of that day, the first day of the week, the doors being shut where the disciples were, for fear of the Jews, Jesus came and stood among them and said to them, "Peace be with you." ²⁰When he had said this, he showed them his hands and his side. Then the disciples were glad when they saw the Lord. ²¹Jesus said to them again, "Peace be with you. As the Father has sent me, even so I send you." ²²And when he had said this, he breathed on them, and said to them, "Receive the Holy Spirit. ²³If you forgive the sins of any, they are forgiven; if you retain the sins of any, they are retained."

Jesus and Thomas

24 Now Thomas, one of the Twelve, called the Twin, was not with them when Jesus came. ²⁵So the other disciples told him, "We have seen the Lord." But he said to them, "Unless I see in his hands the print of the nails, and place my finger in the mark of the nails, and place my hand in his side, I will not believe."

26 Eight days later, his disciples were again in the house, and Thomas was with them. The doors were shut, but Jesus came and stood among them, and said, "Peace be with you." ²⁷Then he said to Thomas, "Put your finger here, and see my hands; and put out your hand, and place it in my side; do not be faithless, but believing." ²⁸Thomas answered him, "My Lord and my God!" ²⁹Jesus said to him, "You have believed because you have seen me. Blessed are those who have not seen and yet believe."

The Purpose of This Book

30 Now Jesus did many other signs in the presence of the disciples, which are not written in this book; ³¹but these are written that you may believe that Jesus is the Christ, the Son of God, and that believing you may have life in his name.

19:39: Jn 3:1; 7:50.
19:40: Mk 16:1; 14:8.
20:1–10: Mt 28:1–8; Mk 16:1–8; Lk 24:1–10.
20:3–10: Lk 24:11–12.
20:9: Lk 24:26, 46.
20:12: Lk 24:4; Mt 28:5; Mk 16:5.
20:13: Jn 20:2.
20:14: Mt 28:9; Jn 21:4.
20:17: Jn 20:27; Mt 28:10; Jn 7:33.
20:18: Lk 24:10, 23.
20:19–20: Lk 24:36–39.
20:21: Jn 17:18; Mt 28:19.
20:22: Acts 2:4, 33.
20:23: Mt 16:19; 18:18.
20:24: Jn 11:16.
20:27: Lk 24:40.
20:29: 1 Pet 1:8.
20:30: Jn 21:25.
20:31: Jn 3:15.

* 20:17: The death and resurrection of Jesus had put an end to the ordinary familiar relationships of human life, and the time of lasting companionship had not yet come.

Jesus Appears to Disciples by the Sea of Tiberias

21 * After this Jesus revealed himself again to the disciples by the Sea of Tibe′ri-as; and he revealed himself in this way. [2]Simon Peter, Thomas called the Twin, Nathan′a-el of Cana in Galilee, the sons of Zeb′edee, and two others of his disciples were together. [3]Simon Peter said to them, "I am going fishing." They said to him, "We will go with you." They went out and got into the boat; but that night they caught nothing.

4 Just as day was breaking, Jesus stood on the beach; yet the disciples did not know that it was Jesus. [5]Jesus said to them, "Children, have you any fish?" They answered him, "No." [6]He said to them, "Cast the net on the right side of the boat, and you will find some." So they cast it, and now they were not able to haul it in, for the quantity of fish. [7]That disciple whom Jesus loved † said to Peter, "It is the Lord!" When Simon Peter heard that it was the Lord, he put on his clothes, for he was stripped for work, and sprang into the sea. [8]But the other disciples came in the boat, dragging the net full of fish, for they were not far from the land, but about a hundred yards[m] off.

9 When they got out on land, they saw a charcoal fire there, with fish lying on it, and bread. [10]Jesus said to them, "Bring some of the fish that you have just caught." [11]So Simon Peter went aboard and hauled the net ashore, full of large fish, a hundred and fifty-three of them; and although there were so many, the net was not torn. [12]Jesus said to them, "Come and have breakfast." Now none of the disciples dared ask him, "Who are you?" They knew it was the Lord. [13]Jesus came and took the bread and gave it to them, and so with the fish. [14]This was now the third time that Jesus was revealed to the disciples after he was raised from the dead.

Peter Is Given a Command

(15) ‡ When they had finished breakfast, Jesus said to Simon Peter, "Simon, son of John, do you love me more than these?" He said to him, "Yes, Lord; you know that I love you." He said to him, "Feed my lambs." [16]A second time he said to him, "Simon, son of John, do you love me?" He said to him, "Yes, Lord; you know that I love you." He said to him, "Tend my sheep." [17]He said to him the third time, "Simon, son of John, do you love me?" Peter was grieved because he said to him the third time, "Do you love me?" And he said to him, "Lord, you know everything; you know that I love you." Jesus said to him, "Feed my sheep. [18]Truly, truly, I say to you, when you were young, you fastened your own belt and walked where you would; but when you are old, you will stretch out your hands, and another will fasten your belt for you and carry you where you do not wish to go." [19](This he said to show by what death he was to glorify God.) And after this he said to him, "Follow me."

Jesus and the Beloved Disciple

20 Peter turned and saw following them the disciple whom Jesus loved, who had lain close to his breast at the supper and had said, "Lord, who is it that is going to betray you?" [21]When Peter saw him, he said to Jesus, "Lord, what about this man?" [22]Jesus said to him, "If it is my will that he remain until I come, what is that to you? Follow me!" [23]The saying spread abroad among the brethren that this disciple was not to die; yet Jesus did not say to him that he was not to die, but, "If it is my will that he remain until I come, what is that to you?"

24 This is the disciple who is bearing witness to these things, and who has written these things; and we know that his testimony is true.

25 But there are also many other things which Jesus did; were every one of them to be written, I suppose that the world itself could not contain the books that would be written.

---

[m] Greek *two hundred cubits.*
21:2: Jn 11:16; 1:45; Lk 5:10.
21:3–6: Lk 5:3–7.
21:4: Jn 20:14; Lk 24:16.
21:5: Lk 24:41.
21:7: Jn 13:23; 19:26; 20:2; 21:20.
21:14: Jn 20:19, 26.
21:15: Jn 1:42; 13:37; Mk 14:29–31; Lk 12:32.
21:16: Mt 2:6; Acts 20:28, 1 Pet 5:2; Rev 7:17.
21:19: 2 Pet 1:14; Mk 1:17.
21:20: Jn 13:25.
21:22: 1 Cor 4:5; Jas 5:7; Rev 2:25; Mt 16:28.
21:24: Jn 15:27; 19:35.
21:25: Jn 20:30.
* 21:1–25: This chapter was added later, either by the evangelist or by a disciple; cf. 20:3–31 and 21:24.
† 21:7: John remembered a similar miracle before; cf. Lk 5:6.
‡ 21:15–17: The threefold question addressed to Peter alone corresponds to the threefold denial. Jesus gives Peter charge over his flock.

THE
ACTS OF THE APOSTLES

The Promise of the Holy Spirit

1 In the first book, * O Theoph′ilus, I have dealt with all that Jesus began to do and teach, ²until the day when he was taken up, after he had given commandment through the Holy Spirit to the apostles whom he had chosen. ³To them he presented himself alive after his passion by many proofs, appearing to them during forty days, and speaking of the kingdom of God. ⁴And while staying ª with them he charged them not to depart from Jerusalem, but to wait for the promise of the Father, which, he said, "you heard from me, ⁵for John baptized with water, but before many days you shall be baptized with the Holy Spirit."

The Ascension of Jesus

6 So when they had come together, they asked him, "Lord, will you at this time restore the kingdom to Israel?" ⁷He said to them, "It is not for you to know times or seasons which the Father has fixed by his own authority. ⁸But you shall receive power when the Holy Spirit has come upon you; and you shall be my witnesses in Jerusalem and in all Judea and Samar′ia and to the end of the earth." ⁹And when he had said this, as they were looking on, he was lifted up, and a cloud took him out of their sight. ¹⁰And while they were gazing into heaven as he went, behold, two men stood by them in white robes, ¹¹and said, "Men of Galilee, why do you stand looking into heaven? This Jesus, who was taken up from you into heaven, will come in the same way as you saw him go into heaven."

Matthias Chosen to Replace Judas

12 Then they returned to Jerusalem from the mount called Olivet, which is near Jerusalem, a sabbath day's journey away; ¹³and when they had entered, they went up to the upper room, where they were staying, Peter and John and James and Andrew, Philip and Thomas, Bartholomew and Matthew, James the son of Alphae′us and Simon the Zealot and Judas the son of James. ¹⁴All these with one accord devoted themselves to prayer, together with the women and Mary the mother of Jesus, and with his brethren. †

15 In those days Peter stood up among the brethren (the company of persons was in all about a hundred and twenty), and said, ¹⁶"Brethren, the Scripture had to be fulfilled, which the Holy Spirit spoke beforehand by the mouth of David, concerning Judas who was guide to those who arrested Jesus. ¹⁷For he was numbered among us, and was allotted his share in this ministry. ¹⁸(Now this man bought a field with the reward of his wickedness; and falling headlong ᵇ he burst open in the middle and all his bowels gushed out. ¹⁹And it became known to all the inhabitants of Jerusalem, so that the field was called in their language Akel′dama, that is, Field of Blood.) ²⁰For it is written in the book of Psalms,

'Let his habitation become desolate, and let there be no one to live in it';

and

'His office let another take.'

²¹So one of the men who have accompanied us during all the time that the Lord Jesus went in and out among us, ²²beginning from the baptism of John until the day when he was taken up from us—one of these men must become with us a witness to his resurrection." ‡ ²³And they put forward two, Joseph called Barsab′bas, who was surnamed Justus, and Matthi′as. ²⁴And they prayed and said, "Lord, you know the hearts of all men, show which one of these two you have chosen ²⁵to take the place in this ministry and apostleship from which Judas turned aside, to go to his own place." ²⁶And they cast lots for them, and the lot fell on Matthi′as; and he was enrolled with the eleven apostles.

The Coming of the Holy Spirit

2 When the day of Pentecost had come, they were all together in one place. ²And suddenly a sound came from heaven like the rush of a mighty wind, and it filled all the house where they were sitting. ³And there appeared to them tongues as of fire, distributed and resting on each one of them. ⁴And they were all filled with the Holy Spirit and began to speak in other tongues, as the Spirit gave them utterance.

5 Now there were dwelling in Jerusalem Jews, devout men from every nation under heaven. ⁶And

---

ª Or *eating.*
ᵇ Or *swelling up.*
1:1: Lk 1:1–4.
1:4: Lk 24:49.
1:8: Lk 24:48–49.
1:9–12: Lk 24:50–53.
1:13: Mt 10:2–4; Mk 3:16–19; Lk 6:14–16.
1:16–19: Mt 27:3–10.
1:20: Ps 69:25; 109:8.
* 1:1, *the first book:* i.e., St. Luke's Gospel.
† 1:14, *brethren:* See note on Mt 12:46.
‡ 1:22: An apostle must be a witness to Christ's resurrection.

at this sound the multitude came together, and they were bewildered, because each one heard them speaking in his own language. ⁷And they were amazed and wondered, saying, "Are not all these who are speaking Galileans? ⁸And how is it that we hear, each of us in his own native language? ⁹Par′thians and Medes and E′lamites and residents of Mesopota′mia, Judea and Cappado′cia, Pontus and Asia, ¹⁰Phryg′ia and Pamphyl′ia, Egypt and the parts of Libya belonging to Cyre′ne, and visitors from Rome, both Jews and proselytes, ¹¹Cretans and Arabians, we hear them telling in our own tongues the mighty works of God." ¹²And all were amazed and perplexed, saying to one another, "What does this mean?" ¹³But others mocking said, "They are filled with new wine."

Peter Addresses the Crowd

14 But Peter, * standing with the Eleven, lifted up his voice and addressed them, "Men of Judea and all who dwell in Jerusalem, let this be known to you, and give ear to my words. ¹⁵For these men are not drunk, as you suppose, since it is only the third hour of the day; ¹⁶but this is what was spoken by the prophet Joel:

¹⁷'And in the last days it shall be, God declares,
  that I will pour out my Spirit upon all flesh,
  and your sons and your daughters shall
      prophesy,
  and your young men shall see visions,
  and your old men shall dream dreams;
¹⁸yes, and on my menservants and my
      maidservants in those days
  I will pour out my Spirit; and they shall
      prophesy.
¹⁹And I will show wonders in the heaven above
  and signs on the earth beneath,
  blood, and fire, and vapor of smoke;
²⁰the sun shall be turned into darkness
  and the moon into blood,
  before the day of the Lord comes,
  the great and manifest day.
²¹And it shall be that whoever calls on the name
  of the Lord shall be saved.'

22 "Men of Israel, hear these words: Jesus of Nazareth, a man attested to you by God with mighty works and wonders and signs which God did through him in your midst, as you yourselves know—²³this Jesus, delivered up according to the definite plan and foreknowledge of God, you crucified and killed by the hands of lawless men. ²⁴But God raised him up, having loosed the pangs of death, because it was not possible for him to be held by it. ²⁵For David says concerning him,

'I saw the Lord always before me,
  for he is at my right hand that I may not be
      shaken;
²⁶therefore my heart was glad, and my tongue
      rejoiced;
  moreover my flesh will dwell in hope.

²⁷For you will not abandon my soul to Hades,
  nor let your Holy One see corruption.
²⁸You have made known to me the ways of life;
  you will make me full of gladness with your
      presence.'

29 "Brethren, I may say to you confidently of the patriarch David that he both died and was buried, and his tomb is with us to this day. ³⁰Being therefore a prophet, and knowing that God had sworn with an oath to him that he would set one of his descendants upon his throne, ³¹he foresaw and spoke of the resurrection of the Christ, that he was not abandoned to Hades, nor did his flesh see corruption. ³²This Jesus God raised up, and of that we all are witnesses. ³³Being therefore exalted at the right hand of God, and having received from the Father the promise of the Holy Spirit, he has poured out this which you see and hear. ³⁴For David did not ascend into the heavens; but he himself says,

'The Lord said to my Lord, Sit at my right
      hand,
³⁵till I make your enemies a stool for your feet.'

³⁶Let all the house of Israel therefore know assuredly that God has made him both Lord and Christ, this Jesus whom you crucified."

The First Converts

37 Now when they heard this they were cut to the heart, and said to Peter and the rest of the apostles, "Brethren, what shall we do?" ³⁸And Peter said to them, "Repent, and be baptized every one of you in the name of Jesus Christ for the forgiveness of your sins; and you shall receive the gift of the Holy Spirit. ³⁹For the promise is to you and to your children and to all that are far off, every one whom the Lord our God calls to him." ⁴⁰And he testified with many other words and exhorted them, saying, "Save yourselves from this crooked generation." ⁴¹So those who received his word were baptized, and there were added that day about three thousand souls. ⁴²And they held steadfastly to the apostles' teaching and fellowship, to the breaking of the bread and to the prayers.

Life among the Believers

43 And fear came upon every soul; and many wonders and signs were done through the apostles. ⁴⁴And all who believed were together and had all things in common; ⁴⁵and they sold their possessions and goods and distributed them to all, as any had need. ⁴⁶And day by day,

---

2:17–21: Joel 2:28–32.
2:25–28: Ps 16:8–11.
2:30: Ps 132:11.
2:31: Ps 16:10.
2:34–35: Ps 110:1.
2:39: Is 57:19; Joel 2:32.
2:44–45: Acts 4:32–35.
* 2:14: Peter assumes the leadership in public. In this discourse we have the earliest form of the apostolic preaching.

attending the temple together and breaking bread in their homes, they partook of food with glad and generous hearts, ⁴⁷praising God and having favor with all the people. And the Lord added to their number day by day those who were being saved.

Peter Heals a Lame Beggar

3 Now Peter and John were going up to the temple at the hour of prayer, the ninth hour. * ²And a man lame from birth was being carried, whom they laid daily at that gate of the temple which is called Beautiful to ask alms of those who entered the temple. ³Seeing Peter and John about to go into the temple, he asked for alms. ⁴And Peter directed his gaze at him, with John, and said, "Look at us." ⁵And he fixed his attention upon them, expecting to receive something from them. ⁶But Peter said, "I have no silver and gold, but I give you what I have; in the name of Jesus Christ of Nazareth, rise and walk." ⁷And he took him by the right hand and raised him up; and immediately his feet and ankles were made strong. ⁸And leaping up he stood and walked and entered the temple with them, walking and leaping and praising God. ⁹And all the people saw him walking and praising God, ¹⁰and recognized him as the one who sat for alms at the Beautiful Gate of the temple; and they were filled with wonder and amazement at what had happened to him.

Peter Addresses the People
in Solomon's Portico

11 While he clung to Peter and John, all the people ran together to them in the portico called Solomon's, astounded. ¹²And when Peter saw it he addressed the people, "Men of Israel, why do you wonder at this, or why do you stare at us, as though by our own power or piety we had made him walk? ¹³The God of Abraham and of Isaac and of Jacob, the God of our fathers, glorified his servant ᶜ Jesus, whom you delivered up and denied in the presence of Pilate, when he had decided to release him. ¹⁴But you denied the Holy and Righteous One, and asked for a murderer to be granted to you, ¹⁵and killed the Author of life, whom God raised from the dead. To this we are witnesses. ¹⁶And his name, by faith in his name, has made this man strong whom you see and know; and the faith which is through Jesus ᵈ has given the man this perfect health in the presence of you all.

17 "And now, brethren, I know that you acted in ignorance, as did also your rulers. ¹⁸But what God foretold by the mouth of all the prophets, that his Christ should suffer, he thus fulfilled. ¹⁹Repent therefore, and turn again, that your sins may be blotted out, that times of refreshing may come from the presence of the Lord, ²⁰and that he may send the Christ appointed for you, Jesus, ²¹whom

heaven must receive until the time for establishing all that God spoke by the mouth of his holy prophets from of old. ²²Moses said, 'The Lord God will raise up for you a prophet from your brethren as he raised me up. You shall listen to him in whatever he tells you. ²³And it shall be that every soul that does not listen to that prophet shall be destroyed from the people.' ²⁴And all the prophets who have spoken, from Samuel and those who came afterwards, also proclaimed these days. ²⁵You are the sons of the prophets and of the covenant which God gave to your fathers, saying to Abraham, 'And in your posterity shall all the families of the earth be blessed.' ²⁶God, having raised up his servant, ᶜ sent him to you first, to bless you in turning every one of you from your wickedness."

Peter and John before the Council

4 And as they were speaking to the people, the priests and the captain of the temple and the Sad'ducees came upon them, ²annoyed because they were teaching the people and proclaiming in Jesus the resurrection from the dead. † ³And they arrested them and put them in custody until the next day, for it was already evening. ⁴But many of those who heard the word believed; and the number of the men came to about five thousand.

5 On the next day their rulers and elders and scribes were gathered together in Jerusalem, ⁶with Annas the high priest and Cai'aphas and John and Alexander, and all who were of the high-priestly family. ⁷And when they had set them in their midst, they inquired, "By what power or by what name did you do this?" ⁸Then Peter, filled with the Holy Spirit, said to them, "Rulers of the people and elders, ⁹if we are being examined today concerning a good deed done to a cripple, by what means this man has been healed, ¹⁰be it known to you all, and to all the people of Israel, that by the name of Jesus Christ of Nazareth, whom you crucified, whom God raised from the dead, by him this man is standing before you well. ¹¹This is the stone which was rejected by you builders, but which has become the cornerstone. ¹²And there is salvation in no one else, for there is no other name under heaven given among men by which we must be saved."

13 Now when they saw the boldness of Peter and John, and perceived that they were uneducated, common men, they wondered; and they

---

ᶜ Or *child*.
ᵈ Greek *him*.
3:13: Ex 3:6; Is 52:13.
3:22: Deut 18:15–16.
3:23: Deut 18:19; Lev 23:29.
3:25: Gen 22:18.
4:11: Ps 118:22.
* 3:1: In the early days, the first Christians observed the prescriptions of the Jewish law.
† 4:2: The Sadducees did not believe in the resurrection of the dead.

recognized that they had been with Jesus. [14]But seeing the man that had been healed standing beside them, they had nothing to say in opposition. [15]But when they had commanded them to go aside out of the council, they conferred with one another, [16]saying, "What shall we do with these men? For that a notable sign has been performed through them is manifest to all the inhabitants of Jerusalem, and we cannot deny it. [17]But in order that it may spread no further among the people, let us warn them to speak no more to any one in this name." [18]So they called them and charged them not to speak or teach at all in the name of Jesus. [19]But Peter and John answered them, "Whether it is right in the sight of God to listen to you rather than to God, you must judge; [20]for we cannot but speak of what we have seen and heard." [21]And when they had further threatened them, they let them go, finding no way to punish them, because of the people; for all men praised God for what had happened. [22]For the man on whom this sign of healing was performed was more than forty years old.

The Believers Pray for Boldness

23 When they were released they went to their friends and reported what the chief priests and the elders had said to them. [24]And when they heard it, they lifted their voices together to God and said, "Sovereign Lord, who made the heaven and the earth and the sea and everything in them, [25]who by the mouth of our father David, your servant, [c] said by the Holy Spirit,

'Why did the Gentiles rage,
  and the peoples imagine vain things?
[26]The kings of the earth set themselves in array,
  and the rulers were gathered together,
    against the Lord and against his Anointed'— [e]
[27]for truly in this city there were gathered together against your holy servant [c] Jesus, whom you anointed, both Herod and Pontius Pilate, with the Gentiles and the peoples of Israel, [28]to do whatever your hand and your plan had predestined to take place. [29]And now, Lord, look upon their threats, and grant to your servants [f] to speak your word with all boldness, [30]while you stretch out your hand to heal, and signs and wonders are performed through the name of your holy servant [c] Jesus." [31]And when they had prayed, the place in which they were gathered together was shaken; and they were all filled with the Holy Spirit and spoke the word of God with boldness.

The Believers Share Their Possessions

32 Now the company of those who believed were of one heart and soul, and no one said that any of the things which he possessed was his own, but they had everything in common. * [33]And with great power the apostles gave their testimony to the resurrection of the Lord Jesus, and

great grace was upon them all. [34]There was not any one needy among them, for as many as were possessors of lands or houses sold them, and brought the proceeds of what was sold [35]and laid it at the apostles' feet; and distribution was made to each as any had need. [36]Thus Joseph who was surnamed by the apostles Barnabas (which means, Son of encouragement), a Levite, a native of Cyprus, [37]sold a field which belonged to him, and brought the money and laid it at the apostles' feet.

Ananias and Sapphira

5 But a man named Anani′as with his wife Sapphi′ra sold a piece of property, [2]and with his wife's knowledge he kept back some of the proceeds, and brought only a part and laid it at the apostles' feet. [3]But Peter said, "Anani′as, why has Satan filled your heart to lie to the Holy Spirit and to keep back part of the proceeds of the land? [4]While it remained unsold, did it not remain your own? And after it was sold, was it not at your disposal? How is it that you have contrived this deed in your heart? You have not lied to men but to God." [5]When Anani′as heard these words, he fell down and died. And great fear came upon all who heard of it. [6]The young men rose and wrapped him up and carried him out and buried him.

7 After an interval of about three hours his wife came in, not knowing what had happened. [8]And Peter said to her, "Tell me whether you sold the land for so much." And she said, "Yes, for so much." [9]But Peter said to her, "How is it that you have agreed together to tempt the Spirit of the Lord? Listen, the feet of those that have buried your husband are at the door, and they will carry you out." [10]Immediately she fell down at his feet and died. When the young men came in they found her dead, and they carried her out and buried her beside her husband. [11]And great fear came upon the whole Church, † and upon all who heard of these things.

The Apostles Heal Many

12 Now many signs and wonders were done among the people by the hands of the apostles. And they were all together in Solomon's Portico. [13]None of the rest dared join them, but the people held them in high honor. [14]And more than ever believers were added to the Lord, multitudes both of men and women, [15]so that they even carried

---

e Or *Christ*.
c Or *child*.
f Or *slaves*.
4:24: Ex 20:11; Ps 146:6.
4:25–26: Ps 2:1–2.
4:27: Ps 2:2; 2:1.
4:32-35: Acts 2:44–45.
* 4:32, *everything in common*: They freely shared what was theirs individually; cf. Acts 5:4.
† 5:11, *Church*: i.e., the Christian and Messianic community; a term borrowed from the Old Testament.

out the sick into the streets, and laid them on beds and pallets, that as Peter came by at least his shadow might fall on some of them. [16]The people also gathered from the towns around Jerusalem, bringing the sick and those afflicted with unclean spirits, and they were all healed.

The Apostles Are Imprisoned and Brought before the Council

17 But the high priest rose up and all who were with him, that is, the party of the Sad'ducees, and filled with jealousy [18]they arrested the apostles and put them in the common prison. [19]But at night an angel of the Lord opened the prison doors and brought them out and said, [20]"Go and stand in the temple and speak to the people all the words of this Life." * [21]And when they heard this, they entered the temple at daybreak and taught.

Now the high priest came and those who were with him and called together the council and all the senate of Israel, and sent to the prison to have them brought. [22]But when the officers came, they did not find them in the prison, and they returned and reported, [23]"We found the prison securely locked and the sentries standing at the doors, but when we opened it we found no one inside." [24]Now when the captain of the temple and the chief priests heard these words, they were much perplexed about them, wondering what this would come to. [25]And some one came and told them, "The men whom you put in prison are standing in the temple and teaching the people." [26]Then the captain with the officers went and brought them, but without violence, for they were afraid of being stoned by the people.

27 And when they had brought them, they set them before the council. And the high priest questioned them, [28]saying, "We strictly charged you not to teach in this name, yet here you have filled Jerusalem with your teaching and you intend to bring this man's blood upon us." [29]But Peter and the apostles answered, "We must obey God rather than men. [30]The God of our fathers raised Jesus whom you killed by hanging him on a tree. [31]God exalted him at his right hand as Leader and Savior, to give repentance to Israel and forgiveness of sins. [32]And we are witnesses to these things, and so is the Holy Spirit whom God has given to those who obey him."

33 When they heard this they were enraged and wanted to kill them. [34]But a Pharisee in the council named Gama'li-el, † a teacher of the law, held in honor by all the people, stood up and ordered the men to be put outside for a while. [35]And he said to them, "Men of Israel, take care what you do with these men. [36]For before these days Theu'das arose, claiming to be somebody, and a number of men, about four hundred, joined him; but he was slain and all who followed him were dispersed and came to nothing. [37]After him

Judas the Galilean arose in the days of the census and drew away some of the people after him; he also perished, and all who followed him were scattered. [38]So in the present case I tell you, keep away from these men and let them alone; for if this plan or this undertaking is of men, it will fail; [39]but if it is of God, you will not be able to overthrow them. You might even be found opposing God!"

40 So they took his advice, and when they had called in the apostles, they beat them and charged them not to speak in the name of Jesus, and let them go. [41]Then they left the presence of the council, rejoicing that they were counted worthy to suffer dishonor for the name. [42]And every day in the temple and at home they did not cease teaching and preaching Jesus as the Christ.

Seven Chosen to Serve

6 Now in these days when the disciples were increasing in number, the Hellenists ‡ murmured against the Hebrews because their widows were neglected in the daily distribution. [2]And the Twelve summoned the body of the disciples and said, "It is not right that we should give up preaching the word of God to serve tables. [3]Therefore, brethren, pick out from among you seven men of good repute, full of the Spirit and of wisdom, whom we may appoint to this duty. [4]But we will devote ourselves to prayer and to the ministry of the word." [5]And what they said pleased the whole multitude, and they chose Stephen, a man full of faith and of the Holy Spirit, and Philip, and Proch'orus, and Nica'nor, and Ti'mon, and Par'menas, and Nicola'us, a proselyte of Antioch. [6]These they set before the apostles, and they prayed and laid their hands upon them.

7 And the word of God increased; and the number of the disciples multiplied greatly in Jerusalem, and a great many of the priests were obedient to the faith.

The Arrest of Stephen

8 And Stephen, full of grace and power, did great wonders and signs among the people. [9]Then some of those who belonged to the synagogue of the Freedmen (as it was called), and of the Cyre'nians, and of the Alexandrians, and of those from Cili'cia and Asia, arose and disputed with Stephen. [10]But they could not withstand the wisdom and the Spirit with which he spoke. [11]Then they secretly instigated men, who said, "We have heard him speak blasphemous words against Moses and God." [12]And they stirred up the people and the elders and the scribes, and they came upon him and seized him and brought him before the council, [13]and set up false witnesses who said,

---

5:30, *Life:* Deut 21:22–23.

* 5:20, *Life:* cf. Acts 9:2, "the Way." These terms recall the words of Jesus, "I am the way, and the truth, and the life" (Jn 14:6).

† 5:34, *Gamaliel:* Teacher of St. Paul; cf. Acts 22:3.

‡ 6:1, *Hellenists:* Greek-speaking Jews of the Dispersion, who had their own synagogues in Jerusalem and read the Scriptures in Greek.

"This man never ceases to speak words against this holy place and the law; [14]for we have heard him say that this Jesus of Nazareth will destroy this place, and will change the customs which Moses delivered to us." [15]And gazing at him, all who sat in the council saw that his face was like the face of an angel.

Stephen's Speech to the Council

7 And the high priest said, "Is this so?" [2]And Stephen said:

"Brethren and fathers, hear me. The God of glory appeared to our father Abraham, when he was in Mesopota'mia, before he lived in Haran, [3]and said to him, 'Depart from your land and from your kindred and go into the land which I will show you.' [4]Then he departed from the land of the Chalde'ans, and lived in Haran. And after his father died, God removed him from there into this land in which you are now living; [5]yet he gave him no inheritance in it, not even a foot's length, but promised to give it to him in possession and to his posterity after him, though he had no child. [6]And God spoke to this effect, that his posterity would be aliens in a land belonging to others, who would enslave them and ill-treat them four hundred years. [7]But I will judge the nation which they serve,' said God, 'and after that they shall come out and worship me in this place.' [8]And he gave him the covenant of circumcision. And so Abraham became the father of Isaac, and circumcised him on the eighth day; and Isaac became the father of Jacob, and Jacob of the twelve patriarchs.

9 "And the patriarchs, jealous of Joseph, sold him into Egypt; but God was with him, [10]and rescued him out of all his afflictions, and gave him favor and wisdom before Pharaoh, king of Egypt, who made him governor over Egypt and over all his household. [11]Now there came a famine throughout all Egypt and Canaan, and great affliction, and our fathers could find no food. [12]But when Jacob heard that there was grain in Egypt, he sent forth our fathers the first time. [13]And at the second visit Joseph made himself known to his brothers, and Joseph's family became known to Pharaoh. [14]And Joseph sent and called to him Jacob his father and all his kindred, seventy-five souls; [15]and Jacob went down into Egypt. And he died, himself and our fathers, [16]and they were carried back to She'chem and laid in the tomb that Abraham had bought for a sum of silver from the sons of Hamor in Shechem.

17 "But as the time of the promise drew near, which God had granted to Abraham, the people grew and multiplied in Egypt [18]till there arose over Egypt another king who had not known Joseph. [19]He dealt craftily with our race and forced our fathers to expose their infants, that they might not be kept alive. [20]At this time Moses was born,

and was beautiful before God. And he was brought up for three months in his father's house; [21]and when he was exposed, Pharaoh's daughter adopted him and brought him up as her own son. [22]And Moses was instructed in all the wisdom of the Egyptians, and he was mighty in his words and deeds.

23 "When he was forty years old, it came into his heart to visit his brethren, the sons of Israel. [24]And seeing one of them being wronged, he defended the oppressed man and avenged him by striking the Egyptian. [25]He supposed that his brethren understood that God was giving them deliverance by his hand, but they did not understand. [26]And on the following day he appeared to them as they were quarreling and would have reconciled them, saying, 'Men, you are brethren, why do you wrong each other?' [27]But the man who was wronging his neighbor thrust him aside, saying, 'Who made you a ruler and a judge over us? [28]Do you want to kill me as you killed the Egyptian yesterday?' [29]At this retort Moses fled, and became an exile in the land of Mid'ian, where he became the father of two sons.

30 "Now when forty years had passed, an angel appeared to him in the wilderness of Mount Sinai, in a flame of fire in a bush. [31]When Moses saw it he wondered at the sight; and as he drew near to look, the voice of the Lord came, [32]'I am the God of your fathers, the God of Abraham and of Isaac and of Jacob.' And Moses trembled and did not dare to look. [33]And the Lord said to him, 'Take off the shoes from your feet, for the place where you are standing is holy ground. [34]I have surely seen the ill-treatment of my people that are in Egypt and heard their groaning, and I have come down to deliver them. And now come, I will send you to Egypt.'

35 "This Moses whom they refused, saying, 'Who made you a ruler and a judge?' God sent as both ruler and deliverer by the hand of the angel

---

7:2: Ps 29:3; Gen 11:31; 15:7.
7:3: Gen 12:1.
7:4: Gen 11:31; 15:7; 12:5.
7:5: Deut 2:5; Gen 12:7; 17:8.
7:6–7: Gen 15:13–14.
7:7: Ex 3:12.
7:8: Gen 17:10–14; 21:2–4; 25:26; 29:31–35; 30:1–24; 35:16–18; 35:23–26.
7:9: Gen 37:11, 28; 45:4.
7:9–10: Gen 39:2–3, 21.
7:10: Gen 41:40–46; Ps 105:21.
7:11: Gen 41:54–55; 42:5.
7:12: Gen 42:2.
7:13: Gen 45:1–4.
7:14: Gen 45:9–10.
7:14–15: Deut 10:22.
7:16: Josh 24:32; Gen 50:13.
7:17–18: Ex 1:7–8.
7:19: Ex 1:10–11, 15–22.
7:20: Ex 2:2.
7:21: Ex 2:5–6, 10.
7:23–29: Ex 2:11–15.
7:29: Ex 2:22; 18:3–4.
7:30–34: Ex 3:1–10.
7:35: Ex 2:14.

that appeared to him in the bush. ³⁶He led them out, having performed wonders and signs in Egypt and at the Red Sea, and in the wilderness for forty years. ³⁷This is the Moses who said to the Israelites, 'God will raise up for you a prophet from your brethren as he raised me up.' ³⁸This is he who was in the congregation in the wilderness with the angel who spoke to him at Mount Sinai, and with our fathers; and he received living oracles to give to us. ³⁹Our fathers refused to obey him, but thrust him aside, and in their hearts they turned to Egypt, ⁴⁰saying to Aaron, 'Make for us gods to go before us; as for this Moses who led us out from the land of Egypt, we do not know what has become of him.' ⁴¹And they made a calf in those days, and offered a sacrifice to the idol and rejoiced in the works of their hands. ⁴²But God turned and gave them over to worship the host of heaven, as it is written in the book of the prophets:

'Did you offer to me slain beasts and sacrifices,
  forty years in the wilderness, O house of
    Israel?
⁴³And you took up the tent of Mo'loch,
  and the star of the god Re'phan,
  the figures which you made to worship;
  and I will remove you beyond Babylon.'

44 "Our fathers had the tent of witness in the wilderness, even as he who spoke to Moses directed him to make it, according to the pattern that he had seen. ⁴⁵Our fathers in turn brought it in with Joshua when they dispossessed the nations which God thrust out before our fathers. So it was until the days of David, ⁴⁶who found favor in the sight of God and asked leave to find a habitation for the God of Jacob. ⁴⁷But it was Solomon who built a house for him. ⁴⁸Yet the Most High does not dwell in houses made with hands; as the prophet says,

⁴⁹"Heaven is my throne,
  and earth my footstool.
What house will you build for me, says the
    Lord,
  or what is the place of my rest?
⁵⁰ Did not my hand make all these things?'

51 "You stiff-necked people, uncircumcised in heart and ears, you always resist the Holy Spirit. As your fathers did, so do you. ⁵²Which of the prophets did not your fathers persecute? And they killed those who announced beforehand the coming of the Righteous One, whom you have now betrayed and murdered, ⁵³you who received the law as delivered by angels and did not keep it."

The Stoning of Stephen

54 Now when they heard these things they were enraged, and they ground their teeth against him. ⁵⁵But he, full of the Holy Spirit, gazed into heaven and saw the glory of God, and Jesus standing at the right hand of God; ⁵⁶and he said, "Behold, I see the heavens opened, and the Son of man standing at the right hand of God." ⁵⁷But they cried out with a loud voice and stopped their ears and rushed together upon him. ⁵⁸Then they cast him out of the city and stoned him; and the witnesses laid down their garments at the feet of a young man named Saul. ⁵⁹And as they were stoning Stephen, he prayed, "Lord Jesus, receive my spirit." ⁶⁰And he knelt down and cried with a loud voice, "Lord, do not hold this sin against them." And when he had said 8 this, he fell asleep. ¹And Saul was consenting to his death.

Saul Persecutes the Church

And on that day a great persecution arose against the Church in Jerusalem; and they were all scattered throughout the region of Judea and Sama'ria, except the apostles. ²Devout men buried Stephen, and made great lamentation over him. ³But Saul laid waste the Church, and entering house after house, he dragged off men and women and committed them to prison.

Philip Preaches in Samaria

4 Now those who were scattered went about preaching the word. ⁵Philip went down to a city of Samar'ia, and proclaimed to them the Christ. ⁶And the multitudes with one accord gave heed to what was said by Philip, when they heard him and saw the signs which he did. ⁷For unclean spirits came out of many who were possessed, crying with a loud voice; and many who were paralyzed or lame were healed. ⁸So there was much joy in that city.

Simon the Magician

9 But there was a man named Simon who had previously practiced magic in the city and amazed the nation of Samar'ia, saying that he himself was somebody great. ¹⁰They all listened to him, from the least to the greatest, saying, "This man is that power of God which is called Great." ¹¹And they listened to him, because for a long time he had amazed them with his magic. ¹²But when they believed Philip as he preached good news about the kingdom of God and the name of Jesus Christ, they were baptized, both men and women. ¹³Even Simon himself believed, and after being baptized he continued with Philip. And seeing

7:36: Ex 7:3; 14:21; Num 14:33.
7:37: Deut 18:15, 18.
7:38: Ex 19.
7:39: Num 14:3–4.
7:40: Ex 32:1, 23.
7:41: Ex 32:4, 6.
7:42: Jer 19:13.
7:42–43: Amos 5:25–27.
7:44: Ex 25:9, 40.
7:45: Josh 3:14–17; Deut 32:49.
7:46: 2 Sam 7:8–16; Ps 132:1–5.
7:47: 1 Kings 6.
7:49–50: Is 66:1–2.
7:51: Ex 33:3, 5; Jer 9:26; 6:10; Is 63:10.
8:1: Acts 11:19.

signs and great miracles performed, he was amazed.

14 Now when the apostles at Jerusalem heard that Samar′ia had received the word of God, they sent to them Peter and John, [15]who came down and prayed for them that they might receive the Holy Spirit; [16]for the Spirit had not yet fallen on any of them, but they had only been baptized in the name of the Lord Jesus. [17]Then they laid their hands on them and they received the Holy Spirit. [18]Now when Simon saw that the Spirit was given through the laying on of the apostles' hands, he offered them money, [19]saying, "Give me also this power, that any one on whom I lay my hands may receive the Holy Spirit." [20]But Peter said to him, "Your silver perish with you, because you thought you could obtain the gift of God with money! * [21]You have neither part nor lot in this matter, for your heart is not right before God. [22]Repent therefore of this wickedness of yours, and pray to the Lord that, if possible, the intent of your heart may be forgiven you. [23]For I see that you are in the gall of bitterness and in the bond of iniquity." [24]And Simon answered, "Pray for me to the Lord, that nothing of what you have said may come upon me."

25 Now when they had testified and spoken the word of the Lord, they returned to Jerusalem, preaching the gospel to many villages of the Samaritans.

Philip and the Ethiopian Eunuch

26 But an angel of the Lord said to Philip, "Rise and go toward the south [g] to the road that goes down from Jerusalem to Gaza." This is a desert road. [27]And he rose and went. And behold, an Ethiopian, a eunuch, a minister of Canda′ce the queen of the Ethiopians, in charge of all her treasure, had come to Jerusalem to worship [28]and was returning; seated in his chariot, he was reading the prophet Isaiah. [29]And the Spirit said to Philip, "Go up and join this chariot." [30]So Philip ran to him, and heard him reading Isaiah the prophet, and asked, "Do you understand what you are reading?" [31]And he said, "How can I, unless some one guides me?" And he invited Philip to come up and sit with him. [32]Now the passage of the Scripture which he was reading was this:

"As a sheep led to the slaughter
or a lamb before its shearer is silent,
so he opens not his mouth.
[33]In his humiliation justice was denied him.
Who can describe his generation?
For his life is taken up from the earth."

[34]And the eunuch said to Philip, "Please, about whom does the prophet say this, about himself or about some one else?" [35]Then Philip opened his mouth, and beginning with this Scripture he told him the good news of Jesus. [36]And as they went along the road they came to some water, and the eunuch said, "See, here is water! What is to prevent my being baptized?" [h] [38]And he commanded the chariot to stop, and they both went down into the water, Philip and the eunuch, and he baptized him. [39]And when they came up out of the water, the Spirit of the Lord caught up Philip; and the eunuch saw him no more, and went on his way rejoicing. [40]But Philip was found at Azo′tus, and passing on he preached the gospel to all the towns till he came to Caesare′a.

The Conversion of Saul

9 But Saul, still breathing threats and murder against the disciples of the Lord, went to the high priest [2]and asked him for letters to the synagogues at Damascus, so that if he found any belonging to the Way, men or women, he might bring them bound to Jerusalem. [3]Now as he journeyed he approached Damascus, and suddenly a light from heaven flashed about him. [4]And he fell to the ground and heard a voice saying to him, "Saul, Saul, why do you persecute me?" [5]And he said, "Who are you, Lord?" And he said, "I am Jesus, whom you are persecuting; † [6]but rise and enter the city, and you will be told what you are to do." [7]The men who were traveling with him stood speechless, hearing the voice but seeing no one. [8]Saul arose from the ground; and when his eyes were opened, he could see nothing; so they led him by the hand and brought him into Damascus. [9]And for three days he was without sight, and neither ate nor drank.

10 Now there was a disciple at Damascus named Anani′as. The Lord said to him in a vision, "Ananias." And he said, "Here I am, Lord." [11]And the Lord said to him, "Rise and go to the street called Straight, and inquire in the house of Judas for a man of Tarsus named Saul; for behold, he is praying, [12]and he has seen a man named Anani′as come in and lay his hands on him so that he might regain his sight." [13]But Anani′as answered, "Lord, I have heard from many about this man, how much evil he has done to your saints ‡ at Jerusalem; [14]and here he has authority from the chief priests to bind all who call upon your name." [15]But the Lord said to him, "Go, for he is a chosen instrument of mine to carry my name before the Gentiles and kings and the sons of Israel; [16]for I will show him how much he must suffer for the sake of my name." [17]So Anani′as departed and

---

[g] Or *at noon.*
[h] Other ancient authorities add all or most of verse 37, *And Philip said, "If you believe with all your heart, you may." And he replied, "I believe that Jesus Christ is the Son of God."*
8:21: Ps 78:37.
8:23: Is 58:6.
8:32–33: Is 53:7–8.
9:1–19: Acts 22:4–16; 26:9–18.
* 8:20: Hence the word "simony," meaning "buying and selling spiritual powers and privileges."
† 9:5: Jesus identifies himself with his followers.
‡ 9:13, *saints:* i.e., Christians, made holy by baptism.

entered the house. And laying his hands on him he said, "Brother Saul, the Lord Jesus who appeared to you on the road by which you came, has sent me that you may regain your sight and be filled with the Holy Spirit." [18]And immediately something like scales fell from his eyes and he regained his sight. Then he rose and was baptized, [19]and took food and was strengthened.

Saul Preaches in Damascus

For several days he was with the disciples at Damascus. [20]And in the synagogues immediately he proclaimed Jesus, saying, "He is the Son of God." [21]And all who heard him were amazed, and said, "Is not this the man who made havoc in Jerusalem of those who called on this name? And he has come here for this purpose, to bring them bound before the chief priests." [22]But Saul increased all the more in strength, and confounded the Jews who lived in Damascus by proving that Jesus was the Christ.

Saul Escapes from the Jews

23 When many days had passed, the Jews plotted to kill him, [24]but their plot became known to Saul. They were watching the gates day and night, to kill him; [25]but his disciples took him by night and let him down over the wall, lowering him in a basket.

Saul in Jerusalem

26 And when he had come to Jerusalem he attempted to join the disciples; and they were all afraid of him, for they did not believe that he was a disciple. [27]But Barnabas took him, and brought him to the apostles, and declared to them how on the road he had seen the Lord, who spoke to him, and how at Damascus he had preached boldly in the name of Jesus. [28]So he went in and out among them at Jerusalem, [29]preaching boldly in the name of the Lord. And he spoke and disputed against the Hellenists; but they were seeking to kill him. [30]And when the brethren knew it, they brought him down to Caesare′a, and sent him off to Tarsus.

31 So the Church throughout all Judea and Galilee and Samar′ia had peace and was built up; and walking in the fear of the Lord and in the comfort of the Holy Spirit it was multiplied.

Peter Heals Aeneas in Lydda

32 Now as Peter went here and there among them all, he came down also to the saints that lived at Lydda. [33]There he found a man named Aene′as, who had been bedridden for eight years and was paralyzed. [34]And Peter said to him, "Aene′as, Jesus Christ heals you; rise and make your bed." And immediately he rose. [35]And all the residents of Lydda and Sharon saw him, and they turned to the Lord.

Peter in Joppa

36 Now there was at Joppa a disciple named Tabitha, which means Dorcas or Gazelle. She was full of good works and acts of charity. [37]In those days she fell sick and died; and when they had washed her, they laid her in an upper room. [38]Since Lydda was near Joppa, the disciples, hearing that Peter was there, sent two men to him entreating him, "Please come to us without delay." [39]So Peter rose and went with them. And when he had come, they took him to the upper room. All the widows stood beside him weeping, and showing coats and garments which Dorcas made while she was with them. [40]But Peter put them all outside and knelt down and prayed; then turning to the body he said, "Tabitha, rise." And she opened her eyes, and when she saw Peter she sat up. [41]And he gave her his hand and lifted her up. Then calling the saints and widows he presented her alive. [42]And it became known throughout all Joppa, and many believed in the Lord. [43]And he stayed in Joppa for many days with one Simon, a tanner.

Peter and Cornelius

10 At Caesare′a there was a man named Cornelius, a centurion of what was known as the Italian Cohort, [2]a devout man who feared God with all his household, gave alms liberally to the people, and prayed constantly to God. [3]About the ninth hour of the day he saw clearly in a vision an angel of God coming in and saying to him, "Cornelius." [4]And he stared at him in terror, and said, "What is it, Lord?" And he said to him, "Your prayers and your alms have ascended as a memorial before God. [5]And now send men to Joppa, and bring one Simon who is called Peter; [6]he is lodging with Simon, a tanner, whose house is by the seaside." [7]When the angel who spoke to him had departed, he called two of his servants and a devout soldier from among those that waited on him, [8]and having related everything to them, he sent them to Joppa.

9 The next day, as they were on their journey and coming near the city, Peter went up on the housetop to pray, about the sixth hour. [10]And he became hungry and desired something to eat; but while they were preparing it, he fell into a trance [11]and saw the heaven opened, and something descending, like a great sheet, let down by four corners upon the earth. [12]In it were all kinds of animals and reptiles and birds of the air. [13]And there came a voice to him, "Rise, Peter; kill and eat." [14]But Peter said, "No, Lord; for I have never eaten anything that is common or unclean." [15]And the voice came to him again a second time, "What God has cleansed, you must not call common." [16]This happened three times, and the thing was taken up at once to heaven. *

9:24–25: 2 Cor 11:32–33.
10:1–48: Acts 11:4–17.
* 10:16: The vision was to prepare Peter for his reception of Cornelius the Gentile and his household into the Church; cf. also Acts 15.

17 Now while Peter was inwardly perplexed as to what the vision which he had seen might mean, behold, the men that were sent by Cornelius, having made inquiry for Simon's house, stood before the gate ¹⁸and called out to ask whether Simon who was called Peter was lodging there. ¹⁹And while Peter was pondering the vision, the Spirit said to him, "Behold, three men are looking for you. ²⁰Rise and go down, and accompany them without hesitation; for I have sent them." ²¹And Peter went down to the men and said, "I am the one you are looking for; what is the reason for your coming?" ²²And they said, "Cornelius, a centurion, an upright and God-fearing man, who is well spoken of by the whole Jewish nation, was directed by a holy angel to send for you to come to his house, and to hear what you have to say." ²³So he called them in to be his guests.

The next day he rose and went off with them, and some of the brethren from Joppa accompanied him. ²⁴And on the following day they entered Caesare′a. Cornelius was expecting them and had called together his kinsmen and close friends. ²⁵When Peter entered, Cornelius met him and fell down at his feet and worshiped him. ²⁶But Peter lifted him up, saying, "Stand up; I too am a man." ²⁷And as he talked with him, he went in and found many persons gathered; ²⁸and he said to them, "You yourselves know how unlawful it is for a Jew to associate with or to visit any one of another nation; but God has shown me that I should not call any man common or unclean. ²⁹So when I was sent for, I came without objection. I ask then why you sent for me."

30 And Cornelius said, "Four days ago, about this hour, I was keeping the ninth hour of prayer in my house; and behold, a man stood before me in bright apparel, ³¹saying, 'Cornelius, your prayer has been heard and your alms have been remembered before God. ³²Send therefore to Joppa and ask for Simon who is called Peter; he is lodging in the house of Simon, a tanner, by the seaside.' ³³So I sent to you at once, and you have been kind enough to come. Now therefore we are all here present in the sight of God, to hear all that you have been commanded by the Lord."

Gentiles Hear the Good News

34 And Peter opened his mouth and said: "Truly I perceive that God shows no partiality, ³⁵but in every nation any one who fears him and does what is right is acceptable to him. ³⁶You know the word which he sent to the sons of Israel, preaching good news of peace by Jesus Christ (he is Lord of all), ³⁷the word which was proclaimed throughout all Judea, beginning from Galilee after the baptism which John preached: ³⁸how God anointed Jesus of Nazareth with the Holy Spirit and with power; how he went about doing good and healing all that were oppressed by the devil,

for God was with him. ³⁹And we are witnesses to all that he did both in the country of the Jews and in Jerusalem. They put him to death by hanging him on a tree; ⁴⁰but God raised him on the third day and made him manifest; ⁴¹not to all the people but to us who were chosen by God as witnesses, who ate and drank with him after he rose from the dead. ⁴²And he commanded us to preach to the people, and to testify that he is the one ordained by God to be judge of the living and the dead. ⁴³To him all the prophets bear witness that every one who believes in him receives forgiveness of sins through his name."

The Gentiles Receive the Holy Spirit

44 While Peter was still saying this, the Holy Spirit fell on all who heard the word. ⁴⁵And the believers from among the circumcised who came with Peter were amazed, because the gift of the Holy Spirit had been poured out even on the Gentiles. ⁴⁶For they heard them speaking in tongues and extolling God. Then Peter declared, ⁴⁷"Can any one forbid water for baptizing these people who have received the Holy Spirit just as we have?" ⁴⁸And he commanded them to be baptized in the name of Jesus Christ. Then they asked him to remain for some days.

Peter's Report to the Church at Jerusalem

11 Now the apostles and the brethren who were in Judea heard that the Gentiles also had received the word of God. ²So when Peter went up to Jerusalem, the circumcision party criticized him, ³saying, "Why did you go to uncircumcised men and eat with them?" ⁴But Peter began and explained to them in order: ⁵"I was in the city of Joppa praying; and in a trance I saw a vision, something descending, like a great sheet, let down from heaven by four corners; and it came down to me. ⁶Looking at it closely I observed animals and beasts of prey and reptiles and birds of the air. ⁷And I heard a voice saying to me, 'Rise, Peter; kill and eat.' ⁸But I said, 'No, Lord; for nothing common or unclean has ever entered my mouth.' ⁹But the voice answered a second time from heaven, 'What God has cleansed you must not call common.' ¹⁰This happened three times, and all was drawn up again into heaven. ¹¹At that very moment three men arrived at the house in which we were, sent to me from Caesare′a. ¹²And the Spirit told me to go with them, making no distinction. These six brethren also accompanied me, and we entered the man's house. ¹³And he told us how he had seen the angel standing in his house and saying, 'Send to Joppa and bring Simon called Peter; ¹⁴he will declare to you a message by which you will be saved, you and all your household.' ¹⁵As I began to speak, the Holy Spirit fell on

11:4-17: Acts 10:1-48.

them just as on us at the beginning. [16]And I remembered the word of the Lord, how he said, 'John baptized with water, but you shall be baptized with the Holy Spirit.' [17]If then God gave the same gift to them as he gave to us when we believed in the Lord Jesus Christ, who was I that I could withstand God?" [18]When they heard this they were silenced. And they glorified God, saying, "Then to the Gentiles also God has granted repentance unto life."

The Church in Antioch

19 Now those who were scattered because of the persecution that arose over Stephen traveled as far as Phoeni'cia and Cyprus and Antioch, speaking the word to none except Jews. [20]But there were some of them, men of Cyprus and Cyre'ne, who on coming to Antioch spoke to the Greeks [1] also, preaching the Lord Jesus. [21]And the hand of the Lord was with them, and a great number that believed turned to the Lord. [22]News of this came to the ears of the Church in Jerusalem, and they sent Barnabas to Antioch. [23]When he came and saw the grace of God, he was glad; and he exhorted them all to remain faithful to the Lord with steadfast purpose; [24]for he was a good man, full of the Holy Spirit and of faith. And a large company was added to the Lord. [25]So Barnabas went to Tarsus to look for Saul; [26]and when he had found him, he brought him to Antioch. For a whole year they met with [3] the Church, and taught a large company of people; and in Antioch the disciples were for the first time called Christians.

27 Now in these days prophets came down from Jerusalem to Antioch. [28]And one of them named Ag'abus stood up and foretold by the Spirit that there would be a great famine over all the world; and this took place in the days of Claudius. [29]And the disciples determined, every one according to his ability, to send relief to the brethren who lived in Judea; [30]and they did so, sending it to the elders by the hand of Barnabas and Saul.

James Killed and Peter Imprisoned by Herod

12 About that time Herod the king laid violent hands upon some who belonged to the Church. * [2]He killed James the brother of John with the sword; [3]and when he saw that it pleased the Jews, he proceeded to arrest Peter also. This was during the days of Unleavened Bread. [4]And when he had seized him, he put him in prison, and delivered him to four squads of soldiers to guard him, intending after the Passover to bring him out to the people. [5]So Peter was kept in prison; but earnest prayer for him was made to God by the Church.

An Angel Rescues Peter from Prison

6 The very night when Herod was about to bring him out, Peter was sleeping between two soldiers, bound with two chains, and sentries before the door were guarding the prison; [7]and behold, an angel of the Lord appeared, and a light shone in the cell; and he struck Peter on the side and woke him, saying, "Get up quickly." And the chains fell off his hands. [8]And the angel said to him, "Dress yourself and put on your sandals." And he did so. And he said to him, "Wrap your cloak around you and follow me." [9]And he went out and followed him; he did not know that what was done by the angel was real, but thought he was seeing a vision. [10]When they had passed the first and the second guard, they came to the iron gate leading into the city. It opened to them of its own accord, and they went out and passed on through one street; and immediately the angel left him. [11]And Peter came to himself, and said, "Now I am sure that the Lord has sent his angel and rescued me from the hand of Herod and from all that the Jewish people were expecting."

12 When he realized this, he went to the house of Mary, the mother of John whose other name was Mark, where many were gathered together and were praying. [13]And when he knocked at the door of the gateway, a maid named Rhoda came to answer. [14]Recognizing Peter's voice, in her joy she did not open the gate but ran in and told that Peter was standing at the gate. [15]They said to her, "You are mad." But she insisted that it was so. They said, "It is his angel!" [16]But Peter continued knocking; and when they opened, they saw him and were amazed. [17]But motioning to them with his hand to be silent, he described to them how the Lord had brought him out of the prison. And he said, "Tell this to James and to the brethren." Then he departed and went to another place.

18 Now when day came, there was no small stir among the soldiers over what had become of Peter. [19]And when Herod had sought for him and could not find him, he examined the sentries and ordered that they should be put to death. Then he went down from Judea to Caesare'a, and remained there.

The Death of Herod

20 Now Herod was angry with the people of Tyre and Si'don; and they came to him in a body, and having persuaded Blastus, the king's chamberlain, they asked for peace, because their country depended on the king's country for food. [21]On an appointed day Herod put on his royal robes, took his seat upon the throne, and made an oration to them. [22]And the people shouted, "The voice of a god, and not of man!" [23]Immediately an angel of the Lord struck him, because he did not give

---

[1] Other ancient authorities read *Hellenists*.
[3] Or *were guests of.*
11:16: Acts 1:5.
11:19: Acts 8:4.
* **12:1:** The second wave of persecution: cf. Acts 8:1.

God the glory; and he was eaten by worms and died.

24 But the word of God grew and multiplied.

25 And Barnabas and Saul returned from [k] Jerusalem when they had fulfilled their mission, bringing with them John whose other name was Mark.

Barnabas and Saul Commissioned

13 Now in the Church at Antioch there were prophets and teachers, Barnabas, Symeon who was called Ni′ger, Lucius of Cyre′ne, Man′a-en a member of the court of Herod the tetrarch, and Saul. [2]While they were worshiping the Lord and fasting, the Holy Spirit said, "Set apart for me Barnabas and Saul for the work to which I have called them." [3]Then after fasting and praying they laid their hands on them and sent them off.

The Apostles Preach in Cyprus

4 So, being sent out by the Holy Spirit, they went down to Seleu′cia; and from there they sailed to Cyprus. [5]When they arrived at Sal′amis, they proclaimed the word of God in the synagogues of the Jews. And they had John to assist them. [6]When they had gone through the whole island as far as Pa′phos, they came upon a certain magician, a Jewish false prophet, named Bar-Jesus. [7]He was with the proconsul, Sergius Paulus, a man of intelligence, who summoned Barnabas and Saul and sought to hear the word of God. [8]But El′ymas the magician (for that is the meaning of his name) withstood them, seeking to turn away the proconsul from the faith. [9]But Saul, who is also called Paul, filled with the Holy Spirit, looked intently at him [10]and said, "You son of the devil, you enemy of all righteousness, full of all deceit and villainy, will you not stop making crooked the straight paths of the Lord? [11]And now, behold, the hand of the Lord is upon you, and you shall be blind and unable to see the sun for a time." Immediately mist and darkness fell upon him and he went about seeking people to lead him by the hand. [12]Then the proconsul believed, when he saw what had occurred, for he was astonished at the teaching of the Lord.

Paul and Barnabas in Antioch of Pisid′ia

13 Now Paul and his company set sail from Pa′phos, and came to Perga in Pamphyl′ia. And John left them and returned to Jerusalem; [14]but they passed on from Perga and came to Antioch of Pisid′ia. And on the sabbath day they went into the synagogue and sat down. [15]After the reading of the law and the prophets, the rulers of the synagogue sent to them, saying, "Brethren, if you have any word of exhortation for the people, say it." [16]So Paul stood up, and motioning with his hand said: *

"Men of Israel, and you that fear God, listen. [17]The God of this people Israel chose our fathers and made the people great during their stay in the land of Egypt, and with uplifted arm he led them out of it. [18]And for about forty years he bore with [m] them in the wilderness. [19]And when he had destroyed seven nations in the land of Canaan, he gave them their land as an inheritance, for about four hundred and fifty years. [20]And after that he gave them judges until Samuel the prophet. [21]Then they asked for a king; and God gave them Saul the son of Kish, a man of the tribe of Benjamin, for forty years. [22]And when he had removed him, he raised up David to be their king; of whom he testified and said, 'I have found in David, the son of Jesse, a man after my heart, who will do all my will.' [23]Of this man's posterity God has brought to Israel a Savior, Jesus, as he promised. [24]Before his coming John had preached a baptism of repentance to all the people of Israel. [25]And as John was finishing his course, he said, 'What do you suppose that I am? I am not he. No, but after me one is coming, the sandals of whose feet I am not worthy to untie.'

26 "Brethren, sons of the family of Abraham, and those among you that fear God, to us has been sent the message of this salvation. [27]For those who live in Jerusalem and their rulers, because they did not recognize him nor understand the utterances of the prophets which are read every sabbath, fulfilled these by condemning him. [28]Though they could charge him with nothing deserving death, yet they asked Pilate to have him killed. [29]And when they had fulfilled all that was written of him, they took him down from the tree, and laid him in a tomb. [30]But God raised him from the dead; [31]and for many days he appeared to those who came up with him from Galilee to Jerusalem, who are now his witnesses to the people. [32]And we bring you the good news that what God promised to the fathers, [33]this he has fulfilled to us their children by raising Jesus; as also it is written in the second psalm,

'You are my Son,
today I have begotten you.'

[34]And as for the fact that he raised him from the dead, no more to return to corruption, he spoke in this way,

'I will give you the holy and sure blessings of David.'

[k] Other ancient authorities read *to*.
[m] Other ancient authorities read *cared for* (Deut 1:31).
13:10: Hos 14:9.
13:17: Ex 6:1,6.
13:18: Deut 1:31.
13:19: Deut 7:1; Josh 14:1.
13:22: Ps 89:20; 1 Sam 13:14; Is 44:28.
13:24: Mk 1:1–4.
13:25: Jn 1:20; Mt 3:11; Mk 1:7; Lk 3:16.
13:26: Ps 107:20.
13:33: Ps 2:7.
13:34: Is 55:3.
* 13:16–41: This first recorded sermon of Paul is similar to that of Peter in Acts 2:14–36.

³⁵Therefore he says also in another psalm,

'You will not let your Holy One see corruption.'
³⁶For David, after he had served the counsel of God in his own generation, fell asleep, and was laid with his fathers, and saw corruption; ³⁷but he whom God raised up saw no corruption. ³⁸Let it be known to you therefore, brethren, that through this man forgiveness of sins is proclaimed to you, ³⁹and by him every one that believes is freed from everything from which you could not be freed by the law of Moses. ⁴⁰Beware, therefore, lest there come upon you what is said in the prophets:
⁴¹'Behold, you scoffers, and wonder, and perish;

for I do a deed in your days,

a deed you will never believe, if one declares it

to you.'"

42 As they went out, the people begged that these things might be told them the next sabbath. ⁴³And when the meeting of the synagogue broke up, many Jews and devout converts to Judaism followed Paul and Barnabas, who spoke to them and urged them to continue in the grace of God.

44 The next sabbath almost the whole city gathered together to hear the word of God. ⁴⁵But when the Jews saw the multitudes, they were filled with jealousy, and contradicted what was spoken by Paul, and reviled him. ⁴⁶And Paul and Barnabas spoke out boldly, saying, "It was necessary that the word of God should be spoken first to you. Since you thrust it from you, and judge yourselves unworthy of eternal life, behold, we turn to the Gentiles. ⁴⁷For so the Lord has commanded us, saying,

'I have set you to be a light for the Gentiles,

that you may bring salvation to the uttermost

parts of the earth.'"

48 And when the Gentiles heard this, they were glad and glorified the word of God; and as many as were ordained to eternal life believed. ⁴⁹And the word of the Lord spread throughout all the region. ⁵⁰But the Jews incited the devout women of high standing and the leading men of the city, and stirred up persecution against Paul and Barnabas, and drove them out of their district. ⁵¹But they shook off the dust from their feet against them, and went to Ico'nium. ⁵²And the disciples were filled with joy and with the Holy Spirit.

Paul and Barnabas in Iconium

14 Now at Ico'nium they entered together into the Jewish synagogue, and so spoke that a great company believed, both of Jews and of Greeks. ²But the unbelieving Jews stirred up the Gentiles and poisoned their minds against the brethren. ³So they remained for a long time, speaking boldly for the Lord, who bore witness to the word of his grace, granting signs and wonders to be done by their hands. ⁴But the people of the city were divided; some sided with the Jews, and some with the apostles. ⁵When an attempt

was made by both Gentiles and Jews, with their rulers, to molest them and to stone them, ⁶they learned of it and fled to Lystra and Der'be, cities of Lycao'nia, and to the surrounding country; ⁷and there they preached the gospel.

Paul and Barnabas in Lystra and Derbe

8 Now at Lystra there was a man sitting, who could not use his feet; he was a cripple from birth, who had never walked. ⁹He listened to Paul speaking; and Paul, looking intently at him and seeing that he had faith to be made well, ¹⁰said in a loud voice, "Stand upright on your feet." And he sprang up and walked. ¹¹And when the crowds saw what Paul had done, they lifted up their voices, saying in Lycao'nian, "The gods have come down to us in the likeness of men!" ¹²Barnabas they called Zeus, and Paul, because he was the chief speaker, they called Hermes. ¹³And the priest of Zeus, whose temple was in front of the city, brought oxen and garlands to the gates and wanted to offer sacrifice with the people. ¹⁴But when the apostles Barnabas and Paul heard of it, they tore their garments and rushed out among the multitude, crying, ¹⁵"Men, why are you doing this? We also are men, of like nature with you, and bring you good news, that you should turn from these vain things to a living God who made the heaven and the earth and the sea and all that is in them. ¹⁶In past generations he allowed all the nations to walk in their own ways; ¹⁷yet he did not leave himself without witness, for he did good and gave you from heaven rains and fruitful seasons, satisfying your hearts with food and gladness." ¹⁸With these words they scarcely restrained the people from offering sacrifice to them.

19 But Jews came there from Antioch and Ico'nium; and having persuaded the people, they stoned Paul and dragged him out of the city, supposing that he was dead. ²⁰But when the disciples gathered about him, he rose up and entered the city; and on the next day he went on with Barnabas to Derbe. ²¹When they had preached the gospel to that city and had made many disciples, they returned to Lystra and to Ico'nium and to Antioch, ²²strengthening the souls of the disciples, exhorting them to continue in the faith, and saying that through many tribulations we must enter the kingdom of God. ²³And when they had appointed elders for them in every church, with prayer and fasting, they committed them to the Lord in whom they believed.

The Return to Antioch in Syria

24 Then they passed through Pisid'ia, and came to Pamphyl'ia. ²⁵And when they had spoken

13:35: Ps 16:10.
13:41: Hab 1:5.
13:47: Is 49:6.
14:15: Ex 20:11; Ps 146:6.
14:19: 2 Cor 11:25.

the word in Perga, they went down to Attali'a; [26]and from there they sailed to Antioch, where they had been commended to the grace of God for the work which they had fulfilled. [27]And when they arrived, they gathered the Church together and declared all that God had done with them, and how he had opened a door of faith to the Gentiles. [28]And they remained no little time with the disciples.

The Council at Jerusalem

15 But some men came down from Judea and were teaching the brethren, "Unless you are circumcised according to the custom of Moses, you cannot be saved." [2]And when Paul and Barnabas had no small dissension and debate with them, Paul and Barnabas and some of the others were appointed to go up to Jerusalem to the apostles and the elders about this question. [3]So, being sent on their way by the Church, they passed through both Phoeni'cia and Samar'ia, reporting the conversion of the Gentiles, and they gave great joy to all the brethren. [4]When they came to Jerusalem, they were welcomed by the Church and the apostles and the elders, and they declared all that God had done with them. [5]But some believers who belonged to the party of the Pharisees rose up, and said, "It is necessary to circumcise them, and to charge them to keep the law of Moses."

6 The apostles and the elders were gathered together to consider this matter. [7]And after there had been much debate, Peter rose and said to them, "Brethren, you know that in the early days God made choice among you, that by my mouth the Gentiles should hear the word of the gospel and believe. [8]And God who knows the heart bore witness to them, giving them the Holy Spirit just as he did to us; [9]and he made no distinction between us and them, but cleansed their hearts by faith. [10]Now therefore why do you make trial of God by putting a yoke upon the neck of the disciples which neither our fathers nor we have been able to bear? [11]But we believe that we shall be saved through the grace of the Lord Jesus, just as they will."

12 And all the assembly kept silence; and they listened to Barnabas and Paul as they related what signs and wonders God had done through them among the Gentiles. [13]After they finished speaking, James replied, "Brethren, listen to me. [14]Symeon has related how God first visited the Gentiles, to take out of them a people for his name. [15]And with this the words of the prophets agree, as it is written,

[16]'After this I will return,
  and I will rebuild the dwelling of David, which
    has fallen;
I will rebuild its ruins,
  and I will set it up,

[17]that the rest of men may seek the Lord,
  and all the Gentiles who are called by my
    name,
[18]says the Lord, who has made these things
    known from of old.'

[19]Therefore my judgment is that we should not trouble those of the Gentiles who turn to God, [20]but should write to them to abstain from the pollutions of idols and from unchastity and from what is strangled [n] and from blood. [21]For from early generations Moses has had in every city those who preach him, for he is read every sabbath in the synagogues."

The Council's Letter to the Gentile Believers

22 Then it seemed good to the apostles and the elders, with the whole Church, to choose men from among them and send them to Antioch with Paul and Barnabas. They sent Judas called Barsab'bas, and Silas, leading men among the brethren, [23]with the following letter: "The brethren, both the apostles and the elders, to the brethren who are of the Gentiles in Antioch and Syria and Cili'cia, greeting. [24]Since we have heard that some persons from us have troubled you with words, unsettling your minds, although we gave them no instructions, [25]it has seemed good to us in assembly to choose men and send them to you with our beloved Barnabas and Paul, [26]men who have risked their lives for the sake of our Lord Jesus Christ. [27]We have therefore sent Judas and Silas, who themselves will tell you the same things by word of mouth. [28]For it has seemed good to the Holy Spirit and to us to lay upon you no greater burden than these necessary things: [29]that you abstain from what has been sacrificed to idols and from blood and from what is strangled [n] and from unchastity. If you keep yourselves from these, you will do well. Farewell."

30 So when they were sent off, they went down to Antioch; and having gathered the congregation together, they delivered the letter. [31]And when they read it, they rejoiced at the exhortation. [32]And Judas and Silas, who were themselves prophets, exhorted the brethren with many words and strengthened them. [33]And after they had spent some time, they were sent off in peace by the brethren to those who had sent them. [o] [35]But Paul and Barnabas remained in Antioch, teaching and preaching the word of the Lord, with many others also.

Paul and Barnabas Separate

36 And after some days Paul said to Barnabas, "Come, let us return and visit the brethren in every city where we proclaimed the word of the

---

[n] Other early authorities omit *and from what is strangled*.
[o] Other ancient authorities insert verse 34, *But it seemed good to Silas to remain there.*
15:1–30: Gal 2:1–10.
15:16–18: Amos 9:11–12; Jer 12:15; Is 45:21.

Lord, and see how they are." [37]And Barnabas wanted to take with them John called Mark. [38]But Paul thought best not to take with them one who had withdrawn from them in Pamphyl'ia, and had not gone with them to the work. [39]And there arose a sharp contention, so that they separated from each other; Barnabas took Mark with him and sailed away to Cyprus, [40]but Paul chose Silas and departed, being commended by the brethren to the grace of the Lord. [41]And he went through Syria and Cili'cia, strengthening the churches.

Timothy Accompanies Paul and Silas

16 And he came also to Derbe and to Lystra. A disciple was there, named Timothy, the son of a Jewish woman who was a believer; but his father was a Greek. [2]He was well spoken of by the brethren at Lystra and Ico'nium. [3]Paul wanted Timothy to accompany him; and he took him and circumcised him because of the Jews that were in those places, for they all knew that his father was a Greek. [4]As they went on their way through the cities, they delivered to them for observance the decisions which had been reached by the apostles and elders who were at Jerusalem. [5]So the churches were strengthened in the faith, and they increased in numbers daily.

Paul's Vision of the Man of Macedonia

[6] And they went through the region of Phry'gia and Galatia, having been forbidden by the Holy Spirit to speak the word in Asia. [7]And when they had come opposite My'sia, they attempted to go into Bithyn'ia, but the Spirit of Jesus did not allow them; [8]so, passing by My'sia, they went down to Troas. [9]And a vision appeared to Paul in the night: a man of Macedonia was standing pleading with him and saying, "Come over to Macedonia and help us." [10]And when he had seen the vision, immediately we sought to go on into Macedonia, concluding that God had called us to preach the gospel to them. *

The Conversion of Lydia and Her Household

[11] Setting sail therefore from Troas, we made a direct voyage to Sam'othrace, and the following day to Ne-ap'olis, [12]and from there to Philip'pi, which is the leading city of the district * of Macedonia, and a Roman colony. We remained in this city some days; [13]and on the sabbath day we went outside the gate to the riverside, where we supposed there was a place of prayer; † and we sat down and spoke to the women who had come together. [14]One who heard us was a woman named Lydia, from the city of Thyati'ra, a seller of purple goods, who was a worshiper of God. The Lord opened her heart to listen to what was said by Paul. [15]And when she was baptized, with her household, she begged us, saying, "If you have judged me to be faithful to the Lord, come to my house and stay." And she prevailed upon us.

Paul and Silas Beaten and Imprisoned

[16] As we were going to the place of prayer, we were met by a slave girl who had a spirit of divination and brought her owners much gain by soothsaying. [17]She followed Paul and us, crying, "These men are servants of the Most High God, who proclaim to you the way of salvation." [18]And this she did for many days. But Paul was annoyed, and turned and said to the spirit, "I charge you in the name of Jesus Christ to come out of her." And it came out that very hour.

[19] But when her owners saw that their hope of gain was gone, they seized Paul and Silas and dragged them into the market place before the rulers; [20]and when they had brought them to the magistrates they said, "These men are Jews and they are disturbing our city. [21]They advocate customs which it is not lawful for us Romans to accept or practice." [22]The crowd joined in attacking them; and the magistrates tore the garments off them and gave orders to beat them with rods. [23]And when they had inflicted many blows upon them, they threw them into prison, charging the jailer to keep them safely. [24]Having received this charge, he put them into the inner prison and fastened their feet in the stocks.

[25] But about midnight Paul and Silas were praying and singing hymns to God, and the prisoners were listening to them, [26]and suddenly there was a great earthquake, so that the foundations of the prison were shaken; and immediately all the doors were opened and every one's chains were unfastened. [27]When the jailer woke and saw that the prison doors were open, he drew his sword and was about to kill himself, supposing that the prisoners had escaped. [28]But Paul cried with a loud voice, "Do not harm yourself, for we are all here." [29]And he called for lights and rushed in, and trembling with fear he fell down before Paul and Silas, [30]and brought them out and said, "Men, what must I do to be saved?" [31]And they said, "Believe in the Lord Jesus, and you will be saved, you and your household." [32]And they spoke the word of the Lord to him and to all that were in his house. [33]And he took them the same hour of the night, and washed their wounds, and he was baptized at once, with all his family. [34]Then he brought them up into his house, and set food before them; and he rejoiced with all his household that he had believed in God.

[35] But when it was day, the magistrates sent the police, saying, "Let those men go." [36]And the

---

* The Greek text is uncertain.

16:22–23: 2 Cor 11:25.

* 16:10: This is the first of the passages in Acts in which the story is told in the first person plural, indicating that Luke, the author, was there. The manuscript Codex Bezae, however, has a "we" passage in 11:28.

† 16:13: Being a Roman colony, Philippi had no synagogue within its walls.

jailer reported the words to Paul, saying, "The magistrates have sent to let you go; now therefore come out and go in peace." [37]But Paul said to them, "They have beaten us publicly, uncondemned, men who are Roman citizens, and have thrown us into prison; and do they now cast us out secretly? No! let them come themselves and take us out." [38]The police reported these words to the magistrates, and they were afraid when they heard that they were Roman citizens; [39]so they came and apologized to them. And they took them out and asked them to leave the city. [40]So they went out of the prison, and visited Lydia; and when they had seen the brethren, they exhorted them and departed.

The Uproar in Thessalonica

17 Now when they had passed through Amphip′olis and Apollo′nia, they came to Thessaloni′ca, where there was a synagogue of the Jews. [2]And Paul went in, as was his custom, and for three weeks[p] he argued with them from the Scriptures, [3]explaining and proving that it was necessary for the Christ to suffer and to rise from the dead, and saying, "This Jesus, whom I proclaim to you, is the Christ." [4]And some of them were persuaded, and joined Paul and Silas; as did a great many of the devout Greeks and not a few of the leading women. [5]But the Jews were jealous, and taking some wicked fellows of the rabble, they gathered a crowd, set the city in an uproar, and attacked the house of Jason, seeking to bring them out to the people. [6]And when they could not find them, they dragged Jason and some of the brethren before the city authorities, crying, "These men who have turned the world upside down have come here also, [7]and Jason has received them; and they are all acting against the decrees of Caesar, saying that there is another king, Jesus." [8]And the people and the city authorities were disturbed when they heard this. [9]And when they had taken security from Jason and the rest, they let them go.

Paul and Silas in Beroea

10 The brethren immediately sent Paul and Silas away by night to Beroe′a; and when they arrived they went into the Jewish synagogue. [11]Now these Jews were more noble than those in Thessaloni′ca, for they received the word with all eagerness, examining the Scriptures daily to see if these things were so. [12]Many of them therefore believed, with not a few Greek women of high standing as well as men. [13]But when the Jews of Thessaloni′ca learned that the word of God was proclaimed by Paul at Beroe′a also, they came there too, stirring up and inciting the crowds. [14]Then the brethren immediately sent Paul off on his way to the sea, but Silas and Timothy remained there. [15]Those who conducted Paul brought him as far as Athens; and receiving a command for Silas and Timothy to come to him as soon as possible, they departed.

Paul in Athens

16 Now while Paul was waiting for them at Athens, his spirit was provoked within him as he saw that the city was full of idols. [17]So he argued in the synagogue with the Jews and the devout persons, and in the market place every day with those who chanced to be there. [18]Some also of the Epicurean and Stoic philosophers met him. And some said, "What would this babbler say?" Others said, "He seems to be a preacher of foreign divinities"—because he preached Jesus and the resurrection. [19]And they took hold of him and brought him to the Are-op′agus, saying, "May we know what this new teaching is which you present? [20]For you bring some strange things to our ears; we wish to know therefore what these things mean." [21]Now all the Athenians and the foreigners who lived there spent their time in nothing except telling or hearing something new.

22 So Paul, standing in the middle of the Are-op′agus, said: "Men of Athens, I perceive that in every way you are very religious. [23]For as I passed along, and observed the objects of your worship, I found also an altar with this inscription, 'To an unknown god.' What therefore you worship as unknown, this I proclaim to you. [24]The God who made the world and everything in it, being Lord of heaven and earth, does not live in shrines made by man, [25]nor is he served by human hands, as though he needed anything, since he himself gives to all men life and breath and everything. [26]And he made from one every nation of men to live on all the face of the earth, having determined allotted periods and the boundaries of their habitation, [27]that they should seek God, in the hope that they might feel after him and find him. Yet he is not far from each one of us, [28]for

'In him we live and move and have our being';

as even some of your poets have said,

'For we are indeed his offspring.'

[29]Being then God's offspring, we ought not to think that the Deity is like gold, or silver, or stone, a representation by the art and imagination of man. [30]The times of ignorance God overlooked, but now he commands all men everywhere to repent, [31]because he has fixed a day on which he will judge the world in righteousness by a man whom he has appointed, and of this he has given assurance to all men by raising him from the dead."

32 Now when they heard of the resurrection of the dead, some mocked; but others said, "We will hear you again about this." [33]So Paul went out

---

[p] Or sabbaths.
17:24–25: Is 42:5.
17:28: Epimenides; Aratus, *Phaenomena*, 5.
17:31: Ps 9:8; 96:13; 98:9.

from among them. [34]But some men joined him and believed, among them Dionys′ius the Are-op′agite and a woman named Dam′aris and others with them.

Paul in Corinth

18 After this he left Athens and went to Corinth. [2]And he found a Jew named Aqui′la, a native of Pontus, lately come from Italy with his wife Priscilla, because Claudius had commanded all the Jews to leave Rome. And he went to see them; [3]and because he was of the same trade he stayed with them, and they worked, for by trade they were tentmakers. [4]And he argued in the synagogue every sabbath, and persuaded Jews and Greeks.

5 When Silas and Timothy arrived from Macedonia, Paul was occupied with preaching, testifying to the Jews that the Christ was Jesus. [6]And when they opposed and reviled him, he shook out his garments and said to them, "Your blood be upon your heads! I am innocent. From now on I will go to the Gentiles." [7]And he left there and went to the house of a man named Titius �q Justus, a worshiper of God; his house was next door to the synagogue. [8]Crispus, the ruler of the synagogue, believed in the Lord, together with all his household; and many of the Corinthians hearing Paul believed and were baptized. [9]And the Lord said to Paul one night in a vision, "Do not be afraid, but speak and do not be silent; [10]for I am with you, and no man shall attack you to harm you; for I have many people in this city." [11]And he stayed a year and six months, teaching the word of God among them.

12 But when Gallio was proconsul of Acha′ia, the Jews made a united attack upon Paul and brought him before the tribunal, [13]saying, "This man is persuading men to worship God contrary to the law." [14]But when Paul was about to open his mouth, Gallio said to the Jews, "If it were a matter of wrongdoing or vicious crime, I should have reason to bear with you, O Jews; [15]but since it is a matter of questions about words and names and your own law, see to it yourselves; I refuse to be a judge of these things." [16]And he drove them from the tribunal. [17]And they all seized Sos′thenes, the ruler of the synagogue, and beat him in front of the tribunal. But Gallio paid no attention to this.

Paul's Return to Antioch

18 After this Paul stayed many days longer, and then took leave of the brethren and sailed for Syria, and with him Priscilla and Aqui′la. At Cen′chre-ae he cut his hair, for he had a vow. [19]And they came to Ephesus, and he left them there; but he himself went into the synagogue and argued with the Jews. [20]When they asked him to stay for a longer period, he declined; [21]but on taking leave of them he said, "I will return to you if God wills," and he set sail from Ephesus.

22 When he had landed at Caesare′a, he went up and greeted the Church, and then went down to Antioch. [23]After spending some time there he departed and went from place to place through the region of Galatia and Phryg′ia, strengthening all the disciples.

Ministry of Apollos

24 Now a Jew named Apol′los, a native of Alexandria, came to Ephesus. He was an eloquent man, well versed in the Scriptures. [25]He had been instructed in the way of the Lord; and being fervent in spirit, he spoke and taught accurately the things concerning Jesus, though he knew only the baptism of John. [26]He began to speak boldly in the synagogue; but when Priscilla and Aqui′la heard him, they took him and expounded to him the way of God more accurately. [27]And when he wished to cross to Acha′ia, the brethren encouraged him, and wrote to the disciples to receive him. When he arrived, he greatly helped those who through grace had believed, [28]for he powerfully confuted the Jews in public, showing by the Scriptures that the Christ was Jesus.

Paul in Ephesus

19 While Apol′los was at Corinth, Paul passed through the upper country and came to Ephesus. There he found some disciples. [2]And he said to them, "Did you receive the Holy Spirit when you believed?" And they said, "No, we have never even heard that there is a Holy Spirit." [3]And he said, "Into what then were you baptized?" They said, "Into John's baptism." [4]And Paul said, "John baptized with the baptism of repentance, telling the people to believe in the one who was to come after him, that is, Jesus." [5]On hearing this, they were baptized in the name of the Lord Jesus. [6]And when Paul had laid his hands upon them, the Holy Spirit came on them; and they spoke with tongues and prophesied. [7]There were about twelve of them in all.

8 And he entered the synagogue and for three months spoke boldly, arguing and pleading about the kingdom of God; [9]but when some were stubborn and disbelieved, speaking evil of the Way before the congregation, he withdrew from them, taking the disciples with him, and argued daily in the hall of Tyran′nus. ᵣ [10]This continued for two years, so that all the residents of Asia heard the word of the Lord, both Jews and Greeks.

The Sons of Sceva

11 And God did extraordinary miracles by the hands of Paul, [12]so that handkerchiefs or aprons were carried away from his body to the sick, and diseases left them and the evil spirits came out of them. [13]Then some of the itinerant Jewish

---

q Other early authorities read *Titus*.
r Other ancient authorities add *from the fifth hour to the tenth*.
18:9–10: Is 43:5; Jer 1:8.

exorcists undertook to pronounce the name of the Lord Jesus over those who had evil spirits, saying, "I adjure you by the Jesus whom Paul preaches." ¹⁴Seven sons of a Jewish high priest named Sceva were doing this. ¹⁵But the evil spirit answered them, "Jesus I know, and Paul I know; but who are you?" ¹⁶And the man in whom the evil spirit was leaped on them, mastered all of them, and overpowered them, so that they fled out of that house naked and wounded. ¹⁷And this became known to all residents of Ephesus, both Jews and Greeks; and fear fell upon them all; and the name of the Lord Jesus was extolled. ¹⁸Many also of those who were now believers came, confessing and divulging their practices. ¹⁹And a number of those who practiced magic arts brought their books together and burned them in the sight of all; and they counted the value of them and found it came to fifty thousand pieces of silver. ²⁰So the word of the Lord grew and prevailed mightily.

The Riot in Ephesus

21 Now after these events Paul resolved in the Spirit to pass through Macedonia and Acha'ia and go to Jerusalem, saying, "After I have been there, I must also see Rome." ²²And having sent into Macedonia two of his helpers, Timothy and Eras'tus, he himself stayed in Asia for a while.

23 About that time there arose no little stir concerning the Way. ²⁴For a man named Deme'trius, a silversmith, who made silver shrines of Ar'temis, brought no little business to the craftsmen. ²⁵These he gathered together, with the workmen of like occupation, and said, "Men, you know that from this business we have our wealth. ²⁶And you see and hear that not only at Ephesus but almost throughout all Asia this Paul has persuaded and turned away a considerable company of people, saying that gods made with hands are not gods. ²⁷And there is danger not only that this trade of ours may come into disrepute but also that the temple of the great goddess Ar'temis may count for nothing, and that she may even be deposed from her magnificence, she whom all Asia and the world worship."

28 When they heard this they were enraged, and cried out, "Great is Ar'temis of the Ephesians!" ²⁹So the city was filled with the confusion; and they rushed together into the theater, dragging with them Ga'ius and Aristar'chus, Macedonians who were Paul's companions in travel. ³⁰Paul wished to go in among the crowd, but the disciples would not let him; ³¹some of the A'siarchs also, who were friends of his, sent to him and begged him not to venture into the theater. ³²Now some cried one thing, some another; for the assembly was in confusion, and most of them did not know why they had come together. ³³Some of the crowd prompted Alexander, whom the Jews

had put forward. And Alexander motioned with his hand, wishing to make a defense to the people. ³⁴But when they recognized that he was a Jew, for about two hours they all with one voice cried out, "Great is Ar'temis of the Ephesians!" ³⁵And when the town clerk had quieted the crowd, he said, "Men of Ephesus, what man is there who does not know that the city of the Ephesians is temple keeper of the great Ar'temis, and of the sacred stone * that fell from the sky? ^{g 36}Seeing then that these things cannot be contradicted, you ought to be quiet and do nothing rash. ³⁷For you have brought these men here who are neither sacrilegious nor blasphemers of our goddess. ³⁸If therefore Deme'trius and the craftsmen with him have a complaint against any one, the courts are open, and there are proconsuls; let them bring charges against one another. ³⁹But if you seek anything further, ^t it shall be settled in the regular assembly. ⁴⁰For we are in danger of being charged with rioting today, there being no cause that we can give to justify this commotion." ⁴¹And when he had said this, he dismissed the assembly.

Paul Goes to Macedonia and Greece

20 After the uproar ceased, Paul sent for the disciples and having exhorted them took leave of them and departed for Macedonia. ²When he had gone through these parts and had given them much encouragement, he came to Greece. ³There he spent three months, and when a plot was made against him by the Jews as he was about to set sail for Syria, he determined to return through Macedonia. ⁴Sop'ater of Beroe'a, the son of Pyrrhus, accompanied him; and of the Thessalo'nians, Aristar'chus and Secun'dus; and Ga'ius of Derbe, and Timothy; and the Asians, Tych'icus and Troph'imus. ⁵These went on and were waiting for us at Troas, ⁶but we sailed away from Philip'pi after the days of Unleavened Bread, and in five days we came to them at Troas, where we stayed for seven days.

Paul Preaches and Heals Eutychus in Troas

7 On the first day of the week, when we were gathered together to break bread, † Paul talked with them, intending to depart on the next day; and he prolonged his speech until midnight. ⁸There were many lights in the upper chamber where we were gathered. ⁹And a young man named Eu'tychus was sitting in the window. He sank into a deep sleep as Paul talked still longer; and being overcome by sleep, he fell down from the third story and was taken up dead. ¹⁰But Paul

went down and bent over him, and embracing him said, "Do not be alarmed, for his life is in him." ¹¹And when Paul had gone up and had broken bread and eaten, he conversed with them a long while, until daybreak, and so departed. ¹²And they took the lad away alive, and were not a little comforted.

13 But going ahead to the ship, we set sail for Assos, intending to take Paul aboard there; for so he had arranged, intending himself to go by land. ¹⁴And when he met us at Assos, we took him on board and came to Mityle'ne. ¹⁵And sailing from there we came the following day opposite Chi'os; the next day we touched at Sa'mos; and ᵘ the day after that we came to Mile'tus. ¹⁶For Paul had decided to sail past Ephesus, so that he might not have to spend time in Asia; for he was hastening to be at Jerusalem, if possible, on the day of Pentecost.

Paul Speaks to the Elders of Ephesus

17 And from Mile'tus he sent to Ephesus and called to him the elders of the Church. ¹⁸And when they came to him, he said to them:

"You yourselves know how I lived among you all the time from the first day that I set foot in Asia, ¹⁹serving the Lord with all humility and with tears and with trials which befell me through the plots of the Jews; ²⁰how I did not shrink from declaring to you anything that was profitable, and teaching you in public and from house to house, ²¹testifying both to Jews and to Greeks of repentance to God and of faith in our Lord Jesus Christ. ²²And now, behold, I am going to Jerusalem, bound in the Spirit, not knowing what shall befall me there; ²³except that the Holy Spirit testifies to me in every city that imprisonment and afflictions await me. ²⁴But I do not account my life of any value nor as precious to myself, if only I may accomplish my course and the ministry which I received from the Lord Jesus, to testify to the gospel of the grace of God. ²⁵And now, behold, I know that all you among whom I have gone about preaching the kingdom will see my face no more. ²⁶Therefore I testify to you this day that I am innocent of the blood of all of you, ²⁷for I did not shrink from declaring to you the whole counsel of God. ²⁸Take heed to yourselves and to all the flock, in which the Holy Spirit has made you guardians, to feed the Church of the Lord ᵛ which he obtained with his own blood. ᵂ ²⁹I know that after my departure fierce wolves will come in among you, not sparing the flock; ³⁰and from among your own selves will arise men speaking perverse things, to draw away the disciples after them. ³¹Therefore be alert, remembering that for three years I did not cease night or day to admonish every one with tears. ³²And now I commend you to God and to the word of his grace, which is able to build you

up and to give you the inheritance among all those who are sanctified. ³³I coveted no one's silver or gold or apparel. ³⁴You yourselves know that these hands ministered to my necessities, and to those who were with me. * ³⁵In all things I have shown you that by so toiling one must help the weak, remembering the words of the Lord Jesus, how he said, 'It is more blessed to give than to receive.'"

36 And when he had spoken thus, he knelt down and prayed with them all. ³⁷And they all wept and embraced Paul and kissed him, ³⁸sorrowing most of all because of the word he had spoken, that they should see his face no more. And they brought him to the ship.

Paul's Journey to Jerusalem

21 And when we had parted from them and set sail, we came by a straight course to Cos, and the next day to Rhodes, and from there to Pat'ara. ˣ ²And having found a ship crossing to Phoeni'cia, we went aboard, and set sail. ³When we had come in sight of Cyprus, leaving it on the left we sailed to Syria, and landed at Tyre; for there the ship was to unload its cargo. ⁴And having sought out the disciples, we stayed there for seven days. Through the Spirit they told Paul not to go † on to Jerusalem. ⁵And when our days there were ended, we departed and went on our journey; and they all, with wives and children, brought us on our way till we were outside the city; and kneeling down on the beach we prayed and bade one another farewell. ⁶Then we went on board the ship, and they returned home.

7 When we had finished the voyage from Tyre, we arrived at Ptolema'is; and we greeted the brethren and stayed with them for one day. ⁸The next day we departed and came to Caesare'a; and we entered the house of Philip the evangelist, who was one of the seven, and stayed with him. ⁹And he had four unmarried daughters, who prophesied. ¹⁰While we were staying for some days, a prophet named Ag'abus came down from Judea. ¹¹And coming to us he took Paul's belt and bound his own feet and hands, and said, "Thus says the Holy Spirit, 'So shall the Jews at Jerusalem bind the man who owns this belt and deliver him into the hands of the Gentiles.'" ¹²When we heard this, we and the people there begged him not to go up to Jerusalem. ¹³Then Paul answered, "What are you doing, weeping and breaking my

---

ᵘ Other ancient authorities add *after remaining at Trogyllium.*
ᵛ Other ancient authorities read *of God.*
ᵂ Or *with the blood of his Own.*
ˣ Other ancient authorities add *and Myra.*
* 20:34: Paul insisted on working for his living, though recognizing the apostle's right to support by the faithful; cf. 1 Cor 9:4–7.
† 21:4, *told Paul not to go*: This was not a command. The Holy Spirit enlightened them about what lay before Paul and they naturally wished to spare him; cf. verse 11.

heart? For I am ready not only to be imprisoned but even to die at Jerusalem for the name of the Lord Jesus." [14]And when he would not be persuaded, we ceased and said, "The will of the Lord be done."

15 After these days we made ready and went up to Jerusalem. [16]And some of the disciples from Caesare′a went with us, bringing us to the house of Mnason of Cyprus, an early disciple, with whom we should lodge.

Paul Visits James at Jerusalem

17 When we had come to Jerusalem, the brethren received us gladly. [18]On the following day Paul went in with us to James; and all the elders were present. [19]After greeting them, he related one by one the things that God had done among the Gentiles through his ministry. [20]And when they heard it, they glorified God. And they said to him, "You see, brother, how many thousands there are among the Jews of those who have believed; they are all zealous for the law, [21]and they have been told about you that you teach all the Jews who are among the Gentiles to forsake Moses, telling them not to circumcise their children or observe the customs. [22]What then is to be done? They will certainly hear that you have come. [23]Do therefore what we tell you. We have four men who are under a vow; [24]take these men and purify yourself along with them and pay their expenses, so that they may shave their heads. Thus all will know that there is nothing in what they have been told about you but that you yourself live in observance of the law. [25]But as for the Gentiles who have believed, we have sent a letter with our judgment that they should abstain from what has been sacrificed to idols and from blood and from what is strangled [y] and from unchastity." [26]Then Paul took the men, and the next day he purified himself with them and went into the temple, to give notice when the days of purification would be fulfilled and the offering presented for every one of them.

Paul Arrested in the Temple

27 When the seven days were almost completed, the Jews from Asia, who had seen him in the temple, stirred up all the crowd, and laid hands on him, [28]crying out, "Men of Israel, help! This is the man who is teaching men everywhere against the people and the law and this place; moreover he also brought Greeks into the temple, and he has defiled this holy place." [29]For they had previously seen Troph′imus the Ephesian with him in the city, and they supposed that Paul had brought him into the temple. [30]Then all the city was aroused, and the people ran together; they seized Paul and dragged him out of the temple, and at once the gates were shut. [31]And as they were trying to kill him, word came to the tribune of the cohort that all Jerusalem was in confusion. [32]He at once took soldiers and centurions, and ran down to them; and when they saw the tribune and the soldiers, they stopped beating Paul. [33]Then the tribune came up and arrested him, and ordered him to be bound with two chains. He inquired who he was and what he had done. [34]Some in the crowd shouted one thing, some another; and as he could not learn the facts because of the uproar, he ordered him to be brought into the barracks. [35]And when he came to the steps, he was actually carried by the soldiers because of the violence of the crowd; [36]for the mob of the people followed, crying, "Away with him!"

Paul Defends Himself

37 As Paul was about to be brought into the barracks, he said to the tribune, "May I say something to you?" And he said, "Do you know Greek? [38]Are you not the Egyptian, then, who recently stirred up a revolt and led the four thousand men of the Assassins out into the wilderness?" [39]Paul replied, "I am a Jew, from Tarsus in Cili′cia, a citizen of no mean city; I beg you, let me speak to the people." [40]And when he had given him leave, Paul, standing on the steps, motioned with his hand to the people; and when there was a great hush, he spoke to them in the Hebrew language, saying:

22 "Brethren and fathers, hear the defense which I now make before you."

2 And when they heard that he addressed them in the Hebrew language, they were the more quiet. And he said:

3 "I am a Jew, born at Tarsus in Cili′cia, but brought up in this city at the feet of Gama′li-el, educated according to the strict manner of the law of our fathers, being zealous for God as you all are this day. [4]I persecuted this Way to the death, binding and delivering to prison both men and women, [5]as the high priest and the whole council of elders bear me witness. From them I received letters to the brethren, and I journeyed to Damascus to take those also who were there and bring them in bonds to Jerusalem to be punished.

Paul Tells of His Conversion

6 "As I made my journey and drew near to Damascus, about noon a great light from heaven suddenly shone about me. [7]And I fell to the ground and heard a voice saying to me, 'Saul, Saul, why do you persecute me?' [8]And I answered, 'Who are you, Lord?' And he said to me, 'I am Jesus of Nazareth whom you are persecuting.' [9]Now those who were with me saw the light but did not hear the voice of the one who was speaking to me. [10]And I said, 'What shall I do, Lord?' And the Lord said to me, 'Rise, and go into Damascus, and there you will be told all that is appointed for you

---

y Other early authorities omit *and from what is strangled*.
22:4-16: Acts 9:1–19; 26:9–18; Gal 1:14.

to do.' [11]And when I could not see because of the brightness of that light, I was led by the hand by those who were with me, and came into Damascus.

12 "And one Anani'as, a devout man according to the law, well spoken of by all the Jews who lived there, [13]came to me, and standing by me said to me, 'Brother Saul, receive your sight.' And in that very hour I received my sight and saw him. [14]And he said, 'The God of our fathers appointed you to know his will, to see the Just One and to hear a voice from his mouth; [15]for you will be a witness for him to all men of what you have seen and heard. [16]And now why do you wait? Rise and be baptized, and wash away your sins, calling on his name.'

Paul Tells How He Was Sent to the Gentiles

17 "When I had returned to Jerusalem and was praying in the temple, I fell into a trance [18]and saw him saying to me, 'Make haste and get quickly out of Jerusalem, because they will not accept your testimony about me.' [19]And I said, 'Lord, they themselves know that in every synagogue I imprisoned and beat those who believed in you. [20]And when the blood of Stephen your witness * was shed, I also was standing by and approving, and keeping the garments of those who killed him.' [21]And he said to me, 'Depart; for I will send you far away to the Gentiles.' "

Paul and the Roman Tribune

22 Up to this word they listened to him; then they lifted up their voices and said, "Away with such a fellow from the earth! For he ought not to live." [23]And as they cried out and waved their garments and threw dust into the air, [24]the tribune commanded him to be brought into the barracks, and ordered him to be examined by scourging, to find out why they shouted thus against him. [25]But when they had tied him up with the thongs, Paul said to the centurion who was standing by, "Is it lawful for you to scourge a man who is a Roman citizen, and uncondemned?" [26]When the centurion heard that, he went to the tribune and said to him, "What are you about to do? For this man is a Roman citizen." [27]So the tribune came and said to him, "Tell me, are you a Roman citizen?" And he said, "Yes." [28]The tribune answered, "I bought this citizenship for a large sum." Paul said, "But I was born a citizen." [29]So those who were about to examine him withdrew from him instantly; and the tribune also was afraid, for he realized that Paul was a Roman citizen and that he had bound him.

Paul before the Chief Priests and Council

30 But the next day, desiring to know the real reason why the Jews accused him, he unbound him, and commanded the chief priests and all the council to meet, and he brought Paul down and set him before them.

23 And Paul, looking intently at the council, said, "Brethren, I have lived before God in all good conscience up to this day." [2]And the high priest Anani'as commanded those who stood by him to strike him on the mouth. [3]Then Paul said to him, "God shall strike you, you whitewashed wall! Are you sitting to judge me according to the law, and yet contrary to the law you order me to be struck?" [4]Those who stood by said, "Would you revile God's high priest?" [5]And Paul said, "I did not know, brethren, that he was the high priest; for it is written, 'You shall not speak evil of a ruler of your people.' "

6 But when Paul perceived that one part were Sad'ducees and the other Pharisees, he cried out in the council, "Brethren, I am a Pharisee, a son of Pharisees; with respect to the hope and the resurrection of the dead I am on trial." [7]And when he had said this, a dissension arose between the Pharisees and the Sad'ducees; and the assembly was divided. [8]For the Sad'ducees say that there is no resurrection, nor angel, nor spirit; but the Pharisees acknowledge them all. [9]Then a great clamor arose; and some of the scribes of the Pharisees' party stood up and contended, "We find nothing wrong in this man. What if a spirit or an angel spoke to him?" [10]And when the dissension became violent, the tribune, afraid that Paul would be torn in pieces by them, commanded the soldiers to go down and take him by force from among them and bring him into the barracks.

11 The following night the Lord stood by him and said, "Take courage, for as you have testified about me at Jerusalem, so you must bear witness also at Rome."

The Plot to Kill Paul

12 When it was day, the Jews made a plot and bound themselves by an oath neither to eat nor drink till they had killed Paul. [13]There were more than forty who made this conspiracy. [14]And they went to the chief priests and elders, and said, "We have strictly bound ourselves by an oath to taste no food till we have killed Paul. [15]You therefore, along with the council, give notice now to the tribune to bring him down to you, as though you were going to determine his case more exactly. And we are ready to kill him before he comes near."

16 Now the son of Paul's sister heard of their ambush; so he went and entered the barracks and told Paul. [17]And Paul called one of the centurions and said, "Take this young man to the tribune; for he has something to tell him." [18]So he took him and brought him to the tribune and said, "Paul

---

23:5: Ex 22:28.
* 22:20, *your witness*: Greek, "martyr." Witnessing by one's death (i.e., martyrdom) is the supreme example.

the prisoner called me and asked me to bring this young man to you, as he has something to say to you." [19]The tribune took him by the hand, and going aside asked him privately, "What is it that you have to tell me?" [20]And he said, "The Jews have agreed to ask you to bring Paul down to the council tomorrow, as though they were going to inquire somewhat more closely about him. [21]But do not yield to them; for more than forty of their men lie in ambush for him, having bound themselves by an oath neither to eat nor drink till they have killed him; and now they are ready, waiting for the promise from you." [22]So the tribune dismissed the young man, charging him, "Tell no one that you have informed me of this."

Paul Is Brought to Felix the Governor

23 Then he called two of the centurions and said, "At the third hour of the night get ready two hundred soldiers with seventy horsemen and two hundred spearmen to go as far as Caesare'a. [24]Also provide mounts for Paul to ride, and bring him safely to Felix the governor." [25]And he wrote a letter to this effect:

26 "Claudius Lys'ias to his Excellency the governor Felix, greeting. [27]This man was seized by the Jews, and was about to be killed by them, when I came upon them with the soldiers and rescued him, having learned that he was a Roman citizen. [28]And desiring to know the charge on which they accused him, I brought him down to their council. [29]I found that he was accused about questions of their law, but charged with nothing deserving death or imprisonment. [30]And when it was disclosed to me that there would be a plot against the man, I sent him to you at once, ordering his accusers also to state before you what they have against him."

31 So the soldiers, according to their instructions, took Paul and brought him by night to Antip'atris. [32]And the next day they returned to the barracks, leaving the horsemen to go on with him. [33]When they came to Caesare'a and delivered the letter to the governor, they presented Paul also before him. [34]On reading the letter, he asked to what province he belonged. When he learned that he was from Cili'cia [35]he said, "I will hear you when your accusers arrive." And he commanded him to be guarded in Herod's praetorium.

Paul before Felix at Caesarea

24 And after five days the high priest Anani'as came down with some elders and a spokesman, one Tertul'lus. They laid before the governor their case against Paul; [2]and when he was called, Tertul'lus began to accuse him, saying:

"Since through you we enjoy much peace, and since by your provision, most excellent Felix, reforms are introduced on behalf of this nation, [3]in every way and everywhere we accept this with all gratitude. [4]But, to detain you no further, I beg you in your kindness to hear us briefly. [5]For we have found this man a pestilent fellow, an agitator among all the Jews throughout the world, and a ringleader of the sect of the Nazarenes. [6]He even tried to profane the temple, but we seized him. [z] [8]By examining him yourself you will be able to learn from him about everything of which we accuse him."

9 The Jews also joined in the charge, affirming that all this was so.

Paul's Defense before Felix

10 And when the governor had motioned to him to speak, Paul replied:

"Realizing that for many years you have been judge over this nation, I cheerfully make my defense. [11]As you may ascertain, it is not more than twelve days since I went up to worship at Jerusalem; [12]and they did not find me disputing with any one or stirring up a crowd, either in the temple or in the synagogues, or in the city. [13]Neither can they prove to you what they now bring up against me. [14]But this I admit to you, that according to the Way, which they call a sect, I worship the God of our fathers, believing everything laid down by the law or written in the prophets, [15]having a hope in God which these themselves accept, that there will be a resurrection of both the just and the unjust. [16]So I always take pains to have a clear conscience toward God and toward men. [17]Now after some years I came to bring to my nation alms and offerings. [18]As I was doing this, they found me purified in the temple, without any crowd or tumult. But some Jews from Asia— [19]they ought to be here before you and to make an accusation, if they have anything against me. [20]Or else let these men themselves say what wrongdoing they found when I stood before the council, [21]except this one thing which I cried out while standing among them, 'With respect to the resurrection of the dead I am on trial before you this day.'"

22 But Felix, having a rather accurate knowledge of the Way, put them off, saying, "When Lys'ias the tribune comes down, I will decide your case." [23]Then he gave orders to the centurion that he should be kept in custody but should have some liberty, and that none of his friends should be prevented from attending to his needs.

Paul Held in Custody

24 After some days Felix came with his wife Drusil'la, who was Jewish; and he sent for Paul and heard him speak upon faith in Christ Jesus. [25]And as he argued about justice and self-control and future judgment, Felix was alarmed and said,

---

[z] Other ancient authorities add *and we would have judged him according to our law.* [7]*But the chief captain Lysias came and with great violence took him out of our hands,* [8]*commanding his accusers to come before you.*

"Go away for the present; when I have an opportunity I will summon you." [26]At the same time he hoped that money would be given him by Paul. So he sent for him often and conversed with him. [27]But when two years had elapsed, Felix was succeeded by Por′cius Festus; and desiring to do the Jews a favor, Felix left Paul in prison.

Paul Appeals to Caesar

25 Now when Festus had come into his province, after three days he went up to Jerusalem from Caesare′a. [2]And the chief priests and the principal men of the Jews informed him against Paul; and they urged him, [3]asking as a favor to have the man sent to Jerusalem, planning an ambush to kill him on the way. [4]Festus replied that Paul was being kept at Caesare′a, and that he himself intended to go there shortly. [5]"So," said he, "let the men of authority among you go down with me, and if there is anything wrong about the man, let them accuse him."

6 When he had stayed among them not more than eight or ten days, he went down to Caesare′a; and the next day he took his seat on the tribunal and ordered Paul to be brought. [7]And when he had come, the Jews who had gone down from Jerusalem stood about him, bringing against him many serious charges which they could not prove. [8]Paul said in his defense, "Neither against the law of the Jews, nor against the temple, nor against Caesar have I offended at all." [9]But Festus, wishing to do the Jews a favor, said to Paul, "Do you wish to go up to Jerusalem, and there be tried on these charges before me?" [10]But Paul said, "I am standing before Caesar's tribunal, where I ought to be tried; to the Jews I have done no wrong, as you know very well. [11]If then I am a wrongdoer, and have committed anything for which I deserve to die, I do not seek to escape death; but if there is nothing in their charges against me, no one can give me up to them. I appeal to Caesar." [12]Then Festus, when he had conferred with his council, answered, "You have appealed to Caesar; to Caesar you shall go."

Festus Consults King Agrippa

13 Now when some days had passed, Agrippa the king and Bernice arrived at Caesare′a to welcome Festus. [14]And as they stayed there many days, Festus laid Paul's case before the king, saying, "There is a man left prisoner by Felix; [15]and when I was at Jerusalem, the chief priests and the elders of the Jews gave information about him, asking for sentence against him. [16]I answered them that it was not the custom of the Romans to give up any one before the accused met the accusers face to face, and had opportunity to make his defense concerning the charge laid against him. [17]When therefore they came together here, I made no delay, but on the next day took my seat on the tribunal and ordered the man to be brought in.

[18]When the accusers stood up, they brought no charge in his case of such evils as I supposed; [19]but they had certain points of dispute with him about their own superstition and about one Jesus, who was dead, but whom Paul asserted to be alive. [20]Being at a loss how to investigate these questions, I asked whether he wished to go to Jerusalem and be tried there regarding them. [21]But when Paul had appealed to be kept in custody for the decision of the emperor, I commanded him to be held until I could send him to Caesar." [22]And Agrippa said to Festus, "I should like to hear the man myself." "Tomorrow," said he, "you shall hear him."

Paul Is Brought before Agrippa

23 So the next day Agrippa and Bernice came with great pomp, and they entered the audience hall with the military tribunes and the prominent men of the city. Then by command of Festus Paul was brought in. [24]And Festus said, "King Agrippa and all who are present with us, you see this man about whom the whole Jewish people petitioned me, both at Jerusalem and here, shouting that he ought not to live any longer. [25]But I found that he had done nothing deserving death; and as he himself appealed to the emperor, I decided to send him. [26]But I have nothing definite to write to my lord about him. Therefore I have brought him before you, and, especially before you, King Agrippa, that, after we have examined him, I may have something to write. [27]For it seems to me unreasonable, in sending a prisoner, not to indicate the charges against him."

Paul Makes His Defense before Agrippa

26 Agrippa said to Paul, "You have permission to speak for yourself." Then Paul stretched out his hand and made his defense:

2 "I think myself fortunate that it is before you, King Agrippa, I am to make my defense today against all the accusations of the Jews, [3]because you are especially familiar with all customs and controversies of the Jews; therefore I beg you to listen to me patiently.

4 "My manner of life from my youth, spent from the beginning among my own nation and at Jerusalem, is known by all the Jews. [5]They have known for a long time, if they are willing to testify, that according to the strictest party of our religion I have lived as a Pharisee. [6]And now I stand here on trial for hope in the promise made by God to our fathers, [7]to which our twelve tribes hope to attain, as they earnestly worship night and day. And for this hope I am accused by Jews, O king! [8]Why is it thought incredible by any of you that God raises the dead?

9 "I myself was convinced that I ought to do many things in opposing the name of Jesus of

26:9–18: Acts 9:1–8; 22:4–16.

Nazareth. [10]And I did so in Jerusalem; I not only shut up many of the saints in prison, by authority from the chief priests, but when they were put to death I cast my vote against them. [11]And I punished them often in all the synagogues and tried to make them blaspheme; and in raging fury against them, I persecuted them even to foreign cities.

Paul Tells of His Conversion

12 "Thus I journeyed to Damascus with the authority and commission of the chief priests. [13]At midday, O king, I saw on the way a light from heaven, brighter than the sun, shining round me and those who journeyed with me. [14]And when we had all fallen to the ground, I heard a voice saying to me in the Hebrew language, 'Saul, Saul, why do you persecute me? It hurts you to kick against the goads.' [15]And I said, 'Who are you, Lord?' And the Lord said, 'I am Jesus whom you are persecuting. [16]But rise and stand upon your feet; for I have appeared to you for this purpose, to appoint you to serve and bear witness to the things in which you have seen me and to those in which I will appear to you, [17]delivering you from the people and from the Gentiles—to whom I send you [18]to open their eyes, that they may turn from darkness to light and from the power of Satan to God, that they may receive forgiveness of sins and a place among those who are sanctified by faith in me.'

Paul Tells of His Preaching

19 "Wherefore, O King Agrippa, I was not disobedient to the heavenly vision, [20]but declared first to those at Damascus, then at Jerusalem and throughout all the country of Judea, and also to the Gentiles, that they should repent and turn to God and perform deeds worthy of their repentance. [21]For this reason the Jews seized me in the temple and tried to kill me. [22]To this day I have had the help that comes from God, and so I stand here testifying both to small and great, saying nothing but what the prophets and Moses said would come to pass: [23]that the Christ must suffer, and that, by being the first to rise from the dead, he would proclaim light both to the people and to the Gentiles."

Paul Appeals to Agrippa to Believe

24 And as he thus made his defense, Festus said with a loud voice, "Paul, you are mad; your great learning is turning you mad." [25]But Paul said, "I am not mad, most excellent Festus, but I am speaking the sober truth. [26]For the king knows about these things, and to him I speak freely; for I am persuaded that none of these things has escaped his notice, for this was not done in a corner. [27]King Agrippa, do you believe the prophets? I know that you believe." [28]And Agrippa said to Paul, "In a short time you think to make me a Christian!" [29]And Paul said, "Whether short or long, I would to God that not only you but also all who hear me this day might become such as I am—except for these chains."

30 Then the king rose, and the governor and Bernice and those who were sitting with them; [31]and when they had withdrawn, they said to one another, "This man is doing nothing to deserve death or imprisonment." [32]And Agrippa said to Festus, "This man could have been set free if he had not appealed to Caesar."

Paul Sails for Rome

27 And when it was decided that we should sail for Italy, they delivered Paul and some other prisoners to a centurion of the Augustan Cohort, named Julius. [2]And embarking in a ship of Adramyt'tium, which was about to sail to the ports along the coast of Asia, we put to sea, accompanied by Aristar'chus, a Macedonian from Thessaloni'ca. [3]The next day we put in at Si'don; and Julius treated Paul kindly, and gave him leave to go to his friends and be cared for. [4]And putting to sea from there we sailed under the lee of Cyprus, because the winds were against us. [5]And when we had sailed across the sea which is off Cili'cia and Pamphyl'ia, we came to Myra in Ly'cia. [6]There the centurion found a ship of Alexandria sailing for Italy, and put us on board. [7]We sailed slowly for a number of days, and arrived with difficulty off Cni'dus, and as the wind did not allow us to go on, we sailed under the lee of Crete off Salmo'ne. [8]Coasting along it with difficulty, we came to a place called Fair Havens, near which was the city of Lase'a.

9 As much time had been lost, and the voyage was already dangerous because the fast had already gone by, Paul advised them, [10]saying, "Sirs, I perceive that the voyage will be with injury and much loss, not only of the cargo and the ship, but also of our lives." [11]But the centurion paid more attention to the captain and to the owner of the ship than to what Paul said. [12]And because the harbor was not suitable to winter in, the majority advised to put to sea from there, on the chance that somehow they could reach Phoenix, a harbor of Crete, looking northeast and southeast, [a] and winter there.

The Storm at Sea

13 And when the south wind blew gently, supposing that they had obtained their purpose, they weighed anchor and sailed along Crete, close inshore. [14]But soon a tempestuous wind, called the northeaster, struck down from the land; [15]and when the ship was caught and could not face the wind, we gave way to it and were driven. [16]And running under the lee of a small island called

---

[a] Or *southwest and northwest.*
26:16–17: Ezek 2:1, 3.
26:18: Is 42:7, 16.

Cau'da,^b we managed with difficulty to secure the boat; ¹⁷after hoisting it up, they took measures^c to undergird the ship; then, fearing that they should run on the Syr'tis, they lowered the gear, and so were driven. ¹⁸As we were violently storm-tossed, they began next day to throw the cargo overboard; ¹⁹and the third day they cast out with their own hands the tackle of the ship. ²⁰And when neither sun nor stars appeared for many a day, and no small tempest lay on us, all hope of our being saved was at last abandoned.

21 As they had been long without food, Paul then came forward among them and said, "Men, you should have listened to me, and should not have set sail from Crete and incurred this injury and loss. ²²I now bid you take heart; for there will be no loss of life among you, but only of the ship. ²³For this very night there stood by me an angel of the God to whom I belong and whom I worship, ²⁴and he said, 'Do not be afraid, Paul; you must stand before Caesar; and behold, God has granted you all those who sail with you.' ²⁵So take heart, men, for I have faith in God that it will be exactly as I have been told. ²⁶But we shall have to run on some island."

27 When the fourteenth night had come, as we were drifting across the sea of A'dria, about midnight the sailors suspected that they were nearing land. ²⁸So they sounded and found twenty fathoms; a little farther on they sounded again and found fifteen fathoms. ²⁹And fearing that we might run on the rocks, they let out four anchors from the stern, and prayed for day to come. ³⁰And as the sailors were seeking to escape from the ship, and had lowered the boat into the sea, under pretense of laying out anchors from the bow, ³¹Paul said to the centurion and the soldiers, "Unless these men stay in the ship, you cannot be saved." ³²Then the soldiers cut away the ropes of the boat, and let it go.

33 As day was about to dawn, Paul urged them all to take some food, saying, "Today is the fourteenth day that you have continued in suspense and without food, having taken nothing. ³⁴Therefore I urge you to take some food; it will give you strength, since not a hair is to perish from the head of any of you." ³⁵And when he had said this, he took bread, and giving thanks to God in the presence of all, he broke it and began to eat. ³⁶Then they all were encouraged and ate some food themselves. ³⁷(We were in all two hundred and seventy-six^d persons in the ship.) ³⁸And when they had eaten enough, they lightened the ship, throwing out the wheat into the sea.

The Shipwreck

39 Now when it was day, they did not recognize the land, but they noticed a bay with a beach, on which they planned if possible to bring the ship ashore. ⁴⁰So they cast off the anchors and left them in the sea, at the same time loosening the ropes that tied the rudders; then hoisting the foresail to the wind they made for the beach. ⁴¹But striking a shoal^e they ran the vessel aground; the bow stuck and remained immovable, and the stern was broken up by the surf. ⁴²The soldiers' plan was to kill the prisoners, lest any should swim away and escape; ⁴³but the centurion, wishing to save Paul, kept them from carrying out their purpose. He ordered those who could swim to throw themselves overboard first and make for the land, ⁴⁴and the rest on planks or on pieces of the ship. And so it was that all escaped to land.

Paul on the Island of Malta

28 After we had escaped, we then learned that the island was called Malta. ²And the natives showed us unusual kindness, for they kindled a fire and welcomed us all, because it had begun to rain and was cold. ³Paul had gathered a bundle of sticks and put them on the fire, when a viper came out because of the heat and fastened on his hand. ⁴When the natives saw the creature hanging from his hand, they said to one another, "No doubt this man is a murderer. Though he has escaped from the sea, justice has not allowed him to live." ⁵He, however, shook off the creature into the fire and suffered no harm. ⁶They waited, expecting him to swell up or suddenly fall down dead; but when they had waited a long time and saw no misfortune come to him, they changed their minds and said that he was a god.

7 Now in the neighborhood of that place were lands belonging to the chief man of the island, named Pub'lius, who received us and entertained us hospitably for three days. ⁸It happened that the father of Pub'lius lay sick with fever and dysentery; and Paul visited him and prayed, and putting his hands on him healed him. ⁹And when this had taken place, the rest of the people on the island who had diseases also came and were cured. ¹⁰They presented many gifts to us;^f and when we sailed, they put on board whatever we needed.

Paul Comes to Rome

11 After three months we set sail in a ship which had wintered in the island, a ship of Alexandria, with the Twin Brothers as figurehead. ¹²Putting in at Syracuse, we stayed there for three days. ¹³And from there we made a circuit and arrived at Rhe'gium; and after one day a south wind sprang up, and on the second day we came to Pute'oli. ¹⁴There we found brethren, and were invited to stay with them for seven days. And so we came to Rome. ¹⁵And the brethren there, when

---

^b Other ancient authorities read *Clauda.*
^c Greek *helps.*
^d Other ancient authorities read *seventy-six* or *about seventy-six.*
^e Greek *place of two seas.*
^f Or *honored us with many honors.*

they heard of us, came as far as the Forum of Ap'pius and Three Taverns to meet us. On seeing them Paul thanked God and took courage. [16]And when we came into Rome, Paul was allowed to stay by himself, with the soldier that guarded him.

Paul and Jewish Leaders in Rome

17 After three days he called together the local leaders of the Jews; and when they had gathered, he said to them, "Brethren, though I had done nothing against the people or the customs of our fathers, yet I was delivered prisoner from Jerusalem into the hands of the Romans. [18]When they had examined me, they wished to set me at liberty, because there was no reason for the death penalty in my case. [19]But when the Jews objected, I was compelled to appeal to Caesar—though I had no charge to bring against my nation. [20]For this reason therefore I have asked to see you and speak with you, since it is because of the hope of Israel that I am bound with this chain." [21]And they said to him, "We have received no letters from Judea about you, and none of the brethren coming here has reported or spoken any evil about you. [22]But we desire to hear from you what your views are; for with regard to this sect we know that everywhere it is spoken against."

Paul Preaches in Rome

23 When they had appointed a day for him, they came to him at his lodging in great numbers. And he expounded the matter to them from morning till evening, testifying to the kingdom of God and trying to convince them about Jesus both from the law of Moses and from the prophets. [24]And some were convinced by what he said, while others disbelieved. [25]So, as they disagreed among themselves, they departed, after Paul had made one statement: "The Holy Spirit was right in saying to your fathers through Isaiah the prophet: [26]'Go to this people, and say,

You shall indeed hear but never understand,
	and you shall indeed see but never perceive.
[27]For this people's heart has grown dull,
	and their ears are heavy of hearing,
	and their eyes they have closed;
lest they should perceive with their eyes,
	and hear with their ears,
	and understand with their heart,
	and turn for me to heal them.'

[28]Let it be known to you then that this salvation of God has been sent to the Gentiles; they will listen." [g]

30 And he lived there two whole years at his own expense, [h] and welcomed all who came to him, [31]preaching the kingdom of God and teaching about the Lord Jesus Christ quite openly and unhindered.

---

[g] Other ancient authorities add verse 29, *And when he had said these words, the Jews departed, holding much dispute among themselves.*
[h] Or *in his own hired dwelling.*
28:26–27: Is 6:9–10.
28:28: Ps 67:2.

THE LETTER OF PAUL TO THE

ROMANS

Salutation

1 * Paul, a servant ^a of Jesus Christ, called to be an apostle, set apart for the gospel of God ²which he promised beforehand through his prophets in the holy Scriptures, ³the gospel concerning his Son, who was descended from David according to the flesh ⁴and designated ^{a2} Son of God in power according to the Spirit of holiness by his resurrection from the dead, Jesus Christ our Lord, ⁵through whom we have received grace and apostleship to bring about the obedience of faith for the sake of his name among all the nations, ⁶including yourselves who are called to belong to Jesus Christ;

7 To all God's beloved in Rome, who are called to be saints:

Grace to you and peace from God our Father and the Lord Jesus Christ.

Prayer of Thanksgiving

8 First, I thank my God through Jesus Christ for all of you, because your faith is proclaimed in all the world. ⁹For God is my witness, whom I serve with my spirit in the gospel of his Son, that without ceasing I mention you always in my prayers, ¹⁰asking that somehow by God's will I may now at last succeed in coming to you. † ¹¹For I long to see you, that I may impart to you some spiritual gift to strengthen you, ¹²that is, that we may be mutually encouraged by each other's faith, both yours and mine. ¹³I want you to know, brethren, that I have often intended to come to you (but thus far have been prevented), in order that I may reap some harvest ‡ among you as well as among the rest of the Gentiles. ¹⁴I am under obligation both to Greeks and to barbarians, both to the wise and to the foolish: ¹⁵so I am eager to preach the gospel to you also who are in Rome.

The Power of the Gospel

16 For I am not ashamed of the gospel: it is the power of God for salvation to every one who has faith, to the Jew first and also to the Greek. ¹⁷For in it the righteousness of God is revealed through faith for faith; as it is written, "He who through faith is righteous shall live." ^b

God's Wrath against Man's Wickedness

18 For the wrath of God is revealed from heaven against all ungodliness and wickedness of men who by their wickedness suppress the truth. ¹⁹For what can be known about God is plain to them, because God has shown it to them. ²⁰Ever since the creation of the world his invisible nature, namely, his eternal power and deity, has been clearly perceived in the things that have been made. So they are without excuse; ²¹for although they knew God they did not honor him as God or give thanks to him, but they became futile in their thinking and their senseless minds were darkened. ²²Claiming to be wise, they became fools, ²³and exchanged the glory of the immortal God for images resembling mortal man or birds or animals or reptiles.

24 Therefore God gave them up in the lusts of their hearts to impurity, to the dishonoring of their bodies among themselves, ²⁵because they exchanged the truth about God for a lie and worshiped and served the creature rather than the Creator, who is blessed for ever! Amen.

26 For this reason God gave them up to dishonorable passions. Their women exchanged natural relations for unnatural, ²⁷and the men likewise gave up natural relations with women and were consumed with passion for one another, men committing shameless acts with men and receiving in their own persons the due penalty for their error.

28 And since they did not see fit to acknowledge God, God gave them up to a base mind and to improper conduct. ²⁹They were filled with all manner of wickedness, evil, covetousness, malice. Full of envy, murder, strife, deceit, malignity, they are gossips, ³⁰slanderers, haters of God, insolent, haughty, boastful, inventors of evil, disobedient

---

^a Or *slave.*
^{a2} Or *constituted.*
^b Or *The righteous shall live by faith.*
1:1: Acts 9:15; 13:2; 1 Cor 1:1; 2 Cor 1:1; Gal 1:15.
1:5: Acts 26:16–18; Rom 15:18; Gal 2:7, 9.
1:7: 1 Cor 1:3; 2 Cor 1:2; Gal 1:3; Eph 1:2; Phil 1:2; Col 1:2; 1 Thess 1:2; 2 Thess 1:2; 1 Tim 1:2; 2 Tim 1:2; Tit 1:4; Philem 3; 2 Jn 3.
1:8: Rom 16:19.
1:10: Rom 15:23, 32; Acts 19:21.
1:13: Rom 15:22.
1:14: 1 Cor 9:16.
1:16: 1 Cor 1:18, 24.
1:17: Rom 3:21; Gal 3:11; Phil 3:9; Heb 10:38; Hab 2:4.
1:18: Eph 5:6; Col 3:6.
1:20: Ps 19:1–4.
1:21: Eph 4:17–18.
1:23: Acts 17:29.
* 1:1–7: The opening address and salutation are very much in the style of contemporary letter-writing, giving the name of the sender and recipient, and following this with greetings.
† 1:10: Paul did not found the church at Rome.
‡ 1:13, *harvest:* Perhaps those who founded the church at Rome had confined themselves largely to Jews and had not made much headway with Gentiles.

to parents, [31]foolish, faithless, heartless, ruthless. [32]Though they know God's decree that those who do such things deserve to die, they not only do them but approve those who practice them.

The Righteous Judgment of God

2 Therefore you have no excuse, O man, whoever you are, when you judge another; for in passing judgment upon him you condemn yourself, because you, the judge, are doing the very same things. [2]We know that the judgment of God rightly falls upon those who do such things. [3]Do you suppose, O man, that when you judge those who do such things and yet do them yourself, you will escape the judgment of God? [4]Or do you presume upon the riches of his kindness and forbearance and patience? Do you not know that God's kindness is meant to lead you to repentance? [5]But by your hard and impenitent heart you are storing up wrath for yourself on the day of wrath when God's righteous judgment will be revealed. [6]For he will render to every man according to his works: [7]to those who by patience in well-doing seek for glory and honor and immortality, he will give eternal life; [8]but for those who are factious and do not obey the truth, but obey wickedness, there will be wrath and fury. [9]There will be tribulation and distress for every human being who does evil, the Jew first and also the Greek, [10]but glory and honor and peace for every one who does good, the Jew first and also the Greek. [11]For God shows no partiality.

12 All who have sinned without the law will also perish without the law, and all who have sinned under the law will be judged by the law. [13]For it is not the hearers of the law who are righteous before God, but the doers of the law who will be justified. [14]When Gentiles who have not the law do by nature what the law requires, they are a law to themselves, even though they do not have the law. [15]They show that what the law requires is written on their hearts, while their conscience also bears witness and their conflicting thoughts accuse or perhaps excuse them [16]on that day when, according to my gospel, God judges the secrets of men by Christ Jesus.

The Jews and the Law

17 But if you call yourself a Jew and rely upon the law and boast of your relation to God [18]and know his will and approve what is excellent, because you are instructed in the law, [19]and if you are sure that you are a guide to the blind, a light to those who are in darkness, [20]a corrector of the foolish, a teacher of children, having in the law the embodiment of knowledge and truth—[21]you then who teach others, will you not teach yourself? While you preach against stealing, do you steal? [22]You who say that one must not commit adultery, do you commit adultery?

You who abhor idols, do you rob temples? [23]You who boast in the law, do you dishonor God by breaking the law? [24]For, as it is written, "The name of God is blasphemed among the Gentiles because of you."

25 Circumcision indeed is of value if you obey the law; but if you break the law, your circumcision becomes uncircumcision. [26]So, if a man who is uncircumcised keeps the precepts of the law, will not his uncircumcision be regarded as circumcision? [27]Then those who are physically uncircumcised but keep the law will condemn you who have the written code and circumcision but break the law. [28]For he is not a real Jew who is one outwardly, nor is true circumcision something external and physical. [29]He is a Jew who is one inwardly, and real circumcision is a matter of the heart, spiritual and not literal. His praise is not from men but from God.

3 Then what advantage has the Jew? Or what is the value of circumcision? [2]Much in every way. To begin with, the Jews are entrusted with the oracles of God. [3]What if some were unfaithful? Does their faithlessness nullify the faithfulness of God? [4]By no means! Let God be true though every man be false, as it is written,

"That you may be justified in your words,
   and prevail when you are judged."

[5]But if our wickedness serves to show the justice of God, what shall we say? That God is unjust to inflict wrath on us? (I speak in a human way.) [6]By no means! For then how could God judge the world? [7]But if through my falsehood God's truthfulness abounds to his glory, why am I still being condemned as a sinner? [8]And why not do evil that good may come?—as some people slanderously charge us with saying. Their condemnation is just.

None Is Righteous

9 What then? Are we Jews any better off? [c] No, not at all; for I [d] have already charged that all

---

[c] Or at any disadvantage?
[d] Greek we.

2:1: Rom 14:22.
2:4: Eph 1:7; 2:7; Phil 4:19; Col 1:27.
2:6: Mt 16:27; 1 Cor 3:8; 2 Cor 5:10; Rev 22:12.
2:11: Deut 10:17; 2 Chron 19:7; Gal 2:6; Eph 6:9; Col 3:25; 1 Pet 1:17.
2:12: Rom 3:19; 1 Cor 9:21.
2:13: Jas 1:22–23, 25.
2:16: Eccles 12:14; Rom 16:25; 1 Cor 4:5.
2:18: Phil 1:10.
2:20: Rom 6:17; 2 Tim 1:13.
2:21: Mt 23:3–4.
2:24: Is 52:5.
2:25: Jer 9:25.
2:26: 1 Cor 7:19; Acts 10:35.
2:27: Mt 12:41.
2:28: Mt 3:9; Jn 8:39; Rom 9:6–7; Gal 6:15.
2:29: 2 Cor 3:6; Phil 3:3; Col 2:11; 1 Pet 3:4.
3:2: Ps 147:19; Rom 9:4.
3:4: Ps 51:4.
3:5: Rom 5:9; 6:19; 1 Cor 9:8; Gal 3:15.
3:8: Rom 6:1, 15.
3:9: Rom 1:18–32; 2:1–29; 11:32; 3:23.

men, both Jews and Greeks, are under the power of sin, [10]as it is written:

"None is righteous, no, not one;
[11]no one understands, no one seeks for God.
[12]All have turned aside, together they have gone
    wrong;
no one does good, not even one."
[13]"Their throat is an open grave,
    they use their tongues to deceive."
"The venom of asps is under their lips."
[14]"Their mouth is full of curses and bitterness."
[15]"Their feet are swift to shed blood,
[16]in their paths are ruin and misery,
[17]and the way of peace they do not know."
[18]"There is no fear of God before their eyes."

19 Now we know that whatever the law says it speaks to those who are under the law, so that every mouth may be stopped, and the whole world may be held accountable to God. [20]For no human being will be justified in his sight by works of the law, since through the law comes knowledge of sin.

Righteousness through Faith

21 But now the righteousness of God has been manifested apart from law, although the law and the prophets bear witness to it, [22]the righteousness of God through faith in Jesus Christ for all who believe. For there is no distinction; [23]since all have sinned and fall short of the glory of God, [24]they are justified by his grace as a gift, through the redemption which is in Christ Jesus, [25]whom God put forward as an expiation by his blood, to be received by faith. This was to show God's righteousness, because in his divine forbearance he had passed over former sins; [26]it was to prove at the present time that he himself is righteous and that he justifies him who has faith in Jesus.

27 Then what becomes of our boasting? It is excluded. On what principle? On the principle of works? No, but on the principle of faith. * [28]For we hold that a man is justified by faith apart from works of law. [29]Or is God the God of Jews only? Is he not the God of Gentiles also? Yes, of Gentiles also, [30]since God is one; and he will justify the circumcised on the ground of their faith and the uncircumcised through their faith. [31]Do we then overthrow the law by this faith? By no means! On the contrary, we uphold the law.

The Example of the Faith of Abraham

4 What then shall we say about [e] Abraham, our forefather according to the flesh? [2]For if Abraham was justified by works, he has something to boast about, but not before God. [3]For what does the Scripture say? "Abraham believed God, and it was reckoned to him as righteousness." [4]Now to one who works, his wages are not reckoned as a gift but as his due. [5]And to one who does not work but trusts him who justifies the ungodly, his faith is reckoned as righteousness.

[6]So also David pronounces a blessing upon the man to whom God reckons righteousness apart from works:

[7]"Blessed are those whose iniquities are
    forgiven, and whose sins are covered;
[8]blessed is the man against whom the Lord will
    not reckon his sin."

9 Is this blessing pronounced only upon the circumcised, or also upon the uncircumcised? We say that faith was reckoned to Abraham as righteousness. [10]How then was it reckoned to him? Was it before or after he had been circumcised? It was not after, but before he was circumcised. [11]He received circumcision as a sign or seal of the righteousness which he had by faith while he was still uncircumcised. The purpose was to make him the father of all who believe without being circumcised and who thus have righteousness reckoned to them, [12]and likewise the father of the circumcised who are not merely circumcised but also follow the example of the faith which our father Abraham had before he was circumcised.

God's Promise Realized through Faith

13 The promise to Abraham and his descendants, that they should inherit the world, did not come through the law but through the righteousness of faith. [14]If it is the adherents of the law who are to be the heirs, faith is null and the promise is void. [15]For the law brings wrath, but where there is no law there is no transgression.

16 That is why it depends on faith, in order that the promise may rest on grace and be guaranteed to all his descendants—not only to the adherents of the law but also to those who share the faith of Abraham, for he is the father of us all, [17]as it is written, "I have made you the father of many nations"—in the presence of the God in whom he believed, who gives life to the dead and

---

* Other ancient authorities read *was gained by.*
3:10–12: Ps 14:1–3; 53:1–3.
3:13: Ps 5:9; 140:3.
3:14: Ps 10:7.
3:15–17: Is 59:7–8.
3:18: Ps 36:1.
3:19: Rom 2:12.
3:20: Ps 143:2; Acts 13:39; Gal 2:16; 3:11; Rom 7:7.
3:21: Rom 1:17; Phil 3:9; 2 Pet 1:1.
3:22: Rom 4:5; 9:30; 10:12; Gal 2:16.
3:23: Rom 3:9.
3:24: Rom 4:16; 5:9; Eph 2:8; Tit 3:7; Eph 1:7; Col 1:14; Heb 9:15.
3:26: 1 Jn 2:2; Col 1:20.
3:28: Acts 13:39; Rom 5:1; Eph 2:9.
3:29: Rom 9:24; Acts 10:34–35.
3:30: Rom 4:11–12, 16.
3:31: Rom 8:4; Mt 5:17.
4:2: 1 Cor 1:31.
4:3: Gen 15:6; Rom 4:9, 22; Gal 3:6; Jas 2:23.
4:4: Rom 11:6.
4:5: Rom 3:22.
4:7: Ps 32:1–2.
4:11: Gen 17:10; Rom 3:22, 30.
4:13: Gen 17:4–6; 22:17–18; Gal 3:29.
4:14: Gal 3:18.
4:15: Gal 3:10.
4:17: Gen 17:5; Jn 5:21.
* 3:27: Above all, it is faith, not works alone, that will justify both Jew and Gentile, and (as is made clear later) faith in Jesus.

calls into existence the things that do not exist. [18]In hope he believed against hope, that he should become the father of many nations; as he had been told, "So shall your descendants be." [19]He did not weaken in faith when he considered his own body, which was as good as dead because he was about a hundred years old, or when he considered the barrenness of Sarah's womb. [20]No distrust made him waver concerning the promise of God, but he grew strong in his faith as he gave glory to God, [21]fully convinced that God was able to do what he had promised. [22]That is why his faith was "reckoned to him as righteousness." [23]But the words, "it was reckoned to him," were written not for his sake alone, [24]but for ours also. It will be reckoned to us who believe in him that raised from the dead Jesus our Lord, [25]who was put to death for our trespasses and raised for our justification.

Results of Justification

5 Therefore, since we are justified by faith, we [f] have peace with God through our Lord Jesus Christ. [2]Through him we have obtained access [g] to this grace in which we stand, and we [h] rejoice in our hope of sharing the glory of God. [3]More than that, we [h] rejoice in our sufferings, knowing that suffering produces endurance, [4]and endurance produces character, and character produces hope, [5]and hope does not disappoint us, because God's love has been poured into our hearts through the Holy Spirit who has been given to us.

6 While we were yet helpless, at the right time Christ died for the ungodly. [7]Why, one will hardly die for a righteous man—though perhaps for a good man one will dare even to die. [8]But God shows his love for us in that while we were yet sinners Christ died for us. [9]Since, therefore, we are now justified by his blood, much more shall we be saved by him from the wrath of God. [10]For if while we were enemies we were reconciled to God by the death of his Son, much more, now that we are reconciled, shall we be saved by his life. [11]Not only so, but we also rejoice in God through our Lord Jesus Christ, through whom we have now received our reconciliation.

Adam and Christ

12 Therefore as sin came into the world through one man and death through sin, and so death spread to all men because all men sinned *—[13]sin indeed was in the world before the law was given, but sin is not counted where there is no law. [14]Yet death reigned from Adam to Moses, even over those whose sins were not like the transgression of Adam, who was a type of the one who was to come.

15 But the free gift is not like the trespass. For if many died through one man's trespass, much more have the grace of God and the free gift in the grace of that one man Jesus Christ abounded for many. † [16]And the free gift is not like the effect of that one man's sin. For the judgment following one trespass brought condemnation, but the free gift following many trespasses brings justification. [17]If, because of one man's trespass, death reigned through that one man, much more will those who receive the abundance of grace and the free gift of righteousness reign in life through the one man Jesus Christ.

18 Then as one man's trespass led to condemnation for all men, so one man's act of righteousness leads to acquittal and life for all men. [19]For as by one man's disobedience many were made sinners, so by one man's obedience many will be made righteous. [20]Law came in, to increase the trespass; but where sin increased, grace abounded all the more, [21]so that, as sin reigned in death, grace also might reign through righteousness to eternal life through Jesus Christ our Lord.

Dying and Rising with Christ

6 What shall we say then? Are we to continue in sin that grace may abound? [2]By no means! How can we who died to sin still live in it? [3]Do you not know that all of us who have been baptized into Christ Jesus were baptized into his death? [4]We were buried ‡ therefore with him by baptism into death, so that as Christ was raised from the dead by the glory of the Father, we too might walk in newness of life.

5 For if we have been united with him in a death like his, we shall certainly be united with him in a resurrection like his. [6]We know that our former man was crucified with him so that the

---

f Other ancient authorities read *let us.*
g Other ancient authorities add *by faith.*
h Or *let us.*
4:18: Gen 15:5.
4:19: Heb 11:12; Gen 17:17; 18:11.
4:22: Rom 4:3.
4:23-24: Rom 15:4; 1 Cor 9:10; 10:11.
4:25: Rom 8:32.
5:1: Rom 3:28.
5:2: Eph 2:18; 3:12; Heb 10:19–20.
5:3: Rom 5:11; 2 Cor 12:10; Jas 1:3.
5:5: Ps 119:116; Acts 2:33; Phil 1:20.
5:8: Jn 15:13; Rom 8:32; 1 Pet 3:18; 1 Jn 3:16; 4:10.
5:9: Rom 3:5, 24–25; Eph 1:7; 1 Thess 1:10.
5:10: Col 1:21.
5:11: Rom 5:3.
5:12: 1 Cor 15:21–22; Rom 6:23; Jas 1:15.
5:14: 1 Cor 15:22, 45.
5:15: Acts 15:11.
5:16: Rom 8:1.
5:19: Phil 2:8.
5:20: Rom 7:7–8; Gal 3:19; 1 Tim 1:14.
5:21: Rom 6:23.
6:1: Rom 3:8; 6:15.
6:2: Rom 7:4, 6; Gal 2:19; 1 Pet 2:24.
6:3: Acts 2:38; 8:16; 19:5.
6:4: Col 2:12.
6:5: 2 Cor 4:10; Col 2:12.
6:6: Rom 7:24; Col 2:13.
* 5:12: Physical death is a sign of spiritual death; though physical death remains after justification.
† 5:15: The *felix culpa* praised in the *Exsultet* at the Easter Vigil.
‡ 6:4, *buried*: Immersed in the water of baptism.

sinful body might be destroyed, and we might no longer be enslaved to sin. [7]For he who has died is freed from sin. [8]But if we have died with Christ, we believe that we shall also live with him. [9]For we know that Christ being raised from the dead will never die again; death no longer has dominion over him. [10]The death he died he died to sin, once for all, but the life he lives he lives to God. [11]So you also must consider yourselves dead to sin and alive to God in Christ Jesus.

12 Let not sin therefore reign in your mortal bodies, to make you obey their passions. [13]Do not yield your members to sin as instruments of wickedness, but yield yourselves to God as men who have been brought from death to life, and your members to God as instruments of righteousness. [14]For sin will have no dominion over you, since you are not under law but under grace.

Slaves of Sin or of Righteousness

15 What then? Are we to sin because we are not under law but under grace? By no means!* [16]Do you not know that if you yield yourselves to any one as obedient slaves, you are slaves of the one whom you obey, either of sin, which leads to death, or of obedience, which leads to righteousness? [17]But thanks be to God, that you who were once slaves of sin have become obedient from the heart to the standard of teaching to which you were committed, [18]and, having been set free from sin, have become slaves of righteousness. [19]I am speaking in human terms, because of your natural limitations. For just as you once yielded your members to impurity and to greater and greater iniquity, so now yield your members to righteousness for sanctification.

20 When you were slaves of sin, you were free in regard to righteousness. [21]But then what return did you get from the things of which you are now ashamed? The end of those things is death. [22]But now that you have been set free from sin and have become slaves of God, the return you get is sanctification and its end, eternal life. [23]For the wages of sin is death, but the free gift of God is eternal life in Christ Jesus our Lord.

The Analogy with Marriage

7 Do you not know, brethren—for I am speaking to those who know the law—that the law is binding on a person only during his life? [2]Thus a married woman is bound by law to her husband as long as he lives; but if her husband dies she is discharged from the law concerning the husband. [3]Accordingly, she will be called an adulteress if she lives with another man while her husband is alive. But if her husband dies she is free from that law, and if she marries another man she is not an adulteress.

4 Likewise, my brethren, you have died to the law through the body of Christ, so that you may belong to another, to him who has been raised from the dead in order that we may bear fruit for God. [5]While we were living in the flesh, our sinful passions, aroused by the law, were at work in our members to bear fruit for death. [6]But now we are discharged from the law, dead to that which held us captive, so that we serve not under the old written code but in the new life of the Spirit.

The Law and Sin

7 What then shall we say? That the law is sin? By no means! Yet, if it had not been for the law, I should not have known sin. I should not have known what it is to covet if the law had not said, "You shall not covet." [8]But sin, finding opportunity in the commandment, wrought in me all kinds of covetousness. Apart from the law sin lies dead. [9]I was once alive apart from the law, but when the commandment came, sin revived and I died; [10]the very commandment which promised life proved to be death to me. [11]For sin, finding opportunity in the commandment, deceived me and by it killed me. [12]So the law is holy, and the commandment is holy and just and good.

The Interior Conflict
between Good and Evil

13 Did that which is good, then, bring death to me? † By no means! It was sin, working death in me through what is good, in order that sin might be shown to be sin, and through the commandment might become sinful beyond measure. [14]We know that the law is spiritual; but I am carnal, sold under sin. [15]I do not understand my own actions. For I do not do what I want, but I do the very thing I hate. [16]Now if I do what I do not want, I agree that the law is good. [17]So then it is no longer I that do it, but sin which dwells within me. [18]For I know that nothing good dwells within me, that is, in my flesh. I can will what is right, but I cannot do it. [19]For I do not do the good I

6:7: 1 Pet 4:1.
6:8: 2 Tim 2:11.
6:9: Acts 2:24; Rev 1:18.
6:11: Rom 7:4, 6; Gal 2:19; 1 Pet 2:24.
6:13: Rom 6:19; 7:5; 12:1.
6:14: Rom 8:2.
6:15: Rom 3:8; 6:1.
6:16: Mt 6:24; Jn 8:34; Rom 12:1.
6:18: Rom 8:2.
6:19: Rom 3:5; 6:13; 12:1.
6:20: Mt 6:24; Jn 8:34.
6:21: Rom 7:5; 8:6, 13, 21.
6:23: Rom 5:12, 21; Gal 6:7, 8.
7:2: 1 Cor 7:39.
7:4: Rom 6:2, 11; Gal 2:19; Col 1:22.
7:5: Rom 6:13, 21; 8:8; Jas 1:15.
7:7: Rom 3:20; 5:20; Ex 20:17; Deut 5:21.
7:8: 1 Cor 15:56.
7:10: Lev 18:5; Rom 10:5.
7:12: 1 Tim 1:8.
7:14: 1 Cor 3:1.
7:15: Gal 5:17.
* 6:15: As before, in the case of the law (Rom 2:17–29), so now, in the case of grace, Paul says it is not a license to sin.
† 7:13–25: Man under the law of Moses and perhaps man under the natural law too.

want, but the evil I do not want is what I do. [20]Now if I do what I do not want, it is no longer I that do it, but sin which dwells within me.

21 So I find it to be a law that when I want to do right, evil lies close at hand. [22]For I delight in the law of God, in my inmost self, [23]but I see in my members another law at war with the law of my mind and making me captive to the law of sin which dwells in my members. [24]Wretched man that I am! Who will deliver me from this body of death? [25]Thanks be to God through Jesus Christ our Lord! So then, I of myself serve the law of God with my mind, but with my flesh I serve the law of sin.

Life in the Spirit

8 There is therefore now no condemnation for those who are in Christ Jesus. [2]For the law of the Spirit of life in Christ Jesus has set me free from the law of sin and death. [3]For God has done what the law, weakened by the flesh, could not do: sending his own Son in the likeness of sinful flesh and for sin, [i] he condemned sin in the flesh, [4]in order that the just requirement of the law might be fulfilled in us, who walk not according to the flesh but according to the Spirit. [5]For those who live according to the flesh set their minds on the things of the flesh, but those who live according to the Spirit set their minds on the things of the Spirit. [6]To set the mind on the flesh is death, but to set the mind on the Spirit is life and peace. [7]For the mind that is set on the flesh is hostile to God; it does not submit to God's law, indeed it cannot; [8]and those who are in the flesh cannot please God.

9 But you are not in the flesh, you are in the Spirit, if the Spirit of God really dwells in you. Any one who does not have the Spirit of Christ does not belong to him. [10]But if Christ is in you, although your bodies are dead because of sin, your spirits are alive because of righteousness. [11]If the Spirit of him who raised Jesus from the dead dwells in you, he who raised Christ Jesus from the dead will give life to your mortal bodies also through his Spirit who dwells in you.

12 So then, brethren, we are debtors, not to the flesh, to live according to the flesh—[13]for if you live according to the flesh you will die, but if by the Spirit you put to death the deeds of the body you will live. [14]For all who are led by the Spirit of God are sons of God. [15]For you did not receive the spirit of slavery to fall back into fear, but you have received the spirit of sonship. When we cry, "Abba! Father!" [16]it is the Spirit himself bearing witness with our spirit that we are children of God, [17]and if children, then heirs, heirs of God and fellow heirs with Christ, provided we suffer with him in order that we may also be glorified with him.

The Glory to Be Revealed

18 I consider that the sufferings of this present time are not worth comparing with the glory that is to be revealed to us. [19]For the creation waits with eager longing for the revealing of the sons of God; * [20]for the creation was subjected to futility, not of its own will but by the will of him who subjected it in hope; [21]because the creation itself will be set free from its bondage to decay and obtain the glorious liberty of the children of God. [22]We know that the whole creation has been groaning with labor pains together until now; [23]and not only the creation, but we ourselves, who have the first fruits of the Spirit, groan inwardly as we wait for adoption as sons, the redemption of our bodies. [24]For in this hope we were saved. Now hope that is seen is not hope. For who hopes for what he sees? [25]But if we hope for what we do not see, we wait for it with patience.

26 Likewise the Spirit helps us in our weakness; for we do not know how to pray as we ought, but the Spirit himself intercedes for us with sighs too deep for words. [27]And he who searches the hearts of men knows what is the mind of the Spirit, because [j] the Spirit intercedes for the saints according to the will of God.

28 We know that in everything God works for good [k] with those who love him, [l] who are called according to his purpose. [29]For those whom he foreknew he also predestined to be conformed to the image of his Son, in order that he might be the first-born among many brethren. [30]And those whom he predestined he also called; and those

---

[i] Or and as a sin offering.
[j] Or that.
[k] Other ancient authorities read in everything he works for good, or everything works for good.
[l] Greek God.
7:22: Ps 1:2.
7:23: Gal 5:17.
7:24: Rom 6:6; Col 2:11.
8:1: Rom 5:16.
8:2: 1 Cor 15:45; Rom 6:14, 18.
8:3: Acts 13:39; Heb 7:18; 10:1–2; Phil 2:7; Heb 2:14.
8:4: Rom 3:31; Gal 5:16, 25.
8:5: Gal 5:19–25.
8:6: Rom 6:21; 8:13, 27; Gal 6:8.
8:8: Rom 7:5.
8:9: 1 Cor 3:16; 6:19; 2 Cor 6:16; 2 Tim 1:14.
8:10: Gal 2:20; Eph 3:17.
8:11: Jn 5:21.
8:13: Rom 8:6; Col 3:5.
8:14: Gal 5:18.
8:15: Rom 9:4; Gal 4:5–7; Mk 14:36.
8:16: Acts 5:32.
8:17: Gal 3:29; 4:7; 2 Cor 1:5, 7; 2 Tim 2:12; 1 Pet 4:13.
8:18: 2 Cor 4:17; Col 3:4; 1 Pet 5:1.
8:19: 1 Pet 1:7, 13; 1 Jn 3:2.
8:20: Eccles 1:2.
8:21: Acts 3:21; Rom 6:21; 2 Pet 3:13; Rev 21:1.
8:22: Jer 12:4, 11.
8:23: 2 Cor 1:22; 5:2, 4; Gal 5:5.
8:24: 2 Cor 5:7; Heb 11:1.
8:27: Ps 139:1–2; Lk 16:15; Rev 2:23; Rom 8:6, 34.
8:29: Rom 9:23; 11:2; 1 Pet 1:2, 20; Eph 1:5, 11.
* 8:19: Material creation, too, shares man's destiny, made as it was for him. Many ancient philosophers thought matter to be evil and that the spirit should be freed from it.

whom he called he also justified; and those whom he justified he also glorified.

God's Love in Christ Jesus

31 What then shall we say to this? If God is for us, who is against us? [32]He who did not spare his own Son but gave him up for us all, will he not also give us all things with him? [33]Who shall bring any charge against God's elect? It is God who justifies; [34]who is to condemn? Is it Christ Jesus, who died, yes, who was raised from the dead, who is at the right hand of God, who indeed intercedes for us? [m] [35]Who shall separate us from the love of Christ? Shall tribulation, or distress, or persecution, or famine, or nakedness, or peril, or sword? [36]As it is written,

"For your sake we are being killed all the day
    long;
we are regarded as sheep to be slaughtered."
[37]No, in all these things we are more than conquerors through him who loved us. [38]For I am sure that neither death, nor life, nor angels, nor principalities, nor things present, nor things to come, nor powers, [39]nor height, nor depth, nor anything else in all creation, will be able to separate us from the love of God in Christ Jesus our Lord.

God's Election of Israel

9 I am speaking the truth in Christ, I am not lying; my conscience bears me witness in the Holy Spirit, [2]that I have great sorrow and unceasing anguish in my heart. [3]For I could wish that I myself were accursed and cut off from Christ for the sake of my brethren, my kinsmen according to the flesh. [4]They are Israelites, and to them belong the sonship, the glory, the covenants, the giving of the law, the worship, and the promises; [5]to them belong the patriarchs, and of their race, according to the flesh, is the Christ, who is God over all, blessed for ever. [n] Amen.

6 But it is not as though the word of God had failed. For not all who are descended from Israel belong to Israel, [7]and not all are children of Abraham because they are his descendants; but "Through Isaac shall your descendants be named." [8]This means that it is not the children of the flesh who are the children of God, but the children of the promise are reckoned as descendants. [9]For this is what the promise said, "About this time I will return and Sarah shall have a son." [10]And not only so, but also when Rebecca had conceived children by one man, our forefather Isaac, [11]though they were not yet born and had done nothing either good or bad, in order that God's purpose of election might continue, not because of works but because of his call, [12]she was told, "The elder will serve the younger." [13]As it is written, "Jacob I loved, but Esau I hated."

14 What shall we say then? Is there injustice on God's part? By no means! [15]For he says to Moses, "I will have mercy on whom I have mercy, and I will have compassion on whom I have compassion." [16]So it depends not upon man's will or exertion, but upon God's mercy. [17]For the Scripture says to Pharaoh, "I have raised you up for the very purpose of showing my power in you, so that my name may be proclaimed in all the earth." [18]So then he has mercy upon whomever he wills, and he hardens the heart of whomever he wills.

God's Wrath and Mercy

19 * You will say to me then, "Why does he still find fault? For who can resist his will?" [20]But who are you, a man, to answer back to God? Will what is molded say to its molder, "Why have you made me thus?" [21]Has the potter no right over the clay, to make out of the same lump one vessel for beauty and another for menial use? [22]What if God, desiring to show his wrath and to make known his power, has endured with much patience the vessels of wrath made for destruction, [23]in order to make known the riches of his glory for the vessels of mercy, which he has prepared beforehand for glory, [24]even us whom he has called, not from the Jews only but also from the Gentiles?

[25]As indeed he says in Hose'a,

"Those who were not my people
I will call 'my people,'
and her who was not beloved
I will call 'my beloved.'"
[26]"And in the very place where it was said to
    them, 'You are not my people,'
they will be called 'sons of the living God.'"

27 And Isaiah cries out concerning Israel: "Though the number of the sons of Israel be as

---

[m] Or It is Christ Jesus . . . for us.
[n] Or Christ. God who is over all be blessed for ever.
8:31: Ps 118:6.
8:32: Jn 3:16; Rom 4:25; 5:8.
8:33: Lk 18:7; Is 50:8–9.
8:34: Rom 8:27.
8:36: Ps 44:22.
8:37: 1 Cor 15:57.
9:3: Ex 32:32.
9:4: Rom 3:2; 8:15.
9:6: Rom 2:28–29.
9:7: Gen 21:12; Heb 11:18.
9:8: Gal 3:29; 4:28.
9:9: Gen 18:10.
9:10: Gen 25:21.
9:12: Gen 25:23.
9:13: Mal 1:2–3.
9:14: 2 Chron 19:7.
9:15: Ex 33:19.
9:17: Ex 9:16.
9:18: Rom 11:7.
9:20: Is 29:16; 45:9.
9:21: 2 Tim 2:20.
9:22: Prov 16:4.
9:23: Rom 8:29.
9:24: Rom 3:29.
9:25: Hos 2:23; 1 Pet 2:10.
9:26: Hos 1:10.
9:27: Is 10:22–23; Gen 22:17; Hos 1:10; Rom 11:5; 2 Kings 19:4; Is 11:11.
* 9:19–24: Paul's words here, taken by themselves, seem to leave no room for moral responsibility, but they must be taken in conjunction with other passages; see chapters 1 and 2.

the sand of the sea, only a remnant of them will be saved; [28]for the Lord will execute his sentence upon the earth with rigor and dispatch." [29]And as Isaiah predicted,

"If the Lord of hosts had not left us children,
we would have fared like Sodom and been
    made like Gomor′rah."

Israel's Lack of Faith

30 What shall we say, then? That Gentiles who did not pursue righteousness have attained it, that is, righteousness through faith; [31]but that Israel who pursued the righteousness which is based on law did not succeed in fulfilling that law. [32]Why? Because they did not pursue it through faith, but as if it were based on works. They have stumbled over the stumbling stone, [33]as it is written,

"Behold, I am laying in Zion a stone that will
    make men stumble,
a rock that will make them fall;
and he who believes in him will not be put to
    shame."

10 Brethren, my heart's desire and prayer to God for them is that they may be saved. * [2]I bear them witness that they have a zeal for God, but it is not enlightened. [3]For, being ignorant of the righteousness that comes from God, and seeking to establish their own, they did not submit to God's righteousness. [4]For Christ is the end of the law, that every one who has faith may be justified.

Salvation Is for Believers in Christ

5 Moses writes that the man who practices the righteousness which is based on the law shall live by it. [6]But the righteousness based on faith says, Do not say in your heart, "Who will ascend into heaven?" (that is, to bring Christ down) [7]or "Who will descend into the abyss?" (that is, to bring Christ up from the dead). [8]But what does it say? The word is near you, on your lips and in your heart (that is, the word of faith which we preach); [9]because, if you confess with your lips that Jesus is Lord and believe in your heart that God raised him from the dead, you will be saved. [10]For man believes with his heart and so is justified, and he confesses with his lips and so is saved. [11]The Scripture says, "No one who believes in him will be put to shame." [12]For there is no distinction between Jew and Greek; the same Lord is Lord of all and bestows his riches upon all who call upon him. [13]For, "every one who calls upon the name of the Lord will be saved."

14 But how are men to call upon him in whom they have not believed? And how are they to believe in him of whom they have never heard? And how are they to hear without a preacher? [15]And how can men preach unless they are sent? As it is written, "How beautiful are the feet of those who

preach good news!" [16]But they have not all heeded the gospel; for Isaiah says, "Lord, who has believed what he has heard from us?" [17]So faith comes from what is heard, and what is heard comes by the preaching of Christ.

18 But I ask, have they not heard? Indeed they have; for

"Their voice has gone out to all the earth,
and their words to the ends of the world."

[19]Again I ask, did Israel not understand? First Moses says,

"I will make you jealous of those who are not a
    nation;
with a foolish nation I will make you angry."

[20]Then Isaiah is so bold as to say,

"I have been found by those who did not seek
    me;
I have shown myself to those who did not ask
    for me."

[21]But of Israel he says, "All day long I have held out my hands to a disobedient and contrary people."

Israel's Rejection Is Not Final

11 I ask, then, has God rejected his people? By no means! I myself am an Israelite, a descendant of Abraham, a member of the tribe of Benjamin. [2]God has not rejected his people whom he foreknew. Do you not know what the Scripture says of Eli′jah, how he pleads with God against Israel? [3]"Lord, they have killed your prophets, they have demolished your altars, and I alone am left, and they seek my life." [4]But what is God's reply to him? "I have kept for myself seven thousand men who have not bowed the knee to Ba′al." [5]So too at the present time there is a remnant, chosen by grace. [6]But if it is by grace, it is no longer on the basis of works; otherwise grace would no longer be grace.

9:29: Is 1:9.
9:30: Rom 3:22; 10:6, 20; Gal 2:16; 3:24; Phil 3:9; Heb 11:7.
9:31: Is 51:1; Rom 10:2–3; 11:7.
9:32: 1 Pet 2:8.
9:33: Is 28:16; Rom 10:11.
10:2–4: Rom 9:31.
10:3: Rom 1:17.
10:4: Gal 3:24; Rom 3:22; 7:1–4.
10:5: Lev 18:5; Neh 9:29; Ezek 20:11, 13, 21; Rom 7:10.
10:6: Deut 30:12–13; Rom 9:30.
10:8: Deut 30:14.
10:9: Mt 10:32; Lk 12:8; Acts 16:31.
10:11: Is 28:16; Rom 9:33.
10:12: Rom 3:22, 29; Gal 3:28; Col 3:11; Acts 10:36.
10:13: Joel 2:32; Acts 2:21.
10:15: Is 52:7.
10:16: Is 53:1; Jn 12:38.
10:18: Ps 19:4; Col 1:6, 23.
10:19: Deut 32:21; Rom 11:11, 14.
10:20: Is 65:1; Rom 9:30.
10:21: Is 65:2.
11:1: 1 Sam 12:22; Jer 31:37; 33:24–26; 2 Cor 11:22; Phil 3:5.
11:2: Ps 94:14; 1 Kings 19:10.
11:4: 1 Kings 19:18.
11:5: 2 Kings 19:4; Is 11:11; Rom 9:27.
11:6: Rom 4:4.
* 10:1: Paul is afraid he has spoken too strongly of their sins, so he declares his love for Israel.

7 What then? Israel failed to obtain what it sought. The elect obtained it, but the rest were hardened, [8]as it is written,

"God gave them a spirit of stupor,
eyes that should not see and ears that should
not hear,
down to this very day."

[9]And David says,

"Let their feast become a snare and a trap,
a pitfall and a retribution for them;
[10]let their eyes be darkened so that they cannot
see,
and bend their backs for ever."

The Salvation of the Gentiles

11 So I ask, have they stumbled so as to fall? By no means! But through their trespass salvation has come to the Gentiles, so as to make Israel jealous. [12]Now if their trespass means riches for the world, and if their failure means riches for the Gentiles, how much more will their full inclusion mean!

13 Now I am speaking to you Gentiles. Inasmuch then as I am an apostle to the Gentiles, I magnify my ministry [14]in order to make my fellow Jews jealous, and thus save some of them. [15]For if their rejection means the reconciliation of the world, what will their acceptance mean but life from the dead? [16]If the dough offered as first fruits is holy, so is the whole batch; and if the root is holy, so are the branches.

17 But if some of the branches were broken off, and you, a wild olive shoot, were grafted in their place to share the richness[o] of the olive tree, [18]do not boast over the branches. If you do boast, remember it is not you that support the root, but the root that supports you. [19]You will say, "Branches were broken off so that I might be grafted in." [20]That is true. They were broken off because of their unbelief, but you stand fast only through faith. So do not become proud, but stand in awe. [21]For if God did not spare the natural branches, neither will he spare you. [22]Note then the kindness and the severity of God: severity toward those who have fallen, but God's kindness to you, provided you continue in his kindness; otherwise you too will be cut off. [23]And even the others, if they do not persist in their unbelief, will be grafted in, for God has the power to graft them in again. [24]For if you have been cut from what is by nature a wild olive tree, and grafted, contrary to nature, into a cultivated olive tree, how much more will these natural branches be grafted back into their own olive tree.

Israel Will Be Saved

25 Lest you be wise in your own conceits, I want you to understand this mystery, brethren: a hardening has come upon part of Israel, until the full number of the Gentiles come in, [26]and so all Israel will be saved; as it is written,

"The Deliverer will come from Zion,
he will banish ungodliness from Jacob";
[27]"and this will be my covenant with them
when I take away their sins."

[28]As regards the gospel they are enemies of God, for your sake; but as regards election they are beloved for the sake of their forefathers. [29]For the gifts and the call of God are irrevocable. [30]Just as you were once disobedient to God but now have received mercy because of their disobedience, [31]so they have now been disobedient in order that by the mercy shown to you they also may[p] receive mercy. [32]For God has consigned all men to disobedience, that he may have mercy upon all.

33 O the depth of the riches and wisdom and knowledge of God! How unsearchable are his judgments and how inscrutable his ways! [34]"For who has known the mind of the Lord, or who has been his counselor?" [35]"Or who has given a gift to him that he might be repaid?" [36]For from him and through him and to him are all things. To him be glory for ever. Amen.

The New Life in Christ

12 I appeal to you therefore, brethren, by the mercies of God, to present your bodies as a living sacrifice, holy and acceptable to God, which is your spiritual worship. [2]Do not be conformed to this world[q] but be transformed by the renewal of your mind, that you may prove what is the will of God, what is good and acceptable and perfect.[r]

3 For by the grace given to me I bid every one among you not to think of himself more highly than he ought to think, but to think with sober judgment, each according to the measure of faith which God has assigned him. [4]For as in one body we have many members, and all the members do not have the same function, [5]so we, though many, are one body in Christ, and individually members

---

[o] Other ancient authorities read *rich root.*
[p] Other ancient authorities add *now.*
[q] Greek *age.*
[r] Or *what is the good and acceptable and perfect will of God.*
11:7: Rom 10:19, 31; 11:25.
11:8: Is 29:10; Deut 29:4; Mt 13:13–14.
11:9: Ps 69:22–23.
11:11: Rom 10:19; 11:14.
11:13: Acts 9:15.
11:14: Rom 10:19; 11:11; 1 Cor 9:22.
11:15: Lk 15:24, 32.
11:20: 2 Cor 1:24.
11:25: 1 Cor 2:7–10; Eph 3:3–5, 9; Rom 9:18; 11:7; Lk 21:24.
11:26: Is 59:20–21.
11:27: Jer 31:33; Is 27:9.
11:32: Rom 3:9; Gal 3:22–29.
11:33: Col 2:3.
11:34: Is 40:13–14; 1 Cor 2:16.
11:35: Job 35:7; 41:11.
11:36: 1 Cor 8:6; 11:12; Col 1:16; Heb 2:10.
12:1: Rom 6:13, 16, 19; 1 Pet 2:5.
12:2: 1 Jn 2:15; Eph 4:23; 5:10.
12:4: 1 Cor 12:12–14; Eph 4:4, 16.
12:5: 1 Cor 10:17; 12:20, 27; Eph 4:25.

one of another. [6]Having gifts that differ according to the grace given to us, let us use them: if prophecy, in proportion to our faith; [7]if service, in our serving; he who teaches, in his teaching; [8]he who exhorts, in his exhortation; he who contributes, in liberality; he who gives aid, with zeal; he who does acts of mercy, with cheerfulness.

Marks of the True Christian

9 Let love be genuine; hate what is evil, hold fast to what is good; [10]love one another with brotherly affection; outdo one another in showing honor. [11]Never flag in zeal, be aglow with the Spirit, serve the Lord. [12]Rejoice in your hope, be patient in tribulation, be constant in prayer. [13]Contribute to the needs of the saints, practice hospitality.

14 Bless those who persecute you; bless and do not curse them. [15]Rejoice with those who rejoice, weep with those who weep. [16]Live in harmony with one another; do not be haughty, but associate with the lowly; [s] never be conceited. [17]Repay no one evil for evil, but take thought for what is noble in the sight of all. [18]If possible, so far as it depends upon you, live peaceably with all. [19]Beloved, never avenge yourselves, but leave it [t] to the wrath of God; for it is written, "Vengeance is mine, I will repay, says the Lord." [20]No, "if your enemy is hungry, feed him; if he is thirsty, give him drink; for by so doing you will heap burning coals upon his head." [21]Do not be overcome by evil, but overcome evil with good.

Being Subject to Authorities

13 Let every person be subject to the governing authorities. For there is no authority except from God, and those that exist have been instituted by God. [2]Therefore he who resists the authorities resists what God has appointed, and those who resist will incur judgment. [3]For rulers are not a terror to good conduct, but to bad. Would you have no fear of him who is in authority? Then do what is good, and you will receive his approval; [4]for he is God's servant for your good. But if you do wrong, be afraid, for he does not bear the sword in vain; he is the servant of God to execute his wrath on the wrongdoer. [5]Therefore one must be subject, not only to avoid God's wrath but also for the sake of conscience. [6]For the same reason you also pay taxes, for the authorities are ministers of God, attending to this very thing. [7]Pay all of them their dues, taxes to whom taxes are due, revenue to whom revenue is due, respect to whom respect is due, honor to whom honor is due.

Love for One Another

8 Owe no one anything, except to love one another; for he who loves his neighbor has fulfilled the law. [9]The commandments, "You shall not commit adultery, You shall not kill, You shall not steal, You shall not covet," and any other commandment, are summed up in this sentence, "You shall love your neighbor as yourself." [10]Love does no wrong to a neighbor; therefore love is the fulfilling of the law.

An Urgent Appeal

11 Besides this you know what hour it is, how it is full time now for you to wake from sleep. For salvation is nearer to us now than when we first believed; [12]the night is far gone, the day is at hand. Let us then cast off the works of darkness and put on the armor of light; [13]let us conduct ourselves becomingly as in the day, not in reveling and drunkenness, not in debauchery and licentiousness, not in quarreling and jealousy. [14]But put on the Lord Jesus Christ, and make no provision for the flesh, to gratify its desires.

Do Not Judge One Another

14 * As for the man who is weak in faith, welcome him, but not for disputes over opinions. [2]One believes he may eat anything, while the weak man eats only vegetables. [3]Let not him who eats despise him who abstains, and let not him who abstains pass judgment on him who eats; for God has welcomed him. [4]Who are you to pass judgment on the servant of another? It is before his own master that he stands or falls. And he will be upheld, for the Master is able to make him stand.

5 One man esteems one day as better than another, while another man esteems all days alike. Let every one be fully convinced in his own mind. [6]He who observes the day, observes it in honor of the Lord. He also who eats, eats in honor of the Lord, since he gives thanks to God; while he who abstains, abstains in honor of the Lord and gives thanks to God. [7]None of us lives to himself, and none of us dies to himself. [8]If we live, we live to the Lord, and if we die, we die to the Lord; so

---

[s] Or give yourselves to humble tasks.
[t] Greek give place.
12:6–8: 1 Cor 7:7; 12:4–11; 1 Pet 4:10–11.
12:12: Acts 1:14; Rom 5:2; 1 Thess 5:17.
12:14: Mt 5:44; Lk 6:28.
12:16: Rom 11:25; 15:5; 1 Cor 1:10; 2 Cor 13:11; Phil 2:2; 4:2; Prov 3:7, 26:12.
12:17: Prov 20:22; 2 Cor 8:21; 1 Thess 5:15.
12:18: Mk 9:50; Rom 14:19.
12:19: Lev 19:18; Deut 32:35; Heb 10:30.
12:20: Prov 25:21–22; Mt 5:44; Lk 6:27.
13:1: Tit 3:1; 1 Pet 2:13–14; Prov 8:15; Jn 19:11.
13:3: 1 Pet 2:14.
13:4: 1 Thess 4:6.
13:7: Mt 22:21; Mk 12:17; Lk 20:25.
13:8: Mt 22:39–40; Rom 13:10; Gal 5:14; Col 3:14; Jas 2:8.
13:9: Ex 20:13–14; Deut 5:17–18; Lev 19:18; Mt 19:19.
13:10: Mt 22:39–40; Rom 13:8; Gal 5:14; Jas 2:8.
13:11: Eph 5:14; 1 Thess 5:6.
13:12: 1 Jn 2:8; Eph 5:11; 1 Thess 5:8.
13:13: 1 Thess 4:12; Gal 5:19–21.
13:14: Gal 3:27; 5:16.
14:3: Col 2:16.
14:5: Gal 4:10.
14:7: Gal 2:20; 2 Cor 5:15.
14:8: Phil 1:20.
* 14:1—15:13: Paul is tolerant of the Jewish Christians' reluctance to abandon the ritual prescriptions of the law of Moses, while being equally insistent that these shall not be forced on Gentile Christians.

then, whether we live or whether we die, we are the Lord's. [9]For to this end Christ died and lived again, that he might be Lord both of the dead and of the living.

10 Why do you pass judgment on your brother? Or you, why do you despise your brother? For we shall all stand before the judgment seat of God; [11]for it is written,

"As I live, says the Lord, every knee shall bow
to me,
and every tongue shall give praise [u] to God."
[12]So each of us shall give account of himself to God.

Do Not Hinder a Brother

13 Then let us no more pass judgment on one another, but rather decide never to put a stumbling block or hindrance in the way of a brother. [14]I know and am persuaded in the Lord Jesus that nothing is unclean in itself; but it is unclean for any one who thinks it unclean. * [15]If your brother is being injured by what you eat, you are no longer walking in love. Do not let what you eat cause the ruin of one for whom Christ died. [16]So do not let what is good to you be spoken of as evil. [17]For the kingdom of God does not mean food and drink but righteousness and peace and joy in the Holy Spirit; [18]he who thus serves Christ is acceptable to God and approved by men. [19]Let us then pursue what makes for peace and for mutual upbuilding. [20]Do not, for the sake of food, destroy the work of God. Everything is indeed clean, but it is wrong for any one to make others fall by what he eats; [21]it is right not to eat meat or drink wine or do anything that makes your brother stumble. [v] [22]The faith that you have, keep between yourself and God; happy is he who has no reason to judge himself for what he approves. [23]But he who has doubts is condemned, if he eats, because he does not act from faith; for whatever does not proceed from faith is sin. [w]

Please Others, Not Yourselves

15 We who are strong ought to bear with the failings of the weak, and not to please ourselves; [2]let each of us please his neighbor for his good, to edify him. [3]For Christ did not please himself; but, as it is written, "The reproaches of those who reproached you fell on me." [4]For whatever was written in former days was written for our instruction, that by steadfastness and by the encouragement of the Scriptures we might have hope. [5]May the God of steadfastness and encouragement grant you to live in such harmony with one another, in accord with Christ Jesus, [6]that together you may with one voice glorify the God and Father of our Lord Jesus Christ.

The Gospel for Jews and Gentiles Alike

7 Welcome one another, therefore, as Christ has welcomed you, for the glory of God. [8]For I tell you that Christ became a servant to the circumcised to show God's truthfulness, in order to confirm the promises given to the patriarchs, [9]and in order that the Gentiles might glorify God for his mercy. As it is written,

"Therefore I will praise you among the Gentiles,
and sing to your name";
[10]and again it is said,
"Rejoice, O Gentiles, with his people";
[11]and again,
"Praise the Lord, all Gentiles,
and let all the peoples praise him";
[12]and further Isaiah says,
"The root of Jesse shall come,
he who rises to rule the Gentiles;
in him shall the Gentiles hope."
[13]May the God of hope fill you with all joy and peace in believing, so that by the power of the Holy Spirit you may abound in hope.

Paul's Reason for Writing So Boldly

14 I myself am satisfied about you, my brethren, that you yourselves are full of goodness, filled with all knowledge, and able to instruct one another. [15]But on some points I have written to you very boldly by way of reminder, because of the grace given me by God [16]to be a minister of Christ Jesus to the Gentiles in the priestly service of the gospel of God, so that the offering of the Gentiles may be acceptable, sanctified by the Holy Spirit. † [17]In Christ Jesus, then, I have reason to be proud of my work for God. [18]For I will not venture to speak of anything except what Christ has wrought through me to win obedience from the Gentiles, by word and deed, [19]by the power of signs and wonders, by the power of the Holy Spirit, so that from Jerusalem and as far round as Illyr'icum I have fully preached the gospel of Christ, [20]thus making it my ambition to preach the gospel, not where Christ has already been named, lest I build on another man's foundation, [21]but as it is written,

---

u Or *confess.*
v Other ancient authorities add *or be upset or be weakened.*
w Other authorities, some ancient, insert here Ch. 16:25–27.
14:10: 2 Cor 5:10.
14:11: Is 45:23; Phil 2:10–11.
14:13: Mt 7:1; 1 Cor 8:13.
14:15: Rom 14:20; 1 Cor 8:11.
14:16: 1 Cor 10:30.
14:19: Mk 9:50; Rom 12:18; 1 Thess 5:11.
14:20: Rom 14:15; 1 Cor 8:9–12.
14:21: 1 Cor 8:13.
14:22: Rom 2:1.
15:3: Ps 69:9.
15:4: Rom 4:23–24; 1 Cor 9:10; 2 Tim 3:16.
15:5: Rom 12:16; 1 Cor 1:10; 2 Cor 13:11; Phil 2:2; 4:2.
15:9: Ps 18:49; 2 Sam 22:50.
15:10: Deut 32:43.
15:11: Ps 117:1.
15:12: Is 11:10; Mt 12:21.
15:16: Acts 9:15.
15:18: Rom 1:5; Acts 15:12; 21:19.
15:19: Acts 19:11; 2 Cor 12:12.
15:20: 2 Cor 10:15–16.
15:21: Is 52:15.
* 14:14: Conscience is the ultimate guide.
† 15:15–16: Paul again justifies his writing to a church he did not found.

"They shall see who have never been told of him, and they shall understand who have never heard of him."

Paul's Plan to Visit Rome

22 This is the reason why I have so often been hindered from coming to you. [23]But now, since I no longer have any room for work in these regions, and since I have longed for many years to come to you, [24]I hope to see you in passing as I go to Spain, and to be sped on my journey there by you, once I have enjoyed your company for a little. [25]At present, however, I am going to Jerusalem with aid for the saints. [26]For Macedonia and Acha'ia have been pleased to make some contribution for the poor among the saints at Jerusalem; [27]they were pleased to do it, and indeed they are in debt to them, for if the Gentiles have come to share in their spiritual blessings, they ought also to be of service to them in material blessings. [28]When therefore I have completed this, and have delivered to them what has been raised,[x] I shall go on by way of you to Spain; [29]and I know that when I come to you I shall come in the fulness of the blessing[y] of Christ.

30 I appeal to you, brethren, by our Lord Jesus Christ and by the love of the Spirit, to strive together with me in your prayers to God on my behalf, [31]that I may be delivered from the unbelievers in Judea, and that my service for Jerusalem may be acceptable to the saints, [32]so that by God's will I may come to you with joy and be refreshed in your company. [33]The God of peace be with you all. Amen.

Personal Greetings

16 I commend to you our sister Phoebe, a deaconess of the Church at Cen'chre-ae, [2]that you may receive her in the Lord as befits the saints, and help her in whatever she may require from you, for she has been a helper of many and of myself as well.

3 Greet Prisca and Aqui'la, my fellow workers in Christ Jesus, [4]who risked their necks for my life, to whom not only I but also all the churches of the Gentiles give thanks; [5]greet also the church in their house. Greet my beloved Epae'netus, who was the first convert in Asia for Christ. [6]Greet Mary, who has worked hard among you. [7]Greet Andron'icus and Ju'nias, my kinsmen and my fellow prisoners; they are men of note among the apostles, and they were in Christ before me. [8]Greet Amplia'tus, my beloved in the Lord. [9]Greet Urba'nus, our fellow worker in Christ, and my beloved Stachys. [10]Greet Apel'les, who is approved in Christ. Greet those who belong to the family of Aristob'ulus. [11]Greet my kinsman Hero'dion. Greet those in the Lord who belong to the family of Narcis'sus. [12]Greet those workers in the Lord, Tryphae'na and Trypho'sa. Greet the beloved Persis, who has worked hard in the Lord. [13]Greet Rufus, eminent in the Lord, also his mother and mine. [14]Greet Asyn'critus, Phlegon, Hermes, Patro'bas, Hermas, and the brethren who are with them. [15]Greet Philol'ogus, Julia, Nereus and his sister, and Olympas, and all the saints who are with them. [16]Greet one another with a holy kiss. All the churches of Christ greet you.[*]

Final Instructions

17 I appeal to you, brethren, to take note of those who create dissensions and difficulties, in opposition to the doctrine which you have been taught; avoid them. [18]For such persons do not serve our Lord Christ, but their own appetites,[z] and by fair and flattering words they deceive the hearts of the simple-minded. [19]For while your obedience is known to all, so that I rejoice over you, I would have you wise as to what is good and guileless as to what is evil; [20]then the God of peace will soon crush Satan under your feet. The grace of our Lord Jesus Christ be with you.[a]

21 Timothy, my fellow worker, greets you; so do Lucius and Jason and Sosip'ater, my kinsmen.

22 I Tertius, the writer of this letter, greet you in the Lord.

23 Ga'ius, who is host to me and to the whole Church, greets you. Eras'tus, the city treasurer, and our brother Quartus, greet you.[b]

Final Doxology

25 Now to him who is able to strengthen you according to my gospel and the preaching of Jesus Christ, according to the revelation of the mystery which was kept secret for long ages [26]but is now disclosed and through the prophetic writings is made known to all nations, according to the command of the eternal God, to bring about the obedience of faith—[27]to the only wise God be glory for evermore through Jesus Christ! Amen.

---

[x] Greek *sealed to them this fruit*.
[y] Other ancient authorities insert *of the gospel*.
[z] Greek *their own belly* (Phil 3:19).
[a] Other ancient authorities omit this sentence.
[b] Other ancient authorities insert verse 24, *The grace of our Lord Jesus Christ be with you all. Amen*.
15:22: Rom 1:13.
15:23: Acts 19:21; Rom 1:10–11; 15:32.
15:24: Rom 15:28.
15:25: Acts 19:21; 24:17; 15:31.
15:26: 2 Cor 8:1–5; 9:2; 1 Thess 1:7–8.
15:27: 1 Cor 9:11.
15:28: Rom 15:24.
15:29: Acts 19:21.
15:31: 2 Thess 3:2; Rom 15:25–26; 2 Cor 8:4; 9:1.
15:32: Rom 1:10; Acts 19:21.
15:33: 2 Cor 13:11; Phil 4:9.
16:3: Acts 18:2.
16:5: 1 Cor 16:19.
16:16: 2 Cor 13:12; 1 Thess 5:26; 1 Pet 5:14.
16:17: Gal 1:8–9; 2 Thess 3:6, 14; 2 Jn 10.
16:19: Rom 1:8; 1 Cor 14:20.
16:20: 1 Cor 16:23; 2 Cor 13:14; Gal 6:18; Phil 4:23; 1 Thess 5:28; 2 Thess 3:18; Rev 22:21.
16:21: Acts 16:1.
16:23: 1 Cor 1:14.
* 16:16, *All the churches of Christ greet you:* A remarkable salutation, not used elsewhere.

THE FIRST LETTER OF PAUL TO THE

CORINTHIANS

Salutation

1 Paul, called by the will of God to be an apostle of Christ Jesus, and our brother Sos'thenes,

2 To the Church of God which is at Corinth, to those sanctified in Christ Jesus, called to be saints * together with all those who in every place call on the name of our Lord Jesus Christ, both their Lord and ours:

3 Grace to you and peace from God our Father and the Lord Jesus Christ.

4 I give thanks to God a always for you because of the grace of God which was given you in Christ Jesus, 5that in every way you were enriched in him with all speech and all knowledge—6even as the testimony to Christ was confirmed among you—7so that you are not lacking in any spiritual gift, as you wait for the revealing of our Lord Jesus Christ; 8who will sustain you to the end, guiltless in the day of our Lord Jesus Christ. 9God is faithful, by whom you were called into the fellowship of his Son, Jesus Christ our Lord.

Dissension in the Church

10 I appeal to you, brethren, by the name of our Lord Jesus Christ, that all of you agree and that there be no dissensions among you, but that you be united in the same mind and the same judgment. 11For it has been reported to me by Chlo'e's people that there is quarreling among you, my brethren. 12What I mean is that each one of you says, "I belong to Paul," or "I belong to Apol'los," or "I belong to Ce'phas," † or "I belong to Christ." 13Is Christ divided? Was Paul crucified for you? Or were you baptized in the name of Paul? 14I am thankful b that I baptized none of you except Crispus and Ga'ius; 15lest any one should say that you were baptized in my name. 16(I did baptize also the household of Steph'anas. Beyond that, I do not know whether I baptized any one else.) 17For Christ did not send me to baptize but to preach the gospel, and not with eloquent wisdom, lest the cross of Christ be emptied of its power.

Christ the Power and Wisdom of God

18 For the word of the cross is folly to those who are perishing, but to us who are being saved it is the power of God. 19For it is written,

"I will destroy the wisdom of the wise,
and the cleverness of the clever I will thwart."

20Where is the wise man? Where is the scribe? Where is the debater of this age? Has not God made foolish the wisdom of the world? 21For since, in the wisdom of God, the world did not know God through wisdom, it pleased God through the folly of what we preach to save those who believe. 22For Jews demand signs and Greeks seek wisdom, 23but we preach Christ crucified, a stumbling block to Jews and folly to Gentiles, 24but to those who are called, both Jews and Greeks, Christ the power of God and the wisdom of God. 25For the foolishness of God is wiser than men, and the weakness of God is stronger than men.

26 For consider your call, brethren; not many of you were wise according to the flesh, not many were powerful, not many were of noble birth; 27but God chose what is foolish in the world to shame the wise, God chose what is weak in the world to shame the strong, 28God chose what is low and despised in the world, even things that are not, to bring to nothing things that are, 29so that no flesh might boast in the presence of God. 30He is the source of your life in Christ Jesus, whom God made our wisdom, our righteousness and sanctification and redemption; 31therefore, as it is written, "Let him who boasts, boast of the Lord."

Proclaiming Christ Crucified

2 When I came to you, brethren, I did not come proclaiming to you the testimony c of God in

---

a Other ancient authorities read my God.
b Other ancient authorities read I thank God.
c Other ancient authorities read mystery (or secret).
1:1: Rom 1:1; Acts 18:17.
1:2: Acts 18:1.
1:3: Rom 1:7.
1:4: Rom 1:8.
1:8: 1 Cor 5:5; 2 Cor 1:14.
1:9: Rom 8:28; 1 Jn 1:3.
1:12: 1 Cor 3:4; Acts 18:24; 1 Cor 3:22; Jn 1:42; 1 Cor 9:5; 15:5.
1:13: Mt 28:19; Acts 2:38.
1:14: Acts 18:8; Rom 16:23.
1:16: 1 Cor 16:15.
1:17: Jn 4:2; Acts 10:48; 1 Cor 2:1; 4:13.
1:19: Is 29:14.
1:22: Mt 12:38.
1:23: 1 Cor 2:2; Gal 3:1; 5:11.
1:27: Jas 2:5.
1:28: Rom 4:17.
1:29: Eph 2:9.
1:30: 1 Cor 4:15; Rom 8:1; 2 Cor 5:21; 1 Cor 6:11; 1 Thess 5:23; Eph 1:7, 14; Col 1:14; Rom 3:24.
1:31: Jer 9:24; 2 Cor 10:17.
2:1: 1 Cor 1:17.
* 1:2, saints: A word commonly used for Christians in Paul's letters and in Acts.
† 1:12, Cephas: i.e., Peter. It does not follow from this that he had even been to Corinth, but it does indicate his authority there.

lofty words or wisdom. ²For I decided to know nothing among you except Jesus Christ and him crucified. * ³And I was with you in weakness and in much fear and trembling; ⁴and my speech and my message were not in plausible words of wisdom, but in demonstration of the Spirit and of power, ⁵that your faith might not rest in the wisdom of men but in the power of God.

The True Wisdom of God

6 Yet among the mature we do impart wisdom, although it is not a wisdom of this age or of the rulers of this age, who are doomed to pass away. ⁷But we impart a secret and hidden wisdom of God, which God decreed before the ages for our glorification. ⁸None of the rulers of this age understood this; for if they had, they would not have crucified the Lord of glory. ⁹But, as it is written,

"What no eye has seen, nor ear heard,
  nor the heart of man conceived,
 what God has prepared for those who love
      him,"

¹⁰God has revealed to us through the Spirit. For the Spirit searches everything, even the depths of God. ¹¹For what person knows a man's thoughts except the spirit of the man which is in him? So also no one comprehends the thoughts of God except the Spirit of God. ¹²Now we have received not the spirit of the world, but the Spirit which is from God, that we might understand the gifts bestowed on us by God. ¹³And we impart this in words not taught by human wisdom but taught by the Spirit, interpreting spiritual truths to those who possess the Spirit. ᵈ

14 The unspiritual ᵉ man does not receive the gifts of the Spirit of God, for they are folly to him, and he is not able to understand them because they are spiritually discerned. ¹⁵The spiritual man judges all things, but is himself to be judged by no one. ¹⁶"For who has known the mind of the Lord so as to instruct him?" But we have the mind of Christ.

On Dissension in the Corinthian Church

3 But I, brethren, could not address you as spiritual men, but as men of the flesh, as infants in Christ. ²I fed you with milk, not solid food; for you were not ready for it; and even yet you are not ready, ³for you are still of the flesh. For while there is jealousy and strife among you, are you not of the flesh, and behaving like ordinary men? ⁴For when one says, "I belong to Paul," and another, "I belong to Apol'los," are you not merely men?

5 What then is Apol'los? What is Paul? Servants through whom you believed, as the Lord assigned to each. ⁶I planted, Apol'los watered, but God gave the growth. ⁷So neither he who plants nor he who waters is anything, but only God who gives the growth. ⁸He who plants and he who waters are equal, and each shall receive his wages according to his labor. ⁹For we are God's fellow workers; ᶠ you are God's field, God's building.

10 According to the commission of God given to me, like a skilled master builder I laid a foundation, and another man is building upon it. Let each man take care how he builds upon it. ¹¹For no other foundation can any one lay than that which is laid, which is Jesus Christ. ¹²Now if any one builds on the foundation with gold, silver, precious stones, wood, hay, straw—¹³each man's work will become manifest; for the Day † will disclose it, because it will be revealed with fire, and the fire will test what sort of work each one has done. ¹⁴If the work which any man has built on the foundation survives, he will receive a reward. ¹⁵If any man's work is burned up, he will suffer loss, though he himself will be saved, but only as through fire.

16 Do you not know that you are God's temple ‡ and that God's Spirit dwells in you? ¹⁷If any one destroys God's temple, God will destroy him. For God's temple is holy, and that temple you are.

18 Let no one deceive himself. If any one among you thinks that he is wise in this age, let him become a fool that he may become wise. ¹⁹For the wisdom of this world is folly with God. For it is written, "He catches the wise in their craftiness," ²⁰and again, "The Lord knows that the thoughts of the wise are futile." ²¹So let no one

---

ᵈ Or interpreting spiritual truths in spiritual language; or comparing spiritual things with spiritual.
ᵉ Or natural.
ᶠ Or fellow workers for God.
2:2: Gal 6:14; 1 Cor 1:23.
2:3: Acts 18:1, 6, 12; 1 Cor 4:10; 2 Cor 11:30.
2:4: Rom 15:19; 1 Cor 4:20.
2:5: 2 Cor 4:7; 6:7; 1 Cor 12:9.
2:6: Eph 4:13.
2:7: Rom 8:29–30.
2:8: Acts 7:2; Jas 2:1.
2:9: Is 64:4; 65:17.
2:10: Mt 11:25; 13:11; 16:17; Eph 3:3, 5.
2:12: Rom 8:15.
2:13: 1 Cor 1:17.
2:14: 1 Cor 1:18; Jas 3:15.
2:15: 1 Cor 3:1; 14:37; Gal 6:1.
2:16: Is 40:13; Rom 11:34.
3:1: Rom 7:14; Heb 5:13.
3:2: Heb 5:12–13; 1 Pet 2:2.
3:4: 1 Cor 1:12.
3:5: 2 Cor 6:4; Eph 3:7; Col 1:25.
3:6: Acts 18:4–11, 24–27; 1 Cor 1:12.
3:9: Is 61:3; Eph 2:20–22; 1 Pet 2:5.
3:10: Rom 12:3; 1 Cor 15:10.
3:11: Eph 2:20.
3:13: 2 Thess 1:7–10.
3:15: Job 23:10.
3:16: 1 Cor 6:19; 2 Cor 6:16.
3:18: Is 5:21; 1 Cor 8:2; Gal 6:3.
3:19: Job 5:13; 1 Cor 1:20.
3:20: Ps 94:11.
3:21: 1 Cor 4:6; Rom 8:32.
* 2:1–2: Paul's failure at Athens convinced him that lofty words and worldly wisdom were less effective than Jesus crucified.
† 3:13, the Day: i.e., the day of the Lord, God's searching judgment.
‡ 3:16, God's temple: The dignity of the Christians.

boast of men. For all things are yours, [22]whether Paul or Apol'los or Ce'phas or the world or life or death or the present or the future, all are yours; [23]and you are Christ's; and Christ is God's.

The Ministry of the Apostles

4 This is how one should regard us, as servants of Christ and stewards of the mysteries of God. [2]Moreover it is required of stewards that they be found trustworthy. [3]But with me it is a very small thing that I should be judged by you or by any human court. I do not even judge myself. [4]I am not aware of anything against myself, but I am not thereby acquitted. It is the Lord who judges me. [5]Therefore do not pronounce judgment before the time, before the Lord comes, who will bring to light the things now hidden in darkness and will disclose the purposes of the heart. Then every man will receive his commendation from God.

6 I have applied all this to myself and Apol'los for your benefit, brethren, that you may learn by us not to go beyond what is written, that none of you may be puffed up in favor of one against another. [7]For who sees anything different in you? What have you that you did not receive? If then you received it, why do you boast as if it were not a gift?

8 Already you are filled! Already you have become rich! Without us you have become kings! And would that you did reign, so that we might share the rule with you! [9]For I think that God has exhibited us apostles as last of all, like men sentenced to death; because we have become a spectacle to the world, to angels and to men. [10]We are fools for Christ's sake, but you are wise in Christ. We are weak, but you are strong. You are held in honor, but we are in disrepute. [11]To the present hour we hunger and thirst, we are poorly clothed and buffeted and homeless, [12]and we labor, working with our own hands. When reviled, we bless; when persecuted, we endure; [13]when slandered, we try to conciliate; we have become, and are now, as the refuse of the world, the dregs of all things.

Fatherly Admonition

14 I do not write this to make you ashamed, but to admonish you as my beloved children. [15]For though you have countless guides in Christ, you do not have many fathers. For I became your father in Christ Jesus through the gospel. [16]I urge you, then, be imitators of me. [17]Therefore I sent [g] to you Timothy, my beloved and faithful child in the Lord, to remind you of my ways in Christ, as I teach them everywhere in every church. [18]Some are arrogant, as though I were not coming to you. [19]But I will come to you soon, if the Lord wills, and I will find out not the talk of these arrogant people but their power. [20]For the kingdom of God does not consist in talk but in power. [21]What do

you wish? Shall I come to you with a rod, or with love in a spirit of gentleness?

Sexual Immorality Defiles the Church

5 It is actually reported that there is immorality among you, and of a kind that is not found even among pagans; for a man is living with his father's wife. [*] [2]And you are arrogant! Ought you not rather to mourn? Let him who has done this be removed from among you.

3 For though absent in body I am present in spirit, and as if present, I have already pronounced judgment [4]in the name of the Lord Jesus on the man who has done such a thing. When you are assembled, and my spirit is present, with the power of our Lord Jesus, [5]you are to deliver this man to Satan [†] for the destruction of the flesh, that his spirit may be saved in the day of the Lord Jesus. [h]

6 Your boasting is not good. Do you not know that a little leaven leavens all the dough? [7]Cleanse out the old leaven that you may be new dough, as you really are unleavened. For Christ, our Paschal Lamb, has been sacrificed. [8]Let us, therefore, celebrate the festival, not with the old leaven, the leaven of malice and evil, but with the unleavened bread of sincerity and truth.

Immorality and Judgment

9 I wrote to you in my letter not to associate with immoral men; [‡] [10]not at all meaning the immoral [‡] of this world, or the greedy and robbers, or idolaters, since then you would need to go out of the world. [11]But rather I wrote [i] to you not to associate with any one who bears the name of brother if he is guilty of immorality [§] or greed, or is an idolater, reviler, drunkard, or robber—not even to eat with such a one. [12]For what have I to do with judging outsiders? Is it not those inside

---

[g] Or *am sending.*
[h] Other ancient authorities omit *Jesus.*
[i] Or *now I write.*
3:22: 1 Cor 1:12; Rom 8:38.
4:1: 1 Cor 9:17; Rom 11:25; 16:25.
4:4: 2 Cor 1:12.
4:5: Rom 2:16; 1 Cor 3:13; 2 Cor 10:18; Rom 2:29.
4:6: 1 Cor 1:19, 31; 3:19–20; 1:12; 3:4.
4:9: 1 Cor 15:31; 2 Cor 11:23; Rom 8:36; Heb 10:33.
4:10: 1 Cor 1:18; 2 Cor 11:19; 1 Cor 3:18; 2 Cor 13:9; 1 Cor 2:3.
4:11: Rom 8:35; 2 Cor 11:23–27.
4:12: Acts 18:3; 1 Pet 3:9.
4:15: 1 Cor 1:30; Philem 10.
4:17: 1 Cor 16:10; Acts 16:1; 1 Cor 7:17.
4:21: 2 Cor 1:23.
5:1: Deut 22:30; 27:20.
5:3: Col 2:5.
5:4: 2 Thess 3:6.
5:5: Mt 4:10; 1 Cor 1:8.
5:6: Gal 5:9.
5:8: Ex 12:19; 13:7; Deut 16:3.
5:9: 2 Cor 6:14.
5:10: 1 Cor 10:27.
5:11: 2 Thess 3:6; 1 Cor 10:7, 14, 20–21.
5:12: Mk 4:11.
* 5:1, *father's wife*: Evidently his stepmother.
† 5:5, *to Satan*: Not only excommunicated, but in some sense given over to suffering, for his own good.
‡ 5:9–10, *immoral*: Literally, "fornicators."
§ 5:11, *guilty of immorality*: Literally, "a fornicator."

the Church whom you are to judge? [13]God judges those outside. " Drive out the wicked person from among you."

Lawsuits among Believers

6 When one of you has a grievance against a brother, does he dare go to law before the unrighteous * instead of the saints? [2]Do you not know that the saints will judge the world? And if the world is to be judged by you, are you incompetent to try trivial cases? [3]Do you not know that we are to judge angels? How much more, matters pertaining to this life! [4]If then you have such cases, why do you lay them before those who are least esteemed by the Church? [5]I say this to your shame. Can it be that there is no man among you wise enough to decide between members of the brotherhood, [6]but brother goes to law against brother, and that before unbelievers?

7 To have lawsuits at all with one another is defeat for you. Why not rather suffer wrong? Why not rather be defrauded? [8]But you yourselves wrong and defraud, and that even your own brethren.

9 Do you not know that the unrighteous will not inherit the kingdom of God? Do not be deceived; neither the immoral, † nor idolaters, nor adulterers, nor homosexuals, [j] ‡ [10]nor thieves, nor the greedy, nor drunkards, nor revilers, nor robbers will inherit the kingdom of God. [11]And such were some of you. But you were washed, you were sanctified, you were justified in the name of the Lord Jesus Christ and in the Spirit of our God.

Glorifying God in the Body

12 "All things are lawful for me," but not all things are helpful. "All things are lawful for me," § but I will not be enslaved by anything. [13]"Food is meant for the stomach and the stomach for food"—and God will destroy both one and the other. The body is not meant for immorality, ** but for the Lord, and the Lord for the body. [14]And God raised the Lord and will also raise us up by his power. [15]Do you not know that your bodies are members of Christ? Shall I therefore take the members of Christ and make them members of a prostitute? Never! [16]Do you not know that he who joins himself to a prostitute becomes one body with her? For, as it is written, "The two shall become one." [k] [17]But he who is united to the Lord becomes one spirit with him. [18]Shun immorality. ** Every other sin which a man commits is outside the body; but the immoral man sins against his own body. [19]Do you not know that your body is a temple of the Holy Spirit within you, which you have from God? You are not your own; [20]you were bought with a price. So glorify God in your body.

Concerning Marriage

7 Now concerning the matters about which you wrote. It is well for a man not to touch a woman. [2]But because of the temptation to immo-

rality, each man should have his own wife and each woman her own husband. †† [3]The husband should give to his wife her conjugal rights, and likewise the wife to her husband. [4]For the wife does not rule over her own body, but the husband does; likewise the husband does not rule over his own body, but the wife does. [5]Do not refuse one another except perhaps by agreement for a season, that you may devote yourselves to prayer; but then come together again, lest Satan tempt you through lack of self-control. [6]I say this by way of concession, not of command. [7]I wish that all were as I myself am. But each has his own special gift from God, one of one kind and one of another.

8 To the unmarried and the widows I say that it is well for them to remain single as I do. [9]But if they cannot exercise self-control, they should marry. For it is better to marry than to be aflame with passion.

10 To the married I give charge, not I but the Lord, that the wife should not separate from her husband [11](but if she does, let her remain single or else be reconciled to her husband)—and that the husband should not divorce his wife.

12 To the rest I say, not the Lord, that if any brother has a wife who is an unbeliever, and she consents to live with him, he should not divorce her. [13]If any woman has a husband who is an unbeliever, and he consents to live with her, she should not divorce him. [14]For the unbelieving husband is consecrated through his wife, and the unbelieving wife is consecrated through her husband. Otherwise, your children would be unclean, but as it is they are holy. [15]But if the unbelieving partner desires to separate, let it be so; in such a

---

[j] Two Greek words are rendered by this expression.
[k] Greek *one flesh.*
5:13: Deut 17:7; 1 Cor 5:2.
6:1: Mt 18:17.
6:7: Mt 5:39–40.
6:9: 1 Cor 15:50.
6:11: Acts 22:16; Rom 8:30.
6:12: 1 Cor 10:23.
6:15: Rom 12:5; 1 Cor 12:27.
6:16: Gen 2:24; Mt 19:5; Mk 10:8; Eph 5:31.
6:17: Jn 17:21–23; Rom 8:9; Gal 2:20.
6:19: 1 Cor 3:16; Jn 2:21.
6:20: 1 Cor 7:23; Acts 20:28; Rom 12:1.
7:5: Ex 19:15.
7:7: 1 Cor 7:8; 9:5.
7:9: 1 Tim 5:14.
7:12: 2 Cor 11:17.
* 6:1, *the unrighteous*: i.e., civil courts in which the judges were, of course, pagan.
† 6:9: *the immoral:* literally, "fornicators."
‡ 6:9: *homosexuals:* Greek has "effeminate nor sodomites." The apostle condemns, not the inherent tendencies of such, but the indulgence of them.
§ 6:12: This saying is possibly an exaggeration of the freedom from the Mosaic law that Christians enjoyed. The saying has been applied to sinful practices, as is clear from the following verses.
** 6:13, 18, *immorality:* i.e., sexual immorality.
†† 7:2: Note Paul's insistence on equality of man and woman in certain aspects of Christian marriage, and his recognition that the unmarried state is also a gift from God.

case the brother or sister is not bound. For God has called us[1] to peace. [16]Wife, how do you know whether you will save your husband? Husband, how do you know whether you will save your wife?

Leading the Life the Lord Has Assigned

17 Only, let every one lead the life which the Lord has assigned to him, and in which God has called him. This is my rule in all the churches. [18]Was any one at the time of his call already circumcised? Let him not seek to remove the marks of circumcision. Was any one at the time of his call uncircumcised? Let him not seek circumcision. [19]For neither circumcision counts for anything nor uncircumcision, but keeping the commandments of God. [20]Every one should remain in the state in which he was called. [21]Were you a slave when called? Never mind. But if you can gain your freedom, avail yourself of the opportunity. [*] [22]For he who was called in the Lord as a slave is a freedman of the Lord. Likewise he who was free when called is a slave of Christ. [23]You were bought with a price; do not become slaves of men. [24]So, brethren, in whatever state each was called, there let him remain with God.

More concerning Marriage

25 Now concerning the unmarried, [*2] I have no command of the Lord, but I give my opinion as one who by the Lord's mercy is trustworthy. [26]I think that in view of the impending distress[m] it is well for a person to remain as he is. [27]Are you bound to a wife? Do not seek to be free. Are you free from a wife? Do not seek marriage. [28]But if you marry, you do not sin, and if a girl [m2] marries she does not sin. Yet those who marry will have worldly troubles, and I would spare you that. [29]I mean, brethren, the appointed time has grown very short; from now on, let those who have wives live as though they had none, [30]and those who mourn as though they were not mourning, and those who rejoice as though they were not rejoicing, and those who buy as though they had no goods, [31]and those who deal with the world as though they had no dealings with it. For the form of this world is passing away.

32 I want you to be free from anxieties. The unmarried man is anxious about the affairs of the Lord, how to please the Lord; [33]but the married man is anxious about worldly affairs, how to please his wife, [34]and his interests are divided. And the unmarried woman or virgin is anxious about the affairs of the Lord, how to be holy in body and spirit; but the married woman is anxious about worldly affairs, how to please her husband. [35]I say this for your own benefit, not to lay any restraint upon you, but to promote good order and to secure your undivided devotion to the Lord.

36 If any one thinks that he is not behaving properly toward his betrothed, [m2] if his passions are strong, and it has to be, let him do as he wishes: let them marry—it is no sin. [37]But whoever is firmly established in his heart, being under no necessity but having his desire under control, and has determined this in his heart, to keep her as his betrothed, [m2] he will do well. [38]So that he who marries his betrothed [m2] does well; and he who refrains from marriage will do better.

39 A wife is bound to her husband as long as he lives. If the husband dies, she is free to be married to whom she wishes, only in the Lord. [40]But in my judgment she is happier if she remains as she is. And I think that I have the Spirit of God.

Food Offered to Idols

8 Now concerning food offered to idols: [*] we know that "all of us possess knowledge." "Knowledge" puffs up, but love builds up. [2]If any one imagines that he knows something, he does not yet know as he ought to know. [3]But if one loves God, one is known by him.

4 Hence, as to the eating of food offered to idols, we know that "an idol has no real existence," and that "there is no God but one." [5]For although there may be so-called gods in heaven or on earth—as indeed there are many "gods" and many "lords"—[6]yet for us there is one God, the Father, from whom are all things and for whom we exist, and one Lord, Jesus Christ, through whom are all things and through whom we exist.

7 However, not all possess this knowledge. But some, through being until now accustomed to idols, eat food as really offered to an idol; and their conscience, being weak, is defiled. [8]Food will not commend us to God. We are no worse off if we do not eat, and no better off if we do. [9]Only take care lest this liberty of yours somehow become a stumbling block to the weak. [10]For if any one sees you, a man of knowledge, at table in an

---

[1] Other ancient authorities read *you.*
[*] Or *make use of your present condition instead.*
[*2] Greek *virgins.*
[m] Or *present.*
[m2] Greek *virgin.*
7:16: 1 Pet 3:1.
7:17: Rom 12:3; 1 Cor 14:33; 2 Cor 8:18; 11:28.
7:18: 1 Mac 1:15; Acts 15:1–8.
7:19: Gal 5:6; 6:15; Rom 2:25.
7:22: Jn 8:32, 36.
7:23: 1 Cor 6:20.
7:29: Rom 13:11–12; 1 Cor 7:31.
7:32: 1 Tim 5:5.
7:39: Rom 7:2.
7:40: 1 Cor 7:25.
8:1: Rom 15:14.
8:2: 1 Cor 3:18; 13:8, 9, 12.
8:3: Gal 4:9; Rom 8:29.
8:4: 1 Cor 10:19; Deut 6:4.
8:6: Mal 2:10; Eph 4:6; Rom 11:36; 1 Cor 1:2; Eph 4:5; Jn 1:3; Col 1:16.
8:7: 1 Cor 8:4–5.
8:8: Rom 14:17.
8:9: 1 Cor 8:10–11; Rom 14:1.
[*] 8:1–13: Animals sacrificed to pagan gods were often sold as meat in the market. Could Christians buy such meat? Paul allows it so long as scandal is avoided.

idol's temple, might he not be encouraged, if his conscience is weak, to eat food offered to idols? [11]And so by your knowledge this weak man is destroyed, the brother for whom Christ died. [12]Thus, sinning against your brethren and wounding their conscience when it is weak, you sin against Christ. [13]Therefore, if food is a cause of my brother's falling, I will never eat meat, lest I cause my brother to fall.

The Rights of an Apostle

9 Am I not free? Am I not an apostle? Have I not seen Jesus our Lord? Are you not my workmanship in the Lord? [2]If to others I am not an apostle, at least I am to you; for you are the seal of my apostleship in the Lord.

3 This is my defense to those who would examine me. * [4]Do we not have the right to our food and drink? [5]Do we not have the right to be accompanied by a wife, [n] † as the other apostles and the brethren ‡ of the Lord and Cephas? [6]Or is it only Barnabas and I who have no right to refrain from working for a living? [7]Who serves as a soldier at his own expense? Who plants a vineyard without eating any of its fruit? Who tends a flock without getting some of the milk?

8 Do I say this on human authority? Does not the law say the same? [9]For it is written in the law of Moses, "You shall not muzzle an ox when it is treading out the grain." Is it for oxen that God is concerned? [10]Does he not speak entirely for our sake? It was written for our sake, because the plowman should plow in hope and the thresher thresh in hope of a share in the crop. [11]If we have sown spiritual good among you, is it too much if we reap your material benefits? [12]If others share this rightful claim upon you, do not we still more?

Nevertheless, we have not made use of this right, but we endure anything rather than put an obstacle in the way of the gospel of Christ. [13]Do you not know that those who are employed in the temple service get their food from the temple, and those who serve at the altar share in the sacrificial offerings? [14]In the same way, the Lord commanded that those who proclaim the gospel should get their living by the gospel.

15 But I have made no use of any of these rights, nor am I writing this to secure any such provision. For I would rather die than have any one deprive me of my ground for boasting. [16]For if I preach the gospel, that gives me no ground for boasting. For necessity is laid upon me. Woe to me if I do not preach the gospel! [17]For if I do this of my own will, I have a reward; but if not of my own will, I am entrusted with a commission. [18]What then is my reward? Just this: that in my preaching I may make the gospel free of charge, not making full use of my right in the gospel.

The Responsibilities of the Apostle

19 For though I am free from all men, I have made myself a slave to all, that I might win the more. [20]To the Jews I became as a Jew, in order to win Jews; to those under the law I became as one under the law—though not being myself under the law—that I might win those under the law. [21]To those outside the law I became as one outside the law—not being without law toward God but under the law of Christ—that I might win those outside the law. [22]To the weak I became weak, that I might win the weak. I have become all things to all men, that I might by all means save some. [23]I do it all for the sake of the gospel, that I may share in its blessings.

24 Do you not know that in a race all the runners compete, but only one receives the prize? So run that you may obtain it. [25]Every athlete exercises self-control in all things. They do it to receive a perishable wreath, but we an imperishable. [26]Well, I do not run aimlessly, I do not box as one beating the air; [27]but I pommel my body and subdue it, lest after preaching to others I myself should be disqualified.

Warnings from Israel's History

10 I want you to know, brethren, that our fathers were all under the cloud, and all passed through the sea, [2]and all were baptized into Moses in the cloud and in the sea, [3]and all ate the same supernatural° food [4]and all drank the same supernatural° drink. For they drank from the supernatural° Rock which followed them,

---

[n] Greek *woman, sister.*
° Greek *spiritual.*
8:11: Rom 14:15, 20.
8:12: Mt 18:6; Rom 14:20.
8:13: Rom 14:21.
9:1: 1 Cor 9:19; 2 Cor 12:12; 1 Thess 2:6; Acts 9:3, 17; 1 Cor 15:8.
9:4: 1 Cor 9:14.
9:5: 1 Cor 7:7–8; Mt 12:46; 8:14; Jn 1:42.
9:6: Acts 4:36.
9:9: Deut 25:4; 1 Tim 5:18.
9:10: 2 Tim 2:6.
9:11: Rom 15:27.
9:12: 2 Cor 6:3.
9:13: Deut 18:1.
9:14: Mt 10:10; Lk 10:7–8.
9:15: 2 Cor 11:10.
9:17: 1 Cor 4:1; Gal 2:7.
9:18: 2 Cor 11:7.
9:20: Rom 11:14.
9:21: Rom 2:12, 14.
9:22: 2 Cor 11:29; Rom 15:1; 1 Cor 10:33; Rom 11:14.
9:24: Heb 12:1.
9:25: 2 Tim 2:5; 4:8; Jas 1:12; 1 Pet 5:4.
10:1: Rom 1:13; Ex 13:21; 14:22, 29.
10:2: Rom 6:3; Gal 3:27.
10:3: Ex 16:4, 35.
10:4: Ex 17:6; Num 20:11.
* 9:3: Paul set great store by the fact that he has earned his living and waived his right to support by the faithful. He used this as an authentication of his apostolate.
† 9:5, *wife*: Greek, a "woman," a "sister." This could mean either a woman who is a Christian or a wife who is a Christian. There were pious women who ministered to the apostles (Lk 8:3). As many of the apostles must have been married, they may have been ministered to by their wives, though it is possible they had left their wives in answer to the Lord's command to leave all (Lk 18:28–29).
‡ 9:5, *brethren*: See note on Mt 12:46.

and the Rock was Christ. [5]Nevertheless with most of them God was not pleased; for they were overthrown in the wilderness.

6 Now these things are warnings for us, not to desire evil as they did. [7]Do not be idolaters as some of them were; as it is written, "The people sat down to eat and drink and rose up to dance." [8]We must not indulge in immorality as some of them did, and twenty-three thousand fell in a single day. [9]We must not put the Lord [p] to the test, as some of them did and were destroyed by serpents; [10]nor grumble, as some of them did and were destroyed by the Destroyer. [11]Now these things happened to them as a warning, but they were written down for our instruction, upon whom the end of the ages has come. [12]Therefore let any one who thinks that he stands take heed lest he fall. [13]No temptation has overtaken you that is not common to man. God is faithful, and he will not let you be tempted beyond your strength, but with the temptation will also provide the way of escape, that you may be able to endure it.

14 Therefore, my beloved, shun the worship of idols. [15]I speak as to sensible men; judge for yourselves what I say. [16]The cup of blessing which we bless, is it not a participation [q] in the blood of Christ? The bread which we break, is it not a participation [q] in the body of Christ? [17]Because there is one bread, we who are many are one body, for we all partake of the one bread. [18]Consider the people of Israel; are not those who eat the sacrifices partners in the altar? [19]What do I imply then? That food offered to idols is anything, or that an idol is anything? [20]No, I imply that what pagans sacrifice they offer to demons and not to God. I do not want you to be partners with demons. * [21]You cannot drink the cup of the Lord and the cup of demons. You cannot partake of the table of the Lord and the table of demons. [22]Shall we provoke the Lord to jealousy? Are we stronger than he?

All to the Glory of God

23 "All things are lawful," but not all things are helpful. "All things are lawful," but not all things build up. [24]Let no one seek his own good, but the good of his neighbor. [25]Eat whatever is sold in the meat market without raising any question on the ground of conscience. [26]For "the earth is the Lord's, and everything in it." [27]If one of the unbelievers invites you to dinner and you are disposed to go, eat whatever is set before you without raising any question on the ground of conscience. [28](But if some one says to you, "This has been offered in sacrifice," then out of consideration for the man who informed you, and for conscience' sake—[29]I mean his conscience, not yours—do not eat it.) For why should my liberty be determined by another man's scruples? [30]If I

partake with thankfulness, why am I denounced because of that for which I give thanks?

31 So, whether you eat or drink, or whatever you do, do all to the glory of God. [32]Give no offense to Jews or to Greeks or to the Church of God, [33]just as I try to please all men in everything I do, not seeking my own advantage, but that of many, that they may be saved. [1]Be imitators of me, as I am of Christ.

11

Head Coverings

2 I commend you because you remember me in everything and maintain the traditions even as I have delivered them to you. [3]But I want you to understand that the head of every man is Christ, the head of a woman is her husband, and the head of Christ is God. [4]Any man who prays or prophesies with his head covered dishonors his head, [5]but any woman who prays or prophesies with her head unveiled dishonors her head—it is the same as if her head were shaven. [6]For if a woman will not veil herself, then she should cut off her hair; but if it is disgraceful for a woman to be shorn or shaven, let her wear a veil. [7]For a man ought not to cover his head, since he is the image and glory of God; but woman is the glory of man. [8](For man was not made from woman, but woman from man. [9]Neither was man created for woman, but woman for man.) [10]That is why a woman ought to have a veil [r] on her head, because of the angels. [11](Nevertheless, in the Lord woman is not independent of man nor man of woman; [12]for as woman was made from man, so man is now born of woman. And all things are from God.) [13]Judge for yourselves; is it proper for a

[p] Other ancient authorities read *Christ*.
[q] Or *communion*.
[r] Greek *authority* (the veil being a symbol of this).
10:5: Num 14:29–30.
10:6: Num 11:4, 34.
10:7: Ex 32:4, 6.
10:8: Num 25:1–18.
10:9: Num 21:5–6.
10:10: Num 16:41, 49.
10:13: 1 Cor 1:9.
10:14: 1 Jn 5:21.
10:16: Mt 26:27–28; Acts 2:42.
10:17: Rom 12:5.
10:18: Lev 7:6.
10:20: Deut 32:17.
10:21: 2 Cor 6:16.
10:22: Deut 32:21; Eccles 6:10; Is 45:9.
10:23: 1 Cor 6:12; Phil 2:21.
10:26: Ps 24:1; 50:12.
10:28: 1 Cor 8:7, 10–12.
10:32: 1 Cor 8:13.
10:33: 1 Cor 9:22; Rom 15:2; 1 Cor 13:5.
11:1: 1 Cor 4:16.
11:2: 2 Thess 2:15.
11:3: Eph 1:22; 4:15; 5:23; Col 1:8; 2:19.
11:5: Lk 2:36; Acts 21:9; 1 Cor 14:34.
11:7: Gen 1:26.
11:8: Gen 2:21–23.
11:9: Gen 2:18.
11:12: 2 Cor 5:18; Rom 11:36.
* 10:20: Paul appears to forbid partaking in sacrificial meals. In verse 27 he says they may eat meat offered to idols if it is at an ordinary meal, unless it would cause scandal to anyone present.

woman to pray to God with her head uncovered? [14]Does not nature itself teach you that for a man to wear long hair is degrading to him, [15]but if a woman has long hair, it is her pride? For her hair is given to her for a covering. [16]If any one is disposed to be contentious, we recognize no other practice, nor do the churches of God.

Abuses at the Lord's Supper

17 But in the following instructions I do not commend you, because when you come together it is not for the better but for the worse. [18]For, in the first place, when you assemble as a Church, I hear that there are divisions among you; and I partly believe it, [19]for there must be factions among you in order that those who are genuine among you may be recognized. [20]When you meet together, it is not the Lord's supper that you eat. * [21]For in eating, each one goes ahead with his own meal, and one is hungry and another is drunk. [22]What! Do you not have houses to eat and drink in? Or do you despise the Church of God and humiliate those who have nothing? What shall I say to you? Shall I commend you in this? No, I will not.

The Institution of the Eucharist

23 For I received from the Lord what I also delivered to you, that the Lord Jesus on the night when he was betrayed took bread, [24]and when he had given thanks, he broke it, and said, "This is my body which is for ⁼ you. Do this in remembrance of me." [25]In the same way also the chalice, after supper, saying, "This chalice is the new covenant in my blood. Do this, as often as you drink it, in remembrance of me." [26]For as often as you eat this bread and drink the chalice, you proclaim the Lord's death until he comes.

Partaking of the Eucharist Unworthily

27 Whoever, therefore, eats the bread or drinks the cup of the Lord in an unworthy manner will be guilty of profaning the body and blood of the Lord. [28]Let a man examine himself, and so eat of the bread and drink of the cup. [29]For any one who eats and drinks without discerning the body eats and drinks judgment upon himself. [30]That is why many of you are weak and ill, and some have died. ᵗ [31]But if we judged ourselves truly, we should not be judged. [32]But when we are judged by the Lord, we are chastened ᵘ so that we may not be condemned along with the world.

33 So then, my brethren, when you come together to eat, wait for one another—[34]if any one is hungry, let him eat at home—lest you come together to be condemned. About the other things I will give directions when I come.

Spiritual Gifts

12 Now concerning spiritual gifts, brethren, I do not want you to be uninformed. † [2]You know that when you were heathen, you were led astray to mute idols, however you may have been moved. [3]Therefore I want you to understand that

no one speaking by the Spirit of God ever says "Jesus be cursed!" and no one can say "Jesus is Lord" except by the Holy Spirit.

4 Now there are varieties of gifts, but the same Spirit; [5]and there are varieties of service, but the same Lord; [6]and there are varieties of working, but it is the same God who inspires them all in every one. [7]To each is given the manifestation of the Spirit for the common good. [8]To one is given through the Spirit the utterance of wisdom, and to another the utterance of knowledge according to the same Spirit, [9]to another faith by the same Spirit, to another gifts of healing by the one Spirit, [10]to another the working of miracles, to another prophecy, to another the ability to distinguish between spirits, to another various kinds of tongues, to another the interpretation of tongues. [11]All these are inspired by one and the same Spirit, who apportions to each one individually as he wills.

One Body with Many Members

12 For just as the body is one and has many members, and all the members of the body, though many, are one body, so it is with Christ. [13]For by one Spirit we were all baptized into one body—Jews or Greeks, slaves or free—and all were made to drink of one Spirit.

14 For the body does not consist of one member but of many. [15]If the foot should say, "Because I am not a hand, I do not belong to the body," that would not make it any less a part of the body. [16]And if the ear should say, "Because I am not an eye, I do not belong to the body," that would not make it any less a part of the body. [17]If the whole body were an eye, where would be the hearing? If the whole body were an ear, where would be the sense of smell? [18]But as it is, God arranged the organs in the body, each one of them, as he chose. [19]If all were a single organ, where would the body be? [20]As it is, there are many parts, yet one body. [21]The eye cannot say to the hand, "I have no need of you," nor again the head to the feet, "I have no need of you." [22]On the contrary, the parts of the body which seem to be weaker

---

ᵃ Other ancient authorities read *broken for.*

ᵗ Greek *have fallen asleep* (as in 15:6, 20).

ᵘ Or *when we are judged we are being chastened by the Lord.*

11:16: 1 Cor 7:17.
11:18: 1 Cor 1:10.
11:23: 1 Cor 15:3.
11:23–25: Mt 26:26–28; Mk 14:22–24; Lk 22:17–19; 1 Cor 10:16.
11:25: 2 Cor 3:6; Lk 22:20.
11:26: 1 Cor 4:5.
11:32: 1 Cor 1:20.
11:34: 1 Cor 4:19.
12:2: Eph 2:11–12.
12:3: Rom 10:9.
12:10: 1 Cor 14:26.
12:12: Rom 12:4.
12:13: Gal 3:28; Col 3:11; Eph 2:13–18; Jn 7:37–39.

* 11:20: There was apparently a common meal before the Eucharist at which food and drink were to be shared. Paul condemns the abuses that had crept in.

† 12:1: The spiritual gifts here referred to were common in the first age of the Church and helped to establish it on a firm basis.

are indispensable, [23]and those parts of the body which we think less honorable we invest with the greater honor, and our unpresentable parts are treated with greater modesty, [24]which our more presentable parts do not require. But God has so composed the body, giving the greater honor to the inferior part, [25]that there may be no discord in the body, but that the members may have the same care for one another. [26]If one member suffers, all suffer together; if one member is honored, all rejoice together.

27 Now you are the body of Christ and individually members of it. [28]And God has appointed in the Church first apostles, second prophets, third teachers, then workers of miracles, then healers, helpers, administrators, speakers in various kinds of tongues. [29]Are all apostles? Are all prophets? Are all teachers? Do all work miracles? [30]Do all possess gifts of healing? Do all speak with tongues? Do all interpret? [31]But earnestly desire the higher gifts.

And I will show you a still more excellent way. *

The Way of Love

13 If I speak in the tongues of men and of angels, but have not love, I am a noisy gong or a clanging cymbal. [2]And if I have prophetic powers, and understand all mysteries and all knowledge, and if I have all faith, so as to remove mountains, but have not love, I am nothing. [3]If I give away all I have, and if I deliver my body to be burned,[v] but have not love, I gain nothing.

4 Love is patient and kind; love is not jealous or boastful; [5]it is not arrogant or rude. Love does not insist on its own way; it is not irritable or resentful; [6]it does not rejoice at wrong, but rejoices in the right. [7]Love bears all things, believes all things, hopes all things, endures all things.

8 Love never ends; as for prophecies, they will pass away; as for tongues, they will cease; as for knowledge, it will pass away. [9]For our knowledge is imperfect and our prophecy is imperfect; [10]but when the perfect comes, the imperfect will pass away. [11]When I was a child, I spoke like a child, I thought like a child, I reasoned like a child; when I became a man, I gave up childish ways. [12]For now we see in a mirror dimly, but then face to face. Now I know in part; then I shall understand fully, even as I have been fully understood. [13]So faith, hope, love abide, these three; but the greatest of these is love.

Gifts of Prophecy and Tongues

14 Make love your aim, and earnestly desire the spiritual gifts, especially that you may prophesy. [2]For one who speaks in a tongue speaks not to men but to God; for no one understands him, but he utters mysteries in the Spirit. [3]On the other hand, he who prophesies speaks to

men for their upbuilding and encouragement and consolation. [4]He who speaks in a tongue edifies himself, but he who prophesies edifies the Church. [5]Now I want you all to speak in tongues, but even more to prophesy. He who prophesies is greater than he who speaks in tongues, unless some one interprets, so that the Church may be edified.

6 Now, brethren, if I come to you speaking in tongues, how shall I benefit you unless I bring you some revelation or knowledge or prophecy or teaching? [7]If even lifeless instruments, such as the flute or the harp, do not give distinct notes, how will any one know what is played? [8]And if the bugle gives an indistinct sound, who will get ready for battle? [9]So with yourselves; if you in a tongue utter speech that is not intelligible, how will any one know what is said? For you will be speaking into the air. [10]There are doubtless many different languages in the world, and none is without meaning; [11]but if I do not know the meaning of the language, I shall be a foreigner to the speaker and the speaker a foreigner to me. [12]So with yourselves; since you are eager for manifestations of the Spirit, strive to excel in building up the Church.

13 Therefore, he who speaks in a tongue should pray for the power to interpret. [14]For if I pray in a tongue, my spirit prays but my mind is unfruitful. [15]What am I to do? I will pray with the spirit and I will pray with the mind also; I will sing with the spirit and I will sing with the mind also. [16]Otherwise, if you bless[w] with the spirit, how can any one in the position of an outsider[x] say the "Amen" to your thanksgiving when he does not know what you are saying? [17]For you may give thanks well enough, but the other man is not edified. [18]I thank God that I speak in tongues more than you all; [19]nevertheless, in church I would rather speak five words with my mind, in order to instruct others, than ten thousand words in a tongue.

20 Brethren, do not be children in your thinking; be infants in evil, but in thinking be mature. [21]In the law it is written, "By men of strange tongues and by the lips of foreigners will I speak to this people, and even then they will not listen to me, says the Lord." [22]Thus, tongues are a sign not

---

[v] Other ancient authorities read *body that I may glory*.
[w] That is, *give thanks to God*.
[x] Or *him that is without gifts*.
12:27: Eph 1:23; Col 1:18, 24; Eph 5:30; Rom 12:5.
12:28: Eph 4:11; 2:20; 3:5.
13:1: Ps 150:5.
13:2: 1 Cor 14:2; Mt 17:20; 21:21.
13:5: 1 Cor 10:24.
13:7: 1 Cor 9:12.
14:15: Eph 5:19; Col 3:16.
14:16: 1 Chron 16:36; Ps 106:48; Mt 15:36.
14:20: Eph 4:14.
14:21: Is 28:11–12.
* 12:31: Love, however, is far superior to these gifts.

for believers but for unbelievers, while prophecy is not for unbelievers but for believers. [23]If, therefore, the whole Church assembles and all speak in tongues, and outsiders or unbelievers enter, will they not say that you are mad? [24]But if all prophesy, and an unbeliever or outsider enters, he is convicted by all, he is called to account by all, [25]the secrets of his heart are disclosed; and so, falling on his face, he will worship God and declare that God is really among you.

Orderly Worship

26 What then, brethren? When you come together, each one has a hymn, a lesson, a revelation, a tongue, or an interpretation. Let all things be done for edification. [27]If any speak in a tongue, let there be only two or at most three, and each in turn; and let one interpret. [28]But if there is no one to interpret, let each of them keep silence in church and speak to himself and to God. [29]Let two or three prophets speak, and let the others weigh what is said. [30]If a revelation is made to another sitting by, let the first be silent. [31]For you can all prophesy one by one, so that all may learn and all be encouraged; [32]and the spirits of prophets are subject to prophets. [33]For God is not a God of confusion but of peace.

As in all the churches of the saints, [34]the women should keep silence in the churches. For they are not permitted to speak, but should be subordinate, as even the law says. [35]If there is anything they desire to know, let them ask their husbands at home. For it is shameful for a woman to speak in church. [36]What! Did the word of God originate with you, or are you the only ones it has reached?

37 If any one thinks that he is a prophet, or spiritual, he should acknowledge that what I am writing to you is a command of the Lord. [38]If any one does not recognize this, he is not recognized. [39]So, my brethren, earnestly desire to prophesy, and do not forbid speaking in tongues; [40]but all things should be done decently and in order.

The Resurrection of Christ

15 Now I would remind you, brethren, in what terms I preached to you the gospel, which you received, in which you stand, [2]by which you are saved, if you hold it fast—unless you believed in vain.

3 For I delivered to you as of first importance what I also received, that Christ died for our sins in accordance with the Scriptures, [4]that he was buried, that he was raised on the third day in accordance with the Scriptures, [5]and that he appeared to Ce'phas, then to the Twelve. [6]Then he appeared to more than five hundred brethren at one time, most of whom are still alive, though some have fallen asleep. [7]Then he appeared to James, then to all the apostles. [8]Last of all, as to one untimely born, he appeared also to me. [9]For I am the least of the apostles, unfit to be called an apostle, because I persecuted the Church of God. [10]But by the grace of God I am what I am, and his grace toward me was not in vain. On the contrary, I worked harder than any of them, though it was not I, but the grace of God which is with me. [11]Whether then it was I or they, so we preach and so you believed.

The Resurrection of the Dead

12 Now if Christ is preached as raised from the dead, how can some of you say that there is no resurrection of the dead? [13]But if there is no resurrection of the dead, then Christ has not been raised; * [14]if Christ has not been raised, then our preaching is in vain and your faith is in vain. [15]We are even found to be misrepresenting God, because we testified of God that he raised Christ, whom he did not raise if it is true that the dead are not raised. [16]For if the dead are not raised, then Christ has not been raised. [17]If Christ has not been raised, your faith is futile and you are still in your sins. [18]Then those also who have fallen asleep in Christ have perished. [19]If for this life only we have hoped in Christ, we are of all men most to be pitied.

20 But in fact Christ has been raised from the dead, the first fruits of those who have fallen asleep. [21]For as by a man came death, by a man has come also the resurrection of the dead. [22]For as in Adam all die, so also in Christ shall all be made alive. [23]But each in his own order: Christ the first fruits, then at his coming those who belong to Christ. [24]Then comes the end, when he delivers the kingdom to God the Father after destroying every rule and every authority and power. [25]For he must reign until he has put all his enemies under his feet. [26]The last enemy to be destroyed is death. [27]"For God ᶻ has put all things in subjection under his feet." But when it says, "All things are put in subjection under him," it is plain that he is excepted who put all things under him. [28]When all things are subjected to him, then the Son himself will also be subjected to him who put all things under him, that God may be everything to every one.

ᶻ Greek *he*.
14:26: Eph 5:19.
14:34: 1 Tim 2:11–12; 1 Pet 3:1.
15:3: 1 Cor 11:23; 1 Pet 2:24; Is 53:5–12.
15:4: Mt 16:21; Ps 16:8–9.
15:5: Lk 24:34; Mt 28:17.
15:8: 1 Cor 9:1; Gal 1:16; Acts 9:3–6.
15:9: Acts 8:3.
15:14: 1 Thess 4:14.
15:18: 1 Thess 4:16.
15:21: Rom 5:12.
15:22: Rom 5:14–18.
15:23: 1 Thess 2:19.
15:25: Ps 110:1.
15:27: Ps 8:6; Eph 1:22.
15:28: Phil 3:21.
* 15:13: Again, the resurrection of the dead is linked with Christ's resurrection; cf. Rom 8:11.

29 Otherwise, what do people mean by being baptized on behalf of the dead? If the dead are not raised at all, why are people baptized on their behalf? * [30]Why am I in peril every hour? [31]I protest, brethren, by my pride in you which I have in Christ Jesus our Lord, I die every day! [32]What do I gain if, humanly speaking, I fought with beasts at Ephesus? If the dead are not raised, "Let us eat and drink, for tomorrow we die." [33]Do not be deceived: "Bad company ruins good morals." [34]Come to your right mind, and sin no more. For some have no knowledge of God. I say this to your shame.

The Resurrection of the Body

35 But some one will ask, "How are the dead raised? With what kind of body do they come?" [36]You foolish man! What you sow does not come to life unless it dies. [37]And what you sow is not the body which is to be, but a bare kernel, perhaps of wheat or of some other grain. [38]But God gives it a body as he has chosen, and to each kind of seed its own body. [39]For not all flesh is alike, but there is one kind for men, another for animals, another for birds, and another for fish. [40]There are celestial bodies and there are terrestrial bodies; but the glory of the celestial is one, and the glory of the terrestrial is another. [41]There is one glory of the sun, and another glory of the moon, and another glory of the stars; for star differs from star in glory.

42 So is it with the resurrection of the dead. What is sown is perishable, what is raised is imperishable. [43]It is sown in dishonor, it is raised in glory. It is sown in weakness, it is raised in power. [44]It is sown a physical body, it is raised a spiritual body. If there is a physical body, there is also a spiritual body. [45]Thus it is written, "The first man Adam became a living soul"; the last Adam became a life-giving spirit. [46]But it is not the spiritual which is first but the physical, and then the spiritual. [47]The first man was from the earth, a man of dust; the second man is from heaven. [48]As was the man of dust, so are those who are of the dust; and as is the man of heaven, so are those who are of heaven. [49]Just as we have borne the image of the man of dust, we shall [a] also bear the image of the man of heaven. [50]I tell you this, brethren: flesh and blood cannot inherit the kingdom of God, nor does the perishable inherit the imperishable.

51 Behold! I tell you a mystery. We shall not all sleep, but we shall all be changed, [52]in a moment, in the twinkling of an eye, at the last trumpet. For the trumpet will sound, and the dead will be raised imperishable, and we shall be changed. [53]For this perishable nature must put on the imperishable, and this mortal nature must put on immortality. [54]When the perishable puts on the imperishable, and the mortal puts on immortality, then shall come to pass the saying that is written:

"Death is swallowed up in victory."
[55]"O death, where is your victory?
O death, where is your sting?"
[56]The sting of death is sin, and the power of sin is the law. [57]But thanks be to God, who gives us the victory through our Lord Jesus Christ.

58 Therefore, my beloved brethren, be steadfast, immovable, always abounding in the work of the Lord, knowing that in the Lord your labor is not in vain.

The Contribution for the Saints

16 Now concerning the contribution for the saints: † as I directed the churches of Galatia, so you also are to do. [2]On the first day of every week, each of you is to put something aside and store it up, as he may prosper, so that contributions need not be made when I come. [3]And when I arrive, I will send those whom you accredit by letter to carry your gift to Jerusalem. [4]If it seems advisable that I should go also, they will accompany me.

Plans for Travel

5 I will visit you after passing through Macedonia, for I intend to pass through Macedonia, [6]and perhaps I will stay with you or even spend the winter, so that you may speed me on my journey, wherever I go. [7]For I do not want to see you now just in passing; I hope to spend some time with you, if the Lord permits. [8]But I will stay in Ephesus until Pentecost, [9]for a wide door for effective work has opened to me, and there are many adversaries.

10 When Timothy comes, see that you put him at ease among you, for he is doing the work of the Lord, as I am. [11]So let no one despise him. Speed him on his way in peace, that he may return to me; for I am expecting him with the brethren.

---

a Other ancient authorities read *let us.*
15:30: 2 Esdr 7:89.
15:31: Rom 8:36.
15:32: 2 Cor 1:8, 9; Is 22:13.
15:33: Menander, *Thais.*
15:34: Rom 13:11.
15:36: Jn 12:24.
15:38: Gen 1:11.
15:42: Dan 12:3.
15:45: Gen 2:7.
15:51-52: 1 Thess 4:15-17.
15:54: Is 25:8.
15:55: Hos 13:14.
16:1: Acts 24:17.
16:2: Acts 20:7; 2 Cor 9:4-5.
16:3: 2 Cor 8:18-19.
16:5: Rom 15:26; Acts 19:21.
16:7: Acts 18:21.
16:8: Acts 18:19.
16:9: Acts 19:9.
16:10: Acts 16:1.
* 15:29: Apparently a custom of vicarious baptism for those who had died without it. Paul mentions it without approving it.
† 16:1: The collection to be made everywhere for the poor Christians in Jerusalem.

12 As for our brother Apol'los, I strongly urged him to visit you with the other brethren, but it was not at all his will [b] to come now. He will come when he has opportunity.

Final Message and Greeting

13 Be watchful, stand firm in your faith, be courageous, be strong. [14]Let all that you do be done in love.

15 Now, brethren, you know that the household of Steph'anas were the first converts in Acha'ia, and they have devoted themselves to the service of the saints; [16]I urge you to be subject to such men and to every fellow worker and laborer. [17]I rejoice at the coming of Steph'anas and Fortuna'tus and Acha'icus, because they have made up for your absence; [18]for they refreshed my spirit as well as yours. Give recognition to such men.

19 The churches of Asia send greetings. Aqui'la and Prisca, together with the church in their house, send you hearty greetings in the Lord. [20]All the brethren send greetings. Greet one another with a holy kiss.

21 I, Paul, write this greeting with my own hand. [22]If any one has no love for the Lord, let him be accursed. Our Lord, come! [c] [23]The grace of the Lord Jesus be with you. [24]My love be with you all in Christ Jesus. Amen.

---

[b] Or *God's will for him.*
[c] Greek *Maranatha.*
16:12: Acts 18:24.
16:13: Ps 31:24; Eph 6:10.
16:19: Acts 18:2; Rom 16:5.
16:20: Rom 16:16.
16:21: Col 4:18; Gal 6:11; 2 Thess 3:17.
16:22: Rom 9:3.
16:23: Rom 16:20.

THE SECOND LETTER OF PAUL TO THE

CORINTHIANS

Salutation

1 Paul, an apostle of Christ Jesus by the will of God, and Timothy our brother.

To the Church of God which is at Corinth, with all the saints who are in the whole of Acha′ia:

2 Grace to you and peace from God our Father and the Lord Jesus Christ.

Paul's Thanksgiving after Affliction

3 Blessed be the God and Father of our Lord Jesus Christ, the Father of mercies and God of all comfort, [4]who comforts us in all our affliction, so that we may be able to comfort those who are in any affliction, with the comfort with which we ourselves are comforted by God. [5]For as we share abundantly in Christ's sufferings, so through Christ we share abundantly in comfort too. [a] [6]If we are afflicted, it is for your comfort and salvation; and if we are comforted, it is for your comfort, which you experience when you patiently endure the same sufferings that we suffer. [7]Our hope for you is unshaken; for we know that as you share in our sufferings, you will also share in our comfort.

8 For we do not want you to be ignorant, brethren, of the affliction * we experienced in Asia; for we were so utterly, unbearably crushed that we despaired of life itself. [9]Why, we felt that we had received the sentence of death; but that was to make us rely not on ourselves but on God who raises the dead; [10]he delivered us from so deadly a peril, and he will deliver us; on him we have set our hope that he will deliver us again. [11]You also must help us by prayer, so that many will give thanks on our behalf for the blessing granted us in answer to many prayers.

12 For our boast is this, the testimony of our conscience that we have behaved in the world, and still more toward you, with holiness and godly sincerity, not by earthly wisdom but by the grace of God. [13]For we write you nothing but what you can read and understand; I hope you will understand fully, [14]as you have understood in part, that you can be proud of us as we can be of you, on the day of the Lord Jesus.

The Postponement of Paul's Visit

15 Because I was sure of this, I wanted to come to you first, so that you might have a double pleasure; [b] [16]I wanted to visit you on my way to Macedonia, and to come back to you from Macedonia and have you send me on my way to Judea.

[17]Was I vacillating when I wanted to do this? Do I make my plans like a worldly man, ready to say Yes and No at once? [18]As surely as God is faithful, our word to you has not been Yes and No. [19]For the Son of God, Jesus Christ, whom we preached among you, Silva′nus and Timothy and I, was not Yes and No; but in him it is always Yes. [20]For all the promises of God find their Yes in him. That is why we utter the Amen through him, to the glory of God. [21]But it is God who establishes us with you in Christ, and has commissioned us; [22]he has put his seal upon us and given us his Spirit in our hearts as a guarantee.

23 But I call God to witness against me—it was to spare you that I refrained from coming to Corinth. [24]Not that we lord it over your faith; we work with you for your joy, for you stand firm in

2 your faith. [1]For I made up my mind not to make you another painful visit. [2]For if I cause you pain, who is there to make me glad but the one whom I have pained? [3]And I wrote as I did, so that when I came I might not suffer pain from those who should have made me rejoice, for I felt sure of all of you, that my joy would be the joy of you all. [4]For I wrote you out of much affliction and anguish of heart and with many tears, not to cause you pain but to let you know the abundant love that I have for you.

Forgiveness for the Offender

5 But if any one has caused pain, he has caused it not to me, but in some measure—not to put it too severely—to you all. [6]For such a one this punishment by the majority is enough; [7]so you should rather turn to forgive and comfort him, or he may be overwhelmed by excessive sorrow. [8]I beg you to reaffirm your love for him. [9]For this is why I wrote, that I might test you and know whether you are obedient in everything. [10]Any one whom you forgive, I also forgive. What I have forgiven, if I have forgiven anything, has been for

---

[a] Or For as the sufferings of Christ abound for us, so also our comfort abounds through Christ.
[b] Other ancient authorities read favor.
1:1: Eph 1:1; Col 1:1; 2 Cor 1:19; Acts 16:1; 18:1.
1:2: Rom 1:7.
1:3: Eph 1:3; 1 Pet 1:3; Rom 15:5.
1:4: 2 Cor 7:6, 7, 13.
1:16: Acts 19:21.
1:19: 1 Thess 1:1; Acts 15:22.
1:20: 1 Cor 14:16; Rev 3:14.
* **1:8,** *affliction:* Possibly the disturbance at Ephesus (Acts 19:23–41), or perhaps a serious illness.

your sake in the presence of Christ, [11]to keep Satan from gaining the advantage over us; for we are not ignorant of his designs.

Paul's Anxiety in Troas

12 When I came to Troas to preach the gospel of Christ, a door was opened for me in the Lord; [13]but my mind could not rest because I did not find my brother Titus there. So I took leave of them and went on to Macedonia.

14 But thanks be to God, who in Christ always leads us in triumph, and through us spreads the fragrance of the knowledge of him everywhere. [15]For we are the aroma of Christ to God among those who are being saved and among those who are perishing, [16]to one a fragrance from death to death, to the other a fragrance from life to life. Who is sufficient for these things? [17]For we are not, like so many, peddlers of God's word; but as men of sincerity, as commissioned by God, in the sight of God we speak in Christ.

Ministers of the New Covenant

3 Are we beginning to commend ourselves again? Or do we need, as some do, letters of recommendation to you, or from you? [2]You yourselves are our letter of recommendation, written on your [c] hearts, to be known and read by all men; [3]and you show that you are a letter from Christ delivered by us, written not with ink but with the Spirit of the living God, not on tablets of stone but on tablets of human hearts.

4 Such is the confidence that we have through Christ toward God. [5]Not that we are sufficient of ourselves to claim anything as coming from us; our sufficiency is from God, [6]who has qualified us to be ministers of a new covenant, not in a written code but in the Spirit; for the written code kills, but the Spirit gives life.

7 Now if the dispensation of death, carved in letters on stone, came with such splendor that the Israelites could not look at Moses' face because of its brightness, fading as this was, [8]will not the dispensation of the Spirit be attended with greater splendor? [9]For if there was splendor in the dispensation of condemnation, the dispensation of righteousness must far exceed it in splendor. [10]Indeed, in this case, what once had splendor has come to have no splendor at all, because of the splendor that surpasses it. [11]For if what faded away came with splendor, what is permanent must have much more splendor.

12 Since we have such a hope, we are very bold, [13]not like Moses, who put a veil over his face so that the Israelites might not see the end of the fading splendor. [14]But their minds were hardened; for to this day, when they read the old covenant, that same veil remains unlifted, because only through Christ is it taken away. [15]Yes, to this day whenever Moses is read a veil lies over their minds; [16]but when a man turns to the Lord the veil is removed. [17]Now the Lord is the Spirit, and where the Spirit of the Lord is, there is freedom. [18]And we all, with unveiled face, beholding [d] the glory of the Lord, are being changed into his likeness from one degree of glory to another; for this comes from the Lord who is the Spirit. *

4 Therefore, having this ministry by the mercy of God, [e] we do not lose heart. [2]We have renounced disgraceful, underhanded ways; we refuse to practice cunning or to tamper with God's word, but by the open statement of the truth we would commend ourselves to every man's conscience in the sight of God. [3]And even if our gospel is veiled, it is veiled only to those who are perishing. [4]In their case the god of this world has blinded the minds of the unbelievers, to keep them from seeing the light of the gospel of the glory of Christ, who is the likeness of God. [5]For what we preach is not ourselves, but Jesus Christ as Lord, with ourselves as your servants [f] for Jesus' sake. [6]For it is the God who said, "Let light shine out of darkness," who has shone in our hearts to give the light of the knowledge of the glory of God in the face of Christ.

Treasure in Earthen Vessels

7 But we have this treasure † in earthen vessels, to show that the transcendent power belongs to God and not to us. [8]We are afflicted in every way, but not crushed; perplexed, but not driven to despair; [9]persecuted, but not forsaken; struck down, but not destroyed; [10]always carrying in the body the death of Jesus, so that the life of Jesus may also be manifested in our bodies. [11]For while we live we are always being given up to death for Jesus' sake, so that the life of Jesus may be manifested in our mortal flesh. [12]So death is at work in us, but life in you. ‡

13 Since we have the same spirit of faith as he had who wrote, "I believed, and so I spoke," we too believe, and so we speak, [14]knowing that he who raised the Lord Jesus will raise us also with Jesus and bring us with you into his presence. [15]For it is all for your sake, so that as grace

---

[c] Other ancient authorities read *our*.
[d] Or *reflecting*.
[e] Greek *as we have received mercy*.
[f] Or *slaves*.
2:12: Acts 16:8.
3:1: Acts 18:27; Rom 16:1; 1 Cor 16:3.
3:3: Ex 24:12; 31:18; 32:15–16; Jer 31:33.
3:6: Jer 31:31.
3:7: Ex 34:29–35.
3:17: Is 61:1–2.
4:4: Jn 12:31; Col 1:15.
4:6: Gen 1:3.
4:13: Ps 116:10.
4:14: 1 Thess 4:14.
* 3:18: Cleansed in baptism through the power of the Holy Spirit, our soul shines with the reflected glory of God.
† 4:7, *this treasure*: i.e., the apostolate.
‡ 4:12: i.e., we suffer, if necessary, even unto death, that you may have (spiritual) life.

extends to more and more people it may increase thanksgiving, to the glory of God.

Living by Faith

16 So we do not lose heart. Though our outer man is wasting away, our inner man is being renewed every day. [17]For this slight momentary affliction is preparing for us an eternal weight of glory beyond all comparison, [18]because we look not to the things that are seen but to the things that are unseen; for the things that are seen are transient, but the things that are unseen are eternal.

5 For we know that if the earthly tent we live in is destroyed, we have a building from God, a house not made with hands, eternal in the heavens. [2]Here indeed we groan, and long to put on our heavenly dwelling, [3]so that by putting it on we may not be found naked. [4]For while we are still in this tent, we sigh with anxiety; not that we would be unclothed, but that we would be further clothed, so that what is mortal may be swallowed up by life. [5]He who has prepared us for this very thing is God, who has given us the Spirit as a guarantee.

6 So we are always of good courage; we know that while we are at home in the body we are away from the Lord, [7]for we walk by faith, not by sight. [8]We are of good courage, and we would rather be away from the body and at home with the Lord. [9]So whether we are at home or away, we make it our aim to please him. [10]For we must all appear before the judgment seat of Christ, so that each one may receive good or evil, according to what he has done in the body.

The Ministry of Reconciliation

11 Therefore, knowing the fear of the Lord, we persuade men; but what we are is known to God, and I hope it is known also to your conscience. [12]We are not commending ourselves to you again but giving you cause to be proud of us, so that you may be able to answer those who pride themselves on a man's position and not on his heart. [13]For if we are beside ourselves, it is for God; if we are in our right mind, it is for you. [14]For the love of Christ urges us on, because we are convinced that one has died for all; therefore all have died. [15]And he died for all, that those who live might live no longer for themselves but for him who for their sake died and was raised.

16 From now on, therefore, we regard no one according to the flesh; even though we once regarded Christ according to the flesh, we regard him thus no longer. [17]Therefore, if any one is in Christ, he is a new creation; [g] the old has passed away, behold, the new has come. [18]All this is from God, who through Christ reconciled us to himself and gave us the ministry of reconciliation; [19]that is, in Christ God was reconciling [h] the world to

himself,[*] not counting their trespasses against them, and entrusting to us the message of reconciliation. [20]So we are ambassadors for Christ, God making his appeal through us. We beg you on behalf of Christ, be reconciled to God. [21]For our sake he made him to be sin † who knew no sin, so that in him we might become the righteousness of God.

6 Working together with him, then, we entreat you not to accept the grace of God in vain. [2]For he says,

"At the acceptable time I have listened to you,
and helped you on the day of salvation."

Behold, now is the acceptable time; behold, now is the day of salvation. [3]We put no obstacle in any one's way, so that no fault may be found with our ministry, [4]but as servants of God we commend ourselves in every way: through great endurance, in afflictions, hardships, calamities, [5]beatings, imprisonments, tumults, labors, watching, hunger; [6]by purity, knowledge, forbearance, kindness, the Holy Spirit, genuine love, [7]truthful speech, and the power of God; with the weapons of righteousness for the right hand and for the left; [8]in honor and dishonor, in ill repute and good repute. We are treated as impostors, and yet are true; [9]as unknown, and yet well known; as dying, and behold we live; as punished, and yet not killed; [10]as sorrowful, yet always rejoicing; as poor, yet making many rich; as having nothing, and yet possessing everything.

11 Our mouth is open to you, Corinthians; our heart is wide. [12]You are not restricted by us, but you are restricted in your own affections. [13]In return—I speak as to children—widen your hearts also.

The Temple of the Living God

14 Do not be mismated with unbelievers. For what partnership have righteousness and iniquity? Or what fellowship has light with darkness? [15]What accord has Christ with Be'lial? [i] Or what has a believer in common with an unbeliever? [16]What agreement has the temple of God with

[g] Or creature.
[h] Or God was in Christ reconciling.
[i] Greek Beliar.
5:10: Mt 16:27.
5:12: 2 Cor 3:1.
5:14: Rom 5:15; 6:6–7.
5:17: Rom 6:7; Gal 6:15.
5:18: 1 Cor 11:12; Col 1:20; Rom 5:10.
5:20: Eph 6:20.
5:21: Heb 4:15; 7:25; 1 Pet 2:22; 1 Jn 3:5; Acts 3:14.
6:2: Is 49:8.
6:4: 2 Cor 4:8–11; 11:23–27.
6:5: Acts 16:23.
6:7: 2 Cor 10:4; Rom 13:12; Eph 6:11–12.
6:9: Rom 8:36.
6:10: Rom 8:32; 1 Cor 3:21.
6:11: Ezek 33:22; Is 60:5.
6:16: 1 Cor 10:21; 3:16; Ex 25:8; 29:45; Lev 26:12; Ezek 37:27; Jer 31:1.
* 5:19: Or, "God was reconciling the world to himself through Christ."
† 5:21, made him to be sin: i.e., "sending his own Son in the likeness of sinful flesh and for sin, he condemned sin in the flesh" (Rom 8:3).

idols? For we are the temple of the living God; as God said,

"I will live in them and move among them,
and I will be their God,
and they shall be my people.

[17]Therefore come out from them,
and be separate from them, says the Lord,
and touch nothing unclean;
then I will welcome you,

[18]and I will be a father to you,
and you shall be my sons and daughters,
says the Lord Almighty."

7 Since we have these promises, beloved, let us cleanse ourselves from every defilement of body and spirit, and make holiness perfect in the fear of God.

Paul's Joy at the Corinthians' Repentance and Zeal

2 Open your hearts to us; we have wronged no one, we have corrupted no one, we have taken advantage of no one. [3]I do not say this to condemn you, for I said before that you are in our hearts, to die together and to live together. [4]I have great confidence in you; I have great pride in you; I am filled with comfort. With all our affliction, I am overjoyed.

5 For even when we came into Macedonia, our bodies had no rest but we were afflicted at every turn—fighting without and fear within. [6]But God, who comforts the downcast, comforted us by the coming of Titus, [7]and not only by his coming but also by the comfort with which he was comforted in you, as he told us of your longing, your mourning, your zeal for me, so that I rejoiced still more. [8]For even if I made you sorry with my letter, I do not regret it (though I did regret it), for I see that that letter grieved you, though only for a while. [9]As it is, I rejoice, not because you were grieved, but because you were grieved into repenting; for you felt a godly grief, so that you suffered no loss through us. [10]For godly grief produces a repentance that leads to salvation and brings no regret, but worldly grief produces death. [11]For see what earnestness this godly grief has produced in you, what eagerness to clear yourselves, what indignation, what alarm, what longing, what zeal, what punishment! At every point you have proved yourselves guiltless in the matter. [12]So although I wrote to you, it was not on account of the one who did the wrong, nor on account of the one who suffered the wrong, but in order that your zeal for us might be revealed to you in the sight of God. [13]Therefore we are comforted.

And besides our own comfort we rejoiced still more at the joy of Titus, because his mind has been set at rest by you all. [14]For if I have expressed to him some pride in you, I was not put to shame; but just as everything we said to you was true, so our boasting before Titus has proved

true. [15]And his heart goes out all the more to you, as he remembers the obedience of you all, and the fear and trembling with which you received him. [16]I rejoice, because I have perfect confidence in you.

Encouragement to Be Generous

8 We want you to know, brethren, about the grace of God which has been shown in the churches of Macedonia, [2]for in a severe test of affliction, their abundance of joy and their extreme poverty have overflowed in a wealth of liberality on their part. [3]For they gave according to their means, as I can testify, and beyond their means, of their own free will, [4]begging us earnestly for the favor of taking part in the relief of the saints—[5]and this, not as we expected, but first they gave themselves to the Lord and to us by the will of God. [6]Accordingly we have urged Titus that as he had already made a beginning, he should also complete among you this gracious work. [7]Now as you excel in everything—in faith, in utterance, in knowledge, in all earnestness, and in your love for us—see that you excel in this gracious work also.

8 I say this not as a command, but to prove by the earnestness of others that your love also is genuine. [9]For you know the grace of our Lord Jesus Christ, that though he was rich, yet for your sake he became poor, so that by his poverty you might become rich. [10]And in this matter I give my advice: it is best for you now to complete what a year ago you began not only to do but to desire, [11]so that your readiness in desiring it may be matched by your completing it out of what you have. [12]For if the readiness is there, it is acceptable according to what a man has, not according to what he has not. [13]I do not mean that others should be eased and you burdened, [14]but that as a matter of equality your abundance at the present time should supply their want, so that their abundance may supply your want, that there may be equality. [15]As it is written, "He who gathered much had nothing over, and he who gathered little had no lack."

Commendation of Titus

16 But thanks be to God who puts the same earnest care for you into the heart of Titus. [17]For he not only accepted our appeal, but being

6:17: Is 52:11.
6:18: Hos 1:10; Is 43:6.
7:2: 2 Cor 6:12–13.
7:3: 2 Cor 6:11–12.
7:5: 2 Cor 2:13; 4:8.
7:6: 2 Cor 2:13; 7:13–14.
7:8: 2 Cor 2:2.
7:12: 2 Cor 7:8; 2:3, 9.
8:3: 1 Cor 16:2.
8:4: Acts 24:17; Rom 15:31.
8:6: 2 Cor 8:16, 23; 2:13.
8:9: 2 Cor 6:10.
8:10: 2 Cor 9:2; 1 Cor 16:2–3.
8:15: Ex 16:18.

himself very earnest he is going to you of his own accord. [18]With him we are sending the brother who is famous among all the churches for his preaching of the gospel; [19]and not only that, but he has been appointed by the churches to travel with us in this gracious work which we are carrying on, for the glory of the Lord and to show our good will. [20]We intend that no one should blame us about this liberal gift which we are administering, [21]for we aim at what is honorable not only in the Lord's sight but also in the sight of men. [22]And with them we are sending our brother whom we have often tested and found earnest in many matters, but who is now more earnest than ever because of his great confidence in you. [23]As for Titus, he is my partner and fellow worker in your service; and as for our brethren, they are messengers [j] of the churches, the glory of Christ. [24]So give proof, before the churches, of your love and of our boasting about you to these men.

Generosity in Giving

9 Now it is superfluous * for me to write to you about the offering for the saints, [2]for I know your readiness, of which I boast about you to the people of Macedonia, saying that Acha′ia has been ready since last year; and your zeal has stirred up most of them. [3]But I am sending the brethren so that our boasting about you may not prove vain in this case, so that you may be ready, as I said you would be; [4]lest if some Macedonians come with me and find that you are not ready, we be humiliated—to say nothing of you—for being so confident. [5]So I thought it necessary to urge the brethren to go on to you before me, and arrange in advance for this gift you have promised, so that it may be ready not as an exaction but as a willing gift.

6 The point is this: he who sows sparingly will also reap sparingly, and he who sows bountifully will also reap bountifully. [7]Each one must do as he has made up his mind, not reluctantly or under compulsion, for God loves a cheerful giver. [8]And God is able to provide you with every blessing in abundance, so that you may always have enough of everything and may provide in abundance for every good work. [9]As it is written,

"He scatters abroad, he gives to the poor;
  his righteousness [k] endures for ever."

[10]He who supplies seed to the sower and bread for food will supply and multiply your resources [l] and increase the harvest of your righteousness. [k] [11]You will be enriched in every way for great generosity, which through us will produce thanksgiving to God; [12]for the rendering of this service not only supplies the wants of the saints but also overflows in many thanksgivings to God. [13]Under the test of this service, you [m] will glorify God by your obedience in acknowledging the gospel of Christ, and by the generosity of your contribution for them and for all others; [14]while they long for you and pray for you, because of the surpassing grace of God in you. [15]Thanks be to God for his inexpressible gift!

Paul Defends His Ministry

10 I, Paul, myself entreat you, by the meekness and gentleness of Christ—I who am humble when face to face with you, but bold to you when I am away! †—[2]I beg of you that when I am present I may not have to show boldness with such confidence as I count on showing against some who suspect us of acting in worldly fashion. [3]For though we live in the world we are not carrying on a worldly war, [4]for the weapons of our warfare are not worldly but have divine power to destroy strongholds. [5]We destroy arguments and every proud obstacle to the knowledge of God, and take every thought captive to obey Christ, [6]being ready to punish every disobedience, when your obedience is complete.

7 Look at what is before your eyes. If any one is confident that he is Christ's, let him remind himself that as he is Christ's, so are we. [8]For even if I boast a little too much of our authority, which the Lord gave for building you up and not for destroying you, I shall not be put to shame. [9]I would not seem to be frightening you with letters. [10]For they say, "His letters are weighty and strong, but his bodily presence is weak, and his speech of no account." [11]Let such people understand that what we say by letter when absent, we do when present. [12]Not that we venture to class or compare ourselves with some of those who commend themselves. But when they measure themselves by one another, and compare themselves with one another, they are without understanding.

13 But we will not boast beyond limit, but will keep to the limits God has apportioned us, to reach even to you. [14]For we are not overextending ourselves, as though we did not reach you; we

---

[j] Greek *apostles.*
[k] Or *benevolence.*
[l] Greek *sowing.*
[m] Or *they.*

8:18: 2 Cor 12:18.
8:19: 1 Cor 16:3–4.
9:1: 2 Cor 8:4.
9:2: Rom 15:26; 2 Cor 8:10.
9:3: 1 Cor 16:2.
9:7: Prov 22:8 Septuagint.
9:8: Eph 3:20.
9:9: Ps 112:9.
9:10: Is 55:10; Hos 10:12.
9:13: 2 Cor 8:4; Rom 15:31.
9:15: Rom 5:15–16.
10:1: 2 Cor 10:10.
10:2: 2 Cor 13:2, 10; 1 Cor 4:21.
10:6: 2 Cor 2:9.
10:7: 1 Cor 1:12.
10:10: 1 Cor 2:3.

* 9:1, *superfluous:* Yet Paul goes on to do so at some length, exhorting them to be generous.
† 10:1: Paul is referring ironically to what some people are saying about him; see verse 10.

were the first to come all the way to you with the gospel of Christ. [15]We do not boast beyond limit, in other men's labors; but our hope is that as your faith increases, our field among you may be greatly enlarged, [16]so that we may preach the gospel in lands beyond you, without boasting of work already done in another's field. [17]"Let him who boasts, boast of the Lord." [18]For it is not the man who commends himself that is accepted, but the man whom the Lord commends.

Paul and the False Apostles

11 I wish you would bear with me in a little foolishness. Do bear with me! [2]I feel a divine jealousy for you, for I betrothed you to Christ to present you as a pure bride to her one husband. [3]But I am afraid that as the serpent deceived Eve by his cunning, your thoughts will be led astray from a sincere and pure devotion to Christ. [4]For if some one comes and preaches another Jesus than the one we preached, or if you receive a different spirit from the one you received, or if you accept a different gospel from the one you accepted, you submit to it readily enough. [5]I think that I am not in the least inferior to these superlative apostles. [6]Even if I am unskilled in speaking, I am not in knowledge; in every way we have made this plain to you in all things.

7 Did I commit a sin in abasing myself so that you might be exalted, because I preached God's gospel without cost to you? [8]I robbed other churches by accepting support from them in order to serve you. [9]And when I was with you and was in want, I did not burden any one, for my needs were supplied by the brethren who came from Macedonia. So I refrained and will refrain from burdening you in any way. [10]As the truth of Christ is in me, this boast of mine shall not be silenced in the regions of Acha′ia. [11]And why? Because I do not love you? God knows I do!

12 And what I do I will continue to do, in order to undermine the claim of those who would like to claim that in their boasted mission they work on the same terms as we do. [13]For such men are false apostles, deceitful workmen, disguising themselves as apostles of Christ. [14]And no wonder, for even Satan disguises himself as an angel of light. [15]So it is not strange if his servants also disguise themselves as servants of righteousness. Their end will correspond to their deeds.

Paul's Sufferings as an Apostle

16 I repeat, let no one think me foolish; but even if you do, accept me as a fool, so that I too may boast a little. [17](What I am saying I say not with the Lord's authority but as a fool, in this boastful confidence; [18]since many boast of worldly things, I too will boast.) [19]For you gladly bear with fools, being wise yourselves! [20]For you bear it if a man makes slaves of you, or preys upon you, or takes advantage of you, or puts on

airs, or strikes you in the face. [21]To my shame, I must say, we were too weak for that!

But whatever any one dares to boast of—I am speaking as a fool—I also dare to boast of that. [22]Are they Hebrews? So am I. Are they Israelites? So am I. Are they descendants of Abraham? So am I. [23]Are they servants of Christ? I am a better one—I am talking like a madman—with far greater labors, far more imprisonments, with countless beatings, and often near death. [24]Five times I have received at the hands of the Jews the forty lashes less one. [25]Three times I have been beaten with rods; once I was stoned. Three times I have been shipwrecked; a night and a day I have been adrift at sea; [26]on frequent journeys, in danger from rivers, danger from robbers, danger from my own people, danger from Gentiles, danger in the city, danger in the wilderness, danger at sea, danger from false brethren; [27]in toil and hardship, through many a sleepless night, in hunger and thirst, often without food, in cold and exposure. [28]And, apart from other things, there is the daily pressure upon me of my anxiety for all the churches. [29]Who is weak, and I am not weak? Who is made to fall, and I am not indignant?

30 If I must boast, I will boast of the things that show my weakness. [31]The God and Father of the Lord Jesus, he who is blessed for ever, knows that I do not lie. [32]At Damascus, the governor under King Ar′etas guarded the city of Damascus in order to seize me, [33]but I was let down in a basket through a window in the wall, and escaped his hands.

Paul's Visions and Revelations

12 I must boast; there is nothing to be gained by it, but I will go on to visions and revelations of the Lord. [2]I know a man in Christ who fourteen years ago was caught up to the third heaven—whether in the body or out of the body I do not know, God knows. [3]And I know that this man was caught up into Paradise—whether in the body or out of the body I do not know, God

10:15: Rom 15:20.
10:17: Jer 9:24.
11:1: 2 Cor 11:21.
11:2: Hos 2:19–20; Eph 5:26–27.
11:3: Gen 3:4.
11:4: Gal 1:6.
11:5: 2 Cor 12:11; Gal 2:6.
11:6: 1 Cor 1:17.
11:7: 2 Cor 12:13; 1 Cor 9:18.
11:8: Phil 4:15, 18.
11:10: 1 Cor 9:15.
11:11: 2 Cor 12:15.
11:12: 1 Cor 9:12.
11:17: 1 Cor 7:12, 25.
11:19: 1 Cor 4:10.
11:23: Acts 16:23; 2 Cor 6:5.
11:24: Deut 25:3.
11:25: Acts 16:22; 14:19.
11:26: Acts 9:23; 14:5.
11:27: 1 Cor 4:11.
11:29: 1 Cor 9:22.
11:32–33: Acts 9:24–25.

knows—⁴and he heard things that cannot be told, which man may not utter. ⁵On behalf of this man I will boast, but on my own behalf I will not boast, except of my weaknesses. ⁶Though if I wish to boast, I shall not be a fool, for I shall be speaking the truth. But I refrain from it, so that no one may think more of me than he sees in me or hears from me. ⁷And to keep me from being too elated by the abundance of revelations, a thorn* was given me in the flesh, a messenger of Satan, to harass me, to keep me from being too elated. ⁸Three times I begged the Lord about this, that it should leave me; ⁹but he said to me, "My grace is sufficient for you, for my power is made perfect in weakness." I will all the more gladly boast of my weaknesses, that the power of Christ may rest upon me. ¹⁰For the sake of Christ, then, I am content with weaknesses, insults, hardships, persecutions, and calamities; for when I am weak, then I am strong.

Paul's Concern for the Corinthian Church

11 I have been a fool! You forced me to it, for I ought to have been commended by you. For I am not at all inferior to these superlative apostles, even though I am nothing. ¹²The signs of a true apostle were performed among you in all patience, with signs and wonders and mighty works. ¹³For in what were you less favored than the rest of the churches, except that I myself did not burden you? Forgive me this wrong! †

14 Here for the third time I am ready to come to you. And I will not be a burden, for I seek not what is yours but you; for children ought not to lay up for their parents, but parents for their children. ¹⁵I will most gladly spend and be spent for your souls. If I love you the more, am I to be loved the less? ¹⁶But granting that I myself did not burden you, I was crafty, you say, and got the better of you by guile. ¹⁷Did I take advantage of you through any of those whom I sent to you? ¹⁸I urged Titus to go, and sent the brother with him. Did Titus take advantage of you? Did we not act in the same spirit? Did we not take the same steps?

19 Have you been thinking all along that we have been defending ourselves before you? It is in the sight of God that we have been speaking in Christ, and all for your upbuilding, beloved. ²⁰For I fear that perhaps I may come and find you not what I wish, and that you may find me not what you wish; that perhaps there may be quarreling, jealousy, anger, selfishness, slander, gossip, conceit, and disorder. ²¹I fear that when I come again my God may humble me before you, and I may have to mourn over many of those who sinned before and have not repented of the impurity, immorality, and licentiousness which they have practiced.

Further Warning

13 This is the third time I am coming to you. Any charge must be sustained by the evidence of two or three witnesses. ²I warned those who sinned before and all the others, and I warn them now while absent, as I did when present on my second visit, that if I come again I will not spare them—³since you desire proof that Christ is speaking in me. He is not weak in dealing with you, but is powerful in you. ⁴For he was crucified in weakness, but lives by the power of God. For we are weak in him, but in dealing with you we shall live with him by the power of God.

5 Examine yourselves, to see whether you are holding to your faith. Test yourselves. Do you not realize that Jesus Christ is in you?—unless indeed you fail to meet the test! ⁶I hope you will find out that we have not failed. ⁷But we beg God that you may not do wrong—not that we may appear to have met the test, but that you may do what is right, though we may seem to have failed. ⁸For we cannot do anything against the truth, but only for the truth. ⁹For we are glad when we are weak and you are strong. What we pray for is your improvement. ¹⁰I write this while I am away from you, in order that when I come I may not have to be severe in my use of the authority which the Lord has given me for building up and not for tearing down.

Final Greetings and Benediction

11 Finally, brethren, rejoice. Mend your ways, heed my appeal, agree with one another, live in peace, and the God of love and peace will be with you. ¹²Greet one another with a holy kiss. ¹³All the saints greet you.

14 The grace of the Lord Jesus Christ and the love of God and the fellowship of ⁿ the Holy Spirit be with you all.

ⁿ Or *and participation in.*
12:4: Lk 23:43.
12:7: Job 2:6.
12:10: Rom 5:3; 2 Cor 6:4–5.
12:11: 2 Cor 11:5.
12:13: 2 Cor 11:7.
12:16: 2 Cor 11:9.
12:18: 2 Cor 2:13; 8:18.
12:20: 2 Cor 2:1–4; 1 Cor 1:11; 3:3.
13:1: 2 Cor 12:14; Deut 19:15.
13:4: Phil 2:7–8; Rom 6:8.
13:10: 2 Cor 2:3.
13:12: Rom 16:16.
13:13: Phil 4:22.
13:14: Rom 16:20.
* 12:7, *a thorn:* Perhaps some form of sickness or disability, or the opposition of Israel to his teaching.
† 12:13: Paul ironically asks forgiveness for not being a charge on them as the other apostles were.

THE LETTER OF PAUL TO THE
GALATIANS

Salutation

1 Paul an apostle—not from men nor through man, but through Jesus Christ and God the Father, who raised him from the dead—²and all the brethren who are with me,

To the churches of Galatia:

3 Grace to you and peace from God the Father and our Lord Jesus Christ, ⁴who gave himself for our sins to deliver us from the present evil age, according to the will of our God and Father; ⁵to whom be the glory for ever and ever. Amen.

There Is No Other Gospel

6 I am astonished that you are so quickly deserting him who called you in the grace of Christ and turning to a different gospel— * ⁷not that there is another gospel, but there are some who trouble you and want to pervert the gospel of Christ. ⁸But even if we, or an angel from heaven, should preach to you a gospel contrary to that which we preached to you, let him be accursed. ⁹As we have said before, so now I say again, If any one is preaching to you a gospel contrary to that which you received, let him be accursed.

10 Am I now seeking the favor of men, or of God? Or am I trying to please men? If I were still pleasing men, I should not be a servant ᵃ of Christ. †

Paul's Vindication of His Apostleship

11 Brethren, I would have you know that the gospel which was preached by me is not man's ᵇ gospel. ¹²For I did not receive it from man, nor was I taught it, but it came through a revelation of Jesus Christ. ¹³For you have heard of my former life in Judaism, how I persecuted the Church of God violently and tried to destroy it; ¹⁴and I advanced in Judaism beyond many of my own age among my people, so extremely zealous was I for the traditions of my fathers. ¹⁵But when he who had set me apart before I was born, and had called me through his grace, ¹⁶was pleased to reveal his Son to ᶜ me, in order that I might preach him among the Gentiles, I did not confer with flesh and blood, ¹⁷nor did I go up to Jerusalem to those who were apostles before me, but I went away into Arabia; and again I returned to Damascus.

18 Then after three years I went up to Jerusalem to visit Ce'phas, and remained with him fifteen days. ¹⁹But I saw none of the other apostles except James the Lord's brother. ‡ ²⁰(In what I am

writing to you, before God, I do not lie!) ²¹Then I went into the regions of Syria and Cili'cia. ²²And I was still not known by sight to the churches of Christ in Judea; ²³they only heard it said, "He who once persecuted us is now preaching the faith he once tried to destroy." ²⁴And they glorified God because of me.

Paul and the Other Apostles

2 Then after fourteen years I went up again to Jerusalem with Barnabas, taking Titus along with me. ²I went up by revelation; and I laid before them (but privately before those who were of repute) the gospel which I preach among the Gentiles, lest somehow I should be running or had run in vain. ³But even Titus, who was with me, was not compelled to be circumcised, though he was a Greek. ⁴But because of false brethren secretly brought in, who slipped in to spy out our freedom which we have in Christ Jesus, that they might bring us into bondage—⁵to them we did not yield submission even for a moment, that the truth of the gospel might be preserved for you. ⁶And from those who were reputed to be something (what they were makes no difference to me; God shows no partiality)—those, I say, who were of repute added nothing to me; ⁷but on the contrary, when they saw that I had been entrusted with the gospel to the uncircumcised, just as Peter had been entrusted with the gospel to the circumcised ⁸(for he who worked through Peter for the mission to the circumcised worked through me also for the Gentiles), ⁹and when they perceived the grace that was given to me, James and Ce'phas and John, who were reputed to be pillars,

---

ᵃ Or *slave.*
ᵇ Greek *according to man.*
ᶜ Greek *in.*
1:3: Rom 1:7.
1:4: Gal 2:20; 1 Tim 2:6.
1:5: Rom 16:27.
1:8: 2 Cor 11:4.
1:10: 1 Thess 2:4.
1:11: Rom 1:16–17.
1:13: Acts 8:3.
1:14: Acts 22:3.
1:15: Acts 9:1–19; Is 49:1; Jer 1:5.
1:18: Acts 9:26–30; 11:30.
2:1: Acts 15:2.
2:5: Acts 15:23–29.
2:6: Deut 10:17.
* 1:6: After the greeting there is no commendation, as was usual, but rather strong rebuke.
† 1:10: No doubt Paul was accused of exempting Gentile converts from the law of Moses in order to curry favor.
‡ 1:19: *Lord's brother:* See the note on *brethren* at Mt 12:46 above.

gave to me and Barnabas the right hand of fellowship, that we should go to the Gentiles and they to the circumcised; [10]only they would have us remember the poor, which very thing I was eager to do.

Paul Rebukes Peter at Antioch

[11] But when Cephas came to Antioch I opposed him to his face, because he stood condemned. [12]For before certain men came from James, he ate with the Gentiles; but when they came he drew back and separated himself, fearing the circumcision party. [13]And with him the rest of the Jews acted insincerely, so that even Barnabas was carried away by their insincerity. [14]But when I saw that they were not straightforward about the truth of the gospel, I said to Cephas before them all, "If you, though a Jew, live like a Gentile and not like a Jew, how can you compel the Gentiles to live like Jews?" [15]We ourselves, who are Jews by birth and not Gentile sinners, [16]yet who know that a man is not justified [d] by works of the law * but through faith in Jesus Christ, even we have believed in Christ Jesus, in order to be justified by faith in Christ, and not by works of the law, because by works of the law shall no flesh be justified. [17]But if, in our endeavor to be justified in Christ, we ourselves were found to be sinners, is Christ then an agent of sin? Certainly not! [18]But if I build up again those things which I tore down, then I prove myself a transgressor. [19]For I through the law died to the law, that I might live to God. [20]I have been crucified with Christ; it is no longer I who live, but Christ who lives in me; and the life I now live in the flesh I live by faith in the Son of God, who loved me and gave himself for me. [21]I do not nullify the grace of God; for if justification [e] were through the law, then Christ died to no purpose.

Law or Faith

3 O foolish Galatians! Who has bewitched you, before whose eyes Jesus Christ was publicly portrayed as crucified? [2]Let me ask you only this: Did you receive the Spirit † by works of the law, or by hearing with faith? [3]Are you so foolish? Having begun with the Spirit, are you now ending with the flesh? [4]Did you experience so many things in vain?—if it really is in vain. [5]Does he who supplies the Spirit to you and works miracles among you do so by works of the law, or by hearing with faith?

[6] Thus Abraham "believed God, and it was reckoned to him as righteousness." [7]So you see that it is men of faith who are the sons of Abraham. [8]And the Scripture, foreseeing that God would justify the Gentiles by faith, preached the gospel beforehand to Abraham, saying, "In you shall all the nations be blessed." [9]So then, those who are men of faith are blessed with Abraham who had faith.

[10] For all who rely on works of the law are under a curse; for it is written, "Cursed be every one who does not abide by all things written in the book of the law, and do them." [11]Now it is evident that no man is justified before God by the law; for "He who through faith is righteous shall live"; [f] [12]but the law does not rest on faith, for "He who does them shall live by them." [13]Christ redeemed us from the curse of the law, having become a curse for us—for it is written, "Cursed be every one who hangs on a tree"—[14]that in Christ Jesus the blessing of Abraham might come upon the Gentiles, that we might receive the promise of the Spirit through faith.

The Promise to Abraham

[15] To give a human example, brethren: no one annuls even a man's will, [g] or adds to it, once it has been ratified. [16]Now the promises were made to Abraham and to his offspring. It does not say, "And to offsprings," referring to many; but, referring to one, "And to your offspring," which is Christ. [17]This is what I mean: the law, which came four hundred and thirty years afterward, does not annul a covenant previously ratified by God, so as to make the promise void. [18]For if the inheritance is by the law, it is no longer by promise; but God gave it to Abraham by a promise.

The Purpose of the Law

[19] Why then the law? It was added because of transgressions, till the offspring should come to whom the promise had been made; and it was ordained by angels through an intermediary. [20]Now an intermediary implies more than one; but God is one.

[21] Is the law then against the promises of God? Certainly not; for if a law had been given which could make alive, then righteousness would indeed be by the law. [22]But the Scripture consigned all things to sin, that what was promised to faith in Jesus Christ might be given to those who believe.

---

[d] Or *reckoned righteous*; and so elsewhere.
[e] Or *righteousness*.
[f] Or *the righteous shall live by faith*.
[g] Or *covenant* (as in verse 17).
2:11: Acts 11:19–26.
2:16: Ps 143:2; Rom 3:20.
2:20: Gal 1:4.
3:6: Gen 15:6; Rom 4:3.
3:8: Gen 12:3; 18:18; Acts 3:25.
3:9: Rom 4:16.
3:10: Deut 27:26.
3:11: Hab 2:4; Rom 1:17; Heb 10:38.
3:12: Lev 18:5; Rom 10:5.
3:13: Deut 21:23.
3:16: Gen 12:7.
3:17: Ex 12:40.
3:18: Rom 11:6.
3:19: Rom 5:20.
3:21: Rom 8:2–4.
3:22: Rom 3:9–19; 11:32.
* 2:16, *works of the law*: Paul is contrasting not faith with good works but faith in Jesus Christ with observance of the law of Moses.
† 3:2, *Spirit*: He probably refers to the outward manifestations of the Spirit, such as the gift of tongues.

23 Now before faith came, we were confined under the law, kept under restraint until faith should be revealed. 24So that the law was our custodian until Christ came, that we might be justified by faith. 25But now that faith has come, we are no longer under a custodian; 26for in Christ Jesus you are all sons of God, through faith. 27For as many of you as were baptized into Christ have put on Christ. 28There is neither Jew nor Greek, there is neither slave nor free, there is neither male nor female; for you are all one in Christ Jesus. 29And if you are Christ's, then you are Abraham's offspring, heirs according to promise.

4 I mean that the heir, as long as he is a child, is no better than a slave, though he is the owner of all the estate; 2but he is under guardians and trustees until the date set by the father. 3So with us; when we were children, we were slaves to the elemental spirits of the universe. 4But when the time had fully come, God sent forth his Son, born of woman, born under the law, 5to redeem those who were under the law, so that we might receive adoption as sons. 6And because you are sons, God has sent the Spirit of his Son into our hearts, crying, "Abba! Father!" 7So through God you are no longer a slave but a son, and if a son then an heir.

Paul Reproves the Galatians

8 Formerly, when you did not know God, you were in bondage to beings that by nature are no gods; 9but now that you have come to know God, or rather to be known by God, how can you turn back again to the weak and beggarly elemental spirits, whose slaves you want to be once more? 10You observe days, and months, and seasons, and years! 11I am afraid I have labored over you in vain.

12 Brethren, I beg you, become as I am, for I also have become as you are. You did me no wrong; 13you know it was because of a bodily ailment that I preached the gospel to you at first; 14and though my condition was a trial to you, you did not scorn or despise me, but received me as an angel of God, as Christ Jesus. 15What has become of the satisfaction you felt? For I bear you witness that, if possible, you would have plucked out your eyes and given them to me. 16Have I then become your enemy by telling you the truth? h 17They make much of you, but for no good purpose; they want to shut you out, that you may make much of them. 18For a good purpose it is always good to be made much of, and not only when I am present with you. 19My little children, with whom I am again in travail until Christ be formed in you! 20I could wish to be present with you now and to change my tone, for I am perplexed about you.

The Allegory of Hagar and Sarah

21 Tell me, you who desire to be under law, do you not hear the law? 22For it is written that Abraham had two sons, one by a slave and one by a free woman. 23But the son of the slave was born according to the flesh, the son of the free woman through promise. 24Now this is an allegory: these women are two covenants. One is from Mount Sinai, bearing children for slavery; she is Hagar. 25Now Hagar is Mount Sinai in Arabia; i she corresponds to the present Jerusalem, for she is in slavery with her children. 26But the Jerusalem above is free, and she is our mother. 27For it is written,

"Rejoice, O barren one who does not bear;
break forth and shout, you who are not with
    labor pains;
for the desolate has more children
than she who has a husband."

28Now we, j brethren, like Isaac, are children of promise. 29But as at that time he who was born according to the flesh persecuted him who was born according to the Spirit, so it is now. 30But what does the Scripture say? "Cast out the slave and her son; for the son of the slave shall not inherit with the son of the free woman." 31So, brethren, we are not children of the slave but of the free woman.

Christian Freedom

5 For freedom Christ has set us free; stand fast therefore, and do not submit again to a yoke of slavery.

2 Now I, Paul, say to you that if you receive circumcision, Christ will be of no advantage to you. 3I testify again to every man who receives circumcision that he is bound to keep the whole law. 4You are severed from Christ, you who would be justified by the law; you have fallen away from grace. 5For through the Spirit, by faith, we wait for the hope of righteousness. 6For in Christ Jesus neither circumcision nor uncircumcision is of any avail, but faith working through love. 7You were running well; who hindered you from obeying the truth? 8This persuasion is not from him who called you. 9A little leaven leavens all the dough. 10I have confidence in the Lord that you will take no other view than mine; and he who is troubling you will bear his judgment, whoever he is. 11But if I, brethren, still preach circumcision, why am I still persecuted? In that case the stumbling block

h Or by dealing truly with you.
i Other ancient authorities read For Sinai is a mountain in Arabia.
j Other ancient authorities read you.
3:28: Rom 10:12.
4:3: Col 2:20.
4:6: Rom 8:15.
4:13: Acts 16:6.
4:19: 1 Cor 4:15.
4:22: Gen 16:15; 21:2, 9.
4:23: Rom 9:7–9.
4:27: Is 54:1.
4:29: Gen 21:9.
4:30: Gen 21:10–12.
5:6: 1 Cor 7:19; Gal 6:15.
5:9: 1 Cor 5:6.

of the cross * has been removed. [12]I wish those who unsettle you would mutilate themselves!

13 For you were called to freedom, brethren; only do not use your freedom as an opportunity for the flesh, but through love be servants of one another. [14]For the whole law is fulfilled in one word, "You shall love your neighbor as yourself." [15]But if you bite and devour one another take heed that you are not consumed by one another.

The Works of the Flesh and the Fruit of the Spirit

16 But I say, walk by the Spirit, and do not gratify the desires of the flesh. [17]For the desires of the flesh are against the Spirit, and the desires of the Spirit are against the flesh; for these are opposed to each other, to prevent you from doing what you would. [18]But if you are led by the Spirit you are not under the law. [19]Now the works of the flesh are plain: immorality, impurity, licentiousness, [20]idolatry, sorcery, enmity, strife, jealousy, anger, selfishness, dissension, party spirit, [21]envy, [k] drunkenness, carousing, and the like. I warn you, as I warned you before, that those who do such things shall not inherit the kingdom of God. [22]But the fruit of the Spirit is love, joy, peace, patience, kindness, goodness, faithfulness, [23]gentleness, self-control; against such there is no law. [24]And those who belong to Christ Jesus have crucified the flesh with its passions and desires.

25 If we live by the Spirit, let us also walk by the Spirit. [26]Let us have no self-conceit, no provoking of one another, no envy of one another.

Bear One Another's Burdens

6 Brethren, if a man is overtaken in any trespass, you who are spiritual should restore him in a spirit of gentleness. Look to yourself, lest you too be tempted. [2]Bear one another's burdens, and so fulfil the law of Christ. [3]For if any one thinks he is something, when he is nothing, he deceives himself. [4]But let each one test his own work, and then his reason to boast will be in himself alone and not in his neighbor. [5]For each man will have to bear his own load.

6 Let him who is taught the word share all good things with him who teaches.

7 Do not be deceived; God is not mocked, for whatever a man sows, that he will also reap. [8]For he who sows to his own flesh will from the flesh reap corruption; but he who sows to the Spirit will from the Spirit reap eternal life. [9]And let us not grow weary in well-doing, for in due season we shall reap, if we do not lose heart. [10]So then, as we have opportunity, let us do good to all men, and especially to those who are of the household of faith.

Final Admonitions and Benediction

11 See with what large letters I am writing to you with my own hand. [12]It is those who want to make a good showing in the flesh that would compel you to be circumcised, and only in order that they may not be persecuted for the cross of Christ. [13]For even those who receive circumcision do not themselves keep the law, but they desire to have you circumcised that they may glory in your flesh. [14]But far be it from me to glory except in the cross of our Lord Jesus Christ, by which [1] the world has been crucified to me, and I to the world. [15]For neither circumcision counts for anything, nor uncircumcision, but a new creation. [16]Peace and mercy be upon all who walk by this rule, upon the Israel of God.

17 Henceforth let no man trouble me; for I bear on my body the marks of Jesus.

18 The grace of our Lord Jesus Christ be with your spirit, brethren. Amen.

---

[k] Other ancient authorities add *murder*.
[1] Or *through whom*.
5:14: Lev 19:18; Rom 13:8–10.
5:17: Rom 7:15–23.
5:19: Rom 1:28.
6:11: 1 Cor 16:21.
6:16: Ps 125:5.
* 5:11, *stumbling block of the cross*: So far as the Jews were concerned, this would consist largely in the exemption of converts from the obligations of the law of Moses.

THE LETTER OF PAUL TO THE

EPHESIANS

Salutation

1 Paul, an apostle of Christ Jesus by the will of God,

To the saints who are * also faithful [a] in Christ Jesus:

2 Grace to you and peace from God our Father and the Lord Jesus Christ.

Spiritual Blessings in Christ

3 Blessed be the God and Father of our Lord Jesus Christ, who has blessed us in Christ with every spiritual blessing in the heavenly places, [4]even as he chose us in him before the foundation of the world, that we should be holy and blameless before him. [5]He destined us in love [b] to be his sons through Jesus Christ, according to the purpose of his will, [6]to the praise of his glorious grace which he freely bestowed on us in the Beloved. [7]In him we have redemption through his blood, the forgiveness of our trespasses, according to the riches of his grace [8]which he lavished upon us. [9]For he has made known to us in all wisdom and insight the mystery of his will, according to his purpose which he set forth in Christ [10]as a plan for the fulness of time, to unite † all things in him, things in heaven and things on earth.

11 In him, according to the purpose of him who accomplishes all things according to the counsel of his will, [12]we who first hoped in Christ have been destined and appointed to live for the praise of his glory. [13]In him you also, who have heard the word of truth, the gospel of your salvation, and have believed in him, were sealed with the promised Holy Spirit, [14]who is the guarantee of our inheritance until we acquire possession of it, to the praise of his glory.

Paul's Prayer

15 For this reason, because I have heard of your faith in the Lord Jesus and your love [c] toward all the saints, [16]I do not cease to give thanks for you, remembering you in my prayers, [17]that the God of our Lord Jesus Christ, the Father of glory, may give you a spirit of wisdom and of revelation in the knowledge of him, [18]having the eyes of your hearts enlightened, that you may know what is the hope to which he has called you, what are the riches of his glorious inheritance in the saints, [19]and what is the immeasurable greatness of his power in us who believe, according to the working of his great might [20]which he accomplished in Christ when he raised him from the dead and made him sit at his right hand in the heavenly places, [21]far above all rule and authority and power and dominion, and above every name that is named, not only in this age but also in that which is to come; [22]and he has put all things under his feet and has made him the head over all things for the Church, [23]which is his body, the fulness of him who fills all in all.

From Death to Life with Christ

2 And you he made alive, when you were dead through the trespasses and sins [2]in which you once walked, following the course of this world, following the prince of the power of the air, the spirit that is now at work in the sons of disobedience. [3]Among these we all once lived in the passions of our flesh, following the desires of body and mind, and so we were by nature children of wrath, like the rest of mankind. [4]But God, who is rich in mercy, out of the great love with which he loved us, [5]even when we were dead through our trespasses, made us alive together with Christ (by grace you have been saved), [6]and raised us up with him, and made us sit with him in the heavenly places in Christ Jesus, [7]that in the coming ages he might show the immeasurable riches of his grace in kindness toward us in Christ Jesus. [8]For by grace you have been saved through faith; and this is not your own doing, it is the gift of God—[9]not because of works, lest any man should boast. [10]For we are his workmanship, created in Christ Jesus for good works, which God prepared beforehand, that we should walk in them.

---

[a] Other ancient authorities read *who are at Ephesus and faithful.*
[b] Or *before him in love, having destined us.*
[c] Other ancient authorities omit *your love.*
1:3: 2 Cor 1:3.
1:6: Col 1:13.
1:7: Col 1:14.
1:10: Gal 4.4.
1:14: 2 Cor 1:22.
1:15: Col 1:9.
1:16: Col 1:3.
1:18: Deut 33:3.
1:20: Ps 110:1.
1:21: Col 1:6; 2:10, 15.
1:22: Ps 8:6; Col 1:19.
1:23: Rom 12:5; Col 2:17.
2:2: Col 1:13.
2:8: Gal 2:16.
* 1:1, *To the saints who are*: The addition "at Ephesus" is doubtful. The letter may have been a form of encyclical.
† 1:10, *to unite*: Or, "to sum up." This is one of the chief themes of the letter. Men are to be under Christ as head of the Mystical Body, and even irrational creatures must be in some way under him as the cornerstone of creation.

One in Christ

11 Therefore remember that at one time you Gentiles in the flesh, called the uncircumcision by what is called the circumcision, which is made in the flesh by hands—[12]remember that you were at that time separated from Christ, alienated from the commonwealth of Israel, and strangers to the covenants of promise, having no hope and without God in the world. [13]But now in Christ Jesus you who once were far off have been brought near in the blood of Christ. [14]For he is our peace, who has made us both one, and has broken down the dividing wall * of hostility, [15]by abolishing in his flesh the law of commandments and ordinances, that he might create in himself one new man in place of the two, so making peace, [16]and might reconcile us both to God in one body through the cross, thereby bringing the hostility to an end. [17]And he came and preached peace to you who were far off and peace to those who were near; [18]for through him we both have access in one Spirit to the Father. [19]So then you are no longer strangers and sojourners, but you are fellow citizens with the saints and members of the household of God, [20]built upon the foundation of the apostles and prophets, Christ Jesus himself being the cornerstone, [21]in whom the whole structure is joined together and grows into a holy temple in the Lord; [22]in whom you also are built into it for a dwelling place of God in the Spirit.

Paul's Ministry to the Gentiles

3 For this reason I, Paul, a prisoner for Christ Jesus on behalf of you Gentiles—[2]assuming that you have heard of the stewardship of God's grace that was given to me for you, [3]how the mystery † was made known to me by revelation, as I have written briefly. [4]When you read this you can perceive my insight into the mystery of Christ, [5]which was not made known to the sons of men in other generations as it has now been revealed to his holy apostles and prophets by the Spirit; [6]that is, how the Gentiles are fellow heirs, members of the same body, and partakers of the promise in Christ Jesus through the gospel.

7 Of this gospel I was made a minister according to the gift of God's grace which was given me by the working of his power. [8]To me, though I am the very least of all the saints, this grace was given, to preach to the Gentiles the unsearchable riches of Christ, [9]and to make all men see what is the plan of the mystery hidden for ages in [d] God who created all things; [10]that through the Church the manifold wisdom of God might now be made known to the principalities and powers in the heavenly places. [11]This was according to the eternal purpose which he has realized in Christ Jesus our Lord, [12]in whom we have boldness and confidence of access through our faith in him. [13]So I

ask you not to [e] lose heart over what I am suffering for you, which is your glory.

Prayer for the Ephesians

14 For this reason I bow my knees before the Father, [15]from whom every family in heaven and on earth is named, [16]that according to the riches of his glory he may grant you to be strengthened with might through his Spirit in the inner man, [17]and that Christ may dwell in your hearts through faith; that you, being rooted and grounded in love, [18]may have power to comprehend with all the saints what is the breadth and length and height and depth, [19]and to know the love of Christ which surpasses knowledge, that you may be filled with all the fulness of God.

20 Now to him who by the power at work within us is able to do far more abundantly than all that we ask or think, [21]to him be glory in the Church and in Christ Jesus to all generations, for ever and ever. Amen.

Unity in the Body of Christ

4 I therefore, a prisoner for the Lord, beg you to walk in a manner worthy of the calling to which you have been called, [2]with all lowliness and meekness, with patience, forbearing one another in love, [3]eager to maintain the unity of the Spirit in the bond of peace. [4]There is one body and one Spirit, just as you were called to the one hope that belongs to your call, [5]one Lord, one faith, one baptism, [6]one God and Father of us all, who is above all and through all and in all. [7]But grace was given to each of us according to the measure of Christ's gift. [8]Therefore it is said,

"When he ascended on high he led a host of captives,
and he gave gifts to men."

[9](In saying, "He ascended," what does it mean but that he had also descended into the lower parts of the earth? [10]He who descended is he who also ascended far above all the heavens, that he might fill all things.) [11]And his gifts were that some should be apostles, some prophets, some evangelists, some pastors and teachers, [12]to equip the saints for the work of ministry, for building up the body of Christ, [13]until we all attain to the unity of the faith and of the knowledge of the Son of God, to mature manhood, to the measure of the stature of the fulness of Christ; [14]so that

---

[d] Or by.
[e] Or I ask that I may not.
2:12: Is 57:19.
2:17: Is 57:19.
3:2: Col 1:25.
3:6: Col 1:27.
3:9: Col 1:26.
4:2: Col 3:12–13.
4:8: Ps 68:18.
* 2:14, dividing wall: A metaphor taken from the wall that divided the court of the Gentiles from the court of the Israelites in the temple.
† 3:3, the mystery: i.e., that the Gentiles were to be admitted to the Church on the basis of equality.

we may no longer be children, tossed back and forth and carried about with every wind of doctrine, by the cunning of men, by their craftiness in deceitful wiles. [15]Rather, speaking the truth in love, we are to grow up in every way into him who is the head, into Christ, [16]from whom the whole body, joined and knit together by every joint with which it is supplied, when each part is working properly, makes bodily growth and upbuilds itself in love.

The Old Life and the New

17 Now this I affirm and testify in the Lord, that you must no longer walk as the Gentiles walk, in the futility of their minds; [18]they are darkened in their understanding, alienated from the life of God because of the ignorance that is in them, due to their hardness of heart; [19]they have become callous and have given themselves up to licentiousness, greedy to practice every kind of uncleanness. [20]You did not so learn Christ! — [21]assuming that you have heard about him and were taught in him, as the truth is in Jesus. [22]Put off the old man that belongs to your former manner of life and is corrupt through deceitful lusts, [23]and be renewed in the spirit of your minds, [24]and put on the new man, created after the likeness of God in true righteousness and holiness.

Rules for the New Life

25 Therefore, putting away falsehood, let every one speak the truth with his neighbor, for we are members one of another. [26]Be angry but do not sin; do not let the sun go down on your anger, [27]and give no opportunity to the devil. [28]Let the thief no longer steal, but rather let him labor, doing honest work with his hands, so that he may be able to give to those in need. [29]Let no evil talk come out of your mouths, but only such as is good for edifying, as fits the occasion, that it may impart grace to those who hear. [30]And do not grieve the Holy Spirit of God, in whom you were sealed for the day of redemption. [31]Let all bitterness and wrath and anger and clamor and slander be put away from you, with all malice, [32]and be kind to one another, tenderhearted, forgiving one another, as God in Christ forgave you.

5 Therefore be imitators of God, as beloved children. [2]And walk in love, as Christ loved us and gave himself up for us, a fragrant offering and sacrifice to God.

Renounce Pagan Ways

3 But immorality and all impurity or covetousness must not even be named among you, as is fitting among saints. [4]Let there be no filthiness, nor silly talk, nor levity, which are not fitting; but instead let there be thanksgiving. [5]Be sure of this, that no immoral or impure man, or one who is covetous (that is, an idolater), has any inheritance in the kingdom of Christ and of God. [6]Let no one deceive you with empty words, for it is because of

these things that the wrath of God comes upon the sons of disobedience. [7]Therefore do not associate with them, [8]for once you were darkness, but now you are light in the Lord; walk as children of light [9](for the fruit of light is found in all that is good and right and true), [10]and try to learn what is pleasing to the Lord. [11]Take no part in the unfruitful works of darkness, but instead expose them. [12]For it is a shame even to speak of the things that they do in secret; [13]but when anything is exposed by the light it becomes visible, for anything that becomes visible is light. [14]Therefore it is said,

"Awake, O sleeper, and arise from the dead,
 and Christ shall give you light." *

15 Look carefully then how you walk, not as unwise men but as wise, [16]making the most of the time, because the days are evil. [17]Therefore do not be foolish, but understand what the will of the Lord is. [18]And do not get drunk with wine, for that is debauchery; but be filled with the Spirit, [19]addressing one another in psalms and hymns and spiritual songs, singing and making melody to the Lord with all your heart, [20]always and for everything giving thanks in the name of our Lord Jesus Christ to God the Father.

The Christian Household

21 Be subject to one another out of reverence for Christ. [22]Wives, be subject to your husbands, as to the Lord. [23]For the husband is the head of the wife as Christ is the head of the Church, his body, and is himself its Savior. [24]As the Church is subject to Christ, so let wives also be subject in everything to their husbands. [25]Husbands, love your wives, as Christ loved the Church and gave himself up for her, [26]that he might sanctify her, having cleansed her by the washing of water with the word, [27]that he might present the Church to himself in splendor, without spot or wrinkle or any such thing, that she might be holy and without blemish. [28]Even so husbands should love their wives as their own bodies. He who loves his wife loves himself. [29]For no man ever hates his own flesh, but nourishes and cherishes it, as Christ does the Church, [30]because we are members of his body. [31]"For this reason a man shall leave his father and mother and be joined to his wife, and the two shall become one flesh." [32]This is a great mystery, and I mean in reference to Christ and the Church; [33]however, let each one of you love his wife as himself, and let the wife see that she respects her husband.

4:15: Col 1:18.
4:16: Col 2:19.
4:25: Zech 8:16; Rom 12:5.
5:2: Ex 29:18; Ezek 20:41.
5:16: Col 4:5.
5:19: Col 3:16–17.
5:22—6:9: Col 3:18—4:1.
5:31: Gen 2:24.
* 5:14: Apparently a fragment of an early Christian hymn; cf. 1 Tim 3:16.

Children and Parents

6 Children, obey your parents in the Lord, for this is right. [2]"Honor your father and mother" (this is the first commandment with a promise), [3]"that it may be well with you and that you may live long on the earth." [4]Fathers, do not provoke your children to anger, but bring them up in the discipline and instruction of the Lord.

Slaves and Masters

5 Slaves, be obedient to those who are your earthly masters, with fear and trembling, in singleness of heart, as to Christ; [6]not in the way of eye-service, as men-pleasers, but as servants [f] of Christ, doing the will of God from the heart, [7]rendering service with a good will as to the Lord and not to men, [8]knowing that whatever good any one does, he will receive the same again from the Lord, whether he is a slave or free. [9]Masters, do the same to them, and forbear threatening, knowing that he who is both their Master and yours is in heaven, and that there is no partiality with him.

The Whole Armor of God

10 Finally, be strong in the Lord and in the strength of his might. [11]Put on the whole armor of God, that you may be able to stand against the wiles of the devil. [12]For we are not contending against flesh and blood, but against the principalities, against the powers, against the world rulers of this present darkness, against the spiritual hosts of wickedness in the heavenly places. [13]Therefore take the whole armor of God, that you may be able to withstand in the evil day, and having done all, to stand. [14]Stand therefore, having fastened the belt of truth around your waist, and having put on the breastplate of righteousness, [15]and having shod your feet with the equipment of the gospel of peace; [16]besides all these, taking the shield of faith, with which you can quench all the flaming darts of the Evil One. [17]And take the helmet of salvation, and the sword of the Spirit, which is the word of God. [18]Pray at all times in the Spirit, with all prayer and supplication. To that end keep alert with all perseverance, making supplication for all the saints, [19]and also for me, that utterance may be given me in opening my mouth boldly to proclaim the mystery of the gospel, [20]for which I am an ambassador in chains; that I may declare it boldly, as I ought to speak.

Personal Matters and Benediction

21 Now that you also may know how I am and what I am doing, Tych′icus the beloved brother and faithful minister in the Lord will tell you everything. [22]I have sent him to you for this very purpose, that you may know how we are, and that he may encourage your hearts.

23 Peace be to the brethren, and love with faith, from God the Father and the Lord Jesus Christ. [24]Grace be with all who love our Lord Jesus Christ with love undying.

---

f Or slaves.
6:2: Ex 20:12.
6:3: Deut 5:16.
6:14: Is 11:5; 59:17; 1 Thess 5:8.
6:15: Is 52:7.
6:21–22: Col 4:7–8.

THE LETTER OF PAUL TO THE

PHILIPPIANS

Salutation

1 Paul and Timothy, servants [a] of Christ Jesus,
To all the saints in Christ Jesus who are at Philip'pi, with the bishops [b] and deacons:

2 Grace to you and peace from God our Father and the Lord Jesus Christ.

Paul's Prayer for the Philippians

3 I thank my God in all my remembrance of you, [4]always in every prayer of mine for you all making my prayer with joy, [5]thankful for your partnership in the gospel from the first day until now. [6]And I am sure that he who began a good work in you will bring it to completion at the day of Jesus Christ. [7]It is right for me to feel this way about you all, because I hold you in my heart, for you are all partakers with me of grace, both in my imprisonment and in the defense and confirmation of the gospel. [8]For God is my witness, how I yearn for you all with the affection of Christ Jesus. [9]And it is my prayer that your love may abound more and more, with knowledge and all discernment, [10]so that you may approve what is excellent, and may be pure and blameless for the day of Christ, [11]filled with the fruits of righteousness which come through Jesus Christ, to the glory and praise of God.

Paul's Present Circumstances

12 I want you to know, brethren, that what has happened to me has really served to advance the gospel, [13]so that it has become known throughout the whole praetorian guard [c] and to all the rest that my imprisonment is for Christ; [14]and most of the brethren have been made confident in the Lord because of my imprisonment, * and are much more bold to speak the word of God without fear.

15 Some indeed preach Christ from envy and rivalry, but others from good will. [16]The latter do it out of love, knowing that I am put here for the defense of the gospel; [17]the former proclaim Christ out of partisanship, not sincerely but thinking to afflict me in my imprisonment. [18]What then? Only that in every way, whether in pretense or in truth, Christ is proclaimed; and in that I rejoice.

To Live Is Christ

19 Yes, and I shall rejoice. For I know that through your prayers and the help of the Spirit of Jesus Christ this will turn out for my deliverance, [20]as it is my eager expectation and hope that I shall not be at all ashamed, but that with full courage now as always Christ will be honored in my body, † whether by life or by death. [21]For to me to live is Christ, and to die is gain. [22]If it is to be life in the flesh, that means fruitful labor for me. Yet which I shall choose I cannot tell. [23]I am hard pressed between the two. My desire is to depart and be with Christ, for that is far better. [24]But to remain in the flesh is more necessary on your account. [25]Convinced of this, I know that I shall remain and continue with you all, for your progress and joy in the faith, [26]so that in me you may have ample cause to glory in Christ Jesus, because of my coming to you again.

27 Only let your manner of life be worthy of the gospel of Christ, so that whether I come and see you or am absent, I may hear of you that you stand firm in one spirit, with one mind striving side by side for the faith of the gospel, [28]and not frightened in anything by your opponents. This is a clear omen to them of their destruction, but of your salvation, and that from God. [29]For it has been granted to you that for the sake of Christ you should not only believe in him but also suffer for his sake, [30]engaged in the same conflict which you saw and now hear to be mine.

Imitating Christ's Humility

2 So if there is any encouragement in Christ, any incentive of love, any participation in the Spirit, any affection and sympathy, [2]complete my joy by being of the same mind, having the same love, being in full accord and of one mind. [3]Do nothing from selfishness or conceit, but in humility count others better than yourselves. [4]Let each of you look not only to his own interests, but also to the interests of others. [5]Have this mind among yourselves, which was in Christ Jesus,

---

[a] Or *slaves*.
[b] Or *overseers*.
[c] Greek *in the whole praetorium*.
1:1: Acts 16:1, 12–40; Rom 1:1; 2 Cor 1:1; Gal 1:10; Col 1:1; 1 Thess 1:1; 2 Thess 5:1; Philem 1.
1:2: Rom 1:7.
1:6, 10: 1 Cor 1:8.
1:7: Acts 21:33; 2 Cor 7:3; Eph 6:20.
1:12: Lk 21:13.
1:13: Acts 28:30; 2 Tim 2:9.
1:19: Acts 16:7; 2 Cor 1:11.
1:20: Rom 14:8.
1:21: Gal 2:20.
1:28: 2 Thess 1:5.
1:30: Acts 16:19–40; 1 Thess 2:2.
2:1: 2 Cor 13:14.
2:3–4: Rom 12:10; 15:1–2.
* 1:14, *because of my imprisonment*: i.e., because I continue to preach in their midst, though in prison.
† 1:20, *honored in my body*: i.e., through my sufferings.

⁶who, though he was in the form of God, * did not count equality with God a thing to be grasped, ⁷but emptied himself, † taking the form of a servant, ᵈ being born in the likeness of men. ⁸And being found in human form he humbled himself and became obedient unto death, even death on a cross. ⁹Therefore God has highly exalted him and bestowed on him the name which is above every name, ¹⁰that at the name of Jesus every knee should bow, in heaven and on earth and under the earth, ¹¹and every tongue confess that Jesus Christ is Lord, to the glory of God the Father.

Shining as Lights in the World

12 Therefore, my beloved, as you have always obeyed, so now, not only as in my presence but much more in my absence, work out your own salvation with fear and trembling; ¹³for God is at work in you, both to will and to work for his good pleasure.

14 Do all things without grumbling or questioning, ¹⁵that you may be blameless and innocent, children of God without blemish in the midst of a crooked and perverse generation, among whom you shine as lights in the world, ¹⁶holding fast the word of life, so that in the day of Christ I may be proud that I did not run in vain or labor in vain. ¹⁷Even if I am to be poured as a libation upon the sacrificial offering of your faith, I am glad and rejoice with you all. ¹⁸Likewise you also should be glad and rejoice with me.

Timothy and Epaphroditus

19 I hope in the Lord Jesus to send Timothy to you soon, so that I may be cheered by news of you. ²⁰I have no one like him, who will be genuinely anxious for your welfare. ²¹They all look after their own interests, not those of Jesus Christ. ²²But Timothy's worth you know, how as a son with a father he has served with me in the gospel. ²³I hope therefore to send him just as soon as I see how it will go with me; ²⁴and I trust in the Lord that shortly I myself shall come also.

25 I have thought it necessary to send to you Epaphrodi'tus my brother and fellow worker and fellow soldier, and your messenger and minister to my need, ²⁶for he has been longing for you all, and has been distressed because you heard that he was ill. ²⁷Indeed he was ill, near to death. But God had mercy on him, and not only on him but on me also, lest I should have sorrow upon sorrow. ²⁸I am the more eager to send him, therefore, that you may rejoice at seeing him again, and that I may be less anxious. ²⁹So receive him in the Lord with all joy; and honor such men, ³⁰for he nearly died for the work of Christ, risking his life to complete your service to me.

Loss of All to Gain Christ

3 Finally, my brethren, rejoice in the Lord. To write the same things to you is not irksome to me, and is safe for you.

2 Look out for the dogs, look out for the evil-workers, look out for those who mutilate the flesh. ³For we are the true circumcision, who worship God in spirit, ᵉ and glory in Christ Jesus, and put no confidence in the flesh. ⁴Though I myself have reason for confidence in the flesh also. If any other man thinks he has reason for confidence in the flesh, I have more: ⁵circumcised on the eighth day, of the people of Israel, of the tribe of Benjamin, a Hebrew born of Hebrews; as to the law a Pharisee, ⁶as to zeal a persecutor of the Church, as to righteousness under the law blameless. ⁷But whatever gain I had, I counted as loss for the sake of Christ. ⁸Indeed I count everything as loss because of the surpassing worth of knowing Christ Jesus my Lord. For his sake I have suffered the loss of all things, and count them as refuse, in order that I may gain Christ ⁹and be found in him, not having a righteousness of my own, based on law, but that which is through faith in Christ, the righteousness from God that depends on faith; ¹⁰that I may know him and the power of his resurrection, and may share his sufferings, becoming like him in his death, ¹¹that if possible I may attain the resurrection from the dead.

Pressing toward the Goal

12 Not that I have already obtained this or am already perfect; but I press on to make it my own, because Christ Jesus has made me his own. ‡ ¹³Brethren, I do not consider that I have made it my own; but one thing I do, forgetting what lies behind and straining forward to what lies ahead, ¹⁴I press on toward the goal for the prize of the upward call of God in Christ Jesus. ¹⁵Let those of us who are mature be thus minded; and if in anything you are otherwise minded, God will reveal that also to you. ¹⁶Only let us hold true to what we have attained.

17 Brethren, join in imitating me, and mark those who so walk as you have an example in us. ¹⁸For many, of whom I have often told you and now tell you even with tears, walk as enemies of the cross of Christ. ¹⁹Their end is destruction, their god is the belly, and they glory in their shame, with minds set on earthly things. § ²⁰But our commonwealth is in heaven, and from it we

---

ᵈ Or slave.
ᵉ Other ancient authorities read worship by the Spirit of God.
2:5–8: Mt 11:29; 20:28; Jn 1:1; 2 Cor 8:9; Heb 5:8.
2:9–11: Rom 10:9; 14:9; Eph 1:20–21.
2:13: 1 Cor 15:10.
2:15: Mt 5:45, 48.
3:3: Rom 2:28–29; Gal 6:14–15.
3:4–7: Acts 8:3; 22:3–21; 23:6; 26:4–23; Rom 11:1; 2 Cor 11:18–31.
3:17: 1 Cor 4:15–17.
* 2:6, in the form of God: The Greek shows that divine attributes, and therefore nature, are implied here. It is not the divine nature he set no store by, but equality of treatment and recognition of his divinity.
† 2:7, emptied himself of this external recognition, which was his right.
‡ 3:12, made me his own: On the road to Damascus.
§ 3:19: These Judaizers made holiness a question of distinction of foods and set great store by circumcision.

await a Savior, the Lord Jesus Christ, [21]who will change our lowly body to be like his glorious body, by the power which enables him even to subject all things to himself.

Exhortations

4 Therefore, my brethren, whom I love and long for, my joy and crown, stand firm in this way in the Lord, my beloved.

2 I entreat Eu-o′dia and I entreat Syn′tyche to agree in the Lord. [3]And I also ask you, who are a true co-worker, help these women, for they have labored side by side with me in the gospel together with Clement and the rest of my fellow workers, whose names are in the book of life.

4 Rejoice in the Lord always; again I will say, Rejoice. [5]Let all men know your forbearance. The Lord is at hand. [6]Have no anxiety about anything, but in everything by prayer and supplication with thanksgiving let your requests be made known to God. [7]And the peace of God, which passes all understanding, will keep your hearts and your minds in Christ Jesus.

8 Finally, brethren, whatever is true, whatever is honorable, whatever is just, whatever is pure, whatever is lovely, whatever is gracious, if there is any excellence, if there is anything worthy of praise, think about these things. [9]What you have learned and received and heard and seen in me, do; and the God of peace will be with you.

Acknowledgment of the Philippians′ Gifts

10 I rejoice in the Lord greatly that now at length you have revived your concern for me; you were indeed concerned for me, but you had no opportunity. [11]Not that I complain of want; for I have learned, in whatever state I am, to be content. [12]I know how to be abased, and I know how to abound; in any and all circumstances I have learned the secret of facing plenty and hunger, abundance and want. [13]I can do all things in him who strengthens me.

14 Yet it was kind of you to share my trouble. [15]And you Philippians yourselves know that in the beginning of the gospel, when I left Macedonia, no church entered into partnership with me in giving and receiving except you only; [16]for even in Thessaloni′ca you sent me help [f] once and again. [17]Not that I seek the gift; but I seek the fruit which increases to your credit. [18]I have received full payment, and more; I am filled, having received from Epaphrodi′tus the gifts you sent, a fragrant offering, a sacrifice acceptable and pleasing to God. [19]And my God will supply every need of yours according to his riches in glory in Christ Jesus. [20]To our God and Father be glory for ever and ever. Amen.

Final Greetings and Benediction

21 Greet every saint in Christ Jesus. The brethren who are with me greet you. [22]All the saints greet you, especially those of Caesar's household.

23 The grace of the Lord Jesus Christ be with your spirit.

---

[f] Other ancient authorities read *money for my needs.*
3:21: 1 Cor 15:35–58; Col 3:4.
4:3: Lk 10:20.
4:6: Mt 6:25–34.
4:9: Rom 15:33.
4:10: 2 Cor 11:9.
4:13: 2 Cor 12:9.
4:16: Acts 17:1–9; 1 Thess 2:9.
4:23: Gal 6:18; Philem 25.

COLOSSIANS

Salutation

1 Paul, an apostle of Christ Jesus by the will of God, and Timothy our brother,

2 To the saints and faithful brethren in Christ at Colos'sae:

Grace to you and peace from God our Father.

Gratitude for the Colossians' Faith

3 We always thank God, the Father of our Lord Jesus Christ, when we pray for you, [4]because we have heard of your faith in Christ Jesus and of the love which you have for all the saints, [5]because of the hope laid up for you in heaven. Of this you have heard before in the word of the truth, the gospel [6]which has come to you, as indeed in the whole world it is bearing fruit and growing—so among yourselves, from the day you heard and understood the grace of God in truth, [7]as you learned it from Ep'aphras our beloved fellow servant. He is a faithful minister of Christ on our [a] behalf [8]and has made known to us your love in the Spirit.

9 And so, from the day we heard of it, we have not ceased to pray for you, asking that you may be filled with the knowledge of his will in all spiritual wisdom and understanding, [10]to lead a life worthy of the Lord, fully pleasing to him, bearing fruit in every good work and increasing in the knowledge of God. [11]May you be strengthened with all power, according to his glorious might, for all endurance and patience with joy, [12]giving thanks to the Father, who has qualified us [b] to share in the inheritance of the saints in light. [13]He has delivered us from the dominion of darkness and transferred us to the kingdom of his beloved Son, [14]in whom we have redemption, the forgiveness of sins.

The Supremacy of Christ

15 He is the image of the invisible God, the first-born * of all creation; [16]for in him all things were created, in heaven and on earth, visible and invisible, whether thrones or dominions or principalities or authorities—all things were created through him and for him. [17]He is before all things, and in him all things hold together. [18]He is the head of the body, the Church; he is the beginning, the first-born from the dead, that in everything he † might be pre-eminent. [19]For in him all the fulness of God was pleased to dwell, [20]and through him to reconcile to himself all things, whether on earth or in heaven, making peace by the blood of his cross.

21 And you, who once were estranged and hostile in mind, doing evil deeds, [22]he has now reconciled in his body of flesh by his death, in order to present you holy and blameless and irreproachable before him, [23]provided that you continue in the faith, stable and steadfast, not shifting from the hope of the gospel which you heard, which has been preached to every creature under heaven, and of which I, Paul, became a minister.

Paul's Sufferings and Ministry

24 Now I rejoice in my sufferings for your sake, and in my flesh I complete what is lacking ‡ in Christ's afflictions for the sake of his body, that is, the Church, [25]of which I became a minister according to the divine office which was given to me for you, to make the word of God fully known, [26]the mystery hidden for ages and generations [c] but now made manifest to his saints. [27]To them God chose to make known how great among the Gentiles are the riches of the glory of this mystery, which is Christ in you, the hope of glory. [28]Him we proclaim, warning every man and teaching every man in all wisdom, that we may present every man mature in Christ. [29]For this I toil, striving with all the energy which he mightily inspires within me.

2 For I want you to know how greatly I strive for you, and for those at La-odice'a, and for all who have not seen my face, [2]that their hearts may be encouraged as they are knit together in love, to have all the riches of assured understanding and the knowledge of God's mystery, of Christ, [3]in whom are hidden all the treasures of wisdom and knowledge. [4]I say this in order that no one may delude you with beguiling

---

[a] Other ancient authorities read *your*.
[b] Other ancient authorities read *you*.
[c] Or *from angels and men*.
1:2: Rom 1:7.
1:3: Eph 1:16.
1:7: Col 4:12; Philem 23.
1:9: Eph 1:15–17.
1:13: Eph 1:21; 2:2.
1:15: 2 Cor 4:4.
1:17: Prov 8:22–31.
1:18: Eph 4:15.
1:25: Eph 3:2.
1:26: Eph 3:9.
2:3: Is 45:3.
* 1:15, *first-born*: Born of the Father before all ages. The reference here is to the divine person of the Word; see verse 16.
† 1:18: His human nature.
‡ 1:24, *what is lacking*: Christ's sufferings were, of course, sufficient for our redemption, but all of us may add ours to his, in order that the fruits of his redemption be applied to the souls of men.

speech. ⁵For though I am absent in body, yet I am with you in spirit, rejoicing to see your good order and the firmness of your faith in Christ.

Fulness of Life in Christ

6 As therefore you received Christ Jesus the Lord, so live in him, ⁷rooted and built up in him and established in the faith, just as you were taught, abounding in thanksgiving.

Warnings against False Teachers

8 See to it that no one makes a prey of you by philosophy and empty deceit, according to human tradition, according to the elemental spirits of the universe, and not according to Christ. ⁹For in him the whole fulness of deity dwells bodily, ¹⁰and you have come to fulness of life in him, who is the head of all rule and authority. ¹¹In him also you were circumcised with a circumcision made without hands, by putting off the body of flesh in the circumcision of Christ; ¹²and you were buried with him in baptism, in which you were also raised with him through faith in the working of God, who raised him from the dead. ¹³And you, who were dead in trespasses and the uncircumcision of your flesh, God made alive together with him, having forgiven us all our trespasses, ¹⁴having canceled the bond which stood against us with its legal demands; this he set aside, nailing it to the cross. ¹⁵He disarmed the principalities and powers and made a public example of them, triumphing over them in him. ᵈ

16 Therefore let no one pass judgment on you in questions of food and drink or with regard to a festival or a new moon or a sabbath. ¹⁷These are only a shadow of what is to come; but the substance belongs to Christ. ¹⁸Let no one disqualify you, insisting on self-abasement and worship of angels, taking his stand on visions, puffed up without reason by his sensuous mind, ¹⁹and not holding fast to the Head, from whom the whole body, nourished and knit together through its joints and ligaments, grows with a growth that is from God.

20 If with Christ you died to the elemental spirits of the universe, why do you live as if you still belonged to the world? Why do you submit to regulations, ²¹"Do not handle, Do not taste, Do not touch" ²²(referring to things which all perish as they are used), according to human precepts and doctrines? ²³These have indeed an appearance of wisdom in promoting rigor of devotion and self-abasement and severity to the body, but they are of no value in checking the indulgence of the flesh. ᵉ

New Life in Christ

3 If then you have been raised with Christ, seek the things that are above, where Christ is, seated at the right hand of God. ²Set your minds on things that are above, not on things that are on earth. ³For you have died, and your life is hidden with Christ in God. ⁴When Christ who is our life appears, then you also will appear with him in glory.

5 Put to death therefore what is earthly in you: immorality, impurity, passion, evil desire, and covetousness, which is idolatry. ⁶On account of these the wrath of God is coming. ᶠ ⁷In these you once walked, when you lived in them. ⁸But now put them all away: anger, wrath, malice, slander, and foul talk from your mouth. ⁹Do not lie to one another, seeing that you have put off the old man with his practices ¹⁰and have put on the new man, who is being renewed in knowledge after the image of his creator. ¹¹Here there cannot be Greek and Jew, circumcised and uncircumcised, barbarian, Scyth′ian, slave, free man, but Christ is all, and in all.

12 Put on then, as God's chosen ones, holy and beloved, compassion, kindness, lowliness, meekness, and patience, ¹³forbearing one another and, if one has a complaint against another, forgiving each other; as the Lord has forgiven you, so you also must forgive. ¹⁴And over all these put on love, which binds everything together in perfect harmony. ¹⁵And let the peace of Christ rule in your hearts, to which indeed you were called in the one body. And be thankful. ¹⁶Let the word of Christ dwell in you richly, as you teach and admonish one another in all wisdom, and as you sing psalms and hymns and spiritual songs with thankfulness in your hearts to God. ¹⁷And whatever you do, in word or deed, do everything in the name of the Lord Jesus, giving thanks to God the Father through him.

Rules for Christian Households

18 * Wives, be subject to your husbands, as is fitting in the Lord. ¹⁹Husbands, love your wives, and do not be harsh with them. ²⁰Children, obey your parents in everything, for this pleases the Lord. ²¹Fathers, do not provoke your children, lest they become discouraged. ²²Slaves, obey in everything those who are your earthly masters, not with eyeservice, as men-pleasers, but in singleness of heart, fearing the Lord. ²³Whatever your task, work heartily, as serving the Lord and not men, ²⁴knowing that from the Lord you

---

ᵈ Or *in it* (that is, the cross).
ᵉ Or *are of no value, serving only to indulge the flesh*.
ᶠ Other ancient authorities add *upon the sons of disobedience*.
2:10: Eph 1:21–22.
2:15: Eph 1:21.
2:16: Rom 14:1–12.
2:17: Eph 1:23.
2:19: Eph 1:22; 4:16.
2:20: Gal 4:3.
2:22: Is 29:13; Mk 7:7.
3:1: Ps 110:1.
3:10: Gen 1:26.
3:12–13: Eph 4:2.
3:16–17: Eph 5:19.
3:18–4:1: Eph 5:22—6:9.
3:23: Rom 12:11.
* 3:18—4:5: The whole passage corresponds closely to Eph 5:22—6:9.

will receive the inheritance as your reward; you are serving the Lord Christ. [25]For the wrongdoer will be paid back for the wrong he has done, and there is no partiality.

4 Masters, treat your slaves justly and fairly, knowing that you also have a Master in heaven.

Further Instructions

2 Continue steadfastly in prayer, being watchful in it with thanksgiving; [3]and pray for us also, that God may open to us a door for the word, to declare the mystery of Christ, on account of which I am in prison, [4]that I may make it clear, as I ought to speak.

5 Conduct yourselves wisely toward outsiders, making the most of the time. [6]Let your speech always be gracious, seasoned with salt, so that you may know how you ought to answer every one.

Final Greetings and Benediction

7 Tych'icus will tell you all about my affairs; he is a beloved brother and faithful minister and fellow servant in the Lord. [8]I have sent him to you for this very purpose, that you may know how we are and that he may encourage your hearts, [9]and with him Ones'imus, the faithful and beloved brother, who is one of yourselves. They will tell you of everything that has taken place here.

10 Aristar'chus my fellow prisoner greets you, and Mark the cousin of Barnabas * (concerning whom you have received instructions—if he comes to you, receive him), [11]and Jesus who is

called Justus. These are the only men of the circumcision among my fellow workers for the kingdom of God, and they have been a comfort to me. [12]Ep'aphras, who is one of yourselves, a servant ᵍ of Christ Jesus, greets you, always remembering you earnestly in his prayers, that you may stand mature and fully assured in all the will of God. [13]For I bear him witness that he has worked hard for you and for those in La-odice'a and in Hierap'olis. [14]Luke the beloved physician † and Demas greet you. [15]Give my greetings to the brethren at La-odice'a, and to Nympha and the church in her house. [16]And when this letter has been read among you, have it read also in the Church of the La-odice'ans; and see that you read also the letter from La-odice'a. [17]And say to Archip'pus, "See that you fulfil the ministry which you have received in the Lord."

18 I, Paul, write this greeting with my own hand. Remember my chains. Grace be with you.

ᵍ Or slave.
4:1: Lev 25:43, 53.
4:2: Rom 12:12.
4:5: Eph 5:16.
4:7–8: Eph 6:21–22.
4:9: Philem 10.
4:10–11: Acts 19:29; 27:2; Philem 24.
4:12: Col 1:7; Philem 23.
4:14: 2 Tim 4:10–11; Philem 24.
4:18: 1 Cor 16:21.
* 4:10: Mark, the evangelist, and, probably, the John Mark of Acts 12:12, 25.
† 4:14: Luke, the evangelist.

THE FIRST LETTER OF PAUL TO THE
THESSALONIANS

Salutation

1 Paul, Silva'nus, and Timothy, *
To the Church of the Thessalo'nians in God the Father and the Lord Jesus Christ:
Grace to you and peace.

The Thessalonians' Faith and Example

2 We give thanks to God always for you all, constantly mentioning you in our prayers, ³remembering before our God and Father your work of faith and labor of love and steadfastness of hope in our Lord Jesus Christ. ⁴For we know, brethren beloved by God, that he has chosen you; ⁵for our gospel came to you not only in word, but also in power and in the Holy Spirit and with full conviction. You know what kind of men we proved to be among you for your sake. ⁶And you became imitators of us and of the Lord, for you received the word in much affliction, with joy inspired by the Holy Spirit; ⁷so that you became an example to all the believers in Macedonia and in Acha'ia. ⁸For not only has the word of the Lord sounded forth from you in Macedonia and Acha'ia, but your faith in God has gone forth everywhere, so that we need not say anything. ⁹For they themselves report concerning us what a welcome we had among you, and how you turned to God from idols, to serve a living and true God, ¹⁰and to wait for his Son from heaven, whom he raised from the dead, Jesus who delivers us from the wrath to come.

Paul's Ministry in Thessalonica

2 For you yourselves know, brethren, that our visit to you was not in vain; ²but though we had already suffered and been shamefully treated at Philip'pi, as you know, we had courage in our God to declare to you the gospel of God in the face of great opposition. ³For our appeal does not spring from error or uncleanness, nor is it made with guile; ⁴but just as we have been approved by God to be entrusted with the gospel, so we speak, not to please men, but to please God who tests our hearts. ⁵For we never used either words of flattery, as you know, or a cloak for greed, as God is witness; ⁶nor did we seek glory from men, whether from you or from others, though we might have made demands as apostles of Christ. ⁷But we were gentle ᵃ among you, like a nurse taking care of her children. ⁸So, being affectionately desirous of you, we were ready to share with you not only the gospel of God but

also our own selves, because you had become very dear to us.

9 For you remember our labor and toil, brethren; we worked night and day, that we might not burden any of you, while we preached to you the gospel of God. ¹⁰You are witnesses, and God also, how holy and righteous and blameless was our behavior to you believers; ¹¹for you know how, like a father with his children, we exhorted each one of you and encouraged you and charged you ¹²to walk in a manner worthy of God, who calls you into his own kingdom and glory.

13 And we also thank God constantly for this, that when you received the word of God which you heard from us, you accepted it not as the word of men but as what it really is, the word of God, which is at work in you believers. ¹⁴For you, brethren, became imitators of the churches of God in Christ Jesus which are in Judea; for you suffered the same things from your own countrymen as they did from the Jews, ¹⁵who killed both the Lord Jesus and the prophets, and drove us out, and displease God and oppose all men ¹⁶by hindering us from speaking to the Gentiles that they may be saved—so as always to fill up the measure of their sins. But God's wrath has come upon them at last! ᵇ

Paul's Desire to Visit
the Thessalonians Again

17 But since we were deprived of you, brethren, for a short time, in person not in heart, we

---

ᵃ Other ancient authorities read *infants.*
ᵇ Or *completely,* or *for ever.*
1:1: 2 Thess 1:1; 2 Cor 1:19; Acts 16:1; 17:1; Rom 1:7.
1:2: 2 Thess 1:3; 2:13; Rom 1:9.
1:3: 2 Thess 1:11; 1:3; Rom 8:25; 15:4; Gal 1:4.
1:4: 2 Thess 2:13; Rom 1:7; 2 Pet 1:10.
1:5: 2 Thess 2:14; Rom 15:19.
1:6: Col 2:2; 1 Thess 2:10; 1 Cor 4:16; 11:1; Acts 17:5–10; 13:52.
1:7: Rom 15:26; Acts 18:12.
1:8: 2 Thess 3:1; Rom 1:8.
1:10: Mt 3:7.
2:2: Acts 16:19–24; 17:1–9; Rom 1:1.
2:5: Acts 20:33.
2:6: 1 Cor 9:1.
2:7: 1 Thess 2:11; Gal 4:19.
2:8: 2 Cor 12:15; 1 Jn 3:16.
2:11: 1 Cor 4:14.
2:12: 1 Pet 5:10.
2:13: 1 Thess 1:2.
2:14: 1 Thess 1:6; 1 Cor 7:17; Gal 1:22; Acts 17:5; 2 Thess 1:4.
2:15: Lk 24:20; Acts 2:23; 7:52.
2:16: Acts 9:23; 13:45, 50; 14:2, 5, 19; 17:5, 13; 18:12; 21:21, 27; 25:2, 7; 1 Cor 10:33; Gen 15:16; 1 Thess 1:10.
2:17: 1 Cor 5:3.
* 1:1: Paul joins with himself two who had evangelized Thessalonica with him.

endeavored the more eagerly and with great desire to see you face to face; [18]because we wanted to come to you—I, Paul,* again and again—but Satan hindered us. [19]For what is our hope or joy or crown of boasting before our Lord Jesus at his coming? Is it not you? [20]For you are our glory and joy.

3 Therefore when we could bear it no longer, we were willing to be left behind at Athens alone, [2]and we sent Timothy, our brother and God's servant in the gospel of Christ, to establish you in your faith and to exhort you, [3]that no one be moved by these afflictions. You yourselves know that this is to be our lot. [4]For when we were with you, we told you beforehand that we were to suffer affliction; just as it has come to pass, and as you know. [5]For this reason, when I could bear it no longer, I sent that I might know your faith, for fear that somehow the tempter had tempted you and that our labor would be in vain.

Timothy's Good Report

6 But now that Timothy has come to us from you, and has brought us the good news of your faith and love and reported that you always remember us kindly and long to see us, as we long to see you—[7]for this reason, brethren, in all our distress and affliction we have been comforted about you through your faith; [8]for now we live, if you stand fast in the Lord. [9]For what thanksgiving can we render to God for you, for all the joy which we feel for your sake before our God, [10]praying earnestly night and day that we may see you face to face and supply what is lacking in your faith?

11 Now may our God and Father himself, and our Lord Jesus, direct our way to you; [12]and may the Lord make you increase and abound in love to one another and to all men, as we do to you, [13]so that he may establish your hearts unblamable in holiness before our God and Father, at the coming of our Lord Jesus with all his saints.

A Life Pleasing to God

4 Finally, brethren, we beg and exhort you in the Lord Jesus, that as you learned from us how you ought to walk and to please God, just as you are doing, you do so more and more. [2]For you know what instructions we gave you through the Lord Jesus. [3]For this is the will of God, your sanctification: † that you abstain from immorality; ‡ [4]that each one of you know how to control his own body in holiness and honor, [5]not in the passion of lust like heathens who do not know God; [6]that no man transgress, and wrong his brother in this matter, [c] because the Lord is an avenger in all these things, as we solemnly forewarned you. [7]For God has not called us for uncleanness, but in holiness. [8]Therefore whoever disregards this, disregards not man but God, who gives his Holy Spirit to you.

9 But concerning love of the brethren you have no need to have any one write to you, for you yourselves have been taught by God to love one another; [10]and indeed you do love all the brethren throughout Macedonia. But we exhort you, brethren, to do so more and more, [11]to aspire to live quietly, to mind your own affairs, and to work with your hands, as we charged you; § [12]so that you may command the respect of outsiders, and be dependent on nobody.

The Coming of the Lord

13 But we would not have you ignorant, brethren, concerning those who are asleep, that you may not grieve as others do who have no hope. ** [14]For since we believe that Jesus died and rose again, even so, through Jesus, God will bring with him those who have fallen asleep. [15]For this we declare to you by the word of the Lord, that we who are alive, who are left until the coming of the Lord, shall not precede those who have fallen asleep. [16]For the Lord himself will descend from heaven with a cry of command, with the archangel's call, and with the sound of the trumpet of God. And the dead in Christ will rise first; [17]then we who are alive, who are left, shall be caught up together with them in the clouds to meet the Lord in the air; and so we shall always be with the Lord. †† [18]Therefore comfort one another with these words.

5 But as to the times and the seasons, brethren, you have no need to have anything written to you. [2]For you yourselves know well that the day of the Lord will come like a thief in the night. [3]When people say, "There is peace and security," then sudden destruction will come upon them as labor pains come upon a woman with child,

---

[c] Or *defraud his brother in business.*
2:19: Phil 4:1; 1 Thess 3:13; 4:15; 5:23; Mt 16:27; Mk 8:38.
2:20: 2 Cor 1:14.
3:1: Phil 2:19; Acts 17:15.
3:2: 2 Cor 1:1; Col 1:1.
3:3: Acts 14:22.
3:4: 1 Thess 2:14.
3:5: Mt 4:3; Phil 2:16.
3:6: Acts 18:5.
3:13: 1 Cor 1:8; 1 Thess 2:19; 4:17.
4:3: 1 Cor 6:18.
4:4: 1 Cor 7:2; 1 Pet 3:7.
4:11: 2 Thess 3:12; Eph 4:28; 2 Thess 3:10–12.
4:13: Eph 2:12.
4:14: 2 Cor 4:14.
4:16: Mt 24:31; 1 Cor 15:23; 2 Thess 2:1.
5:1: Acts 1:7.
5:2: 1 Cor 1:8.
5:3: 2 Thess 1:9.
* 2:18, *I, Paul:* He distinguishes himself from Silvanus and Timothy.
† 4:3, *sanctification:* With special reference to the practice of purity, especially difficult to those newly converted from paganism.
‡ 4:3, *immorality:* i.e., sexual immorality.
§ 4:11: The Thessalonians thought that the second Coming of Christ was at hand and tended to neglect their daily duties. He corrects this misconception.
** 4:13: Paul tells them that those who died before Christ's second Coming are no worse off than those who will still be alive at his coming.
†† 4:17: i.e., we who are alive shall go out to meet him and accompany him back on his return to this earth.

and there will be no escape. [4]But you are not in darkness, brethren, for that day to surprise you like a thief. [5]For you are all sons of light and sons of the day; we are not of the night or of darkness. [6]So then let us not sleep, as others do, but let us keep awake and be sober. [7]For those who sleep sleep at night, and those who get drunk are drunk at night. [8]But, since we belong to the day, let us be sober, and put on the breastplate of faith and love, and for a helmet the hope of salvation. [9]For God has not destined us for wrath, but to obtain salvation through our Lord Jesus Christ, [10]who died for us so that whether we wake or sleep we might live with him. [11]Therefore encourage one another and build one another up, just as you are doing.

Final Exhortations, Greetings, and Benediction

[12]But we beg you, brethren, to respect those who labor among you and are over you in the Lord and admonish you, [13]and to esteem them very highly in love because of their work. Be at peace among yourselves. [c2] [14]And we exhort you, brethren, admonish the idle, encourage the fainthearted, help the weak, be patient with them all. [15]See that none of you repays evil for evil, but always seek to do good to one another and to all. [16]Rejoice always, [17]pray constantly, [18]give thanks in all circumstances; for this is the will of God in Christ Jesus for you. [19]Do not quench the Spirit, [20]do not despise prophesying, [21]but test every-

thing; hold fast what is good, [22]abstain from every form of evil.

23 May the God of peace himself sanctify you wholly; and may your spirit and soul and body be kept sound and blameless at the coming of our Lord Jesus Christ. [24]He who calls you is faithful, and he will do it.

25 Brethren, pray for us.

26 Greet all the brethren with a holy kiss.

27 I adjure you by the Lord that this letter be read to all the brethren.

28 The grace of our Lord Jesus Christ be with you.

---

c2 Or *with them.*
5:4: 1 Jn 2:8; Acts 26:18.
5:5: Lk 16:8.
5:6: Rom 13:11; 1 Pet 1:13.
5:7: Acts 2:15; 2 Pet 2:13.
5:8: Eph 6:14, 23, 17; Rom 8:24.
5:9: 1 Thess 1:10; 2 Thess 2:13; Rom 14:9.
5:12: 1 Cor 16:18; 1 Tim 5:17; 1 Cor 16:16; Rom 16:6, 12; 1 Cor 15:10; Heb 13:17.
5:13: Mk 9:50.
5:14: Is 35:4; Rom 14:1; 1 Cor 8:7; 2 Thess 3:6, 7, 11.
5:15: Rom 12:17; 1 Pet 3:9.
5:16: Phil 4:4.
5:17: Eph 6:18.
5:18: Eph 5:20.
5:19: Eph 4:30.
5:20: 1 Cor 14:31.
5:21: 1 Cor 14:29; 1 Jn 4:1.
5:23: Rom 15:33.
5:26: Rom 16:16.
5:27: Col 4:16.
5:28: Rom 16:20; 2 Thess 3:18.

THE SECOND LETTER OF PAUL TO THE
THESSALONIANS

Salutation

1 Paul, Silva'nus, and Timothy,
To the Church of the Thessalo'nians in God our Father and the Lord Jesus Christ:

2 Grace to you and peace from God the Father and the Lord Jesus Christ.

Thanksgiving

3 We are bound to give thanks to God always for you, brethren, as is fitting, because your faith is growing abundantly, and the love of every one of you for one another is increasing. ⁴Therefore we ourselves boast of you in the churches of God for your steadfastness and faith in all your persecutions and in the afflictions which you are enduring.

The Judgment at Christ's Coming

5 This is evidence of the righteous judgment of God, that you may be made worthy of the kingdom of God, for which you are suffering—⁶since indeed God deems it just to repay with affliction those who afflict you, ⁷and to grant rest with us to you who are afflicted, when the Lord Jesus is revealed from heaven with his mighty angels in flaming fire, ⁸inflicting vengeance upon those who do not know God and upon those who do not obey the gospel of our Lord Jesus. ⁹They shall suffer the punishment of eternal destruction and exclusion from the presence of the Lord and from the glory of his might, ¹⁰when he comes on that day to be glorified in his saints, and to be marveled at in all who have believed, because our testimony to you was believed. ¹¹To this end we always pray for you, that our God may make you worthy of his call, and may fulfil every good resolve and work of faith by his power, ¹²so that the name of our Lord Jesus may be glorified in you, and you in him, according to the grace of our God and the Lord Jesus Christ.

The Man of Lawlessness

2 Now concerning the coming of our Lord Jesus Christ and our assembling to meet him, we beg you, brethren, ²not to be quickly shaken in mind or excited, either by spirit or by word, or by letter purporting to be from us, to the effect that the day of the Lord has come. * ³Let no one deceive you in any way; for that day will not come, unless the rebellion comes first, and the man of lawlessness ª † is revealed, the son of perdition, ⁴who opposes and exalts himself against every so-called god or object of worship, so that he

takes his seat in the temple of God, proclaiming himself to be God. ⁵Do you not remember that when I was still with you I told you this? ⁶And you know what is restraining him now so that he may be revealed in his time. ⁷For the mystery of lawlessness is already at work; only he who now restrains it will do so until he is out of the way. ‡ ⁸And then the lawless one will be revealed, and the Lord Jesus will slay him with the breath of his mouth and destroy him by his appearing and his coming. ⁹The coming of the lawless one by the activity of Satan will be with all power and with pretended signs and wonders, ¹⁰and with all wicked deception for those who are to perish, because they refused to love the truth and so be saved. ¹¹Therefore God sends upon them a strong delusion, to make them believe what is false, ¹²so that all may be condemned who did not believe the truth but had pleasure in unrighteousness.

Chosen for Salvation

13 But we are bound to give thanks to God always for you, brethren beloved by the Lord, because God chose you from the beginning ᵇ to be saved through sanctification by the Spirit ᶜ and belief in the truth. ¹⁴To this he called you through our gospel, so that you may obtain the glory of our Lord Jesus Christ. ¹⁵So then, brethren, stand firm and hold to the traditions which you were taught by us, either by word of mouth or by letter.

16 Now may our Lord Jesus Christ himself, and God our Father, who loved us and gave us eternal comfort and good hope through grace,

---

ª Other ancient authorities read *sin.*
ᵇ Other ancient authorities read *as the first converts.*
ᶜ Or *of spirit.*
1:1: 1 Thess 1:1; 2 Cor 1:19; Acts 16:1.
1:2: Rom 1:7.
1:3: 1 Thess 1:2.
1:8: Gal 4:8.
1:11: 1 Thess 1:3.
2:1: 1 Thess 4:15–17.
2:2: 2 Thess 3:17.
2:3: Eph 5:6–8; Dan 7:25; 8:25; 11:36; Rev 13:5; Jn 17:12.
2:4: Ezek 28:2.
2:5: 1 Thess 3:4.
2:8: Is 11:4.
2:9: Mt 24:24; Jn 4:48.
2:11: Rom 1:28.
2:13: 2 Thess 1:3; Eph 1:4; 1 Pet 1:2.
2:15: 1 Cor 16:13; 11:2.
2:16: 1 Thess 3:11; 1 Pet 1:3.
* 2:2: Paul warns against over-eagerness to expect the second Coming, and specifies various signs to be looked for first.
† 2:3, *the man of lawlessness*: i.e., Antichrist.
‡ 2:7: Evil will operate secretly till the final unmasking.

[17]comfort your hearts and establish them in every good work and word.

Request for Prayer

3 Finally, brethren, pray for us, that the word of the Lord may speed on and triumph, as it did among you, [2]and that we may be delivered from wicked and evil men; for not all have faith. [3]But the Lord is faithful; he will strengthen you and guard you from evil. [a] [4]And we have confidence in the Lord about you, that you are doing and will do the things which we command. [5]May the Lord direct your hearts to the love of God and to the steadfastness of Christ.

Warning against Idleness

6 Now we command you, brethren, in the name of our Lord Jesus Christ, that you keep away from any brother who is walking in idleness and not in accord with the tradition that you received from us. [7]For you yourselves know how you ought to imitate us; we were not idle when we were with you, [8]we did not eat any one's bread without paying, but with toil and labor we worked night and day, that we might not burden any of you. [9]It was not because we have not that right, but to give you in our conduct an example to imitate. [10]For even when we were with you, we gave you this command: If any one will not work, let him not eat. [11]For we hear that some of you are walking in idleness, mere busybodies, not doing any work.

[12]Now such persons we command and exhort in the Lord Jesus Christ to do their work in quietness and to earn their own living. [13]Brethren, do not be weary in well-doing.

14 If any one refuses to obey what we say in this letter, note that man, and have nothing to do with him, that he may be ashamed. [15]Do not look on him as an enemy, but warn him as a brother.

Final Greetings and Benediction

16 Now may the Lord of peace himself give you peace at all times in all ways. The Lord be with you all.

17 I, Paul, write this greeting with my own hand. This is the mark in every letter of mine; it is the way I write. [18]The grace of our Lord Jesus Christ be with you all.

---

[a] Or *the Evil One.*
3:1: 1 Thess 5:25; 1:8.
3:2: Rom 15:31.
3:3: 1 Cor 1:9; 1 Thess 5:24.
3:6: 1 Cor 5:4, 5, 11; 1 Thess 5:14.
3:7: 1 Thess 1:6, 9.
3:8: 1 Thess 2:9; Acts 18:3; Eph 4:28.
3:9: 2 Thess 3:7.
3:10: 1 Thess 4:11.
3:11: 2 Thess 3:6.
3:12: 1 Thess 4:1, 11.
3:13: Gal 6:9.
3:16: Ruth 2:4.
3:17: 1 Cor 16:21.
3:18: Rom 16:20; 1 Thess 5:28.

TIMOTHY

Salutation

1 Paul, an apostle of Christ Jesus by command of God our Savior and of Christ Jesus our hope,

2 To Timothy, my true child in the faith: *

Grace, mercy, and peace from God the Father and Christ Jesus our Lord.

Warning against False Teachers

3 As I urged you when I was going to Macedonia, remain at Ephesus that you may charge certain persons not to teach any different doctrine, [4]nor to occupy themselves with myths and endless genealogies † which promote speculations rather than the divine training [a] that is in faith; [5]whereas the aim of our charge is love that issues from a pure heart and a good conscience and sincere faith. [6]Certain persons by swerving from these have wandered away into vain discussion, [7]desiring to be teachers of the law, without understanding either what they are saying or the things about which they make assertions.

8 Now we know that the law is good, if any one uses it lawfully, [9]understanding this, that the law is not laid down for the just but for the lawless and disobedient, for the ungodly and sinners, for the unholy and profane, for murderers of fathers and murderers of mothers, for manslayers, [10]immoral persons, sodomites, kidnapers, liars, perjurers, and whatever else is contrary to sound doctrine, [11]in accordance with the glorious gospel of the blessed God with which I have been entrusted.

Gratitude for Mercy

12 I thank him who has given me strength for this, Christ Jesus our Lord, because he judged me faithful by appointing me to his service, [13]though I formerly blasphemed and persecuted and insulted him; but I received mercy because I had acted ignorantly in unbelief, [14]and the grace of our Lord overflowed for me with the faith and love that are in Christ Jesus. [15]The saying is sure and worthy of full acceptance, that Christ Jesus came into the world to save sinners. And I am the foremost of sinners; [16]but I received mercy for this reason, that in me, as the foremost, Jesus Christ might display his perfect patience for an example to those who were to believe in him for eternal life. [17]To the King of ages, immortal, invisible, the only God, be honor and glory for ever and ever. [b] Amen.

18 This charge I commit to you, Timothy, my son, in accordance with the prophetic utterances which pointed to you, that inspired by them you may wage the good warfare, [19]holding faith and a good conscience. By rejecting conscience, certain persons have made shipwreck of their faith, [20]among them Hymenae′us and Alexander, whom I have delivered to Satan ‡ that they may learn not to blaspheme.

Instructions concerning Prayer

2 First of all, then, I urge that supplications, prayers, intercessions, and thanksgivings be made for all men, [2]for kings and all who are in high positions, that we may lead a quiet and peaceable life, godly and respectful in every way. [3]This is good, and it is acceptable in the sight of God our Savior, [4]who desires all men to be saved and to come to the knowledge of the truth. [5]For there is one God, and there is one mediator between God and men, the man Christ Jesus, [6]who gave himself as a ransom for all, § the testimony to which was given at the proper time. [7]For this I was appointed a preacher and apostle (I am telling the truth, I am not lying), a teacher of the Gentiles in faith and truth.

8 I desire then that in every place the men should pray, lifting holy hands without anger or quarreling; [9]also that women should adorn themselves modestly and sensibly in seemly apparel, not with braided hair or gold or pearls or costly attire [10]but by good deeds, as befits women who profess religion. [11]Let a woman learn in silence with all submissiveness. [12]I permit no woman to teach or to have authority over men; she is to keep silent. [13]For Adam was formed first, then Eve; [14]and Adam was not deceived, but the woman was deceived and became a transgressor. [15]Yet woman will be saved through bearing children, [c] if she continues [d] in faith and love and holiness, with modesty.

---

[a] Or *stewardship*, or *order*.
[b] Greek *to the ages of ages*.
[c] Or *by the birth of the child*.
[d] Greek *they continue*.
2:13: Gen 2:7, 21–22.
2:14: Gen 3:1–6.
* 1:2: Timothy, son of a Greek father and a Jewish mother, was already a Christian when Paul met him (Acts 16:1). A close association ensued.
† 1:4, *myths and endless genealogies*: A reference to the Jewish legends and spurious pedigrees added by false Judaizers to the Biblical narratives; cf. the Book of Jubilees.
‡ 1:20, *delivered to Satan*: A form of excommunication; see note on 1 Cor 5:5.
§ 2:6, *ransom for all*: This is why Paul wants prayers for all (verse 1).

Qualifications of Bishops

3 The saying is sure: If any one aspires to the office of bishop,* he desires a noble task. [2]Now a bishop must be above reproach, the husband of one wife, temperate, sensible, dignified, hospitable, an apt teacher, [3]no drunkard, not violent but gentle, not quarrelsome, and no lover of money. [4]He must manage his own household well, keeping his children submissive and respectful in every way; [5]for if a man does not know how to manage his own household, how can he care for God's Church? [6]He must not be a recent convert, or he may be puffed up with conceit and fall into the condemnation of the devil; [f] [7]moreover he must be well thought of by outsiders, or he may fall into reproach and the snare of the devil. [f]

Qualifications of Deacons

8 Deacons likewise must be serious, not double-tongued, not addicted to much wine, not greedy for gain; [9]they must hold the mystery of the faith with a clear conscience. [10]And let them also be tested first; then if they prove themselves blameless let them serve as deacons. [11]The women † likewise must be serious, no slanderers, but temperate, faithful in all things. [12]Let deacons be the husband of one wife, and let them manage their children and their households well; [13]for those who serve well as deacons gain a good standing for themselves and also great confidence in the faith which is in Christ Jesus.

The Mystery of Our Religion

14 I hope to come to you soon, but I am writing these instructions to you so that, [15]if I am delayed, you may know how one ought to behave in the household of God, which is the Church of the living God, the pillar and bulwark of the truth. [16]Great indeed, we confess, is the mystery of our religion:

He [h] was manifested in the flesh,
vindicated [i] in the Spirit,
seen by angels,
preached among the nations,
believed on in the world,
taken up in glory.

False Asceticism

4 Now the Spirit expressly says that in later times some will depart from the faith by giving heed to deceitful spirits and doctrines of demons, [2]through the pretensions of liars whose consciences are seared, [3]who forbid marriage ‡ and enjoin abstinence from foods § which God created to be received with thanksgiving by those who believe and know the truth. [4]For everything created by God is good, and nothing is to be rejected if it is received with thanksgiving; [5]for then it is consecrated by the word of God and prayer.

A Good Minister of Jesus Christ

6 If you put these instructions before the brethren, you will be a good minister of Christ Jesus, nourished on the words of the faith and of the good doctrine which you have followed. [7]Have nothing to do with godless and silly myths. Train yourself in godliness; [8]for while bodily training is of some value, godliness is of value in every way, as it holds promise for the present life and also for the life to come. [9]The saying is sure and worthy of full acceptance. [10]For to this end we toil and strive, [j] because we have our hope set on the living God, who is the Savior of all men, especially of those who believe.

11 Command and teach these things. [12]Let no one despise your youth, but set the believers an example in speech and conduct, in love, in faith, in purity. [13]Till I come, attend to the public reading of Scripture, to preaching, to teaching. [14]Do not neglect the gift you have, which was given you by prophetic utterance when the elders laid their hands upon you. [15]Practice these duties, devote yourself to them, so that all may see your progress. [16]Take heed to yourself and to your teaching; hold to that, for by so doing you will save both yourself and your hearers.

Duties toward Believers

5 Do not rebuke an older man but exhort him as you would a father; treat younger men like brothers, [2]older women like mothers, younger women like sisters, in all purity.

3 Honor widows who are real widows.** [4]If a widow has children or grandchildren, let them first learn their religious duty to their own family and make some return to their parents; for this is acceptable in the sight of God. [5]She who is a real widow, and is left all alone, has set her hope on God and continues in supplications and prayers night and day; [6]whereas she who is self-indulgent is dead even while she lives. [7]Command this, so that they may be without reproach. [8]If any one does not provide for his relatives, and especially for his own family, he has disowned the faith and is worse than an unbeliever.

9 Let a widow be enrolled if she is not less than sixty years of age, having been the wife of one husband; [10]and she must be well attested for her good deeds, as one who has brought up children, shown hospitality, washed the feet of the saints, relieved the afflicted, and devoted herself to doing good in every way. [11]But refuse to enrol younger widows; for when they grow wanton against Christ they desire to marry, [12]and so they incur condemnation for having violated their first

---

[f] Or *slanderer*.
[h] Greek *Who*; other ancient authorities read *God*; others, *Which*.
[i] Or *justified*.
[j] Other ancient authorities read *suffer reproach*.
* 3:1, *bishop*: At this time an office probably not distinct from that of priest.
† 3:11, *women*: i.e., deaconesses.
‡ 4:3, *forbid marriage*: As some Gnostics did.
§ 4:3, *abstinence from foods*: As practiced by Judaizers.
** 5:3, *real widows*: i.e., with no one to help and support them.

pledge. * ¹³Besides that, they learn to be idlers, gadding about from house to house, and not only idlers but gossips and busybodies, saying what they should not. ¹⁴So I would have younger widows marry, bear children, rule their households, and give the enemy no occasion to revile us. ¹⁵For some have already strayed after Satan. ¹⁶If any believing woman ¹ has relatives who are widows, let her assist them; let the Church not be burdened, so that it may assist those who are real widows.

17 Let the elders who rule well be considered worthy of double honor, especially those who labor in preaching and teaching; ¹⁸for the Scripture says, "You shall not muzzle an ox when it is treading out the grain," and, "The laborer deserves his wages." ¹⁹Never admit any charge against an elder except on the evidence of two or three witnesses. ²⁰As for those who persist in sin, rebuke them in the presence of all, so that the rest may stand in fear. ²¹In the presence of God and of Christ Jesus and of the elect angels I charge you to keep these rules without favor, doing nothing from partiality. ²²Do not be hasty in the laying on of hands, nor participate in another man's sins; keep yourself pure.

23 No longer drink only water, but use a little wine for the sake of your stomach and your frequent ailments.

Men's Deeds, False Teaching, and True Riches

24 The sins of some men are conspicuous, pointing to judgment, but the sins of others appear later. ²⁵So also good deeds are conspicuous; and even when they are not, they cannot remain hidden.

6 Let all who are under the yoke of slavery regard their masters as worthy of all honor, so that the name of God and the teaching may not be defamed. ²Those who have believing masters must not be disrespectful on the ground that they are brethren; rather they must serve all the better since those who benefit by their service are believers and beloved.

Teach and urge these duties. ³If any one teaches otherwise and does not agree with the sound words of our Lord Jesus Christ and the teaching which accords with godliness, ⁴he is puffed up with conceit, he knows nothing; he has a morbid craving for controversy and for disputes about words, which produce envy, dissension, slander, base suspicions, ⁵and wrangling among men who are depraved in mind and bereft of the truth,

imagining that godliness is a means of gain. ⁶There is great gain in godliness with contentment; ⁷for we brought nothing into the world, and ᵐ we cannot take anything out of the world; ⁸but if we have food and clothing, with these we shall be content. ⁹But those who desire to be rich fall into temptation, into a snare, into many senseless and hurtful desires that plunge men into ruin and destruction. ¹⁰For the love of money is the root of all evils; it is through this craving that some have wandered away from the faith and pierced their hearts with many pangs.

The Good Fight of Faith

11 But as for you, man of God, shun all this; aim at righteousness, godliness, faith, love, steadfastness, gentleness. ¹²Fight the good fight of the faith; take hold of the eternal life to which you were called when you made the good confession in the presence of many witnesses. ¹³In the presence of God who gives life to all things, and of Christ Jesus who in his testimony before Pontius Pilate made the good confession, ¹⁴I charge you to keep the commandment unstained and free from reproach until the appearing of our Lord Jesus Christ; ¹⁵and this will be made manifest at the proper time by the blessed and only Sovereign, the King of kings and Lord of lords, ¹⁶who alone has immortality and dwells in unapproachable light, whom no man has ever seen or can see. To him be honor and eternal dominion. Amen.

17 As for the rich in this world, charge them not to be haughty, nor to set their hopes on uncertain riches but on God who richly furnishes us with everything to enjoy. ¹⁸They are to do good, to be rich in good deeds, liberal and generous, ¹⁹thus laying up for themselves a good foundation for the future, so that they may take hold of the life which is life indeed.

Personal Instructions and Benediction

20 O Timothy, guard what has been entrusted to you. Avoid the godless chatter and contradictions of what is falsely called knowledge, ²¹for by professing it some have missed the mark as regards the faith.

Grace be with you.

---

¹ Other ancient authorities read *man or woman*; others, simply *man*.
ᵐ Other ancient authorities insert *it is certain that*.
5:18: Deut 25:4; 1 Cor 9:9; Mt 10:10; Lk 10:7; 1 Cor 9:14.
5:19: Deut 19:15.
6:13: Jn 18:37.
* 5:12: Paul had no objection to widows marrying again; cf. 1 Cor 7:8–9. But the widows here had clearly made some sort of vow or promise to serve the Church in singleness. Paul recommended that younger widows should marry again (verse 14).

THE SECOND LETTER OF PAUL TO

TIMOTHY

Salutation

1 Paul, an apostle of Christ Jesus by the will of God according to the promise of the life which is in Christ Jesus,

2 To Timothy, my beloved child:

Grace, mercy, and peace from God the Father and Christ Jesus our Lord.

Thanksgiving and Encouragement

3 I thank God whom I serve with a clear conscience, as did my fathers, when I remember you constantly in my prayers. [4]As I remember your tears, I long night and day to see you, that I may be filled with joy. [5]I am reminded of your sincere faith, a faith that dwelt first in your grandmother Lois and your mother Eunice and now, I am sure, dwells in you. [6]For this reason I remind you to rekindle the gift of God that is within you through the laying on of my hands; [7]for God did not give us a spirit of timidity but a spirit of power and love and self-control.

8 Do not be ashamed then of testifying to our Lord, nor of me his prisoner, but take your share of suffering for the gospel in the power of God, [9]who saved us and called us with a holy calling, not in virtue of our works but in virtue of his own purpose and the grace which he gave us in Christ Jesus ages ago, [10]and now has manifested through the appearing of our Savior Christ Jesus, who abolished death and brought life and immortality to light through the gospel. [11]For this gospel I was appointed a preacher and apostle and teacher, [12]and therefore I suffer as I do. But I am not ashamed, for I know whom I have believed, and I am sure that he is able to guard until that Day what has been entrusted to me. [a] [13]Follow the pattern of the sound words which you have heard from me, in the faith and love which are in Christ Jesus; [14]guard the truth that has been entrusted to you by the Holy Spirit who dwells within us.

15 You are aware that all who are in Asia* turned away from me, and among them Phy'gelus and Hermog'enes. [16]May the Lord grant mercy to the household of Onesiph'orus, for he often refreshed me; he was not ashamed of my chains, [17]but when he arrived in Rome he searched for me eagerly and found me—[18]may the Lord grant him to find mercy from the Lord on that Day—and you well know all the service he rendered at Ephesus.

A Good Soldier of Christ

2 You then, my son, be strong in the grace that is in Christ Jesus, [2]and what you have heard from me before many witnesses entrust to faithful men who will be able to teach others also. [3]Take your share of suffering as a good soldier of Christ Jesus. [4]No soldier on service gets entangled in civilian pursuits, since his aim is to satisfy the one who enlisted him. [5]An athlete is not crowned unless he competes according to the rules. [6]It is the hard-working farmer who ought to have the first share of the crops. [7]Think over what I say, for the Lord will grant you understanding in everything.

8 Remember Jesus Christ, risen from the dead, descended from David, as preached in my gospel, [9]the gospel for which I am suffering and wearing chains like a criminal. But the word of God is not chained. [10]Therefore I endure everything for the sake of the elect, that they also may obtain the salvation which in Christ Jesus goes with eternal glory. [11]The saying is sure:

If we have died with him, we shall also live with him;

[12]if we endure, we shall also reign with him;

if we deny him, he also will deny us;

[13]if we are faithless, he remains faithful—

for he cannot deny himself.

A Workman Approved by God

14 Remind them of this, and charge them before the Lord [b] to avoid disputing about words, which does no good, but only ruins the hearers. [15]Do your best to present yourself to God as one approved, a workman who has no need to be ashamed, rightly handling the word of truth. [16]Avoid such godless chatter, for it will lead people into more and more ungodliness, [17]and their talk will eat its way like gangrene. Among them are Hymenae'us and Phile'tus, [18]who have swerved from the truth by holding that the resurrection is past already. † They are upsetting the faith of some. [19]But God's firm foundation stands, bearing this seal: "The Lord knows those who are his," and, "Let every one who names the name of the Lord depart from iniquity."

20 In a great house there are not only vessels of gold and silver but also of wood and earthenware, and some for noble use, some for ignoble.

---

[a] Or *what I have entrusted to him.*
[b] Other ancient authorities read *God.*
1:5: Acts 16:1.
2:19: Num 16:5; Is 26:13.
* 1:15, *Asia:* The Roman province of that name, now in western Turkey.
† 2:18: They explained the resurrection by saying it was the rising to newness of life in baptism, thus ignoring a bodily resurrection, a doctrine the Greeks found very hard to accept; cf. Acts 17:32.

[21]If any one purifies himself from what is ignoble, then he will be a vessel for noble use, consecrated and useful to the master of the house, ready for any good work. [22]So shun youthful passions and aim at righteousness, faith, love, and peace, along with those who call upon the Lord from a pure heart. [23]Have nothing to do with stupid, senseless controversies; you know that they breed quarrels. [24]And the Lord's servant must not be quarrelsome but kindly to every one, an apt teacher, forbearing, [25]correcting his opponents with gentleness. God may perhaps grant that they will repent and come to know the truth, [26]and they may escape from the snare of the devil, after being captured by him to do his will. [c]

Godlessness in the Last Days

3 But understand this, that in the last days there will come times of stress. [2]For men will be lovers of self, lovers of money, proud, arrogant, abusive, disobedient to their parents, ungrateful, unholy, [3]inhuman, implacable, slanderers, profligates, fierce, haters of good, [4]treacherous, reckless, swollen with conceit, lovers of pleasure rather than lovers of God, [5]holding the form of religion but denying the power of it. Avoid such people. [6]For among them are those who make their way into households and capture weak women, burdened with sins and swayed by various impulses, [7]who will listen to anybody and can never arrive at a knowledge of the truth. [8]As Jan'nes and Jam'bres opposed Moses, so these men also oppose the truth, men of corrupt mind and counterfeit faith; [9]but they will not get very far, for their folly will be plain to all, as was that of those two men.

Paul's Charge to Timothy

10 Now you have observed my teaching, my conduct, my aim in life, my faith, my patience, my love, my steadfastness, [11]my persecutions, my sufferings, what befell me at Antioch, at Ico'nium, and at Lystra, what persecutions I endured; yet from them all the Lord rescued me. [12]Indeed all who desire to live a godly life in Christ Jesus will be persecuted, [13]while evil men and impostors will go on from bad to worse, deceivers and deceived. [14]But as for you, continue in what you have learned and have firmly believed, knowing from whom you learned it [15]and how from childhood you have been acquainted with the Sacred Writings which are able to instruct you for salvation through faith in Christ Jesus. [16]All Scripture is inspired by God and [d] profitable for teaching, for reproof, for correction, and for training in righteousness, * [17]that the man of God may be complete, equipped for every good work.

4 I charge you in the presence of God and of Christ Jesus who is to judge the living and the dead, and by his appearing and his kingdom: [2]preach the word, be urgent in season and out of season, convince, rebuke, and exhort, be unfailing in patience and in teaching. [3]For the time is coming when people will not endure sound teaching, but having itching ears they will accumulate for themselves teachers to suit their own likings, [4]and will turn away from listening to the truth and wander into myths. [5]As for you, always be steady, endure suffering, do the work of an evangelist, fulfil your ministry.

6 For I am already on the point of being sacrificed; † the time of my departure has come. [7]I have fought the good fight, I have finished the race, I have kept the faith. [8]From now on there is laid up for me the crown of righteousness, which the Lord, the righteous judge, will award to me on that Day, and not only to me but also to all who have loved his appearing.

Personal Instructions

9 Do your best to come to me soon. [10]For Demas, in love with this present world, has deserted me and gone to Thessaloni'ca; Crescens has gone to Galatia, [e] Titus to Dalmatia. [11]Luke alone is with me. Get Mark and bring him with you; for he is very useful in serving me. [12]Tych'icus I have sent to Ephesus. [13]When you come, bring the cloak that I left with Carpus at Tro'as, also the books, and above all the parchments. [14]Alexander the coppersmith did me great harm; the Lord will pay him back for his deeds. [15]Beware of him yourself, for he strongly opposed our message. [16]At my first defense no one took my part; all deserted me. May it not be charged against them! [17]But the Lord stood by me and gave me strength to proclaim the word fully, that all the Gentiles might hear it. So I was rescued from the lion's mouth. [18]The Lord will rescue me from every evil and save me for his heavenly kingdom. To him be the glory for ever and ever. Amen.

Final Greetings and Benediction

19 Greet Prisca and Aqui'la, and the household of Onesiph'orus. [20]Eras'tus remained at Corinth; Troph'imus I left ill at Mile'tus. [21]Do your best to come before winter. Eubu'lus sends greetings to you, as do Pudens and Linus ‡ and Claudia and all the brethren.

22 The Lord be with your spirit. Grace be with you.

---

[c] Or *by him, to do his* (that is, God's) *will.*
[d] Or *Every Scripture inspired by God is also.*
[e] Other ancient authorities read *Gaul.*
3:8: Ex 7:11.
3:11: Acts 13:14–52; 14:1–20; 16:1–5.
* 3:16: Paul refers to the Old Testament Scriptures.
† 4:6, *on the point of being sacrificed*: Literally, "poured out in sacrifice" as a drink-offering or libation.
‡ 4:21, *Linus:* According to tradition, the successor of Peter in the see of Rome.

THE LETTER OF PAUL TO

TITUS

Salutation

1 Paul, a servant [a] of God and an apostle of Jesus Christ, to further the faith of God's elect and their knowledge of the truth which accords with godliness, [2]in hope of eternal life which God, who never lies, promised ages ago [3]and at the proper time manifested in his word through the preaching with which I have been entrusted by command of God our Savior;

4 To Titus, my true child in a common faith:

Grace and peace from God the Father and Christ Jesus our Savior.

Titus in Crete

5 This is why I left you in Crete, that you might amend what was defective, and appoint elders * in every town as I directed you, [6]if any man is blameless, the husband of one wife, and his children are believers and not open to the charge of debauchery and not being insubordinate. [7]For a bishop, as God's steward, must be blameless; he must not be arrogant or quick-tempered or a drunkard or violent or greedy for gain, [8]but hospitable, a lover of goodness, master of himself, upright, holy, and self-controlled; [9]he must hold firm to the sure word as taught, so that he may be able to give instruction in sound doctrine and also to confute those who contradict it. [10]For there are many insubordinate men, empty talkers and deceivers, especially the circumcision party; [11]they must be silenced, since they are upsetting whole families by teaching for base gain what they have no right to teach. [12]One of themselves, a prophet of their own, said, "Cretans are always liars, evil beasts, lazy gluttons." [13]This testimony is true. Therefore rebuke them sharply, that they may be sound in the faith, [14]instead of giving heed to Jewish myths or to commands of men who reject the truth. [15]To the pure all things are pure, but to the corrupt and unbelieving nothing is pure; their very minds and consciences are corrupted. [16]They profess to know God, but they deny him by their deeds; they are detestable, disobedient, unfit for any good deed.

Teach Sound Doctrine

2 But as for you, teach what befits sound doctrine. [2]Bid the older men be temperate, serious, sensible, sound in faith, in love, and in steadfastness. [3]Bid the older women likewise to be reverent in behavior, not to be slanderers or slaves to drink; they are to teach what is good, [4]and so train the young women to love their husbands and children, [5]to be sensible, chaste, domestic, kind, and submissive to their husbands, that the word of God may not be discredited. [6]Likewise urge the younger men to control themselves. [7]Show yourself in all respects a model of good deeds, and in your teaching show integrity, gravity, [8]and sound speech that cannot be censured, so that an opponent may be put to shame, having nothing evil to say of us. [9]Bid slaves to be submissive to their masters and to give satisfaction in every respect; they are not to talk back, [10]nor to pilfer, but to show entire and true fidelity, so that in everything they may adorn the doctrine of God our Savior.

11 For the grace of God has appeared for the salvation of all men, [12]training us to renounce irreligion and worldly passions, and to live sober, upright, and godly lives in this world, [13]awaiting our blessed hope, the appearing of the glory of our great God and Savior [c] † Jesus Christ, [14]who gave himself for us to redeem us from all iniquity and to purify for himself a people of his own who are zealous for good deeds.

15 Declare these things; exhort and reprove with all authority. Let no one disregard you.

Maintain Good Deeds

3 Remind them to be submissive to rulers and authorities, to be obedient, to be ready for any honest work, [2]to speak evil of no one, to avoid quarreling, to be gentle, and to show perfect courtesy toward all men. [3]For we ourselves were once foolish, disobedient, led astray, slaves to various passions and pleasures, passing our days in malice and envy, hated by men and hating one another; [4]but when the goodness and loving kindness of God our Savior appeared, [5]he saved us, not because of deeds done by us in righteousness, but in virtue of his own mercy, by the washing of regeneration and renewal in the Holy Spirit, [6]which he poured out upon us richly through Jesus Christ our Savior, [7]so that we might be justified by his grace and become heirs in hope of eternal life. ‡ [8]The saying is sure.

---

[a] Or *slave.*
[c] Or *of the great God and our Savior.*
1:12: Epimenides.
2:14: Ps 130:8; Ezek 37:23; Deut 14:2.
* 1:5, *elders:* Each Christian community was ruled by a body of elders.
† 2:13, *God and Savior:* Both terms appear to refer to Jesus Christ.
‡ 3:5–7: A brief and clear statement of the doctrine of justification.

I desire you to insist on these things, so that those who have believed in God may be careful to apply themselves to good deeds; [d] these are excellent and profitable to men. [9]But avoid stupid controversies, genealogies, dissensions, and quarrels over the law, for they are unprofitable and futile. [10]As for a man who is factious, after admonishing him once or twice, have nothing more to do with him, [11]knowing that such a person is perverted and sinful; he is self-condemned.

Final Messages and Benediction

[12] When I send Ar'temas or Tych'icus to you, do your best to come to me at Nicop'olis, for I have decided to spend the winter there. [13]Do your best to speed Ze'nas the lawyer and Apol'los on their way; see that they lack nothing. [14]And let our people learn to apply themselves to good deeds, [d] so as to help cases of urgent need, and not to be unfruitful.

[15] All who are with me send greetings to you. Greet those who love us in the faith.

Grace be with you all.

---

[d] Or *enter honorable occupations.*

THE LETTER OF PAUL TO

PHILEMON

Salutation

1 Paul, a prisoner for Christ Jesus, and Timothy our brother,

To Phile'mon our beloved fellow worker [2]and Ap'phia our sister and Archip'pus our fellow soldier, and the church in your house:

3 Grace to you and peace from God our Father and the Lord Jesus Christ.

Philemon's Love and Faith

4 I thank my God always when I remember you in my prayers, [5]because I hear of your love and of the faith which you have toward the Lord Jesus and all the saints, [6]and I pray that the sharing of your faith may promote the knowledge of all the good that is ours in Christ. [7]For I have derived much joy and comfort from your love, my brother, because the hearts of the saints have been refreshed through you.

Paul's Plea for Onesimus

8 Accordingly, though I am bold enough in Christ to command you to do what is required, [9]yet for love's sake I prefer to appeal to you—I, Paul, an ambassador [a] and now a prisoner also for Christ Jesus—[10]I appeal to you for my child, Ones'imus, [b] whose father I have become in my imprisonment. [11](Formerly he was useless to you, but now he is indeed useful to you and to me.) [12]I am sending him back to you, sending my very heart. [13]I would have been glad to keep him with me, in order that he might serve me on your behalf during my imprisonment for the gospel; [14]but I preferred to do nothing without your consent in order that your goodness might not be by compulsion but of your own free will.

15 Perhaps this is why he was parted from you for a while, that you might have him back for ever, [16]no longer as a slave but more than a slave, as a beloved brother, especially to me but how much more to you, both in the flesh and in the Lord. [17]So if you consider me your partner, receive him as you would receive me. [18]If he has wronged you at all, or owes you anything, charge that to my account. [19]I, Paul, write this with my own hand, I will repay it—to say nothing of your owing me even your own self. [20]Yes, brother, I want some benefit from you in the Lord. Refresh my heart in Christ.

21 Confident of your obedience, I write to you, knowing that you will do even more than I say. [22]At the same time, prepare a guest room for me, for I am hoping through your prayers to be granted to you.

Final Greetings and Benediction

23 Ep'aphras, my fellow prisoner in Christ Jesus, sends greetings to you, [24]and so do Mark, Aristar'chus, Demas, and Luke, my fellow workers.

25 The grace of the Lord Jesus Christ be with your spirit.

---

[a] Or an old man.
[b] The name Onesimus means useful or (compare verse 20) beneficial.
3: Rom 1:7.
4: Rom 1:8.
10: Col 4:9.
23: Col 1:7; 4:12.
24: Col 4:10, 14.

HEBREWS

God Has Spoken by His Son

1 In many and various ways God spoke of old to our fathers by the prophets; ²but in these last days he has spoken to us by a Son, whom he appointed the heir of all things, through whom also he created the ages. ³He reflects the glory of God and bears the very stamp of his nature, upholding the universe by his word of power. When he had made purification for sins, he sat down at the right hand of the Majesty on high, ⁴having become as much superior to angels as the name he has obtained is more excellent than theirs. *

The Son's Superiority to Angels

5 For to what angel did God ever say,
"You are my Son,
today I have begotten you"?
Or again,
"I will be to him a father,
and he shall be to me a son"?
⁶And again, when he brings the first-born into the world, he says,
"Let all God's angels worship him."
⁷Of the angels he says,
"Who makes his angels winds,
and his servants flames of fire."
⁸But of the Son he says,
"Your throne, O God, ᵃ is for ever and ever,
the righteous scepter is the scepter of your ᵇ
kingdom.
⁹You have loved righteousness and hated
lawlessness;
therefore God, your God, has anointed you
with the oil of gladness beyond your
comrades."
¹⁰And,
"You, Lord, founded the earth in the beginning,
and the heavens are the work of your hands;
¹¹they will perish, but you remain;
they will all grow old like a garment,
¹²like a cloak you will roll them up,
and they will be changed. ᶜ
But you are the same,
and your years will never end."
¹³But to what angel has he ever said,
"Sit at my right hand,
till I make your enemies
a stool for your feet"?
¹⁴Are they not all ministering spirits sent forth to serve, for the sake of those who are to obtain salvation?

Warning to Pay Attention

2 Therefore we must pay the closer attention to what we have heard, lest we drift away from it. ²For if the message declared by angels † was valid and every transgression or disobedience received a just retribution, ³how shall we escape if we neglect such a great salvation? It was declared at first by the Lord, and it was attested to us by those who heard him, ⁴while God also bore witness by signs and wonders and various miracles and by gifts of the Holy Spirit distributed according to his own will.

Exaltation through Suffering

5 For it was not to angels that God subjected the world to come, of which we are speaking. ⁶It has been testified somewhere,
"What is man that you are mindful of him,
or the son of man, that you care for him?
⁷You made him for a little while lower than the
angels,
you have crowned him with glory and honor, ᵈ
⁸putting everything in subjection under his
feet."
Now in putting everything in subjection to him, he left nothing outside his control. As it is, we do not yet see everything in subjection to him. ⁹But we see Jesus, who for a little while was made lower than the angels, crowned with glory and honor because of the suffering of death, so that by the grace of God he might taste death for every one.

10 For it was fitting that he, for whom and by whom all things exist, in bringing many sons to glory, should make the pioneer of their salvation perfect through suffering. ‡ ¹¹For he who

---

ᵃ Or *God is your throne.*
ᵇ Other ancient authorities read *his.*
ᶜ Other ancient authorities add *like a garment.*
ᵈ Other ancient authorities insert *and set him over the works of your hands.*
1:5: Ps 2:7; 2 Sam 7:14.
1:6: Deut 32:43 Septuagint; Ps 97:7.
1:7: Ps 104:4.
1:8–9: Ps 45:6–7.
1:10–12: Ps 102:25–27.
1:13: Ps 110:1.
2:6–9: Ps 8:4–6.
* 1:1–4: A contrast between the progressive and piecemeal revelation of the old dispensation and the complete revelation of the new given by a single representative—no mere prophet but the Son of God himself.
† 2:2, *angels:* The covenant of Sinai was thought to have been given through the angels.
‡ 2:10, *suffering:* The divinely appointed means of progress toward God; cf. verse 18.

sanctifies and those who are sanctified have all one origin. That is why he is not ashamed to call them brethren, [12]saying,

"I will proclaim your name to my brethren,
in the midst of the congregation I will praise
  you."

[13]And again,

"I will put my trust in him."

And again,

"Here am I, and the children God has given me."

14 Since therefore the children share in flesh and blood, he himself likewise partook of the same nature, that through death he might destroy him who has the power of death, that is, the devil, [15]and deliver all those who through fear of death were subject to lifelong bondage. [16]For surely it is not with angels that he is concerned but with the descendants of Abraham. [17]Therefore he had to be made like his brethren in every respect, so that he might become a merciful and faithful high priest in the service of God, to make expiation for the sins of the people. [18]For because he himself has suffered and been tempted, he is able to help those who are tempted.

Moses a Servant, Christ a Son

3 Therefore, holy brethren, who share in a heavenly call, consider Jesus, the apostle and high priest of our confession. [2]He was faithful to him who appointed him, just as Moses also was faithful in [e] God's house. [3]Yet Jesus has been counted worthy of as much more glory than Moses as the builder of a house has more honor than the house. [4](For every house is built by some one, but the builder of all things is God.) [5]Now Moses was faithful in all God's house as a servant, to testify to the things that were to be spoken later, [6]but Christ was faithful over God's [f] house as a son. And we are his house if we hold fast our confidence and pride in our hope. [g]

Warning against Unbelief

7 Therefore, as the Holy Spirit says,

"Today, when you hear his voice,
[8]do not harden your hearts as in the rebellion,
  on the day of testing in the wilderness,
[9]where your fathers put me to the test
  and saw my works for forty years.
[10]Therefore I was provoked with that generation,
  and said, 'They always go astray in their
    hearts;
they have not known my ways.'
[11]As I swore in my wrath,
'They shall never enter my rest.' " *

[12]Take care, brethren, lest there be in any of you an evil, unbelieving heart, leading you to fall away from the living God. [13]But exhort one another every day, as long as it is called "today," that none of you may be hardened by the deceitfulness of sin. [14]For we share in Christ, if only we hold our first confidence firm to the end, [15]while it is said,

"Today, when you hear his voice,
do not harden your hearts as in the rebellion."

[16]Who were they that heard and yet were rebellious? Was it not all those who left Egypt under the leadership of Moses? [17]And with whom was he provoked forty years? Was it not with those who sinned, whose bodies fell in the wilderness? [18]And to whom did he swear that they should never enter his rest, but to those who were disobedient? [19]So we see that they were unable to enter because of unbelief.

The Rest That God Promised

4 Therefore, while the promise of entering his rest remains, let us fear lest any of you be judged to have failed to reach it. [2]For good news came to us just as to them; but the message which they heard did not benefit them, because it did not meet with faith in the hearers. [h] [3]For we who have believed enter that rest, as he has said,

"As I swore in my wrath,
'They shall never enter my rest,' "

although his works were finished from the foundation of the world. [4]For he has somewhere spoken of the seventh day in this way, "And God rested on the seventh day from all his works." [5]And again in this place he said,

"They shall never enter my rest."

[6]Since therefore it remains for some to enter it, and those who formerly received the good news failed to enter because of disobedience, [7]again he sets a certain day, "Today," saying through David so long afterward, in the words already quoted,

"Today, when you hear his voice,
do not harden your hearts."

[8]For if Joshua had given them rest, God [i] would not speak later of another day. [9]So then, there remains a sabbath rest for the people of God; [10]for whoever enters God's rest also ceases from his labors as God did from his.

11 Let us therefore strive to enter that rest, that no one fall by the same sort of disobedience.

---

e Other ancient authorities insert *all*.
f Greek *his*.
g Other ancient authorities insert *firm to the end*.
h Other manuscripts read *they were not united in faith with the hearers*.
i Greek *he*.
2:12: Ps 22:22.
2:13: Is 8:17–18.
2:16: Is 41:8–9.
3:2: Num 12:7.
3:5: Num 12:7.
3:7–11: Ps 95:7–11.
3:15: Ps 95:7–8.
3:16–19: Num 14:1–35.
3:17: Num 14:29.
4:3: Ps 95:11.
4:4: Gen 2:2.
4:5: Ps 95:11.
4:7: Ps 95:7–8.
4:10: Gen 2:2.
* 3:11: Those who murmured against God in the desert were excluded from the promised land (the "rest"). Christians should beware lest, by offending God, they be excluded from heaven, the true rest, of which the promised land was a type.

[12]For the word of God is living and active, sharper than any two-edged sword, piercing to the division of soul and spirit, of joints and marrow, and discerning the thoughts and intentions of the heart. [13]And before him no creature is hidden, but all are open and laid bare to the eyes of him with whom we have to do.

Jesus the Great High Priest

14 Since then we have a great high priest who has passed through the heavens, Jesus, the Son of God, let us hold fast our confession. [15]For we have not a high priest who is unable to sympathize with our weaknesses, but one who in every respect has been tempted as we are, yet without sinning. [16]Let us then with confidence draw near to the throne of grace, that we may receive mercy and find grace to help in time of need.

5 For every high priest chosen from among men is appointed to act on behalf of men in relation to God, to offer gifts and sacrifices for sins. [2]He can deal gently with the ignorant and wayward, since he himself is beset with weakness. [3]Because of this he is bound to offer sacrifice for his own sins as well as for those of the people. [4]And one does not take the honor upon himself, but he is called by God, just as Aaron was.

5 So also Christ did not exalt himself to be made a high priest, but was appointed by him who said to him,

"You are my Son,
today I have begotten you"; *

[6]as he says also in another place,

"You are a priest for ever,
according to the order of Melchiz′edek."

7 In the days of his flesh, Jesus [j] offered up prayers and supplications, with loud cries and tears, to him who was able to save him from death, and he was heard for his godly fear. [8]Although he was a Son, he learned obedience through what he suffered; [9]and being made perfect he became the source of eternal salvation to all who obey him, [10]being designated by God a high priest according to the order of Melchiz′edek.

Spiritual Growth

11 About this we have much to say which is hard to explain, since you have become dull of hearing. [12]For though by this time you ought to be teachers, you need some one to teach you again the first principles of God's word. You need milk, not solid food; [13]for every one who lives on milk is unskilled in the word of righteousness, for he is a child. [14]But solid food is for the mature, for those who have their faculties trained by practice to distinguish good from evil.

The Peril of Falling Away

6 Therefore let us leave the elementary doctrines of Christ and go on to maturity, not laying again a foundation of repentance from dead works and of faith toward God, [2]with instruction [k] about baptisms, the laying on of hands, the resurrection of the dead, and eternal judgment. [3]And this we will do if God permits. [l] [4]For it is impossible † to restore again to repentance those who have once been enlightened, who have tasted the heavenly gift, and have become partakers of the Holy Spirit, [5]and have tasted the goodness of the word of God and the powers of the age to come, [6]if they then commit apostasy, since they crucify the Son of God on their own account and hold him up to contempt. [7]For land which has drunk the rain that often falls upon it, and brings forth vegetation useful to those for whose sake it is cultivated, receives a blessing from God. [8]But if it bears thorns and thistles, it is worthless and near to being cursed; its end is to be burned.

9 Though we speak thus, yet in your case, beloved, we feel sure of better things that belong to salvation. [10]For God is not so unjust as to overlook your work and the love which you showed for his sake in serving the saints, as you still do. [11]And we desire each one of you to show the same earnestness in realizing the full assurance of hope until the end, [12]so that you may not be sluggish, but imitators of those who through faith and patience inherit the promises.

The Certainty of God's Promise

13 For when God made a promise to Abraham, since he had no one greater by whom to swear, he swore by himself, [14]saying, "Surely I will bless you and multiply you." [15]And thus Abraham, [m] having patiently endured, obtained the promise. [16]Men indeed swear by a greater than themselves, and in all their disputes an oath is final for confirmation. [17]So when God desired to show more convincingly to the heirs of the promise the unchangeable character of his purpose, he interposed with an oath, [18]so that through two unchangeable things, in which it is impossible that God should prove false, we who have fled for refuge might have strong encouragement to seize the hope set before us. [19]We have this as a sure and steadfast anchor of the

---

[j] Greek *he*.
[k] Other ancient authorities read *of instruction*.
[l] Other ancient authorities read *let us do this if God permits*.
[m] Greek *he*.
5:5: Ps 2:7.
5:6: Ps 110:4.
5:7: Mt 26:36–46; Mk 14:32–42; Lk 22:40–46.
5:9: Is 45:17.
5:10: Ps 110:4.
6:8: Gen 3:17–18.
6:13–14: Gen 22:16–17.
6:19: Lev 16:2.
* 5:1–5: If Jesus was to be mediator, he had to have a human nature like ours, and, moreover, he could not appoint himself, but had to be appointed by God.
† 6:4, *impossible*: The apostasy referred to in verse 6 is clearly thought of as so deliberate as to preclude any real possibility of repentance; or there may be a reference here to the impossibility of being baptized a second time.

soul, a hope that enters into the inner shrine behind the curtain, [20]where Jesus has gone as a forerunner on our behalf, having become a high priest for ever according to the order of Melchiz′edek.

The Priestly Order of Melchizedek

7 For this Melchiz′edek, king of Salem, priest of the Most High God, met Abraham returning from the slaughter of the kings and blessed him; [2]and to him Abraham apportioned a tenth part of everything. He is first, by translation of his name, king of righteousness, and then he is also king of Salem, that is, king of peace. [3]He is without father * or mother or genealogy, and has neither beginning of days nor end of life, † but resembling the Son of God he continues a priest for ever.

4 See how great he is! Abraham the patriarch gave him a tithe of the spoils. [5]And those descendants of Levi who receive the priestly office have a commandment in the law to take tithes from the people, that is, from their brethren, though these also are descended from Abraham. [6]But this man who has not their genealogy received tithes from Abraham and blessed him who had the promises. [7]It is beyond dispute that the inferior is blessed by the superior. [8]Here tithes are received by mortal men; there, by one of whom it is testified that he lives. [9]One might even say that Levi himself, who receives tithes, paid tithes through Abraham, [10]for he was still in the loins of his ancestor when Melchiz′edek met him.

Another Priest, according to the Order of Melchizedek

11 Now if perfection had been attainable through the Levitical priesthood (for under it the people received the law), what further need would there have been for another priest to arise according to the order of Melchiz′edek, rather than one named according to the order of Aaron? [12]For when there is a change in the priesthood, there is necessarily a change in the law as well. [13]For the one of whom these things are spoken belonged to another tribe, from which no one has ever served at the altar. [14]For it is evident that our Lord was descended from Judah, and in connection with that tribe Moses said nothing about priests.

15 This becomes even more evident when another priest arises in the likeness of Melchiz′edek, [16]who has become a priest, not according to a legal requirement concerning bodily descent but by the power of an indestructible life. [17]For it is witnessed of him,

"You are a priest for ever,
according to the order of Melchiz′edek."

[18]On the one hand, a former commandment is set aside because of its weakness and uselessness [19](for the law made nothing perfect); on the other

hand, a better hope is introduced, through which we draw near to God.

20 And it was not without an oath. [21]Those who formerly became priests took their office without an oath, but this one was addressed with an oath,

"The Lord has sworn
and will not change his mind,
'You are a priest for ever.'"

[22]This makes Jesus the surety of a better covenant.

23 The former priests were many in number, because they were prevented by death from continuing in office; [24]but he holds his priesthood permanently, because he continues for ever. [25]Consequently he is able for all time to save those who draw near to God through him, since he always lives to make intercession for them.

26 For it was fitting that we should have such a high priest, holy, blameless, unstained, separated from sinners, exalted above the heavens. [27]He has no need, like those high priests, to offer sacrifices daily, first for his own sins and then for those of the people; he did this once for all when he offered up himself. [28]Indeed, the law appoints men in their weakness as high priests, but the word of the oath, which came later than the law, appoints a Son who has been made perfect for ever.

Mediator of a New Covenant

8 Now the point in what we are saying is this: we have such a high priest, one who is seated at the right hand of the throne of the Majesty in heaven, [2]a minister in the sanctuary and the true tent [n] which is set up not by man but by the Lord. [3]For every high priest is appointed to offer gifts and sacrifices; hence it is necessary for this priest also to have something to offer. [4]Now if he were on earth, he would not be a priest at all, since there are priests who offer gifts according to the law. [5]They serve a copy and shadow of the heavenly sanctuary; for when Moses was about to erect the tent, [n] he was instructed by God, saying, "See that you make everything according to the pattern which was shown you on the mountain." [6]But as it is, Christ [o] has obtained a ministry which is as much more excellent than the old as the covenant he mediates is better, since it is enacted on better promises. [7]For if that first

---

[n] Or tabernacle.
[o] Greek he.
6:20: Ps 110:4.
7:1–10: Gen 14:17–20.
7:11, 15, 17, 21, 28: Ps 110:4.
8:1: Ps 110:1.
8:5: Ex 25:40.
* 7:3, without father: i.e., the father is not mentioned in Scripture.
† 7:3, neither beginning of days nor end of life: So too here, they are not mentioned in Scripture either. Thus his priesthood can be taken to foreshadow or symbolize the Christian priesthood. "You are a priest for ever according to the order of Melchizedek" (Ps 110:4; cf. Heb 7:17).

covenant had been faultless, there would have been no occasion for a second.

8 For he finds fault with them when he says:

"The days will come, says the Lord,
when I will establish a new covenant with the
house of Israel
and with the house of Judah;
[9]not like the covenant that I made with their
fathers
on the day when I took them by the hand
to lead them out of the land of Egypt;
for they did not continue in my covenant,
and so I paid no heed to them, says the Lord.
[10]This is the covenant that I will make with the
house of Israel
after those days, says the Lord:
I will put my laws into their minds,
and write them on their hearts,
and I will be their God,
and they shall be my people.
[11]And they shall not teach every one his fellow
or every one his brother, saying, 'Know the
Lord,'
for all shall know me,
from the least of them to the greatest. *
[12]For I will be merciful toward their iniquities,
and I will remember their sins no more."

[13]In speaking of a new covenant he treats the first as obsolete. And what is becoming obsolete and growing old is ready to vanish away.

The Earthly and the Heavenly Sanctuary

9 Now even the first covenant had regulations for worship and an earthly sanctuary. [2]For a tent [p] was prepared, the outer one, in which were the lampstand and the table and the bread of offering; [q] it is called the Holy Place. [3]Behind the second curtain stood a tent [p] called the Holy of Holies, [4]having the golden altar of incense and the ark of the covenant covered on all sides with gold, which contained a golden urn holding the manna, and Aaron's rod that budded, and the tables of the covenant; [5]above it were the cherubim of glory overshadowing the mercy seat. Of these things we cannot now speak in detail.

6 These preparations having thus been made, the priests go continually into the outer tent, [p] performing their ritual duties; [7]but into the second only the high priest goes, and he but once a year, and not without taking blood which he offers for himself and for the errors of the people. [8]By this the Holy Spirit indicates that the way into the sanctuary is not yet opened as long as the outer tent [p] is still standing [9](which is symbolic for the present age). According to this arrangement, gifts and sacrifices are offered which cannot perfect the conscience of the worshiper, [10]but deal only with food and drink and various baptisms, regulations for the body imposed until the time of reformation.

11 But when Christ appeared as a high priest of the good things that have come, [r] then through the greater and more perfect tent [p] (not made with hands, that is, not of this creation) [12]he entered once for all into the Holy Place, taking [s] not the blood of goats and calves but his own blood, thus securing an eternal redemption. [13]For if the sprinkling of defiled persons with the blood of goats and bulls and with the ashes of a heifer sanctifies for the purification of the flesh, [14]how much more shall the blood of Christ, who through the eternal Spirit offered himself without blemish to God, purify your [t] conscience from dead works to serve the living God.

15 Therefore he is the mediator of a new covenant, so that those who are called may receive the promised eternal inheritance, since a death has occurred which redeems them from the transgressions under the first covenant. [u] [16]For where a will [u] is involved, the death of the one who made it must be established. [17]For a will [u] takes effect only at death, since it is not in force as long as the one who made it is alive. [18]Hence even the first covenant was not ratified without blood. [19]For when every commandment of the law had been declared by Moses to all the people, he took the blood of calves and goats, with water and scarlet wool and hyssop, and sprinkled both the book itself and all the people, [20]saying, "This is the blood of the covenant which God commanded you." [21]And in the same way he sprinkled with the blood both the tent [p] and all the vessels used in worship. [22]Indeed, under the law almost everything is purified with blood, and without the shedding of blood there is no forgiveness of sins.

Christ's Sacrifice Takes Away Sin

23 Thus it was necessary for the copies of the heavenly things to be purified with these rites, but the heavenly things themselves with better sacrifices than these. [24]For Christ has entered, not into a sanctuary made with hands, a copy of the true one, but into heaven itself, now to appear in the presence of God on our behalf. [25]Nor was it to offer himself repeatedly, as the high priest enters the Holy Place yearly with blood not his own; [26]for then he would have had to suffer repeatedly since

[p] Or tabernacle.
[q] Or the Presence. Greek the presentation of the loaves.
[r] Other manuscripts read good things to come.
[s] Greek through.
[t] Other manuscripts read our.
[u] The Greek word here used means both covenant and will.
8:8-12: Jer 31:31-34.
9:1-10: Ex 25:10-40.
9:2: Lev 24:5.
9:3: Ex 26:31-33.
9:4: Ex 30:1-5; 16:32-33; Num 17:8-10.
9:7: Lev 16.
9:13: Lev 16:6, 16; Num 19:9, 17-18.
9:19-20: Ex 24:6-8.
* 8:11: This verse means merely that knowledge of God will be commonly shared. It does not exclude the existence of a ministry of teaching in the Messianic times.

188

the foundation of the world. But as it is, he has appeared once for all at the end of the age to put away sin by the sacrifice of himself. [27]And just as it is appointed for men to die once, and after that comes judgment, [28]so Christ, having been offered once to bear the sins of many, will appear a second time, not to deal with sin but to save those who are eagerly waiting for him.

Christ's Sacrifice Once for All

10 * For since the law has but a shadow of the good things to come instead of the true form of these realities, it can never, by the same sacrifices which are continually offered year after year, make perfect those who draw near. [2]Otherwise, would they not have ceased to be offered? If the worshipers had once been cleansed, they would no longer have any consciousness of sin. [3]But in these sacrifices there is a reminder of sin year after year. [4]For it is impossible that the blood of bulls and goats should take away sins.

5 Consequently, when Christ[v] came into the world, he said,

"Sacrifices and offerings you have not desired,
  but a body have you prepared for me;
[6]in burnt offerings and sin offerings you have
    taken no pleasure.
[7]Then I said, 'Behold, I have come to do your
    will, O God,'
as it is written of me in the roll of the book."

[8]When he said above, "You have neither desired nor taken pleasure in sacrifices and offerings and burnt offerings and sin offerings" (these are offered according to the law), [9]then he added, "Behold, I have come to do your will." He abolishes the first in order to establish the second. [10]And by that will we have been sanctified through the offering of the body of Jesus Christ once for all.

11 And every priest stands daily at his service, offering repeatedly the same sacrifices, which can never take away sins. [12]But when Christ[w] had offered for all time a single sacrifice for sins, he sat down at the right hand of God, [13]then to wait until his enemies should be made a stool for his feet. [14]For by a single offering he has perfected for all time those who are sanctified. [15]And the Holy Spirit also bears witness to us; for after saying,

[16]"This is the covenant that I will make with
    them
after those days, says the Lord:
I will put my laws on their hearts,
  and write them on their minds,"

[17]then he adds,

"I will remember their sins and their misdeeds
    no more."

[18]Where there is forgiveness of these, there is no longer any offering for sin.

A Call to Persevere

19 Therefore, brethren, since we have confidence to enter the sanctuary by the blood of Jesus,

[20]by the new and living way which he opened for us through the curtain, that is, through his flesh, [21]and since we have a great priest over the house of God, [22]let us draw near with a true heart in full assurance of faith, with our hearts sprinkled clean from an evil conscience and our bodies washed with pure water. [23]Let us hold fast the confession of our hope without wavering, for he who promised is faithful; [24]and let us consider how to stir up one another to love and good works, [25]not neglecting to meet together, as is the habit of some, but encouraging one another, and all the more as you see the Day drawing near.

26 For if we sin deliberately after receiving the knowledge of the truth, there no longer remains a sacrifice for sins, [27]but a fearful prospect of judgment, and a fury of fire which will consume the adversaries. [28]A man who has violated the law of Moses dies without mercy at the testimony of two or three witnesses. [29]How much worse punishment do you think will be deserved by the man who has spurned the Son of God, and profaned the blood of the covenant by which he was sanctified, and outraged the Spirit of grace? [30]For we know him who said, "Vengeance is mine, I will repay." And again, "The Lord will judge his people." [31]It is a fearful thing to fall into the hands of the living God.

32 But recall the former days when, after you were enlightened, you endured a hard struggle with sufferings, [33]sometimes being publicly exposed to abuse and affliction, and sometimes being partners with those so treated. [34]For you had compassion on the prisoners, and you joyfully accepted the plundering of your property, since you knew that you yourselves had a better possession and an abiding one. [35]Therefore do not throw away your confidence, which has a great reward. [36]For you have need of endurance, so that you may do the will of God and receive what is promised. [37]"For yet a little while,

and the coming one shall come and shall not
    tarry;
[38]but my righteous one shall live by faith,
  and if he shrinks back,
  my soul has no pleasure in him."

---

[v] Greek *he.*
[w] Greek *this one.*
10:5–9: Ps 40:6–8.
10:12–13: Ps 110:1.
10:16–17: Jer 31:33–34.
10:27: Is 26:11.
10:28: Deut 17:2–6.
10:29: Ex 24:8.
10:30: Deut 32:35–36.
10:37: Is 26:20 Septuagint.
10:37–38: Hab 2:3–4.
* 10:1ff.: The sacrifices of the old law, being imperfect, were repeated and did at least keep alive a sense of sin. Contrast with Christ's sacrifice (verse 14).

39But we are not of those who shrink back and are destroyed, but of those who have faith and keep their souls.

The Meaning of Faith

11 Now faith is the assurance of things hoped for, the conviction of things not seen. 2For by it the men of old received divine approval. 3By faith we understand that the world was created by the word of God, so that what is seen was made out of things which do not appear.

The Examples of Abel, Enoch, and Noah

4 By faith Abel offered to God a more acceptable sacrifice than Cain, through which he received approval as righteous, God bearing witness by accepting his gifts; he died, but through his faith he is still speaking. 5By faith E'noch was taken up so that he should not see death; and he was not found, because God had taken him. Now before he was taken he was attested as having pleased God. 6And without faith it is impossible to please him. For whoever would draw near to God must believe that he exists and that he rewards those who seek him. * 7By faith Noah, being warned by God concerning events as yet unseen, took heed and constructed an ark for the saving of his household; by this he condemned the world and became an heir of the righteousness which comes by faith.

The Faith of Abraham

8 By faith Abraham obeyed when he was called to go out to a place which he was to receive as an inheritance; and he went out, not knowing where he was to go. 9By faith he sojourned in the land of promise, as in a foreign land, living in tents with Isaac and Jacob, heirs with him of the same promise. 10For he looked forward to the city which has foundations, whose builder and maker is God. 11By faith Sarah herself received power to conceive, even when she was past the age, since she considered him faithful who had promised. 12Therefore from one man, and him as good as dead, were born descendants as many as the stars of heaven and as the innumerable grains of sand by the seashore.

13 These all died in faith, not having received what was promised, but having seen it and greeted it from afar, and having acknowledged that they were strangers and exiles on the earth. 14For people who speak thus make it clear that they are seeking a homeland. 15If they had been thinking of that land from which they had gone out, they would have had opportunity to return. 16But as it is, they desire a better country, that is, a heavenly one. Therefore God is not ashamed to be called their God, for he has prepared for them a city.

17 By faith Abraham, when he was tested, offered up Isaac, and he who had received the promises was ready to offer up his only-begotten son, 18of whom it was said, "Through Isaac shall your descendants be named." 19He considered that God was able to raise men even from the dead; hence he did receive him back and this was a symbol. 20By faith Isaac invoked future blessings on Jacob and Esau. 21By faith Jacob, when dying, blessed each of the sons of Joseph, bowing in worship over the head of his staff. 22By faith Joseph, at the end of his life, made mention of the exodus of the Israelites and gave directions concerning his burial. *

The Faith of Moses

23 By faith Moses, when he was born, was hidden for three months by his parents, because they saw that the child was beautiful; and they were not afraid of the king's edict. 24By faith Moses, when he was grown up, refused to be called the son of Pharaoh's daughter, 25choosing rather to share ill-treatment with the people of God than to enjoy the fleeting pleasures of sin. 26He considered abuse suffered for the Christ greater wealth than the treasures of Egypt, for he looked to the reward. 27By faith he left Egypt, not being afraid of the anger of the king; for he endured as seeing him who is invisible. 28By faith he kept the Passover and sprinkled the blood, so that the Destroyer of the first-born might not touch them.

The Faith of Other Heroes in Israel's History

29 By faith the people crossed the Red Sea as if on dry land; but the Egyptians, when they attempted to do the same, were drowned. 30By faith the walls of Jericho fell down after they had been encircled for seven days. 31By faith Rahab the harlot did not perish with those who were disobedient, because she had given friendly welcome to the spies.

32 And what more shall I say? For time would fail me to tell of Gideon, Barak, Samson,

---

* Greek bones.
11:4: Gen 4:3–10.
11:5: Gen 5:21–24.
11:7: Gen 6:13–22.
11:8–9: Gen 12:1–8.
11:11: Gen 17:19; 18:11–14; 21:2.
11:12: Gen 15:5–6; 22:17; 32:12.
11:13: Ps 39:12; Gen 23:4.
11:16: Ex 3:6, 15; 4:5.
11:17: Gen 22:1–10.
11:18: Gen 21:12.
11:20: Gen 27:27–29, 39–40.
11:21: Gen 48; 47:31 Septuagint.
11:22: Gen 50:24–25; Ex 13:19.
11:23: Ex 2:2; 1:22.
11:24: Ex 2:10, 11–15.
11:27: Ex 2:15.
11:28: Ex 12:21–28, 29–30.
11:29: Ex 14:21–31.
11:30: Josh 6:12–21.
11:31: Josh 2:1–21; 6:22–25.
11:32: Judg 6–8; 4–5; 13–16; 11–12; 1 Sam 16–30; 2 Sam 1–24; 1 Kings 1:1—2:11; 1 Sam 1–12; 15; 16:1–13.
* 11:6: Here is stated the minimum necessary for salvation.

Jephthah, of David and Samuel and the prophets—[33]who through faith conquered kingdoms, enforced justice, received promises, stopped the mouths of lions, [34]quenched raging fire, escaped the edge of the sword, won strength out of weakness, became mighty in war, put foreign armies to flight. [35]Women received their dead by resurrection. Some were tortured, refusing to accept release, that they might rise again to a better life. [36]Others suffered mocking and scourging, and even chains and imprisonment. [37]They were stoned, they were sawn in two,[y] they were killed with the sword; they went about in skins of sheep and goats, destitute, afflicted, ill-treated—[38]of whom the world was not worthy—wandering over deserts and mountains, and in dens and caves of the earth.

39 And all these, though well attested by their faith, did not receive what was promised, [40]since God had foreseen something better for us, that apart from us they should not be made perfect.

The Example of Jesus

12 Therefore, since we are surrounded by so great a cloud of witnesses, let us also lay aside every weight, and sin which clings so closely, and let us run with perseverance the race that is set before us,[*] [2]looking to Jesus the pioneer and perfecter of our faith, who for the joy that was set before him endured the cross, despising the shame, and is seated at the right hand of the throne of God.

3 Consider him who endured from sinners such hostility against himself, so that you may not grow weary or fainthearted. [4]In your struggle against sin you have not yet resisted to the point of shedding your blood. [5]And have you forgotten the exhortation which addresses you as sons?—

"My son, do not regard lightly the discipline of
  the Lord,
nor lose courage when you are punished by
  him.
[6]For the Lord disciplines him whom he loves,
and chastises every son whom he receives."

[7]It is for discipline that you have to endure. God is treating you as sons; for what son is there whom his father does not discipline? [8]If you are left without discipline, in which all have participated, then you are illegitimate children and not sons. [9]Besides this, we have had earthly fathers to discipline us and we respected them. Shall we not much more be subject to the Father of spirits and live? [10]For they disciplined us for a short time at their pleasure, but he disciplines us for our good, that we may share his holiness. [11]For the moment all discipline seems painful rather than pleasant; later it yields the peaceful fruit of righteousness to those who have been trained by it.

Exhortation to Be Strong and Avoid Sin

12 Therefore lift your drooping hands and strengthen your weak knees, [13]and make straight paths for your feet, so that what is lame may not be put out of joint but rather be healed. [14]Strive for peace with all men, and for the holiness without which no one will see the Lord. [15]See to it that no one fail to obtain the grace of God; that no "root of bitterness" spring up and cause trouble, and by it the many become defiled; [16]that no one be immoral or irreligious like Esau, who sold his birthright for a single meal. [17]For you know that afterward, when he desired to inherit the blessing, he was rejected, for he found no chance to repent, though he sought it with tears.

18 For you have not come to what may be touched, a blazing fire, and darkness, and gloom, and a tempest, [19]and the sound of a trumpet, and a voice whose words made the hearers entreat that no further messages be spoken to them. [20]For they could not endure the order that was given, "If even a beast touches the mountain, it shall be stoned." [21]Indeed, so terrifying was the sight that Moses said, "I tremble with fear." [22]But you have come to Mount Zion and to the city of the living God, the heavenly Jerusalem, and to innumerable angels in festal gathering, [23]and to the assembly[z] of the first-born who are enrolled in heaven, and to a judge who is God of all, and to the spirits of just men made perfect, [24]and to Jesus, the mediator of a new covenant, and to the sprinkled blood that speaks more graciously than the blood of Abel.

25 See that you do not refuse him who is speaking. For if they did not escape when they refused him who warned them on earth, much less shall we escape if we reject him who warns from heaven. [26]His voice then shook the earth; but now he has promised, "Yet once more I will shake not only the earth but also the heaven." [27]This phrase, "Yet once more," indicates the removal of what is shaken, as of what has been made, in order that what cannot be shaken may remain. [28]Therefore

---

y Other manuscripts add *they were tempted.*
z Or *angels, and to the festal gathering and assembly.*
11:33: Dan 6.
11:34: Dan 3.
11:35: 1 Kings 17:17–24; 2 Kings 4:25–37.
12:2: Ps 110:1.
12:5–8: Prov 3:11–12.
12:12: Is 35:3.
12:13: Prov 4:26 Septuagint.
12:15: Deut 29:18 Septuagint.
12:16: Gen 25:29–34.
12:17: Gen 27:30–40.
12:18–19: Ex 19:12–22; 20:18–21; Deut 4:11–12; 5:22–27.
12:20: Ex 19:12–13.
12:21: Deut 9:19.
12:24: Gen 4:10.
12:25: Ex 20:19.
12:26: Hag 2:6.
* 12:1ff.: After explaining in the preceding chapters how we are redeemed through faith in Jesus Christ, the author now exhorts his readers to run the race with perseverance.

let us be grateful for receiving a kingdom that cannot be shaken, and thus let us offer to God acceptable worship, with reverence and awe; [29]for our God is a consuming fire.

Sacrifices Well-Pleasing to God

13 * Let brotherly love continue. [2]Do not neglect to show hospitality to strangers, for thereby some have entertained angels unawares. [3]Remember those who are in prison, as though in prison with them; and those who are ill-treated, since you also are in the body. [4]Let marriage be held in honor among all, and let the marriage bed be undefiled; for God will judge the immoral and adulterous. [5]Keep your life free from love of money, and be content with what you have; for he has said, "I will never fail you nor forsake you." [6]Hence we can confidently say,

"The Lord is my helper,
I will not be afraid;
what can man do to me?"

7 Remember your leaders, those who spoke to you the word of God; consider the outcome of their life, and imitate their faith. [8]Jesus Christ is the same yesterday and today and for ever. [9]Do not be led away by diverse and strange teachings; for it is well that the heart be strengthened by grace, not by foods, which have not benefited their adherents. † [10]We have an altar from which those who serve the tent [a] have no right to eat. [11]For the bodies of those animals whose blood is brought into the sanctuary by the high priest as a sacrifice for sin are burned outside the camp. [12]So Jesus also suffered outside the gate in order to sanctify the people through his own blood. [13]Therefore let us go forth to him outside the camp, bearing abuse for him. ‡ [14]For here we have no lasting city, but we seek the city which is to come. [15]Through him then let us continually offer up a sacrifice of praise to God, that is, the fruit of lips that acknowledge his name. [16]Do not neglect to do good and to share what you have, for such sacrifices are pleasing to God.

17 Obey your leaders and submit to them; for they are keeping watch over your souls, as men who will have to give account. Let them do this joyfully, and not sadly, for that would be of no advantage to you.

18 Pray for us, for we are sure that we have a clear conscience, desiring to act honorably in all things. [19]I urge you the more earnestly to do this in order that I may be restored to you the sooner.

Benediction

20 Now may the God of peace who brought again from the dead our Lord Jesus, the great shepherd of the sheep, by the blood of the eternal covenant, [21]equip you with everything good that you may do his will, working in you [b] that which is pleasing in his sight, through Jesus Christ; to whom be glory for ever and ever. Amen.

Final Exhortation and Greetings

22 I appeal to you, brethren, bear with my word of exhortation, for I have written to you briefly. [23]You should understand that our brother Timothy has been released, with whom I shall see you if he comes soon. [24]Greet all your leaders and all the saints. Those who come from Italy send you greetings. [25]Grace be with all of you. Amen.

---

[a] Or *tabernacle*.
[b] Other ancient authorities read *us*.
12:29: Deut 4:24.
13:2: Gen 18:1–8; 19:1–3.
13:5: Deut 31:6, 8; Josh 1:5.
13:6: Ps 118:6.
13:11, 13: Lev 16:27.
13:15: Lev 7:12; Is 57:19; Hos 14:2.
13:20: Is 63:11; Zech 9:11; Is 55:3; Ezek 37:26.
* 13:1ff.: Moral exhortation.
† 13:9: Again the warning against false doctrine, especially the Judaizers' teachings; cf. Phil 3:19; 1 Tim 1:4; 4:3.
‡ 13:13: i.e., "Let us leave the observance of Judaism behind us."

THE LETTER OF

JAMES

Salutation

1 James, a servant of God and of the Lord Jesus Christ,

To the twelve tribes * in the Dispersion: Greeting.

Faith and Wisdom

2 Count it all joy, my brethren, when you meet various trials, ³for you know that the testing of your faith produces steadfastness. ⁴And let steadfastness have its full effect, that you may be perfect and complete, lacking in nothing.

5 If any of you lacks wisdom, let him ask God, who gives to all men generously and without reproaching, and it will be given him. ⁶But let him ask in faith, with no doubting, for he who doubts is like a wave of the sea that is driven and tossed by the wind. ⁷, ⁸For that person must not suppose that a double-minded man, unstable in all his ways, will receive anything from the Lord.

Poverty and Riches

9 Let the lowly brother boast in his exaltation, ¹⁰and the rich in his humiliation, because like the flower of the grass he will pass away. ¹¹For the sun rises with its scorching heat and withers the grass; its flower falls, and its beauty perishes. So will the rich man fade away in the midst of his pursuits.

Trial and Temptation

12 Blessed is the man who endures trial, for when he has stood the test he will receive the crown of life which God has promised to those who love him. ¹³Let no one say when he is tempted, "I am tempted by God"; for God cannot be tempted with evil and he himself tempts no one; ¹⁴but each person is tempted when he is lured and enticed by his own desire. ¹⁵Then desire when it has conceived gives birth to sin; and sin when it is full-grown brings forth death.

16 Do not be deceived, my beloved brethren. ¹⁷Every good endowment and every perfect gift is from above, coming down from the Father of lights with whom there is no variation or shadow due to change. ª ¹⁸Of his own will he brought us forth by the word of truth that we should be a kind of first fruits of his creatures.

19 Know this, my beloved brethren. Let every man be quick to hear, slow to speak, slow to anger, ²⁰for the anger of man does not work the righteousness of God. ²¹Therefore put away all filthiness and rank growth of wickedness and receive with meekness the implanted word, which is able to save your souls.

22 But be doers of the word, and not hearers only, deceiving yourselves. † ²³For if any one is a hearer of the word and not a doer, he is like a man who observes his natural face in a mirror; ²⁴for he observes himself and goes away and at once forgets what he was like. ²⁵But he who looks into the perfect law, the law of liberty, and perseveres, being no hearer that forgets but a doer that acts, he shall be blessed in his doing.

26 If any one thinks he is religious, and does not bridle his tongue but deceives his heart, this man's religion is vain. ²⁷Religion that is pure and undefiled before God and the Father is this: to visit orphans and widows in their affliction, and to keep oneself unstained from the world.

Warning against Partiality

2 ‡ My brethren, show no partiality as you hold the faith of our Lord Jesus Christ, the Lord of glory. ²For if a man with gold rings and in fine clothing comes into your assembly, and a poor man in shabby clothing also comes in, ³and you pay attention to the one who wears the fine clothing and say, "Have a seat here, please," while you say to the poor man, "Stand there," or, "Sit at my feet," ⁴have you not made distinctions among yourselves, and become judges with evil thoughts? ⁵Listen, my beloved brethren. Has not God chosen those who are poor in the world to be rich in faith and heirs of the kingdom which he has promised to those who love him? ⁶But you have dishonored the poor man. Is it not the rich who oppress you, is it not they who drag you into court? ⁷Is it not they who blaspheme that honorable name by which you are called?

8 If you really fulfil the royal law, according to the Scripture, "You shall love your neighbor as yourself," you do well. ⁹But if you show partiality, you commit sin, and are convicted by the law as transgressors. ¹⁰For whoever keeps the whole law but fails in one point has become guilty of all

---

ª Other ancient authorities read *variation due to a shadow of turning*.
1:10–11: Is 40:6–7.
2:8: Lev 19:18.
* 1:1, *twelve tribes*: i.e., Jewish Christians outside Palestine.
† 1:22: This is the main theme of the letter.
‡ 2:1–7: These are hard words, but no harder than those of Jesus.

of it. * [11]For he who said, "Do not commit adultery," said also, "Do not kill." If you do not commit adultery but do kill, you have become a transgressor of the law. [12]So speak and so act as those who are to be judged under the law of liberty. [13]For judgment is without mercy to one who has shown no mercy; yet mercy triumphs over judgment.

Faith without Works Is Dead

[14] What does it profit, my brethren, if a man says he has faith but has not works? Can his faith save him? † [15]If a brother or sister is poorly clothed and in lack of daily food, [16]and one of you says to them, "Go in peace, be warmed and filled," without giving them the things needed for the body, what does it profit? [17]So faith by itself, if it has no works, is dead.

[18] But some one will say, "You have faith and I have works." Show me your faith apart from your works, and I by my works will show you my faith. [19]You believe that God is one; you do well. Even the demons believe—and shudder. [20]Do you want to be shown, you foolish fellow, that faith apart from works is barren? [21]Was not Abraham our father justified by works, when he offered his son Isaac upon the altar? [22]You see that faith was active along with his works, and faith was completed by works, [23]and the Scripture was fulfilled which says, "Abraham believed God, and it was reckoned to him as righteousness"; and he was called the friend of God. [24]You see that a man is justified by works and not by faith alone. [25]And in the same way was not also Ra′hab the harlot justified by works when she received the messengers and sent them out another way? [26]For as the body apart from the spirit is dead, so faith apart from works is dead.

Taming the Tongue

3 Let not many of you become teachers, my brethren, for you know that we who teach shall be judged with greater strictness. [2]For we all make many mistakes, and if any one makes no mistakes in what he says he is a perfect man, able to bridle the whole body also. [3]If we put bits into the mouths of horses that they may obey us, we guide their whole bodies. [4]Look at the ships also; though they are so great and are driven by strong winds, they are guided by a very small rudder wherever the will of the pilot directs. [5]So the tongue is a little member and boasts of great things. How great a forest is set ablaze by a small fire!

[6] And the tongue is a fire. The tongue is an unrighteous world among our members, staining the whole body, setting on fire the cycle of nature, [b] and set on fire by hell. [c] [7]For every kind of beast and bird, of reptile and sea creature, can be tamed and has been tamed by mankind, [8]but no human being can tame the tongue—a restless evil, full of deadly poison. [9]With it we bless the Lord and Father, and with it we curse men, who are made in the likeness of God. [10]From the same mouth come blessing and cursing. My brethren, this ought not to be so. [11]Does a spring pour forth from the same opening fresh water and brackish? [12]Can a fig tree, my brethren, yield olives, or a grapevine figs? No more can salt water yield fresh.

Two Kinds of Wisdom

[13] Who is wise and understanding among you? By his good life let him show his works in the meekness of wisdom. [14]But if you have bitter jealousy and selfish ambition in your hearts, do not boast and be false to the truth. [15]This wisdom is not such as comes down from above, but is earthly, unspiritual, devilish. [16]For where jealousy and selfish ambition exist, there will be disorder and every vile practice. [17]But the wisdom from above is first pure, then peaceable, gentle, open to reason, full of mercy and good fruits, without uncertainty or insincerity. [18]And the harvest of righteousness is sown in peace by those who make peace.

Friendship with the World

4 What causes wars, and what causes fightings among you? Is it not your passions that are at war in your members? [2]You desire and do not have; so you kill. And you covet [d] and cannot obtain; so you fight and wage war. You do not have, because you do not ask. [3]You ask and do not receive, because you ask wrongly, to spend it on your passions. [4]Unfaithful creatures! Do you not know that friendship with the world is enmity with God? Therefore whoever wishes to be a friend of the world makes himself an enemy of God. [5]Or do you suppose it is in vain that the Scripture says, "He yearns jealously over the spirit which he has made to dwell in us"? [6]But he gives more grace; therefore it says, "God opposes the proud, but gives grace to the humble." [7]Submit yourselves therefore to God. Resist the devil and he will flee from you. [8]Draw near to God and he will draw near to you. Cleanse your hands, you sinners, and purify your hearts, you men of double mind. [9]Be wretched and mourn and weep. Let your laughter be turned to mourning and your joy to dejection. [10]Humble yourselves before the Lord and he will exalt you.

Warning against Judging Another

[11] Do not speak evil against one another, brethren. He that speaks evil against a brother or

---

[b] Or wheel of birth.
[c] Greek Gehenna.
[d] Or you kill and you covet.
2:11: Ex 20:13–14; Deut 5:17–18.
2:21: Gen 22:1–14.
2:23: Gen 15:6; Is 41:8; 2 Chron 20:7.
2:25: Josh 2:1–21.
4:6: Prov 3:34.
* 2:10: In keeping the law, we must keep the whole law. We cannot pick and choose.
† 2:14: Good works are necessary besides faith.

judges his brother, speaks evil against the law and judges the law. But if you judge the law, you are not a doer of the law but a judge. [12]There is one lawgiver and judge, he who is able to save and to destroy. But who are you that you judge your neighbor?

Boasting about Tomorrow

13 Come now, you who say, "Today or tomorrow we will go into such and such a town and spend a year there and trade and get gain"; [14]whereas you do not know about tomorrow. What is your life? For you are a mist that appears for a little time and then vanishes. [15]Instead you ought to say, "If the Lord wills, we shall live and we shall do this or that." [16]As it is, you boast in your arrogance. All such boasting is evil. [17]Whoever knows what is right to do and fails to do it, for him it is sin.

Warning to Rich Oppressors

5 Come now, you rich, weep and howl for the miseries that are coming upon you. [2]Your riches have rotted and your garments are motheaten. [3]Your gold and silver have rusted, and their rust will be evidence against you and will eat your flesh like fire. You have laid up treasure ●* for the last days. [4]Behold, the wages of the laborers who mowed your fields, which you kept back by fraud, cry out; and the cries of the harvesters have reached the ears of the Lord of hosts. [5]You have lived on the earth in luxury and in pleasure; you have fattened your hearts in a day of slaughter. [6]You have condemned, you have killed the righteous man; he does not resist you.

Patience in Suffering

7 Be patient, therefore, brethren, until the coming of the Lord. Behold, the farmer waits for the precious fruit of the earth, being patient over it until it receives the early and the late rain. [8]You also be patient. Establish your hearts, for the coming of the Lord is at hand. [9]Do not grumble, brethren, against one another, that you may not be judged; behold, the Judge is standing at the doors.

[10]As an example of suffering and patience, brethren, take the prophets who spoke in the name of the Lord. [11]Behold, we call those happy who were steadfast. You have heard of the steadfastness of Job, and you have seen the purpose of the Lord, how the Lord is compassionate and merciful.

12 But above all, my brethren, do not swear, either by heaven or by earth or with any other oath, but let your yes be yes and your no be no, that you may not fall under condemnation.

The Prayer of Faith

13 † Is any one among you suffering? Let him pray. Is any cheerful? Let him sing praise. [14]Is any among you sick? Let him call for the elders of the Church, and let them pray over him, anointing him with oil in the name of the Lord; [15]and the prayer of faith will save the sick man, and the Lord will raise him up; and if he has committed sins, he will be forgiven. [16]Therefore confess your sins to one another, and pray for one another, that you may be healed. The prayer of a righteous man has great power in its effects. [17]Eli′jah was a man of like nature with ourselves and he prayed fervently that it might not rain, and for three years and six months it did not rain on the earth. [18]Then he prayed again and the heaven gave rain, and the earth brought forth its fruit.

19 My brethren, if any one among you wanders from the truth and some one brings him back, [20]let him know that whoever brings back a sinner from the error of his way will save his soul from death and will cover a multitude of sins.

● Or *will eat your flesh, since you have stored up fire.*
5:11: Job 1:21–22; 2:10; Ps 103:8; 111:4.
5:12: Mt 5:37.
5:17: 1 Kings 17:1; 18:1; Luke 4:25.
5:18: 1 Kings 18:42.
* 5:3: The "treasure" they have laid up is described in the following verses.
† 5:13–15: This passage is the scriptural basis for the sacrament of anointing the sick.

THE FIRST LETTER OF

PETER

Salutation

1 * Peter, an apostle of Jesus Christ,
  To the exiles of the Dispersion in Pontus, Galatia, Cappado'cia, Asia, and Bithyn'ia, [2]chosen and destined by God the Father and sanctified by the Spirit for obedience to Jesus Christ and for sprinkling with his blood:
  May grace and peace be multiplied to you.

A Living Hope

3 Blessed be the God and Father of our Lord Jesus Christ! By his great mercy we have been born anew to a living hope through the resurrection of Jesus Christ from the dead, [4]and to an inheritance which is imperishable, undefiled, and unfading, kept in heaven for you, [5]who by God's power are guarded through faith for a salvation ready to be revealed in the last time. [6]In this you rejoice, [a] though now for a little while you may have to suffer various trials, [7]so that the genuineness of your faith, more precious than gold which though perishable is tested by fire, may redound to praise and glory and honor at the revelation of Jesus Christ. [8]Without having seen [b] him you [c] love him; though you do not now see him you believe in him and rejoice with unutterable and exalted joy. [9]As the outcome of your faith you obtain the salvation of your souls.

10 The prophets who prophesied of the grace that was to be yours searched and inquired about this salvation; [11]they inquired what person or time was indicated by the Spirit of Christ † within them when predicting the sufferings of Christ and the subsequent glory. [12]It was revealed to them that they were serving not themselves but you, in the things which have now been announced to you by those who preached the good news to you through the Holy Spirit sent from heaven, things into which angels long to look.

A Call to Holy Living

13 Therefore gird up your minds, be sober, set your hope fully upon the grace that is coming to you at the revelation of Jesus Christ. [14]As obedient children, do not be conformed to the passions of your former ignorance, [15]but as he who called you is holy, be holy yourselves in all your conduct; [16]since it is written, "You shall be holy, for I am holy." [17]And if you invoke as Father him who judges each one impartially according to his deeds, conduct yourselves with fear throughout the time of your exile. [18]You know that you

were ransomed from the futile ways inherited from your fathers, not with perishable things such as silver or gold, [19]but with the precious blood of Christ, like that of a lamb without blemish or spot. [20]He was destined before the foundation of the world but was made manifest at the end of the times for your sake. [21]Through him you have confidence in God, who raised him from the dead and gave him glory, so that your faith and hope are in God. [d]

22 Having purified your souls by your obedience to the truth for a sincere love of the brethren, love one another earnestly from the heart. [23]You have been born anew, not of perishable seed but of imperishable, through the living and abiding word of God; [24]for

"All flesh is like grass
and all its glory like the flower of grass.
The grass withers, and the flower falls,
[25]but the word of the Lord abides for ever."

That word is the good news which was preached to you.

The Living Stone and a Chosen People

2 So put away all malice and all guile and insincerity and envy and all slander. [2]Like newborn infants, long for the pure spiritual milk, that by it you may grow up to salvation; [3]for you have tasted the kindness of the Lord.

4 Come to him, to that living stone, rejected by men but in God's sight chosen and precious; [5]and like living stones be yourselves built into a spiritual house, to be a holy priesthood, to offer spiritual sacrifices acceptable to God through Jesus Christ. [6]For it stands in Scripture:

"Behold, I am laying in Zion a stone,
    a cornerstone chosen and precious,
and he who believes in him will not be put to
    shame."

---

[a] Or *Rejoice in this.*
[b] Other ancient authorities read *known.*
[c] Or omit *you.*
[d] Or *so that your faith is hope in God.*
1:16: Lev 11:44–45.
1:24–25: Is 40:6–9.
2:3: Ps 34:8.
2:4: Ps 118:22; Is 28:16.
2:6: Is 28:16.
* 1:1: See note on Jas 1:1. Baptism is the main theme of this letter which, in fact, may have been a baptismal address.
† 1:11, *Spirit of Christ*: Christ, as the eternally existing Word, is envisaged as inspiring the prophets of old.

[7]To you therefore who believe, he is precious, but for those who do not believe,

"The very stone which the builders rejected
has become the cornerstone,"

[8]and

"A stone that will make men stumble,
a rock that will make them fall";

for they stumble because they disobey the word, as they were destined to do.

9 But you are a chosen race, a royal priesthood, a holy nation, God's own people, [e] that you may declare the wonderful deeds of him who called you out of darkness into his marvelous light. [10]Once you were no people but now you are God's people; once you had not received mercy but now you have received mercy.

Live as Servants of God

11 Beloved, I beg you as aliens and exiles to abstain from the passions of the flesh that wage war against your soul. [12]Maintain good conduct among the Gentiles, so that in case they speak against you as wrongdoers, they may see your good deeds and glorify God on the day of visitation.

13 Be subject for the Lord's sake to every human institution, [f] whether it be to the emperor as supreme, [14]or to governors as sent by him to punish those who do wrong and to praise those who do right. [15]For it is God's will that by doing right you should put to silence the ignorance of foolish men. [16]Live as free men, yet without using your freedom as a pretext for evil; but live as servants of God. [17]Honor all men. Love the brotherhood. Fear God. Honor the emperor.

The Example of Christ's Suffering

18 Servants, be submissive to your masters with all respect, not only to the kind and gentle but also to the overbearing. [19]For one is approved if, mindful of God, he endures pain while suffering unjustly. [20]For what credit is it, if when you do wrong and are beaten for it you take it patiently? But if when you do right and suffer for it you take it patiently, you have God's approval. [21]For to this you have been called, because Christ also suffered for you, leaving you an example, that you should follow in his steps. [22]He committed no sin; no guile was found on his lips. [23]When he was reviled, he did not revile in return; when he suffered, he did not threaten; but he trusted to him who judges justly. [24]He himself bore our sins in his body on the tree, [g] that we might die to sin and live to righteousness. By his wounds you have been healed. [25]For you were straying like sheep, but have now returned to the Shepherd and Guardian of your souls.

Wives and Husbands

3 * Likewise you wives, be submissive to your husbands, so that some, though they do not obey the word, may be won without a word by the behavior of their wives, [2]when they see your reverent and chaste behavior. [3]Let not yours be the outward adorning with braiding of hair, decoration of gold, and wearing of robes, [4]but let it be the hidden person of the heart with the imperishable jewel of a gentle and quiet spirit, which in God's sight is very precious. [5]So once the holy women who hoped in God used to adorn themselves and were submissive to their husbands, [6]as Sarah obeyed Abraham, calling him lord. And you are now her children if you do right and let nothing terrify you.

7 Likewise you husbands, live considerately with your wives, bestowing honor on the woman as the weaker sex, since you are joint heirs of the grace of life, in order that your prayers may not be hindered.

Suffering for Doing Right

8 Finally, all of you, have unity of spirit, sympathy, love of the brethren, a tender heart and a humble mind. [9]Do not return evil for evil or reviling for reviling; but on the contrary bless, for to this you have been called, that you may obtain a blessing. [10]For

"He that would love life
and see good days,
let him keep his tongue from evil
and his lips from speaking guile;
[11]let him turn away from evil and do right;
let him seek peace and pursue it.
[12]For the eyes of the Lord are upon the righteous,
and his ears are open to their prayer.
But the face of the Lord is against those that
do evil."

13 Now who is there to harm you if you are zealous for what is right? [14]But even if you do suffer for righteousness' sake, you will be blessed. Have no fear of them, nor be troubled, [15]but in your hearts reverence Christ as Lord. Always be prepared to make a defense to any one who calls you to account for the hope that is in you, yet do it with gentleness and reverence; [16]and keep your conscience clear, so that, when you are abused, those who revile your good behavior in Christ may be put to shame. [17]For it is better to suffer for doing right, if that should be God's will, than for doing wrong. [18]For Christ also

[e] Greek *a people for his possession.*
[f] Or *every institution ordained for men.*
[g] Or *carried up . . . to the tree.*
2:7: Ps 118:22.
2:8: Is 8:14–15.
2:9: Ex 19:5–6.
2:10: Hos 2:23.
2:22: Is 53:9.
2:24: Is 53:12 Septuagint.
2:24–25: Is 53:5–6.
3:6: Gen 18:12.
3:10–12: Ps 34:12–16.
3:14–15: Is 8:12–13.
* 3:1–6: Peter's teaching on the behavior and status of women corresponds to that of Paul, though without Paul's forthrightness.

died[h] for sins once for all, the righteous for the unrighteous, that he might bring us to God, being put to death in the flesh but made alive in the spirit; [19]in which he went and preached to the spirits in prison, [20]who formerly did not obey, when God's patience waited in the days of Noah, during the building of the ark, in which a few, that is, eight persons, were saved through water. [21]Baptism, which corresponds to this, now saves you, not as a removal of dirt from the body but as an appeal to God for a clear conscience, through the resurrection of Jesus Christ, [22]who has gone into heaven and is at the right hand of God, with angels, authorities, and powers subject to him.

Good Stewards of God's Grace

4 Since therefore Christ suffered in the flesh,[i] arm yourselves with the same thought, for whoever has suffered in the flesh has ceased from sin, * [2]so as to live for the rest of the time in the flesh no longer by human passions but by the will of God. [3]Let the time that is past suffice for doing what the Gentiles like to do, living in licentiousness, passions, drunkenness, revels, carousing, and lawless idolatry. [4]They are surprised that you do not now join them in the same wild debauchery, and they abuse you; [5]but they will give account to him who is ready to judge the living and the dead. [6]For this is why the gospel was preached even to the dead, that though judged in the flesh like men, they might live in the spirit like God.

7 The end of all things is at hand; therefore keep sane and sober for your prayers. [8]Above all hold unfailing your love for one another, since love covers a multitude of sins. [9]Practice hospitality ungrudgingly to one another. [10]As each has received a gift, employ it for one another, as good stewards of God's varied grace: [11]whoever speaks, as one who utters oracles of God; whoever renders service, as one who renders it by the strength which God supplies; in order that in everything God may be glorified through Jesus Christ. To him belong glory and dominion for ever and ever. Amen.

Suffering as a Christian

12 Beloved, do not be surprised at the fiery ordeal which comes upon you to prove you, as though something strange were happening to you. [13]But rejoice in so far as you share Christ's sufferings, that you may also rejoice and be glad when his glory is revealed. [14]If you are reproached for the name of Christ, you are blessed, because the spirit of glory[j] and of God rests upon you. [15]But let none of you suffer as a murderer, or a thief, or a wrongdoer, or a mischief-maker; [16]yet if one suffers as a Christian, let him not be ashamed, but under that name let him glorify God. [17]For the time has come for judgment to begin with the

household of God; and if it begins with us, what will be the end of those who do not obey the gospel of God? [18]And

"If the righteous man is scarcely saved,
   where will the impious and sinner appear?"

[19]Therefore let those who suffer according to God's will do right and entrust their souls to a faithful Creator.

Tending the Flock of Christ

5 So I exhort the elders among you, as a fellow elder and a witness of the sufferings of Christ as well as a partaker in the glory that is to be revealed. [2]Tend the flock of God that is your charge,[k] not by constraint but willingly,[l] not for shameful gain but eagerly, [3]not as domineering over those in your charge but being examples to the flock. [4]And when the chief Shepherd is manifested you will obtain the unfading crown of glory. [5]Likewise you that are younger be subject to the elders. Clothe yourselves, all of you, with humility toward one another, for "God opposes the proud, but gives grace to the humble."

6 Humble yourselves therefore under the mighty hand of God, that in due time he may exalt you. [7]Cast all your anxieties on him, for he cares about you. [8]Be sober, be watchful. Your adversary the devil prowls around like a roaring lion, seeking some one to devour. [9]Resist him, firm in your faith, knowing that the same experience of suffering is required of your brotherhood throughout the world. [10]And after you have suffered a little while, the God of all grace, who has called you to his eternal glory in Christ, will himself restore, establish, and strengthen[m] you. [11]To him be the dominion for ever and ever. Amen.

Final Greetings and Benediction

12 By Silva'nus, a faithful brother as I regard him, I have written briefly to you, exhorting and declaring that this is the true grace of God; stand fast in it. [13]She who is at Babylon,† who is likewise chosen, sends you greetings; and so does my son Mark. [14]Greet one another with the kiss of love.

Peace to all of you that are in Christ.

---

h Other ancient authorities read *suffered*.
i Other ancient authorities add *for us*; some *for you*.
j Other ancient authorities insert *and of power*.
k Other ancient authorities add *exercising the oversight*.
l Other ancient authorities add *as God would have you*.
m Other ancient authorities read *restore, establish, strengthen, and settle*.
3:20: Gen 6–8.
4:14: Is 11:2.
4:18: Prov 11:31 Septuagint.
5:5: Prov 3:34.
5:7: Ps 55:22.
* 4:1, *ceased from sin*: Peter means that a continual acceptance of suffering is incompatible with a proneness to sin.
† 5:13, *Babylon*: Rome was as full of iniquity as ancient Babylon; cf. Rev 17:9.

THE SECOND LETTER OF

PETER

Salutation

1 Simon Peter, a servant and apostle of Jesus Christ,

To those who have obtained a faith of equal standing with ours in the righteousness of our God and Savior Jesus Christ: ᵃ

2 May grace and peace be multiplied to you in the knowledge of God and of Jesus our Lord.

The Christian's Call and Election

3 His divine power has granted to us all things that pertain to life and godliness, through the knowledge of him who called us to ᵇ his own glory and excellence, ⁴by which he has granted to us his precious and very great promises, that through these you may escape from the corruption that is in the world because of passion, and become partakers of the divine nature. * ⁵For this very reason make every effort to supplement your faith with virtue, and virtue with knowledge, ⁶and knowledge with self-control, and self-control with steadfastness, and steadfastness with godliness, ⁷and godliness with brotherly affection, and brotherly affection with love. ⁸For if these things are yours and abound, they keep you from being ineffective or unfruitful in the knowledge of our Lord Jesus Christ. ⁹For whoever lacks these things is blind and shortsighted and has forgotten that he was cleansed from his old sins. ¹⁰Therefore, brethren, be the more zealous to confirm your call and election, for if you do this you will never fall; ¹¹so there will be richly provided for you an entrance into the eternal kingdom of our Lord and Savior Jesus Christ.

12 Therefore I intend always to remind you of these things, though you know them and are established in the truth that you have. ¹³I think it right, as long as I am in this body, ᶜ to arouse you by way of reminder, ¹⁴since I know that the putting off of my body ᶜ will be soon, as our Lord Jesus Christ showed me. ¹⁵And I will see to it that after my departure you may be able at any time to recall these things.

Eyewitnesses of Christ's Glory

16 † For we did not follow cleverly devised myths when we made known to you the power and coming of our Lord Jesus Christ, but we were eyewitnesses of his majesty. ¹⁷For when he received honor and glory from God the Father and the voice was borne to him by the Majestic Glory, "This is my beloved Son, ᵈ with whom I am well pleased," ¹⁸we heard this voice borne from heaven, for we were with him on the holy mountain. ¹⁹And we have the prophetic word made more sure. You will do well to pay attention to this as to a lamp shining in a dark place, until the day dawns and the morning star rises in your hearts. ²⁰First of all you must understand this, that no prophecy of Scripture is a matter of one's own interpretation, ²¹because no prophecy ever came by the impulse of man, but men moved by the Holy Spirit spoke from God. ᵉ

False Prophets and Their Punishment

2 But false prophets also arose among the people, just as there will be false teachers among you, who will secretly bring in destructive heresies, even denying the Master who bought them, bringing upon themselves swift destruction. ²And many will follow their licentiousness, and because of them the way of truth will be reviled. ³And in their greed they will exploit you with false words; from of old their condemnation has not been idle, and their destruction has not been asleep. ‡

4 For if God did not spare the angels when they sinned, but cast them into hell ᶠ and committed them to pits of deepest darkness to be kept until the judgment; ⁵if he did not spare the ancient world, but preserved Noah, a herald of righteousness, with seven other persons, when he brought a flood upon the world of the ungodly; ⁶if by turning the cities of Sodom and Gomor'rah to ashes he condemned them to extinction and made them an example to those who were to be ungodly; ⁷and if he rescued righteous Lot, greatly distressed by the licentiousness of the wicked ⁸(for by what that righteous man saw and heard as he lived among them, he was vexed in his

---

ᵃ Or *of our God and the Savior Jesus Christ.*
ᵇ Or *by.*
ᶜ Greek *tent.*
ᵈ Or *my Son, my* (or *the*) *Beloved.*
ᵉ Other authorities read *moved by the Holy Spirit holy men of God spoke.*
ᶠ Greek *Tartarus.*
1:17–18: Mt 17:1–8; Mk 9:2–8; Lk 9:28–36.
2:1–18: Jude 4–16.
2:5: Gen 8:18; 6:6–8.
2:6: Gen 19:24.
2:7: Gen 19:16, 29.
* 1:4, *partakers of the divine nature*: A strong expression to describe the transformation of human nature by divine grace.
† 1:16–18: A reference to the transfiguration.
‡ 2:3: Much of the material of this chapter appears to be from the Letter of Jude.

righteous soul day after day with their lawless deeds), [9]then the Lord knows how to rescue the godly from trial, and to keep the unrighteous under punishment until the day of judgment, [10]and especially those who indulge in the lust of defiling passion and despise authority.

Bold and wilful, they are not afraid to revile the glorious ones, [11]whereas angels, though greater in might and power, do not pronounce a reviling judgment upon them before the Lord. [12]But these, like irrational animals, creatures of instinct, born to be caught and killed, reviling in matters of which they are ignorant, will be destroyed in the same destruction with them, [13]suffering wrong for their wrongdoing. They count it pleasure to revel in the daytime. They are blots and blemishes, reveling in their dissipation, [g] carousing with you. [14]They have eyes full of adultery, insatiable for sin. They entice unsteady souls. They have hearts trained in greed. Accursed children! [15]Forsaking the right way they have gone astray; they have followed the way of Balaam, the son of Beor, who loved gain from wrongdoing, [16]but was rebuked for his own transgression; a speechless donkey spoke with human voice and restrained the prophet's madness.

17 These are waterless springs and mists driven by a storm; for them the deepest gloom of darkness has been reserved. [18]For, uttering loud boasts of folly, they entice with licentious passions of the flesh men who have barely escaped from those who live in error. [19]They promise them freedom, but they themselves are slaves of corruption; for whatever overcomes a man, to that he is enslaved. [20]For if, after they have escaped the defilements of the world through the knowledge of our Lord and Savior Jesus Christ, they are again entangled in them and overpowered, the last state has become worse for them than the first. [21]For it would have been better for them never to have known the way of righteousness than after knowing it to turn back from the holy commandment delivered to them. [22]It has happened to them according to the true proverb, The dog turns back to his own vomit, and the sow is washed only to wallow in the mire.

The Promise of the Lord's Coming

3 This is now the second letter that I have written to you, beloved, and in both of them I have aroused your sincere mind by way of reminder; [2]that you should remember the predictions of the holy prophets and the commandment of the Lord and Savior through your apostles. [3]First of all you must understand this, that scoffers will come in the last days with scoffing, following their own passions [4]and saying, "Where is the promise of his coming? For ever since the fathers fell asleep, all things have continued as they were from the beginning of creation." [5]They

deliberately ignore this fact, that by the word of God heavens existed long ago, and an earth formed out of water and by means of water, [6]through which the world that then existed was deluged with water and perished. [7]But by the same word the heavens and earth that now exist have been stored up for fire, being kept until the day of judgment and destruction of ungodly men.

8 But do not ignore this one fact, beloved, that with the Lord one day is as a thousand years, and a thousand years as one day. [9]The Lord is not slow about his promise as some count slowness, but is forbearing toward you, [h] not wishing that any should perish, but that all should reach repentance. [10]But the day of the Lord will come like a thief, and then the heavens will pass away with a loud noise, and the elements will be dissolved with fire, and the earth and the works that are upon it will be burned up.

11 Since all these things are thus to be dissolved, what sort of persons ought you to be in lives of holiness and godliness, [12]waiting for and hastening [i] the coming of the day of God, because of which the heavens will be kindled and dissolved, and the elements will melt with fire! [13]But according to his promise we wait for new heavens and a new earth in which righteousness dwells.

Final Exhortation and Doxology

14 Therefore, beloved, since you wait for these, be zealous to be found by him without spot or blemish, and at peace. [15]And count the forbearance of our Lord as salvation. So also our beloved brother Paul wrote to you according to the wisdom given him, [16]speaking of this * as he does in all his letters. There are some things in them hard to understand, which the ignorant and unstable twist to their own destruction, as they do the other Scriptures. [17]You therefore, beloved, knowing this beforehand, beware lest you be carried away with the error of lawless men and lose your own stability. [18]But grow in the grace and knowledge of our Lord and Savior Jesus Christ. To him be the glory both now and to the day of eternity. Amen.

---

[g] Other ancient authorities read love feasts.
[h] Other ancient authorities read on your account.
[i] Or earnestly desiring.
2:15: Num 22:5, 7.
2:16: Num 22:21, 23, 28, 30–31.
2:22: Prov 26:11.
3:5–6: Gen 1:6–8; 7:11.
3:8: Ps 90:4.
3:12: Is 34:4.
3:13: Is 65:17; 66:22.
* 3:16, this seems to refer to the theme of the end of the world and the second Coming of Christ, about which Paul had written in his letters to the Thessalonians.

THE FIRST LETTER OF

JOHN

The Word of Life

1 * That which was from the beginning, which we have heard, which we have seen with our eyes, which we have looked upon and touched with our hands, concerning the word of life—[2]the life was made manifest, and we saw it, and testify to it, and proclaim to you the eternal life which was with the Father and was made manifest to us—[3]that which we have seen and heard we proclaim also to you, so that you may have fellowship † with us; and our fellowship is with the Father and with his Son Jesus Christ. [4]And we are writing this that our [a] joy may be complete.

God Is Light

5 This is the message we have heard from him and proclaim to you, that God is light and in him is no darkness ‡ at all. [6]If we say we have fellowship with him while we walk in darkness, we lie and do not live according to the truth; [7]but if we walk in the light, as he is in the light, we have fellowship with one another, and the blood of Jesus his Son cleanses us from all sin. [8]If we say we have no sin, we deceive ourselves, and the truth is not in us. [9]If we confess our sins, he is faithful and just, and will forgive our sins and cleanse us from all unrighteousness. [10]If we say we have not sinned, we make him a liar, and his word is not in us.

Christ Is Our Advocate

2 My little children, I am writing this to you so that you may not sin; but if any one does sin, we have an advocate with the Father, Jesus Christ the righteous; [2]and he is the expiation for our sins, and not for ours only but also for the sins of the whole world. [3]And by this we may be sure that we know him, if we keep his commandments. § [4]He who says "I know him" but disobeys his commandments is a liar, and the truth is not in him; [5]but whoever keeps his word, in him truly love for God is perfected. By this we may be sure that we are in him: [6]he who says he abides in him ought to walk in the same way in which he walked.

A New Commandment

7 Beloved, I am writing you no new commandment, but an old commandment which you had from the beginning; the old commandment is the word which you have heard. [8]Yet I am writing you a new commandment, which is true in him and in you, because [b] the darkness is passing away and the true light is already shining. [9]He who says he is in the light and hates his brother is in the darkness still. [10]He who loves his brother abides in the light, and in it [c] there is no cause for stumbling. [11]But he who hates his brother is in the darkness and walks in the darkness, and does not know where he is going, because the darkness has blinded his eyes.

12 I am writing to you, little children, because your sins are forgiven for his sake. [13]I am writing to you, fathers, because you know him who is from the beginning. I am writing to you, young men, because you have overcome the Evil One. I write to you, children, because you know the Father. [14]I write to you, fathers, because you know him who is from the beginning. I write to you, young men, because you are strong, and the word of God abides in you, and you have overcome the Evil One.

15 Do not love the world or the things in the world. If any one loves the world, love for the Father is not in him. [16]For all that is in the world, the lust of the flesh and the lust of the eyes and the pride of life, is not of the Father but is of the world. [17]And the world passes away, and the lust of it; but he who does the will of God abides for ever.

Warning against the Antichrist

18 Children, it is the last hour; ** and as you have heard that antichrist is coming, so now

---

[a] Other ancient authorities read *your.*
[b] Or *that.*
[c] Or *him.*
1:1–2: Lk 24:39; Jn 1:1; 4:14; 15:27; 20:20, 25; Acts 4:20; 1 Jn 2:13.
1:4: Jn 15:11; 2 Jn 12.
1:5: 1 Jn 3:11.
1:6–8: Jn 3:21; 1 Jn 2:4, 11.
1:7: Rev 1:5.
1:10: 1 Jn 5:10.
2:1: Jn 14:16.
2:2: Jn 1:29; 3:14–16; 11:51–52; 1 Jn 4:10.
2:3: Jn 15:10.
2:4: 1 Jn 1:6–8; 4:20.
2:5: Jn 14:21, 23; 1 Jn 5:3.
2:6: Jn 13:15.
2:7: Jn 13:34.
2:8: Jn 8:12.
2:10–11: Jn 11:9–10; 1 Jn 1:6.
2:13: Jn 1:1; 1 Jn 1:1.
2:18: 1 Jn 4:3.
* **1:1–7:** Note the likeness with John's Gospel 1:1–18.
† **1:3,** *fellowship*: A Johannine theme.
‡ **1:5,** *light ... darkness*: Another familiar theme in John's Gospel.
§ **2:3:** Cf. the words of Jesus, "If you love me, you will keep my commandments" (Jn 14:15).
** **2:18,** *the last hour*: John exhorts his readers to hold fast, as though the end were at hand.

many antichrists have come; therefore we know that it is the last hour. [19]They went out from us, but they were not of us; for if they had been of us, they would have continued with us; but they went out, that it might be plain that they all are not of us. [20]But you have been anointed by the Holy One, and you all know. [d] [21]I write to you, not because you do not know the truth, but because you know it, and know that no lie is of the truth. [22]Who is the liar but he who denies that Jesus is the Christ? This is the antichrist, he who denies the Father and the Son. [23]Any one who denies the Son does not have the Father. He who confesses the Son has the Father also. [24]Let what you heard from the beginning abide in you. If what you heard from the beginning abides in you, then you will abide in the Son and in the Father. [25]And this is what he has promised us, [e] eternal life.

26 I write this to you about those who would deceive you; [27]but the anointing which you received from him abides in you, and you have no need that any one should teach you; as his anointing teaches you about everything, and is true, and is no lie, just as it has taught you, abide in him.

Children of God

28 And now, little children, abide in him, so that when he appears we may have confidence and not shrink from him in shame at his coming. [29]If you know that he is righteous, you may be sure that every one who does right is born of him.

3 See what love the Father has given us, that we should be called children of God; and so we are. The reason why the world does not know us is that it did not know him. [2]Beloved, we are God's children now; it does not yet appear what we shall be, but we know that when he appears we shall be like him, for we shall see him as he is. [3]And every one who thus hopes in him purifies himself as he is pure.

4 Every one who commits sin is guilty of lawlessness; sin is lawlessness. [5]You know that he appeared to take away sins, and in him there is no sin. [6]Any one who abides in him does not sin; * any one who sins has not seen him, nor has he known him. [7]Little children, let no one deceive you. He who does right is righteous, as he is righteous. [8]He who commits sin is of the devil; for the devil has sinned from the beginning. The reason the Son of God appeared was to destroy the works of the devil. [9]Any one born of God does not commit sin; for God's [f] seed abides in him, and he cannot sin because he is [g] born of God. [10]By this it may be seen who are the children of God, and who are the children of the devil: whoever does not do right is not of God, nor he who does not love his brother.

Love One Another

11 For this is the message which you have heard from the beginning, that we should love one

another, [12]and not be like Cain who was of the Evil One and murdered his brother. And why did he murder him? Because his own deeds were evil and his brother's righteous. [13]Do not wonder, brethren, that the world hates you. [14]We know that we have passed out of death into life, because we love the brethren. He who does not love remains in death. [15]Any one who hates his brother is a murderer, and you know that no murderer has eternal life abiding in him. [16]By this we know love, that he laid down his life for us; and we ought to lay down our lives for the brethren. [17]But if any one has the world's goods and sees his brother in need, yet closes his heart against him, how does God's love abide in him? [18]Little children, let us not love in word or speech but in deed and in truth.

19 By this we shall know that we are of the truth, and reassure our hearts before him [20]whenever our hearts condemn us; for God is greater than our hearts, and he knows everything. [21]Beloved, if our hearts do not condemn us, we have confidence before God; [22]and we receive from him whatever we ask, because we keep his commandments and do what pleases him. [23]And this is his commandment, that we should believe in the name of his Son Jesus Christ and love one another, just as he has commanded us. [24]All who keep his commandments abide in him, and he in them. And by this we know that he abides in us, by the Spirit which he has given us.

Testing the Spirits

4 Beloved, do not believe every spirit, but test the spirits † to see whether they are of God; for many false prophets have gone out into the world. [2]By this you know the Spirit of God: every spirit which confesses that Jesus Christ has come in the flesh is of God, [3]and every spirit which does not confess Jesus is not of God. This is the

---

[d] Other ancient authorities read *you know everything.*
[e] Other ancient authorities read *you.*
[f] Greek *his.*
[g] Or *for the offspring of God abide in him, and they cannot sin because they are.*
2:22: 2 Jn 7.
2:23: 1 Jn 4:15; 2 Jn 9.
2:27: Jn 14:26.
2:28: 1 Jn 4:17.
2:29: 1 Jn 3:7–10; 4:7.
3:1: Jn 1:12; 16:3.
3:5: Jn 1:29.
3:8: Jn 8:34, 44.
3:9: 1 Jn 5:18.
3:11: 1 Jn 1:5.
3:13: Jn 15:18–19.
3:14: Jn 5:24.
3:15: Jn 8:44.
3:16: Jn 13:1; 15:13.
3:18: Jas 1:22.
3:21: 1 Jn 5:14.
3:23: Jn 6:29; 13:34; 15:17.
3:24: 1 Jn 4:13.
4:3: 1 Jn 2:18.
* 3:6, *sins:* i.e., remains in sin, or has a habit of sin.
† 4:1, *test the spirits:* i.e., examine those who claim to have special gifts from the Holy Spirit; cf. 1 Cor 14:32.

spirit of antichrist, of which you heard that it was coming, and now it is in the world already. [4]Little children, you are of God, and have overcome them; for he who is in you is greater than he who is in the world. [5]They are of the world, therefore what they say is of the world, and the world listens to them. [6]We are of God. Whoever knows God listens to us, and he who is not of God does not listen to us. By this we know the spirit of truth and the spirit of error.

God Is Love

7 Beloved, let us love one another; for love is of God, and he who loves is born of God and knows God. [8]He who does not love does not know God; for God is love. [9]In this the love of God was made manifest among us, that God sent his only-begotten Son into the world, so that we might live through him. [10]In this is love, not that we loved God but that he loved us and sent his Son to be the expiation for our sins. [11]Beloved, if God so loved us, we also ought to love one another. [12]No man has ever seen God; if we love one another, God abides in us and his love is perfected in us.

13 By this we know that we abide in him and he in us, because he has given us of his own Spirit. [14]And we have seen and testify that the Father has sent his Son as the Savior of the world. [15]Whoever confesses that Jesus is the Son of God, God abides in him, and he in God. [16]So we know and believe the love God has for us. God is love, and he who abides in love abides in God, and God abides in him. [17]In this is love perfected with us, that we may have confidence for the day of judgment, because as he is so are we in this world. [18]There is no fear in love, but perfect love casts out fear. For fear has to do with punishment, and he who fears is not perfected in love. [19]We love, because he first loved us. [20]If any one says, "I love God," and hates his brother, he is a liar; for he who does not love his brother whom he has seen, cannot [h] love God whom he has not seen. [21]And this commandment we have from him, that he who loves God should love his brother also.

Faith Conquers the World

5 Every one who believes that Jesus is the Christ has been born of God, and every one who loves the parent loves the one begotten by him. [2]By this we know that we love the children of God, when we love God and obey his commandments. [3]For this is the love of God, that we keep his commandments. And his commandments are not burdensome. [4]For whatever is born of God overcomes the world; and this is the victory that overcomes the world, our faith. [5]Who is it that overcomes the world but he who believes that Jesus is the Son of God?

Testimony concerning the Son of God

6 This is he who came by water and blood, Jesus Christ, not with the water only but with the water and the blood. [7]And the Spirit is the witness, because the Spirit is the truth. [8]There are three witnesses, the Spirit, the water, and the blood; and these three agree. * [9]If we receive the testimony of men, the testimony of God is greater; for this is the testimony of God that he has borne witness to his Son. [10]He who believes in the Son of God has the testimony in himself. He who does not believe God has made him a liar, because he has not believed in the testimony that God has borne to his Son. [11]And this is the testimony, that God gave us eternal life, and this life is in his Son. [12]He who has the Son has life; he who has not the Son of God has not life.

Epilogue

13 I write this to you who believe in the name of the Son of God, that you may know that you have eternal life. [14]And this is the confidence which we have in him, that if we ask anything according to his will he hears us. [15]And if we know that he hears us in whatever we ask, we know that we have obtained the requests made of him. [16]If any one sees his brother committing what is not a deadly sin, he will ask, and God [i] will give him life for those whose sin is not deadly. There is sin which is deadly; I do not say that one is to pray for that. [17]All wrongdoing is sin, but there is sin which is not deadly.

18 We know that any one born of God does not sin, but He who was born of God keeps him, and the Evil One does not touch him.

19 We know that we are of God, and the whole world is in the power of the Evil One.

20 And we know that the Son of God has come and has given us understanding, to know him who is true; and we are in him who is true, in his Son Jesus Christ. This is the true God and eternal life. [21]Little children, keep yourselves from idols.

---

[h] Other ancient authorities read how can he.
[i] Greek he.
4:5: Jn 15:19.
4:6: Jn 8:47.
4:7: 1 Jn 2:29.
4:9: Jn 3:16.
4:10: Jn 15:12; 1 Jn 4:19; 2:2.
4:12: Jn 1:18.
4:13: 1 Jn 3:24.
4:14: Jn 4:42; 3:17.
4:17: 1 Jn 2:28.
4:19: 1 Jn 4:10.
4:20: 1 Jn 2:4.
5:1: Jn 8:42.
5:3: Jn 14:15; 1 Jn 2:5; 2 Jn 6.
5:4: Jn 16:33.
5:6-8: Jn 19:34; 4:23; 15:26.
5:9: Jn 5:32, 36; 8:18.
5:10: 1 Jn 1:10.
* 5:8: This reads as follows in the Vulgate: " [7]There are three who give testimony in heaven: the Father, the Word, and the Holy Spirit; and these three are one. [8]And there are three that give testimony on earth: the spirit, and the water, and the blood; and these three are one." The "Three Heavenly Witnesses," as the first sentence is called, is first found in the Latin (fourth century) and does not appear in any Greek manuscript until the fifteenth century. It is probably a marginal gloss that found its way into the text.

JOHN

Salutation

1 The elder * to the elect lady † and her children, whom I love in the truth, and not only I but also all who know the truth, [2]because of the truth which abides in us and will be with us for ever:

3 Grace, mercy, and peace will be with us, from God the Father and from Jesus Christ the Father's Son, in truth and love.

Truth and Love

4 I rejoiced greatly to find some of your children following the truth, just as we have been commanded by the Father. [5]And now I beg you, lady, not as though I were writing you a new commandment, but the one we have had from the beginning, that we love one another. [6]And this is love, that we follow his commandments; this is the commandment, as you have heard from the beginning, that you follow love. [7]For many deceivers have gone out into the world, men who will not acknowledge the coming of Jesus Christ in the flesh; such a one is the deceiver and the antichrist. [8]Look to yourselves, that you may not lose what you [a] have worked for, but may win a full reward.

[9]Any one who goes ahead and does not abide in the doctrine of Christ does not have God; he who abides in the doctrine has both the Father and the Son. [10]If any one comes to you and does not bring this doctrine, do not receive him into the house or give him any greeting; [11]for he who greets him shares his wicked work.

Final Greetings

12 Though I have much to write to you, I would rather not use paper and ink, but I hope to come to see you and talk with you face to face, so that our joy may be complete.

13 The children ‡ of your elect sister greet you.

---

[a] Other ancient authorities read we.
1: 3 Jn 1.
5: Jn 13:34.
6: 1 Jn 5:3.
7: 1 Jn 2:22.
12: 1 Jn 1:4; 3 Jn 13.
* 1, The elder: Perhaps the head of the group or "college" of elders that presided over each Christian community. John was head not only of the Ephesus community but of all the communities in the province of Asia.
† 1, the elect lady: Probably not an individual lady but a particular church or community in Asia.
‡ 13, children: i.e., the Christians of Ephesus.

THE THIRD LETTER OF

JOHN

Salutation

1 The elder to the beloved Ga′ius, whom I love in the truth.

Gaius Commended for His Service

2 Beloved, I pray that all may go well with you and that you may be in health; I know that it is well with your soul. [3]For I greatly rejoiced when some of the brethren arrived and testified to the truth of your life, as indeed you do follow the truth. [4]No greater joy can I have than this, to hear that my children follow the truth.

5 Beloved, it is a loyal thing you do when you render any service to the brethren, especially to strangers, [6]who have testified to your love before the Church. You will do well to send them on their journey as befits God's service. [7]For they have set out for his sake and have accepted nothing from the heathen. [8]So we ought to support such men, that we may be fellow workers in the truth.

Diotrephes and Demetrius

9 I have written something to the Church; but Diot′rephes, who likes to put himself first, does not acknowledge my authority. [10]So if I come, I will bring up what he is doing, accusing me falsely with evil words. And not content with that, he refuses himself to welcome the brethren, and also stops those who want to welcome them and puts them out of the Church.

11 Beloved, do not imitate evil but imitate good. He who does good is of God; he who does evil has not seen God. [12]Deme′trius * has testimony from every one, and from the truth itself; I testify to him too, and you know my testimony is true.

Final Greetings

13 I had much to write to you, but I would rather not write with pen and ink; [14]I hope to see you soon, and we will talk together face to face.

15 Peace be to you. The friends greet you. Greet the friends, every one of them.

1: Acts 19:29; 2 Jn 1.
12: Jn 21:24.
13: 2 Jn 12.
* 12, *Demetrius*: Evidently a leading Christian, recommended to Gaius.

THE LETTER OF
JUDE

Salutation

1 Jude, a servant of Jesus Christ and brother of James,

To those who are called, beloved in God the Father and kept for Jesus Christ:

2 May mercy, peace, and love be multiplied to you.

Occasion of the Letter

3 Beloved, being very eager to write to you of our common salvation, I found it necessary to write appealing to you to contend for the faith which was once for all delivered to the saints. 4For admission has been secretly gained by some who long ago were designated for this condemnation, ungodly persons who pervert the grace of our God into licentiousness and deny our only Master and Lord, Jesus Christ. a

Judgment on the Ungodly

5 Now I desire to remind you, though you were once for all fully informed, that he b who saved a people out of the land of Egypt, afterward destroyed those who did not believe. 6And the angels that did not keep their own position but left their proper dwelling have been kept by him in eternal chains in the deepest darkness until the judgment of the great day; * 7just as Sodom and Gomor′rah and the surrounding cities, which likewise acted immorally and indulged in unnatural lust, serve as an example by undergoing a punishment of eternal fire.

8 Yet in like manner these men in their dreamings defile the flesh, reject authority, and revile the glorious ones. c 9But when the archangel Michael, contending with the devil, disputed about the body of Moses, he did not presume to pronounce a reviling judgment upon him, but said, "The Lord rebuke you." † 10But these men revile whatever they do not understand, and by those things that they know by instinct as irrational animals do, they are destroyed. 11Woe to them! For they walk in the way of Cain, and abandon themselves for the sake of gain to Balaam's error, and perish in Ko′rah's rebellion. 12These are blemishes d on your love feasts, as they boldly carouse together, looking after themselves; waterless clouds, carried along by winds; fruitless trees in late autumn, twice dead, uprooted; 13wild waves of the sea, casting up the foam of their own shame; wandering stars for whom the deepest darkness has been reserved for ever.

14 It was of these also that Enoch in the seventh generation from Adam prophesied, saying, "Behold, the Lord came with myriads of his holy ones, 15to execute judgment on all, and to convict all the ungodly of all their deeds of ungodliness which they have committed in such an ungodly way, and of all the harsh things which ungodly sinners have spoken against him." 16These are grumblers, malcontents, following their own passions, loud-mouthed boasters, flattering people to gain advantage.

Warnings and Exhortations

17 But you must remember, beloved, the predictions of the apostles of our Lord Jesus Christ; 18they said to you, "In the last time there will be scoffers, following their own ungodly passions." 19It is these who set up divisions, worldly people, devoid of the Spirit. 20But you, beloved, build yourselves up on your most holy faith; pray in the Holy Spirit; 21keep yourselves in the love of God; wait for the mercy of our Lord Jesus Christ unto eternal life. 22And convince some, who doubt; 23save some, by snatching them out of the fire; on some have mercy with fear, hating even the garment spotted by the flesh. e

Benediction

24 Now to him who is able to keep you from falling and to present you without blemish before the presence of his glory with rejoicing, 25to the only God, our Savior through Jesus Christ our Lord, be glory, majesty, dominion, and authority, before all time and now and for ever. Amen.

---

a Or *the only Master and our Lord Jesus Christ.*
b Ancient authorities read *Jesus* or *the Lord* or *God.*
c Greek *glories.*
d Or *reefs.*
e The Greek text in this sentence is uncertain at several points.
4–16: 2 Pet 2:1–18.
7: Gen 19.
9: Zech 3:2.
11: Gen 4:3–8; Num 22–24; 16.
14–15: Enoch 1:9.
23: Zech 3:3–4.
* 6: It is not clear to what Jude refers. Perhaps Gen 6:2 or the apocryphal Enoch 6–15.
† 9: Apparently a reference to another apocryphal work, the Assumption of Moses.

THE
REVELATION TO JOHN
(THE APOCALYPSE)

Introduction and Salutation

1 The revelation of Jesus Christ, which God gave him to show to his servants what must soon take place; and he made it known by sending his angel to his servant John, [2]who bore witness to the word of God and to the testimony of Jesus Christ, even to all that he saw. [3]Blessed is he who reads aloud the words of the prophecy, and blessed are those who hear, and who keep what is written therein; for the time is near.

4 John to the seven churches that are in Asia: *

Grace to you and peace from him who is and who was and who is to come, and from the seven spirits who are before his throne, [5]and from Jesus Christ the faithful witness, the first-born of the dead, and the ruler of kings on earth.

To him who loves us and has freed us from our sins by his blood [6]and made us a kingdom, priests to his God and Father, to him be glory and dominion for ever and ever. Amen. [7]Behold, he is coming with the clouds, and every eye will see him, every one who pierced him; and all tribes of the earth will wail on account of him. Even so. Amen.

8 "I am the Alpha and the Omega," says the Lord God, who is and who was and who is to come, the Almighty.

A Vision of Christ

9 I John, your brother, who share with you in Jesus the tribulation and the kingdom and the patient endurance, was on the island called Patmos on account of the word of God and the testimony of Jesus. [10]I was in the Spirit on the Lord's day, and I heard behind me a loud voice like a trumpet [11]saying, "Write what you see in a book and send it to the seven churches, to Ephesus and to Smyrna and to Per'gamum and to Thyati'ra and to Sardis and to Philadelphia and to La·odice'a."

12 Then I turned to see the voice that was speaking to me, and on turning I saw seven golden lampstands, [13]and in the midst of the lampstands one like a Son of man, † clothed with a long robe and with a golden sash across his chest; [14]his head and his hair were white as white wool, white as snow; his eyes were like a flame of fire, [15]his feet were like burnished bronze, refined as in a furnace, and his voice was like the sound of many waters; [16]in his right hand he held seven stars, from his mouth issued a sharp two-edged sword, and his face was like the sun shining in full strength.

17 When I saw him, I fell at his feet as though dead. But he laid his right hand upon me, saying, "Fear not, I am the first and the last, [18]and the living one; I died, and behold I am alive for evermore, and I have the keys of Death and Hades. [19]Now write what you see, what is and what is to take place hereafter. [20]As for the mystery of the seven stars which you saw in my right hand, and the seven golden lampstands, the seven stars are the angels of the seven churches and the seven lampstands are the seven churches.

The Message to Ephesus

2 "To the angel of the Church in Ephesus write: 'The words of him who holds the seven stars in his right hand, who walks among the seven golden lampstands.

2 "'I know your works, your toil and your patient endurance, and how you cannot bear evil men but have tested those who call themselves apostles but are not, and found them to be false; [3]I know you are enduring patiently and bearing up for my name's sake, and you have not grown weary. [4]But I have this against you, that you have abandoned the love you had at first. [5]Remember then from what you have fallen, repent and do the works you did at first. If not, I will come to you and remove your lampstand from its place, unless you repent. [6]Yet this you have, you hate the works of the Nicola'itans, which I also hate. [7]He who has an ear, let him hear what the Spirit says to the churches. To him who conquers I will grant to eat of the tree of life, which is in the paradise of God.'

1:4: Ex 3:14.
1:5: Ps 89:27.
1:6: Ex 19:6; Is 61:6.
1:7: Dan 7:13; Mt 24:30; Mk 14:62; Zech 12:10.
1:8: Ex 3:14.
1:13: Dan 7:13; 10:5.
1:15: Ezek 1:24.
1:16: Ex 34:29.
1:17: Is 44:2, 6.
2:7: Gen 2:9.
* 1:4–8: Describes the glorious coming and reign of the Messiah.
† 1:13, *Son of man* refers to Dan 7:13. The Messiah is described in symbolic terms.

The Message to Smyrna

8 "And to the angel of the Church in Smyrna write: 'The words of the first and the last, who died and came to life.

9 "'I know your tribulation and your poverty (but you are rich) and the slander of those who say that they are Jews and are not, but are a synagogue of Satan. [10]Do not fear what you are about to suffer. Behold, the devil is about to throw some of you into prison, that you may be tested, and for ten days * you will have tribulation. Be faithful unto death, and I will give you the crown of life. [11]He who has an ear, let him hear what the Spirit says to the churches. He who conquers shall not be hurt by the second death.'

The Message to Pergamum

12 "And to the angel of the Church in Per'gamum write: 'The words of him who has the sharp two-edged sword.

13 "'I know where you dwell, where Satan's throne is; you hold fast my name and you did not deny my faith even in the days of An'tipas my witness, my faithful one, who was killed among you, where Satan dwells. [14]But I have a few things against you: you have some there who hold the teaching of Balaam, who taught Balak to put a stumbling block before the sons of Israel, that they might eat food sacrificed to idols and practice immorality. [15]So you also have some who hold the teaching of the Nicola'itans. [16]Repent then. If not, I will come to you soon and war against them with the sword of my mouth. [17]He who has an ear, let him hear what the Spirit says to the churches. To him who conquers I will give some of the hidden manna, and I will give him a white stone, with a new name written on the stone which no one knows except him who receives it.'

The Message to Thyatira

18 "And to the angel of the Church in Thyati'ra write: 'The words of the Son of God, who has eyes like a flame of fire, and whose feet are like burnished bronze.

19 "'I know your works, your love and faith and service and patient endurance, and that your latter works exceed the first. [20]But I have this against you, that you tolerate the woman Jez'ebel, who calls herself a prophetess and is teaching and beguiling my servants to practice immorality † and to eat food sacrificed to idols. [21]I gave her time to repent, but she refuses to repent of her immorality. † [22]Behold, I will throw her on a sickbed, and those who commit adultery with her I will throw into great tribulation, unless they repent of her doings; [23]and I will strike her children dead. And all the churches shall know that I am he who searches mind and heart, and I will give to each of you as your works deserve. [24]But to the rest of you in Thyati'ra, who do not hold this teaching, who have not learned what some call

the deep things of Satan, ‡ to you I say, I do not lay upon you any other burden; [25]only hold fast what you have, until I come. [26]He who conquers and who keeps my works until the end, I will give him power over the nations, [27]and he shall rule them with a rod of iron, as when earthen pots are broken in pieces, even as I myself have received power from my Father; [28]and I will give him the morning star. § [29]He who has an ear, let him hear what the Spirit says to the churches.'

The Message to Sardis

3 "And to the angel of the Church in Sardis write: 'The words of him who has the seven spirits of God and the seven stars.

"'I know your works; you have the name of being alive, and you are dead. [2]Awake, and strengthen what remains and is on the point of death, for I have not found your works perfect in the sight of my God. [3]Remember then what you received and heard; keep that, and repent. If you will not awake, I will come like a thief, and you will not know at what hour I will come upon you. [4]Yet you have still a few names in Sardis, people who have not soiled their garments; and they shall walk with me in white, for they are worthy. [5]He who conquers shall be clothed like them in white garments, and I will not blot his name out of the book of life; I will confess his name before my Father and before his angels. [6]He who has an ear, let him hear what the Spirit says to the churches.'

The Message to Philadelphia

7 "And to the angel of the Church in Philadelphia write: 'The words of the holy one, the true one, who has the key of David, who opens and no one shall shut, who shuts and no one opens.

8 "'I know your works. Behold, I have set before you an open door, which no one is able to shut; I know that you have but little power, and yet you have kept my word and have not denied my name. [9]Behold, I will make those of the synagogue of Satan who say that they are Jews and are not, but lie—behold, I will make them come and bow down before your feet, and learn that I have loved you. [10]Because you have kept my word of patient endurance, I will keep you from the hour of trial which is coming on the whole world,

---

2:8: Is 44:6.
2:10: Dan 1:12.
2:14: Num 31:16; 25:1–2.
2:17: Ps 78:24; Is 62:2.
2:18: Dan 10:6.
2:20: 1 Kings 16:31; 2 Kings 9:22, 30; Num 25:1.
2:23: Jer 17:10; Ps 62:12.
2:26: Ps 2:8–9.
3:5: Ex 32:32; Ps 69:28; Dan 12:1; Mt 10:32.
3:7: Is 22:22.
3:9: Is 60:14; 49:23; 43:4.
* 2:10, *ten days*: Not literally. It means the persecution will be short.
† 2:20–21, *immorality* here seems to mean idolatry rather than sexual excess.
‡ 2:24, *deep things of Satan*: The doctrines of the Nicolaitans. *They* called them the "deep things of God."
§ 2:28, *morning star*: Probably Christ himself.

to try those who dwell upon the earth. [11]I am coming soon; hold fast what you have, so that no one may seize your crown. [12]He who conquers, I will make him a pillar in the temple of my God; never shall he go out of it, and I will write on him the name of my God, and the name of the city of my God, the new Jerusalem which comes down from my God out of heaven, and my own new name. * [13]He who has an ear, let him hear what the Spirit says to the churches.'

The Message to La-odicea

14 "And to the angel of the Church in La-odice'a write: 'The words of the Amen, the faithful and true witness, the beginning of God's creation.

15 " 'I know your works: you are neither cold nor hot. Would that you were cold or hot! [16]So, because you are lukewarm, and neither cold nor hot, I will spew you out of my mouth. [17]For you say, I am rich, I have prospered, and I need nothing; not knowing that you are wretched, pitiable, poor, blind, and naked. [18]Therefore I counsel you to buy from me gold refined by fire, that you may be rich, and white garments to clothe you and to keep the shame of your nakedness from being seen, and salve to anoint your eyes, that you may see. [19]Those whom I love, I reprove and chasten; so be zealous and repent. [20]Behold, I stand at the door and knock; if any one hears my voice and opens the door, I will come in to him and eat with him, and he with me. [21]He who conquers, I will grant him to sit with me on my throne, as I myself conquered and sat down with my Father on his throne. [22]He who has an ear, let him hear what the Spirit says to the churches.' "

The Heavenly Worship

4 After this I looked, and behold, in heaven an open door! And the first voice, which I had heard speaking to me like a trumpet, said, "Come up here, and I will show you what must take place after this." [2]At once I was in the Spirit, and behold, a throne stood in heaven, with one seated on the throne! [3]And he who sat there appeared like jasper and carnelian, and round the throne was a rainbow that looked like an emerald. † [4]Round the throne were twenty-four thrones, and seated on the thrones were twenty-four elders, ‡ clothed in white garments, with golden crowns upon their heads. [5]From the throne issue flashes of lightning, and voices and peals of thunder, and before the throne burn seven torches of fire, which are the seven spirits of God; [6]and before the throne there is as it were a sea of glass, like crystal.

And round the throne, on each side of the throne, are four living creatures, § full of eyes in front and behind: [7]the first living creature like a lion, the second living creature like an ox, the third living creature with the face of a man, and the fourth living creature like a flying eagle. [8]And the four living creatures, each of them with six wings, are full of eyes all round and within, and day and night they never cease to sing,

"Holy, holy, holy, ** is the Lord God Almighty,
    who was and is and is to come!"

[9]And whenever the living creatures give glory and honor and thanks to him who is seated on the throne, who lives for ever and ever, [10]the twenty-four elders fall down before him who is seated on the throne and worship him who lives for ever and ever; they cast their crowns before the throne, singing,

[11]"Worthy are you, our Lord and God,
    to receive glory and honor and power,
    for you created all things,
    and by your will they existed and were
        created."

The Scroll and the Lamb

5 And I saw in the right hand of him who was seated on the throne a scroll †† written within and on the back, sealed with seven seals; [2]and I saw a strong angel proclaiming with a loud voice, "Who is worthy to open the scroll and break its seals?" [3]And no one in heaven or on earth or under the earth was able to open the scroll or to look into it, [4]and I wept much that no one was found worthy to open the scroll or to look into it. [5]Then one of the elders said to me, "Weep not; behold, the Lion of the tribe of Judah, the Root of David, has conquered, so that he can open the scroll and its seven seals."

6 And between the throne and the four living creatures and among the elders, I saw a Lamb standing, as though it had been slain, with seven horns and with seven eyes, §§ which are the seven spirits of God sent out into all the earth; [7]and he went and took the scroll from the right hand of him who was seated on the throne. [8]And when he

3:12: Is 62:2; Ezek 48:35; Rev 21:2.
3:14: Ps 89:28; Prov 8:22; Jn 1:1–3.
3:17: Hos 12:8.
3:19: Prov 3:12.
4:1: Ex 19:16, 24.
4:2: Ezek 1:26–28.
4:5: Ex 19:16; Zech 4:2.
4:6: Ezek 1:5, 18.
4:7: Ezek 1:10.
4:8: Is 6:2–3.
4:9: Ps 47:8.
5:1: Ezek 2:9; Is 29:11.
5:5: Gen 49:9.
5:6: Is 53:7; Zech 4:10.
5:8: Ps 141:2.

* 3:12, *new name*: cf. Is 62:2. Perhaps it was "the Word," or perhaps it is not to be revealed till the last day.
† 4:3: John describes God in symbolic terms.
‡ 4:4, *elders*: They perform a priestly and royal task, since they praise God and share in the government of the world.
§ 4:6, *four living creatures*: cf. Ezek 1:4–25: the four angels who preside over the government of the world. But in Christian tradition these symbols are used for the four evangelists.
** 4:8, *Holy, holy, holy*: Quoted in the *Sanctus* at Mass.
†† 5:1, *a scroll*: This contained God's designs, kept secret till now; being written on both sides, nothing could be added.
§§ 5:6: The seven horns and seven eyes symbolize Christ's full power and knowledge.

had taken the scroll, the four living creatures and the twenty-four elders fell down before the Lamb, each holding a harp, and with golden bowls full of incense, which are the prayers of the saints; [9]and they sang a new song, saying,

"Worthy are you to take the scroll and to open
    its seals,
for you were slain and by your blood you
    ransomed men for God
from every tribe and tongue and people and
    nation,
[10]and have made them a kingdom and priests to
    our God,
and they shall reign on earth."

[11]Then I looked, and I heard around the throne and the living creatures and the elders the voice of many angels, numbering myriads of myriads and thousands of thousands, [12]saying with a loud voice, "Worthy is the Lamb who was slain, to receive power and wealth and wisdom and might and honor and glory and blessing!" [13]And I heard every creature in heaven and on earth and under the earth and in the sea, and all therein, saying, "To him who sits upon the throne and to the Lamb be blessing and honor and glory and might for ever and ever!" [14]And the four living creatures said, "Amen!" and the elders fell down and worshiped.

The Seven Seals

6 * Now I saw when the Lamb opened one of the seven seals, and I heard one of the four living creatures say, as with a voice of thunder, "Come!" [2]And I saw, and behold, a white horse, and its rider had a bow; and a crown was given to him, and he went out conquering and to conquer.

3 When he opened the second seal, I heard the second living creature say, "Come!" [4]And out came another horse, bright red; its rider was permitted to take peace from the earth, so that men should slay one another; and he was given a great sword.

5 When he opened the third seal, I heard the third living creature say, "Come!" And I saw, and behold, a black horse, and its rider had a balance † in his hand; [6]and I heard what seemed to be a voice in the midst of the four living creatures saying, "A quart of wheat for a denarius, [a] and three quarts of barley for a denarius; [a] but do not harm oil and wine!"

7 When he opened the fourth seal, I heard the voice of the fourth living creature say, "Come!" [8]And I saw, and behold, a pale horse, and its rider's name was Death, and Hades followed him; and they were given power over a fourth of the earth, to kill with sword and with famine and with pestilence and by wild beasts of the earth.

9 When he opened the fifth seal, I saw under the altar the souls of those who had been slain for the word of God and for the witness they had

borne; [10]they cried out with a loud voice, "O Sovereign Lord, holy and true, how long before you will judge and avenge our blood on those who dwell upon the earth?" [11]Then they were each given a white robe and told to rest a little longer, until the number of their fellow servants and their brethren should be complete, who were to be killed as they themselves had been.

12 When he opened the sixth seal, I looked, and behold, there was a great earthquake; and the sun became black as sackcloth, the full moon became like blood, [13]and the stars of the sky fell to the earth as the fig tree sheds its winter fruit when shaken by a gale; [14]the sky vanished like a scroll that is rolled up, and every mountain and island was removed from its place. [15]Then the kings of the earth and the great men and the generals and the rich and the strong, and every one, slave and free, hid in the caves and among the rocks of the mountains, [16]calling to the mountains and rocks, "Fall on us and hide us from the face of him who is seated on the throne, and from the wrath of the Lamb; [17]for the great day of their wrath has come, and who can stand before it?"

The 144,000 of Israel Sealed

7 After this I saw four angels standing at the four corners of the earth, holding back the four winds of the earth, that no wind might blow on earth or sea or against any tree. [2]Then I saw another angel ascend from the rising of the sun, with the seal of the living God, and he called with a loud voice to the four angels who had been given power to harm earth and sea, [3]saying, "Do not harm the earth or the sea or the trees, till we have sealed the servants of our God upon their foreheads." [4]And I heard the number of the sealed, a hundred and forty-four thousand ‡ sealed, out of every tribe of the sons of Israel, [5]twelve thousand sealed out of the tribe of Judah, twelve thousand of the tribe of Reuben, twelve thousand of the tribe of Gad, [6]twelve thousand of the tribe of Asher, twelve thousand of the

---

ᵃ The denarius was a day's wage for a laborer.
5:9: Ps 33:3.
5:10: Ex 19:6; Is 61:6.
5:11: Dan 7:10.
6:2: Zech 1:8; 6:1–3.
6:6: 2 Kings 6:25.
6:8: Hos 13:14; Ezek 5:12.
6:10: Zech 1:12; Ps 79:5; Gen 4:10.
6:12: Joel 2:31; Acts 2:20.
6:13: Is 34:4.
6:15: Is 2:10.
6:16: Hos 10:8.
6:17: Joel 2:11; Mal 3:2.
7:1: Zech 6:5.
7:3: Ezek 9:4.
* 6:1: Begins the account of the destruction of the Roman Empire (chapters 6–9).
† 6:5, *balance*: Symbol of famine. The balance was to measure rations.
‡ 7:4, *a hundred and forty-four thousand*: A symbolic number, i.e., twelve (the sacred number) squared and multiplied by 1,000 to denote a multitude. It is the Church, the spiritual Israel, that is meant.

tribe of Naph'tali, twelve thousand of the tribe of Manas'seh, [7]twelve thousand of the tribe of Simeon, twelve thousand of the tribe of Levi, twelve thousand of the tribe of Is'sachar, [8]twelve thousand of the tribe of Zeb'ulun, twelve thousand of the tribe of Joseph, twelve thousand sealed out of the tribe of Benjamin.

The Multitude from Every Nation

9 After this I looked, and behold, a great multitude which no man could number, from every nation, from all tribes and peoples and tongues, standing before the throne and before the Lamb, clothed in white robes, with palm branches in their hands, [10]and crying out with a loud voice, "Salvation belongs to our God who sits upon the throne, and to the Lamb!" [11]And all the angels stood round the throne and round the elders and the four living creatures, and they fell on their faces before the throne and worshiped God, [12]saying, "Amen! Blessing and glory and wisdom and thanksgiving and honor and power and might be to our God for ever and ever! Amen."

13 Then one of the elders addressed me, saying, "Who are these, clothed in white robes, and from where have they come?" [14]I said to him, "Sir, you know." And he said to me, "These are they who have come out of the great tribulation; * they have washed their robes and made them white in the blood of the Lamb.

[15]Therefore are they before the throne of God,
and serve him day and night within his
temple;
and he who sits upon the throne will shelter
them with his presence.
[16]They shall hunger no more, neither thirst any
more;
the sun shall not strike them, nor any
scorching heat.
[17]For the Lamb in the midst of the throne will be
their shepherd,
and he will guide them to springs of living
water;
and God will wipe away every tear from their
eyes."

The Seventh Seal and the Golden Censer

8 When the Lamb opened the seventh seal, there was silence in heaven for about half an hour. [2]Then I saw the seven angels who stand before God, and seven trumpets were given to them. [3]And another angel came and stood at the altar with a golden censer; and he was given much incense to mingle with the prayers of all the saints upon the golden altar before the throne; [4]and the smoke of the incense rose with the prayers of the saints from the hand of the angel before God. [5]Then the angel took the censer and filled it with fire from the altar and threw it on the earth; † and there were peals of thunder, loud noises, flashes of lightning, and an earthquake.

The Seven Angels and Seven Trumpets

6 Now the seven angels who had the seven trumpets made ready to blow them.

7 The first angel blew his trumpet, and there followed hail and fire, mixed with blood, which fell on the earth; and a third of the earth was burnt up, and a third of the trees were burnt up, and all green grass was burnt up.

8 The second angel blew his trumpet, and something like a great mountain, burning with fire, was thrown into the sea; [9]and a third of the sea became blood, a third of the living creatures in the sea died, and a third of the ships were destroyed.

10 The third angel blew his trumpet, and a great star fell from heaven, blazing like a torch, and it fell on a third of the rivers and on the fountains of water. [11]The name of the star is Wormwood. A third of the waters became wormwood, and many men died of the water, because it was made bitter.

12 The fourth angel blew his trumpet, and a third of the sun was struck, and a third of the moon, and a third of the stars, so that a third of their light was darkened; a third of the day was kept from shining, and likewise a third of the night.

13 Then I looked, and I heard an eagle crying with a loud voice, as it flew in midheaven, "Woe, woe, woe to those who dwell on the earth, at the blasts of the other trumpets which the three angels are about to blow!"

9 And the fifth angel blew his trumpet, and I saw a star ‡ fallen from heaven to earth, and he was given the key of the shaft of the bottomless pit; [2]he opened the shaft of the bottomless pit, and from the shaft rose smoke like the smoke of a great furnace, and the sun and the air were darkened with the smoke from the shaft. [3]Then from the smoke came locusts on the earth, and they were given power like the power of scorpions of the earth; [4]they were told not to harm the grass of the earth or any green growth or any tree, but only those of mankind who have not the seal of God upon their foreheads; [5]they were allowed to torture them for five months, but not to kill them, and their torture was like the torture of

---

7:14: Dan 12:1; Gen 49:11.
7:16: Is 49:10; Ps 121:6.
7:17: Ezek 34:23; Ps 23:2; Is 25:8.
8:3: Amos 9:1; Ps 141:2.
8:5: Lev 16:12; Ezek 10:2.
8:7: Ex 9:23–25.
8:8: Jer 51:25.
8:10: Is 14:12.
9:2: Gen 19:28; Ex 19:18; Joel 2:10.
9:3: Ex 10:12–15.
9:4: Ezek 9:4.
* 7:14, *the great tribulation*: The Neronian persecution?
† 8:5: Coals from the altar of burnt offering were brought to the altar of incense.
‡ 9:1, *star*: A fallen angel.

a scorpion, when it stings a man. [6]And in those days men will seek death and will not find it; they will long to die, and death will fly from them.

7 In appearance the locusts were like horses arrayed for battle; on their heads were what looked like crowns of gold; their faces were like human faces, [8]their hair like women's hair, and their teeth like lions' teeth; [9]they had scales like iron breastplates, and the noise of their wings was like the noise of many chariots with horses rushing into battle. [10]They have tails like scorpions, and stings, and their power of hurting men for five months lies in their tails. [11]They have as king over them the angel of the bottomless pit; his name in Hebrew is Abad'don, and in Greek he is called Apol'lyon. [b]

12 The first woe has passed; behold, two woes are still to come.

13 Then the sixth angel blew his trumpet, and I heard a voice from the four horns of the golden altar before God, [14]saying to the sixth angel who had the trumpet, "Release the four angels who are bound at the great river Euphra'tes." * [15]So the four angels were released, who had been held ready for the hour, the day, the month, and the year, to kill a third of mankind. [16]The number of the troops of cavalry was twice ten thousand times ten thousand; I heard their number. [17]And this was how I saw the horses in my vision: the riders wore breastplates the color of fire and of sapphire [c] and of sulphur, and the heads of the horses were like lions' heads, and fire and smoke and sulphur issued from their mouths. [18]By these three plagues a third of mankind was killed, by the fire and smoke and sulphur issuing from their mouths. [19]For the power of the horses is in their mouths and in their tails; their tails are like serpents, with heads, and by means of them they wound.

20 The rest of mankind, who were not killed by these plagues, did not repent of the works of their hands nor give up worshiping demons and idols of gold and silver and bronze and stone and wood, which cannot either see or hear or walk; [21]nor did they repent of their murders or their sorceries or their immorality † or their thefts.

The Angel with the Little Scroll

10 Then I saw another mighty angel coming down from heaven, wrapped in a cloud, with a rainbow over his head, and his face was like the sun, and his legs like pillars of fire. [2]He had a little scroll open in his hand. And he set his right foot on the sea, and his left foot on the land, [3]and called out with a loud voice, like a lion roaring; when he called out, the seven thunders sounded. [4]And when the seven thunders had sounded, I was about to write, but I heard a voice from heaven saying, "Seal up what the seven thunders have said, and do not write it down."

[5]And the angel whom I saw standing on sea and land lifted up his right hand to heaven [6]and swore by him who lives for ever and ever, who created heaven and what is in it, the earth and what is in it, and the sea and what is in it, that there should be no more delay, [7]but that in the days of the trumpet call to be sounded by the seventh angel, the mystery of God, ‡ as he announced to his servants the prophets, should be fulfilled.

8 Then the voice which I had heard from heaven spoke to me again, saying, "Go, take the scroll which is open in the hand of the angel who is standing on the sea and on the land." [9]So I went to the angel and told him to give me the little scroll; and he said to me, "Take it and eat; it will be bitter to your stomach, but sweet § as honey in your mouth." [10]And I took the little scroll from the hand of the angel and ate it; it was sweet as honey in my mouth, but when I had eaten it my stomach was made bitter. [11]And I was told, "You must again prophesy about many peoples and nations and tongues and kings."

The Two Witnesses

11 ** Then I was given a measuring rod like a staff, and I was told: "Rise and measure the temple of God and the altar and those who worship there, [2]but do not measure the court outside the temple; leave that out, for it is given over to the nations, and they will trample over the holy city for forty-two months. †† [3]And I will grant my two witnesses ‡‡ power to prophesy for one thousand two hundred and sixty days, clothed in sackcloth."

4 These are the two olive trees and the two lampstands which stand before the Lord of the earth. [5]And if any one would harm them, fire pours from their mouth and consumes their foes; if any one would harm them, thus he is doomed to

---

[b] Or Destroyer.
[c] Greek hyacinth.
9:6: Job 3:21.
9:7: Joel 2:4.
9:8: Joel 1:6.
9:9: Joel 2:5.
9:13: Ex 30:1–3.
9:20: Is 17:8; Ps 115:4–7; 135:15–17.
10:5: Deut 32:40; Dan 12:7.
10:9: Ezek 2:8; 3:1–3.
10:11: Jer 1:10.
11:1: Ezek 40:3.
11:2: Zech 12:3; Is 63:18; Lk 21:24.
11:4: Zech 4:3, 11–14.
11:5: 2 Kings 1:10; Jer 5:14.
* 9:14, Euphrates: The region of the Parthians.
† 9:21, immorality: See note on 2:20–21.
‡ 10:7, mystery of God: i.e., the establishment of the kingdom of God following on the destruction of Israel's enemies.
§ 10:9, bitter . . . sweet: The scroll related both the sufferings and the victories of Christ's Church.
** 11:1–9: The Jerusalem here described stands for the Church, which is to be persecuted by the Romans.
†† 11:2: The three and a half years' persecution of the Jews by Antiochus Epiphanes, 168–165 B.C., had become the standard time of a persecution. Three and a half years equals 42 months equals 1,260 days (verse 3).
‡‡ 11:3, two witnesses: As they have yet to die, possibly they are Elijah and Enoch.

be killed. [6]They have power to shut the sky, that no rain may fall during the days of their prophesying, and they have power over the waters to turn them into blood, and to afflict the earth with every plague, as often as they desire. [7]And when they have finished their testimony, the beast that ascends from the bottomless pit will make war upon them and conquer them and kill them, [8]and their dead bodies will lie in the street of the great city * which is allegorically [d] called Sodom and Egypt, where their Lord was crucified. [9]For three days and a half men from the peoples and tribes and tongues and nations gaze at their dead bodies and refuse to let them be placed in a tomb, [10]and those who dwell on the earth will rejoice over them and make merry and exchange presents, because these two prophets had been a torment to those who dwell on the earth. [11]But after the three and a half days a breath of life from God entered them, and they stood up on their feet, and great fear fell on those who saw them. [12]Then they heard a loud voice from heaven saying to them, "Come up here!" And in the sight of their foes they went up to heaven in a cloud. [13]And at that hour there was a great earthquake, and a tenth of the city fell; seven thousand people were killed in the earthquake, and the rest were terrified and gave glory to the God of heaven.

14 The second woe has passed; behold, the third woe is soon to come.

The Seventh Trumpet

15 Then the seventh angel blew his trumpet, and there were loud voices in heaven, saying, "The kingdom of the world has become the kingdom of our Lord and of his Christ, and he shall reign for ever and ever." [16]And the twenty-four elders who sit on their thrones before God fell on their faces and worshiped God, [17]saying,

"We give thanks to you, Lord God Almighty,
    who are and who were,
    that you have taken your great power and
        begun to reign.
[18]The nations raged, but your wrath came,
    and the time for the dead to be judged,
for rewarding your servants, the prophets and
        saints,
    and those who fear your name, both small
        and great,
and for destroying the destroyers of the earth."

19 Then God's temple in heaven was opened, and the ark of his covenant was seen within his temple; and there were flashes of lightning, loud noises, peals of thunder, an earthquake, and heavy hail.

The Woman and the Dragon

12 † And a great sign appeared in heaven, a woman clothed with the sun, with the moon under her feet, and on her head a crown of twelve stars; [2]she was with child and she cried

out in her pangs of birth, in anguish for delivery. [3]And another sign appeared in heaven; behold, a great red dragon, with seven heads and ten horns, and seven diadems upon his heads. [4]His tail swept down a third of the stars of heaven, and cast them to the earth. And the dragon stood before the woman who was about to bear a child, that he might devour her child when she brought it forth; [5]she brought forth a male child, one who is to rule all the nations with a rod of iron, but her child was caught up to God and to his throne, [6]and the woman fled into the wilderness, where she has a place prepared by God, in which to be nourished for one thousand two hundred and sixty days.

Michael Defeats the Dragon

7 Now war arose in heaven, Michael and his angels fighting against the dragon; and the dragon and his angels fought, [8]but they were defeated and there was no longer any place for them in heaven. [9]And the great dragon was thrown down, that ancient serpent, who is called the Devil and Satan, the deceiver of the whole world—he was thrown down to the earth, and his angels were thrown down with him. [10]And I heard a loud voice in heaven, saying, "Now the salvation and the power and the kingdom of our God and the authority of his Christ have come, for the accuser of our brethren has been thrown down, who accuses them day and night before our God. [11]And they have conquered him by the blood of the Lamb and by the word of their testimony, for they loved not their lives even unto death. [12]Rejoice then, O heaven and you that dwell therein! But woe to you, O earth and sea, for the devil has come down to you in great wrath, because he knows that his time is short!"

The Dragon Makes War against the Woman's Offspring

13 And when the dragon saw that he had been thrown down to the earth, he pursued the woman who had borne the male child. [14]But the woman was given the two wings of the great

---

[d] Greek *spiritually*.
11:6: 1 Kings 17:1; Ex 7:17, 19.
11:7: Dan 7:3, 7, 21.
11:8: Is 1:9.
11:11: Ezek 37:5, 10.
11:12: 2 Kings 2:11.
11:15: Ps 22:28; Dan 7:14, 27.
11:18: Ps 2:1.
11:19: 1 Kings 8:1–6; 2 Mac 2:4–8.
12:2: Mic 4:10.
12:3: Dan 7:7.
12:4: Dan 8:10.
12:5: Is 66:7; Ps 2:9.
12:7: Dan 10:13.
12:9: Gen 3:1, 14–15; Zech 3:1.
12:10: Job 1:9–11.
12:12: Is 44:23; 49:13.
12:14: Dan 7:25; 12:7.
* 11:8, *the great city:* i.e., Rome.
† 12:1–6: The *child* brought forth is the Messiah; the *dragon* is the devil; the *woman* who gave birth to the Messiah is Israel, and then becomes the Christian Church, which continually gives birth to the faithful.

eagle that she might fly from the serpent into the wilderness, to the place where she is to be nourished for a time, and times, and half a time.* [15]The serpent poured water like a river out of his mouth after the woman, to sweep her away with the flood. [16]But the earth came to the help of the woman, and the earth opened its mouth and swallowed the river which the dragon had poured from his mouth. [17]Then the dragon was angry with the woman, † and went off to make war on the rest of her offspring, on those who keep the commandments of God and bear testimony to Jesus. And he stood [e] on the sand of the sea.

The Beast from the Sea

13 And I saw a beast ‡ rising out of the sea, with ten horns and seven heads, with ten diadems upon its horns and a blasphemous name upon its heads. [2]And the beast that I saw was like a leopard, its feet were like a bear's, and its mouth was like a lion's mouth. And to it the dragon gave his power and his throne and great authority. [3]One of its heads seemed to have a mortal wound, but its mortal wound was healed, and the whole earth followed the beast with wonder. [4]Men worshiped the dragon, for he had given his authority to the beast, and they worshiped the beast, saying, "Who is like the beast, and who can fight against it?"

5 And the beast was given a mouth uttering haughty and blasphemous words, and it was allowed to exercise authority for forty-two months; [6]it opened its mouth to utter blasphemies against God, blaspheming his name and his dwelling, that is, those who dwell in heaven. [7]Also it was allowed to make war on the saints and to conquer them. [f] And authority was given it over every tribe and people and tongue and nation, [8]and all who dwell on earth will worship it, every one whose name has not been written before the foundation of the world in the book of life of the Lamb that was slain. [9]If any one has an ear, let him hear:

[10]If any one is to be taken captive,
    to captivity he goes;
if any one slays with the sword,
    with the sword must he be slain.
Here is a call for the endurance and faith of the saints.

The Beast from the Earth

11 Then I saw another beast § which rose out of the earth; it had two horns like a lamb and it spoke like a dragon. [12]It exercises all the authority of the first beast in its presence, and makes the earth and its inhabitants worship the first beast, whose mortal wound was healed. [13]It works great signs, even making fire come down from heaven to earth in the sight of men; [14]and by the signs which it is allowed to work in the presence of the beast, it deceives those who dwell

on earth, bidding them make an image for the beast which was wounded by the sword and yet lived; [15]and it was allowed to give breath to the image of the beast so that the image of the beast should even speak, and to cause those who would not worship the image of the beast to be slain. [16]Also it causes all, both small and great, both rich and poor, both free and slave, to be marked on the right hand or the forehead, [17]so that no one can buy or sell unless he has the mark, that is, the name of the beast or the number of its name. [18]This calls for wisdom: let him who has understanding reckon the number of the beast, for it is a human number, its number is six hundred and sixty-six. [g] **

The Lamb and the 144,000

14 Then I looked, and behold, on Mount Zion stood the Lamb, and with him a hundred and forty-four thousand who had his name and his Father's name written on their foreheads. [2]And I heard a voice from heaven like the sound of many waters and like the sound of loud thunder; the voice I heard was like the sound of harpists playing on their harps, [3]and they sing a new song before the throne and before the four living creatures and before the elders. No one could learn that song except the hundred and forty-four thousand who had been redeemed from the earth. [4]It is these who have not defiled themselves with women, for they are chaste; [h] †† it is these who follow the Lamb wherever he goes; these have been redeemed from mankind as first fruits for God and the Lamb, [5]and in their mouth no lie was found, for they are spotless.

The Messages of the Three Angels

6 Then I saw another angel flying in mid-heaven, with an eternal gospel to proclaim to those who dwell on earth, to every nation and tribe and tongue and people; [7]and he said with a

---

[e] Other ancient authorities read *And I stood*, connecting the sentence with 13:1.
[f] Other ancient authorities omit this sentence.
[g] Other ancient authorities read *six hundred and sixteen*.
[h] Greek *virgins*.
13:1: Dan 7:1–6.
13:5: Dan 7:8.
13:7: Dan 7:21.
13:9: Mk 4:23.
13:10: Jer 15:2.
13:14: Deut 13:1–5.
13:15: Dan 3:5.
14:1: Ezek 9:4.
* 12:14, *a time, and times, and half a time*: This is the three and a half years of 11:2.
† 12:17: Mary, the mother of the Messiah, must also be included in the meaning.
‡ 13:1, *a beast*: This symbolizes the material forces of evil, arrayed against the Church.
§ 13:11, *another beast*: i.e., the false prophets.
** 13:18, *six hundred and sixty-six*: The letters of Nero's name plus the title of Caesar, given their numerical meaning in Hebrew and added together, make 666.
†† 14:4: Although tradition tends to take this literally, the context and Old Testament metaphor suggest that it means they have kept free from idolatry.

loud voice, "Fear God and give him glory, for the hour of his judgment has come; and worship him who made heaven and earth, the sea and the fountains of water."

8 Another angel, a second, followed, saying, "Fallen, fallen is Babylon * the great, she who made all nations drink the wine of her impure passion."

9 And another angel, a third, followed them, saying with a loud voice, "If any one worships the beast and its image, and receives a mark on his forehead or on his hand, [10]he also shall drink the wine of God's wrath, poured unmixed into the cup of his anger, and he shall be tormented with fire and brimstone in the presence of the holy angels and in the presence of the Lamb. [11]And the smoke of their torment goes up for ever and ever; and they have no rest, day or night, these worshipers of the beast and its image, and whoever receives the mark of its name."

12 Here is a call for the endurance of the saints, those who keep the commandments of God and the faith of Jesus.

13 And I heard a voice from heaven saying, "Write this: Blessed are the dead who from now on die in the Lord." "Blessed indeed," says the Spirit, "that they may rest from their labors, for their deeds follow them!"

Reaping the Earth's Harvest

14 Then I looked, and behold, a white cloud, and seated on the cloud one like a son of man, with a golden crown on his head, and a sharp sickle in his hand. [15]And another angel came out of the temple, calling with a loud voice to him who sat upon the cloud, "Put in your sickle, and reap, for the hour to reap has come, for the harvest of the earth is fully ripe." [16]So he who sat upon the cloud swung his sickle on the earth, and the earth was reaped.

17 And another angel came out of the temple in heaven, and he too had a sharp sickle. [18]Then another angel came out from the altar, the angel who has power over fire, and he called with a loud voice to him who had the sharp sickle, "Put in your sickle, and gather the clusters of the vine of the earth, for its grapes are ripe." [19]So the angel swung his sickle on the earth and gathered the vintage of the earth, and threw it into the great wine press of the wrath of God; [20]and the wine press was trodden outside the city, and blood flowed from the wine press, as high as a horse's bridle, for one thousand six hundred stadia. [i]

The Angels with the Seven Last Plagues

15 Then I saw another sign in heaven, great and wonderful, seven angels with seven plagues, which are the last, for with them the wrath of God is ended.

2 And I saw what appeared to be a sea of glass mingled with fire, and those who had conquered the beast and its image and the number of its name, standing beside the sea of glass with harps of God in their hands. [3]And they sing the song of Moses, † the servant of God, and the song of the Lamb, saying,

"Great and wonderful are your deeds,
O Lord God the Almighty!
Just and true are your ways,
O King of the ages! [j]
[4]Who shall not fear and glorify your name, O
    Lord?
For you alone are holy.
All nations shall come and worship you,
for your judgments have been revealed."

5 After this I looked, and the temple of the tent of witness in heaven was opened, [6]and out of the temple came the seven angels with the seven plagues, robed in pure bright linen, and with golden sashes across their chests. [7]And one of the four living creatures gave the seven angels seven golden bowls full of the wrath of God who lives for ever and ever; [8]and the temple was filled with smoke from the glory of God and from his power, and no one could enter the temple until the seven plagues of the seven angels were ended.

The Bowls of God's Wrath

16 Then I heard a loud voice from the temple telling the seven angels, "Go and pour out on the earth the seven bowls of the wrath of God."

2 So the first angel went and poured his bowl on the earth, and foul and evil sores came upon the men who bore the mark of the beast and worshiped its image.

3 The second angel poured his bowl into the sea, and it became like the blood of a dead man, and every living thing died that was in the sea.

4 The third angel poured his bowl into the rivers and the fountains of water, and they became blood. [5]And I heard the angel of water say,

"Just are you in these your judgments,
you who are and were, O Holy One!
[6]For men have shed the blood of saints and
    prophets,

---

[i] About two hundred miles.
[j] Other ancient authorities read the nations.
14:8: Is 21:9.
14:10: Jer 51:7; Gen 19:24.
14:11: Is 34:10.
14:14: Dan 7:13.
14:15: Joel 3:13; Mt 13:30.
14:20: Joel 3:13.
15:1: Lev 26:21.
15:3: Ex 15:1; Ps 145:17.
15:4: Jer 10:7; Ps 86:9–10.
15:5: Ex 40:34.
15:8: 1 Kings 8:10; Is 6:4; Ezek 44:4.
16:1: Is 66:6; Ps 69:24.
16:2: Ex 9:10–11; Deut 28:35.
16:3–4: Ex 7:17–21.
16:6: Ps 79:3.
* 14:8, Babylon: i.e., Rome.
† 15:3–4: The song of Moses in Ex 15:1–18 celebrated victory over Pharaoh. This is seen as foreshadowing the triumph of the Lamb.

and you have given them blood to drink.
It is their due!"
[7] And I heard the altar cry,
"Yes, Lord God the Almighty,
true and just are your judgments!"

8 The fourth angel poured his bowl on the sun, and it was allowed to scorch men with fire; [9] men were scorched by the fierce heat, and they cursed the name of God who had power over these plagues, and they did not repent and give him glory.

10 The fifth angel poured his bowl on the throne of the beast, and its kingdom was in darkness; men gnawed their tongues in anguish [11] and cursed the God of heaven for their pain and sores, and did not repent of their deeds.

12 The sixth angel poured his bowl on the great river Euphra'tes, and its water was dried up, to prepare the way for the kings from the east. [13] And I saw, issuing from the mouth of the dragon and from the mouth of the beast and from the mouth of the false prophet, three foul spirits like frogs; [14] for they are demonic spirits, performing signs, who go abroad to the kings of the whole world, to assemble them for battle on the great day * of God the Almighty. [15] ("Behold, I am coming like a thief! Blessed is he who is awake, keeping his garments that he may not go naked and be seen exposed!") [16] And they assembled them at the place which is called in Hebrew Armaged'don. †

17 The seventh angel poured his bowl into the air, and a great voice came out of the temple, from the throne, saying, "It is done!" [18] And there were flashes of lightning, loud noises, peals of thunder, and a great earthquake such as had never been since men were on the earth, so great was that earthquake. [19] The great city was split into three parts, and the cities of the nations fell, and God remembered great Babylon, to make her drain the cup of the fury of his wrath. [20] And every island fled away, and no mountains were to be found; [21] and great hailstones, heavy as a hundredweight, dropped on men from heaven, till men cursed God for the plague of the hail, so fearful was that plague.

The Great Whore and the Beast

17 Then one of the seven angels who had the seven bowls came and said to me, "Come, I will show you the judgment of the great harlot ‡ who is seated upon many waters, [2] with whom the kings of the earth have committed fornication, and with the wine of whose fornication § the dwellers on earth have become drunk." [3] And he carried me away in the Spirit into a wilderness, and I saw a woman sitting on a scarlet beast which was full of blasphemous names, and it had seven heads and ten horns. [4] The woman was clothed in purple and scarlet, and adorned with gold and jewels and pearls, holding in her hand a golden cup full of abominations and the impurities of her fornication; [5] and on her forehead was written a name of mystery: "Babylon the great, mother of harlots and of earth's abominations." [6] And I saw the woman, drunk with the blood of the saints and the blood of the martyrs of Jesus.

When I saw her I marveled greatly. [7] But the angel said to me, "Why marvel? I will tell you the mystery of the woman, and of the beast with seven heads and ten horns that carries her. [8] The beast that you saw was, and is not, and is to ascend from the bottomless pit and go to perdition; and the dwellers on earth whose names have not been written in the book of life from the foundation of the world, will marvel to behold the beast, because it was and is not and is to come. [9] This calls for a mind with wisdom: the seven heads are seven hills on which the woman is seated; [10] they are also seven kings, five of whom have fallen, one is, the other has not yet come, and when he comes he must remain only a little while. [11] As for the beast that was and is not, it is an eighth but it belongs to the seven, and it goes to perdition. [12] And the ten horns that you saw are ten kings who have not yet received royal power, but they are to receive authority as kings for one hour, together with the beast. [13] These are of one mind and give over their power and authority to the beast; [14] they will make war on the Lamb, and the Lamb will conquer them, for he is Lord of lords and King of kings, and those with him are called and chosen and faithful."

15 And he said to me, "The waters that you saw, where the harlot is seated, are peoples and multitudes and nations and tongues. [16] And the ten horns that you saw, they and the beast will hate the harlot; they will make her desolate and naked, and devour her flesh and burn her up with fire, [17] for God has put it into their hearts to carry out his purpose by being of one mind and giving over their royal power to the beast, until the words of God shall be fulfilled. [18] And the woman that

16:7: Ps 119:137.
16:10: Ex 10:21.
16:12: Is 11:15–16.
16:13: 1 Kings 22:21–23; Ex 8:3.
16:15: 1 Thess 5:2.
16:16: 2 Kings 9:27.
16:17: Is 66:6.
16:18: Ex 19:16; Dan 12:1.
16:21: Ex 9:23.
17:1: Jer 51:13.
17:2: Is 23:17; Jer 25:15–16.
17:4: Jer 51:7.
17:8: Dan 7:3; Rev 3:5.
17:12: Dan 7:20–24.
17:14: Dan 2:47.
* 16:14, *the great day*: On which all the Gentile armies shall be gathered to give battle.
† 16:16, *Armageddon*: i.e., Megiddo, where Josiah was defeated by the king of Egypt, cf. 2 Kings 23:29.
‡ 17:1, *great harlot*: i.e., Rome.
§ 17:2, *fornication*: i.e., idolatry.

you saw is the great city which has dominion over the kings of the earth."

The Fall of Babylon

18 After this I saw another angel coming down from heaven, having great authority; and the earth was made bright with his splendor. [2]And he called out with a mighty voice,
"Fallen, fallen is Babylon the great!
It has become a dwelling place of demons,
a haunt of every foul spirit,
a haunt of every foul and hateful bird;
[3]for all nations have drunk * the wine of her
impure passion,
and the kings of the earth have committed
fornication with her,
and the merchants of the earth have grown
rich with the wealth of her wantonness."
[4]Then I heard another voice from heaven saying,
"Come out of her, my people,
lest you take part in her sins,
lest you share in her plagues;
[5]for her sins are heaped high as heaven,
and God has remembered her iniquities.
[6]Render to her as she herself has rendered,
and repay her double for her deeds;
mix a double draught for her in the cup she
mixed.
[7]As she glorified herself and played the
wanton,
so give her a like measure of torment and
mourning.
Since in her heart she says, 'A queen I sit,
I am no widow, mourning I shall never see,'
[8]so shall her plagues come in a single day,
pestilence and mourning and famine,
and she shall be burned with fire;
for mighty is the Lord God who judges her."

9 And the kings of the earth, who committed fornication and were wanton with her, will weep and wail over her when they see the smoke of her burning; [10]they will stand far off, in fear of her torment, and say,
"Alas! alas! you great city,
you mighty city, Babylon!
In one hour has your judgment come."

11 * And the merchants of the earth weep and mourn for her, since no one buys their cargo any more, [12]cargo of gold, silver, jewels and pearls, fine linen, purple, silk and scarlet, all kinds of scented wood, all articles of ivory, all articles of costly wood, bronze, iron and marble, [13]cinnamon, spice, incense, myrrh, frankincense, wine, oil, fine flour and wheat, cattle and sheep, horses and chariots, and slaves, that is, human souls.
[14]"The fruit for which your soul longed has gone
from you,
and all your delicacies and your splendor are
lost to you, never to be found again!"

[15]The merchants of these wares, who gained wealth from her, will stand far off, in fear of her torment, weeping and mourning aloud,
[16]"Alas, alas, for the great city
that was clothed in fine linen, in purple and
scarlet,
adorned with gold, with jewels, and with
pearls!
[17]In one hour all this wealth has been laid waste."
And all shipmasters and seafaring men, sailors and all whose trade is on the sea, stood far off [18]and cried out as they saw the smoke of her burning,
"What city was like the great city?"
[19]And they threw dust on their heads, as they wept and mourned, crying out,
"Alas, alas, for the great city
where all who had ships at sea grew rich by
her wealth!
In one hour she has been laid waste.
[20]Rejoice over her, O heaven,
O saints and apostles and prophets,
for God has given judgment for you against
her!"

21 Then a mighty angel took up a stone like a great millstone and threw it into the sea, saying,
"So shall Babylon the great city be thrown
down with violence,
and shall be found no more;
[22]and the sound of harpists and minstrels, of
flute players and trumpeters,
shall be heard in you no more;
and a craftsman of any craft
shall be found in you no more;
and the sound of the millstone
shall be heard in you no more;
[23]and the light of a lamp
shall shine in you no more;
and the voice of bridegroom and bride
shall be heard in you no more;
for your merchants were the great men of the
earth,
and all nations were deceived by your
sorcery.

---

* Other ancient authorities read *fallen by.*
18:2: Is 21:9; Jer 50:39.
18:3: Jer 25:15, 27.
18:4: Is 48:20; Jer 50:8.
18:5: Jer 51:9.
18:6: Ps 137:8.
18:7: Is 47:8–9.
18:9: Ezek 26:16–17.
18:11: Ezek 27:36.
18:12: Ezek 27:12–13, 22.
18:15: Ezek 27:36, 31.
18:17: Is 23:14; Ezek 27:26–30.
18:19: Ezek 27:30–34.
18:20: Is 44:23; Jer 51:48.
18:21: Jer 51:63; Ezek 26:21.
18:22: Is 24:8; Ezek 26:13.
18:23: Jer 25:10.
* 18:11–20: The description abruptly assumes the language of Ezekiel's prophecy of the destruction of Tyre, another city notorious for its sins (Ezek 27:1—28:19).

[24]And in her was found the blood of prophets
and of saints,
and of all who have been slain on earth."

The Rejoicing in Heaven

19 After this I heard what seemed to be the mighty voice of a great multitude in heaven, crying,

"Hallelujah! Salvation and glory and power
belong to our God,
[2]for his judgments are true and just;
he has judged the great harlot who corrupted
the earth with her fornication,
and he has avenged on her the blood of his
servants."

[3]Once more they cried,

"Hallelujah! The smoke from her goes up for
ever and ever."

[4]And the twenty-four elders and the four living creatures fell down and worshiped God who is seated on the throne, saying, "Amen. Hallelujah!" [5]And from the throne came a voice crying,

"Praise our God, all you his servants,
you who fear him, small and great."

[6]Then I heard what seemed to be the voice of a great multitude, like the sound of many waters and like the sound of mighty thunderpeals, crying,

"Hallelujah! For the Lord our God the Almighty
reigns.
[7]Let us rejoice and exult and give him the
glory,
for the marriage of the Lamb * has come,
and his Bride has made herself ready;
[8]it was granted her to be clothed with fine linen,
bright and pure"—

for the fine linen is the righteous deeds of the saints.

9 And the angel said[1] to me, "Write this: Blessed are those who are invited to the marriage supper of the Lamb." And he said to me, "These are true words of God." [10]Then I fell down at his feet to worship him, but he said to me, "You must not do that! I am a fellow servant with you and your brethren who hold the testimony of Jesus. Worship God." For the testimony of Jesus is the spirit of prophecy.

The Rider on the White Horse

11 Then I saw heaven opened, and behold, a white horse! He who sat upon it is called Faithful and True, and in righteousness he judges and makes war. [12]His eyes are like a flame of fire, and on his head are many diadems; and he has a name inscribed which no one knows but himself. [13]He is clothed in a robe dipped in [m] blood, and the name by which he is called is The Word of God. [14]And the armies of heaven, wearing fine linen, white and pure, followed him on white horses. [15]From his mouth issues a sharp sword with which to strike the nations, and he will rule them with a rod of iron; he will tread the wine press of the

fury of the wrath of God the Almighty. [16]On his robe and on his thigh he has a name inscribed, King of kings and Lord of lords.

The Beast and Its Armies Defeated

17 Then I saw an angel standing in the sun, and with a loud voice he called to all the birds that fly in midheaven, "Come, gather for the great supper of God, [18]to eat the flesh of kings, the flesh of captains, the flesh of mighty men, the flesh of horses and their riders, and the flesh of all men, both free and slave, both small and great." [19]And I saw the beast and the kings of the earth with their armies gathered to make war against him who sits upon the horse and against his army. [20]And the beast was captured, and with it the false prophet who in its presence had worked the signs by which he deceived those who had received the mark of the beast and those who worshiped its image. These two were thrown alive into the lake of fire that burns with brimstone. [21]And the rest were slain by the sword of him who sits upon the horse, the sword that issues from his mouth; and all the birds were gorged with their flesh.

The Thousand Years

20 Then I saw an angel coming down from heaven, holding in his hand the key of the bottomless pit and a great chain. [2]And he seized the dragon, that ancient serpent, who is the Devil and Satan, and bound him for a thousand years, [3]and threw him into the pit, and shut it and sealed it over him, that he should deceive the nations no more, till the thousand years were ended. † After that he must be let out for a little while.

4 Then I saw thrones, and seated on them were those to whom judgment was committed. Also I saw the souls of those who had been beheaded for their testimony to Jesus and for the word of God, and who had not worshiped the beast or its image and had not received its mark on their foreheads or their hands. They came to life, and reigned with Christ a thousand years. [5]The rest of the dead did not come to life until the thousand years were ended. This is the first resurrection.

---

[1] Greek *he said*.
[m] Other ancient authorities read *sprinkled with*.
18:24: Jer 51:49.
19:2: Deut 32:43.
19:3: Is 34:10.
19:5: Ps 115:13.
19:7: Ps 118:24.
19:11: Ezek 1:1.
19:12: Dan 10:6.
19:15: Ps 2:9.
19:16: Deut 10:17; Dan 2:47.
19:17: Ezek 39:4, 17–20.
20:4: Dan 7:9, 22, 27.
* 19:7, *marriage of the Lamb*: i.e., final establishment of the kingdom of God. The spouse is the Church.
† 20:3: The destruction of the dragon must coincide in time with that of the beast (19:20), so that the first resurrection with the reign of the martyrs refers to the revival and expansion of the Church after the years of persecution.

[6]Blessed and holy is he who shares in the first resurrection! Over such the second death has no power, but they shall be priests of God and of Christ, and they shall reign with him a thousand years.

Satan's Doom

7 And when the thousand years are ended, Satan will be released from his prison [8]and will come out to deceive the nations which are at the four corners of the earth, that is, Gog and Ma'gog, to gather them for battle; their number is like the sand of the sea. [9]And they marched up over the broad earth and surrounded the camp of the saints and the beloved city; but fire came down from heaven [n] and consumed them, [10]and the devil who had deceived them was thrown into the lake of fire and brimstone where the beast and the false prophet were, and they will be tormented day and night for ever and ever.

The Dead Are Judged

11 Then I saw a great white throne and him who sat upon it; from his presence earth and sky fled away, and no place was found for them. [12]And I saw the dead, great and small, standing before the throne, and books were opened. Also another book was opened, which is the book of life. And the dead were judged by what was written in the books, by what they had done. [13]And the sea gave up the dead in it, Death and Hades gave up the dead in them, and all were judged by what they had done. [14]Then Death and Hades were thrown into the lake of fire. This is the second death, the lake of fire; [15]and if any one's name was not found written in the book of life, he was thrown into the lake of fire.

The New Heaven and the New Earth

21 Then I saw a new heaven and a new earth; for the first heaven and the first earth had passed away, and the sea was no more. * [2]And I saw the holy city, new Jerusalem, coming down out of heaven from God, prepared as a bride adorned for her husband; [3]and I heard a great voice from the throne saying, "Behold, the dwelling of God is with men. He will dwell with them, and they shall be his people, [o] and God himself will be with them; [p] [4]he will wipe away every tear from their eyes, and death shall be no more, neither shall there be mourning nor crying nor pain any more, for the former things have passed away."

5 And he who sat upon the throne said, "Behold, I make all things new." Also he said, "Write this, for these words are trustworthy and true." [6]And he said to me, "It is done! I am the Alpha and the Omega, the beginning and the end. To the thirsty I will give water without price from the fountain of the water of life. [7]He who conquers shall have this heritage, and I will be his God and he shall be my son. [8]But as for the cowardly, the faithless, the polluted, as for murderers, fornicators, sorcerers, idolaters, and all liars, their lot shall be in the lake that burns with fire and brimstone, which is the second death." †

Vision of the New Jerusalem

9 Then came one of the seven angels who had the seven bowls full of the seven last plagues, and spoke to me, saying, "Come, I will show you the Bride, the wife of the Lamb." [10]And in the Spirit he carried me away to a great, high mountain, and showed me the holy city Jerusalem coming down out of heaven from God, [11]having the glory of God, its radiance like a most rare jewel, like a jasper, clear as crystal. [12]It had a great, high wall, with twelve gates, and at the gates twelve angels, and on the gates the names of the twelve tribes of the sons of Israel were inscribed; [13]on the east three gates, on the north three gates, on the south three gates, and on the west three gates. [14]And the wall of the city had twelve foundations, and on them the twelve names of the twelve apostles of the Lamb.

15 And he who talked to me had a measuring rod of gold to measure the city and its gates and walls. [16]The city lies foursquare, its length the same as its breadth; and he measured the city with his rod, twelve thousand stadia; [q] its length and breadth and height are equal. [17]He also measured its wall, a hundred and forty-four cubits by a man's measure, that is, an angel's. [18]The wall was built of jasper, while the city was pure gold, clear as glass. [19]The foundations of the wall of the city were adorned with every jewel; the first was jasper, the second sapphire, the third agate, the fourth emerald, [20]the fifth onyx, the sixth carnelian, the seventh chrysolite, the eighth beryl, the ninth topaz, the tenth chrysoprase, the eleventh jacinth, the twelfth amethyst. [21]And the twelve gates were twelve pearls, each of the gates made of a single pearl, and the street of the city was pure gold, transparent as glass.

---

[n] Other ancient authorities read *from God, out of heaven,* or *out of heaven from God.*
[o] Other ancient authorities read *peoples.*
[p] Other ancient authorities add *and be their God.*
[q] About fifteen hundred miles.
20:8: Ezek 38:2, 9, 15.
20:9: 2 Kings 1:10–12.
20:11–12: Dan 7:9–10.
20:15: Rev 3:5.
21:1: Is 66:22.
21:2: Rev 3:12.
21:3: Ezek 37:27.
21:4: Is 25:8; 35:10.
21:5: Is 43:19.
21:6: Is 55:1.
21:7: Ps 89:27–28.
21:8: Is 30:33.
21:10: Ezek 40:2.
21:12: Ezek 48:30–35; Ex 28:21.
21:15: Ezek 40:5.
21:19: Is 54:11–12.
* 21:1: Creation will be renewed one day, freed from corruption and illumined by God's glory.
† 21:8, *second death*: i.e., eternal damnation.

22 And I saw no temple in the city, for its temple is the Lord God the Almighty and the Lamb. 23 And the city has no need of sun or moon to shine upon it, for the glory of God is its light, and its lamp is the Lamb. 24 By its light shall the nations walk; and the kings of the earth shall bring their glory into it, 25 and its gates shall never be shut by day—and there shall be no night there; 26 they shall bring into it the glory and the honor of the nations. 27 But nothing unclean shall enter it, nor any one who practices abomination or falsehood, but only those who are written in the Lamb's book of life.

River of the Water of Life

22 Then he showed me the river of the water of life, bright as crystal, flowing from the throne of God and of the Lamb 2 through the middle of the street of the city; also, on either side of the river, the tree of life ᶠ with its twelve kinds of fruit, yielding its fruit each month; and the leaves of the tree were for the healing of the nations. 3 There shall no more be anything accursed, but the throne of God and of the Lamb shall be in it, and his servants shall worship him; 4 they shall see his face, and his name shall be on their foreheads. 5 And night shall be no more; they need no light of lamp or sun, for the Lord God will be their light, and they shall reign for ever and ever.

6 And he said to me, "These words are trustworthy and true. And the Lord, the God of the spirits of the prophets, has sent his angel to show his servants what must soon take place. 7 And behold, I am coming soon."

Blessed is he who keeps the words of the prophecy of this book.

Epilogue and Benediction

8 I John am he who heard and saw these things. And when I heard and saw them, I fell down to worship at the feet of the angel who showed them to me; 9 but he said to me, "You must not do that! I am a fellow servant with you and your brethren the prophets, and with those who keep the words of this book. Worship God."

10 And he said to me, "Do not seal up the words of the prophecy of this book, for the time is near. 11 Let the evildoer still do evil, and the filthy still be filthy, and the righteous still do right, and the holy still be holy."

12 "Behold, I am coming soon, bringing my recompense, to repay every one for what he has done. 13 I am the Alpha and the Omega, the first and the last, the beginning and the end."

14 Blessed are those who wash their robes, ᵍ that they may have the right to the tree of life and that they may enter the city by the gates. 15 Outside are the dogs and sorcerers and fornicators and murderers and idolaters, and every one who loves and practices falsehood.

16 "I Jesus have sent my angel to you with this testimony for the churches. I am the root and the offspring of David, the bright morning star."

17 The Spirit and the Bride say, "Come." And let him who hears say, "Come." And let him who is thirsty come, let him who desires take the water of life without price.

18 I warn every one who hears the words of the prophecy of this book: if any one adds to them, God will add to him the plagues described in this book, 19 and if any one takes away from the words of the book of this prophecy, God will take away his share in the tree of life and in the holy city, which are described in this book.

20 He who testifies to these things says, "Surely I am coming soon." Amen. Come, Lord Jesus!

21 The grace of the Lord Jesus be with all the saints. ᵗ Amen.

ᶠ Or the Lamb. In the midst of the street of the city, and on either side of the river, was the tree of life, etc.
ᵍ Other ancient authorities read do his commandments.
ᵗ Other ancient authorities omit all; others omit the saints.

21:23: Is 24:23; 60:1, 19.
21:25: Is 60:11.
21:27: Is 52:1; Rev 3:5.
22:2: Gen 2:9.
22:3: Zech 14:11.
22:4: Ps 17:15.
22:11: Dan 12:10.
22:12: Is 40:10; Jer 17:10.
22:13: Is 44:6; 48:12.
22:14: Gen 2:9; 3:22.
22:16: Is 11:1, 10.
22:17: Is 55:1.
22:21: 2 Thess 3:18.

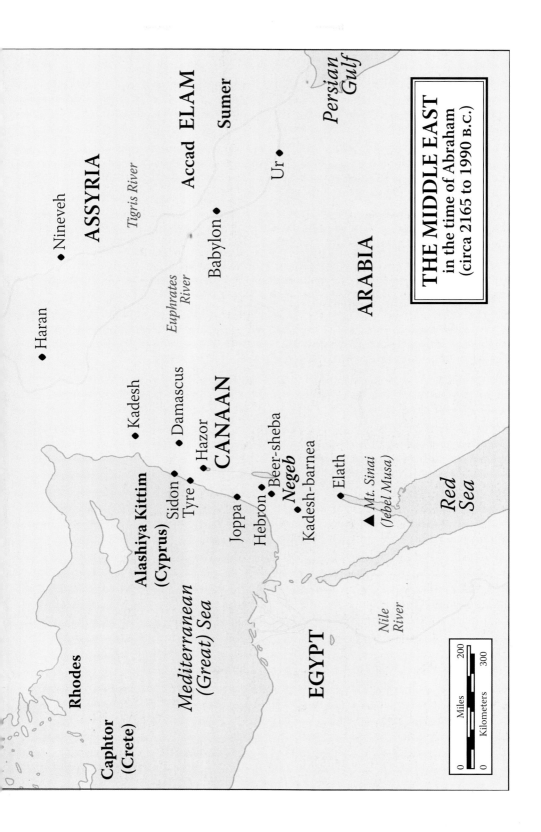

Rhodes

Caphtor
(Crete)

Mediterranean
(Great) Sea

Alashiya Kittim
(Cyprus)

Sidon •
Tyre •

Joppa •

Hebron •
• Beer-sheba
Negeb
• Kadesh-barnea

• Elath

▲ Mt. Sinai
(Jebel Musa)

Red
Sea

Nile
River

EGYPT

• Kadesh

• Damascus

• Hazor
CANAAN

ARABIA

• Haran

ASSYRIA

• Nineveh

Tigris River

Euphrates
River

Babylon •

Accad ELAM

Sumer

Ur •

Persian
Gulf

THE MIDDLE EAST
in the time of Abraham
(circa 2165 to 1990 B.C.)

0 —— Miles —— 200

0 —— Kilometers —— 300

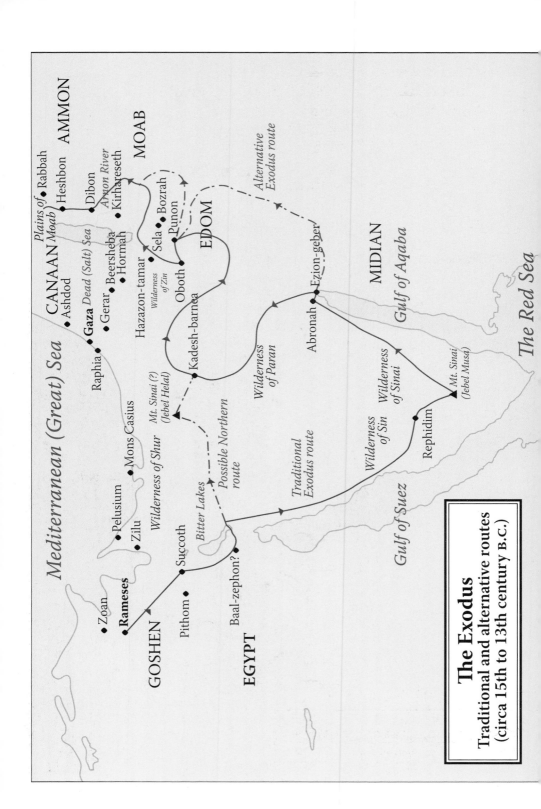

Mediterranean (Great) Sea

AMMON

• Rabbah

Plains of Moab

Heshbon •
Dibon •

Amon River

Kirhareseth •

MOAB

Bozrah •

Sela • • Punon

EDOM

Alternative Exodus route

CANAAN

Ashdod •

Dead (Salt) Sea

Gaza •

Gerar • • Beersheba

• Hormah

Hazazon-tamar

Wilderness of Zin

Oboth •

Kadesh-barnea •

Wilderness of Paran

Raphia •

Mt. Sinai (?) (Jebel Helal)

Wilderness of Shur

Mons Casius •

Pelusium •

Possible Northern route

Abronah •

Ezion-geber •

MIDIAN

Gulf of Aqaba

Zilu •

Bitter Lakes

Succoth •

Wilderness of Sinai

Traditional Exodus route

Wilderness of Sin

Mt. Sinai (Jebel Musa)

Zoan •

Rameses •

GOSHEN

Pithom •

Baal-zephon? •

EGYPT

• Rephidim

Gulf of Suez

The Red Sea

The Exodus
Traditional and alternative routes
(circa 15th to 13th century B.C.)

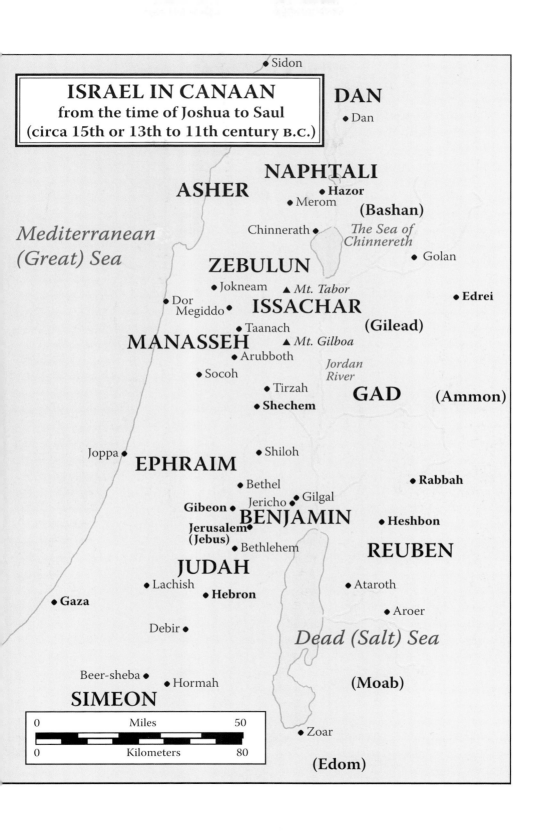

ISRAEL IN CANAAN
from the time of Joshua to Saul
(circa 15th or 13th to 11th century B.C.)

• Sidon

DAN

• Dan

NAPHTALI

ASHER

• **Hazor**

• Merom

(Bashan)

Mediterranean (Great) Sea

Chinnerath •

The Sea of Chinnereth

• Golan

ZEBULUN

• Jokneam ▲ *Mt. Tabor*

• Dor

Megiddo •

ISSACHAR

• **Edrei**

• Taanach

(Gilead)

MANASSEH

▲ *Mt. Gilboa*

• Arubboth

• Socoh

Jordan River

• Tirzah

• **Shechem**

GAD

(Ammon)

Joppa •

EPHRAIM

• Shiloh

• Bethel

• **Rabbah**

Gibeon •

Jericho •• Gilgal

BENJAMIN

Jerusalem•
(Jebus)

• Bethlehem

• **Heshbon**

REUBEN

JUDAH

• Lachish

• **Hebron**

• Ataroth

• **Gaza**

• Aroer

Debir •

Dead (Salt) Sea

Beer-sheba •

• Hormah

(Moab)

SIMEON

0	Miles	50
0	Kilometers	80

• Zoar

(Edom)

THE KINGDOM
in the time of Saul, David and Solomon
(11th to 10th century B.C.)

SIDONIANS   MAACAH

IX   • Hazor   BASHAN
   • Merom
• Acco   VIII   GESHUR

Mediterranean   ARGOB
(Great) Sea   *The Sea of*
   Chinnereth

IV   • Jokneam   X   HAVVOTH
• Dor   -JAIR   VI
   • Megiddo   • Rogelim
   • Taanach
   V
III   • Arubboth   *Jordan*
   River   VII
• Socoh   • Thebez   GILEAD

• Shechem

I

AMMON

Joppa •

   • Bethel   XII   • **Rabbah**
   • Gilgal
Gibeon • • Jericho •
II   XI   • Heshbon
   • **Jerusalem**

   • Bethlehem   MOAB

PHILISTINES
   • Libnah?   • Ataroth

• **Gaza**   • Hebron   • Aroer

Debir •   *Dead (Salt) Sea*

Beer-sheba •

   • **Kir-hareseth**

0	Miles	50
0	Kilometers	80

1-XII = Solomon's
administrative districts

EDOM

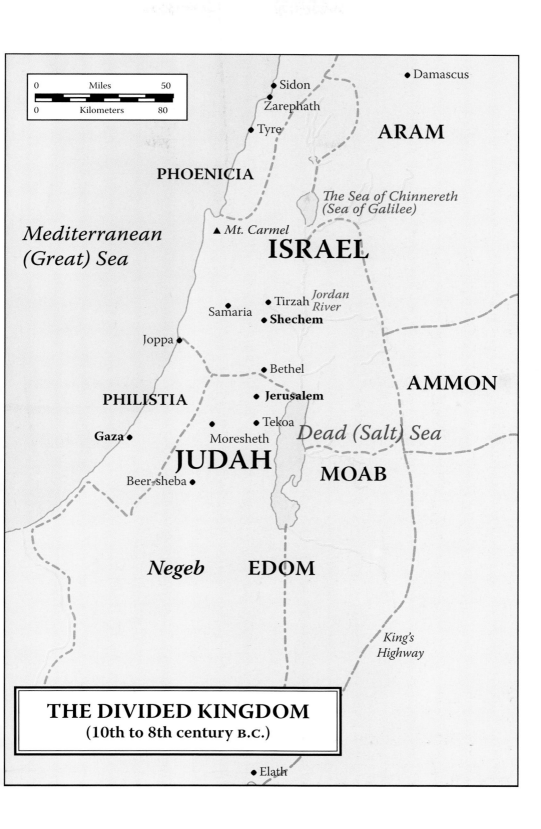

0 Miles 50
0 Kilometers 80

• Damascus

• Sidon
Zarephath
• Tyre

ARAM

PHOENICIA

*The Sea of Chinnereth
(Sea of Galilee)*

*Mediterranean
(Great) Sea*

▲ *Mt. Carmel*

ISRAEL

*Jordan
River*

• Tirzah
Samaria
• **Shechem**

Joppa •

• Bethel

AMMON

PHILISTIA

• **Jerusalem**

Gaza •

• Tekoa
Moresheth

Dead (Salt) Sea

JUDAH

MOAB

Beer-sheba •

Negeb

EDOM

*King's
Highway*

THE DIVIDED KINGDOM
(10th to 8th century B.C.)

• Elath

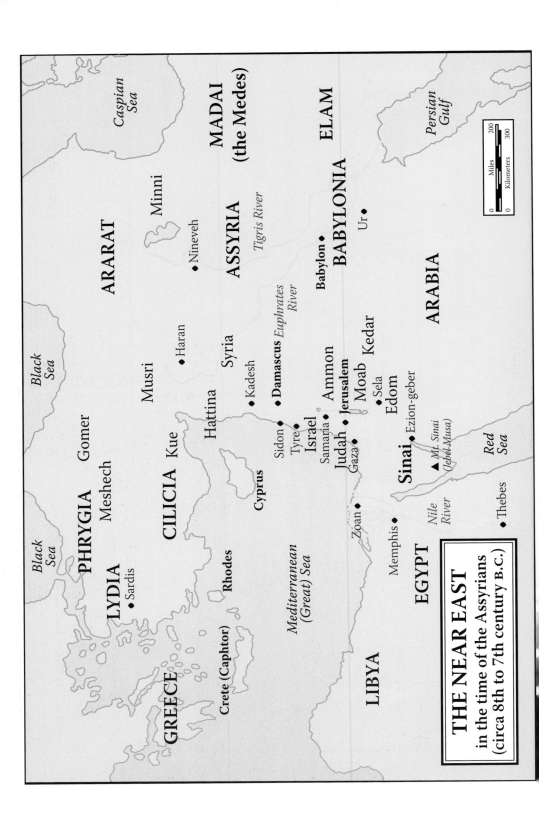

THE NEAR EAST
in the time of the Assyrians
(circa 8th to 7th century B.C.)

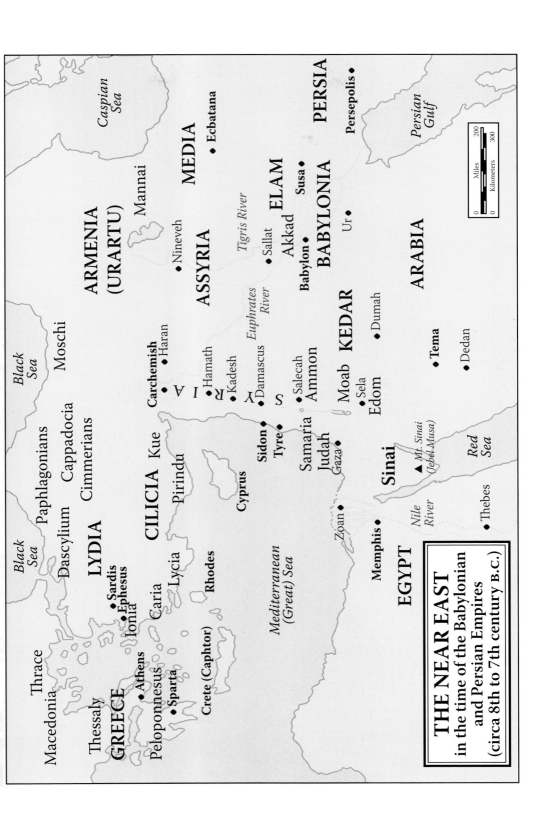

THE NEAR EAST
in the time of the Babylonian
and Persian Empires
(circa 8th to 7th century B.C.)

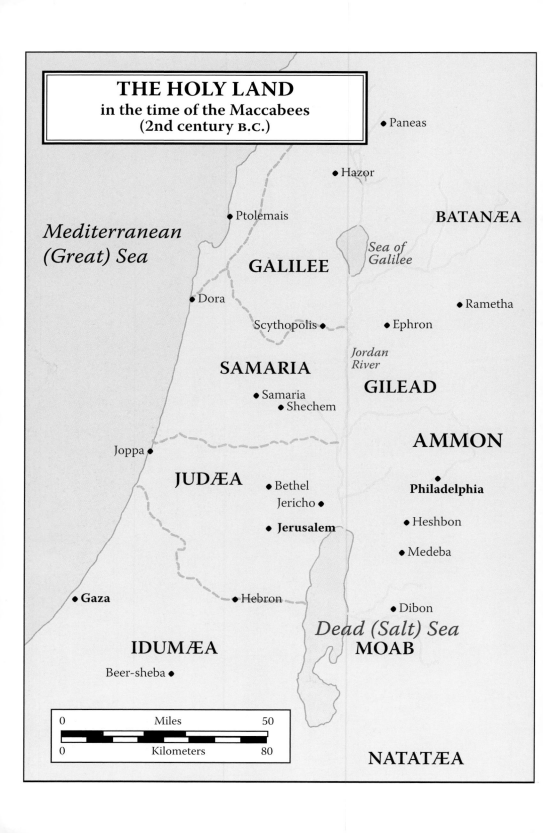

THE HOLY LAND
in the time of the Maccabees
(2nd century B.C.)

• Paneas

• Hazor

BATANÆA

Mediterranean (Great) Sea

• Ptolemais

GALILEE

Sea of Galilee

• Dora

• Rametha

Scythopolis •

• Ephron

Jordan River

SAMARIA

GILEAD

• Samaria
• Shechem

AMMON

Joppa •

JUDÆA

• Bethel
Jericho •

• **Philadelphia**

• **Jerusalem**

• Heshbon

• Medeba

• **Gaza**

• Hebron

• Dibon

Dead (Salt) Sea

IDUMÆA

MOAB

Beer-sheba •

0	Miles	50
0	Kilometers	80

NATATÆA

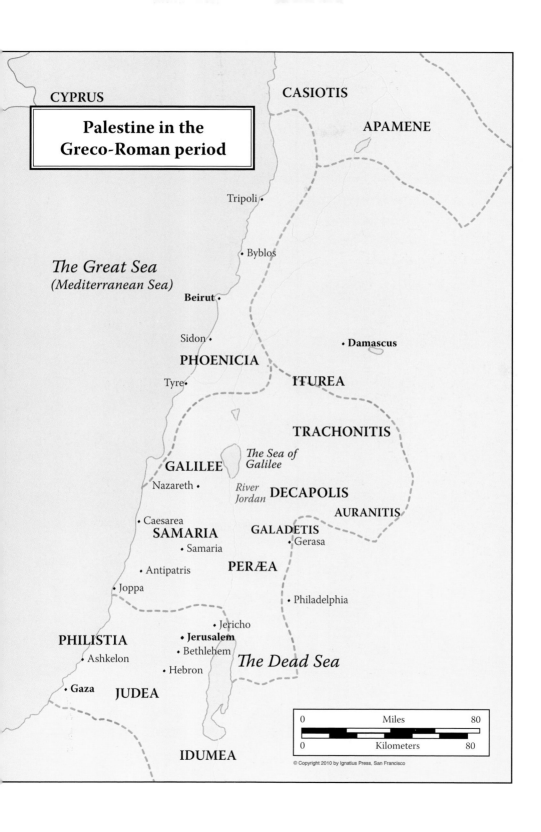

CYPRUS

CASIOTIS

APAMENE

Palestine in the Greco-Roman period

Tripoli •

• Byblos

The Great Sea
(Mediterranean Sea)

Beirut •

Sidon •

PHOENICIA

• **Damascus**

Tyre •

ITUREA

TRACHONITIS

The Sea of Galilee

GALILEE

Nazareth •

River Jordan

DECAPOLIS

AURANITIS

• Caesarea

SAMARIA

• Samaria

GALADETIS

• Gerasa

• Antipatris

PERÆA

• Joppa

• Philadelphia

• Jericho

PHILISTIA

• **Jerusalem**

• Bethlehem

The Dead Sea

• Ashkelon

• Hebron

• **Gaza**

JUDEA

| 0 | Miles | 80 |
| 0 | Kilometers | 80 |

IDUMEA

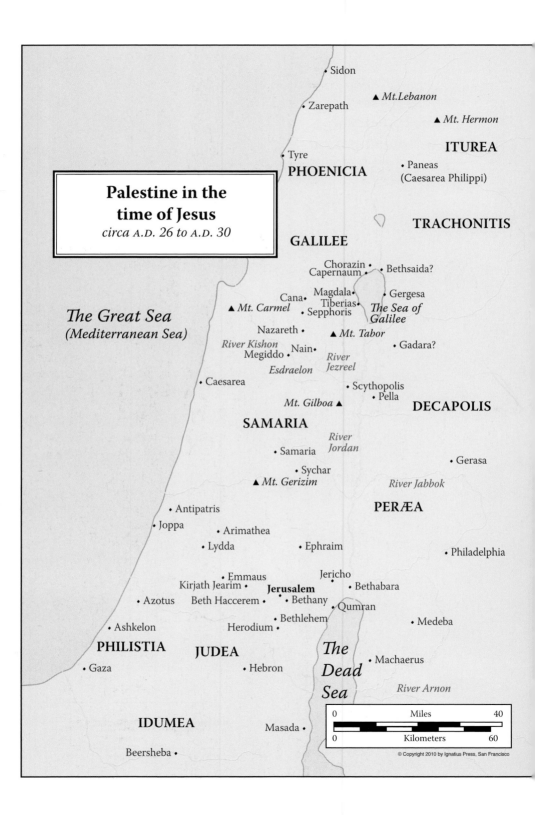

Palestine in the time of Jesus
circa A.D. 26 to A.D. 30

Sidon

▲ *Mt.Lebanon*

Zarepath

▲ *Mt. Hermon*

ITUREA

Tyre

PHOENICIA

Paneas
(Caesarea Philippi)

TRACHONITIS

GALILEE

Chorazin
Capernaum

Bethsaida?

Magdala

Gergesa

Cana

Tiberias

▲ *Mt. Carmel*

Sepphoris

The Sea of Galilee

The Great Sea
(Mediterranean Sea)

Nazareth

▲ *Mt. Tabor*

River Kishon

Nain

Gadara?

Megiddo

River Jezreel

Esdraelon

Caesarea

Scythopolis

Pella

Mt. Gilboa ▲

DECAPOLIS

SAMARIA

River Jordan

Samaria

Gerasa

Sychar

▲ *Mt. Gerizim*

River Jabbok

PERÆA

Antipatris

Joppa

Arimathea

Ephraim

Philadelphia

Lydda

Emmaus

Jericho

Kirjath Jearim

Jerusalem

Bethabara

Azotus

Beth Haccerem

Bethany

Qumran

Medeba

Bethlehem

Ashkelon

Herodium

PHILISTIA

JUDEA

The Dead Sea

Machaerus

Gaza

Hebron

River Arnon

IDUMEA

Masada

0	Miles	40
0	Kilometers	60

Beersheba

© Copyright 2010 by Ignatius Press, San Francisco

The Holy Land in Modern Times

Tripoli

LEBANON

SYRIA

• Beirut

• Sidon

• Damascus

UN Buffer Zone
1973 Line
1967 Cease Fire Line

Tyre •
Qiryat Shemona • Dan •
• Quneitra

Mediterranean Sea

Nahariyya •
Akko •
Safad •
GOLAN HEIGHTS

Haifa •
Tiberias • *The Sea of Galilee*
Nazareth •
• Dera
• Ramtha

• Afula

• Beth Shean
River Jordan

Hadera •
Netanya •
Tulkarm •
• Jarash

Herzliyya •
Tel Aviv •
Yafo
• Petah Tiqwa
• Nablus

Rishon le Zion • • Lod
WEST BANK
• **Amman**

Ramla •
• Ramalah
• Jericho

Ashdod •
Jerusalem •

Ashqelon •
• Bethlehem
• Madaba

Qiryat Gat •
Gaza •
• Hebron
En Gedi •
• Dhiban

The Dead Sea

Al-Arish •
• Beersheba
• Karak

ISRAEL
JORDAN

EGYPT

Negev
Arabah

Sinai

Area occupied by
Israel since June, 1967

0	Miles	50
0	Kilometers	75

Elat • • Aqaba
Gulf of Arabia

© Copyright 2010 by Ignatius Press, San Francisco

BRITANNIA

Oceanus Atlanticus

Oceanus Gallicus

GERMANIA INFERIOR

BELGICA

LUGDUNENSIS

GERMANIA SUPERIOR

NORIC

Avaricum•

RÆTIA

Oceanus Cantabrius AQUATANIA

ALPINA

ITALIA

NARBONENSIS

Sinus Gallicus

Mare Ligusticum

LUSITANIA

TARRACONENSIS

CORSICA

R

•Osilipo

Neapo

•Sanguntum

• Libisosa

SARDINIA

BAETICA

SICILI

• Carteia

• Iol

• Utica

MAURETANIA TINGITANA

MAURETANIA CAESARIENSIS

NUMIDIA

• Thapsus

AFRICA

| 0 | Miles | 500 |
| 0 | Kilometers | 750 |

The Roman Empire in New Testament times
circa A.D. 60 to A.D. 85

PANNONIA

Pontus Euxinus
(The Black Sea)

ILLYRICUM **MOESIA**

Mare
Hadriaticum

THRACIA

• Byzantium

BITHYNIA PONTUS

MACEDONIA

• Thessalonica

CAPPADOCIA

EPIRIUS

Mare
Ionium

Mare
Aegum

ASIA

GALATIA

• Lystra

CILICA

• Athenae

LYCIA

ACHÆA

• Sparta

• Antiochia

SYRIA

• Rhodus

RHODES

CYPRUS

• Damascus

Mare Internum
(The Great Sea)

CRETA

JUDÆA

• Jerusalem

Cyrene •

Gaza •

Alexandria •

ARABIA
PETRÆA

CYRENAICA

ÆGYPTUS

Sinus
Arabicus

Jerusalem
from David to Christ
main features at the time of Christ

Suggested extent of the
City of David
Suggested extent of
Solomon's expansion
Suggested extent of
Hezekiah's expansion
Suggested extent of
Nehemiahs expansion

To Samaria

To Jericho

Mount of Olives

To Antipatris

Antonia
Fortress
(Praetorium?}

Pools of Bethzatha (Bethesda)

Kidron Valley

Sheep Gate

• Gethsemane

Christ's Tomb •

Golgotha/Calvary •

Gate of
Ephraim

Gate of
Benjamin

To Bethany

Horse Gate

To Joppa

Temple

Royal Palace

Suggested extent of
the City at the time
of Christ
City Walls

Herod's Palace
(Praetorium?}

Ophel

Kidron Valley

Spring of Gihon

Caiphas'
House?

City of
David

Hezekiah's Tunnel

■ Cenacle

Stepped
Street

Fountain Gate

Caiphas' House? ■

Kidron Valley

Pool of
Siloam

Essene Gate

Refuse Gate

To Bethlehem,
Hebron and Gaza

Valley of Hinnom

0	Yards	500

feet

700
600
500
400
300
200
100
0

*Valley of
Hinnom*

*Mount of
Olives*

*Kidron
Valley*

© Copyright 2010 by Ignatius Press, San Francisco

Paul's Journeys

*Acts 13–14; 15:39–18:22;
18:23–21:16; 27–28:16*

——— 1st missionary journey with Barnabas
and Mark c. A.D. 46–49

——— 2nd missionary journey with Silas
c. A.D. 50–52

– – – 3rd missionary journey c. A.D. 53–58
Antioch to Jerusalem

– – – 4th missionary journey c. A.D. 59–60
Jerusalem to Rome

© Copyright 2010 by Ignatius Press. San Francisco

MACEDONIA
THRACE
THE BLACK SEA
BITHYNIA
GALATIA
PONTUS
CAPPADOCIA
PHYRGIA
PISIDIA
PAMPHYLIA
LYCIA
CILICIA
SYRIA
CYPRUS
PALESTINE
ACHAIA
CRETE
ITALY
SICILY
MALTA

The Great Sea
(Mediterranean Sea)

Adriatic Sea

Rome
Three Taverns
Appii Forum
Puteoli
Rhegium
Syracuse
Fair Havens

Philippi
Amphipolis
Neapolis
Thessalonica
Apollonia
Beroea
Athens
Corinth

Troas
Assos
Mytilene
Chios
Samos
Ephesus
Miletus
Cos
Cnidus
Rhodes

Antioch
Iconium
Lystra
Derbe
Perga
Attalia
Myra
Patara

Tarsus
Antioch
(in Syria)
Seleucia
Sidon
Tyre
Ptolemais
Caesarea
Jerusalem

Salamis
Paphos

Miles
Kilometers
0   300
0   500

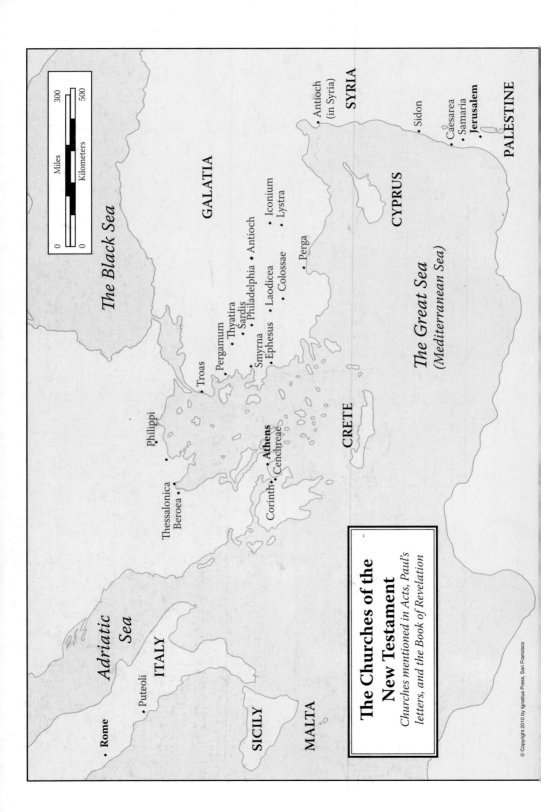

The Churches of the New Testament

Churches mentioned in Acts, Paul's letters, and the Book of Revelation

© Copyright 2010 by Ignatius Press, San Francisco